G(

BASEBALL CARD
Price Guide

Revised 6th Edition

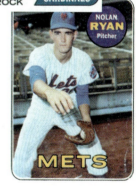

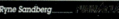
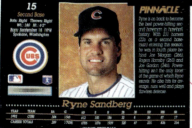

Collector Books
A Division of Schroeder Publishing Co., Inc.

The current values in this book should be used only as a guide. They are not intended to set prices, which vary from one section of the country to another. Auction prices as well as dealer prices vary greatly and are affected by condition as well as demand. Neither the Author nor the Publisher assumes responsibility for any losses that might be incurred as a result of consulting this guide. Baseball cards illustrated are for identification purposes and have been photographed from the author's collection.

Additional copies of this book may be ordered from:

Collector Books
P.O. Box 3009
Paducah, KY 42002-3009

or

May 1 – October 31	November 1 – April 30
Gene Florence	Gene Florence
P.O. Box 22186	Box 64
Lexington, KY 40522	Astatula, FL 34705

@ $9.95 Add $2.00 for postage and handling.

Copyright: Gene Florence, 1994

This book or any part thereof may not be reproduced without the written consent of the Author and Publisher.

Printed by IMAGE GRAPHICS, INC., Paducah, Kentucky

FOREWORD

My baseball card collecting has graduated from a hobby to a major portion of my antique business. When I opened my Grannie Bear Antiques shop in July 1976, one of the first things I stocked along with Depression era glassware and comic books were baseball cards. I knew if I could get the kids to come into my shop the parents would have to bring them and spend some time with the antiques while the kids were shopping. I started several new glass collectors as well as baseball card collectors. My shop is now called Grannie Bear Antiques and Baseball Cards.

From that beginning I started to attend baseball card shows on the West coast and later to sell at these shows including the first and second National shows in California and Michigan. Unfortunately, my books on glassware and other collectibles began to take more of my time and conflict with some of the major baseball card shows. Consequently, I have only been able to attend a few shows each year.

This book explores the world of baseball cards from the beginning of the modern era of bubble gum cards (1948) to the present day cards containing holograms to foil reproductions. I will pass along my thoughts on collecting and grading from the standpoint of dealer and collector since I wear both hats. I hope you enjoy this book which is my forty-sixth book on collectibles since 1972.

ACKNOWLEDGMENTS

Bob McGinnis of Texas helped me change data base programs for the last book and using FileMaker Pro has made my life simpler. Simpler it may be in working with the cards, but this book will still consume more than 360 hours of work by the time it is finally sent to press. An upgrade to 32 K of Ram memory to work with the 33,000 Topps cards was a time-saver, but time is only one consideration in producing a book. I needed a larger time-saver.

A special thanks to Sherry Kraus of Collector Books for working all these card listings into book pages. Now that she has been stuck with my book, she even attended some Florida Spring Training games to check out the Cardinals this year while I slaved in Florida at my computer! We have kept the overnight delivery services in business the last few months with signatures of my three new books traveling from Florida to Kentucky and Lexington to Paducah. Without Collector Books' dedicated editorial staff, I might still be working instead of completing this sixth baseball book.

Cathy, my wife, has endured stacks of cards, boxes and printouts practically taking over the Florida house not to mention all her typing of new sets from our Kentucky office. I have used over 71,000 listings in this book. That new laptop computer certainly came in handy for both Cathy and me to add all the new listings. Just finding the right card to insert into alphabetical listings from all these sets is a major undertaking. My Mom, Grannie Bear, and my Dad spent days opening cards and putting sets together, so I could list the new cards.

Few people ever realize the magnitude of work that goes into producing a book. In my case, it's always been a collective effort. I could never have written any of my books without a wonderful support system. Thank you everyone!

Identification Section

Bowman, 1948, 2 1/16" x 2 1/2"

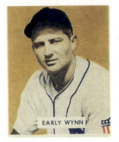

Bowman, 1949, 2 1/16" x 2 1/2"

Bowman, 1950, 2 1/16" x 2 1/2"

Bowman, 1951, 2 1/16" x 3 1/8"

Bowman, 1953BW, 2 1/2" x 3 3/4"

Bowman, 1952, 2 1/16" x 3 1/8"

4

Bowman, 1953BC, 2½" x 3¾"

Bowman, 1954, 2½" x 3¾"

Bowman, 1989, 2½" x 3¾"

Bowman, 1955, 2½" x 3¾"

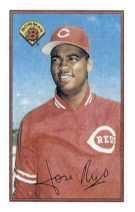

Bowman, 1990, 2½" x 3½"

Bowman, 1991, 2½" x 3½"   Bowman, 1992, 2½" x 3½"   Donruss, 1981, 2½" x 3½"

 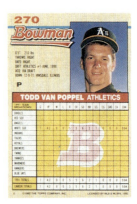 

Donruss, 1982, 2½" x 3½"

Donruss, 1983, 2½" x 3½"

Donruss, 1984, 2½" x 3½"

Donruss, 1985, 2½" x 3½"

Donruss, 1986, 2½" x 3½"

 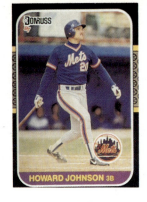 

Donruss, Rookies, 1986, 2½" x 3½"　　Donruss, 1987, 2½" x 3½"　　Donruss, Rookies, 1987, 2½" x 3½"

 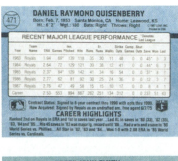 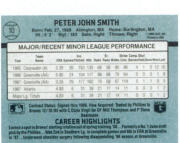 

Donruss, 1988, 2½" x 3½"　　　　　　　　　　　　　　　Donruss, Rookies, 1988, 2½" x 3½"

Donruss, 1989, 2½" x 3½"

Donruss, Traded, 1989, 2½" x 3½"

Donruss, Rookies, 1989, 2½" x 3½"

Donruss, 1990, 2½" x 3½"

Donruss, Rookies, 1990, 2½" x 3½"

Donruss, Leaf, 1990, 2½" x 3½"   Donruss, 1991, 2½" x 3½"   Donruss, Leaf, 1991, 2½" x 3½"

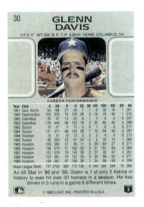  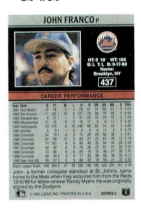

Donruss, Leaf Studio, 1991, 2½" x 3½"

10

Donruss, Rookies, 1991, 2½" x 3½"

Donruss, 1992, 2½" x 3½"

Donruss, Rookies, 1992, 2½" x 3½"

Donruss, Leaf, 1992, 2½" x 3½"

Donruss, Leaf Studio, 1992, 2½" x 3½"

  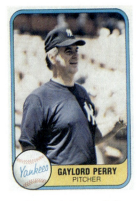

Donruss, 1993, 2½" x 3½" **Donruss, Leaf 1993, 2½" x 3½"** **Fleer, 1981, 2½" x 3½"**

Fleer, 1982, 2½" x 3½"

Fleer, 1983, 2½" x 3½"   Fleer, 1984, 2½" x 3½"   Fleer, 1985, 2½" x 3½"

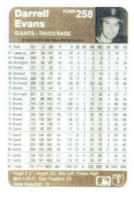 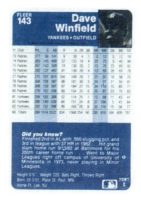 

Fleer, 1986, 2½" x 3½"

 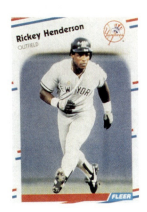 

Fleer, 1987, 2½" x 3½"   Fleer, 1988, 2½" x 3½"   Fleer, 1989, 2½" x 3½"

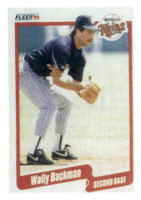 

Fleer, 1990, 2½" x 3½"

  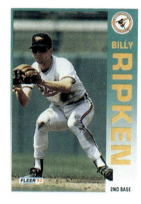

Fleer, 1991, 2½" x 3½"   Fleer, Ultra, 1991, 2½" x 3½"   Fleer, 1992, 2½" x 3½"

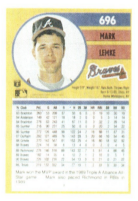  

Fleer, Ultra, 1992, 2½" x 3½"   Fleer, 1993, 2½" x 3½"

Score, 1988, 2½" x 3½" Score, Traded, 1988, 2½" x 3½" Score, 1989, 2½" x 3½"

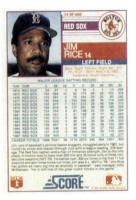 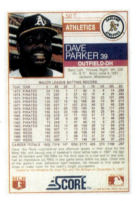 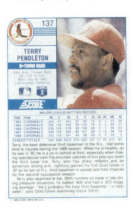

Score, Traded, 1989, 2½" x 3½"

Score, 1990, 2½" x 3½"   Score, Traded, 1990, 2½" x 3½"   Score, 1991, 2½" x 3½"

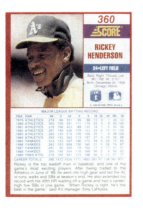 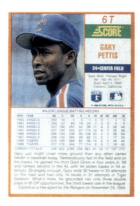 

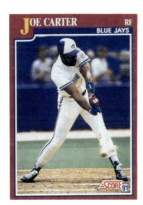 

Score, Traded, 1991, 2½" x 3½"

Score, 1992, 2½" x 3½"   Score, Pinnacle, 1992, 2½" x 3½"   Score, 1993, 2½" x 3½"

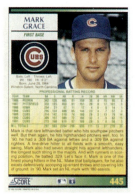  

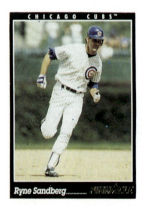 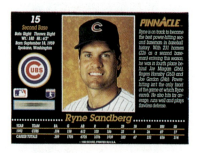

Score, Pinnacle, 1993, 2½" x 3½"

Score, Score Select, 1993, 2½" x 3½"

Topps, Red Back 1951, 2" x 2⅝"

Topps, Blue Back 1951, 2" x 2⅝"

Topps, 1953, 2⅝" x 3¾"

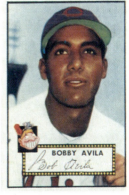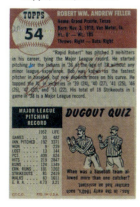

Topps, 1952, 2⅝" x 3¾"

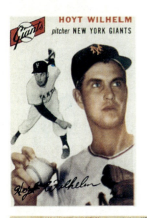

Topps, 1954, 2⅝" x 3¾"

Topps, 1955, 2⅝" x 3¾"

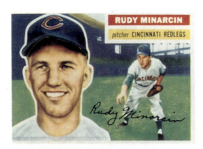

Topps, 1956, 2⅝" x 3¾"

Topps, 1957, 2½" x 3½"

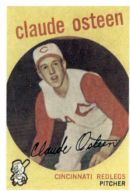

Topps, 1958, 2½" x 3½"   Topps, 1959, 2½" x 3½"

Topps, 1960, 2½" x 3½"   Topps, 1961, 2½" x 3½"   Topps, 1962, 2½" x 3½"

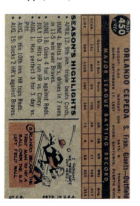

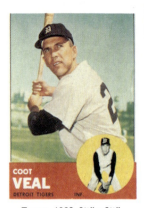

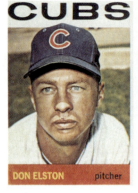

Topps, 1963, 2½" x 3½" Topps, 1964, 2½" x 3½"

Topps, 1965, 2½" x 3½" Topps, 1966, 2½" x 3½" Topps, 1967, 2½" x 3½"

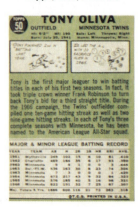

 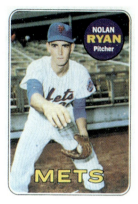 

Topps, 1968, 2½" x 3½"   Topps, 1969, 2½" x 3½"   Topps, 1970, 2½" x 3½"

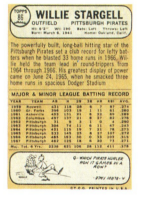  

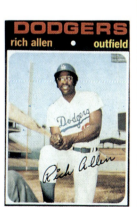  

Topps, 1971, 2½" x 3½"   Topps, 1972, 2½" x 3½"

Topps, 1973, 2½" x 3½"   Topps, 1974, 2½" x 3½"   Topps, 1975, 2½" x 3½"

Topps, 1976, 2½" x 3½"   Topps, 1977, 2½" x 3½"

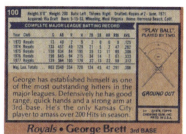

Topps, 1978, 2½" x 3½"   Topps, 1979, 2½" x 3½"

Topps, 1980, 2½" x 3½"   Topps, 1981, 2½" x 3½"   Topps, Traded, 1981, 2½" x 3½"

25

Topps, 1982, 2½" x 3½" Topps, 1983, 2½" x 3½"

Topps, 1984, 2½" x 3½" Topps, 1985, 2½" x 3½" Topps, 1986, 2½" x 3½"

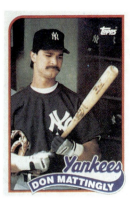

Topps, 1987, 2½" x 3½"   Topps, 1988, 2½" x 3½"   Topps, 1989, 2½" x 3½"

Topps, 1990, 2½" x 3½"   Topps, 1991, 2½" x 3½"

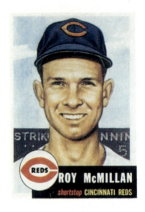 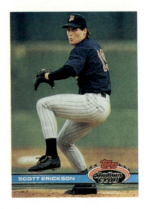 

Topps Archives, 1991, 2½" x 3½"   Topps, 1991, Stadium Club, 2½" x 3½"   Topps, 1992, 2½" x 3½"

 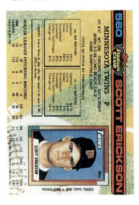

 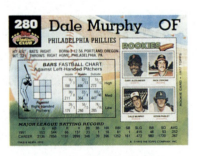

Topps, Stadium Club, 1992, 2½" x 3½"

28

Topps, 1993, 2½" x 3½"   Topps, Stadium Club, 1993, 2½" x 3½"

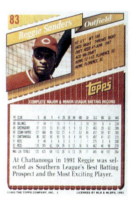 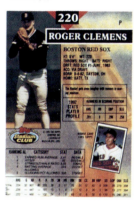

Upper Deck, 1989, 2½" x 3½"

Upper Deck, 1990, 2½" x 3½"

Upper Deck, 1991, 2½" x 3½"

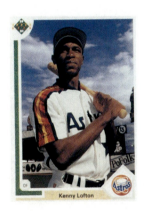 

Upper Deck, Final, 1991, 2½" x 3½"

Upper Deck, 1992, 2½" x 3½"

Upper Deck, 1993, 2½" x 3½"

INTRODUCTION

There are over 10,000 new listings this year making a total of 71,000 listings in this book. Over 2,000 cards have been deleted including all Sportflics and other discontinued series such as Donruss Baseball's Best.

I have not included any of the "chaser" cards in my listings. These cards are the insert cards that are randomly distributed in packs to entice you into buying more cards than you need to complete a set. These cards were avidly sought when first started by Donruss (with Leaf Preview cards) in their factory sets of 1990. In fact, those cards practically rendered the Donruss sets of 1990 worthless since the four cards became more valuable than the sets themselves. Set prices with those cards removed were selling for less than $10.00. Since all the companies are now including these inserts, their value has become tarnished, and they continue to devalue basic sets!

Now, these "chaser" cards are very "hot" when first issued, but rapidly "cool" and drop in price. This even includes the Donruss Diamond Kings which used to be a part of the Donruss set, but are now difficult to assemble. In opening eight boxes of both series of 1993 Donruss, I did not complete one full set! I am still including the Diamond Kings for now, but only because they have been listed since their inception in 1982.

You would think the sixth book in any series of books would be easier to write than the first five. That has never held true for writing glass books, and now I know it does not hold true for baseball card books either. Although things went more smoothly since I have 32K of RAM now, the magnitude of the listings of cards has gotten out of control. File Maker Pro solved the numerical listing problems I have had in the past, and to some extent helped in getting all the players different first names combined into one listing. Dick and Richie Allen are always a disaster to keep together with all the other Allen's in between!

There are six columns for each entry, and each of these can lead to a problem if entered incorrectly. Errors on cards of players who only have one card in the listing are the most difficult to find. I will not even mention the typing mistakes that were missed until the third or later proofing! If you find errors of omission or of any other kind, please let me know. The 71,000 listings with six columns each make over 420,000 entries to be written and proofed!

I first seriously thought about writing a baseball guide in the late 1970's. However, it soon became apparent that I didn't have the necessary equipment to handle all the sorting of data, and there weren't enough hours in my life to do it manually! So, I put the ideas on hold.

In 1980 my publisher approached me about doing a baseball card book; but again, the idea was dropped due to the lack of a computer that could handle the alphabetical listings I felt were needed. The following year my first computer came; and I wrote my next ten books on it; but sorting on it was almost slower than by hand. It took five minutes to sort through two hundred listings and then it would throw out several at the end of the list—unsorted. Needless to say, that computer would not do what I needed for a card book of this magnitude.

"Macintosh II" arrived in April 1988 and with it the reality that thousands of Topps' listings could be sorted! However, I did not know that 16 hour days would be the norm and an occasional one lasting 19 or more would occur. After 360+ hours of work, I am beginning to wonder if this book is really worth all this time! Of course, it has also taken five years to gain the user knowledge that takes the computer only minutes to sort. Increased memory has helped, but as the card lists continue to grow at 10,000 entries a year, we are going to have to re-evaluate the way I am now doing this book!

I'm pleased to report that the present format has been so well received that I am now getting cards and calls from fans wanting to know when to expect the next book! While I certainly hesitate to tamper with sucess, I am considering eliminating the sections by companies and entering all cards in one gigantic listing. This may prove more problems than the 33,000 Topps' listings are beginning to cause, so it is only an idea for now. Let me know if you would like to see all the listings for Cal Ripken in one place instead of under separate headings by company.

HOW TO USE THIS BOOK

Traditionally, the trouble I found with other baseball card guides was that it took too long to find a card of a specific player in them—and you had to have quite a bit of prior knowledge about the card itself before you could hope to find it. Also, you had to flip through pages searching from year to year for all the cards of a specific player. I have had numerous dealers in collectibles tell me that they have avoided buying baseball cards because the guides were impossible to use for someone with little or no knowledge of cards. Therefore, I tried to make a book that's "user friendly" as they say in computer circles.

The format of this book is designed to be easily used by baseball card dealers and collectors as well as those who are just beginning to learn about the magic of card collecting. All listings are alphabetical by player as well as divided alphabetically by company of issue. It is not necessary to know the year of manufacture to find the value of a card listed in this book! The name of the player is all you have to find!

FINDING A CARD'S VALUE
This section is for someone who knows a little about cards.

Pick a card. Look at the name of the manufacturer (Bowman, Donruss, Fleer, Score, Topps or Upper Deck) on the card to determine in which section to look up the name. Turn to that company's section of the book—also listed alphabetically. Find the name of the player on the card. Under each player's name will be a listing of one or more cards. Find the number on the card and match it with a number listed in the book under the No. column. (On very rare occasions a player will have the same number for more than one year. In that case look at the statistical data listed. If 1961 is the last date listed in the record of the player, it is likely the card is 1962).

If you are confused about the year a card was made, turn to the color section that will help identify any cards you can not figure out by year. This section will familiarize you with the different colored backs and fronts of each year shown in this book (1948 – 93). Every card of each player is listed in one place so that you can get a checklist of any player by card company manufacturer. This is especially handy for dealers who are constantly asked for a "Don Gullett" or a "Joe Nuxhall" card. Finding a "rookie" card is simple. It will be the first listing for that player under each company. Since true "rookie" card status is debated among dealers and collectors alike, most people consider the first regular issued card (available to the public in retail outlets) as the true "rookie" card that eliminates "Traded" and "Update" cards as rookie cards.

All players' cards are listed even if the player is only one of several players shown on the card.
There are two prices listed for every one of the 71,000+ listings. The first price column is **VG** which is a very good condition card, and the next column is **EX/MT** which is excellent to mint. **ALL PRICES IN THIS BOOK ARE RETAIL.** (There will be an explanation of grading following this section.)

A STEP BY STEP GUIDE TO FINDING A CARD'S VALUE
This is for someone who knows absolutely nothing about cards.

1. Pick a card.

2. Determine manufacturer of card. There are several different manufacturers of baseball cards and here is the best way to determine each:

BOWMAN – All cards copyrighted Bowman or B.G.H.L.I. on the back except some 1950 cards that say "No. 181 – 252 in the series of Baseball Picture Cards." 1989 and later cards say "Bowman" on the front with a red "B" over a green baseball diamond. (See page 36.)

DONRUSS – All Donruss cards have a Donruss logo on front. (See pages 70 – 71.)

FLEER – 1981 – 84 Fleer name found on back of card and from 1985 Fleer name on the front also. (See page 162.)

SCORE – Score written on the front of each year. (See page 250.)

TOPPS – 1951 cards are baseball game pieces with red or blue backs and no other identification. Topps is written somewhere on the back of all cards from 1952 – 1970 except 1958, 1959, 1960 which along with 1971 – 1975 have only copyright **T.G.C.** on the back. 1976–1978 all have Topps copyright on back and 1979 to date all have a Topps logo on the front. (See pages 299-301.)

UPPER DECK – All cards have Upper Deck logo on front and Upper Deck hologram on back. (See page 559.)

3. Turn to the alphabetical listing of the company determined in No. **2** above and find the player's name. Now look at the number of the card (found on the back of the card, usually in upper left). Find the card's number in the No. column in the book. Follow this line to give you the year and price in VG (very good) and EX/MT (excellent/mint) condition of the card. (An explanation of grading follows this section.)

4. In case of a number being the same in two years (which rarely happened) there are three choices. You can turn to the color section (pages 4 – 31) to locate the card year. You can look for a copyright, or you can look at statistical information of the previous year on the card. The latter does not always work as often the card will only say last year or lifetime stats. After a while the knowledge of which year a card was issued will become the easiest part of learning about the cards!

GRADING

Everyone thinks he has excellent or better cards, but usually those you put in the cigar or shoe box as a youngster fit the VG category *if you took some care with them.* The latest cards in an accumulation of several years are generally the ones in the best condition. It seems the older you got, the better you treated your "treasures."

There are more arguments between buyer and seller over grading than any other idea in collecting. *The grade of a card does not change whether the buyer or the seller owns the card.*

This book only prices cards in two grades because most of the cards collected over the years fit the grades VG or EX/MT.

VG — very good means a card that has been handled but not torn, cut or flawed. There may be some slight rounding of the corners and there may be gum or wax stains on the card. There may even be a hairline crease caused during manufacture. The original luster is usually gone, but there should be no tack holes, ink stains, rubber band marks or tape. The card may be slightly off center but not cut badly by the factory.

EX/MT — excellent/mint means a card that is almost perfect. The card may have a slight wear overall and may have an ever so slightly rounded corner or yellowing of the border. There should be no gum or wax stains visible. The card should be nicely centered. Early cards have to pass the same criteria as newer cards. Many forty-year-old people are in better shape than others. The same can be said for cards! Age of the card is no excuse for lowering grading standards.

There are other grades. *MINT* grading is a field unto itself. There are special boxes to measure centering. It reminds me of the old days of coin grading; so I can only say that a mint card has to be perfect in every way by today's grading standards. Most of the sets I put away as "mint" in the late 1970's would have a difficult time being graded mint today!

Cards that are less than very good are not sought by collectors or dealers unless they are harder to find cards or cards of well-known players. They have little value.

COLLECTING, SELLING and PRICING

I am often asked what to collect. In the past I have suggested buying the factory sets that most companies issued. However, only Topps has issued a 1993 set, and there may not be any others. (This is a major blow to collectors in my thinking!) If you buy the Topps factory set, *leave it sealed! Do not open it!* If you want to look at your set and play with it, then buy a regular set. The factory sets that are sealed will be like the sealed proof coins of yesteryear. If sealed, they sold repeatedly. Everyone assumed that they were perfect. If opened, there was a possibility of tarnished coins that lowered the value. The same holds true with a factory sealed baseball set. If unopened, all cards are assumed to be there in mint condition. If someone opens the set, and disproves that all the cards are there or that some are badly off-center, then the set value is greatly reduced.

Selling your cards is another story. Find a reliable dealer who will even show you what your cards are worth. Remember, a dealer has to make a profit to stay in business. Most dealers will pay from fifty to sixty percent of the retail price for star cards and cards they need. They will pay very little for cards not needed for stock or common cards. Condition of the cards is a main concern! Personally, I do not buy newer cards in less than EX/MT condition and few cards in less than VG no matter what the age. It is easier to sell mint sets of the later years, but it usually takes (waiting time) about five years to make a handsome profit. The volume of cards printed today may make that even longer for some sets. Buy any company's regular sets. The little boxed sets issued for specific stores rarely have lasting collector demand.

There are only so many of the older cards available. If you have some baseball cards packed away in a shoe box in the attic, basement or your closet, you better remove all those rubber bands and look up the values of the treasures you stored. It's time to start taking better care of them!

BOWMAN GUM, INC. 1948 – 1955; 1989 – 1993

The Bowman Company produced a black and white set of 48 cards in 1948. These cards were packed with Blony bubble gum. For a penny you got a piece of bubble gum and one card. As a child, I hated these older cards when I started collecting, because they were black and white.

The 1954 set is the easiest to complete for a new collector if card #66 is collected as Jimmy Piersall and not Ted Williams. There are two #66 cards with the Ted Williams card considered scarce. In my travels I have come to believe it is only scarce in Mint condition.

The 1955 Bowman set is the most popular and the next easiest to assemble. If you collect either the 1954 or 1955 sets in less than excellent condition, you should be able to complete either set without much difficulty.

Topps surprised the baseball card collecting world in 1989 when they announced that they were bringing back the Bowman name on a set of 484 cards measuring the same 2½" x 3½" used on many of the Bowman sets before Topps bought out the Bowman company in 1955. The Bowman name had not been used since then. The listing for these newer Bowman cards is separate from the original Bowman cards of 1948 – 55. In 1990 Topps announced that there would be a Bowman set, but that the cards would be of the standard 2½" x 3½" size. This size was continued in 1991 and 1992. 1993 Bowman cards were unavailable as we went to press.

1948 – 48 black and white cards measuring 2 1/16" x 2½" (Bowman copyright 1948 on back)
1949 – 240 cards with black and white photo on pastel background measuring 2 1/16" x 2½" (Bowman copyright 1949 on back)
1950 – 252 color cards measuring 2 1/16" x 2½" (Bowman copyright 1950 on back of most cards; some cards only say "No. 181–252 in the series of Baseball Picture Cards")
1951 – 324 color cards measuring 2 1/16" x 3⅛" (copyright Bowman 1951 back of card)
1952 – 252 color cards measuring 2 1/16" x 3⅛" (copyright 1952 Bowman Gum Division, Haelan Laboratories, Inc. back of card)
1953BC – 160 color cards measuring 2½" x 3¾" (copyright B.G.H.L.I. on back lower left corner)
1953BW – 64 black and white cards measuring 2½" x 3¾" (copyright B.G.H.L.I. on back lower left corner)
1954 – 224 color cards measuring 2½" x 3¾" (copyright B.G.H.L.I. on back top left corner)
1955 – 320 color (TV screen) cards measuring 2½" x 3¾" (copyright B.G.H.L.I. on back lower left corner)
1989 – 484 color cards measuring 2½" x 3¾" (Bowman on front with a large red B over a baseball diamond; copyright 1989 Bowman Gum, Inc. on back right corner)
1990 – 528 color cards measuring 2½" x 3½" (Bowman on front with a large red B over a baseball diamond; copyright 1990 Bowman Gum, Inc. on back right corner)
1991 – 704 color cards measuring 2½" x 3½" (Bowman on front with a large red B over a baseball diamond; copyright 1991 The Topps Company, Inc. on back right side)
1992 – 705 color cards measuring 2½" x 3½" (Bowman on front with a large red B over blue colored stripe; copyright 1992 The Topps Company, Inc. on back left side)

The only abbreviation used in the Bowman section of card listings is in the 1953 cards. As shown above I have used **BC** and **BW** to distinguish between the color and black and white cards of that year.

Although the original Bowman name was used until 1955 (nine sets issued – two in 1953), these baseball cards with a piece of bubble gum enclosed marked the beginning of many kids' fantasies of being in the Major Leagues and one day having their own picture on a card. Little did we know that Topps would again use the name that they bought out 34 years ago!

The listing for each card shown appears immediately following the photograph.

BOWMAN

Player	Year	No.	VG	EX/MT
Aaron, Hank	55B	179	$62.50	$250.00
Aber, Al	55B	24	$2.00	$8.00
Abrams, Cal	51B	152	$3.50	$14.00
Abrams, Cal	52B	86	$3.75	$15.00
Abrams, Cal	53BC	160	$20.00	$80.00
Abrams, Cal	54B	91	$2.00	$8.00
Abrams, Cal	55B	55	$2.00	$8.00
Adams, Bobby	51B	288	$15.00	$60.00
Adams, Bobby	52B	166	$3.75	$15.00
Adams, Bobby	53BC	108	$7.50	$30.00
Adams, Bobby	54B	108	$2.00	$8.00
Adams, Bobby	55B	118	$1.75	$7.00
Adcock, Joe	51B	323	$22.50	$90.00
Adcock, Joe	52B	69	$5.50	$22.00
Adcock, Joe	53BC	151	$12.50	$50.00
Adcock, Joe	54B	96	$2.50	$10.00
Adcock, Joe	55B	218	$2.00	$10.00
Addis, Bob	53BC	94	$7.50	$30.00
Aloma, Luis	51B	231	$3.50	$14.00
Aloma, Luis	54B	134	$3.50	$14.00
Alston, Tom	55B	257	$3.75	$15.00
Amalfitano, Joe	55B	269	$5.00	$20.00
Antonelli, Johnny	50B	74	$6.25	$25.00
Antonelli, Johnny	51B	243	$3.50	$14.00
Antonelli, Johnny	54B	208	$3.50	$14.00
Antonelli, Johnny	55B	124	$1.75	$7.00
Appling, Luke	49B	175	$37.50	150.00
Appling, Luke	50B	37	$20.00	$80.00
Arft, Hank	49B	139	$3.75	$15.00
Arft, Hank	51B	173	$3.50	$14.00
Arft, Hank	52B	229	$7.50	$30.00
Ashburn, Richie	49B	214	$125.00	$500.00
Ashburn, Richie	50B	84	$22.50	$90.00
Ashburn, Richie	51B	186	$15.00	$60.00
Ashburn, Richie	52B	53	$12.50	$50.00
Ashburn, Richie	53BC	10	$20.00	$80.00
Ashburn, Richie	54B	15	$7.50	$30.00
Ashburn, Richie	55B	130	$6.00	$24.00
Astroth, Joe	51B	298	$15.00	$60.00
Astroth, Joe	52B	170	$3.75	$15.00
Astroth, Joe	53BC	82	$7.50	$30.00
Astroth, Joe	54B	131	$3.50	$14.00
Astroth, Joe	55B	119	$1.75	$7.00
Atwell, Toby	53BC	112	$7.50	$30.00
Atwell, Toby	54B	123	$2.50	$10.00
Atwell, Toby	55B	164	$1.75	$7.00
Avila, Bobby	51B	188	$4.25	$17.00
Avila, Bobby	52B	167	$3.75	$15.00
Avila, Bobby	53BC	29	$7.50	$30.00
Avila, Bobby	54B	68	$2.00	$8.00
Avila, Bobby "Roberto"	55B	19	$2.00	$8.00
Baczewski, Fred	54B	60	$2.00	$8.00
Baczewski, Fred	55B	190	$1.75	$7.00
Baker, Floyd	49B	119	$3.75	$15.00
Baker, Floyd	50B	146	$4.50	$18.00
Baker, Floyd	51B	87	$3.50	$14.00
Baker, Floyd	53BW	49	$8.00	$32.00
Baker, Gene	55B	7	$2.00	$8.00
Ballanfant, E. Lee	55B	295	$6.25	$25.00
Bankhead, Dan	51B	225	$3.50	$14.00
Banks, Ernie	55B	242	$90.00	$360.00
Banta, Jack	50B	224	$4.50	$18.00
Barlick, Albert J.	55B	265	$18.75	$75.00
Barney, Rex	48B	41	$9.00	$28.00
Barney, Rex	49B	61	$6.00	$18.00
Barney, Rex	50B	76	$4.50	$18.00
Barney, Rex	51B	153	$3.50	$14.00
Barrett, Red	49B	213	$18.75	$75.00
Bartell, Dick	55B	234	$5.00	$20.00
Batts, Matt	51B	129	$3.50	$14.00
Batts, Matt	52B	216	$3.75	$15.00
Batts, Matt	53BW	22	$8.00	$32.00
Batts, Matt	54B	183	$3.50	$14.00
Batts, Matt	55B	161	$1.75	$7.00
Bauer, Hank	50B	219	$20.00	$80.00
Bauer, Hank	51B	183	$7.50	$30.00
Bauer, Hank	52B	65	$6.25	$25.00
Bauer, Hank	53BC	44	$112.50	$450.00
Bauer, Hank	53BC	84	$12.50	$50.00
Bauer, Hank	54B	129	$4.50	$18.00
Bauer, Hank	55B	246	$9.00	$36.00
Baumholtz, Frank	49B	21	$5.25	$16.00

Player	Year	No.	VG	EX/MT
Baumholtz, Frank	52B	195	$3.75	$15.00
Baumholtz, Frank	54B	221	$3.50	$14.00
Baumholtz, Frank	55B	227	$3.75	$15.00
Beard, Ralph	55B	206	$1.75	$7.00
Beard, Ted	51B	308	$15.00	$60.00
Bearden, Gene	49B	57	$6.00	$18.00
Bearden, Gene	50B	93	$4.50	$18.00
Bearden, Gene	51B	284	$15.00	$60.00
Bearden, Gene	52B	173	$3.75	$15.00
Belardi, Wayne	55B	36	$2.00	$8.00
Bell, Dave "Gus"	51B	40	$6.25	$25.00
Bell, Gus	53BW	1	$20.00	$110.00
Bell, Gus	54B	124	$2.50	$10.00
Bell, Gus	55B	243	$3.75	$15.00
Berardino, John	51B	245	$5.00	$20.00
Bernier, Carlos	54B	171	$3.50	$14.00
Berra, Larry "Yogi"	48B	6	$135.00	$550.00
Berra, Yogi	49B	60	$80.00	$325.00
Berra, Yogi	50B	46	$100.00	$400.00
Berra, Yogi	51B	2	$112.50	$450.00
Berra, Yogi	52B	1	$100.00	$600.00
Berra, Yogi	53BC	44	$112.50	$450.00
Berra, Yogi	53BC	121	$137.50	$550.00
Berra, Yogi	54B	161	$45.00	$180.00
Berra, Yogi	55B	168	$25.00	$100.00
Berry, Charles	55B	281	$6.25	$25.00
Berry, Connie "Neil"	49B	180	$18.75	$75.00
Berry, Neil	50B	241	$4.50	$18.00
Berry, Neil	51B	213	$3.50	$14.00
Berry, Neil	52B	219	$7.50	$30.00
Bevan, Hal	53BW	43	$8.00	$32.00
Bevins, Floyd	48B	22	$8.50	$35.00
Bickford, Vern	49B	1	$10.00	$85.00
Bickford, Vern	50B	57	$12.50	$50.00
Bickford, Vern	51B	42	$3.50	$14.00

BOWMAN

Player	Year	No.	VG	EX/MT
Bickford, Vern	52B	48	$3.75	$15.00
Bickford, Vern	54B	176	$3.50	$14.00
Bilko, Steve	51B	265	$15.00	$60.00
Bilko, Steve	54B	206	$3.50	$14.00
Bilko, Steve	55B	88	$2.00	$8.00
Blackburn, Jim	49B	160	$18.75	$75.00
Blackburn, Jim	51B	287	$15.00	$60.00
Blackwell, Ewell	48B	2	$12.50	$45.00
Blackwell, Ewell	50B	63	$15.00	$60.00
Blackwell, Ewell	51B	24	$6.25	$25.00
Blatnick, Johnny	49B	123	$3.75	$15.00
Blaylock, Marv	55B	292	$3.75	$15.00
Bloodworth, Jimmy	51B	185	$3.50	$14.00
Bockman, Eddie	49B	195	$18.75	$75.00
Boggess, L. R. "Dusty"	55B	297	$6.25	$25.00
Bolling, Frank	55B	204	$1.75	$7.00
Bolling, Milt	54B	130	$3.50	$14.00
Bolling, Milt	55B	48	$2.00	$8.00
Bollweg, Don	54B	115	$2.50	$10.00
Bollweg, Don	55B	54	$2.00	$8.00
Bonham, Ernie	49B	77	$3.75	$15.00
Boone, Ray	51B	54	$6.25	$25.00
Boone, Ray	52B	214	$3.75	$15.00
Boone, Ray	53BC	79	$7.50	$30.00
Borowy, Hank	49B	134	$3.75	$15.00
Borowy, Hank	50B	177	$4.50	$18.00
Borowy, Hank	51B	250	$3.50	$14.00
Boudreau, Lou	49B	11	$16.25	$65.00
Boudreau, Lou	50B	94	$12.50	$50.00
Boudreau, Lou	51B	62	$11.25	$45.00
Boudreau, Lou	53BC	57	$12.50	$50.00
Boudreau, Lou	55B	89	$5.00	$20.00
Bowman, Roger	55B	115	$1.75	$7.00
Boyd, Bob	54B	118	$2.50	$10.00
Boyer, Cloyd	51B	228	$3.50	$14.00
Boyer, Cloyd	53BC	115	$12.50	$50.00
Boyer, Cloyd	55B	149	$1.75	$7.00
Branca, Ralph	49B	194	$27.50	$110.00
Branca, Ralph	50B	59	$15.00	$60.00
Branca, Ralph	51B	56	$6.25	$25.00
Branca, Ralph	52B	96	$4.50	$18.00
Branca, Ralph	53BW	52	$8.00	$32.00
Brazle, Al	49B	126	$3.75	$15.00
Brazle, Al	50B	126	$4.50	$18.00
Brazle, Al	51B	157	$3.50	$14.00
Brazle, Al	52B	134	$3.75	$15.00
Brazle, Alpha	53BC	140	$11.25	$45.00
Brazle, Al	54B	142	$3.50	$14.00
Brazle, Al	55B	230	$3.75	$15.00
Brecheen, Harry	49B	158	$20.00	$80.00
Brecheen, Harry	50B	90	$4.50	$18.00
Brecheen, Harry	51B	86	$3.50	$14.00
Brecheen, Harry	52B	176	$3.75	$15.00
Brewer, Tom	55B	178	$1.75	$7.00
Brideweser, Jim	53BC	136	$11.25	$45.00
Brideweser, Jim	55B	151	$1.75	$7.00
Bridges, Rocky	53BW	32	$8.00	$32.00
Bridges, Rocky	54B	156	$3.50	$14.00
Bridges, Rocky	55B	136	$1.75	$7.00
Brissie, Leland "Lou"	49B	41	$6.00	$18.00
Brissie, Lou	50B	48	$12.50	$50.00
Brissie, Lou	51B	155	$3.50	$14.00
Brissie, Lou	52B	79	$3.75	$15.00
Brosnan, Jim	55B	229	$5.00	$20.00
Brown, Bobby	49B	19	$13.75	$55.00
Brown, Bobby	50B	101	$7.50	$30.00
Brown, Bobby	51B	110	$7.50	$30.00
Brown, Bobby	52B	105	$6.25	$25.00
Brown, Hector "Skinny"	55B	221	$1.75	$7.00
Brown, Tom	49B	178	$18.75	$75.00
Brown, Tommy	52B	236	$7.50	$30.00
Brown, Tommy	53BC	42	$7.50	$30.00
Bruton, Bill	54B	224	$10.00	$40.00
Bruton, Bill	55B	11	$2.00	$8.00
Bucha, Johnny	54B	215	$3.50	$14.00
Buhl, Bob	55B	43	$2.00	$8.00
Burdette, Lou	52B	244	$15.00	$60.00
Burdette, Lou	53BW	51	$12.50	$50.00
Burdette, Lou	54B	192	$4.50	$18.00
Burdette, Lou	55B	70	$2.50	$10.00
Burgess, Forrest	51B	317	$20.00	$80.00
Burgess, Forrest "Smokey"	52B	112	$4.50	$18.00
Burgess, Forrest "Smoky"	53BC	28	$8.75	$35.00
Burgess, Forrest "Smokey"	54B	31	$2.50	$10.00
Burgess, Forrest "Smoky"	55B	209	$2.00	$8.00
Burtschy, Ed	55B	120	$1.75	$7.00
Busby, Jim	51B	302	$15.00	$60.00
Busby, Jim	52B	68	$3.75	$15.00
Busby, Jim	53BC	15	$7.50	$30.00
Busby, Jim	54B	8	$2.00	$8.00
Busby, Jim	55B	166	$1.75	$7.00
Byrd, Harry	53BC	38	$7.50	$30.00
Byrd, Harry	54B	49	$2.00	$8.00
Byrd, Harry	55B	159	$1.75	$7.00
Byrne, Tommy	51B	73	$3.50	$14.00
Byrne, Tommy	52B	61	$3.75	$15.00
Byrne, Tommy	55B	300	$3.75	$15.00
Cain, Bob	50B	236	$4.50	$18.00
Cain, Bob	51B	197	$3.50	$14.00
Cain, Bob	52B	19	$4.50	$18.00
Cain, Bob	53BC	56	$7.50	$30.00
Cain, Bob	54B	195	$3.50	$14.00
Campanella, Roy	49B	84	$175.00	$700.00
Campanella, Roy	50B	75	$70.00	$280.00
Campanella, Roy	51B	31	$65.00	$260.00
Campanella, Roy	52B	44	$50.00	$200.00

Player	Year	No.	VG	EX/MT
Campanella, Roy	**53BC**	**46**	**$62.50**	**$250.00**
Campanella, Roy	54B	90	$35.00	$140.00
Campanella, Roy	55B	22	$25.00	$100.00
Candini, Milo	51B	255	$15.00	$60.00
Carrasquel, Alfonso Chico	51B	60	$6.25	$25.00
Carrasquel, Chico	52B	41	$3.75	$15.00
Carrasquel, Chico	53BC	54	$7.50	$30.00

BOWMAN

Player	Year	No.	VG	EX/MT	Player	Year	No.	VG	EX/MT
Carrasquel, Chico	54B	54	$2.00	$8.00	Cooper, Walker	48B	9	$7.00	$20.00
Carrasquel, Al "Chico"	55B	173	$1.75	$7.00	Cooper, Walker	49B	117	$3.75	$15.00
Casey, Hugh	49B	179	$18.75	$75.00	Cooper, Walker	50B	111	$4.50	$18.00
Castiglione, Pete	51B	17	$6.00	$20.00	Cooper, Walker	51B	135	$3.50	$14.00
Castiglione, Pete	52B	47	$3.75	$15.00	Cooper, Walker	52B	208	$3.75	$15.00
Castiglione, Pete	54B	174	$3.50	$14.00	Cooper, Walker	53BW	30	$8.00	$32.00
Cavarretta, Phil	49B	6	$6.25	$20.00	Corwin, Al	52B	121	$3.75	$15.00
Cavarretta (Cavaretta), Phil	50B	195	$5.00	$20.00	Corwin, Al	53BC	126	$12.50	$50.00
Cavarretta, Phil	51B	138	$4.25	$17.00	Corwin, Al	53BC	149	$11.25	$45.00
Cavarretta, Phil	52B	126	$4.50	$18.00	Corwin, Al	54B	137	$3.50	$14.00
Cavarretta, Phil	53BC	30	$8.75	$35.00	Corwin, Al	55B	122	$1.75	$7.00
Cavarretta, Phil	55B	282	$5.00	$20.00	Courtney, Clint	53BC	70	$7.50	$30.00
Cerv, Bob	55B	306	$5.50	$22.00	Courtney, Clint	54B	69	$2.00	$8.00
Chakales, Bob	55B	148	$1.75	$7.00	Courtney, Clint	55B	34	$2.00	$8.00
Chambers, Cliff	50B	202	$4.50	$18.00	Cox, Billy	49B	73	$7.50	$30.00
Chambers, Cliff	51B	131	$3.50	$14.00	Cox, Billy	50B	194	$5.00	$20.00
Chambers, Cliff	52B	14	$4.50	$18.00	Cox, Billy	51B	224	$4.00	$16.00
Chambers, Cliff	54B	126	$2.50	$10.00	Cox, Billy	52B	152	$3.75	$15.00
Chapman, Sam	49B	112	$3.75	$15.00	Cox, Billy	53BW	60	$10.00	$40.00
Chapman, Sam	50B	104	$4.50	$18.00	Cox, Billy	54B	26	$2.50	$10.00
Chapman, Sam	51B	9	$6.00	$20.00	Cox, Billy	55B	56	$2.00	$8.00
Chesnes, Bob	49B	13	$5.25	$16.00	Crandall, Del	50B	56	$15.00	$60.00
Chesnes, Bob	50B	70	$12.50	$50.00	Crandall, Del	51B	20	$6.00	$20.00
Chipman, Bob	49B	184	$18.75	$75.00	Crandall, Del	54B	32	$2.00	$8.00
Chipman, Bob	50B	192	$4.50	$18.00	Crandall, Del	55B	217	$1.75	$7.00
Chipman, Bob	52B	228	$7.50	$30.00	Crawford, Rufus	55B	121	$1.75	$7.00
Chiti, Harry	53BC	7	$7.50	$30.00	Crosetti, Frank	52B	252	$30.00	$160.00
Chiti, Harry	55B	304	$3.75	$15.00	Cusick, John	52B	192	$3.75	$15.00
Christman, Mark	49B	121	$3.75	$15.00	Daniels, Jack	53BC	83	$7.50	$30.00
Church, Emory "Bubba"	51B	149	$3.50	$14.00	Dark, Al	49B	67	$7.50	$30.00
Church, Bubba	52B	40	$3.75	$15.00	Dark, Al	50B	64	$15.00	$60.00
Church, Bubba	53BC	138	$11.25	$45.00	Dark, Al	51B	14	$6.25	$25.00
Church, Bubba	55B	273	$3.75	$15.00	Dark, Al	52B	34	$6.00	$24.00
Chylak, Nestor	55B	283	$6.25	$25.00	Dark, Al	53BC	19	$8.75	$35.00
Clark, Allie	49B	150	$18.75	$75.00	Dark, Al	54B	41	$2.50	$10.00
Clark, Allie	50B	233	$4.50	$18.00	Dark, Al "Alwin"	55B	2	$2.50	$10.00
Clark, Allie	51B	29	$6.00	$20.00	Darnell, Bob	55B	39	$2.00	$8.00
Clark, Allie	52B	130	$3.75	$15.00	Dascoli, Frank	55B	291	$6.25	$25.00
Clark, Allie	53BC	155	$11.25	$45.00	De Maestri, Joe	54B	147	$3.50	$14.00
Clark, Mel	53BC	67	$7.50	$30.00	De Maestri, Joe	55B	176	$1.75	$7.00
Clark, Mel	54B	175	$3.50	$14.00	Delock, Ivan	52B	250	$7.50	$30.00
Clark, Mel	55B	41	$2.00	$8.00	Delock, Ivan	55B	276	$3.75	$15.00
Coan, Gil	49B	90	$3.75	$15.00	Delsing, Jim	51B	279	$15.00	$60.00
Coan, Gil	50B	54	$12.50	$50.00	Delsing, Jim	52B	157	$3.75	$15.00
Coan, Gil	51B	18	$6.00	$20.00	Delsing, Jim	53BW	44	$8.00	$32.00
Coan, Gil	52B	51	$3.75	$15.00	Delsing, Jim	54B	55	$2.00	$8.00
Coan, Gil	53BC	34	$7.50	$30.00	Delsing, Jim	55B	274	$3.75	$15.00
Coan, Gil	54B	40	$2.00	$8.00	DeMars, Billy	50B	252	$15.00	$60.00
Coan, Gil	55B	78	$2.00	$8.00	DeMars, Billy	51B	43	$3.50	$14.00
Cole, Dave	52B	132	$3.75	$15.00	Dente, Sam	50B	107	$4.50	$18.00
Cole, Dave	53BW	38	$8.00	$32.00	Dente, Sam	51B	133	$3.50	$14.00
Cole, Dick	54B	27	$2.00	$8.00	Dente, Sam	53BC	137	$11.25	$45.00
Cole, Dick	55B	28	$2.00	$8.00	Dickey, Bill	51B	290	$43.75	$175.00
Coleman, Gerry (Jerry)	49B	225	$22.50	$90.00	Dickson, Murry	49B	8	$5.25	$16.00
Coleman, Jerry	50B	47	$15.00	$60.00	Dickson, Murry	50B	34	$12.50	$50.00
Coleman, Jerry	51B	49	$3.50	$14.00	Dickson, Murry	51B	167	$3.50	$14.00
Coleman, Jerry	52B	73	$3.75	$15.00	Dickson, Murry	52B	59	$3.75	$15.00
Coleman, Jerry	54B	81	$2.00	$8.00	Dickson, Murry	54B	111	$2.00	$8.00
Coleman, Jerry	55B	99	$1.75	$7.00	Dickson, Murry	55B	236	$3.75	$15.00
Coleman, Joe	50B	141	$4.50	$18.00	Diering, Charles "Chuck"	50B	179	$4.50	$18.00
Coleman, Joe	51B	120	$3.50	$14.00	Diering, Chuck	51B	158	$3.50	$14.00
Coleman, Joe	55B	3	$2.00	$8.00	Diering, Chuck	52B	198	$3.75	$15.00
Coleman, Ray	50B	250	$4.50	$18.00	Dillinger, Bob	49B	143	$5.00	$20.00
Coleman, Ray	51B	136	$3.50	$14.00	Dillinger, Bob	50B	105	$4.50	$18.00
Coleman, Ray	52B	201	$3.75	$15.00	Dillinger, Bob	51B	63	$3.50	$14.00
Collins, Joe	52B	181	$3.75	$15.00	DiMaggio, Dom	49B	64	$7.50	$30.00
Collum, Jack	54B	204	$3.50	$14.00	DiMaggio, Dom	50B	3	$16.25	$65.00
Collum, Jack	55B	189	$1.75	$7.00	Ditmar, Art	55B	90	$2.00	$8.00
Conlan, J. B. "Jocko"	55B	303	$22.50	$90.00	Dittmer, Jack	54B	48	$2.00	$8.00
Consuegra, Sandalio	51B	96	$3.50	$14.00	Dittmer, Jack	55B	212	$1.75	$7.00
Consuegra, Sandalio	52B	143	$3.75	$15.00	Dixon, Hal H.	55B	309	$6.25	$25.00
Consuegra, "Sandy"	53BC	89	$7.50	$30.00	Dixon, John "Sonny"	55B	211	$1.75	$7.00
Consuegra, Sandy	54B	166	$3.50	$14.00	Dobernic, Jess	49B	200	$18.75	$75.00
Consuegra, Sandy	55B	116	$1.75	$7.00	Dobson, Joe	49B	7	$5.25	$16.00
Coogan, Dale	50B	244	$4.50	$18.00	Dobson, Joe	50B	44	$12.50	$50.00

BOWMAN

Player	Year	No.	VG	EX/MT	Player	Year	No.	VG	EX/MT
Dobson, Joe	51B	36	$6.00	$20.00	Evers, Walter	53BC	25	$7.50	$30.00
Dobson, Joe	53BC	88	$7.50	$30.00	Evers, Walter "Hoot"	54B	18	$2.00	$8.00
Doby, Larry	49B	233	$40.00	$160.00	Fain, Ferris	48B	21	$7.00	$20.00
Doby, Larry	50B	39	$16.25	$65.00	Fain, Ferris	49B	9	$5.25	$16.00
Doby, Larry	51B	151	$6.25	$25.00	Fain, Ferris	50B	13	$12.50	$50.00
Doby, Larry	52B	115	$6.00	$24.00	Fain, Ferris	52B	154	$3.75	$15.00
Doby, Larry	53BC	40	$11.25	$45.00	Fain, Ferris	54B	214	$3.50	$14.00
Doby, Larry	54B	84	$3.50	$14.00	Fannin, Cliff	49B	120	$3.75	$15.00
Doerr, Bobby	49B	23	$16.25	$65.00	Fannin, Cliff	50B	106	$4.50	$18.00
Doerr, Bobby	50B	43	$22.50	$90.00	Fannin, Cliff	51B	244	$3.50	$14.00
Donatelli, A. J.	55B	313	$8.75	$35.00	Feller, Bob	48B	5	$65.00	$225.00
Donnelly, Sylvester	49B	145	$18.75	$75.00	Feller, Bob	49B	27	$45.00	$180.00
Donnelly, Sylvester	50B	176	$4.50	$18.00	Feller, Bob	50B	6	$50.00	$200.00
Donnelly, Sylvester "Blix"	51B	208	$3.50	$14.00	Feller, Bob	51B	30	$33.75	$135.00
Dorish, Harry	51B	266	$15.00	$60.00	Feller, Bob	52B	43	$30.00	$120.00
Dorish, Harry	54B	86	$2.00	$8.00	Feller, Bob	53BC	114	$80.00	$320.00
Dorish, Harry	55B	248	$3.75	$15.00	Feller, Bob	54B	132	$22.50	$90.00
Dressen, Charlie	51B	259	$18.75	$75.00	Feller, Bob	55B	134	$15.00	$60.00
Dressen, Charlie	52B	188	$3.75	$15.00	Fernandez, Chico	55B	270	$3.75	$15.00
Dressen, Charlie	53BC	124	$15.00	$60.00	Ferrick, Tom	51B	182	$3.50	$14.00
Drews, Karl	49B	188	$18.75	$75.00	Ferriss, Boo	49B	211	$18.75	$75.00
Drews, Karl	53BC	113	$12.50	$50.00	Fitzgerald, Ed	49B	109	$3.75	$15.00
Drews, Karl	54B	191	$3.50	$14.00	Fitzgerald, Ed	50B	178	$4.50	$18.00
Dropo, Walt	50B	246	$6.25	$25.00	Fitzgerald, Ed	52B	180	$3.75	$15.00
Dropo, Walt	52B	169	$3.75	$15.00	Fitzgerald, Ed	54B	168	$3.50	$14.00
Dropo, Walt	53BC	45	$7.50	$30.00	Fitzgerald, Eddy	55B	208	$1.75	$7.00
Dropo, Walt	54B	7	$2.00	$8.00	Fitzsimmons, Fred	52B	234	$7.50	$30.00
Dropo, Walt	55B	285	$3.75	$15.00	Flaherty, John	55B	272	$6.25	$25.00
Dubiel, Walt	51B	283	$15.00	$60.00	Flowers, Bennett	55B	254	$3.75	$15.00
Durocher, Leo	50B	220	$15.00	$60.00	Fondy, Dee	52B	231	$7.50	$30.00
Durocher, Leo	51B	233	$12.50	$50.00	Fondy, Dee	53BW	5	$8.00	$32.00
Durocher, Leo	52B	146	$12.00	$48.00	Fondy, Dee	54B	173	$3.50	$14.00
Durocher, Leo	53BC	55	$12.50	$50.00	Fondy, Dee	55B	224	$1.75	$7.00
Dusak, Erv	51B	310	$15.00	$60.00	Ford, Ed "Whitey"	51B	1	$312.50	$1250.00
Dyck, Jim	53BC	111	$7.50	$30.00	Ford, Ed "Whitey"	53BC	153	$110.00	$440.00
Dyck, Jim	54B	85	$2.00	$8.00	Ford, Ed "Whitey"	54B	177	$27.50	$110.00
Dykes, Jimmy	51B	226	$4.00	$16.00	Ford, Ed "Whitey"	55B	59	$17.50	$70.00
Dykes, Jimmy	52B	98	$4.50	$18.00	Fornieles, Mike	55B	266	$3.75	$15.00
Dykes, Jimmy	53BC	31	$8.75	$35.00	Fowler, Dick	49B	171	$18.75	$75.00
Early, Jake	49B	106	$3.75	$15.00	Fowler, Dick	50B	214	$4.50	$18.00
Easter, Luke	51B	258	$17.50	$70.00	Fowler, Dick	52B	190	$3.75	$15.00
Easter, Luke	52B	95	$3.75	$15.00	Fox, Howard "Howie"	50B	80	$4.50	$18.00
Easter, Luke	53BC	104	$7.50	$30.00	Fox, Howie	51B	180	$3.50	$14.00
Easter, Luke	54B	116	$2.50	$10.00	Fox, Howie	52B	125	$3.75	$15.00
Edwards, Bruce	48B	43	$9.00	$28.00	Fox, Howie	53BC	158	$11.25	$45.00
Edwards, Bruce	49B	206	$18.75	$75.00	Fox, Nelson "Nellie"	51B	232	$32.50	$130.00
Edwards, Bruce	50B	165	$4.50	$18.00	Fox, Nellie	52B	21	$11.25	$45.00
Edwards, Bruce	51B	116	$3.50	$14.00	Fox, Nellie	53BC	18	$15.00	$60.00
Edwards, Bruce	52B	88	$3.75	$15.00	Fox, Nellie	54B	6	$4.00	$20.00
Edwards, Hank	49B	136	$3.75	$15.00	Fox, Nellie	55B	33	$4.00	$20.00
Edwards, Hank	50B	169	$4.50	$18.00	Freeman, Hershell	55B	290	$3.75	$15.00
Edwards, Hank	52B	141	$3.75	$15.00	Freese, George	55B	84	$2.00	$8.00
Elliott, Bob	48B	1	30.00	$100.00	Fricano, Marion	54B	3	$2.00	$8.00
Elliott, Bob	49B	58	$6.00	$18.00	Fricano, Marion	55B	316	$3.75	$15.00
Elliott, Bob	50B	20	$12.50	$50.00	Friend, Bob	52B	191	$5.00	$20.00
Elliott, Bob	51B	66	$3.50	$14.00	Friend, Bob	53BC	16	$8.75	$35.00
Engeln, William R.	55B	301	$6.25	$25.00	Friend, Bob	54B	43	$3.25	$11.00
Ennis, Del	50B	31	$15.00	$60.00	Friend, Bob	55B	57	$2.00	$8.00
Ennis, Del	51B	4	$6.00	$20.00	Friend, Owen	50B	189	$4.50	$18.00
Ennis, Del	52B	76	$3.75	$15.00	Friend, Owen	51B	101	$3.50	$14.00
Ennis, Del	53BC	103	$7.50	$30.00	Friend, Owen	54B	212	$3.50	$14.00
Ennis, Del	54B	127	$2.50	$10.00	Friend, Owen	55B	256	$3.75	$15.00
Ennis, Del	55B	17	$2.00	$8.00	Frisch, Frank	50B	229	$11.25	$45.00
Erskine, Carl	51B	260	$30.00	$120.00	Frisch, Frank	51B	282	$22.50	$90.00
Erskine, Carl	52B	70	$6.25	$25.00	Furillo, Carl	49B	70	$17.50	$70.00
Erskine, Carl	53BC	12	$10.00	$40.00	Furillo, Carl	50B	58	$15.00	$60.00
Erskine, Carl	54B	10	$3.50	$14.00	Furillo, Carl	51B	81	$8.75	$35.00
Erskine, Carl	55B	170	$4.00	$16.00	Furillo, Carl	52B	24	$8.00	$32.00
Evans, Al	49B	132	$3.75	$15.00	Furillo, Carl	53BC	78	$12.50	$50.00
Evans, Al	50B	144	$4.50	$18.00	Furillo, Carl	54B	122	$4.50	$18.00
Evans, Al	51B	38	$3.50	$14.00	Furillo, Carl	55B	169	$4.00	$16.00
Evers, Hoot	49B	42	$6.00	$18.00	Galan, Augie	48B	39	$9.00	$28.00
Evers, Walter	50B	41	$12.50	$50.00	Galan, Augie	49B	230	$18.75	$75.00
Evers, Walter	51B	23	$6.00	$20.00	Garagiola, Joe	51B	122	$35.00	$140.00
Evers, Walter	52B	111	$3.75	$15.00	Garagiola, Joe	52B	27	$17.50	$70.00

BOWMAN

Player	Year	No.	VG	EX/MT
Garagiola, Joe	53BC	21	$17.50	$70.00
Garagiola, Joe	54B	141	$11.25	$45.00
Garcia, Mike	50B	147	$4.50	$18.00
Garcia, Mike	51B	150	$3.50	$14.00
Garcia, Mike	52B	7	$4.50	$18.00
Garcia, Mike	53BC	43	$7.50	$30.00
Garcia, Mike	54B	100	$2.50	$10.00
Garcia, Mike	55B	128	$1.75	$7.00
Gardner, Billy	55B	249	$6.25	$25.00
Garver, Ned	49B	15	$5.25	$16.00
Garver, Ned	50B	51	$12.50	$50.00
Garver, Ned	51B	172	$3.50	$14.00
Garver, Ned	52B	29	$4.50	$18.00
Garver, Ned	53BC	47	$7.50	$30.00
Garver, Ned	54B	39	$3.25	$11.00
Garver, Ned	55B	188	$1.75	$7.00
Gernert, Dick	53BW	11	$8.00	$32.00
Gernert, Dick	54B	146	$3.50	$14.00
Gettel, Allen	51B	304	$15.00	$60.00
Giel, Paul	55B	125	$1.75	$7.00
Gilbert, Harold	50B	235	$4.50	$18.00
Gilliam, James "Junior"	54B	74	$4.50	$18.00
Gilliam, Junior	55B	98	$4.00	$16.00
Ginsberg, Joe	53BC	6	$7.50	$30.00
Ginsberg, Joe	54B	52	$2.00	$8.00
Glaviano, Tommy	51B	301	$15.00	$60.00
Goetz, Lawrence J.	55B	311	$6.25	$25.00
Goliat, Mike	50B	205	$4.50	$18.00
Goliat, Mike	51B	77	$3.50	$14.00
Goodman, Billy	49B	39	$6.00	$18.00
Goodman, Billy	50B	99	$4.50	$18.00
Goodman, Billy	51B	237	$3.50	$14.00
Goodman, Billy	52B	81	$3.75	$15.00
Goodman, Billy	53BC	148	$12.00	$48.00
Goodman, Billy	54B	82	$2.00	$8.00
Goodman, Billy	55B	126	$1.75	$7.00
Gordon, Joe	49B	210	$25.00	$100.00
Gordon, Joe	50B	129	$5.00	$20.00
Gordon, Sid	48B	27	$7.00	$20.00
Gordon, Sid	49B	101	$3.75	$15.00
Gordon, Sid	50B	109	$4.50	$18.00
Gordon, Sid	51B	19	$6.00	$20.00
Gordon, Sid	52B	60	$3.75	$15.00
Gordon, Sid	53BC	5	$7.50	$30.00
Gordon, Sid	54B	11	$2.00	$8.00
Gordon, Sid	55B	163	$1.75	$7.00
Gore, Arthur J.	55B	289	$6.25	$25.00
Gorman, Thomas D.	55B	293	$6.25	$25.00
Gorman, Tom	53BW	61	$8.00	$32.00
Gorman, Tom	54B	17	$2.00	$8.00
Graham, Jack	50B	145	$4.50	$18.00
Grammas, Alex	55B	186	$1.75	$7.00
Grasso, Mickey	51B	205	$3.50	$14.00
Grasso, Mickey	52B	174	$3.75	$15.00
Grasso, Mickey	53BC	77	$7.50	$30.00
Grasso, Mickey	54B	184	$3.50	$14.00
Gray, Ted	49B	10	$5.25	$10.00
Gray, Ted	50B	210	$4.50	$18.00
Gray, Ted	51B	178	$3.50	$14.00
Gray, Ted	52B	199	$3.75	$15.00
Gray, Ted	53BC	72	$7.50	$30.00
Gray, Ted	54B	71	$2.00	$8.00
Gray, Ted	55B	86	$2.00	$8.00
Greengrass, Jim	54B	28	$2.00	$8.00
Greengrass, Jim	55B	49	$2.00	$8.00
Greenwood, Bob	55B	42	$2.00	$8.00
Grieve, William T.	55B	275	$6.25	$25.00
Grim, Bob	55B	167	$2.50	$10.00
Grimm, Charlie	53BC	69	$8.75	$35.00
Grimm, Charlie	55B	298	$5.00	$20.00
Grissom, Marv	55B	123	$1.75	$7.00
Gromek, Steve	49B	198	$18.75	$75.00
Gromek, Steve	50B	131	$4.50	$18.00
Gromek, Steve	51B	115	$3.50	$14.00
Gromek, Steve	52B	203	$3.75	$15.00
Gromek, Steve	53BW	63	$8.00	$32.00
Gromek, Steve	54B	199	$3.50	$14.00
Gromek, Steve	55B	203	$1.75	$7.00
Groth, Johnny	50B	243	$4.50	$18.00
Groth, Johnny	51B	249	$3.50	$14.00
Groth, Johnny	52B	67	$3.75	$15.00
Groth, Johnny	54B	165	$3.50	$14.00
Groth, Johnny	55B	117	$1.75	$7.00
Guerra, Mickey "Mike"	49B	155	$18.75	$75.00
Guerra, Mike	50B	157	$4.50	$18.00
Guerra, Mike	51B	202	$3.50	$14.00
Gumbert, Harry	49B	192	$18.75	$75.00
Gumbert, Harry	50B	171	$4.50	$18.00
Gumpert, Randy	49B	87	$3.75	$15.00
Gumpert, Randy	50B	184	$4.50	$18.00

RANDY GUMPERT

Gumpert, Randy	51B	59	$3.50	$14.00
Gumpert, Randy	52B	106	$3.75	$15.00
Gustine, Frank	49B	99	$3.75	$15.00
Hacker, Warren	51B	318	$15.00	$60.00
Hacker, Warren	53BC	144	$11.25	$45.00
Hacker, Warren	54B	125	$2.50	$10.00
Hacker, Warren	55B	8	$2.00	$8.00
Haefner, Mickey	49B	144	$3.75	$15.00
Haefner, Mickey	50B	183	$4.50	$18.00
Hall, Bob	55B	113	$1.75	$7.00
Hamner, Granny	50B	204	$4.50	$18.00
Hamner, Granny	51B	148	$3.50	$14.00
Hamner, Granny	52B	35	$4.50	$18.00
Hamner, Granny	53BC	60	$7.50	$30.00
Hamner, Granny	54B	47	$2.00	$8.00
Hamner, "Granville" Granny	55B	112	$1.75	$7.00
Hamner, Ralph	49B	212	$18.75	$75.00
Hansen, Andy	53BW	64	$12.50	$50.00
Harris, Bucky	51B	275	$20.00	$80.00
Harris, Bucky	52B	158	$6.25	$25.00
Harris, Bucky	53BW	46	$12.50	$50.00
Harris, Mickey	49B	151	$18.75	$75.00
Harris, Mickey	50B	160	$4.50	$18.00
Harris, Mickey	51B	311	$15.00	$60.00
Harris, Mickey	52B	135	$3.75	$15.00

BOWMAN

Player	Year	No.	VG	EX/MT
Hartsfield, Roy	51B	277	$15.00	$60.00
Hartsfield, Roy	52B	28	$4.50	$18.00
Hartung, Clint	48B	37	$9.00	$28.00
Hartung, Clint	49B	154	$18.75	$75.00
Hartung, Clint	50B	118	$4.50	$18.00
Hartung, Clint	51B	234	$3.50	$14.00
Hatfield, Fred	52B	153	$3.75	$15.00
Hatfield, Fred	53BC	125	$12.50	$50.00
Hatfield, Fred	54B	119	$2.50	$10.00
Hatfield, Fred	55B	187	$1.75	$7.00
Hatten, Joe	49B	116	$3.75	$15.00
Hatten, Joe	50B	166	$4.50	$18.00
Hatten, Joe	51B	190	$3.50	$14.00
Hatten, Joe	52B	144	$3.75	$15.00
Hatton, Grady	49B	62	$6.00	$18.00
Hatton, Grady	50B	26	$12.50	$50.00
Hatton, Grady	51B	47	$3.50	$14.00
Hawes, Roy Lee	55B	268	$3.75	$15.00
Haynes, Joe	49B	191	$18.75	$75.00
Haynes, Joe	51B	240	$3.50	$14.00
Haynes, Joe	52B	103	$3.75	$15.00
Hearn, Jim	49B	190	$18.75	$75.00
Hearn, Jim	50B	208	$4.50	$18.00
Hearn, Jim	51B	61	$3.50	$14.00
Hearn, Jim	52B	49	$3.75	$15.00
Hearn, Jim	53BC	76	$7.50	$30.00
Hearn, Jim	55B	220	$1.75	$7.00
Heath, Jeff	49B	169	$18.75	$75.00
Hegan, Jim	50B	7	$12.50	$50.00
Hegan, Jim	51B	79	$3.50	$14.00
Hegan, Jim	52B	187	$3.75	$15.00
Hegan, Jim	53BC	102	$7.50	$30.00
Heintzelman, Ken	49B	108	$3.75	$15.00
Heintzelman, Ken	50B	85	$4.50	$18.00
Heintzelman, Ken	51B	147	$3.50	$14.00
Heintzelman, Ken	52B	148	$3.75	$15.00
Henrich, Tommy	49B	69	$7.50	$30.00
Henrich, Tommy	50B	10	$15.00	$60.00
Henrich, Tommy	51B	291	$17.50	$70.00
Henry, Bill	55B	264	$3.75	$15.00
Hermanski, Gene	49B	20	$5.25	$16.00
Hermanski, Gene	50B	113	$4.50	$18.00
Hermanski, Gene	51B	55	$3.50	$14.00
Hermanski, Gene	52B	136	$3.75	$15.00
Higbe, Kirby	49B	215	$18.75	$75.00
Higbe, Kirby	50B	200	$4.50	$18.00
Hiller, Frank	52B	114	$3.75	$15.00
Hitchcock, Billy	51B	191	$3.50	$14.00
Hitchcock, Billy	52B	89	$3.75	$15.00
Hoak, Don	55B	21	$2.50	$10.00
Hoderlein, Mel	54B	120	$2.50	$10.00
Hodges, Gil	49B	100	$55.00	$220.00
Hodges, Gil	50B	112	$22.50	$90.00
Hodges, Gil	51B	7	$20.00	$80.00
Hodges, Gil	52B	80	$16.25	$65.00
Hodges, Gil	53BC	92	$30.00	$120.00
Hodges, Gil	54B	138	$16.25	$65.00
Hodges, Gil	55B	158	$10.00	$40.00
Hoeft, Billy	53BW	18	$10.00	$40.00
Hoeft, Billy	54B	167	$3.50	$14.00
Hoffman, Bobby	49B	223	$18.75	$75.00
Holcombe, Ken	51B	267	$15.00	$60.00
Holmes, Tommy	49B	72	$6.00	$18.00
Holmes, Tommy	50B	110	$4.50	$18.00
Honochick, George "Jim"	55B	267	$17.75	$75.00
Hooper, Bob	51B	33	$6.00	$20.00
Hooper, Bob	52B	10	$4.50	$18.00
Hooper, Bob	54B	4	$2.00	$8.00
Hooper, Bob	55B	271	$3.75	$15.00
Hopp, Johnny	49B	207	$22.50	$90.00
Hopp, Johnny	50B	122	$4.50	$18.00
Hopp, Johnny	51B	146	$3.50	$14.00
Houtteman, Art	50B	42	$12.50	$50.00
Houtteman, Art	51B	45	$3.50	$14.00
Houtteman, Art	53BC	4	$7.50	$30.00
Houtteman, Art	54B	20	$2.00	$8.00
Houtteman, Art	55B	144	$1.75	$7.00
Howard, Elston	55B	68	$15.00	$60.00
Howell, Homer "Dixie"	51B	252	$3.50	$14.00
Howell, Homer "Dixie"	52B	222	$7.50	$30.00
Howerton, Bill	50B	239	$4.50	$18.00
Howerton, Bill	51B	229	$3.50	$14.00
Howerton, Bill	52B	119	$3.75	$15.00
Hubbard, Cal	55B	315	$22.50	$90.00
Hudson, Sid	50B	17	$12.50	$50.00
Hudson, Sid	51B	169	$3.50	$14.00
Hudson, Sid	52B	123	$3.75	$15.00
Hudson, Sid	53BW	29	$8.00	$32.00
Hudson, Sid	54B	194	$3.50	$14.00
Hudson, Sid	55B	318	$3.75	$15.00
Hughes, Jim	55B	156	$1.75	$7.00
Hughson, Tex	49B	199	$18.75	$75.00
Hunter, Bill	54B	5	$2.00	$8.00
Hunter, Bill	55B	69	$2.00	$8.00
Hurley, Edwin H.	55B	260	$6.25	$25.00
Hutchinson, Fred	49B	196	$25.00	$100.00
Hutchinson, Fred	50B	151	$5.00	$20.00
Hutchinson, Fred	51B	141	$4.25	$17.00
Hutchinson, Fred	52B	3	$5.50	$22.00
Hutchinson, Fred	53BC	132	$12.00	$48.00
Irvin, Monte	51B	198	$25.00	$100.00
Irvin, Monte	52B	162	$10.00	$40.00
Irvin, Monte	53BC	51	$12.50	$50.00
Jackowski, William A.	55B	284	$6.25	$25.00
Jackson, Ransom "Randy"	52B	175	$3.75	$15.00
Jackson, Randy	53BW	12	$8.00	$32.00
Jackson, Randy	54B	189	$3.50	$14.00
Jackson, Randy	55B	87	$2.00	$8.00
Janowicz, Vic	54B	203	$4.50	$18.00
Janowicz, Vic	55B	114	$2.25	$9.00
Jansen, Larry	48B	23	$7.00	$20.00

Player	Year	No.	VG	EX/MT
Hemus, Solly	**52B**	**212**	**$3.75**	**$15.00**
Hemus, Solly	53BC	85	$7.50	$30.00
Hemus, Solly	54B	94	$2.00	$8.00
Hemus, Solly	55B	107	$1.75	$7.00
Henrich, Tommy	48B	19	$7.50	$30.00

BOWMAN

Player	Year	No.	VG	EX/MT	Player	Year	No.	VG	EX/MT
Jansen, Larry	49B	202	$22.50	$90.00	Keller, Charlie	51B	177	$3.50	$14.00
Jansen, Larry	50B	66	$12.50	$50.00	Kellner, Alex	49B	222	$18.75	$75.00
Jansen, Larry	51B	162	$3.50	$14.00	Kellner, Alex	50B	14	$12.50	$50.00
Jansen, Larry	52B	90	$3.75	$15.00	Kellner, Alex	51B	57	$3.50	$14.00
Jansen, Larry	53BW	40	$8.00	$32.00	Kellner, Alex	52B	226	$7.50	$30.00
Jansen, Larry	54B	169	$3.50	$14.00	Kellner, Alex	53BC	107	$7.50	$30.00
Jeffcoat, Hal	51B	211	$3.50	$14.00	Kellner, Alex	54B	51	$2.00	$8.00
Jeffcoat, Hal	52B	104	$3.75	$15.00	Kellner, Alex	55B	53	$2.00	$8.00
Jeffcoat, Hal	53BW	37	$8.00	$32.00	Keltner, Ken	49B	125	$3.75	$15.00
Jeffcoat, Hal	54B	205	$3.50	$14.00	Keltner, Ken	50B	186	$4.50	$18.00
Jeffcoat, Hal	55B	223	$1.75	$7.00	Kemmerer, Russ	55B	222	$1.75	$7.00
Jensen, Jackie	51B	254	$35.00	$140.00	Kennedy, Bill	49B	105	$3.75	$15.00
Jensen, Jackie	52B	161	$7.50	$30.00	Kennedy, Bob	51B	296	$15.00	$60.00
Jensen, Jackie	53BC	24	$10.00	$40.00	Kennedy, Monte	49B	237	$18.75	$75.00
Jensen, Jackie	54B	2	$3.50	$14.00	Kennedy, Monte	50B	175	$4.50	$18.00
Jethroe, Sam	50B	248	$5.00	$20.00	Kennedy, Monte	51B	163	$3.50	$14.00
Jethroe, Sam	51B	242	$3.50	$14.00	Kennedy, Monte	52B	213	$3.75	$15.00
Jethroe, Sam	52B	84	$3.75	$15.00	Keriazakos, Gus	55B	14	$2.00	$8.00
Jethroe, Sam	53BC	3	$7.50	$30.00	Kerr, Buddy	48B	20	$8.50	$35.00
Johnson, Billy	48B	33	$7.00	$20.00	Kerr, Buddy	49B	186	$18.75	$75.00
Johnson, Billy	49B	129	$3.75	$15.00	Kerr, Buddy	50B	55	$12.50	$50.00
Johnson, Billy	50B	102	$4.50	$18.00	Kerr, John "Buddy"	51B	171	$3.50	$14.00
Johnson, Billy	51B	74	$3.50	$14.00	Kinder, Ellis	50B	152	$5.00	$20.00
Johnson, Billy	52B	122	$3.75	$15.00	Kinder, Ellis	51B	128	$3.50	$14.00
Johnson, Don	53BW	55	$8.00	$32.00	Kinder, Ellis	54B	98	$2.00	$8.00
Johnson, Don	55B	101	$1.75	$7.00	Kiner, Ralph	48B	3	$45.00	$175.00
Johnson, Earl	49B	231	$18.75	$75.00	Kiner, Ralph	49B	29	$22.50	$90.00
Johnson, Earl	50B	188	$4.50	$18.00	Kiner, Ralph	50B	33	$30.00	$120.00
Johnson, Earl	51B	321	$15.00	$60.00	Kiner, Ralph	52B	11	$16.25	$65.00
Johnson, Ernie	54B	144	$4.50	$18.00	Kiner, Ralph	53BC	80	$20.00	$80.00
Johnson, Ernie	55B	157	$1.75	$7.00	Kiner, Ralph	54B	45	$10.00	$40.00
Johnson, Ken	51B	293	$15.00	$60.00	Kiner, Ralph	55B	197	$7.00	$28.00
Jok, Stan	55B	251	$3.75	$15.00	King, Charles	55B	133	$1.75	$7.00
Jolly, Dave	55B	71	$2.00	$8.00	King, Clyde	51B	299	$15.00	$60.00
Jones, Sheldon	48B	34	$8.50	$35.00	King, Clyde	52B	56	$3.75	$15.00
Jones, Sheldon	49B	68	$6.00	$18.00	Klaus, Bill	55B	150	$1.75	$7.00
Jones, Sheldon	50B	83	$4.50	$18.00	Klippstein, Johnny	51B	248	$3.50	$14.00
Jones, Sheldon	51B	199	$3.50	$14.00	Klippstein, Johnny	54B	29	$2.00	$8.00
Jones, Ray "Sheldon"	52B	215	$3.75	$15.00	Klippstein, Johnny	55B	152	$1.75	$7.00
Jones, Vernal	50B	238	$4.50	$18.00	Kluszewski, Ted	50B	62	$20.00	$80.00
Jones, Willie	49B	92	$3.75	$15.00	Kluszewski, Ted	51B	143	$10.00	$40.00
Jones, Willie	50B	67	$12.50	$50.00	Kluszewski, Ted	53BC	62	$15.00	$60.00
Jones, Willie	51B	112	$3.50	$14.00	Kokos, Dick	49B	31	$5.25	$16.00
Jones, Willie	52B	20	$4.50	$18.00	Kokos, Dick	50B	50	$12.50	$50.00
Jones, Willie	53BC	133	$11.25	$45.00	Kokos, Dick	51B	68	$3.50	$14.00
Jones, Willie	54B	143	$3.50	$14.00	Kokos, Dick	54B	37	$2.00	$8.00
Jones, Willie	55B	172	$1.75	$7.00	Kolloway, Don	49B	28	$5.25	$16.00
Joost, Eddie	48B	15	$7.00	$20.00	Kolloway, Don	50B	133	$4.50	$18.00
Joost, Eddie	49B	55	$6.00	$18.00	Kolloway, Don	51B	105	$3.50	$14.00
Joost, Eddie	50B	103	$4.50	$18.00	Kolloway, Don	52B	91	$3.75	$15.00
Joost, Eddie	51B	119	$3.50	$14.00	Konstanty, Jim	50B	226	$7.50	$30.00
Joost, Eddie	52B	26	$4.50	$18.00	Konstanty, Jim	51B	27	$6.25	$25.00
Joost, Eddie	53BC	105	$7.50	$30.00	Konstanty, Jim	53BW	58	$10.00	$40.00
Joost, Eddie	54B	35	$2.00	$8.00	Konstanty, Jim	55B	231	$5.00	$20.00
Joost, Eddie	55B	263	$3.75	$15.00	Koshorek, Clem	53BC	147	$11.25	$45.00
Judson, Howie	50B	185	$4.50	$18.00	Koslo, Dave "George"	48B	48	$15.00	$60.00
Judson, Howie	51B	123	$3.50	$14.00	Koslo, Dave	49B	34	$5.25	$16.00
Judson, Howie	52B	149	$3.75	$15.00	Koslo, Dave	50B	65	$12.50	$50.00
Judson, Howie	53BW	42	$8.00	$32.00	Koslo, Dave	51B	90	$3.50	$14.00
Judson, Howie	55B	193	$1.75	$7.00	Koslo, Dave	52B	182	$3.75	$15.00
Kaline, Al	55B	23	$35.00	$140.00	Kozar, Al	49B	16	$5.25	$16.00
Katt, Ray	54B	121	$2.50	$10.00	Kozar, Al	50B	15	$12.50	$50.00
Katt, Ray	55B	183	$1.75	$7.00	Kramer, Jack	49B	53	$6.00	$18.00
Kazak, Eddie	50B	36	$12.50	$50.00	Kramer, Jack	50B	199	$4.50	$18.00
Kazak, Eddie	51B	85	$3.50	$14.00	Kramer, Jack	51B	200	$3.50	$14.00
Kell, Everett	52B	242	$7.50	$30.00	Kretlow, Lou	52B	221	$7.50	$30.00
Kell, George	49B	26	$12.50	$50.00	Kretlow, Lou	53BC	50	$7.50	$30.00
Kell, George	50B	8	$25.00	$100.00	Kretlow, Lou	54B	197	$3.50	$14.00
Kell, George	51B	46	$12.50	$50.00	Kretlow, Lou	55B	108	$1.75	$7.00
Kell, George	52B	75	$10.00	$40.00	Kryhoski, Dick	49B	218	$18.75	$75.00
Kell, George	53BC	61	$15.00	$60.00	Kryhoski, Dick	50B	242	$4.50	$18.00
Kell, George	54B	50	$8.00	$32.00	Kryhoski, Dick	52B	133	$3.75	$15.00
Kell, George	55B	213	$5.50	$22.00	Kryhoski, Dick	53BC	127	$12.50	$50.00
Keller, Charlie	49B	209	$25.00	$100.00	Kryhoski, Dick	54B	117	$2.50	$10.00
Keller, Charlie	50B	211	$4.50	$18.00	Kuenn, Harvey	54B	23	$7.50	$30.00

BOWMAN

Player	Year	No.	VG	EX/MT
Kuenn (Kueen), Harvey	55B	132	$3.00	$12.00
Kuzava, Bob	50B	5	$12.50	$50.00
Kuzava, Bob	51B	97	$3.50	$14.00
Kuzava, Bob	52B	233	$7.50	$30.00
Kuzava, Bob	53BW	33	$8.00	$32.00
Kuzava, Bob	55B	215	$1.75	$7.00
La Palme, Paul	53BW	19	$8.00	$32.00
La Palme, Paul	54B	107	$2.00	$8.00
La Palme, Paul	55B	61	$2.00	$8.00
Labine, Clem	54B	106	$2.50	$10.00
Lade, Doyle	49B	168	$18.75	$75.00
Lade, Doyle	50B	196	$4.50	$18.00
Lade, Doyle	51B	139	$3.50	$14.00
Lake, Eddie	49B	107	$3.75	$15.00
Lake, Eddie	50B	240	$4.50	$18.00
Lake, Eddie	51B	140	$3.50	$14.00
LaManno, Ray	49B	113	$3.75	$15.00
Landrith, Hobie	54B	220	$3.50	$14.00
Landrith, Hobie	55B	50	$2.00	$8.00
Lanier, Max	50B	207	$4.50	$18.00
Lanier, Max	51B	230	$3.50	$14.00
Lanier, Max	52B	110	$3.75	$15.00
Larsen, Don	54B	101	$10.00	$40.00
Larsen, Don	55B	67	$4.50	$18.00
Lary, Frank	55B	154	$2.50	$10.00
Law, Vernon	51B	203	$6.25	$25.00
Law, Vernon	52B	71	$5.50	$22.00
Law, Vernon	54B	187	$3.50	$14.00
Law, Vernon	55B	199	$1.75	$7.00
Lawrence, Brooks	55B	75	$2.50	$10.00
Lehman, Ken	55B	310	$3.75	$15.00
Lehner, Paul	49B	131	$3.75	$15.00
Lehner, Paul	50B	158	$4.50	$18.00
Lehner, Paul	51B	8	$6.00	$20.00
Lemon, Bob	49B	238	$62.50	$250.00
Lemon, Bob	50B	40	$26.25	$105.00
Lemon, Bob	51B	53	$12.50	$50.00
Lemon, Bob	52B	23	$12.50	$50.00
Lemon, Bob	53BW	27	$30.00	$120.00
Lemon, Bob	54B	196	$9.00	$36.00
Lemon, Bob	55B	191	$6.25	$25.00
Lemon, Jim	55B	262	$3.75	$15.00
Lenhardt, Don	53BC	20	$7.50	$30.00
Lenhardt, Don	54B	53	$2.00	$8.00
Leonard, Dutch	48B	24	$8.50	$35.00
Leonard, Dutch	49B	115	$3.75	$15.00
Leonard, Dutch	50B	170	$4.50	$18.00
Leonard, Dutch	51B	102	$3.50	$14.00
Leonard, Dutch	52B	159	$3.75	$15.00
Leonard, Dutch	53BW	50	$8.00	$32.00
Leonard, Emil "Dutch"	55B	247	$3.75	$15.00
Lepcio, Ted	54B	162	$3.50	$14.00
Liddle, Don	55B	146	$1.75	$7.00
Limmer, Lou	55B	80	$2.00	$8.00
Lindell, Johnny	48B	11	$7.00	$20.00
Lindell, Johnny	49B	197	$18.75	$75.00
Lindell, Johnny	50B	209	$4.50	$18.00
Lindell, Johnny	54B	159	$3.50	$14.00
Lint, Royce	55B	62	$2.00	$8.00
Lipon, Johnny	51B	285	$15.00	$60.00
Lipon, Johnny	52B	163	$3.75	$15.00
Lipon, Johnny	53BC	123	$12.50	$50.00
Littlefield, Dick	52B	209	$3.75	$15.00
Littlefield, Dick	54B	213	$3.50	$14.00
Littlefield, Dick	55B	200	$1.75	$7.00
Litwhiler, Danny	49B	97	$3.75	$15.00
Litwhiler, Danny	50B	198	$4.50	$18.00
Litwhiler, Danny	51B	179	$3.50	$14.00
Lockman, Carroll "Whitey"	48B	30	$10.00	$40.00
Lockman, Whitey	49B	2	$5.25	$16.00
Lockman, Whitey	50B	82	$4.50	$18.00
Lockman, Whitey	51B	37	$3.50	$14.00
Lockman, Whitey	52B	38	$3.75	$15.00
Lockman, Whitey	53BC	128	$12.50	$50.00
Lockman, Whitey	54B	153	$3.50	$14.00
Lockman, Whitey	55B	219	$1.75	$7.00
Loes, Billy	52B	240	$8.75	$35.00
Loes, Billy	53BC	14	$8.75	$35.00
Loes, Billy	54B	42	$2.50	10.00
Loes, Billy	55B	240	$3.75	$15.00
Logan, Johnny	54B	80	$3.00	$12.00
Logan, Johnny	55B	180	$1.75	$7.00
Lohrke, Jack	48B	16	$8.50	$35.00
Lohrke, Jack	49B	59	$6.00	$18.00
Lohrke, Jack	51B	235	$3.50	$14.00
Lohrke, Jack	52B	251	$7.50	$30.00
Lohrke, Jack	53BW	47	$8.00	$32.00
Lollar, Sherman	50B	142	$5.00	$20.00
Lollar, Sherman	51B	100	$3.50	$14.00
Lollar, Sherman	52B	237	$7.50	$30.00
Lollar, Sherman	53BC	157	$12.00	$80.00
Lollar, Sherman	54B	182	$3.50	$14.00
Lollar, Sherman	55B	174	$1.75	$7.00
Lombardi, Vic	51B	204	$3.50	$14.00
Lopat, Ed	49B	229	$35.00	$140.00

Player	Year	No.	VG	EX/MT
Lopat, Ed	50B	215	$8.00	$32.00
Lopat, Ed	51B	218	$7.50	$30.00
Lopat, Ed	52B	17	$7.50	$30.00
Lopata, Stan	49B	177	$18.75	$75.00
Lopata, Stan	50B	206	$4.50	$18.00
Lopata, Stan	51B	76	$7.50	$30.00
Lopata, Stan	54B	207	$3.50	$14.00
Lopata, Stan	55B	18	$2.00	$8.00
Lopez, Al	51B	295	$27.50	$110.00
Lopez, Al	53BC	143	$15.00	$60.00
Lopez, Al	55B	308	$11.25	$45.00
Lown, Omar	52B	16	$4.50	$18.00
Lown, Omar "Turk"	53BC	154	$11.25	$45.00
Lown, Turk	54B	157	$3.50	$14.00
Lowrey, Harry	49B	22	$5.25	$16.00
Lowrey, Harry	50B	172	$4.50	$18.00
Lowrey, Harry "Peanuts"	51B	194	$3.50	$14.00
Lowrey, Peanuts	52B	102	$3.75	$15.00
Luna, Memo	54B	222	$3.50	$14.00
Lund, Don	54B	87	$2.00	$8.00
Lupien, Ulysses	49B	141	$3.75	$15.00
MacDonald, Bill	51B	239	$3.50	$14.00
Maddern, Clarence	49B	152	$18.75	$75.00
Maglie, Sal	51B	127	$11.25	$45.00
Maglie, Sal	52B	66	$5.50	$22.00
Maglie, Sal	53BC	96	$11.25	$45.00
Maglie, Sal	54B	105	$3.50	$14.00
Maglie, Sal	55B	95	$2.50	$10.00
Majeski, Hank	49B	127	$5.00	$20.00

BOWMAN

Player	Year	No.	VG	EX/MT	Player	Year	No.	VG	EX/MT
Majeski, Hank	50B	92	$4.50	$18.00	McDermott, Maury	54B	56	$3.75	$15.00
Majeski, Hank	51B	12	$6.00	$20.00	McDermott, Maury	55B	165	$1.75	$7.00
Majeski, Hank	52B	58	$3.75	$15.00	McDonald, Jim	55B	77	$2.00	$8.00
Majeski, Hank	55B	127	$1.75	$7.00	McDougald, Gil	52B	33	$15.00	$60.00
Malzone, Frank	55B	302	$7.00	$28.00	McDougald, Gil	53BC	63	$15.00	$60.00
Mantle, Mickey	51B	253	$1750.00	$7000.00	McDougald, Gil	54B	97	$4.50	$18.00
Mantle, Mickey	52B	101	$550.00	$2200.00	McDougald, Gil	55B	9	$4.00	$16.00
Mantle, Mickey	53BC	44	$112.50	$450.00	McKinley, W. F.	55B	226	$6.25	$25.00
Mantle, Mickey	53BC	59	$550.00	$2200.00	McMillan, Roy	52B	238	$8.00	$32.00
Mantle, Mickey	54B	65	$225.00	$900.00	McMillan, Roy	53BC	26	$7.50	$30.00
Mantle, Mickey	55B	202	$135.00	$540.00	McMillan, Roy	54B	12	$2.00	$8.00
Mapes, Cliff	50B	218	$4.50	$18.00	McQuinn, George	49B	232	$18.75	$75.00
Mapes, Cliff	51B	289	$15.00	$60.00	Mele, Sam	49B	118	$3.75	$15.00
Mapes, Cliff	52B	13	$4.50	$18.00	Mele, Sam	50B	52	$12.50	$50.00
Marchildon, Phil	49B	187	$18.75	$75.00	Mele, Sam	51B	168	$3.50	$14.00
Marion, Marty	48B	40	$18.50	$75.00	Mele, Sam	52B	15	$4.50	$18.00
Marion, Marty	49B	54	$6.50	$26.00	Mele, Sam	54B	22	$2.00	$8.00
Marion, Marty	50B	88	$5.00	$20.00	Mele, Sam	55B	147	$1.75	$7.00
Marion, Marty	51B	34	$6.25	$25.00	Merriman, Lloyd	50B	173	$4.50	$18.00
Marion, Marty	52B	85	$4.50	$18.00	Merriman, Lloyd	51B	72	$3.50	$14.00
Marion, Marty	53BC	52	$7.50	$30.00	Merriman, Lloyd	52B	78	$3.75	$15.00
Marlowe, Dick	55B	91	$2.00	$8.00	Merriman, Lloyd	55B	135	$1.75	$7.00
Marrero, Conrado	51B	206	$3.50	$14.00	Metkovich, George	51B	274	$15.00	$60.00
Marrero, Conrado	54B	200	$3.50	$14.00	Metkovich, George	52B	108	$3.75	$15.00
Marshall, Willard	48B	13	$8.50	$35.00	Meyer, Billy	51B	272	$15.00	$60.00
Marshall, Willard	49B	48	$6.00	$18.00	Meyer, Billy	52B	155	$3.75	$15.00
Marshall, Willard	50B	73	$4.50	$18.00	Meyer, Russ	51B	75	$3.50	$14.00
Marshall, Willard	51B	98	$3.50	$14.00	Meyer, Russ	52B	220	$7.50	$30.00
Marshall, Willard	52B	97	$3.75	$15.00	Meyer, Russ	53BC	129	$11.25	$45.00
Marshall, Willard	53BC	58	$7.50	$30.00	Meyer, Russ	54B	186	$3.50	$14.00
Marshall, Willard	54B	70	$2.00	$8.00	Meyer, Russ	55B	196	$1.75	$7.00
Marshall, Willard	55B	131	$1.75	$7.00	Michaels, Cass	49B	12	$5.25	$16.00
Martin, Babe	49B	167	$18.75	$75.00	Michaels, Cass	50B	91	$4.50	$18.00
Martin, Billy	53BC	93	$50.00	$200.00	Michaels, Cass	51B	132	$3.50	$14.00
Martin, Billy	53BC	118	$75.00	$300.00	Michaels, Cass	52B	36	$4.50	$18.00
Martin, Billy	54B	145	$16.25	$65.00	Michaels, Cass	53BC	130	$11.25	$45.00
Martin, Morris	53BW	53	$8.00	$32.00	Michaels, Cass	54B	150	$3.50	$14.00
Martin, Morris	54B	179	$3.50	$14.00	Michaels, Cass	55B	85	$2.00	$8.00
Masi, Phil	49B	153	$18.75	$75.00	Miggins, Larry	53BC	142	$11.25	$45.00
Masi, Phil	50B	128	$4.50	$18.00	Miksis, Eddie	51B	117	$3.50	$14.00
Masi, Phil	51B	160	$3.50	$14.00	Miksis, Eddie	52B	32	$4.50	$18.00
Masterson, Walt	49B	157	$18.75	$75.00	Miksis, Eddie	54B	61	$2.00	$8.00
Masterson, Walt	50B	153	$4.50	$18.00	Miksis, Eddie	55B	181	$1.75	$7.00
Masterson, Walt	51B	307	$15.00	$60.00	Miller, Bill	53BW	54	$8.00	$32.00
Masterson, Walt	52B	205	$3.75	$15.00	Miller, Bill	55B	245	$3.75	$15.00
Masterson, Walt	53BW	9	$8.00	$32.00	Miller, Bob	50B	227	$4.50	$18.00
Mathews, Eddie	53BC	97	$45.00	$180.00	Miller, Bob	51B	220	$3.50	$14.00
Mathews, Eddie	54B	64	$15.00	$60.00	Miller, Bob	55B	110	$1.75	$7.00
Mathews, Eddie	55B	103	$12.50	$50.00	Miller, Stu	53BW	16	$10.00	$40.00
Mauch, Gene	51B	312	$20.00	$80.00	Miller, Stu	54B	158	$3.50	$14.00
Maxwell, Charlie	55B	162	$1.75	$7.00	Minner, Paul	52B	211	$3.75	$15.00
Mayo, Eddie	49B	75	$3.75	$15.00	Minner, Paul	53BC	71	$7.50	$30.00
Mayo, Jackie	49B	228	$18.75	$75.00	Minner, Paul	54B	13	$2.00	$8.00
Mays, Willie	51B	305	$800.00	$3200.00	Minoso, Orestes	52B	5	$21.25	$85.00
Mays, Willie	52B	218	$300.00	$1200.00	Minoso, Orestes "Minnie"	53BC	36	$12.50	$50.00
Maye, Willie	54B	89	$100.00	$400.00	Minoso, Minnie	54B	38	$4.50	$18.00
Mays, Willie	55B	184	$62.50	$250.00	Minoso, Minnie	55B	25	$4.00	$16.00
McBride, Tom	49B	74	$3.75	$15.00	Miranda, Willie	55B	79	$2.00	$8.00
McCahan, Bill	48B	31	$7.00	$20.00	Mitchell, Dale	49B	43	$6.00	$18.00
McCahan, Bill	49B	80	$3.75	$15.00	Mitchell, Dale	50B	130	$4.50	$18.00
McCarthy, Johnny	49B	220	$18.75	$75.00	Mitchell, Dale	51B	5	$6.00	$20.00
McCormick, Frank	49B	239	$18.75	$75.00	Mitchell, Dale	52B	239	$7.50	$30.00
McCormick, Mike	49B	146	$18.75	$75.00	Mitchell, Dale	53BC	119	$12.50	$50.00
McCosky, Barney	48B	25	$7.00	$20.00	Mitchell, Dale	54B	148	$3.50	$14.00
McCosky, Barney	49B	203	$18.75	$75.00	Mitchell, Dale	55B	314	$3.75	$15.00
McCosky, Barney	51B	84	$3.50	$14.00	Mize, Johnny	48B	4	$25.00	$100.00
McCullough, Clyde	49B	163	$18.75	$75.00	Mize, Johnny	49B	85	$20.00	$80.00
McCullough, Clyde	50B	124	$4.50	$18.00	Mize, Johnny	50B	139	$16.25	$65.00
McCullough, Clyde	51B	94	$3.50	$14.00	Mize, Johnny	51B	50	$13.75	$55.00
McCullough, Clyde	52B	99	$3.75	$15.00	Mize, Johnny	52B	145	$12.50	$50.00
McCullough, Clyde	55B	280	$3.75	$15.00	Mize, Johnny	53BW	15	$30.00	$120.00
McDermott, Maurice	50B	97	$4.50	$18.00	Mizell, Wilmer	53BW	23	$10.00	$40.00
McDermott, Maurice	51B	16	$6.00	$20.00	Moore, Terry	49B	174	$25.00	$100.00
McDermott, Maurice "Maury"	52B	25	$4.50	$18.00	Morgan, Bobby	50B	222	$4.50	$18.00
McDermott, Maury	53BC	35	$7.50	$30.00	Morgan, Bobby	53BC	135	$11.25	$45.00

45

BOWMAN

Player	Year	No.	VG	EX/MT	Player	Year	No.	VG	EX/MT
Morgan, Bobby	55B	81	$2.00	$8.00	Nuxhall, Joe	55B	194	$1.75	$7.00
Morgan, Tom	52B	109	$3.75	$15.00	O'Connell, Danny	51B	93	$3.50	$14.00
Morgan, Tom	55B	100	$1.75	$7.00	O'Connell, Danny	54B	160	$3.50	$14.00
Moryn, Walt	55B	261	$3.75	$15.00	O'Connell, Danny	55B	44	$2.00	$8.00
Moses, Wally	51B	261	$15.00	$60.00	O'Neill, Steve	51B	201	$3.50	$14.00
Moses, Wally	53BC	95	$7.50	$30.00	Ostermueller, Fritz	49B	227	$18.75	$75.00
Moses, Wally	55B	294	$3.75	$15.00	Overmire, Frank	51B	280	$15.00	$60.00
Moss, John "Lester"	50B	251	$4.50	$18.00	Owen, Mickey	50B	78	$4.50	$18.00
Moss, Les	51B	210	$3.50	$14.00	Owen, Mickey	51B	174	$3.50	$14.00
Moss, Les	54B	181	$3.50	$14.00	Pafko, Andy	49B	63	$6.00	$18.00
Mossi, Don	55B	259	$6.25	$25.00	Pafko, Andy	50B	60	$12.50	$50.00
Moulder, Glen	49B	159	$18.75	$75.00	Pafko, Andy	51B	103	$3.50	$14.00
Mrozinski, Ron	55B	287	$3.75	$15.00	Pafko, Andy	52B	204	$3.75	$15.00
Mueller, Don	50B	221	$7.50	$30.00	Pafko, Andy	53BW	57	$8.00	$32.00
Mueller, Don	51B	268	$17.50	$70.00	Pafko, Andy	54B	112	$2.00	$8.00
Mueller, Don	52B	18	$4.50	$18.00	Pafko, Andy	55B	12	$2.00	$8.00
Mueller, Don	53BC	74	$7.50	$30.00	Page, Joe	48B	29	$12.00	$48.00
Mueller, Don	54B	73	$2.00	$8.00	Page, Joe	49B	82	$6.00	$24.00
Mueller, Ray	51B	313	$15.00	$60.00	Page, Joe	50B	12	$15.00	$60.00
Mullin, Pat	49B	56	$6.00	$18.00	Page, Joe	51B	217	$4.25	$17.00
Mullin, Pat	50B	135	$4.50	$18.00	Paige, Satchell	49B	224	$325.00	$1300.00
Mullin, Pat	51B	106	$3.50	$14.00	Palica, Erv	51B	189	$3.50	$14.00
Mullin, Pat	52B	183	$3.75	$15.00	Palica, Erv	55B	195	$1.75	$7.00
Mullin, Pat	53BW	4	$8.00	$32.00	Papai, Al	50B	245	$4.50	$18.00
Mullin, Pat	54B	151	$3.50	$14.00	Paparella, J. A.	55B	235	$6.25	$25.00
Muncrief, Bob	49B	221	$18.75	$75.00	Parnell, Mel	50B	1	$30.00	$180.00
Munger, George	49B	40	$6.00	$18.00	Parnell, Mel	52B	241	$7.50	$30.00
Munger, George	50B	89	$4.50	$18.00	Parnell, Mel	53BC	66	$7.50	$30.00
Munger, George "Red"	51B	11	$6.00	$20.00	Partee, Roy	49B	149	$18.75	$75.00
Munger, Red	52B	243	$7.50	$30.00	Peck, Hall	49B	182	$18.75	$75.00
Murray, Ray	52B	118	$3.75	$15.00	Pellagrini, Eddie	49B	172	$18.75	$75.00
Murray, Ray	53BW	6	$8.00	$32.00	Pellagrini, Eddie	51B	292	$15.00	$60.00
Murray, Ray	54B	83	$2.00	$8.00	Perkowski, Harry	52B	202	$3.75	$15.00
Murtaugh, Danny	49B	124	$4.00	$16.00	Perkowski, Harry	53BC	87	$7.50	$30.00
Murtaugh, Danny	50B	203	$4.50	$18.00	Perkowski, Harry	54B	44	$2.00	$8.00
Murtaugh, Danny	51B	273	$15.00	$60.00	Pesky, Johnny	49B	86	$5.00	$20.00
Musial, Stan	48B	36	$200.00	$800.00	Pesky, Johnny	50B	137	$5.00	$20.00
Musial, Stan	49B	24	$137.50	$550.00	Pesky, Johnny	51B	15	$6.25	$25.00
Musial, Stan	52B	196	$125.00	$500.00	Pesky, Johnny	52B	45	$5.00	$20.00
Musial, Stan	53BC	32	$125.00	$500.00	Pesky, Johnny	53BC	134	$12.00	$48.00
Napp, Larry	55B	250	$6.25	$25.00	Pesky, Johnny	54B	135	$4.00	$16.00
Naragon, Hal	55B	129	$1.75	$7.00	Pesky, Johnny	55B	241	$5.00	$20.00
Narleski, Ray	55B	96	$2.50	$10.00	Peterson, Kent	51B	215	$3.50	$14.00
Neal, Charles	55B	278	$7.50	$28.00	Philley, Dave	49B	44	$6.00	$18.00
Newcombe, Don	50B	23	$32.50	$130.00	Philley, Dave	50B	127	$4.50	$18.00
Newcombe, Don	51B	6	$10.00	$40.00	Philley, Dave	51B	297	$15.00	$60.00
Newcombe, Don	52B	128	$7.00	$28.00	Philley, Dave	54B	163	$4.50	$18.00
Newcombe, Don	54B	154	$5.00	$20.00	Phillips, John M.	55B	228	$3.75	$15.00
Newcombe, Don	55B	143	$4.00	$16.00	Pierce, Billy	51B	196	$6.25	$25.00
Niarhos, Gus	49B	181	$18.75	$75.00	Pierce, Billy	52B	54	$5.50	$22.00
Niarhos, Gus	50B	154	$4.50	$18.00	Pierce, Billy	53BC	73	$10.00	$40.00
Niarhos, Gus	51B	124	$3.50	$14.00	Pierce, Billy	54B	102	$2.50	$10.00
Niarhos, Gus	52B	129	$3.75	$15.00	Pierce, Billy	55B	214	$2.00	$10.00
Nichols, Chet	52B	120	$3.75	$15.00	Pieretti, Marino	49B	217	$18.75	$75.00
Nichols, Chet	55B	72	$2.00	$8.00	Pieretti, Marino	50B	181	$4.50	$18.00
Nicholson, Bill	49B	76	$5.00	$20.00	Piersall, Jim	51B	306	$25.00	$100.00
Nicholson, Bill	50B	228	$4.50	$18.00	Piersall, Jim	52B	189	$4.50	$18.00
Nicholson, Bill	51B	113	$3.50	$14.00	Piersall, Jim	53BW	36	$10.00	$40.00
Nicholson, Bill	53BW	14	$8.00	$32.00	Piersall, Jim	54B	66	$25.00	$100.00
Nieman, Bob	55B	145	$1.75	$7.00	Piersall, Jim	54B	210	$4.50	$18.00
Nixon, Willard	51B	270	$15.00	$60.00	Piersall, Jim	55B	16	$2.50	$10.00
Nixon, Willard	53BW	2	$8.00	$32.00	Pillette, Duane	51B	316	$15.00	$60.00
Nixon, Willard	54B	114	$2.50	$10.00	Pillette, Duane	53BW	59	$8.00	$32.00
Nixon, Willard	55B	177	$1.75	$7.00	Pillette, Duane	54B	133	$3.50	$14.00
Noble, Ray	51B	269	$15.00	$60.00	Pillette, Duane	55B	244	$3.75	$15.00
Noren, Irv	50B	247	$5.50	$22.00	Pinelli, R. A. "Babe"	55B	307	$6.25	$25.00
Noren, Irv	51B	241	$3.50	$14.00	Platt, Mizell	49B	89	$3.75	$15.00
Noren, Irv	52B	63	$3.75	$15.00	Poat, Ray	48B	42	$9.00	$28.00
Noren, Irv	53BW	45	$8.00	$32.00	Podbielan, Clarence "Bud"	53BW	21	$8.00	$32.00
Noren, Irv	55B	63	$2.00	$8.00	Podres, John	55B	97	$4.00	$16.00
Northey, Ron	49B	79	$3.75	$15.00	Poholsky, Tom	55B	76	$2.00	$8.00
Northey, Ron	50B	81	$4.50	$18.00	Pollet, Howie	49B	95	$3.50	$18.00
Northey, Ron	51B	70	$3.50	$14.00	Pollet, Howie	50B	72	$12.50	$50.00
Nuxhall, Joe	53BC	90	$8.75	$35.00	Pollet, Howie	51B	263	$15.00	$60.00
Nuxhall, Joe	54B	76	$2.00	$8.00	Pollet, Howie	52B	83	$3.75	$15.00

BOWMAN

Player	Year	No.	VG	EX/MT
Pope, Dave	55B	198	$1.75	$7.00
Porterfield, Bob	49B	3	$5.25	$16.00
Porterfield, Bob	50B	216	$4.50	$18.00
Porterfield, Bob	52B	194	$3.75	$15.00
Porterfield, Bob	53BC	22	$7.50	$30.00
Porterfield, Bob	54B	24	$2.00	$8.00
Porterfield, Bob	55B	104	$1.75	$7.00
Post, Wally	55B	32	$2.50	$10.00
Pramesa, Johnny	51B	324	$25.00	$100.00
Pramesa, Johnny	52B	247	$7.50	$30.00
Presko, Joe	52B	62	$3.75	$15.00
Presko, Joe	54B	190	$3.50	$14.00
Priddy, Jerry	49B	4	$5.25	$16.00
Priddy, Jerry (Gerry)	50B	212	$4.50	$18.00
Priddy, Jerry	51B	71	$3.50	$14.00
Priddy, Jerry	52B	139	$3.75	$15.00
Queen, Mel	51B	309	$15.00	$60.00
Queen, Mel	52B	171	$3.75	$15.00
Quinn, Frank	51B	276	$15.00	$60.00
Raffensberger, Ken	49B	176	$18.75	$75.00
Raffensberger, Ken	51B	48	$3.50	$14.00
Raffensberger, Ken	52B	55	$3.75	$15.00
Raffensberger, Ken	53BC	106	$7.50	$30.00
Raffensberger, Ken	54B	92	$2.00	$8.00
Ramazotti, Bob	51B	247	$3.50	$14.00
Ramazotti, Bob	53BW	41	$8.00	$32.00
Ramsdell, Willard	51B	251	$3.50	$14.00
Ramsdell, Willard	52B	22	$4.50	$18.00
Raschi, Vic	49B	35	$11.75	$45.00
Raschi, Vic	50B	100	$7.50	$30.00
Raschi, Vic	51B	25	$10.00	$30.00
Raschi, Vic	52B	37	$5.50	$22.00
Raschi, Vic	53BC	27	$10.00	$40.00
Raschi, Vic	54B	33	$5.00	$20.00
Raschi, Vic	55B	185	$2.50	$10.00
Reese, Harold "Pee Wee"	49B	36	$55.00	$220.00
Reese, Pee Wee	50B	21	$50.00	$200.00
Reese, Pee Wee	51B	80	$35.00	$140.00
Reese, Pee Wee	52B	8	$27.50	$110.00
Reese, Pee Wee	53BC	33	$112.50	$450.00
Reese, Pee Wee	54B	58	$17.50	$70.00
Reese, Pee Wee	55B	37	$18.75	$75.00
Regalado, Rudy	55B	142	$1.75	$7.00
Reiser, Pete	48B	7	$15.00	$60.00
Reiser, Pete	49B	185	$22.50	$90.00
Reiser, Pete	50B	193	$5.00	$20.00
Reiser, Pete	51B	238	$4.25	$17.00
Repulski, Rip	54B	46	$2.00	$8.00
Repulski, Rip	55B	205	$1.75	$7.00
Restelli, Dino	50B	123	$4.50	$18.00
Reynolds, Allie	48B	14	$12.50	$50.00
Reynolds, Allie	49B	114	$7.50	$30.00
Reynolds, Allie	50B	138	$7.50	$30.00
Reynolds, Allie	51B	109	$7.50	$30.00
Reynolds, Allie	53BC	68	$11.25	$45.00
Reynolds, Allie	54B	113	$4.50	$18.00
Reynolds, Allie	55B	201	$4.00	$16.00
Rice, Del	50B	125	$4.50	$18.00
Rice, Del	51B	156	$3.50	$14.00
Rice, Del	52B	107	$3.75	$15.00
Rice, Del	53BC	53	$7.50	$30.00
Rice, Del	54B	30	$2.00	$8.00
Rice, Del	55B	106	$1.75	$7.00
Rice, Hal	51B	300	$15.00	$60.00
Rice, Hal	54B	219	$3.50	$14.00
Rice, Hal	55B	52	$2.00	$8.00
Richards, Paul	51B	195	$5.00	$20.00
Richards, Paul	52B	93	$3.75	$15.00
Richards, Paul	53BC	39	$7.50	$30.00
Richards, Paul	55B	225	$3.75	$15.00
Richmond, Don	51B	264	$15.00	$60.00
Ridzik, Steve	53BW	48	$8.00	$32.00
Ridzik, Steve	54B	223	$3.50	$14.00
Ridzik, Steve	55B	111	$1.75	$7.00
Rigney, Bill	48B	32	$7.00	$20.00
Rigney, Bill	49B	170	$18.75	$75.00
Rigney, Bill	50B	117	$4.50	$18.00
Rigney, Bill	51B	125	$3.50	$14.00
Rigney, Bill	53BW	3	$8.00	$32.00
Rizzuto, Phil	48B	8	$65.00	$225.00
Rizzuto, Phil	49B	98	$18.75	100.00
Rizzuto, Phil	50B	11	$40.00	$160.00
Rizzuto, Phil	51B	26	$26.25	$105.00
Rizzuto, Phil	52B	52	$20.00	$80.00
Rizzuto, Phil	53BC	9	$27.50	$110.00
Rizzuto, Phil	53BC	93	$50.00	$200.00
Rizzuto, Phil	54B	1	$20.00	$125.00
Rizzuto, Phil	55B	10	$13.75	$55.00
Roberts, Robin	49B	46	$65.00	$260.00
Roberts, Robin	50B	32	$37.50	$150.00
Roberts, Robin	51B	3	$20.00	$80.00
Roberts, Robin	52B	4	$15.00	$60.00
Roberts, Robin	53BC	65	$20.00	$80.00
Roberts, Robin	54B	95	$9.00	$36.00
Roberts, Robin	55B	171	$7.00	$28.00
Robertson, Al	54B	211	$3.50	$14.00
Robertson, Jim	55B	5	$2.00	$8.00
Robertson, Sherry	50B	161	$4.50	$18.00
Robertson, Sherry	51B	95	$3.50	$14.00
Robinson, Aaron	49B	133	$3.75	$15.00
Robinson, Aaron	50B	95	$4.50	$18.00
Robinson, Aaron	51B	142	$3.50	$14.00
Robinson, Eddie	50B	18	$12.50	$50.00
Robinson, Eddie	51B	88	$3.50	$14.00
Robinson, Eddie	52B	77	$3.75	$15.00
Robinson, Eddie	53BW	20	$8.00	$32.00
Robinson, Eddie	54B	193	$3.50	$14.00
Robinson, Eddie	55B	153	$1.75	$7.00
Robinson, Jackie	49B	50	$200.00	$800.00
Robinson, Jackie	50B	22	$175.00	$700.00
Rodriquez, Hector	53BC	98	$7.50	$30.00
Roe, Elwin "Preacher"	49B	162	$35.00	$140.00
Roe, Preacher	50B	167	$7.50	$30.00
Roe, Preacher	51B	118	$7.50	$30.00
Roe, Preacher	52B	168	$6.25	$25.00

BOWMAN

Player	Year	No.	VG	EX/MT	Player	Year	No.	VG	EX/MT
Roe, Preacher	53BW	26	$12.50	$50.00	Schoendienst, Red	50B	71	$25.00	$100.00
Roe, Preacher	54B	218	$4.50	$18.00	Schoendienst, Red	51B	10	$16.25	$65.00
Roe, Preacher	55B	216	$2.00	$10.00	Schoendienst, Red	52B	30	$15.00	$60.00
Rogovin, Saul	52B	165	$3.75	$15.00	Schoendienst, Red	53BC	101	$20.00	$80.00
Rogovin, Saul	53BC	75	$7.50	$30.00	Schoendienst, Red	54B	110	$9.00	$36.00
Rogovin, Saul	54B	140	$3.50	$14.00	Schoendienst, Red	55B	29	$6.25	$25.00
Rojek, Stan	49B	135	$3.75	$15.00	Schroll, Albert B.	55B	319	$3.75	$15.00
Rojek, Stan	50B	86	$4.50	$18.00	Schultz, Bob	54B	59	$2.00	$8.00
Rojek, Stan	51B	166	$3.50	$14.00	Secory, Frank E.	55B	286	$6.25	$25.00
Rojek, Stan	52B	137	$3.75	$15.00	Seminick, Andy	49B	30	$5.25	$16.00
Rolfe, Red	51B	319	$17.50	$70.00	Seminick, Andy	50B	121	$4.50	$18.00
Rommel, Edwin A.	55B	239	$6.25	$25.00	Seminick, Andy	51B	51	$3.50	$14.00
Rosar, Buddy	48B	10	$7.00	$20.00	Seminick, Andy	53BW	7	$8.00	$32.00
Rosar, Buddy "Warren"	49B	138	$3.75	$15.00	Seminick, Andy	54B	172	$3.50	$14.00
Rosar, Warren	50B	136	$4.50	$18.00	Seminick, Andy	55B	93	$2.00	$8.00
Rosar, Warren	51B	236	$3.50	$14.00	Serena, Bill	50B	230	$4.50	$18.00
Rosen, Al "Flip"	50B	232	$15.00	$60.00	Serena, Bill	51B	246	$3.50	$14.00
Rosen, Al "Flip"	51B	187	$6.25	$25.00	Serena, Bill	53BC	122	$12.50	$50.00
Rosen, Al "Flip"	52B	151	$5.50	$22.50	Serena, Bill	54B	93	$2.00	$8.00
Rosen, Al "Flip"	53BC	8	$12.50	$50.00	Serena, Bill	55B	233	$3.75	$15.00
Rotblatt, Marv	51B	303	$15.00	$60.00	Sewell, Luke	51B	322	$15.00	$60.00
Rowe, Schoolboy	49B	216	$22.50	$90.00	Sewell, Luke	52B	94	$3.75	$15.00
Roy, Norman	51B	278	$15.00	$60.00	Sewell, Rip	49B	234	$18.75	$75.00
Runge, Ed	55B	277	$6.25	$25.00	Shantz, Billy	55B	139	$2.25	$9.00
Runnels, Pete	53BC	139	$12.00	$48.00	Shantz, Billy "Wilmer"	55B	175	$1.75	$7.00
Runnels, Pete	55B	255	$3.75	$15.00	Shantz, Bobby	50B	234	$7.50	$30.00
Rush, Bob	50B	61	$12.50	$50.00	Shantz (Schantz), Bobby	51B	227	$4.00	$16.00
Rush, Bob	51B	212	$3.50	$14.00	Shantz, Bobby	53BC	11	$9.00	$36.00
Rush, Bob	53BC	110	$7.50	$30.00	Shantz, Bobby	54B	19	$2.50	$10.00
Rush, Bob	54B	77	$2.00	$8.00	Shantz, Bobby	55B	139	$2.25	$9.00
Rush, Bob	55B	182	$1.75	$7.00	Shantz, Bobby	55B	140	$1.75	$7.00
Russell, Jim	49B	235	$18.75	$75.00	Shea, Frank	48B	26	$8.50	$35.00
Russell, Jimmy	50B	223	$4.50	$18.00	Shea, Frank	49B	49	$6.00	$20.00
Ryan, Connie	51B	216	$3.50	$14.00	Shea, Frank	50B	155	$4.50	$18.00
Ryan, Connie	52B	164	$3.75	$15.00	Shea, Frank	52B	230	$7.50	$30.00
Ryan, Connie	53BC	131	$11.25	$45.00	Shea, Frank	53BC	141	$11.25	$45.00
Saffell, Tom	51B	130	$3.50	$14.00	Shea, Frank	54B	104	$2.00	$8.00
Sain, Johnny	48B	12	$12.50	$50.00	Shea, Frank	55B	207	$1.75	$7.00
Sain, Johnny	49B	47	$8.00	$32.50	Shuba, George	53BC	145	$12.00	$48.00
Sain, Johnny	51B	314	$20.00	$80.00	Shuba, George	54B	202	$3.50	$14.00
Sain, Johnny	53BW	25	$12.50	$50.00	Shuba, George	55B	66	$2.00	$8.00
Salkeld, Bill	49B	88	$3.75	$15.00	Sievers, Roy	50B	16	$15.00	$60.00
Salkeld, Bill	50B	237	$4.50	$18.00	Sievers, Roy	51B	67	$3.50	$14.00
Sanford, Fred	49B	236	$18.75	$75.00	Silvera, Charlie	52B	197	$3.75	$15.00
Sanford, Fred	50B	156	$4.50	$18.00	Silvestri, Ken	51B	256	$15.00	$60.00
Sanford, Fred	51B	145	$3.50	$14.00	Silvestri, Ken	52B	200	$3.75	$15.00
Sarni, Bill	55B	30	$2.00	$8.00	Simmons, Curt	49B	14	$7.00	$28.00
Sauer, Hank	48B	45	$10.00	$40.00	Simmons, Curt	50B	68	$15.00	$60.00
Sauer, Hank	49B	5	$6.50	$22.00	Simmons, Curt	51B	111	$3.50	$14.00
Sauer, Hank	50B	25	$15.00	$60.00	Simmons, Curt	52B	184	$3.75	$15.00
Sauer, Hank	51B	22	$6.25	$25.00	Simmons, Curt	53BC	64	$8.75	$35.00
Sauer, Hank	53BC	48	$7.50	$30.00	Simmons, Curt	54B	79	$2.00	$8.00
Savage, Bob	49B	204	$18.75	$75.00	Simmons, Curt	55B	64	$2.00	$8.00
Sawyer, Eddie	50B	225	$4.50	$18.00	Simpson, Harry	52B	223	$7.50	$30.00
Sawyer, Eddie	51B	184	$3.50	$14.00	Simpson, Harry	53BC	86	$7.50	$30.00
Scarborough, Ray	49B	140	$3.75	$15.00	Singleton, Bert	49B	147	$18.75	$75.00
Scarborough, Rae (Ray)	50B	108	$4.50	$18.00	Sisler, Dick	49B	205	$18.75	$75.00
Scarborough, Ray	51B	39	$3.50	$14.00	Sisler, Dick	50B	119	$4.50	$18.00
Scarborough, Ray	52B	140	$3.75	$15.00	Sisler, Dick	51B	52	$3.50	$14.00
Scheffing, Bob	49B	83	$3.75	$15.00	Sisler, Dick	52B	127	$3.75	$15.00
Scheffing, Bob	50B	168	$4.50	$18.00	Sisler, Dick	53BW	10	$8.00	$32.00
Scheib, Carl	49B	25	$5.25	$16.00	Sisti, Sibby	49B	201	$18.75	$75.00
Scheib, Carl	50B	213	$4.50	$18.00	Sisti, Sibby	50B	164	$4.50	$18.00
Scheib, Carl	51B	83	$3.50	$14.00	Sisti, Sibby	51B	170	$3.50	$14.00
Scheib, Carl	52B	46	$3.75	$15.00	Sisti, Sibby	52B	100	$3.75	$15.00
Scheib, Carl	53BC	150	$11.25	$45.00	Skowron, Bill	55B	160	$5.00	$20.00
Scheib, Carl	54B	67	$2.00	$8.00	Slaughter, Enos	48B	17	$25.00	$100.00
Schmees, George	52B	245	$7.50	$30.00	Slaughter, Enos	49B	65	$22.50	$90.00
Schmitz, Johnny	49B	52	$6.00	$18.00	Slaughter, Enos	50B	35	$30.00	$120.00
Schmitz, Johnny	50B	24	$12.50	$50.00	Slaughter, Enos	51B	58	$13.75	$55.00
Schmitz, Johnny	51B	69	$3.50	$14.00	Slaughter, Enos	52B	232	$25.00	$100.00
Schmitz, Johnny	52B	224	$7.50	$30.00	Slaughter, Enos	53BC	81	$20.00	$80.00
Schmitz, Johnny	55B	105	$1.75	$7.00	Slaughter, Enos	54B	62	$10.00	$40.00
Schoendienst, Al "Red"	48B	38	$37.50	$150.00	Slaughter, Enos	55B	60	$7.00	$28.00
Schoendienst, Red	49B	111	$18.75	$80.00	Smalley, Roy	50B	115	$4.50	$18.00

BOWMAN

Player	Year	No.	VG	EX/MT
Smalley, Roy	51B	44	$3.50	$14.00
Smalley, Roy	52B	64	$3.75	$15.00
Smalley, Roy	53BW	56	$8.00	$32.00
Smalley, Roy	54B	109	$2.00	$8.00
Smalley, Roy	55B	252	$3.75	$15.00
Smith, Al	55B	20	$2.00	$8.00
Smith, Dick	55B	288	$3.75	$15.00
Smith, Frank	52B	186	$3.75	$15.00
Smith, Frank	54B	188	$3.50	$14.00
Snider, Duke	49B	226	$300.00	$1200.00
Snider, Duke	50B	77	$70.00	$280.00
Snider, Duke	51B	32	$65.00	$260.00
Snider, Duke	52B	116	$50.00	$200.00
Snider, Duke	53BC	117	$137.50	$550.00
Snider, Duke	54B	170	$40.00	$160.00
Snyder, Jerry	52B	246	$7.50	$30.00
Snyder, Jerry	54B	216	$3.50	$14.00
Snyder, Jerry	55B	74	$2.00	$8.00
Soar, Hank	55B	279	$6.25	$25.00
Souchock, Steve	52B	235	$7.50	$30.00
Souchock, Steve	53BC	91	$7.50	$30.00
Souchock, Steve	54B	103	$2.00	$8.00
Southworth, Billy	51B	207	$3.50	$14.00
Spahn, Warren	48B	18	$75.00	$300.00
Spahn, Warren	49B	33	$43.75	$175.00
Spahn, Warren	50B	19	$50.00	$200.00
Spahn, Warren	51B	134	$30.00	$120.00
Spahn, Warren	52B	156	$25.00	$100.00
Spahn, Warren	53BC	99	$45.00	$180.00
Spence, Stan	49B	102	$3.75	$15.00
Spencer, Daryl	54B	185	$3.50	$14.00
St. Claire, Ebba	52B	172	$3.75	$15.00
St. Claire, Ebba	53BW	34	$8.00	$32.00
St. Claire, Ebba	54B	128	$2.50	$10.00
Staley, Gerry	51B	121	$3.50	$14.00
Staley, Gerry	52B	50	$3.75	$15.00
Staley, Gerry	53BC	17	$7.50	$30.00
Staley, Gerry	54B	14	$2.00	$8.00
Staley, Gerry	55B	155	$1.75	$7.00
Stallcup, Virgil	49B	81	$3.75	$15.00
Stallcup, Virgil "Red"	50B	116	$4.50	$18.00
Stallcup, Virgil	51B	108	$3.50	$14.00
Stallcup, Virgil "Red"	52B	6	$4.50	$18.00
Stanky, Ed	49B	104	$6.25	$25.00
Stanky, Eddie	50B	29	$15.00	$60.00
Stanky, Ed	51B	13	$6.00	$20.00
Stanky, Eddie	52B	160	$3.75	$15.00
Stanky, Eddie	53BC	49	$8.75	$35.00
Stanky, Eddie	55B	238	$5.00	$20.00
Starr, Dick	50B	191	$4.50	$18.00
Starr, Dick	51B	137	$3.50	$14.00
Stengel, Casey	50B	217	$35.00	$140.00
Stengel, Casey	51B	181	$22.50	$90.00
Stengel, Casey	52B	217	$40.00	$160.00
Stengel, Casey	53BW	39	$75.00	$300.00
Stephens, Vern	49B	71	$6.00	$18.00
Stephens, Vern	50B	2	$15.00	$60.00
Stephens, Vern	51B	92	$3.50	$14.00
Stephens, Vern	52B	9	$4.50	$18.00
Stephens, Vern	55B	109	$1.75	$7.00
Stevens, Ed	49B	93	$3.75	$15.00
Stevens, John W.	55B	258	$6.25	$25.00
Stewart, Eddie	49B	173	$18.75	$75.00
Stewart, Eddie	50B	143	$4.50	$18.00
Stewart, Eddie	51B	159	$3.50	$14.00
Stewart, Eddie	52B	185	$3.75	$15.00
Stirnweiss, George	48B	35	$7.00	$20.00
Stirnweiss, George "Snuffy"	49B	165	$18.75	$75.00
Stirnweiss, George "Snuffy"	50B	249	$4.50	$18.00
Stirnweiss, Snuffy	51B	21	$6.00	$20.00
Strickland, George	52B	207	$3.75	$15.00
Strickland, George	54B	36	$2.00	$8.00
Strickland, George	55B	192	$1.75	$7.00
Stringer, Lou	49B	183	$18.75	$75.00
Stringer, Lou	50B	187	$4.50	$18.00

Player	Year	No.	VG	EX/MT
Stuart, Marlin	52B	147	$3.75	$15.00
Stuart, Marlin	53BC	120	$12.50	$50.00
Suder, Pete	50B	140	$4.50	$18.00
Suder, Pete	51B	154	$3.50	$14.00
Suder, Pete	52B	179	$3.75	$15.00
Suder, Pete	53BW	8	$8.00	$32.00
Suder, Pete	54B	99	$2.00	$8.00
Suder, Pete	55B	6	$2.00	$8.00
Sukeforth, Clyde	52B	227	$7.50	$30.00
Sullivan, Frank	55B	15	$2.00	$8.00
Summers, William R.	55B	317	$6.25	$25.00
Surkont, Max	52B	12	$4.50	$18.00
Surkont, Max	53BC	156	$11.25	$45.00
Surkont, Max	54B	75	$2.00	$8.00
Surkont, Max	55B	83	$2.00	$8.00
Susce Jr., George	55B	320	$10.00	$50.00
Swift, Bob	49B	148	$18.75	$75.00
Swift, Bob	50B	149	$4.50	$18.00
Swift, Bob	51B	214	$3.50	$14.00
Swift, Bob	52B	131	$3.75	$15.00
Talbot, Bob	55B	137	$1.75	$7.00
Tappe, Elvin	55B	51	$2.00	$8.00
Taylor, Zack	51B	315	$15.00	$60.00
Tebbetts, Birdie	51B	257	$15.00	$60.00
Tebbetts, George "Birdie"	52B	124	$3.75	$15.00
Tebbetts, Birdie	55B	232	$3.75	$15.00
Temple, Johnny	55B	31	$2.50	$10.00
Terwilliger, Wayne	50B	114	$4.50	$18.00
Terwilliger, Wayne	51B	175	$3.50	$14.00
Thomas, Frank	54B	155	$3.75	$15.00
Thomas, Frank	55B	58	$2.50	$10.00
Thomas, Keith	53BW	62	$8.00	$32.00
Thompson, Henry	50B	174	$5.00	$20.00
Thompson, Henry	51B	89	$3.75	$14.00
Thompson, Henry	52B	249	$7.50	$30.00
Thompson, Henry	54B	217	$3.50	$14.00
Thompson, Henry "Hank"	55B	94	$2.00	$8.00
Thompson, Jocko	49B	161	$18.75	$75.00
Thompson, John "Jocko"	50B	120	$4.50	$18.00
Thompson, John	51B	294	$15.00	$60.00

Player	Year	No.	VG	EX/MT
Thomson, Bobby	**48B**	**47**	**$20.00**	**$80.00**
Thomson, Bobby	49B	18	$7.50	$30.00
Thomson, Bobby	50B	28	$15.00	$60.00
Thomson, Bobby	51B	126	$7.50	$30.00
Thomson, Bobby	52B	2	$7.50	$30.00
Thomson, Bobby	54B	201	$4.50	$18.00
Thomson, Bobby	55B	102	$3.00	$12.00
Tipton, Joe	49B	103	$3.75	$15.00
Tipton, Joe	50B	159	$4.50	$18.00

BOWMAN

Player	Year	No.	VG	EX/MT
Tipton, Joe	51B	82	$3.50	$14.00
Tipton, Joe	53BW	13	$8.00	$32.00
Tipton, Joe	54B	180	$3.50	$14.00
Torgeson, Earl	49B	17	$5.25	$16.00
Torgeson, Earl	50B	163	$4.50	$18.00
Torgeson, Earl	51B	99	$3.50	$14.00
Torgeson, Earl	52B	72	$3.75	$15.00
Torgeson, Earl	54B	63	$2.00	$8.00
Torgeson, Earl	55B	210	$1.75	$7.00
Tresh, Mike	49B	166	$18.75	$75.00
Trinkle, Ken	49B	193	$18.75	$75.00
Trout, Dizzy	49B	208	$22.50	$90.00
Trout, Paul "Dizzy"	50B	134	$4.50	$18.00
Trucks, Virgil	49B	219	$18.75	$75.00
Trucks, Virgil	50B	96	$4.50	$18.00
Trucks, Virgil	51B	104	$3.50	$14.00
Trucks, Virgil	53BW	17	$8.00	$32.00
Trucks, Virgil	54B	198	$3.50	$14.00
Trucks, Virgil	55B	26	$2.00	$8.00
Tucker, Thurman	51B	222	$3.50	$14.00
Tuttle, Bill	55B	35	$2.00	$8.00
Umont, Frank	55B	305	$6.25	$25.00
Umphlett, Tom	54B	88	$2.00	$8.00
Umphlett, Tom	55B	45	$2.00	$8.00
Usher, Bob	51B	286	$15.00	$60.00
Valo, Elmer	49B	66	$6.00	$18.00
Valo, Elmer	50B	49	$12.50	$50.00
Valo, Elmer	52B	206	$3.75	$15.00
VanderMeer, Johnny	49B	128	$5.00	$20.00
VanderMeer, Johnny	50B	79	$5.50	$22.00
VanderMeer, Johnny	51B	223	$5.00	$20.00
Verban, Emil	48B	28	$8.50	$35.00
Verban, Emil	49B	38	$6.00	$18.00
Vernon, Mickey	49B	94	$7.50	$30.00
Vernon, Mickey	50B	132	$5.00	$20.00
Vernon, Mickey	51B	65	$3.50	$14.00
Vernon, Mickey	52B	87	$3.75	$15.00
Vernon, Mickey	53BC	159	$12.00	$48.00
Vernon, Mickey	54B	152	$3.50	$14.00
Vernon, Mickey "James"	55B	46	$2.00	$8.00
Vico, George	49B	122	$3.75	$15.00
Vico, George	50B	150	$4.50	$18.00
Virdon, Bill	55B	296	$8.75	$35.00
Vollmer, Clyde	50B	53	$12.50	$50.00
Vollmer, Clyde	51B	91	$3.50	$14.00
Vollmer, Clyde	52B	57	$3.75	$15.00
Vollmer, Clyde	53BC	152	$11.25	$45.00
Vollmer, Clyde	54B	136	$3.50	$14.00
Vollmer, Clyde	55B	13	$2.00	$8.00
Waitkus, Eddie	49B	142	$3.75	$15.00
Waitkus, Eddie	50B	30	$12.50	$50.00
Waitkus, Eddie	51B	28	$6.00	$20.00
Waitkus, Eddie	52B	92	$3.75	$15.00
Waitkus, Eddie	55B	4	$2.00	$8.00
Wakefield, Dick	49B	91	$3.75	$15.00
Walker, Harry	49B	130	$3.75	$15.00
Walker, Harry	50B	180	$4.50	$18.00
Walls, Lee	55B	82	$2.00	$8.00
Ward, Preston	50B	231	$4.50	$18.00
Ward, Preston	54B	139	$3.50	$14.00
Ward, Preston	55B	27	$2.00	$8.00
Warneke, Lonnie	55B	299	$6.25	$25.00
Wehmeier, Herman	48B	46	$9.00	$28.00
Wehmeier, Herman	49B	51	$6.00	$18.00
Wehmeier, Herman	50B	27	$12.50	$50.00
Wehmeier, Herman	51B	144	$3.50	$14.00
Wehmeier, Herman	52B	150	$3.75	$15.00
Wehmeier, Herman	53BC	23	$7.50	$30.00
Werle, Bill	50B	87	$4.50	$18.00
Werle, Bill	51B	64	$3.50	$14.00
Werle, Bill	52B	248	$7.50	$30.00
Wertz, Vic	49B	164	$18.75	$100.00
Wertz, Vic	50B	9	$12.50	$50.00
Wertz, Vic	51B	176	$3.50	$14.00
Wertz, Vic	52B	39	$3.75	$15.00
Wertz, Vic	53BC	2	$7.50	$30.00
Wertz, Vic	54B	21	$2.00	$8.00
Wertz, Vic	55B	40	$2.00	$8.00
Westlake, Wally	49B	45	$6.00	$18.00
Westlake, Wally	50B	69	$12.50	$50.00
Westrum, Wes	51B	161	$4.25	$17.00
Westrum, Wes	52B	74	$3.75	$15.00
Westrum, Wes	54B	25	$2.00	$8.00
Westrum, Wes	55B	141	$1.75	$7.00
White, Hal	51B	320	$15.00	$60.00
White, Sammy	53BC	41	$7.50	$30.00
White, Sammy	54B	34	$2.00	$8.00
White, Sammy	55B	47	$2.00	$8.00
Whitman, Dick	51B	221	$3.50	$14.00
Widmar, Al	51B	281	$15.00	$60.00
Wight, Bill	50B	38	$12.50	$50.00
Wight, Bill	51B	164	$3.50	$14.00
Wight, Bill	52B	117	$3.75	$15.00
Wight, Bill	53BC	100	$7.50	$30.00
Wight, Bill	55B	312	$3.75	$15.00
Wilber, Del	52B	225	$7.50	$30.00
Wilber, Del	53BW	24	$8.00	$32.00
Wilber, Del	54B	178	$3.50	$14.00
Wilhelm, Hoyt	53BW	28	$30.00	$120.00
Wilhelm, Hoyt	54B	57	$7.50	$30.00
Wilhelm, Hoyt	55B	1	$20.00	$90.00
Wilks, Ted	49B	137	$3.75	$15.00
Wilks, Ted	51B	193	$3.50	$14.00
Wilks, Ted	52B	138	$3.75	$15.00
Williams, Davey	52B	178	$4.50	$18.00
Williams, Davey	53BC	1	$20.00	$90.00
Williams, Davey	54B	9	$2.00	$8.00
Williams, Davey	55B	138	$1.75	$7.00
Williams, Ted	50B	98	$200.00	$800.00
Williams, Ted	51B	165	$165.00	$660.00
Williams, Ted	54B	66	$1125.00	$4500.00
Wilson, Archie	52B	210	$3.75	$15.00
Wilson, Jim	53BC	37	$7.50	$30.00
Wilson, Jim	54B	16	$2.00	$8.00
Wilson, Jim	55B	253	$3.75	$15.00
Wood, Ken	50B	190	$4.50	$18.00
Wood, Ken	51B	209	$3.50	$14.00
Wood, Ken	53BC	109	$7.50	$30.00
Woodling, Gene	51B	219	$8.50	$34.00
Woodling, Gene	52B	177	$5.00	$20.00
Woodling, Gene	53BW	31	$12.50	$50.00
Woodling, Gene	54B	209	$4.50	$18.00

BOWMAN

Player	Year	No.	VG	EX/MT	Player	Year	No.	VG	EX/MT
Wooten, Earl	49B	189	$18.75	$75.00	Yost, Eddie	52B	31	$4.50	$18.00
Wright, Taft	49B	96	$3.75	$15.00	Yost, Eddie	53BC	116	$12.50	$50.00
Wright, Tommy	51B	271	$15.00	$60.00	Yost, Eddie	54B	72	$2.00	$8.00
Wynn, Early	49B	110	$32.50	$130.00	Yost, Eddie	55B	73	$2.00	$8.00
Wynn, Early	50B	148	$16.25	$65.00	Young, Babe	49B	240	$30.00	$130.00
Wynn, Early	51B	78	$12.50	$50.00	Young, Bobby	52B	193	$3.75	$15.00
Wynn, Early	52B	142	$11.25	$45.00	Young, Bobby	54B	149	$3.50	$14.00
Wynn, Early	53BC	146	$27.50	$110.00	Yvars, Sal	54B	78	$2.00	$8.00
Wynn, Early	54B	164	$11.25	$45.00	Zarilla, Al	49B	156	$18.75	$75.00
Wynn, Early	55B	38	$6.25	$25.00	Zarilla, Al	50B	45	$12.50	$50.00
Wyrostek, Johnny	48B	44	$9.00	$28.00	Zarilla, Al	51B	35	$6.00	$20.00
Wyrostek, Johnny	49B	37	$6.00	$18.00	Zarilla, Al	52B	113	$3.75	$15.00
Wyrostek, Johnny	50B	197	$4.50	$18.00	Zernial, Gus	50B	4	$16.25	$65.00
Wyrostek, Johnny	51B	107	$3.50	$14.00	Zernial, Gus	51B	262	$18.75	$70.00
Wyrostek, Johnny	52B	42	$3.75	$15.00	Zernial, Gus	52B	82	$4.50	$18.00
Wyrostek, Johnny	53BW	35	$8.00	$32.00	Zernial, Gus	53BC	13	$7.50	$30.00
Wyrostek, Johnny	55B	237	$3.75	$15.00	Zimmer, Don	55B	65	$7.00	$28.00
Wyse, Hank	51B	192	$3.50	$14.00	Zoldak, Sam	49B	78	$3.75	$15.00
Yost, Eddie	49B	32	$5.75	$20.00	Zoldak, Sam	50B	182	$4.50	$18.00
Yost, Eddie	50B	162	$4.50	$18.00	Zoldak, Sam	51B	114	$3.50	$14.00
Yost, Eddie	51B	41	$3.50	$14.00	Zuverink, George	55B	92	$2.00	$8.00

1989, 1990, 1991, 1992
BOWMAN

Player	Year	No.	VG	EX/MT	Player	Year	No.	VG	EX/MT
Abbott, Jim	89B	39	$ .10	$1.00	Andersen, Larry	91B	660	$ .01	$ .04
Abbott, Jim	90B	288	$ .01	$ .15	Anderson, Allan	89B	149	$ .01	$ .03
Abbott, Jim	91B	200	$ .01	$ .10	Anderson, Allan	90B	409	$ .01	$ .04
Abbott, Jim	92B	185	$ .10	$1.00	Anderson, Allan	91B	327	$ .01	$ .04
Abbott, Jim	92B	572	$ .10	$1.00	Anderson, Brady	89B	18	$ .10	$ .50
Abbott, Kyle	90B	287	$ .01	$ .15	Anderson, Brady	90B	258	$ .01	$ .10
Abbott, Kyle	91B	187	$ .01	$ .04	Anderson, Brady	91B	100	$ .01	$ .04
Abbott, Kyle	92B	310	$ .05	$ .25	Anderson, Dave	92B	394	$ .05	$ .20
Abbott, Paul	91B	329	$ .01	$ .10	Anderson, Garret	92B	298	$ .05	$ .25
Afenir, Troy	92B	509	$ .05	$ .20	Anderson, Kent	91B	194	$ .01	$ .04
Agosto, Juan	89B	321	$ .01	$ .03	Andrews, Shane	91B	452	$ .05	$ .20
Agosto, Juan	91B	402	$ .01	$ .04	Ansley, Willie	89B	332	$ .01	$ .10
Aguayo, Luis	89B	88	$ .01	$ .03	Ansley, Willie	91B	549	$ .01	$ .04
Aguilera, Rick	90B	405	$ .01	$ .04	Anthony, Eric	90B	81	$ .05	$ .25
Aguilera, Rick	91B	334	$ .01	$ .04	Anthony, Eric	91B	540	$ .01	$ .15
Aguilera, Rick	92B	89	$ .05	$ .20	Anthony, Mark	92B	449	$ .05	$ .20
Akerfelds, Darrel	91B	493	$ .01	$ .04	Appier, Kevin	90B	367	$ .05	$ .25
Aldred, Scott	90B	344	$ .01	$ .15	Appier, Kevin	91B	309	$ .01	$ .04
Aldred, Scott	91B	147	$ .01	$ .04	Appier, Kevin	92B	640	$ .05	$ .25
Aldrete, Mike	89B	368	$ .01	$ .03	Ard, Johnny	89B	153	$ .01	$ .10
Alexander, Doyle	89B	94	$ .01	$ .03	Ard, Johnny	90B	406	$ .01	$ .04
Alexander, Manny	92B	41	$ .10	$ .50	Ard, Johnny	91B	634	$ .01	$ .04
Allanson, Andy	89B	83	$ .01	$ .03	Armas, Tony	89B	51	$ .01	$ .03
Allison, Dana	91B	238	$ .01	$ .10	Armstrong, Jack	91B	679	$ .01	$ .04
Allred, Beau	91B	80	$ .01	$ .04	Armstrong, Jack	92B	252	$ .05	$ .20
Alomar, Roberto	89B	258	$ .05	$ .35	Arneberg, Brad	91B	279	$ .01	$ .04
Alomar, Roberto	89B	458	$ .10	$ .75	Ashby, Alan	89B	327	$ .01	$ .03
Alomar, Roberto	90B	221	$ .05	$ .35	Ashby, Andy	91B	485	$ .01	$ .10
Alomar, Roberto	91B	9	$ .01	$ .15	Ashby, Andy	92B	286	$ .05	$ .35
Alomar, Roberto	92B	20	$ .20	$2.00	Ashley, Billy	92B	168	$ .20	$2.00
Alomar, Sandy	89B	258	$ .05	$ .35	Assenmacher, Paul	89B	265	$ .01	$ .03
Alomar Jr., Sandy	89B	454	$ .05	$ .35	Assenmacher, Paul	91B	431	$ .01	$ .04
Alomar, Sandy	90B	337	$ .01	$ .10	Astacio, Pedro	92B	689	$ .10	$1.00
Alomar, Sandy	91B	57	$ .01	$ .04	August, Don	89B	130	$ .01	$ .03
Alomar, Sandy	92B	140	$ .05	$ .20	Ausanio, Joe	91B	528	$ .01	$ .10
Alou, Moises	90B	178	$ .05	$ .35	Avery, Steve	89B	268	$ .10	$1.00
Alvarez, Tavo	92B	165	$ .10	$ .50	Avery, Steve	90B	9	$ .10	$ .50
Alvarez, Wilson	91B	354	$ .01	$ .10	Avery, Steve	91B	566	$ .01	$ .15
Alvarez, Wilson	92B	69	$ .05	$ .20	Avery, Steve	91B	180	$ .10	$1.00
Amaral, Rich	92B	386	$ .05	$ .35	Azocar, Oscar	91B	652	$ .01	$ .04
Amaro, Ruben	91B	208	$ .01	$ .10	Backman, Wally	89B	159	$ .01	$ .03
Amaro, Ruben	92B	184	$ .05	$ .20	Backman, Wally	90B	177	$ .01	$ .04
Andersen, Larry	89B	325	$ .01	$ .03	Backman, Wally	91B	490	$ .01	$ .04
Andersen, Larry	90B	67	$ .01	$ .04	Baerga, Carlos	90B	339	$ .10	$1.00

BOWMAN

Player	Year	No.	VG	EX/MT
Baerga, Carlos	91B	69	$ .01	$ .15
Baerga, Carlos	92B	531	$ .75	$3.00

Player	Year	No.	VG	EX/MT
Bagwell, Jeff	91B	183	$ .10	$1.00
Bagwell, Jeff	92B	200	$ .75	$3.00
Bailes, Scott	91B	205	$ .01	$ .04
Baines, Harold	89B	72	$ .01	$ .10
Baines, Harold	90B	501	$ .01	$ .04
Baines, Harold	91B	231	$ .01	$ .04
Baines, Harold	92B	171	$ .05	$ .20
Balboni, Steve	90B	436	$ .01	$ .04
Ballard, Jeff	89B	7	$ .01	$ .03
Ballard, Jeff	90B	244	$ .01	$ .04
Ballard, Jeff	91B	98	$ .01	$ .04
Bankhead, Scott	89B	203	$ .01	$ .03
Bankhead, Scott	90B	466	$ .01	$ .04
Bankhead, Scott	91B	254	$ .01	$ .04
Banks, Willie	90B	411	$ .05	$ .25
Banks, Willie	91B	341	$ .01	$ .04
Banks, Willie	92B	553	$ .10	$ .75
Bannister, Floyd	89B	112	$ .01	$ .03
Bannister, Floyd	91B	190	$ .01	$ .04
Barber, Brian	92B	29	$ .10	$ .75
Barberie, Bret	92B	467	$ .05	$ .20
Barfield, Jesse	89B	257	$ .01	$ .10
Barfield, Jesse	90B	433	$ .01	$ .04
Barfield, Jesse	91B	169	$ .01	$ .04
Barfield, Jesse	92B	295	$ .05	$ .20
Barnes, Brian	91B	438	$ .01	$ .10
Barnes, Brian	92B	501	$ .05	$ .20
Barrett, Marty	89B	28	$ .01	$ .03
Barrett, Marty	90B	282	$ .01	$ .04
Barrett, Marty	91B	648	$ .01	$ .04
Bass, Kevin	90B	240	$ .01	$ .04
Bass, Kevin	91B	625	$ .01	$ .04
Bathe, Bill	90B	234	$ .01	$ .04
Batiste, Kim	91B	488	$ .01	$ .15
Batiste, Kim	92B	44	$ .05	$ .25
Battle, Howard	92B	183	$ .10	$ .50
Bautista, Jose	89B	3	$ .01	$ .03
Bearse, Kevin	90B	330	$ .01	$ .10
Beatty, Blaine	90B	130	$ .01	$ .10
Becker, Rich	92B	330	$ .10	$1.00
Beckett, Robbie	91B	655	$ .01	$ .15

Player	Year	No.	VG	EX/MT
Beckett, Robbie	92B	508	$ .05	$ .20
Bedrosian, Steve	89B	395	$ .01	$ .10
Bedrosian, Steve	90B	226	$ .01	$ .04
Bedrosian, Steve	91B	317	$ .01	$ .04
Belcher, Tim	89B	336	$ .01	$ .10
Belcher, Tim	90B	85	$ .01	$ .04
Belcher, Tim	91B	605	$ .01	$ .04
Belcher, Tim	92B	319	$ .05	$ .20
Belcher, Tim	92B	664	$ .05	$ .20
Belinda, Stan	92B	455	$ .05	$ .20
Bell, Buddy	89B	229	$ .01	$ .10
Bell, Derek	92B	237	$ .10	$ .50
Bell, Derek	92B	559	$ .10	$1.00
Bell, George	89B	256	$ .01	$ .10
Bell, George	90B	515	$ .01	$ .04
Bell, George	91B	418	$ .01	$ .04
Bell, Jay	90B	174	$ .01	$ .04
Bell, Jay	91B	522	$ .01	$ .04
Bell, Jay	92B	519	$ .05	$ .20
Bell, Juan	89B	11	$ .01	$ .10
Bell, Juan	91B	96	$ .01	$ .04
Belle, Joey "Albert"	90B	333	$ .10	$ .50
Belle, Albert	91B	81	$ .01	$ .10
Belle, Albert	92B	329	$ .75	$3.00
Belliard, Rafael	91B	578	$ .01	$ .04
Belliard, Rafael	92B	75	$ .05	$ .20
Beltre, Esteban	92B	458	$ .05	$ .25
Benavides, Freddie	91B	672	$ .01	$ .04
Bene, Bill	89B	340	$ .01	$ .03
Benedict, Bruce	89B	271	$ .01	$ .03
Benes, Andy	89B	448	$ .10	$ .50
Benes, Andy	90B	207	$ .01	$ .15
Benes, Andy	91B	665	$ .01	$ .04
Benes, Andy	92B	249	$ .05	$ .25
Benes, Andy	92B	599	$ .10	$ .50
Benzinger, Todd	89B	312	$ .01	$ .03
Benzinger, Todd	90B	55	$ .01	$ .04
Benzinger, Todd	92B	141	$ .05	$ .20
Bere, Jason	92B	358	$ .10	$1.00
Berenguer, Juan	89B	152	$ .01	$ .03
Berenguer, Juan	90B	410	$ .01	$ .04
Berenguer, Juan	91B	572	$ .01	$ .04
Bergman, Dave	90B	355	$ .01	$ .04
Bernazard, Tony	91B	143	$ .01	$ .04
Bernhardt, Cesar	91B	360	$ .01	$ .10
Berroa, Geronimo	89B	279	$ .01	$ .03
Berryhill, Damon	89B	288	$ .01	$ .10
Berryhill, Damon	90B	33	$ .01	$ .04
Bichette, Dante	91B	31	$ .01	$ .04
Bichette, Dante	92B	264	$ .05	$ .20
Bielecki, Mike	90B	22	$ .01	$ .04
Bielecki, Mike	91B	422	$ .01	$ .04
Biggio, Craig	90B	78	$ .01	$ .10
Biggio, Craig	91B	556	$ .01	$ .10
Biggio, Craig	92B	484	$ .05	$ .20
Birkbeck, Mike	89B	132	$ .01	$ .03
Bittiger, Jeff	89B	60	$ .01	$ .03
Black, Bud	89B	82	$ .01	$ .03
Black, Bud	91B	639	$ .01	$ .04
Black, Bud	92B	692	$ .05	$ .20
Blair, Willie	90B	504	$ .01	$ .10
Blankenship, Kevin	90B	24	$ .01	$ .04
Blauser, Jeff	90B	15	$ .01	$ .04
Blosser, Greg	90B	278	$ .05	$ .25
Blosser, Greg	91B	115	$ .01	$ .10
Blosser, Greg	92B	251	$ .05	$ .35
Blowers, Mike	90B	441	$ .01	$ .10
Blyleven, Bert	89B	41	$ .01	$ .10
Blyleven, Bert	90B	285	$ .01	$ .04
Bockus, Randy	89B	96	$ .01	$ .03
Boddicker, Mike	89B	21	$ .01	$ .03
Boddicker, Mike	90B	267	$ .01	$ .04
Boddicker, Mike	91B	296	$ .01	$ .04
Boddicker, Mike	92B	132	$ .05	$ .20
Boever, Joe	91B	502	$ .01	$ .04

BOWMAN

Player	Year	No.	VG	EX/MT
Boggs, Wade	89B	32	$ .05	$ .25
Boggs, Wade	90B	281	$ .01	$ .15
Boggs, Wade	91B	129	$ .01	$ .10
Boggs, Wade	92B	70	$ .10	$1.00
Bohanon, Brian	90B	489	$ .05	$ .20
Bohr, Greg	91B	142	$ .01	$ .04
Bolick, Frank	91B	534	$ .01	$ .10
Bolton, Rod	92B	240	$ .05	$ .35
Bolton, Tom	91B	114	$ .01	$ .04
Bonds, Barry	89B	426	$ .05	$ .35
Bonds, Barry	90B	181	$ .05	$ .25
Bonds, Barry	91B	380	$ .01	$ .10
Bonds, Barry	91B	513	$ .01	$ .15
Bonds, Barry	92B	60	$ .75	$3.00
Bonds, Barry	92B	590	$1.25	$5.00
Bones, Ricky	91B	643	$ .01	$ .15
Bonilla, Bobby	89B	422	$ .05	$ .20
Bonilla, Bobby	90B	169	$ .01	$ .10
Bonilla, Bobby	91B	381	$ .01	$ .10
Bonilla, Bobby	91B	525	$ .01	$ .10
Bonilla, Bobby	92B	235	$ .05	$ .35
Boone, Bob	89B	119	$ .01	$ .03
Boone, Bob	90B	373	$ .01	$ .04
Boone, Bret	91B	261	$ .10	$ .50
Boone, Bret	92B	511	$ .15	$1.50
Borders, Pat	90B	521	$ .01	$ .04
Borders, Pat	91B	14	$ .01	$ .04
Borders, Pat	92B	646	$ .05	$ .20
Bordick, Mike	92B	350	$ .05	$ .25
Bosio, Chris	89B	134	$ .01	$ .03
Bosio, Chris	90B	389	$ .01	$ .04
Bosio, Chris	91B	43	$ .01	$ .04
Boston, Daryl	89B	70	$ .01	$ .03
Boston, Daryl	90B	317	$ .01	$ .04
Boston, Daryl	91B	476	$ .01	$ .04
Bottenfield, Kent	92B	478	$ .05	$ .35
Boucher, Denis	91B	29	$ .01	$ .10
Bowen, Ryan	91B	539	$ .01	$ .10
Bowen, Ryan	92B	401	$ .10	$ .40
Boyd, Dennis	90B	102	$ .01	$ .04
Boyd, Dennis	91B	456	$ .01	$ .04
Bradley, Phil	89B	17	$ .01	$ .03
Bradley, Phil	90B	261	$ .01	$ .04
Bradley, Scott	89B	209	$ .01	$ .03
Bradley, Scott	90B	483	$ .01	$ .04
Bradley, Scott	91B	239	$ .01	$ .04
Braggs, Glenn	89B	145	$ .01	$ .03
Braggs, Glenn	90B	403	$ .01	$ .04
Braggs, Glenn	91B	669	$ .01	$ .04
Branca, Ralph	91B	410	$ .01	$ .10
Branson, Jeff	90B	52	$ .01	$ .10
Branson, Jeff	92B	512	$ .05	$ .20
Brantley, Cliff	92B	120	$ .05	$ .20
Brantley, Jeff	91B	620	$ .01	$ .04
Bream, Sid	89B	419	$ .01	$ .03
Bream, Sid	90B	175	$ .01	$ .04
Bream, Sid	91D	505	$ .01	$ .04
Bream, Sid	92B	356	$ .05	$ .20
Brenly, Bob	89B	249	$ .01	$ .03
Brett, George	89B	121	$ .01	$ .15
Brett, George	90B	382	$ .01	$ .10
Brett, George	91B	300	$ .01	$ .10
Brett, George	92B	500	$ .10	$1.00
Briley, Greg	90B	482	$ .01	$ .10
Briley, Greg	91B	256	$ .01	$ .04
Brock, Greg	89B	143	$ .01	$ .03
Brock, Greg	90B	395	$ .01	$ .04
Brock, Greg	91B	41	$ .01	$ .04
Brock, Tarrik	92B	345	$ .05	$ .35
Brogna, Ricco "Rico"	89B	102	$ .05	$ .20
Brogna, Rico	90B	351	$ .01	$ .10
Brogna, Rico	91B	134	$ .01	$ .10
Brogna, Rico	92B	256	$ .05	$ .20
Brooks, Hubie	89B	367	$ .01	$ .03
Brooks, Hubie	90B	100	$ .01	$ .04
Brooks, Hubie	91B	461	$ .01	$ .04
Brooks, Hubie	92B	97	$ .05	$ .20
Brosius, Scott	92B	527	$ .05	$ .20
Bross, Terry	90B	129	$ .01	$ .10
Brower, Bob	89B	182	$ .01	$ .03
Brown, Chris	89B	106	$ .01	$ .03
Brown, Kevin	90B	127	$ .01	$ .10
Brown, Kevin	90B	488	$ .01	$ .10
Brown, Kevin	91B	49	$ .01	$ .04
Brown, Kevin	91B	274	$ .01	$ .04
Brown, Kevin	92B	191	$ .05	$ .20
Browne, Jerry	89B	85	$ .01	$ .03
Browne, Jerry	90B	332	$ .01	$ .04
Browne, Jerry	91B	71	$ .01	$ .04
Browning, Tom	89B	306	$ .01	$ .10
Browning, Tom	90B	43	$ .01	$ .10
Browning, Tom	91B	684	$ .01	$ .04
Browning, Tom	92B	161	$ .05	$ .20
Bruett, J.T.	92B	112	$ .05	$ .25
Brunansky, Tom	89B	444	$ .01	$ .03
Brunansky, Tom	90B	202	$ .01	$ .04
Brunansky, Tom	91B	125	$ .01	$ .04
Bryant, Scott	90B	59	$ .01	$ .10
Buechele, Steve	89B	232	$ .01	$ .03
Buechele, Steve	90B	493	$ .01	$ .04
Buechele, Steve	91B	268	$ .01	$ .04
Buechele, Steve	92B	335	$ .05	$ .20
Buford, Damon	92B	224	$ .05	$ .25
Buhner, Jay	89B	219	$ .01	$ .10
Buhner, Jay	90B	477	$ .01	$ .04
Buhner, Jay	91B	247	$ .01	$ .04
Buhner, Jay	92B	248	$ .05	$ .20
Bullett, Scott	92B	321	$ .05	$ .35
Bullock, Eric	91B	457	$ .01	$ .04
Burba, Dave	91B	263	$ .01	$ .10
Burba, Dave	92B	190	$ .05	$ .20
Burke, Tim	89B	360	$ .01	$ .03
Burke, Tim	90B	103	$ .01	$ .04
Burkett, John	91B	637	$ .01	$ .04
Burks, Ellis	89B	36	$ .01	$ .10
Burks, Ellis	90B	280	$ .01	$ .10
Burks, Ellis	91B	109	$ .01	$ .04
Burks, Ellis	91B	373	$ .01	$ .04
Burks, Ellis	92B	570	$ .05	$ .20
Burnitz, Jeromy	91B	474	$ .05	$ .25
Burnitz, Jeromy	92B	189	$ .10	$ .50
Burns, Todd	91B	221	$ .01	$ .04
Burton, Darren	92B	424	$ .05	$ .25
Bush, Randy	89B	164	$ .01	$ .03
Bush, Randy	90B	416	$ .01	$ .04
Butler, Brett	89B	480	$ .01	$ .03
Butler, Brett	90B	237	$ .01	$ .04
Butler, Brett	91B	597	$ .01	$ .04
Butler, Brett	92B	597	$ .05	$ .20
Butler, Robert	92B	603	$ .05	$ .35
Byrd, Paul	92B	349	$ .10	$ .40
Cadaret, Greg	91B	157	$ .01	$ .04
Cadaret, Greg	92B	231	$ .05	$ .20
Calderon, Ivan	89B	68	$ .01	$ .03
Calderon, Ivan	90B	316	$ .01	$ .04
Calderon, Ivan	91B	440	$ .01	$ .04
Calderon, Ivan	92B	179	$ .05	$ .20
Camacho, Ernie	90B	229	$ .01	$ .04
Caminiti, Ken	90B	73	$ .01	$ .04
Caminiti, Ken	91B	543	$ .01	$ .04
Caminiti, Ken	92B	538	$ .05	$ .20
Campanis, Jim	92B	144	$ .05	$ .20
Canale, George	90B	392	$ .01	$ .10
Candaele, Casey	91B	559	$ .01	$ .04
Candelaria, John	89B	171	$ .01	$ .03
Candiotti, Tom	89B	80	$ .01	$ .03
Candiotti, Tom	90B	324	$ .01	$ .04
Candiotti, Tom	91B	62	$ .01	$ .04
Candiotti, Tom	92B	606	$ .05	$ .20
Cangelosi, John	92B	442	$ .05	$ .20

BOWMAN

Player	Year	No.	VG	EX/MT	Player	Year	No.	VG	EX/MT
Cano, Jose	90B	68	$ .01	$ .04	Clancy, Jim	89B	324	$ .01	$ .03
Canseco, Jose	89B	201	$ .05	$ .35	Clancy, Jim	91B	554	$ .01	$ .04
Canseco, Jose	90B	460	$ .05	$ .25	Clark, Jack	89B	456	$ .01	$ .03
Canseco, Jose	91B	227	$ .01	$ .15	Clark, Jack	90B	214	$ .01	$ .04
Canseco, Jose	91B	372	$ .01	$ .10	Clark, Jack	91B	122	$ .01	$ .04
Canseco, Jose	92B	600	$ .15	$1.50	Clark, Jack	92B	233	$ .05	$ .20
Caraballo, Gary	92B	54	$ .10	$ .30	Clark, Jerald	89B	462	$ .01	$ .10
Caraballo, Ramon	91B	584	$ .01	$ .10	Clark, Jerald	91B	658	$ .01	$ .04
Carew, Rod	91B	1	$ .05	$ .20	Clark, Jerald	92B	323	$ .05	$ .20
Carew, Rod	91B	2	$ .01	$ .15	Clark, Mark	92B	109	$ .05	$ .20
Carew, Rod	91B	3	$ .01	$ .15	Clark, Will	89B	476	$ .05	$ .35
Carew, Rod	91B	4	$ .01	$ .15	Clark, Will	90B	231	$ .05	$ .25
Carew, Rod	91B	5	$ .01	$ .15	Clark, Will	91B	616	$ .01	$ .15
Carman, Don	89B	392	$ .01	$ .03	Clark, Will	92B	260	$ .20	$2.00
Carmona, Greg	91B	392	$ .01	$ .10	Clark, Will	92B	673	$ .25	$2.50
Carreon, Mark	89B	389	$ .01	$ .03	Clayton, Royce	89B	472	$ .05	$ .35
Carreon, Mark	92B	111	$ .05	$ .20	Clayton, Royce	91B	641	$ .01	$ .15
Carter, Gary	89B	379	$ .01	$ .03	Clayton, Royce	92B	212	$ .10	$1.00
Carter, Gary	90B	236	$ .01	$ .10	Clemens, Roger	89B	26	$ .05	$ .30
Carter, Gary	91B	598	$ .01	$ .04	Clemens, Roger	90B	268	$ .05	$ .35
Carter, Gary	92B	385	$ .05	$ .20	Clemens, Roger	91B	118	$ .05	$ .20
Carter, Jeff	91B	348	$ .01	$ .10	Clemens, Roger	92B	691	$ .20	$2.00
Carter, Joe	89B	91	$ .05	$ .20	Clements, Pat	89B	452	$ .01	$ .03
Carter, Joe	90B	220	$ .01	$ .10	Clements, Pat	92B	533	$ .05	$ .20
Carter, Joe	91B	11	$ .01	$ .10	Coffman, Kevin	89B	282	$ .01	$ .03
Carter, Joe	92B	573	$ .10	$1.00	Colbrunn, Greg	91B	449	$ .05	$ .25
Carter, Joe	92B	667	$ .20	$2.00	Cole, Alex	91B	64	$ .01	$ .04
Carter, Michael	92B	243	$ .05	$ .20	Cole, Alex	92B	173	$ .05	$ .20
Carter, Steve	90B	179	$ .01	$ .10	Cole, Victor	92B	239	$ .10	$ .50
Cary, Chuck	91B	176	$ .01	$ .04	Coleman, Paul	90B	199	$ .01	$ .10
Casian, Larry	91B	325	$ .01	$ .04	Coleman, Paul	91B	385	$ .01	$ .04
Castellano, Pete	92B	271	$ .10	$ .40	Coleman, Vince	89B	443	$ .01	$ .10
Castellano, Pete	92B	649	$ .10	$ .75	Coleman, Vince	90B	198	$ .01	$ .04
Castillo, Braulio	92B	104	$ .05	$ .35	Coleman, Vince	91B	471	$ .01	$ .10
Castillo, Joe	89B	244	$ .01	$ .03	Coleman, Vince	92B	613	$ .05	$ .20
Cedeno, Andujar	90B	77	$ .05	$ .20	Coles, Darnell	89B	217	$ .01	$ .03
Cedeno, Andujar	91B	563	$ .01	$ .10	Coles, Darnell	90B	480	$ .01	$ .04
Cedeno, Andujar	92B	9	$ .05	$ .20	Coles, Darnell	92B	382	$ .05	$ .20
Cepicky, Scott	92B	297	$ .10	$ .40	Colon, Cris	92B	405	$ .05	$ .25
Cepicky, Scott	92B	614	$ .10	$ .50	Combs, Pat	89B	398	$ .01	$ .10
Cerone, Rick	90B	435	$ .01	$ .04	Combs, Pat	90B	148	$ .01	$ .04
Cerone, Rick	91B	468	$ .01	$ .04	Combs, Pat	91B	498	$ .01	$ .04
Cerutti, John	89B	247	$ .01	$ .03	Comstock, Keith	90B	467	$ .01	$ .04
Cerutti, John	90B	507	$ .01	$ .04	Cone, David	89B	375	$ .01	$ .10
Cerutti, John	91B	139	$ .01	$ .04	Cone, David	90B	125	$ .01	$ .10
Chamberlain, Wes	91B	505	$ .01	$ .15	Cone, David	91B	460	$ .01	$ .10
Chamberlain, Wes	92B	412	$ .05	$ .35	Cone, David	92B	238	$ .05	$ .35
Charlton, Norm	91B	690	$ .01	$ .04	Conine, Jeff	91B	184	$ .05	$ .35
Checklist, Cards (1-121)	89B	481	$ .01	$ .03	Cook, Dennis	92B	497	$ .05	$ .20
Checklist, Cards (122-242)	89B	482	$ .01	$ .03	Cooke, Steve	92B	274	$ .10	$ .50
Checklist, Cards (243-363)	89B	483	$ .01	$ .03	Coolbaugh, Scott	90B	494	$ .01	$ .10
Checklist, Cards (364-484)	89B	484	$ .01	$ .03	Coolbaugh, Scott	91B	649	$ .01	$ .10
Checklist, Cards (1-132)	90B	525	$ .01	$ .04	Cooper, Scott	90B	277	$ .05	$ .25
Checklist, Cards (133-264)	90B	526	$ .01	$ .04	Cooper, Scott	92B	129	$ .10	$1.00
Checklist, Cards (265-396)	90B	527	$ .01	$ .04	Cora, Joey	90B	211	$ .01	$ .04
Checklist, Cards (397-528)	90B	528	$ .01	$ .04	Cordero, Wilfredo	91B	436	$ .10	$ .50
Checklist, Cards (1-122)	91B	699	$ .01	$ .04	Cordero, Wil	92B	194	$ .75	$3.00
Checklist, Cards (123-244)	91B	700	$ .01	$ .04	Cormier, Rheal	91B	396	$ .01	$ .10
Checklist, Cards (245-366)	91B	701	$ .01	$ .04	Cormier, Rheal	92B	473	$ .10	$ .75
Checklist, Cards (367-471)	91B	702	$ .01	$ .04	Cornelius, Reid	91B	458	$ .01	$ .10
Checklist, Cards (472-593)	91B	703	$ .01	$ .04	Costo, Tim	91B	79	$ .01	$ .15
Checklist, Cards (594-704)	91B	704	$ .01	$ .04	Costo, Tim	92B	489	$ .05	$ .25
Checklist, Cards (1-141)	92B	701	$ .05	$ .20	Cotto, Henry	90B	476	$ .01	$ .04
Checklist, Cards (142-282)	92B	702	$ .05	$ .20	Cotto, Henry	91B	244	$ .01	$ .04
Checklist, Cards (283-423)	92B	703	$ .05	$ .20	Crespo, Felipe	92B	77	$ .05	$ .25
Checklist, Cards (424-564)	92B	704	$ .05	$ .20	Crim, Chuck	89B	136	$ .01	$ .03
Checklist, Cards (565-705)	92B	705	$ .05	$ .20	Crim, Chuck	91B	51	$ .01	$ .04
Cheetham, Sean	91B	414	$ .01	$ .10	Cromartie, Warren	91B	315	$ .01	$ .04
Chiamparino, Scott	91B	282	$ .01	$ .04	Cruz, Ivan	91B	153	$ .01	$ .10
Chitren, Steve	91B	214	$ .01	$ .10	Cruz, Ivan	92B	170	$ .05	$ .25
Chitren, Steve	92B	506	$ .05	$ .20	Cunningham, Earl	90B	34	$ .01	$ .10
Christopher, Mike	92B	374	$ .05	$ .20	Cunningham, Earl	91B	420	$ .01	$ .04
Christopherson, Eric	91B	635	$ .01	$ .10	Cunningham, Earl	92B	81	$ .05	$ .20
Christopherson, Eric	92B	38	$ .05	$ .20	Curtis, Chad	92B	627	$ .75	$3.00
Cianfrocco, Archi	92B	450	$ .05	$ .25	Cuyler, Milt	90B	358	$ .01	$ .15

BOWMAN

Player	Year	No.	VG	EX/MT
Cuyler, Milt	91B	141	$.01	$.04
Cuyler, Milt	92B	196	$.10	$.50
Daniels, Kal	89B	314	$.01	$.10
Daniels, Kal	90B	99	$.01	$.04
Daniels, Kal	91B	600	$.01	$.04
Daniels, Kal	92B	487	$.05	$.20
Darling, Ron	89B	372	$.01	$.10
Darling, Ron	91B	483	$.01	$.04

Player	Year	No.	VG	EX/MT
Darling, Ron	92B	30	$.05	$.20
Darwin, Danny	90B	66	$.01	$.04
Darwin, Danny	91B	111	$.01	$.04
Dascenzo, Doug	92B	287	$.05	$.20
Daugherty, Jack	90B	503	$.01	$.10
Daugherty, Jack	91B	277	$.01	$.04
Daulton, Darren	90B	158	$.01	$.04
Daulton, Darren	91B	507	$.01	$.04
Daulton, Darren	92B	440	$.10	$.50
Dauphin, Phil	92B	169	$.05	$.25
Davis, Alvin	89B	215	$.01	$.03
Davis, Alvin	90B	479	$.01	$.04
Davis, Alvin	91B	258	$.01	$.04
Davis, Alvin	92B	341	$.05	$.20
Davis, Chili	89B	50	$.01	$.03
Davis, Chili	90B	301	$.01	$.04
Davis, Chili	91B	331	$.01	$.04
Davis, Chili	92B	195	$.05	$.20
Davis, Doug	92B	490	$.05	$.20
Davis, Eric	89B	316	$.01	$.10
Davis, Eric	90B	58	$.01	$.10
Davis, Eric	91B	686	$.01	$.04
Davis, Eric	92B	671	$.05	$.20
Davis, Glenn	89B	331	$.01	$.10
Davis, Glenn	90B	80	$.01	$.10
Davis, Glenn	91B	83	$.01	$.04
Davis, Glenn	92B	428	$.05	$.20
Davis, Jody	89B	270	$.01	$.03
Davis, Mark	89B	447	$.01	$.03
Davis, Mark	90B	369	$.01	$.04
Davis, Mark	91B	306	$.01	$.04
Davis, Mike	89B	352	$.01	$.03
Davis, Storm	89B	192	$.01	$.03
Davis, Storm	90B	368	$.01	$.04
Davis, Storm	91B	293	$.01	$.04

Player	Year	No.	VG	EX/MT
Dawson, Andre	89B	298	$.01	$.10
Dawson, Andre	90B	39	$.01	$.10
Dawson, Andre	91B	429	$.01	$.10
Dawson, Andre	92B	625	$.10	$.50
Dayley, Ken	89B	428	$.01	$.03
Dayley, Ken	90B	191	$.01	$.04
Dayley, Ken	91B	27	$.01	$.04
De Los Santos, Luis	91B	152	$.01	$.04
Decker, Steve	91B	622	$.01	$.10
Deer, Rob	89B	146	$.01	$.10
Deer, Rob	90B	401	$.01	$.04
Deer, Rob	91B	132	$.01	$.04
Deer, Rob	92B	363	$.05	$.20
DeLeon, Jose	89B	431	$.01	$.03
DeLeon, Jose	90B	186	$.01	$.04
DeLeon, Jose	91B	400	$.01	$.04
DeLeon, Jose	92B	265	$.05	$.20
Delgado, Carlos	92B	127	$2.50	$10.00
DeLucia, Rich	91B	242	$.01	$.04
DeLucia, Rich	92B	665	$.05	$.20
Dempsey, Rick	89B	343	$.01	$.03
Deshaies, Jim	89B	320	$.01	$.03
Deshaies, Jim	90B	70	$.01	$.04
Deshaies, Jim	91B	541	$.01	$.04
DeShields, Delino	90B	119	$.10	$.50
DeShields, Delino	91B	445	$.01	$.15
DeShields, Delino	92B	47	$.10	$.75
DeSilva, John	91B	148	$.01	$.15
DeSilva, John	92B	229	$.05	$.20
Devereaux, Mike	90B	260	$.01	$.04
Devereaux, Mike	91B	93	$.01	$.04
Devereaux, Mike	92B	688	$.05	$.20
Diaz, Bo	89B	307	$.01	$.03
Dibble, Rob	89B	305	$.05	$.20
Dibble, Rob	90B	42	$.01	$.10
Dibble, Rob	91B	667	$.01	$.10
Dibble, Rob	92B	242	$.05	$.20
Dickson, Lance	91B	411	$.01	$.10
Dickson, Lance	92B	316	$.05	$.20
DiPino, Frank	89B	434	$.01	$.03
DiPino, Frank	90B	187	$.01	$.04
DiPoto, Jerry	92B	92	$.05	$.25
DiSarcina, Gary	90B	290	$.01	$.15
DiSarcina, Gary	92B	159	$.05	$.20
Distefano, Benny	92B	414	$.05	$.20
Dodson, Bo	91B	38	$.01	$.10
Doherty, John	92B	518	$.10	$.50
Donnels, Chris	91B	465	$.01	$.10
Doorneweerd, Dave	92B	146	$.05	$.35
Dopson, John	89B	24	$.01	$.03
Doran, Bill	89B	329	$.01	$.03
Doran, Bill	90B	76	$.01	$.04
Doran, Bill	91B	682	$.01	$.04
Doran, Bill	92B	234	$.05	$.20
Downing, Brian	89B	53	$.01	$.03
Downing, Brian	90B	294	$.01	$.04
Downs, Kelly	89B	465	$.01	$.03
Downs, Kelly	91B	633	$.01	$.04
Downs, Kelly	92B	343	$.05	$.20
Dozier, D.J.	91B	478	$.01	$.10
Dozier, D.J.	92B	219	$.05	$.20
Drabek, Doug	89B	416	$.01	$.03
Drabek, Doug	90B	164	$.01	$.04
Drabek, Doug	91B	515	$.01	$.04
Drabek, Doug	92B	465	$.05	$.20
Drahman, Brian	91B	363	$.01	$.10
Dressendorfer, Kirk	91B	235	$.01	$.10
Dressendorfer, Kirk	92B	91	$.05	$.20
Drew, Cameron	89B	334	$.01	$.03
DuBois, Brian	90B	349	$.01	$.10
Duncan, Mariano	91B	675	$.01	$.04
Dunston, Shawon	89B	294	$.01	$.10
Dunston, Shawon	90B	38	$.01	$.04
Dunston, Shawon	91B	424	$.01	$.04
DuVall, Brad	89B	430	$.01	$.03

BOWMAN

Player	Year	No.	VG	EX/MT	Player	Year	No.	VG	EX/MT
Dykstra, Len	90B	152	$ .01	$ .04	Fielder, Cecil	90B	357	$ .05	$ .25
Dykstra, Len	91B	501	$ .01	$ .04	Fielder, Cecil	91B	136	$ .01	$ .10
Dykstra, Len	92B	635	$ .05	$ .20	Fielder, Cecil	91B	367	$ .01	$ .10
Easley, Damion	92B	672	$ .20	$2.00	Fielder, Cecil	92B	90	$ .10	$ .75
Eave, Gary	90B	471	$ .01	$ .10	Filer, Tom	90B	385	$ .01	$ .04
Eckersley, Dennis	89B	190	$ .01	$ .15	Finley, Chuck	89B	37	$ .01	$ .03
Eckersley, Dennis	90B	451	$ .01	$ .10	Finley, Chuck	90B	289	$ .01	$ .04
Eckersley, Dennis	91B	237	$ .01	$ .10	Finley, Chuck	91B	196	$ .01	$ .04
Eckersley, Dennis	92B	431	$ .05	$ .35	Finley, Chuck	92B	32	$ .05	$ .20
Edwards, Wayne	90B	309	$ .01	$ .10	Finley, Steve	89B	15	$ .05	$ .25
Edwards, Wayne	91B	364	$ .01	$ .04	Finley, Steve	91B	561	$ .01	$ .10
Eenhoorn, Robert	91B	172	$ .01	$ .10	Finley, Steve	92B	574	$ .05	$ .20
Eenhoorn, Robert	92B	278	$ .05	$ .20	Fireovid, Steve	92B	334	$ .05	$ .20
Egloff, Bruce	91B	78	$ .01	$ .10	Fischer, Tom	89B	20	$ .01	$ .03
Eisenreich, Jim	90B	374	$ .01	$ .04	Fisher, Brian	89B	415	$ .01	$ .03
Eisenreich, Jim	91B	304	$ .01	$ .04	Fisk, Carlton	89B	62	$ .01	$ .10
Eldred, Cal	90B	387	$ .10	$ .60	Fisk, Carlton	90B	314	$ .01	$ .10
Eldred, Cal	91B	56	$ .05	$ .25	Fisk, Carlton	91B	345	$ .01	$ .10
Eldred, Cal	92B	299	$ .75	$3.00	Fisk, Carlton	92B	585	$ .10	$ .50
Elster, Kevin	89B	383	$ .01	$ .03	Fitzgerald, Mike	91B	453	$ .01	$ .04
Elster, Kevin	90B	137	$ .01	$ .04	Fitzgerald, Mike	92B	186	$ .05	$ .20
Elster, Kevin	91B	469	$ .01	$ .04	Flanagan, Mike	89B	241	$ .01	$ .03
Elvira, Narciso	91B	47	$ .01	$ .10	Flannery, Tim	89B	457	$ .01	$ .03
Embree, Alan	92B	387	$ .10	$ .50	Fleming, Dave	91B	249	$ .10	$ .60
Ericks, John	89B	433	$ .01	$ .10	Fleming, Dave	92B	624	$ .20	$2.00
Ericks, John	90B	190	$ .01	$ .04	Fletcher, Darrin	91B	496	$ .01	$ .04
Ericks, John	91B	393	$ .01	$ .04	Fletcher, Darrin	92B	609	$ .05	$ .20
Ericks, John	92B	48	$ .05	$ .35	Fletcher, Scott	89B	230	$ .01	$ .03
Erickson, Scott	91B	335	$ .01	$ .15	Fletcher, Scott	90B	319	$ .01	$ .04
Erickson, Scott	92B	53	$ .05	$ .20	Fletcher, Scott	91B	359	$ .01	$ .04
Esasky, Nick	89B	31	$ .01	$ .03	Fletcher, Scott	92B	7	$ .05	$ .20
Esasky, Nick	90B	20	$ .01	$ .04	Flora, Kevin	92B	283	$ .05	$ .25
Escobar, Jose	91B	74	$ .01	$ .10	Floyd, Cliff	92B	678	$2.50	$10.00
Eshelman, Vaughn	92B	318	$ .05	$ .35	Foley, Tom	90B	120	$ .01	$ .04
Espinoza, Alvaro	90B	431	$ .01	$ .04	Ford, Curt	89B	408	$ .01	$ .03
Espinoza, Alvaro	91B	163	$ .01	$ .04	Fordyce, Brook	92B	56	$ .05	$ .25
Espy, Cecil	89B	236	$ .01	$ .03	Franco, John	89B	301	$ .01	$ .10
Espy, Cecil	90B	502	$ .01	$ .04	Franco, John	90B	128	$ .01	$ .04
Estes, Shawn	92B	151	$ .10	$ .40	Franco, John	91B	475	$ .01	$ .04
Evans, Darrell	89B	275	$ .01	$ .10	Franco, John	92B	546	$ .05	$ .20
Evans, Dwight	89B	35	$ .01	$ .03	Franco, Julio	89B	228	$ .01	$ .10
Evans, Dwight	90B	279	$ .01	$ .04	Franco, Julio	90B	497	$ .01	$ .04
Evans, Dwight	91B	103	$ .01	$ .04	Franco, Julio	91B	265	$ .01	$ .04
Everett, Carl	91B	156	$ .01	$ .15	Franco, Julio	91B	368	$ .01	$ .04
Everett, Carl	92B	258	$ .05	$ .25	Franco, Julio	92B	206	$ .05	$ .20
Fabregas, Jorge	92B	8	$ .05	$ .35	Fraser, Willie	91B	6	$ .01	$ .04
Fajardo, Hector	92B	22	$ .05	$ .35	Frey, Steve	91B	451	$ .01	$ .04
Faries, Paul	91B	664	$ .01	$ .10	Fryman, Travis	90B	360	$ .15	$1.25
Fariss, Monty	89B	233	$ .05	$ .20	Fryman, Travis	91B	145	$ .10	$ .50
Fariss, Monty	90B	500	$ .01	$ .10	Fryman, Travis	92B	37	$ .75	$3.00
Fariss, Monty	91B	285	$ .01	$ .04	Gaetti, Gary	89B	158	$ .01	$ .03
Farmer, Howard	90B	107	$ .01	$ .10	Gaetti, Gary	90B	417	$ .01	$ .04
Farr, Steve	89B	114	$ .01	$ .03	Gaetti, Gary	91B	207	$ .01	$ .04
Farr, Steve	90B	366	$ .01	$ .04	Gaetti, Gary	92B	564	$ .05	$ .20
Farr, Steve	91B	168	$ .01	$ .04	Gagne, Greg	89B	161	$ .01	$ .03
Farr, Steve	92B	622	$ .05	$ .20	Gagne, Greg	90B	414	$ .01	$ .04
Farrell, John	89B	74	$ .01	$ .03	Gagne, Greg	91B	338	$ .01	$ .04
Farrell, John	91B	82	$ .01	$ .04	Gagne, Greg	92B	660	$ .05	$ .20
Farrell, Jon	92B	393	$ .05	$ .35	Gakeler, Dan	91B	144	$ .01	$ .04
Felder, Mike	92B	93	$ .05	$ .20	Galarraga, Andres	89B	365	$ .01	$ .10
Felix, Junior	90B	522	$ .01	$ .10	Galarraga, Andres	90B	113	$ .01	$ .04
Felix, Junior	91B	201	$ .01	$ .04	Galarraga, Andres	91B	446	$ .01	$ .10
Felix, Junior	92B	404	$ .05	$ .20	Galarraga, Andres	92B	320	$ .05	$ .20
Fermin, Felix	90B	334	$ .01	$ .04	Gallagher, Dave	89B	71	$ .01	$ .10
Fernandez, Alex	91B	351	$ .01	$ .10	Gallego, Mike	90B	459	$ .01	$ .04
Fernandez, Alex	92B	201	$ .05	$ .20	Gallego, Mike	91B	219	$ .01	$ .04
Fernandez, Sid	89B	377	$ .01	$ .03	Gallego, Mike	92B	273	$ .05	$ .20
Fernandez, Sid	90B	131	$ .01	$ .04	Gant, Ron	89B	274	$ .05	$ .30
Fernandez, Sid	91B	462	$ .01	$ .04	Gant, Ron	91B	583	$ .01	$ .10
Fernandez, Sid	92B	296	$ .05	$ .20	Gant, Ron	92B	534	$ .05	$ .25
Fernandez, Tony	89B	254	$ .01	$ .03	Gantner, Jim	89B	141	$ .01	$ .03
Fernandez, Tony	90B	524	$ .01	$ .04	Gantner, Jim	90B	400	$ .01	$ .04
Fernandez, Tony	91B	642	$ .01	$ .04	Gantner, Jim	91B	48	$ .01	$ .04
Fernandez, Tony	92B	293	$ .05	$ .20	Gantner, Jim	92B	301	$ .05	$ .20
Fetters, Mike	90B	286	$ .01	$ .10	Garces, Rich	91B	324	$ .01	$ .10

BOWMAN

Player	Year	No.	VG	EX/MT	Player	Year	No.	VG	EX/MT
Garcia, Carlos	91B	531	$ .05	$ .25	Gonzalez, Juan	91B	180	$ .05	$ .25
Garcia, Carlos	92B	576	$ .10	$1.00	Gonzalez, Juan	92B	84	$1.50	$6.00
Gardella, Mike	92B	52	$ .05	$ .35	Gonzalez, Luis	91B	550	$ .01	$ .15
Gardner, Chris	92B	457	$ .05	$ .25	Gonzalez, Luis	92B	145	$ .05	$ .35
Gardner, Mark	90B	106	$ .01	$ .10	Gooden, Doc	89B	376	$ .01	$ .10
Gardner, Mark	92B	562	$ .05	$ .20	Gooden, Doc	90B	126	$ .01	$ .10
Gardner, Wes	89B	23	$ .01	$ .03	Gooden, Doc	91B	472	$ .01	$ .10
Gardner, Wes	90B	266	$ .01	$ .04	Gooden, Doc	92B	480	$ .05	$ .20
Gardner, Wes	91B	653	$ .01	$ .04	Goodwin, Tom	90B	96	$ .01	$ .10
Garrelts, Scott	89B	467	$ .01	$ .03	Goodwin, Tom	91B	608	$ .01	$ .04
Garrelts, Scott	90B	228	$ .01	$ .04	Gordon, Tom	89B	115	$ .05	$ .20
Garrelts, Scott	91B	626	$ .01	$ .04	Gordon, Tom	90B	365	$ .01	$ .10
Garrett, Clifton	92B	51	$ .05	$ .35	Gordon, Tom	91B	311	$ .01	$ .10
Gedman, Rich	89B	27	$ .01	$ .03	Gordon, Tom	92B	477	$ .05	$ .20
George, Chris	91B	35	$ .01	$ .10	Gossage, Rich	91B	271	$ .01	$ .04
George, Chris	92B	213	$ .05	$ .20	Gott, Jim	89B	411	$ .01	$ .03
Geren, Bob	90B	438	$ .01	$ .04	Grace, Mark	89B	291	$ .05	$ .25
Gibson, Kirk	89B	351	$ .01	$ .10	Grace, Mark	90B	29	$ .05	$ .20
Gibson, Kirk	90B	97	$ .01	$ .04	Grace, Mark	91B	433	$ .01	$ .10
Gibson, Kirk	91B	302	$ .01	$ .04	Grace, Mark	92B	580	$ .10	$ .50
Gibson, Paul	89B	99	$ .01	$ .03	Grebeck, Craig	90B	318	$ .01	$ .15
Gideon, Brett	90B	105	$ .01	$ .10	Greene, Rick	92B	563	$ .10	$ .50
Gil, Benji	92B	339	$ .20	$2.00	Greene, Tommy	90B	1	$ .01	$ .10
Gilkey, Bernard	91B	408	$ .01	$ .15	Greene, Tommy	92B	227	$ .05	$ .20
Gilkey, Bernard	92B	403	$ .05	$ .20	Greene, Willie	90B	173	$ .05	$ .35
Girardi, Joe	91B	415	$ .01	$ .04	Greene, Willie	91B	448	$ .01	$ .15
Girardi, Joe	92B	636	$ .05	$ .20	Greene, Willie	92B	429	$ .10	$1.00
Gladden, Danny	89B	163	$ .01	$ .03	Greenwell, Mike	89B	34	$ .01	$ .10
Gladden, Danny	90B	420	$ .01	$ .04	Greenwell, Mike	90B	274	$ .01	$ .10
Gladden, Danny	91B	318	$ .01	$ .04	Greenwell, Mike	91B	116	$ .01	$ .04
Glavine, Tom	89B	267	$ .10	$ .50	Greenwell, Mike	92B	615	$ .05	$ .20
Glavine, Tom	90B	2	$ .05	$ .25	Griffey Jr., Ken	89B	220	$1.00	$4.00
Glavine, Tom	91B	576	$ .01	$ .15	Griffey Jr., Ken	89B	259	$ .10	$1.00
Glavine, Tom	92B	699	$ .10	$ .75	Griffey Jr., Ken	90B	481	$ .15	$1.25
Goff, Jerry	90B	112	$ .01	$ .10	Griffey Jr., Ken	91B	246	$ .10	$ .50
Gohr, Greg	90B	347	$ .05	$ .25	Griffey Jr., Ken	92B	100	$1.50	$6.00
Gohr, Greg	92B	453	$ .05	$ .25	Griffey, Ken	89B	259	$ .10	$1.00
Gomez, Leo	90B	262	$ .05	$ .25	Griffey, Ken	90B	60	$ .01	$ .04
Gomez, Leo	91B	88	$ .01	$ .10	Griffey, Ken	91B	255	$ .01	$ .04
					Griffin, Alfredo	89B	345	$ .01	$ .03
					Griffin, Alfredo	90B	95	$ .01	$ .04
					Griffin, Alfredo	91B	592	$ .01	$ .04
					Griffin, Ty	89B	289	$ .01	$ .10
					Griffin, Ty	90B	37	$ .01	$ .04
					Grimsley, Jason	90B	151	$ .01	$ .10
					Grissom, Marquis	90B	115	$ .10	$ .50
					Grissom, Marquis	91B	435	$ .01	$ .15
					Grissom, Marquis	92B	14	$ .10	$ .75
					Gross, Kevin	89B	355	$ .01	$ .03
					Gross, Kevin	90B	109	$ .01	$ .04
					Gross, Kevin	91B	611	$ .01	$ .04
					Gruber, Kelly	89B	251	$ .01	$ .03
					Gruber, Kelly	90B	519	$ .01	$ .10
					Gruber, Kelly	91B	18	$ .01	$ .04
					Gruber, Kelly	91B	369	$ .01	$ .04
					Gruber, Kelly	92B	510	$ .05	$ .20
					Gubicza, Mark	89B	117	$ .01	$ .03
					Gubicza, Mark	90B	363	$ .01	$ .04
					Gubicza, Mark	92B	215	$ .05	$ .20
					Guerrero, Pedro	89B	440	$ .01	$ .10
					Guerrero, Pedro	90B	201	$ .01	$ .04
					Guerrero, Pedro	91B	403	$ .01	$ .04
					Guerrero, Pedro	92B	377	$ .05	$ .20
					Guggiana, Todd	91B	697	$ .01	$ .10
					Guillen, Ozzie	89B	64	$ .01	$ .03
					Guillen, Ozzie	90B	315	$ .01	$ .04
					Guillen, Ozzie	91B	356	$ .01	$ .04
					Guillen, Ozzie	92B	565	$ .05	$ .20
					Gullickson, Bill	90B	65	$ .01	$ .04
					Gullickson, Bill	91B	133	$ .01	$ .04
					Gullickson, Bill	92B	558	$ .05	$ .20
Gomez, Leo	**92B**	**344**	**$ .05**	**$ .35**	Gunderson, Eric	90B	225	$ .01	$ .10
Gonzales, Rene	91B	25	$ .01	$ .04	Gunderson, Eric	91B	628	$ .01	$ .04
Gonzalez, Alex	92B	596	$ .10	$ .50	Gutierrez, Ricky	92B	103	$ .10	$ .50
Gonzalez, Juan	90B	492	$ .20	$2.00	Guzman, Jose	92B	668	$ .05	$ .20

LEO GOMEZ

BOWMAN

Player	Year	No.	VG	EX/MT
Guzman, Juan	92B	294	$1.00	$4.00
Gwynn, Tony	89B	461	$.05	$.25
Gwynn, Tony	90B	217	$.01	$.10
Gwynn, Tony	91B	647	$.01	$.10
Gwynn, Tony	92B	50	$.10	$.75
Haas, Dave	91B	151	$.01	$.10
Habyan, John	91B	167	$.01	$.04
Hall, Drew	89B	221	$.01	$.03
Hall, Mel	90B	437	$.01	$.04
Hall, Mel	91B	179	$.01	$.04
Hall, Mel	92B	425	$.05	$.20
Hamelin, Bob	90B	379	$.01	$.10
Hamelin, Bob	91B	310	$.01	$.04
Hamilton, Darryl	90B	397	$.01	$.10
Hamilton, Darryl	92B	74	$.05	$.20
Hamilton, Jeff	90B	94	$.01	$.04
Hammond, Chris	91B	680	$.01	$.10
Hammond, Chris	92B	328	$.05	$.20
Hammonds, Jeffrey	92B	617	$2.00	$8.00
Hampton, Mike	92B	638	$.05	$.35
Haney, Chris	91B	443	$.01	$.10
Hansell, Greg	92B	314	$.10	$.40
Hansen, Dave	90B	93	$.01	$.10
Hansen, Elston	92B	548	$.10	$1.00
Hanson, Erik	89B	206	$.05	$.25
Hanson, Erik	90B	469	$.01	$.10
Hanson, Erik	91B	260	$.01	$.04
Hanson, Erik	92B	583	$.05	$.20
Harkey, Mike	89B	286	$.01	$.10
Harkey, Mike	90B	28	$.01	$.10
Harkey, Mike	91B	417	$.01	$.04
Harnisch, Pete	89B	4	$.01	$.15
Harnisch, Pete	90B	247	$.01	$.04
Harnisch, Peter	91B	555	$.01	$.04
Harnisch, Pete	92B	514	$.05	$.20
Harper, Brian	89B	155	$.01	$.03
Harper, Brian	91B	333	$.01	$.04
Harper, Brian	92B	149	$.05	$.20
Harris, Donald	90B	499	$.01	$.10
Harris, Donald	91B	269	$.01	$.04
Harris, Donald	92B	332	$.05	$.20
Harris, Greg W.	91B	657	$.01	$.04
Harris, Greg W.	92B	269	$.05	$.20
Harris, Lenny	91B	607	$.01	$.04
Harris, Reggie	90B	446	$.01	$.10
Hartley, Mike	90B	87	$.01	$.10
Harvey, Bryan	89B	40	$.05	$.25
Harvey, Bryan	91B	211	$.01	$.04
Harvey, Bryan	92B	172	$.05	$.20
Hassey, Ron	89B	194	$.01	$.03
Hassey, Ron	90B	464	$.01	$.04
Hatcher, Billy	91B	670	$.01	$.04
Hatcher, Mickey	89B	347	$.01	$.03
Hatteberg, Scott	92B	83	$.05	$.35
Hawblitzel, Ryan	92B	138	$.10	$.50
Hawkins, Andy	89B	166	$.01	$.03
Hayes, Charlie	91B	508	$.01	$.04
Hayes, Charlie	92B	147	$.05	$.20
Hayes, Von	89B	406	$.01	$.10
Hayes, Von	90B	160	$.01	$.04
Hayes, Von	91B	487	$.01	$.04
Hayes, Von	92B	197	$.05	$.35
Heath, Mike	90B	352	$.01	$.04
Heath, Mike	91B	589	$.01	$.04
Heep, Danny	90B	276	$.01	$.04
Heinkel, Don	89B	427	$.01	$.03
Helling, Rick	92B	641	$.10	$.75
Hemond, Scott	90B	453	$.01	$.10
Hemond, Scott	91B	232	$.01	$.04
Henderson, Dave	89B	200	$.01	$.03
Henderson, Dave	90B	458	$.01	$.04
Henderson, Dave	91B	226	$.01	$.04
Henderson, Dave	92B	488	$.05	$.20
Henderson, Rickey	89B	181	$.05	$.25
Henderson, Rickey	90B	457	$.05	$.20
Henderson, Rickey	91B	213	$.01	$.10
Henderson, Rickey	91B	371	$.01	$.10
Henderson, Rickey	91B	692	$.01	$.10
Henderson, Rickey	92B	166	$.10	$1.00
Henke, Tom	89B	246	$.01	$.03
Henke, Tom	90B	506	$.01	$.04
Henke, Tom	91B	16	$.01	$.04
Henneman, Mike	89B	98	$.01	$.03
Henneman, Mike	90B	345	$.01	$.04
Henneman, Mike	92B	441	$.05	$.20
Henry, Butch	92B	502	$.05	$.25
Hentgen, Pat	91B	23	$.05	$.25
Hentgen, Pat	92B	696	$.10	$1.00
Hernandez, Carlos	92B	5	$.05	$.25
Hernandez, Jeremy	92B	73	$.05	$.35
Hernandez, Keith	89B	385	$.01	$.10
Hernandez, Keith	90B	342	$.01	$.04
Hernandez, Kiki	92B	637	$.10	$.40
Hernandez, Roberto	91B	343	$.05	$.20
Hernandez, Roberto	92B	133	$.10	$.50
Hernandez, Xavier	91B	545	$.01	$.04
Herr, Tom	89B	403	$.01	$.03

Player	Year	No.	VG	EX/MT
Herr, Tom	90B	159	$.01	$.04
Herr, Tom	91B	480	$.01	$.04
Hershiser, Orel	89B	341	$.01	$.10
Hershiser, Orel	90B	84	$.01	$.10
Hershiser, Orel	91B	595	$.01	$.04
Hershiser, Orel	92B	517	$.05	$.20
Hiatt, Phil	92B	529	$.75	$3.00
Hibbard, Greg	90B	303	$.01	$.15
Hibbard, Greg	92B	325	$.05	$.20
Higuera, Teddy	89B	129	$.01	$.03
Higuera, Teddy	90B	384	$.01	$.04
Higuera, Teddy	91B	54	$.01	$.04
Higuera, Teddy	92B	223	$.05	$.20
Hill, Glenallen	90B	514	$.01	$.10
Hill, Glenallen	91B	24	$.01	$.04
Hill, Glenallen	92B	659	$.05	$.20
Hill, Ken	91B	390	$.01	$.04
Hill, Ken	92B	507	$.05	$.20
Hillegas, Shawn	89B	58	$.01	$.03
Hillman, Eric	92B	326	$.10	$.50
Hilton, Howard	90B	189	$.01	$.10

BOWMAN

Player	Year	No.	VG	EX/MT	Player	Year	No.	VG	EX/MT
Hirtensteiner, Rick	92B	658	$ .10	$ .50	Jackson, Danny	90B	44	$ .01	$ .04
Hoffman, Trevor	92B	11	$ .05	$ .35	Jackson, Danny	91B	412	$ .01	$ .04
Hoiles, Chris	90B	259	$ .05	$ .35	Jackson, Danny	92B	142	$ .05	$ .20
Hoiles, Chris	91B	99	$ .01	$ .10	Jackson, Darrin	92B	456	$ .05	$ .20
Hoiles, Chris	92B	472	$ .05	$ .25	Jackson, Jeff	90B	157	$ .01	$ .10
Holbert, Aaron	91B	399	$ .01	$ .10	Jackson, Jeff	91B	491	$ .01	$ .04
Hollins, Dave	90B	161	$ .10	$ .50	Jackson, Jeff	92B	72	$ .05	$ .20
Hollins, Dave	92B	6	$ .20	$2.00	Jackson, Mike	89B	207	$ .01	$ .03
Hollins, Jessie	91B	423	$ .01	$ .10	Jackson, Mike	92B	513	$ .05	$ .20
Holman, Brian	89B	357	$ .01	$ .10	Jacoby, Brook	89B	86	$ .01	$ .03
Holman, Brian	91B	240	$ .01	$ .04	Jacoby, Brook	90B	341	$ .01	$ .04
Holton, Brian	89B	2	$ .01	$ .03	Jacoby, Brook	91B	59	$ .01	$ .04
Honeycutt, Rick	89B	187	$ .01	$ .03	Jaha, John	92B	399	$ .10	$1.00
Honeycutt, Rick	90B	450	$ .01	$ .04	Jaha, John	92B	542	$ .20	$2.00
Horn, Sam	92B	177	$ .05	$ .20	James, Chris	89B	404	$ .01	$ .03
Horton, Ricky	89B	338	$ .01	$ .03	James, Chris	90B	340	$ .01	$ .04
Hosey, Steve	90B	242	$ .05	$ .35	James, Chris	91B	67	$ .01	$ .04
Hosey, Steve	91B	629	$ .01	$ .10	James, Dion	89B	277	$ .01	$ .03
Hosey, Steve	92B	544	$ .10	$ .75	James, Dion	90B	331	$ .01	$ .04
Hough, Charlie	89B	224	$ .01	$ .03	James, Dion	92B	494	$ .05	$ .20
Hough, Charlie	91B	355	$ .01	$ .04	Javier, Stan	91B	599	$ .01	$ .04
Hough, Charlie	92B	153	$ .05	$ .20	Jean, Domingo	92B	130	$ .10	$1.00
House, Howard	92B	581	$ .10	$ .50	Jeffcoat, Mike	91B	278	$ .01	$ .04
Houston, Tyler	90B	14	$ .01	$ .10	Jeffereis, Gregg	91B	481	$ .01	$ .04
Houston, Tyler	91B	581	$ .01	$ .04	Jefferies, Gregg	89B	381	$ .05	$ .20
Howard, Chris	92B	309	$ .05	$ .20	Jefferies, Gregg	90B	140	$ .01	$ .10
Howard, David	91B	295	$ .01	$ .10	Jefferies, Gregg	92B	13	$ .05	$ .20
Howard, David	92B	307	$ .05	$ .20	Jefferson, Reggie	90B	51	$ .05	$ .35
Howard, Thomas	90B	212	$ .01	$ .10	Jefferson, Reggie	91B	678	$ .01	$ .15
Howard, Thomas	91B	644	$ .01	$ .04	Jefferson, Reggie	92B	25	$ .10	$1.00
Howard, Tim	91B	538	$ .01	$ .10	Jefferson, Stan	89B	180	$ .01	$ .03
Howell, Jack	89B	48	$ .01	$ .03	Jennings, Lance	92B	633	$ .05	$ .25
Howell, Jack	90B	296	$ .01	$ .04	Johnson, Charles	92B	661	$ .75	$3.00
Howell, Jay	89B	335	$ .01	$ .03	Johnson, Chris	91B	45	$ .01	$ .10
Howell, Jay	90B	83	$ .01	$ .04	Johnson, Howard	90B	133	$ .01	$ .04
Howell, Jay	91B	603	$ .01	$ .04	Johnson, Howard	91B	464	$ .01	$ .04
Howell, Jay	92B	408	$ .05	$ .20	Johnson, Howard	92B	10	$ .05	$ .20
Howell, Ken	89B	394	$ .01	$ .03	Johnson, Jeff	91B	159	$ .01	$ .10
Howell, Ken	90B	147	$ .01	$ .04	Johnson, Jeff	92B	362	$ .05	$ .20
Howitt, Dann	91B	229	$ .01	$ .04	Johnson, Lance	91B	349	$ .01	$ .04
Howitt, Dann	92B	521	$ .05	$ .20	Johnson, Lance	92B	208	$ .05	$ .20
Hoy, Peter	92B	292	$ .05	$ .20	Johnson, Randy	90B	468	$ .01	$ .10
Hrbek, Kent	89B	157	$ .01	$ .10	Johnson, Randy	91B	253	$ .01	$ .04
Hrbek, Kent	90B	418	$ .01	$ .04	Johnson, Randy	92B	178	$ .05	$ .20
Hrbek, Kent	91B	321	$ .01	$ .10	Johnston, Joel	91B	297	$ .01	$ .10
Hrbek, Kent	92B	445	$ .05	$ .20	Johnston, Joel	92B	199	$ .05	$ .20
Hubbard, Glenn	89B	199	$ .01	$ .03	Jones, Barry	91B	439	$ .01	$ .04
Hudler, Rex	89B	364	$ .01	$ .03	Jones, Bobby	92B	389	$ .20	$2.00
Hudler, Rex	91B	409	$ .01	$ .04	Jones, Chipper	91B	569	$ .10	$1.00
Huff, Mike	91B	73	$ .01	$ .04	Jones, Chipper	92B	28	$1.25	$5.00
Huisman, Rick	92B	217	$ .10	$ .50	Jones, Chris	91B	676	$ .01	$ .04
Humphreys, Mike	91B	162	$ .01	$ .15	Jones, Doug	89B	78	$ .01	$ .03
Hundley, Todd	90B	142	$ .01	$ .15	Jones, Doug	90B	328	$ .01	$ .04
Hundley, Todd	91B	467	$ .01	$ .04	Jones, Doug	91B	77	$ .01	$ .04
Hundley, Todd	92B	101	$ .05	$ .20	Jones, Jimmy	89B	169	$ .01	$ .03
Hunter, Brian	92B	662	$ .05	$ .35	Jones, Jimmy	91B	553	$ .01	$ .04
Hurst, Bruce	89B	451	$ .01	$ .03	Jones, Kiki	90B	86	$ .01	$ .10
Hurst, Bruce	90B	208	$ .01	$ .04	Jones, Ron	89B	407	$ .01	$ .10
Hurst, Bruce	91B	661	$ .01	$ .04	Jones, Tim	89B	439	$ .01	$ .03
Hurst, Bruce	92B	187	$ .05	$ .20	Jones, Todd	92B	202	$ .10	$ .50
Hurst, Jonathan	92B	388	$ .05	$ .35	Jones, Tracy	89B	479	$ .01	$ .03
Huskey, Butch	92B	539	$ .10	$ .75	Jordan, Brian	92B	464	$ .10	$1.00
Huson, Jeff	91B	273	$ .01	$ .04	Jordan, Ricky	89B	401	$ .01	$ .04
Hutton, Mark	92B	598	$ .10	$ .50	Jordan, Ricky	90B	156	$ .01	$ .04
Hyzdu, Adam	91B	617	$ .01	$ .10	Jordan, Ricky	91B	494	$ .01	$ .04
Ignasiak, Mike	92B	15	$ .05	$ .25	Jose, Felix	90B	455	$ .05	$ .25
Incaviglia, Pete	89B	238	$ .01	$ .10	Jose, Felix	91B	401	$ .01	$ .04
Incaviglia, Pete	90B	491	$ .01	$ .04	Jose, Felix	92B	176	$ .05	$ .20
Incaviglia, Pete	91B	131	$ .01	$ .04	Joyner, Wally	89B	47	$ .01	$ .10
Incaviglia, Pete	92B	43	$ .05	$ .20	Joyner, Wally	90B	299	$ .01	$ .10
Infante, Alexis	90B	17	$ .01	$ .04	Joyner, Wally	91B	195	$ .01	$ .10
Ingram, Riccardo	92B	164	$ .05	$ .25	Joyner, Wally	92B	435	$ .05	$ .20
Jackson, Bo	89B	126	$ .05	$ .25	Juden, Jeff	90B	64	$ .05	$ .25
Jackson, Bo	90B	378	$ .01	$ .15	Juden, Jeff	91B	547	$ .01	$ .04
Jackson, Danny	89B	304	$ .01	$ .03	Juden, Jeff	92B	188	$ .10	$ .40

BOWMAN

Player	Year	No.	VG	EX/MT
Justice, David	91B	574	$ .05	$ .20
Justice, David	92B	312	$ .20	$2.00
Karros, Eric	91B	604	$ .15	$1.50
Karros, Eric	92B	288	$1.50	$6.00
Karsay, Steve	91B	12	$ .05	$ .20
Karsay, Steve	92B	158	$ .10	$ .50
Kelly, Pat	91B	155	$ .01	$ .10
Kelly, Pat	92B	535	$ .05	$ .25
Kelly, Roberto	89B	183	$ .01	$ .10
Kelly, Roberto	90B	444	$ .01	$ .15
Kelly, Roberto	91B	166	$ .01	$ .10
Kelly, Roberto	92B	12	$ .05	$ .25
Kennedy, Terry	89B	470	$ .01	$ .03
Kennedy, Terry	90B	241	$ .01	$ .04
Kennedy, Terry	91B	631	$ .01	$ .04
Key, Jimmy	89B	243	$ .01	$ .10
Key, Jimmy	90B	509	$ .01	$ .04
Key, Jimmy	91B	19	$ .01	$ .10
Key, Jimmy	92B	588	$ .05	$ .20
Kiecker, Dana	91B	108	$ .01	$ .04
Kiefer, Mark	92B	674	$ .05	$ .35
Kile, Darryl	90B	61	$ .01	$ .15
Kile, Darryl	91B	548	$ .01	$ .04
Kile, Darryl	92B	601	$ .05	$ .25
Kilgus, Paul	89B	285	$ .01	$ .03
Kilgus, Paul	90B	508	$ .01	$ .04
King, Eric	90B	304	$ .01	$ .04
King, Eric	91B	63	$ .01	$ .04
King, Eric	92B	317	$ .05	$ .20
King, Jeff	91B	520	$ .01	$ .04
Kipper, Bob	89B	414	$ .01	$ .03
Kittle, Ron	89B	69	$ .01	$ .10
Klesko, Ryan	91B	590	$ .10	$1.00
Klesko, Ryan	92B	549	$1.00	$4.00
Klesko, Ryan	92B	623	$1.25	$5.00
Kmak, Joe	92B	545	$ .05	$ .20
Knoblauch, Chuck	90B	415	$ .10	$ .75
Knoblauch, Chuck	91B	330	$ .05	$ .35
Knoblauch, Chuck	92B	24	$ .10	$1.00
Koelling, Brian	92B	65	$ .10	$ .40
Kramer, Randy	92B	398	$ .05	$ .20
Kreuter, Chad	92B	515	$ .05	$ .20
Krueger, Bill	91B	248	$ .01	$ .04
Kruk, John	89B	460	$ .01	$ .10
Kruk, John	90B	154	$ .01	$ .04
Kruk, John	91B	503	$ .01	$ .04
Kruk, John	92B	541	$ .05	$ .20
Kunkel, Jeff	89B	231	$ .01	$ .03
Lake, Steve	89B	399	$ .01	$ .03
Landrum, Bill	90B	166	$ .01	$ .04
Landrum, Bill	91B	523	$ .01	$ .04
Lane, Brian	90B	48	$ .01	$ .10
Langston, Mark	89B	205	$ .01	$ .10
Langston, Mark	90B	284	$ .01	$ .04
Langston, Mark	91B	202	$ .01	$ .04
Langston, Mark	92B	520	$ .05	$ .20
Lankford, Ray	90B	192	$ .10	$ .75
Lankford, Ray	91B	388	$ .05	$ .25
Lankford, Ray	92B	643	$ .10	$1.00
Lansford, Carney	89B	198	$ .01	$ .03
Lansford, Carney	90B	452	$ .01	$ .04
Lansford, Carney	92B	78	$ .05	$ .20
LaPoint, Dave	89B	165	$ .01	$ .03
Larkin, Barry	89B	311	$ .05	$ .20
Larkin, Barry	90B	50	$ .01	$ .10
Larkin, Barry	91B	379	$ .01	$ .10
Larkin, Barry	91B	673	$ .01	$ .10
Larkin, Barry	92B	353	$ .10	$ .75
Larkin , Barry	92B	694	$ .20	$2.00
Larkin, Gene	89B	160	$ .01	$ .03
Larkin, Gene	92B	479	$ .05	$ .20
Laudner, Tim	89B	154	$ .01	$ .03
LaValliere, Mike	89B	417	$ .01	$ .03
LaValliere, Mike	90B	172	$ .01	$ .04
Lavalliere, Mike	91B	514	$ .01	$ .04
LaValliere, Mike	92B	245	$ .05	$ .20
Law, Vance	89B	293	$ .01	$ .03
Law, Vance	91B	222	$ .01	$ .04
Lawless, Tom	89B	255	$ .01	$ .03
Layana, Tim	90B	41	$ .01	$ .10
Layana, Tim	91B	689	$ .01	$ .04
Leach, Rick	89B	234	$ .01	$ .03
Leach, Terry	91B	340	$ .01	$ .04
Leary, Tim	89B	339	$ .01	$ .03
Leary, Tim	90B	429	$ .01	$ .04
Lee, Derek	92B	210	$ .05	$ .20
Lee, Manny	90B	512	$ .01	$ .04
Lee, Manny	91B	21	$ .01	$ .04
Lee, Manuel	92B	421	$ .05	$ .20
Lee, Terry	91B	683	$ .01	$ .04
Lefferts, Craig	89B	464	$ .01	$ .03
Lefferts, Craig	90B	206	$ .01	$ .04
Lefferts, Craig	91B	650	$ .01	$ .04
Lefferts, Craig	92B	105	$ .05	$ .20
Leibrandt, Charlie	89B	116	$ .01	$ .03
Leibrandt, Charlie	90B	8	$ .01	$ .04
Leibrandt, Charlie	91B	573	$ .01	$ .04
Leiter, Al	89B	170	$ .01	$ .03
Leiter, Mark	91B	138	$ .01	$ .10
Leiter, Mark	92B	476	$ .05	$ .20
Leius, Scott	90B	423	$ .05	$ .25
Leius, Scott	91B	337	$ .01	$ .04
Leius, Scott	92B	209	$ .05	$ .20
Lemke, Mark	90B	11	$ .01	$ .04
Lemke, Mark	92B	663	$ .05	$ .20
Lemon, Chet	89B	108	$ .01	$ .03
Lemon, Chet	90B	354	$ .01	$ .04
Lennon, Patrick	91B	250	$ .01	$ .10
Lennon, Patrick	92B	192	$ .05	$ .20
Leonard, Jeffrey	89B	218	$ .01	$ .03

Player	Year	No.	VG	EX/MT
Leonard, Jeffrey	90B	472	$ .01	$ .04
Leonard, Mark	91B	624	$ .01	$ .10
Lewis, Darren	90B	463	$ .05	$ .25
Lewis, Darren	92B	683	$ .05	$ .20
Lewis, Mark	89B	87	$ .10	$ .40
Lewis, Mark	90B	338	$ .01	$ .10
Lewis, Mark	91B	70	$ .01	$ .10
Lewis, Mark	92B	439	$ .05	$ .20

BOWMAN

Player	Year	No.	VG	EX/MT	Player	Year	No.	VG	EX/MT
Lewis, Scott	91B	192	$.01	$.10	Martinez, Dave	90B	121	$.01	$.04
Leyritz, Jim	91B	171	$.01	$.04	Martinez, Dave	91B	455	$.01	$.04
Lieberthal, Mike	91B	506	$.01	$.15	Martinez, Dave	92B	220	$.05	$.20
Lilliquist, Derek	89B	264	$.01	$.10	Martinez, Denny	89B	359	$.01	$.03
Lilliquist, Derek	90B	7	$.01	$.04	Martinez, Denny	90B	111	$.01	$.04
Lind, Jose	89B	421	$.01	$.03	Martinez, Denny	91B	434	$.01	$.04
Lind, Jose	90B	170	$.01	$.04	Martinez, Denny	92B	305	$.05	$.20
Lind, Jose	91B	530	$.01	$.04	Martinez, Edgar	89B	216	$.05	$.25
Lind, Jose	92B	351	$.05	$.20	Martinez, Edgar	91B	243	$.01	$.04
Linskey, Mike	91B	105	$.01	$.10	Martinez, Edgar	92B	33	$.05	$.20
Linton, Doug	92B	277	$.05	$.20	Martinez, Pedro	92B	82	$.10	$1.00
Liriano, Nelson	90B	518	$.01	$.04	Martinez, Ramon	90B	88	$.01	$.15
Listach, Pat	92B	526	$1.25	$5.00	Martinez, Ramon	91B	610	$.01	$.10
Litton, Greg	91B	621	$.01	$.04	Martinez, Ramon	92B	255	$.05	$.20
Livernois, Derek	91B	123	$.01	$.10	Martinez, Tino	89B	211	$.05	$.25
Livingstone, Scott	92B	3	$.10	$.40	Martinez, Tino	90B	484	$.01	$.15
Lockett, Ron	92B	303	$.05	$.20	Martinez, Tino	91B	257	$.01	$.10
Lofton, Kenny	91B	565	$.10	$1.00	Martinez, Tino	92B	483	$.05	$.25
Lofton, Kenny	92B	110	$1.00	$4.00	Martinez, Tino	92B	626	$.10	$.50
Long, Bill	89B	56	$.01	$.03	Marzano, John	91B	119	$.01	$.04
Long, Ryan	92B	79	$.05	$.25	Mattingly, Don	89B	176	$.05	$.25
Longmire, Tony	91B	489	$.01	$.10	Mattingly, Don	90B	443	$.05	$.25
Lopez, Javier	91B	587	$.10	$.50	Mattingly, Don	91B	178	$.01	$.10
Lopez, Javier	92B	452	$.75	$3.00	Mattingly, Don	92B	340	$.10	$.75
Lovullo, Torey	91B	175	$.01	$.04	Maurer, Rob	92B	437	$.05	$.25
Lowe, Derek	92B	98	$.10	$.40	Mayne, Brent	90B	372	$.01	$.10
Luecken, Rick	90B	5	$.01	$.04	McAndrew, Jamie	91B	601	$.01	$.10
Lusader, Scott	91B	174	$.01	$.04	McAndrew, Jamie	92B	591	$.05	$.20
Lynn, Fred	90B	216	$.01	$.04	McCaskill, Kirk	89B	38	$.01	$.03
Lyons, Barry	90B	139	$.01	$.04	McCaskill, Kirk	90B	283	$.01	$.04
Lyons, Steve	89B	63	$.01	$.03	McCaskill, Kirk	92B	2	$.05	$.20
Lyons, Steve	90B	321	$.01	$.04	McClendon, Lloyd	89B	287	$.01	$.03
Maas, Kevin	90B	440	$.05	$.25	McClendon, Lloyd	90B	36	$.01	$.04
Maas, Kevin	91B	158	$.01	$.10	McClure, Bob	89B	43	$.01	$.03
Maas, Kevin	92B	205	$.05	$.20	McConnell, Chad	92B	587	$.15	$1.50
Macfarlane, Mike	89B	118	$.01	$.10	McCray, Eric	91B	281	$.01	$.10
Macfarlane, Mike	91B	301	$.01	$.04	McCullers, Lance	89B	168	$.01	$.03
Macfarlane, Mike	92B	589	$.05	$.20	McDonald, Ben	90B	243	$.05	$.35
Machado, Julio	91B	50	$.01	$.04	McDonald, Ben	91B	86	$.01	$.10
Mack, Shane	91B	326	$.01	$.04	McDonald, Ben	92B	359	$.05	$.25
Mack, Shane	92B	592	$.05	$.20	McDowell, Jack	89B	61	$.05	$.25
Maddux, Greg	89B	284	$.05	$.25	McDowell, Jack	90B	305	$.01	$.15
Maddux, Greg	90B	27	$.05	$.25	McDowell, Jack	91B	352	$.01	$.10
Maddux, Greg	91B	426	$.01	$.10	McDowell, Jack	92B	371	$.10	$.50
Maddux, Greg	92B	148	$.10	$.75	McDowell, Jack	92B	605	$.10	$.75
Maddux, Mike	89B	391	$.01	$.03	McDowell, Oddibe	89B	90	$.01	$.03
Magadan, Dave	89B	384	$.01	$.03	McDowell, Oddibe	90B	13	$.01	$.04
Magadan, Dave	91B	484	$.01	$.04	McDowell, Roger	90B	146	$.01	$.04
Magadan, Dave	92B	263	$.05	$.20	McDowell, Roger	91B	500	$.01	$.04
Magallanes, Ever	91B	61	$.01	$.10	McDowell, Roger	92B	657	$.05	$.20
Magrane, Joe	89B	432	$.01	$.10	McElroy, Chuck	90B	150	$.01	$.10
Magrane, Joe	90B	183	$.01	$.04	McGaffigan, Andy	89B	356	$.01	$.03
Mahler, Rick	89B	302	$.01	$.03	McGarity, Jeremy	92B	26	$.05	$.25
Mahomes, Pat	92B	131	$.10	$1.00	McGee, Willie	89B	442	$.01	$.03
Maldonado, Candy	89B	478	$.01	$.03	McGee, Willie	90B	194	$.01	$.04
Maldonado, Candy	90B	335	$.01	$.04	McGee, Willie	91B	640	$.01	$.04
Malone, Chuck	90B	144	$.01	$.10	McGee, Willie	92B	604	$.05	$.20
Malone, Chuck	91B	497	$.01	$.04	McGehee, Kevin	92B	616	$.05	$.20
Manahan, Austin	89B	420	$.01	$.10	McGriff, Fred	89B	253	$.01	$.15
Manahan, Austin	91B	527	$.01	$.04	McGriff, Fred	90B	513	$.01	$.10
Manrique, Fred	89B	66	$.01	$.03	McGriff, Fred	91B	659	$.01	$.10
Manto, Jeff	91B	75	$.01	$.04	McGriff, Fred	92B	650	$.10	$.75
Manwaring, Kirt	89B	469	$.01	$.03	McGwire, Mark	89B	197	$.05	$.35
Manwaring, Kirt	92B	361	$.05	$.20	McGwire, Mark	90B	454	$.05	$.25
Marshall, Mike	89B	350	$.01	$.03	McGwire, Mark	91B	234	$.05	$.15
Marshall, Mike	90B	132	$.01	$.04	McGwire, Mark	92B	384	$.20	$2.00
Martel, Ed	92B	607	$.05	$.20	McGwire, Mark	92B	620	$.75	$3.00
Martin, Chris	92B	493	$.05	$.20	McIntosh, Tim	90B	394	$.01	$.10
Martin, Norberto	91B	346	$.01	$.10	McIntosh, Tim	91B	36	$.01	$.04
Martin, Steve	91B	662	$.01	$.10	McIntosh, Tom	92B	402	$.05	$.20
Martinez, Carlos	90B	322	$.01	$.04	McLemore, Mark	92B	446	$.05	$.20
Martinez, Carmelo	89B	459	$.01	$.03	McNeely, Jeff	91B	113	$.01	$.10
Martinez, Carmelo	90B	162	$.01	$.04	McNeely, Jeffrey	92B	193	$.05	$.35
Martinez, Chito	92B	19	$.05	$.20	McRae, Brian	91B	292	$.01	$.15
Martinez, Dave	89B	370	$.01	$.03	McRae, Brian	92B	66	$.05	$.20

BOWMAN

Player	Year	No.	VG	EX/MT	Player	Year	No.	VG	EX/MT
McReynolds, Kevin	89B	388	$ .01	$ .10	Morris, Hal	91B	691	$ .01	$ .04
McReynolds, Kevin	90B	138	$ .01	$ .04	Morris, Hal	92B	468	$ .05	$ .20
McReynolds, Kevin	91B	479	$ .01	$ .04	Morris, Jack	89B	93	$ .01	$ .10
McReynolds, Kevin	92B	337	$ .05	$ .20	Morris, Jack	91B	319	$ .01	$ .10
McWilliams, Larry	89B	397	$ .01	$ .03	Morris, Jack	92B	16	$ .05	$ .25
Meacham, Rusty	91B	149	$ .01	$ .10	Morris, John	92B	474	$ .05	$ .20
Meacham, Rusty	92B	486	$ .05	$ .20	Morton, Kevin	91B	130	$ .01	$ .10
Medvin, Scott	89B	412	$ .01	$ .03	Moseby, Lloyd	90B	362	$ .01	$ .04
Melvin, Bob	89B	8	$ .01	$ .03	Moseby, Lloyd	91B	135	$ .01	$ .04
Melvin, Bob	91B	89	$ .01	$ .04	Mota, Domingo	91B	696	$ .01	$ .10
Merced, Orlando	91B	512	$ .01	$ .15	Moyer, Jamie	89B	223	$ .01	$ .03
Merced, Orlando	92B	291	$ .05	$ .25	Moyer, Jamie	91B	391	$ .01	$ .04
Mercedes, Luis	91B	94	$ .01	$ .10	Mulholland, Terry	91B	504	$ .01	$ .04
Mercedes, Luis	92B	163	$ .05	$ .35	Mulholland, Terry	92B	39	$ .05	$ .20
Mercker, Kent	90B	6	$ .01	$ .10	Mulliniks, Rance	89B	250	$ .01	$ .03
Mercker, Kent	91B	568	$ .01	$ .04	Munoz, Pedro	91B	336	$ .05	$ .25
Mesa, Jose	91B	91	$ .01	$ .04	Munoz, Roberto	92B	523	$ .05	$ .20
Meulens, Hensley	91B	181	$ .01	$ .04	Murphy, Dale	89B	276	$ .01	$ .10
Meulens, Hensley	92B	338	$ .05	$ .20	Murphy, Dale	90B	19	$ .01	$ .10
Meyer, Brian	89B	319	$ .01	$ .03	Murphy, Dale	91B	486	$ .01	$ .10
Meyer, Joey	89B	138	$ .01	$ .03	Murphy, Dale	92B	684	$ .05	$ .20
Mieske, Matt	91B	694	$ .05	$ .20	Murphy, Rob	89B	22	$ .01	$ .03
Mieske, Matt	92B	608	$ .10	$ .50	Murphy, Rob	90B	269	$ .01	$ .04
Milacki, Bob	91B	101	$ .01	$ .04	Murray, Calvin	92B	652	$ .75	$3.00
Milacki, Bob	92B	61	$ .05	$ .20	Murray, Eddie	89B	346	$ .01	$ .10
Milchin, Mike	91B	397	$ .01	$ .10	Murray, Eddie	90B	101	$ .01	$ .10
Milchin, Mike	92B	567	$ .05	$ .20	Murray, Eddie	91B	376	$ .01	$ .10
Militello, Sam	91B	693	$ .10	$ .50	Murray, Eddie	91B	614	$ .01	$ .10
Militello, Sam	92B	21	$ .10	$1.00	Murray, Eddie	92B	433	$ .10	$ .50
Miller, Brent	92B	150	$ .05	$ .20	Murray, Glenn	92B	289	$ .10	$ .40
Miller, Keith	89B	380	$ .01	$ .03	Musselman, Jeff	89B	240	$ .01	$ .03
Miller, Keith	90B	136	$ .01	$ .04	Mussina, Mike	91B	97	$ .15	$1.25
Miller, Keith	92B	285	$ .05	$ .20	Mussina, Mike	92B	612	$1.50	$6.00
Miller, Kurt	91B	521	$ .01	$ .15	Myers, Chris	90B	250	$ .01	$ .10
Miller, Orlando	92B	555	$ .05	$ .20	Myers, Greg	90B	520	$ .01	$ .04
Miller, Paul	92B	686	$ .05	$ .25	Myers, Randy	89B	374	$ .01	$ .03
Milligan, Randy	89B	10	$ .01	$ .03	Myers, Randy	90B	47	$ .01	$ .04
Milligan, Randy	90B	257	$ .01	$ .04	Myers, Randy	91B	666	$ .01	$ .04
Mills, Alan	90B	428	$ .01	$ .10	Myers, Randy	92B	154	$ .05	$ .20
Mills, Alan	92B	342	$ .05	$ .20	Nabholz, Chris	91B	459	$ .01	$ .10
Minutelli, Gino	91B	677	$ .01	$ .10	Naehring, Tim	91B	127	$ .01	$ .10
Miranda, Angel	91B	53	$ .01	$ .04	Naehring, Tim	92B	416	$ .05	$ .20
Miranda, Angel	92B	63	$ .05	$ .25	Nagy, Charles	89B	73	$ .10	$ .50
Mitchell, Keith	91B	575	$ .01	$ .15	Nagy, Charles	91B	65	$ .01	$ .15
Mitchell, Keith	92B	62	$ .05	$ .25	Nagy, Charles	92B	203	$ .10	$ .40
Mitchell, Kevin	89B	474	$ .01	$ .15	Nagy, Charles	92B	566	$ .10	$1.00
Mitchell, Kevin	90B	232	$ .01	$ .10	Navarro, Jaime	90B	388	$ .01	$ .10
Mitchell, Kevin	91B	636	$ .01	$ .10	Navarro, Jaime	91B	42	$ .01	$ .10
Mitchell, Kevin	92B	276	$ .05	$ .20	Navarro, Jaime	92B	167	$ .05	$ .20
Mlicki, Dave	92B	413	$ .05	$ .35	Navarro, Tito	92B	139	$ .05	$ .25
Molitor, Paul	89B	140	$ .01	$ .10	Neagle, Denny	91B	323	$ .01	$ .10
Molitor, Paul	90B	399	$ .01	$ .10	Neagle, Denny	92B	485	$ .05	$ .25
Molitor, Paul	91B	32	$ .01	$ .10	Neill, Mike	92B	266	$ .10	$1.00
Molitor, Paul	92B	375	$ .05	$ .20	Nelson, Gene	89B	185	$ .01	$ .03
Molitor, Paul	92B	645	$ .10	$ .40	Nelson, Rob	90B	213	$ .01	$ .04
Mondesi, Raul	91B	593	$ .10	$ .50	Nen, Robb	90B	487	$ .01	$ .04
Mondesi, Raul	92B	64	$ .10	$1.00	Nen, Robb	91B	270	$ .01	$ .04
Montalvo, Rafael	91B	189	$ .01	$ .10	Nevers, Tom	91B	542	$ .01	$ .10
Montgomery, Jeff	89B	113	$ .01	$ .03	Nevers, Tom	92B	226	$ .05	$ .20
Montgomery, Jeff	90B	370	$ .01	$ .04	Nevin, Phil	92B	670	$2.25	$9.00
Montgomery, Jeff	91B	308	$ .01	$ .04	Newfield, Marc	91B	698	$ .10	$ .40
Montgomery, Jeff	92B	122	$ .05	$ .20	Newfield, Marc	92B	406	$ .10	$1.00
Moore, Kerwin	91B	312	$ .01	$ .10	Newman, Al	89B	156	$ .01	$ .03
Moore, Kerwin	92B	593	$ .05	$ .20	Newman, Al	90B	419	$ .01	$ .04
Moore, Mike	89B	189	$ .01	$ .03	Newman, Alan	92B	221	$ .05	$ .25
Moore, Mike	90B	445	$ .01	$ .04	Nezelek, Andy	90B	3	$ .01	$ .04
Moore, Mike	91B	212	$ .01	$ .04	Nied, David	92B	504	$3.50	$14.00
Moore, Mike	92B	216	$ .05	$ .20	Niedenfuer, Tom	89B	204	$ .01	$ .03
Moore, Vince	92B	443	$ .05	$ .20	Nieves, Juan	89B	131	$ .01	$ .03
Morandini, Mickey	90B	153	$ .05	$ .20	Nieves, Melvin	92B	143	$ .20	$2.00
Morandini, Mickey	91B	492	$ .01	$ .10	Nilsson, Dave	92B	653	$ .10	$1.00
Morandini, Mickey	92B	628	$ .05	$ .20	Nixon, Donell	89B	477	$ .01	$ .03
Moreland, Keith	89B	109	$ .01	$ .03	Nixon, Otis	89B	366	$ .01	$ .03
Morgan, Mike	92B	647	$ .05	$ .20	Nixon, Otis	91B	571	$ .01	$ .04
Morris, Hal	90B	57	$ .01	$ .15	Nixon, Otis	92B	669	$ .05	$ .20

BOWMAN

Player	Year	No.	VG	EX/MT
Nokes, Matt	89B	101	$ .01	$ .03
Nokes, Matt	91B	164	$ .01	$ .04
Nokes, Matt	92B	540	$ .05	$ .20
Nunez, Clemente	92B	417	$ .10	$ .50
Nunez, Ed	91B	40	$ .01	$ .04
Nutting, Robert	92B	85	$ .05	$ .25
O'Brien, Charlie	91B	473	$ .01	$ .04
O'Brien, Pete	89B	84	$ .01	$ .03
O'Brien, Pete	90B	475	$ .01	$ .04
O'Brien, Pete	91B	259	$ .01	$ .04
O'Brien, Pete	92B	313	$ .05	$ .20
O'Neill, Paul	89B	313	$ .01	$ .10
O'Neill, Paul	90B	49	$ .01	$ .04
O'Neill, Paul	91B	685	$ .01	$ .04
O'Neill, Paul	92B	267	$ .05	$ .20
Oberkfell, Ken	89B	418	$ .01	$ .03
Oberkfell, Ken	90B	74	$ .01	$ .04
Ochoa, Alex	92B	250	$ .10	$ .40
Oester, Ron	89B	310	$ .01	$ .03
Offerman, Jose	90B	92	$ .05	$ .25
Offerman, Jose	91B	182	$ .01	$ .10
Offerman, Jose	92B	304	$ .05	$ .20
Ojeda, Bob	89B	371	$ .01	$ .03
Ojeda, Bob	91B	591	$ .01	$ .04
Ojeda, Bob	92B	379	$ .05	$ .20
Olander, Jim	92B	575	$ .10	$ .40
Olerud, John	90B	510	$ .10	$ .50
Olerud, John	91B	7	$ .01	$ .15
Olerud, John	92B	644	$ .20	$2.00
Olin, Steve	90B	326	$ .01	$ .10
Olin, Steve	92B	236	$ .05	$ .20
Oliva, Jose	92B	55	$ .10	$ .50
Olivares, Omar	92B	420	$ .05	$ .20
Oliver, Joe	90B	54	$ .01	$ .10
Oliver, Joe	91B	671	$ .01	$ .04
Oliver, Joe	92B	594	$ .05	$ .20
Olson, Greg	91B	577	$ .01	$ .04
Olson, Greg	92B	577	$ .05	$ .20
Olson, Gregg	92B	629	$ .05	$ .20
Olson, Gregg	92B	677	$ .05	$ .20
Ontiveros, Steve	90B	145	$ .01	$ .04
Opperman, Dan	91B	606	$ .01	$ .10
Oquendo, Jose	89B	438	$ .01	$ .03
Oquendo, Jose	90B	200	$ .01	$ .04
Oquendo, Jose	91B	395	$ .01	$ .04
Orosco, Jesse	89B	81	$ .01	$ .03
Orosco, Jesse	91B	72	$ .01	$ .04
Orsulak, Joe	90B	252	$ .01	$ .04
Orsulak, Joe	91B	84	$ .01	$ .04
Orsulak, Joe	92B	432	$ .05	$ .20
Ortiz, Javier	91B	562	$ .01	$ .04
Ortiz, Junior	91B	328	$ .01	$ .04
Ortiz, Luis	92B	306	$ .05	$ .25
Orton, John	90B	298	$ .01	$ .10
Osborne, Donovan	91B	406	$ .05	$ .35
Osborne, Donovan	92B	96	$ .10	$1.00
Osuna, Al	92B	639	$ .05	$ .20
Otto, Dave	90B	448	$ .01	$ .04
Otto, Dave	92B	619	$ .05	$ .20
Owen, Dave	91B	110	$ .01	$ .04
Owen, Spike	89B	363	$ .01	$ .03
Owen, Spike	90B	116	$ .01	$ .04
Owen, Spike	91B	454	$ .01	$ .04
Owen, Spike	92B	121	$ .05	$ .20
Pagliarulo, Mike	89B	175	$ .01	$ .03
Pagliarulo, Mike	90B	219	$ .01	$ .04
Pagliarulo, Mike	91B	339	$ .01	$ .04
Pagliarulo, Mike	92B	685	$ .05	$ .20
Pagnozzi, Tom	91B	389	$ .01	$ .04
Pagnozzi, Tom	92B	241	$ .05	$ .20
Palacios, Rey	90B	381	$ .01	$ .04
Pall, Donn	92B	380	$ .05	$ .20
Palmeiro, Rafael	89B	237	$ .01	$ .10
Palmeiro, Rafael	90B	496	$ .01	$ .10
Palmeiro, Rafael	91B	286	$ .01	$ .10
Palmeiro, Rafael	92B	610	$ .05	$ .20
Palmer, Dean	91B	288	$ .01	$ .10
Palmer, Dean	92B	107	$ .20	$2.00
Pappas, Erik	91B	432	$ .01	$ .04
Paquette, Craig	91B	236	$ .01	$ .15
Paquette, Craig	92B	94	$ .05	$ .25
Parker, Clay	92B	366	$ .05	$ .20
Parker, Dave	89B	202	$ .01	$ .10
Parker, Dave	90B	398	$ .01	$ .04
Parker, Dave	91B	199	$ .01	$ .04
Parker, Dave	91B	375	$ .01	$ .04
Parks, Derek	90B	422	$ .01	$ .10
Parrett, Jeff	89B	390	$ .01	$ .03
Parrett, Jeff	90B	149	$ .01	$ .04
Parrish, Lance	89B	45	$ .01	$ .03
Parrish, Lance	90B	295	$ .01	$ .04
Parrish, Lance	91B	188	$ .01	$ .04
Parrish, Lance	91B	374	$ .01	$ .04
Pasqua, Dan	89B	67	$ .01	$ .03
Pasqua, Dan	90B	313	$ .01	$ .04
Pasqua, Dan	91B	361	$ .01	$ .04
Patterson, Bob	90B	168	$ .01	$ .04
Patterson, John	92B	67	$ .05	$ .25
Paulino, Elvin	92B	95	$ .05	$ .25
Pecota, Bill	90B	377	$ .01	$ .04
Pedrique, Al	89B	104	$ .01	$ .03
Peltier, Dan	91B	266	$ .01	$ .10
Pena, Alejandro	90B	124	$ .01	$ .04
Pena, Tony	89B	435	$ .01	$ .10
Pena, Tony	90B	271	$ .01	$ .04
Pena, Tony	91B	124	$ .01	$ .04
Pena, Tony	92B	364	$ .05	$ .20
Pendleton, Terry	89B	437	$ .01	$ .10
Pendleton, Terry	90B	197	$ .01	$ .10
Pendleton, Terry	91B	570	$ .01	$ .10
Pendleton, Terry	92B	254	$ .05	$ .25
Pennington, Brad	92B	136	$ .10	$1.00
Pennyfeather, William	91B	517	$ .01	$ .15

Olson, Gregg	89B	6	$ .05	$ .35
Olson, Gregg	90B	249	$ .01	$ .10
Olson, Gregg	91B	92	$ .01	$ .10

BOWMAN

Player	Year	No.	VG	EX/MT	Player	Year	No.	VG	EX/MT
Pennyfeather, William	92B	17	$ .05	$ .25	Randa, Joe	92B	560	$ .10	$ .40
Peraza, Oswald	89B	1	$ .01	$ .03	Randolph, Willie	89B	344	$ .01	$ .03
Percival, Troy	92B	290	$ .10	$ .50	Randolph, Willie	90B	90	$ .01	$ .04
Perez, Melido	89B	59	$ .01	$ .10	Randolph, Willie	91B	46	$ .01	$ .04
Perez, Melido	90B	310	$ .01	$ .04	Randolph, Willie	92B	681	$ .05	$ .20
Perez, Melido	91B	344	$ .01	$ .04	Rasmussen, Dennis	89B	450	$ .01	$ .03
Perez, Melido	92B	365	$ .05	$ .20	Rasmussen, Dennis	90B	205	$ .01	$ .04
Perez, Pascual	89B	354	$ .01	$ .10	Ratliff, Darryl	92B	71	$ .05	$ .25
Perez, Pascual	90B	430	$ .01	$ .04	Rawley, Shane	89B	151	$ .01	$ .03
Perezchica, Tony	90B	235	$ .01	$ .04	Ray, Johnny	89B	49	$ .01	$ .03
Perona, Joe	92B	246	$ .05	$ .20	Ray, John	90B	302	$ .01	$ .04
Perry, Gerald	89B	273	$ .01	$ .03	Ready, Randy	91B	495	$ .01	$ .04
Perry, Gerald	90B	383	$ .01	$ .04	Reardon, Jeff	89B	148	$ .01	$ .03
Perry, Gerald	91B	405	$ .01	$ .04	Reardon, Jeff	90B	265	$ .01	$ .04
Perschke, Greg	92B	282	$ .05	$ .20	Reardon, Jeff	91B	107	$ .01	$ .04
Petagine, Roberto	92B	31	$ .05	$ .25	Reardon, Jeff	92B	475	$ .05	$ .20
Peters, Don	91B	224	$ .01	$ .04	Redfield, Joe	92B	438	$ .05	$ .20
Peters, Don	92B	244	$ .05	$ .20	Redus, Gary	89B	425	$ .01	$ .03
Peterson, Adam	90B	307	$ .01	$ .04	Redus, Gary	90B	180	$ .01	$ .04
Petralli, Geno	90B	495	$ .01	$ .04	Redus, Gary	91B	516	$ .01	$ .04
Petralli, Geno	91B	284	$ .01	$ .04	Reed, Bobby	92B	522	$ .05	$ .20
Petry, Dan	91B	146	$ .01	$ .04	Reed, Darren	92B	537	$ .05	$ .20
Pettis, Gary	90B	498	$ .01	$ .04	Reed, Jody	89B	30	$ .01	$ .03
Pettis, Gary	91B	276	$ .01	$ .04	Reed, Jody	90B	272	$ .01	$ .04
Phelps, Ken	89B	177	$ .01	$ .03	Reed, Jody	91B	120	$ .01	$ .04
Phelps, Ken	90B	462	$ .01	$ .04	Reed, Jody	92B	642	$ .05	$ .20
Phillips, J.R.	92B	59	$ .05	$ .25	Reese, Calvin	92B	86	$ .10	$ .50
Phillips, Tony	90B	359	$ .01	$ .04	Reese, Jimmie	91B	186	$ .01	$ .04
Phillips, Tony	91B	137	$ .01	$ .04	Reimer, Kevin	92B	115	$ .05	$ .20
Phillips, Tony	92B	272	$ .05	$ .20	Remlinger, Mike	90B	227	$ .01	$ .10
Piazza, Mike	92B	461	$3.50	$14.00	Renteria, Rich	89B	212	$ .01	$ .03
Pina, Mickey	90B	270	$ .01	$ .04	Reuschel, Rick	89B	466	$ .01	$ .03
Pirkl, Greg	92B	654	$ .10	$ .50	Reuschel, Rick	90B	223	$ .01	$ .04
Pittman, Park	90B	408	$ .01	$ .10	Reuss, Jerry	89B	57	$ .01	$ .03
Plantier, Phil	91B	117	$ .10	$ .50	Revenig, Todd	92B	198	$ .05	$ .20
Plantier, Phil	92B	459	$ .10	$ .75	Reyes, Gilberto	91B	447	$ .01	$ .04
Plesac, Dan	89B	133	$ .01	$ .03	Reynolds, Craig	89B	328	$ .01	$ .03
Plesac, Dan	90B	386	$ .01	$ .04	Reynolds, Harold	89B	210	$ .01	$ .03
Plesac, Dan	91B	34	$ .01	$ .04	Reynolds, Harold	90B	478	$ .01	$ .04
Plunk, Eric	89B	191	$ .01	$ .03	Reynolds, Harold	91B	252	$ .01	$ .04
Polonia, Luis	91B	209	$ .01	$ .04	Reynolds, Harold	92B	503	$ .05	$ .20
Polonia, Luis	92B	582	$ .05	$ .20	Reynolds, Shane	92B	327	$ .05	$ .25
Portugal, Mark	89B	318	$ .01	$ .03	Rhoden, Rick	89B	323	$ .01	$ .03
Portugal, Mark	90B	63	$ .01	$ .04	Rhodes, Arthur	91B	95	$ .05	$ .25
Portugal, Mark	91B	552	$ .01	$ .04	Rhodes, Arthur	92B	631	$ .10	$ .75
Portugal, Mark	92B	656	$ .05	$ .20	Rhodes, Karl	90B	79	$ .05	$ .04
Powell, Colin	91B	533	$ .01	$ .10	Rhodes, Karl	91B	544	$ .01	$ .04
Powell, Dennis	92B	426	$ .05	$ .20	Rice, Jim	89B	33	$ .01	$ .10
Power, Ted	91B	688	$ .01	$ .04	Richardson, Jeff	91B	198	$ .01	$ .10
Presley, Jim	89B	214	$ .01	$ .03	Riesgo, Nikco	91B	536	$ .01	$ .10
Presley, Jim	90B	18	$ .01	$ .04	Righetti, Dave	89B	167	$ .01	$ .03
Presley, Jim	91B	646	$ .01	$ .04	Righetti, Dave	90B	426	$ .01	$ .04
Price, Joe	90B	245	$ .01	$ .04	Righetti, Dave	91B	632	$ .01	$ .04
Prince, Tom	90B	176	$ .01	$ .04	Righetti, Dave	92B	324	$ .05	$ .20
Proctor, Dave	89B	378	$ .01	$ .03	Rijo, Jose	89B	300	$ .01	$ .10
Puckett, Kirby	89B	162	$ .05	$ .25	Rijo, Jose	90B	45	$ .01	$ .04
Puckett, Kirby	90B	424	$ .05	$ .25	Rijo, Jose	91B	681	$ .01	$ .04
Puckett, Kirby	91B	320	$ .05	$ .25	Rijo, Jose	92B	680	$ .05	$ .20
Puckett, Kirby	92B	80	$ .20	$2.00	Riles, Ernie	89B	475	$ .01	$ .03
Puleo, Charlie	89B	263	$ .01	$ .03	Riles, Ernie	90B	239	$ .01	$ .04
Pulliam, Harvey	91B	303	$ .01	$ .10	Riles, Ernie	91B	217	$ .01	$ .04
Quantrill, Paul	92B	23	$ .05	$ .35	Ripken, Billy	89B	12	$ .01	$ .03
Quinones, Rey	89B	213	$ .01	$ .03	Ripken, Billy	90B	256	$ .01	$ .04
Quintana, Carlos	91B	126	$ .01	$ .04	Ripken, Billy	91B	87	$ .01	$ .04
Quirk, Jamie	89B	173	$ .01	$ .03	Ripken, Billy	92B	373	$ .05	$ .20
Radinsky, Scott	90B	308	$ .01	$ .10	Ripken, Cal	89B	9	$ .10	$ .50
Radinsky, Scott	91B	365	$ .01	$ .04	Ripken Jr., Cal	92B	260	$ .05	$ .20
Raines, Rock	89B	369	$ .01	$ .10	Ripken, Cal	90B	255	$ .05	$ .25
Raines, Rock	90B	118	$ .01	$ .04	Ripken, Cal	91B	104	$ .05	$ .25
Raines, Rock	91B	362	$ .01	$ .04	Ripken, Cal	92B	400	$ .75	$3.00
Raines, Rock	92B	204	$ .05	$ .20	Ripken Sr., Cal	89B	260	$ .05	$ .20
Ramirez, Manny	92B	532	$1.00	$4.00	Ritchie, Todd	91B	332	$ .01	$ .15
Ramirez, Manny	92B	676	$1.75	$7.00	Ritchie, Todd	92B	524	$ .05	$ .25
Ramirez, Rafael	89B	330	$ .01	$ .03	Ritz, Kevin	90B	350	$ .01	$ .10
Ramirez, Rafael	91B	564	$ .01	$ .04	Ritz, Kevin	92B	419	$ .05	$ .20

BOWMAN

Player	Year	No.	VG	EX/MT
Rivera, Ben	91B	579	.05	$ .20
Rivera, Hector	91B	444	$ .01	$ .10
Rivera, Luis	89B	29	$ .01	$ .03
Rivera, Luis	92B	355	$ .05	$ .20
Rivera, Mariano	92B	302	$ .05	$ .25
Roberts, Bip	90B	222	$ .01	$ .04
Roberts, Bip	91B	654	$ .01	$ .04
Roberts, Bip	92B	525	$ .05	$ .20
Roberts, Chris	92B	569	$ .10	$1.00
Robertson, Mike	92B	687	$ .10	$ .40
Robinson, Don	89B	463	$ .01	$ .03
Robinson, Don	91B	384	$ .01	$ .04
Robinson, Don	91B	619	$ .01	$ .04
Robinson, Jeff D.	89B	410	$ .01	$ .03
Robinson, Jeff D.	90B	427	$ .01	$ .04
Robinson, Jeff D.	91B	193	$ .01	$ .04
Robinson, Jeff M.	89B	97	$ .01	$ .03
Robinson, Jeff M.	91B	90	$ .01	$ .04
Robinson, Napoleon	92B	34	$ .05	$ .25
Robinson, Ron	89B	303	$ .01	$ .03
Robinson, Ron	91B	39	$ .01	$ .04
Rochford, Mike	90B	264	$ .01	$ .04
Rodriguez, Frank	92B	45	$ .10	$ .75
Rodriguez, Henry	91B	185	$ .01	$ .15
Rodriguez, Henry	92B	108	$ .05	$ .35
Rodriguez, Ivan	91B	272	$ .10	$1.00
Rodriguez, Ivan	92B	1	$ .75	$3.00
Rodriguez, Rosario	92B	498	$ .05	$ .20
Rogers, Kenny	91B	290	$ .01	$ .04
Rogers, Kevin	91B	638	$ .05	$ .20
Rogers, Kevin	92B	415	$ .05	$ .25
Rohde, Dave	90B	75	$ .01	$ .04
Rohde, Dave	91B	558	$ .01	$ .04
Rojas, Mel	90B	108	$ .01	$ .10
Romero, Ed	90B	361	$ .01	$ .04
Romine, Kevin	90B	273	$ .01	$ .04
Roomes, Rolando	90B	56	$ .01	$ .04
Roper, John	92B	528	$ .10	$ .50
Rose, Bobby	90B	293	$ .01	$ .10
Rose, Bobby	91B	206	$ .01	$ .04
Roseboro, Jaime	90B	134	$ .01	$ .10
Rossy, Rico	92B	390	$ .05	$ .20
Royer, Stan	89B	195	$ .01	$ .10
Ruffcorn, Scott	92B	88	$ .20	$2.00
Ruffin, Bruce	89B	393	$ .01	$ .03
Ruffin, Bruce	92B	354	$ .05	$ .20
Ruffin, Johnny	91B	347	$ .01	$ .15
Ruffin, Johnny	92B	451	$ .05	$ .35
Ruskin, Scott	90B	167	$ .01	$ .10
Russell, Jeff	89B	226	$ .01	$ .03
Russell, Jeff	90B	485	$ .01	$ .04
Russell, Jeff	91B	267	$ .01	$ .04
Russell, Jeff	92B	218	$ .05	$ .20
Russo, Paul	91B	695	$ .01	$ .15
Ryan, Nolan	89B	225	$ .10	$ .50
Ryan, Nolan	90B	486	$ .10	$ .50
Ryan, Nolan	91B	280	$ .10	$ .50
Ryan, Nolan	92B	222	$1.50	$6.00
Saberhagen, Bret	89B	111	$ .01	$ .10
Saberhagen, Bret	90B	364	$ .01	$ .04
Saberhagen, Bret	91B	291	$ .01	$ .04
Saberhagen, Bret	92B	586	$ .05	$ .20
Sabo, Chris	89B	309	$ .05	$ .30
Sabo, Chris	90B	53	$ .01	$ .10
Sabo, Chris	91B	674	$ .01	$ .04
Sabo, Chris	92B	595	$ .05	$ .35
Salazar, Luis	90B	40	$ .01	$ .04
Salazar, Luis	91B	428	$ .01	$ .04
Salkeld, Roger	90B	465	$ .05	$ .25
Salkeld, Roger	91B	262	$ .01	$ .04
Salkeld, Roger	92B	369	$ .05	$ .20
Salmon, Tim	91B	203	$ .10	$1.00
Salmon, Tim	92B	259	$1.75	$7.00
Sampen, Bill	90B	104	$ .01	$ .10
Sampen, Bill	92B	348	$ .05	$ .20

Player	Year	No.	VG	EX/MT
Samuel, Juan	89B	405	$ .01	$ .03
Samuel, Juan	90B	91	$ .01	$ .04
Samuel, Juan	91B	596	$ .01	$ .04
Samuel, Juan	92B	253	$ .05	$ .20
Sanchez, Alex	89B	245	$ .01	$ .03
Sandberg, Ryne	89B	290	$ .05	$ .35
Sandberg, Ryne	90B	30	$ .05	$ .35
Sandberg, Ryne	91B	377	$ .01	$ .10
Sandberg, Ryne	91B	416	$ .05	$ .20

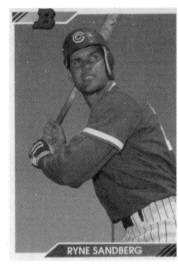

Player	Year	No.	VG	EX/MT
Sandberg, Ryne	92B	300	$ .20	$2.00
Sanders, Deion	91B	588	$ .01	$ .15
Sanders, Deion	92B	160	$ .10	$1.00
Sanders, Reggie	91B	537	$ .10	$ .75
Sanders, Reggie	92B	118	$ .20	$2.00
Sanders, Tracy	92B	42	$ .10	$ .50
Sanderson, Scott	90B	447	$ .01	$ .04
Sanderson, Scott	91B	177	$ .01	$ .04
Sanford, Mo	92B	281	$ .05	$ .25
Santana, Andres	90B	230	$ .01	$ .10
Santana, Rafael	89B	174	$ .01	$ .03
Santiago, Benny	89B	453	$ .01	$ .10
Santiago, Benny	90B	218	$ .01	$ .04
Santiago, Benny	91B	383	$ .01	$ .04
Santiago, Benny	91B	656	$ .01	$ .04
Santiago, Benny	92B	395	$ .05	$ .20
Santovonia, Nelson	89B	361	$ .01	$ .10
Sax, Steve	89B	178	$ .01	$ .03
Sax, Steve	90B	442	$ .01	$ .04
Sax, Steve	91B	170	$ .01	$ .04
Sax, Steve	92B	469	$ .05	$ .20
Schatzeder, Dan	90B	69	$ .01	$ .04
Schilling, Curt	90B	246	$ .01	$ .10
Schilling, Curt	91B	560	$ .01	$ .04
Schmidt, Dave	89B	5	$ .01	$ .03
Schmidt, Dave	90B	110	$ .01	$ .04
Schmidt, Mike	89B	402	$ .05	$ .35
Schofield, Dick	89B	46	$ .01	$ .03
Schofield, Dick	90B	291	$ .01	$ .04
Schofield, Dick	91B	191	$ .01	$ .04
Schooler, Mike	90B	470	$ .01	$ .04
Schooler, Mike	91B	241	$ .01	$ .04
Schooler, Mike	92B	336	$ .05	$ .20
Schourek, Pete	91B	482	$ .01	$ .10
Schroeder, Bill	89B	44	$ .01	$ .03

BOWMAN

Player	Year	No.	VG	EX/MT
Schunk, Jerry	91B	20	$ .01	$ .10
Scioscia, Mike	89B	342	$ .01	$ .03
Scioscia, Mike	90B	89	$ .01	$ .04
Scioscia, Mike	91B	613	$ .01	$ .04
Scioscia, Mike	92B	368	$ .05	$ .20
Scott, Gary	91B	535	$ .01	$ .10
Scott, Gary	92B	128	$ .05	$ .20
Scott, Mike	89B	322	$ .01	$ .03
Scott, Mike	90B	71	$ .01	$ .04
Scott, Mike	91B	546	$ .01	$ .04
Scott, Tim	92B	454	$ .05	$ .35
Scruggs, Tony	91B	289	$ .01	$ .10
Scudder, Scott	90B	46	$ .01	$ .10
Scudder, Scott	92B	571	$ .05	$ .20
Searcy, Steve	89B	95	$ .01	$ .10
Segui, David	90B	251	$ .01	$ .10
Segui, David	91B	102	$ .01	$ .04
Seitzer, Kevin	89B	123	$ .01	$ .10
Seitzer, Kevin	90B	380	$ .01	$ .04
Seitzer, Kevin	91B	305	$ .01	$ .04
Seitzer, Kevin	92B	126	$ .05	$ .20
Sele, Aaron	92B	311	$ .20	$2.00
Sellers, Jeff	89B	299	$ .01	$ .03
Seminara, Frank	92B	561	$ .10	$ .50
Servais, Scott	92B	463	$ .05	$ .20
Service, Scott	90B	143	$ .01	$ .04
Sharperson, Mike	89B	348	$ .01	$ .03
Sharperson, Mike	91B	602	$ .01	$ .04
Shaw, Curtis	92B	174	$ .05	$ .25
Shaw, Jeff	90B	329	$ .01	$ .10
Shaw, Jeff	92B	410	$ .05	$ .20
Sheets, Larry	89B	16	$ .01	$ .03
Sheffield, Gary	89B	142	$ .20	$2.00
Sheffield, Gary	90B	391	$ .10	$ .50
Sheffield, Gary	91B	52	$ .05	$ .25
Sheffield, Gary	92B	214	$ .20	$2.00
Shelby, John	89B	349	$ .01	$ .03
Shelton, Ben	92B	568	$ .10	$ .40
Sheridan, Pat	89B	107	$ .01	$ .03
Shinall, Zakary	91B	612	$ .01	$ .10
Show, Eric	89B	446	$ .01	$ .03
Show, Eric	90B	209	$ .01	$ .04
Show, Eric	91B	223	$ .01	$ .04
Shumpert, Terry	91B	314	$ .01	$ .04
Shumpert, Terry	92B	157	$ .05	$ .20
Sierra, Ruben	89B	235	$ .05	$ .25
Sierra, Ruben	90B	490	$ .05	$ .20
Sierra, Ruben	91B	283	$ .01	$ .10
Sierra, Ruben	92B	225	$ .10	$1.00
Silvestri, Dave	92B	87	$ .05	$ .35
Simms, Mike	91B	551	$ .01	$ .10
Simons, Doug	91B	463	$ .01	$ .10
Sinatro, Matt	92B	462	$ .05	$ .20
Singleton, Duane	92B	679	$ .05	$ .35
Skalski, Joe	90B	323	$ .01	$ .04
Slaught, Don	89B	172	$ .01	$ .03
Slaught, Don	90B	182	$ .01	$ .04
Slaught, Don	91B	532	$ .01	$ .04
Slocumb, Heathcliff	91B	421	$ .01	$ .04
Slusarski, Joe	91B	233	$ .01	$ .04
Slusarski, Joe	92B	58	$ .05	$ .20
Smiley, John	89B	413	$ .01	$ .10
Smiley, John	91B	509	$ .01	$ .04
Smiley, John	92B	257	$ .05	$ .20
Smith, Bryn	89B	353	$ .01	$ .03
Smith, Bryn	90B	184	$ .01	$ .04
Smith, Bryn	91B	407	$ .01	$ .04
Smith, Dan	91B	275	$ .01	$ .15
Smith, Dan	92B	391	$ .10	$ .40
Smith, Dave	89B	317	$ .01	$ .03
Smith, Dave	90B	62	$ .01	$ .04
Smith, Dave	91B	425	$ .01	$ .04
Smith, Dave	92B	333	$ .05	$ .20
Smith, Dwight	89B	297	$ .01	$ .10
Smith, Dwight	90B	32	$ .01	$ .10
Smith, Greg	90B	31	$ .01	$ .10
Smith, Greg	91B	594	$ .01	$ .04
Smith, Lee	89B	19	$ .01	$ .03
Smith, Lee	90B	263	$ .01	$ .04
Smith, Lee	91B	387	$ .01	$ .04
Smith, Lee	92B	505	$ .05	$ .20
Smith, Lonnie	89B	278	$ .01	$ .03
Smith, Lonnie	90B	12	$ .01	$ .04
Smith, Lonnie	91B	567	$ .01	$ .04
Smith, Mark	92B	556	$ .10	$ .50
Smith, Ozzie	89B	436	$ .01	$ .10
Smith, Ozzie	90B	195	$ .01	$ .10

Player	Year	No.	VG	EX/MT
Smith, Ozzie	91B	398	$ .01	$ .10
Smith, Ozzie	92B	675	$ .10	$ .50
Smith, Pete	89B	269	$ .01	$ .10
Smith, Tom	92B	383	$ .05	$ .20
Smith, Willie	90B	425	$ .01	$ .10
Smith, Willie	91B	160	$ .01	$ .04
Smith, Zane	89B	262	$ .01	$ .10
Smith, Zane	91B	524	$ .01	$ .04
Smith, Zane	92B	409	$ .05	$ .20
Smithberg, Roger	90B	203	$ .01	$ .10
Smoltz, John	89B	266	$ .10	$ .50
Smoltz, John	90B	10	$ .05	$ .25
Smoltz, John	91B	580	$ .01	$ .10
Smoltz, John	92B	347	$ .10	$ .50
Snyder, Cory	89B	89	$ .01	$ .10
Snyder, Cory	90B	336	$ .01	$ .04
Snyder, Cory	91B	357	$ .01	$ .04
Snyder, Cory	92B	492	$ .05	$ .20
Sojo, Luis	90B	517	$ .01	$ .10
Sojo, Luis	91B	197	$ .01	$ .04
Sojo, Luis	92B	418	$ .05	$ .20
Sondrini, Joe	92B	211	$ .05	$ .20
Sorrento, Paul	90B	421	$ .05	$ .20
Sosa, Sammy	90B	312	$ .05	$ .25
Sosa, Sammy	91B	350	$ .01	$ .04
Sosa, Sammy	92B	116	$ .05	$ .35
Spehr, Tim	91B	298	$ .01	$ .10
Spencer, Stan	91B	441	$ .01	$ .10
Spiers, Billy	90B	402	$ .01	$ .10
Spiers, Billy	92B	536	$ .05	$ .20
Sprague, Ed	89B	252	$ .05	$ .25
Sprague, Ed	90B	511	$ .01	$ .04

BOWMAN

Player	Year	No.	VG	EX/MT	Player	Year	No.	VG	EX/MT
Sprague, Ed	91B	26	$ .01	$ .15	Tapani, Kevin	90B	407	$ .05	$ .25
Springer, Russ	92B	308	$ .10	$ .50	Tapani, Kevin	91B	322	$ .01	$ .10
Stahoviak, Scott	92B	360	$ .10	$ .50	Tapani, Kevin	92B	552	$ .05	$ .20
Stairs, Matt	92B	434	$ .10	$ .40	Tartabull, Danny	89B	128	$ .01	$ .10
Stairs, Matt	92B	602	$ .10	$ .50	Tartabull, Danny	90B	375	$ .01	$ .04
Stanicek, Pete	89B	14	$ .01	$ .03	Tartabull, Danny	91B	294	$ .01	$ .04
Stankeiwicz, Andy	92B	482	$ .05	$ .35	Tartabull, Danny	92B	550	$ .05	$ .20
Stanley, Bob	89B	25	$ .01	$ .03	Tatar, Kevin	92B	621	$ .05	$ .20
Stanley, Mike	92B	370	$ .05	$ .20	Taubensee, Eddie	92B	697	$ .10	$ .40
Stanton, Mike	90B	4	$ .01	$ .10	Taylor, Brien	92B	124	$2.50	$10.00
Staton, Dave	91B	645	$ .01	$ .15	Taylor, Scott	91B	121	$ .01	$ .10
Staton, Dave	92B	499	$ .05	$ .35	Taylor, Scott	92B	618	$ .05	$ .20
Steinbach, Terry	89B	193	$ .01	$ .03	Taylor, Wade	91B	165	$ .01	$ .04
Steinbach, Terry	90B	456	$ .01	$ .04	Tejada, Wil	89B	468	$ .01	$ .03
Steinbach, Terry	91B	216	$ .01	$ .04	Templeton, Garry	89B	455	$ .01	$ .03
Steinbach, Terry	92B	392	$ .05	$ .20	Templeton, Garry	90B	215	$ .01	$ .04
Stevens, Lee	90B	300	$ .01	$ .10	Terrell, Walt	89B	445	$ .01	$ .03
Stevens, Lee	92B	427	$ .05	$ .20	Terrell, Walt	90B	165	$ .01	$ .04
Stewart, Dave	89B	188	$ .01	$ .15	Tettleton, Mickey	90B	254	$ .01	$ .04
Stewart, Dave	90B	449	$ .01	$ .10	Tettleton, Mickey	91B	140	$ .01	$ .04
Stewart, Dave	91B	225	$ .01	$ .04	Tettleton, Mickey	92B	117	$ .05	$ .20
Stewart, Dave	92B	280	$ .05	$ .20	Teufel, Tim	89B	382	$ .01	$ .03
Stieb, Dave	89B	239	$ .01	$ .03	Tewksbury, Bob	91B	394	$ .01	$ .04
Stieb, Dave	90B	505	$ .01	$ .04	Thigpen, Bobby	89B	55	$ .01	$ .03
Stieb, Dave	91B	22	$ .01	$ .04	Thigpen, Bobby	90B	306	$ .01	$ .04
Stieb, Dave	92B	376	$ .05	$ .20	Thigpen, Bobby	91B	342	$ .01	$ .04
Stillwell, Kurt	89B	120	$ .01	$ .03	Thigpen, Bobby	92B	36	$ .05	$ .20
Stillwell, Kurt	90B	376	$ .01	$ .04	Thomas, Andres	89B	272	$ .01	$ .03
Stillwell, Kurt	91B	307	$ .01	$ .04	Thomas, Frank	90B	320	$ .75	$3.00
Stillwell, Kurt	92B	135	$ .05	$ .20	Thomas, Frank	91B	366	$ .10	$1.00
Stone, Eric	90B	348	$ .01	$ .10	Thomas, Frank	92B	114	$3.50	$14.00
Stottlemyre Jr., Mel	89B	110	$ .01	$ .03	Thomas, Frank	92B	551	$9.00	$36.00
Stottlemyre Jr., Mel	89B	261	$ .01	$ .10	Thome, Jim	91B	68	$ .01	$ .15
Stottlemyre Sr., Mel	89B	261	$ .01	$ .10	Thome, Jim	92B	460	$ .10	$ .50
Stottlemyre, Todd	89B	242	$ .01	$ .10	Thompson, Justin	92B	543	$ .10	$ .40
Stottlemyre, Todd	91B	10	$ .01	$ .04	Thompson, Milt	89B	441	$ .01	$ .03
Stottlemyre, Todd	92B	18	$ .05	$ .20	Thompson, Milt	90B	196	$ .01	$ .04
Strange, Doug	92B	322	$ .05	$ .20	Thompson, Milt	91B	386	$ .01	$ .04
Strawberry, Darryl	89B	387	$ .05	$ .25	Thompson, Robby	89B	473	$ .01	$ .03
Strawberry, Darryl	90B	141	$ .05	$ .20	Thompson, Robby	90B	233	$ .01	$ .04
Strawberry, Darryl	91B	382	$ .01	$ .10	Thompson, Robby	91B	623	$ .01	$ .04
Strawberry, Darryl	91B	609	$ .01	$ .10	Thompson, Robby	92B	448	$ .05	$ .20
Strawberry, Darryl	92B	40	$ .10	$ .75	Thomson, Bobby	91B	410	$ .01	$ .10
Stubbs, Franklin	91B	37	$ .01	$ .04	Thon, Dickie	89B	400	$ .01	$ .03
Stubbs, Franklin	92B	49	$ .05	$ .20	Thon, Dickie	90B	155	$ .01	$ .04
Suero, William	91B	8	$ .01	$ .10	Thon, Dickie	91B	499	$ .01	$ .04
Suero, William	92B	181	$ .05	$ .20	Thon, Dickie	92B	162	$ .05	$ .20
Sundberg, Jim	89B	227	$ .01	$ .03	Thurman, Gary	91B	316	$ .01	$ .04
Surhoff, B.J.	89B	137	$ .01	$ .10	Timlin, Mike	91B	15	$ .01	$ .10
Surhoff, B.J.	90B	393	$ .01	$ .04	Toliver, Fred	89B	147	$ .01	$ .03
Surhoff, B.J.	91B	44	$ .01	$ .04	Tomlin, Randy	91B	518	$ .01	$ .15
Surhoff, B.J.	92B	481	$ .05	$ .20	Tomlin, Randy	92B	495	$ .05	$ .20
Sutcliffe, Rick	89B	281	$ .01	$ .10	Torres, Salomon	92B	4	$ .10	$ .50
Sutcliffe, Rick	90B	21	$ .01	$ .04	Torres, Salomon	92B	584	$ .10	$ .75
Sutcliffe, Rick	91B	430	$ .01	$ .04	Traber, Jim	89B	13	$ .01	$ .03
Sutcliffe, Rick	92B	106	$ .05	$ .20	Trammell, Alan	89B	105	$ .01	$ .10
Sutherland, Alex	92B	123	$ .05	$ .20	Trammell, Alan	90B	353	$ .01	$ .04
Sutko, Glenn	91B	668	$ .01	$ .04	Trammell, Alan	91B	154	$ .01	$ .10
Sveum, Dale	89B	139	$ .01	$ .03	Trammell, Alan	91B	370	$ .01	$ .04
Sveum, Dale	92B	367	$ .05	$ .20	Trammell, Alan	92B	690	$ .05	$ .20
Swan, Russ	90B	224	$ .01	$ .10	Treadway, Jeff	91B	586	$ .01	$ .04
Swan, Russ	92B	378	$ .05	$ .20	Trevino, Alex	89B	326	$ .01	$ .03
Swift, Bill	92B	182	$ .05	$ .20	Trillo, Manny	89B	308	$ .01	$ .03
Swift, Bill	92B	611	$ .05	$ .20	Trlicek, Ricky	92B	76	$ .05	$ .25
Swindell, Greg	89B	76	$ .01	$ .10	Trombley, Mike	92B	102	$ .10	$ .50
Swindell, Greg	90B	325	$ .01	$ .04	Tucker, Michael	92B	682	$1.25	$5.00
Swindell, Greg	91B	58	$ .01	$ .10	Tudor, John	90B	188	$ .01	$ .04
Swindell, Greg	92B	46	$ .05	$ .20	Turner, Ryan	92B	346	$ .10	$ .50
Swindell, Greg	92B	578	$ .05	$ .20	Urbina, Ugueth	92B	261	$ .05	$ .25
Swinton, Jermaine	92B	137	$ .05	$ .25	Uribe, Jose	89B	471	$ .01	$ .03
Tabler, Pat	89B	125	$ .01	$ .03	Uribe, Jose	91B	627	$ .01	$ .04
Tabler, Pat	91B	28	$ .01	$ .04	Valdez, Efrain	91B	60	$ .01	$ .04
Tackett, Jeff	91B	106	$ .01	$ .10	Valdez, Rafael	90B	210	$ .01	$ .10
Tanana, Frank	89B	92	$ .01	$ .03	Valdez, Rafael	91B	663	$ .01	$ .04
Tanana, Frank	90B	343	$ .01	$ .04	Valenzuela, Fernando	89B	337	$ .01	$ .10

BOWMAN

Player	Year	No.	VG	EX/MT
Valera, Julio	90B	123	$ .01	$ .10
Valera, Julio	92B	422	$ .05	$ .20
Valle, Dave	89B	208	$ .01	$ .03
Valle, Dave	90B	473	$ .01	$ .04
Valle, Dave	91B	251	$ .01	$ .04
Valle, Dave	92B	134	$ .05	$ .20
Van Poppel, Todd	91B	218	$ .10	$ .50
Van Poppel, Todd	92B	270	$ .10	$ .75
Van Slyke, Andy	89B	424	$ .01	$ .10
Van Slyke, Andy	90B	171	$ .01	$ .10
Van Slyke, Andy	91B	529	$ .01	$ .04
Van Slyke, Andy	92B	35	$ .05	$ .35
Vander Wal, John	92B	232	$ .10	$ .50
Varsho, Gary	91B	510	$ .01	$ .04
Vasquez, Julian	92B	357	$ .05	$ .20
Vaughn, Greg	90B	396	$ .05	$ .25
Vaughn, Greg	91B	33	$ .01	$ .10
Vaughn, Greg	92B	496	$ .05	$ .20
Vaughn, Maurice	90B	275	$ .10	$ .50
Vaughn, Mo	91B	112	$ .01	$ .15
Vaughn, Mo	92B	397	$ .10	$ .75
Velarde, Randy	90B	434	$ .01	$ .04
Velarde, Randy	92B	207	$ .05	$ .20
Velasquez, Guillermo	92B	698	$ .05	$ .25
Ventura, Robin	89B	65	$ .10	$ .75
Ventura, Robin	90B	311	$ .10	$ .50
Ventura, Robin	91B	358	$ .01	$ .15
Ventura, Robin	92B	275	$ .10	$1.00
Ventura, Robin	92B	655	$ .75	$3.00
Veres, Randy	90B	390	$ .01	$ .04
Viola, Frank	89B	150	$ .01	$ .10
Viola, Frank	90B	122	$ .01	$ .04
Viola, Frank	91B	477	$ .01	$ .04
Viola, Frank	92B	491	$ .05	$ .20
Vitko, Joe	92B	516	$ .10	$ .50
Vizcaino, Jose	90B	98	$ .01	$ .10
Vizcaino, Jose	91B	427	$ .01	$ .04
Vizquel, Omar	90B	474	$ .01	$ .04
Vizquel, Omar	91B	245	$ .01	$ .04

Player	Year	No.	VG	EX/MT
Vizquel, Omar	92B	423	$ .05	$ .20
Wagner, Hector	91B	299	$ .01	$ .04
Wainhouse, Dave	89B	358	$ .01	$ .10
Walden, Ronnie	91B	615	$ .01	$ .04
Walk, Bob	89B	409	$ .01	$ .03

Player	Year	No.	VG	EX/MT
Walk, Bob	90B	163	$ .01	$ .04
Walk, Bob	91B	526	$ .01	$ .04
Walk, Bob	92B	666	$ .05	$ .20
Walker, Hugh	89B	127	$ .01	$ .10
Walker, Hugh	91B	313	$ .01	$ .04
Walker, Larry	90B	117	$ .10	$1.00
Walker, Larry	91B	442	$ .05	$ .25
Walker, Larry	92B	648	$ .10	$1.00
Walker, Mike	89B	77	$ .01	$ .03
Wallace, B.J.	92B	554	$ .75	$3.00
Wallach, Tim	89B	362	$ .01	$ .03
Wallach, Tim	90B	114	$ .01	$ .04
Wallach, Tim	91B	437	$ .01	$ .04
Wallach, Tim	92B	372	$ .05	$ .20
Wallach, Tim	92B	557	$ .05	$ .20
Walling, Denny	92B	530	$ .05	$ .20
Walton, Jerome	89B	295	$ .01	$ .10
Walton, Jerome	90B	35	$ .01	$ .10
Walton, Jerome	91B	413	$ .01	$ .04
Walton, Jerome	92B	27	$ .05	$ .20
Wapnick, Steve	90B	346	$ .01	$ .10
Ward, Turner	91B	76	$ .01	$ .10
Washington, Claudell	89B	52	$ .01	$ .03
Washington, Claudell	90B	297	$ .01	$ .04
Watson, Allen	92B	634	$ .75	$3.00
Webster, Mitch	89B	296	$ .01	$ .03
Webster, Mitch	91B	66	$ .01	$ .04
Wegman, Bill	89B	135	$ .01	$ .03
Wegman, Bill	92B	447	$ .05	$ .20
Wehner, John	92B	444	$ .05	$ .20
Weiss, Walt	89B	196	$ .01	$ .10
Weiss, Walt	90B	461	$ .01	$ .04
Weiss, Walt	91B	228	$ .01	$ .04
Weiss, Walt	92B	651	$ .05	$ .20
Welch, Bob	89B	186	$ .01	$ .03
Welch, Bob	91B	215	$ .01	$ .04
Wells, David	92B	352	$ .05	$ .20
Wendell, Turk	92B	693	$ .05	$ .35
West, Dave	90B	413	$ .01	$ .04
Wetteland, John	90B	82	$ .01	$ .15
Wetteland, John	92B	68	$ .05	$ .20
Whitaker, Lou	89B	103	$ .01	$ .10
Whitaker, Lou	90B	356	$ .01	$ .04
Whitaker, Lou	91B	150	$ .01	$ .10
Whitaker, Lou	92B	630	$ .05	$ .20
White, Devon	89B	54	$ .01	$ .03
White, Devon	90B	292	$ .01	$ .04
White, Devon	91B	30	$ .01	$ .04
White, Devon	92B	547	$ .05	$ .20
White, Frank	89B	122	$ .01	$ .03
White, Frank	90B	371	$ .01	$ .04
White, Gabe	92B	279	$ .10	$ .75
White, Rondell	91B	450	$ .10	$ .40
White, Rondell	92B	436	$ .20	$2.00
Whitehurst, Wally	89B	373	$ .01	$ .10
Whitehurst, Wally	91B	470	$ .01	$ .04
Whiten, Mark	91B	13	$ .01	$ .10
Whiten, Mark	92B	57	$ .05	$ .20
Whitson, Eddie	89B	449	$ .01	$ .03
Whitson, Eddie	90B	204	$ .01	$ .04
Whitson, Eddie	91B	651	$ .01	$ .04
Whitt, Ernie	89B	248	$ .01	$ .03
Whitt, Ernie	90B	16	$ .01	$ .04
Wickander, Kevin	89B	75	$ .01	$ .03
Wickander, Kevin	90B	327	$ .01	$ .04
Wickander, Kevin	92B	430	$ .05	$ .20
Wickman, Bob	91B	353	$ .05	$ .35
Wilkerson, Curt	89B	292	$ .01	$ .03
Wilkerson, Curt	91B	511	$ .01	$ .04
Wilkins, Dean	90B	26	$ .01	$ .04
Wilkins, Rick	91B	419	$ .01	$ .10
Wilkins, Rick	92B	156	$ .05	$ .20
Willard, Jerry	92B	470	$ .05	$ .20
Williams, Bernie	90B	439	$ .05	$ .25
Williams, Bernie	91B	173	$ .01	$ .10

BOWMAN

Player	Year	No.	VG	EX/MT
Williams, Bernie	92B	407	$ .10	$ .75
Williams, Brian	92B	125	$ .10	$ .75
Williams, Eddie	92B	331	$ .05	$ .25
Williams, Frank	89B	100	$ .01	$.03
Williams, Gerald	91B	161	$ .05	$ .25
Williams, Gerald	92B	113	$ .05	$ .35
Williams, Jeff	92B	284	$ .05	$ .20
Williams, Matt	90B	238	$ .01	$ .10
Williams, Matt	91B	378	$ .01	$ .04
Williams, Matt	91B	618	$ .01	$ .04
Williams, Matt	92B	175	$ .10	$ .75
Williams, Matt	92B	579	$ .15	$1.50
Williams, Mike	92B	152	$ .10	$ .40
Williams, Mitch	89B	283	$ .01	$ .03
Williams, Mitch	90B	25	$ .01	$ .04
Williams, Mitch	92B	247	$ .05	$ .20
Williamson, Mark	90B	248	$ .01	$ .04
Williamson, Mark	91B	85	$ .01	$ .04
Willis, Carl	92B	466	$ .05	$ .20
Wilson, Brandon	92B	632	$ .05	$ .25
Wilson, Dan	91B	687	$ .01	$ .10
Wilson, Mookie	89B	386	$ .01	$ .03
Wilson, Mookie	90B	516	$ .01	$ .04
Wilson, Nigel	92B	228	$2.50	$10.00
Wilson, Steve	89B	280	$ .01	$ .03
Wilson, Steve	90B	23	$ .01	$ .04
Wilson, Trevor	91B	630	$ .01	$ .04
Wilson, Trevor	92B	119	$ .05	$ .20
Wilson, Willie	89B	124	$ .01	$ .10
Wilson, Willie	91B	230	$ .01	$ .04
Winfield, Dave	89B	179	$ .05	$ .20
Winfield, Dave	90B	432	$ .01	$ .10
Winfield, Dave	91B	210	$ .01	$ .10
Winfield, Dave	92B	315	$ .10	$1.00
Witt, Bobby	89B	222	$ .01	$ .03
Witt, Bobby	91B	287	$ .01	$ .04
Witt, Bobby	92B	230	$ .05	$ .20
Witt, Mike	89B	42	$ .01	$ .03
Wohlers, Mark	91B	582	$ .01	$ .15
Wohlers, Mark	92B	396	$ .05	$ .25
Wood, Jason	92B	262	$ .05	$ .25
Woodson, Kerry	91B	264	$ .01	$ .15
Woodson, Kerry	92B	411	$ .05	$ .25
Worrell, Todd	89B	429	$ .01	$ .10
Worrell, Todd	90B	185	$ .01	$ .04
Worthington, Craig	90B	253	$ .01	$ .04
Yelding, Eric	91B	557	$ .01	$ .04
Yett, Rich	89B	79	$ .01	$ .03
Yett, Rich	90B	412	$ .01	$ .04
Youmans, Floyd	89B	396	$ .01	$ .10
Young, Anthony	91B	466	$ .01	$ .10
Young, Anthony	92B	268	$ .05	$ .20
Young, Cliff	91B	204	$ .01	$ .04
Young, Curt	89B	184	$ .01	$ .03
Young, Curt	91B	220	$ .01	$ .04
Young, Gerald	89B	333	$ .01	$ .03
Young, Gerald	90B	72	$ .01	$ .04
Young, Kevin	92B	155	$ .75	$3.00
Young, Matt	91B	128	$ .01	$ .04
Youngblood, Joel	89B	315	$ .01	$ .03
Yount, Robin	89B	144	$ .01	$ .15
Yount, Robin	90B	404	$ .01	$ .10
Yount, Robin	91B	55	$ .01	$ .10
Yount, Robin	92B	700	$ .10	$1.00
Zancanaro, David	92B	99	$ .05	$ .20
Zeile, Todd	90B	193	$ .01	$ .15
Zeile, Todd	91B	404	$ .01	$ .04
Zeile, Todd	92B	695	$ .05	$ .20
Zimmerman, Mike	91B	519	$ .01	$ .10
Zinter, Alan	90B	135	$ .01	$ .10
Zosky, Eddie	90B	523	$ .01	$ .15
Zosky, Eddie	91B	17	$ .01	$ .04
Zosky, Eddie	92B	381	$ .05	$ .20

DAN WILSON

Player	Year	No.	VG	EX/MT
Wilson, Dan	**92B**	**471**	**$ .05**	**$ .25**
Wilson, Glenn	89B	423	$ .01	$ .03

DONRUSS-LEAF INC. 1981 – 1993

Donruss baseball cards first made their appearance on the collecting scene in 1981. At first they contained bubble gum in the wax packs; but in 1982, after being sued successfully by Topps, a puzzle piece was included in each pack instead of bubble gum. In 1990 Donruss entered the premium card market with their Leaf set. These 1990 cards were very successful, but in 1991 and 1992 their popularity dimmed with collectors due to lack of originality. As I write this, the first series of 1993 Leaf has just taken the card collecting arena by storm. With most of the super stars to come in the second series, Leaf may be the 1993 set of the year.

Several abbreviations are used in the Donruss section that need some explanation:

D#A & D#B refer to bonus cards numbered with A and B in the wax packs of 1984
DAS – Donruss All-Star card first issued in 1990 sets
DBC – DONRUSS BONUS CARDS were issued starting in 1988. These cards (BC1-BC26) are randomly distributed in the wax, rack and cello packs.
DK – From 1983 until 1991 the first 26 cards of the Donruss sets were designated DIAMOND KINGS. In 1992 and 1993 these were randomly inserted in packs and not a part of the numbered set. These cards feature the art of Dick Perez of Perez-Steele Galleries.
DL – Donruss Leaf set started in 1990 to compete with Upper Deck quality.
DLP – Donruss Leaf Prototype packed four per factory set beginning in 1991 with 26 in set
DLS – Donruss Leaf Studio issued as 264 black and white card set in 1991 and changed to color in 1992.
DMVP – Most valuable players of each team originally began as BC cards but incorporated into sets beginning in 1991.
DR – Donruss issues a boxed 56 card set of DONRUSS ROOKIES at the end of the year. This was started in 1986 and changed to 132 card set issued only in foil packs in 1992.
DRR – Beginning with the 1984 set, a group of top rookies are designated DONRUSS RATED ROOKIES.
DTR – Donruss issued a 56 traded card set only in 1989.

There are many unnumbered checklists in the early Donruss sets. Since there are no numbers on the cards themselves, they are numbered as **"0"** in the listing of cards.

All Donruss cards are 2½" x 3½" and in full color.

1981 – 600 cards plus five unnumbered checklists w/white border w/Donruss logo '81 (copyright 1981 Donruss back upper right)
1982 – 653 cards plus seven unnumbered checklists w/white border w/Donruss logo '82 (copyright 1982 Donruss back upper right
1983 – 653 cards plus seven unnumbered checklists w/white border w/Donruss logo '83 (copyright 1982 Donruss back upper right)
1984 – 651 cards plus seven unnumbered checklists and two cards (A & B) w/white border w/ Donruss logo '84 (copyright 1983 Donruss back upper right)
1985 – 653 cards plus seven unnumbered checklists w/black border w/five red stripes on sides w/ Donruss logo '85 (copyright 1984 Donruss back upper right)
1986 – 653 cards plus seven unnumbered checklists w/blue border w/thin black stripes w/Donruss '86 (copyright 1985 Leaf-Donruss back upper right)
1987 – 660 cards w/black border with brown baseball filled strip inside yellow bands on each side w/Donruss '87 (copyright 1986 Leaf, Inc. back upper right)
1988 – 660 cards plus 26 BC cards w/blue border with black and red shadings w/Donruss '88 (copyright 1987 Leaf, Inc. back upper right)
1989 – 660 cards plus 26 BC cards w/black striped side borders and multi-colored top and bottoms w/Donruss '89 (copyright 1988 Leaf, Inc. back upper right)
1990 – 716 cards plus 26 BC cards w/red borders with Donruss '90 on top left and orange backs (copyright 1989 Leaf, Inc. back upper left.)
1991 – 792 cards plus 22 BC cards issued in two series of 396 cards. Series I is blue bordered and Series II is green bordered with Donruss '91 on top left (copyright 1990 Leaf, Inc. back upper right).
1992 – 792 cards plus eight BC cards issued in two series of 396 cards. Series I and Series II are both white bordered with Donruss '92 across top (copyright 1991 Leaf, Inc. back upper left.)
1993 – 792 cards issued in two series of 396 cards. Series I and Series II are both white bordered with Donruss '93 across top (copyright 1992 Leaf, Inc. back lower right).

DONRUSS

Player	Year	No.	VG	EX/MT
Aaron, Hank	86DK	602	$ .05	$ .20
Aase, Don	81D	411	$ .01	$ .06
Aase, Don	82D	267	$ .01	$ .06
Aase, Don	83D	38	$ .01	$ .06
Aase, Don	85D	255	$ .01	$ .10
Aase, Don	86D	392	$ .01	$ .08
Aase, Don	87D	231	$ .01	$ .05
Abbott, Glenn	81D	47	$ .01	$ .06
Abbott, Glenn	82D	302	$ .01	$ .06
Abbott, Jim	89DR	16	$ .15	$1.25
Abbott, Jim	90D	108	$ .05	$ .20
Abbott, Jim	90DL	31	$1.25	$5.00

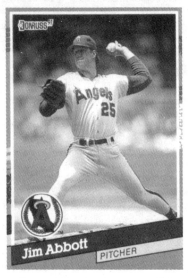

Player	Year	No.	VG	EX/MT
Abbott, Jim	**91D**	**78**	**$ .01**	**$ .10**
Abbott, Jim	91DL	162	$ .05	$ .35
Abbott, Jim	91DLS	22	$ .05	$ .35
Abbott, Jim	92D	130	$ .01	$ .10
Abbott, Jim	92DL	1	$ .05	$ .25
Abbott, Jim	92DLS	141	$ .05	$ .20
Abbott, Jim	93D	35	$ .01	$ .10
Abbott, Kyle	92DL	495	$ .01	$ .15
Abbott, Kyle	92DR	1	$ .01	$ .10
Abbott, Kyle	92DRR	3	$ .01	$ .05
Abbott, Kyle	93D	676	$ .01	$ .05
Abbott, Paul	91D	639	$ .01	$ .10
Abner, Shawn	88DR	5	$ .01	$ .15
Abner, Shawn	88DRR	33	$ .05	$ .20
Abner, Shawn	89D	323	$ .01	$ .10
Abner, Shawn	91D	561	$ .01	$ .04
Abner, Shawn	91DL	381	$ .01	$ .08
Abner, Shawn	92D	736	$ .01	$ .04
Abner, Shawn	93D	651	$ .01	$ .05
Abrego, Johnny	86DRR	32	$ .01	$ .10
Acker, Jim	84D	146	$ .05	$ .20
Acker, Jim	86D	363	$ .01	$ .08
Acker, Jim	87D	659	$ .01	$ .05
Acker, Jim	90D	558	$ .01	$ .04
Acker, Jim	91D	368	$ .01	$ .04
Adams, Glenn	81D	566	$ .01	$ .06
Adams, Glenn	82D	431	$ .01	$ .06
Adams, Rick	84D	85	$ .05	$ .20
Adduci, Jim	87D	495	$ .01	$ .05
Afenir, Troy	92DL	525	$ .01	$ .06
Afenir, Troy	92DR	2	$ .01	$ .05
Agosto, Juan	84D	208	$ .05	$ .20
Agosto, Juan	85D	526	$ .01	$ .10
Agosto, Juan	86D	488	$ .01	$ .08
Agosto, Juan	89D	354	$ .01	$ .04
Agosto, Juan	90D	477	$ .01	$ .04
Agosto, Juan	91D	531	$ .01	$ .04
Agosto, Juan	91DL	404	$ .01	$ .08
Agosto, Juan	92D	37	$ .01	$ .04
Aguayo, Luis	82D	622	$ .01	$ .06
Aguayo, Luis	83D	546	$ .01	$ .06
Aguayo, Luis	85D	503	$ .01	$ .10
Aguayo, Luis	86D	503	$ .01	$ .08
Aguayo, Luis	88D	185	$ .01	$ .04
Aguayo, Luis	89D	551	$ .01	$ .04
Aguilera, Rick	86D	441	$ .15	$1.50
Aguilera, Rick	87D	620	$ .01	$ .15
Aguilera, Rick	88D	446	$ .01	$ .04
Aguilera, Rick	89D	526	$ .01	$ .04
Aguilera, Rick	90D	391	$ .01	$ .04
Aguilera, Rick	90DL	38	$ .05	$ .25
Aguilera, Rick	91D	172	$ .01	$ .04
Aguilera, Rick	91DL	471	$ .01	$ .08
Aguilera, Rick	91DLS	81	$ .01	$ .08
Aguilera, Rick	92D	95	$ .01	$ .04
Aguilera, Rick	92DL	34	$ .01	$ .06
Aguilera, Rick	92DLS	201	$ .01	$ .06
Aguilera, Rick	93D	19	$ .01	$ .05
Aguilera, Rick	93DL	32	$ .01	$ .15
Aikens, Willie	81D	220	$ .01	$ .06
Aikens, Willie	82D	412	$ .01	$ .06
Aikens, Willie	83D	212	$ .01	$ .06
Aikens, Willie	84D	155	$ .05	$ .20
Ainge, Danny	81D	569	$ .20	$2.00
Ainge, Danny	82D	638	$ .10	$1.00
Akerfelds, Darrel	90DL	526	$ .05	$ .25
Akerfelds, Darrel	91D	110	$ .01	$ .04
Aldred, Scott	91DRR	422	$ .01	$ .15
Aldred, Scott	92D	486	$ .01	$ .04
Aldred, Scott	93D	733	$ .01	$ .05
Aldrete, Mike	87D	450	$ .01	$ .05
Aldrete, Mike	88D	362	$ .01	$ .04
Aldrete, Mike	89D	140	$ .01	$ .04
Aldrete, Mike	89DTR	25	$ .01	$ .05
Aldrete, Mike	92D	621	$ .01	$ .04
Aldrich, Jay	88D	460	$ .01	$ .04
Alexander, Doyle	81D	448	$ .01	$ .15
Alexander, Doyle	82D	96	$ .01	$ .06
Alexander, Doyle	83D	451	$ .01	$ .06
Alexander, Doyle	84D	439	$ .05	$ .20
Alexander, Doyle	85D	561	$ .01	$ .10
Alexander, Doyle	86D	390	$ .01	$ .08
Alexander, Doyle	87D	657	$ .01	$ .05
Alexander, Doyle	88D	584	$ .01	$ .04
Alexander, Doyle	89D	178	$ .01	$ .04
Alexander, Doyle	90D	62	$ .01	$ .04
Alexander, Gary	81D	200	$ .01	$ .06
Alexander, Gerald	91DRR	419	$ .01	$ .10
Alexander, Gerald	92D	578	$ .01	$ .04
Alexander, Manny	93D	11	$ .01	$ .15
Alicea, Luis	88DR	52	$ .01	$ .15
Alicea, Luis	89D	466	$ .01	$ .10
Alicea, Luis	92D	560	$ .01	$ .04
Alicea, Luis	93D	416	$ .01	$ .05
Allanson, Andy	86DR	43	$ .01	$ .10
Allanson, Andy	87D	95	$ .01	$ .05
Allanson, Andy	88D	465	$ .01	$ .04
Allanson, Andy	89D	138	$ .01	$ .04
Allanson, Andy	91DL	455	$ .01	$ .08
Allanson, Andy	92D	42	$ .01	$ .04
Allanson, Andy	92DL	510	$ .01	$ .06
Allen, Jamie	84D	267	$ .05	$ .20
Allen, Neil	81D	276	$ .01	$ .06
Allen, Neil	82D	506	$ .01	$ .06
Allen, Neil	83D	98	$ .01	$ .06
Allen, Neil	84D	109	$ .05	$ .20

DONRUSS

Player	Year	No.	VG	EX/MT	Player	Year	No.	VG	EX/MT
Allen, Neil	85D	205	$ .01	$ .10	Andersen, Larry	87D	640	$ .01	$ .05
Allen, Neil	86D	610	$ .01	$ .08	Andersen, Larry	89D	359	$ .01	$ .04
Allen, Neil	87D	507	$ .01	$ .05	Andersen, Larry	90D	359	$ .01	$ .04
Allen, Neil	88D	597	$ .01	$ .04	Andersen, Larry	90DL	386	$ .05	$ .25
Allen, Neil	89D	196	$ .01	$ .04	Andersen, Larry	91D	665	$ .01	$ .04
Allenson, Gary	81D	455	$ .01	$ .06	Andersen, Larry	91DL	407	$ .01	$ .08
Allenson, Gary	82D	386	$ .01	$ .06	Andersen, Larry	91DLS	241	$ .01	$ .08
Allenson, Gary	83D	30	$ .01	$ .06	Andersen, Larry	92D	687	$ .01	$ .04
Allenson, Gary	84D	335	$ .05	$ .20	Anderson, Allan	86DR	3	$ .05	$ .20
Allred, Beau	90D	691	$ .01	$ .15	Anderson, Allan	87D	368	$ .01	$ .15
Allred, Beau	91DL	316	$ .01	$ .15	Anderson, Allan	89D	419	$ .01	$ .10
Almon, Bill	82D	637	$ .01	$ .06	Anderson, Allan	90D	64	$ .01	$ .04
Almon, Bill	83D	356	$ .01	$ .06	Anderson, Allan	90DL	5	$ .05	$ .25
Almon, Bill	84D	467	$ .05	$ .20	Anderson, Allan	91D	527	$ .01	$ .04
Almon, Bill	85D	589	$ .01	$ .10	Anderson, Allan	91DL	259	$ .01	$ .08
Almon, Bill	86D	479	$ .01	$ .08	Anderson, Brady	88DR	14	$ .15	$1.50
Almon, Bill	87D	326	$ .01	$ .05	Anderson, Brady	89D	519	$ .10	$ .50
Almon, Bill	88D	487	$ .01	$ .04	Anderson, Brady	90D	638	$ .05	$ .25
Alomar, Roberto	88DR	35	$3.00	$12.00	Anderson, Brady	91D	668	$ .10	$ .50
Alomar, Roberto	88DRR	34	$1.00	$4.00	Anderson, Brady	92DL	343	$ .01	$ .06
Alomar, Roberto	89D	246	$ .10	$ .75	Anderson, Brady	92DLS	121	$ .01	$ .06
Alomar, Roberto	90D	111	$ .05	$ .35	Anderson, Brady	93D	89	$ .01	$ .05
Alomar, Roberto	90DL	75	$1.50	$6.00	Anderson, Brady	93DK	23	$ .15	$1.50
Alomar, Roberto	91D	682	$ .05	$ .20	Anderson, Brady	93DL	177	$ .05	$ .25
Alomar, Roberto	91DK	12	$ .01	$ .10	Anderson, Bud	84D	590	$ .05	$ .20
Alomar, Roberto	91DL	267	$ .10	$1.00	Anderson, Dave	84D	642	$ .05	$ .25
Alomar, Roberto	91DLS	131	$ .10	$1.00	Anderson, Dave	85D	275	$ .01	$ .10
Alomar, Roberto	92D	58	$ .01	$ .15	Anderson, Dave	88D	475	$ .01	$ .04
Alomar, Roberto	92DAS	28	$ .01	$ .05	Anderson, Dave	89D	434	$ .01	$ .04
Alomar, Roberto	92DL	233	$ .10	$ .50	Anderson, Dave	90D	486	$ .01	$ .04
Alomar, Roberto	92DLS	251	$ .10	$ .50	Anderson, Dave	91DLS	251	$ .01	$ .08
Alomar, Roberto	93D	425	$ .05	$ .20	Anderson, Dave	92D	759	$ .01	$ .04
Alomar, Roberto	93DK	20	$1.25	$5.00	Anderson, Jim	81D	165	$ .01	$ .06
AlomarJr., Sandy	89DR	21	$ .05	$ .35	Anderson, Jim	82D	181	$ .01	$ .06
AlomarJr., Sandy	89DRR	28	$ .05	$ .35	Anderson, Kent	90D	490	$ .01	$ .04
Alomar, Sandy	90DL	232	$ .10	$ .50	Anderson, Kent	91D	525	$ .01	$ .04
Alomar, Sandy	90DR	1	$ .01	$ .05	Andersen (son), Larry	82D	428	$ .01	$ .06
AlomarJr., Sandy	90DRR	30	$ .01	$ .10	Anderson, Larry	88D	332	$ .01	$ .04
Alomar, Sandy	91D	489	$ .01	$ .10	Anderson, Sparky	81D	370	$ .01	$ .06
Alomar, Sandy	91D	693	$ .01	$ .10	Anderson, Sparky	82D	29	$ .05	$ .20
Alomar, Sandy	91DAS	51	$ .01	$ .15	Anderson, Sparky	83D	533	$ .05	$ .20
Alomar, Sandy	91DK	13	$ .01	$ .10	Anderson, Sparky	91DLS	261	$ .01	$ .10
Alomar, Sandy	91DL	189	$ .01	$ .15	Andujar, Joaquin	81D	381	$ .01	$ .06
AlomarJr., Sandy	91DL	528	$ .01	$ .10	Andujar, Joaquin	82D	607	$ .01	$ .06
Alomar, Sandy	91DLP	17	$ .20	$2.00	Andujar, Joaquin	83D	316	$ .01	$ .06
Alomar, Sandy	91DLS	41	$ .01	$ .08	Andujar, Joaquin	84D	181	$ .05	$ .20
Alomar, Sandy	92D	203	$ .01	$ .10	Andujar, Joaquin	85D	449	$ .01	$ .10
Alomar, Sandy	92DAS	29	$ .01	$ .05	Andujar, Joaquin	85DK	13	$ .03	$ .10
Alomar, Sandy	92DL	9	$ .01	$ .06	Andujar, Joaquin	86D	231	$ .01	$ .08
Alomar, Jr., Sandy	92DLS	161	$ .01	$ .06	Andujar, Joaquin	87D	548	$ .01	$ .05
Alomar, Jr., Sandy	93D	39	$ .01	$ .05	Anthony, Eric	90DL	82	$ .75	$3.00
Alomar, Jr., Sandy	93DL	83	$ .05	$ .20	Anthony, Eric	90DR	49	$ .05	$ .35
Alou, Felipe	82D	650	$ .01	$ .06	Anthony, Eric	90DRR	34	$ .05	$ .25
Alou, Moises	91DLS	191	$ .10	$ .40	Anthony, Eric	91D	333	$ .01	$ .10
Alou, Moises	91DRR	38	$ .05	$ .20	Anthony, Eric	91DL	181	$ .01	$ .08
Alou, Moises	92DL	426	$ .05	$ .20	Anthony, Eric	91DLS	171	$ .01	$ .08
Alou, Moises	93D	510	$ .01	$ .05	Anthony, Eric	93D	8	$ .01	$ .05
Alou, Moises	93DL	147	$ .05	$ .35	Anthony, Eric	93DL	218	$ .05	$ .25
Alston, Dell	81D	322	$ .01	$ .06	Aponte, Luis	83D	109	$ .01	$ .06
Altobelli, Joe	84D	88	$ .05	$ .20	Aponte, Luis	84D	371	$ .05	$ .20
Alvarez, Jose	89D	405	$ .01	$ .10	Appier, Kevin	90DR	21	$ .05	$ .20
Alvarez, Jose	90D	389	$ .01	$ .04	Appier, Kevin	91D	740	$ .01	$ .10
Alvarez, Wilson	92D	495	$ .01	$ .04	Appier, Kevin	92D	455	$ .01	$ .04
Alvarez, Wilson	92D	630	$ .01	$ .10	Appier, Kevin	92DL	31	$ .01	$ .06
Alvarez, Wilson	92DL	78	$ .01	$ .06	Appier, Kevin	93D	43	$ .01	$ .05
Alvarez, Wilson	93D	37	$ .01	$ .05	Appier, Kevin	93DL	101	$ .01	$ .15
Amalfitano, Joe	81D	522	$ .01	$ .06	Aquino, Luis	87D	655	$ .01	$ .05
Amaral, Rich	92DR	3	$ .01	$ .05	Aquino, Luis	89D	534	$ .01	$ .04
Amaro, Ruben	92D	733	$ .01	$ .10	Aquino, Luis	90D	179	$ .01	$ .04
Amaro, Ruben	92DL	339	$ .01	$ .06	Aquino, Luis	91D	718	$ .01	$ .04
Amaro, Ruben	92DR	4	$ .01	$ .05	Aquino, Luis	92D	544	$ .01	$ .04
Amaro, Ruben	93D	488	$ .01	$ .05	Arias, Alex	93D	4	$ .01	$ .15
Andersen, Larry	83D	181	$ .01	$ .06	Arias, Alex	93D	780	$ .01	$ .10
Andersen, Larry	85D	570	$ .01	$ .10	Armas, Tony	81D	239	$ .01	$ .06
Andersen, Larry	86D	355	$ .01	$ .08	Armas, Tony	82D	365	$ .01	$ .06

73

DONRUSS

Player	Year	No.	VG	EX/MT	Player	Year	No.	VG	EX/MT
Armas, Tony	83D	71	$ .01	$ .06	Assenmacher, Paul	86DR	28	$ .01	$ .15
Armas, Tony	84D	294	$ .05	$ .20	Assenmacher, Paul	87D	290	$ .01	$ .15
Armas, Tony	85D	249	$ .01	$ .10	Assenmacher, Paul	89D	357	$ .01	$ .04
Armas, Tony	86D	127	$ .01	$ .08	Assenmacher, Paul	90D	459	$ .01	$ .04
Armas, Tony	86DK	5	$ .01	$ .10	Assenmacher, Paul	90DL	493	$ .05	$ .25
Armas, Tony	87D	498	$ .01	$ .05	Assenmacher, Paul	91D	144	$ .01	$ .04
Armas, Tony	89D	580	$ .01	$ .04	Assenmacher, Paul	91DL	53	$ .01	$ .08
Armas, Tony	90D	525	$ .01	$ .04	Assenmacher, Paul	92D	159	$ .01	$ .04
Armstrong, Jack	89D	493	$ .01	$ .10	Assenmacher, Paul	92DL	117	$ .01	$ .06
Armstrong, Jack	90D	544	$ .01	$ .10	Assenmacher, Paul	93D	54	$ .01	$ .05
Armstrong, Jack	90DL	374	$ .05	$ .25	Astacio, Pedro	92DR	6	$ .05	$ .35
Armstrong, Jack	91D	571	$ .01	$ .04	Astacio, Pedro	93D	407	$ .05	$ .20
Armstrong, Jack	91DAS	439	$ .01	$ .03	Astacio, Pedro	93DL	71	$ .10	$ .50
Armstrong, Jack	91DL	459	$ .01	$ .08	Atherton, Keith	84D	497	$ .05	$ .20
Armstrong, Jack	92D	762	$ .01	$ .04	Atherton, Keith	85D	340	$ .05	$ .10
Armstrong, Jack	92DL	247	$ .01	$ .06	Atherton, Keith	87D	272	$ .01	$ .05
					Atherton, Keith	88D	318	$ .01	$ .04
					Atherton, Keith	89D	273	$ .01	$ .04
					August, Don	88D	602	$ .01	$ .15
					August, Don	89D	410	$ .01	$ .04
					August, Don	90D	617	$ .01	$ .04
					August, Don	92D	140	$ .01	$ .04
					Augustine, Jerry	81D	445	$ .01	$ .06
					Augustine, Jerry	82D	332	$ .01	$ .06
					Ausmus, Brad	93D	773	$ .01	$ .10
					Austin, Jim	92DR	7	$ .01	$ .10
					Austin, Jim	93D	659	$ .01	$ .05
					Austin, Jim	93DL	12	$ .01	$ .15
					Avery, Steve	90DL	481	$2.50	$10.00
					Avery, Steve	90DR	42	$ .10	$ .75
					Avery, Steve	90DRR	39	$ .10	$ .50
					Avery, Steve	91D	187	$ .05	$ .25
					Avery, Steve	91DL	510	$ .10	$ .75
					Avery, Steve	91DLS	141	$ .10	$1.00
					Avery, Steve	92D	81	$ .01	$ .15
					Avery, Steve	92DL	59	$ .05	$ .35
					Avery, Steve	92DLS	1	$ .05	$ .35
					Avery, Steve	93D	26	$ .01	$ .10
					Avery, Steve	93DL	121	$ .05	$ .25
					Ayala, Benny	81D	236	$ .01	$ .06
					Ayala, Benny	82D	581	$ .01	$ .06
					Ayala, Benny	83D	331	$ .01	$ .06
					Ayala, Benny	84D	270	$ .05	$ .20
					Ayala, Bobby	93D	30	$ .05	$ .20
					Ayrault, Robert	92DR	8	$ .01	$ .15
					Ayrault, Bob	93D	16	$ .01	$ .10
					Azocar, Oscar	91D	331	$ .01	$ .04
					Babcock, Bob	82D	565	$ .01	$ .06

Player	Year	No.	VG	EX/MT	Player	Year	No.	VG	EX/MT
Armstrong, Jack	92DLS	162	$ .01	$ .06	Babitt, Shooty	82D	556	$ .01	$ .06
Armstrong, Jack	93D	69	$ .01	$ .05	Backman, Wally	83D	618	$ .05	$ .20
Armstrong, Jack	93D	777	$ .01	$ .05	Backman, Wally	85D	319	$ .01	$ .10
Armstrong, Mike	84D	217	$ .05	$ .20	Backman, Wally	86D	238	$ .01	$ .08
Armstrong, Mike	85D	602	$ .01	$ .10	Backman, Wally	87D	316	$ .01	$ .05
Arnsberg, Brad	90DL	495	$ .05	$ .25	Backman, Wally	88D	241	$ .01	$ .04
Arnsberg, Brad	91D	633	$ .01	$ .04	Backman, Wally	89D	383	$ .01	$ .04
Arocha, Rene	93D	572	$ .05	$ .35	Backman, Wally	89DTR	10	$ .01	$ .05
Arroyo, Fernando	82D	177	$ .01	$ .06	Backman, Wally	90D	155	$ .01	$ .04
Asadoor, Randy	87D	574	$ .01	$ .05	Backman, Wally	90DL	341	$ .05	$ .25
Ashby, Alan	81D	259	$ .01	$ .06	Backman, Wally	91D	177	$ .01	$ .04
Ashby, Alan	82D	317	$ .01	$ .06	Backman, Wally	91DL	482	$ .01	$ .08
Ashby, Alan	83D	144	$ .01	$ .06	Backman, Wally	92D	478	$ .01	$ .04
Ashby, Alan	84D	539	$ .05	$ .20	Baerga, Carlos	90DL	443	$3.00	$12.00
Ashby, Alan	85D	283	$ .01	$ .10	Baerga, Carlos	90DR	19	$ .15	$1.50
Ashby, Alan	86D	405	$ .01	$ .08	Baerga, Carlos	91D	274	$ .05	$ .25
Ashby, Alan	87D	332	$ .01	$ .05	Baerga, Carlos	91DL	225	$ .10	$1.00
Ashby, Alan	88D	163	$ .01	$ .04	Baerga, Carlos	92D	120	$ .05	$ .20
Ashby, Alan	89D	88	$ .01	$ .04	Baerga, Carlos	92DL	202	$ .10	$ .50
Ashby, Andy	92DL	405	$ .01	$ .15	Baerga, Carlos	92DLS	163	$ .10	$ .50
Ashby, Andy	92DRR	11	$ .01	$ .05	Baerga, Carlos	93D	405	$ .01	$ .15
Ashby, Andy	93D	743	$ .01	$ .05	Baerga, Carlos	93DK	13	$ .75	$3.00
Ashley, Billy	92DR	5	$ .10	$ .50	Baez, Kevin	92DR	9	$ .01	$ .10
Ashley, Billy	93D	56	$ .05	$ .25	Baez, Kevin	93D	361	$ .01	$ .10
Ashley, Billy	93DL	100	$ .10	$ .50	Bagwell, Jeff	91DLBC	14	$2.50	$10.00
Asselstine, Brian	81D	186	$ .01	$ .06	Bagwell, Jeff	91DLS	172	$ .75	$3.00
Asselstine, Brian	82D	184	$ .01	$ .06	Bagwell, Jeff	91DR	30	$ .10	$1.00

DONRUSS

Player	Year	No.	VG	EX/MT	Player	Year	No.	VG	EX/MT
Bagwell, Jeff	92D	358	$.05	$.25	Bando, Chris	83D	33	$.01	$.06
Bagwell, Jeff	92DBC	6	$.10	$.50	Bando, Chris	84D	224	$.05	$.20
Bagwell, Jeff	92DK	11	$.75	$3.00	Bando, Chris	85D	520	$.01	$.10
Bagwell, Jeff	92DL	28	$.10	$.50	Bando, Chris	86D	373	$.01	$.08
Bagwell, Jeff	92DLS	31	$.10	$.50	Bando, Chris	87D	501	$.01	$.05
Bagwell, Jeff	93D	428	$.01	$.15	Bando, Chris	88D	95	$.01	$.04
Bagwell, Jeff	93DL	125	$.10	$.50	Bando, Sal	81D	84	$.01	$.15
Bahnsen, Stan	81D	452	$.01	$.06	Bando, Sal	82D	592	$.01	$.06
Bahnsen, Stan	82D	392	$.01	$.06	Bankhead, Scott	86DR	36	$.01	$.15
Bailes, Scott	86DR	25	$.05	$.25	Bankhead, Scott	88D	70	$.01	$.04
Bailes, Scott	87D	227	$.01	$.05	Bankhead, Scott	89D	463	$.01	$.04
Bailes, Scott	88D	104	$.01	$.04	Bankhead, Scott	90D	261	$.01	$.04
Bailes, Scott	89D	202	$.01	$.04	Bankhead, Scott	90DL	127	$.05	$.25
Bailes, Scott	90D	468	$.01	$.04	Bankhead, Scott	91D	189	$.01	$.04
Bailes, Scott	90DL	380	$.05	$.25	Bankhead, Scott	91DL	345	$.01	$.08
Bailes, Scott	92D	357	$.01	$.04	Bankhead, Scott	92D	304	$.01	$.04
Bailey, Howard	84D	212	$.05	$.20	Bankhead, Scott	92DL	485	$.01	$.06
Bailey, Mark	85D	450	$.01	$.10	Bankhead, Scott	93D	690	$.01	$.05
Bailey, Mark	86D	354	$.01	$.08	Banks, Willie	91DLBC	5	$.20	$2.00
Bailey, Mark	87D	235	$.01	$.05	Banks, Willie	92D	760	$.01	$.10
Bailor, Bob	81D	389	$.01	$.06	Banks, Willie	93D	79	$.01	$.05
Bailor, Bob	82D	308	$.01	$.06	Bannister, Alan	82D	159	$.01	$.06
Bailor, Bob	83D	506	$.01	$.06	Bannister, Alan	83D	285	$.01	$.06
Bailor, Bob	84D	595	$.05	$.20	Bannister, Alan	84D	154	$.05	$.20
Bailor, Bob	85D	397	$.01	$.10	Bannister, Alan	86D	525	$.01	$.08
Baines, Harold	82D	568	$.10	$1.00	Bannister, Floyd	81D	286	$.01	$.06
Baines, Harold	83D	143	$.10	$.50	Bannister, Floyd	82D	100	$.01	$.06
Baines, Harold	84D	58	$.10	$.75	Bannister, Floyd	83D	50	$.01	$.06
Baines, Harold	85D	58	$.05	$.35	Bannister, Floyd	83DK	21	$.01	$.10
Baines, Harold	86D	180	$.01	$.15	Bannister, Floyd	84D	366	$.05	$.20
Baines, Harold	86DK	13	$.01	$.10	Bannister, Floyd	85D	379	$.01	$.10
Baines, Harold	87D	429	$.05	$.20	Bannister, Floyd	86D	244	$.01	$.08
Baines, Harold	88D	211	$.01	$.04	Bannister, Floyd	87D	211	$.01	$.05
Baines, Harold	89D	148	$.01	$.04	Bannister, Floyd	88D	383	$.01	$.04
Baines, Harold	90D	402	$.01	$.10	Bannister, Floyd	89D	262	$.01	$.04
Baines, Harold	90DAS	660	$.05	$.25	Bannister, Floyd	91DL	439	$.01	$.08
Baines, Harold	90DL	126	$.05	$.25	Barberie, Bret	92D	449	$.01	$.10
Baines, Harold	91D	748	$.01	$.04	Barberie, Bret	92DL	288	$.01	$.06
Baines, Harold	91DL	196	$.01	$.08	Barberie, Bret	92DLS	51	$.01	$.06
Baines, Harold	91DLSP	8	$.20	$2.00	Barberie, Bret	93D	12	$.01	$.05
Baines, Harold	92D	68	$.01	$.04	Barberie, Bret	93D	759	$.01	$.05
Baines, Harold	92DK	14	$.10	$1.00	Barfield, Jesse	83D	595	$.05	$.25
Baines, Harold	92DL	126	$.01	$.06	Barfield, Jesse	84D	193	$.10	$.40
Baines, Harold	92DLS	221	$.01	$.06	Barfield, Jesse	85D	195	$.05	$.25
Baines, Harold	93D	725	$.01	$.05	Barfield, Jesse	86D	193	$.05	$.20
Bair, Doug	81D	64	$.01	$.06	Barfield, Jesse	87D	121	$.01	$.15
Bair, Doug	83D	372	$.01	$.06	Barfield, Jesse	88D	442	$.01	$.15
Bair, Doug	84D	369	$.05	$.20	Barfield, Jesse	89D	425	$.01	$.04
Bair, Doug	85D	369	$.01	$.10	Barfield, Jesse	90D	74	$.01	$.04
Baker, Dusty	81D	179	$.01	$.10	Barfield, Jesse	90DL	201	$.05	$.25
Baker, Dusty	82D	336	$.01	$.06	Barfield, Jesse	91D	498	$.01	$.04
Baker, Dusty	83D	462	$.01	$.06	Barfield, Jesse	91DL	308	$.01	$.08
Baker, Dusty	84D	226	$.05	$.20	Barfield, Jesse	91DLS	91	$.01	$.08
Baker, Dusty	85D	445	$.01	$.10	Barfield, Jesse	92D	316	$.01	$.04
Baker, Dusty	86D	467	$.01	$.08	Barfield, John	91D	688	$.01	$.10
Balboni, Steve	83D	73	$.01	$.06	Barfield, John	92D	168	$.01	$.04
Balboni, Steve	85D	419	$.01	$.10	Barker, Len	81D	320	$.01	$.06
Balboni, Steve	86D	222	$.01	$.08	Barker, Len	82D	137	$.01	$.00
Balboni, Steve	87D	102	$.01	$.05	Barker, Len	82DK	6	$.01	$.15
Balboni, Steve	88D	424	$.01	$.04	Barker, Len	83D	111	$.01	$.06
Balboni, Steve	89D	143	$.01	$.04	Barker, Len	84D	443	$.05	$.20
Balboni, Steve	89DTR	48	$.01	$.05	Barker, Len	85D	165	$.01	$.10
Balboni, Steve	90D	315	$.01	$.04	Barker, Len	86D	409	$.01	$.08
Balboni, Steve	90DL	373	$.05	$.25	Barnes, Brian	91DLS	192	$.05	$.20
Balboni, Steve	91D	650	$.01	$.04	Barnes, Brian	91DRR	415	$.01	$.15
Ballard, Jeff	88D	520	$.01	$.15	Barnes, Brian	92D	117	$.01	$.04
Ballard, Jeff	89D	495	$.01	$.04	Barnes, Brian	93D	88	$.01	$.05
Ballard, Jeff	90D	51	$.01	$.04	Barnes, Richard	84D	608	$.05	$.20
Ballard, Jeff	90DL	118	$.05	$.25	Barnes, Skeeter	85D	530	$.01	$.15
Ballard, Jeff	91D	279	$.01	$.04	Barnes, Skeeter	92D	749	$.01	$.04
Ballard, Jeff	91DL	522	$.01	$.08	Barnes, Skeeter	93D	437	$.01	$.05
Ballard, Jeff	92D	74	$.01	$.04	Barojas, Salome	83D	67	$.01	$.06
Baller, Jay	86D	613	$.01	$.08	Barojas, Salome	84D	570	$.05	$.20
Baller, Jay	93D	356	$.01	$.05	Barojas, Salome	85D	605	$.01	$.10
Bando, Chris	82D	551	$.01	$.06	Barr, Jim	81D	412	$.01	$.06

DONRUSS

Player	Year	No.	VG	EX/MT
Barr, Jim	83D	398	$ .01	$ .06
Barr, Jim	84D	79	$ .05	$ .20
Barrett, Marty	85D	127	$ .05	$ .25
Barrett, Marty	86D	294	$ .01	$ .08
Barrett, Marty	87D	523	$ .01	$ .05
Barrett, Marty	88D	276	$ .01	$ .04
Barrett, Marty	89D	184	$ .01	$ .04
Barrett, Marty	90D	240	$ .01	$ .04
Barrett, Marty	91DL	474	$ .01	$ .08
Barton, Shawn	93D	53	$ .01	$ .15
Bass, Kevin	84D	450	$ .05	$ .20
Bass, Kevin	85D	136	$ .01	$ .10
Bass, Kevin	86D	548	$ .01	$ .08
Bass, Kevin	87D	410	$ .01	$ .05
Bass, Kevin	88D	286	$ .01	$ .04
Bass, Kevin	89D	325	$ .01	$ .04
Bass, Kevin	90D	589	$ .01	$ .04
Bass, Kevin	90DL	305	$ .05	$ .25
Bass, Kevin	91D	630	$ .01	$ .04
Bass, Kevin	91DL	365	$ .01	$ .08
Bass, Kevin	92D	373	$ .01	$ .04
Bass, Kevin	92DL	76	$ .01	$ .06
Bass, Kevin	92DLS	111	$ .01	$ .06
Bass, Kevin	93D	745	$ .01	$ .05
Bass, Randy	82D	439	$ .01	$ .06
Bathe, Bill	86DR	41	$ .01	$ .10
Bathe, Bill	87D	281	$ .01	$ .05
Bathe, Bill	90D	680	$ .01	$ .04
Batiste, Kim	92DL	421	$ .01	$ .06
Batiste, Kim	92DLS	71	$ .01	$ .06
Batiste, Kim	92DRR	402	$ .01	$ .05
Batiste, Kim	93D	148	$ .01	$ .05
Baumgarten, Ross	81D	41	$ .01	$ .06
Baumgarten, Ross	82D	104	$ .01	$ .06
Bautista, Jose	88DR	41	$ .01	$ .07
Bautista, Jose	89D	451	$ .01	$ .10
Baylor, Don	81D	413	$ .05	$ .20
Baylor, Don	82D	493	$ .05	$ .20
Baylor, Don	83D	493	$ .01	$ .15
Baylor, Don	84D	152	$ .05	$ .20
Baylor, Don	85D	173	$ .05	$ .20
Baylor, Don	86D	347	$ .01	$ .08
Baylor, Don	87D	339	$ .01	$ .05
Beane, Billy	86D	647	$ .01	$ .08
Beard, Dave	83D	113	$ .01	$ .06
Beard, Dave	84D	218	$ .05	$ .20
Beattie, Jim	81D	166	$ .01	$ .06
Beattie, Jim	82D	478	$ .01	$ .06
Beattie, Jim	83D	176	$ .01	$ .06
Beattie, Jim	84D	191	$ .05	$ .20
Beattie, Jim	85D	313	$ .01	$ .10
Beattie, Jim	86D	196	$ .01	$ .08
Beck, Rod	92D	461	$ .01	$ .10
Beck, Rod	93D	420	$ .01	$ .05
Beckwith, Joe	84D	337	$ .05	$ .20
Beckwith, Joe	85D	541	$ .01	$ .10
Bedrosian, Steve	82D	401	$ .10	$ .50
Bedrosian, Steve	83D	173	$ .01	$ .15
Bedrosian, Steve	84D	565	$ .05	$ .30
Bedrosian, Steve	85D	628	$ .01	$ .15
Bedrosian, Steve	86D	199	$ .01	$ .15
Bedrosian, Steve	87D	185	$ .01	$ .15
Bedrosian, Steve	88D	62	$ .01	$ .04
Bedrosian, Steve	89D	75	$ .01	$ .10
Bedrosian, Steve	89DK	24	$ .01	$ .10
Bedrosian, Steve	90D	295	$ .01	$ .04
Bedrosian, Steve	90DL	3	$ .05	$ .25
Bedrosian, Steve	91D	207	$ .01	$ .04
Bedrosian, Steve	91DL	505	$ .01	$ .08
Bedrosian, Steve	91DLS	82	$ .01	$ .08
Bedrosian, Steve	92D	184	$ .01	$ .04
Behenna, Rick	84D	346	$ .05	$ .25
Belanger, Mark	81D	472	$ .01	$ .15
Belanger, Mark	83D	514	$ .01	$ .06
Belcher, Kevin	91DLS	121	$ .01	$ .15
Belcher, Kevin	91DRR	46	$ .01	$ .15
Belcher, Tim	88D	587	$ .05	$ .25
Belcher, Tim	88DR	28	$ .05	$ .20
Belcher, Tim	89D	203	$ .01	$ .04
Belcher, Tim	90D	79	$ .01	$ .04
Belcher, Tim	90DL	200	$ .05	$ .25
Belcher, Tim	91D	70	$ .01	$ .04
Belcher, Tim	91DL	508	$ .01	$ .08
Belcher, Tim	92D	78	$ .01	$ .04
Belcher, Tim	92DL	417	$ .01	$ .06
Belcher, Tim	93D	82	$ .01	$ .05
Belinda, Stan	90DL	486	$ .10	$ .40
Belinda, Stan	91D	699	$ .01	$ .10
Belinda, Stan	92D	501	$ .01	$ .04
Belinda, Stan	92DL	287	$ .01	$ .06
Belinda, Stan	93D	490	$ .01	$ .05
Bell, Bill	93D	18	$ .01	$ .05
Bell, Buddy	81D	145	$ .05	$ .20
Bell, Buddy	82D	368	$ .05	$ .20
Bell, Buddy	82DK	23	$ .05	$ .20
Bell, Buddy	83D	215	$ .05	$ .20
Bell, Buddy	84D	56	$ .05	$ .25
Bell, Buddy	85D	56	$ .05	$ .20
Bell, Buddy	86D	447	$ .05	$ .20
Bell, Buddy	87D	556	$ .01	$ .15
Bell, Buddy	88D	206	$ .01	$ .15
Bell, Derek	91DRR	32	$ .05	$ .25
Bell, Derek	92D	581	$ .01	$ .10
Bell, Derek	92DL	243	$ .05	$ .25
Bell, Derek	92DLS	252	$ .05	$ .20
Bell, Derek	93D	557	$ .01	$ .05
Bell, Derek	93DL	179	$ .05	$ .30
Bell, Eric	87DR	2	$ .01	$ .07
Bell, Eric	87DRR	39	$ .01	$ .05
Bell, Eric	88D	125	$ .01	$ .04
Bell, Eric	92DL	379	$ .01	$ .06
Bell, George (Jorge)	82D	54	$1.50	$6.00
Bell, George	84D	73	$ .75	$3.00
Bell, George	85D	146	$ .10	$ .75
Bell, George	86D	71	$ .10	$ .40
Bell, George	86DK	4	$ .05	$ .25
Bell, George	87D	271	$ .05	$ .25

KEVIN BASS RF

DONRUSS

Player	Year	No.	VG	EX/MT	Player	Year	No.	VG	EX/MT
Bell, George	88D	656	$ .05	$ .20	Benes, Andy	93D	22	$ .01	$ .05
Bell, George	88DBC	19	$ .01	$ .10	Benes, Andy	93DL	192	$ .01	$ .15
Bell, George	89D	149	$ .01	$ .10	Beniquez, Juan	81D	518	$ .01	$ .06
Bell, George	90D	206	$ .01	$ .10	Beniquez, Juan	82D	587	$ .01	$ .06
Bell, George	90DBC	13	$ .01	$ .10	Beniquez, Juan	83D	640	$ .01	$ .06
Bell, George	90DL	185	$ .10	$ .50	Beniquez, Juan	84D	207	$ .05	$ .20
Bell, George	91D	642	$ .01	$ .04	Beniquez, Juan	85D	573	$ .01	$ .10
Bell, George	91DL	389	$ .01	$ .15	Beniquez, Juan	86D	352	$ .01	$ .08
Bell, George	91DLS	151	$ .01	$ .08	Beniquez, Juan	87D	371	$ .01	$ .05
Bell, George	92D	127	$ .01	$ .04	Benjamin, Mike	91DLS	252	$ .01	$ .08
Bell, George	92DK	7	$ .10	$1.00	Benjamin, Mike	91DRR	432	$ .01	$ .03
Bell, George	92DL	462	$ .01	$ .06	Benjamin, Mike	93D	472	$ .01	$ .05
Bell, George	92DLS	151	$ .01	$ .06	Benzinger, Todd	87DR	30	$ .05	$ .20
Bell, George	93D	95	$ .01	$ .05	Benzinger, Todd	88D	297	$ .01	$ .15
Bell, George	93DL	217	$ .05	$ .25	Benzinger, Todd	89D	358	$ .01	$ .10
Bell, Jay	88D	637	$ .05	$ .35	Benzinger, Todd	89DTR	47	$ .01	$ .05
Bell, Jay	89D	350	$ .01	$ .10	Benzinger, Todd	90D	257	$ .01	$ .04
Bell, Jay	90D	488	$ .01	$ .04	Benzinger, Todd	90DL	15	$ .05	$ .25
Bell, Jay	90DL	248	$ .05	$ .25	Benzinger, Todd	91D	640	$ .01	$ .04
Bell, Jay	91D	289	$ .01	$ .04	Benzinger, Todd	92D	536	$ .01	$ .04
Bell, Jay	91DL	130	$ .01	$ .08	Benzinger, Todd	92DL	257	$ .01	$ .06
Bell, Jay	91DLS	221	$ .01	$ .08	Benzinger, Todd	93D	562	$ .01	$ .05
Bell, Jay	92D	100	$ .01	$ .04	Berenguer, Juan	82D	580	$ .01	$ .06
Bell, Jay	92DK	17	$ .10	$1.00	Berenguer, Juan	84D	125	$ .05	$ .20
Bell, Jay	92DL	143	$ .01	$ .06	Berenguer, Juan	85D	272	$ .01	$ .10
Bell, Jay	92DLS	81	$ .01	$ .06	Berenguer, Juan	87D	616	$ .01	$ .05
Bell, Jay	93DL	116	$ .01	$ .15	Berenguer, Juan	88D	395	$ .01	$ .04
Bell, Juan	91DL	262	$ .01	$ .08	Berenguer, Juan	89D	81	$ .01	$ .04
Bell, Juan	91DLSP	1	$ .20	$2.00	Berenguer, Juan	90D	301	$ .01	$ .04
Bell, Juan	92D	479	$ .01	$ .04	Berenguer, Juan	90DL	169	$ .05	$ .25
Bell, Juan	93D	200	$ .01	$ .05	Berenguer, Juan	91D	340	$ .01	$ .04
Bell, Juan	93DL	205	$ .01	$ .15	Berenguer, Juan	91DL	526	$ .01	$ .08
Bell, Kevin	81D	39	$ .01	$ .06	Berenguer, Juan	92D	205	$ .01	$ .04
Belle, Joey "Albert"	90D	390	$ .10	$ .75	Berenyi, Bruce	83D	103	$ .01	$ .06
Belle, Joey "Albert"	90DL	180	$3.50	$14.00	Berenyi, Bruce	84D	487	$ .05	$ .20
Belle, Albert	91DL	239	$ .10	$ .75	Berenyi, Bruce	85D	625	$ .01	$ .10
Belle, Albert	92D	500	$ .01	$ .10	Bergman, Dave	81D	139	$ .01	$ .06
Belle, Albert	92DL	350	$ .05	$ .35	Bergman, Dave	82D	146	$ .01	$ .06
Belle, Albert	92DLS	164	$ .05	$ .35	Bergman, Dave	83D	550	$ .01	$ .06
Belle, Albert	93D	435	$ .01	$ .10	Bergman, Dave	84D	624	$ .05	$ .20
Belle, Albert	93DL	18	$ .10	$ .40	Bergman, Dave	85D	537	$ .01	$ .10
Belliard, Rafael	87D	538	$ .01	$ .15	Bergman, Dave	86D	471	$ .01	$ .08
Belliard, Rafael	90D	252	$ .01	$ .04	Bergman, Dave	87D	420	$ .01	$ .05
Belliard, Rafael	91DL	453	$ .01	$ .08	Bergman, Dave	88D	373	$ .01	$ .04
Belliard, Rafael	92D	107	$ .01	$ .04	Bergman, Dave	89D	389	$ .01	$ .04
Belliard, Rafael	92DL	310	$ .01	$ .06	Bergman, Dave	90D	445	$ .01	$ .04
Belliard, Rafael	93D	398	$ .01	$ .05	Bergman, Dave	90DL	244	$ .05	$ .25
Beltre, Esteban (Estaban)	92DR	10	$ .01	$ .10	Bergman, Dave	91D	342	$ .01	$ .04
Beltre, Este	93D	595	$ .01	$ .05	Bergman, Dave	91DL	92	$ .01	$ .08
Benavides, Freddie	92D	573	$ .01	$ .04	Bernard, Dwight	83D	28	$ .01	$ .06
Benavides, Freddie	93D	746	$ .01	$ .05	Bernazard, Tony	81D	449	$ .01	$ .06
Bench, Johnny	81D	62	$ .20	$2.00	Bernazard, Tony	82D	143	$ .01	$ .06
Bench, Johnny	81D	182	$ .20	$2.00	Bernazard, Tony	83D	482	$ .01	$ .06
Bench, Johnny	82D	400	$ .15	$1.50	Bernazard, Tony	84D	240	$ .05	$ .20
Bench, Johnny	82D	628	$ .10	$1.00	Bernazard, Tony	85D	102	$ .01	$ .10
Bench, Johnny	83D	15	$ .15	$1.25	Bernazard, Tony	86D	520	$ .01	$ .08
Bench, Johnny	83DK	22	$ .10	$ .50	Bernazard, Tony	87D	377	$ .01	$ .05
Bench, Johnny	84D#B	0	$2.50	$10.00	Bernazard, Tony	88D	344	$ .01	$ .04
Benedict, Bruce	81D	208	$ .01	$ .06	Berra, Dale	81D	253	$ .01	$ .06
Benedict, Bruce	82D	375	$ .01	$ .06	Berra, Dale	82D	250	$ .01	$ .06
Benedict, Bruce	83D	299	$ .01	$ .06	Berra, Dale	83D	185	$ .01	$ .06
Benedict, Bruce	84D	409	$ .05	$ .20	Berra, Dale	84D	430	$ .05	$ .20
Benedict, Bruce	85D	261	$ .01	$ .10	Berra, Dale	85D	444	$ .01	$ .10
Benedict, Bruce	85D	263	$ .01	$ .10	Berra, Dale	86D	295	$ .01	$ .08
Benedict, Bruce	86D	554	$ .01	$ .08	Berra, Yogi	81D	351	$ .05	$ .30
Benedict, Bruce	87D	448	$ .01	$ .05	Berra, Yogi	82D	387	$ .05	$ .35
Benedict, Bruce	89D	475	$ .01	$ .04	Berroa, Geronimo	88D	659	$ .05	$ .20
Benes, Andy	90DL	56	$ .75	$3.00	Berroa, Geronimo	89DR	19	$ .01	$ .05
Benes, Andy	90DRR	41	$ .05	$ .20	Berroa, Geronimo	90D	104	$ .01	$ .04
Benes, Andy	91D	627	$ .01	$ .10	Berroa, Geronimo	93D	214	$ .01	$ .05
Benes, Andy	91DL	275	$ .05	$ .20	Berry, Sean	92D	651	$ .01	$ .04
Benes, Andy	91DLS	242	$ .05	$ .25	Berry, Sean	93D	275	$ .01	$ .05
Benes, Andy	92D	524	$ .01	$ .04	Berryhill, Damon	88D	639	$ .05	$ .20
Benes, Andy	92DL	74	$ .01	$ .06	Berryhill, Damon	88DR	31	$ .05	$ .20
Benes, Andy	92DLS	101	$ .01	$ .06	Berryhill, Damon	89D	275	$ .01	$ .10

DONRUSS

Player	Year	No.	VG	EX/MT	Player	Year	No.	VG	EX/MT
Berryhill, Damon	90D	167	$ .01	$ .10	Black, Bud	91D	719	$ .01	$ .04
Berryhill, Damon	91D	631	$ .01	$ .04	Black, Bud	91DL	312	$ .01	$ .08
Berryhill, Damon	91DL	156	$ .01	$ .08	Black, Bud	91DLS	260	$ .01	$ .08
Berryhill, Damon	92D	771	$ .01	$ .04	Black, Bud	92D	93	$ .01	$ .04
Berryhill, Damon	92DL	423	$ .01	$ .06	Black, Bud	92DL	3	$ .01	$ .06
Berryhill, Damon	93D	78	$ .01	$ .05	Black, Bud	93D	50	$ .01	$ .05
Berryhill, Damon	93DL	196	$ .01	$ .15	Black, Bud	93DL	212	$ .01	$ .15
Best, Karl	86D	511	$ .01	$ .08	Blackwell, Tim	81D	559	$ .01	$ .06
Best, Karl	87D	198	$ .01	$ .05	Blackwell, Tim	82D	99	$ .01	$ .06
Bevacqua, Kurt	84D	80	$ .05	$ .20	Blackwell, Tim	83D	214	$ .01	$ .06
Bevacqua, Kurt	85D	647	$ .01	$ .10	Blair, Willie	90DL	449	$ .05	$ .25
Bevacqua, Kurt	86D	528	$ .01	$ .08	Blair, Willie	90DR	29	$ .01	$ .05
Biancalana, Buddy	86D	605	$ .01	$ .08	Blair, Willie	91D	267	$ .01	$ .04
Biancalana, Buddy	87D	527	$ .01	$ .05	Blair, Willie	93D	740	$ .01	$ .05
Bibby, Jim	81D	134	$ .01	$ .06	Blankenship, Kevin	89D	658	$ .01	$ .04
Bibby, Jim	82D	171	$ .01	$ .06	Blankenship, Lance	89D	621	$ .05	$ .10
Bichette, Dante	89D	634	$ .05	$ .25	Blankenship, Lance	91D	701	$ .01	$ .04
Bichette, Dante	89DR	29	$ .01	$ .05	Blankenship, Lance	92D	768	$ .01	$ .04
Bichette, Dante	90DL	340	$ .10	$ .50	Blankenship, Lance	92DL	410	$ .01	$ .06
Bichette, Dante	91D	303	$ .01	$ .04	Blankenship, Lance	93D	23	$ .01	$ .05
Bichette, Dante	91DL	242	$ .01	$ .08	Blauser, Jeff	88D	513	$ .05	$ .20
Bichette, Dante	92D	347	$ .01	$ .04	Blauser, Jeff	89D	592	$ .01	$ .04
Bichette, Dante	92DL	134	$ .01	$ .06	Blauser, Jeff	90D	271	$ .01	$ .04
Bichette, Dante	92DLS	191	$ .01	$ .06	Blauser, Jeff	90DL	191	$ .05	$ .25
Bichette, Dante	93D	45	$ .01	$ .05	Blauser, Jeff	91D	229	$ .01	$ .04
Bichette, Dante	93D	783	$ .01	$ .05	Blauser, Jeff	91DL	115	$ .01	$ .08
Bielecki, Mike	85DRR	28	$ .05	$ .25	Blauser, Jeff	92D	228	$ .01	$ .04
Bielecki, Mike	87D	415	$ .01	$ .05	Blauser, Jeff	92DL	147	$ .01	$ .06
Bielecki, Mike	88D	484	$ .01	$ .04	Blauser, Jeff	93D	134	$ .01	$ .05
Bielecki, Mike	89D	512	$ .01	$ .04	Blauser, Jeff	93DL	86	$ .05	$ .20
Bielecki, Mike	90D	373	$ .01	$ .04	Blowers, Mike	90D	656	$ .01	$ .10
Bielecki, Mike	90DK	9	$ .01	$ .05	Blowers, Mike	90DL	109	$ .05	$ .25
Bielecki, Mike	90DL	45	$ .05	$ .25	Blowers, Mike	90DR	26	$ .01	$ .05
Bielecki, Mike	91D	87	$ .01	$ .04	Blowers, Mike	91D	63	$ .01	$ .04
Bielecki, Mike	92D	776	$ .01	$ .04	Blue, Vida	81D	433	$ .01	$ .15
Bielecki, Mike	92DL	505	$ .01	$ .06	Blue, Vida	82D	222	$ .01	$ .06
Biggio, Craig	89D	561	$ .05	$ .25	Blue, Vida	82DK	4	$ .01	$ .15
Biggio, Craig	90D	306	$ .01	$ .10	Blue, Vida	83D	34	$ .01	$ .06
Biggio, Craig	90DL	37	$ .10	$ .75	Blue, Vida	83D	648	$ .05	$ .35
Biggio, Craig	91D	595	$ .01	$ .04	Blue, Vida	86D	509	$ .01	$ .08
Biggio, Craig	91DK	2	$ .01	$ .05	Blue, Vida	87D	362	$ .01	$ .05
Biggio, Craig	91DL	12	$ .05	$ .20	Blyleven, Bert	81D	135	$ .05	$ .30
Biggio, Craig	91DLP	4	$ .20	$2.00	Blyleven, Bert	82D	111	$ .05	$ .25
Biggio, Craig	91DLS	173	$ .01	$ .15	Blyleven, Bert	83D	589	$ .05	$ .25
Biggio, Craig	92D	75	$ .01	$ .04	Blyleven, Bert	84D	129	$ .10	$ .75
Biggio, Craig	92DL	315	$ .01	$ .06	Blyleven, Bert	85D	224	$ .05	$ .25
Biggio, Craig	92DLS	32	$ .01	$ .06	Blyleven, Bert	85DK	4	$ .01	$ .15
Biggio, Craig	93D	84	$ .01	$ .05	Blyleven, Bert	86D	649	$ .05	$ .20
Biggio, Craig	93DK	24	$ .15	$1.50	Blyleven, Bert	87D	71	$ .01	$ .10
Biittner, Larry	81D	515	$ .01	$ .06	Blyleven, Bert	88D	71	$ .01	$ .04
Biittner, Larry	82D	43	$ .01	$ .06	Blyleven, Bert	89D	119	$ .01	$ .04
Biittner, Larry	83D	440	$ .01	$ .06	Blyleven, Bert	89DTR	35	$ .01	$ .15
Biittner, Larry	84D	342	$ .05	$ .20	Blyleven, Bert	90D	331	$ .01	$ .04
Bilardello, Dann	84D	408	$ .05	$ .20	Blyleven, Bert	90DL	63	$ .05	$ .25
Bilardello, Dann	85D	243	$ .01	$ .10	Blyleven, Bert	91D	453	$ .01	$ .04
Bilardello, Dann	92DL	348	$ .01	$ .06	Blyleven, Bert	91DLS	23	$ .01	$ .08
Bilkey, Bernard	92DL	502	$ .01	$ .15	Bochte, Bruce	81D	403	$ .01	$ .06
Bird, Doug	82D	504	$ .01	$ .06	Bochte, Bruce	82D	505	$ .01	$ .06
Bird, Doug	83D	48	$ .01	$ .06	Bochte, Bruce	83D	127	$ .01	$ .06
Birkbeck, Mike	87DR	19	$ .05	$ .20	Bochte, Bruce	85D	253	$ .01	$ .10
Birkbeck, Mike	87DRR	33	$ .05	$ .25	Bochte, Bruce	86D	400	$ .01	$ .08
Birkbeck, Mike	88D	49	$ .01	$ .04	Bochy, Bruce	81D	20	$ .01	$ .06
Birkbeck, Mike	89D	501	$ .01	$ .04	Bochy, Bruce	85D	505	$ .01	$ .10
Birtsas, Tim	86D	462	$ .01	$ .08	Bochy, Bruce	86D	551	$ .01	$ .08
Birtsas, Tim	90D	493	$ .01	$ .10	Bochy, Bruce	87D	311	$ .01	$ .05
Bitker, Joe	91D	624	$ .01	$ .10	Boddicker, Mike	84D	123	$ .05	$ .25
Black, Bud	83D	322	$ .05	$ .35	Boddicker, Mike	85D	291	$ .01	$ .10
Black, Bud	84D	130	$ .05	$ .20	Boddicker, Mike	86D	47	$ .01	$ .08
Black, Bud	85D	100	$ .01	$ .10	Boddicker, Mike	86DK	8	$ .01	$ .10
Black, Bud	86D	374	$ .01	$ .08	Boddicker, Mike	87D	125	$ .01	$ .05
Black, Bud	87D	404	$ .01	$ .05	Boddicker, Mike	88D	89	$ .01	$ .04
Black, Bud	88D	301	$ .01	$ .04	Boddicker, Mike	89D	612	$ .01	$ .04
Black, Bud	89D	556	$ .01	$ .04	Boddicker, Mike	90D	280	$ .01	$ .04
Black, Bud	90D	556	$ .01	$ .04	Boddicker, Mike	90DL	19	$ .05	$ .25
Black, Bud	90DL	451	$ .05	$ .25	Boddicker, Mike	91D	680	$ .01	$ .04

DONRUSS

Player	Year	No.	VG	EX/MT	Player	Year	No.	VG	EX/MT
Boddicker, Mike	91DL	330	$ .01	$ .08	Bonilla, Bobby	90D	290	$ .01	$ .15
Boddicker, Mike	91DLS	61	$ .01	$ .08	Bonilla, Bobby	90DBC	16	$ .01	$ .10
Boddicker, Mike	92D	176	$ .01	$ .04	Bonilla, Bobby	90DL	196	$ .10	$1.00
Boddicker, Mike	92DL	268	$ .01	$ .06	Bonilla, Bobby	91D	325	$ .01	$ .10
Boddicker, Mike	93D	469	$ .01	$ .05	Bonilla, Bobby	91DL	357	$ .05	$ .25
Boever, Joe	89D	168	$ .01	$ .04	Bonilla, Bobby	91DLS	223	$ .05	$ .20
Boever, Joe	90D	357	$ .01	$ .04	Bonilla, Bobby	92D	610	$ .01	$ .10
Boever, Joe	90DL	349	$ .05	$ .25	Bonilla, Bobby	92DAS	427	$ .01	$ .10
Boever, Joe	91D	578	$ .01	$ .04	Bonilla, Bobby	92DL	308	$ .01	$ .15
Boever, Joe	91DL	68	$ .01	$ .08	Bonilla, Bobby	92DLS	61	$ .01	$ .15
Boever, Joe	92D	493	$ .01	$ .04	Bonilla, Bobby	93D	594	$ .01	$ .10
Boever, Joe	92DL	491	$ .01	$ .06	Bonilla, Juan	82D	220	$ .01	$ .06
Boever, Joe	93D	504	$ .01	$ .05	Bonilla, Juan	83D	346	$ .01	$ .06
Boggs, Tommy	81D	597	$ .01	$ .06	Bonilla, Juan	84D	234	$ .05	$ .20
Boggs, Tommy	82D	249	$ .01	$ .06	Bonnell, Barry	81D	272	$ .01	$ .06
Boggs, Tommy	83D	349	$ .01	$ .06	Bonnell, Barry	82D	432	$ .01	$ .06
Boggs, Wade	83D	586	$6.00	$24.00	Bonnell, Barry	83D	430	$ .01	$ .06
Boggs, Wade	84D	151	$3.75	$15.00	Bonnell, Barry	84D	559	$ .05	$ .20
Boggs, Wade	84DK	26	$1.00	$4.00	Bonnell, Barry	85D	191	$ .01	$ .10
Boggs, Wade	85D	172	$1.25	$5.00	Bonner, Bob	82D	610	$ .01	$ .06
Boggs, Wade	86D	371	$ .75	$3.00	Booker, Greg	88D	311	$ .01	$ .04
Boggs, Wade	87D	252	$ .10	$ .75	Boone, Bob	81D	262	$ .01	$ .06
Boggs, Wade	88D	153	$ .05	$ .25	Boone, Bob	82D	471	$ .01	$ .06
Boggs, Wade	88DBC	7	$ .01	$ .15	Boone, Bob	83D	192	$ .01	$ .06
Boggs, Wade	89D	68	$ .05	$ .30	Boone, Bob	84D	158	$ .05	$ .20
Boggs, Wade	90D	68	$ .05	$ .20	Boone, Bob	85D	230	$ .01	$ .10
Boggs, Wade	90DAS	712	$ .01	$ .10	Boone, Bob	86D	230	$ .01	$ .08
Boggs, Wade	90DL	51	$ .20	$2.00	Boone, Bob	86DK	17	$ .01	$ .10
Boggs, Wade	91D	178	$ .01	$ .15	Boone, Bob	87D	233	$ .01	$ .05
Boggs, Wade	91DAS	55	$ .01	$ .10	Boone, Bob	88D	305	$ .01	$ .04
Boggs, Wade	91DL	273	$ .10	$ .50	Boone, Bob	89D	170	$ .01	$ .04
Boggs, Wade	91DLP	14	$1.25	$5.00	Boone, Bob	89DTR	5	$ .01	$ .15
Boggs, Wade	91DLS	11	$ .10	$ .50	Boone, Bob	90D	326	$ .01	$ .04
Boggs, Wade	92D	210	$ .01	$ .10	Boone, Bob	90DL	46	$ .05	$ .25
Boggs, Wade	92DAS	23	$ .01	$ .10	Boone, Bob	91D	356	$ .01	$ .04
Boggs, Wade	92DK	9	$ .20	$2.00	Boone, Bret	93D	188	$ .01	$ .15
Boggs, Wade	92DL	286	$ .05	$ .25	Boone, Danny	82D	187	$ .01	$ .06
Boggs, Wade	92DLS	131	$ .05	$ .25	Borders, Pat	88DR	12	$ .10	$ .40
Boggs, Wade	93D	619	$ .01	$ .10	Borders, Pat	89D	560	$ .05	$ .20
Bogner, Terry	83D	520	$ .01	$ .06	Borders, Pat	90D	560	$ .01	$ .04
Bohanon, Brian	90DR	13	$ .01	$ .05	Borders, Pat	90DL	343	$ .10	$ .50
Bohanon, Brian	92DR	11	$ .01	$ .05					
Bohanon, Brian	93D	27	$ .01	$ .05					
Bolton, Tom	89D	539	$ .01	$ .04					
Bolton, Tom	91D	609	$ .01	$ .04					
Bolton, Tom	91DL	47	$ .01	$ .08					
Bomback, Mark	82D	559	$ .01	$ .06					
Bonds, Barry	86DR	11	$4.00	$16.00					
Bonds, Barry	87D	361	$2.25	$9.00					
Bonds, Barry	88D	326	$ .10	$ .50					
Bonds, Barry	89D	92	$ .10	$ .40					
Bonds, Barry	90D	126	$ .05	$ .25					
Bonds, Barry	90DL	91	$1.00	$4.00					
Bonds, Barry	91D	495	$ .05	$ .20					
Bonds, Barry	91DK	4	$ .05	$ .20					
Bonds, Barry	91DL	261	$ .10	$ .75					
Bonds, Barry	91DL	364	$ .01	$ .15					
Bonds, Barry	91DLP	9	$2.00	$8.00					
Bonds, Barry	91DLS	222	$ .10	$ .75					
Bonds, Barry	91DMVP	762	$ .01	$ .10					
Bonds, Barry	92D	243	$ .01	$ .15					
Bonds, Barry	92DL	275	$ .10	$ .50					
Bonds, Barry	92DLS	82	$ .10	$ .50					
Bonds, Barry	93D	678	$ .05	$ .20					
Bonds, Bobby	81D	71	$ .01	$ .06					
Bones, Ricky	92D	545	$ .01	$ .10					
Bones, Ricky	92DL	500	$ .01	$ .15					
Bones, Ricky	92DLS	192	$ .01	$ .06					
Bones, Ricky	93D	413	$ .01	$ .05					
Bones, Ricky	93DL	122	$ .01	$ .15					
Bonilla, Bobby	86DR	30	$1.25	$5.00					
Bonilla, Bobby	87D	558	$ .75	$3.00					
Bonilla, Bobby	88D	238	$ .05	$ .20					
Bonilla, Bobby	89D	151	$ .01	$ .15	**Borders, Pat**	**91D**	**317**	**$ .01**	**$ .10**
Bonilla, Bobby	89DK	2	$ .01	$ .05	Borders, Pat	91DL	23	$ .01	$ .08

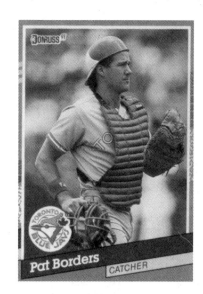

DONRUSS

Player	Year	No.	VG	EX/MT	Player	Year	No.	VG	EX/MT
Borders, Pat	92D	379	$ .01	$ .04	Bradford, Larry	81D	584	$ .01	$ .06
Borders, Pat	92DL	324	$ .01	$ .06	Bradford, Larry	82D	553	$ .01	$ .06
Borders, Pat	92DLS	253	$ .01	$ .06	Bradley, Phil	85D	631	$ .05	$ .25
Borders, Pat	93D	115	$ .01	$ .05	Bradley, Phil	86D	191	$ .05	$ .25
Borders, Pat	93DL	157	$ .01	$ .15	Bradley, Phil	86DK	22	$ .05	$ .20
Bordi, Rich	85D	289	$ .01	$ .10	Bradley, Phil	87D	270	$ .01	$ .05
Bordi, Rich	86D	518	$ .01	$ .08	Bradley, Phil	88D	243	$ .01	$ .04
Bordi, Rich	87D	213	$ .01	$ .05	Bradley, Phil	89D	369	$ .01	$ .04
Bordick, Mike	92D	505	$ .01	$ .04	Bradley, Phil	89DTR	41	$ .01	$ .05
Bordick, Mike	92DL	364	$ .01	$ .06	Bradley, Phil	90D	259	$ .01	$ .04
Bordick, Mike	93D	83	$ .01	$ .05	Bradley, Phil	90DL	138	$ .05	$ .25
Bordick, Mike	93DL	117	$ .01	$ .15	Bradley, Phil	91D	646	$ .01	$ .04
Borgmann, Glenn	81D	159	$ .01	$ .06	Bradley, Scott	85DRR	37	$ .01	$ .15
Bosetti, Rick	81D	152	$ .01	$ .06	Bradley, Scott	86D	396	$ .01	$ .08
Bosetti, Rick	82D	626	$ .01	$ .06	Bradley, Scott	87D	440	$ .01	$ .05
Bosio, Chris	87D	478	$ .05	$ .35	Bradley, Scott	88D	147	$ .01	$ .04
Bosio, Chris	87DR	20	$ .05	$ .25	Bradley, Scott	89D	261	$ .01	$ .04
Bosio, Chris	88D	117	$ .01	$ .04	Bradley, Scott	90D	581	$ .01	$ .04
Bosio, Chris	89D	412	$ .01	$ .04	Bradley, Scott	90DL	404	$ .05	$ .25
Bosio, Chris	90D	57	$ .01	$ .04	Bradley, Scott	91D	287	$ .01	$ .04
Bosio, Chris	90DK	20	$ .01	$ .05	Bradley, Scott	91DL	99	$ .01	$ .08
Bosio, Chris	90DL	26	$ .05	$ .25	Bradley, Scott	92D	713	$ .01	$ .04
Bosio, Chris	91D	160	$ .01	$ .04	Braggs, Glenn	87D	337	$ .01	$ .10
Bosio, Chris	91DL	518	$ .01	$ .08	Braggs, Glenn	88D	240	$ .01	$ .04
Bosio, Chris	92D	471	$ .01	$ .04	Braggs, Glenn	89D	103	$ .01	$ .04
Bosio, Chris	92DL	266	$ .01	$ .06	Braggs, Glenn	90D	264	$ .01	$ .04
Bosio, Chris	93D	499	$ .01	$ .05	Braggs, Glenn	90DL	466	$ .05	$ .25
Boskie, Shawn	90DL	519	$ .10	$ .50	Braggs, Glenn	91D	253	$ .01	$ .04
Boskie, Shawn	90DR	18	$ .01	$ .15	Braggs, Glenn	91DL	362	$ .01	$ .08
Boskie, Shawn	91D	241	$ .01	$ .04	Braggs, Glenn	92D	363	$ .01	$ .04
Boskie, Shawn	91DL	221	$ .01	$ .08	Branson, Jeff	92DR	13	$ .05	$ .20
Boskie, Shawn	91DLS	152	$ .01	$ .08	Branson, Jeff	93D	138	$ .01	$ .10
Boskie, Shawn	92DL	162	$ .01	$ .06	Brantley, Cliff	92D	722	$ .01	$ .15
Boskie, Shawn	93D	500	$ .01	$ .05	Brantley, Cliff	92DL	434	$ .01	$ .06
Bosley, Thad	81D	162	$ .01	$ .06	Brantley, Cliff	93D	250	$ .01	$ .05
Bosley, Thad	85D	388	$ .01	$ .10	Brantley, Jeff	89DR	41	$ .01	$ .05
Bosley, Thad	86D	483	$ .01	$ .08	Brantley, Jeff	90D	466	$ .01	$ .04
Bosley, Thad	87D	191	$ .01	$ .05	Brantley, Jeff	90DL	357	$ .05	$ .25
Bosley, Thad	88D	348	$ .01	$ .04	Brantley, Jeff	91D	319	$ .01	$ .04
Boston, Daryl	85DRR	33	$ .05	$ .25	Brantley, Jeff	91DL	136	$ .01	$ .08
Boston, Daryl	86D	86	$ .01	$ .08	Brantley, Jeff	92D	295	$ .01	$ .04
Boston, Daryl	87D	137	$ .01	$ .05	Brantley, Jeff	92DL	56	$ .01	$ .06
Boston, Daryl	89D	455	$ .01	$ .04	Brantley, Jeff	92DLS	112	$ .01	$ .06
Boston, Daryl	90DL	514	$ .05	$ .25	Brantley, Jeff	93D	100	$ .01	$ .05
Boston, Daryl	91D	210	$ .01	$ .04	Brantley, Jeff	93DL	102	$ .01	$ .15
Boston, Daryl	91DL	202	$ .01	$ .08	Brantley, Mickey	87D	656	$ .01	$ .15
Boston, Daryl	91DLS	201	$ .01	$ .08	Brantley, Mickey	87DR	27	$ .01	$ .07
Boston, Daryl	92D	612	$ .01	$ .04	Brantley, Mickey	88D	610	$ .01	$ .15
Boston, Daryl	93D	38	$ .01	$ .10	Brantley, Mickey	89D	212	$ .01	$ .04
Bottenfield, Kent	92DR	12	$ .01	$ .10	Braun, Steve	82D	418	$ .01	$ .06
Bottenfield, Kent	93D	484	$ .01	$ .10	Braun, Steve	86D	534	$ .01	$ .08
Boucher, Denis	91DR	45	$ .01	$ .10	Bream, Sid	85D	470	$ .10	$1.00
Boucher, Denis	92D	604	$ .01	$ .04	Bream, Sid	86D	566	$ .01	$ .08
Boucher, Denis	93D	755	$ .01	$ .05	Bream, Sid	87D	79	$ .01	$ .05
Bournigal, Rafael	93D	10	$ .01	$ .15	Bream, Sid	88D	188	$ .01	$ .04
Bowa, Larry	81D	142	$ .05	$ .20	Bream, Sid	89D	252	$ .01	$ .04
Bowa, Larry	82D	63	$ .01	$ .15	Bream, Sid	90D	329	$ .01	$ .04
Bowa, Larry	83D	435	$ .01	$ .06	Bream, Sid	91D	644	$ .01	$ .04
Bowa, Larry	84D	239	$ .05	$ .25	Bream, Sid	91DL	379	$ .01	$ .08
Bowa, Larry	85D	361	$ .05	$ .20	Bream, Sid	91DLS	142	$ .01	$ .08
Bowen, Ryan	92D	671	$ .01	$ .10	Bream, Sid	92D	202	$ .01	$ .04
Bowen, Ryan	92DL	385	$ .01	$ .15	Bream, Sid	92DL	242	$ .01	$ .06
Bowen, Ryan	93D	372	$ .01	$ .05	Bream, Sid	92DLS	2	$ .01	$ .06
Boyd, Dennis	84D	457	$ .10	$ .50	Bream, Sid	93D	526	$ .01	$ .05
Boyd, Dennis "Oil Can"	85D	151	$ .01	$ .10	Bream, Sid	93DL	178	$ .01	$ .15
Boyd, Oil Can	86D	50	$ .01	$ .15	Breining, Fred	82D	186	$ .01	$ .06
Boyd, Oil Can	87D	51	$ .01	$ .05	Breining, Fred	83D	503	$ .01	$ .06
Boyd, Oil Can	88D	462	$ .01	$ .04	Breining, Fred	84D	387	$ .05	$ .20
Boyd, Oil Can	89D	476	$ .01	$ .04	Brenly, Bob	82D	574	$ .05	$ .20
Boyd, Oil Can	90D	633	$ .01	$ .04	Brenly, Bob	83D	377	$ .01	$ .06
Boyd, Oil Can	90DL	159	$ .05	$ .25	Brenly, Bob	84D	616	$ .05	$ .20
Boyd, Oil Can	91D	194	$ .01	$ .04	Brenly, Bob	85D	187	$ .01	$ .10
Boyd, Oil Can	91DL	167	$ .01	$ .08	Brenly, Bob	85DK	26	$ .03	$ .10
Boyd, Oil Can	91DLS	193	$ .01	$ .08	Brenly, Bob	86D	323	$ .01	$ .08
Boyd, Oil Can	92D	447	$ .01	$ .04	Brenly, Bob	87D	485	$ .01	$ .05

DONRUSS

Player	Year	No.	VG	EX/MT
Brenly, Bob	88D	189	$ .01	$ .04
Brenly, Bob	89D	453	$ .01	$ .04
Brennan, Tom	84D	102	$ .05	$ .20
Brennan, William	89D	589	$ .01	$ .04
Brett, George	81D	100	$ .90	$3.60
Brett, George	81D	491	$ .20	$2.00
Brett, George	81D	537	$ .20	$2.00
Brett, George	82D	34	$ .75	$3.00
Brett, George	82DK	15	$ .15	$1.50
Brett, George	83D	338	$ .20	$2.00
Brett, George	84D	53	$2.25	$9.00
Brett, George	85D	53	$ .75	$3.00
Brett, George	86D	53	$ .20	$2.00
Brett, George	87D	54	$ .10	$ .50
Brett, George	87DK	15	$ .05	$ .25
Brett, George	88D	102	$ .05	$ .25
Brett, George	89D	204	$ .05	$ .20
Brett, George	89DBC	7	$ .01	$ .15
Brett, George	90D	144	$ .01	$ .15
Brett, George	90DL	178	$ .15	$1.50
Brett, George	91D	201	$ .01	$ .10
Brocail, Doug	92DR	16	$ .01	$ .10
Brocail, Doug	93D	418	$ .01	$ .05
Brock, Greg	83D	579	$ .01	$ .06
Brock, Greg	84D	296	$ .05	$ .20
Brock, Greg	86D	296	$ .01	$ .08
Brock, Greg	88D	337	$ .01	$ .04
Brock, Greg	89D	57	$ .01	$ .04
Brock, Greg	90D	293	$ .01	$ .04
Brock, Greg	90DL	454	$ .05	$ .25
Brock, Greg	91D	572	$ .01	$ .04
Brogna, Rico	91DLBC	11	$ .15	$1.50
Brogna, Rico	92DR	17	$ .01	$ .10
Brogna, Rico	93D	41	$ .01	$ .10
Brookens, Tom	81D	6	$ .01	$ .06
Brookens, Tom	82D	202	$ .01	$ .06
Brookens, Tom	83D	454	$ .01	$ .06
Brookens, Tom	84D	578	$ .05	$ .20
Brookens, Tom	85D	593	$ .01	$ .10
Brookens, Tom	86D	537	$ .01	$ .08
Brookens, Tom	87D	296	$ .01	$ .05
Brookens, Tom	88D	107	$ .01	$ .04
Brookens, Tom	89D	508	$ .01	$ .04
Brookens, Tom	89DTR	53	$ .01	$ .05
Brookens, Tom	91D	658	$ .01	$ .04
Brooks, Hubie	82D	476	$ .10	$ .40
Brooks, Hubie	83D	49	$ .01	$ .15
Brooks, Hubie	84D	607	$ .05	$ .25
Brooks, Hubie	85D	197	$ .01	$ .10
Brooks, Hubie	86D	55	$ .01	$ .08
Brooks, Hubie	87D	88	$ .01	$ .05
Brooks, Hubie	87DK	17	$ .01	$ .05
Brooks, Hubie	88D	468	$ .01	$ .04
Brooks, Hubie	89D	220	$ .01	$ .04
Brooks, Hubie	90D	130	$ .01	$ .04
Brooks, Hubie	90DL	16	$ .05	$ .25
Brooks, Hubie	91D	349	$ .01	$ .04
Brooks, Hubie	91DL	295	$ .01	$ .08
Brooks, Hubie	92D	64	$ .01	$ .04
Brooks, Hubie	92DL	378	$ .01	$ .06
Brooks, Hubie	92DLS	142	$ .01	$ .06
Brooks, Hubie	93D	563	$ .01	$ .05
Brosius, Scott	92D	591	$ .01	$ .10
Brosius, Scott	93D	419	$ .01	$ .05
Bross, Terry	90D	502	$ .01	$ .10
Bross, Terry	91DRR	34	$ .01	$ .10
Brouhard, Mark	82D	154	$ .01	$ .06
Brouhard, Mark	83D	532	$ .01	$ .06
Brouhard, Mark	84D	211	$ .05	$ .20
Brouhard, Mark	85D	149	$ .01	$ .10
Brower, Bob	87D	651	$ .05	$ .20
Brower, Bob	87DR	49	$ .01	$ .07
Brower, Bob	88D	346	$ .01	$ .04
Brower, Bob	89D	411	$ .01	$ .04
Brown, Bobby	81D	469	$ .01	$ .06

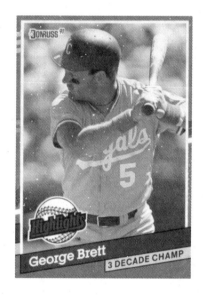

Player	Year	No.	VG	EX/MT
Brett, George	91DBC	19	$ .01	$ .10
Brett, George	91DL	264	$ .01	$ .15
Brett, George	91DL	335	$ .05	$ .25
Brett, George	91DLS	62	$ .05	$ .25
Brett, George	91DMVP	396	$ .01	$ .10
Brett, George	92D	143	$ .01	$ .10
Brett, George	92DL	255	$ .05	$ .20
Brett, George	92DLS	181	$ .05	$ .25
Brett, George	93DL	146	$ .10	$ .40
Brett, Ken	82D	364	$ .01	$ .06
Brewer, Tony	85DRR	31	$ .01	$ .15
Briley, Greg	90D	463	$ .01	$ .10
Briley, Greg	90DL	391	$ .05	$ .25
Briley, Greg	91D	352	$ .01	$ .04
Briley, Greg	91DL	194	$ .01	$ .08
Briley, Greg	92D	487	$ .01	$ .04
Briley, Greg	92DL	65	$ .01	$ .06
Briley, Greg	93D	695	$ .01	$ .05
Brink, Brad	92DR	14	$ .01	$ .10
Briscoe, John	92DR	15	$ .01	$ .10
Bristol, Dave	81D	436	$ .01	$ .06
Brown, Bobby	82D	552	$ .01	$ .06
Brown, Bobby	84D	478	$ .05	$ .20
Brown, Bobby	85D	383	$ .01	$ .10
Brown, Chris	86D	553	$ .05	$ .25
Brown, Chris	87D	80	$ .01	$ .05
Brown, Chris	87DK	11	$ .05	$ .20
Brown, Chris	88D	483	$ .01	$ .04
Brown, Chris	89D	183	$ .01	$ .04
Brown, Chris	89DTR	9	$ .01	$ .05
Brown, Darrell	85D	558	$ .01	$ .10
Brown, Jarvis	92D	770	$ .01	$ .10
Brown, Keith	89D	115	$ .01	$ .04
Brown, Kevin	87D	627	$ .20	$2.00
Brown, Kevin	89D	613	$ .05	$ .25
Brown, Kevin	89DR	44	$ .05	$ .25
Brown, Kevin	90D	343	$ .01	$ .10
Brown, Kevin	90DL	47	$ .10	$1.00
Brown, Kevin	91D	314	$ .01	$ .04
Brown, Kevin	91D	674	$ .01	$ .10
Brown, Kevin	91DL	250	$ .01	$ .08
Brown, Kevin	91DL	475	$ .01	$ .08

DONRUSS

Player	Year	No.	VG	EX/MT	Player	Year	No.	VG	EX/MT
Brown, Kevin	92D	55	$ .01	$ .04	Buechele, Steve	88D	224	$ .01	$ .04
Brown, Kevin	92DL	326	$ .01	$ .06	Buechele, Steve	89D	174	$ .01	$ .04
Brown, Kevin	93D	377	$ .01	$ .05	Buechele, Steve	90D	107	$ .01	$ .04
Brown, Kevin	93DL	202	$ .01	$ .15	Buechele, Steve	90DL	179	$ .05	$ .25
Brown, Marty	90DR	39	$ .01	$ .05	Buechele, Steve	91D	357	$ .01	$ .04
Brown, Mike C.	84D	517	$ .05	$ .20	Buechele, Steve	92D	699	$ .01	$ .04
Brown, Mike C.	84DRR	42	$ .05	$ .25	Buechele, Steve	92DL	91	$ .01	$ .06
Brown, Mike C.	85D	207	$ .01	$ .10	Buechele, Steve	92DLS	83	$ .01	$ .06
Brown, Mike C.	86D	642	$ .01	$ .08	Buechele, Steve	93D	104	$ .01	$ .05
Brown, Mike C.	87D	168	$ .01	$ .05	Buechele, Steve	93DL	106	$ .05	$ .20
Brown, Mike C.	87D	563	$ .01	$ .05	Buhner, Jay	88D	545	$ .05	$ .35
Browne, Jerry	87DR	29	$ .05	$ .25	Buhner, Jay	88DR	11	$ .10	$ .50
Browne, Jerry	87DRR	41	$ .05	$ .20	Buhner, Jay	89D	581	$ .01	$ .15
Browne, Jerry	88D	408	$ .01	$ .04	Buhner, Jay	90D	448	$ .01	$ .04
Browne, Jerry	89D	529	$ .01	$ .04	Buhner, Jay	90DL	114	$ .05	$ .35
Browne, Jerry	89DTR	44	$ .01	$ .15	Buhner, Jay	91D	509	$ .01	$ .04
Browne, Jerry	90D	138	$ .01	$ .04	Buhner, Jay	91DL	62	$ .01	$ .08
Browne, Jerry	90DL	48	$ .05	$ .25	Buhner, Jay	92D	61	$ .01	$ .04
Browne, Jerry	91D	162	$ .01	$ .04	Buhner, Jay	92DL	128	$ .01	$ .06
Browne, Jerry	91DL	43	$ .01	$ .08	Buhner, Jay	92DLS	231	$ .01	$ .06
Browne, Jerry	93D	447	$ .01	$ .05	Buhner, Jay	93D	111	$ .01	$ .05
Browne, Jerry	93DL	150	$ .01	$ .15	Buice, DeWayne	87DR	6	$ .01	$ .07
Browning, Tom	85D	634	$ .10	$1.00	Buice, DeWayne	88D	58	$ .01	$ .04
Browning, Tom	86D	384	$ .10	$ .40	Bulling, Terry	82D	612	$ .01	$ .06
Browning, Tom	87D	63	$ .01	$ .15	Bulling, Terry	83D	226	$ .01	$ .06
Browning, Tom	88D	63	$ .01	$ .10	Bullinger, Jim	92DR	20	$ .01	$ .05
Browning, Tom	89D	71	$ .01	$ .10	Bullinger, Jim	93D	556	$ .01	$ .05
Browning, Tom	90D	308	$ .01	$ .04	Bullinger, Jim	93DL	31	$ .01	$ .15
Browning, Tom	90DL	110	$ .05	$ .35	Bullock, Eric	91DL	470	$ .01	$ .08
Browning, Tom	91D	528	$ .01	$ .04	Bullock, Eric	92D	683	$ .01	$ .04
Browning, Tom	91DL	88	$ .01	$ .08	Bumbry, Al	81D	355	$ .01	$ .06
Browning, Tom	91DLS	161	$ .01	$ .08	Bumbry, Al	82D	153	$ .01	$ .06
Browning, Tom	92D	136	$ .01	$ .04	Bumbry, Al	83D	383	$ .01	$ .06
Browning, Tom	92DL	46	$ .01	$ .06	Bumbry, Al	84D	210	$ .05	$ .20
Browning, Tom	93D	190	$ .01	$ .05	Bumbry, Al	85D	350	$ .01	$ .10
Bruett, J. T.	92DR	18	$ .01	$ .10	Burba, Dave	91DR	12	$ .01	$ .05
Brumfield, Jacob	92D	499	$ .01	$ .06	Burba, Dave	92D	566	$ .01	$ .04
Brumfield, Jacob	92DR	19	$ .01	$ .05	Burba, Dave	92DL	471	$ .01	$ .06
Brumley, Mike	88D	609	$ .01	$ .15	Burba, Dave	93D	128	$ .01	$ .05
Brumley, Mike	89D	302	$ .01	$ .04	Burgmeier, Tom	81D	97	$ .01	$ .06
Brumley, Mike	89DR	39	$ .01	$ .05	Burgmeier, Tom	82D	361	$ .01	$ .06
Brumley, Mike	90D	533	$ .01	$ .04	Burgmeier, Tom	83D	235	$ .01	$ .06
Brummer, Glenn	83D	418	$ .01	$ .06	Burgmeier, Tom	84D	522	$ .05	$ .20
Brummer, Glenn	84D	138	$ .05	$ .20	Burgmeier, Tom	85D	400	$ .01	$ .10
Brummer, Glenn	85D	290	$ .01	$ .10	Burke, Tim	86D	421	$ .05	$ .20
Brunansky, Tom	83D	555	$ .05	$ .35	Burke, Tim	87D	222	$ .01	$ .05
Brunansky, Tom	84D	242	$ .05	$ .35	Burke, Tim	88D	98	$ .01	$ .04
Brunansky, Tom	85D	364	$ .05	$ .25	Burke, Tim	89D	274	$ .01	$ .04
Brunansky, Tom	86D	192	$ .05	$ .20	Burke, Tim	90D	334	$ .01	$ .04
Brunansky, Tom	86DK	24	$ .05	$ .20	Burke, Tim	90DL	28	$ .05	$ .25
Brunansky, Tom	87D	194	$ .01	$ .05	Burke, Tim	91D	125	$ .01	$ .04
Brunansky, Tom	88D	245	$ .05	$ .20	Burke, Tim	91DL	124	$ .01	$ .08
Brunansky, Tom	89D	112	$ .01	$ .04	Burke, Tim	92D	366	$ .01	$ .04
Brunansky, Tom	90D	399	$ .01	$ .04	Burke, Tim	92DL	44	$ .01	$ .06
Brunansky, Tom	90DL	447	$ .05	$ .25	Burke, Tim	92DLS	62	$ .01	$ .06
Brunansky, Tom	91D	513	$ .01	$ .04	Burkett, John	90DL	384	$ .05	$ .25
Brunansky, Tom	91DL	164	$ .01	$ .08	Burkett, John	90DR	51	$ .01	$ .15
Brunansky, Tom	92D	490	$ .01	$ .04	Burkett, John	91D	638	$ .01	$ .04
Brunansky, Tom	93D	693	$ .01	$ .05	Burkett, John	91DL	56	$ .01	$ .08
Brusstar, Warren	84D	442	$ .05	$ .20	Burkett, John	91DLS	253	$ .01	$ .08
Brusstar, Warren	85D	533	$ .01	$ .10	Burkett, John	92D	257	$ .01	$ .04
Brusstar, Warren	86D	555	$ .01	$ .08	Burkett, John	92DL	179	$ .01	$ .06
Bryant, Ralph	87D	587	$ .01	$ .05	Burkett, John	92DLS	113	$ .01	$ .06
Buckner, Bill	81D	482	$ .01	$ .15	Burkett, John	93D	156	$ .01	$ .05
Buckner, Bill	82D	403	$ .01	$ .06	Burks, Ellis	87DR	5	$ .10	$1.00
Buckner, Bill	83D	99	$ .01	$ .15	Burks, Ellis	88D	174	$ .05	$ .25
Buckner, Bill	83DK	14	$ .01	$ .10	Burks, Ellis	89D	303	$ .01	$ .10
Buckner, Bill	84D	117	$ .05	$ .20	Burks, Ellis	90D	228	$ .01	$ .10
Buckner, Bill	85D	416	$ .05	$ .20	Burks, Ellis	90DK	23	$ .01	$ .05
Buckner, Bill	86D	151	$ .01	$ .15	Burks, Ellis	90DL	261	$ .05	$ .35
Buckner, Bill	87D	462	$ .01	$ .05	Burks, Ellis	91D	235	$ .01	$ .10
Buckner, Bill	88D	456	$ .01	$ .15	Burks, Ellis	91DL	121	$ .01	$ .15
Buckner, Bill	90D	474	$ .01	$ .04	Burks, Ellis	91DLS	12	$ .01	$ .08
Buechele, Steve	86D	544	$ .10	$ .75	Burks, Ellis	92D	234	$ .01	$ .04
Buechele, Steve	87D	180	$ .01	$ .05	Burks, Ellis	92DL	314	$ .01	$ .06

DONRUSS

Player	Year	No.	VG	EX/MT	Player	Year	No.	VG	EX/MT
Burks, Ellis	93D	33	$ .01	$ .05	Butcher, John	85D	314	$ .01	$ .10
Burleson, Rick	81D	454	$ .01	$ .06	Butcher, John	86D	120	$ .01	$ .08
Burleson, Rick	82D	342	$ .01	$ .06	Butcher, Mike	93D	665	$ .01	$ .05
Burleson, Rick	83D	318	$ .01	$ .06	Butera, Sal	81D	530	$ .01	$ .06
Burnitz, Jeromy	93D	787	$ .01	$ .10	Butera, Sal	82D	532	$ .01	$ .06
Burns, Britt	81D	279	$ .01	$ .06	Butler, Brett	82D	275	$ .20	$2.00
Burns, Britt	82D	230	$ .01	$ .06	Butler, Brett	83D	636	$ .10	$ .50
Burns, Britt	83D	193	$ .01	$ .06	Butler, Brett	84D	141	$ .10	$ .75
Burns, Britt	83DK	23	$ .01	$ .10	Butler, Brett	85D	216	$ .05	$ .25
Burns, Britt	84D	424	$ .05	$ .20	Butler, Brett	86D	102	$ .01	$ .10
Burns, Britt	85D	257	$ .01	$ .10	Butler, Brett	86DK	12	$ .01	$ .10
Burns, Britt	86D	58	$ .01	$ .08	Butler, Brett	87D	219	$ .01	$ .10
Burns, Todd	89D	564	$ .05	$ .10	Butler, Brett	88D	279	$ .01	$ .10
Burns, Todd	90D	446	$ .01	$ .04	Butler, Brett	89D	217	$ .01	$ .04
Burns, Todd	90DL	458	$ .05	$ .25	Butler, Brett	90D	249	$ .01	$ .04
Burns, Todd	91D	479	$ .01	$ .04	Butler, Brett	90DL	251	$ .05	$ .25
Burns, Todd	93D	641	$ .01	$ .05	Butler, Brett	91D	143	$ .01	$ .04
Burris, Ray	81D	524	$ .01	$ .06	Butler, Brett	91DL	411	$ .01	$ .08
Burris, Ray	82D	414	$ .01	$ .06	Butler, Brett	91DLS	181	$ .01	$ .08
Burris, Ray	83D	36	$ .01	$ .06	Butler, Brett	92D	369	$ .01	$ .04
Burris, Ray	84D	331	$ .05	$ .20	Butler, Brett	92DK	18	$ .10	$1.00
Burris, Ray	85D	218	$ .01	$ .10	Butler, Brett	92DL	186	$ .01	$ .06
Burris, Ray	86D	107	$ .01	$ .08	Butler, Brett	92DLS	41	$ .01	$ .06
Burroughs, Jeff	81D	66	$ .01	$ .06	Butler, Brett	93D	86	$ .01	$ .05
Burroughs, Jeff	82D	379	$ .01	$ .06	Byers, Randall	88D	605	$ .01	$ .15
Burroughs, Jeff	83D	323	$ .01	$ .06	Bystrom, Marty	82D	93	$ .01	$ .06
Burroughs, Jeff	84D	156	$ .05	$ .20	Bystrom, Martin "Marty"	83D	93	$ .01	$ .06
Burroughs, Jeff	85D	542	$ .01	$ .10	Bystrom, Marty	84D	259	$ .05	$ .20
Bush, Randy	84D	513	$ .05	$ .25	Bystrom, Marty	86D	591	$ .01	$ .08
Bush, Randy	85D	633	$ .01	$ .10	Cabell, Enos	81D	138	$ .01	$ .06
Bush, Randy	87D	441	$ .01	$ .05	Cabell, Enos	82D	272	$ .01	$ .06
Bush, Randy	88D	272	$ .01	$ .04	Cabell, Enos	83D	202	$ .01	$ .06
Bush, Randy	89D	537	$ .01	$ .04	Cabell, Enos	84D	456	$ .05	$ .20
Bush, Randy	90D	199	$ .01	$ .04	Cabell, Enos	85D	110	$ .01	$ .10
Bush, Randy	90DL	83	$ .05	$ .25	Cabell, Enos	86D	418	$ .01	$ .08
Bush, Randy	91D	382	$ .01	$ .04	Cabrera, Francisco	90D	646	$ .01	$ .10
Bush, Randy	91DL	26	$ .01	$ .08	Cabrera, Francisco	91D	341	$ .01	$ .04
Bush, Randy	92D	728	$ .01	$ .04	Cabrera, Francisco	92D	482	$ .01	$ .04
Bush, Randy	92DL	467	$ .01	$ .06	Cabrera, Francisco	93D	184	$ .01	$ .05
Bush, Randy	93D	781	$ .01	$ .05	Cadaret, Greg	88D	528	$ .01	$ .15
					Cadaret, Greg	89D	479	$ .01	$ .04
					Cadaret, Greg	90D	545	$ .01	$ .04
					Cadaret, Greg	91D	236	$ .01	$ .04
					Cadaret, Greg	91DL	415	$ .01	$ .08
					Cadaret, Greg	92D	628	$ .01	$ .04
					Cadaret, Greg	92DL	24	$ .01	$ .06
					Cadaret, Greg	93D	610	$ .01	$ .05
					Calderon, Ivan	86D	435	$ .15	$1.50
					Calderon, Ivan	88D	182	$ .05	$ .25
					Calderon, Ivan	88DBC	5	$ .01	$ .10
					Calderon, Ivan	88DK	25	$ .01	$ .05
					Calderon, Ivan	89D	371	$ .01	$ .04
					Calderon, Ivan	90D	294	$ .01	$ .04
					Calderon, Ivan	90DL	89	$ .05	$ .25
					Calderon, Ivan	91D	203	$ .01	$ .04
					Calderon, Ivan	91DL	338	$ .01	$ .08
					Calderon, Ivan	91DLS	194	$ .01	$ .08
					Calderon, Ivan	92D	48	$ .01	$ .04
					Calderon, Ivan	92DAS	431	$ .01	$ .05
					Calderon, Ivan	92DL	283	$ .01	$ .06
					Calderon, Ivan	92DLS	52	$ .01	$ .06
					Calderon, Ivan	93D	196	$ .01	$ .05
					Caldwell, Mike	81D	86	$ .01	$ .06
					Caldwell, Mike	82D	330	$ .01	$ .06
					Caldwell, Mike	83D	154	$ .01	$ .06
					Caldwell, Mike	84D	237	$ .05	$ .20
					Caldwell, Mike	85D	490	$ .01	$ .10
					Calhoun, Jeff	86D	426	$ .01	$ .08
					Calhoun, Jeff	87D	578	$ .01	$ .05
					Calhoun, Jeff	88D	509	$ .01	$ .04
					Camacho, Ernie	85D	129	$ .01	$ .10
					Camacho, Ernie	87D	350	$ .01	$ .05
Buskey, Tom	81D	270	$ .01	$ .06	Campbell, Bill	83D	504	$ .01	$ .06
Butcher, John	83D	37	$ .01	$ .06	Caminiti, Ken	88D	308	$ .05	$ .25
Butcher, John	84D	220	$ .05	$ .20	Caminiti, Ken	89D	542	$ .01	$ .10

TOM BUSKEY PITCHER

DONRUSS

Player	Year	No.	VG	EX/MT	Player	Year	No.	VG	EX/MT
Caminiti, Ken	90D	424	$ .01	$ .04	Candelaria, John	87D	551	$ .01	$ .05
Caminiti, Ken	90DL	253	$ .05	$ .25	Candelaria, John	88D	608	$ .01	$ .15
Caminiti, Ken	91D	221	$ .01	$ .04	Candelaria, John	89D	192	$ .10	$ .75
Caminiti, Ken	91DL	502	$ .01	$ .08	Candelaria, John	90DL	492	$ .05	$ .25
Caminiti, Ken	91DLS	174	$ .01	$ .08	Candelaria, John	91DL	324	$ .01	$ .08
Caminiti, Ken	92D	66	$ .01	$ .04	Candelaria, John	92D	125	$ .01	$ .04
Caminiti, Ken	92DL	140	$ .01	$ .06	Candiotti, Tom	84D	393	$ .10	$1.00
Caminiti, Ken	92DLS	33	$ .01	$ .06	Candiotti, Tom	87D	342	$ .01	$ .05
					Candiotti, Tom	88D	377	$ .01	$ .04
					Candiotti, Tom	89D	256	$ .01	$ .04
					Candiotti, Tom	90D	256	$ .01	$ .04
					Candiotti, Tom	90DL	55	$ .05	$ .25
					Candiotti, Tom	91D	115	$ .01	$ .04
					Candiotti, Tom	91DL	79	$ .01	$ .08
					Candiotti, Tom	91DLS	132	$ .01	$ .08
					Candiotti, Tom	92D	459	$ .01	$ .04
					Candiotti, Tom	92DL	409	$ .01	$ .06
					Candiotti, Tom	92DLS	42	$ .01	$ .06
					Candiotti, Tom	93D	142	$ .01	$ .05
					Cangelosi, John	86DR	51	$ .01	$ .10
					Cangelosi, John	87D	162	$ .01	$ .05
					Cangelosi, John	88D	435	$ .01	$ .04
					Cangelosi, John	90D	565	$ .01	$ .04
					Canseco, Jose	86DR	22	$2.50	$10.00
					Canseco, Jose	86DRR	39	$15.00	$60.00
					Canseco, Jose	87D	97	$1.25	$5.00
					Canseco, Jose	87DK	6	$ .10	$1.00
					Canseco, Jose	88D	302	$ .10	$ .50
					Canseco, Jose	89D	91	$ .10	$ .50
					Canseco, Jose	89D	643	$ .05	$ .25
					Canseco, Jose	89DBC	5	$ .05	$ .20
					Canseco, Jose	90D	125	$ .05	$ .25
					Canseco, Jose	90DL	108	$ .90	$3.60
					Canseco, Jose	91D	536	$ .05	$ .20
					Canseco, Jose	91DAS	50	$ .01	$ .15
					Canseco, Jose	91DL	182	$ .10	$ .75
					Canseco, Jose	91DLS	101	$ .10	$ .75
					Canseco, Jose	92D	548	$ .01	$ .15
					Canseco, Jose	92DL	267	$ .10	$ .50
Caminiti, Ken	93D	140	$ .01	$ .05	Canseco, Jose	92DLS	222	$ .10	$ .50
Camp, Rick	81D	197	$ .01	$ .06	Canseco, Jose	93D	159	$ .01	$ .10
Camp, Rick	82D	223	$ .01	$ .06	Canseco, Ozzie	90DL	516	$ .10	$ .50
Camp, Rick	83D	149	$ .01	$ .06	Canseco, Ozzie	93D	336	$ .01	$ .05
Camp, Rick	84D	165	$ .05	$ .20	Capel, Mike	88DR	46	$ .01	$ .07
Camp, Rick	85D	409	$ .01	$ .10	Capilla, Doug	81D	587	$ .01	$ .06
Camp, Rick	86D	385	$ .01	$ .08	Card, History	92DL	528	$ .01	$ .10
Campaneris, Bert	81D	50	$ .01	$ .06	Card, History	92DLS	264	$ .01	$ .10
Campaneris, Bert	82D	593	$ .01	$ .06	Card, The Leaf	91DL	1	$ .01	$ .08
Campanis, Jim	92D	647	$ .01	$ .10	Carew, Rod	81D	49	$ .20	$2.00
Campbell, Bill	82D	487	$ .01	$ .06	Carew, Rod	81D	169	$ .20	$2.00
Campbell, Bill	84D	555	$ .05	$ .20	Carew, Rod	81D	537	$ .20	$2.00
Campbell, Bill	85D	163	$ .01	$ .10	Carew, Rod	82D	216	$ .15	$1.25
Campbell, Bill	86D	571	$ .01	$ .08	Carew, Rod	82DK	8	$ .10	$ .75
Campbell, Kevin	92DR	21	$ .01	$ .05	Carew, Rod	83D	90	$ .10	$1.00
Campbell, Kevin	93D	155	$ .01	$ .05	Carew, Rod	84D	352	$1.25	$5.00
Campbell, Mike	88DR	2	$ .01	$ .15	Carew, Rod	85D	85	$ .15	$1.50
Campbell, Mike	88DRR	30	$ .01	$ .05	Carew, Rod	86D	280	$ .10	$ .75
Campbell, Mike	89D	497	$ .01	$ .04	Carlton, Steve	81D	33	$ .20	$2.00
Campusano, Sil	88DR	42	$ .01	$ .10	Carlton, Steve	81D	481	$ .10	$ .75
Campusano, Sil	89D	584	$ .01	$ .15	Carlton, Steve	82D	42	$ .15	$1.25
Canale, George	90D	699	$ .01	$ .10	Carlton, Steve	83D	219	$ .10	$1.00
Candaele, Casey	87D	549	$ .01	$ .05	Carlton, Steve	83DK	16	$ .10	$ .50
Candaele, Casey	87DR	33	$ .01	$ .07	Carlton, Steve	84D	111	$1.00	$4.00
Candaele, Casey	88D	179	$ .01	$ .04	Carlton, Steve	85D	305	$ .15	$1.50
Candaele, Casey	91D	324	$ .01	$ .04	Carlton, Steve	86D	183	$ .10	$ .75
Candaele, Casey	91DL	114	$ .01	$ .08	Carlton, Steve	87D	617	$ .05	$ .35
Candaele, Casey	92D	150	$ .01	$ .04	Carman, Don	86D	427	$ .05	$ .20
Candaele, Casey	93D	536	$ .01	$ .05	Carman, Don	87D	432	$ .01	$ .15
Candaele, Casey	93DL	15	$ .01	$ .15	Carman, Don	88D	385	$ .01	$ .04
Candelaria, John	81D	374	$ .05	$ .20	Carman, Don	89D	396	$ .01	$ .04
Candelaria, John	82D	297	$ .01	$ .15	Carman, Don	90D	604	$ .01	$ .04
Candelaria, John	83D	549	$ .01	$ .15	Carman, Don	91D	377	$ .01	$ .04
Candelaria, John	84D	357	$ .05	$ .20	Carpenter, Cris	88DR	50	$ .05	$ .20
Candelaria, John	85D	430	$ .01	$ .10	Carpenter, Cris	89DR	40	$ .01	$ .05
Candelaria, John	86D	499	$ .01	$ .08	Carpenter, Cris	89DRR	39	$ .01	$ .10

KEN CAMINITI 3B

DONRUSS

Player	Year	No.	VG	EX/MT	Player	Year	No.	VG	EX/MT
Carpenter, Cris	90D	634	$.01	$.10	Castillo, Carmen	87D	588	$.01	$.05
Carpenter, Cris	91DL	507	$.01	$.08	Castillo, Carmen	88D	403	$.01	$.04
Carpenter, Cris	92D	79	$.01	$.04	Castillo, Carmen	89D	374	$.01	$.04
Carpenter, Cris	93D	734	$.01	$.05	Castillo, Carmen	90D	554	$.01	$.04
Carr, Chuck	93D	124	$.01	$.05	Castillo, Frank	91DR	20	$.01	$.15
Carr, Chuck	93D	762	$.01	$.05	Castillo, Frank	92D	492	$.01	$.10
Carreon, Mark	89DR	18	$.01	$.05	Castillo, Frank	92DL	290	$.01	$.15
Carreon, Mark	90D	454	$.01	$.04	Castillo, Frank	93D	400	$.01	$.05
Carreon, Mark	90DL	488	$.05	$.25	Castillo, Frank	93DL	141	$.05	$.20
Carreon, Mark	91D	731	$.01	$.04	Castillo, Juan	87D	249	$.01	$.05
Carreon, Mark	92D	465	$.01	$.04	Castillo, Juan	88D	363	$.01	$.04
Carreon, Mark	92DL	259	$.01	$.06	Castillo, Juan	89D	530	$.01	$.04
Carreon, Mark	93D	71	$.01	$.05	Castillo, Manny	83D	253	$.01	$.06
Carter, Gary	81D	90	$.10	$.75	Castillo, Marty	84D	247	$.05	$.20
Carter, Gary	82D	114	$.10	$1.00	Castillo, Marty	85D	394	$.01	$.10
Carter, Gary	82DK	2	$.10	$.45	Castillo, Tony	89DR	12	$.01	$.05
Carter, Gary	83D	340	$.10	$.50	Castillo, Tony	90D	592	$.01	$.04
Carter, Gary	84D	55	$.15	$1.50	Castillo, Tony	92D	739	$.01	$.04
Carter, Gary	85D	55	$.10	$.50	Castino, John	81D	488	$.01	$.06
Carter, Gary	86D	68	$.05	$.25	Castino, John	82D	256	$.01	$.06
Carter, Gary	87D	69	$.05	$.20	Castino, John	83D	303	$.01	$.06
Carter, Gary	88D	199	$.05	$.20	Castino, John	84D	120	$.05	$.20
Carter, Gary	89D	53	$.01	$.15	Castino, John	84DK	4	$.05	$.25
Carter, Gary	90D	147	$.01	$.04	Castro, Bill	81D	578	$.01	$.06
Carter, Gary	90DL	134	$.05	$.25	Caudill, Bill	81D	586	$.01	$.06
Carter, Gary	91D	151	$.01	$.04	Caudill, Bill	82D	426	$.01	$.06
Carter, Gary	91DBC	8	$.01	$.03	Caudill, Bill	83D	302	$.01	$.06
Carter, Gary	91DL	457	$.01	$.08	Caudill, Bill	84D	118	$.05	$.20
Carter, Gary	91DLS	182	$.01	$.08	Caudill, Bill	85D	96	$.01	$.10
Carter, Gary	92D	36	$.01	$.04	Caudill, Bill	86D	317	$.01	$.08
Carter, Gary	92DL	442	$.01	$.06	Cecena, Jose	88DR	6	$.01	$.07
Carter, Gary	92DLS	53	$.01	$.06	Cedeno, Andujar	91DLBC	20	$.20	$2.00
Carter, Joe	84DRR	41	$12.00	$48.00	Cedeno, Andujar	91DLSP	12	$.20	$2.00
Carter, Joe	85D	616	$1.50	$6.00	Cedeno, Andujar	92D	549	$.01	$.10
Carter, Joe	86D	224	$.20	$2.00	Cedeno, Andujar	92DL	341	$.01	$.06
Carter, Joe	87D	156	$.10	$.75	Cedeno, Andujar	92DLS	34	$.01	$.06
Carter, Joe	88D	254	$.05	$.20	Cedeno, Andujar	93D	456	$.01	$.05
Carter, Joe	88DBC	9	$.01	$.10	Cedeno, Andujar	93DL	108	$.01	$.15
Carter, Joe	89D	83	$.05	$.20	Cedeno, Cesar	81D	263	$.01	$.06
Carter, Joe	89DBC	3	$.01	$.10	Cedeno, Cesar	82D	118	$.01	$.15
Carter, Joe	90D	114	$.01	$.15	Cedeno, Cesar	83D	43	$.01	$.06
Carter, Joe	90DL	379	$.15	$1.50	Cedeno, Cesar	84D	306	$.05	$.20
Carter, Joe	91D	298	$.01	$.10	Cedeno, Cesar	85D	447	$.01	$.10
Carter, Joe	91DL	353	$.05	$.35	Cedeno, Cesar	86D	648	$.01	$.08
Carter, Joe	91DLS	133	$.05	$.25	Cerone, Rick	81D	346	$.01	$.06
Carter, Joe	91DMVP	409	$.01	$.03	Cerone, Rick	82D	199	$.01	$.06
Carter, Joe	92D	677	$.01	$.04	Cerone, Rick	83D	577	$.01	$.06
Carter, Joe	92D	693	$.01	$.10	Cerone, Rick	84D	492	$.05	$.20
Carter, Joe	92DK	3	$.20	$2.00	Cerone, Rick	85D	274	$.01	$.10
Carter, Joe	92DL	375	$.05	$.25	Cerone, Rick	86D	310	$.01	$.08
Carter, Joe	92DLS	254	$.05	$.25	Cerone, Rick	88D	351	$.01	$.04
Carter, Joe	93D	615	$.01	$.10	Cerone, Rick	89D	398	$.01	$.04
Carter, Larry	93D	76	$.01	$.15	Cerone, Rick	90D	305	$.01	$.04
Carter, Steve	89DR	8	$.01	$.05	Cerone, Rick	91DL	493	$.01	$.08
Carter, Steve	91DRR	418	$.01	$.03	Cerone, Rick	92D	335	$.01	$.04
Cary, Chuck	87D	461	$.01	$.15	Cerone, Rick	92DL	523	$.01	$.06
Cary, Chuck	90D	429	$.01	$.04	Cerutti, John	86DR	20	$.05	$.25
Cary, Chuck	90DL	50	$.05	$.25	Cerutti, John	87D	442	$.05	$.25
Cary, Chuck	91D	179	$.01	$.04	Cerutti, John	88D	321	$.01	$.04
Cary, Chuck	91DL	66	$.01	$.08	Cerutti, John	89D	467	$.01	$.04
Cash, Dave	81D	121	$.01	$.06	Cerutti, John	90D	645	$.01	$.04
Casian, Larry	91DL	481	$.01	$.15	Cerutti, John	90DL	27	$.05	$.25
Casian, Larry	93D	343	$.01	$.05	Cerutti, John	91D	467	$.01	$.04
Castellano, Pedro	92DR	22	$.01	$.15	Cerutti, John	91DL	270	$.01	$.08
Castellano, Pedro	93D	761	$.01	$.10	Cerutti, John	92D	709	$.01	$.04
Castilla, Vinny	93D	102	$.01	$.05	Cey, Ron	81D	296	$.01	$.15
Castilla, Vinny	93D	770	$.01	$.05	Cey, Ron	82D	210	$.01	$.06
Castillo, Bobby	81D	298	$.01	$.06	Cey, Ron	83D	84	$.01	$.06
Castillo, Bobby	82D	236	$.01	$.06	Cey, Ron	84D	361	$.05	$.20
Castillo, Bobby	83D	102	$.01	$.06	Cey, Ron	85D	320	$.01	$.10
Castillo, Bobby	84D	436	$.05	$.20	Cey, Ron	86D	198	$.01	$.08
Castillo, Braulio	92D	753	$.01	$.15	Chadwick, Ray	87D	505	$.01	$.05
Castillo, Braulio	93D	386	$.01	$.05	Chalk, Dave	81D	101	$.01	$.06
Castillo, Carmen	85D	590	$.01	$.10	Chalk, Dave	82D	590	$.01	$.06
Castillo, Carmen	86D	460	$.01	$.08	Chamberlain, Wes	91DL	178	$.10	$.50

DONRUSS

Player	Year	No.	VG	EX/MT	Player	Year	No.	VG	EX/MT
Chamberlain, Wes	91DLS	211	$ .10	$ .50	Checklist, Cards (1-26)	87DK	27	$ .01	$ .10
Chamberlain, Wes	91DR	3	$ .05	$ .25	Checklist, Cards (1-56)	87DR	56	$ .01	$ .10
Chamberlain, Wes	91DRR	423	$ .05	$ .25	Checklist, Cards (28-137)	88D	100	$ .01	$ .05
Chamberlain, Wes	92D	384	$ .05	$ .20	Checklist, Cards (138-247)	88D	200	$ .01	$ .05
Chamberlain, Wes	92DL	453	$ .01	$ .06	Checklist, Cards (248-357)	88D	300	$ .01	$ .05
Chamberlain, Wes	92DLS	72	$ .01	$ .06	Checklist, Cards (358-467)	88D	400	$ .01	$ .05
Chamberlain, Wes	93D	304	$ .01	$ .05	Checklist, Cards (468-577)	88D	500	$ .01	$ .05
Chambers, Al	83D	649	$ .01	$ .06	Checklist, Cards (578-660)	88D	600	$ .01	$ .05
Chambers, Al	85D	389	$ .01	$ .10	Checklist, Cards (BC1-26)	88D	600	$ .01	$ .05
Chambliss, Chris	81D	219	$ .01	$ .06	Checklist, Cards (1-26)	88DK	27	$ .01	$ .03
Chambliss, Chris	82D	47	$ .01	$ .06	Checklist, Cards (1-56)	88DR	56	$ .01	$ .07
Chambliss, Chris	83D	123	$ .01	$ .06	Checklist, Cards (28-137)	89D	100	$ .01	$ .04
Chambliss, Chris	84D	537	$ .05	$ .20	Checklist, Cards (138-247)	89D	200	$ .01	$ .04
Chambliss, Chris	85D	287	$ .01	$ .10	Checklist, Cards (248-357)	89D	300	$ .01	$ .04
Chambliss, Chris	86D	618	$ .01	$ .08	Checklist, Cards (358-467)	89D	400	$ .01	$ .04
Chapin, Darrin	92D	745	$ .01	$ .10	Checklist, Cards (468-577)	89D	500	$ .01	$ .04
Chapman, Kelvin	85D	626	$ .01	$ .10	Checklist, Cards (578-660)	89D	600	$ .01	$ .04
Charboneau, Joe	81D	82	$ .01	$ .15	Checklist, Cards (1-26)	89DK	27	$ .01	$ .03
Charboneau, Joe	82D	363	$ .01	$ .06	Checklist, Cards (1-56)	89DR	56	$ .01	$ .05
Charlton, Norm	89D	544	$ .01	$ .15	Checklist, Cards (1-56)	89DTR	56	$ .01	$ .05
Charlton, Norm	90D	426	$ .01	$ .04	Checklist, Cards (28-129)	90D	100	$ .01	$ .04
Charlton, Norm	90DL	334	$ .05	$ .35	Checklist, Cards (130-231)	90D	200	$ .01	$ .04
Charlton, Norm	91D	384	$ .01	$ .04	Checklist, Cards (232-333)	90D	300	$ .01	$ .04
Charlton, Norm	91DL	414	$ .01	$ .08	Checklist, Cards (334-435)	90D	400	$ .01	$ .04
Charlton, Norm	92D	102	$ .01	$ .04	Checklist, Cards (436-537)	90D	500	$ .01	$ .04
Charlton, Norm	92DL	120	$ .01	$ .06	Checklist, Cards (538-639)	90D	600	$ .01	$ .04
Charlton, Norm	92DLS	21	$ .01	$ .06	Checklist, Cards (640-720)	90D	700	$ .01	$ .04
Charlton, Norm	93D	238	$ .01	$ .05	Checklist, Cards (1-26)	90DK	27	$ .01	$ .03
Checklist, Cards (1-120)	81D	0	$ .01	$ .15	Checklist, Cards (1-88)	90DL	84	$ .05	$ .35
Checklist, Cards (121-240)	81D	0	$ .01	$ .15	Checklist, Cards (89-176)	90DL	174	$ .05	$ .25
Checklist, Cards (241-360)	81D	0	$ .01	$ .15	Checklist, Cards (177-264)	90DL	264	$ .10	$ .50
Checklist, Cards (361-480)	81D	0	$ .01	$ .15	Checklist, Cards (265-352)	90DL	364	$ .05	$ .30
Checklist, Cards (481-600)	81D	0	$ .01	$ .15	Checklist, Cards (353-440)	90DL	444	$ .05	$ .35
Checklist, Cards (131-234)	82D	0	$ .01	$ .15	Checklist, Cards (441-528)	90DL	528	$ .05	$ .35
Checklist, Cards (235-338)	82D	0	$ .01	$ .15	Checklist, Cards (1-56)	90DR	56	$ .01	$ .05
Checklist, Cards (27-130)	82D	0	$ .01	$ .15	Checklist, Cards (28 -103)	91D	100	$ .01	$ .04
Checklist, Cards (339-442)	82D	0	$ .01	$ .15	Checklist, Cards (104-179)	91D	200	$ .01	$ .04
Checklist, Cards (443-544)	82D	0	$ .01	$ .15	Checklist, Cards (180-255)	91D	300	$ .01	$ .04
Checklist, Cards (545-653)	82D	0	$ .01	$ .15	Checklist, Cards (256-331)	91D	386	$ .01	$ .04
Checklist, Cards (1-26)	82DK	0	$ .05	$ .25	Checklist, Cards (332-408)	91D	500	$ .01	$ .04
Checklist, Cards (131-234)	83D	0	$ .01	$ .15	Checklist, Cards (409-506)	91D	600	$ .01	$ .04
Checklist, Cards (235-338)	83D	0	$ .01	$ .15					
Checklist, Cards (27-130)	83D	0	$ .01	$ .15					
Checklist, Cards (339-442)	83D	0	$ .01	$ .15					
Checklist, Cards (443-546)	83D	0	$ .01	$ .15					
Checklist, Cards (547-653)	83D	0	$ .01	$ .15					
Checklist, Cards (1-26)	83DK	0	$ .05	$ .30					
Checklist, Cards (131-234)	84D	0	$ .05	$ .25					
Checklist, Cards (235-338)	84D	0	$ .05	$ .25					
Checklist, Cards (27-130)	84D	0	$ .05	$ .25					
Checklist, Cards (339-442)	84D	0	$ .05	$ .25					
Checklist, Cards (443-546)	84D	0	$ .05	$ .25					
Checklist, Cards (547-651)	84D	0	$ .05	$ .25					
Checklist, Cards (1-26)	84DK	0	$ .05	$ .30					
Checklist, Cards (131-234)	85D	0	$ .01	$ .15					
Checklist, Cards (235-338)	85D	0	$ .01	$ .15					
Checklist, Cards (27-130)	85D	0	$ .01	$ .15					
Checklist, Cards (339-442)	85D	0	$ .01	$ .15					
Checklist, Cards (443-546)	85D	0	$ .01	$ .15					
Checklist, Cards (547-653)	85D	0	$ .01	$ .15					
Checklist, Cards (1-26)	85DK	0	$ .01	$ .15					
Checklist, Cards (131-234)	86D	0	$ .01	$ .15					
Checklist, Cards (235-338)	86D	0	$ .01	$ .15					
Checklist, Cards (27-130)	86D	0	$ .01	$ .15					
Checklist, Cards (339-442)	86D	0	$ .01	$ .15					
Checklist, Cards (443-546)	86D	0	$ .01	$ .15					
Checklist, Cards (547-653)	86D	0	$ .01	$ .15					
Checklist, Cards (1-26)	86DK	0	$ .01	$ .10					
Checklist, Cards (1-56)	86DR	56	$ .01	$ .15					
Checklist, Cards (28-133)	87D	100	$ .01	$ .10					
Checklist, Cards (134-239)	87D	200	$ .01	$ .10					
Checklist, Cards (240-345)	87D	300	$ .01	$ .10					
Checklist, Cards (346-451)	87D	400	$ .01	$ .10					
Checklist, Cards (452-557)	87D	500	$ .01	$ .10					
Checklist, Cards (558-660)	87D	600	$ .01	$ .10					

| Checklist, Cards (507-604) | 91D | 700 | $ .01 | $ .04 |

DONRUSS

Player	Year	No.	VG	EX/MT	Player	Year	No.	VG	EX/MT
Checklist, Cards (605-702)	91D	760	$.01	$.04	Clancy, Jim	83D	101	$.01	$.06
Checklist, Cards (703-770)	91D	770	$.01	$.04	Clancy, Jim	84D	119	$.05	$.20
Checklist, Cards (BC1-22)	91D	770	$.01	$.04	Clancy, Jim	84DK	19	$.05	$.25
Checklist, Cards (1-26)	91DK	27	$.01	$.05	Clancy, Jim	85D	439	$.01	$.10
Checklist, Cards (1-92)	91DL	84	$.01	$.15	Clancy, Jim	86D	268	$.01	$.08
Checklist, Cards (93-184)	91DL	174	$.01	$.15	Clancy, Jim	87D	639	$.01	$.05
Checklist, Cards(185-264)	91DL	264	$.01	$.15	Clancy, Jim	88D	74	$.01	$.04
Checklist, Cards (BC1-12)	91DL	264	$.01	$.15	Clancy, Jim	89D	268	$.01	$.04
Checklist, Cards (265-356)	91DL	364	$.01	$.15	Clancy, Jim	89DTR	32	$.01	$.05
Checklist, Cards (357-448)	91DL	444	$.01	$.15	Clancy, Jim	90D	69	$.01	$.04
Checklist, Cards (449-528)	91DL	528	$.01	$.10	Clancy, Jim	92D	639	$.01	$.04
Checklist, Cards (BC13-26)	91DL	528	$.01	$.10	Clark, Bobby	81D	572	$.01	$.06
Checklist, Cards (1-88)	91DLS	261	$.01	$.10	Clark, Bobby	82D	318	$.01	$.06
Checklist, Cards (89-176)	91DLS	262	$.01	$.10	Clark, Bobby	83D	444	$.01	$.06
Checklist, Cards (177-263)	91DLS	263	$.01	$.10	Clark, Bobby	84D	524	$.05	$.20
Checklist, Cards (1-56)	91DR	56	$.01	$.05	Clark, Bobby	85D	481	$.01	$.10
Checklist, Cards (1-79)	92D	80	$.01	$.04	Clark, Bryan	82D	596	$.01	$.06
Checklist, Cards (80-157)	92D	160	$.01	$.04	Clark, Bryan	83D	603	$.01	$.06
Checklist, Cards (158-237)	92D	240	$.01	$.04	Clark, Bryan	84D	562	$.05	$.20
Checklist, Cards (238-316)	92D	320	$.01	$.04	Clark, Dave	87D	623	$.05	$.20
Checklist, Cards (317-396)	92D	396	$.01	$.04	Clark, Dave	88D	473	$.01	$.04
Checklist, Cards (397-477)	92D	476	$.01	$.04	Clark, Dave	89D	585	$.01	$.04
Checklist, Cards (478-555)	92D	556	$.01	$.04	Clark, Dave	90D	492	$.01	$.04
Checklist, Cards (556-635)	92D	636	$.01	$.04	Clark, Dave	91D	616	$.01	$.04
Checklist, Cards (636-716)	92D	716	$.01	$.04	Clark, Jack	81D	315	$.05	$.30
Checklist, Cards (714-784)	92D	784	$.01	$.04	Clark, Jack	82D	46	$.05	$.30
Checklist, Cards (1-27)	92DK	27	$.10	$.50	Clark, Jack	83D	222	$.05	$.25
Checklist, Cards (1-88)	92DL	67	$.01	$.06	Clark, Jack	84D	65	$.05	$.35
Checklist, Cards (89-176)	92DL	133	$.01	$.06	Clark, Jack	84DK	7	$.05	$.35
Checklist, Cards (177-264)	92DL	199	$.01	$.06	Clark, Jack	85D	65	$.05	$.30
Checklist, Cards (265-352)	92DL	331	$.01	$.06	Clark, Jack	86D	168	$.05	$.25
Checklist, Cards (353-440)	92DL	397	$.01	$.06	Clark, Jack	87D	111	$.05	$.20
Checklist, Cards (441-528)	92DL	463	$.01	$.06	Clark, Jack	88D	183	$.05	$.20
Checklist, Rod Carew	92DLS	261	$.01	$.10	Clark, Jack	88DBC	15	$.01	$.15
Checklist, Red Schoendienst	92DLS	262	$.01	$.10	Clark, Jack	89D	311	$.05	$.10
Checklist, Billy Williams	92DLS	263	$.01	$.10	Clark, Jack	89DTR	2	$.01	$.15
Checklist, Cards (1-66)	92DR	131	$.01	$.05	Clark, Jack	90D	128	$.01	$.04
Checklist, Cards (67-132)	92DR	132	$.01	$.05	Clark, Jack	90DL	287	$.05	$.25
Checklist, Cards (1-80)	93D	122	$.01	$.05	Clark, Jack	91D	618	$.01	$.04
Checklist, Cards (81-159	93D	132	$.01	$.05	Clark, Jack	91DL	201	$.01	$.08
Checklist, Cards (160-238)	93D	254	$.01	$.05	Clark, Jack	91DLS	13	$.05	$.08
Checklist, Cards (239-317)	93D	264	$.01	$.05	Clark, Jack	92D	169	$.01	$.04
Checklist, Cards (318-396)	93D	396	$.01	$.05	Clark, Jack	92DL	366	$.01	$.06
Checklist, Cards (397-476)	93D	518	$.01	$.05	Clark, Jack	93D	63	$.01	$.05
Checklist, Cards (477-555)	93D	528	$.01	$.05	Clark, Jerald	89D	599	$.01	$.15
Checklist, Cards (556-634)	93D	650	$.01	$.05	Clark, Jerald	90D	593	$.01	$.04
Checklist, Cards (635-713)	93D	660	$.01	$.05	Clark, Jerald	90DL	510	$.10	$.40
Checklist, Cards (714-792)	93D	715	$.01	$.05	Clark, Jerald	90DR	48	$.01	$.05
Checklist, Cards (1-31)	93DK	31	$.15	$1.50	Clark, Jerald	91D	74	$.01	$.04
Checklist, Cards (1-74)	93DL	110	$.01	$.15	Clark, Jerald	91DL	265	$.01	$.08
Checklist, Cards (75-148)	93DL	120	$.01	$.15	Clark, Jerald	92D	144	$.01	$.04
Checklist, Cards (149-220)	93DL	220	$.01	$.15	Clark, Jerald	92DL	55	$.01	$.06
Chiamparino, Scott	91DL	401	$.01	$.15	Clark, Jerald	92DLS	102	$.01	$.06
Chiamparino, Scott	91DLS	122	$.01	$.08	Clark, Jerald	93D	74	$.01	$.05
Chiamparino, Scott	91DRR	42	$.01	$.10	Clark, Jerald	93D	790	$.01	$.05
Chiamparino, Scott	93D	738	$.01	$.05	Clark, Jerry	89D	607	$.01	$.04
Chicken, San Diego	82D	531	$.15	$1.50	Clark, Mark	92DR	25	$.01	$.05
Chicken, San Diego	83D	645	$.05	$.35	Clark, Mark	93D	152	$.01	$.10
Chicken, San Diego	84D	651	$.05	$.35	Clark, Mark	93DL	172	$.05	$.25
Chiffer, Floyd	83D	44	$.01	$.06	Clark, Phil	93D	391	$.01	$.05
Childress, Rocky	88D	554	$.01	$.04	Clark, Will	86DR	32	$3.00	$12.00
Chitren, Steve	91DL	486	$.01	$.15	Clark, Will	87D	66	$2.00	$8.00
Chitren, Steve	91DRR	431	$.01	$.15	Clark, Will	88D	204	$.10	$.50
Chitren, Steve	92D	385	$.01	$.04	Clark, Will	88DBC	24	$.10	$.40
Chitren, Steve	92DL	32	$.01	$.06	Clark, Will	88DK	21	$.05	$.25
Christensen, John	86D	360	$.01	$.08	Clark, Will	89D	249	$.05	$.35
Christenson, Larry	82D	219	$.01	$.06	Clark, Will	89DBC	22	$.05	$.20
Christenson, Larry	83D	345	$.01	$.06	Clark, Will	90D	230	$.05	$.25
Christiansen, Clay	85D	396	$.01	$.10	Clark, Will	90DAS	707	$.05	$.20
Christopher, Mike	92DR	23	$.01	$.05	Clark, Will	90DL	172	$.75	$3.00
Cianfrocco, Archi	92DL	493	$.01	$.15	Clark, Will	90DL	444	$.05	$.35
Cianfrocco, Archi	92DR	24	$.05	$.25	Clark, Will	91D	86	$.01	$.15
Cianfrocco, Archi	93D	246	$.01	$.10	Clark, Will	91DAS	441	$.01	$.10
Citarella, Ralph	85D	504	$.01	$.10	Clark, Will	91DL	238	$.10	$1.00
Clancy, Jim	82D	227	$.01	$.06	Clark, Will	91DLP	12	1.50	$6.00

DONRUSS

Player	Year	No.	VG	EX/MT
Clark, Will	91DLS	254	$ .10	$ .75
Clark, Will	92D	214	$ .01	$ .15
Clark, Will	92DAS	428	$ .01	$ .10
Clark, Will	92DK	2	$ .75	$3.00
Clark, Will	92DL	241	$ .10	$ .50
Clark, Will	92DLS	114	$ .10	$ .50
Clark, Will	93D	446	$ .01	$ .15
Clary, Marty	86DRR	36	$ .01	$ .10
Clary, Marty	90D	381	$ .01	$ .04
Clayton, Royce	92DL	272	$ .05	$ .25
Clayton, Royce	92DLS	115	$ .05	$ .25
Clayton, Royce	92DRR	397	$ .05	$ .20
Clayton, Royce	93D	208	$ .01	$ .10
Clayton, Royce	93DL	176	$ .01	$ .15
Clear, Mark	81D	291	$ .01	$ .06
Clear, Mark	82D	452	$ .01	$ .06
Clear, Mark	83D	361	$ .01	$ .06
Clear, Mark	84D	611	$ .05	$ .20
Clear, Mark	85D	538	$ .01	$ .10
Clear, Mark	86D	493	$ .01	$ .08
Clear, Mark	87D	355	$ .01	$ .05
Clear, Mark	88D	372	$ .01	$ .04
Clear, Mark	89D	528	$ .01	$ .04
Clemens, Roger	85D	273	$15.00	$60.00
Clemens, Roger	86D	172	$3.00	$12.00
Clemens, Roger	87D	276	$ .20	$2.00
Clemens, Roger	87DK	2	$ .10	$ .75
Clemens, Roger	88D	51	$ .10	$ .50
Clemens, Roger	89D	280	$ .05	$ .35
Clemens, Roger	90D	184	$ .05	$ .35
Clemens, Roger	90DL	12	$1.00	$4.00
Clemens, Roger	91D	81	$ .05	$ .20
Clemens, Roger	91DK	9	$ .01	$ .10
Clemens, Roger	91DL	174	$ .01	$ .15
Clemens, Roger	91DL	488	$ .10	$ .75
Clemens, Roger	91DLS	14	$ .10	$ .75
Clemens, Roger	91DLSP	2	$2.00	$8.00
Clemens, Roger	91DMVP	395	$ .01	$ .10
Clemens, Roger	92D	244	$ .05	$ .25
Clemens, Roger	92DBC	3	$ .10	$ .40
Clemens, Roger	92DL	19	$ .10	$ .50
Clemens, Roger	92DLS	132	$ .10	$ .75
Clemens, Roger	93D	119	$ .01	$ .15
Clemens, Roger	93DK	3	$1.50	$6.00
Clemente, Roberto	87D	612	$ .05	$ .20
Clements, Pat	86D	600	$ .01	$ .08
Clements, Pat	87D	390	$ .01	$ .05
Clements, Pat	88D	52	$ .01	$ .04
Cleveland, Reggie	81D	206	$ .01	$ .06
Cleveland, Reggie	82D	456	$ .01	$ .06
Cliburn, Stu	86D	301	$ .01	$ .08
Cliburn, Stu	87D	530	$ .01	$ .05
Cliburn, Stu	89D	462	$ .01	$ .04
Clutterbuck, Bryan	87D	397	$ .01	$ .05
Cobb, Ty	83D	653	$ .05	$ .20
Cocanower, Jaime	85D	455	$ .01	$ .10
Cocanower, Jaime	86D	393	$ .01	$ .08
Cochrane, Dave	92D	539	$ .01	$ .04
Cochrane, Dave	92DL	398	$ .01	$ .06
Cochrane, Dave	93D	481	$ .01	$ .05
Codiroli, Chris	84D	345	$ .05	$ .20
Codiroli, Chris	85D	462	$ .01	$ .10
Codiroli, Chris	86D	278	$ .01	$ .08
Codiroli, Chris	87D	226	$ .01	$ .05
Coffman, Kevin	88D	49	$ .01	$ .07
Colbert, Craig	92DR	26	$ .01	$ .05
Colbrunn, Greg	91DRR	425	$ .05	$ .20
Colbrunn, Greg	92D	557	$ .01	$ .04
Colbrunn, Greg	93D	328	$ .01	$ .05
Colbrunn, Greg	93DL	55	$ .01	$ .15
Cole, Alex	91D	383	$ .01	$ .10
Cole, Alex	91DL	108	$ .01	$ .15
Cole, Alex	92D	220	$ .01	$ .04
Cole, Alex	92DL	307	$ .01	$ .06
Cole, Alex	92DLS	165	$ .01	$ .06
Cole, Alex	93D	70	$ .01	$ .05
Cole, Alex	93D	786	$ .01	$ .05
Cole, Victor	92DR	27	$ .01	$ .10
Cole, Victor	93D	120	$ .01	$ .10
Coleman, Vince	86D	181	$ .20	$2.00
Coleman, Vince	86D	651	$ .05	$ .35
Coleman, Vince	87D	263	$ .05	$ .20
Coleman, Vince	88D	293	$ .01	$ .10
Coleman, Vince	89D	181	$ .01	$ .10
Coleman, Vince	89DK	19	$ .01	$ .05

Player	Year	No.	VG	EX/MT
Coleman, Vince	90D	279	$ .01	$ .10
Coleman, Vince	90DL	90	$ .10	$ .50
Coleman, Vince	91D	487	$ .01	$ .04
Coleman, Vince	91DL	427	$ .01	$ .15
Coleman, Vince	91DLS	202	$ .01	$ .08
Coleman, Vince	92D	218	$ .01	$ .04
Coleman, Vince	92DL	42	$ .01	$ .06
Coleman, Vince	92DLS	63	$ .01	$ .06
Coleman, Vince	93D	618	$ .01	$ .05
Coleman, Vince	93DL	57	$ .01	$ .15
Coles, Darnell	84D	630	$ .10	$ .50
Coles, Darnell	85D	118	$ .01	$ .10
Coles, Darnell	86D	557	$ .01	$ .08
Coles, Darnell	87D	230	$ .01	$ .05
Coles, Darnell	88D	572	$ .01	$ .04
Coles, Darnell	89D	566	$ .01	$ .04
Coles, Darnell	90D	212	$ .01	$ .04
Collins, Dave	81D	185	$ .01	$ .06
Collins, Dave	82D	169	$ .01	$ .06
Collins, Dave	83D	234	$ .01	$ .06
Collins, Dave	84D	650	$ .05	$ .20
Collins, Dave	85D	241	$ .01	$ .10
Collins, Dave	86D	218	$ .01	$ .08
Collins, Dave	87D	215	$ .01	$ .05
Colon, Cris	93D	353	$ .01	$ .10
Combs, Pat	90DL	78	$ .05	$ .25
Combs, Pat	90DR	3	$ .01	$ .05
Combs, Pat	90DRR	44	$ .01	$ .15
Combs, Pat	91D	60	$ .01	$ .04
Combs, Pat	91DL	32	$ .01	$ .08
Combs, Pat	92D	76	$ .01	$ .04
Comer, Steve	82D	341	$ .01	$ .06

DONRUSS

Player	Year	No.	VG	EX/MT	Player	Year	No.	VG	EX/MT
Comer, Steve	83D	163	$ .01	$ .06	Cordero, Wil	91DLBC	3	$1.25	$5.00
Comstock, Keith	90DL	522	$ .05	$ .25	Cordero, Wil	92DRR	2	$ .05	$ .25
Comstock, Keith	91D	246	$ .01	$ .04	Cordero, Wil	93D	432	$ .01	$ .10
Concepcion, Dave	81D	181	$ .05	$ .20	Cordero, Wil	93DL	37	$ .10	$1.00
Concepcion, Dave	82D	421	$ .05	$ .30	Cormier, Rheal	92D	712	$ .05	$ .20
Concepcion, Dave	83D	148	$ .05	$ .20	Cormier, Rheal	92DL	469	$ .01	$ .15
Concepcion, Dave	84D	121	$ .05	$ .20	Cormier, Rheal	93D	228	$ .01	$ .05
Concepcion, Dave	84DK	2	$ .05	$ .35	Cormier, Rheal	93DL	209	$ .05	$ .25
Concepcion, Dave	85D	155	$ .01	$ .10	Corrales, Pat	83D	626	$ .01	$ .06
Concepcion, Dave	85D	203	$ .05	$ .20	Correa, Ed	86DR	4	$ .01	$ .15
Concepcion, Dave	86D	243	$ .05	$ .20	Correa, Ed	87D	57	$ .01	$ .05
Concepcion, Dave	88D	329	$ .01	$ .04	Correa, Ed	88D	57	$ .01	$ .04
Concepcion, Onix	83D	516	$ .01	$ .06	Corsi, Jim	90D	422	$ .01	$ .04
Concepcion, Onix	84D	95	$ .05	$ .20	Corsi, Jim	92D	467	$ .01	$ .04
Concepcion, Onix	86D	252	$ .01	$ .08	Corsi, Jim	93D	741	$ .01	$ .05
Cone, David	87D	502	$ .75	$3.00	Costello, John	89D	518	$ .01	$ .04
Cone, David	87DR	35	$ .20	$2.00	Costello, John	90D	555	$ .01	$ .04
Cone, David	88D	653	$ .10	$ .40	Costo, Tim	91DLBC	18	$ .20	$2.00
Cone, David	89D	388	$ .05	$ .25	Costo, Tim	92DR	29	$ .01	$ .10
Cone, David	89DK	9	$ .01	$ .10	Costo, Tim	93D	270	$ .01	$ .10
Cone, David	90D	265	$ .01	$ .10	Cotto, Henry	85D	411	$ .01	$ .15
Cone, David	90DL	40	$ .10	$1.00	Cotto, Henry	89D	109	$ .01	$ .04
Cone, David	91D	154	$ .01	$ .10	Cotto, Henry	90D	644	$ .01	$ .04
Cone, David	91DL	253	$ .05	$ .20	Cotto, Henry	91D	343	$ .01	$ .04
Cone, David	92D	97	$ .01	$ .04	Cotto, Henry	91DL	113	$ .01	$ .08
Cone, David	92DL	92	$ .01	$ .06	Cotto, Henry	92D	356	$ .01	$ .04
Cone, David	93D	712	$ .01	$ .05	Cotto, Henry	92DL	472	$ .01	$ .06
Conine, Jeff	91DLS	63	$ .10	$ .75	Cotto, Henry	93D	705	$ .01	$ .05
Conine, Jeff	91DRR	427	$ .05	$ .25	Cowens, Al	81D	369	$ .01	$ .06
Conine, Jeff	93D	101	$ .01	$ .05	Cowens, Al	82D	207	$ .01	$ .06
Conine, Jeff	93D	765	$ .01	$ .05	Cowens, Al	83D	554	$ .01	$ .06
Conroy, Tim	84D	340	$ .05	$ .20	Cowens, Al	84D	511	$ .05	$ .20
Conroy, Tim	85D	156	$ .01	$ .10	Cowens, Al	85D	196	$ .01	$ .10
Cook, Dennis	89D	646	$ .05	$ .25	Cowens, Al	86D	389	$ .01	$ .08
Cook, Dennis	90D	193	$ .01	$ .04	Cowley, Joe	85D	613	$ .01	$ .10
Cook, Dennis	90DL	342	$ .05	$ .25	Cowley, Joe	86D	608	$ .01	$ .08
Cook, Dennis	91D	657	$ .01	$ .10	Cowley, Joe	87D	552	$ .01	$ .05
Cook, Dennis	91DL	257	$ .01	$ .08	Cox, Bobby	81D	426	$ .01	$ .06
Cook, Dennis	92DL	503	$ .01	$ .06	Cox, Danny	84D	449	$ .05	$ .35
Cook, Dennis	93D	625	$ .01	$ .05	Cox, Danny	85D	571	$ .01	$ .10
Cook, Dennis	93DL	193	$ .01	$ .15	Cox, Danny	86D	382	$ .01	$ .08
Cooke, Steve	92DR	28	$ .05	$ .25	Cox, Danny	87D	553	$ .01	$ .05
Cooke, Steve	93D	150	$ .01	$ .15	Cox, Danny	88D	60	$ .01	$ .04
Coolbaugh, Scott	90DL	363	$ .05	$ .25	Cox, Danny	89D	348	$ .01	$ .04
Coolbaugh, Scott	90DR	32	$ .05	$ .05	Cox, Danny	91DL	350	$ .01	$ .08
Coolbaugh, Scott	90DRR	43	$ .01	$ .15	Cox, Danny	92D	614	$ .01	$ .04
Coolbaugh, Scott	91DL	397	$ .01	$ .08	Cox, Danny	93D	466	$ .01	$ .05
Cooper, Cecil	81D	83	$ .01	$ .10	Cox, Jeff	81D	230	$ .01	$ .06
Cooper, Cecil	82D	258	$ .01	$ .10	Cox, Larry	81D	285	$ .01	$ .06
Cooper, Cecil	83D	106	$ .01	$ .10	Cox, Ted	81D	283	$ .01	$ .06
Cooper, Cecil	84D	351	$ .05	$ .20	Craig, Rodney	81D	288	$ .01	$ .06
Cooper, Cecil	85D	170	$ .05	$ .20	Craig, Rodney	83D	515	$ .01	$ .06
Cooper, Cecil	86D	170	$ .01	$ .08	Crandall, Del	84D	632	$ .05	$ .20
Cooper, Cecil	86DK	7	$ .05	$ .20	Crawford, Steve	82D	564	$ .01	$ .06
Cooper, Cecil	87D	363	$ .01	$ .05	Crawford, Steve	85D	395	$ .01	$ .10
Cooper, Gary	92D	774	$ .01	$ .10	Crawford, Steve	86D	416	$ .01	$ .04
Cooper, Scott	91D	496	$ .01	$ .15	Crawford, Steve	87D	309	$ .01	$ .05
Cooper, Scott	92D	570	$ .01	$ .10	Crawford, Steve	90DL	494	$ .05	$ .25
Cooper, Scott	92DL	182	$ .05	$ .20	Creel, Keith	83D	574	$ .01	$ .06
Cooper, Scott	93D	135	$ .01	$ .05	Crews, Tim	88D	464	$ .01	$ .04
Cooper, Scott	93DL	175	$ .01	$ .15	Crews, Tim	88DR	20	$ .01	$ .07
Cora, Joey	90D	538	$ .01	$ .04	Crews, Tim	89D	486	$ .01	$ .04
Cora, Joey	90DL	366	$ .05	$ .25	Crews, Tim	90D	550	$ .01	$ .04
Cora, Joey	91DL	375	$ .01	$ .08	Crews, Tim	91D	294	$ .01	$ .04
Cora, Joey	92D	108	$ .01	$ .04	Crews, Tim	91DL	141	$ .01	$ .08
Cora, Joey	93D	697	$ .01	$ .05	Crews, Tim	92D	437	$ .01	$ .04
Corbett, Doug	81D	546	$ .01	$ .06	Crim, Chuck	87DR	18	$ .01	$ .07
Corbett, Doug	82D	53	$ .01	$ .06	Crim, Chuck	88D	355	$ .01	$ .04
Corbett, Doug	85D	474	$ .01	$ .10	Crim, Chuck	89D	617	$ .01	$ .04
Corbett, Doug	87D	333	$ .01	$ .05	Crim, Chuck	90D	221	$ .01	$ .04
Corbett, Sherman	89D	407	$ .01	$ .10	Crim, Chuck	90DL	58	$ .05	$ .25
Corbin, Archie	92DRR	400	$ .01	$ .05	Crim, Chuck	91D	684	$ .01	$ .04
Corcoran, Tim	81D	367	$ .01	$ .06	Crim, Chuck	91DL	28	$ .01	$ .08
Corcoran, Tim	85D	381	$ .01	$ .10	Crim, Chuck	92D	103	$ .01	$ .04
Corcoran, Tim	86D	381	$ .01	$ .08	Crim, Chuck	92DL	312	$ .01	$ .06

DONRUSS

Player	Year	No.	VG	EX/MT
Crim, Chuck	93D	649	$ .01	$ .05
Cromartie, Warren	81D	332	$ .01	$ .06
Cromartie, Warren	82D	340	$ .01	$ .06
Cromartie, Warren	83D	466	$ .01	$ .06
Cromartie, Warren	91DL	458	$ .01	$ .08
Cromartie, Warren	91DLS	64	$ .01	$ .08
Cron, Chris	92D	698	$ .01	$ .10
Crowley, Terry	81D	507	$ .01	$ .06
Crowley, Terry	82D	383	$ .01	$ .06
Crowley, Terry	83D	457	$ .01	$ .06
Cruz, Hector	82D	57	$ .01	$ .06
Cruz, Jose	81D	383	$ .01	$ .06
Cruz, Jose	82D	244	$ .01	$ .06
Cruz, Jose	83D	41	$ .01	$ .06
Cruz, Jose	84D	182	$ .05	$ .20
Cruz, Jose	85D	304	$ .01	$ .10
Cruz, Jose	85DK	20	$ .03	$ .10
Cruz, Jose	86D	60	$ .01	$ .08
Cruz, Jose	87D	85	$ .01	$ .05
Cruz, Julio	81D	163	$ .01	$ .06
Cruz, Julio	82D	50	$ .01	$ .06
Cruz, Julio	83D	379	$ .01	$ .06
Cruz, Julio	84D	379	$ .05	$ .20
Cruz, Julio	85D	452	$ .01	$ .10
Cruz, Julio	86D	257	$ .01	$ .08
Cruz, Todd	83D	505	$ .01	$ .06
Cruz, Todd	84D	148	$ .05	$ .20
Cruz, Victor	81D	321	$ .01	$ .06
Cubbage, Mike	81D	492	$ .01	$ .06
Cummings, Steve	90D	698	$ .01	$ .10
Curtis, Chad	92DLS	143	$ .10	$ .50
Curtis, Chad	92DR	30	$ .05	$ .35
Curtis, Chad	93D	93	$ .01	$ .10
Curtis, John	83D	170	$ .01	$ .06
Cuyler, Milt	91DL	251	$ .05	$ .20
Cuyler, Milt	91DLS	51	$ .01	$ .15
Cuyler, Milt	91DR	6	$ .01	$ .05
Cuyler, Milt	91DRR	40	$ .01	$ .15
Cuyler, Milt	92D	232	$ .01	$ .10
Cuyler, Milt	92DL	75	$ .01	$ .06
Cuyler, Milt	92DLS	171	$ .01	$ .06
Cuyler, Milt	93D	173	$ .01	$ .05
Cuyler, Milt	93DL	38	$ .01	$ .15
Daniels, Kal	86DRR	27	$ .10	$1.00
Daniels, Kal	87D	142	$ .05	$ .20
Daniels, Kal	88D	289	$ .01	$ .15
Daniels, Kal	88DK	14	$ .01	$ .15
Daniels, Kal	89D	198	$ .01	$ .10
Daniels, Kal	89DBC	18	$ .01	$ .05
Daniels, Kal	90D	432	$ .01	$ .04
Daniels, Kal	90DL	313	$ .05	$ .25
Daniels, Kal	91D	336	$ .01	$ .04
Daniels, Kal	91DL	112	$ .01	$ .08
Daniels, Kal	92D	343	$ .01	$ .04
Darling, Ron	84DRR	30	$ .75	$3.00
Darling, Ron	85D	434	$ .05	$ .35
Darling, Ron	86D	563	$ .05	$ .20
Darling, Ron	87D	192	$ .05	$ .20
Darling, Ron	88D	76	$ .01	$ .15
Darling, Ron	88DK	6	$ .01	$ .15
Darling, Ron	89D	171	$ .01	$ .10
Darling, Ron	90D	289	$ .01	$ .04
Darling, Ron	90DL	304	$ .05	$ .25
Darling, Ron	91D	472	$ .01	$ .04
Darling, Ron	91DL	378	$ .01	$ .08
Darling, Ron	92D	723	$ .01	$ .04
Darling, Ron	92DL	447	$ .01	$ .06
Darling, Ron	93D	700	$ .01	$ .05
Darling, Ron	93DL	182	$ .01	$ .15
Darwin, Danny	81D	147	$ .01	$ .06
Darwin, Danny	82D	321	$ .01	$ .06
Darwin, Danny	83D	289	$ .01	$ .06
Darwin, Danny	84D	544	$ .05	$ .20
Darwin, Danny	85D	98	$ .01	$ .10
Darwin, Danny	86D	149	$ .01	$ .08
Darwin, Danny	87D	508	$ .01	$ .05
Darwin, Danny	88D	358	$ .01	$ .04
Darwin, Danny	89D	390	$ .01	$ .04
Darwin, Danny	90D	561	$ .01	$ .04
Darwin, Danny	90DL	346	$ .05	$ .25
Darwin, Danny	91D	165	$ .01	$ .04
Darwin, Danny	91DL	405	$ .01	$ .08
Darwin, Danny	91DMVP	401	$ .01	$ .03
Darwin, Danny	92D	87	$ .01	$ .04
Darwin, Danny	93D	647	$ .01	$ .05
Dascenzo, Doug	89D	491	$ .01	$ .10
Dascenzo, Doug	91D	749	$ .01	$ .04
Dascenzo, Doug	91DL	483	$ .01	$ .08
Dascenzo, Doug	92D	38	$ .01	$ .04
Dascenzo, Doug	92DL	51	$ .01	$ .06
Dascenzo, Doug	92DLS	11	$ .01	$ .06
Dascenzo, Doug	93D	212	$ .01	$ .05
Dauer, Rich	81D	232	$ .01	$ .06
Dauer, Rich	82D	257	$ .01	$ .06
Dauer, Rich	83D	455	$ .01	$ .06
Dauer, Rich	84D	350	$ .05	$ .20
Dauer, Rich	85D	106	$ .01	$ .10
Daugherty, Jack	90D	461	$ .01	$ .10
Daugherty, Jack	90DL	521	$ .05	$ .25
Daugherty, Jack	91D	576	$ .01	$ .04
Daugherty, Jack	91DL	17	$ .01	$ .08
Daugherty, Jack	92D	569	$ .01	$ .04
Daulton, Darren	86D	477	$1.00	$4.00
Daulton, Darren	87D	262	$ .10	$ .50
Daulton, Darren	88D	309	$ .01	$ .15
Daulton, Darren	89D	549	$ .01	$ .04
Daulton, Darren	90D	194	$ .01	$ .04
Daulton, Darren	90DL	369	$ .10	$ .50
Daulton, Darren	91D	316	$ .01	$ .04
Daulton, Darren	91DL	192	$ .01	$ .08
Daulton, Darren	91DLS	212	$ .01	$ .08
Daulton, Darren	92D	198	$ .01	$ .04
Daulton, Darren	92DL	335	$ .01	$ .06
Daulton, Darren	92DLS	73	$ .01	$ .06
Daulton, Darren	93D	92	$ .01	$ .05
Daulton, Darren	93DK	17	$ .15	$1.50
Daulton, Darren	93DL	95	$ .10	$ .40
David, Andre	87D	519	$ .01	$ .05
Davidson, Mark	87DR	22	$ .01	$ .07

DONRUSS

Player	Year	No.	VG	EX/MT	Player	Year	No.	VG	EX/MT
Davidson, Mark	88D	519	$.01	$.04	Davis, Glenn	93DL	45	$.01	$.15
Davidson, Mark	91D	540	$.01	$.04	Davis, Jerry	85D	162	$.01	$.10
Davidson, Mark	91DL	143	$.01	$.08	Davis, Jerry	86D	429	$.01	$.08
Davis, Alvin	85D	69	$.10	$.50	Davis, Jody	82D	225	$.01	$.15
Davis, Alvin	85DK	18	$.05	$.25	Davis, Jody	83D	183	$.01	$.06
Davis, Alvin	86D	69	$.01	$.15	Davis, Jody	84D	433	$.05	$.20
Davis, Alvin	87D	75	$.01	$.15	Davis, Jody	85D	76	$.01	$.10
Davis, Alvin	88D	193	$.01	$.15	Davis, Jody	86D	289	$.01	$.08
Davis, Alvin	88DBC	25	$.01	$.10	Davis, Jody	87D	269	$.01	$.05
Davis, Alvin	89D	345	$.01	$.04	Davis, Jody	88D	119	$.01	$.04
Davis, Alvin	89DBC	25	$.01	$.05	Davis, Jody	89D	650	$.01	$.04
Davis, Alvin	90D	109	$.01	$.10	Davis, Joel	86D	623	$.01	$.08
Davis, Alvin	90DBC	9	$.01	$.10	Davis, Joel	87D	124	$.01	$.05
Davis, Alvin	90DL	35	$.05	$.25	Davis, John	88D	594	$.01	$.15
Davis, Alvin	91D	482	$.01	$.04	Davis, John	88DR	48	$.01	$.07
Davis, Alvin	91DL	429	$.01	$.08	Davis, Mark	84D	201	$.10	$1.00
Davis, Alvin	91DLS	111	$.01	$.08	Davis, Mark	85D	553	$.05	$.20
Davis, Alvin	92D	124	$.01	$.04	Davis, Mark	86D	265	$.01	$.15
Davis, Alvin	92DL	168	$.01	$.06	Davis, Mark	87D	313	$.01	$.15
Davis, Bob	81D	30	$.01	$.06	Davis, Mark	88D	64	$.01	$.15
Davis, Butch	84D	277	$.05	$.20	Davis, Mark	89D	65	$.01	$.04
Davis, Charles "Chili"	83D	348	$.10	$.40	Davis, Mark	90D	302	$.01	$.04
Davis, Chili	84D	114	$.10	$.50	Davis, Mark	90DL	468	$.05	$.25
Davis, Chili	85D	480	$.05	$.20	Davis, Mark	91D	560	$.01	$.04
Davis, Chili	86D	65	$.01	$.15	Davis, Mark	91DL	16	$.01	$.08
Davis, Chili	86DK	6	$.01	$.10	Davis, Mark	92D	54	$.01	$.04
Davis, Chili	87D	268	$.01	$.05	Davis, Mark	92DL	163	$.01	$.06
Davis, Chili	88D	313	$.01	$.04	Davis, Mark	93D	52	$.01	$.05
Davis, Chili	89D	449	$.01	$.04	Davis, Mike	81D	470	$.05	$.20
Davis, Chili	90D	136	$.01	$.04	Davis, Mike	84D	298	$.05	$.20
Davis, Chili	90DBC	20	$.01	$.04	Davis, Mike	85D	223	$.01	$.10
Davis, Chili	90DL	288	$.05	$.25	Davis, Mike	86D	96	$.01	$.08
Davis, Chili	91D	580	$.01	$.04	Davis, Mike	86DK	14	$.01	$.10
Davis, Chili	91DL	374	$.01	$.08	Davis, Mike	87D	133	$.01	$.05
Davis, Chili	92D	115	$.01	$.04	Davis, Mike	88D	281	$.01	$.04
Davis, Chili	92DL	395	$.01	$.06	Davis, Mike	89D	316	$.01	$.04
Davis, Chili	93D	679	$.01	$.05	Davis, Mike	90D	552	$.01	$.04
Davis, Dick	81D	528	$.01	$.06	Davis, Ron	81D	467	$.01	$.06
Davis, Dick	82D	147	$.01	$.06	Davis, Ron	82D	451	$.01	$.06
Davis, Dick	83D	647	$.01	$.06	Davis, Ron	83D	228	$.01	$.06
Davis, Doug	92DR	31	$.01	$.05	Davis, Ron	84D	269	$.05	$.20
Davis, Eric	85D	325	$2.00	$8.00	Davis, Ron	85D	120	$.01	$.10
Davis, Eric	86D	164	$.10	$1.00	Davis, Ron	86D	364	$.01	$.08
Davis, Eric	87D	265	$.10	$.50	Davis, Ron	87D	438	$.01	$.05
Davis, Eric	87DK	22	$.05	$.25	Davis, Storm	83D	619	$.05	$.25
Davis, Eric	88D	369	$.01	$.15	Davis, Storm	84D	585	$.05	$.20
Davis, Eric	88DBC	2	$.01	$.15	Davis, Storm	85D	454	$.01	$.10
Davis, Eric	89D	80	$.01	$.15	Davis, Storm	86D	169	$.01	$.08
Davis, Eric	90D	233	$.01	$.10	Davis, Storm	87D	273	$.01	$.05
Davis, Eric	90DAS	695	$.01	$.10	Davis, Storm	88D	595	$.01	$.04
Davis, Eric	90DBC	23	$.01	$.10	Davis, Storm	89D	210	$.01	$.04
Davis, Eric	90DL	189	$.10	$.50	Davis, Storm	90D	479	$.01	$.04
Davis, Eric	91D	84	$.01	$.15	Davis, Storm	90DL	362	$.05	$.25
Davis, Eric	91DL	37	$.01	$.15	Davis, Storm	91D	185	$.01	$.04
Davis, Eric	91DLS	162	$.01	$.15	Davis, Storm	91DL	161	$.01	$.08
Davie, Eric	91DLSP	11	$.20	$2.00	Davis, Storm	91DLS	65	$.01	$.08
Davis, Eric	92D	503	$.01	$.10	Davis, Storm	92D	629	$.01	$.04
Davis, Eric	92DL	430	$.01	$.06	Davis, Storm	92DL	465	$.01	$.06
Davis, Eric	92DLS	43	$.01	$.06	Davis, Storm	93D	769	$.01	$.05
Davis, Eric	93D	482	$.01	$.05	Davis, Tommy	82D	648	$.01	$.06
Davis, Glenn	86D	380	$.10	$1.00	Dawley, Bill	84D	328	$.05	$.20
Davis, Glenn	87D	61	$.05	$.25	Dawley, Bill	85D	354	$.01	$.10
Davis, Glenn	88D	184	$.01	$.15	Dawley, Bill	86D	283	$.01	$.08
Davis, Glenn	89D	236	$.01	$.10	Dawley, Bill	87D	628	$.01	$.05
Davis, Glenn	89DK	25	$.01	$.10	Dawley, Bill	88D	331	$.01	$.04
Davis, Glenn	90D	118	$.01	$.04	Dawson, Andre	81D	212	$.20	$1.75
Davis, Glenn	90DBC	21	$.01	$.04	Dawson, Andre	82D	88	$.20	$2.00
Davis, Glenn	90DL	30	$.05	$.25	Dawson, Andre	83D	518	$.15	$1.50
Davis, Glenn	91D	474	$.01	$.04	Dawson, Andre	84D	97	$1.25	$5.00
Davis, Glenn	91DL	398	$.01	$.08	Dawson, Andre	85D	421	$.20	$2.00
Davis, Glenn	91DLS	1	$.01	$.08	Dawson, Andre	86D	87	$.10	$1.00
Davis, Glenn	92D	597	$.01	$.04	Dawson, Andre	86DK	25	$.10	$.50
Davis, Glenn	92DL	316	$.01	$.06	Dawson, Andre	87D	458	$.10	$.50
Davis, Glenn	92DLS	122	$.01	$.06	Dawson, Andre	88D	269	$.01	$.15
Davis, Glenn	93D	163	$.01	$.05	Dawson, Andre	88DBC	10	$.01	$.10

DONRUSS

Player	Year	No.	VG	EX/MT	Player	Year	No.	VG	EX/MT
Dawson, Andre	88DK	9	$ .01	$ .15	DeLeon, Jose	86D	235	$ .01	$ .08
Dawson, Andre	89D	167	$ .01	$ .15	DeLeon, Jose	87D	457	$ .01	$ .05
Dawson, Andre	89DBC	8	$ .01	$ .10	DeLeon, Jose	88D	59	$ .01	$ .04
Dawson, Andre	90D	223	$ .01	$ .10	DeLeon, Jose	89D	437	$ .01	$ .04
Dawson, Andre	90DL	177	$ .10	$1.00	DeLeon, Jose	90D	536	$ .01	$ .04
Dawson, Andre	91D	129	$ .01	$ .10	DeLeon, Jose	90DL	485	$ .05	$ .25
Dawson, Andre	91DAS	435	$ .01	$ .10	DeLeon, Jose	91D	128	$ .01	$ .04
Dawson, Andre	91DL	400	$ .05	$ .20	DeLeon, Jose	91DL	190	$ .01	$ .08
Dawson, Andre	91DLS	153	$ .05	$ .20	DeLeon, Jose	92D	246	$ .01	$ .04
Dawson, Andre	92D	119	$ .01	$ .10	DeLeon, Jose	92DL	227	$ .01	$ .06
Dawson, Andre	92DAS	422	$ .01	$ .10	DeLeon, Jose	93D	464	$ .01	$ .05
Dawson, Andre	92DL	183	$ .01	$ .15	DeLeon, Luis	82D	588	$ .01	$ .06
Dawson, Andre	92DLS	12	$ .01	$ .15	DeLeon, Luis	83D	296	$ .01	$ .06
Dawson, Andre	93D	632	$ .01	$ .10	DeLeon, Luis	84D	162	$ .05	$ .20
Dayett, Brian	84DRR	45	$ .05	$ .25	DeLeon, Luis	85D	406	$ .01	$ .10
Dayett, Brian	85D	152	$ .01	$ .10	DeLucia, Rich	91DL	222	$ .05	$ .25
Dayett, Brian	88D	416	$ .01	$ .04	DeLucia, Rich	91DR	2	$ .01	$ .10
Dayley, Ken	82D	501	$ .05	$ .20	DeLucia, Rich	91DRR	426	$ .01	$ .15
Dayley, Ken	83D	375	$ .01	$ .06	DeLucia, Rich	92D	118	$ .01	$ .04
Dayley, Ken	84D	199	$ .05	$ .20	DeLucia, Rich	92DL	155	$ .01	$ .06
Dayley, Ken	86D	303	$ .01	$ .08	DeLucia, Rich	93D	185	$ .01	$ .05
Dayley, Ken	87D	357	$ .01	$ .05	Dempsey, Rick	81D	113	$ .01	$ .06
Dayley, Ken	88D	357	$ .01	$ .04	Dempsey, Rick	82D	77	$ .01	$ .06
Dayley, Ken	89D	299	$ .01	$ .04	Dempsey, Rick	83D	329	$ .01	$ .06
Dayley, Ken	90D	281	$ .01	$ .04	Dempsey, Rick	84D	413	$ .05	$ .20
Dayley, Ken	90DL	275	$ .05	$ .25	Dempsey, Rick	85D	332	$ .01	$ .10
Dayley, Ken	91D	735	$ .01	$ .04	Dempsey, Rick	86D	106	$ .01	$ .08
Dayley, Ken	91DLS	134	$ .01	$ .08	Dempsey, Rick	87D	294	$ .01	$ .05
De Los Santos, Luis	89D	562	$ .01	$ .15	Dempsey, Rick	89D	432	$ .01	$ .04
De Los Santos, Luis	89DR	33	$ .01	$ .05	Dempsey, Rick	90D	557	$ .01	$ .04
DeCinces, Doug	81D	352	$ .01	$ .06	Dempsey, Rick	91DL	484	$ .01	$ .08
DeCinces, Doug	82D	279	$ .01	$ .06	Denny, John	82D	572	$ .01	$ .06
DeCinces, Doug	83D	216	$ .01	$ .06	Denny, John	83D	237	$ .01	$ .15
DeCinces, Doug	84D	230	$ .05	$ .20	Denny, John	84D	407	$ .05	$ .20
DeCinces, Doug	85D	179	$ .01	$ .10	Denny, John	85D	111	$ .01	$ .10
DeCinces, Doug	85DK	2	$ .01	$ .15	Denny, John	86D	204	$ .01	$ .08
DeCinces, Doug	86D	57	$ .01	$ .08	Denny, John	87D	329	$ .01	$ .05
DeCinces, Doug	87D	356	$ .01	$ .05	Dent, Bucky	81D	465	$ .01	$ .06
Decker, Steve	91DL	441	$ .10	$ .40	Dent, Bucky	82D	209	$ .01	$ .06
Decker, Steve	91DLS	260	$ .01	$ .08	Dent, Bucky	84D	300	$ .05	$ .20
Decker, Steve	91DLSP	16	$ .20	$2.00	Dernier, Bob	83D	189	$ .01	$ .06
Decker, Steve	91DRR	428	$ .05	$ .25	Dernier, Bob	84D	541	$ .05	$ .20
Decker, Steve	92D	389	$ .01	$ .15	Dernier, Bob	85D	510	$ .01	$ .10
Decker, Steve	93D	260	$ .01	$ .05	Dernier, Bob	86D	266	$ .01	$ .08
Decker, Steve	93D	768	$ .01	$ .05	Dernier, Bob	87D	146	$ .01	$ .05
Dedmon, Jeff	85D	554	$ .01	$ .10	Dernier, Bob	88D	392	$ .01	$ .04
Dedmon, Jeff	86D	443	$ .01	$ .08	Dernier, Bob	89D	430	$ .01	$ .04
Dedmon, Jeff	87D	314	$ .01	$ .05	DeSa, Joe	86D	546	$ .01	$ .08
Dedmon, Jeff	88D	325	$ .01	$ .04	Deshaies, Jim	86DR	34	$ .05	$ .20
Deer, Rob	87D	274	$ .05	$ .20	Deshaies, Jim	87D	184	$ .05	$ .20
Deer, Rob	88D	274	$ .01	$ .04	Deshaies, Jim	88D	85	$ .01	$ .04
Deer, Rob	89D	173	$ .01	$ .04	Deshaies, Jim	89D	241	$ .01	$ .04
Deer, Rob	90D	55	$ .01	$ .04	Deshaies, Jim	90D	187	$ .01	$ .04
Deer, Rob	90DL	322	$ .05	$ .25	Deshaies, Jim	90DK	7	$ .01	$ .05
Deer, Rob	91D	729	$ .01	$ .04	Deshaies, Jim	90DL	168	$ .05	$ .25
Deer, Rob	91DL	237	$ .01	$ .08	Deshaies, Jim	91D	652	$ .01	$ .04
Deer, Rob	91DLS	52	$ .01	$ .08	Deshaies, Jim	91DL	49	$ .01	$ .08
Deer, Rob	92D	532	$ .01	$ .04	Deshaies, Jim	91DLS	175	$ .01	$ .08
Deer, Rob	92DL	193	$ .01	$ .06	Deshaies, Jim	92D	515	$ .01	$ .04
Deer, Rob	92DLS	172	$ .01	$ .06	DeShields, Delino	90DL	193	$1.25	$5.00
Deer, Rob	93D	231	$ .01	$ .05	DeShields, Delino	90DR	6	$ .10	$ .50
DeJesus, Ivan	81D	483	$ .01	$ .06	DeShields, Delino	90DRR	42	$ .10	$ .50
DeJesus, Ivan	82D	48	$ .01	$ .06	DeShields, Delino	91D	555	$ .01	$ .15
DeJesus, Ivan	82DK	14	$ .01	$ .15	DeShields, Delino	91DBC	16	$ .01	$ .10
DeJesus, Ivan	83D	399	$ .01	$ .06	DeShields, Delino	91DK	11	$ .01	$ .10
DeJesus, Ivan	84D	427	$ .05	$ .20	DeShields, Delino	91DL	139	$ .10	$ .40
DeJesus, Ivan	85D	204	$ .01	$ .10	DeShields, Delino	91DLS	195	$ .10	$ .40
DeJesus, Ivan	86D	449	$ .01	$ .08	DeShields, Delino	92D	277	$ .01	$ .15
DeJesus, Jose	89D	558	$ .01	$ .10	DeShields, Delino	92DL	138	$ .05	$ .20
DeJesus, Jose	90DL	415	$ .05	$ .25	DeShields, Delino	92DLS	54	$ .05	$ .20
DeJesus, Jose	91D	596	$ .01	$ .04	DeShields, Delino	93D	564	$ .01	$ .10
DeJesus, Jose	91DL	200	$ .01	$ .08	Devereaux, Mike	88D	546	$ .10	$ .75
DeJesus, Jose	92D	300	$ .01	$ .04	Devereaux, Mike	89D	603	$ .01	$ .15
DeLeon, Jose	84D	628	$ .05	$ .35	Devereaux, Mike	89DR	51	$ .05	$ .25
DeLeon, Jose	85D	308	$ .01	$ .10	Devereaux, Mike	89DTR	30	$ .05	$ .25

DONRUSS

Player	Year	No.	VG	EX/MT
Devereaux, Mike	90D	282	$ .01	$ .04
Devereaux, Mike	90DL	223	$ .10	$ .75
Devereaux, Mike	91D	444	$ .01	$ .04
Devereaux, Mike	91DL	138	$ .01	$ .08
Devereaux, Mike	92D	354	$ .01	$ .04
Devereaux, Mike	92DL	79	$ .01	$ .06
Devereaux, Mike	92DLS	123	$ .01	$ .06
Devereaux, Mike	93D	455	$ .01	$ .05
Devereaux, Mike	93DL	67	$ .01	$ .15
Diaz, Bo	81D	517	$ .01	$ .06
Diaz, Bo	82D	263	$ .01	$ .15
Diaz, Bo	83D	147	$ .01	$ .06
Diaz, Bo	84D	137	$ .05	$ .20
Diaz, Bo	86D	530	$ .01	$ .08
Diaz, Bo	87D	246	$ .01	$ .05
Diaz, Bo	88D	186	$ .01	$ .04
Diaz, Bo	89D	242	$ .01	$ .04
Diaz, Bo	90D	139	$ .01	$ .04
Diaz, Carlos	83D	562	$ .01	$ .06
Diaz, Carlos	84D	600	$ .05	$ .20
Diaz, Carlos	86D	348	$ .01	$ .08
Diaz, Edgar	90DL	335	$ .05	$ .25

Player	Year	No.	VG	EX/MT
Diaz, Edgar	**91D**	**197**	**$ .01**	**$ .04**
Diaz, Mario	91DL	363	$ .01	$ .08
Diaz, Mario	92D	149	$ .01	$ .04
Diaz, Mike	87D	267	$ .01	$ .05
Diaz, Mike	88D	267	$ .01	$ .04
Diaz, Mike	89D	655	$ .01	$ .04
Dibble, Rob	89D	426	$ .05	$ .25
Dibble, Rob	90D	189	$ .01	$ .15
Dibble, Rob	90DL	57	$ .10	$ .50
Dibble, Rob	91D	321	$ .01	$ .04
Dibble, Rob	91DL	282	$ .01	$ .08
Dibble, Rob	91DLS	163	$ .01	$ .08
Dibble, Rob	92D	139	$ .01	$ .04
Dibble, Rob	92DL	69	$ .01	$ .06
Dibble, Rob	92DLS	22	$ .01	$ .06
Dibble, Rob	93D	322	$ .01	$ .05
Dickson, Lance	91DLS	154	$ .05	$ .25
Dickson, Lance	91DRR	424	$ .01	$ .10
Dickson, Lance	92DRR	421	$ .01	$ .05
Dillard, Steve	81D	502	$ .01	$ .06
Dillard, Steve	82D	174	$ .01	$ .06
Dilone, Miguel	81D	441	$ .01	$ .06

Player	Year	No.	VG	EX/MT
Dilone, Miguel	82D	515	$ .01	$ .06
Dilone, Miguel	83D	85	$ .01	$ .06
Dilone, Miguel	85D	453	$ .01	$ .10
DiPino, Frank	84D	502	$ .05	$ .20
DiPino, Frank	85D	232	$ .01	$ .10
DiPino, Frank	86D	304	$ .01	$ .08
DiPino, Frank	87D	416	$ .01	$ .05
DiPino, Frank	88D	570	$ .01	$ .04
DiPino, Frank	89D	393	$ .01	$ .04
DiPino, Frank	90D	518	$ .01	$ .04
DiPino, Frank	90DL	103	$ .05	$ .25
DiPino, Frank	91D	360	$ .01	$ .04
DiSarcina, Gary	92D	497	$ .01	$ .04
DiSarcina, Gary	92DL	48	$ .01	$ .06
DiSarcina, Gary	92DLS	144	$ .01	$ .06
DiSarcina, Gary	92DR	32	$ .01	$ .05
DiSarcina, Gary	93D	121	$ .01	$ .05
Distefano, Benny	85D	166	$ .01	$ .10
Distefano, Benny	86D	78	$ .01	$ .08
Distefano, Benny	87D	514	$ .01	$ .05
Dixon, Ken	85D	270	$ .01	$ .10
Dixon, Ken	86D	148	$ .01	$ .08
Dixon, Ken	87D	171	$ .01	$ .05
Dixon, Ken	88D	48	$ .01	$ .04
Dodson, Pat	87DRR	44	$ .05	$ .25
Doherty, John	92DR	33	$ .01	$ .10
Doherty, John	93D	277	$ .01	$ .05
Donnels, Chris	91DL	447	$ .05	$ .20
Donnels, Chris	92D	619	$ .01	$ .10
Donnels, Chris	93D	747	$ .01	$ .05
Donohue, Tom	81D	51	$ .01	$ .06
Dopson, John	88DR	43	$ .05	$ .25
Dopson, John	89D	392	$ .01	$ .10
Dopson, John	89DTR	7	$ .01	$ .05
Dopson, John	90D	162	$ .01	$ .04
Dopson, John	90DL	130	$ .05	$ .25
Dopson, John	91D	193	$ .01	$ .04
Doran, Bill	84D	580	$ .10	$ .75
Doran, Bill	85D	84	$ .05	$ .20
Doran, Bill	86D	110	$ .01	$ .08
Doran, Bill	86DK	10	$ .01	$ .10
Doran, Bill	87D	286	$ .01	$ .05
Doran, Bill	88D	235	$ .01	$ .15
Doran, Bill	89D	306	$ .01	$ .04
Doran, Bill	90D	236	$ .01	$ .04
Doran, Bill	90DL	161	$ .05	$ .25
Doran, Bill	91D	756	$ .01	$ .04
Doran, Bill	91DL	197	$ .01	$ .08
Doran, Bill	92D	293	$ .01	$ .04
Doran, Bill	92DL	231	$ .01	$ .06
Doran, Bill	93D	370	$ .01	$ .05
Dotson, Rich	81D	280	$ .05	$ .20
Dotson, Rich	82D	356	$ .01	$ .06
Dotson, Rich	83D	319	$ .01	$ .06
Dotson, Rich	84D	180	$ .05	$ .20
Dotson, Rich	85D	302	$ .01	$ .10
Dotson, Rich	85DK	3	$ .01	$ .15
Dotson, Rich	86D	160	$ .01	$ .08
Dotson, Rich	87D	383	$ .01	$ .05
Dotson, Richard	88D	124	$ .01	$ .04
Dotson, Rich	89D	277	$ .01	$ .04
Downing, Brian	81D	410	$ .01	$ .06
Downing, Brian	82D	115	$ .01	$ .06
Downing, Brian	83D	367	$ .01	$ .06
Downing, Brian	84D	423	$ .05	$ .20
Downing, Brian	85D	158	$ .01	$ .10
Downing, Brian	86D	108	$ .01	$ .08
Downing, Brian	87D	86	$ .01	$ .05
Downing, Brian	88D	258	$ .01	$ .04
Downing, Brian	89D	254	$ .01	$ .04
Downing, Brian	90D	352	$ .01	$ .04
Downing, Brian	90DK	10	$ .01	$ .05
Downing, Brian	91DL	269	$ .01	$ .08
Downing, Brian	92D	167	$ .01	$ .04
Downing, Brian	92DL	440	$ .01	$ .06

DONRUSS

Player	Year	No.	VG	EX/MT	Player	Year	No.	VG	EX/MT
Downs, Kelly	87D	573	$ .01	$ .15	Dunston, Shawon	86D	311	$ .05	$ .25
Downs, Kelly	88D	145	$ .01	$ .04	Dunston, Shawon	87D	119	$ .05	$ .20
Downs, Kelly	89D	367	$ .01	$ .04	Dunston, Shawon	88D	146	$ .01	$ .15
Downs, Kelly	90D	177	$ .01	$ .04	Dunston, Shawon	89D	137	$ .01	$ .04
Downs, Kelly	91D	738	$ .01	$ .04	Dunston, Shawon	90D	49	$ .01	$ .04
Downs, Kelly	92D	303	$ .01	$ .04	Dunston, Shawon	90DL	229	$ .05	$ .25
Dozier, D.J.	92DRR	20	$ .01	$ .05	Dunston, Shawon	91D	686	$ .01	$ .04
Dozier, D. J.	93D	90	$ .01	$ .05	Dunston, Shawon	91DL	25	$ .01	$ .08
Drabek, Doug	86DR	31	$ .15	$1.50	Dunston, Shawon	91DLS	155	$ .01	$ .08
Drabek, Doug	87D	251	$ .15	$ 1.25	Dunston, Shawon	92D	613	$ .01	$ .04
Drabek, Doug	88D	79	$ .01	$ .15	Dunston, Shawon	92DL	249	$ .01	$ .06
Drabek, Doug	89D	211	$ .01	$ .04	Dunston, Shawon	93D	268	$ .01	$ .05
Drabek, Doug	90D	92	$ .01	$ .04	Durham, Leon	81D	427	$ .01	$ .06
Drabek, Doug	90DL	296	$ .10	$ .40	Durham, Leon	82D	151	$ .01	$ .06
Drabek, Doug	91D	269	$ .01	$ .04	Durham, Leon	83D	477	$ .01	$ .06
Drabek, Doug	91D	750	$ .01	$ .04	Durham, Leon	84D	67	$ .05	$ .20
Drabek, Doug	91DL	516	$ .01	$ .08	Durham, Leon	84DK	5	$ .05	$ .25
Drabek, Doug	91DLS	224	$ .01	$ .08	Durham, Leon	85D	189	$ .01	$ .10
Drabek, Doug	91DLSP	15	$ .20	$2.00	Durham, Leon	86D	320	$ .01	$ .08
Drabek, Doug	91DMVP	411	$ .01	$ .03	Durham, Leon	87D	242	$ .01	$ .05
Drabek, Doug	92D	209	$ .01	$ .04	Durham, Leon	88D	191	$ .01	$ .04
Drabek, Doug	92DL	11	$ .01	$ .06	Dwyer, Jim	81D	577	$ .01	$ .06
Drabek, Doug	92DLS	84	$ .01	$ .06	Dwyer, Jim	82D	611	$ .01	$ .06
Drabek, Doug	93D	622	$ .01	$ .05	Dwyer, Jim	83D	583	$ .01	$ .06
Drago, Dick	81D	336	$ .01	$ .06	Dwyer, Jim	84D	454	$ .05	$ .20
Drahman, Brian	93D	672	$ .01	$ .05	Dwyer, Jim	86D	413	$ .01	$ .08
Draper, Mike	92DR	34	$ .01	$ .15	Dwyer, Jim	87D	418	$ .01	$ .05
Dravecky, Dave	84D	551	$ .10	$ .50	Dwyer, Jim	88D	459	$ .01	$ .04
Dravecky, Dave	84DK	8	$ .05	$ .25	Dwyer, Jim	90D	484	$ .01	$ .04
Dravecky, Dave	85D	112	$ .01	$ .10	Dybzinski, Jerry	81D	438	$ .01	$ .06
Dravecky, Dave	86D	162	$ .01	$ .08	Dybzinski, Jerry	82D	647	$ .01	$ .06
Dravecky, Dave	87D	187	$ .01	$ .05	Dybzinski, Jerry	83D	576	$ .01	$ .06
Dravecky, Dave	88D	485	$ .01	$ .04	Dybzinski, Jerry	84D	160	$ .05	$ .20
Dressendorfer, Kirk	91DLBC	13	$ .10	$1.00	Dyer, Duffy	81D	7	$ .01	$ .06
Dressendorfer, Kirk	91DR	24	$ .01	$ .15	Dyer, Mike	90D	642	$ .01	$ .10
Dressendorfer, Kirk	92D	594	$ .01	$ .10					
Dressler, Rob	81D	406	$ .01	$ .06					
Drew, Cameron	89DRR	30	$ .01	$ .15					
Driessen, Dan	81D	301	$ .01	$ .06					
Driessen, Dan	82D	248	$ .01	$ .06					
Driessen, Dan	83D	274	$ .01	$ .06					
Driessen, Dan	84D	243	$ .05	$ .20					
Driessen, Dan	85D	619	$ .01	$ .10					
Driessen, Dan	86D	641	$ .01	$ .08					
Drummond, Tim	90D	510	$ .01	$ .10					
Drummond, Tim	90DR	50	$ .01	$ .05					
Drummond, Tim	91D	694	$ .01	$ .04					
Drumright, Keith	82D	616	$ .01	$ .06					
DuBois, Brian	90DL	266	$ .05	$ .25					
DuBois, Brian	90DR	4	$ .01	$ .05					
DuBois, Brian	90DRR	38	$ .01	$ .10					
Ducey, Rob	91D	705	$ .01	$ .04					
Ducey, Rob	92D	466	$ .01	$ .04					
Ducey, Rob	93D	489	$ .01	$ .05					
Dunbar, Tommy	84DRR	28	$ .05	$ .25					
Dunbar, Tommy	85D	159	$ .01	$ .10					
Dunbar, Tommy	86D	221	$ .01	$ .08					
Duncan, Mariano	86D	128	$ .10	$ .50					
Duncan, Mariano	87D	253	$ .01	$ .15					
Duncan, Mariano	88D	155	$ .01	$ .04					
Duncan, Mariano	90D	684	$ .01	$ .10					
Duncan, Mariano	90DL	202	$ .05	$ .25					
Duncan, Mariano	91D	309	$ .01	$ .04					
Duncan, Mariano	91DL	494	$ .01	$ .08					
Duncan, Mariano	91DLS	164	$ .01	$ .08					
Duncan, Mariano	92D	540	$ .01	$ .04					
Duncan, Mariano	92DL	311	$ .01	$ .06					
Duncan, Mariano	92DLS	74	$ .01	$ .06	Dykstra, Lenny	86D	482	$ .20	$2.00
Duncan, Mariano	93D	382	$ .01	$ .05	Dykstra, Lenny	87D	611	$ .05	$ .20
Duncan, Mariano	93DL	187	$ .05	$ .20	Dykstra, Lenny	88D	364	$ .01	$ .15
Dunne, Mike	87DR	38	$ .05	$ .30	Dykstra, Lenny	89D	353	$ .01	$ .10
Dunne, Mike	88D	390	$ .01	$ .15	Dykstra, Lenny	90D	313	$ .01	$ .10
Dunne, Mike	89D	269	$ .01	$ .04	Dykstra, Len	90DL	262	$ .05	$ .25
Dunne, Mike	90DL	418	$ .05	$ .25	Dykstra, Len	91D	523	$ .01	$ .04
Dunston, Shawon	85DRR	39	$ .15	$1.50	Dykstra, Len	91D	744	$ .01	$ .15

DONRUSS

Player	Year	No.	VG	EX/MT	Player	Year	No.	VG	EX/MT
Dykstra, Len	91DAS	434	$.01	$.03	Eisenreich, Jim	93D	722	$.01	$.05
Dykstra, Len	91DK	7	$.01	$.05	Eldred, Cal	92D	718	$.10	$.40
Dykstra, Len	91DL	163	$.01	$.08	Eldred, Cal	92DL	2	$.10	$.75
Dykstra, Len	91DLP	8	$.15	$1.25	Eldred, Cal	93D	131	$.01	$.15
Dykstra, Lenny	91DLS	213	$.01	$.08	Eldred, Cal	93DL	34	$.10	$1.00
Dykstra, Len	91DMVP	410	$.01	$.03	Elia, Lee	83D	614	$.01	$.06
Dykstra, Lenny	92D	57	$.01	$.04	Ellis, John	81D	26	$.01	$.06
Dykstra, Lenny	92DL	504	$.01	$.06	Ellis, John	82D	642	$.01	$.06
Dykstra, Lenny	92DLS	75	$.01	$.06	Ellsworth, Steve	88DR	54	$.01	$.07
Dykstra, Lenny	93D	544	$.01	$.05	Elster, Kevin	87D	635	$.01	$.15
Dykstra, Lenny	93DL	59	$.01	$.15	Elster, Kevin	88DR	34	$.01	$.10
Earl, Scottie	85D	491	$.01	$.10	Elster, Kevin	88DRR	37	$.01	$.15
Easler, Mike	81D	256	$.01	$.06	Elster, Kevin	89D	289	$.01	$.04
Easler, Mike	82D	221	$.01	$.06	Elster, Kevin	90D	152	$.01	$.04
Easler, Mike	83D	221	$.01	$.06	Elster, Kevin	90DL	8	$.05	$.25
Easler, Mike	84D	444	$.05	$.20	Elster, Kevin	91D	304	$.01	$.04
Easler, Mike	85D	213	$.01	$.10	Elster, Kevin	91DL	305	$.01	$.08
Easler, Mike	86D	395	$.01	$.08	Elster, Kevin	92D	307	$.01	$.04
Easler, Mike	87D	277	$.01	$.05	Embree, Alan	93D	333	$.01	$.15
Easley, Damion	93D	457	$.01	$.15	Engel, Steve	86D	510	$.01	$.08
Easterly, Jamie	82D	623	$.01	$.06	Engle, Dave	82D	102	$.01	$.06
Easterly, Jamie	83D	280	$.01	$.06	Engle, Dave	84D	598	$.05	$.20
Easterly, Jamie	86D	582	$.01	$.08	Engle, Dave	85D	72	$.01	$.10
Eave, Gary	90D	713	$.01	$.10	Engle, Dave	86D	438	$.01	$.08
Eckersley, Dennis	81D	96	$.20	$2.00	Engle, Ralph	83D	646	$.01	$.06
Eckersley, Dennis	82D	30	$.15	$1.25	Erickson, Roger	81D	549	$.01	$.06
Eckersley, Dennis	83D	487	$.10	$1.00	Erickson, Roger	82D	303	$.01	$.06
Eckersley, Dennis	84D	639	$1.00	$4.00	Erickson, Scott	91D	767	$.05	$.25
Eckersley, Dennis	85D	442	$.15	$1.50	Erickson, Scott	91DL	527	$.10	$.50
Eckersley, Dennis	86D	239	$.10	$.75	Erickson, Scott	91DLS	83	$.10	$.50
Eckersley, Dennis	87D	365	$.05	$.25	Erickson, Scott	92D	463	$.01	$.10
Eckersley, Dennis	88D	349	$.01	$.10	Erickson, Scott	92DK	21	$.20	$2.00
Eckersley, Dennis	89D	67	$.01	$.15	Erickson, Scott	92DL	166	$.01	$.10
Eckersley, Dennis	90D	210	$.01	$.10	Erickson, Scott	92DLS	202	$.01	$.15
Eckersley, Dennis	90DL	29	$.10	$.75	Erickson, Scott	93D	211	$.01	$.05
Eckersley, Dennis	91D	270	$.01	$.10	Erickson, Scott	93DL	142	$.01	$.15
Eckersley, Dennis	91DL	285	$.01	$.15	Esasky, Nick	84D	602	$.05	$.35
Eckersley, Dennis	91DLS	102	$.01	$.15	Esasky, Nick	85D	121	$.01	$.15
Eckersley, Dennis	92D	147	$.01	$.15	Esasky, Nick	86D	286	$.01	$.08
Eckersley, Dennis	92DL	100	$.01	$.15	Esasky, Nick	87D	166	$.01	$.05
Eckersley, Dennis	92DLS	223	$.01	$.15	Esasky, Nick	88D	413	$.01	$.04
Eckersley, Dennis	93D	215	$.01	$.05	Esasky, Nick	89D	189	$.01	$.04
Eckersley, Dennis	93DL	72	$.05	$.20	Esasky, Nick	89DTR	18	$.01	$.05
Edens, Tom	91D	590	$.01	$.10	Esasky, Nick	90D	303	$.01	$.04
Edens, Tom	93D	729	$.01	$.05	Esasky, Nick	90DL	164	$.05	$.25
Edwards, Dave	81D	595	$.01	$.06	Esasky, Nick	91DLS	143	$.01	$.08
Edwards, Dave	82D	247	$.01	$.06	Escarrega, Ernesto	83D	291	$.01	$.06
Edwards, Dave	83D	565	$.01	$.06	Espino, Juan	84D	92	$.05	$.20
Edwards, Marshall	83D	406	$.01	$.06	Espinoza, Alvaro	90D	245	$.01	$.04
Edwards, Marshall	84D	490	$.05	$.20	Espinoza, Alvaro	90DL	240	$.05	$.25
Edwards, Mike	81D	497	$.01	$.06	Espinoza, Alvaro	91D	226	$.01	$.04
Edwards, Wayne	90DL	352	$.05	$.25	Espinoza, Alvaro	91DL	198	$.01	$.08
Edwards, Wayne	90DR	17	$.01	$.05	Espinoza, Alvaro	92D	474	$.01	$.04
Edwards, Wayne	91D	327	$.01	$.04	Espy, Cecil	88DR	9	$.01	$.15
Edwards, Wayne	91DL	454	$.01	$.08	Espy, Cecil	89D	292	$.01	$.15
Eichelberger, Juan	82D	422	$.01	$.06	Espy, Cecil	90D	260	$.01	$.04
Eichelberger, Juan	83D	422	$.01	$.06	Espy, Cecil	92D	678	$.01	$.04
Eichelberger, Juan	84D	398	$.05	$.20	Essian, Jim	81D	503	$.01	$.06
Eichhorn, Mark	86DR	13	$.01	$.10	Essian, Jim	82D	369	$.01	$.06
Eichhorn, Mark	87D	321	$.01	$.05	Essian, Jim	83D	478	$.01	$.06
Eichhorn, Mark	88D	121	$.01	$.04	Essian, Jim	84D	629	$.05	$.20
Eichhorn, Mark	90DL	472	$.05	$.25	Eufemia, Frank	86D	513	$.01	$.08
Eichhorn, Mark	91D	318	$.01	$.04	Evans, Barry	82D	271	$.01	$.06
Eichhorn, Mark	92D	181	$.01	$.04	Evans, Darrell	81D	192	$.05	$.20
Eichhorn, Mark	92DL	97	$.01	$.06	Evans, Darrell	82D	398	$.05	$.25
Eiland, Dave	89D	481	$.01	$.10	Evans, Darrell	83D	251	$.01	$.15
Eiland, Dave	91D	354	$.01	$.04	Evans, Darrell	84D	431	$.05	$.25
Eiland, Dave	91DL	184	$.01	$.08	Evans, Darrell	85D	227	$.03	$.10
Eiland, Dave	92DL	488	$.01	$.06	Evans, Darrell	86D	369	$.01	$.08
Eisenreich, Jim	88D	343	$.01	$.04	Evans, Darrell	87D	398	$.01	$.05
Eisenreich, Jim	90D	238	$.01	$.04	Evans, Darrell	88D	250	$.01	$.04
Eisenreich, Jim	90DL	278	$.05	$.25	Evans, Darrell	89D	533	$.01	$.04
Eisenreich, Jim	91D	448	$.01	$.04	Evans, Dwight	81D	458	$.05	$.35
Eisenreich, Jim	92D	297	$.01	$.04	Evans, Dwight	82D	109	$.05	$.25
Eisenreich, Jim	92DL	295	$.01	$.06	Evans, Dwight	82DK	7	$.01	$.15

DONRUSS

Player	Year	No.	VG	EX/MT	Player	Year	No.	VG	EX/MT
Evans, Dwight	83D	452	$ .05	$ .20	Ferguson, Joe	83D	604	$ .01	$ .06
Evans, Dwight	84D	395	$ .10	$ .50	Fermin, Felix	88D	144	$ .01	$ .04
Evans, Dwight	85D	294	$ .05	$ .20	Fermin, Felix	89D	565	$ .01	$ .04
Evans, Dwight	86D	249	$ .05	$ .20	Fermin, Felix	89DTR	33	$ .01	$ .05
Evans, Dwight	87D	129	$ .01	$ .10	Fermin, Felix	90D	191	$ .01	$ .04
Evans, Dwight	88D	216	$ .01	$ .15	Fermin, Felix	91D	537	$ .01	$ .04
Evans, Dwight	88DK	16	$ .01	$ .15	Fermin, Felix	91DL	137	$ .01	$ .08
Evans, Dwight	89D	240	$ .01	$ .04	Fermin, Felix	92D	242	$ .01	$ .04
Evans, Dwight	90D	122	$ .01	$ .04	Fermin, Felix	93D	597	$ .01	$ .05
Evans, Dwight	90DL	235	$ .05	$ .25	Fermin, Felix	93DL	215	$ .01	$ .15
Evans, Dwight	91D	122	$ .01	$ .04	Fernandez, Alex	91D	59	$ .05	$ .20
Evans, Dwight	91DL	266	$ .01	$ .08	Fernandez, Alex	91DL	296	$ .05	$ .25
Evans, Dwight	91DLS	2	$ .01	$ .08	Fernandez, Alex	91DLS	31	$ .05	$ .35
Evans, Dwight	92D	502	$ .01	$ .04	Fernandez, Alex	92D	191	$ .01	$ .05
Fahey, Bill	81D	361	$ .01	$ .06	Fernandez, Alex	92DL	85	$ .01	$ .06
Fahey, Bill	83D	281	$ .01	$ .06	Fernandez, Alex	92DLS	152	$ .01	$ .06
Fajardo, Hector	92DRR	419	$ .01	$ .10	Fernandez, Alex	93D	139	$ .01	$ .05
Falcone, Pete	81D	395	$ .01	$ .06	Fernandez, Alex	93DL	41	$ .01	$ .15
Falcone, Pete	82D	380	$ .01	$ .06	Fernandez, Sid	84DRR	44	$1.25	$5.00
Falcone, Pete	83D	182	$ .01	$ .06	Fernandez, Sid	85D	563	$ .10	$ .50
Falcone, Pete	84D	385	$ .05	$ .20	Fernandez, Sid	86D	625	$ .05	$ .20
Fanning, Jim	82D	492	$ .01	$ .06	Fernandez, Sid	87D	323	$ .01	$ .15
Faries, Paul	91DLS	243	$ .01	$ .08	Fernandez, Sid	88D	118	$ .01	$ .10
Faries, Paul	91DR	16	$ .01	$ .05	Fernandez, Sid	89D	471	$ .01	$ .10
Fariss, Monty	92DL	354	$ .01	$ .15	Fernandez, Sid	90D	572	$ .01	$ .04
Fariss, Monty	92DR	35	$ .01	$ .05	Fernandez, Sid	90DL	66	$ .05	$ .25
Fariss, Monty	93D	245	$ .01	$ .05	Fernandez, Sid	91D	97	$ .01	$ .04
Fariss, Monty	93D	753	$ .01	$ .05	Fernandez, Sid	92D	719	$ .01	$ .04
Farmer, Ed	81D	40	$ .01	$ .06	Fernandez, Sid	92DL	519	$ .01	$ .06
Farmer, Ed	82D	482	$ .01	$ .06	Fernandez, Sid	93D	566	$ .01	$ .05
Farmer, Ed	83D	471	$ .01	$ .06	Fernandez , Sid	93DL	2	$ .01	$ .15
Farmer, Howard	91D	734	$ .01	$ .10	Fernandez, Tony	84DRR	32	$1.25	$5.00
Farmer, Howard	92D	779	$ .01	$ .04	Fernandez, Tony	85D	390	$ .10	$ .50
Farr, Steve	85D	653	$ .10	$ .50	Fernandez, Tony	86D	119	$ .05	$ .20
Farr, Steve	86D	588	$ .01	$ .08	Fernandez, Tony	87D	72	$ .01	$ .15
Farr, Steve	87D	301	$ .01	$ .05	Fernandez, Tony	88D	319	$ .01	$ .15
Farr, Steve	88D	378	$ .01	$ .04	Fernandez, Tony	88DK	12	$ .01	$ .15
Farr, Steve	89D	356	$ .01	$ .04	Fernandez, Tony	89D	206	$ .01	$ .04
Farr, Steve	90D	356	$ .01	$ .04	Fernandez, Tony	90D	149	$ .01	$ .04
Farr, Steve	91D	365	$ .01	$ .04	Fernandez, Tony	90DL	53	$ .05	$ .25
Farr, Steve	91DL	348	$ .01	$ .08	Fernandez, Tony	91D	524	$ .01	$ .08
Farr, Steve	91DLS	92	$ .01	$ .08	Fernandez, Tony	91DL	315	$ .01	$ .08
Farr, Steve	92D	735	$ .01	$ .04	Fernandez, Tony	91DLS	244	$ .01	$ .08
Farr, Steve	92DL	20	$ .01	$ .06	Fernandez, Tony	92D	362	$ .01	$ .08
Farr, Steve	93D	21	$ .01	$ .05	Fernandez, Tony	92DL	187	$ .01	$ .06
Farrell, John	88DRR	42	$ .01	$ .15	Fernandez, Tony	92DLS	103	$ .01	$ .06
Farrell, John	89D	320	$ .01	$ .10	Fernandez, Tony	93D	674	$ .01	$ .05
Farrell, John	90D	232	$ .01	$ .05	Fetters, Mike	90DRR	35	$ .01	$ .10
Farrell, John	90DL	22	$ .05	$ .25	Fetters, Mike	91D	565	$ .01	$ .04
Farrell, John	91D	106	$ .01	$ .04	Fetters, Mike	92D	491	$ .01	$ .04
Farrell, John	91DLS	42	$ .01	$ .08	Fetters, Mike	92DL	460	$ .01	$ .06
Farris, Monty	91D	455	$ .01	$ .10	Fetters, Mike	93D	573	$ .01	$ .05
Fassero, Jeff	91DR	28	$ .01	$ .05	Fidrych, Mark	81D	8	$ .01	$ .06
Fassero, Jeff	92D	717	$ .01	$ .04	Fielder, Cecil	86D	512	$6.50	$26.00
Fassero, Jeff	93D	642	$ .01	$ .05	Fielder, Cecil	88D	565	$ .05	$ .35
Fassero, Jeff	93DL	91	$ .01	$ .15	Fielder, Cecil	89D	442	$ .05	$ .35
Felder, Mike	86D	634	$ .01	$ .15	Fielder, Cecil	90DL	165	$ .20	$2.00
Felder, Mike	87D	295	$ .01	$ .05	Fielder, Cecil	91D	451	$ .01	$ .15
Felder, Mike	88D	397	$ .01	$ .04	Fielder, Cecil	91DBC	5	$ .01	$ .10
Felder, Mike	90D	609	$ .01	$ .04	Fielder, Cecil	91DK	3	$ .01	$ .10
Felder, Mike	90DL	480	$ .05	$ .25	Fielder, Cecil	91DL	106	$ .10	$ .50
Felder, Mike	91D	535	$ .01	$ .04	Fielder, Cecil	91DLP	18	$1.25	$5.00
Felder, Mike	91DL	445	$ .01	$ .08	Fielder, Cecil	91DLS	53	$ .10	$ .50
Felder, Mike	92D	182	$ .01	$ .04	Fielder, Cecil	91DMVP	397	$ .01	$ .15
Felix, Junior	89DR	55	$ .05	$ .20	Fielder, Cecil	92D	206	$ .01	$ .15
Felix, Junior	90D	70	$ .05	$ .20	Fielder, Cecil	92DAS	27	$ .01	$ .15
Felix, Junior	90DL	422	$ .10	$ .50	Fielder, Cecil	92DL	153	$ .05	$ .25
Felix, Junior	91D	323	$ .01	$ .04	Fielder, Cecil	92DLS	173	$ .10	$ .40
Felix, Junior	91DL	435	$ .01	$ .08	Fielder, Cecil	93D	541	$ .01	$ .10
Felix, Junior	92D	217	$ .01	$ .04	Fielder, Cecil	93DK	15	$ .75	$3.00
Felix, Junior	92DL	118	$ .01	$ .06	Fields, Bruce	87DRR	47	$ .01	$ .05
Felix, Junior	93D	197	$ .01	$ .05	Figueroa, Ben	92DR	36	$ .01	$ .05
Felix, Junior	93D	771	$ .01	$ .05	Figueroa, Jesus	81D	556	$ .01	$ .06
Felton, Terry	83D	354	$ .01	$ .06	Filer, Tom	86D	439	$ .01	$ .08
Ferguson, Joe	81D	177	$ .01	$ .06	Filer, Tom	90D	687	$ .01	$ .04

DONRUSS

Player	Year	No.	VG	EX/MT
Filson, Pete	84D	194	$ .05	$ .20
Filson, Pete	85D	607	$ .01	$ .10
Filson, Pete	86D	436	$ .01	$ .08
Fimple, Jack	84D	372	$ .05	$ .20
Fingers, Rollie	81D	2	$ .10	$1.00
Fingers, Rollie	82D	28	$ .10	$ .75
Fingers, Rollie	83D	78	$ .10	$ .50
Fingers, Rollie	83DK	2	$ .05	$ .25
Fingers, Rollie	84D#A	0	$1.25	$5.00
Fingers, Rollie	85D	292	$ .05	$ .35
Fingers, Rollie	86D	229	$ .05	$ .35
Finley, Chuck	87D	407	$ .10	$ .50
Finley, Chuck	88D	530	$ .01	$ .10
Finley, Chuck	89D	226	$ .01	$ .10
Finley, Chuck	90D	344	$ .01	$ .04
Finley, Chuck	90DL	162	$ .05	$ .35
Finley, Chuck	91D	692	$ .01	$ .04
Finley, Chuck	91DK	26	$ .01	$ .05
Finley, Chuck	91DL	45	$ .01	$ .08
Finley, Chuck	91DLP	15	$ .10	$1.00
Finley, Chuck	91DLS	24	$ .01	$ .08
Finley, Chuck	92D	255	$ .01	$ .04
Finley, Chuck	92DL	450	$ .01	$ .06
Finley, Chuck	92DLS	145	$ .01	$ .06
Finley, Chuck	93D	225	$ .01	$ .05
Finley, Steve	89DR	47	$ .05	$ .35
Finley, Steve	90D	215	$ .01	$ .10
Finley, Steve	90DL	329	$ .10	$ .50
Finley, Steve	91D	355	$ .01	$ .04
Finley, Steve	91DL	231	$ .01	$ .08
Finley, Steve	91DLS	176	$ .01	$ .08
Finley, Steve	92D	197	$ .01	$ .04
Finely, Steve	92DL	66	$ .01	$ .06
Finley, Steve	92DLS	35	$ .01	$ .06
Finley, Steve	93D	192	$ .01	$ .05
Fischlin, Mike	83D	489	$ .01	$ .06
Fischlin, Mike	85D	495	$ .01	$ .10
Fishel, John	89D	443	$ .01	$ .10
Fisher, Brian	86D	492	$ .05	$ .25
Fisher, Brian	87D	340	$ .01	$ .05
Fisher, Brian	88D	415	$ .01	$ .04
Fisher, Brian	89D	126	$ .01	$ .04
Fisk, Carlton	81D	335	$ .20	$1.75
Fisk, Carlton	82D	495	$ .15	$1.50
Fisk, Carlton	82DK	20	$ .10	$ .50
Fisk, Carlton	83D	104	$ .10	$1.00
Fisk, Carlton	84D	302	$1.25	$5.00
Fisk, Carlton	85D	208	$ .15	$1.50
Fisk, Carlton	86D	366	$ .10	$ .75
Fisk, Carlton	87D	247	$ .05	$ .25
Fisk, Carlton	88D	260	$ .01	$ .15
Fisk, Carlton	89D	101	$ .01	$ .15
Fisk, Carlton	89DK	7	$ .01	$ .10
Fisk, Carlton	90D	58	$ .01	$ .10
Fisk, Carlton	90DBC	19	$ .01	$ .10
Fisk, Carlton	90DL	10	$ .10	$1.00
Fisk, Carlton	90DL	174	$ .05	$ .26
Fisk, Carlton	91D	108	$ .01	$ .10
Fisk, Carlton	91DBC	6	$ .01	$ .10
Fisk, Carlton	91DL	384	$ .05	$ .25
Fisk, Carlton	91DLP	16	$ .75	$3.00
Fisk, Carlton	91DLS	32	$ .05	$ .25
Fisk, Carlton	92D	543	$ .01	$ .10
Fisk, Carlton	92DL	303	$ .01	$ .15
Fisk, Carlton	93D	519	$ .01	$ .10
Fitzgerald, Mike	84D	482	$ .05	$ .20
Fitzgerald, Mike	85D	238	$ .01	$ .10
Fitzgerald, Mike	86D	97	$ .01	$ .08
Fitzgerald, Mike	87D	345	$ .01	$ .05
Fitzgerald, Mike	88D	159	$ .01	$ .04
Fitzgerald, Mike	89D	456	$ .01	$ .04
Fitzgerald, Mike	90D	392	$ .01	$ .04
Fitzgerald, Mike	91D	82	$ .01	$ .04
Fitzgerald, Mike	91DLS	196	$ .01	$ .08
Fitzgerald, Mike	92DL	371	$ .01	$ .06

Player	Year	No.	VG	EX/MT
Fitzgerald, Mike	93D	757	$ .01	$ .05
Flaherty, John	92DL	439	$ .01	$ .15
Flaherty, John	92DR	37	$ .01	$ .05
Flaherty, John	93D	561	$ .01	$ .05
Flanagan, Mike	81D	234	$ .01	$ .06
Flanagan, Mike	82D	329	$ .01	$ .06
Flanagan, Mike	83D	105	$ .01	$ .06
Flanagan, Mike	84D	169	$ .05	$ .20
Flanagan, Mike	85D	88	$ .01	$ .10
Flanagan, Mike	86D	576	$ .01	$ .08
Flanagan, Mike	87D	459	$ .01	$ .05
Flanagan, Mike	88D	636	$ .01	$ .04
Flanagan, Mike	89D	324	$ .01	$ .04
Flanagan, Mike	90D	324	$ .01	$ .04
Flanagan, Mike	91DL	479	$ .01	$ .08
Flanagan, Mike	92D	196	$ .01	$ .04
Flannery, Tim	82D	61	$ .01	$ .06

Flannery, Tim	83D	472	$ .01	$ .06
Flannery, Tim	84D	202	$ .05	$ .20
Flannery, Tim	85D	551	$ .01	$ .10
Flannery, Tim	86D	383	$ .01	$ .08
Flannery, Tim	87D	287	$ .01	$ .05
Flannery, Tim	88D	328	$ .01	$ .04
Flannery, Tim	89D	364	$ .01	$ .04
Fleming, Dave	92DL	494	$ .10	$ .50
Fleming, Dave	92DRR	404	$ .05	$ .35
Fleming, Dave	93D	243	$ .01	$ .10
Fletcher, Darrin	91DRR	47	$ .01	$ .15
Fletcher, Darrin	92D	319	$ .01	$ .04
Fletcher, Darrin	92DL	264	$ .01	$ .06
Fletcher, Darrin	93D	378	$ .01	$ .05
Fletcher, Darrin	93DL	165	$ .01	$ .15
Fletcher, Scott	82D	554	$ .05	$ .25
Fletcher, Scott	84D	452	$ .05	$ .20
Fletcher, Scott	85D	330	$ .01	$ .10
Fletcher, Scott	86D	282	$ .01	$ .08
Fletcher, Scott	87D	304	$ .01	$ .05
Fletcher, Scott	88D	180	$ .01	$ .04
Fletcher, Scott	88DK	11	$ .01	$ .05
Fletcher, Scott	89D	142	$ .01	$ .04
Fletcher, Scott	90D	455	$ .01	$ .04
Fletcher, Scott	90DL	141	$ .05	$ .25
Fletcher, Scott	91D	276	$ .01	$ .04

DONRUSS

Player	Year	No.	VG	EX/MT	Player	Year	No.	VG	EX/MT
Fletcher, Scott	91DL	306	$ .01	$ .08	Fowlkes, Alan	83D	46	$ .01	$ .06
Fletcher, Scott	91DLS	33	$ .01	$ .08	Fox, Eric	92DR	39	$ .01	$ .05
Fletcher, Scott	92DL	234	$ .01	$ .06	Fox, Eric	93D	287	$ .01	$ .10
Fletcher, Scott	92DLS	193	$ .01	$ .06	Franco, John	85D	164	$ .10	$1.00
Fletcher, Scott	93D	631	$ .01	$ .05	Franco, John	86D	487	$ .05	$ .20
Flynn, Doug	81D	394	$ .01	$ .06	Franco, John	87D	289	$ .01	$ .10
Flynn, Doug	82D	427	$ .01	$ .06	Franco, John	88D	123	$ .01	$ .04
Flynn, Doug	83D	240	$ .01	$ .06	Franco, John	89D	233	$ .01	$ .10
Flynn, Doug	84D	254	$ .05	$ .20	Franco, John	90D	124	$ .01	$ .10
Flynn, Doug	85D	463	$ .01	$ .10	Franco, John	90DK	14	$ .01	$ .05
Foley, Marvis	81D	399	$ .01	$ .06	Franco, John	90DL	356	$ .05	$ .25
Foley, Marvis	83D	652	$ .01	$ .06	Franco, John	91D	322	$ .01	$ .04
Foley, Marvis	85D	500	$ .01	$ .10	Franco, John	91DL	437	$ .01	$ .08
Foley, Tom	84D	81	$ .05	$ .20	Franco, John	91DLS	203	$ .01	$ .08
Foley, Tom	85D	569	$ .01	$ .10	Franco, John	92D	186	$ .01	$ .04
Foley, Tom	86D	549	$ .01	$ .08	Franco, John	92DL	174	$ .01	$ .06
Foley, Tom	87D	504	$ .01	$ .05	Franco, John	92DLS	64	$ .01	$ .06
Foley, Tom	88D	303	$ .01	$ .04	Franco, John	93D	146	$ .01	$ .05
Foley, Tom	89D	342	$ .01	$ .04	Franco, John	93DL	112	$ .01	$ .15
Foley, Tom	90D	274	$ .01	$ .04	Franco, Julio	83D	525	$1.50	$6.00
Foley, Tom	90DL	292	$ .05	$ .25	Franco, Julio	84D	216	$ .75	$3.00
Foley, Tom	91D	180	$ .01	$ .04	Franco, Julio	85D	94	$ .10	$1.00
Foley, Tom	91DLSP	13	$ .20	$2.00	Franco, Julio	86D	216	$ .10	$ .50
Foley, Tom	92D	538	$ .01	$ .04	Franco, Julio	87D	131	$ .05	$ .20
Foley, Tom	92DL	372	$ .01	$ .06	Franco, Julio	88D	156	$ .01	$ .10
Foley, Tom	93D	727	$ .01	$ .05	Franco, Julio	88DK	10	$ .01	$ .10
Foli, Tim	81D	13	$ .01	$ .06	Franco, Julio	89D	310	$ .01	$ .10
Foli, Tim	82D	376	$ .01	$ .06	Franco, Julio	89DTR	31	$ .05	$ .20
Foli, Tim	83D	342	$ .01	$ .06	Franco, Julio	90D	142	$ .01	$ .10
Foli, Tim	84D	474	$ .05	$ .20	Franco, Julio	90DAS	701	$ .01	$ .10
Fontenot, Ray	84D	370	$ .05	$ .20	Franco, Julio	90DBC	14	$ .01	$ .10
Fontenot, Ray	85D	248	$ .01	$ .10	Franco, Julio	90DL	205	$ .05	$ .35
Fontenot, Ray	86D	361	$ .01	$ .08	Franco, Julio	91D	192	$ .01	$ .04
Foote, Barry	81D	558	$ .01	$ .06	Franco, Julio	91DL	228	$ .01	$ .15
Foote, Barry	82D	83	$ .01	$ .06	Franco, Julio	91DLS	123	$ .01	$ .08
Ford, Curt	87D	454	$ .01	$ .05	Franco, Julio	92D	741	$ .01	$ .10
Ford, Curt	88D	417	$ .01	$ .04	Franco, Julio	92DK	4	$ .10	$1.00
Ford, Curt	90D	694	$ .01	$ .04	Franco, Julio	92DL	119	$ .01	$ .06
Ford, Dan	81D	54	$ .01	$ .06	Franco, Julio	92DLS	241	$ .01	$ .06
Ford, Dan	82D	468	$ .01	$ .06	Franco, Julio	93D	451	$ .01	$ .05
Ford, Dan	83D	509	$ .01	$ .06	Franco, Julio	93DL	27	$ .01	$ .15
Ford, Dan	84D	367	$ .05	$ .20	Francona, Terry	82D	627	$ .01	$ .06
Ford, Dan	85D	489	$ .01	$ .10	Francona, Terry	83D	592	$ .01	$ .06
Ford, Dave	81D	552	$ .01	$ .06	Francona, Terry	84D	463	$ .05	$ .20
Ford, Dave	82D	597	$ .01	$ .06	Francona, Terry	85D	132	$ .01	$ .10
Forsch, Bob	81D	69	$ .01	$ .06	Francona, Terry	86D	401	$ .01	$ .08
Forsch, Bob	82D	91	$ .01	$ .06	Fraser, Will	87DR	9	$ .01	$ .07
Forsch, Bob	83D	64	$ .01	$ .06	Fraser, Will	87DRR	40	$ .01	$ .05
Forsch, Bob	84D	168	$ .05	$ .20	Fraser, Willie	88D	135	$ .01	$ .04
Forsch, Bob	86D	353	$ .01	$ .08	Fraser, Willie	89D	567	$ .01	$ .04
Forsch, Bob	87D	540	$ .01	$ .05	Fraser, Willie	90D	587	$ .01	$ .04
Forsch, Bob	88D	111	$ .01	$ .04	Fraser, Willie	91D	379	$ .01	$ .04
Forsch, Bob	89D	118	$ .01	$ .04	Fraser, Willie	92D	755	$ .01	$ .04
Forsch, Ken	81D	141	$ .01	$ .06	Frazier, George	81D	310	$ .01	$ .06
Forsch, Ken	82D	393	$ .01	$ .06	Frazier, George	82D	584	$ .01	$ .06
Forsch, Ken	83D	164	$ .01	$ .06	Frazier, George	83D	535	$ .01	$ .06
Forsch, Ken	84D	280	$ .05	$ .20	Frazier, George	84D	591	$ .05	$ .20
Forster, Terry	82D	362	$ .01	$ .06	Frazier, George	85D	167	$ .01	$ .10
Forster, Terry	83D	453	$ .01	$ .06	Frazier, George	86D	411	$ .01	$ .08
Forster, Terry	86D	432	$ .01	$ .08	Frazier, George	87D	564	$ .01	$ .05
Fortugno, Tim	92DR	38	$ .01	$ .05	Frazier, George	88D	443	$ .01	$ .04
Fortugno, Tim	93D	299	$ .01	$ .10	Freeman, Marvin	87D	576	$ .01	$ .15
Fossas, Tony	90D	457	$ .01	$ .04	Freeman, Marvin	89D	631	$ .01	$ .04
Fossas, Tony	91DL	276	$ .01	$ .08	Freeman, Marvin	91D	619	$ .01	$ .04
Fossas, Tony	92D	645	$ .01	$ .04	Freeman, Marvin	92D	603	$ .01	$ .04
Fossas, Tony	93D	195	$ .01	$ .05	Freeman, Marvin	93D	662	$ .01	$ .05
Foster, George	81D	65	$ .05	$ .20	Freeman, Marvin	93DL	11	$ .01	$ .15
Foster, George	82D	274	$ .05	$ .20	Fregosi, Jim	81D	414	$ .01	$ .06
Foster, George	83D	427	$ .05	$ .20	Frey, Jim	81D	464	$ .01	$ .06
Foster, George	83DK	6	$ .05	$ .20	Frey, Steve	91D	292	$ .01	$ .04
Foster, George	84D	312	$ .05	$ .35	Frey, Steve	91DL	153	$ .01	$ .08
Foster, George	85D	603	$ .03	$ .10	Frey, Steve	92D	660	$ .01	$ .04
Foster, George	86D	116	$ .01	$ .15	Frey, Steve	92DL	418	$ .01	$ .06
Foster, Steve	92DRR	420	$ .01	$ .10	Frey, Steve	93D	533	$ .01	$ .05
Foster, Steve	93D	666	$ .01	$ .05					

DONRUSS

Player	Year	No.	VG	EX/MT	Player	Year	No.	VG	EX/MT
Frobel, Doug	84DRR	38	$ .05	$ .25	Gagne, Greg	88D	441	$ .01	$ .04
Frohwirth, Todd	88DR	3	$ .01	$ .07	Gagne, Greg	89D	318	$ .01	$ .04
Frohwirth, Todd	89D	587	$ .01	$ .04	Gagne, Greg	90D	237	$ .01	$ .04
Frohwirth, Todd	90D	631	$ .01	$ .04	Gagne, Greg	90DL	302	$ .05	$ .25
Frohwirth, Todd	92D	317	$ .01	$ .04	Gagne, Greg	91D	284	$ .01	$ .04
Frohwirth, Todd	93D	513	$ .01	$ .05	Gagne, Greg	91DL	426	$ .01	$ .08
Frost, Dave	81D	52	$ .01	$ .06	Gagne, Greg	91DLS	84	$ .01	$ .08
Frost, Dave	82D	290	$ .01	$ .06	Gagne, Greg	92D	204	$ .01	$ .04
Frye, Jeff	92DR	40	$ .01	$ .05	Gagne, Greg	92DL	146	$ .01	$ .06
Frye, Jeff	93D	724	$ .01	$ .05	Gagne, Greg	92DLS	203	$ .01	$ .06
Fryman, Travis	91D	768	$ .10	$ .50	Gagne, Greg	93D	633	$ .01	$ .05
Fryman, Travis	91DL	149	$ .75	$3.00	Gainey, Ty	86DRR	31	$ .01	$ .10
Fryman, Travis	91DLS	54	$ .75	$3.00	Gainey, Ty	87D	533	$ .01	$ .05
Fryman, Travis	92D	349	$ .05	$ .35	Gainey, Ty	88D	578	$ .01	$ .04
Fryman, Travis	92DL	304	$ .10	$1.00	Galarraga, Andres	86DR	7	$ .10	$1.00
Fryman, Travis	92DLS	174	$ .10	$ .75	Galarraga, Andres	86DRR	33	$ .20	$2.00
Fryman, Travis	93D	127	$ .01	$ .10	Galarraga, Andres	87D	303	$ .05	$ .20
Fryman, Travis	93DL	16	$ .10	$1.00	Galarraga, Andres	88D	282	$ .01	$ .15
Fryman, Woodie	81D	331	$ .01	$ .06	Galarraga, Andres	89D	130	$ .01	$ .10
Fryman, Woodie	82D	68	$ .01	$ .06	Galarraga, Andres	89DBC	16	$ .01	$ .05
Fryman, Woodie	83D	162	$ .01	$ .06	Galarraga, Andres	89DK	14	$ .01	$ .00
Fuentes, Mike	84DRR	40	$ .05	$ .25	Galarraga, Andres	90D	97	$ .01	$ .04
Fulgham, John	81D	70	$ .01	$ .06	Galarraga, Andres	90DL	450	$ .05	$ .25
Funderburk, Mark	86D	630	$ .01	$ .08	Galarraga, Andres	91D	68	$ .01	$ .04
Gaetti, Gary	83D	53	$ .10	$ .50	Galarraga, Andres	91DL	110	$ .01	$ .08
Gaetti, Gary	84D	314	$ .10	$ .50	Galarraga, Andres	91DLS	197	$ .01	$ .08
Gaetti, Gary	85D	242	$ .05	$ .25	Galarraga, Andres	92D	355	$ .01	$ .04
Gaetti, Gary	86D	314	$ .05	$ .25	Galarraga, Andres	92DL	449	$ .01	$ .06
Gaetti, Gary	87D	122	$ .01	$ .05	Galarraga, Andres	93D	764	$ .01	$ .05
Gaetti, Gary	88D	194	$ .01	$ .15	Gale, Rich	81D	462	$ .01	$ .06
Gaetti, Gary	88DK	19	$ .01	$ .05	Gale, Rich	82D	138	$ .01	$ .06
Gaetti, Gary	89D	64	$ .01	$ .10	Gale, Rich	83D	172	$ .01	$ .06
Gaetti, Gary	90D	151	$ .01	$ .04	Gale, Rich	84D	140	$ .05	$ .20
Gaetti, Gary	90DL	97	$ .05	$ .25	Gallagher, Dave	88DR	7	$ .05	$ .20
Gaetti, Gary	91D	547	$ .01	$ .04	Gallagher, Dave	89D	384	$ .01	$ .10
Gaetti, Gary	91DL	303	$ .01	$ .08	Gallagher, Dave	90D	219	$ .01	$ .04
Gaetti, Gary	91DLS	25	$ .01	$ .08	Gallagher, Dave	92D	377	$ .01	$ .04
Gaetti, Gary	92D	96	$ .01	$ .04	Gallagher, Dave	92DL	224	$ .01	$ .06
Gaetti, Gary	92DL	107	$ .01	$ .06	Gallagher, Dave	93D	170	$ .01	$ .05
Gaetti, Gary	93D	517	$ .01	$ .05	Gallego, Mike	86D	156	$ .01	$ .15
Gaff, Brent	83D	553	$ .01	$ .06	Gallego, Mike	88D	379	$ .01	$ .04
Gagne, Greg	84DRR	39	$ .10	$ .75	Gallego, Mike	89D	422	$ .01	$ .04
Gagne, Greg	86D	558	$ .01	$ .10	Gallego, Mike	90D	361	$ .01	$ .04
					Gallego, Mike	90DL	121	$ .05	$ .25
					Gallego, Mike	91D	158	$ .01	$ .04
					Gallego, Mike	91DL	78	$ .01	$ .08
					Gallego, Mike	92D	314	$ .01	$ .04
					Gallego, Mike	92DL	236	$ .01	$ .06
					Gallego, Mike	92DLS	211	$ .01	$ .06
					Gallego, Mike	93D	81	$ .01	$ .05
					Gallego, Mike	93DL	96	$ .01	$ .15
					Gamble, Oscar	81D	229	$ .01	$ .06
					Gamble, Oscar	82D	360	$ .01	$ .06
					Gamble, Oscar	83D	461	$ .01	$ .06
					Gant, Ron	88D	654	$ .20	$2.00
					Gant, Ron	88DR	47	$ .25	$2.50
					Gant, Ron	89D	50	$ .10	$ .40
					Gant, Ron	90D	475	$ .05	$ .25
					Gant, Ron	90DL	376	$ .20	$2.00
					Gant, Ron	91D	507	$ .01	$ .10
					Gant, Ron	91DK	10	$ .01	$ .05
					Gant, Ron	91DL	129	$ .05	$ .35
					Gant, Ron	91DLS	144	$ .05	$ .25
					Gant, Ron	92D	284	$ .01	$ .10
					Gant, Ron	92DL	15	$ .01	$ .15
					Gant, Ron	92DLS	3	$ .01	$ .15
					Gant, Ron	93D	210	$ .01	$ .05
					Gantner, Jim	81D	204	$ .01	$ .06
					Gantner, Jim	82D	406	$ .01	$ .06
					Gantner, Jim	83D	232	$ .01	$ .06
					Gantner, Jim	84D	115	$ .05	$ .20
					Gantner, Jim	85D	229	$ .01	$ .10
					Gantner, Jim	86D	115	$ .01	$ .08
					Gantner, Jim	87D	172	$ .01	$ .05
					Gantner, Jim	88D	214	$ .01	$ .04

| Gagne, Greg | 87D | 395 | $ .01 | $ .05 |

DONRUSS

Player	Year	No.	VG	EX/MT
Gantner, Jim	89D	264	$ .01	$ .04
Gantner, Jim	90D	291	$ .01	$ .04
Gantner, Jim	91D	703	$ .01	$ .04
Gantner, Jim	91DL	145	$ .01	$ .08
Gantner, Jim	92D	574	$ .01	$ .04
Garber, Gene	81D	77	$ .01	$ .06
Garber, Gene	82D	123	$ .01	$ .06
Garber, Gene	83D	223	$ .01	$ .06
Garber, Gene	84D	287	$ .05	$ .20
Garber, Gene	87D	414	$ .01	$ .05
Garber, Gene	88D	618	$ .01	$ .15
Garbey, Barbaro	85D	456	$ .01	$ .10
Garbey, Barbaro	86D	349	$ .01	$ .08
Garces, Rich	91DRR	420	$ .01	$ .10
Garces, Rich	92D	516	$ .01	$ .04
Garcia, Carlos	92DRR	14	$ .01	$ .05
Garcia, Carlos	93D	598	$ .01	$ .05
Garcia, Damaso	81D	269	$ .01	$ .10
Garcia, Damaso	82D	479	$ .01	$ .06
Garcia, Damaso	83D	54	$ .01	$ .06
Garcia, Damaso	84D	241	$ .05	$ .20
Garcia, Damaso	85D	315	$ .01	$ .10
Garcia, Damaso	86D	241	$ .01	$ .08
Garcia, Damaso	87D	614	$ .01	$ .05
Garcia, Damaso	88D	414	$ .01	$ .04
Garcia, Dave	81D	442	$ .01	$ .06
Garcia, Dave	82D	337	$ .01	$ .06
Garcia, Kiko	81D	514	$ .01	$ .06
Garcia, Kiko	82D	470	$ .01	$ .06
Garcia, Kiko	83D	569	$ .01	$ .06
Garcia, Kiko	84D	545	$ .05	$ .20
Garcia, Miguel	89D	622	$ .01	$ .04
Garcia, Ramon	91DR	13	$ .01	$ .10
Garcia, Ramon	92D	658	$ .01	$ .04
Garcia, Ramon	92DR	41	$ .01	$ .05
Gardenhire, Ron	82D	649	$ .01	$ .06
Gardenhire, Ron	83D	175	$ .01	$ .06
Gardenhire, Ron	85D	360	$ .01	$ .10
Gardiner, Mike	91DR	46	$ .01	$ .10
Gardiner, Mike	91DRR	417	$ .01	$ .10
Gardiner, Mike	92D	290	$ .01	$ .04
Gardiner, Mike	92DL	482	$ .01	$ .06
Gardiner, Mike	93D	515	$ .01	$ .05
Gardner, Billy	82D	591	$ .01	$ .06
Gardner, Chris	92DL	8	$ .01	$ .15
Gardner, Chris	92DRR	413	$ .01	$ .10
Gardner, Jeff	93D	470	$ .01	$ .05
Gardner, Mark	90DL	371	$ .10	$ .50
Gardner, Mark	90DR	20	$ .01	$ .05
Gardner, Mark	90DRR	40	$ .01	$ .10
Gardner, Mark	91D	443	$ .01	$ .04
Gardner, Mark	92D	238	$ .01	$ .04
Gardner, Mark	92DL	512	$ .01	$ .06
Gardner, Mark	93D	64	$ .01	$ .05
Gardner, Wes	88D	634	$ .01	$ .15
Gardner, Wes	89D	541	$ .01	$ .04
Gardner, Wes	90D	541	$ .01	$ .04
Gardner, Wes	90DL	407	$ .05	$ .25
Garland, Wayne	81D	440	$ .01	$ .06
Garland, Wayne	82D	489	$ .01	$ .06
Garner, Phil	81D	372	$ .01	$ .06
Garner, Phil	82D	544	$ .01	$ .06
Garner, Phil	83D	270	$ .01	$ .06
Garner, Phil	84D	354	$ .05	$ .20
Garner, Phil	85D	161	$ .01	$ .10
Garner, Phil	86D	527	$ .01	$ .08
Garner, Phil	87D	358	$ .01	$ .05
Garrelts, Scott	84D	646	$ .05	$ .35
Garrelts, Scott	86D	309	$ .01	$ .08
Garrelts, Scott	87D	116	$ .01	$ .05
Garrelts, Scott	88D	80	$ .01	$ .04
Garrelts, Scott	89D	295	$ .01	$ .04
Garrelts, Scott	90D	217	$ .01	$ .04
Garrelts, Scott	90DL	41	$ .05	$ .25
Garrelts, Scott	91D	311	$ .01	$ .04

Player	Year	No.	VG	EX/MT
Garrelts, Scott	91DL	5	$ .01	$ .08
Garrelts, Scott	91DLS	255	$ .01	$ .08
Garvey, Steve	81D	56	$ .10	$ .75
Garvey, Steve	81D	176	$ .10	$ .75
Garvey, Steve	82D	84	$ .10	$ .50
Garvey, Steve	82DK	3	$ .05	$ .35

Player	Year	No.	VG	EX/MT
Garvey, Steve	83D	488	$ .10	$ .40
Garvey, Steve	84D	63	$ .10	$1.00
Garvey, Steve	85D	307	$ .05	$ .35
Garvey, Steve	86D	63	$ .05	$ .35
Garvey, Steve	87D	81	$ .05	$ .25
Garvin, Jerry	81D	150	$ .01	$ .06
Garvin, Jerry	82D	430	$ .01	$ .06
Garvin, Jerry	83D	227	$ .01	$ .06
Gates, Brent	92DR	42	$ .10	$ .40
Gates, Mike	83D	114	$ .01	$ .06
Gedman, Rich	82D	512	$ .05	$ .20
Gedman, Rich	83D	156	$ .01	$ .06
Gedman, Rich	84D	579	$ .05	$ .20
Gedman, Rich	85D	457	$ .01	$ .10
Gedman, Rich	86D	273	$ .01	$ .08
Gedman, Rich	87D	153	$ .01	$ .05
Gedman, Rich	88D	129	$ .01	$ .04
Gedman, Rich	89D	162	$ .01	$ .04
Gedman, Rich	90D	346	$ .01	$ .04
Gedman, Rich	90DL	478	$ .05	$ .25
Gedman, Rich	91DL	418	$ .01	$ .08
Gedman, Rich	92D	553	$ .01	$ .04
Gehrig, Lou	85D	635	$ .05	$ .25
Geisel, Dave	82D	633	$ .01	$ .06
Geisel, Dave	84D	645	$ .05	$ .20
George, Chris	92D	746	$ .01	$ .10
Gerber, Craig	86D	545	$ .01	$ .08
Geren, Bob	89DR	11	$ .01	$ .05
Geren, Bob	90D	395	$ .01	$ .05
Geren, Bob	90DL	182	$ .05	$ .25
Geren, Bob	91D	114	$ .01	$ .04
Gerhart, Ken	87DR	24	$ .01	$ .07
Gerhart, Ken	87DRR	30	$ .01	$ .05
Gerhart, Ken	88D	213	$ .01	$ .04
Geronimo, Cesar	81D	305	$ .01	$ .06
Geronimo, Cesar	82D	322	$ .01	$ .06
Geronimo, Cesar	83D	448	$ .01	$ .06
Geronimo, Cesar	84D	252	$ .05	$ .20

DONRUSS

Player	Year	No.	VG	EX/MT	Player	Year	No.	VG	EX/MT
Giamatti, Bart	90D	716	$.05	$.15	Glavine, Tom	93D	554	$.01	$.10
Gibbons, John	85D	116	$.01	$.10	Glavine, Tom	93DK	19	$.20	$2.00
Gibbons, John	87D	626	$.01	$.05	Gleaton, Jerry	88D	547	$.01	$.04
Gibson, Bob	84D	246	$.05	$.20	Gleaton, Jerry Don	89D	444	$.01	$.04
Gibson, Bob	85D	393	$.01	$.10	Gleaton, Jerry Don	91D	661	$.01	$.04
Gibson, Bob	86D	271	$.01	$.08	Gleaton, Jerry Don	91DL	135	$.01	$.08
Gibson, Kirk	82D	407	$.10	$1.00	Gleaton, Jerry Don	92D	607	$.01	$.04
Gibson, Kirk	83D	459	$.05	$.30	Glynn, Ed	83D	537	$.01	$.06
Gibson, Kirk	84D	593	$.10	$1.00	Goff, Jerry	90DL	476	$.05	$.25
Gibson, Kirk	85D	471	$.05	$.35	Goff, Jerry	91D	499	$.01	$.04
Gibson, Kirk	86D	125	$.05	$.25	Gohr, Greg	93D	605	$.01	$.10
Gibson, Kirk	86DK	1	$.05	$.25	Goltz, Dave	82D	604	$.01	$.06
Gibson, Kirk	87D	50	$.05	$.20	Gomez, Leo	91DL	35	$.10	$.75
Gibson, Kirk	88D	275	$.01	$.15	Gomez, Leo	91DLP	13	$.20	$2.00
Gibson, Kirk	89D	132	$.01	$.10	Gomez, Leo	91DLS	3	$.10	$.50
Gibson, Kirk	89DK	15	$.01	$.10	Gomez, Leo	91DRR	35	$.05	$.25
Gibson, Kirk	90D	368	$.01	$.04	Gomez, Leo	92D	199	$.01	$.10
Gibson, Kirk	90DL	173	$.05	$.25	Gomez, Leo	92DL	87	$.01	$.10
Gibson, Kirk	91D	445	$.01	$.04	Gomez, Leo	93D	31	$.01	$.05
Gibson, Kirk	91DL	249	$.01	$.08	Gomez, Leo	93DL	155	$.01	$.15
Gibson, Kirk	91DLS	66	$.01	$.08	Gomez, Luis	81D	88	$.01	$.06
Gibson, Kirk	92D	39	$.01	$.04	Gomez, Pat	93D	266	$.01	$.15
Gibson, Paul	88DR	19	$.01	$.07	Gonzales, Julio	82D	645	$.01	$.06
Gibson, Paul	89D	445	$.01	$.04	Gonzales, Rene	88D	582	$.01	$.15
Gibson, Paul	90D	657	$.01	$.04	Gonzales, R. C.	89D	377	$.01	$.04
Gibson, Paul	90DL	298	$.05	$.25	Gonzales, Rene	90D	401	$.01	$.04
Gibson, Paul	91D	353	$.01	$.04	Gonzales, Rene	91DL	490	$.01	$.08
Gibson, Paul	91DL	55	$.01	$.08	Gonzales, Rene	92D	274	$.01	$.04
Gibson, Paul	92D	375	$.01	$.04	Gonzales, Rene	93D	785	$.01	$.05
Gibson, Paul	92DL	461	$.01	$.06	Gonzalez, Denny	85D	600	$.01	$.10
Giles, Brian	84D	563	$.05	$.20	Gonzalez, Denny	86D	410	$.01	$.04
Gilkey, Bernard	90DL	353	$.15	$1.50	Gonzalez, German	89D	590	$.01	$.04
Gilkey, Bernard	91DL	286	$.05	$.20	Gonzalez, German	89DR	24	$.01	$.05
Gilkey, Bernard	91DLS	231	$.05	$.25	Gonzalez, Jose	87D	525	$.05	$.25
Gilkey, Bernard	91DRR	30	$.01	$.15	Gonzalez, Jose	88D	341	$.01	$.04
Gilkey, Bernard	92D	376	$.01	$.10	Gonzalez, Jose	90D	314	$.01	$.04
Gilkey, Bernard	93D	284	$.01	$.05	Gonzalez, Jose	91D	543	$.01	$.04
Gilkey, Bernard	93DL	99	$.05	$.25	Gonzalez, Juan	90DRR	33	$.20	$2.00
Girardi, Joe	89DR	23	$.01	$.05	Gonzalez, Juan	91D	371	$.05	$.35
Girardi, Joe	90D	404	$.01	$.05	Gonzalez, Juan	91DL	119	$1.00	$4.00
Girardi, Joe	90DL	289	$.05	$.25	Gonzalez, Juan	91DLS	124	$1.00	$4.00
Girardi, Joe	91D	184	$.01	$.04	Gonzalez, Juan	92D	393	$.10	$.50
Girardi, Joe	91DL	258	$.01	$.08	Gonzalez, Juan	92DL	62	$.15	$1.25
Girardi, Joe	91DLS	156	$.01	$.08	Gonzalez, Juan	92DLS	242	$.15	$1.50
Girardi, Joe	92D	175	$.01	$.04	Gonzalez, Juan	93D	555	$.05	$.25
Girardi, Joe	92DL	72	$.01	$.06	Gonzalez, Juan	93DK	7	$2.00	$8.00
Girardi, Joe	92DLS	13	$.01	$.06	Gonzalez, Juan	93DL	170	$.15	$1.50
Girardi, Joe	93D	736	$.01	$.05	Gonzalez, Luis	91D	690	$.05	$.35
Gladden, Dan	85D	567	$.10	$.45	Gonzalez, Luis	91DLBC	2	$.20	$2.00
Gladden, Dan	86D	187	$.01	$.08	Gonzalez, Luis	91DR	17	$.05	$.35
Gladden, Dan	87D	189	$.01	$.05	Gonzalez, Luis	92D	270	$.01	$.15
Gladden, Dan	88D	491	$.01	$.04	Gonzalez, Luis	92DL	160	$.01	$.06
Gladden, Dan	89D	391	$.01	$.04	Gonzalez, Luis	93D	404	$.01	$.05
Gladden, Dan	90D	182	$.01	$.04	Gonzalez, Luis	93DL	90	$.05	$.25
Gladden, Dan	90DK	22	$.01	$.05	Gooden, Dwight	85D	190	$2.00	$8.00
Gladden, Dan	90DL	254	$.05	$.25	Gooden, Dwight	86D	75	$.10	$1.00
Gladden, Dan	91D	228	$.01	$.04	Gooden, Dwight	86DK	26	$.10	$.40
Gladden, Dan	91DL	76	$.01	$.08	Gooden, Dwight	87D	199	$.10	$.40
Gladden, Dan	91DLS	85	$.01	$.08	Gooden, Dwight	88D	69	$.05	$.20
Gladden, Dan	92D	585	$.01	$.04	Gooden, Dwight	89D	270	$.01	$.15
Gladden, Dan	92DL	239	$.01	$.06	Gooden, Dwight	90D	171	$.01	$.10
Gladden, Dan	93D	467	$.01	$.05	Gooden, Dwight	90DL	139	$.10	$.50
Gladden, Dan	93DL	60	$.01	$.15	Gooden, Dwight	91D	266	$.10	$.10
Glavine, Tom	88D	644	$.20	$2.00	Gooden, Dwight	91DL	165	$.01	$.15
Glavine, Tom	89D	381	$.10	$.50	Gooden, Dwight	91DLP	7	$.20	$2.00
Glavine, Tom	90D	145	$.05	$.25	Gooden, Dwight	91DLS	204	$.01	$.15
Glavine, Tom	90DL	13	$1.75	$7.00	Gooden, Dwight	91DLSP	14	$.20	$2.00
Glavine, Tom	91D	132	$.05	$.20	Gooden, Dwight	92D	446	$.01	$.10
Glavine, Tom	91DL	172	$.10	$.75	Gooden, Dwight	92DK	15	$.10	$1.00
Glavine, Tom	91DLS	145	$.10	$.50	Gooden, Dwight	92DL	112	$.01	$.06
Glavine, Tom	92D	629	$.01	$.15	Gooden, Dwight	92DLS	65	$.01	$.06
Glavine, Tom	92DAS	426	$.01	$.10	Gooden, Dwight	93D	462	$.01	$.05
Glavine, Tom	92DBC	4	$.05	$.20	Gooden, Dwight	93DL	203	$.01	$.15
Glavine, Tom	92DL	279	$.05	$.25	Goodwin, Danny	81D	494	$.01	$.06
Glavine, Tom	92DLS	4	$.05	$.25	Goodwin, Danny	82D	305	$.01	$.06

DONRUSS

Player	Year	No.	VG	EX/MT	Player	Year	No.	VG	EX/MT
Goodwin, Tom	92DR	43	$ .01	$ .05	Green, Dallas	81D	415	$ .01	$ .06
Goodwin, Tom	93D	640	$ .01	$ .05	Green, David	83D	166	$ .01	$ .06
Gordon, Tom	89DR	4	$ .05	$ .20	Green, David	84D	425	$ .05	$ .20
Gordon, Tom	89DRR	45	$ .01	$ .15	Green, David	84D	625	$ .10	$ .75
Gordon, Tom	90D	297	$ .01	$ .10	Green, David	85D	303	$ .01	$ .10
Gordon, Tom	90DL	14	$ .05	$ .35	Green, David	86D	114	$ .01	$ .08
Gordon, Tom	91D	242	$ .01	$ .04	Greene, Tommy	90D	576	$ .05	$ .20
Gordon, Tom	91DL	132	$ .01	$ .08	Greene, Tommy	91D	635	$ .01	$ .10
Gordon, Tom	92D	250	$ .01	$ .04	Greene, Tommy	91DL	524	$ .01	$ .15
Gordon, Tom	92DL	68	$ .01	$ .06	Greene, Tommy	92D	94	$ .01	$ .04
Gordon, Tom	92DLS	182	$ .01	$ .06	Greene, Tommy	92D	109	$ .01	$ .04
Gordon, Tom	93D	497	$ .01	$ .05	Greene, Tommy	92DL	292	$ .01	$ .06
Gordon, Tom	93DL	211	$ .01	$ .15	Greene, Tommy	93D	568	$ .01	$ .05
Goryl, John	81D	527	$ .01	$ .06	Greene, Tommy	93DL	132	$ .01	$ .15
Gossage, Rich	81D	347	$ .05	$ .20	Greene, Willie	93D	143	$ .01	$ .15
Gossage, Rich	82D	283	$ .05	$ .20	Greenwell, Mike	87D	585	$ .15	$1.25
Gossage, Rich	83D	157	$ .05	$ .20	Greenwell, Mike	87DR	4	$ .10	$1.00
Gossage, Goose	84D	396	$ .10	$ .50	Greenwell, Mike	88D	339	$ .05	$ .20
Gossage, Goose	85D	185	$ .05	$ .25	Greenwell, Mike	89D	186	$ .01	$ .10
Gossage, Goose	86D	185	$ .05	$ .25	Greenwell, Mike	89DBC	13	$ .01	$ .10
Gossage, Goose	86DK	2	$ .05	$ .20	Greenwell, Mike	89DK	1	$ .01	$ .10
Gossage, Goose "Rich"	87D	483	$ .01	$ .10	Greenwell, Mike	90D	66	$ .01	$ .10
Gossage, Rich	88D	434	$ .01	$ .15	Greenwell, Mike	90DBC	17	$ .01	$ .10
Gossage, Rich	89D	158	$ .01	$ .04	Greenwell, Mike	90DL	143	$ .10	$ .75
Gossage, Goose	90D	678	$ .01	$ .04	Greenwell, Mike	91D	553	$ .01	$ .10
Gossage, Rich	91DL	236	$ .01	$ .08	Greenwell, Mike	91DL	19	$ .01	$ .10
Gossage, Rich	91DLS	125	$ .01	$ .08	Greenwell, Mike	91DLS	15	$ .01	$ .15
Gossage, Goose	92D	555	$ .05	$ .25	Greenwell, Mike	92D	523	$ .01	$ .10
Gossage, Rich	92DL	474	$ .01	$ .06	Greenwell, Mike	92DL	89	$ .01	$ .06
Gott, Jim	83D	353	$ .05	$ .20	Greenwell, Mike	93D	223	$ .01	$ .05
Gott, Jim	84D	268	$ .05	$ .20	Greenwell, Mike	93DL	197	$ .01	$ .15
Gott, Jim	85D	632	$ .01	$ .10	Gregg, Tommy	88D	203	$ .01	$ .15
Gott, Jim	86D	358	$ .01	$ .08	Gregg, Tommy	89D	121	$ .01	$ .04
Gott, Jim	88D	606	$ .01	$ .15	Gregg, Tommy	90D	239	$ .01	$ .04
Gott, Jim	89D	362	$ .01	$ .04	Gregg, Tommy	90DL	86	$ .05	$ .25
Gott, Jim	90D	605	$ .01	$ .04	Gregg, Tommy	91D	244	$ .01	$ .04
Gott, Jim	91D	601	$ .01	$ .04	Gregg, Tommy	91DL	144	$ .01	$ .08
Gott, Jim	91DL	229	$ .01	$ .08	Gregg, Tommy	92D	485	$ .01	$ .04
Gott, Jim	92D	601	$ .01	$ .04	Grich, Bobby	81D	289	$ .01	$ .06
Gott, Jim	93D	670	$ .01	$ .05	Grich, Bobby	82D	90	$ .01	$ .06
Gozzo, Mauro	90D	655	$ .01	$ .10	Grich, Bobby	83D	468	$ .01	$ .06
Grace, Mark	88DR	1	$ .20	$2.00	Grich, Bobby	84D	179	$ .05	$ .20
Grace, Mark	88DRR	40	$ .15	$1.25	Grich, Bobby	85D	280	$ .01	$ .10
Grace, Mark	89D	255	$ .05	$ .25	Grich, Bobby	86D	207	$ .01	$ .08
Grace, Mark	89DK	17	$ .01	$ .10	Grich, Bobby	87D	456	$ .01	$ .05
Grace, Mark	90D	577	$ .05	$ .20	Griffey Jr., Ken	89DR	3	$2.00	$8.00
Grace, Mark	90DL	137	$ .20	$2.00	Griffey Jr., Ken	89DRR	33	$1.00	$4.00
Grace, Mark	91D	199	$ .01	$ .10	Griffey Jr., Ken	90D	365	$ .15	$1.25
Grace, Mark	91DL	170	$ .05	$ .20	Griffey Jr., Ken	90DK	4	$ .10	$ .50
Grace, Mark	91DLS	157	$ .05	$ .35	Griffey Jr., Ken	90DL	245	$6.25	$25.00
Grace, Mark	92D	281	$ .01	$ .10	Griffey Jr., Ken	91D	77	$ .10	$ .50
Grace, Mark	92DL	26	$ .01	$ .15	Griffey Jr., Ken	91DAS	49	$ .05	$ .25
Grace, Mark	92DLS	14	$ .01	$ .15	Griffey Jr., Ken	91DL	372	$ .20	$2.00
Grace, Mark	93D	532	$ .01	$ .05	Griffey Jr., Ken	91DLS	112	$ .20	$2.00
Grace, Mark	93DL	198	$ .05	$ .35	Griffey Jr., Ken	91DMVP	392	$ .10	$ .25
Graham, Dan	81D	233	$ .01	$ .06	Griffey Jr., Ken	92D	165	$ .10	$ .50
Graham, Dan	82D	455	$ .01	$ .06	Griffey Jr., Ken	92DAS	24	$ .05	$ .35
Grahe, Joe	91D	737	$ .05	$ .10	Griffey Jr., Ken	92DL	392	$ .15	$1.50
Grahe, Joe	92D	445	$ .01	$ .04	Griffey Jr., Ken	92DLS	232	$ .15	$1.50
Grahe, Joe	92DL	137	$ .01	$ .06	Griffey Jr., Ken	93D	553	$ .10	$ .50
Grahe, Joe	93D	401	$ .01	$ .05	Griffey Jr., Ken	93DK	1	$2.50	$10.00
Grant, Mark	85D	601	$ .01	$ .10	Griffey, Ken	81D	184	$ .05	$ .35
Grant, Mark	87D	644	$ .01	$ .05	Griffey, Ken	82D	634	$ .05	$ .25
Grant, Mark	88D	511	$ .01	$ .04	Griffey, Ken	83D	486	$ .05	$ .25
Grant, Mark	90D	441	$ .01	$ .04	Griffey, Ken	84D	613	$ .05	$ .35
Grant, Mark	91D	361	$ .01	$ .04	Griffey, Ken	85D	347	$ .05	$ .20
Gray, Gary	83D	637	$ .01	$ .06	Griffey, Ken	86D	126	$ .01	$ .08
Gray, Jeff	91D	721	$ .01	$ .10	Griffey, Ken	87D	513	$ .01	$ .05
Gray, Jeff	91DL	356	$ .01	$ .08	Griffey, Ken	88D	202	$ .01	$ .15
Gray, Jeff	92D	122	$ .01	$ .04	Griffey, Ken	90D	469	$ .01	$ .04
Grebeck, Craig	90DR	9	$ .01	$ .05	Griffey Sr., Ken	91D	452	$ .01	$ .04
Grebeck, Craig	91D	378	$ .01	$ .04	Griffey Sr., Ken	91DL	503	$ .01	$ .08
Grebeck, Craig	92D	546	$ .01	$ .04	Griffey Sr., Ken	91DLS	113	$ .01	$ .08
Grebeck, Craig	92DL	344	$ .01	$ .06	Griffin, Alfredo	81D	149	$ .01	$ .06
Grebeck, Craig	93D	199	$ .01	$ .05	Griffin, Alfredo	82D	101	$ .01	$ .06

DONRUSS

Player	Year	No.	VG	EX/MT
Griffin, Alfredo	83D	180	$ .01	$ .06
Griffin, Alfredo	84D	605	$ .05	$ .20
Griffin, Alfredo	85D	73	$ .01	$ .10
Griffin, Alfredo	86D	101	$ .01	$ .08
Griffin, Alfredo	87D	256	$ .01	$ .05
Griffin, Alfredo	88D	226	$ .01	$ .04
Griffin, Alfredo	89D	79	$ .01	$ .04
Griffin, Alfredo	90D	195	$ .01	$ .04
Griffin, Alfredo	90DL	95	$ .05	$ .25
Griffin, Alfredo	91D	488	$ .01	$ .04
Griffin, Alfredo	91DL	344	$ .01	$ .08
Griffin, Alfredo	92D	692	$ .01	$ .04
Griffin, Mike	82D	533	$ .01	$ .06
Griffin, Mike	88D	494	$ .01	$ .04
Griffin, Tom	81D	75	$ .01	$ .06
Griffin, Tom	82D	474	$ .01	$ .06
Grimsley, Jason	91D	653	$ .01	$ .10
Grimsley, Jason	91DL	288	$ .01	$ .15
Grimsley, Jason	92D	599	$ .01	$ .04
Grissom, Marquis	90DL	107	$1.25	$5.00
Grissom, Marquis	90DR	45	$ .10	$ .50
Grissom, Marquis	90DRR	36	$ .10	$ .50
Grissom, Marquis	91D	307	$ .01	$ .10
Grissom, Marquis	91DL	22	$ .10	$ .40
Grissom, Marquis	91DLS	198	$ .10	$ .40
Grissom, Marquis	92D	137	$ .01	$ .10
Grissom, Marquis	92DL	273	$ .01	$ .15
Grissom, Marquis	92DLS	55	$ .05	$ .20
Grissom, Marquis	93D	300	$ .01	$ .10
Grissom, Marquis	93DL	129	$ .10	$ .40
Groom, Buddy	92DR	44	$ .01	$ .05
Groom, Buddy	93D	569	$ .01	$ .05
Gross, Greg	81D	598	$ .01	$ .06
Gross, Greg	82D	371	$ .01	$ .06
Gross, Greg	83D	441	$ .01	$ .06
Gross, Greg	84D	285	$ .05	$ .20
Gross, Greg	85D	407	$ .01	$ .10
Gross, Greg	86D	163	$ .01	$ .08
Gross, Greg	87D	385	$ .01	$ .05
Gross, Greg	88D	412	$ .01	$ .04
Gross, Kevin	84D	381	$ .10	$ .50
Gross, Kevin	85D	477	$ .01	$ .10
Gross, Kevin	86D	529	$ .01	$ .08
Gross, Kevin	87D	236	$ .01	$ .05
Gross, Kevin	88D	113	$ .01	$ .04
Gross, Kevin	89D	194	$ .01	$ .04
Gross, Kevin	89DBC	12	$ .01	$ .05
Gross, Kevin	89DTR	3	$ .01	$ .05
Gross, Kevin	90D	248	$ .01	$ .04
Gross, Kevin	90DL	61	$ .05	$ .25
Gross, Kevin	91D	569	$ .01	$ .04
Gross, Kevin	91DL	279	$ .01	$ .08
Gross, Kevin	92D	279	$ .01	$ .04
Gross, Kevin	92DL	33	$ .01	$ .06
Gross, Kevin	93D	458	$ .01	$ .05
Gross, Kevin	93DL	181	$ .01	$ .15
Gross, Kip	93D	194	$ .01	$ .05
Gross, Wayne	81D	237	$ .01	$ .06
Gross, Wayne	82D	139	$ .01	$ .06
Gross, Wayne	83D	591	$ .01	$ .06
Gross, Wayne	84D	375	$ .05	$ .20
Gross, Wayne	85D	228	$ .01	$ .10
Gross, Wayne	86D	535	$ .01	$ .08
Grotewold, Jeff	92DR	45	$ .05	$ .20
Grubb, John	81D	148	$ .01	$ .06
Grubb, John	82D	467	$ .01	$ .06
Grubb, John	83D	341	$ .01	$ .06
Grubb, John	84D	90	$ .05	$ .20
Grubb, John	85D	578	$ .01	$ .10
Grubb, John	86D	615	$ .01	$ .08
Grubb, John	87D	476	$ .01	$ .05
Gruber, Kelly	86DR	16	$ .10	$ .50
Gruber, Kelly	87D	444	$ .10	$ .50
Gruber, Kelly	88D	244	$ .05	$ .20
Gruber, Kelly	89D	113	$ .01	$ .15
Gruber, Kelly	90D	113	$ .01	$ .15
Gruber, Kelly	90DK	12	$ .01	$ .05
Gruber, Kelly	90DL	106	$ .05	$ .25

Player	Year	No.	VG	EX/MT
Gruber, Kelly	91D	149	$ .01	$ .04
Gruber, Kelly	91DL	9	$ .01	$ .08
Gruber, Kelly	91DLS	135	$ .01	$ .08
Gruber, Kelly	92D	65	$ .01	$ .04
Gruber, Kelly	92DL	27	$ .01	$ .06
Gruber, Kelly	92DLS	255	$ .01	$ .06
Gruber, Kelly	93D	453	$ .01	$ .05
Guante, Cecilio	84D	78	$ .05	$ .20
Guante, Cecilio	85D	357	$ .01	$ .10
Guante, Cecilio	86D	142	$ .01	$ .08
Guante, Cecilio	87D	238	$ .01	$ .05
Guante, Cecilio	89D	260	$ .01	$ .04
Guante, Cecilio	90D	403	$ .01	$ .04
Guante, Cecilio	90DL	365	$ .05	$ .25
Guante, Matt	83D	423	$ .01	$ .06
Gubicza, Mark	85D	344	$ .10	$ .50
Gubicza, Mark	86D	583	$ .01	$ .15
Gubicza, Mark	87D	466	$ .01	$ .05
Gubicza, Mark	88D	54	$ .01	$ .04
Gubicza, Mark	89D	179	$ .01	$ .04
Gubicza, Mark	90D	204	$ .01	$ .04
Gubicza, Mark	90DL	145	$ .05	$ .25
Gubicza, Mark	91D	145	$ .01	$ .04
Gubicza, Mark	91DLS	67	$ .01	$ .08
Gubicza, Mark	92D	282	$ .01	$ .04
Gubicza, Mark	92DL	332	$ .01	$ .06
Gubicza, Mark	92DLS	183	$ .01	$ .06
Gubicza, Mark	93D	703	$ .01	$ .05
Guerrero, Juan	92DL	428	$ .01	$ .15
Guerrerc, Juan	92DR	46	$ .05	$ .25
Guerrero, Juan	93D	240	$ .01	$ .10
Guerrero, Pedro	82D	136	$ .05	$ .35
Guerrero, Pedro	83D	110	$ .05	$ .30
Guerrero, Pedro	84D	174	$ .10	$ .50
Guerrero, Pedro	84DK	24	$ .05	$ .25
Guerrero, Pedro	85D	174	$ .05	$ .25
Guerrero, Pedro	86D	174	$ .05	$ .25
Guerrero, Pedro	87D	53	$ .05	$ .20
Guerrero, Pedro	88D	278	$ .01	$ .04
Guerrero, Pedro	88DBC	16	$ .01	$ .10
Guerrero, Pedro	89D	418	$ .01	$ .10

DONRUSS

Player	Year	No.	VG	EX/MT
Guerrero, Pedro	90D	63	$ .01	$ .04
Guerrero, Pedro	90DAS	674	$ .01	$ .04
Guerrero, Pedro	90DBC	6	$ .01	$ .04
Guerrero, Pedro	90DL	44	$ .05	$ .25
Guerrero, Pedro	91D	558	$ .01	$ .04
Guerrero, Pedro	91DK	25	$ .01	$ .05
Guerrero, Pedro	91DL	204	$ .01	$ .08
Guerrero, Pedro	91DLS	232	$ .01	$ .08
Guerrero, Pedro	92D	158	$ .01	$ .04
Guerrero, Pedro	92DL	18	$ .01	$ .06
Guerrero, Pedro	92DLS	91	$ .01	$ .06
Guerrero, Pedro	93D	600	$ .01	$ .05
Guetterman, Lee	87D	322	$ .01	$ .15
Guetterman, Lee	88D	270	$ .01	$ .04
Guetterman, Lee	90D	127	$ .01	$ .04
Guetterman, Lee	90DL	333	$ .05	$ .25
Guetterman, Lee	91D	124	$ .01	$ .04
Guetterman, Lee	91DL	52	$ .01	$ .08
Guetterman, Lee	92D	507	$ .01	$ .04
Guetterman, Lee	92DL	320	$ .01	$ .06
Guetterman, Lee	93D	542	$ .01	$ .05
Guidry, Ron	81D	227	$ .05	$ .20
Guidry, Ron	82D	548	$ .05	$ .25
Guidry, Ron	82D	558	$ .05	$ .20
Guidry, Ron	83D	31	$ .05	$ .25
Guidry, Ron	83DK	17	$ .05	$ .20
Guidry, Ron	84D	173	$ .05	$ .35
Guidry, Ron	85D	214	$ .05	$ .20
Guidry, Ron	86D	103	$ .05	$ .25
Guidry, Ron	87D	93	$ .05	$ .20
Guidry, Ron	88D	175	$ .01	$ .15
Guillen, Ozzie	86D	208	$ .10	$ .75
Guillen, Ozzie	87D	87	$ .01	$ .15
Guillen, Ozzie	88D	137	$ .01	$ .04
Guillen, Ozzie	89D	176	$ .01	$ .04
Guillen, Ozzie	89DBC	23	$ .01	$ .05
Guillen, Ozzie	90D	135	$ .01	$ .04
Guillen, Ozzie	90DK	15	$ .01	$ .05
Guillen, Ozzie	90DL	128	$ .05	$ .25
Guillen, Ozzie	91D	577	$ .01	$ .04
Guillen, Ozzie	91DL	331	$ .01	$ .08
Guillen, Ozzie	92D	229	$ .01	$ .04
Guillen, Ozzie	92DL	149	$ .01	$ .06
Guillen, Ozzie	93D	255	$ .01	$ .05
Guillen, Ozzie	93DL	85	$ .01	$ .15
Gulden, Brad	85D	365	$ .01	$ .10
Gullickson, Bill	81D	91	$ .10	$ .75
Gullickson, Bill	82D	162	$ .05	$ .25
Gullickson, Bill	83D	288	$ .05	$ .15
Gullickson, Bill	84D	401	$ .05	$ .20
Gullickson, Bill	85D	97	$ .01	$ .10
Gullickson, Bill	86D	331	$ .01	$ .08
Gullickson, Bill	87D	369	$ .01	$ .05
Gullickson, Bill	88D	586	$ .01	$ .04
Gullickson, Bill	91DL	402	$ .01	$ .08
Gullickson, Bill	91DLS	55	$ .01	$ .08
Gullickson, Bill	92D	131	$ .01	$ .04
Gullickson, Bill	92DL	61	$ .01	$ .06
Gullickson, Bill	93D	523	$ .01	$ .05
Gullickson, Bill	93DL	103	$ .01	$ .15
Gulliver, Glenn	83D	131	$ .01	$ .06
Gunderson, Eric	91DRR	416	$ .01	$ .10
Gura, Larry	81D	461	$ .01	$ .06
Gura, Larry	82D	338	$ .01	$ .06
Gura, Larry	83D	160	$ .01	$ .06
Gura, Larry	84D	100	$ .05	$ .20
Gura, Larry	85D	217	$ .01	$ .10
Guthrie, Mark	90D	622	$ .01	$ .10
Guthrie, Mark	91D	64	$ .01	$ .04
Guthrie, Mark	91DL	171	$ .01	$ .08
Guthrie, Mark	92D	691	$ .01	$ .04
Guthrie, Mark	92DL	263	$ .01	$ .06
Guthrie, Mark	93D	714	$ .01	$ .05
Gutierrez, Jackie	85D	335	$ .01	$ .10
Gutierrez, Jackie	86D	335	$ .01	$ .08
Gutierrez, Jackie	87D	601	$ .01	$ .05
Guzman, Johnny	92DR	47	$ .05	$ .25
Guzman, Jose	86DR	24	$ .10	$ .40
Guzman, Jose	86DRR	30	$ .10	$ .75
Guzman, Jose	87D	101	$ .01	$ .05
Guzman, Jose	88D	136	$ .01	$ .04
Guzman, Jose	89D	284	$ .01	$ .04
Guzman, Jose	92D	271	$ .01	$ .04
Guzman, Jose	92DL	222	$ .01	$ .06
Guzman, Jose	92DLS	243	$ .01	$ .06
Guzman, Jose	93D	687	$ .01	$ .05
Guzman, Juan	92D	534	$ .10	$ .50
Guzman, Juan	92DL	35	$ .15	$1.50
Guzman, Juan	92DLS	256	$ .15	$1.50
Guzman, Juan	93D	189	$ .01	$ .15
Guzman, Juan	93DL	3	$ .10	$ .75
Gwosdz, Doug	84D	383	$ .05	$ .20
Gwynn, Chris	90DL	411	$ .05	$ .25

Player	Year	No.	VG	EX/MT
Gwynn, Chris	91D	598	$ .01	$ .04
Gwynn, Chris	92D	648	$ .01	$ .04
Gwynn, Chris	92DL	518	$ .01	$ .06
Gwynn, Chris	93D	657	$ .01	$ .05
Gwynn, Tony	83D	598	$5.50	$22.00
Gwynn, Tony	84D	324	$4.00	$16.00
Gwynn, Tony	85D	63	$1.25	$5.00
Gwynn, Tony	85DK	25	$ .75	$3.00
Gwynn, Tony	86D	112	$ .75	$3.00
Gwynn, Tony	87D	64	$ .10	$ .75
Gwynn, Tony	88D	164	$ .05	$ .25
Gwynn, Tony	88DBC	6	$ .01	$ .15
Gwynn, Tony	89D	128	$ .05	$ .20
Gwynn, Tony	89DBC	20	$ .01	$ .15
Gwynn, Tony	89DK	6	$ .01	$ .10
Gwynn, Tony	90D	86	$ .05	$ .20
Gwynn, Tony	90DAS	705	$ .01	$ .10
Gwynn, Tony	90DBC	4	$ .01	$ .15
Gwynn, Tony	90DL	154	$ .20	$2.00
Gwynn, Tony	91D	243	$ .01	$ .10
Gwynn, Tony	91DL	290	$ .05	$ .35
Gwynn, Tony	91DLP	11	$1.25	$5.00
Gwynn, Tony	91DLS	245	$ .05	$ .35
Gwynn, Tony	92D	441	$ .01	$ .10
Gwynn, Tony	92DAS	425	$ .01	$ .10

DONRUSS

Player	Year	No.	VG	EX/MT
Gwynn, Tony	92DL	206	$ .05	$ .25
Gwynn, Tony	92DLS	104	$ .05	$ .35
Gwynn, Tony	93D	126	$ .01	$ .10
Gwynn, Tony	93DL	28	$ .05	$ .35
Haas, Dave	93D	335	$ .01	$ .10
Haas, Moose	81D	85	$ .01	$ .06
Haas, Moose	82D	206	$ .01	$ .06
Haas, Moose	83D	204	$ .01	$ .06
Haas, Moose	84D	368	$ .05	$ .20
Haas, Moose	85D	473	$ .01	$ .10
Haas, Moose	86D	237	$ .01	$ .08
Haas, Moose	87D	528	$ .01	$ .05
Habyan, John	86DRR	45	$ .01	$ .10
Habyan, John	87D	494	$ .01	$ .05
Habyan, John	88D	354	$ .01	$ .04
Habyan, John	91DL	480	$ .01	$ .08
Habyan, John	92D	32	$ .01	$ .04
Habyan, John	92DL	189	$ .01	$ .06
Habyan, John	93D	107	$ .01	$ .05
Habyan, John	93DL	162	$ .01	$ .15
Haddix, Harvey	82D	651	$ .01	$ .06
Hairston, Jerry	83D	616	$ .01	$ .06
Hairston, Jerry	84D	86	$ .05	$ .20
Hairston, Jerry	85D	135	$ .01	$ .10
Hairston, Jerry	86D	424	$ .01	$ .08
Hairston, Jerry	87D	285	$ .01	$ .05
Hairston, Jerry	88D	285	$ .01	$ .04
Hale, Chip	90D	690	$ .01	$ .10
Halicki, Ed	81D	53	$ .01	$ .06
Hall, Albert	88D	290	$ .01	$ .04
Hall, Drew	87D	594	$ .01	$ .05
Hall, Drew	89D	522	$ .01	$ .04
Hall, Drew	90DL	423	$ .05	$ .25
Hall, Mel	83D	126	$ .15	$1.25
Hall, Mel	84D	411	$ .05	$ .25
Hall, Mel	85D	338	$ .01	$ .15
Hall, Mel	86D	276	$ .01	$ .08
Hall, Mel	87D	473	$ .01	$ .05
Hall, Mel	88D	342	$ .01	$ .04
Hall, Mel	89D	73	$ .01	$ .04
Hall, Mel	89DTR	36	$ .01	$ .15
Hall, Mel	90D	598	$ .01	$ .04
Hall, Mel	90DL	227	$ .05	$ .25
Hall, Mel	91D	442	$ .01	$ .04
Hall, Mel	91DL	283	$ .01	$ .08
Hall, Mel	92D	248	$ .01	$ .04
Hall, Mel	92DL	88	$ .01	$ .06
Hamilton, Darryl	91D	517	$ .01	$ .04
Hamilton, Darryl	92D	593	$ .01	$ .04
Hamilton, Darryl	92DL	12	$ .01	$ .06
Hamilton, Darryl	93D	527	$ .01	$ .05
Hamilton, Darryl	93DL	199	$ .01	$ .15
Hamilton, Jeff	87D	464	$ .05	$ .25
Hamilton, Jeff	88D	525	$ .01	$ .04
Hamilton, Jeff	89D	550	$ .01	$ .04
Hamilton, Jeff	90D	321	$ .01	$ .04
Hamilton, Jeff	90DL	300	$ .05	$ .25
Hamilton, Jeff	91DL	509	$ .01	$ .08
Hammaker, Atlee	83D	298	$ .01	$ .06
Hammaker, Atlee	84D	236	$ .05	$ .20
Hammaker, Atlee	85D	509	$ .01	$ .10
Hammaker, Atlee	86D	445	$ .01	$ .08
Hammaker, Atlee	88D	450	$ .01	$ .04
Hammaker, Atlee	89D	414	$ .01	$ .04
Hammaker, Atlee	90D	532	$ .01	$ .04
Hammaker, Atlee	91D	707	$ .01	$ .04
Hammaker, Atlee	91DLS	246	$ .01	$ .08
Hammond, Chris	91D	759	$ .01	$ .10
Hammond, Chris	91DL	373	$ .01	$ .15
Hammond, Chris	91DLS	165	$ .01	$ .15
Hammond, Chris	91DR	19	$ .01	$ .05
Hammond, Chris	92D	172	$ .01	$ .04
Hammond, Chris	92DL	178	$ .01	$ .06
Hammond, Chris	93D	246	$ .01	$ .05
Hancock, Garry	82D	608	$ .01	$ .06
Haney, Chris	91DR	44	$ .01	$ .10
Haney, Chris	92D	291	$ .01	$ .10
Haney, Chris	93D	279	$ .01	$ .05
Haney, Todd	93D	342	$ .01	$ .15
Hanna, Preston	81D	523	$ .01	$ .06
Hansen, Dave	91DRR	45	$ .01	$ .10
Hansen, Dave	92D	506	$ .01	$ .04
Hansen, Dave	92DL	389	$ .01	$ .06
Hansen, Dave	93D	244	$ .01	$ .05
Hanson, Eric	89DR	49	$ .05	$ .20
Hanson, Eric	89DRR	32	$ .05	$ .20
Hanson, Eric	91DLS	114	$ .01	$ .08
Hanson, Erik	90D	345	$ .01	$ .10
Hanson, Erik	90DL	430	$ .10	$1.00
Hanson, Erik	91D	550	$ .01	$ .10
Hanson, Erik	91DL	142	$ .01	$ .08
Hanson, Erik	92D	138	$ .01	$ .04
Hanson, Erik	92DL	23	$ .01	$ .06
Hanson, Erik	92DLS	233	$ .01	$ .06
Hanson, Erik	93D	317	$ .01	$ .05
Hare, Shawn	92DR	48	$ .01	$ .05
Hare, Shawn	93D	305	$ .01	$ .10
Hargrove, Mike	81D	78	$ .01	$ .06
Hargrove, Mike	82D	389	$ .01	$ .06
Hargrove, Mike	83D	450	$ .01	$ .06
Hargrove, Mike	84D	495	$ .05	$ .20
Hargrove, Mike	85D	398	$ .01	$ .10
Hargrove, Mike	86D	590	$ .01	$ .08
Harkey, Mike	89DRR	43	$ .01	$ .10
Harkey, Mike	90D	522	$ .01	$ .04
Harkey, Mike	90DL	309	$ .05	$ .25
Harkey, Mike	90DR	22	$ .01	$ .15
Harkey, Mike	91D	447	$ .01	$ .04
Harkey, Mike	91DL	90	$ .01	$ .08
Harkey, Mike	92D	241	$ .01	$ .04
Harkey, Mike	93D	450	$ .01	$ .05
Harnisch, Pete	89DRR	44	$ .01	$ .15
Harnisch, Pete	90D	596	$ .01	$ .04
Harnisch, Pete	90DL	39	$ .10	$ .50
Harnisch, Pete	91D	181	$ .01	$ .04
Harnisch, Pete	91DL	245	$ .01	$ .08
Harnisch, Pete	91DLS	177	$ .01	$ .08
Harnisch, Pete	92D	235	$ .01	$ .04
Harnisch, Pete	92DL	77	$ .01	$ .06
Harnisch, Pete	92DLS	36	$ .01	$ .06
Harnisch, Pete	93D	272	$ .01	$ .05
Harnisch, Pete	93DL	51	$ .01	$ .15
Harper, Brian	84D	142	$ .15	$1.50
Harper, Brian	85D	566	$ .05	$ .25
Harper, Brian	86D	547	$ .01	$ .15
Harper, Brian	89D	641	$ .01	$ .04
Harper, Brian	90D	355	$ .01	$ .04
Harper, Brian	90DL	479	$ .05	$ .25
Harper, Brian	91D	582	$ .01	$ .04
Harper, Brian	91DK	22	$ .01	$ .05
Harper, Brian	91DL	54	$ .01	$ .08
Harper, Brian	91DLS	86	$ .01	$ .08
Harper, Brian	91DMVP	398	$ .01	$ .03
Harper, Brian	92D	83	$ .01	$ .04
Harper, Brian	92DL	131	$ .01	$ .06
Harper, Brian	92DLS	204	$ .01	$ .06
Harper, Brian	93D	547	$ .01	$ .05
Harper, Brian	93DL	186	$ .01	$ .15
Harper, Terry	83D	607	$ .01	$ .06
Harper, Terry	86D	627	$ .01	$ .08
Harrah, Toby	81D	318	$ .01	$ .06
Harrah, Toby	82D	72	$ .01	$ .06
Harrah, Toby	83D	337	$ .01	$ .06
Harrah, Toby	83DK	13	$ .01	$ .10
Harrah, Toby	84D	251	$ .05	$ .20
Harrah, Toby	86D	159	$ .01	$ .08
Harrah, Toby	87D	408	$ .01	$ .05
Harris, Donald	92D	652	$ .01	$ .10
Harris, Donald	93D	291	$ .01	$ .05
Harris, Gene	90D	247	$ .01	$ .04

DONRUSS

Player	Year	No.	VG	EX/MT	Player	Year	No.	VG	EX/MT
Harris, Gene	90DL	378	$ .05	$ .25	Hatcher, Billy	89D	187	$ .01	$ .04
Harris, Gene	91D	651	$ .01	$ .04	Hatcher, Billy	90D	616	$ .01	$ .04
Harris, Gene	93D	494	$ .01	$ .05	Hatcher, Billy	90DL	241	$ .05	$ .25
Harris, Greg A.	83D	295	$ .01	$ .06	Hatcher, Billy	91D	196	$ .01	$ .04
Harris, Greg A.	86D	465	$ .01	$ .08	Hatcher, Billy	91D	763	$ .01	$ .04
Harris, Greg A.	87D	382	$ .01	$ .05	Hatcher, Billy	91DL	205	$ .01	$ .08
Harris, Greg A.	88D	427	$ .01	$ .04	Hatcher, Billy	91DLS	166	$ .01	$ .08
Harris, Greg A.	89D	548	$ .01	$ .04	Hatcher, Billy	92D	537	$ .01	$ .04
Harris, Greg A.	90D	582	$ .01	$ .04	Hatcher, Billy	93D	754	$ .01	$ .05
Harris, Greg A.	90DL	499	$ .05	$ .25	Hatcher, Billy	93DL	109	$ .01	$ .15
Harris, Greg A.	91D	306	$ .01	$ .04	Hatcher, Mickey	81D	526	$ .01	$ .06
Harris, Greg A.	91DL	83	$ .01	$ .08	Hatcher, Mickey	82D	480	$ .01	$ .06
Harris, Greg A.	92D	113	$ .01	$ .04	Hatcher, Mickey	83D	615	$ .01	$ .06
Harris, Greg A.	92DL	154	$ .01	$ .06	Hatcher, Mickey	84D	147	$ .05	$ .20
Harris, Greg A.	92DLS	133	$ .01	$ .06	Hatcher, Mickey	85D	194	$ .01	$ .10
Harris, Greg A.	93D	663	$ .01	$ .05	Hatcher, Mickey	86D	269	$ .01	$ .08
Harris, Greg A.	93DL	131	$ .01	$ .15	Hatcher, Mickey	87D	491	$ .01	$ .05
Harris, Greg W.	89DR	46	$ .01	$ .05	Hatcher, Mickey	88D	299	$ .01	$ .04
Harris, Greg W.	89DRR	34	$ .01	$ .15	Hatcher, Mickey	89D	346	$ .01	$ .04
Harris, Greg W.	90D	65	$ .01	$ .04	Hatcher, Mickey	90D	439	$ .01	$ .04
Harris, Greg W.	90DL	452	$ .05	$ .25	Hatcher, Mickey	90DL	332	$ .05	$ .25
Harris, Greg W.	91D	131	$ .01	$ .04	Hathaway, Hilly	93D	329	$ .05	$ .25
Harris, Greg W.	91DL	422	$ .01	$ .08	Hausman, Tom	81D	396	$ .01	$ .06
Harris, Greg W.	92D	49	$ .01	$ .04	Hausman, Tom	82D	301	$ .01	$ .06
Harris, Greg W.	92DL	10	$ .01	$ .06	Havens, Brad	82D	382	$ .01	$ .06
Harris, Greg W.	92DLS	105	$ .01	$ .06	Havens, Brad	83D	480	$ .01	$ .06
Harris, Greg W.	93D	154	$ .01	$ .05	Havens, Brad	86D	599	$ .01	$ .08
Harris, Greg W.	93DL	82	$ .01	$ .15	Hawblitzel, Ryan	92DR	49	$ .01	$ .15
Harris, John	82D	444	$ .01	$ .06	Hawkins, Andy	85D	528	$ .05	$ .25
Harris, Lenny	90D	434	$ .01	$ .04	Hawkins, Andy	86D	284	$ .01	$ .08
Harris, Lenny	90DL	437	$ .05	$ .25	Hawkins, Andy	87D	264	$ .01	$ .05
Harris, Lenny	91D	224	$ .01	$ .04	Hawkins, Andy	89D	583	$ .01	$ .04
Harris, Lenny	92D	226	$ .01	$ .04	Hawkins, Andy	89DTR	52	$ .01	$ .05
Harris, Lenny	92DL	213	$ .01	$ .06	Hawkins, Andy	90D	159	$ .01	$ .04
Harris, Lenny	93D	590	$ .01	$ .05	Hawkins, Andy	90DL	281	$ .05	$ .25
Harris, Lenny	93DL	127	$ .01	$ .15	Hawkins, Andy	91D	611	$ .01	$ .04
Harris, Reggie	91D	704	$ .01	$ .10	Hawkins, Andy	91DBC	12	$ .01	$ .03
Harris, Reggie	92D	781	$ .01	$ .04	Hayes, Charlie	90D	548	$ .01	$ .10
Hartley, Mike	90DR	34	$ .01	$ .15	Hayes, Charlie	90DL	131	$ .10	$ .50
Hartley, Mike	91D	545	$ .01	$ .04	Hayes, Charlie	91D	278	$ .01	$ .04
Hartley, Mike	92D	726	$ .01	$ .04	Hayes, Charlie	91DL	214	$ .01	$ .08
Hartley, Mike	93D	596	$ .01	$ .05	Hayes, Charlie	91DLS	214	$ .01	$ .08
Hartsock, Jeff	93D	160	$ .01	$ .10	Hayes, Charlie	92D	547	$ .01	$ .04
Harvey, Bryan	88DR	53	$ .10	$ .50	Hayes, Charlie	92DL	220	$ .01	$ .06
Harvey, Bryan	89D	525	$ .01	$ .15	Hayes, Charlie	92DLS	212	$ .01	$ .06
Harvey, Bryan	90D	372	$ .01	$ .04	Hayes, Charlie	93D	181	$ .01	$ .05
Harvey, Bryan	90DL	116	$ .05	$ .25	Hayes, Charlie	93D	776	$ .01	$ .05
Harvey, Bryan	91D	206	$ .01	$ .04	Hayes, Von	82D	237	$ .10	$ .40
Harvey, Bryan	91DL	213	$ .01	$ .08	Hayes, Von	83D	324	$ .01	$ .15
Harvey, Bryan	92D	211	$ .01	$ .04	Hayes, Von	84D	477	$ .05	$ .25
Harvey, Bryan	92DL	309	$ .01	$ .06	Hayes, Von	85D	326	$ .05	$ .20
Harvey, Bryan	92DLS	146	$ .01	$ .06	Hayes, Von	86D	305	$ .01	$ .08
Harvey, Bryan	93D	728	$ .01	$ .05	Hayes, Von	87D	113	$ .01	$ .05
Haselman, Bill	91D	679	$ .01	$ .10	Hayes, Von	87DK	12	$ .01	$ .05
Hassey, Ron	81D	80	$ .01	$ .06	Hayes, Von	88D	207	$ .01	$ .04
Hassey, Ron	82D	463	$ .01	$ .06	Hayes, Von	89D	160	$ .01	$ .04
Hassey, Ron	83D	159	$ .01	$ .06	Hayes, Von	90D	278	$ .01	$ .04
Hassey, Ron	84D	460	$ .05	$ .20	Hayes, Von	90DBC	25	$ .01	$ .04
Hassey, Ron	86D	370	$ .01	$ .08	Hayes, Von	90DL	52	$ .05	$ .25
Hassey, Ron	87D	532	$ .01	$ .05	Hayes, Von	91D	222	$ .01	$ .04
Hassey, Ron	88D	580	$ .01	$ .04	Hayes, Von	91DL	280	$ .01	$ .08
Hassey, Ron	89D	361	$ .01	$ .04	Hayes, Von	92D	580	$ .01	$ .04
Hassey, Ron	90D	450	$ .01	$ .04	Hayes, Von	92DL	177	$ .01	$ .06
Hassey, Ron	90DL	326	$ .05	$ .25	Hayes, Von	92DLS	147	$ .01	$ .06
Hassey, Ron	91D	476	$ .01	$ .04	Hayward, Ray	87D	632	$ .01	$ .05
Hassey, Ron	91DL	359	$ .01	$ .08	Hayward, Ray	89D	521	$ .01	$ .04
Hassler, Andy	81D	581	$ .01	$ .06	Hearn, Ed	86DR	54	$ .01	$ .10
Hassler, Andy	82D	519	$ .01	$ .06	Hearn, Ed	87D	446	$ .01	$ .05
Hassler, Andy	83D	290	$ .01	$ .06	Hearn, Ed	89D	297	$ .01	$ .04
Hassler, Andy	84D	255	$ .05	$ .20	Hearron, Jeff	87D	490	$ .01	$ .05
Hatcher, Billy	85DRR	41	$ .10	$ .50	Heath, Mike	81D	120	$ .01	$ .06
Hatcher, Billy	86D	433	$ .05	$ .25	Heath, Mike	82D	413	$ .05	$ .06
Hatcher, Billy	87D	481	$ .01	$ .05	Heath, Mike	83D	517	$ .01	$ .06
Hatcher, Billy	88D	261	$ .01	$ .04	Heath, Mike	84D	223	$ .05	$ .20
Hatcher, Billy	88DK	23	$ .01	$ .05	Heath, Mike	85D	298	$ .01	$ .10

DONRUSS

Player	Year	No.	VG	EX/MT	Player	Year	No.	VG	EX/MT
Heath, Mike	86D	253	$ .01	$ .08	Henderson, Steve	81D	157	$ .01	$ .06
Heath, Mike	87D	496	$ .01	$ .05	Henderson, Steve	82D	183	$ .01	$ .06
Heath, Mike	88D	338	$ .01	$ .04	Henderson, Steve	83D	252	$ .01	$ .06
Heath, Mike	89D	271	$ .01	$ .04	Henderson, Steve	84D	389	$ .05	$ .20
Heath, Mike	90D	209	$ .01	$ .04	Henderson, Steve	85D	145	$ .01	$ .10
Heath, Mike	90DL	60	$ .05	$ .25	Henderson, Steve	86D	375	$ .01	$ .08
Heath, Mike	91D	230	$ .01	$ .04	Hendrick, George	81D	430	$ .01	$ .06
Heath, Mike	91DL	320	$ .01	$ .08	Hendrick, George	82D	40	$ .01	$ .06
Heathcock, Jeff	86D	182	$ .01	$ .08	Hendrick, George	82DK	9	$ .01	$ .15
Heaton, Neal	84D	373	$ .05	$ .35	Hendrick, George	83D	404	$ .01	$ .06
Heaton, Neal	85D	373	$ .01	$ .10	Hendrick, George	84D	475	$ .05	$ .20
Heaton, Neal	86D	338	$ .01	$ .08	Hendrick, George	85D	181	$ .01	$ .10
Heaton, Neal	87D	615	$ .01	$ .05	Hendrick, George	88D	479	$ .01	$ .04
Heaton, Neal	88D	134	$ .01	$ .04	Hengel, Dave	88D	629	$ .01	$ .15
Heaton, Neal	89D	224	$ .01	$ .04	Henke, Tom	84D	134	$ .20	$2.00
Heaton, Neal	90D	658	$ .01	$ .04	Henke, Tom	85D	403	$ .05	$ .35
Heaton, Neal	90DL	460	$ .10	$ .75	Henke, Tom	86D	437	$ .05	$ .25
Heaton, Neal	91D	475	$ .01	$ .04	Henke, Tom	87D	197	$ .01	$ .05
Heaton, Neal	92D	522	$ .01	$ .04	Henke, Tom	88D	490	$ .01	$ .04
Heaverlo, Dave	81D	407	$ .01	$ .06	Henke, Tom	89D	385	$ .01	$ .04
Hebner, Richie	81D	125	$ .01	$ .06	Henke, Tom	90D	349	$ .01	$ .04
Hebner, Richie	82D	328	$ .01	$ .06	Henke, Tom	90DL	158	$ .05	$ .25
Hebner, Richie	85D	564	$ .01	$ .10	Henke, Tom	91D	205	$ .01	$ .04
Heep, Danny	83D	443	$ .01	$ .06	Henke, Tom	91DL	517	$ .01	$ .08
Heep, Danny	84D	434	$ .05	$ .20	Henke, Tom	92D	141	$ .01	$ .04
Heep, Danny	85D	556	$ .01	$ .10	Henke, Tom	92DL	159	$ .01	$ .06
Heep, Danny	86D	556	$ .01	$ .08	Henke, Tom	93D	723	$ .01	$ .05
Heep, Danny	87D	649	$ .01	$ .05	Henneman, Mike	87DR	32	$ .05	$ .35
Heep, Danny	89D	368	$ .01	$ .04	Henneman, Mike	88D	420	$ .05	$ .20
Heep, Danny	90D	358	$ .01	$ .04	Henneman, Mike	89D	327	$ .01	$ .04
Heffernan, Bert	92DR	50	$ .01	$ .10	Henneman, Mike	90D	296	$ .01	$ .04
Heimueller, Gorman	84D	131	$ .05	$ .20					
Hemond, Scott	92D	637	$ .01	$ .04					
Hemond, Scott	93D	623	$ .01	$ .05					
Henderson, Dave	84D	557	$ .10	$ .75					
Henderson, Dave	86D	318	$ .05	$ .25					
Henderson, Dave	87D	622	$ .05	$ .20					
Henderson, Dave	89D	450	$ .01	$ .10					
Henderson, Dave	89DK	20	$ .01	$ .05					
Henderson, Dave	90D	243	$ .01	$ .04					
Henderson, Dave	91D	326	$ .01	$ .04					
Henderson, Dave	91DL	232	$ .01	$ .08					
Henderson, Dave	91DLS	103	$ .05	$ .35					
Henderson, Dave	92D	311	$ .01	$ .04					
Henderson, Dave	92DAS	21	$ .01	$ .05					
Henderson, Dave	92DL	232	$ .01	$ .06					
Henderson, Dave	92DLS	224	$ .01	$ .06					
Henderson, Dave	93D	373	$ .01	$ .05					
Henderson, Dave	93DL	139	$ .01	$ .15					
Henderson, Rickey	81D	119	$2.50	$10.00					
Henderson, Rickey	82D	113	$1.00	$4.00					
Henderson, Rickey	83D	35	$ .75	$3.00					
Henderson, Rickey	83DK	11	$ .15	$1.50					
Henderson, Rickey	84D	54	$3.00	$12.00					
Henderson, Rickey	85D	176	$1.00	$4.00					
Henderson, Rickey	86D	51	$ .20	$2.00					
Henderson, Rickey	87D	220	$ .10	$ .76					
Henderson, Rickey	88D	277	$ .05	$ .25					
Henderson, Rickey	89D	245	$ .05	$ .25					
Henderson, Rickey	90D	304	$ .05	$ .20					
Henderson, Rickey	90DL	84	$ .05	$ .35					
Henderson, Rickey	90DL	160	$ .20	$2.00					

MIKE HENNEMAN P

Player	Year	No.	VG	EX/MT
Henderson, Rickey	91D	648	$ .01	$ .15
Henderson, Rickey	91DAS	53	$ .01	$ .10
Henderson, Rickey	91DL	101	$ .10	$ .50
Henderson, Rickey	91DLBC	26	$ .15	$1.50
Henderson, Rickey	91DLP	23	$1.00	$4.00
Henderson, Rickey	91DLS	104	$ .10	$ .50
Henderson, Rickey	91DMVP	387	$ .01	$ .15
Henderson, Rickey	91DMVP	761	$ .01	$ .10
Henderson, Rickey	92D	193	$ .01	$ .15
Henderson, Rickey	92D	215	$ .01	$ .10
Henderson, Rickey	92DAS	30	$ .01	$ .10
Henderson, Rickey	92DL	116	$ .05	$ .20
Henderson, Rickey	93D	315	$ .01	$ .10

Player	Year	No.	VG	EX/MT
Henneman, Mike	90DL	2	$ .05	$ .25
Henneman, Mike	91D	76	$ .01	$ .04
Henneman, Mike	91DL	18	$ .01	$ .08
Henneman, Mike	92D	253	$ .01	$ .04
Henneman, Mike	92DL	325	$ .01	$ .06
Henneman, Mike	92DLS	175	$ .01	$ .06
Henneman, Mike	93D	259	$ .01	$ .05
Henneman, Mike	93DL	81	$ .01	$ .15
Henry, Butch	92DL	435	$ .01	$ .15
Henry, Butch	92DLS	37	$ .01	$ .15
Henry, Butch	92DR	51	$ .01	$ .10
Henry, Butch	93D	348	$ .01	$ .10
Henry, Butch	93D	767	$ .01	$ .05

DONRUSS

Player	Year	No.	VG	EX/MT
Henry, Doug	92D	663	$ .01	$ .15
Henry, Doug	92DL	80	$ .05	$ .25
Henry, Doug	93D	471	$ .01	$ .05
Henry, Dwayne	86D	603	$ .01	$ .08
Henry, Dwayne	87D	637	$ .01	$ .05
Henry, Dwayne	91DL	329	$ .01	$ .08
Henry, Dwayne	92D	114	$ .01	$ .04
Henry, Dwayne	92DL	433	$ .01	$ .06
Henry, Dwayne	93D	478	$ .01	$ .05
Hentgen, Pat	92D	704	$ .01	$ .10
Hentgen, Pat	93D	247	$ .01	$ .10
Heredia, Gil	92D	737	$ .01	$ .10
Hernandez, Carlos	90DR	37	$ .01	$ .05
Hernandez, Carlos	91D	711	$ .01	$ .04
Hernandez, Carlos	92D	778	$ .01	$ .04
Hernandez, Carlos	92DL	54	$ .01	$ .06
Hernandez, Carlos	93D	406	$ .01	$ .10
Hernandez, Cesar	92DR	52	$ .01	$ .15
Hernandez, Cesar	93D	558	$ .01	$ .05
Hernandez, Guillermo	89D	62	$ .01	$ .04
Hernandez, Guillermo	90D	610	$ .01	$ .04
Hernandez, Jeremy	92D	756	$ .01	$ .15
Hernandez, Jeremy	93D	180	$ .01	$ .10
Hernandez, Jose	92D	530	$ .01	$ .10
Hernandez, Keith	81D	67	$ .05	$ .35
Hernandez, Keith	82D	278	$ .05	$ .25
Hernandez, Keith	83D	152	$ .05	$ .25
Hernandez, Keith	83DK	20	$ .05	$ .20
Hernandez, Keith	84D	238	$ .10	$ .50
Hernandez, Keith	85D	68	$ .05	$ .25
Hernandez, Keith	86D	190	$ .05	$ .25

Player	Year	No.	VG	EX/MT
Hernandez, Keith	**87D**	**76**	**$ .01**	**$ .15**
Hernandez, Keith	88D	316	$ .01	$ .15
Hernandez, Keith	89D	117	$ .01	$ .10
Hernandez, Keith	90D	388	$ .01	$ .10
Hernandez, Keith	90DL	470	$ .05	$ .25
Hernandez, Manny	38D	481	$ .01	$ .04
Hernandez, Roberto	92DRR	19	$ .01	$ .10
Hernandez, Roberto	93D	403	$ .01	$ .05
Hernandez, Willie	81D	589	$ .01	$ .10
Hernandez, Willie	83D	174	$ .01	$ .10
Hernandez, Willie	84D	163	$ .05	$ .25
Hernandez, Willie	85D	212	$ .01	$ .10
Hernandez, Willie	86D	227	$ .01	$ .08

Player	Year	No.	VG	EX/MT
Hernandez, Willie	87D	522	$ .01	$ .05
Hernandez, Willie	88D	398	$ .01	$ .04
Hernandez, Xavier	90D	682	$ .01	$ .10
Hernandez, Xavier	90DL	517	$ .05	$ .25
Hernandez, Xavier	90DR	33	$ .01	$ .05
Hernandez, Xavier	91D	708	$ .01	$ .04
Hernandez, Xavier	91DL	462	$ .01	$ .08
Hernandez, Xavier	92D	782	$ .01	$ .04
Hernandez, Xavier	93D	636	$ .01	$ .05
Herndon, Larry	81D	196	$ .01	$ .06
Herndon, Larry	82D	172	$ .01	$ .06
Herndon, Larry	83D	585	$ .01	$ .06
Herndon, Larry	84D	349	$ .05	$ .20
Herndon, Larry	85D	150	$ .01	$ .10
Herndon, Larry	86D	593	$ .01	$ .08
Herndon, Larry	88D	353	$ .01	$ .04
Herr, Tom	81D	68	$ .01	$ .06
Herr, Tom	82D	530	$ .01	$ .06
Herr, Tom	83D	217	$ .01	$ .06
Herr, Tom	84D	596	$ .05	$ .20
Herr, Tom	85D	425	$ .01	$ .10
Herr, Tommy	86D	83	$ .01	$ .08
Herr, Tommy	87D	140	$ .01	$ .05
Herr, Tommy	88D	208	$ .01	$ .04
Herr, Tommy	89D	301	$ .01	$ .04
Herr, Tommy	89DTR	4	$ .01	$ .05
Herr, Tommy	90D	75	$ .01	$ .04
Herr, Tommy	90DK	21	$ .01	$ .05
Herr, Tom	90DL	184	$ .05	$ .25
Herr, Tom	91D	610	$ .01	$ .04
Herr, Tom	91DL	48	$ .01	$ .08
Herr, Tom	91DLS	205	$ .01	$ .08
Hershiser, Orel	85D	581	$1.00	$4.00
Hershiser, Orel	86D	226	$ .10	$ .50
Hershiser, Orel	86DK	18	$ .05	$ .25
Hershiser, Orel	87D	106	$ .05	$ .20
Hershiser, Orel	88D	94	$ .05	$ .20
Hershiser, Orel	89D	197	$ .01	$ .15
Hershiser, Orel	89D	648	$ .05	$ .25
Hershiser, Orel	89DBC	4	$ .01	$ .10
Hershiser, Orel	90D	197	$ .01	$ .10
Hershiser, Orel	90DBC	5	$ .01	$ .10
Hershiser, Orel	90DL	280	$ .05	$ .25
Hershiser, Orel	91D	280	$ .01	$ .04
Hershiser, Orel	91DL	243	$ .01	$ .15
Hershiser, Orel	91DLS	183	$ .01	$ .08
Hershiser, Orel	92D	247	$ .01	$ .04
Hershiser, Orel	92DL	81	$ .01	$ .06
Hershiser, Orel	92DLS	44	$ .01	$ .06
Hershiser, Orel	93D	274	$ .01	$ .05
Hershiser, Orel	93DK	14	$ .15	$1.50
Hershisher, Orel	93DL	53	$ .01	$ .15
Herzog, Whitey	82D	190	$ .01	$ .15
Herzog, Whitey	83D	530	$ .01	$ .06
Hesketh, Joe	85D	157	$ .05	$ .20
Hesketh, Joe	86D	341	$ .01	$ .08
Hesketh, Joe	87D	134	$ .01	$ .05
Hesketh, Joe	88D	504	$ .01	$ .04
Hesketh, Joe	89D	460	$ .01	$ .04
Hesketh, Joe	90D	511	$ .01	$ .04
Hesketh, Joe	90DL	507	$ .05	$ .25
Hesketh, Joe	92D	611	$ .01	$ .04
Hesketh, Joe	92DL	22	$ .01	$ .06
Hetzel, Eric	89D	660	$ .01	$ .10
Hetzel, Eric	90D	539	$ .01	$ .04
Hiatt, Phil	93D	393	$ .01	$ .15
Hibbard, Greg	90D	384	$ .01	$ .15
Hibbard, Greg	90DL	523	$ .10	$ .75
Hibbard, Greg	91D	159	$ .01	$ .04
Hibbard, Greg	91DL	438	$ .01	$ .08
Hibbard, Greg	91DLS	34	$ .01	$ .08
Hibbard, Greg	92D	178	$ .01	$ .04
Hibbard, Greg	92DL	169	$ .01	$ .06
Hibbard, Greg	92DLS	153	$ .01	$ .06
Hibbard, Greg	93D	271	$ .01	$ .05

DONRUSS

Player	Year	No.	VG	EX/MT	Player	Year	No.	VG	EX/MT
Hickerson, Bryan	92D	783	$ .01	$ .10	Hoiles, Chris	91DL	131	$ .05	$ .20
Hickerson, Bryan	92DL	280	$ .01	$ .06	Hoiles, Chris	91DLS	4	$ .05	$ .20
Hickerson, Bryan	93D	496	$ .01	$ .05	Hoiles, Chris	92D	156	$ .01	$ .10
Hickey, Kevin	82D	631	$ .01	$ .06	Hoiles, Chris	92DL	211	$ .01	$ .06
Hickey, Kevin	83D	445	$ .01	$ .06	Hoiles, Chris	92DLS	124	$ .01	$ .06
Hickey, Kevin	84D	135	$ .05	$ .20	Hoiles, Chris	93D	323	$ .01	$ .10
Hickey, Kevin	90D	583	$ .01	$ .04	Hoiles, Chris	93DL	133	$ .05	$ .25
Higuera, Ted	86D	351	$ .05	$ .25	Holland, Al	82D	377	$ .01	$ .06
Higuera, Ted	87D	49	$ .05	$ .20	Holland, Al	83D	146	$ .01	$ .06
Higuera, Ted	87DK	16	$ .05	$ .20	Holland, Al	84D	204	$ .05	$ .20
Higuera, Teddy	88D	90	$ .05	$ .20	Holland, Al	85D	427	$ .01	$ .10
Higuera, Ted	89D	175	$ .01	$ .04	Holland, Al	86D	573	$ .01	$ .08
Higuera, Ted	90D	339	$ .01	$ .04	Hollins, Dave	90DR	47	$ .10	$ .75
Higuera, Ted	90DL	506	$ .05	$ .25	Hollins, Dave	92D	685	$ .01	$ .04
Higuera, Ted	91D	629	$ .01	$ .04	Hollins, Dave	92DL	278	$ .05	$ .25
Higuera, Ted	91DLSP	6	$ .20	$2.00	Hollins, Dave	93D	68	$ .01	$ .10
Higuera, Ted	92D	294	$ .01	$ .04	Hollins, Jessie	93D	368	$ .01	$ .10
Hill, Donnie	84D	96	$ .05	$ .20	Holman, Brian	89D	511	$ .01	$ .15
Hill, Donnie	85D	375	$ .01	$ .10	Holman, Brian	90D	143	$ .01	$ .04
Hill, Donnie	86D	340	$ .01	$ .08	Holman, Brian	90DL	273	$ .05	$ .25
Hill, Donnie	87D	405	$ .01	$ .05	Holman, Brian	91D	539	$ .01	$ .04
Hill, Donnie	88D	87	$ .01	$ .04	Holman, Brian	91DL	11	$ .01	$ .08
Hill, Donnie	91D	376	$ .01	$ .04	Holman, Brian	91DLS	115	$ .01	$ .08
Hill, Donnie	91DL	177	$ .01	$ .08	Holman, Brian	92D	43	$ .01	$ .04
Hill, Donnie	92DL	498	$ .01	$ .06	Holman, Brian	93D	385	$ .01	$ .05
Hill, Glenallen	87D	561	$ .05	$ .20	Holman, Scott	83D	224	$ .01	$ .06
Hill, Glenallen	90D	627	$ .01	$ .10	Holmes, Darren	91D	669	$ .01	$ .10
Hill, Glenallen	90DL	317	$ .05	$ .25	Holmes, Darren	91DL	387	$ .05	$ .20
Hill, Glenallen	90DR	24	$ .01	$ .05	Holmes, Darren	92D	504	$ .01	$ .04
Hill, Glenallen	91D	380	$ .01	$ .04	Holmes, Darren	93D	149	$ .01	$ .05
Hill, Glenallen	91DL	311	$ .01	$ .08	Holmes, Darren	93D	779	$ .01	$ .05
Hill, Glenallen	91DLS	43	$ .01	$ .08	Holton, Brian	87D	598	$ .01	$ .15
Hill, Glenallen	92D	643	$ .01	$ .04	Holton, Brian	87DR	54	$ .01	$ .07
Hill, Glenallen	92DL	70	$ .01	$ .06	Holton, Brian	88D	402	$ .01	$ .04
Hill, Glenallen	92DLS	166	$ .01	$ .06	Holton, Brian	89D	439	$ .01	$ .04
Hill, Glenallen	93D	201	$ .01	$ .05	Holton, Brian	89DTR	20	$ .01	$ .05
Hill, Glenallen	93DL	128	$ .01	$ .15	Holton, Brian	90D	635	$ .01	$ .04
Hill, Ken	89D	536	$ .05	$ .25	Holton, Brian	90DL	487	$ .05	$ .25
Hill, Ken	89DR	31	$ .05	$ .35	Honeycutt, Rick	81D	46	$ .01	$ .06
Hill, Ken	90D	397	$ .01	$ .10	Honeycutt, Rick	82D	494	$ .01	$ .06
Hill, Ken	91D	670	$ .01	$ .04	Honeycutt, Rick	83D	415	$ .01	$ .06
Hill, Ken	91DL	376	$ .01	$ .08	Honeycutt, Rick	84D	494	$ .05	$ .20
Hill, Ken	92D	31	$ .01	$ .04	Honeycutt, Rick	85D	215	$ .01	$ .10
Hill, Ken	92DL	468	$ .01	$ .06	Honeycutt, Rick	86D	372	$ .01	$ .08
Hill, Ken	92DLS	56	$ .01	$ .06	Honeycutt, Rick	87D	402	$ .01	$ .05
Hill, Ken	93D	220	$ .01	$ .05	Honeycutt, Rick	88D	590	$ .01	$ .04
Hill, Ken	93DL	201	$ .05	$ .20	Honeycutt, Rick	89D	328	$ .01	$ .04
Hill, Marc	83D	230	$ .01	$ .06	Honeycutt, Rick	90D	386	$ .01	$ .04
Hill, Marc	84D	330	$ .05	$ .20	Honeycutt, Rick	90DL	372	$ .05	$ .25
Hill, Marc	85D	160	$ .01	$ .10	Honeycutt, Rick	91D	373	$ .01	$ .04
Hill, Milt	92D	659	$ .01	$ .10	Honeycutt, Rick	91DL	210	$ .01	$ .08
Hill, Milt	93D	502	$ .01	$ .05	Honeycutt, Rick	91DLS	105	$ .01	$ .08
Hillegas, Shawn	88DRR	35	$ .01	$ .15	Honeycutt, Rick	92D	269	$ .01	$ .04
Hillegas, Shawn	89D	503	$ .01	$ .04	Hood, Don	83D	390	$ .01	$ .06
Hillegas, Shawn	90D	619	$ .01	$ .04	Hooton, Burt	81D	541	$ .01	$ .06
Hillegas, Shawn	91D	589	$ .01	$ .04	Hooton, Burt	82D	32	$ .01	$ .06
Hillegas, Shawn	91DL	513	$ .01	$ .08	Hooton, Burt	83D	32	$ .01	$ .06
Hillegas, Shawn	92D	72	$ .01	$ .04	Hooton, Burt	84D	459	$ .05	$ .20
Hinzo, Tommy	88D	526	$ .01	$ .04	Hooton, Burt	85D	104	$ .01	$ .10
Hisle, Larry	81D	87	$ .01	$ .06	Hooton, Burt	86D	300	$ .01	$ .08
Hisle, Larry	82D	358	$ .01	$ .06	Horn, Sam	88D	498	$ .01	$ .15
Hitchcock, Sterling	93D	345	$ .01	$ .05	Horn, Sam	91D	733	$ .01	$ .04
Hobson, Butch	81D	542	$ .01	$ .06	Horn, Sam	91DL	332	$ .01	$ .08
Hobson, Butch	82D	577	$ .01	$ .06	Horn, Sam	91DLS	5	$ .01	$ .08
Hodges, Ron	83D	476	$ .01	$ .06	Horn, Sam	92D	278	$ .01	$ .04
Hodges, Ron	84D	603	$ .05	$ .20	Horn, Sam	92DL	219	$ .01	$ .06
Hoffman, Glenn	81D	95	$ .01	$ .06	Horn, Sam	92DLS	125	$ .01	$ .06
Hoffman, Glenn	82D	460	$ .01	$ .06	Horn, Sam	93D	617	$ .01	$ .05
Hoffman, Glenn	83D	282	$ .01	$ .06	Horner, Bob	81D	99	$ .01	$ .06
Hoffman, Glenn	84D	606	$ .05	$ .20	Horner, Bob	82D	173	$ .01	$ .06
Hoffman, Glenn	86D	457	$ .01	$ .08	Horner, Bob	83D	58	$ .01	$ .06
Hoffman, Glenn	90D	407	$ .01	$ .04	Horner, Bob	84D	535	$ .05	$ .20
Hoffman, Guy	88D	452	$ .01	$ .04	Horner, Bob	84DK	14	$ .05	$ .25
Hoiles, Chris	90DL	513	$ .25	$2.50	Horner, Bob	85D	77	$ .01	$ .10
Hoiles, Chris	91D	358	$ .01	$ .10	Horner, Bob	86D	188	$ .01	$ .05

109

DONRUSS

Player	Year	No.	VG	EX/MT
Horner, Bob	87D	389	$ .01	$ .05
Horsman, Vince	92DL	487	$ .01	$ .15
Horsman, Vince	92DR	53	$ .01	$ .05
Horsman, Vince	93D	347	$ .01	$ .10
Horton, Ricky	85D	83	$ .05	$ .25
Horton, Ricky	86D	138	$ .01	$ .08
Horton, Ricky	87D	234	$ .01	$ .05
Horton, Ricky	88D	430	$ .01	$ .04
Horton, Ricky	89D	582	$ .01	$ .04
Horton, Ricky	90D	666	$ .01	$ .04
Hosey, Steve	92DR	54	$ .05	$ .25
Hosey, Steve	93D	704	$ .01	$ .10
Hosey, Steve	93DL	48	$ .10	$ .40
Hostetler, Dave	83D	89	$ .01	$ .06
Hostetler, Dave	84D	159	$ .05	$ .20
Hough, Charlie	82D	447	$ .01	$ .06
Hough, Charlie	83D	69	$ .01	$ .06
Hough, Charlie	84D	638	$ .05	$ .20
Hough, Charlie	85D	422	$ .01	$ .10
Hough, Charlie	86D	342	$ .01	$ .08
Hough, Charlie	87D	470	$ .01	$ .05
Hough, Charlie	87DK	7	$ .01	$ .15
Hough, Charlie	88D	99	$ .01	$ .04
Hough, Charlie	89D	165	$ .01	$ .04
Hough, Charlie	90D	411	$ .01	$ .04
Hough, Charlie	90DL	390	$ .05	$ .25
Hough, Charlie	91D	146	$ .01	$ .04
Hough, Charlie	91DL	472	$ .01	$ .08
Hough, Charlie	91DLS	35	$ .01	$ .08
Hough, Charlie	92D	69	$ .01	$ .04
Hough, Charlie	92DL	39	$ .01	$ .06
Houk, Ralph	82D	282	$ .01	$ .06
Householder, Paul	81D	303	$ .01	$ .06
Householder, Paul	82D	314	$ .01	$ .06
Householder, Paul	83D	566	$ .01	$ .06
Householder, Paul	86D	414	$ .01	$ .08
Howard, Dave	91D	325	$ .05	$ .20
Howard, Dave	92D	567	$ .01	$ .04
Howard, Dave	92DL	4	$ .01	$ .06
Howard, Thomas	91D	746	$ .01	$ .10
Howard, Thomas	92D	266	$ .01	$ .04
Howard, Thomas	92DL	84	$ .01	$ .06
Howard, Thomas	92DL	456	$ .01	$ .06
Howard, Thomas	93D	257	$ .01	$ .05
Howe, Art	81D	258	$ .01	$ .06
Howe, Art	82D	92	$ .01	$ .06
Howe, Art	83D	396	$ .01	$ .06
Howe, Steve	81D	511	$ .01	$ .06
Howe, Steve	82D	158	$ .01	$ .06
Howe, Steve	83D	630	$ .01	$ .06
Howe, Steve	88D	593	$ .01	$ .04
Howe, Steve	91DL	440	$ .01	$ .08
Howe, Steve	91DLS	93	$ .01	$ .08
Howe, Steve	92D	106	$ .01	$ .04
Howe, Steve	93D	763	$ .01	$ .05
Howell, Jack	86D	524	$ .05	$ .30
Howell, Jack	87D	305	$ .01	$ .05
Howell, Jack	88D	333	$ .01	$ .04
Howell, Jack	89D	288	$ .01	$ .04
Howell, Jack	90D	254	$ .01	$ .04
Howell, Jack	90DL	327	$ .05	$ .25
Howell, Jack	91D	247	$ .01	$ .04
Howell, Jack	92D	646	$ .01	$ .04
Howell, Jay	83D	587	$ .01	$ .06
Howell, Jay	85D	103	$ .01	$ .10
Howell, Jay	86D	223	$ .01	$ .08
Howell, Jay	87D	503	$ .01	$ .05
Howell, Jay	88D	55	$ .01	$ .04
Howell, Jay	89D	610	$ .01	$ .04
Howell, Jay	90D	203	$ .01	$ .04
Howell, Jay	90DL	42	$ .05	$ .25
Howell, Jay	91D	486	$ .01	$ .04
Howell, Jay	91DL	98	$ .01	$ .08
Howell, Jay	92D	395	$ .01	$ .04
Howell, Jay	93D	538	$ .01	$ .05

Player	Year	No.	VG	EX/MT
Howell, Ken	85D	592	$ .05	$ .25
Howell, Ken	86D	275	$ .01	$ .08
Howell, Ken	87D	229	$ .01	$ .05
Howell, Ken	88D	130	$ .01	$ .04
Howell, Ken	90D	430	$ .01	$ .04
Howell, Ken	90DL	316	$ .05	$ .25
Howell, Ken	91D	204	$ .01	$ .04
Howell, Pat	92DR	55	$ .01	$ .15
Howell, Pat	93D	116	$ .01	$ .10
Howell, Roy	81D	392	$ .01	$ .06
Howell, Roy	82D	204	$ .01	$ .06
Howell, Roy	83D	358	$ .01	$ .06
Howell, Roy	85D	577	$ .01	$ .10
Howitt, Dann	92D	751	$ .01	$ .04
Howitt, Dann	93D	349	$ .01	$ .05
Howser, Dick	83D	590	$ .01	$ .06
Hoy, Peter	92DL	515	$ .01	$ .15
Hoy, Peter	92DR	56	$ .01	$ .05
Hoyt, LaMarr	81D	160	$ .05	$ .20
Hoyt, LaMarr	82D	117	$ .01	$ .06
Hoyt, LaMarr	83D	632	$ .01	$ .06
Hoyt, LaMarr	84D	488	$ .05	$ .20
Hoyt, LaMarr	85D	86	$ .01	$ .10
Hoyt, LaMarr	86D	139	$ .01	$ .08
Hoyt, LaMarr	87D	434	$ .01	$ .05
Hrabosky, Al	81D	550	$ .01	$ .06
Hrabosky, Al	82D	97	$ .01	$ .06
Hrabosky, Al	83D	475	$ .01	$ .06
Hrbek, Kent	82D	557	$ .25	$2.50
Hrbek, Kent	83D	179	$ .10	$ .50
Hrbek, Kent	83DK	19	$ .05	$ .25
Hrbek, Kent	84D	70	$ .10	$ .75
Hrbek, Kent	85D	70	$ .05	$ .35
Hrbek, Kent	86D	70	$ .05	$ .25
Hrbek, Kent	87D	73	$ .01	$ .15
Hrbek, Kent	88D	320	$ .01	$ .15
Hrbek, Kent	89D	199	$ .01	$ .10
Hrbek, Kent	90D	81	$ .01	$ .04
Hrbek, Kent	90DL	228	$ .05	$ .25
Hrbek, Kent	91D	95	$ .01	$ .04
Hrbek, Kent	91DL	313	$ .01	$ .08
Hrbek, Kent	91DLS	87	$ .01	$ .08

DONRUSS

Player	Year	No.	VG	EX/MT	Player	Year	No.	VG	EX/MT
Hrbek, Kent	92D	326	$.01	$.04	Hurst, Bruce	91D	83	$.01	$.04
Hrbek, Kent	92DL	362	$.01	$.06	Hurst, Bruce	91DL	469	$.01	$.08
Hrbek, Kent	92DLS	205	$.01	$.06	Hurst, Bruce	92D	123	$.01	$.04
Hrbek, Kent	93D	283	$.01	$.05	Hurst, Bruce	92DL	216	$.01	$.06
Hrbek, Kent	93DL	76	$.01	$.15	Hurst, Bruce	93D	576	$.01	$.05
Hubbard, Glenn	81D	459	$.01	$.06	Hurst, Jon	92DR	57	$.05	$.25
Hubbard, Glenn	82D	436	$.01	$.06	Huskey, Butch	93D	506	$.05	$.20
Hubbard, Glenn	83D	184	$.01	$.06	Huson, Jeff	90D	693	$.01	$.10
Hubbard, Glenn	84D	432	$.05	$.20	Huson, Jeff	90DL	285	$.05	$.25
Hubbard, Glenn	85D	199	$.01	$.10	Huson, Jeff	90DR	11	$.01	$.05
Hubbard, Glenn	86D	141	$.01	$.08	Huson, Jeff	91D	305	$.01	$.04
Hubbard, Glenn	87D	634	$.01	$.05	Huson, Jeff	91DL	134	$.01	$.08
Hubbard, Glenn	88D	314	$.01	$.04	Huson, Jeff	92D	456	$.01	$.04
Hubbard, Glenn	88DK	22	$.01	$.05	Huson, Jeff	92DL	251	$.01	$.06
Hubbard, Glenn	89D	568	$.01	$.04	Huson, Jeff	93D	583	$.01	$.05
Hudler, Rex	85D	469	$.01	$.15	Huson, Jeff	93DL	137	$.05	$.20
Hudler, Rex	89D	452	$.01	$.04	Hutton, Mark	92DR	58	$.05	$.25
Hudler, Rex	90D	366	$.01	$.04	Hutton, Mark	93D	671	$.01	$.10
Hudler, Rex	90DL	439	$.05	$.25	Hutton, Tommy	81D	93	$.01	$.06
Hudler, Rex	91D	599	$.01	$.04	Incaviglia, Pete	86DR	23	$.10	$.50
Hudler, Rex	91DL	212	$.01	$.08	Incaviglia, Pete	87D	224	$.05	$.35
Hudler, Rex	91DLS	233	$.01	$.08	Incaviglia, Pete	88D	304	$.05	$.25
Hudler, Rex	92D	438	$.01	$.04	Incaviglia, Pete	89D	56	$.01	$.10
Hudler, Rex	92DL	25	$.01	$.06	Incaviglia, Pete	89DK	3	$.01	$.05
Hudler, Rex	92DLS	92	$.01	$.06	Incaviglia, Pete	90D	48	$.01	$.10
Hudler, Rex	93D	96	$.01	$.05	Incaviglia, Pete	90DL	231	$.05	$.25
Hudson, Charlie	84D	448	$.05	$.20	Incaviglia, Pete	91D	464	$.01	$.04
Hudson, Charlie	85D	355	$.01	$.10	Incaviglia, Pete	91DL	366	$.01	$.08
Hudson, Charlie	86D	622	$.01	$.08	Incaviglia, Pete	92DL	458	$.01	$.06
Hudson, Charlie	87D	630	$.01	$.05	Incaviglia, Pete	93D	480	$.01	$.05
Hudson, Charlie	88D	374	$.01	$.04	Infante, Alexis	89DR	30	$.01	$.05
Hudson, Charles	89D	514	$.01	$.04	Innis, Jeff	90D	408	$.01	$.10
Hudson, Charles	89DTR	50	$.01	$.05	Innis, Jeff	92D	587	$.01	$.04
Huff, Mike	91DLBC	22	$.10	$1.00	Innis, Jeff	93D	330	$.01	$.05
Huff, Mike	92D	579	$.01	$.04	Iorg, Dane	81D	311	$.01	$.06
Huff, Michael	92DL	342	$.01	$.06	Iorg, Dane	82D	166	$.01	$.06
Huff, Michael	93D	788	$.01	$.05	Iorg, Dane	83D	469	$.01	$.06
Hughes, Keith	88D	643	$.01	$.15	Iorg, Dane	84D	571	$.05	$.20
Huismann, Mark	84D	339	$.05	$.20	Iorg, Dane	85D	252	$.01	$.10
Huismann, Mark	85D	583	$.01	$.10	Iorg, Garth	82D	353	$.01	$.06
Hulett, Tim	85D	645	$.01	$.10	Iorg, Garth	83D	306	$.01	$.06
Hulett, Tim	86D	404	$.01	$.08	Iorg, Garth	84D	561	$.05	$.20
Hulett, Tim	87D	260	$.01	$.05	Iorg, Garth	85D	363	$.01	$.10
Hulett, Tim	91D	706	$.01	$.04	Iorg, Garth	86D	640	$.01	$.08
Hulett, Tim	93D	661	$.01	$.05	Iorg, Garth	87D	394	$.01	$.05
Hulse, David	93D	706	$.01	$.10	Iorg, Garth	88D	444	$.01	$.04
Hume, Tom	82D	229	$.01	$.06	Ivie, Mike	81D	312	$.01	$.06
Hume, Tom	83D	229	$.01	$.06	Ivie, Mike	82D	396	$.01	$.06
Hume, Tom	84D	550	$.05	$.20	Ivie, Mike	83D	485	$.01	$.06
Hume, Tom	85D	408	$.01	$.10	Jackson, Bo	86DR	38	$1.50	$6.00
Hume, Tom	86D	365	$.01	$.08	Jackson, Bo	87DR	14	$.20	$2.00
Humphreys, Mike	92D	769	$.05	$.04	Jackson, Bo	87DRR	35	$1.00	$4.00
Hundley, Todd	91D	641	$.01	$.10	Jackson, Bo	88D	220	$.05	$.35
Hundley, Todd	92D	568	$.01	$.04	Jackson, Bo	89D	208	$.05	$.35
Hundley, Todd	92DLS	66	$.01	$.06	Jackson, Bo	90D	61	$.05	$.20
Hundley, Todd	93D	66	$.01	$.05	Jackson, Bo	90DAS	650	$.05	$.20
Hundley, Todd	93DL	75	$.01	$.15	Jackson, Bo	90DBC	1	$.05	$.20
Hunt, Randy	87D	625	$.01	$.05	Jackson, Bo	90DK	1	$.05	$.20
Hunter, Brian	91DR	9	$.05	$.20	Jackson, Bo	90DL	125	$.20	$2.00
Hunter, Brian	92D	163	$.10	$.50	Jackson, Bo	91D	632	$.01	$.15
Hunter, Brian	92DL	374	$.05	$.20	Jackson, Bo	91DBC	10	$.01	$.10
Hunter, Brian	93D	290	$.01	$.05	Jackson, Bo	91DLP	19	$1.25	$5.00
Hurdle, Clint	81D	224	$.01	$.06	Jackson, Bo	92D	470	$.01	$.15
Hurdle, Clint	82D	516	$.01	$.06	Jackson, Chuck	87DR	55	$.01	$.07
Hurdle, Clint	86D	434	$.01	$.08	Jackson, Danny	84D	461	$.10	$.40
Hurst, Bruce	83D	134	$.10	$.40	Jackson, Danny	85D	374	$.01	$.15
Hurst, Bruce	84D	213	$.05	$.20	Jackson, Danny	86D	95	$.01	$.15
Hurst, Bruce	85D	493	$.01	$.10	Jackson, Danny	87D	157	$.01	$.05
Hurst, Bruce	86D	517	$.01	$.08	Jackson, Danny	88D	132	$.01	$.04
Hurst, Bruce	87D	174	$.01	$.05	Jackson, Danny	89D	124	$.01	$.10
Hurst, Bruce	88D	252	$.01	$.04	Jackson, Danny	90D	80	$.01	$.10
Hurst, Bruce	89D	423	$.01	$.04	Jackson, Danny	90DL	279	$.05	$.25
Hurst, Bruce	89DTR	45	$.01	$.05	Jackson, Danny	91D	96	$.01	$.04
Hurst, Bruce	90D	183	$.01	$.04	Jackson, Danny	91DL	678	$.01	$.04
Hurst, Bruce	90DL	23	$.05	$.25	Jackson, Danny	91DL	268	$.01	$.08

111

DONRUSS

Player	Year	No.	VG	EX/MT	Player	Year	No.	VG	EX/MT
Jackson, Danny	92D	91	$ .01	$ .04	James, Chris	92DL	497	$ .01	$ .06
Jackson, Danny	92DL	381	$ .01	$ .06	James, Chris	93D	604	$ .01	$ .05
Jackson, Danny	93D	202	$ .01	$ .05	James, Dion	84DRR	31	$ .10	$ .50
Jackson, Darrell	81D	547	$ .01	$ .06	James, Dion	85D	211	$ .01	$ .15
Jackson, Darrell	82D	179	$ .01	$ .06	James, Dion	86D	89	$ .01	$ .15
Jackson, Darrin	88DR	45	$ .10	$ .50	James, Dion	88D	190	$ .01	$ .04
Jackson, Darrin	90D	641	$ .01	$ .04	James, Dion	89D	340	$ .01	$ .04
Jackson, Darrin	91DL	346	$ .01	$ .08	James, Dion	90D	428	$ .01	$ .04
Jackson, Darrin	92D	292	$ .01	$ .04	James, Dion	91D	348	$ .01	$ .04
Jackson, Darrin	92DL	129	$ .01	$ .06	James, Dion	92DL	365	$ .01	$ .06
Jackson, Darrin	93D	230	$ .01	$ .05	James, Dion	93D	735	$ .01	$ .05
Jackson, Darrin	93DL	140	$ .01	$ .15	Javier, Stan	86D	584	$ .05	$ .20
Jackson, Grant	81D	15	$ .01	$ .06	Javier, Stan	87D	590	$ .01	$ .05
Jackson, Grant	82D	518	$ .01	$ .06	Javier, Stan	89D	185	$ .01	$ .04
Jackson, Mike	87DR	36	$ .05	$ .25	Javier, Stan	90D	568	$ .01	$ .04
Jackson, Mike	88D	139	$ .01	$ .10	Javier, Stan	90DL	445	$ .05	$ .25
Jackson, Mike	89D	652	$ .01	$ .04	Javier, Stan	91D	239	$ .01	$ .04
Jackson, Mike	90DL	351	$ .05	$ .25	Javier, Stan	91DL	155	$ .01	$ .08
Jackson, Mike	91D	676	$ .01	$ .04	Javier, Stan	92D	322	$ .01	$ .04
Jackson, Mike	91DL	452	$ .01	$ .08	Javier, Stan	93D	280	$ .01	$ .05
Jackson, Mike	92D	584	$ .01	$ .04	Jeffcoat, Mike	84DRR	43	$ .05	$ .25
Jackson, Mike	92DL	481	$ .01	$ .06	Jeffcoat, Mike	85D	251	$ .01	$ .10
Jackson, Mike	92DLS	116	$ .01	$ .06	Jeffcoat, Mike	90D	521	$ .01	$ .04
Jackson, Mike	93D	314	$ .01	$ .05	Jeffcoat, Mike	90DL	416	$ .05	$ .25
Jackson, Mike	93DL	84	$ .01	$ .15	Jeffcoat, Mike	91DL	386	$ .01	$ .08
Jackson, Reggie	81D	228	$ .75	$3.00	Jeffcoat, Mike	92D	351	$ .01	$ .04
Jackson, Reggie	81D	348	$ .25	$2.50	Jeffereis, Gregg	92DL	215	$ .01	$ .06
Jackson, Reggie	81D	468	$ .25	$2.50	Jefferies, Gregg	88D	657	$ .10	$1.00
Jackson, Reggie	82D	535	$ .20	$1.75	Jefferies, Gregg	89DR	2	$ .05	$ .25
Jackson, Reggie	82D	575	$ .15	$1.50	Jefferies, Gregg	89DRR	35	$ .05	$ .25
Jackson, Reggie	83D	115	$ .15	$1.50	Jefferies, Gregg	90D	270	$ .01	$ .10
Jackson, Reggie	83DK	3	$ .10	$ .60	Jefferies, Gregg	90DL	171	$ .10	$1.00
Jackson, Reggie	84D	57	$1.75	$7.00	Jefferies, Gregg	91D	79	$ .01	$ .10
Jackson, Reggie	85D	57	$ .15	$1.50	Jefferies, Gregg	91DL	465	$ .05	$ .25
Jackson, Reggie	86D	377	$ .10	$1.00	Jefferies, Gregg	91DLS	206	$ .05	$ .20
Jackson, Reggie	87D	210	$ .10	$ .40	Jefferies, Gregg	92D	372	$ .01	$ .10
Jackson, Ron	81D	489	$ .01	$ .06	Jefferies, Gregg	92DLS	184	$ .01	$ .06
Jackson, Ron	82D	602	$ .01	$ .06	Jefferies, Gregg	93D	307	$ .01	$ .05
Jackson, Ron	83D	639	$ .01	$ .06	Jefferson, Reggie	91DL	514	$ .10	$ .50
Jackson, Ron	84D	133	$ .05	$ .20	Jefferson, Reggie	91DR	55	$ .05	$ .20
Jackson, Roy Lee	81D	36	$ .01	$ .06	Jefferson, Reggie	92DL	86	$ .05	$ .20
Jackson, Roy Lee	82D	541	$ .01	$ .06	Jefferson, Reggie	92DRR	12	$ .05	$ .25
Jackson, Roy Lee	83D	479	$ .01	$ .06	Jefferson, Reggie	93D	303	$ .01	$ .05
Jackson, Roy Lee	84D	195	$ .05	$ .20	Jefferson, Stan	87D	642	$ .01	$ .15
Jackson, Roy Lee	85D	606	$ .01	$ .10	Jefferson, Stan	87DR	43	$ .01	$ .07
Jacoby, Brook	84D	542	$ .10	$ .50	Jefferson, Stan	88D	187	$ .01	$ .04
Jacoby, Brook	85D	154	$ .05	$ .25	Jeltz, Steve	85DRR	44	$ .01	$ .15
Jacoby, Brook	86D	154	$ .01	$ .15	Jeltz, Steve	87D	359	$ .01	$ .05
Jacoby, Brook	87D	104	$ .01	$ .05	Jeltz, Steve	88D	576	$ .01	$ .04
Jacoby, Brook	87DK	8	$ .01	$ .05	Jeltz, Steve	89D	431	$ .01	$ .04
Jacoby, Brook	88D	131	$ .01	$ .04	Jeltz, Steve	90D	133	$ .01	$ .04
Jacoby, Brook	89D	114	$ .01	$ .04	Jenkins, Fergie (Ferguson)	81D	146	$ .10	$ .50
Jacoby, Brook	90D	83	$ .01	$ .04	Jenkins, Fergie	82D	643	$ .10	$ .50
Jacoby, Brook	90DL	74	$ .05	$ .25	Jenkins, Fergie	83D	300	$ .05	$ .25
Jacoby, Brook	91D	176	$ .01	$ .04	Jenkins, Fergie	84D	189	$ .10	$1.00
Jacoby, Brook	91DL	421	$ .01	$ .08	Jennings, Doug	88DR	13	$ .01	$ .15
Jacoby, Brook	91DLS	44	$ .01	$ .08	Jennings, Doug	89D	505	$ .01	$ .10
Jacoby, Brook	92D	670	$ .01	$ .04	Jeter, Shawn	92DR	59	$ .01	$ .15
Jacoby, Brook	93D	493	$ .01	$ .05	Jimenez, Houston	85D	269	$ .01	$ .10
Jaha, John	92DRR	398	$ .05	$ .35	John, Tommy	81D	107	$ .05	$ .20
Jaha, John	93D	207	$ .01	$ .15	John, Tommy	82D	409	$ .05	$ .20
James, Bob	84D	87	$ .05	$ .20	John, Tommy	82D	558	$ .05	$ .20
James, Bob	85D	279	$ .01	$ .10	John, Tommy	83D	570	$ .05	$ .20
James, Bob	86D	379	$ .01	$ .08	John, Tommy	84D	301	$ .05	$ .35
James, Bob	87D	493	$ .01	$ .05	John, Tommy	85D	423	$ .05	$ .25
James, Bob	88D	507	$ .01	$ .04	John, Tommy	88D	401	$ .01	$ .15
James, Chris	87DRR	42	$ .05	$ .20	John, Tommy	88DK	17	$ .01	$ .15
James, Chris	88D	453	$ .01	$ .10	Johnson, Anthony	83D	629	$ .01	$ .06
James, Chris	89D	312	$ .01	$ .04	Johnson, Bob	83D	494	$ .01	$ .06
James, Chris	90D	323	$ .01	$ .04	Johnson, Bob	84D	500	$ .05	$ .20
James, Chris	90DL	319	$ .05	$ .25	Johnson, Cliff	81D	484	$ .01	$ .06
James, Chris	91D	227	$ .01	$ .04	Johnson, Cliff	82D	339	$ .01	$ .06
James, Chris	91DL	175	$ .01	$ .08	Johnson, Cliff	83D	601	$ .01	$ .06
James, Chris	91DLS	45	$ .01	$ .08	Johnson, Cliff	84D	512	$ .05	$ .20
James, Chris	92D	82	$ .01	$ .04	Johnson, Cliff	85D	512	$ .01	$ .10

DONRUSS

Player	Year	No.	VG	EX/MT
Johnson, Cliff	86D	639	$.01	$.08
Johnson, Cliff	87D	645	$.01	$.05
Johnson, Dave	90D	702	$.01	$.04
Johnson, Dave	90DL	434	$.05	$.25
Johnson, Dave	91D	126	$.01	$.04
Johnson, Dave	91DL	248	$.01	$.08
Johnson, Howard	83D	328	$1.25	$5.00
Johnson, Howard	85D	247	$.15	$1.50
Johnson, Howard	86D	312	$.10	$.50
Johnson, Howard	87D	646	$.05	$.25
Johnson, Howard	88D	569	$.01	$.15
Johnson, Howard	89D	235	$.01	$.15
Johnson, Howard	90D	99	$.01	$.10
Johnson, Howard	90DAS	654	$.05	$.20
Johnson, Howard	90DBC	2	$.01	$.10
Johnson, Howard	90DK	18	$.01	$.05
Johnson, Howard	90DL	272	$.10	$.50
Johnson, Howard	91D	454	$.01	$.10
Johnson, Howard	91DL	34	$.01	$.15
Johnson, Howard	91DLS	207	$.01	$.15
Johnson, Howard	92D	341	$.01	$.10
Johnson, Howard	92DL	132	$.01	$.06

Howard Johnson
New York Mets

Player	Year	No.	VG	EX/MT
Johnson, Howard	92DLS	67	$.01	$.06
Johnson, Howard	93D	434	$.01	$.05
Johnson, Howard	93DL	39	$.01	$.15
Johnson, Jeff	91DR	47	$.01	$.15
Johnson, Jeff	92D	275	$.01	$.10
Johnson, Joe	86D	624	$.01	$.08
Johnson, Joe	87D	650	$.01	$.05
Johnson, John Henry	82D	550	$.01	$.06
Johnson, John Henry	84D	91	$.05	$.20
Johnson, Lamar	81D	38	$.01	$.06
Johnson, Lamar	82D	269	$.01	$.06
Johnson, Lamar	83D	142	$.01	$.06
Johnson, Lance	88DRR	31	$.01	$.15
Johnson, Lance	89D	606	$.01	$.04
Johnson, Lance	90D	573	$.01	$.04
Johnson, Lance	90DL	259	$.05	$.25
Johnson, Lance	91D	259	$.01	$.04
Johnson, Lance	91DL	403	$.01	$.08
Johnson, Lance	92D	267	$.01	$.04
Johnson, Lance	92DL	237	$.01	$.06

Player	Year	No.	VG	EX/MT
Johnson, Lance	92DLS	154	$.01	$.06
Johnson, Lance	93D	301	$.01	$.05
Johnson, Randy	83D	305	$.01	$.06
Johnson, Randy	84D	321	$.05	$.20
Johnson, Randy	85D	531	$.01	$.10
Johnson, Randy	89DR	43	$.05	$.20
Johnson, Randy	89DRR	42	$.05	$.25
Johnson, Randy	90D	379	$.01	$.04
Johnson, Randy	90DL	483	$.10	$1.00
Johnson, Randy	91D	134	$.01	$.04
Johnson, Randy	91DBC	2	$.01	$.03
Johnson, Randy	91DL	319	$.01	$.08
Johnson, Randy	91DLS	116	$.01	$.08
Johnson, Randy	92D	207	$.01	$.04
Johnson, Randy	92DL	302	$.01	$.06
Johnson, Randy	92DLS	234	$.01	$.06
Johnson, Randy	93D	581	$.01	$.05
Johnson, Roy	83D	492	$.01	$.06
Johnson, Wallace	89D	484	$.01	$.04
Johnson, Wallace	90D	570	$.01	$.04
Johnson, Wallace	90DL	344	$.05	$.25
Johnston, Joel	92DR	60	$.01	$.05
Johnstone, Jay	81D	300	$.01	$.06
Johnstone, Jay	82D	262	$.01	$.06
Johnstone, Jay	83D	561	$.01	$.06
Johnstone, Jay	84D	540	$.05	$.20
Johnstone, Joel	93D	791	$.01	$.05
Johnstone, John	93D	784	$.05	$.20
Jones, Al	85D	404	$.01	$.10
Jones, Barry	87D	602	$.05	$.25
Jones, Barry	89D	647	$.01	$.04
Jones, Barry	90DL	431	$.05	$.25
Jones, Barry	91D	534	$.01	$.04
Jones, Barry	91DL	406	$.01	$.08
Jones, Barry	92D	155	$.01	$.04
Jones, Barry	92DL	484	$.01	$.06
Jones, Bobby	85D	134	$.01	$.10
Jones, Calvin	92D	690	$.01	$.10
Jones, Calvin	92DL	71	$.01	$.06
Jones, Calvin	93D	749	$.01	$.05
Jones, Chipper	93D	721	$.05	$.25
Jones, Chris	91DR	50	$.01	$.05
Jones, Chris	92D	464	$.01	$.04
Jones, Chris	92DL	444	$.01	$.06
Jones, Doug	88D	588	$.05	$.25
Jones, Doug	89D	438	$.01	$.10
Jones, Doug	90D	320	$.01	$.04
Jones, Doug	90DL	153	$.05	$.25
Jones, Doug	91D	232	$.01	$.04
Jones, Doug	91DL	57	$.01	$.08
Jones, Doug	91DLS	46	$.01	$.08
Jones, Doug	92D	674	$.01	$.04
Jones, Doug	92DL	253	$.01	$.06
Jones, Doug	92DLS	38	$.01	$.06
Jones, Doug	93D	296	$.01	$.05
Jones, Doug	93DL	161	$.01	$.15
Jones, Jeff	82D	213	$.01	$.06
Jones, Jeff	83D	651	$.01	$.06
Jones, Jeff	84D	262	$.05	$.20
Jones, Jimmy	87D	557	$.01	$.15
Jones, Jimmy	88D	141	$.01	$.04
Jones, Jimmy	89D	247	$.01	$.04
Jones, Jimmy	91DL	371	$.01	$.08
Jones, Jimmy	92D	272	$.01	$.04
Jones, Jimmy	93D	324	$.01	$.05
Jones, Lynn	82D	542	$.01	$.06
Jones, Lynn	86D	466	$.01	$.08
Jones, Mike	85D	640	$.01	$.10
Jones, Mike	86D	419	$.01	$.08
Jones, Odell	84D	256	$.05	$.20
Jones, Odell	85D	525	$.01	$.10
Jones, Odell	87D	582	$.01	$.05
Jones, Randy	81D	122	$.01	$.06
Jones, Ron	89DR	42	$.01	$.05
Jones, Ron	89DRR	40	$.01	$.10

DONRUSS

Player	Year	No.	VG	EX/MT
Jones, Ron	90D	487	$ .01	$ .04
Jones, Ron	92D	738	$ .01	$ .04
Jones, Ruppert	81D	349	$ .01	$ .06
Jones, Ruppert	82D	346	$ .01	$ .06
Jones, Ruppert	83D	373	$ .01	$ .06
Jones, Ruppert	84D	261	$ .05	$ .20
Jones, Ruppert	85D	612	$ .01	$ .10
Jones, Ruppert	86D	423	$ .01	$ .08
Jones, Ruppert	87D	428	$ .01	$ .05
Jones, Tim	89D	555	$ .01	$ .10
Jones, Tim	89DR	28	$ .01	$ .05
Jones, Tim	90D	686	$ .01	$ .04
Jones, Tim	91D	66	$ .01	$ .04
Jones, Tim	93D	624	$ .01	$ .05
Jones, Tracy	86DR	2	$ .05	$ .20
Jones, Tracy	87D	413	$ .01	$ .10
Jones, Tracy	88D	310	$ .01	$ .10
Jones, Tracy	89D	574	$ .01	$ .04
Jones, Tracy	90D	636	$ .01	$ .04
Jones, Tracy	91D	594	$ .01	$ .04
Jones, Tracy	92D	519	$ .01	$ .04
Jordan, Brian	92DL	337	$ .10	$ .40
Jordan, Brian	92DLS	93	$ .10	$ .50
Jordan, Brian	93D	442	$ .01	$ .10
Jordan, Ricky	89D	624	$ .01	$ .10
Jordan, Ricky	90D	76	$ .01	$ .05
Jordan, Ricky	90DL	236	$ .05	$ .25
Jordan, Ricky	91D	466	$ .01	$ .04
Jordan, Ricky	91DLS	215	$ .01	$ .08
Jordan, Ricky	92D	458	$ .01	$ .04
Jordan, Ricky	93D	514	$ .01	$ .05
Jordan, Ricky	93DL	169	$ .01	$ .15
Jordan, Scott	89D	609	$ .01	$ .10
Jorgensen, Mike	81D	274	$ .01	$ .06
Jorgensen, Mike	82D	224	$ .01	$ .06
Jorgensen, Terry	93D	151	$ .01	$ .05
Jose, Felix	89DRR	38	$ .10	$ .75
Jose, Felix	90D	564	$ .05	$ .25
Jose, Felix	90DL	385	$ .20	$2.00
Jose, Felix	90DR	5	$ .10	$1.00
Jose, Felix	91D	656	$ .01	$ .10
Jose, Felix	91DL	392	$ .05	$ .20
Jose, Felix	92D	233	$ .01	$ .10
Jose, Felix	92DK	13	$ .10	$1.00
Jose, Felix	92DL	63	$ .01	$ .06
Jose, Felix	92DLS	94	$ .01	$ .06
Jose, Felix	93D	574	$ .01	$ .05
Joyner, Wally	86DR	1	$ .20	$2.00
Joyner, Wally	87D	135	$ .15	$1.50
Joyner, Wally	87DK	1	$ .05	$ .35
Joyner, Wally	88D	110	$ .01	$ .15
Joyner, Wally	88DBC	13	$ .01	$ .10
Joyner, Wally	89D	52	$ .01	$ .10
Joyner, Wally	89DBC	21	$ .01	$ .10
Joyner, Wally	90D	94	$ .01	$ .10
Joyner, Wally	90DL	24	$ .10	$ .75
Joyner, Wally	91D	677	$ .01	$ .04
Joyner, Wally	91DL	31	$ .01	$ .15
Joyner, Wally	91DLS	26	$ .01	$ .15
Joyner, Wally	92D	333	$ .01	$ .10
Joyner, Wally	92DL	438	$ .01	$ .06
Joyner, Wally	92DLS	185	$ .01	$ .06
Joyner, Wally	93D	129	$ .01	$ .05
Joyner, Wally	93DK	8	$ .20	$2.00
Juden, Jeff	92DRR	405	$ .01	$ .05
Jurak, Ed	84D	127	$ .05	$ .20
Jurak, Ed	85D	579	$ .01	$ .10
Justice, Dave	90D	704	$ .15	$1.50
Justice, Dave	90DL	297	$3.75	$15.00
Justice, Dave	90DR	14	$ .15	$1.25
Justice, Dave	91D	548	$ .05	$ .35
Justice, Dave	91D	683	$ .05	$ .20
Justice, Dave	91DL	77	$ .20	$2.00
Justice, Dave	91DL	84	$ .01	$ .15
Justice, Dave	91DLP	1	$2.00	$8.00
Justice, David	91DLS	146	$ .20	$2.00
Justice, Dave	91DLSP	10	$1.75	$7.00
Justice, Dave	91DMVP	402	$ .01	$ .15
Justice, Dave	92D	327	$ .05	$ .20
Justice, David	92DK	6	$ .75	$13.00
Justice, David	92DL	404	$ .10	$ .50
Justice, Dave	92DLS	5	$ .10	$ .50
Justice, David	93D	580	$ .01	$ .10
Justice, David	93DL	50	$ .10	$ .40
Kaat, Jim	81D	536	$ .05	$ .25
Kaat, Jim	82D	217	$ .05	$ .20
Kaat, Jim	83D	343	$ .05	$ .20
Kamieniecki, Scott	91DR	51	$ .01	$ .10

Player	Year	No.	VG	EX/MT
Kamieniecki, Scott	92D	195	$ .01	$ .10
Kamieniecki, Scott	93D	681	$ .01	$ .05
Karkovice, Ron	87D	334	$ .01	$ .05
Karkovice, Ron	90D	413	$ .01	$ .04
Karkovice, Ron	90DL	307	$ .05	$ .25
Karkovice, Ron	91D	220	$ .01	$ .04
Karkovice, Ron	91DL	515	$ .01	$ .08
Karkovice, Ron	92D	374	$ .01	$ .04
Karkovice, Ron	92DL	105	$ .01	$ .06
Karkovice, Ron	93D	331	$ .01	$ .05
Karkovice, Ron	93DL	63	$ .01	$ .15
Karros, Eric	92DL	293	$ .15	$1.50
Karros, Eric	92DLS	45	$ .15	$1.50
Karros, Eric	92DRR	16	$ .10	$ .50
Karros, Eric	93D	430	$ .05	$ .20
Karros, Eric	93DK	30	$1.00	$4.00
Kaufman, Curt	85D	524	$ .01	$ .10
Kearney, Bob	83D	539	$ .01	$ .06
Kearney, Bob	84D	462	$ .05	$ .20
Kearney, Bob	85D	362	$ .01	$ .10
Kearney, Bob	86D	74	$ .01	$ .08
Kearney, Bob	87D	445	$ .01	$ .05
Keeton, Rickey	82D	618	$ .01	$ .06
Kelleher, Mick	81D	513	$ .01	$ .06
Kelleher, Mick	82D	601	$ .01	$ .06
Kelly, Pat	81D	600	$ .01	$ .15
Kelly, Pat	91DLBC	17	$ .20	$2.00
Kelly, Pat	91DR	1	$ .01	$ .15
Kelly, Pat	92D	370	$ .01	$ .10

DONRUSS

Player	Year	No.	VG	EX/MT	Player	Year	No.	VG	EX/MT
Kelly, Pat	92DL	104	$.01	$.15	Kiefer, Steve	88D	542	$.01	$.04
Kelly, Pat	92DLS	213	$.01	$.06	Kiely, John	93D	203	$.01	$.10
Kelly, Pat	93D	503	$.01	$.05	Kile, Darryl	91DLS	178	$.05	$.25
Kelly, Roberto	88D	635	$.10	$1.00	Kile, Darryl	91DR	5	$.01	$.10
Kelly, Roberto	88DR	16	$.10	$1.00	Kile, Darryl	92D	309	$.01	$.10
Kelly, Roberto	89D	433	$.05	$.25	Kile, Darryl	92DL	198	$.01	$.06
Kelly, Roberto	90D	192	$.01	$.10	Kile, Darryl	92DLS	39	$.01	$.15
Kelly, Roberto	90DL	17	$.10	$1.00	Kile, Darryl	93D	668	$.01	$.05
Kelly, Roberto	91D	538	$.01	$.04	Kile, Darryl	93DL	143	$.01	$.15
Kelly, Roberto	91DL	38	$.01	$.15	Kilgus, Paul	88D	469	$.01	$.04
Kelly, Roberto	91DLS	94	$.01	$.15	Kilgus, Paul	89D	283	$.01	$.04
Kelly, Roberto	91DMVP	400	$.01	$.03	Kilgus, Paul	89DTR	42	$.01	$.05
Kelly, Roberto	92D	73	$.01	$.04	Kilgus, Paul	90D	276	$.01	$.04
Kelly, Roberto	92DL	156	$.01	$.15	King, Eric	86DR	27	$.05	$.20
Kelly, Roberto	92DLS	214	$.01	$.06	King, Eric	87D	250	$.05	$.20
Kelly, Roberto	93D	313	$.01	$.05	King, Eric	88D	50	$.01	$.04
Kelly, Roberto	93DK	12	$.20	$2.00	King, Eric	89D	535	$.01	$.04
Kemp, Steve	81D	249	$.01	$.06	King, Eric	89DTR	37	$.01	$.05
Kemp, Steve	82D	594	$.01	$.06	King, Eric	90D	337	$.01	$.04
Kemp, Steve	83D	269	$.01	$.06	King, Eric	90DL	43	$.05	$.25
Kemp, Steve	84D	469	$.05	$.20	King, Eric	91D	271	$.01	$.04
Kemp, Steve	85D	225	$.01	$.10	King, Eric	91DL	382	$.01	$.08
Kemp, Steve	86D	200	$.01	$.08	King, Eric	91DLS	47	$.01	$.08
Kennedy, Junior	81D	424	$.01	$.06	King, Jeff	90D	480	$.01	$.04
Kennedy, Junior	82D	188	$.01	$.06	King, Jeff	90DL	163	$.05	$.25
Kennedy, Junior	83D	529	$.01	$.06	King, Jeff	91D	233	$.01	$.04
Kennedy, Terry	81D	428	$.01	$.06	King, Jeff	91DL	71	$.01	$.08
Kennedy, Terry	82D	121	$.01	$.06	King, Jeff	92D	468	$.01	$.04
Kennedy, Terry	83D	220	$.01	$.06	King, Jeff	92DL	420	$.01	$.06
Kennedy, Terry	83DK	26	$.01	$.10	King, Jeff	93D	252	$.01	$.05
Kennedy, Terry	84D	112	$.05	$.20	King, Jeff	93DL	207	$.01	$.15
Kennedy, Terry	85D	429	$.01	$.10	Kingery, Mike	87D	424	$.01	$.15
Kennedy, Terry	86D	356	$.01	$.08	Kingery, Mike	88D	322	$.01	$.04
Kennedy, Terry	87D	205	$.01	$.05	Kingery, Mike	90D	601	$.01	$.04
Kennedy, Terry	88D	150	$.01	$.04	Kingery, Mike	91D	573	$.01	$.04
Kennedy, Terry	89D	141	$.01	$.04	Kingery, Mike	91DL	224	$.01	$.08
Kennedy, Terry	90D	602	$.01	$.04	Kingman, Brian	81D	360	$.01	$.06
Kennedy, Terry	90DL	67	$.05	$.25	Kingman, Brian	82D	87	$.01	$.06
Kennedy, Terry	91D	94	$.01	$.04	Kingman, Dave	81D	553	$.05	$.20
Kennedy, Terry	91DL	216	$.01	$.08	Kingman, Dave	82D	182	$.01	$.15
Kent, Jeff	92DL	445	$.05	$.35	Kingman, Dave	82DK	17	$.05	$.20
Kent, Jeff	92DR	61	$.05	$.25	Kingman, Dave	83D	301	$.01	$.15
Kent, Jeff	93D	302	$.01	$.10	Kingman, Dave	84D	360	$.05	$.25
Kent, Jeff	93DL	185	$.01	$.15	Kingman, Dave	85D	54	$.03	$.10
Keough, Matt	81D	358	$.01	$.06	Kingman, Dave	86D	54	$.01	$.08
Keough, Matt	82D	71	$.01	$.06	Kingman, Dave	87D	425	$.01	$.05
Keough, Matt	83D	239	$.01	$.06	Kinney, Dennis	81D	363	$.01	$.06
Keough, Matt	84D	627	$.05	$.20	Kipper, Bob	86DR	46	$.01	$.10
Kepshire, Kurt	85D	382	$.01	$.10	Kipper, Bob	86DRR	44	$.01	$.10
Kepshire, Kurt	86D	504	$.01	$.08	Kipper, Bob	87D	572	$.01	$.05
Kerfeld, Charlie	86DR	6	$.01	$.15	Kipper, Bob	88D	115	$.01	$.04
Kerfeld, Charlie	87D	209	$.01	$.05	Kipper, Bob	89D	409	$.01	$.04
Kern, Jim	81D	27	$.01	$.06	Kipper, Bob	90D	362	$.01	$.04
Kern, Jim	82D	89	$.01	$.06	Kipper, Bob	91D	720	$.01	$.04
Kern, Jim	83D	355	$.01	$.06	Kipper, Bob	92D	622	$.01	$.04
Key, Jimmy	85D	559	$.20	$2.00	Kipper, Bob	92DL	506	$.01	$.06
Key, Jimmy	86D	561	$.05	$.25	Kirby, Wayne	93D	380	$.01	$.10
Key, Jimmy	87D	244	$.01	$.05	Kison, Bruce	82D	66	$.01	$.06
Key, Jimmy	88D	72	$.01	$.15	Kison, Bruce	83D	267	$.01	$.06
Key, Jimmy	89D	188	$.01	$.04	Kison, Bruce	84D	499	$.05	$.20
Key, Jimmy	90D	231	$.01	$.04	Kison, Bruce	85D	377	$.01	$.10
Key, Jimmy	90DL	211	$.05	$.25	Kison, Bruce	86D	616	$.01	$.08
Key, Jimmy	91D	98	$.01	$.04	Kittle, Ron	84D	244	$.05	$.35
Key, Jimmy	91DL	103	$.01	$.08	Kittle, Ron	84DK	18	$.05	$.25
Key, Jimmy	92D	219	$.01	$.04	Kittle, Ron	85D	180	$.05	$.20
Key, Jimmy	92DL	111	$.01	$.06	Kittle, Ron	86D	526	$.01	$.08
Key, Jimmy	93D	710	$.01	$.05	Kittle, Ron	87D	351	$.01	$.05
Khalifa, Sam	86D	308	$.01	$.08	Kittle, Ron	88D	422	$.01	$.04
Kiecker, Dana	90DL	525	$.05	$.25	Kittle, Ron	89D	428	$.01	$.04
Kiecker, Dana	90DR	28	$.01	$.15	Kittle, Ron	89DTR	51	$.01	$.05
Kiecker, Dana	91D	347	$.01	$.04	Kittle, Ron	90D	148	$.01	$.04
Kiecker, Dana	91DL	341	$.01	$.08	Kittle, Ron	90DL	405	$.05	$.25
Kiefer, Mark	93D	263	$.01	$.15	Kittle, Ron	91D	613	$.01	$.04
Kiefer, Steve	85DRR	35	$.01	$.15	Klesko, Ryan	91DLBC	21	$2.50	$10.00
Kiefer, Steve	86D	420	$.01	$.08	Klesko, Ryan	92DRR	13	$.10	$.50

DONRUSS

Player	Year	No.	VG	EX/MT
Klesko, Ryan	93D	422	$ .05	$ .25
Klink, Joe	90DL	503	$ .05	$ .25
Klink, Joe	91D	591	$ .01	$ .04
Klink, Joe	91DL	461	$ .01	$ .08
Klink, Joe	92D	183	$ .01	$ .04
Klutts, Mickey	81D	110	$ .01	$ .06
Klutts, Mickey	83D	465	$ .01	$ .06
Knackert, Brent	90DR	52	$ .01	$ .15
Knackert, Brent	91D	662	$ .01	$ .04
Knackert, Brent	92D	608	$ .01	$ .04
Knapp, Chris	81D	173	$ .01	$ .06
Knepper, Bob	81D	194	$ .01	$ .06
Knepper, Bob	82D	41	$ .01	$ .06
Knepper, Robert	83D	92	$ .01	$ .06
Knepper, Bob	84D	572	$ .05	$ .20
Knepper, Bob	85D	476	$ .01	$ .10
Knepper, Bob	86D	161	$ .01	$ .08
Knepper, Bob	87D	112	$ .01	$ .05
Knepper, Bob	88D	138	$ .01	$ .04
Knepper, Bob	89D	123	$ .01	$ .04
Knepper, Bob	90D	485	$ .01	$ .04
Knicely, Alan	83D	620	$ .01	$ .06
Knight, Ray	81D	61	$ .01	$ .06
Knight, Ray	82D	374	$ .01	$ .06
Knight, Ray	83D	522	$ .01	$ .06
Knight, Ray	84D	232	$ .05	$ .20
Knight, Ray	84DK	12	$ .05	$ .25
Knight, Ray	85D	617	$ .01	$ .10
Knight, Ray	86D	597	$ .01	$ .08
Knight, Ray	87D	586	$ .01	$ .05
Knight, Ray	88D	108	$ .01	$ .04
Knoblauch, Chuck	91DL	396	$ .15	$1.50
Knoblauch, Chuck	91DR	39	$ .05	$ .35
Knoblauch, Chuck	91DRR	421	$ .10	$ .50
Knoblauch, Chuck	92D	390	$ .01	$ .15
Knoblauch, Chuck	92DBC	5	$ .05	$ .25
Knoblauch, Chuck	92DL	230	$ .10	$ .40
Knoblauch, Chuck	93D	415	$ .01	$ .15
Knoblauch, Chuck	93DL	98	$ .05	$ .25
Knorr, Randy	93D	717	$ .01	$ .05
Knudsen, Kurt	92DR	62	$ .01	$ .05
Knudsen, Kurt	93D	145	$ .01	$ .05
Knudson, Mark	88D	495	$ .01	$ .04
Knudson, Mark	90D	575	$ .01	$ .04
Knudson, Mark	90DL	348	$ .05	$ .25
Knudson, Mark	91D	328	$ .01	$ .04
Knudson, Mark	91DL	159	$ .01	$ .08
Komminsk, Brad	84DRR	36	$ .05	$ .25
Komminsk, Brad	85D	321	$ .01	$ .10
Komminsk, Brad	88D	583	$ .01	$ .04
Komminsk, Brad	90D	350	$ .01	$ .04
Komminsk, Brad	90DL	303	$ .05	$ .25
Koosman, Jerry	81D	531	$ .01	$ .15
Koosman, Jerry	82D	603	$ .01	$ .15
Koosman, Jerry	83D	39	$ .01	$ .15
Koosman, Jerry	84D	501	$ .05	$ .20
Koosman, Jerry	85D	233	$ .05	$ .20
Koosman, Jerry	86DK	23	$ .05	$ .20
Koslofski, Kevin	92DR	63	$ .01	$ .15
Koslofski, Kevin	93D	205	$ .01	$ .10
Kraemer, Joe	90DR	10	$ .01	$ .05
Kramer, Randy	89D	480	$ .01	$ .04
Kramer, Randy	89DR	48	$ .01	$ .05
Kramer, Randy	90D	409	$ .01	$ .04
Kravec, Ken	82D	378	$ .01	$ .06
Kremers, Jimmy	91D	739	$ .01	$ .10
Krenchicki, Wayne	83D	314	$ .01	$ .06
Krenchicki, Wayne	84D	334	$ .05	$ .20
Krenchicki, Wayne	85D	140	$ .01	$ .10
Krenchicki, Wayne	86D	140	$ .01	$ .08
Krenchicki, Wayne	87D	406	$ .01	$ .05
Kreuter, Chad	89D	579	$ .01	$ .10
Kreuter, Chad	90D	520	$ .01	$ .04
Kreuter, Chad	92DL	496	$ .01	$ .06
Kreuter, Chad	93D	673	$ .01	$ .05

Player	Year	No.	VG	EX/MT
Krueger, Bill	85D	467	$ .01	$ .10
Krueger, Bill	86D	298	$ .01	$ .08
Krueger, Bill	90DL	421	$ .05	$ .25
Krueger, Bill	91D	647	$ .01	$ .04
Krueger, Bill	92D	672	$ .01	$ .04
Krueger, Bill	92DL	477	$ .01	$ .06
Krueger, Bill	93D	352	$ .01	$ .05
Kruk, John	86DR	42	$ .20	$2.00
Kruk, John	87D	328	$ .15	$1.25
Kruk, John	88D	205	$ .01	$ .10
Kruk, John	89D	86	$ .01	$ .04
Kruk, John	90D	160	$ .01	$ .04
Kruk, John	90DL	284	$ .10	$ .40
Kruk, John	91D	260	$ .01	$ .04
Kruk, John	91DL	278	$ .01	$ .08
Kruk, John	92D	230	$ .01	$ .04
Kruk, John	92DK	12	$ .10	$1.00
Kruk, John	92DL	313	$ .01	$ .06
Kruk, John	92DLS	76	$ .01	$ .06
Kruk, John	93D	436	$ .01	$ .05
Krukow, Mike	82D	351	$ .01	$ .06
Krukow, Mike	83D	119	$ .01	$ .06
Krukow, Mike	84D	509	$ .05	$ .20
Krukow, Mike	85D	630	$ .01	$ .10
Krukow, Mike	86D	143	$ .01	$ .08

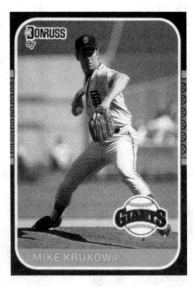

Player	Year	No.	VG	EX/MT
Krukow, Mike	87D	609	$ .01	$ .05
Krukow, Mike	88D	116	$ .01	$ .04
Krukow, Mike	89D	258	$ .01	$ .04
Kuenn, Harvey	82D	578	$ .01	$ .06
Kuenn, Harvey	83D	608	$ .01	$ .06
Kuiper, Duane	81D	319	$ .01	$ .06
Kuiper, Duane	82D	198	$ .01	$ .06
Kuiper, Duane	84D	553	$ .05	$ .20
Kunkel, Jeff	85D	587	$ .01	$ .10
Kunkel, Jeff	89D	496	$ .01	$ .04
Kunkel, Jeff	90D	496	$ .01	$ .04
Kunkel, Jeff	91DLS	126	$ .01	$ .08
Kuntz, Rusty	81D	282	$ .01	$ .06
Kuntz, Rusty	85D	516	$ .01	$ .10
Kutcher, Randy	87D	547	$ .01	$ .05
Kutzler, Jerry	90D	503	$ .01	$ .04
Kutzler, Jerry	90DR	25	$ .01	$ .05
Lacey, Bob	81D	240	$ .01	$ .06

DONRUSS

Player	Year	No.	VG	EX/MT	Player	Year	No.	VG	EX/MT
Lachmann, Rene	82D	600	$.01	$.06	Landrum, Bill	91DLS	225	$.01	$.08
LaCock, Pete	81D	344	$.01	$.06	Landrum, Bill	92D	221	$.01	$.04
LaCorte, Frank	81D	143	$.01	$.06	Landrum, Bill	92DL	333	$.01	$.06
LaCorte, Frank	82D	270	$.01	$.06	Landrum, Ced	91DR	11	$.01	$.10
LaCorte, Frank	83D	218	$.01	$.06	Landrum, Ced	92D	662	$.01	$.04
LaCorte, Frank	84D	283	$.05	$.20	Landrum, Tito	82D	292	$.01	$.06
LaCoss, Mike	81D	183	$.01	$.06	Landrum, Tito	83D	498	$.01	$.06
LaCoss, Mike	82D	440	$.01	$.06	Landrum, Tito	85D	168	$.01	$.10
LaCoss, Mike	83D	344	$.01	$.06	Landrum, Tito	86D	425	$.01	$.08
LaCoss, Mike	84D	206	$.05	$.20	Landrum, Tito	87D	386	$.01	$.05
LaCoss, Mike	85D	405	$.01	$.10	Langford, Rick	81D	238	$.01	$.06
LaCoss, Mike	87D	636	$.01	$.05	Langford, Rick	82D	161	$.01	$.06
LaCoss, Mike	88D	436	$.01	$.04	Langford, Rick	83D	365	$.01	$.06
LaCoss, Mike	89D	602	$.01	$.04	Langston, Mark	85D	557	$1.00	$4.00
LaCoss, Mike	90D	652	$.01	$.04	Langston, Mark	86D	118	$.10	$.50
LaCoss, Mike	90DL	463	$.05	$.25	Langston, Mark	87D	568	$.05	$.20
LaCoss, Mike	91DL	309	$.01	$.08	Langston, Mark	88D	317	$.01	$.10
Lacy, Lee	81D	376	$.01	$.06	Langston, Mark	88DK	20	$.01	$.10
Lacy, Lee	82D	276	$.01	$.06	Langston, Mark	89D	227	$.01	$.15
Lacy, Lee	83D	276	$.01	$.06	Langston, Mark	90D	338	$.01	$.04
Lacy, Lee	84D	479	$.05	$.20	Langston, Mark	90DL	155	$.05	$.25
Lacy, Lee	85D	508	$.01	$.10	Langston, Mark	91D	190	$.01	$.04
Lacy, Lee	86D	228	$.01	$.08	Langston, Mark	91DBC	1	$.01	$.05
Lacy, Lee	87D	336	$.01	$.05	Langston, Mark	91DL	67	$.01	$.08
Ladd, Pete	84D	124	$.05	$.20	Langston, Mark	91DLS	27	$.01	$.08
Ladd, Peter	85D	271	$.01	$.10	Langston, Mark	92D	531	$.01	$.04
Ladd, Pete	87D	660	$.01	$.15	Langston, Mark	92DK	20	$.10	$1.00
LaFrancois, Roger	83D	534	$.01	$.06	Langston, Mark	92DL	229	$.01	$.06
Laga, Mike	84D	491	$.05	$.20	Langston, Mark	92DLS	148	$.01	$.06
Laga, Mike	86D	578	$.01	$.08	Langston, Mark	93D	593	$.01	$.05
Laga, Mike	87D	293	$.01	$.05	Lankford, Ray	91DL	523	$.15	$1.50
Lahti, Jeff	84D	327	$.05	$.20	Lankford, Ray	91DLP	10	$1.25	$5.00
Lahti, Jeff	86D	475	$.01	$.08	Lankford, Ray	91DLS	234	$.15	$1.25
Lahti, Jeff	87D	577	$.01	$.05	Lankford, Ray	91DR	8	$.05	$.25
Lake, Steve	84D	198	$.05	$.20	Lankford, Ray	91DRR	43	$.05	$.35
Lake, Steve	87D	604	$.01	$.05	Lankford, Ray	92D	350	$.01	$.15
Lake, Steve	88D	510	$.01	$.04	Lankford, Ray	92DL	195	$.10	$.40
Lake, Steve	90D	431	$.01	$.04	Lankford, Ray	93D	366	$.01	$.10
Lake, Steve	90DL	395	$.05	$.25	Lansford, Carney	81D	409	$.05	$.25
Lake, Steve	91D	334	$.01	$.04	Lansford, Carney	82D	82	$.05	$.25
Lake, Steve	91DL	385	$.01	$.08	Lansford, Carney	83D	408	$.01	$.06
Lake, Steve	91DLS	216	$.01	$.08	Lansford, Carney	84D	176	$.05	$.20
Laker, Tim	93D	440	$.01	$.15	Lansford, Carney	85D	345	$.01	$.10
Lamp, Dennis	81D	573	$.01	$.06	Lansford, Carney	85DK	8	$.03	$.10
Lamp, Dennis	82D	619	$.01	$.06	Lansford, Carney	86D	131	$.01	$.08
Lamp, Dennis	83D	165	$.01	$.06	Lansford, Carney	87D	158	$.01	$.05
Lamp, Dennis	84D	526	$.05	$.20	Lansford, Carney	88D	178	$.01	$.04
Lamp, Dennis	85D	119	$.01	$.10	Lansford, Carney	89D	243	$.10	$.04
Lamp, Dennis	86D	626	$.01	$.08	Lansford, Carney	90D	95	$.01	$.04
Lamp, Dennis	89D	633	$.01	$.04	Lansford, Carney	90DL	213	$.05	$.25
Lamp, Dennis	90D	423	$.01	$.04	Lansford, Carney	91D	273	$.01	$.04
Lamp, Dennis	90DL	315	$.05	$.25	Lansford, Carney	92D	775	$.01	$.04
Lamp, Dennis	91D	138	$.01	$.04	Lansford, Carney	92DL	148	$.01	$.06
Lampkin, Tom	89D	639	$.01	$.04	Lansford, Carney	92DLS	225	$.01	$.06
Lampkin, Tom	91DL	512	$.01	$.08	LaPoint, Dave	83D	544	$.05	$.30
Lampkin, Tom	93D	654	$.01	$.05	LaPoint, Dave	84D	290	$.05	$.20
Lancaster, Les	87DR	10	$.05	$.25	LaPoint, Dave	85D	138	$.01	$.10
Lancaster, Lester	88D	561	$.05	$.20	LaPoint, Dave	86D	387	$.01	$.08
Lancaster, Les	89D	341	$.01	$.04	LaPoint, Dave	87D	607	$.01	$.05
Lancaster, Les	90D	628	$.01	$.04	LaPoint, Dave	88D	552	$.01	$.04
Lancaster, Les	90DL	361	$.05	$.25	LaPoint, Dave	89D	488	$.01	$.04
Lancaster, Les	91D	256	$.01	$.04	LaPoint, Dave	89DTR	27	$.01	$.05
Lancaster, Les	92D	296	$.01	$.04	LaPoint, Dave	90D	72	$.01	$.04
Lancaster, Les	92DL	402	$.01	$.06	LaPoint, Dave	91D	481	$.01	$.04
Landestoy, Rafael	81D	19	$.01	$.06	Larkin, Barry	87D	492	$1.00	$4.00
Landreaux, Ken	81D	565	$.01	$.06	Larkin, Barry	88D	492	$.05	$.35
Landreaux, Ken	82D	388	$.01	$.06	Larkin, Barry	89D	257	$.05	$.20
Landreaux, Ken	83D	236	$.01	$.06	Larkin, Barry	90D	71	$.01	$.10
Landreaux, Ken	84D	470	$.05	$.20	Larkin, Barry	90DL	18	$.15	$1.25
Landreaux, Ken	85D	494	$.01	$.10	Larkin, Barry	91D	471	$.01	$.10
Landreaux, Ken	86D	470	$.01	$.08	Larkin, Barry	91DK	5	$.01	$.05
Landreaux, Ken	87D	352	$.01	$.05	Larkin, Barry	91DL	168	$.05	$.25
Landrum, Bill	90D	668	$.01	$.04	Larkin, Barry	91DLP	3	$.75	$3.00
Landrum, Bill	90DL	222	$.05	$.25	Larkin, Barry	91DLS	167	$.05	$.20
Landrum, Bill	91D	350	$.01	$.04	Larkin, Barry	92D	185	$.01	$.10

DONRUSS

Player	Year	No.	VG	EX/MT	Player	Year	No.	VG	EX/MT
Larkin, Barry	92DL	73	$ .05	$ .25	LaValliere, Mike	92DL	228	$ .01	$ .06
Larkin, Barry	92DLS	23	$ .05	$ .20	LaValliere, Mike	92DLS	85	$ .01	$ .06
Larkin, Barry	93D	426	$ .01	$ .10	LaValliere, Mike	93D	306	$ .01	$ .05
Larkin, Gene	87DR	23	$ .05	$ .20	Lavelle, Gary	81D	314	$ .01	$ .06
Larkin, Gene	88D	564	$ .01	$ .15	Lavelle, Gary	82D	60	$ .01	$ .06
Larkin, Gene	89D	355	$ .01	$ .04	Lavelle, Gary	83D	60	$ .01	$ .06
Larkin, Gene	90D	436	$ .01	$ .04	Lavelle, Gary	84D	573	$ .05	$ .20
Larkin, Gene	90DL	215	$ .05	$ .25	Lavelle, Gary	85D	265	$ .01	$ .10
Larkin, Gene	91D	152	$ .01	$ .04	Lavelle, Gary	86D	621	$ .01	$ .08
Larkin, Gene	91DL	157	$ .01	$ .08	Law, Rudy	81D	180	$ .01	$ .06
Larkin, Gene	92D	496	$ .01	$ .04	Law, Rudy	83D	521	$ .01	$ .06
Larkin, Gene	92DL	415	$ .01	$ .06	Law, Rudy	84D	257	$ .05	$ .20
					Law, Rudy	85D	244	$ .01	$ .10
					Law, Rudy	86D	632	$ .01	$ .08
					Law, Rudy	87D	343	$ .01	$ .05
					Law, Vance	82D	582	$ .05	$ .20
					Law, Vance	83D	117	$ .01	$ .06
					Law, Vance	84D	546	$ .05	$ .20
					Law, Vance	85D	122	$ .01	$ .10
					Law, Vance	86D	132	$ .01	$ .08
					Law, Vance	87D	212	$ .01	$ .05
					Law, Vance	88D	212	$ .01	$ .04
					Law, Vance	89D	276	$ .01	$ .04
					Law, Vance	90D	629	$ .01	$ .04
					Law, Vance	91DL	355	$ .01	$ .15
					Lawless, Tom	83D	400	$ .01	$ .06
					Lawless, Tom	90D	681	$ .01	$ .04
					Layana, Tim	90DL	410	$ .05	$ .25
					Layana, Tim	90DR	23	$ .01	$ .15
					Layana, Tim	91D	516	$ .01	$ .10
					Lazorko, Jack	86D	628	$ .01	$ .08
					Lazorko, Jack	88D	160	$ .01	$ .04
					Lea, Charlie	82D	320	$ .01	$ .06
					Lea, Charlie	83D	414	$ .01	$ .06
					Lea, Charlie	84D	376	$ .05	$ .20
					Lea, Charlie	85D	177	$ .01	$ .10
					Lea, Charlie	85DK	21	$ .03	$ .10
					Lea, Charlie	86D	376	$ .01	$ .08
					Lea, Charlie	89D	473	$ .01	$ .04
					Leach, Rick	82D	583	$ .01	$ .06
					Leach, Rick	83D	81	$ .01	$ .06
					Leach, Rick	87D	567	$ .01	$ .05
					Leach, Rick	88D	518	$ .01	$ .04
Larkin, Gene	93D	575	$ .01	$ .05	Leach, Rick	89D	638	$ .01	$ .04
Laroche, Dave	82D	569	$ .01	$ .06	Leach, Rick	90D	613	$ .01	$ .04
Larussa, Tony	81D	402	$ .01	$ .06	Leach, Rick	90DL	436	$ .05	$ .25
Larussa, Tony	82D	319	$ .01	$ .06	Leach, Terry	83D	634	$ .05	$ .25
Larussa, Tony	83D	571	$ .01	$ .06	Leach, Terry	88D	603	$ .01	$ .15
Larussa, Tony	91DLS	263	$ .01	$ .10	Leach, Terry	89D	502	$ .01	$ .04
Laskey, Bill	83D	424	$ .01	$ .06	Leach, Terry	90D	534	$ .01	$ .04
Laskey, Bill	84D	358	$ .05	$ .20	Leach, Terry	90DL	360	$ .05	$ .25
Laskey, Bill	85D	387	$ .01	$ .10	Leach, Terry	91D	715	$ .01	$ .04
Laskey, Bill	86D	585	$ .01	$ .08	Leach, Terry	92D	484	$ .01	$ .04
LaSorda, Tom	81D	420	$ .01	$ .06	Leach, Terry	92DL	486	$ .01	$ .06
LaSorda, Tom	82D	110	$ .05	$ .20	Leach, Terry	93D	720	$ .01	$ .05
LaSorda, Tom	83D	136	$ .01	$ .15	Leaf Set, Introduction	90DL	1	$ .05	$ .25
LaSorda, Tom	91DLS	262	$ .01	$ .10	Leaf Studio, Title Card	91DLSP	0	$ .10	$1.00
Laudner, Tim	82D	549	$ .05	$ .25	Leal, Luis	82D	255	$ .01	$ .06
Laudner, Tim	83D	177	$ .01	$ .06	Leal, Luis	83D	129	$ .01	$ .06
Laudner, Tim	85D	652	$ .01	$ .10	Leal, Luis	84D	485	$ .05	$ .20
Laudner, Tim	86D	391	$ .01	$ .08	Leal, Luis	85D	317	$ .01	$ .10
Laudner, Tim	87D	320	$ .01	$ .05	Leal, Luis	86D	315	$ .01	$ .08
Laudner, Tim	88D	631	$ .01	$ .04	Leary, Tim	86D	577	$ .05	$ .35
Laudner, Tim	89D	615	$ .01	$ .04	Leary, Tim	87D	232	$ .01	$ .05
Laudner, Tim	90D	419	$ .01	$ .04	Leary, Tim	89D	552	$ .01	$ .04
LaValliere, Mike	86DR	35	$ .05	$ .25	Leary, Tim	90D	670	$ .01	$ .04
LaValliere, Mike	87D	331	$ .05	$ .20	Leary, Tim	90DL	148	$ .05	$ .25
LaValliere, Mike	88D	312	$ .01	$ .04	Leary, Tim	91D	67	$ .01	$ .04
LaValliere, Mike	89D	244	$ .01	$ .04	Leary, Tim	91DL	206	$ .01	$ .08
LaValliere, Mike	90D	211	$ .01	$ .04	Leary, Tim	91DLS	95	$ .01	$ .08
LaValliere, Mike	90DL	32	$ .05	$ .25	Leary, Tim	92D	433	$ .01	$ .04
LaValliere, Mike	91D	121	$ .01	$ .04	Leary, Tim	93D	289	$ .01	$ .05
LaValliere, Mike	91DL	15	$ .01	$ .08	Lee, Bill	81D	211	$ .01	$ .06
LaValliere, Mike	91DLS	226	$ .01	$ .08	Lee, Bill	82D	194	$ .01	$ .06
LaValliere, Mike	92D	121	$ .01	$ .04	Lee, Manny	87D	518	$ .01	$ .05

118

DONRUSS

Player	Year	No.	VG	EX/MT	Player	Year	No.	VG	EX/MT
Lee, Manny	88D	650	$.01	$.15	Lemke, Mark	90DR	43	$.01	$.05
Lee, Manny	89D	504	$.01	$.04	Lemke, Mark	91D	604	$.01	$.04
Lee, Manny	90D	620	$.01	$.04	Lemke, Mark	92D	606	$.01	$.04
Lee, Manny	90DL	370	$.05	$.25	Lemke, Mark	92DL	94	$.01	$.06
Lee, Manny	91D	211	$.01	$.04	Lemke, Mark	92DLS	6	$.01	$.06
Lee, Manny	91DL	399	$.01	$.08	Lemke, Mark	93D	316	$.01	$.05
Lee, Manuel "Manny"	92D	499	$.01	$.04	Lemke, Mark	93DL	68	$.01	$.15
Lee, Manuel	92DL	382	$.01	$.06	Lemon, Bob	82D	635	$.01	$.15
Lee, Manuel	93D	688	$.01	$.05	Lemon, Chet	81D	281	$.01	$.06
Lee, Mark	91DL	343	$.01	$.15	Lemon, Chet	82D	291	$.01	$.06
Lee, Mark	92D	313	$.01	$.04	Lemon, Chet	83D	511	$.01	$.06
Lee, Terry	91D	752	$.01	$.10	Lemon, Chet	84D	171	$.05	$.20
Leeper, Dave	86D	461	$.01	$.08	Lemon, Chet	85D	90	$.01	$.10
Lefebvre, Joe	81D	571	$.01	$.06	Lemon, Chet	86D	90	$.01	$.08
Lefebvre, Joe	82D	373	$.01	$.06	Lemon, Chet	87D	353	$.01	$.05
Lefebvre, Joe	83D	523	$.01	$.06	Lemon, Chet	88D	215	$.01	$.04
Lefebvre, Joe	84D	82	$.05	$.20	Lemon, Chet	89D	209	$.01	$.04
Lefebvre, Joe	85D	285	$.01	$.10	Lemon, Chet	90D	60	$.01	$.04
Lefferts, Craig	84D	388	$.10	$.75	Lemon, Chet	90DL	133	$.05	$.25
Lefferts, Craig	85D	261	$.01	$.10	Lemon, Chet	91D	301	$.01	$.04
Lefferts, Craig	86D	307	$.01	$.08	Lennon, Pat	92DRR	17	$.05	$.20
Lefferts, Craig	87D	387	$.01	$.05	Lentine, Jim	81D	250	$.01	$.06
Lefferts, Craig	88D	515	$.01	$.04	Leon, Danny	92DR	64	$.01	$.05
Lefferts, Craig	89D	59	$.01	$.04	Leon, Danny	93D	387	$.01	$.10
Lefferts, Craig	90D	376	$.01	$.04	Leonard, Dennis	81D	102	$.01	$.06
Lefferts, Craig	90DL	339	$.05	$.25	Leonard, Dennis	82D	264	$.01	$.06
Lefferts, Craig	91D	515	$.01	$.04	Leonard, Dennis	83D	412	$.01	$.06
Lefferts, Craig	91DL	390	$.01	$.08	Leonard, Jeff	81D	264	$.01	$.06
Lefferts, Craig	92D	162	$.01	$.04	Leonard, Jeff	82D	438	$.01	$.06
Lefferts, Craig	92DL	408	$.01	$.06	Leonard, Jeff	83D	474	$.01	$.06
Lefferts, Craig	93D	1	$.01	$.05	Leonard, Jeff	84D	567	$.05	$.20
LeFlore, Ron	81D	576	$.01	$.06	Leonard, Jeff	85D	358	$.01	$.10
LeFlore, Ron	82D	165	$.01	$.06	Leonard, Jeff	86D	79	$.01	$.08
LeFlore, Ron	83D	543	$.01	$.06	Leonard, Jeff	87D	391	$.01	$.05
Leibrandt, Charlie	81D	421	$.10	$1.00	Leonard, Jeffrey	88D	327	$.01	$.04
Leibrandt, Charlie	83D	421	$.01	$.06	Leonard, Jeffrey	89D	457	$.01	$.04
Leibrandt, Charlie	85D	399	$.01	$.10	Leonard, Jeffrey	89DTR	1	$.01	$.05
Leibrandt, Charlie	86D	297	$.01	$.08	Leonard, Jeffrey	90D	93	$.01	$.04
Leibrandt, Charlie	87D	220	$.01	$.05	Leonard, Jeffrey	90DL	219	$.05	$.25
Leibrandt, Charlie	88D	157	$.01	$.04	Leonard, Mark	91D	526	$.01	$.10
Leibrandt, Charlie	89D	89	$.01	$.04	Leonard, Mark	91DL	369	$.05	$.25
Leibrandt, Charlie	90D	208	$.01	$.04	Leonard, Mark	92D	761	$.01	$.04
Leibrandt, Charlie	90DL	428	$.05	$.25	Leonard, Mark	93D	288	$.01	$.05
Leibrandt, Charlie	91D	562	$.01	$.04	Lerch, Randy	81D	574	$.01	$.06
Leibrandt, Charlie	91DL	209	$.01	$.08	Lerch, Randy	82D	595	$.01	$.06
Leibrandt, Charlie	92D	84	$.01	$.04	Lerch, Randy	85D	309	$.01	$.10
Leibrandt, Charlie	92DL	113	$.01	$.06	Lesley, Brad	83D	547	$.01	$.06
Leibrandt, Charlie	93D	630	$.01	$.05	Levis, Jesse	92DR	65	$.01	$.15
Leiper, Dave	87D	472	$.01	$.05	Levis, Jesse	93D	669	$.01	$.10
Leiper, Dave	88D	557	$.01	$.04	Lewis, Darren	91DR	35	$.01	$.15
Leiper, Dave	89D	465	$.01	$.04	Lewis, Darren	92D	615	$.01	$.04
Leiter, Al	88DR	27	$.01	$.07	Lewis, Darren	92DL	441	$.01	$.06
Leiter, Al	88DRR	43	$.01	$.15	Lewis, Darren	92DLS	117	$.01	$.06
Leiter, Al	89D	315	$.01	$.04	Lewis, Darren	93D	392	$.01	$.05
Leiter, Al	90D	543	$.01	$.04	Lewis, Mark	91DL	289	$.05	$.35
Leiter, Al	91D	697	$.01	$.04	Lewis, Mark	91DLS	48	$.05	$.35
Leiter, Mark	91DR	29	$.01	$.10	Lewis, Mark	91DR	42	$.01	$.15
Leiter, Mark	92D	633	$.01	$.04	Lewis, Mark	91DRR	29	$.01	$.10
Leiter, Mark	92DL	207	$.01	$.06	Lewis, Mark	92D	273	$.01	$.10
Leiter, Mark	93D	495	$.01	$.05	Lewis, Mark	92DL	49	$.01	$.06
Leius, Scott	91DLBC	1	$.10	$1.00	Lewis, Mark	92DLS	167	$.01	$.06
Leius, Scott	91DR	4	$.01	$.05	Lewis, Mark	93D	125	$.01	$.05
Leius, Scott	92D	359	$.01	$.04	Lewis, Richie	93D	265	$.01	$.15
Leius, Scott	92DL	214	$.01	$.06	Lewis, Scott	93D	167	$.01	$.05
Leius, Scott	92DLS	206	$.01	$.06	Leyritz, Jim	90DL	465	$.05	$.35
Leius, Scott	93D	369	$.01	$.05	Leyritz, Jim	91D	219	$.01	$.10
Leius, Scott	93DL	208	$.01	$.15	Leyritz, Jim	92D	649	$.01	$.04
Lemanczyk, Dave	81D	292	$.01	$.06	Leyritz, Jim	93D	477	$.01	$.05
Lemaster, Johnnie	81D	432	$.01	$.06	Lezcano, Carlos	81D	521	$.01	$.06
Lemaster, Johnnie	82D	524	$.01	$.06	Lezcano, Sixto	81D	207	$.01	$.06
Lemaster, Johnnie	83D	125	$.01	$.06	Lezcano, Sixto	82D	64	$.01	$.06
Lemaster, Johnnie	84D	649	$.05	$.20	Lezcano, Sixto	83D	499	$.01	$.06
Lemaster, Johnnie	85D	114	$.01	$.10	Lezcano, Sixto	85D	529	$.01	$.10
Lemke, Mark	89D	523	$.01	$.10	Lilliquist, Derek	89D	653	$.01	$.10
Lemke, Mark	90D	624	$.01	$.04	Lilliquist, Derek	89DR	54	$.01	$.05

119

DONRUSS

Player	Year	No.	VG	EX/MT
Lilliquist, Derek	90D	286	$ .01	$ .05
Lilliquist, Derek	91D	570	$ .01	$ .04
Lilliquist, Derek	92DL	451	$ .01	$ .06
Lilliquist, Derek	93D	9	$ .01	$ .05
Lillis, Bob	84D	84	$ .05	$ .20
Linares, Rufino	82D	310	$ .01	$ .06
Linares, Rufino	83D	275	$ .01	$ .06
Lind, Jose	88DRR	38	$ .05	$ .20
Lind, Jose	89D	290	$ .01	$ .10
Lind, Jose	90D	172	$ .01	$ .04
Lind, Jose	90DL	77	$ .05	$ .25
Lind, Jose	91D	58	$ .01	$ .04
Lind, Jose	91DL	146	$ .01	$ .08
Lind, Jose	91DLS	227	$ .01	$ .08
Lind, Jose	92D	189	$ .01	$ .04

Jose Lind 2B

Player	Year	No.	VG	EX/MT
Lind, Jose	92DL	175	$ .01	$ .06
Lind, Jose	92DLS	86	$ .01	$ .06
Lind, Jose	93D	675	$ .01	$ .05
Lindeman, Jim	87DR	41	$ .01	$ .07
Lindeman, Jim	87DRR	37	$ .01	$ .05
Lindeman, Jim	88D	540	$ .01	$ .04
Lindeman, Jim	92D	701	$ .01	$ .04
Linton, Doug	93D	321	$ .01	$ .10
Liriano, Nelson	88DRR	32	$ .01	$ .15
Liriano, Nelson	89D	627	$ .01	$ .04
Liriano, Nelson	90D	267	$ .01	$ .04
Liriano, Nelson	91D	603	$ .01	$ .04
Listach, Pat	92DL	370	$ .15	$1.50
Listach, Pat	93D	309	$ .05	$ .25
Listach, Pat	93DK	29	$1.00	$4.00
Littell, Mark	81D	580	$ .01	$ .06
Littell, Mark	82D	442	$ .01	$ .06
Little, Bryan	84D	157	$ .05	$ .20
Little, Bryan	86D	452	$ .01	$ .08
Littlefield, John	81D	309	$ .01	$ .06
Littlefield, John	82D	145	$ .01	$ .06
Littlejohn, Dennis	81D	313	$ .01	$ .06
Litton, Greg	90D	453	$ .01	$ .10
Litton, Greg	90DL	331	$ .05	$ .25
Litton, Greg	91D	198	$ .01	$ .04
Litton, Greg	93D	340	$ .01	$ .05
Livingstone, Scott	92D	675	$ .01	$ .15
Livingstone, Scott	92DL	127	$ .01	$ .15
Livingstone, Scott	93D	409	$ .01	$ .05

Player	Year	No.	VG	EX/MT
Lockwood, Skip	81D	217	$ .01	$ .06
Lofton, Kenny	92DLS	168	$ .10	$ .75
Lofton, Kenny	92DRR	5	$ .05	$ .35
Lofton, Kenny	93D	537	$ .05	$ .25
Lofton, Kenny	93DL	40	$ .10	$1.00
Lollar, Tim	83D	61	$ .01	$ .06
Lollar, Tim	84D	284	$ .05	$ .20
Lollar, Tim	85D	324	$ .01	$ .10
Lollar, Tlm	86D	620	$ .01	$ .08
Loman, Doug	85DRR	46	$ .01	$ .15
Lombardi, Phil	87D	401	$ .01	$ .05
Lombardozzi, Steve	86D	598	$ .01	$ .08
Lombardozzi, Steve	86DR	18	$ .01	$ .10
Lombardozzi, Steve	87D	318	$ .01	$ .05
Lombardozzi, Steve	88D	196	$ .01	$ .04
Lombardozzi, Steve	89D	554	$ .01	$ .04
Lombardozzi, Steve	90D	688	$ .01	$ .04
Long, Bill	87DR	48	$ .01	$ .07
Long, Bill	88D	306	$ .01	$ .15
Long, Bill	89D	573	$ .01	$ .04
Lopes, Davey	81D	416	$ .01	$ .15
Lopes, Davey	82D	327	$ .01	$ .06
Lopes, Davey	83D	339	$ .01	$ .06
Lopes, Davey	84D	400	$ .05	$ .20
Lopes, Davey	85D	604	$ .01	$ .10
Lopes, Davey	86D	388	$ .01	$ .08
Lopes, Davey	86DK	9	$ .01	$ .10
Lopes, Davey	87D	455	$ .01	$ .05
Lopez, Aurelio	82D	359	$ .01	$ .06
Lopez, Aurelio	84D	516	$ .05	$ .20
Lopez, Aurelio	85D	349	$ .01	$ .10
Lopez, Aurelio	86D	293	$ .01	$ .08
Lopez, Aurelio	87D	629	$ .01	$ .05
Lopez, Javy	93D	782	$ .05	$ .25
Lovullo, Torey	89DR	17	$ .01	$ .05
Lowenstein, John	81D	235	$ .01	$ .06
Lowenstein, John	82D	599	$ .01	$ .06
Lowenstein, John	83D	153	$ .01	$ .06
Lowenstein, John	84D	228	$ .05	$ .20
Lowenstein, John	85D	245	$ .01	$ .10
Lowry, Dwight	87D	338	$ .01	$ .05
Loynd, Mike	87D	506	$ .01	$ .05
Loynd, Mike	88D	550	$ .01	$ .04
Lozado, Willie	85D	595	$ .01	$ .10
Lubratich, Steve	84D	377	$ .05	$ .20
Lucas, Gary	81D	243	$ .01	$ .06
Lucas, Gary	82D	296	$ .01	$ .06
Lucas, Gary	83D	187	$ .01	$ .06
Lucas, Gary	84D	307	$ .05	$ .20
Lucas, Gary	85D	498	$ .01	$ .10
Lucas, Gary	86D	453	$ .01	$ .08
Lucas, Gary	87D	618	$ .01	$ .05
Lucas, Gary	88D	579	$ .01	$ .04
Luecken, Rick	90D	562	$ .01	$ .10
Lugo, Urbano	86D	329	$ .01	$ .08
Lum, Mike	82D	300	$ .01	$ .06
Lusader, Scott	88D	615	$ .01	$ .15
Lusader, Scott	90D	696	$ .01	$ .04
Luzinski, Greg	81D	175	$ .05	$ .20
Luzinski, Greg	82D	193	$ .01	$ .15
Luzinski, Greg	83D	395	$ .01	$ .06
Luzinski, Greg	84D	122	$ .05	$ .20
Luzinski, Greg	85D	546	$ .01	$ .10
Lyle, Sparky	81D	284	$ .01	$ .15
Lyle, Sparky	82D	189	$ .01	$ .06
Lynch, Ed	82D	641	$ .01	$ .06
Lynch, Ed	83D	308	$ .01	$ .06
Lynch, Ed	84D	75	$ .05	$ .20
Lynch, Ed	85D	623	$ .01	$ .10
Lynch, Ed	86D	631	$ .01	$ .08
Lynch, Ed	87D	516	$ .01	$ .05
Lynch, Ed	88D	77	$ .01	$ .04
Lynn, Fred	81D	218	$ .05	$ .20
Lynn, Fred	82D	367	$ .05	$ .20
Lynn, Fred	83D	241	$ .05	$ .20

DONRUSS

Player	Year	No.	VG	EX/MT	Player	Year	No.	VG	EX/MT
Lynn, Fred	84D	108	$ .05	$ .35	Maddux, Greg	90D	158	$ .05	$ .20
Lynn, Fred	84DK	17	$ .05	$ .25	Maddux, Greg	90DL	25	$1.25	$5.00
Lynn, Fred	85D	133	$ .05	$ .20	Maddux, Greg	91D	374	$ .01	$ .10
Lynn, Fred	86D	245	$ .05	$ .20	Maddux, Greg	91DL	127	$ .05	$ .35
Lynn, Fred	87D	108	$ .05	$ .25	Maddux, Greg	92D	520	$ .01	$ .04
Lynn, Fred	87DK	9	$ .05	$ .20	Maddux, Greg	92DL	294	$ .01	$ .15
Lynn, Fred	88D	248	$ .01	$ .04	Maddux, Greg	92DLS	15	$ .05	$ .20
Lynn, Fred	89D	563	$ .01	$ .10	Maddux, Greg	93D	608	$ .01	$ .10
Lynn, Fred	90DL	188	$ .05	$ .25	Maddux, Mike	87D	535	$ .05	$ .25
Lynn, Fred	91D	673	$ .01	$ .04	Maddux, Mike	89D	487	$ .01	$ .04
Lyons, Barry	88D	619	$ .05	$ .20	Maddux, Mike	90D	312	$ .01	$ .04
Lyons, Barry	89D	572	$ .01	$ .04	Maddux, Mike	91DL	300	$ .01	$ .08
Lyons, Barry	90D	526	$ .01	$ .04	Maddux, Mike	92D	450	$ .01	$ .04
Lyons, Barry	90DL	119	$ .05	$ .25	Maddux, Mike	92DL	393	$ .01	$ .06
Lyons, Steve	85DRR	29	$ .01	$ .15	Maddux, Mike	93D	286	$ .01	$ .05
Lyons, Steve	86D	579	$ .01	$ .08	Madlock, Bill	81D	252	$ .05	$ .30
Lyons, Steve	87D	409	$ .01	$ .05	Madlock, Bill	82D	653	$ .05	$ .20
Lyons, Steve	88D	532	$ .01	$ .04	Madlock, Bill	83D	311	$ .01	$ .15
Lyons, Steve	89D	253	$ .01	$ .04	Madlock, Bill	84D	113	$ .05	$ .25
Lyons, Steve	90D	651	$ .01	$ .04	Madlock, Bill	84DK	20	$ .05	$ .25
Lyons, Steve	92D	758	$ .01	$ .04	Madlock, Bill	85D	200	$ .03	$ .10
Lysander, Rick	84D	560	$ .05	$ .20	Madlock, Bill	86D	617	$ .01	$ .15
Lysander, Rick	85D	560	$ .01	$ .10	Madlock, Bill	87D	155	$ .01	$ .05
Maas, Kevin	90DL	446	$ .10	$1.00	Madlock, Bill	88D	496	$ .01	$ .04
Maas, Kevin	91D	554	$ .01	$ .10	Madrid, Alex	89D	604	$ .01	$ .04
Maas, Kevin	91DL	393	$ .05	$ .20	Magadan, Dave	87D	575	$ .05	$ .25
Maas, Kevin	91DLS	96	$ .01	$ .15	Magadan, Dave	87DR	34	$ .05	$ .20
Maas, Kevin	92D	153	$ .01	$ .10	Magadan, Dave	88D	323	$ .05	$ .20
Maas, Kevin	92DL	284	$ .01	$ .06	Magadan, Dave	89D	408	$ .01	$ .10
Maas, Kevin	92DLS	215	$ .01	$ .06	Magadan, Dave	90D	383	$ .01	$ .04
Maas, Kevin	93D	635	$ .01	$ .05	Magadan, Dave	90DL	330	$ .05	$ .25
Maas, Kevin	93DL	206	$ .01	$ .15	Magadan, Dave	91D	362	$ .01	$ .04
MacDonald, Bob	91D	636	$ .01	$ .10	Magadan, Dave	91DK	17	$ .01	$ .05
MacDonald, Bob	92D	588	$ .01	$ .04	Magadan, Dave	91DL	20	$ .01	$ .08
MacDonald, Bob	93D	689	$ .01	$ .05	Magadan, Dave	91DLS	208	$ .01	$ .08
Macfarlane, Mike	88DR	55	$ .05	$ .35	Magadan, Dave	92D	45	$ .01	$ .04
Macfarlane, Mike	89D	416	$ .01	$ .15	Magadan, Dave	92DL	306	$ .01	$ .06
Macfarlane, Mike	90D	498	$ .01	$ .04	Magadan, Dave	93D	486	$ .01	$ .05
Macfarlane, Mike	90DL	389	$ .05	$ .25	Magnante, Mike	92D	706	$ .01	$ .10
Macfarlane, Mike	91D	313	$ .01	$ .04	Magrane, Joe	87DR	40	$ .05	$ .20
Macfarlane, Mike	91DL	30	$ .01	$ .08	Magrane, Joe	88D	140	$ .01	$ .10
Macfarlane, Mike	92D	161	$ .01	$ .04	Magrane, Joe	89D	201	$ .01	$ .10
Macfarlane, Mike	92DL	83	$ .01	$ .06	Magrane, Joe	90D	163	$ .01	$ .04
Macfarlane, Mike	93D	525	$ .01	$ .05	Magrane, Joe	90DL	13	$ .01	$ .05
Macha, Ken	81D	540	$ .01	$ .06	Magrane, Joe	90DL	11	$ .05	$ .25
Machado, Julio	90DR	41	$ .01	$ .05	Magrane, Joe	91D	295	$ .01	$ .04
Machado, Julio	90DRR	47	$ .01	$ .15	Magrane, Joe	91DLS	235	$ .01	$ .08
Machado, Julio	91D	764	$ .01	$ .04	Magrane, Joe	92D	767	$ .01	$ .04
Machado, Julio	91DL	247	$ .01	$ .08	Magrane, Joe	93D	492	$ .01	$ .05
Machado, Julio	92D	262	$ .01	$ .04	Magrann, Tom	90D	374	$ .01	$ .10
Mack, Shane	87DR	42	$ .10	$1.00	Mahler, Rick	82D	349	$ .01	$ .15
Mack, Shane	88D	411	$ .05	$ .25	Mahler, Rick	83D	527	$ .01	$ .06
Mack, Shane	89D	538	$ .01	$ .04	Mahler, Rick	85D	385	$ .01	$ .10
Mack, Shane	90DL	136	$ .10	$1.00	Mahler, Rick	86D	77	$ .01	$ .08
Mack, Shane	91D	320	$ .01	$ .04	Mahler, Rick	86DK	21	$ .01	$ .10
Mack, Shane	91DL	40	$ .01	$ .08	Mahler, Rick	87D	190	$ .01	$ .05
Mack, Shane	91DLS	88	$ .01	$ .08	Mahler, Rick	88D	380	$ .01	$ .04
Mack, Shane	92D	345	$ .01	$ .04	Mahler, Rick	89D	222	$ .01	$ .04
Mack, Shane	92DL	82	$ .01	$ .06	Mahler, Rick	89DTR	24	$ .01	$ .05
Mack, Shane	92DLS	207	$ .01	$ .06	Mahler, Rick	90D	375	$ .01	$ .05
Mack, Shane	93D	395	$ .01	$ .05	Mahler, Rick	91DL	284	$ .01	$ .08
Mackanin, Pete	82D	354	$ .01	$ .06	Mahomes, Pat	92DLS	208	$ .10	$ .50
Macko, Steve	81D	535	$ .01	$ .06	Mahomes, Pat	92DRR	403	$ .05	$ .25
Madden, Mike	84D	161	$ .05	$ .20	Mahomes, Pat	93D	357	$ .01	$ .10
Maddox, Elliott	81D	397	$ .01	$ .06	Mahomes, Pat	93DL	54	$ .01	$ .15
Maddox, Garry	81D	55	$ .01	$ .06	Maldonado, Candy	83D	262	$ .10	$ .75
Maddox, Garry	82D	315	$ .01	$ .06	Maldonado, Candy	84D	93	$ .05	$ .35
Maddox, Garry	83D	63	$ .01	$ .06	Maldonado, Candy	85D	250	$ .01	$ .10
Maddox, Garry	84D	305	$ .05	$ .20	Maldonado, Candy	87D	327	$ .01	$ .05
Maddox, Garry	85D	137	$ .01	$ .10	Maldonado, Candy	88D	391	$ .05	$ .20
Maddox, Garry	86D	407	$ .01	$ .08	Maldonado, Candy	89D	177	$ .01	$ .04
Maddux, Greg	87DR	52	$1.25	$5.00	Maldonado, Candy	90D	611	$ .01	$ .04
Maddux, Greg	87DRR	36	$1.50	$6.00	Maldonado, Candy	90DL	338	$ .05	$ .25
Maddux, Greg	88D	539	$ .10	$ .40	Maldonado, Candy	91D	480	$ .01	$ .04
Maddux, Greg	89D	373	$ .05	$ .25	Maldonado, Candy	91DL	434	$ .01	$ .08

121

DONRUSS

Player	Year	No.	VG	EX/MT
Maldonado, Candy	91DLS	72	$ .01	$ .08
Maldonado, Candy	91DMVP	391	$ .01	$ .03
Maldonado, Candy	92D	664	$ .01	$ .04
Maldonado, Candy	93D	684	$ .01	$ .05
Mallicoat, Rob	92D	673	$ .01	$ .04
Mann, Kelly	90DRR	46	$ .01	$ .10
Mann, Kelly	91D	736	$ .01	$ .04
Mann, Kelly	91DLS	147	$ .01	$ .15
Manning, Rick	81D	202	$ .01	$ .06
Manning, Rick	82D	85	$ .01	$ .06
Manning, Rick	83D	198	$ .01	$ .06
Manning, Rick	84D	170	$ .05	$ .20
Manning, Rick	85D	237	$ .01	$ .10
Manning, Rick	86D	368	$ .01	$ .08
Manning, Rick	87D	521	$ .01	$ .05
Manning, Rick	88D	486	$ .01	$ .04
Manrique, Fred	88D	493	$ .01	$ .04

Player	Year	No.	VG	EX/MT
Manrique, Fred	**89D**	**489**	**$ .01**	**$ .04**
Manrique, Fred	90D	165	$ .01	$ .05
Manrique, Fred	90DL	518	$ .05	$ .25
Manto, Jeff	91D	602	$ .01	$ .10
Manuel, Barry	92DRR	401	$ .01	$ .05
Manwaring, Kirt	88DRR	39	$ .05	$ .20
Manwaring, Kirt	89D	494	$ .01	$ .04
Manwaring, Kirt	90D	59	$ .01	$ .04
Manwaring, Kirt	92D	494	$ .01	$ .04
Manwaring, Kirt	92DL	208	$ .01	$ .06
Manwaring, Kirt	93D	364	$ .01	$ .05
Manwaring, Kirt	93DL	66	$ .01	$ .15
Marak, Paul	91DL	260	$ .01	$ .15
Marak, Paul	91DRR	413	$ .01	$ .10
Marlins, Florida	92DBC	8	$ .10	$ .50
Marsh, Tom	92DR	66	$ .01	$ .05
Marshall, Mike	82D	562	$ .05	$ .25
Marshall, Mike	83D	362	$ .05	$ .25
Marshall, Mike	84D	348	$ .05	$ .20
Marshall, Mike	85D	296	$ .01	$ .10
Marshall, Mike	85DK	12	$ .03	$ .10
Marshall, Mike	86D	52	$ .01	$ .08
Marshall, Mike	87D	176	$ .01	$ .05
Marshall, Mike	88D	229	$ .01	$ .04
Marshall, Mike	89D	110	$ .01	$ .04
Marshall, Mike	90D	84	$ .01	$ .04
Marshall, Mike	90DL	224	$ .05	$ .25

Player	Year	No.	VG	EX/MT
Marshall, Mike	91D	625	$ .01	$ .04
Martel, Ed	92DR	67	$ .01	$ .10
Martin, Al	92DR	68	$ .10	$ .75
Martin, Al	93D	716	$ .05	$ .20
Martin, Al	93DL	189	$ .10	$ .50
Martin, Billy	81D	479	$ .05	$ .20
Martin, Billy	82D	491	$ .05	$ .20
Martin, Billy	83D	575	$ .01	$ .15
Martin, Jerry	81D	555	$ .01	$ .06
Martin, Jerry	82D	298	$ .01	$ .06
Martin, Jerry	83D	138	$ .01	$ .06
Martin, John	82D	343	$ .01	$ .06
Martin, John	83D	617	$ .01	$ .06
Martin, Renie	81D	103	$ .01	$ .06
Martin, Renie	82D	238	$ .01	$ .06
Martin, Renie	83D	272	$ .01	$ .06
Martin, Renie	84D	445	$ .05	$ .20
Martinez, Alfredo	81D	172	$ .01	$ .06
Martinez, Buck	81D	444	$ .01	$ .06
Martinez, Buck	82D	561	$ .01	$ .06
Martinez, Buck	83D	178	$ .01	$ .06
Martinez, Buck	84D	612	$ .05	$ .20
Martinez, Carlos	89DR	14	$ .01	$ .05
Martinez, Carlos	90D	531	$ .01	$ .15
Martinez, Carlos	90DL	438	$ .05	$ .25
Martinez, Carlos	91D	465	$ .01	$ .10
Martinez, Carlos	92D	521	$ .01	$ .04
Martinez, Carlos	93D	682	$ .01	$ .05
Martinez, Carmelo	84D	623	$ .10	$ .40
Martinez, Carmelo	85D	478	$ .01	$ .10
Martinez, Carmelo	86D	324	$ .01	$ .08
Martinez, Carmelo	88D	287	$ .01	$ .04
Martinez, Carmelo	89D	601	$ .01	$ .04
Martinez, Carmelo	90D	482	$ .01	$ .04
Martinez, Carmelo	90DL	448	$ .05	$ .25
Martinez, Carmelo	91DL	160	$ .01	$ .08
Martinez, Carmelo	91DL	467	$ .01	$ .08
Martinez, Chito	91DR	54	$ .05	$ .20
Martinez, Chito	92D	558	$ .01	$ .15
Martinez, Chito	92DL	300	$ .01	$ .06
Martinez, Chito	93D	221	$ .01	$ .05
Martinez, Dave	87D	488	$ .05	$ .35
Martinez, Dave	88D	438	$ .01	$ .04
Martinez, Dave	89D	102	$ .01	$ .04
Martinez, Dave	90D	452	$ .01	$ .04
Martinez, Dave	90DL	318	$ .05	$ .25
Martinez, Dave	91D	237	$ .01	$ .04
Martinez, Dave	91DL	8	$ .01	$ .08
Martinez, Dave	92D	732	$ .01	$ .04
Martinez, Dave	92DL	457	$ .01	$ .06
Martinez, Dave	93D	534	$ .01	$ .05
Martinez, Dennis	81D	533	$ .05	$ .30
Martinez, Dennis	82D	79	$ .05	$ .25
Martinez, Dennis	83D	231	$ .01	$ .06
Martinez, Dennis	84D	633	$ .05	$ .20
Martinez, Dennis	85D	514	$ .01	$ .10
Martinez, Dennis	86D	454	$ .01	$ .08
Martinez, Dennis	88D	549	$ .01	$ .04
Martinez, Dennis	89D	106	$ .01	$ .04
Martinez, Dennis	90D	156	$ .01	$ .04
Martinez, Dennis	90DL	54	$ .05	$ .25
Martinez, Dennis	91D	139	$ .01	$ .04
Martinez, Dennis	91DL	274	$ .01	$ .08
Martinez, Dennis	92D	276	$ .01	$ .04
Martinez, Dennis	92D	686	$ .01	$ .04
Martinez, Dennis	92DK	24	$ .10	$1.00
Martinez, Dennis	92DL	190	$ .01	$ .06
Martinez, Dennis	92DLS	57	$ .01	$ .06
Martinez, Dennis	93D	168	$ .01	$ .05
Martinez, Domingo	93D	363	$ .05	$ .20
Martinez, Edgar	88DR	36	$ .20	$2.00
Martinez, Edgar	89D	645	$ .05	$ .35
Martinez, Edgar	89DR	15	$ .10	$ .40
Martinez, Edgar	90DL	299	$ .20	$2.00
Martinez, Edgar	91D	606	$ .01	$ .04

DONRUSS

Player	Year	No.	VG	EX/MT	Player	Year	No.	VG	EX/MT
Martinez, Edgar	91DK	16	$ .01	$ .05	Mattingly, Don	87D	52	$ .10	$1.00
Martinez, Edgar	91DL	477	$ .05	$ .20	Mattingly, Don	88D	217	$ .05	$ .25
Martinez, Edgar	91DLS	117	$ .05	$ .20	Mattingly, Don	88DBC	21	$ .05	$ .20
Martinez, Edgar	92D	286	$ .01	$ .04	Mattingly, Don	89D	74	$ .05	$ .25
Martinez, Edgar	92DL	197	$ .01	$ .06	Mattingly, Don	89DK	26	$ .01	$ .15
Martinez, Edgar	92DLS	235	$ .01	$ .06	Mattingly, Don	90D	190	$ .05	$ .20
Martinez, Edgar	93D	421	$ .01	$ .05	Mattingly, Don	90DL	69	$ .20	$2.00
Martinez, Pedro	92DR	69	$ .05	$ .25	Mattingly, Don	91D	107	$ .01	$ .15
Martinez, Pedro	93D	326	$ .01	$ .15	Mattingly, Don	91DL	425	$ .05	$ .35
Martinez, Pedro	93DL	163	$ .05	$ .20	Mattingly, Don	91DLP	22	$1.00	$4.00
Martinez, Ramon	89D	464	$ .10	$ .50	Mattingly, Don	91DLS	97	$ .05	$ .35
Martinez, Ramon	89DR	45	$ .10	$ .50	Mattingly, Don	92D	596	$ .01	$ .10
Martinez, Ramon	90D	685	$ .01	$ .15	Mattingly, Don	92DL	57	$ .05	$ .25
Martinez, Ramon	90DL	147	$ .20	$2.00	Mattingly, Don	92DLS	216	$ .05	$ .25
Martinez, Ramon	91D	557	$ .01	$ .10	Mattingly, Don	93D	609	$ .01	$ .10
Martinez, Ramon	91DK	15	$ .01	$ .05	Matula, Rick	81D	317	$ .01	$ .06
Martinez, Ramon	91DL	61	$ .05	$ .20	Matuszek, Len	84D	549	$ .05	$ .20
Martinez, Ramon	91DLP	5	$ .20	$2.00	Matuszek, Len	85D	259	$ .01	$ .10
Martinez, Ramon	91DLS	184	$ .05	$ .20	Matuszek, Len	86D	494	$ .01	$ .08
Martinez, Ramon	92D	656	$ .01	$ .10	Matuszek, Len	87D	423	$ .01	$ .05
Martinez, Ramon	92DL	297	$ .01	$ .06	Mauch, Gene	82D	141	$ .01	$ .06
Martinez, Ramon	92DLS	46	$ .01	$ .06	Maurer, Rob	92D	703	$ .01	$ .10
Martinez, Ramon	93D	298	$ .01	$ .05	Maurer, Rob	93D	584	$ .01	$ .05
Martinez, Silvio	81D	429	$ .01	$ .06	May, Derrick	91DRR	36	$ .01	$ .10
Martinez, Silvio	82D	469	$ .01	$ .06	May, Derrick	92DR	70	$ .01	$ .05
Martinez, Tino	91DLP	24	$ .20	$2.00	May, Derrick	93D	318	$ .01	$ .05
Martinez, Tino	91DLS	118	$ .05	$ .20	May, Derrick	93DL	200	$ .01	$ .15
Martinez, Tino	91DRR	28	$ .01	$ .10	May, Lee	82D	570	$ .01	$ .06
Martinez, Tino	92DL	329	$ .01	$ .10	May, Lee	83D	538	$ .01	$ .06
Martinez, Tino	92DLS	236	$ .01	$ .06	May, Milt	81D	193	$ .01	$ .06
Martinez, Tino	92DRR	410	$ .01	$ .05	May, Milt	82D	503	$ .01	$ .06
Martinez, Tino	93D	217	$ .01	$ .05	May, Milt	83D	312	$ .01	$ .06
Martinez, Tippy	81D	354	$ .01	$ .06	May, Milt	84D	386	$ .05	$ .20
Martinez, Tippy	82D	205	$ .01	$ .06	May, Milt	85D	410	$ .01	$ .10
Martinez, Tippy	83D	357	$ .01	$ .06	May, Rudy	82D	325	$ .01	$ .06
Martinez, Tippy	84D	472	$ .05	$ .20	May, Rudy	83D	135	$ .01	$ .06
Martinez, Tippy	85D	210	$ .01	$ .10	May, Rudy	84D	626	$ .05	$ .20
Martinez, Tippy	86D	514	$ .01	$ .08	May, Scott	89D	636	$ .01	$ .04
Martz, Randy	82D	126	$ .01	$ .06	Mayberry, John	81D	29	$ .01	$ .06
Martz, Randy	83D	151	$ .01	$ .06	Mayberry, John	82D	306	$ .01	$ .06
Marzano, John	88D	421	$ .05	$ .20	Mayberry, John	82DK	25	$ .01	$ .15
Marzano, John	91D	346	$ .01	$ .04	Mayne, Brent	91D	617	$ .01	$ .10
Marzano, John	91DL	179	$ .01	$ .08	Mayne, Brent	91DR	43	$ .01	$ .05
Marzano, John	92D	448	$ .01	$ .04	Mayne, Brent	92D	265	$ .01	$ .04
Marzano, John	93D	487	$ .01	$ .05	Mayne, Brent	92DL	200	$ .01	$ .06
Mason, Mike	85D	281	$ .01	$ .10	Mayne, Brent	92DLS	186	$ .01	$ .06
Mason, Mike	86D	422	$ .01	$ .08	Mayne, Brent	93D	261	$ .01	$ .05
Mason, Mike	87D	284	$ .01	$ .05	Mayne, Brent	93DL	36	$ .01	$ .15
Mason, Roger	86D	633	$ .01	$ .15	Maysey, Matt	92DR	71	$ .01	$ .05
Mason, Roger	87D	204	$ .01	$ .05	Mazzilli, Lee	81D	34	$ .01	$ .06
Mason, Roger	92D	715	$ .01	$ .04	Mazzilli, Lee	82D	49	$ .01	$ .06
Mason, Roger	92DL	454	$ .01	$ .06	Mazzilli, Lee	83D	638	$ .01	$ .06
Mason, Roger	93D	358	$ .01	$ .05	Mazzilli, Lee	84D	166	$ .05	$ .20
Mata, Vic	85D	629	$ .01	$ .10	Mazzilli, Lee	85D	386	$ .01	$ .10
Mathews, Greg	86DR	26	$ .01	$ .10	Mazzilli, Lee	86D	288	$ .01	$ .08
Mathews, Greg	87D	208	$ .01	$ .05	Mazzilli, Lee	87D	562	$ .01	$ .05
Mathews, Greg	88D	84	$ .01	$ .04	Mazzilli, Lee	88D	614	$ .01	$ .15
Mathews, Greg	89D	281	$ .01	$ .04	Mazzilli, Lee	90D	584	$ .01	$ .04
Mathews, Terry	92D	694	$ .01	$ .10	McAndrew, Jamie	93D	774	$ .01	$ .05
Matlack, Jon	81D	266	$ .01	$ .06	McBride, Bake	81D	404	$ .05	$ .20
Matlack, Jon	82D	215	$ .01	$ .06	McBride, Bake	82D	497	$ .01	$ .06
Matlack, Jon	83D	195	$ .01	$ .06	McCaskill, Kirk	86D	474	$ .05	$ .25
Matlack, Jon	84D	378	$ .05	$ .20	McCaskill, Kirk	87D	381	$ .01	$ .15
Matthews, Gary	81D	306	$ .01	$ .15	McCaskill, Kirk	88D	381	$ .01	$ .04
Matthews, Gary	82D	441	$ .01	$ .06	McCaskill, Kirk	89D	136	$ .01	$ .04
Matthews, Gary	83D	420	$ .01	$ .06	McCaskill, Kirk	90D	170	$ .01	$ .04
Matthews, Gary	84D	233	$ .05	$ .20	McCaskill, Kirk	90DL	247	$ .05	$ .25
Matthews, Gary	85D	239	$ .01	$ .10	McCaskill, Kirk	91D	637	$ .01	$ .04
Matthews, Gary	86D	76	$ .01	$ .08	McCaskill, Kirk	91DL	199	$ .01	$ .08
Mattick, Bobby	81D	570	$ .01	$ .06	McCaskill, Kirk	91DLS	28	$ .01	$ .08
Mattingly, Don	84D	248	$12.50	$50.00	McCaskill, Kirk	92D	340	$ .01	$ .04
Mattingly, Don	85D	295	$1.50	$6.00	McCaskill, Kirk	92DL	517	$ .01	$ .06
Mattingly, Don	85D	651	$ .75	$3.00	McCaskill, Kirk	92DLS	155	$ .01	$ .06
Mattingly, Don	85DK	7	$ .25	$2.50	McCaskill, Kirk	93D	227	$ .01	$ .05
Mattingly, Don	86D	173	$ .25	$2.50	McCaskill, Kirk	93DL	151	$ .01	$ .15

DONRUSS

Player	Year	No.	VG	EX/MT	Player	Year	No.	VG	EX/MT
McCatty, Steve	81D	478	$ .01	$ .06	McGaffigan, Andy	89D	338	$ .01	$ .04
McCatty, Steve	82D	35	$ .01	$ .06	McGaffigan, Andy	90D	574	$ .01	$ .04
McCatty, Steve	83D	491	$ .01	$ .06	McGee, Willie	83D	190	$ .75	$3.00
McCatty, Steve	84D	420	$ .05	$ .20	McGee, Willie	84D	353	$ .10	$1.00
McCatty, Steve	85D	497	$ .01	$ .10	McGee, Willie	84D	625	$ .10	$1.00
McClellan, Paul	92D	700	$ .01	$ .04	McGee, Willie	85D	475	$ .10	$ .50
McClendon, Lloyd	89D	595	$ .01	$ .04	McGee, Willie	86D	109	$ .05	$ .20
McClendon, Lloyd	90D	341	$ .01	$ .04	McGee, Willie	86D	651	$ .10	$ .40
McClendon, Lloyd	92D	338	$ .01	$ .04	McGee, Willie	86DK	3	$ .05	$ .20
McClendon, Lloyd	93D	384	$ .01	$ .05	McGee, Willie	87D	84	$ .01	$ .15
McClure, Bob	81D	510	$ .01	$ .06	McGee, Willie	88D	307	$ .01	$ .04
McClure, Bob	83D	582	$ .01	$ .06	McGee, Willie	89D	161	$ .01	$ .04
McClure, Bob	84D	359	$ .05	$ .20	McGee, Willie	90D	632	$ .01	$ .04
McClure, Bob	85D	536	$ .01	$ .10	McGee, Willie	90DL	367	$ .05	$ .25
McClure, Bob	90D	470	$ .01	$ .04	McGee, Willie	91D	666	$ .01	$ .04
McClure, Bob	92D	661	$ .01	$ .04	McGee, Willie	91DBC	22	$ .01	$ .03
McClure, Rob	88D	529	$ .01	$ .04	McGee, Willie	91DL	360	$ .01	$ .08
McCullers, Lance	86DRR	41	$ .05	$ .25	McGee, Willie	91DLS	256	$ .01	$ .08
McCullers, Lance	87D	237	$ .01	$ .05	McGee, Willie	92D	60	$ .01	$ .04
McCullers, Lance	88D	451	$ .01	$ .04	McGee, Willie	92DL	47	$ .01	$ .06
McCullers, Lance	89D	129	$ .01	$ .04	McGee, Willie	93D	355	$ .01	$ .05
McCullers, Lance	89DTR	13	$ .01	$ .05	McGinnis, Russ	92DR	72	$ .01	$ .05
McCullers, Lance	90D	433	$ .01	$ .04	McGlothen, Lynn	81D	562	$ .01	$ .06
McCullers, Lance	90DL	456	$ .05	$ .25	McGraw, Tug	81D	273	$ .01	$ .15
McCullers, Lance	91D	133	$ .01	$ .04	McGraw, Tug	82D	420	$ .01	$ .06
McDonald, Ben	90DL	249	$ .75	$3.00	McGraw, Tug	83D	371	$ .01	$ .15
McDonald, Ben	90DR	30	$ .10	$ .50	McGraw, Tug	84D	547	$ .05	$ .20
McDonald, Ben	90DRR	32	$ .10	$ .50	McGregor, Scott	81D	114	$ .01	$ .06
McDonald, Ben	91D	485	$ .01	$ .10	McGregor, Scott	82D	331	$ .01	$ .06
McDonald, Ben	91DL	117	$ .05	$ .20	McGregor, Scott	83D	483	$ .01	$ .06
McDonald, Ben	91DLS	6	$ .05	$ .25	McGregor, Scott	84D	594	$ .05	$ .20
McDonald, Ben	92D	436	$ .01	$ .10	McGregor, Scott	85D	413	$ .01	$ .10
McDonald, Ben	92DL	145	$ .01	$ .15	McGregor, Scott	86D	291	$ .01	$ .08
McDonald, Ben	92DLS	126	$ .01	$ .10	McGregor, Scott	87D	520	$ .01	$ .05
McDonald, Ben	93D	249	$ .01	$ .05	McGriff, Fred	86DRR	28	$7.00	$28.00
McDonald, Ben	93DL	1	$ .05	$ .20	McGriff, Fred	87D	621	$ .75	$3.00
McDowell, Jack	88DR	40	$ .20	$2.00	McGriff, Fred	87DR	31	$ .25	$2.50
McDowell, Jack	88DRR	47	$ .10	$1.00	McGriff, Fred	88D	195	$ .05	$ .35
McDowell, Jack	89D	531	$ .05	$ .25	McGriff, Fred	89D	70	$ .05	$ .20
McDowell, Jack	91D	57	$ .01	$ .10	McGriff, Fred	89DBC	19	$ .01	$ .10
McDowell, Jack	91DL	340	$ .05	$ .25	McGriff, Fred	89DK	16	$ .01	$ .10
McDowell, Jack	91DLS	36	$ .05	$ .25	McGriff, Fred	90D	188	$ .01	$ .15
McDowell, Jack	92D	352	$ .01	$ .04	McGriff, Fred	90DL	132	$ .20	$2.00
McDowell, Jack	92DL	422	$ .01	$ .15	McGriff, Fred	91D	261	$ .01	$ .10
McDowell, Jack	93D	433	$ .01	$ .05	McGriff, Fred	91DL	342	$ .05	$ .35
McDowell, Oddibe	86D	56	$ .05	$ .25	McGriff, Fred	91DLS	247	$ .05	$ .35
McDowell, Oddibe	87D	161	$ .01	$ .05	McGriff, Fred	91DMVP	389	$ .01	$ .10
McDowell, Oddibe	88D	382	$ .01	$ .04	McGriff, Fred	92D	283	$ .01	$ .10
McDowell, Oddibe	89D	378	$ .01	$ .04	McGriff, Fred	92DK	26	$ .20	$2.00
McDowell, Oddibe	89DTR	49	$ .01	$ .05	McGriff, Fred	92DK	274	$ .05	$ .25
McDowell, Oddibe	90D	340	$ .01	$ .04	McGriff, Fred	92DLS	106	$ .05	$ .25
McDowell, Oddibe	90DL	112	$ .05	$ .25	McGriff, Fred	93D	390	$ .01	$ .10
McDowell, Oddibe	91D	450	$ .01	$ .04	McGriff, Fred	93DL	46	$ .10	$ .40
McDowell, Roger	86D	629	$ .05	$ .35	McGriff, Terry	87D	512	$ .01	$ .15
McDowell, Roger	87D	241	$ .01	$ .15	McGriff, Terry	88D	556	$ .01	$ .04
McDowell, Roger	88D	651	$ .01	$ .15	McGwire, Mark	87DR	1	$1.50	$6.00
McDowell, Roger	89D	265	$ .01	$ .04	McGwire, Mark	87DRR	46	$2.50	$10.00
McDowell, Roger	90D	251	$ .01	$ .04	McGwire, Mark	88D	256	$ .10	$ .50
McDowell, Roger	90DL	20	$ .05	$ .25	McGwire, Mark	88DBC	23	$ .10	$ .40
McDowell, Roger	91D	166	$ .01	$ .04	McGwire, Mark	88DK	1	$ .05	$ .35
McDowell, Roger	91DL	410	$ .01	$ .08	McGwire, Mark	89D	95	$ .10	$ .40
McDowell, Roger	91DLS	217	$ .01	$ .08	McGwire, Mark	90D	185	$ .05	$ .25
McDowell, Roger	92D	750	$ .01	$ .04	McGwire, Mark	90DAS	697	$ .01	$ .10
McDowell, Roger	92DL	58	$ .01	$ .06	McGwire, Mark	90DL	62	$ .75	$3.00
McDowell, Roger	93D	350	$ .01	$ .05	McGwire, Mark	91D	105	$ .05	$ .20
McElroy, Chuck	91D	709	$ .01	$ .04	McGwire, Mark	91DAS	56	$ .01	$ .10
McElroy, Chuck	91DR	49	$ .01	$ .05	McGwire, Mark	91DBC	9	$ .01	$ .10
McElroy, Chuck	92D	650	$ .01	$ .04	McGwire, Mark	91DL	487	$ .10	$ .75
McElroy, Chuck	92DL	158	$ .01	$ .06	McGwire, Mark	91DLS	106	$ .10	$ .75
McElroy, Chuck	92DLS	16	$ .01	$ .06	McGwire, Mark	92D	348	$ .05	$ .20
McElroy, Chuck	93D	236	$ .01	$ .05	McGwire, Mark	92DL	16	$ .10	$ .50
McGaffigan, Andy	84D	309	$ .05	$ .20	McGwire, Mark	92DLS	226	$ .10	$ .50
McGaffigan, Andy	85D	646	$ .01	$ .10	McGwire, Mark	93D	479	$ .01	$ .15
McGaffigan, Andy	87D	380	$ .01	$ .05	McGwire, Mark	93DK	18	$1.25	$5.00
McGaffigan, Andy	88D	380	$ .01	$ .04	McIntosh, Tim	91DLS	71	$ .01	$ .08

DONRUSS

Player	Year	No.	VG	EX/MT
McIntosh, Tim	91DRR	414	$ .01	$ .10
McIntosh, Tim	92DR	73	$ .01	$ .05
McIntosh, Tim	93D	367	$ .01	$ .05
McIntosh, Tim	93DL	78	$ .01	$ .15
McKay, Dave	81D	350	$ .01	$ .06
McKay, Dave	82D	391	$ .01	$ .06
McKay, Dave	83D	213	$ .01	$ .06
McKeon, Joel	86DR	55	$ .01	$ .10
McLaughlin, Byron	81D	287	$ .01	$ .06
McLaughlin, Joey	81D	271	$ .01	$ .06
McLaughlin, Joey	82D	507	$ .01	$ .06
McLaughlin, Joey	83D	255	$ .01	$ .06
McLaughlin, Joey	84D	617	$ .05	$ .20
McLemore, Mark	86DRR	35	$ .01	$ .10
McLemore, Mark	87D	479	$ .01	$ .05
McLemore, Mark	87DR	7	$ .01	$ .07
McLemore, Mark	88D	181	$ .01	$ .04
McLemore, Mark	89D	94	$ .01	$ .04
McLemore, Mark	91DL	86	$ .01	$ .08
McLemore, Mark	92DL	427	$ .01	$ .06
McLemore, Mark	93D	485	$ .01	$ .05
McMurtry, Craig	84D	599	$ .05	$ .20
McMurtry, Craig	85D	188	$ .01	$ .10
McMurtry, Craig	89D	520	$ .01	$ .04
McNamara, Jim	92DL	514	$ .01	$ .06
McNamara, Jim	92DR	74	$ .01	$ .05
McNamara, John	82D	526	$ .01	$ .06
McNeely, Jeff	92DR	75	$ .05	$ .25
McRae, Brian	91D	575	$ .05	$ .20
McRae, Brian	91DL	235	$ .10	$ .50
McRae, Brian	91DLS	68	$ .10	$ .50
McRae, Brian	91DR	31	$ .05	$ .25
McRae, Brian	92D	387	$ .05	$ .20
McRae, Brian	92DK	16	$ .10	$1.00
McRae, Brian	92DL	123	$ .01	$ .15
McRae, Brian	92DLS	187	$ .01	$ .06
McRae, Brian	93D	411	$ .01	$ .05
McRae, Brian	93DL	58	$ .05	$ .20
McRae, Hal	81D	463	$ .01	$ .15
McRae, Hal	82D	196	$ .01	$ .06
McRae, Hal	83D	238	$ .01	$ .06
McRae, Hal	84D	297	$ .05	$ .20
McRae, Hal	84DK	11	$ .05	$ .25
McRae, Hal	85D	588	$ .01	$ .10
McRae, Hal	86D	521	$ .01	$ .08
McRae, Hal	87D	471	$ .01	$ .05
McReynolds, Kevin	84DRR	34	$ .75	$3.00
McReynolds, Kevin	85D	139	$ .10	$ .40
McReynolds, Kevin	86D	80	$ .05	$ .20
McReynolds, Kevin	87D	451	$ .05	$ .20
McReynolds, Kevin	87DK	14	$ .01	$ .15
McReynolds, Kevin	88D	617	$ .01	$ .10
McReynolds, Kevin	89D	99	$ .01	$ .10
McReynolds, Kevin	90D	218	$ .01	$ .10
McReynolds, Kevin	90DL	198	$ .05	$ .25
McReynolds, Kevin	91D	191	$ .01	$ .04
McReynolds, Kevin	91DL	151	$ .01	$ .08
McReynolds, Kevin	91DLS	209	$ .01	$ .08
McReynolds, Kevin	92D	288	$ .01	$ .04
McReynolds, Kevin	92DL	522	$ .01	$ .06
McReynolds, Kevin	92DLS	188	$ .01	$ .06
McReynolds, Kevin	93D	233	$ .01	$ .05
McReynolds, Kevin	93DL	80	$ .01	$ .15
McWilliams, Larry	82D	527	$ .01	$ .06
McWilliams, Larry	83D	45	$ .01	$ .06
McWilliams, Larry	84D	566	$ .05	$ .20
McWilliams, Larry	85D	78	$ .01	$ .10
McWilliams, Larry	86D	264	$ .01	$ .08
McWilliams, Larry	89D	516	$ .01	$ .04
McWilliams, Larry	90D	709	$ .01	$ .04
Meacham, Bobby	84D	336	$ .05	$ .20
Meacham, Bobby	85D	126	$ .01	$ .10
Meacham, Bobby	86D	638	$ .01	$ .08
Meacham, Bobby	88D	616	$ .01	$ .15
Meacham, Rusty	91DR	53	$ .01	$ .10
Meacham, Rusty	92D	654	$ .01	$ .10
Meacham, Rusty	92DR	76	$ .01	$ .05
Meacham, Rusty	93D	439	$ .01	$ .05
Meacham, Rusty	93DL	14	$ .01	$ .15
Meads, Dave	87DR	46	$ .01	$ .07
Meads, David	88D	455	$ .01	$ .04
Meads, Dave	89D	424	$ .01	$ .04
Medich, Doc	81D	386	$ .01	$ .06
Medich, Doc	82D	142	$ .01	$ .06
Medina, Luis	89DR	20	$ .01	$ .05
Medina, Luis	89DRR	36	$ .01	$ .15
Medvin, Scott	89D	597	$ .01	$ .04
Meier, Dave	85D	147	$ .01	$ .10
Mejias, Sam	82D	295	$ .01	$ .06
Melendez, Francisco	89D	611	$ .01	$ .15
Melendez, Jose	91DR	23	$ .01	$ .10
Melendez, Jose	92D	572	$ .01	$ .04
Melendez, Jose	92DL	507	$ .01	$ .06
Melendez, Jose	93D	626	$ .01	$ .05
Melvin, Bob	86D	456	$ .01	$ .08
Melvin, Bob	87D	239	$ .01	$ .05
Melvin, Bob	88D	638	$ .01	$ .15
Melvin, Bob	90D	451	$ .01	$ .04
Melvin, Bob	90DL	382	$ .05	$ .25
Melvin, Bob	91D	335	$ .01	$ .04
Melvin, Bob	91DL	240	$ .01	$ .08
Melvin, Bob	92D	231	$ .01	$ .04
Mendoza, Mario	81D	45	$ .01	$ .06
Mendoza, Mario	82D	394	$ .01	$ .06
Menendez, Tony	92DR	77	$ .01	$ .05
Mercado, Orlando	84D	318	$ .05	$ .20
Merced, Orlando	91DL	489	$ .10	$ .50
Merced, Orlando	91DR	22	$ .05	$ .20
Merced, Orlando	92D	310	$ .01	$ .15
Merced, Orlando	92DL	363	$ .01	$ .06
Merced, Orlando	93D	282	$ .01	$ .05
Merced, Orlando	93DL	97	$ .01	$ .15

Player	Year	No.	VG	EX/MT
Mercedes, Henry	92DR	78	$ .01	$ .10
Mercedes, Henry	93D	551	$ .01	$ .10
Mercedes, Luis	92DL	130	$ .01	$ .15
Mercedes, Luis	92DRR	6	$ .05	$ .25
Mercedes, Luis	93D	645	$ .01	$ .05
Mercker, Kent	90DRR	31	$ .01	$ .15
Mercker, Kent	91D	299	$ .01	$ .04

DONRUSS

Player	Year	No.	VG	EX/MT	Player	Year	No.	VG	EX/MT
Mercker, Kent	91DL	41	$ .01	$ .08	Mills, Alan	93D	691	$ .01	$ .05
Mercker, Kent	92D	116	$ .01	$ .04	Mills, Alan	93DL	111	$ .01	$ .15
Mercker, Kent	92D	616	$ .01	$ .10	Mills, Brad	83D	366	$ .01	$ .06
Mercker, Kent	93D	2	$ .01	$ .05	Milner, Eddie	83D	169	$ .01	$ .06
Meridith, Ron	86D	533	$ .01	$ .08	Milner, Eddie	84D	365	$ .05	$ .20
Merullo, Matt	89DR	50	$ .01	$ .05	Milner, Eddie	85D	428	$ .01	$ .10
Merullo, Matt	92D	264	$ .01	$ .04	Milner, Eddie	86D	325	$ .01	$ .08
Mesa, Jose	88D	601	$ .01	$ .15	Milner, Eddie	87D	433	$ .01	$ .05
Mesa, Jose	91D	765	$ .01	$ .04	Milner, John	81D	377	$ .01	$ .06
Mesa, Jose	91DL	166	$ .01	$ .08	Milner, John	82D	266	$ .01	$ .06
Mesa, Jose	92D	773	$ .01	$ .04	Minor, Blas	92DR	81	$ .01	$ .10
Mesa, Jose	92DL	351	$ .01	$ .06	Minton, Greg	81D	579	$ .01	$ .06
Mesa, Jose	93D	465	$ .01	$ .05	Minton, Greg	82D	348	$ .01	$ .06
Meulens, Hensley	89D	547	$ .05	$ .20	Minton, Greg	83D	186	$ .01	$ .06
Meulens, Hensley	91DL	349	$ .01	$ .08	Minton, Greg	84D	187	$ .05	$ .20
Meulens, Hensley	91DLS	98	$ .01	$ .08	Minton, Greg	85D	143	$ .01	$ .10
Meulens, Hensley	91DRR	31	$ .01	$ .10	Minton, Greg	86D	480	$ .01	$ .08
Meulens, Hensley	92D	711	$ .01	$ .04	Minton, Greg	88D	505	$ .01	$ .04
Meyer, Brian	89D	640	$ .01	$ .04	Minton, Greg	89D	490	$ .01	$ .04
Meyer, Brian	90D	648	$ .01	$ .04	Minton, Greg	90D	116	$ .01	$ .04
Meyer, Dan	81D	43	$ .01	$ .06	Mirabella, Paul	81D	151	$ .01	$ .06
Meyer, Dan	82D	176	$ .01	$ .06	Mirabella, Paul	82D	629	$ .01	$ .06
Meyer, Dan	83D	413	$ .01	$ .06	Mirabella, Paul	83D	541	$ .01	$ .06
Meyer, Joey	87D	460	$ .05	$ .30	Mirabella, Paul	89D	654	$ .01	$ .04
Meyer, Joey	88DR	38	$ .01	$ .15	Mitchell, Charlie	85DRR	40	$ .01	$ .15
Meyer, Joey	88DRR	36	$ .05	$ .25	Mitchell, John	87DR	37	$ .01	$ .07
Meyer, Joey	89D	339	$ .01	$ .04	Mitchell, John	91D	710	$ .01	$ .04
Michael, Gene	81D	500	$ .01	$ .06	Mitchell, Keith	92D	508	$ .01	$ .10
Mielke, Gary	90D	679	$ .01	$ .10	Mitchell, Kevin	86DR	17	$ .75	$3.00
Milacki, Bob	89D	651	$ .01	$ .15	Mitchell, Kevin	87D	599	$ .20	$2.00
Milacki, Bob	89DR	22	$ .01	$ .05	Mitchell, Kevin	88D	66	$ .05	$ .25
Milacki, Bob	90D	333	$ .01	$ .10	Mitchell, Kevin	89D	485	$ .05	$ .15
Milacki, Bob	90DL	402	$ .05	$ .25	Mitchell, Kevin	90D	98	$ .01	$ .15
Milacki, Bob	91D	69	$ .01	$ .04	Mitchell, Kevin	90DAS	715	$ .01	$ .10
Milacki, Bob	92D	101	$ .01	$ .04	Mitchell, Kevin	90DBC	11	$ .01	$ .10
Milacki, Bob	92DL	262	$ .01	$ .06	Mitchell, Kevin	90DK	11	$ .01	$ .05
Milacki, Bob	93D	587	$ .01	$ .05	Mitchell, Kevin	90DL	120	$ .10	$ .75
Milbourne, Larry	81D	486	$ .01	$ .06	Mitchell, Kevin	91D	255	$ .01	$ .10
Milbourne, Larry	82D	614	$ .01	$ .06	Mitchell, Kevin	91DAS	438	$ .01	$ .06
Milbourne, Larry	83D	411	$ .01	$ .06	Mitchell, Kevin	91DL	85	$ .01	$ .15
Militello, Sam	92DRR	407	$ .05	$ .25	Mitchell, Kevin	91DLS	257	$ .01	$ .15
Militello, Sam	93D	371	$ .01	$ .15	Mitchell, Kevin	91DMVP	407	$ .01	$ .10
Militello, Sam	93DL	52	$ .10	$ .40	Mitchell, Kevin	92D	583	$ .01	$ .10
Miller, Darrell	85D	644	$ .01	$ .10	Mitchell, Kevin	92DL	185	$ .01	$ .06
Miller, Darrell	88D	551	$ .01	$ .04	Mitchell, Kevin	92DLS	237	$ .01	$ .06
Miller, Eddie	82D	425	$ .01	$ .06	Mitchell, Kevin	93D	157	$ .01	$ .05
Miller, Keith	88D	562	$ .01	$ .10	Mitchell, Paul	81D	205	$ .01	$ .06
Miller, Keith	89D	623	$ .01	$ .04	Mizerock, John	84D	380	$ .05	$ .20
Miller, Keith	90D	507	$ .01	$ .04	Mizerock, John	86D	502	$ .01	$ .08
Miller, Keith	90DL	462	$ .05	$ .25	Mizerock, John	87D	653	$ .01	$ .05
Miller, Keith	91D	248	$ .01	$ .06	Mlicki, Dave	93D	273	$ .01	$ .10
Miller, Keith	92D	657	$ .01	$ .04	Mmahat, Kevin	90D	481	$ .01	$ .10
Miller, Keith	92DL	459	$ .01	$ .06	Moeller, Dennis	92DR	82	$ .01	$ .15
Miller, Keith	92DLS	189	$ .01	$ .06	Moeller, Dennis	93D	648	$ .01	$ .05
Miller, Keith	93D	543	$ .01	$ .05	Moffitt, Randy	81D	195	$ .01	$ .06
Miller, Keith	93DL	168	$ .01	$ .15	Moffitt, Randy	83D	545	$ .01	$ .06
Miller, Mike	84D	493	$ .05	$ .20	Moffitt, Randy	84D	390	$ .05	$ .20
Miller, Paul	92DL	492	$ .01	$ .15	Mohorcic, Dale	87D	531	$ .01	$ .05
Miller, Paul	92DR	79	$ .01	$ .05	Mohorcic, Dale	88D	470	$ .01	$ .04
Miller, Rick	81D	294	$ .01	$ .06	Mohorcic, Dale	89D	630	$ .01	$ .04
Miller, Rick	82D	334	$ .01	$ .06	Molinaro, Bobby	82D	417	$ .01	$ .06
Miller, Rick	83D	82	$ .01	$ .06	Molinaro, Bobby	83D	596	$ .01	$ .06
Miller, Rick	85D	517	$ .01	$ .10	Molitor, Paul	81D	203	$ .10	$1.00
Millette, Joe	92DR	80	$ .01	$ .05	Molitor, Paul	82D	78	$ .10	$1.00
Milligan, Randy	88DR	32	$ .05	$ .25	Molitor, Paul	83D	484	$ .10	$ .75
Milligan, Randy	90D	519	$ .01	$ .04	Molitor, Paul	84D	107	$ .25	$2.50
Milligan, Randy	90DL	92	$ .05	$ .25	Molitor, Paul	85D	359	$ .10	$ .75
Milligan, Randy	91D	542	$ .01	$ .04	Molitor, Paul	86D	124	$ .05	$ .35
Milligan, Randy	91DL	109	$ .01	$ .08	Molitor, Paul	87D	117	$ .01	$ .15
Milligan, Randy	91DLS	7	$ .01	$ .08	Molitor, Paul	88D	249	$ .01	$ .10
Milligan, Randy	92D	222	$ .01	$ .04	Molitor, Paul	88DBC	3	$ .01	$ .10
Milligan, Randy	93D	191	$ .01	$ .05	Molitor, Paul	88DK	7	$ .01	$ .15
Mills, Alan	90DL	491	$ .10	$ .40	Molitor, Paul	89D	291	$ .01	$ .10
Mills, Alan	90DR	44	$ .01	$ .05	Molitor, Paul	89DBC	9	$ .01	$ .10
Mills, Alan	91D	338	$ .01	$ .10	Molitor, Paul	90D	103	$ .01	$ .10

DONRUSS

Player	Year	No.	VG	EX/MT
Molitor, Paul	90DBC	15	$.01	$.04
Molitor, Paul	90DL	242	$.10	$.50
Molitor, Paul	91D	85	$.01	$.10
Molitor, Paul	91DL	302	$.01	$.15
Molitor, Paul	91DLP	20	$.75	$3.00
Molitor, Paul	91DLS	73	$.01	$.15
Molitor, Paul	92D	51	$.01	$.04
Molitor, Paul	92DK	1	$.10	$1.00
Molitor, Paul	92DL	238	$.01	$.06
Molitor, Paul	92DLS	194	$.01	$.06
Molitor, Paul	93D	75	$.01	$.05
Monday, Rick	81D	60	$.01	$.06
Monday, Rick	82D	514	$.01	$.06
Monday, Rick	83D	643	$.01	$.06
Mondesi, Raul	92DR	83	$.05	$.25
Money, Don	81D	443	$.01	$.06
Money, Don	82D	384	$.01	$.06

Player	Year	No.	VG	EX/MT
Money, Don	**83D**	**132**	**$.01**	**$.06**
Monge, Sid	81D	81	$.01	$.06
Monge, Sid	82D	620	$.01	$.06
Monge, Sid	83D	245	$.01	$.06
Monge, Sid	84D	139	$.05	$.20
Montefusco, John	81D	434	$.01	$.06
Montefusco, John	03D	313	$.01	$.06
Montefusco, John	84D	126	$.05	$.20
Montefusco, John	85D	580	$.01	$.10
Monteleone, Rich	90D	462	$.01	$.04
Monteleone, Rich	92DL	352	$.01	$.06
Monteleone, Rich	93D	445	$.01	$.05
Montgomery, Jeff	89D	440	$.01	$.10
Montgomery, Jeff	90D	380	$.01	$.04
Montgomery, Jeff	90DL	520	$.05	$.25
Montgomery, Jeff	91D	505	$.01	$.04
Montgomery, Jeff	92D	666	$.01	$.04
Montgomery, Jeff	92DL	136	$.01	$.06
Montgomery, Jeff	92DLS	190	$.01	$.06
Montgomery, Jeff	93D	175	$.01	$.05
Montgomery, Jeff	93DL	124	$.01	$.15
Mooneyham, Bill	86DR	50	$.01	$.10
Mooneyham, Bill	87D	302	$.01	$.05
Moore, Charlie	81D	324	$.01	$.06
Moore, Charlie	82D	280	$.01	$.06
Moore, Charlie	83D	206	$.01	$.06

Player	Year	No.	VG	EX/MT
Moore, Charlie	84D	292	$.05	$.20
Moore, Charlie	85D	351	$.01	$.10
Moore, Charlie	86D	246	$.01	$.08
Moore, Charlie	87D	372	$.01	$.05
Moore, Donnie	85D	650	$.01	$.10
Moore, Donnie	86D	255	$.01	$.08
Moore, Donnie	87D	110	$.01	$.05
Moore, Donnie	88D	621	$.01	$.15
Moore, Kelvin	82D	534	$.01	$.06
Moore, Kelvin	83D	87	$.01	$.06
Moore, Mike	83D	428	$.10	$.75
Moore, Mike	84D	634	$.05	$.35
Moore, Mike	85D	440	$.05	$.25
Moore, Mike	86D	240	$.01	$.08
Moore, Mike	87D	70	$.01	$.05
Moore, Mike	88D	75	$.01	$.04
Moore, Mike	89D	448	$.01	$.04
Moore, Mike	89DTR	21	$.01	$.05
Moore, Mike	90D	214	$.01	$.04
Moore, Mike	90DL	293	$.05	$.25
Moore, Mike	91D	161	$.01	$.04
Moore, Mike	91DL	218	$.01	$.08
Moore, Mike	92D	337	$.01	$.04
Moore, Mike	92DL	164	$.01	$.06
Moore, Mike	92DLS	227	$.01	$.06
Moore, Mike	93D	683	$.01	$.05
Morales, Jerry	82D	309	$.01	$.06
Morales, Jose	81D	495	$.01	$.06
Morales, Jose	82D	203	$.01	$.06
Morales, Jose	84D	275	$.05	$.30
Morandini, Mickey	91DL	383	$.05	$.20
Morandini, Mickey	91DLS	218	$.05	$.20
Morandini, Mickey	91DRR	44	$.01	$.15
Morandini, Mickey	92D	669	$.01	$.04
Morandini, Mickey	92DL	330	$.01	$.06
Morandini, Mickey	92DLS	77	$.01	$.06
Morandini, Mickey	93D	224	$.01	$.05
Morandini, Mickey	93DL	77	$.01	$.15
Moreland, Keith	81D	382	$.05	$.30
Moreland, Keith	82D	119	$.01	$.06
Moreland, Keith	83D	309	$.01	$.06
Moreland, Keith	84D	483	$.05	$.20
Moreland, Keith	85D	117	$.01	$.10
Moreland, Keith	86D	167	$.01	$.08
Moreland, Keith	87D	169	$.01	$.05
Moreland, Keith	87DK	24	$.01	$.05
Moreland, Keith	88D	201	$.01	$.04
Moreland, Keith	89D	111	$.01	$.04
Moreno, Omar	81D	17	$.01	$.06
Moreno, Omar	82D	347	$.01	$.06
Moreno, Omar	83D	347	$.01	$.06
Moreno, Omar	84D	637	$.05	$.20
Moreno, Omar	85D	591	$.01	$.10
Morgan, Joe	81D	18	$.10	$1.00
Morgan, Joe	82D	312	$.10	$.60
Morgan, Joe	83D	438	$.10	$.50
Morgan, Joe	83D	648	$.05	$.35
Morgan, Joe	83DK	24	$.10	$.40
Morgan, Joe	84D	355	$.15	$1.50
Morgan, Joe	85D	584	$.10	$.50
Morgan, Mike	83D	108	$.05	$.35
Morgan, Mike	87D	366	$.01	$.05
Morgan, Mike	88D	120	$.01	$.04
Morgan, Mike	89D	164	$.01	$.04
Morgan, Mike	90D	132	$.01	$.04
Morgan, Mike	90DL	358	$.05	$.25
Morgan, Mike	91D	182	$.01	$.04
Morgan, Mike	91DL	193	$.01	$.08
Morgan, Mike	92D	200	$.01	$.04
Morgan, Mike	92DL	204	$.01	$.06
Morgan, Mike	92DLS	17	$.01	$.06
Morgan, Mike	93D	394	$.01	$.05
Morgan, Mike	93DL	123	$.01	$.15
Morman, Russ	87D	306	$.05	$.25
Morman, Russ	91DL	263	$.01	$.08

DONRUSS

Player	Year	No.	VG	EX/MT	Player	Year	No.	VG	EX/MT
Morris, Hal	89D	545	$ .05	$ .25	Motley, Darryl	84D	344	$ .05	$ .20
Morris, Hal	90D	514	$ .01	$ .10	Motley, Darryl	85D	461	$ .01	$ .10
Morris, Hal	90DL	321	$ .10	$1.00	Motley, Darryl	86D	217	$ .01	$ .08
Morris, Hal	91D	141	$ .01	$ .15	Moyer, Jamie	87D	315	$ .05	$ .30
Morris, Hal	91DL	51	$ .05	$ .20	Moyer, Jamie	88D	169	$ .01	$ .04
Morris, Hal	91DLS	168	$ .05	$ .20	Moyer, Jamie	89D	157	$ .01	$ .04
Morris, Hal	92D	258	$ .01	$ .04	Moyer, Jamie	89DTR	39	$ .01	$ .05
Morris, Hal	92DK	19	$ .10	$1.00	Moyer, Jamie	90D	378	$ .01	$ .04
Morris, Hal	92DL	205	$ .01	$ .06	Mulholland, Terry	87D	515	$ .10	$ .50
Morris, Hal	92DLS	24	$ .01	$ .06	Mulholland, Terry	90D	515	$ .01	$ .04
Morris, Hal	93D	294	$ .01	$ .05	Mulholland, Terry	90DL	474	$ .05	$ .25
Morris, Jack	81D	127	$ .20	$2.00	Mulholland, Terry	91D	541	$ .01	$ .04
Morris, Jack	82D	107	$ .15	$1.25	Mulholland, Terry	91DBC	14	$ .01	$ .03
Morris, Jack	83D	107	$ .10	$1.00	Mulholland, Terry	91DL	46	$ .01	$ .08
Morris, Jack	83DK	5	$ .10	$ .50	Mulholland, Terry	91DLS	219	$ .01	$ .08
Morris, Jack	84D	415	$ .75	$3.00	Mulholland, Terry	92D	268	$ .01	$ .04
Morris, Jack	85D	415	$ .10	$1.00	Mulholland, Terry	92DL	464	$ .01	$ .06
Morris, Jack	86D	105	$ .10	$ .50	Mulholland, Terry	92DLS	78	$ .01	$ .06
Morris, Jack	87D	173	$ .05	$ .25	Mulholland, Terry	93D	172	$ .01	$ .05
Morris, Jack	87DK	13	$ .05	$ .20	Mulholland, Terry	93DL	22	$ .01	$ .15
Morris, Jack	88D	127	$ .05	$ .20	Mulliniks, Rance	81D	504	$ .01	$ .06
Morris, Jack	88D	480	$ .01	$ .04	Mulliniks, Rance	82D	630	$ .01	$ .06
Morris, Jack	89D	234	$ .01	$ .10	Mulliniks, Rance	83D	432	$ .01	$ .06
Morris, Jack	90D	639	$ .01	$ .10	Mulliniks, Rance	84D	584	$ .05	$ .20
Morris, Jack	90DL	482	$ .10	$ .75	Mulliniks, Rance	85D	485	$ .01	$ .10
Morris, Jack	91D	492	$ .01	$ .10	Mulliniks, Rance	86D	606	$ .01	$ .08
Morris, Jack	91DL	294	$ .01	$ .15	Mulliniks, Rance	87D	319	$ .01	$ .05
Morris, Jack	91DLS	89	$ .01	$ .08	Mulliniks, Rance	88D	197	$ .01	$ .04
Morris, Jack	92D	216	$ .01	$ .10	Mulliniks, Rance	89D	87	$ .01	$ .04
Morris, Jack	92DAS	25	$ .01	$ .05	Mulliniks, Rance	90D	607	$ .01	$ .04
Morris, Jack	92DL	425	$ .01	$ .10	Mulliniks, Rance	91D	663	$ .01	$ .04
Morris, Jack	92DLS	257	$ .01	$ .06	Mulliniks, Rance	92D	542	$ .01	$ .04
Morris, Jack	93D	351	$ .01	$ .05	Mumphrey, Jerry	81D	124	$ .01	$ .06
Morris, Jack	93DL	113	$ .05	$ .20	Mumphrey, Jerry	82D	261	$ .01	$ .06
Morris, John	85DRR	32	$ .01	$ .15	Mumphrey, Jerry	83D	360	$ .01	$ .06
Morris, John	87D	480	$ .01	$ .05	Mumphrey, Jerry	84D	426	$ .05	$ .20
Morris, John	90D	516	$ .01	$ .04	Mumphrey, Jerry	85D	206	$ .01	$ .10
Morris, John	91DL	496	$ .01	$ .08	Mumphrey, Jerry	86D	84	$ .01	$ .08
Morris, John	92D	92	$ .01	$ .04	Mumphrey, Jerry	87D	324	$ .01	$ .05
Morrison, Jim	81D	158	$ .01	$ .06	Mumphrey, Jerry	88D	447	$ .01	$ .04
Morrison, Jim	82D	395	$ .01	$ .06	Munoz, Mike	90DR	8	$ .01	$ .05
Morrison, Jim	83D	150	$ .01	$ .06	Munoz, Mike	93D	627	$ .01	$ .05
Morrison, Jim	84D	322	$ .05	$ .20	Munoz, Mike	93DL	191	$ .05	$ .20
Morrison, Jim	85D	532	$ .01	$ .10	Munoz, Pedro	91D	758	$ .05	$ .20
Morrison, Jim	86D	386	$ .01	$ .08	Munoz, Pedro	91DL	186	$ .10	$ .50
Morrison, Jim	87D	484	$ .01	$ .05	Munoz, Pedro	91DR	21	$ .05	$ .20
Morrison, Jim	88D	543	$ .01	$ .04	Munoz, Pedro	92D	305	$ .01	$ .10
Morton, Kevin	91DR	40	$ .01	$ .05	Munoz, Pedro	92DL	53	$ .01	$ .10
Morton, Kevin	91DRR	37	$ .01	$ .15	Munoz, Pedro	93D	311	$ .01	$ .05
Morton, Kevin	92D	330	$ .01	$ .10	Munoz, Pedro	93DL	219	$ .05	$ .25
Moseby, Lloyd	82D	129	$ .10	$ .45	Mura, Steve	81D	362	$ .01	$ .06
Moseby, Lloyd	83D	556	$ .01	$ .06	Mura, Steve	82D	523	$ .01	$ .06
Moseby, Lloyd	84D	363	$ .05	$ .20	Mura, Steve	83D	292	$ .01	$ .06
Moseby, Lloyd	85D	437	$ .03	$ .10	Murcer, Bobby	81D	111	$ .01	$ .06
Moseby, Lloyd	86D	73	$ .01	$ .08	Murcer, Bobby	82D	486	$ .01	$ .06
Moseby, Lloyd	87D	74	$ .01	$ .05	Murcer, Bobby	83D	261	$ .01	$ .06
Moseby, Lloyd	87DK	21	$ .01	$ .05	Murphy, Dale	81D	437	$ .10	$1.00
Moseby, Lloyd	88D	367	$ .01	$ .04	Murphy, Dale	82D	299	$ .10	$1.00
Moseby, Lloyd	89D	231	$ .01	$ .04	Murphy, Dale	83D	47	$ .10	$ .75
Moseby, Lloyd	90D	504	$ .01	$ .04	Murphy, Dale	83DK	12	$ .05	$ .35
Moseby, Lloyd	90DL	377	$ .05	$ .25	Murphy, Dale	84D	66	$ .20	$2.00
Moseby, Lloyd	91D	188	$ .01	$ .04	Murphy, Dale	85D	66	$ .10	$ .75
Moseby, Lloyd	91DL	223	$ .01	$ .08	Murphy, Dale	86D	66	$ .10	$ .50
Moseby, Lloyd	91DLS	56	$ .01	$ .08	Murphy, Dale	87D	78	$ .05	$ .20
Moseby, Lloyd	92D	443	$ .01	$ .04	Murphy, Dale	87DK	3	$ .01	$ .15
Moses, John	84D	74	$ .05	$ .20	Murphy, Dale	88D	78	$ .01	$ .10
Moses, John	87D	393	$ .01	$ .05	Murphy, Dale	88DBC	14	$ .01	$ .10
Moses, John	88D	440	$ .01	$ .04	Murphy, Dale	89D	104	$ .01	$ .10
Moses, John	89D	626	$ .01	$ .04	Murphy, Dale	90D	168	$ .01	$ .10
Moses, John	90D	590	$ .01	$ .04	Murphy, Dale	90DL	243	$ .10	$ .50
Moses, John	90DL	433	$ .05	$ .25	Murphy, Dale	91D	484	$ .01	$ .10
Moskau, Paul	82D	355	$ .01	$ .06	Murphy, Dale	91D	744	$ .01	$ .15
Mota, Andy	92D	598	$ .01	$ .10	Murphy, Dale	91DL	412	$ .01	$ .15
Mota, Manny	81D	299	$ .01	$ .15	Murphy, Dale	91DLS	220	$ .01	$ .15
Motley, Darryl	82D	390	$ .01	$ .06	Murphy, Dale	92D	146	$ .01	$ .10

DONRUSS

Player	Year	No.	VG	EX/MT
Murphy, Dale	92DL	527	$.01	$.06
Murphy, Dale	92DLS	79	$.01	$.06
Murphy, Dale	93D	646	$.01	$.05
Murphy, Dwayne	81D	359	$.01	$.06
Murphy, Dwayne	82D	239	$.01	$.06
Murphy, Dwayne	83D	161	$.01	$.06
Murphy, Dwayne	84D	101	$.05	$.20
Murphy, Dwayne	84DK	3	$.05	$.20
Murphy, Dwayne	85D	420	$.01	$.10
Murphy, Dwayne	86D	176	$.01	$.08
Murphy, Dwayne	87D	379	$.01	$.05
Murphy, Dwayne	88D	405	$.01	$.04
Murphy, Rob	87D	452	$.05	$.20
Murphy, Rob	88D	82	$.01	$.04
Murphy, Rob	89D	139	$.01	$.04
Murphy, Rob	89DTR	15	$.01	$.05
Murphy, Rob	90D	186	$.01	$.04
Murphy, Rob	90DL	183	$.05	$.25
Murphy, Rob	91D	250	$.01	$.04
Murphy, Rob	92D	329	$.01	$.04
Murphy, Rob	93D	588	$.01	$.05
Murray, Dale	83D	381	$.01	$.06
Murray, Dale	84D	577	$.05	$.20
Murray, Eddie	81D	112	$.75	$2.75
Murray, Eddie	82D	483	$.20	$2.00
Murray, Eddie	83D	405	$.15	$1.50
Murray, Eddie	84D	47	$1.25	$5.00
Murray, Eddie	84DK	22	$.15	$1.50
Murray, Eddie	85D	47	$.20	$2.00
Murray, Eddie	86D	88	$.10	$1.00
Murray, Eddie	87D	48	$.05	$.35
Murray, Eddie	88D	231	$.01	$.15
Murray, Eddie	89D	96	$.01	$.15
Murray, Eddie	89DTR	12	$.05	$.25

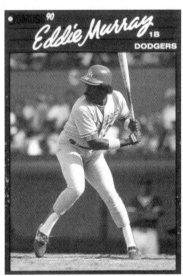

Murray, Eddie	90D	77	$.01	$.10
Murray, Eddie	90DL	181	$.10	$.75
Murray, Eddie	91D	502	$.01	$.10
Murray, Eddie	91DBC	18	$.01	$.10
Murray, Eddie	91DL	126	$.05	$.20
Murray, Eddie	91DLS	185	$.05	$.20
Murray, Eddie	91DMVP	405	$.01	$.10
Murray, Eddie	92D	392	$.01	$.10
Murray, Eddie	92DL	396	$.05	$.20

Player	Year	No.	VG	EX/MT
Murray, Eddie	92DLS	68	$.05	$.20
Murray, Eddie	93D	278	$.01	$.05
Murray, Eddie	93DK	25	$.20	$2.00
Murray, Eddie	93DL	167	$.05	$.20
Musial, Stan	88D	641	$.01	$.15
Musselman, Jeff	87D	591	$.05	$.30
Musselman, Jeff	87DR	53	$.01	$.07
Musselman, Jeff	88D	630	$.01	$.15
Musselman, Jeff	89D	656	$.01	$.04
Musselman, Jeff	90D	623	$.01	$.04
Mussina, Mike	91DLBC	12	$3.00	$12.00
Mussina, Mike	92D	632	$.10	$.50
Mussina, Mike	92DL	13	$.15	$1.50
Mussina, Mike	92DLS	127	$.15	$1.50
Mussina, Mike	93D	427	$.05	$.25
Mutis, Jeff	92DRR	411	$.01	$.05
Myers, Greg	88D	624	$.05	$.20
Myers, Greg	90D	706	$.01	$.04
Myers, Greg	90DL	527	$.05	$.25
Myers, Greg	91D	494	$.01	$.04
Myers, Greg	91DL	256	$.01	$.08
Myers, Greg	92D	342	$.01	$.04
Myers, Greg	92DL	192	$.01	$.06
Myers, Greg	93D	269	$.01	$.05
Myers, Randy	87DRR	29	$.05	$.35
Myers, Randy	88D	620	$.01	$.15
Myers, Randy	89D	336	$.01	$.10
Myers, Randy	90D	336	$.01	$.10
Myers, Randy	90DL	149	$.05	$.25
Myers, Randy	91D	209	$.01	$.04
Myers, Randy	91DL	504	$.01	$.08
Myers, Randy	92D	624	$.01	$.04
Nabholz, Chris	91D	667	$.01	$.15
Nabholz, Chris	91DL	416	$.05	$.20
Nabholz, Chris	92D	170	$.01	$.04
Nabholz, Chris	92DL	327	$.01	$.06
Nabholz, Chris	93D	114	$.01	$.05
Nabholz, Chris	93DL	73	$.01	$.15
Naehring, Tim	91D	367	$.01	$.10
Naehring, Tim	91DL	150	$.01	$.15
Naehring, Tim	91DLS	16	$.01	$.15
Naehring, Tim	92D	742	$.01	$.04
Naehring, Tim	92DL	235	$.01	$.06
Naehring, Tim	92DLS	134	$.01	$.06
Naehring, Tim	93D	399	$.01	$.05
Nagy, Charles	91D	592	$.05	$.25
Nagy, Charles	91DR	18	$.05	$.25
Nagy, Charles	92D	315	$.01	$.10
Nagy, Charles	92DL	115	$.01	$.15
Nagy, Charles	93D	141	$.01	$.05
Nagy, Charles	93DL	171	$.20	$2.00
Narron, Jerry	81D	405	$.01	$.06
Narron, Jerry	82D	433	$.01	$.06
Narron, Jerry	85D	643	$.01	$.10
Narron, Jerry	86D	451	$.01	$.08
Narron, Jerry	87D	603	$.01	$.05
Natal, Rob	92DR	81	$.01	$.15
Natal, Rob	93D	744	$.01	$.05
Navarro, Jaime	90D	640	$.05	$.20
Navarro, Jaime	90DL	85	$.20	$2.00
Navarro, Jaime	91D	216	$.01	$.04
Navarro, Jaime	91DL	409	$.01	$.08
Navarro, Jaime	92D	705	$.01	$.10
Navarro, Jaime	92DL	144	$.01	$.06
Navarro, Jaime	92DLS	195	$.01	$.06
Navarro, Jaime	93D	281	$.01	$.05
Neagle, Denny	91DL	466	$.05	$.35
Neagle, Denny	92D	605	$.01	$.15
Neagle, Denny	92DLS	87	$.01	$.06
Neagle, Denny	93D	226	$.01	$.05
Neagle, Denny	93DL	42	$.01	$.15
Neel, Troy	92DR	85	$.10	$.50
Neel, Troy	93D	308	$.01	$.15
Neidlinger, Jim	91D	713	$.01	$.10
Nelson, Gene	82D	513	$.01	$.06

DONRUSS

Player	Year	No.	VG	EX/MT
Nelson, Gene	83D	55	$ .01	$ .06
Nelson, Gene	85D	615	$ .01	$ .10

Player	Year	No.	VG	EX/MT
Nelson, Gene	86D	501	$ .01	$ .08
Nelson, Gene	87D	580	$ .01	$ .05
Nelson, Gene	88D	133	$ .01	$ .04
Nelson, Gene	89D	540	$ .01	$ .04
Nelson, Gene	90D	540	$ .01	$ .04
Nelson, Gene	90DL	477	$ .05	$ .25
Nelson, Gene	91D	385	$ .01	$ .04
Nelson, Gene	91DL	328	$ .01	$ .08
Nelson, Gene	92D	696	$ .01	$ .04
Nelson, Jeff	92DRR	408	$ .01	$ .05
Nelson, Jeff	93D	685	$ .01	$ .05
Nelson, Ricky	84D	636	$ .05	$ .20
Nelson, Rob	87D	595	$ .01	$ .05
Nelson, Rob	88D	574	$ .01	$ .04
Nettles, Graig	81D	105	$ .05	$ .20
Nettles, Graig	82D	335	$ .05	$ .20
Nettles, Graig	83D	83	$ .05	$ .20
Nettles, Graig	84D	518	$ .05	$ .25
Nettles, Graig	85D	234	$ .05	$ .20
Nettles, Graig	86D	478	$ .05	$ .20
Newell, Tom	88D	604	$ .01	$ .15
Newman, Al	86DR	9	$ .01	$ .10
Newman, Al	87D	426	$ .01	$ .05
Newman, Al	88D	645	$ .01	$ .15
Newman, Al	89D	436	$ .01	$ .04
Newman, Al	90D	506	$ .01	$ .04
Newman, Al	90DL	347	$ .05	$ .25
Newman, Al	91D	208	$ .01	$ .04
Newman, Al	91DL	446	$ .01	$ .08
Newman, Al	92D	339	$ .01	$ .04
Newman, Al	92DL	511	$ .01	$ .06
Newman, Jeff	81D	477	$ .01	$ .06
Newman, Jeff	82D	517	$ .01	$ .06
Newman, Jeff	83D	635	$ .01	$ .06
Newman, Jeff	84D	249	$ .05	$ .20
Newson, Warren	91DR	15	$ .01	$ .15
Newson, Warren	92D	668	$ .01	$ .10
Newson, Warren	93D	463	$ .01	$ .05
Nezelek, Andy	89D	616	$ .01	$ .10
Nezelek, Andy	90D	523	$ .01	$ .04
Nichols, Carl	88D	477	$ .01	$ .04
Nichols, Carl	88DR	39	$ .01	$ .07
Nichols, Carl	91DL	217	$ .01	$ .08
Nichols, Reid	82D	632	$ .01	$ .06
Nichols, Reid	83D	460	$ .01	$ .06
Nichols, Reid	84D	614	$ .05	$ .20
Nichols, Reid	85D	636	$ .01	$ .10
Nichols, Reid	86D	574	$ .01	$ .08
Nichols, Rod	89D	649	$ .01	$ .04
Nichols, Rod	90D	546	$ .01	$ .04
Nichols, Rod	92D	194	$ .01	$ .04
Nichols, Rod	93D	521	$ .01	$ .05
Nicosia, Steve	81D	373	$ .01	$ .06
Nicosia, Steve	82D	45	$ .01	$ .06
Nicosia, Steve	83D	528	$ .01	$ .06
Nied, David	92DR	86	$ .75	$3.00
Nied, David	93D	792	$ .10	$1.00
Nied, David	93DK	28	$1.75	$7.00
Niedenfuer, Tom	83D	536	$ .01	$ .06
Niedenfuer, Tom	84D	128	$ .05	$ .20
Niedenfuer, Tom	85D	153	$ .01	$ .10
Niedenfuer, Tom	86D	397	$ .01	$ .08
Niedenfuer, Tom	87D	218	$ .01	$ .05
Niedenfuer, Tom	88D	294	$ .01	$ .04
Niedenfuer, Tom	89D	282	$ .01	$ .04
Niedenfuer, Tom	89DTR	54	$ .01	$ .05
Niekro, Joe	81D	380	$ .05	$ .20
Niekro, Joe	82D	167	$ .01	$ .10
Niekro, Joe	83D	470	$ .01	$ .06
Niekro, Joe	83D	613	$ .05	$ .30
Niekro, Joe	83DK	10	$ .01	$ .15
Niekro, Joe	84D	110	$ .05	$ .20
Niekro, Joe	86D	601	$ .01	$ .08
Niekro, Joe	86D	645	$ .05	$ .25
Niekro, Joe	87D	217	$ .01	$ .05
Niekro, Phil	81D	328	$ .10	$ .50
Niekro, Phil	82D	475	$ .10	$ .40
Niekro, Phil	82DK	10	$ .05	$ .20
Niekro, Phil	83D	97	$ .10	$ .40
Niekro, Phil	83D	613	$ .05	$ .30
Niekro, Phil	84D	188	$ .10	$1.00
Niekro, Phil	85D	182	$ .01	$ .10
Niekro, Phil	85D	458	$ .05	$ .35
Niekro, Phil	86D	580	$ .05	$ .25
Niekro, Phil	86D	645	$ .05	$ .25
Niekro, Phil	87D	465	$ .05	$ .20
Nielsen, Jerry	92DR	87	$ .01	$ .15
Nielsen, Jerry	93D	359	$ .01	$ .10
Nielsen, Scott	87D	597	$ .01	$ .15
Niemann, Randy	82D	473	$ .01	$ .06
Nieto, Tom	85D	596	$ .01	$ .10
Nieto, Tom	86D	327	$ .01	$ .08
Nieto, Tom	88D	612	$ .01	$ .15
Nieves, Juan	86DR	12	$ .01	$ .10
Nieves, Juan	86DRR	40	$ .05	$ .20
Nieves, Juan	87D	90	$ .01	$ .05
Nieves, Juan	88D	126	$ .01	$ .04
Nieves, Juan	89D	575	$ .01	$ .04
Nieves, Melvin	93D	320	$ .05	$ .25
Nilsson, Dave	92DRR	4	$ .05	$ .20
Nilsson, Dave	93D	235	$ .01	$ .10
Nipper, Al	85D	614	$ .01	$ .10
Nipper, Al	86D	538	$ .01	$ .08
Nipper, Al	87D	297	$ .01	$ .05
Nipper, Al	88D	523	$ .01	$ .04
Nipper, Al	89D	394	$ .01	$ .04
Nixon, Donell	90D	571	$ .01	$ .04
Nixon, Otis	90D	456	$ .01	$ .04
Nixon, Otis	91D	626	$ .01	$ .04
Nixon, Otis	91DL	395	$ .01	$ .08
Nixon, Otis	92D	33	$ .01	$ .04
Nixon, Otis	92D	41	$ .01	$ .04
Nixon, Otis	92DL	358	$ .01	$ .06
Nixon, Otis	93D	262	$ .01	$ .05
Nixon, Otis	93DL	180	$ .01	$ .15

DONRUSS

Player	Year	No.	VG	EX/MT	Player	Year	No.	VG	EX/MT
Noboa, Junior	91D	726	$.01	$.04	O'Malley, Tom	83D	96	$.01	$.06
Noboa, Junior	91DL	255	$.01	$.08	O'Malley, Tom	84D	601	$.05	$.20
Noboa, Junior	92D	765	$.01	$.04	O'Neal, Randy	86D	394	$.01	$.08
Noboa, Junior	92DL	403	$.01	$.06	O'Neal, Randy	87D	584	$.01	$.05
Noce, Paul	87DR	51	$.01	$.07	O'Neill, Paul	86DRR	37	$.25	$2.50
Noce, Paul	88D	315	$.01	$.04	O'Neill, Paul	88D	433	$.01	$.15
Nokes, Matt	87DR	12	$.10	$.50	O'Neill, Paul	89D	360	$.01	$.10
Nokes, Matt	88D	152	$.05	$.20	O'Neill, Paul	90D	198	$.01	$.10
Nokes, Matt	89D	116	$.01	$.04	O'Neill, Paul	90DL	70	$.05	$.25
Nokes, Matt	90D	178	$.01	$.04	O'Neill, Paul	91D	583	$.01	$.04
Nokes, Matt	90DL	192	$.05	$.25	O'Neill, Paul	91DL	219	$.01	$.08
Nokes, Matt	90DL	314	$.05	$.25	O'Neill, Paul	91DLS	169	$.01	$.08
Nokes, Matt	91D	170	$.01	$.04	O'Neill, Paul	92D	63	$.01	$.04
Nokes, Matt	91DL	89	$.01	$.08	O'Neill, Paul	92DL	99	$.01	$.06
Nokes, Matt	92D	126	$.01	$.04	O'Neill, Paul	92DLS	25	$.01	$.06
Nokes, Matt	92DL	102	$.01	$.06	O'Neill, Paul	93D	696	$.01	$.05
Nokes, Matt	92DLS	217	$.01	$.06	Oberkfell, Ken	81D	583	$.01	$.06
Nokes, Matt	93D	239	$.01	$.05	Oberkfell, Ken	82D	404	$.01	$.06
Nolan, Joe	81D	302	$.01	$.06	Oberkfell, Ken	83D	246	$.01	$.06
Nolan, Joe	82D	62	$.01	$.06	Oberkfell, Ken	84D	504	$.05	$.20
Nolan, Joe	83D	79	$.01	$.06	Oberkfell, Ken	85D	432	$.01	$.10
Nolan, Joe	84D	489	$.05	$.20	Oberkfell, Ken	86D	531	$.01	$.08
Nolan, Joe	85D	594	$.01	$.10	Oberkfell, Ken	87D	437	$.01	$.05
Noles, Dick	81D	568	$.01	$.06	Oberkfell, Ken	88D	67	$.01	$.04
Noles, Dickie	83D	426	$.01	$.06	Oberkfell, Ken	89D	506	$.01	$.04
Noles, Dickie	84D	266	$.05	$.20	Oberkfell, Ken	90D	494	$.01	$.04
Noles, Dickie	86D	587	$.01	$.08	Oberkfell, Ken	90DL	294	$.05	$.25
Nolte, Eric	88D	534	$.01	$.04	Oberkfell, Ken	91D	109	$.01	$.04
Nordhagen, Wayne	81D	401	$.01	$.06	Oelkers, Bryan	84D	486	$.05	$.20
Nordhagen, Wayne	82D	67	$.01	$.06	Oelkers, Bryan	87D	596	$.01	$.05
Norman, Fred	81D	92	$.01	$.06	Oester, Ron	81D	423	$.01	$.06
Norman, Nelson	81D	509	$.01	$.06	Oester, Ron	82D	500	$.01	$.06
Norris, Jim	81D	388	$.01	$.06	Oester, Ron	83D	526	$.01	$.06
Norris, Mike	81D	118	$.01	$.06	Oester, Ron	84D	62	$.05	$.20
Norris, Mike	82D	197	$.01	$.06	Oester, Ron	85D	81	$.01	$.10
Norris, Mike	82DK	19	$.01	$.15	Oester, Ron	86D	81	$.01	$.08
Norris, Mike	83D	139	$.01	$.06	Oester, Ron	87D	206	$.01	$.05
North, Bill	81D	76	$.01	$.06	Oester, Ron	88D	246	$.01	$.04
Norwood, Willie	81D	516	$.01	$.06	Oester, Ron	89D	553	$.01	$.04
Nunez, Ed	84D	435	$.05	$.20	Oester, Ron	90D	317	$.01	$.04
Nunez, Ed	85D	484	$.01	$.10	Oester, Ron	91D	628	$.01	$.04
Nunez, Ed	86D	145	$.01	$.08	Offerman, Jose	90DL	464	$.10	$1.00
Nunez, Ed	87D	243	$.01	$.05	Offerman, Jose	91DLS	186	$.01	$.15
Nunez, Ed	88D	445	$.01	$.04	Offerman, Jose	91DRR	33	$.01	$.10
Nunez, Edwin	90D	563	$.01	$.04	Offerman, Jose	92D	721	$.01	$.04
Nunez, Edwin	90DL	397	$.05	$.25	Offerman, Jose	92DL	322	$.01	$.06
Nunez, Edwin	91D	620	$.01	$.04	Offerman, Jose	92DLS	47	$.01	$.06
Nunez, Edwin	91DL	352	$.01	$.08	Offerman, Jose	93D	376	$.01	$.05
Nunez, Edwin	92D	541	$.01	$.04	Offerman, Jose	93DL	17	$.05	$.25
Nunez, Jose	88D	611	$.01	$.15	Office, Rowland	81D	213	$.01	$.06
Nunez, Jose	90D	467	$.01	$.04	Oglivie, Ben	81D	446	$.01	$.06
O'Berry, Mike	82D	538	$.01	$.06	Oglivie, Ben	82D	484	$.01	$.06
O'Brien, Charlie	90D	410	$.01	$.04	Oglivie, Ben	83D	384	$.01	$.06
O'Brien, Charlie	90DL	375	$.05	$.25	Oglivie, Ben	84D	229	$.05	$.20
O'Brien, Charlie	91D	623	$.01	$.04	Oglivie, Ben	85D	333	$.01	$.10
O'Brien, Charlie	91DL	122	$.01	$.08	Oglivie, Ben	86D	333	$.01	$.08
O'Brien, Charlie	92D	777	$.01	$.04	Oglivie, Ben	87D	419	$.01	$.05
O'Brien, Charlie	93D	698	$.01	$.05	Ojeda, Bob	82D	540	$.10	$.40
O'Brien, Pete	84D	281	$.10	$.50	Ojeda, Bob	83D	260	$.01	$.06
O'Brien, Pete	85D	178	$.01	$.10	Ojeda, Bob	84D	538	$.05	$.20
O'Brien, Pete	86D	99	$.01	$.08	Ojeda, Bob	85D	371	$.01	$.10
O'Brien, Pete	87D	259	$.01	$.05	Ojeda, Bob	86D	636	$.01	$.08
O'Brien, Pete	88D	284	$.01	$.04	Ojeda, Bob	87D	364	$.01	$.05
O'Brien, Pete	89D	107	$.01	$.04	Ojeda, Bob	88D	632	$.01	$.15
O'Brien, Pete	89DTR	16	$.01	$.05	Ojeda, Bob	89D	218	$.01	$.04
O'Brien, Pete	90D	202	$.01	$.04	Ojeda, Bob	90D	117	$.01	$.04
O'Brien, Pete	90DK	24	$.01	$.05	Ojeda, Bob	91D	584	$.01	$.04
O'Brien, Pete	90DL	9	$.05	$.25	Ojeda, Bobby	91DL	476	$.01	$.08
O'Brien, Pete	91D	119	$.01	$.04	Ojeda, Bobby	91DLS	187	$.01	$.08
O'Brien, Pete	91DL	244	$.01	$.08	Ojeda, Bobby	92D	157	$.01	$.04
O'Brien, Pete	92D	86	$.01	$.04	Ojeda, Bobby	92DL	345	$.01	$.06
O'Brien, Pete	92DL	260	$.01	$.06	Ojeda, Bobby	93D	614	$.01	$.05
O'Brien, Pete	92DLS	238	$.01	$.06	Olander, Jim	92D	766	$.01	$.10
O'Brien, Pete	93D	613	$.01	$.05	Olerud, John	90D	711	$.10	$.75
O'Connor, Jack	83D	51	$.01	$.06	Olerud, John	90DL	237	$1.25	$5.00

DONRUSS

Player	Year	No.	VG	EX/MT
Olerud, John	90DR	2	$ .10	$ .50
Olerud, John	91D	530	$ .01	$ .10
Olerud, John	91DL	125	$ .10	$ .50
Olerud, John	91DLS	136	$ .05	$ .35
Olerud, John	92D	98	$ .01	$ .15
Olerud, John	92DL	60	$ .05	$ .25
Olerud, John	92DLS	258	$ .05	$ .20
Olerud, John	93D	483	$ .01	$ .10
Olerud, John	93DL	47	$ .05	$ .25
Olin, Steve	90D	438	$ .01	$ .10
Olin, Steve	91D	339	$ .01	$ .04
Olin, Steve	91DL	94	$ .01	$ .08
Olin, Steve	92D	151	$ .01	$ .04
Olin, Steve	92DL	141	$ .01	$ .06
Olin, Steve	93D	567	$ .01	$ .05
Olivares, Omar	91D	503	$ .01	$ .10
Olivares, Omar	92D	481	$ .01	$ .04
Olivares, Omar	92DL	282	$ .01	$ .06
Olivares, Omar	93D	388	$ .01	$ .05
Oliver, Al	81D	387	$ .05	$ .20
Oliver, Al	82D	116	$ .01	$ .15
Oliver, Al	83D	140	$ .05	$ .20
Oliver, Al	84D	177	$ .05	$ .25
Oliver, Al	84DK	9	$ .05	$ .25
Oliver, Al	85D	598	$ .03	$ .10
Oliver, Al	86D	485	$ .01	$ .08
Oliver, Joe	90D	586	$ .01	$ .15
Oliver, Joe	90DL	453	$ .05	$ .25
Oliver, Joe	91D	381	$ .01	$ .04
Oliver, Joe	91DL	73	$ .01	$ .08
Oliver, Joe	92D	261	$ .01	$ .04
Oliver, Joe	92DL	7	$ .01	$ .06
Oliver, Joe	93D	586	$ .01	$ .05
Oliveras, Francisco	89DR	9	$ .01	$ .05
Oliveras, Francisco	90DL	515	$ .05	$ .25
Oliveras, Francisco	91D	469	$ .01	$ .04
Oliveras, Francisco	92D	702	$ .01	$ .04
Olson, Greg	90DL	323	$ .10	$ .40
Olson, Greg	90DR	46	$ .01	$ .15
Olson, Greg	91D	285	$ .01	$ .04
Olson, Greg	91DL	158	$ .01	$ .08
Olson, Greg	92D	386	$ .01	$ .04
Olson, Greg	92DL	226	$ .01	$ .06
Olson, Greg	92DLS	7	$ .01	$ .06
Olson, Greg	93D	530	$ .01	$ .05
Olson, Gregg	89DR	35	$ .10	$ .50
Olson, Gregg	89DRR	46	$ .05	$ .25
Olson, Gregg	90D	377	$ .01	$ .10
Olson, Gregg	90DL	7	$ .15	$1.25
Olson, Gregg	91D	111	$ .01	$ .04
Olson, Gregg	91DK	23	$ .01	$ .05
Olson, Gregg	91DL	519	$ .01	$ .08
Olson, Gregg	91DLS	8	$ .01	$ .08
Olson, Gregg	91DMVP	393	$ .01	$ .03
Olson, Gregg	92D	110	$ .01	$ .04
Olson, Gregg	92DL	277	$ .01	$ .06
Olson, Gregg	92DLS	128	$ .01	$ .06
Olson, Gregg	93D	117	$ .01	$ .05
Olson, Gregg	93DL	23	$ .01	$ .15
Olwine, Ed	87D	560	$ .01	$ .05
Ontiveros, Steve	86D	589	$ .01	$ .08
Ontiveros, Steve	87D	221	$ .01	$ .05
Ontiveros, Steve	88D	467	$ .01	$ .04
Ontiveros, Steve	89D	596	$ .01	$ .04
Ontiveros, Steve	89DTR	11	$ .01	$ .05
Oquendo, Jose	84D	643	$ .05	$ .35
Oquendo, Jose	87D	510	$ .01	$ .05
Oquendo, Jose	88D	234	$ .01	$ .04
Oquendo, Jose	89D	319	$ .01	$ .04
Oquendo, Jose	90D	161	$ .01	$ .04
Oquendo, Jose	90DL	129	$ .05	$ .25
Oquendo, Jose	91D	281	$ .01	$ .04
Oquendo, Jose	91DL	58	$ .01	$ .08
Oquendo, Jose	91DLS	236	$ .01	$ .08
Oquendo, Jose	92D	280	$ .01	$ .04
Oquendo, Jose	92DL	289	$ .01	$ .06
Oquendo, Jose	93D	46	$ .01	$ .05
Oquendo, Jose	93DL	26	$ .01	$ .15
Orosco, Jesse	82D	646	$ .05	$ .20
Orosco, Jesse	83D	434	$ .01	$ .06
Orosco, Jesse	84D	197	$ .05	$ .20
Orosco, Jesse	85D	75	$ .01	$ .10
Orosco, Jesse	85DK	22	$ .05	$ .20
Orosco, Jesse	86D	646	$ .01	$ .08
Orosco, Jesse	87D	439	$ .01	$ .05
Orosco, Jesse	88D	192	$ .01	$ .04
Orosco, Jesse	89D	228	$ .01	$ .04
Orosco, Jesse	89DTR	26	$ .01	$ .05
Orosco, Jesse	90D	154	$ .01	$ .04
Orosco, Jesse	90DL	101	$ .05	$ .25
Orosco, Jesse	91D	171	$ .01	$ .04
Orosco, Jesse	92D	473	$ .01	$ .04
Orosco, Jesse	92DL	524	$ .01	$ .06
Orsulak, Joe	86D	444	$ .05	$ .20
Orsulak, Joe	87D	291	$ .01	$ .05
Orsulak, Joe	89D	287	$ .01	$ .04
Orsulak, Joe	90D	287	$ .01	$ .04
Orsulak, Joe	90DL	355	$ .05	$ .25
Orsulak, Joe	91D	654	$ .01	$ .04
Orsulak, Joe	91DL	152	$ .01	$ .08
Orsulak, Joe	92D	475	$ .01	$ .04
Orsulak, Joe	92DL	36	$ .01	$ .06
Orsulak, Joe	93D	751	$ .01	$ .05
Orta, Jorge	81D	439	$ .01	$ .06
Orta, Jorge	82D	211	$ .01	$ .06
Orta, Jorge	83D	388	$ .01	$ .06
Orta, Jorge	84D	317	$ .05	$ .20
Orta, Jorge	85D	130	$ .01	$ .10
Orta, Jorge	86D	339	$ .01	$ .08
Orta, Jorge	87D	348	$ .01	$ .05
Ortiz, Javier	91D	643	$ .01	$ .10
Ortiz, Javier	92D	551	$ .01	$ .04

JUNIOR ORTIZ c

Player	Year	No.	VG	EX/MT
Ortiz, Junior	84D	319	$ .05	$ .20
Ortiz, Junior	86D	508	$ .01	$ .08
Ortiz, Junior	87D	449	$ .01	$ .05
Ortiz, Junior	88D	168	$ .01	$ .04
Ortiz, Junior	89D	387	$ .01	$ .04

DONRUSS

Player	Year	No.	VG	EX/MT	Player	Year	No.	VG	EX/MT
Ortiz, Junior	91D	659	$.01	$.04	Pagnozzi, Tom	93DL	136	$.01	$.15
Ortiz, Junior	91DL	498	$.01	$.08	Palacios, Vicente	88DRR	45	$.01	$.15
Ortiz, Junior	92D	684	$.01	$.04	Palacios, Vicente	91D	732	$.01	$.04
Ortiz, Junior	93D	699	$.01	$.05	Palacios, Vicente	91DL	442	$.01	$.08
Orton, John	90DL	511	$.05	$.25	Palacios, Vicente	92D	365	$.01	$.04
Orton, John	90DR	54	$.01	$.05	Pall, Donn	89DR	7	$.01	$.05
Orton, John	91D	714	$.01	$.04	Pall, Donn	90D	606	$.01	$.04
Orton, John	91DL	191	$.01	$.08	Pall, Donn	90DL	392	$.05	$.25
Orton, John	93D	431	$.01	$.05	Pall, Donn	91D	215	$.01	$.04
Osborne, Donovan	92DLS	95	$.10	$.40	Pall, Donn	91DL	468	$.01	$.08
Osborne, Donovan	92DR	88	$.05	$.25	Pall, Donn	92D	56	$.01	$.04
Osborne, Donovan	93D	178	$.01	$.10	Pall, Donn	93D	667	$.01	$.05
Osborne, Donovan	93DL	62	$.10	$.75	Palmeiro, Rafael	87DR	47	$.25	$2.50
Osuna, Al	91DL	492	$.05	$.20	Palmeiro, Rafael	87DRR	43	$1.00	$4.00
Osuna, Al	91DR	52	$.01	$.10	Palmeiro, Rafael	88D	324	$.05	$.25
Osuna, Al	92D	318	$.01	$.04	Palmeiro, Rafael	89D	49	$.05	$.25
Osuna, Al	92DL	209	$.01	$.06	Palmeiro, Rafael	89DTR	6	$.10	$.50
Osuna, Al	93D	216	$.01	$.05	Palmeiro, Rafael	90D	225	$.01	$.10
Otis, Amos	81D	104	$.01	$.06	Palmeiro, Rafael	90DL	100	$.10	$1.00
Otis, Amos	82D	70	$.01	$.06	Palmeiro, Rafael	91D	521	$.01	$.10
Otis, Amos	83D	364	$.01	$.06	Palmeiro, Rafael	91DK	19	$.01	$.05
Ott, Ed	81D	133	$.01	$.06	Palmeiro, Rafael	91DL	347	$.05	$.20
Ott, Ed	82D	192	$.01	$.06	Palmeiro, Rafael	91DLS	127	$.01	$.15
Otto, Dave	92D	730	$.01	$.04	Palmeiro, Rafael	91DMVP	394	$.01	$.03
Otto, Dave	92DL	218	$.01	$.06	Palmeiro, Rafael	92D	46	$.01	$.10
Owchinko, Bob	81D	563	$.01	$.06	Palmeiro, Rafael	92DL	296	$.01	$.06
Owchinko, Bob	82D	287	$.01	$.06	Palmeiro, Rafael	92DLS	244	$.01	$.06
Owchinko, Bob	83D	265	$.01	$.06	Palmeiro, Rafael	93D	365	$.01	$.05
Owchinko, Bob	85D	506	$.01	$.10	Palmeiro, Rafael	93DL	49	$.05	$.20
Owen, Dave	85D	483	$.01	$.10	Palmer, Dave	81D	451	$.01	$.06
Owen, Spike	84D	313	$.10	$.50	Palmer, Dave	83D	68	$.01	$.06
Owen, Spike	85D	435	$.01	$.10	Palmer, Dave	85D	341	$.01	$.10
Owen, Spike	86D	362	$.01	$.08	Palmer, David	86D	254	$.01	$.08
Owen, Spike	87D	633	$.01	$.05	Palmer, David	87D	325	$.01	$.05
Owen, Spike	88D	544	$.01	$.04	Palmer, David	88D	266	$.01	$.04
Owen, Spike	89D	593	$.01	$.04	Palmer, David	89D	133	$.01	$.04
Owen, Spike	89DTR	14	$.01	$.05	Palmer, Dean	90D	529	$.10	$.50
Owen, Spike	90D	102	$.01	$.04	Palmer, Dean	91DR	48	$.05	$.25
Owen, Spike	90DL	186	$.05	$.25	Palmer, Dean	92D	177	$.05	$.20
Owen, Spike	91D	251	$.01	$.04	Palmer, Dean	92DL	225	$.05	$.35
Owen, Spike	91DL	36	$.01	$.08	Palmer, Dean	92DLS	245	$.05	$.35
Owen, Spike	92D	518	$.01	$.04	Palmer, Dean	93D	339	$.01	$.10
Owen, Spike	92DL	455	$.01	$.06	Palmer, Dean	93DL	159	$.10	$.50
Owen, Spike	92DLS	58	$.01	$.06	Palmer, Jim	81D	353	$.15	$1.50
Owen, Spike	93D	732	$.01	$.05	Palmer, Jim	81D	473	$.15	$1.50
Pacella, John	83D	130	$.01	$.06	Palmer, Jim	82D	231	$.10	$1.00
Pacillo, Pat	88D	536	$.01	$.04	Palmer, Jim	83D	77	$.10	$1.00
Paciorek, Tom	81D	408	$.01	$.06	Palmer, Jim	83DK	4	$.10	$.50
Paciorek, Tom	82D	253	$.01	$.06	Palmer, Jim	84D	576	$1.00	$4.00
Paciorek, Tom	83D	243	$.01	$.06	Pankovits, Jim	85D	502	$.01	$.10
Paciorek, Tom	84D	282	$.05	$.20	Pankovits, Jim	86D	450	$.01	$.08
Paciorek, Tom	85D	488	$.01	$.10	Pankovits, Jim	87D	605	$.01	$.05
Page, Mitchell	81D	480	$.01	$.06	Papi, Stan	81D	246	$.01	$.06
Pagliarulo, Mike	85D	539	$.05	$.25	Papi, Stan	82D	333	$.01	$.06
Pagliarulo, Mike	86D	152	$.01	$.05	Pardo, Al	86D	489	$.01	$.08
Pagliarulo, Mike	87D	298	$.01	$.15	Paredes, Johnny	88DR	29	$.01	$.07
Pagliarulo, Mike	88D	105	$.01	$.15	Paredes, Johnny	89D	570	$.01	$.04
Pagliarulo, Mike	89D	127	$.01	$.04	Parent, Mark	88DR	8	$.01	$.15
Pagliarulo, Mike	90D	364	$.01	$.04	Parent, Mark	89D	420	$.01	$.10
Pagliarulo, Mike	90DL	320	$.05	$.25	Parent, Mark	90D	229	$.01	$.04
Pagliarulo, Mike	91D	140	$.01	$.04	Parent, Mark	90DL	497	$.05	$.25
Pagliarulo, Mike	91DL	339	$.01	$.08	Parent, Mark	91D	506	$.01	$.04
Pagliarulo, Mike	92D	62	$.01	$.06	Paris, Kelly	84D	384	$.01	$.20
Pagliarulo, Mike	92DL	346	$.01	$.06	Parker, Clay	89DR	52	$.01	$.05
Pagliarulo, Mike	93D	707	$.01	$.05	Parker, Clay	90D	363	$.01	$.04
Pagnozzi, Tom	88D	577	$.05	$.20	Parker, Clay	91D	605	$.01	$.04
Pagnozzi, Tom	89D	399	$.01	$.04	Parker, Dave	81D	136	$.10	$.50
Pagnozzi, Tom	90D	591	$.01	$.04	Parker, Dave	82D	95	$.10	$.50
Pagnozzi, Tom	90DL	498	$.05	$.20	Parker, Dave	82DK	12	$.05	$.30
Pagnozzi, Tom	91D	337	$.01	$.04	Parker, Dave	83D	473	$.01	$.35
Pagnozzi, Tom	91DL	72	$.01	$.08	Parker, Dave	84D	288	$.10	$1.00
Pagnozzi, Tom	92D	254	$.01	$.04	Parker, Dave	85D	62	$.05	$.30
Pagnozzi, Tom	92DL	359	$.01	$.06	Parker, Dave	86D	203	$.05	$.25
Pagnozzi, Tom	92DLS	96	$.01	$.06	Parker, Dave	87D	388	$.05	$.20
Pagnozzi, Tom	93D	360	$.01	$.05	Parker, Dave	88D	388	$.01	$.15

DONRUSS

Player	Year	No.	VG	EX/MT
Parker, Dave	89D	150	$ .01	$ .04
Parker, Dave	90D	328	$ .01	$ .04
Parker, Dave	90DL	190	$ .05	$ .25
Parker, Dave	91D	142	$ .01	$ .04
Parker, Dave	91DK	6	$ .01	$ .05
Parker, Dave	91DL	334	$ .01	$ .08
Parker, Dave	91DLSP	3	$ .20	$2.00
Parker, Dave	91DMVP	390	$ .01	$ .03
Parker, Rick	90DL	398	$ .05	$ .25
Parks, Derek	93D	237	$ .01	$ .05
Parrett, Jeff	88D	406	$ .01	$ .15
Parrett, Jeff	89D	334	$ .01	$ .04
Parrett, Jeff	89DTR	55	$ .01	$ .05
Parrett, Jeff	90D	369	$ .01	$ .04
Parrett, Jeff	90DL	210	$ .05	$ .25
Parrett, Jeff	91D	660	$ .01	$ .04
Parrett, Jeff	92DL	520	$ .01	$ .06
Parrett, Jeff	93D	241	$ .01	$ .05
Parrish, Lance	81D	366	$ .05	$ .30
Parrish, Lance	82D	281	$ .05	$ .25
Parrish, Lance	83D	407	$ .05	$ .20
Parrish, Lance	84D	49	$ .10	$ .50
Parrish, Lance	84DK	15	$ .05	$ .35
Parrish, Lance	85D	49	$ .05	$ .25
Parrish, Lance	86D	334	$ .05	$ .20
Parrish, Lance	87D	91	$ .05	$ .20
Parrish, Lance	88D	359	$ .01	$ .04
Parrish, Lance	89D	278	$ .01	$ .04
Parrish, Lance	90D	213	$ .01	$ .04
Parrish, Lance	90DL	195	$ .05	$ .25
Parrish, Lance	91D	135	$ .01	$ .04
Parrish, Lance	91DL	368	$ .01	$ .08
Parrish, Lance	91DLS	29	$ .01	$ .08
Parrish, Lance	91DMVP	388	$ .01	$ .03
Parrish, Lance	92D	166	$ .01	$ .04
Parrish, Lance	92DL	269	$ .01	$ .06
Parrish, Lance	92DLS	149	$ .01	$ .06
Parrish, Lance	93D	85	$ .01	$ .05
Parrish, Larry	81D	89	$ .01	$ .06
Parrish, Larry	82D	466	$ .01	$ .06
Parrish, Larry	83D	467	$ .01	$ .06
Parrish, Larry	84D	422	$ .05	$ .20
Parrish, Larry	84DK	21	$ .05	$ .25
Parrish, Larry	85D	300	$ .01	$ .10
Parrish, Larry	86D	178	$ .01	$ .08
Parrish, Larry	87D	469	$ .01	$ .05
Parrish, Larry	88D	347	$ .01	$ .04
Parrott, Mike	82D	226	$ .01	$ .06
Pashnick, Larry	83D	233	$ .01	$ .06
Pashnick, Larry	84D	394	$ .05	$ .20
Pasqua, Dan	85D	637	$ .05	$ .35
Pasqua, Dan	86D	417	$ .05	$ .20
Pasqua, Dan	87D	474	$ .05	$ .20
Pasqua, Dan	88D	463	$ .01	$ .04
Pasqua, Dan	89D	294	$ .01	$ .04
Pasqua, Dan	90D	176	$ .01	$ .04
Pasqua, Dan	90DL	274	$ .05	$ .25
Pasqua, Dan	91D	103	$ .01	$ .04
Pasqua, Dan	91DL	428	$ .01	$ .08
Pasqua, Dan	92D	142	$ .01	$ .04
Pasqua, Dan	92DL	369	$ .01	$ .06
Pasqua, Dan	93D	491	$ .01	$ .05
Pasqua, Dan	93DL	20	$ .01	$ .15
Pastore, Frank	82D	122	$ .01	$ .06
Pastore, Frank	83D	62	$ .01	$ .06
Pastore, Frank	84D	164	$ .05	$ .20
Pastore, Frank	85D	550	$ .01	$ .10
Pate, Bob	81D	545	$ .01	$ .06
Patek, Fred	81D	170	$ .01	$ .06
Patek, Fred	82D	241	$ .01	$ .06
Patterson, Bob	91D	345	$ .01	$ .04
Patterson, Bob	92D	590	$ .01	$ .04
Patterson, Bob	93D	174	$ .01	$ .05
Patterson, John	92DR	89	$ .01	$ .10
Patterson, John	93D	193	$ .01	$ .05

Player	Year	No.	VG	EX/MT
Patterson, John	93DL	160	$ .01	$ .15
Patterson, Ken	89DR	37	$ .01	$ .05
Patterson, Ken	90D	371	$ .01	$ .04
Patterson, Ken	91D	522	$ .01	$ .04
Patterson, Ken	92D	457	$ .01	$ .04
Patterson, Ken	92DL	509	$ .01	$ .06

Player	Year	No.	VG	EX/MT
Patterson, Ken	**93D**	**742**	**$ .01**	**$ .05**
Pattin, Marty	81D	343	$ .01	$ .06
Pavlik, Roger	92DR	90	$ .01	$ .15
Pavlik, Roger	93D	113	$ .01	$ .10
Pawlowski, John	88D	457	$ .01	$ .04
Pecota, Bill	88D	466	$ .01	$ .10
Pecota, Bill	91D	672	$ .01	$ .04
Pecota, Bill	92D	361	$ .01	$ .04
Pecota, Bill	92DL	244	$ .01	$ .06
Pecota, Bill	93D	248	$ .01	$ .05
Pedrique, Al	88D	361	$ .01	$ .04
Peltier, Dan	92DR	91	$ .01	$ .15
Peltier, Dan	93D	473	$ .01	$ .05
Pena, Alejandro	84D	250	$ .10	$ .50
Pena, Alejandro	85D	337	$ .03	$ .10
Pena, Alejandro	88D	598	$ .01	$ .04
Pena, Alejandro	89D	557	$ .01	$ .04
Pena, Alejandro	90D	664	$ .01	$ .04
Pena, Alejandro	90DL	403	$ .05	$ .25
Pena, Alejandro	91D	566	$ .01	$ .04
Pena, Alejandro	91DL	70	$ .01	$ .08
Pena, Alejandro	92D	616	$ .01	$ .10
Pena, Alejandro	92D	772	$ .01	$ .04
Pena, Alejandro	92DL	489	$ .01	$ .06
Pena, Geronimo	91D	712	$ .01	$ .10
Pena, Geronimo	92D	533	$ .01	$ .04
Pena, Geronimo	93D	310	$ .01	$ .05
Pena, Geronimo	93DL	118	$ .05	$ .25
Pena, Hipolito	89D	598	$ .01	$ .04
Pena, Jim	92DR	92	$ .01	$ .05
Pena, Jim	93D	628	$ .01	$ .05
Pena, Tony	82D	124	$ .05	$ .25
Pena, Tony	83D	59	$ .01	$ .15
Pena, Tony	84D	186	$ .05	$ .30
Pena, Tony	85D	64	$ .05	$ .20
Pena, Tony	85DK	24	$ .03	$ .10

DONRUSS

Player	Year	No.	VG	EX/MT	Player	Year	No.	VG	EX/MT
Pena, Tony	86D	64	$ .05	$ .20	Perry, Gerald	86D	165	$ .01	$ .08
Pena, Tony	87D	115	$ .01	$ .05	Perry, Gerald	88D	437	$ .01	$ .04
Pena, Tony	88D	170	$ .01	$ .04	Perry, Gerald	89D	239	$ .01	$ .04
Pena, Tony	89D	163	$ .01	$ .04	Perry, Gerald	89DBC	24	$ .01	$ .05
Pena, Tony	90D	181	$ .01	$ .04	Perry, Gerald	89DK	22	$ .01	$ .05
Pena, Tony	90DL	104	$ .05	$ .25	Perry, Gerald	90D	153	$ .01	$ .04
Pena, Tony	91D	456	$ .01	$ .04	Perry, Gerald	90DL	441	$ .05	$ .25
Pena, Tony	91DL	33	$ .01	$ .08	Perry, Gerald	91D	130	$ .01	$ .04
Pena, Tony	91DLS	17	$ .01	$ .08	Perry, Gerald	91DL	272	$ .01	$ .08
Pena, Tony	92D	208	$ .01	$ .04	Perry, Gerald	92D	634	$ .01	$ .04
Pena, Tony	92DL	323	$ .01	$ .06	Perry, Gerald	92DL	122	$ .01	$ .06
Pena, Tony	92DLS	135	$ .01	$ .06	Perry, Gerald	93D	468	$ .01	$ .05
Pena, Tony	93D	297	$ .01	$ .05	Perry, Pat	86D	596	$ .01	$ .08
Pena, Tony	93DL	43	$ .01	$ .15	Perry, Pat	87D	430	$ .01	$ .05
Pendleton, Jeff "Terry"	85D	534	$2.00	$8.00	Perry, Pat	88D	626	$ .01	$ .15
Pendleton, Terry	86D	205	$ .10	$1.00	Perry, Pat	89D	404	$ .01	$ .04
Pendleton, Terry	87D	183	$ .10	$ .40	Peterek, Jeff	90D	530	$ .01	$ .10
Pendleton, Terry	88D	454	$ .01	$ .15	Peters, Rick	81D	10	$ .01	$ .06
Pendleton, Terry	89D	230	$ .01	$ .10	Peters, Rick	82D	155	$ .01	$ .06
Pendleton, Terry	90D	299	$ .01	$ .10	Peters, Steve	88DR	22	$ .01	$ .07
Pendleton, Terry	90DL	260	$ .10	$ .50	Peterson, Adam	89D	619	$ .01	$ .10
Pendleton, Terry	91D	446	$ .01	$ .10	Petralli, Geno	83D	623	$ .01	$ .06
Pendleton, Terry	91DL	304	$ .01	$ .15	Petralli, Geno	87D	619	$ .01	$ .05
Pendleton, Terry	91DLS	148	$ .01	$ .15	Petralli, Geno	88D	506	$ .01	$ .04
Pendleton, Terry	92D	237	$ .01	$ .04	Petralli, Geno	89D	343	$ .01	$ .04
Pendleton, Terry	92DBC	2	$ .01	$ .15	Petralli, Geno	90D	56	$ .01	$ .04
Pendleton, Terry	92DL	245	$ .01	$ .06	Petralli, Geno	90DL	73	$ .05	$ .25
Pendleton, Terry	92DLS	8	$ .01	$ .15	Petralli, Geno	91D	137	$ .01	$ .04
Pendleton, Terry	93D	234	$ .01	$ .05	Petralli, Geno	91DL	148	$ .01	$ .08
Pennyfeather, William	92DR	93	$ .05	$ .25	Petralli, Geno	92D	550	$ .01	$ .04
Pennyfeather, William	93D	702	$ .01	$ .05	Petralli, Geno	92DL	357	$ .01	$ .06
Peraza, Oswald	89D	524	$ .01	$ .10	Petralli, Geno	93D	319	$ .01	$ .05
Perconte, Jack	83D	463	$ .01	$ .06	Petry, Dan	81D	128	$ .01	$ .06
Perconte, Jack	85D	74	$ .01	$ .10	Petry, Dan	82D	133	$ .01	$ .06
Perez, Melido	88D	589	$ .05	$ .35	Petry, Dan	83D	359	$ .01	$ .06
Perez, Melido	88DR	21	$ .10	$ .40	Petry, Dan	84D	105	$ .05	$ .20
Perez, Melido	89D	58	$ .01	$ .15	Petry, Dan	85D	334	$ .01	$ .10
Perez, Melido	90D	101	$ .01	$ .04	Petry, Dan	86D	212	$ .01	$ .08
Perez, Melido	90DL	36	$ .05	$ .25	Petry, Dan	87D	373	$ .01	$ .05
Perez, Melido	91D	164	$ .01	$ .04	Petry, Dan	88D	476	$ .01	$ .04
Perez, Melido	91DBC	13	$ .01	$ .03	Petry, Dan	89D	344	$ .01	$ .04
Perez, Melido	92D	509	$ .01	$ .04	Petry, Dan	90DL	508	$ .05	$ .25
Perez, Melido	92DL	479	$ .01	$ .06	Petry, Dan	91D	675	$ .01	$ .04
Perez, Melido	92DLS	218	$ .01	$ .06	Pettis, Gary	84D	647	$ .05	$ .35
Perez, Melido	93D	709	$ .01	$ .05	Pettis, Gary	85D	499	$ .01	$ .10
Perez, Melido	93DL	74	$ .05	$ .20	Pettis, Gary	86D	158	$ .01	$ .08
Perez, Mike	91D	615	$ .01	$ .10	Pettis, Gary	87D	160	$ .01	$ .05
Perez, Mike	92DR	94	$ .01	$ .05	Pettis, Gary	88D	210	$ .01	$ .04
Perez, Mike	93D	256	$ .01	$ .05	Pettis, Gary	89D	60	$ .01	$ .04
Perez, Pascual	83D	557	$ .05	$ .25	Pettis, Gary	90D	661	$ .01	$ .04
Perez, Pascual	84D	507	$ .05	$ .35	Pettis, Gary	90DL	469	$ .05	$ .25
Perez, Pascual	85D	507	$ .01	$ .10	Pettis, Gary	91D	512	$ .01	$ .04
Perez, Pascual	88D	591	$ .01	$ .04	Pettis, Gary	91DLSP	9	$ .20	$2.00
Perez, Pascual	89D	248	$ .01	$ .04	Pettis, Gary	92DL	466	$ .01	$ .06
Perez, Pascual	90D	342	$ .01	$ .04	Phelps, Ken	85D	318	$ .05	$ .20
Perez, Pascual	91DL	293	$ .01	$ .08	Phelps, Ken	87D	317	$ .01	$ .05
Perez, Pascual	92D	695	$ .01	$ .04	Phelps, Ken	88D	489	$ .01	$ .04
Perez, Tony	81D	334	$ .10	$ .50	Phelps, Ken	89D	363	$ .01	$ .04
Perez, Tony	82D	408	$ .05	$ .30	Phelps, Ken	90D	675	$ .01	$ .04
Perez, Tony	83D	578	$ .05	$ .25	Phillips, Mike	81D	188	$ .01	$ .06
Perez, Tony	84D	503	$ .10	$ .75	Phillips, Tony	84D	278	$ .25	$2.50
Perez, Tony	86D	428	$ .05	$ .25	Phillips, Tony	85D	101	$ .01	$ .10
Perez, Tony	86DK	15	$ .05	$ .20	Phillips, Tony	86D	542	$ .01	$ .08
Perez, Yorkis	92D	754	$ .01	$ .10	Phillips, Tony	87D	103	$ .01	$ .05
Perezchica, Tony	91DR	10	$ .01	$ .05	Phillips, Tony	88D	221	$ .01	$ .04
Perkins, Broderick	81D	525	$ .01	$ .06	Phillips, Tony	90D	91	$ .01	$ .04
Perkins, Broderick	82D	397	$ .01	$ .06	Phillips, Tony	90DL	324	$ .05	$ .25
Perkins, Broderick	83D	121	$ .01	$ .06	Phillips, Tony	91D	286	$ .01	$ .04
Perkins, Broderick	84D	276	$ .05	$ .20	Phillips, Tony	91DL	4	$ .01	$ .08
Perry, Gaylord	81D	471	$ .10	$ .50	Phillips, Tony	92D	328	$ .01	$ .04
Perry, Gaylord	82D	543	$ .10	$ .40	Phillips, Tony	92DK	25	$ .10	$1.00
Perry, Gaylord	83D	307	$ .10	$ .40	Phillips, Tony	92DL	40	$ .01	$ .06
Perry, Gaylord	84D#A	0	$1.25	$5.00	Phillips, Tony	92DLS	176	$ .01	$ .06
Perry, Gerald	84D	263	$ .10	$ .50	Phillips, Tony	93D	701	$ .01	$ .05
Perry, Gerald	85D	443	$ .01	$ .10	Phillips, Tony	93DL	126	$ .01	$ .15

DONRUSS

Player	Year	No.	VG	EX/MT
Piatt, Doug	92D	640	$ .01	$ .04
Piazza, Mike	93D	209	$ .10	$ .40

Player	Year	No.	VG	EX/MT
Piazza, Mike	93DL	35	$2.00	$8.00
Picciolo, Rob	81D	357	$ .01	$ .06
Picciolo, Rob	82D	465	$ .01	$ .06
Picciolo, Rob	83D	456	$ .01	$ .06
Picciolo, Rob	84D	455	$ .05	$ .20
Picciolo, Rob	86D	497	$ .01	$ .08
Pichardo, Hipolito	92DR	95	$ .01	$ .15
Pichardo, Hipolito	93D	571	$ .01	$ .05
Pico, Jeff	89D	513	$ .01	$ .10
Pico, Jeff	90D	585	$ .01	$ .04
Pierce, Eddie	93D	147	$ .01	$ .10
Piniella, Lou	81D	109	$ .05	$ .20
Piniella, Lou	82D	135	$ .05	$ .20
Piniella, Lou	83D	335	$ .01	$ .06
Piniella, Lou	84D	274	$ .05	$ .20
Pinson, Vada	82D	445	$ .05	$ .20
Pirkl, Greg	92DR	96	$ .01	$ .15
Pirkl, Grel	93D	589	$ .01	$ .10
Pittaro, Chris	86D	150	$ .01	$ .08
Pittman, Joe	82D	218	$ .01	$ .06
Pittman, Joe	83D	247	$ .01	$ .06
Plantier, Phil	91DLS	18	$ .10	$1.00
Plantier, Phil	91DRR	41	$ .10	$ .50
Plantier, Phil	92D	488	$ .01	$ .10
Plantier, Phil	92DL	50	$ .05	$ .25
Plantier, Phil	92DLS	136	$ .05	$ .25
Plantier, Phil	93D	3	$ .01	$ .10
Plesac, Dan	86DR	14	$ .05	$ .20
Plesac, Dan	87D	214	$ .05	$ .20
Plesac, Dan	88D	109	$ .01	$ .04
Plesac, Dan	89D	382	$ .01	$ .04
Plesac, Dan	90D	175	$ .01	$ .04
Plesac, Dan	90DL	216	$ .05	$ .25
Plesac, Dan	91D	104	$ .01	$ .04
Plesac, Dan	91DL	287	$ .01	$ .08
Plesac, Dan	92D	682	$ .01	$ .04
Plesac, Dan	93D	677	$ .01	$ .05
Plunk, Eric	86DR	40	$ .05	$ .25
Plunk, Eric	87D	178	$ .01	$ .05
Plunk, Eric	88D	503	$ .01	$ .04
Plunk, Eric	89D	125	$ .01	$ .04
Plunk, Eric	90D	196	$ .01	$ .04
Plunk, Eric	90DL	504	$ .05	$ .25
Plunk, Eric	91D	593	$ .01	$ .04
Plunk, Eric	92D	554	$ .01	$ .04
Pocoroba, Biff	83D	436	$ .01	$ .06
Pocoroba, Biff	84D	77	$ .05	$ .20
Podres, Johnny	82D	566	$ .01	$ .06
Polidor, Gus	87D	579	$ .01	$ .05
Polidor, Gus	88D	356	$ .01	$ .04
Polidor, Gus	90D	412	$ .01	$ .04
Polonia, Luis	87DR	25	$ .10	$ .50
Polonia, Luis	88D	425	$ .05	$ .25
Polonia, Luis	89D	386	$ .01	$ .04
Polonia, Luis	90D	547	$ .01	$ .04
Polonia, Luis	90DL	295	$ .05	$ .25
Polonia, Luis	91D	93	$ .01	$ .04
Polonia, Luis	91DL	81	$ .01	$ .08
Polonia, Luis	92D	252	$ .01	$ .04
Polonia, Luis	92DL	45	$ .01	$ .06
Polonia, Luis	93D	461	$ .01	$ .05
Polonia, Luis	93DK	26	$ .15	$1.50
Ponce, Carlos	86D	595	$ .01	$ .08
Poole, Jimmy	91D	655	$ .01	$ .10
Poole, Jimmy	92D	600	$ .01	$ .04
Poole, Jimmy	93D	295	$ .01	$ .05
Porter, Chuck	84D	333	$ .05	$ .20
Porter, Chuck	85D	115	$ .01	$ .10
Porter, Darrell	81D	505	$ .01	$ .06
Porter, Darrell	82D	498	$ .05	$ .20
Porter, Darrell	83D	278	$ .01	$ .06
Porter, Darrell	84D	303	$ .05	$ .20
Porter, Darrell	85D	353	$ .01	$ .10
Porter, Darrell	86D	290	$ .01	$ .08
Porter, Darrell	87D	593	$ .01	$ .05
Portugal, Mark	86DR	44	$ .01	$ .15
Portugal, Mark	87D	566	$ .01	$ .15
Portugal, Mark	90D	542	$ .01	$ .04
Portugal, Mark	90DL	399	$ .05	$ .25
Portugal, Mark	91D	268	$ .01	$ .04
Portugal, Mark	91DL	63	$ .01	$ .08
Portugal, Mark	92D	188	$ .01	$ .04
Portugal, Mark	93D	612	$ .01	$ .05
Powell, Alonzo	91DL	521	$ .01	$ .15
Powell, Alonzo	92D	213	$ .01	$ .10
Powell, Dennis	86D	250	$ .01	$ .08
Powell, Dennis	87D	499	$ .01	$ .05
Powell, Hosken	81D	567	$ .01	$ .06
Powell, Hosken	82D	228	$ .01	$ .06
Powell, Hosken	83D	644	$ .01	$ .06
Power, Ted	84D	447	$ .05	$ .20
Power, Ted	85D	286	$ .01	$ .10
Power, Ted	86D	408	$ .01	$ .08
Power, Ted	87D	536	$ .01	$ .05
Power, Ted	88D	142	$ .01	$ .04
Power, Ted	89D	153	$ .01	$ .04
Power, Ted	90D	653	$ .01	$ .04
Power, Ted	90DL	473	$ .05	$ .25
Power, Ted	91D	608	$ .01	$ .04
Power, Ted	92D	586	$ .01	$ .04
Power, Ted	93D	766	$ .01	$ .05
Power, Ted	93DL	61	$ .01	$ .15
Pratt, Todd	93D	620	$ .01	$ .10
Presley, Jim	85D	240	$ .10	$1.00
Presley, Jim	86D	313	$ .01	$ .15
Presley, Jim	87D	120	$ .01	$ .10
Presley, Jim	87DK	23	$ .01	$ .05
Presley, Jim	88D	366	$ .01	$ .15
Presley, Jim	89D	379	$ .01	$ .04
Presley, Jim	90D	497	$ .01	$ .04
Presley, Jim	90DL	277	$ .05	$ .25
Presley, Jim	91D	173	$ .01	$ .04
Price, Joe	82D	481	$ .01	$ .06
Price, Joe	83D	481	$ .01	$ .06
Price, Joe	84D	506	$ .05	$ .20

DONRUSS

Player	Year	No.	VG	EX/MT	Player	Year	No.	VG	EX/MT
Price, Joe	85D	627	$.01	$.10	Quintana, Carlos	91D	568	$.01	$.04
Price, Joe	86D	506	$.01	$.08	Quintana, Carlos	91DL	473	$.01	$.08
Price, Joe	88D	655	$.01	$.15	Quintana, Carlos	92D	609	$.01	$.04
Price, Joe	89D	376	$.01	$.04	Quirk, Jamie	81D	341	$.01	$.06
Prince, Tom	88D	538	$.01	$.04	Quirk, Jamie	82D	212	$.01	$.06
Prince, Tom	89D	527	$.01	$.04	Quirk, Jamie	88D	404	$.01	$.04
Proly, Mike	81D	596	$.01	$.06	Quirk, Jamie	91D	588	$.01	$.04
Proly, Mike	82D	345	$.01	$.06	Quirk, Jamie	91DL	431	$.01	$.08
Proly, Mike	83D	225	$.01	$.06	Quirk, Jamie	92D	472	$.01	$.04
Proly, Mike	84D	320	$.05	$.20	Quisenberry, Dan	81D	222	$.05	$.30
Pryor, Greg	81D	278	$.01	$.06	Quisenberry, Dan	82D	112	$.01	$.15
Pryor, Greg	82D	521	$.01	$.06	Quisenberry, Dan	83D	70	$.01	$.15
Pryor, Greg	83D	264	$.01	$.06	Quisenberry, Dan	84D	583	$.05	$.25
Pryor, Greg	84D	374	$.05	$.20	Quisenberry, Dan	85D	95	$.05	$.20
Pryor, Greg	85D	277	$.01	$.10	Quisenberry, Dan	85DK	6	$.05	$.20
Pryor, Greg	86D	344	$.01	$.08	Quisenberry, Dan	86D	541	$.05	$.20
Pryor, Greg	87D	378	$.01	$.05	Quisenberry, Dan	87D	177	$.01	$.05
Puckett, Kirby	85D	438	$12.00	$48.00	Quisenberry, Dan	88D	471	$.01	$.15
Puckett, Kirby	86D	72	$2.50	$10.00	Quisenberry, Dan	90D	437	$.01	$.04
Puckett, Kirby	87D	149	$.20	$2.00	Rabb, John	84D	143	$.05	$.20
Puckett, Kirby	87DK	19	$.10	$.75	Rabb, John	85D	236	$.01	$.10
Puckett, Kirby	88D	368	$.05	$.35	Raczka, Mike	93D	183	$.01	$.15
Puckett, Kirby	88DBC	15	$.05	$.35	Rader, Dave	81D	512	$.01	$.06
Puckett, Kirby	89D	182	$.05	$.25	Radinsky, Scott	90DL	484	$.10	$.50
Puckett, Kirby	89DBC	1	$.01	$.15	Radinsky, Scott	90DR	40	$.01	$.15
Puckett, Kirby	90D	269	$.05	$.25	Radinsky, Scott	91D	332	$.01	$.10
Puckett, Kirby	90DAS	683	$.01	$.15	Radinsky, Scott	91DL	463	$.01	$.08
Puckett, Kirby	90DBC	8	$.05	$.20	Radinsky, Scott	92D	299	$.01	$.04
Puckett, Kirby	90DL	123	$.75	$3.00	Radinsky, Scott	92DL	281	$.01	$.06
Puckett, Kirby	91D	490	$.05	$.20	Radinsky, Scott	93D	169	$.01	$.05
Puckett, Kirby	91DL	208	$.10	$.75	Raines, Dale	91DL	413	$.01	$.08
Puckett, Kirby	91DLP	21	$1.50	$6.00	Raines, Tim	81D	538	$1.25	$5.00
Puckett, Kirby	91DLS	90	$.10	$.50	Raines, Tim	82D	214	$.15	$1.50
Puckett, Kirby	92D	617	$.05	$.20	Raines, Tim	83D	540	$.10	$.60
Puckett, Kirby	92DL	98	$.10	$.50	Raines, Tim	84D	299	$.15	$1.25
Puckett, Kirby	92DLS	209	$.10	$.50	Raines, Tim	85D	299	$.05	$.35
Puckett, Kirby	93D	607	$.01	$.15	Raines, Tim	86D	177	$.05	$.30
Puckett, Kirby	93DK	4	$1.50	$6.00	Raines, Tim	87D	56	$.05	$.20
Pugh, Tim	93D	162	$.05	$.25	Raines, Tim	88D	345	$.01	$.10
Puhl, Terry	81D	24	$.01	$.06	Raines, Tim	88DBC	18	$.01	$.10
Puhl, Terry	82D	370	$.01	$.06	Raines, Tim	88DK	2	$.05	$.25
Puhl, Terry	83D	167	$.01	$.06	Raines, Tim	89D	97	$.01	$.10
Puhl, Terry	84D	476	$.05	$.20	Raines, Tim	90D	216	$.01	$.10
Puhl, Terry	85D	426	$.01	$.10	Raines, Tim	90DBC	7	$.01	$.10
Puhl, Terry	86D	206	$.01	$.08	Raines, Tim	90DL	212	$.05	$.35
Puhl, Terry	87D	431	$.01	$.05	Raines, Tim	91D	457	$.01	$.04
Puhl, Terry	88D	533	$.01	$.04	Raines, Tim "Rock"	91DLS	37	$.01	$.08
Puhl, Terry	89D	472	$.01	$.04	Raines, Tim	91DLSP	4	$.20	$2.00
Puhl, Terry	90D	354	$.01	$.04	Raines, Tim	92D	312	$.01	$.04
Pujols, Luis	81D	379	$.01	$.06	Raines, Tim	92DL	37	$.01	$.06
Pujols, Luis	82D	576	$.01	$.06	Raines, Tim	92DLS	156	$.01	$.06
Pujols, Luis	83D	642	$.01	$.06	Raines, Tim	93D	565	$.01	$.05
Puleo, Charlie	83D	128	$.01	$.06	Rainey, Chuck	83D	334	$.01	$.06
Puleo, Charlie	84D	530	$.05	$.20	Rainey, Chuck	84D	76	$.05	$.20
Puleo, Charlie	88D	537	$.01	$.04	Rainey, Chuck	85D	618	$.01	$.10
Puleo, Charlie	89D	286	$.01	$.04	Rajsich, Dave	81D	267	$.01	$.06
Pulido, Alfonso	85DRR	34	$.01	$.15	Rajsich, Gary	83D	599	$.01	$.06
Pulliam, Henry	92DR	97	$.01	$.05	Ramirez, Allan	84D	332	$.05	$.20
Putnam, Pat	81D	265	$.01	$.06	Ramirez, Manny	92DR	98	$.10	$.75
Putnam, Pat	82D	520	$.01	$.06	Ramirez, Mario	86D	568	$.01	$.08
Putnam, Pat	84D	145	$.05	$.20	Ramirez, Rafael	82D	546	$.01	$.06
Pyznarski, Tim	87D	654	$.01	$.05	Ramirez, Rafael	83D	310	$.01	$.06
Quantrill, Paul	93D	327	$.01	$.10	Ramirez, Rafael	84D	589	$.05	$.20
Quinlan, Tom	93D	161	$.01	$.05	Ramirez, Rafael	85D	141	$.01	$.10
Quinones, Luis	88D	365	$.01	$.04	Ramirez, Rafael	86D	263	$.01	$.08
Quinones, Luis	90D	595	$.01	$.04	Ramirez, Rafael	87D	202	$.01	$.05
Quinones, Luis	91D	459	$.01	$.04	Ramirez, Rafael	88D	448	$.01	$.04
Quinones, Luis	91DL	233	$.01	$.08	Ramirez, Rafael	89D	509	$.01	$.04
Quinones (nez), Rey	86DR	48	$.01	$.10	Ramirez, Rafael	90D	241	$.01	$.04
Quinones (nez), Rey	87D	638	$.01	$.05	Ramirez, Rafael	90DL	135	$.05	$.25
Quinones, Rey	88D	198	$.01	$.04	Ramirez, Rafael	91D	586	$.01	$.04
Quinones, Rey	89D	330	$.01	$.04	Ramos, Bobby	84D	209	$.05	$.20
Quintana, Carlos	89DRR	37	$.05	$.20	Ramos, Domingo	84D	440	$.05	$.20
Quintana, Carlos	90D	517	$.01	$.10	Ramos, Domingo	88D	622	$.01	$.15
Quintana, Carlos	90DL	394	$.05	$.25	Ramos, Domingo	90D	491	$.01	$.04

DONRUSS

Player	Year	No.	VG	EX/MT	Player	Year	No.	VG	EX/MT
Ramos, Domingo	90DL	440	$ .05	$ .25	Ready, Randy	92D	179	$ .01	$ .04
Ramos, John	92DRR	15	$ .05	$ .20	Ready, Randy	92DL	246	$ .01	$ .06
Ramsey, Fernando	93D	539	$ .01	$ .15	Ready, Randy	92DLS	228	$ .01	$ .06
Ramsey, Mike	82D	316	$ .01	$ .06	Reardon, Jeff	81D	156	$1.25	$5.00
Ramsey, Mike	83D	568	$ .01	$ .06	Reardon, Jeff	82D	547	$ .15	$1.50
Ramsey, Mike	84D	382	$ .05	$ .20	Reardon, Jeff	83D	194	$ .10	$1.00
Randle, Lenny	81D	485	$ .01	$ .06	Reardon, Jeff	84D	279	$ .25	$2.50
Randle, Lenny	82D	307	$ .01	$ .06	Reardon, Jeff	85D	331	$ .10	$ .50
Randolph, Willie	81D	345	$ .05	$ .20	Reardon, Jeff	86D	209	$ .05	$ .35
Randolph, Willie	82D	461	$ .01	$ .15	Reardon, Jeff	87D	98	$ .05	$ .20
Randolph, Willie	83D	283	$ .01	$ .06	Reardon, Jeff	88D	122	$ .01	$ .10
Randolph, Willie	84D	417	$ .05	$ .20	Reardon, Jeff	89D	155	$ .01	$ .04
Randolph, Willie	85D	92	$ .01	$ .10	Reardon, Jeff	90D	119	$ .01	$ .04
Randolph, Willie	86D	92	$ .01	$ .08	Reardon, Jeff	90DL	276	$ .05	$ .25
Randolph, Willie	86DK	16	$ .01	$ .10	Reardon, Jeff	91D	369	$ .01	$ .04
Randolph, Willie	87D	154	$ .01	$ .05	Reardon, Jeff	91DL	252	$ .01	$ .08
Randolph, Willie	88D	228	$ .01	$ .04	Reardon, Jeff	91DLS	19	$ .01	$ .08
Randolph, Willie	89D	395	$ .01	$ .04	Reardon, Jeff	92D	89	$ .01	$ .04
Randolph, Willie	89DTR	8	$ .01	$ .10	Reardon, Jeff	92DL	151	$ .01	$ .10
Randolph, Willie	90D	250	$ .01	$ .04	Reardon, Jeff	92DLS	137	$ .01	$ .06
Randolph, Willie	90DK	19	$ .01	$ .05	Reardon, Jeff	93D	739	$ .01	$ .05
Randolph, Willie	90DL	345	$ .05	$ .25	Reboulet, Jeff	92DR	100	$ .01	$ .05
Randolph, Willie	91D	217	$ .01	$ .04	Reboulet, Jeff	93D	179	$ .01	$ .05
Randolph, Willie	91D	766	$ .01	$ .04	Redfern, Pete	81D	548	$ .01	$ .06
Randolph, Willie	91DL	419	$ .01	$ .08	Redfern, Pete	82D	51	$ .01	$ .06
Randolph, Willie	91DLS	74	$ .01	$ .08	Redfern, Pete	83D	256	$ .01	$ .06
Randolph, Willie	92D	625	$ .01	$ .04	Redus, Gary	84D	184	$ .10	$ .50
Randolph, Willie	92DL	240	$ .01	$ .06	Redus, Gary	85D	306	$ .01	$ .10
Randolph, Willie	93D	644	$ .01	$ .05	Redus, Gary	86D	306	$ .01	$ .08
Rapp, Pat	92DR	99	$ .01	$ .15	Redus, Gary	87D	288	$ .01	$ .05
Rasmussen, Dennis	84D	446	$ .05	$ .35	Redus, Gary	88D	370	$ .01	$ .04
Rasmussen, Dennis	85D	518	$ .01	$ .10	Redus, Gary	89D	605	$ .01	$ .04
Rasmussen, Dennis	86D	336	$ .01	$ .08	Redus, Gary	90D	597	$ .01	$ .04
Rasmussen, Dennis	87D	175	$ .01	$ .05	Redus, Gary	90DL	209	$ .05	$ .25
Rasmussen, Dennis	88D	575	$ .01	$ .15	Redus, Gary	91D	587	$ .01	$ .04
Rasmussen, Dennis	89D	559	$ .01	$ .04	Redus, Gary	91DL	254	$ .01	$ .08
Rasmussen, Dennis	90D	420	$ .01	$ .10	Redus, Gary	92D	67	$ .01	$ .04
Rasmussen, Dennis	90DL	471	$ .05	$ .25	Redus, Gary	92DL	223	$ .01	$ .06
Rasmussen, Dennis	91D	458	$ .01	$ .04	Redus, Gary	93D	516	$ .01	$ .05
Rasmussen, Dennis	92D	245	$ .01	$ .04	Reed, Darren	92DR	101	$ .01	$ .05
Rasmussen, Dennis	93D	778	$ .01	$ .05	Reed, Darren	93D	105	$ .01	$ .05
Rasmussen, Eric	81D	123	$ .01	$ .06	Reed, Jeff	85DRR	30	$ .01	$ .15
Rawley, Shane	81D	167	$ .01	$ .06	Reed, Jeff	88D	88	$ .01	$ .04
Rawley, Shane	82D	352	$ .01	$ .06	Reed, Jeff	89D	469	$ .01	$ .04
Rawley, Shane	83D	513	$ .01	$ .06	Reed, Jeff	90D	351	$ .01	$ .04
Rawley, Shane	84D	295	$ .05	$ .20	Reed, Jeff	90DL	505	$ .05	$ .25
Rawley, Shane	85D	599	$ .01	$ .10	Reed, Jeff	91D	741	$ .01	$ .04
Rawley, Shane	86D	233	$ .01	$ .08	Reed, Jeff .	91DL	102	$ .01	$ .08
Rawley, Shane	87D	83	$ .01	$ .05	Reed, Jeff	92D	451	$ .01	$ .04
Rawley, Shane	88D	83	$ .01	$ .04	Reed, Jerry	88D	517	$ .01	$ .04
Rawley, Shane	88DK	13	$ .01	$ .05	Reed, Jerry	89D	657	$ .01	$ .04
Rawley, Shane	89D	251	$ .01	$ .04	Reed, Jerry	90D	614	$ .01	$ .04
Rawley, Shane	90D	537	$ .01	$ .04	Reed, Jerry	90DL	368	$ .05	$ .25
Ray, Johnny	82D	528	$ .05	$ .20	Reed, Jody	88DR	44	$ .10	$ .40
Ray, Johnny	83D	437	$ .05	$ .20	Reed, Jody	88DRR	41	$ .05	$ .25
Ray, Johnny	84D	308	$ .05	$ .20	Reed, Jody	89D	305	$ .01	$ .10
Ray, Johnny	85D	186	$ .01	$ .10	Reed, Jody	90D	398	$ .01	$ .04
Ray, Johnny	86D	186	$ .05	$ .20	Reed, Jody	90DL	150	$ .05	$ .25
Ray, Johnny	86DK	19	$ .01	$ .10	Reed, Jody	91D	123	$ .01	$ .04
Ray, Johnny	87D	144	$ .01	$ .05	Reed, Jody	91DL	69	$ .01	$ .08
Ray, Johnny	88D	428	$ .01	$ .04	Reed, Jody	92D	47	$ .01	$ .04
Ray, Johnny	89D	331	$ .01	$ .04	Reed, Jody	92DL	413	$ .01	$ .06
Ray, Johnny	89DK	12	$ .01	$ .05	Reed, Jody	92DLS	138	$ .01	$ .06
Ray, Johnny	90D	234	$ .01	$ .04	Reed, Jody	93D	165	$ .01	$ .05
Ray, Johnny	90DL	208	$ .05	$ .25	Reed, Rick	90D	527	$ .01	$ .10
Ray, Johnny	91D	622	$ .05	$ .20	Reed, Rick	90DL	427	$ .05	$ .25
Rayford, Floyd	85D	576	$ .01	$ .10	Reed, Ron	81D	44	$ .01	$ .06
Rayford, Floyd	86D	332	$ .01	$ .08	Reed, Ron	82D	399	$ .01	$ .06
Ready, Randy	86D	481	$ .01	$ .08	Reed, Ron	83D	567	$ .01	$ .06
Ready, Randy	88D	264	$ .01	$ .04	Reed, Ron	84D	529	$ .05	$ .20
Ready, Randy	89D	365	$ .01	$ .04	Reed, Ron	85D	282	$ .01	$ .10
Ready, Randy	90D	396	$ .01	$ .04	Reed, Steve	93D	375	$ .01	$ .10
Ready, Randy	90DL	500	$ .05	$ .25	Reese, Jimmy	91DLS	21	$ .01	$ .08
Ready, Randy	91D	148	$ .01	$ .04	Reimer, Kevin	91D	80	$ .01	$ .10
Ready, Randy	91DL	82	$ .01	$ .08	Reimer, Kevin	92D	251	$ .01	$ .04

DONRUSS

Player	Year	No.	VG	EX/MT
Reimer, Kevin	92DL	93	$.01	$.06
Reimer, Kevin	93D	55	$.01	$.05
Reitz, Ken	81D	307	$.01	$.06
Reitz, Ken	82D	277	$.01	$.06
Remlinger, Mike	91DR	37	$.01	$.05
Remlinger, Mike	92D	336	$.01	$.10
Remmerswaal, Win	81D	98	$.01	$.06
Remy, Jerry	81D	215	$.01	$.06
Remy, Jerry	82D	156	$.01	$.06
Remy, Jerry	83D	74	$.01	$.06
Remy, Jerry	84D	172	$.05	$.20
Renko, Steve	81D	337	$.01	$.06
Renko, Steve	82D	38	$.01	$.06
Renko, Steve	83D	393	$.01	$.06
Reuschel, Rick	81D	561	$.01	$.10
Reuschel, Rick	82D	157	$.01	$.06
Reuschel, Rick	86D	532	$.01	$.05
Reuschel, Rick	87D	188	$.01	$.05
Reuschel, Rick	88D	613	$.01	$.04
Reuschel, Rick	89D	335	$.01	$.04

Reuschel, Rick	89DK	11	$.01	$.05
Reuschel, Rick	90D	112	$.01	$.04
Reuschel, Rick	90DAS	663	$.01	$.04
Reuschel, Rick	91D	518	$.01	$.04
Reuss, Jerry	81D	417	$.01	$.06
Reuss, Jerry	82D	284	$.01	$.06
Reuss, Jerry	83D	158	$.01	$.06
Reuss, Jerry	84D	418	$.05	$.20
Reuss, Jerry	85D	226	$.01	$.10
Reuss, Jerry	86D	104	$.01	$.15
Reuss, Jerry	89D	413	$.01	$.04
Reuss, Jerry	90D	528	$.01	$.04
Revering, Dave	81D	117	$.01	$.06
Revering, Dave	82D	234	$.01	$.06
Reyes, Gilberto	86D	581	$.01	$.15
Reyes, Gilberto	91DL	451	$.01	$.08
Reyes, Gilberto	92D	381	$.01	$.04
Reynolds, Craig	81D	378	$.01	$.06
Reynolds, Craig	82D	344	$.01	$.06
Reynolds, Craig	83D	317	$.01	$.06
Reynolds, Craig	84D	405	$.05	$.20
Reynolds, Craig	85D	328	$.01	$.10
Reynolds, Craig	86D	232	$.01	$.08

Player	Year	No.	VG	EX/MT
Reynolds, Craig	87D	384	$.01	$.05
Reynolds, Craig	88D	209	$.01	$.04
Reynolds, Craig	89D	477	$.01	$.04
Reynolds, Harold	86D	484	$.10	$.65
Reynolds, Harold	87D	489	$.01	$.10
Reynolds, Harold	88D	563	$.01	$.04
Reynolds, Harold	89D	93	$.01	$.04
Reynolds, Harold	89DK	21	$.01	$.05
Reynolds, Harold	90D	227	$.01	$.04
Reynolds, Harold	90DL	140	$.05	$.25
Reynolds, Harold	91D	175	$.01	$.04
Reynolds, Harold	91DL	297	$.01	$.08
Reynolds, Harold	91DLS	119	$.01	$.08
Reynolds, Harold	92D	239	$.01	$.04
Reynolds, Harold	92DL	38	$.01	$.06
Reynolds, Harold	92DLS	239	$.01	$.06
Reynolds, Harold	93D	639	$.01	$.05
Reynolds, R. J.	85D	128	$.05	$.25
Reynolds, R. J.	86D	552	$.01	$.08
Reynolds, R. J.	87D	65	$.01	$.05
Reynolds, R. J.	88D	65	$.01	$.04
Reynolds, R. J.	89D	134	$.01	$.04
Reynolds, R. J.	90D	447	$.01	$.04
Reynolds, R. J.	90DL	381	$.05	$.25
Reynolds, R. J.	91D	101	$.01	$.04
Reynolds, Shane	92DR	102	$.01	$.10
Reynolds, Shane	93D	164	$.01	$.10
Reynoso, Armando	93D	752	$.01	$.05
Rhoden, Rick	82D	423	$.01	$.06
Rhoden, Rick	83D	250	$.01	$.06
Rhoden, Rick	84D	552	$.05	$.20
Rhoden, Rick	85D	552	$.01	$.10
Rhoden, Rick	86D	166	$.01	$.08
Rhoden, Rick	87D	435	$.01	$.05
Rhoden, Rick	87DK	10	$.01	$.05
Rhoden, Rick	88D	128	$.01	$.04
Rhoden, Rick	89D	429	$.01	$.04
Rhoden, Rick	89DTR	40	$.01	$.05
Rhodes, Arthur	91DLBC	6	$.75	$3.00
Rhodes, Arthur	92D	727	$.01	$.15
Rhodes, Arthur	92DL	394	$.05	$.25
Rhodes, Arthur	93D	133	$.01	$.10
Rhodes, Karl	91D	698	$.01	$.10
Rhodes, Karl	91DL	195	$.01	$.15
Rice, Jim	81D	338	$.05	$.35
Rice, Jim	82D	200	$.05	$.25
Rice, Jim	83D	208	$.05	$.30
Rice, Jim	84D	50	$.10	$.50
Rice, Jim	85D	50	$.05	$.25
Rice, Jim	85DK	15	$.05	$.20
Rice, Jim	86D	213	$.05	$.25
Rice, Jim	87D	92	$.01	$.15
Rice, Jim	88D	399	$.01	$.15
Rice, Jim	89D	122	$.01	$.15
Richard, J.R.	81D	140	$.01	$.15
Richards, Gene	81D	4	$.01	$.06
Richards, Gene	82D	499	$.01	$.00
Richards, Gene	83D	271	$.01	$.06
Richards, Gene	84D	429	$.05	$.20
Richardt, Mike	83D	368	$.01	$.06
Righetti, Dave	82D	73	$.10	$.75
Righetti, Dave	83D	199	$.05	$.20
Righetti, Dave	84D	103	$.05	$.35
Righetti, Dave	84DK	10	$.05	$.25
Righetti, Dave	85D	336	$.05	$.20
Righetti, Dave	86D	214	$.01	$.08
Righetti, Dave	87D	128	$.01	$.05
Righetti, Dave	88D	93	$.01	$.15
Righetti, Dave	89D	78	$.01	$.04
Righetti, Dave	90D	311	$.01	$.04
Righetti, Dave	91D	275	$.01	$.04
Righetti, Dave	91DK	21	$.01	$.05
Righetti, Dave	91DL	301	$.01	$.08
Righetti, Dave	91DLS	258	$.01	$.08
Righetti, Dave	92D	174	$.01	$.04

DONRUSS

Player	Year	No.	VG	EX/MT
Righetti, Dave	92DL	135	$ .01	$ .06
Righetti, Dave	93D	552	$ .01	$ .05
Rijo, Jose	85D	492	$ .75	$3.00
Rijo, Jose	86D	522	$ .10	$ .50
Rijo, Jose	87D	55	$ .05	$ .20
Rijo, Jose	88D	548	$ .01	$ .15
Rijo, Jose	89D	375	$ .01	$ .04
Rijo, Jose	90D	115	$ .01	$ .04
Rijo, Jose	90DL	282	$ .10	$ .50
Rijo, Jose	91D	723	$ .01	$ .04
Rijo, Jose	91D	742	$ .01	$ .04
Rijo, Jose	91DL	326	$ .01	$ .08
Rijo, Jose	92D	223	$ .01	$ .04
Rijo, Jose	92DL	139	$ .01	$ .10
Rijo, Jose	92DLS	26	$ .01	$ .06
Rijo, Jose	93D	454	$ .01	$ .05
Riles, Ernest	86D	359	$ .05	$ .25
Riles, Ernest	87D	151	$ .01	$ .05
Riles, Ernest	88D	478	$ .01	$ .04
Riles, Ernest	89D	625	$ .01	$ .04
Riles, Ernest	90D	131	$ .01	$ .04
Riles, Ernest	91D	461	$ .01	$ .04
Riles, Ernest	91DL	358	$ .01	$ .08
Riley, George	81D	588	$ .01	$ .06
Ripken, Billy	87DR	16	$ .05	$ .20
Ripken, Billy	88D	336	$ .01	$ .10
Ripken, Billy	88D	625	$ .05	$ .20
Ripken, Billy	89D	259	$ .01	$ .04
Ripken, Billy	90D	164	$ .01	$ .04
Ripken, Billy	90DL	271	$ .05	$ .25
Ripken, Billy	91D	167	$ .01	$ .04
Ripken, Billy	91DL	7	$ .01	$ .08
Ripken, Billy	92D	734	$ .01	$ .04
Ripken, Billy	92DL	184	$ .01	$ .06
Ripken, Billy	93D	59	$ .01	$ .05
Ripken Jr., Cal	82D	405	$12.50	$50.00
Ripken Jr., Cal	83D	279	$4.00	$16.00
Ripken Jr., Cal	84D	106	$7.50	$30.00
Ripken Jr., Cal	85D	169	$2.50	$10.00
Ripken Jr., Cal	85DK	14	$1.00	$4.00
Ripken Jr., Cal	86D	210	$1.25	$5.00
Ripken Jr., Cal	87D	89	$ .15	$1.50
Ripken Jr., Cal	88D	171	$ .10	$ .50
Ripken Jr., Cal	88D	625	$ .05	$ .20
Ripken Jr., Cal	88DBC	1	$ .05	$ .35
Ripken Jr., Cal	88DK	26	$ .05	$ .35
Ripken Jr., Cal	89D	51	$ .10	$ .50
Ripken Jr., Cal	89DBC	15	$ .05	$ .25
Ripken, Cal	90D	96	$ .05	$ .35
Ripken, Cal	90DAS	676	$ .01	$ .15
Ripken, Cal	90DBC	18	$ .05	$ .25
Ripken, Cal	90DL	197	$1.25	$5.00
Ripken, Cal	91D	223	$ .05	$ .25
Ripken, Cal	91DAS	52	$ .01	$ .15
Ripken, Cal	91DBC	17	$ .05	$ .20
Ripken, Cal	91DL	430	$ .15	$1.25
Ripken Jr., Cal	91DLS	9	$ .10	$1.00
Ripken, Cal	92D	35	$ .05	$ .35
Ripken, Cal	92DAS	22	$ .01	$ .15
Ripken, Cal	92DBC	1	$ .10	$ .40
Ripken, Cal	92DK	5	$1.25	$5.00
Ripken, Cal	92DL	52	$ .10	$ .75
Ripken Jr., Cal	92DLS	129	$ .10	$ .75
Ripken Jr., Cal	93D	559	$ .05	$ .25
Ripken Sr., Cal	82D	579	$ .01	$ .15
Ripken Sr., Cal	88D	625	$ .05	$ .20
Ripley, Allen	82D	125	$ .01	$ .06
Ripley, Allen	83D	57	$ .01	$ .06
Risley, Bill	92DR	103	$ .01	$ .05
Ritchie, Wally	88D	555	$ .01	$ .04
Ritchie, Wally	92D	631	$ .01	$ .04
Ritchie, Wally	92DL	443	$ .01	$ .06
Ritz, Kevin	90D	415	$ .01	$ .10
Ritz, Kevin	92DL	386	$ .01	$ .06
Ritz, Kevin	93D	99	$ .01	$ .05

Player	Year	No.	VG	EX/MT
Rivera, Ben	92DR	104	$ .01	$ .15
Rivera, Ben	93D	412	$ .01	$ .05
Rivera, Bombo	81D	593	$ .01	$ .06
Rivera, German	85D	638	$ .01	$ .10
Rivera, Luis	89D	578	$ .01	$ .04
Rivera, Luis	90D	421	$ .01	$ .04
Rivera, Luis	90DL	283	$ .05	$ .25
Rivera, Luis	91D	234	$ .01	$ .04
Rivera, Luis	91DL	408	$ .01	$ .08
Rivera, Luis	92D	332	$ .01	$ .04
Rivera, Luis	92DL	355	$ .01	$ .06
Rivera, Luis	93D	591	$ .01	$ .05
Rivers, Mickey	81D	496	$ .01	$ .15
Rivers, Mickey	82D	242	$ .01	$ .15
Rivers, Mickey	83D	394	$ .01	$ .06
Rivers, Mickey	84D	465	$ .05	$ .20
Rivers, Mickey	85D	465	$ .01	$ .10
Robbins, Bruce	81D	129	$ .01	$ .06
Roberge, Bert	83D	496	$ .01	$ .06
Roberge, Bert	86D	575	$ .01	$ .08
Roberts, Leon (Bip)	86DR	33	$ .15	$1.50
Roberts, Leon (Bip)	87D	114	$ .10	$ .75
Roberts, Bip	90D	347	$ .01	$ .04
Roberts, Bip	90DL	233	$ .05	$ .25
Roberts, Bip	91D	195	$ .01	$ .04
Roberts, Bip	91DL	478	$ .01	$ .08
Roberts, Bip	91DLS	248	$ .01	$ .08
Roberts, Bip	92D	371	$ .01	$ .04

Roberts, Bip	92DL	252	$ .01	$ .06
Roberts, Bip	92DLS	27	$ .01	$ .06
Roberts, Bip	93D	106	$ .01	$ .05
Roberts, Bip	93DK	11	$ .20	$2.00
Roberts, Dave	81D	490	$ .01	$ .06
Roberts, Dave	81D	501	$ .01	$ .06
Roberts, Dave	82D	625	$ .01	$ .06
Roberts, Dave	83D	273	$ .01	$ .06
Roberts, Leon	81D	48	$ .01	$ .06
Roberts, Leon	82D	415	$ .01	$ .06
Roberts, Leon	84D	399	$ .05	$ .25
Robertson, Andre	83D	387	$ .01	$ .06
Robertson, Andre	84D	347	$ .05	$ .20
Robertson, Andre	86D	469	$ .01	$ .08
Robidoux, Billy	86D	515	$ .01	$ .08

DONRUSS

Player	Year	No.	VG	EX/MT	Player	Year	No.	VG	EX/MT
Robidoux, Billy	87D	240	$ .01	$ .05	Roenicke, Ron	84D	484	$ .05	$ .20
Robinson, Bill	81D	137	$ .01	$ .06	Roenicke, Ron	87D	412	$ .01	$ .05
Robinson, Bill	82D	402	$ .01	$ .06	Rogers, Kenny	89DR	13	$ .01	$ .05
Robinson, Don	81D	375	$ .01	$ .06	Rogers, Kenny	90D	283	$ .01	$ .10
Robinson, Don	83D	171	$ .01	$ .06	Rogers, Kenny	90DL	311	$ .05	$ .25
Robinson, Don	84D	532	$ .05	$ .20	Rogers, Kenny	91D	258	$ .01	$ .04
Robinson, Don	85D	262	$ .01	$ .10	Rogers, Kenny	91DL	105	$ .01	$ .08
Robinson, Don	85D	264	$ .01	$ .10	Rogers, Kenny	92D	368	$ .01	$ .04
Robinson, Don	86D	357	$ .01	$ .08	Rogers, Kenny	92DL	173	$ .01	$ .06
Robinson, Don	87D	608	$ .01	$ .05	Rogers, Kenny	93D	509	$ .01	$ .05
Robinson, Don	88D	573	$ .01	$ .04	Rogers, Kenny	93DL	92	$ .01	$ .15
Robinson, Don	89D	571	$ .01	$ .04	Rogers, Steve	81D	330	$ .01	$ .06
Robinson, Don	90D	258	$ .01	$ .04	Rogers, Steve	82D	36	$ .01	$ .06
Robinson, Don	90DL	267	$ .05	$ .25	Rogers, Steve	83D	320	$ .01	$ .06
Robinson, Don	91D	581	$ .01	$ .04	Rogers, Steve	83DK	18	$ .01	$ .10
Robinson, Don	91DL	188	$ .01	$ .08	Rogers, Steve	84D	219	$ .05	$ .20
Robinson, Frank	82D	424	$ .05	$ .25	Rogers, Steve	85D	219	$ .01	$ .10
Robinson, Frank	83D	564	$ .05	$ .25	Rohde, Dave	91D	743	$ .01	$ .10
Robinson, Frank	83D	648	$ .05	$ .35	Rohde, Dave	91DL	424	$ .05	$ .25
Robinson, Jeff D.	85D	201	$ .05	$ .25	Rojas, Mel	91D	681	$ .01	$ .10
Robinson, Jeff D.	87D	559	$ .01	$ .05	Rojas, Mel	92D	435	$ .01	$ .04
Robinson, Jeff D.	88D	558	$ .01	$ .04	Rojas, Mel	93D	408	$ .01	$ .05
Robinson, Jeff D.	89D	370	$ .01	$ .04	Romanick, Ron	85D	451	$ .01	$ .10
Robinson, Jeff D.	90D	134	$ .01	$ .04	Romanick, Ron	86D	85	$ .01	$ .08
Robinson, Jeff D.	90DL	412	$ .05	$ .25	Romero, Ed	82D	536	$ .01	$ .06
Robinson, Jeff D.	91D	291	$ .01	$ .04	Romero, Ed	83D	584	$ .01	$ .06
Robinson, Jeff D.	91DL	307	$ .01	$ .08	Romero, Ed	84D	89	$ .05	$ .20
Robinson, Jeff D.	92D	59	$ .01	$ .04	Romero, Ed	85D	515	$ .01	$ .10
Robinson, Jeff M.	87DR	13	$ .05	$ .25	Romero, Ed	86D	455	$ .01	$ .08
Robinson, Jeff M.	88D	296	$ .01	$ .15	Romero, Ed	87D	606	$ .01	$ .05
Robinson, Jeff M.	89D	470	$ .01	$ .04	Romero, Ed	88D	623	$ .01	$ .15
Robinson, Jeff M.	89DK	18	$ .01	$ .05	Romero, Ramon	86D	495	$ .01	$ .08
Robinson, Jeff M.	90D	417	$ .01	$ .04	Romine, Kevin	90D	476	$ .01	$ .04
Robinson, Jeff M.	90DL	429	$ .05	$ .25	Romine, Kevin	90DL	414	$ .05	$ .25
Robinson, Jeff M.	91D	245	$ .01	$ .04	Romine, Kevin	91D	290	$ .01	$ .04
Robinson, Jeff M.	91DL	464	$ .01	$ .08	Romo, Enrique	81D	255	$ .01	$ .06
Robinson, Jeff M.	92D	77	$ .01	$ .04	Romo, Enrique	82D	59	$ .01	$ .06
Robinson, Ron	85D	649	$ .01	$ .15	Roof, Phil	82D	615	$ .01	$ .15
Robinson, Ron	86D	121	$ .01	$ .08	Roomes, Rolando	89D	577	$ .01	$ .10
Robinson, Ron	87D	310	$ .01	$ .05	Roomes, Rolando	90D	360	$ .01	$ .04
Robinson, Ron	88D	166	$ .01	$ .04	Rose, Bobby	92D	90	$ .01	$ .04
Robinson, Ron	89D	308	$ .01	$ .04	Rose, Bobby	92DL	250	$ .01	$ .06
Robinson, Ron	90D	553	$ .01	$ .04	Rose, Pete	81D	131	$ .20	$2.00
Robinson, Ron	90DL	467	$ .05	$ .25	Rose, Pete	81D	251	$ .20	$2.00
Robinson, Ron	91D	254	$ .01	$ .04	Rose, Pete	81D	371	$ .20	$1.75
Robinson, Ron	91DL	14	$ .01	$ .08	Rose, Pete	82D	168	$ .15	$1.50
Robinson, Ron	91DLS	75	$ .01	$ .08	Rose, Pete	82D	585	$ .10	$1.00
Rockies, Colorado	92DBC	7	$ .10	$ .50	Rose, Pete	82DK	1	$ .20	$2.00
Rodgers, Bob	81D	327	$ .01	$ .06	Rose, Pete	83D	42	$ .15	$1.25
Rodgers, Bob	82D	232	$ .01	$ .06	Rose, Pete	84D	61	$1.00	$4.00
Rodriguez, Aurelio	83D	369	$ .01	$ .06	Rose, Pete	85D	254	$ .15	$1.50
Rodriguez, Carlos	91DR	41	$ .01	$ .10	Rose, Pete	85D	641	$ .20	$2.00
Rodriguez, Henry	91DLBC	8	$ .20	$2.00	Rose, Pete	86D	62	$ .10	$1.00
Rodriguez, Henry	92DR	105	$ .01	$ .05	Rose, Pete	86D	644	$ .10	$ .50
Rodriguez, Henry	93D	218	$ .01	$ .10	Rose, Pete	86DK	653	$ .10	$1.00
Rodriguez, Ivan	91DR	33	$ .10	$1.00	Rose, Pete	87D	186	$ .10	$ .50
Rodriguez, Ivan	92D	289	$ .05	$ .25	Rosello, Dave	81D	79	$ .01	$ .06
Rodriguez, Ivan	92DL	194	$ .10	$ .75	Rosello, Dave	82D	617	$ .01	$ .06
Rodriguez, Ivan	92DLS	246	$ .10	$ .75	Rosenberg, Steve	89D	219	$ .01	$ .04
Rodriguez, Ivan	93D	187	$ .01	$ .15	Rosenberg, Steve	90D	253	$ .01	$ .04
Rodriguez, Ivan	93DL	5	$ .01	$ .15	Rossy, Rico	92DR	106	$ .01	$ .05
Rodriguez, Rich	91D	769	$ .01	$ .10	Rowdon, Wade	85D	642	$ .01	$ .10
Rodriguez, Rich	91DL	448	$ .01	$ .15	Rowland, Rich	93D	77	$ .01	$ .10
Rodriguez, Rich	92D	388	$ .01	$ .04	Royer, Stan	92D	602	$ .01	$ .04
Rodriguez, Rich	92DL	319	$ .01	$ .06	Royer, Stan	93D	680	$ .01	$ .05
Rodriguez, Rich	93D	338	$ .01	$ .05	Royster, Jerry	81D	339	$ .01	$ .06
Rodriguez, Rosario	92D	748	$ .01	$ .04	Royster, Jerry	82D	555	$ .01	$ .06
Rodriguez, Vic	85D	535	$ .01	$ .10	Royster, Jerry	83D	425	$ .01	$ .06
Roenicke, Gary	81D	116	$ .01	$ .06	Royster, Jerry	84D	531	$ .05	$ .20
Roenicke, Gary	82D	509	$ .01	$ .06	Royster, Jerry	86D	446	$ .01	$ .08
Roenicke, Gary	83D	27	$ .01	$ .06	Royster, Jerry	87D	534	$ .01	$ .05
Roenicke, Gary	85D	123	$ .01	$ .10	Royster, Jerry	88D	660	$ .01	$ .15
Roenicke, Gary	86D	472	$ .01	$ .08	Rozema, Dave	81D	9	$ .01	$ .06
Roenicke, Ron	83D	327	$ .01	$ .06	Rozema, Dave	82D	259	$ .01	$ .06
Roenicke, Ron	84D	392	$ .05	$ .20	Rozema, Dave	83D	133	$ .01	$ .06

141

DONRUSS

Player	Year	No.	VG	EX/MT	Player	Year	No.	VG	EX/MT
Rozema, Dave	84D	272	$ .05	$ .20	Ryan, Nolan	90DL	264	$ .10	$ .50
Rozema, Dave	85D	125	$ .01	$ .10	Ryan, Nolan	90DL	265	$1.00	$4.00
Rozema, Dave	86D	343	$ .01	$ .08	Ryan, Nolan	91D	89	$ .05	$ .35
Rucker, Dave	83D	641	$ .01	$ .06	Ryan, Nolan	91DBC	3	$ .05	$ .35
Rucker, Dave	84D	260	$ .05	$ .20	Ryan, Nolan	91DBC	15	$ .05	$ .35
Rucker, Dave	85D	260	$ .01	$ .10	Ryan, Nolan	91DL	423	$ .20	$2.00
Rucker, Dave	86D	448	$ .01	$ .08	Ryan, Nolan	91DLBC	25	$1.00	$4.00
Rudi, Joe	81D	174	$ .01	$ .06	Ryan, Nolan	91DLP	25	$4.50	$18.00
Rudi, Joe	82D	586	$ .01	$ .06	Ryan, Nolan	91DLS	128	$ .25	$2.50
Rudi, Joe	83D	287	$ .01	$ .06	Ryan, Nolan	92D	154	$ .05	$ .25
Ruffin, Bruce	87D	555	$ .05	$ .25	Ryan, Nolan	92D	555	$ .05	$ .25
Ruffin, Bruce	88D	165	$ .01	$ .15	Ryan, Nolan	92D	707	$ .10	$ .50
Ruffin, Bruce	89D	515	$ .01	$ .04	Ryan, Nolan	92DL	41	$ .15	$1.25
Ruffin, Bruce	90DL	151	$ .05	$ .25	Ryan, Nolan	92DLS	248	$ .15	$1.50
Ruffin, Bruce	92D	680	$ .01	$ .04	Ryan, Nolan	93D	423	$ .10	$ .50
Ruffin, Bruce	92DL	414	$ .01	$ .06	Ryan, Nolan	93D	115	$ .20	$2.00
Ruffin, Johnny	92DR	107	$ .01	$ .15	Saberhagen, Bret	85D	222	$1.25	$5.00
Ruhle, Vern	81D	261	$ .01	$ .06	Saberhagen, Bret	86D	100	$ .10	$ .75
Ruhle, Vern	82D	293	$ .01	$ .06	Saberhagen, Bret	86DK	11	$ .05	$ .35
Ruhle, Vern	83D	627	$ .01	$ .06	Saberhagen, Bret	87D	132	$ .05	$ .20
Ruhle, Vern	84D	564	$ .05	$ .20	Saberhagen, Bret	88D	96	$ .01	$ .15
Ruhle, Vern	85D	380	$ .01	$ .10	Saberhagen, Bret	89D	144	$ .01	$ .10
Runnells, Tom	86D	569	$ .01	$ .15	Saberhagen, Bret	90D	89	$ .01	$ .10
Ruskin, Scott	90DL	512	$ .05	$ .25	Saberhagen, Bret	90DL	72	$ .10	$ .50
Ruskin, Scott	90DR	27	$ .01	$ .15	Saberhagen, Bret	91D	88	$ .01	$ .04
Ruskin, Scott	91D	612	$ .01	$ .04	Saberhagen, Bret	91DL	118	$ .01	$ .15
Ruskin, Scott	92D	394	$ .01	$ .04	Saberhagen, Bret	91DLS	69	$ .01	$ .08
Ruskin, Scott	92DL	521	$ .01	$ .06	Saberhagen, Bret	92D	128	$ .01	$ .04
Russell, Bill	81D	57	$ .01	$ .06	Saberhagen, Bret	92D	434	$ .01	$ .04
Russell, Bill	82D	453	$ .01	$ .06	Saberhagen, Bret	92DL	376	$ .01	$ .06
Russell, Bill	83D	210	$ .01	$ .06	Saberhagen, Bret	92DLS	69	$ .01	$ .06
Russell, Bill	84D	587	$ .05	$ .20	Saberhagen, Bret	93D	222	$ .01	$ .05
Russell, Bill	85D	93	$ .01	$ .10	Saberhagen, Bret	93DL	93	$ .01	$ .15
Russell, Bill	86D	153	$ .01	$ .08	Sabo, Chris	88D	30	$ .10	$ .75
Russell, Jeff	84D	569	$ .10	$ .75	Sabo, Chris	89D	317	$ .05	$ .25
Russell, Jeff	85D	487	$ .01	$ .15	Sabo, Chris	89DK	4	$ .01	$ .10
Russell, Jeff	86D	586	$ .01	$ .08	Sabo, Chris	90D	242	$ .01	$ .10
Russell, Jeff	87D	550	$ .01	$ .05	Sabo, Chris	90DL	146	$ .05	$ .35
Russell, Jeff	88D	531	$ .01	$ .04	Sabo, Chris	91D	153	$ .01	$ .10
Russell, Jeff	89D	403	$ .01	$ .04	Sabo, Chris	91DAS	440	$ .01	$ .03
Russell, Jeff	90D	284	$ .01	$ .04	Sabo, Chris	91DL	65	$ .01	$ .15
Russell, Jeff	90DL	152	$ .05	$ .25	Sabo, Chris	91DLS	170	$ .01	$ .15
Russell, Jeff	90DL	442	$ .05	$ .25	Sabo, Chris	91DMVP	412	$ .01	$ .03
Russell, Jeff	91D	202	$ .01	$ .04	Sabo, Chris	92D	50	$ .01	$ .04
Russell, Jeff	91DL	291	$ .01	$ .08	Sabo, Chris	92DAS	424	$ .01	$ .10
Russell, Jeff	92D	129	$ .01	$ .04	Sabo, Chris	92DL	271	$ .01	$ .06
Russell, Jeff	92DL	90	$ .01	$ .06	Sabo, Chris	92DLS	28	$ .01	$ .06
Russell, Jeff	92DLS	247	$ .01	$ .06	Sabo, Chris	93D	58	$ .01	$ .05
Russell, Jeff	93D	711	$ .01	$ .05	Sadek, Mike	81D	498	$ .01	$ .06
Russell, John	85D	648	$ .01	$ .10	Sakata, Lenn	81D	499	$ .01	$ .06
Russell, John	86D	82	$ .01	$ .08	Sakata, Lenn	82D	644	$ .01	$ .06
Russell, John	87D	207	$ .01	$ .05	Sakata, Lenn	83D	205	$ .01	$ .06
Russell, John	90D	458	$ .01	$ .04	Sakata, Lenn	84D	620	$ .05	$ .20
Ruthven, Dick	81D	153	$ .01	$ .06	Salas, Mark	85D	547	$ .01	$ .10
Ruthven, Dick	82D	525	$ .01	$ .06	Salas, Mark	86D	316	$ .01	$ .08
Ruthven, Dick	83D	497	$ .01	$ .06	Salas, Mark	91D	65	$ .01	$ .04
Ruthven, Dick	84D	510	$ .05	$ .20	Salas, Mark	92D	512	$ .01	$ .04
Ruthven, Dick	86D	564	$ .01	$ .08	Salazar, Angel	84DRR	33	$ .05	$ .25
Ryal, Mark	87D	583	$ .01	$ .05	Salazar, Angel	85D	523	$ .01	$ .10
Ryan, Ken	93D	383	$ .05	$ .20	Salazar, Angel	87D	624	$ .01	$ .05
Ryan, Nolan	81D	260	$2.00	$8.00	Salazar, Angel	88D	502	$ .01	$ .04
Ryan, Nolan	82D	419	$2.00	$8.00	Salazar, Luis	82D	472	$ .01	$ .10
Ryan, Nolan	82DK	13	$1.00	$4.00	Salazar, Luis	83D	548	$ .01	$ .06
Ryan, Nolan	83D	118	$1.50	$6.00	Salazar, Luis	84D	356	$ .05	$ .20
Ryan, Nolan	84D	60	$6.25	$25.00	Salazar, Luis	85D	568	$ .01	$ .10
Ryan, Nolan	85D	60	$2.50	$10.00	Salazar, Luis	86D	302	$ .01	$ .08
Ryan, Nolan	86D	258	$1.25	$5.00	Salazar, Luis	89D	352	$ .01	$ .04
Ryan, Nolan	87D	138	$ .20	$2.00	Salazar, Luis	90D	513	$ .01	$ .04
Ryan, Nolan	88D	61	$ .10	$ .75	Salazar, Luis	90DL	388	$ .05	$ .25
Ryan, Nolan	89D	154	$ .10	$ .50	Salazar, Luis	91D	372	$ .01	$ .04
Ryan, Nolan	89DTR	19	$ .20	$2.00	Salazar, Luis	91DL	185	$ .01	$ .08
Ryan, Nolan	90D	166	$ .10	$ .50	Salazar, Luis	92D	152	$ .01	$ .04
Ryan, Nolan	90DAS	659	$ .10	$ .50	Salkeld, Roger	91DLBC	19	$ .20	$2.00
Ryan, Nolan	90DK	665	$ .10	$1.00	Salkeld, Roger	92DRR	7	$ .05	$ .25
Ryan, Nolan	90DL	21	$2.00	$8.00	Salmon, Tim	93D	176	$ .10	$1.00

DONRUSS

Player	Year	No.	VG	EX/MT
Sambito, Joe	81D	21	$ .01	$ .06
Sambito, Joe	82D	65	$ .01	$ .06
Sambito, Joe	83D	244	$ .01	$ .06
Sambito, Joe	85D	572	$ .01	$ .10
Sambito, Joe	87D	421	$ .01	$ .05
Sampen, Bill	90DR	12	$ .01	$ .15
Sampen, Bill	91D	351	$ .01	$ .10
Sampen, Bill	91DL	318	$ .01	$ .08
Sampen, Bill	91DLS	199	$ .01	$ .08
Sampen, Bill	92D	571	$ .01	$ .04
Sampen, Bill	93D	337	$ .01	$ .05
Sample, Billy	81D	268	$ .01	$ .06
Sample, Billy	82D	69	$ .01	$ .06
Sample, Billy	83D	242	$ .01	$ .06
Sample, Billy	84D	403	$ .05	$ .20
Sample, Billy	85D	464	$ .01	$ .10
Sample, Billy	86D	539	$ .01	$ .08
Sample, Billy	87D	143	$ .01	$ .05
Samuel, Juan	85D	183	$ .05	$ .25
Samuel, Juan	85DK	23	$ .05	$ .25
Samuel, Juan	86D	326	$ .05	$ .20
Samuel, Juan	87D	165	$ .01	$ .15
Samuel, Juan	88D	288	$ .05	$ .20
Samuel, Juan	89D	76	$ .01	$ .04
Samuel, Juan	90D	53	$ .01	$ .04
Samuel, Juan	90DL	226	$ .05	$ .25
Samuel, Juan	91D	62	$ .01	$ .04
Samuel, Juan	91DL	10	$ .01	$ .08
Samuel, Juan	91DLS	188	$ .01	$ .08
Samuel, Juan	92D	105	$ .01	$ .04
Samuel, Juan	92DL	125	$ .01	$ .06
Sanchez, Alejandro	85DRR	43	$ .01	$ .15
Sanchez, Alejandro	86D	415	$ .01	$ .08
Sanchez, Alex	89DRR	47	$ .01	$ .15
Sanchez, Alex	90DRR	45	$ .01	$ .10
Sanchez, Israel	89D	474	$ .01	$ .10
Sanchez, Luis	83D	519	$ .01	$ .06
Sanchez, Luis	84D	597	$ .05	$ .20
Sanchez, Luis	85D	352	$ .01	$ .10
Sanchez, Orlando	82D	636	$ .01	$ .06
Sanchez, Rey	92DRR	412	$ .01	$ .05
Sanchez, Rey	93D	424	$ .01	$ .05
Sanchez, Rey	93DL	88	$ .01	$ .15
Sandberg, Ryne	83D	277	$10.00	$40.00
Sandberg, Ryne	84D	311	$7.00	$28.00
Sandberg, Ryne	85D	67	$2.25	$9.00
Sandberg, Ryne	85DK	1	$1.00	$4.00
Sandberg, Ryne	86D	67	$1.00	$4.00
Sandberg, Ryne	87D	77	$ .15	$1.25
Sandberg, Ryne	88D	242	$ .10	$ .50
Sandberg, Ryne	89D	105	$ .05	$ .35
Sandberg, Ryne	90D	105	$ .05	$ .35
Sandberg, Ryne	90DAS	692	$ .01	$ .15
Sandberg, Ryne	90DBC	10	$ .05	$ .20
Sandberg, Ryne	90DL	98	$1.00	$4.00
Sandberg, Ryne	90DL	528	$ .05	$ .35
Sandberg, Ryne	91D	504	$ .05	$ .25
Sandberg, Ryne	91DAS	433	$ .01	$ .10
Sandberg, Ryne	91DBC	7	$ .01	$ .15
Sandberg, Ryne	91DK	14	$ .01	$ .10
Sandberg, Ryne	91DL	207	$ .10	$1.00
Sandberg, Ryne	91DLP	2	$2.50	$10.00
Sandberg, Ryne	91DLS	158	$ .10	$1.00
Sandberg, Ryne	91DMVP	404	$ .01	$ .10
Sandberg, Ryne	92D	576	$ .05	$ .25
Sandberg, Ryne	92DAS	429	$ .01	$ .10
Sandberg, Ryne	92DL	317	$ .10	$ .50
Sandberg, Ryne	92DLS	18	$ .10	$ .50
Sandberg, Ryne	93D	344	$ .01	$ .15
Sandberg, Ryne	93DK	2	$1.50	$6.00
Sanders, Deion	89DR	6	$ .50	$2.00
Sanders, Deion	90D	427	$ .10	$ .50
Sanders, Deion	90DL	359	$1.75	$7.00
Sanders, Deion	91DL	436	$ .10	$ .50
Sanders, Deion	92D	564	$ .05	$ .20
Sanders, Deion	92DL	448	$ .05	$ .25
Sanders, Deion	92DLS	9	$ .05	$ .25
Sanders, Deion	93D	158	$ .01	$ .10
Sanders, Reggie	91DLBC	10	$1.25	$5.00
Sanders, Reggie	92DL	360	$ .10	$ .50
Sanders, Reggie	92DLS	29	$ .10	$ .50
Sanders, Reggie	92DRR	415	$ .05	$ .25
Sanders, Reggie	93D	402	$ .01	$ .15
Sanderson, Scott	81D	450	$ .01	$ .06
Sanderson, Scott	82D	288	$ .01	$ .06
Sanderson, Scott	83D	446	$ .01	$ .06
Sanderson, Scott	84D	341	$ .05	$ .20
Sanderson, Scott	85D	266	$ .01	$ .10
Sanderson, Scott	86D	442	$ .01	$ .08
Sanderson, Scott	87D	447	$ .01	$ .05
Sanderson, Scott	88D	646	$ .01	$ .15

Player	Year	No.	VG	EX/MT
Sanderson, Scott	89D	629	$ .01	$ .04
Sanderson, Scott	90D	647	$ .01	$ .04
Sanderson, Scott	90DL	194	$ .05	$ .25
Sanderson, Scott	91D	533	$ .01	$ .04
Sanderson, Scott	91DL	169	$ .01	$ .08
Sanderson, Scott	91DLS	99	$ .01	$ .08
Sanderson, Scott	92D	227	$ .01	$ .04
Sanderson, Scott	92DK	10	$ .10	$1.00
Sanderson, Scott	92DL	152	$ .01	$ .06
Sanderson, Scott	92DLS	219	$ .01	$ .06
Sanderson, Scott	93D	726	$ .01	$ .05
Sanford, Mo	92DRR	417	$ .05	$ .20
Sanford, Mo	93D	760	$ .01	$ .05
Sanguillen, Manny	81D	14	$ .01	$ .06
Santana, Rafael	85D	610	$ .03	$ .10
Santana, Rafael	86D	319	$ .01	$ .08
Santana, Rafael	87D	569	$ .01	$ .05
Santana, Rafael	88D	633	$ .01	$ .15
Santana, Rafael	89D	309	$ .01	$ .04
Santiago, Benito	87DR	44	$ .10	$ .50
Santiago, Benito	87DRR	31	$ .10	$ .50
Santiago, Benito	88D	114	$ .01	$ .15
Santiago, Benito	88DK	3	$ .05	$ .25
Santiago, Benito	89D	205	$ .01	$ .10
Santiago, Benito	90D	465	$ .01	$ .04
Santiago, Benito	90DAS	708	$ .01	$ .04
Santiago, Benito	90DL	207	$ .05	$ .25

DONRUSS

Player	Year	No.	VG	EX/MT	Player	Year	No.	VG	EX/MT
Santiago, Benito	91D	449	$ .01	$ .04	Schilling, Curt	93D	118	$ .01	$ .05
Santiago, Benito	91DL	432	$ .01	$ .08	Schilling, Curt	93DL	4	$ .01	$ .15
Santiago, Benito	91DLS	249	$ .01	$ .08	Schiraldi, Calvin	85DRR	38	$ .05	$ .25
Santiago, Benito	92D	40	$ .01	$ .04	Schiraldi, Calvin	86D	652	$ .01	$ .08
Santiago, Benito	92DAS	430	$ .01	$ .05	Schiraldi, Calvin	87D	641	$ .01	$ .05
Santiago, Benito	92DL	321	$ .01	$ .06	Schiraldi, Calvin	88D	375	$ .01	$ .04
Santiago, Benito	92DLS	107	$ .01	$ .06	Schiraldi, Calvin	89D	285	$ .01	$ .04
Santiago, Benito	93D	522	$ .01	$ .05	Schiraldi, Calvin	90D	672	$ .01	$ .04
Santovenia, Nelson	89D	366	$ .01	$ .10	Schiraldi, Calvin	91D	308	$ .01	$ .04
Santovenia, Nelson	90D	224	$ .01	$ .04	Schmidt, Dave	83D	321	$ .01	$ .15
Santovenia, Nelson	90DL	502	$ .05	$ .25	Schmidt, Dave	84D	586	$ .05	$ .20
Sarimento, Manny	83D	502	$ .01	$ .06	Schmidt, Dave	85D	586	$ .01	$ .10
Sarmiento, Manny	84D	200	$ .05	$ .20	Schmidt, Dave	86D	378	$ .01	$ .08
Sasser, Mackey	88DR	51	$ .01	$ .15	Schmidt, Dave	87D	182	$ .01	$ .05
Sasser, Mackey	88DRR	28	$ .05	$ .20	Schmidt, Dave	89D	215	$ .01	$ .04
Sasser, Mackey	89D	454	$ .01	$ .04	Schmidt, Dave	89DK	13	$ .01	$ .05
Sasser, Mackey	90D	471	$ .01	$ .10	Schmidt, Dave	90D	524	$ .01	$ .04
Sasser, Mackey	90DL	435	$ .05	$ .25	Schmidt, Dave	90DL	457	$ .05	$ .25
Sasser, Mackey	91D	136	$ .01	$ .04	Schmidt, Mike	81D	11	$ .75	$3.00
Sasser, Mackey	91DL	361	$ .01	$ .08	Schmidt, Mike	81D	590	$ .15	$1.50
Sasser, Mackey	92D	256	$ .01	$ .04	Schmidt, Mike	82D	294	$ .25	$2.25
Sasser, Mackey	92DL	108	$ .01	$ .06	Schmidt, Mike	82D	585	$ .10	$1.00
Sasser, Mackey	93D	512	$ .01	$ .05	Schmidt, Mike	83D	168	$ .20	$2.00
Saucier, Kevin	82D	485	$ .01	$ .06	Schmidt, Mike	84D	183	$3.75	$15.00
Savage, Jack	89D	618	$ .01	$ .10	Schmidt, Mike	84DK	23	$1.00	$4.00
Sax, Dave	84D	519	$ .05	$ .20	Schmidt, Mike	85D	61	$1.25	$5.00
Sax, Dave	87D	647	$ .01	$ .05	Schmidt, Mike	86D	61	$ .20	$2.00
Sax, Steve	82D	624	$ .75	$3.00	Schmidt, Mike	87D	139	$ .10	$1.00
Sax, Steve	83D	336	$ .10	$ .50	Schmidt, Mike	88D	330	$ .05	$ .35
Sax, Steve	84D	104	$ .10	$1.00	Schmidt, Mike	88D	371	$ .05	$ .35
Sax, Steve	85D	418	$ .05	$ .35	Schmidt, Mike	88DBC	4	$ .05	$ .20
Sax, Steve	86D	540	$ .01	$ .15	Schmidt, Mike	89D	193	$ .05	$ .35
Sax, Steve	87D	278	$ .01	$ .15	Schmidt, Mike	90D	643	$ .05	$ .25
Sax, Steve	87DK	26	$ .01	$ .05	Schoendienst, Red	81D	431	$ .01	$ .15
Sax, Steve	88D	176	$ .01	$ .10	Schofield, Dick	84DRR	35	$ .10	$ .40
Sax, Steve	89D	84	$ .01	$ .15	Schofield, Dick	85D	329	$ .01	$ .10
Sax, Steve	89DTR	23	$ .01	$ .05	Schofield, Dick	86D	133	$ .01	$ .08
Sax, Steve	90D	78	$ .01	$ .10	Schofield, Dick	87D	283	$ .01	$ .05
Sax, Steve	90DBC	22	$ .01	$ .04	Schofield, Dick	88D	233	$ .01	$ .04
Sax, Steve	90DK	2	$ .01	$ .05	Schofield, Dick	89D	108	$ .01	$ .04
Sax, Steve	90DL	96	$ .05	$ .25	Schofield, Dick	90D	288	$ .01	$ .04
Sax, Steve	91D	163	$ .01	$ .04	Schofield, Dick	90DL	419	$ .05	$ .25
Sax, Steve	91DAS	48	$ .01	$ .04	Schofield, Dick	91D	262	$ .01	$ .04
Sax, Steve	91DL	220	$ .01	$ .08	Schofield, Dick	91DL	59	$ .01	$ .08
Sax, Steve	91DLS	100	$ .01	$ .08	Schofield, Dick	92D	44	$ .01	$ .04
Sax, Steve	92D	729	$ .01	$ .04	Schofield, Dick	92DL	419	$ .01	$ .06
Sax, Steve	92DL	217	$ .01	$ .06	Schooler, Mike	89D	637	$ .01	$ .15
Sax, Steve	92DLS	157	$ .01	$ .06	Schooler, Mike	90D	330	$ .01	$ .04
Sax, Steve	93D	123	$ .01	$ .05	Schooler, Mike	90DL	258	$ .05	$ .25
Sax, Steve	93DL	107	$ .01	$ .15	Schooler, Mike	91D	302	$ .01	$ .04
Scanlan, Bob	91DL	520	$ .01	$ .15	Schooler, Mike	91DL	230	$ .01	$ .08
Scanlan, Bob	92D	454	$ .01	$ .04	Schooler, Mike	92D	444	$ .01	$ .04
Scanlan, Bob	92DL	437	$ .01	$ .06	Schooler, Mike	93D	449	$ .01	$ .05
Scanlan, Bob	93D	292	$ .01	$ .05	Schourek, Pete	91DLBC	15	$ .10	$1.00
Scanlan, Bob	93DL	13	$ .01	$ .15	Schourek, Pete	92D	535	$ .01	$ .04
Scarsone, Steve	92DR	108	$ .01	$ .15	Schourek, Pete	92DL	176	$ .01	$ .06
Scarsone, Steve	93D	381	$ .01	$ .05	Schourek, Pete	93D	198	$ .01	$ .05
Schaefer, Jeff	92D	525	$ .01	$ .04	Schroeder, Bill	84D	515	$ .05	$ .20
Schaefer, Jeff	92DL	513	$ .01	$ .06	Schroeder, Bill	85D	124	$ .01	$ .10
Schatzeder, Dan	81D	248	$ .01	$ .06	Schroeder, Bill	86D	211	$ .01	$ .08
Schatzeder, Dan	82D	385	$ .01	$ .06	Schroeder, Bill	87D	486	$ .01	$ .05
Schatzeder, Dan	84D	132	$ .05	$ .20	Schroeder, Bill	88D	419	$ .01	$ .04
Schatzeder, Dan	85D	543	$ .01	$ .10	Schroeder, Bill	89D	644	$ .01	$ .04
Schatzeder, Dan	87D	482	$ .01	$ .05	Schroeder, Bill	90D	567	$ .01	$ .04
Schatzeder, Dan	90D	594	$ .01	$ .04	Schrom, Ken	84D	72	$ .05	$ .20
Schatzeder, Dan	91D	497	$ .01	$ .04	Schrom, Ken	85D	486	$ .01	$ .10
Scherrer, Bill	84D	203	$ .05	$ .20	Schrom, Ken	86D	635	$ .01	$ .08
Scherrer, Bill	86D	516	$ .01	$ .08	Schrom, Ken	87D	403	$ .01	$ .05
Schilling, Curt	89D	635	$ .05	$ .35	Schrom, Ken	88D	501	$ .01	$ .04
Schilling, Curt	90D	667	$ .01	$ .15	Schu, Rick	85D	448	$ .03	$ .10
Schilling, Curt	91D	556	$ .01	$ .04	Schu, Rick	86D	570	$ .01	$ .08
Schilling, Curt	91DL	292	$ .01	$ .08	Schu, Rick	87D	509	$ .01	$ .05
Schilling, Curt	91DLS	179	$ .01	$ .08	Schu, Rick	88D	432	$ .01	$ .04
Schilling, Curt	92D	757	$ .01	$ .04	Schu, Rick	89D	406	$ .01	$ .04
Schilling, Curt	92DL	516	$ .01	$ .06	Schu, Rick	90D	599	$ .01	$ .04

DONRUSS

Player	Year	No.	VG	EX/MT
Schultz, Jeff	91D	687	$.01	$.10
Schulze, Don	85D	639	$.01	$.10
Scioscia, Mike	82D	598	$.10	$.40
Scioscia, Mike	83D	75	$.01	$.06
Scioscia, Mike	85D	459	$.01	$.10
Scioscia, Mike	86D	93	$.01	$.08
Scioscia, Mike	87D	130	$.01	$.05
Scioscia, Mike	88D	106	$.01	$.04
Scioscia, Mike	89D	77	$.01	$.04
Scioscia, Mike	90D	316	$.01	$.04
Scioscia, Mike	90DL	49	$.05	$.25
Scioscia, Mike	91D	112	$.01	$.04
Scioscia, Mike	91DAS	436	$.01	$.03
Scioscia, Mike	91DL	24	$.01	$.08
Scioscia, Mike	91DLS	189	$.01	$.08
Scioscia, Mike	92D	480	$.01	$.04
Scioscia, Mike	92DL	165	$.01	$.06
Scioscia, Mike	92DLS	48	$.01	$.06
Scioscia, Mike	93D	508	$.01	$.05
Sconiers, Daryl	83D	141	$.01	$.06
Sconiers, Daryl	84D	451	$.05	$.20
Sconiers, Daryl	85D	620	$.01	$.10
Scott, Donnie	85D	544	$.01	$.10
Scott, Gary	91DLBC	4	$.10	$1.00
Scott, Gary	91DLS	159	$.05	$.20
Scott, Gary	92DL	6	$.01	$.06
Scott, Gary	92DLS	19	$.01	$.06
Scott, Gary	93D	750	$.01	$.05
Scott, Mike	81D	37	$.05	$.35
Scott, Mike	82D	128	$.05	$.20
Scott, Mike	84D	136	$.05	$.25
Scott, Mike	85D	258	$.01	$.15
Scott, Mike	86D	476	$.01	$.10
Scott, Mike	87D	163	$.01	$.10
Scott, Mike	87DK	18	$.01	$.05
Scott, Mike	88D	112	$.01	$.04
Scott, Mike	88DBC	12	$.01	$.10
Scott, Mike	89D	69	$.01	$.10
Scott, Mike	89DBC	2	$.01	$.05
Scott, Mike	90D	207	$.01	$.10
Scott, Mike	90DL	4	$.05	$.25
Scott, Mike	91D	483	$.01	$.04

Player	Year	No.	VG	EX/MT
Scott, Rodney	81D	209	$.01	$.06
Scott, Rodney	82D	240	$.01	$.06
Scott, Tim	92DR	109	$.01	$.05
Scott, Tim	93D	362	$.01	$.10
Scott, Tim	93DL	174	$.01	$.15
Scott, Tony (Anthony)	81D	191	$.01	$.06
Scott, Tony	82D	522	$.01	$.06
Scott, Tony	83D	293	$.01	$.06
Scott, Tony	84D	527	$.05	$.20
Scudder, Scott	90D	435	$.01	$.15
Scudder, Scott	90DL	413	$.05	$.35
Scudder, Scott	91D	265	$.01	$.04
Scudder, Scott	91DL	183	$.01	$.08
Scudder, Scott	92D	306	$.01	$.04
Scudder, Scott	92DL	429	$.01	$.06
Scudder, Scott	93D	653	$.01	$.05
Scurry, Rod	82D	185	$.01	$.06
Scurry, Rod	83D	376	$.01	$.06
Scurry, Rod	84D	235	$.05	$.20
Scurry, Rod	85D	142	$.01	$.10
Scurry, Rod	87D	374	$.01	$.05
Seanez, Rudy	90D	417	$.10	$.40
Seanez, Rudy	91D	218	$.01	$.10
Seanez, Rudy	92D	552	$.01	$.04
Seanez, Rudy	93D	758	$.01	$.05
Searage, Ray	86D	536	$.01	$.08
Searage, Ray	88D	429	$.01	$.04
Searage, Ray	90D	649	$.01	$.04
Searcy, Steve	89DRR	29	$.01	$.05
Searcy, Steve	91D	549	$.01	$.04
Searcy, Steve	91DL	187	$.01	$.08
Seaver, Tom	81D	422	$.20	$2.00
Seaver, Tom	81D	425	$.20	$2.00
Seaver, Tom	82D	148	$.15	$1.50
Seaver, Tom	82D	628	$.10	$1.00
Seaver, Tom	82DK	16	$.10	$.75
Seaver, Tom	83D	122	$.15	$1.25
Seaver, Tom	84D	116	$1.75	$7.00
Seaver, Tom	85D	424	$.20	$1.75
Seaver, Tom	86D	609	$.15	$1.25
Seaver, Tom	87D	375	$.10	$.50
Sebra, Bob	87D	468	$.01	$.05
Sebra, Bob	88D	458	$.01	$.04
Segui, David	91D	730	$.01	$.10
Segui, David	91DLS	10	$.01	$.08
Segui, David	92D	321	$.01	$.04
Segui, David	93D	397	$.01	$.05
Seitzer, Kevin	87DR	15	$.05	$.35
Seitzer, Kevin	88D	280	$.05	$.20
Seitzer, Kevin	88DBC	17	$.01	$.10
Seitzer, Kevin	89D	238	$.01	$.10
Seitzer, Kevin	89DK	10	$.01	$.10
Seitzer, Kevin	90D	85	$.01	$.10
Seitzer, Kevin	90DL	230	$.05	$.25
Seitzer, Kevin	91D	73	$.01	$.04
Seitzer, Kevin	91DL	133	$.01	$.08
Seitzer, Kevin	91DLSP	6	$.20	$2.00
Seitzer, Kevin	92D	577	$.01	$.04
Seitzer, Kevin	92DL	399	$.01	$.06
Seitzer, Kevin	93D	603	$.01	$.05
Sellers, Jeff	86DR	29	$.01	$.10
Sellers, Jeff	87D	544	$.01	$.15
Sellers, Jeff	88D	585	$.01	$.04
Sellers, Jeff	89D	517	$.01	$.04
Seminara, Frank	92DRR	10	$.01	$.05
Seminara, Frank	93D	550	$.01	$.05
Seminara, Frank	93DL	64	$.01	$.15
Senteney, Steven	83D	52	$.01	$.06
Serna, Paul	82D	567	$.01	$.06
Servais, Scott	92D	763	$.01	$.10
Servais, Scott	92DL	121	$.01	$.06
Servais, Scott	93D	108	$.01	$.05
Servais, Scott	93DL	33	$.01	$.15
Sexton, Jimmy	83D	449	$.01	$.06
Sharperson, Mike	87D	565	$.01	$.15

Scott, Mike	91DLS	180	$.01	$.08

DONRUSS

Player	Year	No.	VG	EX/MT
Sharperson, Mike	90D	603	$ .01	$ .04
Sharperson, Mike	90DL	490	$ .05	$ .25
Sharperson, Mike	91D	168	$ .01	$ .04
Sharperson, Mike	92D	526	$ .01	$ .04
Sharperson, Mike	92DL	318	$ .01	$ .06
Sharperson, Mike	92DLS	49	$ .01	$ .06
Sharperson, Mike	93D	166	$ .01	$ .05
Shaw, Jeff	90DR	53	$ .01	$ .05
Shaw, Jeff	92D	595	$ .01	$ .04
Sheets, Larry	85DRR	36	$ .05	$ .25
Sheets, Larry	86D	350	$ .01	$ .08
Sheets, Larry	87D	248	$ .01	$ .05
Sheets, Larry	88D	273	$ .01	$ .04
Sheets, Larry	89D	333	$ .01	$ .04
Sheets, Larry	90D	495	$ .01	$ .04
Sheets, Larry	90DL	350	$ .05	$ .25
Sheffield, Gary	89DR	1	$ .75	$3.00
Sheffield, Gary	89DRR	31	$ .20	$2.00
Sheffield, Gary	90D	501	$ .10	$ .50
Sheffield, Gary	90DL	157	$3.00	$12.00
Sheffield, Gary	91D	751	$ .05	$ .20
Sheffield, Gary	91DL	173	$ .15	$1.25
Sheffield, Gary	91DLS	76	$ .10	$1.00
Sheffield, Gary	92D	192	$ .05	$ .25
Sheffield, Gary	92DL	446	$ .10	$ .75
Sheffield, Gary	92DLS	108	$ .10	$ .50
Sheffield, Gary	93D	444	$ .05	$ .20
Sheffield, Gary	93DK	21	$ .75	$3.00
Shelby, John	84D	291	$ .10	$ .40
Shelby, John	85D	472	$ .01	$ .10
Shelby, John	86D	643	$ .01	$ .08
Shelby, John	87D	354	$ .01	$ .05
Shelby, John	88D	352	$ .01	$ .04
Shelby, John	89D	314	$ .01	$ .04
Shelby, John	91D	563	$ .01	$ .04
Shepherd, Keith	93D	332	$ .01	$ .15
Sheridan, Pat	84D	588	$ .05	$ .25
Sheridan, Pat	85D	339	$ .01	$ .10
Sheridan, Pat	86D	155	$ .01	$ .08
Sheridan, Pat	88D	522	$ .01	$ .04
Sheridan, Pat	89D	417	$ .01	$ .04
Sheridan, Pat	90D	367	$ .01	$ .04
Shifflett, Steve	92DR	110	$ .01	$ .05
Shifflett, Steve	93D	73	$ .01	$ .10
Shines, Razor	85D	401	$ .01	$ .10
Shipanoff, Dave	86DRR	34	$ .01	$ .10
Shipley, Craig	92D	667	$ .01	$ .10
Shipley, Craig	93D	206	$ .01	$ .05
Shirley, Bob	81D	242	$ .01	$ .06
Shirley, Bob	82D	120	$ .01	$ .06
Shirley, Bob	84D	214	$ .05	$ .20
Shirley, Bob	85D	370	$ .01	$ .10
Shirley, Bob	86D	458	$ .01	$ .08
Shirley, Bob	87D	463	$ .01	$ .05
Show, Eric	83D	439	$ .05	$ .25
Show, Eric	84D	406	$ .05	$ .20
Show, Eric	85D	202	$ .01	$ .10
Show, Eric	86D	234	$ .01	$ .08
Show, Eric	87D	164	$ .01	$ .05
Show, Eric	88D	387	$ .01	$ .04
Show, Eric	89D	482	$ .01	$ .04
Show, Eric	90D	559	$ .01	$ .04
Show, Eric	90DL	115	$ .05	$ .35
Show, Eric	91DL	354	$ .01	$ .08
Show, Eric	91DLS	108	$ .01	$ .08
Shumpert, Terry	90DL	409	$ .05	$ .25
Shumpert, Terry	90DR	55	$ .01	$ .05
Shumpert, Terry	91D	297	$ .01	$ .04
Shumpert, Terry	91DL	104	$ .01	$ .08
Shumpert, Terry	92D	562	$ .01	$ .04
Shumpert, Terry	92DL	347	$ .01	$ .06
Shumpert, Terry	93D	601	$ .01	$ .05
Sierra, Ruben	86DR	52	$2.50	$10.00
Sierra, Ruben	87D	346	$1.50	$6.00
Sierra, Ruben	88D	223	$ .10	$ .40
Sierra, Ruben	88DBC	26	$ .05	$ .35
Sierra, Ruben	89D	48	$ .05	$ .25
Sierra, Ruben	89DBC	26	$ .01	$ .15
Sierra, Ruben	90D	174	$ .05	$ .20
Sierra, Ruben	90DAS	673	$ .01	$ .10
Sierra, Ruben	90DK	3	$ .05	$ .35
Sierra, Ruben	90DL	257	$ .20	$2.00

Player	Year	No.	VG	EX/MT
Sierra, Ruben	91D	567	$ .01	$ .10
Sierra, Ruben	91DL	97	$ .10	$ .50
Sierra, Ruben	91DLS	129	$ .05	$ .35
Sierra, Ruben	92D	298	$ .01	$ .10
Sierra, Ruben	92DL	383	$ .05	$ .25
Sierra, Ruben	92DLS	249	$ .10	$ .40
Sierra, Ruben	93D	637	$ .01	$ .10
Sierra, Ruben	93DL	29	$ .10	$ .50
Silvestri, Dave	92DR	111	$ .01	$ .15
Simmons, Nelson	86D	272	$ .01	$ .08
Simmons, Ted	81D	308	$ .05	$ .20
Simmons, Ted	82D	106	$ .01	$ .15
Simmons, Ted	83D	332	$ .01	$ .06
Simmons, Ted	84D	473	$ .05	$ .20
Simmons, Ted	85D	414	$ .05	$ .20
Simmons, Ted	86D	292	$ .05	$ .20
Simmons, Ted	87D	537	$ .01	$ .05
Simmons, Ted	88D	560	$ .01	$ .04
Simms, Mike	92D	747	$ .01	$ .04
Simms, Mike	93D	32	$ .01	$ .05
Simons, Doug	91DR	26	$ .01	$ .05
Simons, Doug	92D	688	$ .01	$ .04
Simons, Doug	93D	276	$ .01	$ .05
Simpson, Joe	81D	168	$ .01	$ .06
Simpson, Joe	82D	55	$ .01	$ .06
Simpson, Joe	84D	496	$ .05	$ .20
Sinatro, Matt	82D	149	$ .01	$ .06
Sinatro, Matt	83D	622	$ .01	$ .06
Singleton, Ken	81D	115	$ .01	$ .15
Singleton, Ken	82D	105	$ .01	$ .06
Singleton, Ken	82DK	24	$ .01	$ .15
Singleton, Ken	83D	257	$ .01	$ .06
Singleton, Ken	84D	610	$ .05	$ .20
Sisk, Doug	84D	615	$ .05	$ .20
Sisk, Doug	85D	441	$ .01	$ .10
Sisk, Doug	88D	642	$ .01	$ .15

DONRUSS

Player	Year	No.	VG	EX/MT	Player	Year	No.	VG	EX/MT
Skinner, Joel	84DRR	27	$ .05	$ .25	Smith, Bryn	92D	323	$ .01	$ .04
Skinner, Joel	85D	574	$ .01	$ .10	Smith, Bryn	92DL	157	$ .01	$ .06
Skinner, Joel	86D	330	$ .01	$ .08	Smith, Chris	84DRR	46	$ .05	$ .25
Skinner, Joel	87D	545	$ .01	$ .05	Smith, Dave	81D	23	$ .10	$ .40
Skinner, Joel	88D	474	$ .01	$ .04	Smith, Dave	82D	191	$ .10	$ .06
Skinner, Joel	89D	427	$ .01	$ .04	Smith, Dave	83D	370	$ .01	$ .06
Skinner, Joel	89DTR	22	$ .01	$ .05	Smith, Dave	84D	548	$ .05	$ .20
Skinner, Joel	90D	73	$ .01	$ .04	Smith, Dave	85D	548	$ .01	$ .10
Skinner, Joel	90DL	286	$ .05	$ .25	Smith, Dave	86D	328	$ .01	$ .08
Skinner, Joel	91D	120	$ .01	$ .04	Smith, Dave	87D	308	$ .01	$ .05
Skinner, Joel	91DL	211	$ .01	$ .08	Smith, Dave	88D	410	$ .01	$ .04
Skinner, Joel	92D	99	$ .01	$ .04	Smith, Dave	89D	272	$ .01	$ .04
Skinner, Joel	92DL	181	$ .01	$ .06	Smith, Dave	90D	88	$ .01	$ .04
Slaton, Jim	81D	447	$ .01	$ .06	Smith, Dave	90DL	122	$ .05	$ .25
Slaton, Jim	82D	80	$ .01	$ .06	Smith, Dave	91D	212	$ .01	$ .04
Slaton, Jim	83D	330	$ .01	$ .06	Smith, Dave	91DL	456	$ .01	$ .08
Slaton, Jim	84D	481	$ .05	$ .20	Smith, Dave	91DLS	160	$ .01	$ .08
Slaton, Jim	85D	545	$ .01	$ .10	Smith, Dave	92D	53	$ .01	$ .04
Slaton, Jim	86D	402	$ .01	$ .08	Smith, Dave	92DL	30	$ .01	$ .06
Slaught, Don	83D	196	$ .10	$ .50	Smith, Dwight	89DR	32	$ .01	$ .05
Slaught, Don	84D	419	$ .05	$ .35	Smith, Dwight	90D	393	$ .01	$ .10
Slaught, Don	85D	496	$ .01	$ .10	Smith, Dwight	90DL	255	$ .05	$ .25
Slaught, Don	86D	281	$ .01	$ .08	Smith, Dwight	91D	559	$ .01	$ .04
Slaught, Don	87D	136	$ .01	$ .05	Smith, Dwight	92D	561	$ .01	$ .04
Slaught, Don	89D	190	$ .01	$ .04	Smith, Dwight	93D	476	$ .01	$ .05
Slaught, Don	90D	277	$ .01	$ .04	Smith, Greg	91D	574	$ .01	$ .04
Slaught, Don	90DL	354	$ .05	$ .25	Smith, Jimmy	83D	402	$ .01	$ .06
Slaught, Don	91D	213	$ .01	$ .04	Smith, Keith	81D	539	$ .01	$ .06
Slaught, Don	91DL	29	$ .01	$ .08	Smith, Lee	82D	252	$1.75	$7.00
Slaught, Don	91DLS	228	$ .01	$ .08	Smith, Lee	83D	403	$ .25	$2.50
Slaught, Don	92D	653	$ .01	$ .04	Smith, Lee	84D	289	$ .25	$2.50
Slaught, Don	92DL	124	$ .01	$ .06	Smith, Lee	85D	311	$ .10	$1.00
Slaught, Don	93D	438	$ .01	$ .05	Smith, Lee	86D	144	$ .10	$ .50
Slaught, Don	93DL	6	$ .01	$ .15	Smith, Lee	87D	292	$ .01	$ .15
Slocumb, Heath (cliff)	91DL	370	$ .01	$ .15	Smith, Lee	88D	292	$ .01	$ .10
Slocumb, Heathcliff	91DR	25	$ .01	$ .10	Smith, Lee	89D	66	$ .01	$ .04
Slocumb, Heathcliff	92D	334	$ .01	$ .10	Smith, Lee	90D	110	$ .01	$ .10
Slocumb, Heathcliff	93D	664	$ .01	$ .05	Smith, Lee	90DL	524	$ .10	$ .50
Slusarski, Joe	92D	626	$ .01	$ .04	Smith, Lee	91D	169	$ .01	$ .04
Slusarski, Joe	92DL	431	$ .01	$ .06	Smith, Lee	91DL	44	$ .01	$ .08
Smalley, Roy	81D	487	$ .01	$ .06	Smith, Lee	91DLS	237	$ .01	$ .08
Smalley, Roy	82D	573	$ .01	$ .06	Smith, Lee	91DMVP	403	$ .01	$ .03
Smalley, Roy	82DK	22	$ .01	$ .15	Smith, Lee	92D	112	$ .01	$ .04
Smalley, Roy	83D	209	$ .01	$ .06	Smith, Lee	92DL	254	$ .01	$ .06
Smalley, Roy	84D	225	$ .05	$ .20	Smith, Lee	92DLS	97	$ .01	$ .06
Smalley, Roy	85D	622	$ .01	$ .10	Smith, Lee	93D	548	$ .01	$ .05
Smalley, Roy	86D	486	$ .01	$ .08	Smith, Lee	93DL	154	$ .05	$ .20
Smalley, Roy	87D	443	$ .01	$ .05	Smith, Lonnie	81D	295	$ .05	$ .25
Smalley, Roy	88D	566	$ .01	$ .04	Smith, Lonnie	82D	606	$ .05	$ .25
Smiley, John	87DR	39	$ .10	$1.00	Smith, Lonnie	83D	91	$ .05	$ .20
Smiley, John	88D	449	$ .05	$ .35	Smith, Lonnie	84D	231	$ .05	$ .25
Smiley, John	89D	329	$ .01	$ .04	Smith, Lonnie	84D	625	$ .10	$1.00
Smiley, John	90D	54	$ .01	$ .10	Smith, Lonnie	85D	231	$ .01	$ .10
Smiley, John	90DK	17	$ .01	$ .05	Smith, Lonnie	86D	399	$ .01	$ .08
Smiley, John	90DL	328	$ .05	$ .25	Smith, Lonnie	87D	225	$ .01	$ .05
Smiley, John	91D	664	$ .01	$ .04	Smith, Lonnie	88D	527	$ .01	$ .04
Smiley, John	91DL	123	$ .01	$ .08	Smith, Lonnie	90D	222	$ .01	$ .04
Smiley, John	91DLS	229	$ .01	$ .08	Smith, Lonnie	90DL	217	$ .05	$ .25
Smiley, John	92D	331	$ .01	$ .04	Smith, Lonnie	91D	364	$ .01	$ .04
Smiley, John	92DL	526	$ .01	$ .06	Smith, Lonnie	91DL	13	$ .01	$ .08
Smiley, John	92DLS	210	$ .01	$ .06	Smith, Lonnie	92D	517	$ .01	$ .04
Smiley, John	93D	475	$ .01	$ .05	Smith, Lonnie	92DL	480	$ .01	$ .06
Smith, Dan	93D	374	$ .01	$ .10	Smith, Lonnie	93D	658	$ .01	$ .05
Smith, Bryn	83D	88	$ .05	$ .20	Smith, Ozzie	81D	1	$ .75	$3.00
Smith, Bryn	84D	453	$ .05	$ .20	Smith, Ozzie	82D	94	$ .20	$2.00
Smith, Bryn	85D	209	$ .01	$ .10	Smith, Ozzie	82DK	21	$ .10	$1.00
Smith, Bryn	86D	299	$ .01	$ .08	Smith, Ozzie	83D	120	$ .15	$1.50
Smith, Bryn	87D	159	$ .01	$ .05	Smith, Ozzie	84D	59	$1.25	$5.00
Smith, Bryn	88D	335	$ .01	$ .04	Smith, Ozzie	84D	625	$ .10	$1.00
Smith, Bryn	89D	216	$ .01	$ .04	Smith, Ozzie	85D	59	$ .15	$1.50
Smith, Bryn	90D	106	$ .01	$ .04	Smith, Ozzie	86D	59	$ .10	$ .75
Smith, Bryn	90DK	25	$ .01	$ .05	Smith, Ozzie	87D	60	$ .05	$ .35
Smith, Bryn	90DL	393	$ .05	$ .25	Smith, Ozzie	87DK	5	$ .05	$ .20
Smith, Bryn	91D	113	$ .01	$ .04	Smith, Ozzie	88D	263	$ .01	$ .15
Smith, Bryn	91DL	226	$ .01	$ .08	Smith, Ozzie	88DBC	22	$ .01	$ .10

DONRUSS

Player	Year	No.	VG	EX/MT	Player	Year	No.	VG	EX/MT
Smith, Ozzie	89D	63	$.01	$.15	Snyder, Cory	91DL	506	$.01	$.08
Smith, Ozzie	89DBC	14	$.01	$.10	Snyder, Cory	92DL	188	$.01	$.06
Smith, Ozzie	90D	201	$.01	$.10	Snyder, Cory	93D	656	$.01	$.05
Smith, Ozzie	90DAS	710	$.01	$.10	Soderholm, Eric	81D	106	$.01	$.06
Smith, Ozzie	90DL	142	$.10	$.75	Soff, Ray	87D	631	$.01	$.05
Smith, Ozzie	90DL	364	$.05	$.30	Sofield, Rick	81D	592	$.01	$.06
Smith, Ozzie	91D	240	$.01	$.10	Sojo, Luis	90DL	291	$.10	$.40
Smith, Ozzie	91DAS	437	$.01	$.10	Sojo, Luis	91D	579	$.01	$.04
Smith, Ozzie	91DL	80	$.05	$.25	Sojo, Luis	91DL	367	$.01	$.08
Smith, Ozzie	91DLS	238	$.05	$.20	Sojo, Luis	92D	302	$.01	$.04
Smith, Ozzie	92D	432	$.01	$.10	Sojo, Luis	92DL	5	$.01	$.06
Smith, Ozzie	92DAS	423	$.01	$.05	Sojo, Luis	93D	137	$.01	$.05
Smith, Ozzie	92DL	400	$.05	$.20	Solomon, Eddie	81D	16	$.01	$.06
Smith, Ozzie	92DLS	98	$.01	$.15	Solomon, Eddie	82D	437	$.01	$.06
Smith, Ozzie	93D	520	$.01	$.10	Sorensen, Lary	81D	325	$.01	$.06
Smith, Pete	88D	571	$.10	$.50	Sorensen, Lary	82D	246	$.01	$.06
Smith, Pete	88DR	10	$.10	$.75	Sorensen, Lary	83D	363	$.01	$.06
Smith, Pete	89D	263	$.01	$.04	Sorensen, Lary	84D	635	$.05	$.20
Smith, Pete	90D	499	$.01	$.04	Sorensen, Lary	85D	131	$.01	$.10
Smith, Pete	90DL	144	$.10	$.75	Sorrento, Paul	90D	626	$.05	$.25
Smith, Pete	93D	498	$.01	$.05	Sorrento, Paul	91D	745	$.01	$.04
Smith, Pete	93DL	214	$.05	$.25	Sorrento, Paul	92D	752	$.01	$.04
Smith, Reggie	81D	59	$.01	$.06	Sorrento, Paul	92DL	401	$.01	$.06
Smith, Reggie	82D	488	$.01	$.06	Sorrento, Paul	92DLS	169	$.01	$.06
Smith, Reggie	83D	611	$.01	$.06	Sorrento, Paul	93D	229	$.01	$.05
Smith, Roy	85D	611	$.01	$.10	Sorrento, Paul	93DL	105	$.05	$.20
Smith, Roy	86D	468	$.01	$.08	Sosa, Elias	81D	599	$.01	$.06
Smith, Roy	90D	273	$.01	$.04	Sosa, Elias	82D	446	$.01	$.06
Smith, Roy	90DL	400	$.05	$.25	Sosa, Elias	83D	259	$.01	$.06
Smith, Roy	91D	470	$.01	$.04	Sosa, Sammy	90D	489	$.05	$.25
Smith, Zane	86D	565	$.05	$.25	Sosa, Sammy	90DL	220	$.20	$2.00
Smith, Zane	87D	167	$.01	$.05	Sosa, Sammy	91D	147	$.01	$.10
Smith, Zane	88D	167	$.01	$.04	Sosa, Sammy	91DL	321	$.01	$.15
Smith, Zane	89D	499	$.01	$.04	Sosa, Sammy	91DLS	38	$.01	$.08
Smith, Zane	90D	460	$.01	$.04	Sosa, Sammy	92D	740	$.01	$.04
Smith, Zane	90DL	238	$.05	$.25	Sosa, Sammy	92DL	412	$.01	$.06
Smith, Zane	91D	532	$.01	$.04	Sosa, Sammy	92DLS	20	$.01	$.06
Smith, Zane	91DL	495	$.01	$.08	Sosa, Sammy	93D	186	$.01	$.05
Smith, Zane	92D	360	$.01	$.04	Sosa, Sammy	93DL	70	$.05	$.25
Smith, Zane	92DL	96	$.01	$.06	Soto, Mario	81D	63	$.05	$.20
Smith, Zane	93D	94	$.01	$.05	Soto, Mario	82D	103	$.01	$.06
Smith, Zane	93DL	152	$.01	$.15	Soto, Mario	83D	248	$.01	$.15
Smithson, Mike	84D	221	$.05	$.20	Soto, Mario	84D	428	$.05	$.20
Smithson, Mike	85D	316	$.01	$.10	Soto, Mario	85D	184	$.03	$.10
Smithson, Mike	86D	147	$.01	$.08	Soto, Mario	85DK	19	$.03	$.10
Smithson, Mike	87D	245	$.01	$.05	Soto, Mario	86D	184	$.01	$.08
Smithson, Mike	89D	628	$.01	$.04	Soto, Mario	87D	82	$.01	$.05
Smithson, Mike	90D	464	$.01	$.04	Spahn, Warren	89D	588	$.01	$.10
Smoltz, John	89D	642	$.10	$.50	Speck, Cliff	87D	571	$.01	$.05
Smoltz, John	90D	121	$.05	$.20	Spehr, Tim	92D	689	$.01	$.10
Smoltz, John	90DBC	12	$.05	$.35	Spehr, Tim	93D	15	$.01	$.05
Smoltz, John	90DK	8	$.01	$.15	Speier, Chris	81D	329	$.01	$.06
Smoltz, John	90DL	59	$1.25	$5.00	Speier, Chris	82D	366	$.01	$.06
Smoltz, John	91D	75	$.01	$.10	Speier, Chris	83D	266	$.01	$.06
Smoltz, John	91DL	27	$.05	$.35	Speier, Chris	84D	523	$.05	$.20
Smoltz, John	91DLS	149	$.05	$.35	Speier, Chris	87D	392	$.01	$.05
Smoltz, John	92D	442	$.01	$.10	Speier, Chris	88D	239	$.01	$.04
Smoltz, John	92DL	191	$.05	$.20	Speier, Chris	89D	532	$.01	$.04
Smoltz, John	92DLS	10	$.05	$.20	Spencer, Jim	81D	226	$.01	$.06
Smoltz, John	93D	130	$.01	$.10	Spencer, Jim	82D	265	$.01	$.06
Smoltz, John	93DL	104	$.05	$.25	Spiers, Bill	89DR	5	$.01	$.05
Snell, Nate	86D	367	$.01	$.08	Spiers, Bill	90D	382	$.01	$.10
Snell, Nate	87D	396	$.01	$.05	Spiers, Bill	90DL	203	$.05	$.25
Snider, Duke	84D	648	$.05	$.25	Spiers, Bill	91D	310	$.01	$.04
Snider, Van	89D	586	$.01	$.10	Spiers, Bill	91DL	111	$.01	$.08
Snow, J. T.	93D	110	10	$.50	Spiers, Bill	92D	364	$.01	$.04
Snyder, Cory	86DR	15	$.05	$.25	Spiers, Bill	92DL	106	$.01	$.06
Snyder, Cory	86DRR	29	$.10	$.50	Spillner, Dan	82D	411	$.01	$.06
Snyder, Cory	87D	526	$.01	$.15	Spillner, Dan	83D	137	$.01	$.06
Snyder, Cory	88D	350	$.01	$.10	Spillner, Dan	84D	582	$.05	$.20
Snyder, Cory	89D	191	$.01	$.10	Spillner, Dan	86D	122	$.01	$.04
Snyder, Cory	89DK	8	$.01	$.05	Spilman, Harry	81D	304	$.01	$.06
Snyder, Cory	90D	272	$.01	$.04	Spilman, Harry	83D	65	$.01	$.06
Snyder, Cory	90DL	187	$.05	$.25	Spilman, Harry	84D	258	$.05	$.20
Snyder, Cory	91D	288	$.01	$.04	Spilman, Harry	88D	607	$.01	$.10

DONRUSS

Player	Year	No.	VG	EX/MT
Splittorff, Paul	81D	342	$ .01	$ .06
Splittorff, Paul	82D	464	$ .01	$ .06
Splittorff, Paul	83D	286	$ .01	$ .06
Splittorff, Paul	84D	521	$ .05	$ .20
Sprague, Ed	91DL	485	$ .10	$ .40
Sprague, Ed	91DR	14	$ .05	$ .20
Sprague, Ed	92D	187	$ .01	$ .10
Sprague, Ed	93D	219	$ .01	$ .05
Springer, Russ	93D	285	$ .01	$ .10
Squires, Mike	81D	398	$ .01	$ .06
Squires, Mike	82D	39	$ .01	$ .06
Squires, Mike	83D	495	$ .01	$ .06
Squires, Mike	84D	404	$ .05	$ .20
Squires, Mike	85D	501	$ .01	$ .10
St. Claire, Randy	85D	575	$ .01	$ .10
St. Claire, Randy	86D	463	$ .01	$ .08
St. Claire, Randy	88D	426	$ .01	$ .04
Stairs, Matt	92DR	112	$ .01	$ .15
Stairs, Matt	93D	460	$ .01	$ .05
Stanhouse, Don	81D	557	$ .01	$ .06
Stanicek, Pete	88D	541	$ .01	$ .04
Stanicek, Pete	88DR	15	$ .01	$ .07
Stanicek, Pete	89D	169	$ .01	$ .04
Stankiewicz, Andy	92DL	470	$ .01	$ .06
Stankiewicz, Andy	93D	213	$ .01	$ .10
Stankiewicz, Andy	93DL	9	$ .01	$ .15
Stanley, Bob	81D	456	$ .01	$ .06
Stanley, Bob	82D	134	$ .01	$ .06
Stanley, Bob	83D	386	$ .01	$ .06
Stanley, Bob	84D	644	$ .05	$ .20
Stanley, Bob	85D	91	$ .01	$ .10
Stanley, Bob	86D	91	$ .01	$ .08
Stanley, Bob	87D	216	$ .01	$ .05
Stanley, Bob	88D	92	$ .01	$ .04
Stanley, Bob	89D	421	$ .01	$ .04
Stanley, Fred	81D	585	$ .01	$ .06
Stanley, Fred	82D	449	$ .01	$ .06
Stanley, Fred	83D	197	$ .01	$ .06
Stanley, Mike	87D	592	$ .01	$ .10
Stanley, Mike	87DR	28	$ .01	$ .07
Stanley, Mike	88D	259	$ .01	$ .04
Stanley, Mike	89D	166	$ .01	$ .04
Stanley, Mike	90D	579	$ .01	$ .04
Stanley, Mike	92D	582	$ .01	$ .04
Stanley, Mike	92DL	367	$ .01	$ .06
Stanley, Mike	93D	718	$ .01	$ .05
Stanley, Mike	93DL	184	$ .01	$ .15
Stanton, Mike	82D	285	$ .01	$ .06
Stanton, Mike	83D	433	$ .01	$ .06
Stanton, Mike	85D	562	$ .01	$ .10
Stanton, Mike	90D	508	$ .01	$ .15
Stanton, Mike	90DR	7	$ .01	$ .05
Stanton, Mike	91D	716	$ .01	$ .04
Stanton, Mike	91DL	491	$ .01	$ .08
Stanton, Mike	92D	780	$ .01	$ .04
Stanton, Mike	92DL	377	$ .01	$ .06
Stanton, Mike	93D	474	$ .01	$ .05
Stapleton, Dave	81D	544	$ .01	$ .15
Stapleton, Dave	82D	208	$ .01	$ .06
Stapleton, Dave	83D	200	$ .01	$ .06
Stapleton, Dave	84D	273	$ .05	$ .20
Stapleton, Dave	88D	521	$ .01	$ .04
Stapleton, Dave	88DR	4	$ .01	$ .07
Stargell, Willie	81D	12	$ .10	$ .75
Stargell, Willie	81D	132	$ .10	$ .75
Stargell, Willie	82D	639	$ .10	$ .50
Stargell, Willie	83D	610	$ .10	$ .50
Stargell, Willie	83DK	8	$ .05	$ .35
Stargell, Willie	91D	702	$ .01	$ .10
Stark, Matt	91D	747	$ .01	$ .15
Staton, Dave	93D	325	$ .01	$ .10
Staub, Rusty	82D	56	$ .01	$ .15
Staub, Rusty	83D	350	$ .01	$ .06
Staub, Rusty	84D	554	$ .05	$ .25
Staub, Rusty	84DK	6	$ .05	$ .25

Player	Year	No.	VG	EX/MT
Stearns, John	81D	35	$ .01	$ .06
Stearns, John	82D	434	$ .01	$ .06
Stearns, John	83D	380	$ .01	$ .06
Steels, James	87DR	50	$ .01	$ .07

Player	Year	No.	VG	EX/MT
Steels, James	88D	360	$ .01	$ .04
Stefero, John	84D	622	$ .05	$ .20
Stefero, John	87D	541	$ .01	$ .05
Stein, Bill	81D	543	$ .01	$ .06
Stein, Bill	82D	37	$ .01	$ .06
Stein, Bill	83D	594	$ .01	$ .06
Stein, Bill	85D	621	$ .01	$ .10
Stein, Bill	86D	403	$ .01	$ .08
Steinbach, Terry	87DR	26	$ .05	$ .20
Steinbach, Terry	87DRR	34	$ .05	$ .35
Steinbach, Terry	88D	158	$ .05	$ .20
Steinbach, Terry	89D	267	$ .01	$ .04
Steinbach, Terry	90D	268	$ .01	$ .10
Steinbach, Terry	90DL	252	$ .05	$ .25
Steinbach, Terry	90DAS	637	$ .01	$ .10
Steinbach, Terry	91D	329	$ .01	$ .04
Steinbach, Terry	91DL	87	$ .01	$ .08
Steinbach, Terry	92D	104	$ .01	$ .04
Steinbach, Terry	92DL	501	$ .01	$ .06
Steinbach, Terry	92DLC	220	$ .01	$ .06
Steinbach, Terry	93D	505	$ .01	$ .05
Steinbach, Terry	93DL	7	$ .01	$ .15
Stenhouse, Mike	84DRR	29	$ .05	$ .25
Stenhouse, Mike	85D	376	$ .01	$ .10
Stennett, Rennie	81D	72	$ .01	$ .06
Stennett, Rennie	82D	563	$ .01	$ .06
Stephans, Russ	85DRR	42	$ .01	$ .15
Stephens, Ray	92D	764	$ .01	$ .04
Stephenson, Phil	89DR	36	$ .01	$ .05
Stevens, Lee	90D	449	$ .01	$ .15
Stevens, Lee	91D	754	$ .01	$ .04
Stevens, Lee	92D	460	$ .01	$ .10
Stevens, Lee	92DL	361	$ .01	$ .06
Stevens, Lee	92DLS	150	$ .01	$ .06
Stevens, Lee	93D	65	$ .01	$ .05
Stewart, Dave	82D	410	$ .75	$3.00
Stewart, Dave	83D	588	$ .10	$ .75
Stewart, Dave	84D	343	$ .15	$1.25

DONRUSS

Player	Year	No.	VG	EX/MT
Stewart, Dave	85D	343	$ .05	$ .35
Stewart, Dave	86D	619	$ .05	$ .20
Stewart, Dave	87D	648	$ .05	$ .20
Stewart, Dave	88D	472	$ .01	$ .15
Stewart, Dave	89D	214	$ .01	$ .04
Stewart, Dave	90D	150	$ .01	$ .10
Stewart, Dave	90DAS	703	$ .01	$ .10
Stewart, Dave	90DBC	3	$ .01	$ .10
Stewart, Dave	90DK	6	$ .01	$ .05
Stewart, Dave	90DL	81	$ .05	$ .25
Stewart, Dave	91D	102	$ .01	$ .04
Stewart, Dave	91DBC	4	$ .01	$ .03
Stewart, Dave	91DL	417	$ .01	$ .08
Stewart, Dave	91DLS	107	$ .01	$ .08
Stewart, Dave	92D	225	$ .01	$ .04
Stewart, Dave	92DL	258	$ .01	$ .06
Stewart, Dave	92DLS	230	$ .01	$ .06
Stewart, Dave	93D	611	$ .01	$ .05
Stewart, Sammy	81D	474	$ .01	$ .06
Stewart, Sammy	82D	457	$ .01	$ .06
Stewart, Sammy	83D	203	$ .01	$ .06
Stewart, Sammy	84D	514	$ .05	$ .20
Stewart, Sammy	85D	148	$ .01	$ .10
Stewart, Sammy	86D	270	$ .01	$ .08
Stewart, Sammy	87D	658	$ .01	$ .05
Stewart, Sammy	88D	596	$ .01	$ .04
Stieb, Dave	81D	582	$ .10	$ .50
Stieb, Dave	82D	52	$ .05	$ .30
Stieb, Dave	83D	507	$ .05	$ .25
Stieb, Dave	83DK	9	$ .01	$ .15
Stieb, Dave	84D	71	$ .10	$ .50
Stieb, Dave	85D	193	$ .05	$ .20
Stieb, Dave	86D	146	$ .05	$ .20
Stieb, Dave	87D	195	$ .01	$ .15
Stieb, Dave	88D	148	$ .01	$ .04
Stieb, Dave	89D	349	$ .01	$ .04
Stieb, Dave	90D	87	$ .01	$ .04
Stieb, Dave	90DL	79	$ .05	$ .25
Stieb, Dave	91D	551	$ .01	$ .04
Stieb, Dave	91DBC	21	$ .01	$ .03
Stieb, Dave	91DK	1	$ .01	$ .05
Stieb, Dave	91DL	96	$ .01	$ .08
Stieb, Dave	91DLP	26	$ .10	$1.00
Stieb, Dave	91DLS	137	$ .01	$ .08
Stieb, Dave	92D	724	$ .01	$ .04
Stieb, Dave	92DL	291	$ .01	$ .06
Stieb, Dave	93D	708	$ .01	$ .05
Stillwell, Kurt	87D	123	$ .05	$ .25
Stillwell, Kurt	88D	265	$ .01	$ .10
Stillwell, Kurt	89D	322	$ .01	$ .04
Stillwell, Kurt	90D	120	$ .01	$ .04
Stillwell, Kurt	90DL	256	$ .05	$ .25
Stillwell, Kurt	91D	520	$ .01	$ .04
Stillwell, Kurt	91DK	24	$ .01	$ .05
Stillwell, Kurt	91DL	2	$ .01	$ .08
Stillwell, Kurt	91DLS	70	$ .01	$ .08
Stillwell, Kurt	92D	440	$ .01	$ .04
Stillwell, Kurt	92DL	142	$ .01	$ .06
Stillwell, Kurt	92DLS	109	$ .01	$ .06
Stillwell, Kurt	93D	258	$ .01	$ .05
Stillwell, Kurt	93DL	138	$ .01	$ .15
Stoddard, Bob	84D	619	$ .05	$ .20
Stoddard, Tim	81D	475	$ .01	$ .06
Stoddard, Tim	82D	131	$ .01	$ .06
Stoddard, Tim	83D	581	$ .01	$ .06
Stoddard, Tim	84D	245	$ .05	$ .20
Stoddard, Tim	85D	144	$ .01	$ .10
Stoddard, Tim	86D	406	$ .01	$ .08
Stoddard, Tim	87D	497	$ .01	$ .05
Stoddard, Tim	88D	497	$ .01	$ .04
Stone, Jeff	85D	624	$ .05	$ .20
Stone, Jeff	86D	259	$ .01	$ .08
Stone, Jeff	87D	309	$ .01	$ .05
Stone, Jeff	88D	482	$ .01	$ .04
Stone, Steve	81D	476	$ .01	$ .06

Player	Year	No.	VG	EX/MT
Stone, Steve	81D	591	$ .01	$ .15
Stone, Steve	82D	357	$ .01	$ .06
Stottlemyre, Mel	90DL	310	$ .05	$ .25
Stottlemyre, Mel	91D	257	$ .01	$ .10
Stottlemyre, Todd	88D	658	$ .10	$ .40
Stottlemyre, Todd	88DR	37	$ .10	$ .40
Stottlemyre, Todd	89D	620	$ .01	$ .10
Stottlemyre, Todd	90D	669	$ .01	$ .04
Stottlemyre, Todd	90DL	475	$ .10	$ .40
Stottlemyre, Todd	91D	155	$ .01	$ .04
Stottlemyre, Todd	91DL	227	$ .01	$ .08
Stottlemyre, Todd	92D	263	$ .01	$ .04
Stottlemyre, Todd	92DL	167	$ .01	$ .06
Stottlemyre, Todd	93D	585	$ .01	$ .05
Stottlemyre, Todd	93DL	25	$ .01	$ .15
Strain, Joe	81D	73	$ .01	$ .06
Straker, Les	87DR	21	$ .01	$ .07
Straker, Les	88D	73	$ .01	$ .04
Strange, Doug	90D	535	$ .01	$ .10
Strange, Doug	92DL	476	$ .01	$ .06
Strange, Doug	93D	136	$ .01	$ .05
Strawberry, Darryl	84D	68	$10.00	$40.00
Strawberry, Darryl	85D	312	$1.75	$7.00
Strawberry, Darryl	86D	197	$ .20	$2.00
Strawberry, Darryl	87D	118	$ .10	$ .75
Strawberry, Darryl	87DK	4	$ .10	$ .50
Strawberry, Darryl	88D	439	$ .05	$ .25
Strawberry, Darryl	88DBC	20	$ .05	$ .20
Strawberry, Darryl	89D	147	$ .05	$ .25
Strawberry, Darryl	89DBC	6	$ .01	$ .15

Player	Year	No.	VG	EX/MT
Strawberry, Darryl	90D	235	$ .05	$ .20
Strawberry, Darryl	90D	250	$ .20	$2.00
Strawberry, Darryl	91D	696	$ .01	$ .15
Strawberry, Darryl	91DL	377	$ .05	$ .35
Strawberry, Darryl	91DL	444	$ .01	$ .15
Strawberry, Darryl	91DLS	190	$ .05	$ .35
Strawberry, Darryl	91DMVP	408	$ .01	$ .10
Strawberry, Darryl	92D	559	$ .01	$ .10
Strawberry, Darryl	92DL	29	$ .05	$ .20
Strawberry, Darryl	92DLS	50	$ .05	$ .25
Strawberry, Darryl	93D	112	$ .01	$ .10
Strawberry, Darryl	93DL	210	$ .05	$ .25
Stubbs, Franklin	85D	348	$ .05	$ .35

DONRUSS

Player	Year	No.	VG	EX/MT	Player	Year	No.	VG	EX/MT
Stubbs, Franklin	86D	592	$ .05	$ .20	Sutton, Don	85D	107	$ .05	$ .30
Stubbs, Franklin	87D	299	$ .01	$ .05	Sutton, Don	85DK	16	$ .05	$ .25
Stubbs, Franklin	88D	218	$ .01	$ .04	Sutton, Don	86D	611	$ .05	$ .25
Stubbs, Franklin	89D	321	$ .01	$ .04	Sutton, Don	87D	181	$ .05	$ .20
Stubbs, Franklin	90D	615	$ .01	$ .04	Sutton, Don	88D	407	$ .01	$ .15
Stubbs, Franklin	90DL	425	$ .05	$ .25	Sveum, Dale	86DR	37	$ .10	$ .10
Stubbs, Franklin	91D	99	$ .01	$ .04	Sveum, Dale	87D	542	$ .01	$ .05
Stubbs, Franklin	91DL	277	$ .01	$ .08	Sveum, Dale	88D	232	$ .01	$ .04
Stubbs, Franklin	91DLS	77	$ .01	$ .08	Sveum, Dale	89D	146	$ .01	$ .04
Stubbs, Franklin	92D	618	$ .01	$ .04	Sveum, Dale	92D	452	$ .01	$ .04
Stubbs, Franklin	92DL	328	$ .01	$ .06	Sveum, Dale	92DL	473	$ .01	$ .06
Stubbs, Franklin	92DLS	196	$ .01	$ .06	Swaggerty, Bill	85D	392	$ .01	$ .10
Stubbs, Franklin	93D	177	$ .01	$ .05	Swaggerty, Bill	86D	594	$ .01	$ .08
Stuper, John	83D	621	$ .01	$ .06	Swan, Craig	81D	155	$ .01	$ .06
Stuper, John	84D	412	$ .05	$ .20	Swan, Craig	82D	589	$ .01	$ .06
Suero, William	92DL	475	$ .01	$ .06	Swan, Craig	83D	254	$ .01	$ .06
Suero, William	92DR	113	$ .01	$ .05	Swan, Craig	84D	441	$ .05	$ .20
Sularz, Guy	83D	605	$ .01	$ .06	Swan, Russ	91D	621	$ .01	$ .04
Sullivan, Marc	86D	614	$ .01	$ .08	Swan, Russ	92D	382	$ .01	$ .04
Sullivan, Marc	87D	643	$ .01	$ .05	Swan , Russ	92DL	203	$ .01	$ .06
Summers, Champ	81D	130	$ .01	$ .06	Swan, Russ	93D	713	$ .01	$ .05
Summers, Champ	82D	81	$ .01	$ .06	Sweet, Rick	83D	352	$ .01	$ .06
Sundberg, Jim	81D	385	$ .01	$ .06	Sweet, Rick	84D	196	$ .05	$ .20
Sundberg, Jim	82D	268	$ .01	$ .06	Swift, Billy	86D	562	$ .10	$ .40
Sundberg, Jim	83D	609	$ .01	$ .06	Swift, Bill	87D	517	$ .05	$ .20
Sundberg, Jim	83DK	7	$ .01	$ .15	Swift, Billy	90D	566	$ .05	$ .20
Sundberg, Jim	84D	178	$ .05	$ .20	Swift, Bill	91D	564	$ .05	$ .20
Sundberg, Jim	85D	89	$ .01	$ .10	Swift, Bill	91DL	380	$ .05	$ .25
Sundberg, Jim	86D	277	$ .01	$ .08	Swift, Billy	92D	260	$ .01	$ .10
Sundberg, Jim	87D	280	$ .01	$ .05	Swift, Bill	92DL	407	$ .01	$ .06
Sundberg, Jim	88D	488	$ .01	$ .04	Swift, Bill	92DLS	118	$ .01	$ .06
Surhoff, B.J.	87DR	17	$ .05	$ .20	Swift, Bill	93D	232	$ .01	$ .05
Surhoff, B.J.	87DRR	28	$ .05	$ .25	Swift, Bill	93DK	5	$ .15	$1.50
Surhoff, B.J.	88D	172	$ .01	$ .15	Swift, Bill	93DL	194	$ .01	$ .15
Surhoff, B.J.	89D	221	$ .01	$ .04	Swindell, Greg	87DRR	32	$ .10	$1.00
Surhoff, B.J.	90D	173	$ .01	$ .04	Swindell, Greg	88D	227	$ .01	$ .15
Surhoff, B.J.	90DL	290	$ .05	$ .25	Swindell, Greg	89D	232	$ .01	$ .10
Surhoff, B.J.	91D	460	$ .01	$ .04	Swindell, Greg	90D	310	$ .01	$ .10
Surhoff, B.J.	91DL	42	$ .01	$ .08	Swindell, Greg	90DBC	24	$ .01	$ .10
Surhoff, B.J.	91DLS	78	$ .01	$ .08	Swindell, Greg	90DL	206	$ .10	$ .40
Surhoff, B.J.	92D	70	$ .01	$ .04	Swindell, Greg	91D	546	$ .01	$ .04
Surhoff, B. J.	92DL	212	$ .01	$ .06	Swindell, Greg	91DLS	49	$ .01	$ .08
Surhoff, B. J.	92DLS	197	$ .01	$ .06	Swindell, Greg	92D	483	$ .01	$ .04
Surhoff, B. J.	93D	545	$ .01	$ .05	Swindell, Greg	92DK	23	$ .10	$1.00
Surhoff, B. J.	93DL	166	$ .01	$ .15	Swindell, Greg	92DK	23	$ .10	$1.00
Surhoff, Rick	86DRR	42	$ .01	$ .10	Swindell, Greg	92DL	384	$ .01	$ .06
Sutcliffe, Rick	81D	418	$ .05	$ .25	Swindell, Greg	92DLS	30	$ .01	$ .06
Sutcliffe, Rick	83D	72	$ .05	$ .20	Swindell, Greg	93D	634	$ .01	$ .05
Sutcliffe, Rick	84D	338	$ .05	$ .25	Swindell, Scott	91DL	6	$ .01	$ .08
Sutcliffe, Rick	85D	433	$ .03	$ .10	Swisher, Steve	83D	633	$ .01	$ .06
Sutcliffe, Rick	86D	189	$ .05	$ .20	Sykes, Bob	82D	640	$ .01	$ .06
Sutcliffe, Rick	87D	68	$ .01	$ .05	Tabler, Pat	82D	529	$ .05	$ .20
Sutcliffe, Rick	88D	68	$ .01	$ .04	Tabler, Pat	83D	552	$ .01	$ .06
Sutcliffe, Rick	89D	223	$ .01	$ .04	Tabler, Pat	84D	536	$ .05	$ .20
Sutcliffe, Rick	90D	157	$ .01	$ .04	Tabler, Pat	85D	460	$ .01	$ .10
Sutcliffe, Rick	90DL	6	$ .05	$ .25	Tabler, Pat	86D	129	$ .01	$ .08
Sutcliffe, Rick	91D	462	$ .01	$ .04	Tabler, Pat	87D	254	$ .01	$ .06
Sutcliffe, Rick	92D	642	$ .01	$ .04	Tabler, Pat	88D	219	$ .01	$ .04
Sutcliffe, Rick	92DL	508	$ .01	$ .06	Tabler, Pat	89D	326	$ .01	$ .04
Sutcliffe, Rick	92DLS	130	$ .01	$ .06	Tabler, Pat	90D	444	$ .01	$ .04
Sutcliffe, Rick	93D	719	$ .01	$ .05	Tabler, Pat	91DL	443	$ .01	$ .08
Sutcliffe, Rick	93DL	89	$ .01	$ .15	Tackett, Jeff	92DL	411	$ .01	$ .06
Sutherland, Leo	81D	42	$ .01	$ .06	Tackett, Jeff	92DR	114	$ .01	$ .05
Sutter, Bruce	81D	560	$ .05	$ .20	Tackett, Jeff	93D	529	$ .01	$ .05
Sutter, Bruce	82D	372	$ .05	$ .20	Tamargo, John	81D	210	$ .01	$ .06
Sutter, Bruce	83D	40	$ .05	$ .15	Tanana, Frank	81D	171	$ .05	$ .20
Sutter, Bruce	84D	534	$ .05	$ .35	Tanana, Frank	82D	326	$ .01	$ .06
Sutter, Bruce	84DK	13	$ .05	$ .25	Tanana, Frank	83D	447	$ .01	$ .06
Sutter, Bruce	85D	109	$ .05	$ .20	Tanana, Frank	84D	98	$ .05	$ .20
Sutter, Bruce	86D	321	$ .01	$ .08	Tanana, Frank	85D	220	$ .01	$ .10
Sutter, Bruce	89D	458	$ .01	$ .04	Tanana, Frank	85DK	9	$ .03	$ .10
Sutton, Don	81D	58	$ .10	$ .50	Tanana, Frank	86D	491	$ .01	$ .08
Sutton, Don	82D	443	$ .10	$ .40	Tanana, Frank	87D	152	$ .01	$ .05
Sutton, Don	83D	531	$ .05	$ .35	Tanana, Frank	88D	461	$ .01	$ .04
Sutton, Don	84D	414	$ .10	$1.00	Tanana, Frank	89D	90	$ .01	$ .04

DONRUSS

Player	Year	No.	VG	EX/MT	Player	Year	No.	VG	EX/MT
Tanana, Frank	90D	180	$ .01	$ .04	Tenace, Gene	82D	152	$ .01	$ .06
Tanana, Frank	90DL	87	$ .05	$ .25	Tenace, Gene	83D	442	$ .01	$ .06
Tanana, Frank	91D	508	$ .01	$ .04	Tenace, Gene	84D	264	$ .05	$ .20
Tanana, Frank	91DL	497	$ .01	$ .08	Terrell, Walt	84D	640	$ .05	$ .35
Tanana, Frank	91DLS	57	$ .01	$ .08	Terrell, Walt	85D	597	$ .01	$ .10
Tanana, Frank	92D	111	$ .01	$ .04	Terrell, Walt	86D	247	$ .01	$ .08
Tanana, Frank	92DL	21	$ .01	$ .06	Terrell, Walt	87D	275	$ .01	$ .05
Tanana, Frank	92DLS	177	$ .01	$ .06	Terrell, Walt	88D	91	$ .01	$ .04
Tanana, Frank	93D	599	$ .01	$ .05	Terrell, Walt	89D	296	$ .01	$ .04
Tanner, Chuck	81D	257	$ .01	$ .06	Terrell, Walt	89DTR	28	$ .01	$ .05
Tanner, Chuck	82D	150	$ .01	$ .06	Terrell, Walt	90D	309	$ .01	$ .04
Tanner, Chuck	83D	124	$ .01	$ .06	Terrell, Walt	91D	717	$ .01	$ .04
Tapani, Kevin	90D	473	$ .05	$ .35	Terrell, Walt	92D	565	$ .01	$ .04
Tapani, Kevin	90DL	269	$ .20	$2.00	Terrell, Walt	93D	772	$ .01	$ .05
Tapani, Kevin	90DR	35	$ .05	$ .35	Terry, Scott	88D	647	$ .01	$ .15
Tapani, Kevin	91D	116	$ .01	$ .10	Terry, Scott	89D	397	$ .01	$ .04
Tapani, Kevin	91DL	128	$ .05	$ .20	Terry, Scott	90D	418	$ .01	$ .04
Tapani, Kevin	92D	236	$ .01	$ .10	Terry, Scott	90DL	234	$ .05	$ .25
Tapani, Kevin	92DL	14	$ .01	$ .06	Terry, Scott	92D	655	$ .01	$ .04
Tapani, Kevin	93D	443	$ .01	$ .05	Tettleton, Mickey	86D	345	$ .20	$2.00
Tartabull, Danny	85DRR	27	$2.25	$9.00	Tettleton, Mickey	87D	349	$ .05	$ .20
Tartabull, Danny	86DR	45	$ .20	$1.75	Tettleton, Mickey	88D	103	$ .01	$ .15
Tartabull, Danny	86DRR	38	$ .15	$1.50	Tettleton, Mickey	89D	401	$ .01	$ .04
Tartabull, Danny	87D	147	$ .05	$ .35	Tettleton, Mickey	90D	169	$ .01	$ .10
Tartabull, Danny	88D	177	$ .01	$ .15	Tettleton, Mickey	90DK	5	$ .01	$ .05
Tartabull, Danny	88DK	5	$ .01	$ .15	Tettleton, Mickey	90DL	65	$ .05	$ .25
Tartabull, Danny	89D	61	$ .01	$ .10	Tettleton, Mickey	91D	597	$ .01	$ .04
Tartabull, Danny	90D	322	$ .01	$ .10	Tettleton, Mickey	91DL	322	$ .01	$ .08
Tartabull, Danny	90DL	99	$ .10	$ .50	Tettleton, Mickey	91DLS	58	$ .01	$ .08
Tartabull, Danny	91D	463	$ .01	$ .04	Tettleton, Mickey	92D	85	$ .01	$ .04
Tartabull, Danny	91DL	147	$ .01	$ .15	Tettleton, Mickey	92DL	285	$ .01	$ .06
Tartabull, Danny	92D	676	$ .01	$ .04	Tettleton, Mickey	92DLS	178	$ .01	$ .06
Tartabull, Danny	92DAS	26	$ .01	$ .05	Tettleton, Mickey	93D	13	$ .01	$ .05
Tartabull, Danny	92DL	406	$ .01	$ .15	Tettleton, Mickey	93DL	213	$ .01	$ .15
Tartabull, Danny	92DLS	220	$ .01	$ .06	Teufel, Tim	84DRR	37	$ .05	$ .35
Tartabull, Danny	93D	549	$ .01	$ .05	Teufel, Tim	85D	192	$ .01	$ .10
Tartabull, Danny	93DL	119	$ .01	$ .15	Teufel, Tim	86D	242	$ .01	$ .08
Tatum, Jim	93D	341	$ .01	$ .15	Teufel, Tim	87D	581	$ .01	$ .05
Taubensee, Eddie	92DLS	40	$ .05	$ .20	Teufel, Tim	88D	648	$ .01	$ .15
Taubensee, Eddie	92DR	115	$ .01	$ .05	Teufel, Tim	89D	507	$ .01	$ .04
Taubensee, Eddie	92DRR	18	$ .05	$ .20	Teufel, Tim	90D	618	$ .01	$ .04
Taubensee, Eddie	93D	560	$ .01	$ .05	Teufel, Tim	90DL	383	$ .05	$ .25
Taveras, Frank	81D	154	$ .01	$ .06	Teufel, Tim	91D	370	$ .01	$ .04
Taveras, Frank	82D	98	$ .01	$ .06	Teufel, Tim	91DL	314	$ .01	$ .08
Taylor, Scott	93D	267	$ .01	$ .10	Teufel, Tim	92D	171	$ .01	$ .04
Taylor, Wade	91DLBC	16	$ .10	$1.00	Teufel, Tim	92DL	261	$ .01	$ .06
Taylor, Wade	91DR	34	$ .01	$ .10	Teufel, Tim	92DLS	110	$ .01	$ .06
Taylor, Wade	92D	527	$ .01	$ .04	Teufel, Tim	93D	98	$ .01	$ .05
Tejada, Wilfredo	87D	529	$ .01	$ .05	Teufel, Tim	93DL	10	$ .01	$ .15
Tekulve, Kent	81D	254	$ .01	$ .06	Tewksbury, Bob	86DR	8	$ .10	$ .75
Tekulve, Kent	82D	311	$ .01	$ .06	Tewksbury, Bob	87D	422	$ .10	$ .50
Tekulve, Kent	83D	297	$ .01	$ .06	Tewksbury, Bob	90D	714	$ .01	$ .04
Tekulve, Kent	84D	410	$ .05	$ .20	Tewksbury, Bob	90DL	406	$ .05	$ .25
Tekulve, Kent	85D	479	$ .01	$ .10	Tewksbury, Bob	91D	183	$ .01	$ .04
Tekulve, Kent	86D	111	$ .01	$ .08	Tewksbury, Bob	91DL	460	$ .01	$ .08
Tekulve, Kent	87D	453	$ .01	$ .05	Tewksbury, Bob	92D	201	$ .01	$ .04
Tekulve, Kent	88D	535	$ .01	$ .04	Tewksbury, Bob	92DL	95	$ .01	$ .06
Telford, Anthony	91D	501	$ .01	$ .10	Tewksbury, Bob	93D	204	$ .01	$ .05
Telford, Anthony	92D	623	$ .01	$ .04	Tewksbury, Bob	93DK	22	$ .15	$1.50
Telford, Anthony	93D	789	$ .01	$ .05	Tewksbury, Bob	93DL	44	$ .01	$ .15
Tellmann, Tom	84D	149	$ .05	$ .20	Thigpen, Bobby	87D	370	$ .10	$ .50
Tellmann, Tom	85D	246	$ .01	$ .10	Thigpen, Bobby	88D	247	$ .01	$ .15
Templeton, Garry	81D	187	$ .01	$ .06	Thigpen, Bobby	89D	266	$ .01	$ .10
Templeton, Garry	82D	545	$ .01	$ .06	Thigpen, Bobby	90D	266	$ .01	$ .04
Templeton, Garry	83D	145	$ .01	$ .06	Thigpen, Bobby	90DL	175	$ .05	$ .25
Templeton, Garry	84D	185	$ .05	$ .20	Thigpen, Bobby	91D	90	$ .01	$ .04
Templeton, Garry	85D	356	$ .01	$ .10	Thigpen, Bobby	91DBC	20	$ .01	$ .03
Templeton, Garry	86D	202	$ .01	$ .08	Thigpen, Bobby	91DK	8	$ .01	$ .05
Templeton, Garry	87D	141	$ .01	$ .05	Thigpen, Bobby	91DL	336	$ .01	$ .08
Templeton, Garry	88D	649	$ .01	$ .04	Thigpen, Bobby	91DLS	39	$ .01	$ .08
Templeton, Garry	89D	483	$ .01	$ .04	Thigpen, Bobby	91DMVP	399	$ .01	$ .03
Templeton, Garry	90D	246	$ .01	$ .04	Thigpen, Bobby	92D	708	$ .01	$ .04
Templeton, Garry	90DL	102	$ .05	$ .25	Thigpen, Bobby	92DL	210	$ .01	$ .06
Templeton, Garry	91D	252	$ .01	$ .04	Thigpen, Bobby	92DLS	158	$ .01	$ .06
Tenace, Gene	81D	241	$ .01	$ .06	Thigpen, Bobby	93D	67	$ .01	$ .05

DONRUSS

Player	Year	No.	VG	EX/MT	Player	Year	No.	VG	EX/MT
Thigpen, Bobby	93DL	30	$ .01	$ .15	Thon, Dickie	91D	91	$ .01	$ .04
Thigpen, Bobby	93DL	173	$ .01	$ .15	Thon, Dickie	91DL	60	$ .01	$ .08
Thomas, Andres	86DR	10	$ .05	$ .20	Thon, Dickie	92D	510	$ .01	$ .04
Thomas, Andres	87D	266	$ .05	$ .20	Thon, Dickie	92DL	180	$ .01	$ .06
Thomas, Andres	88D	627	$ .01	$ .15	Thon, Dickie	92DLS	250	$ .01	$ .06
Thomas, Andres	89D	576	$ .01	$ .04	Thornton, Andre	81D	198	$ .01	$ .06
Thomas, Andres	90D	263	$ .01	$ .04	Thornton, Andre	82D	324	$ .01	$ .06
Thomas, Andres	90DL	33	$ .05	$ .25	Thornton, Andre	83D	211	$ .01	$ .06
Thomas, Andres	91D	491	$ .01	$ .04	Thornton, Andre	84DK	25	$ .05	$ .25
Thomas, Derrel	81D	419	$ .01	$ .06	Thornton, Andre	85D	468	$ .01	$ .10
Thomas, Derrel	82D	537	$ .01	$ .06	Thornton, Andre	86D	251	$ .01	$ .08
Thomas, Derrel	84D	397	$ .05	$ .20	Thornton, Andre	87D	279	$ .01	$ .05
Thomas, Frank	90DL	300	$15.00	$60.00	Thornton, Andy	84D	94	$ .05	$ .20
Thomas, Frank	91D	477	$ .10	$1.00	Thurman, Gary	88DR	33	$ .01	$ .15
Thomas, Frank	91DL	281	$1.50	$6.00	Thurman, Gary	88DRR	44	$ .01	$ .15
Thomas, Frank	91DLS	40	$1.50	$6.00	Thurman, Gary	89D	498	$ .01	$ .10
Thomas, Frank	92D	592	$ .10	$1.00	Thurman, Gary	90D	416	$ .01	$ .04
Thomas, Frank	92DK	8	$2.50	$110.00	Thurman, Gary	92D	346	$ .01	$ .04
Thomas, Frank	92DL	349	$ .75	$3.00	Thurman, Gary	93D	629	$ .01	$ .05
Thomas, Frank	92DLS	159	$ .75	$3.00	Thurmond, Mark	84D	505	$ .05	$ .20
Thomas, Frank	93D	7	$ .05	$ .35	Thurmond, Mark	85D	284	$ .01	$ .10
Thomas, Frank	93DL	195	$1.25	$5.00	Thurmond, Mark	86D	261	$ .01	$ .08
Thomas, Gorman	81D	326	$ .01	$ .06	Thurmond, Mark	87D	543	$ .01	$ .05
Thomas, Gorman	82D	132	$ .01	$ .06	Thurmond, Mark	88D	599	$ .01	$ .04
Thomas, Gorman	82DK	26	$ .01	$ .15	Thurmond, Mark	90D	612	$ .01	$ .04
Thomas, Gorman	83D	510	$ .01	$ .06	Tiant, Luis	81D	231	$ .05	$ .20
Thomas, Gorman	84D	574	$ .05	$ .20	Tiant, Luis	83D	542	$ .01	$ .06
Thomas, Gorman	86D	440	$ .01	$ .08	Tibbs, Jay	85D	262	$ .01	$ .10
Thomasson, Gary	81D	534	$ .01	$ .06	Tibbs, Jay	86D	262	$ .01	$ .08
Thome, Jim	92DL	299	$ .05	$ .20	Tibbs, Jay	87D	282	$ .01	$ .05
Thome, Jim	92DRR	406	$ .01	$ .10	Tidrow, Dick	81D	551	$ .01	$ .06
Thome, Jim	93D	171	$ .01	$ .05	Tidrow, Dick	82D	477	$ .01	$ .06
Thompson, Jason	81D	293	$ .01	$ .06	Timlin, Mike	91DL	525	$ .05	$ .25
Thompson, Jason	82D	502	$ .01	$ .06	Timlin, Mike	91DR	27	$ .01	$ .10
Thompson, Jason	83D	95	$ .01	$ .06					
Thompson, Jason	84D	64	$ .05	$ .20					
Thompson, Jason	85D	322	$ .01	$ .10					
Thompson, Jason	86D	322	$ .01	$ .08					
Thompson, Milt	86D	507	$ .05	$ .20					
Thompson, Milt	87D	330	$ .01	$ .05					
Thompson, Milt	88D	236	$ .01	$ .15					
Thompson, Milt	89D	313	$ .01	$ .04					
Thompson, Milt	89DTR	43	$ .01	$ .05					
Thompson, Milt	90D	82	$ .01	$ .04					
Thompson, Milt	90DL	308	$ .05	$ .35					
Thompson, Milt	91D	225	$ .01	$ .04					
Thompson, Milt	91DL	176	$ .01	$ .08					
Thompson, Milt	91DLS	239	$ .01	$ .08					
Thompson, Milt	92D	513	$ .01	$ .04					
Thompson, Milt	92DL	150	$ .01	$ .06					
Thompson, Milt	93D	775	$ .01	$ .05					
Thompson, Rob	86DR	39	$ .05	$ .35					
Thompson, Rob	87D	145	$ .05	$ .25					
Thompson, Rob	88D	268	$ .01	$ .04					
Thompson, Rob	89D	98	$ .01	$ .04					
Thompson, Robby	90D	140	$ .01	$ .04					
Thompson, Robby	90DL	199	$ .05	$ .25					
Thompson, Robby	91D	363	$ .01	$ .04					
Thompson, Robby	91DL	107	$ .01	$ .08					
Thompson, Robby	92D	52	$ .01	$ .04					
Thompson, Robby	92DL	109	$ .01	$ .06					
Thompson, Robby	92DLS	119	$ .01	$ .06					
Thompson, Robby	93D	524	$ .01	$ .05					
Thompson, Ryan	93D	242	$ .05	$ .20					
Thompson, Scot	81D	519	$ .01	$ .06					
Thompson, Scot	83D	378	$ .01	$ .06					
Thompson, Scot	84D	167	$ .05	$ .20					
Thon, Dickie	81D	290	$ .01	$ .15	**Timlin, Mike**	**92D**	**301**	**$ .01**	**$ .04**
Thon, Dickie	83D	191	$ .01	$ .06	Timlin, Mike	93D	87	$ .01	$ .05
Thon, Dickie	84D	304	$ .05	$ .20	Tingley, Ron	92D	287	$ .01	$ .04
Thon, Dickie	86D	572	$ .01	$ .08	Tingley, Ron	93D	621	$ .01	$ .05
Thon, Dickie	87D	261	$ .01	$ .05	Tobik, Dave	82D	511	$ .01	$ .06
Thon, Dickie	89D	441	$ .01	$ .04	Tobik, Dave	83D	385	$ .01	$ .06
Thon, Dickie	90D	549	$ .01	$ .04	Todd, Jackson	81D	31	$ .01	$ .06
Thon, Dickie	90DL	105	$ .05	$ .25	Todd, Jackson	82D	178	$ .01	$ .06

DONRUSS

Player	Year	No.	VG	EX/MT	Player	Year	No.	VG	EX/MT
Tolentino, Jose	92D	589	$ .01	$ .10	Trammell, Alan	90D	90	$ .01	$ .10
Toliver, Fred	86D	612	$ .01	$ .08	Trammell, Alan	90DBC	26	$ .01	$ .10
Toliver, Fred	89D	510	$ .01	$ .04	Trammell, Alan	90DL	218	$ .10	$ .50
Tolleson, Wayne	83D	573	$ .01	$ .10	Trammell, Alan	91D	118	$ .01	$ .04
Tolleson, Wayne	84D	464	$ .05	$ .20	Trammell, Alan	91DL	351	$ .01	$ .15
Tolleson, Wayne	85D	378	$ .01	$ .10	Trammell, Alan	91DLS	59	$ .01	$ .08
Tolleson, Wayne	86D	134	$ .01	$ .08	Trammell, Alan	92D	164	$ .01	$ .04
Tolleson, Wayne	87D	524	$ .01	$ .05	Trammell, Alan	92DL	172	$ .01	$ .06
Tolleson, Wayne	88D	154	$ .01	$ .04	Trammell, Alan	92DLS	179	$ .01	$ .06
Tolleson, Wayne	89D	659	$ .01	$ .04	Trammell, Alan	93D	655	$ .01	$ .05
Tomlin, Randy	91D	725	$ .01	$ .15	Trautwein, John	88DR	24	$ .01	$ .07
Tomlin, Randy	91DL	203	$ .10	$ .50	Travers, Bill	81D	508	$ .01	$ .06
Tomlin, Randy	92D	367	$ .01	$ .04	Traxler, Brian	90DR	38	$ .01	$ .05
Tomlin, Randy	92DL	256	$ .01	$ .06	Treadway, Jeff	88DR	17	$ .01	$ .15
Tomlin, Randy	92DLS	88	$ .01	$ .06	Treadway, Jeff	88DRR	29	$ .05	$ .20
Tomlin, Randy	93D	570	$ .01	$ .05	Treadway, Jeff	89D	351	$ .01	$ .10
Tomlin, Randy	93DL	24	$ .05	$ .25	Treadway, Jeff	90D	50	$ .01	$ .04
Torre, Joe	81D	506	$ .01	$ .06	Treadway, Jeff	90DL	455	$ .05	$ .25
Torre, Joe	83D	628	$ .01	$ .06	Treadway, Jeff	91D	117	$ .01	$ .04
Torre, Joe	91DLSP	17	$ .20	$2.00	Treadway, Jeff	91DL	246	$ .01	$ .08
Torrez, Mike	81D	216	$ .01	$ .06	Treadway, Jeff	91DLS	150	$ .01	$ .08
Torrez, Mike	82D	235	$ .01	$ .06	Treadway, Jeff	92D	324	$ .01	$ .04
Torrez, Mike	83D	512	$ .01	$ .06	Treadway, Jeff	93D	448	$ .01	$ .05
Torrez, Mike	84D	556	$ .05	$ .20	Trevino, Alex	82D	350	$ .01	$ .06
Traber, Jim	85DRR	45	$ .05	$ .25	Trevino, Alex	83D	374	$ .01	$ .06
Traber, Jim	87D	477	$ .10	$ .40	Trevino, Alex	84D	286	$ .05	$ .20
Traber, Jim	90D	569	$ .01	$ .04	Trevino, Alex	85D	565	$ .01	$ .10
Tracy, Jim	81D	520	$ .01	$ .06	Trevino, Alex	87D	546	$ .01	$ .05
Trammell, Alan	81D	5	$ .10	$1.00	Trevino, Alex	88D	376	$ .01	$ .04
Trammell, Alan	82D	76	$ .10	$ .75	Trevino, Alex	90D	443	$ .01	$ .04
Trammell, Alan	82DK	5	$ .10	$ .40	Trevino, Alex	90DL	432	$ .05	$ .25
Trammell, Alan	83D	207	$ .10	$ .50	Trillo, Manny	81D	22	$ .01	$ .06
Trammell, Alan	84D	293	$ .20	$2.00	Trillo, Manny	82D	245	$ .01	$ .06
Trammell, Alan	85D	171	$ .10	$ .50	Trillo, Manny	83D	294	$ .01	$ .06
Trammell, Alan	86D	171	$ .10	$ .50	Trillo, Manny	84D	575	$ .05	$ .20
Trammell, Alan	87D	127	$ .05	$ .25	Trillo, Manny	85D	431	$ .01	$ .10
					Trillo, Manny	86D	201	$ .01	$ .08
					Trillo, Manny	87D	570	$ .01	$ .05
					Trillo, Manny	88D	516	$ .01	$ .04
					Trillo, Manny	89D	608	$ .01	$ .04
					Trlicek, Rick	92DR	116	$ .01	$ .10
					Trombley, Mike	93D	47	$ .01	$ .15
					Trout, Steve	81D	400	$ .01	$ .06
					Trout, Steve	82D	243	$ .01	$ .06
					Trout, Steve	83D	417	$ .01	$ .06
					Trout, Steve	84D	533	$ .05	$ .20
					Trout, Steve	85D	198	$ .01	$ .10
					Trout, Steve	86D	117	$ .01	$ .08
					Trout, Steve	87D	201	$ .01	$ .05
					Trout, Steve	88D	524	$ .01	$ .04
					Trujillo, Mike	87D	613	$ .01	$ .05
					Tucker, Scooter	92DR	117	$ .01	$ .05
					Tucker, Scooter	93D	60	$ .01	$ .10
					Tudor, John	81D	457	$ .05	$ .35
					Tudor, John	82D	260	$ .05	$ .25
					Tudor, John	83D	563	$ .05	$ .25
					Tudor, John	84D	416	$ .05	$ .25
					Tudor, John	85D	235	$ .03	$ .10
					Tudor, John	86D	260	$ .01	$ .08
					Tudor, John	87D	170	$ .01	$ .05
					Tudor, John	88D	553	$ .01	$ .04
					Tudor, John	89D	195	$ .01	$ .04
					Tudor, John	90DL	176	$ .05	$ .25
					Tunnell, Lee	84D	592	$ .05	$ .20
					Tunnell, Lee	85D	288	$ .01	$ .06
					Turner, Jerry	81D	244	$ .01	$ .06
					Turner, Jerry	82D	609	$ .01	$ .06
					Turner, Shane	92DR	118	$ .01	$ .05
					Tyson, Mike	82D	435	$ .01	$ .06
					Ujdur, Jerry	83D	600	$ .01	$ .06
					Ullger, Scott	84D	438	$ .05	$ .20
					Underwood, Pat	81D	368	$ .01	$ .06
					Underwood, Pat	83D	29	$ .01	$ .06
					Underwood, Tom	81D	108	$ .01	$ .06
					Underwood, Tom	82D	323	$ .01	$ .06

Alan Trammell SS

Trammell, Alan	88D	230	$ .01	$ .15
Trammell, Alan	88DBC	11	$ .01	$ .15
Trammell, Alan	88DK	4	$ .01	$ .15
Trammell, Alan	89D	180	$ .01	$ .15
Trammell, Alan	89DBC	17	$ .01	$ .10

DONRUSS

Player	Year	No.	VG	EX/MT	Player	Year	No.	VG	EX/MT
Underwood, Tom	83D	391	$.01	$.06	Van Slyke, Andy	88D	291	$.01	$.10
Underwood, Tom	84D	253	$.05	$.20	Van Slyke, Andy	88DBC	8	$.01	$.10
Unser, Del	81D	164	$.01	$.06	Van Slyke, Andy	88DK	18	$.01	$.05
Unser, Del	82D	273	$.01	$.06	Van Slyke, Andy	89D	54	$.01	$.15
Upshaw, Willie	82D	652	$.01	$.06	Van Slyke, Andy	89DBC	10	$.01	$.05
Upshaw, Willie	83D	558	$.01	$.06	Van Slyke, Andy	90D	244	$.01	$.10
Upshaw, Willie	84D	315	$.05	$.20	Van Slyke, Andy	90DL	117	$.10	$.50
Upshaw, Willie	85D	71	$.01	$.10	Van Slyke, Andy	91D	552	$.01	$.10
Upshaw, Willie	85DK	10	$.03	$.10	Van Slyke, Andy	91DL	310	$.01	$.15
Upshaw, Willie	86D	195	$.01	$.08	Van Slyke, Andy	91DLS	230	$.05	$.20
Upshaw, Willie	87D	367	$.01	$.05	Van Slyke, Andy	92D	383	$.01	$.04
Upshaw, Willie	88D	271	$.01	$.04	Van Slyke, Andy	92DL	43	$.01	$.06
Upshaw, Willie	89D	492	$.01	$.04	Van Slyke, Andy	92DLS	89	$.01	$.06
Uribe, Jose	86D	236	$.05	$.20	Van Slyke, Andy	93D	414	$.01	$.05
Uribe, Jose	87D	436	$.01	$.05	Van Slyke, Andy	93DK	9	$.20	$2.00
Uribe, Jose	88D	559	$.01	$.04	Van Slyke, Andy	93DL	79	$.05	$.20
Uribe, Jose	89D	131	$.01	$.04	Vande Berg, Ed	83D	100	$.01	$.06
Uribe, Jose	90D	335	$.01	$.04	Vande Berg, Ed	84D	604	$.05	$.20
Uribe, Jose	90DL	225	$.05	$.25	Vande Berg, Ed	85D	511	$.01	$.10
Uribe, Jose	91D	375	$.01	$.04	Vande Berg, Ed	86D	637	$.01	$.08
Uribe, Jose	91DL	433	$.01	$.08	Vande Berg, Ed	87D	376	$.01	$.05
Uribe, Jose	92D	453	$.01	$.04	Vander Wal, John	92DL	416	$.05	$.20
Urrea, John	81D	190	$.01	$.06	Vander Wal, John	92DRR	414	$.01	$.15
Urrea, John	82D	313	$.01	$.06	Vander Wal, John	93D	144	$.01	$.10
Vail, Mike	81D	554	$.01	$.06	Vander Wal, John	93DL	19	$.05	$.35
Vail, Mike	83D	597	$.01	$.06	Varsho, Gary	91D	671	$.01	$.04
Valasquez, Guillermo	93D	312	$.01	$.15	Varsho, Gary	91DL	500	$.01	$.08
Valdez, Julio	82D	560	$.01	$.06	Varsho, Gary	92D	644	$.01	$.04
Valdez, Sergio	90D	405	$.01	$.10	Varsho, Gary	92DL	388	$.01	$.06
Valdez, Sergio	90DL	496	$.05	$.25	Varsho, Gary	92DLS	90	$.01	$.06
Valdez, Sergio	91D	344	$.01	$.04	Varsho, Gary	93D	42	$.01	$.05
Valentin, John	93D	251	$.01	$.10	Vatcher, Jim	91D	753	$.01	$.10
Valentin, John	93DL	87	$.10	$.40	Vatcher, Jim	92D	563	$.01	$.04
Valentine, Ellis	82D	605	$.01	$.06	Vaughn, DeWayne	88DR	25	$.01	$.07
Valenzuela, Fernando	82D	462	$.10	$.50	Vaughn, Greg	90DL	111	$.10	$1.00
Valenzuela, Fernando	83D	284	$.05	$.20	Vaughn, Greg	90DR	16	$.05	$.20
Valenzuela, Fernando	83DK	1	$.05	$.35	Vaughn, Greg	90DRR	37	$.05	$.20
Valenzuela, Fernando	84D	52	$.05	$.35	Vaughn, Greg	91D	478	$.01	$.15
Valenzuela, Fernando	85D	52	$.05	$.20	Vaughn, Greg	91DLS	79	$.05	$.20
Valenzuela, Fernando	86D	215	$.05	$.20	Vaughn, Greg	92D	224	$.01	$.04
Valenzuela, Fernando	87D	94	$.05	$.25	Vaughn, Greg	92DL	276	$.01	$.06
Valenzuela, Fernando	88D	53	$.05	$.25	Vaughn, Greg	92DLS	198	$.01	$.06
Valenzuela, Fernando	89D	250	$.01	$.10	Vaughn, Greg	93D	103	$.01	$.05
Valenzuela, Fernando	90D	625	$.01	$.10	Vaughn, Greg	93DL	56	$.05	$.20
Valenzuela, Fernando	90DL	68	$.05	$.25	Vaughn, Mo	91DLBC	7	$1.25	$5.00
Valenzuela, Fernando	91D	127	$.01	$.04	Vaughn, Mo	91DLS	20	$.10	$.75
Valenzuela, Fernando	91DBC	11	$.01	$.03	Vaughn, Mo	91DR	36	$.05	$.35
Valera, Julio	91DRR	39	$.01	$.15	Vaughn, Mo	91DRR	430	$.05	$.25
Valera, Julio	92DL	490	$.01	$.15	Vaughn, Mo	92D	514	$.01	$.10
Valera, Julio	92DR	119	$.01	$.05	Vaughn, Mo	92DL	103	$.05	$.20
Valera, Julio	93D	5	$.01	$.05	Vaughn, Mo	92DLS	139	$.05	$.20
Valle, Dave	87D	610	$.01	$.05	Vaughn, Mo	93D	429	$.01	$.05
Valle, Dave	88D	393	$.01	$.04	Vega, Jesus	83D	650	$.01	$.06
Valle, Dave	89D	614	$.01	$.04	Velarde, Randy	90D	630	$.01	$.04
Valle, Dave	90D	129	$.01	$.04	Velarde, Randy	92D	679	$.01	$.04
Valle, Dave	90DL	166	$.05	$.25	Velarde, Randy	92DL	368	$.01	$.06
Valle, Dave	91D	366	$.01	$.04	Velarde, Randy	93D	163	$.01	$.05
Valle, Dave	91DL	511	$.01	$.08	Velez, Otto	81D	391	$.01	$.06
Valle, Dave	92D	462	$.01	$.04	Velez, Otto	82D	304	$.01	$.06
Valle, David	91DLS	120	$.01	$.08	Venable, Max	84D	323	$.05	$.20
Valle, David	92DL	170	$.01	$.06	Venable, Max	86D	650	$.01	$.08
Valle, David	92DLS	240	$.01	$.06	Venable, Max	90DL	459	$.05	$.25
Valle, David	93D	507	$.01	$.05	Venable, Max	91D	510	$.01	$.04
Van Gorder, Dave	83D	188	$.01	$.06	Ventura, Robin	90DL	167	$2.50	$10.00
Van Gorder, Dave	85D	384	$.01	$.10	Ventura, Robin	90DR	15	$.10	$.75
Van Gorder, Dave	86D	550	$.01	$.08	Ventura, Robin	90DRR	28	$.10	$.75
Van Poppel, Todd	91DLBC	9	$1.00	$4.00	Ventura, Robin	91D	315	$.01	$.15
Van Poppel, Todd	91DLS	109	$.20	$2.00	Ventura, Robin	91DL	271	$.10	$1.00
Van Poppel, Todd	91DR	7	$.10	$.50	Ventura, Robin	92D	145	$.05	$.20
Van Poppel, Todd	92DL	248	$.10	$.40	Ventura, Robin	92D	17	$.10	$.50
Van Poppel, Todd	92DRR	9	$.05	$.20	Ventura, Robin	92DLS	160	$.10	$.40
Van Slyke, Andy	84D	83	$2.50	$10.00	Ventura, Robin	93D	535	$.01	$.10
Van Slyke, Andy	85D	327	$.20	$2.00	Ventura, Robin	93DK	10	$.75	$3.00
Van Slyke, Andy	86D	412	$.10	$.75	Veres, Randy	91D	755	$.01	$.04
Van Slyke, Andy	87D	417	$.05	$.35	Verhoeven, John	81D	564	$.01	$.06

DONRUSS

Player	Year	No.	VG	EX/MT	Player	Year	No.	VG	EX/MT
Veryzer, Tom	81D	199	$ .01	$ .06	Walk, Bob	86D	430	$ .01	$ .08
Veryzer, Tom	82D	450	$ .01	$ .06	Walk, Bob	87D	203	$ .01	$ .05
Villanueva, Hector	90DL	401	$ .05	$ .25	Walk, Bob	88D	514	$ .01	$ .04
Villanueva, Hector	91D	296	$ .01	$ .04	Walk, Bob	89D	172	$ .01	$ .04
Villanueva, Hector	91DL	75	$ .01	$ .08	Walk, Bob	90D	370	$ .01	$ .04
Villanueva, Hector	92D	725	$ .01	$ .04	Walk, Bob	90DL	64	$ .05	$ .25
Villanueva, Hector	93D	80	$ .01	$ .05	Walk, Bob	91D	157	$ .01	$ .04
Viola, Frank	83D	382	$ .75	$3.00	Walk, Bob	91DL	450	$ .01	$ .08
Viola, Frank	84D	364	$ .15	$1.50	Walk, Bob	92D	88	$ .01	$ .04
Viola, Frank	85D	436	$ .05	$ .35	Walk, Bob	92DL	353	$ .01	$ .06
Viola, Frank	85DK	17	$ .05	$ .35					
Viola, Frank	86D	194	$ .05	$ .35					
Viola, Frank	87D	196	$ .05	$ .20					
Viola, Frank	88D	149	$ .01	$ .15					
Viola, Frank	89D	237	$ .01	$ .10					
Viola, Frank	89DK	23	$ .01	$ .10					
Viola, Frank	90D	353	$ .01	$ .10					
Viola, Frank	90DL	93	$ .05	$ .25					
Viola, Frank	91D	529	$ .01	$ .10					
Viola, Frank	91DL	180	$ .01	$ .08					
Viola, Frank	91DLS	210	$ .01	$ .08					
Viola, Frank	92D	498	$ .01	$ .04					
Viola, Frank	92DL	221	$ .01	$ .06					
Viola, Frank	92DLS	140	$ .01	$ .06					
Viola, Frank	93D	91	$ .01	$ .05					
Viola, Frank	93DL	21	$ .05	$ .20					
Virdon, Bill	81D	384	$ .01	$ .06					
Virdon, Bill	82D	144	$ .01	$ .06					
Virgil, Ozzie	83D	606	$ .01	$ .06					
Virgil, Ozzie	84D	326	$ .05	$ .20					
Virgil, Ozzie	85D	82	$ .01	$ .10					
Virgil, Ozzie	86D	137	$ .01	$ .08					
Virgil, Ozzie	87D	67	$ .01	$ .05					
Virgil, Ozzie	88D	143	$ .01	$ .04					
Virgil, Ozzie	89D	145	$ .01	$ .04					
Vitko, Joe	93D	354	$ .01	$ .15					
Vizcaino, Jose	91D	722	$ .01	$ .04					
Vizcaino, Jose	91DL	323	$ .01	$ .08					
Vizcaino, Jose	92D	212	$ .01	$ .04					
Vizcaino, Jose	92DL	270	$ .01	$ .06					
Vizcaino, Jose	93D	582	$ .01	$ .05					
Vizquel, Omar	89DR	53	$ .01	$ .05					
Vizquel, Omar	90D	483	$ .01	$ .04					
Vizquel, Omar	90DL	88	$ .05	$ .35	Walk, Bob	93D	546	$ .01	$ .05
Vizquel, Omar	91D	231	$ .01	$ .04	Walk, Bob	93DL	134	$ .01	$ .15
Vizquel, Omar	91DL	91	$ .01	$ .08	Walker, Chico	87D	539	$ .01	$ .05
Vizquel, Omar	92D	641	$ .01	$ .04	Walker, Chico	91DL	501	$ .01	$ .08
Vizquel, Omar	92DL	265	$ .01	$ .06	Walker, Chico	92D	439	$ .01	$ .04
Vizquel, Omar	93D	25	$ .01	$ .05	Walker, Chico	93D	410	$ .01	$ .05
Von Ohlen, Dave	84D	205	$ .05	$ .20	Walker, Chico	93DL	149	$ .01	$ .15
Von Ohlen, Dave	85D	412	$ .01	$ .10	Walker, Duane	83D	624	$ .01	$ .06
Vuckovich, Pete	81D	189	$ .01	$ .06	Walker, Duane	84D	325	$ .05	$ .20
Vuckovich, Pete	82D	458	$ .05	$ .20	Walker, Duane	85D	608	$ .01	$ .10
Vuckovich, Pete	83D	80	$ .01	$ .06	Walker, Duane	86D	500	$ .01	$ .08
Vuckovich, Pete	86D	473	$ .01	$ .08	Walker, Greg	84D	609	$ .10	$ .55
Vukovich, George	83D	315	$ .01	$ .06	Walker, Greg	85D	366	$ .01	$ .10
Vukovich, George	84D	468	$ .05	$ .20	Walker, Greg	86D	135	$ .05	$ .20
Vukovich, George	85D	276	$ .01	$ .10	Walker, Greg	87D	59	$ .01	$ .05
Vukovich, George	86D	346	$ .01	$ .08	Walker, Greg	87DK	25	$ .01	$ .05
Waddel, Tom	85D	582	$ .01	$ .10	Walker, Greg	88D	162	$ .01	$ .04
Waddel, Tom	86D	94	$ .01	$ .08	Walker, Greg	89D	135	$ .01	$ .04
Wagner, Mark	81D	126	$ .01	$ .06	Walker, Larry	90D	578	$ .10	$1.00
Wagner, Mark	82D	163	$ .01	$ .06	Walker, Larry	90DL	325	$2.25	$9.00
Wagner, Mark	83D	268	$ .01	$ .06	Walker, Larry	91D	359	$ .05	$ .20
Wagner, Paul	92DR	120	$ .01	$ .05	Walker, Larry	91DL	241	$ .10	$ .75
Wagner, Paul	93D	334	$ .01	$ .10	Walker, Larry	92D	259	$ .01	$ .15
Waits, Rick	81D	201	$ .01	$ .06	Walker, Larry	92DL	201	$ .05	$ .35
Waits, Rick	82D	33	$ .01	$ .06	Walker, Larry	92DLS	59	$ .05	$ .35
Waits, Rick	83D	263	$ .01	$ .06	Walker, Larry	93D	540	$ .01	$ .15
Waits, Rick	85D	368	$ .01	$ .10	Walker, Larry	93DK	6	$ .75	$3.00
Wakefield, Tim	92DR	121	$ .20	$2.00	Walker, Mike	91D	61	$ .01	$ .04
Wakefield, Tim	93D	61	$ .05	$ .35	Walker, Mike	92DR	122	$ .01	$ .05
Walewander, Jim	89D	415	$ .01	$ .04	Wallach, Tim	82D	140	$ .10	$1.00
Walk, Bob	81D	393	$ .05	$ .25	Wallach, Tim	83D	392	$ .05	$ .20
Walk, Bob	83D	401	$ .01	$ .06	Wallach, Tim	84D	421	$ .05	$ .35

156

DONRUSS

Player	Year	No.	VG	EX/MT	Player	Year	No.	VG	EX/MT
Wallach, Tim	85D	87	$.05	$.20	Washington, Claudell	88D	340	$.01	$.04
Wallach, Tim	86D	219	$.01	$.15	Washington, Claudell	89D	72	$.01	$.04
Wallach, Tim	87D	179	$.01	$.05	Washington, Claudell	89DTR	46	$.01	$.05
Wallach, Tim	88D	222	$.01	$.04	Washington, Claudell	90D	52	$.01	$.04
Wallach, Tim	89D	156	$.01	$.04	Washington, Ron	83D	431	$.01	$.06
Wallach, Tim	90D	220	$.01	$.04	Washington, Ron	84D	391	$.05	$.20
Wallach, Tim	90DL	80	$.05	$.25	Washington, Ron	85D	391	$.01	$.10
Wallach, Tim	91D	514	$.01	$.04	Washington, Ron	86D	560	$.01	$.08
Wallach, Tim	91DL	388	$.01	$.08	Washington, Ron	89D	468	$.01	$.04
Wallach, Tim	91DLP	6	$.15	$1.25	Washington, U.L.	81D	460	$.01	$.06
Wallach, Tim	91DLS	200	$.01	$.08	Washington, U.L.	82D	160	$.01	$.06
Wallach, Tim	91DMVP	406	$.01	$.03	Washington, U.L.	83D	490	$.01	$.06
Wallach, Tim	92D	34	$.01	$.04	Washington, U.L.	84D	543	$.05	$.20
Wallach, Tim	92DL	298	$.01	$.06	Washington, U.L.	85D	521	$.01	$.10
Wallach, Tim	92DLS	60	$.01	$.06	Washington, U.L.	86D	498	$.01	$.08
Wallach, Tim	93D	36	$.01	$.05	Wathan, John	81D	221	$.01	$.06
Walling, Dennis	81D	144	$.01	$.06	Wathan, John	82D	86	$.01	$.06
Walling, Denny	82D	496	$.01	$.06	Wathan, John	83D	86	$.01	$.06
Walling, Denny	83D	419	$.01	$.06	Wathan, John	84D	466	$.05	$.20
Walling, Denny	84D	641	$.05	$.25	Wathan, John	85D	466	$.01	$.10
Walling, Denny	85D	527	$.01	$.10	Wathan, John	86D	496	$.01	$.08
Walling, Denny	86D	136	$.01	$.08	Watson, Bob	81D	225	$.01	$.06
Walling, Denny	87D	554	$.01	$.05	Watson, Bob	82D	108	$.01	$.06
Walling, Denny	88D	384	$.01	$.04	Watson, Bob	83D	551	$.01	$.06
Walling, Denny	89D	279	$.01	$.04	Wayne, Gary	89DR	27	$.01	$.05
Walling, Denny	90D	677	$.01	$.04	Wayne, Gary	90D	318	$.01	$.04
Walter, Gene	86DR	47	$.01	$.10	Wayne, Gary	91D	757	$.01	$.04
Walter, Gene	87D	511	$.01	$.05	Wayne, Gary	92DL	424	$.01	$.06
Walters, Dan	93D	48	$.01	$.05	Weathers, David	92DRR	418	$.01	$.05
Walters, Dan	93DL	156	$.01	$.15	Weathers, Dave	93D	731	$.01	$.05
Walton, Bruce	92DR	123	$.01	$.05	Weaver, Earl	81D	356	$.01	$.06
Walton, Jerome	89DR	26	$.01	$.05	Weaver, Earl	82D	27	$.01	$.15
Walton, Jerome	90D	285	$.01	$.10	Webster, Lenny	92DR	124	$.01	$.05
Walton, Jerome	90DL	124	$.05	$.35	Webster, Lenny	93D	694	$.01	$.05
Walton, Jerome	91D	72	$.01	$.10	Webster, Mitch	86D	523	$.05	$.25
Walton, Jerome	91DL	39	$.01	$.08	Webster, Mitch	87D	335	$.01	$.05
Walton, Jerome	92D	528	$.01	$.04	Webster, Mitch	88D	257	$.01	$.04
Wapnick, Steve	92D	743	$.01	$.10	Webster, Mitch	89D	459	$.01	$.04
Ward, Colby	91D	330	$.01	$.10	Webster, Mitch	90D	137	$.01	$.04
Ward, Duane	87DRR	45	$.05	$.35	Webster, Mitch	90DL	312	$.05	$.25
Ward, Duane	88D	567	$.01	$.04	Webster, Mitch	91D	283	$.01	$.04
Ward, Duane	89D	543	$.01	$.04	Webster, Mitch	92D	714	$.01	$.04
Ward, Duane	90D	307	$.01	$.04	Webster, Mitch	93D	62	$.01	$.05
Ward, Duane	90DL	501	$.05	$.25	Wedge, Eric	93D	44	$.01	$.15
Ward, Duane	91D	92	$.01	$.04	Wegman, Bill	86D	490	$.10	$.40
Ward, Duane	91DL	154	$.01	$.08	Wegman, Bill	87D	109	$.01	$.05
Ward, Duane	92D	308	$.01	$.04	Wegman, Bill	88D	151	$.01	$.04
Ward, Duane	92DL	101	$.01	$.06	Wegman, Bill	89D	293	$.01	$.04
Ward, Duane	93D	379	$.01	$.05	Wegman, Bill	92D	378	$.01	$.04
Ward, Duane	93DL	135	$.01	$.15	Wegman, Bill	92DL	196	$.01	$.06
Ward, Gary	81D	594	$.01	$.06	Wegman, Bill	92DLS	199	$.01	$.06
Ward, Gary	82D	571	$.01	$.06	Wegman, Bill	93D	17	$.01	$.05
Ward, Gary	83D	429	$.01	$.06	Wegman, Bill	93DL	144	$.01	$.15
Ward, Gary	84D	192	$.05	$.20	Wehner, John	92D	731	$.01	$.10
Ward, Gary	85D	342	$.01	$.10	Weiss, Walt	88DR	18	$.05	$.25
Ward, Gary	86D	98	$.01	$.08	Weiss, Walt	89D	446	$.05	$.10
Ward, Gary	86DK	20	$.01	$.10	Weiss, Walt	90D	67	$.01	$.10
Ward, Gary	87D	427	$.01	$.05	Weiss, Walt	90DL	239	$.05	$.25
Ward, Gary	88D	251	$.01	$.04	Weiss, Walt	91D	214	$.01	$.04
Ward, Gary	90D	621	$.01	$.04	Weiss, Walt	91DL	50	$.01	$.08
Ward, Gary	90DL	113	$.05	$.25	Weiss, Walt	92D	71	$.01	$.04
Ward, Gary	91D	728	$.01	$.04	Weiss, Walt	92DL	380	$.01	$.06
Ward, Kevin	92DL	338	$.01	$.06	Weiss, Walt	93D	109	$.01	$.05
Ward, Turner	91DL	449	$.01	$.15	Weiss, Walt	93D	756	$.01	$.05
Ward, Turner	91DLS	138	$.01	$.15	Welch, Bob	81D	178	$.10	$.40
Ward, Turner	91DRR	429	$.01	$.15	Welch, Bob	82D	75	$.05	$.25
Ward, Turner	93D	293	$.01	$.05	Welch, Bob	83D	410	$.05	$.25
Warren, Mike	84D	631	$.05	$.20	Welch, Bob	84D	153	$.10	$.50
Warren, Mike	85D	278	$.01	$.10	Welch, Bob	85D	372	$.01	$.15
Washington, Claudell	82D	58	$.01	$.06	Welch, Bob	86D	459	$.01	$.10
Washington, Claudell	83D	249	$.01	$.06	Welch, Bob	87D	475	$.01	$.10
Washington, Claudell	84D	310	$.05	$.20	Welch, Bob	88D	253	$.01	$.04
Washington, Claudell	85D	310	$.01	$.10	Welch, Bob	88DK	24	$.01	$.05
Washington, Claudell	85DK	11	$.03	$.10	Welch, Bob	89D	332	$.01	$.04
Washington, Claudell	86D	287	$.01	$.08	Welch, Bob	90D	332	$.01	$.04

157

DONRUSS

Player	Year	No.	VG	EX/MT	Player	Year	No.	VG	EX/MT
Welch, Bob	91D	645	$.01	$.04	White, Devon	93D	29	$.01	$.05
Welch, Bob	91D	727	$.01	$.04	White, Devon	93DL	69	$.01	$.15
Welch, Bob	91DAS	54	$.01	$.03	White, Frank	81D	340	$.01	$.06
Welch, Bob	91DK	20	$.01	$.05	White, Frank	82D	286	$.01	$.06
Welch, Bob	91DL	64	$.01	$.08	White, Frank	83D	464	$.01	$.06
Welch, Bob	91DLS	110	$.01	$.08	White, Frank	84D	222	$.05	$.20
Welch, Bob	92D	190	$.01	$.04	White, Frank	85D	175	$.01	$.10
Welch, Bob	92DL	390	$.01	$.06	White, Frank	86D	130	$.01	$.08
Welch, Bob	93D	579	$.01	$.05	White, Frank	87D	255	$.01	$.05
Welch, Bob	93DL	94	$.01	$.15	White, Frank	88D	225	$.01	$.04
Wellman, Brad	84D	265	$.05	$.20	White, Frank	89D	85	$.01	$.04
Wellman, Brad	86D	431	$.01	$.08	White, Frank	90D	262	$.01	$.04
Wellman, Brad	89D	380	$.01	$.04	White, Frank	90DL	204	$.05	$.25
Wells, David	88D	640	$.05	$.20	White, Jerry	81D	333	$.01	$.06
Wells, David	88DR	26	$.01	$.15	White, Jerry	82D	621	$.01	$.06
Wells, David	89D	307	$.01	$.04	White, Jerry	83D	602	$.01	$.06
Wells, David	90D	425	$.01	$.04	Whitehouse, Len	84D	558	$.05	$.20
Wells, David	91D	473	$.01	$.04	Whitehouse, Len	85D	513	$.01	$.10
Wells, David	91DL	140	$.01	$.08	Whitehurst, Wally	91D	511	$.01	$.04
Wells, David	92D	620	$.01	$.04	Whitehurst, Wally	91DL	333	$.01	$.08
Wells, David	92DL	483	$.01	$.06	Whitehurst, Wally	92D	134	$.01	$.06
Wells, David	93D	511	$.01	$.05	Whitehurst, Wally	93D	602	$.01	$.05
Welsh, Chris	82D	44	$.01	$.06	Whiten, Mark	90DL	396	$.15	$1.50
Welsh, Chris	83D	94	$.01	$.06	Whiten, Mark	91D	607	$.01	$.10
Welsh, Chris	84D	498	$.05	$.20	Whiten, Mark	91DL	234	$.05	$.25
Welsh, Chris	86D	464	$.01	$.08	Whiten, Mark	91DLS	50	$.05	$.25
Werner, Don	83D	593	$.01	$.06	Whiten, Mark	91DR	32	$.01	$.15
Werth, Dennis	81D	466	$.01	$.06	Whiten, Mark	92D	325	$.01	$.15
West, Dave	89DRR	41	$.01	$.10	Whiten, Mark	92DL	334	$.01	$.06
West, David	90D	387	$.01	$.04	Whiten, Mark	92DLS	170	$.01	$.06
West, David	90DL	387	$.05	$.25	Whiten, Mark	93D	97	$.01	$.05
West, David	91D	264	$.01	$.04	Whitfield, Terry	81D	435	$.01	$.06
West, Dave	92D	638	$.01	$.04	Whitfield, Terry	85D	540	$.01	$.10
West, Dave	93D	501	$.01	$.05	Whitfield, Terry	86D	337	$.01	$.08
Wetteland, John	90D	671	$.01	$.15	Whitson, Ed	81D	74	$.01	$.06
Wetteland, John	91D	614	$.01	$.04	Whitson, Ed	82D	251	$.01	$.06
Wetteland, John	92D	627	$.01	$.04	Whitson, Ed	83D	389	$.01	$.06
Wetteland, John	92DL	478	$.01	$.06	Whitson, Ed	84D	528	$.05	$.20
Wetteland, John	93D	592	$.01	$.05	Whitson, Ed	85D	446	$.01	$.10
Wetteland, John	93DL	183	$.01	$.15	Whitson, Ed	86D	225	$.01	$.08
Whisenton, Larry	83D	501	$.01	$.06	Whitson, Ed	87D	360	$.01	$.05
Whitaker, Lou	81D	365	$.10	$.75	Whitson, Ed	88D	81	$.01	$.04
Whitaker, Lou	82D	454	$.10	$.40	Whitson, Ed	89D	229	$.01	$.04
Whitaker, Lou	83D	333	$.05	$.35	Whitson, Ed	90D	205	$.01	$.10
Whitaker, Lou	84D	227	$.15	$1.50	Whitson, Ed	90DK	26	$.01	$.05
Whitaker, Lou	85D	293	$.05	$.35	Whitson, Ed	90DL	246	$.05	$.25
Whitaker, Lou	85DK	5	$.05	$.25	Whitson, Ed	91D	186	$.01	$.04
Whitaker, Lou	86D	49	$.05	$.25	Whitson, Ed	91DL	337	$.01	$.08
Whitaker, Lou	87D	107	$.05	$.20	Whitson, Ed	91DLS	250	$.01	$.08
Whitaker, Lou	88D	173	$.01	$.15	Whitson, Ed	92D	380	$.01	$.04
Whitaker, Lou	89D	298	$.01	$.15	Whitt, Ernie	81D	390	$.01	$.06
Whitaker, Lou	90D	298	$.01	$.10	Whitt, Ernie	82D	381	$.01	$.06
Whitaker, Lou	90DK	16	$.01	$.05	Whitt, Ernie	83D	304	$.01	$.06
Whitaker, Lou	90DL	34	$.05	$.25	Whitt, Ernie	84D	437	$.05	$.20
Whitaker, Lou	91D	174	$.01	$.04	Whitt, Ernie	85D	268	$.01	$.10
Whitaker, Lou	91DL	120	$.01	$.08	Whitt, Ernie	86D	559	$.01	$.08
Whitaker, Lou	91DLS	60	$.01	$.08	Whitt, Ernie	87D	148	$.01	$.05
Whitaker, Lou	92D	285	$.01	$.04	Whitt, Ernie	88D	394	$.01	$.04
Whitaker, Lou	92DL	391	$.01	$.06	Whitt, Ernie	89D	591	$.01	$.04
Whitaker, Lou	92DLS	180	$.01	$.06	Whitt, Ernie	90D	385	$.01	$.04
Whitaker, Lou	93D	686	$.01	$.05	Whitt, Ernie	90DL	408	$.05	$.25
Whitaker, Lou	93DL	148	$.05	$.20	Whitt, Ernie	91DL	391	$.01	$.08
White, Devon	87DR	8	$.05	$.35	Wickander, Kevin	90DR	36	$.01	$.05
White, Devon	87DRR	38	$.10	$.75	Wickander, Kevin	91D	649	$.01	$.04
White, Devon	88D	283	$.01	$.10	Wickander, Kevin	93D	389	$.01	$.05
White, Devon	88DK	8	$.01	$.15	Wickman, Bob	92DR	125	$.10	$.40
White, Devon	89D	213	$.01	$.10	Wickman, Bob	93D	417	$.01	$.15
White, Devon	90D	226	$.01	$.10	Wiggins, Alan	83D	397	$.01	$.06
White, Devon	90DL	76	$.05	$.25	Wiggins, Alan	84D	568	$.05	$.20
White, Devon	91D	150	$.01	$.04	Wiggins, Alan	85D	80	$.01	$.10
White, Devon	91DL	394	$.01	$.08	Wiggins, Alan	86D	607	$.01	$.08
White, Devon	91DLS	139	$.01	$.08	Wilcox, Milt	81D	247	$.01	$.06
White, Devon	92D	180	$.01	$.04	Wilcox, Milt	82D	233	$.01	$.06
White, Devon	92DL	114	$.01	$.06	Wilcox, Milt	83D	155	$.01	$.06
White, Devon	92DLS	259	$.01	$.06	Wilcox, Milt	84D	471	$.05	$.20

DONRUSS

Player	Year	No.	VG	EX/MT
Wilcox, Milt	85D	105	$ .01	$ .10
Wilfong, Rob	81D	493	$ .01	$ .06
Wilfong, Rob	82D	130	$ .01	$ .06
Wilfong, Rob	83D	612	$ .01	$ .06
Wilfong, Rob	84D	329	$ .05	$ .20
Wilfong, Rob	85D	402	$ .01	$ .10
Wilfong, Rob	87D	258	$ .01	$ .05
Wilkerson, Curt	84D	99	$ .05	$ .20
Wilkerson, Curt	85D	99	$ .01	$ .10
Wilkerson, Curtis	86D	256	$ .01	$ .08
Wilkerson, Curtis	87D	223	$ .01	$ .05
Wilkerson, Curtis	88D	592	$ .01	$ .04
Wilkerson, Curtis	89D	402	$ .01	$ .04
Wilkerson, Curtis	89DTR	34	$ .01	$ .05
Wilkerson, Curt	90D	608	$ .01	$ .04
Wilkerson, Curtis	91DL	317	$ .01	$ .08
Wilkerson, Curtis	92D	489	$ .01	$ .04
Wilkerson, Curtis	92DL	387	$ .01	$ .06
Wilkins, Rick	91DR	38	$ .01	$ .15
Wilkins, Rick	92D	249	$ .01	$ .10
Wilkins, Rick	92DL	336	$ .01	$ .06
Wilkins, Rick	93D	28	$ .01	$ .05
Wilkins, Rick	93DL	216	$ .01	$ .15
Wilkinson, Bill	88D	568	$ .01	$ .04
Willard, Gerry "Jerry"	84D	520	$ .05	$ .20
Willard, Jerry	85D	346	$ .01	$ .10
Willard, Jerry	86D	398	$ .01	$ .08
Willard, Jerry	87D	467	$ .01	$ .05
Willard, Jerry	91D	634	$ .01	$ .04
Williams, Al	82D	429	$ .01	$ .06
Williams, Eddie	89DTR	29	$ .01	$ .05
Williams, Frank	85D	323	$ .05	$ .25
Williams, Frank	88D	512	$ .01	$ .04
Williams, Frank	89D	478	$ .01	$ .04
Williams, Frank	90D	327	$ .01	$ .04
Williams, Gerald	92D	697	$ .01	$ .15
Williams, Gerald	93D	49	$ .01	$ .05
Williams, Ken	87DR	11	$ .01	$ .10
Williams, Ken	88D	334	$ .01	$ .10
Williams, Ken	89D	337	$ .01	$ .04
Williams, Ken	89DTR	17	$ .01	$ .05
Williams, Matt	87DR	45	$1.00	$4.00
Williams, Matt	88D	628	$ .10	$1.00
Williams, Matt	89D	594	$ .01	$ .15
Williams, Matt	90D	348	$ .01	$ .10
Williams, Matt	90DL	94	$ .10	$1.00
Williams, Matt	91D	685	$ .01	$ .10
Williams, Matt	91DK	18	$ .01	$ .05
Williams, Matt	91DL	93	$ .05	$ .20
Williams, Matt	91DLS	259	$ .01	$ .15
Williams, Matt	92D	135	$ .01	$ .10
Williams, Matt	92DL	373	$ .01	$ .06
Williams, Matt	92DLS	120	$ .01	$ .06
Williams, Matt	93D	182	$ .01	$ .05
Williams, Matt	93DL	158	$ .05	$ .35
Williams, Mike	92DR	126	$ .01	$ .05
Williams, Mitch	86DR	19	$ .05	$ .35
Williams, Mitch	87D	347	$ .05	$ .35
Williams, Mitch	88D	161	$ .01	$ .15
Williams, Mitch	89D	225	$ .01	$ .04
Williams, Mitch	89DTR	38	$ .01	$ .15
Williams, Mitch	90D	275	$ .01	$ .04
Williams, Mitch	90DL	156	$ .05	$ .25
Williams, Mitch	91D	312	$ .01	$ .04
Williams, Mitch	91DL	420	$ .01	$ .08
Williams, Mitch	92D	353	$ .01	$ .04
Williams, Mitch	92DL	301	$ .01	$ .06
Williams, Mitch	92DLS	80	$ .01	$ .06
Williams, Mitch	93D	40	$ .01	$ .05
Williams, Mitch	93DL	114	$ .05	$ .20
Williams, Reggie	86DR	5	$ .01	$ .10
Williams, Reggie	87D	341	$ .01	$ .05
Williams, Reggie	93D	253	$ .01	$ .10
Williamson, Mark	87DR	3	$ .01	$ .07
Williamson, Mark	88D	418	$ .01	$ .04
Williamson, Mark	90D	406	$ .01	$ .04
Williamson, Mark	90DL	461	$ .05	$ .25
Williamson, Mark	91D	238	$ .01	$ .04
Williamson, Mark	91DL	21	$ .01	$ .08
Williamson, Mark	92D	511	$ .01	$ .04
Willis, Carl	92D	665	$ .01	$ .04
Willis, Carl	92DL	452	$ .01	$ .06
Willis, Carl	93DL	164	$ .01	$ .15
Wills, Bump	81D	25	$ .01	$ .06
Wills, Bump	82D	289	$ .01	$ .06
Wills, Bump	83D	351	$ .01	$ .06
Wills, Frank	91D	691	$ .01	$ .04
Wilson, Craig	91D	544	$ .01	$ .04
Wilson, Craig	91DL	95	$ .01	$ .15
Wilson, Craig	92D	744	$ .01	$ .04
Wilson, Dan	92DRR	399	$ .01	$ .05
Wilson, Dan	93D	6	$ .01	$ .10
Wilson, Glenn	83D	580	$ .05	$ .25
Wilson, Glenn	84D	618	$ .05	$ .20
Wilson, Glenn	85D	609	$ .01	$ .10
Wilson, Glenn	86D	285	$ .01	$ .08
Wilson, Glenn	87D	62	$ .01	$ .05
Wilson, Glenn	88D	262	$ .01	$ .04
Wilson, Glenn	89D	447	$ .01	$ .04
Wilson, Glenn	90D	472	$ .01	$ .04
Wilson, Glenn	90DL	268	$ .05	$ .25
Wilson, Glenn	91D	156	$ .01	$ .04
Wilson, Mookie	81D	575	$ .10	$ .60
Wilson, Mookie	82D	175	$ .01	$ .10
Wilson, Mookie	83D	56	$ .01	$ .10

Player	Year	No.	VG	EX/MT
Williams, Al	**83D**	**508**	**$ .01**	**$ .06**
Williams, Al	84D	316	$ .05	$ .20
Williams, Bernie	90D	689	$ .05	$ .25
Williams, Bernie	91DLSP	7	$ .75	$3.00
Williams, Bernie	92D	344	$ .01	$ .15
Williams, Bernie	93D	577	$ .01	$ .05
Williams, Bernie	93DL	130	$ .05	$ .25
Williams, Brian	92DRR	416	$ .05	$ .25
Williams, Brian	93D	692	$ .01	$ .10
Williams, Dick	81D	453	$ .01	$ .06
Williams, Dick	83D	625	$ .01	$ .06
Williams, Eddie	88DRR	46	$ .01	$ .15

DONRUSS

Player	Year	No.	VG	EX/MT	Player	Year	No.	VG	EX/MT
Wilson, Mookie	84D	190	$ .05	$ .20	Witt, Bobby	89D	461	$ .01	$ .04
Wilson, Mookie	85D	482	$ .01	$ .10	Witt, Bobby	90D	292	$ .01	$ .04
Wilson, Mookie	86D	604	$ .01	$ .08	Witt, Bobby	90DL	337	$ .05	$ .25
Wilson, Mookie	88D	652	$ .01	$ .15	Witt, Bobby	91D	249	$ .01	$ .04
Wilson, Mookie	89D	152	$ .01	$ .04	Witt, Bobby	91DL	3	$ .01	$ .08
Wilson, Mookie	90D	442	$ .01	$ .04	Witt, Bobby	91DLS	130	$ .01	$ .08
Wilson, Mookie	90DL	263	$ .05	$ .25	Witt, Bobby	92D	391	$ .01	$ .04
Wilson, Mookie	91D	585	$ .01	$ .04	Witt, Bobby	92DL	305	$ .01	$ .06
Wilson, Mookie	91DLS	140	$ .01	$ .08	Witt, Bobby	93D	51	$ .01	$ .05
Wilson, Nigel	93D	737	$ .10	$1.00	Witt, Bobby	93DL	204	$ .01	$ .15
Wilson, Nigel	93DK	27	$1.75	$7.00	Witt, Mike	82D	416	$ .05	$ .25
Wilson, Steve	89DR	10	$ .01	$ .05	Witt, Mike	83D	416	$ .05	$ .20
Wilson, Steve	90D	394	$ .01	$ .04	Witt, Mike	85D	108	$ .01	$ .10
Wilson, Steve	90DL	420	$ .05	$ .25	Witt, Mike	86D	179	$ .01	$ .08
Wilson, Steve	91D	519	$ .01	$ .04	Witt, Mike	87D	58	$ .05	$ .20
Wilson, Steve	92D	710	$ .01	$ .04	Witt, Mike	88D	86	$ .01	$ .04
Wilson, Steve	92DL	161	$ .01	$ .06	Witt, Mike	89D	372	$ .01	$ .04
Wilson, Steve	93D	34	$ .01	$ .05	Witt, Mike	90D	580	$ .01	$ .04
Wilson, Steve	93DL	145	$ .01	$ .15	Witt, Mike	91D	282	$ .01	$ .04
Wilson, Trevor	90D	414	$ .01	$ .10	Witt, Mike	91DBC	1	$ .01	$ .03
Wilson, Trevor	90DL	489	$ .05	$ .25	Witt, Mike	91DL	74	$ .01	$ .08
Wilson, Trevor	91D	263	$ .01	$ .04	Wockenfuss, John	81D	245	$ .01	$ .06
Wilson, Trevor	92D	575	$ .01	$ .04	Wockenfuss, John	82D	459	$ .01	$ .06
Wilson, Trevor	92DL	340	$ .01	$ .06	Wockenfuss, John	83D	76	$ .01	$ .06
Wilson, Trevor	93D	578	$ .01	$ .05	Wockenfuss, John	84D	150	$ .05	$ .20
Wilson, Willie	81D	223	$ .01	$ .15	Wockenfuss, John	85D	549	$ .01	$ .10
Wilson, Willie	82D	448	$ .05	$ .20	Wohlers, Mark	92D	616	$ .01	$ .10
Wilson, Willie	83D	112	$ .05	$ .20	Wohlers, Mark	92DRR	1	$ .01	$ .10
Wilson, Willie	83DK	15	$ .05	$ .20	Wohlers, Mark	93D	606	$ .01	$ .05
Wilson, Willie	84D	175	$ .05	$ .25	Wohlford, Jim	81D	316	$ .01	$ .06
Wilson, Willie	85D	297	$ .01	$ .10	Wohlford, Jim	83D	524	$ .01	$ .06
Wilson, Willie	86D	175	$ .01	$ .08	Wohlford, Jim	85D	585	$ .01	$ .10
Wilson, Willie	87D	96	$ .01	$ .05	Wohlford, Jim	86D	157	$ .01	$ .08
Wilson, Willie	87D	487	$ .01	$ .05	Wojna, Ed	86D	505	$ .01	$ .08
Wilson, Willie	88D	255	$ .01	$ .04	Wojna, Ed	87D	589	$ .01	$ .05
Wilson, Willie	89D	120	$ .01	$ .04	Wood, Ted	92D	681	$ .01	$ .15
Wilson, Willie	90D	440	$ .01	$ .04	Wood, Ted	93D	24	$ .01	$ .05
Wilson, Willie	90DL	336	$ .05	$ .25	Woodard, Mike	86DRR	46	$ .01	$ .10
Wilson, Willie	91DL	299	$ .01	$ .08	Woods, Al	81D	32	$ .01	$ .06
Wine, Robbie	88D	508	$ .01	$ .04	Woods, Al	82D	180	$ .01	$ .06
Winfield, Dave	81D	364	$ .75	$3.00	Woods, Gary	83D	631	$ .01	$ .06
Winfield, Dave	82D	31	$ .20	$2.00	Woods, Gary	84D	144	$ .05	$ .20
Winfield, Dave	82D	575	$ .15	$1.50	Woods, Gary	85D	555	$ .01	$ .10
Winfield, Dave	82DK	18	$ .10	$1.00	Woodson, Kerry	92DR	127	$ .01	$ .10
Winfield, Dave	83D	409	$ .20	$2.00	Woodson, Kerry	93D	748	$ .01	$ .10
Winfield, Dave	84D	51	$2.00	$8.00	Woodson, Tracy	88D	499	$ .01	$ .10
Winfield, Dave	85D	51	$ .75	$3.00	Woodson, Tracy	93D	652	$ .01	$ .05
Winfield, Dave	85D	651	$ .75	$3.00	Woodward, Rob	86DR	53	$ .01	$ .10
Winfield, Dave	86D	248	$ .15	$1.50	Woodward, Rob	87D	652	$ .01	$ .05
Winfield, Dave	87D	105	$ .10	$ .50	Worrell, Todd	86DR	21	$ .05	$ .20
Winfield, Dave	87DK	20	$ .05	$ .25	Worrell, Todd	86DRR	43	$ .05	$ .20
Winfield, Dave	88D	298	$ .05	$ .20	Worrell, Todd	87D	307	$ .01	$ .10
Winfield, Dave	89D	159	$ .01	$ .15	Worrell, Todd	88D	386	$ .01	$ .10
Winfield, Dave	89DBC	11	$ .01	$ .10	Worrell, Todd	89D	82	$ .01	$ .04
Winfield, Dave	90D	551	$ .01	$ .15	Worrell, Todd	90D	319	$ .01	$ .04
Winfield, Dave	90DL	426	$ .15	$1.50	Worrell, Todd	92DL	436	$ .01	$ .06
Winfield, Dave	91D	468	$ .01	$ .10	Worrell, Todd	92DLS	99	$ .01	$ .06
Winfield, Dave	91DL	499	$ .05	$ .20	Worrell, Todd	93D	72	$ .01	$ .05
Winfield, Dave	91DLS	30	$ .05	$ .20	Wortham, Rich	81D	161	$ .01	$ .06
Winfield, Dave	92D	133	$ .01	$ .10	Worthington, Craig	88DR	23	$ .01	$ .15
Winfield, Dave	92DL	171	$ .01	$ .15	Worthington, Craig	89D	569	$ .01	$ .10
Winfield, Dave	92DLS	260	$ .05	$ .20	Worthington, Craig	89DR	25	$ .01	$ .05
Winfield, Dave	93D	643	$ .01	$ .10	Worthington, Craig	90D	141	$ .01	$ .04
Winn, Jim	87D	312	$ .01	$ .05	Worthington, Craig	90DL	170	$ .05	$ .25
Winn, Jim	88D	409	$ .01	$ .04	Worthington, Craig	91D	293	$ .01	$ .04
Winningham, Herm	86D	279	$ .01	$ .15	Worthington, Craig	91DL	298	$ .01	$ .08
Winningham, Herm	88D	581	$ .01	$ .04	Wright, George	83D	116	$ .01	$ .06
Winningham, Herm	89D	435	$ .01	$ .04	Wright, George	84D	525	$ .05	$ .20
Winningham, Herm	90D	478	$ .01	$ .04	Wright, George	85D	256	$ .01	$ .10
Winningham, Herm	91D	695	$ .01	$ .04	Wright, George	86D	220	$ .01	$ .08
Wise, Rick	81D	3	$ .01	$ .06	Wright, Jim	82D	490	$ .01	$ .06
Wise, Rick	82D	170	$ .01	$ .06	Wrona, Rick	89DR	38	$ .01	$ .05
Witt, Bobby	86DR	49	$ .10	$ .50	Wrona, Rick	90D	512	$ .01	$ .15
Witt, Bobby	87D	99	$ .05	$ .35	Wynegar, Butch	81D	529	$ .01	$ .06
Witt, Bobby	88D	101	$ .01	$ .15	Wynegar, Butch	82D	508	$ .01	$ .06

DONRUSS

Player	Year	No.	VG	EX/MT	Player	Year	No.	VG	EX/MT
Wynegar, Butch	83D	325	$.01	$.06	Young, Matt	93D	459	$.01	$.05
Wynegar, Butch	84D	458	$.05	$.20	Young, Matt	93DL	153	$.01	$.15
Wynegar, Butch	85D	417	$.01	$.10	Young, Mike	84D	621	$.05	$.20
Wynegar, Butch	86D	274	$.01	$.08	Young, Mike	85D	367	$.01	$.10
Wynne, Marvell	84D	508	$.05	$.20	Young, Mike	86D	123	$.01	$.08
Wynne, Marvell	85D	113	$.01	$.10	Young, Mike	87D	150	$.01	$.05
Wynne, Marvell	86D	113	$.01	$.08	Young, Mike	88D	396	$.01	$.04
Wynne, Marvell	87D	411	$.01	$.05	Young, Mike	89D	632	$.01	$.04
Wynne, Marvell	88D	237	$.01	$.04	Young, Pete	92DR	130	$.01	$.10
Wynne, Marvell	89D	347	$.01	$.04	Young, Pete	93D	616	$.01	$.05
Wynne, Marvell	90D	255	$.01	$.04	Youngblood, Joel	81D	277	$.01	$.06
Wynne, Marvell	90DL	270	$.05	$.25	Youngblood, Joel	82D	613	$.01	$.06
Yastrzemski, Carl	81D	94	$.20	$2.00	Youngblood, Joel	83D	572	$.01	$.06
Yastrzemski, Carl	81D	214	$.20	$2.00	Youngblood, Joel	84D	480	$.05	$.20
Yastrzemski, Carl	82D	74	$.15	$1.50	Youngblood, Joel	85D	79	$.01	$.10
Yastrzemski, Carl	83D	326	$.10	$1.00	Youngblood, Joel	86D	567	$.01	$.04
Yastrzemski, Carl	83DK	25	$.10	$.75	Yount, Robin	81D	323	$.90	$3.60
Yastrzemski, Carl	84D#B	0	$2.50	$10.00	Yount, Robin	82D	510	$.25	$2.50
Yastrzemski, Carl	90D	588	$.01	$.10	Yount, Robin	83D	258	$.20	$2.00
Yeager, Steve	81D	297	$.01	$.15	Yount, Robin	84D	48	$2.25	$9.00
Yeager, Steve	82D	201	$.01	$.06	Yount, Robin	84DK	1	$1.00	$4.00
Yeager, Steve	83D	201	$.01	$.06	Yount, Robin	85D	48	$.75	$3.00
Yeager, Steve	84D	581	$.05	$.20	Yount, Robin	86D	48	$.20	$2.00
Yeager, Steve	85D	519	$.01	$.10	Yount, Robin	87D	126	$.10	$.75
Yeager, Steve	86D	519	$.01	$.08	Yount, Robin	88D	295	$.05	$.20
Yelding, Eric	89DR	34	$.01	$.05	Yount, Robin	89D	55	$.05	$.20
Yelding, Eric	90D	123	$.01	$.04	Yount, Robin	89DK	5	$.01	$.10
Yelding, Eric	90DL	301	$.05	$.25	Yount, Robin	90D	146	$.01	$.10
Yelding, Eric	91D	277	$.01	$.04	Yount, Robin	90DL	71	$.20	$2.00
Yelding, Eric	91DL	100	$.01	$.08	Yount, Robin	91D	272	$.01	$.10
Yelding, Eric	92D	148	$.01	$.04	Yount, Robin	91DL	116	$.05	$.25
Yett, Rich	89D	546	$.01	$.04	Yount, Robin	91DLS	80	$.05	$.25
Yett, Rich	90D	509	$.01	$.04	Yount, Robin	92D	173	$.01	$.10
Yost, Ned	83D	458	$.01	$.06	Yount , Robin	92DL	64	$.05	$.25
Yost, Ned	84D	271	$.05	$.20	Yount, Robin	92DLS	200	$.05	$.25
Yost, Ned	85D	221	$.01	$.10	Yount, Robin	93D	441	$.01	$.10
Youmans, Floyd	86D	543	$.10	$.60	Yount, Robin	93DK	16	$.75	$3.00
Youmans, Floyd	87D	257	$.01	$.15	Yount, Robin	93DL	188	$.05	$.35
Youmans, Floyd	88D	56	$.01	$.15	Zachry, Pat	81D	275	$.01	$.06
Young, Anthony	91DLBC	23	$.15	$1.50	Zachry, Pat	82D	254	$.01	$.06
Young, Anthony	92DL	356	$.01	$.06	Zachry, Pat	83D	560	$.01	$.06
Young, Anthony	92DLS	70	$.01	$.06	Zachry, Pat	84D	215	$.05	$.20
Young, Anthony	92DRR	409	$.01	$.05	Zahn, Geoff (Jeff)	81D	532	$.01	$.06
Young, Anthony	93D	14	$.01	$.05	Zahn, Geoff	82D	164	$.01	$.06
Young, Curt	85D	522	$.10	$.50	Zahn, Geoff	83D	66	$.01	$.06
Young, Curt	87D	344	$.01	$.05	Zahn, Geoff	84D	402	$.05	$.20
Young, Curt	88D	97	$.01	$.04	Zahn, Geoff	85D	301	$.01	$.10
Young, Curt	89D	304	$.01	$.04	Zavaras, Clint	90D	662	$.01	$.10
Young, Curt	90D	505	$.01	$.04	Zeile, Todd	90DL	221	$.10	$1.00
Young, Curt	90DL	424	$.05	$.25	Zeile, Todd	90DR	31	$.05	$.30
Young, Curt	91D	724	$.01	$.04	Zeile, Todd	90DRR	29	$.05	$.20
Young, Curt	92D	469	$.01	$.04	Zeile, Todd	91D	71	$.01	$.10
Young, Dmitri	93D	638	$.01	$.15	Zeile, Todd	91DL	327	$.01	$.15
Young, Eric	92DR	128	$.10	$.40	Zeile, Todd	91DLS	240	$.01	$.15
Young, Eric	93D	730	$.01	$.15	Zeile, Todd	92D	132	$.01	$.10
Young, Gerald	88D	431	$.05	$.20	Zeile, Todd	92DL	432	$.01	$.06
Young, Gerald	89D	207	$.01	$.04	Zeile, Todd	92DLS	100	$.01	$.06
Young, Gerald	90D	325	$.01	$.04	Zeile, Todd	93D	20	$.01	$.05
Young, Gerald	90DL	214	$.05	$.25	Zeile, Todd	93DL	8	$.01	$.15
Young, Gerald	91D	689	$.01	$.04	Zimmer, Don	82D	195	$.01	$.06
Young, Gerald	92D	477	$.01	$.04	Zisk, Richie	81D	28	$.01	$.06
Young, Kevin	92DR	129	$.10	$.75	Zisk, Richie	82D	127	$.01	$.06
Young, Kevin	93D	452	$.01	$.15	Zisk, Richie	82DK	11	$.01	$.15
Young, Matt	84D	362	$.05	$.20	Zisk, Richie	83D	559	$.01	$.06
Young, Matt	84DK	16	$.05	$.25	Zisk, Richie	84D	69	$.05	$.20
Young, Matt	85D	267	$.01	$.10	Zosky, Eddie	92DRR	8	$.01	$.05
Young, Matt	86D	267	$.01	$.08	Zosky, Eddie	93D	57	$.01	$.05
Young, Matt	87D	193	$.01	$.05	Zosky, Eddie	93DL	190	$.05	$.25
Young, Matt	88D	423	$.01	$.04	Zozky, Eddie	91DLBC	24	$.10	$1.00
Young, Matt	90DL	509	$.05	$.25	Zupcic, Bob	92D	720	$.05	$.20
Young, Matt	91D	493	$.01	$.04	Zupcic, Bob	93D	531	$.01	$.05
Young, Matt	91DL	215	$.01	$.08	Zupcic, Bob	93DL	65	$.10	$.40
Young, Matt	92D	635	$.01	$.04					

FLEER CORPORATION 1981 – 1993

The Fleer Company issued a baseball card set in 1981 to compete with Topps and the newly released Donruss cards. Fleer also issued these cards in wax packs with bubble gum but was forced to issue the cards without bubble gum in 1982 as Topps was able to stop the bubble gum format through a lawsuit. Fleer has chosen to issue their wax packs with a peel off sticker since 1982. Fleer began issuing factory sets in 1984. Unlike Donruss, the sets are not in numerical order. Beginning in 1988, Fleer attached a factory seal to the box to show if it has been opened. This seal is a significant breakthrough in my way of thinking.

Abbreviations used in the Fleer section include the following:
F – Fleer used for all cards in this section
FLL – Fleer League Leader
FPD – Player of decade ten card subset issued in 1990 with one card per year of Fleer's first ten years back in the baseball card business.
FRS – Fleer Record Setter
FU – Update card issued at end of year in sets of 132 since 1984
FUL – Fleer Ultra first issued as a 400 card premium set in 1991 to compete with Upper Deck
FULU – Update Ultra cards issued at end of 1991 in a set of 120

All Fleer cards are 2½" x 3½" and in full color.

1981 – 660 cards w/white border and player's team in baseball on left (Fleer found on back to right of card number but no date on card)
1982 – 660 cards w/white border and player's name, team and position in oval design (Fleer name found under card's number on the back but no date on card)
1983 – 660 cards w/beige border (copyright 1983 Fleer above statistical information on back)
1984 – 660 cards w/white border and blue stripes inside border top and bottom (copyright 1984 Fleer above statistical information on back)
1985 – 660 cards w/gray border and Fleer in white at lower right (copyright 1985 Fleer on back above statistical information)
1986 – 660 cards w/dark blue border w/Fleer in white on top right (copyright 1986 Fleer on back bottom)
1987 – 660 cards w/sky blue and white border w/Fleer in white on colored strip at bottom (copyright 1987 Fleer top right on back)
1988 – 660 cards w/white border w/blue and red stripes and Fleer in blue box at bottom right (copyright 1988 Fleer on back above statistical breakdown)
1989 – 660 cards w/gray border w/white vertical stripes and Fleer in black print on lower right (copyright 1989 Fleer on back lower left side)
1990 – 660 cards w/white borders; player encircled by a colored banner and Fleer '90 in upper left corner (copyright 1990 Fleer Corp. on back at bottom)
1991 – 720 cards w/yellow borders; player in rectangular black bordered box with Fleer '91 in lower right corner (copyright 1991 Fleer Corp. on back under circular photo of player)
1992 – 720 cards w/green to white borders; player's last name in bold letters down right side of card with Fleer '92 in lower left corner (copyright 1992 Fleer Corp. on back under rectangular photo of player)
1993 – 720 cards w/silver borders issued in two series of 360 each; player's name and team up left side of card with Fleer '93 in lower right corner (copyright 1993 Fleer Corp. on back right bottom)

The listing for each card shown appears immediately following the photograph.

FLEER

Player	Year	No.	VG	EX/MT
Aase, Don	81F	286	$.01	$.06
Aase, Don	82F	450	$.01	$.06
Aase, Don	83F	76	$.01	$.06
Aase, Don	85F	293	$.01	$.06
Aase, Don	85FU	1	$.01	$.10
Aase, Don	86F	268	$.01	$.06
Aase, Don	87F	461	$.01	$.06
Aase, Don	87F	627	$.01	$.10
Aase, Don	88F	553	$.01	$.05
Aase, Don	89FU	100	$.01	$.05
Aase, Don	90F	196	$.01	$.04
Aase, Don	91F	193	$.01	$.04
Abbott, Glenn	81F	615	$.01	$.06
Abbott, Glenn	82F	502	$.01	$.06
Abbott, Glenn	84F	74	$.01	$.08
Abbott, Jim	89FU	11	$.15	$1.50
Abbott, Jim	90F	125	$.05	$.20
Abbott, Jim	91F	305	$.01	$.10
Abbott, Jim	91FUL	43	$.05	$.20
Abbott, Jim	92F	50	$.01	$.10
Abbott, Jim	92FUL	321	$.05	$.35
Abbott, Jim	93F	187	$.01	$.10
Abbott, Kyle	92F	51	$.01	$.04
Abbott, Kyle	93F	483	$.01	$.04
Abbott, Kyle	93FUL	82	$.01	$.10
Abbott, Paul	92F	667	$.01	$.04
Abner, Shawn	88F	576	$.01	$.10
Abner, Shawn	91F	522	$.01	$.04
Abner, Shawn	91FUL	300	$.01	$.07
Abner, Shawn	93F	579	$.01	$.04
Acker, Jim	84F	145	$.01	$.10
Acker, Jim	85F	96	$.01	$.06
Acker, Jim	86F	50	$.01	$.06
Acker, Jim	87F	509	$.01	$.06
Acker, Jim	88F	531	$.01	$.05
Acker, Jim	91F	167	$.01	$.04
Acker, Jim	92F	322	$.01	$.04
Adams, Glenn	81F	562	$.01	$.06
Adams, Glenn	82F	545	$.01	$.06
Adduci, Jim	89F	176	$.01	$.04
Afenir, Troy	91F	1	$.01	$.10
Afenir, Troy	92F	248	$.01	$.04
Agosto, Juan	84F	50	$.01	$.08
Agosto, Juan	85F	506	$.01	$.06
Agosto, Juan	86F	197	$.01	$.06
Agosto, Juan	88F	437	$.01	$.05
Agosto, Juan	89F	348	$.01	$.04
Agosto, Juan	90F	220	$.01	$.04
Agosto, Juan	91F	497	$.01	$.04
Agosto, Juan	92F	574	$.01	$.04
Agosto, Juan	92FUL	562	$.01	$.10
Aguayo, Luis	82F	238	$.01	$.06
Aguayo, Luis	86F	433	$.01	$.06
Aguayo, Luis	87F	169	$.01	$.06
Aguayo, Luis	88F	297	$.01	$.05
Aguayo, Luis	89F	249	$.01	$.04
Aguilera, Rick	86F	74	$.15	$1.50
Aguilera, Rick	87F	1	$.05	$.35
Aguilera, Rick	88F	127	$.01	$.05
Aguilera, Rick	89F	27	$.01	$.04
Aguilera, Rick	90F	365	$.01	$.04
Aguilera, Rick	91F	602	$.01	$.04
Aguilera, Rick	91FUL	185	$.01	$.07
Aguilera, Rick	92F	195	$.01	$.04
Aguilera, Rick	92FUL	88	$.01	$.10
Aguilera, Rick	93F	261	$.01	$.04
Aguilera, Rick	93FUL	228	$.01	$.10
Aikens, Willie	81F	43	$.01	$.06
Aikens, Willie	82F	404	$.01	$.06
Aikens, Willie	83F	104	$.01	$.06
Aikens, Willie	84F	341	$.01	$.08
Aikens, Willie	84FU	1	$.10	$.50
Aikens, Willie	85F	97	$.01	$.06
Ainge, Dan	81F	418	$.20	$2.00
Ainge, Danny	82F	608	$.10	$1.00

Player	Year	No.	VG	EX/MT
Akerfelds, Darrel	90FU	41	$.01	$.05
Akerfelds, Darrel	91F	386	$.01	$.04
Aldred, Scott	92F	127	$.01	$.04
Aldrete, Mike	86FU	1	$.01	$.15
Aldrete, Mike	87F	264	$.05	$.25
Aldrete, Mike	88F	76	$.01	$.10
Aldrete, Mike	89F	323	$.01	$.04
Aldrete, Mike	89FU	95	$.01	$.05
Aldrete, Mike	91F	224	$.01	$.04
Aldrete, Mike	92F	102	$.01	$.04
Aldrich, Jay	88F	155	$.01	$.10
Alexander, Doyle	81F	255	$.01	$.10
Alexander, Doyle	82F	383	$.01	$.10
Alexander, Doyle	84F	146	$.01	$.08
Alexander, Doyle	85F	98	$.01	$.06
Alexander, Doyle	86F	51	$.01	$.06
Alexander, Doyle	87F	510	$.01	$.06
Alexander, Doyle	88F	51	$.01	$.05
Alexander, Doyle	89F	128	$.01	$.04
Alexander, Doyle	90F	599	$.01	$.04
Alexander, Gary	81F	398	$.01	$.06
Alexander, Gary	82F	475	$.01	$.06
Alexander, Gerald	91F	278	$.01	$.10
Alexander, Gerald	92F	297	$.01	$.04
Alicea, Luis	88FU	116	$.01	$.10
Alicea, Luis	89F	443	$.01	$.15
Alicea, Luis	93F	507	$.01	$.04
All-Star Game, Cleveland	82F	628	$.01	$.06
Allanson, Andy	86FU	2	$.01	$.15
Allanson, Andy	87F	241	$.01	$.10
Allanson, Andy	88FU	21	$.01	$.06
Allanson, Andy	89F	396	$.01	$.04
Allanson, Andy	90F	483	$.01	$.04
Allanson, Andy	92F	128	$.01	$.04
Allen, Jamie	84F	604	$.01	$.08
Allen, Kim	81F	612	$.01	$.06
Allen, Neil	81F	322	$.01	$.06
Allen, Neil	82F	520	$.01	$.06
Allen, Neil	83F	536	$.01	$.06
Allen, Neil	84F	318	$.01	$.08

Allen, Neil	85F	219	$.01	$.06
Allen, Neil	86F	98	$.01	$.06
Allen, Neil	86FU	3	$.01	$.08

FLEER

Player	Year	No.	VG	EX/MT
Allen, Neil	87F	484	$ .01	$ .06
Allen, Neil	89F	250	$ .01	$ .04
Allen, Rod	89F	397	$ .01	$ .04
Allenson, Gary	82F	287	$ .01	$ .06
Allenson, Gary	83F	177	$ .01	$ .06
Allenson, Gary	84F	388	$ .01	$ .08
Allenson, Gary	85F	148	$ .01	$ .06
Allred, Beau	90FU	88	$ .01	$ .10
Allred, Beau	91F	358	$ .01	$ .10
Allred, Beau	91FUL	101(104)	$ .01	$ .10
Almon, Bill	81F	332	$ .01	$ .06
Almon, Bill	82F	335	$ .01	$ .06
Almon, Bill	83F	228	$ .01	$ .06
Almon, Bill	84F	436	$ .01	$ .08
Almon, Bill	85F	414	$ .01	$ .06
Almon, Bill	85FU	2	$ .01	$ .10
Almon, Bill	86F	602	$ .01	$ .06
Almon, Bill	87F	601	$ .01	$ .06
Alomar, Roberto	88FU	122	$2.50	$10.00
Alomar, Roberto	89F	299	$ .10	$ .75
Alomar, Roberto	89F	630	$ .10	$ .40
Alomar, Roberto	90F	149	$ .05	$ .35
Alomar, Roberto	91F	523	$ .05	$ .25
Alomar, Roberto	91FU	63	$ .01	$ .15
Alomar, Roberto	91FUL	358	$ .10	$ .50
Alomar, Roberto	92F	323	$ .01	$ .15
Alomar, Roberto	92F	698	$ .01	$ .10
Alomar, Roberto	92FUL	143	$ .10	$1.00
Alomar, Roberto	93F	330	$ .05	$ .20
Alomar, Roberto	93F	357	$ .01	$ .15
Alomar Jr., Sandy	89F	300	$ .05	$ .25
Alomar Jr., Sandy	89F	630	$ .10	$ .40
Alomar Jr., Sandy	90F	150	$ .01	$ .15
Alomar Jr., Sandy	90FU	89	$ .01	$ .10
Alomar Jr., Sandy	91F	359	$ .01	$ .15
Alomar Jr., Sandy	91FUL	105	$ .01	$ .10
Alomar Jr., Sandy	92F	103	$ .01	$ .10
Alomar Jr., Sandy	92F	698	$ .01	$ .10
Alomar Jr., Sandy	92FUL	45	$ .01	$ .10
Alomar Jr., Sandy	93F	212	$ .01	$ .04

Player	Year	No.	VG	EX/MT
Alomar Jr., Sandy	93FUL	182	$ .01	$ .10
Alou, Moises	90F	650	$ .05	$ .35
Alou, Moises	92FU	95	$ .10	$ .50

Player	Year	No.	VG	EX/MT
Alou, Moises	92FUL	511	$ .05	$ .35
Alou, Moises	93F	70	$ .01	$ .04
Alou, Moises	93FUL	61	$ .01	$ .15
Altamirano, Porfirio	83F	153	$ .01	$ .06
Altobelli, Joe	84F	643	$ .01	$ .08
Alvarez, Jose	88FU	70	$ .01	$ .10
Alvarez, Jose	89F	585	$ .01	$ .15
Alvarez, Jose	90F	574	$ .01	$ .04
Alvarez, Wilson	91FULU	13	$ .10	$ .50
Alvarez, Wilson	92F	74	$ .01	$ .10
Alvarez, Wilson	92FRS	684	$ .01	$ .10
Alvarez, Wilson	92FUL	32	$ .01	$ .10
Alvarez, Wilson	93F	199	$ .01	$ .04
Alvarez, Wilson	93FUL	170	$ .01	$ .15
Amaral, Rich	92FUL	430	$ .01	$ .10
Amaral, Rich	93FUL	265	$ .01	$ .10
Amaro, Jr., Ruben	92F	52	$ .01	$ .10
Amaro, Ruben	92FUL	540	$ .05	$ .20
Amaro, Jr., Ruben	93F	97	$ .01	$ .04
Amaro, Jr., Ruben	93FUL	83	$ .01	$ .10
Andersen, Larry	83F	470	$ .01	$ .06
Andersen, Larry	85F	244	$ .01	$ .06
Andersen, Larry	86F	434	$ .01	$ .06
Andersen, Larry	87F	49	$ .01	$ .06
Andersen, Larry	88F	438	$ .01	$ .05
Andersen, Larry	89F	349	$ .01	$ .04
Andersen, Larry	90F	221	$ .01	$ .04
Andersen, Larry	91F	83	$ .01	$ .04
Andersen, Larry	91FU	120	$ .01	$ .05
Andersen, Larry	92F	597	$ .01	$ .04
Andersen, Larry	93F	518	$ .01	$ .04
Anderson, Allan	87F	533	$ .01	$ .15
Anderson, Allan	88FU	41	$ .01	$ .10
Anderson, Allan	89F	102	$ .01	$ .15
Anderson, Allan	90F	366	$ .01	$ .04
Anderson, Allan	91F	603	$ .01	$ .04
Anderson, Allan	92F	196	$ .01	$ .04
Anderson, Brady	89F	606	$ .10	$ .50
Anderson, Brady	90F	172	$ .01	$ .15
Anderson, Brady	91F	466	$ .01	$ .15
Anderson, Brady	92F	1	$ .01	$ .10
Anderson, Brady	92FUL	301	$ .05	$ .20
Anderson, Brady	93F	163	$ .01	$ .04
Anderson, Brady	93FUL	138	$ .01	$ .10
Anderson, Dave	84F	533	$ .01	$ .08
Anderson, Dave	85F	366	$ .01	$ .06
Anderson, Dave	86F	123	$ .01	$ .06
Anderson, Dave	87F	436	$ .01	$ .06
Anderson, Dave	88F	508	$ .01	$ .05
Anderson, Dave	89F	53	$ .01	$ .04
Anderson, Dave	90FU	59	$ .01	$ .05
Anderson, Dave	91F	252	$ .01	$ .04
Anderson, Dave	91FUL	314	$ .01	$ .07
Anderson, Dave	92F	625	$ .01	$ .04
Anderson, Jim	81F	598	$ .01	$ .06
Anderson, Jim	82F	503	$ .01	$ .06
Anderson, Kent	91F	306	$ .01	$ .04
Anderson, Rick	87F	2	$ .01	$ .06
Anderson, Scott	91F	225	$ .01	$ .10
Anderson, Sparky	81F	460	$ .01	$ .10
Anderson, Sparky	85F	628	$ .01	$ .06
Andujar, Joaquin	81F	63	$ .01	$ .10
Andujar, Joaquin	82F	110	$ .01	$ .10
Andujar, Joaquin	83F	1	$ .01	$ .10
Andujar, Joaquin	84F	319	$ .01	$ .10
Andujar, Joaquin	85F	220	$ .01	$ .06
Andujar, Joaquin	86F	26	$ .01	$ .10
Andujar, Joaquin	86FU	4	$ .01	$ .08
Andujar, Joaquin	87F	385	$ .01	$ .06
Anthony, Eric	90F	222	$ .05	$ .35
Anthony, Eric	91F	498	$ .01	$ .10
Anthony, Eric	91FUL	131	$ .01	$ .07
Anthony, Eric	92F	424	$ .01	$ .04
Anthony, Eric	93F	45	$ .01	$ .04
Aponte, Luis	83F	178	$ .01	$ .06

FLEER

Player	Year	No.	VG	EX/MT	Player	Year	No.	VG	EX/MT
Aponte, Luis	84F	389	$.01	$.08	August, Don	88FU	37	$.01	$.10
Aponte, Luis	84FU	2	$.10	$.50	August, Don	89F	177	$.01	$.10
Aponte, Luis	85F	437	$.01	$.06	August, Don	92FUL	78	$.01	$.10
Appier, Kevin	89FU	35	$.10	$1.00	Augustine, Jerry	82F	133	$.01	$.06
Appier, Kevin	90F	100	$.05	$.25	Augustine, Jerry	83F	26	$.01	$.06
Appier, Kevin	91F	549	$.01	$.04	Augustine, Jerry	84F	194	$.01	$.08
Appier, Kevin	91FUL	143	$.01	$.07	Ault, Doug	81F	424	$.01	$.06
Appier, Kevin	92F	150	$.01	$.04	Austin, James	92FU	33	$.05	$.25
Appier, Kevin	92FUL	66	$.01	$.10	Austin, James	93FUL	217	$.01	$.10
Appier, Kevin	93F	235	$.01	$.04	Avery, Steve	90FU	1	$.10	$.75
Aquino, Luis	89F	275	$.01	$.04	Avery, Steve	91F	681	$.05	$.25
Aquino, Luis	90F	101	$.01	$.04	Avery, Steve	91FUL	1	$.10	$.75
Aquino, Luis	91F	550	$.01	$.04	Avery, Steve	92F	349	$.01	$.15
Aquino, Luis	92F	151	$.01	$.04	Avery, Steve	92FUL	157	$.10	$.50
Aquino, Luis	93F	615	$.01	$.04	Avery, Steve	93F	1	$.01	$.10
Arias, Alex	92FU	72	$.10	$1.00	Avery, Steve	93FUL	1	$.05	$.35
Armas, Tony	81F	575	$.01	$.10	Aviles, Ramon	81F	23	$.01	$.06
Armas, Tony	82F	85	$.01	$.10	Aviles, Ramon	82F	239	$.01	$.06
Armas, Tony	83F	513	$.05	$.20	Ayala, Benny	81F	185	$.01	$.06
Armas, Tony	84F	390	$.01	$.08	Ayala, Benny	82F	157	$.01	$.06
Armas, Tony	85F	149	$.01	$.06	Ayala, Benny	83F	52	$.01	$.06
Armas, Tony	86F	339	$.01	$.06	Ayala, Bobby	93F	29	$.05	$.35
Armas, Tony	87F	26	$.01	$.06	Ayrault, Bob	93F	484	$.01	$.04
Armas, Tony	88F	484	$.01	$.05	Azocar, Oscar	90FU	111	$.01	$.10
Armas, Tony	89F	467	$.01	$.04	Azocar, Oscar	91F	655	$.01	$.10
Armas, Tony	90F	126	$.01	$.04	Azocar, Oscar	92F	598	$.01	$.04
Armstrong, Jack	90F	412	$.01	$.10	Babbitt, Shooty	82F	86	$.01	$.06
Armstrong, Jack	91F	55	$.01	$.04	Backman, Wally	81F	336	$.01	$.15
Armstrong, Jack	92F	398	$.01	$.04	Backman, Wally	83F	537	$.01	$.06
Armstrong, Jack	92FUL	344	$.01	$.10	Backman, Wally	85F	72	$.01	$.06
Armstrong, Jack	93F	417	$.01	$.04	Backman, Wally	86F	75	$.01	$.06
Armstrong, Mike	81F	503	$.01	$.06	Backman, Wally	87F	3	$.01	$.06
Armstrong, Mike	83F	105	$.01	$.06	Backman, Wally	88F	128	$.01	$.05
Armstrong, Mike	84F	342	$.01	$.08	Backman, Wally	89F	28	$.01	$.04
Armstrong, Mike	85F	120	$.01	$.06	Backman, Wally	89FU	43	$.01	$.05
Arnsberg, Brad	88F	202	$.01	$.15	Backman, Wally	90F	367	$.01	$.04
Arnsberg, Brad	91F	279	$.01	$.04	Backman, Wally	90FU	47	$.01	$.05
Arnsberg, Brad	91FUL	346	$.01	$.07	Backman, Wally	91F	29	$.01	$.04
Arnsberg, Brad	92F	298	$.01	$.04	Backman, Wally	91FU103(106)		$.01	$.05
Arroyo, Fernando	82F	546	$.01	$.06	Backman, Wally	91FULU	98	$.01	$.10
Asadoor, Randy	87F	650	$.05	$.35	Baerga, Carlos	90FU	90	$.10	$1.00
Ashby, Alan	81F	64	$.01	$.06	Baerga, Carlos	91F	360	$.05	$.25
Ashby, Alan	82F	212	$.01	$.06	Baerga, Carlos	91FUL	106	$.10	$.50
Ashby, Alan	83F	445	$.01	$.06	Baerga, Carlos	92F	104	$.05	$.20
Ashby, Alan	84F	220	$.01	$.08	Baerga, Carlos	92FUL	46	$.10	$1.00
Ashby, Alan	85F	343	$.01	$.06	Baerga, Carlos	93F	213	$.01	$.15
Ashby, Alan	86F	292	$.01	$.06	Baerga, Carlos	93F	357	$.01	$.15
Ashby, Alan	87F	50	$.01	$.06	Baerga, Carlos	93FUL	183	$.10	$.50
Ashby, Alan	88F	439	$.01	$.05	Bagwell, Jeff	91F	87	$.10	$1.00
Ashby, Alan	89F	350	$.01	$.04	Bagwell, Jeff	91FULU	79	$2.00	$8.00
Ashby, Andy	91FU	105	$.01	$.10	Bagwell, Jeff	92F	425	$.05	$.35
Ashby, Andy	92F	521	$.01	$.10	Bagwell, Jeff	92FUL	198	$.10	$1.00
Ashby, Andy	92FUL	541	$.05	$.20	Bagwell, Jeff	93F	46	$.01	$.15
Ashby, Andy	93F	401	$.01	$.04	Bahnsen, Stan	81F	156	$.01	$.06
Asselstine, Brian	81F	256	$.01	$.06	Bahnsen, Stan	82F	183	$.01	$.06
Asselstine, Brian	82F	428	$.01	$.06	Bailes, Scott	86FU	6	$.01	$.15
Assenmacher, Paul	86FU	6	$.01	$.15	Bailes, Scott	87F	242	$.01	$.10
Assenmacher, Paul	87F	511	$.01	$.06	Bailes, Scott	88F	600	$.01	$.05
Assenmacher, Paul	88F	532	$.01	$.05	Bailes, Scott	89F	398	$.01	$.04
Assenmacher, Paul	89F	586	$.01	$.06	Bailes, Scott	90F	484	$.01	$.04
Assenmacher, Paul	90F	25	$.01	$.04	Bailes, Scott	92F	53	$.01	$.04
Assenmacher, Paul	91F	413	$.01	$.04	Bailey, Howard	84F	75	$.01	$.08
Assenmacher, Paul	92F	375	$.01	$.04	Bailey, Mark	84FU	3	$.10	$.50
Assenmacher, Paul	92FUL	172	$.01	$.10	Bailey, Mark	85F	344	$.01	$.06
Assenmacher, Paul	93F	17	$.01	$.04	Bailey, Mark	86F	293	$.01	$.06
Assenmacher, Paul	93FUL	14	$.01	$.10	Bailor, Bob	81F	409	$.01	$.06
Astacio, Pedro	93F	57	$.05	$.25	Bailor, Bob	82F	521	$.01	$.06
Astacio, Pedro	93FUL	49	$.10	$.50	Bailor, Bob	83F	538	$.01	$.06
Atherton, Keith	84F	437	$.01	$.08	Bailor, Bob	84F	580	$.01	$.08
Atherton, Keith	85F	415	$.01	$.06	Bailor, Bob	84FU	4	$.10	$.50
Atherton, Keith	86F	410	$.01	$.06	Bailor, Bob	85F	367	$.01	$.06
Atherton, Keith	87F	534	$.01	$.06	Bailor, Bob	86F	124	$.01	$.06
Atherton, Keith	88F	1	$.01	$.05	Baines, Harold	81F	346	$.25	$2.50
Atherton, Keith	89F	103	$.01	$.04	Baines, Harold	82F	336	$.10	$.50
Atherton, Keith	89FU	24	$.01	$.05	Baines, Harold	83F	229	$.05	$.35

FLEER

Player	Year	No.	VG	EX/MT	Player	Year	No.	VG	EX/MT
Baines, Harold	84F	51	$ .10	$ .50	Bannister, Floyd	84F	52	$ .01	$ .08
Baines, Harold	85F	507	$ .05	$ .25	Bannister, Floyd	85F	508	$ .01	$ .06
Baines, Harold	86F	198	$ .01	$ .15	Bannister, Floyd	86F	199	$ .01	$ .06
Baines, Harold	87F	485	$ .05	$ .20	Bannister, Floyd	87F	486	$ .01	$ .06
Baines, Harold	87F	643	$ .01	$ .06	Bannister, Floyd	88F	392	$ .01	$ .05
Baines, Harold	88F	391	$ .01	$ .10	Bannister, Floyd	89F	276	$ .01	$ .04
Baines, Harold	89F	491	$ .01	$ .04	Bannister, Floyd	91FU	8	$ .01	$ .05
Baines, Harold	90F	290	$ .01	$ .04	Bannister, Floyd	92FUL	437	$ .01	$ .10
Baines, Harold	91F	2	$ .01	$ .04	Bannister, Steve	84FU	7	$ .10	$ .50
Baines, Harold	91FULU	45	$ .01	$ .10	Barberie, Bret	91FULU	90	$ .05	$ .35
Baines, Harold	92F	249	$ .01	$ .04	Barberie, Bret	92F	472	$ .01	$ .10
Baines, Harold	92F	707	$ .01	$ .04	Barberie, Bret	92FUL	512	$ .05	$ .20
Baines, Harold	92FUL	109	$ .01	$ .10	Barberie, Bret	93F	418	$ .01	$ .04
Baines, Harold	93F	659	$ .01	$ .04	Barfield, Jesse	83F	424	$ .05	$ .25
Bair, Doug	81F	213	$ .01	$ .06	Barfield, Jesse	84F	147	$ .05	$ .25
Bair, Doug	83F	2	$ .01	$ .06	Barfield, Jesse	85F	99	$ .05	$ .25
Bair, Doug	84F	76	$ .01	$ .08	Barfield, Jesse	86F	52	$ .05	$ .20
Bair, Doug	85F	1	$ .01	$ .10	Barfield, Jesse	87F	219	$ .01	$ .10
Bair, Doug	87F	386	$ .01	$ .06	Barfield, Jesse	87F	643	$ .01	$ .06
Baker, Chuck	81F	500	$ .01	$ .06	Barfield, Jesse	88F	102	$ .01	$ .10
Baker, Chuck	82F	561	$ .01	$ .06	Barfield, Jesse	89F	225	$ .01	$ .04
Baker, Doug	90F	368	$ .01	$ .10	Barfield, Jesse	89FU	46	$ .01	$ .10
Baker, Dusty	81F	115	$ .01	$ .10	Barfield, Jesse	90F	437	$ .01	$ .04
Baker, Dusty	82F	1	$ .01	$ .10	Barfield, Jesse	91F	657	$ .01	$ .04
Baker, Dusty	83F	201	$ .01	$ .06	Barfield, Jesse	91FUL	228	$ .01	$ .07
Baker, Dusty	84F	96	$ .01	$ .08	Barfield, Jesse	92F	221	$ .01	$ .04
Baker, Dusty	84FU	5	$ .10	$ .50	Barfield, Jesse	92FUL	99	$ .01	$ .10
Baker, Dusty	85F	602	$ .01	$ .06	Barfield, John	91FU	58	$ .01	$ .10
Baker, Dusty	85FU	3	$ .01	$ .10	Barker, Len	81F	408	$ .01	$ .06
Baker, Dusty	86F	411	$ .01	$ .06	Barker, Len	82F	360	$ .01	$ .06
Baker, Dusty	87F	387	$ .01	$ .06	Barker, Len	82F	639	$ .01	$ .06
Balboni, Steve	84FU	6	$ .10	$ .50	Barker, Len	83F	402	$ .01	$ .06
Balboni, Steve	85F	196	$ .01	$ .06	Barker, Len	83F	642	$ .01	$ .06
Balboni, Steve	86F	1	$ .01	$ .10	Barker, Len	84F	170	$ .01	$ .08
Balboni, Steve	87F	362	$ .01	$ .06	Barker, Len	85F	318	$ .01	$ .06
Balboni, Steve	88F	251	$ .01	$ .05	Barker, Len	86F	507	$ .01	$ .06
Balboni, Steve	89F	538	$ .01	$ .04	Barnes, Brian	92F	473	$ .01	$ .04
Balboni, Steve	89FU	45	$ .01	$ .05	Barnes, Brian	93F	457	$ .01	$ .04
Balboni, Steve	90F	436	$ .01	$ .04	Barnes, Skeeter	92FUL	358	$ .01	$ .10
Balboni, Steve	91F	656	$ .01	$ .04	Barnes, Skeeter	93F	603	$ .01	$ .04
Ballard, Jeff	88F	554	$ .05	$ .20	Barojas, Salome	83F	230	$ .01	$ .06
Ballard, Jeff	89F	607	$ .01	$ .04	Barojas, Salome	84F	53	$ .01	$ .08
Ballard, Jeff	90F	173	$ .01	$ .04	Barojas, Salome	85F	482	$ .01	$ .06
Ballard, Jeff	91F	467	$ .01	$ .04	Barr, Jim	81F	287	$ .01	$ .06
Baller, Jay	86FU	7	$ .01	$ .08	Barr, Jim	83F	252	$ .01	$ .06
Bando, Chris	83F	400	$ .01	$ .06	Barr, Jim	84F	365	$ .01	$ .04
Bando, Chris	84F	534	$ .01	$ .08	Barrett, Marty	84FU	8	$ .10	$1.00
Bando, Chris	85F	438	$ .01	$ .06	Barrett, Marty	85F	150	$ .05	$ .25
Bando, Chris	86F	579	$ .01	$ .06	Barrett, Marty	86F	340	$ .01	$ .06
Bando, Chris	87F	243	$ .01	$ .06	Barrett, Marty	87F	27	$ .01	$ .10
Bando, Chris	88F	601	$ .01	$ .05	Barrett, Marty	88F	343	$ .01	$ .05
Bando, Sal	81F	510	$ .01	$ .06	Barrett, Marty	89F	78	$ .01	$ .04
Bando, Sal	82F	134	$ .01	$ .06	Barrett, Marty	90F	266	$ .01	$ .04
Bankhead, Scott	86FU	8	$ .01	$ .15	Barrett, Marty	91F	84	$ .01	$ .04
Bankhead, Scott	87F	363	$ .05	$ .25	Barrios, Francisco	81F	352	$ .01	$ .06
Bankhead, Scott	87FU	1	$ .01	$ .06	Bass, Kevin	84F	221	$ .05	$ .25
Bankhead, Scott	88F	368	$ .01	$ .05	Bass, Kevin	85F	345	$ .01	$ .10
Bankhead, Scott	89F	539	$ .01	$ .04	Bass, Kevin	86F	294	$ .01	$ .10
Bankhead, Scott	90F	505	$ .01	$ .04	Bass, Kevin	87F	51	$ .01	$ .10
Bankhead, Scott	91F	442	$ .01	$ .04	Bass, Kevin	88F	440	$ .01	$ .05
Bankhead, Scott	92FU	78	$ .05	$ .25	Bass, Kevin	89F	351	$ .01	$ .04
Bankhead, Scott	92FUL	478	$ .01	$ .10	Bass, Kevin	90F	223	$ .01	$ .04
Bankhead, Scott	93F	386	$ .01	$ .04	Bass, Kevin	90FU	60	$ .01	$ .05
Banks, Willie	91FUL	373	$ .10	$ .40	Bass, Kevin	91F	253	$ .01	$ .04
Banks, Willie	92F	657	$ .01	$ .10	Bass, Kevin	91FULU	315	$ .01	$ .07
Banks, Willie	92FUL	393	$ .05	$ .35	Bass, Kevin	92F	626	$ .01	$ .04
Banks, Willie	93F	637	$ .01	$ .04	Bass, Kevin	92FUL	284	$ .01	$ .10
Bannister, Alan	82F	359	$ .01	$ .06	Bass, Kevin	93F	466	$ .01	$ .04
Bannister, Alan	83F	401	$ .01	$ .06	Bass, Randy	82F	566	$ .01	$ .06
Bannister, Alan	84F	535	$ .01	$ .08	Bathe, Bill	86FU	9	$ .01	$ .08
Bannister, Alan	85F	555	$ .01	$ .06	Batiste, Kim	92F	522	$ .01	$ .10
Bannister, Alan	86F	556	$ .01	$ .06	Batiste, Kim	92FUL	542	$ .05	$ .20
Bannister, Floyd	81F	599	$ .01	$ .06	Batiste, Kim	93F	485	$ .01	$ .04
Bannister, Floyd	82F	504	$ .01	$ .06	Baumgarten, Ross	82F	337	$ .01	$ .06
Bannister, Floyd	83F	471	$ .01	$ .06	Baumgarten, Ross	83F	302	$ .01	$ .06

FLEER

Player	Year	No.	VG	EX/MT	Player	Year	No.	VG	EX/MT
Bautista, Jose	88FU	1	$ .01	$ .10	Bell, Buddy	86F	172	$ .01	$ .10
Bautista, Jose	89F	608	$ .01	$ .10	Bell, Buddy	87F	193	$ .01	$ .10
Bautista, Jose	92F	2	$ .01	$ .04	Bell, Buddy	88F	227	$ .01	$ .10
Baylor, Don	81F	271	$ .05	$ .20	Bell, Buddy	89F	352	$ .01	$ .04
Baylor, Don	82F	451	$ .01	$ .10	Bell, Derek	91F	168	$ .05	$ .25
Baylor, Don	83F	77	$ .01	$ .10	Bell, Derek	92F	324	$ .01	$ .10
Baylor, Don	84F	119	$ .01	$ .10	Bell, Derek	92FUL	448	$ .10	$ .50
Baylor, Don	85F	121	$ .05	$ .20	Bell, Derek	93F	331	$ .01	$ .10
Baylor, Don	86F	99	$ .01	$ .10	Bell, Derek	93FUL	286	$ .05	$ .20
Baylor, Don	86F	631	$ .05	$ .25	Bell, Eric	87FU	2	$ .01	$ .10
Baylor, Don	86FU	10	$ .01	$ .10	Bell, Eric	88F	555	$ .01	$ .05
Baylor, Don	87F	28	$ .01	$ .10	Bell, George (Jorge)	82F	609	$1.50	$6.00
Baylor, Don	88F	2	$ .01	$ .10	Bell, George	84F	148	$ .15	$1.50
Baylor, Don	89F	1	$ .01	$ .04	Bell, George	85F	100	$ .01	$ .75
Beane, Billy	86FU	11	$ .01	$ .08	Bell, George	86F	53	$ .05	$ .35
Beane, Billy	87F	535	$ .01	$ .06	Bell, George	87F	220	$ .10	$ .40
Beard, Dave	82F	87	$ .01	$ .06	Bell, George	88F	103	$ .01	$ .10
Beard, Dave	83F	514	$ .01	$ .06	Bell, George	88F	623	$ .01	$ .10
Beard, Dave	84F	438	$ .01	$ .08	Bell, George	89F	226	$ .01	$ .10
Beard, Dave	84FU	9	$ .10	$ .50	Bell, George	90F	76	$ .01	$ .10
Beard, Dave	85F	483	$ .01	$ .06	Bell, George	90FPD	628	$ .01	$ .15
Bearse, Kevin	90FU	91	$ .01	$ .10	Bell, George	91F	169	$ .01	$ .04
Bearse, Kevin	91F	361	$ .01	$ .10	Bell, George	91FU	77	$ .01	$ .05
Beasley, Chris	92F	54	$ .01	$ .10	Bell, George	91FUL	55	$ .01	$ .07
Beattie, Jim	83F	472	$ .01	$ .06	Bell, George	92F	376	$ .01	$ .04
Beattie, Jim	84F	605	$ .01	$ .08	Bell, George	92FU	12	$ .05	$ .25
Beattie, Jim	85F	484	$ .01	$ .06	Bell, George	92FUL	173	$ .01	$ .10
Beatty, Blaine	90F	197	$ .01	$ .10	Bell, George	92FUL	332	$ .05	$ .20
Beck, Rod	92F	627	$ .01	$ .10	Bell, George	93F	200	$ .01	$ .04
Beck, Rod	92FUL	586	$ .10	$ .40	Bell, George	93FUL	171	$ .01	$ .10
Beck, Rod	93F	150	$ .01	$ .04	Bell, Jay	88F	602	$ .10	$ .75
Beck, Rod	93FUL	126	$ .01	$ .10	Bell, Jay	90F	459	$ .01	$ .04
Beckwith, Joe	83F	202	$ .01	$ .06	Bell, Jay	91F	31	$ .01	$ .04
Beckwith, Joe	84F	97	$ .01	$ .08	Bell, Jay	91FUL	274	$ .01	$ .07
Beckwith, Joe	84FU	10	$ .10	$ .50	Bell, Jay	92F	549	$ .01	$ .04
Beckwith, Joe	85F	197	$ .01	$ .06	Bell, Jay	92FUL	250	$ .01	$ .10
Beckwith, Joe	86F	2	$ .01	$ .06	Bell, Jay	93F	111	$ .01	$ .04
Bedrosian, Steve	83F	129	$ .05	$ .20					
Bedrosian, Steve	84F	171	$ .01	$ .10					
Bedrosian, Steve	85F	319	$ .01	$ .10					
Bedrosian, Steve	86F	508	$ .01	$ .10					
Bedrosian, Steve	86FU	12	$ .01	$ .10					
Bedrosian, Steve	87F	170	$ .01	$ .10					
Bedrosian, Steve	88F	298	$ .01	$ .05					
Bedrosian, Steve	88F	627	$ .01	$ .10					
Bedrosian, Steve	89F	562	$ .01	$ .04					
Bedrosian, Steve	90F	50	$ .01	$ .04					
Bedrosian, Steve	91F	254	$ .01	$ .04					
Bedrosian, Steve	92F	197	$ .01	$ .04					
Belanger, Mark	81F	175	$ .01	$ .06					
Belanger, Mark	82F	158	$ .01	$ .06					
Belcher, Kevin	91F	280	$ .01	$ .10					
Belcher, Tim	88F	509	$ .05	$ .35					
Belcher, Tim	89F	54	$ .01	$ .10					
Belcher, Tim	90F	389	$ .01	$ .04					
Belcher, Tim	91F	194	$ .01	$ .04					
Bolohor, Tim	91FUL	159	$ .01	$ .07					
Belcher, Tim	92F	447	$ .01	$ .04					
Belcher, Tim	92FU	79	$ .05	$ .25					
Belcher, Tim	92FUL	479	$ .01	$ .10					
Belcher, Tim	93F	30	$ .01	$ .04					
Belcher, Tim	93FUL	26	$ .01	$ .10					
Belinda, Stan	90FU	48	$ .01	$ .10					
Belinda, Stan	91F	30	$ .01	$ .04					
Belinda, Stan	91FUL	273	$ .01	$ .07					
Belinda, Stan	92F	548	$ .01	$ .04					
Belinda, Stan	92FUL	550	$ .01	$ .10					
Belinda, Stan	93F	110	$ .01	$ .04					
Belinda, Stan	93FUL	95	$ .01	$ .10					
Bell, Buddy	81F	625	$ .05	$ .20	**Bell, Jay**	**93FUL**	**96**	**$ .01**	**$ .10**
Bell, Buddy	82F	313	$ .05	$ .20	Bell, Juan	91F	468	$ .01	$ .10
Bell, Buddy	83F	562	$ .05	$ .20	Bell, Juan	92F	3	$ .01	$ .04
Bell, Buddy	83F	632	$ .10	$ .50	Bell, Juan	92FU	108	$ .05	$ .25
Bell, Buddy	84F	413	$ .05	$ .20	Bell, Juan	93F	98	$ .01	$ .04
Bell, Buddy	85F	556	$ .05	$ .20	Bell, Juan	93FUL	84	$ .01	$ .10

FLEER

Player	Year	No.	VG	EX/MT
Bell, Kevin	81F	343	$ .01	$ .06
Bell, Mike	91F	682	$ .01	$ .10
Bell, Mike	92F	350	$ .01	$ .04
Bellaird, Rafael	91FULU	65	$ .01	$ .10
Bellaird, Rafael	92FUL	158	$ .01	$ .10
Belle, Joey	89FU	25	$ .75	$3.00
Belle, Joey "Albert"	90F	485	$ .10	$ .50
Belle, Albert	91FU	16	$ .05	$ .20
Belle, Albert	91FUL	107	$ .10	$ .50
Belle, Albert	92F	105	$ .01	$ .15
Belle, Albert	92FUL	47	$ .10	$ .75
Belle, Albert	93F	590	$ .01	$ .15
Belle, Albert	93F	712	$ .01	$ .10
Belliard, Rafael	87F	602	$ .05	$ .25
Belliard, Rafael	88F	321	$ .01	$ .05
Belliard, Rafael	89F	201	$ .01	$ .04
Belliard, Rafael	90F	460	$ .01	$ .04
Belliard, Rafael	91F	32	$ .01	$ .04
Belliard, Rafael	91FU	70	$ .01	$ .05
Belliard, Rafael	92F	351	$ .01	$ .04
Belliard, Rafael	93F	361	$ .01	$ .04
Belliard, Rafael	93FUL	2	$ .01	$ .10
Beltre, Esteban	92F	75	$ .01	$ .15
Beltre, Esteban	92FUL	333	$ .05	$ .20
Benavides, Freddie	91FU	84	$ .01	$ .05
Benavides, Freddie	92F	399	$ .01	$ .04
Benavides, Freddie	92FUL	480	$ .01	$ .10
Benavides, Freddie	93F	402	$ .01	$ .04
Bench, Johnny	81F	196	$ .20	$2.00
Bench, Johnny	82F	57	$ .15	$1.50

Dynamic Duo!
BENCH & SEAVER

Player	Year	No.	VG	EX/MT
Bench, Johnny	**82F**	**634**	**$ .15**	**$1.50**
Bench, Johnny	83F	584	$ .10	$1.00
Bench, Johnny	84F	462	$ .75	$3.00
Bench, Johnny	84F	640	$ .75	$3.00
Benedict, Bruce	81F	248	$ .01	$ .06
Benedict, Bruce	82F	429	$ .01	$ .06
Benedict, Bruce	83F	130	$ .01	$ .06
Benedict, Bruce	84F	172	$ .01	$ .08
Benedict, Bruce	85F	320	$ .01	$ .06
Benedict, Bruce	86F	509	$ .01	$ .06
Benedict, Bruce	87F	512	$ .01	$ .06
Benedict, Bruce	89F	587	$ .01	$ .04
Benes, Andy	90F	151	$ .05	$ .25

Player	Year	No.	VG	EX/MT
Benes, Andy	91F	524	$ .01	$ .10
Benes, Andy	91FUL	301	$ .01	$ .10
Benes, Andy	92F	599	$ .01	$ .04
Benes, Andy	92FUL	274	$ .05	$ .25
Benes, Andy	93F	519	$ .01	$ .04
Benes, Andy	93FUL	116	$ .01	$ .10
Beniquez, Juan	81F	596	$ .01	$ .06
Beniquez, Juan	82F	452	$ .01	$ .06
Beniquez, Juan	83F	78	$ .01	$ .06
Beniquez, Juan	84F	508	$ .01	$ .08
Beniquez, Juan	85F	294	$ .01	$ .06
Beniquez, Juan	86F	148	$ .01	$ .06
Beniquez, Juan	86FU	13	$ .01	$ .08
Beniquez, Juan	87F	462	$ .01	$ .06
Beniquez, Juan	87FU	3	$ .01	$ .06
Beniquez, Juan	88F	104	$ .01	$ .05
Benjamin, Mike	90F	51	$ .01	$ .10
Benjamin, Mike	93F	526	$ .01	$ .04
Benjamin, Mike	93FUL	127	$ .01	$ .10
Benzinger, Todd	88F	344	$ .05	$ .20
Benzinger, Todd	88F	630	$ .05	$ .20
Benzinger, Todd	89F	79	$ .01	$ .15
Benzinger, Todd	89FU	83	$ .01	$ .05
Benzinger, Todd	90F	413	$ .01	$ .04
Benzinger, Todd	91F	56	$ .01	$ .04
Benzinger, Todd	91FUL	87	$ .01	$ .07
Benzinger, Todd	91FULU	25	$ .01	$ .10
Benzinger, Todd	92F	152	$ .01	$ .04
Benzinger, Todd	92FUL	499	$ .01	$ .10
Benzinger, Todd	93F	58	$ .01	$ .04
Berenguer, Juan	84F	77	$ .01	$ .08
Berenguer, Juan	85F	2	$ .01	$ .06
Berenguer, Juan	86F	221	$ .01	$ .06
Berenguer, Juan	87F	265	$ .01	$ .06
Berenguer, Juan	87FU	4	$ .01	$ .06
Berenguer, Juan	88F	3	$ .01	$ .05
Berenguer, Juan	89F	104	$ .01	$ .04
Berenguer, Juan	90F	369	$ .01	$ .04
Berenguer, Juan	91F	604	$ .01	$ .04
Berenguer, Juan	91FU	71	$ .01	$ .05
Berenguer, Juan	91FULU	66	$ .01	$ .10
Berenguer, Juan	92F	352	$ .01	$ .04
Berenguer, Juan	92FUL	455	$ .01	$ .10
Berenyi, Bruce	82F	58	$ .01	$ .06
Berenyi, Bruce	83F	585	$ .01	$ .06
Berenyi, Bruce	84F	463	$ .01	$ .08
Berenyi, Bruce	85F	73	$ .01	$ .06
Bergman, Dave	81F	76	$ .01	$ .06
Bergman, Dave	83F	253	$ .01	$ .06
Bergman, Dave	84F	366	$ .01	$ .08
Bergman, Dave	84FU	11	$ .10	$ .50
Bergman, Dave	85F	3	$ .01	$ .06
Bergman, Dave	86F	222	$ .01	$ .06
Bergman, Dave	87F	144	$ .01	$ .06
Bergman, Dave	88F	52	$ .01	$ .05
Bergman, Dave	89F	129	$ .01	$ .04
Bergman, Dave	90F	600	$ .01	$ .04
Bergman, Dave	91F	331	$ .01	$ .04
Bergman, Dave	91FUL	120	$ .01	$ .07
Bergman, Dave	92FUL	56	$ .01	$ .10
Bernard, Dwight	83F	27	$ .01	$ .06
Bernazard, Tony	81F	168	$ .01	$ .06
Bernazard, Tony	82F	338	$ .01	$ .06
Bernazard, Tony	83F	231	$ .01	$ .06
Bernazard, Tony	84F	606	$ .01	$ .08
Bernazard, Tony	84FU	12	$ .10	$ .50
Bernazard, Tony	85F	439	$ .01	$ .06
Bernazard, Tony	86F	580	$ .01	$ .06
Bernazard, Tony	87F	244	$ .01	$ .06
Bernazard, Tony	88F	275	$ .01	$ .05
Berra, Dale	81F	369	$ .01	$ .06
Berra, Dale	82F	476	$ .01	$ .06
Berra, Dale	83F	303	$ .01	$ .06
Berra, Dale	84F	245	$ .01	$ .08
Berra, Dale	85F	461	$ .01	$ .06

FLEER

Player	Year	No.	VG	EX/MT	Player	Year	No.	VG	EX/MT
Berra, Dale	85FU	4	$.01	$.10	Black, Bud	85F	198	$.01	$.06
Berra, Dale	86F	100	$.01	$.06	Black, Bud	86F	4	$.01	$.06
Berroa, Geronimo	89FU	72	$.01	$.10	Black, Bud	87F	365	$.01	$.06
Berroa, Geronimo	90F	575	$.01	$.04	Black, Bud	88F	252	$.01	$.05
Berry, Sean	92F	680	$.01	$.04	Black, Bud	90F	486	$.01	$.04
Berry, Sean	93F	458	$.01	$.04	Black, Bud	91FU	128	$.01	$.05
Berryhill, Damon	88F	642	$.10	$.75	Black, Bud	91FULU	115	$.01	$.10
Berryhill, Damon	88FU	75	$.05	$.30	Black, Bud	92F	628	$.01	$.04
Berryhill, Damon	89F	418	$.01	$.10	Black, Bud	93F	151	$.01	$.04
Berryhill, Damon	90F	26	$.01	$.04	Blackwell, Tim	81F	304	$.01	$.06
Berryhill, Damon	91F	414	$.01	$.04	Blackwell, Tim	82F	587	$.01	$.06
Berryhill, Damon	91FUL	56	$.01	$.07	Blair, Willie	90FU	126	$.01	$.10
Berryhill, Damon	92FUL	456	$.01	$.10	Blair, Willie	91F	170	$.01	$.10
Berryhill, Damon	93F	362	$.01	$.04	Blair, Willie	92F	106	$.01	$.04
Berryhill, Damon	93FUL	3	$.01	$.10	Blair, Willie	93F	404	$.01	$.04
Best, Karl	85FU	5	$.01	$.10	Blankenship, Kevin	90F	28	$.01	$.04
Best, Karl	86F	459	$.01	$.06	Blankenship, Lance	89F	2	$.01	$.15
Best, Karl	87F	579	$.01	$.06	Blankenship, Lance	90F	1	$.01	$.04
Bevacqua, Kurt	81F	382	$.01	$.06	Blankenship, Lance	91F	3	$.01	$.04
Bevacqua, Kurt	82F	477	$.01	$.06	Blankenship, Lance	92F	250	$.01	$.04
Bevacqua, Kurt	83F	352	$.01	$.06	Blankenship, Lance	92FUL	418	$.01	$.10
Bevacqua, Kurt	84F	294	$.01	$.08	Blankenship, Lance	93F	290	$.01	$.04
Bevacqua, Kurt	85F	26	$.01	$.06	Blankenship, Lance	93FUL	253	$.01	$.10
Bevacqua, Kurt	86F	315	$.01	$.06	Blauser, Jeff	88F	533	$.10	$.50
Biancalana, Buddy	86F	3	$.01	$.06	Blauser, Jeff	89F	588	$.01	$.04
Biancalana, Buddy	87F	364	$.01	$.06	Blauser, Jeff	90F	576	$.01	$.04
Bibby, Jim	81F	370	$.01	$.06	Blauser, Jeff	91F	683	$.01	$.04
Bibby, Jim	82F	478	$.01	$.06	Blauser, Jeff	91FUL	2	$.01	$.07
Bibby, Jim	84F	246	$.01	$.08	Blauser, Jeff	92F	353	$.01	$.04
Bichette, Dante	89F	468	$.05	$.20	Blauser, Jeff	92FUL	159	$.01	$.10
Bichette, Dante	90F	127	$.01	$.04	Blauser, Jeff	93F	364	$.01	$.04
Bichette, Dante	91F	307	$.01	$.04	Blocker, Terry	89F	589	$.01	$.04
Bichette, Dante	91FU	29	$.01	$.05	Blowers, Mike	90F	438	$.01	$.10
Bichette, Dante	92F	173	$.01	$.04	Blue, Vida	81F	432	$.01	$.10
Bichette, Dante	92FUL	79	$.01	$.10	Blue, Vida	82F	384	$.01	$.10
Bichette, Dante	93F	403	$.01	$.04	Blue, Vida	83F	106	$.01	$.06
Bielecki, Mike	85F	650	$.05	$.35	Blue, Vida	83F	643	$.01	$.06
Bielecki, Mike	86F	603	$.01	$.06	Blue, Vida	85FU	7	$.01	$.10
Bielecki, Mike	87F	603	$.01	$.06	Blue, Vida	86F	533	$.01	$.06
Bielecki, Mike	89F	419	$.01	$.04	Blue, Vida	87F	266	$.01	$.06
Bielecki, Mike	90F	27	$.01	$.04	Blyleven, Bert	81F	383	$.10	$.40
Bielecki, Mike	91F	415	$.01	$.04	Blyleven, Bert	82F	361	$.05	$.25
Bielecki, Mike	91FUL	57	$.01	$.07	Blyleven, Bert	84F	536	$.10	$.40
Bielecki, Mike	92FUL	457	$.01	$.10	Blyleven, Bert	85F	440	$.05	$.25
Bielecki, Mike	93F	363	$.01	$.04	Blyleven, Bert	86F	386	$.01	$.10
Biggio, Craig	88FU	89	$.10	$1.00	Blyleven, Bert	87F	536	$.01	$.10
Biggio, Craig	89F	353	$.10	$.40	Blyleven, Bert	88F	4	$.01	$.10
Biggio, Craig	90F	224	$.01	$.15	Blyleven, Bert	89F	105	$.01	$.10
Biggio, Craig	91F	499	$.01	$.04	Blyleven, Bert	89FU	12	$.01	$.10
Biggio, Craig	91FUL	132	$.01	$.10	Blyleven, Bert	90F	128	$.01	$.10
Biggio, Craig	92F	426	$.01	$.04	Blyleven, Bert	91F	308	$.01	$.04
Biggio, Craig	92FUL	199	$.01	$.10	Blyleven, Bert	93F	568	$.01	$.04
Biggio, Craig	93F	47	$.01	$.04	Bobbicker, Mike	86F	269	$.01	$.10
Biggio, Craig	93FUL	37	$.01	$.10	Bochte, Bruce	81F	600	$.01	$.06
Biittner, Larry	81F	314	$.01	$.06	Bochte, Bruce	82F	505	$.01	$.06
Biittner, Larry	82F	59	$.01	$.06	Bochte, Bruce	83F	473	$.01	$.06
Biittner, Larry	83F	586	$.01	$.06	Bochte, Bruce	84FU	13	$.10	$.50
Biittner, Larry	84F	414	$.01	$.08	Bochte, Bruce	85F	416	$.01	$.06
Bilardello, Dann	84F	464	$.01	$.08	Bochte, Bruce	86F	413	$.01	$.06
Bilardello, Dann	87F	313	$.01	$.06	Bochte, Bruce	87F	388	$.01	$.06
Bird, Doug	81F	106	$.01	$.06	Bochy, Bruce	81F	69	$.01	$.06
Bird, Doug	82F	586	$.01	$.06	Bochy, Bruce	87F	411	$.01	$.06
Bird, Doug	83F	490	$.01	$.06	Bockus, Randy	87FU	6	$.01	$.06
Bird, Doug	84F	391	$.01	$.08	Bockus, Randy	88FU	127	$.01	$.06
Birkbeck, Mike	87FU	5	$.01	$.06	Boddicker, Mike	84F	1	$.05	$.25
Birkbeck, Mike	89F	178	$.01	$.04	Boddicker, Mike	84F	645	$.01	$.08
Birtsas, Tim	85FU	6	$.01	$.10	Boddicker, Mike	85F	170	$.01	$.06
Birtsas, Tim	86F	412	$.01	$.10	Boddicker, Mike	87F	463	$.01	$.06
Birtsas, Tim	88FU	82	$.01	$.06	Boddicker, Mike	88F	556	$.01	$.05
Birtsas, Tim	89F	152	$.01	$.04	Boddicker, Mike	88FU	5	$.01	$.06
Birtsas, Tim	90F	414	$.01	$.04	Boddicker, Mike	89F	80	$.01	$.04
Bitker, Joe	91F	281	$.01	$.10	Boddicker, Mike	90F	267	$.01	$.04
Black, Bud	83F	107	$.05	$.35	Boddicker, Mike	91F	85	$.01	$.04
Black, Bud	83F	644	$.01	$.06	Boddicker, Mike	92F	153	$.01	$.04
Black, Bud	84F	343	$.01	$.08	Boddicker, Mike	92FUL	67	$.01	$.10

FLEER

Player	Year	No.	VG	EX/MT	Player	Year	No.	VG	EX/MT
Boddicker, Mike	93F	616	$ .01	$ .04	Bonnell, Barry	81F	413	$ .01	$ .06
Boddicker, Mike	93FUL	205	$ .01	$ .10	Bonnell, Barry	82F	611	$ .01	$ .06
Boever, Joe	88F	534	$ .01	$ .10	Bonnell, Barry	83F	425	$ .01	$ .06
Boever, Joe	90F	577	$ .01	$ .04	Bonnell, Barry	84F	149	$ .01	$ .08
Boever, Joe	91F	387	$ .01	$ .04	Bonnell, Barry	84FU	14	$ .10	$ .50
Boever, Joe	92F	523	$ .01	$ .04	Bonnell, Barry	85F	485	$ .01	$ .06
Boever, Joe	93F	48	$ .01	$ .04	Bonnell, Barry	86F	460	$ .01	$ .06
Boggs, Tommy	81F	261	$ .01	$ .06	Bonner, Bob	83F	53	$ .01	$ .06
Boggs, Tommy	82F	430	$ .01	$ .06	Booker, Greg	85F	27	$ .01	$ .10
Boggs, Tommy	83F	131	$ .01	$ .06	Booker, Greg	88F	577	$ .01	$ .05
Boggs, Wade	83F	179	$6.00	$24.00	Booker, Rod	87FU	7	$ .01	$ .15
Boggs, Wade	84F	392	$2.50	$10.00	Booker, Rod	91F	388	$ .01	$ .04
Boggs, Wade	84F	630	$ .20	$2.00	Boone, Bob	81F	4	$ .01	$ .06
Boggs, Wade	85F	151	$1.25	$5.00	Boone, Bob	82F	240	$ .01	$ .06
Boggs, Wade	86F	341	$ .75	$3.00	Boone, Bob	83F	79	$ .01	$ .06
Boggs, Wade	86F	634	$ .10	$1.00	Boone, Bob	84F	509	$ .01	$ .08
Boggs, Wade	86F	639	$ .10	$1.00	Boone, Bob	84F	637	$ .01	$ .08
Boggs, Wade	87F	29	$ .15	$1.50	Boone, Bob	85F	295	$ .01	$ .06
Boggs, Wade	87F	637	$ .05	$ .25	Boone, Bob	86F	149	$ .01	$ .06
Boggs, Wade	88F	345	$ .10	$ .50	Boone, Bob	87F	73	$ .01	$ .06
Boggs, Wade	89F	81	$ .05	$ .25	Boone, Bob	88F	485	$ .01	$ .05
Boggs, Wade	89F	633	$ .01	$ .10	Boone, Bob	89F	469	$ .01	$ .04
Boggs, Wade	90F	268	$ .05	$ .20	Boone, Bob	89FU	36	$ .01	$ .05
Boggs, Wade	90F	632	$ .01	$ .10	Boone, Bob	90F	102	$ .01	$ .04
Boggs, Wade	91F	86	$ .01	$ .15	Boone, Bob	91F	551	$ .01	$ .04
Boggs, Wade	91FUL	27	$ .05	$ .25	Boone, Bret	92FU	54	$ .20	$2.00
Boggs, Wade	92F	32	$ .01	$ .15	Boone, Bret	93F	304	$ .05	$ .25
Boggs, Wade	92F	707	$ .01	$ .04	Boone, Bret	93FUL	266	$ .10	$ .50
Boggs, Wade	92FUL	311	$ .10	$ .50	Boone, Danny	82F	568	$ .01	$ .06
Boggs, Wade	93F	554	$ .01	$ .10	Borders, Pat	88FU	65	$ .10	$ .50
Bohanon, Brian	90FU	122	$ .01	$ .10	Borders, Pat	89F	227	$ .05	$ .25
Bolton, Tom	88F	346	$ .01	$ .10	Borders, Pat	90F	77	$ .01	$ .04
Bolton, Tom	91F	87	$ .01	$ .04	Borders, Pat	91F	171	$ .01	$ .04
Bolton, Tom	91FUL	28	$ .01	$ .07	Borders, Pat	91FUL	359	$ .01	$ .07
Bolton, Tom	92F	33	$ .01	$ .04	Borders, Pat	92F	325	$ .01	$ .04
Bomback, Mark	81F	323	$ .01	$ .06	Borders, Pat	92FUL	144	$ .01	$ .10
Bomback, Mark	82F	610	$ .01	$ .06	Borders, Pat	93F	332	$ .01	$ .04
Bonds, Barry	86FU	14	$3.00	$12.00	Borders, Pat	93FUL	287	$ .01	$ .10
Bonds, Barry	87F	604	$7.00	$28.00	Bordi, Rich	85F	49	$ .01	$ .06
Bonds, Barry	88F	322	$ .15	$1.50	Bordi, Rich	85FU	8	$ .01	$ .10
Bonds, Barry	89F	202	$ .10	$ .40	Bordi, Rich	86F	101	$ .01	$ .06
Bonds, Barry	90F	461	$ .05	$ .25	Bordi, Rich	86FU	16	$ .01	$ .08
Bonds, Barry	91F	33	$ .05	$ .20	Bordi, Rich	87F	465	$ .01	$ .06
Bonds, Barry	91F	710	$ .05	$ .25	Bordick, Mike	92F	251	$ .01	$ .04
Bonds, Barry	91FUL	275	$ .10	$ .40	Bordick, Mike	92FUL	419	$ .05	$ .20
Bonds, Barry	91FUL	391	$ .05	$ .20	Bordick, Mike	93F	291	$ .01	$ .04
Bonds, Barry	92F	550	$ .05	$ .25	Bordick, Mike	93FUL	254	$ .01	$ .10
Bonds, Barry	92FUL	251	$ .10	$1.00	Bosetti, Rick	82F	88	$ .01	$ .06
Bonds, Barry	93F	112	$ .05	$ .25	Bosio, Chris	87F	338	$ .10	$1.00
Bonds, Barry	93F	350	$ .01	$ .15	Bosio, Chris	88F	156	$ .01	$ .10
Bonds, Bobby	81F	548	$ .01	$ .10	Bosio, Chris	89F	179	$ .01	$ .04
Bonds, Bobby	82F	588	$ .01	$ .06	Bosio, Chris	90F	316	$ .01	$ .04
Bones, Ricky	92F	600	$ .01	$ .10	Bosio, Chris	91F	576	$ .01	$ .04
Bones, Ricky	92FUL	378	$ .05	$ .20	Bosio, Chris	92FUL	379	$ .01	$ .10
Bones, Ricky	93F	247	$ .01	$ .04	Bosio, Chris	93F	628	$ .01	$ .04
Bonham, Bill	81F	215	$ .01	$ .06	Boskie, Shawn	90FU	7	$ .01	$ .10
Bonilla, Bobby	86FU	15	$1.00	$4.00	Boskie, Shawn	91F	416	$ .01	$ .10
Bonilla, Bobby	87F	605	$1.25	$5.00	Boskie, Shawn	92F	377	$ .01	$ .04
Bonilla, Bobby	88F	323	$ .10	$ .50	Boskie, Shawn	92FUL	466	$ .01	$ .10
Bonilla, Bobby	89F	203	$ .05	$ .20	Boskie, Shawn	93F	373	$ .01	$ .04
Bonilla, Bobby	89F	637	$ .05	$ .20	Bosley, Thad	81F	353	$ .01	$ .06
Bonilla, Bobby	90F	462	$ .01	$ .15	Bosley, Thad	86F	361	$ .01	$ .06
Bonilla, Bobby	91F	34	$ .01	$ .10	Bosley, Thad	87F	555	$ .01	$ .06
Bonilla, Bobby	91F	711	$ .05	$ .20	Bosley, Thad	87FU	8	$ .01	$ .06
Bonilla, Bobby	91FUL	276	$ .05	$ .20	Bosley, Thad	88F	253	$ .01	$ .06
Bonilla, Bobby	92F	551	$ .01	$ .10	Boston, Daryl	85FU	9	$ .05	$ .20
Bonilla, Bobby	92F	699	$ .01	$ .10	Boston, Daryl	87F	487	$ .01	$ .06
Bonilla, Bobby	92F	699	$ .01	$ .10	Boston, Daryl	88F	393	$ .01	$ .05
Bonilla, Bobby	92FU	101	$ .05	$ .25	Boston, Daryl	89F	492	$ .01	$ .04
Bonilla, Bobby	92FUL	527	$ .05	$ .25	Boston, Daryl	90FU	33	$ .01	$ .05
Bonilla, Bobby	93F	84	$ .01	$ .10	Boston, Daryl	91F	140	$ .01	$ .04
Bonilla, Juan	82F	567	$ .01	$ .06	Boston, Daryl	91FUL	211	$ .01	$ .07
Bonilla, Juan	83F	353	$ .01	$ .06	Boston, Daryl	92F	495	$ .01	$ .04
Bonilla, Juan	84F	295	$ .01	$ .08	Boston, Daryl	92FUL	227	$ .01	$ .10
Bonilla, Juan	87F	464	$ .01	$ .06	Boston, Daryl	93F	85	$ .01	$ .04

FLEER

Player	Year	No.	VG	EX/MT
Bottenfield, Kent	93FUL	62	$ .05	$ .20
Boucher, Denis	93F	405	$ .01	$ .04
Bournigal, Rafael	93FUL	50	$ .10	$ .50
Bowa, Larry	81F	2	$ .01	$ .10
Bowa, Larry	81F	645	$ .15	$1.50
Bowa, Larry	82F	241	$ .01	$ .10
Bowa, Larry	83F	491	$ .01	$ .10
Bowa, Larry	84F	486	$ .01	$ .10
Bowa, Larry	85F	50	$ .01	$ .10
Bowen, Ryan	92FUL	488	$ .05	$ .20
Bowen, Ryan	93F	419	$ .01	$ .04
Bower, Bob	89F	514	$ .01	$ .04
Boyd, Dennis "Oil Can"	84F	393	$ .05	$ .25
Boyd, Dennis	85F	152	$ .05	$ .20
Boyd, Dennis	86F	342	$ .01	$ .06
Boyd, Dennis	87F	30	$ .01	$ .06
Boyd, Dennis	88F	347	$ .01	$ .05
Boyd, "Oil Can"	89F	82	$ .01	$ .04
Boyd, Dennis	90FU	26	$ .01	$ .05
Boyd, Dennis	91F	226	$ .01	$ .04
Boyd, Dennis	91FUL	197	$ .01	$ .07
Bradford, Larry	81F	265	$ .01	$ .06
Bradford, Larry	82F	431	$ .01	$ .06
Bradley, Mark	84F	581	$ .01	$ .08
Bradley, Phil	84FU	15	$ .15	$1.50
Bradley, Phil	85F	486	$ .05	$ .25
Bradley, Phil	86F	461	$ .05	$ .20
Bradley, Phil	87F	581	$ .01	$ .10
Bradley, Phil	88F	369	$ .01	$ .10
Bradley, Phil	88FU	107	$ .01	$ .06
Bradley, Phil	89F	563	$ .01	$ .04
Bradley, Phil	89FU	1	$ .01	$ .05
Bradley, Phil	90F	174	$ .01	$ .04
Bradley, Phil	91F	114	$ .01	$ .04
Bradley, Scott	87F	580	$ .01	$ .06
Bradley, Scott	88F	370	$ .01	$ .05
Bradley, Scott	89F	540	$ .01	$ .04
Bradley, Scott	90F	506	$ .01	$ .04
Bradley, Scott	91F	443	$ .01	$ .04
Bradley, Scott	91FUL	332	$ .01	$ .07
Bradley, Scott	92F	273	$ .01	$ .04
Braggs, Glenn	87F	339	$ .05	$ .25
Braggs, Glenn	88F	157	$ .01	$ .10
Braggs, Glenn	89F	180	$ .01	$ .04
Braggs, Glenn	90F	317	$ .01	$ .04
Braggs, Glenn	90FU	11	$ .01	$ .05
Braggs, Glenn	91F	57	$ .01	$ .04
Braggs, Glenn	91FUL	88	$ .01	$ .07
Braggs, Glenn	92F	400	$ .01	$ .04
Braggs, Glenn	92FUL	185	$ .01	$ .10
Branson, Jeff	93F	31	$ .01	$ .10
Branson, Jeff	93FUL	27	$ .01	$ .10
Brantley, Cliff	92F	662	$ .01	$ .15
Brantley, Cliff	92FUL	543	$ .01	$ .10
Brantley, Cliff	93F	486	$ .01	$ .04
Brantley, Jeff	89FU	127	$ .01	$ .15
Brantley, Jeff	00F	52	$ .01	$ .10
Brantley, Jeff	91F	255	$ .01	$ .04
Brantley, Jeff	91FUL	316	$ .01	$ .07
Brantley, Jeff	92F	629	$ .01	$ .04
Brantley, Jeff	92FUL	285	$ .01	$ .10
Brantley, Jeff	93F	152	$ .01	$ .04
Brantley, Jeff	93FUL	128	$ .01	$ .10
Brantley, Mickey	86F	651	$ .05	$ .25
Brantley, Mickey	87F	582	$ .01	$ .06
Brantley, Mickey	88F	371	$ .01	$ .05
Brantley, Mickey	89F	541	$ .01	$ .04
Braun, Steve	81F	427	$ .01	$ .06
Braun, Steve	82F	111	$ .01	$ .06
Braun, Steve	83F	3	$ .01	$ .06
Braun, Steve	84F	320	$ .01	$ .08
Braun, Steve	85F	221	$ .01	$ .06
Braun, Steve	86F	27	$ .01	$ .06
Bream, Sid	86F	604	$ .01	$ .06
Bream, Sid	87F	606	$ .01	$ .06
Bream, Sid	88F	324	$ .01	$ .05
Bream, Sid	89F	204	$ .01	$ .04
Bream, Sid	90F	463	$ .01	$ .04
Bream, Sid	91F	35	$ .01	$ .04
Bream, Sid	91FU	72	$ .01	$ .05
Bream, Sid	92F	354	$ .01	$ .04
Bream, Sid	92FUL	160	$ .01	$ .10
Bream, Sid	93F	2	$ .01	$ .04
Bream, Sid	93FUL	4	$ .01	$ .10
Breining, Fred	82F	385	$ .01	$ .06
Breining, Fred	83F	254	$ .01	$ .06
Breining, Fred	84F	367	$ .01	$ .08
Breining, Fred	84FU	16	$ .10	$ .50
Breining, Fred	85F	392	$ .01	$ .06
Brenly, Bob	83F	255	$ .01	$ .06
Brenly, Bob	84F	368	$ .01	$ .08
Brenly, Bob	85F	603	$ .01	$ .06
Brenly, Bob	86F	534	$ .01	$ .06
Brenly, Bob	87F	267	$ .01	$ .06
Brenly, Bob	88F	77	$ .01	$ .05
Brennan, Tom	83F	403	$ .01	$ .06
Brennan, Tom	84F	537	$ .01	$ .04
Brett, George	81F	28	$1.00	$4.00
Brett, George	81F	655	$ .75	$3.00
Brett, George	82F	405	$ .25	$2.50
Brett, George	83F	108	$ .20	$2.00
Brett, George	84F	344	$1.25	$5.00
Brett, George	84F	638	$ .10	$1.00
Brett, George	85F	199	$ .75	$3.00
Brett, George	86F	5	$ .20	$2.00
Brett, George	86F	634	$ .10	$1.00
Brett, George	87F	366	$ .10	$1.00
Brett, George	88F	254	$ .10	$ .50
Brett, George	89F	277	$ .05	$ .20
Brett, George	90F	103	$ .01	$ .15
Brett, George	90FPD	621	$ .01	$ .15
Brett, George	91F	552	$ .01	$ .10
Brett, George	91FUL	144	$ .05	$ .20

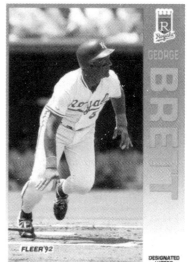

Player	Year	No.	VG	EX/MT
Brett, George	92F	154	$ .01	$ .10
Brett, George	92FUL	68	$ .10	$ .50
Brett, George	93F	236	$ .01	$ .10
Brett, George	93FUL	206	$ .05	$ .35
Brett, Ken	82F	406	$ .01	$ .06

FLEER

Player	Year	No.	VG	EX/MT
Briley, Greg	89FU	57	$ .01	$ .15
Briley, Greg	90F	507	$ .01	$ .10
Briley, Greg	91F	444	$ .01	$ .04
Briley, Greg	92F	274	$ .01	$ .04
Briley, Greg	92FUL	120	$ .01	$ .10
Briley, Greg	93F	670	$ .01	$ .04
Brock, Greg	83F	203	$ .10	$ .40
Brock, Greg	84F	98	$ .01	$ .08
Brock, Greg	85F	368	$ .01	$ .06
Brock, Greg	86F	125	$ .01	$ .06
Brock, Greg	87F	437	$ .01	$ .06
Brock, Greg	87FU	9	$ .01	$ .06
Brock, Greg	88F	158	$ .01	$ .05
Brock, Greg	89F	181	$ .01	$ .04
Brock, Greg	90F	318	$ .01	$ .04
Brock, Greg	91F	577	$ .01	$ .04
Brock, Greg	91FUL	172	$ .01	$ .07
Brogna, Rico	92FU	19	$ .05	$ .25
Brohamer, Jack	81F	393	$ .01	$ .06
Brookens, Tom	81F	473	$ .01	$ .06
Brookens, Tom	82F	263	$ .01	$ .06
Brookens, Tom	83F	327	$ .01	$ .06
Brookens, Tom	84F	78	$ .01	$ .08
Brookens, Tom	85F	4	$ .01	$ .06
Brookens, Tom	86F	223	$ .01	$ .06
Brookens, Tom	87F	145	$ .01	$ .06
Brookens, Tom	88F	53	$ .01	$ .05
Brookens, Tom	89F	132	$ .01	$ .15
Brookens, Tom	90F	439	$ .01	$ .04
Brookens, Tom	91F	362	$ .01	$ .04
Brooks, Hubie	82F	522	$ .05	$ .35
Brooks, Hubie	83F	539	$ .01	$ .15
Brooks, Hubie	84F	582	$ .05	$ .20
Brooks, Hubie	85F	74	$ .01	$ .10
Brooks, Hubie	85FU	10	$ .05	$ .20
Brooks, Hubie	86F	244	$ .01	$ .10
Brooks, Hubie	87F	314	$ .01	$ .10
Brooks, Hubie	88F	179	$ .01	$ .10
Brooks, Hubie	89F	371	$ .01	$ .04
Brooks, Hubie	90F	341	$ .01	$ .04
Brooks, Hubie	90FU	19	$ .01	$ .05
Brooks, Hubie	91F	195	$ .01	$ .04
Brooks, Hubie	91FU	100	$ .01	$ .05

Player	Year	No.	VG	EX/MT
Brooks, Hubie	91FULU	94	$ .01	$ .10
Brooks, Hubie	92F	496	$ .01	$ .04
Brooks, Hubie	92FUL	322	$ .01	$ .10
Brosius, Scott	92F	671	$ .01	$ .10
Bross, Terry	92F	653	$ .01	$ .04
Brosus, Scott	92FUL	420	$ .01	$ .10
Brouhard, Mark	82F	135	$ .01	$ .06
Brouhard, Mark	83F	28	$ .01	$ .06
Brouhard, Mark	84F	195	$ .01	$ .08
Brouhard, Mark	85F	576	$ .01	$ .06
Brower, Bob	87FU	10	$ .01	$ .10
Brower, Bob	88F	461	$ .01	$ .05
Brown, Bobby	81F	95	$ .01	$ .06
Brown, Bobby	82F	30	$ .01	$ .06
Brown, Bobby	84F	296	$ .01	$ .08
Brown, Bobby	85F	28	$ .01	$ .06
Brown, Chris	85FU	11	$ .05	$ .20
Brown, Chris	86F	535	$ .05	$ .20
Brown, Chris	87F	268	$ .05	$ .20
Brown, Chris	87FU	11	$ .01	$ .10
Brown, Chris	88F	578	$ .01	$ .10
Brown, Chris	89F	301	$ .01	$ .04
Brown, Darrell	84F	556	$ .01	$ .08
Brown, Darrell	85F	270	$ .01	$ .06
Brown, Jarvis	92F	669	$ .01	$ .10
Brown, Jarvis	92FUL	394	$ .05	$ .20
Brown, Keith	89F	154	$ .01	$ .15
Brown, Keith	91F	58	$ .01	$ .04
Brown, Kevin	89F	641	$ .10	$ .75
Brown, Kevin	89FU	63	$ .05	$ .20
Brown, Kevin	90F	291	$ .01	$ .10
Brown, Kevin	91F	282	$ .01	$ .04
Brown, Kevin	91FUL	347	$ .01	$ .07
Brown, Kevin	92F	174	$ .01	$ .04
Brown, Kevin	92F	299	$ .01	$ .04
Brown, Kevin	92FUL	438	$ .01	$ .10
Brown, Kevin	93F	317	$ .01	$ .04
Brown, Kevin	93FUL	276	$ .01	$ .10
Brown, Marty	89F	645	$ .01	$ .15
Brown, Mike	84F	394	$ .01	$ .08
Brown, Mike	84FU	17	$ .10	$ .50
Brown, Mike	85F	296	$ .01	$ .06
Brown, Mike	86F	605	$ .01	$ .06
Brown, Mike	87F	583	$ .01	$ .06
Brown, Mike	87F	607	$ .01	$ .06
Brown, Scott	82F	60	$ .01	$ .06
Browne, Jerry	87F	647	$ .05	$ .25
Browne, Jerry	87FU	12	$ .01	$ .06
Browne, Jerry	88F	462	$ .01	$ .05
Browne, Jerry	89FU	26	$ .01	$ .10
Browne, Jerry	90F	487	$ .01	$ .04
Browne, Jerry	91F	363	$ .01	$ .04
Browne, Jerry	91FUL	108	$ .01	$ .07
Browne, Jerry	92F	107	$ .01	$ .04
Browne, Jerry	92FU	47	$ .05	$ .25
Browne, Jerry	92FUL	48	$ .01	$ .10
Browne, Jerry	93F	292	$ .01	$ .04
Browne, Jerry	93FUL	255	$ .01	$ .10
Browning, Tom	85FU	12	$ .10	$1.00
Browning, Tom	86F	173	$ .10	$ .50
Browning, Tom	87F	194	$ .05	$ .25
Browning, Tom	88F	228	$ .01	$ .15
Browning, Tom	89F	153	$ .01	$ .10
Browning, Tom	89F	629	$ .01	$ .10
Browning, Tom	90F	415	$ .01	$ .10
Browning, Tom	91F	59	$ .01	$ .04
Browning, Tom	91FUL	89	$ .01	$ .07
Browning, Tom	92F	401	$ .01	$ .04
Browning, Tom	92FUL	186	$ .01	$ .10
Browning, Tom	93F	387	$ .01	$ .04
Bruett, J.T.	93FUL	229	$ .01	$ .10
Brumfield, Jacob	92FUL	481	$ .05	$ .20
Brumley, Mike	89F	302	$ .01	$ .04
Brumley, Mike	89FU	30	$ .01	$ .05
Brumley, Mike	91F	445	$ .01	$ .04

FLEER

Player	Year	No.	VG	EX/MT	Player	Year	No.	VG	EX/MT
Brummer, Glenn	83F	4	$ .01	$ .06	Burke, Tim	85FU	14	$ .05	$ .25
Brummer, Glenn	84F	321	$ .01	$ .08	Burke, Tim	86F	245	$ .05	$ .20
Brummer, Glenn	86F	557	$ .01	$ .06	Burke, Tim	87F	315	$ .01	$ .06
Brunansky, Tom	83F	607	$ .05	$ .35	Burke, Tim	88F	180	$ .01	$ .05
Brunansky, Tom	84F	557	$ .05	$ .25	Burke, Tim	89F	372	$ .01	$ .04
Brunansky, Tom	85F	271	$ .05	$ .20	Burke, Tim	90F	342	$ .01	$ .04
Brunansky, Tom	86F	387	$ .01	$ .10	Burke, Tim	91F	227	$ .01	$ .04
Brunansky, Tom	87F	537	$ .01	$ .06	Burke, Tim	91FUL	198	$ .01	$ .07
Brunansky, Tom	88F	5	$ .01	$ .10	Burke, Tim	91FULU	95	$ .01	$ .10
Brunansky, Tom	88FU	117	$ .01	$ .10	Burke, Tim	92F	497	$ .01	$ .04
Brunansky, Tom	89F	444	$ .01	$ .10	Burke, Tim	92FUL	228	$ .01	$ .10
Brunansky, Tom	90F	242	$ .01	$ .04	Burke, Tim	93F	647	$ .01	$ .04
Brunansky, Tom	90FU	70	$ .01	$ .05	Burkett, John	88F	651	$ .10	$ .50
Brunansky, Tom	91F	88	$ .01	$ .04	Burkett, John	90FU	61	$ .01	$ .15
Brunansky, Tom	91FUL	29	$ .01	$ .07	Burkett, John	91F	256	$ .01	$ .10
Brunansky, Tom	92F	34	$ .01	$ .04	Burkett, John	91FUL	317	$ .01	$ .07
Brunansky, Tom	92FUL	12	$ .01	$ .10	Burkett, John	92F	630	$ .01	$ .04
Brunansky, Tom	93F	555	$ .01	$ .04	Burkett, John	92FUL	286	$ .01	$ .10
Brusstar, Warren	82F	242	$ .01	$ .06	Burkett, John	93F	153	$ .01	$ .04
Brusstar, Warren	84F	487	$ .01	$ .08	Burkett, John	93FUL	129	$ .01	$ .10
Brusstar, Warren	85F	51	$ .01	$ .06	Burks, Ellis	87FU	15	$ .10	$ .75
Brusstar, Warren	86F	362	$ .01	$ .06	Burks, Ellis	88F	348	$ .10	$ .75
Bryant, Ralph	87F	649	$ .05	$ .25	Burks, Ellis	88F	630	$ .05	$ .20
Bryant, Ralph	87FU	13	$ .01	$ .06	Burks, Ellis	89F	83	$ .01	$ .15
Bryant, Ralph	88F	510	$ .01	$ .05	Burks, Ellis	90F	269	$ .01	$ .10
Buckner, Bill	81F	292	$ .01	$ .10	Burks, Ellis	91F	89	$ .01	$ .10
Buckner, Bill	82F	589	$ .01	$ .10	Burks, Ellis	91FUL	30	$ .01	$ .10
Buckner, Bill	83F	492	$ .01	$ .10	Burks, Ellis	92F	35	$ .01	$ .04
Buckner, Bill	84F	488	$ .01	$ .08	Burks, Ellis	92FUL	13	$ .01	$ .10
Buckner, Bill	84FU	18	$ .10	$ .50	Burks, Ellis	93F	176	$ .01	$ .04
Buckner, Bill	85F	153	$ .01	$ .06	Burleson, Rick	81F	225	$ .01	$ .06
Buckner, Bill	86F	343	$ .01	$ .10	Burleson, Rick	82F	453	$ .01	$ .06
Buckner, Bill	87F	31	$ .01	$ .06	Burleson, Rick	83F	80	$ .01	$ .06
Buckner, Bill	88F	486	$ .01	$ .05	Burleson, Rick	84F	510	$ .01	$ .08
Buckner, Bill	89F	278	$ .01	$ .04	Burleson, Rick	87F	74	$ .01	$ .06
Buechele, Steve	86F	558	$ .10	$ .75	Burmeier, Tom	81F	228	$ .01	$ .06
Buechele, Steve	87F	121	$ .01	$ .06	Burns, Britt	81F	342	$ .05	$ .25
Buechele, Steve	88F	463	$ .01	$ .05	Burns, Britt	82F	339	$ .01	$ .06
Buechele, Steve	89F	515	$ .01	$ .04	Burns, Britt	83F	232	$ .01	$ .06
Buechele, Steve	90F	292	$ .01	$ .04	Burns, Britt	84F	54	$ .01	$ .08
Buechele, Steve	91F	283	$ .01	$ .04	Burns, Britt	85F	509	$ .01	$ .06
Buechele, Steve	92F	552	$ .01	$ .04	Burns, Britt	86F	200	$ .01	$ .06
Buechele, Steve	92FUL	252	$ .01	$ .10	Burns, Todd	88FU	52	$ .05	$ .25
Buechele, Steve	93F	18	$ .01	$ .04	Burns, Todd	89F	3	$ .01	$ .15
Buechele, Steve	93FUL	15	$ .01	$ .15	Burns, Todd	90F	2	$ .01	$ .04
Buhner, Jay	89F	542	$ .01	$ .10	Burns, Todd	91F	4	$ .01	$ .04
Buhner, Jay	90F	508	$ .01	$ .04	Burns, Todd	91FUL	243	$ .01	$ .07
Buhner, Jay	91F	446	$ .01	$ .04	Burns, Todd	93F	318	$ .01	$ .04
Buhner, Jay	91FULU	49	$ .01	$ .10	Burnside, Sheldon	81F	220	$ .01	$ .06
Buhner, Jay	92F	275	$ .01	$ .04	Burris, Ray	81F	328	$ .01	$ .06
Buhner, Jay	92FUL	121	$ .01	$ .10	Burris, Ray	82F	184	$ .01	$ .06
Buhner, Jay	93F	305	$ .01	$ .04	Burris, Ray	83F	277	$ .01	$ .06
Buhner, Jay	93FUL	267	$ .01	$ .10	Burris, Ray	84F	270	$ .01	$ .08
Buice, DeWayne	87FU	14	$ .01	$ .06	Burris, Ray	84FU	19	$ .10	$ .50
Buice, DeWayne	88F	487	$ .01	$ .05	Burris, Ray	85F	418	$ .01	$ .06
Bullett, Scott	92FUL	551	$ .05	$ .20	Burris, Ray	85FU	15	$ .01	$ .10
Bulling, Terry	83F	630	$ .01	$ .10	Burris, Ray	86F	482	$ .01	$ .00
Bullinger, Jim	92FU	73	$ .05	$ .25	Burroughs, Jeff	81F	245	$ .01	$ .06
Bullinger, Jim	93F	374	$ .01	$ .04	Burroughs, Jeff	82F	506	$ .01	$ .06
Bullock, Eric	89F	106	$ .01	$ .10	Burroughs, Jeff	83F	515	$ .01	$ .06
Bullock, Eric	92F	474	$ .01	$ .04	Burroughs, Jeff	84F	440	$ .01	$ .08
Bumbry, Al	81F	172	$ .01	$ .06	Burroughs, Jeff	85FU	16	$ .01	$ .10
Bumbry, Al	82F	159	$ .01	$ .06	Burroughs, Jeff	86F	54	$ .01	$ .06
Bumbry, Al	83F	54	$ .01	$ .06	Busby, Steve	81F	33	$ .01	$ .06
Bumbry, Al	84F	2	$ .01	$ .08	Bush, Randy	84F	558	$ .01	$ .08
Bumbry, Al	85F	171	$ .01	$ .06	Bush, Randy	85F	272	$ .01	$ .06
Bumbry, Al	85FU	13	$ .01	$ .10	Bush, Randy	86F	388	$ .01	$ .06
Bumbry, Al	86F	316	$ .01	$ .06	Bush, Randy	87F	538	$ .01	$ .06
Burba, Dave	91F	447	$ .01	$ .10	Bush, Randy	88F	6	$ .01	$ .05
Burba, Dave	92FUL	587	$ .01	$ .10	Bush, Randy	89F	107	$ .01	$ .04
Burba, Dave	93F	527	$ .01	$ .04	Bush, Randy	90F	370	$ .01	$ .04
Burgmeier, Tom	82F	288	$ .01	$ .06	Bush, Randy	91F	605	$ .01	$ .04
Burgmeier, Tom	83F	180	$ .01	$ .06	Bush, Randy	91FULU	34	$ .01	$ .10
Burgmeier, Tom	84F	439	$ .01	$ .08	Bush, Randy	92F	198	$ .01	$ .04
Burgmeier, Tom	85F	417	$ .01	$ .06	Bush, Randy	93F	638	$ .01	$ .04

FLEER

Player	Year	No.	VG	EX/MT
Butcher, John	81F	635	$ .01	$ .06
Butcher, John	83F	563	$ .01	$ .06
Butcher, John	84F	415	$ .01	$ .08
Butcher, John	84FU	20	$ .10	$ .50
Butcher, John	85F	273	$ .01	$ .06
Butcher, John	86F	389	$ .01	$ .06
Butcher, John	87F	245	$ .01	$ .06
Butcher, Mike	92FU	7	$ .10	$ .40
Butcher, Mike	93F	569	$ .01	$ .04
Butera, Sal	81F	570	$ .01	$ .06
Butera, Sal	82F	548	$ .01	$ .06
Butera, Sal	87F	195	$ .01	$ .06
Butler, Brett	83F	132	$ .10	$ .50
Butler, Brett	84F	173	$ .10	$ .50
Butler, Brett	84FU	21	$ .75	$3.00
Butler, Brett	85F	441	$ .05	$ .35
Butler, Brett	86F	581	$ .01	$ .15
Butler, Brett	87F	246	$ .01	$ .15
Butler, Brett	88F	603	$ .01	$ .10
Butler, Brett	88FU	128	$ .01	$ .10
Butler, Brett	89F	324	$ .01	$ .04
Butler, Brett	90F	53	$ .01	$ .04
Butler, Brett	91F	257	$ .01	$ .04
Butler, Brett	91FU	91	$ .01	$ .05
Butler, Brett	91FULU	85	$ .01	$ .10
Butler, Brett	92F	448	$ .01	$ .04
Butler, Brett	92F	702	$ .01	$ .04
Butler, Brett	92FUL	209	$ .01	$ .10
Butler, Brett	93F	59	$ .01	$ .04
Butler, Brett	93FUL	51	$ .01	$ .10
Byers, Randell	88F	653	$ .10	$ .40
Bystrom, Marty	83F	154	$ .01	$ .06
Bystrom, Marty	84F	24	$ .01	$ .08
Bystrom, Marty	85F	122	$ .01	$ .06
Bystrom, Marty	86F	102	$ .01	$ .06
Cabell, Enos	81F	58	$ .01	$ .06
Cabell, Enos	82F	386	$ .01	$ .06
Cabell, Enos	83F	328	$ .01	$ .06
Cabell, Enos	84F	79	$ .01	$ .08
Cabell, Enos	84FU	22	$ .10	$ .50
Cabell, Enos	85F	346	$ .01	$ .06
Cabell, Enos	86F	126	$ .01	$ .06
Cabell, Enos	87F	438	$ .01	$ .06
Cabrera, Francisco	89FU	68	$ .05	$ .25
Cabrera, Francisco	90FU	2	$ .01	$ .10
Cabrera, Francisco	91F	684	$ .01	$ .04
Cabrera, Francisco	91FUL	3	$ .01	$ .07
Cabrera, Francisco	92F	355	$ .01	$ .04
Cabrera, Francisco	93F	365	$ .01	$ .04
Cadaret, Greg	89F	4	$ .01	$ .04
Cadaret, Greg	91F	658	$ .01	$ .04
Cadaret, Greg	91FUL	229	$ .01	$ .07
Cadaret, Greg	92F	222	$ .01	$ .04
Cadaret, Greg	92FUL	404	$ .01	$ .10
Caderet, Greg	90F	440	$ .01	$ .04
Calderon, Ivan	85FU	17	$ .15	$1.50
Calderon, Ivan	86F	462	$ .15	$1.50
Calderon, Ivan	87F	488	$ .05	$ .20
Calderon, Ivan	88F	394	$ .01	$ .15
Calderon, Ivan	89F	493	$ .01	$ .04
Calderon, Ivan	90F	529	$ .01	$ .04
Calderon, Ivan	91F	115	$ .01	$ .04
Calderon, Ivan	91FU	97	$ .01	$ .05
Calderon, Ivan	91FUL	199	$ .01	$ .07
Calderon, Ivan	92F	475	$ .01	$ .04
Calderon, Ivan	92FUL	513	$ .01	$ .10
Calderon, Ivan	93F	71	$ .01	$ .04
Caldwell, Mike	81F	512	$ .01	$ .06
Caldwell, Mike	82F	136	$ .01	$ .06
Caldwell, Mike	83F	29	$ .01	$ .06
Caldwell, Mike	84F	196	$ .01	$ .08
Caldwell, Mike	85F	577	$ .01	$ .06
Calhoun, Jeff	85FU	18	$ .01	$ .10
Calhoun, Jeff	86F	295	$ .01	$ .06
Calhoun, Jeff	87F	52	$ .01	$ .06
Calhoun, Jeff	88F	299	$ .01	$ .05
Camacho, Ernie	85F	442	$ .01	$ .06
Camacho, Ernie	86F	582	$ .01	$ .06
Camacho, Ernie	87F	247	$ .01	$ .06
Caminiti, Ken	88F	441	$ .10	$ .50
Caminiti, Ken	90F	225	$ .01	$ .04
Caminiti, Ken	91F	500	$ .01	$ .04
Caminiti, Ken	91FUL	133	$ .01	$ .07
Caminiti, Ken	92F	427	$ .01	$ .04
Caminiti, Ken	92FUL	200	$ .01	$ .10
Caminiti, Ken	93F	432	$ .01	$ .04
Caminiti, Ken	93FL	38	$ .01	$ .10
Camp, Rick	81F	246	$ .01	$ .06
Camp, Rick	82F	432	$ .01	$ .06
Camp, Rick	83F	133	$ .01	$ .06
Camp, Rick	84F	174	$ .01	$ .08
Camp, Rick	85F	321	$ .01	$ .06
Camp, Rick	86F	510	$ .01	$ .06
Campaneris, Bert	81F	280	$ .01	$ .06
Campaneris, Bert	82F	454	$ .01	$ .06
Campaneris, Bert	84F	120	$ .01	$ .08
Campbell, Bill	81F	240	$ .01	$ .06
Campbell, Bill	82F	289	$ .01	$ .06
Campbell, Bill	83F	493	$ .01	$ .06
Campbell, Bill	84F	489	$ .01	$ .08
Campbell, Bill	84FU	23	$ .10	$ .50
Campbell, Bill	85F	245	$ .01	$ .06
Campbell, Bill	85FU	19	$ .01	$ .10
Campbell, Bill	86F	28	$ .01	$ .06
Campbell, Bill	86FU	17	$ .01	$ .08
Campbell, Bill	87F	146	$ .01	$ .06
Campbell, Jim	89F	646	$ .05	$ .20
Campbell, Kevin	92FU	48	$ .05	$ .25
Campbell, Kevin	93F	660	$ .01	$ .04
Campbell, Mike	88F	372	$ .01	$ .10
Campbell, Mike	89F	543	$ .01	$ .04
Campusano, Sil	88FU	66	$ .05	$ .20
Campusano, Sil	91F	389	$ .01	$ .04
Canale, George	90F	641	$ .05	$ .25
Canale, George	91F	578	$ .01	$ .04
Candaele, Casey	87FU	16	$ .01	$ .10
Candaele, Casey	88F	181	$ .01	$ .05
Candaele, Casey	91F	501	$ .01	$ .04

FLEER

Player	Year	No.	VG	EX/MT	Player	Year	No.	VG	EX/MT
Candaele, Casey	91FUL	134	$.01	$.07	Carlton, Steve	83F	155	$.10	$1.00
Candaele, Casey	92F	428	$.01	$.04	Carlton, Steve	84F	25	$.25	$2.50
Candaele, Casey	92FUL	489	$.01	$.10	Carlton, Steve	84F	642	$.10	$.50
Candaele, Casey	93F	49	$.01	$.04	Carlton, Steve	85F	246	$.20	$2.00
Candelaria, John	81F	375	$.01	$.10	Carlton, Steve	86F	435	$.10	$.75
Candelaria, John	82F	479	$.01	$.06	Carlton, Steve	87F	490	$.10	$.75
Candelaria, John	83F	304	$.01	$.06	Carlton, Steve	87F	635	$.05	$.20
Candelaria, John	84F	247	$.01	$.08	Carlton, Steve	87FU	17	$.10	$.40
Candelaria, John	85F	462	$.01	$.06	Carlton, Steve	88F	7	$.05	$.25
Candelaria, John	86F	150	$.01	$.06	Carman, Don	85FU	20	$.01	$.10
Candelaria, John	87F	75	$.01	$.06	Carman, Don	86F	436	$.05	$.25
Candelaria, John	88FU	46	$.01	$.06	Carman, Don	87F	171	$.01	$.06
Candelaria, John	89F	251	$.01	$.04	Carman, Don	88F	300	$.01	$.05
Candelaria, John	91FU	92	$.01	$.05	Carman, Don	89F	564	$.01	$.04
Candelaria, John	92F	449	$.01	$.04	Carman, Don	90F	552	$.01	$.04
Candelaria, John	92FUL	500	$.01	$.10	Carman, Don	91F	390	$.01	$.04
Candelaria, John	93F	443	$.01	$.04	Carpenter, Cris	89FU	117	$.05	$.20
Candiotti, Tom	84F	197	$.10	$1.00	Carpenter, Cris	90F	243	$.01	$.10
Candiotti, Tom	86FU	18	$.01	$.15	Carpenter, Cris	91F	628	$.01	$.04
Candiotti, Tom	87F	248	$.01	$.06	Carpenter, Cris	91FULU	105	$.01	$.10
Candiotti, Tom	88F	604	$.01	$.05	Carpenter, Cris	92F	575	$.01	$.04
Candiotti, Tom	89F	399	$.01	$.04	Carpenter, Cris	92FUL	563	$.01	$.10
Candiotti, Tom	90F	488	$.01	$.04	Carpenter, Cris	93F	420	$.01	$.04
Candiotti, Tom	91F	364	$.01	$.04	Carr, Chuck	90FU	34	$.05	$.20
Candiotti, Tom	91FU	64	$.01	$.10	Carr, Chuck	91F	141	$.01	$.10
Candiotti, Tom	91FUL	109	$.01	$.07	Carr, Chuck	93F	421	$.01	$.04
Candiotti, Tom	91FULU	59	$.01	$.10	Carreon, Mark	88F	129	$.01	$.15
Candiotti, Tom	92F	326	$.01	$.04	Carreon, Mark	89F	29	$.01	$.04
Candiotti, Tom	92FU	89	$.05	$.25	Carreon, Mark	90F	198	$.01	$.10
Candiotti, Tom	92FUL	501	$.01	$.10	Carreon, Mark	91F	142	$.01	$.04
Candiotti, Tom	93F	60	$.01	$.04	Carreon, Mark	92F	498	$.01	$.04
Candiotti, Tom	93FUL	52	$.01	$.10	Carreon, Mark	92FUL	359	$.01	$.10
Cangelosi, John	86FU	19	$.01	$.15	Carreon, Mark	93F	604	$.01	$.04
Cangelosi, John	87F	489	$.01	$.10	Carter, Gary	81F	142	$.10	$.75
Cangelosi, John	88F	325	$.01	$.05	Carter, Gary	82F	185	$.10	$.75
Cangelosi, John	92FUL	439	$.01	$.10	Carter, Gary	82F	635	$.05	$.25
Canseco, Jose	86F	649	$10.00	$40.00	Carter, Gary	82F	638	$.05	$.25
Canseco, Jose	86FU	20	$1.75	$7.00	Carter, Gary	83F	278	$.10	$.50
Canseco, Jose	87F	389	$2.50	$10.00	Carter, Gary	83F	637	$.01	$.10
Canseco, Jose	87F	625	$.10	$.50	Carter, Gary	83F	638	$.05	$.25
Canseco, Jose	87F	628	$.10	$1.00	Carter, Gary	84F	271	$.10	$.75
Canseco, Jose	87F	633	$.10	$1.00	Carter, Gary	85F	393	$.10	$.40
Canseco, Jose	88F	276	$.20	$2.00	Carter, Gary	85F	631	$.10	$.75
Canseco, Jose	88F	624	$.10	$1.00	Carter, Gary	85F	632	$.01	$.10
Canseco, Jose	89F	5	$.10	$.50	Carter, Gary	85FU	21	$.10	$1.00
Canseco, Jose	89F	628	$.05	$.25	Carter, Gary	86F	76	$.05	$.30
Canseco, Jose	89F	634	$.05	$.25	Carter, Gary	87F	4	$.05	$.30
Canseco, Jose	90F	3	$.05	$.25	Carter, Gary	87F	629	$.10	$.50
Canseco, Jose	90FPD	629	$.01	$.15	Carter, Gary	87F	634	$.10	$.50
Canseco, Jose	91F	5	$.01	$.15	Carter, Gary	88F	130	$.01	$.15
Canseco, Jose	91FUL	244	$.10	$.50	Carter, Gary	88F	636	$.05	$.25
Canseco, Jose	92F	252	$.05	$.20	Carter, Gary	89F	30	$.01	$.15
Canseco, Jose	92FLL	688	$.01	$.15	Carter, Gary	90F	199	$.01	$.10
Canseco, Jose	92FU	59	$.20	$2.00	Carter, Gary	90FU	62	$.01	$.10
Canseco, Jose	92FUL	110	$.10	$1.00	Carter, Gary	91F	258	$.01	$.04
Canseco, Jose	93F	319	$.05	$.20	Carter, Gary	91FU	93	$.01	$.05
Canseco, Ozzie	90FU	117	$.01	$.10	Carter, Gary	01FULU	86	$.01	$.10
Capel, Mike	89F	643	$.05	$.20	Carter, Gary	92F	450	$.01	$.04
Capel, Mike	92F	429	$.01	$.04	Carter, Gary	92FUL	514	$.01	$.10
Capilla, Doug	81F	309	$.01	$.06	Carter, Joe	85F	443	$2.25	$9.00
Cappuzzello, George	82F	264	$.01	$.06	Carter, Joe	86F	583	$.20	$2.00
Capra, Nick	89F	279	$.01	$.04	Carter, Joe	87F	249	$.15	$1.50
Carew, Rod	81F	268	$.20	$2.00	Carter, Joe	88F	605	$.10	$.50
Carew, Rod	82F	455	$.15	$1.25	Carter, Joe	89F	400	$.05	$.20
Carew, Rod	83F	81	$.10	$1.00	Carter, Joe	90F	489	$.01	$.15
Carew, Rod	84F	511	$.25	$2.50	Carter, Joe	90FU	55	$.05	$.20
Carew, Rod	84F	629	$.10	$.50	Carter, Joe	91F	525	$.01	$.10
Carew, Rod	85F	297	$.15	$1.50	Carter, Joe	91FU	65	$.01	$.10
Carew, Rod	86F	151	$.10	$.75	Carter, Joe	91FUL	360	$.05	$.20
Carew, Rod	86F	629	$.10	$.40	Carter, Joe	92F	327	$.01	$.10
Carlton, Steve	81F	6	$.20	$2.00	Carter, Joe	92F	703	$.01	$.15
Carlton, Steve	81F	660	$.20	$2.00	Carter, Joe	92FRS	685	$.01	$.10
Carlton, Steve	82F	243	$.15	$1.25	Carter, Joe	92FUL	145	$.10	$.50
Carlton, Steve	82F	632	$.10	$.75	Carter, Joe	93F	333	$.01	$.10
Carlton, Steve	82F	641	$.10	$.75	Carter, Joe	93F	713	$.01	$.10

FLEER

Player	Year	No.	VG	EX/MT	Player	Year	No.	VG	EX/MT
Carter, Joe	93FUL	288	$ .05	$ .25	Cerone, Rick	88F	203	$ .01	$ .05
Carter, Steve	91FUL	374	$ .01	$ .07	Cerone, Rick	88FU	6	$ .01	$ .06
Cary, Chuck	86FU	21	$ .01	$ .10	Cerone, Rick	89F	84	$ .01	$ .04
Cary, Chuck	87F	147	$ .01	$ .06	Cerone, Rick	90F	270	$ .01	$ .04
Cary, Chuck	91F	659	$ .01	$ .04	Cerone, Rick	91F	660	$ .01	$ .04
Cash, Dave	81F	492	$ .01	$ .06	Cerone, Rick	91FU	101	$ .01	$ .05
Casian, Larry	92F	199	$ .01	$ .04	Cerone, Rick	91FULU	96	$ .01	$ .10
Castilla, Vinny	92F	666	$ .01	$ .15	Cerutti, John	86FU	24	$ .01	$ .15
Castilla, Vinny	93F	406	$ .01	$ .04	Cerutti, John	87F	222	$ .05	$ .25
Castillo, Bobby	83F	608	$ .01	$ .06	Cerutti, John	88F	105	$ .01	$ .10
Castillo, Bobby	84F	559	$ .01	$ .08	Cerutti, John	89F	228	$ .01	$ .10
Castillo, Bobby	85F	274	$ .01	$ .06	Cerutti, John	90F	78	$ .01	$ .04
Castillo, Bobby	85FU	22	$ .01	$ .10	Cerutti, John	91F	172	$ .01	$ .04
Castillo, Bobby	86F	127	$ .01	$ .06	Cerutti, John	91FU	101	$ .01	$ .05
Castillo, Braulio	93F	407	$ .01	$ .10	Cerutti, John	92F	129	$ .01	$ .04
Castillo, Carmelo	83F	404	$ .01	$ .06	Cey, Ron	81F	126	$ .05	$ .20
Castillo, Carmelo	85F	444	$ .01	$ .06	Cey, Ron	82F	3	$ .01	$ .10
Castillo, Carmelo "Carmen"	86F	584	$ .01	$ .06	Cey, Ron	83F	204	$ .01	$ .10
Castillo, Carmelo	87F	250	$ .01	$ .06	Cey, Ron	84F	490	$ .01	$ .08
Castillo, Carmelo	88F	606	$ .01	$ .05	Cey, Ron	85F	52	$ .01	$ .06
Castillo, Carmen	89F	401	$ .01	$ .04	Cey, Ron	86F	363	$ .01	$ .10
Castillo, Carmen	90F	371	$ .01	$ .04	Cey, Ron	87F	556	$ .01	$ .06
Castillo, Carmen	91F	606	$ .01	$ .04	Chalk, Dave	81F	35	$ .01	$ .06
Castillo, Frank	92F	378	$ .01	$ .10	Chalk, Dave	82F	407	$ .01	$ .06
Castillo, Frank	92FUL	467	$ .05	$ .20	Chamberlain, Wes	91F	391	$ .05	$ .20
Castillo, Frank	93F	375	$ .01	$ .04	Chamberlain, Wes	91FUL	258	$ .10	$ .50
Castillo, Frank	93FUL	16	$ .01	$ .10	Chamberlain, Wes	92F	524	$ .01	$ .10
Castillo, Juan	86FU	22	$ .01	$ .08	Chamberlain, Wes	92FUL	239	$ .01	$ .10
Castillo, Juan	87FU	18	$ .01	$ .06	Chamberlain, Wes	93F	99	$ .01	$ .04
Castillo, Juan	88F	159	$ .01	$ .05	Chamberlain, Wes	93FUL	85	$ .01	$ .10
Castillo, Manny	83F	474	$ .01	$ .06	Chambliss, Chris	81F	252	$ .01	$ .06
Castillo, Manny	84F	607	$ .01	$ .08	Chambliss, Chris	82F	433	$ .01	$ .06
Castillo, Marty	82F	265	$ .01	$ .06	Chambliss, Chris	83F	134	$ .01	$ .06
Castillo, Marty	85F	5	$ .01	$ .06	Chambliss, Chris	84F	175	$ .01	$ .08
Castillo, Robert	81F	137	$ .01	$ .06	Chambliss, Chris	85F	322	$ .01	$ .06
Castillo, Robert	82F	2	$ .01	$ .06	Chambliss, Chris	86F	512	$ .01	$ .06
Castillo, Tony	91F	685	$ .01	$ .04	Chambliss, Chris	87F	513	$ .01	$ .06
Castillo, Tony	92F	499	$ .01	$ .04	Chapman, Kelvin	85F	75	$ .01	$ .06
Castino, John	81F	554	$ .01	$ .06	Charboneau, Joe	81F	397	$ .01	$ .10
Castino, John	82F	549	$ .01	$ .06	Charboneau, Joe	82F	362	$ .01	$ .06
Castino, John	83F	609	$ .01	$ .06	Charland, Colin	90F	640	$ .01	$ .15
Castino, John	84F	560	$ .01	$ .08	Charlton, Norm	89F	155	$ .05	$ .20
Castro, Bill	81F	517	$ .01	$ .06	Charlton, Norm	90F	416	$ .01	$ .10
Castro, Bill	83F	109	$ .01	$ .06	Charlton, Norm	91F	60	$ .01	$ .04
Caudill, Bill	81F	306	$ .01	$ .06	Charlton, Norm	91FUL	90	$ .01	$ .07
Caudill, Bill	82F	590	$ .01	$ .06	Charlton, Norm	92F	402	$ .01	$ .04
Caudill, Bill	83F	475	$ .01	$ .06	Charlton, Norm	92FUL	482	$ .01	$ .10
Caudill, Bill	84F	608	$ .01	$ .08	Charlton, Norm	93F	32	$ .01	$ .04
Caudill, Bill	84FU	24	$ .10	$ .50	Checklist, Cards (1-50)	81F	641	$ .01	$ .10
Caudill, Bill	85F	419	$ .01	$ .06	Checklist, Cards (51-109)	81F	642	$ .01	$ .10
Caudill, Bill	85FU	23	$ .01	$ .10	Checklist, Cards (110-168)	81F	643	$ .01	$ .10
Caudill, Bill	86F	55	$ .01	$ .06	Checklist, Cards (169-220)	81F	644	$ .01	$ .10
Caudill, Bill	87F	221	$ .01	$ .06	Checklist, Cards (221-267)	81F	646	$ .01	$ .10
Cecena, Jose	88FU	62	$ .01	$ .15	Checklist, Cards (268-315)	81F	647	$ .01	$ .10
Cecena, Jose	89F	516	$ .01	$ .10	Checklist, Cards (316-359)	81F	648	$ .01	$ .10
Cedeno, Andujar	91F	502	$ .01	$ .15	Checklist, Cards (360-408)	81F	649	$ .01	$ .10
Cedeno, Andujar	91FUL	135	$ .05	$ .35	Checklist, Cards (409-458)	81F	651	$ .01	$ .10
Cedeno, Andujar	92F	430	$ .01	$ .10	Checklist, Cards (459-506)	81F	652	$ .01	$ .10
Cedeno, Andujar	92FUL	201	$ .01	$ .10	Checklist, Cards (507-550)	81F	654	$ .01	$ .10
Cedeno, Andujar	93F	433	$ .01	$ .04	Checklist, Cards (551-593)	81F	656	$ .01	$ .10
Cedeno, Cesar	81F	59	$ .01	$ .10	Checklist, Cards (594-637)	81F	658	$ .01	$ .10
Cedeno, Cesar	82F	213	$ .01	$ .06	Checklist, Teams (640-660)	81F	659	$ .01	$ .10
Cedeno, Cesar	83F	587	$ .01	$ .10	Checklist, Cards (1-56)	82F	647	$ .01	$ .10
Cedeno, Cesar	84F	465	$ .01	$ .08	Checklist, Cards (57-109)	82F	648	$ .01	$ .10
Cedeno, Cesar	85F	531	$ .01	$ .06	Checklist, Cards (110-156)	82F	649	$ .01	$ .10
Cedeno, Cesar	86F	29	$ .01	$ .06	Checklist, Cards (157-211)	82F	650	$ .01	$ .10
Cerone, Rick	81F	83	$ .01	$ .06	Checklist, Cards (212-262)	82F	651	$ .01	$ .10
Cerone, Rick	82F	31	$ .01	$ .06	Checklist, Cards (263-312)	82F	652	$ .01	$ .10
Cerone, Rick	83F	376	$ .01	$ .06	Checklist, Cards (313-358)	82F	653	$ .01	$ .10
Cerone, Rick	84F	121	$ .01	$ .08	Checklist, Cards (359-403)	82F	654	$ .01	$ .10
Cerone, Rick	85F	123	$ .01	$ .06	Checklist, Cards (404-449)	82F	655	$ .01	$ .10
Cerone, Rick	85FU	24	$ .01	$ .10	Checklist, Cards (450-501)	82F	656	$ .01	$ .10
Cerone, Rick	86F	511	$ .01	$ .06	Checklist, Cards (502-544)	82F	657	$ .01	$ .10
Cerone, Rick	86FU	23	$ .01	$ .08	Checklist, Cards (545-585)	82F	658	$ .01	$ .10
Cerone, Rick	87F	340	$ .01	$ .06	Checklist, Cards (586-627)	82F	659	$ .01	$ .10

FLEER

Player	Year	No.	VG	EX/MT
Checklist, Teams (628-660)	82F	660	$ .01	$ .15
Checklist, Cards (1-51)	83F	647	$ .01	$ .10
Checklist, Cards (52-103)	83F	648	$ .01	$ .10
Checklist, Cards (104-152)	83F	649	$ .01	$ .10
Checklist, Cards (153-200)	83F	650	$ .01	$ .10
Checklist, Cards (201-251)	83F	651	$ .01	$ .10
Checklist, Cards (252-301)	83F	652	$ .01	$ .10
Checklist, Cards (302-351)	83F	653	$ .01	$ .10
Checklist, Cards (352-399)	83F	654	$ .01	$ .10
Checklist, Cards (400-444)	83F	655	$ .01	$ .10
Checklist, Cards (445-489)	83F	656	$ .01	$ .10
Checklist, Cards (490-535)	83F	657	$ .01	$ .10
Checklist, Cards (536-583)	83F	658	$ .01	$ .10
Checklist, Cards (584-628)	83F	659	$ .01	$ .10
Checklist, Cards (629-660)	83F	660	$ .01	$ .10
Checklist, Cards (1-23)	84F	647	$ .01	$ .15
Checklist, Cards (341-364)	84F	647	$ .01	$ .15
Checklist, Cards (24-49)	84F	648	$ .01	$ .15
Checklist, Cards (365-387)	84F	648	$ .01	$ .15
Checklist, Cards (388-412)	84F	649	$ .01	$ .15
Checklist, Cards (50-73)	84F	649	$ .01	$ .15
Checklist, Cards (413-435)	84F	650	$ .01	$ .15
Checklist, Cards (74-95)	84F	650	$ .01	$ .15
Checklist, Cards (436-461)	84F	651	$ .01	$ .15
Checklist, Cards (96-118)	84F	651	$ .01	$ .15
Checklist, Cards (119-144)	84F	652	$ .01	$ .15
Checklist, Cards (462-485)	84F	652	$ .01	$ .15
Checklist, Cards (145-169)	84F	653	$ .01	$ .15
Checklist, Cards (486-507)	84F	653	$ .01	$ .15
Checklist, Cards (170-193)	84F	654	$ .01	$ .15
Checklist, Cards (508-532)	84F	654	$ .01	$ .15
Checklist, Cards (194-219)	84F	655	$ .01	$ .15
Checklist, Cards (533-555)	84F	655	$ .01	$ .15
Checklist, Cards (220-244)	84F	656	$ .01	$ .15
Checklist, Cards (556-579)	84F	656	$ .01	$ .15
Checklist, Cards (245-269)	84F	657	$ .01	$ .15
Checklist, Cards (580-603)	84F	657	$ .01	$ .15
Checklist, Cards (270-293)	84F	658	$ .01	$ .15
Checklist, Cards (604-625)	84F	658	$ .01	$ .15
Checklist, Cards (294-317)	84F	659	$ .01	$ .15
Checklist, Cards (626-646)	84F	659	$ .01	$ .15
Checklist, Cards (318-340)	84F	660	$ .01	$ .15
Checklist, Teams (1-660)	84F	660	$ .01	$ .15
Checklist, Cards (1-132)	84FU	132	$ .10	$ .50
Checklist, Cards (1-95)	85F	654	$ .01	$ .10
Checklist, Cards (96-195)	85F	655	$ .01	$ .10
Checklist, Cards (196-292)	85F	656	$ .01	$ .10
Checklist, Cards (293-391)	85F	657	$ .01	$ .10
Checklist, Cards (392-481)	85F	658	$ .01	$ .10
Checklist, Cards (482-575)	85F	659	$ .01	$ .10
Checklist, Cards (576-660)	85F	660	$ .01	$ .10
Checklist, Cards (1-132)	85FU	132	$ .01	$ .10
Checklist, Cards (1-97)	86F	654	$ .01	$ .10
Checklist, Cards (98-196)	86F	655	$ .01	$ .10
Checklist, Cards (197-291)	86F	656	$ .01	$ .10
Checklist, Cards (292-385)	86F	657	$ .01	$ .10
Checklist, Cards (386-481)	86F	658	$ .01	$ .10
Checklist, Cards (482-578)	86F	659	$ .01	$ .10
Checklist, Cards (579-660)	86F	660	$ .01	$ .10
Checklist, Cards (1-132)	86FU	132	$ .01	$ .10
Checklist, Cards (1-95)	87F	654	$ .01	$ .10
Checklist, Cards (96-192)	87F	655	$ .01	$ .10
Checklist, Cards (193-288)	87F	656	$ .01	$ .10
Checklist, Cards (289-384)	87F	657	$ .01	$ .10
Checklist, Cards (385-483)	87F	658	$ .01	$ .10
Checklist, Cards (484-532)	87F	659	$ .01	$ .10
Checklist, Cards (579-660)	87F	660	$ .01	$ .10
Checklist, Cards (1-132)	87FU	132	$ .01	$ .10
Checklist, Cards (1-101)	88F	654	$ .01	$ .05
Checklist, Cards (102-201)	88F	655	$ .01	$ .05
Checklist, Cards (202-296)	88F	656	$ .01	$ .05
Checklist, Cards (297-390)	88F	657	$ .01	$ .05
Checklist, Cards (391-483)	88F	658	$ .01	$ .05
Checklist, Cards (484-575)	88F	659	$ .01	$ .05
Checklist, Cards (576-660)	88F	660	$ .01	$ .05
Checklist, Cards (1-132)	88FU	132	$ .01	$ .06
Checklist, Cards (1-101)	89F	654	$ .01	$ .04
Checklist, Cards (102-200)	89F	655	$ .01	$ .04
Checklist, Cards (201-298)	89F	656	$ .01	$ .04
Checklist, Cards (299-395)	89F	657	$ .01	$ .04
Checklist, Cards (396-490)	89F	658	$ .01	$ .04
Checklist, Cards (491-584)	89F	659	$ .01	$ .04
Checklist, Cards (585-660)	89F	660	$ .01	$ .04
Checklist, Cards (1-132)	89FU	132	$ .01	$ .10
Checklist, Cards (1-99)	90F	654	$ .01	$ .04
Checklist, Cards (100-195)	90F	655	$ .01	$ .04
Checklist, Cards (196-289)	90F	656	$ .01	$ .04
Checklist, Cards (290-388)	90F	657	$ .01	$ .04
Checklist, Cards (389-482)	90F	658	$ .01	$ .04
Checklist, Cards (483-573)	90F	659	$ .01	$ .04
Checklist, Cards (574-660)	90F	660	$ .01	$ .04
Checklist, Cards (1-132)	90FU	132	$ .01	$ .05
Checklist, Cards (1-113)	91F	714	$ .01	$ .05
Checklist, Cards (114-223)	91F	715	$ .01	$ .05
Checklist, Cards (224-330)	91F	716	$ .01	$ .05
Checklist, Cards (331-441)	91F	717	$ .01	$ .05
Checklist, Cards (442-548)	91F	718	$ .01	$ .05
Checklist, Cards (549-654)	91F	719	$ .01	$ .05
Checklist, Cards (709-720)	91F	720	$ .01	$ .05
Checklist, Cards (1-132)	91FU	132	$ .01	$ .05
Checklist, Cards (1-103)	91FUL	397	$ .01	$ .07
Checklist, Cards (104-210)	91FUL	398	$ .01	$ .07
Checklist, Cards (211-313)	91FUL	399	$ .01	$ .07
Checklist, Cards (314-400)	91FUL	400	$ .01	$ .15
Checklist, Cards (1-120)	91FULU	120	$ .01	$ .10
Checklist, Cards (1-101)	92F	714	$ .01	$ .04
Checklist, Cards (102-194)	92F	715	$ .01	$ .04
Checklist, Cards (195-296)	92F	716	$ .01	$ .04
Checklist, Cards (297-397)	92F	717	$ .01	$ .04
Checklist, Cards (398-494)	92F	718	$ .01	$ .04
Checklist, Cards (495-596)	92F	719	$ .01	$ .04
Checklist, Cards (597-720)	92F	720	$ .01	$ .04
Checklist, Cards (1-132)	92FU	132	$ .05	$ .25
Checklist, Cards (1-108)	92FUL	298	$ .01	$ .10
Checklist, Cards (109-208)	92FUL	299	$ .01	$ .10
Checklist, Cards (209-300)	92FUL	300	$ .01	$ .10
Checklist, Cards (301-403)	92FUL	598	$ .01	$ .10
Checklist, Cards (404-498)	92FUL	599	$ .01	$ .10

FLEER

Player	Year	No.	VG	EX/MT	Player	Year	No.	VG	EX/MT
Checklist, Cards (499-600)	92FUL	600	$ .01	$ .10	Clark, Mark	92FUL	564	$ .05	$ .20
Checklist, Cards (1-123)	93F	358	$ .01	$ .04	Clark, Mark	93F	508	$ .01	$ .04
Checklist, Cards (124-246)	93F	359	$ .01	$ .04	Clark, Phil	91F	332	$ .01	$ .15
Checklist, Cards (247-360)	93F	360	$ .01	$ .04	Clark, Terry	89F	470	$ .01	$ .04
Checklist, Cards (361-482)	93F	718	$ .01	$ .04	Clark, Will	86FU	25	$2.50	$10.00
Checklist, Cards (483-602)	93F	719	$ .01	$ .04	Clark, Will	87F	269	$5.00	$20.00
Checklist, Cards (603-720)	93F	720	$ .01	$ .04	Clark, Will	88F	78	$ .15	$1.50
Checklist, Cards (1-94)	93FUL	298	$ .01	$ .10	Clark, Will	89F	325	$ .05	$ .35
Checklist, Cards (95-193)	93FUL	299	$ .01	$ .10	Clark, Will	89F	631	$ .05	$ .25
Checklist, Cards (194-300)	93FUL	300	$ .01	$ .10	Clark, Will	89F	632	$ .05	$ .25
Chiamparino, Scott	91FUL	375	$ .01	$ .10	Clark, Will	90F	54	$ .05	$ .25
Chiamparino, Scott	93F	422	$ .01	$ .04	Clark, Will	90F	637	$ .01	$ .10
Chiffer, Floyd	83F	354	$ .01	$ .06	Clark, Will	90FPD	630	$ .01	$ .15
Childress, Rocky	88F	442	$ .01	$ .10	Clark, Will	91F	259	$ .05	$ .20
Chitren, Steve	91FUL	376	$ .01	$ .10	Clark, Will	91FUL	318	$ .10	$ .50
Chitren, Steve	92F	253	$ .01	$ .04	Clark, Will	92F	631	$ .05	$ .25
Christensen, John	89F	108	$ .01	$ .04	Clark, Will	92FUL	287	$ .10	$1.00
Christenson, Larry	81F	8	$ .01	$ .06	Clark, Will	93F	154	$ .01	$ .15
Christenson, Larry	82F	244	$ .01	$ .06	Clark, Will	93FUL	130	$ .10	$ .50
Christenson, Larry	83F	156	$ .01	$ .06	Clary, Marty	88F	535	$ .01	$ .05
Christopher, Mike	92F	654	$ .01	$ .10	Clary, Martin	90F	578	$ .01	$ .04
Cianfrocco, Archi	92FUL	515	$ .05	$ .25	Clary, Marty	91F	686	$ .01	$ .04
Cianfrocco, Archi	93F	72	$ .01	$ .15	Clay, Danny	88FU	108	$ .01	$ .06
Cianfrocco, Archi	93FUL	63	$ .01	$ .10	Clay, Ken	81F	633	$ .01	$ .06
Clancy, Jim	81F	412	$ .01	$ .06	Clay, Ken	82F	508	$ .01	$ .06
Clancy, Jim	82F	612	$ .01	$ .06	Clayton, Royce	92F	632	$ .01	$ .15
Clancy, Jim	83F	426	$ .01	$ .06	Clayton, Royce	92FUL	288	$ .10	$ .50
Clancy, Jim	84F	150	$ .01	$ .08	Clayton, Royce	93F	155	$ .01	$ .04
Clancy, Jim	85F	101	$ .01	$ .06	Clayton, Royce	93FUL	131	$ .01	$ .10
Clancy, Jim	86F	56	$ .01	$ .06	Clear, Mark	82F	290	$ .01	$ .06
Clancy, Jim	87F	223	$ .01	$ .06	Clear, Mark	83F	181	$ .01	$ .06
Clancy, Jim	88F	106	$ .01	$ .05	Clear, Mark	83F	629	$ .10	$ .75
Clancy, Jim	89F	229	$ .01	$ .04	Clear, Mark	84F	395	$ .01	$ .08
Clancy, Jim	89FU	88	$ .01	$ .05	Clear, Mark	85F	154	$ .01	$ .06
Clancy, Jim	90F	226	$ .01	$ .04	Clear, Mark	86F	344	$ .01	$ .06
Clark, Bob	82F	456	$ .01	$ .06	Clear, Mark	86FU	26	$ .01	$ .08
Clark, Bobby	83F	82	$ .01	$ .06	Clear, Mark	87F	341	$ .01	$ .06
Clark, Bobby	84F	512	$ .01	$ .08	Clear, Mark	88F	160	$ .01	$ .05
Clark, Bobby	84FU	25	$ .10	$ .50	Clear, Mark	89F	182	$ .01	$ .04
Clark, Bobby	85F	578	$ .01	$ .06	Clemens, Roger	84FU	27	$100.00	$400.00
Clark, Bryan	82F	507	$ .01	$ .06	Clemens, Roger	85F	155	$13.75	$55.00
Clark, Bryan	83F	476	$ .01	$ .06	Clemens, Roger	86F	345	$3.00	$12.00
Clark, Bryan	84F	609	$ .01	$ .08	Clemens, Roger	87F	32	$1.00	$4.00
Clark, Bryan	84FU	26	$ .10	$ .50	Clemens, Roger	87F	634	$ .10	$ .50
Clark, Dave	87F	644	$ .75	$3.00	Clemens, Roger	87F	640	$ .10	$1.00
Clark, Dave	89F	402	$ .01	$ .04	Clemens, Roger	88F	349	$ .10	$1.00
Clark, Dave	90F	490	$ .01	$ .04	Clemens, Roger	89F	85	$ .10	$ .40
Clark, Dave	91F	417	$ .01	$ .04	Clemens, Roger	90F	271	$ .05	$ .35
Clark, Jack	81F	433	$ .05	$ .25	Clemens, Roger	90FPD	627	$ .01	$ .15
Clark, Jack	82F	387	$ .05	$ .25	Clemens, Roger	91F	90	$ .05	$ .20
Clark, Jack	83F	256	$ .05	$ .25	Clemens, Roger	91FUL	31	$ .10	$ .50
Clark, Jack	84F	369	$ .05	$ .25	Clemens, Roger	92F	37	$ .05	$ .25
Clark, Jack	85F	604	$ .05	$ .20	Clemens, Roger	92FUL	15	$ .15	$1.50
Clark, Jack	85FU	25	$ .05	$ .25	Clemens, Roger	93F	177	$ .05	$ .25
Clark, Jack	86F	30	$ .05	$ .20	Clemens, Roger	93F	348	$ .01	$ .10
Clark, Jack	87F	289	$ .05	$ .20	Clemens, Roger	93F	717	$ .01	$ .15
Clark, Jack	88F	26	$ .05	$ .20	Clements, Pat	85FU	26	$ .01	$ .15
Clark, Jack	88FU	47	$ .01	$ .10	Clements, Pat	86F	606	$ .05	$ .20
Clark, Jack	89F	252	$ .01	$ .10	Clements, Pat	87F	608	$ .01	$ .06
Clark, Jack	89FU	123	$ .01	$ .10	Clements, Pat	88F	204	$ .01	$ .05
Clark, Jack	90F	152	$ .01	$ .04	Clements, Pat	90F	153	$ .01	$ .04
Clark, Jack	91F	526	$ .01	$ .04	Clements, Pat	92F	602	$ .01	$ .04
Clark, Jack	91FU	4	$ .01	$ .05	Cleveland, Reggie	81F	523	$ .01	$ .06
Clark, Jack	91FULU	5	$ .01	$ .10	Cleveland, Reggie	82F	137	$ .01	$ .06
Clark, Jack	92F	36	$ .01	$ .04	Cliburn, Stewart	85FU	27	$ .01	$ .10
Clark, Jack	92FUL	14	$ .01	$ .10	Cliburn, Stewart	86F	152	$ .01	$ .06
Clark, Jack	93F	556	$ .01	$ .04	Cliburn, Stew	89F	471	$ .01	$ .04
Clark, Jack	93FUL	148	$ .01	$ .10	Clutterbuck, Bryan	87F	342	$ .01	$ .06
Clark, Jerald	89F	642	$ .05	$ .20	Cocanower, Jaime	84FU	28	$ .10	$ .50
Clark, Jerald	91F	121	$ .01	$ .05	Cocanower, Jaime	85F	579	$ .01	$ .06
Clark, Jerald	91FULU	110	$ .01	$ .10	Cocanower, Jaime	86F	483	$ .01	$ .06
Clark, Jerald	92F	601	$ .01	$ .04	Cochrane, Dave	92FUL	431	$ .01	$ .10
Clark, Jerald	92FUL	275	$ .01	$ .10	Cochrane, Dave	93F	671	$ .01	$ .04
Clark, Jerald	93F	137	$ .01	$ .04	Codiroli, Chris	84F	441	$ .01	$ .08
Clark, Mark	92FU	118	$ .05	$ .25	Codiroli, Chris	85F	420	$ .01	$ .06

FLEER

Player	Year	No.	VG	EX/MT
Codiroli, Chris	86F	414	$.01	$.06
Codiroli, Chris	87F	390	$.01	$.06
Coffman, Kevin	88F	536	$.01	$.10
Colbert, Craig	92FUL	588	$.01	$.15
Colbert, Craig	93F	528	$.01	$.04
Colbrunn, Greg	92FU	96	$.10	$.40
Colbrunn, Greg	93FUL	64	$.01	$.10
Cole, Alex	90F	244	$.05	$.20
Cole, Alex	91F	365	$.01	$.10
Cole, Alex	91FUL	110	$.01	$.10
Cole, Alex	92F	108	$.01	$.04
Cole, Alex	92FUL	345	$.01	$.10
Cole, Alex	93F	408	$.01	$.04
Cole, Victor	92FU	113	$.10	$.50
Coleman, Vince	85FU	28	$1.00	$4.00
Coleman, Vince	86F	31	$.20	$2.00
Coleman, Vince	86F	636	$.05	$.35
Coleman, Vince	86F	637	$.05	$.35
Coleman, Vince	87F	290	$.05	$.25
Coleman, Vince	88F	27	$.01	$.10
Coleman, Vince	88F	634	$.01	$.15
Coleman, Vince	89F	445	$.01	$.10
Coleman, Vince	90F	245	$.01	$.04
Coleman, Vince	91F	629	$.01	$.04
Coleman, Vince	91FU	102	$.01	$.05
Coleman, Vince	91FUL	212	$.01	$.10
Coleman, Vince	92F	500	$.01	$.10
Coleman, Vince	92FUL	229	$.01	$.10
Coleman, Vince	93F	467	$.01	$.04
Coles, Darnell	86FU	27	$.01	$.08
Coles, Darnell	87F	148	$.01	$.06
Coles, Darnell	89F	544	$.01	$.04
Coles, Darnell	90F	509	$.01	$.04
Coles, Darnell	91F	333	$.01	$.04
Coles, Darnell	93F	388	$.01	$.04
Collins, Dave	81F	201	$.01	$.06
Collins, Dave	82F	61	$.01	$.06
Collins, Dave	83F	377	$.01	$.06
Collins, Dave	84F	151	$.01	$.08
Collins, Dave	85F	102	$.01	$.06
Collins, Dave	85FU	29	$.01	$.10
Collins, Dave	86F	415	$.01	$.06
Collins, Dave	86FU	28	$.01	$.08
Collins, Dave	87F	149	$.01	$.06
Combe, Geoff	82F	62	$.01	$.06
Combs, Pat	90F	553	$.01	$.10
Combs, Pat	91F	392	$.01	$.04
Combs, Pat	91FUL	259	$.01	$.07
Combs, Pat	92F	525	$.01	$.04
Comer, Steve	82F	314	$.01	$.06
Comer, Steve	83F	564	$.01	$.06
Comstock, Keith	88F	579	$.01	$.10
Comstock, Keith	90F	510	$.01	$.04
Concepcion, Dave	81F	197	$.05	$.20
Concepcion, Dave	82F	63	$.05	$.20
Concepcion, Dave	82F	630	$.01	$.06
Concepcion, Dave	83F	588	$.01	$.06
Concepcion, Dave	83F	631	$.01	$.10
Concepcion, Dave	84F	466	$.01	$.08
Concepcion, Dave	85F	532	$.01	$.06
Concepcion, Dave	86F	174	$.01	$.10
Concepcion, Dave	87F	196	$.01	$.10
Concepcion, Dave	88F	229	$.01	$.05
Concepcion, Dave	89F	156	$.01	$.04
Concepcion, Onix	83F	110	$.01	$.06
Concepcion, Onix	84F	345	$.01	$.08
Concepcion, Onix	85F	200	$.01	$.06
Concepcion, Onix	86F	6	$.01	$.06
Cone, David	88F	131	$.10	$1.00
Cone, David	89F	31	$.01	$.15
Cone, David	89F	636	$.01	$.15
Cone, David	90F	200	$.01	$.10
Cone, David	91F	143	$.01	$.10
Cone, David	91FUL	213	$.01	$.15
Cone, David	92F	501	$.01	$.04

Player	Year	No.	VG	EX/MT
Cone, David	92FRS	687	$.01	$.04
Cone, David	92FU	63	$.05	$.25
Cone, David	92FUL	230	$.01	$.10
Cone, David	93F	691	$.01	$.04
Conine, Jeff	91F	553	$.05	$.25
Conine, Jeff	91FUL	145	$.10	$.50
Conine, Jeff	93F	423	$.01	$.04
Connally, Fritz	85FU	30	$.01	$.10
Conroy, Tim	84F	442	$.01	$.08
Conroy, Tim	85F	421	$.01	$.06
Conroy, Tim	86FU	29	$.01	$.08
Conroy, Tim	87F	291	$.01	$.06
Cook, Dennis	89F	652	$.10	$.40
Cook, Dennis	89FU	104	$.01	$.05
Cook, Dennis	90F	554	$.01	$.10
Cook, Dennis	91F	196	$.01	$.04
Cook, Dennis	92F	451	$.01	$.04
Cook, Dennis	92FUL	346	$.01	$.10

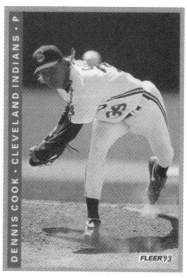

Cook, Dennis	**93F**	**214**	**$.01**	**$.04**
Cook, Mike	89F	472	$.01	$.04
Coolbaugh, Scott	89F	293	$.01	$.10
Coolbaugh, Scott	91FU	122	$.01	$.05
Cooper, Cecil	81F	639	$.01	$.10
Cooper, Cecil	82F	138	$.01	$.10
Cooper, Cecil	83F	30	$.01	$.10
Cooper, Cecil	84F	198	$.01	$.10
Cooper, Cecil	85F	580	$.05	$.20
Cooper, Cecil	86F	484	$.01	$.10
Cooper, Cecil	87F	343	$.01	$.10
Cooper, Cecil	88F	161	$.01	$.04
Cooper, Don	82F	550	$.01	$.06
Cooper, Scott	91F	91	$.05	$.20
Cooper, Scott	92FUL	312	$.05	$.35
Cooper, Scott	93F	178	$.01	$.04
Cooper, Scott	93FUL	149	$.01	$.10
Cora, Joey	88F	580	$.01	$.10
Cora, Joey	90F	154	$.01	$.10
Cora, Joey	91F	527	$.01	$.04
Cora, Joey	91FU	11	$.01	$.05
Cora, Joey	92F	76	$.01	$.04
Cora, Joey	92FUL	334	$.01	$.10
Cora, Joey	93F	580	$.01	$.04
Cora, Joey	93FUL	172	$.01	$.10

FLEER

Player	Year	No.	VG	EX/MT
Corbett, Doug	81F	555	$ .01	$ .06
Corbett, Doug	82F	551	$ .01	$ .06
Corbett, Doug	83F	83	$ .01	$ .06
Corbett, Doug	85F	298	$ .01	$ .06
Corbett, Doug	87F	76	$ .01	$ .06
Corbett, Sherman	88FU	11	$ .01	$ .10
Corbett, Sherman	89F	473	$ .01	$ .04
Corcoran, Tim	81F	479	$ .01	$ .06
Corcoran, Tim	85F	247	$ .01	$ .06
Corcoran, Tim	86F	437	$ .01	$ .06
Cordero, Wil	92FU	97	$ .75	$3.00
Cordero, Wil	93F	73	$ .01	$ .04
Cordero, Wil	93FUL	65	$ .05	$ .35
Corey, Mark	81F	193	$ .01	$ .06
Cormier, Rheal	92FU	119	$ .10	$ .75
Cormier, Rheal	93F	124	$ .01	$ .04
Corrales, Pat	81F	623	$ .01	$ .06
Correa, Ed	86FU	30	$ .01	$ .15
Correa, Ed	87F	122	$ .01	$ .10
Correa, Ed	88F	464	$ .01	$ .05
Corsi, Jim	89F	649	$ .01	$ .15
Corsi, Jim	90F	4	$ .01	$ .04
Corsi, Jim	91FULU	80	$ .01	$ .10
Corsi, Jim	92F	431	$ .01	$ .04
Corsi, Jim	93F	424	$ .01	$ .04
Costello, John	88FU	118	$ .01	$ .10
Costello, John	89F	446	$ .01	$ .10
Costello, John	90F	246	$ .01	$ .04
Cotto, Henry	85F	53	$ .01	$ .10
Cotto, Henry	85FU	31	$ .01	$ .10
Cotto, Henry	88F	205	$ .01	$ .05
Cotto, Henry	88FU	58	$ .01	$ .06
Cotto, Henry	89F	545	$ .01	$ .04
Cotto, Henry	90F	511	$ .01	$ .04
Cotto, Henry	91F	448	$ .01	$ .04
Cotto, Henry	91FUL	333	$ .01	$ .07
Cotto, Henry	92F	276	$ .01	$ .04
Cotto, Henry	92FUL	432	$ .01	$ .10
Cotto, Henry	93F	672	$ .01	$ .04
Cowens, Al	81F	471	$ .01	$ .06
Cowens, Al	82F	266	$ .01	$ .06
Cowens, Al	83F	477	$ .01	$ .06
Cowens, Al	84F	610	$ .01	$ .08
Cowens, Al	85F	487	$ .01	$ .06
Cowens, Al	86F	463	$ .01	$ .06
Cowley, Joe	85F	124	$ .01	$ .06
Cowley, Joe	86F	103	$ .01	$ .06
Cowley, Joe	86FU	31	$ .01	$ .08
Cowley, Joe	87F	491	$ .01	$ .06
Cox, Bob	81F	247	$ .01	$ .06
Cox, Danny	85F	222	$ .05	$ .20
Cox, Danny	86F	32	$ .01	$ .10
Cox, Danny	87F	292	$ .01	$ .06
Cox, Danny	88F	28	$ .01	$ .10
Cox, Danny	89F	447	$ .01	$ .04
Cox, Danny	92F	526	$ .01	$ .04
Cox, Danny	93F	499	$ .01	$ .04
Cox, Larry	81F	604	$ .01	$ .06
Cox, Ted	81F	602	$ .01	$ .06
Craig, Rodney	81F	597	$ .01	$ .06
Crawford, Steve	82F	291	$ .01	$ .06
Crawford, Steve	85F	156	$ .01	$ .06
Crawford, Steve	86F	346	$ .01	$ .06
Crawford, Steve	87F	33	$ .01	$ .06
Crawford, Steve	88F	350	$ .01	$ .05
Crawford, Steve	91F	554	$ .01	$ .04
Creel, Keith	84F	346	$ .01	$ .08
Crews, Tim	88F	511	$ .01	$ .10
Crews, Tim	90F	390	$ .01	$ .04
Crews, Tim	91F	197	$ .01	$ .04
Crews, Tim	91FULU	87	$ .01	$ .10
Crews, Tim	92F	452	$ .01	$ .04
Crews, Tim	92FUL	502	$ .01	$ .10
Crews, Tim	93F	444	$ .01	$ .04
Crim, Chuck	87FU	19	$ .01	$ .10
Crim, Chuck	88F	162	$ .01	$ .10
Crim, Chuck	89F	183	$ .01	$ .04
Crim, Chuck	90F	319	$ .01	$ .04
Crim, Chuck	91F	579	$ .01	$ .04
Crim, Chuck	91FUL	173	$ .01	$ .07
Crim, Chuck	92F	175	$ .01	$ .04
Crim, Chuck	93F	570	$ .01	$ .04
Cromartie, Warren	81F	144	$ .01	$ .06
Cromartie, Warren	83F	279	$ .01	$ .06
Cromartie, Warren	84F	272	$ .01	$ .08
Cromartie, Warren	91FU	25	$ .01	$ .05
Cromartie, Wayne	82F	186	$ .01	$ .06
Cron, Chris	92F	656	$ .01	$ .10
Cron, Chris	93F	581	$ .01	$ .04
Crowley, Terry	81F	190	$ .01	$ .06
Crowley, Terry	82F	160	$ .01	$ .06
Crowley, Terry	83F	55	$ .01	$ .06
Cruz, Hector	81F	206	$ .01	$ .06
Cruz, Hector	82F	591	$ .01	$ .06
Cruz, Jose	81F	60	$ .01	$ .10
Cruz, Jose	82F	214	$ .01	$ .10
Cruz, Jose	83F	446	$ .01	$ .10
Cruz, Jose	84F	222	$ .01	$ .10
Cruz, Jose	85F	347	$ .01	$ .10
Cruz, Jose	86F	201	$ .01	$ .10
Cruz, Jose	86F	296	$ .01	$ .10
Cruz, Jose	87F	53	$ .01	$ .10
Cruz, Jose	88F	443	$ .01	$ .05
Cruz, Julio	81F	601	$ .01	$ .06
Cruz, Julio	82F	509	$ .01	$ .06
Cruz, Julio	83F	478	$ .01	$ .06
Cruz, Julio	84F	55	$ .01	$ .08
Cruz, Julio	85F	510	$ .01	$ .06
Cruz, Julio	87F	492	$ .01	$ .06
Cruz, Todd	81F	341	$ .01	$ .06
Cruz, Todd	83F	479	$ .01	$ .06
Cruz, Todd	84F	3	$ .01	$ .08
Cruz, Todd	85F	172	$ .01	$ .08
Cruz, Victor	81F	407	$ .01	$ .06
Cruz, Victor	82F	480	$ .01	$ .06
Cubbage, Mike	81F	566	$ .01	$ .06
Cubbage, Mike	82F	523	$ .01	$ .06
Cubs, Chicago	85F	642	$ .01	$ .06

FLEER

Player	Year	No.	VG	EX/MT	Player	Year	No.	VG	EX/MT
Curry, Steve	89F	86	$ .01	$ .15	Daulton, Darren	92F	527	$ .01	$ .04
Curtis, Chad	92FU	8	$ .20	$2.00	Daulton, Darren	92FUL	240	$ .01	$ .10
Curtis, Chad	92FUL	323	$ .10	$1.00	Daulton, Darren	93F	100	$ .01	$ .04
Curtis, Chad	93F	571	$ .01	$ .15	Daulton, Darren	93F	352	$ .01	$ .04
Curtis, Chad	93FUL	159	$ .05	$ .35	Daulton, Darren	93F	705	$ .01	$ .04
Curtis, John	81F	491	$ .01	$ .06	Daulton, Darren	93F	715	$ .01	$ .10
Curtis, John	82F	569	$ .01	$ .06	Daulton, Darren	93FUL	86	$ .01	$ .15
Curtis, John	83F	84	$ .01	$ .06	Davalillo, Vic	81F	132	$ .01	$ .06
Curtis, John	84F	513	$ .01	$ .08	Davidson, Mark	87FU	20	$ .01	$ .10
Cuyler, Milt	91F	334	$ .01	$ .15	Davidson, Mark	88F	8	$ .01	$ .10
Cuyler, Milt	91FULU	22	$ .05	$ .25	Davidson, Mark	89F	109	$ .01	$ .04
Cuyler, Milt	92F	130	$ .01	$ .10	Davidson, Mark	91F	504	$ .01	$ .04
Cuyler, Milt	92FUL	57	$ .01	$ .10	Davidson, Mark	91FUL	136	$ .01	$ .07
Cuyler, Milt	93F	224	$ .01	$ .04	Davidson, Mark	92F	432	$ .01	$ .04
Cuyler, Milt	93FUL	194	$ .01	$ .10	Davis, Alvin	84FU	30	$ .20	$2.00
D'Acquisto, John	81F	163	$ .01	$ .06	Davis, Alvin	85F	488	$ .05	$ .20
D'Acquisto, John	83F	516	$ .01	$ .06	Davis, Alvin	86F	464	$ .05	$ .20
Dalton, Mike	92F	131	$ .01	$ .10	Davis, Alvin	87F	584	$ .01	$ .06
Daniels, Kal	86F	646	$ .75	$3.00	Davis, Alvin	88F	373	$ .01	$ .10
Daniels, Kal	87F	197	$ .01	$ .10	Davis, Alvin	89F	546	$ .01	$ .10
Daniels, Kal	88F	230	$ .01	$ .10	Davis, Alvin	90F	512	$ .01	$ .04
Daniels, Kal	89F	157	$ .01	$ .10	Davis, Alvin	91F	449	$ .01	$ .04
Daniels, Kal	90FU	20	$ .01	$ .10	Davis, Alvin	91FUL	334	$ .01	$ .07
Daniels, Kal	91F	198	$ .01	$ .04	Davis, Alvin	92F	277	$ .01	$ .04
Daniels, Kal	91FUL	160	$ .01	$ .07	Davis, Alvin	92FUL	324	$ .01	$ .10
Daniels, Kal	92F	453	$ .01	$ .04	Davis, Bob	81F	428	$ .01	$ .06
Daniels, Kal	92FUL	210	$ .01	$ .10	Davis, Chili	83F	257	$ .10	$ .40
Darling, Ron	84FU	29	$2.25	$9.00	Davis, Chili	84F	370	$ .05	$ .25
Darling, Ron	85F	76	$ .10	$ .50	Davis, Chili	85F	605	$ .01	$ .15
Darling, Ron	86F	77	$ .05	$ .20	Davis, Chili	86F	536	$ .05	$ .10
Darling, Ron	87F	5	$ .01	$ .15	Davis, Chili	87F	270	$ .01	$ .10
Darling, Ron	88F	132	$ .01	$ .10	Davis, Chili	88F	79	$ .01	$ .10
Darling, Ron	89F	32	$ .01	$ .04	Davis, Chili	88FU	12	$ .01	$ .06
Darling, Ron	90F	201	$ .01	$ .04	Davis, Chili	89F	474	$ .01	$ .04
Darling, Ron	91F	144	$ .01	$ .04	Davis, Chili	90F	129	$ .01	$ .04
Darling, Ron	91FUL	214	$ .01	$ .07	Davis, Chili	91F	309	$ .01	$ .04
Darling, Ron	92F	254	$ .01	$ .04	Davis, Chili	91FU	36	$ .01	$ .05
Darling, Ron	92FUL	111	$ .01	$ .10	Davis, Chili	91FULU	35	$ .01	$ .10
Darling, Ron	93F	661	$ .01	$ .04	Davis, Chili	92F	200	$ .01	$ .04
Darling, Ron	93FUL	256	$ .01	$ .10	Davis, Chili	92FUL	89	$ .01	$ .10
Darwin, Danny	81F	632	$ .01	$ .06	Davis, Chili	93F	262	$ .01	$ .04
Darwin, Danny	82F	315	$ .01	$ .06	Davis, Dick	81F	527	$ .01	$ .06
Darwin, Danny	83F	565	$ .01	$ .06	Davis, Dick	82F	245	$ .01	$ .06
Darwin, Danny	84F	416	$ .01	$ .08	Davis, Dick	83F	305	$ .01	$ .06
Darwin, Danny	85F	557	$ .01	$ .06	Davis, Eric	85F	533	$2.00	$8.00
Darwin, Danny	85FU	32	$ .01	$ .10	Davis, Eric	86F	175	$ .10	$1.00
Darwin, Danny	86F	485	$ .01	$ .06	Davis, Eric	87F	198	$ .10	$ .50
Darwin, Danny	87F	54	$ .01	$ .06	Davis, Eric	88F	231	$ .01	$ .15
Darwin, Danny	88F	444	$ .01	$ .05	Davis, Eric	88F	637	$ .05	$ .20
Darwin, Danny	89F	354	$ .01	$ .04	Davis, Eric	89F	158	$ .01	$ .15
Darwin, Danny	90F	227	$ .01	$ .04	Davis, Eric	89F	639	$ .01	$ .15
Darwin, Danny	91F	503	$ .01	$ .04	Davis, Eric	90F	417	$ .01	$ .15
Darwin, Danny	91FU	5	$ .01	$ .05	Davis, Eric	91F	61	$ .01	$ .10
Darwin, Danny	92F	38	$ .01	$ .04	Davis, Eric	91FUL	91	$ .01	$ .15
Darwin, Danny	93F	179	$ .01	$ .04	Davis, Eric	92F	403	$ .01	$ .10
Darwin, Danny	93FUL	150	$ .01	$ .10	Davis, Eric	92FU	90	$ .05	$ .25
Dascenzo, Doug	89F	420	$ .01	$ .10	Davis, Eric	92FUL	503	$ .01	$ .10
Dascenzo, Doug	91F	418	$ .01	$ .04	Davis, Eric	93F	445	$ .01	$ .04
Dascenzo, Doug	93F	376	$ .01	$ .04	Davis, Eric	93FUL	53	$ .01	$ .10
Dauer, Rich	81F	182	$ .01	$ .06	Davis, Glenn	85F	652	$ .75	$3.00
Dauer, Rich	82F	161	$ .01	$ .06	Davis, Glenn	86F	297	$ .10	$1.00
Dauer, Rich	83F	57	$ .01	$ .06	Davis, Glenn	87F	55	$ .05	$ .30
Dauer, Rich	84F	4	$ .01	$ .08	Davis, Glenn	87F	636	$ .05	$ .20
Dauer, Rich	85F	173	$ .01	$ .06	Davis, Glenn	88F	445	$ .01	$ .15
Dauer, Rich	86F	270	$ .01	$ .06	Davis, Glenn	89F	355	$ .01	$ .15
Daugherty, Jack	90F	294	$ .01	$ .10	Davis, Glenn	90F	228	$ .01	$ .10
Daugherty, Jack	91F	284	$ .01	$ .04	Davis, Glenn	91F	505	$ .01	$ .10
Daugherty, Jack	92F	300	$ .01	$ .04	Davis, Glenn	91FU	1	$ .01	$ .05
Daugherty, Jack	93F	682	$ .01	$ .04	Davis, Glenn	91FUL	14	$ .01	$ .07
Daulton, Darren	85FU	33	$2.50	$10.00	Davis, Glenn	92F	4	$ .01	$ .04
Daulton, Darren	86F	438	$1.00	$4.00	Davis, Glenn	92FUL	1	$ .01	$ .10
Daulton, Darren	87F	172	$ .10	$1.00	Davis, Glenn	93F	164	$ .01	$ .04
Daulton, Darren	90F	555	$ .01	$ .04	Davis, Glenn	93FUL	139	$ .01	$ .10
Daulton, Darren	91F	393	$ .01	$ .04	Davis, Jerry	85FU	34	$ .01	$ .10
Daulton, Darren	91FUL	260	$ .01	$ .07	Davis, Jerry	86F	317	$ .01	$ .06

FLEER

Player	Year	No.	VG	EX/MT	Player	Year	No.	VG	EX/MT
Davis, Jody	82F	592	$ .05	$ .20	Dawson, Andre	91FUL	58	$ .05	$ .20
Davis, Jody	83F	494	$ .01	$ .10	Dawson, Andre	92F	379	$ .01	$ .10
Davis, Jody	84F	491	$ .01	$ .08	Dawson, Andre	92FUL	468	$ .05	$ .25
Davis, Jody	85F	54	$ .01	$ .06	Dawson, Andre	93F	377	$ .01	$ .10
Davis, Jody	86F	364	$ .01	$ .10	Dayett, Brian	85F	125	$ .01	$ .06
Davis, Jody	87F	557	$ .01	$ .10	Dayett, Brian	85FU	35	$ .01	$ .10
Davis, Jody	88F	414	$ .01	$ .05	Dayett, Brian	87FU	25	$ .01	$ .06
Davis, Jody	89F	421	$ .01	$ .04	Dayett, Brian	88F	416	$ .01	$ .05
Davis, Jody	90F	579	$ .01	$ .04	Dayley, Ken	83F	135	$ .01	$ .06
Davis, Joel	86F	202	$ .01	$ .10	Dayley, Ken	84F	176	$ .01	$ .08
Davis, John	88F	255	$ .01	$ .15	Dayley, Ken	86F	33	$ .01	$ .06
Davis, John	88FU	15	$ .01	$ .06	Dayley, Ken	87F	293	$ .01	$ .06
Davis, Mark	84F	371	$ .05	$ .20	Dayley, Ken	88F	30	$ .01	$ .05
Davis, Mark	85F	606	$ .01	$ .06	Dayley, Ken	89F	448	$ .01	$ .04
Davis, Mark	86F	537	$ .01	$ .06	Dayley, Ken	90F	247	$ .01	$ .04
Davis, Mark	87F	271	$ .01	$ .06	Dayley, Ken	91F	630	$ .01	$ .04
Davis, Mark	87FU	21	$ .01	$ .06	De Los Santos, Luis	89F	646	$ .05	$ .20
Davis, Mark	88F	581	$ .01	$ .05	De Los Santos, Luis	89FU	37	$ .01	$ .10
Davis, Mark	89F	303	$ .01	$ .04	De Los Santos, Luis	90F	105	$ .01	$ .10
Davis, Mark	89F	635	$ .01	$ .15	DeCinces, Doug	81F	173	$ .01	$ .10
Davis, Mark	89FU	18	$ .01	$ .05	DeCinces, Doug	81F	195	$ .01	$ .10
Davis, Mark	90F	155	$ .01	$ .04	DeCinces, Doug	82F	162	$ .01	$ .10
Davis, Mark	90F	631	$ .01	$ .04	DeCinces, Doug	83F	85	$ .01	$ .06
Davis, Mark	90FU	101	$ .01	$ .05	DeCinces, Doug	84F	514	$ .01	$ .08
Davis, Mark	91F	555	$ .01	$ .04	DeCinces, Doug	85F	299	$ .01	$ .06
Davis, Mark	92FUL	369	$ .01	$ .10	DeCinces, Doug	86F	153	$ .01	$ .06
Davis, Mike	81F	586	$ .05	$ .25	DeCinces, Doug	87F	77	$ .01	$ .06
Davis, Mike	84F	443	$ .10	$1.00	DeCinces, Doug	88F	31	$ .01	$ .05
Davis, Mike	85F	422	$ .01	$ .10	Decker, Steve	91F	260	$ .01	$ .10
Davis, Mike	86F	416	$ .01	$ .06	Decker, Steve	91FUL	319	$ .05	$ .35
Davis, Mike	87F	391	$ .01	$ .06	Decker, Steve	92F	633	$ .01	$ .10
Davis, Mike	88F	277	$ .01	$ .05	Decker, Steve	92FUL	289	$ .01	$ .10
Davis, Mike	89F	55	$ .01	$ .04	Decker, Steve	93F	425	$ .01	$ .04
Davis, Mike	90F	391	$ .01	$ .04	Dedmon, Jeff	85F	323	$ .01	$ .06
Davis, Ron	81F	86	$ .01	$ .06	Dedmon, Jeff	86F	513	$ .01	$ .06
Davis, Ron	82F	32	$ .01	$ .06	Dedmon, Jeff	87F	514	$ .01	$ .06
Davis, Ron	83F	610	$ .01	$ .06	Dedmon, Jeff	88F	537	$ .01	$ .05
Davis, Ron	84F	561	$ .01	$ .08	Deer, Rob	85F	648	$ .75	$3.00
Davis, Ron	85F	275	$ .01	$ .06	Deer, Rob	86F	538	$ .10	$ .40
Davis, Ron	86F	390	$ .01	$ .06	Deer, Rob	86FU	33	$ .10	$ .40
Davis, Ron	87F	558	$ .01	$ .06	Deer, Rob	87F	344	$ .05	$ .25
Davis, Storm	83F	56	$ .05	$ .25	Deer, Rob	88F	163	$ .01	$ .10
Davis, Storm	84F	5	$ .01	$ .15	Deer, Rob	89F	184	$ .01	$ .04
Davis, Storm	85F	174	$ .01	$ .10	Deer, Rob	90F	320	$ .01	$ .04
Davis, Storm	86F	271	$ .01	$ .06	Deer, Rob	91F	580	$ .01	$ .04
Davis, Storm	87F	466	$ .01	$ .06	Deer, Rob	91FU	23	$ .01	$ .05
Davis, Storm	87FU	22	$ .01	$ .06	Deer, Rob	92F	132	$ .01	$ .04
Davis, Storm	88F	278	$ .01	$ .05	Deer, Rob	92FUL	58	$ .01	$ .10
Davis, Storm	89F	6	$ .01	$ .04	Deer, Rob	93F	225	$ .01	$ .04
Davis, Storm	90F	5	$ .01	$ .10	Deer, Rob	93FUL	195	$ .01	$ .10
Davis, Storm	90FU	102	$ .01	$ .05	DeJesus, Ivan	81F	297	$ .01	$ .06
Davis, Storm	91F	556	$ .01	$ .04	DeJesus, Ivan	82F	593	$ .01	$ .06
Davis, Storm	91FULU	26	$ .01	$ .10	DeJesus, Ivan	83F	157	$ .01	$ .06
Davis, Storm	92F	155	$ .01	$ .04	DeJesus, Ivan	84F	26	$ .01	$ .08
Davis, Storm	93F	541	$ .01	$ .04	DeJesus, Ivan	85F	248	$ .01	$ .06
Dawley, Bill	84F	223	$ .01	$ .08	DeJesus, Ivan	86F	34	$ .01	$ .06
Dawley, Bill	85F	348	$ .01	$ .06	DeJesus, Jose	89F	280	$ .01	$ .10
Dawley, Bill	86F	298	$ .01	$ .06	DeJesus, Jose	90F	104	$ .01	$ .04
Dawley, Bill	86FU	32	$ .01	$ .08	DeJesus, Jose	90FU	42	$ .01	$ .10
Dawley, Bill	87F	493	$ .01	$ .06	DeJesus, Jose	91F	394	$ .01	$ .04
Dawley, Bill	87FU	23	$ .01	$ .06	DeJesus, Jose	91FUL	261	$ .01	$ .07
Dawley, Bill	88F	29	$ .01	$ .05	DeJesus, Jose	92F	528	$ .01	$ .04
Dawson, Andre	81F	145	$ .20	$2.00	DeLeon, Jose	84F	248	$ .05	$ .35
Dawson, Andre	82F	187	$ .20	$2.00	DeLeon, Jose	85F	463	$ .01	$ .06
Dawson, Andre	83F	280	$ .15	$1.50	DeLeon, Jose	86F	607	$ .01	$ .06
Dawson, Andre	84F	273	$1.00	$4.00	DeLeon, Jose	87F	494	$ .01	$ .06
Dawson, Andre	85F	394	$ .20	$2.00	DeLeon, Jose	88F	395	$ .01	$ .05
Dawson, Andre	86F	246	$ .10	$1.00	DeLeon, Jose	88FU	119	$ .01	$ .06
Dawson, Andre	87F	316	$ .10	$ .75	DeLeon, Jose	89F	449	$ .01	$ .04
Dawson, Andre	87FU	24	$ .10	$ .50	DeLeon, Jose	90F	248	$ .01	$ .04
Dawson, Andre	88F	415	$ .10	$ .40	DeLeon, Jose	91F	631	$ .01	$ .04
Dawson, Andre	89F	422	$ .01	$ .15	DeLeon, Jose	91FUL	288	$ .01	$ .07
Dawson, Andre	90F	29	$ .01	$ .10	DeLeon, Jose	92F	576	$ .01	$ .04
Dawson, Andre	91F	419	$ .01	$ .10	DeLeon, Jose	92FUL	565	$ .01	$ .10
Dawson, Andre	91F	713	$ .01	$ .10	DeLeon, Jose	93F	487	$ .01	$ .04

FLEER

Player	Year	No.	VG	EX/MT
DeLeon, Luis	83F	355	$.01	$.06
DeLeon, Luis	84F	297	$.01	$.08
DeLeon, Luis	85F	29	$.01	$.06
DeLeon, Luis	86F	318	$.01	$.06
DeLucia, Rich	91FU	52	$.01	$.10
DeLucia, Rich	91FULU	50	$.01	$.15
DeLucia, Rich	92F	278	$.01	$.04
DeLucia, Rich	92FUL	122	$.01	$.10
DeLucia, Rich	93F	673	$.01	$.04

Player	Year	No.	VG	EX/MT
Dempsey, Rick	81F	177	$.01	$.10
Dempsey, Rick	82F	163	$.01	$.06
Dempsey, Rick	83F	58	$.01	$.06
Dempsey, Rick	84F	6	$.01	$.10
Dempsey, Rick	85F	175	$.01	$.06
Dempsey, Rick	86F	272	$.01	$.06
Dempsey, Rick	87F	467	$.01	$.06
Dempsey, Rick	87FU	26	$.01	$.06
Dempsey, Rick	90F	392	$.01	$.04
Denny, John	82F	363	$.01	$.06
Denny, John	83F	158	$.01	$.10
Denny, John	84F	27	$.01	$.10
Denny, John	85F	249	$.01	$.06
Denny, John	86F	439	$.01	$.06
Denny, John	86FU	34	$.01	$.08
Denny, John	87F	199	$.01	$.06
Dent, Bucky	81F	80	$.01	$.06
Dent, Bucky	82F	33	$.01	$.06
Dent, Bucky	82F	629	$.01	$.06
Dent, Bucky	83F	566	$.01	$.06
Dent, Bucky	84F	417	$.01	$.08
Dernier, Bob	83F	159	$.01	$.06
Dernier, Bob	84F	28	$.01	$.08
Dernier, Bob	84FU	31	$.10	$.50
Dernier, Bob	85F	55	$.01	$.06
Dernier, Bob	86F	365	$.01	$.06
Dernier, Bob	87F	559	$.01	$.06
Dernier, Bob	88F	417	$.01	$.05
Dernier, Bob	89F	565	$.01	$.04
Deshaies, Jim	86FU	35	$.05	$.25
Deshaies, Jim	87F	56	$.05	$.35
Deshaies, Jim	88F	446	$.01	$.05
Deshaies, Jim	89F	356	$.01	$.04
Deshaies, Jim	90F	229	$.01	$.04
Deshaies, Jim	91F	506	$.01	$.04
Deshaies, Jim	91FUL	137	$.01	$.07
Deshaies, Jim	93F	520	$.01	$.04
DeShields, Delino	90F	653	$.10	$.50
DeShields, Delino	90FU	27	$.10	$.50
DeShields, Delino	91F	228	$.05	$.20
DeShields, Delino	91FUL	200	$.05	$.35
DeShields, Delino	92F	476	$.01	$.10
DeShields, Delino	92FUL	220	$.10	$.40
DeShields, Delino	93F	74	$.01	$.04
DeShields, Delino	93FUL	66	$.05	$.25
Devereaux, Mike	88F	512	$.20	$2.00
Devereaux, Mike	89F	56	$.01	$.15
Devereaux, Mike	89FU	2	$.05	$.20
Devereaux, Mike	90F	175	$.01	$.04
Devereaux, Mike	91F	469	$.01	$.04
Devereaux, Mike	91FUL	15	$.01	$.07
Devereaux, Mike	92F	5	$.01	$.04
Devereaux, Mike	92FUL	2	$.01	$.10
Devereaux, Mike	93F	165	$.01	$.04
Dewey, Mark	93F	468	$.01	$.04
Diaz, Bo	81F	404	$.05	$.20
Diaz, Bo	82F	364	$.01	$.10
Diaz, Bo	82F	639	$.01	$.10
Diaz, Bo	83F	160	$.01	$.10
Diaz, Bo	83F	637	$.01	$.10
Diaz, Bo	84F	29	$.01	$.10
Diaz, Bo	85F	250	$.01	$.10
Diaz, Bo	86F	176	$.01	$.06
Diaz, Bo	87F	200	$.01	$.06
Diaz, Bo	88F	232	$.01	$.05
Diaz, Bo	89F	159	$.01	$.04
Diaz, Carlos	83F	540	$.01	$.06
Diaz, Carlos	84F	583	$.01	$.08
Diaz, Carlos	84FU	32	$.10	$.50
Diaz, Carlos	85F	369	$.01	$.06
Diaz, Carlos	86F	128	$.01	$.06
Diaz, Edgar	90FU	105	$.01	$.10
Diaz, Edgar	91F	581	$.01	$.04
Diaz, Mario	88F	649	$.05	$.25
Diaz, Mario	92F	301	$.01	$.04
Diaz, Marion	88FU	59	$.01	$.10
Diaz, Marion	89F	547	$.01	$.04
Diaz, Mike	87F	609	$.01	$.10
Diaz, Mike	88F	326	$.01	$.05
Diaz, Mike	89F	494	$.01	$.04
Dibble, Rob	88FU	83	$.10	$.75
Dibble, Rob	89F	160	$.05	$.25
Dibble, Rob	90F	418	$.01	$.15
Dibble, Rob	91F	62	$.01	$.04
Dibble, Rob	91FUL	92	$.01	$.07
Dibble, Rob	92F	404	$.01	$.04
Dibble, Rob	92FUL	187	$.01	$.10
Dibble, Rob	93F	389	$.01	$.04
Dillard, Steve	81F	298	$.01	$.06
Dillard, Steve	82F	594	$.01	$.06
Dilone, Miguel	81F	391	$.01	$.06
Dilone, Miguel	82F	365	$.01	$.06
Dilone, Miguel	83F	405	$.01	$.06
Dilone, Miguel	85F	395	$.01	$.06
DiPino, Frank	84F	224	$.01	$.08
DiPino, Frank	85F	349	$.01	$.06
DiPino, Frank	86F	299	$.01	$.06
DiPino, Frank	87F	560	$.01	$.06
DiPino, Frank	88F	418	$.01	$.05
DiPino, Frank	89F	423	$.01	$.04
DiPino, Frank	89FU	118	$.01	$.05
DiPino, Frank	90F	249	$.01	$.04
DiPino, Frank	91F	632	$.01	$.04
DiSarcina, Gary	92F	664	$.01	$.10
DiSarcina, Gary	92FUL	24	$.01	$.10
DiSarcina, Gary	93F	188	$.01	$.04
DiSarcina, Gary	93FUL	160	$.01	$.10
Distefano, Benny	89F	205	$.01	$.04
Distefano, Benny	90F	464	$.01	$.04

FLEER

Player	Year	No.	VG	EX/MT
Dixon, Ken	85FU	36	$ .01	$ .10
Dixon, Ken	86F	273	$ .01	$ .06
Dixon, Ken	87F	468	$ .01	$ .06
Dixon, Ken	88F	557	$ .01	$ .05
Doherty, John	92FU	20	$ .10	$ .75
Doherty, John	92FUL	360	$ .05	$ .35
Doherty, John	93F	226	$ .01	$ .10
Doherty, John	93FUL	196	$ .01	$ .10
Donnels, Chris	93F	426	$ .01	$ .04
Donohue, Tom	81F	281	$ .01	$ .06
Dopson, John	88FU	99	$ .01	$ .10
Dopson, John	89F	373	$ .01	$ .10
Dopson, John	89FU	8	$ .01	$ .15
Dopson, John	90F	272	$ .01	$ .04
Dopson, John	91F	92	$ .01	$ .04
Dopson, John	93F	557	$ .01	$ .04
Dopson, John	93FUL	151	$ .01	$ .10
Doran, Bill	84F	225	$ .10	$ .75
Doran, Bill	85F	350	$ .05	$ .20
Doran, Bill	86F	300	$ .01	$ .10
Doran, Bill	87F	57	$ .01	$ .10
Doran, Bill	88F	447	$ .01	$ .05
Doran, Bill	89F	357	$ .01	$ .04
Doran, Bill	90F	230	$ .01	$ .04
Doran, Bill	91F	63	$ .01	$ .10
Doran, Bill	91FULU	93	$ .01	$ .07
Doran, Bill	92F	405	$ .01	$ .04
Doran, Bill	92FUL	188	$ .01	$ .10
Doran, Bill	93F	390	$ .01	$ .04
Doran, Bill	93FUL	28	$ .01	$ .10
Dorsett, Brian	88F	607	$ .01	$ .15
Dotson, Richard	81F	356	$ .05	$ .25
Dotson, Richard	82F	340	$ .01	$ .10
Dotson, Richard	83F	233	$ .01	$ .06
Dotson, Richard	84F	56	$ .01	$ .08
Dotson, Richard	85F	511	$ .01	$ .06
Dotson, Richard	86F	203	$ .01	$ .06
Dotson, Richard	87F	495	$ .01	$ .06

Player	Year	No.	VG	EX/MT
Dotson, Richard	88F	396	$ .01	$ .05
Dotson, Richard	88FU	48	$ .01	$ .06
Dotson, Richard	89F	253	$ .01	$ .04
Dowell, Ken	87FU	27	$ .01	$ .06
Downing, Brian	81F	282	$ .01	$ .06

Player	Year	No.	VG	EX/MT
Downing, Brian	82F	457	$ .01	$ .06
Downing, Brian	83F	86	$ .01	$ .06
Downing, Brian	84F	515	$ .01	$ .08
Downing, Brian	85F	300	$ .01	$ .06
Downing, Brian	86F	154	$ .01	$ .06
Downing, Brian	87F	78	$ .01	$ .06
Downing, Brian	88F	488	$ .01	$ .05
Downing, Brian	89F	475	$ .01	$ .04
Downing, Brian	90F	130	$ .01	$ .04
Downing, Brian	91F	310	$ .01	$ .04
Downing, Brian	91FULU	54	$ .01	$ .10
Downing, Brian	92F	302	$ .01	$ .04
Downing, Brian	92FUL	440	$ .01	$ .10
Downs, Kelly	87F	272	$ .05	$ .20
Downs, Kelly	88F	80	$ .01	$ .10
Downs, Kelly	89F	326	$ .01	$ .04
Downs, Kelly	90F	55	$ .01	$ .04
Downs, Kelly	91F	261	$ .01	$ .04
Downs, Kelly	91FULU	116	$ .01	$ .10
Downs, Kelly	92F	634	$ .01	$ .04
Downs, Kelly	92FUL	290	$ .01	$ .10
Downs, Kelly	93F	662	$ .01	$ .04
Doyle, Brian	81F	104	$ .01	$ .06
Drabek, Doug	86FU	36	$ .20	$2.00
Drabek, Doug	87F	96	$ .20	$2.00
Drabek, Doug	88F	327	$ .05	$ .25
Drabek, Doug	89F	206	$ .01	$ .10
Drabek, Doug	90F	465	$ .01	$ .10
Drabek, Doug	91F	36	$ .01	$ .04
Drabek, Doug	91FULU	277	$ .01	$ .07
Drabek, Doug	92F	553	$ .01	$ .04
Drabek, Doug	92FUL	253	$ .01	$ .10
Drabek, Doug	93F	500	$ .01	$ .04
Drago, Dick	81F	239	$ .01	$ .06
Drago, Dick	82F	510	$ .01	$ .06
Drahman, Brian	92F	77	$ .01	$ .10
Dravecky, Dave	83F	356	$ .10	$ .50
Dravecky, Dave	84F	298	$ .05	$ .25
Dravecky, Dave	85F	30	$ .01	$ .06
Dravecky, Dave	86F	319	$ .01	$ .06
Dravecky, Dave	87F	412	$ .01	$ .06
Dravecky, Dave	87FU	28	$ .01	$ .06
Dravecky, Dave	88F	81	$ .01	$ .05
Dravecky, Dave	89F	327	$ .01	$ .04
Drees, Tom	90F	644	$ .01	$ .10
Dressendorfer, Kirk	91FU	50	$ .01	$ .10
Drew, Cameron	89F	640	$ .01	$ .15
Driessen, Dan	81F	205	$ .01	$ .10
Driessen, Dan	82F	64	$ .01	$ .06
Driessen, Dan	82F	630	$ .01	$ .06
Driessen, Dan	83F	589	$ .01	$ .06
Driessen, Dan	84F	467	$ .01	$ .08
Driessen, Dan	85F	396	$ .01	$ .06
Driessen, Dan	86F	539	$ .01	$ .06
Drummond, Tim	90FU	107	$ .01	$ .10
Drummond, Tim	91F	607	$ .01	$ .04
Drumright, Keith	82F	89	$ .01	$ .06
Dubois, Brian	90F	601	$ .01	$ .10
Ducey, Rob	88F	107	$ .01	$ .15
Ducey, Rob	92F	328	$ .01	$ .04
Dunbar, Tommy	85FU	37	$ .01	$ .10
Duncan, Mariano	85FU	38	$ .10	$1.00
Duncan, Mariano	86F	129	$ .10	$ .50
Duncan, Mariano	87F	439	$ .01	$ .06
Duncan, Mariano	88F	513	$ .01	$ .05
Duncan, Mariano	90FU	12	$ .01	$ .05
Duncan, Mariano	91F	64	$ .01	$ .04
Duncan, Mariano	91FUL	94	$ .01	$ .07
Duncan, Mariano	92F	406	$ .01	$ .04
Duncan, Mariano	92FU	109	$ .05	$ .25
Duncan, Mariano	92FUL	544	$ .01	$ .10
Duncan, Mariano	93F	101	$ .01	$ .04
Duncan, Mariano	93FUL	87	$ .01	$ .10
Dunne, Mike	87FU	29	$ .10	$ .50
Dunne, Mike	88F	328	$ .01	$ .10

FLEER

Player	Year	No.	VG	EX/MT
Dunne, Mike	89F	207	$.01	$.04
Dunston, Shawon	85F	649	$.15	$1.50
Dunston, Shawon	86F	366	$.05	$.20
Dunston, Shawon	87F	561	$.01	$.10
Dunston, Shawon	88F	419	$.01	$.10
Dunston, Shawon	89F	424	$.01	$.04
Dunston, Shawon	90F	30	$.01	$.04
Dunston, Shawon	91F	420	$.01	$.04
Dunston, Shawon	91FUL	59	$.01	$.07
Dunston, Shawon	92F	380	$.01	$.04
Dunston, Shawon	92FUL	174	$.01	$.10
Dunston, Shawon	93F	19	$.01	$.04
Dunston, Shawon	93FUL	17	$.01	$.10
Durham, Leon	81F	540	$.01	$.10
Durham, Leon	82F	595	$.01	$.06
Durham, Leon	83F	495	$.01	$.10
Durham, Leon	84F	492	$.01	$.05
Durham, Leon	85F	56	$.01	$.06
Durham, Leon	86F	367	$.01	$.06
Durham, Leon	87F	562	$.01	$.06
Durham, Leon	88F	420	$.01	$.05
Dwyer, Jim	81F	235	$.01	$.06
Dwyer, Jim	82F	164	$.01	$.06
Dwyer, Jim	83F	59	$.01	$.06
Dwyer, Jim	84F	7	$.01	$.08
Dwyer, Jim	85F	176	$.01	$.06
Dwyer, Jim	86F	274	$.01	$.06
Dwyer, Jim	88F	558	$.01	$.05
Dwyer, Kim	87F	469	$.01	$.06
Dybzinski, Jerry	81F	399	$.01	$.06
Dybzinski, Jerry	82F	366	$.01	$.06
Dybzinski, Jerry	83F	406	$.01	$.06
Dybzinski, Jerry	84F	57	$.01	$.08
Dybzinski, Jerry	85F	512	$.01	$.06
Dyer, Mike	90F	372	$.01	$.10
Dykstra, Len	86F	78	$.20	$2.00
Dykstra, Len	87F	6	$.05	$.25
Dykstra, Len	88F	133	$.01	$.15
Dykstra, Len	89F	33	$.01	$.15
Dykstra, Lenny	89FU	105	$.01	$.15
Dykstra, Lenny	90F	556	$.01	$.10
Dykstra, Len	91F	395	$.01	$.04
Dykstra, Len	91FUL	262	$.01	$.07
Dykstra, Lenny	92F	529	$.01	$.04
Dykstra, Lenny	92FUL	241	$.01	$.10
Dykstra, Lenny	93F	488	$.01	$.04
Easler, Mike	81F	372	$.01	$.06
Easler, Mike	82F	481	$.01	$.06
Easler, Mike	83F	306	$.01	$.06
Easler, Mike	84F	249	$.01	$.08
Easler, Mike	84FU	33	$.10	$.50
Easler, Mike	85F	157	$.01	$.06
Easler, Mike	86F	347	$.01	$.06
Easler, Mike	86FU	37	$.01	$.08
Easler, Mike	87F	97	$.01	$.06
Easler, Mike	88F	206	$.01	$.05
Easley, Damion	92FU	9	$.20	$2.00
Easley, Damion	93F	189	$.05	$.20
Easley, Damion	93FUL	161	$.10	$.50
Easterly, Jamie	82F	139	$.01	$.06
Easterly, Jamie	83F	31	$.01	$.06
Easterly, Jamie	84F	538	$.01	$.08
Easterly, Jamie	85F	445	$.01	$.06
Easterly, Jamie	86F	585	$.01	$.06
Eastwick, Rawly	82F	596	$.01	$.06
Eckersley, Dennis	81F	226	$.20	$2.00
Eckersley, Dennis	82F	292	$.15	$1.25
Eckersley, Dennis	83F	182	$.10	$1.00
Eckersley, Dennis	83F	629	$.10	$.75
Eckersley, Dennis	84F	396	$.75	$3.00
Eckersley, Dennis	84FU	34	$5.00	$20.00
Eckersley, Dennis	85F	57	$.15	$1.50
Eckersley, Dennis	86F	368	$.10	$.75
Eckersley, Dennis	87F	563	$.10	$.50
Eckersley, Dennis	87FU	30	$.10	$.40
Eckersley, Dennis	88F	279	$.05	$.25
Eckersley, Dennis	89F	7	$.01	$.15
Eckersley, Dennis	90F	6	$.01	$.10
Eckersley, Dennis	91F	6	$.01	$.10
Eckersley, Dennis	91FUL	245	$.01	$.15
Eckersley, Dennis	92F	255	$.01	$.10
Eckersley, Dennis	92FUL	421	$.05	$.25
Eckersley, Dennis	93F	293	$.01	$.10
Eckersley, Dennis	93F	717	$.01	$.15
Eckersley, Dennis	93FUL	257	$.05	$.20
Edelen, Joe	82F	65	$.01	$.06
Edens, Tom	91F	582	$.01	$.10
Edens, Tom	92FU	39	$.05	$.25
Edens, Tom	93F	434	$.01	$.04
Edler, Dave	81F	610	$.01	$.06
Edwards, Dave	81F	568	$.01	$.06
Edwards, Dave	83F	357	$.01	$.06
Edwards, Marshall	82F	140	$.01	$.06
Edwards, Marshall	83F	32	$.01	$.06
Edwards, Wayne	90F	652	$.01	$.10
Edwards, Wayne	90FU	83	$.01	$.05
Edwards, Wayne	91F	116	$.01	$.04
Eichelberger, Juan	82F	570	$.01	$.06
Eichelberger, Juan	83F	358	$.01	$.06
Eichelberger, Juan	84F	539	$.01	$.08
Eichhorn, Mark	86FU	38	$.01	$.15
Eichhorn, Mark	87F	224	$.05	$.20
Eichhorn, Mark	88F	108	$.01	$.10
Eichhorn, Mark	89F	230	$.01	$.04
Eichhorn, Mark	90F	580	$.01	$.04
Eichhorn, Mark	90FU	77	$.01	$.05
Eichhorn, Mark	91F	311	$.01	$.04
Eichhorn, Mark	92F	55	$.01	$.04
Eiland, Dave	92F	223	$.01	$.04
Eiland, Dave	92FUL	575	$.01	$.10
Eiland, David	91F	661	$.01	$.04
Eisenreich, Jim	89FU	38	$.01	$.05
Eisenreich, Jim	90F	106	$.01	$.04
Eisenreich, Jim	91F	557	$.01	$.04
Eisenreich, Jim	91FUL	146	$.01	$.07
Eisenreich, Jim	92F	156	$.01	$.04
Eisenreich, Jim	92FUL	69	$.01	$.10
Eisenreich, Jim	93F	617	$.01	$.04
Eldred, Cal	92F	679	$.05	$.35
Eldred, Cal	92FUL	380	$.15	$1.50
Eldred, Cal	93F	248	$.05	$.20
Eldred, Cal	93FUL	218	$.10	$.40
Ellis, John	82F	316	$.01	$.06
Elster, Kevin	87F	7	$.01	$.15
Elster, Kevin	88FU	104	$.01	$.10
Elster, Kevin	89F	34	$.01	$.04
Elster, Kevin	90F	202	$.01	$.04
Elster, Kevin	91F	145	$.01	$.04
Elster, Kevin	91FUL	215	$.01	$.07
Elster, Kevin	92F	502	$.01	$.04
Elster, Kevin	92FUL	231	$.01	$.10
Elster, Kevin	93F	469	$.01	$.04
Engle, Dave	82F	552	$.01	$.06
Engle, Dave	84F	562	$.01	$.08
Engle, Dave	85F	276	$.01	$.06
Engle, Dave	86F	391	$.01	$.06
Engle, Dave	86FU	39	$.01	$.08
Eppard, Jim	88F	645	$.10	$.40
Eppard, Jim	88FU	13	$.01	$.06
Eppard, Jim	89F	476	$.01	$.04
Erickson, Roger	81F	561	$.01	$.06
Erickson, Roger	82F	553	$.01	$.06
Erickson, Roger	83F	378	$.01	$.06
Erickson, Scott	91F	608	$.05	$.25
Erickson, Scott	91FULU	36	$.10	$.75
Erickson, Scott	92F	201	$.05	$.20
Erickson, Scott	92FLL	693	$.01	$.10
Erickson, Scott	92FUL	90	$.05	$.20
Erickson, Scott	93F	263	$.01	$.04
Erickson, Scott	93FUL	230	$.01	$.10

FLEER

Player	Year	No.	VG	EX/MT	Player	Year	No.	VG	EX/MT
Esasky, Nick	84F	468	$ .05	$ .25	Farr, Steve	87F	367	$ .01	$ .06
Esasky, Nick	85F	534	$ .05	$ .20	Farr, Steve	88F	256	$ .01	$ .05
Esasky, Nick	86F	177	$ .01	$ .06	Farr, Steve	89F	281	$ .01	$ .04
Esasky, Nick	87F	201	$ .01	$ .06	Farr, Steve	90F	107	$ .01	$ .04
Esasky, Nick	88F	233	$ .01	$ .05	Farr, Steve	91F	558	$ .01	$ .04
Esasky, Nick	89F	161	$ .01	$ .04	Farr, Steve	92F	225	$ .01	$ .04
Esasky, Nick	89FU	9	$ .01	$ .05	Farr, Steve	92FUL	405	$ .01	$ .10
Esasky, Nick	90F	273	$ .01	$ .04	Farr, Steve	93F	276	$ .01	$ .04
Esasky, Nick	90FU	3	$ .01	$ .05	Farrell, John	88F	608	$ .05	$ .20
Esasky, Nick	91F	687	$ .01	$ .04	Farrell, John	89F	403	$ .01	$ .10
Escarrega, Ernesto	83F	234	$ .01	$ .06	Farrell, John	90F	491	$ .01	$ .04
Espinosa, Nino	81F	20	$ .01	$ .06	Farrell, John	91F	366	$ .01	$ .04
Espinoza, Alvaro	89FU	47	$ .01	$ .10	Farrell, John	91FUL	111	$ .01	$ .07
Espinoza, Alvaro	90F	441	$ .01	$ .15	Fassero, Jeff	92F	477	$ .01	$ .04
Espinoza, Alvaro	91F	662	$ .01	$ .04	Fassero, Jeff	92FUL	516	$ .01	$ .10
Espinoza, Alvaro	91FUL	230	$ .01	$ .07	Fassero, Jeff	93F	459	$ .01	$ .04
Espinoza, Alvaro	92F	224	$ .01	$ .04	Felder, Mike	88F	164	$ .01	$ .05
Espinoza, Alvaro	92FUL	100	$ .01	$ .10	Felder, Mike	90F	321	$ .01	$ .04
Espy, Cecil	88F	465	$ .01	$ .15	Felder, Mike	91F	583	$ .01	$ .04
Espy, Cecil	89F	517	$ .01	$ .04	Felder, Mike	91FU	129	$ .01	$ .05
Espy, Cecil	90F	295	$ .01	$ .04	Felder, Mike	91FULU	117	$ .01	$ .10
Espy, Cecil	92FUL	552	$ .01	$ .10	Felder, Mike	92F	635	$ .01	$ .04
Essian, Jim	81F	593	$ .01	$ .06	Felder, Mike	92FUL	291	$ .01	$ .10
Essian, Jim	82F	341	$ .01	$ .06	Felder, Mike	93F	529	$ .01	$ .04
Essian, Jim	84F	540	$ .01	$ .08	Felix, Junior	89FU	69	$ .05	$ .25
Essian, Jim	84FU	35	$ .10	$ .50	Felix, Junior	90F	79	$ .01	$ .15
Essian, Jim	85F	423	$ .01	$ .06	Felix, Junior	91F	173	$ .01	$ .10
Eufemia, Frank	86F	392	$ .01	$ .06	Felix, Junior	92FUL	325	$ .01	$ .10
Evans, Barry	81F	499	$ .01	$ .06	Felix, Junior	93F	190	$ .01	$ .04
Evans, Barry	82F	571	$ .01	$ .06	Felton, Terry	83F	612	$ .01	$ .06
Evans, Darrell	81F	436	$ .01	$ .10	Ferguson, Joe	81F	124	$ .01	$ .06
Evans, Darrell	82F	388	$ .01	$ .10	Ferguson, Joe	83F	87	$ .01	$ .06
Evans, Darrell	83F	258	$ .01	$ .10	Fermin, Felix	88F	643	$ .05	$ .25
Evans, Darrell	84F	372	$ .01	$ .10	Fermin, Felix	89F	208	$ .01	$ .04
Evans, Darrell	84FU	36	$ .10	$ .60	Fermin, Felix	89FU	27	$ .01	$ .05
Evans, Darrell	85F	6	$ .01	$ .10	Fermin, Felix	90F	492	$ .01	$ .04
Evans, Darrell	86F	224	$ .01	$ .10	Fermin, Felix	91F	367	$ .01	$ .04
Evans, Darrell	87F	150	$ .01	$ .10	Fermin, Felix	91FUL	112	$ .01	$ .07
Evans, Darrell	88F	54	$ .01	$ .10	Fermin, Felix	92F	109	$ .01	$ .04
Evans, Darrell	90F	581	$ .01	$ .04	Fermin, Felix	92FUL	49	$ .01	$ .10
Evans, Dwight	81F	232	$ .05	$ .25	Fermin, Felix	93F	591	$ .01	$ .04
Evans, Dwight	82F	293	$ .05	$ .25	Fermin, Felix	93FUL	184	$ .01	$ .04
Evans, Dwight	82F	642	$ .01	$ .06	Fernandez, Alex	90F	84	$ .10	$ .50
Evans, Dwight	83F	183	$ .01	$ .15	Fernandez, Alex	91F	117	$ .01	$ .15
Evans, Dwight	84F	397	$ .05	$ .35	Fernandez, Alex	91FULU	14	$ .10	$ .50
Evans, Dwight	85F	158	$ .05	$ .20	Fernandez, Alex	92F	78	$ .01	$ .10
Evans, Dwight	86F	348	$ .01	$ .10	Fernandez, Alex	92FUL	335	$ .01	$ .10
Evans, Dwight	87F	34	$ .01	$ .15	Fernandez, Alex	93F	201	$ .01	$ .04
Evans, Dwight	88F	351	$ .01	$ .10	Fernandez, Alex	93FUL	173	$ .01	$ .10
Evans, Dwight	89F	87	$ .01	$ .04	Fernandez, Sid	85F	77	$ .10	$ .50
Evans, Dwight	90F	274	$ .01	$ .04	Fernandez, Sid	86F	79	$ .05	$ .20
Evans, Dwight	91F	93	$ .01	$ .04	Fernandez, Sid	87F	8	$ .05	$ .20
Evans, Dwight	91FU	2	$ .01	$ .05	Fernandez, Sid	87F	629	$ .10	$ .50
Evans, Dwight	91FULU	1	$ .01	$ .10	Fernandez, Sid	88F	134	$ .01	$ .10
Evans, Dwight	92F	6	$ .01	$ .04	Fernandez, Sid	89F	35	$ .01	$ .04
Evans, Dwight	92FUL	3	$ .01	$ .10	Fernandez, Sid	90F	203	$ .01	$ .04
Faedo, Lenny	83F	611	$ .01	$ .06	Fernandez, Sid	91F	146	$ .01	$ .04
Faedo, Lenny	84F	563	$ .01	$ .08	Fernandez, Sid	91FUL	216	$ .01	$ .07
Fahey, Bill	81F	490	$ .01	$ .06	Fernandez, Sid	92F	503	$ .01	$ .04
Falcone, Pete	81F	327	$ .01	$ .06	Fernandez, Sid	92FUL	528	$ .01	$ .10
Falcone, Pete	82F	524	$ .01	$ .06	Fernandez, Sid	93F	86	$ .01	$ .04
Falcone, Pete	83F	541	$ .01	$ .06	Fernandez, Sid	93FUL	72	$ .01	$ .10
Falcone, Pete	84F	177	$ .01	$ .08	Fernandez, Tony	84F	152	$ .90	$3.60
Fallon, Bob	85FU	39	$ .01	$ .10	Fernandez, Tony	85F	103	$ .10	$ .50
Faries, Paul	91F	528	$ .01	$ .15	Fernandez, Tony	86F	57	$ .05	$ .20
Faries, Paul	91FUL	302	$ .01	$ .07	Fernandez, Tony	87F	225	$ .01	$ .15
Faries, Paul	92F	603	$ .01	$ .04	Fernandez, Tony	88F	109	$ .01	$ .10
Fariss, Monty	92F	668	$ .01	$ .04	Fernandez, Tony	88F	635	$ .05	$ .35
Fariss, Monty	92FUL	441	$ .05	$ .20	Fernandez, Tony	89F	231	$ .01	$ .04
Fariss, Monty	93F	427	$ .01	$ .04	Fernandez, Tony	90F	80	$ .01	$ .10
Farmer, Ed	81F	339	$ .01	$ .06	Fernandez, Tony	90F	634	$ .01	$ .10
Farmer, Ed	82F	342	$ .01	$ .06	Fernandez, Tony	91F	174	$ .01	$ .04
Farmer, Ed	83F	161	$ .01	$ .06	Fernandez, Tony	91FU	123	$ .01	$ .05
Farr, Steve	85F	446	$ .10	$ .50	Fernandez, Tony	91FULU	111	$ .01	$ .10
Farr, Steve	86F	7	$ .01	$ .06	Fernandez, Tony	92F	604	$ .01	$ .04

FLEER

Player	Year	No.	VG	EX/MT
Fernandez, Tony	92FUL	276	$ .01	$ .10
Fernandez, Tony	93F	470	$ .01	$ .04
Fetters, Mike	90F	131	$ .01	$ .15
Fetters, Mike	91F	312	$ .01	$ .04
Fetters, Mike	92F	56	$ .01	$ .04
Fetters, Mike	93F	249	$ .01	$ .04
Fidrych, Mark	81F	462	$ .01	$ .06
Fielder, Cecil	86F	653	$5.00	$20.00
Fielder, Cecil	87FU	31	$ .15	$1.50
Fielder, Cecil	88F	110	$ .10	$ .75
Fielder, Cecil	89F	232	$ .05	$ .35
Fielder, Cecil	90FU	95	$ .05	$ .25
Fielder, Cecil	91F	335	$ .01	$ .15
Fielder, Cecil	91F	709	$ .05	$ .20
Fielder, Cecil	91FUL	121	$ .05	$ .35
Fielder, Cecil	91FUL	392	$ .05	$ .20
Fielder, Cecil	92F	133	$ .05	$ .20
Fielder, Cecil	92F	705	$ .01	$ .15
Fielder, Cecil	92FLL	692	$ .01	$ .10
Fielder, Cecil	92FUH	4	$1.25	$5.00
Fielder, Cecil	92FUL	59	$ .10	$ .75
Fielder, Cecil	93F	227	$ .01	$ .10
Fielder, Cecil	93F	345	$ .01	$ .10
Fielder, Cecil	93F	711	$ .01	$ .10
Fielder, Cecil	93F	714	$ .05	$ .25
Figueroa, Ed	81F	624	$ .01	$ .06
Filer, Tom	86F	58	$ .01	$ .06
Filer, Tom	89F	185	$ .01	$ .04
Filer, Tom	90F	322	$ .01	$ .04
Filson, Pete	84F	564	$ .01	$ .08
Filson, Pete	85F	277	$ .01	$ .06
Filson, Pete	86F	393	$ .01	$ .06
Fimple, Jack	84F	99	$ .01	$ .08
Fingers, Rollie	81F	485	$ .10	$1.00
Fingers, Rollie	82F	141	$ .10	$ .75
Fingers, Rollie	82F	644	$ .05	$ .35
Fingers, Rollie	83F	33	$ .10	$ .50
Fingers, Rollie	84F	199	$ .10	$1.00
Fingers, Rollie	85F	581	$ .10	$ .50
Fingers, Rollie	86F	486	$ .05	$ .25
Finley, Chuck	87F	79	$ .10	$1.00
Finley, Chuck	88F	489	$ .05	$ .20
Finley, Chuck	89F	477	$ .01	$ .10
Finley, Chuck	90F	132	$ .01	$ .10
Finley, Chuck	91F	313	$ .01	$ .04
Finley, Chuck	91FUL	44	$ .01	$ .07
Finley, Chuck	92F	57	$ .01	$ .04
Finley, Chuck	92FUL	25	$ .01	$ .10
Finley, Chuck	93F	191	$ .01	$ .04
Finley, Chuck	93FUL	162	$ .01	$ .10
Finley, Steve	89FU	3	$ .05	$ .35
Finley, Steve	90F	176	$ .01	$ .10
Finley, Steve	91F	470	$ .01	$ .04
Finley, Steve	91FU	88	$ .01	$ .05
Finley, Steve	91FULU	81	$ .01	$ .10
Finley, Steve	92F	433	$ .01	$ .04
Finley, Steve	92FUL	202	$ .01	$ .10
Finley, Steve	93F	50	$ .01	$ .04
Finley, Steve	93FUL	39	$ .01	$ .10
Fireovid, Steve	87F	653	$ .01	$ .06
Fischlin, Mike	83F	407	$ .01	$ .06
Fischlin, Mike	84F	541	$ .01	$ .08
Fischlin, Mike	85F	447	$ .01	$ .06
Fischlin, Mike	86FU	40	$ .01	$ .08
Fischlin, Mike	87F	98	$ .01	$ .06
Fishel, John	88FU	88	$ .01	$ .10
Fishel, John	89F	358	$ .01	$ .10
Fisher, Brian	85FU	40	$ .01	$ .10
Fisher, Brian	86F	104	$ .05	$ .25
Fisher, Brian	87F	99	$ .01	$ .06
Fisher, Brian	87FU	32	$ .01	$ .06
Fisher, Brian	88F	329	$ .01	$ .05
Fisher, Brian	89F	209	$ .01	$ .04
Fisher, Brian	93F	674	$ .01	$ .04
Fisk, Carlton	81F	224	$ .20	$2.00
Fisk, Carlton	82F	343	$ .15	$1.25
Fisk, Carlton	82F	632	$ .10	$ .75
Fisk, Carlton	83F	235	$ .10	$1.00
Fisk, Carlton	83F	638	$ .05	$ .25
Fisk, Carlton	84F	58	$ .75	$3.00
Fisk, Carlton	85F	513	$ .15	$1.50
Fisk, Carlton	86F	204	$ .10	$1.00
Fisk, Carlton	86F	643	$ .01	$ .10
Fisk, Carlton	87F	496	$ .10	$ .75
Fisk, Carlton	88F	397	$ .05	$ .35
Fisk, Carlton	89F	495	$ .05	$ .20
Fisk, Carlton	90F	530	$ .01	$ .10
Fisk, Carlton	91F	118	$ .01	$ .10
Fisk, Carlton	91FUL	72	$ .05	$ .20
Fisk, Carlton	92F	79	$ .01	$ .10
Fisk, Carlton	92FUL	33	$ .10	$ .40
Fisk, Carlton	93F	582	$ .01	$ .10
Fitzgerald, Mike	84FU	37	$ .10	$ .50
Fitzgerald, Mike	85F	78	$ .01	$ .06

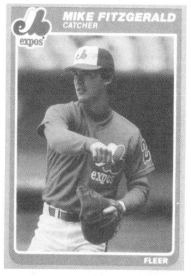

Player	Year	No.	VG	EX/MT
Fitzgerald, Mike	**85FU**	**41**	**$ .01**	**$ .10**
Fitzgerald, Mike	86F	247	$ .01	$ .06
Fitzgerald, Mike	87F	317	$ .01	$ .06
Fitzgerald, Mike	88F	182	$ .01	$ .05
Fitzgerald, Mike	89F	374	$ .01	$ .04
Fitzgerald, Mike	90F	343	$ .01	$ .04
Fitzgerald, Mike	91F	229	$ .01	$ .04
Fitzgerald, Mike	91FUL	201	$ .01	$ .07
Fitzgerald, Mike	92F	478	$ .01	$ .04
Flaherty, John	92FUL	313	$ .05	$ .25
Flanagan, Mike	81F	171	$ .01	$ .10
Flanagan, Mike	82F	165	$ .01	$ .06
Flanagan, Mike	83F	60	$ .01	$ .06
Flanagan, Mike	84F	8	$ .01	$ .10
Flanagan, Mike	85F	177	$ .01	$ .06
Flanagan, Mike	86F	275	$ .01	$ .06
Flanagan, Mike	87F	470	$ .01	$ .06
Flanagan, Mike	88FU	67	$ .01	$ .06
Flanagan, Mike	89F	233	$ .01	$ .04
Flanagan, Mike	90F	81	$ .01	$ .04
Flanagan, Mike	92F	7	$ .01	$ .04
Flannery, Tim	81F	493	$ .01	$ .06
Flannery, Tim	82F	572	$ .01	$ .06

FLEER

Player	Year	No.	VG	EX/MT	Player	Year	No.	VG	EX/MT
Flannery, Tim	83F	359	$ .01	$ .06	Foli, Tim	82F	482	$ .01	$ .06
Flannery, Tim	84F	299	$ .01	$ .08	Foli, Tim	83F	88	$ .01	$ .06
Flannery, Tim	85F	31	$ .01	$ .06	Foli, Tim	84F	516	$ .01	$ .08
Flannery, Tim	86F	320	$ .01	$ .06	Foli, Tim	84FU	38	$ .10	$ .50
Flannery, Tim	87F	413	$ .01	$ .06	Foli, Tim	85F	126	$ .01	$ .06
Flannery, Tim	88F	582	$ .01	$ .05	Fontenot, Ray	84F	122	$ .01	$ .08
Fleming, Dave	92FU	55	$ .15	$1.50	Fontenot, Ray	85F	127	$ .01	$ .06
Fleming, Dave	93F	306	$ .05	$ .20	Fontenot, Ray	85FU	42	$ .01	$ .10
Fleming, Dave	93FUL	268	$ .05	$ .35	Fontenot, Ray	86F	369	$ .01	$ .06
Fletcher, Darrin	91FU	107	$ .01	$ .05	Foote, Barry	81F	313	$ .01	$ .06
Fletcher, Darrin	91FUL	377	$ .01	$ .07	Foote, Barry	82F	34	$ .01	$ .06
Fletcher, Darrin	92F	530	$ .01	$ .04	Ford, Curt	86F	648	$ .05	$ .30
Fletcher, Darrin	92FUL	517	$ .01	$ .10	Ford, Curt	87F	294	$ .01	$ .06
Fletcher, Darrin	93F	460	$ .01	$ .04	Ford, Curt	88F	32	$ .01	$ .05
Fletcher, Darrin	93FUL	67	$ .01	$ .10	Ford, Curt	89F	450	$ .01	$ .04
Fletcher, Scott	84F	59	$ .01	$ .10	Ford, Curt	90F	557	$ .01	$ .04
Fletcher, Scott	· 85F	514	$ .01	$ .06	Ford, Dan	81F	273	$ .01	$ .06
Fletcher, Scott	86F	205	$ .01	$ .06	Ford, Dan	82F	458	$ .01	$ .06
Fletcher, Scott	86FU	41	$ .01	$ .08	Ford, Dan	83F	61	$ .01	$ .06
Fletcher, Scott	87F	123	$ .01	$ .06	Ford, Dan	84F	9	$ .01	$ .08
Fletcher, Scott	88F	466	$ .01	$ .05	Ford, Dan	85F	178	$ .01	$ .06
Fletcher, Scott	89F	518	$ .01	$ .04	Ford, Dave	81F	192	$ .01	$ .06
Fletcher, Scott	90F	531	$ .01	$ .04	Ford, Dave	82F	166	$ .01	$ .06
Fletcher, Scott	91F	119	$ .01	$ .04	Forsch, Bob	81F	537	$ .01	$ .06
Fletcher, Scott	91FUL	73	$ .01	$ .07	Forsch, Bob	82F	112	$ .01	$ .06
Fletcher, Scott	92F	80	$ .01	$ .04	Forsch, Bob	83F	5	$ .01	$ .06
Fletcher, Scott	92FU	34	$ .05	$ .25	Forsch, Bob	84F	322	$ .01	$ .08
Fletcher, Scott	92FUL	381	$ .01	$ .10	Forsch, Bob	84F	639	$ .01	$ .08
Fletcher, Scott	93F	629	$ .01	$ .04	Forsch, Bob	85F	223	$ .01	$ .06
Flynn, Doug	81F	330	$ .01	$ .06	Forsch, Bob	86F	35	$ .01	$ .06
Flynn, Doug	82F	525	$ .01	$ .06	Forsch, Bob	87F	295	$ .01	$ .06
Flynn, Doug	83F	282	$ .01	$ .06	Forsch, Bob	88F	33	$ .01	$ .05
					Forsch, Bob	90F	231	$ .01	$ .04
					Forsch, Ken	81F	52	$ .01	$ .06
					Forsch, Ken	82F	459	$ .01	$ .06
					Forsch, Ken	83F	89	$ .01	$ .06
					Forsch, Ken	84F	517	$ .01	$ .08
					Forsch, Ken	85F	301	$ .01	$ .06
					Forsch, Ken	86F	155	$ .01	$ .06
					Forster, Terry	81F	119	$ .01	$ .06
					Forster, Terry	82F	4	$ .01	$ .06
					Forster, Terry	83F	205	$ .01	$ .06
					Forster, Terry	84F	178	$ .01	$ .08
					Forster, Terry	85F	324	$ .01	$ .06
					Forster, Terry	86F	514	$ .01	$ .06
					Forster, Terry	86FU	42	$ .01	$ .08
					Forster, Terry	87F	80	$ .01	$ .06
					Fortugno, Tim	93F	572	$ .01	$ .04
					Fortugno, Tim	93FUL	163	$ .01	$ .10
					Fossas, Tony	90F	323	$ .01	$ .10
					Fossas, Tony	93F	180	$ .01	$ .04
					Foster, George	81F	202	$ .05	$ .25
					Foster, George	81F	216	$ .05	$ .30
					Foster, George	82F	66	$ .05	$ .25
					Foster, George	82F	630	$ .01	$ .10
					Foster, George	83F	542	$ .05	$ .20
					Foster, George	84F	584	$ .05	$ .20
					Foster, George	85F	79	$ .05	$ .20
					Foster, George	86F	80	$ .01	$ .15
					Foster, Steve	92FU	80	$ .05	$ .25
					Foster, Steve	93F	33	$ .01	$ .10
					Fowlkes, Alan	83F	259	$ .01	$ .06
					Fox, Eric	93F	663	$ .01	$ .04
					Franco, John	84FU	39	$2.50	$10.00

Doug Flynn
SECOND BASE • SHORTSTOP

Flynn, Doug	84F	274	$ .01	$ .08	Franco, John	85F	536	$ .10	$1.00
Flynn, Doug	85F	397	$ .01	$ .06	Franco, John	86F	178	$ .01	$ .15
Foley, Tom	85F	535	$ .01	$ .06	Franco, John	87F	202	$ .01	$ .10
Foley, Tom	86F	440	$ .01	$ .06	Franco, John	87F	631	$ .01	$ .10
Foley, Tom	87F	318	$ .01	$ .06	Franco, John	88F	234	$ .01	$ .10
Foley, Tom	88F	183	$ .01	$ .05	Franco, John	88F	627	$ .01	$ .10
Foley, Tom	89F	375	$ .01	$ .04	Franco, John	89F	162	$ .01	$ .10
Foley, Tom	90F	344	$ .01	$ .04	Franco, John	90F	419	$ .01	$ .10
Foley, Tom	91F	230	$ .01	$ .04	Franco, John	90FU	35	$ .01	$ .05
Foley, Tom	92FUL	221	$ .01	$ .10	Franco, John	91F	147	$ .01	$ .04
Foli, Tim	81F	379	$ .01	$ .06	Franco, John	91F	712	$ .01	$ .10

FLEER

Player	Year	No.	VG	EX/MT
Franco, John	91FUL	217	$ .01	$ .07
Franco, John	92F	504	$ .01	$ .04
Franco, John	92FUL	529	$ .01	$ .10
Franco, John	93F	471	$ .01	$ .04
Franco, John	93FUL	73	$ .01	$ .10
Franco, Julio	84F	542	$ .20	$2.00
Franco, Julio	85F	448	$ .10	$ .75
Franco, Julio	86F	586	$ .05	$ .35
Franco, Julio	87F	251	$ .10	$ .40
Franco, Julio	88F	609	$ .01	$ .10
Franco, Julio	89F	404	$ .01	$ .10
Franco, Julio	89FU	64	$ .01	$ .10
Franco, Julio	90F	296	$ .01	$ .10
Franco, Julio	91F	285	$ .01	$ .04
Franco, Julio	91FUL	348	$ .01	$ .10
Franco, Julio	92F	303	$ .01	$ .10
Franco, Julio	92FLL	690	$ .01	$ .04
Franco, Julio	92FUL	131	$ .01	$ .10
Franco, Julio	93F	320	$ .01	$ .04
Franco, Julio	93FUL	277	$ .01	$ .10
Francona, Terry	82F	188	$ .05	$ .20
Francona, Terry	83F	281	$ .01	$ .06
Francona, Terry	84F	275	$ .01	$ .08
Francona, Terry	85F	398	$ .01	$ .06
Francona, Terry	86F	248	$ .01	$ .06
Francona, Terry	86FU	43	$ .01	$ .08
Francona, Terry	87F	564	$ .01	$ .06
Fraser, Willie	87F	646	$ .15	$1.50
Fraser, Willie	87FU	33	$ .01	$ .06
Fraser, Willie	88F	490	$ .01	$ .05
Fraser, Willie	89F	478	$ .01	$ .04
Fraser, Willie	90F	133	$ .01	$ .04
Fraser, Willie	91F	314	$ .01	$ .04
Frazier, George	82F	35	$ .01	$ .06
Frazier, George	83F	379	$ .01	$ .06
Frazier, George	84F	123	$ .01	$ .08
Frazier, George	84FU	40	$ .10	$ .50
Frazier, George	85F	58	$ .01	$ .06
Frazier, George	86F	370	$ .01	$ .06
Frazier, George	87F	539	$ .01	$ .06
Frazier, George	88F	9	$ .01	$ .05
Freeman, Marvin	87F	651	$ .10	$ .40
Freeman, Marvin	89F	566	$ .01	$ .04
Freeman, Marvin	91FU	73	$ .01	$ .05
Freeman, Marvin	92F	356	$ .01	$ .04
Freeman, Marvin	92FUL	458	$ .01	$ .10
Freeman, Marvin	93F	366	$ .01	$ .04
Fregosi, Jim	81F	274	$ .01	$ .06
Frey, Steve	90F	649	$ .01	$ .10
Frey, Steve	90FU	28	$ .01	$ .05
Frey, Steve	91F	231	$ .01	$ .04
Frey, Steve	91FUL	202	$ .01	$ .07
Frey, Steve	92F	479	$ .01	$ .04
Frey, Steve	92FUL	222	$ .01	$ .10
Frey, Steve	93F	573	$ .01	$ .04
Frias, Pepe	81F	134	$ .01	$ .06
Frobol, Doug	05F	404	$ .01	$ .06
Frohwirth, Todd	88F	301	$ .01	$ .05
Frohwirth, Todd	89F	567	$ .01	$ .04
Frohwirth, Todd	92FU	1	$ .05	$ .25
Frohwirth, Todd	92FUL	302	$ .01	$ .10
Frohwirth, Todd	93F	166	$ .01	$ .04
Frost, Dave	81F	275	$ .01	$ .06
Frost, Dave	82F	460	$ .01	$ .06
Frost, Dave	83F	111	$ .01	$ .06
Frye, Jeff	92FU	60	$ .05	$ .25
Frye, Jeff	93F	321	$ .01	$ .04
Frye, Jeff	93FUL	278	$ .01	$ .10
Fryman, Travis	90FU	96	$ .15	$1.25
Fryman, Travis	91F	336	$ .10	$ .50
Fryman, Travis	91FUL	122	$ .75	$3.00
Fryman, Travis	92F	134	$ .05	$ .35
Fryman, Travis	92FUL	60	$ .15	$1.50
Fryman, Travis	93F	228	$ .05	$ .25
Fryman, Travis	93FUL	197	$ .10	$1.00
Fryman, Woodie	81F	159	$ .01	$ .06
Fryman, Woodie	82F	189	$ .01	$ .06
Fryman, Woodie	83F	283	$ .01	$ .06
Funderburk, Mark	86F	652	$ .01	$ .10
Gaetti, Gary	83F	613	$ .10	$ .50
Gaetti, Gary	84F	565	$ .05	$ .25
Gaetti, Gary	85F	278	$ .05	$ .20
Gaetti, Gary	86F	394	$ .01	$ .10
Gaetti, Gary	87F	540	$ .01	$ .10
Gaetti, Gary	88F	10	$ .01	$ .10
Gaetti, Gary	89F	110	$ .01	$ .10
Gaetti, Gary	90F	373	$ .01	$ .04
Gaetti, Gary	91F	609	$ .01	$ .04
Gaetti, Gary	91FU	9	$ .01	$ .05
Gaetti, Gary	91FULU	8	$ .01	$ .10
Gaetti, Gary	92F	58	$ .01	$ .04
Gaetti, Gary	92FUL	26	$ .01	$ .10
Gaetti, Gary	93F	574	$ .01	$ .04
Gaff, Brent	85F	80	$ .01	$ .06
Gagne, Greg	85FU	43	$ .05	$ .35
Gagne, Greg	86F	395	$ .01	$ .10
Gagne, Greg	87F	541	$ .01	$ .06
Gagne, Greg	88F	11	$ .01	$ .05
Gagne, Greg	89F	111	$ .01	$ .04
Gagne, Greg	90F	374	$ .01	$ .04
Gagne, Greg	91F	610	$ .01	$ .04
Gagne, Greg	91FUL	186	$ .01	$ .07
Gagne, Greg	92F	202	$ .01	$ .04
Gagne, Greg	92FUL	395	$ .01	$ .10
Gagne, Greg	93F	264	$ .01	$ .04
Gainey, Ty	88F	448	$ .01	$ .05
Gakeler, Dan	92F	135	$ .01	$ .10
Galarraga, Andres	86F	647	$ .20	$2.00
Galarraga, Andres	86FU	44	$ .10	$ .50
Galarraga, Andres	87F	319	$ .01	$ .15
Galarraga, Andres	88F	184	$ .05	$ .25
Galarraga, Andres	89F	376	$ .01	$ .15
Galarraga, Andres	89F	638	$ .01	$ .04
Galarraga, Andres	90F	345	$ .01	$ .10
Galarraga, Andres	91F	232	$ .01	$ .04
Galarraga, Andres	91FUL	203	$ .01	$ .07
Galarraga, Andres	92F	480	$ .01	$ .04
Galarraga, Andres	93F	409	$ .01	$ .10
Gale, Rich	81F	40	$ .01	$ .06
Gale, Rich	82F	408	$ .01	$ .06
Gale, Rich	83F	260	$ .01	$ .06
Gale, Rich	84F	469	$ .01	$ .08
Gale, Rich	84FU	41	$ .10	$ .50
Gallagher, Dave	88FU	16	$ .01	$ .10
Gallagher, Dave	89F	496	$ .01	$ .10
Gallagher, Dave	90F	532	$ .01	$ .04
Gallagher, Dave	91F	471	$ .01	$ .04
Gallagher, Dave	91FULU	9	$ .01	$ .10
Gallagher, Dave	92F	59	$ .01	$ .04
Gallagher, Dave	92FUL	530	$ .01	$ .10
Gallagher, Dave	93F	472	$ .01	$ .04
Gallagher, Dave	93FUL	74	$ .01	$ .10
Gallego, Mike	89F	8	$ .01	$ .04
Gallego, Mike	90F	7	$ .01	$ .04
Gallego, Mike	91F	7	$ .01	$ .04
Gallego, Mike	91FUL	246	$ .01	$ .07
Gallego, Mike	92F	256	$ .01	$ .04
Gallego, Mike	92FUL	112	$ .01	$ .10
Gallego, Mike	92FUL	406	$ .01	$ .10
Gallego, Mike	93F	648	$ .01	$ .04
Gallego, Mike	93FUL	240	$ .01	$ .10
Gamble, Oscar	81F	98	$ .01	$ .06
Gamble, Oscar	82F	36	$ .01	$ .06
Gamble, Oscar	83F	380	$ .01	$ .06
Gamble, Oscar	84F	124	$ .01	$ .08
Gamble, Oscar	85FU	44	$ .01	$ .10
Gant, Ron	88F	538	$1.00	$4.00
Gant, Ron	89F	590	$ .10	$ .40
Gant, Ron	90F	582	$ .10	$ .40
Gant, Ron	91F	688	$ .01	$ .10

FLEER

Player	Year	No.	VG	EX/MT
Gant, Ron	91FUL	4	$ .05	$ .35
Gant, Ron	92F	357	$ .01	$ .10
Gant, Ron	92FUL	161	$ .05	$ .20
Gant, Ron	93F	3	$ .01	$ .04
Gant, Ron	93FUL	5	$ .01	$ .10
Gantner, Jim	81F	522	$ .01	$ .06
Gantner, Jim	82F	142	$ .01	$ .06
Gantner, Jim	83F	34	$ .01	$ .06
Gantner, Jim	84F	200	$ .01	$ .08
Gantner, Jim	85F	582	$ .01	$ .06
Gantner, Jim	86F	487	$ .01	$ .06
Gantner, Jim	87F	345	$ .01	$ .06
Gantner, Jim	88F	165	$ .01	$ .05
Gantner, Jim	89F	186	$ .01	$ .04
Gantner, Jim	90F	324	$ .01	$ .04
Gantner, Jim	91F	584	$ .01	$ .04
Gantner, Jim	91FUL	174	$ .01	$ .07
Gantner, Jim	92F	176	$ .01	$ .04
Gantner, Jim	92FUL	382	$ .01	$ .10
Gantner, Jim	93F	630	$ .01	$ .04
Garber, Gene	81F	249	$ .01	$ .06
Garber, Gene	82F	434	$ .01	$ .06
Garber, Gene	83F	136	$ .01	$ .06
Garber, Gene	84F	179	$ .01	$ .08
Garber, Gene	85F	325	$ .01	$ .06
Garber, Gene	86F	515	$ .01	$ .06
Garber, Gene	87F	515	$ .01	$ .06
Garber, Gene	88F	257	$ .01	$ .05
Garbey, Barbaro	84FU	42	$ .10	$ .50
Garbey, Barbaro	85F	7	$ .01	$ .06
Garbey, Barbaro	86F	225	$ .01	$ .10
Garces, Rich	91FUL	378	$ .01	$ .10
Garcia, Carlos	91F	37	$ .05	$ .35
Garcia, Carlos	91FUL	278	$ .10	$ .50
Garcia, Carlos	93F	501	$ .01	$ .10
Garcia, Damaso	81F	415	$ .05	$ .20
Garcia, Damaso	82F	613	$ .01	$ .06
Garcia, Damaso	83F	427	$ .01	$ .06
Garcia, Damaso	84F	153	$ .01	$ .08
Garcia, Damaso	85F	104	$ .01	$ .06
Garcia, Damaso	86F	59	$ .01	$ .06
Garcia, Damaso	87F	226	$ .01	$ .06
Garcia, Damaso	90F	346	$ .01	$ .04
Garcia, Kiko	81F	191	$ .01	$ .06
Garcia, Kiko	82F	215	$ .01	$ .06
Garcia, Kiko	83F	447	$ .01	$ .06
Garcia, Kiko	84F	30	$ .01	$ .08
Garcia, Miguel	89F	647	$ .05	$ .20
Gardenhire, Ron	83F	543	$ .01	$ .06
Gardenhire, Ron	85F	81	$ .01	$ .06
Gardiner, Mike	93F	558	$ .01	$ .04
Gardner, Jeff	92F	675	$ .01	$ .10
Gardner, Mark	90F	646	$ .01	$ .15
Gardner, Mark	90FU	29	$ .01	$ .05
Gardner, Mark	91F	233	$ .01	$ .04
Gardner, Mark	92F	481	$ .01	$ .04
Gardner, Mark	93F	75	$ .01	$ .04
Gardner, Wes	88F	352	$ .01	$ .15
Gardner, Wes	89F	88	$ .01	$ .04
Gardner, Wes	90F	275	$ .01	$ .04
Gardner, Wes	91F	94	$ .01	$ .04
Garland, Wayne	81F	394	$ .01	$ .06
Garland, Wayne	82F	367	$ .01	$ .06
Garner, Phil	81F	364	$ .01	$ .06
Garner, Phil	82F	216	$ .01	$ .06
Garner, Phil	83F	448	$ .01	$ .06
Garner, Phil	84F	226	$ .01	$ .08
Garner, Phil	85F	351	$ .01	$ .06
Garner, Phil	86F	301	$ .01	$ .06
Garner, Phil	87F	58	$ .01	$ .06
Garrelts, Scott	86F	540	$ .01	$ .06
Garrelts, Scott	87F	273	$ .01	$ .06
Garrelts, Scott	88F	82	$ .01	$.05
Garrelts, Scott	89F	328	$ .01	$ .04
Garrelts, Scott	90F	56	$ .01	$ .04

Player	Year	No.	VG	EX/MT
Garrelts, Scott	91F	262	$ .01	$ .04
Garrelts, Scott	91FUL	320	$ .01	$ .07
Garrelts, Scott	92F	636	$ .01	$ .04
Garvey, Steve	81F	110	$ .10	$ .75
Garvey, Steve	81F	606	$ .10	$ .75
Garvey, Steve	82F	5	$ .10	$ .50
Garvey, Steve	83F	206	$ .05	$ .35
Garvey, Steve	84F	300	$ .10	$ .50
Garvey, Steve	84F	628	$ .05	$ .25
Garvey, Steve	85F	32	$ .10	$ .40
Garvey, Steve	85F	631	$ .10	$ .75
Garvey, Steve	85F	633	$ .01	$ .10
Garvey, Steve	86F	321	$ .05	$ .30
Garvey, Steve	86F	640	$ .05	$ .25
Garvey, Steve	87F	414	$ .05	$ .25
Garvin, Jerry	81F	429	$ .01	$ .06
Garvin, Jerry	82F	614	$ .01	$ .06
Garvin, Jerry	83F	428	$ .01	$ .06
Gedman, Rich	82F	294	$ .05	$ .20

Rich Gedman CATCHER

Player	Year	No.	VG	EX/MT
Gedman, Rich	83F	184	$ .01	$ .10
Gedman, Rich	84F	398	$ .01	$ .10
Gedman, Rich	85F	159	$ .01	$ .06
Gedman, Rich	86F	349	$ .01	$ .10
Gedman, Rich	86F	643	$ .01	$ .10
Gedman, Rich	87F	35	$ .01	$ .04
Gedman, Rich	88F	353	$ .01	$ .05
Gedman, Rich	89F	89	$ .01	$ .04
Gedman, Rich	90F	276	$ .01	$ .04
Gedman, Rich	92F	577	$ .01	$ .04
Gedman, Rich	92FUL	566	$ .01	$ .10
Geisel, Dave	84F	154	$ .01	$ .08
Gerber, Craig	86F	156	$ .01	$ .06
Geren, Bob	89FU	48	$ .01	$ .10
Geren, Bob	90F	442	$ .01	$ .10
Geren, Bob	91F	663	$ .01	$ .04
Geren, Bob	91FUL	231	$ .01	$ .07
Geren, Bob	92F	226	$ .01	$ .04
Gerhart, Ken	87FU	34	$ .01	$ .10
Gerhart, Ken	88F	559	$ .01	$ .05
Gerhart, Ken	89F	609	$ .01	$ .04
Geronimo, Cesar	82F	409	$ .01	$ .06
Geronimo, Cesar	83F	112	$ .01	$ .06
Gibson, Bob	84F	201	$ .01	$ .08

FLEER

Player	Year	No.	VG	EX/MT
Gibson, Bob	86F	488	$.01	$.06
Gibson, Kirk	81F	481	$.75	$3.00
Gibson, Kirk	82F	267	$.10	$.75
Gibson, Kirk	83F	329	$.10	$.40
Gibson, Kirk	84F	80	$.10	$.75
Gibson, Kirk	85F	8	$.05	$.30
Gibson, Kirk	86F	226	$.05	$.25
Gibson, Kirk	87F	151	$.05	$.20
Gibson, Kirk	88F	55	$.01	$.15
Gibson, Kirk	88FU	93	$.01	$.10
Gibson, Kirk	89F	57	$.01	$.15
Gibson, Kirk	90F	393	$.01	$.04
Gibson, Kirk	91F	199	$.01	$.04
Gibson, Kirk	91FU	26	$.01	$.05
Gibson, Kirk	91FULU	27	$.01	$.10
Gibson, Kirk	92F	157	$.01	$.04
Gibson, Paul	88FU	26	$.01	$.10
Gibson, Paul	89F	131	$.01	$.10
Gibson, Paul	90F	602	$.01	$.04
Gibson, Paul	91F	337	$.01	$.04
Gibson, Paul	91FULU	23	$.01	$.10
Gibson, Paul	92F	136	$.01	$.10
Gibson, Paul	92FUL	531	$.01	$.10
Gibson, Paul	93F	473	$.01	$.04
Gideon, Brett	88F	330	$.01	$.15
Giles, Brian	83F	544	$.01	$.06
Giles, Brian	84F	585	$.01	$.08
Gilkey, Bernard	91F	633	$.01	$.10
Gilkey, Bernard	92F	578	$.01	$.04
Gilkey, Bernard	92FUL	567	$.05	$.20
Gilkey, Bernard	93F	125	$.01	$.04
Gilkey, Bernard	93FUL	106	$.01	$.15
Girardi, Joe	89F	644	$.05	$.20
Girardi, Joe	90F	31	$.01	$.10
Girardi, Joe	91F	421	$.01	$.04
Girardi, Joe	91FUL	60	$.01	$.07
Girardi, Joe	92FUL	469	$.01	$.10
Girardi, Joe	93F	410	$.01	$.04
Gladden, Dan	85F	607	$.05	$.35
Gladden, Dan	86F	541	$.01	$.06
Gladden, Dan	87F	274	$.01	$.06
Gladden, Dan	87FU	36	$.01	$.06
Gladden, Dan	88F	12	$.01	$.05
Gladden, Dan	89F	112	$.01	$.04
Gladden, Dan	90F	375	$.01	$.04
Gladden, Dan	91F	611	$.01	$.04
Gladden, Dan	91FUL	187	$.01	$.07
Gladden, Dan	92F	203	$.01	$.04
Gladden, Dan	92FU	21	$.05	$.25
Gladden, Dan	92FUL	361	$.01	$.10
Gladden, Dan	93F	605	$.01	$.04
Gladden, Dan	93FUL	198	$.01	$.10
Glavine, Tom	88F	539	$2.25	$9.00
Glavine, Tom	89F	591	$.10	$.50
Glavine, Tom	90F	583	$.05	$.25
Glavine, Tom	91F	689	$.05	$.20
Glavine, Tom	91FLU	5	$.10	$.50
Glavine, Tom	92F	358	$.01	$.10
Glavine, Tom	92FLL	694	$.01	$.10
Glavine, Tom	92FUL	162	$.05	$.35
Glavine, Tom	93F	4	$.01	$.04
Glavine, Tom	93FUL	6	$.05	$.35
Gleaton, Jerry	88F	258	$.01	$.05
Gleaton, Jerry	89F	282	$.01	$.04
Gleaton, Jerry Don	91F	338	$.01	$.04
Glynn, Ed	83F	408	$.01	$.06
Goltz, Dave	81F	127	$.01	$.06
Goltz, Dave	82F	6	$.01	$.06
Goltz, Dave	83F	90	$.01	$.06
Gomez, Leo	91F	472	$.01	$.15
Gomez, Leo	91FUL	16	$.05	$.35
Gomez, Leo	92F	8	$.01	$.15
Gomez, Leo	92FUL	4	$.05	$.20
Gomez, Leo	93F	167	$.01	$.04
Gomez, Leo	93FUL	140	$.01	$.10

Player	Year	No.	VG	EX/MT
Gomez, Luis	81F	253	$.01	$.06
Gonzales, Rene	88F	560	$.01	$.15
Gonzales, Rene	91F	473	$.01	$.04
Gonzales, Rene	93FUL	164	$.01	$.10
Gonzalez, Denny	86F	608	$.01	$.06
Gonzalez, German	89F	113	$.01	$.15
Gonzalez, German	90F	376	$.01	$.04
Gonzalez, Jose	87F	649	$.05	$.25
Gonzalez, Jose	90F	394	$.01	$.04
Gonzalez, Juan	90F	297	$.20	$2.00
Gonzalez, Juan	91F	286	$.05	$.35
Gonzalez, Juan	91FULU	55	$4.50	$18.00
Gonzalez, Juan	92F	304	$.10	$.40
Gonzalez, Juan	92FUL	132	$.75	$3.00
Gonzalez, Juan	93F	322	$.05	$.25
Gonzalez, Juan	93F	709	$.01	$.15
Gonzalez, Juan	93FUL	279	$.10	$1.00
Gonzalez, Julio	81F	73	$.01	$.06
Gonzalez, Luis	91F	507	$.05	$.25
Gonzalez, Luis	91FULU	82	$.10	$1.00
Gonzalez, Luis	92F	434	$.05	$.20
Gonzalez, Luis	92FUL	203	$.01	$.10
Gonzalez, Luis	93F	51	$.01	$.04
Gonzalez, Luis	93FUL	40	$.01	$.15
Gonzalez, Orlando	81F	585	$.01	$.06
Gooden, Dwight	84FU	43	$20.00	$80.00
Gooden, Dwight	85F	82	$2.00	$8.00
Gooden, Dwight	85F	634	$.10	$.40
Gooden, Dwight	86F	81	$.10	$1.00
Gooden, Dwight	86F	626	$.05	$.35
Gooden, Dwight	86F	638	$.10	$.75
Gooden, Dwight	86F	641	$.05	$.20
Gooden, Dwight	87F	9	$.10	$.50
Gooden, Dwight	87F	629	$.10	$.50
Gooden, Dwight	87F	640	$.10	$1.00
Gooden, Dwight	88F	135	$.01	$.15
Gooden, Dwight	89F	36	$.01	$.15
Gooden, Dwight	89F	635	$.01	$.15
Gooden, Dwight	90F	204	$.01	$.10
Gooden, Dwight	91F	148	$.01	$.10
Gooden, Dwight	91FUL	218	$.01	$.15
Gooden, Dwight	92F	505	$.01	$.10
Gooden, Dwight	92FUL	232	$.05	$.20
Gooden, Dwight	93F	474	$.01	$.04
Goodwin, Danny	82F	554	$.01	$.06
Goodwin, Tom	92F	652	$.05	$.20
Goodwin, Tom	93F	446	$.01	$.04
Gordon, Don	89F	405	$.01	$.04
Gordon, Tom	89F	284	$.01	$.15
Gordon, Tom	90F	108	$.01	$.15
Gordon, Tom	91F	559	$.01	$.04
Gordon, Tom	91FUL	147	$.01	$.07
Gordon, Tom	92F	158	$.01	$.04
Gordon, Tom	92FUL	370	$.01	$.10
Gordon, Tom	93F	237	$.01	$.04
Gordon, Tom	93FUL	207	$.01	$.10
Gorman, Tom	85F	00	$.01	$.06
Gorman, Tom	86F	82	$.01	$.06
Gossage, Goose "Rich"	81F	89	$.05	$.25
Gossage, Goose	82F	37	$.05	$.25
Gossage, Goose	83F	381	$.05	$.20
Gossage, Goose	84F	125	$.05	$.20
Gossage, Goose	84FU	44	$.10	$1.00
Gossage, Goose	85F	33	$.05	$.20
Gossage, Goose	85F	633	$.01	$.10
Gossage, Goose	86F	322	$.05	$.20
Gossage, Goose	87F	415	$.01	$.10
Gossage, Goose	88F	583	$.01	$.10
Gossage, Goose	88FU	76	$.01	$.06
Gossage, Goose	89F	425	$.01	$.04
Gossage, Rich	91FU	59	$.01	$.05
Gossage, Rich	92F	305	$.01	$.04
Gott, Jim	84F	155	$.05	$.25
Gott, Jim	85F	105	$.01	$.06
Gott, Jim	85FU	45	$.01	$.10

FLEER

Player	Year	No.	VG	EX/MT	Player	Year	No.	VG	EX/MT
Gott, Jim	86F	542	$ .01	$ .06	Grich, Bobby	86F	157	$ .01	$ .06
Gott, Jim	87FU	35	$ .01	$ .06	Grich, Bobby	87F	81	$ .01	$ .06
Gott, Jim	88FU	112	$ .01	$ .06	Griffey, Ken	81F	199	$ .05	$ .35
Gott, Jim	89F	210	$ .01	$ .04	Griffey, Ken	82F	67	$ .05	$ .25
Gott, Jim	90F	466	$ .01	$ .04	Griffey, Ken	83F	382	$ .05	$ .25
Gott, Jim	91F	200	$ .01	$ .04	Griffey, Ken	84F	126	$ .05	$ .25
Gott, Jim	92F	454	$ .01	$ .04	Griffey, Ken	85F	128	$ .05	$ .20
Gott, Jim	92FUL	504	$ .01	$ .10	Griffey, Ken	86F	105	$ .01	$ .10
Gott, Jim	93F	447	$ .01	$ .04	Griffey, Ken	87F	516	$ .01	$ .10
Gozzo, Mauro	90F	82	$ .01	$ .15	Griffey, Ken	88F	540	$ .01	$ .05
Grace, Mark	88F	641	$1.00	$4.00	Griffey, Ken	89FU	84	$ .01	$ .10
Grace, Mark	88FU	77	$ .20	$2.00	Griffey, Ken	90F	420	$ .01	$ .05
Grace, Mark	89F	426	$ .05	$ .25	Griffey, Ken	91FUL	335	$ .01	$ .07
Grace, Mark	90F	32	$ .01	$ .15	Griffey, Jr., Ken	89F	548	$1.50	$6.00
Grace, Mark	91F	422	$ .01	$ .10	Griffey, Jr., Ken	90F	513	$ .15	$1.50
Grace, Mark	91FUL	61	$ .05	$ .20	Griffey, Jr., Ken	91F	450	$ .10	$ .50
Grace, Mark	92F	381	$ .01	$ .10	Griffey, Jr., Ken	91F	710	$ .05	$ .25
Grace, Mark	92FUL	175	$ .05	$ .25	Griffey, Jr., Ken	91FUL	336	$ .20	$1.75
Grace, Mark	93F	20	$ .01	$ .04	Griffey, Jr., Ken	92F	279	$ .10	$ .75
Grace, Mark	93FUL	18	$ .01	$ .15	Griffey, Jr., Ken	92F	709	$ .10	$ .50
Graham, Dan	81F	189	$ .01	$ .06	Griffey Jr., Ken	92FUH	1	$4.05	$18.00
Graham, Dan	82F	167	$ .01	$ .06	Griffey, Jr., Ken	92FUL	123	$ .75	$3.00
Grahe, Joe	93F	192	$ .01	$ .04	Griffey, Jr., Ken	93F	307	$ .10	$ .50
Grahe, Joe	93FUL	165	$ .01	$ .10	Griffin, Alfredo	81F	430	$ .01	$ .06
Grant, Mark	88F	584	$ .01	$ .05	Griffin, Alfredo	82F	615	$ .01	$ .06
Grant, Mark	89F	304	$ .01	$ .04	Griffin, Alfredo	83F	429	$ .01	$ .06
Grant, Mark	90F	156	$ .01	$ .04	Griffin, Alfredo	84F	156	$ .01	$ .08
Grant, Mark	91F	690	$ .01	$ .04	Griffin, Alfredo	85F	106	$ .01	$ .06
Grant, Mark	93F	675	$ .01	$ .04	Griffin, Alfredo	85FU	47	$ .01	$ .10
Gray, Gary	81F	402	$ .01	$ .06	Griffin, Alfredo	86F	417	$ .01	$ .06
Gray, Gary	82F	511	$ .01	$ .06	Griffin, Alfredo	87F	392	$ .01	$ .06
Gray, Gary	83F	480	$ .01	$ .06	Griffin, Alfredo	88F	280	$ .01	$ .05
Gray, Jeff	91F	95	$ .01	$ .10	Griffin, Alfredo	88FU	94	$ .01	$ .06
Grebeck, Craig	90FU	85	$ .01	$ .10	Griffin, Alfredo	89F	58	$ .01	$ .04
Grebeck, Craig	91F	120	$ .01	$ .10	Griffin, Alfredo	90F	395	$ .01	$ .04
Grebeck, Craig	91FULU	15	$ .01	$ .10	Griffin, Alfredo	91F	201	$ .01	$ .04
Grebeck, Craig	92F	81	$ .01	$ .04	Griffin, Alfredo	91FUL	161	$ .01	$ .07
Grebeck, Craig	92FUL	34	$ .01	$ .10	Griffin, Alfredo	92F	455	$ .01	$ .04
Grebeck, Craig	93F	202	$ .01	$ .04	Griffin, Alfredo	93F	692	$ .01	$ .04
Green, David	83F	6	$ .01	$ .06	Griffin, Mike	81F	107	$ .01	$ .06
Green, David	84F	323	$ .01	$ .08	Griffin, Mike	88F	561	$ .01	$ .05
Green, David	85F	224	$ .01	$ .06	Griffin, Tom	81F	456	$ .01	$ .06
Green, David	85FU	46	$ .01	$ .10	Griffin, Tom	82F	389	$ .01	$ .06
Green, David	86F	543	$ .01	$ .06	Grimsley, Jason	90F	653	$ .10	$ .50
Green, David	88F	34	$ .01	$ .05	Grimsley, Jason	91F	396	$ .01	$ .04
Greene, Tommy	90F	584	$ .05	$ .20	Grimsley, Jason	92F	532	$ .01	$ .04
Greene, Tommy	91FU	108	$ .01	$ .10	Grimsley, Ross	81F	406	$ .01	$ .06
Greene, Tommy	91FULU	99	$ .01	$ .10	Grissom, Marquis	90F	347	$ .10	$ .50
Greene, Tommy	92F	531	$ .01	$ .04	Grissom, Marquis	91F	234	$ .01	$ .15
Greene, Tommy	92FUL	242	$ .01	$ .10	Grissom, Marquis	91FUL	204	$ .05	$ .35
Greene, Tommy	93F	489	$ .01	$ .04	Grissom, Marquis	92F	482	$ .01	$ .10
Greene, Willie	92FU	81	$ .10	$1.00	Grissom, Marquis	92FUL	518	$ .10	$ .40
Greene, Willie	93F	34	$ .01	$ .10	Grissom, Marquis	93F	461	$ .01	$ .10
Greenwell, Mike	87FU	37	$ .10	$1.00	Grissom, Marquis	93F	706	$ .01	$ .10
Greenwell, Mike	88F	354	$ .05	$ .35	Groom, Buddy	92FU	22	$ .10	$ .40
Greenwell, Mike	88F	630	$ .05	$ .20	Gross, Greg	81F	18	$ .01	$ .06
Greenwell, Mike	89F	90	$ .01	$ .10	Gross, Greg	82F	246	$ .01	$ .06
Greenwell, Mike	90F	277	$ .01	$ .10	Gross, Greg	83F	162	$ .01	$ .06
Greenwell, Mike	90F	632	$ .01	$ .10	Gross, Greg	84F	31	$ .01	$ .08
Greenwell, Mike	91F	96	$ .01	$ .10	Gross, Greg	85F	251	$ .01	$ .06
Greenwell, Mike	91FUL	32	$ .01	$ .10	Gross, Greg	86F	441	$ .01	$ .06
Greenwell, Mike	92F	39	$ .01	$ .10	Gross, Greg	87F	173	$ .01	$ .06
Greenwell, Mike	92FUL	16	$ .01	$ .10	Gross, Greg	88F	302	$ .01	$ .05
Greenwell, Mike	93F	559	$ .01	$ .04	Gross, Greg	89F	568	$ .01	$ .04
Greenwell, Mike	93FUL	152	$ .01	$ .10	Gross, Kevin	84F	32	$ .05	$ .25
Gregg, Tommy	88FU	113	$ .01	$ .15	Gross, Kevin	85F	252	$ .01	$ .06
Gregg, Tommy	89F	592	$ .01	$ .04	Gross, Kevin	86F	442	$ .01	$ .06
Gregg, Tommy	90F	585	$ .01	$ .04	Gross, Kevin	87F	174	$ .01	$ .06
Gregg, Tommy	91F	691	$ .01	$ .04	Gross, Kevin	88F	303	$ .01	$ .05
Gregg, Tommy	91FUL	6	$ .01	$ .07	Gross, Kevin	89F	569	$ .01	$ .04
Grich, Bobby	81F	269	$ .01	$ .06	Gross, Kevin	89FU	96	$ .01	$ .05
Grich, Bobby	82F	461	$ .01	$ .06	Gross, Kevin	90F	348	$ .01	$ .04
Grich, Bobby	83F	91	$ .01	$ .06	Gross, Kevin	91F	235	$ .01	$ .04
Grich, Bobby	84F	518	$ .01	$ .08	Gross, Kevin	91FU	94	$ .01	$ .05
Grich, Bobby	85F	302	$ .01	$ .06	Gross, Kevin	92F	456	$ .01	$ .04

FLEER

Player	Year	No.	VG	EX/MT	Player	Year	No.	VG	EX/MT
Gross, Kevin	93F	448	$ .01	$ .04	Gubicza, Mark	90F	633	$ .01	$ .04
Gross, Kip	92F	407	$ .01	$ .10	Gubicza, Mark	91F	560	$ .01	$ .04
Gross, Wayne	81F	587	$ .01	$ .06	Gubicza, Mark	91FUL	148	$ .01	$ .07
Gross, Wayne	82F	90	$ .01	$ .06	Gubicza, Mark	92F	159	$ .01	$ .04
Gross, Wayne	83F	517	$ .01	$ .06	Gubicza, Mark	92FUL	70	$ .01	$ .10
Gross, Wayne	84F	444	$ .01	$ .08	Gubicza, Mark	93F	618	$ .01	$ .04
Gross, Wayne	84FU	45	$ .10	$ .50	Gubicza, Mark	93FUL	208	$ .01	$ .10
Gross, Wayne	85F	179	$ .01	$ .06	Guerrero, Juan	92FU	85	$ .05	$ .35
Gross, Wayne	86F	276	$ .01	$ .06	Guerrero, Juan	92FUL	490	$ .05	$ .20
Grotewold, Jeff	92FU	110	$ .05	$ .25	Guerrero, Juan	93F	435	$ .01	$ .04
Grotewold, Jeff	92FUL	545	$ .05	$ .20	Guerrero, Juan	93FUL	41	$ .01	$ .10
Grotewold, Jeff	93F	490	$ .01	$ .04	Guerrero, Mario	81F	591	$ .01	$ .06
Grubb, John	81F	631	$ .01	$ .06	Guerrero, Pedro	82F	7	$ .05	$ .35
Grubb, John	82F	317	$ .01	$ .06	Guerrero, Pedro	83F	207	$ .05	$ .30
Grubb, John	83F	567	$ .01	$ .06	Guerrero, Pedro	84F	100	$ .05	$ .25
Grubb, John	84F	81	$ .01	$ .08	Guerrero, Pedro	85F	370	$ .05	$ .20
Grubb, John	85F	9	$ .01	$ .06	Guerrero, Pedro	86F	130	$ .05	$ .25
Grubb, John	86F	227	$ .01	$ .06	Guerrero, Pedro	87F	440	$ .01	$ .15
Grubb, John	87F	152	$ .01	$ .06	Guerrero, Pedro	88F	514	$ .01	$ .10
Gruber, Kelly	85F	645	$ .20	$2.00	Guerrero, Pedro	88F	623	$ .01	$ .10
Gruber, Kelly	87F	227	$ .05	$ .25	Guerrero, Pedro	89F	451	$ .01	$ .04
Gruber, Kelly	88F	111	$ .05	$ .25	Guerrero, Pedro	90F	250	$ .01	$ .10
Gruber, Kelly	89F	234	$ .01	$ .15	Guerrero, Pedro	91F	634	$ .01	$ .04
Gruber, Kelly	90F	83	$ .01	$ .04	Guerrero, Pedro	91FUL	289	$ .01	$ .07
Gruber, Kelly	91F	175	$ .01	$ .10	Guerrero, Pedro	92F	579	$ .01	$ .04
Gruber, Kelly	91FUL	361	$ .01	$ .07	Guerrero, Pedro	92FUL	263	$ .01	$ .10
Gruber, Kelly	92F	329	$ .01	$ .04	Guerrero, Pedro	93F	509	$ .01	$ .04
Gruber, Kelly	92FUL	146	$ .01	$ .10	Guetterman, Lee	86FU	45	$ .01	$ .15
Gruber, Kelly	93F	334	$ .01	$ .04	Guetterman, Lee	87F	585	$ .01	$ .10
Guante, Cecilio	84F	250	$ .01	$ .08	Guetterman, Lee	88F	374	$ .01	$ .05
Guante, Cecilio	85F	465	$ .01	$ .06	Guetterman, Lee	90F	443	$ .01	$ .04
Guante, Cecilio	86F	609	$ .01	$ .06	Guetterman, Lee	91F	664	$ .01	$ .04
Guante, Cecilio	87F	610	$ .01	$ .06	Guetterman, Lee	91FUL	232	$ .01	$ .07
Guante, Cecilio	87FU	38	$ .01	$ .06	Guetterman, Lee	92F	227	$ .01	$ .04
Guante, Cecilio	89F	519	$ .01	$ .04	Guetterman, Lee	93F	475	$ .01	$ .04
Guante, Cecilio	90F	298	$ .01	$ .04	Guidry, Ron	81F	88	$ .05	$ .25
Gubicza, Mark	84FU	46	$1.00	$4.00	Guidry, Ron	82F	38	$ .05	$ .25
Gubicza, Mark	85F	201	$ .10	$ .50	Guidry, Ron	83F	383	$ .05	$ .20
Gubicza, Mark	86F	8	$ .01	$ .15	Guidry, Ron	84F	127	$ .05	$ .25
Gubicza, Mark	87F	368	$ .01	$ .06	Guidry, Ron	85F	129	$ .05	$ .20
					Guidry, Ron	86F	106	$ .01	$ .10
					Guidry, Ron	87F	100	$ .01	$ .10
					Guidry, Ron	88F	207	$ .01	$ .10
					Guillen, Ozzie	85FU	48	$ .10	$1.00
					Guillen, Ozzie	86F	206	$ .10	$ .50
					Guillen, Ozzie	87F	497	$ .05	$ .20
					Guillen, Ozzie	88F	398	$ .01	$ .05
					Guillen, Ozzie	89F	497	$ .01	$ .04
					Guillen, Ozzie	90F	533	$ .01	$ .04
					Guillen, Ozzie	91F	121	$ .01	$ .04
					Guillen, Ozzie	91FUL	74	$ .01	$ .07
					Guillen, Ozzie	92F	82	$ .01	$ .04
					Guillen, Ozzie	92F	706	$ .01	$ .04
					Guillen, Ozzie	92FUL	35	$ .01	$ .10
					Guillen, Ozzie	93F	203	$ .01	$ .04
					Gulden, Brad	85F	537	$ .01	$ .06
					Gullickson, Bill	81F	150	$ .10	$ .75
					Gullickson, Bill	82F	190	$ .05	$ .25
					Gullickson, Bill	83F	284	$ .05	$ .15
					Gullickson, Bill	84F	276	$ .01	$ .10
					Gullickson, Bill	85F	399	$ .01	$ .06
					Gullickson, Bill	86F	249	$ .01	$ .06
					Gullickson, Bill	86FU	46	$ .01	$ .08
					Gullickson, Bill	87F	203	$ .01	$ .06
					Gullickson, Bill	88F	208	$ .01	$ .05
					Gullickson, Bill	91F	508	$ .01	$ .04
					Gullickson, Bill	92F	137	$ .01	$ .04
					Gullickson, Bill	92FUL	362	$ .05	$ .20
					Gullickson, Bill	93F	606	$ .01	$ .04
					Gulliver, Glenn	83F	62	$ .01	$ .06
					Gumpert, Dave	87F	565	$ .01	$ .06
					Gunderson, Eric	92F	637	$ .01	$ .04
Gubicza, Mark	88F	259	$ .01	$ .05	Gura, Larry	81F	38	$ .01	$ .06
Gubicza, Mark	89F	283	$ .01	$ .10	Gura, Larry	82F	410	$ .01	$ .06
Gubicza, Mark	90F	109	$ .01	$ .15	Gura, Larry	83F	113	$ .01	$ .06

Mark Gubicza
PITCHER
Royals

FLEER

Player	Year	No.	VG	EX/MT	Player	Year	No.	VG	EX/MT
Gura, Larry	84F	347	$ .01	$ .08	Hall, Mel	89FU	49	$ .01	$ .05
Gura, Larry	85F	202	$ .01	$ .06	Hall, Mel	90F	444	$ .01	$ .04
Guthrie, Mark	91F	612	$ .01	$ .04	Hall, Mel	91F	665	$ .01	$ .04
Guthrie, Mark	92FUL	396	$ .01	$ .10	Hall, Mel	91FUL	233	$ .01	$ .07
Guthrie, Mark	93F	265	$ .01	$ .04	Hall, Mel	92F	229	$ .01	$ .04
Gutierrez, Jackie	84FU	47	$ .10	$ .50	Hall, Mel	92FUL	101	$ .01	$ .10
Gutierrez, Jackie	85F	160	$ .01	$ .06	Hall, Mel	93F	278	$ .01	$ .04
Gutierrez, Jackie	86F	350	$ .01	$ .06	Hamelin, Bob	92F	672	$ .01	$ .10
Gutierrez, Jackie	86FU	47	$ .01	$ .08	Hamilton, Darryl	88FU	38	$ .10	$ .50
Gutierrez, Jackie	87F	471	$ .01	$ .06	Hamilton, Darryl	89F	187	$ .05	$ .25
Guzman, Jose	86F	559	$ .10	$1.00	Hamilton, Darryl	90F	325	$ .01	$ .04
Guzman, Jose	87F	124	$ .01	$ .06	Hamilton, Darryl	91F	585	$ .01	$ .04
Guzman, Jose	88F	467	$ .01	$ .05	Hamilton, Darryl	91FULU	30	$ .05	$ .25
Guzman, Jose	89F	520	$ .01	$ .04	Hamilton, Darryl	92F	177	$ .01	$ .04
Guzman, Jose	91FU	60	$ .01	$ .05	Hamilton, Darryl	92FUL	383	$ .01	$ .10
Guzman, Jose	92F	306	$ .01	$ .04	Hamilton, Darryl	93F	250	$ .01	$ .04
Guzman, Jose	92FUL	442	$ .01	$ .10	Hamilton, Darryl	93FUL	219	$ .01	$ .10
Guzman, Jose	93F	323	$ .01	$ .04	Hamilton, Jeff	88F	515	$ .01	$ .05
Guzman, Juan	91FULU	60	$2.25	$9.00	Hamilton, Jeff	89F	60	$ .01	$ .04
Guzman, Juan	92F	330	$ .10	$ .50	Hamilton, Jeff	90F	396	$ .01	$ .04
Guzman, Juan	92FUL	449	$ .20	$2.00	Hammaker, Atlee	83F	261	$ .01	$ .06
Guzman, Juan	93F	693	$ .05	$ .25	Hammaker, Atlee	84F	373	$ .01	$ .08
Gwynn, Chris	88F	647	$ .10	$ .75	Hammaker, Atlee	85F	608	$ .01	$ .06
Gwynn, Chris	89F	59	$ .01	$ .10	Hammaker, Atlee	86F	544	$ .01	$ .06
Gwynn, Chris	91F	202	$ .01	$ .04	Hammaker, Atlee	87FU	40	$ .01	$ .06
Gwynn, Chris	92F	457	$ .01	$ .04	Hammaker, Atlee	88F	83	$ .01	$ .05
Gwynn, Chris	92FUL	371	$ .01	$ .10	Hammaker, Atlee	89F	329	$ .01	$ .04
Gwynn, Tony	83F	360	$6.00	$24.00	Hammaker, Atlee	90F	57	$ .01	$ .04
Gwynn, Tony	84F	301	$2.75	$11.00	Hammaker, Atlee	91F	530	$ .01	$ .04
Gwynn, Tony	85F	34	$1.25	$5.00	Hammond, Chris	90F	421	$ .05	$ .25
Gwynn, Tony	86F	323	$ .75	$3.00	Hammond, Chris	91F	65	$ .01	$ .10
Gwynn, Tony	87F	416	$ .15	$1.50	Hammond, Chris	91FULU	76	$ .05	$ .20
Gwynn, Tony	88F	585	$ .10	$ .50	Hammond, Chris	92F	408	$ .01	$ .04
Gwynn, Tony	88F	631	$ .01	$ .15	Hammond, Chris	92FUL	189	$ .01	$ .10
Gwynn, Tony	88F	634	$ .01	$ .15	Hammond, Chris	93F	35	$ .01	$ .04
Gwynn, Tony	89F	305	$ .05	$ .25	Hammond, Chris	93FUL	29	$ .01	$ .10
Gwynn, Tony	90F	157	$ .05	$ .20	Hammond, Steve	83F	114	$ .01	$ .06
Gwynn, Tony	91F	529	$ .01	$ .10	Hancock, Garry	81F	229	$ .01	$ .06
Gwynn, Tony	91FUL	303	$ .05	$ .25	Hancock, Garry	82F	295	$ .01	$ .06
Gwynn, Tony	92F	605	$ .01	$ .10	Hancock, Garry	84F	445	$ .01	$ .08
Gwynn, Tony	92FUL	277	$ .10	$ .50	Haney, Chris	92F	483	$ .01	$ .10
Gwynn, Tony	93F	138	$ .01	$ .10	Haney, Chris	92FUL	519	$ .05	$ .20
Haas, Moose	81F	516	$ .01	$ .06	Hanna, Preston	81F	264	$ .01	$ .06
Haas, Moose	82F	143	$ .01	$ .06	Hanna, Preston	82F	435	$ .01	$ .06
Haas, Moose	83F	35	$ .01	$ .06	Hansen, Dave	90F	642	$ .01	$ .15
Haas, Moose	84F	202	$ .01	$ .08	Hansen, Dave	90FU	21	$ .01	$ .10
Haas, Moose	85F	583	$ .01	$ .06	Hansen, Dave	91F	203	$ .01	$ .10
Haas, Moose	86F	489	$ .01	$ .06	Hansen, Dave	92FUL	505	$ .01	$ .10
Haas, Moose	86FU	48	$ .01	$ .08	Hansen, Dave	93F	449	$ .01	$ .04
Haas, Moose	87F	393	$ .01	$ .06	Hanson, Erik	89F	549	$ .05	$ .25
Hayban "Habyan", John	88F	562	$ .01	$ .05	Hanson, Erik	90F	514	$ .01	$ .10
Habyan, John	91FU	42	$ .01	$ .05	Hanson, Erik	91F	451	$ .01	$ .10
Habyan, John	91FULU	40	$ .01	$ .10	Hanson, Erik	91FUL	337	$ .01	$ .07
Habyan, John	92F	228	$ .01	$ .04	Hanson, Erik	92F	280	$ .01	$ .04
Habyan, John	93F	277	$ .01	$ .04	Hanson, Erik	92FUL	124	$ .01	$ .10
Habyan, John	93FUL	241	$ .01	$ .10	Hanson, Erik	93F	308	$ .01	$ .04
Hairston, Jerry	83F	236	$ .01	$ .06	Hare, Shawn	92FU	23	$ .05	$ .25
Hairston, Jerry	84F	60	$ .01	$ .08	Hare, Shawn	92FUL	363	$ .01	$ .10
Hairston, Jerry	85F	515	$ .01	$ .06	Hargesheimer, Alan	81F	457	$ .01	$ .06
Hairston, Jerry	86F	207	$ .01	$ .06	Hargrove, Mike	81F	387	$ .01	$ .06
Hairston, Jerry	87F	498	$ .01	$ .06	Hargrove, Mike	82F	368	$ .01	$ .06
Hall, Albert	85F	326	$ .01	$ .06	Hargrove, Mike	83F	409	$ .01	$ .06
Hall, Albert	87FU	39	$ .01	$ .06	Hargrove, Mike	84F	543	$ .01	$ .08
Hall, Albert	88F	541	$ .01	$ .05	Hargrove, Mike	85F	450	$ .01	$ .06
Hall, Albert	89F	593	$ .01	$ .04	Hargrove, Mike	86F	588	$ .01	$ .06
Hall, Drew	89F	643	$ .05	$ .20	Harkey, Mike	89F	427	$ .01	$ .15
Hall, Drew	90F	299	$ .01	$ .04	Harkey, Mike	90F	33	$ .01	$ .10
Hall, Drew	91F	236	$ .01	$ .04	Harkey, Mike	91F	423	$ .01	$ .04
Hall, Grady	89F	650	$ .05	$ .20	Harkey, Mike	91FUL	62	$ .01	$ .07
Hall, Mel	84F	493	$ .05	$ .25	Harkey, Mike	92F	382	$ .01	$ .04
Hall, Mel	85F	449	$ .05	$ .20	Harkey, Mike	93F	378	$ .01	$ .04
Hall, Mel	86F	587	$ .01	$ .15	Harlow, Larry	81F	289	$ .01	$ .06
Hall, Mel	87F	252	$ .01	$ .06	Harlow, Larry	82F	462	$ .01	$ .06
Hall, Mel	88F	610	$ .01	$ .05	Harnisch, Pete	90F	177	$ .01	$ .10
Hall, Mel	89F	406	$ .01	$ .04	Harnisch, Pete	91F	474	$ .01	$ .04

FLEER

Player	Year	No.	VG	EX/MT
Harnisch, Pete	91FU	89	$ .01	$ .05
Harnisch, Pete	91FULU	83	$ .01	$ .10
Harnisch, Pete	92F	435	$ .01	$ .04
Harnisch, Pete	92FUL	204	$ .01	$ .10
Harnisch, Pete	93F	52	$ .01	$ .04
Harnisch, Pete	93FUL	42	$ .01	$ .10
Harper, Brian	85F	466	$ .10	$ .50
Harper, Brian	86F	36	$ .05	$ .25
Harper, Brian	88FU	42	$ .01	$ .06
Harper, Brian	89F	114	$ .01	$ .04
Harper, Brian	90F	377	$ .01	$ .04
Harper, Brian	91F	613	$ .01	$ .04
Harper, Brian	91FUL	188	$ .01	$ .07
Harper, Brian	92F	204	$ .01	$ .04
Harper, Brian	92FUL	91	$ .01	$ .10
Harper, Brian	93F	266	$ .01	$ .04
Harper, Terry	83F	137	$ .01	$ .06
Harper, Terry	84F	180	$ .01	$ .08
Harper, Terry	85F	327	$ .01	$ .06
Harper, Terry	86F	516	$ .01	$ .06
Harper, Terry	87F	517	$ .01	$ .06
Harper, Terry	88F	331	$ .01	$ .05
Harrah, Toby	81F	389	$ .01	$ .06
Harrah, Toby	82F	369	$ .01	$ .06
Harrah, Toby	83F	410	$ .01	$ .06
Harrah, Toby	83F	635	$ .01	$ .06
Harrah, Toby	84F	544	$ .01	$ .08
Harrah, Toby	84FU	48	$ .10	$ .50
Harrah, Toby	85F	130	$ .01	$ .06
Harrah, Toby	85FU	49	$ .01	$ .10
Harrah, Toby	86F	560	$ .01	$ .06
Harrah, Toby	87F	125	$ .01	$ .06
Harris, Don	92F	660	$ .01	$ .15
Harris, Donald	92FUL	443	$ .05	$ .20
Harris, Gene	89FU	58	$ .01	$ .15
Harris, Gene	90F	515	$ .01	$ .04
Harris, Gene	91F	452	$ .01	$ .04
Harris, Greg A.	83F	590	$ .01	$ .06
Harris, Greg A.	85F	35	$ .01	$ .06
Harris, Greg A.	90FU	71	$ .01	$ .05
Harris, Greg A.	91F	97	$ .01	$ .04
Harris, Greg A.	91FUL	33	$ .01	$ .07
Harris, Greg A.	93F	560	$ .01	$ .04
Harris, Greg W.	88FU	109	$ .01	$ .06
Harris, Greg W.	89F	306	$ .05	$ .20
Harris, Greg W.	90F	158	$ .01	$ .10
Harris, Greg W.	91F	531	$ .01	$ .04
Harris, Greg W.	91FUL	304	$ .01	$ .07
Harris, Greg W.	92F	606	$ .01	$ .04
Harris, Greg W.	92FUL	278	$ .01	$ .10
Harris, Greg W.	93F	139	$ .01	$ .04
Harris, Greg W.	93FUL	117	$ .01	$ .10
Harris, John	82F	463	$ .01	$ .06
Harris, Lenny	89F	645	$ .01	$ .15
Harris, Lenny	90F	397	$ .01	$ .10
Harris, Lenny	91F	204	$ .01	$ .04
Harris, Lenny	91FUL	162	$ .01	$ .07
Harris, Lenny	92F	458	$ .01	$ .04
Harris, Lenny	92FUL	211	$ .01	$ .10
Harris, Lenny	93F	61	$ .01	$ .04
Harris, Lenny	93FUL	54	$ .01	$ .10
Hartley, Mike	90F	651	$ .01	$ .10
Hartley, Mike	90FU	22	$ .01	$ .05
Hartley, Mike	91F	205	$ .01	$ .04
Hartley, Mike	93F	102	$ .01	$ .04
Harvey, Bryan	88FU	14	$ .10	$ .75
Harvey, Bryan	89F	479	$ .05	$ .25
Harvey, Bryan	90F	134	$ .01	$ .04
Harvey, Bryan	91F	315	$ .01	$ .04
Harvey, Bryan	91FUL	45	$ .01	$ .07
Harvey, Bryan	92F	61	$ .01	$ .04
Harvey, Bryan	92FLL	696	$ .01	$ .04
Harvey, Bryan	92FUL	27	$ .01	$ .10
Harvey, Bryan	93F	193	$ .01	$ .04
Haselman, Bill	91F	287	$ .01	$ .15
Hassey, Ron	81F	405	$ .01	$ .06
Hassey, Ron	82F	370	$ .01	$ .06
Hassey, Ron	83F	411	$ .01	$ .06
Hassey, Ron	83F	642	$ .01	$ .06
Hassey, Ron	84F	545	$ .01	$ .08
Hassey, Ron	84FU	49	$ .10	$ .50
Hassey, Ron	85FU	50	$ .01	$ .10
Hassey, Ron	86F	107	$ .01	$ .06
Hassey, Ron	87F	499	$ .01	$ .06
Hassey, Ron	88F	399	$ .01	$ .05
Hassey, Ron	89F	9	$ .01	$ .04
Hassey, Ron	90F	8	$ .01	$ .04
Hassey, Ron	91F	8	$ .01	$ .04
Hassey, Ron	91FU	98	$ .01	$ .05
Hassler, Andy	81F	290	$ .01	$ .06
Hassler, Andy	82F	464	$ .01	$ .06
Hassler, Andy	83F	92	$ .01	$ .06
Hassler, Andy	84F	519	$ .01	$ .08
Hatcher, Billy "Bill"	85F	649	$ .15	$1.50
Hatcher, Billy	86F	371	$ .05	$ .20
Hatcher, Billy	86FU	49	$ .01	$ .08
Hatcher, Billy	87F	59	$ .01	$ .06
Hatcher, Billy	88F	449	$ .01	$ .05
Hatcher, Billy	89F	359	$ .01	$ .04
Hatcher, Billy	90F	467	$ .01	$ .04
Hatcher, Billy	90FU	13	$ .01	$ .05
Hatcher, Billy	91F	66	$ .01	$ .04
Hatcher, Billy	91FUL	95	$ .01	$ .07
Hatcher, Billy	92F	409	$ .01	$ .04
Hatcher, Billy	92FUL	190	$ .01	$ .10
Hatcher, Billy	93F	561	$ .01	$ .04
Hatcher, Mickey	81F	135	$ .01	$ .06
Hatcher, Mickey	83F	614	$ .01	$ .06
Hatcher, Mickey	84F	566	$ .01	$ .08
Hatcher, Mickey	85F	279	$ .01	$ .06
Hatcher, Mickey	86F	396	$ .01	$ .06
Hatcher, Mickey	87F	542	$ .01	$ .06
Hatcher, Mickey	87FU	41	$ .01	$ .06
Hatcher, Mickey	88F	516	$ .01	$ .05

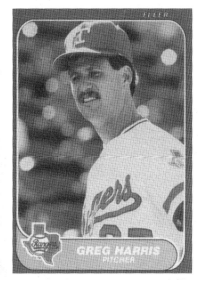

Harris, Greg A.	86F	561	$ .01	$ .06
Harris, Greg A.	87F	126	$ .01	$ .06
Harris, Greg A.	88F	468	$ .01	$ .05
Harris, Greg A.	89F	570	$ .01	$ .04

FLEER

Player	Year	No.	VG	EX/MT
Hatcher, Mickey	90F	398	$ .01	$ .04
Hatcher, Mickey	91F	206	$ .01	$ .04
Hausman, Tom	81F	333	$ .01	$ .06
Hausman, Tom	82F	526	$ .01	$ .06
Havens, Brad	83F	615	$ .01	$ .06
Havens, Brad	87F	472	$ .01	$ .06
Havens, Brad	88F	517	$ .01	$ .05
Havens, Brad	89F	408	$ .01	$ .04
Hawkins, Andy	84F	302	$ .05	$ .35
Hawkins, Andy	85F	36	$ .01	$ .10
Hawkins, Andy	86F	324	$ .01	$ .06
Hawkins, Andy	87F	417	$ .01	$ .06
Hawkins, Andy	88F	586	$ .01	$ .05
Hawkins, Andy	89F	307	$ .01	$ .04
Hawkins, Andy	89FU	50	$ .01	$ .05
Hawkins, Andy	90F	445	$ .01	$ .04
Hawkins, Andy	91F	666	$ .01	$ .04
Hawkins, Andy	91FUL	234	$ .01	$ .07
Hayes, Ben	83F	591	$ .01	$ .06
Hayes, Ben	84F	470	$ .01	$ .08
Hayes, Charlie	89F	330	$ .05	$ .25
Hayes, Charlie	89FU	106	$ .05	$ .25
Hayes, Charlie	90F	558	$ .01	$ .10
Hayes, Charlie	91F	397	$ .01	$ .04
Hayes, Charlie	91FUL	263	$ .01	$ .07
Hayes, Charlie	92F	533	$ .01	$ .04
Hayes, Charlie	92FU	42	$ .05	$ .25
Hayes, Charlie	92FUL	243	$ .01	$ .10
Hayes, Charlie	92FUL	407	$ .01	$ .10
Hayes, Charlie	93F	279	$ .01	$ .04
Hayes, Von	82F	371	$ .10	$ .40
Hayes, Von	83F	412	$ .05	$ .20
Hayes, Von	84F	33	$ .05	$ .20
Hayes, Von	85F	253	$ .05	$ .20
Hayes, Von	86F	443	$ .01	$ .10
Hayes, Von	87F	175	$ .01	$ .10
Hayes, Von	88F	304	$ .01	$ .10
Hayes, Von	89F	571	$ .01	$ .04
Hayes, Von	90F	559	$ .01	$ .04
Hayes, Von	91F	398	$ .01	$ .04
Hayes, Von	91FUL	264	$ .01	$ .07
Hayes, Von	92F	534	$ .01	$ .04
Hayes, Von	92FUL	326	$ .01	$ .10
Hayward, Ray	88FU	63	$ .01	$ .06
Hayward, Ray	89F	521	$ .01	$ .04
Hearn, Ed	87F	10	$ .01	$ .10
Heath, Mike	81F	583	$ .01	$ .06
Heath, Mike	82F	91	$ .01	$ .06
Heath, Mike	83F	518	$ .01	$ .06
Heath, Mike	84F	446	$ .01	$ .08
Heath, Mike	85F	424	$ .01	$ .06
Heath, Mike	86F	418	$ .01	$ .06
Heath, Mike	86FU	50	$ .01	$ .08
Heath, Mike	87FU	42	$ .01	$ .06
Heath, Mike	88F	56	$ .01	$ .05
Heath, Mike	89F	130	$ .01	$ .10
Heath, Mike	90F	603	$ .01	$ .04
Heath, Mike	91F	339	$ .01	$ .04
Heathcock, Jeff	86F	302	$ .01	$ .06
Heathcock, Jeff	88F	450	$ .01	$ .05
Heaton, Neal	84F	546	$ .05	$ .25
Heaton, Neal	85F	451	$ .01	$ .06
Heaton, Neal	86F	589	$ .01	$ .06
Heaton, Neal	87F	543	$ .01	$ .06
Heaton, Neal	87FU	43	$ .01	$ .06
Heaton, Neal	88F	185	$ .01	$ .05
Heaton, Neal	89F	377	$ .01	$ .04
Heaton, Neal	89FU	113	$ .01	$ .05
Heaton, Neal	90F	468	$ .01	$ .04
Heaton, Neal	91F	38	$ .01	$ .04
Heaton, Neal	91FUL	279	$ .01	$ .07
Heaton, Neal	92F	554	$ .01	$ .04
Heaverlo, Dave	81F	594	$ .01	$ .06
Hebner, Richie	81F	474	$ .01	$ .06
Hebner, Richie	82F	268	$ .01	$ .06
Hebner, Richie	83F	307	$ .01	$ .06
Hebner, Richie	84F	251	$ .01	$ .08
Hebner, Richie	84FU	50	$ .10	$ .50
Hebner, Richie	85F	59	$ .01	$ .06
Heep, Danny	81F	72	$ .05	$ .20
Heep, Danny	82F	217	$ .01	$ .06
Heep, Danny	83F	449	$ .01	$ .06
Heep, Danny	84F	586	$ .01	$ .08
Heep, Danny	85F	84	$ .01	$ .06
Heep, Danny	86F	83	$ .01	$ .06
Heep, Danny	87F	11	$ .01	$ .06
Heep, Danny	89F	61	$ .01	$ .04
Heep, Danny	90F	278	$ .01	$ .04
Heinkel, Don	88FU	27	$ .01	$ .10
Heinkel, Don	89F	133	$ .01	$ .15
Hemond, Scott	90F	646	$ .01	$ .15
Hemond, Scott	92FUL	422	$ .01	$ .10
Henderson, Dave	83F	481	$ .10	$ .50

Player	Year	No.	VG	EX/MT
Henderson, Dave	84F	611	$ .05	$ .35
Henderson, Dave	85F	489	$ .05	$ .20
Henderson, Dave	86F	465	$ .05	$ .25
Henderson, Dave	87F	36	$ .01	$ .10
Henderson, Dave	88F	84	$ .01	$ .15
Henderson, Dave	88FU	53	$ .01	$ .10
Henderson, Dave	89F	10	$ .01	$ .10
Henderson, Dave	90F	9	$ .01	$ .10
Henderson, Dave	91F	9	$ .01	$ .04
Henderson, Dave	91FUL	247	$ .01	$ .07
Henderson, Dave	92F	257	$ .01	$ .04
Henderson, Dave	92FUL	113	$ .01	$ .10
Henderson, Dave	93F	664	$ .01	$ .04
Henderson, Rickey	81F	351	$1.75	$7.00
Henderson, Rickey	81F	574	$2.50	$10.00
Henderson, Rickey	82F	92	$1.00	$4.00
Henderson, Rickey	82F	643	$ .20	$2.00
Henderson, Rickey	83F	519	$ .75	$3.00
Henderson, Rickey	83F	639	$ .20	$2.00
Henderson, Rickey	83F	646	$ .15	$1.50
Henderson, Rickey	84F	447	$1.75	$7.00
Henderson, Rickey	85F	425	$1.00	$4.00
Henderson, Rickey	85F	629	$ .15	$1.50
Henderson, Rickey	85FU	51	$1.25	$5.00

FLEER

Player	Year	No.	VG	EX/MT	Player	Year	No.	VG	EX/MT
Henderson, Rickey	86F	108	$ .20	$2.00	Hernandez, Keith	82F	114	$ .05	$ .30
Henderson, Rickey	87F	101	$ .15	$1.50	Hernandez, Keith	83F	8	$ .05	$ .25
Henderson, Rickey	88F	209	$ .10	$ .50	Hernandez, Keith	84F	587	$ .05	$ .30
Henderson, Rickey	89F	254	$ .05	$ .35	Hernandez, Keith	85F	85	$ .05	$ .30
Henderson, Rickey	89FU	54	$ .05	$ .25	Hernandez, Keith	86F	84	$ .05	$ .20
Henderson, Rickey	90F	10	$ .05	$ .20	Hernandez, Keith	87F	12	$ .01	$ .15
Henderson, Rickey	91F	10	$ .01	$ .10	Hernandez, Keith	87F	629	$ .10	$ .50
Henderson, Rickey	91FUL	248	$ .05	$ .25	Hernandez, Keith	87F	637	$ .05	$ .25
Henderson, Rickey	91FUL	393	$ .05	$ .25	Hernandez, Keith	88F	136	$ .05	$ .20
Henderson, Rickey	92F	258	$ .01	$ .10	Hernandez, Keith	88F	639	$ .01	$ .15
Henderson, Rickey	92FRS	681	$ .01	$ .10	Hernandez, Keith	89F	37	$ .01	$ .15
Henderson, Rickey	92FUL	114	$ .10	$ .50	Hernandez, Keith	90F	205	$ .01	$ .10
Henderson, Rickey	93F	294	$ .01	$ .10	Hernandez, Keith	91F	368	$ .01	$ .04
Henderson, Rickey	93FUL	258	$ .05	$ .35	Hernandez, Roberto	92F	677	$ .01	$ .10
Henderson, Steve	81F	321	$ .01	$ .06	Hernandez, Roberto	92FU	13	$ .10	$ .50
Henderson, Steve	82F	597	$ .01	$ .06	Hernandez, Roberto	92FUL	336	$ .05	$ .25
Henderson, Steve	83F	496	$ .01	$ .06	Hernandez, Roberto	93F	583	$ .01	$ .04
Henderson, Steve	84F	612	$ .01	$ .08	Hernandez, Willie	81F	310	$ .05	$ .20
Henderson, Steve	85F	490	$ .01	$ .15	Hernandez, Willie	83F	497	$ .01	$ .10
Henderson, Steve	85FU	52	$ .01	$ .10	Hernandez, Willie	84F	34	$ .01	$ .10
Henderson, Steve	86F	419	$ .01	$ .06	Hernandez, Willie	84FU	51	$ .10	$ .50
Hendrick, George	81F	542	$ .01	$ .06	Hernandez, Willie	85F	10	$ .01	$ .10
Hendrick, George	82F	113	$ .01	$ .06	Hernandez, Willie	86F	228	$ .01	$ .10
Hendrick, George	83F	7	$ .01	$ .06	Hernandez, Willie	87F	153	$ .01	$ .06
Hendrick, George	84F	324	$ .01	$ .08	Hernandez, Willie	88F	58	$ .01	$ .05
Hendrick, George	85F	225	$ .01	$ .06	Hernandez, Xavier	91F	509	$ .01	$ .04
Hendrick, George	85FU	53	$ .01	$ .10	Hernandez, Xavier	92F	437	$ .01	$ .04
Hendrick, George	86F	158	$ .01	$ .06	Hernandez, Xavier	92FUL	205	$ .01	$ .10
Hendrick, George	87F	82	$ .01	$ .06	Hernandez, Xavier	93F	53	$ .01	$ .04
Hengel, Dave	88F	375	$ .01	$ .10	Hernandez, Xavier	93FUL	43	$ .01	$ .10
Henke, Tom	86F	60	$ .10	$ .40	Herndon, Larry	81F	451	$ .01	$ .06
Henke, Tom	87F	228	$ .01	$ .06	Herndon, Larry	82F	390	$ .01	$ .06
Henke, Tom	88F	112	$ .01	$ .05	Herndon, Larry	83F	330	$ .01	$ .06
Henke, Tom	89F	235	$ .01	$ .04	Herndon, Larry	84F	82	$ .01	$ .08
Henke, Tom	90F	84	$ .01	$ .04	Herndon, Larry	85F	11	$ .01	$ .06
Henke, Tom	91F	176	$ .01	$ .04	Herndon, Larry	86F	229	$ .01	$ .06
Henke, Tom	91FUL	362	$ .01	$ .07	Herndon, Larry	87F	154	$ .01	$ .06
Henke, Tom	92F	331	$ .01	$ .04	Herndon, Larry	88F	59	$ .01	$ .05
Henke, Tom	92FUL	450	$ .01	$ .10	Herr, Tom	81F	550	$ .01	$ .10
Henke, Tom	93F	335	$ .01	$ .04	Herr, Tom	82F	115	$ .01	$ .06
Henneman, Mike	87FU	44	$ .05	$ .25	Herr, Tom	83F	9	$ .01	$ .06
Henneman, Mike	88F	57	$ .05	$ .35	Herr, Tom	84F	325	$ .01	$ .08
Henneman, Mike	89F	134	$ .01	$ .04	Herr, Tom	85F	226	$ .01	$ .06
Henneman, Mike	90F	604	$ .01	$ .04	Herr, Tom	86F	37	$ .01	$ .06
Henneman, Mike	91F	340	$ .01	$ .04	Herr, Tom	87F	296	$ .01	$ .06
Henneman, Mike	91FUL	123	$ .01	$ .07	Herr, Tom	88F	35	$ .01	$ .05
Henneman, Mike	92F	138	$ .01	$ .04	Herr, Tom	88FU	43	$ .01	$ .06
Henneman, Mike	92FUL	364	$ .01	$ .10	Herr, Tom	89F	115	$ .01	$ .04
Henneman, Mike	93F	229	$ .01	$ .04	Herr, Tommy	89FU	107	$ .01	$ .05
Henneman, Mike	93FUL	199	$ .01	$ .10	Herr, Tom	90F	560	$ .01	$ .04
Henry, Butch	92FU	86	$ .05	$ .25	Herr, Tom	91F	149	$ .01	$ .04
Henry, Butch	93F	411	$ .01	$ .04	Herr, Tom	91FUL	219	$ .01	$ .07
Henry, Doug	92FUL	384	$ .05	$ .35	Hershiser, Orel	85F	371	$ .75	$3.00
Henry, Doug	93F	251	$ .01	$ .04	Hershiser, Orel	86F	131	$ .10	$ .50
Henry, Doug	93FUL	220	$ .01	$ .10	Hershiser, Orel	87F	441	$ .05	$ .25
Henry, Dwayne	86F	562	$ .01	$ .10	Hershiser, Orel	88F	518	$ .01	$ .10
Henry, Dwayne	91F	692	$ .01	$ .04	Hershiser, Orel	90F	602	$ .01	$ .10
Henry, Dwayne	92F	436	$ .01	$ .04	Hershiser, Orel	89F	62	$ .01	$ .15
Henry, Dwayne	92FUL	483	$ .01	$ .10	Hershiser, Orel	90F	399	$ .01	$ .10
Henry, Dwayne	93F	391	$ .01	$ .04	Hershiser, Orel	91F	208	$ .01	$ .04
Hentgen, Pat	92F	64	$ .10	$1.00	Hershiser, Orel	91FULU	88	$ .01	$ .10
Hentgen, Pat	93F	694	$ .01	$ .04	Hershiser, Orel	92F	459	$ .01	$ .04
Heredia, Gil	92F	665	$ .01	$ .10	Hershiser, Orel	92FUL	507	$ .01	$ .10
Hernandez, Carlos	91F	207	$ .01	$ .10	Hershiser, Orel	93F	63	$ .01	$ .04
Hernandez, Carlos	92FU	91	$ .05	$ .25	Hershiser, Orel	93FUL	55	$ .01	$ .10
Hernandez, Carlos	92FUL	506	$ .01	$ .10	Hesketh, Joe	85F	652	$ .75	$3.00
Hernandez, Carlos	93F	62	$ .01	$ .04	Hesketh, Joe	86F	250	$ .01	$ .06
Hernandez, Cesar	93F	392	$ .01	$ .04	Hesketh, Joe	87F	320	$ .01	$ .06
Hernandez, Guillermo	89F	135	$ .01	$ .04	Hesketh, Joe	89F	378	$ .01	$ .04
Hernandez, Guillermo	90F	605	$ .01	$ .04	Hesketh, Joe	90F	349	$ .01	$ .04
Hernandez, Jeremy	92FU	122	$ .05	$ .25	Hesketh, Joe	92F	40	$ .01	$ .04
Hernandez, Jeremy	92FUL	576	$ .05	$ .25	Hesketh, Joe	92FUL	17	$ .01	$ .10
Hernandez, Jeremy	93F	140	$ .01	$ .04	Hesketh, Joe	93F	562	$ .01	$ .04
Hernandez, Jose	92F	307	$ .01	$ .10	Hetzel, Eric	90F	279	$ .01	$ .10
Hernandez, Keith	81F	545	$ .05	$ .30	Hibbard, Greg	90F	534	$ .01	$ .10

197

FLEER

Player	Year	No.	VG	EX/MT
Hibbard, Greg	91F	122	$ .01	$ .10
Hibbard, Greg	91FUL	75	$ .01	$ .07
Hibbard, Greg	92F	83	$ .01	$ .04
Hibbard, Greg	92FUL	36	$ .01	$ .10
Hibbard, Greg	93F	379	$ .01	$ .04
Hickerson, Bryan	92F	638	$ .01	$ .10
Hickerson, Bryan	92FUL	589	$ .01	$ .10
Hickerson, Bryan	93F	530	$ .01	$ .04
Hickey, Kevin	82F	344	$ .01	$ .06
Hickey, Kevin	83F	237	$ .01	$ .06

Player	Year	No.	VG	EX/MT
Hickey, Kevin	**84F**	**61**	**$ .01**	**$ .08**
Hickey, Kevin	89FU	4	$ .01	$ .05
Hickey, Kevin	90F	178	$ .01	$ .04
Hickey, Kevin	91F	475	$ .01	$ .04
Higuera, Ted "Teddy"	85FU	54	$ .05	$ .35
Higuera, Ted	86F	490	$ .05	$ .25
Higuera, Ted	87F	346	$ .01	$ .10
Higuera, Ted	88F	166	$ .01	$ .10
Higuera, Ted	89F	188	$ .01	$ .04
Higuera, Ted	90F	326	$ .01	$ .04
Higuera, Ted	91F	586	$ .01	$ .04
Higuera, Ted	91FUL	175	$ .01	$ .07
Higuera, Ted	92F	178	$ .01	$ .04
Higuera, Ted	92FUL	80	$ .01	$ .10
Hill, Don "Donnie"	84F	448	$ .01	$ .08
Hill, Donnie	85F	426	$ .01	$ .06
Hill, Donnie	86F	420	$ .01	$ .06
Hill, Donnie	87F	394	$ .01	$ .06
Hill, Donnie	88F	400	$ .01	$ .05
Hill, Donnie	91F	316	$ .01	$ .04
Hill, Donnie	91FUL	46	$ .01	$ .07
Hill, Donnie	92F	60	$ .01	$ .04
Hill, Glenallen	90FU	127	$ .01	$ .10
Hill, Glenallen	91F	177	$ .01	$ .04
Hill, Glenallen	91FUL	17	$ .01	$ .05
Hill, Glenallen	91FUL	363	$ .01	$ .07
Hill, Glenallen	91FULU	19	$ .01	$ .10
Hill, Glenallen	92F	110	$ .01	$ .04
Hill, Glenallen	92FUL	347	$ .01	$ .10
Hill, Glenallen	93F	592	$ .01	$ .04
Hill, Ken	89F	652	$ .10	$ .40
Hill, Ken	89FU	119	$ .05	$ .25

Player	Year	No.	VG	EX/MT
Hill, Ken	90F	251	$ .01	$ .10
Hill, Ken	91F	635	$ .01	$ .04
Hill, Ken	91FULU	106	$ .05	$ .25
Hill, Ken	92F	580	$ .01	$ .04
Hill, Ken	92FU	98	$ .05	$ .25
Hill, Ken	92FUL	520	$ .01	$ .10
Hill, Ken	93F	76	$ .01	$ .04
Hill, Ken	93FUL	68	$ .01	$ .10
Hill, Marc	84F	62	$ .01	$ .08
Hill, Marc	85F	516	$ .01	$ .06
Hill, Milt	93F	36	$ .01	$ .04
Hillegas, Shawn	88F	519	$ .01	$ .15
Hillegas, Shawn	89F	498	$ .01	$ .04
Hillegas, Shawn	90F	535	$ .01	$ .04
Hillegas, Shawn	91FU	18	$ .01	$ .05
Hillegas, Shawn	92F	111	$ .01	$ .04
Hillman, Eric	92FU	102	$ .05	$ .35
Hillman, Eric	93F	87	$ .01	$ .10
Hinzo, Tommy	88F	611	$ .01	$ .10
Hisle, Larry	81F	509	$ .01	$ .06
Hisle, Larry	82F	144	$ .01	$ .06
Hobson, Butch	81F	227	$ .01	$ .06
Hobson, Butch	82F	465	$ .01	$ .06
Hodge, Ed	84FU	52	$ .10	$ .50
Hodge, Ed	85F	280	$ .01	$ .06
Hodges, Ron	82F	527	$ .01	$ .06
Hodges, Ron	83F	545	$ .01	$ .06
Hodges, Ron	84F	588	$ .01	$ .08
Hoffman, Glenn	81F	237	$ .01	$ .06
Hoffman, Glenn	82F	296	$ .01	$ .06
Hoffman, Glenn	83F	185	$ .01	$ .06
Hoffman, Glenn	84F	399	$ .01	$ .08
Hoffman, Glenn	86F	351	$ .01	$ .06
Hoffman, Guy	86FU	51	$ .01	$ .08
Hoffman, Guy	87F	566	$ .01	$ .06
Hoffman, Guy	87FU	45	$ .01	$ .06
Hoffman, Guy	88F	235	$ .01	$ .05
Hoiles, Chris	90FU	65	$ .05	$ .35
Hoiles, Chris	91F	476	$ .01	$ .10
Hoiles, Chris	91FUL	17	$ .05	$ .20
Hoiles, Chris	92F	9	$ .01	$ .04
Hoiles, Chris	92FUL	5	$ .05	$ .20
Hoiles, Chris	93F	168	$ .01	$ .04
Holland, Al	81F	445	$ .01	$ .10
Holland, Al	82F	391	$ .01	$ .06
Holland, Al	83F	262	$ .01	$ .06
Holland, Al	84F	35	$ .01	$ .08
Holland, Al	85F	254	$ .01	$ .06
Holland, Al	85F	637	$ .01	$ .06
Holland, Al	85FU	55	$ .01	$ .10
Holland, Al	86F	159	$ .01	$ .06
Hollins, Dave	90FU	43	$ .10	$ .75
Hollins, David	91F	399	$ .01	$ .10
Hollins, Dave	92F	535	$ .01	$ .04
Hollins, Dave	92FUL	244	$ .10	$ .40
Hollins, Dave	93F	353	$ .01	$ .20
Hollins, Dave	93F	491	$ .05	$ .20
Hollins, Dave	93FUL	88	$ .05	$ .25
Holman, Brian	88FU	100	$ .01	$ .15
Holman, Brian	89F	379	$ .01	$ .15
Holman, Brian	90F	516	$ .01	$ .10
Holman, Brian	91F	453	$ .01	$ .04
Holman, Brian	91FUL	338	$ .01	$ .07
Holman, Brian	92F	281	$ .01	$ .04
Holman, Scott	84F	589	$ .01	$ .08
Holman, Shawn	90F	606	$ .01	$ .10
Holmes, Darren	92F	179	$ .01	$ .04
Holmes, Darren	93F	412	$ .01	$ .04
Holton, Brian	89F	63	$ .01	$ .04
Holton, Brian	89FU	5	$ .01	$ .05
Holton, Brian	90F	179	$ .01	$ .04
Honeycutt, Rick	82F	318	$ .01	$ .06
Honeycutt, Rick	83F	568	$ .01	$ .06
Honeycutt, Rick	84F	101	$ .01	$ .08
Honeycutt, Rick	85F	372	$ .01	$ .06

FLEER

Player	Year	No.	VG	EX/MT
Honeycutt, Rick	86F	132	$.01	$.06
Honeycutt, Rick	87F	442	$.01	$.06
Honeycutt, Rick	88F	281	$.01	$.05
Honeycutt, Rick	89F	11	$.01	$.04
Honeycutt, Rick	90F	11	$.01	$.04
Honeycutt, Rick	91F	11	$.01	$.04
Honeycutt, Rick	91FUL	249	$.01	$.07
Honeycutt, Rick	92F	259	$.01	$.04
Honeycutt, Rick	93F	665	$.01	$.04
Hood, Don	81F	547	$.01	$.06
Hood, Don	83F	115	$.01	$.06
Hood, Don	84F	348	$.01	$.08
Hooton, Burt	81F	113	$.01	$.06
Hooton, Burt	82F	8	$.01	$.06
Hooton, Burt	83F	208	$.01	$.06
Hooton, Burt	84F	102	$.01	$.08
Hooton, Burt	85F	373	$.01	$.06
Hooton, Burt	85FU	56	$.01	$.10
Hooton, Burt	86F	563	$.01	$.06
Horn, Sam	88F	355	$.01	$.15
Horn, Sam	91F	477	$.01	$.04
Horn, Sam	92F	10	$.01	$.04
Horn, Sam	92FUL	6	$.01	$.10
Horn, Sam	93F	542	$.01	$.04
Horner, Bob	81F	244	$.05	$.30
Horner, Bob	82F	436	$.05	$.30
Horner, Bob	83F	138	$.05	$.30
Horner, Bob	84F	181	$.05	$.30
Horner, Bob	85F	328	$.05	$.30
Horner, Bob	86F	517	$.05	$.20
Horner, Bob	86F	635	$.05	$.30
Horner, Bob	87F	518	$.01	$.10
Horner, Bob	87F	632	$.01	$.06
Horner, Bob	88FU	120	$.01	$.10
Horner, Bob	89F	452	$.01	$.04
Horsman, Vince	92FU	49	$.05	$.25
Horsman, Vince	93F	295	$.01	$.10
Horsman, Vince	93FUL	259	$.01	$.10
Horton, Ricky	84FU	53	$.10	$.60
Horton, Ricky	85F	227	$.05	$.30
Horton, Ricky	86F	38	$.01	$.06
Horton, Ricky	87F	297	$.01	$.06
Horton, Ricky	88F	36	$.01	$.05
Horton, Ricky	88FU	17	$.01	$.06
Hosey, Steve	92FU	127	$.10	$1.00
Hosey, Steve	93FUL	132	$.10	$.50
Hostetler, Dave	83F	569	$.01	$.06
Hostetler, Dave	84F	418	$.01	$.08
Hough, Charlie	82F	319	$.01	$.06
Hough, Charlie	83F	570	$.01	$.06
Hough, Charlie	84F	419	$.01	$.08
Hough, Charlie	85F	558	$.01	$.06
Hough, Charlie	86F	564	$.01	$.06
Hough, Charlie	87F	127	$.01	$.06
Hough, Charlie	87F	641	$.01	$.06
Hough, Charlie	88F	469	$.01	$.05
Hough, Charlie	89F	522	$.01	$.04
Hough, Charlie	90F	300	$.01	$.04
Hough, Charlie	91F	288	$.01	$.04
Hough, Charlie	91FU	12	$.01	$.05
Hough, Charlie	92F	84	$.01	$.04
Hough, Charlie	92FUL	37	$.01	$.10
Hough, Charlie	93F	584	$.01	$.04
Householder, Paul	81F	217	$.01	$.06
Householder, Paul	82F	68	$.01	$.06
Householder, Paul	83F	592	$.01	$.06
Householder, Paul	84F	471	$.01	$.08
Householder, Paul	86F	491	$.01	$.06
Housie, Wayne	92FUL	314	$.05	$.20
Howard, David	91FU	27	$.01	$.15
Howard, David	92F	160	$.01	$.10
Howard, David	92FUL	71	$.01	$.10
Howard, David	93F	619	$.01	$.04
Howard, Tom	90FU	56	$.01	$.15
Howard, Thomas	91F	532	$.01	$.10
Howard, Thomas	91FUL	305	$.01	$.07
Howard, Thomas	92F	607	$.01	$.04
Howard, Thomas	92FU	15	$.05	$.25
Howard, Thomas	92FUL	279	$.01	$.10
Howard, Thomas	92FUL	348	$.01	$.10
Howard, Thomas	93F	215	$.01	$.04
Howard, Thomas	93FUL	185	$.01	$.10
Howe, Art	81F	51	$.01	$.06
Howe, Art	82F	218	$.01	$.06
Howe, Art	83F	450	$.01	$.06
Howe, Art	84F	227	$.01	$.08
Howe, Art	84FU	54	$.10	$.50
Howe, Art	85F	228	$.01	$.06
Howe, Steve	81F	136	$.01	$.10
Howe, Steve	82F	9	$.01	$.06
Howe, Steve	83F	209	$.01	$.06
Howe, Steve	84F	103	$.01	$.08
Howe, Steve	91FU	43	$.01	$.05
Howe, Steve	92F	230	$.01	$.04
Howe, Steve	92FUL	408	$.01	$.10
Howell, Jack	87F	83	$.01	$.06
Howell, Jack	88F	491	$.01	$.05
Howell, Jack	89F	480	$.01	$.04
Howell, Jack	90F	135	$.01	$.04
Howell, Jack	91FUL	47	$.01	$.07
Howell, Jay	84F	128	$.01	$.08
Howell, Jay	85F	131	$.01	$.06
Howell, Jay	85FU	57	$.01	$.10
Howell, Jay	86F	421	$.01	$.06
Howell, Jay	87F	395	$.01	$.06
Howell, Jay	88F	282	$.01	$.05
Howell, Jay	88FU	95	$.01	$.06
Howell, Jay	89F	64	$.01	$.04
Howell, Jay	90F	400	$.01	$.04
Howell, Jay	91F	209	$.01	$.04
Howell, Jay	91FUL	163	$.01	$.07
Howell, Jay	92F	460	$.01	$.04
Howell, Jay	93F	450	$.01	$.04
Howell, Ken	85F	374	$.05	$.20
Howell, Ken	86F	133	$.01	$.06
Howell, Ken	87F	443	$.01	$.06
Howell, Ken	88F	520	$.01	$.05
Howell, Ken	89FU	108	$.01	$.05
Howell, Ken	90F	561	$.01	$.04
Howell, Ken	91F	400	$.01	$.04
Howell, Ken	91FUL	265	$.01	$.07
Howell, Pat	92FU	103	$.05	$.35
Howell, Roy	81F	417	$.01	$.06
Howell, Roy	82F	145	$.01	$.06
Howell, Roy	83F	36	$.01	$.06
Howell, Roy	84F	203	$.01	$.08
Howitt, Dann	90F	644	$.01	$.10
Howser, Dick	81F	84	$.05	$.20
Hoy, Peter	92FUL	315	$.05	$.20
Hoyt, LaMarr	82F	345	$.01	$.06
Hoyt, LaMarr	83F	238	$.01	$.06
Hoyt, LaMarr	84F	60	$.01	$.10
Hoyt, LaMarr	85F	517	$.01	$.06
Hoyt, LaMarr	85FU	58	$.01	$.10
Hoyt, LaMarr	86F	325	$.01	$.06
Hoyt, LaMarr	87F	418	$.01	$.06
Hrabosky, Al	81F	262	$.01	$.06
Hrabosky, Al	82F	438	$.01	$.10
Hrbek, Kent	83F	616	$.10	$.75
Hrbek, Kent	83F	633	$.10	$.75
Hrbek, Kent	84F	567	$.10	$.50
Hrbek, Kent	85F	281	$.05	$.30
Hrbek, Kent	86F	397	$.05	$.20
Hrbek, Kent	87F	544	$.05	$.20
Hrbek, Kent	88F	13	$.01	$.10
Hrbek, Kent	89F	116	$.01	$.10
Hrbek, Kent	90F	378	$.01	$.04
Hrbek, Kent	91F	614	$.01	$.04
Hrbek, Kent	91FUL	189	$.01	$.07
Hrbek, Kent	92F	205	$.01	$.04

FLEER

Player	Year	No.	VG	EX/MT	Player	Year	No.	VG	EX/MT
Hrbek, Kent	92FUL	92	$ .01	$ .10	Hurst, Bruce	92F	608	$ .01	$ .04
Hrbek, Kent	93F	267	$ .01	$ .04	Hurst, Bruce	92FUL	280	$ .01	$ .10
Hrbek, Kent	93FUL	231	$ .01	$ .10	Hurst, Bruce	93F	521	$ .01	$ .04
Hubbard, Glenn	81F	260	$ .01	$ .06	Huson, Jeff	90F	350	$ .01	$ .10
Hubbard, Glenn	82F	437	$ .01	$ .06	Huson, Jeff	90FU	123	$ .01	$ .05
Hubbard, Glenn	83F	139	$ .01	$ .06	Huson, Jeff	91F	289	$ .01	$ .04
Hubbard, Glenn	84F	182	$ .01	$ .08	Huson, Jeff	91FUL	349	$ .01	$ .07
Hubbard, Glenn	85F	329	$ .01	$ .06	Huson, Jeff	92F	308	$ .01	$ .04
Hubbard, Glenn	86F	518	$ .01	$ .06	Huson, Jeff	92FUL	133	$ .01	$ .10
Hubbard, Glenn	87F	519	$ .01	$ .06	Huson, Jeff	93F	324	$ .01	$ .04
Hubbard, Glenn	88F	542	$ .01	$ .05	Huson, Jeff	93FUL	280	$ .01	$ .10
Hubbard, Glenn	89F	12	$ .01	$ .04	Hutton, Tommy	81F	164	$ .01	$ .06
Hudler, Rex	88FU	101	$ .01	$ .06	Incaviglia, Pete	86FU	53	$ .05	$ .35
Hudler, Rex	89F	380	$ .01	$ .04	Incaviglia, Pete	87F	128	$ .10	$ .50
Hudler, Rex	91FU	116	$ .01	$ .05	Incaviglia, Pete	87F	625	$ .10	$ .50
Hudler, Rex	92F	581	$ .01	$ .04	Incaviglia, Pete	88F	470	$ .05	$ .20
Hudler, Rex	92FUL	568	$ .01	$ .10	Incaviglia, Pete	89F	523	$ .01	$ .10
Hudler, Rex	93F	510	$ .01	$ .04	Incaviglia, Pete	90F	301	$ .01	$ .10
Hudson, Charles	84F	36	$ .05	$ .25	Incaviglia, Pete	91F	290	$ .01	$ .10
Hudson, Charles	85F	255	$ .01	$ .06	Incaviglia, Pete	92F	139	$ .01	$ .04
Hudson, Charles	86F	444	$ .01	$ .06	Incaviglia, Pete	92FUL	491	$ .01	$ .10
Hudson, Charles	87F	176	$ .01	$ .06	Incaviglia, Pete	93F	436	$ .01	$ .04
Hudson, Charles	87FU	46	$ .01	$ .06	Innis, Jeff	88FU	105	$ .01	$ .10
Hudson, Charles	88F	210	$ .01	$ .05	Innis, Jeff	90F	206	$ .01	$ .10
Huff, Mike	90F	649	$ .01	$ .10	Innis, Jeff	91FU	103	$ .01	$ .05
Huff, Mike	91F	210	$ .01	$ .04	Innis, Jeff	91FULU	97	$ .01	$ .10
Huff, Mike	92F	85	$ .01	$ .04	Innis, Jeff	92F	507	$ .01	$ .04
Huff, Mike	92FUL	337	$ .01	$ .10	Innis, Jeff	92FUL	234	$ .01	$ .10
Hughes, Keith	88F	305	$ .01	$ .15	Innis, Jeff	93F	476	$ .01	$ .04
Huismann, Mark	85F	203	$ .01	$ .06	Iorg, Dane	81F	543	$ .01	$ .06
Huismann, Mark	87F	586	$ .01	$ .06	Iorg, Dane	82F	116	$ .01	$ .06
Hulett, Tim	85FU	59	$ .01	$ .10	Iorg, Dane	83F	10	$ .01	$ .06
Hulett, Tim	86F	208	$ .01	$ .06	Iorg, Dane	84F	326	$ .01	$ .08
Hulett, Tim	87F	500	$ .01	$ .06	Iorg, Dane	84FU	55	$ .10	$ .50
Hulett, Tim	90FU	66	$ .01	$ .05	Iorg, Dane	85F	204	$ .01	$ .06
Hulett, Tim	91F	478	$ .01	$ .04	Iorg, Dane	86F	9	$ .01	$ .06
Hulett, Tim	92F	11	$ .01	$ .04	Iorg, Dane	86FU	54	$ .01	$ .08
Hulett, Tim	93F	543	$ .01	$ .04	Iorg, Garth	81F	423	$ .01	$ .06
Hulse, David	93F	683	$ .01	$ .15	Iorg, Garth	82F	616	$ .01	$ .06
Hume, Tom	81F	211	$ .01	$ .06	Iorg, Garth	83F	430	$ .01	$ .06
Hume, Tom	82F	69	$ .01	$ .06	Iorg, Garth	84F	157	$ .01	$ .08
Hume, Tom	83F	593	$ .01	$ .06	Iorg, Garth	85F	107	$ .01	$ .06
Hume, Tom	84F	472	$ .01	$ .08	Iorg, Garth	86F	61	$ .01	$ .06
Hume, Tom	85F	538	$ .01	$ .06	Iorg, Garth	87F	229	$ .01	$ .06
Hume, Tom	86F	179	$ .01	$ .06	Iorg, Garth	88F	113	$ .01	$ .05
Hume, Tom	86FU	52	$ .01	$ .08	Irvine, Daryl	91F	98	$ .01	$ .10
Hume, Tom	87F	177	$ .01	$ .06	Irvine, Daryl	91FUL	34	$ .01	$ .07
Hume, Tom	88F	236	$ .01	$ .05	Irvine, Daryl	92F	41	$ .01	$ .04
Humphreys, Mike	92F	231	$ .01	$ .10	Ivie, Mike	81F	435	$ .01	$ .06
Hundley, Todd	90FU	36	$ .05	$ .20	Ivie, Mike	83F	331	$ .01	$ .06
Hundley, Todd	91F	150	$ .01	$ .10	Jackson, Bo	87F	369	$1.75	$7.00
Hundley, Todd	91FUL	220	$ .01	$ .07	Jackson, Bo	88F	260	$ .10	$1.00
Hundley, Todd	92F	506	$ .01	$ .10	Jackson, Bo	89F	285	$ .05	$ .25
Hundley, Todd	92FUL	233	$ .01	$ .10	Jackson, Bo	90F	110	$ .05	$ .20
Hundley, Todd	93F	88	$ .01	$ .04	Jackson, Bo	90F	635	$ .01	$ .15
Hundley, Todd	93FUL	75	$ .01	$ .10	Jackson, Bo	91F	561	$ .01	$ .15
Hunter, Brian	91FULU	67	$ .10	$ .50	Jackson, Bo	91FUL	149	$ .05	$ .25
Hunter, Brian	92F	359	$ .01	$ .10	Jackson, Bo	92F	86	$ .05	$ .20
Hunter, Brian	92FUL	163	$ .01	$ .10	Jackson, Bo	92F	701	$ .05	$ .20
Hunter, Brian	93F	5	$ .01	$ .04	Jackson, Chuck	87FU	47	$ .01	$ .10
Hurdle, Clint	81F	45	$ .01	$ .06	Jackson, Danny	85F	205	$ .05	$ .25
Hurdle, Clint	82F	411	$ .01	$ .06	Jackson, Danny	86F	10	$ .05	$ .20
Hurdle, Clint	87F	298	$ .01	$ .06	Jackson, Danny	87F	370	$ .01	$ .10
Hurst, Bruce	82F	297	$ .10	$ .50	Jackson, Danny	88F	261	$ .01	$ .10
Hurst, Bruce	83F	186	$ .01	$ .10	Jackson, Danny	88FU	84	$ .01	$ .10
Hurst, Bruce	84F	400	$ .01	$ .10	Jackson, Danny	89F	163	$ .01	$ .15
Hurst, Bruce	85F	161	$ .01	$ .06	Jackson, Danny	89F	636	$ .01	$ .15
Hurst, Bruce	86F	352	$ .01	$ .10	Jackson, Danny	90F	422	$ .01	$ .10
Hurst, Bruce	87F	37	$ .01	$ .10	Jackson, Danny	91F	67	$ .01	$ .04
Hurst, Bruce	88F	356	$ .01	$ .05	Jackson, Danny	91FU	78	$ .01	$ .05
Hurst, Bruce	89F	91	$ .01	$ .04	Jackson, Danny	91FULU	70	$ .01	$ .10
Hurst, Bruce	89FU	124	$ .01	$ .05	Jackson, Danny	92F	383	$ .01	$ .04
Hurst, Bruce	90F	159	$ .01	$ .04	Jackson, Danny	92FUL	176	$ .05	$ .20
Hurst, Bruce	91F	533	$ .01	$ .04	Jackson, Danny	93F	492	$ .01	$ .04
Hurst, Bruce	91FUL	306	$ .01	$ .07	Jackson, Darrell	81F	567	$ .01	$ .06

FLEER

Player	Year	No.	VG	EX/MT
Jackson, Darrell	82F	555	$ .01	$ .06
Jackson, Darrin	88F	641	$1.00	$4.00
Jackson, Darrin	88FU	78	$ .05	$ .25
Jackson, Darrin	89F	428	$ .01	$ .15
Jackson, Darrin	90F	160	$ .01	$ .04
Jackson, Darrin	91FU	124	$ .01	$ .05
Jackson, Darrin	91FULU	112	$ .01	$ .10
Jackson, Darrin	92F	609	$ .01	$ .04
Jackson, Darrin	93F	141	$ .01	$ .04
Jackson, Darrin	93FUL	118	$ .01	$ .10
Jackson, Grant	81F	378	$ .01	$ .06
Jackson, Grant	82F	191	$ .01	$ .06
Jackson, Mike	87FU	48	$ .05	$ .20
Jackson, Mike	88F	306	$ .01	$ .15
Jackson, Mike	88FU	60	$ .01	$ .06
Jackson, Mike	89F	550	$ .01	$ .04
Jackson, Mike	90F	517	$ .01	$ .04
Jackson, Mike	91F	454	$ .01	$ .04
Jackson, Mike	91FULU	51	$ .01	$ .10
Jackson, Mike	92F	282	$ .01	$ .04
Jackson, Mike	92FU	128	$ .05	$ .25
Jackson, Mike	92FUL	590	$ .01	$ .10
Jackson, Mike	93F	156	$ .01	$ .04
Jackson, Mike	93FUL	133	$ .01	$ .10
Jackson, Reggie	81F	79	$ .25	$2.50
Jackson, Reggie	81F	650	$ .25	$2.50

Player	Year	No.	VG	EX/MT
Jackson, Reggie	**82F**	**39**	**$ .20**	**$2.00**
Jackson, Reggie	82F	646	$ .20	$2.00
Jackson, Reggie	83F	93	$ .15	$1.50
Jackson, Reggie	83F	640	$ .05	$ .35
Jackson, Reggie	83F	645	$ .10	$ .50
Jackson, Reggie	84F	520	$ .75	$3.00
Jackson, Reggie	85F	303	$ .20	$2.00
Jackson, Reggie	85F	639	$ .10	$ .75
Jackson, Reggie	86F	160	$ .10	$1.00
Jackson, Reggie	87F	84	$ .10	$1.00
Jackson, Reggie	87FU	49	$ .10	$ .50
Jackson, Reggie	88F	283	$ .10	$ .50
Jackson, Ron	81F	557	$ .01	$ .06
Jackson, Ron	82F	269	$ .01	$ .06
Jackson, Ron	83F	94	$ .01	$ .06
Jackson, Ron	84F	521	$ .01	$ .08
Jackson, Roy Lee	83F	431	$ .01	$ .06
Jackson, Roy Lee	84F	158	$ .01	$ .08
Jackson, Roy Lee	85F	108	$ .01	$ .06

Player	Year	No.	VG	EX/MT
Jackson, Roy Lee	86F	326	$ .01	$ .06
Jackson, Roy Lee	87F	545	$ .01	$ .06
Jacoby, Brook	84FU	56	$ .20	$2.00
Jacoby, Brook	85F	452	$ .05	$ .30
Jacoby, Brook	86F	590	$ .01	$ .10
Jacoby, Brook	87F	253	$ .01	$ .06
Jacoby, Brook	88F	612	$ .01	$ .05
Jacoby, Brook	89F	407	$ .01	$ .04
Jacoby, Brook	90F	493	$ .01	$ .04
Jacoby, Brook	91F	369	$ .01	$ .04
Jacoby, Brook	91FUL	113	$ .01	$ .07
Jacoby, Brook	91FULU	46	$ .01	$ .10
Jacoby, Brook	92F	260	$ .01	$ .04
Jacoby, Brook	92FUL	349	$ .01	$ .10
Jacoby, Brook	93F	593	$ .01	$ .04
Jaha, John	92FU	35	$ .10	$1.00
Jaha, John	93F	252	$ .01	$ .15
Jaha, John	93FUL	221	$ .05	$ .35
James, Bob	84F	277	$ .05	$ .20
James, Bob	85F	400	$ .01	$ .06
James, Bob	85FU	60	$ .01	$ .10
James, Bob	86F	209	$ .01	$ .06
James, Bob	87F	501	$ .01	$ .06
James, Bob	88F	401	$ .01	$ .05
James, Chris	86FU	55	$ .05	$ .25
James, Chris	87FU	50	$ .01	$ .10
James, Chris	88F	307	$ .01	$ .10
James, Chris	89F	572	$ .01	$ .04
James, Chris	90F	161	$ .01	$ .04
James, Chris	90FU	92	$ .01	$ .05
James, Chris	91F	370	$ .01	$ .04
James, Chris	91FUL111(114)		$ .01	$ .07
James, Chris	92F	112	$ .01	$ .04
James, Chris	93F	531	$ .01	$ .04
James, Dion	84FU	57	$ .10	$ .50
James, Dion	85F	584	$ .05	$ .25
James, Dion	87FU	51	$ .01	$ .06
James, Dion	88F	543	$ .01	$ .05
James, Dion	89F	594	$ .01	$ .04
James, Dion	90F	494	$ .01	$ .04
James, Dion	91F	371	$ .01	$ .04
James, Dion	92FUL	409	$ .01	$ .10
James, Dion	93F	649	$ .01	$ .04
Javier, Stan	86FU	56	$ .01	$ .15
Javier, Stan	87FU	52	$ .01	$ .06
Javier, Stan	89F	13	$ .01	$ .04
Javier, Stan	90F	12	$ .01	$ .04
Javier, Stan	90FU	23	$ .01	$ .05
Javier, Stan	91F	211	$ .01	$ .04
Javier, Stan	92F	461	$ .01	$ .04
Javier, Stan	92FUL	212	$ .01	$ .10
Javier, Stan	93F	493	$ .01	$ .04
Jeffcoat, Mike	84FU	58	$ .10	$ .50
Jeffcoat, Mike	85F	453	$ .01	$ .06
Jeffcoat, Mike	86F	545	$ .01	$ .06
Jeffcoat, Mike	89F	524	$ .01	$ .04
Jeffcoat, Mike	90F	302	$ .01	$ .04
Jeffcoat, Mike	91F	291	$ .01	$ .04
Jeffcoat, Mike	92F	309	$ .01	$ .04
Jeffcoat, Mike	92FUL	134	$ .01	$ .10
Jefferies, Gregg	88F	137	$ .25	$2.50
Jefferies, Gregg	89F	38	$ .05	$ .25
Jefferies, Gregg	90F	207	$ .05	$ .15
Jefferies, Gregg	91F	151	$ .01	$ .10
Jefferies, Gregg	91FUL	221	$ .05	$ .20
Jefferies, Gregg	92F	508	$ .01	$ .10
Jefferies, Gregg	92FU	26	$ .05	$ .25
Jefferies, Gregg	92FUL	372	$ .05	$ .20
Jefferies, Gregg	93F	238	$ .01	$ .10
Jefferies, Gregg	93FUL	209	$ .01	$ .15
Jefferson, Jesse	81F	419	$ .01	$ .06
Jefferson, Jesse	82F	466	$ .01	$ .06
Jefferson, Reggie	91FUL	379	$ .10	$ .50
Jefferson, Reggie	92F	113	$ .01	$ .15
Jefferson, Reggie	92FUL	50	$ .10	$ .40

FLEER

Player	Year	No.	VG	EX/MT	Player	Year	No.	VG	EX/MT
Jefferson, Reggie	93F	594	$ .01	$ .10	Johnson, Lance	92F	87	$ .01	$ .04
Jefferson, Stan	87FU	53	$ .01	$ .10	Johnson, Lance	92FUL	38	$ .01	$ .10
Jefferson, Stan	88F	587	$ .01	$ .05	Johnson, Lance	93F	204	$ .01	$ .04
Jelks, Greg	88F	648	$ .05	$ .30	Johnson, Lance	93FUL	174	$ .01	$ .10
Jeltz, Steve	85F	653	$ .05	$ .20	Johnson, Randy	83F	617	$ .01	$ .06
Jeltz, Steve	87F	178	$ .01	$ .06	Johnson, Randy	84F	183	$ .01	$ .08
Jeltz, Steve	88F	308	$ .01	$ .05	Johnson, Randy	85F	330	$ .01	$ .06
Jeltz, Steve	89F	573	$ .01	$ .04	Johnson, Randy	89F	381	$ .05	$ .35
Jeltz, Steve	90F	562	$ .01	$ .04	Johnson, Randy	89FU	59	$ .01	$ .15
Jenkins, Ferguson "Fergie"	81F	622	$ .10	$ .50	Johnson, Randy	90F	518	$ .01	$ .10
Jenkins, Ferguson	82F	320	$ .05	$ .35	Johnson, Randy	91F	455	$ .01	$ .04
Jenkins, Ferguson	83F	498	$ .10	$ .50	Johnson, Randy	91FUL	339	$ .01	$ .07
Jenkins, Ferguson	84F	494	$ .10	$ .75	Johnson, Randy	92F	283	$ .01	$ .04
Jennings, Doug	88FU	54	$ .05	$ .20	Johnson, Randy	92FUL	125	$ .01	$ .10
Jennings, Doug	89F	14	$ .01	$ .15	Johnson, Randy	93F	676	$ .01	$ .04
Jennings, Doug	91F	12	$ .01	$ .04	Johnson, Randy	93FUL	269	$ .01	$ .10
Jeter, Shawn	92FU	14	$ .05	$ .35	Johnson, Wallace	82F	192	$ .01	$ .06
Jimenez, Cesar	88FU	72	$ .01	$ .06	Johnson, Wallace	83F	285	$ .01	$ .06
Jimenez, Houston	85F	282	$ .01	$ .06	Johnson, Wallace	87F	321	$ .01	$ .06
John, Tommy	81F	81	$ .05	$ .20	Johnson, Wallace	88F	186	$ .01	$ .05
John, Tommy	82F	40	$ .05	$ .20	Johnson, Wallace	89F	382	$ .01	$ .04
John, Tommy	83F	95	$ .05	$ .20	Johnson, Wallace	90F	351	$ .01	$ .04
John, Tommy	84F	522	$ .05	$ .20	Johnston, Joel	92F	673	$ .01	$ .10
John, Tommy	85F	304	$ .05	$ .20	Johnston, Joel	92FUL	72	$ .01	$ .10
John, Tommy	86F	422	$ .05	$ .20	Johnstone, Jay	81F	128	$ .01	$ .06
John, Tommy	86FU	57	$ .05	$ .20	Johnstone, Jay	82F	10	$ .01	$ .06
John, Tommy	87F	102	$ .01	$ .15	Johnstone, Jay	83F	499	$ .01	$ .06
John, Tommy	88F	211	$ .01	$ .10	Johnstone, Jay	84F	495	$ .01	$ .08
John, Tommy	89F	255	$ .01	$ .04	Jones, Barry	87F	611	$ .01	$ .10
Johnson, Bobby	84F	420	$ .01	$ .08	Jones, Barry	88FU	114	$ .01	$ .06
Johnson, Cliff	81F	303	$ .01	$ .06	Jones, Barry	89F	500	$ .01	$ .04
Johnson, Cliff	82F	93	$ .01	$ .06	Jones, Barry	91F	124	$ .01	$ .04
Johnson, Cliff	83F	520	$ .01	$ .06	Jones, Barry	91FULU	91	$ .01	$ .10
Johnson, Cliff	84F	159	$ .01	$ .08	Jones, Barry	92F	484	$ .01	$ .04
Johnson, Cliff	85F	109	$ .01	$ .06	Jones, Barry	92FUL	546	$ .01	$ .10
Johnson, Cliff	85FU	61	$ .01	$ .10	Jones, Bobby	85F	559	$ .01	$ .06
Johnson, Cliff	86F	62	$ .01	$ .06	Jones, Calvin	92FUL	433	$ .01	$ .10
Johnson, Cliff	87F	231	$ .01	$ .06	Jones, Calvin	93F	413	$ .01	$ .04
Johnson, Dave	90FU	67	$ .01	$ .05	Jones, Chris	92F	410	$ .01	$ .10
Johnson, Dave	91F	479	$ .01	$ .04	Jones, Doug	88F	613	$ .10	$ .40
Johnson, Dave	91FUL	18	$ .01	$ .07	Jones, Doug	89F	409	$ .05	$ .35
Johnson, Dave	92F	12	$ .01	$ .04	Jones, Doug	90F	495	$ .01	$ .04
Johnson, Howard	83F	332	$1.25	$5.00	Jones, Doug	91F	372	$ .01	$ .04
Johnson, Howard	85F	12	$ .15	$1.50	Jones, Doug	91FUL	115	$ .01	$ .07
Johnson, Howard	85FU	62	$ .20	$2.00	Jones, Doug	92F	114	$ .01	$ .04
Johnson, Howard	86F	85	$ .10	$ .75	Jones, Doug	92FUL	87	$ .05	$ .25
Johnson, Howard	87F	13	$ .05	$ .35	Jones, Doug	93F	54	$ .01	$ .04
Johnson, Howard	88F	138	$ .01	$ .15	Jones, Doug	93FUL	44	$ .01	$ .10
Johnson, Howard	89F	39	$ .01	$ .15	Jones, Jeff	82F	94	$ .01	$ .06
Johnson, Howard	90F	208	$ .01	$ .10	Jones, Jimmy	87F	650	$ .05	$ .35
Johnson, Howard	90F	639	$ .01	$ .10	Jones, Jimmy	87FU	54	$ .01	$ .06
Johnson, Howard	91F	152	$ .01	$ .04	Jones, Jimmy	88F	588	$ .01	$ .05
Johnson, Howard	91FUL	222	$ .01	$ .15	Jones, Jimmy	89F	308	$ .01	$ .04
Johnson, Howard	92F	509	$ .01	$ .10	Jones, Jimmy	91F	667	$ .01	$ .04
Johnson, Howard	92FLL	689	$ .01	$ .04	Jones, Jimmy	92F	438	$ .01	$ .04
Johnson, Howard	92FUL	235	$ .01	$ .10	Jones, Jimmy	93F	437	$ .01	$ .04
Johnson, Howard	93F	89	$ .01	$ .04	Jones, Lynn	82F	270	$ .01	$ .06
Johnson, Howard	93FUL	76	$ .01	$ .10	Jones, Lynn	83F	333	$ .01	$ .06
Johnson, Jeff	91FU	44	$ .01	$ .15	Jones, Lynn	86F	11	$ .01	$ .06
Johnson, Jeff	92FUL	410	$ .01	$ .10	Jones, Mike	82F	412	$ .01	$ .06
Johnson, Jeff	93F	650	$ .01	$ .04	Jones, Mike	86F	12	$ .01	$ .06
Johnson, Joe	86F	519	$ .01	$ .10	Jones, Odell	84F	421	$ .01	$ .08
Johnson, Joe	87F	230	$ .01	$ .06	Jones, Odell	85F	560	$ .01	$ .06
Johnson, John Henry	82F	321	$ .01	$ .06	Jones, Odell	89F	189	$ .01	$ .04
Johnson, John Henry	84F	401	$ .01	$ .08	Jones, Randy	81F	487	$ .01	$ .06
Johnson, John Henry	85F	162	$ .01	$ .06	Jones, Randy	82F	528	$ .01	$ .06
Johnson, John Henry	87F	347	$ .01	$ .06	Jones, Randy	83F	546	$ .01	$ .06
Johnson, Lamar	81F	350	$ .01	$ .06	Jones, Ron	89F	574	$ .01	$ .10
Johnson, Lamar	82F	346	$ .01	$ .06	Jones, Ron	90F	563	$ .01	$ .10
Johnson, Lamar	83F	571	$ .01	$ .06	Jones, Ross	88F	262	$ .01	$ .10
Johnson, Lance	88F	37	$ .10	$ .40	Jones, Ruppert	81F	101	$ .01	$ .06
Johnson, Lance	89F	499	$ .01	$ .04	Jones, Ruppert	82F	573	$ .01	$ .06
Johnson, Lance	90F	536	$ .01	$ .04	Jones, Ruppert	83F	361	$ .01	$ .06
Johnson, Lance	91F	123	$ .01	$ .04	Jones, Ruppert	84F	303	$ .01	$ .08
Johnson, Lance	91FUL	76	$ .01	$ .07	Jones, Ruppert	84FU	59	$ .10	$ .50

FLEER

Player	Year	No.	VG	EX/MT
Jones, Ruppert	85F	13	$ .05	$ .25
Jones, Ruppert	85FU	63	$ .01	$ .10
Jones, Ruppert	86F	161	$ .01	$ .06
Jones, Ruppert	87F	85	$ .01	$ .06
Jones, Ruppert	88F	492	$ .01	$ .05
Jones, Stacy	92F	701	$ .05	$ .20
Jones, Tim	89F	453	$ .01	$ .04
Jones, Tim	91FU	117	$ .01	$ .05
Jones, Tim	92FUL	569	$ .01	$ .10
Jones, Tracy	86FU	58	$ .05	$ .20
Jones, Tracy	87F	651	$ .10	$ .40
Jones, Tracy	87FU	55	$ .01	$ .10
Jones, Tracy	88F	237	$ .01	$ .05
Jones, Tracy	89F	383	$ .01	$ .04
Jones, Tracy	89FU	31	$ .01	$ .05
Jones, Tracy	90F	607	$ .01	$ .04
Jones, Tracy	91FU	53	$ .01	$ .05
Jones, Tracy	92F	284	$ .01	$ .04
Jordan, Brian	93F	511	$ .01	$ .10
Jordan, Brian	93FUL	107	$ .05	$ .25
Jordan, Ricky	88FU	110	$ .05	$ .25
Jordan, Ricky	89F	575	$ .01	$ .15
Jordan, Ricky	90F	564	$ .01	$ .10
Jordan, Ricky	91F	401	$ .01	$ .04
Jordan, Ricky	91FULU	100	$ .01	$ .10
Jordan, Ricky	92F	536	$ .01	$ .04
Jordan, Ricky	92FUL	245	$ .01	$ .10
Jordan, Ricky	93F	103	$ .01	$ .04
Jordan, Ricky	93FUL	89	$ .01	$ .10
Jorgensen, Mike	81F	324	$ .01	$ .06
Jorgensen, Mike	82F	529	$ .01	$ .06
Jorgensen, Mike	83F	547	$ .01	$ .06
Jorgensen, Mike	85F	229	$ .01	$ .06
Jorgensen, Terry	93F	268	$ .01	$ .04
Jorgensen, Terry	93FUL	232	$ .01	$ .10
Jose, Felix	89F	15	$ .10	$ .75
Jose, Felix	90F	13	$ .05	$ .25
Jose, Felix	91F	636	$ .01	$ .10
Jose, Felix	91FULU	107	$ .05	$ .25
Jose, Felix	92F	582	$ .01	$ .10
Jose, Felix	92FUL	264	$ .05	$ .20
Jose, Felix	93F	126	$ .01	$ .04

Player	Year	No.	VG	EX/MT
Joyner, Wally	87F	628	$ .10	$1.00
Joyner, Wally	88F	493	$ .01	$ .15
Joyner, Wally	88F	622	$ .05	$ .20
Joyner, Wally	89F	481	$ .01	$ .15
Joyner, Wally	90F	136	$ .01	$ .10
Joyner, Wally	91F	317	$ .01	$ .04
Joyner, Wally	91FUL	48	$ .01	$ .10
Joyner, Wally	92F	62	$ .01	$ .10
Joyner, Wally	92FU	27	$ .05	$ .25
Joyner, Wally	92FUL	373	$ .05	$ .20
Joyner, Wally	93F	239	$ .01	$ .10
Joyner, Wally	93FUL	210	$ .01	$ .15
Juden, Jeff	92FUL	492	$ .05	$ .20
Jurak, Ed	84F	402	$ .01	$ .08
Justice, David	90F	586	$ .15	$1.25
Justice, Dave	91F	693	$ .05	$ .25
Justice, Dave	91FUL	7	$ .10	$1.00
Justice, Dave	91FUL	394	$ .05	$ .35
Justice, Dave	92F	360	$ .05	$ .35
Justice, Dave	92F	713	$ .05	$ .25
Justice, Dave	92FUL	164	$ .10	$1.00
Justice, David	93F	367	$ .05	$ .20
Kaat, Jim	81F	536	$ .05	$ .20
Kaat, Jim	82F	117	$ .05	$ .20
Kaat, Jim	83F	11	$ .05	$ .20
Kaiser, Jeff	89F	410	$ .01	$ .04
Kamieniecki, Scott	91FU	45	$ .01	$ .10
Kamieniecki, Scott	92F	232	$ .01	$ .10
Kamieniecki, Scott	93F	651	$ .01	$ .04
Karkovice, Ron	87F	645	$ .05	$ .20
Karkovice, Ron	91F	125	$ .01	$ .04
Karkovice, Ron	91FULU	16	$ .01	$ .10
Karkovice, Ron	92F	88	$ .01	$ .04
Karkovice, Ron	92FUL	39	$ .01	$ .10
Karkovice, Ron	93F	205	$ .01	$ .04
Karkovice, Ron	93FUL	175	$ .01	$ .10
Karros, Eric	91FUL	380	$ .75	$3.00
Karros, Eric	92F	462	$ .10	$ .50
Karros, Eric	92FUL	508	$ .75	$3.00
Karros, Eric	93F	64	$ .05	$ .25
Karros, Eric	93FUL	56	$ .10	$1.00
Kaufman, Curt	85F	305	$ .01	$ .06
Kearney, Bob	84F	449	$ .01	$ .08
Kearney, Bob	84FU	60	$ .10	$ .50
Kearney, Bob	85F	491	$ .01	$ .06
Kearney, Bob	86F	466	$ .01	$ .06
Kearney, Bob	87F	587	$ .01	$ .06
Keeton, Rickey	82F	146	$ .01	$ .06
Kelly, Pat	82F	372	$ .01	$ .06
Kelly, Pat	91FU	46	$ .05	$ .20
Kelly, Pat	91FUL	381	$ .05	$ .35
Kelly, Pat	91FULU	41	$ .10	$ .50
Kelly, Pat	92F	233	$ .01	$ .10
Kelly, Pat	92FUL	102	$ .05	$ .20
Kelly, Pat	93F	280	$ .01	$ .04
Kelly, Pat	93FUL	242	$ .01	$ .10
Kelly, Roberto	88F	212	$ .20	$2.00
Kelly, Roberto	89F	256	$ .01	$ .15
Kelly, Roberto	90F	446	$ .01	$ .10
Kelly, Roberto	91F	668	$ .01	$ .04
Kelly, Roberto	91FUL	235	$ .01	$ .10
Kelly, Roberto	92F	234	$ .01	$ .04
Kelly, Roberto	92FUL	103	$ .05	$ .25
Kelly, Roberto	93F	393	$ .01	$ .10
Kemp, Steve	81F	459	$ .01	$ .06
Kemp, Steve	82F	271	$ .01	$ .06
Kemp, Steve	83F	239	$ .01	$ .06
Kemp, Steve	84F	129	$ .01	$ .08
Kemp, Steve	85F	132	$ .01	$ .06
Kemp, Steve	85FU	64	$ .01	$ .10
Kemp, Steve	86F	610	$ .01	$ .06
Kennedy, Junior	82F	70	$ .01	$ .06
Kennedy, Junior	83F	500	$ .01	$ .06
Kennedy, Terry	81F	203	$ .01	$ .06
Kennedy, Terry	81F	541	$ .01	$ .06

Joyner, Wally	86FU	59	$ .15	$1.50
Joyner, Wally	87F	86	$ .20	$2.00

FLEER

Player	Year	No.	VG	EX/MT
Kennedy, Terry	82F	574	$ .01	$ .06
Kennedy, Terry	83F	362	$ .01	$ .06
Kennedy, Terry	84F	304	$ .01	$ .08
Kennedy, Terry	85F	37	$ .01	$ .06
Kennedy, Terry	86F	327	$ .01	$ .06
Kennedy, Terry	87F	419	$ .01	$ .06
Kennedy, Terry	87FU	56	$ .01	$ .06
Kennedy, Terry	88F	563	$ .01	$ .05
Kennedy, Terry	89F	610	$ .01	$ .04
Kennedy, Terry	89FU	128	$ .01	$ .05
Kennedy, Terry	90F	58	$ .01	$ .04
Kennedy, Terry	91F	263	$ .01	$ .04
Kennedy, Terry	91FUL	321	$ .01	$ .07
Kent, Jeff	92FU	104	$ .10	$1.00
Kent, Jeff	93F	90	$ .01	$ .10
Kent, Jeff	93FUL	77	$ .05	$ .20
Keough, Matt	81F	588	$ .01	$ .06
Keough, Matt	82F	95	$ .01	$ .06
Keough, Matt	83F	521	$ .01	$ .06
Keough, Matt	84F	130	$ .01	$ .08
Kepshire, Kurt	85F	230	$ .01	$ .06
Kepshire, Kurt	86F	39	$ .01	$ .06
Kerfeld, Charlie	86F	303	$ .05	$ .25
Kerfeld, Charlie	87F	60	$ .01	$ .06
Kern, Jim	81F	618	$ .01	$ .06
Kern, Jim	82F	322	$ .01	$ .06
Kern, Jim	83F	240	$ .01	$ .06
Key, Jimmy	84FU	61	$3.50	$14.00
Key, Jimmy	85F	110	$ .20	$2.00
Key, Jimmy	86F	63	$ .05	$ .25
Key, Jimmy	86F	642	$ .01	$ .10
Key, Jimmy	87F	232	$ .01	$ .10
Key, Jimmy	88F	114	$ .01	$ .10
Key, Jimmy	89F	236	$ .01	$ .04
Key, Jimmy	90F	85	$ .01	$ .04
Key, Jimmy	91F	178	$ .01	$ .04
Key, Jimmy	91FUL	364	$ .01	$ .07
Key, Jimmy	92F	332	$ .01	$ .04
Key, Jimmy	92FUL	147	$ .01	$ .10
Key, Jimmy	93F	336	$ .01	$ .04
Khalifa, Sam	86F	611	$ .01	$ .06
Kiecker, Dana	90FU	72	$ .01	$ .15
Kiecker, Dana	91F	99	$ .01	$ .04
Kiecker, Dana	91FULU	6	$ .01	$ .10

Player	Year	No.	VG	EX/MT
Kiefer, Steve	85F	647	$2.00	$8.00
Kiefer, Steve	88F	167	$ .01	$ .05
Kiely, John	92FU	24	$ .05	$ .25
Kiely, John	93F	230	$ .01	$ .10
Kiely, John	93FUL	200	$ .01	$ .10
Kile, Darryl	91FU	90	$ .01	$ .10
Kile, Darryl	91FULU	84	$ .05	$ .35
Kile, Darryl	92F	439	$ .01	$ .10
Kile, Darryl	92FUL	206	$ .01	$ .15
Kile, Darryl	93F	438	$ .01	$ .04
Kilgus, Paul	88F	471	$ .01	$ .10
Kilgus, Paul	89F	525	$ .01	$ .04
Kilgus, Paul	89FU	76	$ .01	$ .05
Kilgus, Paul	90F	34	$ .01	$ .04
Kimm, Bruce	81F	355	$ .01	$ .06
King, Eric	87F	155	$ .05	$ .20
King, Eric	88F	60	$ .01	$ .10
King, Eric	89F	136	$ .01	$ .04
King, Eric	89FU	19	$ .01	$ .05
King, Eric	90F	537	$ .01	$ .04
King, Eric	91F	126	$ .01	$ .04
King, Eric	92F	115	$ .01	$ .04
King, Jeff	88F	653	$ .10	$ .40
King, Jeff	89FU	114	$ .01	$ .10
King, Jeff	90F	469	$ .01	$ .10
King, Jeff	91F	39	$ .01	$ .04
King, Jeff	91FUL	280	$ .01	$ .07
King, Jeff	92F	555	$ .01	$ .04
King, Jeff	92FUL	553	$ .01	$ .10
King, Jeff	93F	113	$ .01	$ .04
King, Jeff	93FUL	97	$ .01	$ .10
Kingery, Mike	87F	371	$ .01	$ .10
Kingery, Mike	87FU	57	$ .01	$ .06
Kingery, Mike	88F	376	$ .01	$ .05
Kingman, Brian	81F	579	$ .01	$ .06
Kingman, Brian	82F	96	$ .01	$ .06
Kingman, Brian	83F	522	$ .01	$ .06
Kingman, Dave	81F	291	$ .05	$ .20
Kingman, Dave	82F	530	$ .05	$ .20
Kingman, Dave	83F	548	$ .01	$ .10
Kingman, Dave	84F	590	$ .01	$ .10
Kingman, Dave	84FU	62	$ .10	$ .50
Kingman, Dave	85F	427	$ .01	$ .10
Kingman, Dave	86F	423	$ .01	$ .10
Kingman, Dave	87F	396	$ .01	$ .10
Kinney, Dennis	81F	505	$ .01	$ .06
Kinzer, Matt	90F	652	$ .01	$ .10
Kipper, Bob	86F	648	$ .05	$ .30
Kipper, Bob	87F	612	$ .01	$ .06
Kipper, Bob	88F	332	$ .01	$ .05
Kipper, Bob	89F	211	$ .01	$ .04
Kipper, Bob	90F	470	$ .01	$ .04
Kipper, Bob	91F	40	$ .01	$ .04
Kipper, Bob	92F	556	$ .01	$ .04
Kirby, Wayne	92F	670	$ .01	$ .10
Kison, Bruce	81F	284	$ .01	$ .06
Kison, Bruce	82F	467	$ .01	$ .06
Kison, Bruce	83F	96	$ .01	$ .06
Kison, Bruce	84F	523	$ .01	$ .08
Kison, Bruce	85F	306	$ .01	$ .06
Kison, Bruce	85FU	65	$ .01	$ .10
Kison, Bruce	86F	353	$ .01	$ .06
Kittle, Ron	83F	241	$ .05	$ .20
Kittle, Ron	84F	64	$ .05	$ .20
Kittle, Ron	85F	518	$ .01	$ .10
Kittle, Ron	86F	210	$ .01	$ .10
Kittle, Ron	87F	103	$ .01	$ .10
Kittle, Ron	88F	213	$ .01	$ .05
Kittle, Ron	89FU	20	$ .01	$ .05
Kittle, Ron	90F	538	$ .01	$ .04
Kittle, Ron	91F	480	$ .01	$ .04
Klesko, Ryan	93F	6	$ .05	$ .25
Klesko, Ryan	93FUL	7	$ .10	$1.00
Klink, Joe	91F	13	$ .01	$ .04
Klutts, Mickey	81F	584	$ .01	$ .06

FLEER

Player	Year	No.	VG	EX/MT
Klutts, Mickey	82F	97	$.01	$.06
Knepper, Bob	81F	447	$.01	$.10
Knepper, Bob	82F	219	$.01	$.06
Knepper, Bob	83F	451	$.01	$.06
Knepper, Bob	84F	228	$.01	$.08
Knepper, Bob	85F	352	$.01	$.06
Knepper, Bob	86F	304	$.01	$.06
Knepper, Bob	87F	61	$.01	$.06
Knepper, Bob	88F	451	$.01	$.05
Knepper, Bob	89F	360	$.01	$.04
Knicely, Alan	83F	452	$.01	$.06
Knicely, Alan	84F	473	$.01	$.08
Knight, Ray	81F	198	$.01	$.10
Knight, Ray	82F	71	$.01	$.10
Knight, Ray	83F	453	$.01	$.10
Knight, Ray	84F	229	$.01	$.10
Knight, Ray	85F	86	$.01	$.10
Knight, Ray	86F	86	$.01	$.06
Knight, Ray	87F	14	$.01	$.06
Knight, Ray	87FU	58	$.01	$.06
Knight, Ray	88F	564	$.01	$.05
Knight, Ray	88FU	28	$.01	$.06
Knoblauch, Chuck	91FU	37	$.10	$.50
Knoblauch, Chuck	91FUL	382	$.10	$1.00
Knoblauch, Chuck	91FULU	37	$.75	$3.00
Knoblauch, Chuck	92F	206	$.05	$.20
Knoblauch, Chuck	92FUL	93	$.10	$.50
Knoblauch, Chuck	93F	357	$.01	$.15
Knoblauch, Chuck	93F	639	$.01	$.15
Knorr, Randy	92FU	65	$.05	$.25
Knorr, Randy	93F	695	$.01	$.10
Knudsen, Kurt	92FU	25	$.05	$.25
Knudsen, Kurt	93F	231	$.01	$.10
Knudson, Mark	90F	327	$.01	$.04
Knudson, Mark	91F	587	$.01	$.04
Knudson, Mark	91FUL	176	$.01	$.07
Komminsk, Brad	84FU	63	$.10	$.50
Komminsk, Brad	85F	331	$.01	$.06
Komminsk, Brad	86F	520	$.01	$.06
Komminsk, Brad	89FU	28	$.01	$.05
Komminsk, Brad	90F	496	$.01	$.04
Koosman, Jerry	81F	552	$.01	$.10
Koosman, Jerry	82F	347	$.01	$.10
Koosman, Jerry	83F	242	$.01	$.10
Koosman, Jerry	84F	65	$.01	$.10
Koosman, Jerry	84FU	64	$.10	$.50
Koosman, Jerry	85F	256	$.01	$.10
Koslofski, Kevin	92FU	28	$.05	$.35
Koslofski, Kevin	93F	240	$.01	$.10
Koslofski, Kevin	93FUL	211	$.01	$.10
Kraemer, Joe	90FU	8	$.01	$.10
Kramer, Randy	89F	647	$.05	$.20
Kramer, Randy	89FU	115	$.01	$.05
Kramer, Randy	90F	471	$.01	$.04
Kremers, Jim	90FU	4	$.01	$.10
Kremers, Jimmy	91F	694	$.01	$.10
Krenchicki, Wayne	82F	168	$.01	$.06
Krenchicki, Wayne	83F	594	$.01	$.06
Krenchicki, Wayne	84F	83	$.01	$.08
Krenchicki, Wayne	84FU	65	$.10	$.50
Krenchicki, Wayne	85F	539	$.01	$.06
Krenchicki, Wayne	86F	180	$.01	$.06
Krenchicki, Wayne	86FU	60	$.01	$.08
Krenchicki, Wayne	87F	322	$.01	$.06
Kreuter, Chad	89F	526	$.05	$.20
Kreuter, Chad	90F	303	$.01	$.04
Kreuter, Chad	92FUL	365	$.01	$.10
Kreuter, Chad	93F	607	$.01	$.04
Kreuter, Chad	93FUL	201	$.01	$.10
Krueger, Bill	84F	450	$.05	$.35
Krueger, Bill	85F	428	$.01	$.06
Krueger, Bill	86F	424	$.01	$.06
Krueger, Bill	90F	328	$.01	$.04
Krueger, Bill	91F	588	$.01	$.04
Krueger, Bill	91FU	54	$.01	$.05
Krueger, Bill	91FULU	52	$.01	$.10
Krueger, Bill	92F	285	$.01	$.04
Krueger, Bill	92FUL	397	$.01	$.10
Kruk, John	86FU	61	$.15	$1.50
Kruk, John	87F	420	$.20	$2.00
Kruk, John	88F	589	$.05	$.25
Kruk, John	89F	309	$.01	$.04
Kruk, John	89FU	109	$.01	$.05
Kruk, John	90F	565	$.01	$.04
Kruk, John	91F	402	$.01	$.04
Kruk, John	91FUL	266	$.01	$.07
Kruk, John	92F	537	$.01	$.04
Kruk, John	92FUL	246	$.01	$.10
Kruk, John	93F	104	$.01	$.04
Kruk, John	93FUL	90	$.01	$.15
Krukow, Mike	81F	312	$.01	$.10
Krukow, Mike	82F	598	$.01	$.06
Krukow, Mike	83F	163	$.01	$.06
Krukow, Mike	84F	374	$.01	$.08
Krukow, Mike	85F	609	$.01	$.06
Krukow, Mike	86F	546	$.01	$.06
Krukow, Mike	87F	275	$.01	$.06
Krukow, Mike	87F	630	$.01	$.10
Krukow, Mike	88F	85	$.01	$.05
Krukow, Mike	89F	331	$.01	$.04
Kuiper, Duane	82F	373	$.01	$.06
Kuiper, Duane	83F	263	$.01	$.06
Kuiper, Duane	84F	375	$.01	$.08
Kuiper, Duane	85F	610	$.01	$.06
Kunkel, Jeff	85F	561	$.01	$.06
Kunkel, Jeff	89F	527	$.01	$.04
Kunkel, Jeff	90F	304	$.01	$.04
Kunkel, Jeff	91F	292	$.01	$.04
Kuntz, Rusty	82F	348	$.01	$.06
Kuntz, Rusty	84F	568	$.01	$.08
Kuntz, Rusty	84FU	66	$.10	$.50
Kuntz, Rusty	85F	14	$.01	$.06
Kutcher, Randy	87F	276	$.01	$.10
Kutcher, Randy	91F	100	$.01	$.04
Lacey, Bob	81F	578	$.01	$.06
Lacey, Bob	85F	611	$.01	$.06
LaCock, Pete	81F	47	$.01	$.06
LaCorte, Frank	81F	55	$.01	$.06
LaCorte, Frank	82F	220	$.01	$.06
LaCorte, Frank	83F	454	$.01	$.06
LaCorte, Frank	84F	230	$.01	$.08
LaCorte, Frank	84FU	67	$.10	$.50
LaCoss, Mike	82F	72	$.01	$.06
LaCoss, Mike	83F	455	$.01	$.06
LaCoss, Mike	84F	231	$.01	$.08
LaCoss, Mike	85F	353	$.01	$.06
LaCoss, Mike	85FU	66	$.01	$.10
LaCoss, Mike	86FU	62	$.01	$.08
LaCoss, Mike	87F	277	$.01	$.06
LaCoss, Mike	88F	86	$.01	$.05
LaCoss, Mike	89FU	129	$.01	$.05
LaCoss, Mike	90F	50	$.01	$.04
LaCoss, Mike	91F	264	$.01	$.04
Lacy, Lee	81F	374	$.01	$.06
Lacy, Lee	82F	483	$.01	$.06
Lacy, Lee	83F	308	$.01	$.06
Lacy, Lee	84F	252	$.01	$.08
Lacy, Lee	85F	467	$.01	$.06
Lacy, Lee	85FU	67	$.01	$.10
Lacy, Lee	86F	277	$.01	$.06
Lacy, Lee	87F	473	$.01	$.06
Lacy, Lee	88F	565	$.01	$.05
Ladd, Pete	83F	37	$.01	$.06
Ladd, Pete	84F	204	$.01	$.08
Ladd, Pete	85F	585	$.01	$.06
Ladd, Pete	86F	492	$.01	$.06
Ladd, Pete	87F	588	$.01	$.06
Ladd, Peter	86FU	63	$.01	$.08
Lahti, Jeff	83F	12	$.01	$.06
Lahti, Jeff	84F	327	$.01	$.08

FLEER

Player	Year	No.	VG	EX/MT	Player	Year	No.	VG	EX/MT
Lahti, Jeff	85F	231	$ .01	$ .06	Lankford, Ray	91FUL	290	$ .10	$ .50
Lahti, Jeff	86F	40	$ .01	$ .06	Lankford, Ray	92F	583	$ .01	$ .10
Lahti, Jeff	87F	299	$ .01	$ .06	Lankford, Ray	92FUL	265	$ .10	$ .75
Lake, Steve	87F	300	$ .01	$ .06	Lankford, Ray	93F	127	$ .01	$ .10
Lake, Steve	88F	38	$ .01	$ .05	Lankford, Ray	93FUL	108	$ .05	$ .25
Lake, Steve	89F	454	$ .01	$ .04	Lansford, Carney	81F	270	$ .05	$ .25
Lake, Steve	90F	566	$ .01	$ .04	Lansford, Carney	82F	298	$ .01	$ .10
Lake, Steve	91F	403	$ .01	$ .04	Lansford, Carney	83F	187	$ .01	$ .10
Laker, Tim	93F	77	$ .01	$ .15	Lansford, Carney	84F	452	$ .01	$ .08
Lamp, Dennis	81F	305	$ .01	$ .06	Lansford, Carney	85F	429	$ .01	$ .06
Lamp, Dennis	82F	349	$ .01	$ .06	Lansford, Carney	86F	426	$ .01	$ .06
Lamp, Dennis	83F	243	$ .01	$ .06	Lansford, Carney	87F	397	$ .01	$ .06
Lamp, Dennis	84F	66	$ .01	$ .08	Lansford, Carney	88F	285	$ .01	$ .05
Lamp, Dennis	84FU	68	$ .10	$ .50	Lansford, Carney	89F	16	$ .01	$ .04
Lamp, Dennis	85F	111	$ .01	$ .06	Lansford, Carney	89F	633	$ .01	$ .10
Lamp, Dennis	86F	64	$ .01	$ .06	Lansford, Carney	90F	14	$ .01	$ .10
Lamp, Dennis	87F	233	$ .01	$ .06	Lansford, Carney	91F	14	$ .01	$ .04
Lamp, Dennis	88F	284	$ .01	$ .05	Lansford, Carney	91FUL	250	$ .01	$ .07
Lamp, Dennis	89F	92	$ .01	$ .04	Lansford, Carney	92F	261	$ .01	$ .04
Lamp, Dennis	90F	280	$ .01	$ .04	Lansford, Carney	92FUL	423	$ .01	$ .10
Lamp, Dennis	91F	101	$ .01	$ .04	LaPoint, Dave	83F	14	$ .10	$ .40
Lamp, Dennis	92F	42	$ .01	$ .04	LaPoint, Dave	84F	328	$ .01	$ .15
Lampkin, Tom	92F	610	$ .01	$ .04	LaPoint, Dave	85F	233	$ .01	$ .10
Lancaster, Les	88F	421	$ .01	$ .15	LaPoint, Dave	85FU	68	$ .01	$ .10
Lancaster, Les	89F	429	$ .01	$ .04	LaPoint, Dave	86F	547	$ .01	$ .06
Lancaster, Les	90F	35	$ .01	$ .04	LaPoint, Dave	86FU	64	$ .01	$ .08
Lancaster, Les	91F	424	$ .01	$ .04	LaPoint, Dave	87F	421	$ .01	$ .06
Lancaster, Les	91FUL	63	$ .01	$ .07	LaPoint, Dave	88F	402	$ .01	$ .05
Lancaster, Les	92F	384	$ .01	$ .04	LaPoint, Dave	89F	212	$ .01	$ .04
Lancaster, Les	92FUL	177	$ .01	$ .10	LaPoint, Dave	91F	669	$ .01	$ .04
Landestoy, Rafael	81F	70	$ .01	$ .06	Larkin, Barry	87F	204	$1.75	$7.00
Landestoy, Rafael	82F	73	$ .01	$ .06	Larkin, Barry	88F	239	$ .10	$ .50
Landestoy, Rafael	83F	595	$ .01	$ .06	Larkin, Barry	89F	164	$ .05	$ .20
Landreaux, Ken	81F	553	$ .01	$ .06	Larkin, Barry	90F	423	$ .01	$ .15
Landreaux, Ken	82F	11	$ .01	$ .06	Larkin, Barry	91F	68	$ .01	$ .10
Landreaux, Ken	83F	210	$ .01	$ .06	Larkin, Barry	91F	711	$ .05	$ .20
Landreaux, Ken	84F	104	$ .01	$ .08	Larkin, Barry	91FUL	96	$ .01	$ .15
Landreaux, Ken	85F	375	$ .01	$ .06	Larkin, Barry	92F	411	$ .01	$ .10
Landreaux, Ken	86F	134	$ .01	$ .06	Larkin, Barry	92F	704	$ .01	$ .10
Landreaux, Ken	87F	444	$ .01	$ .06	Larkin, Barry	92FUL	191	$ .05	$ .35
Landrum, Bill	88F	238	$ .01	$ .10	Larkin, Barry	93F	394	$ .01	$ .10
Landrum, Bill	89FU	116	$ .01	$ .05	Larkin, Barry	93FUL	30	$ .05	$ .25
Landrum, Bill	90F	472	$ .01	$ .04	Larkin, Gene	87FU	59	$ .05	$ .20
Landrum, Bill	91F	41	$ .01	$ .04	Larkin, Gene	88F	14	$ .05	$ .20
Landrum, Bill	91FUL	281	$ .01	$ .07	Larkin, Gene	89F	117	$ .01	$ .04
Landrum, Bill	92F	557	$ .01	$ .04	Larkin, Gene	90F	379	$ .01	$ .04
Landrum, Cedric	92F	385	$ .01	$ .10	Larkin, Gene	91F	615	$ .01	$ .04
Landrum, Terry 'Tito'	81F	539	$ .01	$ .06	Larkin, Gene	91FUL	190	$ .01	$ .07
Landrum, Tito	82F	118	$ .01	$ .06	Larkin, Gene	92F	207	$ .01	$ .04
Landrum, Tito	83F	13	$ .01	$ .06	Larkin, Gene	93F	269	$ .01	$ .04
Landrum, Tito	84FU	69	$ .10	$ .50	LaRoche, Dave	81F	285	$ .01	$ .06
Landrum, Tito	85F	232	$ .01	$ .06	LaRoche, Dave	83F	384	$ .01	$ .06
Landrum, Tito	86F	41	$ .01	$ .06	LaRussa, Tony	81F	344	$ .01	$ .06
Landrum, Tito	87F	301	$ .01	$ .06	Laskey, Bill	83F	264	$ .01	$ .06
Langford, Rick	81F	572	$ .01	$ .06	Laskey, Bill	84F	376	$ .01	$ .08
Langford, Rick	82F	98	$ .01	$ .06	Laskey, Bill	85F	612	$ .01	$ .06
Langford, Rick	83F	523	$ .01	$ .06	Laskey, Bill	86F	251	$ .01	$ .06
Langford, Rick	84F	451	$ .01	$ .08	Lasorda, Tom	81F	116	$ .01	$ .10
Langford, Rick	86F	425	$ .01	$ .06	Laudner, Tim	83F	618	$ .01	$ .06
Langston, Mark	84FU	70	$6.25	$25.00	Laudner, Tim	84F	569	$ .01	$ .08
Langston, Mark	85F	492	$1.00	$4.00	Laudner, Tim	85F	283	$ .01	$ .06
Langston, Mark	86F	467	$ .10	$ .50	Laudner, Tim	86F	398	$ .01	$ .06
Langston, Mark	87F	589	$ .05	$ .35	Laudner, Tim	87F	546	$ .01	$ .06
Langston, Mark	88F	377	$ .01	$ .15	Laudner, Tim	88F	15	$ .01	$ .05
Langston, Mark	89F	551	$ .01	$ .10	Laudner, Tim	89F	118	$ .01	$ .04
Langston, Mark	89FU	97	$ .01	$ .15	Laudner, Tim	90F	380	$ .01	$ .04
Langston, Mark	90F	352	$ .01	$ .10	LaValliere, Mike	86FU	65	$ .05	$ .25
Langston, Mark	90FU	78	$ .01	$ .10	LaValliere, Mike	87F	302	$ .05	$ .25
Langston, Mark	91F	318	$ .01	$ .04	LaValliere, Mike	87FU	60	$ .01	$ .15
Langston, Mark	91FUL	49	$ .01	$ .07	LaValliere, Mike	88F	333	$ .01	$ .05
Langston, Mark	92F	63	$ .01	$ .04	LaValliere, Mike	89F	213	$ .01	$ .04
Langston, Mark	92FUL	327	$ .05	$ .25	LaValliere, Mike	90F	473	$ .01	$ .04
Langston, Mark	93F	194	$ .01	$ .04	LaValliere, Mike	91F	42	$ .01	$ .04
Langston, Mark	93FUL	166	$ .01	$ .10	LaValliere, Mike	91FUL	282	$ .01	$ .07
Lankford, Ray	91F	637	$ .05	$ .35	LaValliere, Mike	92F	558	$ .01	$ .04

FLEER

Player	Year	No.	VG	EX/MT
LaValliere, Mike	92FUL	254	$ .01	$ .10
LaValliere, Mike	93F	114	$ .01	$ .04
LaValliere, Mike	93FUL	98	$ .01	$ .10
Lavelle, Gary	81F	448	$ .01	$ .06
Lavelle, Gary	82F	392	$ .01	$ .06
Lavelle, Gary	83F	265	$ .01	$ .06
Lavelle, Gary	84F	377	$ .01	$ .08
Lavelle, Gary	85F	613	$ .01	$ .06
Lavelle, Gary	85FU	69	$ .01	$ .10
Lavelle, Gary	86F	65	$ .01	$ .06
Law, Rudy	81F	139	$ .01	$ .06
Law, Rudy	83F	244	$ .01	$ .06
Law, Rudy	84F	67	$ .01	$ .08
Law, Rudy	85F	519	$ .01	$ .06
Law, Rudy	86F	211	$ .01	$ .06
Law, Rudy	86FU	66	$ .01	$ .08
Law, Rudy	87F	372	$ .01	$ .06
Law, Vance	82F	484	$ .01	$ .06
Law, Vance	83F	245	$ .01	$ .06
Law, Vance	84F	68	$ .01	$ .08
Law, Vance	85F	520	$ .01	$ .06
Law, Vance	85FU	70	$ .01	$ .10
Law, Vance	86F	252	$ .01	$ .06
Law, Vance	87F	323	$ .01	$ .06
Law, Vance	88F	187	$ .01	$ .05
Law, Vance	88FU	79	$ .01	$ .06
Law, Vance	89F	430	$ .01	$ .04
Law, Vance	90F	36	$ .01	$ .04
Layana, Tim	90FU	14	$ .01	$ .10
Layana, Tim	91F	69	$ .01	$ .10
Lazorko, Jack	87FU	61	$ .01	$ .06
Lazorko, Jack	88F	494	$ .01	$ .05
Lazorko, Jack	89F	482	$ .01	$ .04
Lea, Charlie	81F	165	$ .05	$ .20
Lea, Charlie	82F	193	$ .01	$ .06
Lea, Charlie	83F	286	$ .01	$ .06
Lea, Charlie	84F	278	$ .01	$ .08
Lea, Charlie	85F	401	$ .01	$ .06
Lea, Charlie	85F	632	$ .01	$ .10
Lea, Charlie	86F	253	$ .01	$ .06
Lea, Charlie	88FU	44	$ .01	$ .06
Lea, Charlie	89F	119	$ .01	$ .04
Leach, Rick	82F	272	$ .01	$ .06
Leach, Rick	83F	334	$ .01	$ .06
Leach, Rick	84F	84	$ .01	$ .08
Leach, Rick	84FU	71	$ .10	$ .50
Leach, Rick	85F	112	$ .01	$ .06
Leach, Rick	87F	234	$ .01	$ .06
Leach, Rick	87FU	63	$ .01	$ .06
Leach, Rick	88F	115	$ .01	$ .05
Leach, Rick	89F	237	$ .01	$ .04
Leach, Rick	90F	305	$ .01	$ .04
Leach, Terry	86F	87	$ .01	$ .06
Leach, Terry	87FU	62	$ .01	$ .06
Leach, Terry	88F	139	$ .01	$ .05
Leach, Terry	89F	40	$ .01	$ .04
Leach, Terry	90F	111	$ .01	$ .04
Leach, Terry	91F	616	$ .01	$ .04
Leach, Terry	92F	208	$ .01	$ .04
Leach, Terry	93F	585	$ .01	$ .04
Leal, Luis	82F	617	$ .01	$ .06
Leal, Luis	83F	432	$ .01	$ .06
Leal, Luis	84F	160	$ .01	$ .08
Leal, Luis	85F	113	$ .01	$ .06
Leary, Tim	87F	348	$ .01	$ .06
Leary, Tim	88F	521	$ .01	$ .05
Leary, Tim	89F	65	$ .01	$ .04
Leary, Tim	90F	424	$ .01	$ .04
Leary, Tim	91F	670	$ .01	$ .04
Leary, Tim	91FUL	236	$ .01	$ .07
Leary, Tim	92F	235	$ .01	$ .04
Leary, Tim	92FUL	411	$ .01	$ .10
Leary, Tim	93F	677	$ .01	$ .04
Lee, Bill	81F	157	$ .01	$ .06
Lee, Bill	82F	194	$ .01	$ .06
Lee, Manny	85FU	71	$ .10	$ .50
Lee, Manny	88F	116	$ .01	$ .05
Lee, Manny	89F	238	$ .01	$ .04
Lee, Manny	90F	86	$ .01	$ .04
Lee, Manny	91F	179	$ .01	$ .04
Lee, Manny	91FUL	365	$ .01	$ .07
Lee, Manny	92F	333	$ .01	$ .04
Lee, Manny "Manuel"	92FUL	148	$ .01	$ .10
Lee, Manuel	93F	337	$ .01	$ .04
Lee, Mark	91FU	30	$ .01	$ .15
Lee, Mark	92F	180	$ .01	$ .04
Lee, Terry	91F	70	$ .01	$ .10
Lefebvre, Joe	81F	103	$ .01	$ .06
Lefebvre, Joe	82F	575	$ .01	$ .06
Lefebvre, Joe	83F	363	$ .01	$ .06
Lefebvre, Joe	84F	37	$ .01	$ .08
Lefebvre, Joe	85F	257	$ .01	$ .06
Lefferts, Craig	84F	496	$ .10	$ .75
Lefferts, Craig	84FU	72	$ .10	$1.00
Lefferts, Craig	85F	38	$ .01	$ .06
Lefferts, Craig	86F	328	$ .01	$ .06
Lefferts, Craig	87F	422	$ .01	$ .06
Lefferts, Craig	87FU	64	$ .01	$ .06
Lefferts, Craig	88F	87	$ .01	$ .05
Lefferts, Craig	89F	332	$ .01	$ .04
Lefferts, Craig	90F	60	$ .01	$ .04
Lefferts, Craig	90FU	57	$ .01	$ .05
Lefferts, Craig	91F	534	$ .01	$ .04
Lefferts, Craig	91FUL	307	$ .01	$ .07
Lefferts, Craig	92F	611	$ .01	$ .04
Lefferts, Craig	92FUL	577	$ .01	$ .10
Lefferts, Craig	93F	544	$ .01	$ .04
LeFlore, Ron	81F	154	$ .01	$ .06
LeFlore, Ron	82F	350	$ .01	$ .06
LeFlore, Ron	83F	246	$ .01	$ .06
Leibrandt, Charlie	81F	208	$ .10	$ .75
Leibrandt, Charlie	82F	74	$ .01	$ .10
Leibrandt, Charlie	83F	596	$ .01	$ .06
Leibrandt, Charlie	85F	206	$ .01	$ .06
Leibrandt, Charlie	86F	13	$ .01	$ .06

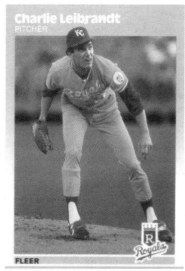

Player	Year	No.	VG	EX/MT
Leibrandt, Charlie	87F	373	$ .01	$ .06
Leibrandt, Charlie	88F	263	$ .01	$ .05
Leibrandt, Charlie	89F	286	$ .01	$ .04

FLEER

Player	Year	No.	VG	EX/MT	Player	Year	No.	VG	EX/MT
Leibrandt, Charlie	90F	112	$ .01	$ .04	Lemon, Chet	91F	341	$ .01	$ .04
Leibrandt, Charlie	91F	695	$ .01	$ .04	Lentine, Jim	81F	476	$ .01	$ .06
Leibrandt, Charlie	92F	361	$ .01	$ .04	Leon, Danito	92FU	61	$ .05	$ .25
Leibrandt, Charlie	92FUL	459	$ .01	$ .10	Leonard, Dennis	81F	42	$ .01	$ .06
Leibrandt, Charlie	93F	7	$ .01	$ .04	Leonard, Dennis	82F	413	$ .01	$ .06
Leiper, David	87F	398	$ .01	$ .10	Leonard, Dennis	83F	116	$ .01	$ .06
Leiper, Dave	88FU	123	$ .01	$ .06	Leonard, Dennis	84F	349	$ .01	$ .08
Leiper, Dave	89F	310	$ .01	$ .04	Leonard, Dennis	86FU	67	$ .01	$ .08
Leiter, Al	88FU	49	$ .01	$ .10	Leonard, Dennis	87F	374	$ .01	$ .06
Leiter, Al	89F	257	$ .01	$ .10	Leonard, Jeff	81F	67	$ .05	$ .20
Leiter, Al	89FU	70	$ .01	$ .10	Leonard, Jeff	84F	379	$ .01	$ .10
Leiter, Al	92F	334	$ .01	$ .04	Leonard, Jeff	85F	615	$ .05	$ .20
Leiter, Mark	92F	140	$ .01	$ .04	Leonard, Jeff	86F	548	$ .01	$ .10
Leiter, Mark	92FUL	366	$ .01	$ .10	Leonard, Jeff	87F	278	$ .01	$ .10
Leiter, Mark	93F	608	$ .01	$ .04	Leonard, Jeff	88F	88	$ .01	$ .05
Leius, Scott	90F	647	$ .05	$ .25	Leonard, Jeff	88FU	39	$ .01	$ .06
Leius, Scott	91FU	38	$ .01	$ .15	Leonard, Jeffrey	89F	190	$ .01	$ .04
Leius, Scott	91FULU	38	$ .05	$ .25	Leonard, Jeffrey	89FU	60	$ .01	$ .05
Leius, Scott	92F	209	$ .01	$ .04	Leonard, Jeffrey	90F	519	$ .01	$ .04
Leius, Scott	92FUL	94	$ .01	$ .10	Leonard, Jeffrey	91F	456	$ .01	$ .04
Leius, Scott	93F	270	$ .01	$ .04	Leonard, Mark	91F	265	$ .01	$ .15
Leius, Scott	93FUL	233	$ .01	$ .10	Leonard, Mark	91FUL	322	$ .01	$ .15
LeMaster, Johnnie	81F	450	$ .01	$ .06	Leonard, Mark	92FUL	591	$ .01	$ .10
LeMaster, Johnnie	82F	393	$ .01	$ .06	Leonard, Mark	93F	532	$ .01	$ .04
LeMaster, Johnnie	83F	266	$ .01	$ .06	Lerch, Randy	81F	25	$ .01	$ .06
LeMaster, Johnnie	84F	378	$ .01	$ .08	Lerch, Randy	82F	147	$ .01	$ .06
LeMaster, Johnnie	85F	614	$ .01	$ .06	Lerch, Randy	83F	287	$ .01	$ .06
Lemke, Mark	90F	587	$ .01	$ .04	Lerch, Randy	84F	380	$ .01	$ .08
Lemke, Mark	91F	696	$ .01	$ .04	Lerch, Randy	85F	616	$ .01	$ .06
Lemke, Mark	92F	362	$ .01	$ .04	Levis, Jesse	92FU	16	$ .10	$ .40
Lemke, Mark	92FUL	165	$ .01	$ .10	Lewis, Darren	91F	15	$ .01	$ .10
Lemke, Mark	93F	368	$ .01	$ .04	Lewis, Darren	91FUL	323	$ .05	$ .25
Lemke, Mark	93FUL	8	$ .01	$ .10	Lewis, Darren	92F	639	$ .01	$ .10
Lemon, Chet	81F	354	$ .01	$ .06	Lewis, Darren	92FUL	292	$ .05	$ .25
Lemon, Chet	82F	351	$ .01	$ .06	Lewis, Darren	93F	157	$ .01	$ .04
Lemon, Chet	83F	335	$ .01	$ .06	Lewis, Darren	93FUL	134	$ .01	$ .10
Lemon, Chet	84F	85	$ .01	$ .08	Lewis, Jim	92F	612	$ .01	$ .10
Lemon, Chet	85F	15	$ .01	$ .06	Lewis, Mark	91FU	19	$ .01	$ .10
Lemon, Chet	86F	230	$ .01	$ .06	Lewis, Mark	92F	116	$ .01	$ .10
Lemon, Chet	87F	156	$ .01	$ .06	Lewis, Mark	92FUL	51	$ .05	$ .35
					Lewis, Mark	93F	216	$ .01	$ .04
					Lewis, Mark	93FUL	186	$ .01	$ .10
					Lewis, Scott	92FUL	328	$ .01	$ .10
					Lewis, Scott	93F	575	$ .01	$ .04
					Leyritz, Jim	90FU	112	$ .01	$ .10
					Leyritz, Jim	91F	671	$ .01	$ .10
					Leyritz, Jim	91FUL	237	$ .01	$ .07
					Leyritz, Jim	92FUL	412	$ .01	$ .10
					Lezcano, Carlos	81F	307	$ .01	$ .06
					Lezcano, Sixto	81F	513	$ .01	$ .06
					Lezcano, Sixto	82F	119	$ .01	$ .06
					Lezcano, Sixto	83F	364	$ .01	$ .06
					Lezcano, Sixto	84F	38	$ .01	$ .08
					Lezcano, Sixto	85F	258	$ .01	$ .06
					Lezcano, Sixto	85FU	72	$ .01	$ .10
					Lilliquist, Derek	89FU	73	$ .01	$ .15
					Lilliquist, Derek	90F	588	$ .01	$ .10
					Lilliquist, Derek	91F	535	$ .01	$ .04
					Lilliquist, Derek	93F	217	$ .01	$ .04
					Lilliquist, Derek	93FUL	187	$ .01	$ .10
					Linares, Rufino	82F	439	$ .01	$ .06
					Linares, Rufino	83F	140	$ .01	$ .06
					Lind, Jose	88F	334	$ .05	$ .25
					Lind, Jose	89F	214	$ .01	$ .10
					Lind, Jose	90F	474	$ .01	$ .04
					Lind, Jose	91F	43	$ .01	$ .04
					Lind, Jose	91FUL	283	$ .01	$ .07
					Lind, Jose	92F	559	$ .01	$ .04
					Lind, Jose	92FUL	255	$ .01	$ .10
					Lind, Jose	93F	115	$ .01	$ .04
					Lindeman, Jim	87FU	65	$ .01	$ .10
					Lindeman, Jim	88F	39	$ .01	$ .10
Lemon, Chet	88F	61	$ .01	$ .05	Lindeman, Jim	92F	538	$ .01	$ .04
Lemon, Chet	89F	137	$ .01	$ .04	Lindsey, Bill	88F	403	$ .01	$ .10
Lemon, Chet	90F	608	$ .01	$ .04	Linskey, Mike	92F	663	$ .01	$ .15

Lemon, Chet
OUTFIELD

FLEER

Player	Year	No.	VG	EX/MT
Liriano, Nelson	88F	117	$.05	$.30
Liriano, Nelson	89F	239	$.01	$.04
Liriano, Nelson	90F	87	$.01	$.04
Liriano, Nelson	91F	617	$.01	$.04
Listach, Pat	92FU	36	$1.25	$5.00
Listach, Pat	92FUL	385	$.75	$3.00
Listach, Pat	93F	253	$.05	$.35
Littell, Mark	81F	544	$.01	$.06
Littell, Mark	82F	120	$.01	$.06
Little, Bryan	84F	279	$.01	$.08
Little, Bryan	85F	402	$.01	$.06
Little, Bryan	86F	212	$.01	$.06
Little, Jeff	83F	619	$.01	$.06
Littlefield, John	81F	535	$.01	$.06
Littlefield, John	82F	576	$.01	$.06
Littlejohn, Dennis	81F	455	$.01	$.06
Litton, Greg	89FU	130	$.01	$.10
Litton, Greg	90F	61	$.01	$.10
Litton, Greg	91F	266	$.01	$.04
Litton, Greg	91FUL	324	$.01	$.07
Litton, Greg	92F	640	$.01	$.04
Litton, Greg	93F	533	$.01	$.04
Livingstone, Scott	92F	141	$.01	$.15
Livingstone, Scott	92FUL	61	$.05	$.25
Livingstone, Scott	93F	232	$.01	$.10
Livingstone, Scott	93FUL	202	$.01	$.10
Lofton, Kenny	92F	655	$.10	$.40
Lofton, Kenny	92FU	17	$1.00	$3.00
Lofton, Kenny	92FUL	350	$.15	$1.50
Lofton, Kenny	93F	218	$.05	$.20
Lofton, Kenny	93F	346	$.01	$.15
Lollar, Tim	81F	108	$.01	$.06
Lollar, Tim	83F	365	$.01	$.06
Lollar, Tim	84F	305	$.01	$.08
Lollar, Tim	85F	39	$.01	$.06
Lollar, Tim	85FU	73	$.01	$.10
Lollar, Tim	86F	354	$.01	$.06
Lollar, Tim	87F	38	$.01	$.06
Lombardi, Phil	87F	648	$.10	$.75
Lombardozzi, Steve	86FU	68	$.01	$.15
Lombardozzi, Steve	87F	547	$.01	$.06
Lombardozzi, Steve	88F	16	$.01	$.05
Lombardozzi, Steve	89F	120	$.01	$.04
Long, Bill	87FU	66	$.01	$.10
Long, Bill	88F	404	$.01	$.15
Long, Bill	89F	501	$.01	$.04
Long, Bill	91F	425	$.01	$.04
Long, Bob	86F	468	$.01	$.06
Lopes, Davey 'Dave'	81F	114	$.01	$.10
Lopes, Davey	82F	12	$.01	$.10
Lopes, Davey	83F	524	$.01	$.10
Lopes, Davey	84F	453	$.01	$.08
Lopes, Davey	85F	60	$.01	$.06
Lopes, Davey	86F	372	$.01	$.06
Lopes, Davey	87F	62	$.01	$.06
Lopez, Aurelio	82F	273	$.01	$.06
Lopez, Aurelio	84F	80	$.01	$.08
Lopez, Aurelio	85F	16	$.01	$.06
Lopez, Aurelio	86F	231	$.01	$.06
Lopez, Aurelio	86FU	69	$.01	$.08
Lopez, Aurelio	87F	63	$.01	$.06
Lopez, Javier	93FUL	9	$.10	$1.00
Lovelace, Vance	89F	651	$.05	$.20
Lovullo, Torey	89F	648	$.05	$.25
Lowenstein, John	81F	186	$.01	$.06
Lowenstein, John	82F	169	$.01	$.06
Lowenstein, John	83F	63	$.01	$.06
Lowenstein, John	84F	10	$.01	$.08
Lowenstein, John	85F	180	$.01	$.06
Lowry, Dwight	87F	157	$.01	$.06
Loynd, Mike	87FU	67	$.01	$.06
Loynd, Mike	88F	472	$.01	$.05
Lozado, Willie	85F	644	$.05	$.06
Lubratich, Steve	84F	524	$.01	$.08
Lucas, Gary	81F	502	$.01	$.06
Lucas, Gary	82F	577	$.01	$.06
Lucas, Gary	83F	366	$.01	$.06
Lucas, Gary	84F	306	$.01	$.08
Lucas, Gary	84FU	73	$.10	$.50
Lucas, Gary	85F	403	$.01	$.06
Lucas, Gary	86F	254	$.01	$.06
Lucas, Gary	87F	87	$.01	$.06
Lucas, Gary	88F	495	$.01	$.05
Luecken, Rick	90F	113	$.01	$.10
Lugo, Urbano	85FU	74	$.01	$.10
Lugo, Urbano	86F	162	$.01	$.06
Lum, Mike	81F	258	$.01	$.06
Lum, Mike	82F	599	$.01	$.06
Lusader, Scott	88F	62	$.01	$.15
Luzinski, Greg	81F	10	$.01	$.10
Luzinski, Greg	82F	352	$.01	$.10
Luzinski, Greg	83F	247	$.01	$.10
Luzinski, Greg	84F	69	$.01	$.08
Luzinski, Greg	85F	521	$.01	$.06
Lyle, Sparky	81F	17	$.01	$.10
Lyle, Sparky	82F	247	$.01	$.10
Lynch, Ed	82F	531	$.01	$.06
Lynch, Ed	83F	549	$.01	$.06
Lynch, Ed	84F	591	$.01	$.08
Lynch, Ed	85F	87	$.01	$.06
Lynch, Ed	86F	88	$.01	$.06
Lynch, Ed	87F	567	$.01	$.06
Lynch, Ed	88F	422	$.01	$.05
Lynn, Fred	81F	223	$.05	$.25
Lynn, Fred	82F	468	$.05	$.20
Lynn, Fred	82F	642	$.01	$.06
Lynn, Fred	83F	97	$.05	$.20
Lynn, Fred	84F	525	$.05	$.20
Lynn, Fred	84F	626	$.01	$.10
Lynn, Fred	85F	307	$.05	$.20
Lynn, Fred	85FU	75	$.05	$.25
Lynn, Fred	86F	278	$.05	$.20
Lynn, Fred	87F	474	$.05	$.20
Lynn, Fred	88F	566	$.01	$.10
Lynn, Fred	89F	138	$.01	$.04
Lynn, Fred	90F	609	$.01	$.04
Lynn, Fred	91F	536	$.01	$.04
Lyons, Barry	88F	140	$.01	$.10
Lyons, Barry	89FU	101	$.01	$.05
Lyons, Barry	90F	209	$.01	$.04
Lyons, Steve	85FU	76	$.01	$.10
Lyons, Steve	86F	355	$.01	$.06
Lyons, Steve	87F	502	$.01	$.06
Lyons, Steve	88F	405	$.01	$.05
Lyons, Steve	89F	502	$.01	$.04
Lyons, Steve	90F	539	$.01	$.04
Lyons, Steve	91F	127	$.01	$.04
Lyons, Steve	91FU	6	$.01	$.05
Lyons, Steve	91FUL	77	$.01	$.07
Lyons, Steve	91FULU	7	$.01	$.10
Lysander, Rick	84F	570	$.01	$.08
Lysander, Rick	85F	284	$.01	$.06
Lysander, Rick	86F	399	$.01	$.06
Maas, Kevin	90F	641	$.05	$.25
Maas, Kevin	90FU	113	$.05	$.25
Maas, Kevin	91F	672	$.01	$.10
Maas, Kevin	91FUL	238	$.01	$.20
Maas, Kevin	92F	236	$.01	$.10
Maas, Kevin	92FUL	104	$.01	$.10
Maas, Kevin	93F	652	$.01	$.10
Maas, Kevin	93FUL	243	$.01	$.10
MacDonald, Bob	91FULU	61	$.01	$.15
MacDonald, Bob	92F	335	$.01	$.04
MacDonald, Bob	93F	696	$.01	$.04
MacDonald, Bob	93FUL	289	$.01	$.10
MacFarlane (f), Mike	88FU	31	$.05	$.35
Macfarlane, Mike	89F	287	$.05	$.20
Macfarlane, Mike	90F	114	$.05	$.04
Macfarlane, Mike	91F	562	$.01	$.04
Macfarlane, Mike	91FUL	151	$.01	$.07

FLEER

Player	Year	No.	VG	EX/MT	Player	Year	No.	VG	EX/MT
Macfarlane, Mike	92F	161	$ .01	$ .04	Mahler, Rick	89FU	85	$ .01	$ .05
Macfarlane, Mike	92FUL	73	$ .01	$ .10	Mahler, Rick	90F	425	$ .01	$ .04
Macfarlane, Mike	93F	241	$ .01	$ .04	Mahler, Rick	91F	71	$ .01	$ .04
Macha, Ken	81F	167	$ .01	$ .06	Mahomes, Pat	92FU	40	$ .10	$1.00
Macha, Ken	82F	618	$ .01	$ .06	Mahomes, Pat	92FUL	398	$ .10	$ .75
Machado, Julio	90FU	37	$ .01	$ .10	Mahomes, Pat	93F	271	$ .01	$ .10
Machado, Julio	91FU	31	$ .01	$ .15	Mahomes, Pat	93FUL	234	$ .05	$ .20
Machado, Julio	92F	181	$ .01	$ .04	Maldonado, Candy	83F	212	$ .10	$ .75
Mack, Shane	88F	590	$ .10	$1.00	Maldonado, Candy	85F	376	$ .01	$ .10
Mack, Shane	91F	618	$ .01	$ .04	Maldonado, Candy	86F	136	$ .01	$ .10
Mack, Shane	91FUL	191	$ .01	$ .07	Maldonado, Candy	86FU	71	$ .01	$ .08
Mack, Shane	92F	210	$ .01	$ .04	Maldonado, Candy	87F	279	$ .01	$ .10
Mack, Shane	92FUL	95	$ .01	$ .10	Maldonado, Candy	88F	89	$ .01	$ .05
Mack, Shane	93F	640	$ .01	$ .04	Maldonado, Candy	89F	333	$ .01	$ .10
Mackanin, Pete	81F	565	$ .01	$ .06	Maldonado, Candy	90F	62	$ .01	$ .04
Mackanin, Pete	82F	556	$ .01	$ .06	Maldonado, Candy	90FU	93	$ .01	$ .05
Madden, Mike	84F	232	$ .01	$ .08	Maldonado, Candy	91F	373	$ .01	$ .04
Maddox, Elliott	81F	326	$ .01	$ .06	Maldonado, Candy	92F	336	$ .01	$ .04
Maddox, Garry	81F	19	$ .01	$ .06	Maldonado, Candy	92FUL	451	$ .01	$ .10
Maddox, Garry	82F	248	$ .01	$ .06	Maldonado, Candy	93F	338	$ .01	$ .04
Maddox, Garry	83F	164	$ .01	$ .06	Mallicoat, Rob	88F	452	$ .01	$ .10
Maddox, Garry	84F	39	$ .01	$ .08	Mallicoat, Rob	92F	440	$ .01	$ .10
Maddox, Garry	85F	259	$ .01	$ .06	Malone, Chuck	91F	404	$ .01	$ .10
Maddox, Garry	86F	445	$ .01	$ .06	Mann, Kelly	90F	642	$ .01	$ .15
Maddux, Greg	87FU	68	$1.25	$5.00	Manning, Rick	81F	403	$ .01	$ .06
Maddux, Greg	88F	423	$ .15	$1.25	Manning, Rick	82F	374	$ .01	$ .06
Maddux, Greg	89F	431	$ .05	$ .35	Manning, Rick	83F	413	$ .01	$ .06
Maddux, Greg	90F	37	$ .05	$ .20	Manning, Rick	84F	205	$ .01	$ .08
Maddux, Greg	91F	426	$ .01	$ .10	Manning, Rick	85F	586	$ .01	$ .06
Maddux, Greg	91FUL	64	$ .05	$ .25	Manning, Rick	86F	493	$ .01	$ .06
Maddux, Greg	92F	386	$ .01	$ .04	Manning, Rick	87F	349	$ .01	$ .06
Maddux, Greg	92FUL	178	$ .05	$ .35	Manning, Rick	88F	168	$ .01	$ .05
Maddux, Greg	93F	380	$ .01	$ .10	Manon, Ramon	90FU	124	$ .01	$ .10
Maddux, Greg	93F	707	$ .01	$ .10	Manrique, Fred	87FU	72	$ .01	$ .10
Maddux, Mike	87F	179	$ .01	$ .06	Manrique, Fred	88F	406	$ .01	$ .15
Maddux, Mike	88F	309	$ .01	$ .05	Manrique, Fred	89F	503	$ .01	$ .04
Maddux, Mike	89F	576	$ .01	$ .04	Manrique, Fred	90F	306	$ .01	$ .04
Maddux, Mike	91FULU	113	$ .01	$ .10	Manto, Jeff	89FU	13	$ .01	$ .15
Maddux, Mike	92F	613	$ .01	$ .04	Manto, Jeff	90F	137	$ .01	$ .10
Maddux, Mike	92FUL	281	$ .01	$ .10	Manto, Jeff	90FU	94	$ .01	$ .05
Maddux, Mike	93F	142	$ .01	$ .04	Manuel, Jerry	82F	195	$ .01	$ .06
Madlock, Bill	81F	381	$ .05	$ .20	Manwaring, Kirt	88F	651	$ .10	$ .50
Madlock, Bill	82F	485	$ .01	$ .10	Manwaring, Kirt	89F	334	$ .01	$ .04
Madlock, Bill	83F	309	$ .01	$ .10	Manwaring, Kirt	90F	63	$ .01	$ .04
Madlock, Bill	84F	253	$ .01	$ .10	Manwaring, Kirt	92F	641	$ .01	$ .04
Madlock, Bill	85F	468	$ .01	$ .10	Manwaring, Kirt	92FUL	293	$ .01	$ .10
Madlock, Bill	86F	135	$ .01	$ .10	Manwaring, Kirt	93F	158	$ .01	$ .04
Madlock, Bill	87F	445	$ .01	$ .10	Manwaring, Kirt	93FUL	135	$ .01	$ .10
Madlock, Bill	87FU	69	$ .01	$ .06	Marsh, Tom	93F	494	$ .01	$ .04
Madlock, Bill	88F	63	$ .01	$ .10	Marshall, Mike	82F	13	$ .05	$ .20
Magadan, Dave	87F	648	$ .10	$ .75	Marshall, Mike	82F	532	$ .01	$ .06
Magadan, Dave	87FU	70	$ .05	$ .20	Marshall, Mike	83F	211	$ .05	$ .20
Magadan, Dave	88F	141	$ .01	$ .15	Marshall, Mike	84F	105	$ .05	$ .20
Magadan, Dave	89F	41	$ .01	$ .04	Marshall, Mike	85F	377	$ .01	$ .10
Magadan, Dave	90F	210	$ .01	$ .04	Marshall, Mike	86F	137	$ .01	$ .10
Magadan, Dave	91F	153	$ .01	$ .04	Marshall, Mike	87F	446	$ .01	$ .10
Magadan, Dave	91FUL	223	$ .01	$ .07	Marshall, Mike	88F	522	$ .01	$ .05
Magadan, Dave	92F	510	$ .01	$ .04	Marshall, Mike	89F	66	$ .01	$ .04
Magadan, Dave	92FUL	236	$ .01	$ .10	Marshall, Mike	90F	401	$ .01	$ .04
Magadan, Dave	93F	477	$ .01	$ .04	Marshall, Mike	91F	102	$ .01	$ .04
Magnante, Mike	93F	620	$ .01	$ .04	Marshall, Mike	91FUL	35	$ .01	$ .07
Magrane, Joe	87FU	71	$ .01	$ .15	Martin, Albert	92FU	114	$ .75	$3.00
Magrane, Joe	88F	40	$ .05	$ .20	Martin, Billy	81F	581	$ .01	$ .15
Magrane, Joe	89F	455	$ .01	$ .15	Martin, Jerry	81F	295	$ .01	$ .06
Magrane, Joe	90F	252	$ .01	$ .04	Martin, Jerry	82F	394	$ .01	$ .06
Magrane, Joe	91F	638	$ .01	$ .04	Martin, Jerry	83F	117	$ .01	$ .06
Magrane, Joe	91FUL	291	$ .01	$ .07	Martin, Jerry	84FU	74	$ .10	$ .50
Mahler, Mickey	85FU	77	$ .01	$ .10	Martin, John	82F	121	$ .01	$ .06
Mahler, Mickey	86FU	70	$ .01	$ .08	Martin, Renie	81F	39	$ .01	$ .06
Mahler, Rick	82F	440	$ .01	$ .15	Martin, Renie	82F	414	$ .01	$ .06
Mahler, Rick	83F	141	$ .01	$ .06	Martin, Renie	83F	267	$ .01	$ .06
Mahler, Rick	85F	332	$ .01	$ .06	Martin, Renie	84F	381	$ .01	$ .08
Mahler, Rick	86F	521	$ .01	$ .06	Martinez, Alfredo	81F	288	$ .01	$ .06
Mahler, Rick	87F	520	$ .01	$ .06	Martinez, Buck	81F	526	$ .01	$ .06
Mahler, Rick	89F	595	$ .01	$ .04	Martinez, Buck	83F	433	$ .01	$ .06

FLEER

Player	Year	No.	VG	EX/MT	Player	Year	No.	VG	EX/MT
Martinez, Buck	84F	161	$.01	$.08	Martinez, Tino	90FU	119	$.05	$.20
Martinez, Buck	85F	114	$.01	$.06	Martinez, Tino	91F	458	$.01	$.15
Martinez, Buck	86F	66	$.01	$.06	Martinez, Tino	91FUL	341	$.05	$.25
Martinez, Buck	87F	235	$.01	$.06	Martinez, Tino	92F	287	$.01	$.10
Martinez, Carlos	90F	540	$.01	$.10	Martinez, Tino	92FUL	127	$.01	$.10
Martinez, Carlos	91F	128	$.01	$.04	Martinez, Tippy	81F	179	$.01	$.06
Martinez, Carlos	92F	117	$.01	$.04	Martinez, Tippy	82F	171	$.01	$.06
Martinez, Carlos	92FUL	52	$.01	$.10	Martinez, Tippy	83F	65	$.01	$.06
Martinez, Carlos	93F	595	$.01	$.04	Martinez, Tippy	84F	12	$.01	$.08
Martinez, Carlos	93FUL	188	$.01	$.10	Martinez, Tippy	84F	635	$.01	$.08
Martinez, Carmelo	84F	497	$.05	$.25	Martinez, Tippy	85F	182	$.01	$.06
Martinez, Carmelo	84FU	75	$.10	$.50	Martinez, Tippy	86F	279	$.01	$.06
Martinez, Carmelo	85F	40	$.01	$.06	Martz, Randy	81F	300	$.01	$.06
Martinez, Carmelo	86F	329	$.01	$.06	Martz, Randy	82F	600	$.01	$.06
Martinez, Carmelo	87F	423	$.01	$.06	Martz, Randy	83F	501	$.01	$.06
Martinez, Carmelo	88F	591	$.01	$.05	Marzano, John	88F	357	$.05	$.20
Martinez, Carmelo	89F	311	$.01	$.04	Marzano, John	91F	103	$.01	$.04
Martinez, Carmelo	90F	162	$.01	$.04	Marzano, John	92FUL	316	$.01	$.10
Martinez, Carmelo	90FU	44	$.01	$.05	Mason, Mike	84FU	76	$.10	$.50
Martinez, Carmelo	91F	44	$.01	$.04	Mason, Mike	85F	562	$.01	$.06
Martinez, Chito	91FULU	2	$.10	$.40	Mason, Mike	86F	565	$.01	$.06
Martinez, Chito	92F	13	$.01	$.10	Mason, Mike	87F	129	$.01	$.06
Martinez, Chito	92FUL	7	$.01	$.10	Mason, Mike	87FU	73	$.01	$.06
Martinez, Chito	93F	545	$.01	$.04	Mason, Roger	86FU	72	$.01	$.15
Martinez, Chito	93FUL	141	$.01	$.10	Mason, Roger	87F	280	$.01	$.06
Martinez, Dave	88F	424	$.01	$.15	Mason, Roger	92FUL	115	$.05	$.25
Martinez, Dave	89F	384	$.01	$.04	Mason, Roger	92FUL	554	$.01	$.10
Martinez, Dave	90F	353	$.01	$.04	Mason, Roger	93F	116	$.01	$.04
Martinez, Dave	91F	237	$.01	$.04	Mata, Vic	85F	644	$.01	$.06
Martinez, Dave	91FUL	205	$.01	$.07	Mathews, Greg	86FU	73	$.01	$.15
Martinez, Dave	92F	485	$.01	$.04	Mathews, Greg	87F	303	$.01	$.10
Martinez, Dave	92FUL	484	$.01	$.10	Mathews, Greg	88F	41	$.01	$.10
Martinez, Dave	93F	395	$.01	$.04	Mathews, Greg	89F	456	$.01	$.04
Martinez, Dennis	81F	180	$.05	$.25	Mathews, Greg	93F	495	$.01	$.04
Martinez, Dennis	82F	170	$.01	$.15	Mathews, Terry	92F	310	$.01	$.10
Martinez, Dennis	83F	64	$.01	$.06	Mathews, Terry	92FUL	135	$.01	$.10
Martinez, Dennis	84F	11	$.01	$.08	Mathews, Terry	93F	684	$.01	$.04
Martinez, Dennis	85F	181	$.01	$.06					
Martinez, Dennis	86F	280	$.01	$.06					
Martinez, Dennis	87F	324	$.01	$.06					
Martinez, Dennis	88F	188	$.01	$.05					
Martinez, Dennis	89F	385	$.01	$.04					
Martinez, Dennis	90F	354	$.01	$.04					
Martinez, Dennis	91F	238	$.01	$.04					
Martinez, Dennis	91FUL	206	$.01	$.07					
Martinez, Dennis	92F	486	$.01	$.04					
Martinez, Dennis	92FLL	695	$.01	$.04					
Martinez, Dennis	92FRS	683	$.01	$.04					
Martinez, Dennis	92FUL	223	$.01	$.10					
Martinez, Dennis	93F	462	$.01	$.04					
Martinez, Edgar	88F	378	$.75	$3.00					
Martinez, Edgar	89F	552	$.05	$.35					
Martinez, Edgar	90F	520	$.05	$.20					
Martinez, Edgar	91F	457	$.01	$.04					
Martinez, Edgar	91FUL	340	$.01	$.15					
Martinez, Edgar	92F	286	$.01	$.04					
Martinez, Edgar	92FUL	126	$.01	$.10					
Martinez, Edgar	93F	309	$.01	$.10					
Martinez, Edgar	93F	344	$.01	$.04					
Martinez, Edgar	93F	716	$.01	$.10					
Martinez, Edgar	93FUL	270	$.01	$.10					
Martinez, Pedro	93F	354	$.01	$.15					
Martinez, Pedro	93FUL	57	$.05	$.25					
Martinez, Ramon	89F	67	$.10	$.50					
Martinez, Ramon	90F	402	$.05	$.20					
Martinez, Ramon	91F	212	$.01	$.15					
Martinez, Ramon	91FUL	164	$.01	$.10					
Martinez, Ramon	92F	463	$.01	$.10					
Martinez, Ramon	92F	706	$.01	$.04					
Martinez, Ramon	92FUL	213	$.01	$.10	Mathis, Ron	85FU	78	$.01	$.10
Martinez, Ramon	93F	65	$.01	$.04	Mathis, Ron	86F	305	$.01	$.06
Martinez, Ramon	93F	354	$.05	$.15	Matlack, Jon	81F	621	$.01	$.06
Martinez, Silvio	81F	546	$.01	$.06	Matlack, Jon	82F	323	$.01	$.06
Martinez, Silvio	82F	122	$.01	$.06	Matlack, Jon	83F	572	$.01	$.06
Martinez, Tilno	93F	310	$.01	$.04	Matlack, Jon	84F	422	$.01	$.08

FLEER

Player	Year	No.	VG	EX/MT
Matthews, Gary	81F	251	$.01	$.10
Matthews, Gary	82F	249	$.01	$.06
Matthews, Gary	83F	165	$.01	$.06
Matthews, Gary	84F	40	$.01	$.08
Matthews, Gary	84FU	77	$.10	$.50
Matthews, Gary	85F	61	$.01	$.06
Matthews, Gary	86F	373	$.01	$.06
Matthews, Gary	87F	568	$.01	$.06
Mattick, Bob	81F	431	$.01	$.06
Mattingly, Don	84F	131	$6.00	$24.00
Mattingly, Don	85F	133	$1.50	$6.00
Mattingly, Don	86F	109	$.20	$2.00
Mattingly, Don	86F	627	$.10	$1.00
Mattingly, Don	86F	639	$.10	$1.00
Mattingly, Don	87F	104	$.15	$1.25
Mattingly, Don	87F	638	$.10	$.75
Mattingly, Don	88F	214	$.10	$.50
Mattingly, Don	89F	258	$.05	$.25
Mattingly, Don	90F	447	$.01	$.15
Mattingly, Don	90F	638	$.01	$.10
Mattingly, Don	90FPD	626	$.01	$.15
Mattingly, Don	91F	673	$.01	$.10
Mattingly, Don	91FUL	239	$.05	$.25
Mattingly, Don	92F	237	$.01	$.15
Mattingly, Don	92FUL	105	$.10	$.50
Mattingly, Don	93F	281	$.01	$.10
Mattingly, Don	93FUL	244	$.05	$.35
Matula, Rick	81F	263	$.01	$.06
Matuszek, Len	84F	41	$.01	$.08
Matuszek, Len	85F	260	$.01	$.06

Player	Year	No.	VG	EX/MT
Matuszek, Len	85FU	79	$.01	$.10
Matuszek, Len	86F	138	$.01	$.06
Matuszek, Len	87F	447	$.01	$.06
Maurer, Rob	92F	659	$.01	$.15
May, Derrick	90F	645	$.05	$.35
May, Derrick	91F	427	$.05	$.20
May, Derrick	91FUL	65	$.05	$.25
May, Derrick	92F	387	$.01	$.10
May, Derrick	93F	21	$.01	$.04
May, Derrick	93FUL	19	$.01	$.10
May, Lee	81F	183	$.01	$.06
May, Lee	82F	415	$.01	$.06
May, Lee	83F	118	$.01	$.06

Player	Year	No.	VG	EX/MT
May, Milt	81F	442	$.01	$.06
May, Milt	82F	395	$.01	$.06
May, Milt	83F	268	$.01	$.06
May, Milt	84F	254	$.01	$.08
May, Rudy	81F	90	$.01	$.06
May, Rudy	82F	41	$.01	$.06
May, Rudy	83F	385	$.01	$.06
Mayberry, John	81F	416	$.01	$.06
Mayberry, John	82F	619	$.01	$.06
Mayberry, John	83F	386	$.01	$.06
Mayne, Brent	91FU	28	$.01	$.15
Mayne, Brent	91FUL	150	$.01	$.10
Mayne, Brent	92F	162	$.01	$.04
Mayne, Brent	92FUL	74	$.01	$.10
Mayne, Brent	93F	621	$.01	$.04
Mayne, Brent	93FUL	212	$.01	$.10
Mazzilli, Lee	81F	316	$.01	$.06
Mazzilli, Lee	82F	533	$.01	$.06
Mazzilli, Lee	83F	387	$.01	$.06
Mazzilli, Lee	84F	255	$.01	$.08
Mazzilli, Lee	85F	469	$.01	$.06
Mazzilli, Lee	86F	612	$.01	$.06
Mazzilli, Lee	87F	15	$.01	$.06
Mazzilli, Lee	90F	88	$.01	$.04
McBride, Bake	81F	9	$.01	$.06
McBride, Bake	82F	250	$.01	$.06
McBride, Bake	83F	414	$.01	$.06
McBride, Bake	84F	547	$.01	$.08
McCament, Randy	90F	64	$.01	$.10
McCarthy, Tom	90F	541	$.01	$.04
McCarver, Tim	81F	27	$.01	$.15
McCaskill, Kirk	86F	163	$.05	$.25
McCaskill, Kirk	87F	88	$.01	$.06
McCaskill, Kirk	88F	496	$.01	$.05
McCaskill, Kirk	89F	483	$.01	$.04
McCaskill, Kirk	90F	138	$.01	$.04
McCaskill, Kirk	91F	319	$.01	$.04
McCaskill, Kirk	91FUL	50	$.01	$.07
McCaskill, Kirk	92F	64	$.01	$.04
McCaskill, Kirk	92FUL	338	$.01	$.10
McCaskill, Kirk	93F	206	$.01	$.04
McCatty, Steve	81F	589	$.01	$.06
McCatty, Steve	82F	99	$.01	$.06
McCatty, Steve	83F	525	$.01	$.04
McCatty, Steve	84F	454	$.01	$.04
McCatty, Steve	85F	430	$.01	$.04
McCatty, Steve	86F	427	$.01	$.04
McClellan, Paul	92F	642	$.01	$.04
McClendon, Lloyd	87FU	74	$.01	$.1
McClendon, Lloyd	89FU	77	$.01	$.1
McClendon, Lloyd	90F	38	$.01	$.04
McClendon, Lloyd	91FU	111	$.01	$.04
McClendon, Lloyd	92F	560	$.01	$.04
McClendon, Lloyd	92FUL	256	$.01	$.1
McClendon, Lloyd	93F	502	$.01	$.04
McClendon, Lloyd	93FUL	99	$.01	$.1
McClure, Bob	81F	520	$.01	$.04
McClure, Bob	83F	38	$.01	$.04
McClure, Bob	84F	206	$.01	$.04
McClure, Bob	85F	587	$.01	$.04
McClure, Bob	86F	494	$.01	$.04
McClure, Bob	87F	325	$.01	$.04
McClure, Bob	88F	189	$.01	$.04
McClure, Bob	89F	42	$.01	$.04
McClure, Bob	89FU	14	$.01	$.1
McClure, Bob	90F	139	$.01	$.04
McClure, Bob	93F	128	$.01	$.04
McCovey, Willie	81F	434	$.10	$1.00
McCullers, Lance	86F	330	$.05	$.25
McCullers, Lance	87F	424	$.01	$.04
McCullers, Lance	88F	592	$.01	$.04
McCullers, Lance	89F	312	$.01	$.04
McCullers, Lance	90F	448	$.01	$.04
McCullers, Lance	91F	342	$.01	$.04
McDaniel, Terry	92F	511	$.01	$.

FLEER

Player	Year	No.	VG	EX/MT	Player	Year	No.	VG	EX/MT
McDonald, Ben	90F	180	$ .10	$ .50	McGraw, Tug	85F	261	$ .01	$ .10
McDonald, Ben	91F	481	$ .01	$ .15	McGregor, Scott	81F	174	$ .01	$ .06
McDonald, Ben	91FUL	19	$ .01	$ .15	McGregor, Scott	82F	172	$ .01	$ .06
McDonald, Ben	92F	14	$ .01	$ .10	McGregor, Scott	83F	66	$ .01	$ .06
McDonald, Ben	92FUL	303	$ .05	$ .20	McGregor, Scott	84F	13	$ .01	$ .08
McDonald, Ben	93F	169	$ .01	$ .04	McGregor, Scott	84F	646	$ .01	$ .08
McDonald, Ben	93FUL	142	$ .01	$ .15	McGregor, Scott	85F	183	$ .01	$ .06
McDowell, Jack	88F	407	$ .75	$3.00	McGregor, Scott	86F	281	$ .01	$ .06
McDowell, Jack	89F	504	$ .05	$ .25	McGregor, Scott	87F	475	$ .01	$ .06
McDowell, Jack	91F	129	$ .01	$ .10	McGriff, Fred	87FU	75	$ .75	$3.00
McDowell, Jack	91FUL	78	$ .05	$ .20	McGriff, Fred	88F	118	$ .15	$1.50
McDowell, Jack	92F	89	$ .01	$ .04	McGriff, Fred	89F	240	$ .05	$ .20
McDowell, Jack	92FUL	40	$ .05	$ .25	McGriff, Fred	90F	89	$ .01	$ .15
McDowell, Jack	93F	207	$ .01	$ .10	McGriff, Fred	91F	180	$ .01	$ .10
McDowell, Jack	93FUL	176	$ .01	$ .15	McGriff, Fred	91FU	125	$ .01	$ .10
McDowell, Oddibe	85FU	80	$ .05	$ .25	McGriff, Fred	91FUL	308	$ .05	$ .20
McDowell, Oddibe	86F	566	$ .05	$ .20	McGriff, Fred	92F	614	$ .01	$ .10
McDowell, Oddibe	87F	130	$ .01	$ .10	McGriff, Fred	92FUL	282	$ .05	$ .35
McDowell, Oddibe	88F	473	$ .01	$ .10	McGriff, Fred	93F	143	$ .01	$ .10
McDowell, Oddibe	89F	528	$ .01	$ .04	McGriff, Fred	93F	349	$ .01	$ .10
McDowell, Oddibe	90F	589	$ .01	$ .04	McGriff, Fred	93FUL	119	$ .05	$ .25
McDowell, Oddibe	91F	697	$ .01	$ .04	McGriff, Terry	88F	240	$ .01	$ .10
McDowell, Oddibe	91FUL	8	$ .01	$ .07	McGuire, Bill	89F	553	$ .01	$ .04
McDowell, Roger	85FU	81	$ .05	$ .35	McGwire, Mark	87FU	76	$1.25	$5.00
McDowell, Roger	86F	89	$ .05	$ .30	McGwire, Mark	88F	286	$ .20	$2.00
McDowell, Roger	87F	16	$ .01	$ .10	McGwire, Mark	88F	624	$ .10	$1.00
McDowell, Roger	88F	142	$ .01	$ .10	McGwire, Mark	88F	629	$ .10	$ .40
McDowell, Roger	89F	43	$ .01	$ .04	McGwire, Mark	88F	633	$ .05	$ .25
McDowell, Roger	89FU	110	$ .01	$ .05	McGwire, Mark	89F	17	$ .10	$ .40
McDowell, Roger	90F	567	$ .01	$ .04	McGwire, Mark	89F	634	$ .05	$ .25
McDowell, Roger	91F	405	$ .01	$ .04	McGwire, Mark	90F	15	$ .05	$ .25
McDowell, Roger	91FUL	267	$ .01	$ .07	McGwire, Mark	90F	638	$ .01	$ .10
McDowell, Roger	92F	464	$ .01	$ .04	McGwire, Mark	91F	17	$ .05	$ .25
McDowell, Roger	92FUL	214	$ .01	$ .10	McGwire, Mark	91FUL	251	$ .10	$ .50
McDowell, Roger	93F	451	$ .01	$ .04	McGwire, Mark	92F	262	$ .05	$ .20
McDowell, Roger	93FUL	58	$ .01	$ .10	McGwire, Mark	92FUL	115	$ .10	$1.00
McElroy, Chuck	90F	650	$ .05	$ .35	McGwire, Mark	93F	296	$ .05	$ .20
McElroy, Chuck	91F	406	$ .01	$ .10	McGwire, Mark	93F	710	$ .01	$ .10
McElroy, Chuck	91FU	79	$ .01	$ .05	McIntosh, Tim	90F	329	$ .01	$ .15
McElroy, Chuck	91FULU	71	$ .01	$ .10	McIntosh, Tim	91F	589	$ .01	$ .10
McElroy, Chuck	92F	388	$ .01	$ .04	McIntosh, Tim	91FUL	177	$ .01	$ .07
McElroy, Chuck	92FUL	470	$ .01	$ .10	McIntosh, Tim	92FUL	386	$ .01	$ .10
McElroy, Chuck	93F	22	$ .01	$ .04	McKay, Dave	81F	592	$ .01	$ .06
McElroy, Chuck	93FUL	20	$ .01	$ .10	McKay, Dave	82F	100	$ .01	$ .06
McGaffigan, Andy	84F	382	$ .01	$ .08	McKay, Dave	83F	526	$ .01	$ .06
McGaffigan, Andy	84FU	78	$ .10	$ .50	McKeon, Joel	86FU	75	$ .01	$ .08
McGaffigan, Andy	85F	540	$ .01	$ .06	McKeon, Joel	87F	503	$ .01	$ .10
McGaffigan, Andy	86F	181	$ .01	$ .06	McLaughlin, Joey	81F	420	$ .01	$ .06
McGaffigan, Andy	86FU	74	$ .01	$ .08	McLaughlin, Joey	82F	620	$ .01	$ .06
McGaffigan, Andy	87F	326	$ .01	$ .06	McLaughlin, Joey	83F	434	$ .01	$ .06
McGaffigan, Andy	88F	190	$ .01	$ .05	McLaughlin, Joey	84F	162	$ .01	$ .08
McGaffigan, Andy	89F	386	$ .01	$ .04	McLaughlin, Joey	84FU	79	$ .10	$ .50
McGaffigan, Andy	90F	355	$ .01	$ .04	McLemore, Mark	86F	650	$ .05	$ .20
McGee, Willie	83F	15	$ .25	$2.50	McLemore, Mark	87FU	77	$ .01	$ .06
McGee, Willie	84F	329	$ .10	$ .75	McLemore, Mark	88F	497	$ .01	$ .05
McGee, Willie	85F	234	$ .05	$ .30	McLemore, Mark	89F	484	$ .01	$ .04
McGee, Willie	86F	42	$ .05	$ .25	McLemore, Mark	92FUL	304	$ .01	$ .10
McGee, Willie	86F	636	$ .05	$ .35	McLemore, Mark	93F	546	$ .01	$ .04
McGee, Willie	87F	304	$ .01	$ .15	McMurtry, Craig	84F	184	$ .01	$ .08
McGee, Willie	88F	42	$ .01	$ .10	McMurtry, Craig	85F	333	$ .01	$ .06
McGee, Willie	89F	457	$ .01	$ .04	McNamara, Jim	92FUL	592	$ .05	$ .20
McGee, Willie	90F	253	$ .01	$ .04	McRae, Brian	91F	563	$ .05	$ .25
McGee, Willie	91F	16	$ .01	$ .04	McRae, Brian	91FUL	152	$ .10	$ .50
McGee, Willie	91FUL	130	$ .01	$ .05	McRae, Brian	92F	163	$ .01	$ .10
McGee, Willie	91FUL	325	$ .01	$ .07	McRae, Brian	92FUL	75	$ .05	$ .20
McGee, Willie	91FULU	118	$ .01	$ .10	McRae, Brian	93F	242	$ .01	$ .04
McGee, Willie	92F	643	$ .01	$ .04	McRae, Brian	93FUL	213	$ .01	$ .10
McGee, Willie	92FUL	294	$ .05	$ .20	McRae, Hal	81F	41	$ .01	$ .10
McGee, Willie	93F	159	$ .04	$ .04	McRae, Hal	82F	416	$ .01	$ .10
McGlothen, Lynn	81F	302	$ .01	$ .06	McRae, Hal	83F	119	$ .01	$ .10
McGraw, Tug	81F	7	$ .01	$ .06	McRae, Hal	84F	350	$ .01	$ .10
McGraw, Tug	81F	657	$ .05	$ .25	McRae, Hal	85F	207	$ .01	$ .06
McGraw, Tug	82F	251	$ .01	$ .10	McRae, Hal	86F	14	$ .01	$ .06
McGraw, Tug	83F	166	$ .01	$ .10	McRae, Hal	87F	375	$ .01	$ .06
McGraw, Tug	84F	42	$ .05	$ .20	McReynolds, Kevin	84F	307	$ .20	$2.00

FLEER

Player	Year	No.	VG	EX/MT	Player	Year	No.	VG	EX/MT
McReynolds, Kevin	85F	41	$ .05	$ .25	Mesa, Jose	91FU	3	$ .01	$ .05
McReynolds, Kevin	86F	331	$ .05	$ .20	Mesa, Jose	92F	17	$ .01	$ .04
McReynolds, Kevin	87F	425	$ .01	$ .10	Mesa, Jose	92FUL	305	$ .01	$ .10
McReynolds, Kevin	87FU	78	$ .01	$ .15	Mesa, Jose	93F	596	$ .01	$ .04
McReynolds, Kevin	88F	143	$ .01	$ .10	Meulens, Hensley	89FU	51	$ .05	$ .20
McReynolds, Kevin	89F	44	$ .01	$ .10	Meulens, Hensley	90F	449	$ .01	$ .10
McReynolds, Kevin	90F	211	$ .01	$ .10	Meulens, Hensley	91FU	47	$ .01	$ .05
McReynolds, Kevin	91F	154	$ .01	$ .04	Meulens, Hensley	91FUL	240	$ .01	$ .07
McReynolds, Kevin	91FUL	224	$ .01	$ .07	Meulens, Hensley	92F	238	$ .01	$ .04
McReynolds, Kevin	92F	512	$ .01	$ .04	Meulens, Hensley	92FUL	106	$ .01	$ .10
McReynolds, Kevin	92FU	29	$ .05	$ .25	Meulens, Hensley	93FUL	245	$ .01	$ .10
McReynolds, Kevin	92FUL	374	$ .01	$ .10	Meyer, Brian	90F	232	$ .01	$ .04
McReynolds, Kevin	93F	622	$ .01	$ .04	Meyer, Brian	91F	510	$ .01	$ .04
McReynolds, Kevin	93FUL	214	$ .01	$ .10	Meyer, Dan	81F	603	$ .01	$ .06
McWilliams, Larry	81F	267	$ .01	$ .06	Meyer, Dan	82F	512	$ .01	$ .06
McWilliams, Larry	83F	310	$ .01	$ .06	Meyer, Dan	83F	527	$ .01	$ .06
McWilliams, Larry	84F	256	$ .01	$ .08	Meyer, Dan	84F	455	$ .01	$ .08
McWilliams, Larry	85F	470	$ .01	$ .06	Meyer, Joey	88F	645	$ .10	$ .40
McWilliams, Larry	86F	613	$ .01	$ .06	Meyer, Joey	88FU	40	$ .01	$ .10
McWilliams, Larry	87F	613	$ .01	$ .06	Meyer, Joey	89F	191	$ .01	$ .10
McWilliams, Larry	89F	458	$ .01	$ .04	Mielke, Gary	90FU	125	$ .01	$ .10
Meacham, Bobby	85F	134	$ .01	$ .06	Mielke, Gary	91F	293	$ .01	$ .04
Meacham, Bobby	86F	110	$ .01	$ .06	Milacki, Bob	89F	649	$ .01	$ .15
Meacham, Bobby	87F	105	$ .01	$ .06	Milacki, Bob	89FU	6	$ .01	$ .15
Meacham, Bobby	88F	215	$ .01	$ .05	Milacki, Bob	90F	182	$ .01	$ .04
Meacham, Rusty	92FU	30	$ .05	$ .25	Milacki, Bob	91F	483	$ .01	$ .04
Meacham, Rusty	93F	243	$ .01	$ .04	Milacki, Bob	92F	18	$ .01	$ .04
Meacham, Rusty	93FUL	215	$ .01	$ .10	Milacki, Bob	92FUL	306	$ .01	$ .10
Meadows, Louie	88FU	92	$ .01	$ .10	Milacki, Bob	93F	548	$ .01	$ .04
Meadows, Louie	89F	361	$ .01	$ .10	Milbourne, Larry	81F	611	$ .01	$ .06
Meads, Dave	87FU	79	$ .01	$ .06	Milbourne, Larry	82F	42	$ .01	$ .06
Meads, Dave	88F	453	$ .01	$ .05	Milbourne, Larry	83F	415	$ .01	$ .06
Meads, Dave	89F	362	$ .01	$ .04	Milbourne, Larry	85F	493	$ .01	$ .06
Medich, Doc	81F	627	$ .01	$ .06	Militello, Sam	92FU	43	$ .10	$1.00
Medich, Doc	82F	324	$ .01	$ .06	Militello, Sam	93F	282	$ .01	$ .10
Medich, Doc	83F	39	$ .01	$ .06	Militello, Sam	93FUL	246	$ .10	$ .75
Medina, Luis	89F	411	$ .01	$ .10	Miller, Darrell	88F	498	$ .01	$ .05
Meier, Dave	85F	285	$ .01	$ .06	Miller, Dyar	82F	534	$ .01	$ .06
Meier, Dave	86F	400	$ .01	$ .06	Miller, Ed	82F	441	$ .01	$ .06
Mejias, Sam	81F	219	$ .01	$ .06	Miller, Keith	88F	144	$ .05	$ .25
Mejias, Sam	82F	75	$ .01	$ .06	Miller, Keith	89F	45	$ .01	$ .04
Melendez, Jose	92F	615	$ .01	$ .10	Miller, Keith	91F	155	$ .01	$ .04
Melendez, Jose	92FUL	578	$ .05	$ .20	Miller, Keith	91FUL	225	$ .01	$ .07
Melendez, Jose	93F	144	$ .01	$ .04	Miller, Keith	92F	513	$ .01	$ .04
Melvin, Bob	87F	281	$ .01	$ .06	Miller, Keith	92FU	31	$ .05	$ .25
Melvin, Bob	88F	91	$ .01	$ .05	Miller, Keith	92FUL	375	$ .01	$ .10
Melvin, Bob	89F	335	$ .01	$ .04	Miller, Keith	93F	244	$ .01	$ .04
Melvin, Bob	90F	181	$ .01	$ .04	Miller, Paul	92FUL	555	$ .05	$ .20
Melvin, Bob	91F	482	$ .01	$ .04	Miller, Rick	81F	279	$ .01	$ .06
Melvin, Bob	91FULU	3	$ .01	$ .10	Miller, Rick	82F	299	$ .01	$ .06
Melvin, Bob	92F	15	$ .01	$ .04	Miller, Rick	83F	188	$ .01	$ .06
Mendoza, Mario	81F	613	$ .01	$ .06	Miller, Rick	84F	403	$ .01	$ .08
Mendoza, Mario	82F	325	$ .01	$ .06	Miller, Rick	85F	163	$ .01	$ .06
Mercado, Orlando	84F	613	$ .01	$ .08	Milligan, Randy	88FU	115	$ .05	$ .35
Merced, Orlando	91FU	112	$ .05	$ .20	Milligan, Randy	89FU	7	$ .01	$ .05
Merced, Orlando	91FUL	284	$ .10	$ .40	Milligan, Randy	90F	183	$ .01	$ .04
Merced, Orlando	92F	561	$ .01	$ .15	Milligan, Randy	91F	484	$ .01	$ .04
Merced, Orlando	92FUL	257	$ .05	$ .25	Milligan, Randy	91FUL	20	$ .01	$ .07
Merced, Orlando	93F	117	$ .01	$ .04	Milligan, Randy	92F	19	$ .01	$ .04
Merced, Orlando	93FUL	100	$ .01	$ .10	Milligan, Randy	92FUL	8	$ .01	$ .10
Mercedes, Henry	92FUL	424	$ .05	$ .25	Milligan, Randy	93F	170	$ .01	$ .04
Mercedes, Luis	92F	16	$ .01	$ .10	Mills, Alan	90FU	114	$ .01	$ .10
Mercedes, Luis	93F	547	$ .01	$ .04	Mills, Alan	92FU	2	$ .05	$ .25
Mercker, Kent	90F	590	$ .01	$ .15	Mills, Alan	93F	171	$ .01	$ .04
Mercker, Kent	91FU	74	$ .01	$ .05	Mills, Alan	93FUL	143	$ .01	$ .10
Mercker, Kent	91FULU	68	$ .01	$ .10	Mills, Brad	82F	196	$ .01	$ .06
Mercker, Kent	92F	363	$ .01	$ .04	Mills, Brad	83F	288	$ .01	$ .06
Mercker, Kent	92F	700	$ .01	$ .10	Milner, Eddie	83F	597	$ .01	$ .10
Mercker, Kent	92FUL	460	$ .01	$ .10	Milner, Eddie	84F	474	$ .01	$ .08
Mercker, Kent	93F	8	$ .01	$ .04	Milner, Eddie	85F	541	$ .01	$ .06
Meredith, Ron	86F	374	$ .01	$ .06	Milner, Eddie	86F	182	$ .01	$ .06
Merullo, Matt	89FU	21	$ .01	$ .10	Milner, Eddie	87F	205	$ .01	$ .06
Merullo, Matt	90F	542	$ .01	$ .10	Milner, Eddie	88F	90	$ .01	$ .05
Merullo, Matt	91FU	13	$ .01	$ .05	Milner, John	81F	386	$ .01	$ .06
Merullo, Matt	92F	90	$ .01	$ .04	Milner, John	82F	197	$ .01	$ .06

FLEER

Player	Year	No.	VG	EX/MT	Player	Year	No.	VG	EX/MT
Milner, John	83F	311	$ .01	$ .06	Monge, Sid	84F	308	$ .01	$ .08
Minor, Blas	92FU	116	$ .05	$ .25	Monge, Sid	85F	17	$ .01	$ .06
Minton, Greg	81F	449	$ .01	$ .06	Montanez, Willy "Willie"	81F	506	$ .01	$ .06
Minton, Greg	82F	396	$ .01	$ .06	Montanez, Willy	82F	486	$ .01	$ .06
Minton, Greg	83F	269	$ .01	$ .06	Montefusco, John	81F	439	$ .01	$ .06
Minton, Greg	84F	383	$ .01	$ .08	Montefusco, John	82F	442	$ .01	$ .06
Minton, Greg	85F	617	$ .01	$ .06	Montefusco, John	83F	367	$ .01	$ .06
Minton, Greg	86F	549	$ .01	$ .06	Montefusco, John	84F	132	$ .01	$ .08
Minton, Greg	87F	282	$ .01	$ .06	Montefusco, John	85F	135	$ .01	$ .06
Minton, Greg	87FU	80	$ .01	$ .06	Montefusco, John	86F	111	$ .01	$ .06
Minton, Greg	88F	499	$ .01	$ .05	Monteleone, Rich	90F	648	$ .01	$ .10
Minton, Greg	89F	485	$ .01	$ .04	Monteleone, Rich	93F	653	$ .01	$ .04
Minton, Greg	90F	140	$ .01	$ .04	Montgomery, Jeff	88F	642	$ .10	$ .75
Mirabella, Paul	83F	573	$ .01	$ .06	Montgomery, Jeff	88FU	32	$ .05	$ .20
Mirabella, Paul	85F	494	$ .01	$ .06	Montgomery, Jeff	89F	288	$ .01	$ .15
Mirabella, Paul	89F	192	$ .01	$ .04	Montgomery, Jeff	90F	115	$ .01	$ .04
Mirabella, Paul	91F	590	$ .01	$ .04	Montgomery, Jeff	91F	564	$ .01	$ .04
Mitchell, Bobby	82F	14	$ .01	$ .06	Montgomery, Jeff	91FUL	153	$ .01	$ .07
Mitchell, Bob	83F	620	$ .01	$ .06	Montgomery, Jeff	92F	164	$ .01	$ .04
Mitchell, Bobby	84F	571	$ .01	$ .08	Montgomery, Jeff	92FUL	76	$ .01	$ .10
Mitchell, John	87FU	81	$ .01	$ .10	Montgomery, Jeff	93F	245	$ .01	$ .04
Mitchell, John	88F	145	$ .05	$ .20	Mooneyham, Bill	86FU	77	$ .01	$ .08
Mitchell, John	91F	485	$ .01	$ .10	Mooneyham, Bill	87F	399	$ .01	$ .06
Mitchell, Keith	92F	364	$ .01	$ .15	Moore, Brad	90FU	45	$ .01	$ .05
Mitchell, Kevin	86FU	76	$ .20	$2.00	Moore, Charlie	81F	521	$ .01	$ .06
Mitchell, Kevin	87F	17	$1.00	$4.00	Moore, Charlie	82F	150	$ .01	$ .06
Mitchell, Kevin	87FU	82	$ .10	$1.00	Moore, Charlie	83F	42	$ .01	$ .06
Mitchell, Kevin	88F	92	$ .05	$ .35	Moore, Charlie	84F	209	$ .01	$ .08
Mitchell, Kevin	89F	336	$ .01	$ .15	Moore, Charlie	85F	589	$ .01	$ .06
Mitchell, Kevin	90F	65	$ .01	$ .15	Moore, Charlie	86F	496	$ .01	$ .06
Mitchell, Kevin	90F	637	$ .01	$ .10	Moore, Charlie	87F	351	$ .01	$ .06
Mitchell, Kevin	91F	267	$ .01	$ .10	Moore, Donnie	84F	185	$ .01	$ .08
Mitchell, Kevin	91FUL	326	$ .01	$ .10	Moore, Donnie	85F	334	$ .01	$ .06
Mitchell, Kevin	92F	644	$ .01	$ .10	Moore, Donnie	85FU	82	$ .01	$ .10
Mitchell, Kevin	92FU	56	$ .05	$ .25	Moore, Donnie	86F	164	$ .01	$ .06
Mitchell, Kevin	92FUL	434	$ .05	$ .25	Moore, Donnie	87F	89	$ .01	$ .06
Mitchell, Kevin	93F	396	$ .01	$ .10	Moore, Donnie	88F	500	$ .01	$ .05
Moffitt, Randy	81F	446	$ .01	$ .06	Moore, Mike	83F	482	$ .10	$ .75
Moffitt, Randy	83F	456	$ .01	$ .06					
Moffitt, Randy	84F	163	$ .01	$ .08					
Mohorcic, Dale	87F	131	$ .01	$ .10					
Mohorcic, Dale	88F	474	$ .01	$ .05					
Mohorcic, Dale	89F	259	$ .01	$ .04					
Mohorcic, Dale	90F	450	$ .01	$ .04					
Mohorcic, Dale	91F	239	$ .01	$ .04					
Molinaro, Bob	81F	340	$ .01	$ .06					
Molinaro, Bob	82F	353	$ .01	$ .06					
Molinaro, Bob	83F	167	$ .01	$ .06					
Molitor, Paul	81F	515	$ .15	$1.50					
Molitor, Paul	82F	148	$ .10	$1.00					
Molitor, Paul	83F	40	$ .10	$ .75					
Molitor, Paul	84F	207	$ .15	$1.50					
Molitor, Paul	85F	588	$ .10	$ .75					
Molitor, Paul	86F	495	$ .05	$ .35					
Molitor, Paul	87F	350	$ .05	$ .35					
Molitor, Paul	88F	169	$ .05	$ .25					
Molitor, Paul	89F	193	$ .01	$ .10					
Molitor, Paul	90F	330	$ .01	$ .10					
Molitor, Paul	91F	591	$ .01	$ .10					
Molitor, Paul	91FUL	178	$ .01	$ .10					
Molitor, Paul	92F	182	$ .01	$ .04					
Molitor, Paul	92F	702	$ .01	$ .04					
Molitor, Paul	92FUL	81	$ .01	$ .10					
Molitor, Paul	93F	254	$ .01	$ .10					
Monday, Rick	81F	122	$ .01	$ .06					
Monday, Rick	82F	15	$ .01	$ .06					
Monday, Rick	83F	213	$ .01	$ .06					
Monday, Rick	84F	106	$ .01	$ .08					
Money, Don	81F	524	$ .01	$ .06					
Money, Don	82F	149	$ .01	$ .06					
Money, Don	83F	41	$ .01	$ .06	Moore, Mike	84F	614	$ .05	$ .25
Money, Don	84F	208	$ .01	$ .08	Moore, Mike	85F	495	$ .01	$ .15
Monge, Sid	81F	395	$ .01	$ .06	Moore, Mike	86F	469	$ .01	$ .06
Monge, Sid	82F	375	$ .01	$ .06	Moore, Mike	87F	590	$ .01	$ .06
Monge, Sid	83F	168	$ .01	$ .06	Moore, Mike	88F	379	$ .01	$ .05

Mike Moore
PITCHER

FLEER

Player	Year	No.	VG	EX/MT
Moore, Mike	89F	554	$ .01	$ .04
Moore, Mike	89FU	55	$ .01	$ .05
Moore, Mike	90F	16	$ .01	$ .04
Moore, Mike	91F	18	$ .01	$ .04
Moore, Mike	91FUL	252	$ .01	$ .07
Moore, Mike	92F	263	$ .01	$ .04
Moore, Mike	92FUL	425	$ .01	$ .10
Moore, Mike	93F	666	$ .01	$ .04
Morales, Jerry	81F	338	$ .01	$ .06
Morales, Jerry	82F	601	$ .01	$ .06
Morales, Jerry	83F	502	$ .01	$ .06
Morales, Jerry	84F	498	$ .01	$ .08
Morales, Jose	81F	571	$ .01	$ .06
Morales, Jose	82F	173	$ .01	$ .06
Morales, Jose	84F	107	$ .01	$ .08
Morandini, Mickey	91F	407	$ .01	$ .15
Morandini, Mickey	91FUL	268	$ .01	$ .15
Morandini, Mickey	92F	539	$ .01	$ .04
Morandini, Mickey	92FUL	247	$ .01	$ .10
Morandini, Mickey	93F	105	$ .01	$ .04
Morandini, Mickey	93FUL	91	$ .01	$ .10
Moreland, Keith	81F	13	$ .05	$ .20
Moreland, Keith	82F	252	$ .01	$ .10
Moreland, Keith	83F	503	$ .01	$ .06
Moreland, Keith	84F	499	$ .01	$ .08
Moreland, Keith	85F	62	$ .01	$ .06
Moreland, Keith	86F	375	$ .01	$ .06
Moreland, Keith	87F	569	$ .01	$ .06
Moreland, Keith	88F	425	$ .01	$ .05
Moreland, Keith	88FU	124	$ .01	$ .06

KEITH MORELAND
FIRST BASE

Player	Year	No.	VG	EX/MT
Moreland, Keith	89F	313	$ .01	$ .04
Moreno, Angel	82F	469	$ .01	$ .06
Moreno, Omar	81F	361	$ .01	$ .06
Moreno, Omar	82F	487	$ .01	$ .06
Moreno, Omar	83F	312	$ .01	$ .06
Moreno, Omar	84F	133	$ .01	$ .08
Moreno, Omar	85F	136	$ .01	$ .06
Moreno, Omar	86F	15	$ .01	$ .06
Moreno, Omar	86FU	78	$ .01	$ .08
Moreno, Omar	87F	521	$ .01	$ .06
Morgan, Joe	81F	78	$ .10	$1.00
Morgan, Joe	82F	397	$ .10	$ .75
Morgan, Joe	83F	270	$ .10	$ .50

Player	Year	No.	VG	EX/MT
Morgan, Joe	84F	43	$ .10	$1.00
Morgan, Joe	84F	636	$ .10	$ .75
Morgan, Joe	84FU	80	$2.50	$10.00
Morgan, Joe	85F	431	$ .10	$ .50
Morgan, Mike	83F	388	$ .05	$ .20
Morgan, Mike	87F	591	$ .01	$ .06
Morgan, Mike	88F	380	$ .01	$ .05
Morgan, Mike	89FU	91	$ .01	$ .05
Morgan, Mike	90F	403	$ .01	$ .04
Morgan, Mike	91F	213	$ .01	$ .04
Morgan, Mike	91FUL	165	$ .01	$ .07
Morgan, Mike	92F	465	$ .01	$ .04
Morgan, Mike	92FU	74	$ .05	$ .25
Morgan, Mike	92FUL	471	$ .01	$ .10
Morgan, Mike	93F	23	$ .01	$ .04
Morgan, Mike	93FUL	21	$ .01	$ .10
Morman, Russ	87F	645	$ .05	$ .20
Morris, Hal	89F	260	$ .10	$ .50
Morris, Hal	90FU	15	$ .01	$ .15
Morris, Hal	91F	72	$ .01	$ .10
Morris, Hal	91FUL	98	$ .01	$ .15
Morris, Hal	92F	412	$ .01	$ .10
Morris, Hal	92FUL	192	$ .01	$ .10
Morris, Hal	93F	37	$ .01	$ .04
Morris, Hal	93FUL	31	$ .01	$ .10
Morris, Jack	81F	475	$ .20	$2.00
Morris, Jack	82F	274	$ .15	$1.50
Morris, Jack	83F	336	$ .10	$1.00
Morris, Jack	84F	87	$ .20	$2.00
Morris, Jack	85F	18	$ .10	$1.00
Morris, Jack	85F	643	$ .01	$ .15
Morris, Jack	86F	232	$ .10	$ .50
Morris, Jack	87F	158	$ .10	$ .50
Morris, Jack	88F	64	$ .01	$ .15
Morris, Jack	88F	626	$ .01	$ .05
Morris, Jack	89F	139	$ .01	$ .15
Morris, Jack	90F	610	$ .01	$ .10
Morris, Jack	91F	343	$ .01	$ .10
Morris, Jack	91FU	39	$ .01	$ .10
Morris, Jack	91FULU	39	$ .01	$ .10
Morris, Jack	92F	211	$ .01	$ .10
Morris, Jack	92FU	66	$ .05	$ .25
Morris, Jack	92FUL	452	$ .01	$ .10
Morris, Jack	93F	347	$ .01	$ .10
Morris, Jack	93F	697	$ .01	$ .04
Morris, Jack	93FUL	290	$ .01	$ .10
Morris, John	87FU	83	$ .01	$ .06
Morris, John	88F	43	$ .01	$ .05
Morris, John	90F	254	$ .01	$ .04
Morris, John	91FU	109	$ .01	$ .05
Morrison, Jim	81F	357	$ .01	$ .06
Morrison, Jim	82F	354	$ .01	$ .06
Morrison, Jim	83F	313	$ .01	$ .06
Morrison, Jim	84F	257	$ .01	$ .06
Morrison, Jim	85F	471	$ .01	$ .06
Morrison, Jim	86F	614	$ .01	$ .06
Morrison, Jim	87F	614	$ .01	$ .06
Morrison, Jim	88F	65	$ .01	$ .05
Moseby, Lloyd	81F	421	$ .05	$ .25
Moseby, Lloyd	82F	621	$ .01	$ .10
Moseby, Lloyd	83F	435	$ .01	$ .10
Moseby, Lloyd	84F	164	$ .01	$ .10
Moseby, Lloyd	85F	115	$ .05	$ .20
Moseby, Lloyd	85F	636	$ .01	$ .10
Moseby, Lloyd	86F	67	$ .01	$ .10
Moseby, Lloyd	87F	236	$ .01	$ .06
Moseby, Lloyd	88F	119	$ .01	$ .10
Moseby, Lloyd	89F	241	$ .01	$ .05
Moseby, Lloyd	90F	90	$ .01	$ .05
Moseby, Lloyd	90FU	97	$ .01	$ .05
Moseby, Lloyd	91F	344	$ .01	$ .05
Moseby, Lloyd	91FUL	124	$ .01	$ .05
Moseby, Lloyd	92F	142	$ .01	$ .05
Moses, John	87F	592	$ .01	$ .05
Moses, John	88F	381	$ .01	$ .05

FLEER

Player	Year	No.	VG	EX/MT	Player	Year	No.	VG	EX/MT
Moses, John	88FU	45	$.01	$.06	Murphy, Dale	88F	639	$.01	$.15
Moses, John	89F	121	$.01	$.04	Murphy, Dale	89F	596	$.01	$.15
Moses, John	90F	381	$.01	$.04	Murphy, Dale	90F	591	$.01	$.10
Moses, John	91F	619	$.01	$.04	Murphy, Dale	90FPD	623	$.01	$.10
Moskau, Paul	81F	207	$.01	$.06	Murphy, Dale	90FU	46	$.01	$.10
Moskau, Paul	82F	76	$.01	$.06	Murphy, Dale	91F	409	$.01	$.10
Mota, Andy	92F	441	$.01	$.10	Murphy, Dale	91FUL	270	$.01	$.10
Mota, Jose	91FU	126	$.01	$.15	Murphy, Dale	92F	541	$.01	$.10
Mota, Jose	92F	616	$.01	$.10	Murphy, Dale	92FUL	249	$.01	$.10
Mota, Manny	81F	141	$.01	$.06	Murphy, Dale	93F	496	$.01	$.04
Motley, Darryl	82F	417	$.01	$.06	Murphy, Dwayne	81F	590	$.01	$.06
Motley, Darryl	84FU	81	$.10	$.50	Murphy, Dwayne	82F	101	$.01	$.06
Motley, Darryl	85F	208	$.01	$.06	Murphy, Dwayne	83F	528	$.01	$.06
Motley, Darryl	86F	16	$.01	$.06	Murphy, Dwayne	84F	456	$.01	$.08
Moyer, Jamie	87F	570	$.01	$.10	Murphy, Dwayne	85F	432	$.01	$.06
Moyer, Jamie	88F	426	$.01	$.05	Murphy, Dwayne	86F	428	$.01	$.06
Moyer, Jamie	89F	432	$.01	$.04	Murphy, Dwayne	87F	400	$.01	$.06
Moyer, Jamie	89FU	65	$.01	$.05	Murphy, Dwayne	88F	287	$.01	$.05
Moyer, Jamie	90F	307	$.01	$.04	Murphy, Dwayne	90F	569	$.01	$.04
Moyer, Jamie	91F	294	$.01	$.04	Murphy, Rob	87F	206	$.05	$.30
Mulholland, Terry	89FU	111	$.01	$.10	Murphy, Rob	88F	241	$.01	$.05
Mulholland, Terry	90F	568	$.01	$.04	Murphy, Rob	89F	165	$.01	$.04
Mulholland, Terry	91F	408	$.01	$.04	Murphy, Rob	89FU	10	$.01	$.05
Mulholland, Terry	91FUL	269	$.01	$.07	Murphy, Rob	90F	281	$.01	$.04
Mulholland, Terry	92F	540	$.01	$.04	Murphy, Rob	91F	104	$.01	$.04
Mulholland, Terry	92FUL	248	$.01	$.10	Murphy, Rob	92F	288	$.01	$.04
Mulholland, Terry	93F	106	$.01	$.04	Murphy, Rob	92FUL	493	$.01	$.10
Mulholland, Terry	93FUL	92	$.01	$.10	Murphy, Rob	93F	439	$.01	$.04
Mulliniks, Rance	81F	48	$.01	$.06	Murray, Dale	83F	437	$.01	$.06
Mulliniks, Rance	82F	418	$.01	$.06	Murray, Dale	84F	134	$.01	$.08
Mulliniks, Rance	83F	436	$.01	$.06	Murray, Dale	85F	137	$.01	$.06
Mulliniks, Rance	84F	165	$.01	$.08	Murray, Eddie	81F	184	$.25	$2.50
Mulliniks, Rance	85F	116	$.01	$.06	Murray, Eddie	82F	174	$.20	$2.00
Mulliniks, Rance	86F	68	$.01	$.06	Murray, Eddie	83F	67	$.15	$1.50
Mulliniks, Rance	87F	237	$.01	$.06	Murray, Eddie	84F	14	$1.00	$4.00
Mulliniks, Rance	88F	120	$.01	$.05	Murray, Eddie	85F	184	$.15	$1.50
Mulliniks, Rance	89F	242	$.01	$.04	Murray, Eddie	86F	282	$.10	$1.00
Mulliniks, Rance	90F	91	$.01	$.04	Murray, Eddie	87F	476	$.10	$.50
Mulliniks, Rance	91F	181	$.01	$.04	Murray, Eddie	87F	636	$.05	$.20
Mulliniks, Rance	91FUL	366	$.01	$.07	Murray, Eddie	88F	567	$.05	$.25
Mulliniks, Rance	92F	337	$.01	$.04	Murray, Eddie	89F	611	$.01	$.15
Mulliniks, Rance	92FUL	149	$.01	$.10	Murray, Eddie	89FU	92	$.01	$.15
Mumphrey, Jerry	81F	494	$.01	$.06	Murray, Eddie	90F	404	$.01	$.10
Mumphrey, Jerry	82F	43	$.01	$.06	Murray, Eddie	91F	214	$.01	$.10
Mumphrey, Jerry	83F	389	$.01	$.06	Murray, Eddie	91FUL	166	$.01	$.15
Mumphrey, Jerry	84F	233	$.01	$.08	Murray, Eddie	92F	466	$.01	$.10
Mumphrey, Jerry	85F	354	$.01	$.06	Murray, Eddie	92FUL	532	$.05	$.35
Mumphrey, Jerry	86F	306	$.01	$.06	Murray, Eddie	93F	91	$.01	$.10
Mumphrey, Jerry	86FU	79	$.01	$.08	Murray, Eddie	93FUL	78	$.05	$.25
Mumphrey, Jerry	87F	571	$.01	$.06	Murray, Rich	81F	452	$.01	$.06
Mumphrey, Jerry	88F	427	$.01	$.05	Musselman, Jeff	87FU	84	$.01	$.10
Munoz, Mike	92FUL	367	$.01	$.10	Musselman, Jeff	88F	121	$.01	$.05
Munoz, Mike	93F	609	$.01	$.04	Musselman, Jeff	89F	243	$.01	$.04
Munoz, Pedro	91F	620	$.05	$.20	Musselman, Jeff	90F	212	$.01	$.04
Munoz, Pedro	91FUL	192	$.10	$.50	Musselman, Ron	85FU	83	$.01	$.10
Munoz, Pedro	92F	212	$.01	$.10	Mussina, Mike	91FULU	4	$2.50	$10.00
Munoz, Pedro	92FUL	399	$.05	$.20	Mussina, Mike	92F	20	$.10	$.60
Munoz, Pedro	93F	272	$.01	$.10	Mussina, Mike	92FUL	9	$.20	$2.00
Munoz, Pedro	93FUL	235	$.01	$.10	Mussina, Mike	93F	172	$.05	$.35
Mura, Steve	81F	496	$.01	$.06	Mussina, Mike	93FUL	144	$.10	$1.00
Mura, Steve	82F	578	$.01	$.06	Myers, Greg	88F	644	$.05	$.20
Mura, Steve	83F	16	$.01	$.06	Myers, Greg	91F	182	$.01	$.04
Murcer, Bobby	81F	94	$.01	$.10	Myers, Greg	91FULU	62	$.01	$.10
Murcer, Bobby	82F	44	$.01	$.10	Myers, Greg	92F	338	$.01	$.04
Murcer, Bobby	83F	390	$.01	$.10	Myers, Greg	92FUL	150	$.01	$.10
Murphy, Dale	81F	243	$.10	$1.00	Myers, Randy	87FU	85	$.05	$.35
Murphy, Dale	82F	443	$.10	$1.00	Myers, Randy	88F	146	$.01	$.15
Murphy, Dale	83F	142	$.10	$.75	Myers, Randy	89F	46	$.01	$.10
Murphy, Dale	84F	186	$.15	$1.25	Myers, Randy	90F	213	$.01	$.04
Murphy, Dale	85F	335	$.10	$.75	Myers, Randy	91F	73	$.01	$.04
Murphy, Dale	86F	522	$.10	$.50	Myers, Randy	91FUL	97	$.01	$.07
Murphy, Dale	86F	635	$.05	$.30	Myers, Randy	92F	413	$.01	$.06
Murphy, Dale	86F	640	$.05	$.25	Myers, Randy	92FU	123	$.05	$.25
Murphy, Dale	87F	522	$.05	$.35	Myers, Randy	92FUL	579	$.01	$.10
Murphy, Dale	88F	544	$.05	$.20	Myers, Randy	93F	522	$.01	$.04

FLEER

Player	Year	No.	VG	EX/MT
Nabholz, Chris	90FU	30	$ .05	$ .20
Nabholz, Chris	91F	240	$ .01	$ .10
Nabholz, Chris	92F	487	$ .01	$ .04
Nabholz, Chris	92FUL	521	$ .01	$ .10
Nabholz, Chris	93F	78	$ .01	$ .04

Player	Year	No.	VG	EX/MT
Nabholz, Chris	93FUL	69	$ .01	$ .10
Naehring, Tim	90FU	73	$ .01	$ .15
Naehring, Tim	91F	105	$ .01	$ .10
Naehring, Tim	91FUL	36	$ .01	$ .10
Naehring, Tim	92FUL	317	$ .05	$ .20
Naehring, Tim	93FUL	153	$ .01	$ .10
Nagy, Charles	91FU	20	$ .05	$ .35
Nagy, Charles	91FULU	20	$ .10	$1.00
Nagy, Charles	92F	118	$ .01	$ .10
Nagy, Charles	92FUL	351	$ .05	$ .25
Nagy, Charles	93F	219	$ .01	$ .15
Nagy, Charles	93FUL	189	$ .05	$ .20
Nahorodny, Bill	81F	254	$ .01	$ .06
Nahorodny, Bill	83F	416	$ .01	$ .06
Narron, Jerry	82F	513	$ .01	$ .06
Natal, Bob	93F	428	$ .01	$ .04
Navarro, Jaime	89FU	39	$ .10	$ .50
Navarro, Jaime	90F	331	$ .01	$ .10
Navarro, Jaime	91F	592	$ .01	$ .04
Navarro, Jaime	91FULU	31	$ .10	$ .50
Navarro, Jaime	92F	183	$ .01	$ .04
Navarro, Jaime	92FUL	82	$ .01	$ .10
Navarro, Jaime	93F	255	$ .01	$ .04
Neagle, Denny	91FUL	383	$ .05	$ .25
Neagle, Denny	92F	213	$ .01	$ .10
Neagle, Denny	92FUL	556	$ .05	$ .20
Neagle, Denny	93F	503	$ .01	$ .04
Neel, Troy	92FU	50	$ .20	$2.00
Neel, Troy	93FUL	260	$ .05	$ .35
Neidlinger, Jim	91F	215	$ .01	$ .10
Nelson, Gene	82F	45	$ .05	$ .25
Nelson, Gene	85F	522	$ .01	$ .06
Nelson, Gene	86F	213	$ .01	$ .06
Nelson, Gene	87F	504	$ .01	$ .06
Nelson, Gene	87FU	86	$ .01	$ .06
Nelson, Gene	88F	288	$ .01	$ .05
Nelson, Gene	89F	18	$ .01	$ .04
Nelson, Gene	90F	17	$ .01	$ .04
Nelson, Gene	91F	19	$ .01	$ .04
Nelson, Gene	92F	264	$ .01	$ .04
Nelson, Gene	92FUL	426	$ .01	$ .10
Nelson, Jeff	92FU	57	$ .05	$ .25
Nelson, Jeff	93F	311	$ .01	$ .10
Nelson, Ricky	84F	615	$ .01	$ .08
Nelson, Rob	87F	653	$ .01	$ .06
Nettles, Graig	81F	87	$ .05	$ .25
Nettles, Graig	82F	46	$ .05	$ .20
Nettles, Graig	83F	391	$ .05	$ .20
Nettles, Graig	84F	135	$ .05	$ .20
Nettles, Graig	84FU	82	$ .10	$1.00
Nettles, Graig	85F	42	$ .05	$ .20
Nettles, Graig	86F	332	$ .01	$ .10
Nettles, Graig	87F	426	$ .01	$ .10
Newell, Tom	88F	648	$ .05	$ .30
Newman, Al	86FU	80	$ .01	$ .08
Newman, Al	87F	327	$ .01	$ .06
Newman, Al	88F	17	$ .01	$ .05
Newman, Al	89F	122	$ .01	$ .04
Newman, Al	90F	382	$ .01	$ .04
Newman, Al	91F	621	$ .01	$ .04
Newman, Al	91FUL	193	$ .01	$ .07
Newman, Al	92F	214	$ .01	$ .04
Newman, Al	93F	685	$ .01	$ .04
Newman, Jeff	81F	577	$ .01	$ .06
Newman, Jeff	82F	102	$ .01	$ .06
Newman, Jeff	83F	529	$ .01	$ .06
Newman, Jeff	84F	404	$ .01	$ .08
Newson, Warren	91FU	14	$ .01	$ .10
Newson, Warren	91FULU	17	$ .05	$ .25
Newson, Warren	92F	91	$ .01	$ .10
Nichols, Carl	89F	612	$ .01	$ .15
Nichols, Reid	82F	300	$ .01	$ .06
Nichols, Reid	83F	189	$ .01	$ .06
Nichols, Reid	84F	405	$ .01	$ .08
Nichols, Reid	85F	164	$ .01	$ .06
Nichols, Reid	86F	214	$ .01	$ .06
Nichols, Reid	87FU	89	$ .01	$ .06
Nichols, Reid	88F	191	$ .01	$ .05
Nichols, Rod	90F	497	$ .01	$ .04
Nichols, Rod	92F	119	$ .01	$ .04
Nichols, Rod	92FUL	352	$ .01	$ .10
Nichols, Rod	93F	597	$ .01	$ .04
Nicosia, Steve	81F	371	$ .01	$ .06
Nicosia, Steve	82F	488	$ .01	$ .06
Nicosia, Steve	83F	314	$ .01	$ .06
Nicosia, Steve	85F	618	$ .01	$ .06
Nied, David	92FU	68	$3.50	$14.00
Nied, David	93F	9	$ .15	$1.50
Niedenfuer, Tom	82F	16	$ .05	$ .30
Niedenfuer, Tom	83F	214	$ .01	$ .06
Niedenfuer, Tom	84F	108	$ .01	$ .08
Niedenfuer, Tom	85F	378	$ .01	$ .06
Niedenfuer, Tom	86F	139	$ .01	$ .06
Niedenfuer, Tom	87F	448	$ .01	$ .06
Niedenfuer, Tom	88F	568	$ .01	$ .05
Niedenfuer, Tom	89F	613	$ .01	$ .04
Niedenfuer, Tom	91F	639	$ .01	$ .04
Niekro, Joe	81F	54	$ .01	$ .10
Niekro, Joe	82F	221	$ .01	$ .10
Niekro, Joe	83F	457	$ .01	$ .10
Niekro, Joe	84F	234	$ .01	$ .10
Niekro, Joe	85F	355	$ .01	$ .10
Niekro, Joe	87F	106	$ .01	$ .10
Niekro, Joe	87FU	87	$ .01	$ .10
Niekro, Joe	88F	18	$ .01	$ .10
Niekro, Phil	81F	242	$ .10	$ .50
Niekro, Phil	82F	444	$ .10	$ .40
Niekro, Phil	83F	143	$ .05	$ .35
Niekro, Phil	84F	187	$ .10	$ .50
Niekro, Phil	84FU	83	$2.00	$8.00
Niekro, Phil	85F	138	$ .05	$ .35
Niekro, Phil	86F	112	$ .05	$ .20
Niekro, Phil	86F	630	$ .05	$ .35

FLEER

Player	Year	No.	VG	EX/MT
Niekro, Phil	86FU	81	$ .05	$ .25
Niekro, Phil	87F	254	$ .05	$ .20
Niekro, Phil	87F	626	$ .01	$ .10
Nielsen, Jerry	93F	654	$ .01	$ .04
Nielson, Scott	89F	261	$ .01	$ .04
Niemann, Randy	81F	77	$ .01	$ .06
Niemann, Randy	86FU	82	$ .01	$ .08
Niemann, Randy	87F	18	$ .01	$ .06
Nieto, Tom	85F	235	$ .01	$ .06
Nieto, Tom	86F	43	$ .01	$ .06
Nieto, Tom	87FU	88	$ .01	$ .06
Nieves, Juan	86FU	83	$ .01	$ .15
Nieves, Juan	87F	352	$ .01	$ .10
Nieves, Juan	88F	170	$ .01	$ .10
Nilsson, Dave	92FU	37	$ .10	$1.00
Nilsson, Dave	93F	631	$ .01	$ .10
Nilsson, Dave	93FUL	222	$ .05	$ .25
Nipper, Al	85F	165	$ .05	$ .25
Nipper, Al	86F	356	$ .01	$ .06
Nipper, Al	87F	39	$ .01	$ .06
Nipper, Al	88F	358	$ .01	$ .05
Nipper, Al	89F	433	$ .01	$ .04
Nixon, Donell	88F	382	$ .01	$ .15
Nixon, Donell	88FU	129	$ .01	$ .06
Nixon, Donell	89F	337	$ .01	$ .04
Nixon, Donell	90F	66	$ .01	$ .04
Nixon, Otis	86F	591	$ .10	$1.00
Nixon, Otis	87F	255	$ .05	$ .35
Nixon, Otis	89F	387	$ .01	$ .04
Nixon, Otis	90F	356	$ .01	$ .04
Nixon, Otis	91F	241	$ .01	$ .04
Nixon, Otis	91FU	75	$ .01	$ .05
Nixon, Otis	91FULU	69	$ .01	$ .10
Nixon, Otis	92FU	69	$ .05	$ .25
Nixon, Otis	92FUL	461	$ .01	$ .10
Nixon, Otis	93F	10	$ .01	$ .04
Noboa, Junior	91F	242	$ .01	$ .04
Noboa, Junior	91FUL	207	$ .01	$ .07
Noboa, Junior	92FUL	533	$ .01	$ .10
Noce, Paul	88F	428	$ .01	$ .10
Nokes, Matt	87FU	90	$ .05	$ .25
Nokes, Matt	88F	66	$ .05	$ .35
Nokes, Matt	88F	638	$ .05	$ .20
Nokes, Matt	89F	140	$ .01	$ .10
Nokes, Matt	90F	611	$ .01	$ .04
Nokes, Matt	90FU	115	$ .01	$ .05
Nokes, Matt	91F	674	$ .01	$ .04
Nokes, Matt	91FULU	42	$ .01	$ .10
Nokes, Matt	92F	239	$ .01	$ .04
Nokes, Matt	92FUL	107	$ .01	$ .10
Nokes, Matt	93F	283	$ .01	$ .04
Nokes, Matt	93FUL	247	$ .01	$ .10
Nolan, Joe	81F	212	$ .01	$ .06
Nolan, Joe	82F	77	$ .01	$ .06
Nolan, Joe	83F	68	$ .01	$ .06
Nolan, Joe	84F	15	$ .01	$ .08
Nolan, Joe	85F	185	$ .01	$ .06
Noles, Dickie	81F	12	$ .01	$ .06
Noles, Dickie	82F	253	$ .01	$ .06
Noles, Dickie	83F	504	$ .01	$ .06
Noles, Dickie	84F	500	$ .01	$ .08
Noles, Dickie	86F	567	$ .01	$ .06
Noles, Dickie	87F	256	$ .01	$ .06
Noles, Dickie	87FU	91	$ .01	$ .06
Nolte, Eric	88F	593	$ .01	$ .15
Nordhagen, Wayne	81F	348	$ .01	$ .06
Nordhagen, Wayne	82F	355	$ .01	$ .06
Nordhagen, Wayne	83F	438	$ .01	$ .06
Norman, Dan	81F	337	$ .01	$ .06
Norman, Dan	83F	289	$ .01	$ .06
Norman, Fred	81F	158	$ .01	$ .06
Norris, Jim	81F	634	$ .01	$ .06
Norris, Mike	81F	573	$ .01	$ .06
Norris, Mike	82F	103	$ .01	$ .06
Norris, Mike	83F	530	$ .01	$ .06
Norris, Mike	84F	457	$ .01	$ .08
North, Bill	81F	441	$ .01	$ .06
Nunez, Edwin	85F	496	$ .01	$ .06
Nunez, Edwin	86F	470	$ .01	$ .06
Nunez, Edwin	87FU	92	$ .01	$ .06
Nunez, Edwin	88F	383	$ .01	$ .05
Nunez, Edwin	90FU	98	$ .01	$ .05
Nunez, Edwin	91F	345	$ .01	$ .04
Nunez, Edwin	91FU	32	$ .01	$ .05
Nunez, Edwin	92F	184	$ .01	$ .04
Nunez, Edwin	92FUL	387	$ .01	$ .10
Nunez, Edwin	93F	686	$ .01	$ .04
Nunez, Jose	87FU	93	$ .01	$ .10
Nunez, Jose	88F	122	$ .01	$ .15
O'Berry, Mike	82F	78	$ .01	$ .06
O'Brien, Charlie	89F	194	$ .01	$ .04
O'Brien, Charlie	90F	332	$ .01	$ .04
O'Brien, Charlie	92F	514	$ .01	$ .04
O'Brien, Charlie	92FUL	534	$ .01	$ .10
O'Brien, Charlie	93F	478	$ .01	$ .04
O'Brien, Pete	84F	423	$ .05	$ .35
O'Brien, Pete	85F	563	$ .05	$ .20
O'Brien, Pete	86F	568	$ .05	$ .20
O'Brien, Pete	87F	132	$ .01	$ .10
O'Brien, Pete	88F	475	$ .01	$ .05
O'Brien, Pete	89F	529	$ .01	$ .04
O'Brien, Pete	89FU	29	$ .01	$ .05
O'Brien, Pete	90F	498	$ .01	$ .04
O'Brien, Pete	91F	459	$ .01	$ .04
O'Brien, Pete	91FUL	342	$ .01	$ .07
O'Brien, Pete	92F	289	$ .01	$ .04
O'Brien, Pete	92FUL	128	$ .01	$ .10
O'Brien, Pete	93F	678	$ .01	$ .04
O'Connor, Jack	83F	621	$ .01	$ .06
O'Malley, Tom	83F	271	$ .01	$ .06
O'Malley, Tom	84F	384	$ .01	$ .08
O'Malley, Tom	87F	477	$ .01	$ .06
O'Malley, Tom	91F	157	$ .01	$ .04
O'Neal, Randy	85F	645	$ .20	$2.00
O'Neal, Randy	86F	233	$ .01	$ .06
O'Neal, Randy	87F	159	$ .01	$ .06
O'Neal, Randy	91F	268	$ .01	$ .04
O'Neill, Paul	86F	646	$ .75	$3.00
O'Neill, Paul	87FU	94	$ .05	$ .25
O'Neill, Paul	88FU	85	$ .01	$ .15
O'Neill, Paul	89F	166	$ .01	$ .15
O'Neill, Paul	90F	427	$ .01	$ .10
O'Neill, Paul	91F	76	$ .01	$ .04
O'Neill, Paul	91FUL	100	$ .01	$ .07
O'Neill, Paul	92F	415	$ .01	$ .04
O'Neill, Paul	92FUL	194	$ .01	$ .10
O'Neill, Paul	93F	39	$ .01	$ .04
Oates, Johnny	81F	99	$ .01	$ .06
Oates, Johnny	82F	47	$ .01	$ .06
Oberkfell, Ken	81F	532	$ .01	$ .06
Oberkfell, Ken	82F	123	$ .01	$ .06
Oberkfell, Ken	83F	17	$ .01	$ .06
Oberkfell, Ken	84F	330	$ .01	$ .08
Oberkfell, Ken	84FU	84	$ .10	$ .50
Oberkfell, Ken	85F	336	$ .01	$ .06
Oberkfell, Ken	86F	523	$ .01	$ .06
Oberkfell, Ken	87F	523	$ .01	$ .06
Oberkfell, Ken	88F	545	$ .01	$ .05
Oberkfell, Ken	90F	67	$ .01	$ .04
Oberkfell, Ken	91F	511	$ .01	$ .04
Oelkers, Bryan	87F	257	$ .01	$ .06
Oester, Ron	81F	218	$ .01	$ .06
Oester, Ron	82F	79	$ .01	$ .06
Oester, Ron	83F	598	$ .01	$ .06
Oester, Ron	84F	475	$ .01	$ .08
Oester, Ron	85F	542	$ .01	$ .06
Oester, Ron	86F	183	$ .01	$ .06
Oester, Ron	87F	207	$ .01	$ .06
Oester, Ron	88F	242	$ .01	$ .05
Oester, Ron	91F	74	$ .01	$ .04

FLEER

Player	Year	No.	VG	EX/MT	Player	Year	No.	VG	EX/MT
Offerman, Jose	90FU	24	$ .01	$ .25	Olson, Greg	93FUL	10	$ .01	$ .10
Offerman, Jose	91F	216	$ .01	$ .10	Olson, Gregg	90F	184	$ .01	$ .15
Offerman, Jose	91FUL	167	$ .01	$ .10	Olson, Gregg	91F	486	$ .01	$ .04
Offerman, Jose	92F	467	$ .01	$ .10	Olson, Gregg	91FUL	21	$ .01	$ .07
Offerman, Jose	92FUL	215	$ .01	$ .10	Olson, Gregg	92F	21	$ .01	$ .04
Offerman, Jose	93F	66	$ .01	$ .04	Olson, Gregg	92FUL	307	$ .01	$ .10
Offerman, Jose	93FUL	59	$ .01	$ .10	Olson, Gregg	93F	173	$ .01	$ .04
Office, Rowland	81F	147	$ .01	$ .06	Olson, Gregg	93FUL	145	$ .01	$ .10
Office, Rowland	82F	198	$ .01	$ .06	Olwine, Ed	87F	524	$ .01	$ .10
Oglivie, Ben	81F	508	$ .01	$ .06	Ontiveros, Steve	86F	429	$ .05	$ .20
Oglivie, Ben	82F	151	$ .01	$ .06	Ontiveros, Steve	87F	401	$ .01	$ .06
Oglivie, Ben	83F	43	$ .01	$ .06	Ontiveros, Steve	88F	289	$ .01	$ .05
Oglivie, Ben	83F	640	$ .05	$ .35	Opperman, Dan	91FUL	384	$ .05	$ .20
Oglivie, Ben	84F	210	$ .01	$ .08	Oquendo, Jose	84F	592	$ .05	$ .25
Oglivie, Ben	85F	590	$ .01	$ .06	Oquendo, Jose	85F	88	$ .01	$ .10
Oglivie, Ben	86F	497	$ .01	$ .06	Oquendo, Jose	87F	305	$ .01	$ .06
Oglivie, Ben	87F	353	$ .01	$ .06	Oquendo, Jose	88F	44	$ .01	$ .05
Ojeda, Bob	82F	301	$ .05	$ .35	Oquendo, Jose	89F	459	$ .01	$ .04
Ojeda, Bob	83F	190	$ .01	$ .10	Oquendo, Jose	90F	255	$ .01	$ .04
Ojeda, Bob	84F	406	$ .01	$ .08	Oquendo, Jose	91F	640	$ .01	$ .04
Ojeda, Bob	85F	166	$ .01	$ .06	Oquendo, Jose	91FUL	292	$ .01	$ .07
Ojeda, Bob	86F	357	$ .01	$ .06	Oquendo, Jose	92F	585	$ .01	$ .04
Ojeda, Bob	86FU	84	$ .01	$ .08	Oquendo, Jose	92FUL	267	$ .01	$ .10
Ojeda, Bob	87F	19	$ .01	$ .06	Oquendo, Jose	93F	513	$ .01	$ .04
Ojeda, Bob	88F	147	$ .01	$ .10	Orosco, Jesse	83F	550	$ .01	$ .10
Ojeda, Bob	89F	47	$ .01	$ .04	Orosco, Jesse	84F	593	$ .01	$ .08
Ojeda, Bob	90F	214	$ .01	$ .04	Orosco, Jesse	85F	89	$ .01	$ .06
Ojeda, Bob	91F	156	$ .01	$ .04	Orosco, Jesse	86F	90	$ .01	$ .06
Ojeda, Bob	91FU	95	$ .01	$ .05	Orosco, Jesse	87F	20	$ .01	$ .06
Ojeda, Bob	91FULU	89	$ .01	$ .10	Orosco, Jesse	88F	148	$ .01	$ .05
Ojeda, Bob	92F	468	$ .01	$ .04	Orosco, Jesse	88FU	96	$ .01	$ .06
Ojeda, Bob	92FUL	509	$ .01	$ .10	Orosco, Jesse	89F	68	$ .01	$ .04
Ojeda, Bob	93F	452	$ .01	$ .04	Orosco, Jesse	90F	500	$ .01	$ .04
Olerud, John	90FU	128	$ .10	$ .75	Orosco, Jesse	91F	375	$ .01	$ .04
Olerud, John	91F	183	$ .01	$ .15	Orosco, Jesse	92F	121	$ .01	$ .04
Olerud, John	91FUL	367	$ .05	$ .35	Orosco, Jesse	93F	632	$ .01	$ .04
Olerud, John	92F	339	$ .01	$ .10	Orosco, Jesse	93FUL	223	$ .01	$ .10
Olerud, John	92FUL	151	$ .05	$ .35	Orsulak, Joe	85FU	85	$ .10	$ .50
Olerud, John	93F	339	$ .01	$ .10	Orsulak, Joe	86F	615	$ .10	$ .40
Olerud, John	93FUL	291	$ .05	$ .20	Orsulak, Joe	87F	615	$ .01	$ .06
Olin, Steve	90F	499	$ .01	$ .10	Orsulak, Joe	88FU	2	$ .01	$ .06
Olin, Steve	91F	374	$ .01	$ .04	Orsulak, Joe	89F	614	$ .01	$ .04
Olin, Steve	91FUL	116	$ .01	$ .07	Orsulak, Joe	90F	185	$ .01	$ .04
Olin, Steve	92F	120	$ .01	$ .04	Orsulak, Joe	91F	487	$ .01	$ .04
Olin, Steve	92FUL	53	$ .01	$ .10	Orsulak, Joe	91FUL	22	$ .01	$ .07
Olin, Steve	93F	220	$ .01	$ .04	Orsulak, Joe	92F	22	$ .01	$ .04
Olivares, Omar	91FULU	108	$ .05	$ .35	Orsulak, Joe	93F	549	$ .01	$ .04
Olivares, Omar	92F	584	$ .01	$ .04	Orta, Jorge	81F	388	$ .01	$ .06
Olivares, Omar	92FUL	266	$ .01	$ .10	Orta, Jorge	82F	376	$ .01	$ .06
Olivares, Omar	93F	512	$ .01	$ .04	Orta, Jorge	83F	215	$ .01	$ .06
Oliver, Al	81F	626	$ .01	$ .10	Orta, Jorge	84F	166	$ .01	$ .08
Oliver, Al	82F	326	$ .01	$ .10	Orta, Jorge	84FU	86	$ .10	$ .50
Oliver, Al	83F	290	$ .01	$ .10	Orta, Jorge	85F	209	$ .01	$ .06
Oliver, Al	84F	280	$ .01	$ .10	Orta, Jorge	86F	17	$ .01	$ .06
Oliver, Al	84F	632	$ .01	$ .08	Orta, Jorge	87F	376	$ .01	$ .06
Oliver, Al	84FU	85	$ .10	$ .75	Ortiz, Javier	90FU	16	$ .01	$ .10
Oliver, Al	85F	262	$ .01	$ .10	Ortiz, Junior	84F	594	$ .01	$ .08
Oliver, Al	85FU	84	$ .01	$ .10	Ortiz, Junior	87F	616	$ .01	$ .06
Oliver, Al	86F	69	$ .01	$ .10	Ortiz, Junior	88F	335	$ .01	$ .05
Oliver, Joe	90F	426	$ .01	$ .10	Ortiz, Junior	89F	215	$ .01	$ .04
Oliver, Joe	91F	75	$ .01	$ .04	Ortiz, Junior	90F	475	$ .01	$ .04
Oliver, Joe	91FUL	99	$ .01	$ .07	Ortiz, Junior	90FU	108	$ .01	$ .05
Oliver, Joe	92F	414	$ .01	$ .04	Ortiz, Junior	91F	622	$ .01	$ .04
Oliver, Joe	92FUL	193	$ .01	$ .10	Ortiz, Junior	91FUL	194	$ .01	$ .07
Oliver, Joe	93F	38	$ .01	$ .04	Ortiz, Junior	92F	215	$ .01	$ .04
Oliver, Joe	93FUL	32	$ .01	$ .10	Ortiz, Junior	92FUL	353	$ .01	$ .10
Oliveras, Francisco	92F	645	$ .01	$ .04	Ortiz, Junior	93F	598	$ .01	$ .04
Oliveras, Francisco	93F	534	$ .01	$ .04	Orton, John	90F	647	$ .05	$ .25
Olson, Greg	90FU	5	$ .01	$ .10	Orton, John	90FU	79	$ .01	$ .05
Olson, Greg	91F	698	$ .01	$ .04	Orton, John	91F	320	$ .01	$ .04
Olson, Greg	91FUL	9	$ .01	$ .07	Orton, John	92F	65	$ .01	$ .04
Olson, Greg	92F	365	$ .01	$ .04	Orton, John	93F	195	$ .01	$ .04
Olson, Greg	92F	701	$ .05	$ .20	Orton, John	93FUL	167	$ .01	$ .10
Olson, Greg	92FUL	166	$ .01	$ .10	Osborne, Donovan	92FU	120	$ .10	$1.00
Olson, Greg	93F	11	$ .01	$ .04	Osborne, Donovan	92FUL	570	$ .10	$ .50

FLEER

Player	Year	No.	VG	EX/MT
Osborne, Donovan	93F	129	$ .01	$ .10
Osborne, Donovan	93FUL	109	$ .05	$ .25
Osuna, Al	92F	442	$ .01	$ .04
Osuna, Al	92FUL	207	$ .01	$ .10
Osuna, Al	93F	440	$ .01	$ .04

Player	Year	No.	VG	EX/MT
Osuna, Al	93FUL	45	$ .01	$ .10
Otis, Amos	81F	32	$ .01	$ .10
Otis, Amos	81F	483	$ .05	$ .30
Otis, Amos	82F	419	$ .01	$ .06
Otis, Amos	83F	120	$ .01	$ .06
Otis, Amos	84F	351	$ .01	$ .10
Otis, Amos	84FU	87	$ .10	$ .50
Ott, Ed	81F	365	$ .01	$ .06
Ott, Ed	82F	470	$ .01	$ .06
Ott, Ed	83F	98	$ .01	$ .06
Otto, Dave	88F	652	$ .05	$ .35
Otto, Dave	91F	20	$ .01	$ .04
Otto, Dave	92FUL	354	$ .01	$ .10
Owchinko, Bob	82F	104	$ .01	$ .06
Owchinko, Bob	83F	531	$ .01	$ .06
Owchinko, Bob	84FU	88	$ .10	$ .50
Owchinko, Bob	85F	543	$ .01	$ .06
Owen, Spike	84F	616	$ .05	$ .35
Owon, Spike	85F	497	$ .01	$ .06
Owen, Spike	86F	471	$ .01	$ .06
Owen, Spike	87F	40	$ .01	$ .06
Owen, Spike	88F	359	$ .01	$ .05
Owen, Spike	89F	93	$ .01	$ .04
Owen, Spike	89FU	98	$ .01	$ .05
Owen, Spike	90F	357	$ .01	$ .04
Owen, Spike	91F	243	$ .01	$ .04
Owen, Spike	91FUL	208	$ .01	$ .07
Owen, Spike	92F	488	$ .01	$ .04
Owen, Spike	92FUL	224	$ .01	$ .10
Owen, Spike	93F	463	$ .01	$ .04
Owens, Paul	84F	643	$ .01	$ .08
Ownbey, Rick	83F	551	$ .01	$ .06
Ownbey, Rick	86FU	85	$ .01	$ .08
Pacella, John	83F	622	$ .01	$ .06
Paciorek, Jim	87FU	95	$ .01	$ .06
Paciorek, Tom	81F	614	$ .01	$ .06
Paciorek, Tom	82F	514	$ .01	$ .06
Paciorek, Tom	83F	248	$ .01	$ .06
Paciorek, Tom	84F	70	$ .01	$ .08
Paciorek, Tom	85F	523	$ .01	$ .06
Paciorek, Tom	86F	91	$ .01	$ .06
Paciorek, Tom	86FU	86	$ .01	$ .08
Paciorek, Tom	87F	133	$ .01	$ .06
Page, Mitchell	81F	580	$ .01	$ .06
Page, Mitchell	82F	105	$ .01	$ .06
Pagliarulo, Mike	85F	139	$ .05	$ .20
Pagliarulo, Mike	86F	113	$ .05	$ .25
Pagliarulo, Mike	87F	107	$ .01	$ .10
Pagliarulo, Mike	88F	216	$ .01	$ .10
Pagliarulo, Mike	89F	262	$ .01	$ .04
Pagliarulo, Mike	90F	163	$ .01	$ .04
Pagliarulo, Mike	91F	537	$ .01	$ .04
Pagliarulo, Mike	91FU	40	$ .01	$ .05
Pagliarulo, Mike	92F	216	$ .01	$ .04
Pagliarulo, Mike	92FUL	96	$ .01	$ .10
Pagliarulo, Mike	93F	641	$ .01	$ .04
Pagnozzi, Tom	91F	641	$ .01	$ .04
Pagnozzi, Tom	91FUL	293	$ .01	$ .07
Pagnozzi, Tom	92F	586	$ .01	$ .04
Pagnozzi, Tom	92FUL	268	$ .01	$ .10
Pagnozzi, Tom	93F	130	$ .01	$ .04
Pagnozzi, Tom	93FUL	110	$ .01	$ .10
Palacios, Robert	89F	648	$ .05	$ .25
Palacios, Vicente	88F	336	$ .01	$ .15
Palacios, Vicente	89F	216	$ .01	$ .04
Palacios, Vicente	91FU	113	$ .01	$ .05
Palacios, Vicente	92FUL	557	$ .01	$ .10
Pall, Donn	89F	505	$ .01	$ .10
Pall, Donn	90F	543	$ .01	$ .04
Pall, Donn	91F	130	$ .01	$ .04
Pall, Donn	92F	92	$ .01	$ .04
Pall, Donn	92FUL	41	$ .01	$ .10
Pall, Donn	93F	586	$ .01	$ .04
Palmeiro, Rafael	88F	429	$ .10	$1.00
Palmeiro, Rafael	89F	434	$ .01	$ .15
Palmeiro, Rafael	89F	631	$ .05	$ .25
Palmeiro, Rafael	89FU	66	$ .01	$ .15
Palmeiro, Rafael	90F	308	$ .01	$ .10
Palmeiro, Rafael	91F	295	$ .01	$ .04
Palmeiro, Rafael	91FUL	350	$ .05	$ .20
Palmeiro, Rafael	92F	311	$ .01	$ .10
Palmeiro, Rafael	92FUL	136	$ .05	$ .25
Palmeiro, Rafael	93F	687	$ .01	$ .04
Palmeiro, Rafael	93FUL	281	$ .01	$ .10
Palmer, Dave "David"	81F	160	$ .01	$ .06
Palmer, David	82F	199	$ .01	$ .06
Palmer, David	83F	291	$ .01	$ .06
Palmer, David	85F	404	$ .01	$ .15
Palmer, David	85F	643	$ .01	$ .15
Palmer, David	86F	255	$ .01	$ .06
Palmer, David	86FU	87	$ .01	$ .08
Palmer, David	87F	525	$ .01	$ .06
Palmer, David	88F	546	$ .01	$ .05
Palmer, David	88FU	111	$ .01	$ .06
Palmer, David	89F	577	$ .01	$ .04
Palmer, Dean	91FU	61	$ .05	$ .20
Palmer, Dean	91FULU	56	$1.00	$4.00
Palmer, Dean	92F	312	$ .01	$ .15
Palmer, Dean	92FUL	137	$ .10	$ .50
Palmer, Dean	93F	325	$ .01	$ .04
Palmer, Dean	93FUL	282	$ .05	$ .25
Palmer, Jim	81F	169	$ .15	$1.50
Palmer, Jim	82F	175	$ .10	$1.00
Palmer, Jim	83F	69	$ .10	$1.00
Palmer, Jim	84F	16	$ .75	$3.00
Pankovits, Jim	86F	307	$ .01	$ .06
Pankovits, Jim	87F	64	$ .01	$ .06
Pankovits, Jim	89F	363	$ .01	$ .04
Papi, Stan	81F	480	$ .01	$ .10
Papi, Stan	82F	280	$ .01	$ .06
Paredes, Johnny	89F	388	$ .01	$ .10
Parent, Mark	88FU	125	$ .01	$ .10
Parent, Mark	89FU	125	$ .01	$ .05

FLEER

Player	Year	No.	VG	EX/MT	Player	Year	No.	VG	EX/MT
Parent, Mark	90F	164	$ .01	$ .04	Pasqua, Dan	92F	93	$ .01	$ .04
Parent, Mark	91F	538	$ .01	$ .04	Pasqua, Dan	92FUL	339	$ .01	$ .10
Paris, Kelly	84F	476	$ .01	$ .08	Pasqua, Dan	93F	587	$ .01	$ .04
Paris, Kelly	89F	506	$ .01	$ .04	Pasque, Dan	90F	544	$ .01	$ .04
Parker, Clay	88F	649	$ .05	$ .25	Pastore, Frank	81F	204	$ .01	$ .06
Parker, Clay	90F	451	$ .01	$ .04	Pastore, Frank	82F	80	$ .01	$ .06
Parker, Clay	91F	346	$ .01	$ .04	Pastore, Frank	83F	599	$ .01	$ .06
Parker, Clay	92FUL	435	$ .01	$ .10	Pastore, Frank	84F	477	$ .01	$ .08
Parker, Dave	81F	360	$ .10	$ .50	Pastore, Frank	85F	545	$ .01	$ .06
Parker, Dave	82F	489	$ .05	$ .25	Pastore, Frank	86F	185	$ .01	$ .06
Parker, Dave	82F	638	$ .05	$ .25	Patek, Fred	81F	283	$ .01	$ .06
Parker, Dave	83F	315	$ .05	$ .35	Patek, Fred	82F	471	$ .01	$ .06
Parker, Dave	84F	258	$ .10	$ .50	Patterson, Bob	88F	337	$ .01	$ .10
Parker, Dave	84FU	89	$1.00	$4.00	Patterson, Bob	90FU	49	$ .01	$ .05
Parker, Dave	85F	544	$ .05	$ .35	Patterson, Bob	91F	45	$ .01	$ .04
Parker, Dave	86F	184	$ .05	$ .25	Patterson, Bob	92F	562	$ .01	$ .04
Parker, Dave	86F	640	$ .05	$ .25	Patterson, Bob	92FUL	558	$ .01	$ .10
Parker, Dave	87F	208	$ .05	$ .20	Patterson, Bob	93F	118	$ .01	$ .04
Parker, Dave	87F	639	$ .05	$ .20	Patterson, John	92FUL	593	$ .05	$ .20
Parker, Dave	88F	243	$ .01	$ .15	Patterson, John	93F	535	$ .01	$ .04
Parker, Dave	88FU	55	$ .01	$ .10	Patterson, Ken	89F	508	$ .01	$ .04
Parker, Dave	89F	19	$ .01	$ .04	Patterson, Ken	90F	545	$ .01	$ .10
Parker, Dave	90F	18	$ .01	$ .10	Patterson, Ken	91F	132	$ .01	$ .04
Parker, Dave	90FU	106	$ .01	$ .10	Patterson, Ken	92F	94	$ .01	$ .04
Parker, Dave	91F	593	$ .01	$ .10	Patterson, Ken	92FUL	472	$ .01	$ .10
Parker, Dave	91FU	10	$ .01	$ .05	Patterson, Ken	93F	381	$ .01	$ .04
Parker, Dave	91FULU	10	$ .01	$ .10	Patterson, Reggie	86F	376	$ .01	$ .06
Parker, Rick	90FU	63	$ .01	$ .10	Pattin, Marty	81F	37	$ .01	$ .06
Parker, Rick	91F	269	$ .01	$ .10	Pavlik, Roger	92FU	62	$ .10	$ .40
Parrett, Jeff	86FU	88	$ .05	$ .20	Pavlik, Roger	93F	688	$ .01	$ .10
Parrett, Jeff	88FU	102	$ .01	$ .10	Pavlik, Roger	93FUL	283	$ .01	$ .15
Parrett, Jeff	89F	389	$ .01	$ .10	Paxton, Mike	81F	401	$ .01	$ .06
Parrett, Jeff	89FU	112	$ .01	$ .05	Pecota, Bill	87FU	97	$ .05	$ .20
Parrett, Jeff	90F	570	$ .01	$ .04	Pecota, Bill	88F	264	$ .01	$ .15
Parrett, Jeff	91F	699	$ .01	$ .04	Pecota, Bill	89F	289	$ .01	$ .04
Parrett, Jeff	93F	297	$ .01	$ .04	Pecota, Bill	91F	565	$ .01	$ .04
Parrett, Jeff	93FUL	261	$ .01	$ .10	Pecota, Bill	91FULU	28	$ .01	$ .10
Parrish, Lance	81F	467	$ .05	$ .35	Pecota, Bill	92F	165	$ .01	$ .04
Parrish, Lance	82F	276	$ .05	$ .25	Pecota, Bill	92FUL	535	$ .01	$ .10
Parrish, Lance	83F	337	$ .05	$ .25	Pecota, Bill	93F	92	$ .01	$ .04
Parrish, Lance	84F	88	$ .05	$ .35	Pedrique, Al	88F	338	$ .01	$ .15
Parrish, Lance	84F	637	$ .01	$ .08	Peguero, Julio	92FUL	547	$ .05	$ .20
Parrish, Lance	85F	19	$ .05	$ .20	Pena, Alejandro	84F	109	$ .10	$ .50
Parrish, Lance	86F	234	$ .05	$ .20	Pena, Alejandro	85F	379	$ .01	$ .06
Parrish, Lance	87F	160	$ .05	$ .20	Pena, Alejandro	86F	140	$ .01	$ .06
Parrish, Lance	87FU	96	$ .01	$ .06	Pena, Alejandro	87F	449	$ .01	$ .06
Parrish, Lance	88F	310	$ .01	$ .10	Pena, Alejandro	88FU	97	$ .01	$ .06
Parrish, Lance	89F	578	$ .01	$ .04	Pena, Alejandro	89F	69	$ .01	$ .04
Parrish, Lance	89FU	15	$ .01	$ .05	Pena, Alejandro	90F	405	$ .01	$ .04
Parrish, Lance	90F	141	$ .01	$ .10	Pena, Alejandro	90FU	38	$ .01	$ .05
Parrish, Lance	91F	321	$ .01	$ .04	Pena, Alejandro	91F	158	$ .01	$ .04
Parrish, Lance	91FUL	51	$ .01	$ .07	Pena, Alejandro	92F	700	$ .01	$ .10
Parrish, Lance	92F	66	$ .01	$ .04	Pena, Alejandro	92FU	70	$ .05	$ .25
Parrish, Lance	92FUL	28	$ .01	$ .10	Pena, Alejandro	92FUL	462	$ .01	$ .10
Parrish, Lance	93F	679	$ .01	$ .04	Pena, Alejandro	93F	369	$ .01	$ .04
Parrish, Larry	81F	146	$ .01	$ .10	Pena, Geronimo	90FU	52	$ .05	$ .20
Parrish, Larry	82F	200	$ .01	$ .10	Pena, Geronimo	91FU	118	$ .01	$ .05
Parrish, Larry	83F	574	$ .01	$ .06	Pena, Geronimo	92F	587	$ .01	$ .04
Parrish, Larry	84F	424	$ .01	$ .08	Pena, Geronimo	93F	131	$ .01	$ .04
Parrish, Larry	85F	564	$ .01	$ .06	Pena, Hipolito	89F	263	$ .01	$ .10
Parrish, Larry	86F	569	$ .01	$ .06	Pena, Jim	92FU	129	$ .05	$ .25
Parrish, Larry	87F	134	$ .01	$ .06	Pena, Jim	93F	536	$ .01	$ .04
Parrish, Larry	88F	476	$ .01	$ .05	Pena, Tony	82F	490	$ .05	$ .20
Parrish, Larry	88FU	7	$ .01	$ .06	Pena, Tony	83F	316	$ .01	$ .15
Parrish, Larry	89F	94	$ .01	$ .04	Pena, Tony	84F	259	$ .05	$ .20
Parsons, Casey	82F	515	$ .01	$ .06	Pena, Tony	85F	472	$ .01	$ .10
Pashnick, Larry	83F	338	$ .01	$ .06	Pena, Tony	86F	616	$ .01	$ .10
Pasqua, Dan	85FU	86	$ .05	$ .35	Pena, Tony	87F	617	$ .01	$ .10
Pasqua, Dan	86F	114	$ .05	$ .20	Pena, Tony	87FU	98	$ .01	$ .10
Pasqua, Dan	87F	108	$ .01	$ .10	Pena, Tony	88F	45	$ .01	$ .10
Pasqua, Dan	88F	217	$ .01	$ .10	Pena, Tony	89F	460	$ .01	$ .04
Pasqua, Dan	88FU	18	$ .01	$ .06	Pena, Tony	90F	256	$ .01	$ .04
Pasqua, Dan	89F	507	$ .01	$ .04	Pena, Tony	90FU	74	$ .01	$ .05
Pasqua, Dan	91F	131	$ .01	$ .04	Pena, Tony	91F	106	$ .01	$ .04
Pasqua, Dan	91FUL	79	$ .01	$ .07	Pena, Tony	91FUL	37	$ .01	$ .07

FLEER

Player	Year	No.	VG	EX/MT	Player	Year	No.	VG	EX/MT
Pena, Tony	92F	43	$ .01	$ .04	Perry, Gerald	86F	525	$ .01	$ .06
Pena, Tony	92FUL	18	$ .01	$ .10	Perry, Gerald	88F	547	$ .01	$ .05
Pena, Tony	93F	563	$ .01	$ .04	Perry, Gerald	89F	597	$ .01	$ .04
Pena, Tony	93FUL	154	$ .01	$ .10	Perry, Gerald	89F	638	$ .01	$ .04
Pendleton, Terry	85F	236	$2.00	$8.00	Perry, Gerald	90F	592	$ .01	$ .04
Pendleton, Terry	86F	44	$ .15	$1.50	Perry, Gerald	90FU	103	$ .01	$ .05
Pendleton, Terry	87F	306	$ .10	$ .75	Perry, Gerald	91F	566	$ .01	$ .04
Pendleton, Terry	88F	46	$ .05	$ .25	Perry, Gerald	91FU	119	$ .01	$ .05
Pendleton, Terry	89F	461	$ .01	$ .10	Perry, Gerald	91FULU	109	$ .01	$ .10
Pendleton, Terry	90F	257	$ .01	$ .10	Perry, Gerald	92F	589	$ .01	$ .04
Pendleton, Terry	91F	642	$ .01	$ .10	Perry, Gerald	92FUL	572	$ .01	$ .10
Pendleton, Terry	91FU	76	$ .01	$ .10	Perry, Gerald	93F	514	$ .01	$ .04
Pendleton, Terry	91FUL	10	$ .01	$ .10	Perry, Pat	86FU	89	$ .01	$ .10
Pendleton, Terry	92F	366	$ .01	$ .04	Perry, Pat	87F	307	$ .01	$ .06
Pendleton, Terry	92FLL	691	$ .01	$ .04	Perry, Pat	88F	244	$ .01	$ .05
Pendleton, Terry	92FUL	167	$ .05	$ .20	Perry, Pat	89F	435	$ .01	$ .04
Pendleton, Terry	93F	12	$ .01	$ .04	Peterek, Jeff	90F	333	$ .01	$ .10
Pendleton, Terry	93FUL	11	$ .01	$ .15	Peters, Rick	81F	470	$ .01	$ .06
Peraza, Oswaldo	89F	615	$ .01	$ .15					
Perconte, Jack	83F	417	$ .01	$ .06					
Perconte, Jack	84FU	90	$ .10	$ .50					
Perconte, Jack	85F	498	$ .01	$ .06					
Perconte, Jack	86F	472	$ .01	$ .06					
Perez, Melido	88F	265	$ .10	$ .50					
Perez, Melido	88FU	19	$ .05	$ .35					
Perez, Melido	89F	509	$ .01	$ .10					
Perez, Melido	90F	546	$ .01	$ .04					
Perez, Melido	91F	133	$ .01	$ .04					
Perez, Melido	91FUL	80	$ .01	$ .07					
Perez, Melido	92F	95	$ .01	$ .04					
Perez, Melido	92FUL	42	$ .01	$ .10					
Perez, Melido	92FUL	413	$ .01	$ .10					
Perez, Melido	93F	284	$ .01	$ .04					
Perez, Melido	93FUL	248	$ .01	$ .10					
Perez, Mike	91F	643	$ .01	$ .10					
Perez, Mike	92F	588	$ .01	$ .04					
Perez, Mike	92FUL	571	$ .01	$ .10					
Perez, Mike	93F	132	$ .01	$ .04					
Perez, Mike	93FUL	111	$ .01	$ .10					
Perez, Pascual	82F	491	$ .05	$ .20					
Perez, Pascual	83F	144	$ .01	$ .06					
Perez, Pascual	84F	188	$ .01	$ .08					
Perez, Pascual	86F	524	$ .01	$ .06					
Perez, Pascual	88F	192	$ .01	$ .05					
Perez, Pascual	89F	390	$ .01	$ .04					
Perez, Pascual	90F	358	$ .01	$ .04					
Perez, Pascual	90FU	116	$ .01	$ .05					
Perez, Pascual	91F	675	$ .01	$ .04					
Perez, Pascual	92F	240	$ .01	$ .04					
Perez, Tony	81F	241	$ .10	$ .50					
Perez, Tony	82F	302	$ .05	$ .35	**Peters, Rick**	**82F**	**277**	**$ .01**	**$ .06**
Perez, Tony	83F	191	$ .05	$ .25	Peters, Ricky	84F	458	$ .01	$ .08
Perez, Tony	84F	44	$ .10	$ .75	Peters, Steve	89F	462	$ .01	$ .04
Perez, Tony	84F	636	$ .10	$ .75	Peterson, Adam	88F	646	$ .05	$ .20
Perez, Tony	84FU	91	$2.00	$8.00	Peterson, Adam	91F	134	$ .01	$ .04
Perez, Tony	85F	546	$ .10	$ .40	Petralli, Gene	83F	439	$ .01	$ .15
Perez, Tony	86F	186	$ .05	$ .25	Petralli, Geno	87F	135	$ .01	$ .06
Perez, Tony	87F	209	$ .05	$ .20	Petralli, Geno	88F	477	$ .01	$ .05
Perezchica, Tony	89F	338	$ .01	$ .04	Petralli, Geno	89F	530	$ .01	$ .04
Perezchica, Tony	92FUL	355	$ .01	$ .10	Petralli, Geno	90F	309	$ .01	$ .04
Perkins, Broderick	81F	498	$ .01	$ .06	Petralli, Geno	91F	296	$ .01	$ .04
Perkins, Broderick	82F	579	$ .01	$ .06	Petralli, Geno	91FUL	351	$ .01	$ .07
Perkins, Broderick	83F	368	$ .01	$ .06	Petralli, Geno	92F	313	$ .01	$ .04
Perkins, Broderick	84F	548	$ .01	$ .08	Petralli, Geno	92FUL	138	$ .01	$ .10
Perlman, Jon	88F	93	$ .01	$ .10	Petralli, Geno	93F	689	$ .01	$ .04
Perlman, Jon	88FU	22	$ .01	$ .06	Petry, Dan	81F	468	$ .01	$ .10
Perry, Gaylord	81F	91	$ .10	$ .50	Petry, Dan	82F	278	$ .01	$ .10
Perry, Gaylord	82F	445	$ .10	$ .50	Petry, Dan	83F	339	$ .01	$ .10
Perry, Gaylord	83F	483	$ .05	$ .35	Petry, Dan	84F	89	$ .01	$ .08
Perry, Gaylord	83F	630	$ .01	$ .10	Petry, Dan	85F	20	$ .01	$ .06
Perry, Gaylord	84F	352	$ .10	$ .50	Petry, Dan	86F	235	$ .01	$ .10
Perry, Gaylord	84F	638	$ .10	$1.00	Petry, Dan	87F	161	$ .01	$ .06
Perry, Gaylord	84F	641	$ .05	$ .35	Petry, Dan	88F	67	$ .01	$ .05
Perry, Gerald	84FU	92	$ .20	$1.75	Petry, Dan	89F	486	$ .01	$ .04
Perry, Gerald	85F	338	$ .01	$ .10	Petry, Dan	90F	142	$ .01	$ .04

FLEER

Player	Year	No.	VG	EX/MT
Petry, Dan	91F	347	$ .01	$ .04
Pettini, Joe	81F	453	$ .01	$ .06

Player	Year	No.	VG	EX/MT
Pettini, Joe	82F	398	$ .01	$ .06
Pettis, Gary	84F	526	$ .05	$ .25
Pettis, Gary	85F	308	$ .01	$ .06
Pettis, Gary	86F	165	$ .01	$ .06
Pettis, Gary	87F	90	$ .01	$ .06
Pettis, Gary	88FU	29	$ .01	$ .06
Pettis, Gary	89F	141	$ .01	$ .04
Pettis, Gary	90F	612	$ .01	$ .04
Pettis, Gary	91F	297	$ .01	$ .04
Pettis, Gary	91FUL	352	$ .01	$ .07
Pettis, Gary	92F	314	$ .01	$ .04
Pettis, Gary	92FUL	580	$ .01	$ .10
Petty, Dan	91FUL	125	$ .01	$ .07
Phelps, Ken	82F	420	$ .01	$ .15
Phelps, Ken	85F	499	$ .01	$ .06
Phelps, Ken	87F	593	$ .01	$ .06
Phelps, Ken	88F	384	$ .01	$ .05
Phelps, Ken	89F	264	$ .01	$ .04
Phillips, Mike	81F	538	$ .01	$ .06
Phillips, Mike	82F	201	$ .01	$ .06
Phillips, Tony	84F	459	$ .15	$1.50
Phillips, Tony	85F	433	$ .01	$ .06
Phillips, Tony	86F	430	$ .01	$ .06
Phillips, Tony	87F	402	$ .01	$ .06
Phillips, Tony	88F	290	$ .01	$ .05
Phillips, Tony	89FU	56	$ .01	$ .05
Phillips, Tony	90F	19	$ .01	$ .04
Phillips, Tony	90FU	99	$ .01	$ .05
Phillips, Tony	91F	348	$ .01	$ .04
Phillips, Tony	91FUL	126	$ .01	$ .07
Phillips, Tony	92F	143	$ .01	$ .04
Phillips, Tony	92FUL	62	$ .01	$ .10
Phillips, Tony	93F	233	$ .01	$ .04
Phillips, Tony	93FUL	203	$ .01	$ .10
Piazza, Mike	92FU	92	$4.50	$18.00
Piazza, Mike	93FUL	60	$1.00	$4.00
Picciolo, Rob	81F	582	$ .01	$ .06
Picciolo, Rob	82F	106	$ .01	$ .06
Pichardo, Hipolito	92FU	32	$ .05	$ .35
Pichardo, Hipolito	93F	246	$ .01	$ .10
Pico, Jeff	88FU	80	$ .01	$ .10
Pico, Jeff	89F	436	$ .01	$ .15
Pico, Jeff	90F	39	$ .01	$ .04
Pico, Jeff	91F	428	$ .01	$ .04
Pierce, Ed	93F	623	$ .01	$ .10
Piniella, Lou	81F	85	$ .01	$ .10
Piniella, Lou	82F	48	$ .01	$ .10
Piniella, Lou	83F	392	$ .01	$ .10
Piniella, Lou	84F	136	$ .01	$ .08
Pittaro, Chris	85FU	87	$ .01	$ .10
Pittman, Joe	82F	222	$ .01	$ .06
Pittman, Joe	83F	369	$ .01	$ .06
Pittman, Park	90FU	109	$ .01	$ .10
Plantier, Phil	91F	107	$ .10	$ .40
Plantier, Phil	91FUL	38	$ .10	$1.00
Plantier, Phil	92F	44	$ .05	$ .20
Plantier, Phil	92FUL	318	$ .10	$ .50
Plantier, Phil	93F	564	$ .01	$ .04
Plesac, Dan	86FU	90	$ .01	$ .15
Plesac, Dan	87F	354	$ .01	$ .10
Plesac, Dan	88F	171	$ .01	$ .10
Plesac, Dan	88F	625	$ .01	$ .05
Plesac, Dan	89F	195	$ .01	$ .04
Plesac, Dan	90F	334	$ .01	$ .04
Plesac, Dan	91F	594	$ .01	$ .04
Plesac, Dan	91FUL	179	$ .01	$ .07
Plesac, Dan	92F	185	$ .01	$ .04
Plesac, Dan	92FUL	388	$ .01	$ .10
Plesac, Dan	93F	633	$ .01	$ .04
Plunk, Eric	86F	649	$10.00	$40.00
Plunk, Eric	87F	403	$ .01	$ .06
Plunk, Eric	88F	291	$ .01	$ .05
Plunk, Eric	89F	20	$ .01	$ .04
Plunk, Eric	90F	452	$ .01	$ .04
Plunk, Eric	91F	676	$ .01	$ .04
Plunk, Eric	91FUL	241	$ .01	$ .07
Plunk, Eric	92F	241	$ .01	$ .04
Plunk, Eric	93F	599	$ .01	$ .04
Pocoroba, Biff	81F	257	$ .01	$ .06
Pocoroba, Biff	82F	446	$ .01	$ .06
Pocoroba, Biff	83F	145	$ .01	$ .06
Pocoroba, Biff	84F	189	$ .01	$ .08
Polidor, Gus	86F	650	$ .05	$ .20
Polidor, Gus	88F	501	$ .01	$ .05
Polonia, Luis	87FU	99	$ .10	$ .50
Polonia, Luis	88F	292	$ .10	$ .50
Polonia, Luis	89F	21	$ .01	$ .04
Polonia, Luis	90FU	80	$ .01	$ .05
Polonia, Luis	91F	322	$ .01	$ .04
Polonia, Luis	91FULU	11	$ .01	$ .10
Polonia, Luis	92F	67	$ .01	$ .04
Polonia, Luis	92FUL	29	$ .01	$ .10
Polonia, Luis	93F	196	$ .01	$ .04
Polonia, Luis	93FUL	168	$ .01	$ .10
Poole, Jim	91F	217	$ .01	$ .10
Poole, Jim	92F	23	$ .01	$ .04
Porter, Chuck	84F	211	$ .01	$ .08
Porter, Chuck	85F	591	$ .01	$ .06
Porter, Darrell	81F	36	$ .01	$ .06
Porter, Darrell	82F	124	$ .01	$ .06
Porter, Darrell	83F	18	$ .01	$ .06
Porter, Darrell	84F	331	$ .01	$ .08
Porter, Darrell	85F	237	$ .01	$ .06
Porter, Darrell	85F	337	$ .01	$ .06
Porter, Darrell	86F	45	$ .01	$ .06
Porter, Darrell	86FU	91	$ .01	$ .08
Porter, Darrell	87F	136	$ .01	$ .06
Portugal, Mark	87F	548	$ .05	$ .25
Portugal, Mark	89F	123	$ .01	$ .04
Portugal, Mark	91F	512	$ .01	$ .04
Portugal, Mark	91FUL	138	$ .01	$ .07
Portugal, Mark	92F	443	$ .01	$ .04
Portugal, Mark	92FUL	494	$ .01	$ .10
Portugal, Mark	93F	441	$ .01	$ .04
Pounders, Brad	89F	642	$ .05	$ .20
Powell, Alonzo	91FU	55	$ .01	$ .10

FLEER

Player	Year	No.	VG	EX/MT	Player	Year	No.	VG	EX/MT
Powell, Alonzo	92F	290	$.01	$.04	Puhl, Terry	84F	235	$.01	$.08
Powell, Dennis	87F	450	$.01	$.06	Puhl, Terry	85F	356	$.01	$.06
Powell, Dennis	89FU	61	$.01	$.05	Puhl, Terry	86F	308	$.01	$.06
Powell, Dennis	90F	521	$.01	$.04	Puhl, Terry	87F	65	$.01	$.06
Powell, Dennis	93F	312	$.01	$.04	Puhl, Terry	88FU	90	$.01	$.06
Powell, Hosken	81F	559	$.01	$.06	Puhl, Terry	89F	364	$.01	$.04
Powell, Hosken	82F	558	$.01	$.06	Puhl, Terry	90F	233	$.01	$.04
Powell, Hosken	83F	440	$.01	$.06	Pujols, Luis	81F	68	$.01	$.06
Power, Ted	82F	17	$.01	$.15	Pujols, Luis	82F	224	$.01	$.06
Power, Ted	84F	478	$.01	$.08	Pujols, Luis	83F	459	$.01	$.06
Power, Ted	85F	547	$.01	$.06	Pujols, Luis	84F	236	$.01	$.08
Power, Ted	86F	187	$.01	$.06	Puleo, Charlie	83F	552	$.01	$.06
Power, Ted	87F	210	$.01	$.06	Puleo, Charlie	84F	480	$.01	$.08
Power, Ted	88F	245	$.01	$.05	Puleo, Charlie	88F	548	$.01	$.05
Power, Ted	88FU	33	$.01	$.06	Puleo, Charlie	89F	598	$.01	$.04
Power, Ted	89F	142	$.01	$.04	Pulliam, Harvey	92F	166	$.01	$.10
Power, Ted	90F	258	$.01	$.04	Putnam, Pat	81F	630	$.01	$.06
Power, Ted	90FU	50	$.01	$.05	Putnam, Pat	82F	327	$.01	$.06
Power, Ted	91F	46	$.01	$.04	Putnam, Pat	84F	617	$.01	$.08
Power, Ted	91FU	85	$.01	$.05	Putnam, Pat	85F	287	$.01	$.06
Power, Ted	92F	416	$.01	$.04	Quantrill, Paul	93F	181	$.01	$.10
Power, Ted	93F	600	$.01	$.04	Quantrill, Paul	93FUL	155	$.01	$.15
Pratt, Todd	93F	497	$.01	$.15	Quinones, Luis	86FU	92	$.01	$.08
Presley, Jim	85F	500	$.10	$.50	Quinones, Luis	90F	428	$.01	$.04
Presley, Jim	86F	473	$.05	$.25	Quinones, Luis	91F	77	$.01	$.04
Presley, Jim	87F	594	$.01	$.10	Quinones, Luis	91FULU	77	$.01	$.10
Presley, Jim	88F	385	$.01	$.10	Quinones, Luis	92F	417	$.01	$.04
Presley, Jim	89F	555	$.01	$.04	Quinones, Rey	87F	595	$.05	$.25
Presley, Jim	90F	522	$.01	$.04	Quinones, Rey	88F	386	$.01	$.05
Presley, Jim	90FU	6	$.01	$.05	Quinones, Rey	89F	556	$.01	$.04
Presley, Jim	91F	700	$.01	$.04	Quinones (z), Rey	86FU	93	$.01	$.15
Price, Joe	81F	210	$.01	$.06	Quintana, Carlos	89F	95	$.01	$.10
Price, Joe	82F	81	$.01	$.06	Quintana, Carlos	90F	283	$.01	$.10
Price, Joe	83F	600	$.01	$.06	Quintana, Carlos	91F	108	$.01	$.04
Price, Joe	84F	479	$.01	$.08	Quintana, Carlos	91FUL	39	$.01	$.07
Price, Joe	85F	548	$.01	$.06	Quintana, Carlos	92F	45	$.01	$.04
Price, Joe	86F	188	$.01	$.06	Quintana, Carlos	92FUL	19	$.01	$.10
Price, Joe	87F	211	$.01	$.06	Quirk, Jamie	81F	50	$.01	$.06
Price, Joe	89F	339	$.01	$.04	Quirk, Jamie	82F	421	$.01	$.06
Price, Joe	90F	282	$.01	$.04	Quirk, Jamie	84F	332	$.01	$.08
Price, Joe	91F	488	$.01	$.04	Quirk, Jamie	87F	377	$.01	$.06
Prince, Tom	89F	217	$.01	$.04	Quirk, Jamie	88F	266	$.01	$.05
Prince, Tom	92FUL	559	$.01	$.10	Quirk, Jamie	89F	290	$.01	$.04
Proly, Mike	81F	358	$.01	$.06	Quirk, Jamie	91F	21	$.01	$.04
Proly, Mike	82F	254	$.01	$.06	Quirk, Jamie	92F	265	$.01	$.04
Proly, Mike	83F	505	$.01	$.06	Quirk, Jamie	93F	667	$.01	$.04
Proly, Mike	84F	501	$.01	$.08	Quisenberry, Dan	81F	31	$.05	$.20
Pryor, Greg	81F	359	$.01	$.06	Quisenberry, Dan	82F	422	$.05	$.20
Pryor, Greg	82F	356	$.01	$.06	Quisenberry, Dan	83F	122	$.05	$.20
Pryor, Greg	83F	121	$.01	$.06	Quisenberry, Dan	84F	354	$.05	$.20
Pryor, Greg	84F	353	$.01	$.08	Quisenberry, Dan	84F	635	$.01	$.08
Pryor, Greg	85F	210	$.01	$.06	Quisenberry, Dan	85F	211	$.05	$.20
Puckett, Kirby	84FU	93	$100.00	$400.00	Quisenberry, Dan	86F	18	$.05	$.20
Puckett, Kirby	85F	286	$11.25	$45.00	Quisenberry, Dan	87F	378	$.01	$.10
Puckett, Kirby	86F	401	$2.50	$10.00	Quisenberry, Dan	88F	267	$.01	$.10
Puckett, Kirby	87F	549	$1.00	$4.00	Quisenberry, Dan	89FU	120	$.01	$.05
Puckett, Kirby	87F	633	$.10	$1.00	Quisenberry, Dan	90F	259	$.01	$.04
Puckett, Kirby	88F	19	$.10	$1.00	Radinsky, Scott	90FU	86	$.01	$.15
Puckett, Kirby	88F	638	$.05	$.20	Radinsky, Scott	91F	135	$.01	$.10
Puckett, Kirby	89F	124	$.05	$.25	Radinsky, Scott	91FULU	18	$.01	$.10
Puckett, Kirby	89F	639	$.01	$.15	Radinsky, Scott	92F	96	$.01	$.04
Puckett, Kirby	90F	383	$.05	$.25	Radinsky, Scott	92FUL	340	$.01	$.10
Puckett, Kirby	90F	635	$.01	$.15	Radinsky, Scott	93F	208	$.01	$.04
Puckett, Kirby	91F	623	$.05	$.20	Radinsky, Scott	93FUL	177	$.01	$.10
Puckett, Kirby	91FUL	195	$.10	$.50	Raines, Tim	82F	202	$.20	$2.00
Puckett, Kirby	92F	217	$.01	$.15	Raines, Tim	83F	292	$.10	$.50
Puckett, Kirby	92F	704	$.05	$.10	Raines, Tim	84F	281	$.10	$1.00
Puckett, Kirby	92FUL	97	$.10	$1.00	Raines, Tim	84F	631	$.10	$.50
Puckett, Kirby	93F	273	$.05	$.20	Raines, Tim	85F	405	$.05	$.35
Puckett, Kirby	93F	355	$.05	$.15	Raines, Tim	86F	256	$.05	$.25
Puckett, Kirby	93FUL	236	$.10	$.50	Raines, Tim	86F	632	$.10	$.50
Pugh, Tim	93F	40	$.05	$.35	Raines, Tim	87F	328	$.05	$.25
Puhl, Terry	81F	62	$.01	$.06	Raines, Tim	87F	642	$.01	$.15
Puhl, Terry	82F	223	$.01	$.06	Raines, Tim	88F	193	$.01	$.15
Puhl, Terry	83F	458	$.01	$.06	Raines, Tim	88F	631	$.01	$.15

FLEER

Player	Year	No.	VG	EX/MT	Player	Year	No.	VG	EX/MT
Raines, Tim	89F	391	$ .01	$ .15	Rawley, Shane	86F	446	$ .01	$ .06
Raines, Tim	90F	359	$ .01	$ .10	Rawley, Shane	86F	456	$ .01	$ .06
Raines, Tim	91F	244	$ .01	$ .04	Rawley, Shane	87F	180	$ .01	$ .06
Raines, Tim	91FU	15	$ .01	$ .05	Rawley, Shane	88F	311	$ .01	$ .05
Raines, Tim	91FUL	81	$ .01	$ .07	Rawley, Shane	89F	579	$ .01	$ .04
Raines, Tim	92F	97	$ .01	$ .04	Rawley, Shane	89FU	44	$ .01	$ .05
Raines, Tim	92FUL	43	$ .01	$ .10	Rawley, Shane	90F	384	$ .01	$ .04
Raines, Tim	93F	209	$ .01	$ .04	Ray, Johnny	82F	492	$ .05	$ .20
Raines, Tim	93FUL	178	$ .01	$ .10	Ray, Johnny	83F	317	$ .01	$ .10
Rainey, Chuck	82F	303	$ .01	$ .06	Ray, Johnny	84F	260	$ .01	$ .10
Rainey, Chuck	83F	192	$ .01	$ .06	Ray, Johnny	85F	473	$ .01	$ .10
Rainey, Chuck	84F	502	$ .01	$ .08	Ray, Johnny	86F	617	$ .01	$ .10
Rajsich, Gary	83F	553	$ .01	$ .06	Ray, Johnny	87F	618	$ .01	$ .10
Ramirez, Mario	84F	309	$ .01	$ .08	Ray, Johnny	88F	502	$ .01	$ .10
Ramirez, Rafael	81F	266	$ .05	$ .25	Ray, Johnny	89F	487	$ .01	$ .04
Ramirez, Rafael	82F	447	$ .01	$ .06	Ray, Johnny	90F	143	$ .01	$ .04
Ramirez, Rafael	83F	146	$ .01	$ .06	Ray, Johnny	91F	323	$ .01	$ .04
Ramirez, Rafael	84F	190	$ .01	$ .08	Rayford, Floyd	84F	334	$ .01	$ .08
Ramirez, Rafael	85F	339	$ .01	$ .06	Rayford, Floyd	84FU	95	$ .10	$ .50
Ramirez, Rafael	86F	526	$ .01	$ .06	Rayford, Floyd	85F	186	$ .01	$ .06
Ramirez, Rafael	87F	526	$ .01	$ .06	Rayford, Floyd	86F	283	$ .01	$ .06
Ramirez, Rafael	88FU	91	$ .01	$ .06	Ready, Randy	85F	592	$ .01	$ .15
Ramirez, Rafael	89F	365	$ .01	$ .04	Ready, Randy	86F	498	$ .01	$ .06
Ramirez, Rafael	90F	234	$ .01	$ .04	Ready, Randy	87FU	100	$ .01	$ .06
Ramirez, Rafael	91F	513	$ .01	$ .04	Ready, Randy	88F	594	$ .01	$ .05
Ramirez, Rafael	91FUL	139	$ .01	$ .07	Ready, Randy	89F	315	$ .01	$ .15
Ramirez, Rafael	92FUL	495	$ .01	$ .10	Ready, Randy	90F	571	$ .01	$ .04
Ramos, Bobby "Roberto"	81F	162	$ .01	$ .06	Ready, Randy	91F	410	$ .01	$ .04
Ramos, Bobby	82F	203	$ .01	$ .06	Ready, Randy	91FUL	271	$ .01	$ .07
Ramos, Bobby	84F	282	$ .01	$ .08	Ready, Randy	92F	542	$ .01	$ .04
Ramos, Domingo	88FU	23	$ .01	$ .06	Ready, Randy	92FUL	427	$ .01	$ .10
Ramos, Domingo	91F	429	$ .01	$ .04	Reardon, Jeff	81F	335	$1.25	$5.00
Ramos, John	91FUL	385	$ .01	$ .10	Reardon, Jeff	82F	204	$ .15	$1.50
Ramos, John	92F	242	$ .01	$ .10	Reardon, Jeff	83F	293	$ .15	$1.25
Ramsey, Mike	81F	549	$ .01	$ .06	Reardon, Jeff	84F	283	$ .15	$1.50
Ramsey, Mike	82F	125	$ .01	$ .06	Reardon, Jeff	85F	407	$ .10	$ .75
Ramsey, Mike	83F	19	$ .01	$ .06	Reardon, Jeff	86F	257	$ .10	$ .50
Ramsey, Mike	84F	333	$ .01	$ .08	Reardon, Jeff	87F	329	$ .05	$ .35
Ramsey, Mike	85F	406	$ .01	$ .06	Reardon, Jeff	87FU	101	$ .01	$ .15
Randle, Lenny	81F	301	$ .01	$ .06	Reardon, Jeff	88F	20	$ .01	$ .15
Randle, Lenny	82F	516	$ .01	$ .06	Reardon, Jeff	89F	125	$ .01	$ .04
Randolph, Willie	81F	109	$ .01	$ .15	Reardon, Jeff	90F	385	$ .01	$ .10
Randolph, Willie	82F	49	$ .01	$ .15	Reardon, Jeff	90FU	75	$ .01	$ .05
Randolph, Willie	83F	393	$ .01	$ .06	Reardon, Jeff	91F	109	$ .01	$ .04
Randolph, Willie	84F	137	$ .01	$ .08	Reardon, Jeff	91FUL	40	$ .01	$ .07
Randolph, Willie	85F	140	$ .01	$ .06	Reardon, Jeff	92F	46	$ .01	$ .04
Randolph, Willie	86F	115	$ .01	$ .06	Reardon, Jeff	92FU	71	$ .05	$ .25
Randolph, Willie	87F	109	$ .01	$ .06	Reardon, Jeff	92FUH	3	$ .15	$1.50
Randolph, Willie	88F	218	$ .01	$ .05	Reardon, Jeff	92FUL	20	$ .01	$ .10
Randolph, Willie	89F	265	$ .01	$ .04	Reardon, Jeff	93F	370	$ .01	$ .10
Randolph, Willie	89FU	93	$ .01	$ .05	Reboulet, Jeff	93F	642	$ .01	$ .04
Randolph, Willie	90F	406	$ .01	$ .04	Redfern, Pete	81F	560	$ .01	$ .06
Randolph, Willie	91F	22	$ .01	$ .04	Redfern, Pete	82F	559	$ .01	$ .06
Randolph, Willie	91FU	33	$ .01	$ .05	Redfern, Pete	83F	623	$ .01	$ .06
Randolph, Willie	91FULU	32	$ .01	$ .10	Redfield, Joe	92F	563	$ .01	$ .10
Randolph, Willie	92F	186	$ .01	$ .04	Redus, Gary	84F	481	$ .05	$ .25
Randolph, Willie	92FUL	536	$ .01	$ .10	Redus, Gary	85F	549	$ .01	$ .06
Randolph, Willie	93F	479	$ .01	$ .04	Redus, Gary	86F	189	$ .01	$ .06
Rapp, Pat	93F	429	$ .01	$ .10	Redus, Gary	86FU	94	$ .01	$ .08
Rasmussen, Dennis	85F	141	$ .05	$ .20	Redus, Gary	87F	181	$ .01	$ .06
Rasmussen, Dennis	87F	110	$ .01	$ .06	Redus, Gary	87FU	102	$ .01	$ .06
Rasmussen, Dennis	88F	246	$ .01	$ .05	Redus, Gary	88F	408	$ .01	$ .05
Rasmussen, Dennis	88FU	126	$ .01	$ .06	Redus, Gary	89F	218	$ .01	$ .04
Rasmussen, Dennis	89F	314	$ .01	$ .04	Redus, Gary	90F	476	$ .01	$ .04
Rasmussen, Dennis	90F	165	$ .01	$ .04	Redus, Gary	91F	47	$ .01	$ .04
Rasmussen, Dennis	91F	539	$ .01	$ .04	Redus, Gary	91FUL	285	$ .01	$ .07
Rasmussen, Dennis	91FUL	309	$ .01	$ .07	Redus, Gary	92F	564	$ .01	$ .04
Rasmussen, Dennis	92F	617	$ .01	$ .04	Redus, Gary	92FUL	560	$ .01	$ .10
Rasmussen, Eric	81F	497	$ .01	$ .06	Redus, Gary	93F	504	$ .01	$ .04
Rau, Doug	81F	133	$ .01	$ .06	Reed, Darren	90FU	39	$ .01	$ .15
Rawley, Shane	82F	517	$ .01	$ .10	Reed, Darren	91F	159	$ .01	$ .10
Rawley, Shane	83F	394	$ .01	$ .06	Reed, Jeff	86FU	95	$ .01	$ .08
Rawley, Shane	84F	138	$ .01	$ .08	Reed, Jeff	87F	550	$ .01	$ .06
Rawley, Shane	84FU	94	$ .10	$ .50	Reed, Jeff	88F	194	$ .01	$ .05
Rawley, Shane	85F	263	$ .01	$ .06	Reed, Jeff	89F	167	$ .01	$ .04

FLEER

Player	Year	No.	VG	EX/MT
Reed, Jeff	90F	429	$ .01	$ .05
Reed, Jeff	91F	78	$ .01	$ .04
Reed, Jeff	91FUL	101	$ .01	$ .07
Reed, Jeff	92F	418	$ .01	$ .04
Reed, Jeff	92FUL	195	$ .01	$ .10
Reed, Jeff	93F	397	$ .01	$ .04
Reed, Jerry	86F	592	$ .01	$ .06
Reed, Jerry	88F	387	$ .01	$ .05
Reed, Jerry	89F	557	$ .01	$ .04

Player	Year	No.	VG	EX/MT
Reed, Jerry	**90F**	**523**	**$ .01**	**$ .04**
Reed, Jerry	90FU	76	$ .01	$ .05
Reed, Jerry	91F	110	$ .01	$ .04
Reed, Jody	88F	360	$ .10	$ .50
Reed, Jody	89F	96	$ .01	$ .04
Reed, Jody	90F	284	$ .01	$ .04
Reed, Jody	91F	111	$ .01	$ .04
Reed, Jody	91FUL	41	$ .01	$ .07
Reed, Jody	92F	47	$ .01	$ .04
Reed, Jody	92FUL	21	$ .01	$ .10
Reed, Jody	93F	182	$ .01	$ .04
Reed, Rick	90F	477	$ .01	$ .10
Reed, Ron	81F	11	$ .01	$ .06
Reed, Ron	82F	255	$ .01	$ .06
Reed, Ron	83F	169	$ .01	$ .06
Reed, Ron	84F	45	$ .01	$ .08
Reed, Ron	84FU	96	$ .10	$ .50
Reed, Ron	85F	524	$ .01	$ .06
Reed, Steve	93F	414	$ .01	$ .10
Reid, Jessie	88F	643	$ .05	$ .25
Reimer, Kevin	89F	641	$ .10	$ .75
Reimer, Kevin	90F	310	$ .01	$ .10
Reimer, Kevin	91F	298	$ .01	$ .10
Reimer, Kevin	91FULU	57	$ .05	$ .25
Reimer, Kevin	92F	315	$ .01	$ .04
Reimer, Kevin	92FUL	444	$ .01	$ .10
Reimer, Kevin	93F	326	$ .01	$ .04
Reitz, Ken	81F	530	$ .01	$ .06
Reitz, Ken	82F	602	$ .01	$ .06
Remllinger, Mike	92F	646	$ .01	$ .04
Remy, Jerry	81F	238	$ .01	$ .06
Remy, Jerry	82F	304	$ .01	$ .06
Remy, Jerry	83F	193	$ .01	$ .06
Remy, Jerry	84F	407	$ .01	$ .08

Player	Year	No.	VG	EX/MT
Remy, Jerry	85F	167	$ .01	$ .06
Renko, Steve	81F	231	$ .01	$ .06
Renko, Steve	82F	472	$ .01	$ .06
Renko, Steve	83F	99	$ .01	$ .06
Renko, Steve	84F	355	$ .01	$ .08
Reuschel, Rick	81F	293	$ .01	$ .10
Reuschel, Rick	82F	50	$ .01	$ .06
Reuschel, Rick	85F	63	$ .01	$ .06
Reuschel, Rick	85FU	88	$ .01	$ .10
Reuschel, Rick	86F	618	$ .01	$ .06
Reuschel, Rick	87F	619	$ .01	$ .06
Reuschel, Rick	88F	94	$ .01	$ .10
Reuschel, Rick	89F	340	$ .01	$ .04
Reuschel, Rick	90F	68	$ .01	$ .04
Reuschel, Rick	91F	270	$ .01	$ .04
Reuss, Jerry	81F	118	$ .01	$ .10
Reuss, Jerry	82F	18	$ .01	$ .06
Reuss, Jerry	83F	216	$ .01	$ .06
Reuss, Jerry	84F	110	$ .01	$ .08
Reuss, Jerry	85F	380	$ .01	$ .06
Reuss, Jerry	86F	141	$ .01	$ .06
Reuss, Jerry	87F	451	$ .01	$ .06
Reuss, Jerry	89F	510	$ .01	$ .04
Reuss, Jerry	90F	335	$ .01	$ .04
Revering, Dave	81F	576	$ .01	$ .06
Revering, Dave	82F	51	$ .01	$ .06
Revering, Dave	83F	484	$ .01	$ .06
Reyes, Gilberto	91FU	99	$ .01	$ .05
Reyes, Gilberto	91FULU	92	$ .01	$ .10
Reyes, Gilberto	92F	489	$ .01	$ .04
Reyes, Gilberto	92FUL	225	$ .01	$ .10
Reynolds, Craig	81F	74	$ .01	$ .06
Reynolds, Craig	82F	225	$ .01	$ .06
Reynolds, Craig	83F	460	$ .01	$ .06
Reynolds, Craig	84F	237	$ .01	$ .08
Reynolds, Craig	85F	357	$ .01	$ .06
Reynolds, Craig	86F	309	$ .01	$ .06
Reynolds, Craig	87F	66	$ .01	$ .06
Reynolds, Craig	88F	454	$ .01	$ .05
Reynolds, Craig	89F	366	$ .01	$ .04
Reynolds, Harold	87F	596	$ .01	$ .15
Reynolds, Harold	88F	388	$ .01	$ .05
Reynolds, Harold	89F	558	$ .01	$ .04
Reynolds, Harold	90F	524	$ .01	$ .04
Reynolds, Harold	91F	460	$ .01	$ .04
Reynolds, Harold	91FUL	343	$ .01	$ .07
Reynolds, Harold	92F	291	$ .01	$ .04
Reynolds, Harold	92FUL	129	$ .01	$ .10
Reynolds, Harold	93F	680	$ .01	$ .04
Reynolds, R.J.	84FU	97	$ .10	$1.00
Reynolds, R.J.	85F	381	$ .01	$ .15
Reynolds, R.J.	86F	619	$ .01	$ .06
Reynolds, R.J.	87F	620	$ .01	$ .06
Reynolds, R.J.	88F	339	$ .01	$ .05
Reynolds, R.J.	89F	219	$ .01	$ .04
Reynolds, R.J.	90F	478	$ .01	$ .04
Reynolds, R.J.	91F	48	$ .01	$ .04
Reynolds, Ronn	86F	92	$ .01	$ .06
Reynoso, Armando	92F	367	$ .01	$ .15
Rhoden, Rick	81F	377	$ .01	$ .10
Rhoden, Rick	82F	493	$ .01	$ .06
Rhoden, Rick	83F	318	$ .01	$ .06
Rhoden, Rick	84F	261	$ .01	$ .08
Rhoden, Rick	85F	474	$ .01	$ .06
Rhoden, Rick	86F	620	$ .01	$ .06
Rhoden, Rick	87F	621	$ .01	$ .06
Rhoden, Rick	87FU	103	$ .01	$ .06
Rhoden, Rick	88F	219	$ .01	$ .10
Rhoden, Rick	89F	266	$ .01	$ .04
Rhoden, Rick	89FU	89	$ .01	$ .05
Rhoden, Rick	90F	235	$ .01	$ .04
Rhodes, Arthur	92F	24	$ .01	$ .10
Rhodes, Arthur	93F	174	$ .01	$ .10
Rhodes, Karl	91F	514	$ .01	$ .10
Rice, Jim	81F	222	$ .05	$ .35

FLEER

Player	Year	No.	VG	EX/MT	Player	Year	No.	VG	EX/MT
Rice, Jim	82F	305	$ .05	$ .30	Rijo, Jose	91F	79	$ .01	$ .04
Rice, Jim	83F	194	$ .05	$ .25	Rijo, Jose	91FUL	102	$ .01	$ .07
Rice, Jim	84F	408	$ .05	$ .25	Rijo, Jose	92F	419	$ .01	$ .04
Rice, Jim	85F	168	$ .05	$ .20	Rijo, Jose	92FUL	196	$ .01	$ .10
Rice, Jim	86F	358	$ .05	$ .20	Rijo, Jose	93F	41	$ .01	$ .04
Rice, Jim	87F	41	$ .01	$ .15	Rijo, Jose	93FUL	33	$ .01	$ .15
Rice, Jim	87F	633	$ .10	$1.00	Riles, Earnie "Earnest"	85FU	89	$ .01	$ .15
Rice, Jim	88F	361	$ .01	$ .15	Riles, Earnie	86F	499	$ .05	$ .25
Rice, Jim	89F	97	$ .01	$ .10	Riles, Earnie	87F	355	$ .01	$ .06
Rice, Pat	92F	658	$ .01	$ .15	Riles, Earnie	88F	172	$ .01	$ .05
Richard, J.R.	81F	56	$ .01	$ .10	Riles, Earnest	88FU	130	$ .01	$ .06
Richard, J.R.	82F	226	$ .01	$ .10	Riles, Earnest	89F	341	$ .01	$ .04
Richards, Gene	81F	486	$ .01	$ .06	Riles, Ernie	90F	69	$ .01	$ .04
Richards, Gene	82F	580	$ .01	$ .06	Riles, Ernest	91F	271	$ .01	$ .04
Richards, Gene	83F	370	$ .01	$ .06	Riles, Ernest	91FU	51	$ .01	$ .05
Richards, Gene	84F	310	$ .01	$ .08	Riles, Ernest	91FULU	47	$ .01	$ .10
Richards, Gene	84FU	98	$ .10	$ .50	Ripken, Bill(y)	88F	569	$ .01	$ .15
Richards, Gene	85F	619	$ .01	$ .06	Ripken, Bill(y)	88F	640	$ .10	$ .40
Richardt, Mike	83F	575	$ .01	$ .06	Ripken, Bill	89F	616	$ .01	$ .15
Rick, Dempsey	84F	644	$ .01	$ .08	Ripken, Bill (obscene bat)	89F	616	$2.00	$8.00
Righetti, Dave	82F	52	$ .10	$ .50	Ripken, Bill	90F	186	$ .01	$ .04
Righetti, Dave	83F	395	$ .05	$ .20	Ripken, Billy	91F	489	$ .01	$ .04
Righetti, Dave	84F	139	$ .05	$ .25	Ripken, Bill	91FUL	23	$ .01	$ .07
Righetti, Dave	84F	639	$ .01	$ .08	Ripken, Billy	92F	25	$ .01	$ .04
Righetti, Dave	85F	142	$ .05	$ .20	Ripken, Billy	92FUL	10	$ .01	$ .10
Righetti, Dave	86F	116	$ .01	$ .15	Ripken, Billy	93F	550	$ .01	$ .04
Righetti, Dave	87F	111	$ .01	$ .10	Ripken, Jr., Cal	82F	176	$12.50	$50.00
Righetti, Dave	87F	627	$ .01	$ .10	Ripken ,Jr., Cal	83F	70	$4.00	$16.00
Righetti, Dave	88F	220	$ .01	$ .10	Ripken, Jr., Cal	84F	17	$4.50	$18.00
Righetti, Dave	88F	625	$ .01	$ .05	Ripken, Jr., Cal	85F	187	$2.50	$10.00
Righetti, Dave	89F	267	$ .01	$ .04	Ripken, Jr., Cal	85F	626	$1.00	$4.00
Righetti, Dave	90F	453	$ .01	$ .04	Ripken, Jr., Cal	85F	641	$ .75	$3.00
Righetti, Dave	91F	677	$ .01	$ .04	Ripken, Jr., Cal	86F	284	$1.25	$5.00
Righetti, Dave	91FU	131	$ .01	$ .05	Ripken, Jr., Cal	86F	633	$ .10	$1.00
Righetti, Dave	92F	647	$ .01	$ .04	Ripken, Jr., Cal	87F	478	$ .75	$3.00
Righetti, Dave	92FUL	594	$ .01	$ .10	Ripken, Jr., Cal	88F	570	$ .10	$1.00
Righetti, Dave	93F	537	$ .01	$ .04	Ripken, Jr., Cal	88F	635	$ .05	$ .35
Rijo, Jose	84FU	99	$7.00	$28.00	Ripken. Jr., Cal	88F	640	$ .10	$ .40
Rijo, Jose	85F	143	$ .75	$3.00	Ripken, Jr., Cal	89F	617	$ .10	$ .50
Rijo, Jose	86F	431	$ .10	$ .50	Ripken, Jr., Cal	90F	187	$ .05	$ .25
					Ripken, Jr., Cal	90F	634	$ .01	$ .10
					Ripken, Jr., Cal	90FPD	624	$ .05	$ .20
					Ripken, Jr., Cal	91F	490	$ .05	$ .25
					Ripken, Jr., Cal	91FUL	24	$ .10	$ .75
					Ripken, Jr., Cal	92F	26	$ .05	$ .35
					Ripken, Jr., Cal	92F	703	$ .01	$ .15
					Ripken, Jr., Cal	92F	711	$ .10	$ .40
					Ripken, Jr., Cal	92FUL	11	$ .15	$1.50
					Ripken, Jr., Cal	93F	551	$ .05	$ .25
					Ripken, Sr., Cal	85F	641	$ .75	$3.00
					Ripley, Allen	81F	454	$ .01	$ .06
					Ripley, Allen	82F	399	$ .01	$ .06
					Ripley, Allen	83F	506	$ .01	$ .06
					Ritchie, Wally	87FU	104	$ .01	$ .06
					Ritchie, Wally	88F	312	$ .01	$ .10
					Ritchie, Wally	92F	543	$ .01	$ .04
					Ritz, Kevin	90F	613	$ .01	$ .15
					Ritz, Kevin	92FUL	368	$ .01	$ .10
					Ritz, Kevin	93F	415	$ .01	$ .04
					Rivera, Ben	92FU	111	$ .10	$1.00
					Rivera, Ben	92FUL	463	$ .05	$ .35
					Rivera, Ben	93F	107	$ .01	$ .10
					Rivera, Ben	93FUL	93	$ .01	$ .10
					Rivera, Bombo	81F	556	$ .01	$ .06
					Rivera, German	85F	382	$ .01	$ .06
					Rivera, Luis	87F	330	$ .01	$ .06
					Rivera, Luis	89F	392	$ .01	$ .04
					Rivera, Luis	90F	285	$ .01	$ .04
					Rivera, Luis	91F	112	$ .01	$ .04
					Rivera, Luis	91FUL	42	$ .01	$ .07
					Rivera, Luis	92F	48	$ .01	$ .04
					Rivera, Luis	92FUL	22	$ .01	$ .10
					Rivera, Luis	93F	565	$ .01	$ .04
					Rivers, Mickey	81F	617	$ .01	$ .06
					Rivers, Mickey	82F	328	$ .01	$ .06

Rijo, Jose	87F	404	$ .05	$ .35
Rijo, Jose	88FU	86	$ .01	$ .15
Rijo, Jose	89F	168	$ .01	$ .10
Rijo, Jose	90F	430	$ .01	$ .15

FLEER

Player	Year	No.	VG	EX/MT	Player	Year	No.	VG	EX/MT
Rivers, Mickey	83F	576	$.01	$.06	Rodriguez, Henry	93F	453	$.01	$.04
Rivers, Mickey	84F	425	$.01	$.08	Rodriguez, Ivan	91FU	62	$.10	$1.00
Rivers, Mickey	85F	565	$.01	$.06	Rodriguez, Ivan	91FULU	58	$1.50	$6.00
Robbins, Bruce	81F	477	$.01	$.06	Rodriguez, Ivan	92F	316	$.10	$.75
Roberge, Bert	83F	461	$.01	$.06	Rodriguez, Ivan	92FUL	139	$.15	$1.50
Roberge, Bert	85F	525	$.01	$.06	Rodriguez, Ivan	93F	327	$.05	$.20
Roberge, Bert	86F	258	$.01	$.06	Rodriguez, Ivan	93F	355	$.01	$.15
Roberts, Bip	86FU	96	$.10	$1.00	Rodriguez, Ivan	93FUL	284	$.10	$.50
Roberts, Bip	87F	427	$.15	$1.50	Rodriguez, Rick	88F	293	$.01	$.15
Roberts, Bip	89FU	126	$.01	$.05	Rodriguez, Richard	91F	541	$.01	$.10
Roberts, Bip	90F	166	$.01	$.10	Rodriguez, Rich	92F	619	$.01	$.04
Roberts, Bip	91F	540	$.01	$.04	Rodriguez, Rich	92FUL	581	$.01	$.10
Roberts, Bip	91FUL	310	$.01	$.07	Rodriguez, Rich	93F	145	$.01	$.04
Roberts, Bip	92F	618	$.01	$.04	Rodriguez, Rich	93FUL	120	$.01	$.10
Roberts, Bip	92FU	82	$.05	$.25	Rodriguez, Rosario	92F	565	$.01	$.04
Roberts, Bip	92FUL	485	$.01	$.10	Roenicke, Gary	81F	187	$.01	$.06
Roberts, Bip	93F	42	$.01	$.04	Roenicke, Gary	83F	71	$.01	$.06
Roberts, Bip	93FUL	34	$.01	$.10	Roenicke, Gary	84F	18	$.01	$.08
Roberts, Dave	81F	607	$.01	$.06	Roenicke, Gary	85F	188	$.01	$.06
Roberts, Dave	81F	636	$.01	$.06	Roenicke, Gary	86F	285	$.01	$.06
Roberts, Dave	82F	227	$.01	$.06	Roenicke, Gary	86FU	98	$.01	$.08
Roberts, Leon	81F	608	$.01	$.06	Roenicke, Gary	87F	112	$.01	$.06
Roberts, Leon	82F	329	$.01	$.06	Roenicke, Ron	82F	19	$.01	$.06
Roberts, Leon	84F	356	$.01	$.08	Roenicke, Ron	82F	177	$.01	$.06
Robertson, Andre	83F	396	$.01	$.06	Roenicke, Ron	83F	217	$.01	$.06
Robertson, Andre	84F	140	$.01	$.08	Roenicke, Ron	84F	618	$.01	$.08
Robertson, Andre	85F	144	$.01	$.06	Roenicke, Ron	86FU	99	$.01	$.08
Robertson, Andre	86F	117	$.01	$.06	Roenicke, Ron	87F	182	$.01	$.06
Robidoux, Billy Joe	86F	652	$.01	$.10	Roesler, Mike	90F	645	$.05	$.35
Robidoux, Billy Joe	86FU	97	$.01	$.08	Rogers, Kenny	90F	311	$.05	$.10
Robidoux, Billy Joe	87F	356	$.01	$.06	Rogers, Kenny	91F	299	$.01	$.04
Robinson, Bill	81F	373	$.01	$.06	Rogers, Kenny	91FUL	353	$.01	$.07
Robinson, Bill	82F	494	$.01	$.06	Rogers, Kenny	92F	317	$.01	$.04
Robinson, Don	81F	366	$.01	$.06	Rogers, Kenny	92FUL	445	$.01	$.10
Robinson, Don	82F	495	$.01	$.06	Rogers, Kenny	93F	328	$.01	$.04
Robinson, Don	83F	319	$.01	$.06	Rogers, Kenny	93FUL	285	$.01	$.10
Robinson, Don	84F	262	$.01	$.08	Rogers, Steve	81F	143	$.01	$.06
Robinson, Don	85F	475	$.01	$.06	Rogers, Steve	82F	205	$.01	$.06
Robinson, Don	86F	621	$.01	$.06	Rogers, Steve	83F	294	$.01	$.06
Robinson, Don	87F	622	$.01	$.06	Rogers, Steve	84F	284	$.01	$.08
Robinson, Don	88F	95	$.01	$.05	Rogers, Steve	85F	408	$.01	$.06
Robinson, Don	89F	342	$.01	$.04	Rohde, Dave	90FU	17	$.01	$.10
Robinson, Don	90F	70	$.01	$.04	Rojas, Mel	91F	245	$.01	$.10
Robinson, Don	91F	272	$.01	$.04	Rojas, Mel	92F	490	$.01	$.04
Robinson, Don	91FUL	327	$.01	$.07	Rojas, Mel	93F	79	$.01	$.04
Robinson, Don	92FUL	329	$.01	$.10	Rojas, Mel	93FUL	70	$.01	$.10
Robinson, Jeff D.	84FU	100	$.10	$.75	Roman, Jose	85F	646	$.01	$.10
Robinson, Jeff D.	85F	620	$.05	$.30	Romanick, Ron	84FU	101	$.10	$.50
Robinson, Jeff D.	87F	283	$.01	$.06	Romanick, Ron	85F	309	$.01	$.06
Robinson, Jeff D.	89F	220	$.01	$.04	Romanick, Ron	86F	166	$.01	$.06
Robinson, Jeff D.	90F	479	$.01	$.04	Romero, Ed	83F	44	$.01	$.06
Robinson, Jeff D.	91F	678	$.01	$.04	Romero, Ed	84F	212	$.01	$.08
Robinson, Jeff M.	87FU	105	$.01	$.10	Romero, Ed	85F	593	$.01	$.06
Robinson, Jeff M.	88F	68	$.01	$.15	Romero, Ed	86F	500	$.01	$.06
Robinson, Jeff M.	89F	143	$.01	$.04	Romero, Ed	87F	42	$.01	$.06
Robinson, Jeff M.	90F	614	$.01	$.04	Romero, Ed	88F	362	$.01	$.05
Robinson, Jeff M.	91F	349	$.01	$.04	Romine, Kevin	88F	363	$.01	$.06
Robinson, Jeff M.	93F	382	$.01	$.04	Romine, Kevin	89F	98	$.01	$.10
Robinson, Ron	83F	170	$.01	$.06	Romine, Kevin	90F	286	$.01	$.04
Robinson, Ron	85F	650	$.05	$.35	Romine, Kevin	91F	113	$.01	$.04
Robinson, Ron	86F	190	$.01	$.06	Romo, Enrique	81F	385	$.01	$.06
Robinson, Ron	87F	212	$.01	$.06	Romo, Enrique	82F	496	$.01	$.06
Robinson, Ron	88F	247	$.01	$.05	Romo, Enrique	83F	320	$.01	$.06
Robinson, Ron	89F	169	$.01	$.04	Romo, Vincente	83F	218	$.01	$.06
Robinson, Ron	90F	431	$.01	$.04	Roof, Gene	83F	20	$.01	$.06
Robinson, Ron	91F	595	$.01	$.04	Rooker, Jim	81F	368	$.01	$.06
Robinson, Ron	92F	187	$.01	$.04	Roomes, Rolando	89F	644	$.05	$.20
Robinson, Ron	93F	634	$.01	$.04	Roomes, Rolando	89FU	86	$.01	$.15
Rochford, Mike	89F	650	$.05	$.20	Roomes, Rolando	90F	432	$.01	$.04
Rodiguez, Rick	88FU	24	$.01	$.06	Rosario, Victor	91F	701	$.01	$.10
Rodriguez, Aurelio	81F	105	$.01	$.06	Rose, Bobby	90F	651	$.01	$.10
Rodriguez, Aurelio	82F	53	$.01	$.06	Rose, Bobby	91F	324	$.01	$.04
Rodriguez, Aurelio	83F	249	$.01	$.06	Rose, Bobby	92F	68	$.01	$.04
Rodriguez, Henry	91FUL	386	$.10	$.40	Rose, Bobby	92FUL	330	$.01	$.10
Rodriguez, Henry	92F	661	$.01	$.10	Rose, Pete	81F	1	$.25	$2.50

FLEER

Player	Year	No.	VG	EX/MT	Player	Year	No.	VG	EX/MT
Rose, Pete	81F	645	$ .15	$1.50	Russell, Jeff	87F	137	$ .01	$ .06
Rose, Pete	82F	256	$ .15	$1.50	Russell, Jeff	88F	478	$ .01	$ .05
Rose, Pete	82F	640	$ .15	$1.50	Russell, Jeff	89F	531	$ .01	$ .04
Rose, Pete	83F	171	$ .15	$1.25	Russell, Jeff	90F	312	$ .01	$ .04
Rose, Pete	83F	634	$ .10	$ .75	Russell, Jeff	90F	633	$ .01	$ .04
Rose, Pete	84F	46	$ .75	$3.00	Russell, Jeff	91F	300	$ .01	$ .04
Rose, Pete	84F	636	$ .10	$ .75	Russell, Jeff	91FUL	354	$ .01	$ .07
Rose, Pete	84FU	102	$5.00	$20.00	Russell, Jeff	92F	319	$ .01	$ .04
Rose, Pete	85F	550	$ .20	$2.00	Russell, Jeff	92FUL	140	$ .01	$ .10
Rose, Pete	85F	640	$ .10	$ .50	Russell, Jeff	93F	668	$ .01	$ .04
Rose, Pete	86F	191	$ .10	$1.00	Russell, John	85F	653	$ .05	$ .20
Rose, Pete	86F	628	$ .10	$ .50	Russell, John	86F	448	$ .01	$ .06
Rose, Pete	86F	638	$ .10	$ .75	Russell, John	86F	458	$ .01	$ .06
Rose, Pete	87F	213	$ .10	$ .75	Russell, John	87F	184	$ .01	$ .06
Rose, Jr., Pete	82F	640	$ .15	$1.50	Russell, John	91F	301	$ .01	$ .04
Rosello, Dave	82F	377	$ .01	$ .06	Ruthven, Dick	81F	16	$ .01	$ .06
Rosenberg, Steve	89FU	22	$ .01	$ .05	Ruthven, Dick	82F	257	$ .01	$ .06
Rosenberg, Steve	90F	547	$ .01	$ .04	Ruthven, Dick	83F	172	$ .01	$ .06
Rosenthal, Wayne	92F	318	$ .01	$ .10	Ruthven, Dick	84F	503	$ .01	$ .08
Rosenthal, Wayne	92FUL	446	$ .01	$ .10	Ruthven, Dick	85F	64	$ .01	$ .06
Rossy, Rico	92F	676	$ .01	$ .10	Ruthven, Dick	86F	377	$ .01	$ .06
Rossy, Rico	92FUL	376	$ .05	$ .20	Ryal, Mark	88F	503	$ .01	$ .05
Rowdon, Wade	88F	430	$ .01	$ .05	Ryan, Nolan	81F	57	$1.75	$7.00
Rowland, Rich	93F	610	$ .01	$ .04	Ryan, Nolan	82F	229	$2.00	$8.00
Royster, Jerry	81F	250	$ .01	$ .06	Ryan, Nolan	83F	463	$1.50	$6.00
Royster, Jerry	82F	448	$ .01	$ .06	Ryan, Nolan	84F	239	$4.00	$16.00
Royster, Jerry	83F	147	$ .01	$ .06	Ryan, Nolan	85F	359	$2.50	$10.00
Royster, Jerry	84F	191	$ .01	$ .08	Ryan, Nolan	86F	310	$1.50	$6.00
Royster, Jerry	85F	340	$ .01	$ .06	Ryan, Nolan	87F	67	$1.00	$4.00
Royster, Jerry	85FU	90	$ .01	$ .10	Ryan, Nolan	88F	455	$ .15	$1.50
Royster, Jerry	86F	333	$ .01	$ .06	Ryan, Nolan	89F	368	$ .10	$ .50
Royster, Jerry	87F	428	$ .01	$ .06	Ryan, Nolan	89FU	67	$ .15	$1.50
Royster, Jerry	88F	221	$ .01	$ .05	Ryan, Nolan	90F	313	$ .10	$ .50
Rozema, Dave	81F	464	$ .01	$ .06	Ryan, Nolan	90F	636	$ .01	$ .15
Rozema, Dave "David"	82F	279	$ .01	$ .06	Ryan, Nolan	90FU	131	$ .10	$ .50
Rozema, Dave	83F	340	$ .01	$ .06	Ryan, Nolan	91F	302	$ .05	$ .35
Rozema, Dave	84F	90	$ .01	$ .08	Ryan, Nolan	91FUL	355	$ .10	$1.00
Rozema, Dave	85F	21	$ .01	$ .06	Ryan, Nolan	91FUL	395	$ .10	$ .50
Rozema, Dave	85FU	91	$ .01	$ .10	Ryan, Nolan	91FUL	400	$ .01	$ .15
Rozema, Dave	86F	570	$ .01	$ .06	Ryan, Nolan	92F	320	$ .10	$ .50
Rucker, Dave	83F	341	$ .01	$ .06	Ryan, Nolan	92F	710	$ .10	$ .50
Rucker, Dave	85F	238	$ .01	$ .06	Ryan, Nolan	92FRS	682	$ .05	$ .25
Rucker, Dave	85FU	92	$ .01	$ .10	Ryan, Nolan	92FUL	141	$ .75	$3.00
Rucker, Dave	86F	447	$ .01	$ .06	Ryan, Nolan	93F	690	$ .10	$ .50
Rudi, Joe	81F	272	$ .01	$ .06	Saberhagen, Bret	84FU	103	$9.00	$36.00
Rudi, Joe	82F	306	$ .01	$ .06	Saberhagen, Bret	85F	212	$1.25	$5.00
Rudi, Joe	83F	532	$ .01	$ .06	Saberhagen, Bret	86F	19	$ .10	$1.00
Ruffin, Bruce	87F	183	$ .01	$ .06	Saberhagen, Bret	87F	379	$ .05	$ .35
Ruffin, Bruce	88F	313	$ .01	$ .10	Saberhagen, Bret	88F	268	$ .05	$ .20
Ruffin, Bruce	89F	581	$ .01	$ .04	Saberhagen, Bret	88F	626	$ .01	$ .05
Ruffin, Bruce	90F	572	$ .01	$ .04	Saberhagen, Bret	89F	291	$ .01	$ .15
Ruffin, Bruce	91F	411	$ .01	$ .04	Saberhagen, Bret	90F	116	$ .01	$ .10
Ruffin, Bruce	92F	544	$ .01	$ .04	Saberhagen, Bret	91F	567	$ .01	$ .04
Ruhle, Vern	81F	53	$ .01	$ .06	Saberhagen, Bret	91FUL	154	$ .01	$ .15
Ruhle, Vern	82F	228	$ .01	$ .06	Saberhagen, Bret	92F	167	$ .01	$ .04
Ruhle, Vern	83F	462	$ .01	$ .06	Saberhagen, Bret	92FUL	537	$ .01	$ .10
Ruhle, Vern	84F	238	$ .01	$ .08	Saberhagen, Bret	93F	93	$ .01	$ .04
Ruhle, Vern	85F	358	$ .01	$ .06	Saberhagen, Bret	93FUL	79	$ .01	$ .05
Ruhle, Vern	85FU	93	$ .01	$ .10	Sabo, Chris	88FU	87	$ .10	$ .75
Ruhle, Vern	86F	593	$ .01	$ .06	Sabo, Chris	89F	170	$ .05	$ .35
Ruhle, Vern	87F	91	$ .01	$ .06	Sabo, Chris	89F	637	$ .05	$ .20
Runge, Paul	88FU	71	$ .01	$ .06	Sabo, Chris	90F	433	$ .01	$ .15
Ruskin, Scott	91F	246	$ .01	$ .10	Sabo, Chris	91F	80	$ .01	$ .10
Ruskin, Scott	91FUL	209	$ .01	$ .07	Sabo, Chris	91FUL	103	$ .01	$ .10
Ruskin, Scott	92F	491	$ .01	$ .04	Sabo, Chris	92F	420	$ .01	$ .10
Ruskin, Scott	92FU	83	$ .05	$ .25	Sabo, Chris	92FUL	197	$ .01	$ .10
Ruskin, Scott	93F	398	$ .01	$ .04	Sabo, Chris	93F	43	$ .01	$ .04
Russell, Bill	81F	117	$ .01	$ .06	Sabo, Chris	93FUL	35	$ .01	$ .10
Russell, Bill	82F	20	$ .01	$ .06	Sakata, Lenn	81F	194	$ .01	$ .06
Russell, Bill	83F	219	$ .01	$ .06	Sakata, Lenn	82F	178	$ .01	$ .06
Russell, Bill	84F	111	$ .01	$ .08	Sakata, Lenn	83F	72	$ .01	$ .06
Russell, Bill	85F	383	$ .01	$ .06	Sakata, Lenn	84F	19	$ .01	$ .08
Russell, Bill	86F	142	$ .01	$ .06	Sakata, Lenn	85F	189	$ .01	$ .06
Russell, Bill	87F	452	$ .01	$ .06	Salas, Mark	85FU	94	$ .01	$ .10
Russell, Jeff	85F	551	$ .01	$ .15	Salas, Mark	86F	402	$ .01	$ .06

FLEER

Player	Year	No.	VG	EX/MT
Salas, Mark	87F	551	$ .01	$ .06
Salas, Mark	87FU	106	$ .01	$ .06
Salas, Mark	89F	511	$ .01	$ .04
Salas, Mark	91F	350	$ .01	$ .04
Salas, Mark	91FUL	127	$ .01	$ .07
Salas, Mark	92F	144	$ .01	$ .04
Salazar, Angel	86FU	100	$ .01	$ .08
Salazar, Angel	87F	380	$ .01	$ .06
Salazar, Angel	88F	269	$ .01	$ .05
Salazar, Luis	81F	501	$ .01	$ .15
Salazar, Luis	82F	581	$ .01	$ .06
Salazar, Luis	83F	371	$ .01	$ .06
Salazar, Luis	84F	311	$ .01	$ .08
Salazar, Luis	85F	43	$ .01	$ .06
Salazar, Luis	85FU	95	$ .01	$ .10
Salazar, Luis	86F	215	$ .01	$ .06
Salazar, Luis	88F	595	$ .01	$ .05
Salazar, Luis	88FU	30	$ .01	$ .06
Salazar, Luis	89F	144	$ .01	$ .04
Salazar, Luis	90FU	9	$ .01	$ .05
Salazar, Luis	91F	430	$ .01	$ .04
Salazar, Luis	91FUL	67	$ .01	$ .07
Salazar, Luis	92FUL	179	$ .01	$ .10
Salazar, Luis	93F	383	$ .01	$ .04
Salmon, Tim	92FU	10	$2.50	$10.00
Salmon, Tim	93F	197	$ .10	$ .75
Sambito, Joe	81F	65	$ .01	$ .06
Sambito, Joe	82F	230	$ .01	$ .06
Sambito, Joe	83F	464	$ .01	$ .06
Sambito, Joe	85F	360	$ .01	$ .06
Sambito, Joe	85FU	96	$ .01	$ .10
Sambito, Joe	86FU	101	$ .01	$ .08
Sambito, Joe	87F	43	$ .01	$ .06
Sambito, Joe	88F	364	$ .01	$ .05
Sampen, Bill	90FU	31	$ .01	$ .10
Sampen, Bill	91F	247	$ .01	$ .10
Sampen, Bill	92F	492	$ .01	$ .04
Sampen, Bill	92FUL	522	$ .01	$ .10
Sampen, Bill	93F	624	$ .01	$ .04
Sample, Billy	81F	637	$ .01	$ .06
Sample, Billy	82F	330	$ .01	$ .06
Sample, Billy	83F	577	$ .01	$ .06
Sample, Billy	84F	426	$ .01	$ .08
Sample, Billy	85F	566	$ .01	$ .06
Sample, Billy	85FU	97	$ .01	$ .10
Sample, Billy	86F	118	$ .01	$ .06
Sample, Billy	86FU	102	$ .01	$ .08
Sample, Billy	87F	527	$ .01	$ .06
Samuel, Juan	84F	47	$ .10	$1.00
Samuel, Juan	85F	264	$ .05	$ .35
Samuel, Juan	85F	634	$ .10	$ .40
Samuel, Juan	86F	449	$ .01	$ .15
Samuel, Juan	87F	185	$ .01	$ .10
Samuel, Juan	87F	642	$ .01	$ .15
Samuel, Juan	88F	314	$ .01	$ .10
Samuel, Juan	88F	580	$ .01	$ .04
Samuel, Juan	89FU	102	$ .01	$ .10
Samuel, Juan	90F	215	$ .01	$ .04
Samuel, Juan	90FU	25	$ .01	$ .05
Samuel, Juan	91F	218	$ .01	$ .04
Samuel, Juan	91FUL	168	$ .01	$ .07
Samuel, Juan	92F	469	$ .01	$ .04
Samuel, Juan	92FUL	216	$ .01	$ .10
Samuels, Roger	88FU	131	$ .01	$ .06
Sanchez, Alejandro "Alex"	85F	648	$ .75	$3.00
Sanchez, Alex	85FU	98	$ .01	$ .10
Sanchez, Alex	86F	236	$ .01	$ .06
Sanchez, Alex	89FU	71	$ .01	$ .10
Sanchez, Alex	90F	92	$ .01	$ .10
Sanchez, Israel	88FU	34	$ .01	$ .10
Sanchez, Luis	83F	100	$ .01	$ .06
Sanchez, Luis	84F	527	$ .01	$ .08
Sanchez, Luis	85F	310	$ .01	$ .06
Sanchez, Orlando	82F	126	$ .01	$ .06
Sanchez, Rey	92FU	75	$ .10	$ .50

Player	Year	No.	VG	EX/MT
Sanchez, Rey	92FUL	180	$ .05	$ .20
Sanchez, Rey	93F	24	$ .01	$ .04
Sandberg, Ryne	83F	507	$10.00	$40.00
Sandberg, Ryne	84F	504	$5.00	$20.00
Sandberg, Ryne	85F	65	$2.50	$10.00
Sandberg, Ryne	85F	630	$ .20	$2.00
Sandberg, Ryne	86F	378	$1.00	$4.00
Sandberg, Ryne	87F	572	$ .25	$2.50
Sandberg, Ryne	87F	639	$ .05	$ .20
Sandberg, Ryne	88F	431	$ .10	$1.00
Sandberg, Ryne	88F	628	$ .05	$ .35
Sandberg, Ryne	89F	437	$ .05	$ .35
Sandberg, Ryne	90F	40	$ .05	$ .35
Sandberg, Ryne	90F	639	$ .01	$ .10
Sandberg, Ryne	90FPD	625	$ .01	$ .15
Sandberg, Ryne	91F	431	$ .05	$ .20
Sandberg, Ryne	91F	709	$ .05	$ .20
Sandberg, Ryne	91F	713	$ .01	$ .10

Sandberg, Ryne	91FUL	66	$ .10	$ .50
Sandberg, Ryne	92F	389	$ .05	$ .25
Sandberg, Ryne	92FUL	181	$ .10	$1.00
Sandberg, Ryne	93F	25	$ .01	$ .15
Sandberg, Ryne	93F	356	$ .01	$ .15
Sanders, Deion	89FU	53	$ .20	$2.00
Sanders, Deion	90F	454	$ .10	$ .40
Sanders, Deion	92F	368	$ .01	$ .10
Sanders, Deion	92FUL	464	$ .10	$ .50
Sanders, Deion	93F	13	$ .01	$ .15
Sanders, Deion	93FUL	12	$ .05	$ .25
Sanders, Reggie	92F	421	$ .05	$ .25
Sanders, Reggie	92FUL	486	$ .10	$1.00
Sanders, Reggie	93F	44	$ .01	$ .15
Sanders, Reggie	93FUL	36	$ .05	$ .35
Sanderson, Scott	81F	166	$ .01	$ .06
Sanderson, Scott	82F	206	$ .01	$ .06
Sanderson, Scott	83F	295	$ .01	$ .06
Sanderson, Scott	84F	285	$ .01	$ .08
Sanderson, Scott	84FU	104	$ .10	$ .50
Sanderson, Scott	85F	66	$ .01	$ .06
Sanderson, Scott	86F	379	$ .01	$ .06
Sanderson, Scott	87F	573	$ .01	$ .06
Sanderson, Scott	88F	432	$ .01	$ .05
Sanderson, Scott	89FU	78	$ .01	$ .05
Sanderson, Scott	90F	41	$ .01	$ .04

FLEER

Player	Year	No.	VG	EX/MT
Sanderson, Scott	90FU	118	$ .01	$ .05
Sanderson, Scott	91F	23	$ .01	$ .04
Sanderson, Scott	91FULU	43	$ .01	$ .10
Sanderson, Scott	92F	243	$ .01	$ .04
Sanderson, Scott	92FUL	414	$ .01	$ .10
Sanderson, Scott	93F	655	$ .01	$ .04
Sanford, Mo	91FU	86	$ .05	$ .20
Sanguillen, Manny	81F	376	$ .01	$ .06
Santana, Andres	91FUL	328	$ .05	$ .20
Santana, Rafael	85F	90	$ .05	$ .20
Santana, Rafael	86F	93	$ .01	$ .06
Santana, Rafael	87F	21	$ .01	$ .06
Santana, Rafael	88F	149	$ .01	$ .05
Santana, Rafael	88FU	50	$ .01	$ .06
Santana, Rafael	89F	268	$ .01	$ .04
Santiago, Benito	86F	644	$1.00	$4.00
Santiago, Benito	87F	429	$ .10	$ .50
Santiago, Benito	88F	596	$ .01	$ .15
Santiago, Benito	89F	316	$ .05	$ .25
Santiago, Benito	90F	167	$ .01	$ .04
Santiago, Benito	91F	542	$ .01	$ .04
Santiago, Benito	91FUL	311	$ .01	$ .07
Santiago, Benito	92F	620	$ .01	$ .04
Santiago, Benito	92FUL	283	$ .01	$ .10
Santiago, Benito	93F	523	$ .01	$ .04
Santovenia, Nelson	88FU	103	$ .01	$ .10
Santovenia, Nelson	89F	393	$ .01	$ .10
Santovenia, Nelson	90F	360	$ .01	$ .04
Santovenia, Nelson	91F	248	$ .01	$ .04
Sarmiento, Manny	83F	321	$ .01	$ .06

Manny Sarmiento
PITCHER

Player	Year	No.	VG	EX/MT
Sarmiento, Manny	84F	263	$ .01	$ .08
Sasser, Mackey	88FU	106	$ .01	$ .15
Sasser, Mackey	89F	48	$ .01	$ .04
Sasser, Mackey	90F	216	$ .01	$ .04
Sasser, Mackey	91F	160	$ .01	$ .04
Sasser, Mackey	91FUL	226	$ .01	$ .07
Sasser, Mackey	92F	515	$ .01	$ .04
Sasser, Mackey	92FUL	237	$ .01	$ .10
Sasser, Mackey	93F	480	$ .01	$ .04
Saucier, Kevin	81F	24	$ .01	$ .06
Saucier, Kevin	82F	275	$ .01	$ .06
Savage, Jack	88F	650	$ .05	$ .25
Sax, Steve	82F	21	$ .20	$2.00
Sax, Steve	83F	220	$ .10	$ .50

Player	Year	No.	VG	EX/MT
Sax, Steve	84F	112	$ .10	$ .50
Sax, Steve	84F	633	$ .01	$ .08
Sax, Steve	85F	384	$ .10	$ .40
Sax, Steve	86F	143	$ .01	$ .15
Sax, Steve	87F	453	$ .01	$ .15
Sax, Steve	88F	523	$ .01	$ .10
Sax, Steve	89F	70	$ .01	$ .15
Sax, Steve	89FU	52	$ .01	$ .10
Sax, Steve	90F	455	$ .01	$ .04
Sax, Steve	91F	679	$ .01	$ .04
Sax, Steve	91FUL	242	$ .01	$ .07
Sax, Steve	92F	244	$ .01	$ .04
Sax, Steve	92FUL	108	$ .01	$ .10
Sax, Steve	92FUL	341	$ .01	$ .10
Sax, Steve	93F	588	$ .01	$ .04
Sax, Steve	93FUL	179	$ .01	$ .10
Scanlan, Bob	92FU	76	$ .05	$ .25
Scanlan, Bob	92FUL	473	$ .01	$ .10
Scanlan, Bob	93F	26	$ .01	$ .04
Scanlan, Bob	93FUL	22	$ .01	$ .10
Schaefer, Jeff	90FU	120	$ .01	$ .10
Schaefer, Jeff	91FU	56	$ .01	$ .05
Schatzeder, Dan	81F	482	$ .01	$ .06
Schatzeder, Dan	82F	281	$ .01	$ .06
Schatzeder, Dan	83F	296	$ .01	$ .06
Schatzeder, Dan	84F	286	$ .01	$ .08
Schatzeder, Dan	85F	409	$ .01	$ .06
Schatzeder, Dan	86F	259	$ .01	$ .06
Schatzeder, Dan	87F	186	$ .01	$ .06
Schatzeder, Dan	88F	21	$ .01	$ .05
Schatzeder, Dan	89FU	90	$ .01	$ .05
Schatzeder, Dan	90F	236	$ .01	$ .04
Scherrer, Bill	84F	482	$ .01	$ .08
Scherrer, Bill	85F	22	$ .01	$ .06
Scherrer, Bill	86F	237	$ .01	$ .06
Schilling, Curt	90FU	68	$ .01	$ .15
Schilling, Curt	91F	491	$ .01	$ .10
Schilling, Curt	92FU	112	$ .05	$ .25
Schilling, Curt	92FUL	208	$ .01	$ .10
Schilling, Curt	92FUL	548	$ .01	$ .10
Schilling, Curt	93F	108	$ .01	$ .04
Schiraldi, Calvin	85FU	99	$ .01	$ .10
Schiraldi, Calvin	87F	44	$ .01	$ .06
Schiraldi, Calvin	88F	365	$ .01	$ .05
Schiraldi, Calvin	89F	438	$ .01	$ .04
Schiraldi, Calvin	90F	168	$ .01	$ .04
Schiraldi, Calvin	91F	543	$ .01	$ .04
Schmidt, Dave	83F	578	$ .01	$ .10
Schmidt, Dave	84F	427	$ .01	$ .08
Schmidt, Dave	85F	567	$ .01	$ .06
Schmidt, Dave	86F	571	$ .01	$ .06
Schmidt, Dave	86FU	103	$ .01	$ .08
Schmidt, Dave	87F	505	$ .01	$ .06
Schmidt, Dave	87FU	107	$ .01	$ .06
Schmidt, Dave	88F	571	$ .01	$ .05
Schmidt, Dave	89F	618	$ .01	$ .04
Schmidt, Dave	90F	188	$ .01	$ .04
Schmidt, Dave	90FU	32	$ .01	$ .05
Schmidt, Dave	91F	249	$ .01	$ .04
Schmidt, Mike	81F	5	$ .75	$3.00
Schmidt, Mike	81F	640	$ .25	$2.50
Schmidt, Mike	81F	645	$ .15	$1.50
Schmidt, Mike	82F	258	$ .20	$2.00
Schmidt, Mike	82F	637	$ .10	$1.00
Schmidt, Mike	82F	641	$ .10	$ .75
Schmidt, Mike	83F	173	$ .20	$2.00
Schmidt, Mike	84F	48	$2.00	$8.00
Schmidt, Mike	85F	265	$1.00	$4.00
Schmidt, Mike	85F	627	$ .20	$2.00
Schmidt, Mike	85F	630	$ .20	$2.00
Schmidt, Mike	86F	450	$ .20	$2.00
Schmidt, Mike	87F	187	$ .15	$1.50
Schmidt, Mike	88F	315	$ .10	$ .75
Schmidt, Mike	88F	636	$ .05	$ .25
Schmidt, Mike	89F	582	$ .05	$ .35

FLEER

Player	Year	No.	VG	EX/MT	Player	Year	No.	VG	EX/MT
Schmidt, Mike	89FU	131	$.10	$.50	Scott, Mike	87F	68	$.01	$.10
Schofield, Dick	84FU	105	$.10	$1.00	Scott, Mike	87F	630	$.01	$.10
Schofield, Dick	85F	311	$.01	$.06	Scott, Mike	88F	456	$.01	$.10
Schofield, Dick	86F	167	$.01	$.06	Scott, Mike	88F	632	$.01	$.10
Schofield, Dick	87F	92	$.01	$.06	Scott, Mike	89F	367	$.01	$.04
Schofield, Dick	88F	504	$.01	$.10	Scott, Mike	90F	237	$.01	$.04
Schofield, Dick	89F	488	$.01	$.04	Scott, Mike	90F	636	$.01	$.15
Schofield, Dick	90F	144	$.01	$.04	Scott, Mike	91F	515	$.01	$.04
Schofield, Dick	91F	325	$.01	$.04	Scott, Mike	91FUL	140	$.01	$.07
Schofield, Dick	91FUL	52	$.01	$.07	Scott, Rodney	81F	155	$.01	$.06
Schofield, Dick	92F	69	$.01	$.04	Scott, Rodney	82F	207	$.01	$.15
Schofield, Dick	92FU	105	$.05	$.25	Scott, Tim	93F	524	$.01	$.04
Schofield, Dick	92FUL	30	$.01	$.10	Scott, Tony	81F	531	$.01	$.06
Schofield, Dick	92FUL	538	$.01	$.10	Scott, Tony	82F	231	$.01	$.06
Schofield, Dick	93F	94	$.01	$.04	Scott, Tony	83F	465	$.01	$.06
Schooler, Mike	89F	559	$.01	$.15	Scott, Tony	84F	241	$.01	$.08
Schooler, Mike	90F	525	$.01	$.04	Scudder, Scott	89FU	87	$.05	$.20
Schooler, Mike	91F	461	$.01	$.04	Scudder, Scott	90F	434	$.01	$.15
Schooler, Mike	92F	292	$.01	$.04	Scudder, Scott	91F	81	$.01	$.04
Schooler, Mike	93F	313	$.01	$.04	Scudder, Scott	92F	422	$.01	$.04
Schooler, Mike	93FUL	271	$.01	$.10	Scudder, Scott	92FUL	356	$.01	$.10
Schourek, Pete	91FU	104	$.01	$.15	Scudder, Scott	93F	601	$.01	$.04
Schourek, Pete	92F	516	$.01	$.04	Scudder, Scott	93FUL	190	$.01	$.10
Schourek, Pete	92FUL	539	$.01	$.10	Scurry, Rod	81F	380	$.01	$.06
Schourek, Pete	93F	95	$.01	$.04	Scurry, Rod	83F	322	$.01	$.06
Schroeder, Bill	85F	594	$.01	$.06	Scurry, Rod	84F	264	$.01	$.08
Schroeder, Bill	86F	501	$.01	$.06	Scurry, Rod	85F	476	$.01	$.06
Schroeder, Bill	87F	357	$.01	$.06	Scurry, Rod	87F	113	$.01	$.06
Schroeder, Bill	88F	173	$.01	$.05	Scurry, Ron	82F	497	$.01	$.06
Schrom, Ken	81F	425	$.05	$.20	Seanez, Rudy	90F	640	$.01	$.15
Schrom, Ken	84F	572	$.01	$.08	Seanez, Rudy	91F	376	$.01	$.04
Schrom, Ken	85F	288	$.01	$.06	Seanez, Rudy	92F	122	$.01	$.04
Schrom, Ken	86F	403	$.01	$.06	Searage, Ray	85F	595	$.01	$.06
Schrom, Ken	86FU	104	$.01	$.08	Searage, Ray	86F	502	$.01	$.06
Schrom, Ken	87F	258	$.01	$.06	Searage, Ray	87F	506	$.01	$.06
Schrom, Ken	88F	614	$.01	$.05	Searage, Ray	88F	409	$.01	$.05
Schu, Rick	85FU	100	$.01	$.10	Searage, Ray	89FU	94	$.01	$.05
Schu, Rick	86F	451	$.01	$.06	Searage, Ray	90F	408	$.01	$.04
Schu, Rick	87F	188	$.01	$.06	Searage, Ray	91F	220	$.01	$.04
Schu, Rick	88F	316	$.01	$.05	Searcy, Steve	89F	145	$.01	$.10
Schu, Rick	89F	619	$.01	$.04	Searcy, Steve	90F	615	$.01	$.04
Schu, Rick	91F	326	$.01	$.04	Searcy, Steve	92F	545	$.01	$.04
Schulz, Jeff	91F	568	$.01	$.10	Seaver, Tom	81F	200	$.20	$2.00
Schulze, Don	85F	454	$.01	$.06	Seaver, Tom	82F	82	$.15	$1.50
Schulze, Don	87F	259	$.01	$.06	Seaver, Tom	82F	634	$.15	$1.50
Schwabe, Mike	89FU	32	$.05	$.20	Seaver, Tom	82F	645	$.10	$.50
Schwabe, Mike	91F	351	$.01	$.10	Seaver, Tom	83F	601	$.15	$1.25
Scioscia, Mike	81F	131	$.10	$.75	Seaver, Tom	84F	595	$1.00	$4.00
Scioscia, Mike	82F	22	$.05	$.25	Seaver, Tom	84FU	106	$6.25	$25.00
Scioscia, Mike	83F	221	$.01	$.06	Seaver, Tom	85F	526	$.15	$1.50
Scioscia, Mike	84F	113	$.01	$.08	Seaver, Tom	86F	216	$.10	$1.00
Scioscia, Mike	85F	385	$.01	$.06	Seaver, Tom	86F	630	$.05	$.35
Scioscia, Mike	86F	144	$.01	$.06	Seaver, Tom	87F	45	$.10	$.75
Scioscia, Mike	87F	454	$.01	$.06	Sebra, Bob	87F	331	$.01	$.06
Scioscia, Mike	88F	524	$.01	$.05	Sebra, Bob	88F	195	$.01	$.05
Scioscia, Mike	89F	71	$.01	$.04	Segui, David	90FU	69	$.01	$.04
Scioscia, Mike	90F	407	$.01	$.04	Segui, David	91F	492	$.01	$.15
Scioscia, Mike	91F	219	$.01	$.04	Segui, David	91FUL	25	$.01	$.07
Scioscia, Mike	91FUL	169	$.01	$.07	Segui, David	92F	27	$.01	$.04
Scioscia, Mike	92F	470	$.01	$.04	Segui, David	92FUL	308	$.01	$.10
Scioscia, Mike	92FUL	217	$.01	$.10	Segui, David	93F	175	$.01	$.04
Scioscia, Mike	93F	67	$.01	$.04	Segui, David	93FUL	146	$.01	$.10
Sconiers, Daryl	84F	528	$.01	$.08	Segura, Jose	88FU	20	$.01	$.10
Sconiers, Daryl	85F	312	$.01	$.06	Seitzer, Kevin	87F	652	$.10	$1.00
Sconiers, Daryl	86F	168	$.01	$.06	Seitzer, Kevin	87FU	108	$.05	$.25
Scott, Donnie	85F	568	$.01	$.06	Seitzer, Kevin	88F	270	$.01	$.06
Scott, Donnie	86F	474	$.01	$.06	Seitzer, Kevin	89F	292	$.01	$.10
Scott, Gary	91FU	80	$.05	$.20	Seitzer, Kevin	90F	117	$.01	$.04
Scott, Gary	91FULU	72	$.05	$.35	Seitzer, Kevin	91F	569	$.01	$.04
Scott, Gary	92FUL	474	$.01	$.10	Seitzer, Kevin	91FUL	155	$.01	$.07
Scott, Mike	82F	535	$.05	$.25	Seitzer, Kevin	92F	168	$.01	$.04
Scott, Mike	83F	554	$.01	$.15	Seitzer, Kevin	92FU	38	$.05	$.25
Scott, Mike	84F	240	$.05	$.20	Seitzer, Kevin	92FUL	389	$.01	$.10
Scott, Mike	85F	361	$.01	$.15	Seitzer, Kevin	93F	256	$.01	$.04
Scott, Mike	86F	311	$.01	$.10	Sellers, Jeff	87F	46	$.01	$.10

FLEER

Player	Year	No.	VG	EX/MT
Sellers, Jeff	88F	366	$ .01	$ .05
Seminara, Frank	92FU	124	$ .10	$ .50
Seminara, Frank	93F	146	$ .01	$ .04
Seminara, Frank	93FUL	121	$ .01	$ .15
Servais, Scott	92F	444	$ .01	$ .10
Servais, Scott	92FUL	496	$ .01	$ .10
Servais, Scott	93F	442	$ .01	$ .04
Service, Scott	89F	653	$ .01	$ .15
Sexton, Jimmy	83F	533	$ .01	$ .06
Sharperson, Mike	88F	525	$ .01	$ .05
Sharperson, Mike	89F	72	$ .01	$ .04
Sharperson, Mike	91F	221	$ .01	$ .04
Sharperson, Mike	91FUL	170	$ .01	$ .07
Sharperson, Mike	92FU	93	$ .05	$ .25
Sharperson, Mike	92FUL	218	$ .01	$ .10
Sharperson, Mike	93F	68	$ .01	$ .04
Sheets, Larry	85FU	101	$ .01	$ .15
Sheets, Larry	86F	286	$ .05	$ .35
Sheets, Larry	87F	479	$ .01	$ .06
Sheets, Larry	88F	572	$ .01	$ .05
Sheets, Larry	89F	620	$ .01	$ .04
Sheets, Larry	90F	189	$ .01	$ .04
Sheets, Larry	90FU	100	$ .01	$ .05
Sheets, Larry	91F	352	$ .01	$ .04
Sheffield, Gary	89F	196	$ .20	$2.00
Sheffield, Gary	90F	336	$ .10	$ .50
Sheffield, Gary	91F	596	$ .05	$ .25
Sheffield, Gary	91FUL	180	$ .10	$ .75
Sheffield, Gary	92F	188	$ .05	$ .25
Sheffield, Gary	92FU	125	$ .20	$2.00
Sheffield, Gary	92FUL	83	$ .10	$1.00
Sheffield, Gary	92FUL	582	$ .10	$1.00
Sheffield, Gary	93F	351	$ .01	$ .15
Sheffield, Gary	93F	356	$ .01	$ .15
Sheffield, Gary	93F	704	$ .01	$ .10
Sheffield, Gary	93FUL	122	$ .10	$ .50
Sheffiled, Gary	93F	147	$ .01	$ .15
Shelby, John	84F	20	$ .05	$ .25
Shelby, John	85F	190	$ .01	$ .06
Shelby, John	86F	287	$ .01	$ .06
Shelby, John	87F	480	$ .01	$ .06
Shelby, John	87FU	109	$ .01	$ .06
Shelby, John	88F	526	$ .01	$ .05
Shelby, John	89F	73	$ .01	$ .04
Shelby, John	91F	353	$ .01	$ .04
Shepherd, Keith	93F	109	$ .01	$ .15
Shepherd, Ron	85FU	102	$ .01	$ .10
Sheridan, Pat	84F	357	$ .01	$ .10
Sheridan, Pat	85F	213	$ .01	$ .06
Sheridan, Pat	86F	20	$ .01	$ .06
Sheridan, Pat	87F	162	$ .01	$ .06
Sheridan, Pat	88F	69	$ .01	$ .05
Sheridan, Pat	89F	146	$ .01	$ .04
Sheridan, Pat	90F	71	$ .01	$ .04
Shields, Steve	86F	527	$ .01	$ .06
Shields, Steve	89F	269	$ .01	$ .04
Shifflett, Steve	93F	625	$ .01	$ .04
Shifflett, Steve	93FUL	216	$ .01	$ .10
Shipanoff, Dave	86F	452	$ .01	$ .06
Shipley, Craig	92F	621	$ .01	$ .10
Shipley, Craig	92FUL	583	$ .01	$ .10
Shipley, Craig	93FUL	123	$ .01	$ .10
Shirley, Bob	81F	495	$ .01	$ .06
Shirley, Bob	82F	127	$ .01	$ .06
Shirley, Bob	83F	602	$ .01	$ .06
Shirley, Bob	84F	141	$ .01	$ .08
Shirley, Bob	85F	145	$ .01	$ .06
Shirley, Bob	86F	119	$ .01	$ .06
Shirley, Bob	87F	114	$ .01	$ .06
Show, Eric	83F	372	$ .01	$ .10
Show, Eric	84F	312	$ .01	$ .08
Show, Eric	85F	44	$ .01	$ .06
Show, Eric	86F	334	$ .01	$ .06
Show, Eric	87F	430	$ .01	$ .06
Show, Eric	88F	597	$ .01	$ .05
Show, Eric	89F	317	$ .01	$ .04
Show, Eric	90F	169	$ .01	$ .04
Show, Eric	91F	544	$ .01	$ .04
Shumpert, Terry	90FU	104	$ .01	$ .10
Shumpert, Terry	91F	570	$ .01	$ .10
Shumpert, Terry	91FUL	156	$ .01	$ .07
Shumpert, Terry	92F	169	$ .01	$ .04
Shumpert, Terry	92FUL	77	$ .01	$ .10
Sierra, Candy	89F	171	$ .01	$ .10
Sierra, Ruben	86FU	105	$1.50	$6.00
Sierra, Ruben	87F	138	$3.00	$12.00
Sierra, Ruben	88F	479	$ .10	$1.00
Sierra, Ruben	89F	532	$ .05	$ .30
Sierra, Ruben	90F	314	$ .05	$ .20
Sierra, Ruben	91F	303	$ .01	$ .10

RUBEN SIERRA — RANGERS OUTFIELD

Player	Year	No.	VG	EX/MT
Sierra, Ruben	91FUL	356	$ .05	$ .35
Sierra, Ruben	92F	321	$ .01	$ .15
Sierra, Ruben	92FU	51	$ .10	$ .75
Sierra, Ruben	92FUL	142	$ .10	$ .50
Sierra, Ruben	93F	298	$ .01	$ .15
Simmons, Nelson	85FU	103	$ .01	$ .10
Simmons, Nelson	86F	238	$ .01	$ .06
Simmons, Ted	81F	528	$ .01	$ .15
Simmons, Ted	82F	152	$ .01	$ .10
Simmons, Ted	83F	45	$ .01	$ .10
Simmons, Ted	84F	213	$ .01	$ .10
Simmons, Ted	85F	596	$ .01	$ .10
Simmons, Ted	86F	503	$ .01	$ .10
Simmons, Ted	86FU	106	$ .01	$ .10
Simmons, Ted	87F	528	$ .01	$ .10
Simmons, Ted	88F	549	$ .01	$ .10
Simmons, Ted	89F	599	$ .01	$ .04
Simmons, Todd	88F	650	$ .05	$ .25
Simmons, Todd	89F	318	$ .01	$ .04
Simms, Mike	91F	516	$ .01	$ .10
Simms, Mike	92F	445	$ .01	$ .10
Simpson, Joe	81F	616	$ .01	$ .06
Simpson, Joe	82F	518	$ .01	$ .06
Simpson, Joe	83F	485	$ .01	$ .06
Simpson, Joe	84F	358	$ .01	$ .08
Singleton, Ken	81F	188	$ .01	$ .10
Singleton, Ken	82F	179	$ .01	$ .10
Singleton, Ken	83F	73	$ .01	$ .06

FLEER

Player	Year	No.	VG	EX/MT	Player	Year	No.	VG	EX/MT
Singleton, Ken	84F	21	$ .01	$ .08	Smith, Bryn	93F	515	$ .01	$ .04
Singleton, Ken	85F	191	$ .01	$ .06	Smith, Dan	93F	329	$ .01	$ .15
Sisk, Doug	84F	596	$ .01	$ .08	Smith, Dave	81F	71	$ .05	$ .30
Sisk, Doug	85F	91	$ .01	$ .06	Smith, Dave	82F	232	$ .01	$ .10
Sisk, Doug	86F	94	$ .01	$ .06	Smith, Dave	83F	466	$ .01	$ .06
Sisk, Doug	87F	22	$ .01	$ .06	Smith, Dave	84F	242	$ .01	$ .08
Sisk, Doug	88F	150	$ .01	$ .05	Smith, Dave	85F	362	$ .01	$ .06
Sisk, Doug	88FU	3	$ .01	$ .06	Smith, Dave	86F	312	$ .01	$ .06
Sisk, Doug	89F	621	$ .01	$ .04	Smith, Dave	87F	69	$ .01	$ .06
Skinner, Joel	85F	646	$ .01	$ .10	Smith, Dave	88F	457	$ .01	$ .05
Skinner, Joel	87F	115	$ .01	$ .06	Smith, Dave	89F	369	$ .01	$ .04
Skinner, Joel	89F	270	$ .01	$ .04	Smith, Dave	90F	238	$ .01	$ .04
Skinner, Joel	90F	501	$ .01	$ .04	Smith, Dave	91F	517	$ .01	$ .04
Skinner, Joel	91F	377	$ .01	$ .04	Smith, Dave	91FU	82	$ .01	$ .05
Skinner, Joel	92F	123	$ .01	$ .04	Smith, Dave	92F	391	$ .01	$ .04
Slaton, Jim	81F	518	$ .01	$ .06	Smith, Dave	92FUL	475	$ .01	$ .10
Slaton, Jim	82F	153	$ .01	$ .06	Smith, Dwight	89FU	79	$ .01	$ .15
Slaton, Jim	83F	46	$ .01	$ .06	Smith, Dwight	90F	42	$ .01	$ .15
Slaton, Jim	84F	214	$ .01	$ .08	Smith, Dwight	91F	432	$ .01	$ .04
Slaton, Jim	84FU	107	$ .10	$ .50	Smith, Dwight	91FUL	68	$ .01	$ .07
Slaton, Jim	85F	313	$ .01	$ .06	Smith, Dwight	92F	392	$ .01	$ .04
Slaton, Jim	86F	169	$ .01	$ .06	Smith, Dwight	93F	384	$ .01	$ .04
Slaton, Jim	87F	163	$ .01	$ .06	Smith, Dwight	93FUL	23	$ .01	$ .10
Slaught, Don	83F	123	$ .10	$ .50	Smith, Greg	90F	643	$ .01	$ .10
Slaught, Don	84F	359	$ .05	$ .25	Smith, Greg	91F	433	$ .01	$ .04
Slaught, Don	85F	214	$ .01	$ .06	Smith, Jim	83F	323	$ .01	$ .06
Slaught, Don	85FU	104	$ .01	$ .10	Smith, Keith	81F	534	$ .01	$ .06
Slaught, Don	86F	572	$ .01	$ .06	Smith, Ken	83F	148	$ .01	$ .06
Slaught, Don	87F	139	$ .01	$ .06	Smith, Lee	82F	603	$1.75	$7.00
Slaught, Don	88FU	51	$ .01	$ .06	Smith, Lee	83F	508	$ .20	$2.00
Slaught, Don	89F	271	$ .01	$ .04	Smith, Lee	84F	505	$ .20	$2.00
Slaught, Don	90F	456	$ .01	$ .04	Smith, Lee	85F	67	$ .10	$1.00
Slaught, Don	90FU	51	$ .01	$ .05	Smith, Lee	86F	380	$ .10	$ .50
Slaught, Don	91F	49	$ .01	$ .04	Smith, Lee	87F	574	$ .05	$ .35
Slaught, Don	91FUL	286	$ .01	$ .07	Smith, Lee	88F	433	$ .05	$ .25
Slaught, Don	92F	566	$ .01	$ .04	Smith, Lee	88FU	8	$ .01	$ .15
Slaught, Don	92FUL	258	$ .01	$ .10	Smith, Lee	89F	99	$ .01	$ .04
Slaught, Don	93F	119	$ .01	$ .04	Smith, Lee	90F	287	$ .01	$ .04
Slocumb, Heathcliff	91FU	81	$ .01	$ .10	Smith, Lee	90FU	53	$ .01	$ .05
Slocumb, Heathcliff	91FULU	73	$ .01	$ .10	Smith, Lee	91F	645	$ .01	$ .04
Slocumb, Heathcliff	92F	390	$ .01	$ .04	Smith, Lee	91FUL	295	$ .01	$ .07
Slusarski, Joe	92F	266	$ .01	$ .10	Smith, Lee	92F	591	$ .01	$ .04
Smalley, Roy	81F	551	$ .01	$ .06	Smith, Lee	92FLL	697	$ .01	$ .04
Smalley, Roy	82F	560	$ .01	$ .06	Smith, Lee	92FUL	270	$ .01	$ .10
Smalley, Roy	83F	397	$ .01	$ .06	Smith, Lee	93F	133	$ .01	$ .04
Smalley, Roy	84F	142	$ .01	$ .08	Smith, Lee	93FUL	112	$ .01	$ .10
Smalley, Roy	85F	527	$ .01	$ .06	Smith, Lonnie	81F	15	$ .01	$ .15
Smalley, Roy	85FU	105	$ .01	$ .10	Smith, Lonnie	82F	259	$ .05	$ .25
Smalley, Roy	86F	404	$ .01	$ .06	Smith, Lonnie	82F	641	$ .10	$ .75
Smalley, Roy	87F	552	$ .01	$ .06	Smith, Lonnie	83F	21	$ .01	$ .15
Smalley, Roy	88F	22	$ .01	$ .05	Smith, Lonnie	83F	636	$ .10	$ .50
Smiley, John	87FU	110	$ .10	$1.00	Smith, Lonnie	84F	335	$ .05	$ .25
Smiley, John	88F	340	$ .10	$1.00	Smith, Lonnie	85F	239	$ .01	$ .06
Smiley, John	89F	221	$ .01	$ .10	Smith, Lonnie	85FU	106	$ .01	$ .10
Smiley, John	90F	480	$ .01	$ .04	Smith, Lonnie	86F	21	$ .01	$ .06
Smiley, John	91F	50	$ .01	$ .04	Smith, Lonnie	87F	381	$ .01	$ .06
Smiley, John	91FULU	102	$ .01	$ .10	Smith, Lonnie	89FU	74	$ .01	$ .05
Smiley, John	92F	567	$ .01	$ .04	Smith, Lonnie	90F	593	$ .01	$ .04
Smiley, John	92FU	41	$ .05	$ .25	Smith, Lonnie	91F	702	$ .01	$ .04
Smiley, John	92FUL	259	$ .01	$ .10	Smith, Lonnie	91FUL	11	$ .01	$ .07
Smiley, John	92FUL	400	$ .01	$ .10	Smith, Lonnie	92F	369	$ .01	$ .04
Smiley, John	93F	643	$ .01	$ .04	Smith, Lonnie	92FUL	168	$ .01	$ .10
Smith, Billy	82F	400	$ .01	$ .06	Smith, Lonnie	93F	371	$ .01	$ .04
Smith, Bryn	83F	297	$ .01	$ .10	Smith, Ozzie	81F	488	$ .25	$2.50
Smith, Bryn	84F	287	$ .01	$ .08	Smith, Ozzie	82F	582	$ .20	$2.00
Smith, Bryn	85F	410	$ .01	$ .06	Smith, Ozzie	83F	22	$ .15	$1.50
Smith, Bryn	86F	260	$ .01	$ .06	Smith, Ozzie	83F	636	$ .10	$ .50
Smith, Bryn	87F	332	$ .01	$ .06	Smith, Ozzie	84F	336	$1.00	$4.00
Smith, Bryn	88F	196	$ .01	$ .05	Smith, Ozzie	85F	240	$ .20	$2.00
Smith, Bryn	89F	394	$ .01	$ .04	Smith, Ozzie	85F	631	$ .10	$ .75
Smith, Bryn	90F	361	$ .01	$ .04	Smith, Ozzie	86F	46	$ .10	$1.00
Smith, Bryn	91F	644	$ .01	$ .04	Smith, Ozzie	87F	308	$ .10	$ .75
Smith, Bryn	91FUL	294	$ .01	$ .07	Smith, Ozzie	88F	47	$ .10	$ .40
Smith, Bryn	92F	590	$ .01	$ .04	Smith, Ozzie	88F	628	$ .05	$ .35
Smith, Bryn	92FUL	269	$ .01	$ .10	Smith, Ozzie	89F	463	$ .01	$ .15

FLEER

Player	Year	No.	VG	EX/MT	Player	Year	No.	VG	EX/MT
Smith, Ozzie	90F	260	$ .01	$ .10	Solano, Julio	85F	363	$ .01	$ .06
Smith, Ozzie	91F	646	$ .01	$ .10	Solomon, Eddie	81F	384	$ .01	$ .06
Smith, Ozzie	91FUL	296	$ .05	$ .20	Solomon, Eddie	82F	498	$ .01	$ .06
Smith, Ozzie	92F	592	$ .01	$ .10	Sorensen, Lary	81F	519	$ .01	$ .06
Smith, Ozzie	92FUL	271	$ .05	$ .25	Sorensen, Lary	82F	128	$ .01	$ .06
Smith, Ozzie	93FUL	113	$ .05	$ .20	Sorensen, Lary	83F	418	$ .01	$ .06
Smith, Peter	88F	647	$ .10	$ .75	Sorensen, Lary	84F	549	$ .01	$ .08
Smith, Pete	88FU	73	$ .10	$ .75	Sorensen, Lary	84FU	109	$ .10	$ .50
Smith, Pete	89F	600	$ .01	$ .04	Sorensen, Lary	85F	434	$ .01	$ .06
Smith, Pete	90F	594	$ .01	$ .04	Sorensen, Lary	85FU	108	$ .01	$ .10
Smith, Pete	91F	703	$ .01	$ .04	Sorensen, Lary	86F	381	$ .01	$ .06
Smith, Pete	92F	370	$ .01	$ .04	Sorensen, Lary	87FU	111	$ .01	$ .06
Smith, Pete	93F	372	$ .01	$ .04	Sorrento, Paul	92F	218	$ .01	$ .04
Smith, Ray	84F	573	$ .01	$ .08	Sorrento, Paul	92FU	18	$ .05	$ .25
Smith, Reggie	81F	111	$ .01	$ .10	Sorrento, Paul	92FUL	357	$ .01	$ .10
Smith, Reggie	82F	23	$ .01	$ .06	Sorrento, Paul	93F	221	$ .01	$ .04
Smith, Reggie	83F	272	$ .01	$ .06	Sorrento, Paul	93FUL	191	$ .01	$ .10
Smith, Roy	85F	455	$ .01	$ .06	Sosa, Elias	81F	151	$ .01	$ .06
Smith, Roy	90F	386	$ .01	$ .10	Sosa, Elias	82F	208	$ .01	$ .06
Smith, Roy	91F	624	$ .01	$ .04	Sosa, Elias	83F	342	$ .01	$ .06
Smith, Roy	92F	28	$ .01	$ .04	Sosa, Elias	84F	313	$ .01	$ .08
Smith, Zane	85F	651	$ .10	$ .50	Sosa, Sammy	90F	548	$ .05	$ .25
Smith, Zane	86F	528	$ .05	$ .25	Sosa, Sammy	91F	136	$ .01	$ .10
Smith, Zane	87F	529	$ .01	$ .10	Sosa, Sammy	91FUL	82	$ .01	$ .07
Smith, Zane	88F	550	$ .01	$ .05	Sosa, Sammy	92F	98	$ .01	$ .04
Smith, Zane	89F	601	$ .01	$ .04	Sosa, Sammy	92FU	77	$ .05	$ .25
Smith, Zane	89FU	99	$ .01	$ .05	Sosa, Sammy	92FUL	476	$ .01	$ .10
Smith, Zane	90F	362	$ .01	$ .04	Sosa, Sammy	93F	27	$ .01	$ .04
Smith, Zane	91F	51	$ .01	$ .04	Sosa, Sammy	93FUL	24	$ .01	$ .10
Smith, Zane	92F	568	$ .01	$ .04	Soto, Mario	81F	214	$ .05	$ .30
Smith, Zane	92FUL	260	$ .01	$ .10	Soto, Mario	82F	83	$ .05	$ .20
Smith, Zane	93F	120	$ .01	$ .04	Soto, Mario	83F	603	$ .05	$ .20
Smith, Zane	93FUL	101	$ .01	$ .10	Soto, Mario	84F	483	$ .01	$ .08
Smithson, Mike	84F	428	$ .01	$ .08	Soto, Mario	85F	552	$ .01	$ .06
Smithson, Mike	84FU	108	$ .10	$ .50	Soto, Mario	86F	192	$ .01	$ .06
Smithson, Mike	85F	289	$ .01	$ .06	Soto, Mario	87F	214	$ .01	$ .06
Smithson, Mike	86F	405	$ .01	$ .06	Spehr, Tim	92F	674	$ .01	$ .10
Smithson, Mike	87F	553	$ .01	$ .06	Speier, Chris	81F	153	$ .01	$ .06
Smithson, Mike	88F	23	$ .01	$ .05	Speier, Chris	82F	209	$ .01	$ .06
Smithson, Mike	88FU	9	$ .01	$ .06	Speier, Chris	83F	298	$ .01	$ .06
Smithson, Mike	89F	100	$ .01	$ .04	Speier, Chris	84F	288	$ .01	$ .08
Smithson, Mike	90F	288	$ .01	$ .04	Speier, Chris	85FU	109	$ .01	$ .10
Smoltz, John	88F	74	$1.25	$5.00	Speier, Chris	86F	382	$ .01	$ .06
Smoltz, John	89F	602	$ .10	$ .75	Speier, Chris	87F	575	$ .01	$ .06
Smoltz, John	90F	595	$ .05	$ .25	Speier, Chris	87FU	112	$ .01	$ .06
Smoltz, John	91F	704	$ .01	$ .10	Speier, Chris	88F	96	$ .01	$ .05
Smoltz, John	91FUL	12	$ .05	$ .25	Speier, Chris	89F	343	$ .01	$ .04
Smoltz, John	92F	371	$ .01	$ .10	Speier, Chris	90F	72	$ .01	$ .04
Smoltz, John	92FUL	169	$ .05	$ .25	Spencer, Jim	81F	96	$ .01	$ .06
Smoltz, John	93F	14	$ .01	$ .04	Spencer, Jim	82F	107	$ .01	$ .06
Snell, Nate	85FU	107	$ .01	$ .10	Spiers, Bill	89FU	40	$ .01	$ .15
Snell, Nate	86F	288	$ .01	$ .06	Spiers, Bill	90F	337	$ .01	$ .15
Snell, Nate	87F	481	$ .01	$ .06	Spiers, Bill	91F	597	$ .01	$ .04
Snell, Nate	88F	70	$ .01	$ .05	Spiers, Bill	91FUL	181	$ .01	$ .07
Snider, Van	89F	172	$ .01	$ .10	Spiers, Bill	92F	189	$ .01	$ .04
Snyder, Cory	86F	653	$5.00	$20.00	Spiers, Bill	92FUL	84	$ .01	$ .10
Snyder, Cory	87F	260	$ .01	$ .15	Spiers, Bill	93F	635	$ .01	$ .04
Snyder, Cory	88F	615	$ .01	$ .10	Spikes, Charlie	81F	259	$ .01	$ .06
Snyder, Cory	88F	622	$ .05	$ .20	Spillner, Dan	81F	392	$ .01	$ .06
Snyder, Cory	89F	412	$ .01	$ .10	Spillner, Dan	82F	378	$ .01	$ .06
Snyder, Cory	90F	502	$ .01	$ .04	Spillner, Dan	83F	419	$ .01	$ .06
Snyder, Cory	91F	378	$ .01	$ .04	Spillner, Dan	84F	550	$ .01	$ .08
Snyder, Cory	91FUL	83	$ .01	$ .07	Spillner, Dan	85F	528	$ .01	$ .06
Snyder, Cory	92FU	130	$ .05	$ .25	Spillner, Dan	86F	217	$ .01	$ .06
Snyder, Cory	92FUL	595	$ .01	$ .10	Spilman, Harry	81F	209	$ .01	$ .06
Snyder, Cory	93F	160	$ .01	$ .04	Spilman, Harry	82F	233	$ .01	$ .06
Soderholm, Eric	81F	92	$ .01	$ .06	Spilman, Harry	83F	467	$ .01	$ .06
Soff, Ray	87F	309	$ .01	$ .06	Spilman, Harry	87F	284	$ .01	$ .06
Sofield, Rick	81F	563	$ .01	$ .06	Spilman, Harry	88F	97	$ .01	$ .05
Sojo, Luis	90FU	129	$ .01	$ .10	Splittorff, Paul	81F	35	$ .01	$ .06
Sojo, Luis	91F	184	$ .01	$ .10	Splittorff, Paul	82F	423	$ .01	$ .06
Sojo, Luis	91FULU	12	$ .01	$ .10	Splittorff, Paul	83F	124	$ .01	$ .06
Sojo, Luis	92F	70	$ .01	$ .04	Splittorff, Paul	84F	360	$ .01	$ .08
Sojo, Luis	92FUL	31	$ .01	$ .10	Sprague, Ed	91FU	66	$ .05	$ .20
Sojo, Luis	93F	198	$ .01	$ .04	Sprague, Ed	91FULU	63	$ .10	$ .50

FLEER

Player	Year	No.	VG	EX/MT	Player	Year	No.	VG	EX/MT
Sprague, Ed	92F	340	$ .01	$ .04	Stanton, Mike	90F	596	$ .01	$ .15
Sprague, Ed	93F	698	$ .01	$ .04	Stanton, Mike	91F	705	$ .01	$ .04
Sprague, Ed	93FUL	292	$ .01	$ .10	Stanton, Mike	92F	372	$ .01	$ .04
Squires, Mike	81F	349	$ .01	$ .06	Stanton, Mike	92FUL	170	$ .01	$ .10
Squires, Mike	82F	357	$ .01	$ .06	Stanton, Mike	93F	15	$ .01	$ .04
Squires, Mike	83F	250	$ .01	$ .06	Stanton, Mike	93FUL	13	$ .01	$ .10
Squires, Mike	84F	71	$ .01	$ .08	Stapleton, Dave	81F	236	$ .01	$ .06
Squires, Mike	85F	529	$ .01	$ .06	Stapleton, Dave	82F	308	$ .01	$ .06
St. Claire, Randy	86F	261	$ .01	$ .06	Stapleton, Dave	83F	196	$ .01	$ .06
St. Claire, Randy	87FU	113	$ .01	$ .06	Stapleton, Dave	84F	410	$ .01	$ .08
St. Claire, Randy	88F	197	$ .01	$ .05	Stargell, Willie	81F	363	$ .10	$ .75
Stairs, Matt	93F	464	$ .01	$ .04	Stargell, Willie	82F	499	$ .10	$ .75
Stanhouse, Don	81F	121	$ .01	$ .06	Stargell, Willie	83F	324	$ .10	$ .50
Stanicek, Pete	88F	573	$ .01	$ .15	Stargell, Willie	83F	634	$ .10	$ .75
Stanicek, Pete	89F	622	$ .01	$ .04	Staub, Rusty	81F	629	$ .01	$ .10
Stanicek, Steve	88F	174	$ .01	$ .10	Staub, Rusty	82F	536	$ .01	$ .10
Stankiewicz, Andy	92FU	44	$ .10	$ .50	Staub, Rusty	83F	555	$ .01	$ .10
Stankiewicz, Andy	92FUL	415	$ .05	$ .20	Staub, Rusty	84F	597	$ .01	$ .10
Stankiewicz, Andy	93F	285	$ .01	$ .10	Staub, Rusty	85F	92	$ .01	$ .10
Stankiewicz, Andy	93FUL	249	$ .01	$ .10	Staub, Rusty	86F	95	$ .01	$ .10
Stanley, Bob	81F	234	$ .01	$ .06	Stearns, John	81F	317	$ .01	$ .06
Stanley, Bob	82F	307	$ .01	$ .06	Stearns, John	82F	537	$ .01	$ .06
Stanley, Bob	83F	195	$ .01	$ .06	Stearns, John	83F	556	$ .01	$ .06
Stanley, Bob	84F	409	$ .01	$ .08	Stearns, John	84F	598	$ .01	$ .08
Stanley, Bob	85F	169	$ .01	$ .06	Steels, Jim	88FU	64	$ .01	$ .06
Stanley, Bob	86F	359	$ .01	$ .06	Stefero, John	87F	652	$ .10	$1.00
Stanley, Bob	87F	47	$ .01	$ .06	Stein, Bill	81F	605	$ .01	$ .06
Stanley, Bob	88F	367	$ .01	$ .05	Stein, Bill	82F	331	$ .01	$ .06
Stanley, Bob	89F	101	$ .01	$ .04	Stein, Bill	83F	579	$ .01	$ .06
Stanley, Bob	90F	289	$ .01	$ .04	Stein, Bill	84F	429	$ .01	$ .08
Stanley, Fred	81F	100	$ .01	$ .06	Steinbach, Terry	87F	405	$ .10	$ .50
Stanley, Fred	82F	108	$ .01	$ .06	Steinbach, Terry	88F	294	$ .01	$ .10
Stanley, Fred	83F	534	$ .01	$ .06	Steinbach, Terry	89F	22	$ .01	$ .10
Stanley, Mike	87F	647	$ .05	$ .25	Steinbach, Terry	89F	634	$ .05	$ .25
Stanley, Mike	88F	480	$ .01	$ .05	Steinbach, Terry	90F	20	$ .01	$ .04
Stanley, Mike	89F	533	$ .01	$ .04	Steinbach, Terry	91F	24	$ .01	$ .04
					Steinbach, Terry	91FUL	253	$ .01	$ .07
					Steinbach, Terry	92F	267	$ .01	$ .04
					Steinbach, Terry	92FUL	116	$ .01	$ .10
					Steinbach, Terry	93F	299	$ .01	$ .04
					Steinbach, Terry	93FUL	262	$ .01	$ .06
					Stenhouse, Mike	85F	411	$ .01	$ .06
					Stenhouse, Mike	85FU	110	$ .01	$ .10
					Stenhouse, Mike	86F	406	$ .01	$ .06
					Stennett, Rennie	81F	438	$ .01	$ .06
					Stennett, Rennie	82F	401	$ .01	$ .06
					Stephenson, Phil	91F	545	$ .01	$ .04
					Stevens, Lee	89FU	16	$ .05	$ .25
					Stevens, Lee	90F	145	$ .01	$ .10
					Stevens, Lee	91F	327	$ .01	$ .50
					Stevens, Lee	91FUL	53	$ .01	$ .15
					Stevens, Lee	92F	71	$ .01	$ .04
					Stevens, Lee	92FUL	331	$ .01	$ .04
					Stevens, Lee	93F	576	$ .01	$ .04
					Stewart, Dave	82F	24	$ .75	$3.00
					Stewart, Dave	83F	222	$ .10	$ .75
					Stewart, Dave	04F	430	$.10	$1.00
					Stewart, Dave	85F	569	$ .10	$ .50
					Stewart, Dave	86F	453	$ .05	$ .30
					Stewart, Dave	87F	406	$ .05	$ .30
					Stewart, Dave	88F	295	$ .01	$ .10
					Stewart, Dave	89F	23	$ .01	$ .10
					Stewart, Dave	90F	21	$ .01	$ .04
					Stewart, Dave	91F	25	$ .01	$ .10
					Stewart, Dave	91FUL	254	$ .01	$ .07
					Stewart, Dave	92F	268	$ .01	$ .04
					Stewart, Dave	92FUL	117	$ .01	$ .10
					Stewart, Dave	93F	669	$ .01	$ .04
Stanley, Mike	92FUL	416	$ .01	$ .10	Stewart, Sammy	81F	181	$ .01	$ .06
Stanley, Mike	93F	656	$ .01	$ .04	Stewart, Sammy	82F	180	$ .01	$ .06
Stanton, Mike	81F	400	$ .01	$ .06	Stewart, Sammy	83F	74	$ .01	$ .06
Stanton, Mike	82F	379	$ .01	$ .06	Stewart, Sammy	84F	22	$ .01	$ .08
Stanton, Mike	83F	486	$ .01	$ .06	Stewart, Sammy	85F	192	$ .01	$ .06
Stanton, Mike	84F	619	$ .01	$ .08	Stewart, Sammy	86F	289	$ .01	$ .06
Stanton, Mike	85F	501	$ .01	$ .06	Stewart, Sammy	86FU	107	$ .01	$ .08

MIKE STANLEY
NEW YORK YANKEES ♦ CATCHER

FLEER

Player	Year	No.	VG	EX/MT	Player	Year	No.	VG	EX/MT
Stewart, Sammy	87F	48	$.01	$.06	Strawberry, Darryl	91FUL	171	$.10	$.40
Stewart, Sammy	88F	616	$.01	$.05	Strawberry, Darryl	92F	471	$.01	$.15
Stieb, Dave	81F	414	$.10	$.40	Strawberry, Darryl	92FUL	219	$.05	$.35
Stieb, Dave	82F	622	$.05	$.25	Strawberry, Darryl	93F	454	$.01	$.10
Stieb, Dave	83F	441	$.05	$.25	Stubbs, Franklin	85F	386	$.05	$.25
Stieb, Dave	84F	167	$.05	$.25	Stubbs, Franklin	87F	455	$.01	$.06
Stieb, Dave	85F	117	$.01	$.15	Stubbs, Franklin	88F	527	$.01	$.05
Stieb, Dave	86F	70	$.01	$.10	Stubbs, Franklin	89F	74	$.01	$.04
Stieb, Dave	86F	642	$.01	$.10	Stubbs, Franklin	91F	518	$.01	$.04
Stieb, Dave	87F	238	$.01	$.10	Stubbs, Franklin	91FU	34	$.01	$.05
Stieb, Dave	88F	123	$.01	$.10	Stubbs, Franklin	92FUL	390	$.01	$.10
Stieb, Dave	89F	244	$.01	$.04	Stubbs, Franklin	93F	636	$.01	$.04
Stieb, Dave	90F	93	$.01	$.04	Stuper, John	83F	23	$.01	$.06
Stieb, Dave	91F	185	$.01	$.10	Stuper, John	84F	337	$.01	$.08
Stieb, Dave	91FUL	368	$.01	$.07	Stuper, John	85FU	112	$.01	$.10
Stieb, Dave	92F	341	$.01	$.04	Stuper, John	86F	193	$.01	$.06
Stieb, Dave	92FUL	152	$.01	$.10	Suero, William	92FUL	391	$.05	$.20
Stieb, Dave	93F	699	$.01	$.04	Sularz, Guy	83F	273	$.01	$.06
Stillwell, Kurt	86FU	108	$.05	$.25	Summers, Champ	81F	466	$.01	$.06
Stillwell, Kurt	87F	215	$.05	$.25	Summers, Champ	82F	282	$.01	$.06
Stillwell, Kurt	88F	248	$.01	$.10	Summers, Champ	83F	274	$.01	$.06
Stillwell, Kurt	88FU	35	$.01	$.10	Summers, Champ	84FU	112	$.10	$.50
Stillwell, Kurt	89F	293	$.01	$.04	Sundberg, Jim	81F	619	$.01	$.06
Stillwell, Kurt	90F	118	$.01	$.04	Sundberg, Jim	82F	332	$.01	$.10
Stillwell, Kurt	91F	571	$.01	$.04	Sundberg, Jim	83F	580	$.01	$.06
Stillwell, Kurt	91FUL	157	$.01	$.07	Sundberg, Jim	84F	431	$.01	$.08
Stillwell, Kurt	92F	170	$.01	$.04	Sundberg, Jim	84FU	113	$.10	$.50
Stillwell, Kurt	92FUL	584	$.01	$.10	Sundberg, Jim	85F	597	$.01	$.06
Stillwell, Kurt	93F	148	$.01	$.04	Sundberg, Jim	85FU	113	$.01	$.10
Stillwell, Kurt	93FUL	124	$.01	$.10	Sundberg, Jim	86F	22	$.01	$.06
Stoddard, Bob	84F	620	$.01	$.08	Sundberg, Jim	87F	382	$.01	$.06
Stoddard, Bob	85F	502	$.01	$.06	Sundberg, Jim	87FU	114	$.01	$.06
Stoddard, Bob	87F	431	$.01	$.06	Sundberg, Jim	88F	434	$.01	$.05
Stoddard, Tim	81F	176	$.01	$.06	Surhoff, B.J.	87FU	115	$.05	$.20
Stoddard, Tim	82F	181	$.01	$.06	Surhoff, B.J.	88F	175	$.01	$.15
Stoddard, Tim	83F	75	$.01	$.06	Surhoff, B.J.	89F	197	$.01	$.04
Stoddard, Tim	84F	23	$.01	$.08	Surhoff, B.J.	90F	338	$.01	$.04
Stoddard, Tim	84FU	110	$.10	$.50	Surhoff, B.J.	91F	598	$.01	$.04
Stoddard, Tim	85F	68	$.01	$.06	Surhoff, B.J.	91FUL	182	$.01	$.07
Stoddard, Tim	85FU	111	$.01	$.10	Surhoff, B.J.	92F	190	$.01	$.04
Stoddard, Tim	86F	335	$.01	$.06	Surhoff, B. J.	92FUL	85	$.01	$.10
Stoddard, Tim	87F	116	$.01	$.06	Surhoff, B. J.	93F	257	$.01	$.04
Stoddard, Tim	88F	222	$.01	$.05	Surhoff, B. J.	93FUL	224	$.01	$.10
Stone, Jeff	84F	111	$.10	$.50	Sutcliff, Rick	92FU	3	$.05	$.25
Stone, Jeff	85F	266	$.05	$.20	Sutcliffe, Rick	81F	125	$.05	$.25
Stone, Jeff	86F	454	$.01	$.06	Sutcliffe, Rick	82F	25	$.05	$.20
Stone, Jeff	87F	189	$.01	$.06	Sutcliffe, Rick	83F	420	$.05	$.25
Stone, Jeff	88F	317	$.01	$.05	Sutcliffe, Rick	84F	551	$.05	$.25
Stone, Steve	81F	170	$.01	$.06	Sutcliffe, Rick	84FU	114	$.10	$1.00
Stone, Steve	82F	182	$.01	$.06	Sutcliffe, Rick	85F	69	$.01	$.10
Stottlemyre, Todd	88FU	68	$.10	$.50	Sutcliffe, Rick	86F	383	$.01	$.10
Stottlemyre, Todd	89F	245	$.01	$.15	Sutcliffe, Rick	87F	576	$.01	$.10
Stottlemyre, Todd	90F	94	$.01	$.04	Sutcliffe, Rick	88F	435	$.01	$.10
Stottlemyre, Todd	91F	186	$.01	$.04	Sutcliffe, Rick	89F	439	$.01	$.10
Stottlemyre, Todd	92F	342	$.01	$.04	Sutcliffe, Rick	90F	43	$.01	$.04
Stottlemyre, Todd	92FUL	153	$.01	$.10	Sutcliffe, Rick	91F	434	$.01	$.04
Stottlemyre, Todd	93F	340	$.01	$.04	Sutcliffe, Rick	92F	393	$.01	$.04
Stottlemyre, Todd	93FUL	293	$.01	$.10	Sutcliffe, Rick	92FUL	309	$.01	$.10
Strain, Joe	81F	458	$.01	$.06	Sutcliffe, Rick	93F	552	$.01	$.04
Straker, Les	88F	24	$.01	$.10	Sutko, Glenn	92F	423	$.01	$.04
Strawberry, Darryl	84F	599	$6.00	$24.00	Sutter, Bruce	81F	294	$.05	$.25
Strawberry, Darryl	85F	93	$1.75	$7.00	Sutter, Bruce	82F	129	$.05	$.20
Strawberry, Darryl	85F	631	$.10	$.75	Sutter, Bruce	82F	631	$.01	$.06
Strawberry, Darryl	86F	96	$.20	$2.00	Sutter, Bruce	83F	24	$.01	$.15
Strawberry, Darryl	86F	632	$.10	$.50	Sutter, Bruce	84F	338	$.05	$.20
Strawberry, Darryl	87F	23	$.15	$1.25	Sutter, Bruce	85F	241	$.01	$.10
Strawberry, Darryl	87F	629	$.10	$.50	Sutter, Bruce	85FU	114	$.01	$.10
Strawberry, Darryl	87F	638	$.10	$.75	Sutter, Bruce	86F	529	$.01	$.10
Strawberry, Darryl	88F	151	$.10	$.50	Sutter, Bruce	87F	530	$.01	$.10
Strawberry, Darryl	88F	637	$.05	$.20	Sutter, Bruce	89F	603	$.01	$.04
Strawberry, Darryl	89F	49	$.05	$.25	Sutton, Don	81F	112	$.10	$.50
Strawberry, Darryl	89F	632	$.05	$.25	Sutton, Don	82F	234	$.05	$.30
Strawberry, Darryl	90F	217	$.05	$.20	Sutton, Don	83F	47	$.05	$.35
Strawberry, Darryl	91F	161	$.01	$.15	Sutton, Don	84F	215	$.10	$.50
Strawberry, Darryl	91FU	96	$.01	$.10	Sutton, Don	85F	598	$.10	$.40

FLEER

Player	Year	No.	VG	EX/MT
Sutton, Don	85FU	115	$ .10	$ .75
Sutton, Don	86F	170	$ .05	$ .20
Sutton, Don	87F	93	$ .01	$ .15
Sutton, Don	87F	626	$ .01	$ .10
Sutton, Don	88F	505	$ .01	$ .15
Sveum, Dale	86FU	109	$ .10	$ .50
Sveum, Dale	87F	358	$ .05	$ .35
Sveum, Dale	88F	176	$ .01	$ .10
Sveum, Dale	89F	198	$ .01	$ .04
Sveum, Dale	92F	191	$ .01	$ .04
Swaggerty, Bill	85F	193	$ .01	$ .06
Swan, Craig	81F	319	$ .01	$ .06
Swan, Craig	82F	538	$ .01	$ .06
Swan, Craig	83F	557	$ .01	$ .06
Swan, Craig	84F	600	$ .01	$ .08
Swan, Craig	84FU	115	$ .10	$ .50
Swan, Russ	91FU	57	$ .01	$ .05
Swan, Russ	92F	293	$ .01	$ .04
Swan, Russ	93F	314	$ .01	$ .04
Swan, Russ	93FUL	272	$ .01	$ .10
Sweet, Rick	83F	487	$ .01	$ .06
Sweet, Rick	84F	621	$ .01	$ .08
Swift, Bill	86F	475	$ .10	$ .40
Swift, Bill	87F	597	$ .01	$ .10
Swift, Bill	88FU	61	$ .01	$ .10
Swift, Bill	89F	560	$ .01	$ .10
Swift, Bill	90F	526	$ .01	$ .04
Swift, Bill	91F	462	$ .05	$ .20
Swift, Bill	91FULU	53	$ .01	$ .10
Swift, Bill	92F	294	$ .01	$ .04
Swift, Bill	92FU	131	$ .05	$ .25
Swift, Bill	92FUL	596	$ .01	$ .10
Swift, Bill	93F	161	$ .01	$ .04
Swift, Bill	93F	708	$ .01	$ .04
Swift, Bill	93FUL	136	$ .01	$ .10
Swindell, Greg	87F	644	$ .75	$3.00
Swindell, Greg	87FU	116	$ .10	$ .75
Swindell, Greg	88F	617	$ .05	$ .25
Swindell, Greg	89F	413	$ .01	$ .15
Swindell, Greg	90F	503	$ .01	$ .10
Swindell, Greg	91F	379	$ .01	$ .04
Swindell, Greg	91FUL	117	$ .01	$ .07
Swindell, Greg	92F	124	$ .01	$ .04
Swindell, Greg	92FU	84	$ .05	$ .25
Swindell, Greg	92FUL	487	$ .01	$ .10
Swindell, Greg	93F	399	$ .01	$ .04
Sykes, Bob	81F	533	$ .01	$ .06
Sykes, Bob	82F	130	$ .01	$ .06
Tabler, Pat	83F	509	$ .05	$ .20
Tabler, Pat	84F	552	$ .01	$ .10
Tabler, Pat	85F	456	$ .01	$ .10
Tabler, Pat	86F	594	$ .01	$ .06
Tabler, Pat	87F	261	$ .01	$ .06
Tabler, Pat	88F	618	$ .01	$ .05
Tabler, Pat	88F	633	$ .05	$ .25
Tabler, Pat	88FU	36	$ .01	$ .06
Tabler, Pat	89F	294	$ .01	$ .04
Tabler, Pat	90F	119	$ .01	$ .04
Tabler, Pat	91FU	67	$ .01	$ .05
Tabler, Pat	93F	700	$ .01	$ .04
Tabor, Greg	88F	644	$ .05	$ .20
Tackett, Jeff	92FUL	310	$ .01	$ .10
Tackett, Jeff	93F	553	$ .01	$ .04
Tackett, Jeff	93FUL	147	$ .01	$ .10
Tamargo, John	81F	152	$ .01	$ .06
Tanana, Frank	81F	276	$ .01	$ .15
Tanana, Frank	82F	309	$ .01	$ .06
Tanana, Frank	83F	581	$ .01	$ .06
Tanana, Frank	84F	432	$ .01	$ .08
Tanana, Frank	85F	570	$ .01	$ .06
Tanana, Frank	86F	239	$ .01	$ .06
Tanana, Frank	87F	164	$ .01	$ .06
Tanana, Frank	88F	71	$ .01	$ .05
Tanana, Frank	89F	147	$ .01	$ .04
Tanana, Frank	90F	616	$ .01	$ .04
Tanana, Frank	91F	354	$ .01	$ .04
Tanana, Frank	91FUL	128	$ .01	$ .07
Tanana, Frank	92F	145	$ .01	$ .04
Tanana, Frank	93F	611	$ .01	$ .04
Tanner, Bruce	85FU	116	$ .01	$ .10
Tanner, Bruce	86F	218	$ .01	$ .10
Tanner, Chuck	81F	367	$ .01	$ .06
Tapani, Kevin	90FU	110	$ .05	$ .35
Tapani, Kevin	91F	625	$ .01	$ .04
Tapani, Kevin	91FUL	196	$ .01	$ .07
Tapani, Kevin	92F	219	$ .01	$ .04
Tapani , Kevin	92FUL	98	$ .01	$ .10
Tapani, Kevin	93F	274	$ .01	$ .04
Tapani, Kevin	93FUL	237	$ .01	$ .10
Tartabull, Danny	85F	647	$2.00	$8.00
Tartabull, Danny	86F	476	$ .20	$2.00
Tartabull, Danny	87F	598	$ .10	$ .50
Tartabull, Danny	87FU	117	$ .05	$ .35
Tartabull, Danny	88F	271	$ .05	$ .25
Tartabull, Danny	89F	295	$ .01	$ .15
Tartabull, Danny	90F	120	$ .01	$ .10
Tartabull, Danny	91F	572	$ .01	$ .04
Tartabull, Danny	91FUL	158	$ .01	$ .10
Tartabull, Danny	92F	171	$ .01	$ .10
Tartabull, Danny	92FU	45	$ .05	$ .25
Tartabull, Danny	92FUL	417	$ .05	$ .20
Tartabull, Danny	93F	286	$ .01	$ .10
Tate, Stu	90F	643	$ .01	$ .10
Tatum, Jim	93F	416	$ .05	$ .20
Taubensee, Ed	92FUL	497	$ .05	$ .25
Taubensee, Eddie	93F	55	$ .01	$ .04
Taubensee, Eddie	93FUL	46	$ .01	$ .10
Taveras, Frank	81F	320	$ .01	$ .06
Taveras, Frank	82F	539	$ .01	$ .06
Taylor, Dorn	87FU	118	$ .01	$ .06
Taylor, Terry	89F	651	$ .05	$ .20
Taylor, Wade	91FU	48	$ .01	$ .15
Taylor, Wade	92F	245	$ .01	$ .10
Tekulve, Kent	81F	362	$ .01	$ .10
Tekulve, Kent	82F	500	$ .01	$ .06
Tekulve, Kent	83F	326	$ .01	$ .06
Tekulve, Kent	84F	265	$ .01	$ .08
Tekulve, Kent	85F	477	$ .01	$ .06
Tekulve, Kent	85FU	117	$ .01	$ .10

FLEER

Player	Year	No.	VG	EX/MT
Tekulve, Kent	86F	455	$ .01	$ .06
Tekulve, Kent	87F	190	$ .01	$ .06
Tekulve, Kent	88F	318	$ .01	$ .05
Tekulve, Kent	89F	583	$ .01	$ .04
Telford, Anthony	91F	493	$ .01	$ .10
Telford, Anthony	92F	29	$ .01	$ .04
Tellmann, Tom	84F	216	$ .01	$ .08
Tellmann, Tom	85F	599	$ .01	$ .06
Templeton, Garry	81F	529	$ .01	$ .10
Templeton, Garry	82F	131	$ .01	$ .10
Templeton, Garry	83F	373	$ .01	$ .10
Templeton, Garry	84F	314	$ .01	$ .10
Templeton, Garry	85F	45	$ .01	$ .10
Templeton, Garry	86F	336	$ .01	$ .06
Templeton, Garry	87F	432	$ .01	$ .06
Templeton, Garry	88F	598	$ .01	$ .05
Templeton, Garry	89F	319	$ .01	$ .04
Templeton, Garry	90F	170	$ .01	$ .04
Templeton, Garry	91F	546	$ .01	$ .04
Templeton, Garry	91FUL	312	$ .01	$ .07
Tenace, Gene	81F	489	$ .01	$ .06
Tenace, Gene	82F	132	$ .01	$ .06
Tenace, Gene	83F	25	$ .01	$ .06
Tenace, Gene	84F	266	$ .01	$ .08
Terrell, Walt	84F	601	$ .05	$ .25
Terrell, Walt	85F	94	$ .01	$ .06
Terrell, Walt	85FU	118	$ .01	$ .10
Terrell, Walt	86F	240	$ .01	$ .06
Terrell, Walt	87F	165	$ .01	$ .06
Terrell, Walt	88F	72	$ .01	$ .05
Terrell, Walt	89F	149	$ .01	$ .04
Terrell, Walt	90F	457	$ .01	$ .04
Terrell, Walt	92F	146	$ .01	$ .04
Terrell, Walt	93F	612	$ .01	$ .04
Terry, Scott	88FU	121	$ .01	$ .10
Terry, Scott	89F	464	$ .01	$ .04
Terry, Scott	90F	261	$ .01	$ .04
Terry, Scott	91F	647	$ .01	$ .04
Terry, Scott	92F	593	$ .01	$ .04
Tettleton, Mickey	85FU	119	$1.25	$5.00
Tettleton, Mickey	86F	432	$ .20	$2.00
Tettleton, Mickey	87F	407	$ .05	$ .35
Tettleton, Mickey	89F	623	$ .01	$ .04
Tettleton, Mickey	90F	190	$ .01	$ .04
Tettleton, Mickey	91F	494	$ .01	$ .04
Tettleton, Mickey	91FU	24	$ .01	$ .05
Tettleton, Mickey	91FULU	24	$ .01	$ .10
Tettleton, Mickey	92F	147	$ .01	$ .04
Tettleton, Mickey	92FUL	63	$ .01	$ .10
Tettleton, Mickey	93F	234	$ .01	$ .04
Teufel, Tim	84F	574	$ .05	$ .35
Teufel, Tim	85F	290	$ .01	$ .06
Teufel, Tim	86F	407	$ .01	$ .06
Teufel, Tim	86FU	110	$ .01	$ .08
Teufel, Tim	87F	24	$ .01	$ .06
Teufel, Tim	88F	152	$ .01	$ .05
Teufel, Tim	89F	50	$ .01	$ .04
Teufel, Tim	90F	218	$ .01	$ .04
Teufel, Tim	91F	162	$ .01	$ .04
Teufel, Tim	91FU	127	$ .01	$ .05
Teufel, Tim	91FULU	114	$ .01	$ .10
Teufel, Tim	92F	622	$ .01	$ .04
Teufel, Tim	92FUL	585	$ .01	$ .10
Teufel, Tim	93F	525	$ .01	$ .04
Tewksbury, Bob	86FU	111	$ .10	$ .75
Tewksbury, Bob	87F	117	$ .10	$1.00
Tewksbury, Bob	91F	648	$ .01	$ .04
Tewksbury, Bob	92F	594	$ .01	$ .04
Tewksbury, Bob	92FUL	573	$ .01	$ .10
Tewksbury, Bob	93F	134	$ .01	$ .04
Tewksbury, Bob	93FUL	114	$ .01	$ .10
Thigpen, Bobby	87F	507	$ .10	$ .75
Thigpen, Bobby	88F	410	$ .05	$ .20
Thigpen, Bobby	89F	512	$ .01	$ .04
Thigpen, Bobby	90F	549	$ .01	$ .04
Thigpen, Bobby	91F	137	$ .01	$ .04
Thigpen, Bobby	91F	712	$ .01	$ .10
Thigpen, Bobby	91FUL	84	$ .01	$ .07
Thigpen, Bobby	91FUL	396	$ .01	$ .07
Thigpen, Bobby	92F	99	$ .01	$ .04
Thigpen, Bobby	92FUL	342	$ .01	$ .10
Thigpen, Bobby	93F	589	$ .01	$ .04
Thigpen, Bobby	93FUL	180	$ .01	$ .10
Thomas, Andres	86FU	112	$ .01	$ .15
Thomas, Andres	87F	531	$ .01	$ .10
Thomas, Andres	88F	551	$ .01	$ .05
Thomas, Andres	89F	604	$ .01	$ .04
Thomas, Andres	90F	597	$ .01	$ .04

Player	Year	No.	VG	EX/MT
Thomas, Andres	91F	706	$ .01	$ .04
Thomas, Derrel	81F	123	$ .01	$ .06
Thomas, Derrel	82F	26	$ .01	$ .06
Thomas, Derrel	83F	223	$ .01	$ .06
Thomas, Derrel	84F	114	$ .01	$ .08
Thomas, Derrel	84FU	116	$ .10	$ .50
Thomas, Derrel	85F	314	$ .01	$ .06
Thomas, Frank	90FU	87	$ .75	$3.00
Thomas, Frank	91F	138	$ .10	$1.00
Thomas, Frank	91FUL	85	$1.25	$5.00
Thomas, Frank	92F	100	$ .10	$1.00
Thomas, Frank	92F	701	$ .05	$ .20
Thomas, Frank	92F	712	$ .15	$1.25
Thomas, Frank	92FUL	44	$1.25	$5.00
Thomas, Frank	93F	210	$ .10	$ .75
Thomas, Frank	93F	714	$ .05	$ .25
Thomas, Frank	93FUL	181	$ .75	$3.00
Thomas, Gorman	81F	507	$ .01	$ .10
Thomas, Gorman	82F	154	$ .01	$ .10
Thomas, Gorman	83F	48	$ .01	$ .10
Thomas, Gorman	84F	553	$ .01	$ .08
Thomas, Gorman	84FU	117	$ .10	$ .50
Thomas, Gorman	85F	503	$ .01	$ .06
Thomas, Gorman	86F	477	$ .01	$ .10
Thomas, Gorman	87F	359	$ .01	$ .06
Thomas, Roy	84F	622	$ .01	$ .08
Thomas, Roy	86F	478	$ .01	$ .06
Thomasson, Gary	81F	138	$ .01	$ .06
Thome, Jim	92F	125	$ .01	$ .10
Thome, Jim	92FUL	54	$ .10	$ .40

FLEER

Player	Year	No.	VG	EX/MT	Player	Year	No.	VG	EX/MT
Thome, Jim	93F	222	$.01	$.10	Tiant, Luis	81F	82	$.01	$.10
Thome, Jim	93FUL	192	$.01	$.10	Tibbs, Jay	85F	553	$.05	$.20
Thompson, Jason	81F	278	$.01	$.06	Tibbs, Jay	86F	194	$.01	$.06
Thompson, Jason	82F	501	$.01	$.06	Tibbs, Jay	86FU	116	$.01	$.08
Thompson, Jason	83F	325	$.01	$.06	Tibbs, Jay	87F	333	$.01	$.06
Thompson, Jason	84F	267	$.01	$.08	Tibbs, Jay	89F	624	$.01	$.04
Thompson, Jason	85F	478	$.01	$.06	Tibbs, Jay	90F	192	$.01	$.04
Thompson, Jason	86F	622	$.01	$.06	Tidrow, Dick	81F	299	$.01	$.06
Thompson, Jason	86FU	113	$.01	$.08	Tidrow, Dick	82F	604	$.01	$.06
Thompson, Milt	86F	530	$.05	$.25	Tidrow, Dick	83F	510	$.01	$.06
Thompson, Milt	86FU	114	$.01	$.10	Tidrow, Dick	84F	72	$.01	$.08
Thompson, Milt	87F	191	$.01	$.10	Timlin, Mike	91FU	68	$.01	$.15
Thompson, Milt	88F	319	$.01	$.05	Timlin, Mike	92F	343	$.01	$.10
Thompson, Milt	89F	584	$.01	$.04	Timlin, Mike	93F	701	$.01	$.04
Thompson, Milt	89FU	121	$.01	$.05	Timlin, Mike	93FUL	294	$.01	$.10
Thompson, Milt	90F	262	$.01	$.04	Tingley, Ron	89F	414	$.01	$.04
Thompson, Milt	91F	649	$.01	$.04	Tingley, Ron	93F	577	$.01	$.04
Thompson, Milt	91FUL	297	$.01	$.07	Tobik, Dave	83F	343	$.01	$.06
Thompson, Milt	92F	595	$.01	$.04	Tobik, Dave	84F	433	$.01	$.08
Thompson, Milt	92FUL	272	$.01	$.10	Todd, Jackson	82F	623	$.01	$.06
Thompson, Rich	85FU	120	$.01	$.10	Toliver, Fred	86F	647	$.10	$.75
Thompson, Rich	86F	595	$.01	$.06	Toliver, Fred	86FU	117	$.01	$.08
Thompson, Rob "Robby"	86FU	115	$.05	$.35	Toliver, Fred	89F	126	$.01	$.04
Thompson, Rob	87F	285	$.10	$.50	Tolleson, Wayne	84F	434	$.01	$.08
Thompson, Rob	88F	98	$.01	$.10	Tolleson, Wayne	85F	571	$.01	$.06
Thompson, Robby	89F	344	$.01	$.04	Tolleson, Wayne	86F	573	$.01	$.06
Thompson, Robby	90F	73	$.01	$.04	Tolleson, Wayne	86FU	118	$.01	$.08
Thompson, Robby	91F	273	$.01	$.04	Tolleson, Wayne	87F	118	$.01	$.06
Thompson, Robby	91FUL	329	$.01	$.07	Tolleson, Wayne	88F	223	$.01	$.05
Thompson, Robby	92F	648	$.01	$.04	Tomlin, Randy	91F	52	$.05	$.20
Thompson, Robby	92FUL	295	$.01	$.10	Tomlin, Randy	91FULU	103	$.10	$.50
Thompson, Robby	93F	538	$.01	$.04	Tomlin, Randy	92F	569	$.01	$.04
Thompson, Robby	93FUL	137	$.01	$.10	Tomlin, Randy	92FUL	261	$.05	$.20
Thompson, Ryan	92FU	106	$.20	$2.00	Tomlin, Randy	93F	121	$.01	$.04
Thompson, Ryan	93F	481	$.05	$.20	Tomlin, Randy	93FUL	102	$.01	$.10
Thompson, Scott	81F	296	$.01	$.06	Torre, Joe	81F	325	$.01	$.10
Thompson, Scott	85F	621	$.01	$.06	Torrez, Mike	81F	233	$.01	$.06
Thompson, Scott	86F	262	$.01	$.06	Torrez, Mike	82F	310	$.01	$.06
Thon, Dickie	81F	277	$.01	$.10	Torrez, Mike	83F	197	$.01	$.06
Thon, Dickie	82F	235	$.01	$.06	Torrez, Mike	84F	602	$.01	$.08
Thon, Dickie	83F	468	$.01	$.06	Torve, Kelvin	90FU	40	$.01	$.05
Thon, Dickie	84F	243	$.01	$.08	Torve, Kelvin	91F	163	$.01	$.04
Thon, Dickie	84F	634	$.01	$.08	Traber, Jim	87F	482	$.01	$.06
Thon, Dickie	85F	364	$.01	$.06	Traber, Jim	89F	625	$.01	$.04
Thon, Dickie	86F	313	$.01	$.06	Traber, Jim	90F	193	$.01	$.04
Thon, Dickie	87F	70	$.01	$.06	Tracy, Jim	81F	308	$.01	$.06
Thon, Dickie	89F	320	$.01	$.04	Tracy, Jim	82F	605	$.01	$.06
Thon, Dickie	90F	573	$.01	$.04	Trammell, Alan	81F	461	$.10	$1.00
Thon, Dickie	91F	412	$.01	$.04	Trammell, Alan	82F	283	$.10	$.50
Thon, Dickie	91FUL	272	$.01	$.07	Trammell, Alan	83F	344	$.10	$.50
Thon, Dickie	92F	546	$.01	$.04	Trammell, Alan	84F	91	$.15	$1.25
Thon, Dickie	92FUL	447	$.01	$.10	Trammell, Alan	85F	23	$.10	$.50
Thornton, Andre	82F	380	$.01	$.10	Trammell, Alan	86F	241	$.10	$.50
Thornton, Andre	83F	421	$.01	$.10	Trammell, Alan	86F	633	$.10	$1.00
Thornton, Andre	83F	635	$.01	$.06	Trammell, Alan	87F	167	$.05	$.35
Thornton, Andre	84F	554	$.01	$.10	Trammell, Alan	88F	74	$.05	$.20
Thornton, Andre	85F	457	$.01	$.06	Trammell, Alan	88F	635	$.05	$.35
Thornton, Andre	86F	596	$.01	$.06	Trammell, Alan	89F	148	$.01	$.15
Thornton, Andre	87F	262	$.01	$.06	Trammell, Alan	90F	617	$.01	$.10
Thornton, Louis	85FU	121	$.01	$.10	Trammell, Alan	91F	355	$.01	$.04
Thornton, Louis	86F	71	$.01	$.10	Trammell, Alan	91FUL	129	$.01	$.10
Thurman, Gary	88F	272	$.01	$.06	Trammell, Alan	92F	148	$.01	$.04
Thurman, Gary	89F	296	$.01	$.10	Trammell, Alan	92FUL	64	$.01	$.04
Thurman, Gary	90F	121	$.01	$.04	Trammell, Alan	93F	613	$.01	$.04
Thurman, Gary	91F	573	$.01	$.04	Trammell, Alan	93FUL	204	$.01	$.10
Thurman, Gary	91FULU	29	$.01	$.10	Trautwein, John	88FU	10	$.01	$.10
Thurman, Gary	92F	172	$.01	$.04	Travers, Billy	81F	514	$.01	$.06
Thurman, Gary	93F	626	$.01	$.04	Travers, Billy	81F	525	$.01	$.06
Thurmond, Mark	84F	315	$.01	$.10	Treadway, Jeff	88F	249	$.01	$.15
Thurmond, Mark	85F	46	$.01	$.06	Treadway, Jeff	89F	173	$.01	$.15
Thurmond, Mark	86F	337	$.01	$.06	Treadway, Jeff	89FU	75	$.01	$.05
Thurmond, Mark	87F	166	$.01	$.06	Treadway, Jeff	90F	598	$.01	$.04
Thurmond, Mark	88F	73	$.01	$.05	Treadway, Jeff	91F	707	$.01	$.04
Thurmond, Mark	90F	191	$.01	$.04	Treadway, Jeff	91FUL	13	$.01	$.07
Thurmond, Mark	91F	274	$.01	$.04	Treadway, Jeff	92F	373	$.01	$.04

FLEER

Player	Year	No.	VG	EX/MT
Treadway, Jeff	92FUL	171	$ .01	$ .10
Trevino, Alex	81F	318	$ .01	$ .06
Trevino, Alex	82F	540	$ .01	$ .06
Trevino, Alex	83F	604	$ .01	$ .06
Trevino, Alex	84F	484	$ .01	$ .08
Trevino, Alex	84FU	118	$ .10	$ .50
Trevino, Alex	85F	341	$ .01	$ .06
Trevino, Alex	85FU	122	$ .01	$ .10
Trevino, Alex	86F	550	$ .01	$ .06
Trevino, Alex	86FU	119	$ .01	$ .08
Trevino, Alex	87F	456	$ .01	$ .06
Trevino, Alex	90F	239	$ .01	$ .04
Trillo, Manny	81F	3	$ .01	$ .06
Trillo, Manny	82F	260	$ .01	$ .06
Trillo, Manny	83F	174	$ .01	$ .06
Trillo, Manny	83F	631	$ .01	$ .10
Trillo, Manny	84F	289	$ .01	$ .08
Trillo, Manny	84F	627	$ .01	$ .08
Trillo, Manny	84FU	119	$ .10	$ .50
Trillo, Manny	85F	622	$ .01	$ .06
Trillo, Manny	86F	551	$ .01	$ .06
Trillo, Manny	86FU	120	$ .01	$ .08
Trillo, Manny	87F	577	$ .01	$ .06
Trillo, Manny	88F	436	$ .01	$ .05
Trillo, Manny	89F	440	$ .01	$ .04
Trombley, Mike	93F	644	$ .01	$ .15
Trout, Steve	81F	345	$ .01	$ .06
Trout, Steve	82F	358	$ .01	$ .06
Trout, Steve	83F	251	$ .01	$ .06
Trout, Steve	84F	506	$ .01	$ .08
Trout, Steve	85F	70	$ .01	$ .06
Trout, Steve	86F	384	$ .01	$ .06
Trout, Steve	87F	578	$ .01	$ .06
Trujillo, Mike	86F	360	$ .01	$ .06
Tucker, Scooter	93FUL	47	$ .01	$ .10
Tudor, John	82F	311	$ .05	$ .35
Tudor, John	83F	198	$ .01	$ .10
Tudor, John	84F	411	$ .01	$ .10
Tudor, John	84FU	120	$ .10	$ .50
Tudor, John	85F	479	$ .01	$ .10
Tudor, John	85FU	123	$ .01	$ .10
Tudor, John	86F	47	$ .01	$ .10
Tudor, John	87F	310	$ .01	$ .10
Tudor, John	88F	48	$ .01	$ .10
Tudor, John	89F	75	$ .01	$ .04
Tudor, John	90FU	54	$ .01	$ .05
Tudor, John	91F	650	$ .01	$ .04
Tunnell, Lee	84F	268	$ .01	$ .08
Tunnell, Lee	85F	480	$ .01	$ .06
Tunnell, Lee	85F	638	$ .01	$ .06
Tunnell, Lee	86F	623	$ .01	$ .06
Tunnell, Lee	87FU	119	$ .01	$ .06
Tunnell, Lee	88F	49	$ .01	$ .05
Turner, Jerry	81F	504	$ .01	$ .06
Turner, Jerry	83F	345	$ .01	$ .06
Turner, Shane	89F	653	$ .01	$ .15
Turner, Shane	92FU	58	$ .05	$ .25
Turner, Shane	93F	681	$ .01	$ .04
Twitty, Jeff	81F	49	$ .01	$ .06
Tyson, Mike	81F	315	$ .01	$ .06
Tyson, Mike	82F	606	$ .01	$ .06
Ujdur, Jerry	83F	346	$ .01	$ .06
Underwood, Pat	81F	469	$ .01	$ .06
Underwood, Pat	83F	347	$ .01	$ .06
Underwood, Tom	81F	97	$ .01	$ .06
Underwood, Tom	82F	109	$ .01	$ .06
Underwood, Tom	83F	535	$ .01	$ .06
Underwood, Tom	84F	460	$ .01	$ .06
Underwood, Tom	84FU	121	$ .10	$ .50
Underwood, Tom	85F	194	$ .01	$ .06
Unser, Del	81F	26	$ .01	$ .06
Unser, Del	82F	261	$ .01	$ .06
Upshaw, Willie	82F	624	$ .01	$ .06
Upshaw, Willie	83F	442	$ .01	$ .06
Upshaw, Willie	84F	168	$ .01	$ .08
Upshaw, Willie	85F	118	$ .01	$ .06
Upshaw, Willie	85F	635	$ .01	$ .10
Upshaw, Willie	86F	72	$ .01	$ .06
Upshaw, Willie	87F	239	$ .01	$ .06
Upshaw, Willie	88F	124	$ .01	$ .05
Upshaw, Willie	88FU	25	$ .01	$ .06
Upshaw, Willie	89F	415	$ .01	$ .04
Uribe, Jose	85FU	124	$ .05	$ .20
Uribe, Jose	86F	552	$ .05	$ .20
Uribe, Jose	87F	286	$ .01	$ .06
Uribe, Jose	88F	99	$ .01	$ .05
Uribe, Jose	89F	345	$ .01	$ .04
Uribe, Jose	90F	74	$ .01	$ .04
Uribe, Jose	91F	275	$ .01	$ .04
Uribe, Jose	91FUL	330	$ .01	$ .07
Uribe, Jose	92F	649	$ .01	$ .04
Uribe, Jose	93F	539	$ .01	$ .04
Urrea, John	82F	583	$ .01	$ .06
Vail, Mike	81F	311	$ .01	$ .06
Vail, Mike	82F	84	$ .01	$ .06
Vail, Mike	83F	605	$ .01	$ .06
Vail, Mike	84F	290	$ .01	$ .08
Vail, Mike	84FU	122	$ .10	$ .50
Valdez, Julio	83F	199	$ .01	$ .06
Valdez, Rafael	90FU	58	$ .01	$ .15
Valdez, Sergio	91F	380	$ .01	$ .04
Valdez, Sergio	93F	465	$ .01	$ .04
Valentin, John	92FU	4	$ .10	$ .75
Valentin, John	93F	183	$ .01	$ .10
Valentine, Ellis	81F	148	$ .01	$ .06
Valentine, Ellis	82F	541	$ .01	$ .06
Valentine, Ellis	83F	558	$ .01	$ .06
Valentine, Ellis	84F	529	$ .01	$ .08
Valenzuela, Fernando	81F	140	$ .20	$2.00
Valenzuela, Fernando	82F	27	$ .05	$ .25
Valenzuela, Fernando	82F	635	$ .05	$ .25
Valenzuela, Fernando	82F	636	$ .05	$ .25
Valenzuela, Fernando	83F	224	$ .05	$ .20
Valenzuela, Fernando	84F	115	$ .05	$ .25
Valenzuela, Fernando	85F	387	$ .05	$ .20
Valenzuela, Fernando	86F	145	$ .05	$ .20
Valenzuela, Fernando	86F	641	$ .05	$ .20
Valenzuela, Fernando	87F	457	$ .01	$ .15

FLEER

Player	Year	No.	VG	EX/MT	Player	Year	No.	VG	EX/MT
Valenzuela, Fernando	87F	631	$.01	$.10	Velarde, Randy	92F	246	$.01	$.04
Valenzuela, Fernando	88F	528	$.01	$.10	Velarde, Randy	93F	287	$.01	$.04
Valenzuela, Fernando	89F	76	$.01	$.15	Velarde, Randy	93FUL	250	$.01	$.10
Valenzuela, Fernando	90F	409	$.01	$.04	Velez, Otto	81F	410	$.01	$.06
Valenzuela, Fernando	90FPD	622	$.01	$.15	Velez, Otto	82F	625	$.01	$.06
Valenzuela, Fernando	91F	222	$.01	$.04	Venable, Max	81F	443	$.01	$.06
Valera, Julio	91F	164	$.01	$.15	Venable, Max	83F	275	$.01	$.06
Valera, Julio	92F	517	$.01	$.04	Venable, Max	84F	385	$.01	$.08
Valera, Julio	92FU	11	$.05	$.25	Venable, Max	86F	196	$.01	$.06
Valera, Julio	93F	578	$.01	$.04	Venable, Max	87F	216	$.01	$.06
Valera, Julio	93FUL	169	$.01	$.10	Ventura, Robin	89FU	23	$.25	$2.50
Valle, Dave	85FU	125	$.05	$.20	Ventura, Robin	90F	550	$.10	$.60
Valle, Dave	88F	389	$.01	$.05	Ventura, Robin	91F	139	$.05	$.25
Valle, Dave	89F	561	$.01	$.04	Ventura, Robin	91FUL	86	$.10	$.75
Valle, Dave	91F	463	$.01	$.04	Ventura, Robin	92F	101	$.01	$.15
Valle, Dave	92F	295	$.01	$.04	Ventura, Robin	92FUL	343	$.10	$.50
Valle, Dave	92FUL	130	$.01	$.10	Ventura, Robin	93F	211	$.01	$.15
Valle, Dave	93F	315	$.01	$.04	Ventura, Robin	93F	716	$.01	$.10
Valle, Dave	93FUL	273	$.01	$.10	Veres, Randy	89FU	42	$.01	$.10
Valle, David	90F	527	$.01	$.04	Veres, Randy	91F	600	$.01	$.04
Valle, David	91FUL	344	$.01	$.07	Verhoeven, John	82F	547	$.01	$.06
Van Gorder, David	86F	195	$.01	$.06	Veryzer, Tom	81F	390	$.01	$.06
Van Poppel, Todd	92F	269	$.05	$.20	Veryzer, Tom	82F	381	$.01	$.06
Van Poppel, Todd	92FUL	118	$.10	$.50	Veryzer, Tom	83F	559	$.01	$.06
Van Slyke, Andy	84F	339	$2.00	$8.00	Villanueva, Hector	90FU	10	$.01	$.10
Van Slyke, Andy	85F	242	$.20	$2.00	Villanueva, Hector	91F	436	$.01	$.10
Van Slyke, Andy	86F	48	$.10	$.50	Villanueva, Hector	91FUL	69	$.01	$.07
Van Slyke, Andy	87F	311	$.10	$.40	Villanueva, Hector	92F	394	$.01	$.04
Van Slyke, Andy	87FU	121	$.05	$.25	Villanueva, Hector	92FUL	477	$.01	$.10
Van Slyke, Andy	88F	341	$.05	$.20	Viola, Frank	83F	625	$.75	$3.00
Van Slyke, Andy	89F	222	$.01	$.10	Viola, Frank	84F	575	$.10	$1.00
Van Slyke, Andy	90F	481	$.01	$.10	Viola, Frank	85F	291	$.10	$.50
Van Slyke, Andy	91F	53	$.01	$.10	Viola, Frank	86F	408	$.10	$.40
Van Slyke, Andy	91FUL	287	$.01	$.15	Viola, Frank	87F	554	$.05	$.35
Van Slyke, Andy	92F	570	$.01	$.04	Viola, Frank	88F	25	$.01	$.10
Van Slyke, Andy	92FUL	262	$.01	$.10	Viola, Frank	89F	127	$.01	$.15
Van Slyke, Andy	93F	122	$.01	$.04	Viola, Frank	90F	219	$.01	$.15
Van Slyke, Andy	93FUL	103	$.01	$.15	Viola, Frank	91F	165	$.01	$.10
Vande Berg, Ed	83F	488	$.01	$.06	Viola, Frank	91FUL	227	$.01	$.07
Vande Berg, Ed	84F	623	$.01	$.08	Viola, Frank	92F	518	$.01	$.04
Vande Berg, Ed	85F	504	$.01	$.06	Viola, Frank	92FU	5	$.05	$.25
Vande Berg, Ed	86F	479	$.01	$.06	Viola, Frank	92FUL	319	$.05	$.20
Vande Berg, Ed	86FU	121	$.01	$.08	Viola, Frank	93F	185	$.01	$.04
Vande Berg, Ed	87F	458	$.01	$.06	Viola, Frank	93FUL	157	$.01	$.15
Vande Berg, Ed	87FU	120	$.01	$.06	Virdon, Bill	81F	61	$.01	$.06
Vande Berg, Ed	88F	619	$.01	$.05	Virgil, Ozzie	83F	175	$.01	$.06
Vande Berg, Ed	89F	534	$.01	$.04	Virgil, Ozzie	84F	49	$.01	$.08
Vander Wal, John	92FU	99	$.05	$.35	Virgil, Ozzie	85F	267	$.01	$.06
Vander Wal, John	92FUL	523	$.05	$.25	Virgil, Ozzie	86FU	122	$.05	$.20
Vander Wal, John	93F	80	$.01	$.10	Virgil, Ozzie	87F	532	$.01	$.06
Varsho, Gary	88FU	81	$.01	$.10	Virgil, Ozzie	88F	552	$.01	$.05
Varsho, Gary	89F	441	$.01	$.10	Virgil, Ozzie	89F	605	$.01	$.04
Varsho, Gary	91F	435	$.01	$.04	Vizcaino, Jose	90F	410	$.01	$.10
Varsho, Gary	91FU	114	$.01	$.05	Vizcaino, Jose	91F	223	$.01	$.04
Varsho, Gary	91FULU	104	$.01	$.10	Vizcaino, Jose	92FUL	182	$.01	$.10
Varsho, Gary	92F	571	$.01	$.04	Vizcaino, Jose	93F	385	$.01	$.04
Varsho, Gary	92FUL	561	$.01	$.10	Vizquel, Omar	89FU	62	$.01	$.15
Vatcher, Jim	91F	708	$.01	$.10	Vizquel, Omar	90F	528	$.01	$.10
Vaughn, Greg	89FU	41	$.10	$1.00	Vizquel, Omar	91F	464	$.01	$.10
Vaughn, Greg	90F	339	$.05	$.25	Vizquel, Omar	91FUL	345	$.01	$.07
Vaughn, Greg	91F	599	$.01	$.15	Vizquel, Omar	92F	296	$.01	$.04
Vaughn, Greg	91FUL	183	$.01	$.15	Vizquel, Omar	92FUL	436	$.01	$.10
Vaughn, Greg	92F	192	$.01	$.04	Vizquel, Omar	93F	316	$.01	$.04
Vaughn, Greg	92FUL	86	$.05	$.25	Vizquel, Omar	93FUL	274	$.01	$.10
Vaughn, Greg	93F	258	$.01	$.04	Von Ohlen, Dave	84F	340	$.01	$.08
Vaughn, Greg	93FUL	225	$.01	$.10	Von Ohlen, Dave	85F	243	$.01	$.06
Vaughn, Mo	91FU	7	$.05	$.25	Von Ohlen, Dave	85FU	126	$.01	$.10
Vaughn, Maurice	91FUL	387	$.10	$.75	Von Ohlen, Dave	86F	597	$.01	$.06
Vaughn, Mo	92F	49	$.01	$.10	Von Ohlen, Dave	87F	408	$.01	$.06
Vaughn, Mo	92F	705	$.01	$.15	Vuckovich, Pete	82F	156	$.01	$.06
Vaughn, Mo	92FUL	23	$.05	$.35	Vuckovich, Pete	83F	49	$.01	$.06
Vaughn, Mo	93F	184	$.01	$.04	Vuckovich, Pete	84F	217	$.01	$.08
Vaughn, Mo	93FUL	156	$.05	$.20	Vuckovich, Pete	86F	504	$.01	$.06
Vega, Jesus	83F	624	$.01	$.06	Vukovich, George	81F	21	$.01	$.06
Velarde, Randy	88F	646	$.05	$.20	Vukovich, George	82F	262	$.01	$.06

FLEER

Player	Year	No.	VG	EX/MT	Player	Year	No.	VG	EX/MT
Vukovich, George	83F	176	$.01	$.06	Walling, Denny	84F	244	$.01	$.08
Vukovich, George	84F	555	$.01	$.08	Walling, Denny	85F	365	$.01	$.06
Vukovich, George	85F	458	$.01	$.06	Walling, Denny	86F	314	$.01	$.06
Vukovich, George	86F	598	$.01	$.06	Walling, Denny	87F	72	$.01	$.06
Vukovich, John	81F	22	$.01	$.06	Walling, Denny	88F	458	$.01	$.05
Waddell, Tom	84FU	123	$.10	$.50	Walling, Denny	89F	465	$.01	$.04
Waddell, Tom	85F	459	$.01	$.06	Walling, Denny	90F	263	$.01	$.04
Waddell, Tom	86F	599	$.01	$.06	Walling, Denny	91F	651	$.01	$.04
Wagner, Mark	81F	478	$.01	$.06	Walter, Gene	86F	644	$1.00	$4.00
Wagner, Mark	82F	333	$.01	$.06	Walter, Gene	86FU	124	$.01	$.08
Wagner, Mark	83F	582	$.01	$.06	Walter, Gene	87F	433	$.01	$.06
Wainhouse, David	92FUL	524	$.05	$.20	Walter, Gene	88F	153	$.01	$.05
Waits, Rick	81F	396	$.01	$.06	Walters, Dan	92FU	126	$.05	$.25
Waits, Rick	82F	382	$.01	$.06	Walters, Dan	93F	149	$.01	$.04
Waits, Rick	83F	422	$.01	$.06	Walters, Dan	93FUL	125	$.01	$.10
Waits, Rick	85F	600	$.01	$.06	Walton, Bruce	92FU	52	$.05	$.25
Waits, Rick	86F	505	$.01	$.06	Walton, Bruce	92FUL	428	$.01	$.10
Wakefield, Tim	92FU	117	$1.75	$7.00	Walton, Jerome	89FU	80	$.01	$.10
Wakefield, Tim	93F	123	$.10	$.50	Walton, Jerome	90F	44	$.01	$.10
Wakefield, Tim	93FUL	104	$.20	$2.00	Walton, Jerome	91F	437	$.01	$.04
Walewander, Jim	89F	150	$.01	$.04	Walton, Jerome	91FUL	70	$.01	$.07
Walk, Bob	81F	14	$.05	$.25	Walton, Jerome	92F	396	$.01	$.04
Walk, Bob	83F	149	$.01	$.06	Walton, Jerome	92FUL	184	$.01	$.10
Walk, Bob	87F	623	$.01	$.06	Walton, Reggie	81F	609	$.01	$.06
Walk, Bob	88F	342	$.01	$.05	Ward, Colby	91F	382	$.01	$.10
Walk, Bob	89F	223	$.01	$.04	Ward, Colin	86F	645	$.01	$.10
Walk, Bob	90F	482	$.01	$.04	Ward, Duane	86FU	125	$.10	$.75
Walk, Bob	91F	54	$.01	$.04	Ward, Duane	88F	125	$.05	$.20
Walk, Bob	92F	572	$.01	$.04	Ward, Duane	89F	246	$.01	$.04
Walk, Bob	93F	505	$.01	$.04	Ward, Duane	90F	95	$.01	$.04
Walker, Chico	91FULU	74	$.01	$.10	Ward, Duane	91F	187	$.01	$.04
Walker, Chico	92F	395	$.01	$.04	Ward, Duane	91FUL	369	$.01	$.07
Walker, Chico	92FU	107	$.05	$.25	Ward, Duane	92F	344	$.01	$.04
Walker, Chico	92FUL	183	$.01	$.10	Ward, Duane	92FUL	154	$.01	$.10
Walker, Chico	93F	482	$.01	$.04	Ward, Duane	93F	341	$.01	$.04
Walker, Chico	93FUL	80	$.01	$.10	Ward, Duane	93FUL	295	$.01	$.10
Walker, Duane	83F	606	$.01	$.06	Ward, Gary	82F	562	$.01	$.06
Walker, Duane	84F	485	$.01	$.08	Ward, Gary	83F	627	$.01	$.06
Walker, Duane	85F	554	$.01	$.06	Ward, Gary	84F	576	$.01	$.08
Walker, Duane	86F	574	$.01	$.06	Ward, Gary	84FU	124	$.10	$.50
Walker, Greg	84F	73	$.10	$.50	Ward, Gary	85F	572	$.01	$.06
Walker, Greg	85F	530	$.01	$.06	Ward, Gary	86F	575	$.01	$.06
Walker, Greg	86F	219	$.01	$.10	Ward, Gary	87F	140	$.01	$.06
Walker, Greg	87F	508	$.01	$.06	Ward, Gary	87FU	122	$.01	$.06
Walker, Greg	88F	411	$.01	$.05	Ward, Gary	88F	224	$.01	$.05
Walker, Greg	90F	551	$.01	$.04	Ward, Gary	89F	273	$.01	$.04
Walker, Larry	90F	363	$.10	$.75	Ward, Gary	89FU	33	$.01	$.05
Walker, Larry	91F	250	$.05	$.20	Ward, Gary	90F	618	$.01	$.04
Walker, Larry	91FULU	93	$.75	$3.00	Ward, Gary	91F	356	$.01	$.04
Walker, Larry	92F	493	$.01	$.15	Ward, Kevin	92F	623	$.01	$.15
Walker, Larry	92FUL	525	$.10	$.50	Ward, Turner	91F	383	$.01	$.15
Walker, Larry	93F	81	$.01	$.15	Ward, Turner	91FUL	118	$.01	$.15
Walker, Larry	93F	715	$.01	$.10	Wardle, Curt	85FU	127	$.01	$.10
Walker, Larry	93FUL	71	$.05	$.35	Wardle, Curt	86F	600	$.01	$.06
Walker, Mike	91F	381	$.01	$.10	Warren, Mike	84F	461	$.01	$.08
Walker, Tony	86FU	123	$.01	$.08	Warren, Mike	84F	639	$.01	$.08
Walker, Tony	87F	71	$.01	$.10	Warren, Mike	85F	435	$.01	$.06
Wallach, Tim	82F	210	$.10	$1.00	Washington, Claudell	81F	329	$.01	$.06
Wallach, Tim	83F	299	$.05	$.20	Washington, Claudell	82F	449	$.01	$.06
Wallach, Tim	84F	291	$.05	$.20	Washington, Claudell	83F	150	$.01	$.06
Wallach, Tim	85F	412	$.05	$.20	Washington, Claudell	84F	192	$.01	$.08
Wallach, Tim	86F	263	$.01	$.06	Washington, Claudell	85F	342	$.01	$.06
Wallach, Tim	87F	334	$.01	$.10	Washington, Claudell	86F	531	$.01	$.06
Wallach, Tim	88F	198	$.01	$.10	Washington, Claudell	87F	119	$.01	$.06
Wallach, Tim	89F	395	$.01	$.04	Washington, Claudell	88F	225	$.01	$.05
Wallach, Tim	90F	364	$.01	$.04	Washington, Claudell	89F	272	$.01	$.04
Wallach, Tim	91F	251	$.01	$.04	Washington, Claudell	89FU	17	$.01	$.05
Wallach, Tim	91FUL	210	$.01	$.07	Washington, Claudell	90F	146	$.01	$.04
Wallach, Tim	92F	494	$.01	$.04	Washington, Ron	83F	626	$.01	$.06
Wallach, Tim	92FUL	226	$.01	$.10	Washington, Ron	84F	577	$.01	$.08
Wallach, Tim	93F	82	$.01	$.04	Washington, Ron	85F	292	$.01	$.06
Waller, Ty	82F	607	$.01	$.06	Washington, Ron	86F	409	$.01	$.06
Walling, Denny	81F	66	$.01	$.06	Washington, Ron	89F	416	$.01	$.04
Walling, Denny	82F	236	$.01	$.06	Washington, U. L.	81F	34	$.01	$.06
Walling, Denny	83F	469	$.01	$.06	Washington, U. L.	82F	424	$.01	$.06

FLEER

Player	Year	No.	VG	EX/MT
Washington, U. L.	83F	125	$ .01	$ .06
Washington, U. L.	84F	361	$ .01	$ .08
Washington, U. L.	85F	215	$ .01	$ .06
Washington, U. L.	85FU	128	$ .01	$ .10
Washington, U. L.	86F	264	$ .01	$ .06
Wasinger, Mark	88F	100	$ .01	$ .15
Wathan, John	81F	46	$ .01	$ .06
Wathan, John	82F	425	$ .01	$ .06
Wathan, John	83F	126	$ .01	$ .06
Wathan, John	84F	362	$ .01	$ .08
Wathan, John	85F	216	$ .01	$ .06
Wathan, John	86F	23	$ .01	$ .06
Watson, Bob	81F	93	$ .01	$ .06
Watson, Bob	82F	54	$ .01	$ .06
Watson, Bob	83F	151	$ .01	$ .06
Watson, Bob	84F	193	$ .01	$ .08
Wayne, Gary	90F	387	$ .01	$ .10
Wayne, Gary	91F	626	$ .01	$ .04
Wayne, Gary	92FUL	401	$ .01	$ .10

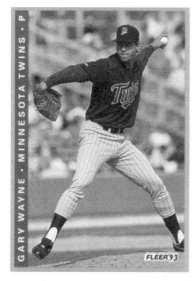

Player	Year	No.	VG	EX/MT
Wayne, Gary	93F	645	$ .01	$ .04
Weathers, Dave	93F	430	$ .01	$ .04
Weaver, Earl	81F	178	$ .01	$ .06
Webster, Lenny	91FU	41	$ .01	$ .10
Webster, Lenny	92F	220	$ .01	$ .04
Webster, Lenny	92FUL	102	$ .01	$ .10
Webster, Lenny	93F	646	$ .01	$ .04
Webster, Lenny	93FUL	238	$ .01	$ .10
Webster, Mitch	86F	265	$ .05	$ .25
Webster, Mitch	87F	335	$ .01	$ .06
Webster, Mitch	88F	199	$ .01	$ .05
Webster, Mitch	89F	442	$ .01	$ .04
Webster, Mitch	90F	45	$ .01	$ .04
Webster, Mitch	91F	384	$ .01	$ .04
Webster, Mitch	91FUL	116(119)	$ .01	$ .07
Webster, Mitch	93F	455	$ .01	$ .04
Wegman, Bill	87F	360	$ .05	$ .20
Wegman, Bill	88F	177	$ .01	$ .05
Wegman, Bill	89F	199	$ .01	$ .04
Wegman, Bill	91FU	35	$ .01	$ .05
Wegman, Bill	91FULU	33	$ .01	$ .10
Wegman, Bill	92F	193	$ .01	$ .04
Wegman, Bill	92FUL	392	$ .01	$ .10
Wegman, Bill	93F	259	$ .01	$ .04

Player	Year	No.	VG	EX/MT
Wegman, Bill	93FUL	226	$ .01	$ .10
Wehner, John	91FU	115	$ .01	$ .10
Wehner, John	92F	573	$ .01	$ .10
Wehner, John	93F	506	$ .01	$ .04
Wehner, John	93FUL	105	$ .01	$ .10
Wehrmeister, Dave	86F	220	$ .01	$ .06
Weiss, Gary	81F	130	$ .01	$ .06
Weiss, Walt	88F	652	$ .05	$ .35
Weiss, Walt	88FU	56	$ .05	$ .25
Weiss, Walt	89F	24	$ .01	$ .10
Weiss, Walt	90F	22	$ .01	$ .10
Weiss, Walt	91F	26	$ .01	$ .04
Weiss, Walt	91FUL	255	$ .01	$ .07
Weiss, Walt	92F	270	$ .01	$ .04
Weiss, Walt	93F	300	$ .01	$ .04
Welch, Bob	81F	120	$ .10	$ .50
Welch, Bob	82F	28	$ .05	$ .25
Welch, Bob	83F	225	$ .05	$ .20
Welch, Bob	84F	116	$ .05	$ .25
Welch, Bob	85F	388	$ .01	$ .15
Welch, Bob	86F	146	$ .01	$ .15
Welch, Bob	87F	459	$ .01	$ .10
Welch, Bob	88F	529	$ .01	$ .05
Welch, Bob	88FU	57	$ .01	$ .06
Welch, Bob	89F	25	$ .01	$ .04
Welch, Bob	90F	23	$ .01	$ .10
Welch, Bob	91F	27	$ .01	$ .04
Welch, Bob	91FUL	256	$ .01	$ .07
Welch, Bob	92F	271	$ .01	$ .04
Welch, Bob	92FUL	119	$ .01	$ .10
Welch, Bob	93F	301	$ .01	$ .04
Welch, Bob	93FUL	263	$ .01	$ .10
Wellman, Brad	84F	386	$ .01	$ .08
Wellman, Brad	85F	623	$ .01	$ .06
Wellman, Brad	86F	553	$ .01	$ .06
Wells, David	88FU	69	$ .05	$ .25
Wells, David	89F	247	$ .01	$ .10
Wells, David	90F	96	$ .01	$ .04
Wells, Dave	91F	188	$ .01	$ .04
Wells, David	91FUL	370	$ .01	$ .07
Wells, David	92F	345	$ .01	$ .04
Wells, David	92FUL	453	$ .01	$ .10
Wells, David	93F	702	$ .01	$ .04
Wells, David	93FUL	296	$ .01	$ .10
Welsh, Chris	82F	584	$ .01	$ .06
Welsh, Chris	83F	374	$ .01	$ .06
Welsh, Chris	84F	292	$ .01	$ .08
Welsh, Chris	86F	576	$ .01	$ .06
Welsh, Chris	87F	217	$ .01	$ .06
Werth, Dennis	81F	102	$ .01	$ .06
Werth, Dennis	82F	55	$ .01	$ .06
West, Dave	89F	51	$ .01	$ .15
West, Dave	90F	388	$ .01	$ .10
West, David	91F	627	$ .01	$ .04
Wetteland, John	90F	411	$ .01	$ .10
Wetteland, John	92FU	100	$ .05	$ .25
Wetteland, John	92FUL	520	$ .01	$ .10
Wetteland, John	93F	83	$ .01	$ .04
Whisenton, Larry	83F	152	$ .01	$ .06
Whitaker, Lou	81F	463	$ .10	$1.00
Whitaker, Lou	82F	284	$ .10	$ .50
Whitaker, Lou	83F	348	$ .05	$ .35
Whitaker, Lou	84F	92	$ .10	$1.00
Whitaker, Lou	85F	24	$ .10	$ .50
Whitaker, Lou	86F	242	$ .05	$ .35
Whitaker, Lou	87F	168	$ .05	$ .25
Whitaker, Lou	88F	75	$ .05	$ .20
Whitaker, Lou	89F	151	$ .01	$ .10
Whitaker, Lou	90F	619	$ .01	$ .10
Whitaker, Lou	91F	357	$ .01	$ .04
Whitaker, Lou	91FUL	130	$ .01	$ .07
Whitaker, Lou	92F	149	$ .01	$ .04
Whitaker, Lou	92FUL	65	$ .01	$ .10
Whitaker, Lou	93F	614	$ .01	$ .04
White, Devon	87F	646	$ .15	$1.50

FLEER

Player	Year	No.	VG	EX/MT	Player	Year	No.	VG	EX/MT
White, Devon	87FU	123	$ .05	$ .35	Wiggins, Alan	86F	290	$ .01	$ .06
White, Devon	88F	506	$ .05	$ .20	Wiggins, Alan	87FU	124	$ .01	$ .06
White, Devon	89F	489	$ .01	$ .10	Wilcox, Milt	81F	465	$ .01	$ .06
White, Devon	90F	147	$ .01	$ .04	Wilcox, Milt	82F	285	$ .01	$ .06
White, Devon	91F	328	$ .01	$ .04	Wilcox, Milt	83F	349	$ .01	$ .06
White, Devon	91FU	69	$ .01	$ .05	Wilcox, Milt	84F	93	$ .01	$ .08
White, Devon	91FULU	64	$ .01	$ .10	Wilcox, Milt	85F	25	$ .01	$ .06
White, Devon	92F	346	$ .01	$ .04	Wilcox, Milt	86F	243	$ .01	$ .06
White, Devon	92FUL	155	$ .01	$ .10	Wilfong, Bob	81F	569	$ .01	$ .06
White, Devon	93F	342	$ .01	$ .04	Wilfong, Rob	82F	563	$ .01	$ .06
White, Devon	93FUL	297	$ .01	$ .10	Wilfong, Rob	83F	101	$ .01	$ .06
White, Frank	81F	44	$ .01	$ .10	Wilfong, Rob	84F	530	$ .01	$ .08
White, Frank	82F	426	$ .01	$ .10	Wilfong, Rob	85F	315	$ .01	$ .06
White, Frank	82F	629	$ .01	$ .06	Wilfong, Rob	87F	94	$ .01	$ .06
White, Frank	83F	127	$ .01	$ .06	Wilkerson, Curtis	84FU	126	$ .10	$ .50
White, Frank	84F	363	$ .01	$ .08	Wilkerson, Curtis	85F	573	$ .01	$ .06
White, Frank	85F	217	$ .01	$ .06	Wilkerson, Curtis	86F	577	$ .01	$ .06
White, Frank	86F	24	$ .01	$ .06	Wilkerson, Curtis	87F	141	$ .01	$ .06
White, Frank	87F	383	$ .01	$ .06	Wilkerson, Curtis	88F	481	$ .01	$ .05
White, Frank	88F	273	$ .01	$ .05	Wilkerson, Curtis	89F	535	$ .01	$ .04
White, Frank	89F	297	$ .01	$ .04	Wilkerson, Curt	90F	46	$ .01	$ .04
White, Frank	90F	122	$ .01	$ .04	Wilkerson, Curtis	91F	438	$ .01	$ .04
White, Frank	91F	574	$ .01	$ .04	Wilkerson, Curtis	92FUL	377	$ .01	$ .10
White, Jerry	81F	161	$ .01	$ .06	Wilkerson, Curtis	93F	627	$ .01	$ .04
White, Jerry	82F	211	$ .01	$ .06	Wilkins, Dean	90F	47	$ .01	$ .10
White, Jerry	83F	300	$ .01	$ .06	Wilkins, Rick	91FU	83	$ .01	$ .15
Whitehouse, Len	84F	578	$ .01	$ .08	Wilkins, Rick	91FULU	75	$ .05	$ .35
Whitehurst, Wally	89FU	103	$ .01	$ .15	Wilkins, Rick	92F	397	$ .01	$ .10
Whitehurst, Wally	91F	166	$ .01	$ .04	Wilkins, Rick	93F	28	$ .01	$ .04
Whitehurst, Wally	92F	519	$ .01	$ .04	Wilkins, Rick	93FUL	25	$ .01	$ .10
Whiten, Mark	90FU	130	$ .10	$ .40	Wilkinson, Bill	87FU	125	$ .01	$ .10
Whiten, Mark	91F	189	$ .01	$ .15	Wilkinson, Bill	88F	390	$ .01	$ .10
Whiten, Mark	91FU	21	$ .01	$ .15	Willard, Jerry	85F	460	$ .01	$ .06
Whiten, Mark	91FUL	371	$ .05	$ .25	Willard, Jerry	86F	601	$ .01	$ .06
Whiten, Mark	91FULU	21	$ .05	$ .35	Willard, Jerry	86FU	126	$ .01	$ .08
Whiten, Mark	92F	126	$ .01	$ .10	Willard, Jerry	87F	409	$ .01	$ .06
Whiten, Mark	92FUL	55	$ .01	$ .10	Williams, Al	82F	564	$ .01	$ .06
Whiten, Mark	93F	223	$ .01	$ .04	Williams, Al	83F	628	$ .01	$ .06
Whiten, Mark	93FUL	193	$ .01	$ .10	Williams, Al	84F	579	$ .01	$ .08
Whitfield, Terry	81F	437	$ .01	$ .06	Williams, Bernie	91F	49	$ .05	$ .20
Whitfield, Terry	84FU	125	$ .10	$ .50	Williams, Bernie	91FULU	44	$ .10	$1.00
Whitfield, Terry	85F	389	$ .01	$ .06	Williams, Bernie	92F	247	$ .01	$ .15
Whitfield, Terry	86F	147	$ .01	$ .06	Williams, Bernie	93F	289	$ .01	$ .04
Whitson, Ed	81F	444	$ .01	$ .06	Williams, Bernie	93FUL	252	$ .01	$ .10
Whitson, Ed	82F	402	$ .01	$ .06	Williams, Brian	92FU	88	$ .10	$ .75
Whitson, Eddie	83F	423	$ .01	$ .06	Williams, Brian	92FUL	498	$ .05	$ .35
Whitson, Ed	84F	316	$ .01	$ .08	Williams, Brian	93F	56	$ .01	$ .04
Whitson, Ed	85F	47	$ .01	$ .06	Williams, Brian	93FUL	48	$ .01	$ .15
Whitson, Ed	85FU	129	$ .01	$ .10	Williams, Dana	90F	648	$ .01	$ .10
Whitson, Ed	86F	120	$ .01	$ .06	Williams, Dick	81F	149	$ .01	$ .10
Whitson, Ed	87F	434	$ .01	$ .06	Williams, Eddie	88F	620	$ .01	$ .15
Whitson, Ed	88F	599	$ .01	$ .05	Williams, Eddie	91F	548	$ .01	$ .04
Whitson, Ed	89F	321	$ .01	$ .04	Williams, Frank	84FU	127	$ .10	$ .50
Whitson, Ed	90F	171	$ .01	$ .04	Williams, Frank	85F	624	$ .05	$ .25
Whitson, Ed	91F	547	$ .01	$ .04	Williams, Frank	86F	554	$ .01	$ .06
Whitson, Ed	91FUL	313	$ .01	$ .07	Williams, Frank	87F	287	$ .01	$ .06
Whitson, Ed	92F	624	$ .01	$ .04	Williams, Frank	87FU	127	$ .01	$ .06
Whitt, Ernie	81F	411	$ .01	$ .06	Williams, Frank	88F	250	$ .01	$ .05
Whitt, Ernie	82F	626	$ .01	$ .06	Williams, Frank	89F	174	$ .01	$ .04
Whitt, Ernie	83F	443	$ .01	$ .06	Williams, Frank	89FU	34	$ .01	$ .05
Whitt, Ernie	84F	169	$ .01	$ .08	Williams, Frank	90F	620	$ .01	$ .04
Whitt, Ernie	85F	119	$ .01	$ .06	Williams, Gerald	91FUL	388	$ .10	$ .50
Whitt, Ernie	86F	73	$ .01	$ .06	Williams, Gerald	93F	657	$ .01	$ .15
Whitt, Ernie	87F	240	$ .01	$ .06	Williams, Ken "Kenny"	87FU	128	$ .01	$ .10
Whitt, Ernie	88F	126	$ .01	$ .05	Williams, Ken	88F	412	$ .01	$ .10
Whitt, Ernie	89F	248	$ .01	$ .04	Williams, Ken	91F	190	$ .01	$ .04
Whitt, Ernie	90F	97	$ .01	$ .04	Williams, Matt	87FU	129	$ .75	$3.00
Wickander, Kevin	91F	385	$ .01	$ .10	Williams, Matt	88F	101	$ .75	$3.00
Wickander, Kevin	93F	602	$ .01	$ .04	Williams, Matt	89F	346	$ .05	$ .20
Wickman, Bob	92FU	46	$ .15	$1.50	Williams, Matt	90F	75	$ .01	$ .15
Wickman, Bob	93F	288	$ .05	$ .20	Williams, Matt	91F	276	$ .01	$ .10
Wickman, Bob	93FUL	251	$ .10	$ .50	Williams, Matt	91FUL	331	$ .01	$ .10
Wiggins, Alan	83F	375	$ .01	$ .10	Williams, Matt	92F	650	$ .01	$ .10
Wiggins, Alan	84F	317	$ .01	$ .08	Williams, Matt	92FUL	296	$ .01	$ .10
Wiggins, Alan	85F	48	$ .01	$ .06	Williams, Matt	93F	540	$ .01	$ .04

FLEER

Player	Year	No.	VG	EX/MT
Williams, Mike	93FUL	94	$ .05	$ .20
Williams, Mitch	86FU	127	$ .10	$ .40
Williams, Mitch	87F	142	$ .10	$ .50
Williams, Mitch	88F	482	$ .01	$ .10
Williams, Mitch	89F	536	$ .01	$ .10
Williams, Mitch	89FU	81	$ .01	$ .10
Williams, Mitch	90F	48	$ .01	$ .04
Williams, Mitch	90F	631	$ .01	$ .04
Williams, Mitch	91F	439	$ .01	$ .04
Williams, Mitch	91FU	110	$ .01	$ .05
Williams, Mitch	91FUL	71	$ .01	$ .07
Williams, Mitch	91FULU	101	$ .01	$ .10
Williams, Mitch	92F	547	$ .01	$ .04
Williams, Mitch	92FUL	549	$ .01	$ .10
Williams, Mitch	93F	498	$ .01	$ .04
Williams, Reggie	86FU	128	$ .01	$ .15
Williams, Reggie	87F	460	$ .01	$ .06
Williamson, Mark	88F	574	$ .01	$ .10
Williamson, Mark	89F	626	$ .01	$ .04
Williamson, Mark	90F	194	$ .01	$ .04
Williamson, Mark	91F	495	$ .01	$ .04
Williamson, Mark	92F	30	$ .01	$ .04
Willis, Carl	87F	218	$ .01	$ .10
Willis, Carl	92FUL	403	$ .01	$ .10
Willis, Carl	93F	275	$ .01	$ .04
Willis, Carl	93FUL	239	$ .01	$ .10
Willis, Mike	81F	426	$ .01	$ .06
Wills, Bump	81F	628	$ .01	$ .06
Wills, Bump	82F	334	$ .01	$ .06
Wills, Bump	83F	511	$ .01	$ .06
Wills, Frank	86F	480	$ .01	$ .06
Wills, Frank	90F	98	$ .01	$ .10
Wills, Frank	91F	191	$ .01	$ .04
Wills, Maury	81F	595	$ .01	$ .06
Wilson, Craig	91F	652	$ .01	$ .10
Wilson, Craig	91FUL	298	$ .01	$ .07
Wilson, Craig	93F	516	$ .01	$ .04
Wilson, Dan	93F	400	$ .01	$ .04
Wilson, Glenn	83F	350	$ .10	$ .40
Wilson, Glenn	84F	94	$ .05	$ .20
Wilson, Glenn	84FU	128	$ .10	$ .50
Wilson, Glenn	85F	268	$ .01	$ .06
Wilson, Glenn	86F	457	$ .01	$ .06
Wilson, Glenn	87F	192	$ .01	$ .10
Wilson, Glenn	88F	320	$ .01	$ .05
Wilson, Glenn	89F	224	$ .01	$ .04
Wilson, Glenn	90F	240	$ .01	$ .04
Wilson, Glenn	91F	519	$ .01	$ .04
Wilson, Mookie	82F	542	$ .01	$ .10
Wilson, Mookie	83F	560	$ .01	$ .10
Wilson, Mookie	84F	603	$ .01	$ .08
Wilson, Mookie	85F	95	$ .01	$ .06
Wilson, Mookie	86F	97	$ .01	$ .06
Wilson, Mookie	87F	25	$ .01	$ .06
Wilson, Mookie	88F	154	$ .01	$ .05
Wilson, Mookie	89F	52	$ .01	$ .04
Wilson, Mookie	90F	99	$ .01	$ .04
Wilson, Mookie	91F	192	$ .01	$ .04
Wilson, Mookie	91FUL	372	$ .01	$ .07
Wilson, Mookie	92F	347	$ .01	$ .04
Wilson, Nigel	93F	431	$ .10	$1.00
Wilson, Steve	89F	640	$ .01	$ .15
Wilson, Steve	89FU	82	$ .01	$ .10
Wilson, Steve	90F	49	$ .01	$ .10
Wilson, Steve	91F	440	$ .01	$ .04
Wilson, Steve	92FUL	510	$ .01	$ .10
Wilson, Steve	93F	456	$ .01	$ .04
Wilson, Trevor	89F	347	$ .01	$ .10
Wilson, Trevor	90FU	64	$ .01	$ .05
Wilson, Trevor	91F	277	$ .01	$ .04
Wilson, Trevor	91FULU	119	$ .01	$ .10
Wilson, Trevor	92F	651	$ .01	$ .04
Wilson, Trevor	92FUL	297	$ .01	$ .10
Wilson, Trevor	93F	162	$ .01	$ .04
Wilson, Willie	81F	29	$ .05	$ .20
Wilson, Willie	81F	653	$ .01	$ .15
Wilson, Willie	82F	427	$ .05	$ .20
Wilson, Willie	83F	128	$ .01	$ .10
Wilson, Willie	84F	364	$ .01	$ .10
Wilson, Willie	85F	218	$ .01	$ .10
Wilson, Willie	86F	25	$ .01	$ .10
Wilson, Willie	87F	384	$ .01	$ .10
Wilson, Willie	88F	274	$ .01	$ .10
Wilson, Willie	89F	298	$ .01	$ .04
Wilson, Willie	90F	123	$ .01	$ .04
Wilson, Willie	91F	575	$ .01	$ .04
Wilson, Willie	91FULU	48	$ .01	$ .10
Wilson, Willie	92FU	53	$ .05	$ .25
Wilson, Willie	92FUL	429	$ .01	$ .10
Wilson, Willie	93F	302	$ .01	$ .04
Wine, Robbie	88F	459	$ .01	$ .15
Winfield, Dave	81F	484	$ .75	$3.00
Winfield, Dave	82F	56	$ .20	$2.00
Winfield, Dave	82F	646	$ .20	$2.00
Winfield, Dave	83F	398	$ .20	$2.00
Winfield, Dave	83F	633	$ .10	$ .75
Winfield, Dave	84F	143	$1.25	$5.00
Winfield, Dave	85F	146	$ .75	$3.00
Winfield, Dave	85F	629	$ .15	$1.50
Winfield, Dave	86F	121	$ .10	$1.00
Winfield, Dave	87F	120	$ .10	$ .75
Winfield, Dave	88F	226	$ .05	$ .35
Winfield, Dave	89F	274	$ .01	$ .15
Winfield, Dave	90F	458	$ .01	$ .15
Winfield, Dave	90FU	81	$ .01	$ .10
Winfield, Dave	91F	329	$ .01	$ .10
Winfield, Dave	91FUL	54	$ .05	$ .20
Winfield, Dave	92F	72	$ .01	$ .10
Winfield, Dave	92FRS	686	$ .01	$ .10
Winfield, Dave	92FU	67	$ .10	$1.00
Winfield, Dave	92FUL	454	$ .05	$ .35
Winfield, Dave	93F	343	$ .01	$ .15
Winn, Jim	86F	624	$ .01	$ .06
Winn, Jim	87F	624	$ .01	$ .06
Winn, Jim	87FU	126	$ .01	$ .06
Winn, Jim	88F	413	$ .01	$ .05
Winningham, Herm	85FU	130	$ .05	$ .20
Winningham, Herm	86F	266	$ .01	$ .10

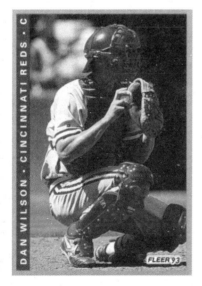

FLEER

Player	Year	No.	VG	EX/MT
Winningham, Herm	87FU	130	$ .01	$ .06

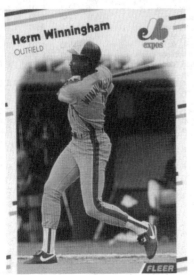

Player	Year	No.	VG	EX/MT
Winningham, Herm	88F	200	$ .01	$ .05
Winningham, Herm	89F	175	$ .01	$ .04
Winningham, Herm	90F	435	$ .01	$ .04
Winningham, Herm	91F	82	$ .01	$ .04
Winningham, Herm	91FULU	78	$ .01	$ .10
Winningham, Herm	93F	566	$ .01	$ .04
Winters, Matt	90F	124	$ .01	$ .10
Wise, Rick	82F	585	$ .01	$ .06
Witt, Mike	82F	473	$ .05	$ .20
Witt, Bobby	86FU	129	$ .05	$ .35
Witt, Bobby	87F	143	$ .10	$ .75
Witt, Bobby	88F	483	$ .01	$ .05
Witt, Bobby	89F	537	$ .01	$ .04
Witt, Bobby	90F	315	$ .01	$ .15
Witt, Bobby	91F	304	$ .01	$ .04
Witt, Bobby	91FUL	357	$ .01	$ .07
Witt, Bobby	93F	303	$ .01	$ .04
Witt, Bobby	93FUL	264	$ .01	$ .10
Witt, Mike	83F	102	$ .05	$ .25
Witt, Mike	84F	531	$ .05	$ .25
Witt, Mike	85F	316	$ .01	$ .10
Witt, Mike	85F	643	$ .01	$ .15
Witt, Mike	86F	171	$ .01	$ .10
Witt, Mike	87F	95	$ .01	$ .10
Witt, Mike	87F	641	$ .01	$ .06
Witt, Mike	88F	507	$ .01	$ .05
Witt, Mike	88F	626	$ .01	$ .05
Witt, Mike	89F	490	$ .01	$ .04
Witt, Mike	90F	148	$ .01	$ .04
Witt, Mike	91F	680	$ .01	$ .04
Wockenfuss, John	81F	472	$ .01	$ .06
Wockenfuss, John	82F	286	$ .01	$ .06
Wockenfuss, John	83F	351	$ .01	$ .06
Wockenfuss, John	84F	95	$ .01	$ .08
Wockenfuss, John	84FU	129	$ .10	$ .50
Wockenfuss, John	85F	269	$ .01	$ .06
Wohlers, Mark	92F	374	$ .01	$ .10
Wohlers, Mark	92F	700	$ .01	$ .10
Wohlers, Mark	92FUL	465	$ .05	$ .25
Wohlers, Mark	93F	16	$ .01	$ .04
Wohlford, Jim	81F	440	$ .01	$ .06
Wohlford, Jim	82F	403	$ .01	$ .06
Wohlford, Jim	83F	276	$ .01	$ .06
Wohlford, Jim	84F	293	$ .01	$ .08
Wohlford, Jim	85F	413	$ .01	$ .06
Wohlford, Jim	87F	336	$ .01	$ .06
Wojna, Ed	86F	338	$ .01	$ .10
Wood, Ted	92F	678	$ .01	$ .10
Wood, Ted	92FUL	597	$ .05	$ .20
Woodard, Mike	86F	645	$ .01	$ .10
Woodard, Mike	89F	513	$ .01	$ .04
Woods, Al	81F	422	$ .01	$ .06
Woods, Al	82F	627	$ .01	$ .06
Woods, Al	83F	444	$ .01	$ .06
Woods, Gary	81F	75	$ .01	$ .06
Woods, Gary	82F	237	$ .01	$ .06
Woods, Gary	83F	512	$ .01	$ .06
Woods, Gary	84F	507	$ .01	$ .08
Woods, Gary	85F	71	$ .01	$ .06
Woods, Gary	86F	385	$ .01	$ .06
Woodson, Kerry	93FUL	275	$ .01	$ .15
Woodson, Tracy	88FU	98	$ .01	$ .10
Woodson, Tracy	89F	77	$ .01	$ .04
Woodson, Tracy	93F	517	$ .01	$ .04
Woodward, Rob	86F	651	$ .05	$ .25
Worrell, Todd	86F	49	$ .05	$ .25
Worrell, Todd	87F	312	$ .05	$ .25
Worrell, Todd	88F	50	$ .01	$ .10
Worrell, Todd	89F	466	$ .01	$ .04
Worrell, Todd	90F	264	$ .01	$ .04
Worrell, Todd	91F	653	$ .01	$ .04
Worrell, Todd	92FU	121	$ .05	$ .25
Worrell, Todd	92FUL	574	$ .01	$ .10
Worrell, Todd	93F	135	$ .01	$ .04
Wortham, Richard	81F	347	$ .01	$ .06
Worthington, Craig	88FU	4	$ .01	$ .10
Worthington, Craig	89F	627	$ .01	$ .10
Worthington, Craig	90F	195	$ .01	$ .10
Worthington, Craig	91F	496	$ .01	$ .04
Worthington, Craig	91FUL	26	$ .01	$ .07
Worthington, Craig	92F	31	$ .01	$ .04
Wright, George	83F	583	$ .01	$ .06
Wright, George	84F	435	$ .01	$ .08
Wright, George	85F	574	$ .01	$ .06
Wright, George	86F	578	$ .01	$ .06
Wright, Ricky	83F	226	$ .01	$ .06
Wynegar, Butch	81F	558	$ .01	$ .06
Wynegar, Butch	82F	565	$ .01	$ .06
Wynegar, Butch	83F	399	$ .01	$ .06
Wynegar, Butch	84F	144	$ .01	$ .08
Wynegar, Butch	85F	147	$ .01	$ .06
Wynegar, Butch	86F	122	$ .01	$ .06
Wynne, Marvell	84F	269	$ .01	$ .08
Wynne, Marvell	85F	481	$ .01	$ .06
Wynne, Marvell	86F	625	$ .01	$ .06
Wynne, Marvell	86FU	130	$ .01	$ .08
Wynne, Marvell	87F	435	$ .01	$ .06
Wynne, Marvell	89F	322	$ .01	$ .04
Wynne, Marvell	91F	441	$ .01	$ .04
Yastrzemski, Carl	81F	221	$ .20	$2.00
Yastrzemski, Carl	81F	638	$ .20	$2.00
Yastrzemski, Carl	82F	312	$ .15	$1.25
Yastrzemski, Carl	82F	633	$ .10	$ .75
Yastrzemski, Carl	83F	200	$ .10	$1.00
Yastrzemski, Carl	83F	629	$ .10	$ .75
Yastrzemski, Carl	84F	412	$ .75	$3.00
Yastrzemski, Carl	84F	640	$ .75	$3.00
Yeager, Steve	81F	129	$ .01	$ .06
Yeager, Steve	82F	29	$ .01	$ .06
Yeager, Steve	83F	227	$ .01	$ .06
Yeager, Steve	84F	117	$ .01	$ .08
Yeager, Steve	85F	390	$ .01	$ .06
Yeager, Steve	86F	131	$ .01	$ .08
Yeager, Steve	87F	599	$ .01	$ .06
Yelding, Eric	90FU	18	$ .01	$ .10
Yelding, Eric	91F	520	$ .01	$ .04
Yelding, Eric	91FUL	141	$ .01	$ .07

FLEER

Player	Year	No.	VG	EX/MT	Player	Year	No.	VG	EX/MT
Yett, Rich	85FU	131	$.01	$.10	Youngblood, Joel	84F	387	$.01	$.08
Yett, Rich	87F	263	$.01	$.06	Youngblood, Joel	85F	625	$.01	$0.06
Yett, Rich	88F	621	$.01	$.05	Youngblood, Joel	86F	555	$.01	$.06
Yett, Rich	89F	417	$.01	$.04	Youngblood, Joel	87F	288	$.01	$.06
Yett, Rich	90F	504	$.01	$.04	Yount, Robin	81F	511	$1.00	$4.00
York, Mike	91FUL	389	$.01	$.15	Yount, Robin	82F	155	$.75	$3.00
Yost, Ned	83F	50	$.01	$.06	Yount, Robin	83F	51	$.20	$2.00
Yost, Ned	84F	218	$.01	$.08	Yount, Robin	83F	632	$.10	$.50
Yost, Ned	84FU	130	$.10	$.50	Yount, Robin	84F	219	$1.25	$5.00
Yost, Ned	85F	575	$.01	$.06	Yount, Robin	85F	601	$.75	$3.00
Youmans, Floyd	86F	267	$.10	$.50	Yount, Robin	86F	506	$.20	$2.00
Youmans, Floyd	87F	337	$.01	$.10	Yount, Robin	87F	361	$.10	$1.00
Youmans, Floyd	88F	201	$.01	$.10	Yount, Robin	88F	178	$.10	$.50
Young, Anthony	92F	520	$.01	$.10	Yount, Robin	89F	200	$.05	$.20
Young, Anthony	92FUL	238	$.05	$.20	Yount, Robin	90F	340	$.01	$.10
Young, Anthony	93F	96	$.01	$.04	Yount, Robin	91F	601	$.01	$.10
Young, Anthony	93FUL	81	$.01	$.10	Yount, Robin	91FUL	184	$.05	$.25
Young, Cliff	90FU	82	$.01	$.15	Yount, Robin	92F	194	$.01	$.10
Young, Cliff	91F	330	$.01	$.10	Yount, Robin	92F	708	$.05	$.20
Young, Cliff	92F	73	$.01	$.04	Yount, Robin	92FUH	2	$1.50	$6.00
Young, Curt	85F	436	$.10	$.40	Yount, Robin	92FUL	87	$.10	$.50
Young, Curt	87F	410	$.01	$.06	Yount, Robin	93F	260	$.01	$.10
Young, Curt	88F	296	$.01	$.05	Yount, Robin	93FUL	227	$.05	$.35
Young, Curt	89F	26	$.01	$.04	Zachry, Pat	81F	334	$.01	$.06
Young, Curt	90F	24	$.01	$.04	Zachry, Pat	82F	544	$.01	$.06
Young, Curt	91F	28	$.01	$.04	Zachry, Pat	83F	561	$.01	$.06
Young, Curt	91FUL	257	$.01	$.07	Zachry, Pat	84F	118	$.01	$.08
Young, Curt	92F	272	$.01	$.04	Zachry, Pat	85F	391	$.01	$.06
Young, Curt	93F	658	$.01	$.04	Zahn, Geoff	81F	564	$.01	$.06
Young, Eric	92FU	94	$.75	$3.00	Zahn, Geoff	82F	474	$.01	$.06
Young, Eric	93F	69	$.05	$.20	Zahn, Geoff	83F	103	$.01	$.06
Young, Gerald	88F	460	$.01	$.10	Zahn, Geoff	84F	532	$.01	$.08
Young, Gerald	89F	370	$.01	$.04	Zahn, Geoff	85F	317	$.01	$.06
Young, Gerald	90F	241	$.01	$.04	Zeile, Todd	89FU	122	$.10	$.50
Young, Gerald	91F	521	$.01	$.04	Zeile, Todd	90F	265	$.05	$.20
Young, Gerald	91FUL	142	$.01	$.07	Zeile, Todd	91F	654	$.01	$.04
Young, Gerald	92F	446	$.01	$.04	Zeile, Todd	91FUL	299	$.01	$.15
Young, Matt	84F	624	$.05	$.20	Zeile, Todd	92F	596	$.01	$.10
Young, Matt	85F	505	$.01	$.06	Zeile, Todd	92FUL	273	$.01	$.10
Young, Matt	86F	481	$.01	$.06	Zeile, Todd	93F	136	$.01	$.04
Young, Matt	87F	600	$.01	$.06	Zeile, Todd	93FUL	115	$.01	$.10
Young, Matt	87FU	131	$.01	$.06	Zimmer, Don	81F	230	$.01	$.06
Young, Matt	88F	530	$.05	$.25	Zisk, Richie	81F	620	$.01	$.06
Young, Matt	90FU	121	$.01	$.05	Zisk, Richie	82F	519	$.01	$.06
Young, Matt	91F	465	$.01	$.04	Zisk, Richie	83F	489	$.01	$.06
Young, Matt	92FUL	320	$.01	$.10	Zisk, Richie	84F	625	$.01	$.08
Young, Matt	93F	567	$.01	$.04	Zosky, Eddie	91FUL	390	$.05	$.20
Young, Mike	84FU	131	$.10	$.50	Zosky, Eddie	92F	348	$.01	$.10
Young, Mike	85F	195	$.05	$.20	Zosky, Eddie	92FUL	156	$.01	$.10
Young, Mike	86F	291	$.01	$.06	Zosky, Eddie	93F	703	$.01	$.04
Young, Mike	87F	483	$.01	$.06	Zupcic, Bob	92FU	6	$.10	$1.00
Young, Mike	88F	575	$.01	$.05	Zupcic, Bob	93F	186	$.01	$.04
Youngblood, Joel	81F	331	$.01	$.06	Zupcic, Bob	93FUL	158	$.05	$.20
Youngblood, Joel	82F	543	$.01	$.06	Zuvella, Paul	85F	651	$.10	$.50
Youngblood, Joel	83F	301	$.01	$.06	Zuvella, Paul	86F	532	$.01	$.06
Youngblood, Joel	83F	641	$.01	$.06					

MAJOR LEAGUE MARKETING (SCORE) 1988 – 1993

Score sets produced by Major League Marketing in 1988 are colorful with lots of action shots. The reverse of the cards feature a color close-up portrait photo of the player. Over production has plagued all issues of Score except the 1988 traded and rookie cards.

In 1992 Score issued two series of a premium card line. It was called Pinnacle and introduced a number of "insert" cards. These were highly collectible at first, but now the prices have dropped to half and even less of the prices that were being obtained late in 1992. 1993 saw a new issue of Pinnacle and a new card called Score Select which was made to sell in between the prices of regular Score cards and the highly priced Pinnacle. "Insert" cards abound and many collectors are beginning to write off these gimmicks as quickly as they first embraced them.

Abbreviations used in this section:
SC – Score cards
SCAS – Score All Star (1991)
SCBC – Score Bonus Card (7) (1991 factory sets)
SCDT – Score Dream Team beginning in 1990
SCHL – Score Highlight
SCKM – Score subset K-Man (1991)
SCMB – Score subset of Master Blaster (1991)
SCMVP – Score Most Valuable Player
SCP - Score Pinnacle first made in 1992
SCRM – Score Rifleman subset (1991)
SCS – Score Select cards first made in 1993
SCTF – Score subset The Franchise (1991)
SCTR – Score traded cards beginning in 1988

Both Score and Pinnacle cards measure 2½" x 3½".

1988SC – Score set of 660 cards w/six different colored borders (blue, green, gold, purple, red and yellow) Score logo on front lower right corner (copyright 1988 Score on back lower right)

1989SC – Score set of 660 cards w/white borders w/six different colored inside borders (green, light blue, purple, orange, red and dark blue) Score logo on front right corner (copyright 1989 Score on back lower left)

1990SC – Score set of 704 cards with four different colored borders (red, blue, green and white) whose color scheme is carried onto the back. Score logo on front upper left corner (copyright 1990 Score on back right center)

1991SC – Score cards were issued in two series. Series I has 441 cards, and Series II has 452 cards, but seven additional "Bonus Cards" are in the factory sets making a total of 900.

1992SC – Score cards were issued in two series. Series I has 442 cards, and Series II has 451 cards.

1992SCP – Pinnacle cards were issued in two series of 310 cards each.

1993SC – Score cards were issued in only one series of 660.

1993SCP – Pinnacle cards were only issued in Series I of 310 cards at the time of this writing.

The listings for each card shown appears immediately following the photograph.

SCORE

Player	Year	No.	VG	EX/MT
Aase, Don	88SC	518	$ .01	$ .04
Aase, Don	89SC	524	$ .01	$ .03
Aase, Don	90SC	377	$ .01	$ .04
Aase, Don	90SCTR	29	$ .01	$ .05
Aase, Don	91SC	289	$ .01	$ .04
Abbott, Jim	89SCTR	88	$ .15	$1.50
Abbott, Jim	90SC	330	$ .01	$ .15
Abbott, Jim	91SC	105	$ .01	$ .10
Abbott, Jim	92SC	620	$ .01	$ .10
Abbott, Jim	92SCP	281	$ .10	$ .40
Abbott, Jim	92SCP	539	$ .05	$ .20
Abbott, Jim	93SC	646	$ .01	$ .10
Abbott, Jim	93SCP	11	$ .01	$ .15
Abbott, Jim	93SCS	98	$ .01	$ .15
Abbott, Kyle	90SC	673	$ .05	$ .25
Abbott, Kyle	92SC	849	$ .01	$ .10
Abbott, Kyle	92SCP	432	$ .01	$ .10
Abbott, Kyle	93SC	403	$ .01	$ .03
Abbott, Kyle	93SCS	332	$ .01	$ .05
Abbott, Paul	91SC	363	$ .01	$ .10
Abbott, Paul	92SC	697	$ .01	$ .04
Abner, Shawn	88SC	626	$ .01	$ .04
Abner, Shawn	89SC	411	$ .01	$ .10
Abner, Shawn	90SC	352	$ .01	$ .04
Abner, Shawn	91SC	261	$ .01	$ .04
Abner, Shawn	92SC	616	$ .01	$ .04
Abner, Shawn	93SC	437	$ .01	$ .03
Acker, Jim	88SC	576	$ .01	$ .04
Acker, Jim	91SC	122	$ .01	$ .04
Acker, Jim	92SC	63	$ .01	$ .04
Adduci, Jim	89SC	587	$ .01	$ .03

Player	Year	No.	VG	EX/MT
Adkins, Steve	**91SC**	**716**	**$ .01**	**$ .15**
Afenir, Troy	91SC	745	$ .01	$ .04
Afenir, Troy	92SC	407	$ .01	$ .04
Agosto, Juan	88SC	558	$ .01	$ .04
Agosto, Juan	89SC	283	$ .01	$ .03
Agosto, Juan	90SC	284	$ .01	$ .04
Agosto, Juan	91SC	591	$ .01	$ .04
Agosto, Juan	92SC	329	$ .01	$ .04
Aguayo, Luis	88SC	499	$ .01	$ .04
Aguayo, Luis	89SC	436	$ .01	$ .03
Aguilera, Rick	88SC	521	$ .01	$ .04
Aguilera, Rick	89SC	327	$ .01	$ .03

Player	Year	No.	VG	EX/MT
Aguilera, Rick	90SC	519	$ .01	$ .04
Aguilera, Rick	91SC	170	$ .01	$ .04
Aguilera, Rick	92SC	42	$ .01	$ .04
Aguilera, Rick	92SCP	211	$ .01	$ .05
Aguilera, Rick	93SC	64	$ .01	$ .03
Aguilera, Rick	93SCS	206	$ .01	$ .05
Akerfelds, Darrel	88SC	632	$ .01	$ .04
Akerfelds, Darrel	91SC	223	$ .01	$ .04
Aldred, Scott	91SC	740	$ .01	$ .10
Aldred, Scott	92SC	729	$ .01	$ .04
Aldred, Scott	92SCP	354	$ .01	$ .05
Aldrete, Mike	88SC	556	$ .01	$ .04
Aldrete, Mike	89SC	82	$ .01	$ .03
Aldrete, Mike	89SCTR	68	$ .01	$ .05
Aldrete, Mike	90SC	220	$ .01	$ .04
Aldrete, Mike	91SC	447	$ .01	$ .04
Aldrete, Mike	92SC	351	$ .01	$ .04
Aldrich, Jay	88SC	578	$ .01	$ .04
Alexander, Doyle	88SC	610	$ .01	$ .04
Alexander, Doyle	89SC	129	$ .01	$ .03
Alexander, Doyle	90SC	237	$ .01	$ .04
Alexander, Gerald	91SC	733	$ .01	$ .10
Alexander, Gerald	92SC	163	$ .01	$ .04
Alexander, Manny	93SC	234	$ .01	$ .15
Alexander, Manny	93SCP	244	$ .05	$ .20
Alexander, Manny	93SCS	391	$ .01	$ .15
Alicea, Luis	88SCTR	98	$ .05	$ .25
Alicea, Luis	89SC	231	$ .01	$ .15
Alicea, Luis	92SC	607	$ .01	$ .04
Alicea, Luis	93SC	183	$ .01	$ .03
Allanson, Andy	88SC	586	$ .01	$ .04
Allanson, Andy	89SC	46	$ .01	$ .03
Allanson, Andy	90SC	452	$ .01	$ .04
Allanson, Andy	92SC	537	$ .01	$ .04
Allen, Neil	89SC	375	$ .01	$ .03
Allison, Dana	91SCTR	94	$ .01	$ .05
Allred, Beau	90SCTR	70	$ .01	$ .10
Allred, Beau	91SC	338	$ .01	$ .04
Alomar, Roberto	88SCTR	105	$15.00	$60.00
Alomar, Roberto	89SC	232	$ .10	$ .75
Alomar, Roberto	90SC	12	$ .10	$ .40
Alomar, Roberto	91SC	25	$ .05	$ .25
Alomar, Roberto	91SCDT	887	$ .10	$ .40
Alomar, Roberto	91SCTR	44	$ .05	$ .25
Alomar, Roberto	92SC	15	$ .05	$ .20
Alomar, Roberto	92SCP	45	$ .10	$ .40
Alomar, Roberto	92SCP	306	$ .05	$ .25
Alomar, Roberto	92SCP	586	$ .05	$ .25
Alomar, Roberto	93SC	14	$ .05	$ .20
Alomar, Roberto	93SC	511	$ .01	$ .10
Alomar, Roberto	93SC	542	$ .01	$ .15
Alomar, Roberto	93SCP	30	$ .10	$ .40
Alomar, Roberto	93SCS	8	$ .05	$ .25
Alomar Jr., Sandy	89SC	630	$ .05	$ .35
Alomar Jr., Sandy	90SC	577	$ .01	$ .10
Alomar Jr., Sandy	90SCTR	18	$ .01	$ .10
Alomar Jr., Sandy	91SC	790	$ .01	$ .10
Alomar Jr., Sandy	91SCAS	400	$ .01	$ .04
Alomar Jr., Sandy	91SCMVP	879	$ .01	$ .05
Alomar Jr., Sandy	91SCRM	694	$ .01	$ .10
Alomar Jr., Sandy	91SCTF	851	$ .01	$ .04
Alomar Jr., Sandy	92SC	510	$ .01	$ .04
Alomar, Jr., Sandy	92SCP	436	$ .01	$ .05
Alomar, Sandy	92SCP	586	$ .05	$ .25
Alomar, Jr., Sandy	93SC	116	$ .01	$ .03
Alomar, Jr., Sandy	93SCP	211	$ .01	$ .08
Alomar, Jr., Sandy	93SCS	26	$ .01	$ .05
Alou, Moises	90SC	592	$ .10	$ .40
Alou, Moises	91SC	813	$ .01	$ .15
Alou, Moises	92SCP	572	$ .01	$ .05
Alou, Moises	93SC	187	$ .01	$ .15
Alou, Moises	93SCP	92	$ .01	$ .15
Alou, Moises	93SCS	272	$ .01	$ .05
Alvarez, Jose	90SC	148	$ .01	$ .04
Alvarez, Wilson	92SC	428	$ .01	$ .04

SCORE

Player	Year	No.	VG	EX/MT
Alvarez, Wilson	92SC	760	$ .01	$ .04
Alvarez, Wilson	92SCP	192	$ .01	$ .05
Alvarez, Wilson	93SC	609	$ .01	$ .03
Amaral, Rich	92SCP	581	$ .01	$ .05
Amaral, Rich	93SC	249	$ .01	$ .03
Amaro Jr., Ruben	92SCP	570	$ .01	$ .05
Amaro Jr., Ruben	92SCTR	98	$ .01	$ .05
Amaro Jr., Ruben	93SC	341	$ .01	$ .03
Andersen, Larry	88SC	133	$ .01	$ .04
Andersen, Larry	89SC	523	$ .01	$ .03
Andersen, Larry	90SC	282	$ .01	$ .04
Andersen, Larry	91SC	848	$ .01	$ .04
Andersen, Larry	91SCTR	71	$ .01	$ .05
Andersen, Larry	92SC	263	$ .01	$ .04
Andersen, Larry	92SCP	399	$ .01	$ .05
Andersen, Larry	93SC	445	$ .01	$ .03
Anderson, Allan	89SC	394	$ .01	$ .10
Anderson, Allan	90SC	292	$ .01	$ .04
Anderson, Allan	91SC	135	$ .01	$ .04
Anderson, Allan	92SC	731	$ .01	$ .04
Anderson, Brady	88SCTR	70	$1.75	$7.00
Anderson, Brady	89SC	563	$ .10	$ .50
Anderson, Brady	90SC	33	$ .01	$ .10
Anderson, Brady	91SC	249	$ .01	$ .15
Anderson, Brady	92SC	365	$ .01	$ .04
Anderson, Brady	92SCP	452	$ .01	$ .05
Anderson, Brady	93SC	140	$ .01	$ .03
Anderson, Brady	93SCP	70	$ .01	$ .08
Anderson, Brady	93SCS	56	$ .01	$ .15
Anderson, Dave	88SC	166	$ .01	$ .04
Anderson, Dave	89SC	478	$ .01	$ .03
Anderson, Dave	90SC	238	$ .01	$ .04
Anderson, Dave	91SC	641	$ .01	$ .04
Anderson, Dave	92SC	167	$ .01	$ .04
Anderson, Dave	92SCTR	45	$ .01	$ .05
Anderson, Kent	90SC	412	$ .01	$ .04
Anderson, Kent	91SC	224	$ .01	$ .04
Anderson, Rick	89SC	441	$ .01	$ .03
Anderson, Scott	91SC	734	$ .01	$ .10
Andrews, Shane	91SC	674	$ .05	$ .25
Andujar, Joaquin	88SC	193	$ .01	$ .04
Andujar, Joaquin	89SC	472	$ .01	$ .03
Anthony, Eric	90SC	584	$ .05	$ .25
Anthony, Eric	91SC	146	$ .01	$ .10
Anthony, Eric	92SC	315	$ .01	$ .04
Anthony, Eric	92SCP	363	$ .01	$ .05
Anthony, Eric	93SC	173	$ .01	$ .10
Anthony, Eric	93SCP	84	$ .01	$ .08
Anthony, Eric	93SCS	137	$ .01	$ .15
Appier, Kevin	90SC	625	$ .05	$ .25
Appier, Kevin	91SC	268	$ .01	$ .04
Appier, Kevin	92SC	542	$ .01	$ .04
Appier, Kevin	92SCP	434	$ .01	$ .05
Appier, Kevin	93SC	154	$ .01	$ .03
Appier, Kevin	93SCP	133	$ .01	$ .08
Appier, Kevin	93SCS	102	$ .01	$ .05
Aquino, Luis	90SC	432	$ .01	$ .04
Aquino, Luis	92SC	369	$ .01	$ .04
Aquino, Luis	92SCP	454	$ .01	$ .05
Arias, Alex	93SC	565	$ .01	$ .10
Armas, Tony	88SC	487	$ .01	$ .04
Armas, Tony	89SC	182	$ .01	$ .03
Armas, Tony	90SC	378	$ .01	$ .04
Armstrong, Jack	88SCTR	78	$ .10	$ .75
Armstrong, Jack	89SC	462	$ .01	$ .15
Armstrong, Jack	91SC	231	$ .01	$ .04
Armstrong, Jack	92SC	488	$ .01	$ .04
Armstrong, Jack	92SCTR	58	$ .01	$ .05
Armstrong, Jack	93SC	655	$ .01	$ .03
Arnold, Jamie	93SC	487	$ .01	$ .15
Arnold, Jamie	93SCS	303	$ .05	$ .25
Arnsberg, Brad	91SC	510	$ .01	$ .04
Ashby, Alan	88SC	73	$ .01	$ .04
Ashby, Alan	89SC	366	$ .01	$ .03
Ashby, Andy	92SC	396	$ .01	$ .04
Ashby, Andy	92SCP	265	$ .01	$ .05
Ashley, Billy	93SC	267	$ .05	$ .25
Ashley, Billy	93SCP	281	$ .10	$ .50
Assenmacher, Paul	89SC	373	$ .01	$ .03
Assenmacher, Paul	91SC	147	$ .01	$ .04
Assenmacher, Paul	92SC	360	$ .01	$ .04
Assenmacher, Paul	92SCP	466	$ .01	$ .05
Astacio, Pedro	92SCP	551	$ .10	$ .50
Astacio, Pedro	93SC	231	$ .05	$ .25
Astacio, Pedro	93SCS	325	$ .05	$ .35
Atherton, Keith	88SC	613	$ .01	$ .04
Atherton, Keith	89SC	381	$ .01	$ .03
August, Don	88SCTR	104	$ .01	$ .15
August, Don	89SC	419	$ .01	$ .10
August, Don	90SC	144	$ .01	$ .04
August, Don	92SC	533	$ .01	$ .04
Austin, Jim	92SC	747	$ .01	$ .10
Austin, James	92SCTR	107	$ .01	$ .10
Austin, James	93SC	331	$ .01	$ .03
Austin, James	93SCS	322	$ .01	$ .05
Austin, Pat	90SC	626	$ .01	$ .04
Avery, Steve	90SCTR	109	$ .10	$1.00
Avery, Steve	91SC	80	$ .05	$ .20
Avery, Steve	92SC	241	$ .01	$ .15
Avery, Steve	92SC	797	$ .01	$ .15
Avery, Steve	92SCP	231	$ .05	$ .20
Avery, Steve	92SCP	585	$ .05	$ .20
Avery, Steve	92SCP	612	$ .01	$ .10
Avery, Steve	93SC	169	$ .01	$ .10
Avery, Steve	93SCS	109	$ .01	$ .15
Ayrault, Bob	93SC	289	$ .01	$ .03
Ayrault, Bob	93SCP	229	$ .01	$ .08
Azocar, Oscar	90SCTR	71	$ .01	$ .10
Azocar, Oscar	91SC	72	$ .01	$ .10
Azocar, Oscar	92SC	692	$ .01	$ .04
Backman, Wally	88SC	303	$ .01	$ .04
Backman, Wally	89SC	315	$ .01	$ .03
Backman, Wally	89SCTR	34	$ .01	$ .05
Backman, Wally	90SC	281	$ .01	$ .04
Backman, Wally	90SCTR	37	$ .01	$ .05
Backman, Wally	91SC	16	$ .01	$ .04
Backman, Wally	91SCTR	8	$ .01	$ .05
Backman, Wally	92SC	177	$ .01	$ .04
Baerga, Carlos	90SCTR	74	$ .15	$1.50
Baerga, Carlos	91SC	74	$ .05	$ .25
Baerga, Carlos	92SC	128	$ .05	$ .20
Baerga, Carlos	92SC	3	$ .01	$ .05
Baerga, Carlos	93SC	9	$ .01	$ .15
Baerga, Carlos	93SCP	6	$ .05	$ .25
Baerga, Carlos	93SCS	122	$ .05	$ .25
Bagwell, Jeff	91SCTR	96	$ .10	$1.00
Bagwell, Jeff	92SC	576	$ .05	$ .25
Bagwell, Jeff	92SC	793	$ .01	$ .15
Bagwell, Jeff	92SCP	70	$ .10	$ .40
Bagwell, Jeff	93SC	89	$ .01	$ .15
Bagwell, Jeff	93SCP	10	$ .05	$ .25
Bagwell, Jeff	93SCP	297	$ .05	$ .20
Bagwell, Jeff	93SCS	113	$ .05	$ .25
Bailes, Scott	89SC	424	$ .01	$ .03
Bailes, Scott	90SC	218	$ .01	$ .04
Bailes, Scott	90SCTR	64	$ .01	$ .05
Bailes, Scott	91SC	535	$ .01	$ .04
Bailes, Scott	92SC	331	$ .01	$ .04
Baines, Harold	88SC	590	$ .01	$ .10
Baines, Harold	89SC	128	$ .01	$ .03
Baines, Harold	89SCTR	62	$ .01	$ .10
Baines, Harold	90SC	470	$ .01	$ .04
Baines, Harold	91SC	291	$ .01	$ .04
Baines, Harold	92SC	137	$ .01	$ .04
Baines, Harold	92SCP	41	$ .01	$ .05
Baines, Harold	93SC	585	$ .01	$ .03
Baines, Harold	93SCP	111	$ .01	$ .08
Baines, Harold	93SCS	257	$ .01	$ .05
Bair, Doug	90SC	517	$ .01	$ .04
Balboni, Steve	88SC	273	$ .01	$ .04

SCORE

Player	Year	No.	VG	EX/MT
Balboni, Steve	88SCTR	46	$ .01	$ .15
Balboni, Steve	89SC	353	$ .01	$ .03
Balboni, Steve	89SCTR	27	$ .01	$ .05
Balboni, Steve	90SC	327	$ .01	$ .04
Balboni, Steve	91SC	159	$ .01	$ .04
Ballard, Jeff	89SC	551	$ .01	$ .15
Ballard, Jeff	90SC	349	$ .01	$ .04
Ballard, Jeff	91SC	243	$ .01	$ .04
Ballard, Jeff	92SC	129	$ .01	$ .04
Bando, Chris	88SC	172	$ .01	$ .04
Bankhead, Scott	88SC	238	$ .01	$ .04
Bankhead, Scott	89SC	341	$ .01	$ .03
Bankhead, Scott	90SC	555	$ .01	$ .04
Bankhead, Scott	91SC	817	$ .01	$ .04
Bankhead, Scott	92SC	594	$ .01	$ .04
Bankhead, Scott	92SCP	580	$ .01	$ .05
Bankhead, Scott	92SCTR	47	$ .01	$ .05
Bankhead, Scott	93SC	584	$ .01	$ .03
Bankhead, Scott	93SCS	265	$ .01	$ .05
Banks, Willie	92SCP	575	$ .05	$ .20

Player	Year	No.	VG	EX/MT
Banks, Willie	93SC	235	$ .05	$ .20
Banks, Willie	93SCS	314	$ .01	$ .05
Bannister, Floyd	88SC	622	$ .01	$ .04
Bannister, Floyd	88SCTR	63	$ .01	$ .15
Bannister, Floyd	89SC	249	$ .01	$ .03
Barber, Al	92SC	803	$ .01	$ .15
Barber, Brian	92SCP	298	$ .05	$ .35
Barberie, Bret	92SC	419	$ .01	$ .10
Barberie, Bret	92SCP	93	$ .01	$ .10
Barberie, Bret	93SC	617	$ .01	$ .03
Barfield, Jesse	88SC	8	$ .01	$ .10
Barfield, Jesse	89SC	160	$ .01	$ .10
Barfield, Jesse	89SCTR	22	$ .01	$ .10
Barfield, Jesse	90SC	222	$ .01	$ .10
Barfield, Jesse	91SC	148	$ .01	$ .04
Barfield, Jesse	91SCRM	414	$ .01	$ .05
Barfield, Jesse	92SC	565	$ .01	$ .04
Barfield, Jesse	92SCP	425	$ .01	$ .05
Barfield, John	91SC	573	$ .01	$ .04
Barfield, John	92SC	683	$ .01	$ .04
Barnes, Brian	91SC	708	$ .01	$ .15
Barnes, Brian	92SC	715	$ .01	$ .04
Barnes, Skeeter	92SC	569	$ .01	$ .04

Player	Year	No.	VG	EX/MT
Barnes, Skeeter	92SCP	218	$ .01	$ .05
Barrett, Marty	88SC	155	$ .01	$ .04
Barrett, Marty	89SC	63	$ .01	$ .03
Barrett, Marty	90SC	15	$ .01	$ .04
Barrett, Marty	91SC	228	$ .01	$ .04
Barrett, Tom	90SC	633	$ .01	$ .04
Barton, Shawn	93SCP	250	$ .01	$ .15
Bass, Kevin	88SC	33	$ .01	$ .04
Bass, Kevin	89SC	226	$ .01	$ .03
Bass, Kevin	90SC	279	$ .01	$ .04
Bass, Kevin	90SCTR	2	$ .01	$ .05
Bass, Kevin	91SC	616	$ .01	$ .04
Bass, Kevin	92SC	139	$ .01	$ .04
Bass, Kevin	92SCP	53	$ .01	$ .05
Bass, Kevin	92SCTR	76	$ .01	$ .05
Bass, Kevin	93SC	578	$ .01	$ .03
Bates, Billy	90SC	608	$ .01	$ .10
Batiste, Kim	92SC	833	$ .01	$ .10
Batiste, Kim	92SCP	266	$ .01	$ .10
Batiste, Kim	93SC	191	$ .01	$ .03
Bautista, Jose	89SC	573	$ .01	$ .15
Baylor, Don	88SC	250	$ .01	$ .04
Baylor, Don	88SCTR	55	$ .01	$ .15
Baylor, Don	89SC	205	$ .01	$ .03
Beatty, Blaine	90SC	632	$ .01	$ .10
Beatty, Blaine	92SC	843	$ .01	$ .04
Beck, Rod	92SC	746	$ .01	$ .10
Beck, Rod	92SCP	613	$ .05	$ .20
Beck, Rod	93SC	391	$ .01	$ .03
Beckett, Robbie	91SC	673	$ .01	$ .10
Bedrosian, Steve	88SC	161	$ .01	$ .10
Bedrosian, Steve	88SC	656	$ .01	$ .04
Bedrosian, Steve	89SC	260	$ .01	$ .03
Bedrosian, Steve	89SCTR	49	$ .01	$ .10
Bedrosian, Steve	90SC	379	$ .01	$ .04
Bedrosian, Steve	91SC	459	$ .01	$ .04
Bedrosian, Steve	91SCTR	14	$ .01	$ .05
Bedrosian, Steve	92SC	17	$ .01	$ .04
Belcher, Kevin	91SC	714	$ .01	$ .10
Belcher, Tim	88SCTR	101	$ .10	$ .50
Belcher, Tim	89SC	418	$ .01	$ .15
Belcher, Tim	90SC	126	$ .01	$ .10
Belcher, Tim	91SC	187	$ .01	$ .04
Belcher, Tim	92SC	368	$ .01	$ .04
Belcher, Tim	92SCP	384	$ .01	$ .05
Belcher, Tim	92SCTR	65	$ .01	$ .05
Belcher, Tim	93SC	423	$ .01	$ .03
Belcher, Tim	93SCS	191	$ .01	$ .05
Belinda, Stan	90SC	634	$ .01	$ .10
Belinda, Stan	91SC	296	$ .01	$ .04
Belinda, Stan	92SC	325	$ .01	$ .04
Belinda, Stan	92SCP	370	$ .01	$ .05
Belinda, Stan	93SC	369	$ .01	$ .03
Belinda, Stan	93SCP	142	$ .01	$ .08
Bell, Buddy	88SC	99	$ .01	$ .10
Bell, Buddy	89SC	610	$ .01	$ .03
Bell, Derek	90SCTR	81	$ .10	$ .75
Bell, Derek	92SC	402	$ .01	$ .10
Bell, Derek	92SCP	250	$ .05	$ .20
Bell, Derek	93SC	122	$ .01	$ .03
Bell, Derek	93SCP	171	$ .01	$ .15
Bell, Derek	93SCS	286	$ .01	$ .10
Bell, Eric	88SC	101	$ .01	$ .04
Bell, George	88SC	540	$ .01	$ .10
Bell, George	89SC	347	$ .01	$ .10
Bell, George	90SC	286	$ .01	$ .10
Bell, George	91SC	195	$ .01	$ .10
Bell, George	91SCTR	13	$ .01	$ .10
Bell, George	92SC	45	$ .01	$ .04
Bell, George	92SCP	37	$ .01	$ .05
Bell, George	92SCTR	24	$ .01	$ .05
Bell, George	93SC	387	$ .01	$ .03
Bell, George	93SCS	100	$ .01	$ .10
Bell, Jay	89SC	352	$ .01	$ .10
Bell, Jay	90SC	563	$ .01	$ .04

SCORE

Player	Year	No.	VG	EX/MT
Bell, Jay	91SC	323	$ .01	$ .04
Bell, Jay	92SC	180	$ .01	$ .04
Bell, Jay	92SCP	34	$ .01	$ .05
Bell, Jay	93SC	32	$ .01	$ .03
Bell, Jay	93SCP	48	$ .01	$ .08
Bell, Jay	93SCS	81	$ .01	$ .05
Bell, Juan	90SC	603	$ .01	$ .10
Bell, Juan	92SC	646	$ .01	$ .04
Bell, Juan	93SC	588	$ .01	$ .03
Bell, Mike	91SC	375	$ .01	$ .10
Bell, Mike	92SC	249	$ .01	$ .04
Bellaird, Rafael	93SC	478	$ .01	$ .03
Belle, Joey	89SCTR	106	$ .20	$2.00
Belle, Joey "Albert"	90SC	508	$ .10	$ .50
Belle, Albert	92SC	31	$ .01	$ .15
Belle, Albert	92SCP	31	$ .05	$ .35
Belle, Albert	93SC	84	$ .05	$ .20
Belle, Albert	93SCP	93	$ .05	$ .25
Belle, Albert	93SCS	50	$ .05	$ .20
Belliard, Rafael	88SC	453	$ .01	$ .04
Belliard, Rafael	89SC	379	$ .01	$ .03
Belliard, Rafael	90SC	520	$ .01	$ .04
Belliard, Rafael	91SCTR	76	$ .01	$ .05
Belliard, Rafael	92SC	116	$ .01	$ .04
Belliard, Rafael	92SCP	357	$ .01	$ .05
Belliard, Rafael	93SCS	267	$ .01	$ .05
Beltre, Esteban	92SC	766	$ .01	$ .10
Beltre, Esteban	92SCP	535	$ .01	$ .15
Benavides, Freddie	91SCTR	98	$ .01	$ .10
Benavides, Freddie	92SC	813	$ .01	$ .04
Benavides, Freddie	92SCP	278	$ .01	$ .05
Benavides, Freddie	93SC	627	$ .01	$ .03
Benedict, Bruce	88SC	423	$ .01	$ .04
Benedict, Bruce	89SC	502	$ .01	$ .03
Benes, Andy	90SC	578	$ .05	$ .20
Benes, Andy	91SC	538	$ .01	$ .10
Benes, Andy	92SC	133	$ .01	$ .04
Benes, Andy	92SCP	74	$ .01	$ .05
Benes, Andy	93SC	91	$ .01	$ .03
Benes, Andy	93SCP	42	$ .01	$ .08
Benes, Andy	93SCS	117	$ .01	$ .05
Benjamin, Mike	91SC	345	$ .01	$ .04
Benjamin, Mike	92SC	649	$ .01	$ .04
Benjamin, Mike	93SC	603	$ .01	$ .03
Benzinger, Todd	88SC	546	$ .01	$ .15
Benzinger, Todd	89SC	371	$ .01	$ .03
Benzinger, Todd	89SCTR	15	$ .01	$ .10
Benzinger, Todd	90SC	65	$ .01	$ .04
Benzinger, Todd	91SC	90	$ .01	$ .04
Benzinger, Todd	92SC	563	$ .01	$ .04
Benzinger, Todd	92SCP	438	$ .01	$ .05
Berenguer, Juan	89SC	414	$ .01	$ .03
Berenguer, Juan	90SC	223	$ .01	$ .04
Berenguer, Juan	91SC	111	$ .01	$ .04
Berenguer, Juan	91SCTR	73	$ .01	$ .05
Berenguer, Juan	92SC	216	$ .01	$ .04
Berenguer, Juan	92SCP	515	$ .01	$ .05
Bergman, Dave	88SC	217	$ .01	$ .04
Bergman, Dave	89SC	469	$ .01	$ .03
Bergman, Dave	90SC	254	$ .01	$ .04
Bergman, Dave	91SC	562	$ .01	$ .04
Bergman, Dave	92SC	543	$ .01	$ .04
Bernazard, Tony	88SC	604	$ .01	$ .04
Berroa, Geronimo	89SC	632	$ .01	$ .10
Berroa, Geronimo	90SC	151	$ .01	$ .04
Berry, Sean	91SC	764	$ .01	$ .10
Berry, Sean	92SC	678	$ .01	$ .04
Berry, Sean	92SCP	271	$ .01	$ .10
Berry, Sean	93SC	543	$ .01	$ .03
Berry, Sean	93SCP	212	$ .01	$ .08
Berryhill, Damon	88SCTR	82	$ .10	$ .50
Berryhill, Damon	89SC	336	$ .01	$ .10
Berryhill, Damon	90SC	163	$ .01	$ .10
Berryhill, Damon	91SC	881	$ .01	$ .04
Berryhill, Damon	92SCP	390	$ .01	$ .05
Berryhill, Damon	93SC	373	$ .01	$ .03
Biancalana, Buddy	88SC	383	$ .01	$ .04

Player	Year	No.	VG	EX/MT
Bichette, Dante	91SC	463	$ .01	$ .04
Bichette, Dante	91SCTR	37	$ .01	$ .05
Bichette, Dante	92SC	316	$ .01	$ .04
Bichette, Dante	92SCP	514	$ .01	$ .05
Bichette, Dante	93SC	428	$ .01	$ .03
Bichette, Dante	93SCP	232	$ .01	$ .08
Bichette, Dante	93SCS	114	$ .01	$ .05
Bielecki, Mike	88SC	611	$ .01	$ .04
Bielecki, Mike	90SC	484	$ .01	$ .04
Bielecki, Mike	91SC	453	$ .01	$ .04
Bielecki, Mike	92SCP	566	$ .01	$ .05
Bielecki, Mike	93SC	457	$ .01	$ .03
Biggio, Craig	88SCTR	103	$1.25	$5.00
Biggio, Craig	89SC	237	$ .05	$ .35
Biggio, Craig	90SC	275	$ .01	$ .10
Biggio, Craig	91SC	161	$ .01	$ .04
Biggio, Craig	91SCTF	872	$ .01	$ .04
Biggio, Craig	92SC	460	$ .01	$ .04
Biggio, Craig	92SCDT	888	$ .01	$ .04
Biggio, Craig	92SCP	140	$ .01	$ .05
Biggio, Craig	93SC	18	$ .01	$ .03
Biggio, Craig	93SCP	50	$ .01	$ .08
Biggio, Craig	93SCS	25	$ .01	$ .05
Bilardello, Dann	91SC	659	$ .01	$ .04
Bilardello, Dann	92SC	719	$ .01	$ .04
Birkbeck, Mike	88SC	369	$ .01	$ .04
Birkbeck, Mike	89SC	596	$ .01	$ .03
Birtsas, Tim	89SC	454	$ .01	$ .03
Birtsas, Tim	90SC	408	$ .01	$ .04
Birtsas, Tim	91SC	648	$ .01	$ .04
Bitker, Joe	92SC	743	$ .01	$ .04
Bittiger, Jeff	88SCTR	66	$ .01	$ .15
Bittiger, Jeff	89SC	512	$ .01	$ .10
Black, Bud	88SC	313	$ .01	$ .04
Black, Bud	88SCTR	11	$ .01	$ .15
Black, Bud	89SC	404	$ .01	$ .03
Black, Bud	90SC	197	$ .01	$ .04
Black, Bud	91SCTR	46	$ .01	$ .05
Black, Bud	92SC	358	$ .01	$ .04
Black, Bud	92SCP	202	$ .01	$ .05
Black, Bud	93SC	131	$ .01	$ .03

SCORE

Player	Year	No.	VG	EX/MT	Player	Year	No.	VG	EX/MT
Black, Bud	93SCP	181	$.01	$.08	Bonds, Barry	93SC	560	$.05	$.20
Black, Bud	93SCS	221	$.01	$.05	Bonds, Barry	93SCS	1	$.05	$.25
Blair, Willie	90SCTR	88	$.01	$.10	Bones, Ricky	92SC	758	$.01	$.04
Blair, Willie	91SC	57	$.01	$.04	Bones, Ricky	93SC	470	$.01	$.03
Blair, Willie	92SC	730	$.01	$.04	Bonilla, Bobby	88SC	116	$.05	$.25
Blankenship, Kevin	90SC	646	$.01	$.04	Bonilla, Bobby	89SC	195	$.01	$.15
Blankenship, Lance	89SC	641	$.01	$.10	Bonilla, Bobby	90SC	170	$.01	$.15
Blankenship, Lance	90SC	536	$.01	$.04	Bonilla, Bobby	91SC	315	$.01	$.10
Blankenship, Lance	91SC	303	$.01	$.04	Bonilla, Bobby	91SCAS	670	$.01	$.04
Blankenship, Lance	92SC	279	$.01	$.04	Bonilla, Bobby	91SCMB	402	$.01	$.10
Blauser, Jeff	88SC	562	$.05	$.25	Bonilla, Bobby	92SC	225	$.01	$.10
Blauser, Jeff	89SC	589	$.01	$.03	Bonilla, Bobby	92SCP	310	$.01	$.05
Blauser, Jeff	90SC	178	$.01	$.04	Bonilla, Bobby	92SCP	395	$.01	$.15
Blauser, Jeff	91SC	52	$.01	$.04	Bonilla, Bobby	92SCTR	5	$.01	$.10
Blauser, Jeff	92SC	362	$.01	$.04	Bonilla, Bobby	93SC	8	$.01	$.10
Blauser, Jeff	92SCP	477	$.01	$.05	Bonilla, Bobby	93SCP	43	$.01	$.15
Blauser, Jeff	93SC	142	$.01	$.03	Bonilla, Bobby	93SCS	11	$.01	$.10
Blocker, Terry	89SC	605	$.01	$.03	Booker, Greg	88SC	447	$.01	$.04
Blosser, Greg	90SC	681	$.05	$.25	Booker, Greg	89SC	417	$.01	$.03
Blowers, Mike	90SC	624	$.01	$.10	Boone, Bob	88SC	63	$.01	$.04
Blowers, Mike	91SC	838	$.01	$.04	Boone, Bob	89SC	233	$.01	$.03
Blyleven, Bert	88SC	90	$.01	$.10	Boone, Bob	89SCTR	74	$.01	$.05
Blyleven, Bert	89SC	215	$.01	$.10	Boone, Bob	90SC	60	$.01	$.04
Blyleven, Bert	89SCTR	17	$.01	$.10	Boone, Bret	92SCTR	104	$.10	$.75
Blyleven, Bert	90SC	180	$.01	$.04	Boone, Bret	93SC	335	$.05	$.25
Blyleven, Bert	91SC	235	$.01	$.04	Boone, Bret	93SCP	243	$.10	$.50
Blyleven, Bert	93SC	577	$.01	$.03	Boone, Bret	93SCS	326	$.05	$.35
Blyleven, Bert	93SCP	83	$.01	$.08	Boone, Dan	91SC	715	$.01	$.04
Blyleven, Bert	93SCP	296	$.01	$.08	Borders, Pat	88SCTR	99	$.25	$2.50
Blyleven, Bert	93SCS	252	$.01	$.05	Borders, Pat	89SC	198	$.05	$.25
Bochy, Bruce	88SC	469	$.01	$.04	Borders, Pat	90SC	288	$.01	$.04
Boddicker, Mike	88SC	67	$.01	$.10	Borders, Pat	91SC	425	$.01	$.04
Boddicker, Mike	89SC	549	$.01	$.03	Borders, Pat	92SC	288	$.01	$.04
Boddicker, Mike	90SC	31	$.01	$.04	Borders, Pat	92SCP	421	$.01	$.05
Boddicker, Mike	91SC	232	$.01	$.04	Borders, Pat	93SC	642	$.01	$.03
Boddicker, Mike	91SCTR	45	$.01	$.05	Borders, Pat	93SCP	203	$.01	$.08
Boddicker, Mike	92SC	102	$.01	$.04	Borders, Pat	93SCS	369	$.01	$.05
Boddicker, Mike	92SCP	142	$.01	$.05	Bordick, Mike	91SC	339	$.05	$.35
Boever, Joe	88SC	542	$.01	$.04	Bordick, Mike	92SC	681	$.01	$.04
Boever, Joe	90SC	81	$.01	$.04	Bordick, Mike	92SCP	462	$.01	$.10
Boever, Joe	92SC	647	$.01	$.04	Bordick, Mike	93SC	100	$.01	$.03
Boggs, Wade	88SC	2	$.05	$.25	Bordick, Mike	93SCP	85	$.01	$.08
Boggs, Wade	89SC	175	$.05	$.30	Bordick, Mike	93SCS	208	$.01	$.05
Boggs, Wade	89SC	654	$.01	$.15	Bosio, Chris	88SC	38	$.01	$.04
Boggs, Wade	90SC	245	$.05	$.20	Bosio, Chris	89SC	243	$.01	$.03
Boggs, Wade	90SC	704	$.01	$.10	Bosio, Chris	90SC	283	$.01	$.04
Boggs, Wade	90SCDT	683	$.01	$.10	Bosio, Chris	91SC	43	$.01	$.04
Boggs, Wade	91SC	12	$.01	$.10	Bosio, Chris	92SC	37	$.01	$.04
Boggs, Wade	91SCAS	393	$.01	$.10	Bosio, Chris	92SCP	367	$.01	$.05
Boggs, Wade	91SCBC	1	$.15	$1.50	Bosio, Chris	93SC	616	$.01	$.03
Boggs, Wade	91SCDT	889	$.05	$.20	Boskie, Shawn	90SCTR	94	$.01	$.10
Boggs, Wade	92SC	660	$.01	$.10	Boskie, Shawn	91SC	59	$.01	$.15
Boggs, Wade	92SCAS	434	$.01	$.10	Boskie, Shawn	92SC	713	$.01	$.04
Boggs, Wade	92SCDT	885	$.01	$.15	Boskie, Shawn	92SCP	527	$.01	$.05
Boggs, Wade	92SCP	175	$.05	$.25	Bossy, Mike	93SCP	299	$.01	$.15
Boggs, Wade	92SCP	282	$.01	$.15	Boston, Daryl	88SC	582	$.01	$.04
Boggs, Wade	93SC	592	$.01	$.10	Boston, Daryl	89SC	443	$.01	$.03
Boggs, Wade	93SCS	48	$.01	$.15	Boston, Daryl	90SC	213	$.01	$.04
Bohanon, Brian	92SC	672	$.01	$.04	Boston, Daryl	90SCTR	47	$.01	$.05
Bolton, Tom	89SC	531	$.01	$.03	Boston, Daryl	91SC	618	$.01	$.04
Bolton, Tom	91SC	781	$.01	$.04	Boston, Daryl	92SC	276	$.01	$.04
Bolton, Tom	92SC	99	$.01	$.04	Boston, Daryl	92SCP	343	$.01	$.05
Bolton, Tom	92SCTR	77	$.01	$.05	Boston, Daryl	93SC	447	$.01	$.03
Bonds, Barry	88SC	265	$.10	$.50	Boston Red Sox, A. L. Wins	89SC	660	$.01	$.03
Bonds, Barry	89SC	127	$.10	$.40	Bottenfield, Kent	93SC	312	$.01	$.10
Bonds, Barry	90SC	4	$.05	$.25	Boucher, Denis	92SC	848	$.01	$.04
Bonds, Barry	91SC	330	$.05	$.20	Bournigal, Rafael	93SC	307	$.01	$.15
Bonds, Barry	91SCAS	668	$.01	$.10	Bournigal, Rafael	93SCP	279	$.10	$.40
Bonds, Barry	91SCMVP	876	$.01	$.05	Bowen, Ryan	92SC	762	$.10	$.10
Bonds, Barry	91SCTF	868	$.01	$.04	Bowen, Ryan	92SCP	473	$.01	$.15
Bonds, Barry	92SC	555	$.05	$.25	Boyd, Dennis	88SC	121	$.01	$.04
Bonds, Barry	92SCAS	777	$.01	$.04	Boyd, Dennis	89SC	238	$.01	$.03
Bonds, Barry	92SCP	500	$.10	$.50	Boyd, Dennis	90SC	137	$.01	$.04
Bonds, Barry	93SC	482	$.05	$.20	Boyd, Dennis	90SCTR	24	$.01	$.05
Bonds, Barry	93SC	523	$.01	$.15	Boyd, Dennis	91SC	202	$.01	$.04

SCORE

Player	Year	No.	VG	EX/MT	Player	Year	No.	VG	EX/MT
Boyd, Dennis	92SC	531	$ .01	$ .04	Brennan, Bill	89SC	622	$ .01	$ .03
Bradley, Phil	88SC	66	$ .01	$ .10	Brett, George	88SC	11	$ .05	$ .20
Bradley, Phil	88SCTR	34	$ .01	$ .15	Brett, George	89SC	75	$ .05	$ .25
Bradley, Phil	89SC	79	$ .01	$ .03	Brett, George	90SC	140	$ .01	$ .15
Bradley, Phil	89SCTR	44	$ .01	$ .05	Brett, George	91SC	120	$ .01	$ .10
Bradley, Phil	90SC	24	$ .01	$ .04	Brett, George	91SCBC	5	$ .10	$1.00
Bradley, Phil	90SCTR	44	$ .01	$ .05	Brett, George	91SCHL	769	$ .01	$ .05
Bradley, Phil	91SC	560	$ .01	$ .04	Brett, George	91SCTF	853	$ .01	$ .04
					Brett, George	92SC	650	$ .01	$ .10
					Brett, George	92SCP	60	$ .05	$ .25
					Brett, George	92SCP	282	$ .01	$ .15
					Brett, George	93SC	57	$ .01	$ .10
					Brett, George	93SC	517	$ .01	$ .10
					Brett, George	93SCP	131	$ .05	$ .20
					Brett, George	93SCP	294	$ .01	$ .15
					Brett, George	93SCS	78	$ .01	$ .15
					Brewer, Rod	92SC	864	$ .01	$ .04
					Briley, Greg	88SCTR	74	$ .05	$ .35
					Briley, Greg	90SC	303	$ .01	$ .15
					Briley, Greg	91SC	494	$ .01	$ .04
					Briley, Greg	92SC	387	$ .01	$ .04
					Brink, Brad	93SC	224	$ .01	$ .03
					Briscoe, John	91SCTR	108	$ .01	$ .10
					Brito, Barnardo	93SCP	274	$ .01	$ .08
					Brito, Bernardo	93SC	306	$ .01	$ .03
					Brock, Greg	88SC	234	$ .01	$ .04
					Brock, Greg	89SC	307	$ .01	$ .03
					Brock, Greg	90SC	485	$ .01	$ .04
					Brock, Greg	91SC	522	$ .01	$ .04
					Brogna, Rico	91SC	741	$ .01	$ .10
					Brogna, Rico	93SC	114	$ .01	$ .03
					Brogna, Rico	93SCP	240	$ .01	$ .08
					Brookens, Tom	88SC	233	$ .01	$ .04
					Brookens, Tom	89SC	269	$ .01	$ .03
					Brookens, Tom	89SCTR	73	$ .01	$ .05
					Brookens, Tom	90SC	297	$ .01	$ .04
					Brookens, Tom	91SC	106	$ .01	$ .04
					Brooks, Hubie	88SC	305	$ .01	$ .04
					Brooks, Hubie	89SC	53	$ .01	$ .03
					Brooks, Hubie	90SC	299	$ .01	$ .04
Bradley, Scott	88SC	151	$ .01	$ .04	Brooks, Hubie	90SCTR	34	$ .01	$ .05
Bradley, Scott	89SC	324	$ .01	$ .03	Brooks, Hubie	91SC	196	$ .01	$ .04
Bradley, Scott	90SC	228	$ .01	$ .04	Brooks, Hubie	91SCTR	5	$ .01	$ .05
Bradley, Scott	91SC	113	$ .01	$ .04	Brooks, Hubie	92SC	107	$ .01	$ .04
Bradley, Scott	92SC	304	$ .01	$ .04	Brooks, Hubie	92SCP	449	$ .01	$ .05
Braggs, Glenn	88SC	59	$ .01	$ .04	Brooks, Hubie	92SCTR	69	$ .01	$ .05
Braggs, Glenn	89SC	147	$ .01	$ .03	Brosius, Scott	92SC	846	$ .01	$ .10
Braggs, Glenn	90SC	105	$ .01	$ .04	Brosius, Scott	92SCP	274	$ .01	$ .10
Braggs, Glenn	90SCTR	56	$ .01	$ .05	Bross, Terry	92SC	763	$ .01	$ .04
Braggs, Glenn	91SC	18	$ .01	$ .04	Brower, Bob	88SC	236	$ .01	$ .04
Braggs, Glenn	92SC	393	$ .01	$ .04	Brower, Bob	89SC	344	$ .01	$ .03
Braggs, Glenn	92SCP	502	$ .01	$ .05	Brown, Chris	88SC	363	$ .01	$ .04
Branson, Jeff	92SCP	533	$ .01	$ .05	Brown, Chris	89SC	369	$ .01	$ .03
Branson, Jeff	93SC	308	$ .01	$ .03	Brown, Jarvis	92SC	870	$ .01	$ .10
Brantley, Cliff	92SC	854	$ .01	$ .15	Brown, Jarvis	92SCP	544	$ .01	$ .10
Brantley, Cliff	92SCP	557	$ .01	$ .05	Brown, Kevin	89SCTR	89	$ .05	$ .25
Brantley, Jeff	89SCTR	101	$ .01	$ .15	Brown, Kevin	90SC	210	$ .01	$ .10
Brantley, Jeff	90SC	371	$ .01	$ .10	Brown, Kevin	91SC	846	$ .01	$ .04
Brantley, Jeff	91SC	160	$ .01	$ .04	Brown, Kevin	92SC	709	$ .01	$ .04
Brantley, Jeff	92SC	157	$ .01	$ .04	Brown, Kevin	92SCP	405	$ .01	$ .05
Brantley, Jeff	92SCP	470	$ .01	$ .05	Brown, Kevin	93SC	146	$ .01	$ .03
Brantley, Jeff	93SC	153	$ .01	$ .03	Brown, Kevin	93SCS	204	$ .01	$ .05
Brantley, Mickey	89SC	89	$ .01	$ .03	Browne, Jerry	88SC	278	$ .01	$ .04
Bream, Sid	88SC	260	$ .01	$ .04	Browne, Jerry	90SC	52	$ .01	$ .04
Bream, Sid	89SC	48	$ .01	$ .03	Browne, Jerry	91SC	481	$ .01	$ .04
Bream, Sid	90SC	423	$ .01	$ .04	Browne, Jerry	92SC	496	$ .01	$ .04
Bream, Sid	91SC	304	$ .01	$ .04	Browne, Jerry	92SCP	208	$ .01	$ .05
Bream, Sid	91SCTR	12	$ .01	$ .05	Browne, Jerry	93SC	382	$ .01	$ .03
Bream, Sid	92SC	131	$ .01	$ .04	Browning, Tom	88SC	132	$ .01	$ .15
Bream, Sid	92SCP	446	$ .01	$ .05	Browning, Tom	89SC	554	$ .01	$ .10
Bream, Sid	93SC	396	$ .01	$ .03	Browning, Tom	89SC	658	$ .01	$ .10
Bream, Sid	93SCP	204	$ .01	$ .08	Browning, Tom	90SC	165	$ .01	$ .10
Bream, Sid	93SCS	382	$ .01	$ .05	Browning, Tom	91SC	229	$ .01	$ .04
Brenley, Bob	88SC	134	$ .01	$ .04	Browning, Tom	92SC	642	$ .01	$ .04
Brenly, Bob	89SC	395	$ .01	$ .03	Browning, Tom	92SCP	101	$ .01	$ .05

SCOTT BRADLEY

SCORE

Player	Year	No.	VG	EX/MT	Player	Year	No.	VG	EX/MT
Browning, Tom	93SC	404	$ .01	$ .03	Burns, Todd	88SCTR	106	$ .05	$ .25
Browning, Tom	93SCS	249	$ .01	$ .05	Burns, Todd	89SC	465	$ .01	$ .10
Bruett, J. T.	93SC	275	$ .01	$ .03	Burns, Todd	90SC	64	$ .01	$ .04
Bruett, J. T.	93SCP	241	$ .01	$ .08	Burns, Todd	91SC	41	$ .01	$ .04
Brumfield, Jacob	92SCP	553	$ .01	$ .10	Burns, Todd	92SC	341	$ .01	$ .04
Brumfield, Jacob	93SC	292	$ .01	$ .03	Bush, Randy	88SC	292	$ .01	$ .04
Brumley, Mike	91SC	624	$ .01	$ .04	Bush, Randy	89SC	212	$ .01	$ .03
Brumley, Mike	92SC	363	$ .01	$ .04	Bush, Randy	90SC	278	$ .01	$ .04
Brunansky, Tom	88SC	194	$ .01	$ .04	Bush, Randy	91SC	574	$ .01	$ .04
Brunansky, Tom	88SCTR	5	$ .01	$ .15	Bush, Randy	92SC	377	$ .01	$ .04
Brunansky, Tom	89SC	184	$ .01	$ .03	Butcher, Mike	93SC	277	$ .01	$ .03
Brunansky, Tom	90SC	72	$ .01	$ .04	Butcher, Mike	93SCP	262	$ .01	$ .08
Brunansky, Tom	90SCTR	49	$ .01	$ .05	Butera, Sal	88SC	361	$ .01	$ .04
Brunansky, Tom	91SC	245	$ .01	$ .04	Butler, Brett	88SC	122	$ .01	$ .10
Brunansky, Tom	92SC	46	$ .01	$ .04	Butler, Brett	88SCTR	3	$ .05	$ .35
Brunansky, Tom	92SCP	314	$ .01	$ .05	Butler, Brett	89SC	216	$ .01	$ .03
Brunansky, Tom	93SC	612	$ .01	$ .03	Butler, Brett	90SC	236	$ .01	$ .04
Brunansky, Tom	93SCS	210	$ .01	$ .05	Butler, Brett	91SC	455	$ .01	$ .04
Bryant, Scott	90SC	667	$ .01	$ .10	Butler, Brett	91SCTR	23	$ .01	$ .05
Buckner, Bill	88SC	591	$ .01	$ .04	Butler, Brett	92SC	465	$ .01	$ .04
Buckner, Bill	88SCTR	36	$ .01	$ .15	Butler, Brett	92SCAS	778	$ .01	$ .04
Buckner, Bill	89SC	214	$ .01	$ .03	Butler, Brett	92SCP	133	$ .01	$ .05
Buckner, Bill	90SC	396	$ .01	$ .04	Butler, Brett	92SCP	619	$ .01	$ .05
Buechele, Steve	88SC	306	$ .01	$ .04	Butler, Brett	93SC	20	$ .01	$ .03
Buechele, Steve	89SC	368	$ .01	$ .03	Butler, Brett	93SCP	91	$ .01	$ .08
Buechele, Steve	90SC	221	$ .01	$ .04	Butler, Brett	93SCS	115	$ .01	$ .05
Buechele, Steve	91SC	257	$ .01	$ .04	Cabrera, Francisco	90SCTR	67	$ .01	$ .10
Buechele, Steve	92SC	695	$ .01	$ .04	Cabrera, Francisco	91SC	63	$ .01	$ .04
Buechele, Steve	92SCP	430	$ .01	$ .05	Cabrera, Francisco	92SC	581	$ .01	$ .04
Buechele, Steve	92SCTR	21	$ .01	$ .05	Cabrera, Francisco	93SC	472	$ .01	$ .03
Buechele, Steve	93SC	97	$ .01	$ .03	Cadaret, Greg	89SC	340	$ .01	$ .03
Buechele, Steve	93SCP	176	$ .01	$ .08	Cadaret, Greg	89SCTR	69	$ .01	$ .05
Buechele, Steve	93SCS	129	$ .01	$ .05	Cadaret, Greg	91SC	188	$ .01	$ .04
Buhner, Jay	88SCTR	95	$ .75	$3.00	Cadaret, Greg	92SC	454	$ .01	$ .04
Buhner, Jay	89SC	530	$ .01	$ .15	Cadaret, Greg	92SCP	402	$ .01	$ .05
Buhner, Jay	90SC	521	$ .01	$ .04	Calderon, Ivan	88SC	607	$ .01	$ .04
Buhner, Jay	91SC	125	$ .01	$ .04	Calderon, Ivan	89SC	331	$ .01	$ .03
Buhner, Jay	92SC	64	$ .01	$ .04	Calderon, Ivan	90SC	94	$ .01	$ .04
Buhner, Jay	92SCP	27	$ .01	$ .05	Calderon, Ivan	91SC	254	$ .01	$ .04
Buhner, Jay	92SCP	305	$ .01	$ .05	Calderon, Ivan	91SCTR	6	$ .01	$ .05
Buhner, Jay	93SC	172	$ .01	$ .03	Calderon, Ivan	92SC	83	$ .01	$ .04
Buhner, Jay	93SCP	68	$ .01	$ .08	Calderon, Ivan	92SCP	58	$ .01	$ .05
Buhner, Jay	93SCS	202	$ .01	$ .05	Calderon, Ivan	93SCP	150	$ .01	$ .08
Buice, DeWayne	88SC	376	$ .01	$ .04	Calderon, Ivan	93SCS	125	$ .01	$ .05
Buice, DeWayne	89SC	153	$ .01	$ .03	Calderon, Juan	93SC	95	$ .01	$ .03
Bullinger, Jim	92SCTR	101	$ .01	$ .10	Caminiti, Ken	88SC	164	$ .05	$ .25
Bullinger, Jim	93SC	339	$ .01	$ .03	Caminiti, Ken	90SC	76	$ .01	$ .04
Bullinger, Jim	93SCS	285	$ .01	$ .05	Caminiti, Ken	91SC	186	$ .01	$ .04
Bullock, Eric	92SC	661	$ .01	$ .04	Caminiti, Ken	91SCRM	415	$ .01	$ .05
Burba, Dave	91SC	742	$ .01	$ .10	Caminiti, Ken	92SC	69	$ .01	$ .04
Burba, Dave	92SC	611	$ .01	$ .04	Caminiti, Ken	92SCP	43	$ .01	$ .05
Burba, Dave	92SCP	529	$ .01	$ .05	Caminiti, Ken	93SC	40	$ .01	$ .03
Burba, Dave	92SCTR	51	$ .01	$ .05	Caminiti, Ken	93SCP	59	$ .01	$ .08
Burke, Tim	88SC	187	$ .01	$ .04	Caminiti, Ken	93SCS	47	$ .01	$ .05
Burke, Tim	89SC	228	$ .01	$ .03	Campbell, Kevin	92SC	855	$ .01	$ .15
Burke, Tim	90SC	127	$ .01	$ .04	Campbell, Mike	89SC	568	$ .01	$ .15
Burke, Tim	91SC	181	$ .01	$ .04	Campusano, Sil	88SCTR	93	$ .05	$ .25
Burke, Tim	92SC	651	$ .01	$ .04	Campusano, Sil	89SC	473	$ .01	$ .10
Burke, Tim	92SCP	471	$ .01	$ .05	Campusano, Sil	91SC	847	$ .01	$ .04
Burkett, John	90SCTR	73	$ .01	$ .10	Canale, George	90SC	656	$ .01	$ .10
Burkett, John	91SC	70	$ .01	$ .10	Candaele, Casey	88SC	97	$ .01	$ .04
Burkett, John	92SC	522	$ .01	$ .04	Candaele, Casey	91SC	577	$ .01	$ .04
Burkett, John	92SCP	292	$ .01	$ .05	Candaele, Casey	92SC	147	$ .01	$ .04
Burkett, John	92SCP	578	$ .01	$ .05	Candelaria, John	88SC	293	$ .01	$ .04
Burkett, John	93SC	174	$ .01	$ .03	Candelaria, John	88SCTR	40	$ .01	$ .15
Burks, Ellis	88SC	472	$ .05	$ .25	Candelaria, John	89SC	246	$ .01	$ .03
Burks, Ellis	89SC	9	$ .01	$ .10	Candelaria, John	90SCTR	54	$ .01	$ .05
Burks, Ellis	90SC	340	$ .01	$ .10	Candelaria, John	91SC	791	$ .01	$ .04
Burks, Ellis	91SC	8	$ .01	$ .15	Candelaria, John	91SCTR	32	$ .01	$ .05
Burks, Ellis	92SC	270	$ .01	$ .04	Candelaria, John	92SC	350	$ .01	$ .04
Burks, Ellis	92SCP	26	$ .01	$ .05	Candelaria, John	93SC	448	$ .01	$ .03
Burks, Ellis	93SC	78	$ .01	$ .03	Candiotti, Tom	88SC	595	$ .01	$ .04
Burks, Ellis	93SCP	46	$ .01	$ .08	Candiotti, Tom	89SC	239	$ .01	$ .03
Burks, Ellis	93SCS	68	$ .01	$ .05	Candiotti, Tom	90SC	269	$ .01	$ .04
Burnitz, Jeromy	91SC	380	$ .05	$ .25	Candiotti, Tom	91SC	488	$ .01	$ .04

SCORE

Player	Year	No.	VG	EX/MT	Player	Year	No.	VG	EX/MT
Candiotti, Tom	92SC	575	$ .01	$ .04	Castillo, Braulio	92SC	824	$ .01	$ .10
Candiotti, Tom	92SCP	459	$ .01	$ .05	Castillo, Braulio	93SC	629	$ .01	$ .10
Candiotti, Tom	92SCP	610	$ .01	$ .05	Castillo, Braulio	93SCS	340	$ .01	$ .05
Candiotti, Tom	92SCTR	68	$ .01	$ .05	Castillo, Carmelo	90SC	123	$ .01	$ .04
Candiotti, Tom	93SC	175	$ .01	$ .03	Castillo, Carmelo	91SC	608	$ .01	$ .04
Candiotti, Tom	93SCP	147	$ .01	$ .08	Castillo, Carmen	88SC	581	$ .01	$ .04
Candiotti, Tom	93SCS	143	$ .01	$ .05	Castillo, Carmen	89SC	497	$ .01	$ .03
Cangelosi, John	88SC	418	$ .01	$ .04	Castillo, Carmen	89SCTR	23	$ .01	$ .05
Cangelosi, John	89SC	601	$ .01	$ .03	Castillo, Frank	92SC	399	$ .01	$ .10
Cangelosi, John	90SC	367	$ .01	$ .04	Castillo, Frank	92SCP	504	$ .01	$ .15
Canseco, Jose	88SC	45	$ .10	$ .50	Castillo, Frank	93SC	462	$ .01	$ .03
Canseco, Jose	89SC	1	$ .10	$ .50	Castillo, Frank	93SCP	208	$ .01	$ .08
Canseco, Jose	89SC	655	$ .01	$ .15	Castillo, Tony	91SC	582	$ .01	$ .04
Canseco, Jose	90SC	375	$ .05	$ .25	Castillo, Tony	92SC	682	$ .01	$ .04
Canseco, Jose	91SC	1	$ .05	$ .20	Cedeno, Andujar	91SC	753	$ .01	$ .15
Canseco, Jose	91SCAS	398	$ .01	$ .10	Cedeno, Andujar	92SC	599	$ .01	$ .10
Canseco, Jose	91SCDT	441	$ .15	$1.50	Cedeno, Andujar	92SCP	84	$ .01	$ .10
Canseco, Jose	91SCMB	690	$ .01	$ .10	Cedeno, Andujar	93SC	127	$ .01	$ .03
Canseco, Jose	92SC	500	$ .01	$ .15	Cedeno, Andujar	93SCP	32	$ .01	$ .08
Canseco, Jose	92SCP	130	$ .10	$ .40	Cerone, Rick	88SC	486	$ .01	$ .04
Canseco, Jose	92SCTR	9	$ .10	$ .40	Cerone, Rick	88SCTR	21	$ .01	$ .15
Canseco, Jose	93SC	13	$ .05	$ .20	Cerone, Rick	89SC	396	$ .01	$ .03
Canseco, Jose	93SCP	49	$ .05	$ .35	Cerone, Rick	90SC	139	$ .01	$ .04
Canseco, Jose	93SCS	364	$ .05	$ .25	Cerone, Rick	90SCTR	63	$ .01	$ .05
Canseco, Ozzie	91SC	346	$ .01	$ .10	Cerone, Rick	91SC	580	$ .01	$ .04
Canseco, Ozzie	93SC	241	$ .01	$ .03	Cerone, Rick	91SCTR	41	$ .01	$ .05
Canseco, Ozzie	93SCP	272	$ .01	$ .15	Cerutti, John	88SC	98	$ .01	$ .10
Capel, Mike	92SC	687	$ .01	$ .04	Cerutti, John	89SC	304	$ .01	$ .03
Carew, Rod	92SCP	584	$ .05	$ .20	Cerutti, John	90SC	429	$ .01	$ .04
Carman, Don	88SC	401	$ .01	$ .04	Cerutti, John	91SC	786	$ .01	$ .04
Carman, Don	89SC	222	$ .01	$ .03	Cerutti, John	91SCTR	40	$ .01	$ .05
Carman, Don	91SC	237	$ .01	$ .04	Cerutti, John	92SC	179	$ .01	$ .04
Carpenter, Cris	89SCTR	81	$ .01	$ .15	Chamberlain, Wes	91SC	713	$ .05	$ .25
Carpenter, Cris	92SC	160	$ .01	$ .04	Chamberlain, Wes	92SC	384	$ .01	$ .15
Carpenter, Cris	93SC	633	$ .01	$ .03	Chamberlain, Wes	92SCP	36	$ .01	$ .10
Carr, Chuck	92SC	857	$ .01	$ .04	Chamberlain, Wes	93SC	168	$ .01	$ .03
Carr, Chuck	93SC	545	$ .01	$ .03	Chamberlain, Wes	93SCS	217	$ .01	$ .05
Carreon, Amalio	92SC	867	$ .01	$ .10	Charlton, Norm	89SC	646	$ .05	$ .25
Carreon, Mark	89SCTR	108	$ .01	$ .10	Charlton, Norm	90SC	248	$ .01	$ .10
Carreon, Mark	90SC	363	$ .01	$ .04	Charlton, Norm	91SC	530	$ .01	$ .04
Carreon, Mark	91SC	165	$ .01	$ .04	Charlton, Norm	92SC	267	$ .01	$ .10
Carreon, Mark	92SC	19	$ .01	$ .04	Charlton, Norm	92SCP	216	$ .01	$ .05
Carreon, Mark	92SCP	441	$ .01	$ .05	Charlton, Norm	93SC	375	$ .01	$ .03
Carreon, Mark	92SCTR	37	$ .01	$ .05	Charlton, Norm	93SCS	207	$ .01	$ .05
Carreon, Mark	93SC	366	$ .01	$ .03	Chiamparino, Scott	90SCTR	108	$ .01	$ .10
Carreon, Mark	93SCP	136	$ .01	$ .08	Chiamparino, Scott	91SC	352	$ .01	$ .10
Carter, Gary	88SC	325	$ .01	$ .15	Chiamparino, Scott	92SC	688	$ .01	$ .04
Carter, Gary	89SC	240	$ .01	$ .10	Chiamparino, Scott	93SC	386	$ .01	$ .03
Carter, Gary	90SC	416	$ .01	$ .04	Chitren, Steve	91SC	760	$ .01	$ .10
Carter, Gary	90SCTR	35	$ .01	$ .05	Chitren, Steve	92SC	202	$ .01	$ .04
Carter, Gary	91SC	215	$ .01	$ .04	Chitren, Steve	92SCP	236	$ .01	$ .05
Carter, Gary	91SCTR	26	$ .01	$ .05	Christensen, John	88SC	419	$ .01	$ .04
Carter, Gary	92SC	489	$ .01	$ .04	Christopherson, Eric	91SC	672	$ .01	$ .10
Carter, Gary	92SCP	321	$ .01	$ .05	Cianfrocco, Archi	92SC	510	$ .01	$ .10
Carter, Gary	92SCTR	59	$ .01	$ .05	Cianfrocco, Archi	92SCTR	99	$ .01	$ .10
Carter, Gary	93SCS	55	$ .01	$ .05	Cianfrocco, Archi	93SC	340	$ .01	$ .03
Carter, Jeff	92SC	770	$ .01	$ .04	Clancy, Jim	88SC	530	$ .01	$ .04
Carter, Jeff	92SCP	280	$ .01	$ .05	Clancy, Jim	89SC	538	$ .01	$ .03
Carter, Joe	88SC	80	$ .05	$ .20	Clancy, Jim	89SCTR	42	$ .01	$ .05
Carter, Joe	89SC	213	$ .05	$ .25	Clancy, Jim	90SC	424	$ .01	$ .04
Carter, Joe	90SC	319	$ .05	$ .20	Clancy, Jim	92SC	627	$ .01	$ .04
Carter, Joe	90SCTR	19	$ .05	$ .20	Clark, Dave	88SC	633	$ .01	$ .04
Carter, Joe	91SC	9	$ .01	$ .10	Clark, Dave	90SC	141	$ .01	$ .04
Carter, Joe	91SCTR	11	$ .01	$ .10	Clark, Dave	91SC	542	$ .01	$ .04
Carter, Joe	92SC	90	$ .01	$ .10	Clark, Dave	92SC	657	$ .01	$ .04
Carter, Joe	92SCAS	435	$ .01	$ .10	Clark, Jack	88SC	100	$ .01	$ .15
Carter, Joe	92SCP	148	$ .05	$ .20	Clark, Jack	88SC	650	$ .01	$ .15
Carter, Joe	93SC	506	$ .01	$ .10	Clark, Jack	88SCTR	1	$ .05	$ .20
Carter, Joe	93SC	575	$ .01	$ .10	Clark, Jack	89SC	25	$ .01	$ .10
Carter, Joe	93SCS	96	$ .01	$ .15	Clark, Jack	89SCTR	3	$ .01	$ .10
Carter, Larry	93SC	300	$ .01	$ .15	Clark, Jack	90SC	20	$ .01	$ .04
Cary, Chuck	90SC	393	$ .01	$ .04	Clark, Jack	91SC	523	$ .01	$ .04
Cary, Chuck	91SC	566	$ .01	$ .04	Clark, Jack	91SCTR	4	$ .01	$ .05
Casillo, Juan	88SC	429	$ .01	$ .04	Clark, Jack	92SCP	85	$ .01	$ .05
Castilla, Vinny	92SC	860	$ .01	$ .15	Clark, Jack	93SCP	221	$ .01	$ .08

SCORE

Player	Year	No.	VG	EX/MT
Clark, Jack	93SCS	188	$.01	$.05
Clark, Jerald	89SC	644	$.01	$.10
Clark, Jerald	90SC	660	$.01	$.04
Clark, Jerald	91SC	242	$.01	$.04
Clark, Jerald	92SC	257	$.01	$.04
Clark, Jerald	92SCP	48	$.01	$.05
Clark, Jerald	93SC	405	$.01	$.03
Clark, Jerald	93SCP	234	$.01	$.08
Clark, Joe	92SC	318	$.01	$.04
Clark, Mark	93SC	320	$.01	$.03
Clark, Mark	93SCS	301	$.01	$.05
Clark, Phil	91SC	756	$.01	$.10
Clark, Phil	93SCP	287	$.01	$.08
Clark, Phil	93SCS	335	$.01	$.05
Clark, Terry	89SC	566	$.01	$.03
Clark, Will	88SC	78	$.10	$.50
Clark, Will	89SC	450	$.05	$.35
Clark, Will	90SC	300	$.05	$.25
Clark, Will	90SC	699	$.01	$.15
Clark, Will	90SCDT	684	$.01	$.15
Clark, Will	91SC	7	$.01	$.15
Clark, Will	91SCAS	664	$.01	$.10
Clark, Will	91SCBC	6	$.15	$1.50
Clark, Will	91SCDT	886	$.05	$.35

Player	Year	No.	VG	EX/MT
Clark, Will	91SCTF	871	$.01	$.10
Clark, Will	92SC	3	$.01	$.15
Clark, Will	92SCAS	773	$.01	$.10
Clark, Will	92SCDT	883	$.01	$.15
Clark, Will	92SCP	122	$.10	$.40
Clark, Will	93SC	22	$.05	$.20
Clark, Will	93SCP	16	$.10	$.40
Clark, Will	93SCS	3	$.05	$.25
Clayton, Royce	92SC	841	$.01	$.10
Clayton, Royce	92SCP	268	$.05	$.20
Clayton, Royce	93SC	157	$.01	$.10
Clayton, Royce	93SCS	400	$.01	$.15
Clear, Mark	88SC	446	$.01	$.04
Clear, Mark	89SC	430	$.01	$.03
Clemens, Roger	88SC	110	$.10	$.50
Clemens, Roger	89SC	350	$.05	$.35
Clemens, Roger	90SC	310	$.05	$.35
Clemens, Roger	91SC	655	$.05	$.25
Clemens, Roger	91SCAS	399	$.01	$.10
Clemens, Roger	91SCKM	684	$.01	$.10

Player	Year	No.	VG	EX/MT
Clemens, Roger	91SCTF	850	$.01	$.10
Clemens, Roger	92SC	21	$.05	$.25
Clemens, Roger	92SC	790	$.01	$.10
Clemens, Roger	92SCP	95	$.10	$.75
Clemens, Roger	93SC	7	$.05	$.25
Clemens, Roger	93SCP	25	$.10	$.50
Clemens, Roger	93SCS	14	$.05	$.35
Clements, Pat	88SC	389	$.01	$.04
Clements, Pat	92SC	714	$.01	$.04
Cliburn, Stewart	89SC	445	$.01	$.03
Coachman, Pete	91SC	344	$.01	$.10
Cobb, Ty	92SC	878	$.05	$.25
Cochrane, Dave	92SC	461	$.01	$.04
Colbert, Craig	93SC	255	$.01	$.03
Colbert, Craig	93SCS	338	$.01	$.05
Colbrunn, Greg	93SC	271	$.01	$.03
Colbrunn, Greg	93SCS	295	$.01	$.05
Cole, Alex	91SC	555	$.01	$.10
Cole, Alex	92SC	463	$.01	$.04
Cole, Alex	92SCP	66	$.01	$.05
Cole, Alex	93SC	400	$.01	$.03
Coleman, Paul	90SC	662	$.01	$.15
Coleman, Vince	88SC	68	$.01	$.15
Coleman, Vince	88SC	652	$.01	$.10
Coleman, Vince	89SC	155	$.01	$.10
Coleman, Vince	90SC	260	$.01	$.10
Coleman, Vince	91SC	450	$.01	$.10
Coleman, Vince	91SCTR	57	$.01	$.10
Coleman, Vince	92SC	95	$.01	$.10
Coleman, Vince	92SCP	39	$.01	$.05
Coleman, Vince	93SC	650	$.01	$.03
Coleman, Vince	93SCP	61	$.01	$.10
Coleman, Vince	93SCP	69	$.01	$.08
Coleman, Vince	93SCS	175	$.01	$.05
Coles, Darnell	88SC	554	$.01	$.04
Coles, Darnell	89SC	83	$.01	$.03
Coles, Darnell	90SC	62	$.01	$.04
Coles, Darnell	91SC	629	$.01	$.04
Coles, Darnell	93SC	416	$.01	$.03
Collins, Dave	88SC	371	$.01	$.04
Collins, Dave	89SC	267	$.01	$.03
Coloon, Cris	93SC	314	$.01	$.03
Combs, Pat	90SC	623	$.01	$.10
Combs, Pat	91SC	440	$.01	$.04
Combs, Pat	92SC	106	$.05	$.04
Comstock, Keith	88SC	438	$.01	$.04
Comstock, Keith	91SC	502	$.01	$.04
Concepcion, Dave	88SC	210	$.01	$.04
Concepcion, Dave	89SC	166	$.01	$.03
Cone, David	88SC	49	$.10	$.40
Cone, David	89SC	221	$.01	$.15
Cone, David	90SC	430	$.01	$.10
Cone, David	91SC	549	$.01	$.10
Cone, David	91SCKM	409	$.01	$.05
Cone, David	92SC	680	$.01	$.04
Cone, David	92SC	795	$.01	$.04
Cone, David	92SCP	450	$.01	$.05
Cone, David	92SCP	590	$.01	$.10
Cone, David	92SCP	611	$.01	$.05
Cone, David	92SCTR	27	$.01	$.05
Cone, David	93SC	654	$.01	$.03
Cone, David	93SCS	361	$.01	$.05
Conine, Jeff	91SC	722	$.05	$.25
Conine, Jeff	93SC	402	$.01	$.03
Conine, Jeff	93SCS	321	$.01	$.05
Conroy, Tim	88SC	384	$.01	$.04
Cook, Dennis	90SC	545	$.01	$.04
Cook, Dennis	92SCP	493	$.01	$.05
Cooke, Steve	93SC	296	$.01	$.10
Cooke, Steve	93SCP	260	$.01	$.15
Coolbaugh, Scott	90SC	612	$.05	$.15
Coolbaugh, Scott	92SC	205	$.01	$.04
Cooper, Cecil	88SC	169	$.01	$.04
Cooper, Gary	92SC	840	$.01	$.10
Cooper, Scott	90SC	651	$.05	$.35

SCORE

Player	Year	No.	VG	EX/MT
Cooper, Scott	92SC	876	$ .01	$ .10
Cooper, Scott	92SCP	252	$ .05	$ .20
Cooper, Scott	93SC	198	$ .01	$ .10
Cooper, Scott	93SCS	302	$ .01	$ .05
Cora, Joey	88SC	420	$ .01	$ .10
Cora, Joey	91SC	253	$ .01	$ .04
Cora, Joey	92SC	326	$ .01	$ .04
Cora, Joey	93SC	454	$ .01	$ .03
Cordero, Wil	92SCTR	110	$ .10	$ .40
Cordero, Wil	93SC	334	$ .01	$ .15
Cordero, Wil	93SCP	280	$ .05	$ .25
Cordero, Wil	93SCS	336	$ .01	$ .15
Cormier, Rheal	92SC	851	$ .01	$ .15
Cormier, Rheal	93SC	371	$ .01	$ .03
Correa, Ed	88SC	523	$ .01	$ .04
Corsi, Jim	90SC	553	$ .01	$ .04
Corsi, Jim	92SC	524	$ .01	$ .04
Costello, John	88SCTR	107	$ .01	$ .15
Costello, John	89SC	534	$ .01	$ .10
Costello, John	90SC	347	$ .01	$ .04
Costello, John	92SC	614	$ .01	$ .04
Costo, Tim	91SC	680	$ .01	$ .15
Costo, Tim	93SC	265	$ .01	$ .10
Cotto, Henry	88SC	368	$ .01	$ .04
Cotto, Henry	88SCTR	48	$ .01	$ .15
Cotto, Henry	89SC	209	$ .01	$ .03
Cotto, Henry	90SC	161	$ .01	$ .04
Cotto, Henry	91SC	282	$ .01	$ .04
Cotto, Henry	92SC	390	$ .01	$ .04
Cotto, Henry	92SCP	342	$ .01	$ .05
Cox, Danny	88SC	415	$ .01	$ .04
Cox, Danny	89SC	613	$ .01	$ .03
Cox, Danny	92SC	568	$ .01	$ .04
Crawford, Steve	88SC	289	$ .01	$ .04
Crawford, Steve	91SC	287	$ .01	$ .04
Crawford, Steve	92SC	349	$ .01	$ .04
Crews, Tim	88SC	641	$ .01	$ .10
Crews, Tim	89SC	505	$ .01	$ .03
Crews, Tim	90SC	164	$ .01	$ .04
Crews, Tim	91SC	302	$ .01	$ .04
Crews, Tim	92SC	238	$ .01	$ .04
Crim, Chuck	88SC	402	$ .01	$ .04
Crim, Chuck	89SC	272	$ .01	$ .03
Crim, Chuck	90SC	108	$ .01	$ .04
Crim, Chuck	91SC	99	$ .01	$ .04
Crim, Chuck	92SC	22	$ .01	$ .04
Crim, Chuck	92SCTR	53	$ .01	$ .05
Crim, Chuck	93SC	455	$ .01	$ .03
Cromartie, Warren	92SC	637	$ .01	$ .04
Cron, Chris	92SC	847	$ .01	$ .04
Cruz, Jose	88SC	28	$ .01	$ .04
Cummings, Steve	90SCTR	78	$ .01	$ .10
Cunningham, Earl	90SC	670	$ .01	$ .15
Curry, Steve	88SCTR	81	$ .01	$ .15
Curtis, Chad	92SCP	523	$ .10	$ .50
Curtis, Chad	92SCTR	87	$ .10	$ .50
Curtis, Chad	93SC	354	$ .01	$ .15
Curtis, Chad	93SCS	290	$ .01	$ .15
Cuyler, Milt	90SC	583	$ .05	$ .25
Cuyler, Milt	92SC	26	$ .01	$ .04
Cuyler, Milt	92SCP	174	$ .01	$ .05
Cuyler, Milt	93SC	82	$ .01	$ .03
Cuyler, Milt	93SCP	193	$ .01	$ .08
Cuyler, Milt	93SCS	166	$ .01	$ .05
Daniels, Kal	88SC	86	$ .01	$ .15
Daniels, Kal	89SC	7	$ .01	$ .10
Daniels, Kal	89SCTR	48	$ .01	$ .05
Daniels, Kal	90SC	490	$ .01	$ .04
Daniels, Kal	91SC	20	$ .01	$ .04
Daniels, Kal	92SC	110	$ .01	$ .04
Daniels, Kal	92SCP	374	$ .01	$ .05
Daniels, Kal	92SCTR	70	$ .01	$ .05
Daniels, Kal	93SCS	181	$ .01	$ .05
Darling, Ron	88SC	141	$ .01	$ .10
Darling, Ron	89SC	180	$ .01	$ .03
Darling, Ron	90SC	446	$ .01	$ .04
Darling, Ron	91SC	456	$ .01	$ .04
Darling, Ron	92SC	710	$ .01	$ .04
Darling, Ron	92SCP	378	$ .01	$ .05
Darling, Ron	93SC	619	$ .01	$ .03
Darling, Ron	93SCP	199	$ .01	$ .08
Darling, Ron	93SCS	10	$ .01	$ .05
Darwin, Danny	88SC	184	$ .01	$ .04
Darwin, Danny	89SC	553	$ .01	$ .03
Darwin, Danny	90SC	402	$ .01	$ .04
Darwin, Danny	91SC	51	$ .01	$ .04
Darwin, Danny	91SCTR	24	$ .01	$ .05
Darwin, Danny	92SC	138	$ .01	$ .04
Dascenzo, Doug	89SC	621	$ .01	$ .10
Dascenzo, Doug	91SC	209	$ .01	$ .04
Dascenzo, Doug	92SC	319	$ .01	$ .04
Dascenzo, Doug	92SCP	160	$ .01	$ .05
Dascenzo, Doug	93SC	446	$ .01	$ .03
Daugherty, Jack	90SC	564	$ .01	$ .10
Daugherty, Jack	91SC	309	$ .01	$ .04
Daugherty, Jack	92SC	622	$ .01	$ .04
Daulton, Darren	88SC	473	$ .01	$ .04
Daulton, Darren	89SC	413	$ .01	$ .03
Daulton, Darren	90SC	389	$ .01	$ .04
Daulton, Darren	91SC	246	$ .01	$ .04
Daulton, Darren	92SC	506	$ .01	$ .04
Daulton, Darren	92SCP	241	$ .01	$ .05
Daulton, Darren	93SC	10	$ .01	$ .10
Daulton, Darren	93SC	526	$ .01	$ .03
Daulton, Darren	93SCP	99	$ .01	$ .08
Daulton, Darren	93SCS	13	$ .01	$ .05
Davidson, Mark	88SC	570	$ .01	$ .04
Davidson, Mark	89SC	107	$ .01	$ .03
Davidson, Mark	92SC	289	$ .01	$ .04
Davis, Alvin	88SC	83	$ .01	$ .10

Player	Year	No.	VG	EX/MT
Davis, Alvin	89SC	51	$ .01	$ .10
Davis, Alvin	90SC	205	$ .01	$ .04
Davis, Alvin	91SC	482	$ .01	$ .04
Davis, Alvin	92SC	76	$ .01	$ .04
Davis, Alvin	92SCP	467	$ .01	$ .05
Davis, Chili	88SC	605	$ .01	$ .04
Davis, Chili	88SCTR	28	$ .01	$ .15
Davis, Chili	89SC	54	$ .01	$ .03

SCORE

Player	Year	No.	VG	EX/MT	Player	Year	No.	VG	EX/MT
Davis, Chili	90SC	326	$.01	$.04	De Los Santos, Luis	90SC	659	$.01	$.10
Davis, Chili	91SC	803	$.01	$.04	DeCinces, Doug	88SC	239	$.01	$.04
Davis, Chili	91SCTR	70	$.01	$.05	Decker, Steve	91SC	710	$.01	$.15
Davis, Chili	92SC	94	$.01	$.04	Decker, Steve	92SC	317	$.01	$.10
Davis, Chili	92SCP	46	$.01	$.05	Decker, Steve	92SCP	63	$.01	$.05
Davis, Chili	93SC	583	$.01	$.03	Decker, Steve	93SC	653	$.01	$.03
Davis, Chili	93SCS	238	$.01	$.05	Decker, Steve	93SCP	233·	$.01	$.08
Davis, Eric	88SC	10	$.01	$.10	Dedmon, Jeff	88SC	498	$.01	$.04
Davis, Eric	88SC	649	$.01	$.15	Deer, Rob	88SC	95	$.01	$.04
Davis, Eric	89SC	109	$.01	$.10	Deer, Rob	89SC	72	$.01	$.03
Davis, Eric	90SC	185	$.01	$.10	Deer, Rob	90SC	390	$.01	$.04
Davis, Eric	91SC	137	$.01	$.10	Deer, Rob	91SC	248	$.01	$.04
Davis, Eric	91SCAS	669	$.01	$.10	Deer, Rob	91SCTR	47	$.01	$.05
Davis, Eric	91SCMB	403	$.01	$.10	Deer, Rob	92SC	56	$.01	$.04
Davis, Eric	91SCRM	696	$.01	$.10	Deer, Rob	92SCP	348	$.01	$.05
Davis, Eric	91SCTF	863	$.01	$.10	Deer, Rob	93SC	636	$.01	$.03
Davis, Eric	92SC	44	$.01	$.10	Deer, Rob	93SCP	167	$.01	$.08
Davis, Eric	92SCP	323	$.01	$.05	Deer, Rob	93SCS	186	$.01	$.05
Davis, Eric	92SCP	602	$.01	$.05	DeJesus, Jose	90SC	587	$.01	$.04
Davis, Eric	92SCTR	62	$.01	$.05	DeJesus, Jose	91SC	623	$.01	$.04
Davis, Eric	93SC	570	$.01	$.03	DeJesus, Jose	92SC	380	$.01	$.04
Davis, Eric	93SCS	91	$.01	$.05	DeJesus, Jose	92SCP	172	$.01	$.05
Davis, Glenn	88SC	460	$.01	$.10	DeLeon, Jose	88SC	508	$.01	$.04
Davis, Glenn	89SC	164	$.01	$.10	DeLeon, Jose	88SCTR	7	$.01	$.15
Davis, Glenn	90SC	272	$.01	$.10	DeLeon, Jose	89SC	115	$.01	$.03
Davis, Glenn	91SC	830	$.01	$.04	DeLeon, Jose	90SC	309	$.01	$.04
Davis, Glenn	91SCMB	405	$.01	$.10	DeLeon, Jose	91SC	221	$.01	$.04
Davis, Glenn	91SCTR	7	$.01	$.05	DeLeon, Jose	92SC	81	$.01	$.04
Davis, Glenn	92SC	615	$.01	$.04	DeLeon, Jose	92SCP	341	$.01	$.05
Davis, Glenn	92SCP	138	$.01	$.05	DeLucia, Rich	91SC	728	$.01	$.10
Davis, Glenn	93SC	383	$.01	$.03	DeLucia, Rich	92SC	135	$.01	$.04
Davis, Glenn	93SCP	217	$.01	$.08	DeLucia, Rich	92SCP	388	$.01	$.05
Davis, Glenn	93SCS	378	$.01	$.05	Dempsey, Rick	88SC	262	$.01	$.04
Davis, Jody	88SC	551	$.01	$.04	Dempsey, Rick	88SCTR	32	$.01	$.15
Davis, Jody	89SC	173	$.01	$.03	Dempsey, Rick	89SC	556	$.01	$.03
Davis, Jody	89SCTR	64	$.01	$.05	Dempsey, Rick	90SC	414	$.01	$.04
Davis, Jody	90SC	328	$.01	$.04	Dempsey, Rick	91SC	816	$.01	$.04
Davis, John	88SC	636	$.01	$.04	Dernier, Bob	88SC	451	$.01	$.04
Davis, John	89SC	608	$.01	$.03	Dernier, Bob	88SCTR	45	$.01	$.15
Davis, Mark	88SC	391	$.01	$.04	Dernier, Bob	89SC	357	$.01	$.03
Davis, Mark	89SC	490	$.01	$.03	Deshaies, Jim	88SC	354	$.01	$.04
Davis, Mark	90SC	259	$.01	$.04	Deshaies, Jim	89SC	546	$.01	$.03
Davis, Mark	90SCTR	26	$.01	$.05	Deshaies, Jim	90SC	154	$.01	$.04
Davis, Mark	91SC	136	$.01	$.04	Deshaies, Jim	91SC	193	$.01	$.04
Davis, Mark	92SC	718	$.01	$.04	Deshaies, Jim	92SC	364	$.01	$.04
Davis, Mark	92SCP	359	$.01	$.05	DeShields, Delino	90SC	645	$.10	$.50
Davis, Mike	88SC	211	$.01	$.04	DeShields, Delino	91SC	545	$.01	$.10
Davis, Mike	88SCTR	53	$.01	$.15	DeShields, Delino	92SC	16	$.01	$.10
Davis, Mike	89SC	376	$.01	$.03	DeShields, Delino	92SCP	24	$.05	$.20
Davis, Mike	90SC	437	$.01	$.04	DeShields, Delino	93SC	145	$.01	$.15
Davis, Steve	90SC	187	$.01	$.10	DeShields, Delino	93SCP	121	$.01	$.15
Davis, Storm	89SC	248	$.01	$.03	DeShields, Delino	93SCP	302	$.05	$.25
Davis, Storm	90SC	266	$.01	$.04	DeShields, Delino	93SCS	43	$.01	$.15
Davis, Storm	90SCTR	21	$.01	$.05	Destrade, Orestes	88SCTR	110	$.20	$2.00
Davis, Storm	91SC	511	$.01	$.04	Devereaux, Mike	88SC	637	$.10	$.75
Davis, Storm	92SC	264	$.01	$.04	Devereaux, Mike	90SC	232	$.01	$.04
Davis, Storm	92SCP	312	$.01	$.05	Devereaux, Mike	91SC	250	$.01	$.04
Davis, Storm	92SCTR	34	$.01	$.05	Devereaux, Mike	92SC	36	$.01	$.04
Davis, Storm	93SC	449	$.01	$.03	Devereaux, Mike	92SCP	165	$.01	$.05
Davis, Willie	92SCP	591	$.01	$.15	Devereaux, Mike	93SC	170	$.01	$.03
Dawley, Bill	88SC	328	$.01	$.04	Devereaux, Mike	93SCS	170	$.01	$.05
Dawson, Andre	88SC	4	$.05	$.20	Dewey, Mark	91SC	371	$.01	$.10
Dawson, Andre	89SC	2	$.01	$.10	DeWillis, Jeff	88SC	583	$.01	$.04
Dawson, Andre	90SC	265	$.01	$.10	Diaz, Bo	88SC	206	$.01	$.04
Dawson, Andre	91SC	445	$.01	$.10	Diaz, Bo	89SC	187	$.01	$.03
Dawson, Andre	92SC	75	$.01	$.10	Diaz, Bo	90SC	434	$.01	$.04
Dawson, Andre	92SCP	115	$.05	$.20	Diaz, Edgar	91SC	576	$.01	$.03
Dawson, Andre	93SC	552	$.01	$.10	Diaz, Mike	88SC	143	$.01	$.04
Dawson, Andre	93SCS	9	$.01	$.10	Diaz, Mike	89SC	603	$.01	$.03
Dayett, Brian	88SC	205	$.01	$.04	Dibble, Rob	88SCTR	86	$.75	$3.00
Dayley, Ken	88SC	517	$.01	$.04	Dibble, Rob	89SC	618	$.05	$.25
Dayley, Ken	90SC	556	$.01	$.04	Dibble, Rob	90SC	277	$.05	$.20
Dayley, Ken	91SC	607	$.01	$.04	Dibble, Rob	91SC	17	$.01	$.10
Dayley, Ken	92SC	685	$.01	$.04	Dibble, Rob	91SCKM	407	$.01	$.10
De Los Santos, Luis	89SC	648	$.01	$.10	Dibble, Rob	92SC	455	$.01	$.04

SCORE

Player	Year	No.	VG	EX/MT
Dibble, Rob	92SCDT	891	$ .01	$ .04
Dibble, Rob	92SCP	180	$ .01	$ .05
Dibble, Rob	93SC	651	$ .01	$ .03
Dibble, Rob	93SCP	101	$ .01	$ .08
Dibble, Rob	93SCS	65	$ .01	$ .05
Dickson, Lance	91SC	385	$ .01	$ .15
Dickson, Lance	92SCP	272	$ .01	$ .05
DiPino, Frank	88SC	413	$ .01	$ .04
DiPino, Frank	89SC	146	$ .01	$ .03
DiPino, Frank	90SC	462	$ .01	$ .04
DiPino, Frank	91SC	553	$ .01	$ .04
DiSarcina, Gary	90SCTR	68	$ .05	$ .25
DiSarcina, Gary	91SC	768	$ .01	$ .04
DiSarcina, Gary	92SCP	52	$ .01	$ .05
DiSarcina, Gary	93SC	374	$ .01	$ .03
DiSarcina, Gary	93SCS	281	$ .01	$ .05
Dixon, Ken	88SC	411	$ .01	$ .04
Dodson, Pat	88SC	352	$ .01	$ .04
Doherty, John	92SCP	513	$ .01	$ .05
Doherty, John	92SCTR	81	$ .05	$ .25
Doherty, John	93SC	353	$ .01	$ .03
Doherty, John	93SCS	298	$ .01	$ .05
Donnels, Chris	91SCTR	104	$ .01	$ .10
Donnels, Chris	92SC	212	$ .01	$ .10
Donnels, Chris	92SCP	168	$ .01	$ .05
Dopson, John	88SCTR	88	$ .05	$ .35
Dopson, John	89SC	466	$ .01	$ .15
Dopson, John	89SCTR	40	$ .01	$ .05
Dopson, John	90SC	331	$ .01	$ .04
Dopson, John	91SC	772	$ .01	$ .04
Doran, Bill	88SC	52	$ .01	$ .04
Doran, Bill	89SC	21	$ .01	$ .03
Doran, Bill	90SC	182	$ .01	$ .04
Doran, Bill	91SC	775	$ .01	$ .04
Doran, Bill	92SC	77	$ .01	$ .04
Doran, Bill	92SCP	47	$ .01	$ .05
Dotson, Richard	88SC	480	$ .01	$ .04
Dotson, Richard	88SCTR	60	$ .01	$ .15
Dotson, Richard	89SC	278	$ .01	$ .03
Dotson, Richard	89SCTR	80	$ .01	$ .05
Dotson, Richard	90SC	19	$ .01	$ .04
Downing, Brian	88SC	44	$ .01	$ .04
Downing, Brian	89SC	76	$ .01	$ .03
Downing, Brian	90SC	26	$ .01	$ .04
Downing, Brian	91SC	104	$ .01	$ .04
Downing, Brian	91SCTR	30	$ .01	$ .05
Downing, Brian	92SC	579	$ .01	$ .04
Downing, Brian	92SCP	368	$ .01	$ .05
Downs, Kelly	88SC	27	$ .01	$ .04
Downs, Kelly	89SC	124	$ .01	$ .03
Downs, Kelly	90SC	534	$ .01	$ .04
Downs, Kelly	91SC	654	$ .01	$ .04
Downs, Kelly	92SC	191	$ .01	$ .04
Downs, Kelly	92SCP	492	$ .01	$ .05
Dozier, D. J.	90SCTR	97	$ .05	$ .20
Drabek, Doug	88SC	51	$ .01	$ .15
Drabek, Doug	89SC	117	$ .01	$ .03
Drabek, Doug	90SC	505	$ .01	$ .04
Drabek, Doug	91SC	472	$ .01	$ .04
Drabek, Doug	91SCAS	661	$ .01	$ .04
Drabek, Doug	91SCMVP	878	$ .01	$ .05
Drabek, Doug	92SC	115	$ .01	$ .04
Drabek, Doug	92SCP	96	$ .01	$ .05
Drabek, Doug	93SC	580	$ .01	$ .03
Drabek, Doug	93SCS	153	$ .01	$ .05
Drahman, Brian	91SCTR	81	$ .01	$ .10
Drahman, Brian	92SC	734	$ .01	$ .04
Dravecky, Dave	88SC	564	$ .01	$ .10
Dravecky, Dave	90SC	550	$ .01	$ .10
Dressendorfer, Kirk	91SCTR	97	$ .01	$ .15
Dressendorfer, Kirk	92SC	728	$ .01	$ .10
Dressendorfer, Kirk	92SCP	270	$ .01	$ .05
Drew, Cameron	89SC	643	$ .01	$ .03
Drummond, Tim	90SCTR	103	$ .01	$ .10
Drummond, Tim	91SC	76	$ .01	$ .04
Dubois, Brian	90SC	657	$ .01	$ .10
Ducey, Rob	88SC	629	$ .01	$ .10
Ducey, Rob	91SC	821	$ .01	$ .04
Ducey, Rob	92SC	609	$ .01	$ .04
Duncan, Mariano	88SC	321	$ .01	$ .10
Duncan, Mariano	90SC	506	$ .01	$ .10
Duncan, Mariano	91SC	479	$ .01	$ .04
Duncan, Mariano	92SC	352	$ .01	$ .04
Duncan, Mariano	92SCP	377	$ .01	$ .05
Duncan, Mariano	92SCTR	54	$ .01	$ .05
Duncan, Mariano	93SC	201	$ .01	$ .03
Duncan, Mariano	93SCP	218	$ .01	$ .08
Duncan, Mariano	93SCS	151	$ .01	$ .05
Dunne, Mike	88SC	432	$ .01	$ .10
Dunne, Mike	89SC	285	$ .01	$ .03
Dunston, Shawon	88SC	529	$ .01	$ .10
Dunston, Shawon	89SC	235	$ .01	$ .03
Dunston, Shawon	90SC	169	$ .01	$ .04
Dunston, Shawon	91SC	201	$ .01	$ .04
Dunston, Shawon	91SCRM	413	$ .01	$ .05
Dunston, Shawon	92SC	634	$ .01	$ .04
Dunston, Shawon	92SCP	244	$ .01	$ .05
Dunston, Shawon	93SC	26	$ .01	$ .03
Dunston, Shawon	93SCP	89	$ .01	$ .08
Dunston, Shawon	93SCS	121	$ .01	$ .05
Durham, Leon	88SC	378	$ .01	$ .04
Dwyer, Jim	88SC	229	$ .01	$ .04
Dyer, Mike	90SC	571	$ .01	$ .04

Player	Year	No.	VG	EX/MT
Dykstra, Len	88SC	370	$ .01	$ .10
Dykstra, Lenny	89SC	84	$ .01	$ .10
Dykstra, Lenny	89SCTR	28	$ .01	$ .10
Dykstra, Lenny	90SC	427	$ .01	$ .10
Dykstra, Lenny	91SC	250	$ .01	$ .04
Dykstra, Lenny	91SCTF	867	$ .01	$ .04
Dykstra, Lenny	92SC	560	$ .01	$ .04
Dykstra, Lenny	92SCP	12	$ .01	$ .05
Dykstra, Lenny	93SC	30	$ .01	$ .03
Dykstra, Lenny	93SCP	45	$ .01	$ .08
Dykstra, Lenny	93SCS	59	$ .01	$ .05
Easler, Mike	88SC	220	$ .01	$ .04
Easley, Damion	93SC	222	$ .05	$ .20
Easley, Damion	93SCP	227	$ .05	$ .35
Easley, Damion	93SCS	328	$ .05	$ .25

SCORE

Player	Year	No.	VG	EX/MT	Player	Year	No.	VG	EX/MT
Eave, Gary	90SC	621	$ .01	$ .10	Evans, Darrell	90SC	302	$ .01	$ .04
Eckersley, Dennis	88SC	104	$ .01	$ .10	Evans, Dwight	88SC	65	$ .01	$ .10
Eckersley, Dennis	89SC	276	$ .01	$ .15	Evans, Dwight	89SC	193	$ .01	$ .10
Eckersley, Dennis	90SC	315	$ .01	$ .15	Evans, Dwight	90SC	3	$ .01	$ .04
Eckersley, Dennis	91SC	485	$ .01	$ .10	Evans, Dwight	91SC	225	$ .01	$ .04
Eckersley, Dennis	92SC	190	$ .01	$ .10	Evans, Dwight	91SCTR	62	$ .01	$ .05
Eckersley, Dennis	92SCP	25	$ .01	$ .10	Evans, Dwight	92SC	150	$ .01	$ .04
Eckersley, Dennis	93SC	21	$ .01	$ .10	Evans, Dwight	93SCP	303	$ .05	$ .35
Eckersley, Dennis	93SC	481	$ .01	$ .10	Everett, Carl	91SC	386	$ .05	$ .25
Eckersley, Dennis	93SC	483	$ .01	$ .03	Fajardo, Hector	92SC	842	$ .01	$ .10
Eckersley, Dennis	93SC	509	$ .01	$ .03	Fajardo, Hector	92SCP	573	$ .01	$ .15
Eckersley, Dennis	93SC	513	$ .01	$ .03	Faries, Paul	91SC	711	$ .01	$ .10
Eckersley, Dennis	93SC	540	$ .01	$ .10	Faries, Paul	92SC	509	$ .01	$ .04
Eckersley, Dennis	93SCP	100	$ .01	$ .15	Faries, Paul	92SCP	332	$ .01	$ .05
Eckersley, Dennis	93SCS	38	$ .01	$ .10	Fariss, Monty	92SC	772	$ .01	$ .04
Edens, Tom	91SC	78	$ .01	$ .10	Fariss, Monty	92SCP	560	$ .01	$ .10
Edens, Tom	92SC	720	$ .01	$ .04	Fariss, Monty	93SC	432	$ .01	$ .03
Edens, Tom	93SC	450	$ .01	$ .03	Farmer, Howard	90SCTR	91	$ .01	$ .10
Edwards, Wayne	91SC	66	$ .01	$ .04	Farmer, Howard	91SC	718	$ .01	$ .04
Egloff, Bruce	92SC	751	$ .01	$ .04	Farr, Steve	88SC	466	$ .01	$ .04
Eichhorn, Mark	88SC	198	$ .01	$ .04	Farr, Steve	89SC	183	$ .01	$ .03
Eichhorn, Mark	89SC	152	$ .01	$ .03	Farr, Steve	90SC	356	$ .01	$ .04
Eichhorn, Mark	91SC	504	$ .01	$ .04	Farr, Steve	91SC	172	$ .01	$ .04
Eichhorn, Mark	92SC	221	$ .01	$ .04	Farr, Steve	91SCTR	21	$ .01	$ .05
Eichhorn, Mark	92SCP	353	$ .01	$ .05	Farr, Steve	92SC	47	$ .01	$ .04
Eiland, Dave	90SC	652	$ .01	$ .04	Farr, Steve	92SCP	206	$ .01	$ .05
Eiland, Dave	91SC	826	$ .01	$ .04	Farr, Steve	93SC	162	$ .01	$ .03
Eiland, Dave	92SC	679	$ .01	$ .04	Farr, Steve	93SCP	196	$ .01	$ .08
Eisenreich, Jim	88SC	456	$ .01	$ .04	Farr, Steve	93SCS	172	$ .01	$ .05
Eisenreich, Jim	89SC	594	$ .01	$ .03	Farrell, John	88SC	620	$ .05	$ .25
Eisenreich, Jim	90SC	179	$ .01	$ .04	Farrell, John	89SC	266	$ .01	$ .03
Eisenreich, Jim	91SC	154	$ .01	$ .04	Farrell, John	90SC	103	$ .01	$ .10
Eisenreich, Jim	92SC	158	$ .01	$ .04	Farrell, John	91SC	50	$ .01	$ .04
Eisenreich, Jim	92SCP	468	$ .01	$ .05	Farrell, Jon	92SC	804	$ .01	$ .15
Eisenreich, Jim	93SC	551	$ .01	$ .03	Farrell, Jon	92SCP	299	$ .01	$ .15
Eisenreich, Jim	93SCS	241	$ .01	$ .05	Fassero, Jeff	92SC	738	$ .01	$ .04
Eldred, Cal	90SC	669	$ .10	$1.00	Felder, Mike	88SC	388	$ .01	$ .04
Eldred, Cal	92SC	834	$ .10	$ .40	Felder, Mike	90SC	268	$ .01	$ .04
Eldred, Cal	92SCP	249	$ .10	$ .75	Felder, Mike	91SC	97	$ .01	$ .04
Eldred, Cal	93SC	368	$ .01	$ .15	Felder, Mike	92SC	251	$ .01	$ .04
Eldred, Cal	93SCP	2	$ .05	$ .25	Felder, Mike	92SCP	311	$ .01	$ .05
Eldred, Cal	93SCS	296	$ .05	$ .25	Felder, Mike	93SC	621	$ .01	$ .03
Ellsworth, Steve	88SCTR	83	$ .01	$ .15	Felder, Mike	93SCP	148	$ .01	$ .08
Elster, Kevin	88SC	624	$ .01	$ .10	Felix, Junior	89SCTR	83	$ .05	$ .25
Elster, Kevin	89SC	130	$ .01	$ .10	Felix, Junior	90SC	258	$ .05	$ .20
Elster, Kevin	90SC	443	$ .01	$ .04	Felix, Junior	91SC	203	$ .01	$ .04
Elster, Kevin	91SC	633	$ .01	$ .04	Felix, Junior	91SCTR	20	$ .01	$ .05
Elster, Kevin	92SC	103	$ .01	$ .04	Felix, Junior	92SC	519	$ .01	$ .04
Elster, Kevin	92SCP	89	$ .01	$ .05	Felix, Junior	92SCP	220	$ .01	$ .05
Engle, Dave	88SC	617	$ .01	$ .04	Felix, Junior	93SC	425	$ .01	$ .03
Eppard, Jim	89SC	607	$ .01	$ .10	Felix, Junior	93SCS	28	$ .01	$ .05
Erickson, Scott	91SC	812	$ .05	$ .20	Fermin, Felix	89SC	620	$ .01	$ .03
Erickson, Scott	92SC	60	$ .01	$ .04	Fermin, Felix	89SCTR	78	$ .01	$ .04
Erickson, Scott	92SCAS	438	$ .01	$ .10	Fermin, Felix	90SC	256	$ .01	$ .04
Erickson, Scott	92SCDT	889	$ .05	$ .25	Fermin, Felix	91SC	139	$ .01	$ .04
Erickson, Scott	92SCP	106	$ .01	$ .10	Fermin, Felix	92SC	148	$ .01	$ .04
Erickson, Scott	93SC	208	$ .01	$ .10	Fermin, Felix	92SCP	162	$ .01	$ .05
Erickson, Scott	93SCP	163	$ .01	$ .08	Fermin, Felix	93SCS	256	$ .01	$ .05
Erickson, Scott	93SCS	253	$ .01	$ .05	Fernandez, Alex	92SC	82	$ .01	$ .10
Esasky, Nick	88SC	163	$ .01	$ .04	Fernandez, Alex	92SCP	30	$ .01	$ .05
Esasky, Nick	89SC	64	$ .01	$ .03	Fernandez, Alex	93SC	412	$ .01	$ .03
Esasky, Nick	89SCTR	37	$ .01	$ .10	Fernandez, Sid	88SC	615	$ .01	$ .04
Esasky, Nick	90SC	91	$ .01	$ .04	Fernandez, Sid	89SC	268	$ .01	$ .03
Esasky, Nick	90SCTR	3	$ .01	$ .05	Fernandez, Sid	90SC	18	$ .01	$ .04
Espinoza, Alvaro	90SC	101	$ .01	$ .10	Fernandez, Sid	91SC	180	$ .01	$ .04
Espinoza, Alvaro	91SC	127	$ .01	$ .04	Fernandez, Sid	92SC	675	$ .01	$ .04
Espinoza, Alvaro	92SC	41	$ .01	$ .04	Fernandez, Sid	92SCP	509	$ .01	$ .05
Espy, Cecil	88SCTR	73	$ .05	$ .35	Fernandez, Sid	93SC	556	$ .01	$ .03
Espy, Cecil	89SC	401	$ .01	$ .15	Fernandez, Sid	93SCS	243	$ .01	$ .05
Espy, Cecil	90SC	69	$ .01	$ .10	Fernandez, Tony	88SC	20	$ .01	$ .10
Espy, Cecil	92SC	673	$ .01	$ .04	Fernandez, Tony	88SC	651	$ .05	$ .20
Eusebio, Tony	92SC	858	$ .01	$ .15	Fernandez, Tony	89SC	57	$ .01	$ .03
Evans, Darrell	88SC	75	$ .01	$ .04	Fernandez, Tony	90SC	89	$ .01	$ .10
Evans, Darrell	89SC	171	$ .01	$ .03	Fernandez, Tony	91SC	432	$ .01	$ .04
Evans, Darrell	89SCTR	65	$ .01	$ .10	Fernandez, Tony	91SCTR	66	$ .01	$ .05

SCORE

Player	Year	No.	VG	EX/MT
Fernandez, Tony	92SC	645	$ .01	$ .04
Fernandez, Tony	92SCP	137	$ .01	$ .05
Fernandez, Tony	93SC	572	$ .01	$ .03
Fernandez, Tony	93SCS	93	$ .01	$ .05
Fernanez, Alex	91SC	382	$ .01	$ .15
Fetters, Mike	91SC	497	$ .01	$ .04
Fetters, Mike	92SC	606	$ .01	$ .04
Fetters, Mike	93SC	420	$ .01	$ .03
Fetters, Mike	93SCS	174	$ .01	$ .05
Fielder, Cecil	88SC	399	$ .05	$ .35
Fielder, Cecil	89SC	120	$ .05	$ .25
Fielder, Cecil	90SCTR	9	$ .05	$ .20
Fielder, Cecil	91SC	168	$ .01	$ .15
Fielder, Cecil	91SCAS	395	$ .01	$ .10
Fielder, Cecil	91SCHL	770	$ .01	$ .10
Fielder, Cecil	91SCMB	693	$ .01	$ .10

Fielder, Cecil	92SC	50	$ .01	$ .15
Fielder, Cecil	92SCAS	431	$ .01	$ .10
Fielder, Cecil	92SCP	4	$ .05	$ .25
Fielder, Cecil	93SC	31	$ .01	$ .10
Fielder, Cecil	93SCP	26	$ .05	$ .25
Fielder, Cecil	93SCS	20	$ .01	$ .15
Figueroa, Bien	93SC	281	$ .01	$ .03
Figueroa, Bien	93SCP	263	$ .01	$ .08
Finley, Chuck	89SC	503	$ .01	$ .10
Finley, Chuck	90SC	380	$ .01	$ .10
Finley, Chuck	91SC	100	$ .01	$ .04
Finley, Chuck	92SC	585	$ .01	$ .04
Finley, Chuck	92SCP	42	$ .01	$ .05
Finley, Chuck	93SC	158	$ .01	$ .03
Finley, Chuck	93SCP	201	$ .01	$ .08
Finley, Chuck	93SCS	198	$ .01	$ .05
Finley, Steve	89SCTR	95	$ .10	$ .40
Finley, Steve	90SC	339	$ .01	$ .10
Finley, Steve	91SC	266	$ .01	$ .04
Finley, Steve	92SC	176	$ .01	$ .04
Finley, Steve	92SCP	19	$ .01	$ .05
Finley, Steve	93SC	65	$ .01	$ .03
Finley, Steve	93SCP	172	$ .01	$ .08
Finley, Steve	93SCS	88	$ .01	$ .05
Fischer, Jeff	90SC	654	$ .01	$ .04
Fisher, Brian	88SC	130	$ .01	$ .04
Fisher, Brian	89SC	24	$ .01	$ .03
Fisher, Brian	90SC	547	$ .01	$ .05
Fisk, Carlton	88SC	592	$ .05	$ .25
Fisk, Carlton	89SC	449	$ .01	$ .15
Fisk, Carlton	90SC	290	$ .01	$ .10
Fisk, Carlton	91SC	265	$ .01	$ .10
Fisk, Carlton	91SCHL	421	$ .01	$ .10
Fisk, Carlton	92SC	72	$ .01	$ .10
Fisk, Carlton	92SCP	361	$ .01	$ .15
Fisk, Carlton	93SC	579	$ .01	$ .10
Fisk, Carlton	93SCP	301	$ .05	$ .20
Fisk, Carlton	93SCS	76	$ .01	$ .15
Fitzgerald, Mike	88SC	318	$ .01	$ .04
Fitzgerald, Mike	89SC	511	$ .01	$ .03
Fitzgerald, Mike	90SC	361	$ .01	$ .04
Fitzgerald, Mike	91SC	198	$ .01	$ .04
Fitzgerald, Mike	92SC	667	$ .01	$ .04
Flag, Desert Storm	91SC	737	$ .05	$ .25
Flaherty, John	93SC	278	$ .01	$ .03
Flanagan, Mike	88SC	427	$ .01	$ .04
Flanagan, Mike	89SC	475	$ .01	$ .03
Flanagan, Mike	90SC	67	$ .01	$ .04
Flanagan, Mike	91SCTR	2	$ .01	$ .05
Flanagan, Mike	92SC	333	$ .01	$ .04
Flanagan, Mike	92SC	427	$ .01	$ .04
Flanagan, Mike	92SCP	475	$ .01	$ .05
Flannery, Tim	88SC	483	$ .01	$ .04
Flannery, Tim	89SC	513	$ .01	$ .03
Fleming, Dave	92SCP	275	$ .10	$ .40
Fleming, Dave	92SCTR	85	$ .05	$ .25
Fleming, Dave	93SC	356	$ .01	$ .03
Fleming, Dave	93SCP	5	$ .05	$ .25
Fleming, Dave	93SCS	271	$ .05	$ .20
Fletcher, Darrin	90SC	622	$ .01	$ .10
Fletcher, Darrin	92SC	193	$ .01	$ .04
Fletcher, Darrin	92SCTR	64	$ .01	$ .05
Fletcher, Darrin	93SC	216	$ .01	$ .03
Fletcher, Scott	88SC	251	$ .01	$ .04
Fletcher, Scott	89SC	78	$ .01	$ .03
Fletcher, Scott	89SCTR	47	$ .01	$ .05
Fletcher, Scott	90SC	58	$ .01	$ .04
Fletcher, Scott	91SC	36	$ .01	$ .04
Fletcher, Scott	92SC	203	$ .01	$ .04
Fletcher, Scott	93SC	632	$ .01	$ .03
Fletcher, Scott	93SCS	140	$ .01	$ .05
Floyd, Cliff	92SC	801	$ .10	$1.00
Floyd, Cliff	92SCP	296	$ .20	$2.00
Foley, Tom	88SC	159	$ .01	$ .04
Foley, Tom	89SC	405	$ .01	$ .03
Foley, Tom	90SC	32	$ .01	$ .04
Foley, Tom	91SC	526	$ .01	$ .04
Foley, Tom	92SC	486	$ .01	$ .04
Ford, Curt	88SC	288	$ .01	$ .04
Ford, Curt	90SC	183	$ .01	$ .04
Forsch, Bob	88SC	264	$ .01	$ .04
Forsch, Bob	89SC	525	$ .01	$ .03
Forsch, Bob	90SC	219	$ .01	$ .04
Fortugno, Tim	93SC	262	$ .01	$ .03
Fossas, Tony	90SC	567	$ .01	$ .04
Fossas, Tony	91SC	634	$ .01	$ .04
Fossas, Tony	92SC	389	$ .01	$ .04
Foster, Steve	93SC	284	$ .01	$ .03
Fox, Eric	92SCTR	88	$ .05	$ .20
Fox, Eric	93SC	352	$ .01	$ .03
Fox, Eric	93SCS	313	$ .01	$ .05
Franco, John	88SC	535	$ .01	$ .10
Franco, John	89SC	575	$ .01	$ .10
Franco, John	90SC	273	$ .01	$ .04
Franco, John	90SCTR	15	$ .01	$ .05
Franco, John	91SC	14	$ .01	$ .04
Franco, John	92SC	605	$ .01	$ .04
Franco, John	92SCP	64	$ .01	$ .05
Franco, John	93SC	139	$ .01	$ .03
Franco, John	93SCP	216	$ .01	$ .08
Franco, John	93SCP	310	$ .01	$ .08

SCORE

Player	Year	No.	VG	EX/MT	Player	Year	No.	VG	EX/MT
Franco, John	93SCS	167	$.01	$.05	Gant, Ron	89SC	372	$.05	$.35
Franco, Julio	88SC	60	$.01	$.15	Gant, Ron	91SC	448	$.01	$.10
Franco, Julio	89SC	11	$.01	$.10	Gant, Ron	92SC	25	$.01	$.10
Franco, Julio	89SCTR	35	$.01	$.10	Gant, Ron	92SCP	128	$.01	$.05
Franco, Julio	90SC	160	$.01	$.10	Gant, Ron	93SC	220	$.01	$.03
Franco, Julio	91SC	493	$.01	$.10	Gant, Ron	93SCS	133	$.01	$.05
Franco, Julio	91SCAS	392	$.01	$.04	Gantner, Jim	88SC	197	$.01	$.04
Franco, Julio	92SC	108	$.01	$.04	Gantner, Jim	89SC	313	$.01	$.03
Franco, Julio	92SCAS	432	$.01	$.04	Gantner, Jim	90SC	382	$.01	$.04
Franco, Julio	92SCP	150	$.01	$.05	Gantner, Jim	91SC	532	$.01	$.04
Franco, Julio	93SC	394	$.01	$.03	Gantner, Jim	92SC	246	$.01	$.04
Franco, Julio	93SCP	104	$.01	$.08	Gantner, Jim	92SCP	71	$.01	$.05
Franco, Julio	93SCS	58	$.01	$.05	Gantner, Jim	93SCP	207	$.01	$.08
Francona, Terry	88SC	297	$.01	$.04	Garber, Gene	88SC	565	$.01	$.04
Francona, Terry	89SC	597	$.01	$.03	Garcia, Carlos	92SC	821	$.05	$.20
Francona, Terry	90SC	216	$.01	$.04	Garcia, Carlos	92SCP	264	$.05	$.25
Fraser, Willie	88SC	394	$.01	$.04	Garcia, Carlos	93SC	246	$.01	$.15
Fraser, Willie	89SC	157	$.01	$.03	Garcia, Carlos	93SCS	403	$.01	$.05
Fraser, Willie	90SC	358	$.01	$.04	Garcia, Ramon	92SC	745	$.01	$.04
Fraser, Willie	91SC	96	$.01	$.04	Gardiner, Mike	91SC	721	$.01	$.10
Fraser, Willie	92SC	721	$.01	$.04	Gardiner, Mike	92SC	694	$.01	$.04
Frazier, George	88SC	332	$.01	$.04	Gardiner, Mike	92SCP	505	$.01	$.05
Freeman, Marvin	92SC	307	$.01	$.04	Gardner, Chris	92SCP	599	$.01	$.15
Frey, Steve	91SC	436	$.01	$.04	Gardner, Jeff	92SC	869	$.01	$.10
Frohwirth, Todd	89SC	647	$.01	$.15	Gardner, Mark	90SC	639	$.01	$.15
Frohwirth, Todd	92SC	534	$.01	$.04	Gardner, Mark	91SC	518	$.01	$.04
Frohwirth, Todd	92SCP	411	$.01	$.05	Gardner, Mark	92SC	586	$.01	$.04
Frye, Jeff	93SC	274	$.01	$.03	Gardner, Mark	92SC	785	$.01	$.04
Fryman, Travis	91SC	570	$.10	$.50	Gardner, Mark	92SCP	215	$.01	$.05
Fryman, Travis	92SC	65	$.05	$.35	Gardner, Mark	93SC	390	$.01	$.03
Fryman, Travis	92SCP	110	$.10	$.75	Gardner, Mark	93SCS	185	$.01	$.05
Fryman, Travis	93SC	11	$.05	$.25	Gardner, Wes	89SC	412	$.01	$.03
Fryman, Travis	93SCP	79	$.10	$.50	Gardner, Wes	90SC	348	$.01	$.04
Fryman, Travis	93SCS	44	$.05	$.35	Gardner, Wes	91SC	592	$.01	$.04
Gaetti, Gary	88SC	62	$.01	$.10	Garner, Phil	88SC	431	$.01	$.04
Gaetti, Gary	89SC	8	$.01	$.10	Garrelts, Scott	88SC	533	$.01	$.04
Gaetti, Gary	90SC	145	$.01	$.04	Garrelts, Scott	89SC	258	$.01	$.03
Gaetti, Gary	91SC	325	$.01	$.04	Garrelts, Scott	90SC	246	$.01	$.04
Gaetti, Gary	91SCTR	39	$.01	$.05	Garrelts, Scott	91SC	541	$.01	$.04
Gaetti, Gary	92SC	39	$.01	$.04	Garrelts, Scott	92SC	117	$.01	$.04
Gaetti, Gary	92SCP	81	$.01	$.05	Garvey, Steve	88SC	225	$.01	$.15
Gaetti, Gary	93SC	644	$.01	$.03	Gates, Brent	92SC	805	$.10	$.40
Gaetti, Gary	93SCP	112	$.01	$.08	Gedman, Rich	88SC	241	$.01	$.04
Gaetti, Gary	93SCS	262	$.01	$.05	Gedman, Rich	89SC	345	$.01	$.03
Gagne, Greg	89SC	159	$.01	$.03	Gedman, Rich	90SC	173	$.01	$.04
Gagne, Greg	90SC	102	$.01	$.04	Gedman, Rich	92SC	689	$.01	$.04
Gagne, Greg	91SC	211	$.01	$.04	Gehrig, Lou	92SC	881	$.05	$.35
Gagne, Greg	92SC	182	$.01	$.04	Gehrig, Lou	92SCP	286	$.05	$.25
Gagne, Greg	92SC	262	$.01	$.05	George, Chris	92SC	835	$.01	$.10
Gagne, Greg	92SCP	261	$.01	$.05	Geren, Bob	89SCTR	93	$.01	$.10
Gagne, Greg	93SC	555	$.01	$.03	Geren, Bob	90SC	464	$.01	$.10
Gagne, Greg	93SCS	178	$.01	$.05	Geren, Bob	91SC	435	$.01	$.04
Gakeler, Dan	92SC	831	$.01	$.04	Geren, Bob	92SC	170	$.01	$.04
Galarraga, Andres	88SC	19	$.01	$.10	Gerhart, Ken	88SC	58	$.01	$.10
Galarraga, Andres	89SC	144	$.01	$.10	Gerhart, Ken	89SC	506	$.01	$.03
Galarraga, Andres	90SC	25	$.01	$.10	Gibson, Kirk	88SC	525	$.01	$.10
Galarraga, Andres	91SC	443	$.01	$.04	Gibson, Kirk	88SCTR	10	$.01	$.15
Galarraga, Andres	92SC	35	$.01	$.04	Gibson, Kirk	89SC	210	$.01	$.15
Galarraga, Andres	92SCP	381	$.01	$.05	Gibson, Kirk	90SC	487	$.01	$.04
Galarraga, Andres	92SCTR	60	$.01	$.05	Gibson, Kirk	91SC	800	$.01	$.04
Galarraga, Andres	93SC	649	$.01	$.03	Gibson, Kirk	91SCTR	18	$.01	$.05
Gallagher, Dave	88SCTR	89	$.05	$.25	Gibson, Kirk	92SC	520	$.01	$.04
Gallagher, Dave	89SC	455	$.01	$.10	Gibson, Kirk	92SCP	481	$.01	$.05
Gallagher, Dave	90SC	115	$.01	$.04	Gibson, Paul	89SC	595	$.01	$.03
Gallagher, Dave	92SC	239	$.01	$.04	Gibson, Paul	90SC	261	$.01	$.04
Gallagher, Dave	92SCTR	55	$.01	$.05	Gibson, Paul	91SC	152	$.01	$.04
Gallego, Mike	88SC	428	$.01	$.04	Gibson, Paul	92SC	261	$.01	$.04
Gallego, Mike	89SC	537	$.01	$.03	Gil, Benji	92SC	808	$.05	$.25
Gallego, Mike	90SC	323	$.01	$.04	Gil, Benji	92SCP	302	$.10	$.75
Gallego, Mike	91SC	476	$.01	$.04	Gilkey, Bernard	90SCTR	106	$.05	$.35
Gallego, Mike	92SC	43	$.01	$.04	Gilkey, Bernard	91SC	709	$.01	$.10
Gallego, Mike	92SCP	387	$.01	$.05	Gilkey, Bernard	92SC	544	$.01	$.04
Gallego, Mike	92SCTR	30	$.01	$.05	Gilkey, Bernard	92SCP	88	$.01	$.10
Gallego, Mike	93SCS	220	$.01	$.05	Gilkey, Bernard	93SC	81	$.01	$.03
Gant, Ron	88SC	647	$.15	$1.50	Gilkey, Bernard	93SCP	88	$.01	$.08

SCORE

Player	Year	No.	VG	EX/MT
Gilkey, Bernard	93SCP	304	$ .01	$ .08
Gilkey, Bernard	93SCS	173	$ .01	$ .05
Girardi, Joe	89SCTR	84	$ .01	$ .10
Girardi, Joe	90SC	535	$ .01	$ .15
Girardi, Joe	91SC	585	$ .01	$ .04
Girardi, Joe	92SC	701	$ .01	$ .04
Girardi, Joe	92SCP	498	$ .01	$ .05
Girardi, Joe	93SC	419	$ .01	$ .03
Girardi, Joe	93SCP	236	$ .01	$ .08
Girardi, Joe	93SCS	53	$ .01	$ .05
Gladden, Dan	88SC	324	$ .01	$ .04
Gladden, Dan	89SC	62	$ .01	$ .03
Gladden, Dan	90SC	61	$ .01	$ .04
Gladden, Dan	91SC	163	$ .01	$ .04
Gladden, Dan	92SC	28	$ .01	$ .04
Gladden, Dan	92SCP	318	$ .01	$ .05
Gladden, Dan	92SCTR	28	$ .01	$ .05
Gladden, Dan	93SC	207	$ .01	$ .03
Gladden, Dan	93SCS	244	$ .01	$ .05
Glavine, Tom	88SC	638	$ .20	$2.00
Glavine, Tom	89SC	442	$ .10	$ .50
Glavine, Tom	90SC	481	$ .05	$ .25
Glavine, Tom	91SC	206	$ .05	$ .20
Glavine, Tom	92SC	450	$ .01	$ .10
Glavine, Tom	92SC	791	$ .01	$ .10
Glavine, Tom	92SCDT	890	$ .01	$ .15
Glavine, Tom	92SCP	75	$ .05	$ .25
Glavine, Tom	92SCP	594	$ .01	$ .10
Glavine, Tom	93SC	15	$ .05	$ .25
Glavine, Tom	93SC	539	$ .01	$ .15
Glavine, Tom	93SCP	90	$ .05	$ .35
Glavine, Tom	93SCS	7	$ .05	$ .25
Gleason, Jackie	92SCP	590	$ .01	$ .10
Gleaton, Jerry Don	88SC	343	$ .01	$ .04
Gleaton, Jerry Don	89SC	423	$ .01	$ .03
Gleaton, Jerry Don	91SC	316	$ .01	$ .04
Gleaton, Jerry Don	92SC	375	$ .01	$ .04
Goff, Jerry	91SC	834	$ .01	$ .04
Gohr, Greg	90SC	679	$ .05	$ .25
Gomez, Leo	91SC	725	$ .05	$ .25
Gomez, Leo	92SC	240	$ .01	$ .10
Gomez, Leo	92SCP	356	$ .01	$ .10
Gomez, Leo	93SC	104	$ .01	$ .03
Gomez, Leo	93SCS	66	$ .01	$ .05
Gomez, Pat	93SC	310	$ .01	$ .10
Gonzales, Rene	89SC	585	$ .01	$ .03
Gonzales, Rene	90SC	118	$ .01	$ .04
Gonzales, Rene	91SC	638	$ .01	$ .04
Gonzales, Rene	92SC	582	$ .01	$ .04
Gonzales, Rene	92SCTR	75	$ .01	$ .05
Gonzales, Rene	93SC	604	$ .01	$ .03
Gonzales, Rene	93SCP	55	$ .01	$ .08
Gonzales, Rene	93SCS	379	$ .01	$ .05
Gonzalez, German	90SC	133	$ .01	$ .04
Gonzalez, Jose	88SC	364	$ .01	$ .04
Gonzalez, Jose	90SC	368	$ .01	$ .04
Gonzalez, Jose	91SC	614	$ .01	$ .04
Gonzalez, Jose	92SC	733	$ .01	$ .04
Gonzalez, Juan	90SC	637	$ .20	$2.00
Gonzalez, Juan	91SC	805	$ .10	$ .40
Gonzalez, Juan	92SC	11	$ .10	$ .50
Gonzalez, Juan	92SCP	127	$ .15	$1.50
Gonzalez, Juan	93SC	51	$ .05	$ .35
Gonzalez, Juan	93SCP	191	$ .10	$ .50
Gonzalez, Juan	93SCS	40	$ .10	$ .40
Gonzalez, Luis	91SCTR	99	$ .05	$ .25
Gonzalez, Luis	92SC	210	$ .01	$ .10
Gonzalez, Luis	92SCP	163	$ .01	$ .05
Gonzalez, Luis	93SC	151	$ .01	$ .03
Gonzalez, Luis	93SCS	205	$ .01	$ .05
Gooden, Dwight "Doc"	88SC	350	$ .01	$ .15
Gooden, Doc	89SC	200	$ .01	$ .15
Gooden, Doc	90SC	313	$ .01	$ .10
Gooden, Doc	91SC	540	$ .01	$ .10
Gooden, Doc	91SCKM	685	$ .01	$ .10
Gooden, Doc	91SCTF	866	$ .01	$ .10
Gooden, Doc	92SC	10	$ .01	$ .10
Gooden, Doc	92SCP	111	$ .01	$ .05
Gooden, Doc	93SC	53	$ .01	$ .03
Gooden, Doc	93SCP	96	$ .01	$ .08

Player	Year	No.	VG	EX/MT
Gooden, Doc	93SCS	57	$ .01	$ .05
Goodwin, Tom	90SC	668	$ .01	$ .10
Goodwin, Tom	92SC	830	$ .01	$ .10
Goodwin, Tom	93SCS	349	$ .01	$ .05
Gordon, Don	88SCTR	92	$ .01	$ .15
Gordon, Don	89SC	547	$ .01	$ .03
Gordon, Tom	89SC	634	$ .01	$ .15
Gordon, Tom	90SC	472	$ .01	$ .15
Gordon, Tom	91SC	197	$ .01	$ .04
Gordon, Tom	92SC	130	$ .01	$ .04
Gordon, Tom	92SCP	238	$ .01	$ .05
Gordon, Tom	93SC	184	$ .01	$ .03
Gordon, Tom	93SCP	105	$ .01	$ .08
Gossage, Goose	88SC	331	$ .01	$ .10
Gossage, Goose	88SCTR	14	$ .01	$ .15
Gossage, Goose	89SC	223	$ .01	$ .03
Gossage, Goose	92SC	538	$ .01	$ .04
Gott, Jim	88SC	320	$ .01	$ .04
Gott, Jim	89SC	257	$ .01	$ .03
Gott, Jim	90SC	515	$ .01	$ .04
Gott, Jim	91SC	621	$ .01	$ .04
Gott, Jim	92SC	172	$ .01	$ .04
Gott, Jim	92SCP	228	$ .01	$ .05
Gott, Jim	92SCP	596	$ .01	$ .05
Gott, Jim	93SC	422	$ .01	$ .03
Gozzo, Goose	90SC	610	$ .01	$ .10
Gozzo, Mauro	91SC	843	$ .01	$ .04
Grace, Mark	88SCTR	80	$3.75	$15.00
Grace, Mark	89SC	362	$ .05	$ .35
Grace, Mark	90SC	150	$ .05	$ .20
Grace, Mark	91SC	175	$ .01	$ .10
Grace, Mark	92SC	445	$ .01	$ .04
Grace, Mark	92SCP	136	$ .01	$ .10
Grace, Mark	93SC	50	$ .01	$ .03
Grace, Mark	93SCP	34	$ .01	$ .15
Grace, Mark	93SCS	73	$ .01	$ .10
Grahe, Joe	91SC	367	$ .01	$ .04
Grahe, Joe	92SC	674	$ .01	$ .04

SCORE

Player	Year	No.	VG	EX/MT	Player	Year	No.	VG	EX/MT
Grahe, Joe	92SCP	371	$.01	$.05	Grissom, Marquis	90SC	591	$.10	$.50
Grahe, Joe	93SC	188	$.01	$.03	Grissom, Marquis	91SC	234	$.01	$.10
Grahe, Joe	93SCS	374	$.01	$.05	Grissom, Marquis	92SC	66	$.01	$.10
Grant, Mark	89SC	349	$.01	$.03	Grissom, Marquis	92SCP	129	.05	$.20
Grant, Mark	90SC	466	$.01	$.04	Grissom, Marquis	93SC	28	$.01	$.10
Grant, Mark	91SC	824	$.01	$.04	Grissom, Marquis	93SCS	99	$.01	$.15
Gray, Jeff	91SC	586	$.01	$.10	Groppuso, Mike	92SCP	543	$.01	$.15
Gray, Jeff	92SC	187	$.01	$.04	Gross, Greg	88SC	386	$.01	$.04
Grebeck, Craig	90SCTR	105	$.01	$.15	Gross, Greg	89SC	125	$.01	$.03
Grebeck, Craig	91SC	69	$.01	$.04	Gross, Kevin	88SC	468	$.01	$.04
Grebeck, Craig	92SCP	334	$.01	$.05	Gross, Kevin	89SC	227	$.01	$.03
Grebeck, Craig	93SC	126	$.01	$.03	Gross, Kevin	89SCTR	39	$.01	$.05
Grebeck, Craig	93SCS	389	$.01	$.05	Gross, Kevin	90SC	251	$.01	$.04
Grebek, Craig	92SC	561	$.01	$.04	Gross, Kevin	91SC	22	$.01	$.04
Green, Tyler	92SC	810	$.05	$.25	Gross, Kevin	91SCTR	51	$.01	$.05
Green, Tyler	92SCP	303	$.10	$.50	Gross, Kevin	92SC	34	$.01	$.04
Green, Willie	90SC	682	$.05	$.35	Gross, Kevin	92SCP	344	$.01	$.05
Greene, Tommy	90SC	640	$.05	$.25	Gross, Kevin	93SC	519	$.01	$.03
Greene, Tommy	91SC	808	$.01	$.04	Gross, Kevin	93SCP	177	$.01	$.08
Greene, Tommy	92SC	336	$.01	$.04	Gross, Kip	92SC	740	$.01	$.10
Greene, Tommy	92SC	426	$.01	$.04	Grotewald, Jeff	93SC	305	$.01	$.03
Greene, Tommy	92SCP	155	$.01	$.05	Grubb, John	88SC	199	$.01	$.04
Greene, Tommy	93SC	464	$.01	$.03	Gruber, Kelly	88SC	422	$.01	$.15
Greene, Willie	93SC	250	$.01	$.10	Gruber, Kelly	89SC	194	$.01	$.15
Greene, Willie	93SCP	285	$.05	$.25	Gruber, Kelly	90SC	425	$.01	$.10
Greene, Willie	93SCS	348	$.05	$.25	Gruber, Kelly	91SC	595	$.01	$.10
Greenwell, Mike	88SC	175	$.01	$.15	Gruber, Kelly	92SC	495	$.01	$.04
Greenwell, Mike	89SC	66	$.01	$.15	Gruber, Kelly	92SCP	134	$.01	$.05
Greenwell, Mike	89SC	659	$.01	$.10	Gruber, Kelly	93SC	156	$.01	$.03
Greenwell, Mike	90SC	345	$.01	$.10	Gruber, Kelly	93SCP	198	$.01	$.08
Greenwell, Mike	91SC	130	$.01	$.10	Gruber, Kelly	93SCS	200	$.01	$.05
Greenwell, Mike	92SC	545	$.01	$.04	Guante, Cecilio	89SC	439	$.01	$.03
Greenwell, Mike	92SCP	131	$.01	$.05	Guante, Cecilio	90SC	438	$.01	$.04
Greenwell, Mike	93SC	385	$.01	$.03	Gubicza, Mark	88SC	516	$.01	$.04
Greenwell, Mike	93SCP	102	$.01	$.08	Gubicza, Mark	89SC	291	$.01	$.03
Greenwell, Mike	93SCS	228	$.01	$.05	Gubicza, Mark	90SC	121	$.01	$.04
Greg, Gagne	88SC	214	$.01	$.04	Gubicza, Mark	91SC	212	$.01	$.04
Gregg, Tommy	88SCTR	69	$.05	$.30	Gubicza, Mark	92SC	459	$.01	$.04
Gregg, Tommy	90SC	78	$.01	$.10	Gubicza, Mark	92SCP	102	$.01	$.05
Gregg, Tommy	91SC	606	$.01	$.04	Gubicza, Mark	93SC	581	$.01	$.03
Gregg, Tommy	92SC	623	$.01	$.04	Gubicza, Mark	93SCP	81	$.01	$.08
Griffey, Jr., Ken	89SCTR	100	$1.25	$5.00	Gubicza, Mark	93SCS	227	$.01	$.05
Griffey, Jr., Ken	90SC	560	$.15	$1.25	Guerrero, Juan	92SCP	552	$.01	$.15
Griffey, Jr., Ken	91SC	2	$.10	$.50	Guerrero, Juan	93SC	259	$.01	$.03
Griffey, Jr., Ken	91SC	841	$.10	$.50	Guerrero, Pedro	88SC	9	$.01	$.10
Griffey, Jr., Ken	91SCAS	396	$.05	$.25	Guerrero, Pedro	89SC	564	$.01	$.03
Griffey, Jr., Ken	91SCBC	3	$1.00	$4.00	Guerrero, Pedro	90SC	13	$.01	$.10
Griffey, Jr., Ken	91SCDT	892	$.10	$1.00	Guerrero, Pedro	91SC	140	$.01	$.04
Griffey, Jr., Ken	91SCRM	697	$.05	$.25	Guerrero, Pedro	92SC	376	$.01	$.04
Griffey, Jr., Ken	91SCTF	858	$.05	$.25	Guerrero, Pedro	92SCP	392	$.01	$.05
Griffey, Jr., Ken	92SC	1	$.10	$.50	Guetterman, Lee	88SC	323	$.01	$.04
Griffey, Jr., Ken	92SCAS	436	$.05	$.25	Guetterman, Lee	90SC	294	$.01	$.04
Griffey, Jr., Ken	92SCP	283	$.10	$.75	Guetterman, Lee	91SC	34	$.01	$.04
Griffey, Jr., Ken	92SCP	549	$.15	$1.50	Guetterman, Lee	92SC	244	$.01	$.04
Griffey, Jr., Ken	93SC	1	$.10	$.50	Guetterman, Lee	92SCTR	74	$.01	$.05
Griffey, Jr., Ken	93SC	504	$.05	$.25	Guidry, Ron	88SC	310	$.01	$.04
Griffey, Jr., Ken	93SC	536	$.05	$.25	Guidry, Ron	89SC	342	$.01	$.03
Griffey, Jr., Ken	93SCP	110	$.15	$1.50	Guillen, Ozzie	88SC	603	$.01	$.04
Griffey, Jr., Ken	93SCS	2	$.10	$.75	Guillen, Ozzie	89SC	433	$.01	$.03
Griffey, Sr., Ken	88SC	390	$.01	$.10	Guillen, Ozzie	90SC	6	$.01	$.04
Griffey, Sr., Ken	89SC	609	$.01	$.10	Guillen, Ozzie	91SC	11	$.01	$.04
Griffey, Sr., Ken	90SC	338	$.01	$.04	Guillen, Ozzie	91SCAS	394	$.01	$.05
Griffey, Sr., Ken	91SC	835	$.01	$.04	Guillen, Ozzie	92SC	92	$.01	$.04
Griffey, Sr., Ken	91SC	841	$.10	$.50	Guillen, Ozzie	92SCP	79	$.01	$.05
Griffin, Alfredo	88SC	88	$.01	$.04	Guillen, Ozzie	93SC	94	$.01	$.04
Griffin, Alfredo	88SCTR	37	$.01	$.15	Guillen, Ozzie	93SCP	166	$.01	$.08
Griffin, Alfredo	89SC	167	$.01	$.03	Guillen, Ozzie	93SCS	128	$.01	$.05
Griffin, Alfredo	90SC	156	$.01	$.04	Gullickson, Bill	88SC	585	$.01	$.04
Griffin, Alfredo	91SC	442	$.01	$.04	Gullickson, Bill	91SC	177	$.01	$.04
Griffin, Alfredo	92SC	254	$.01	$.04	Gullickson, Bill	91SCTR	56	$.01	$.05
Grigsby, Benji	93SC	495	$.05	$.15	Gullickson, Bill	92SC	242	$.01	$.04
Grigsby, Benji	93SCS	354	$.05	$.25	Gullickson, Bill	92SCP	87	$.01	$.05
Grimsley, Jason	90SC	649	$.01	$.10	Gullickson, Bill	93SC	643	$.01	$.03
Grimsley, Jason	91SC	818	$.01	$.04	Gullickson, Bill	93SCS	85	$.01	$.04
Grimsley, Jason	92SC	711	$.01	$.04	Gunderson, Eric	90SCTR	99	$.01	$.10

SCORE

Player	Year	No.	VG	EX/MT
Gunderson, Eric	91SC	744	$ .01	$ .04
Guthrie, Mark	91SC	778	$ .01	$ .04
Guthrie, Mark	92SC	164	$ .01	$ .04
Guthrie, Mark	92SCP	511	$ .01	$ .05
Guzman, Johnny	93SC	270	$ .01	$ .03

Player	Year	No.	VG	EX/MT
Guzman, Johnny	93SCP	261	$ .01	$ .15
Guzman, Jose	88SC	322	$ .01	$ .04
Guzman, Jose	89SC	143	$ .01	$ .03
Guzman, Jose	92SC	502	$ .01	$ .04
Guzman, Jose	92SCP	98	$ .01	$ .05
Guzman, Jose	93SC	256	$ .01	$ .03
Guzman, Juan	92SC	424	$ .10	$ .50
Guzman, Juan	92SCP	183	$ .10	$1.00
Guzman, Juan	93SC	372	$ .05	$ .20
Guzman, Juan	93SCS	180	$ .05	$ .25
Gwynn, Chris	88SC	640	$ .01	$ .15
Gwynn, Chris	91SC	178	$ .01	$ .04
Gwynn, Chris	92SC	449	$ .01	$ .04
Gwynn, Chris	92SCTR	56	$ .01	$ .05
Gwynn, Tony	88SC	385	$ .05	$ .25
Gwynn, Tony	89SC	90	$ .05	$ .25
Gwynn, Tony	90SC	255	$ .01	$ .15
Gwynn, Tony	90SCDT	685	$ .01	$ .10
Gwynn, Tony	91SC	500	$ .01	$ .10
Gwynn, Tony	92SC	625	$ .01	$ .10
Gwynn, Tony	92SCAS	779	$ .01	$ .04
Gwynn, Tony	92SCDT	887	$ .01	$ .15
Gwynn, Tony	92SCP	400	$ .05	$ .25
Gwynn, Tony	92SCP	591	$ .01	$ .15
Gwynn, Tony	93SC	24	$ .01	$ .10
Gwynn, Tony	93SC	525	$ .01	$ .10
Gwynn, Tony	93SCP	98	$ .01	$ .15
Gwynn, Tony	93SCP	289	$ .01	$ .15
Gwynn, Tony	93SCS	5	$ .01	$ .10
Haas, David	92SC	825	$ .01	$ .04
Haas, David	93SC	215	$ .01	$ .03
Haas, Moose	88SC	177	$ .01	$ .04
Habyan, John	88SC	353	$ .01	$ .04
Habyan, John	92SC	451	$ .01	$ .04
Habyan, John	92SCP	433	$ .01	$ .05
Habyan, John	93SC	459	$ .01	$ .03
Hagy, Charles	93SC	29	$ .01	$ .03
Hale, Chip	90SC	588	$ .01	$ .04

Player	Year	No.	VG	EX/MT
Hall, Albert	88SC	148	$ .01	$ .04
Hall, Albert	89SC	74	$ .01	$ .03
Hall, Drew	90SC	516	$ .01	$ .04
Hall, Drew	91SC	581	$ .01	$ .04
Hall, Mel	88SC	441	$ .01	$ .04
Hall, Mel	89SC	17	$ .01	$ .03
Hall, Mel	89SCTR	54	$ .01	$ .05
Hall, Mel	90SC	383	$ .01	$ .04
Hall, Mel	91SC	166	$ .01	$ .04
Hall, Mel	92SC	154	$ .01	$ .04
Hall, Mel	92SCP	144	$ .01	$ .05
Hall, Mel	93SCS	89	$ .01	$ .05
Hamilton, Darryl	88SCTR	72	$ .20	$2.00
Hamilton, Darryl	91SC	107	$ .01	$ .04
Hamilton, Darryl	92SC	497	$ .01	$ .04
Hamilton, Darryl	92SCP	151	$ .01	$ .05
Hamilton, Darryl	93SC	118	$ .01	$ .03
Hamilton, Darryl	93SCP	144	$ .01	$ .08
Hamilton, Darryl	93SCS	168	$ .01	$ .05
Hamilton, Jeff	89SC	570	$ .01	$ .03
Hamilton, Jeff	90SC	132	$ .01	$ .04
Hamilton, Jeff	92SC	684	$ .01	$ .04
Hammaker, Atlee	88SC	528	$ .01	$ .04
Hammaker, Atlee	89SC	422	$ .01	$ .03
Hammaker, Atlee	90SC	231	$ .01	$ .04
Hammaker, Atlee	92SC	233	$ .01	$ .04
Hammond, Chris	90SC	629	$ .01	$ .15
Hammond, Chris	92SC	513	$ .01	$ .04
Hammond, Chris	92SCP	335	$ .01	$ .05
Hammond, Chris	93SC	195	$ .01	$ .10
Haney, Chris	92SC	873	$ .01	$ .04
Haney, Chris	92SCP	521	$ .01	$ .10
Hansen, Dave	92SC	754	$ .01	$ .04
Hansen, Dave	93SCP	209	$ .01	$ .08
Hanson, Erik	90SC	530	$ .01	$ .10
Hanson, Erik	91SC	486	$ .01	$ .10
Hanson, Erik	91SCKM	688	$ .01	$ .04
Hanson, Erik	92SC	8	$ .01	$ .04
Hanson, Erik	92SCP	188	$ .01	$ .05
Hanson, Erik	93SC	136	$ .01	$ .03
Hanson, Erik	93SCP	152	$ .01	$ .08
Hare, Shawn	92SC	828	$ .01	$ .10
Hare, Shawn	92SCP	598	$ .01	$ .10
Harkey, Mike	89SC	624	$ .01	$ .10
Harkey, Mike	91SC	322	$ .01	$ .04
Harkey, Mike	92SC	67	$ .01	$ .04
Harkey, Mike	92SCP	197	$ .01	$ .05
Harkey, Mike	93SC	111	$ .01	$ .03
Harkey, Mike	93SCS	397	$ .01	$ .05
Harnandez, Xavier	93SC	417	$ .01	$ .03
Harney, Chris	93SCP	194	$ .01	$ .08
Harnisch, Pete	89SCTR	110	$ .05	$ .25
Harnisch, Pete	90SC	355	$ .01	$ .04
Harnisch, Pete	91SC	492	$ .01	$ .04
Harnisch, Pete	91SCTR	36	$ .01	$ .05
Harnisch, Pete	92SC	224	$ .01	$ .04
Harnisch, Pete	92SCP	196	$ .01	$ .05
Harnisch, Pete	93SC	395	$ .01	$ .03
Harnisch, Pete	93SCP	113	$ .01	$ .08
Harnisch, Pete	93SCS	219	$ .01	$ .05
Harper, Brian	89SC	408	$ .01	$ .03
Harper, Brian	90SC	189	$ .01	$ .04
Harper, Brian	91SC	312	$ .01	$ .04
Harper, Brian	92SC	215	$ .01	$ .04
Harper, Brian	92SCP	73	$ .01	$ .05
Harper, Brian	93SC	72	$ .01	$ .03
Harper, Brian	93SCP	54	$ .01	$ .08
Harper, Brian	93SCS	154	$ .01	$ .05
Harris, Donald	90SC	661	$ .01	$ .15
Harris, Donald	92SCP	597	$ .01	$ .05
Harris, Donald	93SC	254	$ .01	$ .03
Harris, Donald	93SCS	341	$ .01	$ .05
Harris, Gene	90SC	548	$ .01	$ .04
Harris, Gene	91SC	627	$ .01	$ .04
Harris, Greg A.	88SC	179	$ .01	$ .04

SCORE

Player	Year	No.	VG	EX/MT	Player	Year	No.	VG	EX/MT
Harris, Greg A.	89SC	476	$ .01	$ .03	Heath, Mike	88SC	156	$ .01	$ .04
Harris, Greg A.	91SC	109	$ .01	$ .04	Heath, Mike	89SC	131	$ .01	$ .03
Harris, Greg A.	92SC	156	$ .01	$ .04	Heath, Mike	90SC	172	$ .01	$ .04
Harris, Greg A.	93SC	640	$ .01	$ .03	Heath, Mike	91SC	112	$ .01	$ .04
Harris, Greg W.	89SCTR	87	$ .01	$ .15	Heath, Mike	91SCTR	69	$ .01	$ .05
Harris, Greg W.	90SC	257	$ .01	$ .04	Heath, Mike	92SC	344	$ .01	$ .04
Harris, Greg W.	91SC	251	$ .01	$ .04	Heaton, Neal	88SC	430	$ .01	$ .04
Harris, Greg W.	92SC	378	$ .01	$ .04	Heaton, Neal	89SC	253	$ .01	$ .03
Harris, Greg W.	92SCP	169	$ .01	$ .05	Heaton, Neal	91SC	233	$ .01	$ .04
Harris, Greg W.	93SC	599	$ .01	$ .03	Heaton, Neal	92SC	723	$ .01	$ .04
Harris, Lenny	90SC	23	$ .01	$ .04	Heep, Danny	88SC	417	$ .01	$ .04
Harris, Lenny	91SC	144	$ .01	$ .04	Heep, Danny	89SC	343	$ .01	$ .03
Harris, Lenny	92SC	291	$ .01	$ .04	Heep, Danny	89SCTR	57	$ .01	$ .05
Harris, Lenny	92SCP	57	$ .01	$ .05	Heep, Danny	90SC	113	$ .01	$ .04
Harris, Lenny	93SC	546	$ .01	$ .03	Heep, Danny	91SC	827	$ .01	$ .04
Harris, Lenny	93SCP	119	$ .01	$ .08	Heinkel, Don	88SCTR	79	$ .01	$ .15
Harris, Lenny	93SCS	384	$ .01	$ .05	Heinkel, Don	89SC	168	$ .01	$ .10
Harris, Reggie	91SC	643	$ .01	$ .10	Helling, Rick	93SCS	358	$ .01	$ .15
Hartley, Mike	90SC	641	$ .01	$ .10	Hellling, Rick	93SC	491	$ .01	$ .10
Hartley, Mike	91SC	252	$ .01	$ .04	Hemond, Scott	90SC	598	$ .01	$ .10
Hartley, Mike	92SC	670	$ .01	$ .04	Hemond, Scott	92SC	617	$ .01	$ .04
Harvey, Bryan	88SCTR	87	$ .20	$2.00	Henderson, Dave	88SC	228	$ .01	$ .10
Harvey, Bryan	89SC	185	$ .05	$ .20	Henderson, Dave	88SCTR	49	$ .05	$ .25
Harvey, Bryan	90SC	8	$ .01	$ .04	Henderson, Dave	89SC	533	$ .01	$ .03
Harvey, Bryan	91SC	108	$ .01	$ .04	Henderson, Dave	90SC	325	$ .01	$ .04
Harvey, Bryan	92SC	322	$ .01	$ .04	Henderson, Dave	91SC	644	$ .01	$ .04
Harvey, Bryan	92SCP	145	$ .01	$ .05	Henderson, Dave	92SC	5	$ .01	$ .04
Harvey, Bryan	93SC	558	$ .01	$ .03	Henderson, Dave	92SCP	16	$ .01	$ .05
Harvey, Bryan	93SCP	235	$ .01	$ .08	Henderson, Dave	93SC	134	$ .01	$ .03
Harvey, Bryan	93SCS	126	$ .01	$ .05	Henderson, Dave	93SCP	170	$ .01	$ .08
Haselman, Bill	91SC	377	$ .01	$ .10	Henderson, Rickey	88SC	13	$ .05	$ .25
Hassey, Ron	88SCTR	33	$ .01	$ .15	Henderson, Rickey	89SC	70	$ .05	$ .25
Hassey, Ron	89SC	334	$ .01	$ .03	Henderson, Rickey	89SCTR	50	$ .05	$ .30
Hassey, Ron	90SC	168	$ .01	$ .04	Henderson, Rickey	90SC	360	$ .05	$ .20
Hassey, Ron	91SC	806	$ .01	$ .04	Henderson, Rickey	90SC	698	$ .01	$ .15
Hassey, Ron	91SCTR	43	$ .01	$ .05	Henderson, Rickey	90SCDT	686	$ .01	$ .10
Hassey, Ron	92SC	273	$ .01	$ .04	Henderson, Rickey	91SC	10	$ .01	$ .15
Hatcher, Billy	88SC	505	$ .01	$ .04	Henderson, Rickey	91SCAS	397	$ .01	$ .10
Hatcher, Billy	89SC	61	$ .01	$ .03	Henderson, Rickey	91SCBC	4	$ .20	$2.00
Hatcher, Billy	90SC	562	$ .01	$ .04	Henderson, Rickey	91SCDT	890	$ .05	$ .25
Hatcher, Billy	90SCTR	42	$ .01	$ .05	Henderson, Rickey	91SCMVP	875	$ .01	$ .15
Hatcher, Billy	91SC	469	$ .01	$ .04	Henderson, Rickey	91SCTF	857	$ .01	$ .10
Hatcher, Billy	92SC	447	$ .01	$ .04	Henderson, Rickey	92SC	430	$ .01	$ .10
Hatcher, Billy	92SCP	460	$ .01	$ .05	Henderson, Rickey	92SC	480	$ .01	$ .10
Hatcher, Billy	92SCTR	72	$ .01	$ .05	Henderson, Rickey	92SCDT	441	$ .05	$ .20
Hatcher, Billy	93SC	657	$ .01	$ .03	Henderson, Rickey	92SCP	283	$ .10	$ .75
Hatcher, Billy	93SCS	225	$ .01	$ .05	Henderson, Rickey	92SCP	401	$ .05	$ .20
Hatcher, Mickey	88SC	298	$ .01	$ .04	Henderson, Rickey	92SCP	614	$ .05	$ .20
Hatcher, Mickey	89SC	332	$ .01	$ .03	Henderson, Rickey	93SC	71	$ .01	$ .10
Hatcher, Mickey	90SC	359	$ .01	$ .04	Henderson, Rickey	93SCP	29	$ .05	$ .20
Hatcher, Mickey	91SC	153	$ .01	$ .04	Henderson, Rickey	93SCP	308	$ .01	$ .10
Hatteberg, Scott	92SCP	569	$ .01	$ .15	Henderson, Rickey	93SCS	106	$ .01	$ .15
Hawkins, Andy	88SC	347	$ .01	$ .04	Henderson, Steve	88SC	547	$ .01	$ .04
Hawkins, Andy	89SC	118	$ .01	$ .03	Hendrick, George	88SC	308	$ .01	$ .04
Hawkins, Andy	89SCNI	14	$ .01	$ .05	Henke, Tom	88SC	57	$ .01	$ .04
Hawkins, Andy	91SC	47	$ .01	$ .04	Henke, Tom	89SC	310	$ .01	$ .00
Hawkins, Andy	01SCNI	704	$ .01	$ .04	Henke, Tom	89SC	310	$ .01	$ .00
Hawkins, Andy	91SCTR	77	$ .01	$ .05	Henke, Tom	90SC	157	$ .01	$ .04
Hayes, Charlie	89SC	628	$ .05	$ .25	Henke, Tom	91SC	579	$ .01	$ .04
Hayes, Charlie	90SC	507	$ .01	$ .04	Henke, Tom	92SC	385	$ .01	$ .04
Hayes, Charlie	91SC	238	$ .01	$ .04	Henke, Tom	92SCAS	439	$ .01	$ .04
Hayes, Charlie	92SC	301	$ .01	$ .04	Henke, Tom	92SCP	417	$ .01	$ .05
Hayes, Charlie	92SCP	497	$ .01	$ .05	Henke, Tom	93SC	602	$ .01	$ .03
Hayes, Charlie	92SCTR	16	$ .01	$ .05	Henke, Tom	93SCS	211	$ .01	$ .05
Hayes, Charlie	93SC	411	$ .01	$ .03	Henneman, Mike	88SC	520	$ .05	$ .20
Hayes, Charlie	93SCS	194	$ .01	$ .05	Henneman, Mike	89SC	293	$ .01	$ .03
Hayes, Von	88SC	515	$ .01	$ .04	Henneman, Mike	90SC	184	$ .01	$ .04
Hayes, Von	89SC	38	$ .01	$ .03	Henneman, Mike	91SC	142	$ .01	$ .04
Hayes, Von	90SC	36	$ .01	$ .10	Henneman, Mike	92SC	217	$ .01	$ .04
Hayes, Von	91SC	426	$ .01	$ .04	Henneman, Mike	92SCP	164	$ .01	$ .05
Hayes, Von	92SC	207	$ .01	$ .04	Henneman, Mike	93SC	166	$ .01	$ .03
Hayes, Von	92SCP	326	$ .01	$ .05	Henneman, Mike	93SCS	138	$ .01	$ .05
Hayward, Ray	88SCTR	67	$ .01	$ .15	Hennis, Randy	91SC	752	$ .01	$ .10
Hayward, Ray	89SC	514	$ .01	$ .10	Henry, Butch	92SCP	567	$ .01	$ .15
Hearn, Ed	88SC	569	$ .01	$ .04	Henry, Butch	93SC	569	$ .01	$ .03

269

SCORE

Player	Year	No.	VG	EX/MT
Henry, Doug	92SC	421	$ .01	$ .15
Henry, Doug	93SC	177	$ .01	$ .03
Henry, Doug	93SCS	399	$ .01	$ .05
Henry, Dwayne	92SC	204	$ .01	$ .04
Henry, Dwayne	93SC	474	$ .01	$ .03
Hentgen, Pat	92SCP	563	$ .05	$ .20
Hentgen, Pat	92SCTR	96	$ .05	$ .35
Hentgen, Pat	93SC	343	$ .01	$ .03
Hentgen, Pat	93SCS	309	$ .01	$ .05
Heredia, Gil	92SC	771	$ .01	$ .10
Hernandez, Carlos	92SCP	456	$ .01	$ .05
Hernandez, Carlos	92SCTR	91	$ .01	$ .05
Hernandez, Carlos	93SC	348	$ .05	$ .25
Hernandez, Carlos	93SCP	146	$ .01	$ .08
Hernandez, Carlos	93SCS	317	$ .01	$ .05
Hernandez, Cesar	93SC	302	$ .01	$ .03
Hernandez, Guillermo	89SC	275	$ .01	$ .03
Hernandez, Guillermo	90SC	267	$ .01	$ .04
Hernandez, Jose	92SC	866	$ .01	$ .10
Hernandez, Keith	88SC	400	$ .05	$ .25
Hernandez, Keith	89SC	41	$ .01	$ .10
Hernandez, Keith	90SC	193	$ .01	$ .04
Hernandez, Keith	90SCTR	57	$ .01	$ .05
Hernandez, Keith	91SC	89	$ .01	$ .04

Player	Year	No.	VG	EX/MT
Hernandez, Roberto	**92SC**	**874**	**$ .01**	**$ .10**
Hernandez, Roberto	92SCP	253	$ .05	$ .20
Hernandez, Roberto	93SC	376	$ .01	$ .03
Hernandez, Roberto	93SCP	129	$ .01	$ .08
Hernandez, Roberto	93SCS	311	$ .01	$ .05
Hernandez, Willie	88SC	507	$ .01	$ .04
Hernandez, Xavier	91SC	564	$ .01	$ .10
Herndon, Larry	88SC	138	$ .01	$ .04
Herndon, Larry	89SC	279	$ .01	$ .03
Herr, Tom	88SC	84	$ .01	$ .04
Herr, Tom	88SCTR	8	$ .01	$ .15
Herr, Tommy	89SC	191	$ .01	$ .03
Herr, Tom	89SCTR	9	$ .01	$ .05
Herr, Tom	90SC	171	$ .01	$ .04
Herr, Tom	91SC	820	$ .01	$ .04
Hershiser, Orel	88SC	470	$ .01	$ .10
Hershiser, Orel	89SC	370	$ .01	$ .10
Hershiser, Orel	89SC	653	$ .01	$ .15
Hershiser, Orel	90SC	50	$ .01	$ .10
Hershiser, Orel	91SC	550	$ .01	$ .10

Player	Year	No.	VG	EX/MT
Hershiser, Orel	92SC	653	$ .01	$ .05
Hershiser, Orel	92SCP	21	$ .01	$ .05
Hershiser, Orel	92SCP	592	$ .01	$ .05
Hershiser, Orel	93SC	90	$ .01	$ .03
Hershiser, Orel	93SCS	49	$ .01	$ .05
Hesketh, Joe	89SC	498	$ .01	$ .03
Hesketh, Joe	90SC	483	$ .01	$ .04
Hesketh, Joe	92SC	359	$ .01	$ .04
Hesketh, Joe	92SCP	415	$ .01	$ .05
Hesketh, Joe	93SC	467	$ .01	$ .03
Hetzel, Eric	90SC	543	$ .01	$ .04
Hibbard, Greg	90SC	369	$ .05	$ .20
Hibbard, Greg	91SC	128	$ .01	$ .04
Hibbard, Greg	92SC	266	$ .01	$ .04
Hibbard, Greg	92SCP	364	$ .01	$ .05
Hibbard, Greg	93SC	622	$ .01	$ .03
Hibbard, Greg	93SCS	216	$ .01	$ .05
Hickerson, Bryan	92SC	750	$ .01	$ .10
Hickey, Kevin	90SC	214	$ .01	$ .04
Higuera, Teddy	88SC	280	$ .01	$ .04
Higuera, Teddy	89SC	132	$ .01	$ .03
Higuera, Teddy	90SC	305	$ .01	$ .04
Higuera, Teddy	91SC	260	$ .01	$ .04
Higuera, Teddy	92SC	126	$ .01	$ .04
Higuera, Teddy	92SCP	439	$ .01	$ .05
Hill, Donnie	88SC	572	$ .01	$ .04
Hill, Donnie	89SC	583	$ .01	$ .03
Hill, Donnie	92SC	183	$ .01	$ .04
Hill, Glenallen	90SC	601	$ .01	$ .10
Hill, Glenallen	91SC	514	$ .01	$ .04
Hill, Glenallen	92SC	448	$ .01	$ .04
Hill, Glenallen	92SCP	420	$ .01	$ .05
Hill, Glenallen	93SC	398	$ .01	$ .03
Hill, Glenallen	93SCP	123	$ .01	$ .08
Hill, Ken	89SCTR	98	$ .10	$ .50
Hill, Ken	90SC	233	$ .05	$ .20
Hill, Ken	91SC	567	$ .01	$ .04
Hill, Ken	92SC	104	$ .01	$ .04
Hill, Ken	92SCP	486	$ .01	$ .05
Hill, Ken	92SCTR	61	$ .01	$ .05
Hill, Ken	93SC	48	$ .01	$ .03
Hill, Ken	93SCP	66	$ .01	$ .08
Hill, Ken	93SCS	169	$ .01	$ .05
Hill, Milt	92SC	820	$ .01	$ .10
Hill, Tyrone	92SC	807	$ .05	$ .25
Hill, Tyrone	92SCP	301	$ .10	$ .50
Hillegas, Shawn	88SC	612	$ .01	$ .15
Hillegas, Shawn	89SC	488	$ .01	$ .03
Hillegas, Shawn	90SC	329	$ .01	$ .04
Hillegas, Shawn	91SCTR	65	$ .01	$ .05
Hillegas, Shawn	92SC	93	$ .01	$ .04
Hillman, Eric	93SC	280	$ .01	$ .15
Hillman, Eric	93SCS	350	$ .01	$ .15
Hinzo, Tommy	88SC	567	$ .01	$ .04
Hitchcock, Sterling	93SC	311	$ .05	$ .35
Hoffman, Guy	88SC	609	$ .01	$ .04
Hoiles, Chris	90SCTR	96	$ .10	$ .40
Hoiles, Chris	91SC	334	$ .01	$ .10
Hoiles, Chris	92SC	641	$ .01	$ .04
Hoiles, Chris	92SCP	83	$ .01	$ .10
Hoiles, Chris	93SC	54	$ .01	$ .03
Hoiles, Chris	93SCP	186	$ .01	$ .08
Hoiles, Chris	93SCS	144	$ .01	$ .05
Holbert, Aaron	91SC	676	$ .01	$ .10
Hollins, Dave	90SCTR	75	$ .10	$ .75
Hollins, Dave	91SC	61	$ .01	$ .10
Hollins, Dave	92SC	553	$ .01	$ .04
Hollins, Dave	92SCP	67	$ .05	$ .25
Hollins, Dave	93SC	99	$ .01	$ .15
Hollins, Dave	93SCP	127	$ .05	$ .20
Hollins, Dave	93SCS	187	$ .01	$ .05
Holman, Brian	90SC	387	$ .01	$ .04
Holman, Brian	91SC	285	$ .01	$ .04
Holman, Brian	92SC	228	$ .01	$ .04
Holman, Brian	92SCP	520	$ .01	$ .05

SCORE

Player	Year	No.	VG	EX/MT	Player	Year	No.	VG	EX/MT
Holman, Shawn	90SC	620	$ .01	$ .10	Hrbek, Kent	93SCS	80	$ .01	$ .05
Holmes, Darren	92SC	753	$ .01	$ .04	Hubbard, Glenn	88SC	111	$ .01	$ .04
Holmes, Darren	93SC	600	$ .01	$ .03	Hubbard, Glenn	88SCTR	58	$ .01	$ .15
Holton, Brian	88SC	208	$ .01	$ .04	Hubbard, Glenn	89SC	34	$ .01	$ .03
Holton, Brian	89SC	507	$ .01	$ .03	Hudler, Rex	89SC	470	$ .01	$ .03
Holton, Brian	89SCTR	59	$ .01	$ .05	Hudler, Rex	90SC	287	$ .01	$ .04
Holton, Brian	90SC	177	$ .01	$ .04	Hudler, Rex	91SC	589	$ .01	$ .04
Honeycutt, Rick	88SC	87	$ .01	$ .04	Hudler, Rex	92SC	184	$ .01	$ .04
Honeycutt, Rick	89SC	416	$ .01	$ .03	Hudler, Rex	92SCP	315	$ .01	$ .05
Honeycutt, Rick	90SC	317	$ .01	$ .04	Hudler, Rex	92SCP	589	$ .05	$ .20
Honeycutt, Rick	91SC	539	$ .01	$ .04	Hudson, Charles	89SC	415	$ .01	$ .03
Honeycutt, Rick	92SC	456	$ .01	$ .04	Huff, Mike	90SC	597	$ .01	$ .10
Horn, Sam	88SC	201	$ .01	$ .10	Huff, Mike	91SCTR	52	$ .01	$ .05
Horn, Sam	91SC	605	$ .01	$ .04	Huff, Mike	92SC	664	$ .01	$ .04
Horn, Sam	92SC	290	$ .01	$ .04	Huff, Mike	92SCP	485	$ .01	$ .05
Horn, Sam	92SCP	221	$ .01	$ .05	Hughes, Keith	88SC	635	$ .01	$ .04
Horn, Sam	93SCP	128	$ .01	$ .08	Hulett, Tim	91SC	632	$ .01	$ .04
Horner, Bob	89SC	68	$ .01	$ .03	Hulett, Tim	92SC	391	$ .01	$ .04
Horsman, Vince	92SCP	524	$ .01	$ .10	Hulse, David	93SC	293	$ .01	$ .15
Horsman, Vince	92SCTR	106	$ .01	$ .10	Hulse, David	93SCP	269	$ .05	$ .20
Horsman, Vince	93SC	406	$ .01	$ .03	Hume, Tom	88SC	494	$ .01	$ .04
Horsman, Vince	93SCS	316	$ .01	$ .05	Humphreys, Mike	92SC	815	$ .01	$ .04
Horton, Rick	88SC	412	$ .01	$ .04	Humphreys, Mike	92SCP	277	$ .01	$ .05
Horton, Rick	88SCTR	24	$ .01	$ .15	Hundley, Todd	90SCTR	76	$ .01	$ .15
Horton, Rick	89SC	145	$ .01	$ .03	Hundley, Todd	91SC	340	$ .01	$ .10
Hosey, Steve	90SC	666	$ .05	$ .35	Hundley, Todd	92SC	602	$ .01	$ .04
Hosey, Steve	93SC	303	$ .01	$ .15	Hundley, Todd	92SCP	571	$ .01	$ .05
Hosey, Steve	93SCP	253	$ .05	$ .25	Hundley, Todd	93SC	167	$ .01	$ .03
Hosey, Steve	93SCS	346	$ .05	$ .20	Hundley, Todd	93SCP	126	$ .01	$ .08
Hough, Charlie	88SC	140	$ .01	$ .04	Hundley, Todd	93SCS	293	$ .01	$ .05
Hough, Charlie	89SC	295	$ .01	$ .03	Hunter, Brian	92SC	417	$ .05	$ .35
Hough, Charlie	90SC	202	$ .01	$ .04	Hunter, Brian	92SCP	412	$ .01	$ .05
Hough, Charlie	91SC	141	$ .01	$ .04	Hunter, Brian	93SC	549	$ .01	$ .03
Hough, Charlie	92SC	302	$ .01	$ .04	Hunter, Brian	93SCS	189	$ .01	$ .05
Hough, Charlie	92SCP	422	$ .01	$ .05	Hunter, Catfish	92SCP	587	$ .01	$ .05
Hough, Charlie	93SC	223	$ .01	$ .03	Hunter, Jim	92SC	741	$ .01	$ .10
Housie, Wayne	92SC	836	$ .01	$ .10	Hurst, Bruce	88SC	380	$ .01	$ .04
Houston, Tyler	90SC	677	$ .01	$ .10	Hurst, Bruce	89SC	325	$ .01	$ .03
Howard, David	91SCTR	83	$ .01	$ .15	Hurst, Bruce	89SCTR	19	$ .01	$ .10
Howard, David	92SC	704	$ .01	$ .04	Hurst, Bruce	90SC	270	$ .01	$ .04
Howard, David	92SCP	86	$ .01	$ .05	Hurst, Bruce	91SC	145	$ .01	$ .04
Howard, David	93SC	645	$ .01	$ .03	Hurst, Bruce	92SC	111	$ .01	$ .04
Howard, Steve	91SC	364	$ .01	$ .10	Hurst, Bruce	92SCP	40	$ .01	$ .05
Howard, Thomas	91SC	335	$ .01	$ .10	Hurst, Bruce	93SC	133	$ .01	$ .03
Howard, Thomas	92SC	293	$ .01	$ .04	Hurst, Bruce	93SCS	141	$ .01	$ .05
Howard, Thomas	93SC	426	$ .01	$ .03	Hurst, Jonathan	93SC	299	$ .01	$ .10
Howe, Steve	88SC	543	$ .01	$ .04	Hurst, Jonathan	93SCP	242	$ .01	$ .15
Howe, Steve	92SC	275	$ .01	$ .04	Huson, Jeff	90SC	615	$ .01	$ .10
Howe, Steve	92SCP	507	$ .01	$ .05	Huson, Jeff	90SCTR	41	$ .01	$ .05
Howell, Jack	88SC	124	$ .01	$ .04	Huson, Jeff	91SC	263	$ .01	$ .04
Howell, Jack	89SC	261	$ .01	$ .03	Huson, Jeff	92SC	466	$ .01	$ .04
Howell, Jack	90SC	206	$ .01	$ .04	Hyzdu, Adam	91SC	388	$ .01	$ .15
Howell, Jack	91SC	842	$ .01	$ .04	Ignasiak, Mike	92SC	837	$ .01	$ .10
Howell, Jack	92SC	706	$ .01	$ .04	Incaviglia, Pete	88SC	485	$ .01	$ .15
Howell, Jay	88SC	522	$ .01	$ .04	Incaviglia, Pete	89SC	201	$ .01	$ .15
Howell, Jay	88SCTR	35	$ .01	$ .15	Incaviglia, Pete	90SC	93	$ .01	$ .10
Howell, Jay	89SC	378	$ .01	$ .03	Incaviglia, Pete	91SC	278	$ .01	$ .04
Howell, Jay	90SC	227	$ .01	$ .04	Incaviglia, Pete	91SCTR	3	$ .01	$ .05
Howell, Jay	91SC	29	$ .01	$ .04	Incaviglia, Pete	92SC	306	$ .01	$ .04
Howell, Jay	92SC	119	$ .01	$ .04	Incaviglia, Pete	92SCP	325	$ .01	$ .05
Howell, Jay	92SCP	444	$ .01	$ .05	Incaviglia, Pete	92SCTR	17	$ .01	$ .05
Howell, Ken	88SC	406	$ .01	$ .04	Incaviglia, Pete	93SC	568	$ .01	$ .03
Howell, Ken	91SC	458	$ .01	$ .04	Innis, Jeff	92SC	327	$ .01	$ .04
Howitt, Dann	92SC	861	$ .01	$ .04	Innis, Jeff	93SC	409	$ .01	$ .03
Hoy, Peter	92SCP	526	$ .01	$ .10	Iorg, Garth	88SC	204	$ .01	$ .04
Hoy, Peter	93SC	230	$ .01	$ .03	Irvine, Daryl	91SC	333	$ .01	$ .10
Hrbek, Kent	88SC	43	$ .01	$ .10	Irvine, Daryl	92SC	726	$ .01	$ .04
Hrbek, Kent	89SC	382	$ .01	$ .10	Jackson, Bo	88SC	180	$ .05	$ .35
Hrbek, Kent	90SC	381	$ .01	$ .04	Jackson, Bo	89SC	330	$ .05	$ .25
Hrbek, Kent	91SC	292	$ .01	$ .04	Jackson, Bo	90SC	280	$ .05	$ .20
Hrbek, Kent	92SC	530	$ .01	$ .04	Jackson, Bo	90SC	566	$ .05	$ .20
Hrbek, Kent	92SCP	68	$ .01	$ .05	Jackson, Bo	90SC	697	$ .20	$2.00
Hrbek, Kent	93SC	98	$ .01	$ .03	Jackson, Bo	90SCDT	687	$ .05	$ .20
Hrbek, Kent	93SCP	27	$ .01	$ .08	Jackson, Bo	91SC	5	$ .01	$ .15
Hrbek, Kent	93SCP	307	$ .01	$ .08	Jackson, Bo	91SC	773	$ .05	$ .20

SCORE

Player	Year	No.	VG	EX/MT	Player	Year	No.	VG	EX/MT
Jackson, Bo	91SCHL	420	$ .01	$ .10	Jefferies, Gregg	90SC	468	$ .01	$ .10
Jackson, Bo	91SCMB	692	$ .01	$ .10	Jefferies, Gregg	91SC	660	$ .01	$ .10
Jackson, Bo	91SCRM	412	$ .01	$ .10	Jefferies, Gregg	92SC	192	$ .01	$ .04
Jackson, Bo	91SCTR	1	$ .05	$ .20	Jefferies, Gregg	92SCP	330	$ .01	$ .05
Jackson, Bo	92SC	361	$ .01	$ .15	Jefferies, Gregg	92SCTR	39	$ .01	$ .05
Jackson, Chuck	88SC	222	$ .01	$ .04	Jefferies, Gregg	93SC	17	$ .01	$ .03
Jackson, Chuck	89SC	584	$ .01	$ .03	Jefferies, Gregg	93SCP	24	$ .01	$ .10
Jackson, Danny	88SC	398	$ .01	$ .10	Jefferies, Gregg	93SCS	152	$ .01	$ .05
Jackson, Danny	88SCTR	2	$ .01	$ .15	Jefferson, Reggie	92SC	409	$ .01	$ .10
Jackson, Danny	89SC	555	$ .01	$ .10	Jefferson, Reggie	92SCP	476	$ .01	$ .05
Jackson, Danny	90SC	289	$ .01	$ .04	Jefferson, Reggie	93SC	433	$ .01	$ .03
Jackson, Danny	91SC	601	$ .01	$ .04	Jefferson, Reggie	93SCS	330	$ .01	$ .05
Jackson, Danny	91SCTR	17	$ .01	$ .05	Jefferson, Stan	88SC	114	$ .01	$ .04
Jackson, Danny	92SC	120	$ .01	$ .04	Jefferson, Stan	89SC	519	$ .01	$ .03
Jackson, Danny	92SCP	457	$ .01	$ .05	Jeltz, Steve	88SC	435	$ .01	$ .04
Jackson, Danny	93SC	421	$ .01	$ .03	Jeltz, Steve	89SC	355	$ .01	$ .03
Jackson, Danny	93SCS	371	$ .01	$ .05	Jeltz, Steve	90SC	421	$ .01	$ .04
Jackson, Darrin	88SCTR	109	$ .20	$2.00	Jeltz, Steve	90SCTR	59	$ .01	$ .05
Jackson, Darrin	89SC	360	$ .01	$ .15	Jeltz, Steve	91SC	272	$ .01	$ .04
Jackson, Darrin	90SC	541	$ .01	$ .04	Jennings, Doug	89SC	459	$ .01	$ .10
Jackson, Darrin	91SC	169	$ .01	$ .04	Jennings, Doug	91SC	819	$ .01	$ .04
Jackson, Darrin	92SC	521	$ .01	$ .04	Jeter, Derek	93SC	489	$ .05	$ .20
Jackson, Darrin	92SCP	207	$ .01	$ .05	Jeter, Derek	93SCS	360	$ .10	$ .40
Jackson, Darrin	93SC	155	$ .01	$ .03	Jeter, Shawn	93SCP	265	$ .01	$ .08
Jackson, Darrin	93SCP	125	$ .01	$ .08	John, Tommy	88SC	240	$ .01	$ .10
Jackson, Darrin	93SCS	199	$ .01	$ .05	John, Tommy	89SC	477	$ .01	$ .03
Jackson, Jeff	90SC	678	$ .01	$ .10	Johnson, Dave	90SC	528	$ .01	$ .04
Jackson, Mike	88SC	144	$ .01	$ .10	Johnson, Dave	91SC	506	$ .01	$ .04
Jackson, Mike	88SCTR	62	$ .01	$ .15	Johnson, Dave	92SC	604	$ .01	$ .04
Jackson, Mike	89SC	398	$ .01	$ .03					
Jackson, Mike	90SC	546	$ .01	$ .04					
Jackson, Mike	91SC	91	$ .01	$ .10					
Jackson, Mike	92SC	194	$ .01	$ .04					
Jackson, Mike	92SCP	437	$ .01	$ .05					
Jackson, Mike	92SCTR	40	$ .01	$ .05					
Jackson, Reggie #1	88SC	500	$ .05	$ .25					
Jackson, Reggie #2	88SC	501	$ .05	$ .25					
Jackson, Reggie #3	88SC	502	$ .05	$ .25					
Jackson, Reggie #4	88SC	503	$ .05	$ .25					
Jackson, Reggie #5	88SC	504	$ .05	$ .25					
Jacoby, Brook	88SC	39	$ .01	$ .10					
Jacoby, Brook	89SC	19	$ .01	$ .03					
Jacoby, Brook	90SC	56	$ .01	$ .04					
Jacoby, Brook	91SC	162	$ .01	$ .04					
Jacoby, Brook	92SC	577	$ .01	$ .04					
Jacoby, Brook	92SCP	376	$ .01	$ .05					
Jacoby, Brook	93SC	567	$ .01	$ .03					
Jaha, John	93SC	236	$ .05	$ .20					
Jaha, John	93SCP	228	$ .05	$ .35					
Jaha, John	93SCS	308	$ .05	$ .20					
James, Chris	88SC	409	$ .01	$ .04					
James, Chris	89SC	202	$ .01	$ .03					
James, Chris	89SCTR	46	$ .01	$ .05					
James, Chris	90SC	498	$ .01	$ .04					
James, Chris	90SCTR	60	$ .01	$ .05					
James, Chris	91SC	491	$ .01	$ .04					
James, Chris	92SC	262	$ .01	$ .04					
James, Chris	93SCP	120	$ .01	$ .08					
James, Dion	88SC	395	$ .01	$ .04					
James, Dion	89SC	163	$ .01	$ .03					
James, Dion	89SCTR	51	$ .01	$ .05					
James, Dion	90SC	514	$ .01	$ .04	Johnson, Howard	88SC	69	$ .01	$ .15
James, Dion	91SC	131	$ .01	$ .04	Johnson, Howard	89SC	136	$ .01	$ .10
Janicki, Pete	93SC	500	$ .05	$ .25	Johnson, Howard	90SC	124	$ .01	$ .10
Javier, Stan	88SC	367	$ .01	$ .04	Johnson, Howard	91SC	185	$ .01	$ .10
Javier, Stan	89SC	322	$ .01	$ .03	Johnson, Howard	92SC	550	$ .01	$ .04
Javier, Stan	90SC	394	$ .01	$ .04	Johnson, Howard	92SCAS	776	$ .01	$ .04
Javier, Stan	90SCTR	52	$ .01	$ .05	Johnson, Howard	92SCP	15	$ .01	$ .05
Javier, Stan	91SC	281	$ .01	$ .04	Johnson, Howard	93SC	62	$ .01	$ .03
Javier, Stan	92SC	583	$ .01	$ .04	Johnson, Howard	93SCS	101	$ .01	$ .05
Jeffcoat, Mike	90SC	158	$ .01	$ .04	Johnson, J. J.	92SCP	577	$ .05	$ .20
Jeffcoat, Mike	91SC	174	$ .01	$ .04	Johnson, Jeff	91SCTR	110	$ .01	$ .15
Jeffcoat, Mike	92SC	174	$ .01	$ .04	Johnson, Jeff	92SC	523	$ .01	$ .04
Jefferies, Gregg	88SC	645	$ .10	$1.00	Johnson, Jeff	92SCP	464	$ .01	$ .05
Jefferies, Gregg	89SC	600	$ .05	$ .25	Johnson, Lance	90SC	570	$ .01	$ .04

SCORE

Player	Year	No.	VG	EX/MT	Player	Year	No.	VG	EX/MT
Johnson, Lance	91SC	157	$ .01	$ .04	Jordan, Ricky	93SC	141	$ .01	$ .03
Johnson, Lance	92SC	146	$ .01	$ .04	Jordan, Ricky	93SCP	187	$ .01	$ .08
Johnson, Lance	92SCP	373	$ .01	$ .05	Jorgensen, Terry	90SC	655	$ .01	$ .04
Johnson, Lance	93SC	109	$ .01	$ .03	Jorgensen, Terry	93SC	458	$ .01	$ .03
Johnson, Lance	93SCP	137	$ .01	$ .08	Jose, Felix	89SC	629	$ .10	$ .75
Johnson, Lance	93SCS	266	$ .01	$ .05	Jose, Felix	90SC	321	$ .05	$ .20
Johnson, Randy	89SC	645	$ .05	$ .25	Jose, Felix	91SC	784	$ .01	$ .10
Johnson, Randy	89SCTR	77	$ .01	$ .15	Jose, Felix	92SC	40	$ .01	$ .04
Johnson, Randy	90SC	415	$ .01	$ .04	Jose, Felix	92SCP	159	$ .01	$ .05
Johnson, Randy	91SC	290	$ .01	$ .04	Jose, Felix	93SC	110	$ .01	$ .03
Johnson, Randy	91SCNH	700	$ .01	$ .04	Jose, Felix	93SCP	36	$ .01	$ .08
Johnson, Randy	92SC	584	$ .01	$ .04	Jose, Felix	93SCS	131	$ .01	$ .05
Johnson, Randy	92SCP	379	$ .01	$ .05	Joyner, Wally	88SC	7	$ .01	$ .15
Johnson, Randy	92SCP	595	$ .01	$ .05	Joyner, Wally	89SC	65	$ .01	$ .10
Johnson, Randy	93SC	384	$ .01	$ .03	Joyner, Wally	90SC	120	$ .01	$ .10
Johnson, Randy	93SCP	41	$ .01	$ .08	Joyner, Wally	91SC	470	$ .01	$ .10
Johnson, Randy	93SCS	118	$ .01	$ .05	Joyner, Wally	91SCTF	873	$ .01	$ .04
Johnson, Wallace	88SC	433	$ .01	$ .04	Joyner, Wally	92SC	535	$ .01	$ .04
Johnson, Wallace	89SC	196	$ .01	$ .03	Joyner, Wally	92SCP	284	$ .01	$ .05
Johnson, Wallace	90SC	479	$ .01	$ .04	Joyner, Wally	92SCP	537	$ .01	$ .05
Johnston, Joel	92SC	764	$ .01	$ .04	Joyner, Wally	92SCTR	13	$ .01	$ .05
Johnston, Joel	92SCP	259	$ .01	$ .05	Joyner, Wally	93SC	43	$ .01	$ .03
Jones, Barry	89SC	333	$ .01	$ .03	Joyner, Wally	93SCP	51	$ .01	$ .08
Jones, Barry	90SC	152	$ .01	$ .04	Joyner, Wally	93SCS	34	$ .01	$ .05
Jones, Barry	91SC	115	$ .01	$ .04	Justice, Dave	90SC	650	$ .15	$1.50
Jones, Barry	91SCTR	75	$ .01	$ .05	Justice, Dave	91SC	55	$ .05	$ .25
Jones, Barry	92SC	297	$ .01	$ .04	Justice, Dave	91SCMVP	880	$ .05	$ .25
Jones, Bobby	92SCP	548	$ .10	$ .50	Justice, Dave	91SCTF	861	$ .05	$ .20
Jones, Calvin	92SC	868	$ .01	$ .10	Justice, Dave	92SC	4	$ .05	$ .25
Jones, Chipper	91SC	671	$ .10	$1.00	Justice, Dave	92SCP	100	$ .10	$ .40
Jones, Chris	91SCTR	92	$ .01	$ .15	Justice, Dave	92SCP	588	$ .05	$ .20
Jones, Chris	92SC	811	$ .01	$ .04	Justice, Dave	92SCP	604	$ .05	$ .20
Jones, Doug	88SC	594	$ .05	$ .25	Justice, Dave	92SCP	620	$ .05	$ .25
Jones, Doug	89SC	387	$ .01	$ .03	Justice, Dave	93SC	107	$ .01	$ .10
Jones, Doug	89SC	656	$ .01	$ .03	Justice, Dave	93SCS	39	$ .05	$ .25
Jones, Doug	90SC	130	$ .01	$ .04	Kamieniecki, Scott	92SC	415	$ .01	$ .04
Jones, Doug	91SC	45	$ .01	$ .04	Kamieniecki, Scott	93SC	377	$ .01	$ .03
Jones, Doug	91SCDT	884	$ .01	$ .04	Karkovice, Ron	88SC	374	$ .01	$ .04
Jones, Doug	92SC	53	$ .01	$ .04	Karkovice, Ron	90SC	22	$ .01	$ .04
Jones, Doug	92SCP	499	$ .01	$ .05	Karkovice, Ron	91SC	833	$ .01	$ .04
Jones, Doug	92SCTR	38	$ .01	$ .05	Karkovice, Ron	92SC	532	$ .01	$ .04
Jones, Doug	93SC	197	$ .01	$ .03	Karkovice, Ron	92SCP	413	$ .01	$ .05
Jones, Doug	93SCS	67	$ .01	$ .05	Karkovice, Ron	93SC	152	$ .01	$ .03
Jones, Jimmy	88SC	246	$ .01	$ .04	Karkovice, Ron	93SCP	195	$ .01	$ .08
Jones, Jimmy	89SC	294	$ .01	$ .03	Karkovice, Ron	93SCS	381	$ .01	$ .05
Jones, Jimmy	91SC	583	$ .01	$ .04	Karros, Eric	92SC	827	$ .10	$ .50
Jones, Jimmy	92SC	33	$ .01	$ .04	Karros, Eric	92SCP	256	$ .15	$1.50
Jones, Jimmy	93SC	463	$ .01	$ .03	Karros, Eric	93SC	63	$ .05	$ .35
Jones, Keith "Kiki"	90SC	676	$ .01	$ .15	Karros, Eric	93SC	486	$ .05	$ .20
Jones, Odell	89SC	579	$ .01	$ .03	Karros, Eric	93SCP	14	$ .10	$1.00
Jones, Ron	89SC	639	$ .01	$ .10	Karros, Eric	93SCS	278	$ .10	$ .50
Jones, Ron	90SC	364	$ .01	$ .04	Karsay, Steve	91SC	675	$ .05	$ .25
Jones, Ron	91SC	653	$ .01	$ .04	Kelly, Pat	91SCTR	107	$ .01	$ .15
Jones, Ron	92SC	342	$ .01	$ .04	Kelly, Pat	92SC	185	$ .01	$ .10
Jones, Ross	88SC	598	$ .01	$ .04	Kelly, Pat	92SCP	54	$ .01	$ .10
Jones, Ruppert	88SC	333	$ .01	$ .04	Kelly, Pat	93SC	370	$ .01	$ .03
Jones, Stacy	92SC	832	$ .01	$ .10	Kelly, Pat	93SCP	104	$ .01	$ .00
Jones, Tim	89SC	649	$ .01	$ .03	Kelly, Pat	93SCS	255	$ .01	$ .05
Jones, Tim	90SC	579	$ .01	$ .04	Kelly, Roberto	88SC	634	$ .10	$1.00
Jones, Tracy	88SC	326	$ .01	$ .04	Kelly, Roberto	89SC	487	$ .01	$ .15
Jones, Tracy	89SC	510	$ .01	$ .03	Kelly, Roberto	90SC	100	$ .01	$ .10
Jones, Tracy	89SCTR	43	$ .01	$ .05	Kelly, Roberto	91SC	119	$ .01	$ .10
Jones, Tracy	90SC	291	$ .01	$ .04	Kelly, Roberto	92SC	324	$ .01	$ .04
Jones, Tracy	91SC	87	$ .01	$ .04	Kelly, Roberto	92SCP	114	$ .01	$ .10
Jones, Tracy	92SC	206	$ .01	$ .04	Kelly, Roberto	93SC	438	$ .01	$ .10
Jordan, Brian	92SCP	555	$ .05	$ .35	Kelly, Roberto	93SCS	64	$ .01	$ .05
Jordan, Brian	92SCTR	83	$ .05	$ .25	Kendall, Jason	93SC	490	$ .05	$ .20
Jordan, Brian	93SC	217	$ .01	$ .10	Kendall, Jason	93SCS	359	$ .05	$ .25
Jordan, Brian	93SCS	280	$ .01	$ .15	Kennedy, Terry	88SC	123	$ .01	$ .04
Jordan, Ricky	88SCTR	68	$ .10	$ .50	Kennedy, Terry	89SC	123	$ .01	$ .03
Jordan, Ricky	89SC	548	$ .01	$ .10	Kennedy, Terry	89SCTR	30	$ .01	$ .05
Jordan, Ricky	90SC	16	$ .01	$ .10	Kennedy, Terry	90SC	7	$ .01	$ .04
Jordan, Ricky	91SC	15	$ .01	$ .04	Kennedy, Terry	91SC	548	$ .01	$ .04
Jordan, Ricky	92SC	476	$ .01	$ .04	Kennedy, Terry	92SC	503	$ .01	$ .04
Jordan, Ricky	92SCP	530	$ .01	$ .05	Kent, Jeff	92SCP	522	$ .05	$ .35

273

SCORE

Player	Year	No.	VG	EX/MT
Kent, Jeff	92SCTR	84	$ .05	$ .35
Kent, Jeff	93SC	189	$ .01	$ .10
Kent, Jeff	93SCP	155	$ .01	$ .15
Kent, Jeff	93SCS	318	$ .01	$ .05
Kerfeld, Charlie	88SC	479	$ .01	$ .04
Key, Jimmy	88SC	216	$ .01	$ .04
Key, Jimmy	89SC	480	$ .01	$ .03
Key, Jimmy	90SC	407	$ .01	$ .04
Key, Jimmy	91SC	422	$ .01	$ .04
Key, Jimmy	92SC	96	$ .01	$ .04
Key, Jimmy	92SCP	193	$ .01	$ .05
Key, Jimmy	93SC	639	$ .01	$ .03
Key, Jimmy	93SCP	9	$ .01	$ .08
Key, Jimmy	93SCS	376	$ .01	$ .05
Kiecker, Dana	90SCTR	102	$ .01	$ .10
Kiecker, Dana	91SC	77	$ .01	$ .10

Player	Year	No.	VG	EX/MT
Kiecker, Dana	92SC	732	$ .01	$ .04
Kiefer, Steve	88SC	630	$ .01	$ .04
Kile, Darryl	91SCTR	86	$ .01	$ .15
Kile, Darryl	92SC	494	$ .01	$ .04
Kile, Darryl	92SCP	225	$ .01	$ .05
Kile, Darryl	93SC	430	$ .01	$ .03
Kilgus, Paul	88SC	536	$ .01	$ .04
Kilgus, Paul	89SC	271	$ .01	$ .03
Kilgus, Paul	90SC	196	$ .01	$ .04
Kilgus, Paul	92SC	268	$ .01	$ .04
King, Eric	88SC	471	$ .01	$ .04
King, Eric	89SC	471	$ .01	$ .03
King, Eric	89SCTR	26	$ .01	$ .05
King, Eric	90SC	28	$ .01	$ .04
King, Eric	91SC	124	$ .01	$ .04
King, Eric	91SCTR	60	$ .01	$ .05
King, Eric	92SC	144	$ .01	$ .04
King, Eric	92SCP	503	$ .01	$ .05
King, Eric	92SCTR	42	$ .01	$ .05
King, Jeff	90SC	549	$ .01	$ .04
King, Jeff	91SC	244	$ .01	$ .04
King, Jeff	92SC	511	$ .01	$ .04
King, Jeff	92SCP	317	$ .01	$ .05
King, Jeff	93SC	159	$ .01	$ .03
Kingery, Mike	88SC	178	$ .01	$ .04
Kingery, Mike	91SC	547	$ .01	$ .04
Kinzer, Matt	90SC	628	$ .01	$ .04
Kipper, Bob	89SC	354	$ .01	$ .03
Kipper, Bob	91SC	646	$ .01	$ .04
Kipper, Bob	92SC	340	$ .01	$ .04
Kipper, Bob	92SCP	495	$ .01	$ .05
Kirby, Wayne	93SC	328	$ .01	$ .03
Kittle, Ron	88SC	449	$ .01	$ .04
Kittle, Ron	88SCTR	44	$ .01	$ .15
Kittle, Ron	89SC	96	$ .01	$ .03
Kittle, Ron	90SC	529	$ .01	$ .04
Klesko, Ryan	93SC	294	$ .05	$ .35
Klesko, Ryan	93SCP	251	$ .10	$ .50
Klesko, Ryan	93SCS	405	$ .05	$ .35
Klink, Joe	91SC	588	$ .01	$ .04
Klink, Joe	92SC	151	$ .01	$ .04
Knackert, Brent	91SC	774	$ .01	$ .04
Knepper, Bob	88SC	344	$ .01	$ .04
Knepper, Bob	89SC	273	$ .01	$ .03
Knight, Ray	88SC	96	$ .01	$ .04
Knight, Ray	88SCTR	17	$ .01	$ .15
Knight, Ray	89SC	135	$ .01	$ .03
Knoblauch, Chuck	90SC	672	$ .10	$1.00
Knoblauch, Chuck	91SCTR	93	$ .05	$ .35
Knoblauch, Chuck	92SC	572	$ .05	$ .20
Knoblauch, Chuck	92SC	792	$ .01	$ .15
Knoblauch, Chuck	92SCP	119	$ .05	$ .25
Knoblauch, Chuck	92SCP	285	$ .05	$ .20
Knoblauch, Chuck	92SCP	307	$ .01	$ .15
Knoblauch, Chuck	93SC	148	$ .01	$ .15
Knoblauch, Chuck	93SCP	107	$ .05	$ .25
Knoblauch, Chuck	93SCS	36	$ .05	$ .20
Knudsen, Kurt	93SC	264	$ .01	$ .03
Knudsen, Kurt	93SCS	306	$ .01	$ .05
Knudson, Mark	90SC	539	$ .01	$ .04
Knudson, Mark	91SC	239	$ .01	$ .04
Knudson, Mark	92SC	373	$ .01	$ .04
Komminsk, Brad	90SC	496	$ .01	$ .04
Komminsk, Brad	90SCTR	53	$ .01	$ .05
Komminsk, Brad	91SC	259	$ .01	$ .04
Komminsk, Brad	92SC	735	$ .01	$ .04
Koslofski, Kevin	93SC	226	$ .01	$ .03
Koslofski, Kevin	93SCS	394	$ .01	$ .05
Kraemer, Joe	91SC	755	$ .01	$ .04
Kremers, Jimmy	91SC	736	$ .01	$ .04
Kreuter, Chad	89SC	638	$ .01	$ .10
Kreuter, Chad	90SC	406	$ .01	$ .04
Krueger, Bill	90SC	366	$ .01	$ .04
Krueger, Bill	91SC	598	$ .01	$ .10
Krueger, Bill	92SC	253	$ .01	$ .04
Krueger, Bill	92SCP	501	$ .01	$ .05
Kruk, John	88SC	36	$ .01	$ .10
Kruk, John	89SC	148	$ .01	$ .03
Kruk, John	89SCTR	70	$ .01	$ .05
Kruk, John	90SC	467	$ .01	$ .04
Kruk, John	91SC	94	$ .01	$ .04
Kruk, John	92SC	235	$ .01	$ .04
Kruk, John	92SCP	147	$ .01	$ .05
Kruk, John	93SCP	8	$ .01	$ .08
Kruk, John	93SCS	33	$ .01	$ .05
Krukow, Mike	88SC	185	$ .01	$ .04
Krukow, Mike	89SC	190	$ .01	$ .03
Krukow, Mike	90SC	215	$ .01	$ .04
Krux, John	93SC	79	$ .01	$ .03
Kunkel, Jeff	88SC	407	$ .01	$ .04
Kunkel, Jeff	89SC	484	$ .01	$ .03
Kunkel, Jeff	90SC	431	$ .01	$ .04
Kunkel, Jeff	91SC	783	$ .01	$ .04
Kutcher, Randy	90SC	551	$ .01	$ .04
Kutcher, Randy	91SC	837	$ .01	$ .04
Kutzler, Jerry	90SCTR	80	$ .01	$ .10
Kutzler, Jerry	91SC	749	$ .01	$ .04
LaCoss, Mike	88SC	465	$ .01	$ .04
LaCoss, Mike	89SC	500	$ .01	$ .03
LaCoss, Mike	90SC	253	$ .01	$ .04
LaCoss, Mike	91SC	652	$ .01	$ .04

SCORE

Player	Year	No.	VG	EX/MT	Player	Year	No.	VG	EX/MT
Lacy, Lee	88SC	173	$ .01	$ .04	Larkin, Barry	93SCP	306	$ .01	$ .15
Laga, Mike	89SC	536	$ .01	$ .03	Larkin, Barry	93SCS	23	$ .01	$ .15
Lake, Steve	88SC	596	$ .01	$ .04	Larkin, Gene	88SC	276	$ .01	$ .10
Lake, Steve	89SC	363	$ .01	$ .03	Larkin, Gene	89SC	280	$ .01	$ .03
Lake, Steve	89SCTR	12	$ .01	$ .05	Larkin, Gene	90SC	276	$ .01	$ .04
Lake, Steve	90SC	435	$ .01	$ .04	Larkin, Gene	91SC	471	$ .01	$ .04
Lake, Steve	91SC	572	$ .01	$ .04	Larkin, Gene	92SC	272	$ .01	$ .04
Lake, Steve	92SC	467	$ .01	$ .04	Larkin, Gene	92SCP	435	$ .01	$ .05
Lake, Steve	93SC	443	$ .01	$ .03	Larkin, Gene	93SC	444	$ .01	$ .03
Lamp, Dennis	88SC	616	$ .01	$ .04	Laudner, Tim	88SC	153	$ .01	$ .04
Lamp, Dennis	88SCTR	6	$ .01	$ .15	Laudner, Tim	89SC	134	$ .01	$ .03
Lamp, Dennis	89SC	508	$ .01	$ .03	Laudner, Tim	90SC	318	$ .01	$ .04
Lamp, Dennis	90SC	471	$ .01	$ .04	LaValliere, Mike	88SC	421	$ .01	$ .04
Lamp, Dennis	91SC	612	$ .01	$ .04	LaValliere, Mike	89SC	33	$ .01	$ .03
Lamp, Dennis	92SC	335	$ .01	$ .04	LaValliere, Mike	90SC	116	$ .01	$ .04
Lampkin, Tom	91SC	720	$ .01	$ .04	LaValliere, Mike	91SC	222	$ .01	$ .04
Lampkin, Tom	92SC	338	$ .01	$ .04	LaValliere, Mike	92SC	38	$ .01	$ .04
Lancaster, Les	88SC	602	$ .01	$ .10	LaValliere, Mike	92SCP	146	$ .01	$ .05
Lancaster, Les	89SC	60	$ .01	$ .03	LaValliere, Mike	93SC	83	$ .01	$ .03
Lancaster, Les	90SC	413	$ .01	$ .04	LaValliere, Mike	93SCP	219	$ .01	$ .08
Lancaster, Les	91SC	293	$ .01	$ .04	LaValliere, Mike	93SCS	203	$ .01	$ .05
Lancaster, Les	92SC	348	$ .01	$ .04	Law, Vance	88SC	85	$ .01	$ .04
Landreaux, Ken	88SC	247	$ .01	$ .04	Law, Vance	88SCTR	16	$ .01	$ .15
Landrum, Bill	90SC	456	$ .01	$ .04	Law, Vance	89SC	102	$ .01	$ .03
Landrum, Bill	91SC	98	$ .01	$ .04	Law, Vance	90SC	73	$ .01	$ .04
Landrum, Bill	92SC	196	$ .01	$ .04	Layana, Tim	90SCTR	107	$ .01	$ .10
Landrum, Bill	92SCP	116	$ .01	$ .05	Layana, Tim	91SC	64	$ .01	$ .10
Landrum, Ced	92SC	418	$ .01	$ .04	Layana, Tim	92SC	628	$ .01	$ .04
Langston, Mark	88SC	30	$ .01	$ .10	Lazorko, Jack	88SC	437	$ .01	$ .04
Langston, Mark	89SC	161	$ .01	$ .10	Lea, Charlie	89SC	501	$ .01	$ .03
Langston, Mark	89SCTR	25	$ .01	$ .10	Leach, Rick	88SC	257	$ .01	$ .04
Langston, Mark	90SC	401	$ .01	$ .10	Leach, Rick	89SC	540	$ .01	$ .03
Langston, Mark	90SCDT	688	$ .01	$ .10	Leach, Rick	90SC	426	$ .01	$ .04
Langston, Mark	90SCTR	11	$ .01	$ .05	Leach, Terry	88SC	203	$ .01	$ .04
Langston, Mark	91SC	21	$ .01	$ .04	Leach, Terry	89SC	431	$ .01	$ .03
Langston, Mark	91SCKM	411	$ .01	$ .05	Leach, Terry	89SCTR	24	$ .01	$ .05
Langston, Mark	91SCNH	699	$ .01	$ .04	Leach, Terry	90SC	502	$ .01	$ .04
Langston, Mark	92SC	12	$ .01	$ .04	Leach, Terry	90SCTR	43	$ .01	$ .05
Langston, Mark	92SCP	132	$ .01	$ .05	Leach, Terry	91SC	556	$ .01	$ .04
Langston, Mark	93SC	66	$ .01	$ .03	Leach, Terry	92SC	296	$ .01	$ .04
Langston, Mark	93SCP	56	$ .01	$ .08	Leach, Terry	93SC	479	$ .01	$ .03
Langston, Mark	93SCS	52	$ .01	$ .05	Leary, Tim	88SC	224	$ .01	$ .04
Lankford, Ray	90SCTR	84	$ .10	$1.00	Leary, Tim	89SC	429	$ .01	$ .03
Lankford, Ray	91SC	731	$ .05	$ .35	Leary, Tim	89SCTR	52	$ .01	$ .05
Lankford, Ray	92SC	223	$ .01	$ .15	Leary, Tim	90SC	504	$ .01	$ .04
Lankford, Ray	92SCP	126	$ .05	$ .35	Leary, Tim	90SCTR	27	$ .01	$ .05
Lankford, Ray	93SC	56	$ .01	$ .10	Leary, Tim	91SC	631	$ .01	$ .04
Lankford, Ray	93SCP	116	$ .05	$ .25	Leary, Tim	92SC	286	$ .01	$ .04
Lankford, Ray	93SCS	155	$ .01	$ .15	Leary, Tim	92SCP	349	$ .01	$ .05
Lansford, Carney	88SC	253	$ .01	$ .04	Lee, Manny	88SC	561	$ .01	$ .04
Lansford, Carney	89SC	179	$ .01	$ .03	Lee, Manny	89SC	326	$ .01	$ .03
Lansford, Carney	90SC	296	$ .01	$ .04	Lee, Manny	90SC	482	$ .01	$ .04
Lansford, Carney	91SC	630	$ .01	$ .04	Lee, Manny	91SC	534	$ .01	$ .04
Lansford, Carney	92SC	648	$ .01	$ .04	Lee, Manny	92SC	518	$ .01	$ .04
Lansford, Carney	92SCP	455	$ .01	$ .05	Lee, Manuel	92SCP	245	$ .01	$ .05
Lansford, Carney	93SCS	156	$ .01	$ .05	Lee, Manuel	93SC	205	$ .01	$ .03
LaPoint, Dave	88SC	580	$ .01	$ .04	Lee, Manuel	93SCS	380	$ .01	$ .05
LaPoint, Dave	89SC	384	$ .01	$ .03	Lee, Mark	91SC	372	$ .01	$ .10
LaPoint, Dave	89SCTR	4	$ .01	$ .05	Lee, Mark	92SC	277	$ .01	$ .04
LaPoint, Dave	90SC	357	$ .01	$ .04	Lefferts, Craig	88SC	553	$ .01	$ .04
LaPoint, Dave	91SC	218	$ .01	$ .04	Lefferts, Craig	89SC	178	$ .01	$ .03
Larkin, Barry	88SC	72	$ .05	$ .25	Lefferts, Craig	90SC	209	$ .01	$ .04
Larkin, Barry	89SC	31	$ .01	$ .15	Lefferts, Craig	90SCTR	22	$ .01	$ .05
Larkin, Barry	90SC	155	$ .01	$ .15	Lefferts, Craig	91SC	184	$ .01	$ .04
Larkin, Barry	90SCDT	689	$ .01	$ .10	Lefferts, Craig	92SC	175	$ .01	$ .04
Larkin, Barry	91SC	505	$ .01	$ .10	Lefferts, Craig	92SCP	478	$ .01	$ .05
Larkin, Barry	91SCAS	666	$ .01	$ .10	Lefferts, Craig	93SC	435	$ .01	$ .03
Larkin, Barry	91SCBC	2	$ .10	$1.00	Lefferts, Craig	93SCS	373	$ .01	$ .05
Larkin, Barry	91SCDT	888	$ .05	$ .20	Leibrandt, Charlie	88SC	61	$ .01	$ .04
Larkin, Barry	92SC	100	$ .01	$ .10	Leibrandt, Charlie	89SC	133	$ .01	$ .03
Larkin, Barry	92SCAS	775	$ .05	$ .04	Leibrandt, Charlie	90SC	82	$ .01	$ .04
Larkin, Barry	92SCP	5	$ .05	$ .20	Leibrandt, Charlie	91SC	536	$ .01	$ .04
Larkin, Barry	93SC	16	$ .01	$ .10	Leibrandt, Charlie	92SC	105	$ .01	$ .04
Larkin, Barry	93SCP	22	$ .05	$ .20	Leibrandt, Charlie	92SCP	423	$ .01	$ .05
Larkin, Barry	93SCP	300	$ .05	$ .20	Leibrandt, Charlie	93SC	393	$ .01	$ .03

SCORE

Player	Year	No.	VG	EX/MT	Player	Year	No.	VG	EX/MT
Leibrandt, Charlie	93SCP	115	$ .01	$ .08	Liriano, Nelson	91SC	288	$ .01	$ .04
Leibrandt, Charlie	93SCS	209	$ .01	$ .05	Listach, Pat	92SCP	562	$ .15	$1.25
Leiper, Dave	88SC	348	$ .01	$ .04	Listach, Pat	92SCTR	80	$ .15	$1.50
Leiper, Dave	89SC	515	$ .01	$ .03	Listach, Pat	93SC	357	$ .05	$ .35
Leiper, Dave	90SC	212	$ .01	$ .04	Listach, Pat	93SC	485	$ .01	$ .15
Leiter, Al	88SCTR	97	$ .05	$ .25	Listach, Pat	93SCP	33	$ .10	$1.00
Leiter, Al	89SC	580	$ .01	$ .15	Listach, Pat	93SCS	273	$ .10	$ .50
Leiter, Mark	91SC	727	$ .01	$ .10	Litton, Greg	89SCTR	86	$ .01	$ .15
Leiter, Mark	92SC	626	$ .01	$ .04	Litton, Greg	90SC	497	$ .01	$ .04
Leius, Scott	91SC	370	$ .01	$ .10	Litton, Greg	91SC	533	$ .01	$ .04
Leius, Scott	92SC	320	$ .01	$ .04	Litton, Greg	92SC	603	$ .01	$ .04
Leius, Scott	92SCP	365	$ .01	$ .05	Livingstone, Scott	92SC	414	$ .01	$ .10
Leius, Scott	93SC	178	$ .01	$ .03	Livingstone, Scott	92SCP	490	$ .01	$ .10
Leius, Scott	93SCP	192	$ .01	$ .08	Livingstone, Scott	93SC	196	$ .01	$ .03
Leius, Scott	93SCS	251	$ .01	$ .05	Livingstone, Scott	93SCP	106	$ .01	$ .08
Lemke, Mark	90SC	593	$ .01	$ .04	Livingstone, Scott	93SCS	320	$ .01	$ .05
Lemke, Mark	91SC	779	$ .01	$ .04	Livsey, Shawn	92SCP	545	$ .01	$ .10
Lemke, Mark	92SC	386	$ .01	$ .04	Lofton, Kenny	92SC	845	$ .10	$ .40
Lemke, Mark	92SCP	426	$ .01	$ .05	Lofton, Kenny	92SCP	290	$ .05	$ .35
Lemke, Mark	93SC	147	$ .01	$ .03	Lofton, Kenny	92SCP	582	$ .10	$ .50
Lemke, Mark	93SCS	161	$ .01	$ .05	Lofton, Kenny	92SCTR	14	$ .10	$ .75
Lemon, Chet	88SC	119	$ .01	$ .04	Lofton, Kenny	93SC	58	$ .01	$ .15
Lemon, Chet	89SC	44	$ .01	$ .03	Lofton, Kenny	93SCP	40	$ .10	$ .40
Lemon, Chet	90SC	106	$ .01	$ .04	Lofton, Kenny	93SCS	275	$ .05	$ .25
Lemon, Chet	91SC	557	$ .01	$ .04	Lombardozzi, Steve	88SC	174	$ .01	$ .04
Lennon, Patrick	92SCP	542	$ .01	$ .10	Lombardozzi, Steve	89SC	421	$ .01	$ .03
Leonard, Jeffrey	88SC	580	$ .01	$ .04	Long, Bill	88SC	539	$ .01	$ .04
Leonard, Jeff	89SC	557	$ .01	$ .03	Long, Bill	89SC	351	$ .01	$ .03
Leonard, Jeffrey	89SCTR	7	$ .01	$ .05	Long, Bill	90SC	526	$ .01	$ .05
Leonard, Jeffrey	90SC	98	$ .01	$ .04	Long, Bill	90SCTR	62	$ .01	$ .05
Leonard, Jeffrey	91SC	44	$ .01	$ .04	Long, Bill	91SC	559	$ .01	$ .04
Leonard, Mark	91SC	719	$ .01	$ .10	Lopes, Davey	88SC	489	$ .01	$ .04
Leonard, Mark	92SC	499	$ .01	$ .04	Lopez, Luis	91SCTR	109	$ .01	$ .15
Leonard, Mark	92SCP	233	$ .01	$ .05	Lopez, Luis	92SC	716	$ .01	$ .04
Leonard, Mark	93SC	381	$ .01	$ .03	Lowe, Sean	93SC	493	$ .01	$ .15
Levis, Jesse	93SC	330	$ .01	$ .10	Lowe, Sean	93SCS	356	$ .05	$ .25
Levis, Jesse	93SCP	288	$ .01	$ .10	Loynd, Mike	88SC	491	$ .01	$ .04
Lewis, Darren	91SC	350	$ .01	$ .15	Lusader, Scott	90SC	575	$ .01	$ .04
Lewis, Darren	92SC	562	$ .01	$ .04	Lynch, Ed	88SC	506	$ .01	$ .04
Lewis, Darren	92SCP	408	$ .01	$ .05	Lynn, Fred	88SC	42	$ .01	$ .10
Lewis, Darren	93SC	203	$ .01	$ .03	Lynn, Fred	89SC	126	$ .01	$ .03
Lewis, Darren	93SCP	94	$ .01	$ .08	Lynn, Fred	90SC	131	$ .01	$ .04
Lewis, Jim	92SC	852	$ .01	$ .15	Lynn, Fred	90SCTR	20	$ .01	$ .05
Lewis, Mark	91SCTR	106	$ .01	$ .10	Lynn, Fred	91SC	554	$ .01	$ .04
Lewis, Mark	92SC	528	$ .01	$ .04	Lyons, Barry	88SC	387	$ .01	$ .04
Lewis, Mark	92SCP	91	$ .01	$ .05	Lyons, Barry	89SC	456	$ .01	$ .03
Lewis, Mark	93SC	164	$ .01	$ .03	Lyons, Barry	90SC	29	$ .01	$ .04
Lewis, Mark	93SCS	150	$ .01	$ .05	Lyons, Steve	89SC	388	$ .01	$ .04
Lewis, Scott	91SC	759	$ .01	$ .10	Lyons, Steve	90SC	88	$ .01	$ .04
Lewis, Scott	92SC	165	$ .01	$ .04	Lyons, Steve	91SC	269	$ .01	$ .04
Leyritz, Jim	90SCTR	83	$ .01	$ .10	Lyons, Steve	92SC	294	$ .01	$ .04
Leyritz, Jim	91SC	65	$ .01	$ .10	Maas, Kevin	90SC	606	$ .05	$ .25
Lieberthal, Mike	91SC	683	$ .05	$ .20	Maas, Kevin	91SC	600	$ .01	$ .10
Lilliquist, Derek	89SC	631	$ .01	$ .15	Maas, Kevin	92SC	613	$ .01	$ .04
Lilliquist, Derek	90SC	243	$ .01	$ .10	Maas, Kevin	92SCP	90	$ .01	$ .05
Lilliquist, Derek	91SC	571	$ .01	$ .04	Maas, Kevin	93SC	634	$ .01	$ .03
Lilliquist, Derek	92SCTR	44	$ .01	$ .05	Maas, Kevin	93SCP	165	$ .01	$ .08
Lilliquist, Derek	93SC	548	$ .01	$ .03	Maas, Kevin	93SCS	142	$ .01	$ .05
Lind, Jose	88SC	597	$ .01	$ .15	MacDonald, Bob	92SC	405	$ .01	$ .04
Lind, Jose	89SC	87	$ .01	$ .10	Macfarlane, Mike	88SCTR	76	$ .15	$1.50
Lind, Jose	90SC	83	$ .01	$ .10	Macfarlane, Mike	89SC	319	$ .01	$ .15
Lind, Jose	91SC	461	$ .01	$ .04	Macfarlane, Mike	91SC	839	$ .01	$ .04
Lind, Jose	92SC	265	$ .01	$ .04	Macfarlane, Mike	92SC	27	$ .01	$ .04
Lind, Jose	92SCP	49	$ .01	$ .05	Macfarlane, Mike	92SCP	517	$ .01	$ .05
Lind, Jose	92SCP	603	$ .01	$ .05	MacFarlane, Mike	93SC	323	$ .01	$ .03
Lind, Jose	93SC	660	$ .01	$ .03	Machado, Julio	90SCTR	92	$ .01	$ .04
Lind, Jose	93SCP	103	$ .01	$ .08	Mack, Shane	88SC	414	$ .05	$ .25
Lind, Jose	93SCS	105	$ .01	$ .05	Mack, Shane	89SC	270	$ .01	$ .03
Lindeman, Jim	88SC	302	$ .01	$ .04	Mack, Shane	91SC	284	$ .01	$ .04
Lindeman, Jim	92SC	321	$ .01	$ .04	Mack, Shane	92SC	284	$ .01	$ .04
Lindros, Eric	90SCTR	100	$1.75	$7.00	Mack, Shane	92SCP	230	$ .01	$ .05
Linton, Doug	93SC	295	$ .01	$ .03	Mack, Shane	93SC	19	$ .01	$ .04
Liriano, Nelson	88SC	621	$ .01	$ .04	Mack, Shane	93SCP	78	$ .01	$ .08
Liriano, Nelson	89SC	577	$ .01	$ .03	Mack, Shane	93SCS	104	$ .01	$ .05
Liriano, Nelson	90SC	77	$ .01	$ .04	Maddux, Greg	89SC	119	$ .05	$ .25

SCORE

Player	Year	No.	VG	EX/MT
Maddux, Greg	90SC	403	$ .05	$ .20
Maddux, Greg	91SC	317	$ .01	$ .10
Maddux, Greg	92SC	269	$ .01	$ .04
Maddux, Greg	92SCP	65	$ .05	$ .20
Maddux, Greg	92SCP	608	$ .01	$ .10
Maddux, Greg	93SC	484	$ .01	$ .03
Maddux, Greg	93SC	527	$ .01	$ .03
Maddux, Greg	93SC	576	$ .01	$ .10
Maddux, Greg	93SCS	31	$ .01	$ .15
Maddux, Mike	89SC	393	$ .01	$ .03
Maddux, Mike	92SC	313	$ .01	$ .04
Maddux, Mike	92SCP	489	$ .01	$ .05
Maddux, Mike	93SC	451	$ .01	$ .03
Madlock, Bill	88SC	445	$ .01	$ .04
Magadan, Dave	88SC	41	$ .01	$ .10
Magadan, Dave	89SC	312	$ .01	$ .10
Magadan, Dave	90SC	46	$ .01	$ .04
Magadan, Dave	91SC	190	$ .01	$ .04
Magadan, Dave	92SC	201	$ .01	$ .04
Magadan, Dave	92SCP	201	$ .01	$ .05
Magadan, Dave	93SC	631	$ .01	$ .03

Dave Magadan

Player	Year	No.	VG	EX/MT
Magadan, Dave	93SCP	237	$ .01	$ .08
Magadan, Dave	93SCS	149	$ .01	$ .05
Magnante, Mike	92SC	739	$ .01	$ .10
Magrane, Joe	88SC	94	$ .01	$ .10
Magrane, Joe	89SC	460	$ .01	$ .10
Magrane, Joe	90SC	17	$ .01	$ .04
Magrane, Joe	91SC	575	$ .01	$ .04
Magrane, Joe	92SCP	494	$ .01	$ .05
Mahler, Rick	88SC	319	$ .01	$ .04
Mahler, Rick	89SC	229	$ .01	$ .03
Mahler, Rick	89SCTR	79	$ .01	$ .05
Mahler, Rick	90SC	87	$ .01	$ .04
Mahler, Rick	91SC	464	$ .01	$ .04
Mahomes, Pat	92SCP	472	$ .05	$ .35
Mahomes, Pat	92SCTR	102	$ .05	$ .25
Mahomes, Pat	93SC	337	$ .01	$ .15
Mahomes, Pat	93SCS	324	$ .01	$ .15
Maldonado, Candy	88SC	54	$ .01	$ .04
Maldonado, Candy	89SC	47	$ .01	$ .03
Maldonado, Candy	90SC	138	$ .01	$ .04
Maldonado, Candy	90SCTR	8	$ .01	$ .05
Maldonado, Candy	91SC	93	$ .01	$ .04
Maldonado, Candy	91SCTR	28	$ .01	$ .05
Maldonado, Candy	92SC	591	$ .01	$ .04
Maldonado, Candy	93SC	615	$ .01	$ .03
Maldonado, Candy	93SCS	110	$ .01	$ .05
Mallicoat, Rob	92SC	819	$ .01	$ .04
Mallicoat, Rob	93SC	253	$ .01	$ .03
Malone, Chuck	91SC	724	$ .01	$ .04
Mann, Kelly	90SC	627	$ .01	$ .10
Manning, Rick	88SC	593	$ .01	$ .04
Manrique, Fred	88SC	139	$ .01	$ .04
Manrique, Fred	89SC	457	$ .01	$ .03
Manrique, Fred	90SC	166	$ .01	$ .04
Manto, Jeff	91SC	337	$ .01	$ .10
Manto, Jeff	92SC	666	$ .01	$ .04
Manuel, Barry	93SC	225	$ .01	$ .03
Manuel, Barry	93SCP	257	$ .01	$ .08
Manwaring, Kirt	88SC	627	$ .01	$ .10
Manwaring, Kirt	89SC	619	$ .01	$ .03
Manwaring, Kirt	90SC	146	$ .01	$ .04
Manwaring, Kirt	91SC	101	$ .01	$ .04
Manwaring, Kirt	92SC	636	$ .01	$ .04
Manwaring, Kirt	92SCP	181	$ .01	$ .05
Manwaring, Kirt	93SC	179	$ .01	$ .03
Manwaring, Kirt	93SCP	122	$ .01	$ .08
Manwaring, Kirt	93SCS	247	$ .01	$ .05
Manzanillo, Josias	92SC	838	$ .01	$ .10
Marak, Paul	91SC	712	$ .01	$ .04
Marsh, Tom	93SC	263	$ .01	$ .03
Marsh, Tom	93SCP	256	$ .01	$ .08
Marshall, Mike	88SC	135	$ .01	$ .10
Marshall, Mike	89SC	186	$ .01	$ .03
Marshall, Mike	90SC	384	$ .01	$ .04
Marshall, Mike	91SC	617	$ .01	$ .04
Martin, Al	93SC	322	$ .05	$ .20
Martinez, Carlos	89SCTR	103	$ .01	$ .15
Martinez, Carlos	90SC	314	$ .01	$ .04
Martinez, Carlos	91SC	274	$ .01	$ .04
Martinez, Carlos	92SC	593	$ .01	$ .04
Martinez, Carmelo	88SC	181	$ .01	$ .04
Martinez, Carmelo	89SC	517	$ .01	$ .03
Martinez, Carmelo	90SC	114	$ .01	$ .04
Martinez, Carmelo	90SCTR	10	$ .01	$ .05
Martinez, Carmelo	91SC	792	$ .01	$ .04
Martinez, Carmelo	92SC	686	$ .01	$ .04
Martinez, Chito	92SC	400	$ .01	$ .15
Martinez, Chito	92SCP	380	$ .01	$ .05
Martinez, Chito	93SC	638	$ .01	$ .03
Martinez, Chito	93SCP	214	$ .01	$ .08
Martinez, Dave	88SC	223	$ .01	$ .04
Martinez, Dave	89SC	77	$ .01	$ .03
Martinez, Dave	90SC	27	$ .01	$ .04
Martinez, Dave	91SC	82	$ .01	$ .04
Martinez, Dave	92SC	501	$ .01	$ .04
Martinez, Dave	92SCP	397	$ .01	$ .05
Martinez, Dave	92SCTR	33	$ .01	$ .05
Martinez, Dave	93SC	601	$ .01	$ .03
Martinez, Dave	93SCP	132	$ .01	$ .08
Martinez, Dennis	88SC	601	$ .01	$ .04
Martinez, Dennis	89SC	114	$ .01	$ .03
Martinez, Dennis	90SC	47	$ .01	$ .04
Martinez, Dennis	91SC	454	$ .01	$ .04
Martinez, Dennis	92SC	470	$ .01	$ .04
Martinez, Dennis	92SC	783	$ .01	$ .04
Martinez, Dennis	92SC	784	$ .01	$ .04
Martinez, Dennis	92SCP	77	$ .01	$ .05
Martinez, Dennis	93SC	75	$ .01	$ .03
Martinez, Dennis	93SCP	38	$ .01	$ .08
Martinez, Dennis	93SCP	291	$ .01	$ .08
Martinez, Dennis	93SCS	147	$ .01	$ .05
Martinez, Domingo	93SC	257	$ .01	$ .15
Martinez, Edgar	89SC	637	$ .10	$ .50
Martinez, Edgar	90SC	324	$ .05	$ .25
Martinez, Edgar	91SC	264	$ .01	$ .04
Martinez, Edgar	92SC	485	$ .01	$ .04
Martinez, Edgar	92SCP	13	$ .01	$ .05

SCORE

Player	Year	No.	VG	EX/MT	Player	Year	No.	VG	EX/MT
Martinez, Edgar	93SC	49	$ .01	$ .03	McClendon, Lloyd	90SC	176	$ .01	$ .04
Martinez, Edgar	93SC	502	$ .01	$ .03	McClendon, Lloyd	92SC	566	$ .01	$ .04
Martinez, Edgar	93SCP	17	$ .01	$ .08	McClendon, Lloyd	93SC	380	$ .01	$ .03
Martinez, Edgar	93SCS	82	$ .01	$ .05	McClure, Bob	88SC	381	$ .01	$ .04
Martinez, Pedro	93SC	321	$ .01	$ .10	McClure, Bob	89SC	572	$ .01	$ .03
Martinez, Pedro	93SCP	259	$ .05	$ .20	McClure, Bob	89SCTR	58	$ .01	$ .05
Martinez, Ramon	89SC	635	$ .10	$ .50	McClure, Bob	90SC	117	$ .01	$ .04
Martinez, Ramon	90SC	461	$ .05	$ .20	McClure, Bob	92SC	717	$ .01	$ .04
Martinez, Ramon	91SC	300	$ .01	$ .10	McClure, Bob	93SC	434	$ .01	$ .03
Martinez, Ramon	91SCHL	419	$ .01	$ .10	McCray, Rodney	91SC	763	$ .01	$ .04
Martinez, Ramon	91SCKM	408	$ .01	$ .10	McCray, Rodney	92SC	517	$ .01	$ .04
Martinez, Ramon	92SC	610	$ .01	$ .10	McCullers, Lance	88SC	150	$ .01	$ .04
Martinez, Ramon	92SCAS	780	$ .01	$ .04	McCullers, Lance	89SC	158	$ .01	$ .03
Martinez, Ramon	92SCP	429	$ .01	$ .05	McCullers, Lance	89SCTR	63	$ .01	$ .05
Martinez, Ramon	93SC	199	$ .01	$ .03	McCullers, Lance	90SC	186	$ .01	$ .04
Martinez, Ramon	93SCS	213	$ .01	$ .05	McCullers, Lance	91SC	313	$ .01	$ .04
Martinez, Tino	90SC	596	$ .05	$ .20	McDaniel, Terry	92SC	765	$ .01	$ .10
Martinez, Tino	91SC	798	$ .01	$ .10					
Martinez, Tino	92SC	596	$ .01	$ .04					
Martinez, Tino	92SCP	123	$ .01	$ .10					
Martinez, Tino	93SC	76	$ .01	$ .03					
Martinez, Tino	93SCP	213	$ .01	$ .08					
Martinez, Tino	93SCS	246	$ .01	$ .05					
Marzano, John	88SC	584	$ .05	$ .25					
Marzano, John	91SC	831	$ .01	$ .04					
Marzano, John	92SC	539	$ .01	$ .04					
Mason, Roger	92SC	727	$ .01	$ .04					
Mason, Roger	93SC	441	$ .01	$ .03					
Mathews, Greg	88SC	226	$ .01	$ .04					
Mathews, Greg	89SC	286	$ .01	$ .03					
Mathews, Greg	90SC	537	$ .01	$ .04					
Mathews, Terry	92SC	737	$ .01	$ .10					
Matthews, Gary	88SC	599	$ .01	$ .04					
Mattingly, Don	88SC	1	$ .05	$ .25					
Mattingly, Don	88SC	650	$ .01	$ .15					
Mattingly, Don	88SC	658	$ .01	$ .15					
Mattingly, Don	89SC	100	$ .05	$ .25					
Mattingly, Don	90SC	1	$ .05	$ .20					
Mattingly, Don	91SC	23	$ .01	$ .10					
Mattingly, Don	91SCTF	856	$ .01	$ .10					
Mattingly, Don	92SC	23	$ .01	$ .10					
Mattingly, Don	92SCP	23	$ .05	$ .25					
Mattingly, Don	92SCP	584	$ .05	$ .20					
Mattingly, Don	93SC	23	$ .01	$ .10					
Mattingly, Don	93SCP	23	$ .05	$ .20					
Mattingly, Don	93SCS	24	$ .01	$ .15					
Matuszek, Len	88SC	424	$ .01	$ .04					
Maurer, Rob	92SC	767	$ .01	$ .15	McDonald, Ben	90SC	680	$ .10	$ .50
Maurer, Rob	92SCP	273	$ .01	$ .15	McDonald, Ben	91SC	645	$ .01	$ .10
Mauser, Tim	92SC	744	$ .01	$ .10	McDonald, Ben	92SC	658	$ .01	$ .10
May, Derrick	91SC	379	$ .05	$ .20	McDonald, Ben	92SCP	44	$ .01	$ .10
May, Derrick	92SCP	534	$ .01	$ .05	McDonald, Ben	93SC	202	$ .01	$ .03
May, Derrick	93SC	213	$ .01	$ .03	McDonald, Ben	93SCP	72	$ .01	$ .15
May, Derrick	93SCS	402	$ .01	$ .05	McDonald, Ben	93SCS	224	$ .01	$ .10
Mayne, Brent	90SC	664	$ .01	$ .15	McDowell, Jack	88SCTR	85	$3.75	$15.00
Mayne, Brent	91SC	765	$ .01	$ .04	McDowell, Jack	89SC	289	$ .05	$ .35
Mayne, Brent	92SC	84	$ .01	$ .04	McDowell, Jack	91SC	27	$ .01	$ .10
Mayne, Brent	92SCP	469	$ .01	$ .05	McDowell, Jack	92SC	62	$ .01	$ .04
Maysey, Matt	93SC	316	$ .01	$ .03	McDowell, Jack	92SCP	107	$ .01	$ .10
Mazzilli, Lee	88SC	158	$ .01	$ .04	McDowell, Jack	92SCP	291	$ .01	$ .10
Mazzilli, Lee	89SC	217	$ .01	$ .03	McDowell, Jack	92SCP	607	$ .01	$ .05
Mazzilli, Lee	90SC	459	$ .01	$ .04	McDowell, Jack	93SC	70	$ .01	$ .03
McCament, Randy	90SC	580	$ .01	$ .04	McDowell, Jack	93SCP	80	$ .01	$ .08
McCaskill, Kirk	88SC	552	$ .01	$ .04	McDowell, Jack	93SCS	196	$ .01	$ .05
McCaskill, Kirk	89SC	181	$ .01	$ .03	McDowell, Oddibe	88SC	215	$ .01	$ .04
McCaskill, Kirk	90SC	217	$ .01	$ .04	McDowell, Oddibe	89SC	59	$ .01	$ .03
McCaskill, Kirk	91SC	590	$ .01	$ .04	McDowell, Oddibe	89SCTR	72	$ .01	$ .05
McCaskill, Kirk	92SC	79	$ .01	$ .04	McDowell, Oddibe	90SC	476	$ .01	$ .04
McCaskill, Kirk	92SCP	391	$ .01	$ .05	McDowell, Oddibe	91SC	121	$ .01	$ .04
McCaskill, Kirk	92SCTR	29	$ .01	$ .05	McDowell, Roger	88SC	188	$ .01	$ .04
McCaskill, Kirk	93SC	469	$ .01	$ .03	McDowell, Roger	89SC	281	$ .01	$ .03
McCaskill, Kirk	93SCS	387	$ .01	$ .05	McDowell, Roger	89SCTR	53	$ .01	$ .05
McClellan, Paul	91SC	726	$ .01	$ .04	McDowell, Roger	90SC	445	$ .01	$ .04
McClellan, Paul	92SC	703	$ .01	$ .04	McDowell, Roger	91SC	537	$ .01	$ .04
McClendon, Lloyd	89SC	521	$ .01	$ .03					

Player	Year	No.	VG	EX/MT	Player	Year	No.	VG	EX/MT
McDowell, Roger	92SC	597	$ .01	$ .04	Meacham, Rusty	92SCP	600	$ .01	$ .05
McDowell, Roger	92SCP	445	$ .01	$ .05	Meacham, Rusty	93SC	378	$ .01	$ .03
McDowell, Roger	93SC	605	$ .01	$ .03	Meacham, Rusty	93SCP	149	$ .01	$ .08
McDowell, Roger	93SCS	375	$ .01	$ .05	Meacham, Rusty	93SCS	277	$ .01	$ .05
McElroy, Chuck	91SC	374	$ .01	$ .04	Meads, Dave	88SC	243	$ .01	$ .04
McElroy, Chuck	92SC	366	$ .01	$ .04	Meads, Dave	89SC	593	$ .01	$ .03
McElroy, Chuck	92SCP	329	$ .01	$ .05	Medina, Luis	89SC	633	$ .05	$ .30
McElroy, Chuck	93SC	389	$ .01	$ .03	Melendez, Jose	92SC	397	$ .01	$ .04
McGaffigan, Andy	88SC	366	$ .01	$ .04	Melendez, Jose	92SCP	536	$ .01	$ .10
McGaffigan, Andy	89SC	138	$ .01	$ .03	Melvin, Bob	88SC	477	$ .01	$ .04
McGaffigan, Andy	90SC	224	$ .01	$ .04	Melvin, Bob	89SC	617	$ .01	$ .03
McGaffigan, Andy	91SC	619	$ .01	$ .04	Melvin, Bob	89SCTR	61	$ .01	$ .05
McGee, Willie	88SC	40	$ .01	$ .10	Melvin, Bob	90SC	453	$ .01	$ .04
McGee, Willie	89SC	88	$ .01	$ .03	Melvin, Bob	92SC	208	$ .01	$ .04
McGee, Willie	90SC	374	$ .01	$ .04	Melvin, Bob	92SCTR	73	$ .01	$ .05
McGee, Willie	91SC	597	$ .01	$ .04	Merced, Orlando	91SC	747	$ .05	$ .25
McGee, Willie	91SCTR	19	$ .01	$ .05	Merced, Orlando	92SC	153	$ .01	$ .10
McGee, Willie	92SC	112	$ .01	$ .04	Merced, Orlando	92SCP	62	$ .01	$ .10
McGee, Willie	92SCP	7	$ .01	$ .05	Merced, Orlando	93SC	137	$ .01	$ .03
McGee, Willie	93SC	93	$ .01	$ .03	Merced, Orlando	93SCP	160	$ .01	$ .08
McGee, Willie	93SCP	39	$ .01	$ .08	Merced, Orlando	93SCS	183	$ .01	$ .05
McGee, Willie	93SCS	119	$ .01	$ .05	Mercedes, Henry	93SC	290	$ .01	$ .10
McGill, Fred	93SCP	71	$ .05	$ .20	Mercedes, Henry	93SCP	268	$ .01	$ .08
McGregor, Scott	88SC	315	$ .01	$ .04	Mercedes, Luis	92SC	826	$ .01	$ .10
McGriff, Fred	88SC	107	$ .10	$ .40	Mercedes, Luis	92SCP	248	$ .01	$ .10
McGriff, Fred	89SC	6	$ .05	$ .25	Mercedes, Luis	93SCS	331	$ .01	$ .05
McGriff, Fred	90SC	271	$ .05	$ .20	Mercker, Kent	90SCTR	72	$ .01	$ .15
McGriff, Fred	91SC	480	$ .01	$ .10	Mercker, Kent	91SC	79	$ .01	$ .10
McGriff, Fred	91SCMB	404	$ .01	$ .10	Mercker, Kent	92SC	178	$ .01	$ .04
McGriff, Fred	91SCTR	58	$ .01	$ .15	Mercker, Kent	92SC	787	$ .01	$ .04
McGriff, Fred	92SC	7	$ .01	$ .10	Merullo, Matt	90SC	605	$ .01	$ .04
McGriff, Fred	92SCP	112	$ .05	$ .25	Merullo, Matt	92SC	367	$ .01	$ .04
McGriff, Fred	93SC	44	$ .01	$ .15	Mesa, Jose	92SC	707	$ .01	$ .04
McGriff, Fred	93SC	528	$ .01	$ .10	Mesa, Jose	92SCP	496	$ .01	$ .05
McGriff, Fred	93SCS	19	$ .01	$ .15	Mesa, Jose	93SC	424	$ .01	$ .03
McGriff, Terry	88SC	281	$ .01	$ .04	Meulens, Hensley	90SC	636	$ .01	$ .10
McGwire, Mark	88SC	5	$ .10	$ .40	Meulens, Hensley	91SC	828	$ .01	$ .04
McGwire, Mark	88SC	648	$ .05	$ .25	Meulens, Hensley	92SC	89	$ .01	$ .04
McGwire, Mark	88SC	659	$ .05	$ .25	Meulens, Hensley	92SCP	366	$ .01	$ .05
McGwire, Mark	89SC	3	$ .05	$ .35	Meulens, Hensley	93SC	595	$ .01	$ .03
McGwire, Mark	90SC	385	$ .05	$ .25	Meulens, Hensley	93SCP	124	$ .01	$ .08
McGwire, Mark	91SC	324	$ .01	$ .15	Meyer, Joey	88SCTR	75	$ .01	$ .15
McGwire, Mark	92SC	20	$ .05	$ .25	Meyer, Joey	89SC	374	$ .01	$ .03
McGwire, Mark	92SCP	217	$ .10	$ .40	Meyer, Joey	90SC	532	$ .01	$ .04
McGwire, Mark	93SC	557	$ .05	$ .20	Mickey, Brantley	88SC	213	$ .01	$ .04
McGwire, Mark	93SCP	58	$ .10	$ .40	Mielke, Gary	90SC	574	$ .01	$ .04
McGwire, Mark	93SCS	16	$ .05	$ .25	Mielke, Gary	91SC	167	$ .01	$ .04
McIntosh, Tim	91SC	347	$ .01	$ .10	Milacki, Bob	89SC	651	$ .01	$ .15
McIntosh, Tim	92SC	469	$ .01	$ .04	Milacki, Bob	90SC	239	$ .01	$ .04
McIntosh, Tim	93SCS	334	$ .01	$ .05	Milacki, Bob	91SC	512	$ .01	$ .04
McKnight, Jeff	91SC	369	$ .01	$ .10	Milacki, Bob	92SC	314	$ .01	$ .04
McLemore, Mark	88SC	152	$ .01	$ .04	Milacki, Bob	92SC	427	$ .01	$ .04
McLemore, Mark	89SC	208	$ .01	$ .03	Milacki, Bob	92SCP	339	$ .01	$ .05
McLemore, Mark	93SCP	184	$ .01	$ .08	Militello, Sam	92SCTR	82	$ .05	$ .35
McMurtry, Craig	91SC	602	$ .01	$ .04	Militello, Sam	93SC	351	$ .01	$ .15
McRae, Brian	91SC	331	$ .05	$ .20	Militello, Sam	93SCP	225	$ .10	$ .50
McRae, Brian	92SC	478	$ .01	$ .15	Militello, Sam	93SCS	315	$ .05	$ .25
McRae, Brian	92SCP	117	$ .01	$ .10	Miller, Darrell	88SC	463	$ .01	$ .04
McRae, Brian	93SC	128	$ .01	$ .03	Miller, Darrell	89SC	499	$ .01	$ .03
McRae, Brian	93SCS	250	$ .01	$ .05	Miller, Keith	88SC	639	$ .05	$ .20
McReynolds, Kevin	88SC	21	$ .01	$ .10	Miller, Keith	89SC	464	$ .01	$ .03
McReynolds, Kevin	89SC	93	$ .01	$ .03	Miller, Keith	90SC	559	$ .01	$ .04
McReynolds, Kevin	90SC	5	$ .01	$ .04	Miller, Keith	91SC	318	$ .01	$ .04
McReynolds, Kevin	91SC	327	$ .01	$ .04	Miller, Keith	92SC	462	$ .01	$ .04
McReynolds, Kevin	92SC	168	$ .01	$ .04	Miller, Keith	92SCP	403	$ .01	$ .05
McReynolds, Kevin	92SCP	427	$ .01	$ .05	Miller, Keith	92SCTR	50	$ .01	$ .05
McReynolds, Kevin	92SCTR	31	$ .01	$ .05	Miller, Keith	93SC	96	$ .01	$ .03
McReynolds, Kevin	93SC	69	$ .01	$ .03	Miller, Keith	93SCS	54	$ .01	$ .05
McReynolds, Kevin	93SCP	164	$ .01	$ .08	Miller, Kurt	91SC	682	$ .05	$ .25
McReynolds, Kevin	93SCS	176	$ .01	$ .05	Miller, Paul	93SC	239	$ .01	$ .03
McWilliams, Larry	88SCTR	23	$ .01	$ .15	Miller, Paul	93SCP	258	$ .01	$ .08
McWilliams, Larry	89SC	259	$ .01	$ .03	Miller, Trever	92SCP	579	$ .01	$ .15
Meacham, Bobby	88SC	137	$ .01	$ .04	Milligan, Randy	88SC	623	$ .05	$ .25
Meacham, Bobby	89SC	509	$ .01	$ .03	Milligan, Randy	90SC	252	$ .01	$ .04
Meacham, Rusty	92SC	395	$ .01	$ .04	Milligan, Randy	91SC	86	$ .01	$ .04

SCORE

Player	Year	No.	VG	EX/MT
Milligan, Randy	92SC	87	$ .01	$ .04
Milligan, Randy	92SCP	179	$ .01	$ .05
Milligan, Randy	93SC	112	$ .01	$ .03
Milligan, Randy	93SCP	157	$ .01	$ .08
Milligan, Randy	93SCS	212	$ .01	$ .05
Mills, Alan	90SCTR	89	$ .01	$ .15
Mills, Alan	91SC	73	$ .01	$ .10
Mills, Alan	93SC	440	$ .01	$ .03
Mills, Alan	93SCS	367	$ .01	$ .05
Milner, Eddie	88SC	548	$ .01	$ .04
Minor, Blas	93SC	304	$ .01	$ .03
Minor, Blas	93SCP	283	$ .01	$ .08
Minton, Greg	88SC	176	$ .01	$ .04
Minton, Greg	89SC	543	$ .01	$ .03
Minton, Greg	90SC	48	$ .01	$ .04
Minton, Greg	91SC	823	$ .01	$ .04
Minutelli, Gino	92SC	408	$ .01	$ .04
Minutelli, Gino	92SCP	261	$ .01	$ .05
Mirabella, Paul	89SC	569	$ .01	$ .03
Mirabella, Paul	91SC	558	$ .01	$ .04
Mitchell, John	88SC	249	$ .01	$ .04
Mitchell, John	91SC	569	$ .01	$ .04
Mitchell, Keith	92SC	748	$ .01	$ .10
Mitchell, Keith	92SCP	258	$ .01	$ .10
Mitchell, Kevin	88SC	481	$ .05	$ .20
Mitchell, Kevin	89SC	39	$ .01	$ .15
Mitchell, Kevin	90SC	343	$ .01	$ .10
Mitchell, Kevin	91SC	451	$ .01	$ .10
Mitchell, Kevin	91SCMB	406	$ .01	$ .10
Mitchell, Kevin	92SC	640	$ .01	$ .04
Mitchell, Kevin	92SCP	393	$ .01	$ .05
Mitchell, Kevin	92SCTR	18	$ .01	$ .05
Mitchell, Kevin	93SC	407	$ .01	$ .10
Mitchell, Kevin	93SCS	108	$ .01	$ .15
Mlicki, Dave	93SC	285	$ .01	$ .10
Mlicki, Dave	93SCP	275	$ .05	$ .25
Mmahat, Kevin	90SC	643	$ .01	$ .04
Mohorcic, Dale	88SC	452	$ .01	$ .04
Mohorcic, Dale	89SC	420	$ .01	$ .03
Mohorcic, Dale	90SC	191	$ .01	$ .04
Mohorcic, Dale	91SC	596	$ .01	$ .04
Molitor, Paul	88SC	340	$ .01	$ .10
Molitor, Paul	88SC	660	$ .01	$ .10
Molitor, Paul	89SC	565	$ .01	$ .10
Molitor, Paul	90SC	460	$ .01	$ .10
Molitor, Paul	91SC	49	$ .01	$ .10
Molitor, Paul	92SC	61	$ .01	$ .04
Molitor, Paul	92SCP	8	$ .01	$ .05
Molitor, Paul	93SC	598	$ .01	$ .03
Molitor, Paul	93SCS	42	$ .01	$ .05
Monteleone, Rich	89SCTR	92	$ .01	$ .10
Monteleone, Rich	90SC	565	$ .01	$ .04
Monteleone, Rich	92SC	690	$ .01	$ .04
Montgomery, Jeff	88SC	497	$ .05	$ .25
Montgomery, Jeff	88SCTR	71	$ .10	$ .75
Montgomery, Jeff	89SC	367	$ .01	$ .10
Montgomery, Jeff	90SC	365	$ .01	$ .04
Montgomery, Jeff	91SC	143	$ .01	$ .04
Montgomery, Jeff	92SC	14	$ .01	$ .04
Montgomery, Jeff	92SCP	173	$ .01	$ .05
Montgomery, Jeff	93SC	212	$ .01	$ .03
Montgomery, Jeff	93SCS	264	$ .01	$ .05
Moore, Charlie	88SC	444	$ .01	$ .04
Moore, Donnie	88SC	195	$ .01	$ .04
Moore, Donnie	89SC	535	$ .01	$ .03
Moore, Mike	88SC	464	$ .01	$ .04
Moore, Mike	89SC	274	$ .01	$ .03
Moore, Mike	89SCTR	5	$ .01	$ .05
Moore, Mike	90SC	190	$ .01	$ .04
Moore, Mike	91SC	516	$ .01	$ .04
Moore, Mike	92SC	91	$ .01	$ .04
Moore, Mike	92SCP	109	$ .01	$ .05
Moore, Mike	93SC	641	$ .01	$ .03
Moore, Mike	93SCP	202	$ .01	$ .08
Moore, Mike	93SCS	270	$ .01	$ .05

Player	Year	No.	VG	EX/MT
Morandini, Mickey	91SC	376	$ .01	$ .10
Morandini, Mickey	92SC	143	$ .01	$ .04
Morandini, Mickey	92SCP	103	$ .01	$ .05
Morandini, Mickey	93SC	415	$ .01	$ .03
Morandini, Mickey	93SC	512	$ .01	$ .03
Morandini, Mickey	93SCP	156	$ .01	$ .08

Player	Year	No.	VG	EX/MT
Morandini, Mickey	93SCS	245	$ .01	$ .05
Moreland, Keith	88SC	71	$ .01	$ .04
Moreland, Keith	88SCTR	9	$ .01	$ .15
Moreland, Keith	89SC	42	$ .01	$ .03
Moreland, Keith	89SCTR	29	$ .01	$ .05
Moreland, Keith	90SC	444	$ .01	$ .04
Morgan, Mike	88SC	295	$ .01	$ .04
Morgan, Mike	90SC	342	$ .01	$ .04
Morgan, Mike	91SC	276	$ .01	$ .04
Morgan, Mike	92SC	171	$ .01	$ .04
Morgan, Mike	92SCP	414	$ .01	$ .05
Morgan, Mike	92SCTR	66	$ .01	$ .05
Morgan, Mike	93SC	73	$ .01	$ .03
Morgan, Mike	93SCP	63	$ .01	$ .08
Morgan, Mike	93SCS	145	$ .01	$ .05
Morris, Hal	90SC	602	$ .05	$ .20
Morris, Hal	91SC	647	$ .01	$ .10
Morris, Hal	92SC	125	$ .01	$ .10
Morris, Hal	92SCP	22	$ .01	$ .05
Morris, Hal	93SC	38	$ .01	$ .03
Morris, Hal	93SCP	222	$ .01	$ .08
Morris, Hal	93SCS	45	$ .01	$ .05
Morris, Jack	88SC	545	$ .01	$ .10
Morris, Jack	89SC	250	$ .01	$ .10
Morris, Jack	90SC	203	$ .01	$ .10
Morris, Jack	91SC	114	$ .01	$ .10
Morris, Jack	91SCTR	74	$ .01	$ .10
Morris, Jack	92SC	652	$ .01	$ .10
Morris, Jack	92SC	798	$ .01	$ .04
Morris, Jack	92SCP	483	$ .01	$ .10
Morris, Jack	92SCP	585	$ .01	$ .05
Morris, Jack	92SCTR	—15	$ .01	$ .10
Morris, Jack	93SC	37	$ .01	$ .03
Morris, Jack	93SC	508	$ .01	$ .03
Morris, Jack	93SCP	57	$ .01	$ .08
Morris, Jack	93SCP	298	$ .01	$ .15
Morris, Jack	93SCS	158	$ .01	$ .05

SCORE

Player	Year	No.	VG	EX/MT	Player	Year	No.	VG	EX/MT
Morris, John	88SC	346	$.01	$.04	Murray, Eddie	93SCS	29	$.01	$.10
Morris, John	90SC	134	$.01	$.04	Musselman, Jeff	88SC	478	$.01	$.04
Morrison, Jim	88SC	272	$.01	$.04	Musselman, Jeff	89SC	558	$.01	$.03
Morton, Kevin	92SC	420	$.01	$.04	Musselman, Jeff	90SC	525	$.01	$.04
Moseby, Lloyd	88SC	109	$.01	$.04	Musselman, Jeff	91SC	294	$.01	$.04
Moseby, Lloyd	89SC	12	$.01	$.03	Mussina, Mike	91SC	383	$.15	$1.50
Moseby, Lloyd	90SC	404	$.01	$.04	Mussina, Mike	92SC	755	$.10	$.50
Moseby, Lloyd	90SCTR	25	$.01	$.05	Mussina, Mike	92SCP	204	$.15	$1.50
Moseby, Lloyd	91SC	133	$.01	$.04	Mussina, Mike	93SC	27	$.10	$.40
Moseby, Lloyd	92SC	468	$.01	$.04	Mussina, Mike	93SCP	44	$.10	$.75
Moses, John	88SC	309	$.01	$.04	Mussina, Mike	93SCS	92	$.10	$.50
Moses, John	89SC	432	$.01	$.03	Myers, Greg	91SC	88	$.01	$.04
Moses, John	90SC	391	$.01	$.04	Myers, Greg	92SC	471	$.01	$.04
Moses, John	91SC	429	$.01	$.04	Myers, Greg	92SCP	324	$.01	$.05
Mota, Andy	92SC	872	$.01	$.04	Myers, Greg	93SC	468	$.01	$.03
Mota, Andy	92SCP	257	$.01	$.05	Myers, Randy	88SC	336	$.01	$.04
Mota, Jose	92SC	742	$.01	$.04	Myers, Randy	89SC	306	$.01	$.03
Moyer, Jamie	88SC	573	$.01	$.04	Myers, Randy	90SC	351	$.01	$.10
Moyer, Jamie	89SC	263	$.01	$.03	Myers, Randy	90SCTR	16	$.01	$.05
Moyer, Jamie	90SC	107	$.01	$.04	Myers, Randy	91SC	501	$.01	$.04
Moyer, Jamie	91SC	437	$.01	$.04	Myers, Randy	91SCAS	662	$.01	$.04
Mulholland, Terry	89SC	474	$.01	$.10	Myers, Randy	91SCDT	885	$.01	$.04
Mulholland, Terry	90SC	542	$.01	$.04	Myers, Randy	92SC	155	$.01	$.04
Mulholland, Terry	91SC	33	$.01	$.04	Myers, Randy	92SCTR	12	$.01	$.05
Mulholland, Terry	91SCNH	706	$.01	$.04	Myers, Randy	93SC	607	$.01	$.03
Mulholland, Terry	92SC	118	$.01	$.04	Myers, Randy	93SCS	215	$.01	$.05
Mulholland, Terry	92SCP	199	$.01	$.05	Nabholz, Chris	91SC	804	$.01	$.10
Mulholland, Terry	93SC	117	$.01	$.03	Nabholz, Chris	92SC	140	$.01	$.04
Mulholland, Terry	93SCP	73	$.01	$.08	Nabholz, Chris	92SCP	360	$.01	$.05
Mulholland, Terry	93SCS	127	$.01	$.05	Nabholz, Chris	93SC	477	$.01	$.03
Mulliniks, Rance	88SC	235	$.01	$.04	Nachado, Julio	92SC	353	$.01	$.04
Mulliniks, Rance	89SC	385	$.01	$.03	Naehring, Tim	90SCTR	87	$.01	$.15
Mulliniks, Rance	90SC	204	$.01	$.04	Naehring, Tim	91SC	356	$.01	$.10
Mulliniks, Rance	91SC	433	$.01	$.04	Naehring, Tim	92SC	259	$.01	$.04
Mulliniks, Rance	92SC	132	$.01	$.04	Naehring, Tim	92SCP	242	$.01	$.05
Mumphrey, Jerry	88SC	467	$.01	$.04	Naehring, Tim	93SC	452	$.01	$.03
Mumphrey, Jerry	89SC	288	$.01	$.03	Nagy, Charles	90SC	611	$.10	$.50
Munoz, Mike	90SC	653	$.01	$.15	Nagy, Charles	91SC	75	$.05	$.25
Munoz, Mike	93SC	228	$.01	$.03	Nagy, Charles	92SC	330	$.01	$.10
Munoz, Pedro	91SC	332	$.05	$.25	Nagy, Charles	92SCP	383	$.05	$.20
Munoz, Pedro	92SC	514	$.01	$.10	Nagy, Charles	92SCP	609	$.01	$.10
Munoz, Pedro	92SCP	139	$.01	$.10	Nagy, Charles	93SC	538	$.05	$.20
Munoz, Pedro	93SC	130	$.01	$.03	Nagy, Charles	93SCP	65	$.05	$.20
Munoz, Pedro	93SCP	135	$.01	$.08	Nagy, Charles	93SCS	70	$.01	$.10
Munoz, Pedro	93SCS	370	$.01	$.05	Navarro, Jaime	90SC	569	$.01	$.15
Murphy, Dale	88SC	450	$.01	$.15	Navarro, Jaime	91SC	102	$.01	$.04
Murphy, Dale	89SC	30	$.01	$.15	Navarro, Jaime	92SC	231	$.01	$.04
Murphy, Dale	90SC	66	$.01	$.10	Navarro, Jaime	92SCP	212	$.01	$.05
Murphy, Dale	90SCTR	31	$.01	$.05	Navarro, Jaime	93SC	218	$.01	$.10
Murphy, Dale	91SC	650	$.01	$.10	Navarro, Jaime	93SCS	260	$.01	$.05
Murphy, Dale	92SC	80	$.01	$.04	Neagle, Denny	92SCP	556	$.01	$.10
Murphy, Dale	92SCP	124	$.01	$.05	Neagle, Denny	92SCTR	89	$.01	$.05
Murphy, Dale	92SCP	284	$.01	$.05	Neagle, Denny	93SC	350	$.01	$.03
Murphy, Dale	93SC	597	$.01	$.03	Neagle, Denny	93SCS	299	$.01	$.05
Murphy, Dale	93SCS	103	$.01	$.05	Neel, Troy	93SC	326	$.01	$.15
Murphy, Dwayne	88SC	455	$.01	$.04	Neel, Troy	93SCP	246	$.05	$.25
Murphy, Dwayne	89SC	545	$.01	$.03	Neidlinger, Jim	91SC	794	$.01	$.04
Murphy, Rob	88SC	559	$.01	$.04	Nelson, Gene	88SC	588	$.01	$.04
Murphy, Rob	89SC	141	$.01	$.03	Nelson, Gene	89SC	434	$.01	$.03
Murphy, Rob	89SCTR	8	$.01	$.05	Nelson, Gene	90SC	441	$.01	$.04
Murphy, Rob	90SC	181	$.01	$.04	Nelson, Gene	91SC	478	$.01	$.04
Murphy, Rob	91SC	183	$.01	$.04	Nelson, Gene	92SC	383	$.01	$.04
Murphy, Rob	91SCTR	33	$.01	$.05	Nelson, Gene	92SCP	443	$.01	$.05
Murphy, Rob	92SC	492	$.01	$.04	Nelson, Jeff	93SC	272	$.01	$.03
Murray, Eddie	88SC	18	$.01	$.15	Nettles, Graig	88SC	440	$.01	$.04
Murray, Eddie	89SC	94	$.01	$.10	Nettles, Graig	88SCTR	25	$.01	$.15
Murray, Eddie	89SCTR	31	$.01	$.15	Nettles, Graig	89SC	277	$.01	$.03
Murray, Eddie	90SC	80	$.01	$.10	Nevers, Tom	91SC	387	$.01	$.15
Murray, Eddie	91SC	310	$.01	$.10	Newfield, Marc	91SC	391	$.10	$.40
Murray, Eddie	92SC	195	$.01	$.10	Newman, Al	88SC	252	$.01	$.04
Murray, Eddie	92SCP	424	$.05	$.20	Newman, Al	89SC	493	$.01	$.03
Murray, Eddie	92SCTR	11	$.01	$.15	Newman, Al	90SC	128	$.01	$.04
Murray, Eddie	93SC	77	$.01	$.10	Newman, Al	91SC	424	$.01	$.04
Murray, Eddie	93SCP	18	$.01	$.15	Newman, Al	92SC	357	$.01	$.04
Murray, Eddie	93SCP	292	$.01	$.08	Newman, Al	92SCTR	49	$.01	$.05

SCORE

Player	Year	No.	VG	EX/MT
Newson, Warren	92SC	398	$ .01	$ .10
Nichols, Rod	92SC	559	$ .01	$ .04
Nichols, Rod	92SCP	525	$ .01	$ .05
Nied, David	93SC	553	$ .15	$1.50
Nied, David	93SCP	238	$1.00	$4.00
Niedenfuer, Tom	88SC	261	$ .01	$ .04
Niedenfuer, Tom	89SC	252	$ .01	$ .03
Niedenfuer, Tom	91SC	217	$ .01	$ .04
Niekro, Joe	88SC	237	$ .01	$ .04

Player	Year	No.	VG	EX/MT
Niekro, Phil	88SC	555	$ .01	$ .10
Nielsen, Jerry	93SC	268	$ .01	$ .03
Nieves, Juan	88SC	513	$ .01	$ .04
Nieves, Juan	88SC	655	$ .01	$ .04
Nieves, Juan	89SC	410	$ .01	$ .03
Nieves, Mel	93SC	248	$ .10	$ .40
Nieves, Melvin	93SCP	248	$ .10	$ .50
Nilsson, Dave	92SCP	568	$ .05	$ .25
Nilsson, Dave	92SCTR	94	$ .05	$ .25
Nilsson, Dave	93SC	344	$ .01	$ .10
Nilsson, Dave	93SCS	283	$ .01	$ .05
Nipper, Al	88SC	527	$ .01	$ .04
Nipper, Al	89SC	532	$ .01	$ .03
Nixon, Donell	88SC	436	$ .01	$ .04
Nixon, Donell	89SC	481	$ .01	$ .03
Nixon, Donell	90SC	538	$ .01	$ .04
Nixon, Otis	89SC	451	$ .01	$ .03
Nixon, Otis	90SC	241	$ .01	$ .04
Nixon, Otis	91SC	431	$ .01	$ .04
Nixon, Otis	91SCTR	29	$ .01	$ .05
Nixon, Otis	92SC	429	$ .01	$ .04
Nixon, Otis	92SC	443	$ .01	$ .04
Nixon, Otis	92SCP	519	$ .01	$ .05
Nixon, Otis	93SC	87	$ .01	$ .03
Nixon, Otis	93SCP	35	$ .01	$ .08
Nixon, Otis	93SCS	159	$ .01	$ .05
Noboa, Junior	91SC	423	$ .01	$ .04
Noce, Paul	88SC	329	$ .01	$ .04
Nokes, Matt	88SC	15	$ .05	$ .25
Nokes, Matt	88SC	648	$ .05	$ .25
Nokes, Matt	89SC	23	$ .01	$ .03
Nokes, Matt	90SC	55	$ .01	$ .04
Nokes, Matt	90SCTR	38	$ .01	$ .05
Nokes, Matt	91SC	551	$ .01	$ .04
Nokes, Matt	92SC	573	$ .01	$ .04
Nokes, Matt	92SCP	72	$ .01	$ .05
Nokes, Matt	93SC	192	$ .01	$ .03
Nokes, Matt	93SCP	82	$ .01	$ .08
Nokes, Matt	93SCS	368	$ .01	$ .05
Nolte, Eric	88SC	568	$ .01	$ .04
Nosek, Randy	90SC	607	$ .01	$ .10
Novoa, Rafael	91SC	366	$ .01	$ .10
Nunez, Edwin	92SC	676	$ .01	$ .04
Nunez, Jose	88SC	312	$ .01	$ .04
O'Brien, Charlie	89SC	606	$ .01	$ .03
O'Brien, Charlie	91SC	829	$ .01	$ .04
O'Brien, Charlie	92SC	621	$ .01	$ .04
O'Brien, Charlie	92SCP	488	$ .01	$ .05
O'Brien, Pete	89SC	22	$ .01	$ .03
O'Brien, Pete	89SCTR	6	$ .01	$ .05
O'Brien, Pete	90SC	175	$ .01	$ .04
O'Brien, Pete	90SCTR	23	$ .01	$ .05
O'Brien, Pete	91SC	509	$ .01	$ .04
O'Brien, Pete	92SC	141	$ .01	$ .04
O'Brien, Pete	92SCP	125	$ .01	$ .05
O'Brien, Pete	93SC	460	$ .01	$ .03
O'Brien, Pete	93SCP	151	$ .01	$ .08
O'Connor, Jack	88SC	434	$ .01	$ .04
O'Malley, Tom	88SC	534	$ .01	$ .04
O'Malley, Tom	91SC	439	$ .01	$ .04
O'Neill, Paul	88SC	304	$ .01	$ .15
O'Neill, Paul	89SC	206	$ .01	$ .03
O'Neill, Paul	90SC	295	$ .01	$ .10
O'Neill, Paul	91SC	227	$ .01	$ .04
O'Neill, Paul	92SC	57	$ .01	$ .04
O'Neill, Paul	92SCP	154	$ .01	$ .05
O'Neill, Paul	93SC	439	$ .01	$ .03
O'Neill, Paul	93SCS	86	$ .01	$ .05
Oberkfell, Ken	88SC	245	$ .01	$ .04
Oberkfell, Ken	89SC	139	$ .01	$ .03
Oberkfell, Ken	90SC	422	$ .01	$ .04
Oberkfell, Ken	90SCTR	58	$ .01	$ .05
Oberkfell, Ken	91SC	214	$ .01	$ .04
Oester, Ron	88SC	183	$ .01	$ .04
Oester, Ron	89SC	615	$ .01	$ .03
Oester, Ron	90SC	59	$ .01	$ .04
Oester, Ron	91SC	651	$ .01	$ .04
Offerman, Jose	91SC	343	$ .01	$ .10
Offerman, Jose	92SC	699	$ .01	$ .04
Offerman, Jose	92SCP	153	$ .01	$ .05
Offerman, Jose	93SC	129	$ .01	$ .03
Offerman, Jose	93SCS	197	$ .01	$ .05
Ojeda, Bob	88SC	563	$ .01	$ .04
Ojeda, Bob	89SC	116	$ .01	$ .03
Ojeda, Bob	90SC	53	$ .01	$ .04
Ojeda, Bob	91SC	321	$ .01	$ .04
Ojeda, Bob	91SCTR	79	$ .01	$ .05
Ojeda, Bob	92SC	527	$ .01	$ .04
Ojeda, Bob	92SCP	512	$ .01	$ .05
Ojeda, Bob	93SC	589	$ .01	$ .03
Ojeda, Bob	93SCS	263	$ .01	$ .05
Olander, Jim	92SC	839	$ .01	$ .10
Olerud, John	90SC	589	$ .10	$ .50
Olerud, John	91SC	625	$ .01	$ .10
Olerud, John	91SCTF	860	$ .01	$ .10
Olerud, John	92SC	345	$ .01	$ .10
Olerud, John	92SCP	78	$ .05	$ .20
Olerud, John	93SC	68	$ .01	$ .10
Olerud, John	93SCP	86	$ .01	$ .15
Olerud, John	93SCS	124	$ .01	$ .15
Olin, Steve	90SC	590	$ .01	$ .15
Olin, Steve	91SC	496	$ .01	$ .04
Olin, Steve	92SC	644	$ .01	$ .04
Olin, Steve	92SCP	120	$ .01	$ .05
Olin, Steve	93SC	388	$ .01	$ .03
Olin, Steve	93SCS	377	$ .01	$ .05
Olivares, Omar	91SC	748	$ .01	$ .10
Olivares, Omar	92SC	334	$ .01	$ .04
Olivares, Omar	92SCP	186	$ .01	$ .05

SCORE

Player	Year	No.	VG	EX/MT	Player	Year	No.	VG	EX/MT
Oliver, Joe	89SCTR	104	$ .05	$ .20	Owen, Spike	88SC	372	$ .01	$ .04
Oliver, Joe	90SC	576	$ .01	$ .15	Owen, Spike	89SC	218	$ .01	$ .03
Oliver, Joe	91SC	620	$ .01	$ .04	Owen, Spike	89SCTR	13	$ .01	$ .05
Oliver, Joe	92SC	370	$ .01	$ .04	Owen, Spike	90SC	247	$ .01	$ .04
Oliver, Joe	92SCP	331	$ .01	$ .05	Owen, Spike	91SC	452	$ .01	$ .04
Oliver, Joe	93SC	125	$ .01	$ .03	Owen, Spike	92SC	323	$ .01	$ .04
Oliver, Joe	93SCP	190	$ .01	$ .08	Owen, Spike	92SCP	234	$ .01	$ .05
Oliver, Joe	93SCS	235	$ .01	$ .05	Owen, Spike	93SC	554	$ .01	$ .03
Oliveras, Francisco	91SC	635	$ .01	$ .04	Owen, Spike	93SCS	239	$ .01	$ .05
Oliveras, Francisco	92SC	295	$ .01	$ .04	Paciorek, Tom	88SC	531	$ .01	$ .04
Olson, Greg	92SC	474	$ .01	$ .04	Pagliarulo, Mike	88SC	170	$ .01	$ .10
Olson, Greg	92SCP	149	$ .01	$ .05	Pagliarulo, Mike	89SC	189	$ .01	$ .03
Olson, Greg	93SC	209	$ .01	$ .03	Pagliarulo, Mike	89SCTR	11	$ .01	$ .05
Olson, Greg	93SCP	173	$ .01	$ .08	Pagliarulo, Mike	90SC	494	$ .01	$ .04
Olson, Greg	93SCS	233	$ .01	$ .05	Pagliarulo, Mike	91SC	199	$ .01	$ .04
Olson, Gregg	89SCTR	96	$ .10	$ .50	Pagliarulo, Mike	91SCTR	42	$ .01	$ .05
Olson, Gregg	90SC	63	$ .01	$ .10	Pagliarulo, Mike	92SC	173	$ .01	$ .04
Olson, Gregg	90SCTR	69	$ .01	$ .10	Pagliarulo, Mike	92SCP	246	$ .01	$ .05
Olson, Gregg	91SC	56	$ .01	$ .10	Pagnozzi, Tom	88SC	358	$ .05	$ .25
Olson, Gregg	91SC	490	$ .01	$ .10	Pagnozzi, Tom	89SC	483	$ .01	$ .15
Olson, Gregg	92SC	71	$ .01	$ .04	Pagnozzi, Tom	91SC	797	$ .01	$ .04
Olson, Gregg	92SC	427	$ .01	$ .04	Pagnozzi, Tom	92SC	136	$ .01	$ .04
Olson, Gregg	92SCP	61	$ .01	$ .05	Pagnozzi, Tom	92SCP	69	$ .01	$ .05
Olson, Gregg	93SC	80	$ .01	$ .03	Pagnozzi, Tom	93SC	135	$ .01	$ .03
Olson, Gregg	93SCP	97	$ .01	$ .08	Pagnozzi, Tom	93SCP	62	$ .01	$ .08
Olson, Gregg	93SCS	46	$ .01	$ .05	Pagnozzi, Tom	93SCS	37	$ .01	$ .05
Olwine, Ed	88SC	379	$ .01	$ .04	Paige, Satchell	92SC	882	$ .05	$ .20
Ontiveros, Steve	88SC	511	$ .01	$ .04	Palacios, Vicente	88SC	643	$ .01	$ .15
Ontiveros, Steve	89SC	337	$ .01	$ .03	Palacios, Vicente	92SC	109	$ .01	$ .04
Ontiveros, Steve	91SC	832	$ .01	$ .04	Palacios, Vicente	92SCP	386	$ .01	$ .05
Oquendo, Jose	88SC	248	$ .01	$ .10	Palacios, Vicente	93SCP	130	$ .01	$ .08
Oquendo, Jose	89SC	529	$ .01	$ .03	Pall, Donn	89SCTR	102	$ .01	$ .05
Oquendo, Jose	90SC	68	$ .01	$ .04	Pall, Donn	90SC	304	$ .01	$ .04
Oquendo, Jose	91SC	622	$ .01	$ .04	Pall, Donn	91SC	132	$ .01	$ .04
Oquendo, Jose	92SC	305	$ .01	$ .04	Pall, Donn	92SC	484	$ .01	$ .04
Oquendo, Jose	92SCP	239	$ .01	$ .05	Palmeiro, Rafael	88SC	186	$ .05	$ .35
Oquendo, Jose	93SC	163	$ .01	$ .03	Palmeiro, Rafael	89SC	199	$ .01	$ .15
Orosco, Jesse	88SC	495	$ .01	$ .04	Palmeiro, Rafael	89SCTR	1	$ .05	$ .20
Orosco, Jesse	88SCTR	64	$ .01	$ .15	Palmeiro, Rafael	90SC	405	$ .01	$ .10
Orosco, Jesse	89SC	356	$ .01	$ .03	Palmeiro, Rafael	91SC	216	$ .01	$ .10
Orosco, Jesse	90SC	353	$ .01	$ .04	Palmeiro, Rafael	92SC	55	$ .01	$ .04
Orosco, Jesse	91SC	578	$ .01	$ .04	Palmeiro, Rafael	92SCP	35	$ .01	$ .05
Orosco, Jesse	92SC	547	$ .01	$ .04	Palmeiro, Rafael	93SC	74	$ .01	$ .03
Orsulak, Joe	88SCTR	41	$ .01	$ .15	Palmeiro, Rafael	93SCP	220	$ .01	$ .08
Orsulak, Joe	89SC	247	$ .01	$ .03	Palmer, David	88SC	457	$ .01	$ .04
Orsulak, Joe	90SC	41	$ .01	$ .04	Palmer, Dave	89SC	544	$ .01	$ .03
Orsulak, Joe	91SC	508	$ .01	$ .04	Palmer, Dean	90SC	594	$ .10	$ .50
Orsulak, Joe	92SC	551	$ .01	$ .04	Palmer, Dean	92SC	392	$ .01	$ .15
Orsulak, Joe	92SCP	362	$ .01	$ .05	Palmer, Dean	92SCP	351	$ .01	$ .05
Orsulak, Joe	93SC	590	$ .01	$ .03	Palmer, Dean	93SC	138	$ .01	$ .15
Orsulak, Joe	93SCS	234	$ .01	$ .05	Palmer, Dean	93SCP	161	$ .05	$ .20
Ortiz, Javier	92SC	403	$ .01	$ .04	Palmer, Dean	93SCS	248	$ .01	$ .15
Ortiz, Junior	88SC	404	$ .01	$ .04	Palmiero, Rafael	93SCS	162	$ .01	$ .05
Ortiz, Junior	89SC	402	$ .01	$ .03	Pankovits, Jim	89SC	192	$ .01	$ .03
Ortiz, Junior	90SC	143	$ .01	$ .04	Pappas, Erik	91SCTR	95	$ .01	$ .10
Ortiz, Junior	90SCTR	66	$ .01	$ .05	Parent, Mark	89SC	576	$ .01	$ .15
Ortiz, Junior	91SC	438	$ .01	$ .04	Parent, Mark	90SC	119	$ .01	$ .04
Ortiz, Junior	92SC	473	$ .01	$ .04	Parent, Mark	91SC	213	$ .01	$ .04
Orton, John	90SC	582	$ .01	$ .10	Parker, Clay	89SCTR	94	$ .01	$ .15
Orton, John	91SC	467	$ .01	$ .04	Parker, Clay	90SC	316	$ .01	$ .04
Orton, John	92SC	712	$ .01	$ .04	Parker, Dave	88SC	17	$ .05	$ .15
Orton, John	93SC	453	$ .01	$ .03	Parker, Dave	88SCTR	50	$ .05	$ .20
Orton, John	93SCP	197	$ .01	$ .08	Parker, Dave	89SC	108	$ .01	$ .03
Osborne, Donovan	91SC	677	$ .10	$ .50	Parker, Dave	90SC	135	$ .01	$ .10
Osborne, Donovan	92SCP	541	$ .10	$ .40	Parker, Dave	90SCTR	12	$ .01	$ .05
Osborne, Donovan	92SCTR	90	$ .05	$ .35	Parker, Dave	91SC	484	$ .01	$ .05
Osborne, Donovan	93SC	349	$ .01	$ .15	Parker, Dave	91SCTR	31	$ .01	$ .05
Osborne, Donovan	93SCS	276	$ .05	$ .20	Parker, Rick	90SCTR	77	$ .01	$ .10
Osuna, Al	91SCTR	89	$ .01	$ .15	Parker, Rick	91SC	58	$ .01	$ .04
Osuna, Al	92SC	452	$ .01	$ .04	Parker, Rick	92SC	601	$ .01	$ .04
Osuna, Al	92SCP	347	$ .01	$ .05	Parks, Derek	93SC	245	$ .01	$ .03
Osuna, Al	93SC	475	$ .01	$ .03	Parks, Derek	93SCP	267	$ .01	$ .08
Otto, Dave	90SCTR	101	$ .01	$ .10	Parrett, Jeff	89SC	377	$ .01	$ .10
Otto, Dave	92SCP	316	$ .01	$ .05	Parrett, Jeff	89SCTR	33	$ .01	$ .05
Owen, Larry	88SC	230	$ .01	$ .04	Parrett, Jeff	91SC	565	$ .01	$ .04

283

SCORE

Player	Year	No.	VG	EX/MT	Player	Year	No.	VG	EX/MT
Parrett, Jeff	93SC	180	$ .01	$ .03	Pendleton, Terry	93SC	36	$ .01	$ .10
Parrett, Jeff	93SCS	396	$ .01	$ .05	Pendleton, Terry	93SCP	60	$ .01	$ .10
Parrish, Lance	88SC	131	$ .01	$ .10	Pendleton, Terry	93SCS	17	$ .01	$ .05
Parrish, Lance	89SC	95	$ .01	$ .03	Pennyfeather, William	93SC	301	$ .01	$ .03
Parrish, Lance	89SCTR	36	$ .01	$ .10	Peraza, Oswald	88SCTR	77	$ .01	$ .15
Parrish, Lance	90SC	35	$ .01	$ .04	Peraza, Oswald	89SC	571	$ .01	$ .15
Parrish, Lance	91SC	37	$ .01	$ .04	Perez, Melido	88SCTR	108	$ .25	$2.50
Parrish, Lance	92SC	298	$ .01	$ .04	Perez, Melido	89SC	386	$ .01	$ .15
Parrish, Lance	92SCP	105	$ .01	$ .05	Perez, Melido	90SC	311	$ .01	$ .04
Parrish, Lance	93SC	587	$ .01	$ .03	Perez, Melido	91SC	179	$ .01	$ .04
Parrish, Lance	93SCS	388	$ .01	$ .05	Perez, Melido	91SCNH	705	$ .01	$ .04
Parrish, Larry	88SC	191	$ .01	$ .04	Perez, Melido	92SC	29	$ .01	$ .04
Parrish, Larry	88SCTR	65	$ .01	$ .15	Perez, Melido	92SCP	322	$ .01	$ .05
Parrish, Larry	89SC	495	$ .01	$ .03	Perez, Melido	92SCTR	36	$ .01	$ .05
Pasqua, Dan	88SC	196	$ .01	$ .04	Perez, Melido	93SC	86	$ .01	$ .03
Pasqua, Dan	88SCTR	56	$ .01	$ .15	Perez, Melido	93SCP	109	$ .01	$ .08
Pasqua, Dan	89SC	338	$ .01	$ .03	Perez, Melido	93SCS	116	$ .01	$ .05
Pasqua, Dan	90SC	306	$ .01	$ .04	Perez, Mike	91SC	758	$ .01	$ .15
Pasqua, Dan	91SC	85	$ .01	$ .04	Perez, Mike	92SCP	565	$ .01	$ .15
Pasqua, Dan	92SC	237	$ .01	$ .04	Perez, Mike	92SCTR	95	$ .01	$ .05
Pasqua, Dan	92SCP	227	$ .01	$ .05	Perez, Mike	93SC	345	$ .01	$ .03
Pasqua, Dan	93SC	210	$ .01	$ .03	Perez, Mike	93SCP	162	$ .01	$ .08
Patterson, Bob	91SC	636	$ .01	$ .04	Perez, Mike	93SCS	319	$ .01	$ .05
Patterson, Bob	92SC	548	$ .01	$ .04	Perez, Pascual	88SC	459	$ .01	$ .04
Patterson, John	92SCP	532	$ .01	$ .15	Perez, Pascual	89SC	299	$ .01	$ .03
Patterson, John	93SC	279	$ .01	$ .03	Perez, Pascual	90SC	486	$ .01	$ .04
Patterson, Ken	89SCTR	97	$ .01	$ .05	Perez, Pascual	90SCTR	5	$ .01	$ .05
Patterson, Ken	90SC	207	$ .01	$ .04	Perez, Pascual	92SC	88	$ .01	$ .04
Patterson, Ken	92SC	347	$ .01	$ .04	Perez, Pascual	92SCP	182	$ .01	$ .05
Paulik, Roger	93SC	325	$ .01	$ .03	Perezchica, Tony	91SC	735	$ .01	$ .04
Pavlas, Dave	91SC	378	$ .01	$ .10	Perezchica, Tony	92SC	702	$ .01	$ .04
Pawlowski, John	90SC	617	$ .01	$ .04	Perlman, Jon	89SC	591	$ .01	$ .03
Pecota, Bill	88SC	377	$ .01	$ .10	Perry, Gerald	88SC	136	$ .01	$ .04
Pecota, Bill	89SC	339	$ .01	$ .03	Perry, Gerald	89SC	101	$ .01	$ .03
Pecota, Bill	91SC	513	$ .01	$ .04	Perry, Gerald	90SC	249	$ .01	$ .04
Pecota, Bill	92SC	252	$ .01	$ .04	Perry, Gerald	90SCTR	28	$ .01	$ .05
Pecota, Bill	92SCP	319	$ .01	$ .05	Perry, Gerald	91SC	286	$ .01	$ .04
Pecota, Bill	92SCTR	52	$ .01	$ .05					
Pecota, Bill	93SC	365	$ .01	$ .03					
Pedre, Jorge	92SC	844	$ .01	$ .10					
Pedrique, Al	88SC	301	$ .01	$ .04					
Pedrique, Al	89SC	614	$ .01	$ .03					
Peltier, Dan	93SC	240	$ .01	$ .03					
Pena, Alejandro	89SC	389	$ .01	$ .03					
Pena, Alejandro	90SC	39	$ .01	$ .04					
Pena, Alejandro	90SCTR	32	$ .01	$ .05					
Pena, Alejandro	91SC	204	$ .01	$ .04					
Pena, Alejandro	92SC	691	$ .01	$ .04					
Pena, Alejandro	92SC	787	$ .01	$ .04					
Pena, Alejandro	92SCP	528	$ .01	$ .05					
Pena, Alejandro	93SC	625	$ .01	$ .03					
Pena, Geronimo	91SC	717	$ .01	$ .10					
Pena, Geronimo	92SC	516	$ .01	$ .04					
Pena, Geronimo	92SCP	487	$ .05	$ .20					
Pena, Geronimo	93SC	161	$ .01	$ .03					
Pena, Geronimo	93SCP	174	$ .01	$ .08					
Pena, Geronimo	93SCS	372	$ .01	$ .05					
Pena, Jim	93SC	288	$ .01	$ .03					
Pena, Tony	88SC	48	$ .01	$ .04					
Pena, Tony	89SC	36	$ .01	$ .03					
Pena, Tony	90SC	122	$ .01	$ .04					
Pena, Tony	90SCTR	7	$ .01	$ .05					
Pena, Tony	91SC	790	$ .01	$ .04					
Pena, Tony	92SC	446	$ .01	$ .04					
Pena, Tony	92SCP	33	$ .01	$ .05					
Pena, Tony	93SC	261	$ .01	$ .03					
Pena, Tony	93SCS	148	$ .01	$ .05					
Pendleton, Terry	88SC	190	$ .01	$ .10					
Pendleton, Terry	89SC	137	$ .01	$ .10					
Pendleton, Terry	90SC	208	$ .01	$ .10	**Perry, Gerald**	**91SCTR**	**63**	**$ .01**	**$ .05**
Pendleton, Terry	91SC	230	$ .01	$ .10	Perry, Gerald	92SC	491	$ .01	$ .04
Pendleton, Terry	91SCTR	50	$ .01	$ .10	Perry, Pat	88SC	557	$ .01	$ .04
Pendleton, Terry	92SC	18	$ .01	$ .04	Perry, Pat	89SC	364	$ .01	$ .03
Pendleton, Terry	92SC	789	$ .01	$ .04	Perry, Pat	90SC	436	$ .01	$ .04
Pendleton, Terry	92SCP	18	$ .01	$ .10	Perry, Pat	91SC	527	$ .01	$ .04

Player	Year	No.	VG	EX/MT	Player	Year	No.	VG	EX/MT
Peters, Don	91SC	381	$ .01	$ .15	Poole, Jim	91SC	357	$ .01	$ .10
Peterson, Adam	91SC	604	$ .01	$ .04	Poole, Jim	92SC	693	$ .01	$ .04
Petralli, Geno	88SC	373	$ .01	$ .04	Porter, Darrell	88SC	537	$ .01	$ .04
Petralli, Geno	89SC	526	$ .01	$ .03	Portugal, Mark	89SC	482	$ .01	$ .03
Petralli, Geno	90SC	153	$ .01	$ .04	Portugal, Mark	90SC	552	$ .01	$ .04
Petralli, Geno	91SC	191	$ .01	$ .04	Portugal, Mark	91SC	319	$ .01	$ .04
Petralli, Geno	92SC	283	$ .01	$ .04	Portugal, Mark	92SC	243	$ .01	$ .04
Petry, Dan	88SC	461	$ .01	$ .04	Portugal, Mark	92SCP	189	$ .01	$ .05
Petry, Dan	88SCTR	26	$ .01	$ .15	Powell, Alonzo	92SC	413	$ .01	$ .04
Petry, Dan	89SC	122	$ .01	$ .03	Powell, Dennis	90SC	308	$ .01	$ .04
Petry, Dan	90SC	211	$ .01	$ .04	Power, Ted	88SC	242	$ .01	$ .04
Petry, Dan	90SCTR	39	$ .01	$ .05	Power, Ted	89SC	348	$ .01	$ .03
Petry, Dan	91SC	434	$ .01	$ .04	Power, Ted	91SC	255	$ .01	$ .04
Petry, Dean	92SC	705	$ .01	$ .04	Power, Ted	92SC	113	$ .01	$ .04
Pettis, Gary	88SC	255	$ .01	$ .04	Pratt, Todd	93SC	276	$ .01	$ .10
Pettis, Gary	88SCTR	38	$ .01	$ .15	Presley, Jim	88SC	46	$ .01	$ .10
Pettis, Gary	89SC	26	$ .01	$ .03	Presley, Jim	89SC	73	$ .01	$ .03
Pettis, Gary	90SC	136	$ .01	$ .04	Presley, Jim	90SC	34	$ .01	$ .04
Pettis, Gary	90SCTR	6	$ .01	$ .05	Presley, Jim	90SCTR	36	$ .01	$ .05
Pettis, Gary	91SC	182	$ .01	$ .04	Presley, Jim	91SC	771	$ .01	$ .04
Pettis, Gary	92SC	308	$ .01	$ .04	Price, Joe	89SC	444	$ .01	$ .03
Pettis, Gary	93SC	442	$ .01	$ .03	Prince, Tom	89SC	626	$ .01	$ .10
Phelps, Ken	88SC	256	$ .01	$ .04	Prince, Tom	92SC	618	$ .01	$ .04
Phelps, Ken	89SC	242	$ .01	$ .03	Puckett, Kirby	88SC	24	$ .05	$ .35
Phillips, Tony	88SC	294	$ .01	$ .04	Puckett, Kirby	88SC	653	$ .05	$ .25
Phillips, Tony	89SC	156	$ .01	$ .03	Puckett, Kirby	89SC	20	$ .10	$ .40
Phillips, Tony	90SC	84	$ .01	$ .04	Puckett, Kirby	90SC	400	$ .05	$ .25
Phillips, Tony	90SCTR	14	$ .01	$ .05	Puckett, Kirby	90SCDT	690	$ .01	$ .10
Phillips, Tony	91SC	38	$ .01	$ .04	Puckett, Kirby	91SC	200	$ .05	$ .20
Phillips, Tony	92SC	453	$ .01	$ .04	Puckett, Kirby	91SCDT	891	$ .10	$ .40
Phillips, Tony	92SCP	243	$ .01	$ .05	Puckett, Kirby	91SCTF	855	$ .01	$ .10
Phillips, Tony	93SC	614	$ .01	$ .03	Puckett, Kirby	92SC	600	$ .05	$ .20
Phillips, Tony	93SCS	218	$ .01	$ .05	Puckett, Kirby	92SC	796	$ .01	$ .10
Piatt, Doug	92SC	422	$ .01	$ .04	Puckett, Kirby	92SCDT	886	$ .01	$ .15
Piazza, Mike	93SC	286	$ .10	$ .75	Puckett, Kirby	92SCP	20	$ .10	$ .50
Piazza, Mike	93SCP	252	$ .20	$2.00	Puckett, Kirby	92SCP	289	$ .05	$ .25
Piazza, Mike	93SCS	347	$ .15	$1.50	Puckett, Kirby	93SC	505	$ .01	$ .15
Pichardo, Hipolito	92SCTR	103	$ .01	$ .10	Puckett, Kirby	93SC	533	$ .01	$ .10
Pichardo, Hipolito	93SC	336	$ .01	$ .03	Puckett, Kirby	93SC	550	$ .01	$ .15
Pichardo, Hipolito	93SCS	312	$ .01	$ .05	Puckett, Kirby	93SC	606	$ .01	$ .15
Pico, Jeff	88SCTR	94	$ .01	$ .15	Puckett, Kirby	93SCS	4	$ .05	$ .25
Pico, Jeff	89SC	13	$ .01	$ .03	Pugh, Tim	93SC	247	$ .05	$ .25
Pico, Jeff	90SC	428	$ .01	$ .04	Pugh, Tim	93SCP	270	$ .10	$ .50
Pico, Jeff	91SC	326	$ .01	$ .04	Puhl, Terry	88SC	282	$ .01	$ .04
Pina, Mickey	90SCTR	104	$ .01	$ .10	Puhl, Terry	89SC	567	$ .01	$ .03
Plantier, Phil	91SC	348	$ .10	$ .50	Puhl, Terry	90SC	473	$ .01	$ .04
Plantier, Phil	92SC	406	$ .01	$ .15	Puleo, Charlie	88SC	454	$ .01	$ .04
Plantier, Phil	92SCP	51	$ .05	$ .25	Puleo, Charlie	89SC	448	$ .01	$ .03
Plantier, Phil	93SC	176	$ .01	$ .10	Pulliam, Harvey	92SC	761	$ .01	$ .10
Plantier, Phil	93SCS	242	$ .01	$ .10	Pulliam, Harvey	92SCP	279	$ .01	$ .05
Plesac, Dan	88SC	77	$ .01	$ .04	Quantrill, Paul	93SC	221	$ .01	$ .10
Plesac, Dan	89SC	320	$ .01	$ .03	Quantrill, Paul	93SCP	175	$ .01	$ .15
Plesac, Dan	90SC	86	$ .01	$ .04	Quinlan, Tom	93SC	309	$ .01	$ .15
Plesac, Dan	91SC	275	$ .01	$ .04	Quinones, Luis	90SC	499	$ .01	$ .04
Plesac, Dan	92SC	567	$ .01	$ .04	Quinones, Luis	91SC	822	$ .01	$ .04
Plesac, Dan	92SCP	162	$ .01	$ .05	Quinones, Luis	92SC	638	$ .01	$ .04
Plesac, Dan	93SC	450	$ .01	$ .03	Quinones, Rey	89SC	192	$ .01	$ .04
Plunk, Eric	88SC	614	$ .01	$ .04	Quinones, Rey	89SC	361	$ .01	$ .03
Plunk, Eric	89SC	392	$ .01	$ .03	Quintana, Carlos	89SC	623	$ .01	$ .10
Plunk, Eric	91SC	428	$ .01	$ .04	Quintana, Carlos	90SC	658	$ .01	$ .10
Plunk, Eric	92SC	379	$ .01	$ .04	Quintana, Carlos	91SC	149	$ .01	$ .04
Plunk, Eric	93SC	594	$ .01	$ .03	Quintana, Carlos	92SC	189	$ .01	$ .04
Plympton, Jeff	92SC	823	$ .01	$ .10	Quintana, Carlos	92SCP	358	$ .01	$ .05
Polidor, Gus	88SC	341	$ .01	$ .04	Quirk, Jamie	88SC	577	$ .01	$ .04
Polonia, Luis	88SC	64	$ .05	$ .25	Quirk, Jamie	89SC	461	$ .01	$ .03
Polonia, Luis	89SC	380	$ .01	$ .10	Quirk, Jamie	92SC	526	$ .01	$ .04
Polonia, Luis	89SCTR	38	$ .01	$ .05	Quisenberry, Dan	88SC	290	$ .01	$ .04
Polonia, Luis	90SC	442	$ .01	$ .04	Quisenberry, Dan	88SCTR	18	$ .01	$ .15
Polonia, Luis	90SCTR	46	$ .01	$ .05	Quisenberry, Dan	89SC	520	$ .01	$ .03
Polonia, Luis	91SC	587	$ .01	$ .04	Quisenberry, Dan	90SC	475	$ .01	$ .04
Polonia, Luis	92SC	68	$ .01	$ .04	Raczka, Mike	93SCP	277	$ .01	$ .10
Polonia, Luis	92SCP	166	$ .01	$ .05	Radinsky, Scott	90SCTR	90	$ .01	$ .15
Polonia, Luis	93SC	39	$ .01	$ .03	Radinsky, Scott	91SC	62	$ .01	$ .10
Polonia, Luis	93SCP	31	$ .01	$ .08	Radinsky, Scott	92SC	444	$ .01	$ .04
Polonia, Luis	93SCS	74	$ .01	$ .05	Radinsky, Scott	92SCP	389	$ .01	$ .05

SCORE

Player	Year	No.	VG	EX/MT	Player	Year	No.	VG	EX/MT
Radinsky, Scott	93SC	182	$ .01	$ .03	Redus, Gary	92SC	303	$ .01	$ .04
Raines, Tim	88SC	3	$ .01	$ .15	Reed, Darren	91SC	368	$ .01	$ .10
Raines, Tim	88SC	649	$ .01	$ .15	Reed, Jeff	88SC	408	$ .01	$ .04
Raines, Tim	89SC	40	$ .01	$ .10	Reed, Jeff	89SC	99	$ .01	$ .03
Raines, Tim	90SC	409	$ .01	$ .04	Reed, Jeff	90SC	147	$ .01	$ .04
Raines, Tim	91SC	35	$ .01	$ .04	Reed, Jeff	92SC	311	$ .01	$ .04
Raines, Tim	91SCTR	10	$ .01	$ .10	Reed, Jerry	88SC	488	$ .01	$ .04
Raines, Tim	92SC	635	$ .01	$ .04	Reed, Jerry	89SC	427	$ .01	$ .03
Raines, Tim	92SCP	178	$ .01	$ .05	Reed, Jerry	90SC	492	$ .01	$ .04
Raines, Tim	92SCP	605	$ .01	$ .05	Reed, Jody	88SC	625	$ .05	$ .25
Raines, Tim	93SC	658	$ .01	$ .03	Reed, Jody	89SC	486	$ .01	$ .15
Raines, Tim	93SCP	53	$ .01	$ .08	Reed, Jody	90SC	11	$ .01	$ .04
Raines, Tim	93SCS	236	$ .01	$ .05	Reed, Jody	91SC	173	$ .01	$ .04
Ramirez, Manny	92SC	800	$ .10	$ .75	Reed, Jody	92SC	85	$ .01	$ .04
Ramirez, Manny	92SCP	295	$ .15	$1.50	Reed, Jody	92SCP	222	$ .01	$ .05
Ramirez, Rafael	88SC	426	$ .01	$ .04	Reed, Jody	93SC	414	$ .01	$ .03
Ramirez, Rafael	88SCTR	12	$ .01	$ .15	Reed, Jody	93SCS	120	$ .01	$ .05
Ramirez, Rafael	89SC	113	$ .01	$ .03	Reed, Rick	90SC	544	$ .01	$ .10
Ramirez, Rafael	90SC	42	$ .01	$ .04	Reed, Rick	91SC	584	$ .01	$ .04
Ramirez, Rafael	91SC	305	$ .01	$ .04	Reed, Steve	93SC	573	$ .01	$ .10
Ramirez, Rafael	92SC	388	$ .01	$ .04	Reed, Steve	93SCS	351	$ .01	$ .15
Ramos, Domingo	88SC	362	$ .01	$ .04	Reimer, Kevin	91SC	836	$ .01	$ .10
Ramos, Domingo	90SC	489	$ .01	$ .04	Reimer, Kevin	92SC	152	$ .01	$ .04
Ramos, John	92SC	818	$ .01	$ .10	Reimer, Kevin	92SCP	340	$ .01	$ .05
Ramsey, Fernando	93SCP	273	$ .05	$ .20	Reimer, Kevin	93SC	628	$ .01	$ .03
Ramsey, Mike	88SC	267	$ .01	$ .04	Reimer, Kevin	93SCS	268	$ .01	$ .05
Randolph, Willie	88SC	266	$ .01	$ .04	Remlinger, Mike	92SC	410	$ .01	$ .04
Randolph, Willie	89SC	45	$ .01	$ .03	Renfroe, Laddie	92SC	875	$ .01	$ .04
Randolph, Willie	89SCTR	41	$ .01	$ .10	Renteria, Rich	89SC	142	$ .01	$ .03
Randolph, Willie	90SC	395	$ .01	$ .04	Reuschel, Rick	88SC	519	$ .01	$ .04
Randolph, Willie	90SCTR	51	$ .01	$ .05	Reuschel, Rick	89SC	5	$ .01	$ .03
Randolph, Willie	91SC	194	$ .01	$ .04	Reuschel, Rick	90SC	465	$ .01	$ .04
Randolph, Willie	91SCTR	35	$ .01	$ .05	Reuschel, Rick	91SC	544	$ .01	$ .04
Randolph, Willie	92SC	30	$ .01	$ .04	Reuss, Jerry	88SC	270	$ .01	$ .04
Randolph, Willie	92SCP	382	$ .01	$ .05	Reuss, Jerry	88SCTR	61	$ .01	$ .15
Randolph, Willie	92SCTR	35	$ .01	$ .05	Reuss, Jerry	89SC	489	$ .01	$ .03
Randolph, Willie	93SC	613	$ .01	$ .03	Reyes, Gilberto	92SC	229	$ .01	$ .04
Randolph, Willie	93SCS	195	$ .01	$ .05	Reyes, Gilberto	92SCP	428	$ .01	$ .05
Rasmussen, Dennis	88SC	560	$ .01	$ .04	Reynolds, Craig	88SC	207	$ .01	$ .04
Rasmussen, Dennis	89SC	562	$ .01	$ .03	Reynolds, Craig	89SC	468	$ .01	$ .03
Rasmussen, Dennis	90SC	129	$ .01	$ .04	Reynolds, Harold	88SC	277	$ .01	$ .04
Rasmussen, Dennis	91SC	457	$ .01	$ .04	Reynolds, Harold	89SC	310	$ .01	$ .03
Rasmussen, Dennis	92SC	536	$ .01	$ .04	Reynolds, Harold	90SC	167	$ .01	$ .04
Rasmussen, Dennis	93SC	392	$ .01	$ .03	Reynolds, Harold	91SC	48	$ .01	$ .04
Rawley, Shane	88SC	375	$ .01	$ .04	Reynolds, Harold	92SC	250	$ .01	$ .04
Rawley, Shane	89SC	170	$ .01	$ .03	Reynolds, Harold	92SCP	59	$ .01	$ .05
Rawley, Shane	90SC	71	$ .01	$ .04	Reynolds, Harold	93SC	559	$ .01	$ .03
Ray, Johnny	88SC	254	$ .01	$ .04	Reynolds, Harold	93SCS	134	$ .01	$ .05
Ray, Johnny	89SC	14	$ .01	$ .03	Reynolds, R.J.	88SC	34	$ .01	$ .04
Ray, Johnny	90SC	293	$ .01	$ .04	Reynolds, R.J.	89SC	91	$ .01	$ .03
Ray, Johnny	91SC	31	$ .01	$ .04	Reynolds, R.J.	90SC	469	$ .01	$ .04
Rayford, Floyd	88SC	359	$ .01	$ .04	Reynolds, R.J.	91SC	273	$ .01	$ .04
Ready, Randy	88SC	512	$ .01	$ .04	Reynolds, Shane	93SC	282	$ .01	$ .03
Ready, Randy	89SC	426	$ .01	$ .03	Reynolds, Shane	93SCP	254	$ .01	$ .08
Ready, Randy	89SCTR	60	$ .01	$ .05	Reynoso, Armando	92SC	877	$ .01	$ .10
Ready, Randy	90SC	376	$ .01	$ .04	Rhoden, Rick	88SC	74	$ .01	$ .04
Ready, Randy	91SC	615	$ .01	$ .04	Rhoden, Rick	89SC	317	$ .01	$ .03
Ready, Randy	92SC	59	$ .01	$ .04	Rhodes, Arthur Lee	92SC	736	$ .01	$ .10
Reardon, Jeff	88SC	91	$ .01	$ .10	Rhodes, Arthur	92SCP	251	$ .05	$ .20
Reardon, Jeff	89SC	305	$ .01	$ .03	Rhodes, Arthur	93SC	360	$ .01	$ .10
Reardon, Jeff	90SC	522	$ .01	$ .04	Rhodes, Arthur	93SCS	300	$ .01	$ .05
Reardon, Jeff	90SCTR	17	$ .01	$ .05	Rhodes, Karl	91SC	365	$ .01	$ .10
Reardon, Jeff	91SC	164	$ .01	$ .04	Rice, Jim	88SC	14	$ .01	$ .10
Reardon, Jeff	92SC	58	$ .01	$ .04	Rice, Jim	89SC	85	$ .01	$ .10
Reardon, Jeff	92SCP	158	$ .01	$ .05	Rice, Pat	92SC	423	$ .01	$ .10
Reardon, Jeff	92SCTR	46	$ .01	$ .05	Righetti, Dave	88SC	351	$ .01	$ .04
Reardon, Jeff	93SC	514	$ .01	$ .03	Righetti, Dave	89SC	225	$ .01	$ .03
Reardon, Jeff	93SC	564	$ .01	$ .03	Righetti, Dave	90SC	194	$ .01	$ .04
Reardon, Jeff	93SCS	362	$ .01	$ .05	Righetti, Dave	91SC	24	$ .01	$ .04
Reboulet, Jeff	93SC	233	$ .01	$ .03	Righetti, Dave	91SCTR	53	$ .01	$ .05
Redfield, Joe	92SC	412	$ .01	$ .10	Righetti, Dave	92SC	260	$ .01	$ .04
Redus, Gary	88SC	443	$ .01	$ .04	Righetti, Dave	92SCP	82	$ .01	$ .05
Redus, Gary	89SC	177	$ .01	$ .03	Rijo, Jose	88SC	392	$ .01	$ .15
Redus, Gary	90SC	14	$ .01	$ .04	Rijo, Jose	88SCTR	27	$ .10	$ .50
Redus, Gary	91SC	226	$ .01	$ .04	Rijo, Jose	89SC	552	$ .01	$ .15

SCORE

Player	Year	No.	VG	EX/MT	Player	Year	No.	VG	EX/MT
Rijo, Jose	90SC	511	$ .01	$ .04	Rivera, Ben	93SCS	329	$ .01	$ .05
Rijo, Jose	91SC	658	$ .01	$ .04	Rivera, Luis	89SC	169	$ .01	$ .03
Rijo, Jose	92SC	232	$ .01	$ .04	Rivera, Luis	91SC	271	$ .01	$ .04
Rijo, Jose	92SCP	508	$ .01	$ .05	Rivera, Luis	92SC	159	$ .01	$ .04
Rijo, Jose	93SC	105	$ .01	$ .03	Rivera, Luis	92SCP	346	$ .01	$ .05
Rijo, Jose	93SCP	77	$ .01	$ .08	Rivera, Luis	93SCP	159	$ .01	$ .08
Rijo, Jose	93SCS	163	$ .01	$ .05	Roberts, Bip	90SC	51	$ .01	$ .04
Riles, Ernest	88SC	349	$ .01	$ .04	Roberts, Bip	91SC	28	$ .01	$ .04
Riles, Ernest	88SCTR	57	$ .01	$ .15	Roberts, Bip	92SC	123	$ .01	$ .04
Riles, Ernest	89SC	458	$ .01	$ .03	Roberts, Bip	92SCP	404	$ .01	$ .05
Riles, Ernest	90SC	447	$ .01	$ .04	Roberts, Bip	92SCTR	79	$ .01	$ .05
Riles, Ernest	91SC	626	$ .01	$ .04	Roberts, Bip	93SC	85	$ .01	$ .03
Riles, Ernest	91SCTR	55	$ .01	$ .05	Roberts, Bip	93SC	516	$ .01	$ .03
Riles, Ernest	92SC	222	$ .01	$ .04	Roberts, Bip	93SCS	111	$ .01	$ .05
Ripken, Bill	88SC	200	$ .01	$ .10	Roberts, Chris	93SC	499	$ .01	$ .10
Ripken, Bill	89SC	18	$ .01	$ .03	Roberts, Chris	93SCS	297	$ .05	$ .25
Ripken, Bill	90SC	174	$ .01	$ .04	Robidoux, Billy Jo	88SC	334	$ .01	$ .04
Ripken, Bill	91SC	487	$ .01	$ .04	Robinson, Don	88SC	618	$ .01	$ .04
Ripken, Billy	92SC	97	$ .01	$ .04	Robinson, Don	89SC	440	$ .01	$ .03
Ripken, Billy	92SCP	336	$ .01	$ .05	Robinson, Don	90SC	112	$ .01	$ .04
					Robinson, Don	91SC	639	$ .01	$ .04
					Robinson, Don	92SCP	463	$ .01	$ .05
					Robinson, Jeff D.	88SC	439	$ .01	$ .04
					Robinson, Jeff D.	89SC	309	$ .01	$ .03
					Robinson, Jeff D.	91SC	192	$ .01	$ .04
					Robinson, Jeff D.	92SC	274	$ .01	$ .04
					Robinson, Jeff M.	88SC	549	$ .01	$ .15
					Robinson, Jeff M.	89SC	284	$ .01	$ .03
					Robinson, Jeff M.	90SC	333	$ .01	$ .04
					Robinson, Jeff M.	91SC	129	$ .01	$ .04
					Robinson, Jeff M.	92SC	186	$ .01	$ .04
					Robinson, Jeff M.	92SCP	516	$ .01	$ .05
					Robinson, Ron	88SC	476	$ .01	$ .04
					Robinson, Ron	89SC	559	$ .01	$ .03
					Robinson, Ron	90SC	495	$ .01	$ .04
					Robinson, Ron	91SC	517	$ .01	$ .04
					Rochford, Mike	91SC	739	$ .01	$ .04
					Rodriguez, Carlos	92SC	411	$ .01	$ .04
					Rodriguez, Henry	93SC	244	$ .01	$ .03
					Rodriguez, Henry	93SCP	182	$ .01	$ .08
					Rodriguez, Henry	93SCS	404	$ .01	$ .05
					Rodriguez, Ivan	91SCTR	82	$ .10	$1.00
					Rodriguez, Ivan	92SC	700	$ .05	$ .35
					Rodriguez, Ivan	92SCP	156	$ .10	$ .50
					Rodriguez, Ivan	93SC	507	$ .01	$ .15
					Rodriguez, Ivan	93SC	537	$ .01	$ .15
					Rodriguez, Ivan	93SCP	21	$ .10	$ .40
					Rodriguez, Ivan	93SCP	301	$ .05	$ .20
					Rodriguez, Ivan	93SCS	136	$ .05	$ .25
					Rodriguez, Juan	93SC	25	$ .05	$ .25
					Rodriguez, Rich	91SC	593	$ .01	$ .10
					Rodriguez, Rich	92SC	149	$ .01	$ .04

Billy Ripken

Player	Year	No.	VG	EX/MT
Ripken, Billy	93SCP	153	$ .01	$ .08
Ripken, Jr., Cal	88SC	550	$ .10	$ .50
Ripken, Jr., Cal	88SC	651	$ .05	$ .20
Ripken, Jr., Cal	89SC	15	$ .10	$ .50
Ripken, Jr., Cal	90SC	2	$ .05	$ .35
Ripken, Jr., Cal	91SC	95	$ .05	$ .25
Ripken, Jr., Cal	91SCTF	849	$ .01	$ .15
Ripken, Jr., Cal	92SC	540	$ .05	$ .25
Ripken, Jr., Cal	92SC	788	$ .01	$ .15
Ripken, Jr., Cal	92SC	794	$ .05	$ .20
Ripken, Jr., Cal	92SCAS	433	$ .01	$ .10
Ripken, Jr., Cal	92SCDT	884	$ .05	$ .35
Ripken, Jr., Cal	92SCP	200	$ .10	$ .50
Ripken, Jr., Cal	93SC	6	$ .05	$ .35
Ripken, Jr., Cal	93SCP	20	$ .10	$ .50
Ripken, Jr., Cal	93SCP	305	$ .05	$ .25
Ripken, Jr., Cal	93SCS	18	$ .05	$ .35
Ritchie, Todd	91SC	678	$ .05	$ .20
Ritchie, Wally	88SC	526	$ .01	$ .04
Ritchie, Wally	92SC	619	$ .01	$ .04
Ritz, Kevin	90SC	572	$ .01	$ .10
Rivera, Ben	92SCP	554	$ .05	$ .20
Rivera, Ben	93SC	242	$ .01	$ .03

Player	Year	No.	VG	EX/MT
Rodriguez, Rich	93SC	466	$ .01	$ .03
Rodriguez, Rosario	91SC	373	$ .01	$ .10
Roenicke, Gary	88SC	482	$ .01	$ .04
Roenicke, Ron	88SC	566	$ .01	$ .04
Hoesler, Mike	90SC	648	$ .01	$ .04
Rogers, Kenny	89SCTR	107	$ .01	$ .10
Rogers, Kenny	90SC	301	$ .01	$ .04
Rogers, Kenny	91SC	155	$ .01	$ .04
Rogers, Kenny	92SC	101	$ .01	$ .04
Rogers, Kenny	92SCP	482	$ .01	$ .05
Rogers, Kenny	93SC	204	$ .01	$ .03
Rogers, Kevin	93SC	319	$ .01	$ .10
Rojas, Mel	91SC	729	$ .01	$ .10
Rojas, Mel	92SC	725	$ .01	$ .04
Rojas, Mel	93SC	363	$ .01	$ .03
Romero, Ed	88SC	259	$ .01	$ .04
Romine, Kevin	88SC	644	$ .01	$ .04
Romine, Kevin	89SC	541	$ .01	$ .03
Romine, Kevin	90SC	458	$ .01	$ .04
Romine, Kevin	91SC	116	$ .01	$ .04
Roomes, Rolando	89SCTR	109	$ .01	$ .10
Roomes, Rolando	90SC	417	$ .01	$ .04
Rose, Bobby	90SC	604	$ .01	$ .10

SCORE

Player	Year	No.	VG	EX/MT
Rose, Bobby	92SC	558	$ .01	$ .04
Rosenberg, Steve	90SC	523	$ .01	$ .04
Rosenthal, Wayne	92SC	749	$ .01	$ .10
Rossy, Rico	92SC	817	$ .01	$ .04
Rowland, Rich	93SC	283	$ .01	$ .03
Rowland, Rich	93SCP	264	$ .01	$ .08
Royer, Stan	92SC	822	$ .01	$ .04
Royer, Stan	92SCP	263	$ .01	$ .10
Ruffcorn, Scott	92SC	806	$ .05	$ .25
Ruffcorn, Scott	92SCP	300	$ .10	$ .40
Ruffin, Bruce	88SC	492	$ .01	$ .04
Ruffin, Bruce	89SC	328	$ .01	$ .03
Ruffin, Bruce	91SC	524	$ .01	$ .04
Ruffin, Bruce	92SC	161	$ .01	$ .04
Ruffin, Bruce	92SCTR	71	$ .01	$ .05
Ruskin, Scott	91SC	799	$ .01	$ .04
Ruskin, Scott	92SC	121	$ .01	$ .04
Ruskin, Scott	92SCTR	57	$ .01	$ .05

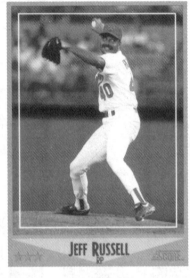

Player	Year	No.	VG	EX/MT
Russell, Jeff	88SC	514	$ .01	$ .04
Russell, Jeff	89SC	438	$ .01	$ .03
Russell, Jeff	90SC	263	$ .01	$ .04
Russell, Jeff	91SC	277	$ .01	$ .04
Russell, Jeff	92SC	124	$ .01	$ .04
Russell, Jeff	92SCP	209	$ .01	$ .05
Russell, Jeff	93SC	413	$ .01	$ .03
Russell, Jeff	93SCS	365	$ .01	$ .05
Russell, John	91SC	802	$ .01	$ .04
Russell, John	92SC	339	$ .01	$ .04
Ruth, Babe	92SC	879	$ .10	$ .40
Ryan, Ken	93SC	329	$ .01	$ .15
Ryan, Ken	93SCP	278	$ .10	$ .40
Ryan, Nolan	88SC	575	$ .10	$ .75
Ryan, Nolan	89SC	300	$ .10	$ .50
Ryan, Nolan	89SCTR	2	$ .15	$1.50
Ryan, Nolan	90SC	250	$ .10	$ .50
Ryan, Nolan	90SC	696	$ .05	$ .25
Ryan, Nolan	91SC	4	$ .05	$ .35
Ryan, Nolan	91SCBC	7	$ .25	$2.50
Ryan, Nolan	91SCHL	417	$ .05	$ .25
Ryan, Nolan	91SCKM	686	$ .05	$ .25
Ryan, Nolan	91SCNH	701	$ .05	$ .25
Ryan, Nolan	92SC	2	$ .10	$ .50
Ryan, Nolan	92SC	425	$ .05	$ .25
Ryan, Nolan	92SCP	50	$ .15	$1.50
Ryan, Nolan	92SCP	281	$ .10	$ .40
Ryan, Nolan	92SCP	294	$ .10	$ .75
Ryan, Nolan	92SCP	618	$ .10	$ .50
Ryan, Nolan	93SC	59	$ .10	$ .50
Ryan, Nolan	93SCP	75	$ .10	$1.00
Ryan, Nolan	93SCP	290	$ .10	$ .50
Ryan, Nolan	93SCS	90	$ .10	$ .50
Saberhagen, Bret	88SC	89	$ .01	$ .15
Saberhagen, Bret	89SC	251	$ .01	$ .10
Saberhagen, Bret	90SC	195	$ .01	$ .10
Saberhagen, Bret	91SC	6	$ .01	$ .04
Saberhagen, Bret	92SC	6	$ .01	$ .04
Saberhagen, Bret	92SC	786	$ .01	$ .04
Saberhagen, Bret	92SCP	442	$ .01	$ .05
Saberhagen, Bret	92SCTR	20	$ .01	$ .05
Saberhagen, Bret	93SC	115	$ .01	$ .03
Saberhagen, Bret	93SCP	185	$ .01	$ .08
Saberhagen, Bret	93SCS	123	$ .01	$ .10
Sabo, Chris	88SCTR	100	$1.00	$4.00
Sabo, Chris	89SC	104	$ .10	$ .40
Sabo, Chris	90SC	70	$ .01	$ .10
Sabo, Chris	91SC	462	$ .01	$ .10
Sabo, Chris	92SC	70	$ .01	$ .04
Sabo, Chris	92SCP	135	$ .01	$ .05
Sabo, Chris	93SC	149	$ .01	$ .03
Sabo, Chris	93SCP	47	$ .01	$ .08
Sabo, Chris	93SCS	135	$ .01	$ .05
Salas, Mark	88SC	232	$ .01	$ .04
Salas, Mark	88SCTR	52	$ .01	$ .15
Salas, Mark	89SC	542	$ .01	$ .03
Salas, Mark	92SC	394	$ .01	$ .04
Salazar, Angel	88SC	330	$ .01	$ .04
Salazar, Angel	89SC	527	$ .01	$ .03
Salazar, Luis	88SC	284	$ .01	$ .04
Salazar, Luis	88SCTR	13	$ .01	$ .15
Salazar, Luis	89SC	316	$ .01	$ .03
Salazar, Luis	90SC	92	$ .01	$ .04
Salazar, Luis	91SC	207	$ .01	$ .04
Salazar, Luis	92SC	508	$ .01	$ .04
Salazar, Luis	92SCP	372	$ .01	$ .05
Salkeld, Roger	90SC	674	$ .10	$ .50
Salmon, Tim	92SCTR	93	$1.00	$4.00
Salmon, Tim	93SC	346	$ .15	$1.25
Salmon, Tim	93SCP	276	$ .20	$2.00
Salmon, Tim	93SCP	303	$ .05	$ .35
Salmon, Tim	93SCS	339	$ .20	$2.00
Sambito, Joe	88SC	314	$ .01	$ .04
Sampen, Bill	90SCTR	79	$ .01	$ .10
Sampen, Bill	91SC	68	$ .01	$ .10
Sampen, Bill	92SC	166	$ .01	$ .04
Samuel, Juan	88SC	32	$ .01	$ .04
Samuel, Juan	89SC	255	$ .01	$ .03
Samuel, Juan	89SCTR	21	$ .01	$ .05
Samuel, Juan	90SC	198	$ .01	$ .04
Samuel, Juan	90SCTR	33	$ .01	$ .05
Samuel, Juan	91SC	446	$ .01	$ .04
Samuel, Juan	92SC	73	$ .01	$ .04
Samuel, Juan	92SCP	99	$ .01	$ .05
Samuel, Juan	93SC	611	$ .01	$ .03
Samuel, Juan	93SCS	237	$ .01	$ .05
Sanchez, Rey	92SCP	550	$ .05	$ .20
Sanchez, Rey	93SC	324	$ .01	$ .03
Sandberg, Ryne	88SC	26	$ .10	$ .50
Sandberg, Ryne	89SC	35	$ .10	$ .40
Sandberg, Ryne	90SC	90	$ .05	$ .35
Sandberg, Ryne	90SC	561	$ .05	$ .25
Sandberg, Ryne	90SCDT	691	$ .01	$ .15
Sandberg, Ryne	91SC	3	$ .05	$ .20
Sandberg, Ryne	91SC	815	$ .05	$ .25
Sandberg, Ryne	91SCAS	665	$ .01	$ .10
Sandberg, Ryne	91SCTF	862	$ .01	$ .15
Sandberg, Ryne	92SC	200	$ .05	$ .25
Sandberg, Ryne	92SCAS	774	$ .01	$ .10
Sandberg, Ryne	92SCDT	442	$ .05	$ .25

SCORE

Player	Year	No.	VG	EX/MT	Player	Year	No.	VG	EX/MT
Sandberg, Ryne	92SCP	10	$.10	$.50	Schatzeder, Dan	90SC	418	$.01	$.04
Sandberg, Ryne	92SCP	617	$.05	$.25	Schilling, Curt	90SC	581	$.01	$.15
Sandberg, Ryne	93SC	4	$.05	$.25	Schilling, Curt	91SC	788	$.01	$.04
Sandberg, Ryne	93SC	530	$.01	$.10	Schilling, Curt	91SCTR	80	$.01	$.05
Sandberg, Ryne	93SCP	15	$.10	$.50	Schilling, Curt	92SC	671	$.01	$.04
Sandberg, Ryne	93SCS	97	$.05	$.25	Schilling, Curt	92SCTR	25	$.01	$.05
Sanders, Deion	90SC	586	$.05	$.35	Schilling, Curt	93SC	52	$.01	$.03
Sanders, Deion	91SCTR	34	$.05	$.20	Schilling, Curt	93SCS	229	$.01	$.05
Sanders, Deion	92SC	571	$.01	$.15	Schiraldi, Calvin	88SC	218	$.01	$.04
Sanders, Deion	92SCP	170	$.05	$.20	Schiraldi, Calvin	88SCTR	39	$.01	$.15
Sanders, Deion	93SC	123	$.01	$.10	Schiraldi, Calvin	89SC	321	$.01	$.03
Sanders, Deion	93SCP	4	$.05	$.25	Schiraldi, Calvin	91SC	611	$.01	$.04
Sanders, Deion	93SCS	84	$.05	$.20	Schmidt, Dave	88SC	103	$.01	$.04
Sanders, Reggie	92SC	829	$.05	$.25	Schmidt, Dave	89SC	292	$.01	$.03
Sanders, Reggie	92SCP	440	$.10	$.40	Schmidt, Dave	90SC	30	$.01	$.04
Sanders, Reggie	93SC	171	$.01	$.15	Schmidt, Dave	91SC	156	$.01	$.04
Sanders, Reggie	93SCP	158	$.01	$.15	Schmidt, Jeff	93SC	501	$.01	$.10
Sanders, Reggie	93SCS	274	$.05	$.20	Schmidt, Mike	88SC	16	$.05	$.35
Sanderson, Scott	88SC	544	$.01	$.04	Schmidt, Mike	88SC	657	$.05	$.25
Sanderson, Scott	90SC	488	$.01	$.04	Schmidt, Mike	89SC	149	$.05	$.35
Sanderson, Scott	90SCTR	61	$.01	$.05	Schofield, Dick	88SC	274	$.01	$.04
Sanderson, Scott	91SC	118	$.01	$.04	Schofield, Dick	89SC	16	$.01	$.03
Sanderson, Scott	91SCTR	78	$.01	$.05	Schofield, Dick	90SC	44	$.01	$.04
Sanderson, Scott	92SC	211	$.01	$.04	Schofield, Dick	91SC	776	$.01	$.04
Sanderson, Scott	92SCP	337	$.01	$.05	Schofield, Dick	92SC	552	$.01	$.04
Sanderson, Scott	92SCP	587	$.01	$.05	Schofield, Dick	92SCP	338	$.01	$.05
Sanderson, Scott	93SC	618	$.01	$.03	Schofield, Dick	92SCTR	26	$.01	$.05
Sanderson, Scott	93SCS	261	$.01	$.05	Schooler, Mike	88SCTR	91	$.10	$.40
Sanford, Mo	92SC	769	$.01	$.15	Schooler, Mike	89SC	528	$.01	$.10
Sanford, Mo	92SCP	254	$.01	$.10	Schooler, Mike	90SC	149	$.01	$.04
Sanford, Mo	93SCP	230	$.01	$.08	Schooler, Mike	91SC	489	$.01	$.04
Santana, Andres	91SC	762	$.01	$.10	Schooler, Mike	92SC	654	$.01	$.04
Santana, Rafael	88SC	316	$.01	$.04	Schooler, Mike	92SCP	171	$.01	$.05
Santana, Rafael	88SCTR	54	$.01	$.15	Schooler, Mike	93SC	544	$.01	$.03
Santana, Rafael	89SC	296	$.01	$.03	Schooler, Mike	93SCS	392	$.01	$.05
Santiago, Benny	88SC	25	$.01	$.15	Schourek, Pete	91SCTR	87	$.01	$.15
Santiago, Benny	88SC	654	$.01	$.10	Schourek, Pete	92SC	332	$.01	$.04
Santiago, Benny	89SC	4	$.01	$.10	Schourek, Pete	92SCP	141	$.01	$.05
Santiago, Benny	90SC	454	$.01	$.04	Schroeder, Bill	88SC	311	$.01	$.04
Santiago, Benny	91SC	810	$.01	$.04	Schroeder, Bill	90SC	362	$.01	$.04
Santiago, Benny	91SCAS	663	$.01	$.04	Schrom, Ken	88SC	574	$.01	$.04
Santiago, Benny	91SCDT	893	$.01	$.10	Schu, Rick	88SC	448	$.01	$.04
Santiago, Benny	91SCRM	416	$.01	$.05	Schu, Rick	89SC	452	$.01	$.03
Santiago, Benny	91SCTF	870	$.01	$.04	Schulz, Jeff	91SC	336	$.01	$.10
Santiago, Benny	92SC	245	$.01	$.04	Scioscia, Mike	88SC	53	$.01	$.04
Santiago, Benito	92SCP	2	$.10	$.40	Scioscia, Mike	89SC	121	$.01	$.03
Santiago, Benito	92SCP	601	$.01	$.05	Scioscia, Mike	90SC	398	$.01	$.04
Santiago, Benito	92SCP	615	$.01	$.05	Scioscia, Mike	91SC	520	$.01	$.04
Santiago, Benito	93SC	591	$.01	$.03	Scioscia, Mike	92SC	226	$.01	$.04
Santiago, Benito	93SCS	269	$.01	$.05	Scioscia, Mike	92SCAS	782	$.01	$.04
Santovenia, Nelson	88SCTR	96	$.05	$.35	Scioscia, Mike	92SCP	210	$.01	$.05
Santovenia, Nelson	89SC	346	$.01	$.15	Scioscia, Mike	93SC	623	$.01	$.03
Santovenia, Nelson	90SC	451	$.01	$.04	Scioscia, Mike	93SCS	69	$.01	$.05
Santovenia, Nelson	91SC	777	$.01	$.04	Scott, Gary	91SCTR	90	$.05	$.20
Sasser, Mackey	88SC	642	$.01	$.10	Scott, Gary	92SCP	269	$.01	$.05
Sasser, Mackey	88SCTR	30	$.05	$.25	Scott, Gary	93SC	547	$.01	$.03
Sasser, Mackey	89SC	303	$.01	$.03	Scott, Mike	88SC	335	$.01	$.04
Sasser, Mackey	90SC	510	$.01	$.04	Scott, Mike	89SC	550	$.01	$.03
Sasser, Mackey	91SC	307	$.01	$.04	Scott, Mike	90SC	40	$.01	$.04
Sasser, Mackey	92SC	472	$.01	$.04	Scott, Mike	90SCDT	692	$.01	$.10
Sasser, Mackey	92SCP	447	$.01	$.05	Scott, Mike	91SC	46	$.01	$.04
Sax, Steve	88SC	35	$.01	$.10	Scott, Tim	93SC	251	$.01	$.03
Sax, Steve	89SC	69	$.01	$.10	Scudder, Scott	89SCTR	99	$.05	$.25
Sax, Steve	89SCTR	20	$.01	$.10	Scudder, Scott	90SC	518	$.01	$.15
Sax, Steve	90SC	125	$.01	$.10	Scudder, Scott	91SC	642	$.01	$.04
Sax, Steve	91SC	32	$.01	$.04	Scudder, Scott	92SC	209	$.01	$.04
Sax, Steve	92SC	475	$.01	$.04	Scudder, Scott	92SCP	480	$.01	$.05
Sax, Steve	92SCP	328	$.01	$.05	Scudder, Scott	92SCTR	67	$.01	$.05
Sax, Steve	92SCTR	4	$.01	$.05	Scurry, Rod	89SC	516	$.01	$.03
Sax, Steve	93SC	418	$.01	$.03	Seanez, Rudy	92SC	696	$.01	$.04
Sax, Steve	93SCS	160	$.01	$.05	Searcy, Steve	89SC	627	$.01	$.10
Scanlan, Bob	91SCTR	102	$.01	$.10	Searcy, Steve	91SC	649	$.01	$.04
Scanlan, Bob	92SC	285	$.01	$.04	Searcy, Steve	92SC	698	$.01	$.04
Scanlan, Bob	93SC	361	$.01	$.03	Sebra, Bob	88SC	337	$.01	$.04
Schaefer, Jeff	92SC	629	$.01	$.04	Segui, David	90SCTR	95	$.01	$.10

SCORE

Player	Year	No.	VG	EX/MT	Player	Year	No.	VG	EX/MT
Segui, David	91SC	362	$ .01	$ .10	Shumpert, Terry	92SCP	203	$ .01	$ .05
Segui, David	92SC	554	$ .01	$ .04	Sierra, Ruben	88SC	113	$ .10	$ .40
Segui, David	92SCP	185	$ .01	$ .05	Sierra, Ruben	89SC	43	$ .05	$ .25
Segui, David	93SC	610	$ .01	$ .03	Sierra, Ruben	90SC	420	$ .05	$ .20
Segura, Jose	92SC	278	$ .01	$ .10	Sierra, Ruben	91SC	495	$ .01	$ .15
Seitzer, Kevin	88SC	6	$ .01	$ .15	Sierra, Ruben	91SCTF	859	$ .01	$ .10
Seitzer, Kevin	89SC	55	$ .01	$ .10	Sierra, Ruben	92SC	490	$ .01	$ .10
Seitzer, Kevin	90SC	199	$ .01	$ .04	Sierra, Ruben	92SCAS	437	$ .01	$ .10
Seitzer, Kevin	91SC	279	$ .01	$ .04	Sierra, Ruben	92SCP	14	$ .05	$ .25
Seitzer, Kevin	92SC	310	$ .01	$ .04	Sierra, Ruben	92SCP	616	$ .05	$ .20
Seitzer, Kevin	92SCP	11	$ .01	$ .05	Sierra, Ruben	92SCTR	63	$ .05	$ .25
Seitzer, Kevin	92SCTR	2	$ .01	$ .05	Sierra, Ruben	93SC	608	$ .01	$ .15
Seitzer, Kevin	93SC	571	$ .01	$ .03	Sierra, Ruben	93SCP	200	$ .05	$ .25
Seitzer, Kevin	93SCP	117	$ .01	$ .08	Sierra, Ruben	93SCS	366	$ .01	$ .15
Seitzer, Kevin	93SCS	87	$ .01	$ .05	Silvestri, Dave	92SCP	531	$ .01	$ .15
Sele, Aaron	92SC	809	$ .05	$ .35	Silvestri, Dave	93SC	252	$ .01	$ .03
Sellers, Jeff	88SC	541	$ .01	$ .04	Silvestri, Dave	93SCP	180	$ .01	$ .08
Sellers, Jeff	89SC	491	$ .01	$ .03	Simmons, Ted	88SC	285	$ .01	$ .04
Seminara, Frank	92SCTR	97	$ .01	$ .15	Simmons, Ted	89SC	611	$ .01	$ .03
Seminara, Frank	93SC	342	$ .01	$ .03	Simms, Mike	91SC	766	$ .01	$ .10
Seminara, Frank	93SCS	305	$ .01	$ .05	Simms, Mike	92SC	632	$ .01	$ .04
Serafini, Dan	93SC	497	$ .01	$ .15	Simons, Doug	91SCTR	91	$ .01	$ .10
Serafini, Dan	93SCS	352	$ .05	$ .25	Simons, Doug	92SC	479	$ .01	$ .04
Servais, Scott	92SC	816	$ .01	$ .04	Sisk, Doug	88SC	227	$ .01	$ .04
Servais, Scott	92SCP	255	$ .01	$ .05	Sisk, Doug	89SC	264	$ .01	$ .03
Sharperson, Mike	89SC	602	$ .01	$ .03	Skalski, Joe	90SC	618	$ .01	$ .04
Sharperson, Mike	91SC	546	$ .01	$ .04	Skinner, Joel	88SC	532	$ .01	$ .04
Sharperson, Mike	92SC	592	$ .01	$ .04	Skinner, Joel	89SC	447	$ .01	$ .03
Sharperson, Mike	92SCP	167	$ .01	$ .05	Skinner, Joel	89SCTR	76	$ .01	$ .05
Sharperson, Mike	93SC	429	$ .01	$ .03	Skinner, Joel	91SC	809	$ .01	$ .04
Sharperson, Mike	93SCP	37	$ .01	$ .08	Skinner, Joel	92SC	227	$ .01	$ .04
Sharperson, Mike	93SCS	157	$ .01	$ .05	Slaught, Don	88SC	268	$ .01	$ .04
Shaw, Jeff	91SC	746	$ .01	$ .10	Slaught, Don	88SCTR	19	$ .01	$ .15
Shaw, Jeff	92SC	624	$ .01	$ .04	Slaught, Don	89SC	561	$ .01	$ .03
Sheets, Larry	88SC	219	$ .01	$ .04					
Sheets, Larry	89SC	81	$ .01	$ .03					
Sheets, Larry	90SC	111	$ .01	$ .04					
Sheets, Larry	90SCTR	65	$ .01	$ .05					
Sheets, Larry	91SC	176	$ .01	$ .04					
Sheffield, Gary	89SC	625	$ .20	$2.00					
Sheffield, Gary	90SC	97	$ .10	$ .50					
Sheffield, Gary	91SC	473	$ .05	$ .25					
Sheffield, Gary	92SC	589	$ .05	$ .25					
Sheffield, Gary	92SCP	235	$ .10	$ .50					
Sheffield, Gary	92SCTR	1	$ .05	$ .35					
Sheffield, Gary	93SC	2	$ .05	$ .35					
Sheffield, Gary	93SC	531	$ .01	$ .10					
Sheffield, Gary	93SC	534	$ .01	$ .15					
Sheffield, Gary	93SCP	1	$ .05	$ .35					
Sheffield, Gary	93SCP	300	$ .05	$ .20					
Sheffield, Gary	93SCS	41	$ .05	$ .25					
Shelby, John	88SC	286	$ .01	$ .10					
Shelby, John	89SC	103	$ .01	$ .03					
Shelby, John	91SC	609	$ .01	$ .04					
Sheridan, Pat	88SC	171	$ .01	$ .04					
Sheridan, Pat	89SC	204	$ .01	$ .03					
Sheridan, Pat	89SCTR	71	$ .01	$ .05					
Sheridan, Pat	90SC	509	$ .01	$ .04					
Sherill, Tim	92SC	404	$ .01	$ .04					
Shields, Steve	88SC	396	$ .01	$ .04					
Shields, Steve	88SCTR	47	$ .01	$ .15					
Shields, Steve	89SC	578	$ .01	$ .03					
Shifflett, Steve	93SC	266	$ .01	$ .03					
Shipley, Craig	92SC	856	$ .01	$ .10					
Shirley, Al	92SC	802	$ .05	$ .20					
Shirley, Al	92SCP	297	$ .01	$ .05					
Show, Eric	88SC	338	$ .01	$ .04					
Show, Eric	89SC	254	$ .01	$ .03	Slaught, Don	90SC	79	$ .01	$ .04
Show, Eric	90SC	493	$ .01	$ .04	Slaught, Don	90SCTR	13	$ .01	$ .05
Show, Eric	91SC	563	$ .01	$ .04	Slaught, Don	91SC	610	$ .01	$ .04
Show, Eric	91SCTR	64	$ .01	$ .05	Slaught, Don	92SC	280	$ .01	$ .04
Show, Eric	92SC	662	$ .01	$ .04	Slaught, Don	92SCP	416	$ .01	$ .05
Shumpert, Terry	90SCTR	110	$ .01	$ .10	Slaught, Don	93SC	181	$ .01	$ .03
Shumpert, Terry	91SC	349	$ .01	$ .10	Slaught, Don	93SCP	188	$ .01	$ .08
Shumpert, Terry	92SC	248	$ .01	$ .04	Slaught, Don	93SCS	171	$ .01	$ .05

SCORE

Player	Year	No.	VG	EX/MT	Player	Year	No.	VG	EX/MT
Slocumb, Heath	91SCTR	84	$.01	$.10	Smith, Roy	92SC	256	$.01	$.04
Slocumb, Heath	92SC	213	$.01	$.04	Smith, Zane	88SC	410	$.01	$.04
Slusarski, Joe	91SCTR	105	$.01	$.10	Smith, Zane	89SC	492	$.01	$.03
Slusarski, Joe	92SC	309	$.01	$.04	Smith, Zane	89SCTR	56	$.01	$.05
Slusarski, Joe	92SCP	187	$.01	$.05	Smith, Zane	90SC	477	$.01	$.04
Smalley, Roy	88SC	606	$.01	$.04	Smith, Zane	91SC	845	$.01	$.04
Smiley, John	88SC	287	$.05	$.35	Smith, Zane	92SC	493	$.01	$.04
Smiley, John	89SC	409	$.01	$.10	Smith, Zane	92SCP	237	$.01	$.05
Smiley, John	90SC	334	$.01	$.10	Smith, Zane	93SC	121	$.01	$.03
Smiley, John	91SC	465	$.01	$.04	Smith, Zane	93SCS	231	$.01	$.05
Smiley, John	92SC	659	$.01	$.04	Smithson, Mike	88SCTR	59	$.01	$.15
Smiley, John	92SCP	184	$.01	$.05	Smithson, Mike	89SC	403	$.01	$.03
Smiley, John	92SCTR	22	$.01	$.05	Smithson, Mike	90SC	512	$.01	$.04
Smiley, John	93SC	624	$.01	$.03	Smoltz, John	89SC	616	$.10	$.50
Smiley, John	93SCS	75	$.01	$.05	Smoltz, John	90SC	370	$.05	$.25
Smith, Bryn	88SC	356	$.01	$.04	Smoltz, John	91SC	208	$.01	$.10
Smith, Bryn	89SC	428	$.01	$.03	Smoltz, John	92SC	287	$.01	$.10
Smith, Bryn	90SC	419	$.01	$.04	Smoltz, John	92SCP	191	$.05	$.20
Smith, Bryn	90SCTR	55	$.01	$.05	Smoltz, John	93SC	61	$.01	$.10
Smith, Bryn	91SC	444	$.01	$.04	Smoltz, John	93SCP	143	$.01	$.15
Smith, Bryn	92SC	529	$.01	$.04	Smoltz, John	93SCP	298	$.01	$.15
Smith, Bryn	92SCP	474	$.01	$.05	Smoltz, John	93SCS	177	$.01	$.10
Smith, Dan	91SC	384	$.05	$.25	Snider, Van	89SC	640	$.01	$.15
Smith, Dave	88SC	365	$.01	$.04	Snow, J. T.	93SC	260	$.15	$1.50
Smith, Dave	89SC	245	$.01	$.03	Snow, J. T.	93SCS	385	$.20	$2.00
Smith, Dave	90SC	45	$.01	$.04	Snyder, Cory	88SC	92	$.01	$.10
Smith, Dave	91SC	314	$.01	$.04	Snyder, Cory	89SC	52	$.01	$.15
Smith, Dave	91SCTR	9	$.01	$.05	Snyder, Cory	90SC	10	$.01	$.04
Smith, Dave	92SC	98	$.01	$.04	Snyder, Cory	91SC	19	$.01	$.04
Smith, Dave	92SCP	94	$.01	$.05	Snyder, Cory	91SCRM	695	$.01	$.04
Smith, Dwight	89SC	642	$.01	$.10	Snyder, Cory	91SCTR	61	$.01	$.05
Smith, Dwight	90SC	240	$.01	$.10	Snyder, Cory	92SC	598	$.01	$.04
Smith, Dwight	91SC	301	$.01	$.04	Snyder, Cory	92SCP	506	$.01	$.05
Smith, Dwight	92SC	612	$.01	$.04	Snyder, Cory	92SCTR	48	$.01	$.05
Smith, Dwight	92SCP	293	$.01	$.05	Snyder, Cory	93SC	574	$.01	$.03
Smith, Dwight	93SC	637	$.01	$.03	Snyder, Cory	93SCS	71	$.01	$.05
Smith, Greg	90SC	614	$.01	$.10	Sojo, Luis	91SC	342	$.01	$.10
Smith, Lee	88SC	31	$.01	$.15	Sojo, Luis	91SCTR	49	$.01	$.05
Smith, Lee	88SCTR	20	$.10	$1.00	Sojo, Luis	92SC	127	$.01	$.04
Smith, Lee	89SC	150	$.01	$.03	Sojo, Luis	92SCP	223	$.01	$.05
Smith, Lee	90SC	37	$.01	$.04	Sojo, Luis	93SC	124	$.01	$.03
Smith, Lee	90SCTR	48	$.01	$.05	Sojo, Luis	93SCS	77	$.01	$.05
Smith, Lee	91SC	81	$.01	$.04	Sorrento, Paul	90SC	647	$.05	$.25
Smith, Lee	92SC	630	$.01	$.04	Sorrento, Paul	91SC	796	$.01	$.04
Smith, Lee	92SCAS	781	$.01	$.04	Sorrento, Paul	93SC	194	$.01	$.03
Smith, Lee	92SCP	195	$.01	$.05	Sorrento, Paul	93SCS	226	$.01	$.05
Smith, Lee	93SC	103	$.01	$.03	Sosa, Sammy	90SC	558	$.05	$.25
Smith, Lee	93SC	529	$.01	$.03	Sosa, Sammy	91SC	256	$.01	$.10
Smith, Lee	93SCS	83	$.01	$.05	Sosa, Sammy	92SC	258	$.01	$.04
Smith, Lonnie	88SC	263	$.01	$.04	Sosa, Sammy	92SCP	369	$.01	$.05
Smith, Lonnie	90SC	399	$.01	$.04	Sosa, Sammy	92SCTR	23	$.01	$.05
Smith, Lonnie	91SC	543	$.01	$.04	Sosa, Sammy	93SC	143	$.01	$.03
Smith, Lonnie	92SC	13	$.01	$.04	Sosa, Sammy	93SCP	145	$.01	$.08
Smith, Lonnie	92SCP	465	$.01	$.05	Sosa, Sammy	93SCS	165	$.01	$.05
Smith, Lonnie	93SC	431	$.01	$.03	Soto, Mario	89SC	588	$.01	$.03
Smith, Mike	90SC	635	$.01	$.04	Spehr, Tim	92SC	416	$.01	$.04
Smith, Ozzio	88SC	12	$.06	$.25	Spoior, Chric	88SC	103	$.01	$.04
Smith, Ozzie	89SC	80	$.01	$.10	Speier, Chris	89SC	297	$.01	$.03
Smith, Ozzie	90SC	285	$.01	$.10	Spiers, Bill	89SCTR	82	$.01	$.10
Smith, Ozzie	91SC	825	$.01	$.10	Spiers, Bill	90SC	449	$.01	$.15
Smith, Ozzie	92SC	590	$.01	$.10	Spiers, Bill	91SC	84	$.01	$.04
Smith, Ozzie	92SCP	6	$.05	$.20	Spiers, Bill	92SC	218	$.01	$.05
Smith, Ozzie	92SCP	285	$.05	$.20	Spiers, Bill	92SCP	177	$.01	$.05
Smith, Ozzie	93SC	522	$.01	$.10	Spiers, Bill	93SC	88	$.01	$.03
Smith, Ozzie	93SC	532	$.01	$.10	Spiers, Bill	93SCS	259	$.01	$.05
Smith, Ozzie	93SC	562	$.01	$.10	Spilman, Harry	88SC	619	$.01	$.04
Smith, Ozzie	93SCS	15	$.01	$.15	Sprague, Ed	91SCTR	101	$.05	$.04
Smith, Pete	88SCTR	84	$.25	$2.50	Sprague, Ed	92SC	504	$.01	$.04
Smith, Pete	89SC	207	$.01	$.03	Sprague, Ed	93SC	214	$.01	$.03
Smith, Pete	90SC	225	$.01	$.04	Sprague, Ed	93SC	520	$.01	$.04
Smith, Pete	91SC	205	$.01	$.04	Sprague, Ed	93SCP	223	$.01	$.15
Smith, Pete	92SC	464	$.01	$.04	Springer, Russ	92SCP	561	$.05	$.20
Smith, Pete	93SC	408	$.01	$.03	Springer, Russ	93SC	238	$.01	$.10
Smith, Roy	90SC	568	$.01	$.04	Springer, Russ	93SCS	337	$.01	$.04
Smith, Roy	91SC	151	$.01	$.04	St. Claire, Randy	88SC	397	$.01	$.04

SCORE

Player	Year	No.	VG	EX/MT	Player	Year	No.	VG	EX/MT
St. Claire, Randy	92SC	708	$ .01	$ .04	Stillwell, Kurt	93SCP	154	$ .01	$ .08
Stairs, Matt	92SCP	583	$ .01	$ .15	Stillwell, Kurt	93SCS	193	$ .01	$ .05
Stairs, Matt	93SC	232	$ .01	$ .03	Stoddard, Tim	88SC	258	$ .01	$ .04
Stairs, Matt	93SCS	327	$ .01	$ .05	Stottlemyre Jr., Mel	91SC	361	$ .01	$ .04
Stanicek, Pete	88SC	628	$ .01	$ .04	Stottlemyre, Todd	88SCTR	90	$ .20	$2.00
Stanicek, Pete	89SC	236	$ .01	$ .03	Stottlemyre, Todd	89SC	453	$ .01	$ .15
Stankiewicz, Andy	92SCP	564	$ .01	$ .10	Stottlemyre, Todd	90SC	554	$ .01	$ .04
Stankiewicz, Andy	92SCTR	100	$ .01	$ .05	Stottlemyre, Todd	91SC	39	$ .01	$ .04
Stankiewicz, Andy	93SC	338	$ .01	$ .03	Stottlemyre, Todd	92SC	74	$ .01	$ .04
Stankiewicz, Andy	93SCS	279	$ .01	$ .05	Stottlemyre, Todd	92SCP	240	$ .01	$ .05
Stanley, Bob	88SC	300	$ .01	$ .04	Stottlemyre, Todd	93SC	186	$ .01	$ .03
Stanley, Bob	89SC	383	$ .01	$ .03	Straker, Les	88SC	108	$ .01	$ .04
Stanley, Mike	88SC	47	$ .01	$ .04	Straker, Les	89SC	244	$ .01	$ .03
Stanley, Mike	89SC	241	$ .01	$ .03	Strawberry, Darryl	88SC	360	$ .05	$ .25
Stanley, Mike	91SC	92	$ .01	$ .04	Strawberry, Darryl	89SC	10	$ .05	$ .25
Stanley, Mike	92SC	549	$ .01	$ .04	Strawberry, Darryl	90SC	200	$ .05	$ .20
Stanton, Mike	90SC	609	$ .01	$ .15	Strawberry, Darryl	91SC	640	$ .05	$ .15
Stanton, Mike	91SC	468	$ .01	$ .04	Strawberry, Darryl	91SCMB	691	$ .01	$ .10
Stanton, Mike	92SC	498	$ .01	$ .04	Strawberry, Darryl	91SCTF	864	$ .01	$ .10
Stanton, Mike	92SCP	350	$ .01	$ .05	Strawberry, Darryl	91SCTR	16	$ .05	$ .20
Stanton, Mike	93SC	317	$ .01	$ .03	Strawberry, Darryl	92SC	9	$ .01	$ .15
Stapleton, Dave	89SC	581	$ .01	$ .10	Strawberry, Darryl	92SCP	80	$ .05	$ .25
Stargell, Willie	92SCP	588	$ .05	$ .20	Strawberry, Darryl	92SCP	308	$ .01	$ .15
Stark, Matt	91SC	751	$ .01	$ .10	Strawberry, Darryl	93SC	42	$ .01	$ .10
Staubach, Roger	92SCP	589	$ .05	$ .20	Strawberry, Darryl	93SCP	64	$ .05	$ .20
Steinbach, Terry	88SC	82	$ .01	$ .15	Strawberry, Darryl	93SCP	309	$ .01	$ .10
Steinbach, Terry	89SC	365	$ .01	$ .10	Strawberry, Darryl	93SCS	21	$ .01	$ .15
Steinbach, Terry	90SC	162	$ .01	$ .04	Stubbs, Franklin	88SC	147	$ .01	$ .04
Steinbach, Terry	90SCDT	693	$ .01	$ .10	Stubbs, Franklin	89SC	599	$ .01	$ .03
Steinbach, Terry	91SC	780	$ .01	$ .04	Stubbs, Franklin	90SC	478	$ .01	$ .04
Steinbach, Terry	92SC	633	$ .01	$ .04	Stubbs, Franklin	90SCTR	40	$ .01	$ .05
Steinbach, Terry	92SCAS	440	$ .01	$ .04	Stubbs, Franklin	91SC	308	$ .01	$ .04
Steinbach, Terry	92SCP	76	$ .01	$ .05	Stubbs, Franklin	91SCTR	59	$ .01	$ .05
Steinbach, Terry	93SC	626	$ .01	$ .03	Stubbs, Franklin	92SC	292	$ .01	$ .04
Steinbach, Terry	93SCP	12	$ .01	$ .08	Stubbs, Franklin	92SCP	320	$ .01	$ .05
Steinbach, Terry	93SCS	132	$ .01	$ .05	Suero, William	93SC	258	$ .01	$ .03
Stephens, Ray	91SC	743	$ .01	$ .04	Suero, William	93SCP	271	$ .01	$ .08
Stephenson, Phil	90SC	642	$ .01	$ .04	Sullivan, Marc	88SC	271	$ .01	$ .04
Stephenson, Phil	91SC	138	$ .01	$ .04	Sundberg, Jim	88SC	244	$ .01	$ .04
Stevens, Lee	91SC	67	$ .01	$ .10	Surhoff, B.J.	88SC	22	$ .01	$ .10
Stevens, Lee	92SC	372	$ .01	$ .04	Surhoff, B.J.	89SC	154	$ .01	$ .10
Stevens, Lee	92SCP	453	$ .01	$ .05	Surhoff, B.J.	90SC	74	$ .01	$ .04
Stevens, Lee	93SCP	169	$ .01	$ .08	Surhoff, B.J.	91SC	477	$ .01	$ .04
Steverson, Todd	93SC	496	$ .01	$ .15	Surhoff, B.J.	92SC	78	$ .01	$ .04
Steverson, Todd	93SCS	353	$ .05	$ .25	Surhoff, B. J.	92SCP	118	$ .01	$ .05
Stewart, Dave	88SC	458	$ .01	$ .15	Surhoff, B. J.	93SC	33	$ .01	$ .03
Stewart, Dave	89SC	32	$ .01	$ .10	Surhoff, B. J.	93SCP	87	$ .01	$ .08
Stewart, Dave	90SC	410	$ .01	$ .10	Surhoff, B. J.	93SCS	62	$ .01	$ .05
Stewart, Dave	91SC	150	$ .01	$ .10	Sutcliffe, Rick	88SC	50	$ .01	$ .10
Stewart, Dave	91SCDT	883	$ .01	$ .04	Sutcliffe, Rick	89SC	407	$ .01	$ .04
Stewart, Dave	91SCNH	702	$ .01	$ .04	Sutcliffe, Rick	90SC	450	$ .01	$ .04
Stewart, Dave	92SC	580	$ .01	$ .04	Sutcliffe, Rick	91SC	785	$ .01	$ .04
Stewart, Dave	92SCP	157	$ .01	$ .05	Sutcliffe, Rick	92SC	665	$ .01	$ .04
Stewart, Dave	93SC	656	$ .01	$ .03	Sutcliffe, Rick	92SCP	398	$ .01	$ .05
Stewart, Dave	93SCS	240	$ .01	$ .05	Sutcliffe, Rick	92SCTR	8	$ .01	$ .05
Stewart, Shannon	93SC	494	$ .01	$ .15	Sutcliffe, Rick	93SC	563	$ .01	$ .05
Stewart, Shannon	93SCS	355	$ .05	$ .25	Sutcliffe, Rick	93SCS	182	$ .01	$ .05
Stieb, Dave	88SC	76	$ .01	$ .04	Sutko, Glenn	91SC	767	$ .01	$ .10
Stieb, Dave	89SC	197	$ .01	$ .03	Sutter, Bruce	89SC	425	$ .01	$ .04
Stieb, Dave	90SC	201	$ .01	$ .04	Sutton, Don	88SC	105	$ .01	$ .10
Stieb, Dave	91SC	30	$ .01	$ .04	Sutton, Don	89SC	400	$ .01	$ .10
Stieb, Dave	91SCNH	707	$ .01	$ .04	Sveum, Dale	88SC	120	$ .01	$ .04
Stieb, Dave	92SC	656	$ .01	$ .04	Sveum, Dale	89SC	256	$ .01	$ .03
Stieb, Dave	92SCP	108	$ .01	$ .05	Sveum, Dale	91SC	814	$ .01	$ .04
Stieb, Dave	93SC	630	$ .01	$ .03	Sveum, Dale	92SC	181	$ .01	$ .04
Stieb, Dave	93SCS	386	$ .01	$ .05	Swan, Russ	92SC	281	$ .01	$ .04
Stillwell, Kurt	88SC	221	$ .01	$ .04	Swan, Russ	92SCP	484	$ .01	$ .05
Stillwell, Kurt	88SCTR	4	$ .01	$ .15	Swift, Bill	89SC	219	$ .10	$ .75
Stillwell, Kurt	89SC	162	$ .01	$ .03	Swift, Bill	91SC	123	$ .01	$ .04
Stillwell, Kurt	90SC	96	$ .01	$ .04	Swift, Bill	92SC	541	$ .01	$ .15
Stillwell, Kurt	91SC	295	$ .01	$ .04	Swift, Bill	92SCP	448	$ .01	$ .05
Stillwell, Kurt	92SC	236	$ .01	$ .04	Swift, Bill	92SCTR	32	$ .01	$ .05
Stillwell, Kurt	92SCP	418	$ .01	$ .05	Swift, Bill	93SC	67	$ .01	$ .03
Stillwell, Kurt	92SCTR	19	$ .01	$ .05	Swift, Bill	93SCS	51	$ .01	$ .05
Stillwell, Kurt	93SC	379	$ .01	$ .03	Swindell, Greg	88SC	154	$ .01	$ .15

SCORE

Player	Year	No.	VG	EX/MT
Swindell, Greg	89SC	282	$ .01	$ .15
Swindell, Greg	90SC	230	$ .01	$ .10
Swindell, Greg	91SC	110	$ .01	$ .04
Swindell, Greg	92SC	371	$ .01	$ .04
Swindell, Greg	92SCP	327	$ .01	$ .05
Swindell, Greg	92SCTR	10	$ .01	$ .10
Swindell, Greg	93SC	566	$ .01	$ .03
Swindell, Greg	93SCS	179	$ .01	$ .05
Tabler, Pat	88SC	23	$ .01	$ .04
Tabler, Pat	88SCTR	22	$ .01	$ .15
Tabler, Pat	89SC	391	$ .01	$ .03
Tabler, Pat	90SC	242	$ .01	$ .04
Tabler, Pat	91SC	811	$ .01	$ .04
Tabler, Pat	91SCTR	22	$ .01	$ .05
Tabler, Pat	92SC	312	$ .01	$ .04
Tackett, Jeff	92SCTR	86	$ .01	$ .05
Tackett, Jeff	93SC	355	$ .01	$ .03
Tackett, Jeff	93SCS	294	$ .01	$ .05
Tanana, Frank	88SC	490	$ .01	$ .04
Tanana, Frank	89SC	112	$ .01	$ .03
Tanana, Frank	90SC	57	$ .01	$ .04
Tanana, Frank	91SC	328	$ .01	$ .04
Tanana, Frank	92SC	271	$ .01	$ .04
Tanana, Frank	92SCP	198	$ .01	$ .05
Tanana, Frank	93SC	652	$ .01	$ .03
Tanana, Frank	93SCS	398	$ .01	$ .05
Tapani, Kevin	90SCTR	82	$ .05	$ .35
Tapani, Kevin	91SC	60	$ .01	$ .04
Tapani, Kevin	92SC	507	$ .01	$ .04
Tapani, Kevin	92SCP	176	$ .01	$ .05
Tapani, Kevin	93SC	45	$ .01	$ .03
Tapani, Kevin	93SCS	130	$ .01	$ .05
Tartabull, Danny	88SC	106	$ .01	$ .15
Tartabull, Danny	89SC	105	$ .01	$ .15
Tartabull, Danny	90SC	244	$ .01	$ .10
Tartabull, Danny	91SC	515	$ .01	$ .10
Tartabull, Danny	92SC	145	$ .01	$ .10
Tartabull, Danny	92SCP	309	$ .01	$ .05
Tartabull, Danny	92SCP	547	$ .01	$ .10
Tartabull, Danny	92SCTR	3	$ .01	$ .05
Tartabull, Danny	93SC	35	$ .01	$ .03
Tartabull, Danny	93SC	515	$ .01	$ .03
Tartabull, Danny	93SCP	168	$ .01	$ .08
Tartabull, Danny	93SCS	12	$ .01	$ .05
Taubensee, Eddie	92SC	871	$ .01	$ .10
Taubensee, Eddie	92SCP	538	$ .01	$ .15
Taubensee, Eddie	93SC	108	$ .01	$ .03
Taubensee, Eddie	93SCP	140	$ .01	$ .08
Taubensee, Eddie	93SCS	333	$ .01	$ .05
Taylor, Wade	91SCTR	100	$ .01	$ .15
Taylor, Wade	92SC	631	$ .01	$ .04
Tekulve, Kent	88SC	425	$ .01	$ .04
Tekulve, Kent	89SC	287	$ .01	$ .03
Telford, Anthony	91SC	354	$ .01	$ .10
Telford, Anthony	92SC	853	$ .01	$ .04
Templeton, Garry	88SC	189	$ .01	$ .04
Templeton, Garry	89SC	176	$ .01	$ .03
Templeton, Garry	90SC	336	$ .01	$ .04
Templeton, Garry	91SC	117	$ .01	$ .04
Templeton, Garry	91SCTR	38	$ .01	$ .05
Templeton, Garry	92SC	588	$ .01	$ .04
Terrell, Walt	88SC	538	$ .01	$ .04
Terrell, Walt	89SC	314	$ .01	$ .03
Terrell, Walt	89SCTR	75	$ .01	$ .05
Terrell, Walt	90SC	463	$ .01	$ .04
Terrell, Walt	91SC	801	$ .01	$ .04
Terrell, Walt	92SC	355	$ .01	$ .04
Terrell, Walt	92SCP	190	$ .01	$ .05
Terry, Scott	89SC	397	$ .01	$ .03
Terry, Scott	90SC	235	$ .01	$ .04
Terry, Scott	91SC	247	$ .01	$ .04
Terry, Scott	92SC	219	$ .01	$ .04
Tettleton, Mickey	88SC	269	$ .01	$ .10
Tettleton, Mickey	88SCTR	31	$ .10	$ .50
Tettleton, Mickey	89SC	358	$ .01	$ .03

Player	Year	No.	VG	EX/MT
Tettleton, Mickey	90SC	322	$ .01	$ .04
Tettleton, Mickey	91SC	270	$ .01	$ .04
Tettleton, Mickey	91SCTR	25	$ .01	$ .05
Tettleton, Mickey	92SC	134	$ .01	$ .04
Tettleton, Mickey	92SCP	226	$ .01	$ .05
Tettleton, Mickey	93SC	60	$ .01	$ .03

Tettleton, Mickey	93SCP	52	$ .01	$ .08
Tettleton, Mickey	93SCS	60	$ .01	$ .05
Teufel, Tim	88SC	128	$ .01	$ .04
Teufel, Tim	89SC	58	$ .01	$ .03
Teufel, Tim	90SC	501	$ .01	$ .04
Teufel, Tim	91SC	427	$ .01	$ .04
Teufel, Tim	91SCTR	67	$ .01	$ .05
Teufel, Tim	92SC	234	$ .01	$ .04
Teufel, Tim	92SCP	313	$ .01	$ .05
Teufel, Tim	93SC	480	$ .01	$ .03
Teufel, Tim	93SCP	183	$ .01	$ .08
Tewksbury, Bob	91SC	499	$ .01	$ .04
Tewksbury, Bob	92SC	282	$ .01	$ .04
Tewksbury, Bob	92SCP	219	$ .01	$ .05
Tewksbury, Bob	92SCP	288	$ .01	$ .05
Tewksbury, Bob	93SC	34	$ .01	$ .03
Tewksbury, Bob	93SCP	13	$ .01	$ .08
Tewksbury, Bob	93SCS	107	$ .01	$ .05
Thigpen, Bobby	88SC	307	$ .01	$ .15
Thigpen, Bobby	89SC	399	$ .01	$ .03
Thigpen, Bobby	90SC	335	$ .01	$ .04
Thigpen, Bobby	90SCDT	694	$ .01	$ .10
Thigpen, Bobby	91SC	280	$ .01	$ .04
Thigpen, Bobby	91SCAS	401	$ .01	$ .04
Thigpen, Bobby	91SCHL	418	$ .01	$ .05
Thigpen, Bobby	92SC	570	$ .01	$ .04
Thigpen, Bobby	92SCP	214	$ .01	$ .05
Thigpen, Bobby	93SC	582	$ .01	$ .03
Thigpen, Bobby	93SCS	232	$ .01	$ .05
Thomas, Andres	88SC	299	$ .01	$ .04
Thomas, Andres	89SC	406	$ .01	$ .03
Thomas, Andres	90SC	99	$ .01	$ .04
Thomas, Andres	91SC	613	$ .01	$ .04
Thomas, Frank	90SC	663	$1.50	$6.00
Thomas, Frank	90SCTR	86	$1.50	$6.00
Thomas, Frank	91SC	840	$ .10	$1.00
Thomas, Frank	91SCTF	874	$ .10	$ .75

SCORE

Player	Year	No.	VG	EX/MT	Player	Year	No.	VG	EX/MT
Thomas, Frank	92SC	505	$ .10	$1.00	Treadway, Jeff	89SCTR	18	$ .01	$ .05
Thomas, Frank	92SCDT	893	$ .10	$ .75	Treadway, Jeff	90SC	95	$ .01	$ .04
Thomas, Frank	92SCP	1	$ .75	$3.00	Treadway, Jeff	91SC	219	$ .01	$ .04
Thomas, Frank	93SC	3	$ .10	$1.00	Treadway, Jeff	92SC	142	$ .01	$ .04
Thomas, Frank	93SC	510	$ .05	$ .35	Treadway, Jeff	93SC	461	$ .01	$ .03
Thomas, Frank	93SC	541	$ .10	$ .50	Trevino, Alex	88SC	182	$ .01	$ .04
Thomas, Frank	93SCP	108	$ .20	$2.00	Trevino, Alex	89SC	574	$ .01	$ .03
Thomas, Frank	93SCS	6	$ .10	$1.00	Trillo, Manny	88SC	524	$ .01	$ .04
Thome, Jim	92SC	859	$ .01	$ .10	Trillo, Manny	89SC	446	$ .01	$ .03
Thome, Jim	92SCP	247	$ .05	$ .20	Trlicek, Rick	93SC	318	$ .01	$ .03
Thome, Jim	93SC	364	$ .01	$ .03	Trlicek, Rick	93SCP	284	$ .01	$ .08
Thome, Jim	93SCS	304	$ .01	$ .05	Trombley, Mike	93SC	287	$ .01	$ .15
Thompson, Milt	88SC	115	$ .01	$ .10	Trout, Steve	88SC	342	$ .01	$ .04
Thompson, Milt	89SC	92	$ .01	$ .03	Trout, Steve	89SC	522	$ .01	$ .03
Thompson, Milt	89SCTR	45	$ .01	$ .05	Tucker, Michael	93SC	498	$ .10	$ .50
Thompson, Milt	90SC	49	$ .01	$ .04	Tucker, Michael	93SCS	291	$ .10	$1.00
Thompson, Milt	91SC	54	$ .01	$ .04	Tucker, Scooter	93SC	237	$ .01	$ .03
Thompson, Milt	92SC	114	$ .01	$ .04	Tucker, Scooter	93SCP	245	$ .01	$ .08
Thompson, Milt	92SCP	345	$ .01	$ .05	Tudor, John	88SC	275	$ .01	$ .04
Thompson, Milt	93SC	397	$ .01	$ .03	Tudor, John	89SC	560	$ .01	$ .03
Thompson, Milt	93SCS	223	$ .01	$ .05	Tudor, John	91SC	53	$ .01	$ .04
Thompson, Robby	88SC	146	$ .01	$ .04	Tunnell, Lee	88SC	587	$ .01	$ .04
Thompson, Robby	89SC	172	$ .01	$ .03	Upshaw, Willie	88SC	279	$ .01	$ .04
Thompson, Robby	90SC	397	$ .01	$ .04	Upshaw, Willie	88SCTR	42	$ .01	$ .15
Thompson, Robby	91SC	26	$ .01	$ .04	Upshaw, Willie	89SC	188	$ .01	$ .03
Thompson, Robby	92SC	247	$ .01	$ .04	Uribe, Jose	88SC	165	$ .01	$ .04
Thompson, Robby	92SCP	143	$ .01	$ .05	Uribe, Jose	89SC	56	$ .01	$ .03
Thompson, Robby	93SC	593	$ .01	$ .03	Uribe, Jose	90SC	455	$ .01	$ .04
Thompson, Robby	93SCS	139	$ .01	$ .05	Uribe, Jose	91SC	628	$ .01	$ .04
Thompson, Ryan	93SC	227	$ .05	$ .20	Uribe, Jose	92SC	546	$ .01	$ .04
Thompson, Ryan	93SCP	249	$ .05	$ .35	Valdez, Efrain	91SC	723	$ .01	$ .04
Thon, Dickie	88SCTR	29	$ .01	$ .15	Valdez, Rafael	90SCTR	93	$ .01	$ .15
Thon, Dickie	89SC	234	$ .01	$ .03	Valdez, Rafael	91SC	360	$ .01	$ .04
Thon, Dickie	89SCTR	55	$ .01	$ .05	Valentin, John	93SC	243	$ .01	$ .10
Thon, Dickie	90SC	142	$ .01	$ .04	Valentin, John	93SCP	224	$ .05	$ .20
Thon, Dickie	91SC	103	$ .01	$ .04	Valentin, John	93SCS	344	$ .05	$ .20
Thon, Dickie	92SC	24	$ .01	$ .04	Valenzuela, Fernando	88SC	600	$ .01	$ .10
Thon, Dickie	92SCP	394	$ .01	$ .05	Valenzuela, Fernando	89SC	437	$ .01	$ .10
Thon, Dickie	92SCTR	41	$ .01	$ .05	Valenzuela, Fernando	90SC	54	$ .01	$ .04
Thornton, Andre	88SC	231	$ .01	$ .04	Valenzuela, Fernando	91SC	449	$ .01	$ .04
Thurman, Gary	88SC	631	$ .01	$ .15	Valenzuela, Fernando	91SCNH	703	$ .01	$ .04
Thurman, Gary	92SC	512	$ .01	$ .04	Valera, Julio	91SC	353	$ .01	$ .10
Thurmond, Mark	88SC	382	$ .01	$ .04					
Thurmond, Mark	90SC	350	$ .01	$ .04					
Tibbs, Jay	88SC	608	$ .01	$ .04					
Tibbs, Jay	89SC	262	$ .01	$ .03					
Tibbs, Jay	90SC	480	$ .01	$ .04					
Timlin, Mike	91SCTR	85	$ .01	$ .15					
Timlin, Mike	92SC	214	$ .01	$ .04					
Timlin, Mike	93SC	410	$ .01	$ .03					
Tingley, Ron	92SC	757	$ .01	$ .04					
Toliver, Fred	89SC	479	$ .01	$ .03					
Tolleson, Wayne	88SC	117	$ .01	$ .04					
Tolleson, Wayne	90SC	386	$ .01	$ .04					
Tomlin, Randy	91SC	782	$ .01	$ .15					
Tomlin, Randy	92SC	86	$ .01	$ .04					
Tomlin, Randy	92SCP	213	$ .01	$ .05					
Tomlin, Randy	92SCP	606	$ .01	$ .05					
Tomlin, Randy	93SC	101	$ .01	$ .03					
Tomlin, Randy	93SCP	74	$ .01	$ .08					
Tomlin, Randy	93SCS	61	$ .01	$ .05					
Torve, Kelvin	91SC	754	$ .01	$ .04					
Traber, Jim	89SC	590	$ .01	$ .03					
Trammell, Alan	88SC	37	$ .01	$ .15					
Trammell, Alan	88SC	651	$ .05	$ .20					
Trammell, Alan	89SC	110	$ .01	$ .10					
Trammell, Alan	90SC	9	$ .01	$ .10					
Trammell, Alan	91SC	40	$ .01	$ .10					
Trammell, Alan	91SCTF	852	$ .01	$ .04					
Trammell, Alan	92SC	515	$ .01	$ .04					
Trammell, Alan	92SCP	113	$ .01	$ .05					
Trammell, Alan	93SC	313	$ .01	$ .03					
Trammell, Alan	93SCS	230	$ .01	$ .05					
Treadway, Jeff	88SC	646	$ .01	$ .10					
Treadway, Jeff	89SC	86	$ .01	$ .10					

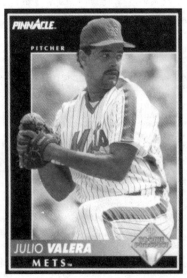

Valera, Julio	92SCP	267	$ .01	$ .10

SCORE

Player	Year	No.	VG	EX/MT	Player	Year	No.	VG	EX/MT
Valera, Julio	93SC	427	$.01	$.03	Viola, Frank	93SCP	76	$.01	$.08
Valera, Julio	93SCP	139	$.01	$.08	Viola, Frank	93SCS	94	$.01	$.05
Valera, Julio	93SCS	288	$.01	$.05	Virgil, Ozzie	88SC	129	$.01	$.04
Valle, Dave	88SC	126	$.01	$.04	Virgil, Ozzie	89SC	111	$.01	$.03
Valle, Dave	89SC	27	$.01	$.03	Vizcaino, Jose	90SC	613	$.01	$.10
Valle, Dave	90SC	109	$.01	$.04	Vizcaino, Jose	91SC	787	$.01	$.04
Valle, Dave	91SC	262	$.01	$.04	Vizcaino, Jose	92SC	169	$.01	$.04
Valle, Dave	92SC	343	$.01	$.04	Vizquel, Omar	89SCTR	105	$.01	$.10
Valle, Dave	92SCP	232	$.01	$.05	Vizquel, Omar	90SC	264	$.01	$.04
Valle, Dave	93SC	200	$.01	$.03	Vizquel, Omar	91SC	299	$.01	$.04
Valle, Dave	93SCP	179	$.01	$.08	Vizquel, Omar	92SC	162	$.01	$.04
Van Poppel, Todd	91SC	389	$.10	$.50	Vizquel, Omar	92SCP	97	$.01	$.05
Van Poppel, Todd	92SC	865	$.05	$.20	Vizquel, Omar	93SC	102	$.01	$.03
Van Poppel, Todd	92SCP	574	$.05	$.20	Vizquel, Omar	93SC	503	$.01	$.03
Van Slyke, Andy	88SC	416	$.01	$.10	Vizquel, Omar	93SCP	95	$.01	$.08
Van Slyke, Andy	89SC	174	$.01	$.10	Vizquel, Omar	93SCS	164	$.01	$.05
Van Slyke, Andy	90SC	440	$.01	$.10	Vosberg, Ed	91SC	757	$.01	$.10
Van Slyke, Andy	91SC	475	$.01	$.10	Wagner, Hector	91SC	730	$.01	$.04
Van Slyke, Andy	91SCRM	698	$.01	$.04	Wagner, Honus	92SC	880	$.05	$.35
Van Slyke, Andy	92SC	655	$.01	$.04	Wagner, Paul	93SC	315	$.01	$.03
Van Slyke, Andy	92SCP	9	$.01	$.05	Wagner, Paul	93SCP	282	$.01	$.08
Van Slyke, Andy	93SC	12	$.01	$.03	Wakamatsu, Don	92SC	814	$.01	$.10
Van Slyke, Andy	93SC	524	$.01	$.03	Wakefield, Tim	92SCTR	92	$.75	$3.00
Van Slyke, Andy	93SC	535	$.01	$.03	Wakefield, Tim	93SC	347	$.10	$.50
Van Slyke, Andy	93SCP	19	$.01	$.08	Wakefield, Tim	93SCS	307	$.10	$.75
Van Slyke, Andy	93SCS	35	$.01	$.05	Walden, Ron	91SC	679	$.01	$.10
Vander Wal, John	92SCP	559	$.05	$.20	Walewander, Jim	88SC	571	$.01	$.04
Vander Wal, John	92SCTR	105	$.05	$.20	Walewander, Jim	89SC	311	$.01	$.03
Vander Wal, John	93SC	359	$.01	$.03	Walk, Bob	88SC	162	$.01	$.04
Vander Wal, John	93SCS	323	$.01	$.05	Walk, Bob	89SC	224	$.01	$.03
Varsho, Gary	89SC	604	$.01	$.15	Walk, Bob	90SC	21	$.01	$.04
Varsho, Gary	91SCTR	72	$.01	$.05	Walk, Bob	91SC	599	$.01	$.04
Varsho, Gary	92SC	481	$.01	$.04	Walk, Bob	92SC	54	$.01	$.04
Vatcher, Jim	91SC	341	$.01	$.10	Walk, Bob	92SCP	410	$.01	$.05
Vaughn, Greg	90SC	585	$.05	$.20	Walk, Bob	93SC	144	$.01	$.03
Vaughn, Greg	91SC	528	$.01	$.10	Walker, Chico	92SC	578	$.01	$.04
Vaughn, Greg	92SC	639	$.01	$.04	Walker, Chico	93SC	399	$.01	$.03
Vaughn, Greg	92SCP	92	$.01	$.05	Walker, Greg	88SC	93	$.01	$.04
Vaughn, Greg	93SC	160	$.01	$.03	Walker, Greg	89SC	37	$.01	$.03
Vaughn, Greg	93SCS	222	$.01	$.05	Walker, Greg	90SC	354	$.01	$.04
Vaughn, Maurice "Mo"	90SC	675	$.15	$1.50	Walker, Larry	90SC	631	$.10	$1.00
Vaughn, Mo	91SC	750	$.05	$.25	Walker, Larry	91SC	241	$.05	$.20
Vaughn, Mo	92SC	556	$.01	$.15	Walker, Larry	92SC	199	$.01	$.15
Vaughn, Mo	92SCP	205	$.05	$.25	Walker, Larry	92SCP	194	$.05	$.25
Vaughn, Mo	93SC	132	$.01	$.03	Walker, Larry	93SC	5	$.01	$.15
Vaughn, Mo	93SCP	189	$.01	$.15	Walker, Larry	93SCP	3	$.05	$.25
Vaughn, Mo	93SCS	214	$.01	$.10	Walker, Larry	93SCP	299	$.01	$.15
Velarde, Randy	90SC	524	$.01	$.04	Walker, Larry	93SCS	27	$.05	$.20
Velarde, Randy	91SC	134	$.01	$.04	Wallace, B. J.	93SC	488	$.05	$.25
Velarde, Randy	92SC	337	$.01	$.04	Wallace, B . J.	93SCS	310	$.10	$.50
Velarde, Randy	93SC	219	$.01	$.03	Wallace, Derek	93SC	492	$.01	$.15
Venable, Max	92SC	477	$.01	$.04	Wallace, Derek	93SCS	357	$.05	$.25
Ventura, Robin	90SC	595	$.10	$.75	Wallach, Tim	88SC	70	$.01	$.10
Ventura, Robin	91SC	320	$.05	$.20	Wallach, Tim	89SC	220	$.01	$.03
Ventura, Robin	92SC	122	$.01	$.15	Wallach, Tim	90SC	192	$.01	$.04
Ventura, Robin	92SCP	121	$.05	$.25	Wallach, Tim	91SC	210	$.01	$.04
Ventura, Robin	92SCP	286	$.05	$.25	Wallach, Tim	91SCTF	865	$.01	$.04
Ventura, Robin	93SC	41	$.01	$.15	Wallach, Tim	92SC	595	$.01	$.04
Ventura, Robin	93SCP	28	$.05	$.25	Wallach, Tim	92SCP	161	$.01	$.05
Ventura, Robin	93SCS	29	$.05	$.25	Wallach, Tim	93SC	211	$.01	$.03
Villanueva, Hector	90SCTR	98	$.01	$.10	Wallach, Tim	93SCP	178	$.01	$.08
Villanueva, Hector	91SC	71	$.01	$.10	Wallach, Tim	93SCS	190	$.01	$.05
Villanueva, Hector	92SC	677	$.01	$.04	Walling, Dennis	88SC	145	$.01	$.04
Villanueva, Hector	92SCP	419	$.01	$.05	Walling, Denny	89SC	49	$.01	$.03
Viola, Frank	88SC	475	$.01	$.15	Walsh, David	91SC	351	$.01	$.10
Viola, Frank	89SC	290	$.01	$.15	Walters, Dan	92SCTR	109	$.01	$.10
Viola, Frank	89SCTR	67	$.01	$.15	Walters, Dan	93SC	332	$.01	$.03
Viola, Frank	90SC	500	$.01	$.10	Walters, Dan	93SCP	215	$.01	$.08
Viola, Frank	91SC	460	$.01	$.10	Walters, Dan	93SCS	289	$.01	$.05
Viola, Frank	91SCDT	882	$.01	$.04	Walton, Bruce	91SCTR	88	$.01	$.10
Viola, Frank	91SCKM	687	$.01	$.04	Walton, Jerome	89SCTR	85	$.01	$.15
Viola, Frank	92SC	220	$.01	$.04	Walton, Jerome	90SC	229	$.01	$.04
Viola, Frank	92SCP	407	$.01	$.05	Walton, Jerome	91SC	13	$.01	$.10
Viola, Frank	92SCTR	6	$.01	$.05	Walton, Jerome	92SC	457	$.01	$.04
Viola, Frank	93SC	55	$.01	$.03	Walton, Jerome	92SCP	224	$.01	$.05

SCORE

Player	Year	No.	VG	EX/MT	Player	Year	No.	VG	EX/MT
Wapnick, Steve	92SC	863	$ .01	$ .15	Wells, David	92SC	49	$ .01	$ .04
Ward, Duane	89SC	359	$ .01	$ .03	Wells, David	92SCP	431	$ .01	$ .05
Ward, Duane	90SC	439	$ .01	$ .04	Wells, David	93SC	648	$ .01	$ .03
Ward, Duane	91SC	561	$ .01	$ .04	Wells, David	93SCP	114	$ .01	$ .08
Ward, Duane	92SC	48	$ .01	$ .04	Wells, Terry	91SC	359	$ .01	$ .10
Ward, Duane	92SCP	385	$ .01	$ .05	West, Dave	89SC	650	$ .01	$ .15
Ward, Duane	93SC	436	$ .01	$ .03	West, Dave	90SC	573	$ .01	$ .04
Ward, Duane	93SCS	258	$ .01	$ .05	West, Dave	91SC	158	$ .01	$ .04
Ward, Gary	88SC	157	$ .01	$ .04	West, Dave	92SC	669	$ .01	$ .04
Ward, Gary	89SC	435	$ .01	$ .03	West, David	92SCP	333	$ .01	$ .05
Ward, Gary	90SC	513	$ .01	$ .04	Weston, Mickey	90SC	616	$ .01	$ .04
Ward, Gary	91SC	637	$ .01	$ .04	Wetherby, Jeff	90SC	540	$ .01	$ .10
Ward, Kevin	92SC	862	$ .01	$ .04	Wetteland, John	89SCTR	90	$ .10	$ .40
Ward, Turner	91SC	732	$ .01	$ .15	Wetteland, John	90SC	388	$ .01	$ .04
Ward, Turner	93SC	473	$ .01	$ .03	Wetteland, John	91SC	267	$ .01	$ .04
Ware, Jeff	92SCP	546	$ .01	$ .15	Wetteland, John	92SCP	461	$ .01	$ .05
Washington, Claudell	88SC	579	$ .01	$ .04	Wetteland, John	92SCP	593	$ .01	$ .05
Washington, Claudell	89SC	211	$ .01	$ .03	Wetteland, John	92SCTR	78	$ .01	$ .05
Washington, Claudell	89SCTR	10	$ .01	$ .05	Wetteland, John	93SC	165	$ .01	$ .03
Washington, Claudell	90SC	298	$ .01	$ .04	Wetteland, John	93SCS	201	$ .01	$ .05
Washington, Claudell	90SCTR	45	$ .01	$ .05	Whitaker, Lou	88SC	56	$ .01	$ .10
Wasinger, Mark	88SC	283	$ .01	$ .04	Whitaker, Lou	89SC	230	$ .01	$ .03
Watson, Allen	92SC	799	$ .05	$ .25	Whitaker, Lou	90SC	75	$ .01	$ .04
Watson, Allen	92SCP	304	$ .10	$ .50	Whitaker, Lou	91SC	297	$ .01	$ .04
Wayne, Edwards	90SCTR	85	$ .01	$ .10	Whitaker, Lou	92SC	255	$ .01	$ .04
Wayne, Gary	89SCTR	91	$ .05	$ .20	Whitaker, Lou	92SCP	29	$ .01	$ .05
Wayne, Gary	90SC	527	$ .01	$ .04	Whitaker, Lou	93SC	596	$ .01	$ .03
Wayne, Gary	91SC	283	$ .01	$ .04	Whitaker, Lou	93SCS	112	$ .01	$ .05
Webster, Lenny	90SC	638	$ .01	$ .10	White, Devon	88SC	212	$ .01	$ .10
Webster, Lenny	92SC	663	$ .01	$ .04	White, Devon	89SC	323	$ .01	$ .10
Webster, Lenny	92SCP	276	$ .01	$ .05	White, Devon	90SC	312	$ .01	$ .04
Webster, Lenny	93SC	471	$ .01	$ .03	White, Devon	91SC	466	$ .01	$ .04
Webster, Mitch	88SC	345	$ .01	$ .04	White, Devon	91SCTR	48	$ .01	$ .05
Webster, Mitch	89SC	71	$ .01	$ .03	White, Devon	92SC	198	$ .01	$ .04
Webster, Mitch	90SC	85	$ .01	$ .04	White, Devon	92SCP	17	$ .01	$ .05
Webster, Mitch	90SCTR	4	$ .01	$ .05	White, Devon	93SC	92	$ .01	$ .03
Webster, Mitch	91SC	594	$ .01	$ .04	White, Devon	93SCP	138	$ .01	$ .08
Webster, Mitch	91SCTR	68	$ .01	$ .05	White, Devon	93SCS	72	$ .01	$ .05
Webster, Mitch	92SC	643	$ .01	$ .04	White, Frank	88SC	79	$ .01	$ .04
Wedge, Eric	93SC	561	$ .05	$ .25	White, Frank	89SC	390	$ .01	$ .03
Wedge, Eric	93SCP	239	$ .10	$ .50	White, Frank	90SC	372	$ .01	$ .04
Wedge, Eric	93SCS	401	$ .05	$ .35	White, Mark	92SC	587	$ .01	$ .04
Wegman, Bill	88SC	296	$ .01	$ .04	White, Rondell	91SC	390	$ .10	$ .50
Wegman, Bill	89SC	335	$ .01	$ .03	Whited, Ed	90SC	644	$ .01	$ .04
Wegman, Bill	90SC	188	$ .01	$ .04	Whitehurst, Wally	90SC	599	$ .01	$ .04
Wegman, Bill	91SC	483	$ .01	$ .04	Whitehurst, Wally	91SC	529	$ .01	$ .04
Wegman, Bill	92SC	374	$ .01	$ .04	Whitehurst, Wally	92SC	299	$ .01	$ .04
Wegman, Bill	92SCP	396	$ .01	$ .05	Whiten, Mark	91SC	358	$ .01	$ .15
Wegman, Bill	93SC	190	$ .01	$ .03	Whiten, Mark	92SCP	355	$ .01	$ .05
Wegman, Bill	93SCS	184	$ .01	$ .05	Whiten, Mark	93SC	106	$ .01	$ .03
Wehner, John	92SC	752	$ .01	$ .10	Whiten, Mark	93SCS	146	$ .01	$ .05
Wehner, John	92SCP	260	$ .01	$ .05	Whitson, Ed	88SC	167	$ .01	$ .04
Weiss, Walt	88SCTR	102	$ .10	$ .50	Whitson, Ed	89SC	329	$ .01	$ .03
Weiss, Walt	89SC	165	$ .01	$ .15	Whitson, Ed	90SC	373	$ .01	$ .04
Weiss, Walt	90SC	110	$ .01	$ .10	Whitson, Ed	91SC	789	$ .01	$ .04
Weiss, Walt	91SC	171	$ .01	$ .04	Whitson, Ed	92SC	564	$ .01	$ .04
Weiss, Walt	92SC	51	$ .01	$ .04	Whitson, Ed	92SCP	104	$ .01	$ .05
Weiss, Walt	92SCP	56	$ .01	$ .05	Whitt, Ernie	88SC	168	$ .01	$ .04
Weiss, Walt	93SC	659	$ .01	$ .03	Whitt, Ernie	89SC	98	$ .01	$ .03
Weiss, Walt	93SCP	231	$ .01	$ .08	Whitt, Ernie	90SC	433	$ .01	$ .04
Weiss, Walt	93SCS	192	$ .01	$ .05	Whitt, Ernie	90SCTR	30	$ .01	$ .05
Welch, Bob	88SC	510	$ .01	$ .04	Whitt, Mike	90SCTR	50	$ .01	$ .05
Welch, Bob	88SCTR	15	$ .01	$ .15	Wickander, Kevin	91SC	355	$ .01	$ .04
Welch, Bob	89SC	308	$ .01	$ .03	Wickander, Kevin	93SC	358	$ .01	$ .03
Welch, Bob	90SC	159	$ .01	$ .04	Wickman, Bob	93SC	291	$ .05	$ .25
Welch, Bob	91SC	311	$ .01	$ .04	Wickman, Bob	93SCP	226	$ .05	$ .35
Welch, Bob	91SC	568	$ .01	$ .04	Wickman, Bob	93SCS	343	$ .05	$ .25
Welch, Bob	91SCMVP	877	$ .01	$ .05	Wiggins, Alan	88SC	291	$ .01	$ .04
Welch, Bob	92SC	300	$ .01	$ .04	Wilkerson, Curt	88SC	127	$ .01	$ .04
Welch, Bob	92SCP	409	$ .01	$ .05	Wilkerson, Curtis	89SC	518	$ .01	$ .03
Welch, Bob	93SC	208	$ .01	$ .03	Wilkerson, Curtis	90SC	474	$ .01	$ .04
Welch, Bob	93SCS	254	$ .01	$ .05	Wilkerson, Curtis	91SC	603	$ .01	$ .04
Wellman, Brad	89SC	504	$ .01	$ .03	Wilkerson, Curtis	92SC	382	$ .01	$ .04
Wells, David	90SC	491	$ .01	$ .04	Wilkins, Dean	90SC	630	$ .01	$ .04
Wells, David	91SC	474	$ .01	$ .04	Wilkins, Rick	91SCTR	103	$ .01	$ .10

SCORE

Player	Year	No.	VG	EX/MT
Wilkins, Rick	92SC	483	$ .01	$ .04
Wilkins, Rick	93SC	185	$ .01	$ .03
Wilkins, Rick	93SCP	206	$ .01	$ .08
Wilkins, Rick	93SCS	390	$ .01	$ .05
Willard, Jerry	92SC	188	$ .01	$ .04
Williams, Bernie	90SC	619	$ .05	$ .25
Williams, Bernie	92SC	401	$ .01	$ .10
Williams, Bernie	92SCP	229	$ .05	$ .20
Williams, Bernie	93SC	120	$ .01	$ .03
Williams, Bernie	93SCP	7	$ .01	$ .08
Williams, Bernie	93SCS	393	$ .01	$ .05
Williams, Brian	92SCP	540	$ .05	$ .25
Williams, Brian	92SCTR	108	$ .05	$ .20
Williams, Brian	93SC	333	$ .01	$ .10
Williams, Brian	93SCS	287	$ .01	$ .10
Williams, Eddie	91SC	552	$ .01	$ .04
Williams, Frank	88SC	317	$ .01	$ .04
Williams, Frank	89SC	485	$ .01	$ .03
Williams, Frank	90SC	341	$ .01	$ .04
Williams, Gerald	93SC	298	$ .01	$ .03
Williams, Gerald	93SCP	266	$ .01	$ .15
Williams, Gerald	93SCS	383	$ .01	$ .10
Williams, Ken	88SC	112	$ .05	$ .20
Williams, Ken	89SC	67	$ .01	$ .03
Williams, Ken	92SC	354	$ .01	$ .04
Williams, Matt	88SC	118	$ .20	$1.75
Williams, Matt	89SC	612	$ .05	$ .25
Williams, Matt	90SC	503	$ .01	$ .10
Williams, Matt	91SC	189	$ .01	$ .10
Williams, Matt	91SCAS	667	$ .01	$ .04
Williams, Matt	91SCMB	689	$ .01	$ .04
Williams, Matt	92SC	230	$ .01	$ .04
Williams, Matt	92SCP	28	$ .01	$ .05
Williams, Matt	93SC	46	$ .01	$ .03
Williams, Matt	93SCP	67	$ .05	$ .20
Williams, Matt	93SCS	95	$ .01	$ .05
Williams, Mitch	88SC	339	$ .01	$ .04
Williams, Mitch	89SC	301	$ .01	$ .03
Williams, Mitch	89SCTR	32	$ .01	$ .05
Williams, Mitch	90SC	262	$ .01	$ .04
Williams, Mitch	90SCDT	695	$ .01	$ .10
Williams, Mitch	91SC	220	$ .01	$ .04
Williams, Mitch	91SCTR	27	$ .01	$ .05
Williams, Mitch	92SC	356	$ .01	$ .04
Williams, Mitch	92SCDT	892	$ .01	$ .04
Williams, Mitch	92SCP	406	$ .01	$ .05
Williams, Mitch	93SC	367	$ .01	$ .03
Williams, Mitch	93SCS	79	$ .01	$ .10
Williamson, Mark	89SC	592	$ .01	$ .10
Williamson, Mark	90SC	332	$ .01	$ .04
Williamson, Mark	91SC	498	$ .01	$ .04
Williamson, Mark	92SC	427	$ .01	$ .04
Williamson, Mark	92SC	487	$ .01	$ .04
Willis, Carl	92SC	482	$ .01	$ .04
Willis, Carl	92SCP	491	$ .01	$ .05
Wills, Frank	91SC	521	$ .01	$ .04
Wilson, Craig	92SC	557	$ .01	$ .04
Wilson, Craig	93SC	476	$ .01	$ .03
Wilson, Dan	91SC	681	$ .01	$ .10
Wilson, Dan	93SC	229	$ .01	$ .03
Wilson, Dan	93SCP	255	$ .05	$ .20
Wilson, Dan	93SCS	345	$ .01	$ .05
Wilson, Glenn	88SC	405	$ .01	$ .04
Wilson, Glenn	89SC	106	$ .01	$ .03
Wilson, Glenn	90SC	346	$ .01	$ .04
Wilson, Glenn	91SC	298	$ .01	$ .04
Wilson, Mookie	88SC	474	$ .01	$ .04
Wilson, Mookie	89SC	302	$ .01	$ .03
Wilson, Mookie	89SCTR	16	$ .05	$ .05
Wilson, Mookie	90SC	448	$ .01	$ .04
Wilson, Mookie	91SC	42	$ .01	$ .04
Wilson, Mookie	92SC	458	$ .01	$ .04
Wilson, Steve	90SC	531	$ .01	$ .04
Wilson, Steve	91SC	306	$ .01	$ .04
Wilson, Steve	92SC	812	$ .01	$ .04

Player	Year	No.	VG	EX/MT
Wilson, Trevor	91SC	657	$ .01	$ .04
Wilson, Trevor	92SC	608	$ .01	$ .04
Wilson , Trevor	92SCP	352	$ .01	$ .05
Wilson, Trevor	93SC	401	$ .01	$ .03
Wilson, Trevor	93SCP	210	$ .01	$ .08
Wilson, Willie	88SC	102	$ .01	$ .04
Wilson, Willie	89SC	28	$ .01	$ .03
Wilson, Willie	90SC	104	$ .01	$ .04
Wilson, Willie	91SCTR	15	$ .01	$ .05
Wilson, Willie	92SC	328	$ .01	$ .04
Wilson, Willie	93SC	647	$ .01	$ .03
Wilson, Willie	93SCP	141	$ .01	$ .08
Wilson, Willie	93SCS	395	$ .01	$ .05
Wine, Jr., Robbie	88SC	496	$ .01	$ .04
Winfield, Dave	88SC	55	$ .05	$ .20
Winfield, Dave	89SC	50	$ .05	$ .20
Winfield, Dave	90SC	307	$ .01	$ .10
Winfield, Dave	90SCTR	1	$ .05	$ .25
Winfield, Dave	91SC	83	$ .01	$ .10
Winfield, Dave	92SC	32	$ .01	$ .10
Winfield, Dave	92SCP	375	$ .05	$ .20
Winfield, Dave	92SCTR	7	$ .05	$ .20
Winfield, Dave	93SC	521	$ .01	$ .10
Winfield, Dave	93SC	620	$ .01	$ .10
Winfield, Dave	93SCS	32	$ .01	$ .15
Winn, Jim	88SC	462	$ .01	$ .04
Winningham, Herm	88SC	142	$ .01	$ .04
Winningham, Herm	88SCTR	43	$ .01	$ .15
Winningham, Herm	89SC	496	$ .01	$ .03
Winningham, Herm	90SC	38	$ .01	$ .04
Winningham, Herm	91SC	656	$ .01	$ .04
Winningham, Herm	92SC	574	$ .01	$ .04
Winningham, Herm	92SCTR	43	$ .01	$ .05
Witt, Bob	88SC	149	$ .01	$ .10
Witt, Bobby	89SC	463	$ .01	$ .03
Witt, Bobby	90SC	457	$ .01	$ .04
Witt, Bobby	91SC	507	$ .01	$ .04
Witt, Bobby	91SCKM	410	$ .01	$ .05
Witt, Bobby	92SC	381	$ .01	$ .04
Witt, Bobby	92SCP	451	$ .01	$ .05

Player	Year	No.	VG	EX/MT
Witt, Bobby	**93SC**	**150**	**$ .01**	**$ .03**
Witt, Bobby	93SCS	363	$ .01	$ .05
Witt, Mike	88SC	81	$ .01	$ .10

SCORE

Player	Year	No.	VG	EX/MT
Witt, Mike	89SC	298	$ .01	$ .03
Witt, Mike	90SC	226	$ .01	$ .04
Witt, Mike	91SC	430	$ .01	$ .04
Witt, Mike	91SCNH	699	$ .01	$ .04
Wohlers, Mark	92SC	759	$ .01	$ .15
Wohlers, Mark	92SC	787	$ .01	$ .04
Wohlers, Mark	92SCP	55	$ .01	$ .05
Wohlers, Mark	93SC	193	$ .01	$ .03
Wohlers, Mark	93SCS	282	$ .01	$ .05

Player	Year	No.	VG	EX/MT
Wood, Ted	92SC	768	$ .01	$ .15
Wood, Ted	93SCP	286	$ .01	$ .08
Woodson, Kerry	93SC	327	$ .01	$ .03
Woodson, Tracy	89SC	586	$ .01	$ .03
Woodson, Tracy	93SC	465	$ .01	$ .03
Woodward, Rob	88SC	403	$ .01	$ .04
World Series, 1988	89SC	582	$ .01	$ .10
World Series '89, Game 1&2	90SC	700	$ .01	$ .10
World Series '89, Lights Out	90SC	701	$ .01	$ .10
World Series '89, Game 3	90SC	702	$ .01	$ .10
World Series '89, Game 4	90SC	703	$ .01	$ .10
World Series '90, Reds' Oct.	91SC	795	$ .01	$ .10
Worrell, Todd	88SC	202	$ .01	$ .04
Worrell, Todd	89SC	265	$ .01	$ .03
Worrell, Todd	90SC	392	$ .01	$ .04
Worrell, Todd	91SC	807	$ .01	$ .04
Worrell, Todd	92SCP	479	$ .01	$ .05
Worrell, Todd	93SC	635	$ .01	$ .03
Worthington, Craig	89SC	636	$ .05	$ .20
Worthington, Craig	90SC	234	$ .01	$ .10
Worthington, Craig	91SC	503	$ .01	$ .04
Worthington, Craig	92SC	724	$ .01	$ .04
Wrigley Field, 1st Night Game	89SC	652	$ .01	$ .10
Wrona, Rick	90SC	557	$ .01	$ .10
Wrona, Rick	91SC	519	$ .01	$ .04
Wynegar, Butch	88SC	355	$ .01	$ .04
Wynegar, Butch	89SC	140	$ .01	$ .03
Wynfield, Dave	93SCP	295	$ .01	$ .15
Wynne, Marvell	88SC	209	$ .01	$ .04
Wynne, Marvell	89SC	203	$ .01	$ .03
Wynne, Marvell	90SC	337	$ .01	$ .04

Player	Year	No.	VG	EX/MT
Wynne, Marvell	91SC	531	$ .01	$ .10
X, Malcolm	93SCP	302	$ .05	$ .25
Yastrzemski, Carl	93SCP	297	$ .05	$ .20
Yelding, Eric	90SC	411	$ .01	$ .10
Yelding, Eric	91SC	329	$ .01	$ .04
Yelding, Eric	92SC	197	$ .01	$ .04
Yett, Rich	88SC	484	$ .01	$ .04
Yett, Rich	89SC	467	$ .01	$ .03
Yett, Rich	90SC	274	$ .01	$ .04
York, Mike	91SC	738	$ .01	$ .04
Youmans, Floyd	88SC	327	$ .01	$ .04
Young, Anthony	92SC	756	$ .01	$ .10
Young, Anthony	92SCP	558	$ .01	$ .05
Young, Anthony	93SC	113	$ .01	$ .03
Young, Anthony	93SCS	284	$ .01	$ .05
Young, Curt	88SC	125	$ .01	$ .10
Young, Curt	89SC	29	$ .01	$ .03
Young, Curt	90SC	533	$ .01	$ .04
Young, Curt	91SC	236	$ .01	$ .04
Young, Curt	92SC	722	$ .01	$ .04
Young, Eric	93SC	586	$ .01	$ .10
Young, Eric	93SCS	342	$ .05	$ .25
Young, Gerald	88SC	442	$ .01	$ .10
Young, Gerald	89SC	97	$ .01	$ .03
Young, Gerald	90SC	43	$ .01	$ .04
Young, Gerald	91SC	844	$ .01	$ .04
Young, Gerald	92SC	346	$ .01	$ .04
Young, Gerald	92SCP	458	$ .01	$ .05
Young, Kevin	93SC	273	$ .05	$ .25
Young, Matt	88SC	357	$ .01	$ .04
Young, Matt	91SC	126	$ .01	$ .04
Young, Matt	91SCTR	54	$ .01	$ .05
Young, Matt	92SC	668	$ .01	$ .04
Young, Matt	92SCP	518	$ .01	$ .05
Young, Mike	88SC	393	$ .01	$ .04
Young, Mike	88SCTR	51	$ .01	$ .15
Young, Mike	89SC	494	$ .01	$ .03
Young, Pete	93SC	269	$ .01	$ .03
Young, Ray	91SC	761	$ .01	$ .15
Youngblood, Joel	88SC	509	$ .01	$ .04
Youngblood, Joel	89SC	539	$ .01	$ .03
Youngblood, Joel	89SCTR	66	$ .01	$ .05
Youngblood, Joel	90SC	344	$ .01	$ .04
Yount, Robin	88SC	160	$ .05	$ .20
Yount, Robin	89SC	151	$ .01	$ .15
Yount, Robin	90SC	320	$ .01	$ .15
Yount, Robin	91SC	525	$ .01	$ .10
Yount, Robin	91SCTF	854	$ .01	$ .04
Yount, Robin	92SC	525	$ .01	$ .10
Yount, Robin	92SCP	38	$ .05	$ .35
Yount, Robin	92SCP	287	$ .01	$ .15
Yount, Robin	93SC	47	$ .01	$ .15
Yount, Robin	93SC	518	$ .01	$ .10
Yount, Robin	93SCP	118	$ .05	$ .25
Yount, Robin	93SCP	293	$ .01	$ .15
Yount, Robin	93SCS	22	$ .01	$ .15
Zeile, Todd	90SC	600	$ .05	$ .20
Zeile, Todd	91SC	240	$ .01	$ .10
Zeile, Todd	91SCTF	869	$ .01	$ .10
Zeile, Todd	92SC	52	$ .01	$ .10
Zeile, Todd	92SCP	32	$ .01	$ .05
Zeile, Todd	93SC	119	$ .01	$ .03
Zeile, Todd	93SCP	205	$ .01	$ .08
Zeile, Todd	93SCS	63	$ .01	$ .05
Zinter, Alan	90SC	671	$ .01	$ .10
Zosky, Eddie	90SC	665	$ .01	$ .15
Zosky, Eddie	93SC	297	$ .01	$ .03
Zosky, Eddie	93SCP	247	$ .01	$ .08
Zupcic, Bob	92SC	850	$ .05	$ .25
Zupcic, Bob	92SCP	576	$ .05	$ .35
Zupcic, Bob	93SC	362	$ .01	$ .10
Zupcic, Bob	93SCS	292	$ .01	$ .05
Zuvella, Paul	89SC	598	$ .01	$ .03

TOPPS CHEWING GUM COMPANY, INC. 1951-1993

The success story of the Topps Chewing Gum Company with billions of cards printed began in 1951 with two game baseball cards that had to be punched out of a perforated piece of cardboard. Those first cards had either blue or red backs and were for use in playing a baseball game. You also received a piece of candy for your penny investment.

Improving on those small cards, Topps produced a baseball card set in 1952 containing 407 cards, Topps was able to control the market after bankruptcy forced its competitor to cease making sets in 1955. Until 1981 there were few challenges to Topps, and they prospered.

In 1991 Topps finally caught on to the collector's acceptance of premium cards and entered this ever increasing field with an issue called Stadium Club cards. These cards have a Stadium Card logo on the front.

Refer to the color section beginning on page 4 to see a representative sample of each year of the Topps cards in color. A brief description of each set follows.

All cards from 1957 to 1993 are 2½" x 3½".

1951bb – 52 cards 2" x 2⅝" white borders with blue and white back (no copyright or date)
1951rb – 52 cards 2" x 2⅝" white borders with red and white back (no copyright or date)
1952 – 407 cards 2⅝" x 3¾" white border (Topps baseball in either red or black printing on back bottom and copyright T.G.C. on lower left)
1953 – 280 card numbers with six numbers not used (253, 261, 267, 268, 272, 275) 2⅝" x 3¾" white border except for black or red name strip on bottom (copyright T.G.C. on back in lower left corner with Topps written in card numbered baseball)
1954 – 250 cards 2⅝" x 3¾" white border with black and white photo insert on front (copyright T.G.C. up right side from bottom with Topps written in card numbered baseball)
1955 – 210 card numbers with four numbers not used (175, 186, 203, 209) 2⅝" x 3¾" white border horizontal card with color insert photo on front (copyright T.G.C. below birth date with Topps written in card numbered baseball)
1956 – 340 cards 2⅝" x 3¾" white border horizontal card with color insert photo on front (copyright T.G.C. up right border on back with Topps written in card numbered baseball)
1957 – 407 cards w/white borders (copyright T.G.C. up right border on back with Topps written in card numbered baseball)
1958 – 495 card numbers (#145 not used) w/white borders (copyright T.G.C. up right border on back and card number in hatted baseball)
1959 – 572 cards w/white borders and green and red or black and red printing on back (copyright T.G.C. up right side on back)
1960 – 572 cards w/white borders horizontal with black and white photo insert on front (copyright T.G.C. up right side on back)
1961 – 589 cards with three numbers not used (426, 587, 588) white border (copyright T.G.C. lower right corner on back with Topps written in card numbered baseball)
1962 – 598 cards w/brown wood grain effect borders (copyright T.G.C. above statistical record on back with Topps written in card numbered baseball)
1963 – 576 cards w/brightly colored name panel at bottom and black and white circular portrait also (copyright T.G.C. on lower back corner with Topps written above card number)
1964 – 587 cards w/white border but bold team name at top of card (copyright T.G.C. above rub-off quiz on back with Topps written in card numbered baseball)
1965 – 598 cards w/white border but pennant waving team name in lower left corner (copyright T.G.C. on back lower right corner with Topps written in card numbered baseball)
1966 – 598 cards w/white border and team name in upper left corner in diagonal strip (copyright T.G.C. on back lower right corner with Topps written in card numbered baseball)

1967 – 609 cards w/white borders and bold team name at bottom (copyright T.G.C. on back lower right corner and Topps written in card numbered baseball)
1968 – 598 cards with brown basketweave borders and team name in brightly colored circle (copyright T.G.C. on back lower right corner with Topps written in card numbered baseball)
1969 – 664 cards w/white border (copyright T.G.C. up right side on back with "T" in Topps encircling the card number)
1970 – 720 cards w/gray border (copyright T.G.C. up right side on back with Topps written in circle above card number)
1971 – 752 cards w/black border and player black and white photo on reverse (copyright T.G.C. up left side on back is only indication of Topps card)
1972 – 787 cards w/white border and arched effect with team name in that arch above the player (copyright T.G.C. on lower right corner on back)
1973 – 660 cards w/white border and back in black bordered design (copyright T.G.C. at bottom on back)
1974 – 660 cards w/white border and pennant-like player name at bottom and team name at top (copyright T.G.C. at bottom on back.)
1975 – 660 cards w/bright colored borders of two colors depending upon team for the colors (copyright 1975 Topps Chewing Gum, Inc. on bottom back)
1976 – 660 cards w/white border plus 44 traded cards issued later with same number and "T" added to number (copyright 1976 Topps Chewing Gum, Inc. up right border on back)
1977 – 660 cards w/white borders (copyright 1977 Topps Chewing Gum, Inc. on bottom back)
1978 – 726 cards w/white borders (copyright 1978 Topps Chewing Gum, Inc. on lower right side of back)
1979 – 726 cards w/white border and Topps logo in baseball on front (copyright 1979 Topps Chewing Gum, Inc. on lower right corner of back)
1980 – 726 cards w/white border (copyright 1980 Topps Chewing Gum, Inc. lower left side on back)
1981 – 726 cards w/white border and Topps logo in baseball on front (copyright 1981 Topps Chewing Gum, Inc. on lower right side of back)
1982 – 792 cards w/white borders and Topps logo above team name on the front lower right side (copyright 1982 Topps Chewing Gum, Inc. on back lower right side)
1983 – 792 cards w/white borders and Topps logo in upper right corner on front (copyright 1983 Topps Chewing Gum, Inc. on bottom of back)
1984 – 792 cards w/white borders, team name vertically down left, and Topps logo in upper right corner on front (copyright 1984 Topps Chewing Gum, Inc. up right side on back)
1985 – 792 cards w/white border and Topps logo in upper left corner on front (copyright 1985 Topps Chewing Gum, Inc. above "Baseball Trivia Quiz" on back)
1986 – 792 cards w/black border across the top and down the sides becoming white and Topps logo on upper right of front (Copyright 1986 Topps Chewing Gum, Inc. on bottom of back)
1987 – 792 cards w/brown wood grain effect similar to 1962 and Topps logo on lower left corner of front (copyright 1987 Topps Chewing Gum, Inc. on back above personal statistical information)
1988 – 792 cards w/white border and Topps logo in lower left corner on front (copyright 1988 Topps Chewing Gum, Inc. up the right side on back)
1989 – 792 cards w/ white border and Topps logo on the front in various locations (copyright 1989 on back in dark pink area inside black border at lower right.)
1990 – 792 cards w/multi-colored borders and Topps logo on front in various locations (copyright 1990 on mustard yellow back right side)
1991– 792 cards w/white border and Topps 40 Years of Baseball logo on front upper left corner (copyright 1991 on reddish colored back at lower right side)
1992 – 792 cards w/white border and Topps written on front usually in upper left corner (copyright 1992 Topps on white back at lower right side)
1993– 792 cards issued in two series of 396 cards w/white border and Topps written on front usually in upper left corner (copyright 1993 Topps on white back at lower left side)

There are abbreviations used throughout the Topps section that need some explanation. All of the following will be found under the year section referring to the type of card that is listed:

T – Topps used for designation of all cards in section
TAS – Topps All Star card of any given year
TATL – Topps All Time Leader up to that time of issue
Tbb – Refers to 1951 Topps blue back cards only
THL – Topps Highlights (usually refers to the previous year accomplishments)
TIA – Topps In Action (another way of including a star more than once)
TMVP – Topps Most Valuable Player
TRB – Topps Record Breaker usually refers to previous year or lifetime accomplishments
Trb – Refers to 1951 Topps red backs only
TRH – Topps Record Holder
TSA – Topps Super Action
TSC – Topps Stadium Club premium cards first issued in 1991 as a two series 600 card set
TTB – Topps Turn Back The Clock refers to happenings of previous years usually in increments of five years
TTR – Topps Traded cards usually numbered 1T-132T, with "T" omitted on the number listing and placed on the year. The Traded cards of 1981 continued the numbers of that year's set and are numbered 727-858.

The listing for each card shown appears immediately following the photograph.

TOPPS

Player	Year	No.	VG	EX/MT
A's, Team	56T	236	$8.00	$32.00
A's, Team	57T	204	$3.00	$12.00
A's, Team	58T	174	$3.50	$14.00
A's, Team	59T	172	$2.50	$10.00
A's, Team	60T	413	$2.00	$8.00
A's, Team	61T	297	$1.75	$7.00
A's, Team	62T	384	$2.50	$10.00
A's, Team	63T	397	$2.00	$8.00
A's, Team	64T	151	$1.00	$4.00
A's, Team	65T	151	$.75	$3.00
A's, Team	66T	492	$2.75	$11.00
A's, Team	67T	262	$1.00	$4.00
A's, Team	68T	554	$1.75	$7.00
A's, Team	70T	631	$1.25	$5.00
A's, Team	71T	624	$1.75	$7.00
A's, Team	72T	454	$.75	$3.00
A's, Team	73T	500	$.50	$2.00
A's, Team	74T	246	$.25	$1.00
A's, Team Checklist	75T	561	$.35	$1.40
A's, Team Checklist	76T	421	$.30	$1.20
A's, Team Checklist	77T	74	$.25	$1.00
A's, Team Checklist	78T	577	$.20	$.80
A's, Team Checklist	79T	328	$.15	$.60
A's, Team Checklist	80T	96	$.10	$.50
A's, Team Checklist	81T	671	$.05	$.25
A's, Team Leaders	86T	216	$.01	$.05
A's, Team Leaders	87T	456	$.01	$.04
A's, Team Leaders	88T	759	$.05	$.25
A's, Team Leaders	89T	639	$.01	$.03
Aaron, Hank	54T	128	$450.00	$1800.00
Aaron, Hank	55T	47	$95.00	$380.00
Aaron, Hank	56T	31	$65.00	$260.00
Aaron, Hank	57T	20	$60.00	$240.00
Aaron, Hank	58T	30	$52.50	$210.00
Aaron, Hank	58T	351	$7.00	$28.00
Aaron, Hank	58T	418	$42.50	$170.00
Aaron, Hank	58TAS	488	$12.50	$50.00
Aaron, Hank	59T	212	$12.00	$48.00
Aaron, Hank	59T	380	$30.00	$120.00
Aaron, Hank	59T	467	$6.00	$24.00
Aaron, Hank	59TAS	561	$30.00	$120.00
Aaron, Hank	60T	300	$30.00	$120.00
Aaron, Hank	60TAS	566	$30.00	$120.00
Aaron, Hank	61T	43	$3.00	$12.00
Aaron, Hank	61T	415	$30.00	$120.00
Aaron, Hank	61TAS	577	$40.00	$160.00
Aaron, Hank	61TMVP	484	$11.25	$45.00
Aaron, Hank	62T	320	$35.00	$140.00
Aaron, Hank	62TAS	394	$11.25	$45.00
Aaron, Hank	63T	1	$8.00	$32.00
Aaron, Hank	63T	3	$5.50	$22.00
Aaron, Hank	63T	242	$9.00	$36.00
Aaron, Hank	63T	390	$40.00	$160.00
Aaron, Hank	64T	7	$2.00	$8.00
Aaron, Hank	64T	9	$4.00	$16.00
Aaron, Hank	64T	11	$1.75	$7.00
Aaron, Hank	64T	300	$30.00	$120.00
Aaron, Hank	64T	423	$27.50	$110.00
Aaron, Hank	65T	2	$2.50	$10.00
Aaron, Hank	65T	170	$21.25	$85.00
Aaron, Hank	66T	215	$7.00	$28.00
Aaron, Hank	66T	500	$30.00	$120.00
Aaron, Hank	67T	242	$2.50	$10.00
Aaron, Hank	67T	244	$2.50	$10.00
Aaron, Hank	67T	250	$22.50	$90.00
Aaron, Hank	68T	3	$1.75	$7.00
Aaron, Hank	68T	5	$1.50	$6.00
Aaron, Hank	68T	110	$16.25	$65.00
Aaron, Hank	68TAS	370	$3.50	$14.00
Aaron, Hank	69T	100	$15.00	$60.00
Aaron, Hank	70T	65	$1.25	$5.00
Aaron, Hank	70T	500	$12.50	$50.00
Aaron, Hank	70TAS	462	$3.50	$14.00
Aaron, Hank	71T	400	$13.75	$55.00
Aaron, Hank	72T	87	$.75	$3.00
Aaron, Hank	72T	89	$.50	$2.00
Aaron, Hank	72T	299	$8.00	$32.00
Aaron, Hank	72TIA	300	$4.00	$16.00
Aaron, Hank	73T	1	$6.75	$27.00
Aaron, Hank	73T	100	$5.50	$22.00
Aaron, Hank	73TATL	473	$1.25	$5.00
Aaron, Hank	74T	1	$8.00	$32.00
Aaron, Hank (54-57)	74T	2	$1.50	$6.00
Aaron, Hank (58-61)	74T	3	$1.50	$6.00
Aaron, Hank (62-65)	74T	4	$1.50	$6.00
Aaron, Hank (66-69)	74T	5	$1.50	$6.00

1970 · HANK AARON SPECIAL · 1971
1972   1973

Player	Year	No.	VG	EX/MT
Aaron, Hank (70-73)	74T	6	$1.50	$6.00
Aaron, Hank	74TAS	332	$.75	$3.00
Aaron, Hank	75T	195	$3.00	$12.00
Aaron, Hank	75T	660	$7.00	$28.00
Aaron, Hank	75THL	1	$7.00	$28.00
Aaron, Hank	76T	550	$5.50	$22.00
Aaron, Hank	76TRB	1	$3.75	$15.00
Aaron, Hank	79T	412	$.15	$.60
Aaron, Hank	79TRH	413	$.20	$.80
Aaron, Hank	89TTB	663	$.01	$.10
Aaron, Hank	91TA53	317	$2.50	$110.00
Aaron, Tommie	63T	46	$.90	$3.60
Aaron, Tommie	64T	454	$1.00	$4.00
Aaron, Tommie	65T	567	$1.40	$5.60
Aaron, Tommie	68T	394	$.35	$1.40
Aaron, Tommie	69T	128	$.35	$1.40
Aaron, Tommie	70T	278	$.35	$1.40
Aaron, Tommie	71T	717	$1.50	$6.00
Aase, Don	76T	597	$.20	$.80
Aase, Don	77T	472	$.05	$.20
Aase, Don	78T	12	$.04	$.16
Aase, Don	79T	368	$.03	$.12
Aase, Don	80T	239	$.01	$.10
Aase, Don	81T	601	$.01	$.08
Aase, Don	82T	199	$.01	$.08
Aase, Don	83T	599	$.01	$.08
Aase, Don	85T	86	$.01	$.08
Aase, Don	85TTR	1	$.01	$.10
Aase, Don	86T	288	$.01	$.05
Aase, Don	87T	766	$.01	$.04
Aase, Don	88T	467	$.01	$.04
Aase, Don	89TTR	1	$.01	$.05

TOPPS

Player	Year	No.	VG	EX/MT	Player	Year	No.	VG	EX/MT
Aase, Don	90T	301	$.01	$.03	Acosta, Cy	75T	634	$.10	$.40
Abarbanel, Mickey	68T	287	$.35	$1.40	Acosta, Ed	71T	343	$.40	$1.60
Abbott, Glenn	74T	602	$.10	$.40	Acosta, Ed	72T	123	$.10	$.40
Abbott, Glenn	75T	591	$.10	$.40	Acosta, Ed	73T	244	$.10	$.40
Abbott, Glenn	76T	322	$.05	$.25	Adair, Jerry	61T	71	$.60	$2.40
Abbott, Glenn	77T	207	$.05	$.20	Adair, Jerry	62T	449	$1.50	$6.00
Abbott, Glenn	78T	31	$.04	$.16	Adair, Jerry	63T	488	$3.00	$12.00
Abbott, Glenn	79T	497	$.03	$.12	Adair, Jerry	64T	22	$.50	$2.00
Abbott, Glenn	80T	166	$.01	$.10	Adair, Jerry	65T	231	$.50	$2.00
Abbott, Glenn	81T	699	$.01	$.08	Adair, Jerry	66T	533	$7.00	$28.00
Abbott, Glenn	82T	336	$.01	$.08	Adair, Jerry	67T	484	$1.50	$6.00
Abbott, Glenn	82T	571	$.01	$.08	Adair, Jerry	68T	346	$.35	$1.40
Abbott, Glenn	84T	356	$.01	$.06	Adair, Jerry	69T	159	$.35	$1.40
Abbott, Jim	88TTR	1	$1.75	$7.00	Adair, Jerry	70T	525	$.35	$1.40
Abbott, Jim	89T	573	$.10	$1.00	Adair, Jerry	73T	179	$.25	$1.00
Abbott, Jim	89TTR	2	$.10	$1.00	Adams, Bobby	52T	249	$7.00	$28.00
Abbott, Jim	90T	675	$.05	$.20	Adams, Bobby	53T	152	$4.00	$16.00
Abbott, Jim	91T	285	$.01	$.10	Adams, Bobby	54T	123	$3.75	$15.00
Abbott, Jim	91TSC	124	$.15	$1.50	Adams, Bobby	55T	178	$6.25	$25.00
Abbott, Jim	92T	530	$.01	$.10	Adams, Bobby	56T	287	$2.50	$10.00
Abbott, Jim	92TAS	406	$.01	$.10	Adams, Bobby	58T	99	$2.00	$8.00
Abbott, Jim	92TSC	210	$.05	$.35	Adams, Bobby	59T	249	$1.00	$4.00
Abbott, Jim	93T	780	$.01	$.10	Adams, Bobby	91TA53	152	$.01	$.15
Abbott, Kyle	90T	444	$.05	$.25	Adams, Glenn	76T	389	$.05	$.25
Abbott, Kyle	92T	763	$.01	$.03	Adams, Glenn	78T	497	$.04	$.16
Abbott, Kyle	92TSC	818	$.01	$.15	Adams, Glenn	79T	193	$.03	$.12
Abbott, Kyle	93T	317	$.01	$.03	Adams, Glenn	80T	604	$.01	$.10
Abbott, Kyle	93TSC	201	$.01	$.10	Adams, Glenn	81T	18	$.01	$.08
Abbott, Paul	92T	781	$.01	$.03	Adams, Glenn	82T	519	$.01	$.08
Abbott, Paul	92TSC	567	$.01	$.10	Adams, Glenn	83T	574	$.01	$.08
Aber, Al	53T	233	$22.50	$90.00	Adams, Mike	74T	573	$.10	$.40
Aber, Al	54T	238	$3.75	$15.00	Adams, Red	73T	569	$1.10	$4.40
Aber, Al	56T	317	$2.50	$10.00	Adams, Red	74T	144	$.50	$2.00
Aber, Al	57T	141	$2.00	$8.00	Adams, Ricky	84T	487	$.01	$.06
Aber, Al	91TA53	233	$.01	$.15	Adams, Ricky	86T	153	$.01	$.05
Abernathy, Ted	57T	293	$5.00	$20.00	Adams, Willie	92TTR	1	$.05	$.20
Abernathy, Ted	59T	169	$1.00	$4.00	Adamson, Joel	93T	613	$.01	$.15
Abernathy, Ted	60T	334	$.75	$3.00	Adamson, Mike	69T	66	$.50	$2.00
Abernathy, Ted	64T	64	$.50	$2.00	Adamson, Mike	71T	362	$.25	$1.00
Abernathy, Ted	65T	332	$.50	$2.00	Adcock, Joe	52T	347	$57.50	$230.00
Abernathy, Ted	66T	2	$.35	$1.40	Adcock, Joe	56T	320	$3.50	$14.00
Abernathy, Ted	67T	597	$4.00	$16.00	Adcock, Joe	57T	117	$2.00	$8.00
Abernathy, Ted	68T	264	$.35	$1.40	Adcock, Joe	58T	325	$1.50	$6.00
Abernathy, Ted	69T	483	$.30	$1.20	Adcock, Joe	58T	351	$7.00	$28.00
Abernathy, Ted	70T	562	$.50	$2.00	Adcock, Joe	59T	315	$1.00	$4.00
Abernathy, Ted	71T	187	$.25	$1.00	Adcock, Joe	60T	3	$.85	$3.40
Abernathy, Ted	72T	519	$.25	$1.00	Adcock, Joe	61T	245	$.75	$3.00
Abernathy, Ted	73T	22	$.10	$.40	Adcock, Joe	62T	265	$.75	$3.00
Abner, Shawn	85T	282	$.01	$.15	Adcock, Joe	63T	170	$.75	$3.00
Abner, Shawn	90T	122	$.01	$.03	Adcock, Joe	67T	563	$6.00	$24.00
Abner, Shawn	91T	697	$.01	$.03	Adcock, Joe	91TA53	285	$.05	$.25
Abner, Shawn	91TSC	291	$.05	$.25	Addis, Bob	52T	259	$12.50	$50.00
Abner, Shawn	92T	339	$.01	$.03	Addis, Bob	53T	157	$4.00	$16.00
Abner, Shawn	92TSC	197	$.01	$.10	Addis, Bob	91TA53	157	$.01	$.15
Abner, Shawn	93T	582	$.01	$.03	Adduci, Jim	89T	338	$.01	$.03
Abrams, Cal	52T	350	$43.75	$175.00	Adlesh, Dave	67T	51	$.40	$1.60
Abrams, Cal	50T	90	$4.00	$10.00	Adlesh, Dave	08T	570	$.70	$2.80
Abrams, Cal	91TA53	98	$.01	$.15	Adlesh, Dave	69T	341	$.30	$1.20
Acker, Jim	84T	359	$.01	$.06	Afenir, Troy	92TSC	613	$.01	$.10
Acker, Jim	85T	101	$.01	$.06	Agee, Tommie	65T	166	$.75	$3.00
Acker, Jim	86T	569	$.01	$.05	Agee, Tommie	66T	164	$.50	$2.00
Acker, Jim	87T	407	$.01	$.04	Agee, Tommie	67T	455	$.60	$2.40
Acker, Jim	88T	678	$.01	$.04	Agee, Tommie	68T	465	$.75	$3.00
Acker, Jim	89T	244	$.01	$.03	Agee, Tommie	69T	364	$.30	$1.20
Acker, Jim	90T	728	$.01	$.03	Agee, Tommie	70T	50	$.20	$.80
Acker, Jim	91T	71	$.01	$.03	Agee, Tommie	71T	310	$.25	$1.00
Acker, Jim	92T	178	$.01	$.03	Agee, Tommie	72T	245	$.10	$.40
Acker, Tom	57T	219	$2.00	$8.00	Agee, Tommie	73T	420	$.25	$1.00
Acker, Tom	58T	149	$1.25	$5.00	Agee, Tommie	74T	630	$.10	$.40
Acker, Tom	59T	201	$1.00	$4.00	Agee, Tommie	74TTR	630	$.10	$.40
Acker, Tom	60T	274	$.75	$3.00	Agganis, Harry	55T	152	$20.00	$80.00
Ackley, Fritz	64T	368	$.65	$2.60	Agosto, Juan	84T	409	$.01	$.06
Ackley, Fritz	65T	477	$130.00	$520.00	Agosto, Juan	85T	351	$.01	$.06
Acosta, Cy	73T	379	$.10	$.40	Agosto, Juan	86T	657	$.01	$.05
Acosta, Cy	74T	22	$.10	$.40	Agosto, Juan	87T	277	$.01	$.04

303

TOPPS

Player	Year	No.	VG	EX/MT
Agosto, Juan	88TTR	2	$ .01	$ .10
Agosto, Juan	89T	559	$ .01	$ .03
Agosto, Juan	90T	181	$ .01	$ .03
Agosto, Juan	91T	703	$ .01	$ .03
Agosto, Juan	91TSC	570	$ .05	$ .25
Agosto, Juan	91TTR	1	$ .01	$ .05
Agosto, Juan	92T	421	$ .01	$ .03
Aguayo, Luis	82T	449	$ .01	$ .08
Aguayo, Luis	83T	252	$ .01	$ .08
Aguayo, Luis	85T	663	$ .01	$ .06
Aguayo, Luis	86T	69	$ .01	$ .05
Aguayo, Luis	87T	755	$ .01	$ .04
Aguayo, Luis	88T	356	$ .01	$ .04
Aguayo, Luis	89T	561	$ .01	$ .03
Aguilera, Rick	86T	599	$ .10	$ .75
Aguilera, Rick	87T	103	$ .01	$ .15
Aguilera, Rick	88T	434	$ .01	$ .04
Aguilera, Rick	89T	257	$ .01	$ .03
Aguilera, Rick	90T	711	$ .01	$ .03
Aguilera, Rick	91T	318	$ .01	$ .03
Aguilera, Rick	91TSC	76	$ .05	$ .25
Aguilera, Rick	92T	44	$ .01	$ .03
Aguilera, Rick	92TSC	726	$ .01	$ .10
Aguilera, Rick	93T	625	$ .01	$ .03
Aguirre, Hank	57T	96	$2.00	$8.00
Aguirre, Hank	58T	337	$1.25	$5.00
Aguirre, Hank	59T	36	$1.10	$4.40
Aguirre, Hank	60T	546	$2.75	$11.00
Aguirre, Hank	61T	324	$ .60	$2.40
Aguirre, Hank	62T	407	$1.25	$5.00
Aguirre, Hank	63T	6	$1.25	$5.00
Aguirre, Hank	63T	257	$ .90	$3.60
Aguirre, Hank	64T	39	$ .50	$2.00
Aguirre, Hank	65T	522	$1.25	$5.00
Aguirre, Hank	66T	113	$ .50	$2.00
Aguirre, Hank	67T	263	$ .50	$2.00
Aguirre, Hank	68T	553	$ .70	$2.80
Aguirre, Hank	69T	94	$ .35	$1.40
Aguirre, Hank	70T	699	$1.25	$5.00
Aguirre, Hank	73T	81	$ .25	$1.00
Aguirre, Hank	74T	354	$ .10	$ .40
Aikens, Willie	80T	368	$ .01	$ .10
Aikens, Willie	81T	524	$ .01	$ .08
Aikens, Willie	82T	35	$ .01	$ .08
Aikens, Willie	83T	136	$ .01	$ .08
Aikens, Willie	84T	685	$ .01	$ .06
Aikens, Willie	84TTR	1	$ .01	$ .15
Aikens, Willie	85T	436	$ .01	$ .06
Ainge, Danny	81TTR	727	$1.50	$6.00
Ainge, Danny	82T	125	$ .15	$1.50
Aker, Jack	66T	287	$ .50	$2.00
Aker, Jack	67T	110	$ .40	$1.60
Aker, Jack	68T	224	$ .35	$1.40
Aker, Jack	69T	612	$ .40	$1.60
Aker, Jack	70T	43	$ .20	$ .80
Aker, Jack	71T	593	$1.00	$4.00
Aker, Jack	72T	769	$1.25	$5.00
Aker, Jack	73T	262	$ .10	$ .40
Aker, Jack	74T	562	$ .10	$ .40
Akerfelds, Darrel	88T	82	$ .01	$ .04
Akerfelds, Darrel	90TTR	1	$ .01	$ .05
Akerfelds, Darrel	91T	524	$ .01	$ .03
Akerfelds, Darrel	91TSC	581	$ .05	$ .25
Akins, Sid	85T	390	$ .01	$ .06
Albury, Vic	72T	778	$3.75	$15.00
Albury, Vic	74T	605	$1.25	$5.00
Albury, Vic	75T	368	$ .10	$ .40
Albury, Vic	76T	336	$ .05	$ .25
Albury, Vic	77T	536	$ .05	$ .20
Alcala, Santo	76T	589	$ .50	$2.00
Alcala, Santo	77T	636	$ .05	$ .20
Alcala, Santo	78T	321	$ .04	$ .16
Alcaraz, Luis	69T	437	$ .30	$1.20
Aldred, Scott	91T	658	$ .01	$ .10
Aldred, Scott	91TSC	429	$ .10	$ .40
Aldred, Scott	92T	198	$ .01	$ .03
Aldred, Scott	92TSC	762	$ .01	$ .10
Aldred, Scott	93T	463	$ .01	$ .03
Aldrete, Mike	87T	71	$ .01	$ .04
Aldrete, Mike	88T	602	$ .01	$ .10
Aldrete, Mike	89T	158	$ .01	$ .03
Aldrete, Mike	90T	589	$ .01	$ .03
Aldrete, Mike	91T	483	$ .01	$ .03
Aldrete, Mike	92T	256	$ .01	$ .03
Aldrete, Mike	92TSC	305	$ .01	$ .10
Aldrich, Jay	88T	616	$ .01	$ .04
Alexander, Doyle	72T	579	$ .75	$3.00
Alexander, Doyle	73T	109	$ .30	$1.20
Alexander, Doyle	74T	282	$ .10	$ .40
Alexander, Doyle	75T	491	$ .15	$ .60
Alexander, Doyle	76T	638	$ .15	$ .60
Alexander, Doyle	77T	254	$ .05	$ .20
Alexander, Doyle	78T	146	$ .05	$ .20
Alexander, Doyle	79T	442	$ .05	$ .20
Alexander, Doyle	80T	67	$ .01	$ .10
Alexander, Doyle	81T	708	$ .01	$ .15
Alexander, Doyle	81TTR	728	$ .05	$ .20
Alexander, Doyle	82T	364	$ .01	$ .15
Alexander, Doyle	82TTR	1	$ .05	$ .20
Alexander, Doyle	83T	512	$ .01	$ .08
Alexander, Doyle	84T	677	$ .01	$ .06
Alexander, Doyle	85T	218	$ .01	$ .06
Alexander, Doyle	86T	196	$ .01	$ .05
Alexander, Doyle	87T	686	$ .01	$ .04
Alexander, Doyle	88T	492	$ .01	$ .04
Alexander, Doyle	89T	77	$ .01	$ .03
Alexander, Doyle	90T	748	$ .01	$ .03
Alexander, Gary	77T	476	$7.50	$30.00
Alexander, Gary	78T	624	$ .04	$ .16
Alexander, Gary	79T	332	$ .03	$ .12

Player	Year	No.	VG	EX/MT
Alexander, Gary	80T	141	$ .01	$ .10
Alexander, Gary	81T	416	$ .01	$ .08
Alexander, Gary	81TTR	729	$ .01	$ .15
Alexander, Gary	82T	11	$ .01	$ .08
Alexander, Gerald	92TSC	185	$ .01	$ .10
Alexander, Manny	92T	551	$ .10	$ .50
Alexander, Manny	93T	587	$ .01	$ .15
Alexander, Matt	76T	382	$ .05	$ .25

TOPPS

Player	Year	No.	VG	EX/MT	Player	Year	No.	VG	EX/MT
Alexander, Matt	77T	644	$ .05	$ .20	Allen, Dick	73T	310	$ .25	$1.00
Alexander, Matt	78T	102	$ .04	$ .16	Allen, Dick	74T	70	$ .15	$ .60
Alexander, Matt	81T	68	$ .01	$ .08	Allen, Dick	74TAS	332	$ .75	$3.00
Alexander, Matt	82T	528	$ .01	$ .08	Allen, Dick	75T	210	$ .40	$1.60
Alfaro, Flavio	85T	391	$ .01	$ .06	Allen, Dick	75T	307	$ .50	$2.00
Alicea, Luis	88TTR	3	$ .01	$ .15	Allen, Dick	75T	400	$ .15	$ .60
Alicea, Luis	89T	588	$ .01	$ .10	Allen, Dick	76T	455	$ .15	$ .60
Alicea, Luis	92TSC	103	$ .01	$ .10	Allenson, Gary	80T	376	$ .01	$ .15
Alicea, Luis	93T	257	$ .01	$ .03	Allenson, Gary	81T	128	$ .01	$ .08
Alicea, Luis	93TSC	178	$ .01	$ .10	Allenson, Gary	82T	686	$ .01	$ .08
Alkire, Jeff	92TTR	2	$ .05	$ .35	Allenson, Gary	83T	472	$ .01	$ .08
Allanson, Andy	86TTR	1	$ .01	$ .15	Allenson, Gary	84T	56	$ .01	$ .06
Allanson, Andy	87T	436	$ .01	$ .04	Allenson, Gary	85T	259	$ .01	$ .06
Allanson, Andy	88T	728	$ .01	$ .04	Alley, Gene	64T	509	$2.00	$8.00
Allanson, Andy	89T	283	$ .01	$ .03	Alley, Gene	65T	121	$ .35	$1.40
Allanson, Andy	90T	514	$ .01	$ .03	Alley, Gene	66T	336	$ .50	$2.00
Allanson, Andy	92T	167	$ .01	$ .03	Alley, Gene	67T	283	$ .50	$2.00
Allanson, Andy	92TSC	238	$ .01	$ .10	Alley, Gene	68T	53	$ .35	$1.40
Allard, Brian	80T	673	$ .01	$ .10	Alley, Gene	68TAS	368	$ .50	$2.00
Allard, Brian	82T	283	$ .01	$ .08	Alley, Gene	69T	436	$ .30	$1.20
Allen, Bernie	62T	596	$15.00	$60.00	Alley, Gene	70T	566	$ .50	$2.00
Allen, Bernie	63T	427	$1.00	$4.00	Alley, Gene	71T	416	$ .50	$2.00
Allen, Bernie	64T	455	$1.00	$4.00	Alley, Gene	72T	286	$ .10	$ .40
Allen, Bernie	65T	237	$ .50	$2.00	Alley, Gene	73T	635	$ .60	$2.40
Allen, Bernie	66T	327	$ .50	$2.00	Allie, Gair	54T	179	$3.75	$15.00
Allen, Bernie	67T	118	$ .40	$1.60	Allie, Gair	55T	59	$2.25	$9.00
Allen, Bernie	68T	548	$ .70	$2.80	Allietta, Bob	76T	623	$ .05	$ .25
Allen, Bernie	69T	27	$ .35	$1.40	Allison, Bob	59T	116	$1.75	$7.00
Allen, Bernie	70T	577	$ .50	$2.00	Allison, Bob	60T	320	$1.25	$5.00
Allen, Bernie	71T	427	$ .50	$2.00	Allison, Bob	61T	355	$ .60	$2.40
Allen, Bernie	72T	644	$ .40	$1.60	Allison, Bob	62T	180	$ .60	$2.40
Allen, Bernie	73T	293	$ .10	$ .40	Allison, Bob	63T	75	$ .50	$2.00
Allen, Bob	61T	452	$1.35	$5.40	Allison, Bob	64T	10	$1.00	$4.00
Allen, Bob	62T	543	$6.00	$24.00	Allison, Bob	64T	290	$ .65	$2.60
Allen, Bob	63T	266	$ .90	$3.60	Allison, Bob	65T	180	$ .35	$1.40
Allen, Bob	64T	209	$ .65	$2.60	Allison, Bob	66T	345	$ .50	$2.00
Allen, Bob	66T	538	$7.00	$28.00	Allison, Bob	67T	194	$ .40	$1.60
Allen, Bob	67T	24	$ .40	$1.60	Allison, Bob	67T	334	$1.10	$4.40
Allen, Bob	68T	176	$ .35	$1.40	Allison, Bob	68T	335	$ .35	$1.40
Allen, Hank	67T	569	$125.00	$500.00	Allison, Bob	69T	30	$ .35	$1.40
Allen, Hank	68T	426	$ .35	$1.40	Allison, Bob	70T	635	$1.25	$5.00
Allen, Hank	69T	623	$ .40	$1.60	Allred, Beau	90T	419	$ .01	$ .10
Allen, Hank	70T	14	$ .20	$ .80	Almon, Billy	77T	490	$ .05	$ .20
Allen, Jamie	84T	744	$ .01	$ .06	Almon, Billy	78T	392	$ .04	$ .16
Allen, Lloyd	71T	152	$ .25	$1.00	Almon, Billy	79T	616	$ .03	$ .12
Allen, Lloyd	72T	102	$ .10	$ .40	Almon, Billy	80T	436	$ .01	$ .10
Allen, Lloyd	73T	267	$ .10	$ .40	Almon, Billy	81T	163	$ .01	$ .08
Allen, Lloyd	74T	539	$ .10	$ .40	Almon, Billy	81TTR	730	$ .01	$ .15
Allen, Neil	80T	94	$ .05	$ .20	Almon, Billy "Bill"	82T	521	$ .01	$ .08
Allen, Neil	81T	322	$ .01	$ .08	Almon, Bill	83T	362	$ .01	$ .08
Allen, Neil	82T	205	$ .01	$ .08	Almon, Bill	83TTR	2	$ .01	$ .10
Allen, Neil	83T	575	$ .01	$ .08	Almon, Bill	84T	241	$ .01	$ .06
Allen, Neil	83TTR	1	$ .01	$ .10	Almon, Bill	85T	273	$ .01	$ .06
Allen, Neil	84T	435	$ .01	$ .06	Almon, Bill	85T	607	$ .01	$ .06
Allen, Neil	85T	731	$ .01	$ .06	Almon, Bill	85TTR	2	$ .01	$ .10
Allen, Neil	86T	663	$ .01	$ .05	Almon, Bill	86T	48	$ .01	$ .05
Allen, Neil	86TTR	2	$ .01	$ .06	Almon, Bill	87T	447	$ .01	$ .04
Allen, Neil	87T	113	$ .01	$ .04	Almon, Bill	87TTR	1	$ .01	$ .05
Allen, Neil	88T	384	$ .01	$ .04	Almon, Bill	88T	787	$ .01	$ .04
Allen, Neil	89T	61	$ .01	$ .03	Aloma, Luis	52T	308	$12.50	$50.00
Allen, Richie	64T	243	$5.00	$20.00	Aloma, Luis	54T	57	$7.50	$30.00
Allen, Richie	65T	460	$4.00	$16.00	Alomar, Roberto	88TTR	4	$2.00	$8.00
Allen, Richie	66T	80	$1.00	$4.00	Alomar, Roberto	89T	206	$ .10	$ .75
Allen, Richie	67T	242	$2.50	$10.00	Alomar, Roberto	90T	517	$ .10	$ .40
Allen, Richie	67T	244	$2.50	$10.00	Alomar, Roberto	91T	315	$ .05	$ .20
Allen, Richie	67T	309	$ .60	$1.20	Alomar, Roberto	91TSC	304	$1.25	$5.00
Allen, Richie	67T	450	$1.50	$6.00	Alomar, Roberto	91TTR	2	$ .05	$ .20
Allen, Richie	68T	225	$1.00	$4.00	Alomar, Roberto	92T	225	$ .05	$ .20
Allen, Richie	69T	6	$1.00	$4.00	Alomar, Roberto	92TSC	159	$ .10	$1.00
Allen, Richie	69T	350	$ .75	$3.00	Alomar, Roberto	93T	50	$ .05	$ .20
Allen, Richie	70T	40	$ .35	$1.40	Alomar, Roberto	93TSC	142	$ .10	$ .50
Allen, Richie	71T	650	$5.50	$22.00	Alomar, Santos "Sandy"	65T	82	$ .75	$3.00
Allen, Richie "Dick"	72T	240	$ .75	$3.00	Alomar, Sandy	66T	428	$ .65	$2.60
Allen, Dick	73T	62	$ .50	$2.00	Alomar, Sandy	67T	561	$6.00	$24.00
Allen, Dick	73T	63	$ .50	$2.00	Alomar, Sandy	68T	541	$ .70	$2.80

TOPPS

Player	Year	No.	VG	EX/MT	Player	Year	No.	VG	EX/M
Alomar, Sandy	69T	283	$ .50	$2.00	Alou, Moises	92TSC	519	$ .01	$ .10
Alomar, Sandy	70T	29	$ .20	$ .80	Alou, Moises	92TTR	4	$ .05	$ .20
Alomar, Sandy	71T	745	$1.50	$6.00	Alou, Moises	93T	123	$ .01	$ .03
Alomar, Sandy	72T	253	$ .10	$ .40	Alou, Moises	93TSC	239	$ .01	$ .10
Alomar, Sandy	73T	123	$ .10	$ .40	Alston, Dell	78T	710	$ .15	$ .60
Alomar, Sandy	74T	347	$ .10	$ .40	Alston, Dell	79T	54	$ .03	$ .12
Alomar, Sandy	75T	266	$ .10	$ .40	Alston, Dell	80T	198	$ .01	$ .10
Alomar, Sandy	76T	629	$ .05	$ .25	Alston, Garvin	93T	661	$ .05	$ .20
Alomar, Sandy	77T	54	$ .05	$ .20	Alston, Walter	56T	8	$9.50	$38.00
Alomar, Sandy	78T	533	$ .04	$ .16	Alston, Walter	58T	314	$6.00	$24.00
Alomar, Sandy	79T	144	$ .03	$ .12	Alston, Walt	60T	212	$2.75	$11.00
Alomar, Jr., Sandy	89T	648	$ .05	$ .25	Alston, Walt	61T	136	$1.25	$5.00
Alomar, Jr., Sandy	90T	353	$ .01	$ .10	Alston, Walt	62T	217	$1.25	$5.00
Alomar, Sandy	90TTR	2	$ .01	$ .10	Alston, Walt	63T	154	$1.00	$4.00
Alomar, Sandy	91T	165	$ .01	$ .10	Alston, Walt	64T	101	$1.00	$4.00
Alomar, Sandy	91TSC	61	$ .05	$ .35	Alston, Walt	65T	217	$1.00	$4.00
Alomar, Sandy	92T	420	$ .01	$ .03	Alston, Walt	66T	116	$ .75	$3.00
Alomar, Sandy	92TSC	740	$ .01	$ .10	Alston, Walt	67T	294	$ .75	$3.00
Alomar, Sandy	93T	85	$ .01	$ .03	Alston, Walt	68T	472	$1.00	$4.00
Alou, Felipe	59T	102	$5.00	$20.00	Alston, Walt	69T	24	$ .55	$2.20
Alou, Felipe	60T	287	$1.50	$6.00	Alston, Walt	70T	242	$ .55	$2.20
Alou, Felipe	61T	565	$10.00	$40.00	Alston, Walt	71T	567	$1.25	$5.00
Alou, Felipe	62T	133	$1.00	$4.00	Alston, Walt	72T	749	$2.00	$8.00
Alou, Felipe	63T	270	$1.25	$5.00	Alston, Walt	73T	569	$1.10	$4.40
Alou, Felipe	64T	65	$ .75	$3.00	Alston, Walt	74T	144	$ .50	$2.00
Alou, Felipe	65T	383	$1.25	$5.00	Altamirano, Porfirio	83T	432	$ .01	$ .08
Alou, Felipe	66T	96	$ .50	$2.00	Altamirano, Porfirio	84T	101	$ .01	$ .06
Alou, Felipe	67T	240	$ .75	$3.00	Altman, George	59T	512	$4.00	$16.00
Alou, Felipe	67T	530	$2.50	$10.00	Altman, George	60T	259	$ .75	$3.00
Alou, Felipe	68T	55	$ .50	$2.00	Altman, George	61T	551	$7.50	$30.00
Alou, Felipe	69T	2	$1.25	$5.00	Altman, George	62T	240	$ .75	$3.00
Alou, Felipe	69T	300	$ .75	$3.00	Altman, George	63T	357	$ .90	$3.60
Alou, Felipe	70T	434	$ .35	$1.40	Altman, George	64T	95	$ .50	$2.00
Alou, Felipe	71T	495	$ .75	$3.00	Altman, George	65T	528	$1.40	$5.60
Alou, Felipe	72T	263	$ .25	$1.00	Altman, George	66T	146	$ .50	$2.00
Alou, Felipe	73T	650	$ .75	$3.00	Altman, George	67T	87	$ .40	$1.60
Alou, Felipe	74T	485	$ .20	$ .80	Altobelli, Joe	78T	256	$ .04	$ .16
Alou, Felipe	74TTR	485	$ .20	$ .80	Altobelli, Joe	83TTR	3	$ .01	$ .10
Alou, Felipe	92TTR	3	$ .01	$ .05	Altobelli, Joe	84T	21	$ .01	$ .06
Alou, Felipe	93T	508	$ .01	$ .03	Altobelli, Joe	85T	574	$ .01	$ .06
Alou, Jesus	64T	47	$ .75	$3.00	Alusik, George	62T	261	$ .75	$3.00
Alou, Jesus	65T	545	$2.50	$10.00	Alusik, George	63T	51	$ .50	$2.00
Alou, Jesus	66T	242	$ .50	$2.00	Alusik, George	64T	431	$1.00	$4.00
Alou, Jesus	67T	332	$ .60	$2.40	Alvarado, Luis	70T	317	$ .35	$1.40
Alou, Jesus	68T	452	$ .35	$1.40	Alvarado, Luis	71T	489	$ .50	$2.00
Alou, Jesus	69T	22	$ .35	$1.40	Alvarado, Luis	72T	774	$1.25	$5.00
Alou, Jesus	70T	248	$ .20	$ .80	Alvarado, Luis	73T	627	$ .60	$2.40
Alou, Jesus	71T	337	$ .25	$1.00	Alvarado, Luis	74T	462	$ .10	$ .40
Alou, Jesus	72T	716	$1.25	$5.00	Alvarez, Jose	89T	253	$ .01	$ .03
Alou, Jesus	73T	93	$ .10	$ .40	Alvarez, Jose	90T	782	$ .01	$ .03
Alou, Jesus	74T	654	$ .25	$1.00	Alvarez, Ossie	59T	504	$1.00	$4.00
Alou, Jesus	75T	253	$ .10	$ .40	Alvarez, Rogelio	63T	158	$ .90	$3.60
Alou, Jesus	76T	468	$ .05	$ .25	Alvarez, Wilson	91T	378	$ .01	$ .15
Alou, Jesus	79T	107	$ .03	$ .12	Alvarez, Wilson	92T	452	$ .01	$ .03
Alou, Jesus	80T	593	$ .01	$ .10	Alvarez, Wilson	92TSC	761	$ .01	$ .10
Alou, Matty	61T	327	$1.75	$7.00	Alvarez, Wilson	93T	737	$ .01	$ .03
Alou, Matty	62T	413	$1.25	$5.00	Alvarez, Wilson	93TSC	181	$ .01	$ .15
Alou, Matty	63T	128	$ .50	$2.00	Alvis, Max	63T	228	$12.50	$50.00
Alou, Matty	64T	204	$ .75	$3.00	Alvis, Max	64T	545	$2.25	$9.00
Alou, Matty	65T	318	$ .50	$2.00	Alvis, Max	65T	185	$ .35	$1.40
Alou, Matty	66T	94	$ .35	$1.40	Alvis, Max	66T	415	$ .65	$2.60
Alou, Matty	67T	10	$ .40	$1.60	Alvis, Max	67T	520	$1.50	$6.00
Alou, Matty	67T	240	$ .75	$3.00	Alvis, Max	68T	340	$ .35	$1.40
Alou, Matty	68T	1	$4.00	$16.00	Alvis, Max	69T	145	$ .35	$1.40
Alou, Matty	68T	270	$ .35	$1.40	Alvis, Max	70T	85	$ .20	$ .80
Alou, Matty	69T	2	$1.25	$5.00	Alyea, Brant	66T	11	$ .35	$1.40
Alou, Matty	69T	490	$ .30	$1.20	Alyea, Brant	69T	48	$ .35	$1.40
Alou, Matty	70T	30	$ .20	$ .80	Alyea, Brant	70T	303	$ .35	$1.40
Alou, Matty	70TAS	460	$ .50	$2.00	Alyea, Brant	71T	449	$ .50	$2.00
Alou, Matty	71T	720	$1.10	$4.40	Alyea, Brant	72T	383	$ .10	$ .40
Alou, Matty	72T	395	$ .20	$ .80	Amalfitano, Joe	55T	144	$2.75	$11.00
Alou, Matty	73T	132	$ .20	$ .80	Amalfitano, Joe	60T	356	$ .75	$3.00
Alou, Matty	74T	430	$ .10	$ .40	Amalfitano, Joe	61T	87	$ .60	$2.40
Alou, Moises	91T	526	$ .05	$ .25	Amalfitano, Joe	62T	456	$1.50	$6.00
Alou, Moises	91TSC	31	$ .20	$2.00	Amalfitano, Joe	63T	199	$ .90	$3.60

TOPPS

Player	Year	No.	VG	EX/MT
Amalfitano, Joe	64T	451	$1.00	$4.00
Amalfitano, Joe	65T	402	$1.00	$4.00
Amalfitano, Joe	73T	252	$ .20	$ .80
Amalfitano, Joe	74T	78	$ .10	$ .40
Amaral, Rich	92TSC	689	$ .01	$ .10
Amaral, Rich	93T	431	$ .01	$ .03
Amaral, Rich	93TSC	264	$ .01	$ .10
Amaro, Ruben	59T	178	$1.00	$4.00
Amaro, Ruben	61T	103	$ .60	$2.40
Amaro, Ruben	62T	284	$ .75	$3.00
Amaro, Ruben	63T	455	$3.00	$12.00
Amaro, Ruben	64T	432	$1.00	$4.00
Amaro, Ruben	65T	419	$1.00	$4.00
Amaro, Ruben	66T	186	$ .50	$2.00
Amaro, Ruben	67T	358	$ .60	$2.40
Amaro, Ruben	68T	138	$ .35	$1.40
Amaro, Ruben	69T	598	$ .40	$1.60
Amaro, Ruben	92T	269	$ .01	$ .10
Amaro, Ruben	92TSC	870	$ .01	$ .10
Amaro, Ruben	92TTR	5	$ .01	$ .05
Amaro, Ruben	93T	43	$ .01	$ .03
Amoros, Sandy	55T	75	$5.50	$22.00
Amoros, Sandy	56T	42	$3.00	$12.00
Amoros, Sandy	57T	201	$2.00	$8.00
Amoros, Sandy	58T	93	$2.00	$8.00
Amoros, Sandy	60T	531	$2.75	$11.00
Andersen, Larry	78T	703	$3.50	$14.00
Andersen, Larry	80T	665	$ .01	$ .10

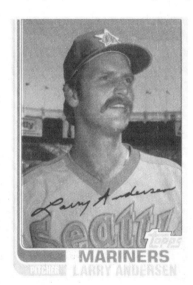

Player	Year	No.	VG	EX/MT
Andersen, Larry	82T	52	$ .01	$ .08
Andersen, Larry	83T	234	$ .01	$ .08
Andersen, Larry	85T	428	$ .01	$ .06
Andersen, Larry	86T	183	$ .01	$ .05
Andersen, Larry	87T	503	$ .01	$ .04
Andersen, Larry	88T	342	$ .01	$ .04
Andersen, Larry	89T	24	$ .01	$ .03
Andersen, Larry	91T	761	$ .01	$ .03
Andersen, Larry	91TSC	390	$ .05	$ .25
Andersen, Larry	92T	616	$ .01	$ .03
Andersen, Larry	92TSC	91	$ .01	$ .10
Anderson, Allan	87T	336	$ .01	$ .04
Anderson, Allan	88T	101	$ .01	$ .04
Anderson, Allan	89T	672	$ .01	$ .03
Anderson, Allan	90T	71	$ .01	$ .03

Player	Year	No.	VG	EX/MT
Anderson, Allan	91T	223	$ .01	$ .03
Anderson, Allan	91TSC	188	$ .05	$ .25
Anderson, Allan	92T	417	$ .01	$ .03
Anderson, Allan	92TSC	204	$ .01	$ .10
Anderson, Allan	92TSC	767	$ .01	$ .10
Anderson, Bob	58T	209	$1.25	$5.00
Anderson, Bob	59T	447	$1.00	$4.00
Anderson, Bob	60T	412	$ .75	$3.00
Anderson, Bob	61T	283	$ .60	$2.40
Anderson, Bob	62T	557	$6.00	$24.00
Anderson, Bob	63T	379	$1.00	$4.00
Anderson, Brady	88TTR	5	$ .10	$1.00
Anderson, Brady	89T	757	$ .10	$ .50
Anderson, Brady	90T	598	$ .01	$ .15
Anderson, Brady	91T	97	$ .01	$ .15
Anderson, Brady	91TSC	410	$ .10	$ .75
Anderson, Brady	92T	268	$ .01	$ .10
Anderson, Brady	92TSC	303	$ .01	$ .10
Anderson, Brady	93T	355	$ .01	$ .03
Anderson, Bud	79T	712	$ .03	$ .12
Anderson, Bud	83T	367	$ .01	$ .08
Anderson, Bud	84T	497	$ .01	$ .06
Anderson, Craig	62T	593	$5.25	$21.00
Anderson, Craig	63T	59	$ .50	$2.00
Anderson, Dave	84T	376	$ .01	$ .06
Anderson, Dave	85T	654	$ .01	$ .06
Anderson, Dave	86T	758	$ .01	$ .05
Anderson, Dave	87T	73	$ .01	$ .04
Anderson, Dave	88T	456	$ .01	$ .04
Anderson, Dave	89T	117	$ .01	$ .03
Anderson, Dave	90T	248	$ .01	$ .03
Anderson, Dave	91T	572	$ .01	$ .03
Anderson, Dwain	72T	268	$ .10	$ .40
Anderson, Dwain	73T	241	$ .10	$ .40
Anderson, Harry	57T	404	$1.75	$7.00
Anderson, Harry	58T	171	$1.25	$5.00
Anderson, Harry	59T	85	$1.50	$6.00
Anderson, Harry	60T	285	$ .75	$3.00
Anderson, Harry	61T	76	$ .60	$2.40
Anderson, Jim	79T	703	$ .05	$ .20
Anderson, Jim	80T	183	$ .01	$ .10
Anderson, Jim	81T	613	$ .01	$ .08
Anderson, Jim	82T	497	$ .01	$ .08
Anderson, Jim	84T	353	$ .01	$ .06
Anderson, John	62T	266	$ .75	$3.00
Anderson, Kent	89TTR	3	$ .01	$ .10
Anderson, Kent	90T	16	$ .01	$ .03
Anderson, Kent	91T	667	$ .01	$ .03
Anderson, Kent	91TSC	241	$ .05	$ .25
Anderson, Larry	76T	593	$ .15	$ .60
Anderson, Larry	77T	487	$ .05	$ .20
Anderson, Mike	72T	14	$ .10	$ .40
Anderson, Mike	73T	147	$ .10	$ .40
Anderson, Mike	74T	619	$ .10	$ .40
Anderson, Mike	75T	118	$ .10	$ .40
Anderson, Mike	76T	527	$ .05	$ .25
Anderson, Mike	76TTR	527	$ .05	$ .25
Anderson, Mike	77T	72	$ .05	$ .20
Anderson, Mike	78T	714	$ .04	$ .16
Anderson, Mike	79T	102	$ .03	$ .12
Anderson, Mike	80T	317	$ .01	$ .10
Anderson, Rick	81T	282	$ .01	$ .08
Anderson, Rick	87T	594	$ .01	$ .04
Anderson, George	59T	338	$11.25	$45.00
Anderson, George "Sparky"	60T	34	$2.50	$10.00
Anderson, Sparky	70T	181	$ .50	$2.00
Anderson, Sparky	71T	688	$4.50	$18.00
Anderson, Sparky	72T	358	$ .50	$2.00
Anderson, Sparky	73T	296	$ .20	$ .80
Anderson, Sparky	74T	326	$ .25	$1.00
Anderson, Sparky	78T	401	$ .05	$ .20
Anderson, Sparky	83T	666	$ .01	$ .08
Anderson, Sparky	84T	259	$ .01	$ .06
Anderson, Sparky	85T	307	$ .01	$ .06
Anderson, Sparky	86T	411	$ .01	$ .05

TOPPS

Player	Year	No.	VG	EX/MT	Player	Year	No.	VG	EX/MT
Anderson, Sparky	87T	218	$.01	$.04	Antonelli, Johnny	60TAS	572	$6.25	$25.00
Anderson, Sparky	88T	14	$.01	$.04	Antonelli, Johnny	61T	115	$.60	$2.40
Anderson, Sparky	89T	193	$.01	$.03	Antonelli, John	91TA53	106	$.01	$.15
Anderson, Sparky	90T	609	$.01	$.03	Antonello, Bill	53T	272	$22.50	$90.00
Anderson, Sparky	91T	519	$.01	$.03	Antonello, Bill	91TA53	272	$.01	$.15
Anderson, Sparky	92T	381	$.01	$.03	Aparicio, Luis	56T	292	$35.00	$140.00
Anderson, Sparky	93T	506	$.01	$.10	Aparicio, Luis	57T	7	$10.00	$40.00
Andrews, Mike	67T	314	$1.75	$7.00	Aparicio, Luis	58T	85	$6.00	$24.00
Andrews, Mike	68T	502	$.75	$3.00	Aparicio, Luis	58TAS	483	$3.00	$12.00
Andrews, Mike	69T	52	$.35	$1.40	Aparicio, Luis	59T	310	$4.50	$18.00
Andrews, Mike	70T	406	$.35	$1.40	Aparicio, Luis	59T	408	$2.00	$8.00
Andrews, Mike	71T	191	$.25	$1.00	Aparicio, Luis	59TAS	560	$7.50	$30.00
Andrews, Mike	72T	361	$.10	$.40	Aparicio, Luis	60T	240	$4.00	$16.00
Andrews, Mike	73T	42	$.10	$.40	Aparicio, Luis	60TAS	559	$6.25	$25.00
Andrews, Rob	76T	568	$.05	$.25	Aparicio, Luis	61T	440	$3.75	$15.00
Andrews, Rob	77T	209	$.05	$.20	Aparicio, Luis	61TAS	574	$11.25	$45.00
Andrews, Rob	78T	461	$.04	$.16	Aparicio, Luis	62T	325	$3.50	$14.00
Andrews, Rob	79T	34	$.03	$.12	Aparicio, Luis	62TAS	469	$2.50	$10.00
Andrews, Rob	80T	279	$.01	$.10	Aparicio, Luis	63T	205	$3.00	$12.00
Andrews, Shane	91T	74	$.05	$.25	Aparicio, Luis	64T	540	$5.00	$20.00
Andujar, Joaquin	77T	67	$.10	$.40	Aparicio, Luis	65T	410	$3.00	$12.00
Andujar, Joaquin	78T	158	$.04	$.16	Aparicio, Luis	66T	90	$1.50	$6.00
Andujar, Joaquin	79T	471	$.05	$.20	Aparicio, Luis	67T	60	$1.50	$6.00
Andujar, Joaquin	80T	617	$.01	$.10	Aparicio, Luis	68T	310	$1.50	$6.00
Andujar, Joaquin	81T	329	$.01	$.08	Aparicio, Luis	69T	75	$1.25	$5.00
Andujar, Joaquin	81TTR	731	$.01	$.15	Aparicio, Luis	70T	315	$1.00	$4.00
Andujar, Joaquin	82T	533	$.01	$.08	Aparicio, Luis	71T	740	$4.50	$18.00
Andujar, Joaquin	83T	228	$.01	$.08	Aparicio, Luis	72T	313	$.75	$3.00
Andujar, Joaquin	83T	561	$.01	$.08	Aparicio, Luis	72TIA	314	$.25	$1.00
Andujar, Joaquin	84T	785	$.01	$.06	Aparicio, Luis	73T	165	$.75	$3.00
Andujar, Joaquin	85T	655	$.01	$.06	Aparicio, Luis	74T	61	$.50	$2.00
Andujar, Joaquin	86T	150	$.01	$.05	Apodaca, Bob	74T	608	$.10	$.40
Andujar, Joaquin	86TTR	3	$.01	$.06	Apodaca, Bob	75T	659	$.10	$.40
Andujar, Joaquin	87T	775	$.01	$.04	Apodaca, Bob	76T	16	$.05	$.25
Andujar, Joaquin	88T	47	$.01	$.04	Apodaca, Bob	77T	225	$.10	$.40
Angelini, Norm	73T	616	$.75	$3.00	Apodaca, Bob	78T	592	$.04	$.16
Angels, Team	62T	132	$1.50	$6.00	Apodaca, Bob	79T	197	$.03	$.12
Angels, Team	63T	39	$1.00	$4.00	Apodaca, Bob	80T	633	$.01	$.10
Angels, Team	64T	213	$1.50	$6.00	Aponte, Luis	83T	577	$.01	$.08
Angels, Team	65T	293	$1.50	$6.00	Aponte, Luis	84T	187	$.01	$.06
Angels, Team	66T	131	$1.00	$4.00	Aponte, Luis	84TTR	2	$.01	$.15
Angels, Team	67T	327	$1.00	$4.00	Appier, Kevin	90T	167	$.05	$.25
Angels, Team	68T	252	$.75	$3.00	Appier, Kevin	91T	454	$.01	$.03
Angels, Team	70T	522	$.75	$3.00	Appier, Kevin	91TSC	501	$.10	$1.00
Angels, Team	71T	442	$.75	$3.00	Appier, Kevin	92T	281	$.01	$.10
Angels, Team	72T	71	$.25	$1.00	Appier, Kevin	92TSC	523	$.01	$.10
Angels, Team	73T	243	$.30	$1.20	Appier, Kevin	93T	76	$.01	$.03
Angels, Team	74T	114	$.25	$1.00	Appling, Luke	60T	461	$1.75	$7.00
Angels, Team Checklist	75T	236	$.35	$1.40	Aquino, Luis	87T	301	$.01	$.04
Angels, Team Checklist	76T	304	$.30	$1.20	Aquino, Luis	89T	266	$.01	$.03
Angels, Team Checklist	77T	34	$.25	$1.00	Aquino, Luis	90T	707	$.01	$.03
Angels, Team Checklist	78T	214	$.20	$.80	Aquino, Luis	91T	169	$.01	$.03
Angels, Team Checklist	79T	424	$.15	$.60	Aquino, Luis	91TSC	451	$.05	$.25
Angels, Team Checklist	80T	214	$.10	$.50	Aquino, Luis	92T	412	$.01	$.03
Angels, Team Checklist	81T	663	$.05	$.25	Aquino, Luis	92TSC	365	$.01	$.10
Angels, Team Leaders	86T	486	$.01	$.05	Aquino, Luis	93T	643	$.01	$.03
Angels, Team Leaders	87T	556	$.01	$.04	Archer, Jim	61T	552	$7.50	$30.00
Angels, Team Leaders	88T	381	$.01	$.04	Archer, Jim	62T	433	$1.25	$5.00
Angels, Team Leaders	89T	51	$.01	$.03	Arcia, Jose	68T	258	$.35	$1.40
Ansley, Willie	89T	607	$.01	$.15	Arcia, Jose	69T	473	$.30	$1.20
Anthony, Eric	90T	608	$.05	$.25	Arcia, Jose	70T	587	$.50	$2.00
Anthony, Eric	91T	331	$.01	$.10	Arcia, Jose	71T	134	$.25	$1.00
Anthony, Eric	91TSC	229	$.05	$.25	Arcia, Jose	73T	466	$.25	$1.00
Anthony, Eric	92TSC	575	$.01	$.10	Arft, Hank	52T	284	$13.75	$55.00
Anthony, Eric	93T	89	$.01	$.03	Arias, Alex	92T	551	$.10	$.50
Anthony, Eric	93TSC	141	$.01	$.15	Arias, Alex	93T	516	$.01	$.15
Anthony, Greg	92T	336	$.01	$.10	Arias, Rodolfo	59T	537	$4.00	$16.00
Antonelli, John	52T	140	$7.00	$28.00	Arlin, Steve	72T	78	$.10	$.40
Antonelli, John	53T	106	$7.50	$30.00	Arlin, Steve	73T	294	$.10	$.40
Antonelli, Johnny	54T	119	$3.75	$15.00	Arlin, Steve	74T	406	$.10	$.40
Antonelli, Johnny	56T	138	$2.50	$10.00	Arlin, Steve	75T	159	$.10	$.40
Antonelli, Johnny	57T	105	$2.00	$8.00	Armas, Tony	77T	492	$0.25	$.80
Antonelli, Johnny	58T	152	$1.25	$5.00	Armas, Tony	78T	298	$.05	$.20
Antonelli, Johnny	59T	377	$1.00	$4.00	Armas, Tony	79T	507	$.05	$.20
Antonelli, Johnny	60T	80	$.85	$3.40	Armas, Tony	80T	391	$.01	$.10

TOPPS

Player	Year	No.	VG	EX/MT
Armas, Tony	81T	629	$.01	$.08
Armas, Tony	82T	60	$.01	$.08
Armas, Tony	82T	162	$.10	$.50
Armas, Tony	83T	435	$.01	$.08
Armas, Tony	83TRB	1	$.01	$.15
Armas, Tony	83TTR	4	$.01	$.10
Armas, Tony	84T	105	$.01	$.06
Armas, Tony	85T	785	$.01	$.06
Armas, Tony	85TAS	707	$.01	$.06
Armas, Tony	86T	255	$.01	$.05
Armas, Tony	87T	535	$.01	$.04
Armas, Tony	88T	761	$.01	$.04
Armas, Tony	89T	332	$.01	$.03
Armas, Tony	90T	603	$.01	$.03
Armbrister, Ed	72T	524	$.25	$1.00
Armbrister, Ed	74T	601	$1.25	$5.00
Armbrister, Ed	75T	622	$2.75	$11.00
Armbrister, Ed	76T	652	$.05	$.25
Armbrister, Ed	77T	203	$.05	$.20
Armbrister, Ed	78T	556	$.04	$.16
Armstrong, Jack	88TTR	6	$.05	$.20
Armstrong, Jack	89T	317	$.01	$.15
Armstrong, Jack	90T	642	$.01	$.10
Armstrong, Jack	91T	175	$.01	$.03
Armstrong, Jack	91TSC	510	$.05	$.25
Armstrong, Jack	92T	77	$.01	$.03
Armstrong, Jack	92TSC	791	$.01	$.10
Armstrong, Jack	92TTR	6	$.01	$.05
Armstrong, Jack	93T	434	$.01	$.10
Armstrong, Mike	82T	731	$.01	$.08
Armstrong, Mike	83T	219	$.01	$.08
Armstrong, Mike	84T	417	$.01	$.06
Armstrong, Mike	84TTR	3	$.01	$.15
Armstrong, Mike	85T	612	$.01	$.06
Arnold, Chris	72T	232	$.10	$.40
Arnold, Chris	73T	584	$.60	$2.40
Arnold, Chris	74T	432	$.10	$.40
Arnold, Chris	77T	591	$.05	$.25
Arnold, Jamie	93T	559	$.05	$.25
Arnsberg, Brad	88T	159	$.01	$.04
Arnsberg, Brad	90TTR	3	$.01	$.05
Arnsberg, Brad	91T	706	$.01	$.03
Arnsberg, Brad	91TSC	540	$.05	$.25
Arnsberg, Brad	92TSC	668	$.01	$.10
Arocha, Rene	93T	742	$.10	$.50
Arrigo, Gerry	64T	516	$1.00	$4.00
Arrigo, Gerry	65T	39	$.35	$1.40
Arrigo, Gerry	66T	357	$.50	$2.00
Arrigo, Gerry	67T	488	$1.50	$6.00
Arrigo, Gerry	68T	302	$.35	$1.40
Arrigo, Gerry	69T	213	$.35	$1.40
Arrigo, Gerry	70T	274	$.35	$1.40
Arroyo, Fernando	76T	614	$.05	$.25
Arroyo, Fernando	78T	607	$.04	$.16
Arroyo, Fernando	81T	408	$.01	$.08
Arroyo, Fernando	82T	18	$.01	$.08
Arroyo, Fernando	82T	396	$.01	$.08
Arroyo, Luis	56T	64	$2.75	$11.00
Arroyo, Luis	57T	394	$1.75	$7.00
Arroyo, Luis	61T	142	$.60	$2.40
Arroyo, Luis	62T	455	$1.50	$6.00
Arroyo, Luis	63T	569	$2.25	$9.00
Ashburn, Richie	51Tbb	3	$43.75	$175.00
Ashburn, Richie	52T	216	$25.00	$100.00
Ashburn, Richie	54T	45	$10.50	$42.00
Ashburn, Richie	56T	120	$8.00	$32.00
Ashburn, Richie	57T	70	$5.50	$22.00
Ashburn, Richie	58T	230	$4.25	$17.00
Ashburn, Richie	59T	300	$3.50	$14.00
Ashburn, Richie	59T	317	$8.00	$32.00
Ashburn, Richie	60T	305	$2.50	$10.00
Ashburn, Richie	61T	88	$2.00	$8.00
Ashburn, Richie	62T	213	$2.50	$10.00
Ashburn, Richie	63T	135	$2.25	$9.00
Ashburn, Richie	91TA53	311	$.10	$.75

Player	Year	No.	VG	EX/MT
Ashby, Alan	76T	209	$.10	$.40
Ashby, Alan	77T	564	$.05	$.20
Ashby, Alan	78T	319	$.04	$.16
Ashby, Alan	79T	36	$.03	$.12
Ashby, Alan	80T	187	$.01	$.10

Player	Year	No.	VG	EX/MT
Ashby, Alan	81T	696	$.01	$.08
Ashby, Alan	82T	433	$.01	$.08
Ashby, Alan	83T	774	$.01	$.08
Ashby, Alan	84T	217	$.01	$.15
Ashby, Alan	85T	564	$.01	$.06
Ashby, Alan	86T	331	$.01	$.05
Ashby, Alan	87T	112	$.01	$.04
Ashby, Alan	88T	48	$.01	$.04
Ashby, Alan	89T	492	$.01	$.03
Ashby, Andy	92T	497	$.01	$.10
Ashby, Andy	92TSC	717	$.05	$.20
Ashby, Andy	93T	794	$.01	$.03
Ashford, Tucker	78T	116	$.04	$.16
Ashford, Tucker	79T	247	$.03	$.12
Ashford, Tucker	84T	492	$.01	$.06
Ashley, Billy	93T	815	$.05	$.25
Aspromonte, Bob	60T	547	$2.75	$11.00
Aspromonte, Bob	61T	396	$1.00	$4.00
Aspromonte, Bob	62T	248	$.75	$3.00
Aspromonte, Bob	63T	45	$.50	$2.00
Aspromonte, Bob	64T	467	$1.00	$4.00
Aspromonte, Bob	65T	175	$.35	$1.40
Aspromonte, Bob	66T	273	$.75	$3.00
Aspromonte, Bob	66T	352	$.50	$2.00
Aspromonte, Bob	67T	274	$.50	$2.00
Aspromonte, Bob	68T	95	$.35	$1.40
Aspromonte, Bob	69T	542	$.40	$1.60
Aspromonte, Bob	70T	529	$.35	$1.40
Aspromonte, Bob	71T	469	$.50	$2.00
Aspromonte, Bob	72T	659	$1.25	$5.00
Aspromonte, Ken	58T	405	$1.00	$4.00
Aspromonte, Ken	59T	424	$1.00	$4.00
Aspromonte, Ken	60T	114	$.75	$3.00
Aspromonte, Ken	61T	176	$.60	$2.40
Aspromonte, Ken	62T	563	$3.50	$14.00
Aspromonte, Ken	63T	464	$3.00	$12.00
Aspromonte, Ken	64T	252	$.65	$2.60
Aspromonte, Ken	72T	784	$1.25	$5.00

TOPPS

Player	Year	No.	VG	EX/MT
Aspromonte, Ken	73T	449	$ .50	$2.00
Aspromonte, Ken	74T	521	$ .10	$ .40
Asselstine, Brian	77T	479	$ .05	$ .20
Asselstine, Brian	78T	372	$ .04	$ .16
Asselstine, Brian	79T	529	$ .03	$ .12
Asselstine, Brian	81T	64	$ .01	$ .08
Asselstine, Brian	82T	214	$ .01	$ .08
Assenmacher, Paul	86TTR	4	$ .01	$ .06
Assenmacher, Paul	87T	132	$ .01	$ .04
Assenmacher, Paul	88T	266	$ .01	$ .04
Assenmacher, Paul	89T	454	$ .01	$ .03
Assenmacher, Paul	90T	644	$ .01	$ .03
Assenmacher, Paul	91T	12	$ .01	$ .03
Assenmacher, Paul	91TSC	586	$ .05	$ .25
Assenmacher, Paul	92T	753	$ .01	$ .03
Assenmacher, Paul	92TSC	731	$ .01	$ .10
Assenmacher, Paul	93T	319	$ .01	$ .03
Astacio, Pedro	93T	93	$ .05	$ .25
Astros, Team	70T	448	$ .50	$2.00
Astros, Team	71T	722	$3.50	$24.00
Astros, Team	72T	282	$ .50	$2.00
Astros, Team	73T	158	$ .30	$1.20
Astros, Team	74T	154	$ .25	$1.00
Astros, Team Checklist	75T	487	$ .35	$1.40
Astros, Team Checklist	76T	147	$ .30	$1.20
Astros, Team Checklist	77T	327	$ .25	$1.00
Astros, Team Checklist	78T	112	$ .20	$ .80
Astros, Team Checklist	79T	381	$ .15	$ .60
Astros, Team Checklist	80T	82	$ .10	$ .50
Astros, Team Checklist	81T	678	$ .05	$ .25
Astros, Team Leaders	86T	186	$ .01	$ .05
Astros, Team Leaders	87T	531	$ .01	$ .10
Astros, Team Leaders	88T	291	$ .01	$ .04
Astros, Team Leaders	89T	579	$ .01	$ .03
Astroth, Joe	52T	290	$13.75	$55.00
Astroth, Joe	53T	103	$4.00	$16.00
Astroth, Joe	56T	106	$2.50	$10.00
Astroth, Joe	91TA53	103	$ .01	$ .15
Atherton, Keith	84T	529	$ .01	$ .06
Atherton, Keith	85T	166	$ .01	$ .06
Atherton, Keith	86T	353	$ .01	$ .05
Atherton, Keith	87T	52	$ .01	$ .04
Atherton, Keith	88T	451	$ .01	$ .04
Atherton, Keith	89T	698	$ .01	$ .03
Atherton, Keith	89TTR	4	$ .01	$ .05
Atkinson, Bill	78T	43	$ .04	$ .16
Atkinson, Bill	80T	415	$ .01	$ .10
Atwell, Toby	52T	356	$43.75	$175.00
Atwell, Toby	53T	23	$4.00	$16.00
Atwell, Toby	56T	232	$3.75	$15.00
Atwell, Toby	91TA53	23	$ .01	$ .15
Auerbach, Rick	72T	153	$ .10	$ .40
Auerbach, Rick	73T	427	$ .25	$1.00
Auerbach, Rick	74T	289	$ .10	$ .40
Auerbach, Rick	75T	588	$ .10	$ .40
Auerbach, Rick	76T	622	$ .05	$ .25
Auerbach, Rick	78T	646	$ .04	$ .16
Auerbach, Rick	79T	174	$ .03	$ .12
Auerbach, Rick	80T	354	$ .01	$ .10
Auerbach, Rick	82T	72	$ .01	$ .08
August, Don	85T	392	$ .10	$ .40
August, Don	88TTR	7	$ .01	$ .10
August, Don	89T	696	$ .01	$ .03
August, Don	90T	192	$ .01	$ .03
Augustine, Dave	74T	598	$6.00	$24.00
Augustine, Dave	75T	616	$6.00	$24.00
Augustine, Jerry	77T	577	$ .05	$ .20
Augustine, Jerry	78T	133	$ .04	$ .16
Augustine, Jerry	79T	357	$ .03	$ .12
Augustine, Jerry	80T	243	$ .01	$ .10
Augustine, Jerry	81T	596	$ .01	$ .08
Augustine, Jerry	82T	46	$ .01	$ .08
Augustine, Jerry	83T	424	$ .01	$ .08
Augustine, Jerry	84T	658	$ .01	$ .06
Ault, Doug	77T	477	$ .05	$ .20
Ault, Doug	78T	267	$ .04	$ .16
Ault, Doug	79T	392	$ .03	$ .12
Ausmus, Brad	92T	58	$ .05	$ .25
Aust, Dennis	66T	179	$ .50	$2.00
Austin, Jim	92TSC	411	$ .01	$ .15
Austin, James	93T	449	$ .01	$ .03
Austin, Rick	71T	41	$ .25	$1.00

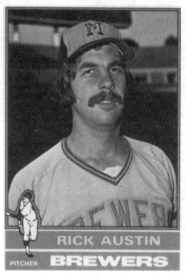

Player	Year	No.	VG	EX/MT
Austin, Rick	76T	269	$ .05	$ .25
Averill, Earl	59T	301	$1.00	$4.00
Averill, Earl	60T	39	$ .85	$3.40
Averill, Earl	61T	358	$ .60	$2.40
Averill, Earl	62T	452	$1.50	$6.00
Averill, Earl	63T	139	$ .50	$2.00
Avery, Steve	89T	784	$ .10	$1.00
Avery, Steve	90TTR	4	$ .10	$ .50
Avery, Steve	91T	227	$ .05	$ .20
Avery, Steve	91TSC	48	$1.00	$4.00
Avery, Steve	92T	574	$ .01	$ .15
Avery, Steve	92TSC	60	$ .10	$ .50
Avery, Steve	92TSC	594	$ .05	$ .25
Avery, Steve	93T	615	$ .01	$ .10
Avila, Bobby	52T	257	$12.50	$50.00
Avila, Bobby	56T	132	$2.50	$10.00
Avila, Bobby	57T	195	$2.00	$8.00
Avila, Bobby	58T	276	$1.25	$5.00
Avila, Bobby	59T	363	$1.00	$4.00
Avila, Bobby	60T	90	$ .85	$3.40
Aviles, Ramon	80T	682	$ .01	$ .10
Aviles, Ramon	81T	644	$ .01	$ .08
Aviles, Ramon	82T	152	$ .01	$ .08
Award, Babe Ruth	72T	626	$ .75	$3.00
Award, Commissioners	72T	621	$ .35	$1.40
Award, Cy Young	72T	623	$ .35	$1.40
Award, Minor L.P. of Yr.	72T	624	$ .35	$1.40
Award, MVP	72T	622	$ .35	$1.40
Award, Rookie of Year	72T	625	$ .35	$1.40
Ayala, Benny	75T	619	$ .10	$ .40
Ayala, Benny	80T	262	$ .01	$ .10
Ayala, Benny	81T	101	$ .01	$ .08
Ayala, Benny	82T	331	$ .01	$ .08
Ayala, Benny	83T	59	$ .01	$ .08
Ayala, Benny	84T	443	$ .01	$ .06
Ayala, Benny	85T	624	$ .01	$ .06

TOPPS

Player	Year	No.	VG	EX/MT	Player	Year	No.	VG	EX/MT
Ayala, Benny	85TTR	3	$.01	$.10	Bailes, Scott	92TSC	167	$.01	$.10
Ayrault, Bob	93T	126	$.01	$.10	Bailey, Bob	63T	228	$12.50	$50.00
Ayrault, Bob	93TSC	4	$.01	$.10	Bailey, Bob	64T	91	$.50	$2.00
Azcue, Joe	62T	417	$1.25	$5.00	Bailey, Bob	65T	412	$1.00	$4.00
Azcue, Joe	63T	501	$3.00	$12.00	Bailey, Bob	66T	485	$1.50	$6.00
Azcue, Joe	64T	199	$.65	$2.60	Bailey, Bob	67T	32	$.40	$1.60
Azcue, Joe	65T	514	$1.25	$5.00	Bailey, Bob	68T	580	$.70	$2.80
Azcue, Joe	66T	452	$1.50	$6.00	Bailey, Bob	69T	399	$.30	$1.20
Azcue, Joe	67T	336	$.60	$2.40	Bailey, Bob	70T	293	$.35	$1.40
Azcue, Joe	68T	443	$.35	$1.40	Bailey, Bob	71T	157	$.25	$1.00
Azcue, Joe	69T	176	$.35	$1.40	Bailey, Bob	72T	493	$.25	$1.00
Azcue, Joe "Jose"	70T	294	$.35	$1.40	Bailey, Bob	72T	526	$.40	$1.60
Azcue, Jose	71T	657	$1.10	$4.40	Bailey, Bob	73T	505	$.25	$1.00
Azocar, Oscar	91T	659	$.01	$.03	Bailey, Bob	74T	97	$.10	$.40
Azocar, Oscar	91TSC	450	$.05	$.25	Bailey, Bob	75T	365	$.10	$.40
Azocar, Oscar	92T	112	$.01	$.03	Bailey, Bob	76T	338	$.05	$.25
Azocar, Oscar	92TSC	552	$.01	$.10	Bailey, Bob	76TTR	338	$.05	$.25
Azocar, Oscar	93TSC	257	$.01	$.10	Bailey, Bob	77T	221	$.05	$.20
Babcock, Bob	81T	41	$.01	$.08	Bailey, Bob	78T	457	$.04	$.16
Babcock, Bob	82T	567	$.01	$.08	Bailey, Bob	79T	549	$.03	$.12
Babitt, Shooty	82T	578	$.01	$.08	Bailey, Ed	53T	206	$6.00	$24.00
Backman, Wally	83T	444	$.01	$.08	Bailey, Ed	54T	184	$4.50	$18.00
Backman, Wally	85T	677	$.01	$.06	Bailey, Ed	55T	69	$2.25	$9.00
Backman, Wally	86T	191	$.01	$.05	Bailey, Ed	57T	128	$2.00	$8.00
Backman, Wally	87T	48	$.01	$.04	Bailey, Ed	58T	330	$1.25	$5.00
Backman, Wally	88T	333	$.01	$.04	Bailey, Ed	58T	386	$2.50	$10.00
Backman, Wally	89T	508	$.01	$.03	Bailey, Ed	58TAS	490	$1.00	$4.00
Backman, Wally	89TTR	5	$.01	$.05	Bailey, Ed	59T	210	$1.00	$4.00
Backman, Wally	90T	218	$.01	$.03	Bailey, Ed	60T	411	$.75	$3.00
Backman, Wally	90TTR	5	$.01	$.05	Bailey, Ed	61T	418	$1.00	$4.00
Backman, Wally	91T	722	$.01	$.03	Bailey, Ed	62T	459	$1.50	$6.00
Backman, Wally	91TSC	368	$.05	$.25	Bailey, Ed	63T	368	$.90	$3.60
Backman, Wally	91TTR	3	$.01	$.05	Bailey, Ed	64T	437	$1.00	$4.00
Backman, Wally	92T	434	$.01	$.03	Bailey, Ed	65T	559	$2.50	$10.00
Backman, Wally	92TSC	4	$.01	$.10	Bailey, Ed	66T	246	$.50	$2.00
Bacsik, Mike	77T	103	$.05	$.20	Bailey, Ed	91TA53	206	$.05	$.25
Bacsik, Mike	80T	453	$.01	$.10	Bailey, Howard	82T	261	$.01	$.08
Baerga, Carlos	90TTR	6	$.10	$1.00	Bailey, Howard	84T	284	$.01	$.06
Baerga, Carlos	91T	147	$.05	$.25	Bailey, Mark	85T	64	$.01	$.04
Baerga, Carlos	91TSC	115	$1.00	$4.00	Bailey, Mark	86T	432	$.01	$.05
Baerga, Carlos	92T	33	$.05	$.20	Bailey, Mark	87T	197	$.01	$.04
Baerga, Carlos	92TSC	143	$.10	$1.00	Bailey, Roger	93T	433	$.10	$.40
Baerga, Carlos	93T	221	$.01	$.10	Bailor, Bob	77T	474	$.10	$.40
Baerga, Carlos	93T	402	$.01	$.10	Bailor, Bob	78T	196	$.04	$.16
Baerga, Carlos	93TSC	61	$.10	$.75	Bailor, Bob	79T	492	$.03	$.12
Baez, Jose	78T	311	$.04	$.16	Bailor, Bob	80T	581	$.01	$.10
Baez, Kevin	92TSC	543	$.01	$.15	Bailor, Bob	81T	297	$.01	$.07
Bagwell, Jeff	91TSC	388	$2.25	$9.00	Bailor, Bob	81TTR	732	$.01	$.15
Bagwell, Jeff	91TTR	4	$.10	$1.00	Bailor, Bob	82T	79	$.01	$.08
Bagwell, Jeff	92T	520	$.05	$.25	Bailor, Bob	83T	343	$.01	$.08
Bagwell, Jeff	92TSC	330	$.10	$1.00	Bailor, Bob	84T	654	$.01	$.06
Bagwell, Jeff	92TSC	606	$.10	$.50	Bailor, Bob	84TTR	4	$.01	$.15
Bagwell, Jeff	93T	227	$.05	$.20	Bailor, Bob	85T	728	$.01	$.06
Bahnsen, Stan	67T	93	$.75	$3.00	Bailor, Bob	86T	522	$.01	$.05
Bahnsen, Stan	68T	214	$.35	$1.40	Baines, Harold	81T	347	$.90	$3.60
Bahnsen, Stan	60T	380	$.30	$1.20	Baines, Harold	82T	684	$.10	$1.00
Bahnsen, Stan	70T	568	$.50	$2.00	Baines, Harold	83T	177	$.10	$.50
Bahnsen, Stan	71T	184	$.25	$1.00	Baines, Harold	84T	434	$.05	$.25
Bahnsen, Stan	72T	662	$1.25	$5.00	Baines, Harold	85T	249	$.05	$.20
Bahnsen, Stan	73T	20	$.10	$.40	Baines, Harold	85T	275	$.01	$.10
Bahnsen, Stan	74T	254	$.10	$.40	Baines, Harold	86T	755	$.01	$.15
Bahnsen, Stan	75T	161	$.10	$.40	Baines, Harold	87T	772	$.01	$.10
Bahnsen, Stan	76T	534	$.05	$.25	Baines, Harold	88T	35	$.01	$.10
Bahnsen, Stan	77T	383	$.05	$.20	Baines, Harold	89T	585	$.01	$.03
Bahnsen, Stan	78T	97	$.04	$.16	Baines, Harold	90T	345	$.01	$.03
Bahnsen, Stan	79T	468	$.03	$.12	Baines, Harold	91T	166	$.01	$.03
Bahnsen, Stan	80T	653	$.01	$.10	Baines, Harold	91TSC	303	$.05	$.25
Bahnsen, Stan	81T	267	$.01	$.08	Baines, Harold	92T	635	$.01	$.03
Bahnsen, Stan	82T	131	$.01	$.08	Baines, Harold	92TSC	536	$.01	$.10
Bailes, Scott	86TTR	5	$.01	$.06	Baines, Harold	93T	345	$.01	$.03
Bailes, Scott	87T	585	$.01	$.04	Bair, Doug	78T	353	$.04	$.16
Bailes, Scott	88T	107	$.01	$.04	Bair, Doug	79T	126	$.03	$.12
Bailes, Scott	89T	339	$.01	$.03	Bair, Doug	80T	449	$.01	$.10
Bailes, Scott	90T	784	$.01	$.03	Bair, Doug	81T	73	$.01	$.08
Bailes, Scott	92T	95	$.01	$.03	Bair, Doug	82T	262	$.01	$.08

311

TOPPS

Player	Year	No.	VG	EX/MT	Player	Year	No.	VG	EX/MT
Bair, Doug	83T	627	$ .01	$ .08	Ballard, Jeff	89T	69	$ .01	$ .03
Bair, Doug	83TTR	5	$ .01	$ .10	Ballard, Jeff	90T	296	$ .01	$ .03
Bair, Doug	84T	536	$ .01	$ .06	Ballard, Jeff	90TAS	394	$ .01	$ .03
Bair, Doug	85T	744	$ .01	$ .06	Ballard, Jeff	91T	546	$ .01	$ .03
Bakenhaster, Dave	64T	479	$1.00	$4.00	Ballard, Jeff	91TSC	283	$ .05	$ .25
Baker, Chuck	79T	456	$ .03	$ .12	Ballard, Jeff	92T	104	$ .01	$ .15
Baker, Chuck	82T	253	$ .01	$ .08	Ballard, Jeff	92TSC	771	$ .01	$ .10
Baker, Del	54T	133	$3.75	$15.00	Baller, Jay	88T	717	$ .01	$ .04
Baker, Del	60T	456	$1.50	$6.00	Bamberger, George	59T	529	$4.50	$18.00
Baker, Doug	85T	269	$ .01	$ .06	Bamberger, George	73T	136	$ .25	$1.00
Baker, Dusty	71T	709	$15.00	$60.00	Bamberger, George	74T	306	$ .15	$ .60
Baker, Dusty	72T	764	$3.00	$12.00	Bamberger, George	83T	246	$ .01	$ .08
Baker, Dusty	73T	215	$ .25	$1.00	Bamberger, George	85TTR	5	$ .01	$ .10
Baker, Dusty	74T	320	$ .25	$1.00	Bamberger, George	86T	21	$ .01	$ .05
Baker, Dusty	75T	33	$ .10	$ .40	Bamberger, George	87T	468	$ .01	$ .04
Baker, Dusty	76T	28	$ .20	$ .80	Bando, Chris	81T	451	$ .01	$ .08
Baker, Dusty	76TTR	28	$ .05	$ .25	Bando, Chris	82T	141	$ .10	$ .40
Baker, Dusty	77T	146	$ .05	$ .20	Bando, Chris	83T	227	$ .01	$ .08
Baker, Dusty	78T	668	$ .05	$ .25	Bando, Chris	84T	431	$ .01	$ .06
Baker, Dusty	79T	562	$ .05	$ .20	Bando, Chris	85T	14	$ .01	$ .06
Baker, Dusty	80T	255	$ .01	$ .10	Bando, Chris	86T	594	$ .01	$ .05
Baker, Dusty	81T	495	$ .01	$ .08	Bando, Chris	87T	322	$ .01	$ .04
Baker, Dusty	82T	311	$ .01	$ .08	Bando, Chris	88T	604	$ .01	$ .04
Baker, Dusty	82T	375	$ .01	$ .08	Bando, Sal	67T	33	$ .75	$3.00
Baker, Dusty	83T	220	$ .01	$ .08	Bando, Sal	68T	146	$ .35	$1.40
Baker, Dusty	84T	40	$ .01	$ .06	Bando, Sal	69T	371	$ .30	$1.20
Baker, Dusty	84TTR	5	$ .05	$ .20	Bando, Sal	69T	556	$ .40	$1.60
Baker, Dusty	85T	165	$ .01	$ .06	Bando, Sal	70T	120	$ .20	$ .80
Baker, Dusty	85TTR	4	$ .01	$ .10	Bando, Sal	71T	285	$ .25	$1.00
Baker, Dusty	86T	645	$ .01	$ .05	Bando, Sal	72T	348	$ .10	$ .40
Baker, Dusty	87T	565	$ .01	$ .04	Bando, Sal	72T	650	$ .35	$1.40
Baker, Dusty	93T	514	$ .01	$ .03	Bando, Sal	73T	155	$ .20	$ .80
Baker, Floyd	52T	292	$13.75	$55.00	Bando, Sal	74T	103	$ .10	$ .40
Baker, Frank	70T	704	$1.25	$5.00	Bando, Sal	75T	380	$ .15	$ .60
Baker, Frank	71T	213	$ .25	$1.00	Bando, Sal	76T	90	$ .05	$ .25
Baker, Frank	71T	689	$1.10	$4.40	Bando, Sal	77T	498	$ .05	$ .20
Baker, Frank	72T	409	$ .25	$1.00	Bando, Sal	78T	265	$ .04	$ .16
Baker, Frank	74T	411	$ .10	$ .40	Bando, Sal	79T	550	$ .03	$ .12
Baker, Gene	56T	142	$2.50	$10.00	Bando, Sal	80T	715	$ .01	$ .10
Baker, Gene	57T	176	$2.00	$8.00	Bando, Sal	81T	623	$ .01	$ .08
Baker, Gene	58T	358	$1.00	$4.00	Bane, Ed	74T	592	$ .10	$ .40
Baker, Gene	59T	238	$1.00	$4.00	Bane, Ed	77T	486	$ .05	$ .20
Baker, Gene	60T	539	$2.75	$11.00	Baney, Dick	70T	88	$ .20	$ .80
Baker, Gene	61T	339	$ .60	$2.40	Baney, Dick	74T	608	$ .10	$ .40
Baker, Steve	83TTR	6	$ .01	$ .10	Bankhead, Scott	85T	393	$ .10	$ .50
Balaz, John	76T	539	$ .05	$ .25	Bankhead, Scott	87T	508	$ .10	$ .50
Balboni, Steve	82T	83	$ .01	$ .15	Bankhead, Scott	87TTR	2	$ .05	$ .25
Balboni, Steve	83T	8	$ .10	$ .50	Bankhead, Scott	88T	738	$ .01	$ .15
Balboni, Steve	84T	782	$ .01	$ .06	Bankhead, Scott	89T	79	$ .01	$ .15
Balboni, Steve	84TTR	6	$ .05	$ .25	Bankhead, Scott	90T	213	$ .01	$ .10
Balboni, Steve	85T	486	$ .01	$ .06	Bankhead, Scott	91T	436	$ .01	$ .10
Balboni, Steve	86T	164	$ .01	$ .05	Bankhead, Scott	91TSC	597	$ .10	$ .50
Balboni, Steve	87T	240	$ .01	$ .04	Bankhead, Scott	92T	155	$ .01	$ .10
Balboni, Steve	88T	638	$ .01	$ .04	Bankhead, Scott	92TSC	375	$ .01	$ .10
Balboni, Steve	89T	336	$ .01	$ .03	Bankhead, Scott	92TSC	701	$ .01	$ .10
Balboni, Steve	89TTR	6	$ .01	$ .05	Bankhead, Scott	92TTR	7	$ .01	$ .05
Balboni, Steve	90T	716	$ .01	$ .03	Bankhead, Scott	93T	361	$ .01	$ .03
Balboni, Steve	91T	511	$ .01	$ .03	Bankhead, Scott	93TSC	145	$ .01	$ .10
Balboni, Steve	91TSC	134	$ .05	$ .25	Banks, Ernie	54T	94	$187.50	$750.00
Baldschun, Jack	62T	46	$ .60	$2.40	Banks, Ernie	55T	28	$55.00	$220.00
Baldschun, Jack	63T	341	$ .90	$3.60	Banks, Ernie	56T	15	$20.00	$80.00
Baldschun, Jack	64T	520	$1.00	$4.00	Banks, Ernie	57T	55	$27.50	$110.00
Baldschun, Jack	65T	555	$2.50	$10.00	Banks, Ernie	58T	310	$22.50	$90.00
Baldschun, Jack	66T	272	$ .50	$2.00	Banks, Ernie	58TAS	482	$6.25	$25.00
Baldschun, Jack	67T	114	$ .40	$1.60	Banks, Ernie	59T	147	$3.00	$12.00
Baldschun, Jack	70T	284	$ .35	$1.40	Banks, Ernie	59T	350	$17.50	$70.00
Baldwin, Dave	68T	231	$ .35	$1.40	Banks, Ernie	59T	469	$4.00	$16.00
Baldwin, Dave	69T	132	$ .35	$1.40	Banks, Ernie	59TAS	559	$12.50	$50.00
Baldwin, Dave	70T	613	$ .50	$2.00	Banks, Ernie	60T	10	$12.50	$50.00
Baldwin, Dave	71T	48	$ .25	$1.00	Banks, Ernie	60TAS	560	$13.75	$55.00
Baldwin, Reggie	80T	678	$ .01	$ .10	Banks, Ernie	61T	43	$3.00	$12.00
Baldwin, Rick	76T	372	$ .05	$ .25	Banks, Ernie	61T	350	$10.00	$40.00
Baldwin, Rick	77T	587	$ .05	$ .20	Banks, Ernie	61TAS	575	$22.50	$90.00
Bales, Wes	67T	51	$ .40	$1.60	Banks, Ernie	61TMVP	485	$7.50	$30.00
Ballard, Jeff	88T	782	$ .01	$ .04	Banks, Ernie	62T	25	$10.00	$40.00

TOPPS

Player	Year	No.	VG	EX/MT
Banks, Ernie	63T	3	$5.50	$22.00
Banks, Ernie	63T	242	$9.00	$36.00
Banks, Ernie	63T	380	$15.00	$60.00
Banks, Ernie	64T	55	$7.50	$30.00
Banks, Ernie	65T	510	$18.75	$75.00
Banks, Ernie	66T	110	$6.25	$25.00
Banks, Ernie	67T	215	$5.00	$20.00
Banks, Ernie	68T	355	$5.50	$22.00
Banks, Ernie	69T	6	$1.00	$4.00
Banks, Ernie	69T	20	$5.00	$20.00
Banks, Ernie	70T	630	$8.75	$35.00
Banks, Ernie	71T	525	$10.00	$40.00
Banks, Ernie	73T	81	$ .25	$1.00
Banks, Ernie	75T	196	$ .30	$1.20
Banks, Ernie	75T	197	$ .30	$1.20
Banks, George	63T	564	$2.25	$9.00
Banks, George	64T	223	$ .65	$2.60
Banks, George	65T	348	$ .50	$2.00
Banks, George	66T	488	$1.50	$6.00
Banks, Willie	92T	747	$ .01	$ .03
Banks, Willie	92TSC	321	$ .05	$ .35
Banks, Willie	93T	226	$ .01	$ .03
Banks, Willie	93TSC	170	$ .01	$ .15
Bannister, Alan	77T	559	$ .05	$ .20
Bannister, Alan	78T	213	$ .04	$ .16
Bannister, Alan	79T	134	$ .03	$ .12
Bannister, Alan	80T	608	$ .01	$ .10
Bannister, Alan	81T	632	$ .01	$ .08
Bannister, Alan	82T	287	$ .01	$ .08
Bannister, Alan	83T	348	$ .01	$ .08
Bannister, Alan	84T	478	$ .01	$ .06
Bannister, Alan	84TTR	7	$ .01	$ .15
Bannister, Alan	85T	76	$ .01	$ .06
Bannister, Alan	86T	784	$ .01	$ .05
Bannister, Floyd	78T	39	$ .25	$1.00
Bannister, Floyd	79T	306	$ .03	$ .12
Bannister, Floyd	80T	699	$ .01	$ .10
Bannister, Floyd	81T	166	$ .01	$ .08
Bannister, Floyd	82T	468	$ .01	$ .08
Bannister, Floyd	83T	545	$ .01	$ .08
Bannister, Floyd	83T	706	$ .01	$ .10
Bannister, Floyd	83TTR	7	$ .01	$ .10
Bannister, Floyd	84T	280	$ .01	$ .06
Bannister, Floyd	85T	274	$ .01	$ .06
Bannister, Floyd	85T	725	$ .01	$ .06
Bannister, Floyd	86T	64	$ .01	$ .05
Bannister, Floyd	87T	737	$ .01	$ .04
Bannister, Floyd	88T	357	$ .01	$ .04
Bannister, Floyd	88TTR	8	$ .01	$ .05
Bannister, Floyd	89T	638	$ .01	$ .03
Bannister, Floyd	90T	116	$ .01	$ .03
Bannister, Floyd	92TSC	743	$ .01	$ .10
Barber, Brian	92T	594	$ .05	$ .20
Barber, Steve	60T	514	$4.00	$16.00
Barber, Steve	61T	125	$ .60	$2.40
Barber, Steve	62T	57	$1.25	$5.00
Barber, Steve	62T	355	$ .75	$3.00
Barber, Steve	63T	12	$ .50	$2.00
Barber, Steve	64T	450	$1.00	$4.00
Barber, Steve	65T	113	$ .35	$1.40
Barber, Steve	66T	477	$1.50	$6.00
Barber, Steve	67T	82	$ .40	$1.60
Barber, Steve	68T	316	$ .35	$1.40
Barber, Steve	69T	233	$ .50	$2.00
Barber, Steve	70T	224	$ .20	$ .80
Barber, Steve	72T	333	$ .10	$ .40
Barber, Steve	73T	36	$ .10	$ .40
Barber, Steve	74T	631	$ .10	$ .40
Barberie, Bret	88TTR	9	$ .10	$ .40
Barberie, Bret	92T	224	$ .01	$ .10
Barberie, Bret	92TSC	427	$ .01	$ .15
Barbieri, Jim	67T	76	$ .40	$1.60
Barclay, Curt	57T	361	$1.75	$7.00
Barclay, Curt	58T	21	$2.00	$8.00
Barclay, Curt	59T	307	$1.00	$4.00
Bare, Ray	76T	507	$ .05	$ .25
Bare, Ray	77T	43	$ .05	$ .20
Barfield, Jesse	82T	203	$ .10	$1.00
Barfield, Jesse	82TTR	2	$ .10	$1.00
Barfield, Jesse	83T	257	$ .05	$ .25
Barfield, Jesse	84T	488	$ .05	$ .20
Barfield, Jesse	85T	24	$ .05	$ .20
Barfield, Jesse	86T	593	$ .01	$ .10
Barfield, Jesse	87T	655	$ .01	$ .10
Barfield, Jesse	88T	140	$ .01	$ .10
Barfield, Jesse	89T	325	$ .01	$ .10
Barfield, Jesse	89TTR	7	$ .01	$ .10
Barfield, Jesse	90T	740	$ .01	$ .03
Barfield, Jesse	91T	85	$ .01	$ .03
Barfield, Jesse	91TSC	103	$ .05	$ .25
Barfield, Jesse	92T	650	$ .01	$ .03
Barfield, Jesse	92TSC	214	$ .01	$ .10
Barfield, John	91T	428	$ .01	$ .10
Barfield, John	92TSC	364	$ .01	$ .10
Bargar, Greg	84T	474	$ .01	$ .06
Barker, Len	77T	489	$ .20	$ .80
Barker, Len	78T	634	$ .04	$ .16
Barker, Len	79T	94	$ .03	$ .12
Barker, Len	80T	227	$ .01	$ .10
Barker, Len	81T	6	$ .05	$ .25
Barker, Len	81T	432	$ .01	$ .08
Barker, Len	82T	166	$ .01	$ .15
Barker, Len	82T	360	$ .01	$ .08
Barker, Len	83T	120	$ .01	$ .08
Barker, Len	84T	614	$ .01	$ .06
Barker, Len	85T	557	$ .01	$ .06

Player	Year	No.	VG	EX/MT
Barker, Len	**86T**	**24**	**$ .01**	**$ .05**
Barker, Ray	61T	428	$1.00	$4.00
Barker, Ray	65T	546	$1.40	$5.60
Barker, Ray	66T	323	$ .50	$2.00
Barker, Ray	67T	583	$4.50	$18.00
Barkley, Jeff	86T	567	$ .01	$ .05
Barlow, Mike	78T	429	$ .04	$ .16
Barlow, Mike	80T	312	$ .01	$ .10
Barlow, Mike	81T	77	$ .01	$ .08
Barnes, Brian	91T	211	$ .01	$ .10
Barnes, Brian	91TSC	114	$ .10	$ .50
Barnes, Brian	92T	73	$ .01	$ .03

TOPPS

Player	Year	No.	VG	EX/MT
Barnes, Brian	92TSC	549	$ .01	$ .10
Barnes, Brian	93T	112	$ .01	$ .03
Barnes, Frank	60T	538	$2.75	$11.00
Barnes, Skeeter	91TTR	5	$ .01	$ .05
Barnes, Skeeter	92T	221	$ .01	$ .03
Barnes, Skeeter	92TSC	585	$ .01	$ .10
Barnes, Skeeter	93T	26	$ .01	$ .03
Barnowski, Ed	66T	442	$ .65	$2.60
Barnowski, Ed	67T	507	$1.50	$6.00
Baron, Jimmy	93T	538	$ .01	$ .15
Barr, Jim	72T	232	$ .10	$ .40
Barr, Jim	73T	387	$ .10	$ .40
Barr, Jim	74T	233	$ .10	$ .40
Barr, Jim	75T	107	$ .10	$ .40
Barr, Jim	76T	308	$ .05	$ .25
Barr, Jim	77T	609	$ .05	$ .20
Barr, Jim	78T	62	$ .04	$ .16
Barr, Jim	79T	461	$ .03	$ .12
Barr, Jim	80T	529	$ .01	$ .10
Barr, Jim	81T	717	$ .01	$ .08
Barr, Jim	83T	133	$ .01	$ .08
Barr, Jim	84T	282	$ .01	$ .06
Barr, Steve	76T	595	$ .05	$ .25
Barragan, Cuno	62T	66	$ .60	$2.40
Barragan, Cuno	63T	557	$2.25	$9.00
Barrett, Marty	84T	683	$ .15	$1.25
Barrett, Marty	85T	298	$ .01	$ .06
Barrett, Marty	86T	734	$ .01	$ .05
Barrett, Marty	87T	39	$ .01	$ .04

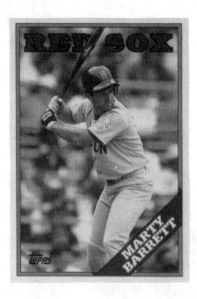

Player	Year	No.	VG	EX/MT
Barrett, Marty	88T	525	$ .01	$ .04
Barrett, Marty	89T	155	$ .01	$ .03
Barrett, Marty	90T	355	$ .01	$ .03
Barrett, Marty	91T	496	$ .01	$ .03
Barrett, Tommy	89T	653	$ .01	$ .03
Barrios, Francisco	77T	222	$ .05	$ .20
Barrios, Francisco	78T	552	$ .04	$ .16
Barrios, Francisco	79T	386	$ .03	$ .12
Barrios, Francisco	80T	107	$ .01	$ .10
Bartirome, Tony	52T	332	$43.75	$175.00
Bartirome, Tony	53T	71	$6.25	$25.00
Bartirome, Tony	91TA53	71	$ .01	$ .15
Barton, Bob	66T	511	$1.50	$6.00

Player	Year	No.	VG	EX/MT
Barton, Bob	67T	462	$1.50	$6.00
Barton, Bob	68T	351	$ .35	$1.40
Barton, Bob	69T	41	$ .35	$1.40
Barton, Bob	70T	352	$ .35	$1.40
Barton, Bob	71T	589	$1.00	$4.00
Barton, Bob	72T	39	$ .10	$ .40
Barton, Bob	72TIA	40	$ .10	$ .40
Barton, Bob	73T	626	$ .60	$2.40
Barton, Shawn	93T	569	$ .01	$ .15
Basgall, Monty	52T	12	$13.75	$55.00
Basgall, Monty	73T	569	$1.10	$4.40
Basgall, Monty	74T	144	$ .50	$2.00
Bass, Kevin	79T	708	$ .25	$1.00
Bass, Kevin	84T	538	$ .01	$ .06
Bass, Kevin	85T	326	$ .01	$ .06
Bass, Kevin	86T	458	$ .01	$ .05
Bass, Kevin	87T	85	$ .01	$ .04
Bass, Kevin	88T	175	$ .01	$ .04
Bass, Kevin	89T	646	$ .01	$ .03
Bass, Kevin	90T	281	$ .01	$ .03
Bass, Kevin	90TTR	7	$ .01	$ .05
Bass, Kevin	91T	752	$ .01	$ .03
Bass, Kevin	91TSC	29	$ .05	$ .25
Bass, Kevin	92T	513	$ .01	$ .03
Bass, Kevin	92TSC	6	$ .01	$ .10
Bass, Kevin	93T	672	$ .01	$ .03
Bass, Norm	62T	122	$ .60	$2.40
Bass, Norm	63T	461	$3.00	$12.00
Bass, Randy	79T	707	$ .03	$ .12
Bass, Randy	82T	307	$ .01	$ .08
Bateman, John	63T	386	$1.00	$4.00
Bateman, John	64T	142	$ .50	$2.00
Bateman, John	65T	433	$1.00	$4.00
Bateman, John	66T	86	$ .35	$1.40
Bateman, John	67T	231	$ .50	$2.00
Bateman, John	68T	592	$ .70	$2.80
Bateman, John	69T	138	$ .35	$1.40
Bateman, John	70T	417	$ .35	$1.40
Bateman, John	71T	628	$1.00	$4.00
Bateman, John	72T	5	$ .10	$ .40
Bates, Jason	93T	579	$ .05	$ .35
Bathe, Bill	91T	679	$ .01	$ .03
Batiste, Kim	92T	514	$ .01	$ .10
Batiste, Kim	92TSC	788	$ .01	$ .15
Batiste, Kim	93T	679	$ .01	$ .03
Battey, Earl	57T	401	$2.00	$8.00
Battey, Earl	58T	364	$1.00	$4.00
Battey, Earl	59T	114	$1.00	$4.00
Battey, Earl	60T	328	$ .75	$3.00
Battey, Earl	61T	315	$ .60	$2.40
Battey, Earl	61TAS	582	$8.00	$32.00
Battey, Earl	62T	371	$1.25	$5.00
Battey, Earl	63T	306	$ .90	$3.60
Battey, Earl	63T	410	$1.00	$4.00
Battey, Earl	64T	90	$ .50	$2.00
Battey, Earl	65T	490	$1.25	$5.00
Battey, Earl	66T	240	$ .50	$2.00
Battey, Earl	67T	15	$ .40	$1.60
Batton, Chris	77T	475	$ .05	$ .20
Batts, Matt	52T	230	$7.00	$28.00
Batts, Matt	54T	88	$3.75	$15.00
Bauer, Hank	51Trb	24	$3.50	$14.00
Bauer, Hank	52T	215	$12.50	$50.00
Bauer, Hank	54T	130	$8.00	$32.00
Bauer, Hank	55T	166	$12.50	$50.00
Bauer, Hank	56T	177	$5.00	$20.00
Bauer, Hank	57T	240	$3.50	$14.00
Bauer, Hank	58T	9	$3.00	$12.00
Bauer, Hank	59T	240	$1.50	$6.00
Bauer, Hank	60T	262	$1.00	$4.00
Bauer, Hank	61T	119	$ .60	$2.40
Bauer, Hank	61T	398	$1.25	$5.00
Bauer, Hank	62T	127	$ .60	$2.40
Bauer, Hank	62T	463	$1.50	$6.00
Bauer, Hank	64T	178	$ .50	$2.00

TOPPS

Player	Year	No.	VG	EX/MT	Player	Year	No.	VG	EX/MT
Bauer, Hank	65T	323	$.50	$2.00	Bearnarth, Larry	63T	386	$1.25	$5.00
Bauer, Hank	66T	229	$.50	$2.00	Bearnarth, Larry	64T	527	$2.25	$9.00
Bauer, Hank	67T	1	$5.00	$20.00	Bearnarth, Larry	65T	258	$.50	$2.00
Bauer, Hank	67T	534	$2.50	$10.00	Bearnarth, Larry	66T	464	$1.50	$6.00
Bauer, Hank	68T	513	$.75	$3.00	Beasley, Chris	92TSC	492	$.01	$.15
Bauer, Hank	69T	124	$.35	$1.40	Beattie, Jim	79T	179	$.03	$.12
Bauer, Hank	91TA53	290	$.05	$.35	Beattie, Jim	80T	334	$.01	$.10
Baugh, Gavin	93T	641	$.05	$.20	Beattie, Jim	81T	443	$.01	$.08
Baumann, Frank	58T	167	$1.25	$5.00	Beattie, Jim	82T	22	$.01	$.08
Baumann, Frank	59T	161	$1.00	$4.00	Beattie, Jim	83T	675	$.01	$.08
Baumann, Frank	60T	306	$.75	$3.00	Beattie, Jim	83T	711	$.01	$.08
Baumann, Frank	61T	46	$.75	$3.00	Beattie, Jim	84T	288	$.01	$.06
Baumann, Frank	61T	550	$7.50	$30.00	Beattie, Jim	85T	505	$.01	$.06
Baumann, Frank	62T	161	$.60	$2.40	Beattie, Jim	86T	729	$.01	$.05
Baumann, Frank	63T	381	$1.00	$4.00	Beattie, Jim	87T	117	$.01	$.04
Baumann, Frank	64T	453	$1.00	$4.00	Beauchamp, Jim	64T	492	$1.25	$5.00
Baumann, Frank	65T	161	$.35	$1.40	Beauchamp, Jim	65T	409	$1.25	$5.00
Baumer, Jim	61T	292	$.60	$2.40	Beauchamp, Jim	66T	84	$.35	$1.40
Baumgarten, Ross	79T	704	$.15	$.60	Beauchamp, Jim	67T	307	$.60	$2.40
Baumgarten, Ross	80T	138	$.01	$.10	Beauchamp, Jim	69T	613	$.40	$1.60
Baumgarten, Ross	81T	398	$.01	$.08	Beauchamp, Jim	71T	322	$.25	$1.00
Baumgarten, Ross	82T	563	$.01	$.08	Beauchamp, Jim	72T	594	$.40	$1.60
Baumgarten, Ross	82TTR	3	$.01	$.10	Beauchamp, Jim	73T	137	$.10	$.40
Baumgarten, Ross	83T	97	$.01	$.08	Beauchamp, Jim	74T	424	$.10	$.40
Baumholtz, Frank	52T	225	$7.00	$28.00	Beck, Rich	66T	234	$1.75	$7.00
Baumholtz, Frank	54T	60	$7.50	$30.00	Beck, Rod	93T	604	$.01	$.03
Baumholtz, Frank	55T	172	$3.00	$12.00	Beck, Rod	93TSC	81	$.01	$.10
Baumholtz, Frank	56T	274	$2.50	$10.00	Becker, Joe	60T	463	$1.25	$5.00
Bauta, Ed	62T	344	$.75	$3.00	Becker, Rich	93T	658	$.05	$.35
Bauta, Ed	63T	336	$.90	$3.60	Beckert, Glenn	65T	549	$4.00	$16.00
Bautista, Jose	88TTR	10	$.01	$.10	Beckert, Glenn	66T	232	$.50	$2.00
Bautista, Jose	89T	469	$.01	$.10	Beckert, Glenn	67T	296	$.60	$2.40
Baxes, Jim	59T	547	$4.00	$16.00	Beckert, Glenn	68T	101	$.35	$1.40
Baxes, Jim	60T	318	$.75	$3.00	Beckert, Glenn	69T	171	$.35	$1.40
Baxes, Mike	58T	302	$1.25	$5.00	Beckert, Glenn	70T	480	$.35	$1.40
Baxes, Mike	59T	381	$1.00	$4.00	Beckert, Glenn	71T	390	$.25	$1.00
Baylor, Don	71T	709	$15.00	$60.00	Beckert, Glenn	72T	45	$.10	$.40
Baylor, Don	72T	474	$1.50	$6.00	Beckert, Glenn	72T	85	$.50	$2.00
Baylor, Don	73T	384	$.50	$3.00	Beckert, Glenn	72TIA	46	$.10	$.40
Baylor, Don	74T	187	$.75	$3.00	Beckert, Glenn	73T	440	$.25	$1.00
Baylor, Don	75T	382	$.50	$2.00	Beckert, Glenn	74T	241	$.10	$.40
Baylor, Don	76T	125	$.25	$1.00	Beckert, Glenn	75T	484	$.10	$.40
Baylor, Don	77T	462	$.25	$1.00	Beckwith, Joe	80T	679	$.01	$.10
Baylor, Don	78T	48	$.25	$1.00	Beckwith, Joe	81T	231	$.01	$.08
Baylor, Don	79T	635	$.15	$.60	Beckwith, Joe	84T	454	$.01	$.06
Baylor, Don	80T	203	$.10	$1.00	Beckwith, Joe	84TTR	9	$.01	$.15
Baylor, Don	80T	285	$.10	$.50	Beckwith, Joe	85T	77	$.01	$.06
Baylor, Don	81T	580	$.01	$.15	Beckwith, Joe	86T	562	$.01	$.05
Baylor, Don	82T	415	$.01	$.15	Becquer, Julio	58T	458	$1.00	$4.00
Baylor, Don	83T	105	$.01	$.10	Becquer, Julio	59T	93	$1.50	$6.00
Baylor, Don	83TTR	8	$.05	$.25	Becquer, Julio	60T	271	$.75	$3.00
Baylor, Don	84T	335	$.01	$.10	Becquer, Julio	61T	329	$.60	$2.40
Baylor, Don	84T	486	$.01	$.06	Bedell, Howie	61T	353	$.60	$2.40
Baylor, Don	85T	70	$.01	$.10	Bedell, Howie	62T	76	$.60	$2.40
Baylor, Don	86T	765	$.01	$.05	Bedrosian, Steve	82T	502	$.25	$2.50
Baylor, Don	86TTR	6	$.01	$.10	Bedrosian, Steve	82TTR	4	$.01	$.10
Baylor, Don	87T	230	$.01	$.04	Bedrosian, Steve	83T	157	$.01	$.15
Baylor, Don	88T	545	$.01	$.04	Bedrosian, Steve	84T	365	$.01	$.06
Baylor, Don	88TTR	11	$.01	$.05	Bedrosian, Steve	85T	25	$.01	$.06
Baylor, Don	89T	673	$.01	$.06	Bedrosian, Steve	86T	648	$.01	$.05
Baylor, Don	93T	504	$.01	$.03	Bedrosian, Steve	86TTR	7	$.01	$.06
Beall, Bob	79T	222	$.03	$.12	Bedrosian, Steve	87T	736	$.01	$.10
Beamon, Charley	59T	192	$1.00	$4.00	Bedrosian, Steve	88T	440	$.01	$.04
Beamon, Charlie	80T	672	$.01	$.10	Bedrosian, Steve	88TAS	407	$.01	$.04
Beane, Billy	87T	114	$.01	$.04	Bedrosian, Steve	89T	20	$.01	$.03
Bean(e), Billy	88T	267	$.01	$.04	Bedrosian, Steve	89TTR	8	$.01	$.05
Beard, Dave	81T	96	$.01	$.08	Bedrosian, Steve	90T	310	$.01	$.03
Beard, Dave	83T	102	$.01	$.08	Bedrosian, Steve	91T	125	$.01	$.03
Beard, Dave	84T	513	$.01	$.06	Bedrosian, Steve	91TSC	531	$.05	$.25
Beard, Dave	84TTR	8	$.01	$.15	Bedrosian, Steve	91TTR	6	$.01	$.05
Beard, Dave	85T	232	$.01	$.06	Bedrosian, Steve	92T	267	$.01	$.03
Beard, Mike	76T	53	$.05	$.25	Beene, Fred	70T	121	$.25	$1.00
Beard, Ted	52T	150	$7.00	$28.00	Beene, Fred	73T	573	$.60	$2.40
Beardon, Gene	52T	229	$7.00	$28.00	Beene, Fred	74T	274	$.10	$.40
Beare, Gary	78T	516	$.04	$.16	Beene, Fred	75T	181	$.10	$.40

TOPPS

Player	Year	No.	VG	EX/MT
Behney, Mel	72T	524	$ .25	$1.00
Behney, Mel	73T	602	$ .75	$3.00
Belanger, Mark	67T	558	$15.00	$60.00
Belanger, Mark	68T	118	$ .35	$1.40
Belanger, Mark	69T	299	$ .50	$2.00
Belanger, Mark	70T	615	$ .50	$2.00
Belanger, Mark	71T	99	$ .25	$1.00
Belanger, Mark	72T	456	$ .20	$ .80
Belanger, Mark	73T	253	$ .10	$ .40
Belanger, Mark	74T	329	$ .10	$ .40
Belanger, Mark	75T	74	$ .10	$ .40
Belanger, Mark	76T	505	$ .05	$ .25
Belanger, Mark	77T	135	$ .05	$ .20
Belanger, Mark	78T	315	$ .04	$ .16
Belanger, Mark	79T	65	$ .03	$ .12
Belanger, Mark	80T	425	$ .01	$ .10
Belanger, Mark	81T	641	$ .01	$ .08
Belanger, Mark	82T	776	$ .01	$ .10
Belanger, Mark	82TTR	5	$ .05	$ .20
Belanger, Mark	83T	273	$ .01	$ .08
Belcher, Tim	85T	281	$ .10	$1.00
Belcher, Tim	88TTR	12	$ .01	$ .15
Belcher, Tim	89T	456	$ .01	$ .03
Belcher, Tim	90T	173	$ .01	$ .10
Belcher, Tim	91T	25	$ .01	$ .03
Belcher, Tim	91TSC	152	$ .05	$ .25
Belcher, Tim	92T	688	$ .01	$ .03
Belcher, Tim	92TSC	842	$ .01	$ .10
Belcher, Tim	92TTR	8	$ .01	$ .05
Belcher, Tim	93T	382	$ .01	$ .03
Belcher, Tim	93TSC	9	$ .01	$ .10
Belinda, Stan	90T	354	$ .01	$ .10
Belinda, Stan	91T	522	$ .01	$ .03
Belinda, Stan	91TSC	453	$ .05	$ .25
Belinda, Stan	92T	466	$ .01	$ .03
Belinda, Stan	92TSC	75	$ .01	$ .10
Belinda, Stan	93T	748	$ .01	$ .03
Belinda, Stan	93TSC	268	$ .01	$ .10
Belinsky, Bo	62T	592	$15.00	$60.00
Belinsky, Bo	63T	33	$ .90	$3.60
Belinsky, Bo	64T	315	$ .65	$2.60
Belinsky, Bo	65T	225	$ .50	$2.00
Belinsky, Bo	66T	506	$1.50	$6.00
Belinsky, Bo	67T	447	$ .60	$2.40
Belinsky, Bo	69T	366	$ .30	$1.20
Bell, Buddy	73T	31	$ .75	$3.00
Bell, Buddy	74T	257	$ .25	$1.00
Bell, Buddy	75T	38	$ .25	$1.00
Bell, Buddy	76T	66	$ .25	$1.00
Bell, Buddy	76T	358	$ .15	$ .60
Bell, Buddy	77T	590	$ .10	$ .40
Bell, Buddy	78T	280	$ .10	$ .40
Bell, Buddy	79T	690	$ .05	$ .20
Bell, Buddy	80T	190	$ .01	$ .15
Bell, Buddy	81T	475	$ .05	$ .20
Bell, Buddy	82T	50	$ .01	$ .15
Bell, Buddy	83T	330	$ .01	$ .15
Bell, Buddy	83T	412	$ .01	$ .08
Bell, Buddy	84T	37	$ .01	$ .06
Bell, Buddy	84T	665	$ .01	$ .15
Bell, Buddy	85T	131	$ .01	$ .10
Bell, Buddy	85T	745	$ .01	$ .10
Bell, Buddy	86T	285	$ .01	$ .10
Bell, Buddy	87T	545	$ .01	$ .04
Bell, Buddy	88T	130	$ .01	$ .04
Bell, Buddy	88TTR	13	$ .01	$ .05
Bell, Buddy	89T	461	$ .01	$ .03
Bell, Derek	91TTR	7	$ .05	$ .25
Bell, Derek	92T	121	$ .01	$ .15
Bell, Derek	92TSC	555	$ .10	$ .50
Bell, Derek	93T	268	$ .01	$ .10
Bell, Eric	87TTR	3	$ .01	$ .05
Bell, Eric	88T	383	$ .01	$ .04
Bell, Gary	59T	327	$1.00	$4.00
Bell, Gary	60T	441	$1.25	$5.00
Bell, Gary	61T	274	$ .60	$2.40
Bell, Gary	62T	273	$ .75	$3.00
Bell, Gary	63T	129	$ .50	$2.00
Bell, Gary	64T	234	$ .65	$2.60
Bell, Gary	65T	424	$1.00	$4.00
Bell, Gary	66T	525	$7.00	$28.00
Bell, Gary	67T	479	$1.50	$6.00
Bell, Gary	68T	43	$ .35	$1.40
Bell, Gary	69T	377	$ .30	$1.20
Bell, George (Jorge)	82T	254	$2.00	$8.00
Bell, George (Jorge)	84T	278	$ .10	$ .75
Bell, George (Jorge)	85T	698	$ .05	$ .35
Bell, George (Jorge)	86T	338	$ .05	$ .20
Bell, George (Jorge)	86TAS	718	$ .01	$ .15
Bell, George	87T	681	$ .05	$ .20
Bell, George	87TAS	612	$ .01	$ .10
Bell, George	88T	590	$ .01	$ .10
Bell, George	88TAS	390	$ .01	$ .10
Bell, George	89T	50	$ .01	$ .10
Bell, George	89TRB	1	$ .01	$ .10
Bell, George	90T	170	$ .01	$ .10
Bell, George	91T	440	$ .01	$ .10
Bell, George	91TSC	504	$ .05	$ .25
Bell, George	91TTR	8	$ .01	$ .10
Bell, George	92T	320	$ .01	$ .03
Bell, George	92TSC	525	$ .01	$ .10
Bell, George	92TSC	840	$ .01	$ .10
Bell, George	92TTR	9	$ .01	$ .05
Bell, George	93T	790	$ .01	$ .03
Bell, Dave (Gus)	51Trb	17	$2.50	$10.00
Bell, Gus	52T	170	$7.00	$28.00
Bell, Gus	53T	118	$4.50	$18.00
Bell, Gus	56T	162	$3.75	$15.00
Bell, Gus	57T	180	$2.00	$8.00
Bell, Gus	58T	75	$2.00	$8.00

Player	Year	No.	VG	EX/MT
Bell, Gus	59T	365	$1.00	$4.00
Bell, Gus	60T	235	$ .75	$3.00
Bell, Gus	60T	352	$1.75	$7.00
Bell, Gus	61T	25	$1.75	$7.00
Bell, Gus	61T	215	$ .60	$2.40
Bell, Gus	62T	408	$1.25	$5.00
Bell, Gus	63T	547	$2.25	$9.00
Bell, Gus	64T	534	$2.25	$9.00

Player	Year	No.	VG	EX/MT	Player	Year	No.	VG	EX/MT
Bell, Gus	76T	66	$ .25	$1.00	Bench, Johnny	82T	400	$ .20	$2.00
Bell, Gus	85T	131	$ .01	$ .10	Bench, Johnny	82TSA	401	$ .10	$1.00
Bell, Gus	91TA53	118	$ .01	$ .15	Bench, Johnny	83T	60	$ .20	$2.00
Bell, Jay	88T	637	$ .05	$ .35	Bench, Johnny	83T	61	$ .10	$1.00
Bell, Jay	89T	144	$ .01	$ .03	Bench, Johnny	84T	6	$ .10	$ .40
Bell, Jay	90T	523	$ .01	$ .03	Bench, Johnny	90TTB	664	$ .01	$ .03
Bell, Jay	91T	293	$ .01	$ .03	Bene, Bill	89T	84	$ .01	$ .03
Bell, Jay	91TSC	84	$ .05	$ .25	Benedict, Bruce	79T	715	$ .05	$ .20
Bell, Jay	92T	779	$ .01	$ .03	Benedict, Bruce	80T	675	$ .01	$ .10
Bell, Jay	92TSC	507	$ .01	$ .10	Benedict, Bruce	81T	108	$ .01	$ .08
Bell, Jay	93T	354	$ .01	$ .03	Benedict, Bruce	82T	424	$ .01	$ .08
Bell, Jay	93TSC	138	$ .01	$ .10	Benedict, Bruce	83T	521	$ .01	$ .08
Bell, Jerry	72T	162	$ .25	$1.00	Benedict, Bruce	84T	255	$ .01	$ .06
Bell, Jerry	73T	92	$ .10	$ .40	Benedict, Bruce	85T	335	$ .01	$ .06
Bell, Jerry	74T	261	$ .10	$ .40	Benedict, Bruce	86T	78	$ .01	$ .05
Bell, Juan	90T	724	$ .01	$ .15	Benedict, Bruce	87T	186	$ .01	$ .04
Bell, Juan	92T	52	$ .01	$ .03	Benedict, Bruce	88T	652	$ .01	$ .04
Bell, Juan	92TSC	835	$ .01	$ .10	Benedict, Bruce	89T	778	$ .01	$ .03
Bell, Juan	93TSC	157	$ .01	$ .10	Benedict, Bruce	90T	583	$ .01	$ .03
Bell, Kevin	77T	83	$ .05	$ .20	Benes, Andy	88TTR	14	$ .75	$3.00
Bell, Kevin	78T	463	$ .04	$ .16	Benes, Andy	89T	437	$ .10	$ .50
Bell, Kevin	79T	662	$ .03	$ .12	Benes, Andy	90T	193	$ .05	$ .20
Bell, Kevin	80T	379	$ .01	$ .10	Benes, Andy	91T	307	$ .01	$ .10
Bella, Zeke	59T	254	$1.00	$4.00	Benes, Andy	91TSC	51	$ .10	$1.00
Belle, Joey "Albert"	90T	283	$ .10	$ .50	Benes, Andy	92T	682	$ .01	$ .03
Belle, Albert	91TSC	465	$1.00	$4.00	Benes, Andy	92TSC	423	$ .01	$ .10
Belle, Albert	92T	785	$ .01	$ .15	Benes, Andy	93T	568	$ .01	$ .03
Belle, Albert	92TSC	220	$ .10	$ .75	Beniquez, Juan	74T	647	$ .15	$ .60
Belle, Albert	93T	635	$ .01	$ .15	Beniquez, Juan	75T	601	$ .10	$ .40
Belle, Albert	93TSC	102	$ .10	$ .50	Beniquez, Juan	76T	496	$ .05	$ .25
Belliard, Rafael	87T	541	$ .01	$ .15	Beniquez, Juan	77T	81	$ .05	$ .20
Belliard, Rafael	88T	221	$ .01	$ .04	Beniquez, Juan	78T	238	$ .04	$ .16
Belliard, Rafael	89T	723	$ .01	$ .03	Beniquez, Juan	79T	478	$ .03	$ .12
Belliard, Rafael	90T	143	$ .01	$ .03	Beniquez, Juan	80T	114	$ .01	$ .10
Belliard, Rafael	91T	487	$ .01	$ .03	Beniquez, Juan	81T	306	$ .01	$ .08
Belliard, Rafael	91TSC	404	$ .05	$ .25	Beniquez, Juan	81TTR	733	$ .01	$ .15
Belliard, Rafael	91TTR	9	$ .01	$ .05	Beniquez, Juan	82T	572	$ .01	$ .08
Belliard, Rafael	92T	367	$ .01	$ .03	Beniquez, Juan	83T	678	$ .01	$ .08
Belliard, Rafael	92TSC	105	$ .01	$ .10	Beniquez, Juan	84T	53	$ .01	$ .06
Belliard, Rafael	93T	62	$ .01	$ .03	Beniquez, Juan	85T	226	$ .01	$ .06
Belliard, Rafael	93TSC	58	$ .01	$ .10	Beniquez, Juan	86T	325	$ .01	$ .05
Belloir, Rob	77T	312	$ .05	$ .20	Beniquez, Juan	86TTR	8	$ .01	$ .06
Belloir, Rob	78T	681	$ .04	$ .16	Beniquez, Juan	87T	688	$ .01	$ .04
Beltre, Esteban	92TSC	611	$ .05	$ .20	Beniquez, Juan	87TTR	4	$ .01	$ .05
Beltre, Esteban	93T	13	$ .01	$ .03	Beniquez, Juan	88T	541	$ .01	$ .04
Benavides, Freddie	92TSC	394	$ .01	$ .10	Benjamin, Mike	91T	791	$ .01	$ .10
Benavides, Freddie	92TTR	10	$ .01	$ .05	Benjamin, Mike	91TSC	143	$ .05	$ .25
Benavides, Freddie	93T	356	$ .01	$ .03	Benjamin, Mike	92TSC	314	$ .01	$ .10
Bench, Johnny	68T	247	$65.00	$260.00	Benjamin, Mike	93T	384	$ .01	$ .03
Bench, Johnny	69T	95	$27.50	$110.00	Bennett, Dave	64T	561	$3.00	$12.00
Bench, Johnny	69TAS	430	$3.50	$14.00	Bennett, Dave	65T	521	$1.25	$5.00
Bench, Johnny	70T	660	$40.00	$160.00	Bennett, Dennis	63T	56	$ .50	$2.00
Bench, Johnny	70TAS	464	$3.50	$14.00	Bennett, Dennis	64T	396	$1.00	$4.00
Bench, Johnny	71T	64	$ .75	$3.00	Bennett, Dennis	65T	147	$ .35	$1.40
Bench, Johnny	71T	66	$1.00	$4.00	Bennett, Dennis	66T	491	$1.50	$6.00
Bench, Johnny	71T	250	$12.50	$50.00	Bennett, Dennis	67T	206	$ .50	$2.00
Bench, Johnny	72T	433	$10.00	$40.00	Benson, Vern	53T	205	$4.50	$18.00
Bench, Johnny	72TIA	434	$5.00	$20.00	Benson, Vern	73T	497	$ .50	$2.00
Bench, Johnny	73T	62	$ .50	$2.00	Benson, Vern	74T	236	$ .10	$ .40
Bench, Johnny	73T	63	$ .50	$2.00	Benson, Vern	91TA53	205	$ .01	$ .15
Bench, Johnny	73T	380	$6.00	$24.00	Benton, Al	52T	374	$43.75	$175.00
Bench, Johnny	74T	10	$4.00	$16.00	Benzinger, Todd	88T	96	$ .01	$ .10
Bench, Johnny	74TAS	331	$1.50	$6.00	Benzinger, Todd	89T	493	$ .01	$1.00
Bench, Johnny	75T	208	$ .25	$1.00	Benzinger, Todd	89TTR	9	$ .01	$ .05
Bench, Johnny	75T	210	$ .40	$1.60	Benzinger, Todd	90T	712	$ .01	$ .03
Bench, Johnny	75T	260	$3.50	$14.00	Benzinger, Todd	91T	334	$ .01	$ .03
Bench, Johnny	75T	308	$ .30	$1.20	Benzinger, Todd	91TSC	113	$ .05	$ .25
Bench, Johnny	76T	195	$ .30	$1.20	Benzinger, Todd	92T	506	$ .01	$ .03
Bench, Johnny	76T	300	$2.50	$10.00	Benzinger, Todd	92TSC	764	$ .01	$ .10
Bench, Johnny	77T	70	$2.25	$9.00	Benzinger, Todd	92TTR	11	$ .01	$ .05
Bench, Johnny	78T	700	$1.25	$5.00	Benzinger, Todd	93T	620	$ .01	$ .03
Bench, Johnny	79T	200	$ .75	$3.00	Berardino, Johnny	52T	253	$13.75	$55.00
Bench, Johnny	80T	100	$1.00	$4.00	Berberet, Lou	56T	329	$2.50	$10.00
Bench, Johnny	81T	600	$ .25	$2.50	Berberet, Lou	57T	315	$5.00	$20.00
Bench, Johnny	81TRB	201	$ .10	$ .75	Berberet, Lou	58T	383	$1.00	$4.00

TOPPS

Player	Year	No.	VG	EX/MT
Berberet, Lou	59T	96	$1.50	$6.00
Berberet, Lou	60T	6	$ .85	$3.40
Berenguer, Juan	79T	721	$ .05	$ .20
Berenguer, Juan	81T	259	$ .15	$1.50
Berenguer, Juan	82T	437	$ .01	$ .08
Berenguer, Juan	84T	174	$ .01	$ .06
Berenguer, Juan	85T	672	$ .01	$ .06
Berenguer, Juan	86T	47	$ .01	$ .05
Berenguer, Juan	86TTR	9	$ .01	$ .06
Berenguer, Juan	87T	303	$ .01	$ .04
Berenguer, Juan	87TTR	5	$ .01	$ .05
Berenguer, Juan	88T	526	$ .01	$ .04
Berenguer, Juan	89T	294	$ .01	$ .03
Berenguer, Juan	90T	709	$ .01	$ .03
Berenguer, Juan	91T	449	$ .01	$ .03
Berenguer, Juan	91TSC	460	$ .05	$ .25
Berenguer, Juan	92T	172	$ .01	$ .03
Berenguer, Juan	92TSC	44	$ .01	$ .10
Berenyi, Bruce	81T	606	$ .01	$ .08
Berenyi, Bruce	82T	459	$ .01	$ .08
Berenyi, Bruce	83T	139	$ .01	$ .08
Berenyi, Bruce	84T	297	$ .01	$ .06
Berenyi, Bruce	84TTR	10	$ .01	$ .15
Berenyi, Bruce	85T	27	$ .01	$ .06
Berenyi, Bruce	86T	339	$ .01	$ .05
Berenyi, Bruce	87T	582	$ .01	$ .04
Bergman, Dave	78T	705	$ .04	$ .16
Bergman, Dave	79T	697	$ .03	$ .12
Bergman, Dave	81T	253	$ .01	$ .08
Bergman, Dave	81TTR	734	$ .01	$ .15
Bergman, Dave	82T	498	$ .01	$ .08
Bergman, Dave	83T	32	$ .01	$ .08
Bergman, Dave	84T	522	$ .01	$ .06
Bergman, Dave	84TTR	11	$ .01	$ .15
Bergman, Dave	85T	368	$ .01	$ .06
Bergman, Dave	86T	101	$ .01	$ .05
Bergman, Dave	87T	700	$ .01	$ .04
Bergman, Dave	88T	289	$ .01	$ .04
Bergman, Dave	89T	631	$ .01	$ .03
Bergman, Dave	90T	77	$ .01	$ .03
Bergman, Dave	91T	412	$ .01	$ .03
Bergman, Dave	91TSC	386	$ .05	$ .25
Bergman, Dave	92T	354	$ .01	$ .03
Bergman, Dave	92TSC	171	$ .01	$ .10
Beringer, Carroll	73T	486	$ .25	$1.00
Beringer, Carroll	74T	119	$ .10	$ .40
Bernard, Dwight	79T	721	$ .05	$ .20
Bernard, Dwight	83T	244	$ .01	$ .08
Bernazard, Tony	80T	680	$ .05	$ .20
Bernazard, Tony	81T	413	$ .01	$ .08
Bernazard, Tony	81TTR	735	$ .01	$ .15
Bernazard, Tony	82T	206	$ .01	$ .08
Bernazard, Tony	83T	698	$ .01	$ .08
Bernazard, Tony	83TTR	9	$ .01	$ .10
Bernazard, Tony	84T	41	$ .01	$ .06
Bernazard, Tony	84TTR	12	$ .01	$ .15
Bernazard, Tony	85T	533	$ .01	$ .06
Bernazard, Tony	86T	354	$ .01	$ .05
Bernazard, Tony	87T	758	$ .01	$ .04
Bernazard, Tony	87TAS	607	$ .01	$ .04
Bernazard, Tony	88T	122	$ .01	$ .04
Bernhardt, Cesar	92T	179	$ .05	$ .20
Bernhardt, Juan	77T	494	$ .35	$1.40
Bernhardt, Juan	78T	698	$ .04	$ .16
Bernhardt, Juan	79T	366	$ .03	$ .12
Bernier, Carlos	53T	243	$11.25	$45.00
Bernier, Carlos	91TA53	243	$ .01	$ .15
Berra, Dale	79T	723	$ .05	$ .20
Berra, Dale	80T	292	$ .01	$ .10
Berra, Dale	81T	147	$ .01	$ .08
Berra, Dale	82T	588	$ .01	$ .08
Berra, Dale	83T	433	$ .01	$ .08
Berra, Dale	84T	18	$ .01	$ .06
Berra, Dale	85T	132	$ .01	$ .15
Berra, Dale	85T	305	$ .01	$ .06
Berra, Dale	85TTR	6	$ .01	$ .10
Berra, Dale	86T	692	$ .01	$ .05
Berra, Larry "Yogi"	51Trb	1	$30.00	$120.00
Berra, Yogi	52T	191	$100.00	$400.00

Player	Year	No.	VG	EX/MT
Berra, Yogi	53T	104	$65.00	$260.00
Berra, Yogi	54T	50	$60.00	$240.00
Berra, Yogi	55T	198	$60.00	$240.00
Berra, Yogi	56T	110	$35.00	$140.00
Berra, Yogi	57T	2	$32.50	$130.00
Berra, Yogi	57T	407	$95.00	$380.00
Berra, Yogi	58T	370	$25.00	$100.00
Berra, Yogi	59T	180	$22.50	$90.00
Berra, Yogi	60T	480	$20.00	$80.00
Berra, Yogi	61T	425	$18.75	$75.00
Berra, Yogi	61TMVP	472	$12.50	$50.00
Berra, Yogi	62T	360	$17.50	$70.00
Berra, Yogi	63T	340	$17.50	$70.00
Berra, Yogi	64T	21	$10.00	$40.00
Berra, Yogi	65T	470	$12.50	$50.00
Berra, Yogi	73T	257	$ .50	$2.00
Berra, Yogi	74T	179	$ .40	$1.60
Berra, Yogi	75T	189	$ .50	$2.00
Berra, Yogi	75T	192	$ .50	$2.00
Berra, Yogi	75T	193	$ .50	$2.00
Berra, Yogi	84TTR	13	$ .10	$ .75
Berra, Yogi	85T	132	$ .01	$ .15
Berra, Yogi	85T	155	$ .05	$ .20
Berra, Yogi	91TA53	104	$ .25	$2.50
Berres, Ray	60T	458	$1.25	$5.00
Berroa, Geronimo	89TTR	10	$ .01	$ .10
Berroa, Geronimo	90T	617	$ .01	$ .03
Berry, Ken	65T	368	$ .50	$2.00
Berry, Ken	66T	127	$ .50	$2.00
Berry, Ken	67T	67	$ .40	$1.60
Berry, Ken	68T	485	$ .75	$3.00
Berry, Ken	69T	494	$ .30	$1.20
Berry, Ken	70T	239	$ .20	$ .80
Berry, Ken	71T	466	$ .50	$2.00
Berry, Ken	72T	379	$ .10	$ .40
Berry, Ken	73T	445	$ .25	$1.00
Berry, Ken	74T	163	$ .10	$ .40
Berry, Ken	75T	432	$ .10	$ .40

TOPPS

Player	Year	No.	VG	EX/MT	Player	Year	No.	VG	EX/MT
Berry, Sean	92TSC	114	$.05	$.25	Bichette, Dante	91TTR	10	$.01	$.05
Berry, Sean	93T	758	$.01	$.03	Bichette, Dante	92T	371	$.01	$.03
Berry, Sean	93TSC	184	$.01	$.10	Bichette, Dante	92TSC	7	$.01	$.10
Berryhill, Damon	88TTR	15	$.05	$.20	Bichette, Dante	93T	644	$.01	$.03
Berryhill, Damon	89T	543	$.01	$.03	Bickford, Vern	52T	252	$12.50	$50.00
Berryhill, Damon	90T	362	$.01	$.03	Bickford, Vern	53T	161	$4.00	$16.00
Berryhill, Damon	91T	188	$.01	$.03	Bickford, Vern	91TA53	161	$.01	$.15
Berryhill, Damon	91TSC	28	$.05	$.25	Bielecki, Mike	86TTR	10	$.01	$.15
Berryhill, Damon	92T	49	$.01	$.03	Bielecki, Mike	87T	394	$.01	$.04
Berryhill, Damon	92TSC	856	$.01	$.10	Bielecki, Mike	88T	436	$.01	$.04
Berryhill, Damon	93T	306	$.01	$.03	Bielecki, Mike	89T	668	$.01	$.03
Berryhill, Damon	93TSC	261	$.01	$.10	Bielecki, Mike	90T	114	$.01	$.03
Bertaina, Frank	65T	396	$1.00	$4.00	Bielecki, Mike	91T	501	$.01	$.03
Bertaina, Frank	66T	579	$4.50	$18.00	Bielecki, Mike	91TSC	109	$.05	$.25
Bertaina, Frank	68T	131	$.35	$1.40	Bielecki, Mike	92T	26	$.01	$.03
Bertaina, Frank	69T	554	$.40	$1.60	Bielecki, Mike	92TSC	656	$.01	$.10
Bertaina, Frank	70T	638	$1.25	$5.00	Bielecki, Mike	93T	251	$.01	$.03
Bertaina, Frank	71T	422	$.50	$2.00	Biercevicz, Greg	79T	712	$.03	$.12
Bertell, Dick	61T	441	$1.00	$4.00	Biercevicz, Greg	81T	282	$.01	$.08
Bertell, Dick	63T	287	$.90	$3.60	Biggio, Craig	89T	49	$.05	$.35
Bertell, Dick	64T	424	$1.00	$4.00	Biggio, Craig	90T	157	$.01	$.15
Bertell, Dick	65T	27	$.35	$1.40	Biggio, Craig	90TAS	404	$.01	$.10
Bertell, Dick	66T	587	$3.75	$15.00	Biggio, Craig	91T	565	$.01	$.10
Bertoia, Reno	54T	131	$3.75	$15.00	Biggio, Craig	91TSC	176	$.10	$.50
Bertoia, Reno	55T	94	$2.25	$9.00	Biggio, Craig	92T	715	$.01	$.03
Bertoia, Reno	57T	390	$1.75	$7.00	Biggio, Craig	92TAS	393	$.01	$.03
Bertoia, Reno	58T	232	$1.25	$5.00	Biggio, Craig	92TSC	200	$.01	$.10
Bertoia, Reno	59T	84	$1.50	$6.00	Biggio, Craig	93T	680	$.01	$.03
Bertoia, Reno	60T	297	$.75	$3.00	Biggio, Craig	93TSC	183	$.01	$.10
Bertoia, Reno	61T	392	$1.00	$4.00	Biittner, Larry	72T	122	$.10	$.40
Berumen, Andres	93T	627	$.01	$.15	Biittner, Larry	73T	249	$.10	$.40
Bessent, Don	56T	184	$3.75	$15.00	Biittner, Larry	75T	543	$.10	$.40
Bessent, Don	57T	178	$2.00	$8.00	Biittner, Larry	76T	238	$.05	$.25
Bessent, Don	58T	401	$1.00	$4.00	Biittner, Larry	77T	64	$.05	$.20
Bessent, Don	59T	71	$1.50	$6.00	Biittner, Larry	78T	346	$.04	$.16
Best, Karl	86T	61	$.01	$.05	Biittner, Larry	79T	433	$.03	$.12
Best, Karl	87T	439	$.01	$.04	Biittner, Larry	80T	639	$.01	$.10
Beswick, Jim	79T	725	$.03	$.12	Biittner, Larry	81T	718	$.01	$.08
Bethke, Jim	65T	533	$8.00	$32.00	Biittner, Larry	81TTR	736	$.01	$.15
Bevacqua, Kurt	72T	193	$.10	$.40	Biittner, Larry	82T	159	$.01	$.08
Bevacqua, Kurt	74T	454	$.10	$.40	Biittner, Larry	83T	527	$.01	$.08
Bevacqua, Kurt	74TTR	454	$.10	$.40	Biittner, Larry	83TTR	10	$.01	$.10
Bevacqua, Kurt	76T	427	$.05	$.25	Biittner, Larry	84T	283	$.01	$.06
Bevacqua, Kurt	76T	564	$.15	$.60	Bilardello, Dann	83TTR	11	$.01	$.10
Bevacqua, Kurt	77T	317	$.05	$.20	Bilardello, Dann	84T	424	$.01	$.06
Bevacqua, Kurt	78T	725	$.04	$.16	Bilardello, Dann	85T	28	$.01	$.06
Bevacqua, Kurt	79T	44	$.03	$.12	Bilardello, Dann	86T	253	$.01	$.05
Bevacqua, Kurt	80T	584	$.01	$.10	Bilardello, Dann	87T	577	$.01	$.04
Bevacqua, Kurt	81T	118	$.01	$.08	Bilardello, Dann	90T	682	$.01	$.03
Bevacqua, Kurt	82T	267	$.01	$.08	Bilardello, Dann	92TSC	254	$.01	$.10
Bevacqua, Kurt	82TTR	6	$.01	$.10	Bilko, Steve	52T	287	$13.75	$55.00
Bevacqua, Kurt	83T	674	$.01	$.08	Bilko, Steve	54T	116	$3.75	$15.00
Bevacqua, Kurt	84T	346	$.01	$.06	Bilko, Steve	55T	93	$2.25	$9.00
Bevacqua, Kurt	85T	478	$.01	$.06	Bilko, Steve	58T	346	$1.25	$5.00
Bevacqua, Kurt	86T	789	$.01	$.05	Bilko, Steve	59T	43	$1.50	$6.00
Bevan, Hal	61T	456	$1.35	$5.40	Bilko, Steve	60T	396	$.75	$3.00
Biancalana, Buddy	85T	387	$.01	$.06	Bilko, Steve	61T	104	$.60	$2.40
Biancalana, Buddy	86T	99	$.01	$.05	Bilko, Steve	62T	422	$1.25	$5.00
Biancalana, Buddy	87T	554	$.01	$.04	Billingham, Jack	68T	228	$.35	$1.40
Bibby, Jim	72T	316	$.10	$.40	Billingham, Jack	69T	92	$.35	$1.40
Bibby, Jim	74T	11	$.10	$.40	Billingham, Jack	70T	701	$1.25	$5.00
Bibby, Jim	75T	155	$.10	$.40	Billingham, Jack	71T	162	$.25	$1.00
Bibby, Jim	76T	324	$.05	$.25	Billingham, Jack	72T	542	$.40	$1.60
Bibby, Jim	77T	501	$.05	$.20	Billingham, Jack	73T	89	$.10	$.40
Bibby, Jim	78T	636	$.04	$.16	Billingham, Jack	74T	158	$.10	$.40
Bibby, Jim	79T	92	$.03	$.12	Billingham, Jack	75T	235	$.10	$.40
Bibby, Jim	80T	229	$.01	$.10	Billingham, Jack	76T	155	$.05	$.25
Bibby, Jim	81T	430	$.01	$.08	Billingham, Jack	77T	512	$.05	$.20
Bibby, Jim	82T	170	$.01	$.08	Billingham, Jack	78T	47	$.04	$.16
Bibby, Jim	83T	355	$.01	$.08	Billingham, Jack	79T	388	$.03	$.12
Bibby, Jim	84T	566	$.01	$.06	Billingham, Jack	80T	603	$.01	$.10
Bichette, Dante	89T	761	$.05	$.25	Billings, Dick	71T	729	$1.10	$4.40
Bichette, Dante	90T	43	$.01	$.03	Billings, Dick	72T	148	$.10	$.40
Bichette, Dante	91T	564	$.01	$.03	Billings, Dick	73T	94	$.10	$.40
Bichette, Dante	91TSC	211	$.05	$.35	Billings, Dick	74T	466	$.10	$.40

TOPPS

Player	Year	No.	VG	EX/MT	Player	Year	No.	VG	EX/MT
Bird, Doug	74T	17	$ .10	$ .40	Blair, Paul	75T	275	$ .10	$ .40
Bird, Doug	75T	364	$ .10	$ .40	Blair, Paul	76T	473	$ .05	$ .25
Bird, Doug	76T	96	$ .05	$ .25	Blair, Paul	77T	313	$ .05	$ .20
Bird, Doug	77T	556	$ .05	$ .20	Blair, Paul	78T	114	$ .04	$ .16
Bird, Doug	78T	183	$ .04	$ .16	Blair, Paul	79T	582	$ .03	$ .12
Bird, Doug	79T	664	$ .03	$ .12	Blair, Paul	80T	281	$ .01	$ .10
Bird, Doug	80T	421	$ .01	$ .10	Blair, Willie	90TTR	8	$ .01	$ .10
Bird, Doug	81T	516	$ .01	$ .08	Blair, Willie	91T	191	$ .01	$ .03
Bird, Doug	81TTR	737	$ .01	$ .15	Blair, Willie	92TSC	813	$ .01	$ .10
Bird, Doug	82T	273	$ .01	$ .08	Blake, Ed	52T	144	$7.00	$28.00
Bird, Doug	83T	759	$ .01	$ .08	Blanchard, John	59T	117	$1.75	$7.00
Bird, Doug	83TTR	12	$ .01	$ .10	Blanchard, John	60T	283	$1.25	$5.00
Bird, Doug	84T	82	$ .01	$ .06	Blanchard, John	61T	104	$ .60	$2.40
Birkbeck, Mike	87T	229	$ .01	$ .04	Blanchard, John	62T	93	$ .60	$2.40
Birkbeck, Mike	88T	692	$ .01	$ .04	Blanchard, John	63T	555	$2.25	$9.00
Birkbeck, Mike	89T	491	$ .01	$ .03	Blanchard, John	64T	118	$ .50	$2.00
Birrer, Babe	56T	84	$2.00	$8.00	Blanchard, John	65T	388	$1.00	$4.00
Birtsas, Tim	88T	501	$ .01	$ .04	Blanchard, John	66T	268	$ .50	$2.00
Birtsas, Tim	89T	103	$ .01	$ .03	Blanco, Gil	65T	566	$2.50	$10.00
Birtsas, Tim	90T	687	$ .01	$ .03	Blanco, Gil	67T	303	$ .60	$2.40
Birtsas, Tim	91T	289	$ .01	$ .03	Blankenship, Lance	90T	132	$ .01	$ .03
Bishop, Charlie	53T	186	$4.50	$18.00	Blankenship, Lance	91T	411	$ .01	$ .03
Bishop, Charlie	55T	96	$2.25	$9.00	Blankenship, Lance	91TSC	437	$ .05	$ .25
Bishop, Charlie	91TA53	186	$ .01	$ .15	Blankenship, Lance	92TSC	897	$ .01	$ .10
Bittiger, Jeff	89T	209	$ .01	$ .03	Blankenship, Lance	93T	548	$ .01	$ .03
Bjorkman, George	84T	116	$ .01	$ .06	Blanks, Larvell	73T	609	$1.00	$4.00
Black, Bud	83T	238	$ .10	$ .40	Blanks, Larvell	75T	394	$ .10	$ .40
Black, Bud	84T	26	$ .01	$ .06	Blanks, Larvell	76T	127	$ .05	$ .25
Black, Bud	85T	412	$ .01	$ .06	Blanks, Larvell	77T	441	$ .05	$ .20
Black, Bud	86T	697	$ .01	$ .05	Blanks, Larvell	78T	61	$ .04	$ .16
Black, Bud	87T	669	$ .01	$ .04	Blanks, Larvell	79T	307	$ .03	$ .12
Black, Bud	88T	301	$ .01	$ .04	Blanks, Larvell	80T	656	$ .01	$ .10
Black, Bud	88TTR	16	$ .01	$ .05	Blasingame, Don	56T	309	$3.00	$12.00
Black, Bud	89T	509	$ .01	$ .03	Blasingame, Don	57T	47	$2.00	$8.00
Black, Bud	90T	144	$ .01	$ .03	Blasingame, Don	58T	199	$1.25	$5.00
Black, Bud	91T	292	$ .01	$ .03	Blasingame, Don	59T	491	$1.00	$4.00
Black, Bud	91TSC	302	$ .05	$ .25	Blasingame, Don	60T	397	$ .75	$3.00
Black, Bud	91TTR	11	$ .01	$ .05	Blasingame, Don	61T	294	$ .60	$2.40
Black, Bud	92T	774	$ .01	$ .03	Blasingame, Don	62T	103	$ .60	$2.40
Black, Bud	92TSC	55	$ .01	$ .10	Blasingame, Don	63T	518	$1.75	$7.00
Black, Bud	93T	498	$ .01	$ .03	Blasingame, Don	64T	327	$ .65	$2.60
Black, Joe	52T	321	$62.50	$250.00	Blasingame, Don	65T	21	$ .35	$1.40
Black, Joe	53T	81	$15.00	$60.00	Blasingame, Wade	65T	44	$ .35	$1.40
Black, Joe	54T	98	$5.50	$22.00	Blasingame, Wade	66T	355	$ .50	$2.00
Black, Joe	55T	156	$8.00	$32.00	Blasingame, Wade	67T	119	$ .40	$1.60
Black, Joe	56T	178	$3.50	$14.00	Blasingame, Wade	68T	507	$ .75	$3.00
Black, Joe	91TA53	81	$ .01	$ .15	Blasingame, Wade	69T	308	$ .50	$2.00
Blackburn, Ron	58T	459	$1.00	$4.00	Blasingame, Wade	71T	79	$ .25	$1.00
Blackburn, Ron	59T	401	$1.00	$4.00	Blasingame, Wade	72T	581	$ .75	$3.00
Blackburn, Ron	60T	209	$ .75	$3.00	Blass, Steve	65T	232	$ .50	$2.00
Blackwell, Ewell	52T	344	$50.00	$200.00	Blass, Steve	66T	344	$ .50	$2.00
Blackwell, Ewell	53T	31	$10.00	$40.00	Blass, Steve	67T	562	$2.25	$9.00
Blackwell, Ewell	91TA53	31	$ .05	$ .20	Blass, Steve	68T	499	$ .75	$3.00
Blackwell, Tim	78T	449	$ .04	$ .16	Blass, Steve	69T	104	$ .35	$1.40
Blackwell, Tim	80T	153	$ .01	$ .10	Blass, Steve	70T	396	$ .35	$1.40
Blackwell, Tim	81T	553	$ .01	$ .08	Blass, Steve	71T	143	$ .25	$1.00
Blackwell, Tim	82T	374	$ .01	$ .08	Blass, Steve	72T	320	$ .10	$ .40
Blackwell, Tim	82TTR	7	$ .01	$ .10	Blass, Steve	73T	95	$ .10	$ .40
Blackwell, Tim	83T	57	$ .01	$ .08	Blass, Steve	74T	595	$ .10	$ .40
Blades, Ray	54T	243	$3.75	$15.00	Blateric, Steve	73T	616	$ .75	$3.00
Bladt, Rich	74T	601	$1.25	$5.00	Blauser, Jeff	89T	83	$ .01	$ .10
Blair, Dennis	75T	521	$ .10	$ .40	Blauser, Jeff	90T	251	$ .01	$ .03
Blair, Dennis	76T	642	$ .05	$ .25	Blauser, Jeff	91T	623	$ .01	$ .03
Blair, Dennis	77T	593	$ .05	$ .20	Blauser, Jeff	91TSC	377	$ .05	$ .25
Blair, Dennis	78T	466	$ .04	$ .16	Blauser, Jeff	92T	199	$ .01	$ .03
Blair, Paul	65T	473	$2.50	$10.00	Blauser, Jeff	92TSC	168	$ .01	$ .10
Blair, Paul	66T	48	$ .35	$1.40	Blauser, Jeff	93T	552	$ .01	$ .03
Blair, Paul	67T	319	$ .60	$2.40	Blaylock, Bob	59T	211	$1.00	$4.00
Blair, Paul	68T	135	$ .35	$1.40	Blaylock, Gary	59T	539	$4.00	$16.00
Blair, Paul	69T	506	$ .30	$1.20	Blaylock, Marv	57T	224	$2.00	$8.00
Blair, Paul	70T	285	$ .35	$1.40	Blefary, Curt	65T	49	$ .75	$3.00
Blair, Paul	71T	53	$ .25	$1.00	Blefary, Curt	66T	460	$1.50	$6.00
Blair, Paul	72T	660	$1.25	$5.00	Blefary, Curt	67T	180	$ .40	$1.60
Blair, Paul	73T	528	$ .25	$1.00	Blefary, Curt	67T	521	$1.50	$6.00
Blair, Paul	74T	92	$ .10	$ .40	Blefary, Curt	68T	312	$ .35	$1.40

TOPPS

Player	Year	No.	VG	EX/MT
Blefary, Curt	69T	458	$ .30	$1.20
Blefary, Curt	70T	297	$ .35	$1.40
Blefary, Curt	71T	131	$ .25	$1.00
Blefary, Curt	72T	691	$1.25	$5.00
Blefary, Curt	72TIA	692	$1.25	$5.00
Blocker, Terry	89T	76	$ .01	$ .03
Blomberg, Ron	72T	203	$ .10	$ .40
Blomberg, Ron	73T	462	$ .25	$1.00
Blomberg, Ron	74T	117	$ .10	$ .40
Blomberg, Ron	75T	68	$ .10	$ .40
Blomberg, Ron	76T	354	$ .05	$ .25
Blomberg, Ron	77T	543	$ .05	$ .20
Blomberg, Ron	78T	506	$ .04	$ .16
Blomberg, Ron	79T	42	$ .03	$ .12
Blomberg, Ron	88TTB	663	$ .01	$ .04
Bloomfield, Bud	64T	532	$2.50	$10.00
Blosser, Greg	93T	798	$ .01	$ .03
Blowers, Mike	90TTR	9	$ .01	$ .10
Blowers, Mike	91T	691	$ .01	$ .03
Blowers, Mike	93TSC	144	$ .01	$ .10
Blue Jays, Team Checklist	77T	113	$ .25	$1.00
Blue Jays, Team Checklist	78T	626	$ .10	$ .40
Blue Jays, Team Checklist	79T	282	$ .15	$ .60
Blue Jays, Team Checklist	80T	577	$ .10	$ .50
Blue Jays, Team Checklist	81T	674	$ .05	$ .25
Blue Jays, Team Leaders	86T	96	$ .01	$ .05
Blue Jays, Team Leaders	87T	106	$ .01	$ .04
Blue Jays, Team Leaders	88T	729	$ .01	$ .04
Blue Jays, Team Leaders	89T	201	$ .01	$ .03
Blue, Vida	70T	21	$1.50	$6.00
Blue, Vida	71T	544	$1.25	$5.00
Blue, Vida	72T	92	$ .60	$2.40
Blue, Vida	72T	94	$ .40	$1.60
Blue, Vida	72T	96	$ .40	$1.60
Blue, Vida	72T	169	$ .25	$1.00
Blue, Vida	72TIA	170	$ .20	$ .80
Blue, Vida	73T	430	$ .25	$1.00
Blue, Vida	74T	290	$ .25	$1.00
Blue, Vida	75T	209	$ .25	$1.00
Blue, Vida	75T	510	$ .25	$1.00
Blue, Vida	76T	140	$ .15	$ .60
Blue, Vida	76T	200	$ .35	$1.40
Blue, Vida	77T	230	$ .20	$ .80
Blue, Vida	78T	680	$ .05	$ .25
Blue, Vida	79T	110	$ .05	$ .20
Blue, Vida	80T	30	$ .05	$ .20
Blue, Vida	81T	310	$ .01	$ .08
Blue, Vida	82T	430	$ .01	$ .08
Blue, Vida	82T	576	$ .01	$ .08
Blue, Vida	82TSA	431	$ .01	$ .07
Blue, Vida	82TTR	8	$ .05	$ .20
Blue, Vida	83T	471	$ .01	$ .08
Blue, Vida	83T	570	$ .01	$ .08
Blue, Vida	86T	770	$ .01	$ .05
Blue, Vida	87T	260	$ .01	$ .04
Blyleven, Bert	71T	26	$15.00	$60.00
Blyleven, Bert	72T	515	$2.50	$10.00
Blyleven, Bert	73T	199	$1.00	$4.00
Blyleven, Bert	74T	98	$ .75	$3.00
Blyleven, Bert	75T	30	$ .50	$2.00
Blyleven, Bert	76T	204	$ .25	$1.00
Blyleven, Bert	76T	235	$ .50	$2.00
Blyleven, Bert	77T	630	$ .50	$2.00
Blyleven, Bert	78T	131	$ .20	$ .80
Blyleven, Bert	79T	308	$ .10	$ .40
Blyleven, Bert	80T	457	$ .10	$ .50
Blyleven, Bert	81T	554	$ .10	$ .50
Blyleven, Bert	81TTR	738	$ .15	$1.50
Blyleven, Bert	82T	559	$ .01	$ .08
Blyleven, Bert	82T	685	$ .10	$ .40
Blyleven, Bert	83T	280	$ .05	$ .35
Blyleven, Bert	84T	716	$ .01	$ .15
Blyleven, Bert	84T	789	$ .05	$ .20
Blyleven, Bert	85T	355	$ .01	$ .10
Blyleven, Bert	86T	445	$ .01	$ .10

Player	Year	No.	VG	EX/MT
Blyleven, Bert	87T	25	$ .01	$ .10
Blyleven, Bert	88T	295	$ .01	$ .10
Blyleven, Bert	89T	555	$ .01	$ .03
Blyleven, Bert	89TTR	11	$ .01	$ .10
Blyleven, Bert	90T	130	$ .01	$ .03
Blyleven, Bert	91T	615	$ .01	$ .03
Blyleven, Bert	91TSC	175	$ .05	$ .25
Blyleven, Bert	92T	375	$ .01	$ .03
Blyleven, Bert	93T	48	$ .01	$ .03
Blyzka, Mike	54T	152	$3.75	$15.00

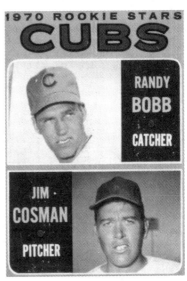

Player	Year	No.	VG	EX/MT
Bobb, Randy	70T	429	$ .35	$1.40
Bobb, Randy	71T	83	$ .25	$1.00
Boccabella, John	64T	192	$ .50	$2.00
Boccabella, John	66T	482	$1.50	$6.00
Boccabella, John	67T	578	$4.00	$16.00
Boccabella, John	68T	542	$ .70	$2.80
Boccabella, John	69T	466	$ .30	$1.20
Boccabella, John	70T	19	$ .20	$ .80
Boccabella, John	71T	452	$ .50	$2.00
Boccabella, John	72T	159	$ .10	$ .40
Boccabella, John	73T	592	$ .60	$2.40
Boccabella, John	74T	253	$ .10	$ .40
Boccabella, John	75T	553	$ .10	$ .40
Bochte, Bruce	75T	392	$ .10	$ .40
Bochte, Bruce	76T	637	$ .05	$ .25
Bochte, Bruce	77T	68	$ .05	$ .20
Bochte, Bruce	78T	537	$ .04	$ .16
Bochte, Bruce	79T	443	$ .03	$ .12
Bochte, Bruce	80T	143	$ .01	$ .10
Bochte, Bruce	81T	723	$ .01	$ .08
Bochte, Bruce	82T	224	$ .01	$ .08
Bochte, Bruce	83T	28	$ .01	$ .08
Bochte, Bruce	83T	711	$ .01	$ .08
Bochte, Bruce	85T	632	$ .01	$ .06
Bochte, Bruce	86T	378	$ .01	$ .05
Bochte, Bruce	87T	496	$ .01	$ .04
Bochtler, Doug	93T	523	$ .01	$ .15
Bochy, Bruce	79T	718	$ .03	$ .12
Bochy, Bruce	80T	289	$ .01	$ .10
Bochy, Bruce	84T	571	$ .01	$ .06
Bochy, Bruce	85T	324	$ .01	$ .06
Bochy, Bruce	86T	608	$ .01	$ .05
Bochy, Bruce	87T	428	$ .01	$ .04

TOPPS

Player	Year	No.	VG	EX/MT	Player	Year	No.	VG	EX/MT
Bochy, Bruce	88T	31	$ .01	$ .04	Bolger, Jim	59T	29	$1.50	$6.00
Bockus, Randy	89T	733	$ .01	$ .03	Bolick, Frank	92T	473	$ .05	$ .25
Boddicker, Mike	81T	399	$ .10	$1.00	Bolin, Bobby	61T	449	$1.35	$5.40
Boddicker, Mike	84T	191	$ .01	$ .15	Bolin, Bobby	62T	329	$ .75	$3.00
Boddicker, Mike	84T	426	$ .10	$1.00	Bolin, Bobby	63T	106	$ .50	$2.00
Boddicker, Mike	85T	225	$ .01	$ .06	Bolin, Bobby	64T	374	$1.00	$4.00
Boddicker, Mike	85TAS	709	$ .01	$ .06	Bolin, Bobby	65T	341	$ .50	$2.00
Boddicker, Mike	86T	575	$ .01	$ .05	Bolin, Bobby	66T	61	$ .35	$1.40
Boddicker, Mike	87T	455	$ .01	$ .10	Bolin, Bobby	67T	252	$ .50	$2.00
Boddicker, Mike	88T	725	$ .01	$ .04	Bolin, Bobby	68T	169	$ .35	$1.40
Boddicker, Mike	89T	71	$ .01	$ .03	Bolin, Bobby	69T	8	$ .75	$3.00
Boddicker, Mike	90T	652	$ .01	$ .03	Bolin, Bobby	69T	505	$ .30	$1.20
Boddicker, Mike	91T	303	$ .01	$ .03	Bolin, Bobby	70T	574	$ .50	$2.00
Boddicker, Mike	91TSC	400	$ .05	$ .25	Bolin, Bobby	71T	446	$ .50	$2.00
Boddicker, Mike	91TTR	12	$ .01	$ .05	Bolin, Bobby	72T	266	$ .10	$ .40
Boddicker, Mike	92T	106	$ .01	$ .03	Bolin, Bobby	73T	541	$ .60	$2.40
Boddicker, Mike	92TSC	39	$ .01	$ .10	Bolin, Bobby	74T	427	$ .10	$ .40
Boddicker, Mike	93T	239	$ .01	$ .03	Bolling, Frank	57T	325	$5.00	$20.00
Boddicker, Mike	93TSC	192	$ .01	$ .10	Bolling, Frank	58T	95	$2.00	$8.00
Boehmer, Len	69T	519	$ .40	$1.60	Bolling, Frank	59T	280	$1.00	$4.00
Boever, Joe	88T	627	$ .01	$ .04	Bolling, Frank	60T	482	$1.25	$5.00
Boever, Joe	89T	586	$ .01	$ .03	Bolling, Frank	61T	335	$ .60	$2.40
Boever, Joe	90T	410	$ .01	$ .03	Bolling, Frank	62T	130	$ .60	$2.40
Boever, Joe	91T	159	$ .01	$ .03	Bolling, Frank	62T	211	$ .75	$3.00
Boever, Joe	91TSC	462	$ .05	$ .25	Bolling, Frank	63T	570	$2.25	$9.00
Boever, Joe	92T	696	$ .01	$ .03	Bolling, Frank	64T	115	$ .50	$2.00
Boever, Joe	92TSC	156	$ .01	$ .10	Bolling, Frank	65T	269	$ .50	$2.00
Boever, Joe	92TSC	639	$ .01	$ .10	Bolling, Milt	53T	280	$50.00	$350.00
Boever, Joe	92TTR	12	$ .01	$ .05	Bolling, Milt	54T	82	$3.75	$15.00
Boever, Joe	93T	792	$ .01	$ .03	Bolling, Milt	55T	91	$2.25	$9.00
Bogatyrev, Ilya	93T	633	$ .05	$ .25	Bolling, Milt	56T	315	$2.50	$10.00
Boggs, Tommy	77T	328	$ .05	$ .20	Bolling, Milt	57T	131	$2.00	$8.00
Boggs, Tommy	78T	518	$ .04	$ .16	Bolling, Milt	58T	188	$1.25	$5.00
Boggs, Tommy	79T	384	$ .03	$ .12	Bolling, Milt	91TA53	280	$ .10	$ .40
Boggs, Tommy	81T	132	$ .01	$ .08	Bollo, Greg	65T	541	$1.40	$5.60
Boggs, Tommy	82T	61	$ .01	$ .08	Bollo, Greg	66T	301	$ .50	$2.00
Boggs, Tommy	83T	649	$ .01	$ .08	Bollweg, Don	52T	128	$7.00	$28.00
Boggs, Wade	83T	498	$9.50	$38.00	Bolton, Tom	88T	442	$ .01	$ .04
Boggs, Wade	84T	30	$1.25	$5.00	Bolton, Tom	89T	269	$ .01	$ .03
Boggs, Wade	84T	131	$ .10	$ .50	Bolton, Tom	91T	37	$ .01	$ .03
Boggs, Wade	84T	786	$ .10	$ .50	Bolton, Tom	91TSC	588	$ .05	$ .25
Boggs, Wade	85T	350	$ .25	$2.50	Bolton, Tom	92T	708	$ .01	$ .03
Boggs, Wade	86T	510	$ .10	$1.00	Bolton, Tom	92TSC	561	$ .01	$ .10
Boggs, Wade	87T	150	$ .10	$ .50	Bomback, Mark	81T	567	$ .01	$ .08
Boggs, Wade	87TAS	608	$ .05	$ .20	Bomback, Mark	81TTR	739	$ .01	$ .15
Boggs, Wade	88T	200	$ .05	$ .20	Bomback, Mark	82T	707	$ .01	$ .08
Boggs, Wade	88TAS	388	$ .01	$ .15	Bond, Walt	60T	552	$2.75	$11.00
Boggs, Wade	89T	600	$ .05	$ .25	Bond, Walt	61T	334	$ .60	$2.40
Boggs, Wade	89TAS	399	$ .01	$ .15	Bond, Walt	63T	493	$3.00	$12.00
Boggs, Wade	89TRB	2	$ .01	$ .10	Bond, Walt	64T	339	$ .65	$2.60
Boggs, Wade	90T	760	$ .05	$ .20	Bond, Walt	65T	109	$ .35	$1.40
Boggs, Wade	90TAS	387	$ .01	$ .15	Bond, Walt	66T	431	$ .65	$2.60
Boggs, Wade	91T	450	$ .01	$ .15	Bond, Walt	67T	224	$ .50	$2.00
Boggs, Wade	91TSC	170	$ .20	$2.00	Bonds, Barry	86TTR	11	$1.75	$7.00
Boggs, Wade	92T	10	$ .01	$ .10	Bonds, Barry	87T	320	$ .25	$2.50
Boggs, Wade	92TAS	399	$ .01	$ .10	Bonds, Barry	88T	450	$ .10	$ .50
Boggs, Wade	92TSC	520	$ .10	$ .50	Bonds, Barry	89T	620	$ .10	$ .40
Boggs, Wade	93T	390	$ .01	$ .10	Bonds, Barry	90T	220	$ .05	$ .25
Boggs, Wade	93TSC	134	$ .05	$ .25	Bonds, Barry	91T	570	$ .05	$ .20
Bohammer, Jack	74T	586	$ .10	$ .40	Bonds, Barry	91TAS	401	$ .01	$ .10
Bohanon, Brian	92T	149	$ .01	$ .10	Bonds, Barry	91TSC	220	$1.00	$4.00
Bohanon, Brian	92TSC	297	$ .05	$ .20	Bonds, Barry	92T	380	$ .01	$ .10
Bohanon, Brian	93T	638	$ .01	$ .03	Bonds, Barry	92TAS	390	$ .01	$ .10
Bohanon, Brian	93TSC	154	$ .01	$ .10	Bonds, Barry	92TSC	604	$ .10	$ .50
Boisclair, Bruce	77T	399	$ .05	$ .20	Bonds, Barry	92TSC	620	$ .10	$1.00
Boisclair, Bruce	78T	277	$ .04	$ .16	Bonds, Barry	93T	2	$ .05	$ .20
Boisclair, Bruce	79T	148	$ .03	$ .12	Bonds, Barry	93T	407	$ .05	$ .20
Boisclair, Bruce	80T	654	$ .01	$ .10	Bonds, Barry	93TSC	51	$ .10	$ .75
Boitano, Danny	80T	668	$ .01	$ .10	Bonds, Bobby	69T	630	$8.75	$35.00
Bokelmann, Dick	53T	204	$4.50	$18.00	Bonds, Bobby	70T	425	$1.75	$7.00
Bokelmann, Dick	91TA53	204	$ .01	$ .15	Bonds, Bobby	71T	295	$1.00	$4.00
Boles, Carl	63T	428	$1.00	$4.00	Bonds, Bobby	72T	711	$4.50	$18.00
Bolger, Jim	55T	179	$6.25	$25.00	Bonds, Bobby	72TIA	712	$2.25	$9.00
Bolger, Jim	57T	289	$5.00	$20.00	Bonds, Bobby	73T	145	$ .50	$2.00
Bolger, Jim	58T	201	$1.25	$5.00	Bonds, Bobby	74T	30	$ .50	$2.00

TOPPS

Player	Year	No.	VG	EX/MT
Bonds, Bobby	75T	55	$.25	$1.00
Bonds, Bobby	76T	380	$.25	$1.00
Bonds, Bobby	76TRB	2	$.15	$.60
Bonds, Bobby	76TTR	380	$.15	$.60
Bonds, Bobby	77T	570	$.20	$.80
Bonds, Bobby	78T	150	$.10	$.40
Bonds, Bobby	79T	285	$.10	$.40
Bonds, Bobby	80T	410	$.01	$.10
Bonds, Bobby	81T	635	$.05	$.20
Bonds, Bobby	81TTR	740	$.10	$.40
Bonds, Bobby	82T	580	$.01	$.15
Bones, Ricky	92T	711	$.01	$.03
Bones, Ricky	92TSC	109	$.05	$.20
Bones, Ricky	92TTR	13	$.01	$.05
Bones, Ricky	93T	71	$.01	$.03
Bones, Ricky	93TSC	225	$.01	$.10
Bonham, Bill	72T	29	$.10	$.40
Bonham, Bill	73T	328	$.10	$.40
Bonham, Bill	74T	528	$.10	$.40
Bonham, Bill	75T	85	$.10	$.40
Bonham, Bill	76T	151	$.05	$.25
Bonham, Bill	77T	446	$.05	$.20
Bonham, Bill	78T	276	$.04	$.16
Bonham, Bill	79T	354	$.03	$.12
Bonham, Bill	80T	47	$.01	$.10
Bonham, Bill	81T	712	$.01	$.08
Bonikowski, Joe	62T	592	$15.00	$60.00
Bonilla, Bobby	86TTR	12	$.20	$2.00
Bonilla, Bobby	87T	184	$.10	$1.00
Bonilla, Bobby	88T	681	$.01	$.15
Bonilla, Bobby	89T	440	$.05	$.20
Bonilla, Bobby	89TAS	388	$.01	$.10
Bonilla, Bobby	90T	273	$.01	$.15
Bonilla, Bobby	91T	750	$.01	$.10
Bonilla, Bobby	91TAS	403	$.01	$.10
Bonilla, Bobby	91TSC	139	$.10	$1.00
Bonilla, Bobby	92T	160	$.01	$.10
Bonilla, Bobby	92TAS	392	$.01	$.10
Bonilla, Bobby	92TSC	608	$.01	$.10
Bonilla, Bobby	92TSC	780	$.05	$.20
Bonilla, Bobby	92TTR	14	$.01	$.10
Bonilla, Bobby	93T	52	$.01	$.10
Bonilla, Bobby	93TSC	163	$.01	$.15

Player	Year	No.	VG	EX/MT
Bonilla, Juan	82T	464	$.01	$.08
Bonilla, Juan	83T	563	$.01	$.08
Bonilla, Juan	84T	168	$.01	$.06
Bonilla, Juan	86TTR	13	$.01	$.06
Bonilla, Juan	87T	668	$.01	$.04
Bonnell, Barry	78T	242	$.04	$.16
Bonnell, Barry	79T	496	$.03	$.12
Bonnell, Barry	80T	632	$.01	$.10
Bonnell, Barry	81T	558	$.01	$.08
Bonnell, Barry	82T	99	$.01	$.08
Bonnell, Barry	83T	766	$.01	$.08
Bonnell, Barry	84T	302	$.01	$.06
Bonnell, Barry	84TTR	14	$.01	$.15
Bonnell, Barry	85T	423	$.01	$.06
Bonnell, Barry	86T	119	$.01	$.05
Bonner, Bob	82T	21	$18.25	$75.00
Booker, Greg	85T	262	$.01	$.06
Booker, Greg	86T	429	$.01	$.05
Booker, Greg	87TTR	6	$.01	$.05
Booker, Greg	88T	727	$.01	$.04
Booker, Greg	89T	319	$.01	$.03
Booker, Jim	76T	243	$.05	$.25
Booker, Rod	88T	483	$.01	$.04
Booker, Rod	91T	186	$.01	$.03
Boone, Bob	73T	613	$11.25	$45.00
Boone, Bob	74T	131	$1.00	$4.00
Boone, Bob	75T	351	$.35	$1.40
Boone, Bob	76T	67	$.15	$.60
Boone, Bob	76T	318	$.25	$1.00
Boone, Bob	77T	545	$.20	$.80
Boone, Bob	78T	161	$.10	$.40
Boone, Bob	79T	90	$.10	$.40
Boone, Bob	80T	470	$.10	$.40
Boone, Bob	81T	290	$.05	$.20
Boone, Bob	82T	615	$.01	$.15
Boone, Bob	82T	616	$.01	$.15
Boone, Bob	82TTR	9	$.05	$.20
Boone, Bob	83T	765	$.01	$.10
Boone, Bob	84T	520	$.01	$.10
Boone, Bob	85T	133	$.01	$.10
Boone, Bob	85T	348	$.01	$.06
Boone, Bob	86T	62	$.01	$.05
Boone, Bob	87T	166	$.01	$.04
Boone, Bob	88T	498	$.01	$.04
Boone, Bob	89T	243	$.01	$.03
Boone, Bob	89TAS	404	$.01	$.05
Boone, Bob	89TTR	12	$.01	$.05
Boone, Bob	90T	671	$.01	$.03
Boone, Bret	93T	808	$.05	$.20
Boone, Danny	82T	407	$.01	$.08
Boone, Ray	51Trb	23	$2.75	$11.00
Boone, Ray	52T	55	$13.75	$55.00
Boone, Ray	53T	25	$7.50	$30.00
Boone, Ray	54T	77	$3.75	$15.00
Boone, Ray	55T	65	$2.25	$9.00
Boone, Ray	56T	6	$2.00	$8.00
Boone, Ray	57T	102	$2.00	$0.00
Boone, Ray	58T	185	$1.25	$5.00
Boone, Ray	59T	252	$1.00	$4.00
Boone, Ray	60T	281	$.75	$3.00
Boone, Ray	76T	67	$.15	$.60
Boone, Ray	85T	133	$.01	$.10
Boone, Ray	91TA53	25	$.01	$.15
Boozer, John	63T	29	$.90	$3.60
Boozer, John	64T	16	$.50	$2.00
Boozer, John	65T	184	$.35	$1.40
Boozer, John	66T	324	$.50	$2.00
Boozer, John	68T	173	$.35	$1.40
Boozer, John	69T	599	$.40	$1.60
Borbon, Pedro	70T	358	$.35	$1.40
Borbon, Pedro	71T	613	$1.00	$4.00
Borbon, Pedro	73T	492	$.25	$1.00
Borbon, Pedro	74T	410	$.10	$.40
Borbon, Pedro	75T	157	$.10	$.40
Borbon, Pedro	76T	77	$.05	$.25

TOPPS

Player	Year	No.	VG	EX/MT	Player	Year	No.	VG	EX/MT
Borbon, Pedro	77T	581	$ .05	$ .20	Boskie, Shawn	91TSC	521	$ .05	$ .25
Borbon, Pedro	78T	220	$ .04	$ .16	Boskie, Shawn	92T	229	$ .01	$ .03
Borbon, Pedro	79T	326	$ .03	$ .12	Boskie, Shawn	92TSC	284	$ .01	$ .10
Borbon, Pedro	80T	627	$ .01	$ .10	Boskie, Shawn	93T	563	$ .01	$ .03
Borders, Pat	88TTR	17	$ .10	$ .50	Bosley, Thad	78T	619	$ .04	$ .16
Borders, Pat	89T	693	$ .05	$ .25	Bosley, Thad	79T	127	$ .03	$ .12
Borders, Pat	90T	191	$ .01	$ .03	Bosley, Thad	80T	412	$ .01	$ .10
Borders, Pat	91T	49	$ .01	$ .03	Bosley, Thad	82T	350	$ .01	$ .15
Borders, Pat	91TSC	266	$ .05	$ .25	Bosley, Thad	84T	657	$ .01	$ .06
Borders, Pat	92T	563	$ .01	$ .03	Bosley, Thad	85T	432	$ .01	$ .06
Borders, Pat	92TSC	77	$ .01	$ .10	Bosley, Thad	86T	512	$ .01	$ .05
Borders, Pat	93T	322	$ .01	$ .03	Bosley, Thad	87T	58	$ .01	$ .04
Borders, Pat	93TSC	1	$ .01	$ .10	Bosley, Thad	87TTR	7	$ .01	$ .05
Bordi, Rich	82T	531	$ .01	$ .08	Bosley, Thad	88T	247	$ .01	$ .04
Bordi, Rich	85T	357	$ .01	$ .06	Bosman, Dick	67T	459	$1.75	$7.00
Bordi, Rich	85TTR	7	$ .01	$ .10	Bosman, Dick	68T	442	$ .35	$1.40
Bordi, Rich	86T	94	$ .01	$ .05	Bosman, Dick	69T	607	$ .40	$1.60
Bordi, Rich	86TTR	14	$ .01	$ .06	Bosman, Dick	70T	68	$ .50	$2.00
Bordi, Rich	87T	638	$ .01	$ .04	Bosman, Dick	70T	175	$ .35	$1.40
Bordick, Mike	92T	317	$ .01	$ .03	Bosman, Dick	71T	60	$ .25	$1.00
Bordick, Mike	92TSC	272	$ .01	$ .15	Bosman, Dick	72T	365	$ .10	$ .40
Bordick, Mike	93T	639	$ .01	$ .03	Bosman, Dick	73T	640	$ .60	$2.40
Bordick, Mike	93TSC	80	$ .01	$ .10	Bosman, Dick	74T	465	$ .10	$ .40
Borgmann, Glenn	73T	284	$ .10	$ .40	Bosman, Dick	75T	354	$ .10	$ .40
Borgmann, Glenn	74T	547	$ .10	$ .40	Bosman, Dick	75THL	7	$1.50	$6.00
Borgmann, Glenn	75T	127	$ .10	$ .40	Bosman, Dick	76T	298	$ .05	$ .25
Borgmann, Glenn	76T	498	$ .05	$ .25	Bosman, Dick	77T	101	$ .05	$ .20
Borgmann, Glenn	77T	87	$ .05	$ .20	Bostock, Lyman	76T	263	$ .10	$ .40
Borgmann, Glenn	78T	307	$ .04	$ .16	Bostock, Lyman	77T	531	$ .05	$ .20
Borgmann, Glenn	79T	431	$ .03	$ .12	Bostock, Lyman	78T	655	$ .04	$ .16
Borgmann, Glenn	80T	634	$ .01	$ .10	Boston, Daryl	85TTR	8	$ .05	$ .25
Borgmann, Glenn	81T	716	$ .01	$ .08	Boston, Daryl	86T	139	$ .01	$ .10
Boris, Paul	83T	266	$ .01	$ .08	Boston, Daryl	87T	482	$ .01	$ .04
Bork, Frank	65T	592	$2.50	$10.00	Boston, Daryl	88T	739	$ .01	$ .04
Bork, Frank	66T	123	$ .50	$2.00	Boston, Daryl	89T	633	$ .01	$ .03
Borkowski, Bob	52T	328	$43.75	$175.00	Boston, Daryl	90T	524	$ .01	$ .03
Borkowski, Bob	53T	7	$4.00	$16.00	Boston, Daryl	90TTR	11	$ .01	$ .05
Borkowski, Bob	54T	138	$3.75	$15.00	Boston, Daryl	91T	83	$ .01	$ .03
Borkowski, Bob	55T	74	$2.25	$9.00	Boston, Daryl	91TSC	125	$ .05	$ .25
Borkowski, Bob	91TA53	7	$ .01	$ .15	Boston, Daryl	92T	227	$ .01	$ .03
Borland, Tom	60T	117	$ .75	$3.00	Boston, Daryl	92TSC	328	$ .01	$ .10
Borland, Tom	61T	419	$1.00	$4.00	Boston, Daryl	93T	399	$ .01	$ .03
Boros, Steve	58T	81	$2.25	$9.00	Boston, Daryl	93TSC	3	$ .01	$ .10
Boros, Steve	59T	331	$1.00	$4.00	Boswell, Dave	67T	575	$5.00	$20.00
Boros, Steve	61T	348	$ .60	$2.40	Boswell, Dave	68T	322	$ .35	$1.40
Boros, Steve	62T	62	$ .60	$2.40	Boswell, Dave	69T	459	$ .30	$1.20
Boros, Steve	62T	72	$ .60	$2.40	Boswell, Dave	70T	70	$ .50	$2.00
Boros, Steve	63T	532	$2.25	$9.00	Boswell, Dave	70T	325	$ .35	$1.40
Boros, Steve	64T	131	$ .50	$2.00	Boswell, Dave	71T	675	$1.10	$4.40
Boros, Steve	65T	102	$ .35	$1.40	Boswell, Ken	69T	402	$ .30	$1.20
Boros, Steve	83TTR	13	$ .01	$ .10	Boswell, Ken	70T	214	$ .20	$ .80
Boros, Steve	84T	531	$ .01	$ .06	Boswell, Ken	71T	492	$ .50	$2.00
Boros, Steve	86TTR	15	$ .01	$ .06	Boswell, Ken	72T	305	$ .10	$ .40
Boros, Steve	87T	143	$ .01	$ .04	Boswell, Ken	72TIA	306	$ .10	$ .40
Bosch, Don	68T	572	$ .70	$2.80	Boswell, Ken	73T	87	$ .10	$ .40
Bosch, Don	69T	578	$ .40	$1.60	Boswell, Ken	74T	645	$ .10	$ .40
Bosch, Don	70T	527	$ .35	$1.40	Boswell, Ken	75T	479	$ .10	$ .40
Bosetti, Rick	78T	710	$ .15	$ .60	Boswell, Ken	76T	379	$ .05	$ .25
Bosetti, Rick	79T	542	$ .03	$ .12	Boswell, Ken	77T	429	$ .05	$ .20
Bosetti, Rick	80T	277	$ .01	$ .10	Bottenfield, Kent	93T	695	$ .01	$ .03
Bosetti, Rick	81T	46	$ .01	$ .08	Bottenfield, Kent	93TSC	101	$ .01	$ .15
Bosetti, Rick	81TTR	741	$ .01	$ .15	Botting, Ralph	80T	663	$ .10	$1.00
Bosetti, Rick	82T	392	$ .01	$ .08	Botting, Ralph	81T	214	$ .01	$ .08
Bosio, Chris	87T	448	$ .05	$ .20	Bouchee, Ed	57T	314	$5.00	$20.00
Bosio, Chris	88T	137	$ .01	$ .04	Bouchee, Ed	59T	39	$1.50	$6.00
Bosio, Chris	89T	311	$ .01	$ .03	Bouchee, Ed	60T	347	$ .75	$3.00
Bosio, Chris	90T	597	$ .01	$ .03	Bouchee, Ed	61T	196	$ .60	$2.40
Bosio, Chris	91T	217	$ .01	$ .03	Bouchee, Ed	62T	497	$1.50	$6.00
Bosio, Chris	91TSC	164	$ .05	$ .25	Boucher, Denis	92TSC	773	$ .01	$ .15
Bosio, Chris	92T	638	$ .01	$ .03	Boucher, Denis	93T	541	$ .01	$ .03
Bosio, Chris	92TSC	578	$ .01	$ .10	Boudreau, Lou	91TA53	304	$ .10	$ .50
Bosio, Chris	93T	775	$ .01	$ .03	Bouldin, Carl	63T	496	$3.00	$12.00
Bosio, Chris	93TSC	79	$ .01	$ .10	Bouldin, Carl	64T	518	$1.00	$4.00
Boskie, Shawn	90TTR	10	$ .01	$ .15	Bourjos, Chris	81T	502	$ .01	$ .08
Boskie, Shawn	91T	254	$ .01	$ .03	Bournigal, Rafael	93T	651	$ .05	$ .20

TOPPS

Player	Year	No.	VG	EX/MT
Bournigal, Rafael	93TSC	197	$.10	$.40
Bourque, Pat	73T	605	$1.00	$4.00
Bourque, Pat	74T	141	$.10	$.40
Bourque, Pat	75T	502	$.10	$.40
Bouton, Jim	62T	592	$15.00	$60.00
Bouton, Jim	63T	401	$2.00	$8.00
Bouton, Jim	64T	4	$1.25	$5.00
Bouton, Jim	64T	219	$.75	$3.00
Bouton, Jim	64T	470	$1.50	$6.00

Player	Year	No.	VG	EX/MT
Bouton, Jim	65T	30	$.75	$3.00
Bouton, Jim	66T	276	$.75	$3.00
Bouton, Jim	67T	393	$1.00	$4.00
Bouton, Jim	68T	562	$1.50	$6.00
Bowa, Larry	70T	539	$1.00	$4.00
Bowa, Larry	71T	233	$.50	$2.00
Bowa, Larry	72T	520	$.50	$2.00
Bowa, Larry	73T	119	$.25	$1.00
Bowa, Larry	74T	255	$.25	$1.00
Bowa, Larry	75T	420	$.25	$1.00
Bowa, Larry	76T	145	$.15	$.60
Bowa, Larry	77T	310	$.05	$.20
Bowa, Larry	78T	90	$.10	$.40
Bowa, Larry	79T	210	$.05	$.20
Bowa, Larry	80T	630	$.01	$.10
Bowa, Larry	81T	120	$.01	$.15
Bowa, Larry	82T	515	$.01	$.15
Bowa, Larry	82TSA	516	$.01	$.07
Bowa, Larry	82TTR	10	$.05	$.20
Bowa, Larry	83T	305	$.01	$.08
Bowa, Larry	84T	705	$.01	$.10
Bowa, Larry	84T	757	$.01	$.06
Bowa, Larry	85T	484	$.01	$.10
Bowa, Larry	87TTR	8	$.01	$.10
Bowa, Larry	88T	284	$.01	$.04
Bowen, Ryan	92T	254	$.01	$.10
Bowen, Ryan	92TSC	101	$.05	$.20
Bowens, Sam	64T	201	$.65	$2.60
Bowens, Sam	65T	188	$.35	$1.40
Bowens, Sam	66T	412	$.65	$2.60
Bowens, Sam	67T	491	$1.50	$6.00
Bowens, Sam	68T	82	$.35	$1.40
Bowman, Bob	57T	332	$5.00	$20.00
Bowman, Bob	58T	415	$1.00	$4.00
Bowman, Bob	59T	221	$1.00	$4.00
Bowman, Ernie	62T	231	$.75	$3.00
Bowman, Ernie	63T	61	$.50	$2.00
Bowman, Ernie	66T	302	$.50	$2.00
Bowsfield, Ted	59T	236	$1.00	$4.00
Bowsfield, Ted	60T	382	$.75	$3.00
Bowsfield, Ted	61T	216	$.60	$2.40
Bowsfield, Ted	62T	369	$.75	$3.00
Bowsfield, Ted	63T	339	$.90	$3.60
Bowsfield, Ted	64T	447	$1.00	$4.00
Boyd, Bob	53T	257	$22.50	$90.00
Boyd, Bob	54T	113	$3.75	$15.00
Boyd, Bob	57T	26	$2.00	$8.00
Boyd, Bob	58T	279	$1.25	$5.00
Boyd, Bob	59T	82	$1.50	$6.00
Boyd, Bob	60T	207	$.75	$3.00
Boyd, Bob	61T	199	$.60	$2.40
Boyd, Bob	91TA53	257	$.01	$.15
Boyd, Dennis	85T	116	$.01	$.15
Boyd, Dennis	86T	605	$.01	$.05
Boyd, Dennis	87T	285	$.01	$.04
Boyd, Dennis	88T	704	$.01	$.04
Boyd, Dennis	89T	326	$.01	$.03
Boyd, Dennis	90T	544	$.01	$.03
Boyd, Dennis	90TTR	12	$.01	$.05
Boyd, Dennis	91T	48	$.01	$.03
Boyd, Dennis	91TSC	142	$.05	$.25
Boyd, Dennis	92T	428	$.01	$.03
Boyd, Dennis	92TSC	99	$.01	$.10
Boyd, Gary	70T	7	$.20	$.80
Boyd, Greg	93T	621	$.05	$.25
Boyer, Cletis	57T	121	$5.50	$22.00
Boyer, Cletis	59T	251	$1.50	$6.00
Boyer, Cletis	60T	109	$1.50	$6.00
Boyer, Cletis	61T	19	$1.25	$5.00
Boyer, Cletis "Clete"	62T	163	$.60	$2.40
Boyer, Clete	62T	490	$2.00	$8.00
Boyer, Clete	63T	361	$1.50	$6.00
Boyer, Clete	64T	69	$.75	$3.00
Boyer, Clete	65T	475	$1.50	$6.00
Boyer, Clete	66T	9	$.55	$2.20
Boyer, Clete	67T	328	$.60	$2.40
Boyer, Clete	68T	550	$.70	$2.80
Boyer, Clete	69T	489	$.30	$1.20
Boyer, Clete	70T	206	$.20	$.80
Boyer, Clete	71T	374	$.25	$1.00
Boyer, Cloyd	52T	280	$12.50	$50.00
Boyer, Cloyd	53T	60	$4.00	$16.00
Boyer, Cloyd	91TA53	60	$.01	$.15
Boyer, Ken	55T	125	$17.50	$70.00
Boyer, Ken	56T	14	$3.75	$15.00
Boyer, Ken	57T	122	$3.50	$14.00
Boyer, Ken	58T	350	$3.00	$12.00
Boyer, Ken	59T	325	$2.00	$8.00
Boyer, Ken	59TAS	557	$6.00	$24.00
Boyer, Ken	60T	100	$13.75	$55.00
Boyer, Ken	60T	485	$3.00	$12.00
Boyer, Ken	61T	43	$3.00	$12.00
Boyer, Ken	61T	375	$1.75	$7.00
Boyer, Ken	61TAS	573	$9.00	$36.00
Boyer, Ken	62T	52	$1.75	$7.00
Boyer, Ken	62T	370	$1.50	$6.00
Boyer, Ken	62TAS	392	$2.00	$8.00
Boyer, Ken	63T	375	$2.00	$8.00
Boyer, Ken	64T	11	$1.75	$7.00
Boyer, Ken	64T	160	$1.25	$5.00
Boyer, Ken	65T	6	$1.25	$5.00
Boyer, Ken	65T	100	$.75	$3.00
Boyer, Ken	66T	385	$1.25	$5.00
Boyer, Ken	67T	105	$.50	$2.00
Boyer, Ken	68T	259	$.50	$2.00
Boyer, Ken	69T	379	$.50	$2.00
Boyer, Ken	75T	202	$.25	$1.00
Boyland, Dorian	80T	683	$.01	$.10

TOPPS

Player	Year	No.	VG	EX/MT
Brabender, Gene	66T	579	$4.50	$18.00
Brabender, Gene	67T	22	$ .40	$1.60
Brabender, Gene	68T	163	$ .35	$1.40
Brabender, Gene	69T	393	$ .30	$1.20
Brabender, Gene	70T	289	$ .35	$1.40
Brabender, Gene	71T	666	$1.50	$6.00
Bradford, Buddy	68T	142	$ .35	$1.40
Bradford, Buddy	69T	97	$ .35	$1.40
Bradford, Buddy	70T	299	$ .35	$1.40
Bradford, Buddy	71T	552	$1.00	$4.00
Bradford, Buddy	74T	357	$ .10	$ .40
Bradford, Buddy	75T	504	$ .10	$ .40
Bradford, Buddy	76T	451	$ .05	$ .25
Bradford, Larry	80T	675	$ .01	$ .10
Bradford, Larry	81T	542	$ .01	$ .08
Bradford, Larry	82T	271	$ .01	$ .08
Bradley, Mark	84T	316	$ .01	$ .06
Bradley, Phil	84TTR	15	$ .10	$ .50
Bradley, Phil	85T	449	$ .05	$ .25
Bradley, Phil	86T	305	$ .01	$ .10
Bradley, Phil	87T	525	$ .01	$ .10
Bradley, Phil	88T	55	$ .01	$ .10
Bradley, Phil	88TTR	18	$ .01	$ .05
Bradley, Phil	89T	608	$ .01	$ .03
Bradley, Phil	89TTR	13	$ .01	$ .05
Bradley, Phil	90T	163	$ .01	$ .03
Bradley, Phil	91T	717	$ .01	$ .03
Bradley, Scott	86T	481	$ .01	$ .05
Bradley, Scott	87T	376	$ .01	$ .04
Bradley, Scott	88T	762	$ .01	$ .04
Bradley, Scott	89T	279	$ .01	$ .03
Bradley, Scott	90T	593	$ .01	$ .03
Bradley, Scott	91T	38	$ .01	$ .03
Bradley, Scott	91TSC	252	$ .05	$ .25
Bradley, Scott	92T	608	$ .01	$ .03
Bradley, Scott	92TSC	146	$ .01	$ .10
Bradley, Tom	71T	588	$1.00	$4.00
Bradley, Tom	72T	248	$ .10	$ .40
Bradley, Tom	73T	336	$ .10	$ .40
Bradley, Tom	74T	455	$ .10	$ .40
Bradley, Tom	75T	179	$ .10	$ .40
Bradley, Tom	76T	644	$ .05	$ .25
Brady, Jim	56T	126	$2.50	$10.00
Bragan, Bobby	60T	463	$1.25	$5.00
Bragan, Bobby	63T	73	$ .75	$3.00
Bragan, Bobby	64T	506	$1.00	$4.00
Bragan, Bobby	65T	346	$ .50	$2.00
Bragan, Bobby	66T	476	$1.50	$6.00
Braggs, Glenn	87T	622	$ .01	$ .15
Braggs, Glenn	88T	263	$ .01	$ .04
Braggs, Glenn	89T	718	$ .01	$ .03
Braggs, Glenn	90T	88	$ .01	$ .03
Braggs, Glenn	90TTR	13	$ .01	$ .05
Braggs, Glenn	91T	444	$ .01	$ .03
Braggs, Glenn	91TSC	187	$ .05	$ .25
Braggs, Glenn	92T	197	$ .01	$ .03
Braggs, Glenn	92TSC	13	$ .01	$ .10
Branca, Ralph	51Tbb	20	$11.25	$45.00
Branca, Ralph	52T	274	$22.50	$90.00
Branca, Ralph	91TA53	293	$ .10	$ .50
Brand, Ron	64T	326	$ .65	$2.60
Brand, Ron	65T	212	$ .50	$2.00
Brand, Ron	66T	394	$ .65	$2.60
Brand, Ron	68T	317	$ .35	$1.40
Brand, Ron	69T	549	$ .40	$1.60
Brand, Ron	70T	221	$ .20	$ .80
Brand, Ron	71T	304	$ .25	$1.00
Brand, Ron	72T	773	$1.25	$5.00
Brandon, Darrell	66T	456	$1.50	$6.00
Brandon, Darrell	67T	117	$ .40	$1.60
Brandon, Darrell	68T	26	$ .35	$1.40
Brandon, Darrell	69T	301	$ .50	$2.00
Brandon, Darrell	72T	283	$ .10	$ .40
Brandon, Darrell	73T	326	$ .10	$ .40
Brandt, Jackie	59T	297	$1.00	$4.00
Brandt, Jackie	60T	53	$ .85	$3.40
Brandt, Jackie	61T	515	$1.35	$5.40
Brandt, Jackie	62T	165	$ .60	$2.40
Brandt, Jackie	63T	65	$ .50	$2.00
Brandt, Jackie	64T	399	$1.00	$4.00
Brandt, Jackie	65T	33	$ .35	$1.40
Brandt, Jackie	66T	383	$ .65	$2.60
Brandt, Jackie	67T	142	$ .40	$1.60
Branson, Jeff	88TTR	19	$ .05	$ .25
Branson, Jeff	92TSC	716	$ .01	$ .10
Branson, Jeff	93T	784	$ .01	$ .15
Branson, Jeff	93TSC	188	$ .01	$ .10
Brantley, Cliff	92T	544	$ .01	$ .10
Brantley, Cliff	92TSC	583	$ .01	$ .10
Brantley, Cliff	93T	773	$ .01	$ .03
Brantley, Cliff	93TSC	253	$ .01	$ .10
Brantley, Jeff	89TTR	14	$ .01	$ .15
Brantley, Jeff	90T	703	$ .01	$ .03
Brantley, Jeff	91T	17	$ .01	$ .03
Brantley, Jeff	91TSC	567	$ .05	$ .25
Brantley, Jeff	92T	491	$ .01	$ .03
Brantley, Jeff	92TSC	294	$ .01	$ .10
Brantley, Jeff	93T	631	$ .01	$ .03

Player	Year	No.	VG	EX/MT
Brantley, Jeff	93TSC	260	$ .01	$ .10
Brantley, Mickey	87T	347	$ .01	$ .04
Brantley, Mickey	88T	687	$ .01	$ .04
Brantley, Mickey	89T	568	$ .01	$ .03
Braun, John	65T	82	$ .75	$3.00
Braun, Steve	72T	244	$ .10	$ .40
Braun, Steve	73T	16	$ .10	$ .40
Braun, Steve	74T	321	$ .10	$ .40
Braun, Steve	75T	273	$ .10	$ .40
Braun, Steve	76T	183	$ .05	$ .25
Braun, Steve	77T	606	$ .05	$ .20
Braun, Steve	78T	422	$ .04	$ .16
Braun, Steve	79T	502	$ .03	$ .12
Braun, Steve	80T	9	$ .01	$ .10
Braun, Steve	82T	316	$ .01	$ .08
Braun, Steve	83T	734	$ .01	$ .08
Braun, Steve	84T	227	$ .01	$ .06
Braun, Steve	85T	152	$ .01	$ .06

TOPPS

Player	Year	No.	VG	EX/MT	Player	Year	No.	VG	EX/MT
Braun, Steve	86T	631	$.01	$.05	Brenly, Bob	89T	52	$.01	$.03
Braves, Team	56T	95	$7.50	$30.00	Brennan, Tom	81T	451	$.01	$.08
Braves, Team	57T	114	$4.50	$18.00	Brennan, Tom	82T	141	$.10	$.40
Braves, Team	58T	377	$3.50	$14.00	Brennan, Tom	83T	524	$.01	$.08
Braves, Team	59T	419	$2.50	$10.00	Brennan, Tom	84T	662	$.01	$.06
Braves, Team	60T	381	$2.00	$8.00	Bressoud, Eddie	58T	263	$1.25	$5.00
Braves, Team	61T	463	$2.00	$8.00	Bressoud, Eddie	59T	19	$1.50	$6.00
Braves, Team	62T	158	$1.50	$6.00	Bressoud, Eddie	60T	253	$.75	$3.00
Braves, Team	63T	503	$9.00	$36.00	Bressoud, Eddie	61T	203	$.60	$2.40
Braves, Team	64T	132	$1.00	$4.00	Bressoud, Eddie	62T	504	$1.50	$6.00
Braves, Team	65T	426	$2.25	$9.00	Bressoud, Eddie	63T	188	$.50	$2.00
Braves, Team	66T	326	$1.25	$5.00	Bressoud, Eddie	64T	352	$.65	$2.60
Braves, Team	67T	477	$2.50	$10.00	Bressoud, Eddie	65T	525	$1.40	$5.60
Braves, Team	68T	221	$.75	$3.00	Bressoud, Eddie	66T	516	$1.50	$6.00
Braves, Team	70T	472	$.75	$3.00	Bressoud, Eddie	67T	121	$.40	$1.60
Braves, Team	71T	652	$2.50	$10.00	Brett, George	75T	228	$50.00	$200.00
Braves, Team	72T	21	$.25	$1.00	Brett, George	76T	19	$13.75	$55.00
Braves, Team	73T	521	$.50	$2.00	Brett, George	77T	1	$1.00	$4.00
Braves, Team	74T	483	$.25	$1.00	Brett, George	77T	580	$8.00	$32.00
Braves, Team Checklist	75T	589	$.35	$1.40	Brett, George	77T	631	$1.25	$5.00
Braves, Team Checklist	76T	631	$.30	$1.20	Brett, George	77TRB	231	$2.25	$9.00
Braves, Team Checklist	77T	442	$.25	$1.00	Brett, George	78T	100	$6.00	$24.00
Braves, Team Checklist	78T	551	$.20	$.80	Brett, George	79T	330	$3.50	$14.00
Braves, Team Checklist	79T	302	$.15	$.60	Brett, George	80T	450	$3.00	$12.00
Braves, Team Checklist	80T	192	$.10	$.50	Brett, George	81T	1	$.20	$2.00
Braves, Team Checklist	81T	675	$.05	$.25	Brett, George	81T	700	$1.25	$5.00
Braves, Team Leaders	86T	456	$.01	$.10	Brett, George	82T	96	$.10	$.50
Braves, Team Leaders	87T	31	$.01	$.04	Brett, George	82T	200	$.75	$3.00
Braves, Team Leaders	88T	549	$.01	$.04	Brett, George	82TAS	549	$.15	$1.50
Braves, Team Leaders	89T	171	$.01	$.03	Brett, George	82TSA	201	$.35	$1.50
Bravo, Angel	70T	283	$.35	$1.40	Brett, George	83T	600	$.75	$3.00
Bravo, Angel	71T	538	$1.00	$4.00	Brett, George	83TAS	388	$.10	$1.00
Brazle, Al	52T	228	$7.00	$28.00	Brett, George	84T	500	$.15	$1.50
Bream, Sid	85T	253	$.10	$.50	Brett, George	84T	710	$.05	$.20
Bream, Sid	86T	589	$.01	$.05	Brett, George	84TAS	399	$.10	$.50
Bream, Sid	87T	35	$.01	$.04	Brett, George	85T	100	$.10	$1.00
Bream, Sid	88T	478	$.01	$.04	Brett, George	85TAS	703	$.10	$.50
Bream, Sid	89T	126	$.01	$.03	Brett, George	86T	300	$.10	$.75
Bream, Sid	90T	622	$.01	$.03	Brett, George	86TAS	714	$.05	$.35
Bream, Sid	91T	354	$.01	$.03	Brett, George	87T	400	$.05	$.35
Bream, Sid	91TSC	427	$.05	$.25	Brett, George	88T	700	$.05	$.25
Bream, Sid	91TTR	13	$.01	$.05	Brett, George	89T	200	$.05	$.20
Bream, Sid	92T	770	$.01	$.03	Brett, George	90T	60	$.01	$.15
Bream, Sid	92TSC	478	$.01	$.10	Brett, George	91T	540	$.01	$.10
Bream, Sid	93T	224	$.01	$.03	Brett, George	91TRB	2	$.01	$.10
Bream, Sid	93TSC	151	$.01	$.10	Brett, George	91TSC	159	$.10	$1.00
Breazeale, Jim	73T	33	$.10	$.40	Brett, George	92T	620	$.01	$.10
Brecheen, Harry	51Tbb	28	$7.50	$30.00	Brett, George	92TSC	150	$.10	$.50
Brecheen, Harry	52T	263	$12.50	$50.00	Brett, George	92TSC	609	$.05	$.25
Brecheen, Harry	54T	203	$3.75	$15.00	Brett, George	93T	397	$.01	$.10
Brecheen, Harry	55T	113	$2.25	$9.00	Brett, Ken	69T	476	$.50	$2.00
Brecheen, Harry	56T	229	$3.75	$15.00	Brett, Ken	71T	89	$.25	$1.00
Brecheen, Harry	60T	455	$1.25	$5.00	Brett, Ken	72T	517	$.25	$1.00
Breeden, Danny	69T	536	$.40	$1.60	Brett, Ken	73T	444	$.25	$1.00
Breeden, Danny	70T	36	$.25	$1.00	Brett, Ken	74T	237	$.10	$.40
Breeden, Hal	72T	684	$1.50	$6.00	Brett, Ken	75T	250	$.10	$.40
Breeden, Hal	73T	173	$.10	$.40	Brett, Ken	76T	401	$.05	$.25
Breeden, Hal	74T	297	$.10	$.40	Brett, Ken	76TTR	401	$.05	$.25
Breeden, Hal	75T	341	$.10	$.40	Brett, Ken	77T	157	$.05	$.20
Breeding, Marv	60T	525	$2.75	$11.00	Brett, Ken	77T	631	$1.25	$5.00
Breeding, Marv	61T	321	$.60	$2.40	Brett, Ken	78T	682	$.04	$.16
Breeding, Marv	62T	6	$.60	$2.40	Brett, Ken	79T	557	$.03	$.12
Breeding, Marv	63T	149	$.50	$2.00	Brett, Ken	80T	521	$.01	$.10
Breining, Fred	82T	144	$.01	$.08	Brett, Ken	81T	47	$.01	$.08
Breining, Fred	83T	747	$.01	$.08	Brett, Ken	82T	397	$.01	$.08
Breining, Fred	84T	428	$.01	$.06	Brewer, Jim	61T	317	$.60	$2.40
Breining, Fred	84TTR	16	$.01	$.15	Brewer, Jim	62T	191	$.60	$2.40
Breining, Fred	85T	36	$.01	$.06	Brewer, Jim	63T	309	$.90	$3.60
Brenly, Bob	82T	171	$.20	$2.00	Brewer, Jim	64T	553	$2.25	$9.00
Brenly, Bob	83T	494	$.01	$.08	Brewer, Jim	65T	416	$1.00	$4.00
Brenly, Bob	84T	378	$.01	$.06	Brewer, Jim	66T	158	$.50	$2.00
Brenly, Bob	85T	215	$.01	$.06	Brewer, Jim	67T	31	$.40	$1.60
Brenly, Bob	86T	625	$.01	$.05	Brewer, Jim	68T	298	$.35	$1.40
Brenly, Bob	87T	125	$.01	$.04	Brewer, Jim	69T	241	$.50	$2.00
Brenly, Bob	88T	703	$.01	$.04	Brewer, Jim	70T	571	$.50	$2.00

TOPPS

Player	Year	No.	VG	EX/MT
Brewer, Jim	71T	549	$1.00	$4.00
Brewer, Jim	72T	151	$.10	$.40
Brewer, Jim	73T	126	$.10	$.40
Brewer, Jim	74T	189	$.10	$.40
Brewer, Jim	75T	163	$.10	$.40
Brewer, Jim	76T	459	$.05	$.25
Brewer, Rod	93T	566	$.01	$.03
Brewer, Tom	55T	83	$2.25	$9.00
Brewer, Tom	56T	34	$2.00	$8.00
Brewer, Tom	57T	112	$2.00	$8.00
Brewer, Tom	58T	220	$1.25	$5.00
Brewer, Tom	59T	55	$1.50	$6.00
Brewer, Tom	59T	346	$1.00	$4.00
Brewer, Tom	60T	439	$.75	$3.00
Brewer, Tom	61T	434	$1.00	$4.00
Brewers, Team	71T	698	$3.50	$14.00
Brewers, Team	72T	106	$.25	$1.00
Brewers, Team	73T	127	$.25	$1.00
Brewers, Team	74T	314	$.25	$1.00
Brewers, Team Checklist	75T	384	$.35	$1.40
Brewers, Team Checklist	76T	606	$.30	$1.20
Brewers, Team Checklist	77T	51	$.25	$1.00
Brewers, Team Checklist	78T	328	$.20	$.80
Brewers, Team Checklist	79T	577	$.15	$.60
Brewers, Team Checklist	80T	659	$.10	$.50
Brewers, Team Checklist	81T	668	$.05	$.25
Brewers, Team Leaders	86T	426	$.01	$.05
Brewers, Team Leaders	87T	56	$.01	$.04
Brewers, Team Leaders	88T	639	$.01	$.04
Brewers, Team Leaders	89T	759	$.01	$.03
Brickell, Fritz	61T	333	$.60	$2.40
Brideweser, Jim	57T	382	$1.75	$7.00
Bridges, Rocky	52T	239	$7.00	$28.00
Bridges, Rocky	56T	324	$2.50	$10.00
Bridges, Rocky	57T	294	$5.00	$20.00
Bridges, Rocky	58T	274	$1.25	$5.00
Bridges, Rocky	59T	318	$1.00	$4.00
Bridges, Rocky	60T	22	$.85	$3.40
Bridges, Rocky	61T	508	$1.35	$5.40
Briggs, Dan	77T	592	$.05	$.20
Briggs, Dan	79T	77	$.03	$.12
Briggs, Dan	80T	352	$.01	$.10
Briggs, Dan	82T	102	$.01	$.08
Briggs, Dan	82TTR	11	$.01	$.10
Briggs, Johnny	59T	177	$1.00	$4.00
Briggs, Johnny	60T	376	$.75	$3.00
Briggs, Johnny	64T	482	$1.00	$4.00
Briggs, Johnny	65T	163	$.35	$1.40
Briggs, Johnny	66T	359	$.50	$2.00
Briggs, Johnny	67T	268	$.50	$2.00
Briggs, Johnny	68T	284	$.35	$1.40
Briggs, Johnny	69T	73	$.35	$1.40
Briggs, Johnny	70T	564	$.50	$2.00
Briggs, Johnny	71T	297	$.25	$1.00
Briggs, Johnny	72T	197	$.10	$.40
Briggs, Johnny	73T	71	$.10	$.40
Briggs, Johnny	74T	218	$.10	$.40
Briggs, Johnny	75T	123	$.10	$.40
Briggs, Johnny	76T	373	$.05	$.25
Bright, Harry	59T	523	$4.00	$16.00
Bright, Harry	60T	277	$.75	$3.00
Bright, Harry	61T	447	$1.35	$5.40
Bright, Harry	62T	551	$3.50	$14.00
Bright, Harry	63T	304	$.90	$3.60
Bright, Harry	64T	259	$.65	$2.60
Bright, Harry	65T	584	$1.40	$5.60
Briles, Nelson	65T	431	$1.25	$5.00
Briles, Nelson	66T	243	$.50	$2.00
Briles, Nelson	67T	404	$.60	$2.40
Briles, Nelson	68T	540	$.70	$2.80
Briles, Nelson	69T	60	$.35	$1.40
Briles, Nelson	70T	435	$.35	$1.40
Briles, Nelson	71T	257	$.25	$1.00
Briles, Nelson	72T	605	$.40	$1.60
Briles, Nelson	73T	303	$.10	$.40

Player	Year	No.	VG	EX/MT
Briles, Nelson	74T	123	$.10	$.40
Briles, Nelson	74TTR	123	$.10	$.40
Briles, Nelson	75T	495	$.10	$.40
Briles, Nelson	76T	569	$.05	$.25
Briles, Nelson	77T	174	$.05	$.20
Briles, Nelson	78T	717	$.04	$.16
Briles, Nelson	79T	262	$.03	$.12
Briley, Greg	89T	781	$.01	$.15
Briley, Greg	90T	288	$.01	$.03
Briley, Greg	91T	133	$.01	$.03
Briley, Greg	91TSC	130	$.05	$.25
Briley, Greg	92T	502	$.01	$.03
Briley, Greg	92TSC	228	$.01	$.10
Briley, Greg	93T	14	$.01	$.03
Brink, Brad	93T	818	$.01	$.03
Brinkman, Charlie "Chuck"	71T	13	$.25	$1.00
Brinkman, Chuck	72T	786	$1.25	$5.00
Brinkman, Chuck	73T	404	$.25	$1.00
Brinkman, Chuck	74T	641	$.10	$.40
Brinkman, Ed	63T	479	$3.00	$12.00
Brinkman, Ed	64T	46	$.50	$2.00
Brinkman, Ed	65T	417	$1.00	$4.00
Brinkman, Ed	66T	251	$.50	$2.00
Brinkman, Ed	67T	311	$.60	$2.40
Brinkman, Ed	68T	49	$.35	$1.40
Brinkman, Ed	69T	153	$.35	$1.40
Brinkman, Ed	70T	711	$1.25	$5.00
Brinkman, Ed	71T	389	$.25	$1.00
Brinkman, Ed	72T	535	$.40	$1.60
Brinkman, Ed	73T	5	$.10	$.40
Brinkman, Ed	74T	138	$.10	$.40
Brinkman, Ed	75T	439	$.10	$.40
Briscoe, John	92TSC	681	$.01	$.10
Brissie, Lou	51Tbb	31	$7.50	$30.00
Brissie, Lou	52T	270	$12.50	$50.00
Bristol, Dave	67T	21	$.40	$1.60
Bristol, Dave	68T	148	$.35	$1.40
Bristol, Dave	69T	234	$.50	$2.00
Bristol, Dave	70T	556	$.30	$1.20
Bristol, Dave	71T	637	$1.00	$4.00
Bristol, Dave	72T	602	$.40	$1.60
Bristol, Dave	73T	377	$.20	$.80
Bristol, Dave	74T	531	$.25	$1.00
Britton, Jim	64T	94	$.50	$2.00
Britton, Jim	68T	76	$.35	$1.40
Britton, Jim	69T	154	$.35	$1.40
Britton, Jim	70T	646	$1.25	$5.00
Britton, Jim	71T	699	$1.10	$4.40
Britton, Jimmy	72T	351	$.10	$.40
Brizzolara, Tony	80T	156	$.01	$.10
Brklyn-Boston, 26 Inning Tie	61T	403	$1.00	$4.00
Broberg, Pete	72T	64	$.10	$.40
Broberg, Pete	73T	162	$.10	$.40
Broberg, Pete	74T	425	$.10	$.40
Broberg, Pete	75T	542	$.10	$.40
Broberg, Pete	76T	39	$.05	$.25
Broberg, Pete	77T	409	$.05	$.20
Broberg, Pete	78T	722	$.04	$.16
Broberg, Pete	79T	578	$.03	$.12
Brocail, Doug	93T	821	$.01	$.15
Brock, Greg	83TTR	14	$.01	$.10
Brock, Greg	84T	555	$.01	$.06
Brock, Greg	85T	753	$.01	$.06
Brock, Greg	86T	368	$.01	$.05
Brock, Greg	87T	26	$.01	$.04
Brock, Greg	87TTR	9	$.01	$.05
Brock, Greg	88T	212	$.01	$.04
Brock, Greg	89T	517	$.01	$.03
Brock, Greg	90T	139	$.01	$.03
Brock, Greg	91T	663	$.01	$.03
Brock, Greg	91TSC	269	$.05	$.25
Brock, Lou	62T	387	$55.00	$220.00
Brock, Lou	63T	472	$35.00	$140.00
Brock, Lou	64T	29	$9.00	$36.00
Brock, Lou	65T	540	$11.25	$45.00

TOPPS

Player	Year	No.	VG	EX/MT
Brock, Lou	66T	125	$6.25	$25.00
Brock, Lou	67T	63	$1.50	$6.00
Brock, Lou	67T	285	$5.50	$22.00
Brock, Lou	68T	520	$6.00	$24.00
Brock, Lou	68TAS	372	$2.50	$10.00
Brock, Lou	69T	85	$5.00	$20.00
Brock, Lou	69TAS	428	$1.50	$6.00
Brock, Lou	70T	330	$2.50	$10.00
Brock, Lou	71T	625	$7.00	$28.00
Brock, Lou	72T	200	$1.50	$6.00
Brock, Lou	73T	64	$ .35	$1.40
Brock, Lou	73T	320	$1.25	$5.00
Brock, Lou	74T	60	$1.25	$5.00
Brock, Lou	74T	204	$ .30	$1.20
Brock, Lou	75T	309	$ .30	$1.20
Brock, Lou	75T	540	$1.25	$5.00
Brock, Lou	75THL	2	$ .75	$3.00
Brock, Lou	76T	10	$1.00	$4.00
Brock, Lou	76T	197	$ .25	$1.00
Brock, Lou	77T	355	$1.00	$4.00
Brock, Lou	78T	170	$ .75	$3.00
Brock, Lou	78TRB	1	$ .75	$3.00
Brock, Lou	79T	665	$ .50	$2.00
Brock, Lou	79TRH	415	$ .15	$ .60
Brock, Lou	80THL	1	$ .25	$2.50

Player	Year	No.	VG	EX/MT
Brock, Lou	89TTB	662	$ .01	$ .05
Brodowski, Dick	52T	404	$43.75	$175.00
Brodowski, Dick	53T	69	$6.25	$25.00
Brodowski, Dick	54T	221	$3.75	$15.00
Brodowski, Dick	55T	171	$6.25	$25.00
Brodowski, Dick	56T	157	$2.50	$10.00
Brodowski, Dick	59T	371	$1.00	$4.00
Brodowski, Dick	91TA53	69	$ .01	$ .15
Broglio, Ernie	59T	296	$1.25	$5.00
Broglio, Ernie	60T	16	$1.25	$5.00
Broglio, Ernie	61T	45	$1.00	$4.00
Broglio, Ernie	61T	47	$ .75	$3.00
Broglio, Ernie	61T	49	$2.00	$8.00
Broglio, Ernie	61T	451	$1.35	$5.40
Broglio, Ernie	62T	507	$1.50	$6.00
Broglio, Ernie	63T	313	$ .90	$3.60
Broglio, Ernie	64T	59	$ .50	$2.00
Broglio, Ernie	65T	565	$2.50	$10.00
Broglio, Ernie	66T	423	$ .65	$2.60

Player	Year	No.	VG	EX/MT
Brogna, Rico	92T	126	$ .10	$1.00
Brogna, Rico	93T	598	$ .01	$ .03
Brohamer, Jack	73T	181	$ .10	$ .40
Brohamer, Jack	75T	552	$ .10	$ .40
Brohamer, Jack	76T	618	$ .05	$ .25
Brohamer, Jack	77T	293	$ .05	$ .20
Brohamer, Jack	78T	416	$ .04	$ .16
Brohamer, Jack	79T	63	$ .03	$ .12
Brohamer, Jack	80T	349	$ .01	$ .10
Brohamer, Jack	81T	462	$ .01	$ .08
Brookens, Tom	80T	416	$ .01	$ .10
Brookens, Tom	81T	251	$ .01	$ .08
Brookens, Tom	82T	753	$ .01	$ .08
Brookens, Tom	83T	119	$ .01	$ .08
Brookens, Tom	84T	14	$ .01	$ .06
Brookens, Tom	85T	512	$ .01	$ .06
Brookens, Tom	86T	643	$ .01	$ .05
Brookens, Tom	87T	713	$ .01	$ .04
Brookens, Tom	88T	474	$ .01	$ .04
Brookens, Tom	89T	342	$ .01	$ .03
Brookens, Tom	91T	268	$ .01	$ .03
Brooks, Bobby	70T	381	$ .35	$1.40
Brooks, Bobby	71T	633	$1.00	$4.00
Brooks, Hubie	81T	259	$ .15	$1.50
Brooks, Hubie	81TTR	742	$ .10	$1.00
Brooks, Hubie	82T	246	$ .05	$ .25
Brooks, Hubie	82T	494	$ .05	$ .25
Brooks, Hubie	83T	134	$ .05	$ .20
Brooks, Hubie	84T	368	$ .01	$ .10
Brooks, Hubie	85T	222	$ .01	$ .06
Brooks, Hubie	85TTR	9	$ .01	$ .10
Brooks, Hubie	86T	555	$ .01	$ .05
Brooks, Hubie	87T	650	$ .01	$ .10
Brooks, Hubie	88T	50	$ .01	$ .04
Brooks, Hubie	89T	485	$ .01	$ .03
Brooks, Hubie	90T	745	$ .01	$ .03
Brooks, Hubie	90TTR	14	$ .01	$ .05
Brooks, Hubie	91T	115	$ .01	$ .03
Brooks, Hubie	91TSC	325	$ .05	$ .25
Brooks, Hubie	91TTR	14	$ .01	$ .05
Brooks, Hubie	92T	457	$ .01	$ .03
Brooks, Hubie	92TSC	754	$ .01	$ .10
Brooks, Hubie	92TTR	15	$ .01	$ .05
Brosius, Scott	93T	796	$ .01	$ .03
Brosius, Scott	93TSC	62	$ .01	$ .10
Brosnan, Jim	57T	155	$2.00	$8.00
Brosnan, Jim	58T	342	$1.25	$5.00
Brosnan, Jim	59T	194	$1.00	$4.00
Brosnan, Jim	60T	449	$1.25	$5.00
Brosnan, Jim	61T	513	$1.35	$5.40
Brosnan, Jim	62T	2	$ .60	$2.40
Brosnan, Jim	63T	116	$ .50	$2.00
Brouhard, Mark	82T	517	$ .01	$ .08
Brouhard, Mark	83T	167	$ .01	$ .08
Brouhard, Mark	84T	528	$ .01	$ .06
Brouhard, Mark	85T	653	$ .01	$ .06
Brouhard, Mark	86T	473	$ .01	$ .05
Brower, Bob	87TTR	10	$ .01	$ .05
Brower, Bob	88T	252	$ .01	$ .04
Brower, Bob	89T	754	$ .01	$ .03
Brown, Bobby	80T	670	$ .01	$ .10
Brown, Bobby	81T	418	$ .01	$ .08
Brown, Bobby	82T	791	$ .01	$ .08
Brown, Bobby	82TTR	12	$ .01	$ .10
Brown, Bobby	83T	287	$ .01	$ .08
Brown, Bobby	84T	261	$ .01	$ .06
Brown, Bobby	85T	583	$ .01	$ .06
Brown, Bobby	86T	182	$ .01	$ .05
Brown, Chris	85TTR	10	$ .01	$ .15
Brown, Chris	86T	383	$ .01	$ .10
Brown, Chris	87T	180	$ .01	$ .04
Brown, Chris	88T	568	$ .01	$ .04
Brown, Chris	89T	481	$ .01	$ .03
Brown, Darrell	84T	193	$ .01	$ .06
Brown, Darrell	85T	767	$ .01	$ .06

TOPPS

Player	Year	No.	VG	EX/MT
Brown, Dick	58T	456	$1.00	$4.00
Brown, Dick	59T	61	$1.50	$6.00
Brown, Dick	60T	256	$ .75	$3.00
Brown, Dick	61T	192	$ .60	$2.40
Brown, Dick	62T	438	$1.25	$5.00
Brown, Dick	63T	112	$ .50	$2.00
Brown, Gates	64T	471	$1.50	$6.00
Brown, Gates	65T	19	$ .35	$1.40
Brown, Gates	66T	362	$ .50	$2.00
Brown, Gates	67T	134	$ .40	$1.60
Brown, Gates	68T	583	$1.25	$5.00
Brown, Gates	69T	256	$ .50	$2.00
Brown, Gates	70T	98	$ .20	$ .80
Brown, Gates	71T	503	$ .50	$2.00
Brown, Gates	72T	187	$ .10	$ .40
Brown, Gates	73T	508	$ .25	$1.00
Brown, Gates	74T	389	$ .10	$ .40
Brown, Gates	75T	371	$ .10	$ .40
Brown, Hal	53T	184	$4.50	$18.00
Brown, Hal	54T	172	$3.75	$15.00
Brown, Hal	55T	148	$2.25	$9.00
Brown, Hal	57T	194	$2.00	$8.00
Brown, Hal	58T	381	$1.00	$4.00
Brown, Hal	59T	487	$1.00	$4.00
Brown, Hal	60T	89	$ .85	$3.40
Brown, Hal	61T	46	$ .75	$3.00
Brown, Hal	61T	218	$ .60	$2.40
Brown, Hal	62T	488	$1.50	$6.00
Brown, Hal	63T	289	$ .90	$3.60
Brown, Hal	64T	56	$ .50	$2.00
Brown, Hal	91TA53	184	$ .01	$ .15
Brown, Ike	70T	152	$ .20	$ .80
Brown, Ike	71T	669	$1.50	$6.00
Brown, Ike	72T	284	$ .10	$ .40
Brown, Ike	73T	633	$ .60	$2.40
Brown, Ike	74T	409	$ .10	$ .40
Brown, Jackie	71T	591	$1.00	$4.00
Brown, Jackie	74T	89	$ .10	$ .40
Brown, Jackie	75T	316	$ .10	$ .40
Brown, Jackie	76T	301	$ .05	$ .25
Brown, Jackie	77T	147	$ .05	$ .20
Brown, Jackie	78T	699	$ .04	$ .16
Brown, Jarvis	92TSC	515	$ .01	$ .10
Brown, Kevin	89TTR	15	$ .05	$ .25
Brown, Kevin	90T	136	$ .01	$ .10
Brown, Kevin	91T	584	$ .01	$ .03
Brown, Kevin	91TSC	56	$ .10	$ .50
Brown, Kevin	92T	297	$ .01	$ .03
Brown, Kevin	92TSC	123	$ .01	$ .10
Brown, Kevin	93T	785	$ .01	$ .03
Brown, Larry	64T	301	$ .65	$2.60
Brown, Larry	65T	468	$1.25	$5.00
Brown, Larry	66T	16	$ .35	$1.40
Brown, Larry	67T	145	$ .40	$1.60
Brown, Larry	68T	197	$ .35	$1.40
Brown, Larry	69T	503	$ .30	$1.20
Brown, Larry	70T	391	$ .35	$1.40
Brown, Larry	71T	539	$1.00	$4.00
Brown, Larry	72T	279	$ .10	$ .40
Brown, Mark	86T	451	$ .01	$ .05
Brown, Mike	83TTR	15	$ .01	$ .10
Brown, Mike	84T	472	$ .01	$ .06
Brown, Mike	84T	643	$ .01	$ .06
Brown, Mike	85T	258	$ .01	$ .06
Brown, Mike	86T	114	$ .01	$ .05
Brown, Mike	87T	271	$ .01	$ .04
Brown, Mike	87T	341	$ .01	$ .04
Brown, Ollie	66T	524	$7.00	$28.00
Brown, Ollie	67T	83	$ .40	$1.60
Brown, Ollie	68T	223	$ .35	$1.40
Brown, Ollie	69T	149	$ .35	$1.40
Brown, Ollie	70T	130	$ .20	$ .80
Brown, Ollie	71T	505	$ .50	$2.00
Brown, Ollie	72T	551	$ .40	$1.60
Brown, Ollie	72TIA	552	$ .40	$1.60
Brown, Ollie	73T	526	$ .25	$1.00
Brown, Ollie	74T	625	$ .10	$ .40
Brown, Ollie	75T	596	$ .10	$ .40
Brown, Ollie	76T	223	$ .05	$ .25
Brown, Ollie	77T	84	$ .05	$ .20
Brown, Oscar	71T	52	$ .25	$1.00
Brown, Oscar	72T	516	$ .25	$1.00
Brown, Oscar	73T	312	$ .10	$ .40
Brown, Paul	62T	181	$ .60	$2.40
Brown, Paul	63T	478	$3.00	$12.00
Brown, Paul	64T	319	$ .65	$2.60
Brown, Scott	82T	351	$ .01	$ .08
Brown, Tom	64T	311	$ .75	$3.00
Brown, Tommy	52T	281	$13.75	$55.00
Brown, Willie	93T	497	$ .05	$ .35
Brown, Winston	61T	391	$1.00	$4.00
Browne, Byron	66T	139	$ .50	$2.00
Browne, Byron	67T	439	$ .60	$2.40
Browne, Byron	68T	296	$ .35	$1.40
Browne, Byron	70T	388	$ .35	$1.40
Browne, Byron	71T	659	$1.50	$6.00
Browne, Jerry	87TTR	11	$ .01	$ .05
Browne, Jerry	88T	139	$ .01	$ .04
Browne, Jerry	89T	532	$ .01	$ .03
Browne, Jerry	89TTR	16	$ .01	$ .05
Browne, Jerry	90T	442	$ .01	$ .03
Browne, Jerry	91T	76	$ .01	$ .03
Browne, Jerry	91TSC	25	$ .05	$ .25
Browne, Jerry	92T	219	$ .01	$ .03
Browne, Jerry	92TSC	251	$ .01	$ .10
Browne, Jerry	92TTR	16	$ .01	$ .05
Browne, Jerry	93T	383	$ .01	$ .03
Browning, Brian	83T	442	$ .01	$ .08
Browning, Tom	85TTR	11	$ .15	$1.25
Browning, Tom	86T	652	$ .05	$ .20
Browning, Tom	87T	65	$ .01	$ .15
Browning, Tom	88T	577	$ .01	$ .10
Browning, Tom	89T	234	$ .01	$ .10
Browning, Tom	90T	418	$ .01	$ .10
Browning, Tom	91T	151	$ .01	$ .03
Browning, Tom	91TSC	235	$ .05	$ .25
Browning, Tom	92T	338	$ .01	$ .03
Browning, Tom	92TSC	624	$ .01	$ .10
Browning, Tom	93T	733	$ .01	$ .03
Brubaker, Bruce	65T	493	$1.25	$5.00
Brubaker, Bruce	67T	276	$ .50	$2.00
Bruce, Bob	60T	118	$ .75	$3.00
Bruce, Bob	61T	83	$ .60	$2.40
Bruce, Bob	62T	419	$1.25	$5.00
Bruce, Bob	63T	24	$ .50	$2.00
Bruce, Bob	64T	282	$ .65	$2.60
Bruce, Bob	65T	240	$ .50	$2.00
Bruce, Bob	66T	64	$ .35	$1.40
Bruce, Bob	67T	417	$ .60	$2.40
Bruett, J. T.	93T	309	$ .01	$ .15
Bruhert, Mike	79T	172	$ .03	$ .12
Brumfield, Jacob	92T	591	$ .05	$ .20
Brumley, Mike	64T	167	$7.50	$30.00
Brumley, Mike	65T	523	$2.50	$10.00
Brumley, Mike	66T	29	$ .35	$1.40
Brumley, Mike	90T	471	$ .01	$ .03
Brummer, Glenn	82T	561	$ .01	$ .08
Brummer, Glenn	83T	311	$ .01	$ .08
Brummer, Glenn	84T	152	$ .01	$ .06
Brummer, Glenn	86T	616	$ .01	$ .05
Brunansky, Tom	82T	653	$ .10	$1.00
Brunansky, Tom	82TTR	13	$ .20	$2.00
Brunansky, Tom	83T	232	$ .05	$ .30
Brunansky, Tom	84T	447	$ .05	$ .20
Brunansky, Tom	85T	122	$ .01	$ .10
Brunansky, Tom	86T	565	$ .01	$ .05
Brunansky, Tom	87T	776	$ .01	$ .04
Brunansky, Tom	88T	375	$ .01	$ .04
Brunansky, Tom	88TTR	20	$ .01	$ .05
Brunansky, Tom	89T	60	$ .01	$ .03

TOPPS

Player	Year	No.	VG	EX/MT
Brunansky, Tom	90T	409	$.01	$.03
Brunansky, Tom	90TTR	15	$.01	$.05
Brunansky, Tom	91T	675	$.01	$.03
Brunansky, Tom	91TSC	297	$.05	$.25
Brunansky, Tom	92T	296	$.01	$.03
Brunansky, Tom	92TSC	464	$.01	$.10
Brunansky, Tom	93T	532	$.01	$.03
Brunet, George	58T	139	$1.25	$5.00
Brunet, George	63T	538	$2.25	$9.00
Brunet, George	64T	322	$.65	$2.60
Brunet, George	65T	242	$.50	$2.00
Brunet, George	66T	393	$.65	$2.60
Brunet, George	67T	122	$.40	$1.60
Brunet, George	68T	347	$.35	$1.40
Brunet, George	69T	645	$.40	$1.60
Brunet, George	70T	328	$.35	$1.40
Brunet, George	71T	73	$.25	$1.00
Bruno, Tom	79T	724	$.15	$.60
Brusstar, Warren	78T	297	$.04	$.16
Brusstar, Warren	79T	653	$.03	$.12
Brusstar, Warren	80T	52	$.01	$.10
Brusstar, Warren	81T	426	$.01	$.08
Brusstar, Warren	82T	647	$.01	$.08
Brusstar, Warren	84T	304	$.01	$.06
Brusstar, Warren	85T	189	$.01	$.06
Brusstar, Warren	86T	564	$.01	$.05
Bruton, Bill	53T	214	$6.00	$24.00
Bruton, Bill	54T	109	$3.75	$15.00
Bruton, Bill	56T	185	$3.75	$15.00
Bruton, Bill	57T	48	$2.25	$9.00
Bruton, Bill	58T	355	$1.00	$4.00
Bruton, Bill	59T	165	$1.00	$4.00
Bruton, Bill	60T	37	$.85	$3.40
Bruton, Bill	61T	251	$.60	$2.40
Bruton, Bill	62T	335	$.75	$3.00
Bruton, Bill	63T	437	$1.00	$4.00
Bruton, Bill	64T	98	$.50	$2.00
Bruton, Bill	91TA53	214	$.01	$.15
Bryan, Bill	63T	236	$.90	$3.60
Bryan, Bill	65T	51	$.35	$1.40
Bryan, Bill	66T	332	$.50	$2.00
Bryan, Bill	67T	601	$4.00	$16.00
Bryan, Bill	68T	498	$.75	$3.00
Bryant, Clay	74T	521	$.10	$.40
Bryant, Derek	80T	671	$.20	$2.00
Bryant, Don	69T	499	$.30	$1.20
Bryant, Don	70T	473	$.35	$1.40
Bryant, Don	74T	403	$.10	$.40
Bryant, Ralph	87TTR	12	$.01	$.05
Bryant, Ron	70T	433	$.35	$1.40
Bryant, Ron	71T	621	$1.00	$4.00
Bryant, Ron	72T	185	$.10	$.40
Bryant, Ron	72TIA	186	$.10	$.40
Bryant, Ron	73T	298	$.10	$.40
Bryant, Ron	74T	104	$.10	$.40
Bryant, Ron	74T	205	$.25	$1.00
Bryant, Ron	75T	265	$.10	$.40
Bryden, T.R.	87T	387	$.01	$.04
Brye, Steve	71T	391	$.25	$1.00
Brye, Steve	72T	28	$.10	$.40
Brye, Steve	73T	353	$.10	$.40
Brye, Steve	74T	232	$.10	$.40
Brye, Steve	75T	151	$.10	$.40
Brye, Steve	76T	519	$.05	$.25
Brye, Steve	77T	424	$.05	$.20
Brye, Steve	78T	673	$.04	$.16
Brye, Steve	79T	28	$.03	$.12
Buchek, Jerry	62T	439	$1.25	$5.00
Buchek, Jerry	64T	314	$.65	$2.60
Buchek, Jerry	65T	397	$1.00	$4.00
Buchek, Jerry	66T	454	$1.50	$6.00
Buchek, Jerry	67T	574	$5.50	$22.00
Buchek, Jerry	68T	277	$.35	$1.40
Buchia, Johnny	52T	19	$13.75	$55.00
Buckley, Travis	93T	732	$.01	$.15

Player	Year	No.	VG	EX/MT
Buckner, Bill	70T	286	$2.00	$8.00
Buckner, Bill	71T	529	$1.25	$5.00
Buckner, Bill	72T	114	$.50	$2.00
Buckner, Bill	73T	368	$.30	$1.20
Buckner, Bill	74T	505	$.25	$1.00
Buckner, Bill	75T	244	$.25	$1.00
Buckner, Bill	76T	253	$.15	$.60
Buckner, Bill	77T	27	$.10	$.40
Buckner, Bill	78T	473	$.10	$.40
Buckner, Bill	79T	346	$.05	$.20
Buckner, Bill	80T	135	$.01	$.10
Buckner, Bill	81T	1	$.20	$2.00
Buckner, Bill	81T	625	$.01	$.15
Buckner, Bill	82T	456	$.01	$.08
Buckner, Bill	82T	760	$.01	$.10
Buckner, Bill	83T	250	$.01	$.10
Buckner, Bill	84T	545	$.01	$.10
Buckner, Bill	84TTR	17	$.05	$.20
Buckner, Bill	85T	65	$.01	$.06
Buckner, Bill	86T	443	$.01	$.05
Buckner, Bill	87T	764	$.01	$.04
Buckner, Bill	88T	147	$.01	$.04
Budaska, Mark	82T	531	$.01	$.08
Buddin, Don	58T	297	$1.25	$5.00
Buddin, Don	59T	32	$1.50	$6.00
Buddin, Don	60T	520	$2.75	$11.00
Buddin, Don	61T	99	$.60	$2.40
Buddin, Don	62T	332	$.75	$3.00
Buechele, Steve	86T	397	$.10	$.40
Buechele, Steve	87T	176	$.01	$.04
Buechele, Steve	88T	537	$.01	$.04
Buechele, Steve	89T	732	$.01	$.03
Buechele, Steve	90T	279	$.01	$.03
Buechele, Steve	91T	464	$.01	$.03

Player	Year	No.	VG	EX/MT
Buechele, Steve	91TSC	337	$.05	$.25
Buechele, Steve	92T	622	$.01	$.03
Buechele, Steve	92TSC	405	$.01	$.10
Buechele, Steve	93T	74	$.01	$.03
Buford, Damon	93T	576	$.10	$.75
Buford, Don	65T	81	$.35	$1.40
Buford, Don	66T	465	$1.50	$6.00
Buford, Don	67T	143	$.40	$1.60
Buford, Don	67T	232	$.50	$2.00

TOPPS

Player	Year	No.	VG	EX/MT	Player	Year	No.	VG	EX/MT
Buford, Don	68T	194	$ .35	$1.40	Bunning, Jim	63T	10	$1.00	$4.00
Buford, Don	69T	478	$ .30	$1.20	Bunning, Jim	63T	218	$ .90	$3.60
Buford, Don	70T	428	$ .35	$1.40	Bunning, Jim	63T	365	$2.25	$9.00
Buford, Don	71T	29	$ .25	$1.00	Bunning, Jim	64T	6	$ .75	$3.00
Buford, Don	72T	370	$ .10	$ .40	Bunning, Jim	64T	265	$1.50	$6.00
Buford, Don	73T	183	$ .10	$ .40	Bunning, Jim	65T	20	$1.25	$5.00
Buhl, Bob	54T	210	$4.50	$18.00	Bunning, Jim	66T	435	$1.75	$7.00
Buhl, Bob	56T	244	$3.75	$15.00	Bunning, Jim	67T	238	$1.50	$6.00
Buhl, Bob	57T	127	$2.00	$8.00	Bunning, Jim	67T	560	$15.00	$60.00
Buhl, Bob	58T	176	$1.25	$5.00	Bunning, Jim	68T	7	$ .55	$2.20
Buhl, Bob	59T	347	$1.00	$4.00	Bunning, Jim	68T	9	$ .75	$3.00
Buhl, Bob	60T	230	$1.75	$7.00	Bunning, Jim	68T	11	$1.00	$4.00
Buhl, Bob	60T	374	$ .75	$3.00	Bunning, Jim	68T	215	$1.00	$4.00
Buhl, Bob	61T	145	$ .60	$2.40	Bunning, Jim	69T	175	$ .75	$3.00
Buhl, Bob	62T	458	$1.50	$6.00	Bunning, Jim	70T	403	$ .75	$3.00
Buhl, Bob	63T	175	$ .50	$2.00	Bunning, Jim	71T	574	$1.25	$5.00
Buhl, Bob	64T	96	$ .50	$2.00	Burba, Dave	92T	728	$ .01	$ .03
Buhl, Bob	65T	264	$ .50	$2.00	Burba, Dave	92TSC	348	$ .01	$ .10
Buhl, Bob	66T	185	$ .50	$2.00	Burba, Dave	92TSC	718	$ .01	$ .10
Buhl, Bob	67T	68	$ .40	$1.60	Burba, Dave	92TTR	18	$ .01	$ .05
Buhner, Jay	88TTR	21	$ .10	$ .50	Burba, Dave	93TSC	245	$ .01	$ .10
Buhner, Jay	89T	223	$ .01	$ .15	Burbach, Bill	69T	658	$ .40	$1.60
Buhner, Jay	90T	554	$ .01	$ .03	Burbach, Bill	70T	167	$ .20	$ .80
Buhner, Jay	91T	154	$ .01	$ .03	Burbach, Bill	71T	683	$1.50	$6.00
Buhner, Jay	91TSC	153	$ .05	$ .25	Burbrink, Nelson	56T	27	$2.00	$8.00
Buhner, Jay	92T	327	$ .01	$ .03	Burchart, Larry	69T	597	$35.00	$140.00
Buhner, Jay	92TSC	213	$ .01	$ .10	Burchart, Larry	70T	412	$ .35	$1.40
Buhner, Jay	93T	718	$ .01	$ .03	Burda, Bob	69T	392	$ .30	$1.20
Buice, DeWayne	87TTR	13	$ .01	$ .05	Burda, Bob	70T	357	$ .35	$1.40
Buice, DeWayne	88T	649	$ .01	$ .04	Burda, Bob	71T	541	$1.00	$4.00
Buice, DeWayne	89T	147	$ .01	$ .03	Burda, Bob	72T	734	$1.25	$5.00
Bullett, Scott	92TSC	288	$ .01	$ .15	Burdette, Fred	64T	408	$1.00	$4.00
Bulling, Terry	78T	432	$ .04	$ .16	Burdette, Lew	56T	219	$5.00	$20.00
Bulling, Terry	82T	98	$ .01	$ .08	Burdette, Lew "Lou"	57T	208	$2.25	$9.00
Bulling, Terry	83T	519	$ .01	$ .08	Burdette, Lou	58T	10	$2.50	$10.00
Bullinger, Jim	92TSC	714	$ .01	$ .15	Burdette, Lou	58T	289	$1.50	$6.00
Bullinger, Jim	92TTR	17	$ .01	$ .10	Burdette, Lou	59T	440	$1.75	$7.00
Bullinger, Jim	93T	101	$ .01	$ .10	Burdette, Lou	60T	70	$1.50	$6.00
Bullinger, Jim	93TSC	118	$ .01	$ .10	Burdette, Lou	60T	230	$1.75	$7.00
Bullock, Eric	92TSC	659	$ .01	$ .10	Burdette, Lou	61T	47	$ .75	$3.00
Bumbry, Alonza "Al"	73T	614	$12.50	$50.00	Burdette, Lou	61T	320	$1.10	$4.40
Bumbry, Al	74T	137	$ .10	$ .40	Burdette, Lou	62T	380	$1.50	$6.00
Bumbry, Al	75T	358	$ .10	$ .40	Burdette, Lou	63T	429	$1.25	$5.00
Bumbry, Al	76T	307	$ .05	$ .25	Burdette, Lou	64T	523	$2.25	$9.00
Bumbry, Al	77T	626	$ .05	$ .20	Burdette, Lou	65T	64	$ .35	$1.40
Bumbry, Al	78T	188	$ .04	$ .16	Burdette, Lou	66T	299	$ .35	$1.40
Bumbry, Al	79T	517	$ .03	$ .12	Burdette, Lou	67T	265	$ .50	$2.00
Bumbry, Al	80T	65	$ .01	$ .10	Burdette, Lew "Lou"	73T	237	$ .30	$1.20
Bumbry, Al	81T	425	$ .01	$ .08	Burdette, Lew	91TA53	310	$ .10	$ .75
Bumbry, Al	82T	265	$ .01	$ .08	Burford, Don	64T	368	$ .65	$2.60
Bumbry, Al	83T	655	$ .01	$ .08	Burgess, Smoky	52T	357	$60.00	$240.00
Bumbry, Al	84T	319	$ .01	$ .06	Burgess, Smoky	53T	10	$12.50	$50.00
Bumbry, Al	85T	726	$ .01	$ .06	Burgess, Smoky	56T	192	$5.00	$20.00
Bumbry, Al	85TTR	12	$ .01	$ .10	Burgess, Smoky	57T	228	$2.00	$8.00
Bumbry, Al	86T	583	$ .01	$ .05	Burgess, Smoky	58T	49	$2.00	$8.00
Bunker, Wally	64T	201	$ .65	$2.60	Burgess, Smoky	59T	432	$1.00	$4.00
Bunker, Wally	65T	9	$ .75	$3.00	Burgess, Smoky	60T	393	$ .75	$3.00
Bunker, Wally	65T	290	$ .50	$2.00	Burgess, Smoky	61T	461	$1.35	$5.40
Bunker, Wally	66T	499	$1.50	$6.00	Burgess, Smoky	62T	389	$1.25	$5.00
Bunker, Wally	67T	585	$4.00	$16.00	Burgess, Smoky	63T	18	$4.50	$18.00
Bunker, Wally	68T	489	$ .75	$3.00	Burgess, Smoky	63T	425	$1.00	$4.00
Bunker, Wally	69T	137	$ .35	$1.40	Burgess, Smoky	64T	37	$ .50	$2.00
Bunker, Wally	70T	266	$ .35	$1.40	Burgess, Smoky	65T	198	$ .50	$2.00
Bunker, Wally	71T	528	$1.00	$4.00	Burgess, Smoky	66T	354	$ .50	$2.00
Bunning, Jim	57T	338	$32.50	$130.00	Burgess, Smoky	67T	506	$1.50	$6.00
Bunning, Jim	58T	115	$4.50	$22.00	Burgess, Smoky	91TA53	10	$ .05	$ .20
Bunning, Jim	59T	149	$3.00	$12.00	Burgmeier, Tom	69T	558	$ .40	$1.60
Bunning, Jim	60T	502	$3.00	$12.00	Burgmeier, Tom	70T	108	$ .20	$ .80
Bunning, Jim	61T	46	$ .75	$3.00	Burgmeier, Tom	71T	431	$ .50	$2.00
Bunning, Jim	61T	50	$ .75	$3.00	Burgmeier, Tom	72T	246	$ .10	$ .40
Bunning, Jim	61T	490	$2.50	$10.00	Burgmeier, Tom	73T	306	$ .10	$ .40
Bunning, Jim	62T	57	$1.25	$5.00	Burgmeier, Tom	75T	478	$ .10	$ .40
Bunning, Jim	62T	59	$ .60	$2.40	Burgmeier, Tom	76T	87	$ .05	$ .25
Bunning, Jim	62T	460	$2.50	$10.00	Burgmeier, Tom	77T	398	$ .05	$ .20
Bunning, Jim	63T	8	$1.00	$4.00	Burgmeier, Tom	78T	678	$ .04	$ .16

TOPPS

Player	Year	No.	VG	EX/MT
Burgmeier, Tom	79T	524	$ .03	$ .12
Burgmeier, Tom	80T	128	$ .01	$ .10
Burgmeier, Tom	81T	320	$ .01	$ .08
Burgmeier, Tom	82T	455	$ .01	$ .08
Burgmeier, Tom	83T	213	$ .01	$ .08
Burgmeier, Tom	83TTR	16	$ .01	$ .10

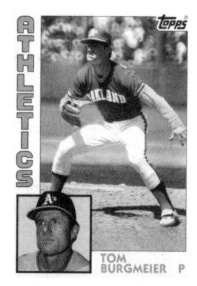

Player	Year	No.	VG	EX/MT
Burgmeier, Tom	**84T**	**33**	**$ .01**	**$ .06**
Burk, Mack	57T	91	$2.00	$8.00
Burk, Mack	58T	278	$1.25	$5.00
Burke, Glenn	78T	562	$ .04	$ .16
Burke, Glenn	79T	163	$ .03	$ .12
Burke, Leo	63T	249	$ .90	$3.60
Burke, Leo	64T	557	$2.25	$9.00
Burke, Leo	65T	202	$ .50	$2.00
Burke, Steve	78T	709	$ .04	$ .16
Burke, Tim	86T	258	$ .01	$ .10
Burke, Tim	87T	624	$ .01	$ .04
Burke, Tim	88T	529	$ .01	$ .04
Burke, Tim	89T	48	$ .01	$ .03
Burke, Tim	90T	195	$ .01	$ .03
Burke, Tim	91T	715	$ .01	$ .03
Burke, Tim	91TSC	514	$ .05	$ .25
Burke, Tim	92T	322	$ .01	$ .03
Burke, Tim	92TSC	392	$ .01	$ .10
Burke, Tim	93T	249	$ .01	$ .03
Burkett, John	90TTR	16	$ .01	$ .10
Burkett, John	91T	447	$ .01	$ .03
Burkett, John	91TSC	119	$ .05	$ .25
Burkett, John	92T	762	$ .01	$ .03
Burkett, John	92TSC	136	$ .01	$ .10
Burkett, John	93T	66	$ .01	$ .03
Burks, Ellis	87TTR	14	$ .10	$ .50
Burks, Ellis	88T	269	$ .05	$ .25
Burks, Ellis	89T	785	$ .01	$ .10
Burks, Ellis	90T	155	$ .01	$ .15
Burks, Ellis	91T	70	$ .01	$ .10
Burks, Ellis	91TSC	108	$ .05	$ .35
Burks, Ellis	92T	416	$ .01	$ .03
Burks, Ellis	92TSC	399	$ .01	$ .10
Burks, Ellis	93TSC	187	$ .01	$ .10
Burks, Todd	93T	279	$ .01	$ .03
Burleson, Rick	75T	302	$ .10	$ .40
Burleson, Rick	76T	29	$ .05	$ .25

Player	Year	No.	VG	EX/MT
Burleson, Rick	77T	585	$ .05	$ .20
Burleson, Rick	78T	245	$ .04	$ .16
Burleson, Rick	79T	125	$ .03	$ .12
Burleson, Rick	80T	645	$ .01	$ .10
Burleson, Rick	81T	455	$ .01	$ .08
Burleson, Rick	81TTR	743	$ .01	$ .15
Burleson, Rick	82T	55	$ .01	$ .08
Burleson, Rick	83T	315	$ .01	$ .08
Burleson, Rick	84T	735	$ .01	$ .06
Burleson, Rick	86TTR	16	$ .01	$ .06
Burleson, Rick	87T	579	$ .01	$ .04
Burnette, Wally	57T	13	$2.00	$8.00
Burnette, Wally	58T	69	$2.00	$8.00
Burnitz, Jeromy	92T	591	$ .05	$ .20
Burnitz, Jeromy	93T	658	$ .05	$ .35
Burns, Britt	81T	412	$ .01	$ .08
Burns, Britt	82T	44	$ .01	$ .08
Burns, Britt	83T	541	$ .01	$ .08
Burns, Britt	84T	125	$ .01	$ .06
Burns, Britt	85T	338	$ .01	$ .06
Burns, Britt	86T	679	$ .01	$ .05
Burns, Todd	89T	174	$ .01	$ .10
Burns, Todd	90T	369	$ .01	$ .03
Burns, Todd	91T	608	$ .01	$ .03
Burns, Todd	91TSC	207	$ .05	$ .25
Burns, Todd	93TSC	210	$ .01	$ .10
Burnside, Pete	58T	211	$1.25	$5.00
Burnside, Pete	59T	354	$1.00	$4.00
Burnside, Pete	60T	261	$ .75	$3.00
Burnside, Pete	61T	507	$1.35	$5.40
Burnside, Pete	62T	207	$ .75	$3.00
Burnside, Pete	63T	19	$ .50	$2.00
Burright, Larry	62T	348	$ .75	$3.00
Burright, Larry	63T	174	$ .50	$2.00
Burris, Ray	74T	161	$ .10	$ .40
Burris, Ray	75T	566	$ .10	$ .40
Burris, Ray	76T	51	$ .05	$ .25
Burris, Ray	77T	190	$ .05	$ .20
Burris, Ray	78T	371	$ .04	$ .16
Burris, Ray	79T	98	$ .03	$ .12
Burris, Ray	80T	364	$ .01	$ .10
Burris, Ray	81T	654	$ .01	$ .08
Burris, Ray	81TTR	744	$ .01	$ .15
Burris, Ray	82T	227	$ .01	$ .08
Burris, Ray	83T	474	$ .01	$ .08
Burris, Ray	84T	552	$ .01	$ .06
Burris, Ray	84TTR	18	$ .01	$ .15
Burris, Ray	85T	758	$ .01	$ .06
Burris, Ray	85TTR	13	$ .01	$ .10
Burris, Ray	86T	106	$ .01	$ .05
Burroughs, Jeff	72T	191	$ .25	$1.00
Burroughs, Jeff	73T	489	$ .25	$1.00
Burroughs, Jeff	74T	223	$ .10	$ .40
Burroughs, Jeff	75T	212	$ .25	$1.00
Burroughs, Jeff	75T	308	$ .30	$1.20
Burroughs, Jeff	75T	470	$ .10	$ .40
Burroughs, Jeff	76T	360	$ .05	$ .25
Burroughs, Jeff	77T	55	$ .05	$ .20
Burroughs, Jeff	78T	130	$ .04	$ .16
Burroughs, Jeff	79T	245	$ .03	$ .12
Burroughs, Jeff	80T	545	$ .01	$ .10
Burroughs, Jeff	81T	20	$ .01	$ .08
Burroughs, Jeff	81TTR	745	$ .01	$ .15
Burroughs, Jeff	82T	440	$ .01	$ .08
Burroughs, Jeff	82TTR	14	$ .01	$ .10
Burroughs, Jeff	83T	648	$ .01	$ .08
Burroughs, Jeff	84T	354	$ .01	$ .06
Burroughs, Jeff	85T	91	$ .01	$ .06
Burroughs, Jeff	85T	272	$ .01	$ .06
Burroughs, Jeff	85TTR	14	$ .01	$ .10
Burroughs, Jeff	86T	168	$ .01	$ .05
Burton, Ellis	59T	231	$1.00	$4.00
Burton, Ellis	60T	446	$1.25	$5.00
Burton, Ellis	63T	262	$ .90	$3.60
Burton, Ellis	64T	269	$ .65	$2.60

TOPPS

Player	Year	No.	VG	EX/MT	Player	Year	No.	VG	EX/MT
Burton, Jim	76T	471	$ .05	$ .25	Butters, Tom	63T	299	$1.00	$4.00
Burwell, Bill	60T	467	$1.25	$5.00	Butters, Tom	64T	74	$ .50	$2.00
Busby, Jim	52T	309	$12.50	$50.00	Butters, Tom	65T	246	$ .50	$2.00
Busby, Jim	56T	330	$2.50	$10.00	Buzhardt, John	59T	118	$1.00	$4.00
Busby, Jim	57T	309	$5.00	$20.00	Buzhardt, John	60T	549	$2.75	$11.00
Busby, Jim	58T	28	$2.00	$8.00	Buzhardt, John	61T	3	$ .60	$2.40
Busby, Jim	59T	185	$1.00	$4.00	Buzhardt, John	62T	555	$6.00	$24.00
Busby, Jim	60T	232	$ .75	$3.00	Buzhardt, John	63T	35	$ .50	$2.00
Busby, Jim	73T	237	$ .30	$1.20	Buzhardt, John	64T	323	$ .65	$2.60
Busby, Jim	74T	634	$ .25	$1.00	Buzhardt, John	65T	458	$1.25	$5.00
Busby, Steve	73T	608	$1.00	$4.00	Buzhardt, John	66T	245	$ .50	$2.00
Busby, Steve	74T	365	$ .10	$ .40	Buzhardt, John	67T	178	$ .40	$1.60
Busby, Steve	75T	120	$ .15	$ .60	Buzhardt, John	68T	403	$ .35	$1.40
Busby, Steve	75THL	7	$1.50	$6.00	Byerly, Bud	52T	161	$7.00	$28.00
Busby, Steve	76T	260	$ .05	$ .25	Byerly, Bud	58T	72	$2.00	$8.00
Busby, Steve	78T	336	$ .04	$ .16	Byerly, Bud	60T	371	$ .75	$3.00
Busby, Steve	80T	474	$ .01	$ .10	Byrd, Harry	53T	131	$4.00	$16.00
Buschhorn, Don	65T	577	$2.50	$10.00	Byrd, Harry	58T	154	$1.25	$5.00
Bush, Randy	83TTR	17	$ .01	$ .10	Byrd, Harry	91TA53	131	$ .01	$ .15
Bush, Randy	84T	429	$ .01	$ .06	Byrd, Jeff	78T	667	$ .04	$ .16
Bush, Randy	85T	692	$ .01	$ .06	Byrne, Tommy	51Tbb	35	$7.50	$30.00
Bush, Randy	86T	214	$ .01	$ .05	Byrne, Tommy	52T	241	$7.00	$28.00
Bush, Randy	87T	364	$ .01	$ .04	Byrne, Tommy	53T	123	$4.00	$16.00
Bush, Randy	88T	73	$ .01	$ .04	Byrne, Tommy	56T	215	$3.75	$15.00
Bush, Randy	89T	577	$ .01	$ .03					
Bush, Randy	90T	747	$ .01	$ .03					
Bush, Randy	91T	124	$ .01	$ .03					
Bush, Randy	92T	476	$ .01	$ .03					
Bush, Randy	92TSC	84	$ .01	$ .10					
Buskey, Tom	75T	403	$ .10	$ .40					
Buskey, Tom	76T	178	$ .05	$ .25					
Buskey, Tom	77T	236	$ .05	$ .20					
Buskey, Tom	80T	506	$ .01	$ .10					
Busse, Ray	72T	101	$ .50	$2.00					
Busse, Ray	73T	607	$ .75	$3.00					
Butcher, John	81T	41	$ .01	$ .08					
Butcher, John	82T	418	$ .01	$ .15					
Butcher, John	83T	534	$ .01	$ .08					
Butcher, John	84T	299	$ .01	$ .06					
Butcher, John	84TTR	19	$ .01	$ .15					
Butcher, John	85T	741	$ .01	$ .06					
Butcher, John	86T	638	$ .01	$ .05					
Butcher, John	87T	107	$ .01	$ .04					
Butcher, Mike	93T	104	$ .01	$ .10					
Butera, Sal	81T	243	$ .01	$ .08					
Butera, Sal	82T	676	$ .01	$ .08					
Butera, Sal	83T	67	$ .01	$ .08					
Butera, Sal	86T	407	$ .01	$ .05					
Butera, Sal	87T	358	$ .01	$ .04					
Butera, Sal	88T	772	$ .01	$ .04					
Butler, Bill	69T	619	$ .40	$1.60					
Butler, Bill	70T	377	$ .35	$1.40					
Butler, Bill	71T	687	$1.10	$4.40					
Butler, Bill	75T	549	$ .10	$ .40					
Butler, Bill	76T	619	$ .05	$ .25					
Butler, Brett	82T	502	$ .25	$2.50	Byrne, Tommy	57T	108	$2.00	$8.00
Butler, Brett	83T	364	$ .10	$ .75	Byrne, Tommy	91TA53	123	$ .01	$ .15
Butler, Brett	84T	77	$ .05	$ .25	Bystrom, Marty	81T	526	$ .01	$ .08
Butler, Brett	84TTR	20	$ .10	$ .75	Bystrom, Marty	82T	416	$ .01	$ .08
Butler, Brett	85T	637	$ .01	$ .15	Bystrom, Marty	83T	199	$ .01	$ .08
Butler, Brett	86T	149	$ .01	$ .10	Bystrom, Marty	84T	511	$ .01	$ .06
Butler, Brett	87T	723	$ .01	$ .10	Bystrom, Marty	85T	284	$ .01	$ .06
Butler, Brett	88T	479	$ .01	$ .10	Bystrom, Marty	86T	723	$ .01	$ .05
Butler, Brett	88TTR	22	$ .01	$ .10	Cabell, Enos	73T	605	$1.00	$4.00
Butler, Brett	89T	241	$ .01	$ .03	Cabell, Enos	75T	247	$ .10	$ .40
Butler, Brett	90T	571	$ .01	$ .03	Cabell, Enos	76T	404	$ .05	$ .25
Butler, Brett	91T	325	$ .01	$ .03	Cabell, Enos	77T	567	$ .05	$ .20
Butler, Brett	91TSC	389	$ .05	$ .25	Cabell, Enos	78T	132	$ .04	$ .16
Butler, Brett	91TTR	15	$ .01	$ .05	Cabell, Enos	79T	515	$ .03	$ .12
Butler, Brett	92T	655	$ .01	$ .03	Cabell, Enos	80T	385	$ .01	$ .10
Butler, Brett	92TSC	292	$ .01	$ .10	Cabell, Enos	81T	45	$ .01	$ .08
Butler, Brett	93T	65	$ .01	$ .03	Cabell, Enos	81TTR	746	$ .01	$ .15
Butler, Brett	93TSC	216	$ .01	$ .10	Cabell, Enos	82T	627	$ .01	$ .08
Butler, Cecil	62T	239	$ .75	$3.00	Cabell, Enos	82TTR	15	$ .01	$ .10
Butler, Cecil	63T	201	$ .90	$3.60	Cabell, Enos	83T	225	$ .01	$ .08

TOPPS

Player	Year	No.	VG	EX/MT	Player	Year	No.	VG	EX/MT
Cabell, Enos	84T	482	$.01	$.06	Callison, Johnny	70T	375	$.10	$.40
Cabell, Enos	84TTR	21	$.01	$.15	Callison, Johnny	71T	12	$.25	$1.00
Cabell, Enos	85T	786	$.01	$.06	Callison, Johnny	72T	364	$.10	$.40
Cabell, Enos	86T	197	$.01	$.05	Callison, Johnny	73T	535	$.60	$2.40
Cabell, Enos	87T	509	$.01	$.04	Calmus, Dick	64T	231	$.65	$2.60
Cabrera, Francisco	90T	254	$.01	$.15	Calmus, Dick	68T	427	$.35	$1.40
Cabrera, Francisco	91T	693	$.01	$.03	Camacho, Ernie	81T	96	$.01	$.08
Cabrera, Francisco	92TSC	797	$.01	$.10	Camacho, Ernie	85T	739	$.01	$.06
Cabrera, Francisco	93T	769	$.01	$.03	Camacho, Ernie	86T	509	$.01	$.05
Cadaret, Greg	88T	328	$.01	$.04	Camacho, Ernie	87T	353	$.01	$.04
Cadaret, Greg	89T	552	$.01	$.03	Cambria, Fred	71T	27	$.25	$1.00
Cadaret, Greg	90T	659	$.01	$.03	Cambria, Fred	72T	392	$.25	$1.00
Cadaret, Greg	91T	187	$.01	$.03	Camilli, Doug	62T	594	$20.00	$80.00
Cadaret, Greg	91TSC	536	$.05	$.25	Camilli, Doug	63T	196	$.50	$2.00
Cadaret, Greg	92T	18	$.01	$.03	Camilli, Doug	64T	249	$.65	$2.60
Cadaret, Greg	92TSC	176	$.01	$.10	Camilli, Doug	65T	77	$.35	$1.40
Cadaret, Greg	93T	478	$.01	$.03	Camilli, Doug	66T	593	$7.00	$28.00
Caffie, Joe	58T	182	$1.25	$5.00	Camilli, Doug	67T	551	$2.25	$9.00
Caffrey, Bob	85T	394	$.01	$.06	Camilli, Doug	73T	131	$.20	$.80
Cage, Wayne	78T	706	$.04	$.16	Camilli, Lou	71T	612	$1.00	$4.00
Cage, Wayne	79T	150	$.03	$.12	Caminiti, Ken	88T	64	$.05	$.25
Cage, Wayne	80T	208	$.01	$.10	Caminiti, Ken	89T	369	$.01	$.03
Cain, Bob	52T	349	$43.75	$175.00	Caminiti, Ken	90T	531	$.01	$.03
Cain, Bob	53T	266	$22.50	$90.00	Caminiti, Ken	91T	174	$.01	$.03
Cain, Bob	54T	61	$7.50	$30.00	Caminiti, Ken	91TSC	520	$.05	$.25
Cain, Bob	91TA53	266	$.01	$.15	Caminiti, Ken	92T	740	$.01	$.03
Cain, Les	69T	324	$.50	$2.00	Caminiti, Ken	92TSC	142	$.01	$.10
Cain, Les	71T	101	$.25	$1.00	Caminiti, Ken	93T	448	$.01	$.03
Cain, Les	72T	783	$1.25	$5.00	Camp, Rick	77T	475	$.05	$.20
Calderon, Ivan	86T	382	$.10	$.50	Camp, Rick	78T	349	$.04	$.16
Calderon, Ivan	87TTR	15	$.01	$.15	Camp, Rick	79T	105	$.03	$.12
Calderon, Ivan	88T	184	$.01	$.10	Camp, Rick	81T	87	$.01	$.08
Calderon, Ivan	89T	656	$.01	$.03	Camp, Rick	82T	637	$.01	$.08
Calderon, Ivan	90T	569	$.01	$.03	Camp, Rick	83T	207	$.01	$.08
Calderon, Ivan	91T	93	$.01	$.03	Camp, Rick	84T	597	$.01	$.06
Calderon, Ivan	91TSC	383	$.05	$.25	Camp, Rick	85T	491	$.01	$.06
Calderon, Ivan	91TTR	16	$.01	$.05	Camp, Rick	86T	319	$.01	$.05
Calderon, Ivan	92T	775	$.01	$.03	Campanella, Roy	52T	314	$500.00	$2000.00
Calderon, Ivan	92TSC	73	$.01	$.10	Campanella, Roy	53T	27	$50.00	$200.00
Calderon, Ivan	93T	540	$.01	$.03	Campanella, Roy	56T	101	$35.00	$140.00
Calderon, Ivan	93TSC	119	$.01	$.10	Campanella, Roy	57T	210	$27.50	$110.00
Calderone, Sam	53T	260	$22.50	$90.00	Campanella, Roy	57T	400	$50.00	$200.00
Calderone, Sammy	54T	68	$7.50	$30.00	Campanella, Roy	59T	550	$40.00	$160.00
Calderone, Sam	91TA53	260	$.01	$.15	Campanella, Roy	61TMVP	480	$8.75	$35.00
Caldwell, Mike	73T	182	$.20	$.80	Campanella, Roy	75T	189	$.50	$2.00
Caldwell, Mike	74T	344	$.10	$.40	Campanella, Roy	75T	191	$.35	$1.40
Caldwell, Mike	75T	347	$.10	$.40	Campanella, Roy	75T	193	$.50	$2.00
Caldwell, Mike	76T	157	$.05	$.25	Campanella, Roy	91TA53	27	$.20	$2.00
Caldwell, Mike	77T	452	$.05	$.20	Campaneris, Bert	65T	266	$1.75	$7.00
Caldwell, Mike	78T	212	$.04	$.16	Campaneris, Bert	66T	175	$.50	$2.00
Caldwell, Mike	79T	651	$.03	$.12	Campaneris, Bert	67T	515	$1.75	$7.00
Caldwell, Mike	80T	515	$.01	$.10	Campaneris, Bert	68T	109	$.35	$1.40
Caldwell, Mike	81T	85	$.01	$.08	Campaneris, Bert	69T	495	$.30	$1.20
Caldwell, Mike	82T	378	$.01	$.08	Campaneris, Bert	69T	556	$.40	$1.60
Caldwell, Mike	83T	142	$.01	$.08	Campaneris, Bert	69TAS	423	$.50	$2.00
Caldwell, Mike	84T	605	$.01	$.06	Campaneris, Bert	70T	205	$.25	$1.00
Caldwell, Mike	85T	419	$.01	$.06	Campaneris, Bert	71T	440	$.25	$1.00
Calhoun, Jeff	86T	534	$.01	$.05	Campaneris, Bert	72T	75	$.20	$.80
Calhoun, Jeff	87T	282	$.01	$.04	Campaneris, Bert	73T	64	$.35	$1.40
Calhoun, Jeff	87TTR	16	$.01	$.05	Campaneris, Bert	73T	295	$.25	$1.00
Calhoun, Jeff	88T	38	$.01	$.04	Campaneris, Bert	74T	155	$.25	$1.00
Callison, John	59T	119	$1.75	$7.00	Campaneris, Bert	74TAS	335	$.15	$.60
Callison, Johnny	60T	17	$1.25	$5.00	Campaneris, Bert	75T	170	$.15	$.60
Callison, Johnny	61T	468	$1.35	$5.40	Campaneris, Bert	76T	580	$.10	$.40
Callison, Johnny	62T	17	$.60	$2.40	Campaneris, Bert	77T	373	$.05	$.20
Callison, Johnny	63T	434	$1.00	$4.00	Campaneris, Bert	78T	260	$.05	$.20
Callison, Johnny	64T	135	$.50	$2.00	Campaneris, Bert	79T	620	$.05	$.20
Callison, Johnny	65T	4	$2.00	$8.00	Campaneris, Bert	80T	505	$.01	$.10
Callison, Johnny	65T	310	$.50	$2.00	Campaneris, Bert	81T	410	$.01	$.08
Callison, Johnny	66T	52	$.50	$2.00	Campaneris, Bert	82T	772	$.01	$.10
Callison, Johnny	66T	230	$.50	$2.00	Campaneris, Bert	83TTR	18	$.05	$.20
Callison, Johnny	67T	85	$.40	$1.60	Campaneris, Bert	84T	139	$.01	$.06
Callison, Johnny	67T	309	$.60	$1.20	Campaneris, Bert	84T	711	$.05	$.20
Callison, Johnny	68T	415	$.35	$1.40	Campaneris, Bert	84T	714	$.01	$.06
Callison, Johnny	69T	133	$.35	$1.40	Campanis, Jim	67T	12	$.40	$1.60

TOPPS

Player	Year	No.	VG	EX/MT
Campanis, Jim	68T	281	$ .35	$1.40
Campanis, Jim	69T	396	$ .30	$1.20
Campanis, Jim	70T	671	$1.25	$5.00
Campanis, Jim	74T	513	$ .10	$ .40
Campanis, Jim	88TTR	23	$ .01	$ .15
Campanis, Jim	92T	58	$ .05	$ .25
Campbell, Bill	74T	26	$ .10	$ .40
Campbell, Bill	75T	226	$ .10	$ .40
Campbell, Bill	76T	288	$ .05	$ .25
Campbell, Bill	77T	8	$ .05	$ .20
Campbell, Bill	77T	166	$ .05	$ .20
Campbell, Bill	78T	208	$ .10	$ .40
Campbell, Bill	78T	545	$ .04	$ .16
Campbell, Bill	79T	375	$ .03	$ .12
Campbell, Bill	80T	15	$ .01	$ .10
Campbell, Bill	81T	396	$ .01	$ .08
Campbell, Bill	82T	619	$ .01	$ .08
Campbell, Bill	82TTR	16	$ .01	$ .10
Campbell, Bill	83T	436	$ .01	$ .08
Campbell, Bill	84T	787	$ .01	$ .06
Campbell, Bill	84TTR	22	$ .01	$ .15
Campbell, Bill	85T	209	$ .01	$ .06
Campbell, Bill	85TTR	15	$ .01	$ .10
Campbell, Bill	86T	112	$ .01	$ .05
Campbell, Bill	86TTR	17	$ .01	$ .06
Campbell, Bill	87T	674	$ .01	$ .04
Campbell, Dave	69T	324	$ .50	$2.00
Campbell, Dave	70T	639	$1.25	$5.00
Campbell, Dave	71T	46	$1.50	$6.00
Campbell, Dave	72T	384	$ .10	$ .40
Campbell, Dave	73T	488	$ .25	$1.00
Campbell, Dave	74T	556	$ .10	$ .40
Campbell, Dave	78T	402	$ .04	$ .16
Campbell, Dave	79T	9	$ .03	$ .12
Campbell, Jim	63T	373	$1.00	$4.00
Campbell, Jim	64T	303	$ .65	$2.60
Campbell, Kevin	92TSC	647	$ .01	$ .15
Campbell, Kevin	92TTR	19	$ .01	$ .10
Campbell, Kevin	93T	236	$ .01	$ .15
Campbell, Kevin	93TSC	235	$ .01	$ .10
Campbell, Mike	88T	246	$ .01	$ .04
Campbell, Mike	89T	143	$ .01	$ .03
Campbell, Ron	67T	497	$1.50	$6.00

Player	Year	No.	VG	EX/MT
Campisi, Sal	70T	716	$1.25	$5.00
Campisi, Sal	71T	568	$1.00	$4.00
Campos, Frank	52T	307	$12.50	$50.00
Campos, Frank	53T	51	$4.00	$16.00
Campos, Frank	91TA53	51	$ .01	$ .15
Campusano, Sil	88TTR	24	$ .01	$ .10
Campusano, Sil	89T	191	$ .01	$ .10
Campusano, Sil	91T	618	$ .01	$ .03
Campusano, Sil	91TSC	484	$ .05	$ .25
Canale, George	90T	344	$ .01	$ .10
Candaele, Casey	87TTR	17	$ .01	$ .05
Candaele, Casey	88T	431	$ .01	$ .04
Candaele, Casey	90TTR	17	$ .01	$ .05
Candaele, Casey	91T	602	$ .01	$ .03
Candaele, Casey	91TSC	434	$ .05	$ .25
Candaele, Casey	92T	161	$ .01	$ .03
Candaele, Casey	92TSC	178	$ .01	$ .10
Candaele, Casey	93T	584	$ .01	$ .03
Candaele, Casey	93TSC	70	$ .01	$ .10
Candelaria, John	76T	317	$ .75	$3.00
Candelaria, John	77T	510	$ .10	$ .40
Candelaria, John	78T	190	$ .05	$ .20
Candelaria, John	78T	207	$ .04	$ .16
Candelaria, John	79T	70	$ .03	$ .12
Candelaria, John	80T	635	$ .01	$ .10
Candelaria, John	81T	265	$ .01	$ .08
Candelaria, John	82T	425	$ .01	$ .15
Candelaria, John	83T	291	$ .01	$ .08
Candelaria, John	83T	755	$ .01	$ .08
Candelaria, John	84T	330	$ .01	$ .10
Candelaria, John	85T	50	$ .01	$ .06
Candelaria, John	86T	140	$ .01	$ .05
Candelaria, John	87T	630	$ .01	$ .04
Candelaria, John	88T	546	$ .01	$ .04
Candelaria, John	88TTR	25	$ .01	$ .05
Candelaria, John	89T	285	$ .01	$ .03
Candelaria, John	90T	485	$ .01	$ .03
Candelaria, John	90TTR	18	$ .01	$ .05
Candelaria, John	91T	777	$ .01	$ .03
Candelaria, John	91TSC	538	$ .05	$ .25
Candelaria, John	91TTR	17	$ .01	$ .05
Candelaria, John	92T	363	$ .01	$ .03
Candelaria, John	92TSC	164	$ .01	$ .10
Candelaria, John	93T	682	$ .01	$ .03
Candiotti, Tom	84T	262	$ .10	$ .40
Candiotti, Tom	86TTR	18	$ .01	$ .15
Candiotti, Tom	87T	463	$ .01	$ .04
Candiotti, Tom	88T	123	$ .01	$ .04
Candiotti, Tom	89T	599	$ .01	$ .03
Candiotti, Tom	90T	743	$ .01	$ .03
Candiotti, Tom	91T	624	$ .01	$ .03
Candiotti, Tom	91TSC	405	$ .05	$ .25
Candiotti, Tom	91TTR	18	$ .01	$ .05
Candiotti, Tom	92T	38	$ .01	$ .03
Candiotti, Tom	92TSC	113	$ .01	$ .10
Candiotti, Tom	92TSC	875	$ .01	$ .10
Candiotti, Tom	92TTR	20	$ .01	$ .05
Candiotti, Tom	93T	365	$ .01	$ .03
Cangelosi, John	86TTR	19	$ .01	$ .06
Cangelosi, John	87T	201	$ .05	$ .30
Cangelosi, John	87TTR	18	$ .01	$ .05
Cangelosi, John	88T	506	$ .01	$ .04
Cangelosi, John	89T	592	$ .01	$ .03
Cangelosi, John	90T	29	$ .01	$ .03
Cannizzaro, Chris	61T	118	$ .60	$2.40
Cannizzaro, Chris	62T	26	$ .60	$2.40
Cannizzaro, Chris	65T	61	$ .35	$1.40
Cannizzaro, Chris	66T	497	$1.50	$6.00
Cannizzaro, Chris	69T	131	$ .35	$1.40
Cannizzaro, Chris	70T	329	$ .35	$1.40
Cannizzaro, Chris	71T	426	$ .50	$2.00
Cannizzaro, Chris	72T	759	$1.25	$5.00
Cannizzaro, Chris	75T	355	$ .10	$ .40
Cannon, Joe	80T	221	$ .01	$ .10
Canseco, Jose	86TTR	20	$1.50	$6.00

| Camper, Cardell | 78T | 711 | $ .04 | $ .16 |

TOPPS

Player	Year	No.	VG	EX/MT	Player	Year	No.	VG	EX/MT
Canseco, Jose	87T	620	$.20	$2.00	Cardinal, Randy	63T	562	$5.00	$20.00
Canseco, Jose	88T	370	$.10	$.50	Cardinals, Team	56T	134	$7.50	$30.00
Canseco, Jose	89T	500	$.05	$.35	Cardinals, Team	57T	243	$3.00	$12.00
Canseco, Jose	89TAS	401	$.01	$.15	Cardinals, Team	58T	216	$3.50	$14.00
Canseco, Jose	90T	250	$.05	$.25	Cardinals, Team	59T	223	$2.50	$10.00
Canseco, Jose	91T	700	$.05	$.25	Cardinals, Team	60T	242	$2.00	$8.00
Canseco, Jose	91TAS	390	$.01	$.10	Cardinals, Team	61T	347	$1.75	$7.00
Canseco, Jose	91TSC	155	$.75	$3.00	Cardinals, Team	62T	61	$1.50	$6.00
Canseco, Jose	92T	100	$.01	$.15	Cardinals, Team	63T	524	$6.25	$25.00
Canseco, Jose	92TAS	401	$.01	$.10	Cardinals, Team	64T	87	$1.25	$5.00
Canseco, Jose	92TSC	370	$.10	$1.00	Cardinals, Team	65T	57	$.75	$3.00
Canseco, Jose	92TSC	597	$.10	$.50	Cardinals, Team	66T	379	$2.00	$8.00
Canseco, Jose	93T	500	$.05	$.20	Cardinals, Team	67T	173	$.75	$3.00
Canseco, Ozzie	91T	162	$.01	$.10	Cardinals, Team	68T	497	$1.50	$6.00
Capel, Mike	89T	767	$.01	$.03	Cardinals, Team	70T	549	$1.25	$5.00
Capilla, Doug	78T	477	$.04	$.16	Cardinals, Team	71T	308	$.50	$2.00
Capilla, Doug	80T	628	$.01	$.10	Cardinals, Team	72T	688	$2.50	$10.00
Capilla, Doug	81T	136	$.01	$.08	Cardinals, Team	73T	219	$.30	$1.20
Capilla, Doug	82T	537	$.01	$.08	Cardinals, Team	74T	36	$.25	$1.00
Cappuzzello, George	82T	137	$.01	$.08	Cardinals, Team Checklist	75T	246	$.35	$1.40
Cappuzzello, George	83T	422	$.01	$.08	Cardinals, Team Checklist	76T	581	$.30	$1.20
Capra, Buzz	72T	141	$.10	$.40	Cardinals, Team Checklist	77T	183	$.25	$1.00
Capra, Buzz	75T	105	$.10	$.40	Cardinals, Team Checklist	78T	479	$.20	$.80
Capra, Buzz	75T	311	$.25	$1.00	Cardinals, Team Checklist	79T	192	$.15	$.60
Capra, Buzz	76T	153	$.05	$.25	Cardinals, Team Checklist	80T	244	$.10	$.50
Capra, Buzz	77T	432	$.05	$.20	Cardinals, Team Checklist	81T	684	$.05	$.25
Capra, Buzz	78T	578	$.04	$.16	Cardinals, Team Leaders	86T	66	$.01	$.05
Caraballo, Ramon	93T	451	$.05	$.25	Cardinals, Team Leaders	87T	181	$.01	$.04
Carbo, Bernie	70T	36	$.25	$1.00	Cardinals, Team Leaders	88T	351	$.01	$.04
Carbo, Bernie	71T	478	$.50	$2.00	Cardinals, Team Leaders	89T	261	$.01	$.03
Carbo, Bernie	72T	463	$.25	$1.00	Cardwell, Don	57T	374	$1.75	$7.00
Carbo, Bernie	73T	171	$.10	$.40	Cardwell, Don	58T	372	$1.00	$4.00
Carbo, Bernie	74T	621	$.10	$.40	Cardwell, Don	59T	314	$1.00	$4.00
Carbo, Bernie	75T	379	$.10	$.40	Cardwell, Don	60T	384	$.75	$3.00
Carbo, Bernie	76T	278	$.05	$.25	Cardwell, Don	61T	393	$1.00	$4.00
Carbo, Bernie	77T	159	$.05	$.20	Cardwell, Don	61T	564	$7.50	$30.00
Carbo, Bernie	78T	524	$.04	$.16	Cardwell, Don	62T	495	$1.50	$6.00
Carbo, Bernie	79T	38	$.03	$.12	Cardwell, Don	63T	575	$2.25	$9.00
Carbo, Bernie	80T	266	$.01	$.10	Cardwell, Don	64T	417	$1.00	$4.00
Cardenal, Jose	65T	374	$1.50	$6.00	Cardwell, Don	65T	502	$1.25	$5.00
Cardenal, Jose	66T	505	$1.50	$6.00	Cardwell, Don	66T	235	$.50	$2.00
Cardenal, Jose	67T	193	$.40	$1.60	Cardwell, Don	67T	555	$4.00	$16.00
Cardenal, Jose	68T	102	$.35	$1.40	Cardwell, Don	68T	437	$.35	$1.40
Cardenal, Jose	69T	325	$.50	$2.00	Cardwell, Don	69T	193	$.35	$1.40
Cardenal, Jose	70T	675	$1.25	$5.00	Cardwell, Don	70T	83	$.20	$.80
Cardenal, Jose	71T	435	$.50	$2.00	Carew, Rod	67T	569	$125.00	$500.00
Cardenal, Jose	72T	12	$.10	$.40	Carew, Rod	68T	80	$32.50	$130.00
Cardenal, Jose	72TTR	757	$1.25	$5.00	Carew, Rod	68TAS	363	$3.50	$14.00
Cardenal, Jose	73T	393	$.10	$.40	Carew, Rod	69T	510	$17.50	$70.00
Cardenal, Jose	74T	185	$.10	$.40	Carew, Rod	69TAS	419	$2.50	$10.00
Cardenal, Jose	75T	15	$.10	$.40	Carew, Rod	70T	62	$.75	$3.00
Cardenal, Jose	76T	430	$.05	$.25	Carew, Rod	70T	290	$12.50	$50.00
Cardenal, Jose	77T	610	$.05	$.20	Carew, Rod	70TAS	453	$1.75	$7.00
Cardenal, Jose	78T	210	$.04	$.16	Carew, Rod	71T	210	$11.25	$45.00
Cardenal, Jose	79T	317	$.03	$.12	Carew, Rod	72T	695	$20.00	$80.00
Cardenal, Jose	80T	512	$.01	$.10	Carew, Rod	72TIA	696	$10.00	$40.00
Cardenal, Jose	81T	473	$.01	$.08	Carew, Rod	73T	61	$.50	$2.00
Cardenas, Chico	60T	119	$.75	$3.00	Carew, Rod	73T	330	$3.50	$14.00
Cardenas, Chico	61T	244	$.60	$2.40	Carew, Rod	74T	50	$3.00	$12.00
Cardenas, Chico	62T	381	$1.25	$5.00	Carew, Rod	74T	201	$1.00	$4.00
Cardenas, Chico	63T	203	$.90	$3.60	Carew, Rod	74TAS	333	$.75	$3.00
Cardenas, Chico	64T	72	$.50	$2.00	Carew, Rod	75T	306	$.30	$1.20
Cardenas, Chico	65T	437	$1.00	$4.00	Carew, Rod	75T	600	$2.50	$10.00
Cardenas, Chico	66T	370	$.50	$2.00	Carew, Rod	76T	192	$.50	$2.00
Cardenas, Chico	67T	325	$.60	$2.40	Carew, Rod	76T	400	$2.00	$8.00
Cardenas, Chico	68T	23	$.35	$1.40	Carew, Rod	77T	120	$2.00	$8.00
Cardenas, Chico	68T	480	$8.00	$32.00	Carew, Rod	78T	201	$.25	$1.00
Cardenas, Chico "Leo"	69T	265	$.50	$2.00	Carew, Rod	78T	580	$1.25	$5.00
Cardenas, Leo	70T	245	$.20	$.80	Carew, Rod	79T	1	$.75	$3.00
Cardenas, Leo	71T	405	$.50	$2.00	Carew, Rod	79T	300	$.75	$3.00
Cardenas, Leo	72T	561	$.40	$1.60	Carew, Rod	80T	700	$.50	$2.00
Cardenas, Leo	72TIA	562	$.40	$1.60	Carew, Rod	81T	100	$.25	$2.50
Cardenas, Leo	73T	522	$.25	$1.00	Carew, Rod	82T	276	$.05	$.25
Cardenas, Leo	75T	518	$.10	$.40	Carew, Rod	82T	500	$.15	$1.50
Cardenas, Leo	76T	587	$.05	$.25	Carew, Rod	82TAS	547	$.10	$1.00

TOPPS

Player	Year	No.	VG	EX/MT
Carew, Rod	82TSA	501	$.10	$.75
Carew, Rod	83T	200	$.15	$1.50
Carew, Rod	83T	201	$.10	$.75
Carew, Rod	83T	651	$.05	$.20
Carew, Rod	83TAS	386	$.10	$1.00
Carew, Rod	84T	276	$.01	$.15
Carew, Rod	84T	600	$.10	$1.00
Carew, Rod	84T	710	$.05	$.20
Carew, Rod	84T	711	$.05	$.20
Carew, Rod	85T	300	$.10	$.50
Carew, Rod	86T	400	$.10	$.50
Carey, Andy	53T	188	$8.00	$32.00
Carey, Andy	54T	105	$4.50	$18.00
Carey, Andy	55T	20	$2.50	$10.00
Carey, Andy	56T	12	$2.00	$8.00
Carey, Andy	57T	290	$5.00	$20.00
Carey, Andy	58T	333	$1.25	$5.00
Carey, Andy	59T	45	$1.50	$6.00
Carey, Andy	60T	196	$.75	$3.00
Carey, Andy	61T	518	$1.35	$5.40
Carey, Andy	62T	418	$1.25	$5.00
Carey, Andy	91TA53	188	$.01	$.15
Carlos, Cisco	68T	287	$.35	$1.40
Carlos, Cisco	69T	54	$.35	$1.40
Carlos, Cisco	70T	487	$.35	$1.40
Carlton, Steve	65T	477	$130.00	$520.00
Carlton, Steve	67T	146	$27.50	$110.00
Carlton, Steve	68T	408	$13.75	$55.00
Carlton, Steve	69T	255	$13.50	$54.00
Carlton, Steve	70T	67	$1.50	$6.00
Carlton, Steve	70T	220	$8.00	$32.00
Carlton, Steve	71T	55	$7.50	$30.00
Carlton, Steve	72T	93	$.75	$3.00
Carlton, Steve	72T	420	$5.50	$22.00
Carlton, Steve	72TTR	751	$15.00	$60.00
Carlton, Steve	73T	65	$.35	$1.40
Carlton, Steve	73T	66	$.35	$1.40
Carlton, Steve	73T	67	$3.00	$12.00
Carlton, Steve	73T	300	$3.50	$14.00
Carlton, Steve	74T	95	$3.00	$12.00
Carlton, Steve	75T	185	$2.25	$9.00
Carlton, Steve	75T	312	$3.00	$12.00
Carlton, Steve	76T	355	$2.00	$8.00
Carlton, Steve	77T	110	$2.00	$8.00
Carlton, Steve	78T	205	$.20	$.80
Carlton, Steve	78T	540	$1.25	$5.00
Carlton, Steve	79T	25	$1.00	$4.00
Carlton, Steve	80T	210	$.90	$3.60
Carlton, Steve	81T	5	$.05	$.25
Carlton, Steve	81T	6	$.05	$.25
Carlton, Steve	81T	630	$.20	$2.00
Carlton, Steve	81TRB	202	$.10	$.75
Carlton, Steve	82T	480	$.15	$1.50
Carlton, Steve	82T	636	$.10	$.50
Carlton, Steve	82THL	1	$.10	$1.00
Carlton, Steve	82TSA	481	$.10	$.75
Carlton, Steve	83T	70	$.20	$2.00
Carlton, Steve	83T	71	$.10	$1.00
Carlton, Steve	83T	229	$.01	$.10
Carlton, Steve	83T	705	$.05	$.25
Carlton, Steve	83T	706	$.01	$.10
Carlton, Steve	83TAS	406	$.10	$.75
Carlton, Steve	84T	1	$.10	$.50
Carlton, Steve	84T	4	$.10	$1.00
Carlton, Steve	84T	136	$.05	$.25
Carlton, Steve	84T	706	$.05	$.25
Carlton, Steve	84T	707	$.10	$1.00
Carlton, Steve	84T	708	$.05	$.20
Carlton, Steve	84T	780	$.10	$1.00
Carlton, Steve	84TAS	395	$.05	$.35
Carlton, Steve	85T	360	$.10	$.50
Carlton, Steve	86T	120	$.05	$.25
Carlton, Steve	87T	718	$.05	$.25
Carlton, Steve	87TTR	19	$.05	$.25
Carman, Don	85TTR	16	$.01	$.15
Carman, Don	86T	532	$.01	$.05
Carman, Don	87T	355	$.01	$.04
Carman, Don	88T	415	$.01	$.04
Carman, Don	89T	154	$.01	$.03
Carman, Don	90T	731	$.01	$.03
Carman, Don	91T	282	$.01	$.03
Carmel, Duke	60T	120	$.75	$3.00
Carmel, Duke	63T	544	$10.00	$40.00
Carmel, Duke	64T	44	$.50	$2.00
Carmel, Duke	65T	261	$.50	$2.00
Carpenter, Cris	89T	282	$.01	$.10
Carpenter, Cris	90T	443	$.01	$.03
Carpenter, Cris	91T	518	$.01	$.03
Carpenter, Cris	91TSC	499	$.05	$.25
Carpenter, Cris	92T	147	$.01	$.03
Carpenter, Cris	92TSC	429	$.01	$.10
Carpenter, Cris	93T	629	$.01	$.03
Carpin, Frank	66T	71	$.35	$1.40
Carr, Chuck	93T	722	$.01	$.03
Carrasquel, Chico	51Tbb	26	$10.00	$40.00
Carrasquel, Chico	52T	251	$12.50	$50.00
Carrasquel, Chico	56T	230	$3.75	$15.00
Carrasquel, Chico	57T	67	$2.00	$8.00
Carrasquel, Chico	58T	55	$2.00	$8.00
Carrasquel, Chico	59T	264	$1.00	$4.00
Carreon, Camilo	60T	121	$.75	$3.00
Carreon, Camilo	61T	509	$1.35	$5.40
Carreon, Camilo	62T	178	$.60	$2.40
Carreon, Camilo	63T	308	$.90	$3.60
Carreon, Camilo	64T	421	$1.00	$4.00
Carreon, Camilo	65T	578	$2.50	$10.00
Carreon, Camilo	66T	513	$1.50	$6.00
Carreon, Mark	90T	434	$.01	$.03
Carreon, Mark	91T	764	$.01	$.03
Carreon, Mark	91TSC	196	$.05	$.25
Carreon, Mark	92T	111	$.01	$.03
Carreon, Mark	92TSC	678	$.01	$.10
Carreon, Mark	92TTR	21	$.01	$.05
Carreon, Mark	93T	567	$.01	$.03
Carrithers, Don	72T	76	$.10	$.40
Carrithers, Don	73T	651	$.60	$2.40
Carrithers, Don	74T	361	$.10	$.40

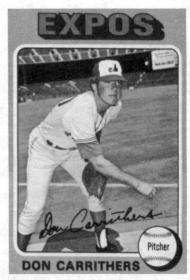

Carrithers, Don	75T	438	$.10	$.40
Carrithers, Don	76T	312	$.05	$.25

TOPPS

Player	Year	No.	VG	EX/MT	Player	Year	No.	VG	EX/MT
Carrithers, Don	77T	579	$ .05	$ .20	Carter, Joe	93TSC	279	$ .05	$ .20
Carrithers, Don	78T	113	$ .04	$ .16	Carter, Steve	90T	482	$ .01	$ .03
Carroll, Clay	65T	461	$12.50	$50.00	Carty, Rico	64T	476	$2.25	$9.00
Carroll, Clay	66T	307	$ .50	$2.00	Carty, Rico	65T	2	$2.50	$10.00
Carroll, Clay	67T	219	$ .50	$2.00	Carty, Rico	65T	305	$1.00	$4.00
Carroll, Clay	68T	412	$ .35	$1.40	Carty, Rico	66T	153	$ .35	$1.40
Carroll, Clay	69T	26	$ .35	$1.40	Carty, Rico	67T	35	$ .40	$1.60
Carroll, Clay	70T	133	$ .20	$ .80	Carty, Rico	67T	240	$ .75	$3.00
Carroll, Clay	71T	394	$ .50	$2.00	Carty, Rico	68T	455	$ .35	$1.40
Carroll, Clay	72T	311	$ .10	$ .40	Carty, Rico	69T	590	$ .40	$1.60
Carroll, Clay	72TIA	312	$ .10	$ .40	Carty, Rico	70T	145	$ .25	$1.00
Carroll, Clay	73T	68	$ .25	$1.00	Carty, Rico	71T	62	$ .50	$2.00
Carroll, Clay	73T	195	$ .10	$ .40	Carty, Rico	71T	270	$ .25	$1.00
Carroll, Clay	74T	111	$ .10	$ .40	Carty, Rico	72T	740	$1.25	$5.00
Carroll, Clay	75T	345	$ .10	$ .40	Carty, Rico	73T	435	$ .25	$1.00
Carroll, Clay	76T	211	$ .05	$ .25	Carty, Rico	75T	655	$ .15	$ .60
Carroll, Clay	76TTR	211	$ .05	$ .25	Carty, Rico	76T	156	$ .10	$ .40
Carroll, Clay	77T	497	$ .05	$ .20	Carty, Rico	77T	465	$ .05	$ .20
Carroll, Clay	78T	615	$ .04	$ .16	Carty, Rico	78T	305	$ .04	$ .16
Carroll, Tom	55T	158	$4.00	$16.00	Carty, Rico	79T	565	$ .05	$ .20
Carroll, Tom	56T	139	$2.50	$10.00	Carty, Rico	80T	46	$ .01	$ .10
Carroll, Tom	57T	164	$2.00	$8.00	Cary, Chuck	87T	171	$ .01	$ .04
Carroll, Tom	59T	513	$4.00	$16.00	Cary, Chuck	89TTR	17	$ .01	$ .10
Carroll, Tom	75T	507	$ .10	$ .40	Cary, Chuck	90T	691	$ .01	$ .03
Carroll, Tom	76T	561	$ .05	$ .25	Cary, Chuck	91T	359	$ .01	$ .03
Carter, Dick	60T	466	$1.25	$5.00	Cary, Chuck	91TSC	40	$ .05	$ .25
Carter, Gary	75T	620	$11.25	$45.00	Casagrande, Tom	55T	167	$6.25	$25.00
Carter, Gary	76T	441	$2.50	$10.00	Casale, Jerry	59T	456	$1.00	$4.00
Carter, Gary	77T	295	$1.50	$6.00	Casale, Jerry	60T	38	$ .85	$3.40
Carter, Gary	78T	120	$1.00	$4.00	Casale, Jerry	61T	195	$ .60	$2.40
Carter, Gary	79T	520	$ .75	$3.00	Casanova, Paul	67T	115	$ .40	$1.60
Carter, Gary	80T	70	$ .20	$2.00	Casanova, Paul	68T	560	$ .70	$2.80
Carter, Gary	81T	660	$ .15	$1.50	Casanova, Paul	69T	486	$ .30	$1.20
Carter, Gary	82T	730	$ .10	$1.00	Casanova, Paul	70T	84	$ .20	$ .80
Carter, Gary	82TAS	344	$ .10	$ .50	Casanova, Paul	71T	139	$ .25	$1.00
Carter, Gary	83T	370	$ .10	$ .75	Casanova, Paul	72T	591	$ .40	$1.60
Carter, Gary	83TAS	404	$ .10	$ .40	Casanova, Paul	73T	452	$ .25	$1.00
Carter, Gary	84T	450	$ .10	$ .50	Casanova, Paul	74T	272	$ .10	$ .40
Carter, Gary	84TAS	393	$ .05	$ .25	Casanova, Paul	75T	633	$ .10	$ .40
Carter, Gary	85T	230	$ .05	$ .25	Case, Michael	93T	661	$ .05	$ .20
Carter, Gary	85TAS	719	$ .01	$ .15	Cash, Dave	70T	141	$ .25	$1.00
Carter, Gary	85TTR	17	$ .10	$1.00	Cash, Dave	71T	582	$1.25	$5.00
Carter, Gary	86T	170	$ .05	$ .25	Cash, Dave	72T	125	$ .10	$ .40
Carter, Gary	86TAS	708	$ .01	$ .15	Cash, Dave	73T	397	$ .25	$1.00
Carter, Gary	87T	20	$ .01	$ .15	Cash, Dave	74T	198	$ .10	$ .40
Carter, Gary	87TAS	602	$ .01	$ .10	Cash, Dave	75T	22	$ .10	$ .40
Carter, Gary	88T	530	$ .01	$ .10	Cash, Dave	76T	295	$ .05	$ .25
Carter, Gary	89T	680	$ .01	$ .03	Cash, Dave	77T	649	$ .05	$ .20
Carter, Gary	89TAS	393	$ .01	$ .05	Cash, Dave	78T	495	$ .04	$ .16
Carter, Gary	89TRB	3	$ .01	$ .05	Cash, Dave	79T	395	$ .03	$ .12
Carter, Gary	90T	790	$ .01	$ .10	Cash, Dave	80T	14	$ .01	$ .10
Carter, Gary	90TTR	19	$ .01	$ .05	Cash, Dave	81T	707	$ .01	$ .08
Carter, Gary	91T	310	$ .01	$ .03	Cash, Norm	59T	509	$15.00	$60.00
Carter, Gary	91TSC	424	$ .05	$ .25	Cash, Norm	60T	488	$2.50	$10.00
Carter, Gary	91TTR	19	$ .01	$ .10	Cash, Norm	61T	95	$1.50	$6.00
Carter, Gary	92T	45	$ .01	$ .03	Cash, Norm	62T	51	$1.50	$6.00
Carter, Gary	92TSC	845	$ .01	$ .10	Cash, Norm	62T	250	$1.50	$0.00
Carter, Gary	92TTR	22	$ .01	$ .05	Cash, Norm	62TAS	466	$2.00	$8.00
Carter, Gary	93T	205	$ .01	$ .03	Cash, Norm	63T	4	$2.00	$8.00
Carter, Jeff	92TSC	381	$ .01	$ .10	Cash, Norm	63T	445	$1.50	$6.00
Carter, Joe	85T	694	$1.00	$4.00	Cash, Norm	64T	331	$30.00	$120.00
Carter, Joe	86T	377	$ .10	$1.00	Cash, Norm	64T	425	$1.25	$5.00
Carter, Joe	87T	220	$ .10	$ .40	Cash, Norm	65T	153	$ .75	$3.00
Carter, Joe	88T	75	$ .05	$ .25	Cash, Norm	66T	218	$ .75	$3.00
Carter, Joe	89T	420	$ .05	$ .25	Cash, Norm	66T	315	$ .75	$3.00
Carter, Joe	90T	580	$ .05	$ .20	Cash, Norm	67T	216	$1.75	$7.00
Carter, Joe	90TTR	20	$ .05	$ .20	Cash, Norm	67T	540	$11.25	$45.00
Carter, Joe	91T	120	$ .01	$ .10	Cash, Norm	68T	256	$1.25	$5.00
Carter, Joe	91TSC	513	$ .10	$1.00	Cash, Norm	69T	80	$ .75	$3.00
Carter, Joe	91TTR	20	$ .01	$ .10	Cash, Norm	70T	611	$1.00	$4.00
Carter, Joe	92T	790	$ .01	$ .15	Cash, Norm	71T	599	$1.25	$5.00
Carter, Joe	92TAS	402	$ .01	$ .10	Cash, Norm	72T	90	$ .50	$2.00
Carter, Joe	92TSC	10	$ .10	$ .50	Cash, Norm	72T	150	$ .20	$ .80
Carter, Joe	93T	350	$ .01	$ .10	Cash, Norm	73T	485	$ .25	$1.00
Carter, Joe	93T	407	$ .01	$ .10	Cash, Norm	74T	367	$ .25	$1.00

TOPPS

Player	Year	No.	VG	EX/MT
Cash, Ron	74T	600	$1.25	$5.00
Casian, Larry	91T	374	$ .01	$ .10
Castiglione, Pete	52T	260	$12.50	$50.00
Castillo, Bobby	79T	641	$ .03	$ .12
Castillo, Bobby	81T	146	$ .01	$ .08
Castillo, Bobby	82T	48	$ .01	$ .08
Castillo, Bobby	82TTR	17	$ .01	$ .10
Castillo, Bobby	83T	327	$ .01	$ .08
Castillo, Bobby	83T	771	$ .01	$ .08
Castillo, Bobby	84T	491	$ .01	$ .06
Castillo, Bobby	85T	588	$ .01	$ .06
Castillo, Bobby	85TTR	18	$ .01	$ .10
Castillo, Bobby	86T	252	$ .01	$ .05
Castillo, Braulio	92T	353	$ .01	$ .10
Castillo, Braulio	92TSC	124	$ .05	$ .25
Castillo, Carmen	85T	184	$ .01	$ .06
Castillo, Carmen	86TTR	21	$ .01	$ .06
Castillo, Carmen	87T	513	$ .01	$ .04
Castillo, Carmen	88T	341	$ .01	$ .04
Castillo, Carmen	89T	637	$ .01	$ .03
Castillo, "Carmen" Carmelo	89TTR	18	$ .01	$ .05
Castillo, Carmelo	91T	266	$ .01	$ .03
Castillo, Frank	92T	196	$ .01	$ .10
Castillo, Frank	92TSC	65	$ .05	$ .25
Castillo, Frank	93T	533	$ .01	$ .03
Castillo, Juan	87TTR	20	$ .01	$ .05
Castillo, Juan	88T	362	$ .01	$ .04
Castillo, Juan	89T	538	$ .01	$ .03
Castillo, Manny	81T	66	$ .01	$ .08
Castillo, Manny	83T	258	$ .01	$ .08
Castillo, Manny	84T	562	$ .01	$ .06
Castillo, Marty	82T	261	$ .01	$ .08
Castillo, Marty	84T	303	$ .01	$ .06
Castillo, Marty	85T	461	$ .01	$ .06
Castillo, Marty	86T	788	$ .01	$ .05
Castillo, Tony	90T	620	$ .01	$ .03
Castillo, Tony	91T	353	$ .01	$ .03
Castino, John	80T	137	$ .01	$ .10
Castino, John	81T	304	$ .01	$ .08
Castino, John	82T	396	$ .01	$ .08
Castino, John	82T	644	$ .01	$ .08
Castino, John	83T	93	$ .01	$ .08
Castino, John	84T	237	$ .01	$ .06
Castino, John	85T	452	$ .01	$ .06
Castleman, Foster	56T	271	$2.50	$10.00
Castleman, Foster	57T	237	$2.00	$8.00
Castleman, Foster	58T	416	$1.00	$4.00
Castro, Bill	76T	293	$ .05	$ .25
Castro, Bill	77T	528	$ .05	$ .20
Castro, Bill	78T	448	$ .04	$ .16
Castro, Bill	79T	133	$ .03	$ .12
Castro, Bill	80T	303	$ .01	$ .10
Castro, Bill	81T	271	$ .01	$ .08
Cater, Danny	64T	482	$1.00	$4.00
Cater, Danny	65T	253	$ .50	$2.00
Cater, Danny	66T	398	$ .65	$2.60
Cater, Danny	67T	157	$ .40	$1.60
Cater, Danny	68T	535	$ .70	$2.80
Cater, Danny	69T	1	$2.75	$11.00
Cater, Danny	69T	44	$ .35	$1.40
Cater, Danny	69T	556	$ .40	$1.60
Cater, Danny	70T	437	$ .35	$1.40
Cater, Danny	71T	358	$ .25	$1.00
Cater, Danny	72T	676	$1.25	$5.00
Cater, Danny	73T	317	$ .10	$ .40
Cater, Danny	74T	543	$ .10	$ .40
Cater, Danny	75T	645	$ .10	$ .40
Cato, Keefe	85T	367	$ .01	$ .06
Caudill, Bill	80T	103	$ .01	$ .10
Caudill, Bill	81T	574	$ .01	$ .08
Caudill, Bill	82T	303	$ .01	$ .08
Caudill, Bill	82TTR	18	$ .01	$ .10
Caudill, Bill	83T	78	$ .01	$ .08
Caudill, Bill	84T	769	$ .01	$ .06
Caudill, Bill	84TTR	23	$ .01	$ .15
Caudill, Bill	85T	685	$ .01	$ .06
Caudill, Bill	85TTR	19	$ .01	$ .10
Caudill, Bill	86T	435	$ .01	$ .05
Caudill, Bill	87T	733	$ .01	$ .04
Causey, Wayne	62T	496	$1.50	$6.00
Causey, Wayne	63T	539	$2.25	$9.00
Causey, Wayne	64T	75	$ .50	$2.00
Causey, Wayne	65T	425	$1.00	$4.00
Causey, Wayne	66T	366	$ .50	$2.00
Causey, Wayne	67T	286	$ .60	$2.40
Causey, Wayne	68T	522	$ .75	$3.00
Causey, Wayne	69T	33	$ .35	$1.40
Cavarretta, Phil	52T	295	$15.00	$60.00
Cavarretta, Phil	54T	55	$8.00	$32.00
Cavarretta, Phil	91TA53	295	$ .05	$ .20
Ceccarelli, Art	58T	191	$1.25	$5.00
Ceccarelli, Art	59T	226	$1.00	$4.00
Ceccarelli, Art	60T	156	$ .75	$3.00
Cecena, Jose	88TTR	26	$ .01	$ .10
Cecena, Jose	89T	683	$ .01	$ .03
Cedeno, Andujar	91T	646	$ .01	$ .15
Cedeno, Andujar	91TSC	476	$ .10	$1.00
Cedeno, Andujar	92T	288	$ .01	$ .10
Cedeno, Andujar	92TSC	310	$ .01	$ .15
Cedeno, Andujar	93T	553	$ .01	$ .03
Cedeno, Andujar	93TSC	207	$ .01	$ .10
Cedeno, Cesar	71T	237	$1.00	$4.00
Cedeno, Cesar	72T	65	$ .25	$1.00
Cedeno, Cesar	73T	290	$ .10	$ .40
Cedeno, Cesar	74T	200	$ .20	$ .80
Cedeno, Cesar	74TAS	331	$ .10	$ .40
Cedeno, Cesar	75T	590	$ .15	$ .60
Cedeno, Cesar	76T	460	$ .10	$ .40
Cedeno, Cesar	77T	90	$ .05	$ .20
Cedeno, Cesar	78T	650	$ .04	$ .16
Cedeno, Cesar	79T	570	$ .05	$ .20
Cedeno, Cesar	80T	370	$ .01	$ .10
Cedeno, Cesar	81T	190	$ .01	$ .08
Cedeno, Cesar	82T	640	$ .01	$ .08
Cedeno, Cesar	82TTR	19	$ .01	$ .10
Cedeno, Cesar	83T	351	$ .01	$ .08
Cedeno, Cesar	83T	475	$ .01	$ .08
Cedeno, Cesar	84T	705	$ .01	$ .10
Cedeno, Cesar	84T	725	$ .01	$ .06

TOPPS

Player	Year	No.	VG	EX/MT
Cedeno, Cesar	85T	54	$.01	$.06
Cedeno, Cesar	86T	224	$.01	$.05
Cepeda, Orlando	58T	343	$20.00	$80.00
Cepeda, Orlando	59T	390	$5.50	$22.00
Cepeda, Orlando	59TAS	553	$6.00	$24.00
Cepeda, Orlando	60T	450	$4.50	$18.00
Cepeda, Orlando	61T	435	$2.75	$11.00
Cepeda, Orlando	62T	40	$2.00	$8.00
Cepeda, Orlando	62T	54	$2.00	$8.00
Cepeda, Orlando	62T	401	$10.00	$40.00
Cepeda, Orlando	62TAS	390	$2.00	$8.00
Cepeda, Orlando	63T	3	$5.50	$22.00
Cepeda, Orlando	63T	520	$5.50	$22.00
Cepeda, Orlando	64T	9	$4.00	$16.00
Cepeda, Orlando	64T	306	$6.50	$26.00
Cepeda, Orlando	64T	390	$2.00	$8.00
Cepeda, Orlando	65T	4	$2.00	$8.00
Cepeda, Orlando	65T	360	$1.75	$7.00
Cepeda, Orlando	66T	132	$1.25	$5.00
Cepeda, Orlando	67T	20	$2.00	$8.00
Cepeda, Orlando	68T	3	$1.75	$7.00
Cepeda, Orlando	68T	200	$1.00	$4.00
Cepeda, Orlando	68TAS	362	$.75	$3.00
Cepeda, Orlando	69T	385	$.90	$3.60
Cepeda, Orlando	70T	555	$1.25	$5.00
Cepeda, Orlando	71T	605	$1.50	$6.00
Cepeda, Orlando	72T	195	$.75	$3.00
Cepeda, Orlando	73T	545	$1.00	$4.00
Cepeda, Orlando	74T	83	$.35	$1.40
Cepeda, Orlando	75T	205	$.25	$1.00
Cerone, Rick	77T	476	$7.50	$30.00
Cerone, Rick	78T	469	$.04	$.16
Cerone, Rick	79T	152	$.03	$.12
Cerone, Rick	80T	591	$.01	$.10
Cerone, Rick	81T	335	$.01	$.08
Cerone, Rick	82T	45	$.01	$.08
Cerone, Rick	83T	254	$.01	$.08
Cerone, Rick	84T	617	$.01	$.06
Cerone, Rick	85T	429	$.01	$.06
Cerone, Rick	85TTR	20	$.01	$.10
Cerone, Rick	86T	747	$.01	$.05
Cerone, Rick	86TTR	22	$.01	$.06
Cerone, Rick	87T	129	$.01	$.04
Cerone, Rick	87TTR	21	$.01	$.05
Cerone, Rick	88T	561	$.01	$.04
Cerone, Rick	88TTR	27	$.01	$.05
Cerone, Rick	89T	96	$.01	$.03
Cerone, Rick	90T	303	$.01	$.03
Cerone, Rick	90TTR	21	$.01	$.05
Cerone, Rick	91T	237	$.01	$.03
Cerone, Rick	91TSC	511	$.05	$.25
Cerone, Rick	91TTR	21	$.01	$.05
Cerone, Rick	92T	643	$.01	$.03
Cerone, Rick	92TSC	705	$.01	$.10
Cerutti, John	86TTR	23	$.01	$.10
Corutti, John	87T	557	$.01	$.04
Cerutti, John	88T	191	$.01	$.04
Cerutti, John	89T	347	$.01	$.03
Cerutti, John	90T	211	$.01	$.03
Cerutti, John	91T	687	$.01	$.03
Cerutti, John	91TSC	445	$.05	$.25
Cerutti, John	92T	487	$.01	$.03
Cerutti, John	92TSC	71	$.01	$.10
Cerv, Bob	53T	210	$7.00	$28.00
Cerv, Bob	56T	288	$6.00	$24.00
Cerv, Bob	57T	269	$5.00	$20.00
Cerv, Bob	58T	329	$1.25	$5.00
Cerv, Bob	59T	100	$1.50	$6.00
Cerv, Bob	60T	415	$.75	$3.00
Cerv, Bob	61T	563	$9.00	$36.00
Cerv, Bob	62T	169	$.60	$2.40
Cerv, Bob	91TA53	210	$.01	$.15
Cey, Ron	72T	761	$6.00	$24.00
Cey, Ron	73T	615	$120.00	$480.00
Cey, Ron	74T	315	$.25	$1.00
Cey, Ron	75T	390	$.20	$.80
Cey, Ron	76T	370	$.15	$.60
Cey, Ron	77T	50	$.10	$.40
Cey, Ron	78T	630	$.10	$.40
Cey, Ron	79T	190	$.10	$.40
Cey, Ron	80T	510	$.05	$.20
Cey, Ron	81T	260	$.05	$.20
Cey, Ron	82T	410	$.01	$.08
Cey, Ron	82TSA	411	$.01	$.07
Cey, Ron	83T	15	$.01	$.08
Cey, Ron	83TTR	19	$.01	$.10
Cey, Ron	84T	357	$.01	$.06
Cey, Ron	85T	768	$.01	$.06
Cey, Ron	86T	669	$.01	$.05
Cey, Ron	87T	767	$.01	$.04
Cey, Ron	87TTR	22	$.01	$.05
Chacon, Elio	60T	543	$2.75	$11.00
Chacon, Elio	62T	256	$.75	$3.00
Chakales, Bob	52T	120	$7.00	$28.00
Chakales, Bob	57T	261	$2.00	$8.00
Chalk, Dave	74T	597	$.15	$.60
Chalk, Dave	75T	64	$.10	$.40
Chalk, Dave	76T	52	$.05	$.25
Chalk, Dave	77T	315	$.05	$.20
Chalk, Dave	78T	178	$.04	$.16
Chalk, Dave	79T	682	$.03	$.12
Chalk, Dave	80T	261	$.01	$.10
Chalk, Dave	82T	462	$.01	$.08
Chamberlain, Craig	80T	417	$.01	$.10
Chamberlain, Craig	81T	274	$.01	$.08
Chamberlain, Wes	91T	603	$.05	$.20
Chamberlain, Wes	91TSC	317	$.10	$1.00
Chamberlain, Wes	92T	14	$.01	$.15
Chamberlain, Wes	92TSC	396	$.01	$.10
Chamberlain, Wes	93T	154	$.01	$.03
Chamberlain, Wes	93TSC	34	$.01	$.10
Chambers, Al	85T	277	$.01	$.06
Chambers, Cliff	51Trb	25	$1.65	$6.60
Chambers, Cliff	52T	68	$13.75	$55.00
Chambliss, Chris	72T	142	$.75	$3.00
Chambliss, Chris	73T	11	$.20	$.80
Chambliss, Chris	74T	384	$.25	$1.00
Chambliss, Chris	75T	585	$.15	$.60
Chambliss, Chris	76T	65	$.10	$.40
Chambliss, Chris	77T	220	$.05	$.20
Chambliss, Chris	78T	485	$.05	$.20
Chambliss, Chris	79T	335	$.05	$.20
Chambliss, Chris	80T	625	$.01	$.10
Chambliss, Chris	81T	155	$.01	$.08
Chambliss, Chris	82T	320	$.01	$.08
Chambliss, Chris	82TSA	321	$.01	$.07
Chambliss, Chris	83T	792	$.05	$.20
Chambliss, Chris	84T	50	$.01	$.06
Chambliss, Chris	85T	518	$.01	$.06
Chambliss, Chris	86T	293	$.01	$.05
Chambliss, Chris	87T	777	$.01	$.04
Champarino, Scott	93T	64	$.01	$.03
Champion, Billy	70T	149	$.20	$.80
Champion, Billy	71T	323	$.25	$1.00
Champion, Billy	72T	599	$.40	$1.60
Champion, Billy	73T	74	$.10	$.40
Champion, Billy	74T	391	$.10	$.40
Champion, Billy	75T	256	$.10	$.40
Champion, Billy	76T	501	$.05	$.25
Champion, Mike	77T	494	$.35	$1.40
Champion, Mike	78T	683	$.04	$.16
Championship, A.L.	75T	459	$.25	$1.00
Championship, A.L.	77T	276	$.10	$.40
Championship, A.L.	78T	411	$.15	$.60
Championship, A.L.	81T	401	$.10	$1.00
Championship, N.L.	75T	460	$.25	$1.00
Championship, N.L.	77T	277	$.25	$1.00
Championship, N.L.	78T	412	$.10	$.40
Championship, N.L.	81T	402	$.05	$.20
Chance, Bob	64T	146	$16.25	$65.00

TOPPS

Player	Year	No.	VG	EX/MT
Chance, Bob	65T	224	$ .50	$2.00
Chance, Bob	66T	564	$7.00	$28.00
Chance, Bob	67T	349	$ .60	$2.40
Chance, Bob	69T	523	$ .40	$1.60
Chance, Dean	62T	194	$ .75	$3.00
Chance, Dean	63T	6	$1.25	$5.00
Chance, Dean	63T	355	$1.00	$4.00
Chance, Dean	64T	32	$ .75	$3.00
Chance, Dean	65T	7	$ .75	$3.00
Chance, Dean	65T	9	$ .75	$3.00
Chance, Dean	65T	11	$ .75	$3.00
Chance, Dean	65T	140	$ .35	$1.40
Chance, Dean	66T	340	$ .50	$2.00
Chance, Dean	67T	380	$ .60	$2.40
Chance, Dean	68T	10	$ .75	$3.00
Chance, Dean	68T	12	$ .55	$2.20
Chance, Dean	68T	255	$ .35	$1.40
Chance, Dean	69T	620	$ .40	$1.60
Chance, Dean	70T	625	$ .50	$2.00
Chance, Dean	71T	36	$ .25	$1.00
Chaney, Darrel	69T	624	$ .75	$3.00
Chaney, Darrel	70T	3	$ .20	$ .80
Chaney, Darrel	71T	632	$1.00	$4.00
Chaney, Darrel	72T	136	$ .10	$ .40
Chaney, Darrel	73T	507	$ .25	$1.00
Chaney, Darrel	74T	559	$ .10	$ .40
Chaney, Darrel	75T	581	$ .10	$ .40
Chaney, Darrel	76T	259	$ .05	$ .25

Chaney, Darrel	**76TTR**	**259**	**$ .05**	**$ .25**
Chaney, Darrel	77T	384	$ .05	$ .20
Chaney, Darrel	78T	443	$ .04	$ .16
Chaney, Darrel	79T	184	$ .03	$ .12
Chapman, Ben	52T	391	$43.75	$175.00
Chapman, Kelvin	85T	751	$ .01	$ .06
Chapman, Kelvin	86T	492	$ .01	$ .05
Chapman, Sam	51Tbb	52	$11.25	$45.00
Chappas, Harry	80T	347	$ .01	$ .10
Charboneau, Joe	81T	13	$ .01	$ .08
Charboneau, Joe	82T	630	$ .01	$ .08
Charles, Ed	62T	595	$5.25	$21.00
Charles, Ed	63T	67	$ .50	$2.00
Charles, Ed	64T	475	$1.00	$4.00
Charles, Ed	65T	35	$ .35	$1.40

Player	Year	No.	VG	EX/MT
Charles, Ed	66T	422	$ .65	$2.60
Charles, Ed	67T	182	$ .40	$1.60
Charles, Ed	68T	563	$ .70	$2.80
Charles, Ed	69T	245	$ .50	$2.00
Charlton, Norm	89T	737	$ .05	$ .25
Charlton, Norm	90T	289	$ .01	$ .10
Charlton, Norm	91T	309	$ .01	$ .03
Charlton, Norm	91TSC	305	$ .05	$ .25
Charlton, Norm	92T	649	$ .01	$ .03
Charlton, Norm	92TSC	530	$ .01	$ .10
Charlton, Norm	93T	57	$ .01	$ .03
Charton, Pete	64T	459	$1.00	$4.00
Charton, Pete	66T	329	$ .50	$2.00
Chavarria, Ossie	67T	344	$ .60	$2.40
Checklist, Cards (1-88)	58T	71	$8.00	$32.00
Checklist, Cards (89-176)	58T	134	$3.50	$14.00
Checklist, Cards (177-264)	58T	158	$3.50	$14.00
Checklist, Cards (89-176)	58T	174	$3.50	$14.00
Checklist, Cards (177-264)	58T	216	$3.50	$14.00
Checklist, Cards (177-264)	58T	246	$12.50	$50.00
Checklist, Cards (265-362)	58T	256	$3.50	$14.00
Checklist, Cards (353-440)	58T	312	$3.50	$14.00
Checklist, Cards (265-352)	58T	327	$3.50	$14.00
Checklist, Cards (265-352)	58T	341	$3.50	$14.00
Checklist, Cards (1-88)	59T	8	$9.00	$36.00
Checklist, Cards (1-88)	59T	48	$5.00	$20.00
Checklist, Cards (89-176)	59T	69	$5.00	$20.00
Checklist, Cards (89-176)	59T	94	$5.00	$20.00
Checklist, Cards (89-176)	59T	111	$3.00	$12.00
Checklist, Cards (177-242)	59T	172	$2.50	$10.00
Checklist, Cards (265-352)	59T	223	$2.50	$10.00
Checklist, Cards (177-264)	59T	248	$2.50	$10.00
Checklist, Cards (265-352)	59T	304	$2.50	$10.00
Checklist, Cards (353-429)	59T	329	$2.50	$10.00
Checklist, Cards (430-495)	59T	397	$2.50	$10.00
Checklist, Cards (353-429)	59T	419	$2.50	$10.00
Checklist, Cards (430-495)	59T	457	$5.00	$20.00
Checklist, Cards (496-572)	59T	476	$2.50	$10.00
Checklist, Cards (496-572)	59T	510	$18.75	$75.00
Checklist, Cards (496-572)	59T	528	$11.25	$45.00
Checklist, Cards (1-88)	60T	18	$5.50	$22.00
Checklist, Cards (1-88)	60T	43	$2.00	$8.00
Checklist, Cards (89-176)	60T	72	$2.00	$8.00
Checklist, Cards (177-264)	60T	151	$2.00	$58.00
Checklist, Cards (177-264)	60T	164	$2.00	$8.00
Checklist, Cards (89-176)	60T	174	$2.00	$8.00
Checklist, Cards (177-264)	60T	208	$2.00	$8.00
Checklist, Cards (265-352)	60T	242	$2.00	$8.00
Checklist, Cards (353-429)	60T	302	$2.00	$8.00
Checklist, Cards (265-332)	60T	332	$7.50	$30.00
Checklist, Cards (353-429)	60T	381	$2.00	$8.00
Checklist, Cards (430-495)	60T	413	$2.00	$8.00
Checklist, Cards (430-495)	60T	484	$6.25	$25.00
Checklist, Cards (496-572)	60T	494	$3.50	$14.00
Checklist, Cards (496-572)	60T	513	$8.00	$32.00
Checklist, Cards (496-572)	60T	537	$8.00	$32.00
Checklist, Cards (1-88)	61T	17	$2.50	$10.00
Checklist, Cards (89-176)	61T	98	$2.50	$10.00
Checklist, Cards (177-264)	61T	189	$2.50	$10.00
Checklist, Cards (265-352)	61T	273	$2.50	$10.00
Checklist, Cards (353-429)	61T	361	$2.50	$10.00
Checklist, Cards (430-506)	61T	437	$3.50	$14.00
Checklist, Cards (507-587)	61T	516	$3.50	$14.00
Checklist, Cards (1-88)	62T	22	$2.50	$10.00
Checklist, Cards (89-176)	62T	98	$2.50	$10.00
Checklist, Cards (177-264)	62T	192	$2.50	$10.00
Checklist, Cards (265-352)	62T	277	$2.50	$10.00
Checklist, Cards (353-429)	62T	367	$2.50	$10.00
Checklist, Cards (430-506)	62T	441	$3.50	$14.00
Checklist, Cards (507-598)	62T	516	$3.50	$14.00
Checklist, Cards (1-88)	63T	79	$2.25	$9.00
Checklist, Cards (89-176)	63T	102	$2.25	$9.00
Checklist, Cards (177-264)	63T	191	$2.25	$9.00
Checklist, Cards (265-352)	63T	274	$2.25	$9.00
Checklist, Cards (353-429)	63T	362	$2.25	$9.00

TOPPS

Player	Year	No.	VG	EX/MT
Checklist, Cards (430-506)	63T	431	$2.25	$9.00
Checklist, Cards (507-576)	63T	509	$5.00	$20.00
Checklist, Cards (1-88)	64T	76	$2.50	$10.00
Checklist, Cards (89-176)	64T	102	$2.50	$10.00
Checklist, Cards (177-264)	64T	188	$2.50	$10.00
Checklist, Cards (265-352)	64T	274	$2.50	$10.00
Checklist, Cards (353-429)	64T	362	$2.50	$10.00
Checklist, Cards (430-506)	64T	438	$3.75	$15.00
Checklist, Cards (507-587)	64T	517	$3.75	$15.00
Checklist, Cards (1-88)	65T	79	$2.25	$9.00
Checklist, Cards (89-176)	65T	104	$2.25	$9.00
Checklist, Cards (177-264)	65T	189	$2.25	$9.00
Checklist, Cards (265-352)	65T	273	$2.25	$9.00
Checklist, Cards (353-429)	65T	361	$1.50	$6.00
Checklist, Cards (430-506)	65T	443	$2.50	$10.00
Checklist, Cards (507-598)	65T	508	$2.50	$10.00
Checklist, Cards (1-88)	66T	34	$2.00	$8.00
Checklist, Cards (89-176)	66T	101	$2.00	$8.00
Checklist, Cards (177-264)	66T	183	$2.00	$8.00
Checklist, Cards (265-352)	66T	279	$2.00	$8.00
Checklist, Cards (353-429)	66T	363	$2.25	$9.00
Checklist, Cards (430-506)	66T	444	$2.25	$9.00
Checklist, Cards (507-598)	66T	517	$3.75	$15.00
Checklist, Cards (1-109)	67T	62	$1.50	$6.00
Checklist, Cards (110-196)	67T	103	$2.25	$9.00
Checklist, Cards (197-283)	67T	191	$1.75	$7.00
Checklist, Cards (284-370)	67T	278	$1.50	$6.00
Checklist, Cards (371-457)	67T	361	$1.50	$6.00
Checklist, Cards (458-533)	67T	454	$2.00	$8.00
Checklist, Cards (534-609)	67T	531	$3.00	$12.00
Checklist, Cards (1-109)	68T	67	$1.25	$5.00
Checklist, Cards (110-196)	68T	107	$1.25	$5.00
Checklist, Cards (197-283)	68T	192	$1.75	$7.00
Checklist, Cards (284-370)	68T	278	$1.25	$5.00
Checklist, Cards (371-457)	68T	356	$1.25	$5.00
Checklist, Cards (458-533)	68T	454	$1.75	$7.00
Checklist, Cards (534 -598)	68T	518	$2.00	$8.00
Checklist, Cards (1-109)	69T	57	$1.25	$5.00
Checklist, Cards (110-218)	69T	107	$1.25	$5.00
Checklist, Cards (219-327)	69T	214	$1.25	$5.00
Checklist, Cards (328-425)	69T	314	$1.25	$5.00
Checklist, Cards (426-512)	69T	412	$2.00	$8.00
Checklist, Cards (513-588)	69T	504	$1.50	$6.00
Checklist, Cards (589-664)	69T	582	$1.25	$5.00
Checklist, Cards (1-132)	70T	9	$1.25	$5.00
Checklist, Cards (133-263)	70T	128	$1.25	$5.00
Checklist, Cards (264-372)	70T	244	$1.25	$5.00
Checklist, Cards (373-459)	70T	343	$1.25	$5.00
Checklist, Cards (460-546)	70T	432	$1.25	$5.00
Checklist, Cards (547 -633)	70T	542	$1.25	$5.00
Checklist, Cards (634-720)	70T	588	$1.25	$5.00
Checklist, Cards (1-132)	71T	54	$1.25	$5.00
Checklist, Cards (122-263)	71T	123	$1.25	$5.00
Checklist, Cards (264-393)	71T	206	$1.25	$5.00
Checklist, Cards (394-523)	71T	369	$1.25	$5.00
Checklist, Cards (524-040)	71T	499	$1.25	$5.00
Checklist, Cards (644-752)	71T	619	$1.25	$5.00
Checklist, Cards (1-132)	72T	4	$1.00	$4.00
Checklist, Cards (133-263)	72T	103	$1.00	$4.00
Checklist, Cards (264-394)	72T	251	$1.00	$4.00
Checklist, Cards (395-525)	72T	378	$1.00	$4.00
Checklist, Cards (526-656)	72T	478	$1.00	$4.00
Checklist, Cards (657-787)	72T	604	$2.00	$8.00
Checklist, Cards (1-132)	73T	54	$.55	$2.20
Checklist, Cards (133-264)	73T	103	$.55	$2.20
Checklist, Cards (265-396)	73T	338	$.55	$2.20
Checklist, Cards (397-528)	73T	453	$.55	$2.20
Checklist, Cards (529-660)	73T	588	$5.00	$20.00
Checklist, Cards (1-132)	74T	126	$.50	$2.00
Checklist, Cards (133-264)	74T	263	$.50	$2.00
Checklist, Cards (265-396)	74T	273	$.50	$2.00
Checklist, Cards (397-528)	74T	414	$.50	$2.00
Checklist, Cards (529-660)	74T	637	$.50	$2.00
Checklist, Cards Traded	74TTR	0	$.25	$1.00
Checklist, Cards (1-132)	75T	126	$.50	$2.00
Checklist, Cards (133-264)	75T	257	$.50	$2.00
Checklist, Cards (265-396)	75T	386	$.50	$2.00
Checklist, Cards (397-528)	75T	517	$.50	$2.00
Checklist, Cards (529-660)	75T	646	$.50	$2.00
Checklist, Cards (1-132)	76T	119	$.35	$1.40
Checklist, Cards (133-264)	76T	262	$.35	$1.40
Checklist, Cards (265-396)	76T	392	$.35	$1.40
Checklist, Cards (397-528)	76T	526	$.35	$1.40
Checklist, Cards (529-660)	76T	643	$.35	$1.40
Checklist, Cards Traded	76TTR	0	$.25	$1.00
Checklist, Cards (1-132)	77T	32	$.25	$1.00
Checklist, Cards (133-264)	77T	208	$.25	$1.00
Checklist, Cards (265-396)	77T	356	$.25	$1.00
Checklist, Cards (397-528)	77T	451	$.25	$1.00
Checklist, Cards (529-660)	77T	562	$.25	$1.00
Checklist, Cards (1-121)	78T	74	$.25	$1.00
Checklist, Cards (122-242)	78T	184	$.25	$1.00
Checklist, Cards (243-363)	78T	289	$.25	$1.00
Checklist, Cards (364-484)	78T	435	$.25	$1.00
Checklist, Cards (485-605)	78T	535	$.25	$1.00
Checklist, Cards (606-726)	78T	652	$.25	$1.00
Checklist, Cards (1-121)	79T	121	$.05	$.20
Checklist, Cards (122-242)	79T	241	$.05	$.20
Checklist, Cards (243-363)	79T	353	$.20	$.80
Checklist, Cards (364-484)	79T	483	$.05	$.20
Checklist, Cards (485-605)	79T	602	$.20	$.80
Checklist, Cards (606-726)	79T	669	$.20	$.80
Checklist, Cards (1-121)	80T	121	$.10	$.50
Checklist, Cards (122-242)	80T	241	$.10	$.50
Checklist, Cards (243-363)	80T	348	$.10	$.50
Checklist, Cards (364-484)	80T	484	$.10	$.50
Checklist, Cards (485-605)	80T	533	$.10	$.50
Checklist, Cards (606-726)	80T	646	$.10	$.50
Checklist, Cards (1-121)	81T	31	$.01	$.15
Checklist, Cards (122-242)	81T	241	$.01	$.15
Checklist, Cards (243-363)	81T	338	$.05	$.25
Checklist, Cards (364-484)	81T	446	$.05	$.25
Checklist, Cards (485-605)	81T	562	$.05	$.25
Checklist, Cards (606-726)	81T	638	$.05	$.25
Checklist, Cards (727-858)	81TTR	858	$.10	$.50
Checklist, Cards (1-132)	82T	129	$.01	$.15
Checklist, Cards (133-264)	82T	226	$.01	$.15
Checklist, Cards (265-396)	82T	394	$.01	$.15
Checklist, Cards (397-528)	82T	491	$.01	$.15
Checklist, Cards (529-660)	82T	634	$.01	$.15
Checklist, Cards (661-792)	82T	789	$.01	$.15
Checklist, Cards (1T-132T)	82TTR	132	$.10	$.50
Checklist, Cards (1-132)	83T	129	$.01	$.15
Checklist, Cards (133-264)	83T	249	$.01	$.15
Checklist, Cards (265-396)	83T	349	$.01	$.15
Checklist, Cards (397-528)	83T	526	$.01	$.15
Checklist, Cards (529-660)	83T	642	$.01	$.15
Checklist, Cards (661-792)	83T	769	$.01	$.15
Checklist, Cards (1T-132T)	83TTR	132	$.10	$.50
Checklist, Cards (1-132)	84T	114	$.01	$.10
Checklist, Cards (133-264)	84T	233	$.01	$.10
Checklist, Cards (133-264)	84T	379	$.01	$.10
Checklist, Cards (397-528)	84T	527	$.01	$.10
Checklist, Cards (529-660)	84T	646	$.01	$.10
Checklist, Cards (661-792)	84T	781	$.01	$.10
Checklist, Cards (1T-132T)	84TTR	132	$.05	$.25
Checklist, Cards (1-132)	85T	121	$.01	$.10
Checklist, Cards (133-264)	85T	261	$.01	$.10
Checklist, Cards (265-396)	85T	377	$.01	$.10
Checklist, Cards (397-528)	85T	527	$.01	$.10
Checklist, Cards (529-660)	85T	659	$.01	$.10
Checklist, Cards (661-792)	85T	784	$.01	$.10
Checklist, Cards (1T-132T)	85TTR	132	$.05	$.20
Checklist, Cards (1-132)	86T	131	$.01	$.10
Checklist, Cards (133-264)	86T	263	$.01	$.10
Checklist, Cards (265-396)	86T	394	$.01	$.10
Checklist, Cards (397-528)	86T	527	$.01	$.10
Checklist, Cards (529-660)	86T	659	$.01	$.10
Checklist, Cards (661-792)	86T	791	$.01	$.10
Checklist, Cards (1T-132T)	86TTR	132	$.05	$.25

TOPPS

Player	Year	No.	VG	EX/MT
Checklist, Cards (1-132)	87T	128	$ .01	$ .04
Checklist, Cards (133-264)	87T	264	$ .01	$ .04
Checklist, Cards (265-396)	87T	392	$ .01	$ .04
Checklist, Cards (397-528)	87T	522	$ .01	$ .04
Checklist, Cards (529-660)	87T	654	$ .01	$ .04
Checklist, Cards (661-792)	87T	792	$ .01	$ .04
Checklist, Cards (1T-132T)	87TTR	132	$ .05	$ .20
Checklist, Cards (1-132)	88T	121	$ .01	$ .04
Checklist, Cards (133-264)	88T	253	$ .01	$ .04
Checklist, Cards (265-396)	88T	373	$ .01	$ .04
Checklist, Cards (397-528)	88T	528	$ .01	$ .04
Checklist, Cards (529-660)	88T	646	$ .01	$ .04
Checklist, Cards (661-792)	88T	776	$ .01	$ .04
Checklist, Cards (1T-132T)	88TTR	132	$ .01	$ .05
Checklist, Cards (1-132)	89T	118	$ .01	$ .03
Checklist, Cards (133-264)	89T	258	$ .01	$ .03
Checklist, Cards (265-396)	89T	378	$ .01	$ .03
Checklist, Cards (397-528)	89T	524	$ .01	$ .03
Checklist, Cards (529-660)	89T	619	$ .01	$ .03
Checklist, Cards (661-792)	89T	782	$ .01	$ .03
Checklist, Cards (1T-132T)	89TTR	132	$ .01	$ .05
Checklist, Cards (1-132)	90T	128	$ .01	$ .03
Checklist, Cards (133-264)	90T	262	$ .01	$ .03
Checklist, Cards (265-396)	90T	376	$ .01	$ .03
Checklist, Cards (397-528)	90T	526	$ .01	$ .03
Checklist, Cards (529-660)	90T	646	$ .01	$ .03
Checklist, Cards (661-792)	90T	783	$ .01	$ .03
Checklist, Cards (1T-132T)	90TTR	132	$ .01	$ .05
Checklist, Cards (1-132)	91T	131	$ .01	$ .03
Checklist, Cards (133-264)	91T	263	$ .01	$ .03
Checklist, Cards (265-396)	91T	366	$ .01	$ .03
Checklist, Cards (397-528)	91T	527	$ .01	$ .03
Checklist, Cards (529-660)	91T	656	$ .01	$ .03
Checklist, Cards (661-792)	91T	787	$ .01	$ .03
Checklist, Cards (1-140)	91TA53	335	$ .05	$ .20
Checklist, Cards (141-280)	91TA53	336	$ .05	$ .20
Checklist, Cards (281-337)	91TA53	337	$ .05	$ .20
Checklist, Cards (1-100)	91TSC	298	$ .05	$ .25
Checklist, Cards (101-200)	91TSC	299	$ .05	$ .25
Checklist, Cards (201-300)	91TSC	300	$ .05	$ .25
Checklist, Cards (301-400)	91TSC	598	$ .05	$ .25
Checklist, Cards (401-500)	91TSC	599	$ .05	$ .25
Checklist, Cards (501-600)	91TSC	600	$ .05	$ .25
Checklist, Cards (1T-132T)	91TTR	132	$ .01	$ .05
Checklist, Cards (1-132)	92T	131	$ .01	$ .03
Checklist, Cards (133-264)	92T	264	$ .01	$ .03
Checklist, Cards (265-396)	92T	366	$ .01	$ .03
Checklist, Cards (397-528)	92T	527	$ .01	$ .03
Checklist, Cards (529-660)	92T	658	$ .01	$ .03
Checklist, Cards (661-792)	92T	787	$ .01	$ .03
Checklist, Cards (1-100)	92TSC	298	$ .01	$ .10
Checklist, Cards (101-200)	92TSC	299	$ .01	$ .10
Checklist, Cards (201-300)	92TSC	300	$ .01	$ .10
Checklist, Cards (301-400)	92TSC	588	$ .01	$ .10
Checklist, Cards (401-500)	92TSC	589	$ .01	$ .10
Checklist, Cards (501-600)	92TSC	590	$ .01	$ .10
Checklist, Cards (601-700)	92TSC	898	$ .01	$ .10
Checlist, Cards (701-800)	92TSC	899	$ .01	$ .10
Checklist, Cards (801-900)	92TSC	900	$ .01	$ .10
Checklist, Cards (1T-132T)	92TTR	132	$ .01	$ .05
Checklist, Cards (1-132)	93T	394	$ .01	$ .03
Checklist, Cards (133-264)	93T	395	$ .01	$ .03
Checklist, Cards (265-396)	93T	396	$ .01	$ .03
Checklist, Cards (397-540)	93T	823	$ .01	$ .03
Checklist, Cards (541-691)	93T	824	$ .01	$ .03
Checklist, Cards (692-825)	93T	825	$ .01	$ .03
Checklist, Cards (1-100)	93TSC	288	$ .01	$ .10
Checklist, Cards (101-200)	93TSC	289	$ .01	$ .10
Checklist, Cards (201-300)	93TSC	290	$ .01	$ .10
Checklist, Coins (1-161)	71T	161	$1.25	$5.00
Cheney, Tom	57T	359	$2.00	$8.00
Cheney, Tom	61T	494	$1.35	$5.40
Chesbro, Jack	61T	407	$1.00	$4.00
Chesbro, Jack	79TRH	416	$ .05	$ .20
Chiamparino, Scott	91T	676	$ .01	$ .15
Chiamparino, Scott	91TSC	384	$ .05	$ .25
Chiamparino, Scott	92T	277	$ .01	$ .03
Chiamparino, Scott	92TSC	896	$ .01	$ .10
Chiamparino, Scott	93T	711	$ .01	$ .03
Chiffer, Floyd	83T	298	$ .01	$ .08
Childress, Rocky	88T	643	$ .01	$ .04
Chiles, Rich	72T	56	$ .10	$ .40
Chiles, Rich	73T	617	$ .60	$2.40
Chiles, Rich	78T	193	$ .04	$ .16
Chiles, Rich	79T	498	$ .03	$ .12
Chipman, Bob	52T	388	$43.75	$175.00
Chiti, Harry	56T	179	$2.50	$10.00
Chiti, Harry	58T	119	$1.25	$5.00
Chiti, Harry	59T	79	$1.50	$6.00
Chiti, Harry	60T	339	$ .75	$3.00
Chiti, Harry	61T	269	$ .60	$2.40
Chiti, Harry	62T	253	$ .75	$3.00
Chitren, Steve	92T	379	$ .01	$ .03
Chitren, Steve	92TSC	518	$ .01	$ .10
Chittum, Nelson	60T	296	$ .75	$3.00
Chlupsa, Bob	71T	594	$1.25	$5.00
Chris, Mike	80T	666	$ .01	$ .10
Chrisley, Neil	57T	320	$5.00	$20.00
Chrisley, Neil	58T	303	$1.25	$5.00
Chrisley, Neil	59T	189	$1.00	$4.00
Chrisley, Neil	60T	273	$ .75	$3.00
Chrisley, Neil	62T	308	$ .75	$3.00
Christensen, John	86T	287	$ .01	$ .05
Christensen, John	87TTR	23	$ .01	$ .05
Christensen, John	88T	413	$ .01	$ .04
Christenson, Larry	74T	587	$ .10	$ .40
Christenson, Larry	75T	551	$ .10	$ .40
Christenson, Larry	76T	634	$ .05	$ .25
Christenson, Larry	77T	59	$ .05	$ .20
Christenson, Larry	78T	247	$ .04	$ .16
Christenson, Larry	79T	493	$ .03	$ .12
Christenson, Larry	80T	161	$ .01	$ .10
Christenson, Larry	81T	346	$ .01	$ .08
Christenson, Larry	82T	544	$ .01	$ .08
Christenson, Larry	83T	668	$ .01	$ .08
Christenson, Larry	84T	252	$ .01	$ .06
Christian, Bob	69T	173	$ .35	$1.40
Christian, Bob	70T	51	$ .20	$ .80
Christian, Eddie	93T	683	$ .05	$ .20
Christiansen, Clay	85T	211	$ .01	$ .06
Christopher, Joe	61T	82	$ .60	$2.40
Christopher, Joe	63T	217	$ .90	$3.60
Christopher, Joe	64T	546	$2.25	$9.00
Christopher, Joe	65T	495	$1.25	$5.00
Christopher, Joe	66T	343	$ .50	$2.00
Christopher, Mike	92TSC	612	$ .01	$ .15
Christopher, Mike	93T	786	$ .05	$ .20
Church, Bubba	52T	323	$43.75	$175.00
Church, Bubba	53T	47	$4.00	$16.00
Church, Bubba	91TA53	47	$ .01	$ .15
Cianfrocco, Archi	92TSC	802	$ .05	$ .20
Cianfrocco, Archi	92TTR	23	$ .01	$ .15
Cianfrocco, Archi	93T	151	$ .01	$ .10
Ciardi, Mark	88T	417	$ .01	$ .04
Cias, Darryl	84T	159	$ .01	$ .06
Cicotte, Al	57T	398	$1.75	$7.00
Cicotte, Al	58T	382	$1.00	$4.00
Cicotte, Al	59T	57	$1.50	$6.00
Cicotte, Al	60T	473	$1.25	$5.00
Cicotte, Al	61T	241	$ .60	$2.40
Cicotte, Al	62T	126	$ .60	$2.40
Cimino, Pete	66T	563	$3.75	$15.00
Cimino, Pete	67T	34	$ .40	$1.60
Cimino, Pete	68T	143	$ .35	$1.40
Cimoli, Gino	57T	319	$5.50	$22.00
Cimoli, Gino	58T	286	$1.25	$5.00
Cimoli, Gino	59T	418	$1.00	$4.00
Cimoli, Gino	60T	58	$ .85	$3.40
Cimoli, Gino	61T	165	$ .60	$2.40
Cimoli, Gino	62T	402	$1.25	$5.00

TOPPS

Player	Year	No.	VG	EX/MT
Cimoli, Gino	63T	321	$ .90	$3.60
Cimoli, Gino	64T	26	$ .50	$2.00
Cimoli, Gino	65T	569	$2.50	$10.00
Cipriani, Frank	62T	333	$ .75	$3.00
Cisco, Galen	62T	301	$1.25	$5.00
Cisco, Galen	63T	93	$ .50	$2.00
Cisco, Galen	64T	202	$ .65	$2.60
Cisco, Galen	65T	364	$ .50	$2.00
Cisco, Galen	67T	596	$2.25	$9.00
Cisco, Galen	69T	211	$ .35	$1.40
Cisco, Galen	73T	593	$ .75	$3.00
Cisco, Galen	74T	166	$ .10	$ .40
Clancy, Jim	78T	496	$ .05	$ .20
Clancy, Jim	79T	131	$ .03	$ .12
Clancy, Jim	80T	249	$ .01	$ .10
Clancy, Jim	81T	19	$ .01	$ .08
Clancy, Jim	82T	665	$ .01	$ .08
Clancy, Jim	83T	345	$ .01	$ .08
Clancy, Jim	84T	575	$ .01	$ .06
Clancy, Jim	85T	746	$ .01	$ .06
Clancy, Jim	86T	412	$ .01	$ .05

Player	Year	No.	VG	EX/MT
Clancy, Jim	87T	122	$ .01	$ .04
Clancy, Jim	88T	54	$ .01	$ .04
Clancy, Jim	89T	219	$ .01	$ .03
Clancy, Jim	89TTR	19	$ .01	$ .05
Clancy, Jim	90T	648	$ .01	$ .03
Clancy, Jim	92T	279	$ .01	$ .03
Clark, Al	52T	278	$12.50	$50.00
Clark, Bob	80T	663	$ .10	$1.00
Clark, Bob	81T	288	$ .01	$ .08
Clark, Bob	82T	74	$ .01	$ .08
Clark, Bob	83T	184	$ .01	$ .08
Clark, Bob	84T	626	$ .01	$ .06
Clark, Bob	84TTR	24	$ .01	$ .15
Clark, Bob	85T	553	$ .01	$ .06
Clark, Bob	86T	452	$ .01	$ .05
Clark, Bryan	82T	632	$ .01	$ .08
Clark, Bryan	83T	789	$ .01	$ .08
Clark, Bryan	84T	22	$ .01	$ .06
Clark, Bryan	84TTR	25	$ .01	$ .15
Clark, Bryan	85T	489	$ .01	$ .06
Clark, Bryan	85TTR	21	$ .01	$ .10
Clark, Dave	88T	49	$ .01	$ .10

Player	Year	No.	VG	EX/MT
Clark, Dave	89T	574	$ .01	$ .03
Clark, Dave	90T	339	$ .01	$ .03
Clark, Dave	91T	241	$ .01	$ .03
Clark, Jack	77T	488	$2.50	$10.00
Clark, Jack	78T	384	$ .50	$2.00
Clark, Jack	79T	512	$ .20	$ .80
Clark, Jack	80T	167	$ .10	$1.00
Clark, Jack	81T	30	$ .10	$ .50
Clark, Jack	82T	460	$ .05	$ .35
Clark, Jack	83T	210	$ .05	$ .25
Clark, Jack	84T	690	$ .05	$ .25
Clark, Jack	85TTR	22	$ .05	$ .35
Clark, Jack	86T	350	$ .01	$ .10
Clark, Jack	87T	520	$ .01	$ .10
Clark, Jack	88T	100	$ .01	$ .10
Clark, Jack	88TAS	397	$ .01	$ .04
Clark, Jack	88TTR	28	$ .01	$ .10
Clark, Jack	89T	410	$ .01	$ .10
Clark, Jack	89TTR	20	$ .01	$ .10
Clark, Jack	90T	90	$ .01	$ .03
Clark, Jack	91T	650	$ .01	$ .03
Clark, Jack	91TSC	500	$ .05	$ .25
Clark, Jack	91TTR	22	$ .01	$ .05
Clark, Jack	92T	207	$ .01	$ .03
Clark, Jack	92TSC	186	$ .01	$ .10
Clark, Jack	93T	781	$ .01	$ .03
Clark, Jack	93TSC	20	$ .01	$ .10
Clark, Jerald	91T	513	$ .01	$ .03
Clark, Jerald	91TSC	468	$ .05	$ .25
Clark, Jerald	92T	749	$ .01	$ .03
Clark, Jerald	92TSC	149	$ .01	$ .10
Clark, Jerald	93T	194	$ .01	$ .03
Clark, Jerald	93T	565	$ .01	$ .03
Clark, Joe	85T	740	$ .01	$ .10
Clark, Mark	93T	339	$ .01	$ .10
Clark, Mark	93TSC	60	$ .01	$ .15
Clark, Mike	53T	193	$4.50	$18.00
Clark, Mike	91TA53	193	$ .01	$ .15
Clark, Phil	58T	423	$1.00	$4.00
Clark, Phil	59T	454	$1.00	$4.00
Clark, Phil	92TTR	24	$ .01	$ .05
Clark, Phil	93T	802	$ .01	$ .03
Clark, Rickey	70T	586	$ .50	$2.00
Clark, Rickey	71T	697	$1.50	$6.00
Clark, Rickey	72T	462	$ .25	$1.00
Clark, Rickey	73T	636	$ .60	$2.40
Clark, Ron	67T	137	$ .50	$2.00
Clark, Ron	68T	589	$ .70	$2.80
Clark, Ron	69T	561	$ .40	$1.60
Clark, Ron	70T	531	$ .35	$1.40
Clark, Terry	89T	129	$ .01	$ .03
Clark, Will	86TTR	24	$1.50	$6.00
Clark, Will	87T	420	$ .20	$2.00
Clark, Will	88T	350	$ .10	$ .50
Clark, Will	89T	660	$ .05	$ .35
Clark, Will	90T	100	$ .05	$ .25
Clark, Will	90TAS	397	$ .01	$ .15
Clark, Will	91T	500	$ .05	$ .20
Clark, Will	91TSC	5	$ .75	$3.00
Clark, Will	92T	330	$ .01	$ .15
Clark, Will	92TAS	386	$ .01	$ .10
Clark, Will	92TSC	460	$ .10	$ .75
Clark, Will	92TSC	598	$ .10	$ .50
Clark, Will	93T	10	$ .01	$ .10
Clarke, Horace	66T	547	$10.00	$40.00
Clarke, Horace	67T	169	$ .40	$1.60
Clarke, Horace	68T	263	$ .35	$1.40
Clarke, Horace	69T	87	$ .35	$1.40
Clarke, Horace	70T	623	$ .50	$2.00
Clarke, Horace	71T	715	$1.50	$6.00
Clarke, Horace	72T	387	$ .10	$ .40
Clarke, Horace	73T	198	$ .10	$ .40
Clarke, Horace	74T	529	$ .10	$ .40
Clarke, Stan	88T	556	$ .01	$ .04
Clary, Ellis	60T	470	$1.25	$5.00

TOPPS

Player	Year	No.	VG	EX/MT
Clary, Marty	90T	304	$ .01	$ .03
Clary, Marty	91T	582	$ .01	$ .03
Clay, Ken	78T	89	$ .04	$ .16
Clay, Ken	79T	434	$ .03	$ .12
Clay, Ken	80T	159	$ .01	$ .10
Clay, Ken	81T	305	$ .01	$ .08
Clay, Ken	81TTR	747	$ .01	$ .15
Clay, Ken	82T	649	$ .01	$ .08
Clayton, Royce	92T	786	$ .01	$ .15
Clayton, Royce	92TSC	630	$ .05	$ .35
Clayton, Royce	93T	542	$ .01	$ .10
Clayton, Royce	93TSC	39	$ .01	$ .15
Clear, Mark	80T	638	$ .01	$ .10
Clear, Mark	81T	12	$ .01	$ .08
Clear, Mark	81TTR	748	$ .01	$ .15
Clear, Mark	82T	421	$ .01	$ .08
Clear, Mark	83T	162	$ .01	$ .08
Clear, Mark	84T	577	$ .01	$ .06
Clear, Mark	85T	207	$ .01	$ .06
Clear, Mark	86T	349	$ .01	$ .05
Clear, Mark	86TTR	25	$ .01	$ .06
Clear, Mark	87T	640	$ .01	$ .04
Clear, Mark	88T	742	$ .01	$ .04
Clear, Mark	89T	63	$ .01	$ .03
Clemens, Doug	67T	489	$1.50	$6.00
Clemens, Roger	85T	181	$6.00	$24.00
Clemens, Roger	86T	661	$1.00	$4.00
Clemens, Roger	87T	340	$ .10	$1.00
Clemens, Roger	87TAS	614	$ .10	$ .50
Clemens, Roger	87TRB	1	$ .05	$ .25
Clemens, Roger	88T	70	$ .10	$ .50
Clemens, Roger	88TAS	394	$ .05	$ .20
Clemens, Roger	89T	450	$ .10	$ .40
Clemens, Roger	89TAS	405	$ .05	$ .20
Clemens, Roger	90T	245	$ .05	$ .35
Clemens, Roger	91T	530	$ .05	$ .25
Clemens, Roger	91TSC	309	$ .75	$3.00
Clemens, Roger	92T	150	$ .05	$ .25
Clemens, Roger	92TAS	405	$ .01	$ .10
Clemens, Roger	92TSC	80	$ .15	$1.50
Clemens, Roger	92TSC	593	$ .10	$1.00
Clemens, Roger	93T	4	$ .05	$ .20
Clemens, Roger	93T	409	$ .01	$ .15
Clemens, Roger	93TSC	220	$ .10	$ .75
Clemente, Roberto	55T	164	$400.00	$1600.00
Clemente, Roberto	56T	33	$100.00	$400.00
Clemente, Bob "Roberto"	57T	76	$55.00	$220.00
Clemente, Bob	58T	52	$45.00	$180.00
Clemente, Bob	59T	478	$28.75	$115.00
Clemente, Roberto	59T	543	$15.00	$60.00
Clemente, Bob	60T	326	$31.25	$125.00
Clemente, Bob	61T	41	$2.25	$9.00
Clemente, Bob	61T	388	$25.00	$100.00
Clemente, Bob	62T	10	$30.00	$120.00
Clemente, Bob	62T	52	$1.75	$7.00
Clemente, Bob	63T	18	$4.50	$18.00
Clemente, Bob	63T	540	$60.00	$240.00
Clemente, Bob	64T	7	$2.00	$8.00
Clemente, Bob	64T	440	$35.00	$140.00
Clemente, Bob	65T	2	$2.50	$10.00
Clemente, Bob	65T	160	$20.00	$80.00
Clemente, Bob	66T	215	$7.00	$28.00
Clemente, Bob	66T	300	$22.50	$90.00
Clemente, Bob	67T	242	$2.50	$10.00
Clemente, Bob	67T	400	$16.25	$65.00
Clemente, Bob	68T	1	$4.00	$16.00
Clemente, Bob	68T	3	$1.75	$7.00
Clemente, Bob	68T	150	$12.50	$50.00
Clemente, Bob	68T	480	$8.00	$32.00
Clemente, Bob	68TAS	374	$3.50	$14.00
Clemente, Bob	69T	50	$12.50	$50.00
Clemente, Bob	70T	61	$1.25	$5.00
Clemente, Roberto	70T	350	$12.50	$50.00
Clemente, Roberto	71T	630	$15.00	$60.00
Clemente, Roberto	72T	309	$8.00	$32.00

Player	Year	No.	VG	EX/MT
Clemente, Roberto	72TIA	310	$4.00	$16.00
Clemente, Roberto	73T	50	$8.25	$33.00
Clemente, Roberto	75T	204	$ .50	$2.00
Clemente, Roberto	87TTB	313	$ .05	$ .20
Clements, Pat	85TR	23	$ .01	$ .10
Clements, Pat	86T	754	$ .01	$ .05
Clements, Pat	87T	16	$ .01	$ .04
Clements, Pat	88T	484	$ .01	$ .04
Clements, Pat	89T	159	$ .01	$ .03
Clements, Pat	90T	548	$ .01	$ .03
Clemons, Lance	72T	372	$ .10	$ .40
Clendenon, Donn	62T	86	$ .75	$3.00
Clendenon, Donn	63T	477	$3.00	$12.00
Clendenon, Donn	64T	163	$ .50	$2.00
Clendenon, Donn	65T	325	$ .50	$2.00
Clendenon, Donn	66T	375	$ .65	$2.60
Clendenon, Donn	67T	266	$1.00	$4.00
Clendenon, Donn	67T	535	$5.00	$20.00
Clendenon, Donn	68T	344	$ .35	$1.40
Clendenon, Donn	69T	208	$ .35	$1.40
Clendenon, Donn	70T	280	$ .35	$1.40
Clendenon, Donn	71T	115	$ .25	$1.00
Clendenon, Donn	72T	671	$1.25	$5.00
Cleveland, Reggie	70T	716	$1.25	$5.00
Cleveland, Reggie	71T	216	$ .25	$1.00
Cleveland, Reggie	72T	375	$ .10	$ .40
Cleveland, Reggie	73T	104	$ .10	$ .40
Cleveland, Reggie	74T	175	$ .10	$ .40
Cleveland, Reggie	74TTR	175	$ .10	$ .40
Cleveland, Reggie	75T	32	$ .10	$ .40
Cleveland, Reggie	76T	419	$ .05	$ .25
Cleveland, Reggie	77T	613	$ .05	$ .20
Cleveland, Reggie	78T	105	$ .04	$ .16
Cleveland, Reggie	79T	209	$ .03	$ .12
Cleveland, Reggie	80T	394	$ .01	$ .10
Cleveland, Reggie	81T	576	$ .01	$ .08
Cleveland, Reggie	82T	737	$ .01	$ .08
Clevenger, Tex	58T	31	$2.00	$8.00
Clevenger, Tex	59T	298	$1.00	$4.00
Clevenger, Tex	60T	392	$ .75	$3.00
Clevenger, Tex	61T	291	$ .60	$2.40
Clevenger, Tex	63T	457	$3.00	$12.00
Cliburn, Stu	86T	179	$ .01	$ .05
Cliburn, Stewart	89T	649	$ .01	$ .03
Cline, Ty	61T	421	$1.00	$4.00
Cline, Ty	62T	362	$ .75	$3.00
Cline, Ty	63T	414	$1.00	$4.00
Cline, Ty	64T	171	$ .50	$2.00
Cline, Ty	65T	63	$ .35	$1.40
Cline, Ty	66T	306	$ .50	$2.00
Cline, Ty	67T	591	$4.00	$16.00
Cline, Ty	68T	469	$ .75	$3.00
Cline, Ty	69T	442	$ .30	$1.20
Cline, Ty	70T	164	$ .20	$ .80
Cline, Ty	71T	319	$ .25	$1.00
Clines, Gene	71T	27	$ .25	$1.00
Clines, Gene	72T	152	$ .10	$ .40
Clines, Gene	73T	333	$ .10	$ .40
Clines, Gene	74T	172	$ .10	$ .40
Clines, Gene	75T	575	$ .10	$ .40
Clines, Gene	76T	417	$ .05	$ .25
Clines, Gene	77T	237	$ .05	$ .20
Clines, Gene	78T	639	$ .04	$ .16
Clines, Gene	79T	171	$ .03	$ .12
Clinkscales, Sherard	93T	706	$ .01	$ .15
Clinton, Lou	60T	533	$2.75	$11.00
Clinton, Lou	62T	457	$1.50	$6.00
Clinton, Lou	63T	96	$ .50	$2.00
Clinton, Lou	64T	526	$2.25	$9.00
Clinton, Lou	64T	527	$2.25	$9.00
Clinton, Lou	65T	229	$ .50	$2.00
Clinton, Lou	67T	426	$ .60	$2.40
Cloninger, Tony	62T	63	$ .75	$3.00
Cloninger, Tony	63T	367	$ .90	$3.60
Cloninger, Tony	64T	575	$2.25	$9.00

TOPPS

Player	Year	No.	VG	EX/MT
Cloninger, Tony	65T	520	$1.25	$5.00
Cloninger, Tony	66T	10	$.35	$1.40
Cloninger, Tony	66T	223	$1.75	$7.00
Cloninger, Tony	67T	396	$.60	$2.40
Cloninger, Tony	67T	490	$1.50	$6.00
Cloninger, Tony	68T	93	$.35	$1.40
Cloninger, Tony	69T	492	$.30	$1.20
Cloninger, Tony	70T	705	$1.25	$5.00
Cloninger, Tony	71T	218	$.25	$1.00
Cloninger, Tony	72T	779	$1.25	$5.00
Closter, Alan	66T	549	$3.75	$15.00
Closter, Alan	69T	114	$.35	$1.40
Closter, Alan	72T	124	$.10	$.40
Closter, Alan	73T	634	$.60	$2.40
Clutterbuck, Bryan	87T	562	$.01	$.04
Clutterbuck, Bryan	89TTR	21	$.01	$.05
Clutterbuck, Bryan	90T	264	$.01	$.03
Clyde, David	74T	133	$.10	$.40
Clyde, David	75T	12	$.10	$.40
Clyde, David	79T	399	$.03	$.12
Clyde, David	80T	697	$.01	$.10
Coan, Gil	52T	291	$13.75	$55.00
Coan, Gil	53T	133	$6.25	$25.00
Coan, Gil	91TA53	133	$.01	$.15
Coates, Jim	59T	525	$4.00	$16.00
Coates, Jim	60T	51	$.85	$3.40
Coates, Jim	61T	531	$7.50	$30.00
Coates, Jim	62T	553	$3.50	$14.00
Coates, Jim	63T	237	$.90	$3.60
Coates, Jim	67T	401	$.60	$2.40
Cobb, Ty	73TATL	471	$1.00	$4.00
Cobb, Ty	73TATL	475	$1.00	$4.00
Cobb, Ty	76TAT	346	$1.50	$6.00
Cobb, Ty	79TRH	411	$.15	$.60
Cobb, Ty	79TRH	414	$.15	$.60
Cocanower, Jaime	84TTR	26	$.01	$.15
Cocanower, Jaime	85T	576	$.01	$.06
Cocanower, Jaime	86T	277	$.01	$.05
Cocanower, Jamie	87T	423	$.01	$.04
Cochrane, Dave	90T	491	$.01	$.10
Cochrane, Dave	92TSC	69	$.01	$.10
Cochrane, Dave	93T	288	$.01	$.03
Cochrane, Mickey	76TAT	348	$.30	$1.20
Cockrell, Alan	92T	591	$.05	$.20
Codiroli, Chris	83TTR	20	$.01	$.10
Codiroli, Chris	84T	61	$.01	$.06
Codiroli, Chris	85T	552	$.01	$.06
Codiroli, Chris	86T	433	$.01	$.05
Codiroli, Chris	87T	217	$.01	$.04
Coffman, Kevin	88TTR	29	$.01	$.05
Coffman, Kevin	89T	488	$.01	$.03
Coggins, Frank	68T	96	$.35	$1.40
Coggins, Rich	73T	611	$.75	$3.00
Coggins, Rich	74T	353	$.10	$.40
Coggins, Rich	75T	167	$.10	$.40
Coggins, Rich	76T	572	$.05	$.25
Cohen, Andy	60T	466	$1.25	$5.00
Coker, Jim	60T	438	$.75	$3.00
Coker, Jim	61T	144	$.60	$2.40
Coker, Jim	63T	456	$3.00	$12.00
Coker, Jim	64T	211	$.65	$2.60
Coker, Jim	65T	192	$.35	$1.40
Coker, Jim	66T	292	$.50	$2.00
Coker, Jimmie	67T	158	$.40	$1.60
Colavito, Rocco (Rocky)	57T	212	$32.50	$130.00
Colavito, Rocky	58T	368	$7.50	$30.00
Colavito, Rocky	59T	166	$1.50	$6.00
Colavito, Rocky	59T	420	$5.00	$20.00
Colavito, Rocky	59T	462	$2.50	$10.00
Colavito, Rocky	60T	260	$1.25	$5.00
Colavito, Rocky	60T	400	$3.00	$12.00
Colavito, Rocky	61T	44	$10.00	$40.00
Colavito, Rocky	61T	330	$3.00	$12.00
Colavito, Rocky	62T	20	$2.25	$9.00
Colavito, Rocky	62T	314	$1.50	$6.00
Colavito, Rocky	62TAS	472	$2.25	$9.00
Colavito, Rocky	63T	4	$2.00	$8.00
Colavito, Rocky	63T	240	$2.50	$10.00
Colavito, Rocky	64T	320	$1.75	$7.00
Colavito, Rocky	65T	380	$1.75	$7.00
Colavito, Rocky	66T	150	$1.00	$4.00
Colavito, Rocky	66T	220	$.75	$3.00
Colavito, Rocky	67T	109	$.60	$2.40
Colavito, Rocky	67T	580	$18.75	$75.00
Colavito, Rocky	68T	99	$.75	$3.00
Colavito, Rocky	73T	449	$.50	$2.00
Colbern, Mike	79T	704	$.15	$.60
Colbern, Mike	80T	664	$.01	$.10
Colbern, Mike	81T	522	$.01	$.08
Colbert, Craig	92TSC	891	$.01	$.15
Colbert, Craig	93T	91	$.01	$.03
Colbert, Nate	66T	596	$4.50	$18.00
Colbert, Nate	69T	408	$.30	$1.20
Colbert, Nate	70T	11	$.20	$.80
Colbert, Nate	71T	235	$.25	$1.00
Colbert, Nate	72T	571	$.40	$1.60
Colbert, Nate	72TIA	572	$.40	$1.60
Colbert, Nate	73T	340	$.10	$.40
Colbert, Nate	74T	125	$.10	$.40
Colbert, Nate	75T	599	$.10	$.40
Colbert, Nate	76T	495	$.05	$.25
Colbert, Nate	77TB	433	$.05	$.20
Colbert, Vince	71T	231	$.25	$1.00
Colbert, Vince	72T	84	$.10	$.40
Colborn, Jim	71T	38	$.25	$1.00

Player	Year	No.	VG	EX/MT
Colborn, Jim	72T	386	$.10	$.40
Colborn, Jim	73T	408	$.25	$1.00
Colborn, Jim	74T	75	$.25	$1.00
Colborn, Jim	75T	305	$.10	$.40
Colborn, Jim	76T	521	$.05	$.25
Colborn, Jim	77T	331	$.05	$.20
Colborn, Jim	78T	129	$.04	$.16
Colborn, Jim	79T	276	$.03	$.12
Colbrunn, Greg	91T	91	$.05	$.25
Colbrunn, Greg	91TSC	215	$.10	$1.00
Colbrunn, Greg	93T	464	$.01	$.03
Cole, Alex	91T	421	$.01	$.10
Cole, Alex	91TSC	392	$.05	$.25

TOPPS

Player	Year	No.	VG	EX/MT	Player	Year	No.	VG	EX/MT
Cole, Alex	92T	170	$ .01	$ .03	Collins, Dave	76T	363	$ .20	$ .80
Cole, Alex	92TSC	437	$ .01	$ .10	Collins, Dave	77T	431	$ .05	$ .20
Cole, Alex	93T	591	$ .01	$ .03	Collins, Dave	78T	254	$ .04	$ .16
Cole, Dick	54T	84	$3.75	$15.00	Collins, Dave	79T	622	$ .03	$ .12
Cole, Dick	57T	234	$2.00	$8.00	Collins, Dave	80T	73	$ .01	$ .10
Cole, Stu	92TSC	553	$ .01	$ .10	Collins, Dave	81T	175	$ .01	$ .08
Cole, Victor	93T	453	$ .01	$ .10	Collins, Dave	82T	595	$ .01	$ .08
Coleman, Claren. Choo Choo	61T	502	$1.50	$6.00	Collins, Dave	82TTR	20	$ .01	$ .10
Coleman, Choo Choo	63T	27	$ .50	$2.00	Collins, Dave	83T	359	$ .01	$ .08
Coleman, Choo Choo	64T	251	$ .65	$2.60	Collins, Dave	83TTR	21	$ .01	$ .10
Coleman, Choo Choo	66T	561	$10.00	$40.00	Collins, Dave	84T	733	$ .01	$ .06
Coleman, Gerry	51Trb	18	$2.50	$10.00	Collins, Dave	85T	463	$ .01	$ .06
Coleman, Gordy	60T	257	$1.25	$5.00	Collins, Dave	85TTR	25	$ .01	$ .10
Coleman, Gordy	61T	194	$ .60	$2.40	Collins, Dave	86T	271	$ .01	$ .05
Coleman, Gordy	62T	508	$1.50	$6.00	Collins, Dave	86TTR	27	$ .01	$ .06
Coleman, Gordy	63T	90	$ .50	$2.00	Collins, Dave	87T	148	$ .01	$ .04
Coleman, Gordy	64T	577	$2.25	$9.00	Collins, Joe	52T	202	$8.75	$35.00
Coleman, Gordy	65T	289	$ .50	$2.00	Collins, Joe	53T	9	$8.00	$32.00
Coleman, Gordy	66T	494	$1.50	$6.00	Collins, Joe	54T	83	$5.00	$20.00
Coleman, Gordy	67T	61	$ .40	$1.60	Collins, Joe	55T	63	$2.50	$10.00
Coleman, Jerry	52T	237	$7.50	$30.00	Collins, Joe	56T	21	$2.00	$8.00
Coleman, Jerry	56T	316	$3.75	$15.00	Collins, Joe	57T	295	$5.00	$20.00
Coleman, Jerry	57T	192	$2.00	$8.00	Collins, Joe	91TA53	9	$ .01	$ .15
Coleman, Joe	53T	279	$11.25	$45.00	Collins, Kevin	65T	581	$37.50	$150.00
Coleman, Joe	54T	156	$3.75	$15.00	Collins, Kevin	69T	127	$ .35	$1.40
Coleman, Joe	55T	162	$6.25	$25.00	Collins, Kevin	70T	707	$1.25	$5.00
Coleman, Joe	66T	333	$ .75	$3.00	Collins, Kevin	71T	553	$1.00	$4.00
Coleman, Joe	67T	167	$ .40	$1.60	Collum, Jackie	57T	268	$5.00	$20.00
Coleman, Joe	68T	573	$ .70	$2.80	Colon, Cris	93T	809	$ .01	$ .15
Coleman, Joe	69T	246	$ .50	$2.00	Colpaert, Dick	73T	608	$1.00	$4.00
Coleman, Joe	70T	127	$ .20	$ .80	Colson, Loyd	71T	111	$ .25	$1.00
Coleman, Joe	71T	403	$ .50	$2.00	Colt .45's, Houston	63T	312	$3.50	$14.00
Coleman, Joe	72T	96	$ .40	$1.60	Colton, Larry	68T	348	$ .35	$1.40
Coleman, Joe	72T	640	$ .40	$1.60	Colton, Larry	69T	454	$ .30	$1.20
Coleman, Joe	73T	120	$ .10	$ .40	Coluccio, Bob	74T	124	$ .10	$ .40
Coleman, Joe	74T	240	$ .10	$ .40	Coluccio, Bob	75T	456	$ .10	$ .40
Coleman, Joe	75T	42	$ .10	$ .40	Coluccio, Bob	76T	333	$ .05	$ .25
Coleman, Joe	76T	68	$ .10	$ .40	Combe, Geoff	81T	606	$ .01	$ .08
Coleman, Joe	76T	456	$ .05	$ .25	Combe, Geoff	82T	351	$ .01	$ .08
Coleman, Joe	77T	219	$ .05	$ .20	Combs, Earle	54T	183	$5.50	$22.00
Coleman, Joe	78T	554	$ .04	$ .16	Combs, Merrill	52T	18	$13.75	$55.00
Coleman, Joe	79T	329	$ .03	$ .12	Combs, Pat	88TTR	30	$ .01	$ .15
Coleman, Joe	80T	542	$ .01	$ .10	Combs, Pat	90T	384	$ .01	$ .10
Coleman, Joe	91TA53	279	$ .01	$ .15	Combs, Pat	91T	571	$ .01	$ .03
Coleman, Jr., Joe	76T	68	$ .10	$ .40	Combs, Pat	91TSC	36	$ .05	$ .25
Coleman, Paul	90T	654	$ .01	$ .15	Combs, Pat	92T	456	$ .01	$ .03
Coleman, Ray	52T	217	$7.00	$28.00	Combs, Pat	92TSC	443	$ .01	$ .10
Coleman, Rip	57T	354	$1.75	$7.00	Comer, Steve	79T	463	$ .03	$ .12
Coleman, Rip	59T	51	$1.50	$6.00	Comer, Steve	80T	144	$ .01	$ .10
Coleman, Rip	60T	179	$ .75	$3.00	Comer, Steve	81T	592	$ .01	$ .08
Coleman, Vince	85TTR	24	$1.00	$4.00	Comer, Steve	82T	16	$ .01	$ .08
Coleman, Vince	86T	370	$ .10	$1.00	Comer, Steve	83T	353	$ .01	$ .08
Coleman, Vince	86TRB	201	$ .05	$ .20	Comer, Steve	85T	788	$ .01	$ .06
Coleman, Vince	87T	590	$ .05	$ .20	Comer, Wayne	69T	346	$ .30	$1.20
Coleman, Vince	88T	260	$ .01	$ .10	Comer, Wayne	70T	323	$ .35	$1.40
Coleman, Vince	88TRB	1	$ .01	$ .10	Compton, Mike	71T	77	$ .25	$1.00
Coleman, Vince	89T	90	$ .01	$ .10	Comstock, Keith	88T	778	$ .01	$ .04
Coleman, Vince	90T	660	$ .01	$ .10	Comstock, Keith	91T	337	$ .01	$ .03
Coleman, Vince	90TRB	6	$ .01	$ .10	Comstock, Keith	91TSC	556	$ .05	$ .25
Coleman, Vince	91T	160	$ .01	$ .03	Concepcion, Dave	71T	14	$5.50	$22.00
Coleman, Vince	91TSC	498	$ .05	$ .35	Concepcion, Dave	72T	267	$ .75	$3.00
Coleman, Vince	91TTR	23	$ .01	$ .05	Concepcion, Dave	73T	554	$1.00	$4.00
Coleman, Vince	92T	500	$ .01	$ .03	Concepcion, Dave	74T	435	$ .50	$2.00
Coleman, Vince	92TSC	40	$ .01	$ .10	Concepcion, Dave	75T	17	$ .50	$2.00
Coleman, Vince	93T	765	$ .01	$ .03	Concepcion, Dave	76T	48	$ .30	$1.20
Coleman, Vince	93TSC	195	$ .01	$ .10	Concepcion, Dave	77T	560	$ .20	$ .80
Coles, Chuck	59T	120	$1.00	$4.00	Concepcion, Dave	78T	180	$ .25	$1.00
Coles, Darnell	85T	108	$ .01	$ .06	Concepcion, Dave	79T	450	$ .20	$ .80
Coles, Darnell	86T	337	$ .01	$ .05	Concepcion, Dave	80T	220	$ .10	$ .50
Coles, Darnell	86TTR	26	$ .01	$ .06	Concepcion, Dave	81T	375	$ .05	$ .20
Coles, Darnell	87T	411	$ .01	$ .04	Concepcion, Dave	82T	660	$ .05	$ .20
Coles, Darnell	88T	46	$ .01	$ .04	Concepcion, Dave	82TAS	340	$ .01	$ .15
Coles, Darnell	89T	738	$ .01	$ .03	Concepcion, Dave	82TSA	661	$ .01	$ .10
Coles, Darnell	90T	232	$ .01	$ .03	Concepcion, Dave	83T	720	$ .01	$ .08
Coles, Darnell	91T	506	$ .01	$ .03	Concepcion, Dave	83TAS	400	$ .01	$ .10

TOPPS

Player	Year	No.	VG	EX/MT
Concepcion, Dave	84T	55	$.01	$.06
Concepcion, Dave	85T	515	$.01	$.06
Concepcion, Dave	86T	195	$.01	$.05
Concepcion, Dave	87T	731	$.01	$.10
Concepcion, Dave	88T	422	$.01	$.10
Concepcion, Onix	83T	52	$.01	$.08
Concepcion, Onix	84T	247	$.01	$.06
Concepcion, Onix	85T	697	$.01	$.06
Concepcion, Onix	86T	596	$.01	$.05
Cone, Dave	87TTR	24	$.15	$1.50
Cone, Dave	88T	181	$.05	$.35
Cone, Dave	89T	710	$.01	$.15
Cone, David	90T	30	$.01	$.15
Cone, David	91T	680	$.01	$.10
Cone, David	91TSC	367	$.10	$.50
Cone, David	92T	195	$.01	$.03
Cone, David	92TSC	17	$.01	$.10
Cone, David	93T	720	$.01	$.03
Conigliaro, Bill	69T	628	$.75	$3.00
Conigliaro, Billy	70T	317	$.35	$1.40
Conigliaro, Billy	71T	114	$.25	$1.00
Conigliaro, Billy	72T	481	$.25	$1.00
Conigliaro, Billy	74T	545	$.10	$.40
Conigliaro, Tony	64T	287	$7.50	$30.00
Conigliaro, Tony	65T	55	$2.00	$8.00
Conigliaro, Tony	66T	218	$.75	$3.00
Conigliaro, Tony	66T	380	$1.75	$7.00
Conigliaro, Tony	67T	280	$1.50	$6.00
Conigliaro, Tony	68T	140	$1.00	$4.00
Conigliaro, Tony	69T	330	$.75	$3.00
Conigliaro, Tony	70T	340	$.35	$1.40
Conigliaro, Tony	71T	63	$.25	$1.00
Conigliaro, Tony	71T	105	$.40	$1.60
Conine, Jeff	91TSC	578	$.20	$2.00
Conine, Jeff	92TSC	683	$.01	$.10
Conine, Jeff	93T	789	$.01	$.03
Conley, Bob	59T	121	$1.00	$4.00
Conley, Gene	53T	215	$6.00	$24.00
Conley, Gene	54T	59	$7.50	$30.00
Conley, Gene	55T	81	$2.25	$9.00
Conley, Gene	56T	17	$2.00	$8.00
Conley, Gene	57T	28	$2.00	$8.00
Conley, Gene	58T	431	$1.00	$4.00
Conley, Gene	59T	492	$1.00	$4.00
Conley, Gene	60T	293	$.75	$3.00
Conley, Gene	61T	193	$.60	$2.40
Conley, Gene	62T	187	$.60	$2.40
Conley, Gene	63T	216	$.90	$3.60
Conley, Gene	64T	571	$2.25	$9.00
Conley, Gene	91TA53	215	$.01	$.15
Connelly, Bill	53T	126	$4.00	$16.00
Connelly, Bill	91TA53	126	$.01	$.15
Connolly, Ed	65T	543	$2.50	$10.00
Connors, Bill	67T	272	$.75	$3.00
Conroy, Tim	84T	156	$.05	$.25
Conroy, Tim	84T	189	$.01	$.06
Conroy, Tim	85T	503	$.01	$.06
Conroy, Tim	86TTR	28	$.01	$.06
Conroy, Tim	87T	338	$.01	$.04
Conroy, Tim	88T	658	$.01	$.04
Consolo, Bill	54T	195	$4.00	$16.00
Consolo, Bill	55T	207	$6.25	$25.00
Consolo, Billy	57T	399	$1.75	$7.00
Consolo, Billy	58T	148	$1.25	$5.00
Consolo, Billy	59T	112	$1.00	$4.00
Consolo, Billy	60T	508	$2.75	$11.00
Consolo, Billy	61T	504	$1.35	$5.40
Constable, Jimmy	59T	451	$1.00	$4.00
Constable, Jim	63T	411	$1.00	$4.00
Consuegra, Sandy	56T	265	$2.50	$10.00
Coogan, Dale	52T	87	$7.00	$28.00
Cook, Cliff	61T	399	$1.00	$4.00
Cook, Cliff	62T	41	$.60	$2.40
Cook, Cliff	63T	566	$2.25	$9.00
Cook, Dennis	90T	633	$.01	$.03
Cook, Dennis	91T	467	$.01	$.03
Cook, Dennis	91TSC	411	$.05	$.25
Cook, Dennis	92TSC	887	$.01	$.10
Cook, Dennis	93T	141	$.01	$.03
Cook, Dennis	93TSC	153	$.01	$.10
Cook, Glen	86T	502	$.01	$.05
Cook, Ron	71T	583	$1.00	$4.00
Cook, Ron	72T	339	$.10	$.40
Cooke, Steve	93T	716	$.01	$.15
Coolbaugh, Scott	90TTR	22	$.01	$.10
Coolbaugh, Scott	91T	277	$.01	$.10
Coolbaugh, Scott	91TSC	493	$.05	$.25
Coolbaugh, Scott	91TTR	24	$.01	$.05
Coombs, Dan	65T	553	$1.40	$5.60
Coombs, Dan	66T	414	$.65	$2.60
Coombs, Dan	67T	464	$1.50	$6.00
Coombs, Dan	68T	547	$.70	$2.80
Coombs, Dan	69T	389	$.30	$1.20
Coombs, Danny	71T	126	$.25	$1.00
Cooney, Johnny	60T	458	$1.25	$5.00
Cooper, Cecil	72T	79	$25.00	$100.00
Cooper, Cecil	74T	523	$.50	$2.00

Player	Year	No.	VG	EX/MT
Cooper, Cecil	75T	489	$.30	$1.20
Cooper, Cecil	76T	78	$.25	$1.00
Cooper, Cecil	77T	235	$.25	$1.00
Cooper, Cecil	78T	154	$.10	$.40
Cooper, Cecil	79T	325	$.20	$.80
Cooper, Cecil	80T	95	$.05	$.20
Cooper, Cecil	81T	3	$.10	$.50
Cooper, Cecil	81T	555	$.01	$.15
Cooper, Cecil	82T	675	$.05	$.25
Cooper, Cecil	82T	703	$.01	$.15
Cooper, Cecil	83T	190	$.01	$.15
Cooper, Cecil	84T	133	$.05	$.20
Cooper, Cecil	84T	420	$.01	$.15
Cooper, Cecil	84T	710	$.05	$.20
Cooper, Cecil	85T	290	$.01	$.10
Cooper, Cecil	86T	385	$.01	$.10
Cooper, Cecil	87T	10	$.01	$.04
Cooper, Cecil	88T	769	$.01	$.04
Cooper, Don	82T	409	$.01	$.08
Cooper, Scott	92T	488	$.01	$.03
Cooper, Scott	92TSC	377	$.05	$.35

TOPPS

Player	Year	No.	VG	EX/MT	Player	Year	No.	VG	EX/MT
Cooper, Scott	93T	655	$.01	$.03	Cosman, Jim	70T	429	$.35	$1.40
Cooper, Walker	52T	294	$13.75	$55.00	Costello, John	89T	184	$.01	$.03
Cooper, Walker	56T	273	$2.50	$10.00	Costello, John	90T	36	$.01	$.03
Cooper, Walker	57T	380	$1.75	$7.00	Costo, Tim	91T	103	$.05	$.20
Cooper, Walker	60T	462	$1.25	$5.00	Costo, Tim	93T	577	$.01	$.10
Cora, Joey	88T	91	$.01	$.15	Cotes, Eugenio	79T	723	$.05	$.20
Cora, Joey	92T	302	$.01	$.03	Cottier, Chuck	60T	417	$1.00	$4.00
Cora, Joey	92TSC	535	$.01	$.10	Cottier, Chuck	61T	13	$.60	$2.40
Cora, Joey	93T	122	$.01	$.03	Cottier, Chuck	62T	27	$.60	$2.40
Cora, Joey	93TSC	54	$.01	$.10	Cottier, Chuck	63T	219	$.90	$3.60
Corbett, Doug	81T	162	$.01	$.08	Cottier, Chuck	64T	397	$1.00	$4.00
Corbett, Doug	82T	560	$.01	$.08	Cottier, Chuck	69T	252	$.50	$2.00
Corbett, Doug	82TTR	21	$.01	$.10	Cottier, Chuck	85T	656	$.01	$.06
Corbett, Doug	83T	27	$.01	$.08	Cottier, Chuck	86T	141	$.01	$.05
Corbett, Doug	85T	682	$.01	$.06	Cotto, Henry	85T	267	$.01	$.06
Corbett, Doug	86T	234	$.01	$.05	Cotto, Henry	87T	174	$.01	$.04
Corbett, Doug	87T	359	$.01	$.04	Cotto, Henry	88T	766	$.01	$.04
Corbett, Sherman	89T	99	$.01	$.03	Cotto, Henry	88TTR	31	$.01	$.05
Corbin, Archie	92TSC	473	$.01	$.15	Cotto, Henry	89T	468	$.01	$.03
Corbin, Ray	72T	66	$.10	$.40	Cotto, Henry	90T	31	$.01	$.03
Corbin, Ray	73T	411	$.25	$1.00	Cotto, Henry	91T	634	$.01	$.03
Corbin, Ray	74T	296	$.10	$.40	Cotto, Henry	91TSC	525	$.05	$.25
Corbin, Ray	75T	78	$.10	$.40	Cotto, Henry	92T	311	$.01	$.03
Corbin, Ray	76T	474	$.05	$.25	Cotto, Henry	92TSC	14	$.01	$.10
Corcoran, Tim	78T	515	$.04	$.16	Cotto, Henry	93T	206	$.01	$.03
Corcoran, Tim	79T	272	$.03	$.12	Coughtry, Marlan	62T	595	$5.25	$21.00
Corcoran, Tim	81T	448	$.01	$.08	Courtney, Clint	53T	127	$4.00	$16.00
Corcoran, Tim	85T	302	$.01	$.06	Courtney, Clint	56T	159	$2.50	$10.00
Corcoran, Tim	86T	664	$.01	$.05	Courtney, Clint	57T	51	$2.00	$8.00
Cordero, Wil	92T	551	$.10	$.50	Courtney, Clint	58T	92	$2.00	$8.00
Cordero, Wil	93T	256	$.01	$.10	Courtney, Clint	59T	483	$1.00	$4.00
Corey, Mark	79T	701	$.03	$.12	Courtney, Clint	60T	344	$.75	$3.00
Corey, Mark	80T	661	$.01	$.10	Courtney, Clint	61T	342	$.60	$2.40
Corey, Mark	81T	399	$.10	$1.00	Courtney, Clint	91TA53	127	$.01	$.15
Corkins, Mike	70T	573	$.50	$2.00	Covington, Wes	57T	283	$5.00	$20.00
Corkins, Mike	71T	179	$.25	$1.00	Covington, Wes	58T	140	$1.25	$5.00
Corkins, Mike	72T	608	$.40	$1.60	Covington, Wes	59T	290	$1.00	$4.00
Corkins, Mike	73T	461	$.25	$1.00	Covington, Wes	59TAS	565	$4.00	$16.00
Corkins, Mike	74T	546	$.10	$.40	Covington, Wes	60T	158	$.75	$3.00
Cormier, Rheal	92T	346	$.01	$.15	Covington, Wes	61T	296	$.60	$2.40
Cormier, Rheal	92TSC	506	$.05	$.25	Covington, Wes	62T	157	$.60	$2.40
Cormier, Rheal	93T	149	$.01	$.03	Covington, Wes	63T	529	$2.25	$9.00
Cormier, Rheal	93TSC	15	$.01	$.10	Covington, Wes	64T	208	$.65	$2.60
Cornell, Jeff	85T	514	$.01	$.06	Covington, Wes	65T	583	$2.50	$10.00
Corrales, Pat	65T	107	$.75	$3.00	Covington, Wes	66T	52	$.50	$2.00
Corrales, Pat	66T	137	$.50	$2.00	Covington, Wes	66T	484	$1.50	$6.00
Corrales, Pat	67T	78	$.40	$1.60	Cowan, Billy	64T	192	$.50	$2.00
Corrales, Pat	69T	382	$.30	$1.20	Cowan, Billy	65T	186	$.35	$1.40
Corrales, Pat	70T	507	$.35	$1.40	Cowan, Billy	69T	643	$.40	$1.60
Corrales, Pat	71T	293	$.25	$1.00	Cowan, Billy	71T	614	$1.00	$4.00
Corrales, Pat	72T	705	$1.25	$5.00	Cowan, Billy	72T	19	$.10	$.40
Corrales, Pat	72TIA	706	$1.25	$5.00	Cowens, Al	75T	437	$.10	$.40
Corrales, Pat	73T	542	$.60	$2.40	Cowens, Al	76T	648	$.05	$.25
Corrales, Pat	74T	498	$.15	$.60	Cowens, Al	77T	262	$.05	$.20
Corrales, Pat	83T	637	$.01	$.08	Cowens, Al	78T	46	$.04	$.16
Corrales, Pat	84T	141	$.01	$.06	Cowens, Al	79T	490	$.03	$.12
Corrales, Pat	85T	119	$.01	$.06	Cowens, Al	80T	330	$.01	$.10
Corrales, Pat	86T	699	$.01	$.05	Cowens, Al	81T	123	$.01	$.08
Corrales, Pat	87T	268	$.01	$.04	Cowens, Al	82T	575	$.01	$.08
Correa, Ed	87T	334	$.01	$.04	Cowens, Al	82TTR	22	$.01	$.10
Correa, Ed	88T	227	$.01	$.04	Cowens, Al	83T	763	$.01	$.08
Correll, Vic	75T	177	$.10	$.40	Cowens, Al	84T	622	$.01	$.06
Correll, Vic	76T	608	$.05	$.25	Cowens, Al	85T	224	$.01	$.06
Correll, Vic	77T	364	$.05	$.20	Cowens, Al	86T	92	$.01	$.05
Correll, Vic	78T	527	$.04	$.16	Cowley, Joe	83T	288	$.01	$.08
Correll, Vic	79T	281	$.03	$.12	Cowley, Joe	85T	769	$.01	$.06
Correll, Vic	80T	419	$.01	$.10	Cowley, Joe	86T	427	$.01	$.05
Correll, Vic	81T	628	$.01	$.08	Cowley, Joe	86TTR	29	$.01	$.06
Corsi, Jim	89T	292	$.01	$.10	Cowley, Joe	87T	27	$.01	$.04
Corsi, Jim	90T	623	$.01	$.03	Cox, Billy	51Tbb	48	$10.00	$40.00
Corsi, Jim	93T	753	$.01	$.03	Cox, Billy	52T	232	$7.50	$30.00
Cosgrove, Mike	75T	96	$.10	$.40	Cox, Bobby	69T	237	$1.25	$5.00
Cosgrove, Mike	76T	122	$.05	$.25	Cox, Bobby	78T	93	$.04	$.16
Cosgrove, Mike	77T	589	$.05	$.20	Cox, Bobby	83T	606	$.01	$.08
Cosman, Jim	67T	384	$.60	$2.40	Cox, Bobby	84T	202	$.01	$.06

350

TOPPS

Player	Year	No.	VG	EX/MT
Cox, Bobby	85T	411	$ .01	$ .06
Cox, Bobby	86T	471	$ .01	$ .05
Cox, Bobby	90TTR	23	$ .01	$ .05
Cox, Bobby	91T	759	$ .01	$ .03
Cox, Bobby	92T	489	$ .01	$ .03
Cox, Bobby	93T	501	$ .01	$ .03
Cox, Casey	66T	549	$3.75	$15.00
Cox, Casey	67T	414	$ .60	$2.40
Cox, Casey	68T	66	$ .35	$1.40
Cox, Casey	69T	383	$ .30	$1.20
Cox, Casey	70T	281	$ .35	$1.40
Cox, Casey	71T	82	$ .25	$1.00
Cox, Casey	72T	231	$ .10	$ .40
Cox, Casey	73T	419	$ .25	$1.00
Cox, Danny	85T	499	$ .05	$ .25
Cox, Danny	86T	294	$ .01	$ .05

Player	Year	No.	VG	EX/MT
Cox, Danny	**87T**	**621**	**$ .01**	**$ .04**
Cox, Danny	88T	59	$ .01	$ .04
Cox, Danny	89T	562	$ .01	$ .03
Cox, Danny	90T	184	$ .01	$ .03
Cox, Danny	91TTR	25	$ .01	$ .05
Cox, Danny	92T	791	$ .01	$ .03
Cox, Danny	92TSC	351	$ .01	$ .10
Cox, Jeff	81T	133	$ .01	$ .08
Cox, Jim	74T	600	$1.25	$5.00
Cox, Larry	77T	379	$ .05	$ .20
Cox, Larry	78T	541	$ .04	$ .16
Cox, Larry	79T	489	$ .03	$ .12
Cox, Larry	80T	116	$ .01	$ .10
Cox, Larry	81T	249	$ .01	$ .08
Cox, Larry	81TTR	749	$ .01	$ .15
Cox, Ted	78T	706	$ .04	$ .16
Cox, Ted	79T	79	$ .03	$ .12
Cox, Ted	80T	252	$ .01	$ .10
Cox, Terry	71T	559	$1.00	$4.00
Crabtree, Tim	93T	742	$ .10	$ .50
Craddock, Walt	59T	281	$1.00	$4.00
Craft, Harry	62T	12	$ .60	$2.40
Craft, Harry	63T	491	$3.00	$12.00
Craft, Harry	64T	298	$ .65	$2.60
Craig, Pete	65T	466	$1.25	$5.00
Craig, Pete	66T	11	$ .35	$1.40
Craig, Pete	67T	459	$1.75	$7.00
Craig, Rodney	80T	672	$ .01	$ .10

Player	Year	No.	VG	EX/MT
Craig, Roger	56T	63	$7.50	$30.00
Craig, Roger	57T	173	$3.50	$14.00
Craig, Roger	58T	194	$2.25	$9.00
Craig, Roger	60T	62	$1.25	$5.00
Craig, Roger	61T	543	$1.00	$40.00
Craig, Roger	62T	183	$1.00	$4.00
Craig, Roger	63T	197	$1.00	$4.00
Craig, Roger	64T	295	$1.00	$4.00
Craig, Roger	65T	411	$1.25	$5.00
Craig, Roger	66T	543	$10.00	$40.00
Craig, Roger	74T	31	$ .10	$ .40
Craig, Roger	81T	282	$ .01	$ .08
Craig, Roger	86T	111	$ .01	$ .05
Craig, Roger	87T	193	$ .01	$ .04
Craig, Roger	88T	654	$ .01	$ .04
Craig, Roger	89T	744	$ .01	$ .03
Craig, Roger	90T	351	$ .01	$ .03
Craig, Roger	91T	579	$ .01	$ .03
Craig, Roger	92T	109	$ .01	$ .03
Cram, Jerry	71T	247	$ .25	$1.00
Crandall, Del	52T	162	$7.00	$28.00
Crandall, Del	53T	197	$4.50	$18.00
Crandall, Del	54T	12	$3.75	$15.00
Crandall, Del	56T	175	$2.50	$10.00
Crandall, Del	57T	133	$2.00	$8.00
Crandall, Del	58T	351	$7.00	$28.00
Crandall, Del	58T	390	$1.00	$4.00
Crandall, Del	59T	425	$1.00	$4.00
Crandall, Del	59TAS	567	$4.00	$16.00
Crandall, Del	60T	170	$ .75	$3.00
Crandall, Del	60TAS	568	$3.50	$14.00
Crandall, Del	61T	390	$1.00	$4.00
Crandall, Del	61TAS	583	$8.00	$32.00
Crandall, Del	62T	351	$1.25	$5.00
Crandall, Del	62T	443	$1.25	$5.00
Crandall, Del	63T	460	$3.00	$12.00
Crandall, Del	64T	169	$ .50	$2.00
Crandall, Del	65T	68	$ .35	$1.40
Crandall, Del	66T	339	$ .50	$2.00
Crandall, Del	73T	646	$ .75	$3.00
Crandall, Del	74T	99	$ .10	$ .40
Crandall, Del	84T	721	$ .01	$ .06
Crandall, Del	91TA53	197	$ .01	$ .15
Crawford, Jim	74T	279	$ .10	$ .40
Crawford, Jim	76T	428	$ .05	$ .25
Crawford, Jim	76TTR	428	$ .05	$ .25
Crawford, Jim	77T	69	$ .05	$ .20
Crawford, Steve	82T	157	$ .01	$ .08
Crawford, Steve	83T	419	$ .01	$ .08
Crawford, Steve	85T	661	$ .01	$ .06
Crawford, Steve	86T	91	$ .01	$ .05
Crawford, Steve	87T	589	$ .01	$ .04
Crawford, Steve	88T	299	$ .01	$ .04
Crawford, Steve	91T	718	$ .01	$ .03
Crawford, Willie	65T	453	$1.25	$5.00
Crawford, Willie	68T	417	$ .35	$1.40
Crawford, Willie	69T	327	$ .50	$2.00
Crawford, Willie	70T	34	$ .20	$ .80
Crawford, Willie	71T	519	$ .50	$2.00
Crawford, Willie	72T	669	$1.25	$5.00
Crawford, Willie	73T	639	$ .60	$2.40
Crawford, Willie	74T	480	$ .10	$ .40
Crawford, Willie	75T	186	$ .10	$ .40
Crawford, Willie	76T	76	$ .05	$ .25
Crawford, Willie	77T	642	$ .05	$ .20
Crawford, Willie	78T	507	$ .04	$ .16
Crews, Tim	88T	57	$ .01	$ .10
Crews, Tim	89T	22	$ .01	$ .03
Crews, Tim	90T	551	$ .01	$ .03
Crews, Tim	91T	737	$ .01	$ .03
Crews, Tim	91TSC	375	$ .05	$ .25
Crews, Tim	92T	642	$ .01	$ .03
Crews, Tim	92TSC	349	$ .01	$ .10
Crider, Jerry	69T	491	$ .30	$1.20
Crider, Jerry	71T	113	$ .25	$1.00

TOPPS

Player	Year	No.	VG	EX/MT
Crim, Chuck	87TTR	25	$ .01	$ .05
Crim, Chuck	88T	286	$ .01	$ .04
Crim, Chuck	89T	466	$ .01	$ .03
Crim, Chuck	90T	768	$ .01	$ .03
Crim, Chuck	91T	644	$ .01	$ .03
Crim, Chuck	91TSC	112	$ .05	$ .25
Crim, Chuck	92T	169	$ .01	$ .03
Crim, Chuck	92TSC	823	$ .01	$ .10
Crim, Chuck	93T	499	$ .01	$ .03
Crimian, Jack	56T	319	$2.50	$10.00
Crimian, Jack	57T	297	$5.00	$20.00
Cromartie, Warren	78T	468	$ .10	$ .40
Cromartie, Warren	79T	76	$ .03	$ .12
Cromartie, Warren	80T	180	$ .01	$ .10
Cromartie, Warren	81T	345	$ .01	$ .08
Cromartie, Warren	82T	526	$ .01	$ .08
Cromartie, Warren	82T	695	$ .01	$ .08
Cromartie, Warren	83T	495	$ .01	$ .08
Cromartie, Warren	84T	287	$ .01	$ .06
Crone, Ray	54T	206	$3.75	$15.00
Crone, Ray	55T	149	$2.25	$9.00
Crone, Ray	56T	76	$2.00	$8.00
Crone, Ray	57T	68	$2.00	$8.00
Crone, Ray	58T	272	$1.25	$5.00
Crosby, Ed	71T	672	$1.50	$6.00
Crosby, Ed	73T	599	$ .60	$2.40
Crosby, Ed	76T	457	$ .05	$ .25
Crosby, Ken	76T	593	$ .15	$ .60
Crosetti, Frank	52T	384	$65.00	$260.00
Crosetti, Frank	60T	465	$3.50	$14.00
Crowe, George	52T	360	$50.00	$200.00
Crowe, George	53T	3	$6.25	$25.00
Crowe, George	56T	254	$3.75	$15.00
Crowe, George	57T	73	$2.00	$8.00
Crowe, George	58T	12	$2.00	$8.00
Crowe, George	59T	337	$1.00	$4.00
Crowe, George	60T	419	$ .75	$3.00
Crowe, George	61T	52	$ .60	$2.40
Crowe, George	91TA53	3	$ .01	$ .15
Crowley, Terry	70T	121	$ .25	$1.00
Crowley, Terry	71T	453	$ .50	$2.00
Crowley, Terry	72T	628	$ .40	$1.60
Crowley, Terry	73T	302	$ .10	$ .40
Crowley, Terry	74T	648	$ .10	$ .40
Crowley, Terry	74TTR	648	$ .10	$ .40
Crowley, Terry	75T	447	$ .10	$ .40
Crowley, Terry	76T	491	$ .05	$ .25
Crowley, Terry	79T	91	$ .03	$ .12
Crowley, Terry	80T	188	$ .01	$ .10
Crowley, Terry	81T	543	$ .01	$ .08
Crowley, Terry	82T	232	$ .01	$ .08
Crowley, Terry	83T	372	$ .01	$ .08
Crowley, Terry	83TTR	22	$ .01	$ .10
Crowley, Terry	84T	732	$ .01	$ .06
Cruz, Hector	76T	598	$ .05	$ .25
Cruz, Hector	77T	624	$ .05	$ .20
Cruz, Hector	78T	257	$ .04	$ .16
Cruz, Hector	79T	436	$ .03	$ .12
Cruz, Hector	80T	516	$ .01	$ .10
Cruz, Hector	81T	52	$ .01	$ .08
Cruz, Hector	81TTR	750	$ .01	$ .15
Cruz, Hector	82T	663	$ .01	$ .08
Cruz, Henry	76T	590	$ .15	$ .60
Cruz, Henry	78T	316	$ .04	$ .16
Cruz, Ivan	93T	423	$ .10	$ .75
Cruz, Jose	72T	107	$ .50	$2.00
Cruz, Jose	73T	292	$ .25	$1.00
Cruz, Jose	74T	464	$ .15	$ .60
Cruz, Jose	75T	514	$ .20	$ .80
Cruz, Jose	76T	321	$ .15	$ .60
Cruz, Jose	77T	42	$ .05	$ .20
Cruz, Jose	78T	625	$ .04	$ .16
Cruz, Jose	79T	289	$ .03	$ .12
Cruz, Jose	80T	722	$ .01	$ .10
Cruz, Jose	81T	105	$ .01	$ .08
Cruz, Jose	82T	325	$ .01	$ .08
Cruz, Jose	83T	585	$ .01	$ .08
Cruz, Jose	84T	66	$ .10	$ .50
Cruz, Jose	84T	422	$ .01	$ .06
Cruz, Jose	85T	95	$ .01	$ .06
Cruz, Jose	86T	640	$ .01	$ .05
Cruz, Jose	87T	670	$ .01	$ .04
Cruz, Jose	88T	278	$ .01	$ .04
Cruz, Julio	78T	687	$ .04	$ .16
Cruz, Julio	79T	583	$ .03	$ .12
Cruz, Julio	80T	32	$ .01	$ .10
Cruz, Julio	81T	397	$ .01	$ .08
Cruz, Julio	82T	130	$ .01	$ .08
Cruz, Julio	83T	414	$ .01	$ .08
Cruz, Julio	83TTR	23	$ .01	$ .10
Cruz, Julio	84T	257	$ .01	$ .06
Cruz, Julio	85T	749	$ .01	$ .06
Cruz, Julio	86T	14	$ .01	$ .05
Cruz, Julio	87T	790	$ .01	$ .04
Cruz, Todd	80T	492	$ .01	$ .10
Cruz, Todd	81T	571	$ .01	$ .08
Cruz, Todd	83T	132	$ .01	$ .08
Cruz, Todd	84T	773	$ .01	$ .06
Cruz, Todd	85T	366	$ .01	$ .06
Cruz, Victor	79T	714	$ .03	$ .12
Cruz, Victor	80T	99	$ .01	$ .10
Cruz, Victor	81T	252	$ .01	$ .08
Cruz, Victor	81TTR	751	$ .01	$ .15
Cruz, Victor	82T	263	$ .01	$ .08
Cubbage, Mike	75T	617	$ .50	$2.00
Cubbage, Mike	76T	615	$ .05	$ .25
Cubbage, Mike	77T	149	$ .05	$ .20
Cubbage, Mike	78T	219	$ .04	$ .16
Cubbage, Mike	79T	362	$ .03	$ .12
Cubbage, Mike	80T	503	$ .01	$ .10
Cubbage, Mike	81T	657	$ .01	$ .08
Cubbage, Mike	81TTR	752	$ .01	$ .15

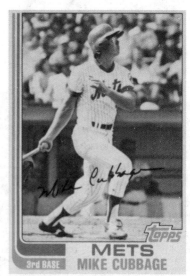

Player	Year	No.	VG	EX/MT
Cubbage, Mike	82T	43	$ .01	$ .08
Cubs, Team	56T	11	$6.00	$24.00
Cubs, Team	57T	183	$3.00	$12.00
Cubs, Team	58T	327	$3.50	$14.00
Cubs, Team	59T	304	$2.50	$10.00

TOPPS

Player	Year	No.	VG	EX/MT	Player	Year	No.	VG	EX/MT
Cubs, Team	60T	513	$8.00	$32.00	Cumberland, John	72T	403	$ .25	$1.00
Cubs, Team	61T	122	$1.75	$7.00	Cummings, Midre	93T	616	$ .05	$ .25
Cubs, Team	62T	552	$12.00	$48.00	Cummings, Steve	90T	374	$ .01	$ .10
Cubs, Team	63T	222	$1.25	$5.00	Cunningham, Earl	90T	134	$ .01	$ .15
Cubs, Team	64T	237	$1.50	$6.00	Cunningham, Joe	55T	37	$2.75	$11.00
Cubs, Team	65T	91	$ .75	$3.00	Cunningham, Joe	57T	304	$5.00	$20.00
Cubs, Team	66T	204	$1.00	$4.00	Cunningham, Joe	58T	168	$1.25	$5.00
Cubs, Team	67T	354	$1.00	$4.00	Cunningham, Joe	59T	285	$1.00	$4.00
Cubs, Team	70T	593	$1.25	$5.00	Cunningham, Joe	60T	40	$ .85	$3.40
Cubs, Team	71T	502	$ .75	$3.00	Cunningham, Joe	60TAS	562	$3.50	$14.00
Cubs, Team	72T	192	$ .25	$1.00	Cunningham, Joe	61T	520	$1.35	$5.40
Cubs, Team	73T	464	$ .50	$2.00	Cunningham, Joe	62T	195	$ .60	$2.40
Cubs, Team	74T	211	$ .25	$1.00	Cunningham, Joe	63T	100	$ .50	$2.00
Cubs, Team Checklist	75T	638	$ .35	$1.40	Cunningham, Joe	64T	340	$ .65	$2.60
Cubs, Team Checklist	76T	277	$ .30	$1.20	Cunningham, Joe	65T	496	$1.25	$5.00
Cubs, Team Checklist	77T	518	$ .25	$1.00	Cunningham, Joe	66T	531	$3.75	$15.00
Cubs, Team Checklist	78T	302	$ .20	$ .80	Curry, Steve	89T	471	$ .01	$ .03
Cubs, Team Checklist	79T	551	$ .15	$ .60	Curry, Tony	60T	541	$2.75	$11.00
Cubs, Team Checklist	80T	381	$ .10	$ .50	Curry, Tony	61T	262	$ .60	$2.40
Cubs, Team Checklist	81T	676	$ .05	$ .25	Curtis, Chad	92TTR	25	$ .05	$ .35
Cubs, Team Leaders	86T	636	$ .01	$ .15	Curtis, Chad	93T	699	$ .01	$ .03
Cubs, Team Leaders	87T	581	$ .01	$ .04	Curtis, Jack	61T	533	$7.50	$30.00
Cubs, Team Leaders	88T	171	$ .01	$ .04	Curtis, Jack	62T	372	$1.25	$5.00
Cubs, Team Leaders	89T	549	$ .01	$ .03	Curtis, John	72T	724	$1.25	$5.00
Cuccinello, Tony	60T	458	$1.25	$5.00	Curtis, John	73T	143	$ .10	$ .40
Cuellar, Bobby	80T	665	$ .01	$ .10	Curtis, John	74T	373	$ .10	$ .40
Cueller (Cuellar), Mike	59T	518	$6.00	$24.00	Curtis, John	74TTR	373	$ .10	$ .40
Cuellar, Mike	60T	398	$ .75	$3.00	Curtis, John	75T	381	$ .10	$ .40
Cuellar, Mike	65T	337	$ .50	$2.00	Curtis, John	76T	239	$ .05	$ .25
Cuellar, Mike	66T	566	$8.00	$323.00	Curtis, John	77T	324	$ .05	$ .20
Cuellar, Mike	67T	97	$ .40	$1.60	Curtis, John	78T	486	$ .04	$ .16
Cuellar, Mike	67T	234	$2.00	$8.00	Curtis, John	79T	649	$ .03	$ .12
Cuellar, Mike	68T	274	$ .35	$1.40	Curtis, John	80T	12	$ .01	$ .10
Cuellar, Mike	69T	453	$ .50	$2.00	Curtis, John	81T	531	$ .01	$ .08
Cuellar, Mike	69T	532	$ .40	$1.60	Curtis, John	82T	219	$ .01	$ .08
Cuellar, Mike	70T	68	$ .50	$2.00	Curtis, John	83T	777	$ .01	$ .08
Cuellar, Mike	70T	70	$ .50	$2.00	Curtis, John	84T	158	$ .01	$ .06
Cuellar, Mike	70T	590	$ .50	$2.00	Cuyler, Milt	91T	684	$ .01	$ .15
Cuellar, Mike	71T	69	$ .50	$2.00	Cuyler, Milt	91TSC	470	$ .10	$ .50
Cuellar, Mike	71T	170	$ .25	$1.00	Cuyler, Milt	92T	522	$ .01	$ .10
Cuellar, Mike	72T	70	$ .20	$ .80	Cuyler, Milt	92TSC	5	$ .05	$ .25
Cuellar, Mike	73T	470	$ .25	$1.00	Cuyler, Milt	93T	429	$ .01	$ .03
Cuellar, Mike	74T	560	$ .20	$ .80	Cuyler, Milt	93TSC	156	$ .01	$ .10
Cueller (Cuellar), Mike	75T	410	$ .10	$ .40	D'Acquisto, John	74T	608	$ .10	$ .40
Cuellar, Mike	76T	285	$ .15	$ .60	D'Acquisto, John	75T	372	$ .10	$ .40
Cuellar, Mike	77T	162	$ .05	$ .20	D'Acquisto, John	76T	628	$ .05	$ .25
Cullen, Jack	63T	54	$1.50	$6.00	D'Acquisto, John	77T	19	$ .05	$ .20
Cullen, Jack	66T	31	$ .35	$1.40	D'Acquisto, John	79T	506	$ .03	$ .12
Cullen, Tim	67T	167	$ .40	$1.60	D'Acquisto, John	80T	339	$ .01	$ .10
Cullen, Tim	68T	209	$ .35	$1.40	D'Acquisto, John	81T	427	$ .01	$ .08
Cullen, Tim	69T	586	$ .40	$1.60	D'Acquisto, John	82T	58	$ .01	$ .08
Cullen, Tim	70T	49	$ .20	$ .80	Daboll, Dennis	65T	561	$3.00	$12.00
Cullen, Tim	71T	566	$1.00	$4.00	Dade, Paul	78T	662	$ .04	$ .16
Cullen, Tim	72T	461	$ .25	$1.00	Dade, Paul	79T	13	$ .03	$ .12
Culp, Ray	63T	29	$ .90	$3.60	Dade, Paul	80T	254	$ .01	$ .10
Culp, Ray	64T	412	$1.00	$4.00	Dade, Paul	81T	496	$ .01	$ .08
Culp, Ray	65T	505	$1.25	$5.00	Dailey, Bill	63T	301	$1.00	$4.00
Culp, Ray	66T	4	$ .35	$1.40	Dailey, Bill	64T	156	$ .50	$2.00
Culp, Ray	67T	168	$ .40	$1.60	Dal Canton, Bruce	69T	468	$ .30	$1.20
Culp, Ray	68T	272	$ .35	$1.40	Dal Canton, Bruce	70T	52	$ .20	$ .80
Culp, Ray	69T	391	$ .30	$1.20	Dal Canton, Bruce	71T	168	$ .25	$1.00
Culp, Ray	70T	144	$ .20	$ .80	Dal Canton, Bruce	72T	717	$1.25	$5.00
Culp, Ray	71T	660	$1.10	$4.40	Dal Canton, Bruce	73T	487	$ .25	$1.00
Culp, Ray	72T	2	$ .10	$ .40	Dal Canton, Bruce	74T	308	$ .10	$ .40
Culver, George	65T	166	$ .75	$3.00	Dal Canton, Bruce	75T	472	$ .10	$ .40
Culver, George	67T	499	$1.50	$6.00	Dal Canton, Bruce	76T	486	$ .05	$ .25
Culver, George	68T	319	$ .35	$1.40	Dal Canton, Bruce	77T	114	$ .05	$ .20
Culver, George	69T	635	$ .40	$1.60	Daley, Bud	58T	222	$1.25	$5.00
Culver, George	70T	92	$ .20	$ .80	Daley, Bud	59T	263	$1.00	$4.00
Culver, George	71T	291	$ .25	$1.00	Daley, Bud	60T	8	$ .85	$3.40
Culver, George	72T	732	$1.25	$5.00	Daley, Bud	61T	48	$ .75	$3.00
Culver, George	73T	242	$ .10	$ .40	Daley, Bud	61T	422	$1.00	$4.00
Culver, George	74T	632	$ .10	$ .40	Daley, Bud	62T	376	$1.25	$5.00
Cumberland, John	69T	114	$ .35	$1.40	Daley, Bud	63T	38	$ .50	$2.00
Cumberland, John	71T	108	$ .25	$1.00	Daley, Bud	64T	164	$ .50	$2.00

TOPPS

Player	Year	No.	VG	EX/MT
Daley, Bud	65T	262	$ .50	$2.00
Daley, Pete	55T	206	$6.25	$25.00
Daley, Pete	57T	388	$1.75	$7.00
Daley, Pete	58T	73	$2.00	$8.00
Daley, Pete	59T	276	$1.00	$4.00
Daley, Pete	60T	108	$ .85	$3.40
Daley, Pete	61T	158	$ .60	$2.40
Dalkowski, Steve	63T	496	$3.00	$12.00
Dalrymple, Clay	60T	523	$2.75	$11.00
Dalrymple, Clay	61T	299	$ .60	$2.40
Dalrymple, Clay	62T	434	$1.25	$5.00
Dalrymple, Clay	63T	192	$ .50	$2.00
Dalrymple, Clay	64T	191	$ .50	$2.00
Dalrymple, Clay	65T	372	$1.00	$4.00
Dalrymple, Clay	66T	202	$ .50	$2.00
Dalrymple, Clay	67T	53	$ .40	$1.60
Dalrymple, Clay	68T	567	$ .70	$2.80
Dalrymple, Clay	69T	151	$ .60	$2.40
Dalrymple, Clayton	70T	319	$ .35	$1.40
Dalrymple, Clay	71T	617	$1.00	$4.00
Daniels, Bennie	58T	392	$1.00	$4.00
Daniels, Bennie	59T	122	$1.00	$4.00
Daniels, Bennie	60T	91	$ .85	$3.40
Daniels, Bennie	61T	368	$ .60	$2.40
Daniels, Bennie	62T	378	$1.25	$5.00
Daniels, Bennie	63T	497	$3.00	$12.00
Daniels, Bennie	64T	587	$3.00	$12.00
Daniels, Bennie	65T	129	$ .35	$1.40
Daniels, Kal	87T	466	$ .01	$ .10
Daniels, Kal	88T	622	$ .01	$ .10
Daniels, Kal	89T	45	$ .01	$ .06
Daniels, Kal	90T	585	$ .01	$ .03
Daniels, Kal	91T	245	$ .01	$ .03
Daniels, Kal	91TSC	116	$ .05	$ .25
Daniels, Kal	92T	767	$ .01	$ .03
Daniels, Kal	92TSC	514	$ .01	$ .10
Daniels, Kal	93T	128	$ .01	$ .03
Darcy, Pat	75T	615	$ .25	$1.00
Darcy, Pat	76T	538	$ .05	$ .25
Dark, Al	52T	351	$57.50	$230.00
Dark, Al	53T	109	$7.50	$30.00
Dark, Al	56T	148	$3.50	$14.00
Dark, Al	57T	98	$2.00	$8.00
Dark, Al	58T	125	$2.00	$8.00
Dark, Al	59T	502	$1.00	$4.00
Dark, Al	60T	472	$1.25	$5.00
Dark, Al	61T	220	$ .60	$2.40
Dark, Al	62T	322	$ .75	$3.00
Dark, Al	63T	258	$ .90	$3.60
Dark, Al	64T	529	$2.25	$9.00
Dark, Al	66T	433	$ .35	$1.40
Dark, Al	67T	389	$ .60	$2.40
Dark, Alvin "Al"	68T	237	$ .35	$1.40
Dark, Al	69T	91	$ .35	$1.40
Dark, Alvin	70T	524	$ .35	$1.40
Dark, Alvin	71T	397	$ .50	$2.00
Dark, Alvin	78T	467	$ .04	$ .16
Dark, Alvin	91TA53	109	$ .05	$ .35
Darling, Ron	84TTR	27	$ .75	$3.00
Darling, Ron	85T	415	$ .01	$ .15
Darling, Ron	86T	225	$ .01	$ .10
Darling, Ron	87T	75	$ .01	$ .10
Darling, Ron	88T	685	$ .01	$ .04
Darling, Ron	89T	105	$ .01	$ .03
Darling, Ron	90T	330	$ .01	$ .06
Darling, Ron	91T	735	$ .01	$ .03
Darling, Ron	91TSC	60	$ .05	$ .25
Darling, Ron	92T	259	$ .01	$ .03
Darling, Ron	92TSC	685	$ .01	$ .10
Darling, Ron	93T	182	$ .01	$ .03
Darwin, Bobby	69T	641	$ .40	$1.60
Darwin, Bobby	73T	228	$ .10	$ .40
Darwin, Bobby	74T	527	$ .10	$ .40
Darwin, Bobby	75T	346	$ .10	$ .40
Darwin, Bobby	76T	63	$ .05	$ .25
Darwin, Bobby	77T	617	$ .05	$ .20
Darwin, Danny	79T	713	$ .15	$ .60
Darwin, Danny	80T	498	$ .01	$ .10
Darwin, Danny	81T	22	$ .01	$ .08
Darwin, Danny	82T	298	$ .01	$ .08
Darwin, Danny	83T	609	$ .01	$ .08
Darwin, Danny	84T	377	$ .01	$ .06
Darwin, Danny	85T	227	$ .01	$ .06
Darwin, Danny	85TTR	26	$ .01	$ .10
Darwin, Danny	86T	519	$ .01	$ .05
Darwin, Danny	87T	157	$ .01	$ .04
Darwin, Danny	88T	461	$ .01	$ .04
Darwin, Danny	89T	719	$ .01	$ .03

DANNY DARWIN

Player	Year	No.	VG	EX/MT
Darwin, Danny	90T	64	$ .01	$ .03
Darwin, Danny	91T	666	$ .01	$ .03
Darwin, Danny	91TSC	394	$ .05	$ .25
Darwin, Danny	91TTR	26	$ .01	$ .05
Darwin, Danny	92T	324	$ .01	$ .03
Darwin, Danny	92TSC	539	$ .01	$ .10
Darwin, Danny	93T	214	$ .01	$ .03
Dascenzo, Doug	89T	149	$ .01	$ .10
Dascenzo, Doug	90T	762	$ .01	$ .03
Dascenzo, Doug	91T	437	$ .01	$ .03
Dascenzo, Doug	92T	509	$ .01	$ .03
Dascenzo, Doug	92TSC	252	$ .01	$ .10
Dascenzo, Doug	93T	211	$ .01	$ .03
Dauer, Rich	77T	477	$ .05	$ .20
Dauer, Rich	78T	237	$ .04	$ .16
Dauer, Rich	79T	666	$ .03	$ .12
Dauer, Rich	80T	102	$ .01	$ .10
Dauer, Rich	81T	314	$ .01	$ .08
Dauer, Rich	82T	8	$ .01	$ .08
Dauer, Rich	83T	579	$ .01	$ .08
Dauer, Rich	84T	723	$ .01	$ .06
Dauer, Rich	85T	494	$ .01	$ .06
Dauer, Rich	86T	251	$ .01	$ .05
Daugherty, Jack	90T	52	$ .01	$ .10
Daugherty, Jack	91T	622	$ .01	$ .03
Daugherty, Jack	91TSC	276	$ .05	$ .25
Daugherty, Jack	92T	344	$ .01	$ .03
Daugherty, Jack	92TSC	634	$ .01	$ .10
Daulton, Darren	86T	264	$ .10	$1.00
Daulton, Darren	87T	636	$ .05	$ .25

TOPPS

Player	Year	No.	VG	EX/MT
Daulton, Darren	88T	468	$ .01	$ .15
Daulton, Darren	89T	187	$ .01	$ .03
Daulton, Darren	90T	542	$ .01	$ .03
Daulton, Darren	91T	89	$ .01	$ .03
Daulton, Darren	91TSC	4	$ .10	$ .40
Daulton, Darren	92T	244	$ .01	$ .03
Daulton, Darren	92TSC	529	$ .01	$ .10
Daulton, Darren	93T	180	$ .01	$ .03
Daulton, Darren	93T	408	$ .01	$ .03
Davalillo, Vic	63T	324	$1.25	$5.00
Davalillo, Vic	64T	435	$1.00	$4.00
Davalillo, Vic	65T	128	$ .35	$1.40
Davalillo, Vic	66T	216	$1.25	$5.00
Davalillo, Vic	66T	325	$ .50	$2.00
Davalillo, Vic	67T	69	$ .40	$1.60
Davalillo, Vic	68T	397	$ .35	$1.40
Davalillo, Vic	69T	275	$ .50	$2.00
Davalillo, Vic	70T	256	$ .20	$ .80
Davalillo, Vic	71T	4	$ .25	$1.00
Davalillo, Vic	72T	785	$1.25	$5.00
Davalillo, Vic	73T	163	$ .10	$ .40
Davalillo, Vic	74T	444	$ .10	$ .40
Davalillo, Vic	78T	539	$ .04	$ .16
Davalillo, Vic	79T	228	$ .03	$ .12
DaVanon, Jerry	69T	637	$ .40	$1.60
DaVanon, Jerry	71T	32	$ .25	$1.00
DaVanon, Jerry	76T	551	$ .05	$ .25
DaVanon, Jerry	77T	283	$ .05	$ .20
Davenport, Adell	93T	494	$ .05	$ .35
Davenport, Jim	58T	413	$1.50	$6.00
Davenport, Jim	59T	198	$1.00	$4.00
Davenport, Jim	60T	154	$ .75	$3.00
Davenport, Jim	61T	55	$ .60	$2.40
Davenport, Jim	62T	9	$ .60	$2.40
Davenport, Jim	63T	388	$1.00	$4.00
Davenport, Jim	64T	82	$ .50	$2.00
Davenport, Jim	65T	213	$ .50	$2.00
Davenport, Jim	66T	176	$ .50	$2.00
Davenport, Jim	67T	441	$ .60	$2.40
Davenport, Jim	68T	525	$ .75	$3.00
Davenport, Jim	69T	102	$ .35	$1.40
Davenport, Jim	70T	378	$ .35	$1.40
Davenport, Jim	85TTR	27	$ .01	$ .10
David, Andre	85T	43	$ .01	$ .06
Davidson, Mark	88T	19	$ .01	$ .04
Davidson, Mark	89T	451	$ .01	$ .03
Davidson, Mark	90T	267	$ .01	$ .03
Davidson, Mark	91T	678	$ .01	$ .03
Davidson, Mark	91TSC	584	$ .05	$ .25
Davidson, Ted	65T	243	$ .75	$3.00
Davidson, Ted	66T	89	$ .35	$1.40
Davidson, Ted	67T	519	$1.50	$6.00
Davidson, Ted	68T	48	$ .35	$1.40
Davie, Jerry	59T	256	$1.00	$4.00
Davie, Jerry	60T	301	$ .75	$3.00
Davis, Alvin	84TTR	28	$ .10	$1.00
Davis, Alvin	85T	145	$ .05	$ .20
Davis, Alvin	86T	440	$ .05	$ .30
Davis, Alvin	87T	235	$ .01	$ .10
Davis, Alvin	88T	785	$ .01	$ .04
Davis, Alvin	89T	687	$ .01	$ .03
Davis, Alvin	90T	373	$ .01	$ .03
Davis, Alvin	91T	515	$ .01	$ .03
Davis, Alvin	91TSC	82	$ .05	$ .25
Davis, Alvin	92T	130	$ .01	$ .03
Davis, Alvin	92TSC	90	$ .01	$ .10
Davis, Alvin	92TSC	617	$ .01	$ .10
Davis, Bill	65T	546	$1.40	$5.60
Davis, Bill	66T	44	$ .35	$1.40
Davis, Bill	67T	253	$ .50	$2.00
Davis, Bill	68T	432	$ .35	$1.40
Davis, Bill	69T	304	$1.75	$7.00
Davis, Bob	61T	246	$ .60	$2.40
Davis, Bob	76T	472	$ .05	$ .25
Davis, Bob	77T	78	$ .05	$ .20
Davis, Bob	78T	713	$ .04	$ .16
Davis, Bob	80T	351	$ .01	$ .10
Davis, Bob	81T	221	$ .01	$ .08
Davis, Brock	63T	553	$60.00	$240.00
Davis, Brock	71T	576	$1.00	$4.00
Davis, Brock	72T	161	$ .10	$ .40
Davis, Brock	73T	366	$ .10	$ .40
Davis, Butch	85T	49	$ .01	$ .06
Davis, Chili	82T	171	$ .20	$2.00
Davis, Chili	82TTR	23	$ .20	$2.00
Davis, Chili	83T	115	$ .10	$ .50
Davis, Chili	84T	494	$ .05	$ .20
Davis, Chili	85T	245	$ .01	$ .15
Davis, Chili	87T	672	$ .01	$ .04
Davis, Chili	88T	15	$ .01	$ .04
Davis, Chili	88TTR	32	$ .01	$ .05
Davis, Chili	89T	525	$ .01	$ .03
Davis, Chili	90T	765	$ .01	$ .03
Davis, Chili	91T	355	$ .01	$ .03
Davis, Chili	91TSC	329	$ .05	$ .25
Davis, Chili	91TTR	27	$ .01	$ .05
Davis, Chili	92T	118	$ .01	$ .03
Davis, Chili	92TSC	18	$ .01	$ .10
Davis, Chili	93T	455	$ .01	$ .03
Davis, Chili	93TSC	222	$ .01	$ .10
Davis, Dick	79T	474	$ .03	$ .12
Davis, Dick	80T	553	$ .01	$ .10
Davis, Dick	81T	183	$ .01	$ .08
Davis, Dick	81TTR	753	$ .01	$ .15
Davis, Dick	82T	352	$ .01	$ .08
Davis, Dick	82TTR	24	$ .01	$ .10
Davis, Dick	83T	667	$ .01	$ .08
Davis, Doug	92TSC	692	$ .01	$ .10
Davis, Eric	85T	627	$1.00	$4.00
Davis, Eric	86T	28	$ .10	$ .50
Davis, Eric	87T	412	$ .05	$ .25
Davis, Eric	88T	150	$ .01	$ .10
Davis, Eric	89T	330	$ .01	$ .15
Davis, Eric	90T	260	$ .01	$ .10
Davis, Eric	90TAS	402	$ .01	$ .10
Davis, Eric	91T	550	$ .01	$ .10
Davis, Eric	91TSC	37	$ .10	$ .50
Davis, Eric	92T	610	$ .01	$ .10
Davis, Eric	92TSC	660	$ .01	$ .10
Davis, Eric	92TTR	26	$ .01	$ .05
Davis, Eric	93T	745	$ .01	$ .03
Davis, Glenn	86T	389	$ .05	$ .35
Davis, Glenn	87T	560	$ .01	$ .10
Davis, Glenn	88T	430	$ .01	$ .10
Davis, Glenn	89T	765	$ .01	$ .03
Davis, Glenn	90T	50	$ .01	$ .03
Davis, Glenn	91T	350	$ .01	$ .03
Davis, Glenn	91TSC	391	$ .05	$ .25
Davis, Glenn	91TTR	28	$ .01	$ .05
Davis, Glenn	92T	190	$ .01	$ .03
Davis, Glenn	92TSC	808	$ .01	$ .10
Davis, Glenn	93T	485	$ .01	$ .03
Davis, Jacke	62T	521	$1.50	$6.00
Davis, Jacke	63T	117	$ .50	$2.00
Davis, Jerry	85TTR	28	$ .01	$ .10
Davis, Jerry	86T	323	$ .01	$ .05
Davis, Jim	55T	68	$2.25	$9.00
Davis, Jim	56T	102	$2.50	$10.00
Davis, Jim	57T	273	$5.00	$20.00
Davis, Jody	82T	508	$ .05	$ .20
Davis, Jody	83T	542	$ .01	$ .08
Davis, Jody	84T	73	$ .01	$ .06
Davis, Jody	85T	384	$ .01	$ .06
Davis, Jody	86T	767	$ .01	$ .05
Davis, Jody	87T	270	$ .01	$ .04
Davis, Jody	88T	615	$ .01	$ .04
Davis, Jody	89T	115	$ .01	$ .03
Davis, Jody	89TTR	22	$ .01	$ .05
Davis, Jody	90T	453	$ .01	$ .03
Davis, Joel	86TTR	30	$ .01	$ .06

TOPPS

Player	Year	No.	VG	EX/MT
Davis, Joel	87T	299	$ .01	$ .04
Davis, Joel	88T	511	$ .01	$ .04
Davis, John	88T	672	$ .01	$ .04
Davis, John	89T	162	$ .01	$ .03
Davis, Mark	82T	231	$ .05	$ .35
Davis, Mark	84T	343	$ .01	$ .06
Davis, Mark	85T	541	$ .01	$ .06
Davis, Mark	86T	138	$ .01	$ .05

Player	Year	No.	VG	EX/MT
Davis, Mark	87T	21	$ .01	$ .04
Davis, Mark	88T	482	$ .01	$ .04
Davis, Mark	89T	59	$ .01	$ .03
Davis, Mark	90T	205	$ .01	$ .03
Davis, Mark	90TAS	407	$ .01	$ .03
Davis, Mark	90TTR	24	$ .01	$ .05
Davis, Mark	91T	116	$ .01	$ .03
Davis, Mark	91TSC	136	$ .05	$ .25
Davis, Mark	92T	766	$ .01	$ .03
Davis, Mark	92TSC	212	$ .01	$ .10
Davis, Mike	81T	364	$ .05	$ .20
Davis, Mike	82T	671	$ .01	$ .08
Davis, Mike	83TTR	24	$ .01	$ .10
Davis, Mike	84T	558	$ .01	$ .06
Davis, Mike	85T	778	$ .01	$ .06
Davis, Mike	86T	165	$ .01	$ .05
Davis, Mike	87T	83	$ .01	$ .04
Davis, Mike	88T	448	$ .01	$ .04
Davis, Mike	88TTR	33	$ .01	$ .05
Davis, Mike	89T	277	$ .01	$ .03
Davis, Mike	90T	697	$ .01	$ .03
Davis, Ron	67T	298	$ .60	$2.40
Davis, Ron	68T	21	$ .35	$1.40
Davis, Ron	69T	553	$ .40	$1.60
Davis, Ron	80T	179	$ .05	$ .20
Davis, Ron	81T	16	$ .01	$ .08
Davis, Ron	82T	635	$ .01	$ .08
Davis, Ron	82THL	2	$ .01	$ .15
Davis, Ron	82TTR	25	$ .01	$ .10
Davis, Ron	83T	380	$ .01	$ .08
Davis, Ron	84T	519	$ .01	$ .06
Davis, Ron	85T	430	$ .01	$ .06
Davis, Ron	86T	265	$ .01	$ .05
Davis, Ron	87T	383	$ .01	$ .04
Davis, Steve	90T	428	$ .01	$ .10

Player	Year	No.	VG	EX/MT
Davis, Storm	83T	268	$ .05	$ .25
Davis, Storm	84T	140	$ .01	$ .10
Davis, Storm	85T	599	$ .01	$ .06
Davis, Storm	86T	469	$ .01	$ .05
Davis, Storm	87T	349	$ .01	$ .04
Davis, Storm	87TTR	26	$ .01	$ .05
Davis, Storm	88T	248	$ .01	$ .04
Davis, Storm	89T	701	$ .01	$ .03
Davis, Storm	90T	606	$ .01	$ .06
Davis, Storm	90TTR	25	$ .01	$ .05
Davis, Storm	91T	22	$ .01	$ .03
Davis, Storm	91TSC	67	$ .05	$ .25
Davis, Storm	92T	556	$ .01	$ .03
Davis, Storm	92TSC	728	$ .01	$ .10
Davis, Storm	93TSC	174	$ .01	$ .10
Davis, Tim	92TTR	27	$ .05	$ .20
Davis, Tommy	60T	509	$6.50	$26.00
Davis, Tommy	61T	168	$1.50	$6.00
Davis, Tommy	62T	358	$1.50	$6.00
Davis, Tommy	63T	1	$8.00	$32.00
Davis, Tommy	63T	310	$1.25	$5.00
Davis, Tommy	64T	7	$2.00	$8.00
Davis, Tommy	64T	180	$ .75	$3.00
Davis, Tommy	65T	370	$ .55	$2.20
Davis, Tommy	66T	75	$ .50	$2.00
Davis, Tommy	67T	370	$ .60	$2.40
Davis, Tommy	68T	265	$ .35	$1.40
Davis, Tommy	69T	135	$ .35	$1.40
Davis, Tommy	70T	559	$ .75	$3.00
Davis, Tommy	71T	151	$ .25	$1.00
Davis, Tommy	72T	41	$ .10	$ .40
Davis, Tommy	72TIA	42	$ .10	$ .40
Davis, Tommy	74T	396	$ .25	$1.00
Davis, Tommy	75T	564	$ .15	$ .60
Davis, Tommy	76T	149	$ .10	$ .40
Davis, Tommy	77T	362	$ .05	$ .20
Davis, Willie	61T	506	$4.00	$16.00
Davis, Willie	62T	108	$ .75	$3.00
Davis, Willie	63T	229	$ .90	$3.60
Davis, Willie	64T	68	$ .50	$2.00
Davis, Willie	65T	435	$1.00	$4.00
Davis, Willie	66T	535	$12.00	$48.00
Davis, Willie	67T	160	$ .40	$1.60
Davis, Willie	68T	208	$ .35	$1.40
Davis, Willie	69T	65	$ .35	$1.40
Davis, Willie	70T	390	$ .35	$1.40
Davis, Willie	71T	585	$1.00	$4.00
Davis, Willie	72T	390	$ .20	$ .80
Davis, Willie	73T	35	$ .20	$ .80
Davis, Willie	74T	165	$ .15	$ .60
Davis, Willie	74TTR	165	$ .15	$ .60
Davis, Willie	75T	10	$ .10	$ .40
Davis, Willie	76T	265	$ .10	$ .40
Davis, Willie	77T	603	$ .05	$ .20
Davison, Mike	71T	276	$2.00	$8.00
Dawley, Bill	84T	248	$ .01	$ .06
Dawley, Bill	85T	634	$ .01	$ .06
Dawley, Bill	86T	376	$ .01	$ .05
Dawley, Bill	87T	54	$ .01	$ .04
Dawley, Bill	88T	509	$ .01	$ .04
Dawson, Andre	77T	473	$17.50	$70.00
Dawson, Andre	78T	72	$6.00	$24.00
Dawson, Andre	79T	348	$3.50	$14.00
Dawson, Andre	80T	235	$2.25	$9.00
Dawson, Andre	81T	125	$ .75	$3.00
Dawson, Andre	82T	540	$ .25	$2.50
Dawson, Andre	82TAS	341	$ .10	$1.00
Dawson, Andre	83T	680	$ .20	$2.00
Dawson, Andre	83TAS	402	$ .10	$ .75
Dawson, Andre	84T	200	$ .10	$1.00
Dawson, Andre	84TAS	392	$ .10	$ .40
Dawson, Andre	85T	420	$ .10	$ .50
Dawson, Andre	86T	760	$ .10	$ .50
Dawson, Andre	87T	345	$ .05	$ .20
Dawson, Andre	87TTR	27	$ .05	$ .30

TOPPS

Player	Year	No.	VG	EX/MT	Player	Year	No.	VG	EX/MT
Dawson, Andre	88T	500	$ .01	$ .15	Decker, Joe	71T	98	$ .25	$1.00
Dawson, Andre	88TAS	401	$ .01	$ .10	Decker, Joe	72T	612	$ .40	$1.60
Dawson, Andre	89T	10	$ .01	$ .10	Decker, Joe	73T	311	$ .10	$ .40
Dawson, Andre	89TAS	391	$ .01	$ .10	Decker, Joe	74T	469	$ .10	$ .40
Dawson, Andre	89TRB	4	$ .01	$ .05	Decker, Joe	75T	102	$ .10	$ .40
Dawson, Andre	90T	140	$ .01	$ .10	Decker, Joe	76T	636	$ .05	$ .25
Dawson, Andre	91T	640	$ .01	$ .10	Decker, Steve	91TSC	569	$ .10	$ .50
Dawson, Andre	91TSC	310	$ .10	$ .75	Decker, Steve	91TTR	29	$ .01	$ .15
Dawson, Andre	92T	460	$ .01	$ .10	Decker, Steve	92T	593	$ .01	$ .10
Dawson, Andre	92TSC	810	$ .05	$ .25	Decker, Steve	92TSC	417	$ .01	$ .10
Dawson, Andre	93T	265	$ .01	$ .10	Decker, Steve	93T	544	$ .01	$ .03
Dawson, Andre	93TSC	203	$ .01	$ .15	Dedeaux, Rod	85T	389	$ .01	$ .06
Day, Boots	70T	654	$1.50	$6.00	Dedmon, Jeff	84TTR	30	$ .01	$ .15
Day, Boots	71T	42	$ .25	$1.00	Dedmon, Jeff	85T	602	$ .01	$ .06
Day, Boots	72T	254	$ .10	$ .40	Dedmon, Jeff	86T	129	$ .01	$ .05
Day, Boots	73T	307	$ .10	$ .40	Dedmon, Jeff	87T	373	$ .01	$ .04
Day, Boots	74T	589	$ .10	$ .40	Dedmon, Jeff	88T	469	$ .01	$ .04
Dayett, Brian	85T	534	$ .01	$ .06	Deer, Rob	86T	249	$ .05	$ .25
Dayett, Brian	85TTR	29	$ .01	$ .10	Deer, Rob	86TTR	31	$ .05	$ .20
Dayett, Brian	86T	284	$ .01	$ .05	Deer, Rob	87T	547	$ .01	$ .15
Dayett, Brian	87T	369	$ .01	$ .04	Deer, Rob	88T	33	$ .01	$ .04
Dayett, Brian	88T	136	$ .01	$ .04	Deer, Rob	89T	364	$ .01	$ .03
Dayley, Ken	83T	314	$ .01	$ .08	Deer, Rob	90T	615	$ .01	$ .03
Dayley, Ken	84T	104	$ .01	$ .06	Deer, Rob	91T	192	$ .01	$ .03
Dayley, Ken	84TTR	29	$ .01	$ .15	Deer, Rob	91TSC	539	$ .05	$ .25
Dayley, Ken	86T	607	$ .01	$ .05	Deer, Rob	91TTR	30	$ .01	$ .05
Dayley, Ken	87T	59	$ .01	$ .04	Deer, Rob	92T	441	$ .01	$ .03
Dayley, Ken	88T	234	$ .01	$ .04	Deer, Rob	92TSC	92	$ .01	$ .10
Dayley, Ken	89T	409	$ .01	$ .03	Deer, Rob	93T	243	$ .01	$ .03
Dayley, Ken	90T	561	$ .01	$ .03	Dees, Charlie	64T	159	$ .50	$2.00
Dayley, Ken	91T	41	$ .01	$ .03	DeFilippis, Art	76T	595	$ .05	$ .25
Dayley, Ken	91TSC	552	$ .05	$ .25	DeFreites, Art	80T	677	$ .01	$ .10
Dayley, Ken	92T	717	$ .01	$ .03	DeJesus, Ivan	78T	152	$ .04	$ .16
Dayley, Ken	92TSC	137	$ .01	$ .10	DeJesus, Ivan	79T	398	$ .03	$ .12
De Jardin, Bobby	92T	179	$ .05	$ .20	DeJesus, Ivan	80T	691	$ .01	$ .10
De la Hoz, Mike	61T	191	$ .60	$2.40	DeJesus, Ivan	81T	54	$ .01	$ .08
De la Hoz, Mike	62T	123	$ .60	$2.40	DeJesus, Ivan	82T	484	$ .01	$ .15
De la Hoz, Mike	63T	561	$2.25	$9.00	DeJesus, Ivan	82TTR	27	$ .01	$ .10
De la Hoz, Mike	64T	216	$ .65	$2.60	DeJesus, Ivan	83T	587	$ .01	$ .08
De la Hoz, Mike	65T	182	$ .35	$1.40	DeJesus, Ivan	84T	279	$ .01	$ .06
De la Hoz, Mike	66T	346	$ .50	$2.00	DeJesus, Ivan	85T	791	$ .01	$ .06
De la Hoz, Mike	67T	372	$ .60	$2.40	DeJesus, Ivan	85TTR	30	$ .01	$ .10
De la Rosa, Francisco	92TSC	61	$ .01	$ .15	DeJesus, Ivan	86T	178	$ .01	$ .05
De Los Santos, Luis	90T	452	$ .01	$ .03	DeJesus, Jose	90T	596	$ .01	$ .03
De Maestri, Joe	52T	286	$13.75	$55.00	DeJesus, Jose	91T	232	$ .01	$ .03
De Maestri, Joe	56T	161	$2.50	$10.00	DeJesus, Jose	91TSC	104	$ .05	$ .25
De Maestri, Joe	57T	44	$2.00	$8.00	DeJesus, Jose	92T	471	$ .01	$ .03
De Maestri, Joe	58T	62	$2.00	$8.00	Del Greco, Bob	52T	353	$43.75	$175.00
De Maestri, Joe	59T	64	$1.50	$6.00	Del Greco, Bob	53T	48	$4.00	$16.00
De Maestri, Joe	60T	358	$ .75	$3.00	Del Greco, Bob	57T	94	$2.00	$8.00
De Maestri, Joe	61T	116	$ .60	$2.40	Del Greco, Bobby	60T	486	$1.25	$5.00
Deal, Cot	54T	192	$3.75	$15.00	Del Greco, Bobby	61T	154	$ .60	$2.40
Deal, Cot	60T	459	$1.25	$5.00	Del Greco, Bobby	62T	548	$3.50	$14.00
Dean, Dizzy	91TA53	326	$ .10	$ .50	Del Greco, Bob	63T	282	$ .90	$3.60
Dean, Tommy	69T	641	$ .40	$1.60	Del Greco, Bob	91TA53	48	$ .01	$ .15
Dean, Tommy	70T	234	$ .20	$ .80	DeLeon, Jose	84T	581	$ .01	$ .10
Dean, Tommy	71T	004	$ .25	$1.00	DeLeon, Jose	85T	305	$ .01	$ .00
DeBusschere, Dave	63T	54	$1.50	$6.00	DeLeon, Jose	86T	75	$ .01	$ .05
DeBusschere, Dave	64T	247	$1.00	$4.00	DeLeon, Jose	87T	421	$ .01	$ .04
DeBusschere, Dave	65T	297	$1.00	$4.00	DeLeon, Jose	88T	634	$ .01	$ .04
DeCinces, Doug	75T	617	$ .50	$2.00	DeLeon, Jose	88TTR	34	$ .01	$ .05
DeCinces, Doug	76T	438	$ .20	$ .80	DeLeon, Jose	89T	107	$ .01	$ .03
DeCinces, Doug	77T	216	$ .05	$ .20	DeLeon, Jose	90T	257	$ .01	$ .03
DeCinces, Doug	78T	9	$ .04	$ .16	DeLeon, Jose	91T	711	$ .01	$ .03
DeCinces, Doug	79T	421	$ .05	$ .20	DeLeon, Jose	91TSC	455	$ .05	$ .25
DeCinces, Doug	80T	615	$ .01	$ .10	DeLeon, Jose	92T	85	$ .01	$ .03
DeCinces, Doug	81T	188	$ .01	$ .08	DeLeon, Jose	92TSC	67	$ .01	$ .10
DeCinces, Doug	82T	564	$ .01	$ .08	DeLeon, Luis	82T	561	$ .01	$ .08
DeCinces, Doug	82TTR	26	$ .01	$ .10	DeLeon, Luis	83T	323	$ .01	$ .08
DeCinces, Doug	83T	341	$ .01	$ .08	DeLeon, Luis	84T	38	$ .01	$ .06
DeCinces, Doug	84T	790	$ .01	$ .06	DeLeon, Luis	85T	689	$ .01	$ .06
DeCinces, Doug	85T	111	$ .01	$ .06	DeLeon, Luis	86T	286	$ .01	$ .05
DeCinces, Doug	86T	257	$ .01	$ .05	Delgado, Carlos	93T	701	$ .15	$1.50
DeCinces, Doug	87T	22	$ .01	$ .04	Delock, Ike	52T	329	$43.75	$175.00
DeCinces, Doug	88T	446	$ .01	$ .04	Delock, Ike	56T	284	$2.50	$10.00

TOPPS

Player	Year	No.	VG	EX/MT	Player	Year	No.	VG	EX/MT
Delock, Ike	57T	63	$2.00	$8.00	Denny, John	84T	135	$ .01	$ .06
Delock, Ike	58T	328	$1.25	$5.00	Denny, John	84T	637	$ .01	$ .06
Delock, Ike	59T	437	$1.00	$4.00	Denny, John	85T	325	$ .01	$ .06
Delock, Ike	60T	336	$ .75	$3.00	Denny, John	86T	556	$ .01	$ .05
Delock, Ike	61T	268	$ .60	$2.40	Denny, John	86TTR	32	$ .01	$ .06
Delock, Ike	62T	201	$ .75	$3.00	Denny, John	87T	644	$ .01	$ .04
Delock, Ike	63T	136	$ .50	$2.00	Dent, Bucky	74T	582	$ .50	$2.00
Delsing, Jim	52T	271	$12.50	$50.00	Dent, Bucky	75T	299	$ .20	$ .80
Delsing, Jim	53T	239	$22.50	$90.00	Dent, Bucky	76T	154	$ .10	$ .40
Delsing, Jim	54T	111	$3.75	$15.00	Dent, Bucky	77T	29	$ .10	$ .40
Delsing, Jim	55T	192	$6.25	$25.00	Dent, Bucky	78T	335	$ .10	$ .40
Delsing, Jim	56T	338	$2.50	$10.00	Dent, Bucky	79T	485	$ .05	$ .20
Delsing, Jim	59T	386	$1.00	$4.00	Dent, Bucky	80T	60	$ .01	$ .10
Delsing, Jim	91TA53	239	$ .01	$ .15	Dent, Bucky	81T	650	$ .01	$ .08
DeLucia, Rich	91TTR	31	$ .01	$ .05	Dent, Bucky	82T	240	$ .01	$ .08
DeLucia, Rich	92T	686	$ .01	$ .03	Dent, Bucky	82TAS	550	$ .01	$ .07
DeLucia, Rich	92TSC	511	$ .01	$ .10	Dent, Bucky	82TSA	241	$ .01	$ .07
DeLucia, Rich	93T	152	$ .01	$ .03	Dent, Bucky	83T	565	$ .01	$ .08
DeMars, Billy	73T	486	$ .25	$1.00	Dent, Bucky	84T	331	$ .01	$ .06
DeMars, Billy	74T	119	$ .10	$ .40	Dent, Bucky	90T	519	$ .01	$ .03
DeMerit, John	61T	501	$1.35	$5.40	Dente, Sam	52T	304	$12.50	$50.00
DeMerit, John	62T	4	$ .60	$2.40	DePino, Frank	91TSC	439	$ .05	$ .25
Demery, Larry	75T	433	$ .10	$ .40	Dernier, Bob	82T	231	$ .05	$ .35
Demery, Larry	76T	563	$ .05	$ .25	Dernier, Bob	82TTR	28	$ .01	$ .10
Demery, Larry	77T	607	$ .05	$ .20	Dernier, Bob	83T	43	$ .01	$ .08
Demery, Larry	78T	138	$ .04	$ .16	Dernier, Bob	84T	358	$ .01	$ .06
Demeter, Don	58T	244	$1.25	$5.00	Dernier, Bob	84TTR	31	$ .01	$ .15
Demeter, Don	59T	324	$1.00	$4.00	Dernier, Bob	85T	589	$ .01	$ .06
Demeter, Don	60T	234	$ .75	$3.00	Dernier, Bob	86T	188	$ .01	$ .05
Demeter, Don	61T	23	$ .60	$2.40	Dernier, Bob	87T	715	$ .01	$ .04
Demeter, Don	62T	146	$ .60	$2.40	Dernier, Bob	88T	642	$ .01	$ .04
Demeter, Don	63T	268	$ .90	$3.60	Dernier, Bob	89T	418	$ .01	$ .03
Demeter, Don	64T	58	$ .50	$2.00	Dernier, Bob	90T	204	$ .01	$ .03
Demeter, Don	65T	429	$1.00	$4.00	Derrington, Jim	58T	129	$1.25	$5.00
Demeter, Don	66T	98	$ .35	$1.40	DeSa, Joe	86T	313	$ .01	$ .05
Demeter, Don	67T	572	$5.50	$22.00	DeSarcina, Gary	93T	157	$ .01	$ .03
DeMola, Don	75T	391	$ .10	$ .40	Deshaies, Jim	87T	167	$ .01	$ .15
DeMola, Don	76T	571	$ .05	$ .25	Deshaies, Jim	87TRB	2	$ .01	$ .04
Dempsey, Con	52T	44	$13.75	$55.00	Deshaies, Jim	88T	24	$ .01	$ .04
Dempsey, Pat	81T	96	$ .01	$ .08	Deshaies, Jim	89T	341	$ .01	$ .03
Dempsey, Rick	72T	778	$3.75	$15.00	Deshaies, Jim	90T	225	$ .01	$ .03
Dempsey, Rick	74T	569	$ .10	$ .40	Deshaies, Jim	91T	782	$ .01	$ .03
Dempsey, Rick	75T	451	$ .15	$ .60	Deshaies, Jim	91TSC	262	$ .05	$ .25
Dempsey, Rick	76T	272	$ .04	$ .15	Deshaies, Jim	92T	415	$ .01	$ .03
Dempsey, Rick	77T	189	$ .05	$ .20	DeShields, Delino	90T	224	$ .10	$ .50
Dempsey, Rick	78T	367	$ .04	$ .16	DeShields, Delino	91T	432	$ .01	$ .15
Dempsey, Rick	79T	593	$ .03	$ .12	DeShields, Delino	91TSC	194	$ .20	$2.00
Dempsey, Rick	80T	91	$ .01	$ .10	DeShields, Delino	92T	515	$ .01	$ .15
Dempsey, Rick	81T	615	$ .01	$ .08	DeShields, Delino	92TSC	505	$ .10	$ .40
Dempsey, Rick	82T	489	$ .01	$ .08	DeShields, Delino	93T	368	$ .01	$ .10
Dempsey, Rick	83T	138	$ .01	$ .10	DeShields, Delino	93TSC	78	$ .05	$ .20
Dempsey, Rick	84T	272	$ .05	$ .20	Destrade, Orestes	89T	27	$ .05	$ .25
Dempsey, Rick	85T	521	$ .01	$ .06	Dettmer, John	91TTR	32	$ .05	$ .25
Dempsey, Rick	86T	358	$ .01	$ .05	Dettore, Tom	75T	469	$ .10	$ .40
Dempsey, Rick	87T	28	$ .01	$ .04	Dettore, Tom	76T	126	$ .05	$ .25
Dempsey, Rick	87TTR	28	$ .01	$ .05	Devereaux, Mike	89TTR	23	$ .05	$ .35
Dempsey, Rick	89T	606	$ .01	$ .03	Devereaux, Mike	90T	127	$ .01	$ .03
Dempsey, Rick	90T	736	$ .01	$ .03	Devereaux, Mike	91T	758	$ .01	$ .03
Dempsey, Rick	91T	427	$ .01	$ .03	Devereaux, Mike	91TSC	555	$ .10	$ .40
Dempsey, Rick	91TSC	553	$ .05	$ .25	Devereaux, Mike	92T	492	$ .01	$ .03
Denehy, Bill	67T	581	$300.00	$1200.00	Devereaux, Mike	92TSC	199	$ .01	$ .10
Denehy, Bill	68T	526	$ .75	$3.00	Devereaux, Mike	93T	741	$ .01	$ .03
Dennis, Don	66T	142	$ .50	$2.00	Devereaux, Mike	93TSC	56	$ .01	$ .10
Dennis, Don	67T	259	$ .50	$2.00	Devine, Adrian	74T	614	$ .10	$ .40
Denny, John	75T	621	$ .15	$ .60	Devine, Adrian	77T	339	$ .05	$ .20
Denny, John	76T	339	$ .05	$ .25	Devine, Adrian	78T	92	$ .04	$ .16
Denny, John	77T	7	$ .05	$ .20	Devine, Adrian	79T	257	$ .03	$ .12
Denny, John	77T	541	$ .05	$ .20	Devine, Adrian	80T	528	$ .01	$ .10
Denny, John	78T	609	$ .04	$ .16	Devine, Adrian	81T	464	$ .01	$ .08
Denny, John	79T	59	$ .03	$ .12	Dewey, Mark	92TSC	817	$ .01	$ .15
Denny, John	80T	464	$ .01	$ .10	Diaz, Bo	78T	708	$3.75	$15.00
Denny, John	81T	122	$ .01	$ .08	Diaz, Bo	79T	61	$ .03	$ .12
Denny, John	82T	773	$ .01	$ .08	Diaz, Bo	80T	483	$ .01	$ .10
Denny, John	83T	211	$ .05	$ .25	Diaz, Bo	81T	362	$ .01	$ .15
Denny, John	84T	17	$ .01	$ .06	Diaz, Bo	82T	258	$ .01	$ .10

TOPPS

Player	Year	No.	VG	EX/MT
Diaz, Bo	82TTR	29	$ .01	$ .10
Diaz, Bo	83T	175	$ .01	$ .08
Diaz, Bo	83T	229	$ .01	$ .08
Diaz, Bo	84T	535	$ .01	$ .06
Diaz, Bo	85T	737	$ .01	$ .06
Diaz, Bo	86T	639	$ .01	$ .05
Diaz, Bo	87T	41	$ .01	$ .04
Diaz, Bo	88T	265	$ .01	$ .04
Diaz, Bo	89T	422	$ .01	$ .03
Diaz, Carlos	84T	524	$ .01	$ .06
Diaz, Carlos	84TTR	32	$ .01	$ .15
Diaz, Carlos	85T	159	$ .01	$ .06
Diaz, Carlos	86T	343	$ .01	$ .05
Diaz, Edgar	90TTR	26	$ .01	$ .10
Diaz, Edgar	91T	164	$ .01	$ .03
Diaz, Mario	89T	309	$ .01	$ .03
Diaz, Mario	90T	781	$ .01	$ .03
Diaz, Mike	87T	469	$ .01	$ .04
Diaz, Mike	88T	567	$ .01	$ .04
Diaz, Mike	89T	142	$ .01	$ .03
Dibble, Rob	89T	264	$ .05	$ .25
Dibble, Rob	90T	46	$ .01	$ .10
Dibble, Rob	91T	662	$ .01	$ .03
Dibble, Rob	91TSC	131	$ .05	$ .25
Dibble, Rob	92T	757	$ .01	$ .03
Dibble, Rob	92TSC	584	$ .01	$ .10
Dibble, Rob	93T	470	$ .01	$ .03
Dickey, Bill	52T	400	$175.00	$700.00
Dickey, Bill	60T	465	$3.50	$14.00
Dickson, Jim	64T	524	$2.25	$9.00
Dickson, Jim	65T	286	$ .50	$2.00
Dickson, Jim	66T	201	$ .50	$2.00
Dickson, Lance	91T	114	$ .01	$ .10
Dickson, Lance	91TSC	44	$ .10	$ .50
Dickson, Lance	92TSC	836	$ .01	$ .10
Dickson, Murry	51Tbb	16	$7.50	$30.00
Dickson, Murry	52T	266	$12.50	$50.00
Dickson, Murry	56T	211	$3.75	$15.00
Dickson, Murry	57T	71	$2.00	$8.00
Dickson, Murry	58T	349	$1.25	$5.00
Dickson, Murry	59T	23	$1.50	$6.00
Didier, Bob	69T	611	$ .75	$3.00
Didier, Bob	70T	232	$ .20	$ .80
Didier, Bob	71T	432	$ .50	$2.00
Didier, Bob	73T	574	$ .60	$2.40
Didier, Bob	74T	482	$ .10	$ .40
Diering, Chuck	52T	265	$12.50	$50.00
Diering, Chuck	55T	105	$2.25	$9.00
Diering, Chuck	56T	19	$2.00	$8.00
Dierker, Larry	65T	409	$1.25	$5.00
Dierker, Larry	66T	228	$ .50	$2.00
Dierker, Larry	67T	498	$1.50	$6.00
Dierker, Larry	68T	565	$ .70	$2.80
Dierker, Larry	69T	411	$ .30	$1.20
Dierker, Larry	70T	15	$ .20	$ .80
Dierker, Larry	71T	540	$1.00	$4.00
Dierker, Larry	72T	155	$ .10	$ .40
Dierker, Larry	73T	375	$ .10	$ .40
Dierker, Larry	74T	660	$ .25	$1.00
Dierker, Larry	75T	49	$ .10	$ .40
Dierker, Larry	76T	75	$ .05	$ .25
Dierker, Larry	77T	350	$ .05	$ .20
Dierker, Larry	78T	195	$ .04	$ .16
Dietz, Dick	67T	341	$ .60	$2.40
Dietz, Dick	68T	104	$ .35	$1.40
Dietz, Dick	69T	293	$ .50	$2.00
Dietz, Dick	70T	135	$ .20	$ .80
Dietz, Dick	71T	545	$1.00	$4.00
Dietz, Dick	72T	295	$ .10	$ .40
Dietz, Dick	72TIA	296	$ .10	$ .40
Dietz, Dick	73T	442	$ .25	$1.00
DiLauro, Jack	70T	382	$ .35	$1.40
DiLauro, Jack	71T	677	$1.50	$6.00
Dillard, Don	59T	123	$1.00	$4.00
Dillard, Don	60T	122	$ .75	$3.00
Dillard, Don	61T	172	$ .60	$2.40
Dillard, Don	63T	298	$ .90	$3.60
Dillard, Steve	77T	142	$ .05	$ .20
Dillard, Steve	78T	597	$ .04	$ .16
Dillard, Steve	79T	217	$ .03	$ .12
Dillard, Steve	80T	452	$ .01	$ .10
Dillard, Steve	81T	78	$ .01	$ .08
Dillard, Steve	82T	324	$ .01	$ .08
Dillman, Bill	67T	558	$15.00	$60.00
Dillman, Bill	68T	466	$ .75	$3.00
Dillman, Bill	69T	141	$ .35	$1.40
Dillman, Bill	70T	386	$ .35	$1.40
Dillon, Steve	64T	556	$2.25	$9.00
Dilone, Miguel	78T	705	$ .04	$ .16
Dilone, Miguel	79T	487	$ .03	$ .12
Dilone, Miguel	80T	541	$ .01	$ .10
Dilone, Miguel	81T	141	$ .01	$ .08
Dilone, Miguel	82T	77	$ .01	$ .08
Dilone, Miguel	83T	303	$ .01	$ .08
Dilone, Miguel	85T	178	$ .01	$ .06
DiMaggio, Dom	51Trb	20	$3.75	$15.00
DiMaggio, Dom	52T	22	$25.00	$100.00
DiMaggio, Dom	53T	149	$8.00	$32.00
DiMaggio, Dom	91TA53	149	$ .10	$ .50
Diorio, Ron	74T	599	$ .15	$ .60
DiPino, Frank	82T	333	$ .01	$ .08
DiPino, Frank	83TTR	25	$ .01	$ .10
DiPino, Frank	84T	172	$ .01	$ .06
DiPino, Frank	85T	532	$ .01	$ .06
DiPino, Frank	86T	26	$ .01	$ .05
DiPino, Frank	87T	662	$ .01	$ .04
DiPino, Frank	88T	211	$ .01	$ .04
DiPino, Frank	89T	439	$ .01	$ .03
DiPino, Frank	89TTR	24	$ .01	$ .05
DiPino, Frank	90T	788	$ .01	$ .03
DiPino, Frank	91T	112	$ .01	$ .03
DiPino, Frank	92TSC	886	$ .01	$ .10
DiSarcina, Gary	92TSC	458	$ .01	$ .10
DiSarcina, Gary	92TTR	28	$ .01	$ .05
DiSarcina, Gary	93TSC	196	$ .01	$ .10
Distaso, Alec	69T	602	$ .40	$1.60
Distefano, Benny	85T	162	$ .01	$ .06
Distefano, Benny	87T	651	$ .01	$ .04

Didier, Bob

TOPPS

Player	Year	No.	VG	EX/MT
Distefano, Benny	89TTR	25	$ .01	$ .05
Ditmar, Art	56T	258	$3.75	$15.00
Ditmar, Art	57T	132	$2.00	$8.00
Ditmar, Art	58T	354	$1.00	$4.00
Ditmar, Art	59T	374	$1.00	$4.00
Ditmar, Art	60T	430	$ .75	$3.00
Ditmar, Art	61T	46	$ .75	$3.00
Ditmar, Art	61T	48	$ .75	$3.00
Ditmar, Art	61T	510	$1.35	$5.40
Ditmar, Art	62T	246	$ .75	$3.00
Dittmer, Jack	53T	212	$4.50	$18.00
Dittmer, Jack	54T	53	$7.50	$30.00
Dittmer, Jack	57T	282	$5.00	$20.00
Dittmer, Jack	91TA53	212	$ .01	$ .15
Dixon, Ken	85TTR	31	$ .01	$ .10
Dixon, Ken	86T	198	$ .01	$ .05
Dixon, Ken	87T	528	$ .01	$ .04
Dixon, Ken	88T	676	$ .01	$ .04
Dixon, Tom	79T	361	$ .03	$ .12
Dixon, Tom	80T	513	$ .01	$ .10
Dobbek, Dan	59T	124	$1.00	$4.00
Dobbek, Dan	60T	123	$ .75	$3.00
Dobbek, Dan	61T	108	$ .60	$2.40
Dobbek, Dan	62T	267	$ .75	$3.00
Dobson, Chuck	66T	588	$3.75	$15.00
Dobson, Chuck	67T	438	$ .60	$2.40
Dobson, Chuck	68T	62	$ .35	$1.40
Dobson, Chuck	69T	397	$ .30	$1.20
Dobson, Chuck	70T	331	$ .35	$1.40
Dobson, Chuck	71T	238	$ .25	$1.00
Dobson, Chuck	72T	523	$ .25	$1.00
Dobson, Chuck	75T	635	$ .10	$ .40
Dobson, Joe	52T	254	$12.50	$50.00
Dobson, Joe	53T	5	$6.25	$25.00
Dobson, Joe	91TA53	5	$ .01	$ .15
Dobson, Pat	67T	526	$1.75	$7.00
Dobson, Pat	68T	22	$ .35	$1.40
Dobson, Pat	69T	231	$ .50	$2.00
Dobson, Pat	70T	421	$ .35	$1.40
Dobson, Pat	71T	547	$1.00	$4.00
Dobson, Pat	72T	140	$ .10	$ .40
Dobson, Pat	73T	34	$ .10	$ .40
Dobson, Pat	74T	463	$ .10	$ .40
Dobson, Pat	75T	44	$ .10	$ .40
Dobson, Pat	76T	296	$ .05	$ .25
Dobson, Pat	76TTR	296	$ .05	$ .25
Dobson, Pat	77T	618	$ .05	$ .20
Dobson, Pat	78T	575	$ .04	$ .16
Doby, Larry	52T	243	$10.00	$40.00
Doby, Larry	54T	70	$16.25	$65.00
Doby, Larry	56T	250	$6.00	$24.00
Doby, Larry	57T	85	$2.50	$10.00
Doby, Larry	58T	424	$1.50	$6.00
Doby, Larry	59T	166	$1.50	$6.00
Doby, Larry	59T	455	$1.50	$6.00
Doby, Larry	73T	377	$ .20	$ .80
Doby, Larry	74T	531	$ .25	$1.00
Doby, Larry	91TA53	333	$ .10	$ .50
Dodgers, Team	56T	166	$40.00	$160.00
Dodgers, Team	57T	324	$30.00	$120.00
Dodgers, Team	58T	71	$11.25	$45.00
Dodgers, Team	59T	457	$5.00	$20.00
Dodgers, Team	60T	18	$5.50	$22.00
Dodgers, Team	61T	86	$1.75	$7.00
Dodgers, Team	62T	43	$1.50	$6.00
Dodgers, Team	63T	337	$3.00	$12.00
Dodgers, Team	64T	531	$5.50	$22.00
Dodgers, Team	65T	126	$1.00	$4.00
Dodgers, Team	66T	238	$1.00	$4.00
Dodgers, Team	67T	503	$3.00	$12.00
Dodgers, Team	68T	168	$ .75	$3.00
Dodgers, Team	70T	411	$ .75	$3.00
Dodgers, Team	71T	402	$ .75	$3.00
Dodgers, Team	72T	522	$ .75	$3.00
Dodgers, Team	73T	91	$ .30	$1.20

Player	Year	No.	VG	EX/MT
Dodgers, Team	74T	643	$ .25	$1.00
Dodgers, Team Checklist	75T	361	$ .35	$1.40
Dodgers, Team Checklist	76T	46	$ .30	$1.20
Dodgers, Team Checklist	77T	504	$ .25	$1.00
Dodgers, Team Checklist	78T	259	$ .20	$ .80
Dodgers, Team Checklist	79T	526	$ .15	$ .60
Dodgers, Team Checklist	80T	302	$ .10	$ .50
Dodgers, Team Checklist	81T	679	$ .05	$ .25
Dodgers, Team Leaders	86T	696	$ .01	$ .05

Player	Year	No.	VG	EX/MT
Dodgers, Team Leaders	87T	431	$ .01	$ .04
Dodgers, Team Leaders	88T	489	$ .01	$ .04
Dodgers, Team Leaders	89T	669	$ .01	$ .03
Dodson, Pat	87T	449	$ .01	$ .04
Doerr, Bobby	51Tbb	37	$25.00	$100.00
Doherty, John	75T	524	$ .10	$ .40
Doherty, John	93T	713	$ .01	$ .03
Donaldson, John	68T	244	$ .35	$1.40
Donaldson, John	69T	217	$ .35	$1.40
Donaldson, John	70T	418	$ .35	$1.40
Donnels, Chris	92T	376	$ .01	$ .10
Donnels, Chris	92TSC	353	$ .01	$ .10
Donnels, Chris	93T	238	$ .01	$ .03
Donohue, Jim	60T	124	$ .75	$3.00
Donohue, Jim	61T	151	$ .60	$2.40
Donohue, Jim	62T	498	$1.50	$6.00
Donohue, Tom	80T	454	$ .01	$ .10
Donohue, Tom	81T	621	$ .01	$ .08
Donovan, Dick	55T	146	$2.75	$11.00
Donovan, Dick	56T	18	$2.00	$8.00
Donovan, Dick	57T	181	$2.00	$8.00
Donovan, Dick	58T	290	$1.25	$5.00
Donovan, Dick	59T	5	$1.50	$6.00
Donovan, Dick	60T	199	$ .75	$3.00
Donovan, Dick	61T	414	$1.00	$4.00
Donovan, Dick	62T	15	$ .60	$2.40
Donovan, Dick	62T	55	$ .60	$2.40
Donovan, Dick	63T	8	$1.00	$4.00
Donovan, Dick	63T	370	$ .90	$3.60
Dopson, John	89T	251	$ .01	$ .03
Dopson, John	89TTR	26	$ .01	$ .10
Dopson, John	90T	733	$ .01	$ .03
Dopson, John	91T	94	$ .01	$ .03
Dopson, John	92TSC	287	$ .01	$ .10

TOPPS

Player	Year	No.	VG	EX/MT	Player	Year	No.	VG	EX/MT
Dopson, John	93T	187	$ .01	$ .03	Downing, Brian	90T	635	$ .01	$ .03
Dopson, John	93TSC	41	$ .01	$ .10	Downing, Brian	91T	255	$ .01	$ .03
Doran, Bill	83TTR	26	$ .10	$1.00	Downing, Brian	91TSC	348	$ .05	$ .25
Doran, Bill	84T	198	$ .05	$ .25	Downing, Brian	91TTR	33	$ .01	$ .05
Doran, Bill	85T	684	$ .01	$ .06	Downing, Brian	92T	173	$ .01	$ .03
Doran, Bill	86T	57	$ .01	$ .10	Downing, Brian	92TSC	494	$ .01	$ .10
Doran, Bill	87T	472	$ .01	$ .04	Downs, Kelly	87T	438	$ .01	$ .10
Doran, Bill	88T	745	$ .01	$ .10	Downs, Kelly	88T	629	$ .01	$ .04
Doran, Bill	89T	226	$ .01	$ .03	Downs, Kelly	89T	361	$ .01	$ .03
Doran, Bill	90T	368	$ .01	$ .03	Downs, Kelly	90T	17	$ .01	$ .03
Doran, Bill	91T	577	$ .01	$ .03	Downs, Kelly	91T	733	$ .01	$ .03
Doran, Bill	91TSC	148	$ .05	$ .25	Downs, Kelly	91TSC	193	$ .05	$ .25
Doran, Bill	92T	136	$ .01	$ .03	Downs, Kelly	92T	573	$ .01	$ .03
Doran, Bill	92TSC	38	$ .01	$ .10	Downs, Kelly	92TSC	517	$ .01	$ .10
Doran, Bill	93T	608	$ .01	$ .03	Doyle, Brian	79T	710	$ .05	$ .20
Dorish, Harry	52T	303	$12.50	$50.00	Doyle, Brian	80T	582	$ .01	$ .10
Dorish, Harry	53T	145	$4.00	$16.00	Doyle, Brian	81T	159	$ .01	$ .08
Dorish, Harry	54T	110	$3.75	$15.00	Doyle, Brian	81TTR	754	$ .01	$ .15
Dorish, Harry	56T	167	$2.50	$10.00	Doyle, Dennis	70T	539	$1.00	$4.00
Dorish, Harry	91TA53	145	$ .01	$ .15	Doyle, Denny	71T	352	$ .25	$1.00
Dorsey, Jim	81T	214	$ .01	$ .08	Doyle, Denny	72T	768	$1.25	$5.00
Dotson, Rich	81T	138	$ .05	$ .20	Doyle, Denny	73T	424	$ .25	$1.00
Dotson, Rich	82T	461	$ .01	$ .08	Doyle, Denny	74T	552	$ .10	$ .40
Dotson, Richard	83T	46	$ .01	$ .08	Doyle, Denny	75T	187	$ .10	$ .40
Dotson, Richard	84T	216	$ .01	$ .15	Doyle, Denny	76T	381	$ .05	$ .25
Dotson, Richard	84T	759	$ .01	$ .06	Doyle, Denny	77T	336	$ .05	$ .20
Dotson, Richard	85T	364	$ .01	$ .06	Doyle, Denny	78T	642	$ .04	$ .16
Dotson, Richard	86T	612	$ .01	$ .05	Doyle, Paul	70T	277	$ .35	$1.40
Dotson, Richard	87T	720	$ .01	$ .04	Doyle, Paul	72T	629	$ .40	$1.60
Dotson, Richard	88T	209	$ .01	$ .04	Dozier, D.J.	92T	591	$ .05	$ .20
Dotson, Richard	88TTR	35	$ .01	$ .05	Drabek, Doug	87T	283	$ .10	$ .50
Dotson, Richard	89T	511	$ .01	$ .03	Drabek, Doug	87TTR	29	$ .05	$ .35
Dotson, Richard	90T	169	$ .01	$ .03	Drabek, Doug	88T	591	$ .01	$ .15
Dotter, Gary	65T	421	$1.00	$4.00	Drabek, Doug	89T	478	$ .01	$ .03
Dotterer, Dutch	58T	396	$1.00	$4.00	Drabek, Doug	90T	197	$ .01	$ .03
Dotterer, Dutch	59T	288	$1.00	$4.00	Drabek, Doug	91T	685	$ .01	$ .03
Dotterer, Dutch	60T	21	$ .85	$3.40	Drabek, Doug	91TAS	405	$ .01	$ .03
Dotterer, Dutch	61T	332	$ .60	$2.40	Drabek, Doug	91TSC	202	$ .05	$ .25
Douglas, Whammy	58T	306	$1.25	$5.00	Drabek, Doug	92T	440	$ .01	$ .03
Douglas, Whammy	59T	431	$1.00	$4.00	Drabek, Doug	92TSC	170	$ .01	$ .10
Dowling, Dave	65T	116	$ .50	$2.00	Drabek, Doug	93T	190	$ .01	$ .03
Dowling, Dave	66T	482	$1.50	$6.00	Drabek, Doug	93TSC	167	$ .01	$ .10
Dowling, Dave	67T	272	$ .75	$3.00	Drabowsky, Moe	57T	84	$2.00	$8.00
Downing, Al	62T	219	$1.25	$5.00	Drabowsky, Moe (Mike)	58T	135	$1.25	$5.00
Downing, Al	64T	86	$ .50	$2.00	Drabowsky, Moe	59T	407	$1.00	$4.00
Downing, Al	64T	219	$ .90	$3.60	Drabowsky, Moe	60T	349	$ .75	$3.00
Downing, Al	65T	11	$ .75	$3.00	Drabowsky, Moe	61T	364	$ .60	$2.40
Downing, Al	65T	598	$4.00	$16.00	Drabowsky, Moe	62T	331	$ .75	$3.00
Downing, Al	66T	384	$ .35	$1.40	Drabowsky, Moe	64T	42	$ .50	$2.00
Downing, Al	67T	308	$ .60	$2.40	Drabowsky, Moe	65T	439	$1.00	$4.00
Downing, Al	68T	105	$ .35	$1.40	Drabowsky, Moe	66T	291	$ .50	$2.00
Downing, Al	69T	292	$ .50	$2.00	Drabowsky, Moe	67T	125	$ .40	$1.60
Downing, Al	70T	584	$ .50	$2.00	Drabowsky, Moe	68T	242	$ .35	$1.40
Downing, Al	71T	182	$ .25	$1.00	Drabowsky, Moe	69T	508	$ .30	$1.20
Downing, Al	72T	93	$ .75	$3.00	Drabowsky, Moe	70T	653	$1.25	$5.00
Downing, Al	72T	460	$ .25	$1.00	Drabowsky, Moe	71T	685	$1.10	$4.40
Downing, Al	73T	324	$ .10	$ .40	Drabowsky, Moe	72T	627	$ .40	$1.60
Downing, Al	74T	620	$ .10	$ .40	Drago, Dick	69T	662	$ .40	$1.60
Downing, Al	75T	498	$ .10	$ .40	Drago, Dick	70T	37	$ .20	$ .80
Downing, Al	76T	605	$ .05	$ .25	Drago, Dick	71T	752	$2.25	$9.00
Downing, Brian	74T	601	$1.25	$5.00	Drago, Dick	72T	205	$ .10	$ .40
Downing, Brian	75T	422	$ .25	$1.00	Drago, Dick	73T	392	$ .10	$ .40
Downing, Brian	76T	23	$ .20	$ .80	Drago, Dick	74T	113	$ .10	$ .40
Downing, Brian	77T	344	$ .10	$ .40	Drago, Dick	75T	333	$ .10	$ .40
Downing, Brian	78T	519	$ .10	$ .40	Drago, Dick	76T	142	$ .05	$ .25
Downing, Brian	79T	71	$ .10	$ .40	Drago, Dick	77T	426	$ .05	$ .20
Downing, Brian	80T	602	$ .01	$ .10	Drago, Dick	78T	567	$ .04	$ .16
Downing, Brian	81T	263	$ .01	$ .08	Drago, Dick	79T	12	$ .03	$ .12
Downing, Brian	82T	158	$ .01	$ .08	Drago, Dick	80T	271	$ .01	$ .10
Downing, Brian	84T	574	$ .01	$ .06	Drago, Dick	81T	647	$ .01	$ .08
Downing, Brian	85T	374	$ .01	$ .06	Drago, Dick	81TTR	755	$ .01	$ .15
Downing, Brian	86T	772	$ .01	$ .05	Drago, Dick	82T	742	$ .01	$ .08
Downing, Brian	87T	782	$ .01	$ .04	Drahman, Brian	92T	231	$ .01	$ .03
Downing, Brian	88T	331	$ .01	$ .04	Drahman, Brian	92TSC	744	$ .01	$ .10
Downing, Brian	89T	17	$ .01	$ .03	Drake, Sammy	62T	162	$ .60	$2.40

TOPPS

Player	Year	No.	VG	EX/MT
Drake, Solly	57T	159	$2.00	$8.00
Drake, Solly	59T	406	$1.00	$4.00
Dravecky, Dave	83T	384	$ .10	$ .75
Dravecky, Dave	84T	290	$ .01	$ .15
Dravecky, Dave	84T	366	$ .01	$ .06
Dravecky, Dave	85T	530	$ .01	$ .06
Dravecky, Dave	86T	735	$ .01	$ .05
Dravecky, Dave	87T	470	$ .01	$ .04
Dravecky, Dave	88T	68	$ .01	$ .04
Dravecky, Dave	89T	601	$ .01	$ .03
Dravecky, Dave	90T	124	$ .01	$ .03
Dreifort, Darren	91TTR	34	$ .10	$ .50
Dreifort, Darren	92TTR	29	$ .05	$ .20
Dressen, Chuck	52T	377	$50.00	$200.00
Dressen, Chuck	53T	50	$6.25	$25.00
Dressen, Chuck	60T	213	$ .75	$3.00
Dressen, Chuck	61T	137	$ .60	$2.40
Dressen, Chuck	64T	443	$1.00	$4.00
Dressen, Chuck	65T	538	$2.50	$10.00
Dressen, Chuck	66T	187	$ .50	$2.00
Dressen, Chuck	91TA53	50	$ .01	$ .15
Dressendorfer, Kirk	91TTR	35	$ .01	$ .15

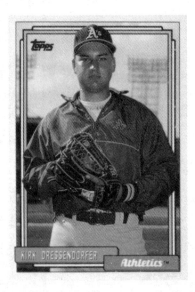

Player	Year	No.	VG	EX/MT
Dressendorfer, Kirk	92T	716	$ .01	$ .10
Dressendorfer, Kirk	92TSC	806	$ .01	$ .10
Dressler, Rob	76T	599	$2.00	$8.00
Dressler, Rob	77T	11	$ .05	$ .20
Dressler, Rob	80T	366	$ .01	$ .10
Dressler, Rob	81T	508	$ .01	$ .08
Drews, Karl	52T	352	$43.75	$175.00
Drews, Karl	53T	59	$4.00	$16.00
Drews, Karl	91TA53	59	$ .01	$ .15
Driessen, Dan	74T	341	$ .25	$1.00
Driessen, Dan	75T	133	$ .10	$ .40
Driessen, Dan	76T	514	$ .15	$ .60
Driessen, Dan	77T	23	$ .05	$ .20
Driessen, Dan	78T	246	$ .05	$ .20
Driessen, Dan	79T	475	$ .03	$ .12
Driessen, Dan	80T	325	$ .01	$ .10
Driessen, Dan	81T	655	$ .01	$ .08
Driessen, Dan	82T	785	$ .01	$ .08
Driessen, Dan	83T	165	$ .01	$ .08
Driessen, Dan	84T	585	$ .01	$ .06
Driessen, Dan	85T	285	$ .01	$ .06

Player	Year	No.	VG	EX/MT
Driessen, Dan	86T	65	$ .01	$ .05
Driscoll, Jim	71T	317	$ .25	$1.00
Dropo, Walt	52T	235	$7.50	$30.00
Dropo, Walt	53T	121	$7.50	$30.00
Dropo, Walt	54T	18	$3.75	$15.00
Dropo, Walt	56T	238	$3.75	$15.00
Dropo, Walt	57T	257	$2.00	$8.00
Dropo, Walt	58T	338	$1.25	$5.00
Dropo, Walt	59T	158	$1.00	$4.00
Dropo, Walt	60T	79	$ .85	$3.40
Dropo, Walt	61T	489	$1.35	$5.40
Dropo, Walt	91TA53	121	$ .01	$ .15
Drott, Dick	58T	80	$2.00	$8.00
Drott, Dick	59T	15	$1.50	$6.00
Drott, Dick	60T	27	$ .85	$3.40
Drott, Dick	61T	231	$ .60	$2.40
Drummond, Tim	90T	713	$ .01	$ .10
Drummond, Tim	91T	46	$ .01	$ .03
Drumright, Keith	82T	673	$ .01	$ .08
Drysdale, Don	57T	18	$52.50	$210.00
Drysdale, Don	58T	25	$18.75	$75.00
Drysdale, Don	59T	262	$2.00	$8.00
Drysdale, Don	59T	387	$10.00	$40.00
Drysdale, Don	60T	475	$11.00	$44.00
Drysdale, Don	60TAS	570	$8.00	$32.00
Drysdale, Don	61T	45	$1.00	$4.00
Drysdale, Don	61T	49	$2.00	$8.00
Drysdale, Don	61T	260	$7.50	$30.00
Drysdale, Don	62T	60	$2.00	$8.00
Drysdale, Don	62T	340	$9.00	$36.00
Drysdale, Don	62TAS	398	$3.50	$14.00
Drysdale, Don	63T	5	$2.00	$8.00
Drysdale, Don	63T	7	$1.25	$5.00
Drysdale, Don	63T	9	$2.00	$8.00
Drysdale, Don	63T	360	$10.00	$40.00
Drysdale, Don	63T	412	$9.00	$36.00
Drysdale, Don	64T	5	$2.00	$8.00
Drysdale, Don	64T	120	$4.50	$18.00
Drysdale, Don	65T	8	$2.25	$9.00
Drysdale, Don	65T	12	$1.00	$4.00
Drysdale, Don	65T	260	$5.00	$20.00
Drysdale, Don	66T	223	$1.75	$7.00
Drysdale, Don	66T	430	$5.00	$20.00
Drysdale, Don	67T	55	$3.50	$14.00
Drysdale, Don	68T	145	$2.50	$10.00
Drysdale, Don	69T	400	$2.50	$10.00
Dubiel, Walt	52T	164	$7.00	$28.00
DuBois, Brian	90T	413	$ .01	$ .10
Ducey, Rob	88T	438	$ .01	$ .10
Ducey, Rob	89T	203	$ .01	$ .03
Ducey, Rob	90T	619	$ .01	$ .03
Ducey, Rob	91T	101	$ .01	$ .03
Ducey, Rob	91TSC	374	$ .05	$ .25
Ducey, Rob	92T	739	$ .01	$ .03
Ducey, Rob	92TSC	422	$ .01	$ .10
Ducey, Rob	93T	293	$ .01	$ .03
Ducey, Rob	93TSC	69	$ .01	$ .10
Dues, Hal	79T	699	$ .03	$ .12
Dues, Hal	81T	71	$ .01	$ .08
Duffalo, Jim	62T	578	$3.50	$14.00
Duffalo, Jim	63T	567	$2.25	$9.00
Duffalo, Jim	64T	573	$2.25	$9.00
Duffalo, Jim	65T	159	$ .35	$1.40
Duffy, Frank	71T	164	$ .25	$1.00
Duffy, Frank	72T	607	$ .40	$1.60
Duffy, Frank	73T	376	$ .10	$ .40
Duffy, Frank	74T	81	$ .10	$ .40
Duffy, Frank	75T	448	$ .10	$ .40
Duffy, Frank	76T	232	$ .05	$ .25
Duffy, Frank	77T	542	$ .05	$ .20
Duffy, Frank	78T	511	$ .04	$ .16
Duffy, Frank	79T	106	$ .03	$ .12
Dukes, Jan	70T	154	$ .20	$ .80
Dukes, Tom	68T	128	$ .35	$1.40
Dukes, Tom	69T	223	$ .50	$2.00

TOPPS

Player	Year	No.	VG	EX/MT	Player	Year	No.	VG	EX/MT
Dukes, Tom	71T	106	$.25	$1.00	Durham, Leon	86T	460	$.01	$.05
Duliba, Bob	60T	401	$.75	$3.00	Durham, Leon	87T	290	$.01	$.04
Duliba, Bob	62T	149	$.60	$2.40	Durham, Leon	88T	65	$.01	$.04
Duliba, Bob	63T	97	$.50	$2.00	Durocher, Leo	52T	315	$82.50	$330.00
Duliba, Bob	64T	441	$1.00	$4.00	Durocher, Leo	67T	481	$3.00	$12.00
Duliba, Bob	66T	53	$.35	$1.40	Durocher, Leo	68T	321	$.50	$2.00
Duliba, Bob	67T	599	$2.25	$9.00	Durocher, Leo	69T	147	$.75	$3.00
Dunbar, Tommy	85T	102	$.01	$.06	Durocher, Leo	70T	291	$.35	$1.40
Dunbar, Tommy	86T	559	$.01	$.05	Durocher, Leo	71T	609	$1.25	$5.00
Duncan, Dave	64T	528	$3.00	$12.00	Durocher, Leo	72T	576	$.75	$3.00
Duncan, Dave	68T	261	$.35	$1.40	Durocher, Leo	73T	624	$1.00	$4.00
Duncan, Dave	69T	68	$.35	$1.40	Durocher, Leo	91TA53	309	$.10	$.50
Duncan, Dave	70T	678	$1.25	$5.00	Dusak, Erv	52T	183	$7.00	$28.00
Duncan, Dave	71T	178	$.30	$1.20	Dustal, Bob	63T	299	$.90	$3.60
Duncan, Dave	72T	17	$.10	$.40	Dwyer, Jim	75T	429	$.10	$.40
Duncan, Dave	73T	337	$.10	$.40	Dwyer, Jim	76T	94	$.05	$.25
Duncan, Dave	74T	284	$.10	$.40	Dwyer, Jim	78T	644	$.04	$.16
Duncan, Dave	75T	238	$.10	$.40	Dwyer, Jim	79T	236	$.03	$.12
Duncan, Dave	76T	49	$.05	$.25	Dwyer, Jim	80T	576	$.01	$.10
Duncan, Dave	77T	338	$.05	$.20	Dwyer, Jim	81T	184	$.01	$.08
Duncan, Mariano	85TTR	32	$.10	$1.00	Dwyer, Jim	81TTR	757	$.01	$.15
Duncan, Mariano	86T	602	$.05	$.25	Dwyer, Jim	82T	359	$.01	$.08
Duncan, Mariano	87T	199	$.01	$.04	Dwyer, Jim	83T	718	$.01	$.08
Duncan, Mariano	88T	481	$.01	$.04	Dwyer, Jim	84T	473	$.01	$.06
Duncan, Mariano	90T	234	$.01	$.03	Dwyer, Jim	85T	56	$.01	$.06
Duncan, Mariano	91T	13	$.01	$.03	Dwyer, Jim	86T	653	$.01	$.05
Duncan, Mariano	91TSC	251	$.05	$.25	Dwyer, Jim	87T	246	$.01	$.04
Duncan, Mariano	92T	589	$.01	$.03	Dwyer, Jim	88T	521	$.01	$.04
Duncan, Mariano	92TSC	614	$.01	$.10	Dybzinski, Jerry	81T	198	$.01	$.08
Duncan, Mariano	92TTR	30	$.01	$.05	Dybzinski, Jerry	82T	512	$.01	$.08
Duncan, Mariano	93T	371	$.01	$.03	Dybzinski, Jerry	83T	289	$.01	$.08
Duncan, Mariano	93TSC	276	$.01	$.10	Dybzinski, Jerry	83TTR	27	$.01	$.10
Duncan, Taylor	79T	658	$.03	$.12	Dybzinski, Jerry	84T	619	$.01	$.06
Dunegan, Jim	71T	121	$.25	$1.00	Dybzinski, Jerry	85T	52	$.01	$.06
Dunlop, Harry	73T	593	$.75	$3.00	Dyck, Jim	53T	177	$4.50	$18.00
Dunlop, Harry	74T	166	$.10	$.40	Dyck, Jim	56T	303	$2.50	$10.00
Dunne, Mike	85T	395	$.05	$.20	Dyck, Jim	91TA53	177	$.01	$.15
Dunne, Mike	87TTR	30	$.01	$.10	Dyer, Duffy	69T	624	$.75	$3.00
Dunne, Mike	88T	619	$.01	$.04	Dyer, Duffy	70T	692	$1.25	$5.00
Dunne, Mike	89T	165	$.01	$.03	Dyer, Duffy	71T	136	$.25	$1.00
Dunne, Mike	90T	522	$.01	$.03	Dyer, Duffy	72T	127	$.10	$.40
Dunne, Mike	91T	238	$.01	$.03	Dyer, Duffy	73T	493	$.25	$1.00
Dunning, Steve	71T	294	$.25	$1.00	Dyer, Duffy	74T	536	$.10	$.40
Dunning, Steve	72T	658	$1.25	$5.00	Dyer, Duffy	75T	538	$.10	$.40
Dunning, Steve	73T	53	$.10	$.40	Dyer, Duffy	76T	88	$.05	$.25
Dunning, Steve	78T	647	$.04	$.16	Dyer, Duffy	77T	318	$.05	$.20
Dunston, Shawon	85T	280	$.10	$.75	Dyer, Duffy	78T	637	$.04	$.16
Dunston, Shawon	86T	72	$.01	$.10	Dyer, Duffy	79T	286	$.03	$.12
Dunston, Shawon	87T	346	$.01	$.10	Dyer, Duffy	80T	446	$.01	$.10
Dunston, Shawon	88T	695	$.01	$.10	Dyer, Duffy	81T	196	$.01	$.08
Dunston, Shawon	89T	140	$.01	$.03	Dyer, Mike	90T	576	$.01	$.10
Dunston, Shawon	90T	415	$.01	$.10	Dykes, Jimmie	60T	214	$1.25	$5.00
Dunston, Shawon	91T	765	$.01	$.03	Dykes, Jimmie	61T	222	$.75	$3.00
Dunston, Shawon	91TSC	3	$.05	$.25	Dykes, Jimmie	91TA53	281	$.05	$.25
Dunston, Shawon	92T	370	$.01	$.03	Dykstra, Len	86T	53	$.10	$1.00
Dunston, Shawon	92TSC	540	$.01	$.03	Dykstra, Len	87T	295	$.01	$.15
Dunston, Shawon	93T	595	$.01	$.03	Dykstra, Len	88T	655	$.01	$.10
Dupree, Mike	77T	491	$1.75	$7.00	Dykstra, Len	89T	435	$.01	$.03
Duren, Ryne	58T	296	$3.50	$14.00	Dykstra, Len	89TTR	27	$.01	$.10
Duren, Ryne	59T	485	$1.25	$5.00	Dykstra, Len	90T	515	$.01	$.03
Duren, Ryne	60T	204	$.75	$3.00	Dykstra, Len	91T	345	$.01	$.03
Duren, Ryne	61T	356	$1.00	$4.00	Dykstra, Len	91TSC	150	$.05	$.25
Duren, Ryne	62T	388	$1.50	$6.00	Dykstra, Len	92T	200	$.01	$.03
Duren, Ryne	63T	17	$.50	$2.00	Dykstra, Len	92TSC	470	$.01	$.10
Duren, Ryne	64T	173	$.50	$2.00	Dykstra, Len	93T	740	$.01	$.03
Duren, Ryne	65T	339	$.50	$2.00	Earley, Arnold	67T	388	$.60	$2.40
Durham, Don	73T	548	$.60	$2.40	Easler, Mike	78T	710	$.15	$.60
Durham, Joe	58T	96	$2.00	$8.00	Easler, Mike	80T	194	$.01	$.10
Durham, Leon	81T	321	$.05	$.20	Easler, Mike	81T	92	$.01	$.08
Durham, Leon	81TTR	756	$.05	$.20	Easler, Mike	82T	235	$.01	$.08
Durham, Leon	82T	607	$.01	$.15	Easler, Mike	83T	385	$.01	$.08
Durham, Leon	83T	51	$.01	$.08	Easler, Mike	84T	589	$.01	$.06
Durham, Leon	83T	125	$.01	$.08	Easler, Mike	84TTR	33	$.01	$.15
Durham, Leon	84T	565	$.01	$.06	Easler, Mike	85T	686	$.01	$.06
Durham, Leon	85T	330	$.01	$.06	Easler, Mike	86T	477	$.01	$.05

TOPPS

Player	Year	No.	VG	EX/MT
Easler, Mike	86TTR	33	$ .01	$ .06
Easler, Mike	87T	135	$ .01	$ .04
Easler, Mike	88T	741	$ .01	$ .04
Easley, Damion	93T	184	$ .01	$ .15
Easley, Damion	93TSC	6	$ .10	$ .50
Easter, Luke	51Trb	26	$2.50	$10.00
Easter, Luke	52T	24	$13.75	$55.00
Easter, Luke	53T	2	$4.00	$16.00
Easter, Luke	54T	23	$3.75	$15.00
Easter, Luke	91TA53	2	$ .01	$ .15
Easterly, Jamie	75T	618	$ .25	$1.00
Easterly, Jamie	76T	511	$ .05	$ .25
Easterly, Jamie	78T	264	$ .04	$ .16
Easterly, Jamie	79T	684	$ .03	$ .12
Easterly, Jamie	82T	122	$ .01	$ .08
Easterly, Jamie	83T	528	$ .01	$ .08
Easterly, Jamie	83TTR	28	$ .01	$ .10
Easterly, Jamie	84T	367	$ .01	$ .06
Easterly, Jamie	85T	764	$ .01	$ .06
Easterly, Jamie	86T	31	$ .01	$ .05
Eastwick, Rawly	75T	621	$ .15	$ .60
Eastwick, Rawly	76T	469	$ .05	$ .25
Eastwick, Rawly	77T	8	$ .05	$ .20
Eastwick, Rawly	77T	45	$ .05	$ .20
Eastwick, Rawly	78T	405	$ .04	$ .16
Eastwick, Rawly	79T	271	$ .03	$ .12
Eastwick, Rawly	80T	692	$ .01	$ .10
Eastwick, Rawly	82T	117	$ .01	$ .08
Eckersley, Dennis	76T	98	$15.00	$60.00
Eckersley, Dennis	76T	202	$1.00	$4.00
Eckersley, Dennis	77T	525	$5.00	$20.00
Eckersley, Dennis	78T	122	$2.50	$10.00
Eckersley, Dennis	79T	40	$1.75	$7.00
Eckersley, Dennis	80T	320	$ .75	$3.00
Eckersley, Dennis	81T	620	$ .20	$2.00
Eckersley, Dennis	82T	490	$ .20	$2.00
Eckersley, Dennis	83T	270	$ .20	$2.00
Eckersley, Dennis	84T	745	$ .10	$1.00
Eckersley, Dennis	84TTR	34	$1.50	$6.00
Eckersley, Dennis	85T	163	$ .10	$ .50
Eckersley, Dennis	86T	538	$ .05	$ .35
Eckersley, Dennis	87T	459	$ .05	$ .20
Eckersley, Dennis	87TTR	31	$ .05	$ .35
Eckersley, Dennis	88T	72	$ .05	$ .20
Eckersley, Dennis	89T	370	$ .01	$ .10
Eckersley, Dennis	90T	670	$ .01	$ .10
Eckersley, Dennis	91T	250	$ .01	$ .10
Eckersley, Dennis	91TSC	332	$ .10	$ .50
Eckersley, Dennis	92T	738	$ .01	$ .15
Eckersley, Dennis	92TSC	190	$ .05	$ .25
Eckersley, Dennis	93T	155	$ .01	$ .03
Eckersley, Dennis	93T	411	$ .01	$ .10
Eckersley, Dennis	93TSC	291	$ .01	$ .15
Eddy, Don	72T	413	$ .25	$1.00
Edens, Tom	91T	118	$ .01	$ .10
Edens, Tom	92TSC	662	$ .01	$ .10
Edge, Bruce	80T	674	$ .01	$ .10
Edler, Dave	82T	711	$ .10	$1.00
Edler, Dave	83T	622	$ .01	$ .08
Edmonds, Jim	93T	799	$ .01	$ .15
Edmondson, Paul	70T	414	$ .35	$1.40
Edred, Cal	92TSC	327	$ .15	$1.50
Edward, Wayne	91T	751	$ .01	$ .03
Edwards, Bruce	51Tbb	42	$7.50	$30.00
Edwards, Bruce	52T	224	$7.00	$28.00
Edwards, Dave	80T	657	$ .01	$ .10
Edwards, Dave	81T	386	$ .01	$ .08
Edwards, Dave	81TTR	758	$ .01	$ .15
Edwards, Dave	82T	151	$ .01	$ .08
Edwards, Dave	83T	94	$ .01	$ .08
Edwards, Doc	62T	594	$20.00	$80.00
Edwards, Doc	63T	296	$ .90	$3.60
Edwards, Doc	64T	174	$ .50	$2.00
Edwards, Doc	65T	239	$ .50	$2.00
Edwards, Doc	88T	374	$ .01	$ .04
Edwards, Doc	89T	534	$ .01	$ .03
Edwards, Hank	52T	176	$7.00	$28.00
Edwards, Hank	53T	90	$4.00	$16.00

Player	Year	No.	VG	EX/MT
Edwards, Hank	91TA53	90	$ .01	$ .15
Edwards, John	62T	302	$ .75	$3.00
Edwards, Johnny	63T	178	$ .50	$2.00
Edwards, Johnny	64T	507	$1.00	$4.00
Edwards, Johnny	65T	418	$1.00	$4.00
Edwards, Johnny	66T	507	$1.50	$6.00
Edwards, Johnny	67T	202	$ .50	$2.00
Edwards, John	68T	558	$ .70	$2.80
Edwards, Johnny	69T	186	$ .35	$1.40
Edwards, Johnny	70T	339	$ .35	$1.40
Edwards, Johnny	71T	44	$ .25	$1.00
Edwards, Johnny	72T	416	$ .25	$1.00
Edwards, Johnny	73T	519	$ .25	$1.00
Edwards, Johnny	74T	635	$ .10	$ .40
Edwards, Marshall	82T	333	$ .01	$ .08
Edwards, Marshall	83T	582	$ .01	$ .08
Edwards, Marshall	84T	167	$ .01	$ .06
Edwards, Mike	79T	613	$ .03	$ .12
Edwards, Mike	79TRB	201	$ .03	$ .12
Edwards, Mike	80T	301	$ .01	$ .10
Edwards, Wayne	90TTR	27	$ .01	$ .10
Edwards, Wayne	91TSC	129	$ .05	$ .25
Edwards, Wayne	92TSC	674	$ .01	$ .10
Egan, Dick	63T	169	$8.00	$32.00
Egan, Dick	64T	572	$2.25	$9.00
Egan, Dick	66T	536	$3.75	$15.00
Egan, Dick	67T	539	$2.25	$9.00
Egan, Tom	65T	486	$1.25	$5.00
Egan, Tom	66T	263	$ .50	$2.00
Egan, Tom	67T	147	$ .40	$1.60
Egan, Tom	69T	407	$ .30	$1.20
Egan, Tom	70T	4	$ .20	$ .80
Egan, Tom	71T	537	$1.00	$4.00
Egan, Tom	72T	207	$ .10	$ .40
Egan, Tom	73T	648	$ .60	$2.40
Egan, Tom	75T	88	$ .10	$ .40
Egloff, Bruce	92TSC	503	$ .01	$ .10
Eichelberger, Juan	81T	478	$ .01	$ .08
Eichelberger, Juan	82T	366	$ .01	$ .08
Eichelberger, Juan	82T	614	$ .01	$ .08

TOPPS

Player	Year	No.	VG	EX/MT
Eichelberger, Juan	83T	168	$ .01	$ .08
Eichelberger, Juan	83TTR	29	$ .01	$ .10
Eichelberger, Juan	84T	226	$ .01	$ .06
Eichhorn, Mark	86TTR	34	$ .01	$ .06
Eichhorn, Mark	87T	371	$ .01	$ .10
Eichhorn, Mark	88T	749	$ .01	$ .04
Eichhorn, Mark	89T	274	$ .01	$ .03
Eichhorn, Mark	90T	513	$ .01	$ .03
Eichhorn, Mark	90TTR	28	$ .01	$ .05
Eichhorn, Mark	91T	129	$ .01	$ .03
Eichhorn, Mark	92T	435	$ .01	$ .03
Eichhorn, Mark	92TSC	857	$ .01	$ .10
Eiland, Dave	89T	8	$ .01	$ .10
Eiland, Dave	91T	611	$ .01	$ .03
Eiland, Dave	91TSC	477	$ .05	$ .25
Eiland, Dave	92TSC	133	$ .01	$ .10
Eiland, Dave	92TSC	879	$ .01	$ .10
Eilers, Dave	66T	534	$3.75	$15.00
Eisenreich, Jim	83T	197	$ .10	$ .50
Eisenreich, Jim	88T	348	$ .01	$ .04
Eisenreich, Jim	89TTR	28	$ .01	$ .05
Eisenreich, Jim	90T	246	$ .01	$ .03
Eisenreich, Jim	91T	707	$ .01	$ .03
Eisenreich, Jim	91TSC	373	$ .05	$ .25
Eisenreich, Jim	92T	469	$ .01	$ .03
Eisenreich, Jim	92TSC	409	$ .01	$ .10
Eisenreich, Jim	93T	22	$ .01	$ .03
Eisenreich, Jim	93TSC	224	$ .01	$ .10
Eldred, Cal	92T	433	$ .05	$ .35
Eldred, Cal	93T	590	$ .05	$ .20
Elia, Lee	66T	529	$5.00	$20.00
Elia, Lee	67T	406	$ .60	$2.40
Elia, Lee	68T	561	$ .70	$2.80
Elia, Lee	69T	312	$ .50	$2.00
Elia, Lee	83T	456	$ .01	$ .08
Elia, Lee	87TTR	32	$ .01	$ .05
Elia, Lee	88T	254	$ .01	$ .04
Ellingsen, Bruce	75T	288	$ .10	$ .40
Elliot, Larry	63T	407	$1.00	$4.00
Elliot, Larry	64T	536	$2.25	$9.00
Elliot, Larry	67T	23	$ .40	$1.60
Elliott, Bob	51Tbb	32	$7.50	$30.00
Elliott, Bob	52T	14	$13.75	$55.00
Elliott, Bob	60T	215	$ .75	$3.00
Elliott, Harry	55T	137	$2.25	$9.00
Elliott, Randy	78T	719	$ .04	$ .16
Ellis, Dock	69T	286	$ .50	$2.00
Ellis, Dock	70T	551	$ .50	$2.00
Ellis, Dock	71T	2	$ .25	$1.00
Ellis, Dock	72T	179	$ .10	$ .40
Ellis, Dock	72TIA	180	$ .10	$ .40
Ellis, Dock	73T	575	$ .60	$2.40
Ellis, Dock	74T	145	$ .10	$ .40
Ellis, Dock	75T	385	$ .10	$ .40
Ellis, Dock	76T	528	$ .05	$ .25
Ellis, Dock	76TTR	528	$ .05	$ .25
Ellis, Dock	77T	71	$ .05	$ .20
Ellis, Dock	78T	209	$ .04	$ .16
Ellis, Dock	79T	691	$ .03	$ .12
Ellis, Dock	80T	117	$ .01	$ .10
Ellis, John	70T	516	$ .35	$1.40
Ellis, John	71T	263	$ .25	$1.00
Ellis, John	72T	47	$ .10	$ .40
Ellis, John	72TIA	48	$ .10	$ .40
Ellis, John	73T	656	$ .60	$2.40
Ellis, John	74T	128	$ .10	$ .40
Ellis, John	75T	605	$ .10	$ .40
Ellis, John	76T	383	$ .05	$ .25
Ellis, John	76TTR	383	$ .05	$ .25
Ellis, John	77T	36	$ .05	$ .20
Ellis, John	78T	438	$ .04	$ .16
Ellis, John	79T	539	$ .03	$ .12
Ellis, John	80T	283	$ .10	$ .10
Ellis, John	81T	339	$ .01	$ .08
Ellis, John	82T	177	$ .01	$ .08

Player	Year	No.	VG	EX/MT
Ellis, Sammy	63T	29	$ .90	$3.60
Ellis, Sammy	64T	33	$ .50	$2.00
Ellis, Sammy	65T	507	$1.25	$5.00
Ellis, Sam	66T	250	$ .50	$2.00
Ellis, Sammy	67T	176	$ .40	$1.60
Ellis, Sammy	68T	453	$ .35	$1.40
Ellis, Sammy	69T	32	$ .35	$1.40
Ellsworth, Dick	60T	125	$1.25	$5.00
Ellsworth, Dick	61T	427	$1.00	$4.00
Ellsworth, Dick	62T	264	$ .75	$3.00
Ellsworth, Dick	63T	399	$1.00	$4.00
Ellsworth, Dick	64T	1	$5.00	$20.00
Ellsworth, Dick	64T	220	$ .65	$2.60
Ellsworth, Dick	65T	165	$ .35	$1.40
Ellsworth, Dick	66T	447	$1.75	$7.00
Ellsworth, Dick	67T	359	$ .60	$2.40
Ellsworth, Dick	68T	406	$ .35	$1.40
Ellsworth, Dick	69T	605	$ .40	$1.60
Ellsworth, Dick	70T	59	$ .20	$ .80
Ellsworth, Dick	71T	309	$ .25	$1.00
Ellsworth, Steve	89T	299	$ .01	$ .03
Elster, Kevin	88T	8	$ .01	$ .10
Elster, Kevin	89T	356	$ .01	$ .03
Elster, Kevin	90T	734	$ .01	$ .03
Elster, Kevin	91T	134	$ .01	$ .03
Elster, Kevin	91TSC	149	$ .05	$ .25
Elster, Kevin	92T	251	$ .01	$ .03
Elster, Kevin	92TSC	201	$ .01	$ .10
Elston, Don	57T	376	$1.75	$7.00
Elston, Don	58T	363	$1.00	$4.00
Elston, Don	59T	520	$4.00	$16.00
Elston, Don	60T	233	$ .75	$3.00
Elston, Don	61T	169	$ .60	$2.40
Elston, Don	62T	446	$1.25	$5.00
Elston, Don	63T	515	$1.75	$7.00
Elston, Don	64T	111	$ .50	$2.00
Elston, Don	65T	436	$1.00	$4.00
Embree, Alan	93T	742	$ .10	$ .50
Engle, Dave	81T	328	$ .01	$ .08
Engle, Dave	82T	738	$ .01	$ .08
Engle, Dave	83T	294	$ .01	$ .08
Engle, Dave	84T	463	$ .01	$ .06
Engle, Dave	85T	667	$ .01	$ .06
Engle, Dave	86T	43	$ .01	$ .05
Engle, Dave	88T	196	$ .01	$ .04
Engle, Eleanor	91TA53	332	$ .15	$1.50
Ennis, Del	51Tbb	4	$9.00	$36.00
Ennis, Del	52T	223	$7.00	$28.00
Ennis, Del	56T	220	$3.75	$15.00
Ennis, Del	57T	260	$2.00	$8.00
Ennis, Del	58T	60	$2.00	$8.00
Ennis, Del	59T	255	$1.00	$4.00
Eppard, Jim	89T	42	$ .01	$ .03
Epstein, Mike	67T	204	$ .50	$2.00
Epstein, Mike	68T	358	$ .35	$1.40
Epstein, Mike	69T	461	$ .30	$1.20
Epstein, Mike	69T	539	$1.50	$6.00
Epstein, Mike	70T	235	$ .20	$ .80
Epstein, Mike	71T	655	$1.50	$6.00
Epstein, Mike	72T	715	$1.25	$5.00
Epstein, Mike	73T	38	$ .10	$ .40
Epstein, Mike	74T	650	$ .10	$ .40
Erautt, Ed	52T	171	$7.00	$28.00
Erautt, Ed	53T	226	$22.50	$90.00
Erautt, Ed	91TA53	226	$ .01	$ .15
Erickson, Roger	79T	81	$ .03	$ .12
Erickson, Roger	80T	256	$ .01	$ .10
Erickson, Roger	81T	434	$ .01	$ .08
Erickson, Roger	82T	153	$ .01	$ .08
Erickson, Roger	82TTR	30	$ .01	$ .10
Erickson, Roger	83T	539	$ .01	$ .08
Erickson, Scott	90TTR	29	$ .10	$ .75
Erickson, Scott	91T	234	$ .05	$ .20
Erickson, Scott	91TSC	560	$ .10	$1.00
Erickson, Scott	92T	605	$ .01	$ .15

365

TOPPS

Player	Year	No.	VG	EX/MT	Player	Year	No.	VG	EX/MT
Erickson, Scott	92TSC	110	$.01	$.15	Estrada, Chuck	73T	549	$1.00	$4.00
Erickson, Scott	93T	90	$.01	$.03	Etchebarren, Andy	66T	27	$.35	$1.40
Ermer, Cal	68T	206	$.35	$1.40					
Erskine, Carl	52T	250	$17.50	$70.00					
Erskine, Carl	56T	233	$7.00	$28.00					
Erskine, Carl	57T	252	$2.75	$11.00					
Erskine, Carl	58T	258	$2.00	$8.00					
Erskine, Carl	59T	217	$1.50	$6.00					
Erskine, Carl	91TA53	308	$.10	$.50					
Esasky, Nick	84T	192	$.01	$.15					
Esasky, Nick	85T	779	$.05	$.25					
Esasky, Nick	86T	677	$.01	$.05					
Esasky, Nick	87T	13	$.01	$.06					
Esasky, Nick	88T	364	$.01	$.04					
Esasky, Nick	89T	554	$.01	$.03					
Esasky, Nick	89TTR	29	$.01	$.05					
Esasky, Nick	90T	206	$.01	$.03					
Esasky, Nick	90TTR	30	$.01	$.05					
Esasky, Nick	91T	418	$.01	$.03					
Esasky, Nick	92TSC	497	$.01	$.10					
Espino, Juan	87T	239	$.01	$.04					
Espinosa, Nino	77T	376	$.05	$.20					
Espinosa, Nino	78T	197	$.04	$.16					
Espinosa, Nino	79T	566	$.03	$.12					
Espinosa, Nino	80T	447	$.01	$.10					
Espinosa, Nino	81T	405	$.01	$.08					
Espinoza, Alvaro	87T	529	$.01	$.10					
Espinoza, Alvaro	89TTR	30	$.01	$.10					
Espinoza, Alvaro	90T	791	$.01	$.03					
Espinoza, Alvaro	91T	28	$.01	$.03					
Espinoza, Alvaro	91TSC	242	$.05	$.25					
Espinoza, Alvaro	92T	243	$.01	$.03					
Espinoza, Alvaro	92TSC	527	$.01	$.10					
Esposito, Sam	57T	301	$5.00	$20.00					
Esposito, Sam	58T	425	$1.00	$4.00	Etchebarren, Andy	67T	457	$.60	$2.40
Esposito, Sam	59T	438	$1.00	$4.00	Etchebarren, Andy	68T	204	$.35	$1.40
Esposito, Sammy	60T	31	$.85	$3.40	Etchebarren, Andy	69T	634	$.40	$1.60
Esposito, Sammy	61T	323	$.60	$2.40	Etchebarren, Andy	70T	213	$.20	$.80
Esposito, Sammy	62T	586	$6.00	$24.00	Etchebarren, Andy	71T	501	$.50	$2.00
Esposito, Sammy	63T	181	$.50	$2.00	Etchebarren, Andy	72T	26	$.10	$.40
Espy, Cecil	88TTR	36	$.01	$.10	Etchebarren, Andy	73T	618	$.60	$2.40
Espy, Cecil	89T	221	$.01	$.03	Etchebarren, Andy	74T	488	$.10	$.40
Espy, Cecil	90T	496	$.01	$.03	Etchebarren, Andy	75T	583	$.10	$.40
Espy, Cecil	92TSC	95	$.01	$.10	Etchebarren, Andy	76T	129	$.05	$.25
Essegian, Chuck	58T	460	$1.00	$4.00	Etchebarren, Andy	77T	454	$.05	$.20
Essegian, Chuck	59T	278	$1.00	$4.00	Etchebarren, Andy	78T	313	$.04	$.16
Essegian, Chuck	60T	166	$.75	$3.00	Etheridge, Bobby	68T	126	$.35	$1.40
Essegian, Chuck	61T	384	$1.00	$4.00	Etheridge, Bobby	69T	604	$.40	$1.60
Essegian, Chuck	62T	379	$1.25	$5.00	Etheridge, Bobby	70T	107	$.20	$.80
Essegian, Chuck	63T	103	$.50	$2.00	Eufemia, Frank	86T	236	$.01	$.05
Essian, Jim	77T	529	$.05	$.20	Eusebio, Tony	92TSC	546	$.01	$.10
Essian, Jim	78T	98	$.04	$.16	Evans, Al	52T	152	$7.00	$28.00
Essian, Jim	79T	458	$.03	$.12	Evans, Barry	81T	72	$.01	$.08
Essian, Jim	80T	341	$.01	$.10	Evans, Barry	82T	541	$.01	$.08
Essian, Jim	81T	178	$.01	$.08	Evans, Darrell	70T	621	$6.00	$24.00
Essian, Jim	81TTR	759	$.01	$.15	Evans, Darrell	72T	171	$.50	$2.00
Essian, Jim	82T	269	$.01	$.08	Evans, Darrell	72TIA	172	$.25	$1.00
Essian, Jim	82TTR	31	$.01	$.10	Evans, Darrell	73T	374	$.25	$1.00
Essian, Jim	83T	646	$.01	$.08	Evans, Darrell	74T	140	$.25	$1.00
Essian, Jim	83TTR	30	$.01	$.10	Evans, Darrell	75T	475	$.25	$1.00
Essian, Jim	84T	737	$.01	$.06	Evans, Darrell	76T	81	$.20	$.80
Essian, Jim	84TTR	35	$.01	$.15	Evans, Darrell	77T	571	$.20	$.80
Essian, Jim	85T	472	$.01	$.06	Evans, Darrell	78T	215	$.05	$.20
Essian, Jim	91TTR	36	$.01	$.05	Evans, Darrell	79T	410	$.05	$.20
Estelle, Dick	65T	282	$.75	$3.00	Evans, Darrell	80T	145	$.01	$.10
Estelle, Dick	66T	373	$.65	$2.60	Evans, Darrell	81T	648	$.01	$.08
Estes, Shawn	92T	624	$.01	$.10	Evans, Darrell	82T	17	$.01	$.15
Estrada, Chuck	60T	126	$1.25	$5.00	Evans, Darrell	83T	448	$.01	$.08
Estrada, Chuck	61T	48	$.75	$3.00	Evans, Darrell	84T	325	$.01	$.06
Estrada, Chuck	61T	395	$1.00	$4.00	Evans, Darrell	84TTR	36	$.01	$.15
Estrada, Chuck	62T	560	$6.00	$24.00	Evans, Darrell	85T	792	$.01	$.10
Estrada, Chuck	63T	465	$3.00	$12.00	Evans, Darrell	86T	515	$.01	$.05
Estrada, Chuck	64T	263	$.65	$2.60	Evans, Darrell	87T	265	$.01	$.10
Estrada, Chuck	65T	378	$1.00	$4.00	Evans, Darrell	88T	630	$.01	$.04
Estrada, Chuck	67T	537	$2.25	$9.00	Evans, Darrell	89TTR	31	$.01	$.10

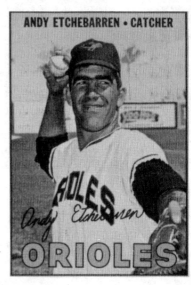

TOPPS

Player	Year	No.	VG	EX/MT	Player	Year	No.	VG	EX/MT
Evans, Darrell	90T	55	$ .01	$ .03	Fahey, Bill	76T	436	$ .05	$ .25
Evans, Dwight	73T	614	$12.50	$50.00	Fahey, Bill	77T	511	$ .05	$ .20
Evans, Dwight	74T	351	$2.50	$10.00	Fahey, Bill	78T	388	$ .04	$ .16
Evans, Dwight	75T	255	$1.50	$6.00	Fahey, Bill	80T	44	$ .01	$ .10
Evans, Dwight	76T	575	$ .75	$3.00	Fahey, Bill	81T	653	$ .01	$ .08
Evans, Dwight	77T	25	$ .75	$3.00	Fahey, Bill	81TTR	760	$ .01	$ .15
Evans, Dwight	78T	695	$ .50	$2.00	Fahey, Bill	82T	286	$ .01	$ .08
Evans, Dwight	79T	155	$ .25	$1.00	Fahey, Bill	83T	196	$ .01	$ .08
Evans, Dwight	80T	405	$ .10	$1.00	Fain, Ferris	51Trb	3	$1.65	$6.60
Evans, Dwight	81T	275	$ .10	$ .50	Fain, Ferris	52T	21	$13.75	$55.00
Evans, Dwight	82T	162	$ .10	$ .50	Fain, Ferris	53T	24	$7.50	$30.00
Evans, Dwight	82T	355	$ .05	$ .20	Fain, Ferris	54T	27	$3.75	$15.00
Evans, Dwight	83T	135	$ .05	$ .25	Fain, Ferris	55T	11	$2.50	$10.00
Evans, Dwight	84T	720	$ .05	$ .20	Fain, Ferris	91TA53	24	$ .01	$ .15
Evans, Dwight	85T	580	$ .01	$ .10	Fairey, Jim	68T	228	$ .35	$1.40
Evans, Dwight	86T	60	$ .01	$ .10	Fairey, Jim	69T	117	$ .35	$1.40
Evans, Dwight	87T	645	$ .01	$ .10	Fairey, Jim	71T	474	$ .50	$2.00
Evans, Dwight	87TRB	3	$ .01	$ .04	Fairey, Jim	72T	653	$ .40	$1.60
Evans, Dwight	88T	470	$ .01	$ .10	Fairey, Jim	73T	429	$ .25	$1.00
Evans, Dwight	89T	205	$ .01	$ .03	Fairly, Ron	59T	125	$1.75	$7.00
Evans, Dwight	90T	375	$ .01	$ .03	Fairly, Ron	60T	321	$1.25	$5.00
Evans, Dwight	91T	155	$ .01	$ .03	Fairly, Ron	61T	492	$1.35	$5.40
Evans, Dwight	91TSC	351	$ .05	$ .25	Fairly, Ron	62T	375	$1.25	$5.00
Evans, Dwight	91TTR	37	$ .01	$ .05	Fairly, Ron	63T	105	$ .50	$2.00
Evans, Dwight	92T	705	$ .01	$ .03	Fairly, Ron	64T	490	$1.00	$4.00
Evans, Dwight	92TSC	463	$ .01	$ .10	Fairly, Ron	65T	196	$ .35	$1.40
Everett, Carl	91T	113	$ .05	$ .25	Fairly, Ron	66T	330	$ .50	$2.00
Evers, Hoot	52T	222	$7.00	$28.00	Fairly, Ron	67T	94	$ .40	$1.60
Evers, Hoot	91TA53	291	$ .05	$ .20	Fairly, Ron	68T	510	$ .75	$3.00
Ewing, Sam	78T	344	$ .04	$ .16	Fairly, Ron	69T	122	$ .35	$1.40
Ewing, Sam	79T	521	$ .03	$ .12	Fairly, Ron	70T	690	$1.25	$5.00
Expos, Team	70T	509	$ .75	$3.00	Fairly, Ron	71T	315	$ .25	$1.00
Expos, Team	71T	674	$2.50	$10.00	Fairly, Ron	72T	405	$ .20	$ .80
Expos, Team	72T	582	$1.25	$5.00	Fairly, Ron	73T	125	$ .20	$ .80
Expos, Team	73T	576	$1.50	$6.00	Fairly, Ron	74T	146	$ .10	$ .40
Expos, Team	74T	508	$ .25	$1.00	Fairly, Ron	75T	270	$ .10	$ .40
Expos, Team Checklist	75T	101	$ .35	$1.40	Fairly, Ron	76T	375	$ .05	$ .25
Expos, Team Checklist	76T	216	$ .30	$1.20	Fairly, Ron	77T	127	$ .05	$ .20
Expos, Team Checklist	77T	647	$ .25	$1.00	Fairly, Ron	78T	85	$ .04	$ .16
Expos, Team Checklist	78T	244	$ 10	$ .40	Fairly, Ron	79T	580	$ .03	$ .12
Expos, Team Checklist	79T	606	$ .15	$ .60	Falcone, Pete	76T	524	$ .05	$ .25
Expos, Team Checklist	80T	479	$ .10	$ .50	Falcone, Pete	76TTR	524	$ .05	$ .25
Expos, Team Checklist	81T	680	$ .05	$ .25	Falcone, Pete	77T	205	$ .05	$ .20
Expos, Team Leaders	86T	576	$ .01	$ .10	Falcone, Pete	78T	669	$ .04	$ .16
Expos, Team Leaders	87T	381	$ .01	$ .04	Falcone, Pete	79T	87	$ .03	$ .12
Expos, Team Leaders	88T	111	$ .01	$ .04	Falcone, Pete	80T	401	$ .01	$ .10
Expos, Team Leaders	89T	81	$ .01	$ .03	Falcone, Pete	81T	117	$ .01	$ .08
Face, Roy	53T	246	$20.00	$80.00	Falcone, Pete	82T	326	$ .01	$ .08
Face, Roy	54T	87	$4.50	$18.00	Falcone, Pete	83T	764	$ .01	$ .08
Face, Roy	56T	13	$2.50	$10.00	Falcone, Pete	83TTR	31	$ .01	$ .10
Face, Roy	57T	166	$2.00	$8.00	Falcone, Pete	84T	521	$ .01	$ .06
Face, Roy	58T	74	$2.00	$8.00	Falcone, Pete	85T	618	$ .01	$ .06
Face, Roy	59T	339	$1.00	$4.00	Fannin, Cliff	51Tbb	36	$7.50	$30.00
Face, Roy	59T	428	$1.00	$4.00	Fannin, Cliff	52T	285	$13.75	$55.00
Face, Roy	60T	20	$1.25	$5.00	Fannin, Cliff	53T	203	$4.50	$18.00
Face, Roy	60T	115	$1.25	$5.00	Fannin, Cliff	91TA53	203	$ .01	$ .15
Face, Roy	61T	250	$ .75	$3.00	Fannin, Jim	05T	750	$ .01	$ .06
Face, Roy	61T	370	$ .75	$3.00	Fanok, Harry	63T	54	$1.50	$6.00
Face, Roy	62T	210	$ .75	$3.00	Fanok, Harry	64T	262	$ .65	$2.60
Face, Roy	62T	423	$1.50	$6.00	Fanzone, Carmen	73T	139	$ .10	$ .40
Face, Roy	63T	409	$1.00	$4.00	Fanzone, Carmen	74T	484	$ .10	$ .40
Face, Roy	64T	539	$2.25	$9.00	Fanzone, Carmen	75T	363	$ .10	$ .40
Face, Roy	65T	347	$ .50	$2.00	Faries, Paul	91TSC	557	$ .05	$ .25
Face, Roy	66T	461	$1.50	$6.00	Faries, Paul	92T	162	$ .01	$ .03
Face, Roy	67T	49	$ .40	$1.60	Faries, Paul	92TSC	513	$ .01	$ .10
Face, Roy	68T	198	$ .35	$1.40	Fariss, Monty	89T	177	$ .05	$ .25
Face, Roy	69T	207	$ .35	$1.40	Fariss, Monty	92T	138	$ .01	$ .03
Face, Roy	91TA53	246	$ .10	$ .50	Fariss, Monty	92TSC	803	$ .05	$ .15
Faedo, Lenny	82T	766	$ .90	$3.60	Fariss, Monty	93T	575	$ .01	$ .03
Faedo, Lenny	83T	671	$ .01	$ .08	Farley, Bob	62T	426	$1.25	$5.00
Faedo, Lenny	84T	84	$ .01	$ .06	Farmer, Billy	70T	444	$ .35	$1.40
Fahey, Bill	72T	334	$ .10	$ .40	Farmer, Ed	72T	116	$ .10	$ .40
Fahey, Bill	73T	186	$ .10	$ .40	Farmer, Ed	73T	272	$ .10	$ .40
Fahey, Bill	74T	558	$ .10	$ .40	Farmer, Ed	74T	506	$ .10	$ .40
Fahey, Bill	75T	644	$ .10	$ .40	Farmer, Ed	80T	702	$ .01	$ .10

TOPPS

Player	Year	No.	VG	EX/MT
Farmer, Ed	81T	36	$ .01	$ .08
Farmer, Ed	82T	328	$ .01	$ .08
Farmer, Ed	82TTR	32	$ .01	$ .10
Farmer, Ed	83T	459	$ .01	$ .08
Farmer, Howard	92TSC	367	$ .01	$ .10
Farr, Steve	85T	664	$ .05	$ .25
Farr, Steve	86TTR	35	$ .01	$ .06
Farr, Steve	87T	473	$ .01	$ .04
Farr, Steve	88T	222	$ .01	$ .04
Farr, Steve	89T	507	$ .01	$ .03
Farr, Steve	90T	149	$ .01	$ .03
Farr, Steve	91T	301	$ .01	$ .03
Farr, Steve	91TSC	419	$ .05	$ .25
Farr, Steve	91TTR	38	$ .01	$ .05
Farr, Steve	92T	46	$ .01	$ .03
Farr, Steve	92TSC	793	$ .01	$ .10
Farr, Steve	93T	717	$ .01	$ .03
Farr, Steve	93TSC	176	$ .01	$ .10
Farrell, Dick	58T	76	$2.00	$8.00
Farrell, Dick	59T	175	$1.00	$4.00
Farrell, Dick	60T	103	$ .85	$3.40
Farrell, Dick	61T	522	$1.35	$5.40
Farrell, Dick	62T	304	$ .75	$3.00
Farrell, Dick	63T	9	$2.00	$8.00
Farrell, Dick	63T	277	$ .90	$3.60
Farrell, Dick	64T	560	$2.25	$9.00
Farrell, Dick	69T	531	$ .40	$1.60
Farrell, John	88T	533	$ .01	$ .04
Farrell, John	89T	227	$ .01	$ .03
Farrell, John	90T	32	$ .01	$ .03
Farrell, John	91T	664	$ .01	$ .03
Farrell, John	91TSC	185	$ .05	$ .25
Farrell, John	92TSC	693	$ .01	$ .10
Farrell, Jon	92T	9	$ .01	$ .15
Farrell, Turk	65T	80	$ .35	$1.40
Farrell, Turk	66T	377	$ .65	$2.60
Farrell, Turk	67T	190	$ .40	$1.60
Farrell, Turk	68T	217	$ .35	$1.40
Fassero, Jeff	91TTR	39	$ .01	$ .10
Fassero, Jeff	92T	423	$ .01	$ .03
Fassero, Jeff	92TSC	469	$ .01	$ .10
Fassero, Jeff	93T	178	$ .01	$ .03
Fast, Darcy	72T	457	$ .25	$1.00
Faul, Bill	63T	558	$3.00	$12.00
Faul, Bill	64T	236	$ .65	$2.60
Faul, Bill	66T	322	$ .50	$2.00
Felder, Kenny	93T	723	$ .10	$ .40
Felder, Mike	87T	352	$ .01	$ .04
Felder, Mike	88T	718	$ .01	$ .04
Felder, Mike	89T	263	$ .01	$ .03
Felder, Mike	90T	159	$ .01	$ .03
Felder, Mike	91T	44	$ .01	$ .03
Felder, Mike	91TSC	307	$ .05	$ .25
Felder, Mike	92T	697	$ .01	$ .03
Felder, Mike	92TSC	194	$ .01	$ .10
Felder, Mike	93T	466	$ .01	$ .03
Felix, Junior	89TTR	32	$ .05	$ .25
Felix, Junior	90T	347	$ .01	$ .10
Felix, Junior	91T	543	$ .01	$ .03
Felix, Junior	91TSC	457	$ .05	$ .25
Felix, Junior	91TTR	40	$ .01	$ .05
Felix, Junior	92T	189	$ .01	$ .03
Felix, Junior	92TSC	141	$ .01	$ .10
Felix, Junior	93T	77	$ .01	$ .03
Feller, Bob	51Trb	22	$13.75	$55.00
Feller, Bob	52T	88	$40.00	$160.00
Feller, Bob	53T	54	$25.00	$100.00
Feller, Bob	56T	200	$35.00	$140.00
Feller, Bob	91TA53	54	$ .10	$1.00
Felske, John	73T	332	$ .10	$ .40
Felske, John	85TTR	33	$ .01	$ .10
Felske, John	86T	621	$ .01	$ .05
Felske, John	87T	443	$ .01	$ .04
Felton, Terry	83T	181	$ .01	$ .08
Fenwick, Bob	72T	679	$1.25	$5.00
Fenwick, Bob	73T	567	$ .60	$2.40
Ferguson, Joe	72T	616	$ .75	$3.00
Ferguson, Joe	73T	621	$ .75	$3.00
Ferguson, Joe	74T	86	$ .10	$ .40
Ferguson, Joe	75T	115	$ .10	$ .40
Ferguson, Joe	76T	329	$ .05	$ .25
Ferguson, Joe	77T	573	$ .05	$ .20
Ferguson, Joe	78T	226	$ .04	$ .16
Ferguson, Joe	79T	671	$ .03	$ .12
Ferguson, Joe	80T	51	$ .01	$ .10
Ferguson, Joe	81T	711	$ .01	$ .08
Ferguson, Joe	82T	514	$ .01	$ .08
Ferguson, Joe	83T	416	$ .01	$ .08
Fermin, Felix	88T	547	$ .01	$ .04
Fermin, Felix	89T	303	$ .01	$ .03
Fermin, Felix	89TTR	33	$ .01	$ .05
Fermin, Felix	90T	722	$ .01	$ .03
Fermin, Felix	91T	193	$ .01	$ .03
Fermin, Felix	91TSC	238	$ .05	$ .25
Fermin, Felix	92T	632	$ .01	$ .03
Fermin, Felix	92TSC	102	$ .01	$ .10

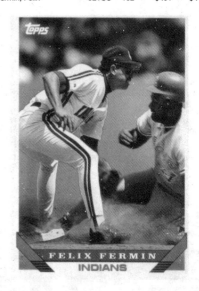

Player	Year	No.	VG	EX/MT
Fermin, Felix	93T	462	$ .01	$ .03
Fermin, Felix	93TSC	139	$ .01	$ .10
Fernandez, Alex	91T	278	$ .05	$ .20
Fernandez, Alex	91TSC	147	$ .10	$ .75
Fernandez, Alex	92T	755	$ .01	$ .10
Fernandez, Alex	92TSC	467	$ .01	$ .10
Fernandez, Alex	93T	41	$ .01	$ .03
Fernandez, Chico	57T	305	$5.00	$20.00
Fernandez, Chico	58T	348	$1.25	$5.00
Fernandez, Chico	59T	452	$1.00	$4.00
Fernandez, Chico	60T	314	$ .75	$3.00
Fernandez, Chico	61T	112	$ .60	$2.40
Fernandez, Chico	62T	173	$ .60	$2.40
Fernandez, Chico	63T	278	$ .90	$3.60
Fernandez, Frank	66T	584	$3.75	$15.00
Fernandez, Frank	68T	214	$ .35	$1.40
Fernandez, Frank	69T	557	$ .40	$1.60
Fernandez, Frank	70T	82	$ .20	$ .80
Fernandez, Frank	71T	468	$ .50	$2.00
Fernandez, Sid	85T	649	$ .05	$ .25
Fernandez, Sid	86T	104	$ .01	$ .15
Fernandez, Sid	87T	570	$ .01	$ .10

TOPPS

Player	Year	No.	VG	EX/MT
Fernandez, Sid	88T	30	$ .01	$ .04
Fernandez, Sid	89T	790	$ .01	$ .03
Fernandez, Sid	90T	480	$ .01	$ .03
Fernandez, Sid	91T	230	$ .01	$ .03
Fernandez, Sid	91TSC	225	$ .05	$ .25
Fernandez, Sid	92T	382	$ .01	$ .03
Fernandez, Sid	92TSC	655	$ .01	$ .10
Fernandez, Sid	93T	188	$ .01	$ .03
Fernandez, Tony	85T	48	$ .10	$ .50
Fernandez, Tony	86T	241	$ .01	$ .10
Fernandez, Tony	87T	485	$ .01	$ .10
Fernandez, Tony	88T	290	$ .01	$ .10
Fernandez, Tony	89T	170	$ .01	$ .10
Fernandez, Tony	90T	685	$ .01	$ .03
Fernandez, Tony	91T	320	$ .01	$ .03
Fernandez, Tony	91TSC	515	$ .05	$ .25
Fernandez, Tony	91TTR	41	$ .01	$ .05
Fernandez, Tony	92T	60	$ .01	$ .03
Fernandez, Tony	92TSC	203	$ .01	$ .10
Fernandez, Tony	93T	465	$ .01	$ .03
Ferrara, Al	64T	337	$1.75	$7.00
Ferrara, Al	65T	331	$ .50	$2.00
Ferrara, Al	66T	487	$1.50	$6.00
Ferrara, Al	67T	557	$4.00	$16.00
Ferrara, Al	68T	34	$ .35	$1.40
Ferrara, Al	69T	452	$ .30	$1.20
Ferrara, Al	70T	345	$ .35	$1.40
Ferrara, Al	71T	214	$ .25	$1.00
Ferrarese, Don	55T	185	$6.25	$25.00
Ferrarese, Don	56T	266	$2.50	$10.00
Ferrarese, Don	57T	146	$2.00	$8.00
Ferrarese, Don	58T	469	$1.00	$4.00
Ferrarese, Don	59T	247	$1.00	$4.00
Ferrarese, Don	60T	477	$1.25	$5.00
Ferrarese, Don	61T	558	$7.50	$30.00
Ferrarese, Don	62T	547	$3.50	$14.00
Ferraro, Mike	68T	539	$ .70	$2.80
Ferraro, Mike	69T	83	$ .35	$1.40
Ferraro, Mike	72T	613	$ .40	$1.60
Ferraro, Mike	83TTR	32	$ .01	$ .10
Ferrer, Sergio	79T	397	$ .03	$ .12
Ferrer, Sergio	80T	619	$ .01	$ .10
Ferrick, Tom	60T	461	$1.75	$7.00
Fetters, Mike	90T	14	$ .01	$ .10
Fetters, Mike	91T	477	$ .01	$ .03
Fetters, Mike	91TSC	228	$ .05	$ .25
Fetters, Mike	92T	602	$ .01	$ .03
Fetters, Mike	92TSC	696	$ .01	$ .10
Fetters, Mike	93T	527	$ .01	$ .03
Fidrych, Mark	77T	7	$ .05	$ .20
Fidrych, Mark	77T	265	$ .25	$1.00
Fidrych, Mark	78T	45	$ .05	$ .20
Fidrych, Mark	79T	625	$ .05	$ .20
Fidrych, Mark	80T	445	$ .01	$ .10
Fidrych, Mark	81T	150	$ .01	$ .08
Fielder, Cecil	86T	386	$1.50	$6.00
Fielder, Cecil	87T	178	$ .10	$1.00
Fielder, Cecil	88T	618	$ .05	$ .35
Fielder, Cecil	89T	541	$ .05	$ .25
Fielder, Cecil	90TTR	31	$ .05	$ .20
Fielder, Cecil	91T	720	$ .01	$ .15
Fielder, Cecil	91TAS	386	$ .01	$ .10
Fielder, Cecil	91TSC	186	$ .20	$2.00
Fielder, Cecil	92T	425	$ .01	$ .10
Fielder, Cecil	92TAS	397	$ .01	$ .10
Fielder, Cecil	92TSC	250	$ .10	$ .50
Fielder, Cecil	92TSC	599	$ .05	$ .35
Fielder, Cecil	93T	80	$ .01	$ .10
Fields, Bruce	89T	556	$ .01	$ .03
Fiesella, Dan	68T	191	$ .35	$1.40
Fife, Dan	74T	421	$ .10	$ .40
Figueroa, Bien	93T	690	$ .01	$ .03
Figueroa, Danny	93T	704	$ .05	$ .20
Figueroa, Ed	75T	476	$ .10	$ .40
Figueroa, Ed	76T	27	$ .05	$ .25
Figueroa, Ed	76TTR	27	$ .05	$ .25
Figueroa, Ed	77T	195	$ .05	$ .20
Figueroa, Ed	78T	365	$ .04	$ .16
Figueroa, Ed	79T	35	$ .03	$ .12
Figueroa, Ed	80T	555	$ .01	$ .10
Figueroa, Ed	81T	245	$ .01	$ .08
Figueroa, Jesus	81T	533	$ .01	$ .08
Filer, Tom	83T	508	$ .01	$ .08
Filer, Tom	86T	312	$ .01	$ .05
Filer, Tom	88TTR	37	$ .01	$ .05
Filer, Tom	89T	419	$ .01	$ .06
Filson, Pete	84T	568	$ .01	$ .06
Filson, Pete	85T	97	$ .01	$ .06
Filson, Pete	86T	122	$ .01	$ .05
Fimple, Jack	84T	263	$ .01	$ .06
Finch, Joel	79T	702	$ .03	$ .12
Finch, Joel	80T	662	$ .01	$ .10
Fingers, Rollie	69T	597	$35.00	$140.00
Fingers, Rollie	70T	502	$8.75	$35.00
Fingers, Rollie	71T	384	$3.75	$15.00
Fingers, Rollie	72T	241	$1.75	$7.00
Fingers, Rollie	73T	84	$1.50	$6.00
Fingers, Rollie	74T	212	$1.25	$5.00
Fingers, Rollie	75T	21	$1.00	$4.00
Fingers, Rollie	76T	405	$ .75	$3.00
Fingers, Rollie	77T	523	$1.00	$4.00
Fingers, Rollie	78T	140	$ .75	$3.00
Fingers, Rollie	78T	208	$ .10	$ .40
Fingers, Rollie	79T	8	$ .10	$ .40
Fingers, Rollie	79T	390	$ .40	$1.60
Fingers, Rollie	80T	651	$ .15	$1.50
Fingers, Rollie	81T	8	$ .05	$ .25
Fingers, Rollie	81T	229	$ .20	$2.00
Fingers, Rollie	81TTR	761	$ .75	$3.00
Fingers, Rollie	82T	168	$ .05	$ .25
Fingers, Rollie	82T	585	$ .10	$ .75
Fingers, Rollie	82TSA	586	$ .05	$ .35
Fingers, Rollie	83T	35	$ .10	$ .75
Fingers, Rollie	83T	36	$ .05	$ .35
Fingers, Rollie	84T	495	$ .10	$ .50
Fingers, Rollie	84T	717	$ .05	$ .20
Fingers, Rollie	84T	718	$ .01	$ .15
Fingers, Rollie	85T	750	$ .05	$ .20
Fingers, Rollie	86T	185	$ .01	$ .15
Finigan, Jim	55T	14	$2.25	$9.00
Finigan, Jim	56T	22	$2.00	$8.00
Finigan, Jim	57T	248	$2.00	$8.00
Finigan, Jim	58T	136	$1.25	$5.00
Finigan, Jim	59T	47	$1.50	$6.00
Finley, Chuck	87T	446	$ .05	$ .25
Finley, Chuck	88T	99	$ .01	$ .15
Finley, Chuck	89T	708	$ .01	$ .10
Finley, Chuck	90T	147	$ .01	$ .10
Finley, Chuck	91T	505	$ .01	$ .03
Finley, Chuck	91TAS	395	$ .01	$ .03
Finley, Chuck	91TSC	81	$ .05	$ .25
Finley, Chuck	92T	247	$ .01	$ .03
Finley, Chuck	92TSC	315	$ .01	$ .10
Finley, Chuck	93T	605	$ .01	$ .03
Finley, Steve	90T	349	$ .01	$ .15
Finley, Steve	91T	212	$ .01	$ .10
Finley, Steve	91TSC	376	$ .05	$ .25
Finley, Steve	91TTR	42	$ .01	$ .05
Finley, Steve	92T	86	$ .01	$ .03
Finley, Steve	92TSC	29	$ .01	$ .10
Finley, Steve	93T	148	$ .01	$ .03
Fiore, Mike	69T	376	$ .30	$1.20
Fiore, Mike	70T	709	$1.25	$5.00
Fiore, Mike	71T	287	$ .25	$1.00
Fiore, Mike	72T	199	$ .10	$ .40
Fiore, Mike	88TTR	38	$ .01	$ .10
Fireovid, Steve	87T	357	$ .01	$ .04
Fischer, Bill	58T	56	$2.00	$8.00
Fischer, Bill	59T	230	$1.00	$4.00
Fischer, Bill	60T	76	$ .85	$3.40

TOPPS

Player	Year	No.	VG	EX/MT	Player	Year	No.	VG	EX/MT
Fischer, Bill	61T	553	$7.50	$30.00	Fisher, Jack	64T	422	$1.00	$4.00
Fischer, Bill	63T	301	$ .90	$3.60	Fisher, Jack	65T	93	$ .35	$1.40
Fischer, Bill	64T	409	$1.00	$4.00	Fisher, Jack	66T	316	$ .50	$2.00
Fischer, Hank	63T	554	$2.25	$9.00	Fisher, Jack	67T	533	$1.50	$6.00
Fischer, Hank	64T	218	$ .65	$2.60	Fisher, Jack	68T	444	$ .35	$1.40
Fischer, Hank	65T	585	$1.40	$5.60	Fisher, Jack	69T	318	$ .50	$2.00
Fischer, Hank	66T	381	$ .65	$2.60	Fisher, Jack	70T	684	$1.25	$5.00
Fischer, Hank	67T	342	$ .60	$2.40	Fisk, Carlton	72T	79	$25.00	$100.00
Fischlin, Mike	79T	718	$ .03	$ .12	Fisk, Carlton	73T	193	$10.00	$40.00
Fischlin, Mike	83T	182	$ .01	$ .08	Fisk, Carlton	74T	105	$6.00	$24.00
Fischlin, Mike	84T	689	$ .01	$ .06	Fisk, Carlton	74TAS	331	$1.50	$6.00
Fischlin, Mike	85T	41	$ .01	$ .06	Fisk, Carlton	75T	80	$5.50	$22.00
Fischlin, Mike	86T	283	$ .01	$ .05	Fisk, Carlton	76T	365	$2.50	$10.00
Fischlin, Mike	87T	434	$ .01	$ .04	Fisk, Carlton	77T	640	$2.25	$9.00
Fisella, Danny	72TIA	294	$ .10	$ .40	Fisk, Carlton	78T	270	$1.75	$7.00
Fisher, Brian	86T	584	$ .01	$ .10	Fisk, Carlton	79T	680	$1.25	$5.00
Fisher, Brian	87T	316	$ .01	$ .04	Fisk, Carlton	80T	40	$1.00	$4.00
Fisher, Brian	87TTR	33	$ .01	$ .05	Fisk, Carlton	81T	480	$ .75	$3.00
Fisher, Brian	88T	193	$ .01	$ .04	Fisk, Carlton	81TTR	762	$1.50	$6.00
Fisher, Brian	89T	423	$ .01	$ .03	Fisk, Carlton	82T	110	$ .20	$2.00
Fisher, Brian	90T	666	$ .01	$ .03	Fisk, Carlton	82TAS	554	$ .10	$ .75
Fisher, Eddie	60T	23	$ .85	$3.40	Fisk, Carlton	82TSA	111	$ .10	$1.00
Fisher, Eddie	61T	366	$ .60	$2.40	Fisk, Carlton	83T	20	$ .20	$2.00
Fisher, Eddie	63T	6	$1.25	$5.00	Fisk, Carlton	83TAS	393	$ .10	$ .75
Fisher, Eddie	63T	223	$ .90	$3.60	Fisk, Carlton	84T	216	$ .01	$ .15
Fisher, Eddie	64T	66	$ .50	$2.00	Fisk, Carlton	84T	560	$ .10	$1.00
Fisher, Eddie	65T	328	$ .50	$2.00	Fisk, Carlton	85T	770	$ .10	$ .75
Fisher, Eddie	66T	85	$ .35	$1.40	Fisk, Carlton	85TRB	1	$ .05	$ .35
Fisher, Eddie	66T	222	$ .75	$3.00	Fisk, Carlton	86T	290	$ .05	$ .25
Fisher, Eddie	67T	434	$ .60	$2.40	Fisk, Carlton	86TAS	719	$ .05	$ .20
Fisher, Eddie	68T	418	$ .35	$1.40	Fisk, Carlton	87T	756	$ .05	$ .20
Fisher, Eddie	69T	315	$ .50	$2.00	Fisk, Carlton	88T	385	$ .05	$ .20
Fisher, Eddie	70T	156	$ .20	$ .80	Fisk, Carlton	89T	695	$ .01	$ .10
Fisher, Eddie	71T	631	$1.00	$4.00	Fisk, Carlton	90T	420	$ .01	$ .10
Fisher, Eddie	72T	689	$1.25	$5.00	Fisk, Carlton	90TAS	392	$ .01	$ .10
					Fisk, Carlton	91T	170	$ .01	$ .10
					Fisk, Carlton	91TAS	393	$ .01	$ .10
					Fisk, Carlton	91TRB	3	$ .01	$ .10
					Fisk, Carlton	91TSC	180	$ .10	$1.00
					Fisk, Carlton	92T	630	$ .01	$ .10
					Fisk, Carlton	92TSC	480	$ .05	$ .25
					Fisk, Carlton	93T	230	$ .01	$ .10
					Fisk, Carlton	93TSC	221	$ .01	$ .15
					Fitzgerald, Ed	52T	236	$7.00	$28.00
					Fitzgerald, Ed	56T	198	$3.75	$15.00
					Fitzgerald, Ed	57T	367	$1.75	$7.00
					Fitzgerald, Ed	58T	236	$1.25	$5.00
					Fitzgerald, Ed	59T	33	$1.50	$6.00
					Fitzgerald, Ed	60T	423	$ .75	$3.00
					Fitzgerald, Mike	84TTR	37	$ .01	$ .15
					Fitzgerald, Mike	85T	104	$ .01	$ .06
					Fitzgerald, Mike	85TTR	34	$ .01	$ .10
					Fitzgerald, Mike	86T	503	$ .01	$ .05
					Fitzgerald, Mike	87T	212	$ .01	$ .04
					Fitzgerald, Mike	88T	674	$ .01	$ .04
					Fitzgerald, Mike	89T	23	$ .01	$ .03
					Fitzgerald, Mike	90T	484	$ .01	$ .03
					Fitzgerald, Mike	91T	317	$ .01	$ .03
					Fitzgerald, Mike	91TSC	128	$ .05	$ .25
					Fitzgerald, Mike	92T	761	$ .01	$ .03
					Fitzgerald, Mike	92TSC	844	$ .01	$ .10
					Fitzgerald, Mike	92TTR	31	$ .01	$ .05
					Fitzmorris, Al	70T	241	$ .20	$ .80
					Fitzmorris, Al	71T	564	$1.00	$4.00
					Fitzmorris, Al	72T	349	$ .10	$ .40
					Fitzmorris, Al	73T	643	$ .60	$2.40
					Fitzmorris, Al	74T	191	$ .10	$ .40

EDDIE FISHER
CHICAGO WHITE SOX   PITCHER

Player	Year	No.	VG	EX/MT	Player	Year	No.	VG	EX/MT
Fisher, Eddie	73T	439	$ .25	$1.00	Fitzmorris, Al	75T	24	$ .10	$ .40
Fisher, Fritz	64T	312	$ .65	$2.60	Fitzmorris, Al	76T	144	$ .05	$ .25
Fisher, Fritz	66T	209	$ .75	$3.00	Fitzmorris, Al	77T	449	$ .05	$ .20
Fisher, Jack	60T	46	$ .85	$3.40	Fitzmorris, Al	78T	227	$ .04	$ .16
Fisher, Jack	60T	399	$ .75	$3.00	Fitzmorris, Al	79T	638	$ .03	$ .12
Fisher, Jack	61T	463	$1.35	$5.40	Fitzpatrick, John	54T	213	$3.75	$15.00
Fisher, Jack	62T	203	$ .75	$3.00	Fitzsimmons, Fred	60T	462	$1.25	$5.00
Fisher, Jack	63T	474	$3.00	$12.00	Flaherty, John	92TTR	32	$ .01	$ .10

TOPPS

Player	Year	No.	VG	EX/MT	Player	Year	No.	VG	EX/MT
Flanagan, Mike	76T	589	$ .50	$2.00	Flores, Gil	78T	268	$ .04	$ .16
Flanagan, Mike	77T	106	$ .10	$ .40	Flores, Gil	80T	478	$ .01	$ .10
Flanagan, Mike	78T	341	$ .10	$ .40	Floyd, Bob	69T	597	$35.00	$140.00
Flanagan, Mike	79T	160	$ .10	$ .40	Floyd, Bobby	70T	101	$ .20	$ .80
Flanagan, Mike	80T	205	$ .05	$ .20	Floyd, Bobby	71T	646	$1.50	$6.00
Flanagan, Mike	80T	640	$ .01	$ .10	Floyd, Bobby	72T	273	$ .10	$ .40
Flanagan, Mike	81T	10	$ .01	$ .08	Floyd, Bobby	74T	41	$ .10	$ .40
Flanagan, Mike	82T	520	$ .01	$ .08	Floyd, Cliff	92T	186	$ .10	$ .75
Flanagan, Mike	83T	445	$ .01	$ .08	Floyd, Cliff	93T	576	$ .10	$ .75
Flanagan, Mike	84T	295	$ .01	$ .06	Flynn, Doug	76T	518	$ .10	$ .40
Flanagan, Mike	85T	780	$ .01	$ .06	Flynn, Doug	77T	186	$ .05	$ .20
Flanagan, Mike	86T	365	$ .01	$ .05	Flynn, Doug	78T	453	$ .04	$ .16
Flanagan, Mike	87T	748	$ .01	$ .04	Flynn, Doug	79T	229	$ .03	$ .12
Flanagan, Mike	88T	623	$ .01	$ .04	Flynn, Doug	80T	58	$ .01	$ .10
Flanagan, Mike	89T	139	$ .01	$ .03	Flynn, Doug	81T	634	$ .01	$ .08
Flanagan, Mike	90T	78	$ .01	$ .03	Flynn, Doug	82T	302	$ .01	$ .08
Flanagan, Mike	92T	218	$ .01	$ .03	Flynn, Doug	82TTR	33	$ .01	$ .10
Flanagan, Mike	92TSC	30	$ .01	$ .10	Flynn, Doug	83T	169	$ .01	$ .08
Flanagan, Mike	93T	381	$ .01	$ .03	Flynn, Doug	84T	749	$ .01	$ .06
Flanagan, Mike	93TSC	123	$ .01	$ .10	Flynn, Doug	85T	554	$ .01	$ .06
Flannery, Tim	80T	685	$ .01	$ .10	Flynn, Doug	86T	436	$ .01	$ .05
Flannery, Tim	81T	579	$ .01	$ .08	Fodge, Gene	58T	449	$1.00	$4.00
Flannery, Tim	82T	249	$ .01	$ .08	Foiles, Henry "Hank"	53T	252	$22.50	$90.00
Flannery, Tim	83T	38	$ .01	$ .08	Foiles, Hank	57T	104	$2.00	$8.00
Flannery, Tim	84T	674	$ .01	$ .06	Foiles, Hank	58T	4	$2.00	$8.00
Flannery, Tim	85T	182	$ .01	$ .06	Foiles, Hank	59T	294	$1.00	$4.00
Flannery, Tim	86T	413	$ .01	$ .05	Foiles, Hank	60T	77	$ .85	$3.40
Flannery, Tim	87T	763	$ .01	$ .04	Foiles, Hank	61T	277	$ .60	$2.40
Flannery, Tim	88T	513	$ .01	$ .04	Foiles, Hank	62T	112	$ .60	$2.40
Flannery, Tim	89T	379	$ .01	$ .03	Foiles, Hank	63T	326	$ .90	$3.60
Fleming, Dave	92T	192	$ .05	$ .20	Foiles, Hank	64T	554	$2.25	$9.00
Fleming, Dave	92TSC	814	$ .15	$ .75	Foiles, Henry	91TA53	252	$ .01	$ .15
Fleming, Dave	93T	410	$ .01	$ .03	Foley, Marvis	81T	646	$ .01	$ .08
Fleming, Dave	93T	45	$ .05	$ .20	Foley, Marvis	83T	409	$ .01	$ .08
Fletcher, Darrin	91T	9	$ .01	$ .10	Foley, Marvis	85T	621	$ .01	$ .06
Fletcher, Darrin	92T	159	$ .01	$ .03	Foley, Tom	84T	632	$ .01	$ .06
Fletcher, Darrin	92TTR	33	$ .01	$ .05	Foley, Tom	85T	107	$ .01	$ .06
Fletcher, Darrin	93T	665	$ .01	$ .03	Foley, Tom	86T	466	$ .01	$ .05
Fletcher, Darrin	93TSC	272	$ .01	$ .10	Foley, Tom	87T	78	$ .01	$ .04
Fletcher, Scott	84T	364	$ .01	$ .06	Foley, Tom	88T	251	$ .01	$ .04
Fletcher, Scott	85T	78	$ .01	$ .06	Foley, Tom	89T	529	$ .01	$ .03
Fletcher, Scott	86T	187	$ .01	$ .05	Foley, Tom	90T	341	$ .01	$ .03
Fletcher, Scott	86TTR	36	$ .01	$ .06	Foley, Tom	91T	773	$ .01	$ .03
Fletcher, Scott	87T	462	$ .01	$ .04	Foley, Tom	92T	666	$ .01	$ .03
Fletcher, Scott	88T	345	$ .01	$ .04	Foley, Tom	92TSC	19	$ .01	$ .10
Fletcher, Scott	89T	295	$ .01	$ .03	Foli, Tim	71T	83	$ .25	$1.00
Fletcher, Scott	90T	565	$ .01	$ .03	Foli, Tim	72T	707	$1.25	$5.00
Fletcher, Scott	91T	785	$ .01	$ .03	Foli, Tim	72TIA	708	$1.25	$5.00
Fletcher, Scott	91TSC	30	$ .05	$ .25	Foli, Tim	73T	19	$ .10	$ .40
Fletcher, Scott	92T	648	$ .01	$ .03	Foli, Tim	74T	217	$ .10	$ .40
Fletcher, Scott	92TSC	116	$ .01	$ .10	Foli, Tim	75T	149	$ .10	$ .40
Fletcher, Scott	92TTR	792	$ .01	$ .10	Foli, Tim	76T	397	$ .05	$ .25
Fletcher, Scott	92TTR	34	$ .01	$ .05	Foli, Tim	77T	76	$ .05	$ .20
Fletcher, Scott	93T	97	$ .01	$ .03	Foli, Tim	78T	167	$ .04	$ .16
Fletcher, Scott	93TSC	112	$ .01	$ .10	Foli, Tim	79T	403	$ .03	$ .12
Flinn, John	79T	701	$ .03	$ .12	Foli, Tim	80T	246	$ .01	$ .10
Flinn, John	81T	659	$ .01	$ .08	Foli, Tim	81T	501	$ .01	$ .08
Floethe, Chris	72T	268	$ .10	$ .40	Foli, Tim	82T	618	$ .01	$ .08
Flood, Curt	58T	464	$5.50	$22.00	Foli, Tim	82TTR	34	$ .01	$ .10
Flood, Curt	59T	353	$1.50	$6.00	Foli, Tim	83T	738	$ .01	$ .08
Flood, Curt	60T	275	$1.25	$5.00	Foli, Tim	84T	342	$ .01	$ .06
Flood, Curt	61T	438	$1.25	$5.00	Foli, Tim	84TFN	38	$ .01	$ .15
Flood, Curt	62T	590	$4.50	$18.00	Foli, Tim	85T	271	$ .01	$ .06
Flood, Curt	63T	505	$5.00	$20.00	Foli, Tim	85T	456	$ .01	$ .06
Flood, Curt	64T	103	$ .75	$3.00	Folkers, Rich	71T	648	$3.00	$12.00
Flood, Curt	65T	415	$1.50	$6.00	Folkers, Rich	73T	649	$ .60	$2.40
Flood, Curt	66T	60	$ .50	$2.00	Folkers, Rich	74T	417	$ .10	$ .40
Flood, Curt	67T	63	$1.50	$6.00	Folkers, Rich	75T	98	$ .10	$ .40
Flood, Curt	67T	245	$ .75	$3.00	Folkers, Rich	76T	611	$ .05	$ .25
Flood, Curt	68T	180	$ .50	$2.00	Folkers, Rich	77T	372	$ .05	$ .20
Flood, Curt	69T	540	$ .75	$3.00	Fondy, Dee	52T	359	$43.75	$175.00
Flood, Curt	69TAS	426	$ .30	$1.20	Fondy, Dee	56T	112	$2.50	$10.00
Flood, Curt	70T	360	$ .35	$1.40	Fondy, Dee	57T	42	$2.00	$8.00
Flood, Curt	71T	535	$1.25	$5.00	Fondy, Dee	58T	157	$1.25	$5.00
Flora, Kevin	93T	521	$ .01	$ .10	Fontenot, Ray	84T	19	$ .01	$ .06

TOPPS

Player	Year	No.	VG	EX/MT	Player	Year	No.	VG	EX/MT
Fontenot, Ray	85T	507	$ .01	$ .06	Forsch, Bob	79T	230	$ .03	$ .12
Fontenot, Ray	85TTR	35	$ .01	$ .10	Forsch, Bob	80T	535	$ .01	$ .10
Fontenot, Ray	86T	308	$ .01	$ .05	Forsch, Bob	81T	140	$ .01	$ .08
Fontenot, Ray	87T	124	$ .01	$ .04	Forsch, Bob	82T	186	$ .05	$ .25
Foor, Jim	72T	257	$ .10	$ .40	Forsch, Bob	82T	775	$ .01	$ .08
Foote, Barry	74T	603	$ .10	$ .40	Forsch, Bob	83T	415	$ .01	$ .08
Foote, Barry	75T	229	$ .10	$ .40	Forsch, Bob	84T	5	$ .01	$ .10
Foote, Barry	76T	42	$ .05	$ .25	Forsch, Bob	84T	75	$ .01	$ .06
Foote, Barry	77T	612	$ .05	$ .20	Forsch, Bob	85T	631	$ .01	$ .06
Foote, Barry	78T	513	$ .04	$ .16	Forsch, Bob	86T	322	$ .01	$ .05
Foote, Barry	79T	161	$ .03	$ .12	Forsch, Bob	87T	257	$ .01	$ .04
Foote, Barry	80T	398	$ .01	$ .10	Forsch, Bob	88T	586	$ .01	$ .04
Foote, Barry	81T	492	$ .01	$ .08	Forsch, Bob	89T	163	$ .01	$ .03
Foote, Barry	81TTR	763	$ .01	$ .15	Forsch, Ken	71T	102	$ .25	$1.00
Foote, Barry	82T	706	$ .01	$ .08	Forsch, Ken	72T	394	$ .10	$ .40
Foote, Barry	83T	697	$ .01	$ .08	Forsch, Ken	73T	589	$ .60	$2.40
Ford, Curt	87T	399	$ .01	$ .04	Forsch, Ken	74T	91	$ .10	$ .40
Ford, Curt	88T	612	$ .01	$ .04	Forsch, Ken	75T	357	$ .10	$ .40
Ford, Curt	89T	132	$ .01	$ .03	Forsch, Ken	76T	357	$ .05	$ .25
Ford, Curt	90T	39	$ .01	$ .03	Forsch, Ken	77T	21	$ .05	$ .20
Ford, Dan	76T	313	$ .05	$ .25	Forsch, Ken	77T	632	$ .05	$ .20
Ford, Dan	77T	555	$ .05	$ .20	Forsch, Ken	78T	181	$ .04	$ .16
Ford, Dan	78T	275	$ .04	$ .16	Forsch, Ken	79T	534	$ .03	$ .12
Ford, Dan	79T	385	$ .03	$ .12	Forsch, Ken	80T	642	$ .01	$ .10
Ford, Dan	80T	20	$ .01	$ .10	Forsch, Ken	81T	269	$ .01	$ .08
Ford, Dan	81T	422	$ .01	$ .08	Forsch, Ken	81TTR	764	$ .01	$ .15
Ford, Dan	82T	134	$ .01	$ .08	Forsch, Ken	82T	276	$ .05	$ .25
Ford, Dan	82TTR	35	$ .01	$ .10	Forsch, Ken	82T	385	$ .01	$ .08
Ford, Dan	83T	683	$ .01	$ .08	Forsch, Ken	83T	625	$ .01	$ .08
Ford, Dan	84T	530	$ .01	$ .06	Forsch, Ken	84T	765	$ .01	$ .06
Ford, Dan	85T	252	$ .01	$ .06	Forsch, Ken	85T	442	$ .01	$ .06
Ford, Dan	86T	753	$ .01	$ .05	Forster, Terry	72T	539	$ .75	$3.00
Ford, Dave	80T	661	$ .01	$ .10	Forster, Terry	73T	129	$ .20	$ .80
Ford, Dave	81T	706	$ .01	$ .08	Forster, Terry	74T	310	$ .10	$ .40
Ford, Dave	82T	174	$ .01	$ .08	Forster, Terry	75T	137	$ .10	$ .40
Ford, Ted	71T	612	$1.00	$4.00	Forster, Terry	75T	313	$ .25	$1.00
Ford, Ted	72T	24	$ .10	$ .40					
Ford, Ted	73T	299	$ .10	$ .40					
Ford, Ted	74T	617	$ .10	$ .40					
Ford, Whitey	53T	207	$40.00	$160.00					
Ford, Whitey	54T	37	$25.00	$100.00					
Ford, Whitey	56T	240	$35.00	$140.00					
Ford, Whitey	57T	25	$15.00	$60.00					
Ford, Whitey	58T	320	$10.00	$40.00					
Ford, Whitey	59T	430	$10.00	$40.00					
Ford, Whitey	60T	35	$10.00	$40.00					
Ford, Whitey	61T	160	$9.00	$36.00					
Ford, Whitey	61TAS	586	$22.50	$90.00					
Ford, Whitey	62T	57	$1.25	$5.00					
Ford, Whitey	62T	59	$ .60	$2.40					
Ford, Whitey	62T	310	$9.00	$36.00					
Ford, Whitey	62T	315	$2.25	$9.00					
Ford, Whitey	62TAS	475	$3.50	$14.00					
Ford, Whitey	63T	6	$1.25	$5.00					
Ford, Whitey	63T	446	$10.00	$40.00					
Ford, Whitey	64T	4	$1.25	$5.00					
Ford, Whitey	64T	380	$7.50	$30.00					
Ford, Whitey	65T	330	$8.00	$32.00					
Ford, Whitey	66T	160	$5.50	$22.00					
Ford, Whitey	67T	5	$5.00	$20.00					
Ford, Whitey	91TA53	207	$ .15	$1.50					
Fordyce, Brook	93T	701	$ .15	$1.50					
Fornieles, Mike	54T	154	$3.75	$15.00					
Fornieles, Mike	57T	116	$2.00	$8.00					
Fornieles, Mike	58T	361	$1.00	$4.00					
Fornieles, Mike	59T	473	$1.00	$4.00					
Fornieles, Mike	60T	54	$ .85	$3.40					
Fornieles, Mike	61T	113	$ .60	$2.40					
Fornieles, Mike	62T	512	$1.50	$6.00	Forster, Terry	76T	437	$ .05	$ .25
Fornieles, Mike	63T	28	$ .50	$2.00	Forster, Terry	77T	271	$ .05	$ .20
Forsch, Bob	75T	51	$ .15	$ .60	Forster, Terry	78T	347	$ .04	$ .16
Forsch, Bob	76T	426	$ .05	$ .25	Forster, Terry	79T	23	$ .03	$ .12
Forsch, Bob	77T	381	$ .05	$ .20	Forster, Terry	80T	605	$ .01	$ .10
Forsch, Bob	77T	632	$ .05	$ .20	Forster, Terry	81T	104	$ .01	$ .08
Forsch, Bob	78T	58	$ .04	$ .16	Forster, Terry	82T	444	$ .01	$ .08

TOPPS

Player	Year	No.	VG	EX/MT	Player	Year	No.	VG	EX/MT
Forster, Terry	83T	583	$.01	$.08	Fowler, Art	55T	3	$2.25	$9.00
Forster, Terry	83TTR	33	$.01	$.10	Fowler, Art	56T	47	$2.00	$8.00
Forster, Terry	84T	791	$.01	$.06	Fowler, Art	57T	233	$2.00	$8.00
Forster, Terry	85T	248	$.01	$.06	Fowler, Art	59T	508	$4.00	$16.00
Forster, Terry	86T	363	$.01	$.05	Fowler, Art	62T	128	$.60	$2.40
Forster, Terry	86TTR	37	$.01	$.06	Fowler, Art	63T	454	$3.00	$12.00
Forster, Terry	87T	652	$.01	$.04	Fowler, Art	64T	349	$.65	$2.60
Fortugno, Tim	93T	320	$.01	$.03	Fowler, Art	73T	323	$.25	$1.00
Fortugno, Tim	93TSC	231	$.01	$.10	Fowler, Art	74T	379	$.25	$1.00
Fosnow, Jerry	65T	529	$2.50	$10.00	Fowler, Dick	52T	210	$7.00	$28.00
Fossas, Tony	90T	34	$.01	$.10	Fowlkes, Alan	83T	543	$.01	$.08
Fossas, Tony	91T	747	$.01	$.03	Fox, Charlie	71T	517	$.50	$2.00
Fossas, Tony	92T	249	$.01	$.03	Fox, Charlie	72T	129	$.10	$.40
Fossas, Tony	92TSC	144	$.01	$.10	Fox, Charlie	73T	252	$.20	$.80
Fossas, Tony	93TSC	247	$.01	$.10	Fox, Charlie	74T	78	$.10	$.40
Fosse, Ray	69T	244	$.75	$3.00	Fox, Eric	93T	46	$.01	$.10
Fosse, Ray	70T	184	$.20	$.80	Fox, Eric	93TSC	131	$.01	$.10
Fosse, Ray	71T	125	$.25	$1.00	Fox, Howie	52T	209	$7.00	$28.00
Fosse, Ray	72T	470	$.25	$1.00	Fox, Howie	53T	22	$6.25	$25.00
Fosse, Ray	73T	226	$.10	$.40	Fox, Howie	54T	246	$3.75	$15.00
Fosse, Ray	74T	420	$.10	$.40	Fox, Howie	91TA53	22	$.01	$.15
Fosse, Ray	75T	486	$.10	$.40	Fox, Nellie	56T	118	$7.50	$30.00
Fosse, Ray	76T	554	$.05	$.25	Fox, Nellie	57T	38	$5.50	$22.00
Fosse, Ray	76TTR	554	$.05	$.25	Fox, Nellie	58T	400	$3.00	$12.00
Fosse, Ray	77T	267	$.05	$.20	Fox, Nellie	58TAS	479	$2.00	$8.00
Fosse, Ray	78T	415	$.04	$.16	Fox, Nellie	59T	30	$4.00	$16.00
Fosse, Ray	79T	51	$.03	$.12	Fox, Nellie	59T	408	$2.00	$8.00
Fosse, Ray	80T	327	$.01	$.10	Fox, Nellie	59TAS	556	$6.00	$24.00
Foster, Alan	69T	266	$.50	$2.00	Fox, Nellie	60T	100	$2.25	$9.00
Foster, Alan	70T	369	$.35	$1.40	Fox, Nellie	60T	429	$1.50	$6.00
Foster, Alan	71T	207	$.25	$1.00	Fox, Nellie	60TAS	555	$4.50	$18.00
Foster, Alan	72T	521	$.25	$1.00	Fox, Nellie	61T	30	$1.75	$7.00
Foster, Alan	73T	543	$.60	$2.40	Fox, Nellie	61TAS	570	$10.00	$40.00
Foster, Alan	74T	442	$.10	$.40	Fox, Nellie	61TMVP	477	$1.75	$7.00
Foster, Alan	75T	296	$.10	$.40	Fox, Nellie	62T	73	$1.50	$6.00
Foster, Alan	76T	266	$.05	$.25	Fox, Nellie	63T	525	$5.00	$20.00
Foster, Alan	77T	108	$.05	$.20	Fox, Nellie	64T	81	$1.75	$7.00
Foster, George	71T	276	$2.00	$8.00	Fox, Nellie	64T	205	$1.25	$5.00
Foster, George	72T	256	$.50	$2.00	Fox, Nellie	65T	485	$2.50	$10.00
Foster, George	73T	399	$.50	$2.00	Fox, Nellie	75T	197	$.30	$1.20
Foster, George	74T	646	$.50	$2.00	Fox, Nellie	91TA53	331	$.10	$.50
Foster, George	75T	87	$.35	$1.40	Fox, Terry	61T	459	$1.35	$5.40
Foster, George	76T	179	$.25	$1.00	Fox, Terry	62T	196	$.60	$2.40
Foster, George	77T	3	$.30	$1.20	Fox, Terry	63T	44	$.50	$2.00
Foster, George	77T	347	$.30	$1.20	Fox, Terry	64T	387	$1.00	$4.00
Foster, George	78T	202	$.05	$.20	Fox, Terry	65T	576	$2.50	$10.00
Foster, George	78T	203	$.05	$.20	Fox, Terry	66T	472	$1.50	$6.00
Foster, George	78T	500	$.20	$.80	Fox, Terry	67T	181	$.40	$1.60
Foster, George	79T	2	$.20	$.80	Foy, Joe	66T	456	$1.50	$6.00
Foster, George	79T	3	$.20	$.80	Foy, Joe	67T	331	$.60	$2.40
Foster, George	79T	600	$.10	$.40	Foy, Joe	68T	387	$.35	$1.40
Foster, George	80T	400	$.05	$.25	Foy, Joe	69T	93	$.35	$1.40
Foster, George	81T	200	$.05	$.20	Foy, Joe	70T	138	$.20	$.80
Foster, George	82T	700	$.05	$.20	Foy, Joe	71T	706	$1.10	$4.40
Foster, George	82TAS	342	$.05	$.20	Foytack, Paul	57T	77	$2.00	$8.00
Foster, George	82TSA	701	$.01	$.15	Foytack, Paul	58T	282	$1.25	$5.00
Foster, George	82TTR	30	$.10	$.50	Foytack, Paul	59T	200	$1.00	$4.00
Foster, George	83T	80	$.05	$.20	Foytack, Paul	60T	364	$.75	$3.00
Foster, George	84T	350	$.01	$.15	Foytack, Paul	61T	171	$.60	$2.40
Foster, George	85T	170	$.01	$.06	Foytack, Paul	62T	349	$.75	$3.00
Foster, George	86T	680	$.01	$.05	Foytack, Paul	63T	327	$.90	$3.60
Foster, Leo	74T	607	$.10	$.40	Foytack, Paul	64T	149	$.50	$2.00
Foster, Leo	75T	418	$.10	$.40	Frailing, Ken	74T	605	$1.25	$5.00
Foster, Leo	77T	458	$.05	$.20	Frailing, Ken	75T	436	$.10	$.40
Foster, Leo	78T	229	$.04	$.16	Francis, Earl	61T	54	$.60	$2.40
Foster, Roy	71T	107	$.25	$1.00	Francis, Earl	62T	252	$.75	$3.00
Foster, Roy	72T	329	$.10	$.40	Francis, Earl	63T	303	$.90	$3.60
Foster, Steve	92T	528	$.01	$.15	Francis, Earl	64T	117	$.50	$2.00
Foster, Steve	92TSC	826	$.01	$.15	Franco, John	85T	417	$.10	$.50
Foster, Steve	93T	193	$.01	$.03	Franco, John	86T	54	$.01	$.15
Foucault, Steve	74T	294	$.10	$.40	Franco, John	87T	305	$.01	$.10
Foucault, Steve	75T	283	$.10	$.40	Franco, John	88T	730	$.01	$.04
Foucault, Steve	76T	303	$.05	$.25	Franco, John	89T	290	$.01	$.03
Foucault, Steve	77T	459	$.05	$.20	Franco, John	90T	120	$.01	$.03
Foucault, Steve	78T	68	$.04	$.16	Franco, John	90TTR	32	$.01	$.05

TOPPS

Player	Year	No.	VG	EX/MT	Player	Year	No.	VG	EX/MT
Franco, John	91T	510	$ .01	$ .03	Frazier, George	86T	431	$ .01	$ .05
Franco, John	91TAS	407	$ .01	$ .03	Frazier, George	87T	207	$ .01	$ .04
Franco, John	91TSC	22	$ .05	$ .25	Frazier, George	88T	709	$ .01	$ .04
Franco, John	92T	690	$ .01	$ .03	Frazier, Joe	55T	89	$2.25	$9.00
Franco, John	92TSC	565	$ .01	$ .10	Frazier, Joe	56T	141	$2.50	$10.00
Franco, John	93T	25	$ .01	$ .03	Fredrickson, Scott	93T	489	$ .01	$ .15
Franco, Julio	83TTR	34	$2.00	$8.00	Freeburg, Ryan	93T	616	$ .05	$ .25
Franco, Julio	84T	48	$ .10	$1.00	Freed, Roger	70T	477	$ .35	$1.40
Franco, Julio	85T	237	$ .05	$ .35	Freed, Roger	71T	362	$ .25	$1.00
Franco, Julio	86T	391	$ .05	$ .20	Freed, Roger	72T	69	$ .10	$ .40
Franco, Julio	87T	160	$ .05	$ .20	Freed, Roger	78T	504	$ .04	$ .16
Franco, Julio	88T	683	$ .01	$ .15	Freed, Roger	79T	111	$ .03	$ .12
Franco, Julio	89T	55	$ .01	$ .10	Freed, Roger	80T	418	$ .01	$ .10
Franco, Julio	89TAS	398	$ .01	$ .10	Freehan, Bill	63T	466	$12.50	$50.00
Franco, Julio	89TTR	34	$ .01	$ .10	Freehan, Bill	64T	407	$1.50	$6.00
Franco, Julio	90T	550	$ .01	$ .10	Freehan, Bill	65T	390	$1.25	$5.00
Franco, Julio	90TAS	386	$ .01	$ .10	Freehan, Bill	66T	145	$ .50	$2.00
Franco, Julio	91T	775	$ .01	$ .10	Freehan, Bill	67T	48	$ .40	$1.60
Franco, Julio	91TAS	387	$ .01	$ .03	Freehan, Bill	68T	470	$1.00	$4.00
Franco, Julio	91TSC	173	$ .10	$ .50	Freehan, Bill	68TAS	375	$ .50	$2.00
Franco, Julio	92T	490	$ .01	$ .10	Freehan, Bill	69T	390	$ .50	$2.00
Franco, Julio	92TAS	398	$ .01	$ .03	Freehan, Bill	69TAS	431	$ .30	$1.20
Franco, Julio	92TSC	440	$ .01	$ .10	Freehan, Bill	70T	335	$ .35	$1.40
Franco, Julio	93T	670	$ .01	$ .03	Freehan, Bill	70TAS	465	$ .50	$2.00
Francona, Terry	82T	118	$ .10	$ .50	Freehan, Bill	71T	575	$1.00	$4.00
Francona, Terry	83T	267	$ .01	$ .08	Freehan, Bill	72T	120	$ .20	$ .80
Francona, Terry	84T	496	$ .01	$ .06	Freehan, Bill	73T	460	$ .25	$1.00
Francona, Terry	85T	134	$ .01	$ .10	Freehan, Bill	74T	162	$ .25	$1.00
Francona, Terry	85T	578	$ .01	$ .06	Freehan, Bill	75T	397	$ .20	$ .80
Francona, Terry	86T	374	$ .01	$ .05	Freehan, Bill	76T	540	$ .05	$ .25
Francona, Terry	86TTR	38	$ .01	$ .06	Freehan, Bill	77T	22	$ .05	$ .20
Francona, Terry	87T	785	$ .01	$ .04	Freeman, Hershell	56T	242	$3.75	$15.00
Francona, Terry	87TTR	34	$ .01	$ .05	Freeman, Hershell "Bud"	57T	32	$2.00	$8.00
Francona, Terry	88T	686	$ .01	$ .04	Freeman, Bud	58T	27	$2.00	$8.00
Francona, Terry	89T	31	$ .01	$ .03	Freeman, Jimmy	73T	610	$1.25	$5.00
Francona, Terry	89TTR	35	$ .01	$ .05	Freeman, Mark	59T	532	$4.00	$16.00
Francona, Terry	90T	214	$ .01	$ .03	Freeman, Marvin	89T	634	$ .01	$ .03
Francona, Tito	57T	184	$2.00	$8.00	Freeman, Marvin	90T	103	$ .01	$ .03
Francona, Tito	58T	316	$1.25	$5.00	Freeman, Marvin	92T	68	$ .01	$ .03
Francona, Tito	59T	268	$1.00	$4.00	Freeman, Marvin	92TSC	264	$ .01	$ .10
Francona, Tito	60T	30	$ .85	$3.40	Freeman, Marvin	93T	583	$ .01	$ .03
Francona, Tito	60T	260	$1.25	$5.00	Freese, Gene	55T	205	$8.00	$32.00
Francona, Tito	61T	503	$1.35	$5.40	Freese, Gene	56T	46	$2.00	$8.00
Francona, Tito	62T	97	$ .60	$2.40	Freese, Gene	58T	293	$1.25	$5.00
Francona, Tito	63T	248	$ .90	$3.60	Freese, Gene	59T	472	$1.00	$4.00
Francona, Tito	63T	392	$1.00	$4.00	Freese, Gene	60T	435	$ .75	$3.00
Francona, Tito	64T	583	$2.25	$9.00	Freese, Gene	61T	175	$ .60	$2.40
Francona, Tito	65T	256	$ .50	$2.00	Freese, Gene	62T	205	$ .75	$3.00
Francona, Tito	66T	163	$ .50	$2.00	Freese, Gene	63T	133	$ .50	$2.00
Francona, Tito	67T	443	$ .60	$2.40	Freese, Gene	64T	266	$ .65	$2.60
Francona, Tito	68T	527	$ .75	$3.00	Freese, Gene	65T	492	$1.25	$5.00
Francona, Tito	69T	398	$ .30	$1.20	Freese, Gene	66T	319	$ .50	$2.00
Francona, Tito	70T	663	$1.25	$5.00	Fregosi, Jim	62T	209	$2.25	$9.00
Francona, Tito	85T	134	$ .01	$ .10	Fregosi, Jim	63T	167	$1.00	$4.00
Franks, Herman	52T	385	$50.00	$200.00	Fregosi, Jim	64T	97	$ .50	$2.00
Franks, Herman	65T	32	$ .35	$1.40	Fregosi, Jim	65T	210	$ .50	$2.00
Franks, Herman	66T	537	$3.75	$15.00	Fregosi, Jim	66T	5	$ .35	$1.40
Franks, Herman	67T	116	$ .40	$1.60	Fregosi, Jim	67T	385	$ .60	$2.40
Franks, Herman	68T	267	$ .35	$1.40	Fregosi, Jim	68T	170	$ .35	$1.40
Franks, Herman	78T	234	$ .04	$ .16	Fregosi, Jim	68TAS	367	$ .50	$2.00
Fraser, Ron	92TTR	35	$ .01	$ .10	Fregosi, Jim	69T	365	$ .30	$1.20
Fraser, Willie	87TTR	35	$ .01	$ .05	Fregosi, Jim	70T	570	$ .50	$2.00
Fraser, Willie	88T	363	$ .01	$ .04	Fregosi, Jim	71T	360	$ .25	$1.00
Fraser, Willie	89T	679	$ .01	$ .03	Fregosi, Jim	72T	115	$ .20	$ .80
Fraser, Willie	90T	477	$ .01	$ .03	Fregosi, Jim	72T	346	$ .10	$ .40
Fraser, Willie	91T	784	$ .01	$ .03	Fregosi, Jim	72TTR	755	$1.25	$5.00
Fraser, Willie	91TSC	496	$ .05	$ .25	Fregosi, Jim	73T	525	$ .25	$1.00
Fraser, Willie	92TSC	33	$ .01	$ .10	Fregosi, Jim	74T	196	$ .10	$ .40
Frazier, George	79T	724	$ .15	$ .60	Fregosi, Jim	75T	339	$ .20	$ .80
Frazier, George	80T	684	$ .10	$ .75	Fregosi, Jim	76T	635	$ .10	$ .40
Frazier, George	82T	349	$ .01	$ .08	Fregosi, Jim	78T	323	$ .04	$ .16
Frazier, George	83T	123	$ .01	$ .08	Fregosi, Jim	86TTR	39	$ .01	$ .06
Frazier, George	84T	539	$ .01	$ .06	Fregosi, Jim	87T	318	$ .01	$ .04
Frazier, George	84TTR	39	$ .01	$ .15	Fregosi, Jim	88T	714	$ .01	$ .04
Frazier, George	85T	19	$ .01	$ .06	Fregosi, Jim	89T	414	$ .01	$ .03

TOPPS

Player	Year	No.	VG	EX/MT
Fregosi, Jim	91TTR	43	$.01	$.05
Fregosi, Jim	92T	669	$.01	$.03
Fregosi, Jim	93T	510	$.01	$.03
Freisleben, Dave	74T	599	$.15	$.60
Freisleben, Dave	75T	37	$.10	$.40
Freisleben, Dave	76T	217	$.05	$.25
Freisleben, Dave	77T	407	$.05	$.20
Freisleben, Dave	78T	594	$.04	$.16
Freisleben, Dave	79T	168	$.03	$.12
Freisleben, Dave	80T	382	$.01	$.10
French, Jim	66T	333	$.75	$3.00
French, Jim	69T	199	$.35	$1.40
French, Jim	70T	617	$.50	$2.00
French, Jim	71T	399	$.50	$2.00
Frey, Jim	73T	136	$.25	$1.00
Frey, Jim	74T	306	$.15	$.60
Frey, Jim	84T	51	$.01	$.06
Frey, Jim	85T	241	$.01	$.06
Frey, Jim	86T	231	$.01	$.05
Frey, Steve	90T	91	$.01	$.10
Frey, Steve	91T	462	$.01	$.03
Frey, Steve	92T	174	$.01	$.03
Frey, Steve	92TSC	572	$.01	$.10
Frey, Steve	93T	728	$.01	$.03
Frias, Pepe	73T	607	$.75	$3.00
Frias, Pepe	74T	468	$.10	$.40
Frias, Pepe	75T	496	$.10	$.40

Player	Year	No.	VG	EX/MT
Frias, Pepe	76T	544	$.05	$.25
Frias, Pepe	77T	199	$.05	$.20
Frias, Pepe	78T	654	$.04	$.16
Frias, Pepe	79T	294	$.03	$.12
Frias, Pepe	80T	87	$.01	$.10
Fricano, Marion	53T	199	$4.50	$18.00
Fricano, Marion	54T	124	$3.75	$15.00
Fricano, Marion	91TA53	199	$.01	$.15
Frick, Ford	59T	1	$17.50	$75.00
Fridley, Jim	52T	399	$43.75	$175.00
Fridley, Jim	53T	187	$4.50	$18.00
Fridley, Jim	91TA53	187	$.01	$.15
Friend, Bob	52T	233	$8.75	$35.00
Friend, Bob	56T	221	$3.75	$15.00
Friend, Bob	57T	150	$2.00	$8.00
Friend, Bob	58T	315	$1.25	$5.00

Player	Year	No.	VG	EX/MT
Friend, Bob	58T	334	$1.25	$5.00
Friend, Bob	58TAS	492	$1.00	$4.00
Friend, Bob	59T	428	$1.00	$4.00
Friend, Bob	59T	460	$1.00	$4.00
Friend, Bob	59TAS	569	$4.00	$16.00
Friend, Bob	60T	437	$.75	$3.00
Friend, Bob	61T	45	$1.00	$4.00
Friend, Bob	61T	270	$.60	$2.40
Friend, Bob	61TAS	585	$8.00	$32.00
Friend, Bob	62T	520	$1.50	$6.00
Friend, Bob	63T	450	$3.00	$12.00
Friend, Bob	64T	1	$5.00	$20.00
Friend, Bob	64T	20	$.50	$2.00
Friend, Bob	65T	392	$1.00	$4.00
Friend, Bob	66T	519	$2.00	$8.00
Friend, Bob	91TA53	298	$.05	$.20
Friend, Owen	52T	160	$7.00	$28.00
Frisella, Dan	69T	343	$.30	$1.20
Frisella, Dan	71T	104	$.25	$1.00
Frisella, Danny	72T	293	$.10	$.40
Frisella, Danny	73T	432	$.25	$1.00
Frisella, Danny	74T	71	$.10	$.40
Frisella, Danny	75T	343	$.10	$.40
Frisella, Danny	76T	32	$.05	$.25
Frisella, Danny	77T	278	$.05	$.20
Frobel, Doug	84T	264	$.01	$.06
Frobel, Doug	85T	587	$.01	$.06
Frohwirth, Todd	88T	378	$.01	$.04
Frohwirth, Todd	89T	542	$.01	$.03
Frohwirth, Todd	90T	69	$.01	$.03
Frohwirth, Todd	92T	158	$.01	$.03
Frohwirth, Todd	92TSC	358	$.01	$.10
Frohwirth, Todd	93T	415	$.01	$.03
Frost, Dave	79T	703	$.05	$.20
Frost, Dave	80T	423	$.01	$.10
Frost, Dave	81T	286	$.01	$.08
Frost, Dave	82T	24	$.01	$.08
Frost, Dave	82TTR	37	$.01	$.10
Frost, Dave	83T	656	$.01	$.08
Fry, Jerry	79T	720	$.25	$1.00
Frye, Jeff	93T	197	$.01	$.03
Frye, Jeff	93TSC	133	$.01	$.10
Fryman, Travis	90TTR	33	$.15	$1.50
Fryman, Travis	91T	128	$.10	$.50
Fryman, Travis	91TSC	355	$3.00	$12.00
Fryman, Travis	92T	750	$.05	$.35
Fryman, Travis	92TSC	59	$.15	$1.50
Fryman, Travis	93T	392	$.05	$.20
Fryman, Travis	93T	404	$.01	$.15
Fryman, Travis	93TSC	298	$.10	$.50
Fryman, Woody	66T	498	$1.50	$6.00
Fryman, Woody	67T	221	$.50	$2.00
Fryman, Woody	68T	112	$.35	$1.40
Fryman, Woody "Woodie"	69T	51	$.35	$1.40
Fryman, Woodie	71T	414	$.50	$2.00
Fryman, Woodie	72T	357	$.10	$.40
Fryman, Woodie	73T	146	$.10	$.40
Fryman, Woodie	74T	555	$.10	$.40
Fryman, Woodie	75T	166	$.10	$.40
Fryman, Woodie	76T	467	$.05	$.25
Fryman, Woodie	77T	28	$.05	$.20
Fryman, Woodie	78T	585	$.04	$.16
Fryman, Woodie	79T	269	$.03	$.12
Fryman, Woodie	80T	607	$.01	$.10
Fryman, Woodie	81T	394	$.01	$.08
Fryman, Woodie	82T	788	$.01	$.08
Fryman, Woodie	83T	137	$.01	$.08
Fuentes, Miguel	70T	88	$.20	$.80
Fuentes, Tito	66T	511	$2.00	$8.00
Fuentes, Tito	67T	177	$.40	$1.60
Fuentes, Tito	70T	42	$.20	$.80
Fuentes, Tito	71T	378	$.25	$1.00
Fuentes, Tito	72T	427	$.25	$1.00
Fuentes, Tito	72TIA	428	$.25	$1.00
Fuentes, Tito	73T	236	$.10	$.40

TOPPS

Player	Year	No.	VG	EX/MT
Fuentes, Tito	74T	305	$ .10	$ .40
Fuentes, Tito	75T	425	$ .10	$ .40
Fuentes, Tito	76T	8	$ .05	$ .25
Fuentes, Tito	77T	63	$ .05	$ .20
Fuentes, Tito	78T	385	$ .04	$ .16
Fulgham, John	80T	152	$ .01	$ .10
Fulgham, John	81T	523	$ .01	$ .08
Fuller, Jim	74T	606	$ .10	$ .40
Fuller, Jim	75T	594	$ .10	$ .40
Fuller, Vern	68T	71	$ .35	$1.40
Fuller, Vern	69T	291	$ .50	$2.00
Fuller, Vern	70T	558	$ .50	$2.00
Funk, Frank	61T	362	$ .60	$2.40
Funk, Frank	62T	587	$6.00	$24.00
Funk, Frank	63T	476	$3.00	$12.00
Funk, Frank	64T	289	$ .65	$2.60
Furillo, Carl	56T	190	$7.00	$28.00
Furillo, Carl	57T	45	$4.00	$16.00
Furillo, Carl	57T	400	$50.00	$200.00
Furillo, Carl	58T	417	$2.25	$9.00
Furillo, Carl	59T	206	$1.50	$6.00
Furillo, Carl	60T	408	$1.25	$5.00
Furillo, Carl	91TA53	305	$ .10	$ .50
Fusselman, Les	52T	378	$43.75	$175.00
Fusselman, Les	53T	218	$4.50	$18.00
Fusselman, Les	91TA53	218	$ .01	$ .15
Gabrielson, Len	63T	253	$ .90	$3.60
Gabrielson, Len	64T	198	$ .65	$2.60
Gabrielson, Len	65T	14	$ .35	$1.40
Gabrielson, Len	66T	395	$ .65	$2.60
Gabrielson, Len	67T	469	$1.50	$6.00
Gabrielson, Len	68T	357	$ .35	$1.40
Gabrielson, Len	69T	615	$ .40	$1.60
Gabrielson, Len	70T	204	$ .20	$ .80
Gaetti, Gary	83T	431	$ .10	$ .50
Gaetti, Gary	84T	157	$ .05	$ .20
Gaetti, Gary	85T	304	$ .01	$ .15
Gaetti, Gary	86T	97	$ .01	$ .15
Gaetti, Gary	87T	710	$ .01	$ .10
Gaetti, Gary	88T	578	$ .01	$ .04
Gaetti, Gary	89T	220	$ .01	$ .03
Gaetti, Gary	90T	630	$ .01	$ .03
Gaetti, Gary	91T	430	$ .01	$ .03
Gaetti, Gary	91TSC	353	$ .05	$ .25
Gaetti, Gary	91TTR	44	$ .01	$ .05
Gaetti, Gary	92T	70	$ .01	$ .03
Gaetti, Gary	92TSC	436	$ .01	$ .10
Gaetti, Gary	93T	139	$ .01	$ .03
Gaff, Brent	85T	546	$ .01	$ .06
Gaff, Brent	86T	18	$ .01	$ .05
Gagliano, Phil	64T	568	$2.25	$9.00
Gagliano, Phil	65T	503	$1.25	$5.00
Gagliano, Phil	66T	418	$ .65	$2.60
Gagliano, Phil	67T	304	$ .60	$2.40
Gagliano, Phil	68T	479	$ .75	$3.00
Gagliano, Phil	69T	609	$ .40	$1.60
Gagliano, Phil	70T	143	$ .20	$ .80
Gagliano, Phil	71T	302	$ .25	$1.00
Gagliano, Phil	72T	472	$ .25	$1.00
Gagliano, Phil	73T	69	$ .10	$ .40
Gagliano, Phil	74T	622	$ .10	$ .40
Gagliano, Ralph	65T	501	$1.25	$5.00
Gagne, Greg	85TTR	36	$ .05	$ .35
Gagne, Greg	86T	162	$ .01	$ .05
Gagne, Greg	87T	558	$ .01	$ .04
Gagne, Greg	88T	343	$ .01	$ .04
Gagne, Greg	89T	19	$ .01	$ .03
Gagne, Greg	90T	448	$ .01	$ .03
Gagne, Greg	91T	216	$ .01	$ .03
Gagne, Greg	91TSC	277	$ .05	$ .25
Gagne, Greg	92T	663	$ .01	$ .03
Gagne, Greg	92TSC	376	$ .01	$ .10
Gagne, Greg	93T	715	$ .01	$ .03
Gaines, Joe	62T	414	$1.25	$5.00
Gaines, Joe	63T	319	$ .90	$3.60
Gaines, Joe	64T	364	$ .65	$2.60
Gaines, Joe	65T	594	$1.40	$5.60
Gaines, Joe	66T	122	$ .50	$2.00
Gakeler, Dan	92T	621	$ .01	$ .03
Gakeler, Dan	92TSC	276	$ .01	$ .10
Galan, Augie	54T	233	$3.75	$15.00
Galarraga, Andres	86TTR	40	$ .10	$ .50
Galarraga, Andres	87T	272	$ .01	$ .10
Galarraga, Andres	88T	25	$ .01	$ .10
Galarraga, Andres	89T	590	$ .01	$ .03
Galarraga, Andres	89TAS	386	$ .01	$ .05
Galarraga, Andres	90T	720	$ .01	$ .03
Galarraga, Andres	91T	610	$ .01	$ .03

Player	Year	No.	VG	EX/MT
Galarraga, Andres	91TSC	69	$ .05	$ .25
Galarraga, Andres	92T	240	$ .01	$ .03
Galarraga, Andres	92TSC	652	$ .01	$ .10
Galarraga, Andres	92TTR	36	$ .01	$ .05
Galarraga, Andres	93T	173	$ .01	$ .10
Galasso, Bob	80T	711	$ .01	$ .10
Galasso, Bob	82T	598	$ .01	$ .08
Gale, Rich	79T	298	$ .03	$ .12
Gale, Rich	80T	433	$ .01	$ .10
Gale, Rich	81T	544	$ .01	$ .08
Gale, Rich	82T	67	$ .01	$ .08
Gale, Rich	82TTR	38	$ .01	$ .10
Gale, Rich	83T	719	$ .01	$ .08
Gale, Rich	83TTR	35	$ .15	$1.25
Gale, Rich	84T	142	$ .01	$ .06
Gale, Rich	84TTR	40	$ .01	$ .15
Gale, Rich	85T	606	$ .01	$ .06
Gallagher, Alan	71T	224	$ .25	$1.00
Gallagher, Alan	72T	693	$1.25	$5.00
Gallagher, Alan	72TIA	694	$1.25	$5.00
Gallagher, Bob	74T	21	$ .10	$ .40
Gallagher, Bob	75T	406	$ .10	$ .40
Gallagher, Dave	89T	156	$ .01	$ .15
Gallagher, Dave	90T	612	$ .01	$ .03
Gallagher, Dave	91T	349	$ .01	$ .03
Gallagher, Dave	91TSC	563	$ .05	$ .25
Gallagher, Dave	92T	552	$ .01	$ .03
Gallagher, Dave	92TSC	841	$ .01	$ .10
Gallagher, Dave	92TTR	37	$ .01	$ .05
Gallagher, Dave	93T	471	$ .01	$ .03

TOPPS

Player	Year	No.	VG	EX/MT
Gallego, Mike	86T	304	$ .01	$ .15
Gallego, Mike	88T	702	$ .01	$ .04
Gallego, Mike	89T	102	$ .01	$ .03
Gallego, Mike	90T	293	$ .01	$ .03
Gallego, Mike	91T	686	$ .01	$ .03
Gallego, Mike	91TSC	151	$ .05	$ .25
Gallego, Mike	92T	76	$ .01	$ .03
Gallego, Mike	92TSC	106	$ .01	$ .10
Gallego, Mike	92TSC	627	$ .01	$ .10
Gallego, Mike	92TTR	38	$ .01	$ .05
Gallego, Mike	93T	287	$ .01	$ .03
Gallego, Mike	93TSC	126	$ .01	$ .10
Gamble, John	74T	597	$ .15	$ .60
Gamble, Oscar	70T	654	$1.50	$6.00
Gamble, Oscar	71T	23	$ .25	$1.00
Gamble, Oscar	72T	423	$ .25	$1.00
Gamble, Oscar	73T	372	$ .10	$ .40
Gamble, Oscar	74T	152	$ .10	$ .40
Gamble, Oscar	75T	213	$ .10	$ .40
Gamble, Oscar	76T	74	$ .05	$ .25
Gamble, Oscar	76TTR	74	$ .05	$ .25
Gamble, Oscar	77T	505	$ .05	$ .20
Gamble, Oscar	78T	390	$ .04	$ .16
Gamble, Oscar	79T	263	$ .03	$ .12
Gamble, Oscar	80T	698	$ .01	$ .10
Gamble, Oscar	81T	139	$ .01	$ .08
Gamble, Oscar	82T	472	$ .01	$ .08
Gamble, Oscar	83T	19	$ .01	$ .08
Gamble, Oscar	84T	512	$ .01	$ .06
Gamble, Oscar	85T	724	$ .01	$ .06
Gamble, Oscar	85TTR	37	$ .01	$ .10
Gandarillas, Gus	93T	719	$ .01	$ .03
Gant, Ron	88TTR	39	$ .20	$2.00
Gant, Ron	89T	296	$ .10	$ .50
Gant, Ron	90T	567	$ .05	$ .25
Gant, Ron	91T	725	$ .01	$ .15
Gant, Ron	91TSC	454	$ .10	$1.00
Gant, Ron	92T	25	$ .01	$ .10
Gant, Ron	92TAS	391	$ .01	$ .10
Gant, Ron	92TSC	730	$ .01	$ .15
Gant, Ron	93T	393	$ .01	$ .10
Gant, Ron	93TSC	28	$ .01	$ .15
Gantner, Jim	77T	494	$ .35	$1.40
Gantner, Jim	79T	154	$ .05	$ .20
Gantner, Jim	80T	374	$ .01	$ .10
Gantner, Jim	81T	482	$ .01	$ .08
Gantner, Jim	82T	613	$ .01	$ .08
Gantner, Jim	83T	88	$ .01	$ .08
Gantner, Jim	84T	298	$ .01	$ .06
Gantner, Jim	85T	781	$ .01	$ .06
Gantner, Jim	86T	582	$ .01	$ .05
Gantner, Jim	87T	108	$ .01	$ .04
Gantner, Jim	88T	337	$ .01	$ .04
Gantner, Jim	89T	671	$ .01	$ .03
Gantner, Jim	90T	417	$ .01	$ .03
Gantner, Jim	91T	23	$ .01	$ .03
Gantner, Jim	91TSC	183	$ .05	$ .25
Gantner, Jim	92T	248	$ .01	$ .03
Gantner, Jim	92TSC	502	$ .01	$ .10
Garagiola, Joe	52T	227	$30.00	$120.00
Garagiola, Joe	91TA53	314	$ .10	$ .50
Garber, Gene	74T	431	$ .25	$1.00
Garber, Gene	75T	444	$ .10	$ .40
Garber, Gene	76T	14	$ .05	$ .25
Garber, Gene	77T	289	$ .05	$ .20
Garber, Gene	78T	177	$ .04	$ .16
Garber, Gene	79T	629	$ .03	$ .12
Garber, Gene	80T	504	$ .01	$ .10
Garber, Gene	81T	307	$ .01	$ .08
Garber, Gene	82T	32	$ .01	$ .08
Garber, Gene	83T	255	$ .01	$ .08
Garber, Gene	83T	256	$ .01	$ .08
Garber, Gene	84T	466	$ .01	$ .06
Garber, Gene	84T	709	$ .01	$ .06
Garber, Gene	85T	129	$ .01	$ .06

Player	Year	No.	VG	EX/MT
Garber, Gene	86T	776	$ .01	$ .05
Garber, Gene	87T	351	$ .01	$ .04
Garber, Gene	88T	597	$ .01	$ .04
Garbey, Barbaro	84TTR	41	$ .01	$ .15
Garbey, Barbaro	85T	243	$ .01	$ .06
Garbey, Barbaro	86T	609	$ .01	$ .05
Garces, Rich	91T	594	$ .01	$ .15
Garces, Rich	91TSC	370	$ .05	$ .25
Garcia, Carlos	93T	27	$ .01	$ .03
Garcia, Damaso	81T	488	$ .05	$ .25
Garcia, Damaso	82T	596	$ .01	$ .08
Garcia, Damaso	83T	202	$ .01	$ .08
Garcia, Damaso	83T	222	$ .01	$ .08
Garcia, Damaso	84T	124	$ .01	$ .06
Garcia, Damaso	85T	645	$ .01	$ .06
Garcia, Damaso	85TAS	702	$ .01	$ .06
Garcia, Damaso	86T	45	$ .01	$ .05
Garcia, Damaso	86TAS	713	$ .01	$ .05
Garcia, Damaso	87T	395	$ .01	$ .04
Garcia, Damaso	88T	241	$ .01	$ .04
Garcia, Damaso	90T	432	$ .01	$ .03
Garcia, Dave	73T	12	$ .20	$ .80
Garcia, Dave	78T	656	$ .04	$ .16
Garcia, Dave	83T	546	$ .01	$ .08
Garcia, Kiko	77T	474	$ .10	$ .40
Garcia, Kiko	78T	287	$ .04	$ .16
Garcia, Kiko	79T	543	$ .03	$ .12
Garcia, Kiko	80T	37	$ .01	$ .10
Garcia, Kiko	81T	688	$ .01	$ .08
Garcia, Kiko	81TTR	765	$ .01	$ .15
Garcia, Kiko	82T	377	$ .01	$ .08
Garcia, Kiko	83T	198	$ .01	$ .08
Garcia, Kiko	83TTR	36	$ .01	$ .10
Garcia, Kiko	84T	458	$ .01	$ .06
Garcia, Kiko	85T	763	$ .01	$ .06
Garcia, Mike	51Trb	40	$2.50	$10.00
Garcia, Mike	52T	272	$12.50	$50.00
Garcia, Mike	53T	75	$7.50	$30.00
Garcia, Mike	56T	210	$3.75	$15.00
Garcia, Mike	57T	300	$5.00	$20.00
Garcia, Mike	58T	196	$1.25	$5.00
Garcia, Mike	59T	516	$4.00	$16.00
Garcia, Mike	60T	532	$3.25	$13.00
Garcia, Mike	91TA53	75	$ .01	$ .15
Garcia, Pedro	73T	609	$1.00	$4.00
Garcia, Pedro	74T	142	$ .10	$ .40
Garcia, Pedro	75T	147	$ .10	$ .40
Garcia, Pedro	76T	187	$ .05	$ .25
Garcia, Pedro	77T	453	$ .05	$ .20
Garcia, Ralph	73T	602	$ .75	$3.00
Garcia, Ramon	92T	176	$ .01	$ .10
Garcia, Ramon	92TSC	866	$ .01	$ .10
Garciaparra, Nomar	92TSC	39	$ .05	$ .35
Gardenhire, Ron	82T	623	$ .05	$ .25
Gardenhire, Ron	82TTR	39	$ .01	$ .10
Gardenhire, Ron	83T	469	$ .01	$ .08
Gardenhire, Ron	85T	144	$ .01	$ .06
Gardenhire, Ron	86T	274	$ .01	$ .05
Gardiner, Mike	92T	694	$ .01	$ .03
Gardiner, Mike	92TSC	732	$ .01	$ .10
Gardiner, Mike	93T	241	$ .01	$ .03
Gardner, Billy	55T	27	$2.25	$9.00
Gardner, Billy	57T	17	$2.00	$8.00
Gardner, Billy	58T	105	$2.00	$8.00
Gardner, Billy	59T	89	$1.50	$6.00
Gardner, Billy	60T	106	$ .85	$3.40
Gardner, Billy	61T	123	$ .60	$2.40
Gardner, Billy	62T	163	$1.25	$5.00
Gardner, Billy	62T	338	$ .75	$3.00
Gardner, Billy	63T	408	$1.00	$4.00
Gardner, Billy	83T	11	$ .01	$ .08
Gardner, Billy	84T	771	$ .01	$ .06
Gardner, Billy	85T	213	$ .01	$ .06
Gardner, Billy	87TTR	36	$ .01	$ .05
Gardner, Jeff	93T	663	$ .01	$ .10

TOPPS

Player	Year	No.	VG	EX/MT	Player	Year	No.	VG	EX/MT
Gardner, Mark	90T	284	$ .01	$ .10	Garrett, Adrian	71T	576	$1.00	$4.00
Gardner, Mark	91T	757	$ .01	$ .03	Garrett, Adrian	74T	656	$ .10	$ .40
Gardner, Mark	91TSC	592	$ .05	$ .25	Garrett, Adrian	76T	562	$ .05	$ .25
Gardner, Mark	92T	119	$ .01	$ .03	Garrett, Greg	70T	642	$1.25	$5.00
Gardner, Mark	92TSC	42	$ .01	$ .10	Garrett, Greg	71T	377	$ .25	$1.00
Gardner, Mark	93T	314	$ .01	$ .03	Garrett, Neil	93T	579	$ .05	$ .35
Gardner, Mark	93TSC	159	$ .01	$ .10	Garrett, Pat	66T	553	$4.00	$16.00
Gardner, Rob	66T	534	$3.75	$15.00	Garrett, Wayne	70T	628	$ .50	$2.00
Gardner, Rob	67T	217	$ .50	$2.00					
Gardner, Rob	68T	219	$ .35	$1.40					
Gardner, Rob	71T	734	$1.50	$6.00					
Gardner, Rob	72T	22	$ .10	$ .40					
Gardner, Rob	73T	222	$ .10	$ .40					
Gardner, Wes	88T	189	$ .01	$ .04					
Gardner, Wes	89T	526	$ .01	$ .03					
Gardner, Wes	90T	38	$ .01	$ .03					
Gardner, Wes	91T	629	$ .01	$ .03					
Garibaldi, Bob	70T	681	$1.25	$5.00					
Garibaldi, Bob	71T	701	$1.10	$4.40					
Garland, Wayne	74T	596	$ .10	$ .40					
Garland, Wayne	76T	414	$ .05	$ .25					
Garland, Wayne	77T	33	$ .05	$ .20					
Garland, Wayne	78T	174	$ .04	$ .16					
Garland, Wayne	79T	636	$ .03	$ .12					
Garland, Wayne	80T	361	$ .01	$ .10					
Garland, Wayne	81T	511	$ .01	$ .08					
Garland, Wayne	82T	446	$ .01	$ .08					
Garman, Mike	71T	512	$ .50	$2.00					
Garman, Mike	72T	79	$25.00	$100.00					
Garman, Mike	73T	616	$ .75	$3.00					
Garman, Mike	75T	584	$ .10	$ .40					
Garman, Mike	76T	34	$ .05	$ .25					
Garman, Mike	77T	302	$ .05	$ .20					
Garman, Mike	78T	417	$ .04	$ .16					
Garman, Mike	79T	181	$ .03	$ .12					
Garner, Phil	75T	623	$5.25	$21.00					
Garner, Phil	76T	57	$ .20	$ .80					
Garner, Phil	77T	261	$ .05	$ .20					
Garner, Phil	78T	53	$ .04	$ .16					
Garner, Phil	79T	383	$ .03	$ .12					
Garner, Phil	80T	118	$ .01	$ .10	**Garrett, Wayne**	**71T**	**228**	**$ .25**	**$1.00**
Garner, Phil	81T	573	$ .01	$ .08	Garrett, Wayne	72T	518	$ .25	$1.00
Garner, Phil	82T	683	$ .01	$ .08	Garrett, Wayne	73T	562	$ .60	$2.40
Garner, Phil	83T	478	$ .01	$ .08	Garrett, Wayne	74T	510	$ .10	$ .40
Garner, Phil	84T	752	$ .01	$ .06	Garrett, Wayne	75T	111	$ .10	$ .40
Garner, Phil	85T	206	$ .01	$ .06	Garrett, Wayne	76T	222	$ .05	$ .25
Garner, Phil	86T	83	$ .01	$ .05	Garrett, Wayne	77T	417	$ .05	$ .20
Garner, Phil	87T	304	$ .01	$ .04	Garrett, Wayne	78T	679	$ .04	$ .16
Garner, Phil	88T	174	$ .01	$ .04	Garrett, Wayne	79T	319	$ .03	$ .12
Garner, Phil	92T	291	$ .01	$ .03	Garrido, Gil	64T	452	$1.50	$6.00
Garner, Phil	93T	508	$ .01	$ .03	Garrido, Gil	69T	331	$ .50	$2.00
Garr, Ralph	70T	172	$ .50	$2.00	Garrido, Gil	70T	48	$ .20	$ .80
Garr, Ralph	71T	494	$ .50	$2.00	Garrido, Gil	71T	173	$ .25	$1.00
Garr, Ralph	72T	85	$ .50	$2.00	Garrido, Gil	72T	758	$1.25	$5.00
Garr, Ralph	72T	260	$ .10	$ .40	Garver, Ned	51Tbb	18	$7.50	$30.00
Garr, Ralph	73T	15	$ .20	$ .80	Garver, Ned	52T	212	$7.00	$28.00
Garr, Ralph	74T	570	$ .10	$ .40	Garver, Ned	53T	112	$4.00	$16.00
Garr, Ralph	75T	306	$ .30	$1.20	Garver, Ned	54T	44	$3.75	$15.00
Garr, Ralph	75T	550	$ .10	$ .40	Garver, Ned	56T	189	$3.75	$15.00
Garr, Ralph	76T	410	$ .05	$ .25	Garver, Ned	57T	285	$5.00	$20.00
Garr, Ralph	76TTR	410	$ .05	$ .25	Garver, Ned	58T	292	$1.25	$5.00
Garr, Ralph	77T	133	$ .05	$ .20	Garver, Ned	59T	245	$1.00	$4.00
Garr, Ralph	78T	628	$ .04	$ .16	Garver, Ned	60T	471	$1.25	$5.00
Garr, Ralph	79T	309	$ .03	$ .12	Garver, Ned	61T	331	$ .60	$2.40
Garr, Ralph	80T	272	$ .01	$ .10	Garver, Ned	91TA53	112	$ .01	$ .15
Garrelts, Scott	85TTR	38	$ .05	$ .20	Garvey, Steve	71T	341	$15.00	$60.00
Garrelts, Scott	86T	395	$ .01	$ .05	Garvey, Steve	72T	686	$17.50	$70.00
Garrelts, Scott	87T	475	$ .01	$ .04	Garvey, Steve	73T	213	$3.00	$12.00
Garrelts, Scott	88T	97	$ .01	$ .04	Garvey, Steve	74T	575	$2.50	$10.00
Garrelts, Scott	89T	703	$ .01	$ .03	Garvey, Steve	75T	140	$2.00	$8.00
Garrelts, Scott	90T	602	$ .01	$ .03	Garvey, Steve	75T	212	$ .25	$1.00
Garrelts, Scott	91T	361	$ .01	$ .03	Garvey, Steve	76T	150	$1.25	$5.00
Garrelts, Scott	91TSC	182	$ .05	$ .25	Garvey, Steve	77T	400	$1.00	$4.00
Garrelts, Scott	92T	558	$ .01	$ .03	Garvey, Steve	78T	350	$ .75	$3.00
Garrelts, Scott	92TSC	832	$ .01	$ .10	Garvey, Steve	79T	50	$ .30	$1.20

TOPPS

Player	Year	No.	VG	EX/MT
Garvey, Steve	80T	290	$.15	$1.50
Garvey, Steve	81T	530	$.10	$1.00
Garvey, Steve	82T	179	$.10	$.75
Garvey, Steve	82TSA	180	$.05	$.35
Garvey, Steve	83T	610	$.10	$.50
Garvey, Steve	83TTR	37	$.15	$1.50
Garvey, Steve	84T	380	$.10	$.50
Garvey, Steve	85T	450	$.05	$.25
Garvey, Steve	85TRB	2	$.05	$.20
Garvey, Steve	86T	660	$.05	$.25
Garvey, Steve	87T	100	$.01	$.15
Garvin, Jerry	78T	419	$.04	$.16
Garvin, Jerry	79T	293	$.03	$.12
Garvin, Jerry	80T	611	$.01	$.10
Garvin, Jerry	81T	124	$.01	$.08
Garvin, Jerry	82T	768	$.01	$.08
Garvin, Jerry	83T	358	$.01	$.08
Gaspar, Rod	70T	371	$.35	$1.40
Gaspar, Rod	71T	383	$.25	$1.00
Gaston, Cito	89TTR	36	$.01	$.05
Gaston, Cito	90T	201	$.01	$.03
Gaston, Cito	91T	81	$.01	$.03
Gaston, Cito	92T	699	$.01	$.03
Gaston, Clarence	69T	304	$1.75	$7.00
Gaston, Clarence	70T	604	$.75	$3.00
Gaston, Clarence	71T	25	$.50	$2.00
Gaston, Clarence	72T	431	$.50	$2.00
Gaston, Clarence	72TIA	432	$.25	$1.00
Gaston, Clarence	73T	159	$.20	$.80
Gaston, Clarence	74T	364	$.20	$.80
Gaston, Clarence	75T	427	$.10	$.40
Gaston, Clarence	76T	558	$.05	$.25
Gaston, Clarence	77T	192	$.05	$.20
Gaston, Clarence	78T	716	$.04	$.16
Gaston, Clarence	79T	208	$.03	$.12
Gates, Brent	92T	216	$.10	$.40
Gates, Brent	93T	451	$.05	$.25
Gates, Mike	83T	657	$.01	$.08
Gatewood, Aubrey	64T	127	$.50	$2.00
Gatewood, Aubrey	65T	422	$1.00	$4.00
Gatewood, Aubrey	66T	42	$.35	$1.40
Gaudet, Jim	79T	707	$.03	$.12
Gebhard, Bob	72T	28	$.10	$.40
Geddes, Jim	73T	561	$.60	$2.40
Gedman, Rich	82T	59	$.05	$.20
Gedman, Rich	83T	602	$.01	$.10
Gedman, Rich	84T	498	$.01	$.10
Gedman, Rich	85T	529	$.01	$.10
Gedman, Rich	86T	375	$.01	$.10
Gedman, Rich	87T	740	$.01	$.04
Gedman, Rich	88T	245	$.01	$.04
Gedman, Rich	89T	652	$.01	$.03
Gedman, Rich	90T	123	$.01	$.03
Gedman, Rich	92TSC	58	$.01	$.10
Gehrig, Lou	61T	405	$5.50	$22.00
Gehrig, Lou	62T	140	$6.00	$24.00
Gehrig, Lou	73TATL	472	$1.25	$5.00
Gehrig, Lou	76TAT	341	$1.50	$6.00
Geiger, Gary	58T	462	$3.00	$12.00
Geiger, Gary	59T	521	$4.00	$16.00
Geiger, Gary	60T	184	$.75	$3.00
Geiger, Gary	61T	33	$.60	$2.40
Geiger, Gary	62T	117	$.60	$2.40
Geiger, Gary	63T	513	$1.75	$7.00
Geiger, Gary	64T	93	$.50	$2.00
Geiger, Gary	65T	452	$1.25	$5.00
Geiger, Gary	66T	286	$.50	$2.00
Geiger, Gary	67T	566	$2.25	$9.00
Geiger, Gary	69T	278	$.50	$2.00
Geisel, Dave	79T	716	$.03	$.12
Geisel, Dave	80T	676	$.01	$.10
Geisel, Dave	84T	256	$.01	$.06
Geishert, Vern	70T	683	$1.50	$6.00
Gelnar, John	65T	143	$.35	$1.40
Gelnar, John	67T	472	$1.50	$6.00
Gelnar, John	70T	393	$.35	$1.40
Gelnar, John	71T	604	$1.00	$4.00
Gentile, Jim	60T	448	$2.50	$10.00
Gentile, Jim	61T	559	$9.00	$36.00
Gentile, Jim	62T	53	$13.75	$55.00
Gentile, Jim	62T	290	$1.25	$5.00
Gentile, Jim	63T	4	$2.00	$8.00
Gentile, Jim	63T	260	$.90	$3.60
Gentile, Jim	64T	196	$.75	$3.00
Gentile, Jim	65T	365	$.50	$2.00
Gentile, Jim	66T	45	$.35	$1.40
Gentry, Gary	69T	31	$.75	$3.00
Gentry, Gary	70T	153	$.20	$.80
Gentry, Gary	71T	725	$1.50	$6.00
Gentry, Gary	72T	105	$.10	$.40
Gentry, Gary	73T	288	$.10	$.40
Gentry, Gary	74T	415	$.10	$.40
Gentry, Gary	75T	393	$.10	$.40
George, Chris	92TSC	354	$.01	$.10
George, Chris	93T	744	$.01	$.03
Gerber, Craig	86T	222	$.01	$.05
Geren, Bob	89TTR	37	$.01	$.10
Geren, Bob	90T	536	$.01	$.03
Geren, Bob	91T	716	$.01	$.03
Geren, Bob	91TSC	171	$.05	$.25
Geren, Bob	92T	341	$.01	$.03
Gerhart, Ken	87TTR	37	$.01	$.05
Gerhart, Ken	88T	271	$.01	$.04
Gerhart, Ken	89T	598	$.01	$.03
Gernert, Dick	52T	343	$43.75	$175.00
Gernert, Dick	57T	202	$2.00	$8.00
Gernert, Dick	58T	38	$2.00	$8.00
Gernert, Dick	59T	13	$1.50	$6.00
Gernert, Dick	59T	519	$4.00	$16.00
Gernert, Dick	60T	86	$.85	$3.40
Gernert, Dick	61T	284	$.60	$2.40
Gernert, Dick	62T	536	$3.50	$14.00
Geronimo, Cesar	71T	447	$.50	$2.00
Geronimo, Cesar	72T	719	$1.25	$5.00
Geronimo, Cesar	73T	156	$.10	$.40
Geronimo, Cesar	74T	181	$.10	$.40
Geronimo, Cesar	75T	41	$.10	$.40
Geronimo, Cesar	76T	24	$.05	$.25
Geronimo, Cesar	77T	535	$.05	$.20
Geronimo, Cesar	78T	354	$.04	$.16
Geronimo, Cesar	79T	220	$.03	$.12
Geronimo, Cesar	80T	475	$.01	$.10
Geronimo, Cesar	81T	390	$.01	$.08
Geronimo, Cesar	81TTR	766	$.01	$.15
Geronimo, Cesar	82T	693	$.01	$.08
Geronimo, Cesar	83T	194	$.01	$.08
Geronimo, Cesar	84T	544	$.01	$.06
Geurrero, Juan	93TSC	16	$.01	$.10
Giallombardo, Bob	59T	321	$1.00	$4.00
Giamatti, A. Bartlett	90T	396	$.05	$.20
Giambi, Jason	91TTR	45	$.10	$.40
Giambi, Jason	92TTR	40	$.01	$.15
Giants, Team	56T	226	$18.00	$72.00
Giants, Team	57T	317	$15.00	$60.00
Giants, Team	58T	19	$8.00	$32.00
Giants, Team	59T	69	$5.00	$20.00
Giants, Team	60T	151	$2.00	$88.00
Giants, Team	61T	167	$1.75	$7.00
Giants, Team	62T	226	$1.50	$6.00
Giants, Team	63T	417	$2.00	$8.00
Giants, Team	64T	257	$1.50	$6.00
Giants, Team	65T	379	$2.25	$9.00
Giants, Team	66T	19	$.75	$3.00
Giants, Team	67T	516	$2.50	$10.00
Giants, Team	70T	696	$2.50	$10.00
Giants, Team	71T	563	$1.75	$7.00
Giants, Team	72T	771	$2.50	$10.00
Giants, Team	73T	434	$.50	$2.00
Giants, Team	74T	281	$.25	$1.00
Giants, Team Checklist	75T	216	$.35	$1.40

TOPPS

Player	Year	No.	VG	EX/MT	Player	Year	No.	VG	EX/MT
Giants, Team Checklist	76T	443	$ .30	$1.20	Gibson, Kirk	87T	765	$ .01	$ .15
Giants, Team Checklist	77T	211	$ .25	$1.00	Gibson, Kirk	88T	605	$ .01	$ .10
Giants, Team Checklist	78T	82	$ .20	$ .80	Gibson, Kirk	88TTR	40	$ .01	$ .15
Giants, Team Checklist	79T	356	$ .15	$ .60	Gibson, Kirk	89T	340	$ .01	$ .10
Giants, Team Checklist	80T	499	$ .10	$ .50	Gibson, Kirk	89TAS	396	$ .01	$ .05
Giants, Team Checklist	81T	686	$ .05	$ .25	Gibson, Kirk	90T	150	$ .01	$ .03
Giants, Team Leaders	86T	516	$ .01	$ .05	Gibson, Kirk	91T	490	$ .01	$ .03
Giants, Team Leaders	87T	231	$ .01	$ .04	Gibson, Kirk	91TSC	344	$ .05	$ .25
Giants, Team Leaders	88T	261	$ .01	$ .04	Gibson, Kirk	91TTR	46	$ .01	$ .05
Giants, Team Leaders	89T	351	$ .01	$ .03	Gibson, Kirk	92T	720	$ .01	$ .03
Gibbon, Joe	60T	512	$2.75	$11.00	Gibson, Kirk	92TSC	495	$ .01	$ .10
Gibbon, Joe	61T	523	$7.50	$30.00	Gibson, Kirk	92TSC	784	$ .01	$ .10
Gibbon, Joe	62T	448	$1.50	$6.00	Gibson, Paul	89T	583	$ .01	$ .03
Gibbon, Joe	63T	101	$ .50	$2.00	Gibson, Paul	90T	11	$ .01	$ .03
Gibbon, Joe	64T	307	$ .65	$2.60	Gibson, Paul	91T	431	$ .01	$ .03
Gibbon, Joe	65T	54	$ .35	$1.40	Gibson, Paul	92T	143	$ .01	$ .03
Gibbon, Joe	66T	457	$1.50	$6.00	Gibson, Paul	92TSC	223	$ .01	$ .10
Gibbon, Joe	67T	541	$4.00	$16.00	Gibson, Paul	92TSC	694	$ .01	$ .10
Gibbon, Joe	68T	32	$ .35	$1.40	Gibson, Paul	93TSC	29	$ .01	$ .10
Gibbon, Joe	69T	158	$ .35	$1.40	Gibson, Russ	67T	547	$2.25	$9.00
Gibbon, Joe	70T	517	$ .35	$1.40	Gibson, Russ	68T	297	$ .35	$1.40
Gibbon, Joe	72T	382	$ .10	$ .40	Gibson, Russ	69T	89	$ .35	$1.40
Gibbs, Jake	62T	281	$ .75	$3.00	Gibson, Russ	70T	237	$ .20	$ .80
Gibbs, Jake	64T	281	$ .65	$2.60	Gibson, Russ	71T	738	$1.50	$6.00
Gibbs, Jake	65T	226	$ .50	$2.00	Gibson, Russ	72T	643	$ .40	$1.60
Gibbs, Jake	66T	117	$ .50	$2.00	Gideon, Jim	77T	478	$ .05	$ .20
Gibbs, Jake	67T	375	$ .60	$2.40	Giel, Paul	58T	308	$1.25	$5.00
Gibbs, Jake	68T	89	$ .35	$1.40	Giel, Paul	59T	9	$1.50	$6.00
Gibbs, Jake	69T	401	$ .30	$1.20	Giel, Paul	60T	526	$2.75	$11.00
Gibbs, Jake	70T	594	$ .50	$2.00	Giel, Paul	61T	374	$1.00	$4.00
Gibbs, Jake	71T	382	$ .25	$1.00	Gigon, Norm	67T	576	$6.00	$24.00
Gibson, Bob	59T	514	$100.00	$400.00	Gil, Benji	92T	534	$ .05	$ .20
Gibson, Bob	60T	73	$16.50	$66.00	Gil, Benji	93T	529	$ .10	$ .50
Gibson, Bob	61T	211	$9.00	$38.00	Gil, Gus	67T	253	$ .50	$2.00
Gibson, Bob	62T	530	$43.75	$175.00	Gil, Gus	69T	651	$ .40	$1.60
Gibson, Bob	63T	5	$2.00	$8.00	Gilbert, Andy	73T	252	$ .20	$ .80
Gibson, Bob	63T	9	$2.00	$8.00	Gilbert, Andy	74T	78	$ .10	$ .40
Gibson, Bob	63T	415	$11.25	$45.00	Gilbert, Buddy	60T	359	$ .75	$3.00
Gibson, Bob	64T	460	$10.00	$40.00	Gilbert, Tookie	52T	61	$13.75	$55.00
Gibson, Bob	65T	12	$1.00	$4.00	Gilbreath, Rod	74T	93	$ .10	$ .40
Gibson, Bob	65T	320	$8.00	$32.00	Gilbreath, Rod	75T	431	$ .10	$ .40
Gibson, Bob	66T	225	$1.75	$7.00	Gilbreath, Rod	76T	306	$ .05	$ .25
Gibson, Bob	66T	320	$7.00	$28.00	Gilbreath, Rod	77T	126	$ .05	$ .20
Gibson, Bob	67T	210	$5.00	$20.00	Gilbreath, Rod	78T	217	$ .04	$ .16
Gibson, Bob	67T	236	$3.75	$15.00	Gilbreath, Rod	79T	572	$ .03	$ .12
Gibson, Bob	68T	100	$6.25	$25.00	Gile, Don	61T	236	$ .60	$2.40
Gibson, Bob	68TAS	378	$2.25	$9.00	Gile, Don	62T	244	$ .75	$3.00
Gibson, Bob	69T	8	$ .75	$3.00	Giles, Brian	83T	548	$ .01	$ .08
Gibson, Bob	69T	10	$1.25	$5.00	Giles, Brian	84T	676	$ .01	$ .06
Gibson, Bob	69T	12	$ .75	$3.00	Giles, Warren	56T	2	$4.50	$18.00
Gibson, Bob	69T	200	$3.50	$14.00	Giles, Warren	57T	100	$2.75	$11.00
Gibson, Bob	69TAS	432	$1.25	$5.00	Giles, Warren	58T	300	$2.00	$8.00
Gibson, Bob	70T	67	$1.50	$6.00	Giles, Warren	59T	200	$1.50	$6.00
Gibson, Bob	70T	71	$ .75	$3.00	Gilkey, Bernard	91T	126	$ .01	$ .15
Gibson, Bob	70T	530	$3.00	$12.00	Gilkey, Bernard	91TSC	402	$ .10	$ .50
Gibson, Bob	71T	70	$ .75	$3.00	Gilkey, Bernard	92T	746	$ .01	$ .03
Gibson, Bob	71T	72	$1.00	$4.00	Gilkey, Bernard	92TSC	234	$ .05	$ .25
Gibson, Bob	71T	450	$3.50	$14.00	Gilkey, Bernard	93T	203	$ .01	$ .03
Gibson, Bob	72T	130	$1.50	$6.00	Gilkey, Bernard	93TSC	230	$ .01	$ .10
Gibson, Bob	73T	190	$1.50	$6.00	Gilliam, Jim	53T	258	$65.00	$260.00
Gibson, Bob	74T	350	$1.25	$5.00	Gilliam, Junior	54T	35	$7.00	$28.00
Gibson, Bob	75T	150	$1.25	$5.00	Gilliam, Jim	55T	5	$4.00	$16.00
Gibson, Bob	75T	206	$ .25	$1.00	Gilliam, Jim	56T	280	$5.00	$20.00
Gibson, Bob	75THL	3	$ .75	$3.00	Gilliam, Jim	57T	115	$3.00	$12.00
Gibson, Bob	84T	349	$ .01	$ .06	Gilliam, Jim	58T	215	$2.25	$9.00
Gibson, Bob	85TTR	39	$ .01	$ .10	Gilliam, Jim	59T	306	$1.50	$6.00
Gibson, Bob	86T	499	$ .01	$ .05	Gilliam, Jim	60T	255	$1.25	$5.00
Gibson, Bob	88TTB	664	$ .01	$ .10	Gilliam, Jim	61T	238	$1.25	$5.00
Gibson, Joel	65T	368	$ .50	$2.00	Gilliam, Jim	62T	486	$2.00	$8.00
Gibson, Kirk	81T	315	$1.00	$4.00	Gilliam, Jim	63T	80	$1.00	$4.00
Gibson, Kirk	82T	105	$ .10	$1.00	Gilliam, Jim	64T	310	$1.00	$4.00
Gibson, Kirk	83T	430	$ .10	$ .50	Gilliam, Jim	73T	569	$1.10	$4.40
Gibson, Kirk	84T	65	$ .05	$ .35	Gilliam, Jim	74T	144	$ .50	$2.00
Gibson, Kirk	85T	565	$ .05	$ .25	Gilliam, Jim	91TA53	258	$ .10	$ .50
Gibson, Kirk	86T	295	$ .01	$ .10	Gilson, Hal	68T	162	$ .35	$1.40

TOPPS

Player	Year	No.	VG	EX/MT
Gilson, Hal	69T	156	$ .35	$1.40
Ginsberg, Joe	57T	236	$2.00	$8.00
Ginsberg, Joe	58T	67	$2.00	$8.00
Ginsberg, Joe	59T	66	$1.50	$6.00
Ginsberg, Joe	60T	304	$ .75	$3.00
Ginsberg, Joe	61T	79	$ .60	$2.40
Ginsberg, Myron	52T	192	$7.00	$28.00
Girardi, Joe	90T	12	$ .01	$ .03
Girardi, Joe	91T	214	$ .01	$ .03
Girardi, Joe	91TSC	247	$ .05	$ .25
Girardi, Joe	92T	529	$ .01	$ .03
Girardi, Joe	92TSC	132	$ .01	$ .10
Girardi, Joe	93T	425	$ .01	$ .03
Giusti, Dave	62T	509	$1.75	$7.00
Giusti, Dave	63T	189	$ .50	$2.00
Giusti, Dave	64T	354	$ .65	$2.60
Giusti, Dave	65T	524	$2.50	$10.00
Giusti, Dave	66T	258	$ .50	$2.00
Giusti, Dave	67T	318	$ .60	$2.40
Giusti, Dave	68T	182	$ .35	$1.40
Giusti, Dave	69T	98	$ .35	$1.40
Giusti, Dave	70T	372	$ .35	$1.40
Giusti, Dave	71T	562	$1.00	$4.00
Giusti, Dave	72T	190	$ .10	$ .40
Giusti, Dave	73T	465	$ .25	$1.00
Giusti, Dave	74T	82	$ .10	$ .40
Giusti, Dave	75T	53	$ .10	$ .40
Giusti, Dave	76T	352	$ .05	$ .25
Giusti, Dave	77T	154	$ .05	$ .20
Gladden, Dan	85T	386	$ .05	$ .25
Gladden, Dan	86T	678	$ .01	$ .05
Gladden, Danny	87T	46	$ .01	$ .04
Gladden, Danny	87TTR	38	$ .01	$ .05
Gladden, Danny	88T	502	$ .01	$ .04
Gladden, Danny	89T	426	$ .01	$ .03
Gladden, Danny	90T	298	$ .01	$ .03
Gladden, Danny	91T	778	$ .01	$ .03
Gladden, Danny	91TSC	54	$ .05	$ .25
Gladden, Danny	92T	177	$ .01	$ .03
Gladden, Danny	92TSC	801	$ .01	$ .10
Gladden, Danny	92TTR	41	$ .01	$ .05
Gladden, Danny	93T	626	$ .01	$ .03
Gladden, Danny	93TSC	191	$ .01	$ .10
Gladding, Fred	64T	312	$ .65	$2.60
Gladding, Fred	65T	37	$ .35	$1.40
Gladding, Fred	66T	337	$ .50	$2.00
Gladding, Fred	67T	192	$ .40	$1.60
Gladding, Fred	68T	423	$ .35	$1.40
Gladding, Fred	69T	58	$ .35	$1.40
Gladding, Fred	70T	208	$ .20	$ .80
Gladding, Fred	71T	381	$ .25	$1.00
Gladding, Fred	72T	507	$ .25	$1.00
Gladding, Fred	73T	17	$ .10	$ .40
Glaviano, Tommy	51Trb	47	$1.75	$7.50
Glaviano, Tommy	52T	56	$13.75	$55.00
Glaviano, Tommy	53T	140	$6.25	$25.00
Glaviano, Tommy	91TA53	140	$ .01	$ .15
Glavine, Tom	88T	779	$ .20	$2.00
Glavine, Tom	89T	157	$ .10	$ .50
Glavine, Tom	90T	506	$ .05	$ .25
Glavine, Tom	91T	82	$ .05	$ .20
Glavine, Tom	91TSC	558	$ .20	$2.00
Glavine, Tom	92T	305	$ .01	$ .15
Glavine, Tom	92TAS	395	$ .01	$ .10
Glavine, Tom	92TSC	395	$ .10	$ .50
Glavine, Tom	93T	280	$ .01	$ .10
Glavine, Tom	93T	410	$ .01	$ .10
Glavine, Tom	93TSC	296	$ .05	$ .20
Gleaton, Jerry Don	80T	673	$ .01	$ .10
Gleaton, Jerry Don	81T	41	$ .01	$ .08
Gleaton, Jerry Don	82T	371	$ .01	$ .08
Gleaton, Jerry Don	85T	216	$ .01	$ .06
Gleaton, Jerry Don	86T	447	$ .01	$ .05
Gleaton, Jerry Don	88T	116	$ .01	$ .04
Gleaton, Jerry Don	89T	724	$ .01	$ .03
Gleaton, Jerry Don	91T	597	$ .01	$ .03
Gleaton, J erry Don	91TSC	574	$ .05	$ .25
Gleaton, Jerry Don	92T	272	$ .01	$ .03
Glynn, Bill	53T	171	$4.50	$18.00
Glynn (Gylnn), Bill	54T	178	$3.75	$15.00
Glynn, Bill	55T	39	$2.25	$9.00
Glynn, Bill	91TA53	171	$ .01	$ .15
Glynn, Ed	77T	487	$ .05	$ .20
Glynn, Ed	79T	343	$ .03	$ .12
Glynn, Ed	80T	509	$ .01	$ .10
Glynn, Ed	81T	93	$ .01	$ .08
Glynn, Ed	83T	614	$ .01	$ .08
Goggin, Chuck	74T	457	$ .10	$ .40
Gogolewski, Bill	71T	559	$1.00	$4.00
Gogolewski, Bill	72T	424	$ .25	$1.00
Gogolewski, Bill	73T	27	$ .10	$ .40
Gogolewski, Bill	74T	242	$ .10	$ .40
Golden, Jim	61T	298	$ .60	$2.40
Golden, Jim	62T	568	$3.50	$14.00
Golden, Jim	63T	297	$ .90	$3.60
Goldsberry, Gordon	52T	46	$13.75	$55.00
Goldsberry, Gordon	53T	200	$4.50	$18.00
Goldsberry, Gordon	91TA53	200	$ .01	$ .15
Goldy, Purnal	63T	516	$1.75	$7.00
Goltz, Dave	73T	148	$ .10	$ .40
Goltz, Dave	74T	636	$ .10	$ .40
Goltz, Dave	75T	419	$ .10	$ .40
Goltz, Dave	76T	136	$ .05	$ .25
Goltz, Dave	77T	321	$ .05	$ .20
Goltz, Dave	78T	205	$ .20	$ .80
Goltz, Dave	78T	249	$ .04	$ .16
Goltz, Dave	79T	27	$ .03	$ .12
Goltz, Dave	80T	193	$ .01	$ .10
Goltz, Dave	81T	548	$ .01	$ .08
Goltz, Dave	82T	674	$ .01	$ .08
Goltz, Dave	83T	468	$ .01	$ .08
Gomez, Leo	91TTR	47	$ .05	$ .20

Player	Year	No.	VG	EX/MT
Gomez, Leo	**92T**	**84**	**$ .01**	**$ .10**
Gomez, Leo	92TSC	664	$ .05	$ .20
Gomez, Leo	93T	164	$ .01	$ .03
Gomez, Luis	77T	13	$ .05	$ .20
Gomez, Luis	78T	573	$ .04	$ .16
Gomez, Luis	79T	254	$ .03	$ .12

TOPPS

Player	Year	No.	VG	EX/MT
Gomez, Luis	80T	169	$ .01	$ .10
Gomez, Luis	81T	477	$ .01	$ .08
Gomez, Luis	82T	372	$ .01	$ .08
Gomez, Preston	69T	74	$ .35	$1.40
Gomez, Preston	70T	513	$ .35	$1.40
Gomez, Preston	71T	737	$1.50	$6.00
Gomez, Preston	72T	637	$ .40	$1.60
Gomez, Preston	73T	624	$1.00	$4.00
Gomez, Preston	74T	31	$ .10	$ .40
Gomez, Ruben	54T	220	$3.75	$15.00
Gomez, Ruben	55T	71	$2.25	$9.00
Gomez, Ruben	56T	9	$2.00	$8.00
Gomez, Ruben	57T	58	$2.00	$8.00
Gomez, Ruben	58T	335	$1.25	$5.00
Gomez, Ruben	59T	535	$4.00	$16.00
Gomez, Ruben	60T	82	$ .85	$3.40
Gomez, Ruben	61T	377	$1.00	$4.00
Gomez, Ruben	67T	427	$ .60	$2.40
Gonder, Jesse	63T	29	$ .90	$3.60
Gonder, Jesse	64T	457	$1.00	$4.00
Gonder, Jesse	65T	423	$1.00	$4.00
Gonder, Jesse	66T	528	$7.00	$28.00
Gonder, Jesse	67T	301	$ .60	$2.40
Gonder, Jesse	69T	617	$ .40	$1.60
Gonzales, Rene	88T	98	$ .01	$ .10
Gonzales, Rene	89T	213	$ .01	$ .03
Gonzales, Rene	90T	787	$ .01	$ .03
Gonzales, Rene	91T	377	$ .01	$ .03
Gonzales, Rene	91TSC	406	$ .05	$ .25
Gonzales, Rene	92T	681	$ .01	$ .03
Gonzales, Rene	92TSC	704	$ .01	$ .10

RENE GONZALES — Angels

Player	Year	No.	VG	EX/MT
Gonzales, Rene	**92TTR**	**42**	**$ .01**	**$ .05**
Gonzales, Rene	93T	266	$ .01	$ .03
Gonzales, Rene	93TSC	121	$ .01	$ .10
Gonzalez, Denny	86T	746	$ .01	$ .05
Gonzalez, Fernando	74T	649	$ .10	$ .40
Gonzalez, Fernando	74TTR	649	$ .10	$ .40
Gonzalez, Fernando	78T	433	$ .04	$ .16
Gonzalez, Fernando	79T	531	$ .03	$ .12
Gonzalez, Fernando	80T	171	$ .01	$ .10
Gonzalez, German	89T	746	$ .01	$ .03
Gonzalez, German	90T	266	$ .01	$ .03
Gonzalez, Jimmy	92T	564	$ .01	$ .10

Player	Year	No.	VG	EX/MT
Gonzalez, Jose	90T	98	$ .01	$ .03
Gonzalez, Jose	91T	279	$ .01	$ .10
Gonzalez, Jose	91TSC	208	$ .05	$ .25
Gonzalez, Jose	92TSC	774	$ .01	$ .10
Gonzalez, Juan	90T	331	$ .20	$2.00
Gonzalez, Juan	91T	224	$ .10	$ .40
Gonzalez, Juan	91TSC	237	$4.50	$18.00
Gonzalez, Juan	92T	27	$ .10	$ .40
Gonzalez, Juan	92TSC	240	$ .75	$3.00
Gonzalez, Juan	93T	34	$ .05	$ .25
Gonzalez, Juan	93TSC	297	$ .10	$ .50
Gonzalez, Julio	78T	389	$ .04	$ .16
Gonzalez, Julio	79T	268	$ .03	$ .12
Gonzalez, Julio	80T	696	$ .01	$ .10
Gonzalez, Julio	82T	503	$ .01	$ .08
Gonzalez, Julio	83T	74	$ .01	$ .08
Gonzalez, Luis	91TSC	576	$ .20	$2.00
Gonzalez, Luis	91TTR	48	$ .05	$ .25
Gonzalez, Luis	92T	12	$ .01	$ .15
Gonzalez, Luis	92TSC	227	$ .05	$ .20
Gonzalez, Luis	93T	362	$ .01	$ .03
Gonzalez, Orlando	77T	477	$ .05	$ .20
Gonzalez, Pedro	63T	537	$212.50	$850.00
Gonzalez, Pedro	64T	581	$2.25	$9.00
Gonzalez, Pedro	65T	97	$ .35	$1.40
Gonzalez, Pedro	66T	266	$ .50	$2.00
Gonzalez, Pedro	67T	424	$ .60	$2.40
Gonzalez, Tony	60T	518	$2.75	$11.00
Gonzalez, Tony	61T	93	$ .60	$2.40
Gonzalez, Tony	62T	534	$4.50	$22.00
Gonzalez, Tony	63T	32	$ .50	$2.00
Gonzalez, Tony	64T	379	$1.00	$4.00
Gonzalez, Tony	65T	72	$ .35	$1.40
Gonzalez, Tony	66T	478	$1.50	$6.00
Gonzalez, Tony	67T	548	$2.25	$9.00
Gonzalez, Tony	68T	1	$4.00	$16.00
Gonzalez, Tony	68T	245	$ .35	$1.40
Gonzalez, Tony	69T	501	$ .30	$1.20
Gonzalez, Tony	70T	105	$ .20	$ .80
Gonzalez, Tony	71T	256	$ .25	$1.00
Gooden, Dwight	84TTR	42	$6.25	$25.00
Gooden, Dwight	85T	620	$ .75	$3.00
Gooden, Dwight	85TRB	3	$ .10	$ .40
Gooden, Dwight	86T	250	$ .10	$ .50
Gooden, Dwight	86TAS	709	$ .05	$ .20
Gooden, Dwight	86TRB	202	$ .05	$ .20
Gooden, Dwight	87T	130	$ .05	$ .25
Gooden, Dwight	87TAS	603	$ .01	$ .15
Gooden, Dwight	88T	480	$ .01	$ .10
Gooden, Dwight	88TAS	405	$ .01	$ .10
Gooden, Dwight "Doc"	89T	30	$ .01	$ .10
Gooden, Dwight	89TTB	661	$ .01	$ .10
Gooden, Doc	90T	510	$ .01	$ .10
Gooden, Doc	91T	330	$ .01	$ .10
Gooden, Doc	91TSC	100	$ .10	$ .50
Gooden, Doc	92T	725	$ .01	$ .10
Gooden, Doc	92TSC	455	$ .01	$ .10
Gooden, Doc	92TSC	602	$ .01	$ .10
Gooden, Doc	93T	640	$ .01	$ .03
Goodman, Billy	51Trb	46	$1.65	$6.60
Goodman, Billy	52T	23	$13.75	$55.00
Goodman, Billy	56T	245	$3.75	$15.00
Goodman, Billy	57T	303	$5.00	$20.00
Goodman, Billy	58T	225	$1.25	$5.00
Goodman, Billy	59T	103	$1.50	$6.00
Goodman, Billy	60T	69	$ .85	$3.40
Goodman, Billy	61T	247	$ .75	$3.00
Goodman, Billy	91TA53	334	$ .05	$ .20
Goodrich, Jon	93T	704	$ .05	$ .20
Goodson, Ed	73T	197	$ .10	$ .40
Goodson, Ed	74T	494	$ .10	$ .40
Goodson, Ed	75T	322	$ .10	$ .40
Goodson, Ed	76T	386	$ .05	$ .25
Goodson, Ed	77T	584	$ .05	$ .20
Goodson, Ed	78T	586	$ .04	$ .16

TOPPS

Player	Year	No.	VG	EX/MT	Player	Year	No.	VG	EX/MT
Goodwin, Danny	79T	322	$ .03	$ .12	Gotay, Julio	62T	489	$1.50	$6.00
Goodwin, Danny	80T	362	$ .01	$ .10	Gotay, Julio	63T	122	$ .50	$2.00
Goodwin, Danny	81T	527	$ .01	$ .08	Gotay, Julio	65T	552	$1.40	$5.60
Goodwin, Danny	82T	123	$ .01	$ .08	Gotay, Julio	68T	41	$ .35	$1.40
Goodwin, Tom	92TSC	322	$ .01	$ .15	Gott, Jim	83T	506	$ .05	$ .20
Goodwin, Tom	93T	228	$ .01	$ .03	Gott, Jim	84T	9	$ .01	$ .06
Goossen, Greg	67T	287	$ .60	$2.40	Gott, Jim	85T	311	$ .01	$ .06
Goossen, Greg	68T	386	$ .35	$1.40	Gott, Jim	85TTR	40	$ .01	$ .10
Goossen, Greg	70T	271	$ .35	$1.40	Gott, Jim	86T	463	$ .01	$ .05
Gorbous, Glen	56T	174	$2.50	$10.00	Gott, Jim	87TTR	39	$ .01	$ .05
Gordon, Don	88T	144	$ .01	$ .04	Gott, Jim	88T	127	$ .01	$ .04
Gordon, Joe	60T	216	$1.25	$5.00	Gott, Jim	89T	752	$ .01	$ .03
Gordon, Joe	61T	224	$ .75	$3.00	Gott, Jim	90T	292	$ .01	$ .03
Gordon, Joe	69T	484	$ .30	$1.20	Gott, Jim	91T	606	$ .01	$ .03
Gordon, Sid	51Trb	2	$1.75	$7.50	Gott, Jim	92T	517	$ .01	$ .03
Gordon, Sid	52T	267	$12.50	$50.00	Gott, Jim	92TSC	483	$ .01	$ .10
Gordon, Sid	53T	117	$4.00	$16.00	Gott, Jim	93T	418	$ .01	$ .03
Gordon, Sid	91TA53	117	$ .01	$ .15	Gozzo, Goose	90T	274	$ .01	$ .10
Gordon, Tom	89TTR	38	$ .01	$ .15	Grabarkewitz, Billy	70T	446	$ .35	$1.40
Gordon, Tom	90T	752	$ .01	$ .03	Grabarkewitz, Billy	71T	85	$ .25	$1.00
Gordon, Tom	91T	248	$ .01	$ .03	Grabarkewitz, Billy	72T	578	$ .40	$1.60
Gordon, Tom	91TSC	254	$ .05	$ .25	Grabarkewitz, Billy	73T	301	$ .10	$ .40
Gordon, Tom	92T	431	$ .01	$ .03	Grabarkewitz, Billy	74T	214	$ .10	$ .40
Gordon, Tom	92TSC	388	$ .01	$ .10	Grabarkewitz, Billy	75T	233	$ .10	$ .40
Gordon, Tom	93T	611	$ .01	$ .03	Grace, Mark	88TTR	42	$ .20	$2.00
Gorinski, Bob	78T	386	$ .04	$ .16	Grace, Mark	89T	465	$ .05	$ .35
Gorman, Tom	56T	246	$3.75	$15.00	Grace, Mark	90T	240	$ .05	$ .20
Gorman, Tom	57T	87	$2.00	$8.00	Grace, Mark	91T	520	$ .01	$ .10
Gorman, Tom	58T	235	$1.25	$5.00	Grace, Mark	91TSC	290	$ .10	$1.00
Gorman, Tom	59T	449	$1.00	$4.00	Grace, Mark	92T	140	$ .01	$ .10
Gorman, Tom	84T	774	$ .01	$ .06	Grace, Mark	92TSC	174	$ .05	$ .25
Gorman, Tom	85T	53	$ .01	$ .06	Grace, Mark	93T	630	$ .01	$ .10
Gorman, Tom	86T	414	$ .01	$ .05	Graff, Milt	57T	369	$1.75	$7.00
Goryl, John	58T	384	$1.00	$4.00	Graff, Milt	58T	192	$1.25	$5.00
Goryl, John	59T	77	$1.50	$6.00	Graff, Milt	59T	182	$1.00	$4.00
Goryl, John	62T	558	$3.50	$14.00	Graham, Dan	80T	669	$ .05	$ .30
Goryl, John	63T	314	$ .90	$3.60	Graham, Dan	81T	161	$ .01	$ .08
Goryl, John	64T	194	$ .50	$2.00	Graham, Dan	82T	37	$ .01	$ .08
Gosger, Jim	63T	553	$60.00	$240.00	Grahe, Joe	91T	426	$ .01	$ .10
Gosger, Jim	66T	114	$ .50	$2.00	Grahe, Joe	92T	496	$ .01	$ .03
Gosger, Jim	67T	17	$ .40	$1.60	Grahe, Joe	92TSC	579	$ .01	$ .10
Gosger, Jim	68T	343	$ .35	$1.40	Grahe, Joe	93T	129	$ .01	$ .03
Gosger, Jim	69T	482	$ .30	$1.20	Grahe, Joe	93TSC	262	$ .01	$ .10
Gosger, Jim	70T	651	$1.25	$5.00	Grammas, Alex	54T	151	$3.75	$15.00
Gosger, Jim	71T	284	$ .25	$1.00	Grammas, Alex	55T	21	$2.25	$9.00
Goss, Howie	62T	598	$17.50	$70.00	Grammas, Alex	56T	37	$2.00	$8.00
Goss, Howie	63T	364	$ .90	$3.60	Grammas, Alex	57T	222	$2.00	$8.00
Gossage, Rich	73T	174	$5.00	$20.00	Grammas, Alex	58T	254	$1.25	$5.00
Gossage, Rich	74T	542	$1.25	$5.00	Grammas, Alex	59T	6	$1.50	$6.00
Gossage, Rich	75T	554	$ .75	$3.00	Grammas, Alex	60T	168	$ .75	$3.00
Gossage, Rich	76T	180	$ .75	$3.00	Grammas, Alex	61T	64	$ .60	$2.40
Gossage, Rich	76T	205	$ .15	$ .60	Grammas, Alex	62T	223	$ .75	$3.00
Gossage, Rich	77T	319	$ .25	$1.00	Grammas, Alex	63T	416	$1.00	$4.00
Gossage, Rich	78T	70	$ .25	$1.00	Grammas, Alex	73T	296	$ .20	$ .80
Gossage, Rich	79T	8	$ .10	$ .40	Grammas, Alex	74T	326	$ .25	$1.00
Gossage, Rich	79T	225	$ .25	$1.00	Granger, Jeff	91TTR	49	$ .10	$ .40
Gossage, Rich	80T	140	$ .25	$1.00	Granger, Jeff	92TTR	43	$ .01	$ .15
Gossage, Rich	81T	460	$ .05	$ .35	Granger, Wayne	69T	551	$ .40	$1.60
Gossage, Rich	82T	770	$ .05	$ .25	Granger, Wayne	70T	73	$ .20	$ .80
Gossage, Rich	82TAS	557	$ .01	$ .15	Granger, Wayne	71T	379	$ .25	$1.00
Gossage, Rich	82TSA	771	$ .01	$ .10	Granger, Wayne	72T	545	$ .40	$1.60
Gossage, Rich	83T	240	$ .05	$ .35	Granger, Wayne	73T	523	$ .25	$1.00
Gossage, Rich	83T	241	$ .01	$ .15	Granger, Wayne	74T	644	$ .10	$ .40
Gossage, Rich	84T	670	$ .01	$ .06	Granger, Wayne	76T	516	$ .05	$ .25
Gossage, Rich	84TTR	43	$ .01	$ .15	Grant, Jim	58T	394	$1.50	$6.00
Gossage, Rich	84TTR	43	$ .10	$ .50	Grant, Jim "Mudcat"	59T	186	$1.00	$4.00
Gossage, Rich	85T	90	$ .01	$ .15	Grant, Jim	60T	14	$ .85	$3.40
Gossage, Rich	86T	530	$ .01	$ .10	Grant, Jim	61T	18	$ .60	$2.40
Gossage, Rich	87T	380	$ .01	$ .10	Grant, Jim	62T	307	$ .75	$3.00
Gossage, Rich	88T	170	$ .01	$ .05	Grant, Jim	63T	227	$ .90	$3.60
Gossage, Rich	88TTR	41	$ .01	$ .10	Grant, Jim	64T	133	$ .50	$2.00
Gossage, Rich	89T	415	$ .01	$ .03	Grant, Jim	65T	432	$1.00	$4.00
Gossage, Rich	92T	215	$ .01	$ .03	Grant, Jim	66T	40	$ .35	$1.40
Gossage, Rich	92TSC	719	$ .01	$ .10	Grant, Jim	66T	224	$ .75	$3.00
Gossage, Rich	93TSC	17	$ .01	$ .10	Grant, Jim	67T	545	$4.00	$16.00

TOPPS

Player	Year	No.	VG	EX/MT	Player	Year	No.	VG	EX/MT
Grant, Jim	68T	398	$ .35	$1.40	Green, Lenny	62T	84	$ .60	$2.40
Grant, Jim	69T	306	$ .50	$2.00	Green, Lenny	63T	198	$ .90	$3.60
Grant, Jim	71T	509	$ .50	$2.00	Green, Lenny	64T	386	$1.00	$4.00
Grant, Jim	72T	111	$ .10	$ .40	Green, Lenny	65T	588	$1.40	$5.60
Grant, Mark	88T	752	$ .01	$ .04	Green, Lenny	66T	502	$1.50	$6.00
Grant, Mark	89T	178	$ .01	$ .03	Green, Pumpsie	60T	317	$ .75	$3.00
Grant, Mark	90T	537	$ .01	$ .03	Green, Pumpsie	61T	454	$1.35	$5.40
Grant, Mark	91T	287	$ .01	$ .03	Green, Pumpsie	62T	153	$ .60	$2.40
Grasso, Mickey	52T	90	$7.00	$28.00	Green, Pumpsie	63T	292	$ .90	$3.60
Grasso, Mickey	53T	148	$6.25	$25.00	Green, Pumpsie	64T	442	$1.00	$4.00
Grasso, Mickey	91TA53	148	$ .01	$ .15	Green, Shawn	92T	276	$ .05	$ .25
Gray, Dave	64T	572	$2.25	$9.00	Green, Tyler	92T	764	$ .05	$ .35
Gray, Dick	58T	146	$1.25	$5.00	Greene, Al	80T	666	$ .01	$ .10
Gray, Dick	59T	244	$1.00	$4.00	Greene, Rick	92TTR	44	$ .05	$ .20
Gray, Dick	60T	24	$ .85	$3.40	Greene, Rick	93T	233	$ .01	$ .10
Gray, Gary	81TTR	767	$ .01	$ .15	Greene, Todd	91TTR	50	$ .05	$ .25
Gray, Gary	82T	523	$ .01	$ .08	Greene, Tommy	91T	486	$ .01	$ .10
Gray, Gary	83T	313	$ .01	$ .08	Greene, Tommy	91TSC	549	$ .05	$ .25
Gray, Jeff	91T	731	$ .01	$ .10	Greene, Tommy	92T	83	$ .01	$ .03
Gray, Jeff	91TSC	271	$ .05	$ .25	Greene, Tommy	92TSC	27	$ .01	$ .10
Gray, Jeff	92TSC	222	$ .01	$ .10	Greene, Tommy	93T	291	$ .01	$ .03
Gray, Johnny	55T	101	$2.25	$9.00	Greene, Willie	93T	764	$ .01	$ .15
Gray, Lorenzo	84T	163	$ .01	$ .06	Greengrass, Jim	53T	209	$4.50	$18.00
Gray, Ted	52T	86	$7.00	$28.00	Greengrass, Jim	54T	22	$3.75	$15.00
Gray, Ted	53T	52	$4.00	$16.00	Greengrass, Jim	56T	275	$2.50	$10.00
Gray, Ted	91TA53	52	$ .01	$ .15	Greengrass, Jim	91TA53	209	$ .01	$ .15
Grba, Eli	60T	183	$ .75	$3.00	Greenwell, Mike	87T	259	$ .10	$ .50
Grba, Eli	61T	121	$ .60	$2.40	Greenwell, Mike	88T	493	$ .01	$ .10
Grba, Eli	62T	96	$ .60	$2.40	Greenwell, Mike	89T	630	$ .01	$ .15
Grba, Eli	63T	231	$ .90	$3.60	Greenwell, Mike	89TAS	402	$ .01	$ .10
Grebeck, Craig	91T	446	$ .01	$ .10	Greenwell, Mike	90T	70	$ .01	$ .10
Grebeck, Craig	91TSC	559	$ .05	$ .25	Greenwell, Mike	91T	792	$ .01	$ .10
Grebeck, Craig	92T	273	$ .01	$ .03	Greenwell, Mike	91TSC	253	$ .10	$ .50
Grebeck, Craig	92TSC	145	$ .01	$ .10	Greenwell, Mike	92T	113	$ .01	$ .03
Grebeck, Craig	93T	259	$ .01	$ .03	Greenwell, Mike	92TSC	446	$ .01	$ .10
Grebeck, Craig	93TSC	136	$ .01	$ .10	Greenwell, Mike	93T	323	$ .01	$ .03
Green, Dallas	60T	366	$2.00	$8.00	Greenwell, Mike	93TSC	86	$ .01	$ .10
Green, Dallas	61T	359	$1.00	$4.00	Greer, Brian	80T	685	$ .01	$ .10
Green, Dallas	62T	111	$ .75	$3.00	Gregg, Hal	52T	318	$43.75	$175.00
Green, Dallas	63T	91	$ .90	$3.60	Gregg, Tommy	89TTR	39	$ .01	$ .15
Green, Dallas	64T	464	$1.25	$5.00	Gregg, Tommy	90T	223	$ .01	$ .03
Green, Dallas	65T	203	$ .50	$2.00	Gregg, Tommy	91T	742	$ .01	$ .03
Green, Dallas	89T	104	$ .01	$ .03	Gregg, Tommy	91TSC	571	$ .05	$ .25
Green, David	83T	578	$ .01	$ .08	Gregg, Tommy	92T	53	$ .01	$ .03
Green, David	84T	362	$ .01	$ .06	Gregg, Tommy	92TSC	244	$ .01	$ .10
Green, David	85T	87	$ .01	$ .06	Greif, Bill	72T	101	$ .50	$2.00
Green, David	85TTR	41	$ .01	$ .10	Greif, Bill	73T	583	$ .60	$2.40
Green, David	86T	727	$ .01	$ .05	Greif, Bill	74T	102	$ .10	$ .40
Green, Dick	64T	466	$1.00	$4.00	Greif, Bill	75T	168	$ .10	$ .40
Green, Dick	65T	168	$ .35	$1.40	Greif, Bill	76T	184	$ .05	$ .25
Green, Dick	66T	545	$7.00	$28.00	Greif, Bill	77T	112	$ .05	$ .20
Green, Dick	67T	54	$ .40	$1.60	Grich, Bob	71T	193	$1.00	$4.00
Green, Dick	68T	303	$ .35	$1.40	Grich, Bob	72T	338	$ .25	$1.00
Green, Dick	69T	515	$ .40	$1.60	Grich, Bob	73T	418	$ .25	$1.00
Green, Dick	70T	311	$ .35	$1.40	Grich, Bob	74T	109	$ .10	$ .40
Green, Dick	71T	258	$ .25	$1.00	Grich, Bob	75T	225	$ .15	$ .60
Green, Dick	72T	780	$1.25	$5.00	Grich, Bob	76T	335	$ .05	$ .25
Green, Dick	73T	456	$ .25	$1.00	Grich, Bob	77T	521	$ .05	$ .20
Green, Dick	74T	392	$ .10	$ .40	Grich, Bob	78T	18	$ .04	$ .16
Green, Dick	75T	91	$ .10	$ .40	Grich, Bob	79T	477	$ .03	$ .12
Green, Fred	60T	272	$ .75	$3.00	Grich, Bob	80T	621	$ .01	$ .10
Green, Fred	61T	181	$ .60	$2.40	Grich, Bob	81T	182	$ .01	$ .08
Green, Gary	85T	396	$ .01	$ .06	Grich, Bob	82T	162	$ .10	$ .50
Green, Gary	91T	184	$ .01	$ .03	Grich, Bob	82T	284	$ .01	$ .08
Green, Gary	91TSC	323	$ .05	$ .25	Grich, Bob	83T	790	$ .01	$ .08
Green, Gene	58T	366	$1.00	$4.00	Grich, Bob	83TAS	387	$ .01	$ .08
Green, Gene	59T	37	$1.50	$6.00	Grich, Bob	84T	315	$ .01	$ .06
Green, Gene	60T	269	$ .75	$3.00	Grich, Bob	85T	465	$ .01	$ .06
Green, Gene	61T	206	$ .60	$2.40	Grich, Bob	86T	155	$ .01	$ .05
Green, Gene	62T	78	$ .60	$2.40	Grich, Bob	87T	677	$ .01	$ .04
Green, Gene	63T	506	$3.00	$12.00	Grieve, Tom	71T	167	$ .40	$1.60
Green, Lenny	58T	471	$1.00	$4.00	Grieve, Tom	72T	609	$ .40	$1.60
Green, Lenny	59T	209	$1.00	$4.00	Grieve, Tom	73T	579	$ .60	$2.40
Green, Lenny	60T	99	$ .85	$3.40	Grieve, Tom	74T	268	$ .10	$ .40
Green, Lenny	61T	4	$ .60	$2.40	Grieve, Tom	75T	234	$ .10	$ .40

TOPPS

Player	Year	No.	VG	EX/MT
Grieve, Tom	76T	106	$ .05	$ .25
Grieve, Tom	77T	403	$ .05	$ .20
Grieve, Tom	78T	337	$ .04	$ .16
Grieve, Tom	79T	277	$ .03	$ .12
Griffey, Ken	74T	598	$6.00	$24.00
Griffey, Ken	75T	284	$1.00	$4.00
Griffey, Ken	76T	128	$ .50	$2.00
Griffey, Ken	77T	320	$ .25	$1.00
Griffey, Ken	78T	80	$ .30	$1.20
Griffey, Ken	79T	420	$ .20	$ .80
Griffey, Ken	80T	550	$ .10	$ .50
Griffey, Ken	81T	280	$ .10	$ .50
Griffey, Ken	82T	620	$ .05	$ .35
Griffey, Ken	82T	756	$ .05	$ .20
Griffey, Ken	82TSA	621	$ .05	$ .20
Griffey, Ken	82TTR	40	$ .10	$ .50
Griffey, Ken	83T	110	$ .05	$ .25
Griffey, Ken	84T	770	$ .01	$ .15
Griffey, Ken	85T	380	$ .01	$ .10
Griffey, Ken	86T	40	$ .01	$ .05
Griffey, Ken	86TTR	41	$ .01	$ .15
Griffey, Ken	87T	711	$ .01	$ .10
Griffey, Ken	88T	443	$ .01	$ .04
Griffey, Ken	89TTR	40	$ .01	$ .10
Griffey, Ken	90T	581	$ .01	$ .03
Griffey, Ken	91T	465	$ .01	$ .03
Griffey, Ken	91TSC	342	$ .05	$ .25
Griffey, Ken	92T	250	$ .01	$ .03
Griffey, Jr., Ken	89TTR	41	$1.00	$4.00
Griffey, Jr., Ken	90T	336	$ .15	$1.50
Griffey, Jr., Ken	91T	790	$ .10	$ .50
Griffey, Jr., Ken	91TAS	392	$ .05	$ .25
Griffey, Jr., Ken	91TSC	270	$3.25	$13.00
Griffey, Jr, Ken	92T	50	$ .10	$ .50
Griffey, Jr., Ken	92TSC	400	$ .75	$3.00
Griffey, Jr., Ken	92TSC	603	$ .15	$1.50
Griffey, Jr., Ken	93T	179	$ .05	$ .35
Griffey, Jr., Ken	93T	405	$ .05	$ .25
Griffin, Alfredo	79T	705	$ .25	$1.00
Griffin, Alfredo	80T	558	$ .01	$ .10
Griffin, Alfredo	81T	277	$ .01	$ .08
Griffin, Alfredo	82T	677	$ .01	$ .08
Griffin, Alfredo	83T	488	$ .01	$ .08
Griffin, Alfredo	84T	76	$ .01	$ .06
Griffin, Alfredo	85T	361	$ .01	$ .06
Griffin, Alfredo	85TTR	42	$ .01	$ .10
Griffin, Alfredo	86T	566	$ .01	$ .05
Griffin, Alfredo	87T	111	$ .01	$ .04
Griffin, Alfredo	88T	726	$ .01	$ .04
Griffin, Alfredo	88TTR	43	$ .01	$ .05
Griffin, Alfredo	89T	62	$ .01	$ .03
Griffin, Alfredo	90T	643	$ .01	$ .03
Griffin, Alfredo	91T	226	$ .01	$ .03
Griffin, Alfredo	91TSC	524	$ .05	$ .25
Griffin, Alfredo	92T	418	$ .01	$ .03
Griffin, Doug	71T	176	$ .25	$1.00
Griffin, Doug	72T	703	$1.25	$5.00
Griffin, Doug	72TIA	704	$1.25	$5.00
Griffin, Doug	73T	96	$ .10	$ .40
Griffin, Doug	74T	219	$ .10	$ .40
Griffin, Doug	75T	454	$ .10	$ .40
Griffin, Doug	76T	654	$ .05	$ .25
Griffin, Doug	77T	191	$ .05	$ .20
Griffin, Mike	81T	483	$ .01	$ .08
Griffin, Mike	82T	146	$ .01	$ .08
Griffin, Tom	69T	614	$ .40	$1.60
Griffin, Tom	70T	578	$ .50	$2.00
Griffin, Tom	71T	471	$ .50	$2.00
Griffin, Tom	73T	468	$ .25	$1.00
Griffin, Tom	74T	256	$ .10	$ .40
Griffin, Tom	75T	188	$ .10	$ .40
Griffin, Tom	76T	454	$ .05	$ .25
Griffin, Tom	77T	39	$ .05	$ .20
Griffin, Tom	78T	318	$ .04	$ .16
Griffin, Tom	79T	291	$ .03	$ .12

Player	Year	No.	VG	EX/MT
Griffin, Tom	80T	649	$ .01	$ .10
Griffin, Tom	81T	538	$ .01	$ .08
Griffin, Tom	82T	777	$ .01	$ .08
Griffin, Ty	88TTR	44	$ .01	$ .10
Griffin, Ty	89T	713	$ .01	$ .10
Griffith, Derrell	65T	112	$ .35	$1.40
Griffith, Derrell	66T	573	$3.75	$15.00
Griffith, Derrell	67T	502	$1.50	$6.00
Griffiths, Brian	93T	483	$ .01	$ .15
Griggs, Hal	58T	455	$1.00	$4.00
Griggs, Hal	59T	434	$1.00	$4.00
Griggs, Hal	60T	244	$ .75	$3.00
Grigsby, Benji	93T	518	$ .01	$ .03
Grilli, Guido	66T	558	$6.00	$24.00
Grilli, Steve	76T	591	$ .05	$ .25
Grilli, Steve	77T	506	$ .05	$ .20
Grim, Bob	55T	80	$3.50	$14.00
Grim, Bob	56T	52	$2.00	$8.00
Grim, Bob	57T	36	$2.00	$8.00
Grim, Bob	58T	224	$1.25	$5.00
Grim, Bob	59T	423	$1.00	$4.00
Grim, Bob	60T	78	$ .85	$3.40
Grim, Bob	62T	564	$3.50	$14.00
Grimm, Charley	60T	217	$1.25	$5.00
Grimm, Charlie	91TA53	321	$ .05	$ .20
Grimsley, Jason	90T	493	$ .01	$ .10
Grimsley, Jason	91T	173	$ .01	$ .03
Grimsley, Jason	91TSC	294	$ .05	$ .25
Grimsley, Jason	92TSC	418	$ .01	$ .10
Grimsley, Ross	72T	99	$ .20	$ .80
Grimsley, Ross	73T	357	$ .10	$ .40
Grimsley, Ross	74T	59	$ .10	$ .40
Grimsley, Ross	74TTR	59	$ .10	$ .40
Grimsley, Ross	75T	458	$ .10	$ .40
Grimsley, Ross	76T	257	$ .05	$ .25
Grimsley, Ross	77T	572	$ .05	$ .20
Grimsley, Ross	78T	691	$ .04	$ .16
Grimsley, Ross	79T	15	$ .03	$ .12
Grimsley, Ross	80T	375	$ .01	$ .10
Grimsley, Ross	81T	170	$ .01	$ .08
Grissom, Marquis	90T	714	$ .10	$ .50
Grissom, Marquis	91T	283	$ .01	$ .15

Player	Year	No.	VG	EX/MT
Grissom, Marquis	91TSC	8	$ .20	$2.00
Grissom, Marquis	92T	647	$ .01	$ .15

TOPPS

Player	Year	No.	VG	EX/MT
Grissom, Marquis	92TSC	120	$ .05	$ .35
Grissom, Marquis	93T	15	$ .01	$ .03
Grissom, Marv	56T	301	$2.50	$10.00
Grissom, Marv	57T	216	$2.00	$8.00
Grissom, Marv	58T	399	$1.00	$4.00
Grissom, Marv	59T	243	$1.00	$4.00
Groat, Dick	52T	369	$80.00	$320.00
Groat, Dick	53T	154	$8.75	$35.00
Groat, Dick	54T	43	$4.50	$18.00
Groat, Dick	55T	26	$2.75	$11.00
Groat, Dick	56T	24	$2.75	$11.00
Groat, Dick	57T	12	$2.50	$10.00
Groat, Dick	58T	45	$2.25	$9.00
Groat, Dick	59T	160	$1.00	$4.00
Groat, Dick	60T	258	$1.50	$6.00
Groat, Dick	61T	1	$5.00	$20.00
Groat, Dick	61T	41	$2.25	$9.00
Groat, Dick	61TMVP	486	$1.35	$5.40
Groat, Dick	62T	270	$ .75	$3.00
Groat, Dick	63T	130	$ .50	$2.00
Groat, Dick	64T	7	$2.00	$8.00
Groat, Dick	64T	40	$ .50	$2.00
Groat, Dick	65T	275	$ .75	$3.00
Groat, Dick	66T	103	$ .50	$2.00
Groat, Dick	67T	205	$ .50	$2.00
Groat, Dick	75T	198	$ .55	$2.20
Groat, Dick	91TA53	154	$ .10	$ .50
Gromek, Steve	52T	258	$12.50	$50.00
Gromek, Steve	56T	310	$2.50	$10.00
Gromek, Steve	57T	258	$2.00	$8.00
Groom, Buddy	93T	353	$ .01	$ .10
Gross, Don	57T	341	$5.00	$20.00
Gross, Don	58T	172	$1.25	$5.00
Gross, Don	59T	228	$1.00	$4.00
Gross, Don	60T	284	$ .75	$3.00
Gross, Greg	75T	334	$ .10	$ .40
Gross, Greg	76T	171	$ .05	$ .25
Gross, Greg	77T	614	$ .05	$ .20
Gross, Greg	78T	397	$ .04	$ .16
Gross, Greg	79T	579	$ .03	$ .12
Gross, Greg	80T	718	$ .01	$ .10
Gross, Greg	81T	459	$ .01	$ .08
Gross, Greg	82T	53	$ .01	$ .08
Gross, Greg	83T	279	$ .01	$ .08
Gross, Greg	84T	613	$ .01	$ .06
Gross, Greg	85T	117	$ .01	$ .06
Gross, Greg	86T	302	$ .01	$ .05
Gross, Greg	87T	702	$ .01	$ .04
Gross, Greg	88T	518	$ .01	$ .04
Gross, Greg	89T	438	$ .01	$ .03
Gross, Kevin	84T	332	$ .05	$ .20
Gross, Kevin	85T	584	$ .01	$ .06
Gross, Kevin	86T	764	$ .01	$ .05
Gross, Kevin	87T	163	$ .01	$ .04
Gross, Kevin	88T	20	$ .01	$ .04
Gross, Kevin	89T	215	$ .01	$ .03
Gross, Kevin	89TTR	42	$ .01	$ .05
Gross, Kevin	90T	465	$ .01	$ .03
Gross, Kevin	91T	674	$ .01	$ .03
Gross, Kevin	92T	334	$ .01	$ .03
Gross, Kevin	92TSC	72	$ .01	$ .10
Gross, Kevin	93T	714	$ .01	$ .03
Gross, Kip	92T	372	$ .01	$ .10
Gross, Kip	92TSC	247	$ .01	$ .15
Gross, Kip	93TSC	7	$ .01	$ .10
Gross, Wayne	77T	479	$ .05	$ .20
Gross, Wayne	78T	139	$ .04	$ .16
Gross, Wayne	79T	528	$ .03	$ .12
Gross, Wayne	80T	363	$ .01	$ .10
Gross, Wayne	81T	86	$ .01	$ .08
Gross, Wayne	82T	692	$ .01	$ .08
Gross, Wayne	83T	233	$ .01	$ .08
Gross, Wayne	84T	741	$ .01	$ .06
Gross, Wayne	84TTR	44	$ .01	$ .15
Gross, Wayne	85T	416	$ .01	$ .06
Gross, Wayne	86T	173	$ .01	$ .05
Grote, Gerald "Jerry"	64T	226	$1.00	$4.00
Grote, Jerry	65T	504	$1.25	$5.00
Grote, Jerry	66T	328	$ .50	$2.00
Grote, Jerry	67T	413	$ .60	$2.40
Grote, Jerry	68T	582	$ .70	$2.80
Grote, Jerry	69T	55	$ .35	$1.40
Grote, Jerry	70T	183	$ .20	$ .80
Grote, Jerry	71T	278	$ .25	$1.00
Grote, Jerry	72T	655	$ .40	$1.60
Grote, Jerry	73T	113	$ .10	$ .40
Grote, Jerry	74T	311	$ .10	$ .40
Grote, Jerry	75T	158	$ .10	$ .40
Grote, Jerry	76T	143	$ .05	$ .25
Grote, Jerry	78T	464	$ .04	$ .16
Grote, Jerry	79T	279	$ .03	$ .12
Grotewold, Jeff	93T	72	$ .01	$ .03
Grotewold, Jeff	93TSC	63	$ .01	$ .10
Groth, Johnny	51Tbb	11	$7.50	$30.00
Groth, Johnny	52T	25	$13.75	$55.00
Groth, Johnny	53T	36	$4.00	$16.00
Groth, Johnny	56T	279	$2.50	$10.00
Groth, Johnny	57T	360	$1.75	$7.00
Groth, Johnny	58T	262	$1.25	$5.00
Groth, Johnny	59T	164	$1.00	$4.00
Groth, Johnny	60T	171	$ .75	$3.00
Groth, Johnny	91TA53	36	$ .01	$ .15
Grove, Lefty	76TAT	350	$ .50	$2.00
Grubb, John	74T	32	$ .10	$ .40
Grubb, Johnny	75T	298	$ .10	$ .40
Grubb, Johnny	76T	422	$ .05	$ .25
Grubb, Johnny	77T	286	$ .05	$ .20
Grubb, Johnny	78T	608	$ .04	$ .16
Grubb, Johnny	79T	198	$ .03	$ .12
Grubb, Johnny	80T	313	$ .01	$ .10
Grubb, Johnny	81T	545	$ .01	$ .08
Grubb, Johnny	82T	496	$ .01	$ .08
Grubb, Johnny	83T	724	$ .01	$ .08
Grubb, Johnny	83TTR	38	$ .01	$ .10
Grubb, Johnny	84T	42	$ .01	$ .06
Grubb, Johnny	85T	643	$ .01	$ .06
Grubb, Johnny	86T	243	$ .01	$ .05

TOPPS

Player	Year	No.	VG	EX/MT	Player	Year	No.	VG	EX/MT
Grubb, Johnny	87T	384	$ .01	$ .04	Guetterman, Lee	93TSC	214	$ .01	$ .10
Grubb, Johnny	88T	128	$ .01	$ .04	Guidry, Ron	76T	599	$2.00	$8.00
Gruber, Kelly	87T	458	$ .05	$ .20	Guidry, Ron	77T	656	$ .50	$2.00
Gruber, Kelly	88T	113	$ .01	$ .15	Guidry, Ron	78T	135	$ .20	$ .80
Gruber, Kelly	89T	29	$ .01	$ .10	Guidry, Ron	79T	5	$ .10	$ .40
Gruber, Kelly	90T	505	$ .01	$ .10	Guidry, Ron	79T	7	$ .03	$ .12
Gruber, Kelly	91T	370	$ .01	$ .10	Guidry, Ron	79T	500	$ .20	$ .80
Gruber, Kelly	91TAS	388	$ .01	$ .03	Guidry, Ron	79TRB	202	$ .05	$ .20
Gruber, Kelly	91TSC	331	$ .05	$ .25	Guidry, Ron	80T	207	$ .01	$ .10
Gruber, Kelly	92T	298	$ .01	$ .03	Guidry, Ron	80T	300	$ .10	$ .50
Gruber, Kelly	92TSC	570	$ .01	$ .10	Guidry, Ron	81T	250	$ .05	$ .35
Gruber, Kelly	93T	628	$ .01	$ .03	Guidry, Ron	82T	9	$ .05	$ .25
Grunwald, Al	60T	427	$ .75	$3.00	Guidry, Ron	82TSA	10	$ .01	$ .15
Grzenda, Joe	69T	121	$ .35	$1.40	Guidry, Ron	83T	440	$ .05	$ .25
Grzenda, Joe	70T	691	$1.25	$5.00	Guidry, Ron	84T	110	$ .05	$ .25
Grzenda, Joe	71T	518	$ .50	$2.00	Guidry, Ron	84T	486	$ .01	$ .06
Grzenda, Joe	72T	13	$ .10	$ .40	Guidry, Ron	84T	717	$ .05	$ .20
Guante, Cecilio	84T	122	$ .01	$ .06	Guidry, Ron	84TAS	406	$ .01	$ .06
Guante, Cecilio	85T	457	$ .01	$ .06	Guidry, Ron	85T	790	$ .05	$ .20
Guante, Cecilio	86T	668	$ .01	$ .05	Guidry, Ron	86T	610	$ .01	$ .10
Guante, Cecilio	87T	219	$ .01	$ .04	Guidry, Ron	86TAS	721	$ .01	$ .05
Guante, Cecilio	87TTR	40	$ .01	$ .05	Guidry, Ron	87T	375	$ .01	$ .10
Guante, Cecilio	88T	84	$ .01	$ .04	Guidry, Ron	88T	535	$ .01	$ .04
Guante, Cecilio	89T	766	$ .01	$ .03	Guidry, Ron	89T	255	$ .01	$ .03
Guante, Cecilio	90T	532	$ .01	$ .03	Guillen, Dave	93T	474	$ .01	$ .03
Gubicza, Mark	84TTR	45	$ .20	$2.00	Guillen, Ozzie	85TTR	43	$ .15	$1.50
Gubicza, Mark	85T	127	$ .05	$ .25	Guillen, Ozzie	86T	254	$ .05	$ .25
Gubicza, Mark	86T	644	$ .01	$ .10	Guillen, Ozzie	87T	89	$ .01	$ .10
Gubicza, Mark	87T	326	$ .01	$ .10	Guillen, Ozzie	88T	585	$ .01	$ .04
Gubicza, Mark	88T	507	$ .01	$ .04	Guillen, Ozzie	89T	195	$ .01	$ .03
Gubicza, Mark	89T	430	$ .01	$ .10	Guillen, Ozzie	90T	365	$ .01	$ .03
Gubicza, Mark	90T	20	$ .01	$ .03	Guillen, Ozzie	91T	620	$ .01	$ .03
Gubicza, Mark	91T	265	$ .01	$ .03	Guillen, Ozzie	91TSC	70	$ .05	$ .25
Gubicza, Mark	91TSC	240	$ .05	$ .25	Guillen, Ozzie	92T	210	$ .01	$ .03
Gubicza, Mark	92T	741	$ .01	$ .03	Guillen, Ozzie	92TSC	20	$ .01	$ .10
Gubicza, Mark	92TSC	542	$ .01	$ .10	Guindon, Bob	65T	509	$1.25	$5.00
Gubicza, Mark	93T	674	$ .01	$ .03	Guinn, Skip	69T	614	$ .40	$1.60
Guerrero, Juan	92TSC	775	$ .01	$ .15	Guinn, Skip	70T	316	$ .35	$1.40
Guerrero, Juan	93T	414	$ .01	$ .03	Guinn, Skip	71T	741	$1.10	$4.40
Guerrero, Mario	73T	607	$ .75	$3.00	Gulden, Brad	80T	670	$ .01	$ .10
Guerrero, Mario	74T	192	$ .10	$ .40	Gulden, Brad	85T	251	$ .01	$ .06
Guerrero, Mario	75T	152	$ .10	$ .40	Gullett, Don	71T	124	$ .25	$1.00
Guerrero, Mario	76T	499	$ .05	$ .25	Gullett, Don	72T	157	$ .10	$ .40
Guerrero, Mario	77T	628	$ .05	$ .20	Gullett, Don	73T	595	$ .55	$2.20
Guerrero, Mario	78T	339	$ .04	$ .16	Gullett, Don	74T	385	$ .10	$ .40
Guerrero, Mario	79T	261	$ .03	$ .12	Gullett, Don	75T	65	$ .10	$ .40
Guerrero, Mario	80T	49	$ .01	$ .10	Gullett, Don	76T	390	$ .10	$ .40
Guerrero, Mario	81T	547	$ .01	$ .08	Gullett, Don	77T	15	$ .05	$ .20
Guerrero, Pedro	79T	719	$1.50	$6.00	Gullett, Don	78T	225	$ .04	$ .16
Guerrero, Pedro	81T	651	$ .10	$1.00	Gullett, Don	79T	140	$ .03	$ .12
Guerrero, Pedro	82T	247	$ .10	$ .50	Gullett, Don	80T	435	$ .01	$ .10
Guerrero, Pedro	83T	425	$ .05	$ .35	Gullickson, Bill	81T	578	$ .10	$1.00
Guerrero, Pedro	83T	681	$ .01	$ .15	Gullickson, Bill	81TRB	203	$ .05	$ .20
Guerrero, Pedro	84T	90	$ .05	$ .25	Gullickson, Bill	82T	172	$ .10	$ .40
Guerrero, Pedro	84T	306	$ .01	$ .15	Gullickson, Bill	82T	526	$ .01	$ .08
Guerrero, Pedro	85T	575	$ .01	$ .15	Gullickson, Bill	83T	31	$ .05	$ .25
Guerrero, Pedro	86T	145	$ .01	$ .10	Gullickson, Bill	84T	318	$ .01	$ .06
Guerrero, Pedro	86TAS	706	$ .01	$ .05	Gullickson, Bill	85T	687	$ .01	$ .06
Guerrero, Pedro	87T	360	$ .01	$ .10	Gullickson, Bill	86T	229	$ .01	$ .05
Guerrero, Pedro	88T	550	$ .01	$ .10	Gullickson, Bill	86TTR	42	$ .01	$ .06
Guerrero, Pedro	89T	780	$ .01	$ .03	Gullickson, Bill	87T	489	$ .01	$ .04
Guerrero, Pedro	90T	610	$ .01	$ .03	Gullickson, Bill	88T	711	$ .01	$ .04
Guerrero, Pedro	91T	20	$ .01	$ .03	Gullickson, Bill	90TTR	34	$ .01	$ .05
Guerrero, Pedro	91TSC	314	$ .05	$ .25	Gullickson, Bill	92T	508	$ .01	$ .03
Guerrero, Pedro	92T	470	$ .01	$ .03	Gullickson, Bill	92TSC	119	$ .01	$ .10
Guerrero, Pedro	92TSC	320	$ .01	$ .10	Gullickson, Bill	93T	325	$ .01	$ .03
Guetterman, Lee	87T	307	$ .01	$ .04	Gulliver, Glenn	83T	293	$ .01	$ .08
Guetterman, Lee	88T	656	$ .01	$ .04	Gumpert, Dave	84T	371	$ .01	$ .06
Guetterman, Lee	89TTR	43	$ .01	$ .05	Gumpert, Dave	87T	487	$ .01	$ .04
Guetterman, Lee	90T	286	$ .01	$ .03	Gumpert, Randy	52T	247	$7.00	$28.00
Guetterman, Lee	91T	62	$ .01	$ .03	Gunderson, Eric	92TSC	397	$ .01	$ .10
Guetterman, Lee	91TSC	361	$ .05	$ .25	Gura, Larry	71T	203	$ .30	$1.20
Guetterman, Lee	92T	578	$ .01	$ .03	Gura, Larry	73T	501	$ .25	$1.00
Guetterman, Lee	92TSC	346	$ .01	$ .10	Gura, Larry	74T	616	$ .10	$ .40
Guetterman, Lee	93T	134	$ .01	$ .03	Gura, Larry	74TTR	616	$ .15	$ .60

TOPPS

Player	Year	No.	VG	EX/MT	Player	Year	No.	VG	EX/MT
Gura, Larry	75T	557	$ .10	$ .40	Haas, Dave	93T	536	$ .01	$ .03
Gura, Larry	76T	319	$ .05	$ .25	Haas, Eddie	59T	126	$1.00	$4.00
Gura, Larry	77T	193	$ .05	$ .20	Haas, Eddie	85TTR	44	$ .01	$ .10
Gura, Larry	78T	441	$ .04	$ .16	Haas, Moose	78T	649	$ .04	$ .16
Gura, Larry	79T	19	$ .03	$ .12	Haas, Moose	79T	448	$ .03	$ .12
Gura, Larry	80T	295	$ .01	$ .10	Haas, Moose	80T	181	$ .01	$ .10
Gura, Larry	81T	130	$ .01	$ .08	Haas, Moose	81T	327	$ .01	$ .08
Gura, Larry	82T	96	$ .10	$ .50	Haas, Moose	82T	12	$ .01	$ .08
Gura, Larry	82T	790	$ .01	$ .08	Haas, Moose	83T	503	$ .01	$ .08
Gura, Larry	83T	340	$ .01	$ .08	Haas, Moose	84T	271	$ .01	$ .06
Gura, Larry	83TAS	395	$ .01	$ .08	Haas, Moose	84T	726	$ .01	$ .06
Gura, Larry	84T	96	$ .01	$ .06	Haas, Moose	85T	151	$ .01	$ .06
Gura, Larry	84T	625	$ .01	$ .06	Haas, Moose	86T	759	$ .01	$ .05
Gura, Larry	85T	595	$ .01	$ .06	Haas, Moose	86TTR	44	$ .01	$ .06
Guthrie, Mark	90T	317	$ .01	$ .10	Haas, Moose	87T	413	$ .01	$ .04
Guthrie, Mark	91T	698	$ .01	$ .03	Haas, Moose	88T	606	$ .01	$ .04
Guthrie, Mark	91TSC	219	$ .05	$ .25	Habholz, Chris	92TSC	318	$ .01	$ .10
Guthrie, Mark	92T	548	$ .01	$ .03	Habyan, John	88T	153	$ .01	$ .04
Guthrie, Mark	92TSC	456	$ .01	$ .10	Habyan, John	91TSC	590	$ .05	$ .25
Guthrie, Mark	93T	777	$ .01	$ .03	Habyan, John	92T	698	$ .01	$ .03
Gutierrez, Cesar	69T	16	$ .35	$1.40	Habyan, John	92TSC	576	$ .01	$ .10
Gutierrez, Cesar	70T	269	$ .35	$1.40	Habyan, John	93T	86	$ .01	$ .03
Gutierrez, Cesar	71T	154	$ .25	$1.00	Hack, Stan	55T	6	$2.75	$11.00
Gutierrez, Cesar	72T	743	$1.25	$5.00	Hacker, Warren	52T	324	$43.75	$175.00
Gutierrez, Jackie	84TTR	46	$ .01	$ .15	Hacker, Warren	56T	282	$2.50	$10.00
Gutierrez, Jackie	85T	89	$ .01	$ .06	Hacker, Warren	57T	370	$1.75	$7.00
Gutierrez, Jackie	86T	633	$ .01	$ .05	Hacker, Warren	58T	251	$1.25	$5.00
Gutierrez, Jackie	87T	276	$ .01	$ .04	Haddix, Harvey	53T	273	$30.00	$120.00
Gutteridge, Don	60T	458	$1.25	$5.00	Haddix, Harvey	54T	9	$3.75	$15.00
Gutteridge, Don	70T	123	$ .20	$ .80	Haddix, Harvey	55T	43	$2.50	$10.00
Guzman, Johnny	92TSC	498	$ .05	$ .35	Haddix, Harvey	56T	77	$2.00	$8.00
Guzman, Johnny	93TSC	284	$ .05	$ .20	Haddix, Harvey	57T	265	$5.00	$20.00
Guzman, Jose	86TTR	43	$ .10	$ .40	Haddix, Harvey	58T	118	$1.25	$5.00
Guzman, Jose	87T	363	$ .01	$ .04	Haddix, Harvey	59T	184	$1.00	$4.00
Guzman, Jose	88T	563	$ .01	$ .04	Haddix, Harvey	60T	340	$ .75	$3.00
Guzman, Jose	89T	462	$ .01	$ .03	Haddix, Harvey	61T	100	$ .60	$2.40
Guzman, Jose	90T	308	$ .01	$ .03	Haddix, Harvey	61T	410	$1.75	$4.00
Guzman, Jose	92T	188	$ .01	$ .03	Haddix, Harvey	62T	67	$ .60	$2.40
Guzman, Jose	92TSC	153	$ .01	$ .10	Haddix, Harvey	63T	239	$ .90	$3.60
Guzman, Jose	93T	253	$ .01	$ .03	Haddix, Harvey	64T	439	$1.00	$4.00
Guzman, Juan	92T	662	$ .10	$ .50	Haddix, Harvey	65T	67	$ .35	$1.40
Guzman, Juan	92TSC	402	$ .20	$2.00	Haddix, Harvey	91TA53	273	$ .10	$ .40
Guzman, Juan	93T	75	$ .05	$ .20	Hadley, Kent	59T	127	$1.00	$4.00
Guzman, Juan	93TSC	244	$ .10	$ .75	Hadley, Kent	60T	102	$ .85	$3.40
Guzman, Santiago	70T	716	$1.25	$5.00	Hagen, Kevin	84T	337	$ .01	$ .06
Guzman, Santiago	72T	316	$ .10	$ .40	Hagen, Mike	71T	415	$ .50	$2.00
Gwosdz, Doug	82T	731	$ .01	$ .08	Hague, Joe	69T	559	$ .40	$1.60
Gwosdz, Doug	84T	753	$ .01	$ .06	Hague, Joe	70T	362	$ .35	$1.40
Gwynn, Chris	90T	456	$ .01	$ .10	Hague, Joe	71T	96	$ .25	$1.00
Gwynn, Chris	91T	99	$ .01	$ .03	Hague, Joe	72T	546	$ .40	$1.60
Gwynn, Chris	91TSC	480	$ .05	$ .25	Hague, Joe	73T	447	$ .25	$1.00
Gwynn, Chris	92T	604	$ .01	$ .03	Hahn, Don	71T	94	$ .25	$1.00
Gwynn, Chris	92TSC	815	$ .01	$ .10	Hahn, Don	72T	269	$ .10	$ .40
Gwynn, Chris	93T	472	$ .01	$ .03	Hahn, Don	74T	291	$ .10	$ .40
Gwynn, Tony	83T	482	$8.75	$35.00	Hahn, Don	75T	182	$ .10	$ .40
Gwynn, Tony	84T	251	$1.25	$5.00	Hairston, Jerry	74T	96	$ .15	$ .60
Gwynn, Tony	85T	660	$ .25	$2.50	Hairston, Jerry	75T	327	$ .10	$ .40
Gwynn, Tony	85TAS	717	$ .10	$ .50	Hairston, Jerry	76T	391	$ .05	$ .25
Gwynn, Tony	86T	10	$ .10	$1.00	Hairston, Jerry	83T	487	$ .01	$ .08
Gwynn, Tony	87T	530	$ .10	$ .40	Hairston, Jerry	84T	177	$ .01	$ .06
Gwynn, Tony	87TAS	599	$ .05	$ .25	Hairston, Jerry	85T	596	$ .01	$ .06
Gwynn, Tony	88T	360	$ .05	$ .25	Hairston, Jerry	86T	778	$ .01	$ .05
Gwynn, Tony	88TAS	402	$ .01	$ .10	Hairston, Jerry	87T	685	$ .01	$ .04
Gwynn, Tony	89T	570	$ .05	$ .25	Hairston, Jerry	88T	281	$ .01	$ .04
Gwynn, Tony	90T	730	$ .01	$ .15	Hale, Bob	56T	231	$3.75	$15.00
Gwynn, Tony	90TAS	403	$ .01	$ .10	Hale, Bob	57T	406	$1.75	$7.00
Gwynn, Tony	91T	180	$ .01	$ .10	Hale, Bob	59T	507	$4.00	$16.00
Gwynn, Tony	91TSC	308	$ .15	$1.50	Hale, Bob	60T	309	$ .75	$3.00
Gwynn, Tony	92T	270	$ .01	$ .10	Hale, Bob	61T	532	$7.50	$30.00
Gwynn, Tony	92TSC	825	$ .10	$ .40	Hale, Chip	90T	704	$ .01	$ .03
Gwynn, Tony	93T	5	$ .01	$ .10	Hale, John	76T	228	$ .05	$ .25
Haas, Bill	63T	544	$10.00	$40.00	Hale, John	77T	253	$ .05	$ .20
Haas, Bill	64T	398	$1.00	$4.00	Hale, John	78T	584	$ .04	$ .16
Haas, Dave	92T	665	$ .01	$ .03	Hale, John	79T	56	$ .03	$ .12
Haas, Dave	92TSC	362	$ .01	$ .10	Halicki, Ed	75T	467	$ .10	$ .40

TOPPS

Player	Year	No.	VG	EX/MT
Halicki, Ed	76T	423	$ .05	$ .25
Halicki, Ed	77T	343	$ .05	$ .20
Halicki, Ed	78T	107	$ .04	$ .16
Halicki, Ed	79T	672	$ .03	$ .12
Halicki, Ed	80T	217	$ .01	$ .10
Halicki, Ed	81T	69	$ .01	$ .08
Hall, Albert	85T	676	$ .01	$ .06
Hall, Albert	87TTR	41	$ .01	$ .05
Hall, Albert	88T	213	$ .01	$ .04
Hall, Albert	89T	433	$ .01	$ .03
Hall, Bill	59T	49	$1.50	$6.00
Hall, Dick	55T	126	$2.25	$9.00
Hall, Dick	56T	331	$2.50	$10.00
Hall, Dick	57T	308	$5.00	$20.00
Hall, Dick	60T	308	$ .75	$3.00
Hall, Dick	61T	197	$ .60	$2.40
Hall, Dick	62T	189	$ .60	$2.40
Hall, Dick	63T	526	$2.25	$9.00
Hall, Dick	67T	508	$1.50	$6.00
Hall, Dick	68T	17	$ .35	$1.40
Hall, Dick	70T	182	$ .20	$ .80
Hall, Dick	71T	417	$ .50	$2.00
Hall, Drew	88T	262	$ .01	$ .04
Hall, Drew	89T	593	$ .01	$ .03
Hall, Drew	90T	463	$ .01	$ .03
Hall, Drew	91T	77	$ .01	$ .03
Hall, Jimmie	64T	73	$ .50	$2.00
Hall, Jimmie	65T	580	$2.50	$10.00
Hall, Jimmie	66T	190	$ .50	$2.00
Hall, Jimmie	67T	432	$ .60	$2.40
Hall, Jimmie	68T	121	$ .35	$1.40
Hall, Jimmie	69T	61	$ .35	$1.40
Hall, Jimmie	70T	649	$1.25	$5.00
Hall, Mel	83TTR	39	$ .20	$2.00
Hall, Mel	84T	508	$ .05	$ .35
Hall, Mel	84TTR	47	$ .05	$ .35
Hall, Mel	85T	263	$ .01	$ .10
Hall, Mel	86T	647	$ .01	$ .10
Hall, Mel	87T	51	$ .01	$ .04
Hall, Mel	88T	318	$ .01	$ .04
Hall, Mel	89T	173	$ .01	$ .03
Hall, Mel	89TTR	44	$ .01	$ .05
Hall, Mel	90T	436	$ .01	$ .03
Hall, Mel	91T	738	$ .01	$ .03
Hall, Mel	91TSC	333	$ .05	$ .25
Hall, Mel	92T	223	$ .01	$ .03
Hall, Mel	92TSC	9	$ .01	$ .10
Hall, Mel	93T	114	$ .01	$ .03
Hall, Tom	69T	658	$ .40	$1.60
Hall, Tom	70T	169	$ .20	$ .80
Hall, Tom	71T	313	$ .25	$1.00
Hall, Tom	72T	417	$ .25	$1.00
Hall, Tom	73T	8	$ .10	$ .40
Hall, Tom	74T	248	$ .10	$ .40
Hall, Tom	75T	108	$ .10	$ .40
Hall, Tom	76T	621	$ .05	$ .25
Haller, Tom	62T	356	$1.00	$4.00
Haller, Tom	63T	85	$ .50	$2.00
Haller, Tom	64T	485	$1.00	$4.00
Haller, Tom	65T	465	$1.25	$5.00
Haller, Tom	66T	308	$ .50	$2.00
Haller, Tom	67T	65	$ .40	$1.60
Haller, Tom	68T	185	$ .35	$1.40
Haller, Tom	69T	310	$ .50	$2.00
Haller, Tom	70T	685	$1.25	$5.00
Haller, Tom	71T	639	$1.00	$4.00
Haller, Tom	72T	175	$ .10	$ .40
Haller, Tom	72TIA	176	$ .10	$ .40
Haller, Tom	73T	454	$ .25	$1.00
Hambright, Roger	72T	124	$ .10	$ .40
Hamilton, Darryl	89T	88	$ .05	$ .20
Hamilton, Darryl	90TTR	35	$ .01	$ .05
Hamilton, Darryl	91T	781	$ .01	$ .03
Hamilton, Darryl	91TSC	234	$ .05	$ .25
Hamilton, Darryl	92T	278	$ .01	$ .03

Player	Year	No.	VG	EX/MT
Hamilton, Darryl	92TSC	253	$ .01	$ .10
Hamilton, Darryl	93T	556	$ .01	$ .03
Hamilton, Dave	73T	214	$ .10	$ .40
Hamilton, Dave	74T	633	$ .10	$ .40
Hamilton, Dave	75T	428	$ .10	$ .40
Hamilton, Dave	76T	237	$ .05	$ .25
Hamilton, Dave	77T	367	$ .05	$ .20
Hamilton, Dave	78T	288	$ .04	$ .16
Hamilton, Dave	79T	147	$ .03	$ .12

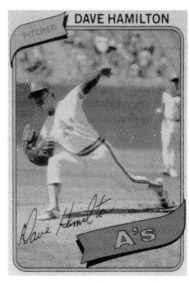

Player	Year	No.	VG	EX/MT
Hamilton, Dave	80T	86	$ .01	$ .10
Hamilton, Jack	62T	593	$5.25	$21.00
Hamilton, Jack	63T	132	$ .50	$2.00
Hamilton, Jack	65T	288	$ .50	$2.00
Hamilton, Jack	66T	262	$ .50	$2.00
Hamilton, Jack	67T	2	$ .40	$1.60
Hamilton, Jack	68T	193	$ .35	$1.40
Hamilton, Jack	69T	629	$ .40	$1.60
Hamilton, Jeff	87T	266	$ .01	$ .10
Hamilton, Jeff	88T	62	$ .01	$ .04
Hamilton, Jeff	89T	736	$ .01	$ .03
Hamilton, Jeff	90T	426	$ .01	$ .03
Hamilton, Jeff	91T	552	$ .01	$ .03
Hamilton, Jeff	91TSC	550	$ .05	$ .25
Hamilton, Jeff	92T	151	$ .01	$ .03
Hamilton, Jeff	92TSC	330	$ .01	$ .10
Hamilton, Steve	63T	171	$ .50	$2.00
Hamilton, Steve	64T	206	$ .65	$2.60
Hamilton, Steve	65T	309	$ .50	$2.00
Hamilton, Steve	66T	503	$1.50	$6.00
Hamilton, Steve	67T	567	$4.00	$16.00
Hamilton, Steve	68T	496	$ .75	$3.00
Hamilton, Steve	69T	69	$ .35	$1.40
Hamilton, Steve	70T	349	$ .35	$1.40
Hamilton, Steve	71T	627	$1.00	$4.00
Hamilton, Steve	72T	766	$1.25	$5.00
Hamlin, Ken	60T	542	$2.75	$11.00
Hamlin, Ken	61T	263	$ .60	$2.40
Hamlin, Ken	62T	296	$ .75	$3.00
Hamlin, Ken	66T	69	$ .35	$1.40
Hamm, Pete	71T	74	$ .25	$1.00
Hamm, Pete	72T	501	$ .25	$1.00
Hammaker, Atlee	82T	471	$ .05	$ .20
Hammaker, Atlee	83T	342	$ .01	$ .08

TOPPS

Player	Year	No.	VG	EX/MT
Hammaker, Atlee	84T	85	$ .01	$ .06
Hammaker, Atlee	84T	137	$ .01	$ .06
Hammaker, Atlee	84T	576	$ .01	$ .06
Hammaker, Atlee	85T	674	$ .01	$ .06
Hammaker, Atlee	86T	223	$ .01	$ .05
Hammaker, Atlee	87T	781	$ .01	$ .04
Hammaker, Atlee	88T	157	$ .01	$ .04
Hammaker, Atlee	89T	572	$ .01	$ .03
Hammaker, Atlee	90T	447	$ .01	$ .03
Hammaker, Atlee	91T	34	$ .01	$ .03
Hammaker, Atlee	91TSC	347	$ .05	$ .25
Hammond, Chris	91T	258	$ .01	$ .10
Hammond, Chris	91TSC	575	$ .10	$ .50
Hammond, Chris	92T	744	$ .01	$ .03
Hammond, Chris	92TSC	751	$ .01	$ .10
Hammond, Chris	93T	437	$ .01	$ .03
Hammond, Chris	93TSC	209	$ .01	$ .10
Hammonds, Jeffrey	91TTR	51	$ .20	$2.00

Player	Year	No.	VG	EX/MT
Hammonds, Jeffrey	**92TTR**	**45**	**$ .10**	**$1.00**
Hamner, Granville "Granny"	51Tbb	29	$7.50	$30.00
Hamner, Granny	52T	221	$7.00	$28.00
Hamner, Granny	53T	146	$6.25	$25.00
Hamner, Granny	54T	24	$3.75	$15.00
Hamner, Granny	56T	197	$3.75	$15.00
Hamner, Granny	57T	335	$5.00	$20.00
Hamner, Granny	58T	268	$1.25	$5.00
Hamner, Granny	59T	436	$1.00	$4.00
Hamner, Granville	91TA53	146	$ .01	$ .15
Hampton, Ike	78T	503	$ .04	$ .16
Hamric, Bert	55T	199	$6.25	$25.00
Hamric, Bert	58T	336	$1.25	$5.00
Hancock, Garry	79T	702	$ .03	$ .12
Hancock, Garry	82T	322	$ .01	$ .08
Hancock, Garry	84T	197	$ .01	$ .06
Hand, Rich	71T	24	$ .25	$1.00
Hand, Rich	72T	317	$ .10	$ .40
Hand, Rich	73T	398	$ .25	$1.00
Hand, Rich	74T	571	$ .10	$ .40
Hands, Bill	66T	392	$1.25	$5.00
Hands, Bill	67T	16	$ .40	$1.60
Hands, Bill	68T	279	$ .35	$1.40
Hands, Bill	69T	115	$ .35	$1.40
Hands, Bill	70T	405	$ .35	$1.40
Hands, Bill	71T	670	$1.10	$4.40
Hands, Bill	72T	335	$ .10	$ .40
Hands, Bill	73T	555	$ .60	$2.40
Hands, Bill	74T	271	$ .10	$ .40
Hands, Bill	75T	412	$ .10	$ .40
Hands, Bill	76T	509	$ .05	$ .25
Hanebrink, Harry	58T	454	$1.00	$4.00
Hanebrink, Harry	59T	322	$1.00	$4.00
Haney, Chris	92T	626	$ .01	$ .10
Haney, Chris	92TSC	449	$ .01	$ .15
Haney, Chris	93T	581	$ .01	$ .03
Haney, Fred	54T	75	$7.50	$30.00
Haney, Fred	58T	475	$4.50	$18.00
Haney, Fred	59TAS	551	$4.00	$16.00
Haney, Fred	91TA53	316	$ .05	$ .20
Haney, Larry	67T	507	$1.50	$6.00
Haney, Larry	68T	42	$ .35	$1.40
Haney, Larry	69T	209	$ .35	$1.40
Haney, Larry	70T	648	$1.25	$5.00
Haney, Larry	73T	563	$ .60	$2.40
Haney, Larry	75T	626	$ .10	$ .40
Haney, Larry	76T	446	$ .05	$ .25
Haney, Larry	77T	12	$ .05	$ .20
Haney, Larry	78T	391	$ .04	$ .16
Hanna, Preston	79T	296	$ .03	$ .12
Hanna, Preston	80T	489	$ .01	$ .10
Hanna, Preston	81T	594	$ .01	$ .08
Hanna, Preston	83T	127	$ .01	$ .08
Hannan, Jim	63T	121	$ .50	$2.00
Hannan, Jim	64T	261	$ .65	$2.60
Hannan, Jim	65T	394	$1.00	$4.00
Hannan, Jim	66T	479	$1.50	$6.00
Hannan, Jim	67T	291	$ .60	$2.40
Hannan, Jim	69T	106	$ .35	$1.40
Hannan, Jim	70T	697	$1.25	$5.00
Hannan, Jim	71T	229	$ .25	$1.00
Hansen, Andy	52T	74	$13.75	$55.00
Hansen, Bob	75T	508	$ .10	$ .40
Hansen, Dave	92TSC	36	$ .01	$ .15
Hansen, Dave	93T	469	$ .01	$ .03
Hansen, Dave	93TSC	263	$ .01	$ .10
Hansen, Ronnie	59T	444	$1.00	$4.00
Hansen, Ron	60T	127	$ .75	$3.00
Hansen, Ron	61T	240	$ .60	$2.40
Hansen, Ron	62T	245	$ .75	$3.00
Hansen, Ron	63T	88	$ .50	$2.00
Hansen, Ron	64T	384	$1.00	$4.00
Hansen, Ron	65T	146	$ .35	$1.40
Hansen, Ron	66T	261	$ .50	$2.00
Hansen, Ron	67T	9	$ .40	$1.60
Hansen, Ron	68T	411	$ .35	$1.40
Hansen, Ron	69T	566	$ .40	$1.60
Hansen, Ron	70T	217	$ .20	$ .80
Hansen, Ron	71T	419	$ .50	$2.00
Hansen, Ron	72T	763	$1.25	$5.00
Hansen, Terrel	92TSC	878	$ .05	$ .20
Hanson, Erik	89TTR	45	$ .05	$ .25
Hanson, Erik	90T	118	$ .01	$ .10
Hanson, Erik	91T	655	$ .01	$ .03
Hanson, Erik	91TSC	9	$ .05	$ .25
Hanson, Erik	92T	71	$ .01	$ .03
Hanson, Erik	92TSC	37	$ .01	$ .10
Hanson, Erik	93T	342	$ .01	$ .03
Harder, Mel	60T	460	$1.75	$7.00
Hardin, Jim	68T	222	$ .35	$1.40
Hardin, Jim	69T	532	$ .40	$1.60
Hardin, Jim	69T	610	$ .40	$1.60
Hardin, Jim	70T	656	$1.25	$5.00
Hardin, Jim	71T	491	$ .50	$2.00
Hardin, Jim	72T	287	$ .10	$ .40
Hardin, Jim	73T	124	$ .10	$ .40
Hardy, Carroll	58T	446	$3.00	$12.00
Hardy, Carroll	59T	168	$1.00	$4.00
Hardy, Carroll	60T	341	$ .75	$3.00
Hardy, Carroll	61T	257	$ .60	$2.40

TOPPS

Player	Year	No.	VG	EX/MT
Hardy, Carroll	62T	101	$ .60	$2.40
Hardy, Carroll	63T	468	$3.00	$12.00
Hardy, Larry	75T	112	$ .10	$ .40
Hare, Shawn	92TSC	465	$ .01	$ .10
Hare, Shawn	93T	491	$ .01	$ .03
Hargan, Steve	66T	508	$2.00	$8.00
Hargan, Steve	67T	233	$ .50	$2.00
Hargan, Steve	67T	440	$ .60	$2.40
Hargan, Steve	68T	35	$ .35	$1.40
Hargan, Steve	69T	348	$ .30	$1.20
Hargan, Steve	70T	136	$ .20	$ .80
Hargan, Steve	71T	375	$ .25	$1.00
Hargan, Steve	72T	615	$ .40	$1.60
Hargan, Steve	75T	362	$ .10	$ .40
Hargan, Steve	76T	463	$ .05	$ .25
Hargan, Steve	77T	37	$ .05	$ .20
Hargesheimer, Al	81T	502	$ .01	$ .08
Hargrove, Mike	75T	106	$ .15	$ .60
Hargrove, Mike	76T	485	$ .05	$ .25
Hargrove, Mike	77T	275	$ .05	$ .20
Hargrove, Mike	78T	172	$ .04	$ .16
Hargrove, Mike	79T	591	$ .03	$ .12
Hargrove, Mike	80T	308	$ .01	$ .10
Hargrove, Mike	81T	74	$ .01	$ .08
Hargrove, Mike	82T	310	$ .01	$ .08
Hargrove, Mike	82T	559	$ .01	$ .08
Hargrove, Mike	83T	660	$ .01	$ .08
Hargrove, Mike	84T	546	$ .01	$ .06

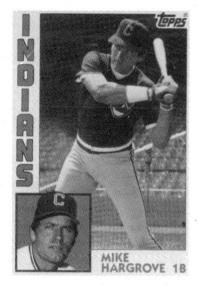

Player	Year	No.	VG	EX/MT
Hargrove, Mike	84T	764	$ .01	$ .06
Hargrove, Mike	85T	425	$ .01	$ .06
Hargrove, Mike	86T	136	$ .01	$ .05
Hargrove, Mike	91TTR	52	$ .01	$ .05
Hargrove, Mike	92T	609	$ .01	$ .03
Hargrove, Mike	93T	505	$ .01	$ .03
Harkey, Mike	89T	742	$ .01	$ .15
Harkey, Mike	90TTR	36	$ .01	$ .10
Harkey, Mike	91T	376	$ .01	$ .03
Harkey, Mike	91TSC	197	$ .05	$ .25
Harkey, Mike	92T	98	$ .01	$ .03
Harkey, Mike	92TSC	501	$ .01	$ .10
Harkey, Mike	93T	657	$ .01	$ .03
Harkness, Tim	62T	404	$1.25	$5.00
Harkness, Tim	63T	436	$1.00	$4.00

Player	Year	No.	VG	EX/MT
Harkness, Tim	64T	57	$ .50	$2.00
Harlow, Larry	78T	543	$ .04	$ .16
Harlow, Larry	79T	314	$ .03	$ .12
Harlow, Larry	80T	68	$ .01	$ .10
Harlow, Larry	81T	121	$ .01	$ .08
Harlow, Larry	82T	257	$ .01	$ .08
Harmon, Chuck	54T	182	$3.75	$15.00
Harmon, Chuck	55T	82	$2.25	$9.00
Harmon, Chuck	56T	308	$2.50	$10.00
Harmon, Chuck	57T	299	$5.00	$20.00
Harmon, Chuck	58T	48	$2.00	$8.00
Harmon, Terry	69T	624	$ .75	$3.00
Harmon, Terry	70T	486	$ .35	$1.40
Harmon, Terry	71T	682	$1.10	$4.40
Harmon, Terry	72T	377	$ .10	$ .40
Harmon, Terry	73T	166	$ .10	$ .40
Harmon, Terry	74T	642	$ .10	$ .40
Harmon, Terry	75T	399	$ .10	$ .40
Harmon, Terry	76T	247	$ .05	$ .25
Harmon, Terry	77T	388	$ .05	$ .20
Harmon, Terry	78T	118	$ .04	$ .16
Harnisch, Pete	90T	324	$ .01	$ .10
Harnisch, Pete	91T	179	$ .01	$ .03
Harnisch, Pete	91TSC	343	$ .05	$ .25
Harnisch, Pete	91TTR	53	$ .01	$ .05
Harnisch, Pete	92T	765	$ .01	$ .03
Harnisch, Pete	92TSC	391	$ .01	$ .10
Harnisch, Pete	93T	195	$ .01	$ .03
Harnisch, Pete	93TSC	110	$ .01	$ .10
Harper, Brian	84T	144	$ .10	$ .50
Harper, Brian	85T	332	$ .01	$ .15
Harper, Brian	86T	656	$ .01	$ .15
Harper, Brian	89T	472	$ .01	$ .03
Harper, Brian	90T	47	$ .01	$ .03
Harper, Brian	91T	554	$ .01	$ .03
Harper, Brian	91TSC	589	$ .05	$ .25
Harper, Brian	92T	217	$ .01	$ .03
Harper, Brian	92TSC	296	$ .01	$ .10
Harper, Brian	93T	389	$ .01	$ .03
Harper, Brian	93T	408	$ .01	$ .03
Harper, Brian	93TSC	95	$ .01	$ .10
Harper, Terry	81T	192	$ .05	$ .20
Harper, Terry	82T	507	$ .01	$ .08
Harper, Terry	83T	339	$ .01	$ .08
Harper, Terry	84T	624	$ .01	$ .06
Harper, Terry	85TTR	45	$ .01	$ .10
Harper, Terry	86T	247	$ .01	$ .05
Harper, Terry	87T	49	$ .01	$ .04
Harper, Terry	87TTR	42	$ .01	$ .05
Harper, Tommy	63T	158	$ .90	$3.60
Harper, Tommy	64T	330	$ .65	$2.60
Harper, Tommy	65T	47	$ .35	$1.40
Harper, Tommy	66T	214	$ .50	$2.00
Harper, Tommy	67T	392	$ .60	$2.40
Harper, Tommy	68T	590	$ .70	$2.80
Harper, Tommy	69T	42	$ .35	$1.40
Harper, Tommy	70T	370	$ .35	$1.40
Harper, Tommy	71T	260	$ .25	$1.00
Harper, Tommy	72T	455	$ .25	$1.00
Harper, Tommy	73T	620	$ .75	$3.00
Harper, Tommy	74T	204	$ .30	$1.20
Harper, Tommy	74T	325	$ .10	$ .40
Harper, Tommy	75T	537	$ .10	$ .40
Harper, Tommy	76T	274	$ .05	$ .25
Harper, Tommy	77T	414	$ .05	$ .20
Harrah, Toby	72T	104	$ .50	$2.00
Harrah, Toby	73T	216	$ .20	$ .80
Harrah, Toby	74T	511	$ .10	$ .40
Harrah, Toby	75T	131	$ .10	$ .40
Harrah, Toby	76T	412	$ .05	$ .25
Harrah, Toby	77T	301	$ .05	$ .20
Harrah, Toby	78T	44	$ .04	$ .16
Harrah, Toby	79T	234	$ .03	$ .12
Harrah, Toby	80T	636	$ .01	$ .10
Harrah, Toby	81T	721	$ .01	$ .08

TOPPS

Player	Year	No.	VG	EX/MT	Player	Year	No.	VG	EX/MT
Harrah, Toby	82T	532	$ .01	$ .08	Harris, Greg A.	89T	627	$ .01	$ .03
Harrah, Toby	83T	141	$ .01	$ .08	Harris, Greg A.	90T	572	$ .01	$ .03
Harrah, Toby	83T	480	$ .01	$ .08	Harris, Greg A.	91T	123	$ .01	$ .03
Harrah, Toby	84T	348	$ .01	$ .06	Harris, Greg A.	91TSC	324	$ .05	$ .25
Harrah, Toby	84TTR	48	$ .01	$ .15	Harris, Greg A.	92T	468	$ .01	$ .03
Harrah, Toby	85T	94	$ .01	$ .06	Harris, Greg A.	92TSC	49	$ .01	$ .10
Harrah, Toby	85TTR	46	$ .01	$ .10	Harris, Greg A.	93T	436	$ .01	$ .03
Harrah, Toby	86T	535	$ .01	$ .05	Harris, Greg W.	89T	194	$ .01	$ .15
Harrah, Toby	87T	152	$ .01	$ .04	Harris, Greg W.	90T	529	$ .01	$ .03
Harrell, Billy	58T	443	$3.00	$12.00	Harris, Greg W.	91T	749	$ .01	$ .03
Harrell, Billy	59T	433	$1.00	$4.00	Harris, Greg W.	91TSC	205	$ .05	$ .25
Harrell, Billy	61T	354	$ .60	$2.40	Harris, Greg W.	92T	636	$ .01	$ .03
Harrell, John	70T	401	$ .35	$1.40	Harris, Greg W.	92TSC	275	$ .01	$ .10
Harrelson, Bill	69T	224	$ .50	$2.00	Harris, Greg W.	93T	78	$ .01	$ .03
Harrelson, Bud	67T	306	$1.00	$4.00	Harris, John	81T	214	$ .01	$ .08
Harrelson, Bud	68T	132	$ .35	$1.40	Harris, John	82T	313	$ .01	$ .08
Harrelson, Bud	69T	456	$ .30	$1.20	Harris, Lenny	90T	277	$ .01	$ .03
Harrelson, Bud	70T	634	$1.25	$5.00	Harris, Lenny	91T	453	$ .01	$ .03
Harrelson, Bud	71T	355	$ .25	$1.00	Harris, Lenny	91TSC	65	$ .05	$ .25
Harrelson, Bud	72T	53	$ .20	$ .80	Harris, Lenny	92T	92	$ .01	$ .03
Harrelson, Bud	72T	496	$ .25	$1.00	Harris, Lenny	92TSC	121	$ .01	$ .10
Harrelson, Bud	72TIA	54	$ .10	$ .40	Harris, Lenny	93T	177	$ .01	$ .03
Harrelson, Bud	73T	223	$ .10	$ .40	Harris, Lenny	93TSC	98	$ .01	$ .10
Harrelson, Bud	74T	380	$ .10	$ .40	Harris, Lum	60T	455	$1.25	$5.00
Harrelson, Bud	75T	395	$ .10	$ .40	Harris, Lum	65T	274	$ .50	$2.00
Harrelson, Bud	76T	337	$ .05	$ .25	Harris, Lum	66T	147	$ .50	$2.00
Harrelson, Bud	77T	44	$ .05	$ .20	Harris, Lum	68T	439	$ .35	$1.40
Harrelson, Bud	78T	403	$ .04	$ .16	Harris, Lum	69T	196	$ .35	$1.40
Harrelson, Bud	79T	118	$ .03	$ .12	Harris, Lum	70T	86	$ .20	$ .80
Harrelson, Bud	80T	566	$ .01	$ .10	Harris, Lum	71T	346	$ .25	$1.00
Harrelson, Bud	81T	694	$ .01	$ .08	Harris, Lum	72T	484	$ .25	$1.00
Harrelson, Bud	90TTR	37	$ .01	$ .05	Harris, Mickey	52T	207	$7.00	$28.00
Harrelson, Bud	91T	261	$ .01	$ .03	Harris, Reggie	91T	177	$ .01	$ .15
Harrelson, Ken	64T	419	$1.25	$5.00	Harris, Reggie	92TSC	158	$ .01	$ .10
Harrelson, Ken	65T	479	$1.50	$6.00	Harris, Vic	73T	594	$ .60	$2.40
Harrelson, Ken	66T	55	$ .35	$1.40	Harris, Vic	74T	157	$ .10	$ .40
Harrelson, Ken	67T	188	$ .40	$1.60	Harris, Vic	75T	658	$ .10	$ .40
Harrelson, Ken	68T	566	$ .70	$2.80	Harris, Vic	78T	436	$ .04	$ .16
Harrelson, Ken	69T	3	$1.00	$4.00	Harris, Vic	79T	338	$ .03	$ .12
Harrelson, Ken	69T	5	$ .75	$3.00	Harrison, Chuck	66T	244	$ .50	$2.00
Harrelson, Ken	69T	240	$ .50	$2.00	Harrison, Chuck	67T	8	$ .40	$1.60
Harrelson, Ken	69TAS	417	$ .50	$2.00	Harrison, Chuck	69T	116	$ .35	$1.40
Harrelson, Ken	70T	545	$ .35	$1.40	Harrison, Roric	72T	474	$1.50	$6.00
Harrelson, Ken	71T	510	$ .30	$1.20	Harrison, Roric	73T	229	$ .10	$ .40
Harridge, William	56T	1	$30.00	$120.00	Harrison, Roric	74T	298	$ .10	$ .40
Harridge, William	57T	100	$2.75	$11.00	Harrison, Roric	75T	287	$ .10	$ .40
Harridge, William	58T	300	$2.00	$8.00	Harrison, Roric	76T	547	$ .05	$ .25
Harris, Alonzo	67T	564	$2.25	$9.00	Harrison, Roric	78T	536	$ .04	$ .16
Harris, Alonzo	68T	128	$ .35	$1.40	Harrist, Earl	52T	402	$43.75	$175.00
Harris, Bill	60T	128	$ .75	$3.00	Harrist, Earl	53T	65	$6.25	$25.00
Harris, Billy	69T	569	$ .40	$1.60	Harrist, Earl	91TA53	65	$ .01	$ .15
Harris, Billy	70T	512	$ .35	$1.40	Harshman, Jack	54T	173	$3.75	$15.00
Harris, Bucky	91TA53	313	$ .10	$ .40	Harshman, Jack	55T	104	$2.25	$9.00
Harris, Buddy	71T	404	$ .50	$2.00	Harshman, Jack	56T	29	$2.00	$8.00
Harris, Donald	90T	314	$ .01	$ .15	Harshman, Jack	57T	152	$2.00	$8.00
Harris, Donald	92T	554	$ .01	$ .10	Harshman, Jack	58T	217	$1.25	$5.00
Harris, Donald	92TSC	691	$ .01	$ .10	Harshman, Jack	59T	475	$1.00	$4.00
Harris, Donald	93T	731	$ .01	$ .03	Harshman, Jack	60T	112	$ .75	$3.00
Harris, Gail	56T	91	$2.00	$8.00	Hart, Jim	64T	452	$1.25	$5.00
Harris, Gail	57T	281	$5.00	$20.00	Hart, Jim	65T	4	$2.00	$8.00
Harris, Gail	58T	309	$1.25	$5.00	Hart, Jim	65T	395	$1.00	$4.00
Harris, Gail	59T	378	$1.00	$4.00	Hart, Jim	66T	295	$ .50	$2.00
Harris, Gail	60T	152	$ .75	$3.00	Hart, Jim	67T	220	$ .50	$2.00
Harris, Gene	89TTR	46	$ .01	$ .15	Hart, Jim	68T	73	$ .35	$1.40
Harris, Gene	90T	738	$ .01	$ .03	Hart, Jim	69T	555	$ .40	$1.60
Harris, Gene	91T	203	$ .01	$ .03	Hart, Jim	70T	176	$ .35	$1.40
Harris, Gene	92TSC	425	$ .01	$ .10	Hart, Jim	71T	461	$ .50	$2.00
Harris, Greg A.	82T	783	$ .01	$ .15	Hart, Jim	72T	733	$1.25	$5.00
Harris, Greg A.	82TTR	41	$ .01	$ .10	Hart, Jim	73T	538	$ .60	$2.40
Harris, Greg A.	83T	296	$ .01	$ .08	Hart, Jim	74T	159	$ .10	$ .40
Harris, Greg A.	85T	242	$ .01	$ .06	Hart, John	90T	141	$ .01	$ .03
Harris, Greg A.	85TTR	47	$ .01	$ .10	Hart, Mike	88T	69	$ .01	$ .04
Harris, Greg A.	86T	586	$ .01	$ .05	Hartenstein, Chuck	68T	13	$ .35	$1.40
Harris, Greg A.	87T	44	$ .01	$ .04	Hartenstein, Chuck	69T	596	$ .40	$1.60
Harris, Greg A.	88T	369	$ .01	$ .04	Hartenstein, Chuck	70T	216	$ .20	$ .80

TOPPS

Player	Year	No.	VG	EX/MT
Hartenstein, Chuck	77T	416	$.05	$.20
Hartley, Mike	91T	199	$.01	$.03
Hartley, Mike	92T	484	$.01	$.03
Hartley, Mike	93T	208	$.01	$.03
Hartley, Mike	93TSC	124	$.01	$.10
Hartman, Bob	59T	128	$1.00	$4.00
Hartman, Bob	60T	129	$.75	$3.00
Hartman, J. C.	63T	442	$1.00	$4.00
Hartsfield, Roy	52T	264	$12.50	$50.00
Hartsfield, Roy	73T	237	$.30	$1.20
Hartsfield, Roy	78T	444	$.04	$.16
Hartung, Clint	52T	141	$7.00	$28.00
Hartzell, Paul	77T	179	$.05	$.20
Hartzell, Paul	78T	529	$.04	$.16
Hartzell, Paul	79T	402	$.03	$.12
Hartzell, Paul	80T	721	$.01	$.10
Harvey, Bryan	88TTR	45	$.10	$.50
Harvey, Bryan	89T	632	$.05	$.20
Harvey, Bryan	90T	272	$.01	$.03
Harvey, Bryan	91T	153	$.01	$.03
Harvey, Bryan	91TSC	98	$.05	$.25
Harvey, Bryan	92T	568	$.01	$.03
Harvey, Bryan	92TAS	407	$.01	$.03
Harvey, Bryan	92TSC	410	$.01	$.10
Harvey, Bryan	93T	439	$.01	$.03
Haselman, Bill	92TSC	574	$.01	$.10
Hassey, Ron	80T	222	$.05	$.30
Hassey, Ron	81T	564	$.01	$.08
Hassey, Ron	82T	54	$.01	$.08
Hassey, Ron	83T	689	$.01	$.08
Hassey, Ron	84T	308	$.01	$.06
Hassey, Ron	84TTR	49	$.01	$.15
Hassey, Ron	85T	742	$.01	$.06
Hassey, Ron	85TTR	48	$.01	$.10
Hassey, Ron	86T	157	$.01	$.05
Hassey, Ron	87T	667	$.01	$.04
Hassey, Ron	88T	458	$.01	$.04
Hassey, Ron	88TTR	46	$.01	$.05
Hassey, Ron	89T	272	$.01	$.03
Hassey, Ron	90T	527	$.01	$.03
Hassey, Ron	91T	327	$.01	$.03
Hassey, Ron	91TSC	490	$.05	$.25
Hassler, Andy	75T	261	$.10	$.40
Hassler, Andy	76T	207	$.05	$.25
Hassler, Andy	77T	602	$.05	$.20
Hassler, Andy	78T	73	$.04	$.16
Hassler, Andy	79T	696	$.03	$.12
Hassler, Andy	80T	353	$.01	$.10
Hassler, Andy	81T	454	$.01	$.08
Hassler, Andy	82T	94	$.01	$.08
Hassler, Andy	83T	573	$.01	$.08
Hassler, Andy	84T	719	$.01	$.06
Hatcher, Billy	86T	46	$.01	$.15
Hatcher, Billy	86TTR	45	$.01	$.06
Hatcher, Billy	87T	578	$.01	$.04
Hatcher, Billy	88T	306	$.01	$.04
Hatcher, Billy	89T	252	$.01	$.03
Hatcher, Billy	90T	119	$.01	$.10
Hatcher, Billy	90TTR	38	$.01	$.05
Hatcher, Billy	91T	604	$.01	$.03
Hatcher, Billy	91TSC	371	$.05	$.35
Hatcher, Billy	92T	432	$.01	$.03
Hatcher, Billy	92TSC	363	$.01	$.10
Hatcher, Billy	93T	725	$.01	$.03
Hatcher, Mickey	80T	679	$.01	$.10
Hatcher, Mickey	81T	289	$.01	$.08
Hatcher, Mickey	81TTR	768	$.01	$.15
Hatcher, Mickey	82T	467	$.01	$.08
Hatcher, Mickey	83T	121	$.01	$.08
Hatcher, Mickey	84T	746	$.01	$.06
Hatcher, Mickey	85T	18	$.01	$.06
Hatcher, Mickey	86T	356	$.01	$.05
Hatcher, Mickey	87T	504	$.01	$.04
Hatcher, Mickey	87TTR	43	$.01	$.05
Hatcher, Mickey	88T	607	$.01	$.04
Hatcher, Mickey	89T	483	$.01	$.03
Hatcher, Mickey	90T	226	$.01	$.03
Hatcher, Mickey	91T	152	$.01	$.03
Hatfield, Fred	52T	354	$43.75	$175.00
Hatfield, Fred	53T	163	$4.00	$16.00
Hatfield, Fred	56T	318	$2.50	$10.00
Hatfield, Fred	57T	278	$5.00	$20.00
Hatfield, Fred	58T	339	$1.25	$5.00
Hatfield, Fred	91TA53	163	$.01	$.15
Hatteberg, Scott	92T	734	$.01	$.10
Hatten, Joe	52T	194	$7.00	$28.00
Hatton, Grady	51Trb	34	$1.75	$7.50
Hatton, Grady	52T	6	$13.75	$55.00
Hatton, Grady	53T	45	$4.00	$16.00
Hatton, Grady	54T	208	$3.75	$15.00
Hatton, Grady	55T	131	$2.25	$9.00
Hatton, Grady	56T	26	$2.00	$8.00
Hatton, Grady	66T	504	$1.50	$6.00
Hatton, Grady	67T	347	$.60	$2.40
Hatton, Grady	68T	392	$.35	$1.40
Hatton, Grady	73T	624	$1.00	$4.00
Hatton, Grady	74T	31	$.10	$.40
Hatton, Grady	91TA53	45	$.01	$.15
Haugstad, Phil	52T	198	$7.00	$28.00
Hausman, Tom	76T	452	$.05	$.26
Hausman, Tom	77T	99	$.05	$.20
Hausman, Tom	79T	643	$.03	$.12
Hausman, Tom	80T	151	$.01	$.10
Hausman, Tom	81T	359	$.01	$.08
Hausman, Tom	82T	524	$.01	$.08
Hausman, Tom	83T	417	$.01	$.08
Havens, Brad	82T	92	$.01	$.08
Havens, Brad	83T	751	$.01	$.08
Havens, Brad	84T	509	$.01	$.06
Havens, Brad	87T	398	$.01	$.04
Havens, Brad	87TTR	44	$.01	$.05
Havens, Brad	88T	698	$.01	$.04
Havens, Brad	89T	204	$.01	$.03
Hawblitzel, Ryan	93T	648	$.01	$.15
Hawkins, Andy	84T	778	$.01	$.10
Hawkins, Andy	85T	299	$.01	$.10
Hawkins, Andy	86T	478	$.01	$.05
Hawkins, Andy	87T	183	$.01	$.04

TOPPS

Player	Year	No.	VG	EX/MT	Player	Year	No.	VG	EX/MT
Hawkins, Andy	88T	9	$ .01	$ .04	Heath, Mike	91T	16	$ .01	$ .03
Hawkins, Andy	89T	533	$ .01	$ .03	Heath, Mike	91TSC	393	$ .05	$ .25
Hawkins, Andy	89TTR	47	$ .01	$ .05	Heath, Mike	92T	512	$ .01	$ .03
Hawkins, Andy	90T	335	$ .01	$ .03	Heath, Mike	92TSC	128	$ .01	$ .10
Hawkins, Andy	91T	635	$ .01	$ .03	Heaton, Neal	87TTR	45	$ .01	$ .05
Hawkins, Andy	91TSC	487	$ .05	$ .25	Heaton, Neal	88T	765	$ .01	$ .04
Hawkins, Wynn	60T	536	$2.75	$11.00	Heaton, Neal	89T	197	$ .01	$ .03
Hawkins, Wynn	61T	34	$ .60	$2.40	Heaton, Neal	90T	539	$ .01	$ .03
Hawkins, Wynn	63T	334	$ .90	$3.60	Heaton, Neal	91T	451	$ .01	$ .03
Haydel, Hal	71T	692	$1.50	$6.00	Heaton, Neal	91TSC	53	$ .05	$ .25
Haydel, Hal	72T	28	$ .10	$ .40	Heaton, Neal	92T	89	$ .01	$ .03
Hayes, Ben	84T	448	$ .01	$ .06	Heaton, Neal	92TSC	357	$ .01	$ .10
Hayes, Charlie	90T	577	$ .01	$ .15	Heaton, Neal	92TSC	877	$ .01	$ .10
Hayes, Charlie	91T	312	$ .01	$ .03	Heaverlo, Dave	76T	213	$ .05	$ .25
Hayes, Charlie	91TSC	163	$ .05	$ .25	Heaverlo, Dave	77T	97	$ .05	$ .20
Hayes, Charlie	92T	754	$ .01	$ .03	Heaverlo, Dave	78T	338	$ .04	$ .16
Hayes, Charlie	92TSC	711	$ .01	$ .10	Heaverlo, Dave	79T	432	$ .03	$ .12
Hayes, Charlie	92TTR	46	$ .01	$ .05	Heaverlo, Dave	80T	177	$ .01	$ .10
Hayes, Charlie	93T	142	$ .01	$ .03	Hebert, Ray	54T	190	$3.75	$15.00
Hayes, Charlie	93T	759	$ .01	$ .03	Hebner, Rich	69T	82	$2.50	$10.00
Hayes, Von	82T	141	$ .10	$ .40	Hebner, Rich	70T	264	$ .35	$1.40
Hayes, Von	82TTR	42	$ .10	$ .75	Hebner, Rich	71T	212	$ .25	$1.00
Hayes, Von	83T	325	$ .05	$ .25	Hebner, Rich	72T	630	$ .40	$1.60
Hayes, Von	83TTR	40	$ .10	$ .75	Hebner, Rich	73T	2	$ .10	$ .40
Hayes, Von	84T	587	$ .01	$ .10	Hebner, Rich	74T	450	$ .10	$ .40
Hayes, Von	85T	68	$ .01	$ .10	Hebner, Rich	75T	492	$ .10	$ .40
Hayes, Von	86T	420	$ .01	$ .05					
Hayes, Von	87T	666	$ .01	$ .04					
Hayes, Von	88T	215	$ .01	$ .04					
Hayes, Von	89T	385	$ .01	$ .03					
Hayes, Von	90T	710	$ .01	$ .03					
Hayes, Von	91T	15	$ .01	$ .03					
Hayes, Von	91TSC	127	$ .05	$ .25					
Hayes, Von	92T	135	$ .01	$ .03					
Hayes, Von	92TSC	880	$ .01	$ .10					
Hayes, Von	92TTR	47	$ .01	$ .05					
Haynes, Joe	52T	145	$7.00	$28.00					
Haynes, Joe	54T	223	$3.75	$15.00					
Hayward, Ray	88TTR	47	$ .01	$ .05					
Hazle, Bob	58T	83	$2.25	$9.00					
Healy, Fran	72T	663	$1.50	$6.00					
Healy, Fran	73T	361	$ .10	$ .40					
Healy, Fran	74T	238	$ .10	$ .40					
Healy, Fran	75T	251	$ .10	$ .40					
Healy, Fran	76T	394	$ .05	$ .25					
Healy, Fran	77T	148	$ .05	$ .20					
Healy, Fran	78T	582	$ .04	$ .16					
Heard, Jehosie	54T	226	$3.75	$15.00					
Hearn, Ed	87T	433	$ .01	$ .04					
Hearn, Ed	88T	56	$ .01	$ .04					
Hearn, Ed	89T	348	$ .01	$ .03					
Hearn, Jim	52T	337	$43.75	$175.00					
Hearn, Jim	53T	38	$4.00	$16.00					
Hearn, Jim	56T	202	$3.75	$15.00					
Hearn, Jim	57T	348	$5.00	$20.00					
Hearn, Jim	58T	298	$1.25	$5.00					
Hearn, Jim	59T	63	$1.50	$6.00					
Hearn, Jim	91TA53	38	$ .01	$ .15					
Hearron, Jeff	87T	274	$ .01	$ .04	Hebner, Rich	76T	376	$ .05	$ .25
Heath, Bill	66T	539	$5.00	$20.00	Hebner, Rich	77T	167	$ .05	$ .20
Heath, Bill	67T	172	$ .40	$1.60	Hebner, Rich	78T	26	$ .04	$ .16
Heath, Bill	70T	541	$ .35	$1.40	Hebner, Rich	79T	567	$ .03	$ .12
Heath, Mike	79T	710	$ .05	$ .20	Hebner, Rich	80T	331	$ .01	$ .10
Heath, Mike	80T	687	$ .01	$ .10	Hebner, Rich	81T	217	$ .01	$ .08
Heath, Mike	81T	437	$ .01	$ .08	Hebner, Rich	82T	603	$ .01	$ .08
Heath, Mike	82T	318	$ .01	$ .08	Hebner, Rich	83T	778	$ .01	$ .08
Heath, Mike	83T	23	$ .01	$ .08	Hebner, Rich	84T	433	$ .01	$ .06
Heath, Mike	84T	567	$ .01	$ .06	Hebner, Rich	84TTR	50	$ .01	$ .15
Heath, Mike	85T	662	$ .01	$ .06	Hebner, Rich	85T	124	$ .01	$ .06
Heath, Mike	86T	148	$ .01	$ .05	Hebner, Rich	86T	19	$ .01	$ .10
Heath, Mike	86TTR	46	$ .01	$ .06	Hedlund, Mike	65T	546	$1.40	$5.60
Heath, Mike	87T	492	$ .01	$ .04	Hedlund, Mike	69T	591	$ .40	$1.60
Heath, Mike	88T	237	$ .01	$ .04	Hedlund, Mike	70T	187	$ .20	$ .80
Heath, Mike	89T	743	$ .01	$ .03	Hedlund, Mike	71T	662	$1.50	$6.00
Heath, Mike	90T	366	$ .01	$ .03	Hedlund, Mike	72T	81	$ .10	$ .40

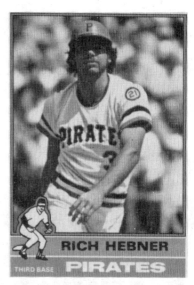

TOPPS

Player	Year	No.	VG	EX/MT
Hedlund, Mike	73T	591	$.60	$2.40
Heep, Danny	81T	82	$.01	$.08
Heep, Danny	82T	441	$.01	$.08
Heep, Danny	83T	538	$.01	$.08
Heep, Danny	83TTR	41	$.01	$.10
Heep, Danny	84T	29	$.01	$.06
Heep, Danny	85T	339	$.01	$.06
Heep, Danny	86T	619	$.01	$.05
Heep, Danny	87T	241	$.01	$.04
Heep, Danny	88T	753	$.01	$.04
Heep, Danny	89T	198	$.01	$.03
Heep, Danny	90T	573	$.01	$.03
Heffner, Bob	64T	79	$.50	$2.00
Heffner, Bob	65T	199	$.50	$2.00
Heffner, Bob	66T	432	$.65	$2.60
Heffner, Don	60T	462	$1.25	$5.00
Heffner, Don	66T	269	$.50	$2.00
Hegan, Jim	51Trb	12	$1.75	$7.50
Hegan, Jim	52T	17	$13.75	$55.00
Hegan, Jim	53T	80	$6.25	$25.00
Hegan, Jim	54T	29	$3.75	$15.00
Hegan, Jim	55T	7	$2.25	$9.00
Hegan, Jim	56T	48	$2.00	$8.00
Hegan, Jim	57T	136	$2.00	$8.00
Hegan, Jim	58T	345	$1.25	$5.00
Hegan, Jim	59T	372	$1.00	$4.00
Hegan, Jim	73T	116	$.20	$.80
Hegan, Jim	76T	69	$.10	$.40
Hegan, Jim	91TA53	80	$.01	$.15
Hegan, Mike	67T	553	$7.50	$30.00
Hegan, Mike	68T	402	$.35	$1.40
Hegan, Mike	69T	577	$.40	$1.60
Hegan, Mike	70T	111	$.20	$.80
Hegan, Mike	72T	632	$.40	$1.60
Hegan, Mike	73T	382	$.10	$.40
Hegan, Mike	74T	517	$.10	$.40
Hegan, Mike	75T	99	$.10	$.40
Hegan, Mike	76T	69	$.10	$.40
Hegan, Mike	76T	377	$.05	$.25
Hegan, Mike	77T	507	$.05	$.20
Heidemann, Jack	71T	87	$.25	$1.00
Heidemann, Jack	72T	374	$.10	$.40
Heidemann, Jack	73T	644	$.60	$2.40
Heidemann, Jack	75T	649	$.10	$.40
Heidemann, Jack	77T	553	$.05	$.20
Heinkel, Don	89T	499	$.01	$.03
Heintzelman, Ken	52T	362	$43.75	$175.00
Heintzelman, Ken	53T	136	$4.00	$16.00
Heintzelman, Ken	91TA53	136	$.01	$.15
Heintzelman, Tom	74T	607	$.10	$.40
Heise, Bob	70T	478	$.35	$1.40
Heise, Bob	71T	691	$1.10	$4.40
Heise, Bobby	72T	402	$.25	$1.00
Heise, Bobby	73T	547	$.60	$2.40
Heise, Bobby	74T	51	$.10	$.40
Heise, Bobby	74TTR	51	$.10	$.40
Heise, Bobby	75T	441	$.10	$.40
Heist, Al	61T	302	$.60	$2.40
Heist, Al	62T	373	$1.25	$5.00
Held, Woody	58T	202	$1.50	$6.00
Held, Woody	59T	266	$1.00	$4.00
Held, Woody	60T	178	$.75	$3.00
Held, Woodie (y)	61T	60	$.60	$2.40
Held, Woody	62T	215	$.75	$3.00
Held, Woody	63T	435	$1.00	$4.00
Held, Woody	64T	105	$.50	$2.00
Held, Woody	65T	336	$.50	$2.00
Held, Woody	66T	136	$.50	$2.00
Held, Woody	67T	251	$.50	$2.00
Held, Woody	68T	289	$.35	$1.40
Held, Woody	69T	636	$.40	$1.60
Helling, Rick	91TTR	54	$.10	$.50
Helling, Rick	92TTR	48	$.05	$.25
Helms, Tommy	65T	243	$.75	$3.00
Helms, Tommy	66T	311	$.35	$1.40

Player	Year	No.	VG	EX/MT
Helms, Tommy	67T	505	$1.75	$7.00
Helms, Tommy	68T	405	$.35	$1.40
Helms, Tommy	69T	70	$.35	$1.40
Helms, Tommy	69TAS	418	$.50	$2.00
Helms, Tommy	70T	159	$.20	$.80
Helms, Tommy	71T	272	$.25	$1.00
Helms, Tommy	72T	204	$.10	$.40
Helms, Tommy	73T	495	$.25	$1.00
Helms, Tommy	74T	67	$.10	$.40
Helms, Tommy	75T	119	$.10	$.40
Helms, Tommy	76T	583	$.05	$.25
Helms, Tommy	76TTR	583	$.05	$.25
Helms, Tommy	77T	402	$.05	$.20
Helms, Tommy	78T	618	$.04	$.16
Helms, Tommy	90T	110	$.01	$.03
Heman, Russ	59T	283	$1.00	$4.00
Hemond, Scott	92TSC	62	$.05	$.25
Hemsley, Rollie	54T	143	$3.75	$15.00
Hemus, Solly	52T	196	$8.00	$32.00
Hemus, Solly	53T	231	$11.25	$45.00
Hemus, Solly	54T	117	$3.75	$15.00
Hemus, Solly	57T	231	$2.00	$8.00
Hemus, Solly	58T	207	$1.25	$5.00
Hemus, Solly	59T	527	$4.00	$16.00
Hemus, Solly	60T	218	$.75	$3.00
Hemus, Solly	61T	139	$.60	$2.40
Hemus, Solly	91TA53	231	$.01	$.15
Henderson, Dave	82T	711	$.10	$1.00
Henderson, Dave	83T	732	$.05	$.35
Henderson, Dave	84T	154	$.01	$.15
Henderson, Dave	85T	344	$.01	$.10
Henderson, Dave	86T	221	$.01	$.05
Henderson, Dave	87T	452	$.01	$.04
Henderson, Dave	88T	628	$.01	$.10
Henderson, Dave	88TTR	48	$.01	$.10
Henderson, Dave	89T	527	$.01	$.03
Henderson, Dave	90T	68	$.01	$.03
Henderson, Dave	91T	144	$.01	$.03
Henderson, Dave	91TSC	284	$.05	$.25
Henderson, Dave	92T	335	$.01	$.03
Henderson, Dave	92TSC	218	$.01	$.10
Henderson, Dave	93T	473	$.01	$.03
Henderson, Joe	77T	487	$.05	$.20
Henderson, Ken	65T	497	$1.25	$5.00
Henderson, Ken	66T	39	$.35	$1.40
Henderson, Ken	67T	383	$.60	$2.40
Henderson, Ken	68T	309	$.35	$1.40
Henderson, Ken	70T	298	$.35	$1.40
Henderson, Ken	71T	155	$.25	$1.00
Henderson, Ken	72T	443	$.25	$1.00
Henderson, Ken	72TIA	444	$.25	$1.00
Henderson, Ken	73T	101	$.10	$.40
Henderson, Ken	74T	394	$.10	$.40
Henderson, Ken	75T	59	$.10	$.40
Henderson, Ken	76T	464	$.05	$.25
Henderson, Ken	76TTR	464	$.05	$.25
Henderson, Ken	77T	242	$.05	$.20
Henderson, Ken	78T	612	$.04	$.16
Henderson, Ken	79T	73	$.03	$.12
Henderson, Ken	80T	523	$.01	$.10
Henderson, Rickey	80T	482	$22.50	$90.00
Henderson, Rickey	81T	4	$.15	$1.50
Henderson, Rickey	81T	261	$3.50	$14.00
Henderson, Rickey	82T	156	$.10	$.50
Henderson, Rickey	82T	164	$.10	$.50
Henderson, Rickey	82T	610	$1.50	$6.00
Henderson, Rickey	83T	180	$1.25	$5.00
Henderson, Rickey	83T	531	$.10	$.40
Henderson, Rickey	83T	704	$.10	$.75
Henderson, Rickey	83TAS	391	$.15	$1.50
Henderson, Rickey	83TRB	2	$.15	$1.50
Henderson, Rickey	84T	2	$.10	$1.00
Henderson, Rickey	84T	134	$.10	$.50
Henderson, Rickey	84T	156	$.05	$.25
Henderson, Rickey	84T	230	$1.00	$4.00

395

TOPPS

Player	Year	No.	VG	EX/MT	Player	Year	No.	VG	EX/MT
Henderson, Rickey	85T	115	$ .15	$1.50	Henke, Tom	92TSC	819	$ .01	$ .10
Henderson, Rickey	85TAS	706	$ .10	$ .50	Henke, Tom	93T	376	$ .01	$ .03
Henderson, Rickey	85TTR	49	$1.25	$5.00	Henneman, Mike	87TTR	46	$ .05	$ .25
Henderson, Rickey	86T	500	$ .10	$1.00	Henneman, Mike	88T	582	$ .05	$ .20
Henderson, Rickey	86TAS	716	$ .05	$ .35	Henneman, Mike	89T	365	$ .01	$ .03
Henderson, Rickey	87T	735	$ .05	$ .35	Henneman, Mike	90T	177	$ .01	$ .03
Henderson, Rickey	87TTB	311	$ .01	$ .15	Henneman, Mike	91T	641	$ .01	$ .03
Henderson, Rickey	88T	60	$ .05	$ .25	Henneman, Mike	91TSC	287	$ .05	$ .25
Henderson, Rickey	89T	380	$ .05	$ .25	Henneman, Mike	92T	293	$ .01	$ .03
Henderson, Rickey	89TTR	48	$ .05	$ .25	Henneman, Mike	92TSC	34	$ .01	$ .10
Henderson, Rickey	90T	450	$ .05	$ .25	Henneman, Mike	93T	756	$ .01	$ .03
Henderson, Rickey	90TRB	7	$ .01	$ .15	Hennigan, Phil	71T	211	$ .25	$1.00
Henderson, Rickey	91T	670	$ .01	$ .15	Hennigan, Phil	72T	748	$1.25	$5.00
Henderson, Rickey	91TAS	391	$ .01	$ .10	Hennigan, Phil	73T	107	$ .10	$ .40
Henderson, Rickey	91TSC	120	$ .20	$2.00	Henninger, Rick	74T	602	$ .10	$ .40
Henderson, Rickey	92T	560	$ .01	$ .15	Henrich, Bob	58T	131	$1.25	$5.00
Henderson, Rickey	92TRB	2	$ .01	$ .10	Henry, Bill	59T	46	$1.50	$6.00
Henderson, Rickey	92TSC	750	$ .05	$ .35	Henry, Bill	60T	524	$2.75	$11.00
Henderson, Rickey	93T	750	$ .01	$ .10	Henry, Bill	61T	66	$ .60	$2.40
Henderson, Steve	78T	134	$ .04	$ .16	Henry, Bill	62T	562	$3.50	$14.00
Henderson, Steve	79T	445	$ .03	$ .12	Henry, Bill	63T	378	$1.00	$4.00
Henderson, Steve	80T	299	$ .05	$ .20	Henry, Bill	64T	49	$ .50	$2.00
Henderson, Steve	81T	619	$ .01	$ .08	Henry, Bill	65T	456	$1.25	$5.00
Henderson, Steve	81TTR	769	$ .01	$ .15	Henry, Bill	66T	115	$ .50	$2.00
Henderson, Steve	82T	89	$ .01	$ .08	Henry, Bill	67T	579	$4.00	$16.00
Henderson, Steve	83T	335	$ .01	$ .08	Henry, Bill	68T	239	$ .35	$1.40
Henderson, Steve	83TTR	42	$ .01	$ .10	Henry, Bill	68T	384	$2.50	$10.00
Henderson, Steve	84T	501	$ .01	$ .06	Henry, Butch	92TSC	742	$ .01	$ .15
Henderson, Steve	85T	640	$ .01	$ .06	Henry, Butch	92TTR	49	$ .01	$ .15
Henderson, Steve	85TTR	50	$ .01	$ .10	Henry, Butch	93T	281	$ .01	$ .10
Henderson, Steve	86T	748	$ .01	$ .05	Henry, Butch	93T	719	$ .01	$ .03
Henderson, Steve	88T	527	$ .01	$ .04	Henry, Doug	92T	776	$ .01	$ .15
Hendley, Bob	61T	372	$1.00	$4.00	Henry, Doug	92TSC	615	$ .05	$ .35
Hendley, Bob	62T	361	$ .75	$3.00	Henry, Doug	93T	343	$ .01	$ .03
Hendley, Bob	63T	62	$ .50	$2.00	Henry, Dwayne	88T	178	$ .01	$ .04
Hendley, Bob	64T	189	$ .50	$2.00	Henry, Dwayne	89T	496	$ .01	$ .03
Hendley, Bob	65T	444	$1.00	$4.00	Henry, Dwayne	91T	567	$ .01	$ .03
Hendley, Bob	66T	82	$ .35	$1.40	Henry, Dwayne	92T	668	$ .01	$ .03
Hendley, Bob	67T	256	$ .50	$2.00	Henry, Dwayne	92TSC	892	$ .01	$ .10
Hendley, Bob	68T	345	$ .35	$1.40	Henry, Dwayne	93T	29	$ .01	$ .03
Hendley, Bob	69T	144	$ .35	$1.40	Hentgen, Pat	93T	752	$ .01	$ .03
Hendrick, George	72T	406	$ .50	$2.00	Hentgen, Pat	93TSC	26	$ .01	$ .10
Hendrick, George	73T	13	$ .20	$ .80	Hepler, Bill	66T	574	$3.75	$15.00
Hendrick, George	74T	303	$ .10	$ .40	Hepler, Bill	67T	144	$ .40	$1.60
Hendrick, George	75T	109	$ .10	$ .40	Herbel, Ron	63T	208	$ .90	$3.60
Hendrick, George	76T	570	$ .05	$ .25	Herbel, Ron	64T	47	$ .75	$3.00
Hendrick, George	77T	330	$ .05	$ .20	Herbel, Ron	65T	84	$ .35	$1.40
Hendrick, George	78T	30	$ .04	$ .16	Herbel, Ron	66T	331	$ .50	$2.00
Hendrick, George	79T	175	$ .03	$ .12	Herbel, Ron	67T	156	$ .40	$1.60
Hendrick, George	80T	350	$ .05	$ .25	Herbel, Ron	68T	333	$ .35	$1.40
Hendrick, George	81T	230	$ .01	$ .08	Herbel, Ron	69T	251	$ .50	$2.00
Hendrick, George	82T	420	$ .01	$ .08	Herbel, Ron	70T	526	$ .35	$1.40
Hendrick, George	83T	650	$ .01	$ .08	Herbel, Ron	71T	387	$ .25	$1.00
Hendrick, George	84T	540	$ .01	$ .06	Herbel, Ron	72T	469	$ .25	$1.00
Hendrick, George	84TAS	386	$ .01	$ .06	Herbert, Ray	55T	138	$2.25	$9.00
Hendrick, George	85T	60	$ .01	$ .06	Herbert, Ray	58T	379	$1.00	$4.00
Hendrick, George	85TTR	51	$ .01	$ .10	Herbert, Ray	59T	154	$1.00	$4.00
Hendrick, George	86T	190	$ .01	$ .05	Herbert, Ray	60T	252	$ .75	$3.00
Hendrick, George	87T	725	$ .01	$ .04	Herbert, Ray	61T	498	$1.35	$5.40
Hendrick, George	88T	304	$ .01	$ .04	Herbert, Ray	62T	8	$ .60	$2.40
Hendricks, Rod	69T	277	$ .75	$3.00	Herbert, Ray	63T	8	$1.00	$4.00
Hendricks, Elrod	70T	528	$ .35	$1.40	Herbert, Ray	63T	560	$2.25	$9.00
Hendricks, Elrod "Ellie"	71T	219	$ .25	$1.00	Herbert, Ray	64T	215	$ .65	$2.60
Hendricks, Ellie	75T	609	$ .10	$ .40	Herbert, Ray	65T	399	$1.00	$4.00
Hendricks, Ellie	76T	371	$ .05	$ .25	Herbert, Ray	66T	121	$ .50	$2.00
Hengel, Dave	89T	531	$ .01	$ .03	Heredia, Gil	92TSC	895	$ .01	$ .15
Henke, Tom	86T	333	$ .05	$ .20	Herman, Billy	52T	394	$70.00	$280.00
Henke, Tom	87T	510	$ .01	$ .04	Herman, Billy	54T	86	$6.50	$26.00
Henke, Tom	88T	220	$ .01	$ .04	Herman, Billy	55T	19	$3.50	$14.00
Henke, Tom	88TAS	396	$ .01	$ .04	Herman, Billy	60T	456	$1.50	$6.00
Henke, Tom	89T	75	$ .01	$ .03	Herman, Billy	65T	251	$ .75	$3.00
Henke, Tom	90T	695	$ .01	$ .03	Herman, Billy	66T	37	$ .50	$2.00
Henke, Tom	91T	110	$ .01	$ .03	Herman, Ed	73T	73	$ .10	$ .40
Henke, Tom	91TSC	24	$ .05	$ .25	Hermann, Ed	75T	219	$ .10	$ .40
Henke, Tom	92T	451	$ .01	$ .03	Hermann, Ed	78T	677	$ .04	$ .16

TOPPS

Player	Year	No.	VG	EX/MT
Hermann, Ed	79T	374	$ .03	$ .12
Hermanski, Gene	51Trb	11	$1.75	$7.50
Hermanski, Gene	52T	16	$13.75	$55.00
Hermanski, Gene	53T	179	$4.50	$18.00
Hermanski, Gene	54T	228	$3.75	$15.00
Hermanski, Gene	91TA53	179	$ .01	$ .15
Hermoso, Angel	70T	147	$ .20	$ .80
Hernandez, Carlos	92TTR	50	$ .01	$ .05
Hernandez, Carlos	93T	589	$ .01	$ .03
Hernandez, Carlos	93TSC	149	$ .01	$ .10
Hernandez, Cesar	92T	618	$ .05	$ .25
Hernandez, Cesar	93T	301	$ .01	$ .10
Hernandez, Enzo	71T	529	$1.25	$5.00
Hernandez, Enzo	72T	7	$ .10	$ .40
Hernandez, Enzo	73T	438	$ .25	$1.00
Hernandez, Enzo	74T	572	$ .10	$ .40
Hernandez, Enzo	75T	84	$ .10	$ .40
Hernandez, Enzo	76T	289	$ .05	$ .25
Hernandez, Enzo	77T	522	$ .05	$ .20
Hernandez, Guillermo	89T	43	$ .01	$ .03
Hernandez, Jackie	68T	352	$ .35	$1.40
Hernandez, Jackie	69T	258	$ .50	$2.00
Hernandez, Jackie	70T	686	$1.25	$5.00
Hernandez, Jackie	71T	144	$ .25	$1.00
Hernandez, Jackie	72T	502	$ .25	$1.00
Hernandez, Jackie	73T	363	$ .10	$ .40
Hernandez, Jackie	74T	566	$ .10	$ .40
Hernandez, Jeremy	92T	211	$ .01	$ .10
Hernandez, Jeremy	92TSC	734	$ .05	$ .20
Hernandez, Jeremy	93T	388	$ .01	$ .03
Hernandez, Jose	92T	237	$ .01	$ .10
Hernandez, Keith	75T	623	$5.25	$21.00
Hernandez, Keith	76T	542	$1.25	$5.00
Hernandez, Keith	77T	95	$ .50	$2.00
Hernandez, Keith	78T	143	$ .50	$2.00
Hernandez, Keith	79T	695	$ .45	$1.80
Hernandez, Keith	80T	201	$ .05	$ .30
Hernandez, Keith	80T	321	$ .10	$1.00
Hernandez, Keith	81T	420	$ .10	$ .50
Hernandez, Keith	82T	186	$ .05	$ .25
Hernandez, Keith	82T	210	$ .10	$ .50
Hernandez, Keith	83T	700	$ .01	$ .15
Hernandez, Keith	83TTR	43	$ .10	$ .50
Hernandez, Keith	84T	120	$ .05	$ .30
Hernandez, Keith	85T	80	$ .01	$ .15
Hernandez, Keith	85TAS	712	$ .01	$ .10
Hernandez, Keith	86T	520	$ .01	$ .10
Hernandez, Keith	86TAS	701	$ .01	$ .10
Hernandez, Keith	86TRB	203	$ .01	$ .10
Hernandez, Keith	87T	350	$ .01	$ .10
Hernandez, Keith	87TAS	595	$ .01	$ .10
Hernandez, Keith	88T	610	$ .01	$ .04
Hernandez, Keith	89T	480	$ .01	$ .03
Hernandez, Keith	90T	230	$ .01	$ .03
Hernandez, Keith	90TTR	39	$ .01	$ .05
Hernandez, Leo	83TTR	44	$ .01	$ .10
Hernandez, Leo	84T	71	$ .01	$ .06
Hernandez, Ramon	67T	576	$6.00	$24.00
Hernandez, Ramon	68T	382	$ .35	$1.40
Hernandez, Ramon	73T	117	$ .10	$ .40
Hernandez, Ramon	74T	222	$ .10	$ .40
Hernandez, Ramon	75T	224	$ .10	$ .40
Hernandez, Ramon	76T	647	$ .05	$ .25
Hernandez, Ramon	77T	468	$ .05	$ .20
Hernandez, Roberto	92T	667	$ .01	$ .10
Hernandez, Roberto	92TSC	356	$ .05	$ .25
Hernandez, Roberto	93T	70	$ .01	$ .03
Hernandez, Roberto	93TSC	21	$ .01	$ .10
Hernandez, Rudy	61T	229	$ .60	$2.40
Hernandez, Willie	78T	99	$ .20	$ .80
Hernandez, Willie	79T	614	$ .03	$ .12
Hernandez, Willie	80T	472	$ .05	$ .25
Hernandez, Willie	81T	238	$ .01	$ .08
Hernandez, Willie	82T	23	$ .01	$ .08
Hernandez, Willie	83T	568	$ .01	$ .08
Hernandez, Willie	83TTR	45	$ .01	$ .10
Hernandez, Willie	84T	199	$ .10	$ .60
Hernandez, Willie	84TTR	51	$ .05	$ .25
Hernandez, Willie	85T	333	$ .01	$ .06
Hernandez, Willie	86T	670	$ .01	$ .05
Hernandez, Willie	87T	515	$ .01	$ .04
Hernandez, Willie	88T	713	$ .01	$ .04
Hernandez, Xavier	91T	194	$ .01	$ .10
Hernandez, Xavier	91TSC	74	$ .05	$ .25
Hernandez, Xavier	92T	640	$ .01	$ .03
Hernandez, Xavier	92TSC	736	$ .01	$ .10
Hernandez, Xavier	93T	252	$ .01	$ .03
Hernandez, Xavier	93TSC	271	$ .01	$ .10
Herndon, Larry	77T	397	$ .05	$ .20
Herndon, Larry	78T	512	$ .04	$ .16
Herndon, Larry	79T	624	$ .03	$ .12
Herndon, Larry	80T	257	$ .01	$ .10
Herndon, Larry	81T	409	$ .01	$ .08
Herndon, Larry	82T	182	$ .01	$ .08
Herndon, Larry	82TTR	43	$ .01	$ .10
Herndon, Larry	83T	13	$ .01	$ .08
Herndon, Larry	83T	261	$ .01	$ .08
Herndon, Larry	84T	333	$ .01	$ .06
Herndon, Larry	85T	591	$ .01	$ .06
Herndon, Larry	86T	688	$ .01	$ .05
Herndon, Larry	87T	298	$ .01	$ .04
Herndon, Larry	88T	743	$ .01	$ .04
Herr, Tom	80T	684	$ .10	$ .75
Herr, Tom	81T	266	$ .01	$ .08

Player	Year	No.	VG	EX/MT
Herr, Tom	82T	27	$ .01	$ .08
Herr, Tom	83T	489	$ .01	$ .08
Herr, Tom	84T	649	$ .01	$ .06
Herr, Tom	85T	113	$ .01	$ .06
Herr, Tom	86T	550	$ .01	$ .05
Herr, Tom	86TAS	702	$ .01	$ .05
Herr, Tom	87T	721	$ .01	$ .04
Herr, Tom	88T	310	$ .01	$ .04
Herr, Tom	88TTR	49	$ .01	$ .05
Herr, Tom	89T	709	$ .01	$ .03
Herr, Tom	89TTR	49	$ .01	$ .05
Herr, Tom	90T	297	$ .01	$ .03
Herr, Tom	91T	64	$ .01	$ .03
Herr, Tom	91TSC	532	$ .05	$ .25

TOPPS

Player	Year	No.	VG	EX/MT
Herrera, Frank "Pancho"	58T	433	$1.25	$5.00
Herrera, Frank	59T	129	$1.00	$4.00
Herrera, Frank	60T	130	$ .75	$3.00
Herrera, Frank	61TAS	569	$8.00	$32.00
Herrera, Jose	69T	378	$ .30	$1.20
Herrmann, Ed	69T	439	$ .30	$1.20
Herrmann, Ed	70T	368	$ .35	$1.40
Herrmann, Ed	71T	169	$ .25	$1.00
Herrmann, Ed	72T	452	$ .25	$1.00
Herrmann, Ed	74T	438	$ .10	$ .40
Herrmann, Ed	76T	406	$ .05	$ .25

Player	Year	No.	VG	EX/MT
Herrmann, Ed	77T	143	$ .05	$ .20
Herrnstein, John	63T	553	$60.00	$240.00
Herrnstein, John	64T	243	$5.00	$20.00
Herrnstein, John	65T	534	$1.40	$5.60
Herrnstein, John	66T	304	$ .50	$2.00
Hershberger, Mike	62T	341	$ .75	$3.00
Hershberger, Mike	63T	254	$ .90	$3.60
Hershberger, Mike	64T	465	$1.00	$4.00
Hershberger, Mike	65T	89	$ .35	$1.40
Hershberger, Mike	66T	236	$ .50	$2.00
Hershberger, Mike	67T	323	$ .60	$2.40
Hershberger, Mike	68T	18	$ .35	$1.40
Hershberger, Mike	69T	655	$ .40	$1.60
Hershberger, Mike	70T	596	$ .50	$2.00
Hershberger, Mike	71T	149	$ .25	$1.00
Hershiser, Orel	85T	493	$ .20	$2.00
Hershiser, Orel	86T	159	$ .05	$ .25
Hershiser, Orel	87T	385	$ .01	$ .15
Hershiser, Orel	88T	40	$ .01	$ .10
Hershiser, Orel	89T	550	$ .01	$ .10
Hershiser, Orel	89TAS	394	$ .01	$ .05
Hershiser, Orel	89TRB		$ .01	$ .10
Hershiser, Orel	90T	780	$ .01	$ .10
Hershiser, Orel	91T	690	$ .01	$ .03
Hershiser, Orel	91TSC	244	$ .05	$ .25
Hershiser, Orel	92T	175	$ .01	$ .03
Hershiser, Orel	92TSC	431	$ .01	$ .10
Hershiser, Orel	93T	255	$ .01	$ .03
Hertz, Steve	64T	544	$2.25	$9.00
Herzog, Whitey	57T	29	$8.00	$32.00
Herzog, Whitey	58T	438	$2.00	$8.00
Herzog, Whitey	59T	392	$1.50	$6.00

Player	Year	No.	VG	EX/MT
Herzog, Whitey	60T	92	$$1.50	$6.00
Herzog, Whitey	61T	106	$1.25	$5.00
Herzog, Whitey	62T	513	$1.75	$7.00
Herzog, Whitey	63T	302	$1.50	$6.00
Herzog, Whitey	73T	549	$1.00	$4.00
Herzog, Whitey	78T	299	$ .05	$ .20
Herzog, Whitey	83T	186	$ .01	$ .08
Herzog, Whitey	84T	561	$ .01	$ .06
Herzog, Whitey	85T	683	$ .01	$ .06
Herzog, Whitey	86T	441	$ .01	$ .05
Herzog, Whitey	87T	243	$ .01	$ .04
Herzog, Whitey	88T	744	$ .01	$ .04
Herzog, Whitey	89T	654	$ .01	$ .03
Herzog, Whitey	90T	261	$ .01	$ .03
Hesketh, Joe	85TTR	52	$ .05	$ .25
Hesketh, Joe	86T	472	$ .01	$ .05
Hesketh, Joe	87T	189	$ .01	$ .04
Hesketh, Joe	88T	371	$ .01	$ .04
Hesketh, Joe	89T	614	$ .01	$ .03
Hesketh, Joe	90T	24	$ .01	$ .03
Hesketh, Joe	90TTR	40	$ .01	$ .05
Hesketh, Joe	91T	269	$ .01	$ .03
Hesketh, Joe	92T	521	$ .01	$ .03
Hesketh, Joe	92TSC	636	$ .01	$ .10
Hesketh, Joe	93T	162	$ .01	$ .03
Hesketh, Joe	93TSC	107	$ .01	$ .10
Hetki, John	53T	235	$11.25	$45.00
Hetki, John	54T	161	$3.75	$15.00
Hetki, John	91TA53	235	$ .01	$ .15
Hetzel, Eric	90T	629	$ .01	$ .03
Hiatt, Jack	65T	497	$1.25	$5.00
Hiatt, Jack	66T	373	$ .65	$2.60
Hiatt, Jack	67T	368	$ .60	$2.40
Hiatt, Jack	68T	419	$ .35	$1.40
Hiatt, Jack	69T	204	$ .35	$1.40
Hiatt, Jack	70T	13	$ .20	$ .80
Hiatt, Jack	71T	371	$ .25	$1.00
Hiatt, Jack	72T	633	$ .40	$1.60
Hiatt, Jack	73T	402	$ .25	$1.00
Hibbard, Greg	90T	769	$ .05	$ .20
Hibbard, Greg	91T	256	$ .01	$ .03
Hibbard, Greg	92T	477	$ .01	$ .03
Hibbard, Greg	92TSC	586	$ .01	$ .10
Hibbard, Greg	93T	313	$ .01	$ .03
Hickerson, Bryan	92T	8	$ .01	$ .10
Hickerson, Bryan	92TSC	686	$ .01	$ .15
Hickerson, Bryan	93T	147	$ .01	$ .03
Hickerson, Bryan	93TSC	217	$ .01	$ .10
Hickey, Kevin	82T	778	$ .01	$ .08
Hickey, Kevin	83T	278	$ .01	$ .08
Hickey, Kevin	84T	459	$ .01	$ .06
Hickey, Kevin	90T	546	$ .01	$ .03
Hickman, Jim	62T	598	$17.50	$70.00
Hickman, Jim	63T	107	$ .50	$2.00
Hickman, Jim	64T	514	$1.00	$4.00
Hickman, Jim	65T	114	$ .35	$1.40
Hickman, Jim	66T	402	$ .65	$2.60
Hickman, Jim	67T	346	$ .60	$2.40
Hickman, Jim	69T	63	$ .35	$1.40
Hickman, Jim	70T	612	$ .50	$2.00
Hickman, Jim	71T	175	$ .25	$1.00
Hickman, Jim	72T	534	$ .40	$1.60
Hickman, Jim	73T	565	$ .60	$2.40
Hicks, Jim	67T	532	$1.50	$6.00
Hicks, Jim	69T	559	$ .40	$1.60
Hicks, Jim	70T	173	$ .20	$ .80
Hicks, Joe	61T	386	$1.00	$4.00
Hicks, Joe	62T	428	$1.25	$5.00
Higgins, Dennis	66T	529	$5.00	$20.00
Higgins, Dennis	67T	52	$ .40	$1.60
Higgins, Dennis	68T	509	$ .75	$3.00
Higgins, Dennis	69T	441	$ .30	$1.20
Higgins, Dennis	70T	257	$ .20	$ .80
Higgins, Dennis	71T	479	$ .50	$2.00
Higgins, Dennis	72T	278	$ .10	$ .40

TOPPS

Player	Year	No.	VG	EX/MT
Higgins, Mike	55T	150	$2.25	$9.00
Higgins, Mike	61T	221	$ .60	$2.40
Higgins, Mike	62T	559	$3.50	$14.00
Higuera, Teddy	85TTR	53	$ .05	$ .25
Higuera, Teddy	86T	347	$ .01	$ .15
Higuera, Teddy	87T	250	$ .01	$ .10
Higuera, Teddy	87TAS	615	$ .01	$ .10
Higuera, Teddy	88T	110	$ .01	$ .04
Higuera, Teddy	89T	595	$ .01	$ .03
Higuera, Teddy	90T	15	$ .01	$ .03
Higuera, Teddy	91T	475	$ .01	$ .03
Higuera, Teddy	91TSC	46	$ .05	$ .25
Higuera, Teddy	92T	265	$ .01	$ .03
Higuera, Teddy	92TSC	208	$ .01	$ .10
Hilgendorf, Tom	70T	482	$ .35	$1.40
Hilgendorf, Tom	74T	13	$ .10	$ .40
Hilgendorf, Tom	75T	377	$ .10	$ .40
Hilgendorf, Tom	76T	168	$ .05	$ .25
Hill, Donnie	84T	265	$ .01	$ .06
Hill, Donnie	85TTR	54	$ .01	$ .10
Hill, Donnie	86T	484	$ .01	$ .05
Hill, Donnie	87T	339	$ .01	$ .04
Hill, Donnie	87TTR	47	$ .01	$ .05
Hill, Donnie	88T	132	$ .01	$ .04
Hill, Donnie	89T	512	$ .01	$ .03
Hill, Donnie	91T	36	$ .01	$ .03
Hill, Donnie	92T	731	$ .01	$ .03
Hill, Donnie	92TSC	702	$ .01	$ .10
Hill, Garry	70T	172	$ .50	$2.00
Hill, Glenallen	90T	194	$ .01	$ .10
Hill, Glenallen	91T	509	$ .01	$ .03
Hill, Glenallen	91TSC	425	$ .05	$ .25
Hill, Glenallen	91TTR	55	$ .01	$ .05
Hill, Glenallen	92T	364	$ .01	$ .03
Hill, Glenallen	92TSC	413	$ .01	$ .10
Hill, Glenallen	93T	666	$ .01	$ .03
Hill, Herman	70T	267	$ .35	$1.40
Hill, Ken	89TTR	50	$ .10	$ .50
Hill, Ken	90T	233	$ .01	$ .15
Hill, Ken	91T	591	$ .01	$ .03
Hill, Ken	91TSC	435	$ .05	$ .25
Hill, Ken	92T	664	$ .01	$ .03
Hill, Ken	92TSC	138	$ .01	$ .10
Hill, Ken	92TSC	735	$ .01	$ .10
Hill, Ken	92TTR	51	$ .01	$ .05
Hill, Ken	93T	495	$ .01	$ .03
Hill, Ken	93TSC	227	$ .01	$ .10
Hill, Marc	75T	620	$11.25	$45.00
Hill, Marc	76T	577	$ .05	$ .25
Hill, Marc	77T	57	$ .05	$ .20
Hill, Marc	78T	359	$ .04	$ .16
Hill, Marc	79T	11	$ .03	$ .12
Hill, Marc	80T	236	$ .01	$ .10
Hill, Marc	81T	486	$ .01	$ .08
Hill, Marc	81TTR	770	$ .01	$ .15
Hill, Marc	82T	748	$ .01	$ .08
Hill, Marc	83T	124	$ .01	$ .08
Hill, Marc	84T	698	$ .01	$ .06
Hill, Marc	85T	312	$ .01	$ .06
Hill, Marc	86T	552	$ .01	$ .05
Hill, Milt	92TSC	733	$ .01	$ .15
Hill, Milt	93T	642	$ .01	$ .03
Hill, Tyrone	92T	444	$ .05	$ .25
Hillegas, Shawn	88T	455	$ .01	$ .04
Hillegas, Shawn	89T	247	$ .01	$ .03
Hillegas, Shawn	90T	93	$ .01	$ .03
Hillegas, Shawn	92T	523	$ .01	$ .03
Hillegas, Shawn	92TSC	76	$ .01	$ .10
Hiller, Chuck	61T	538	$7.50	$30.00
Hiller, Chuck	62T	188	$ .60	$2.40
Hiller, Chuck	63T	185	$ .50	$2.00
Hiller, Chuck	64T	313	$ .65	$2.60
Hiller, Chuck	65T	531	$1.40	$5.60
Hiller, Chuck	66T	154	$ .50	$2.00
Hiller, Chuck	67T	198	$ .50	$2.00

Player	Year	No.	VG	EX/MT
Hiller, Chuck	68T	461	$ .75	$3.00
Hiller, Chuck	73T	549	$1.00	$4.00
Hiller, Frank	52T	156	$7.00	$28.00
Hiller, John	66T	209	$ .75	$3.00
Hiller, John	68T	307	$ .35	$1.40
Hiller, John	69T	642	$ .40	$1.60
Hiller, John	70T	12	$ .20	$ .80
Hiller, John	71T	629	$1.00	$4.00
Hiller, John	73T	448	$ .25	$1.00
Hiller, John	74T	24	$ .10	$ .40
Hiller, John	74T	208	$ .10	$ .40
Hiller, John	75T	415	$ .10	$ .40
Hiller, John	76T	37	$ .05	$ .25
Hiller, John	77T	595	$ .05	$ .20
Hiller, John	78T	258	$ .04	$ .16
Hiller, John	79T	151	$ .03	$ .12
Hiller, John	80T	614	$ .01	$ .10
Hillman, Dave	57T	351	$5.00	$20.00
Hillman, Dave	58T	41	$2.00	$8.00
Hillman, Dave	59T	319	$1.00	$4.00
Hillman, Dave	60T	68	$ .85	$3.40
Hillman, Dave	61T	326	$ .60	$2.40
Hillman, Dave	62T	282	$ .75	$3.00
Hillman, Eric	92TSC	847	$ .05	$ .35
Hillman, Eric	93T	751	$ .01	$ .15
Hilton, Dave	73T	615	$120.00	$480.00
Hilton, Dave	74T	148	$ .10	$ .40
Hilton, Dave	75T	509	$ .10	$ .40
Hilton, Dave	77T	163	$ .05	$ .20

SAM HINDS

Player	Year	No.	VG	EX/MT
Hinds, Sam	**78T**	**303**	**$ .04**	**$ .16**
Hinsley, Jerry	64T	576	$2.25	$9.00
Hinsley, Jerry	65T	449	$1.25	$5.00
Hinton, Chuck	62T	347	$ .75	$3.00
Hinton, Chuck	63T	2	$5.00	$20.00
Hinton, Chuck	63T	330	$ .90	$3.60
Hinton, Chuck	64T	52	$ .50	$2.00
Hinton, Chuck	65T	235	$ .50	$2.00
Hinton, Chuck	66T	391	$ .65	$2.60
Hinton, Chuck	67T	189	$ .40	$1.60
Hinton, Chuck	68T	531	$ .70	$2.80
Hinton, Chuck	69T	644	$ .40	$1.60
Hinton, Chuck	70T	27	$ .20	$ .80
Hinton, Chuck	71T	429	$ .50	$2.00

TOPPS

Player	Year	No.	VG	EX/MT	Player	Year	No.	VG	EX/MT
Hinton, Rich	72T	724	$1.25	$5.00	Hodges, Gil	58T	162	$7.00	$28.00
Hinton, Rich	73T	321	$ .10	$ .40	Hodges, Gil	59T	270	$5.00	$20.00
Hinton, Rich	76T	607	$ .05	$ .25	Hodges, Gil	60T	295	$4.00	$16.00
Hinzo, Tommy	88T	576	$ .01	$ .04	Hodges, Gil	61T	460	$3.50	$14.00
Hippauf, Herb	66T	518	$1.50	$6.00	Hodges, Gil	62T	85	$4.00	$16.00
Hiser, Gene	72T	61	$ .25	$1.00	Hodges, Gil	63T	68	$3.00	$12.00
Hiser, Gene	74T	452	$ .10	$ .40	Hodges, Gil	63T	245	$4.50	$18.00
Hisle, Larry	68T	579	$1.00	$4.00	Hodges, Gil	64T	547	$4.00	$16.00
Hisle, Larry	69T	206	$ .35	$1.40	Hodges, Gil	65T	99	$1.50	$6.00
Hisle, Larry	70T	288	$ .35	$1.40	Hodges, Gil	66T	386	$1.50	$6.00
Hisle, Larry	71T	616	$1.00	$4.00	Hodges, Gil	67T	228	$1.25	$5.00
Hisle, Larry	72T	398	$ .25	$1.00	Hodges, Gil	68T	27	$2.00	$8.00
Hisle, Larry	73T	622	$ .60	$2.40	Hodges, Gil	69T	564	$2.25	$9.00
Hisle, Larry	74T	366	$ .10	$ .40	Hodges, Gil	70T	394	$1.25	$5.00
Hisle, Larry	75T	526	$ .10	$ .40	Hodges, Gil	71T	183	$1.00	$4.00
Hisle, Larry	76T	59	$ .05	$ .25	Hodges, Gil	72T	465	$1.00	$4.00
Hisle, Larry	77T	375	$ .05	$ .20	Hodges, Gil	89TTB	664	$ .01	$ .05
Hisle, Larry	78T	203	$ .05	$ .20	Hodges, Gil	91TA53	296	$ .10	$1.00
Hisle, Larry	78T	520	$ .04	$ .16	Hodges, Ron	74T	448	$ .10	$ .40
Hisle, Larry	79T	180	$ .03	$ .12	Hodges, Ron	75T	134	$ .10	$ .40
Hisle, Larry	80T	430	$ .01	$ .10	Hodges, Ron	77T	329	$ .05	$ .20
Hisle, Larry	81T	215	$ .01	$ .08	Hodges, Ron	78T	653	$ .04	$ .16
Hisle, Larry	82T	93	$ .01	$ .08	Hodges, Ron	79T	46	$ .03	$ .12
Hisle, Larry	83T	773	$ .01	$ .08	Hodges, Ron	80T	172	$ .01	$ .10
Hitchcock, Billy	52T	182	$7.00	$28.00	Hodges, Ron	81T	537	$ .01	$ .08
Hitchcock, Billy	53T	17	$6.25	$25.00	Hodges, Ron	82T	234	$ .01	$ .08
Hitchcock, Billy	60T	461	$1.75	$7.00	Hodges, Ron	83T	713	$ .01	$ .08
Hitchcock, Billy	62T	121	$ .60	$2.40	Hodges, Ron	84T	418	$ .01	$ .06
Hitchcock, Billy	63T	213	$ .90	$3.60	Hodges, Ron	85T	363	$ .01	$ .06
Hitchcock, Billy	67T	199	$ .50	$2.00	Hoeft, Billy	52T	370	$50.00	$200.00
Hitchcock, Billy	91TA53	17	$ .01	$ .15	Hoeft, Billy	53T	165	$6.25	$25.00
Hitchcock, Sterling	93T	530	$ .05	$ .35	Hoeft, Billy	56T	152	$2.50	$10.00
Hoak, Don	53T	176	$6.00	$24.00	Hoeft, Billy	57T	60	$2.00	$8.00
Hoak, Don	54T	211	$4.00	$16.00	Hoeft, Billy	58T	13	$2.00	$8.00
Hoak, Don	55T	40	$2.50	$10.00	Hoeft, Billy	59T	343	$1.00	$4.00
Hoak, Don	56T	335	$2.50	$10.00	Hoeft, Billy	60T	369	$ .75	$3.00
Hoak, Don	57T	274	$5.00	$20.00	Hoeft, Billy	61T	256	$ .60	$2.40
Hoak, Don	58T	160	$1.25	$5.00	Hoeft, Billy	62T	134	$ .60	$2.40
Hoak, Don	59T	25	$1.10	$4.40	Hoeft, Billy	63T	346	$ .90	$3.60
Hoak, Don	60T	373	$ .75	$3.00	Hoeft, Billy	64T	551	$2.25	$9.00
Hoak, Don	61T	230	$ .60	$2.40	Hoeft, Billy	65T	471	$1.25	$5.00
Hoak, Don	62T	95	$ .60	$2.40	Hoeft, Billy	66T	409	$ .65	$2.60
Hoak, Don	63T	305	$ .90	$3.60	Hoeft, Billy	91TA53	165	$ .01	$ .15
Hoak, Don	64T	254	$ .65	$2.60	Hoerner, Joe	64T	544	$2.25	$9.00
Hoak, Don	91TA53	176	$ .05	$ .35	Hoerner, Joe	66T	544	$8.00	$32.00
Hobaugh, Ed	60T	131	$ .75	$3.00	Hoerner, Joe	67T	41	$ .40	$1.60
Hobaugh, Ed	61T	129	$ .60	$2.40	Hoerner, Joe	68T	227	$ .35	$1.40
Hobaugh, Ed	62T	79	$ .60	$2.40	Hoerner, Joe	69T	522	$ .40	$1.60
Hobaugh, Ed	63T	423	$1.00	$4.00	Hoerner, Joe	70T	511	$ .35	$1.40
Hobbie, Glen	58T	467	$1.00	$4.00	Hoerner, Joe	71T	166	$ .25	$1.00
Hobbie, Glen	59T	334	$1.00	$4.00	Hoerner, Joe	72T	482	$ .25	$1.00
Hobbie, Glen	60T	182	$ .75	$3.00	Hoerner, Joe	73T	653	$ .60	$2.40
Hobbie, Glen	61T	264	$ .60	$2.40	Hoerner, Joe	74T	493	$ .10	$ .40
Hobbie, Glen	61T	393	$1.00	$4.00	Hoerner, Joe	75T	629	$ .10	$ .40
Hobbie, Glen	62T	585	$6.00	$24.00	Hoerner, Joe	77T	256	$ .05	$ .20
Hobbie, Glen	63T	212	$ .90	$3.60	Hoffman, Glenn	81T	349	$ .01	$ .08
Hobbie, Glen	64T	578	$2.25	$9.00	Hoffman, Glenn	82T	189	$ .01	$ .08
Hobson, Butch	77T	89	$ .15	$ .60	Hoffman, Glenn	83T	108	$ .01	$ .08
Hobson, Butch	78T	155	$ .04	$ .16	Hoffman, Glenn	84T	523	$ .01	$ .06
Hobson, Butch	79T	270	$ .03	$ .12	Hoffman, Glenn	85T	633	$ .01	$ .06
Hobson, Butch	80T	420	$ .01	$ .10	Hoffman, Glenn	86T	38	$ .01	$ .05
Hobson, Butch	81T	595	$ .01	$ .08	Hoffman, Glenn	87T	374	$ .01	$ .04
Hobson, Butch	81TTR	771	$ .01	$ .15	Hoffman, Glenn	88T	202	$ .01	$ .04
Hobson, Butch	82T	357	$ .01	$ .08	Hoffman, Guy	80T	664	$ .01	$ .10
Hobson, Butch	83T	652	$ .01	$ .08	Hoffman, Guy	87TTR	48	$ .01	$ .05
Hobson, Butch	92TTR	52	$ .01	$ .05	Hoffman, Guy	88T	496	$ .01	$ .04
Hobson, Butch	93T	502	$ .01	$ .03	Hoffman, Trevor	93T	572	$ .01	$ .03
Hodge, Ed	85T	639	$ .01	$ .06	Hofman, Bob	52T	371	$75.00	$225.00
Hodges, Gil	51Trb	31	$8.75	$35.00	Hofman, Bob	53T	182	$4.50	$18.00
Hodges, Gil	52T	36	$40.00	$160.00	Hofman, Bob	54T	99	$3.75	$15.00
Hodges, Gil	54T	102	$20.00	$80.00	Hofman, Bob	91TA53	182	$ .01	$ .15
Hodges, Gil	55T	187	$35.00	$140.00	Hofman, Bobby	55T	17	$2.25	$9.00
Hodges, Gil	56T	145	$12.50	$50.00	Hofman, Bobby	56T	28	$2.00	$8.00
Hodges, Gil	57T	80	$12.50	$50.00	Hogue, Bobby	52T	9	$13.75	$55.00
Hodges, Gil	57T	400	$50.00	$200.00	Hogue, Cal	53T	238	$11.25	$45.00

TOPPS

Player	Year	No.	VG	EX/MT
Hogue, Cal	54T	134	$3.75	$15.00
Hogue, Cal	91TA53	238	$.01	$.15
Hoiles, Chris	91T	42	$.01	$.15
Hoiles, Chris	91TSC	489	$.10	$1.00

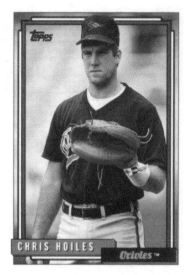

Player	Year	No.	VG	EX/MT
Hoiles, Chris	92T	125	$.01	$.03
Hoiles, Chris	92TSC	161	$.01	$.10
Hoiles, Chris	93T	524	$.01	$.03
Holcombe, Ken	52T	95	$7.00	$28.00
Holdsworth, Fred	74T	596	$.10	$.40
Holdsworth, Fred	75T	323	$.10	$.40
Holdsworth, Fred	77T	466	$.05	$.20
Holland, Al	81T	213	$.01	$.08
Holland, Al	82T	406	$.01	$.08
Holland, Al	83T	58	$.01	$.08
Holland, Al	83TTR	46	$.01	$.10
Holland, Al	84T	138	$.01	$.10
Holland, Al	84T	564	$.01	$.06
Holland, Al	85T	185	$.01	$.06
Holland, Al	85TTR	55	$.01	$.10
Holland, Al	86T	369	$.01	$.05
Hollins, Dave	90TTR	41	$.10	$.75
Hollins, Dave	91T	264	$.01	$.10
Hollins, Dave	92T	383	$.01	$.03
Hollins, Dave	92TSC	246	$.10	$.50
Hollins, Dave	93T	17	$.01	$.03
Hollins, Jessie	93T	487	$.01	$.03
Holloman, Bobo	91TA53	306	$.05	$.20
Holly, Jeff	79T	371	$.03	$.12
Holman, Brian	89TTR	51	$.01	$.15
Holman, Brian	90T	616	$.01	$.03
Holman, Brian	91T	458	$.01	$.03
Holman, Brian	91TSC	106	$.05	$.25
Holman, Brian	92T	239	$.01	$.03
Holman, Brian	92TSC	295	$.01	$.10
Holman, Gary	69T	361	$.30	$1.20
Holman, Scott	84T	13	$.01	$.06
Holmes, Darren	92T	454	$.01	$.03
Holmes, Darren	92TSC	155	$.01	$.15
Holmes, Darren	93T	681	$.01	$.03
Holmes, Tommy	51Trb	52	$4.50	$18.00
Holmes, Tommy	52T	289	$15.00	$60.00
Holt, Jim	71T	7	$.25	$1.00
Holt, Jim	72T	588	$.40	$1.60

Player	Year	No.	VG	EX/MT
Holt, Jim	73T	259	$.10	$.40
Holt, Jim	74T	122	$.10	$.40
Holt, Jim	75T	607	$.10	$.40
Holt, Jim	76T	603	$.05	$.25
Holt, Jim	77T	349	$.05	$.20
Holton, Brian	87TTR	49	$.01	$.05
Holton, Brian	88T	338	$.01	$.04
Holton, Brian	89T	368	$.01	$.03
Holton, Brian	89TTR	52	$.01	$.05
Holton, Brian	90T	179	$.01	$.03
Holtzman, Ken	67T	185	$1.00	$4.00
Holtzman, Ken	68T	60	$.35	$1.40
Holtzman, Ken	68TAS	380	$.50	$2.00
Holtzman, Ken	69T	288	$.50	$2.00
Holtzman, Ken	70T	505	$.35	$1.40
Holtzman, Ken	71T	410	$.50	$2.00
Holtzman, Ken	72T	670	$1.25	$5.00
Holtzman, Ken	73T	60	$.20	$.80
Holtzman, Ken	74T	180	$.10	$.40
Holtzman, Ken	75T	145	$.10	$.40
Holtzman, Ken	76T	115	$.05	$.25
Holtzman, Ken	77T	625	$.05	$.20
Holtzman, Ken	78T	387	$.04	$.16
Holtzman, Ken	79T	522	$.03	$.12
Holtzman, Ken	80T	298	$.01	$.10
Honeycutt, Rick	79T	612	$.15	$.60
Honeycutt, Rick	80T	307	$.01	$.10
Honeycutt, Rick	81T	33	$.01	$.08
Honeycutt, Rick	81TTR	772	$.01	$.15
Honeycutt, Rick	82T	751	$.01	$.08
Honeycutt, Rick	83T	557	$.01	$.08
Honeycutt, Rick	84T	37	$.01	$.06
Honeycutt, Rick	84T	137	$.01	$.06
Honeycutt, Rick	84T	222	$.01	$.06
Honeycutt, Rick	85T	174	$.01	$.06
Honeycutt, Rick	86T	439	$.01	$.05
Honeycutt, Rick	87T	753	$.01	$.04
Honeycutt, Rick	88T	641	$.01	$.04
Honeycutt, Rick	89T	328	$.01	$.03
Honeycutt, Rick	90T	582	$.01	$.03
Honeycutt, Rick	91T	67	$.01	$.03
Honeycutt, Rick	91TSC	415	$.05	$.25
Honeycutt, Rick	92T	202	$.01	$.03
Honeycutt, Rick	92TSC	581	$.01	$.10
Hood, Don	74T	436	$.10	$.40
Hood, Don	75T	516	$.10	$.40
Hood, Don	76T	132	$.05	$.25
Hood, Don	77T	296	$.05	$.20
Hood, Don	78T	398	$.04	$.16
Hood, Don	79T	667	$.03	$.12
Hood, Don	80T	89	$.01	$.10
Hood, Don	83T	443	$.01	$.08
Hood, Don	84T	743	$.01	$.06
Hook, Jay	60T	187	$.75	$3.00
Hook, Jay	61T	162	$.60	$2.40
Hook, Jay	62T	94	$.60	$2.40
Hook, Jay	63T	469	$3.00	$12.00
Hook, Jay	64T	361	$.65	$2.60
Hooper, Bob	52T	340	$43.75	$175.00
Hooper, Bob	53T	84	$4.00	$16.00
Hooper, Bob	91TA53	84	$.01	$.15
Hooten, Leon	77T	478	$.05	$.20
Hooton, Burt	72T	61	$.25	$1.00
Hooton, Burt	73T	367	$.10	$.40
Hooton, Burt	74T	378	$.10	$.40
Hooton, Burt	75T	176	$.10	$.40
Hooton, Burt	76T	280	$.05	$.25
Hooton, Burt	77T	484	$.05	$.20
Hooton, Burt	78T	41	$.04	$.16
Hooton, Burt	79T	694	$.03	$.12
Hooton, Burt	80T	170	$.01	$.10
Hooton, Burt	81T	565	$.01	$.08
Hooton, Burt	82T	311	$.01	$.08
Hooton, Burt	82T	315	$.01	$.08
Hooton, Burt	83T	775	$.01	$.08

TOPPS

Player	Year	No.	VG	EX/MT	Player	Year	No.	VG	EX/MT
Hooton, Burt	84T	15	$ .01	$ .06	Horton, Willie	72T	750	$1.25	$5.00
Hooton, Burt	85T	201	$ .01	$ .06	Horton, Willie	73T	433	$ .25	$1.00
Hooton, Burt	85TTR	56	$ .01	$ .10	Horton, Willie	74T	115	$ .10	$ .40
Hooton, Burt	86T	454	$ .01	$ .05	Horton, Willie	75T	66	$ .10	$ .40
Hoover, John	85T	397	$ .01	$ .06	Horton, Willie	76T	320	$ .05	$ .25
Hopkins, Gail	70T	483	$ .35	$1.40	Horton, Willie	77T	660	$ .10	$ .40
Hopkins, Gail	71T	269	$ .25	$1.00	Horton, Willie	78T	290	$ .04	$ .16
Hopkins, Gail	72T	728	$1.25	$5.00	Horton, Willie	79T	239	$ .03	$ .12
Hopkins, Gail	73T	441	$ .25	$1.00	Horton, Willie	80T	532	$ .01	$ .10
Hopkins, Gail	74T	652	$ .10	$ .40	Hoscheit, Vern	73T	179	$ .25	$1.00
Hopp, Johnny	52T	214	$7.00	$28.00	Hosey, Steve	92T	618	$ .05	$ .25
Hopp, Johnny	54T	193	$3.75	$15.00	Hosey, Steve	93T	653	$ .01	$ .10
Horlen, Joel	62T	479	$2.00	$8.00	Hoskins, Dave	54T	81	$3.75	$15.00
Horlen, Joel	63T	332	$ .90	$3.60	Hoskins, Dave	55T	133	$2.25	$9.00
Horlen, Joel	64T	584	$2.25	$9.00	Hosley, Tim	72T	257	$ .10	$ .40
Horlen, Joel	65T	7	$ .75	$3.00	Hosley, Tim	76T	482	$ .05	$ .25
Horlen, Joel	65T	480	$1.25	$5.00	Hosley, Tim	78T	261	$ .04	$ .16
Horlen, Joel	66T	560	$3.75	$15.00	Hostetler, Dave	83T	584	$ .01	$ .08
Horlen, Joel	67T	107	$ .40	$1.60					
Horlen, Joel	67T	233	$ .50	$2.00					
Horlen, Joe "Joel"	68T	8	$ .55	$2.20					
Horlen, Joe	68T	125	$ .35	$1.40					
Horlen, Joe	68TAS	377	$ .50	$2.00					
Horlen, Joe	69T	328	$ .30	$1.20					
Horlen, Joe	70T	35	$ .20	$ .80					
Horlen, Joe	71T	345	$ .25	$1.00					
Horlen, Joe	72T	685	$1.25	$5.00					
Horn, Sam	88T	377	$ .01	$ .10					
Horn, Sam	90TTR	43	$ .01	$ .15					
Horn, Sam	91T	598	$ .01	$ .03					
Horn, Sam	91TSC	316	$ .05	$ .25					
Horn, Sam	92T	422	$ .01	$ .03					
Horn, Sam	92TSC	269	$ .01	$ .10					
Horn, Sam	93T	109	$ .01	$ .03					
Horner, Bob	79T	586	$ .20	$ .80					
Horner, Bob	80T	108	$ .01	$ .10					
Horner, Bob	81T	355	$ .01	$ .08					
Horner, Bob	82T	145	$ .01	$ .08					
Horner, Bob	83T	50	$ .01	$ .08					
Horner, Bob	84T	760	$ .01	$ .06					
Horner, Bob	85T	276	$ .01	$ .06					
Horner, Bob	85T	410	$ .01	$ .06					
Horner, Bob	86T	220	$ .01	$ .05					
Horner, Bob	87T	660	$ .01	$ .04					
Horner, Bob	88TTR	50	$ .01	$ .05					
Horner, Bob	89T	510	$ .01	$ .03					
Hornsby, Rogers	61T	404	$2.50	$10.00					
Hornsby, Rogers	76TAT	342	$ .75	$3.00					
Hornsby, Rogers	79TRH	414	$ .15	$ .60					
Hornsby, Rogers	91TA53	289	$ .10	$ .75	Hostetler, Dave	84T	62	$ .01	$ .06
Horsman, Vince	92TSC	637	$ .01	$ .15	Hough, Charlie	72T	198	$1.25	$5.00
Horsman, Vince	92TTR	53	$ .01	$ .10	Hough, Charlie	73T	610	$1.25	$5.00
Horsman, Vince	93T	263	$ .01	$ .10	Hough, Charlie	74T	408	$ .20	$ .80
Horsman, Vince	93TSC	256	$ .01	$ .10	Hough, Charlie	75T	71	$ .15	$ .60
Horton, Ricky	84TTR	52	$ .05	$ .30	Hough, Charlie	76T	174	$ .05	$ .25
Horton, Ricky	85T	321	$ .01	$ .10	Hough, Charlie	77T	298	$ .05	$ .20
Horton, Ricky	86T	783	$ .01	$ .05	Hough, Charlie	78T	22	$ .04	$ .16
Horton, Ricky	87T	542	$ .01	$ .04	Hough, Charlie	79T	508	$ .03	$ .12
Horton, Ricky	88T	34	$ .01	$ .04	Hough, Charlie	80T	644	$ .01	$ .10
Horton, Ricky	88TTR	51	$ .01	$ .05	Hough, Charlie	81T	371	$ .01	$ .08
Horton, Ricky	89T	232	$ .01	$ .03	Hough, Charlie	82T	718	$ .01	$ .08
Horton, Ricky	90T	133	$ .01	$ .03	Hough, Charlie	83T	412	$ .01	$ .08
Horton, Willie	64T	512	$2.50	$10.00	Hough, Charlie	83T	479	$ .01	$ .08
Horton, Willie	65T	206	$ .75	$3.00	Hough, Charlie	84T	118	$ .01	$ .06
Horton, Willie	66T	20	$ .35	$1.40	Hough, Charlie	85T	571	$ .01	$ .06
Horton, Willie	66T	218	$ .75	$3.00	Hough, Charlie	86T	275	$ .01	$ .05
Horton, Willie	66T	220	$ .75	$3.00	Hough, Charlie	87T	70	$ .01	$ .04
Horton, Willie	67T	465	$1.50	$6.00	Hough, Charlie	88T	680	$ .01	$ .04
Horton, Willie	68T	360	$ .50	$2.00	Hough, Charlie	89T	345	$ .01	$ .03
Horton, Willie	69T	5	$ .75	$3.00	Hough, Charlie	90T	735	$ .01	$ .03
Horton, Willie	69T	180	$ .35	$1.40	Hough, Charlie	91T	495	$ .01	$ .03
Horton, Willie	69TAS	429	$ .30	$1.20	Hough, Charlie	91TSC	579	$ .05	$ .25
Horton, Willie	70T	520	$ .35	$1.40	Hough, Charlie	91TTR	56	$ .01	$ .05
Horton, Willie	71T	120	$ .25	$1.00	Hough, Charlie	92T	191	$ .01	$ .03
Horton, Willie	72T	494	$ .25	$1.00	Hough, Charlie	92TSC	894	$ .01	$ .10

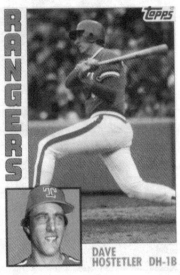

TOPPS

Player	Year	No.	VG	EX/MT	Player	Year	No.	VG	EX/MT
Hough, Charlie	93T	520	$ .01	$ .03	Howard, Elston	66T	405	$1.25	$5.00
Houk, Ralph	52T	200	$16.25	$65.00	Howard, Elston	67T	25	$1.00	$4.00
Houk, Ralph	60T	465	$3.50	$14.00	Howard, Elston	68T	167	$ .75	$3.00
Houk, Ralph	61T	133	$1.25	$5.00	Howard, Elston	73T	116	$ .20	$ .80
Houk, Ralph	62T	88	$ .75	$3.00	Howard, Elston	75T	201	$ .25	$1.00
Houk, Ralph	63T	382	$1.25	$5.00	Howard, Frank	60T	132	$4.00	$16.00
Houk, Ralph	67T	468	$1.50	$6.00	Howard, Frank	61T	280	$1.25	$5.00
Houk, Ralph	68T	47	$ .35	$1.40	Howard, Frank	62T	175	$1.25	$5.00
Houk, Ralph	69T	447	$ .30	$1.20	Howard, Frank	63T	123	$ .90	$3.60
Houk, Ralph	70T	273	$ .35	$1.40	Howard, Frank	64T	371	$1.50	$6.00
Houk, Ralph	71T	146	$ .25	$1.00	Howard, Frank	65T	40	$ .75	$3.00
Houk, Ralph	72T	533	$ .40	$1.60	Howard, Frank	66T	515	$2.00	$8.00
Houk, Ralph	73T	116	$ .20	$ .80	Howard, Frank	67T	255	$ .75	$3.00
Houk, Ralph	74T	578	$ .10	$ .40	Howard, Frank	68T	6	$1.75	$7.00
Houk, Ralph	78T	684	$ .04	$ .16	Howard, Frank	68T	320	$ .50	$2.00
Houk, Ralph	83T	786	$ .01	$ .08	Howard, Frank	69T	3	$1.00	$4.00
Houk, Ralph	84T	381	$ .01	$ .06	Howard, Frank	69T	5	$ .75	$3.00
Houk, Ralph	85T	11	$ .01	$ .06	Howard, Frank	69T	170	$ .60	$2.40
Houk, Ralph	91TA53	282	$ .05	$ .25	Howard, Frank	70T	66	$1.25	$5.00
House, Frank	52T	146	$7.00	$28.00	Howard, Frank	70T	550	$1.00	$4.00
House, Frank	54T	163	$3.75	$15.00	Howard, Frank	71T	63	$ .25	$1.00
House, Frank	55T	87	$2.25	$9.00	Howard, Frank	71T	65	$ .75	$3.00
House, Frank	56T	32	$2.00	$8.00	Howard, Frank	71T	620	$1.25	$5.00
House, Frank	57T	223	$2.00	$8.00	Howard, Frank	72T	350	$ .25	$1.00
House, Frank	58T	318	$1.25	$5.00	Howard, Frank	73T	560	$1.00	$4.00
House, Frank	59T	313	$1.00	$4.00	Howard, Frank	83TTR	47	$ .01	$ .10
House, Frank	60T	372	$ .75	$3.00	Howard, Frank	84T	621	$ .01	$ .06
House, Tom	69T	331	$ .50	$2.00	Howard, Fred	80T	72	$ .01	$ .10
House, Tom	72T	351	$ .10	$ .40	Howard, Larry	71T	102	$ .25	$1.00
House, Tom	74T	164	$ .10	$ .40	Howard, Steve	90TTR	42	$ .01	$ .05
House, Tom	75T	525	$ .10	$ .40	Howard, Thomas	91TSC	403	$ .05	$ .35
House, Tom	76T	231	$ .05	$ .25	Howard, Thomas	92T	539	$ .01	$ .03
House, Tom	76TTR	231	$ .05	$ .25	Howard, Thomas	92TSC	401	$ .01	$ .10
House, Tom	77T	358	$ .05	$ .20	Howard, Thomas	93T	113	$ .01	$ .03
House, Tom	78T	643	$ .04	$ .16	Howard, Wilbur	74T	606	$ .10	$ .40
House, Tom	79T	31	$ .03	$ .12	Howard, Wilbur	75T	563	$ .10	$ .40
Householder, Paul	81T	606	$ .01	$ .08	Howard, Wilbur	76T	97	$ .05	$ .25
Householder, Paul	82T	351	$ .01	$ .08	Howard, Wilbur	77T	248	$ .05	$ .20
Householder, Paul	83T	34	$ .01	$ .08	Howard, Wilbur	78T	534	$ .04	$ .16
Householder, Paul	84T	214	$ .01	$ .06	Howard, Wilbur	79T	642	$ .03	$ .12
Householder, Paul	86T	554	$ .01	$ .05	Howarth, Jimmy	73T	459	$ .25	$1.00
Housie, Wayne	92T	639	$ .01	$ .10	Howarth, Jimmy	74T	404	$ .10	$ .40
Housie, Wayne	92TSC	352	$ .01	$ .10	Howe, Art	78T	13	$ .15	$ .60
Houston, Tyler	90T	564	$ .01	$ .15	Howe, Art	79T	327	$ .03	$ .12
Houtteman, Art	52T	238	$7.00	$28.00	Howe, Art	80T	554	$ .01	$ .10
Houtteman, Art	56T	281	$2.50	$10.00	Howe, Art	81T	129	$ .01	$ .08
Houtteman, Art	57T	385	$1.75	$7.00	Howe, Art	82T	66	$ .10	$1.00
Hovley, Steve	70T	514	$ .35	$1.40	Howe, Art	82T	453	$ .01	$ .08
Hovley, Steve	71T	109	$ .25	$1.00	Howe, Art	83T	639	$ .01	$ .08
Hovley, Steve	72T	683	$1.25	$5.00	Howe, Art	84T	679	$ .01	$ .06
Hovley, Steve	73T	282	$ .10	$ .40	Howe, Art	84TTR	53	$ .01	$ .15
Howard, Bruce	64T	107	$ .50	$2.00	Howe, Art	85T	204	$ .01	$ .06
Howard, Bruce	65T	41	$ .35	$1.40	Howe, Art	89TTR	53	$ .01	$ .05
Howard, Bruce	66T	281	$ .50	$2.00	Howe, Art	90T	579	$ .01	$ .03
Howard, Bruce	67T	159	$ .40	$1.60	Howe, Art	91T	51	$ .01	$ .03
Howard, Bruce	68T	293	$ .35	$1.40	Howe, Art	92T	729	$ .01	$ .03
Howard, Bruce	69T	226	$ .50	$2.00	Howe, Art	93T	506	$ .01	$ .03
Howard, David	92T	641	$ .01	$ .03	Howe, Steve	81T	693	$ .05	$ .20
Howard, David	92TSC	245	$ .01	$ .10	Howe, Steve	82T	14	$ .01	$ .08
Howard, David	93T	519	$ .01	$ .03	Howe, Steve	83T	170	$ .01	$ .08
Howard, Elston	56T	208	$12.50	$50.00	Howe, Steve	84T	425	$ .01	$ .06
Howard, Elston	57T	82	$5.00	$20.00	Howe, Steve	91TSC	401	$ .05	$ .25
Howard, Elston	58T	275	$3.50	$14.00	Howe, Steve	92T	318	$ .01	$ .03
Howard, Elston	59T	395	$2.00	$8.00	Howe, Steve	92TSC	827	$ .01	$ .10
Howard, Elston	60T	65	$1.50	$6.00	Howell, Dixie	52T	135	$7.00	$28.00
Howard, Elston	61T	495	$2.25	$9.00	Howell, Dixie	53T	255	$22.50	$90.00
Howard, Elston	62T	51	$1.50	$6.00	Howell, Dixie	56T	149	$2.50	$10.00
Howard, Elston	62T	400	$2.25	$9.00	Howell, Dixie	57T	221	$2.00	$8.00
Howard, Elston	62TAS	473	$2.00	$8.00	Howell, Dixie	58T	421	$1.00	$4.00
Howard, Elston	63T	60	$1.50	$6.00	Howell, Dixie	91TA53	255	$ .01	$ .15
Howard, Elston	63T	306	$1.00	$4.00	Howell, Jack	86T	127	$ .01	$ .05
Howard, Elston	64T	100	$1.25	$5.00	Howell, Jack	87T	422	$ .01	$ .04
Howard, Elston	65T	1	$3.75	$15.00	Howell, Jack	88T	631	$ .01	$ .04
Howard, Elston	65T	3	$5.50	$22.00	Howell, Jack	89T	216	$ .01	$ .03
Howard, Elston	65T	450	$1.75	$7.00	Howell, Jack	90T	547	$ .01	$ .03

403

TOPPS

Player	Year	No.	VG	EX/MT
Howell, Jack	91T	57	$ .01	$ .03
Howell, Jack	91TSC	198	$ .05	$ .25
Howell, Jack	92T	769	$ .01	$ .03
Howell, Jay	82T	51	$ .05	$ .25
Howell, Jay	84T	239	$ .01	$ .06
Howell, Jay	85T	559	$ .01	$ .06
Howell, Jay	85TTR	57	$ .01	$ .10
Howell, Jay	86T	115	$ .01	$ .05
Howell, Jay	87T	391	$ .01	$ .04
Howell, Jay	88T	690	$ .01	$ .04
Howell, Jay	88TTR	52	$ .01	$ .05
Howell, Jay	89T	425	$ .01	$ .03
Howell, Jay	90T	40	$ .01	$ .03
Howell, Jay	91T	770	$ .01	$ .03
Howell, Jay	91TSC	278	$ .05	$ .25
Howell, Jay	92T	205	$ .01	$ .03
Howell, Jay	92TSC	457	$ .01	$ .10
Howell, Jay	93T	311	$ .01	$ .03
Howell, Ken	85TTR	58	$ .01	$ .10
Howell, Ken	86T	654	$ .01	$ .05
Howell, Ken	87T	477	$ .01	$ .04
Howell, Ken	88T	149	$ .01	$ .04
Howell, Ken	89T	93	$ .01	$ .03
Howell, Ken	89TTR	54	$ .01	$ .05
Howell, Ken	90T	756	$ .01	$ .03
Howell, Ken	91T	209	$ .01	$ .03
Howell, Ken	91TSC	71	$ .05	$ .25
Howell, Pat	93T	215	$ .01	$ .10
Howell, Roy	76T	279	$ .05	$ .25
Howell, Roy	77T	608	$ .05	$ .20
Howell, Roy	78T	394	$ .04	$ .16
Howell, Roy	79T	101	$ .03	$ .12
Howell, Roy	80T	488	$ .01	$ .10
Howell, Roy	81T	581	$ .01	$ .08
Howell, Roy	81TTR	773	$ .01	$ .15
Howell, Roy	82T	68	$ .01	$ .08
Howell, Roy	83T	218	$ .01	$ .08
Howell, Roy	84T	687	$ .01	$ .06
Howell, Roy	85T	372	$ .01	$ .06

Howerton, Bill

	52T	167	$7.00	$28.00
Howser, Dick	61T	416	$2.25	$9.00
Howser, Dick	62T	13	$ .75	$3.00

Player	Year	No.	VG	EX/MT
Howser, Dick	63T	124	$ .90	$3.60
Howser, Dick	64T	478	$1.00	$4.00
Howser, Dick	65T	92	$ .75	$3.00
Howser, Dick	66T	567	$8.00	$32.00
Howser, Dick	67T	411	$ .75	$3.00
Howser, Dick	68T	467	$ .75	$3.00
Howser, Dick	73T	116	$ .20	$ .80
Howser, Dick	83T	96	$ .01	$ .08
Howser, Dick	84T	471	$ .01	$ .06
Howser, Dick	85T	334	$ .01	$ .06
Howser, Dick	86T	199	$ .01	$ .05
Howser, Dick	87T	18	$ .01	$ .04
Howser, Dick	90TTB	661	$ .01	$ .03
Hoyt, LaMarr	81T	164	$ .05	$ .20
Hoyt, LaMarr	82T	428	$ .01	$ .08
Hoyt, LaMarr	83T	591	$ .01	$ .08
Hoyt, LaMarr	83T	618	$ .01	$ .08
Hoyt, LaMarr	83T	705	$ .05	$ .25
Hoyt, LaMarr	84T	97	$ .01	$ .06
Hoyt, LaMarr	84T	135	$ .01	$ .06
Hoyt, LaMarr	84TAS	405	$ .01	$ .06
Hoyt, LaMarr	85T	520	$ .01	$ .06
Hoyt, LaMarr	85TTR	59	$ .01	$ .10
Hoyt, LaMarr	86T	380	$ .01	$ .05
Hoyt, LaMarr	87T	275	$ .01	$ .04
Hrabosky, Al	71T	594	$1.25	$5.00
Hrabosky, Al	73T	153	$ .20	$ .80
Hrabosky, Al	74T	108	$ .10	$ .40
Hrabosky, Al	75T	122	$ .10	$ .40
Hrabosky, Al	76T	205	$ .15	$ .60
Hrabosky, Al	76T	315	$ .05	$ .25
Hrabosky, Al	77T	495	$ .05	$ .20
Hrabosky, Al	78T	230	$ .04	$ .16
Hrabosky, Al	79T	45	$ .03	$ .12
Hrabosky, Al	80T	585	$ .01	$ .10
Hrabosky, Al	81T	636	$ .01	$ .08
Hrabosky, Al	82T	393	$ .01	$ .08
Hrbek, Kent	82T	766	$ .90	$3.60
Hrbek, Kent	82TTR	44	$1.50	$6.00
Hrbek, Kent	83T	690	$ .10	$ .50
Hrbek, Kent	83T	771	$ .10	$ .40
Hrbek, Kent	84T	11	$ .01	$ .10
Hrbek, Kent	84T	345	$ .05	$ .25
Hrbek, Kent	85T	510	$ .05	$ .20
Hrbek, Kent	86T	430	$ .01	$ .15
Hrbek, Kent	87T	679	$ .01	$ .10
Hrbek, Kent	88T	45	$ .01	$ .10
Hrbek, Kent	89T	265	$ .01	$ .10
Hrbek, Kent	90T	125	$ .01	$ .03
Hrbek, Kent	91T	710	$ .01	$ .03
Hrbek, Kent	91TSC	248	$ .05	$ .25
Hrbek, Kent	92T	347	$ .01	$ .03
Hrbek, Kent	92TSC	235	$ .01	$ .10
Hrbek, Kent	93T	9	$ .01	$ .03
Hriniak, Walt	69T	611	$ .75	$3.00
Hriniak, Walt	70T	392	$ .35	$1.40
Hubbard, Glenn	79T	715	$ .05	$ .20
Hubbard, Glenn	81T	247	$ .01	$ .08
Hubbard, Glenn	82T	482	$ .01	$ .08
Hubbard, Glenn	83T	624	$ .01	$ .08
Hubbard, Glenn	84T	25	$ .01	$ .06
Hubbard, Glenn	85T	195	$ .01	$ .06
Hubbard, Glenn	86T	539	$ .01	$ .05
Hubbard, Glenn	87T	745	$ .01	$ .04
Hubbard, Glenn	88T	325	$ .01	$ .04
Hubbard, Glenn	88TTR	53	$ .01	$ .05
Hubbard, Glenn	89T	237	$ .01	$ .03
Hubbs, Ken	62T	461	$5.50	$22.00
Hubbs, Ken	63T	15	$ .90	$3.60
Hubbs, Ken	64T	550	$5.50	$22.00
Hudler, Rex	89T	346	$ .01	$ .03
Hudler, Rex	90T	647	$ .01	$ .03
Hudler, Rex	91T	228	$ .01	$ .03
Hudler, Rex	91TSC	280	$ .05	$ .25
Hudler, Rex	92T	47	$ .01	$ .03

TOPPS

Player	Year	No.	VG	EX/MT	Player	Year	No.	VG	EX/MT
Hudler, Rex	92TSC	851	$.01	$.10	Hundley, Randy	70T	265	$.35	$1.40
Hudler, Rex	93TSC	113	$.01	$.10	Hundley, Randy	71T	592	$1.00	$4.00
Hudson, Charles	85T	379	$.01	$.06	Hundley, Randy	72T	258	$.10	$.40
Hudson, Charles	86T	792	$.01	$.05	Hundley, Randy	73T	21	$.10	$.40
Hudson, Charles	87T	191	$.01	$.04	Hundley, Randy	74T	319	$.10	$.40
Hudson, Charles	87TTR	50	$.01	$.05	Hundley, Randy	74TTR	319	$.10	$.40
Hudson, Charles	88T	636	$.01	$.04	Hundley, Randy	76T	351	$.05	$.25
Hudson, Charles	89T	236	$.01	$.03	Hundley, Randy	77T	502	$.05	$.20
Hudson, Charlie	84T	432	$.01	$.10	Hundley, Todd	90TTR	44	$.05	$.35
Hudson, Jesse	70T	348	$.35	$1.40	Hundley, Todd	91T	457	$.01	$.10
Hudson, Sid	51Trb	44	$1.75	$7.50	Hundley, Todd	91TSC	349	$.05	$.25
Hudson, Sid	52T	60	$13.75	$55.00	Hundley, Todd	92T	673	$.01	$.03
Hudson, Sid	53T	251	$22.50	$90.00	Hundley, Todd	92TSC	290	$.01	$.10
Hudson, Sid	54T	93	$3.75	$15.00	Hundley, Todd	93T	380	$.01	$.03
Hudson, Sid	91TA53	251	$.01	$.15	Hundley, Todd	93TSC	72	$.01	$.10
Huff, Mike	92T	532	$.01	$.03	Hunt, Ken	60T	522	$2.75	$11.00
Huff, Mike	92TSC	329	$.01	$.10	Hunt, Ken	61T	156	$.60	$2.40
Huffman, Phil	80T	142	$.01	$.10	Hunt, Ken	61T	556	$7.50	$30.00
Huffman, Phil	81T	506	$.01	$.08	Hunt, Ken	62T	68	$.60	$2.40
Hughes, Dick	67T	384	$.60	$2.40	Hunt, Ken	62T	364	$.75	$3.00
Hughes, Dick	68T	253	$.35	$1.40	Hunt, Ken	63T	207	$.90	$3.60
Hughes, Dick	69T	39	$.35	$1.40	Hunt, Ken	64T	294	$.65	$2.60
Hughes, Jim	53T	216	$4.50	$18.00	Hunt, Randy	86T	218	$.01	$.05
Hughes, Jim	54T	169	$3.75	$15.00	Hunt, Ron	63T	558	$3.00	$12.00
Hughes, Jim	55T	51	$2.25	$9.00	Hunt, Ron	64T	235	$.65	$2.60
Hughes, Jim	76T	11	$.05	$.25	Hunt, Ron	65T	285	$.50	$2.00
Hughes, Jim	77T	304	$.05	$.20	Hunt, Ron	66T	360	$.50	$2.00
Hughes, Jim	78T	395	$.04	$.16	Hunt, Ron	67T	525	$1.50	$6.00
Hughes, Jim	91TA53	216	$.01	$.15	Hunt, Ron	68T	15	$.35	$1.40
Hughes, Keith	88T	781	$.01	$.04	Hunt, Ron	69T	664	$1.00	$4.00
Hughes, Terry	73T	603	$.75	$3.00	Hunt, Ron	70T	276	$.35	$1.40
Hughes, Terry	74T	604	$1.25	$5.00	Hunt, Ron	71T	578	$1.00	$4.00
Hughes, Terry	75T	612	$.10	$.40	Hunt, Ron	72T	110	$.10	$.40
Huismann, Mark	85T	644	$.01	$.06	Hunt, Ron	73T	149	$.10	$.40
Huismann, Mark	87T	187	$.01	$.04	Hunt, Ron	74T	275	$.10	$.40
Hulett, Tim	85TTR	60	$.01	$.10	Hunt, Ron	75T	610	$.10	$.40
Hulett, Tim	86T	724	$.01	$.05	Hunter, Billy	53T	166	$4.50	$18.00
Hulett, Tim	87T	566	$.01	$.04	Hunter, Billy	54T	48	$3.75	$15.00
Hulett, Tim	88T	158	$.01	$.04	Hunter, Gordon (Billy)	57T	207	$2.00	$8.00
Hulett, Tim	91T	468	$.01	$.03	Hunter, Billy	58T	98	$2.00	$8.00
Hulett, Tim	91TSC	517	$.05	$.25	Hunter, Billy	59T	11	$1.50	$6.00
Hulett, Tim	92TSC	104	$.01	$.10	Hunter, Billy	73T	136	$.25	$1.00
Hulett, Tim	93T	327	$.01	$.03	Hunter, Billy	74T	306	$.15	$.60
Hulett, Tim	93TSC	14	$.01	$.10	Hunter, Billy	78T	548	$.04	$.16
Hulse, David	93T	118	$.01	$.15	Hunter, Bill	91TA53	166	$.01	$.15
Hume, Tom	78T	701	$.04	$.16	Hunter, Brian	92T	611	$.01	$.10
Hume, Tom	79T	301	$.03	$.12	Hunter, Brian	92TSC	432	$.05	$.20
Hume, Tom	80T	149	$.01	$.10	Hunter, Brian	93T	102	$.01	$.03
Hume, Tom	81T	8	$.05	$.25	Hunter, Jim	65T	526	$35.00	$140.00
Hume, Tom	81T	419	$.01	$.08	Hunter, Jim	66T	36	$7.50	$30.00
Hume, Tom	82T	763	$.01	$.08	Hunter, Jim	67T	369	$5.00	$20.00
Hume, Tom	83T	86	$.01	$.08	Hunter, Jim	68T	385	$3.50	$14.00
Hume, Tom	84T	607	$.01	$.06	Hunter, Jim	69T	235	$3.00	$12.00
Hume, Tom	85T	223	$.01	$.06	Hunter, Jim	70T	565	$3.50	$14.00
Hume, Tom	86T	573	$.01	$.05	Hunter, Jim	71T	45	$1.50	$6.00
Hume, Tom	86TTR	47	$.01	$.06	Hunter, Jim	72T	330	$1.25	$5.00
Hume, Tom	87T	719	$.01	$.04	Hunter, Jim	73T	235	$1.00	$4.00
Humphrey, Terry	72T	489	$.25	$1.00	Hunter, Jim	73T	344	$.30	$1.20
Humphrey, Terry	73T	106	$.10	$.40	Hunter, Jim	74T	7	$1.00	$4.00
Humphrey, Terry	76T	552	$.05	$.25	Hunter, Jim	74TAS	339	$.25	$1.00
Humphrey, Terry	77T	369	$.05	$.20	Hunter, Jim	75T	230	$1.00	$4.00
Humphrey, Terry	78T	71	$.04	$.16	Hunter, Jim	75T	310	$.25	$1.00
Humphrey, Terry	79T	503	$.03	$.12	Hunter, Jim	75T	311	$.25	$1.00
Humphreys, Bob	65T	154	$.35	$1.40	Hunter, Jim	76T	100	$.75	$3.00
Humphreys, Bob	66T	342	$.50	$2.00	Hunter, Jim	76T	200	$.35	$1.40
Humphreys, Bob	67T	478	$1.50	$6.00	Hunter, Jim	76T	202	$1.00	$4.00
Humphreys, Bob	68T	268	$.35	$1.40	Hunter, Jim	77T	280	$.50	$2.00
Humphreys, Bob	69T	84	$.35	$1.40	Hunter, Jim	78T	460	$.50	$2.00
Humphreys, Bob	70T	538	$.35	$1.40	Hunter, Jim	79T	670	$.20	$.80
Humphreys, Bob	71T	236	$.25	$1.00	Huntz, Steve	69T	136	$.35	$1.40
Humphreys, Mike	92TSC	319	$.01	$.10	Huntz, Steve	70T	282	$.35	$1.40
Hundley, Randy	66T	392	$1.25	$5.00	Huntz, Steve	71T	486	$.50	$2.00
Hundley, Randy	67T	106	$.40	$1.60	Huntz, Steve	72T	73	$.10	$.40
Hundley, Randy	68T	136	$.35	$1.40	Hurd, Tom	55T	116	$2.25	$9.00
Hundley, Randy	69T	347	$.30	$1.20	Hurd, Tom	56T	256	$3.75	$15.00

TOPPS

Player	Year	No.	VG	EX/MT
Hurdle, Clint	78T	705	$.04	$.16
Hurdle, Clint	79T	547	$.03	$.12
Hurdle, Clint	80T	525	$.01	$.10
Hurdle, Clint	81T	98	$.01	$.08
Hurdle, Clint	82T	297	$.01	$.08
Hurdle, Clint	86T	438	$.01	$.05
Hurdle, Clint	87T	317	$.01	$.04
Hurst, Bruce	81T	689	$.20	$2.00
Hurst, Bruce	82T	381	$.10	$.50
Hurst, Bruce	83T	82	$.01	$.08
Hurst, Bruce	84T	213	$.01	$.06
Hurst, Bruce	85T	451	$.01	$.06
Hurst, Bruce	86T	581	$.01	$.05
Hurst, Bruce	87T	705	$.01	$.04
Hurst, Bruce	88T	125	$.01	$.04
Hurst, Bruce	89T	675	$.01	$.03
Hurst, Bruce	89TTR	55	$.01	$.05
Hurst, Bruce	90T	315	$.01	$.03
Hurst, Bruce	91T	65	$.01	$.03
Hurst, Bruce	91TSC	475	$.05	$.25
Hurst, Bruce	92T	595	$.01	$.03
Hurst, Bruce	92TSC	312	$.01	$.10
Hurst, Bruce	93T	111	$.01	$.03
Hurst, Jonathan	93T	727	$.01	$.15
Huson, Jeff	90T	72	$.01	$.10
Huson, Jeff	90TTR	45	$.01	$.05
Huson, Jeff	91T	756	$.01	$.03
Huson, Jeff	91TSC	160	$.05	$.25
Huson, Jeff	92T	314	$.01	$.03
Huson, Jeff	92TSC	341	$.01	$.10
Huson, Jeff	93T	143	$.01	$.03
Huson, Jeff	93TSC	281	$.01	$.10
Hutchins, Jason	93T	537	$.05	$.20
Hutchinson, Fred	52T	126	$8.00	$32.00
Hutchinson, Fred	53T	72	$8.75	$35.00
Hutchinson, Fred	60T	219	$.75	$3.00
Hutchinson, Fred	61T	135	$.60	$2.40
Hutchinson, Fred	62T	172	$.60	$2.40
Hutchinson, Fred	63T	422	$1.00	$4.00
Hutchinson, Fred	64T	207	$.65	$2.60
Hutchinson, Fred	91TA53	72	$.01	$.15
Hutton, Mark	93T	806	$.01	$.10
Hutton, Tom	67T	428	$.75	$3.00
Hutton, Tom	69T	266	$.50	$2.00
Hutton, Tom	72T	741	$2.50	$10.00
Hutton, Tom	73T	271	$.10	$.40
Hutton, Tom	74T	443	$.10	$.40
Hutton, Tom	75T	477	$.10	$.40
Hutton, Tom	76T	91	$.05	$.25
Hutton, Tom	77T	264	$.05	$.20
Hutton, Tom	78T	568	$.04	$.16
Hutton, Tom	79T	673	$.03	$.12
Hutton, Tom	80T	427	$.01	$.10
Hutton, Tom	81T	374	$.01	$.08
Hyde, Dick	57T	403	$1.75	$7.00
Hyde, Dick	58T	156	$1.25	$5.00
Hyde, Dick	59T	498	$1.00	$4.00
Hyde, Dick	60T	193	$.75	$3.00
Incaviglia, Pete	86TTR	48	$.05	$.25
Incaviglia, Pete	87T	550	$.01	$.15
Incaviglia, Pete	88T	280	$.01	$.04
Incaviglia, Pete	89T	706	$.01	$.03
Incaviglia, Pete	90T	430	$.01	$.03
Incaviglia, Pete	91T	172	$.01	$.03
Incaviglia, Pete	91TSC	78	$.05	$.25
Incaviglia, Pete	91TTR	57	$.01	$.05
Incaviglia, Pete	92T	679	$.01	$.03
Incaviglia, Pete	92TSC	874	$.01	$.10
Incaviglia, Pete	92TTR	54	$.01	$.05
Incaviglia, Pete	93T	7	$.01	$.03
Incaviglia, Pete	93TSC	47	$.01	$.10
Indians, Team	56T	85	$6.00	$24.00
Indians, Team	57T	275	$12.00	$48.00
Indians, Team	58T	158	$3.50	$14.00
Indians, Team	59T	476	$2.50	$10.00
Indians, Team	60T	174	$2.00	$8.00
Indians, Team	61T	467	$2.25	$9.00
Indians, Team	62T	537	$10.00	$40.00
Indians, Team	63T	451	$9.00	$36.00
Indians, Team	64T	172	$1.00	$4.00
Indians, Team	65T	481	$2.50	$10.00
Indians, Team	66T	303	$1.25	$5.00
Indians, Team	67T	544	$8.25	$33.00
Indians, Team	70T	637	$2.50	$10.00
Indians, Team	71T	584	$1.75	$7.00
Indians, Team	72T	547	$1.25	$5.00
Indians, Team	73T	629	$1.50	$6.00
Indians, Team	74T	541	$.25	$1.00
Indians, Team Checklist	75T	331	$.35	$1.40
Indians, Team Checklist	76T	477	$.30	$1.20
Indians, Team Checklist	77T	18	$.25	$1.00
Indians, Team Checklist	78T	689	$.20	$.80
Indians, Team Checklist	79T	96	$.15	$.60
Indians, Team Checklist	80T	451	$.10	$.50
Indians, Team Checklist	81T	665	$.05	$.25
Indians, Team Leaders	86T	336	$.01	$.05
Indians, Team Leaders	87T	11	$.01	$.04
Indians, Team Leaders	88T	789	$.01	$.10
Indians, Team Leaders	89T	141	$.01	$.03
Innis, Jeff	88TTR	54	$.01	$.10

Player	Year	No.	VG	EX/MT
Innis, Jeff	90T	557	$.01	$.10
Innis, Jeff	91T	443	$.01	$.03
Innis, Jeff	91TSC	547	$.05	$.25
Innis, Jeff	92T	139	$.01	$.03
Innis, Jeff	92TSC	863	$.01	$.10
Innis, Jeff	93T	297	$.01	$.03
Iorg, Dane	80T	139	$.01	$.10
Iorg, Dane	81T	334	$.01	$.08
Iorg, Dane	82T	86	$.01	$.08
Iorg, Dane	83T	788	$.01	$.08
Iorg, Dane	84T	416	$.01	$.06
Iorg, Dane	84TTR	54	$.01	$.15
Iorg, Dane	85T	671	$.01	$.06
Iorg, Dane	86T	269	$.01	$.05
Iorg, Dane	86TTR	49	$.01	$.06
Iorg, Dane	87T	690	$.01	$.04
Iorg, Garth	78T	704	$4.50	$18.00
Iorg, Garth	81T	444	$.01	$.08

TOPPS

Player	Year	No.	VG	EX/MT	Player	Year	No.	VG	EX/MT
Iorg, Garth	82T	518	$ .01	$ .08	Jackson, Darrin	89T	286	$ .01	$ .15
Iorg, Garth	83T	326	$ .01	$ .08	Jackson, Darrin	90T	624	$ .01	$ .03
Iorg, Garth	84T	39	$ .01	$ .06	Jackson, Darrin	91T	373	$ .01	$ .03
Iorg, Garth	85T	168	$ .01	$ .06	Jackson, Darrin	92T	88	$ .01	$ .03
Iorg, Garth	86T	694	$ .01	$ .05	Jackson, Darrin	92TSC	226	$ .01	$ .10
Iorg, Garth	87T	751	$ .01	$ .04	Jackson, Darrin	93T	761	$ .01	$ .03
Iorg, Garth	88T	273	$ .01	$ .04	Jackson, Darrin	93TSC	19	$ .01	$ .10
Ireland, Rich	93T	767	$ .01	$ .15	Jackson, Grant	66T	591	$11.25	$45.00
Ireland, Tim	81T	66	$ .01	$ .08	Jackson, Grant	67T	402	$ .60	$2.40
Irvin, Monte	51Trb	50	$10.00	$40.00	Jackson, Grant	68T	512	$ .75	$3.00
Irvin, Monte(y)	52T	26	$27.50	$110.00	Jackson, Grant	69T	174	$ .35	$1.40
Irvin, Monte	53T	62	$10.00	$40.00	Jackson, Grant	70T	6	$ .20	$ .80
Irvin, Monte	54T	3	$8.00	$32.00	Jackson, Grant	71T	392	$ .25	$1.00
Irvin, Monte	55T	100	$7.00	$28.00	Jackson, Grant	72T	212	$ .10	$ .40
Irvin, Monte	56T	194	$8.00	$32.00	Jackson, Grant	73T	396	$ .10	$ .40
Irvin, Monte	91TA53	62	$ .10	$ .50	Jackson, Grant	74T	68	$ .10	$ .40
Irvine, Daryl	91T	189	$ .01	$ .10	Jackson, Grant	75T	303	$ .10	$ .40
Irvine, Daryl	91TSC	122	$ .05	$ .25	Jackson, Grant	76T	233	$ .05	$ .25
Ivie, Mike	72T	457	$ .25	$1.00	Jackson, Grant	77T	49	$ .05	$ .20
Ivie, Mike	73T	613	$11.25	$45.00	Jackson, Grant	78T	661	$ .04	$ .16
Ivie, Mike	76T	134	$ .05	$ .25	Jackson, Grant	79T	117	$ .03	$ .12
Ivie, Mike	77T	325	$ .05	$ .20	Jackson, Grant	80T	426	$ .01	$ .10
Ivie, Mike	78T	445	$ .04	$ .16	Jackson, Grant	81T	518	$ .01	$ .08
Ivie, Mike	79T	538	$ .03	$ .12	Jackson, Grant	82T	779	$ .01	$ .08
Ivie, Mike	80T	62	$ .01	$ .10	Jackson, Grant	82TTR	46	$ .01	$ .10
Ivie, Mike	81T	236	$ .01	$ .08	Jackson, Jeff	90T	74	$ .01	$ .15
Ivie, Mike	81TTR	774	$ .01	$ .15	Jackson, Larry	56T	119	$3.50	$14.00
Ivie, Mike	82T	734	$ .01	$ .08	Jackson, Larry	57T	196	$2.00	$8.00
Ivie, Mike	82TTR	45	$ .01	$ .10	Jackson, Larry	58T	97	$2.00	$8.00
Ivie, Mike	83T	613	$ .01	$ .08	Jackson, Larry	59T	399	$1.00	$4.00
Jablonski, Ray	53T	189	$4.50	$18.00	Jackson, Larry	60T	492	$1.25	$5.00
Jablonski, Ray	54T	26	$3.75	$15.00	Jackson, Larry	61T	75	$ .75	$3.00
Jablonski, Ray	55T	56	$2.25	$9.00	Jackson, Larry	61T	535	$7.50	$30.00
Jablonski, Ray	56T	86	$2.00	$8.00	Jackson, Larry	62T	83	$ .60	$2.40
Jablonski, Ray	57T	218	$2.00	$8.00	Jackson, Larry	62T	306	$ .75	$3.00
Jablonski, Ray	58T	362	$1.00	$4.00	Jackson, Larry	63T	95	$ .50	$2.00
Jablonski, Ray	59T	342	$1.00	$4.00	Jackson, Larry	64T	444	$1.00	$4.00
Jablonski, Ray	91TA53	189	$ .01	$ .15	Jackson, Larry	65T	10	$ .75	$3.00
Jackson, Al	62T	464	$2.00	$8.00	Jackson, Larry	65T	420	$1.00	$4.00
Jackson, Al	63T	111	$ .50	$2.00	Jackson, Larry	66T	595	$3.75	$15.00
Jackson, Al	64T	494	$1.00	$4.00	Jackson, Larry	67T	229	$ .50	$2.00
Jackson, Al	65T	381	$1.00	$4.00	Jackson, Larry	68T	81	$ .35	$1.40
Jackson, Al	66T	206	$ .50	$2.00	Jackson, Lou	59T	130	$1.00	$4.00
Jackson, Al	67T	195	$ .40	$1.60	Jackson, Lou	64T	511	$1.00	$4.00
Jackson, Al	68T	503	$ .75	$3.00	Jackson, Mike	88T	651	$ .01	$ .10
Jackson, Al	69T	649	$ .40	$1.60	Jackson, Mike	89T	169	$ .01	$ .03
Jackson, Al	70T	443	$ .35	$1.40	Jackson, Mike	90T	761	$ .01	$ .03
Jackson, Bo	86TTR	50	$ .75	$3.00	Jackson, Mike	91T	534	$ .01	$ .03
Jackson, Bo	87T	170	$ .10	$1.00	Jackson, Mike	92T	411	$ .01	$ .03
Jackson, Bo	88T	750	$ .05	$ .25	Jackson, Mike	92TSC	653	$ .01	$ .10
Jackson, Bo	89T	540	$ .05	$ .20	Jackson, Mike	93T	283	$ .01	$ .03
Jackson, Bo	90T	300	$ .05	$ .20	Jackson, Randy	52T	322	$43.75	$175.00
Jackson, Bo	91T	600	$ .05	$ .20	Jackson, Randy	56T	223	$3.75	$15.00
Jackson, Bo	91TSC	224	$ .10	$1.00	Jackson, Randy	57T	190	$2.00	$8.00
Jackson, Bo	91TTR	58	$ .05	$ .20	Jackson, Randy	58T	301	$1.25	$5.00
Jackson, Bo	92T	290	$ .01	$ .15	Jackson, Randy	59T	394	$1.00	$4.00
Jackson, Bo	92TSC	654	$ .10	$ .40	Jackson, Reggie	69T	260	$175.00	$700.00
Jackson, Bo	93T	400	$ .01	$ .10	Jackson, Reggie	70T	64	$1.25	$5.00
Jackson, Chuck	88T	94	$ .01	$ .04	Jackson, Reggie	70T	66	$1.25	$5.00
Jackson, Danny	87TTR	51	$ .01	$ .10	Jackson, Reggie	70T	140	$50.00	$200.00
Jackson, Danny	88T	324	$ .01	$ .04	Jackson, Reggie	70TAS	459	$7.00	$28.00
Jackson, Danny	88TTR	55	$ .01	$ .10	Jackson, Reggie	71T	20	$35.00	140.00
Jackson, Danny	89T	730	$ .01	$ .03	Jackson, Reggie	72T	90	$ .50	$2.00
Jackson, Danny	89TAS	395	$ .01	$ .05	Jackson, Reggie	72T	435	$13.75	$55.00
Jackson, Danny	90T	445	$ .01	$ .03	Jackson, Reggie	72TIA	436	$6.75	$27.00
Jackson, Danny	91T	92	$ .01	$ .03	Jackson, Reggie	73T	255	$8.00	$32.00
Jackson, Danny	91TSC	433	$ .05	$ .25	Jackson, Reggie	74T	130	$9.00	$36.00
Jackson, Danny	91TTR	59	$ .01	$ .05	Jackson, Reggie	74T	202	$1.25	$5.00
Jackson, Danny	92T	619	$ .01	$ .03	Jackson, Reggie	74T	203	$1.25	$5.00
Jackson, Danny	92TSC	406	$ .01	$ .10	Jackson, Reggie	74TAS	338	$1.25	$5.00
Jackson, Darrell	79T	246	$ .03	$ .12	Jackson, Reggie	75T	211	$1.25	$5.00
Jackson, Darrell	80T	386	$ .01	$ .10	Jackson, Reggie	75T	300	$7.50	$30.00
Jackson, Darrell	81T	89	$ .01	$ .08	Jackson, Reggie	76T	194	$ .50	$2.00
Jackson, Darrell	82T	193	$ .01	$ .08	Jackson, Reggie	76T	500	$5.50	$22.00
Jackson, Darrin	88TTR	56	$ .10	$ .40	Jackson, Reggie	77T	10	$4.00	$16.00

TOPPS

Player	Year	No.	VG	EX/MT	Player	Year	No.	VG	EX/MT
Jackson, Reggie	78T	200	$3.50	$14.00	Jackson, Roy Lee	86T	634	$ .01	$ .05
Jackson, Reggie	78T	413	$ .75	$3.00	Jackson, Roy Lee	87T	138	$ .01	$ .04
Jackson, Reggie	78TRB	7	$1.25	$5.00	Jackson, Sonny	65T	16	$35.00	$140.00
Jackson, Reggie	79T	700	$ .90	$3.60	Jackson, Sonny	66T	244	$ .50	$2.00
Jackson, Reggie	80T	600	$2.00	$8.00	Jackson, Sonny	67T	415	$ .60	$2.40
Jackson, Reggie	81T	2	$ .10	$ .50	Jackson, Sonny	68T	187	$ .35	$1.40
Jackson, Reggie	81T	400	$ .90	$3.60	Jackson, Sonny	69T	53	$ .35	$1.40
Jackson, Reggie	82T	300	$ .75	$3.00	Jackson, Sonny	70T	413	$ .35	$1.40
Jackson, Reggie	82TAS	551	$ .15	$1.50	Jackson, Sonny	71T	587	$1.00	$4.00
Jackson, Reggie	82TSA	301	$ .15	$1.50	Jackson, Sonny	72T	318	$ .10	$ .40
Jackson, Reggie	82TTR	47	$3.00	$12.00	Jackson, Sonny	73T	403	$ .25	$1.00
Jackson, Reggie	83T	500	$ .20	$2.00	Jackson, Sonny	74T	591	$ .10	$ .40
Jackson, Reggie	83T	501	$ .10	$1.00	Jacobs, Forrest "Spook"	54T	129	$3.75	$15.00
Jackson, Reggie	83T	702	$ .05	$ .25	Jacobs, Spook	55T	61	$2.25	$9.00
Jackson, Reggie	83TAS	390	$ .10	$ .75	Jacobs, Spook	56T	151	$2.50	$10.00
					Jacobs, Tony	55T	183	$6.25	$25.00
					Jacoby, Brook	84TTR	55	$ .10	$ .50
					Jacoby, Brook	85T	327	$ .01	$ .10
					Jacoby, Brook	86T	116	$ .01	$ .05
					Jacoby, Brook	87T	405	$ .01	$ .04
					Jacoby, Brook	88T	555	$ .01	$ .04
					Jacoby, Brook	89T	739	$ .01	$ .03
					Jacoby, Brook	90T	208	$ .01	$ .03
					Jacoby, Brook	91T	47	$ .01	$ .03
					Jacoby, Brook	91TSC	286	$ .05	$ .25
					Jacoby, Brook	92T	606	$ .01	$ .03
					Jacoby, Brook	92TSC	828	$ .01	$ .10
					Jacoby, Brook	93T	303	$ .01	$ .03
					Jaeckel, Paul	65T	386	$1.00	$4.00
					Jaha, John	92T	126	$ .10	$1.00
					Jaha, John	93T	181	$ .01	$ .15
					James, Bob	84T	579	$ .01	$ .10
					James, Bob	85T	114	$ .01	$ .06
					James, Bob	85TTR	61	$ .01	$ .10
					James, Bob	86T	467	$ .01	$ .05
					James, Bob	87T	342	$ .01	$ .04
					James, Bob	88T	232	$ .01	$ .04
					James, Charley	60T	517	$2.75	$11.00
					James, Charley	61T	561	$7.50	$30.00
					James, Charlie	62T	412	$1.25	$5.00
					James, Charley	63T	83	$ .50	$2.00
					James, Charley	64T	357	$ .65	$2.60
					James, Charlie	65T	141	$ .35	$1.40
					James, Chris	87TTR	53	$ .01	$ .15
					James, Chris	88T	572	$ .01	$ .04
					James, Chris	89T	298	$ .01	$ .03
Jackson, Reggie	84T	100	$ .10	$1.00	James, Chris	89TTR	56	$ .01	$ .05
Jackson, Reggie	84T	711	$ .05	$ .20	James, Chris	90T	178	$ .01	$ .03
Jackson, Reggie	84T	712	$ .01	$ .15	James, Chris	90TTR	46	$ .01	$ .05
Jackson, Reggie	84T	713	$ .01	$ .15	James, Chris	91T	494	$ .01	$ .03
Jackson, Reggie	85T	200	$ .10	$ .75	James, Chris	91TSC	422	$ .05	$ .25
Jackson, Reggie	86T	700	$ .04	$ .50	James, Chris	92T	709	$ .01	$ .03
Jackson, Reggie	87T	300	$ .05	$ .25	James, Chris	92TSC	23	$ .01	$ .10
Jackson, Reggie	87TTB	312	$ .01	$ .10	James, Chris	92TSC	747	$ .01	$ .10
Jackson, Reggie	87TTR	52	$ .05	$ .35	James, Chris	93T	38	$ .01	$ .03
Jackson, Ron	55T	66	$2.25	$9.00	James, Cleo	72T	117	$ .10	$ .40
Jackson, Ron	56T	186	$3.75	$15.00	James, Dion	85T	228	$ .01	$ .06
Jackson, Ron	58T	26	$2.00	$8.00	James, Dion	86T	76	$ .01	$ .05
Jackson, Ron	59T	73	$1.50	$6.00	James, Dion	87TTR	54	$ .01	$ .10
Jackson, Ron	60T	426	$ .75	$3.00	James, Dion	88T	408	$ .01	$ .04
Jackson, Ron	77T	153	$ .05	$ .20	James, Dion	89T	678	$ .01	$ .03
Jackson, Ron	78T	718	$ .04	$ .16	James, Dion	90T	319	$ .01	$ .03
Jackson, Ron	79T	339	$ .03	$ .12	James, Dion	91T	117	$ .01	$ .03
Jackson, Ron	80T	18	$ .01	$ .10	James, Dion	92TSC	884	$ .01	$ .10
Jackson, Ron	81T	631	$ .01	$ .08	James, Dion	93TSC	266	$ .01	$ .10
Jackson, Ron	82T	488	$ .01	$ .08	James, Jeff	69T	477	$ .30	$1.20
Jackson, Ron	82TTR	48	$ .01	$ .10	James, Jeff	70T	302	$ .35	$1.40
Jackson, Ron	83T	262	$ .01	$ .08	James, Johnny	60T	499	$1.25	$5.00
Jackson, Ron	84T	548	$ .01	$ .06	James, Johnny	61T	457	$1.35	$5.40
Jackson, Roy Lee	81T	223	$ .01	$ .08	Janeski, Gerry	71T	673	$1.50	$6.00
Jackson, Roy Lee	81TTR	775	$ .01	$ .15	Janowicz, Vic	53T	222	$12.50	$50.00
Jackson, Roy Lee	82T	71	$ .01	$ .08	Janowicz, Vic	54T	16	$4.00	$16.00
Jackson, Roy Lee	83T	427	$ .01	$ .08	Janowicz, Vic	91TA53	222	$ .05	$ .25
Jackson, Roy Lee	84T	339	$ .01	$ .06	Jansen, Larry	51Trb	21	$1.75	$7.50
Jackson, Roy Lee	85T	516	$ .01	$ .06	Jansen, Larry	52T	5	$13.75	$55.00

TOPPS

Player	Year	No.	VG	EX/MT	Player	Year	No.	VG	EX/MT
Jansen, Larry	54T	200	$3.75	$15.00	Jefferson, Jesse	73T	604	$.75	$3.00
Jansen, Larry	73T	81	$.25	$1.00	Jefferson, Jesse	74T	509	$.10	$.40
Jarvis, Pat	67T	57	$.40	$1.60	Jefferson, Jesse	75T	539	$.10	$.40
Jarvis, Pat	68T	134	$.35	$1.40	Jefferson, Jesse	76T	47	$.05	$.25
Jarvis, Pat	69T	282	$.50	$2.00	Jefferson, Jesse	77T	326	$.05	$.20
Jarvis, Pat	70T	438	$.35	$1.40	Jefferson, Jesse	78T	144	$.04	$.16
Jarvis, Pat	71T	623	$1.00	$4.00	Jefferson, Jesse	79T	221	$.03	$.12
Jarvis, Pat	72T	675	$1.25	$5.00	Jefferson, Jesse	80T	467	$.01	$.10
Jarvis, Pat	73T	192	$.10	$.40	Jefferson, Jesse	82T	682	$.01	$.08
Jarvis, Ray	70T	361	$.35	$1.40	Jefferson, Reggie	91TTR	60	$.05	$.20
Jarvis, Ray	71T	526	$1.00	$4.00	Jefferson, Reggie	92T	93	$.01	$.15
Jaster, Larry	67T	356	$.60	$2.40	Jefferson, Reggie	92TSC	335	$.10	$.50
Jaster, Larry	68T	117	$.35	$1.40	Jefferson, Reggie	93T	496	$.01	$.10
Jaster, Larry	69T	496	$.30	$1.20	Jefferson, Stan	87TTR	55	$.01	$.05
Jaster, Larry	70T	124	$.20	$.80	Jefferson, Stan	88T	223	$.01	$.04
Jata, Paul	72T	257	$.10	$.40	Jefferson, Stan	89T	689	$.01	$.03
Javier, Manuel "Julian"	60T	133	$1.50	$6.00	Jeltz, Steve	85TTR	62	$.01	$.10
Javier, Julian	61T	148	$.60	$2.40	Jeltz, Steve	86T	453	$.01	$.05
Javier, Julian	62T	118	$.60	$2.40	Jeltz, Steve	87T	294	$.01	$.04
Javier, Julian	63T	226	$.90	$3.60	Jeltz, Steve	88T	126	$.01	$.04
Javier, Julian	64T	446	$1.00	$4.00	Jeltz, Steve	89T	707	$.01	$.03
Javier, Julian	65T	447	$1.25	$5.00	Jeltz, Steve	90T	607	$.01	$.03
Javier, Julian	66T	436	$.65	$2.60	Jeltz, Steve	91T	507	$.01	$.03
Javier, Julian	67T	226	$.50	$2.00	Jenkins, Ferguson	66T	254	$32.50	$130.00
Javier, Julian	68T	25	$.35	$1.40	Jenkins, Ferguson	67T	333	$8.00	$32.00
Javier, Julian	69T	497	$.30	$1.20	Jenkins, Ferguson	68T	9	$.75	$3.00
Javier, Julian	70T	415	$.35	$1.40	Jenkins, Ferguson	68T	11	$1.00	$4.00
Javier, Julian	71T	185	$.25	$1.00	Jenkins, Ferguson "Fergie"	68T	410	$4.50	$18.00
Javier, Julian	72T	745	$1.25	$5.00	Jenkins, Fergie	69T	12	$.75	$3.00
Javier, Stan	87T	263	$.01	$.04	Jenkins, Fergie	69T	640	$5.50	$22.00
Javier, Stan	89T	622	$.01	$.03	Jenkins, Fergie	70T	69	$1.50	$6.00
Javier, Stan	90T	102	$.01	$.03	Jenkins, Fergie	70T	71	$.75	$3.00
Javier, Stan	90TTR	47	$.01	$.05	Jenkins, Fergie	70T	240	$2.00	$8.00
Javier, Stan	91T	61	$.01	$.03	Jenkins, Fergie	71T	70	$.75	$3.00
Javier, Stan	91TSC	39	$.05	$.25	Jenkins, Fergie	71T	72	$1.00	$4.00
Javier, Stan	92T	581	$.01	$.03	Jenkins, Fergie	71T	280	$2.75	$11.00
Javier, Stan	92TSC	187	$.01	$.10	Jenkins, Fergie	72T	93	$.75	$3.00
Javier, Stan	93T	712	$.01	$.03	Jenkins, Fergie	72T	95	$.75	$3.00
Jay, Joe	54T	141	$4.50	$18.00	Jenkins, Fergie	72T	410	$1.75	$7.00
Jay, Joe	55T	134	$2.25	$9.00	Jenkins, Fergie	73T	180	$1.00	$4.00
Jay, Joe	58T	472	$1.00	$4.00					
Jay, Joe	59T	273	$1.00	$4.00					
Jay, Joe	60T	266	$.75	$3.00					
Jay, Joe	61T	233	$.60	$2.40					
Jay, Joe	62T	58	$1.50	$6.00					
Jay, Joe	62T	263	$.75	$3.00					
Jay, Joe	62T	440	$1.25	$5.00					
Jay, Joe	63T	7	$1.25	$5.00					
Jay, Joe	63T	225	$.90	$3.60					
Jay, Joe	64T	346	$.65	$2.60					
Jay, Joe	65T	174	$.35	$1.40					
Jay, Joe	66T	406	$.65	$2.60					
Jeffcoat, Hal	52T	341	$43.75	$175.00					
Jeffcoat, Hal	53T	29	$6.25	$25.00					
Jeffcoat, Hal	56T	289	$2.50	$10.00					
Jeffcoat, Hal	57T	93	$2.00	$8.00					
Jeffcoat, Hal	58T	294	$1.25	$5.00					
Jeffcoat, Hal	59T	81	$1.50	$6.00					
Jeffcoat, Hal	91TA53	29	$.01	$.15					
Jeffcoat, Mike	84TTR	56	$.01	$.15					
Jeffcoat, Mike	85T	303	$.01	$.06					
Jeffcoat, Mike	86T	571	$.01	$.05					
Jeffcoat, Mike	90T	778	$.01	$.03					
Jeffcoat, Mike	91T	244	$.01	$.03					
Jeffcoat, Mike	91TSC	216	$.05	$.25					
Jeffcoat, Mike	92T	464	$.01	$.03					
Jeffcoat, Mike	92TSC	265	$.01	$.10					
Jefferies, Gregg	89T	233	$.05	$.25					
Jefferies, Gregg	90T	457	$.01	$.10					
Jefferies, Gregg	91T	30	$.01	$.10					
Jefferies, Gregg	91TSC	257	$.10	$.75					
Jefferies, Gregg	92T	707	$.01	$.03					
Jefferies, Gregg	92TSC	737	$.01	$.10					
Jefferies, Gregg	92TTR	55	$.01	$.10	**Jenkins, Fergie**	**74T**	**87**	**$1.00**	**$4.00**
Jefferies, Gregg	93T	105	$.01	$.03	Jenkins, Fergie	75T	60	$1.00	$4.00

TOPPS

Player	Year	No.	VG	EX/MT
Jenkins, Fergie	75T	310	$ .25	$1.00
Jenkins, Fergie	76T	250	$ .75	$3.00
Jenkins, Fergie	76TTR	250	$ .50	$2.00
Jenkins, Fergie	77T	430	$ .50	$2.00
Jenkins, Fergie	78T	720	$ .50	$2.00
Jenkins, Fergie	79T	544	$ .35	$1.40
Jenkins, Fergie	80T	390	$ .15	$1.25
Jenkins, Fergie	81T	158	$ .10	$1.00
Jenkins, Fergie	82T	624	$ .10	$ .50
Jenkins, Fergie	82TTR	49	$ .20	$2.00
Jenkins, Fergie	83T	51	$ .01	$ .08
Jenkins, Fergie	83T	230	$ .10	$ .50
Jenkins, Fergie	83T	231	$ .05	$ .25
Jenkins, Fergie	84T	456	$ .01	$ .06
Jenkins, Fergie	84T	483	$ .05	$ .25
Jenkins, Fergie	84T	706	$ .05	$ .25
Jenkins, Jack	70T	286	$2.00	$8.00
Jennings, Doug	89T	166	$ .01	$ .03
Jensen, Jack	52T	122	$17.50	$70.00
Jensen, Jackie	53T	265	$28.75	$115.00
Jensen, Jackie	54T	80	$5.00	$20.00
Jensen, Jackie	55T	200	$12.50	$50.00
Jensen, Jackie	56T	115	$3.75	$15.00
Jensen, Jackie	57T	220	$2.50	$10.00
Jensen, Jackie	58T	130	$2.50	$10.00
Jensen, Jackie	58TAS	489	$1.00	$4.00
Jensen, Jackie	59T	400	$1.00	$4.00
Jensen, Jackie	61T	173	$ .75	$3.00
Jensen, Jackie	61T	540	$10.00	$40.00
Jensen, Jackie	61TMVP	476	$1.35	$5.40
Jensen, Jackie	75T	196	$ .30	$1.20
Jensen, Jackie	91TA53	265	$ .10	$ .50
Jernigan, Pete	63T	253	$ .90	$3.60
Jestadt, Garry	70T	109	$ .20	$ .80
Jestadt, Garry	71T	576	$1.00	$4.00
Jethroe, Sam	51Tbb	12	$7.50	$30.00
Jethroe, Sam	52T	27	$13.75	$55.00
Jimenez, E. Manny	62T	598	$17.50	$70.00
Jimenez, E. Manny	63T	195	$ .50	$2.00
Jimenez, E. Manny	64T	574	$2.25	$9.00
Jimenez, Elvio "Manny"	65T	226	$ .50	$2.00
Jimenez, E. Manny	66T	458	$1.50	$6.00
Jimenez, E. Manny	67T	586	$4.00	$16.00
Jimenez, E. Manny	68T	538	$ .70	$2.80
Jimenez, Elvio	69T	567	$ .40	$1.60
Jimenez, German	89T	569	$ .01	$ .03
Jimenez, Houston	84T	411	$ .01	$ .06
Jimenez, Houston	85T	562	$ .01	$ .06
John, Tommy	64T	146	$16.25	$65.00
John, Tommy	65T	208	$3.50	$14.00
John, Tommy	66T	486	$3.50	$14.00
John, Tommy	67T	609	$30.00	$120.00
John, Tommy	68T	72	$1.10	$4.40
John, Tommy	69T	465	$1.00	$4.00
John, Tommy	70T	180	$ .75	$3.00
John, Tommy	71T	520	$1.00	$4.00
John, Tommy	72T	264	$ .50	$2.00
John, Tommy	73T	258	$ .50	$2.00
John, Tommy	74T	451	$ .50	$2.00
John, Tommy	75T	47	$ .50	$2.00
John, Tommy	76T	416	$ .35	$1.40
John, Tommy	77T	128	$ .30	$1.20
John, Tommy	78T	375	$ .25	$1.00
John, Tommy	79T	255	$ .25	$1.00
John, Tommy	80T	690	$ .10	$ .50
John, Tommy	81T	550	$ .05	$ .35
John, Tommy	82T	75	$ .05	$ .25
John, Tommy	82T	486	$ .01	$ .15
John, Tommy	83T	735	$ .05	$ .20
John, Tommy	83T	736	$ .01	$ .10
John, Tommy	84T	415	$ .05	$ .20
John, Tommy	84T	715	$ .05	$ .20
John, Tommy	85T	179	$ .05	$ .20
John, Tommy	86T	240	$ .01	$ .10
John, Tommy	87T	236	$ .01	$ .10
John, Tommy	88T	611	$ .01	$ .10
John, Tommy	89T	359	$ .01	$ .03
Johnson, Alex	65T	352	$ .75	$3.00
Johnson, Alex	66T	104	$ .35	$1.40
Johnson, Alex	67T	108	$ .40	$1.60
Johnson, Alex	68T	441	$ .35	$1.40
Johnson, Alex	69T	280	$ .50	$2.00
Johnson, Alex	70T	115	$ .20	$ .80
Johnson, Alex	71T	61	$ .75	$3.00
Johnson, Alex	71T	590	$1.00	$4.00
Johnson, Alex	72T	215	$ .10	$ .40
Johnson, Alex	73T	425	$ .25	$1.00
Johnson, Alex	74T	107	$ .10	$ .40
Johnson, Alex	75T	534	$ .10	$ .40
Johnson, Alex	77T	637	$ .05	$ .20
Johnson, Bart	70T	669	$1.25	$5.00
Johnson, Bart	71T	156	$ .25	$1.00
Johnson, Bart	72T	126	$ .10	$ .40
Johnson, Bart	73T	506	$ .25	$1.00
Johnson, Bart	74T	147	$ .10	$ .40
Johnson, Bart	75T	446	$ .10	$ .40
Johnson, Bart	76T	513	$ .05	$ .25
Johnson, Bart	77T	177	$ .05	$ .20
Johnson, Ben	60T	528	$2.75	$11.00
Johnson, Billy	51Tbb	21	$7.50	$30.00
Johnson, Billy	52T	83	$7.00	$28.00
Johnson, Billy	53T	21	$6.25	$25.00
Johnson, Billy	91TA53	21	$ .01	$ .15
Johnson, Bob D.	71T	71	$ .50	$2.00
Johnson, Bob D.	71T	365	$ .25	$1.00
Johnson, Bob D.	72T	27	$ .10	$ .40
Johnson, Bob D.	73T	657	$ .60	$2.40
Johnson, Bob D.	74T	269	$ .10	$ .40
Johnson, Bob D.	74TTR	269	$ .10	$ .40
Johnson, Bob W.	62T	519	$1.50	$6.00

Jestadt, Garry	72T	143	$ .10	$ .40
Jeter, Derek	93T	98	$ .05	$ .25
Jeter, Johnny	70T	141	$ .25	$1.00
Jeter, Johnny	71T	47	$ .25	$1.00
Jeter, Johnny	72T	288	$ .10	$ .40
Jeter, Johnny	73T	423	$ .25	$1.00
Jeter, Johnny	74T	615	$ .10	$ .40
Jeter, Shawn	93T	800	$ .01	$ .03

TOPPS

Player	Year	No.	VG	EX/MT
Johnson, Bob W.	63T	504	$3.00	$12.00
Johnson, Bob W.	64T	304	$ .65	$2.60
Johnson, Bob W.	65T	363	$ .50	$2.00
Johnson, Bob W.	66T	148	$ .50	$2.00
Johnson, Bob W.	67T	38	$ .40	$1.60
Johnson, Bob W.	68T	338	$ .35	$1.40
Johnson, Bob W.	69T	261	$ .50	$2.00
Johnson, Bob W.	70T	693	$1.25	$5.00
Johnson, Bob W.	70T	702	$1.25	$5.00
Johnson, Bobby	82T	418	$ .01	$ .15
Johnson, Bobby	83TTR	48	$ .01	$ .10
Johnson, Bobby	84T	608	$ .01	$ .06
Johnson, Charles	91TTR	61	$ .10	$ .50
Johnson, Charles	92TTR	56	$ .10	$ .50
Johnson, Cliff	75T	143	$ .10	$ .40
Johnson, Cliff	76T	249	$ .05	$ .25
Johnson, Cliff	77T	514	$ .05	$ .20
Johnson, Cliff	78T	309	$ .04	$ .16
Johnson, Cliff	79T	114	$ .03	$ .12
Johnson, Cliff	80T	612	$ .01	$ .10
Johnson, Cliff	81T	17	$ .01	$ .08
Johnson, Cliff	81TTR	776	$ .01	$ .15
Johnson, Cliff	82T	422	$ .01	$ .08
Johnson, Cliff	83T	762	$ .01	$ .08
Johnson, Cliff	83TTR	49	$ .01	$ .10
Johnson, Cliff	84T	221	$ .01	$ .06
Johnson, Cliff	85T	568	$ .01	$ .06

Player	Year	No.	VG	EX/MT
Johnson, Cliff	85TRB	4	$ .01	$ .06
Johnson, Cliff	85TTR	63	$ .01	$ .10
Johnson, Cliff	86T	348	$ .01	$ .05
Johnson, Cliff	87T	663	$ .01	$ .04
Johnson, Connie	56T	326	$2.50	$10.00
Johnson, Connie	57T	43	$2.00	$8.00
Johnson, Connie	58T	266	$1.25	$5.00
Johnson, Connie	59T	21	$1.50	$6.00
Johnson, Darrell	57T	306	$5.00	$20.00
Johnson, Darrell	58T	61	$2.00	$8.00
Johnson, Darrell	59T	533	$4.00	$16.00
Johnson, Darrell	60T	263	$ .75	$3.00
Johnson, Darrell	62T	16	$ .60	$2.40
Johnson, Darrell	74T	403	$ .10	$ .40
Johnson, Darrell	78T	79	$ .04	$ .16
Johnson, Darrell	83T	37	$ .01	$ .08

Player	Year	No.	VG	EX/MT
Johnson, Dave	65T	473	$2.50	$10.00
Johnson, Dave	66T	579	$4.50	$18.00
Johnson, Dave	67T	363	$ .60	$2.40
Johnson, Dave	68T	273	$ .35	$1.40
Johnson, Dave	69T	203	$ .75	$3.00
Johnson, Dave	70T	45	$ .35	$1.40
Johnson, Dave	71T	595	$1.00	$4.00
Johnson, Dave	72T	680	$1.25	$5.00
Johnson, Dave	73T	550	$ .75	$3.00
Johnson, Dave	74T	45	$ .25	$1.00
Johnson, Dave	75T	57	$ .25	$1.00
Johnson, Dave	77T	478	$ .05	$ .20
Johnson, Dave	78T	317	$ .05	$ .20
Johnson, Dave	78T	627	$ .04	$ .16
Johnson, Dave	79T	513	$ .05	$ .20
Johnson, Dave	84TTR	57	$ .01	$ .15
Johnson, Dave	85T	492	$ .01	$ .06
Johnson, Dave	86T	501	$ .01	$ .05
Johnson, Dave	87T	543	$ .01	$ .04
Johnson, Dave	88T	164	$ .01	$ .04
Johnson, Dave	89T	684	$ .01	$ .03
Johnson, Dave	90T	291	$ .01	$ .03
Johnson, Dave	90T	416	$ .01	$ .03
Johnson, Dave	91T	163	$ .01	$ .03
Johnson, Dave	91TSC	117	$ .05	$ .25
Johnson, Dave	92T	657	$ .01	$ .03
Johnson, Deron	59T	131	$1.75	$7.00
Johnson, Deron	60T	134	$ .75	$3.00
Johnson, Deron	61T	68	$ .60	$2.40
Johnson, Deron	62T	82	$ .60	$2.40
Johnson, Deron	64T	449	$1.00	$4.00
Johnson, Deron	65T	75	$ .35	$1.40
Johnson, Deron	66T	219	$1.75	$7.00
Johnson, Deron	66T	440	$ .65	$2.60
Johnson, Deron	67T	135	$ .40	$1.60
Johnson, Deron	68T	323	$ .35	$1.40
Johnson, Deron	69T	297	$ .50	$2.00
Johnson, Deron	70T	125	$ .20	$ .80
Johnson, Deron	71T	490	$ .50	$2.00
Johnson, Deron	72T	167	$ .10	$ .40
Johnson, Deron	72TIA	168	$ .10	$ .40
Johnson, Deron	73T	590	$ .60	$2.40
Johnson, Deron	74T	312	$ .10	$ .40
Johnson, Deron	76T	529	$ .05	$ .25
Johnson, Don	52T	190	$7.00	$28.00
Johnson, Don	54T	146	$3.75	$15.00
Johnson, Don	55T	165	$6.25	$25.00
Johnson, Ernie	56T	294	$2.50	$10.00
Johnson, Ernie	57T	333	$5.00	$20.00
Johnson, Ernie	58T	78	$2.00	$8.00
Johnson, Ernie	59T	279	$1.00	$4.00
Johnson, Ernie	60T	228	$ .75	$3.00
Johnson, Frank	69T	227	$ .50	$2.00
Johnson, Frank	71T	128	$ .25	$1.00
Johnson, Howard	85T	192	$ .20	$2.00
Johnson, Howard	85TTR	64	$ .20	$2.00
Johnson, Howard	86T	751	$ .10	$ .40
Johnson, Howard	87T	267	$ .05	$ .20
Johnson, Howard	88T	85	$ .01	$ .15
Johnson, Howard	89T	383	$ .01	$ .10
Johnson, Howard	90T	680	$ .01	$ .10
Johnson, Howard	90TAS	399	$ .01	$ .10
Johnson, Howard	91T	470	$ .01	$ .10
Johnson, Howard	91TSC	86	$ .10	$ .50
Johnson, Howard	92T	590	$ .01	$ .03
Johnson, Howard	92TAS	388	$ .01	$ .03
Johnson, Howard	92TSC	430	$ .01	$ .10
Johnson, Howard	92TSC	610	$ .01	$ .10
Johnson, Howard	93T	106	$ .01	$ .03
Johnson, Jeff	91TTR	62	$ .01	$ .15
Johnson, Jeff	92T	449	$ .01	$ .10
Johnson, Jeff	92TSC	471	$ .01	$ .10
Johnson, Jerry	69T	253	$ .50	$2.00
Johnson, Jerry	70T	162	$ .20	$ .80
Johnson, Jerry	71T	412	$ .50	$2.00

TOPPS

Player	Year	No.	VG	EX/MT	Player	Year	No.	VG	EX/MT
Johnson, Jerry	72T	35	$ .10	$ .40	Johnson, Wallace	88T	228	$ .01	$ .04
Johnson, Jerry	72TIA	36	$ .10	$ .40	Johnson, Wallace	89T	138	$ .01	$ .03
Johnson, Jerry	73T	248	$ .10	$ .40	Johnson, Wallace	90T	318	$ .01	$ .03
Johnson, Jerry	75T	218	$ .10	$ .40	Johnson, Walter	61T	409	$2.25	$9.00
Johnson, Jerry	76T	658	$ .05	$ .25	Johnson, Walter	73TATL	476	$ .50	$2.00
Johnson, Jerry	78T	169	$ .04	$ .16	Johnson, Walter	73TATL	478	$ .50	$2.00
Johnson, Joe	87TTR	56	$ .01	$ .05	Johnson, Walter	76TAT	349	$ .75	$3.00
Johnson, Joe	88T	347	$ .01	$ .04	Johnson, Walter	79TRH	417	$ .50	$2.00
Johnson, John Henry	79T	681	$ .03	$ .12	Johnson, Walter	79TRH	418	$ .03	$ .12
Johnson, John Henry	80T	173	$ .01	$ .10	Johnston, Greg	79T	726	$ .05	$ .20
Johnson, John Henry	81T	216	$ .01	$ .08	Johnston, Greg	80T	686	$ .01	$ .10
Johnson, John Henry	82T	527	$ .01	$ .08	Johnston, Greg	81T	328	$ .01	$ .08
Johnson, John Henry	84T	419	$ .01	$ .06	Johnston, Joel	92T	328	$ .01	$ .10
Johnson, John Henry	85T	734	$ .01	$ .06	Johnston, Joel	92TSC	345	$ .01	$ .10
Johnson, John Henry	87T	377	$ .01	$ .04	Johnstone, Jay	67T	213	$ .75	$3.00
Johnson, Ken	60T	135	$ .75	$3.00	Johnstone, Jay	68T	389	$ .35	$1.40
Johnson, Ken	61T	24	$ .60	$2.40	Johnstone, Jay	69T	59	$ .35	$1.40
Johnson, Ken	62T	278	$ .75	$3.00	Johnstone, Jay	70T	485	$ .35	$1.40
Johnson, Ken	63T	352	$ .90	$3.60	Johnstone, Jay	71T	292	$ .25	$1.00
Johnson, Ken	64T	158	$ .50	$2.00	Johnstone, Jay	72T	233	$ .10	$ .40
Johnson, Ken	65T	359	$ .50	$2.00	Johnstone, Jay	75T	242	$ .10	$ .40
Johnson, Ken	66T	466	$1.50	$6.00	Johnstone, Jay	76T	114	$ .05	$ .25
Johnson, Ken	67T	101	$ .40	$1.60	Johnstone, Jay	77T	415	$ .05	$ .20
Johnson, Ken	68T	342	$ .35	$1.40	Johnstone, Jay	78T	675	$ .04	$ .16
Johnson, Ken	69T	238	$ .50	$2.00	Johnstone, Jay	79T	558	$ .03	$ .12
Johnson, Lamar	76T	596	$ .15	$ .60	Johnstone, Jay	80T	31	$ .01	$ .10
Johnson, Lamar	77T	443	$ .05	$ .20	Johnstone, Jay	81T	372	$ .01	$ .08
Johnson, Lamar	78T	693	$ .04	$ .16	Johnstone, Jay	82T	774	$ .01	$ .08
Johnson, Lamar	79T	372	$ .03	$ .12	Johnstone, Jay	82TTR	52	$ .01	$ .10
Johnson, Lamar	80T	242	$ .01	$ .10	Johnstone, Jay	83T	152	$ .01	$ .08
Johnson, Lamar	81T	589	$ .01	$ .08	Johnstone, Jay	84T	249	$ .01	$ .06
Johnson, Lamar	82T	13	$ .01	$ .08	Johnstone, Jay	86T	496	$ .01	$ .05
Johnson, Lamar	82TTR	50	$ .01	$ .10	Johnstone, John	93T	454	$ .01	$ .15
Johnson, Lamar	83T	453	$ .01	$ .08	Jok, Stan	54T	196	$3.75	$15.00
Johnson, Lance	89T	122	$ .01	$ .03	Jolly, Dave	54T	188	$3.75	$15.00
Johnson, Lance	90T	587	$ .01	$ .03	Jolly, Dave	55T	35	$2.25	$9.00
Johnson, Lance	91T	243	$ .01	$ .03	Jolly, Dave	57T	389	$1.75	$7.00
Johnson, Lance	91TSC	199	$ .05	$ .25	Jolly, Dave	58T	183	$1.25	$5.00
Johnson, Lance	92T	736	$ .01	$ .03	Jones, Al	85T	437	$ .01	$ .06
Johnson, Lance	92TSC	444	$ .01	$ .10	Jones, Al	86T	227	$ .01	$ .05
Johnson, Lance	93T	94	$ .01	$ .03	Jones, Barry	87T	494	$ .01	$ .04
Johnson, Lou	60T	476	$1.25	$5.00	Jones, Barry	88T	168	$ .01	$ .04
Johnson, Lou	63T	238	$ .90	$3.60	Jones, Barry	89T	539	$ .01	$ .03
Johnson, Lou	66T	13	$ .35	$1.40	Jones, Barry	90T	243	$ .01	$ .03
Johnson, Lou	67T	410	$ .60	$2.40	Jones, Barry	91T	33	$ .01	$ .03
Johnson, Lou	68T	184	$ .35	$1.40	Jones, Barry	91TSC	551	$ .05	$ .25
Johnson, Lou	69T	367	$ .30	$1.20	Jones, Barry	91TTR	64	$ .01	$ .05
Johnson, Owen	66T	356	$ .50	$2.00	Jones, Barry	92T	361	$ .01	$ .03
Johnson, Randy	89TTR	647	$ .05	$ .35	Jones, Barry	92TSC	671	$ .01	$ .10
Johnson, Randy	89TTR	57	$ .01	$ .15	Jones, Bob	77T	16	$ .05	$ .20
Johnson, Randy	90T	431	$ .01	$ .03	Jones, Bob	84T	451	$ .01	$ .06
Johnson, Randy	91T	225	$ .01	$ .03	Jones, Bob	85T	648	$ .01	$ .06
Johnson, Randy	91TSC	409	$ .05	$ .25	Jones, Bob	86T	142	$ .01	$ .05
Johnson, Randy	92T	525	$ .01	$ .03	Jones, Bobby	93T	817	$ .05	$ .25
Johnson, Randy	92TSC	720	$ .01	$ .10	Jones, Calvin	92TSC	127	$ .05	$ .35
Johnson, Randy	93T	460	$ .01	$ .03	Jones, Calvin	93T	664	$ .01	$ .03
Johnson, Randy G.	83T	596	$ .01	$ .08	Jones, Chipper	91T	333	$ .10	$1.00
Johnson, Randy G.	84T	289	$ .01	$ .06	Jones, Chipper	92T	551	$ .10	$ .50
Johnson, Randy G.	85T	458	$ .01	$ .06	Jones, Chipper	93T	529	$ .10	$ .50
Johnson, Randy S.	82TTR	51	$ .01	$ .10	Jones, Chris	91TTR	65	$ .01	$ .10
Johnson, Randy S.	83T	354	$ .01	$ .08	Jones, Chris	92T	332	$ .01	$ .03
Johnson, Tim	74T	554	$ .10	$ .40	Jones, Chris	92TSC	698	$ .01	$ .10
Johnson, Tim	75T	556	$ .10	$ .40	Jones, Clarence	68T	506	$1.00	$4.00
Johnson, Tim	76T	613	$ .05	$ .25	Jones, Cleon	65T	308	$1.50	$6.00
Johnson, Tim	77T	406	$ .05	$ .20	Jones, Cleon	66T	67	$ .35	$1.40
Johnson, Tim	78T	542	$ .04	$ .16	Jones, Cleon	67T	165	$ .40	$1.60
Johnson, Tim	79T	182	$ .03	$ .12	Jones, Cleon	68T	254	$ .35	$1.40
Johnson, Tim	80T	297	$ .01	$ .10	Jones, Cleon	69T	512	$ .30	$1.20
Johnson, Todd	91TTR	63	$ .05	$ .25	Jones, Cleon	70T	61	$1.25	$5.00
Johnson, Tom	75T	618	$ .25	$1.00	Jones, Cleon	70T	575	$ .50	$2.00
Johnson, Tom	76T	448	$ .05	$ .25	Jones, Cleon	71T	527	$1.00	$4.00
Johnson, Tom	77T	202	$ .05	$ .20	Jones, Cleon	72T	31	$ .10	$ .40
Johnson, Tom	78T	54	$ .04	$ .16	Jones, Cleon	72TIA	32	$ .10	$ .40
Johnson, Tom	79T	162	$ .03	$ .12	Jones, Cleon	73T	540	$ .60	$2.40
Johnson, Wallace	87T	588	$ .01	$ .04	Jones, Cleon	74T	245	$ .10	$ .40

TOPPS

Player	Year	No.	VG	EX/MT
Jones, Cleon	75T	43	$ .10	$ .40
Jones, Dalton	64T	459	$1.00	$4.00
Jones, Dalton	65T	178	$ .35	$1.40
Jones, Dalton	66T	317	$ .50	$2.00
Jones, Dalton	67T	139	$ .40	$1.60
Jones, Dalton	68T	106	$ .35	$1.40
Jones, Dalton	69T	457	$ .30	$1.20
Jones, Dalton	70T	682	$1.25	$5.00
Jones, Dalton	71T	367	$ .25	$1.00
Jones, Dalton	72T	83	$ .10	$ .40
Jones, Dalton	73T	512	$ .25	$1.00
Jones, Darryl	80T	670	$ .01	$ .10
Jones, Deacon	63T	253	$ .90	$3.60
Jones, Doug	88T	293	$ .05	$ .20
Jones, Doug	89T	690	$ .01	$ .06
Jones, Doug	89TRB	6	$ .01	$ .05
Jones, Doug	90T	75	$ .01	$ .03
Jones, Doug	91T	745	$ .01	$ .03
Jones, Doug	91TSC	145	$ .05	$ .25
Jones, Doug	92T	461	$ .01	$ .03
Jones, Doug	92TSC	616	$ .01	$ .10
Jones, Doug	92TTR	57	$ .01	$ .05
Jones, Doug	93T	171	$ .01	$ .03
Jones, Gary	71T	559	$1.00	$4.00
Jones, Gordon	55T	78	$2.25	$9.00
Jones, Gordon	59T	458	$1.00	$4.00
Jones, Gordon	60T	98	$ .85	$3.40
Jones, Gordon	61T	442	$1.00	$4.00
Jones, Hal	62T	49	$ .60	$2.40
Jones, Jeff	81T	687	$ .01	$ .08
Jones, Jeff	82T	139	$ .01	$ .08
Jones, Jeff	83T	259	$ .01	$ .08

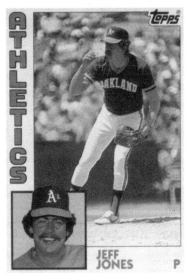

Jones, Jeff	84T	464	$ .01	$ .06
Jones, Jeff	85T	319	$ .01	$ .06
Jones, Jimmy	88T	63	$ .01	$ .04
Jones, Jimmy	89T	748	$ .01	$ .03
Jones, Jimmy	89TTR	58	$ .01	$ .05
Jones, Jimmy	90T	359	$ .01	$ .03
Jones, Jimmy	92T	184	$ .01	$ .03
Jones, Jimmy	92TSC	53	$ .01	$ .10
Jones, Jimmy	93T	477	$ .01	$ .03
Jones, Lynn	80T	123	$ .01	$ .15
Jones, Lynn	81T	337	$ .01	$ .08

Player	Year	No.	VG	EX/MT
Jones, Lynn	82T	64	$ .01	$ .08
Jones, Lynn	83T	483	$ .01	$ .08
Jones, Lynn	84T	731	$ .01	$ .06
Jones, Lynn	84TTR	58	$ .01	$ .15
Jones, Lynn	85T	513	$ .01	$ .06
Jones, Lynn	86T	671	$ .01	$ .05
Jones, Mack	62T	186	$ .60	$2.40
Jones, Mack	63T	137	$ .50	$2.00
Jones, Mack	65T	241	$ .50	$2.00
Jones, Mack	66T	446	$ .65	$2.60
Jones, Mack	67T	435	$ .60	$2.40
Jones, Mack	68T	353	$ .35	$1.40
Jones, Mack	69T	625	$ .40	$1.60
Jones, Mack	70T	38	$ .20	$ .80
Jones, Mack	71T	142	$ .25	$1.00
Jones, Mike	81T	66	$ .01	$ .08
Jones, Mike	82T	471	$ .05	$ .20
Jones, Mike	85T	244	$ .01	$ .06
Jones, Mike	86T	514	$ .01	$ .05
Jones, Nippy	52T	213	$7.00	$28.00
Jones, Odell	78T	407	$ .04	$ .16
Jones, Odell	80T	342	$ .01	$ .10
Jones, Odell	83TTR	50	$ .01	$ .10
Jones, Odell	84T	734	$ .01	$ .06
Jones, Odell	85T	29	$ .01	$ .06
Jones, Randy	74T	173	$ .10	$ .40
Jones, Randy	75T	248	$ .10	$ .40
Jones, Randy	76T	199	$ .25	$1.00
Jones, Randy	76T	201	$ .25	$1.00
Jones, Randy	76T	310	$ .05	$ .25
Jones, Randy	77T	5	$ .15	$ .60
Jones, Randy	77T	550	$ .05	$ .20
Jones, Randy	78T	56	$ .04	$ .16
Jones, Randy	79T	194	$ .03	$ .12
Jones, Randy	80T	305	$ .01	$ .10
Jones, Randy	81T	458	$ .01	$ .08
Jones, Randy	81TTR	777	$ .01	$ .15
Jones, Randy	82T	626	$ .01	$ .08
Jones, Randy	83T	29	$ .01	$ .08
Jones, Rick	77T	118	$ .05	$ .20
Jones, Ron	89T	349	$ .01	$ .10
Jones, Ron	90T	129	$ .01	$ .03
Jones, Ross	88T	169	$ .01	$ .04
Jones, Ruppert	77T	488	$2.50	$10.00
Jones, Ruppert	78T	141	$ .04	$ .16
Jones, Ruppert	79T	422	$ .03	$ .12
Jones, Ruppert	80T	78	$ .01	$ .10
Jones, Ruppert	81T	225	$ .01	$ .08
Jones, Ruppert	81TTR	778	$ .01	$ .15
Jones, Ruppert	82T	511	$ .01	$ .08
Jones, Ruppert	83T	695	$ .01	$ .08
Jones, Ruppert	84T	327	$ .01	$ .06
Jones, Ruppert	84TTR	59	$ .01	$ .15
Jones, Ruppert	85T	126	$ .01	$ .06
Jones, Ruppert	85TTR	65	$ .01	$ .10
Jones, Ruppert	86T	464	$ .01	$ .05
Jones, Ruppert	87T	53	$ .01	$ .04
Jones, Sam	52T	382	$50.00	$200.00
Jones, Sam	53T	6	$6.25	$25.00
Jones, Sam	56T	259	$3.75	$15.00
Jones, Sam	57T	287	$5.00	$20.00
Jones, Sam	58T	287	$1.25	$5.00
Jones, Sam	59T	75	$1.50	$6.00
Jones, Sam	60T	410	$ .75	$3.00
Jones, Sam	61T	49	$2.00	$8.00
Jones, Sam	61T	555	$7.50	$30.00
Jones, Sam	62T	92	$ .60	$2.40
Jones, Sam	91TA53	6	$ .01	$ .15
Jones, Sheldon	52T	130	$7.00	$28.00
Jones, Sherman	61T	161	$ .60	$2.40
Jones, Steve	69T	49	$ .35	$1.40
Jones, Tim	78T	703	$3.50	$14.00
Jones, Tim	90T	533	$ .01	$ .03
Jones, Tim	91T	262	$ .01	$ .03
Jones, Tim	91TSC	121	$ .05	$ .25

TOPPS

Player	Year	No.	VG	EX/MT
Jones, Tim	92TSC	206	$ .01	$ .10
Jones, Tim	93TSC	280	$ .01	$ .10
Jones, Tracy	87T	146	$ .01	$ .04
Jones, Tracy	88T	553	$ .01	$ .04
Jones, Tracy	89T	373	$ .01	$ .03
Jones, Tracy	90T	767	$ .01	$ .03
Jones, Tracy	91T	87	$ .01	$ .03
Jones, Tracy	91TSC	446	$ .05	$ .25
Jones, Tracy	92T	271	$ .01	$ .03
Jones, Willie	51Tbb	43	$7.50	$30.00
Jones, Willie	52T	47	$13.75	$55.00
Jones, Willie	53T	88	$4.00	$16.00
Jones, Willie	54T	41	$3.75	$15.00
Jones, Willie	56T	127	$2.50	$10.00
Jones, Willie	57T	174	$2.00	$8.00
Jones, Willie	58T	181	$1.25	$5.00
Jones, Willie	59T	208	$1.00	$4.00
Jones, Willie	60T	289	$ .75	$3.00
Jones, Willie	61T	497	$1.35	$5.40
Jones, Willie	91TA53	88	$ .01	$ .15
Joost, Eddie	51Tbb	15	$7.50	$30.00
Joost, Eddie	52T	45	$13.75	$55.00
Jordan, Brian	92TTR	58	$ .05	$ .25
Jordan, Brian	93T	754	$ .01	$ .15
Jordan, Ricky	89T	358	$ .01	$ .10
Jordan, Ricky	90T	216	$ .01	$ .10
Jordan, Ricky	91T	712	$ .01	$ .03
Jordan, Ricky	91TSC	192	$ .05	$ .25
Jordan, Ricky	92T	103	$ .01	$ .03
Jordan, Ricky	92TSC	188	$ .01	$ .10
Jordan, Ricky	93T	585	$ .01	$ .03
Jordan, Ricky	93TSC	229	$ .01	$ .10
Jorgensen, Mike	70T	348	$ .35	$1.40
Jorgensen, Mike	71T	596	$1.00	$4.00
Jorgensen, Mike	72T	16	$ .10	$ .40
Jorgensen, Mike	73T	281	$ .10	$ .40
Jorgensen, Mike	74T	549	$ .10	$ .40
Jorgensen, Mike	75T	286	$ .10	$ .40
Jorgensen, Mike	76T	117	$ .05	$ .25
Jorgensen, Mike	77T	368	$ .05	$ .20
Jorgensen, Mike	78T	406	$ .04	$ .16
Jorgensen, Mike	79T	22	$ .03	$ .12
Jorgensen, Mike	80T	213	$ .01	$ .10
Jorgensen, Mike	81T	698	$ .01	$ .08
Jorgensen, Mike	82T	566	$ .01	$ .08
Jorgensen, Mike	83T	107	$ .01	$ .08
Jorgensen, Mike	83TTR	51	$ .01	$ .10
Jorgensen, Mike	84T	313	$ .01	$ .06
Jorgensen, Mike	84TTR	60	$ .01	$ .15
Jorgensen, Mike	85T	783	$ .01	$ .06
Jorgensen, Mike	86T	422	$ .01	$ .05
Jorgensen, Terry	93T	805	$ .01	$ .03
Jose, Felix	90T	238	$ .05	$ .20
Jose, Felix	91T	368	$ .01	$ .10
Jose, Felix	91TSC	366	$ .10	$ .75
Jose, Felix	92T	105	$ .01	$ .10
Jose, Felix	92TSC	407	$ .01	$ .15
Jose, Felix	93T	67	$ .01	$ .03
Joseph, Ricardo	68T	434	$ .35	$1.40
Joseph, Rick	69T	329	$ .30	$1.20
Joseph, Rick	70T	186	$ .20	$ .80
Josephson, Duane	67T	373	$ .60	$2.40
Josephson, Duane	68T	329	$ .35	$1.40
Josephson, Duane	69T	222	$ .50	$2.00
Josephson, Duane	70T	263	$ .20	$ .80
Josephson, Duane	71T	56	$ .25	$1.00
Josephson, Duane	72T	543	$ .40	$1.60
Joshua, Von	71T	57	$ .25	$1.00
Joshua, Von	73T	544	$ .60	$2.40
Joshua, Von	74T	551	$ .10	$ .40
Joshua, Von	75T	547	$ .10	$ .40
Joshua, Von	76T	82	$ .05	$ .25
Joshua, Von	77T	651	$ .05	$ .20
Joshua, Von	78T	108	$ .04	$ .16
Joshua, Von	80T	209	$ .01	$ .10
Joyce, Mike	63T	66	$ .50	$2.00
Joyce, Mike	64T	477	$1.00	$4.00
Joyner, Wally	86TTR	51	$ .10	$1.00
Joyner, Wally	87T	80	$ .10	$ .50
Joyner, Wally	88T	420	$ .01	$ .15
Joyner, Wally	89T	270	$ .01	$ .10
Joyner, Wally	90T	525	$ .01	$ .10
Joyner, Wally	91T	195	$ .01	$ .10

Player	Year	No.	VG	EX/MT
Joyner, Wally	**91TSC**	**2**	**$ .05**	**$ .35**
Joyner, Wally	92T	629	$ .01	$ .10
Joyner, Wally	92TSC	122	$ .01	$ .10
Joyner, Wally	92TSC	710	$ .01	$ .10
Joyner, Wally	92TTR	59	$ .01	$ .05
Joyner, Wally	93T	375	$ .01	$ .03
Juden, Jeff	90T	164	$ .05	$ .25
Juden, Jeff	92T	34	$ .01	$ .10
Juden, Jeff	92TSC	479	$ .05	$ .25
Juden, Jeff	93T	709	$ .01	$ .03
Judson, Howie	52T	169	$7.00	$28.00
Judson, Howie	53T	12	$4.00	$16.00
Judson, Howie	91TA53	12	$ .01	$ .15
Jurak, Ed	84T	628	$ .01	$ .06
Jurak, Ed	85T	233	$ .01	$ .06
Jurak, Ed	86T	749	$ .01	$ .05
Jurges, Billy	60T	220	$ .75	$3.00
Justice, Dave	90TTR	48	$ .10	$1.00
Justice, Dave	91T	329	$ .05	$ .35
Justice, Dave	91TSC	26	$2.25	$9.00
Justice, David	92T	80	$ .05	$ .25
Justice, David	92TSC	182	$ .10	$1.00
Justice, David	92TSC	592	$ .10	$ .40
Justice, David	93T	170	$ .01	$ .10
Jutze, Skip	73T	613	$11.25	$45.00
Jutze, Skip	74T	328	$ .10	$ .40
Jutze, Skip	76T	489	$ .05	$ .25
Jutze, Skip	78T	532	$ .04	$ .16
Kaat, Jim	60T	136	$8.75	$35.00
Kaat, Jim	61T	63	$2.00	$8.00
Kaat, Jim	62T	21	$1.50	$6.00
Kaat, Jim	63T	10	$1.00	$4.00
Kaat, Jim	63T	165	$1.25	$5.00
Kaat, Jim	64T	567	$3.00	$12.00
Kaat (Katt), Jim	65T	62	$1.00	$4.00
Kaat, Jim	66T	224	$ .75	$3.00

TOPPS

Player	Year	No.	VG	EX/MT	Player	Year	No.	VG	EX/MT
Kaat, Jim	66T	445	$1.75	$7.00	Karkovice, Ron	90T	717	$ .01	$ .03
Kaat, Jim	67T	235	$ .75	$3.00	Karkovice, Ron	91T	568	$ .01	$ .03
Kaat, Jim	67T	237	$ .50	$2.00	Karkovice, Ron	91TSC	102	$ .05	$ .25
Kaat, Jim	67T	300	$1.00	$4.00	Karkovice, Ron	92T	153	$ .01	$ .03
Kaat, Jim	68T	450	$1.00	$4.00	Karkovice, Ron	92TSC	257	$ .01	$ .10
Kaat, Jim	69T	290	$1.00	$4.00	Karkovice, Ron	93T	286	$ .01	$ .03
Kaat, Jim	70T	75	$ .50	$2.00	Karros, Eric	92T	194	$ .10	$ .50
Kaat, Jim	71T	245	$ .75	$3.00	Karros, Eric	92TSC	236	$ .75	$3.00
Kaat, Jim	72T	709	$3.50	$14.00	Karros, Eric	93T	11	$ .05	$ .25
Kaat, Jim	72TIA	710	$1.75	$7.00	Karros, Eric	93TSC	292	$ .10	$ .50
Kaat, Jim	73T	530	$1.00	$4.00	Kasko, Eddie	57T	363	$1.75	$7.00
Kaat, Jim	74T	440	$ .50	$2.00	Kasko, Eddie	58T	8	$2.00	$8.00
Kaat, Jim	75T	243	$ .25	$1.00	Kasko, Eddie	59T	232	$1.00	$4.00
Kaat, Jim	76T	80	$ .25	$1.00	Kasko, Eddie	60T	61	$ .85	$3.40
Kaat, Jim	76TTR	80	$ .30	$1.20	Kasko, Eddie	61T	534	$7.50	$30.00
Kaat, Jim	77T	638	$ .20	$ .80	Kasko, Eddie	62T	193	$ .75	$3.00
Kaat, Jim	78T	715	$ .20	$ .80	Kasko, Eddie	63T	498	$3.00	$12.00
Kaat, Jim	79T	136	$ .10	$ .40	Kasko, Eddie	70T	489	$ .35	$1.40
Kaat, Jim	80T	250	$ .10	$ .50	Kasko, Eddie	71T	31	$ .25	$1.00
Kaat, Jim	81T	563	$ .05	$ .25	Kasko, Eddie	72T	218	$ .10	$ .40
Kaat, Jim	82T	367	$ .05	$ .25	Kasko, Eddie	73T	131	$ .20	$ .80
Kaat, Jim	83T	672	$ .05	$ .20	Katt, Ray	57T	331	$5.00	$20.00
Kaat, Jim	83T	673	$ .01	$ .08	Katt, Ray	58T	284	$1.25	$5.00
Kaiser, Don	56T	124	$2.50	$10.00	Katt, Ray	60T	468	$1.25	$5.00
Kaiser, Don	57T	134	$2.00	$8.00	Kaufman, Curt	85T	61	$ .01	$ .06
Kaiser, Jeff	90TTR	49	$ .01	$ .10	Kazak, Eddie	52T	165	$7.00	$28.00
Kaiser, Jeff	91T	576	$ .01	$ .03	Kazak, Eddie	53T	194	$4.50	$18.00
Kaiser, Jeff	92TSC	526	$ .01	$ .10					
Kaline, Al	54T	201	$212.50	$850.00					
Kaline, Al	55T	4	$57.25	$230.00					
Kaline, Al	56T	20	$30.00	$120.00					
Kaline, Al	57T	125	$25.00	$100.00					
Kaline, Al	58T	70	$21.25	$85.00					
Kaline, Al	58T	304	$3.50	$14.00					
Kaline, Al	59T	34	$3.50	$14.00					
Kaline, Al	59T	360	$18.75	$75.00					
Kaline, Al	59T	463	$4.00	$16.00					
Kaline, Al	59TAS	562	$12.50	$50.00					
Kaline, Al	60T	50	$12.00	$48.00					
Kaline, Al	60TAS	561	$13.75	$55.00					
Kaline, Al	61T	429	$11.00	$44.00					
Kaline, Al	61TAS	580	$22.50	$90.00					
Kaline, Al	62T	51	$1.50	$6.00					
Kaline, Al	62T	150	$8.50	$34.00					
Kaline, Al	62TAS	470	$4.50	$18.00					
Kaline, Al	63T	25	$8.00	$32.00					
Kaline, Al	64T	8	$2.00	$8.00					
Kaline, Al	64T	12	$1.25	$5.00					
Kaline, Al	64T	250	$8.00	$32.00					
Kaline, Al	64T	331	$30.00	$120.00					
Kaline, Al	65T	130	$7.50	$28.00					
Kaline, Al	66T	410	$7.50	$30.00					
Kaline, Al	67T	30	$3.75	$15.00					
Kaline, Al	67T	216	$1.75	$7.00					
Kaline, Al	67T	239	$1.25	$5.00					
Kaline, Al	68T	2	$2.25	$9.00					
Kaline, Al	68T	240	$5.50	$22.00					
Kaline, Al	69T	410	$4.50	$18.00					
Kaline, Al	70T	640	$12.50	$50.00					
Kaline, Al	71T	180	$4.50	$18.00	Kazak, Eddie	91TA53	194	$ .01	$ .15
Kaline, Al	72T	600	$5.50	$22.00	Kazanski, Ted	54T	78	$3.75	$15.00
Kaline, Al	73T	280	$1.50	$6.00	Kazanski, Ted	55T	46	$2.25	$9.00
Kaline, Al	74T	215	$1.25	$5.00	Kazanski, Ted	57T	27	$2.00	$8.00
Kaline, Al	75THL	4	$ .75	$3.00	Kazanski, Ted	58T	36	$2.00	$8.00
Kamieniecki, Scott	91TSC	568	$ .05	$ .35	Kazanski, Ted	59T	99	$1.50	$6.00
Kamieniecki, Scott	91TTR	66	$ .01	$ .10	Kealey, Steve	69T	224	$ .50	$2.00
Kamieniecki, Scott	92T	102	$ .01	$ .10	Kealey, Steve	71T	43	$ .25	$1.00
Kamieniecki, Scott	92TSC	649	$ .01	$ .10	Kealey, Steve	72T	146	$ .10	$ .40
Kamieniecki, Scott	93T	749	$ .01	$ .03	Kealey, Steve	73T	581	$ .60	$2.40
Kanehl, Rod	62T	597	$9.00	$36.00	Keane, Johnny	60T	468	$1.25	$5.00
Kanehl, Rod	63T	371	$1.00	$4.00	Keane, Johnny	62T	198	$ .75	$3.00
Kanehl, Rod	64T	582	$2.25	$9.00	Keane, Johnny	63T	166	$ .50	$2.00
Karkovice, Ron	87T	491	$ .01	$ .04	Keane, Johnny	64T	413	$1.00	$4.00
Karkovice, Ron	88T	86	$ .01	$ .04	Keane, Johnny	65T	131	$ .35	$1.40
Karkovice, Ron	89T	308	$ .01	$ .03	Keane, Johnny	66T	296	$ .50	$2.00

TOPPS

Player	Year	No.	VG	EX/MT	Player	Year	No.	VG	EX/MT
Kearney, Bob	83TTR	52	$ .01	$ .10	Kelly, Pat	80T	543	$ .01	$ .10
Kearney, Bob	84T	326	$ .01	$ .06	Kelly, Pat	80T	674	$ .01	$ .10
Kearney, Bob	84TTR	61	$ .01	$ .15	Kelly, Pat	82T	417	$ .01	$ .08
Kearney, Bob	85T	679	$ .01	$ .06	Kelly, Pat	91TSC	381	$ .10	$ .75
Kearney, Bob	86T	13	$ .01	$ .05	Kelly, Pat	91TTR	67	$ .05	$ .20
Kearney, Bob	87T	498	$ .01	$ .04	Kelly, Pat	92T	612	$ .01	$ .10
Keedy, Pat	88T	486	$ .01	$ .04	Kelly, Pat	92TSC	89	$ .05	$ .20
Keegan, Bob	53T	196	$4.50	$18.00	Kelly, Pat	93T	196	$ .01	$ .03
Keegan, Bob	54T	100	$3.75	$15.00	Kelly, Pat	93TSC	155	$ .01	$ .10
Keegan, Bob	55T	10	$2.25	$9.00	Kelly, Roberto	88TTR	57	$ .10	$1.00
Keegan, Bob	56T	54	$2.00	$8.00	Kelly, Roberto	89T	691	$ .01	$ .15
Keegan, Bob	57T	99	$2.00	$8.00	Kelly, Roberto	90T	109	$ .01	$ .10
Keegan, Bob	58T	200	$1.25	$5.00	Kelly, Roberto	91T	11	$ .01	$ .10
Keegan, Bob	59T	86	$1.50	$6.00	Kelly, Roberto	91TSC	319	$ .10	$ .50
Keegan, Bob	60T	291	$ .75	$3.00	Kelly, Roberto	92T	266	$ .01	$ .03
Keegan, Bob	77TB	436	$ .05	$ .20	Kelly, Roberto	92TSC	393	$ .01	$ .10
Keegan, Bob	91TA53	196	$ .01	$ .15	Kelly, Roberto	93T	60	$ .01	$ .03
Keegan, Ed	61T	248	$ .60	$2.40	Kelly, Tom	87T	618	$ .01	$ .04
Keegan, Ed	62T	249	$ .75	$3.00	Kelly, Tom	88T	194	$ .01	$ .04
Keely, Bob	54T	176	$3.75	$15.00	Kelly, Tom	89T	14	$ .01	$ .03
Keeton, Rickey	82T	268	$ .01	$ .08	Kelly, Tom	90T	429	$ .01	$ .03
Kekich, Mike	65T	561	$3.00	$12.00	Kelly, Tom	91T	201	$ .01	$ .03
Kekich, Mike	69T	262	$ .50	$2.00	Kelly, Tom	92T	459	$ .01	$ .03
Kekich, Mike	70T	536	$ .35	$1.40	Kelly, Tom	93T	509	$ .01	$ .03
Kekich, Mike	71T	703	$1.10	$4.40	Kelso, Bill	65T	194	$ .35	$1.40
Kekich, Mike	72T	138	$ .10	$ .40	Kelso, Bill	67T	367	$ .60	$2.40
Kekich, Mike	73T	371	$ .10	$ .40	Kelso, Bill	68T	511	$ .75	$3.00
Kekich, Mike	74T	199	$ .10	$ .40	Kemmerer, Russ	55T	18	$2.25	$9.00
Kekich, Mike	76T	582	$ .05	$ .25	Kemmerer, Russ	58T	137	$1.25	$5.00
Kell, George	52T	246	$20.00	$80.00	Kemmerer, Russ	59T	191	$1.00	$4.00
Kell, George	53T	138	$12.00	$48.00	Kemmerer, Russ	60T	362	$ .75	$3.00
Kell, George	56T	195	$9.00	$36.00	Kemmerer, Russ	61T	56	$ .60	$2.40
Kell, George	57T	230	$5.00	$20.00	Kemmerer, Russ	62T	576	$6.00	$24.00
Kell, George	58T	40	$3.50	$14.00	Kemmerer, Russ	63T	338	$ .90	$3.60
Kell, George	91TA53	138	$ .10	$ .75	Kemp, Steve	77T	492	$0.25	$ .80
Kelleher, Mick	77T	657	$ .05	$ .20	Kemp, Steve	78T	21	$ .04	$ .16
Kelleher, Mick	78T	564	$ .04	$ .16	Kemp, Steve	79T	196	$ .03	$ .12
Kelleher, Mick	79T	53	$ .03	$ .12	Kemp, Steve	80T	315	$ .01	$ .10
Kelleher, Mick	80T	323	$ .01	$ .10	Kemp, Steve	81T	593	$ .01	$ .08
Kelleher, Mick	81T	429	$ .01	$ .08	Kemp, Steve	82T	666	$ .01	$ .08
Kelleher, Mick	81TTR	779	$ .01	$ .15	Kemp, Steve	82T	670	$ .01	$ .08
Kelleher, Mick	82T	184	$ .01	$ .08	Kemp, Steve	82TTR	54	$ .01	$ .10
Kelleher, Mick	82TTR	53	$ .01	$ .10	Kemp, Steve	83T	260	$ .01	$ .08
Kelleher, Mick	83T	79	$ .01	$ .08	Kemp, Steve	83TTR	53	$ .01	$ .10
Kellert, Frank	56T	291	$2.50	$10.00	Kemp, Steve	84T	440	$ .01	$ .06
Kelley, Dick	64T	476	$2.25	$9.00	Kemp, Steve	85T	120	$ .01	$ .06
Kelley, Dick	66T	84	$ .35	$1.40	Kemp, Steve	85TTR	66	$ .01	$ .10
Kelley, Dick	67T	138	$ .40	$1.60	Kemp, Steve	86T	387	$ .01	$ .05
Kelley, Dick	68T	203	$ .35	$1.40	Kendall, Fred	72T	532	$ .40	$1.60
Kelley, Dick	69T	359	$ .30	$1.20	Kendall, Fred	73T	221	$ .10	$ .40
Kelley, Dick	70T	474	$ .35	$1.40	Kendall, Fred	74T	53	$ .10	$ .40
Kelley, Dick	72T	412	$ .25	$1.00	Kendall, Fred	75T	332	$ .10	$ .40
Kelley, Tom	64T	552	$2.25	$9.00	Kendall, Fred	76T	639	$ .05	$ .25
Kelley, Tom	66T	44	$ .35	$1.40	Kendall, Fred	77T	576	$ .05	$ .20
Kelley, Tom	67T	214	$ .50	$2.00	Kendall, Fred	78T	426	$ .04	$ .16
Kelley, Tom	71T	463	$ .50	$2.00	Kendall, Fred	79T	83	$ .03	$ .12
Kelley, Tom	72T	97	$ .10	$ .40	Kendall, Fred	80T	598	$ .01	$ .10
Kellner, Alex	52T	201	$7.00	$28.00	Kendall, Jason	93T	334	$ .05	$ .35
Kellner, Alex	56T	176	$2.50	$10.00	Kendrena, Ken	93T	726	$ .05	$ .20
Kellner, Alex	57T	280	$5.00	$20.00	Kennedy, Bill	52T	102	$7.00	$28.00
Kellner, Alex	58T	3	$2.00	$8.00	Kennedy, Bill	53T	94	$4.00	$16.00
Kellner, Alex	59T	101	$1.50	$6.00	Kennedy, Bob	51Trb	29	$1.75	$7.50
Kelly, Bob	52T	348	$43.75	$175.00	Kennedy, Bob	52T	77	$13.75	$55.00
Kelly, Pat	69T	619	$ .40	$1.60	Kennedy, Bob	53T	33	$4.00	$16.00
Kelly, Pat	70T	57	$ .20	$ .80	Kennedy, Bob	54T	155	$3.75	$15.00
Kelly, Pat	71T	413	$ .50	$2.00	Kennedy, Bob	55T	48	$2.25	$9.00
Kelly, Pat	72T	326	$ .10	$ .40	Kennedy, Bob	56T	38	$2.00	$8.00
Kelly, Pat	73T	261	$ .10	$ .40	Kennedy, Bob	57T	149	$2.00	$8.00
Kelly, Pat	74T	46	$ .10	$ .40	Kennedy, Bob	64T	486	$1.00	$4.00
Kelly, Pat	75T	82	$ .10	$ .40	Kennedy, Bob	65T	457	$1.25	$5.00
Kelly, Pat	76T	212	$ .05	$ .25	Kennedy, Bob	68T	183	$ .35	$1.40
Kelly, Pat	77T	469	$ .05	$ .20	Kennedy, Bob	85T	135	$ .01	$ .10
Kelly, Pat	78T	616	$ .04	$ .16	Kennedy, Bob	91TA53	33	$ .01	$ .15
Kelly, Pat	79T	188	$ .03	$ .12	Kennedy, John	64T	203	$ .65	$2.60
Kelly, Pat	79T	714	$ .03	$ .12	Kennedy, John	65T	119	$ .35	$1.40

416

TOPPS

Player	Year	No.	VG	EX/MT
Kennedy, John	66T	407	$ .65	$2.60
Kennedy, John	67T	111	$ .40	$1.60
Kennedy, John	69T	631	$ .40	$1.60
Kennedy, John	70T	53	$ .20	$ .80
Kennedy, John	71T	498	$ .50	$2.00
Kennedy, John	72T	674	$1.25	$5.00
Kennedy, John	73T	437	$ .25	$1.00
Kennedy, Junior	79T	501	$ .03	$ .12
Kennedy, Junior	80T	377	$ .01	$ .10
Kennedy, Junior	81T	447	$ .01	$ .08
Kennedy, Junior	82T	723	$ .01	$ .08
Kennedy, Junior	82TTR	55	$ .01	$ .10
Kennedy, Junior	83T	204	$ .01	$ .08
Kennedy, Kevin	93T	513	$ .01	$ .03
Kennedy, Monte	52T	124	$7.00	$28.00
Kennedy, Terry	79T	724	$ .15	$ .60
Kennedy, Terry	80T	569	$ .01	$ .10
Kennedy, Terry	81T	353	$ .01	$ .08
Kennedy, Terry	81TTR	780	$ .01	$ .15
Kennedy, Terry	82T	65	$ .01	$ .08
Kennedy, Terry	83T	274	$ .01	$ .08
Kennedy, Terry	83T	742	$ .01	$ .08
Kennedy, Terry	84T	366	$ .01	$ .06
Kennedy, Terry	84T	455	$ .01	$ .06
Kennedy, Terry	85T	135	$ .01	$ .10
Kennedy, Terry	85T	635	$ .01	$ .06
Kennedy, Terry	86T	230	$ .01	$ .05
Kennedy, Terry	87T	540	$ .01	$ .04
Kennedy, Terry	87TTR	57	$ .01	$ .05
Kennedy, Terry	88T	180	$ .01	$ .04
Kennedy, Terry	89T	705	$ .01	$ .03
Kennedy, Terry	89TTR	59	$ .01	$ .05
Kennedy, Terry	90T	372	$ .01	$ .03
Kennedy, Terry	91T	66	$ .01	$ .03
Kennedy, Terry	91TSC	91	$ .05	$ .25
Kennedy, Terry	92T	253	$ .01	$ .03
Kennedy, William	91TA53	94	$ .01	$ .15
Kenney, Gerry (Jerry)	69T	519	$ .40	$1.60
Kenney, Jerry	70T	219	$ .20	$ .80
Kenney, Jerry	71T	572	$1.00	$4.00
Kenney, Jerry	72T	158	$ .10	$ .40
Kenney, Jerry	73T	514	$ .25	$1.00
Kent, Jeff	93T	703	$ .01	$ .10
Kent, Jeff	93TSC	269	$ .05	$ .20
Kenworthy, Dick	68T	63	$ .35	$1.40
Keough, Joe	69T	603	$ .40	$1.60
Keough, Joe	70T	589	$ .50	$2.00
Keough, Joe	71T	451	$ .50	$2.00
Keough, Joe	72T	133	$ .10	$ .40
Keough, Marty	58T	371	$1.00	$4.00
Keough, Marty	59T	303	$1.00	$4.00
Keough, Marty	60T	71	$ .85	$3.40
Keough, Marty	61T	146	$ .60	$2.40
Keough, Marty	62T	258	$ .75	$3.00
Keough, Marty	63T	21	$ .50	$2.00
Keough, Marty	64T	166	$ .50	$2.00
Keough, Marty	65T	263	$ .50	$2.00
Keough, Marty	66T	334	$ .50	$2.00
Keough, Matt	78T	709	$ .04	$ .16
Keough, Matt	79T	554	$ .03	$ .12
Keough, Matt	80T	134	$ .01	$ .10
Keough, Matt	81T	301	$ .01	$ .08
Keough, Matt	82T	87	$ .01	$ .08
Keough, Matt	83T	413	$ .01	$ .08
Keough, Matt	83TTR	54	$ .01	$ .10
Keough, Matt	84T	203	$ .01	$ .06
Kepshire, Kurt	85T	474	$ .01	$ .06
Kepshire, Kurt	86T	256	$ .05	$ .25
Kerfeld, Charlie	86TTR	52	$ .01	$ .06
Kerfeld, Charlie	87T	145	$ .01	$ .04
Kerfeld, Charlie	88T	608	$ .01	$ .04
Kern, Jim	75T	621	$ .15	$ .60
Kern, Jim	77T	41	$ .05	$ .20
Kern, Jim	78T	253	$ .04	$ .16
Kern, Jim	79T	573	$ .03	$ .12
Kern, Jim	80T	369	$ .01	$ .10
Kern, Jim	81T	197	$ .01	$ .08
Kern, Jim	82T	463	$ .01	$ .08
Kern, Jim	82TTR	56	$ .01	$ .10
Kern, Jim	83T	772	$ .01	$ .08
Kernek, George	66T	544	$8.00	$32.00
Kerrigan, Joe	77T	341	$ .05	$ .20
Kerrigan, Joe	78T	549	$ .04	$ .16
Kerrigan, Joe	79T	37	$ .03	$ .12
Kessinger, Don	66T	24	$ .90	$3.60
Kessinger, Don	67T	419	$ .60	$2.40
Kessinger, Don	68T	159	$ .35	$1.40
Kessinger, Don	69T	225	$ .50	$2.00
Kessinger, Don	69TAS	422	$ .50	$2.00
Kessinger, Don	70T	80	$ .20	$ .80
Kessinger, Don	70TAS	456	$ .35	$1.40
Kessinger, Don	71T	455	$ .50	$2.00
Kessinger, Don	72T	145	$ .10	$ .40
Kessinger, Don	73T	285	$ .10	$ .40
Kessinger, Don	74T	38	$ .10	$ .40
Kessinger, Don	75T	315	$ .10	$ .40
Kessinger, Don	76T	574	$ .05	$ .25
Kessinger, Don	77T	229	$ .05	$ .20
Kessinger, Don	78T	672	$ .04	$ .16
Kessinger, Don	79T	467	$ .03	$ .12
Kester, Rick	70T	621	$6.00	$24.00
Kester, Rick	71T	494	$ .50	$2.00
Kester, Rick	72T	351	$ .10	$ .40
Key, Jimmy	84TTR	62	$1.50	$6.00
Key, Jimmy	85T	193	$ .10	$1.00
Key, Jimmy	86T	545	$ .01	$ .15
Key, Jimmy	87T	29	$ .01	$ .10
Key, Jimmy	88T	682	$ .01	$ .10

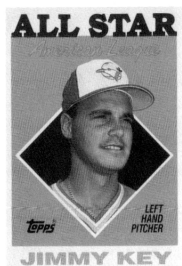

Player	Year	No.	VG	EX/MT
Key, Jimmy	88TAS	395	$ .01	$ .04
Key, Jimmy	89T	229	$ .01	$ .03
Key, Jimmy	90T	371	$ .01	$ .03
Key, Jimmy	91T	741	$ .01	$ .03
Key, Jimmy	91TSC	221	$ .05	$ .25
Key, Jimmy	92T	482	$ .01	$ .03
Key, Jimmy	92TSC	259	$ .01	$ .10
Key, Jimmy	93T	596	$ .01	$ .03
Khalifa, Sammy	86T	316	$ .01	$ .05
Khalifa, Sammy	87T	164	$ .01	$ .04

TOPPS

Player	Year	No.	VG	EX/MT
Kiecker, Dana	90TTR	50	$ .01	$ .10
Kiecker, Dana	91T	763	$ .01	$ .03
Kiecker, Dana	91TSC	140	$ .05	$ .25
Kiecker, Dana	92T	163	$ .01	$ .03
Kiefer, Steve	88T	187	$ .01	$ .04
Kiely, John	92TSC	384	$ .01	$ .10
Kiely, John	93T	107	$ .01	$ .10
Kiely, John	93TSC	212	$ .01	$ .10
Kiely, Leo	52T	54	$13.75	$55.00
Kiely, Leo	54T	171	$3.75	$15.00
Kiely, Leo	55T	36	$2.25	$9.00
Kiely, Leo	58T	204	$1.25	$5.00
Kiely, Leo	59T	199	$1.00	$4.00
Kiely, Leo	60T	94	$ .85	$3.40
Kile, Darryl	91TTR	68	$ .01	$ .10
Kile, Darryl	92T	134	$ .01	$ .03
Kile, Darryl	92TSC	837	$ .01	$ .15
Kile, Darryl	93T	308	$ .01	$ .03
Kilgus, Paul	88T	427	$ .01	$ .04
Kilgus, Paul	89T	276	$ .01	$ .03
Kilgus, Paul	89TTR	60	$ .01	$ .05
Kilgus, Paul	90T	86	$ .01	$ .03
Kilgus, Paul	92TSC	722	$ .01	$ .10
Kilkenny, Mike	69T	544	$ .40	$1.60

Player	Year	No.	VG	EX/MT
Kilkenny, Mike	70T	424	$ .35	$1.40
Kilkenny, Mike	71T	86	$ .25	$1.00
Kilkenny, Mike	72T	337	$ .10	$ .40
Kilkenny, Mike	73T	551	$ .60	$2.40
Killebrew, Harmon	55T	124	$95.00	$380.00
Killebrew, Harmon	56T	164	$40.00	$160.00
Killebrew, Harmon	58T	288	$22.50	$90.00
Killebrew, Harmon	59T	515	$35.00	$140.00
Killebrew, Harmon	60T	210	$8.00	$32.00
Killebrew, Harmon	61T	80	$6.00	$24.00
Killebrew, Harmon	62T	53	$13.75	$55.00
Killebrew, Harmon	62T	70	$5.00	$20.00
Killebrew, Harmon	62T	316	$2.25	$9.00
Killebrew, Harmon	63T	4	$2.00	$8.00
Killebrew, Harmon	63T	500	$32.50	$130.00
Killebrew, Harmon	64T	10	$1.00	$4.00
Killebrew, Harmon	64T	12	$1.25	$5.00
Killebrew, Harmon	64T	81	$1.75	$7.00
Killebrew, Harmon	64T	177	$5.00	$20.00
Killebrew, Harmon	65T	3	$5.50	$22.00
Killebrew, Harmon	65T	5	$5.50	$22.00
Killebrew, Harmon	65T	400	$8.00	$32.00
Killebrew, Harmon	66T	120	$5.00	$20.00
Killebrew, Harmon	67T	241	$1.25	$5.00
Killebrew, Harmon	67T	243	$1.25	$5.00
Killebrew, Harmon	67T	334	$1.10	$4.40
Killebrew, Harmon	67T	460	$12.50	$50.00
Killebrew, Harmon	68T	4	$2.25	$9.00
Killebrew, Harmon	68T	6	$1.75	$7.00
Killebrew, Harmon	68T	220	$3.50	$14.00
Killebrew, Harmon	68T	490	$30.00	$120.00
Killebrew, Harmon	68TAS	361	$1.75	$7.00
Killebrew, Harmon	69T	375	$4.50	$18.00
Killebrew, Harmon	70T	64	$1.25	$5.00
Killebrew, Harmon	70T	66	$1.25	$5.00
Killebrew, Harmon	70T	150	$2.00	$8.00
Killebrew, Harmon	71T	65	$ .75	$3.00
Killebrew, Harmon	71T	550	$5.50	$22.00
Killebrew, Harmon	72T	51	$1.50	$6.00
Killebrew, Harmon	72T	88	$ .75	$3.00
Killebrew, Harmon	72TIA	52	$ .75	$3.00
Killebrew, Harmon	73T	170	$1.25	$5.00
Killebrew, Harmon	74T	400	$1.00	$4.00
Killebrew, Harmon	75T	207	$ .25	$1.00
Killebrew, Harmon	75T	640	$1.00	$4.00
Kimm, Bruce	77T	554	$ .05	$ .20
Kimm, Bruce	81T	272	$ .01	$ .08
Kindall, Jerry	58T	221	$1.50	$6.00
Kindall, Jerry	59T	274	$1.00	$4.00
Kindall, Jerry	60T	444	$1.25	$5.00
Kindall, Jerry	61T	27	$ .60	$2.40
Kindall, Jerry	62T	292	$ .75	$3.00
Kindall, Jerry	63T	36	$ .50	$2.00
Kinder, Ellis	52T	78	$13.75	$55.00
Kinder, Ellis	53T	44	$8.00	$32.00
Kinder, Ellis	54T	47	$3.75	$15.00
Kinder, Ellis	55T	115	$2.25	$9.00
Kinder, Ellis	56T	336	$2.50	$10.00
Kinder, Ellis	57T	352	$5.00	$20.00
Kinder, Ellis	91TA53	44	$ .01	$ .15
Kiner, Ralph	51Trb	15	$7.50	$30.00
Kiner, Ralph	53T	191	$17.50	$70.00
Kiner, Ralph	77TB	437	$ .15	$ .60
Kiner, Ralph	91TA53	191	$ .10	$1.00
King, Chick	59T	538	$4.00	$16.00
King, Clyde	52T	205	$7.00	$28.00
King, Clyde	69T	274	$ .50	$2.00
King, Clyde	70T	624	$ .50	$2.00
King, Clyde	83T	486	$ .01	$ .08
King, Eric	86TTR	53	$ .01	$ .15
King, Eric	87T	36	$ .01	$ .10
King, Eric	88T	499	$ .01	$ .04
King, Eric	89T	238	$ .01	$ .03
King, Eric	89TTR	61	$ .01	$ .05
King, Eric	90T	786	$ .01	$ .03
King, Eric	91T	121	$ .01	$ .03
King, Eric	91TSC	328	$ .05	$ .25
King, Eric	92T	326	$ .01	$ .03
King, Eric	92TSC	125	$ .01	$ .10
King, Eric	92TSC	638	$ .01	$ .10
King, Hal	70T	327	$ .35	$1.40
King, Hal	71T	88	$ .25	$1.00
King, Hal	72T	598	$ .40	$1.60
King, Hal	74T	362	$ .10	$ .40
King, Jeff	90T	454	$ .01	$ .03
King, Jeff	91T	272	$ .01	$ .03
King, Jeff	91TSC	528	$ .05	$ .25
King, Jeff	92T	693	$ .01	$ .03
King, Jeff	92TSC	24	$ .01	$ .10
King, Jeff	93T	136	$ .01	$ .03
King, Jeff	93TSC	93	$ .01	$ .10
King, Jim	56T	74	$2.00	$8.00
King, Jim	57T	186	$2.00	$8.00
King, Jim	58T	332	$1.25	$5.00

TOPPS

Player	Year	No.	VG	EX/MT
King, Jim	61T	351	$ .60	$2.40
King, Jim	62T	42	$ .60	$2.40
King, Jim	63T	176	$ .50	$2.00
King, Jim	64T	217	$ .65	$2.60
King, Jim	65T	38	$ .35	$1.40
King, Jim	66T	369	$ .50	$2.00
King, Jim	67T	509	$1.50	$6.00
King, Nelson	55T	112	$2.25	$9.00
King, Nelson	57T	349	$5.00	$20.00
Kingery, Mike	87T	203	$ .01	$ .04
Kingery, Mike	87TTR	58	$ .01	$ .05
Kingery, Mike	88T	532	$ .01	$ .04
Kingery, Mike	89T	413	$ .01	$ .03
Kingery, Mike	91T	657	$ .01	$ .03
Kingery, Mike	92TSC	862	$ .01	$ .10
Kingman, Brian	80T	671	$ .20	$2.00
Kingman, Brian	81T	284	$ .01	$ .08

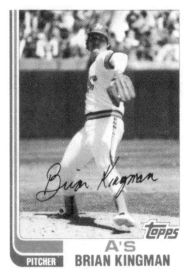

Player	Year	No.	VG	EX/MT
Kingman, Brian	82T	476	$ .01	$ .08
Kingman, Brian	83T	312	$ .01	$ .08
Kingman, Dave	72T	147	$1.50	$6.00
Kingman, Dave	73T	23	$ .35	$1.40
Kingman, Dave	74T	610	$ .25	$1.00
Kingman, Dave	75T	156	$ .25	$1.00
Kingman, Dave	76T	40	$ .20	$ .80
Kingman, Dave	76T	193	$ .50	$2.00
Kingman, Dave	77T	500	$ .10	$ .40
Kingman, Dave	78T	570	$ .10	$ .40
Kingman, Dave	79T	370	$ .05	$ .20
Kingman, Dave	80T	202	$ .05	$ .20
Kingman, Dave	80T	240	$ .05	$ .25
Kingman, Dave	81T	450	$ .01	$ .15
Kingman, Dave	81TTR	781	$ .10	$ .40
Kingman, Dave	82T	690	$ .05	$ .20
Kingman, Dave	83T	160	$ .01	$ .15
Kingman, Dave	83T	161	$ .01	$ .08
Kingman, Dave	83T	702	$ .05	$ .25
Kingman, Dave	84T	573	$ .01	$ .10
Kingman, Dave	84T	703	$ .05	$ .20
Kingman, Dave	84TTR	63	$ .05	$ .20
Kingman, Dave	85T	730	$ .01	$ .06
Kingman, Dave	86T	410	$ .01	$ .05
Kingman, Dave	87T	709	$ .01	$ .04
Kinney, Dennis	81T	599	$ .01	$ .08

Player	Year	No.	VG	EX/MT
Kipp, Fred	59T	258	$1.00	$4.00
Kipp, Fred	60T	202	$ .75	$3.00
Kipper, Bob	86TTR	54	$ .01	$ .06
Kipper, Bob	87T	289	$ .01	$ .04
Kipper, Bob	88T	723	$ .01	$ .04
Kipper, Bob	89T	114	$ .01	$ .03
Kipper, Bob	90T	441	$ .01	$ .03
Kipper, Bob	91T	551	$ .01	$ .03
Kipper, Bob	91TSC	334	$ .05	$ .25
Kipper, Bob	92T	64	$ .01	$ .03
Kipper, Bob	92TSC	752	$ .01	$ .10
Kipper, Thornton	54T	108	$3.75	$15.00
Kipper, Thornton	55T	62	$2.25	$9.00
Kirby, Clay	69T	637	$ .40	$1.60
Kirby, Clay	70T	79	$ .20	$ .80
Kirby, Clay	71T	333	$ .25	$1.00
Kirby, Clay	72T	173	$ .10	$ .40
Kirby, Clay	72TIA	174	$ .10	$ .40
Kirby, Clay	73T	655	$ .60	$2.40
Kirby, Clay	74T	287	$ .10	$ .40
Kirby, Clay	75T	423	$ .10	$ .40
Kirby, Clay	76T	579	$ .05	$ .25
Kirby, Clay	76TTR	579	$ .05	$ .25
Kirby, Wayne	93TSC	35	$ .01	$ .10
Kirkland, Willie	58T	128	$1.25	$5.00
Kirkland, Willie	59T	484	$1.00	$4.00
Kirkland, Willie	60T	172	$ .75	$3.00
Kirkland, Willie	61T	15	$ .60	$2.40
Kirkland, Willie	62T	447	$1.50	$6.00
Kirkland, Willie	63T	187	$ .50	$2.00
Kirkland, Willie	64T	17	$ .50	$2.00
Kirkland, Willie	65T	148	$ .35	$1.40
Kirkland, Willie	66T	434	$ .65	$2.60
Kirkpatrick, Ed	63T	386	$1.00	$4.00
Kirkpatrick, Ed	64T	296	$ .65	$2.60
Kirkpatrick, Ed	65T	393	$1.00	$4.00
Kirkpatrick, Ed	66T	102	$ .35	$1.40
Kirkpatrick, Ed	67T	293	$ .60	$2.40
Kirkpatrick, Ed	68T	552	$ .70	$2.80
Kirkpatrick, Ed	69T	529	$ .40	$1.60
Kirkpatrick, Ed	70T	165	$ .20	$ .80
Kirkpatrick, Ed	71T	299	$ .25	$1.00
Kirkpatrick, Ed	72T	569	$ .40	$1.60
Kirkpatrick, Ed	72TIA	570	$ .40	$1.60
Kirkpatrick, Ed	73T	233	$ .10	$ .40
Kirkpatrick, Ed	74T	262	$ .10	$ .40
Kirkpatrick, Ed	74TTR	262	$ .10	$ .40
Kirkpatrick, Ed	75T	171	$ .10	$ .40
Kirkpatrick, Ed	76T	294	$ .05	$ .25
Kirkpatrick, Ed	77T	582	$ .05	$ .20
Kirkpatrick, Ed	78T	77	$ .04	$ .16
Kirkreit, Daron	92TTR	60	$ .10	$ .40
Kirkwood, Don	76T	108	$ .05	$ .25
Kirkwood, Don	77T	519	$ .05	$ .20
Kirkwood, Don	78T	251	$ .04	$ .16
Kirkwood, Don	79T	632	$ .03	$ .12
Kison, Bruce	72T	72	$ .25	$1.00
Kison, Bruce	73T	141	$ .10	$ .40
Kison, Bruce	75T	598	$ .10	$ .40
Kison, Bruce	76T	161	$ .05	$ .25
Kison, Bruce	77T	563	$ .05	$ .20
Kison, Bruce	78T	223	$ .04	$ .16
Kison, Bruce	79T	661	$ .03	$ .12
Kison, Bruce	80T	28	$ .01	$ .10
Kison, Bruce	81T	340	$ .01	$ .08
Kison, Bruce	82T	442	$ .01	$ .08
Kison, Bruce	83T	712	$ .01	$ .08
Kison, Bruce	84T	201	$ .01	$ .06
Kison, Bruce	85T	544	$ .01	$ .06
Kison, Bruce	85TTR	67	$ .01	$ .10
Kison, Bruce	86T	117	$ .01	$ .05
Kissell, George	73T	497	$ .50	$2.00
Kissell, George	74T	236	$ .10	$ .40
Kittle, Hub	73T	624	$1.00	$4.00
Kittle, Hub	74T	31	$ .10	$ .40

TOPPS

Player	Year	No.	VG	EX/MT
Kittle, Ron	83TTR	55	$ .05	$ .35
Kittle, Ron	84T	480	$ .01	$ .10
Kittle, Ron	85T	105	$ .01	$ .06
Kittle, Ron	86T	574	$ .01	$ .05
Kittle, Ron	87T	584	$ .01	$ .04
Kittle, Ron	88T	259	$ .01	$ .04
Kittle, Ron	88TTR	58	$ .01	$ .05
Kittle, Ron	89T	771	$ .01	$ .03
Kittle, Ron	89TTR	62	$ .01	$ .05
Kittle, Ron	90T	79	$ .01	$ .03
Kittle, Ron	91T	324	$ .01	$ .03
Klages, Fred	67T	373	$ .60	$2.40
Klages, Fred	68T	229	$ .35	$1.40
Klaus, Billy	56T	217	$3.75	$15.00
Klaus, Billy	57T	292	$5.00	$20.00
Klaus, Billy	58T	89	$2.00	$8.00
Klaus, Billy	59T	299	$1.00	$4.00
Klaus, Billy	60T	406	$ .75	$3.00
Klaus, Billy	61T	187	$ .60	$2.40
Klaus, Billy	62T	571	$6.00	$24.00
Klaus, Billy	63T	551	$2.25	$9.00
Klaus, Bobby	64T	524	$2.25	$9.00
Klaus, Bobby	65T	227	$ .50	$2.00
Klaus, Bobby	66T	108	$ .35	$1.40
Klaus, Bobby	69T	387	$ .30	$1.20
Klein, Lou	60T	457	$1.25	$5.00
Klesko, Ryan	92T	126	$ .10	$1.00
Klesko, Ryan	93T	423	$ .10	$ .75
Klimchock, Lou	60T	137	$ .75	$3.00
Klimchock, Lou	61T	462	$1.35	$5.40
Klimchock, Lou	62T	259	$ .75	$3.00
Klimchock, Lou	63T	542	$2.25	$9.00
Klimchock, Lou	65T	542	$1.40	$5.60
Klimchock, Lou	66T	589	$8.00	$32.00
Klimchock, Lou	70T	247	$ .20	$ .80
Klimkowski, Ron	70T	702	$1.25	$5.00
Klimkowski, Ron	71T	28	$ .25	$1.00
Klimkowski, Ron	72T	363	$ .10	$ .40
Kline, Johnny	55T	173	$6.25	$25.00
Kline, Ron	53T	175	$4.50	$18.00
Kline, Ronnie	56T	94	$2.00	$8.00
Kline, Ronnie	57T	256	$2.00	$8.00
Kline, Ronnie	58T	82	$2.00	$8.00
Kline, Ron	59T	265	$1.00	$4.00
Kline, Ron	59T	428	$1.00	$4.00
Kline, Ron	60T	197	$ .75	$3.00
Kline, Ron	61T	127	$ .60	$2.40
Kline, Ron	62T	216	$ .75	$3.00
Kline, Ron	63T	84	$ .50	$2.00
Kline, Ron	64T	358	$ .65	$2.60
Kline, Ron	65T	56	$ .35	$1.40
Kline, Ron	66T	453	$1.50	$6.00
Kline, Ron	67T	133	$ .40	$1.60
Kline, Ron	68T	446	$ .35	$1.40
Kline, Ron "Ronnie"	69T	243	$ .50	$2.00
Kline, Ron	91TA53	175	$ .01	$ .15
Kline, Steve	71T	51	$ .25	$1.00
Kline, Steve	72T	467	$ .25	$1.00
Kline, Steve	73T	172	$ .10	$ .40
Kline, Steve	74T	324	$ .10	$ .40
Kline, Steve	75T	639	$ .10	$ .40
Klink, Joe	90TTR	51	$ .01	$ .10
Klink, Joe	91T	553	$ .01	$ .03
Klink, Joe	92T	678	$ .01	$ .03
Klink, Joe	92TSC	326	$ .01	$ .10
Klippstein, Johnny	52T	148	$7.00	$28.00
Klippstein, Johnny	53T	46	$4.00	$16.00
Klippstein, Johnny	54T	31	$3.75	$15.00
Klippstein, Johnny	56T	249	$3.75	$15.00
Klippstein, Johnny	57T	296	$5.00	$20.00
Klippstein, Johnny	58T	242	$1.25	$5.00
Klippstein, Johnny	59T	152	$1.00	$4.00
Klippstein, Johnny	60T	191	$ .75	$3.00
Klippstein, Johnny	61T	539	$7.50	$30.00
Klippstein, Johnny	62T	151	$ .60	$2.40

Player	Year	No.	VG	EX/MT
Klippstein, Johnny	63T	571	$2.25	$9.00
Klippstein, Johnny	64T	533	$2.25	$9.00
Klippstein, Johnny	65T	384	$1.00	$4.00
Klippstein, Johnny	66T	493	$1.50	$6.00
Klippstein, Johnny	67T	588	$2.25	$9.00
Klippstein, Johnny	91TA53	46	$ .01	$ .15
Kluszewski, Ted	51Trb	39	$4.00	$16.00
Kluszewski, Ted	52T	29	$25.00	$100.00
Kluszewski, Ted	53T	162	$11.25	$45.00
Kluszewski, Ted	54T	7	$7.00	$28.00
Kluszewski, Ted	55T	120	$6.00	$24.00
Kluszewski, Ted	56T	25	$6.00	$24.00
Kluszewski, Ted	57T	165	$8.00	$32.00
Kluszewski, Ted	58T	178	$3.50	$14.00
Kluszewski, Ted	58T	321	$10.00	$40.00
Kluszewski, Ted	59T	17	$1.50	$6.00
Kluszewski, Ted	59T	35	$3.00	$12.00
Kluszewski, Ted	60T	505	$3.00	$12.00
Kluszewski, Ted	61T	65	$1.50	$6.00
Kluszewski, Ted	73T	296	$ .20	$ .80
Kluszewski, Ted	74T	326	$ .25	$1.00
Kluszewski, Ted	91TA53	162	$ .10	$ .75
Klutts, Mickey	77T	490	$ .05	$ .20
Klutts, Mickey	78T	707	$12.50	$50.00
Klutts, Mickey	80T	717	$ .01	$ .10
Klutts, Mickey	81T	232	$ .01	$ .08
Klutts, Mickey	82T	148	$ .01	$ .08
Klutts, Mickey	83T	571	$ .01	$ .08
Klutts, Mickey	83TTR	56	$ .01	$ .10

Player	Year	No.	VG	EX/MT
Kluttz, Clyde	52T	132	$7.00	$28.00
Knackert, Brent	90TTR	52	$ .01	$ .10
Knackert, Brent	91T	563	$ .01	$ .03
Knapp, Chris	77T	247	$ .05	$ .20
Knapp, Chris	78T	361	$ .04	$ .16
Knapp, Chris	79T	453	$ .03	$ .12
Knapp, Chris	80T	658	$ .01	$ .10
Knapp, Chris	81T	557	$ .01	$ .08
Knepper, Bob	78T	589	$ .10	$ .40
Knepper, Bob	79T	486	$ .03	$ .12
Knepper, Bob	80T	111	$ .01	$ .10
Knepper, Bob	81T	279	$ .01	$ .08
Knepper, Bob	81TTR	782	$ .01	$ .15
Knepper, Bob	82T	672	$ .01	$ .08

TOPPS

Player	Year	No.	VG	EX/MT	Player	Year	No.	VG	EX/MT
Knepper, Bob	83T	382	$.01	$.08	Kobel, Kevin	80T	189	$.01	$.10
Knepper, Bob	84T	93	$.01	$.06	Koegel, Pete	71T	633	$1.00	$4.00
Knepper, Bob	85T	455	$.01	$.06	Koegel, Pete	72T	14	$.10	$.40
Knepper, Bob	85TAS	721	$.01	$.06	Kokos, Dick	51Trb	19	$1.75	$7.50
Knepper, Bob	86T	590	$.01	$.05	Kokos, Dick	53T	232	$22.50	$90.00
Knepper, Bob	87T	722	$.01	$.04	Kokos, Dick	54T	106	$3.75	$15.00
Knepper, Bob	88T	151	$.01	$.04	Kokus, Dick	91TA53	232	$.01	$.15
Knepper, Bob	89T	280	$.01	$.03	Kolb, Gary	64T	119	$.50	$2.00
Knepper, Bob	90T	104	$.01	$.03	Kolb, Gary	65T	287	$.50	$2.00
Knicely, Alan	80T	678	$.01	$.10	Kolb, Gary	68T	407	$.35	$1.40
Knicely, Alan	81T	82	$.01	$.08	Kolb, Gary	69T	307	$.50	$2.00
Knicely, Alan	83T	117	$.01	$.08	Kolloway, Don	52T	104	$7.00	$28.00
Knicely, Alan	83TTR	57	$.01	$.10	Kolloway, Don	53T	97	$4.00	$16.00
Knicely, Alan	84T	323	$.01	$.06	Kolloway, Don	91TA53	97	$.01	$.15
Knicely, Alan	85TTR	68	$.01	$.10	Kolstad, Hal	62T	276	$.75	$3.00
Knicely, Alan	86T	418	$.01	$.05	Kolstad, Hal	63T	574	$2.25	$9.00
Knight, Ray	78T	674	$.35	$1.40	Komminsk, Brad	85T	292	$.01	$.06
Knight, Ray	79T	401	$.10	$.40	Komminsk, Brad	86T	698	$.01	$.05
Knight, Ray	80T	174	$.01	$.10	Komminsk, Brad	90T	476	$.01	$.03
Knight, Ray	81T	325	$.01	$.08	Komminsk, Brad	90TTR	53	$.01	$.05
Knight, Ray	82T	525	$.01	$.08	Konieczny, Doug	75T	624	$.10	$.40
Knight, Ray	82TTR	57	$.05	$.25	Konieczny, Doug	76T	602	$.05	$.25
Knight, Ray	83T	275	$.01	$.08	Konstanty, Jim	52T	108	$7.50	$30.00
Knight, Ray	83T	441	$.01	$.08	Konstanty, Jim	56T	321	$3.50	$14.00
Knight, Ray	84T	660	$.01	$.06	Konstanty, Jim	61TMVP	479	$1.35	$5.40
Knight, Ray	85T	590	$.01	$.06	Koonce, Cal	63T	31	$.50	$2.00
Knight, Ray	86T	27	$.01	$.10	Koonce, Cal	65T	34	$.35	$1.40
Knight, Ray	87T	488	$.01	$.04	Koonce, Cal	66T	278	$.50	$2.00
Knight, Ray	87TTR	59	$.01	$.05	Koonce, Cal	67T	171	$.40	$1.60
Knight, Ray	88T	124	$.01	$.04	Koonce, Cal	68T	486	$.75	$3.00
Knight, Ray	88TTR	59	$.01	$.05	Koonce, Cal	69T	303	$.50	$2.00
Knoblauch, Chuck	91TSC	548	$1.25	$5.00	Koonce, Cal	70T	521	$.35	$1.40
Knoblauch, Chuck	91TTR	69	$.10	$.50	Koonce, Cal "Calvin"	71T	254	$.25	$1.00
Knoblauch, Chuck	92T	23	$.01	$.15	Koosman, Jerry	68T	177	$375.00	$1500.00
Knoblauch, Chuck	92TSC	601	$.05	$.35	Koosman, Jerry	69T	90	$1.25	$5.00
Knoblauch, Chuck	92TSC	830	$.10	$.50	Koosman, Jerry	69TAS	434	$.30	$1.20
Knoblauch, Chuck	93T	250	$.01	$.10	Koosman, Jerry	70T	610	$1.00	$4.00
Knoop, Bobby	64T	502	$1.00	$4.00	Koosman, Jerry	70TAS	468	$.50	$2.00
Knoop, Bobby	65T	26	$.35	$1.40	Koosman, Jerry	71T	335	$.60	$2.40
Knoop, Bobby	66T	280	$.50	$2.00	Koosman, Jerry	72T	697	$3.50	$14.00
Knoop, Bobby	67T	175	$.40	$1.60	Koosman, Jerry	72TIA	698	$1.75	$7.00
Knoop, Bobby	68T	271	$.35	$1.40	Koosman, Jerry	73T	184	$.20	$.80
Knoop, Bobby	69T	445	$.30	$1.20	Koosman, Jerry	74T	356	$.15	$.60
Knoop, Bobby	70T	695	$1.25	$5.00	Koosman, Jerry	75T	19	$.15	$.60
Knoop, Bobby	71T	506	$.50	$2.00	Koosman, Jerry	76T	64	$.10	$.40
Knoop, Bobby	72T	664	$1.25	$5.00	Koosman, Jerry	77T	300	$.05	$.20
Knorr, Randy	93T	534	$.01	$.10	Koosman, Jerry	78T	565	$.04	$.16
Knowles, Darold	64T	418	$1.00	$4.00	Koosman, Jerry	79T	655	$.05	$.20
Knowles, Darold	65T	577	$2.50	$10.00	Koosman, Jerry	80T	275	$.01	$.10
Knowles, Darold	66T	27	$.35	$1.40	Koosman, Jerry	81T	476	$.01	$.08
Knowles, Darold	67T	362	$.60	$2.40	Koosman, Jerry	82T	714	$.01	$.08
Knowles, Darold	68T	483	$.75	$3.00	Koosman, Jerry	83T	153	$.01	$.08
Knowles, Darold	70T	106	$.20	$.80	Koosman, Jerry	84T	311	$.01	$.06
Knowles, Darold	71T	261	$.25	$1.00	Koosman, Jerry	84T	716	$.01	$.15
Knowles, Darold	72T	583	$.40	$1.60	Koosman, Jerry	84TTR	64	$.05	$.20
Knowles, Darold	73T	274	$.10	$.40	Koosman, Jerry	85T	15	$.01	$.06
Knowles, Darold	74T	57	$.10	$.40	Koosman, Jerry	OCT	505	$.01	$.05
Knowles, Darold	75T	352	$.10	$.40	Kopacz, George	71T	204	$.25	$1.00
Knowles, Darold	76T	617	$.05	$.25	Koplitz, Howie	62T	114	$.60	$2.40
Knowles, Darold	77T	169	$.05	$.20	Koplitz, Howie	63T	406	$1.00	$4.00
Knowles, Darold	78T	414	$.04	$.16	Koplitz, Howie	64T	372	$1.00	$4.00
Knowles, Darold	79T	581	$.03	$.12	Koplitz, Howie	66T	46	$.35	$1.40
Knowles, Darold	80T	286	$.01	$.10	Koppe, Joe	59T	517	$4.00	$16.00
Knox, John	74T	604	$1.25	$5.00	Koppe, Joe	60T	319	$.75	$3.00
Knox, John	75T	546	$.10	$.40	Koppe, Joe	61T	179	$.60	$2.40
Knox, John	76T	218	$.05	$.25	Koppe, Joe	62T	39	$.60	$2.40
Knudsen, Kurt	93T	272	$.01	$.10	Koppe, Joe	63T	396	$1.00	$4.00
Knudsen, Kurt	93TSC	65	$.01	$.10	Koppe, Joe	64T	279	$.65	$2.60
Knudson, Mark	88T	61	$.01	$.04	Korcheck, Steve	58T	403	$1.00	$4.00
Knudson, Mark	90T	566	$.01	$.03	Korcheck, Steve	59T	284	$1.00	$4.00
Knudson, Mark	91T	267	$.01	$.03	Korcheck, Steve	60T	56	$.85	$3.40
Kobel, Kevin	74T	605	$1.25	$5.00	Korince, George	67T	72	$.40	$1.60
Kobel, Kevin	75T	337	$.10	$.40	Korince, George	67T	526	$1.75	$7.00
Kobel, Kevin	76T	588	$.05	$.25	Korince, George	68T	447	$.35	$1.40
Kobel, Kevin	79T	21	$.03	$.12	Kosco, Andy	66T	264	$.50	$2.00

TOPPS

Player	Year	No.	VG	EX/MT	Player	Year	No.	VG	EX/MT
Kosco, Andy	67T	366	$ .60	$2.40	Kranepool, Ed	77T	201	$ .05	$ .20
Kosco, Andy	68T	524	$ .75	$3.00	Kranepool, Ed	78T	49	$ .04	$ .16
Kosco, Andy	69T	139	$ .35	$1.40	Kranepool, Ed	79T	505	$ .03	$ .12
Kosco, Andy	70T	535	$ .35	$1.40	Kranepool, Ed	80T	641	$ .01	$ .10
Kosco, Andy	71T	746	$1.10	$4.40	Krausse, Lew	63T	104	$ .50	$2.00
Kosco, Andy	72T	376	$ .10	$ .40	Krausse, Lew	64T	334	$ .65	$2.60
Kosco, Andy	74T	34	$ .10	$ .40	Krausse, Lew	65T	462	$1.25	$5.00
Koshorek, Clem	52T	380	$43.75	$175.00	Krausse, Lew	66T	256	$ .50	$2.00
Koshorek, Clem	53T	8	$4.00	$16.00	Krausse, Lew	67T	565	$4.00	$16.00
Koshorek, Clem	91TA53	8	$ .01	$ .15	Krausse, Lew	68T	458	$ .75	$3.00
Koslo, Dave	52T	336	$43.75	$175.00	Krausse, Lew	69T	23	$ .35	$1.40
Koslofski, Kevin	93T	158	$ .01	$ .10	Krausse, Lew	70T	233	$ .20	$ .80
Kostro, Frank	63T	407	$1.00	$4.00	Krausse, Lew	71T	372	$ .25	$1.00
Kostro, Frank	65T	459	$1.25	$5.00	Krausse, Lew	72T	592	$ .40	$1.60
Kostro, Frank	68T	44	$ .35	$1.40	Krausse, Lew	73T	566	$ .60	$2.40
Kostro, Frank	69T	242	$ .50	$2.00					
Kotarski, Mike	93T	621	$ .05	$ .25					
Koufax, Sandy	55T	123	$300.00	$1200.00					
Koufax, Sandy	56T	79	$100.00	$400.00					
Koufax, Sandy	57T	302	$85.00	$340.00					
Koufax, Sandy	58T	187	$50.00	$200.00					
Koufax, Sandy	59T	163	$42.50	$170.00					
Koufax, Sandy	60T	343	$35.00	$140.00					
Koufax, Sandy	61T	49	$2.00	$8.00					
Koufax, Sandy	61T	49	$2.00	$8.00					
Koufax, Sandy	61T	207	$5.00	$20.00					
Koufax, Sandy	61T	344	$22.50	$90.00					
Koufax, Sandy	62T	5	$30.00	$120.00					
Koufax, Sandy	62T	60	$2.00	$8.00					
Koufax, Sandy	63T	5	$2.00	$8.00					
Koufax, Sandy	63T	9	$2.00	$8.00					
Koufax, Sandy	63T	210	$40.00	$160.00					
Koufax, Sandy	63T	412	$9.00	$36.00					
Koufax, Sandy	64T	1	$5.00	$20.00					
Koufax, Sandy	64T	3	$2.50	$10.00					
Koufax, Sandy	64T	5	$2.00	$8.00					
Koufax, Sandy	64T	200	$25.00	$100.00					
Koufax, Sandy	65T	8	$2.25	$9.00					
Koufax, Sandy	65T	300	$30.00	$120.00					
Koufax, Sandy	66T	100	$25.00	$100.00					
Koufax, Sandy	66T	221	$1.75	$7.00					
Koufax, Sandy	66T	223	$1.75	$7.00					
Koufax, Sandy	66T	225	$1.75	$7.00					
Koufax, Sandy	67T	234	$2.00	$8.00					
Koufax, Sandy	67T	236	$3.75	$15.00					
Koufax, Sandy	67T	238	$1.50	$6.00					
Koufax, Sandy	75T	201	$ .25	$1.00					
Koufax, Sandy	90TTB	665	$ .01	$ .06	Krausse, Lew	75T	603	$ .10	$ .40
Kralick, Jack	61T	36	$ .60	$2.40	Kravec, Ken	77T	389	$ .05	$ .20
Kralick, Jack	62T	346	$ .75	$3.00	Kravec, Ken	78T	439	$ .04	$ .16
Kralick, Jack	63T	448	$3.00	$12.00	Kravec, Ken	79T	283	$ .03	$ .12
Kralick, Jack	64T	338	$ .65	$2.60	Kravec, Ken	80T	575	$ .01	$ .10
Kralick, Jack	65T	535	$2.50	$10.00	Kravec, Ken	81T	67	$ .01	$ .08
Kralick, Jack	66T	129	$ .50	$2.00	Kravec, Ken	81TTR	783	$ .01	$ .15
Kralick, Jack	67T	316	$ .60	$2.40	Kravec, Ken	82T	639	$ .01	$ .08
Kraly, Steve	55T	139	$2.25	$9.00	Kravitz, Danny	57T	267	$5.00	$20.00
Kramer, Randy	89T	522	$ .01	$ .03	Kravitz, Danny	58T	444	$1.00	$4.00
Kramer, Randy	90T	126	$ .01	$ .03	Kravitz, Danny	59T	536	$4.00	$16.00
Kranepool, Ed	63T	228	$12.50	$50.00	Kravitz, Danny	60T	238	$ .75	$3.00
Kranepool, Ed	64T	393	$1.50	$6.00	Kravitz, Danny	61T	166	$ .60	$2.40
Kranepool, Ed	64T	566	$3.00	$12.00	Krenchicki, Wayne	80T	661	$ .01	$ .10
Kranepool, Ed	65T	144	$ .35	$1.40	Krenchicki, Wayne	82T	107	$ .01	$ .08
Kranepool, Ed	66T	212	$ .50	$2.00	Krenchicki, Wayne	82TTR	58	$ .01	$ .10
Kranepool, Ed	67T	186	$ .40	$1.60	Krenchicki, Wayne	83T	374	$ .01	$ .08
Kranepool, Ed	67T	452	$ .60	$2.40	Krenchicki, Wayne	84T	223	$ .01	$ .06
Kranepool, Ed	68T	92	$ .35	$1.40	Krenchicki, Wayne	84TTR	65	$ .01	$ .15
Kranepool, Ed	69T	381	$ .30	$1.20	Krenchicki, Wayne	85T	468	$ .01	$ .06
Kranepool, Ed	70T	557	$ .50	$2.00	Krenchicki, Wayne	86T	777	$ .01	$ .05
Kranepool, Ed	71T	573	$1.00	$4.00	Krenchicki, Wayne	86TTR	55	$ .01	$ .06
Kranepool, Ed	72T	181	$ .10	$ .40	Krenchicki, Wayne	87T	774	$ .01	$ .04
Kranepool, Ed	72TIA	182	$ .10	$ .40	Kress, Chuck	54T	219	$3.75	$15.00
Kranepool, Ed	73T	329	$ .10	$ .40	Kress, Red	54T	160	$3.75	$15.00
Kranepool, Ed	74T	561	$ .10	$ .40	Kress, Red	55T	151	$4.00	$16.00
Kranepool, Ed	75T	324	$ .10	$ .40	Kress, Red	60T	460	$1.75	$7.00
Kranepool, Ed	76T	314	$ .05	$ .25	Kretlow, Lou	52T	42	$13.75	$55.00

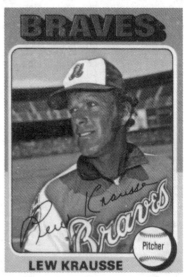

TOPPS

Player	Year	No.	VG	EX/MT
Kretlow, Lou	57T	139	$2.00	$8.00
Kreuter, Chad	89T	432	$ .01	$ .15
Kreuter, Chad	90T	562	$ .01	$ .03
Kreuter, Chad	93T	692	$ .01	$ .03
Kreutzer, Frank	64T	107	$ .50	$2.00
Kreutzer, Frank	65T	371	$1.00	$4.00
Kreutzer, Frank	66T	211	$ .50	$2.00
Kroll, Gary	65T	449	$1.25	$5.00
Kroll, Gary	66T	548	$7.00	$28.00
Krsnich, Mike	62T	289	$ .75	$3.00
Krsnich, Rocky	53T	229	$15.00	$60.00
Krsnich, Rocky	91TA53	229	$ .01	$ .15
Krueger, Bill	84T	178	$ .01	$ .15
Krueger, Bill	85T	528	$ .01	$ .06
Krueger, Bill	86T	58	$ .01	$ .05
Krueger, Bill	87T	238	$ .01	$ .04
Krueger, Bill	90T	518	$ .01	$ .03
Krueger, Bill	91T	417	$ .01	$ .03
Krueger, Bill	91TTR	70	$ .01	$ .05
Krueger, Bill	92T	368	$ .01	$ .10
Krueger, Bill	92TSC	861	$ .01	$ .10
Krueger, Bill	92TTR	61	$ .01	$ .05
Krug, Chris	66T	166	$ .50	$2.00
Kruk, John	86TTR	56	$ .10	$1.00
Kruk, John	87T	123	$ .10	$ .50
Kruk, John	88T	596	$ .01	$ .10
Kruk, John	89T	235	$ .01	$ .03
Kruk, John	89TTR	63	$ .01	$ .05
Kruk, John	90T	469	$ .01	$ .03
Kruk, John	91T	689	$ .01	$ .03
Kruk, John	91TSC	227	$ .05	$ .35
Kruk, John	92T	30	$ .01	$ .03
Kruk, John	92TSC	209	$ .01	$ .10
Kruk, John	93T	340	$ .01	$ .03
Kruk, John	93TSC	83	$ .05	$ .20
Krukow, Mike	77T	493	$0.25	$ .80
Krukow, Mike	78T	17	$ .04	$ .16
Krukow, Mike	79T	592	$ .03	$ .12
Krukow, Mike	80T	431	$ .01	$ .10
Krukow, Mike	81T	176	$ .01	$ .08
Krukow, Mike	82T	215	$ .01	$ .08
Krukow, Mike	82TTR	59	$ .01	$ .10
Krukow, Mike	83T	331	$ .01	$ .08
Krukow, Mike	83TTR	58	$ .01	$ .10
Krukow, Mike	84T	633	$ .01	$ .06
Krukow, Mike	85T	74	$ .01	$ .06
Krukow, Mike	86T	752	$ .01	$ .05
Krukow, Mike	87T	580	$ .01	$ .04
Krukow, Mike	88T	445	$ .01	$ .04
Krukow, Mike	89T	125	$ .01	$ .03
Krukow, Mike	90T	241	$ .01	$ .03
Kryhoski, Dick	52T	149	$7.00	$28.00
Kryhoski, Dick	54T	150	$3.75	$15.00
Kubek, Tony	57T	312	$27.50	$110.00
Kubek, Tony	58T	393	$4.50	$18.00
Kubek, Tony	59T	505	$2.75	$11.00
Kubek, Tony	60T	83	$1.75	$7.00
Kubek, Tony	61T	265	$2.00	$8.00
Kubek, Tony	62T	311	$1.25	$5.00
Kubek, Tony	62T	430	$2.25	$9.00
Kubek, Tony	63T	20	$1.00	$4.00
Kubek, Tony	64T	415	$1.50	$6.00
Kubek, Tony	65T	65	$1.00	$4.00
Kubiak, Ted	68T	79	$ .35	$1.40
Kubiak, Ted	69T	281	$ .50	$2.00
Kubiak, Ted	70T	688	$1.25	$5.00
Kubiak, Ted	71T	516	$ .50	$2.00
Kubiak, Ted	72T	23	$ .10	$ .40
Kubiak, Ted	73T	652	$ .60	$2.40
Kubiak, Ted	74T	228	$ .10	$ .40
Kubiak, Ted	75T	329	$ .10	$ .40
Kubiak, Ted	76T	578	$ .05	$ .25
Kubiak, Ted	77T	158	$ .05	$ .20
Kucab, John	52T	358	$43.75	$175.00
Kucek, John "Jack"	75T	614	$ .10	$ .40

Player	Year	No.	VG	EX/MT
Kucek, Jack	76T	597	$ .20	$ .80
Kucek, Jack	77T	623	$ .05	$ .20
Kucks, Johnny	56T	88	$2.75	$11.00
Kucks, Johnny	57T	185	$2.00	$8.00
Kucks, Johnny	58T	87	$2.00	$8.00
Kucks, Johnny	59T	289	$1.00	$4.00
Kucks, Johnny	60T	177	$ .75	$3.00
Kucks, Johnny	61T	94	$ .60	$2.40
Kucks, Johnny	62T	241	$ .75	$3.00
Kuenn, Harvey	54T	25	$9.00	$36.00
Kuenn, Harvey	56T	155	$4.00	$16.00
Kuenn, Harvey	57T	88	$2.75	$11.00
Kuenn, Harvey	58T	304	$3.50	$14.00
Kuenn, Harvey	58T	434	$1.50	$6.00
Kuenn, Harvey	59T	70	$2.25	$9.00
Kuenn, Harvey	60T	330	$1.25	$5.00
Kuenn, Harvey	60T	429	$1.50	$6.00
Kuenn, Harvey	61T	500	$1.50	$6.00
Kuenn, Harvey	62T	480	$1.75	$7.00
Kuenn, Harvey	63T	30	$ .50	$2.00
Kuenn, Harvey	64T	242	$ .65	$2.60
Kuenn, Harvey	65T	103	$ .35	$1.40
Kuenn, Harvey	66T	372	$ .65	$2.60
Kuenn, Harvey	73T	646	$ .75	$3.00
Kuenn, Harvey	74T	99	$ .10	$ .40
Kuenn, Harvey	83T	726	$ .01	$ .08

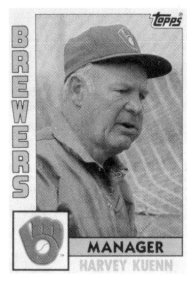

Player	Year	No.	VG	EX/MT
Kuenn, Harvey	84T	321	$ .01	$ .06
Kuenn, Harvey	91TA53	301	$ .10	$ .50
Kuhaulua, Fred	82T	731	$ .01	$ .08
Kuhn, Ken	57T	266	$5.00	$20.00
Kuiper, Duane	76T	508	$ .05	$ .25
Kuiper, Duane	77T	85	$ .05	$ .20
Kuiper, Duane	78T	332	$ .04	$ .16
Kuiper, Duane	79T	146	$ .03	$ .12
Kuiper, Duane	80T	429	$ .01	$ .10
Kuiper, Duane	81T	612	$ .01	$ .08
Kuiper, Duane	82T	233	$ .01	$ .08
Kuiper, Duane	82TTR	60	$ .01	$ .10
Kuiper, Duane	83T	767	$ .01	$ .08
Kuiper, Duane	84T	542	$ .01	$ .06
Kuiper, Duane	85T	22	$ .01	$ .06
Kunkel, Bill	61T	322	$ .60	$2.40
Kunkel, Bill	62T	147	$ .75	$3.00

TOPPS

Player	Year	No.	VG	EX/MT
Kunkel, Bill	63T	523	$2.25	$9.00
Kunkel, Bill	85T	136	$ .01	$ .10
Kunkel, Jeff	85T	136	$ .01	$ .10
Kunkel, Jeff	85T	288	$ .01	$ .06
Kunkel, Jeff	89T	92	$ .01	$ .03
Kunkel, Jeff	90T	174	$ .01	$ .03
Kunkel, Jeff	91T	562	$ .01	$ .03
Kunkel, Jeff	91TSC	580	$ .05	$ .25
Kuntz, Rusty	81T	112	$ .01	$ .15
Kuntz, Rusty	82T	237	$ .01	$ .08
Kuntz, Rusty	84T	598	$ .01	$ .06
Kuntz, Rusty	84TTR	66	$ .01	$ .15

Player	Year	No.	VG	EX/MT
Kuntz, Rusty	85T	73	$ .01	$ .06
Kusick, Craig	75T	297	$ .10	$ .40
Kusick, Craig	77T	38	$ .05	$ .20
Kusick, Craig	78T	137	$ .04	$ .16
Kusick, Craig	79T	472	$ .03	$ .12
Kusick, Craig	80T	693	$ .01	$ .10
Kusnyer, Art	72T	213	$ .20	$ .80
Kutcher, Randy	89TTR	64	$ .01	$ .05
Kutcher, Randy	90T	676	$ .01	$ .03
Kutyna, Marty	60T	516	$2.75	$11.00
Kutyna, Marty	61T	546	$7.50	$30.00
Kutyna, Marty	62T	566	$6.00	$24.00
Kuzava, Bob	51Tbb	22	$7.50	$30.00
Kuzava, Bob	52T	85	$7.00	$28.00
Kuzava, Bob	54T	230	$5.50	$22.00
Labine, Clem	52T	342	$57.50	$230.00
Labine, Clem	53T	14	$5.00	$20.00
Labine, Clem	54T	121	$4.50	$18.00
Labine, Clem	55T	180	$8.00	$32.00
Labine, Clem	56T	295	$3.00	$12.00
Labine, Clem	57T	53	$2.50	$10.00
Labine, Clem	58T	305	$1.25	$5.00
Labine, Clem	59T	262	$2.00	$8.00
Labine, Clem	59T	403	$1.00	$4.00
Labine, Clem	60T	29	$ .85	$3.40
Labine, Clem	61T	22	$ .60	$2.40
Labine, Clem	91TA53	14	$ .01	$ .15
Laboy, Jose	69T	524	$ .40	$1.60
Laboy, Jose	70T	238	$ .20	$ .80
Laboy, Jose	71T	132	$ .25	$1.00
Laboy, Jose	72T	727	$1.25	$5.00
Laboy, Jose	73T	642	$ .60	$2.40
Lacey, Bob	78T	29	$ .04	$ .16
Lacey, Bob	79T	647	$ .03	$ .12
Lacey, Bob	80T	316	$ .01	$ .10
Lacey, Bob	81T	481	$ .01	$ .08
Lacey, Bob	81TTR	784	$ .01	$ .15
Lacey, Bob	82T	103	$ .01	$ .08
Lachemann, Marcel	71T	84	$ .25	$1.00
Lachemann, Rene	65T	526	$35.00	$140.00
Lachemann, Rene	66T	157	$ .50	$2.00
Lachemann, Rene	67T	471	$1.50	$6.00
Lachemann, Rene	68T	422	$ .35	$1.40
Lachemann, Rene	83T	336	$ .01	$ .08
Lachemann, Rene	84TTR	67	$ .01	$ .15
Lachemann, Rene	85T	628	$ .01	$ .06
Lachemann, Rene	93T	505	$ .01	$ .03
LaCock, Pete	75T	494	$ .10	$ .40
LaCock, Pete	76T	101	$ .05	$ .25
LaCock, Pete	77T	561	$ .05	$ .20
LaCock, Pete	78T	157	$ .04	$ .16
LaCock, Pete	79T	248	$ .03	$ .12
LaCock, Pete	80T	389	$ .01	$ .10
LaCock, Pete	81T	9	$ .01	$ .08
LaCorte, Frank	76T	597	$ .20	$ .80
LaCorte, Frank	80T	411	$ .01	$ .10
LaCorte, Frank	81T	513	$ .01	$ .08
LaCorte, Frank	82T	248	$ .01	$ .08
LaCorte, Frank	83T	14	$ .01	$ .08
LaCorte, Frank	84T	301	$ .01	$ .06
LaCorte, Frank	84TTR	68	$ .01	$ .15
LaCorte, Frank	85T	153	$ .01	$ .06
LaCoss, Mike	79T	717	$ .10	$ .40
LaCoss, Mike	80T	199	$ .01	$ .10
LaCoss, Mike	81T	474	$ .01	$ .08
LaCoss, Mike	82T	294	$ .01	$ .08
LaCoss, Mike	82TTR	61	$ .01	$ .10
LaCoss, Mike	83T	92	$ .01	$ .08
LaCoss, Mike	84T	507	$ .01	$ .06
LaCoss, Mike	85T	666	$ .01	$ .06
LaCoss, Mike	85TTR	69	$ .01	$ .10
LaCoss, Mike	86T	359	$ .01	$ .05
LaCoss, Mike	86TTR	57	$ .01	$ .06
LaCoss, Mike	87T	151	$ .01	$ .04
LaCoss, Mike	88T	754	$ .01	$ .04
LaCoss, Mike	89T	417	$ .01	$ .03
LaCoss, Mike	90T	53	$ .01	$ .03
LaCoss, Mike	91T	242	$ .01	$ .03
LaCoss, Mike	91TSC	479	$ .05	$ .25
Lacy, Lee	73T	391	$ .25	$1.00
Lacy, Lee	74T	658	$ .10	$ .40
Lacy, Lee	75T	631	$ .10	$ .40
Lacy, Lee	76T	99	$ .05	$ .25
Lacy, Lee	76TTR	99	$ .05	$ .25
Lacy, Lee	77T	272	$ .05	$ .20
Lacy, Lee	78T	104	$ .04	$ .16
Lacy, Lee	79T	441	$ .03	$ .12
Lacy, Lee	80T	536	$ .01	$ .10
Lacy, Lee	81T	332	$ .01	$ .08
Lacy, Lee	82T	752	$ .01	$ .08
Lacy, Lee	83T	69	$ .01	$ .08
Lacy, Lee	84T	462	$ .01	$ .06
Lacy, Lee	85T	669	$ .01	$ .06
Lacy, Lee	85TTR	70	$ .01	$ .10
Lacy, Lee	86T	226	$ .01	$ .05
Lacy, Lee	87T	182	$ .01	$ .04
Lacy, Lee	88T	598	$ .01	$ .04
Ladd, Pete	80T	678	$ .01	$ .10
Ladd, Pete	84T	243	$ .01	$ .06
Ladd, Pete	85T	471	$ .01	$ .06
Ladd, Pete	86T	163	$ .01	$ .05
Ladd, Pete	86TTR	58	$ .01	$ .06
Ladd, Pete	87T	572	$ .01	$ .04
LaFrancois, Roger	83T	344	$ .01	$ .08
Laga, Mike	86TTR	59	$ .01	$ .06
Laga, Mike	87T	321	$ .01	$ .04

TOPPS

Player	Year	No.	VG	EX/MT	Player	Year	No.	VG	EX/MT
LaGrow, Lerrin	71T	39	$ .25	$1.00	Lampkin, Tom	92TSC	453	$ .01	$ .10
LaGrow, Lerrin	73T	369	$ .10	$ .40	Lampkin, Tom	93T	492	$ .01	$ .03
LaGrow, Lerrin	74T	433	$ .10	$ .40	Lancaster, Les	88T	112	$ .01	$ .04
LaGrow, Lerrin	75T	116	$ .10	$ .40	Lancaster, Les	89T	694	$ .01	$ .03
LaGrow, Lerrin	76T	138	$ .05	$ .25	Lancaster, Les	90T	437	$ .01	$ .03
LaGrow, Lerrin	78T	14	$ .04	$ .16	Lancaster, Les	91T	86	$ .01	$ .03
LaGrow, Lerrin	79T	527	$ .03	$ .12	Lancaster, Les	92T	213	$ .01	$ .03
LaGrow, Lerrin	80T	624	$ .01	$ .10	Lancaster, Les	92TSC	88	$ .01	$ .10
Lahoud, Joe	69T	189	$ .35	$1.40	Landaker, Dave	93T	743	$ .01	$ .15
Lahoud, Joe	70T	78	$ .20	$ .80	Landestoy, Rafael	79T	14	$ .03	$ .12
Lahoud, Joe	71T	622	$1.00	$4.00	Landestoy, Rafael	80T	268	$ .01	$ .10
Lahoud, Joe	72T	321	$ .10	$ .40	Landestoy, Rafael	81T	597	$ .01	$ .08
Lahoud, Joe	73T	212	$ .10	$ .40	Landestoy, Rafael	81TTR	786	$ .01	$ .15
Lahoud, Joe	74T	512	$ .10	$ .40	Landestoy, Rafael	82T	361	$ .01	$ .08
Lahoud, Joe	75T	317	$ .10	$ .40	Landestoy, Rafael	83T	684	$ .01	$ .08
Lahoud, Joe	76T	612	$ .05	$ .25	Landestoy, Rafael	83TTR	59	$ .01	$ .10
Lahoud, Joe	78T	382	$ .04	$ .16	Landestoy, Rafael	84T	477	$ .01	$ .06
Lahti, Jeff	83T	284	$ .01	$ .08	Landis, Bill	68T	189	$ .35	$1.40
Lahti, Jeff	84T	593	$ .01	$ .06	Landis, Bill	69T	264	$ .50	$2.00
Lahti, Jeff	85T	447	$ .01	$ .06	Landis, Jim	57T	375	$1.75	$7.00
Lahti, Jeff	86T	33	$ .01	$ .05	Landis, Jim	58T	108	$2.00	$8.00
Lahti, Jeff	87T	367	$ .01	$ .04	Landis, Jim	59T	493	$1.00	$4.00
Lake, Steve	84T	691	$ .01	$ .06	Landis, Jim	60T	550	$2.75	$11.00
Lake, Steve	85T	98	$ .01	$ .06	Landis, Jim	61T	271	$ .60	$2.40
Lake, Steve	86T	588	$ .01	$ .05	Landis, Jim	62T	540	$6.00	$24.00
Lake, Steve	87T	84	$ .01	$ .04	Landis, Jim	63T	485	$3.00	$12.00
Lake, Steve	88T	208	$ .01	$ .04	Landis, Jim	64T	264	$ .65	$2.60
Lake, Steve	89T	463	$ .01	$ .03	Landis, Jim	65T	376	$1.00	$4.00
Lake, Steve	89TTR	65	$ .01	$ .05	Landis, Jim	66T	128	$ .50	$2.00
Lake, Steve	90T	183	$ .01	$ .03	Landis, Jim	67T	483	$1.50	$6.00
Lake, Steve	91T	661	$ .01	$ .03	Landreaux, Ken	79T	619	$ .05	$ .20
Lake, Steve	91TSC	395	$ .05	$ .25	Landreaux, Ken	80T	88	$ .01	$ .10
Lake, Steve	92T	331	$ .01	$ .03	Landreaux, Ken	81T	219	$ .01	$ .08
Lake, Steve	92TSC	54	$ .01	$ .10	Landreaux, Ken	81TTR	787	$ .01	$ .15
Laker, Tim	93T	816	$ .05	$ .20	Landreaux, Ken	82T	114	$ .01	$ .08
Laker, Tim	93TSC	18	$ .05	$ .35	Landreaux, Ken	83T	376	$ .01	$ .08
Lamabe, Jack	62T	593	$5.25	$21.00	Landreaux, Ken	84T	533	$ .01	$ .06
Lamabe, Jack	63T	251	$ .90	$3.60	Landreaux, Ken	85T	418	$ .01	$ .06
Lamabe, Jack	64T	305	$ .65	$2.60	Landreaux, Ken	86T	782	$ .01	$ .05
Lamabe, Jack	65T	88	$ .35	$1.40	Landreaux, Ken	87T	699	$ .01	$ .04
Lamabe, Jack	66T	577	$7.00	$28.00	Landreaux, Ken	88T	23	$ .01	$ .04
Lamabe, Jack	67T	208	$ .50	$2.00	Landreth, Larry	78T	701	$ .04	$ .16
Lamabe, Jack	68T	311	$ .35	$1.40	Landrith, Hobie	56T	314	$2.50	$10.00
Lamanczyk, Dave	81T	391	$ .01	$ .08	Landrith, Hobie	57T	182	$2.00	$8.00
LaMay, Dick	62T	71	$ .60	$2.40	Landrith, Hobie	58T	24	$2.00	$8.00
Lamb, Ray	70T	131	$ .20	$ .80	Landrith, Hobie	59T	422	$1.00	$4.00
Lamb, Ray	71T	727	$1.50	$6.00	Landrith, Hobie	60T	42	$ .85	$3.40
Lamb, Ray	72T	422	$ .25	$1.00	Landrith, Hobie	61T	114	$ .60	$2.40
Lamb, Ray	73T	496	$ .25	$1.00	Landrith, Hobie	62T	279	$ .75	$3.00
Lamont, Gene	71T	39	$ .25	$1.00	Landrith, Hobie	63T	209	$ .90	$3.60
Lamont, Gene	75T	593	$ .10	$ .40	Landrum, Bill	88T	42	$ .01	$ .10
Lamont, Gene	92TTR	62	$ .01	$ .05	Landrum, Bill	90T	425	$ .01	$ .03
Lamont, Gene	93T	504	$ .01	$ .03	Landrum, Bill	91T	595	$ .01	$ .03
Lamp, Dennis	78T	711	$ .04	$ .16	Landrum, Bill	91TSC	431	$ .05	$ .25
Lamp, Dennis	79T	153	$ .03	$ .12	Landrum, Bill	92T	661	$ .01	$ .03
Lamp, Dennis	80T	54	$ .01	$ .10	Landrum, Bill	92TSC	672	$ .01	$ .10
Lamp, Dennis	81I	331	$ .01	$ .08	Landrum, Ced	92T	81	$ .01	$ .10
Lamp, Dennis	81TTR	785	$ .01	$ .15	Landrum, Ced	92TSC	334	$ .01	$ .10
Lamp, Dennis	82T	216	$ .01	$ .08	Landrum, Don	58T	291	$1.25	$5.00
Lamp, Dennis	82T	622	$ .01	$ .08	Landrum, Don	61T	338	$ .60	$2.40
Lamp, Dennis	83T	434	$ .01	$ .08	Landrum, Don	62T	323	$ .75	$3.00
Lamp, Dennis	84T	541	$ .01	$ .06	Landrum, Don	63T	113	$ .50	$2.00
Lamp, Dennis	84TTR	69	$ .01	$ .15	Landrum, Don	64T	286	$ .65	$2.60
Lamp, Dennis	85T	774	$ .01	$ .06	Landrum, Don	65T	596	$2.50	$10.00
Lamp, Dennis	86T	219	$ .01	$ .05	Landrum, Don	66T	43	$ .35	$1.40
Lamp, Dennis	87T	768	$ .01	$ .04	Landrum, Tito	81T	244	$ .01	$ .08
Lamp, Dennis	89T	188	$ .01	$ .03	Landrum, Tito	82T	658	$ .01	$ .08
Lamp, Dennis	90T	338	$ .01	$ .03	Landrum, Tito	83T	337	$ .01	$ .08
Lamp, Dennis	91T	14	$ .01	$ .03	Landrum, Tito	85T	33	$ .01	$ .06
Lamp, Dennis	92T	653	$ .01	$ .03	Landrum, Tito	86T	498	$ .01	$ .05
Lampard, Keith	70T	492	$ .35	$1.40	Landrum, Tito	87T	288	$ .01	$ .04
Lampard, Keith	71T	728	$1.10	$4.40	Landrum, Tito	88T	581	$ .01	$ .04
Lampard, Keith	72T	489	$ .25	$1.00	Lane, Jerry	54T	97	$3.75	$15.00
Lampkin, Tom	90T	172	$ .01	$ .03	Lang, Chip	77T	132	$ .05	$ .20
Lampkin, Tom	91TSC	530	$ .05	$ .25	Lange, Dick	74T	429	$ .10	$ .40

425

TOPPS

Player	Year	No.	VG	EX/MT	Player	Year	No.	VG	EX/MT
Lange, Dick	75T	114	$ .10	$ .40	LaPoint, Dave	85T	229	$ .01	$ .06
Lange, Dick	76T	176	$ .05	$ .25	LaPoint, Dave	85TTR	71	$ .01	$ .10
Langford, Rick	78T	327	$ .04	$ .16	LaPoint, Dave	86T	551	$ .01	$ .05
Langford, Rick	79T	29	$ .03	$ .12	LaPoint, Dave	86TTR	61	$ .01	$ .06
Langford, Rick	80T	546	$ .01	$ .10	LaPoint, Dave	87T	754	$ .01	$ .04
Langford, Rick	81T	154	$ .01	$ .08					
Langford, Rick	82T	454	$ .01	$ .08					
Langford, Rick	83T	286	$ .01	$ .08					
Langford, Rick	83T	531	$ .10	$ .40					
Langford, Rick	84T	629	$ .01	$ .06					
Langford, Rick	85T	347	$ .01	$ .06					
Langford, Rick	86T	766	$ .01	$ .05					
Langston, Mark	84TTR	70	$2.00	$8.00					
Langston, Mark	85T	625	$ .15	$1.50					
Langston, Mark	86T	495	$ .05	$ .25					
Langston, Mark	87T	215	$ .05	$ .20					
Langston, Mark	88T	80	$ .01	$ .10					
Langston, Mark	89T	355	$ .01	$ .10					
Langston, Mark	89TTR	66	$ .01	$ .10					
Langston, Mark	90T	530	$ .01	$ .10					
Langston, Mark	90TTR	54	$ .01	$ .05					
Langston, Mark	91T	755	$ .01	$ .03					
Langston, Mark	91TSC	27	$ .05	$ .25					
Langston, Mark	92T	165	$ .01	$ .03					
Langston, Mark	92TSC	670	$ .01	$ .10					
Langston, Mark	93T	210	$ .01	$ .03					
Lanier, Hal	65T	118	$ .50	$2.00					
Lanier, Hal	66T	156	$ .50	$2.00					
Lanier, Hal	66T	271	$ .50	$2.00					
Lanier, Hal	67T	4	$ .40	$1.60					
Lanier, Hal	68T	436	$ .35	$1.40					
Lanier, Hal	69T	316	$ .35	$1.40					
Lanier, Hal	70T	583	$ .50	$2.00					
Lanier, Hal	71T	181	$ .25	$1.00					
Lanier, Hal	72T	589	$ .35	$1.40					
Lanier, Hal	73T	479	$ .25	$1.00					
Lanier, Hal	74T	588	$ .10	$ .40					
Lanier, Hal	86TTR	60	$ .01	$ .06	**LaPoint, Dave**	**88T**	**334**	**$ .01**	**$ .04**
Lanier, Hal	87T	343	$ .01	$ .04	LaPoint, Dave	89T	89	$ .01	$ .03
Lanier, Hal	88T	684	$ .01	$ .04	LaPoint, Dave	89TTR	67	$ .01	$ .05
Lanier, Hal	89T	164	$ .01	$ .03	LaPoint, Dave	90T	186	$ .01	$ .03
Lanier, Max	52T	101	$7.00	$28.00	LaPoint, Dave	91T	484	$ .01	$ .03
Lankford, Ray	91T	682	$ .05	$ .35	Larker, Norm	59T	107	$1.50	$6.00
Lankford, Ray	91TSC	537	$1.25	$5.00	Larker, Norm	60T	394	$ .75	$3.00
Lankford, Ray	92T	292	$ .01	$ .10	Larker, Norm	61T	41	$2.25	$9.00
Lankford, Ray	92TSC	8	$ .10	$ .50	Larker, Norm	61T	130	$ .60	$2.40
Lankford, Ray	93T	386	$ .01	$ .15	Larker, Norm	62T	23	$ .60	$2.40
Lankford, Ray	93TSC	49	$ .05	$ .25	Larker, Norm	63T	536	$2.25	$9.00
Lansford, Carney	79T	212	$1.00	$4.00	Larkin, Barry	87T	648	$ .10	$1.00
Lansford, Carney	80T	337	$ .10	$1.00	Larkin, Barry	88T	102	$ .05	$ .25
Lansford, Carney	81T	639	$ .05	$ .25	Larkin, Barry	89T	515	$ .01	$ .15
Lansford, Carney	81TTR	788	$ .10	$ .50	Larkin, Barry	90T	10	$ .01	$ .15
Lansford, Carney	82T	91	$ .01	$ .08	Larkin, Barry	91T	730	$ .01	$ .10
Lansford, Carney	82T	161	$ .01	$ .15	Larkin, Barry	91TAS	400	$ .01	$ .10
Lansford, Carney	82T	786	$ .01	$ .08	Larkin, Barry	91TSC	92	$ .10	$1.00
Lansford, Carney	83T	523	$ .01	$ .08	Larkin, Barry	92T	465	$ .01	$ .10
Lansford, Carney	83TTR	60	$ .01	$ .10	Larkin, Barry	92TAS	389	$ .01	$ .03
Lansford, Carney	84T	767	$ .01	$ .06	Larkin, Barry	92TSC	100	$ .05	$ .35
Lansford, Carney	85T	422	$ .01	$ .06	Larkin, Barry	92TSC	596	$ .05	$ .25
Lansford, Carney	86T	134	$ .01	$ .05	Larkin, Barry	93T	110	$ .01	$ .10
Lansford, Carney	87T	678	$ .01	$ .04	Larkin, Barry	93T	404	$ .01	$ .10
Lansford, Carney	88T	292	$ .01	$ .04	Larkin, Gene	87TTR	60	$ .01	$ .15
Lansford, Carney	89T	47	$ .01	$ .03	Larkin, Gene	88T	746	$ .01	$ .10
Lansford, Carney	90T	316	$ .01	$ .03	Larkin, Gene	89T	318	$ .01	$ .03
Lansford, Carney	91T	502	$ .01	$ .03	Larkin, Gene	90T	556	$ .01	$ .03
Lansford, Carney	91TSC	231	$ .05	$ .25	Larkin, Gene	91T	102	$ .01	$ .03
Lansford, Carney	92T	495	$ .01	$ .03	Larkin, Gene	91TSC	132	$ .05	$ .25
Lansford, Carney	92TSC	45	$ .01	$ .10	Larkin, Gene	92T	284	$ .01	$ .03
Lansford, Carney	93T	127	$ .01	$ .03	Larkin, Gene	92TSC	66	$ .01	$ .10
LaPalme, Paul	52T	166	$7.00	$28.00	Larkin, Gene	93T	61	$ .01	$ .03
LaPalme, Paul	53T	201	$4.50	$18.00	Larkin, Gene	93TSC	42	$ .01	$ .10
LaPalme, Paul	57T	344	$5.00	$20.00	LaRoche, Dave	71T	174	$ .25	$1.00
LaPalme, Paul	91TA53	201	$ .01	$ .15	LaRoche, Dave	72T	352	$ .10	$ .40
LaPoint, Dave	83T	438	$ .05	$ .25	LaRoche, Dave	73T	426	$ .25	$1.00
LaPoint, Dave	84T	627	$ .01	$ .06	LaRoche, Dave	74T	502	$ .10	$ .40

TOPPS

Player	Year	No.	VG	EX/MT	Player	Year	No.	VG	EX/MT
LaRoche, Dave	75T	258	$ .10	$ .40	Lary, Frank	59T	393	$1.00	$4.00
LaRoche, Dave	76T	21	$ .05	$ .25	Lary, Frank	60T	85	$ .85	$3.40
LaRoche, Dave	77T	385	$ .05	$ .20	Lary, Frank	61T	48	$ .75	$3.00
LaRoche, Dave	78T	454	$ .04	$ .16	Lary, Frank	61T	50	$ .75	$3.00
LaRoche, Dave	79T	601	$ .03	$ .12	Lary, Frank	61T	243	$ .60	$2.40
LaRoche, Dave	80T	263	$ .01	$ .10	Lary, Frank	62T	57	$1.25	$5.00
					Lary, Frank	62TAS	474	$1.50	$6.00
					Lary, Frank	63T	140	$ .50	$2.00
					Lary, Frank	63T	218	$ .90	$3.60
					Lary, Frank	64T	197	$ .65	$2.60
					Lary, Frank	65T	127	$ .35	$1.40
					Lasher, Fred	68T	447	$ .35	$1.40
					Lasher, Fred	69T	373	$ .30	$1.20
					Lasher, Fred	70T	356	$ .35	$1.40
					Lasher, Fred	71T	707	$1.10	$4.40
					Laskey, Bill	83T	171	$ .01	$ .08
					Laskey, Bill	83T	518	$ .01	$ .08
					Laskey, Bill	84T	129	$ .01	$ .06
					Laskey, Bill	85T	331	$ .01	$ .06
					Laskey, Bill	86T	603	$ .01	$ .05
					Lasorda, Tom	54T	132	$40.00	$160.00
					Lasorda, Tom	73T	569	$1.10	$4.40
					Lasorda, Tom	74T	144	$ .50	$2.00
					Lasorda, Tom	78T	189	$ .05	$ .25
					Lasorda, Tom	83T	306	$ .01	$ .15
					Lasorda, Tom	84T	681	$ .01	$ .10
					Lasorda, Tom	85T	601	$ .01	$ .06
					Lasorda, Tom	86T	291	$ .01	$ .05
					Lasorda, Tom	87T	493	$ .01	$ .04
					Lasorda, Tom	88T	74	$ .01	$ .04
					Lasorda, Tom	89T	254	$ .01	$ .03
					Lasorda, Tom	90T	669	$ .01	$ .03
					Lasorda, Tom	91T	789	$ .01	$ .03
					Lasorda, Tom	92T	261	$ .01	$ .03
					Lasorda, Tom	93T	507	$ .01	$ .03
					Latman, Barry	59T	477	$1.00	$4.00
					Latman, Barry	60T	41	$ .85	$3.40
					Latman, Barry	61T	560	$7.50	$30.00
					Latman, Barry	62T	37	$ .60	$2.40
LaRoche, Dave	81T	529	$ .01	$ .08	Latman, Barry	62T	145	$ .60	$2.40
LaRoche, Dave	81TTR	789	$ .01	$ .15	Latman, Barry	63T	426	$1.00	$4.00
LaRoche, Dave	82T	142	$ .01	$ .08	Latman, Barry	64T	227	$ .65	$2.60
LaRoche, Dave	83T	333	$ .01	$ .08	Latman, Barry	65T	307	$ .50	$2.00
LaRoche, Dave	83T	334	$ .01	$ .08	Latman, Barry	66T	451	$1.50	$6.00
LaRose, Vic	69T	404	$ .30	$1.20	Latman, Barry	67T	28	$ .40	$1.60
Larsen, Don	56T	332	$10.00	$40.00	Lau, Charlie	58T	448	$2.00	$8.00
Larsen, Don	57T	175	$4.50	$18.00	Lau, Charlie	60T	312	$1.25	$5.00
Larsen, Don	58T	161	$2.75	$11.00	Lau, Charlie	61T	261	$ .60	$2.40
Larsen, Don	59T	205	$1.25	$5.00	Lau, Charlie	62T	533	$6.00	$24.00
Larsen, Don	59T	383	$2.00	$8.00	Lau, Charlie	63T	41	$ .50	$2.00
Larsen, Don	60T	353	$1.25	$5.00	Lau, Charley	64T	229	$ .65	$2.60
Larsen, Don	61T	177	$1.00	$4.00	Lau, Charlie	65T	94	$ .35	$1.40
Larsen, Don	61T	402	$5.00	$20.00	Lau, Charlie	66T	368	$ .50	$2.00
Larsen, Don	62T	33	$ .75	$3.00	Lau, Charley (Charlie)	67T	329	$ .60	$2.40
Larsen, Don	63T	163	$ .90	$3.60	Lau, Charlie	73T	593	$ .75	$3.00
Larsen, Don	64T	513	$1.25	$5.00	Lau, Charlie	74T	166	$ .10	$ .40
Larsen, Don	65T	389	$1.25	$5.00	Laudner, Tim	82T	766	$ .90	$3.60
Larson, Dan	77T	641	$ .05	$ .20	Laudner, Tim	83T	529	$ .01	$ .08
LaRussa, Tony	64T	244	$5.00	$20.00	Laudner, Tim	84T	363	$ .01	$ .06
LaRussa, Tony	68T	571	$1.75	$7.00	Laudner, Tim	85T	71	$ .01	$ .06
LaRussa, Tony	72T	451	$ .50	$2.00	Laudner, Tim	86T	184	$ .01	$ .05
LaRussa, Tony	83T	216	$ .01	$ .08	Laudner, Tim	87T	478	$ .01	$ .04
LaRussa, Tony	84T	591	$ .01	$ .06	Laudner, Tim	88T	671	$ .01	$ .04
LaRussa, Tony	85T	466	$ .01	$ .06	Laudner, Tim	89T	239	$ .01	$ .03
LaRussa, Tony	86T	531	$ .01	$ .05	Laudner, Tim	90T	777	$ .01	$ .03
LaRussa, Tony	87T	68	$ .01	$ .04	Lauzerique, George	69T	358	$ .30	$1.20
LaRussa, Tony	88T	344	$ .01	$ .04	Lauzerique, George	70T	41	$ .20	$ .80
LaRussa, Tony	89T	224	$ .01	$ .03	Lavagetto, Cookie	52T	365	$50.00	$200.00
LaRussa, Tony	90T	639	$ .01	$ .03	Lavagetto, Cookie	59T	74	$1.50	$6.00
LaRussa, Tony	91T	171	$ .01	$ .03	Lavagetto, Cookie	60T	221	$ .75	$3.00
LaRussa, Tony	92T	429	$ .01	$ .03	Lavagetto, Harry "Cookie"	61T	226	$ .60	$2.40
LaRussa, Tony	93T	511	$ .01	$ .03	LaValliere, Mike	87T	162	$ .01	$ .15
Lary, Frank	56T	191	$4.50	$18.00	LaValliere, Mike	87TTR	61	$ .01	$ .05
Lary, Frank	57T	168	$2.00	$8.00	LaValliere, Mike	88T	539	$ .01	$ .04
Lary, Frank	58T	245	$1.25	$5.00	LaValliere, Mike	89T	218	$ .01	$ .03

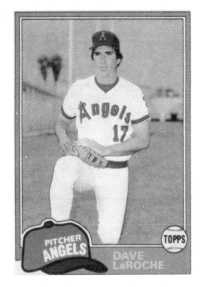

TOPPS

Player	Year	No.	VG	EX/MT
LaValliere, Mike	90T	478	$ .01	$ .03
LaValliere, Mike	91T	665	$ .01	$ .03
LaValliere, Mike	91TSC	279	$ .05	$ .25
LaValliere, Mike	92T	312	$ .01	$ .03
LaValliere, Mike	92TSC	216	$ .01	$ .10
LaValliere, Mike	93T	54	$ .01	$ .03
Lavelle, Gary	75T	624	$ .10	$ .40
Lavelle, Gary	76T	105	$ .05	$ .25
Lavelle, Gary	77T	423	$ .05	$ .20
Lavelle, Gary	78T	671	$ .04	$ .16
Lavelle, Gary	79T	311	$ .03	$ .12
Lavelle, Gary	80T	84	$ .01	$ .10
Lavelle, Gary	81T	588	$ .01	$ .08
Lavelle, Gary	82T	209	$ .01	$ .08
Lavelle, Gary	83T	791	$ .01	$ .08
Lavelle, Gary	84T	145	$ .01	$ .06
Lavelle, Gary	85T	462	$ .01	$ .06
Lavelle, Gary	85TTR	72	$ .01	$ .10
Lavelle, Gary	86T	622	$ .01	$ .05
Law, Rudy	79T	719	$1.50	$6.00
Law, Rudy	81T	127	$ .01	$ .08
Law, Rudy	83T	514	$ .01	$ .08
Law, Rudy	84T	47	$ .01	$ .06
Law, Rudy	85T	286	$ .01	$ .06
Law, Rudy	86T	637	$ .01	$ .05
Law, Rudy	86TTR	62	$ .01	$ .06
Law, Rudy	87T	382	$ .01	$ .04
Law, Vance	81T	551	$ .10	$1.00
Law, Vance	82T	291	$ .05	$ .25
Law, Vance	83T	98	$ .01	$ .08
Law, Vance	84T	667	$ .01	$ .06
Law, Vance	85T	137	$ .01	$ .10
Law, Vance	85T	413	$ .01	$ .06
Law, Vance	85TTR	73	$ .01	$ .10
Law, Vance	86T	787	$ .01	$ .05
Law, Vance	87T	127	$ .01	$ .04
Law, Vance	88T	346	$ .01	$ .04
Law, Vance	88TTR	60	$ .01	$ .05
Law, Vance	89T	501	$ .01	$ .03
Law, Vance	90T	287	$ .01	$ .03
Law, Vern	52T	81	$8.00	$32.00
Law, Vern	54T	235	$3.75	$15.00
Law, Vernon	56T	252	$2.50	$10.00
Law, Vernon	57T	199	$2.00	$8.00
Law, Vernon "Vern"	58T	132	$1.25	$5.00
Law, Vern	59T	12	$1.50	$6.00
Law, Vern	59T	428	$1.00	$4.00
Law, Vern	60T	453	$1.50	$6.00
Law, Vern	61T	47	$ .75	$3.00
Law, Vern	61T	250	$ .75	$3.00
Law, Vern	61T	400	$1.00	$4.00
Law, Vern	62T	295	$ .75	$3.00
Law, Vern	63T	184	$ .50	$2.00
Law, Vern	64T	472	$1.00	$4.00
Law, Vern	65T	515	$1.25	$5.00
Law, Vern	66T	15	$ .35	$1.40
Law, Vern	66T	221	$1.75	$7.00
Law, Vern	67T	351	$ .60	$2.40
Law, Vern	85T	137	$ .01	$ .10
Law, Vern	91TA53	324	$ .05	$ .20
Lawless, Tom	83T	423	$ .01	$ .08
Lawless, Tom	86T	228	$ .01	$ .05
Lawless, Tom	87T	647	$ .01	$ .04
Lawless, Tom	88T	183	$ .01	$ .04
Lawless, Tom	89T	312	$ .01	$ .03
Lawless, Tom	90T	49	$ .01	$ .03
Lawrence, Brooks	56T	305	$2.50	$10.00
Lawrence, Brooks	57T	66	$2.00	$8.00
Lawrence, Brooks	58T	374	$1.00	$4.00
Lawrence, Brooks	59T	67	$1.50	$6.00
Lawrence, Brooks	60T	434	$ .75	$3.00
Lawson, Steve	73T	612	$ .75	$3.00
Lawton, Marcus	90T	302	$ .01	$ .03
Laxton, Bill	77T	394	$ .05	$ .20
Layana, Tim	90TTR	55	$ .01	$ .10
Layana, Tim	91T	627	$ .01	$ .03
Layana, Tim	91TSC	396	$ .05	$ .25
Layana, Tim	92TSC	419	$ .01	$ .10
Lazar, Dan	69T	439	$ .30	$1.20
Lazar, Dan	70T	669	$1.25	$5.00
Lazorko, Jack	85T	317	$ .01	$ .06
Lazorko, Jack	87TTR	62	$ .01	$ .05
Lazorko, Jack	88T	601	$ .01	$ .04
Lazorko, Jack	89T	362	$ .01	$ .03

Player	Year	No.	VG	EX/MT
Lea, Charlie	81T	293	$ .01	$ .08
Lea, Charlie	82T	38	$ .01	$ .08
Lea, Charlie	83T	629	$ .01	$ .08
Lea, Charlie	84T	421	$ .01	$ .06
Lea, Charlie	84T	516	$ .01	$ .06
Lea, Charlie	85T	345	$ .01	$ .06
Lea, Charlie	86T	526	$ .01	$ .05
Leach, Rick	82T	266	$ .01	$ .08
Leach, Rick	83T	147	$ .01	$ .08
Leach, Rick	84T	427	$ .01	$ .06
Leach, Rick	84TTR	71	$ .01	$ .15
Leach, Rick	85T	593	$ .01	$ .06
Leach, Rick	86TTR	63	$ .01	$ .06
Leach, Rick	87T	716	$ .01	$ .04
Leach, Rick	88T	323	$ .01	$ .04
Leach, Rick	89T	682	$ .01	$ .03
Leach, Rick	89TTR	68	$ .01	$ .05
Leach, Rick	90T	27	$ .01	$ .03
Leach, Rick	90TTR	56	$ .01	$ .05
Leach, Terry	82T	623	$ .05	$ .25
Leach, Terry	83T	187	$ .01	$ .08
Leach, Terry	86T	774	$ .01	$ .05
Leach, Terry	87TTR	63	$ .01	$ .05
Leach, Terry	88T	457	$ .01	$ .04
Leach, Terry	89T	207	$ .01	$ .03
Leach, Terry	89TTR	69	$ .01	$ .05
Leach, Terry	90T	508	$ .01	$ .03
Leach, Terry	90TTR	57	$ .01	$ .05
Leach, Terry	91TSC	397	$ .05	$ .25
Leach, Terry	92T	644	$ .01	$ .03
Leach, Terry	92TSC	778	$ .01	$ .10
Leach, Terry	93T	443	$ .01	$ .03
Leahy, Pat	93T	641	$ .05	$ .20
Leal, Luis	81T	577	$ .01	$ .08

TOPPS

Player	Year	No.	VG	EX/MT	Player	Year	No.	VG	EX/MT
Leal, Luis	82T	412	$.01	$.08	Lefebvre, Jim	72T	369	$.10	$.40
Leal, Luis	83T	109	$.01	$.08	Lefebvre, Jim	89TTR	70	$.01	$.05
Leal, Luis	84T	783	$.01	$.06	Lefebvre, Jim	90T	459	$.01	$.03
Leal, Luis	85T	622	$.01	$.06	Lefebvre, Jim	91T	699	$.01	$.03
Leal, Luis	86T	459	$.01	$.05	Lefebvre, Jim	92TTR	63	$.01	$.05
Leary, Tim	82T	623	$.05	$.25	Lefebvre, Jim	93T	502	$.01	$.03
Leary, Tim	86TTR	64	$.01	$.06	Lefebvre, Joe	81T	88	$.01	$.08
Leary, Tim	87T	32	$.01	$.04	Lefebvre, Joe	81TTR	790	$.01	$.15
Leary, Tim	87TTR	64	$.01	$.05	Lefebvre, Joe	82T	434	$.01	$.08
Leary, Tim	88T	367	$.01	$.04	Lefebvre, Joe	83T	644	$.01	$.08
Leary, Tim	89T	249	$.01	$.03	Lefebvre, Joe	83TTR	61	$.01	$.10
Leary, Tim	90T	516	$.01	$.03	Lefebvre, Joe	84T	148	$.01	$.06
Leary, Tim	90TTR	58	$.01	$.05	Lefebvre, Joe	85T	531	$.01	$.06
Leary, Tim	91T	161	$.01	$.03	Lefferts, Craig	84T	99	$.05	$.25
Leary, Tim	91TSC	423	$.05	$.25	Lefferts, Craig	84TTR	72	$.10	$.40
Leary, Tim	92T	778	$.01	$.03	Lefferts, Craig	85T	608	$.01	$.06
Leary, Tim	92TSC	291	$.01	$.10	Lefferts, Craig	86T	244	$.01	$.05
Lee, Bill	70T	279	$.35	$1.40	Lefferts, Craig	87T	501	$.01	$.04
Lee, Bill	71T	58	$.25	$1.00	Lefferts, Craig	88T	734	$.01	$.04
Lee, Bill	72T	636	$.40	$1.60	Lefferts, Craig	89T	372	$.01	$.03
Lee, Bill	73T	224	$.10	$.40	Lefferts, Craig	90T	158	$.01	$.03
Lee, Bill	74T	118	$.10	$.40	Lefferts, Craig	90TTR	59	$.01	$.05
Lee, Bill	75T	128	$.10	$.40	Lefferts, Craig	91T	448	$.01	$.03
Lee, Bill	76T	396	$.05	$.25	Lefferts, Craig	91TSC	533	$.05	$.25
Lee, Bill	77T	503	$.05	$.20	Lefferts, Craig	92T	41	$.01	$.03
Lee, Bill	78T	295	$.04	$.16	Lefferts, Craig	92TSC	618	$.01	$.10
Lee, Bill	79T	455	$.03	$.12	Lefferts, Craig	93T	617	$.01	$.03
Lee, Bill	80T	97	$.01	$.10	LeFlore, Ron	75T	628	$.25	$1.00
Lee, Bill	81T	633	$.01	$.08	LeFlore, Ron	76T	61	$.10	$.40
Lee, Bill	82T	323	$.01	$.08	LeFlore, Ron	77T	240	$.05	$.20
Lee, Bob	64T	502	$1.00	$4.00	LeFlore, Ron	78T	480	$.04	$.16
Lee, Bob	65T	46	$.35	$1.40	LeFlore, Ron	79T	4	$.03	$.12
Lee, Bob	66T	481	$1.50	$6.00	LeFlore, Ron	79T	660	$.03	$.12
Lee, Bob	67T	313	$.60	$2.40	LeFlore, Ron	80T	80	$.01	$.10
Lee, Bob	68T	543	$.70	$2.80	LeFlore, Ron	81T	4	$.15	$1.50
Lee, Don	57T	379	$1.75	$7.00	LeFlore, Ron	81T	710	$.01	$.08
Lee, Don	59T	132	$1.00	$4.00	LeFlore, Ron	81TRB	204	$.01	$.10
Lee, Don	60T	503	$1.25	$5.00	LeFlore, Ron	81TTR	791	$.01	$.15
Lee, Don	61T	153	$.60	$2.40	LeFlore, Ron	82T	140	$.01	$.08
Lee, Don	62T	166	$.60	$2.40	LeFlore, Ron	83T	560	$.01	$.08
Lee, Don	63T	372	$1.00	$4.00	Lehman, Ken	57T	366	$1.75	$7.00
Lee, Don	64T	493	$1.00	$4.00	Lehman, Ken	58T	141	$1.25	$5.00
Lee, Don	65T	595	$1.40	$5.60	Lehman, Ken	59T	31	$1.50	$6.00
Lee, Leron	70T	96	$.50	$2.00	Leibrandt, Charlie	81T	126	$.10	$1.00
Lee, Leron	71T	521	$.50	$2.00	Leibrandt, Charlie	82T	169	$.01	$.08
Lee, Leron	72T	238	$.10	$.40	Leibrandt, Charlie	83T	607	$.01	$.08
Lee, Leron	73T	83	$.10	$.40	Leibrandt, Charlie	85T	459	$.01	$.06
Lee, Leron	74T	651	$.10	$.40	Leibrandt, Charlie	86T	77	$.01	$.05
Lee, Leron	75T	506	$.10	$.40	Leibrandt, Charlie	87T	223	$.01	$.04
Lee, Leron	76T	487	$.05	$.25	Leibrandt, Charlie	88T	569	$.01	$.04
Lee, Manny	86T	23	$.05	$.20	Leibrandt, Charlie	89T	301	$.01	$.03
Lee, Manny	87T	574	$.01	$.04	Leibrandt, Charlie	90T	776	$.01	$.03
Lee, Manny	88T	722	$.01	$.04	Leibrandt, Charlie	90TTR	60	$.01	$.05
Lee, Manny	89T	371	$.01	$.03	Leibrandt, Charlie	91T	456	$.01	$.03
Lee, Manny	90T	113	$.01	$.03	Leibrandt, Charlie	91TSC	527	$.05	$.25
Lee, Manny	91T	297	$.01	$.03	Leibrandt, Charlie	92T	152	$.01	$.03
Lee, Manny	91TSC	168	$.05	$.25	Leibrandt, Charlie	92TSC	366	$.01	$.10
Lee, Manuel "Manny"	92T	634	$.01	$.03	Leibrandt, Charlie	93T	677	$.01	$.03
Lee, Manuel	92TSC	283	$.01	$.10	Leiper, Dave	87T	441	$.01	$.10
Lee, Manuel	93T	488	$.01	$.03	Leiper, Dave	89T	82	$.01	$.03
Lee, Mark	79T	138	$.03	$.12	Leiper, Dave	90T	773	$.01	$.03
Lee, Mark	80T	557	$.01	$.10	Leiter, Al	88T	18	$.03	$.15
Lee, Mark	91T	721	$.01	$.10	Leiter, Al	89T	659	$.01	$.03
Lee, Mark	92T	384	$.01	$.03	Leiter, Al	89TTR	71	$.01	$.10
Lee, Mark	92TSC	32	$.01	$.10	Leiter, Al	90T	138	$.01	$.03
Lee, Mike	60T	521	$2.75	$11.00	Leiter, Al	91T	233	$.01	$.03
Lee, Terry	92T	262	$.01	$.03	Leiter, Al	92TSC	231	$.01	$.10
Leek, Gene	61T	527	$7.50	$30.00	Leiter, Mark	92T	537	$.01	$.03
Lefebvre, Jim	65T	561	$3.00	$12.00	Leiter, Mark	92TSC	889	$.01	$.10
Lefebvre, Jim	66T	57	$.40	$1.60	Leiter, Mark	93T	216	$.01	$.03
Lefebvre, Jim	67T	260	$.50	$2.00	Leiter, Mark	93TSC	116	$.01	$.10
Lefebvre, Jim	68T	457	$.35	$1.40	Leius, Scott	91TSC	338	$.05	$.35
Lefebvre, Jim	69T	140	$.35	$1.40	Leius, Scott	91TTR	71	$.01	$.10
Lefebvre, Jim	70T	553	$.50	$2.00	Leius, Scott	92T	74	$.01	$.03
Lefebvre, Jim	71T	459	$.50	$2.00	Leius, Scott	92TSC	350	$.01	$.10

TOPPS

Player	Year	No.	VG	EX/MT
Leius, Scott	93T	146	$ .01	$ .03
Leius, Scott	93TSC	254	$ .01	$ .10
Leja, Frank	54T	175	$5.00	$20.00
Leja, Frank	55T	99	$2.50	$10.00
LeJohn, Don	66T	41	$ .35	$1.40
Lemanczyk, Dave	75T	571	$ .10	$ .40
Lemanczyk, Dave	76T	409	$ .05	$ .25
Lemanczyk, Dave	77T	611	$ .05	$ .20
Lemanczyk, Dave	78T	33	$ .04	$ .16
Lemanczyk, Dave	79T	207	$ .03	$ .12
Lemanczyk, Dave	80T	124	$ .01	$ .10
Lemaster, Denver	63T	74	$ .50	$2.00
Lemaster, Denver	64T	152	$ .50	$2.00
Lemaster, Denver	65T	441	$1.00	$4.00
Lemaster, Denver	66T	252	$ .50	$2.00
Lemaster, Denver	67T	288	$ .60	$2.40
Lemaster, Denny "Denver"	68T	491	$ .75	$3.00
Lemaster, Denny	69T	96	$ .35	$1.40
Lemaster, Denny	70T	178	$ .20	$ .80
Lemaster, Denny	71T	636	$1.00	$4.00
Lemaster, Denny	72T	371	$ .10	$ .40
LeMaster, Johnnie	76T	596	$ .15	$ .60
LeMaster, Johnnie	77T	151	$ .05	$ .20
LeMaster, Johnnie	78T	538	$ .04	$ .16
LeMaster, Johnnie	79T	284	$ .03	$ .12
LeMaster, Johnnie	80T	434	$ .01	$ .10
LeMaster, Johnnie	81T	84	$ .01	$ .08
LeMaster, Johnnie	82T	304	$ .01	$ .08
LeMaster, Johnnie	83T	154	$ .01	$ .08
LeMaster, Johnnie	84T	663	$ .01	$ .06
LeMaster, Johnnie	85T	772	$ .01	$ .06
LeMaster, Johnnie	85TTR	74	$ .01	$ .10
LeMaster, Johnnie	86T	289	$ .01	$ .05
LeMay, Dick	63T	459	$3.00	$12.00
Lemke, Mark	89T	327	$ .01	$ .15
Lemke, Mark	90T	451	$ .01	$ .03
Lemke, Mark	91T	251	$ .01	$ .03
Lemke, Mark	91TSC	203	$ .05	$ .25
Lemke, Mark	92T	689	$ .01	$ .03
Lemke, Mark	92TSC	316	$ .01	$ .10
Lemon, Bob	57T	120	$5.50	$22.00
Lemon, Bob	58T	2	$5.00	$20.00
Lemon, Bob	60T	460	$1.75	$7.00
Lemon, Bob	61T	44	$10.00	$40.00
Lemon, Bob	71T	91	$ .35	$1.40
Lemon, Bob	72T	449	$ .30	$1.20
Lemon, Bob	78T	574	$ .10	$ .40
Lemon, Bob	91TA53	284	$ .10	$ .50
Lemon, Chet	76T	590	$ .15	$ .60
Lemon, Chet	77T	58	$ .05	$ .20
Lemon, Chet	78T	127	$ .04	$ .16
Lemon, Chet	79T	333	$ .03	$ .12
Lemon, Chet	80T	589	$ .01	$ .10
Lemon, Chet	81T	242	$ .01	$ .08
Lemon, Chet	82T	216	$ .01	$ .08
Lemon, Chet	82T	493	$ .01	$ .08
Lemon, Chet	82TTR	62	$ .01	$ .10
Lemon, Chet	83T	727	$ .01	$ .08
Lemon, Chet	84T	611	$ .01	$ .06
Lemon, Chet	85T	20	$ .01	$ .06
Lemon, Chet	86T	160	$ .01	$ .05
Lemon, Chet	87T	739	$ .01	$ .04
Lemon, Chet	88T	366	$ .01	$ .04
Lemon, Chet	89T	514	$ .01	$ .03
Lemon, Chet	90T	271	$ .01	$ .03
Lemon, Chet	91T	469	$ .01	$ .03
Lemon, Chet	91TSC	23	$ .05	$ .25
Lemon, Don	93T	441	$ .10	$ .40
Lemon, Jim	54T	103	$4.50	$18.00
Lemon, Jim	57T	57	$2.00	$8.00
Lemon, Jim	58T	15	$2.00	$8.00
Lemon, Jim	59T	74	$1.50	$6.00
Lemon, Jim	59T	215	$1.00	$4.00
Lemon, Jim	60T	440	$ .75	$3.00
Lemon, Jim	61T	44	$10.00	$40.00
Lemon, Jim	61T	450	$1.35	$5.40
Lemon, Jim	62T	510	$1.50	$6.00
Lemon, Jim	63T	369	$ .90	$3.60
Lemon, Jim	68T	341	$ .35	$1.40
Lemon, Jim	69T	294	$ .50	$2.00
Lemonds, Dave	71T	458	$ .50	$2.00
Lemonds, Dave	72T	413	$ .25	$1.00
Lemonds, Dave	73T	534	$ .60	$2.40
Lemongello, Mark	77T	478	$ .05	$ .20
Lemongello, Mark	78T	358	$ .04	$ .16
Lemongello, Mark	79T	187	$ .03	$ .12
Lenhardt, Don	51Tbb	33	$7.50	$30.00
Lenhardt, Don	52T	4	$13.75	$55.00
Lenhardt, Don	54T	157	$3.75	$15.00
Lenhardt, Don	73T	131	$ .20	$ .80
Lennon, Bob	55T	119	$2.25	$9.00
Lennon, Bob	56T	104	$2.50	$10.00
Lennon, Bob	57T	371	$1.75	$7.00
Lennon, Patrick	92TSC	679	$ .01	$ .10
Leon, Danny	92TTR	64	$ .01	$ .15
Leon, Eddie	70T	292	$ .35	$1.40
Leon, Eddie	71T	252	$ .25	$1.00
Leon, Eddie	72T	721	$1.25	$5.00
Leon, Eddie	73T	287	$ .10	$ .40
Leon, Eddie	74T	501	$ .10	$ .40
Leon, Eddie	75T	528	$ .10	$ .40
Leon, Maximino	75T	442	$ .10	$ .40
Leon, Maximino	76T	576	$ .05	$ .25
Leon, Maximino	77T	213	$ .05	$ .20
Leonard, Dave	72T	527	$ .40	$1.60
Leonard, Dennis	75T	615	$ .25	$1.00
Leonard, Dennis	76T	334	$ .05	$ .25
Leonard, Dennis	77T	75	$ .05	$ .20
Leonard, Dennis	78T	205	$ .20	$ .80
Leonard, Dennis	78T	665	$ .04	$ .16
Leonard, Dennis	79T	218	$ .03	$ .12
Leonard, Dennis	80T	565	$ .01	$ .10
Leonard, Dennis	81T	185	$ .01	$ .08
Leonard, Dennis	82T	495	$ .01	$ .08
Leonard, Dennis	83T	785	$ .01	$ .08

Player	Year	No.	VG	EX/MT
Lemke, Mark	93T	116	$ .01	$ .03
Lemke, Mark	93TSC	172	$ .01	$ .10
Lemon, Bob	52T	268	$45.00	$180.00
Lemon, Bob	56T	255	$8.75	$35.00

TOPPS

Player	Year	No.	VG	EX/MT
Leonard, Dennis	84T	375	$ .01	$ .06
Leonard, Dennis	86TTR	65	$ .01	$ .06
Leonard, Dennis	87T	38	$ .01	$ .04
Leonard, Dutch	52T	110	$7.00	$28.00
Leonard, Dutch	53T	155	$6.25	$25.00
Leonard, Dutch	79TRH	418	$ .03	$ .12
Leonard, Dutch	91TA53	155	$ .01	$ .15
Leonard, Jeff	80T	106	$ .10	$ .50
Leonard, Jeff	81T	469	$ .05	$ .20
Leonard, Jeff	82T	47	$ .01	$ .08
Leonard, Jeff	83T	309	$ .01	$ .08
Leonard, Jeff	84T	576	$ .01	$ .06
Leonard, Jeff	84T	748	$ .01	$ .06
Leonard, Jeff	85T	619	$ .01	$ .06
Leonard, Jeff	85TAS	718	$ .01	$ .06
Leonard, Jeff	86T	490	$ .01	$ .05
Leonard, Jeffrey	87T	280	$ .01	$ .04
Leonard, Jeffrey	88T	570	$ .01	$ .04
Leonard, Jeffrey	89T	160	$ .01	$ .03
Leonard, Jeffrey	89TTR	72	$ .01	$ .05
Leonard, Jeffrey	90T	455	$ .01	$ .03
Leonard, Jeffrey	91T	55	$ .01	$ .03
Leonard, Mark	92TSC	538	$ .01	$ .10
Leonard, Mark	93T	729	$ .01	$ .03
Leonhard, Dave	68T	56	$ .35	$1.40
Leonhard, Dave	69T	228	$ .50	$2.00
Leonhard, Dave	70T	674	$1.25	$5.00
Leonhard, Dave	71T	716	$1.10	$4.40
Lepcio, Ted	52T	335	$43.75	$175.00
Lepcio, Ted	53T	18	$4.00	$16.00
Lepcio, Ted	54T	66	$7.50	$30.00
Lepcio, Ted	55T	128	$2.25	$9.00
Lepcio, Ted	57T	288	$5.00	$20.00
Lepcio, Ted	58T	29	$2.00	$8.00
Lepcio, Ted	59T	348	$1.00	$4.00
Lepcio, Ted	60T	97	$ .85	$3.40
Lepcio, Ted	61T	234	$ .60	$2.40

Player	Year	No.	VG	EX/MT
Lepcio, Ted	91TA53	18	$ .01	$ .15
Leppert, Don	62T	36	$ .60	$2.40
Leppert, Don	63T	243	$ .90	$3.60
Leppert, Don	64T	463	$1.00	$4.00
Leppert, Don	73T	517	$ .25	$1.00
Leppert, Don	74T	489	$ .10	$ .40

Player	Year	No.	VG	EX/MT
Lerch, Randy	76T	595	$ .05	$ .25
Lerch, Randy	77T	489	$ .20	$ .80
Lerch, Randy	78T	271	$ .04	$ .16
Lerch, Randy	79T	52	$ .03	$ .12
Lerch, Randy	80T	344	$ .01	$ .10
Lerch, Randy	81T	584	$ .01	$ .08
Lerch, Randy	81TTR	792	$ .01	$ .15
Lerch, Randy	82T	466	$ .01	$ .08
Lerch, Randy	83T	686	$ .01	$ .08
Lerch, Randy	85T	103	$ .01	$ .06
Lersch, Barry	69T	206	$ .35	$1.40
Lersch, Barry	71T	739	$1.50	$6.00
Lersch, Barry	72T	453	$ .25	$1.00
Lersch, Barry	73T	559	$ .60	$2.40
Lersch, Barry	74T	313	$ .10	$ .40
Lersch, Barry	74TTR	313	$ .10	$ .40
Leshnock, Donnie	91TTR	72	$ .05	$ .25
Leshnock, Donnie	93T	701	$ .15	$1.50
Leskanic, Curtis	93T	774	$ .01	$ .15
Lesley, Brad	85T	597	$ .01	$ .06
Levis, Jesse	93T	801	$ .01	$ .15
Lewallyn, Denny	82T	356	$ .01	$ .08
Lewis, Darren	91T	239	$ .01	$ .10
Lewis, Darren	91TSC	362	$ .05	$ .35
Lewis, Darren	92T	743	$ .01	$ .03
Lewis, Darren	92TSC	31	$ .01	$ .10
Lewis, Darren	93T	176	$ .01	$ .03
Lewis, Darren	93TSC	143	$ .01	$ .10
Lewis, Johnny	64T	479	$1.00	$4.00
Lewis, Johnny	65T	277	$ .50	$2.00
Lewis, Johnny	66T	282	$ .50	$2.00
Lewis, Johnny	67T	91	$ .40	$1.60
Lewis, Johnny	74T	236	$ .10	$ .40
Lewis, Mark	89T	222	$ .05	$ .25
Lewis, Mark	91TSC	492	$ .10	$ .50
Lewis, Mark	91TTR	73	$ .01	$ .15
Lewis, Mark	92T	446	$ .01	$ .10
Lewis, Mark	92TSC	193	$ .01	$ .15
Lewis, Mark	93T	762	$ .01	$ .03
Lewis, Scott	92TSC	43	$ .05	$ .25
Lewis, Scott	93T	668	$ .01	$ .03
Ley, Terry	72T	506	$ .20	$ .80
Leyland, Jim	86TTR	66	$ .05	$ .25
Leyland, Jim	87T	93	$ .01	$ .10
Leyland, Jim	88T	624	$ .01	$ .04
Leyland, Jim	89T	284	$ .01	$ .03
Leyland, Jim	90T	699	$ .01	$ .03
Leyland, Jim	91T	381	$ .01	$ .03
Leyland, Jim	92T	141	$ .01	$ .03
Leyland, Jim	93T	511	$ .01	$ .03
Leyritz, Jim	90TTR	61	$ .01	$ .10
Leyritz, Jim	91T	202	$ .01	$ .03
Leyritz, Jim	92TSC	198	$ .01	$ .10
Leyritz, Jim	93T	385	$ .01	$ .03
Leyritz, Jim	93TSC	234	$ .01	$ .10
Leyva, Nick	89T	74	$ .01	$ .03
Leyva, Nick	90T	400	$ .01	$ .03
Leyva, Nick	91T	141	$ .01	$ .03
Lezcano, Carlos	81T	381	$ .01	$ .08
Lezcano, Carlos	82T	51	$ .05	$ .25
Lezcano, Sixto	76T	353	$ .10	$ .40
Lezcano, Sixto	77T	185	$ .05	$ .20
Lezcano, Sixto	78T	595	$ .04	$ .16
Lezcano, Sixto	79T	685	$ .03	$ .12
Lezcano, Sixto	80T	215	$ .01	$ .10
Lezcano, Sixto	81T	25	$ .01	$ .08
Lezcano, Sixto	81TTR	793	$ .01	$ .15
Lezcano, Sixto	82T	727	$ .01	$ .08
Lezcano, Sixto	82TTR	63	$ .01	$ .10
Lezcano, Sixto	83T	455	$ .01	$ .08
Lezcano, Sixto	84T	185	$ .01	$ .06
Lezcano, Sixto	85T	556	$ .01	$ .06
Lezcano, Sixto	85TTR	75	$ .01	$ .10
Lezcano, Sixto	86T	278	$ .01	$ .05
Liddle, Don	54T	225	$3.75	$15.00

TOPPS

Player	Year	No.	VG	EX/MT
Liddle, Don	56T	325	$2.50	$10.00
Lieberthal, Mike	91T	471	$ .05	$ .20
Lilliquist, Derek	89TTR	73	$ .01	$ .10
Lilliquist, Derek	90T	282	$ .01	$ .03
Lilliquist, Derek	91T	683	$ .01	$ .03
Lilliquist, Derek	91TSC	268	$ .05	$ .25
Lilliquist, Derek	92TSC	864	$ .01	$ .10
Lilliquist, Derek	93T	31	$ .01	$ .03
Lillis, Bob	59T	133	$1.00	$4.00
Lillis, Bob	60T	354	$ .75	$3.00
Lillis, Bob	61T	38	$ .60	$2.40
Lillis, Bob	62T	74	$ .60	$2.40
Lillis, Bob	63T	119	$ .50	$2.00
Lillis, Bob	64T	321	$ .65	$2.60
Lillis, Bob	74T	31	$ .10	$ .40
Lillis, Bob	83T	66	$ .01	$ .08
Lillis, Bob	84T	441	$ .01	$ .06
Lillis, Bob	85T	186	$ .01	$ .06
Lillis, Bob	86T	561	$ .01	$ .05
Limmer, Lou	54T	232	$3.75	$15.00
Limmer, Lou	55T	54	$2.25	$9.00
Linares, Rufino	82T	244	$ .01	$ .08
Linares, Rufino	83T	467	$ .01	$ .08
Linares, Rufino	85T	167	$ .01	$ .06
Lind, Jose	88T	767	$ .01	$ .15
Lind, Jose	89T	273	$ .01	$ .03
Lind, Jose	90T	168	$ .01	$ .03
Lind, Jose	91T	537	$ .01	$ .03
Lind, Jose	91TSC	233	$ .05	$ .25
Lind, Jose	92T	43	$ .01	$ .03
Lind, Jose	92TSC	859	$ .01	$ .10
Lind, Jose	93T	108	$ .01	$ .03
Lindblad, Paul	66T	568	$3.75	$15.00
Lindblad, Paul	67T	227	$ .50	$2.00
Lindblad, Paul	68T	127	$ .35	$1.40
Lindblad, Paul	69T	449	$ .30	$1.20
Lindblad, Paul	70T	408	$ .35	$1.40
Lindblad, Paul	71T	658	$1.50	$6.00
Lindblad, Paul	72T	396	$ .25	$1.00
Lindblad, Paul	73T	406	$ .25	$1.00
Lindblad, Paul	74T	369	$ .10	$ .40
Lindblad, Paul	75T	278	$ .10	$ .40
Lindblad, Paul	76T	9	$ .05	$ .25
Lindblad, Paul	77T	583	$ .05	$ .20
Lindblad, Paul	78T	314	$ .04	$ .16
Lindblad, Paul	79T	634	$ .03	$ .12
Lindell, Johnny	53T	230	$11.25	$45.00
Lindell, Johnny	54T	51	$7.50	$30.00
Lindell, Johnny	91TA53	230	$ .01	$ .15
Lindeman, Jim	87TTR	65	$ .01	$ .05
Lindeman, Jim	88T	562	$ .01	$ .04
Lindeman, Jim	89T	791	$ .01	$ .03
Lindeman, Jim	92T	258	$ .01	$ .03
Lindeman, Jim	92TSC	893	$ .01	$ .10
Lines, Dick	67T	273	$ .50	$2.00
Lines, Dick	68T	291	$ .35	$1.40
Linton, Doug	93T	159	$ .01	$ .10
Lintz, Larry	74T	121	$ .10	$ .40
Lintz, Larry	75T	416	$ .10	$ .40
Lintz, Larry	76T	109	$ .05	$ .25
Lintz, Larry	77T	323	$ .05	$ .20
Linz, Phil	62T	596	$15.00	$60.00
Linz, Phil	63T	264	$ .90	$3.60
Linz, Phil	64T	344	$ .65	$2.60
Linz, Phil	65T	369	$ .50	$2.00
Linz, Phil	66T	522	$1.50	$6.00
Linz, Phil	67T	14	$ .40	$1.60
Linz, Phil	68T	594	$ .70	$2.80
Linzy, Frank	65T	589	$2.50	$10.00
Linzy, Frank	66T	78	$ .35	$1.40
Linzy, Frank	67T	279	$ .50	$2.00
Linzy, Frank	68T	147	$ .35	$1.40
Linzy, Frank	69T	345	$ .30	$1.20
Linzy, Frank	70T	77	$ .20	$ .80
Linzy, Frank	71T	551	$1.00	$4.00
Linzy, Frank	72T	243	$ .10	$ .40
Linzy, Frank	73T	286	$ .10	$ .40
Lipon, Johnny	52T	89	$7.00	$28.00
Lipon, John	53T	40	$6.25	$25.00
Lipon, Johnny	54T	19	$3.75	$15.00
Lipon, John	91TA53	40	$ .01	$ .15
Lipski, Bob	63T	558	$3.00	$12.00

Player	Year	No.	VG	EX/MT
Liriano, Nelson	88T	205	$ .01	$ .04
Liriano, Nelson	89T	776	$ .01	$ .03
Liriano, Nelson	90T	543	$ .01	$ .03
Liriano, Nelson	91T	18	$ .01	$ .03
Lis, Joe	70T	56	$ .20	$ .80
Lis, Joe	71T	138	$ .25	$1.00
Lis, Joe	74T	659	$ .10	$ .40
Lis, Joe	75T	86	$ .10	$ .40
Lis, Joe	77T	269	$ .05	$ .20
Listach, Pat	92TSC	757	$ .20	$2.00
Listach, Pat	92TTR	65	$ .10	$1.00
Listach, Pat	93T	480	$ .05	$ .25
Listach, Pat	93TSC	293	$ .10	$ .50
Littell, Mark	74T	596	$ .10	$ .40
Littell, Mark	76T	593	$ .15	$ .60
Littell, Mark	77T	141	$ .05	$ .20
Littell, Mark	78T	331	$ .04	$ .16
Littell, Mark	79T	466	$ .03	$ .12
Littell, Mark	80T	631	$ .01	$ .10
Littell, Mark	81T	255	$ .01	$ .08
Littell, Mark	82T	56	$ .01	$ .08
Little, Bryan	83TTR	62	$ .01	$ .10
Little, Bryan	84T	188	$ .01	$ .06
Little, Bryan	85T	257	$ .01	$ .06
Little, Bryan	86T	346	$ .01	$ .05
Little, Jeff	83T	499	$ .01	$ .08
Littlefield, Dick	57T	346	$5.00	$20.00
Littlefield, Dick	58T	241	$1.25	$5.00
Littlefield, John	81T	489	$ .01	$ .08
Littlefield, John	81TTR	794	$ .01	$ .15
Littlefield, John	82T	278	$ .01	$ .08
Littlejohn, Dennis	80T	686	$ .01	$ .10
Littlejohn, Dennis	81T	561	$ .01	$ .08
Litton, Greg	90T	66	$ .01	$ .03
Litton, Greg	91T	628	$ .01	$ .03
Litton, Greg	91TSC	45	$ .05	$ .25

TOPPS

Player	Year	No.	VG	EX/MT
Litton, Greg	92T	238	$ .01	$ .03
Litton, Greg	92TSC	439	$ .01	$ .10
Livingstone, Scott	92T	685	$ .01	$ .10
Livingstone, Scott	92TSC	317	$ .05	$ .20
Livingstone, Scott	93T	298	$ .01	$ .03
Livsey, Shawn	92T	124	$ .01	$ .10
Llenas, Winston	71T	152	$ .25	$1.00
Llenas, Winston	74T	467	$ .10	$ .40
Llenas, Winston	75T	597	$ .10	$ .40
Lock, Don	63T	47	$ .50	$2.00
Lock, Don	64T	114	$ .50	$2.00
Lock, Don	65T	445	$1.00	$4.00
Lock, Don	66T	165	$ .50	$2.00
Lock, Don	67T	376	$ .60	$2.40
Lock, Don	68T	59	$ .35	$1.40
Lock, Don	69T	229	$ .50	$2.00
Locke, Bobby	60T	44	$ .85	$3.40
Locke, Bobby	61T	537	$7.50	$30.00
Locke, Bobby	62T	359	$ .75	$3.00
Locke, Bobby	65T	324	$ .50	$2.00
Locke, Bobby	68T	24	$ .35	$1.40
Locke, Ron	64T	556	$2.25	$9.00
Locke, Ron	65T	511	$1.25	$5.00
Locker, Bob	65T	541	$1.40	$5.60
Locker, Bob	66T	374	$ .65	$2.60
Locker, Bob	67T	338	$ .60	$2.40
Locker, Bob	68T	51	$ .35	$1.40
Locker, Bob	69T	548	$ .40	$1.60
Locker, Bob	70T	249	$ .20	$ .80
Locker, Bob	71T	356	$ .25	$1.00
Locker, Bob	72T	537	$ .40	$1.60
Locker, Bob	73T	645	$ .60	$2.40
Locker, Bob	74T	62	$ .10	$ .40
Locker, Bob	74TTR	62	$ .10	$ .40
Locker, Bob	75T	434	$ .10	$ .40
Locklear, Gene	75T	13	$ .10	$ .40
Locklear, Gene	76T	447	$ .05	$ .25
Lockman, Whitey	51Trb	41	$1.75	$7.50
Lockman, Whitey	56T	205	$3.75	$15.00
Lockman, Whitey	57T	232	$2.00	$8.00
Lockman, Whitey	58T	195	$1.25	$5.00
Lockman, Whitey	59T	411	$1.00	$4.00
Lockman, Whitey	60T	535	$2.75	$11.00
Lockman, Whitey	73T	81	$ .25	$1.00
Lockman, Whitey	74T	354	$ .10	$ .40
Lockman, Whitey	91TA53	292	$ .05	$ .20
Lockwood, Skip	65T	526	$35.00	$140.00
Lockwood, Skip	70T	499	$ .35	$1.40
Lockwood, Skip	71T	433	$ .50	$2.00
Lockwood, Skip	72T	118	$ .10	$ .40
Lockwood, Skip	73T	308	$ .10	$ .40
Lockwood, Skip	74T	532	$ .10	$ .40
Lockwood, Skip	75T	417	$ .10	$ .40
Lockwood, Skip	76T	166	$ .05	$ .25
Lockwood, Skip	77T	65	$ .05	$ .20
Lockwood, Skip	78T	379	$ .04	$ .16
Lockwood, Skip	79T	481	$ .03	$ .12
Lockwood, Skip	80T	567	$ .01	$ .10
Lockwood, Skip	81T	233	$ .01	$ .08
Loes, Billy	52T	20	$28.75	$115.00
Loes, Billy	53T	174	$6.00	$24.00
Loes, Billy	56T	270	$3.75	$15.00
Loes, Billy	57T	244	$2.00	$8.00
Loes, Billy	58T	359	$1.00	$4.00
Loes, Billy	59T	336	$1.00	$4.00
Loes, Billy	60T	181	$ .75	$3.00
Loes, Billy	61T	237	$ .60	$2.40
Lofton, Kenny	92T	69	$ .05	$ .35
Lofton, Kenny	92TSC	695	$ .15	$ 1.25
Lofton, Kenny	92TTR	66	$ .10	$ .40
Lofton, Kenny	93T	331	$ .05	$ .20
Lofton, Kenny	93TSC	277	$ .10	$ .75
Logan, Johnny	53T	158	$8.00	$32.00
Logan, Johnny	54T	122	$3.75	$15.00
Logan, Johnny	56T	136	$2.50	$10.00
Logan, Johnny	57T	4	$2.25	$9.00
Logan, Johnny	58T	110	$2.00	$8.00
Logan, Johnny	59T	225	$1.00	$4.00
Logan, Johnny	60T	205	$ .75	$3.00
Logan, Johnny	61T	524	$9.00	$36.00
Logan, Johnny	62T	573	$3.50	$14.00
Logan, Johnny	63T	259	$ .90	$3.60
Logan, John	91TA53	158	$ .01	$ .15
Lois, Alberto	80T	683	$ .01	$ .10
Lolich, Mickey	64T	128	$4.00	$16.00
Lolich, Mickey	65T	335	$1.25	$5.00
Lolich, Mickey	66T	226	$ .75	$3.00
Lolich, Mickey	66T	455	$2.00	$8.00
Lolich, Mickey	67T	88	$ .75	$3.00
Lolich, Mickey	68T	414	$1.00	$4.00
Lolich, Mickey	69T	270	$1.00	$4.00
Lolich, Mickey	70T	72	$ .50	$2.00
Lolich, Mickey	70T	715	$1.50	$6.00
Lolich, Mickey	71T	71	$ .50	$2.00
Lolich, Mickey	71T	133	$ .40	$1.60
Lolich, Mickey	72T	94	$ .40	$1.60
Lolich, Mickey	72T	96	$ .40	$1.60

MICKEY LOLICH

Player	Year	No.	VG	EX/MT
Lolich, Mickey	72T	450	$ .50	$2.00
Lolich, Mickey	73T	390	$ .25	$1.00
Lolich, Mickey	74T	9	$ .25	$1.00
Lolich, Mickey	75T	245	$ .25	$1.00
Lolich, Mickey	76T	385	$ .25	$1.00
Lolich, Mickey	76TRB	3	$ .05	$ .20
Lolich, Mickey	76TTR	385	$ .15	$ .60
Lolich, Mickey	77T	565	$ .20	$ .80
Lolich, Mickey	79T	164	$ .05	$ .20
Lolich, Mickey	80T	459	$ .01	$ .10
Lolich, Ron	71T	458	$ .50	$2.00
Lollar, Sherman	51Tbb	24	$7.50	$30.00
Lollar, Sherman	52T	117	$7.00	$28.00
Lollar, Sherman	53T	53	$4.50	$18.00
Lollar, Sherm "Sherman"	54T	39	$3.75	$15.00
Lollar, Sherm	55T	201	$6.25	$25.00
Lollar, Sherm	56T	243	$3.75	$15.00
Lollar, Sherm	57T	23	$2.00	$8.00
Lollar, Sherm	58T	267	$1.25	$5.00
Lollar, Sherm	58TAS	491	$1.00	$4.00
Lollar, Sherm	59T	385	$1.00	$4.00
Lollar, Sherm	60T	495	$1.25	$5.00

TOPPS

Player	Year	No.	VG	EX/MT	Player	Year	No.	VG	EX/MT
Lollar, Sherm	60TAS	567	$3.50	$14.00	Lopes, Dave	76T	660	$ .25	$1.00
Lollar, Sherm	61T	285	$ .60	$2.40	Lopes, Dave	76TRB	4	$ .05	$ .20
Lollar, Sherm	62T	514	$1.50	$6.00	Lopes, Dave	77T	4	$ .05	$ .20
Lollar, Sherm	63T	118	$ .50	$2.00					
Lollar, Sherman	91TA53	53	$ .01	$ .15					
Lollar, Tim	81T	424	$ .01	$ .08					
Lollar, Tim	82T	587	$ .01	$ .08					
Lollar, Tim	83T	185	$ .01	$ .08					
Lollar, Tim	83T	742	$ .01	$ .08					
Lollar, Tim	84T	644	$ .01	$ .06					
Lollar, Tim	85T	13	$ .01	$ .06					
Lollar, Tim	85TTR	76	$ .01	$ .10					
Lollar, Tim	86T	297	$ .01	$ .05					
Lollar, Tim	87T	396	$ .01	$ .04					
Lombardi, Phil	88T	283	$ .01	$ .04					
Lombardozzi, Steve	87TTR	66	$ .01	$ .05					
Lombardozzi, Steve	88T	697	$ .01	$ .04					
Lombardozzi, Steve	89T	376	$ .01	$ .03					
Lonborg, Jim	65T	573	$6.00	$24.00					
Lonborg, Jim	66T	93	$ .50	$2.00					
Lonborg, Jim	67T	371	$1.00	$4.00					
Lonborg, Jim	68T	10	$ .75	$3.00					
Lonborg, Jim	68T	12	$ .55	$2.20					
Lonborg, Jim	68T	460	$ .75	$3.00					
Lonborg, Jim	69T	109	$ .35	$1.40					
Lonborg, Jim	70T	665	$1.10	$4.40					
Lonborg, Jim	71T	577	$1.00	$4.00					
Lonborg, Jim	72T	255	$ .10	$ .40					
Lonborg, Jim	73T	3	$ .20	$ .80					
Lonborg, Jim	74T	342	$ .10	$ .40					
Lonborg, Jim	75T	94	$ .10	$ .40					
Lonborg, Jim	76T	271	$ .05	$ .25					
Lonborg, Jim	77T	569	$ .05	$ .20					
Lonborg, Jim	78T	52	$ .04	$ .16					
Lonborg, Jim	79T	446	$ .03	$ .12					
Long, Bill	87TTR	67	$ .01	$ .05	Lopes, Dave	77T	180	$ .05	$ .20
Long, Bill	88T	309	$ .01	$ .04	Lopes, Dave	78T	440	$ .05	$ .20
Long, Bill	89T	133	$ .01	$ .03	Lopes, Dave	79T	290	$ .03	$ .12
Long, Bill	90T	499	$ .01	$ .03	Lopes, Dave	80T	560	$ .01	$ .10
Long, Bill	91T	668	$ .01	$ .03	Lopes, Dave	81T	50	$ .01	$ .08
Long, Bob	82T	291	$ .05	$ .25	Lopes, Dave	82T	740	$ .01	$ .08
Long, Dale	55T	127	$2.50	$10.00	Lopes, Dave	82TAS	338	$ .01	$ .07
Long, Dale	56T	56	$2.00	$8.00	Lopes, Dave	82TSA	741	$ .01	$ .07
Long, Dale	57T	3	$2.00	$8.00	Lopes, Dave	82TTR	64	$ .01	$ .15
Long, Dale	58T	7	$2.00	$8.00	Lopes, Dave	83T	365	$ .01	$ .08
Long, Dale	59T	147	$3.00	$12.00	Lopes, Dave	84T	669	$ .01	$ .10
Long, Dale	59T	414	$1.00	$4.00	Lopes, Dave	84T	714	$ .01	$ .06
Long, Dale	60T	375	$ .75	$3.00	Lopes, Dave	85T	12	$ .01	$ .06
Long, Dale	61T	117	$ .60	$2.40	Lopes, Dave	86T	125	$ .01	$ .15
Long, Dale	62T	228	$ .75	$3.00	Lopes, Dave	87T	445	$ .01	$ .04
Long, Dale	63T	484	$4.00	$16.00	Lopes, Dave	87TRB	4	$ .01	$ .04
Long, Jeoff	64T	497	$1.00	$4.00	Lopes, Dave	88T	226	$ .01	$ .04
Lonnett, Joe	57T	241	$2.00	$8.00	Lopez, Al	60T	222	$1.75	$7.00
Lonnett, Joe	58T	64	$2.00	$8.00	Lopez, Al	61T	132	$1.10	$4.40
Lonnett, Joe	73T	356	$ .20	$ .80	Lopez, Al	61T	337	$1.00	$4.00
Lonnett, Joe	74T	221	$ .10	$ .40	Lopez, Al	62T	286	$1.25	$5.00
Look, Bruce	69T	317	$ .50	$2.00	Lopez, Al	63T	458	$4.50	$18.00
Lopat, Ed	51Tbb	39	$10.50	$42.00	Lopez, Al	64T	232	$1.00	$4.00
Lopat, Ed	52T	57	$25.00	$100.00	Lopez, Al	65T	414	$1.25	$5.00
Lopat, Ed	53T	87	$10.00	$40.00	Lopez, Al	69T	527	$ .75	$3.00
Lopat, Ed	54T	5	$5.50	$22.00	Lopez, Al	91TA53	329	$ .10	$ .50
Lopat, Ed	55T	109	$3.50	$14.00	Lopez, Art	65T	566	$2.50	$10.00
Lopat, Ed	60T	465	$3.50	$14.00	Lopez, Aurelio	79T	444	$ .05	$ .20
Lopat, Ed	63T	23	$ .50	$2.00	Lopez, Aurelio	80T	101	$ .01	$ .10
Lopat, Ed	64T	348	$ .65	$2.60	Lopez, Aurelio	81T	291	$ .01	$ .08
Lopat, Ed	91TA53	87	$ .10	$ .50	Lopez, Aurelio	82T	728	$ .01	$ .08
Lopata, Stan	56T	183	$3.75	$15.00	Lopez, Aurelio	83TTR	63	$ .01	$ .10
Lopata, Stan	57T	119	$2.00	$8.00	Lopez, Aurelio	84T	95	$ .01	$ .06
Lopata, Stan	58T	353	$1.00	$4.00	Lopez, Aurelio	85T	539	$ .01	$ .06
Lopata, Stan	59T	412	$1.00	$4.00	Lopez, Aurelio	86T	367	$ .01	$ .05
Lopata, Stan	60T	515	$2.75	$11.00	Lopez, Aurelio	87T	659	$ .01	$ .04
Lopes, Dave	73T	609	$1.00	$4.00	Lopez, Carlos	77T	492	$ .25	$ .80
Lopes, Dave	74T	112	$ .25	$1.00	Lopez, Carlos	78T	166	$ .04	$ .16
Lopes, Dave	75T	93	$ .25	$1.00	Lopez, Carlos	79T	568	$ .03	$ .12
Lopes, Dave	76T	197	$ .25	$1.00	Lopez, Hector	56T	16	$2.50	$10.00

TOPPS

Player	Year	No.	VG	EX/MT
Lopez, Hector	57T	6	$2.00	$8.00
Lopez, Hector	58T	155	$1.25	$5.00
Lopez, Hector	59T	402	$1.00	$4.00
Lopez, Hector	60T	163	$ .75	$3.00
Lopez, Hector	61T	28	$ .60	$2.40
Lopez, Hector	62T	502	$1.50	$6.00
Lopez, Hector	63T	92	$ .50	$2.00
Lopez, Hector	64T	325	$ .65	$2.60
Lopez, Hector	65T	532	$1.40	$5.60
Lopez, Hector	66T	177	$ .50	$2.00
Lopez, Javy	93T	811	$ .05	$ .25
Lopez, Luis	92TSC	556	$ .01	$ .15
Lopez, Marcelino	63T	549	$2.25	$9.00
Lopez, Marcelino	65T	537	$1.50	$6.00
Lopez, Marcelino	66T	155	$ .50	$2.00
Lopez, Marcelino	67T	513	$1.50	$6.00
Lopez, Marcelino	70T	344	$ .35	$1.40
Lopez, Marcelino	71T	137	$ .25	$1.00
Lopez, Marcelino	72T	652	$ .40	$1.60
Loun, Don	65T	181	$ .35	$1.40
Loviglio, Jay	81T	526	$ .01	$ .08
Loviglio, Jay	82T	599	$ .01	$ .08
Lovitto, Joe	73T	276	$ .10	$ .40
Lovitto, Joe	74T	639	$ .10	$ .40
Lovitto, Joe	75T	36	$ .10	$ .40
Lovitto, Joe	76T	604	$ .05	$ .25
Lovrich, Pete	63T	549	$2.25	$9.00
Lovrich, Pete	64T	212	$ .65	$2.60
Lovullo, Torey	92TSC	809	$ .01	$ .10
Lowe, Sean	93T	191	$ .01	$ .15
Lowenstein, John	71T	231	$ .25	$1.00
Lowenstein, John	72T	486	$ .25	$1.00
Lowenstein, John	73T	327	$ .10	$ .40
Lowenstein, John	74T	176	$ .10	$ .40
Lowenstein, John	75T	424	$ .10	$ .40
Lowenstein, John	76T	646	$ .05	$ .25
Lowenstein, John	77T	393	$ .05	$ .20
Lowenstein, John	78T	87	$ .04	$ .16
Lowenstein, John	79T	173	$ .03	$ .12
Lowenstein, John	80T	287	$ .01	$ .10
Lowenstein, John	81T	591	$ .01	$ .08
Lowenstein, John	82T	747	$ .01	$ .08
Lowenstein, John	83T	473	$ .01	$ .08
Lowenstein, John	84T	604	$ .01	$ .06
Lowenstein, John	85T	316	$ .01	$ .06
Lown, Turk	52T	330	$43.75	$175.00
Lown, Turk	53T	130	$4.00	$16.00
Lown, Turk	57T	247	$2.00	$8.00
Lown, Turk	58T	261	$1.25	$5.00
Lown, Turk	59T	277	$1.00	$4.00
Lown, Turk	60T	57	$ .85	$3.40
Lown, Turk	60T	313	$ .75	$3.00
Lown, Turk	61T	424	$1.00	$4.00
Lown, Turk	62T	528	$3.50	$14.00
Lown, Turk	91TA53	130	$ .01	$ .15
Lowrey, Harry	52T	111	$7.00	$28.00
Lowrey, Harry "Peanuts"	53T	16	$4.00	$16.00
Lowrey, Peanuts	54T	158	$3.75	$15.00
Lowrey, Harry	91TA53	16	$ .01	$ .15
Lowry, Dwight	87T	483	$ .01	$ .04
Loynd, Mike	87T	126	$ .01	$ .04
Loynd, Mike	88T	319	$ .01	$ .04
Lubratich, Steve	84T	266	$ .01	$ .06
Lucas, Gary	81T	436	$ .01	$ .08
Lucas, Gary	82T	120	$ .01	$ .08
Lucas, Gary	83T	761	$ .01	$ .08
Lucas, Gary	84T	7	$ .01	$ .06
Lucas, Gary	84TTR	73	$ .01	$ .15
Lucas, Gary	85T	297	$ .01	$ .06
Lucas, Gary	86T	601	$ .01	$ .05
Lucas, Gary	87T	696	$ .01	$ .04
Lucas, Gary	88T	524	$ .01	$ .04
Lucca, Lou	93T	494	$ .05	$ .35
Lucchesi, Frank	70T	662	$1.25	$5.00
Lucchesi, Frank	71T	119	$ .25	$1.00

Player	Year	No.	VG	EX/MT
Lucchesi, Frank	72T	188	$ .10	$ .40
Lucchesi, Frank	74T	379	$ .25	$1.00
Lucchesi, Frank	88T	564	$ .01	$ .04
Luebber, Steve	72T	678	$1.25	$5.00
Luebber, Steve	77T	457	$ .05	$ .20
Luecken, Rick	90T	87	$ .01	$ .10
Lugo, Urbano	86T	373	$ .01	$ .05
Lugo, Urbano	87T	92	$ .01	$ .04
Lum, Mike	68T	579	$ .75	$3.00
Lum, Mike	69T	514	$ .40	$1.60
Lum, Mike	70T	367	$ .35	$1.40
Lum, Mike	71T	194	$ .25	$1.00
Lum, Mike	72T	641	$ .40	$1.60
Lum, Mike	73T	266	$ .10	$ .40
Lum, Mike	74T	227	$ .10	$ .40
Lum, Mike	75T	154	$ .10	$ .40
Lum, Mike	76T	208	$ .05	$ .25
Lum, Mike	76TTR	208	$ .05	$ .25
Lum, Mike	77T	601	$ .05	$ .20
Lum, Mike	78T	326	$ .04	$ .16
Lum, Mike	79T	556	$ .03	$ .12
Lum, Mike	80T	7	$ .01	$ .10
Lum, Mike	81T	457	$ .01	$ .08
Lum, Mike	81TTR	795	$ .01	$ .15
Lum, Mike	82T	732	$ .01	$ .08
Lumenti, Ralph	58T	369	$1.00	$4.00
Lumenti, Ralph	59T	316	$1.00	$4.00
Lumenti, Ralph	61T	469	$1.35	$5.40
Lumpe, Jerry	58T	193	$2.00	$8.00

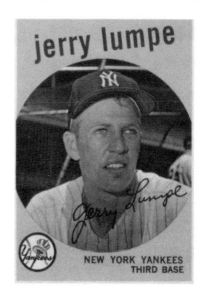

Player	Year	No.	VG	EX/MT
Lumpe, Jerry	59T	272	$1.00	$4.00
Lumpe, Jerry	60T	290	$ .75	$3.00
Lumpe, Jerry	61T	119	$ .60	$2.40
Lumpe, Jerry	61T	365	$ .60	$2.40
Lumpe, Jerry	62T	127	$ .60	$2.40
Lumpe, Jerry	62T	305	$ .75	$3.00
Lumpe, Jerry	63T	256	$ .90	$3.60
Lumpe, Jerry	64T	165	$ .50	$2.00
Lumpe, Jerry	65T	353	$ .50	$2.00
Lumpe, Jerry	66T	161	$ .50	$2.00
Lumpe, Jerry	67T	247	$ .50	$2.00
Lund, Don	53T	277	$22.50	$90.00
Lund, Don	54T	167	$3.75	$15.00

TOPPS

Player	Year	No.	VG	EX/MT	Player	Year	No.	VG	EX/MT
Lund, Don	91TA53	277	$ .01	$ .15	Lyle, Sparky	76T	545	$ .15	$ .60
Lund, Gordon	70T	642	$1.25	$5.00	Lyle, Sparky	77T	598	$ .20	$ .80
Lundstedt, Tom	74T	603	$ .10	$ .40	Lyle, Sparky	78T	35	$ .04	$ .16
Luplow, Al	62T	598	$17.50	$70.00	Lyle, Sparky	78TRB	2	$ .04	$ .16
Luplow, Al	63T	351	$ .90	$3.60	Lyle, Sparky	79T	365	$ .05	$ .20
Luplow, Al	64T	184	$ .50	$2.00	Lyle, Sparky	80T	115	$ .01	$ .10
Luplow, Al	66T	188	$ .50	$2.00	Lyle, Sparky	81T	719	$ .01	$ .08
Luplow, Al	67T	433	$ .60	$2.40	Lyle, Sparky	82T	285	$ .01	$ .08
Lusader, Scott	89T	487	$ .01	$ .03	Lyle, Sparky	83T	693	$ .01	$ .08
Lusader, Scott	90T	632	$ .01	$ .03	Lyle, Sparky	83T	694	$ .01	$ .08
Luttrell, Lyle	57T	386	$1.75	$7.00	Lynch, Ed	82T	121	$ .01	$ .08
Lutz, Joe	73T	449	$ .50	$2.00	Lynch, Ed	83T	601	$ .01	$ .08
Luzinski, Greg	71T	439	$1.00	$4.00	Lynch, Ed	84T	293	$ .01	$ .06
Luzinski, Greg	72T	112	$ .25	$1.00	Lynch, Ed	85T	467	$ .01	$ .06
Luzinski, Greg	73T	189	$ .25	$1.00	Lynch, Ed	86T	68	$ .01	$ .05
Luzinski, Greg	74T	360	$ .15	$ .60	Lynch, Ed	87T	697	$ .01	$ .04
Luzinski, Greg	75T	630	$ .25	$1.00	Lynch, Ed	88T	336	$ .01	$ .04
Luzinski, Greg	76T	193	$ .50	$2.00	Lynch, Jerry	54T	234	$4.50	$18.00
Luzinski, Greg	76T	195	$ .30	$1.20	Lynch, Jerry	55T	142	$2.25	$9.00
Luzinski, Greg	76T	610	$ .15	$ .60	Lynch, Jerry	56T	97	$2.00	$8.00
Luzinski, Greg	77T	30	$ .20	$ .80	Lynch, Jerry	57T	358	$1.75	$7.00
Luzinski, Greg	78T	420	$ .05	$ .20	Lynch, Jerry	58T	103	$2.00	$8.00
Luzinski, Greg	79T	540	$ .05	$ .20	Lynch, Jerry	59T	97	$1.50	$6.00
Luzinski, Greg	80T	120	$ .01	$ .10	Lynch, Jerry	60T	198	$ .75	$3.00
Luzinski, Greg	81T	270	$ .01	$ .15	Lynch, Jerry	60T	352	$1.75	$7.00
Luzinski, Greg	81TTR	796	$ .01	$ .15	Lynch, Jerry	61T	97	$ .60	$2.40
Luzinski, Greg	82T	720	$ .01	$ .15	Lynch, Jerry	62T	487	$1.50	$6.00
Luzinski, Greg	82TSA	721	$ .01	$ .07	Lynch, Jerry	63T	37	$ .50	$2.00
					Lynch, Jerry	64T	193	$ .50	$2.00
					Lynch, Jerry	65T	291	$ .50	$2.00
					Lynch, Jerry	66T	182	$ .50	$2.00
					Lynn, Fred	75T	622	$2.75	$11.00
					Lynn, Fred	76T	50	$ .50	$2.00
					Lynn, Fred	76T	192	$ .50	$2.00
					Lynn, Fred	76T	196	$ .25	$1.00
					Lynn, Fred	77T	210	$ .40	$1.60
					Lynn, Fred	78T	320	$ .25	$1.00
					Lynn, Fred	79T	480	$ .20	$ .80
					Lynn, Fred	80T	110	$ .05	$ .25
					Lynn, Fred	80T	201	$ .05	$ .30
					Lynn, Fred	81T	720	$ .05	$ .20
					Lynn, Fred	81TTR	797	$ .10	$ .50
					Lynn, Fred	82T	251	$ .05	$ .20
					Lynn, Fred	82TSA	252	$ .01	$ .10
					Lynn, Fred	83T	520	$ .01	$ .15
					Lynn, Fred	83TAS	392	$ .01	$ .10
					Lynn, Fred	84T	680	$ .05	$ .20
					Lynn, Fred	85T	220	$ .01	$ .15
					Lynn, Fred	85TTR	77	$ .01	$ .15
					Lynn, Fred	86T	55	$ .01	$ .10
					Lynn, Fred	87T	370	$ .01	$ .10
					Lynn, Fred	88T	707	$ .01	$ .10
					Lynn, Fred	89T	416	$ .01	$ .03
					Lynn, Fred	90T	107	$ .01	$ .03
					Lynn, Fred	90TTB	663	$ .01	$ .03
					Lynn, Fred	90TTR	62	$ .01	$ .05
					Lynn, Fred	91T	586	$ .01	$ .03
					Lyons, Barry	87TTR	68	$ .01	$ .05
					Lyons, Barry	88T	633	$ .01	$ .04
					Lyons, Barry	89T	412	$ .01	$ .03
					Lyons, Barry	90T	258	$ .01	$ .03
Luzinski, Greg	**83T**	**310**	**$ .01**	**$ .08**	Lyons, Steve	86T	233	$ .01	$ .05
Luzinski, Greg	83T	591	$ .01	$ .08	Lyons, Steve	86TTR	67	$ .01	$ .06
Luzinski, Greg	84T	20	$ .01	$ .06	Lyons, Steve	88T	108	$ .01	$ .04
Luzinski, Greg	84T	712	$ .01	$ .15	Lyons, Steve	89T	334	$ .01	$ .03
Luzinski, Greg	85T	650	$ .01	$ .06	Lyons, Steve	90T	751	$ .01	$ .03
Luzinski, Ryan	93T	481	$ .05	$ .35	Lyons, Steve	91T	612	$ .01	$ .03
Lyle, Sparky	69T	311	$3.00	$12.00	Lyons, Steve	92T	349	$ .01	$ .03
Lyle, Sparky	70T	116	$ .30	$1.20	Lysander, Rick	84T	639	$ .01	$ .06
Lyle, Sparky	71T	649	$3.00	$12.00	Lysander, Rick	85T	383	$ .01	$ .06
Lyle, Sparky	72T	259	$ .25	$1.00	Lysander, Rick	86T	482	$ .01	$ .05
Lyle, Sparky	73T	68	$ .25	$1.00	Lyttle, Jim	70T	516	$ .35	$1.40
Lyle, Sparky	73T	394	$ .25	$1.00	Lyttle, Jim	71T	234	$ .25	$1.00
Lyle, Sparky	74T	66	$ .25	$1.00	Lyttle, Jim	72T	648	$ .40	$1.60
Lyle, Sparky	75T	485	$ .15	$ .60	Lyttle, Jim	74T	437	$ .10	$ .40

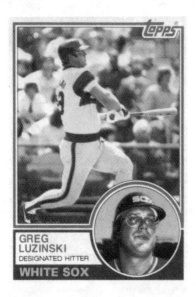

TOPPS

Player	Year	No.	VG	EX/MT
Maas, Duke	56T	57	$2.00	$8.00
Maas, Duke	57T	405	$1.75	$7.00
Maas, Duke	58T	228	$1.25	$5.00
Maas, Duke	59T	167	$1.00	$4.00
Maas, Duke	60T	421	$ .75	$3.00
Maas, Duke	61T	387	$1.00	$4.00
Maas, Kevin	90TTR	63	$ .05	$ .25
Maas, Kevin	91T	435	$ .01	$ .10
Maas, Kevin	91TRB	4	$ .01	$ .10
Maas, Kevin	91TSC	282	$ .10	$ .40
Maas, Kevin	92T	710	$ .01	$ .10
Maas, Kevin	92TSC	35	$ .01	$ .10
Maas, Kevin	93T	168	$ .01	$ .03
Mabe, Bob	59T	356	$1.00	$4.00
Mabe, Bob	60T	288	$ .75	$3.00
MacDonald, Bill	52T	138	$7.00	$28.00
MacDonald, Bob	91TSC	585	$ .05	$ .25
MacDonald, Bob	92T	87	$ .01	$ .10
MacDonald, Bob	92TSC	372	$ .01	$ .10
MacDonald, Bob	93T	427	$ .01	$ .03
Macfarlane, Mike	88TTR	62	$ .05	$ .35
Macfarlane, Mike	89T	479	$ .01	$ .15
Macfarlane, Mike	90T	202	$ .01	$ .03
Macfarlane, Mike	91T	638	$ .01	$ .03
Macfarlane, Mike	91TSC	15	$ .05	$ .25
Macfarlane, Mike	92T	42	$ .01	$ .03
Macfarlane, Mike	92TSC	74	$ .01	$ .10
Macfarlane, Mike	93T	768	$ .01	$ .03
Macha, Ken	78T	483	$ .04	$ .16
Macha, Ken	82T	282	$ .01	$ .08
Machado, Julio	90T	684	$ .01	$ .10
Machado, Julio	91T	434	$ .01	$ .03
Machado, Julio	92T	208	$ .01	$ .03
Mack, Shane	85T	398	$ .75	$3.00
Mack, Shane	87TTR	69	$ .10	$ .50
Mack, Shane	88T	548	$ .05	$ .35
Mack, Shane	90TTR	64	$ .01	$ .05
Mack, Shane	91T	672	$ .01	$ .03
Mack, Shane	91TSC	259	$ .10	$ .50
Mack, Shane	92T	164	$ .01	$ .03
Mack, Shane	92TSC	47	$ .01	$ .10
Mack, Shane	93T	282	$ .01	$ .03
Mackanin, Pete	74T	597	$ .15	$ .60
Mackanin, Pete	76T	287	$ .05	$ .25
Mackanin, Pete	77T	156	$ .05	$ .20
Mackanin, Pete	78T	399	$ .04	$ .16
Mackanin, Pete	81T	509	$ .01	$ .08
Mackanin, Pete	82T	438	$ .01	$ .08
MacKenzie, Ken	60T	534	$2.75	$11.00
MacKenzie, Ken	61T	496	$1.35	$5.40
MacKenzie, Ken	62T	421	$1.25	$5.00
MacKenzie, Ken	63T	393	$1.00	$4.00
MacKenzie, Ken	64T	297	$ .65	$2.60
Macko, Steve	80T	676	$ .01	$ .10
Macko, Steve	81T	381	$ .01	$ .08
MacWhorter, Keith	81T	689	$ .20	$2.00
Madden, Mike	83TTR	64	$ .01	$ .10
Madden, Mike	84T	127	$ .01	$ .06
Madden, Mike	85T	479	$ .01	$ .06
Madden, Mike	86T	691	$ .01	$ .05
Maddox, Elliott	71T	11	$ .25	$1.00
Maddox, Elliott	72T	277	$ .10	$ .40
Maddox, Elliott	73T	658	$ .60	$2.40
Maddox, Elliott	74T	401	$ .10	$ .40
Maddox, Elliott	75T	113	$ .10	$ .40
Maddox, Elliott	76T	503	$ .05	$ .25
Maddox, Elliott	77T	332	$ .05	$ .20
Maddox, Elliott	78T	442	$ .04	$ .16
Maddox, Elliott	79T	69	$ .03	$ .12
Maddox, Elliott	80T	707	$ .01	$ .10
Maddox, Elliott	81T	299	$ .01	$ .08
Maddox, Garry	73T	322	$ .25	$1.00
Maddox, Garry	74T	178	$ .10	$ .40
Maddox, Garry	75T	240	$ .10	$ .40
Maddox, Garry	76T	38	$ .05	$ .25
Maddox, Garry	77T	520	$ .05	$ .20
Maddox, Garry	78T	610	$ .04	$ .16
Maddox, Garry	79T	470	$ .03	$ .12
Maddox, Garry	80T	380	$ .01	$ .10
Maddox, Garry	81T	160	$ .01	$ .08
Maddox, Garry	82T	20	$ .01	$ .08
Maddox, Garry	83T	615	$ .01	$ .08
Maddox, Garry	84T	755	$ .01	$ .06
Maddox, Garry	85T	235	$ .01	$ .06
Maddox, Garry	86T	585	$ .01	$ .05
Maddux, Greg	87TTR	70	$ .75	$3.00
Maddux, Greg	88T	361	$ .10	$ .75
Maddux, Greg	89T	240	$ .05	$ .25
Maddux, Greg	90T	715	$ .05	$ .20
Maddux, Greg	91T	35	$ .01	$ .10
Maddux, Greg	91TSC	126	$ .15	$1.50
Maddux, Greg	92T	580	$ .01	$ .03
Maddux, Greg	92TSC	665	$ .05	$ .25
Maddux, Greg	93T	183	$ .01	$ .10
Maddux, Greg	93T	409	$ .01	$ .10
Maddux, Greg	93TSC	2	$ .05	$ .20
Maddux, Mike	87T	553	$ .01	$ .04
Maddux, Mike	88T	756	$ .01	$ .04
Maddux, Mike	89T	39	$ .01	$ .03
Maddux, Mike	90T	154	$ .01	$ .06
Maddux, Mike	92T	438	$ .01	$ .03

Maddux, Mike	92TSC	26	$ .01	$ .10
Maddux, Mike	93T	329	$ .01	$ .03
Maddux, Mike	93TSC	103	$ .01	$ .10
Madison, Dave	52T	366	$43.75	$175.00
Madison, Dave	53T	99	$6.25	$25.00
Madison, Dave	91TA53	99	$ .01	$ .15
Madison, Scotti	88TTR	63	$ .01	$ .05
Madlock, Bill	74T	600	$1.25	$5.00
Madlock, Bill	75T	104	$ .30	$1.20
Madlock, Bill	76T	191	$ .25	$1.00
Madlock, Bill	76T	640	$ .30	$1.20
Madlock, Bill	77T	1	$1.00	$4.00
Madlock, Bill	77T	250	$ .25	$1.00
Madlock, Bill	78T	410	$ .10	$ .40
Madlock, Bill	79T	195	$ .10	$ .40
Madlock, Bill	80T	55	$ .05	$ .25
Madlock, Bill	81T	715	$ .05	$ .20

TOPPS

Player	Year	No.	VG	EX/MT
Madlock, Bill	82T	161	$ .01	$ .15
Madlock, Bill	82T	365	$ .01	$ .15
Madlock, Bill	82T	696	$ .01	$ .08
Madlock, Bill	83T	291	$ .01	$ .08
Madlock, Bill	83T	645	$ .01	$ .08
Madlock, Bill	84T	131	$ .10	$ .50
Madlock, Bill	84T	250	$ .01	$ .10
Madlock, Bill	84T	696	$ .01	$ .06
Madlock, Bill	84T	701	$ .05	$ .30
Madlock, Bill	85T	560	$ .01	$ .10
Madlock, Bill	86T	470	$ .01	$ .05
Madlock, Bill	87T	734	$ .01	$ .04
Madlock, Bill	87TTR	71	$ .01	$ .10
Madlock, Bill	88T	145	$ .01	$ .04
Magadan, Dave	87T	512	$ .05	$ .20
Magadan, Dave	88T	58	$ .01	$ .10
Magadan, Dave	89T	655	$ .01	$ .03
Magadan, Dave	90T	135	$ .01	$ .03
Magadan, Dave	91T	480	$ .01	$ .10

Player	Year	No.	VG	EX/MT
Magadan, Dave	91TSC	210	$ .05	$ .25
Magadan, Dave	92T	745	$ .01	$ .03
Magadan, Dave	92TSC	118	$ .01	$ .10
Magadan, Dave	93T	578	$ .01	$ .03
Maglie, Sal	57T	5	$2.50	$10.00
Maglie, Sal	58T	43	$2.50	$10.00
Maglie, Sal	59T	309	$1.25	$5.00
Maglie, Sal	60T	456	$1.50	$6.00
Maglie, Sal	91TA53	303	$ .10	$ .75
Magnante, Mike	92T	597	$ .01	$ .10
Magnante, Mike	92TSC	448	$ .05	$ .20
Magnante, Mike	93T	186	$ .01	$ .03
Magnante, Mike	93TSC	12	$ .01	$ .10
Magnuson, Jim	72T	597	$ .40	$1.60
Magrane, Joe	87TTR	72	$ .01	$ .10
Magrane, Joe	88T	380	$ .01	$ .10
Magrane, Joe	89T	657	$ .01	$ .03
Magrane, Joe	90T	578	$ .01	$ .03
Magrane, Joe	90TAS	406	$ .01	$ .03
Magrane, Joe	91T	185	$ .01	$ .03
Magrane, Joe	91TSC	85	$ .05	$ .25
Magrane, Joe	92T	783	$ .01	$ .03
Magrane, Joe	92TSC	622	$ .01	$ .10

Player	Year	No.	VG	EX/MT
Magrini, Pete	66T	558	$6.00	$24.00
Mahaffey, Art	60T	138	$ .75	$3.00
Mahaffey, Art	61T	433	$1.00	$4.00
Mahaffey, Art	62T	550	$6.00	$24.00
Mahaffey, Art	63T	7	$1.25	$5.00
Mahaffey, Art	63T	385	$1.00	$4.00
Mahaffey, Art	64T	104	$ .50	$2.00
Mahaffey, Art	65T	446	$1.00	$4.00
Mahaffey, Art	66T	570	$7.00	$28.00
Mahlberg, Greg	80T	673	$ .01	$ .10
Mahler, Mickey	78T	703	$3.50	$14.00
Mahler, Mickey	79T	331	$ .03	$ .12
Mahler, Mickey	86TTR	68	$ .01	$ .06
Mahler, Rick	82T	126	$ .01	$ .08
Mahler, Rick	82T	579	$ .05	$ .20
Mahler, Rick	83T	76	$ .01	$ .08
Mahler, Rick	85T	79	$ .01	$ .06
Mahler, Rick	86T	437	$ .01	$ .05
Mahler, Rick	87T	242	$ .01	$ .04
Mahler, Rick	88T	706	$ .01	$ .04
Mahler, Rick	89T	621	$ .01	$ .03
Mahler, Rick	89TTR	74	$ .01	$ .05
Mahler, Rick	90T	151	$ .01	$ .03
Mahler, Rick	91T	363	$ .01	$ .03
Mahomes, Pat	92T	676	$ .05	$ .35
Mahomes, Pat	93T	684	$ .01	$ .10
Mahoney, Bob	52T	58	$13.75	$55.00
Mahoney, Jim	73T	356	$ .20	$ .80
Mahoney, Jim	74T	221	$ .10	$ .40
Main, Forrest	52T	397	$43.75	$175.00
Main, Forrest	53T	198	$4.50	$18.00
Main, Forrest	91TA53	198	$ .01	$ .15
Majeski, Hank	51Tbb	2	$7.50	$30.00
Majeski, Henry	52T	112	$7.00	$28.00
Maldonado, Candy	84T	244	$ .05	$ .20
Maldonado, Candy	85T	523	$ .01	$ .06
Maldonado, Candy	86T	87	$ .01	$ .05
Maldonado, Candy	86TTR	69	$ .01	$ .06
Maldonado, Candy	87T	335	$ .01	$ .04
Maldonado, Candy	88T	190	$ .01	$ .04
Maldonado, Candy	89T	495	$ .01	$ .03
Maldonado, Candy	90T	628	$ .01	$ .03
Maldonado, Candy	90TTR	65	$ .01	$ .05
Maldonado, Candy	91T	723	$ .01	$ .03
Maldonado, Candy	91TSC	350	$ .05	$ .25
Maldonado, Candy	91TTR	74	$ .01	$ .05
Maldonado, Candy	92T	507	$ .01	$ .03
Maldonado, Candy	92TSC	179	$ .01	$ .10
Maldonado, Candy	93T	213	$ .01	$ .03
Maldonado, Carlos	92TSC	569	$ .01	$ .15
Maler, Jim	83T	54	$ .01	$ .08
Maler, Jim	84T	461	$ .01	$ .06
Malkmus, Bob	58T	356	$1.00	$4.00
Malkmus, Bob	59T	151	$1.00	$4.00
Malkmus, Bobby	60T	251	$ .75	$3.00
Malkmus, Bobby	61T	530	$7.50	$30.00
Mallicoat, Rob	92T	501	$ .01	$ .10
Maloney, Jim	61T	436	$2.50	$10.00
Maloney, Jim	63T	444	$1.50	$6.00
Maloney, Jim	64T	3	$2.50	$10.00
Maloney, Jim	64T	5	$2.00	$8.00
Maloney, Jim	64T	420	$1.00	$4.00
Maloney, Jim	65T	530	$1.40	$5.60
Maloney, Jim	66T	140	$ .50	$2.00
Maloney, Jim	67T	80	$ .40	$1.60
Maloney, Jim	68T	425	$ .35	$1.40
Maloney, Jim	69T	362	$ .30	$1.20
Maloney, Jim	70T	320	$ .35	$1.40
Maloney, Jim	71T	645	$1.50	$6.00
Maloney, Jim	72T	645	$ .40	$1.60
Malzone, Frank	56T	304	$4.50	$18.00
Malzone, Frank	57T	355	$1.75	$7.00
Malzone, Frank	58T	260	$1.25	$5.00
Malzone, Frank	58TAS	481	$1.00	$4.00
Malzone, Frank	59T	220	$1.00	$4.00

TOPPS

Player	Year	No.	VG	EX/MT
Malzone, Frank	59T	519	$4.00	$16.00
Malzone, Frank	59TAS	558	$4.00	$16.00
Malzone, Frank	60T	310	$.75	$3.00
Malzone, Frank	60TAS	557	$3.50	$14.00
Malzone, Frank	61T	173	$.75	$3.00
Malzone, Frank	61T	445	$1.00	$4.00
Malzone, Frank	62T	225	$.75	$3.00
Malzone, Frank	63T	232	$.90	$3.60
Malzone, Frank	64T	60	$.50	$2.00
Malzone, Frank	65T	315	$.75	$3.00
Malzone, Frank	66T	152	$.50	$2.00
Mangual, Angel	70T	654	$1.50	$6.00
Mangual, Angel	71T	317	$.25	$1.00
Mangual, Angel	72T	6	$.10	$.40
Mangual, Angel	72T	62	$.10	$.40
Mangual, Angel	73T	625	$.60	$2.40
Mangual, Angel	75T	452	$.10	$.40
Mangual, Pepe	75T	616	$6.00	$24.00
Mangual, Pepe	76T	164	$.05	$.25
Mangual, Pepe	77T	552	$.05	$.20
Mankowski, Phil	77T	477	$.05	$.20
Mankowski, Phil	78T	559	$.04	$.16
Mankowski, Phil	79T	93	$.03	$.12
Mankowski, Phil	80T	216	$.01	$.10
Mann, Kelly	90T	744	$.01	$.10
Manning, Rick	76T	275	$.05	$.25
Manning, Rick	77T	115	$.05	$.20
Manning, Rick	78T	11	$.04	$.16
Manning, Rick	79T	425	$.03	$.12
Manning, Rick	80T	564	$.01	$.10
Manning, Rick	81T	308	$.01	$.08
Manning, Rick	82T	202	$.01	$.08
Manning, Rick	83T	757	$.01	$.08
Manning, Rick	83TTR	65	$.01	$.10
Manning, Rick	84T	128	$.01	$.06
Manning, Rick	85T	603	$.01	$.06
Manning, Rick	86T	49	$.01	$.05
Manning, Rick	87T	706	$.01	$.04
Manning, Rick	88T	441	$.01	$.04
Manrique, Fred	88T	437	$.01	$.04
Manrique, Fred	89T	108	$.01	$.03
Manrique, Fred	90T	242	$.01	$.03
Manrique, Fred	90TTR	66	$.01	$.05
Mantilla, Felix	57T	188	$2.00	$8.00
Mantilla, Felix	58T	17	$2.00	$8.00
Mantilla, Felix	59T	157	$1.00	$4.00
Mantilla, Felix	60T	19	$.85	$3.40
Mantilla, Felix	61T	164	$.60	$2.40
Mantilla, Felix	62T	436	$1.25	$5.00
Mantilla, Felix	63T	447	$3.00	$12.00
Mantilla, Felix	64T	228	$.65	$2.60
Mantilla, Felix	65T	29	$.35	$1.40
Mantilla, Felix	66T	557	$7.00	$28.00
Mantilla, Felix	67T	524	$1.50	$6.00
Mantle, Mickey	52T	311	$6000.00	$24000.00
Mantle, Mickey	53T	82	$800.00	$3200.00
Mantle, Mickey	56T	135	$300.00	$1200.00
Mantle, Mickey	57T	95	$275.00	$1100.00
Mantle, Mickey	57T	407	$95.00	$380.00
Mantle, Mickey	58T	150	$150.00	$600.00
Mantle, Mickey	58T	418	$42.50	$170.00
Mantle, Mickey	58TAS	487	$27.50	$110.00
Mantle, Mickey	59T	10	$120.00	$480.00
Mantle, Mickey	59T	461	$12.50	$50.00
Mantle, Mickey	59TAS	564	$70.00	$280.00
Mantle, Mickey	60T	160	$13.75	$55.00
Mantle, Mickey	60T	350	$97.50	$390.00
Mantle, Mickey	60TAS	563	$70.00	$280.00
Mantle, Mickey	61T	44	$10.00	$40.00
Mantle, Mickey	61T	300	$100.00	$400.00
Mantle, Mickey	61T	406	$12.50	$50.00
Mantle, Mickey	61TAS	578	$100.00	$400.00
Mantle, Mickey	61TMVP	475	$30.00	$120.00
Mantle, Mickey	62T	18	$30.00	$120.00
Mantle, Mickey	62T	53	$13.75	$55.00

Player	Year	No.	VG	EX/MT
Mantle, Mickey	62T	200	$135.00	$540.00
Mantle, Mickey	62T	318	$16.25	$65.00
Mantle, Mickey	62TAS	471	$40.00	$160.00
Mantle, Mickey	63T	2	$5.00	$20.00
Mantle, Mickey	63T	173	$20.00	$80.00
Mantle, Mickey	63T	200	$120.00	$480.00
Mantle, Mickey	64T	50	$60.00	$240.00
Mantle, Mickey	64T	331	$30.00	$120.00
Mantle, Mickey	65T	3	$5.50	$22.00
Mantle, Mickey	65T	5	$5.50	$22.00
Mantle, Mickey	65T	350	$112.50	$450.00
Mantle, Mickey	66T	50	$50.00	$200.00
Mantle, Mickey	67T	150	$65.00	$260.00
Mantle, Mickey	68T	280	$60.00	$240.00
Mantle, Mickey	68T	490	$30.00	$120.00
Mantle, Mickey	69T	500	$65.00	$260.00
Mantle, Mickey	75T	194	$1.50	$6.00
Mantle, Mickey	75T	195	$3.00	$12.00
Mantle, Mickey	75T	200	$1.50	$6.00
Mantle, Mickey	91TA53	82	$6.00	$24.00
Manto, Jeff	91T	488	$.01	$.03
Manto, Jeff	91TSC	582	$.05	$.25
Manto, Jeff	92TSC	699	$.01	$.10
Manual, Jerry	76T	596	$.15	$.60
Manuel, Chuck	70T	194	$.20	$.80
Manuel, Chuck	71T	744	$1.50	$6.00
Manush, Heinie	54T	187	$6.00	$24.00
Manwaring, Kirt	88TTR	64	$.01	$.10
Manwaring, Kirt	89T	506	$.01	$.03
Manwaring, Kirt	90T	678	$.01	$.03
Manwaring, Kirt	91T	472	$.01	$.03
Manwaring, Kirt	92T	726	$.01	$.03
Manwaring, Kirt	92TSC	271	$.01	$.10
Manwaring, Kirt	93T	337	$.01	$.03
Manzanillo, Josias	92TSC	504	$.05	$.20
Mapes, Cliff	52T	103	$7.00	$28.00
Marak, Paul	91T	753	$.01	$.10
Maranda, Georges	60T	479	$1.25	$5.00
Margoneri, Joe	57T	191	$2.00	$8.00
Marichal, Juan	61T	417	$30.00	$120.00
Marichal, Juan	62T	505	$10.00	$40.00
Marichal, Juan	63T	440	$7.00	$28.00
Marichal, Juan	64T	3	$2.50	$10.00
Marichal, Juan	64T	280	$3.50	$14.00
Marichal, Juan	65T	10	$.75	$3.00
Marichal, Juan	65T	50	$2.75	$11.00
Marichal, Juan	66T	221	$1.75	$7.00
Marichal, Juan	66T	420	$.03	$12.00
Marichal, Juan	67T	234	$2.00	$8.00
Marichal, Juan	67T	236	$3.75	$15.00
Marichal, Juan	67T	500	$5.50	$22.00
Marichal, Juan	68T	205	$2.25	$9.00
Marichal, Juan	69T	10	$1.25	$5.00
Marichal, Juan	69T	370	$2.00	$8.00
Marichal, Juan	69T	572	$3.00	$12.00
Marichal, Juan	70T	67	$1.50	$6.00
Marichal, Juan	70T	69	$1.50	$6.00
Marichal, Juan	70T	210	$1.50	$6.00
Marichal, Juan	70TAS	466	$1.00	$4.00
Marichal, Juan	71T	325	$1.50	$6.00
Marichal, Juan	72T	567	$1.75	$7.00
Marichal, Juan	72TIA	568	$.90	$3.60
Marichal, Juan	73T	480	$1.00	$4.00
Marichal, Juan	74T	330	$.75	$3.00
Marichal, Juan	74TTR	330	$.50	$2.00
Mariners, Team Checklist	77T	597	$.25	$1.00
Mariners, Team Checklist	78T	499	$.20	$.80
Mariners, Team Checklist	79T	659	$.15	$.60
Mariners, Team Checklist	80T	282	$.10	$.50
Mariners, Team Checklist	81T	672	$.05	$.25
Mariners, Team Leaders	86T	546	$.01	$.05
Mariners, Team Leaders	87T	156	$.01	$.04
Mariners, Team Leaders	88T	519	$.01	$.04
Mariners, Team Leaders	89T	459	$.01	$.03
Marion, Marty	91TA53	302	$.05	$.35

439

TOPPS

Player	Year	No.	VG	EX/MT
Maris, Roger	58T	47	$112.50	$450.00
Maris, Roger	59T	202	$37.50	$150.00
Maris, Roger	60T	377	$30.00	$120.00
Maris, Roger	60TAS	565	$27.50	$110.00
Maris, Roger	61T	2	$42.50	$170.00
Maris, Roger	61T	44	$10.00	$40.00
Maris, Roger	61TAS	576	$37.50	$150.00
Maris, Roger	61TMVP	478	$10.00	$40.00
Maris, Roger	62T	1	$55.00	$220.00
Maris, Roger	62T	53	$13.75	$55.00
Maris, Roger	62T	313	$5.50	$22.00
Maris, Roger	62T	401	$10.00	$40.00
Maris, Roger	63T	4	$2.00	$8.00
Maris, Roger	63T	120	$15.00	$60.00
Maris, Roger	64T	225	$15.00	$60.00
Maris, Roger	64T	331	$30.00	$120.00
Maris, Roger	65T	155	$14.00	$56.00
Maris, Roger	66T	365	$15.00	$60.00
Maris, Roger	67T	45	$10.50	$42.00
Maris, Roger	68T	330	$9.00	$36.00
Maris, Roger	75T	198	$ .55	$2.20
Maris, Roger	75T	199	$ .75	$3.00
Maris, Roger	79TRH	413	$ .20	$ .80
Maris, Roger	86TTB	405	$ .01	$ .15
Marone, Lou	70T	703	$1.25	$5.00
Marquess, Mark	88TTR	65	$ .01	$ .05
Marquez, Gonzalo	73T	605	$1.00	$4.00
Marquez, Gonzalo	74T	422	$ .10	$ .40
Marrero, Connie	52T	317	$50.00	$200.00
Marrero, Connie	53T	13	$4.00	$16.00
Marrero, Connie	91TA53	13	$ .01	$ .15
Marsh, Fred	52T	8	$13.75	$55.00
Marsh, Freddie	53T	240	$22.50	$90.00
Marsh, Fred	54T	218	$3.75	$15.00
Marsh, Fred	55T	13	$2.25	$9.00
Marsh, Freddie	56T	23	$2.00	$8.00
Marsh, Freddie	91TA53	240	$ .01	$ .15
Marsh, Tom	93T	649	$ .01	$ .03
Marshall, Clarence	52T	174	$7.00	$28.00
Marshall, Dave	69T	464	$ .30	$1.20
Marshall, Dave	70T	58	$ .20	$ .80
Marshall, Dave	71T	259	$ .25	$1.00
Marshall, Dave	72T	673	$1.25	$5.00
Marshall, Dave	73T	513	$ .25	$1.00
Marshall, Jim	58T	441	$1.00	$4.00
Marshall, Jim	59T	153	$1.00	$4.00
Marshall, Jim	60T	267	$ .75	$3.00
Marshall, Jim	61T	188	$ .60	$2.40
Marshall, Jim	62T	337	$ .75	$3.00
Marshall, Jim	74T	354	$ .10	$ .40
Marshall, Mike	68T	201	$ .50	$2.00
Marshall, Mike	69T	17	$ .35	$1.40
Marshall, Mike	71T	713	$1.50	$6.00
Marshall, Mike	72T	505	$ .20	$ .80
Marshall, Mike	73T	355	$ .20	$ .80
Marshall, Mike	74T	73	$ .15	$ .60
Marshall, Mike	74T	208	$ .10	$ .40
Marshall, Mike	74TTR	73	$ .15	$ .60
Marshall, Mike	75T	313	$ .25	$1.00
Marshall, Mike	75T	330	$ .10	$ .40
Marshall, Mike	75THL	6	$ .15	$ .60
Marshall, Mike	76T	465	$ .10	$ .40
Marshall, Mike	77T	263	$ .05	$ .20
Marshall, Mike	82T	681	$1.25	$5.00
Marshall, Mike	83T	324	$ .01	$ .15
Marshall, Mike	84T	634	$ .01	$ .10
Marshall, Mike	85T	85	$ .01	$ .06
Marshall, Mike	86T	728	$ .01	$ .10
Marshall, Mike	87T	664	$ .01	$ .10
Marshall, Mike	88T	249	$ .01	$ .04
Marshall, Mike	89T	582	$ .01	$ .03
Marshall, Mike	90T	198	$ .01	$ .03
Marshall, Mike	90TTR	67	$ .01	$ .05
Marshall, Mike	91T	356	$ .01	$ .03
Marshall, Mike	91TSC	226	$ .05	$ .25
Marshall, Willard	52T	96	$7.00	$28.00
Marshall, Willard	53T	95	$4.00	$16.00
Marshall, Willard	91TA53	95	$ .01	$ .15
Martin, Al	93T	623	$ .05	$ .25
Martin, Billy	52T	175	$90.00	$360.00

Player	Year	No.	VG	EX/MT
Martin, Billy	53T	86	$35.00	$140.00
Martin, Billy	54T	13	$17.50	$70.00
Martin, Billy	56T	181	$25.00	$100.00
Martin, Billy	57T	62	$12.50	$50.00
Martin, Billy	58T	271	$5.00	$20.00
Martin, Billy	59T	295	$4.00	$16.00
Martin, Billy	60T	173	$2.50	$10.00
Martin, Billy	61T	89	$2.00	$8.00
Martin, Billy	62T	208	$2.00	$8.00
Martin, Billy	69T	547	$1.50	$6.00
Martin, Billy	71T	208	$ .75	$3.00
Martin, Billy	72T	33	$ .75	$3.00
Martin, Billy	72TIA	34	$ .25	$1.00
Martin, Billy	73T	323	$ .25	$1.00
Martin, Billy	74T	379	$ .25	$1.00
Martin, Billy	78T	721	$ .15	$ .60
Martin, Billy	83T	156	$ .01	$ .15
Martin, Billy	83TTR	66	$ .05	$ .25
Martin, Billy	84T	81	$ .01	$ .15
Martin, Billy	85TTR	78	$ .01	$ .15
Martin, Billy	86T	651	$ .01	$ .10
Martin, Billy	91TA53	86	$ .15	$1.50
Martin, Gene	70T	599	$ .75	$3.00
Martin, J. C.	60T	346	$ .75	$3.00
Martin, J. C.	61T	124	$ .60	$2.40
Martin, J. C.	62T	91	$ .60	$2.40
Martin, J. C.	63T	499	$3.00	$12.00
Martin, J. C.	64T	148	$ .50	$2.00
Martin, J. C.	65T	382	$1.00	$4.00
Martin, J. C.	66T	47	$ .35	$1.40
Martin, J. C.	67T	538	$4.00	$16.00
Martin, J. C.	68T	211	$ .35	$1.40
Martin, J. C.	69T	112	$ .35	$1.40
Martin, J. C.	70T	488	$ .35	$1.40
Martin, J. C.	71T	704	$1.50	$6.00
Martin, J. C.	72T	639	$ .40	$1.60
Martin, J. C.	73T	552	$ .60	$2.40
Martin, J. C.	74T	354	$ .10	$ .40

TOPPS

Player	Year	No.	VG	EX/MT	Player	Year	No.	VG	EX/MT
Martin, Jake	56T	129	$2.50	$10.00	Martinez, Denny	79T	211	$ .35	$1.40
Martin, Jerry	77T	596	$ .05	$ .20	Martinez, Denny	80T	10	$ .10	$ .50
Martin, Jerry	78T	222	$ .04	$ .16	Martinez, Denny	81T	367	$ .05	$ .25
Martin, Jerry	79T	382	$ .03	$ .12	Martinez, Denny	82T	165	$ .01	$ .15
Martin, Jerry	80T	493	$ .01	$ .10	Martinez, Denny	82T	712	$ .05	$ .25
Martin, Jerry	81T	103	$ .01	$ .08	Martinez, Denny	83T	553	$ .01	$ .08
Martin, Jerry	81TTR	798	$ .01	$ .15	Martinez, Denny	84T	631	$ .01	$ .06
Martin, Jerry	82T	722	$ .01	$ .08	Martinez, Denny	85T	199	$ .01	$ .06
Martin, Jerry	82TTR	65	$ .01	$ .10	Martinez, Denny	86T	416	$ .01	$ .05
Martin, Jerry	83T	626	$ .01	$ .08	Martinez, Denny	87T	252	$ .01	$ .04
Martin, Jerry	84T	74	$ .01	$ .06	Martinez, Denny	88T	76	$ .01	$ .04
Martin, Jerry	84TTR	74	$ .01	$ .15	Martinez, Denny	89T	313	$ .01	$ .03
Martin, Jerry	85T	517	$ .01	$ .06	Martinez, Denny	90T	763	$ .01	$ .03
Martin, John	82T	236	$ .01	$ .08	Martinez, Denny	91T	528	$ .01	$ .03
Martin, John	83T	721	$ .01	$ .08	Martinez, Denny	91TSC	273	$ .05	$ .25
Martin, John	84T	24	$ .01	$ .06	Martinez, Denny	92T	15	$ .01	$ .03
Martin, Morrie	52T	131	$7.00	$28.00	Martinez, Denny	92TAS	394	$ .01	$ .03
Martin, Morrie	53T	227	$22.50	$90.00	Martinez, Denny	92TSC	860	$ .01	$ .10
Martin, Morrie	54T	168	$3.75	$15.00	Martinez, Denny	93T	610	$ .01	$ .03
Martin, Morrie	58T	53	$2.00	$8.00	Martinez, Denny	93TSC	140	$ .01	$ .10
Martin, Morrie	59T	38	$1.50	$6.00	Martinez, Domingo	93T	810	$ .05	$ .20
Martin, Morrie	91TA53	227	$ .01	$ .15	Martinez, Edgar	90T	148	$ .05	$ .25
Martin, Renie	80T	667	$ .20	$2.00	Martinez, Edgar	91T	607	$ .01	$ .03
Martin, Renie	81T	452	$ .01	$ .08	Martinez, Edgar	91TSC	47	$ .10	$1.00
Martin, Renie	82T	594	$ .01	$ .08	Martinez, Edgar	92T	553	$ .01	$ .03
Martin, Renie	82TTR	66	$ .01	$ .10	Martinez, Edgar	92TSC	267	$ .01	$ .10
Martin, Renie	83T	263	$ .01	$ .08	Martinez, Edgar	93T	315	$ .01	$ .03
Martin, Renie	84T	603	$ .01	$ .06	Martinez, Edgar	93T	403	$ .01	$ .03
Martinez, Buck	70T	609	$ .75	$3.00	Martinez, Fred	81T	227	$ .01	$ .08
Martinez, Buck	71T	163	$ .25	$1.00	Martinez, Fred	82T	659	$ .01	$ .08
Martinez, Buck	72T	332	$ .10	$ .40	Martinez, Jose	70T	8	$ .25	$1.00
Martinez, Buck	75T	314	$ .10	$ .40	Martinez, Jose	71T	712	$1.10	$4.40
Martinez, Buck	76T	616	$ .05	$ .25	Martinez, Orlando "Marty"	67T	504	$1.50	$6.00
Martinez, Buck	77T	46	$ .05	$ .20	Martinez, Orlando	68T	578	$ .70	$2.80
Martinez, Buck	78T	571	$ .04	$ .16	Martinez, Marty	69T	337	$ .30	$1.20
Martinez, Buck	79T	243	$ .03	$ .12	Martinez, Marty	70T	126	$ .20	$ .80
Martinez, Buck	80T	477	$ .01	$ .10	Martinez, Marty	71T	602	$1.00	$4.00
Martinez, Buck	81T	56	$ .01	$ .08	Martinez, Marty	72T	336	$ .10	$ .40
Martinez, Buck	81TTR	799	$ .01	$ .15	Martinez, Pedro	93T	557	$ .01	$ .15
Martinez, Buck	82T	314	$ .01	$ .08	Martinez, Ramon	89T	225	$ .10	$ .50
Martinez, Buck	83T	733	$ .01	$ .08	Martinez, Ramon	90T	62	$ .05	$ .20
Martinez, Buck	84T	179	$ .01	$ .06	Martinez, Ramon	91T	340	$ .01	$ .10
Martinez, Buck	85T	673	$ .01	$ .06	Martinez, Ramon	91TSC	516	$ .10	$ .50
Martinez, Buck	86T	518	$ .01	$ .05	Martinez, Ramon	92T	730	$ .01	$ .10
Martinez, Carlos	90T	461	$ .01	$ .03	Martinez, Ramon	92TSC	207	$ .01	$ .15
Martinez, Carlos	91T	156	$ .01	$ .03	Martinez, Ramon	93T	120	$ .01	$ .03
Martinez, Carlos	92T	280	$ .01	$ .03	Martinez, Ramon	93TSC	71	$ .01	$ .10
Martinez, Carlos	92TSC	482	$ .01	$ .10	Martinez, Silvio	79T	609	$ .03	$ .12
Martinez, Carlos	93T	59	$ .01	$ .03	Martinez, Silvio	80T	496	$ .01	$ .10
Martinez, Carlos	93TSC	255	$ .01	$ .10	Martinez, Silvio	81T	586	$ .01	$ .08
Martinez, Carmelo	84T	267	$ .05	$ .25	Martinez, Silvio	82T	181	$ .01	$ .08
Martinez, Carmelo	84TTR	75	$ .01	$ .15	Martinez, Ted	71T	648	$3.00	$12.00
Martinez, Carmelo	85T	558	$ .01	$ .06	Martinez, Ted	72T	544	$ .40	$1.60
Martinez, Carmelo	86T	67	$ .01	$ .05	Martinez, Ted	73T	161	$ .10	$ .40
Martinez, Carmelo	87T	348	$ .01	$ .04	Martinez, Ted	74T	487	$ .10	$ .40
Martinez, Carmelo	88T	148	$ .01	$ .04	Martinez, Ted	75T	637	$ .10	$ .40
Martinez, Carmelo	89T	449	$ .01	$ .03	Martinez, Ted	76T	356	$ .05	$ .25
Martinez, Carmelo	90T	686	$ .01	$ .03	Martinez, Ted	78T	546	$ .04	$ .16
Martinez, Carmelo	90TTR	68	$ .01	$ .05	Martinez, Ted	79T	128	$ .03	$ .12
Martinez, Carmelo	91T	779	$ .01	$ .03	Martinez, Ted	80T	191	$ .01	$ .10
Martinez, Chito	92T	479	$ .01	$ .15	Martinez, Tino	88TTR	66	$ .10	$1.00
Martinez, Chito	92TSC	438	$ .01	$ .10	Martinez, Tino	91T	482	$ .01	$ .15
Martinez, Chito	93T	772	$ .01	$ .03	Martinez, Tino	91TSC	179	$ .10	$ .75
Martinez, Dave	87TTR	73	$ .01	$ .15	Martinez, Tino	92T	481	$ .01	$ .10
Martinez, Dave	88T	439	$ .01	$ .15	Martinez, Tino	92TSC	573	$ .01	$ .15
Martinez, Dave	89T	763	$ .01	$ .03	Martinez, Tino	93T	232	$ .01	$ .03
Martinez, Dave	90T	228	$ .01	$ .03	Martinez, Tino	93TSC	273	$ .01	$ .10
Martinez, Dave	91T	24	$ .01	$ .03	Martinez, Tippy	76T	41	$ .10	$ .40
Martinez, Dave	91TSC	346	$ .05	$ .25	Martinez, Tippy	77T	238	$ .05	$ .20
Martinez, Dave	92T	309	$ .01	$ .03	Martinez, Tippy	78T	393	$ .04	$ .16
Martinez, Dave	92TSC	723	$ .01	$ .10	Martinez, Tippy	79T	491	$ .03	$ .12
Martinez, Dave	92TTR	67	$ .01	$ .05	Martinez, Tippy	80T	706	$ .01	$ .10
Martinez, Dave	93T	671	$ .01	$ .03	Martinez, Tippy	81T	119	$ .01	$ .08
Martinez, Denny	77T	491	$1.75	$7.00	Martinez, Tippy	82T	583	$ .01	$ .08
Martinez, Denny	78T	119	$ .50	$2.00	Martinez, Tippy	83T	631	$ .01	$ .08

TOPPS

Player	Year	No.	VG	EX/MT	Player	Year	No.	VG	EX/MT
Martinez, Tippy	84T	215	$ .01	$ .06	Mathews, Ed	64T	35	$4.50	$18.00
Martinez, Tippy	85T	445	$ .01	$ .06	Mathews, Ed	65T	500	$8.00	$32.00
Martinez, Tippy	86T	82	$ .01	$ .05	Mathews, Ed	66T	200	$3.00	$12.00
Martinez, Tippy	87T	728	$ .01	$ .04	Mathews, Ed	67T	166	$3.00	$12.00
Martinez, Tony	63T	466	$12.50	$50.00	Mathews, Ed	68T	58	$2.75	$11.00
Martinez, Tony	64T	404	$1.00	$4.00	Mathews, Eddie	73T	237	$ .30	$1.20
Martinez, Tony	66T	581	$3.75	$15.00	Mathews, Eddie	74T	634	$ .25	$1.00
Marting, Tim	71T	423	$ .50	$2.00	Mathews, Ed	91TA53	37	$ .20	$2.00
Martyn, Bob	58T	39	$2.00	$8.00	Mathews, Greg	87T	567	$ .01	$ .04
Martyn, Bob	59T	41	$1.50	$6.00	Mathews, Greg	88T	133	$ .01	$ .04
Martz, Randy	81T	381	$ .01	$ .08	Mathews, Greg	89T	97	$ .01	$ .03
Martz, Randy	82T	188	$ .01	$ .08	Mathews, Greg	90T	209	$ .01	$ .03
Martz, Randy	82T	456	$ .01	$ .08	Mathews, Nelson	64T	366	$ .65	$2.60
Martz, Randy	83T	22	$ .01	$ .08	Mathews, Nelson	65T	87	$ .35	$1.40
Marzano, John	85T	399	$ .01	$ .15	Mathewson, Christy	61T	408	$2.25	$9.00
Marzano, John	88T	757	$ .01	$ .04	Mathias, Carl	60T	139	$ .75	$3.00
Marzano, John	90TTR	69	$ .01	$ .05	Mathis, Ron	85TTR	79	$ .01	$ .10
Marzano, John	91T	574	$ .01	$ .03	Mathis, Ron	86T	476	$ .01	$ .05
Marzano, John	91TSC	201	$ .05	$ .25	Matias, John	70T	444	$ .35	$1.40
Marzano, John	92T	677	$ .01	$ .03	Matias, John	71T	546	$1.00	$4.00
Marzano, John	92TSC	424	$ .01	$ .10	Matlack, Jon	71T	648	$3.00	$12.00
Marzano, John	93TSC	73	$ .01	$ .10	Matlack, Jon	72T	141	$ .10	$ .40
Mashore, Clyde	71T	376	$ .25	$1.00	Matlack, Jon	73T	55	$ .20	$ .80
Mashore, Clyde	73T	401	$ .25	$1.00	Matlack, Jon	74T	153	$ .10	$ .40
Masi, Phil	51Tbb	19	$7.50	$30.00	Matlack, Jon	75T	290	$ .10	$ .40
Masi, Phil	52T	283	$13.75	$55.00	Matlack, Jon	76T	190	$ .05	$ .25
Mason, Don	66T	524	$7.00	$28.00	Matlack, Jon	77T	440	$ .05	$ .20
Mason, Don	69T	584	$ .40	$1.60	Matlack, Jon	78T	25	$ .04	$ .16
Mason, Don	71T	548	$1.00	$4.00	Matlack, Jon	79T	315	$ .03	$ .12
Mason, Don	72T	739	$1.25	$5.00	Matlack, Jon	80T	592	$ .01	$ .10
Mason, Henry	60T	331	$ .75	$3.00	Matlack, Jon	81T	656	$ .01	$ .08
Mason, Jim	72T	334	$ .10	$ .40	Matlack, Jon	82T	239	$ .01	$ .08
Mason, Jim	73T	458	$ .25	$1.00	Matlack, Jon	83T	749	$ .01	$ .08
Mason, Jim	74T	618	$ .10	$ .40	Matlack, Jon	84T	149	$ .01	$ .06
Mason, Jim	74TTR	618	$ .10	$ .40	Matthews, Gary	73T	606	$1.00	$4.00
Mason, Jim	75T	136	$ .10	$ .40	Matthews, Gary	74T	386	$ .25	$1.00
Mason, Jim	77T	212	$ .05	$ .20	Matthews, Gary	75T	79	$ .15	$ .60
Mason, Jim	78T	588	$ .04	$ .16					
Mason, Jim	79T	67	$ .03	$ .12					
Mason, Jim	80T	497	$ .01	$ .10					
Mason, Mike	84TTR	76	$ .01	$ .15					
Mason, Mike	85T	464	$ .01	$ .06					
Mason, Mike	86T	189	$ .01	$ .05					
Mason, Mike	87T	646	$ .01	$ .04					
Mason, Mike	88T	87	$ .01	$ .04					
Mason, Roger	86TTR	70	$ .01	$ .06					
Mason, Roger	87T	526	$ .01	$ .04					
Mason, Roger	92TSC	266	$ .01	$ .10					
Masse, Billy	88TTR	67	$ .05	$ .20					
Masterson, Walt	52T	186	$7.00	$28.00					
Matchick, John (Tom)	67T	72	$ .40	$1.60					
Matchick, Tom	68T	113	$ .35	$1.40					
Matchick, Tom	69T	344	$ .30	$1.20					
Matchick, Tom	70T	647	$1.25	$5.00					
Matchick, Tom	71T	321	$ .25	$1.00					
Matchick, Tom	73T	631	$ .60	$2.40					
Mathew, Nelson	63T	54	$1.50	$6.00					
Mathews, Byron	93T	612	$ .01	$ .10					
Mathews, Ed	52T	407	$625.00	$2500.00					
Mathews, Ed	53T	37	$25.00	$100.00					
Mathews, Ed	54T	30	$23.75	$95.00					
Mathews, Ed	55T	155	$30.00	$120.00					
Mathews, Ed	56T	107	$15.00	$60.00					
Mathews, Ed	57T	250	$11.00	$44.00					
Mathews, Ed	58T	351	$7.00	$28.00					
Mathews, Ed	58T	440	$9.00	$36.00					
Mathews, Ed	58TAS	480	$3.50	$14.00					
Mathews, Ed	59T	212	$12.00	$48.00					
Mathews, Ed	59T	450	$7.50	$30.00					
Mathews, Ed	60T	420	$8.00	$32.00	Matthews, Gary	76T	133	$ .05	$ .25
Mathews, Ed	60TAS	558	$8.00	$32.00	Matthews, Gary	77T	194	$ .05	$ .20
Mathews, Ed	61T	43	$3.00	$12.00	Matthews, Gary	78T	475	$ .04	$ .16
Mathews, Ed	61T	120	$7.00	$28.00	Matthews, Gary	79T	85	$ .03	$ .12
Mathews, Ed	62T	30	$4.00	$20.00	Matthews, Gary	80T	355	$ .01	$ .10
Mathews, Ed	63T	275	$5.00	$20.00	Matthews, Gary	81T	528	$ .01	$ .08

TOPPS

Player	Year	No.	VG	EX/MT	Player	Year	No.	VG	EX/MT
Matthews, Gary	81TTR	800	$.01	$.15	Maxwell, Charley	57T	205	$2.00	$8.00
Matthews, Gary	82T	680	$.01	$.08	Maxwell, Charley	58T	380	$1.00	$4.00
Matthews, Gary	83T	780	$.01	$.08	Maxwell, Charlie	59T	34	$3.50	$14.00
Matthews, Gary	84T	70	$.01	$.06	Maxwell, Charley	59T	481	$1.00	$4.00
Matthews, Gary	84T	637	$.01	$.06	Maxwell, Charlie	60T	443	$1.25	$5.00
Matthews, Gary	84TTR	77	$.01	$.15	Maxwell, Charlie	61T	37	$.60	$2.40
Matthews, Gary	85T	210	$.01	$.06	Maxwell, Charley	62T	506	$1.50	$6.00
Matthews, Gary	86T	485	$.01	$.05	Maxwell, Charley	63T	86	$.50	$2.00
Matthews, Gary	87T	390	$.01	$.04	Maxwell, Charlie	64T	401	$1.00	$4.00
Matthews, Gary	88T	156	$.01	$.04	May, Carlos	69T	654	$.75	$3.00
Matthews, Mike	93T	787	$.05	$.20	May, Carlos	70T	18	$.20	$.80
Mattingly, Don	84T	8	$3.00	$12.00	May, Carlos	71T	243	$.25	$1.00
Mattingly, Don	85T	665	$.75	$3.00	May, Carlos	72T	525	$.25	$1.00
Mattingly, Don	86T	180	$.10	$1.00	May, Carlos	73T	105	$.10	$.40
Mattingly, Don	86TAS	712	$.05	$.35	May, Carlos	74T	195	$.10	$.40
Mattingly, Don	87T	500	$.10	$.50	May, Carlos	75T	480	$.10	$.40
Mattingly, Don	87TAS	606	$.05	$.20	May, Carlos	76T	110	$.05	$.25
Mattingly, Don	88T	300	$.05	$.25	May, Carlos	77T	568	$.05	$.20
Mattingly, Don	88TAS	386	$.01	$.15	May, Carlos	77T	633	$.05	$.20
Mattingly, Don	88TRB	2	$.01	$.10	May, Dave	68T	56	$.35	$1.40
Mattingly, Don	89T	700	$.05	$.20	May, Dave	69T	113	$.35	$1.40
Mattingly, Don	89TAS	397	$.01	$.15	May, Dave	70T	81	$.20	$.80
Mattingly, Don	90T	200	$.01	$.15	May, Dave	71T	493	$.50	$2.00
Mattingly, Don	91T	100	$.01	$.15	May, Dave	72T	549	$.40	$1.60
Mattingly, Don	91TSC	21	$.15	$1.50	May, Dave	73T	152	$.10	$.40
Mattingly, Don	92T	300	$.01	$.10	May, Dave	74T	12	$.10	$.40
Mattingly, Don	92TSC	420	$.10	$.50	May, Dave	75T	650	$.10	$.40
Mattingly, Don	93T	32	$.01	$.10	May, Dave	76T	281	$.05	$.25
Matula, Rick	80T	596	$.01	$.10	May, Dave	78T	362	$.04	$.16
Matula, Rick	81T	611	$.01	$.08	May, Derrick	91T	288	$.01	$.15
Matuszek, Len	83T	357	$.01	$.08	May, Derrick	91TSC	73	$.10	$.75
Matuszek, Len	84T	275	$.01	$.06	May, Derrick	92TSC	148	$.01	$.10
Matuszek, Len	85T	688	$.01	$.06	May, Derrick	92TTR	68	$.01	$.05
Matuszek, Len	85TTR	80	$.01	$.10	May, Derrick	93T	391	$.01	$.03
Matuszek, Len	86T	109	$.01	$.05	May, Derrick	93TSC	109	$.01	$.10
Matuszek, Len	87T	457	$.01	$.04	May, Jerry	65T	143	$.35	$1.40
Matuszek, Len	88T	92	$.01	$.04	May, Jerry	66T	123	$.50	$2.00
Mauch, Gene	57T	342	$6.00	$24.00	May, Jerry	67T	379	$.60	$2.40
Mauch, Gene	61T	219	$.75	$3.00	May, Jerry	68T	598	$1.25	$5.00
Mauch, Gene	62T	374	$1.25	$5.00	May, Jerry	69T	263	$.50	$2.00
Mauch, Gene	63T	318	$.90	$3.60	May, Jerry	70T	423	$.35	$1.40
Mauch, Gene	64T	157	$.50	$2.00	May, Jerry	71T	719	$1.50	$6.00
Mauch, Gene	65T	489	$1.25	$5.00	May, Jerry	72T	109	$.10	$.40
Mauch, Gene	66T	411	$.65	$2.60	May, Jerry	73T	558	$.60	$2.40
Mauch, Gene	67T	248	$.50	$2.00	May, Lee	66T	424	$1.75	$7.00
Mauch, Gene	68T	122	$.35	$1.40	May, Lee	67T	222	$.50	$2.00
Mauch, Gene	69T	606	$.40	$1.60	May, Lee	68T	487	$1.00	$4.00
Mauch, Gene	70T	442	$.35	$1.40	May, Lee	69T	405	$.30	$1.20
Mauch, Gene	71T	59	$.25	$1.00	May, Lee	70T	65	$1.25	$5.00
Mauch, Gene	72T	276	$.20	$.80	May, Lee	70T	225	$.20	$.80
Mauch, Gene	73T	377	$.20	$.80	May, Lee	71T	40	$.25	$1.00
Mauch, Gene	74T	531	$.25	$1.00	May, Lee	72T	89	$.50	$2.00
Mauch, Gene	78T	601	$.04	$.16	May, Lee	72T	480	$.20	$.80
Mauch, Gene	83T	276	$.01	$.08	May, Lee	73T	135	$.20	$.80
Mauch, Gene	85TTR	81	$.01	$.10	May, Lee	74T	500	$.25	$1.00
Mauch, Gene	86T	81	$.01	$.05	May, Lee	75T	25	$.15	$.60
Mauch, Gene	87T	518	$.01	$.04	May, Lee	76T	210	$.05	$.25
Mauch, Gene	88T	774	$.01	$.04	May, Lee	77T	3	$.30	$1.20
Maurer, Rob	92TSC	462	$.05	$.20	May, Lee	77T	380	$.05	$.20
Maurer, Rob	93T	763	$.01	$.03	May, Lee	77T	633	$.05	$.20
Mauser, Tim	92TSC	558	$.01	$.15	May, Lee	78T	640	$.04	$.16
Maxie, Larry	64T	94	$.50	$2.00	May, Lee	79T	10	$.03	$.12
Maxvill, Dal	63T	49	$.90	$3.60	May, Lee	80T	490	$.01	$.10
Maxvill, Dal	64T	563	$2.25	$9.00	May, Lee	82T	132	$.01	$.08
Maxvill, Dal	65T	78	$.35	$1.40	May, Lee	83T	377	$.01	$.08
Maxvill, Dal	66T	338	$.50	$2.00	May, Lee	83T	378	$.01	$.08
Maxvill, Dal	67T	421	$.60	$2.40	May, Milt	71T	343	$.40	$1.60
Maxvill, Dal	68T	141	$.35	$1.40	May, Milt	72T	247	$.10	$.40
Maxvill, Dal	69T	320	$.50	$2.00	May, Milt	73T	529	$.60	$2.40
Maxvill, Dal	70T	503	$.35	$1.40	May, Milt	74T	293	$.10	$.40
Maxvill, Dal	71T	476	$.50	$2.00	May, Milt	75T	279	$.10	$.40
Maxvill, Dal	72T	206	$.10	$.40	May, Milt	76T	532	$.05	$.25
Maxvill, Dal	73T	483	$.25	$1.00	May, Milt	76TTR	532	$.05	$.25
Maxvill, Dal	74T	358	$.10	$.40	May, Milt	77T	98	$.05	$.20
Maxwell, Charley	52T	180	$8.00	$32.00	May, Milt	78T	176	$.04	$.16

TOPPS

Player	Year	No.	VG	EX/MT	Player	Year	No.	VG	EX/MT
May, Milt	79T	316	$ .03	$ .12	Mays, Willie	59TAS	563	$30.00	$120.00
May, Milt	80T	647	$ .01	$ .10	Mays, Willie	60T	7	$5.00	$20.00
May, Milt	81T	463	$ .01	$ .08	Mays, Willie	60T	200	$30.00	$120.00
May, Milt	82T	242	$ .01	$ .08	Mays, Willie	60TAS	564	$30.00	$120.00
May, Milt	82T	576	$ .01	$ .08	Mays, Willie	61T	41	$2.25	$9.00
May, Milt	83T	84	$ .01	$ .08	Mays, Willie	61T	150	$30.00	$120.00
May, Milt	84T	788	$ .01	$ .06	Mays, Willie	61TAS	579	$40.00	$160.00
May, Milt	85T	509	$ .01	$ .06	Mays, Willie	61TMVP	482	$11.25	$45.00
May, Rudy	65T	537	$1.50	$6.00	Mays, Willie	62T	18	$30.00	$120.00
May, Rudy	70T	203	$ .20	$ .80	Mays, Willie	62T	54	$2.00	$8.00
May, Rudy	71T	318	$ .25	$1.00	Mays, Willie	62T	300	$37.50	$150.00
May, Rudy	72T	656	$ .40	$1.60	Mays, Willie	62TAS	395	$11.25	$45.00
May, Rudy	73T	102	$ .10	$ .40	Mays, Willie	63T	3	$5.50	$22.00
May, Rudy	74T	302	$ .10	$ .40	Mays, Willie	63T	138	$8.75	$35.00
May, Rudy	75T	321	$ .10	$ .40	Mays, Willie	63T	300	$45.00	$180.00
May, Rudy	76T	481	$ .05	$ .25	Mays, Willie	64T	9	$4.00	$16.00
May, Rudy	77T	56	$ .05	$ .20	Mays, Willie	64T	150	$25.00	$100.00
May, Rudy	78T	262	$ .04	$ .16	Mays, Willie	64T	306	$6.50	$26.00
May, Rudy	79T	603	$ .03	$ .12	Mays, Willie	64T	423	$27.50	$110.00
May, Rudy	80T	539	$ .01	$ .10	Mays, Willie	65T	4	$2.00	$8.00
May, Rudy	81T	7	$ .05	$ .20	Mays, Willie	65T	6	$1.25	$5.00
May, Rudy	81T	179	$ .01	$ .08	Mays, Willie	65T	250	$25.00	$100.00
May, Rudy	82T	735	$ .01	$ .08	Mays, Willie	66T	1	$35.00	$140.00
May, Rudy	83T	408	$ .01	$ .08	Mays, Willie	66T	215	$7.00	$28.00
May, Rudy	84T	652	$ .01	$ .06	Mays, Willie	66T	217	$4.00	$16.00
Mayberry, John	70T	227	$ .30	$1.20	Mays, Willie	66T	219	$1.75	$7.00
Mayberry, John	71T	148	$ .25	$1.00	Mays, Willie	67T	200	$22.50	$90.00
Mayberry, John	72T	373	$ .10	$ .40	Mays, Willie	67T	244	$2.50	$10.00
Mayberry, John	73T	118	$ .20	$ .80	Mays, Willie	67T	423	$6.00	$24.00
Mayberry, John	74T	150	$ .10	$ .40	Mays, Willie	68T	50	$17.50	$70.00
Mayberry, John	75T	95	$ .10	$ .40	Mays, Willie	68T	490	$30.00	$120.00
Mayberry, John	76T	194	$ .50	$2.00	Mays, Willie	69T	190	$15.00	$60.00
Mayberry, John	76T	196	$ .25	$1.00	Mays, Willie	70T	600	$18.25	$75.00
Mayberry, John	76T	440	$ .05	$ .25	Mays, Willie	71T	600	$22.50	$00.00
Mayberry, John	77T	244	$ .05	$ .20	Mays, Willie	72T	49	$7.00	$28.00
Mayberry, John	78T	550	$ .04	$ .16	Mays, Willie	72TIA	50	$3.50	$14.00
Mayberry, John	79T	380	$ .03	$ .12	Mays, Willie	73T	1	$6.75	$27.00
Mayberry, John	80T	643	$ .01	$ .10	Mays, Willie	73T	305	$8.75	$35.00
Mayberry, John	81T	169	$ .01	$ .08	Mays, Willie	75T	192	$ .50	$2.00
Mayberry, John	82T	470	$ .01	$ .08	Mays, Willie	75T	203	$ .35	$1.40
Mayberry, John	82T	606	$ .01	$ .10	Mays, Willie	86TTB	403	$ .01	$ .15
Mayberry, John	82TTR	67	$ .01	$ .10	Mays, Willie	91TA53	244	$3.00	$12.00
Mayberry, John	83T	45	$ .01	$ .08	Mazeroski, Bill	57T	24	$15.00	$60.00
Maye, Lee	60T	246	$ .75	$3.00	Mazeroski, Bill	58T	238	$3.50	$14.00
Maye, Lee	61T	84	$ .60	$2.40	Mazeroski, Bill	59T	415	$1.75	$7.00
Maye, Lee	62T	518	$1.50	$6.00	Mazeroski, Bill	59TAS	555	$6.00	$24.00
Maye, Lee	63T	109	$ .50	$2.00	Mazeroski, Bill	60T	55	$1.75	$7.00
Maye, Lee	64T	416	$1.00	$4.00	Mazeroski, Bill	61T	430	$9.00	$36.00
Maye, Lee	65T	407	$1.00	$4.00	Mazeroski, Bill	61TAS	571	$10.00	$40.00
Maye, Lee	66T	162	$ .50	$2.00	Mazeroski, Bill	62T	353	$1.75	$7.00
Maye, Lee	67T	258	$ .50	$2.00	Mazeroski, Bill	62TAS	391	$2.00	$8.00
Maye, Lee	68T	94	$ .35	$1.40	Mazeroski, Bill	63T	323	$1.50	$6.00
Maye, Lee	69T	595	$ .40	$1.60	Mazeroski, Bill	64T	570	$3.00	$12.00
Maye, Lee	70T	439	$ .35	$1.40	Mazeroski, Bill	65T	95	$ .75	$3.00
Maye, Lee	71T	733	$1.50	$6.00	Mazeroski, Bill	66T	210	$1.00	$4.00
Mayer, Ed	58T	461	$1.00	$4.00	Mazeroski, Bill	67T	510	$3.00	$12.00
Mayne, Brent	91T	776	$ .01	$ .15	Mazeroski, Bill	68T	390	$ .75	$3.00
Mayne, Brent	91TSC	418	$ .05	$ .25	Mazeroski, Bill	69T	335	$ .75	$3.00
Mayne, Brent	92T	183	$ .01	$ .03	Mazeroski, Bill	70T	440	$ .50	$2.00
Mayne, Brent	92TSC	229	$ .01	$ .10	Mazeroski, Bill	71T	110	$ .40	$1.60
Mayne, Brent	93T	294	$ .01	$ .03	Mazeroski, Bill	72T	760	$2.00	$8.00
Mayne, Brent	93TSC	25	$ .01	$ .10	Mazeroski, Bill	73T	517	$ .25	$1.00
Mayo, Eddie	54T	247	$3.75	$15.00	Mazeroski, Bill	74T	489	$ .10	$ .40
Mays, Willie	52T	261	$700.00	$2800.00	Mazzilli, Lee	77T	488	$2.50	$10.00
Mays, Willie	53T	244	$625.00	$2500.00	Mazzilli, Lee	78T	147	$ .04	$ .16
Mays, Willie	54T	90	$125.00	$500.00	Mazzilli, Lee	79T	355	$ .03	$ .12
Mays, Willie	55T	194	$130.00	$520.00	Mazzilli, Lee	80T	25	$ .01	$ .10
Mays, Willie	56T	130	$90.00	$360.00	Mazzilli, Lee	81T	510	$ .01	$ .08
Mays, Willie	57T	10	$60.00	$240.00	Mazzilli, Lee	82T	465	$ .01	$ .08
Mays, Willie	58T	5	$50.00	$200.00	Mazzilli, Lee	82TTR	68	$ .01	$ .10
Mays, Willie	58T	436	$17.50	$70.00	Mazzilli, Lee	83T	685	$ .01	$ .08
Mays, Willie	58TAS	486	$12.50	$50.00	Mazzilli, Lee	83TTR	67	$ .01	$ .10
Mays, Willie	59T	50	$40.00	$160.00	Mazzilli, Lee	84T	225	$ .01	$ .06
Mays, Willie	59T	317	$8.00	$32.00	Mazzilli, Lee	85T	748	$ .01	$ .06
Mays, Willie	59T	464	$6.50	$26.00	Mazzilli, Lee	86T	578	$ .01	$ .05

TOPPS

Player	Year	No.	VG	EX/MT
Mazzilli, Lee	87T	198	$ .01	$ .04
Mazzilli, Lee	88T	308	$ .01	$ .04
Mazzilli, Lee	89T	58	$ .01	$ .03
Mazzilli, Lee	90T	721	$ .01	$ .03
McAnally, Ernie	71T	376	$ .25	$1.00
McAnally, Ernie	72T	58	$ .10	$ .40
McAnally, Ernie	73T	484	$ .25	$1.00
McAnally, Ernie	74T	322	$ .10	$ .40
McAnally, Ernie	75T	318	$ .10	$ .40
McAndrew, Jamie	93T	412	$ .01	$ .03
McAndrew, Jim	69T	321	$ .50	$2.00
McAndrew, Jim	70T	246	$ .20	$ .80
McAndrew, Jim	71T	428	$ .50	$2.00
McAndrew, Jim	72T	781	$1.25	$5.00
McAndrew, Jim	73T	436	$ .25	$1.00
McAuliffe, Dick	62T	527	$4.50	$18.00
McAuliffe, Dick	63T	64	$ .50	$2.00
McAuliffe, Dick	64T	363	$ .65	$2.60
McAuliffe, Dick	65T	53	$ .35	$1.40
McAuliffe, Dick	66T	495	$1.50	$6.00
McAuliffe, Dick	67T	170	$ .40	$1.60
McAuliffe, Dick	68T	285	$ .35	$1.40
McAuliffe, Dick	69T	305	$ .50	$2.00
McAuliffe, Dick	70T	475	$ .35	$1.40
McAuliffe, Dick	71T	3	$ .25	$1.00
McAuliffe, Dick	72T	725	$1.25	$5.00
McAuliffe, Dick	73T	349	$ .10	$ .40

Player	Year	No.	VG	EX/MT
McAuliffe, Dick	74T	495	$ .10	$ .40
McBean, Al	62T	424	$1.25	$5.00
McBean, Al	63T	387	$1.00	$4.00
McBean, Al	64T	525	$2.25	$9.00
McBean, Al	65T	25	$ .35	$1.40
McBean, Al	66T	353	$ .50	$2.00
McBean, Al	67T	203	$ .50	$2.00
McBean, Al	68T	514	$ .75	$3.00
McBean, Al	69T	14	$ .35	$1.40
McBean, Al	70T	641	$1.25	$5.00
McBride, Bake	74T	601	$1.25	$5.00
McBride, Bake	75T	174	$ .10	$ .40
McBride, Bake	76T	135	$ .05	$ .25
McBride, Bake	77T	516	$ .05	$ .20
McBride, Bake	78T	340	$ .04	$ .16
McBride, Bake	79T	630	$ .05	$ .20
McBride, Bake	80T	495	$ .01	$ .10

Player	Year	No.	VG	EX/MT
McBride, Bake	81T	90	$ .01	$ .15
McBride, Bake	82T	745	$ .01	$ .08
McBride, Bake	82TTR	69	$ .01	$ .10
McBride, Bake	83T	248	$ .01	$ .08
McBride, Bake	84T	569	$ .01	$ .06
McBride, Ken	60T	276	$ .75	$3.00
McBride, Ken	61T	209	$ .60	$2.40
McBride, Ken	62T	268	$ .75	$3.00
McBride, Ken	63T	510	$1.75	$7.00
McBride, Ken	64T	405	$1.00	$4.00
McBride, Ken	65T	268	$ .50	$2.00
McCabe, Joe	64T	564	$2.25	$9.00
McCabe, Joe	65T	181	$ .35	$1.40
McCall, Windy	55T	42	$2.25	$9.00
McCall, Windy	56T	44	$2.00	$8.00
McCall, Windy	57T	291	$5.00	$20.00
McCament, Randy	90T	361	$ .01	$ .10
McCarthy, Tom	89TTR	75	$ .01	$ .10
McCarthy, Tom	90T	326	$ .01	$ .03
McCarver, Tim	62T	167	$8.00	$32.00
McCarver, Tim	63T	394	$3.50	$14.00
McCarver, Tim	64T	429	$2.00	$8.00
McCarver, Tim	65T	294	$1.25	$5.00
McCarver, Tim	66T	275	$1.25	$5.00
McCarver, Tim	67T	485	$5.50	$22.00
McCarver, Tim	68T	275	$ .75	$3.00
McCarver, Tim	68TAS	376	$ .75	$3.00
McCarver, Tim	69T	475	$ .75	$3.00
McCarver, Tim	70T	90	$ .25	$1.00
McCarver, Tim	71T	465	$ .50	$2.00
McCarver, Tim	72T	139	$ .25	$1.00
McCarver, Tim	73T	269	$ .25	$1.00
McCarver, Tim	74T	520	$ .20	$ .80
McCarver, Tim	75T	586	$ .25	$1.00
McCarver, Tim	76T	502	$ .20	$ .80
McCarver, Tim	77T	357	$ .20	$ .80
McCarver, Tim	78T	235	$ .05	$ .20
McCarver, Tim	79T	675	$ .05	$ .20
McCarver, Tim	80T	178	$ .05	$ .25
McCaskill, Kirk	86T	628	$ .01	$ .15
McCaskill, Kirk	87T	194	$ .01	$ .04
McCaskill, Kirk	88T	16	$ .01	$ .04
McCaskill, Kirk	89T	421	$ .01	$ .03
McCaskill, Kirk	90T	215	$ .01	$ .03
McCaskill, Kirk	91T	532	$ .01	$ .03
McCaskill, Kirk	91TSC	313	$ .05	$ .25
McCaskill, Kirk	92T	301	$ .01	$ .03
McCaskill, Kirk	92TSC	688	$ .01	$ .10
McCaskill, Kirk	92TTR	69	$ .01	$ .05
McCaskill, Kirk	93T	175	$ .01	$ .03
McCaskill, Kirk	93TSC	166	$ .01	$ .10
McCatty, Steve	78T	701	$ .04	$ .16
McCatty, Steve	80T	231	$ .01	$ .10
McCatty, Steve	81T	503	$ .01	$ .08
McCatty, Steve	82T	113	$ .01	$ .08
McCatty, Steve	82T	156	$ .10	$ .50
McCatty, Steve	82T	165	$ .01	$ .15
McCatty, Steve	82T	167	$ .15	$1.50
McCatty, Steve	83T	493	$ .01	$ .08
McCatty, Steve	84T	369	$ .01	$ .06
McCatty, Steve	85T	63	$ .01	$ .06
McCatty, Steve	86T	624	$ .01	$ .05
McClain, Joe	61T	488	$1.35	$5.40
McClain, Joe	62T	324	$ .75	$3.00
McClain, Joe	63T	311	$ .90	$3.60
McClellan, Paul	92T	424	$ .01	$ .03
McClellan, Paul	92TSC	566	$ .01	$ .10
McClendon, Lloyd	88T	172	$ .01	$ .04
McClendon, Lloyd	89T	644	$ .01	$ .03
McClendon, Lloyd	89TTR	76	$ .01	$ .05
McClendon, Lloyd	90T	337	$ .01	$ .03
McClendon, Lloyd	91TSC	385	$ .05	$ .25
McClendon, Lloyd	92T	209	$ .01	$ .03
McClendon, Lloyd	92TSC	302	$ .01	$ .10
McClendon, Lloyd	93T	81	$ .01	$ .03

TOPPS

Player	Year	No.	VG	EX/MT
McClendon, Lloyd	93TSC	66	$ .01	$ .10
McClure, Bob	76T	599	$2.00	$8.00
McClure, Bob	77T	472	$ .05	$ .20
McClure, Bob	78T	243	$ .04	$ .16
McClure, Bob	79T	623	$ .03	$ .12
McClure, Bob	80T	357	$ .01	$ .10
McClure, Bob	81T	156	$ .01	$ .08
McClure, Bob	82T	487	$ .01	$ .08
McClure, Bob	83T	62	$ .01	$ .08
McClure, Bob	84T	582	$ .01	$ .06
McClure, Bob	85T	203	$ .01	$ .06
McClure, Bob	86T	684	$ .01	$ .05
McClure, Bob	86TTR	71	$ .01	$ .06
McClure, Bob	87T	707	$ .01	$ .04
McClure, Bob	88T	313	$ .01	$ .04
McClure, Bob	89T	182	$ .01	$ .03
McClure, Bob	90T	458	$ .01	$ .03
McClure, Bob	91T	84	$ .01	$ .03
McClure, Bob	92TSC	484	$ .01	$ .10
McClure, Jack	65T	553	$1.40	$5.60
McConnell, Chad	92TTR	70	$ .10	$ .50
McConnell, Chad	93T	161	$ .05	$ .25
McCool, Bill	64T	356	$ .65	$2.60
McCool, Bill	65T	18	$ .35	$1.40
McCool, Bill	66T	459	$1.50	$6.00
McCool, Bill	67T	353	$ .60	$2.40
McCool, Bill	68T	597	$ .70	$2.80
McCool, Bill	69T	129	$ .35	$1.40
McCool, Bill	70T	314	$ .35	$1.40
McCormick, Mike	58T	37	$2.50	$10.00
McCormick, Mike	59T	148	$1.00	$4.00
McCormick, Mike	60T	530	$2.75	$11.00
McCormick, Mike	61T	45	$1.00	$4.00
McCormick, Mike	61T	305	$ .60	$2.40
McCormick, Mike	61T	383	$1.00	$4.00
McCormick, Mike	62T	56	$1.50	$6.00
McCormick, Mike	62T	107	$ .60	$2.40
McCormick, Mike	62T	319	$ .75	$3.00
McCormick, Mike	63T	563	$2.25	$9.00
McCormick, Mike	64T	487	$1.00	$4.00
McCormick, Mike	65T	343	$ .50	$2.00
McCormick, Mike	66T	118	$ .50	$2.00
McCormick, Mike	67T	86	$ .40	$1.60
McCormick, Mike	68T	9	$ .75	$3.00
McCormick, Mike	68T	400	$ .35	$1.40
McCormick, Mike	69T	517	$ .40	$1.60
McCormick, Mike	70T	337	$ .35	$1.40
McCormick, Mike	71T	438	$ .50	$2.00
McCormick, Mike	72T	682	$1.25	$5.00
McCosky, Barney	52T	300	$13.75	$55.00
McCovey, Willie	60T	316	$56.25	$225.00
McCovey, Willie	60TAS	554	$15.00	$60.00
McCovey, Willie	61T	517	$13.75	$55.00
McCovey, Willie	62T	544	$35.00	$140.00
McCovey, Willie	63T	490	$35.00	$140.00
McCovey, Willie	64T	9	$4.00	$16.00
McCovey, Willie	64T	41	$1.25	$5.00
McCovey, Willie	64T	350	$7.00	$28.00
McCovey, Willie	65T	176	$5.00	$20.00
McCovey, Willie	66T	217	$4.00	$16.00
McCovey, Willie	66T	550	$27.50	$110.00
McCovey, Willie	67T	423	$6.00	$24.00
McCovey, Willie	67T	480	$8.75	$35.00
McCovey, Willie	68T	5	$1.50	$6.00
McCovey, Willie	68T	290	$3.00	$12.00
McCovey, Willie	69T	4	$1.00	$4.00
McCovey, Willie	69T	6	$1.00	$4.00
McCovey, Willie	69T	440	$4.00	$16.00
McCovey, Willie	69T	572	$3.00	$12.00
McCovey, Willie	69TAS	416	$1.50	$6.00
McCovey, Willie	70T	63	$ .75	$3.00
McCovey, Willie	70T	65	$1.25	$5.00
McCovey, Willie	70T	250	$2.50	$10.00
McCovey, Willie	70TAS	450	$1.25	$5.00
McCovey, Willie	71T	50	$2.25	$9.00
McCovey, Willie	72T	280	$1.50	$6.00
McCovey, Willie	73T	410	$1.25	$5.00
McCovey, Willie	74T	250	$1.25	$5.00
McCovey, Willie	75T	207	$ .25	$1.00
McCovey, Willie	75T	450	$1.00	$4.00
McCovey, Willie	76T	520	$1.00	$4.00
McCovey, Willie	77T	547	$1.00	$4.00
McCovey, Willie	78T	34	$ .75	$3.00
McCovey, Willie	78TRB	3	$ .25	$1.00
McCovey, Willie	79T	215	$ .75	$3.00
McCovey, Willie	80T	335	$ .20	$1.75
McCovey, Willie	80THL	2	$ .10	$1.00
McCraken, Quinton	93T	451	$ .05	$ .25
McCraw, Tommy	64T	283	$ .75	$3.00
McCraw, Tommy	65T	586	$2.50	$10.00
McCraw, Tom	66T	141	$ .50	$2.00
McCraw, Tommy	67T	29	$ .40	$1.60
McCraw, Tommy	68T	413	$ .35	$1.40
McCraw, Tom	69T	388	$ .30	$1.20
McCraw, Tom	70T	561	$ .50	$2.00
McCraw, Tom	71T	373	$ .25	$1.00
McCraw, Tom	72T	767	$1.25	$5.00
McCraw, Tom	73T	86	$ .10	$ .40
McCraw, Tom	74T	449	$ .10	$ .40
McCraw, Tom	75T	482	$ .10	$ .40
McCray, Rodney	91T	523	$ .01	$ .10
McCray, Rodney	92TSC	829	$ .01	$ .10
McCullers, Lance	86T	44	$ .01	$ .05
McCullers, Lance	87T	559	$ .01	$ .04
McCullers, Lance	88T	197	$ .01	$ .04
McCullers, Lance	89T	307	$ .01	$ .03
McCullers, Lance	89TTR	77	$ .01	$ .05
McCullers, Lance	90T	259	$ .01	$ .03
McCullough, Clyde	52T	218	$7.00	$28.00
McDaniel, Jim	59T	134	$1.00	$4.00
McDaniel, Lindy	57T	79	$2.75	$11.00
McDaniel, Lindy	58T	180	$1.25	$5.00
McDaniel, Lindy	59T	479	$1.00	$4.00
McDaniel, Lindy	60T	195	$ .75	$3.00
McDaniel, Lindy	61T	75	$ .60	$2.40
McDaniel, Lindy	61T	266	$ .60	$2.40
McDaniel, Lindy	62T	306	$ .75	$3.00
McDaniel, Lindy	62T	522	$1.50	$6.00
McDaniel, Lindy	63T	329	$ .90	$3.60
McDaniel, Lindy	64T	510	$1.00	$4.00
McDaniel, Lindy	65T	244	$ .50	$2.00
McDaniel, Lindy	66T	496	$1.50	$6.00
McDaniel, Lindy	67T	46	$ .40	$1.60
McDaniel, Lindy	68T	545	$ .70	$2.80
McDaniel, Lindy	69T	191	$ .35	$1.40
McDaniel, Lindy	70T	493	$ .35	$1.40
McDaniel, Lindy	71T	303	$ .25	$1.00
McDaniel, Lindy	72T	513	$ .25	$1.00
McDaniel, Lindy	73T	46	$ .10	$ .40
McDaniel, Lindy	74T	182	$ .10	$ .40
McDaniel, Lindy	74TTR	182	$ .10	$ .40
McDaniel, Lindy	75T	652	$ .10	$ .40
McDaniel, Von	58T	65	$2.25	$9.00
McDermott, Maurice	51Trb	43	$1.75	$7.50
McDermott, Maurice	52T	119	$7.00	$28.00
McDermott, Maurice	53T	55	$4.00	$16.00
McDermott, Mickey "Maurice"	56T	340	$11.25	$45.00
McDermott, Mickey	57T	318	$5.00	$20.00
McDermott, Maurice	91TA53	55	$ .01	$ .15
McDevitt, Danny	58T	357	$1.00	$4.00
McDevitt, Danny	59T	364	$1.00	$4.00
McDevitt, Danny	60T	333	$ .75	$3.00
McDevitt, Danny	61T	349	$ .60	$2.40
McDevitt, Danny	62T	493	$1.50	$6.00
McDonald, Ben	90T	774	$ .05	$ .35
McDonald, Ben	90TTR	70	$ .10	$ .40
McDonald, Ben	91T	497	$ .01	$ .10
McDonald, Ben	91TSC	264	$ .10	$1.00
McDonald, Ben	92T	540	$ .01	$ .10
McDonald, Ben	92TSC	490	$ .01	$ .15

TOPPS

Player	Year	No.	VG	EX/MT
McDonald, Ben	93T	218	$ .01	$ .10
McDonald, Ben	93TSC	259	$ .01	$ .15
McDonald, Dave	70T	189	$25.00	$100.00
McDonald, Jason	91TTR	75	$ .05	$ .20
McDougald, Gil	52T	372	$80.00	$320.00
McDougald, Gil	53T	43	$12.00	$48.00
McDougald, Gil	56T	225	$7.00	$28.00
McDougald, Gil	57T	200	$3.50	$14.00
McDougald, Gil	58T	20	$3.00	$12.00
McDougald, Gil	59T	237	$1.75	$7.00
McDougald, Gil	59T	345	$2.00	$8.00
McDougald, Gil	60T	247	$1.25	$5.00
McDougald, Gil	91TA53	43	$ .05	$ .35
McDowell, Jack	88TTR	68	$ .20	$2.00
McDowell, Jack	89T	486	$ .05	$ .25
McDowell, Jack	90TTR	71	$ .05	$ .20
McDowell, Jack	91T	219	$ .01	$ .15
McDowell, Jack	91TSC	87	$ .10	$1.00
McDowell, Jack	92T	11	$ .01	$ .03
McDowell, Jack	92TSC	52	$ .05	$ .25
McDowell, Jack	93T	344	$ .01	$ .03
McDowell, Jack	93TSC	75	$ .01	$ .15
McDowell, Oddibe	85T	400	$ .05	$ .20
McDowell, Oddibe	85TTR	82	$ .01	$ .15
McDowell, Oddibe	86T	480	$ .01	$ .10
McDowell, Oddibe	87T	95	$ .01	$ .04
McDowell, Oddibe	88T	617	$ .01	$ .04
McDowell, Oddibe	89T	183	$ .01	$ .03
McDowell, Oddibe	89TTR	78	$ .01	$ .05
McDowell, Oddibe	90T	329	$ .01	$ .03
McDowell, Oddibe	91T	533	$ .01	$ .03
McDowell, Roger	85TTR	83	$ .10	$ .50
McDowell, Roger	86T	547	$ .01	$ .15
McDowell, Roger	87T	185	$ .01	$ .04
McDowell, Roger	88T	355	$ .01	$ .04
McDowell, Roger	89T	735	$ .01	$ .03
McDowell, Roger	89TTR	79	$ .01	$ .05
McDowell, Roger	90T	625	$ .01	$ .03
McDowell, Roger	91T	43	$ .01	$ .03
McDowell, Roger	91TSC	506	$ .05	$ .25
McDowell, Roger	92T	713	$ .01	$ .03
McDowell, Roger	92TSC	804	$ .01	$ .10
McDowell, Roger	93T	39	$ .01	$ .03
McDowell, Roger	93TSC	251	$ .01	$ .10
McDowell, Sam	62T	591	$12.50	$50.00
McDowell, Sam	63T	317	$1.25	$5.00
McDowell, Sam	64T	391	$1.00	$4.00
McDowell, Sam	65T	76	$ .35	$1.40
McDowell, Sam	66T	222	$ .75	$3.00
McDowell, Sam	66T	226	$ .75	$3.00
McDowell, Sam	66T	470	$1.50	$6.00
McDowell, Sam	67T	237	$ .50	$2.00
McDowell, Sam	67T	295	$ .60	$2.40
McDowell, Sam	67T	463	$1.50	$6.00
McDowell, Sam	68T	12	$ .55	$2.20
McDowell, Sam	60T	115	$ .35	$1.40
McDowell, Sam	69T	7	$ .75	$3.00
McDowell, Sam	69T	11	$ .75	$3.00
McDowell, Sam	69T	220	$ .35	$1.40
McDowell, Sam	69TAS	435	$ .30	$1.20
McDowell, Sam	70T	72	$ .50	$2.00
McDowell, Sam	70T	650	$1.25	$5.00
McDowell, Sam	70TAS	469	$ .50	$2.00
McDowell, Sam	71T	71	$ .50	$2.00
McDowell, Sam	71T	150	$ .25	$1.00
McDowell, Sam	72T	720	$1.25	$5.00
McDowell, Sam	73T	342	$ .10	$ .40
McDowell, Sam	73T	511	$ .25	$1.00
McDowell, Sam	74T	550	$ .20	$ .80
McElroy, Chuck	91TSC	407	$ .05	$ .25
McElroy, Chuck	92T	727	$ .01	$ .03
McElroy, Chuck	92TSC	474	$ .01	$ .10
McElroy, Chuck	93T	346	$ .01	$ .03
McEnaney, Will	75T	481	$ .10	$ .40
McEnaney, Will	76T	362	$ .05	$ .25
McEnaney, Will	77T	160	$ .05	$ .20
McEnaney, Will	78T	603	$ .01	$ .16
McEnaney, Will	80T	563	$ .01	$ .10
McFadden, Leon	69T	156	$ .35	$1.40
McFadden, Leon	70T	672	$1.25	$5.00
McFarlane, Jesus "Orlando"	62T	229	$ .75	$3.00
McFarlane, Orlando	64T	509	$2.00	$8.00
McFarlane, Orlando	66T	569	$7.00	$28.00
McFarlane, Orlando	67T	496	$1.50	$6.00
McGaffigan, Andy	82T	83	$ .01	$ .15
McGaffigan, Andy	83TTR	68	$ .01	$ .10

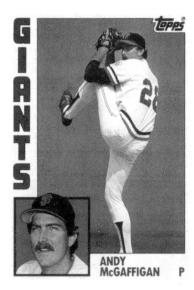

Player	Year	No.	VG	EX/MT
McGaffigan, Andy	84T	31	$ .01	$ .06
McGaffigan, Andy	84TTR	78	$ .01	$ .15
McGaffigan, Andy	85T	323	$ .01	$ .06
McGaffigan, Andy	86T	133	$ .01	$ .05
McGaffigan, Andy	86TTR	72	$ .01	$ .06
McGaffigan, Andy	87T	742	$ .01	$ .04
McGaffigan, Andy	88T	488	$ .01	$ .04
McGaffigan, Andy	89T	278	$ .01	$ .03
McGaffigan, Andy	90T	559	$ .01	$ .03
McGaffigan, Andy	91T	671	$ .01	$ .03
McGaha, Mel	62T	242	$ .75	$3.00
McGaha, Mel	65T	391	$1.00	$4.00
McGee, Willie	83T	49	$1.00	$4.00
McGee, Willie	84T	310	$ .05	$ .25
McGee, Willie	85T	757	$ .05	$ .25
McGee, Willie	86T	580	$ .01	$ .15
McGee, Willie	86TAS	707	$ .01	$ .05
McGee, Willie	87T	440	$ .01	$ .10
McGee, Willie	88T	160	$ .01	$ .10
McGee, Willie	89T	640	$ .01	$ .03
McGee, Willie	90T	285	$ .01	$ .03
McGee, Willie	91T	380	$ .01	$ .03
McGee, Willie	91TSC	335	$ .05	$ .25
McGee, Willie	91TTR	76	$ .01	$ .10
McGee, Willie	92T	65	$ .01	$ .03
McGee, Willie	92TSC	239	$ .01	$ .10
McGee, Willie	93T	435	$ .01	$ .03
McGee, Willie	93TSC	91	$ .01	$ .10
McGhee, Ed	53T	195	$4.50	$18.00
McGhee, Ed	54T	215	$3.75	$15.00
McGhee, Ed	55T	32	$2.25	$9.00

TOPPS

Player	Year	No.	VG	EX/MT
McGhee, Ed	91TA53	195	$ .01	$ .15
McGilberry, Randy	79T	707	$ .03	$ .12
McGinn, Dan	69T	646	$ .40	$1.60
McGinn, Dan	70T	364	$ .35	$1.40
McGinn, Dan	71T	21	$ .25	$1.00
McGinn, Dan	72T	473	$ .25	$1.00
McGinn, Dan	73T	527	$ .05	$ .25
McGlothen, Lynn	73T	114	$ .05	$ .25
McGlothen, Lynn	75T	272	$ .10	$ .40
McGlothen, Lynn	76T	478	$ .05	$ .25
McGlothen, Lynn	77T	47	$ .05	$ .20
McGlothen, Lynn	78T	581	$ .04	$ .16
McGlothen, Lynn	79T	323	$ .03	$ .12
McGlothen, Lynn	80T	716	$ .01	$ .10
McGlothen, Lynn	81T	609	$ .01	$ .07
McGlothen, Lynn	82T	85	$ .01	$ .06
McGlothlin, Jim	66T	417	$ .65	$2.60
McGlothlin, Jim	67T	19	$ .40	$1.60
McGlothlin, Jim	68T	493	$ .75	$3.00
McGlothlin, Jim	69T	386	$ .30	$1.20
McGlothlin, Jim	70T	132	$ .10	$ .40
McGlothlin, Jim	71T	556	$1.00	$4.00
McGlothlin, Jim	72T	236	$ .10	$ .40
McGlothlin, Jim	73T	318	$ .05	$ .25
McGlothlin, Jim	74T	557	$ .10	$ .40
McGraw, Tug	65T	533	$8.00	$32.00
McGraw, Tug	66T	124	$1.00	$4.00
McGraw, Tug	67T	348	$ .75	$3.00
McGraw, Tug	68T	236	$ .75	$3.00
McGraw, Tug	69T	601	$1.00	$4.00
McGraw, Tug	70T	26	$ .30	$1.20
McGraw, Tug	71T	618	$1.25	$5.00
McGraw, Tug	72T	163	$ .25	$1.00
McGraw, Tug	72TIA	164	$ .25	$ .50
McGraw, Tug	73T	30	$ .25	$1.00
McGraw, Tug	74T	265	$ .25	$1.00
McGraw, Tug	75T	67	$ .20	$ .80
McGraw, Tug	76T	565	$ .10	$ .40
McGraw, Tug	77T	164	$ .10	$ .40
McGraw, Tug	78T	446	$ .05	$ .25
McGraw, Tug	79T	345	$ .05	$ .20
McGraw, Tug	80T	655	$ .01	$ .10
McGraw, Tug	81T	40	$ .01	$ .15
McGraw, Tug	82T	250	$ .01	$ .08
McGraw, Tug	83T	510	$ .01	$ .08
McGraw, Tug	83T	511	$ .01	$ .08
McGraw, Tug	84T	709	$ .01	$ .06
McGraw, Tug	84T	728	$ .01	$ .06
McGraw, Tug	85T	157	$ .01	$ .06
McGregor, Scott	75T	618	$ .25	$1.00
McGregor, Scott	77T	475	$ .05	$ .20
McGregor, Scott	78T	491	$ .04	$ .16
McGregor, Scott	79T	393	$ .03	$ .12
McGregor, Scott	80T	237	$ .01	$ .10
McGregor, Scott	81T	65	$ .01	$ .08
McGregor, Scott	82T	617	$ .01	$ .08
McGregor, Scott	82TAS	555	$ .01	$ .07
McGregor, Scott	83T	745	$ .01	$ .08
McGregor, Scott	84T	260	$ .01	$ .06
McGregor, Scott	85T	550	$ .01	$ .06
McGregor, Scott	86T	110	$ .01	$ .05
McGregor, Scott	87T	708	$ .01	$ .04
McGregor, Scott	88T	419	$ .01	$ .04
McGriff, Fred	87TTR	74	$ .20	$2.00
McGriff, Fred	88T	463	$ .10	$ .50
McGriff, Fred	89T	745	$ .05	$ .25
McGriff, Fred	90T	295	$ .01	$ .15
McGriff, Fred	90TAS	385	$ .01	$ .10
McGriff, Fred	91T	140	$ .01	$ .10
McGriff, Fred	91TSC	357	$ .10	$1.00
McGriff, Fred	91TTR	77	$ .01	$ .10
McGriff, Fred	92T	660	$ .01	$ .10
McGriff, Fred	92TSC	580	$ .10	$ .50
McGriff, Fred	93T	30	$ .01	$ .10
McGriff, Fred	93T	401	$ .05	$ .35
McGriff, Terry	88T	644	$ .01	$ .10
McGriff, Terry	89T	151	$ .01	$ .03
McGwire, Mark	85T	401	$7.00	$28.00
McGwire, Mark	87T	366	$ .20	$2.00
McGwire, Mark	88T	580	$ .10	$ .50
McGwire, Mark	88TRB	3	$ .05	$ .20
McGwire, Mark	89T	70	$ .10	$ .40

Player	Year	No.	VG	EX/MT
McGwire, Mark	90T	690	$ .05	$ .25
McGwire, Mark	91T	270	$ .05	$ .20
McGwire, Mark	91TSC	399	$ .75	$3.00
McGwire, Mark	92T	450	$ .05	$ .20
McGwire, Mark	92TSC	475	$ .10	$1.00
McGwire, Mark	93T	100	$ .01	$ .15
McIntosh, Joe	76T	497	$ .05	$ .25
McIntosh, Joe	76TTR	497	$ .05	$ .25
McIntosh, Tim	91T	561	$ .01	$ .10
McIntosh, Tim	91TSC	321	$ .05	$ .25
McIntosh, Tim	92TSC	477	$ .01	$ .10
McIntosh, Tim	93T	234	$ .01	$ .05
McKay, Dave	76T	592	$2.00	$8.00
McKay, Dave	77T	377	$ .05	$ .20
McKay, Dave	79T	608	$ .03	$ .12
McKay, Dave	81T	461	$ .01	$ .08
McKay, Dave	82T	534	$ .01	$ .08
McKay, Dave	83T	47	$ .01	$ .08
McKeon, Jack	73T	593	$ .75	$3.00
McKeon, Jack	74T	166	$ .10	$ .40
McKeon, Jack	88TT	69	$ .01	$ .05
McKeon, Jack	89T	624	$ .01	$ .03
McKeon, Jack	90T	231	$ .01	$ .03
McKeon, Joel	88T	409	$ .01	$ .04
McKinney, Rich	71T	37	$ .25	$1.00
McKinney, Rich	72T	619	$ .40	$1.60
McKinney, Rich	73T	587	$ .60	$2.40
McKinnon, Tom	92T	96	$ .01	$ .10
McKnight, Jeff	91T	319	$ .01	$ .10
McKnight, Jeff	92TSC	633	$ .01	$ .10
McKnight, Jim	62T	597	$9.00	$36.00
McLain, Dennis	65T	236	$6.00	$24.00
McLain, Dennis	66T	226	$ .75	$3.00
McLain, Denny	66T	540	$17.50	$70.00
McLain, Denny	67T	235	$ .75	$3.00
McLain, Dennis	67T	420	$1.50	$6.00

TOPPS

Player	Year	No.	VG	EX/MT	Player	Year	No.	VG	EX/MT
McLain, Denny	68T	40	$2.50	$10.00	McMillan, Roy	74T	179	$ .40	$1.60
McLain, Denny	69T	9	$ .75	$3.00	McMillan, Roy	91TA53	259	$ .01	$ .15
McLain, Denny	69T	11	$ .75	$3.00	McMillan, Tommy	77T	490	$ .05	$ .20
McLain, Denny	69T	150	$1.00	$4.00	McMillon, Billy	91TTR	78	$ .05	$ .25
McLain, Denny	69TAS	433	$ .50	$2.00	McMullen, Ken	63T	537	$212.50	$850.00
McLain, Denny	70T	70	$ .50	$2.00	McMullen, Ken	64T	214	$ .65	$2.60
McLain, Denny	70T	400	$ .50	$2.00	McMullen, Ken	65T	319	$ .50	$2.00
McLain, Denny	70TAS	467	$ .50	$2.00	McMullen, Ken	66T	401	$ .65	$2.60
McLain, Denny	71T	750	$4.00	$16.00	McMullen, Ken	67T	47	$ .40	$1.60
McLain, Denny	72T	210	$ .25	$1.00	McMullen, Ken	68T	116	$ .35	$1.40
McLain, Denny	72TTR	753	$3.00	$12.00	McMullen, Ken	69T	319	$ .50	$2.00
McLain, Denny	73T	630	$1.00	$4.00	McMullen, Ken	70T	420	$ .35	$1.40
McLain, Denny	75T	206	$ .25	$1.00	McMullen, Ken	71T	485	$ .50	$2.00
McLaughlin, Bo	77T	184	$ .05	$ .20	McMullen, Ken	72T	765	$1.25	$5.00
McLaughlin, Bo	78T	437	$ .04	$ .16	McMullen, Ken	73T	196	$ .10	$ .40
McLaughlin, Bo	80T	326	$ .01	$ .10	McMullen, Ken	74T	434	$ .10	$ .40
McLaughlin, Bo	82T	217	$ .01	$ .08	McMullen, Ken	75T	473	$ .10	$ .40
McLaughlin, Byron	79T	712	$ .03	$ .12	McMullen, Ken	76T	566	$ .05	$ .25
McLaughlin, Byron	80T	197	$ .01	$ .10	McMullen, Ken	77T	181	$ .05	$ .20
McLaughlin, Byron	81T	344	$ .01	$ .08	McMurtry, Craig	83TTR	69	$ .01	$ .10
McLaughlin, Byron	84T	442	$ .01	$ .06	McMurtry, Craig	84T	126	$ .01	$ .15
McLaughlin, Joey	80T	384	$ .01	$ .10	McMurtry, Craig	84T	543	$ .01	$ .06
McLaughlin, Joey	81T	248	$ .01	$ .08	McMurtry, Craig	85T	362	$ .01	$ .06
McLaughlin, Joey	82T	739	$ .01	$ .08	McMurtry, Craig	86T	194	$ .01	$ .05
McLaughlin, Joey	83T	9	$ .01	$ .08	McMurtry, Craig	87T	461	$ .01	$ .04
McLaughlin, Joey	84T	556	$ .01	$ .06	McMurtry, Craig	89T	779	$ .01	$ .03
McLaughlin, Joey	85T	678	$ .01	$ .06	McMurtry, Craig	90T	294	$ .01	$ .03
McLemore, Mark	87TTR	75	$ .01	$ .10	McNally, Dave	63T	562	$5.00	$20.00
McLemore, Mark	88T	162	$ .01	$ .04	McNally, Dave	64T	161	$ .75	$3.00
McLemore, Mark	89T	547	$ .01	$ .03	McNally, Dave	65T	249	$ .50	$2.00
McLemore, Mark	93T	55	$ .01	$ .03	McNally, Dave	66T	193	$ .50	$2.00
McLish, Cal	57T	364	$1.75	$7.00	McNally, Dave	67T	382	$ .60	$2.40
McLish, Cal	58T	208	$1.25	$5.00	McNally, Dave	68T	478	$ .35	$1.40
McLish, Cal	59T	445	$1.00	$4.00	McNally, Dave	69T	7	$ .75	$3.00
McLish, Cal	60T	110	$ .85	$3.40	McNally, Dave	69T	9	$ .75	$3.00
McLish, Cal	61T	157	$ .60	$2.40	McNally, Dave	69T	340	$ .30	$1.20
McLish, Cal	62T	453	$1.50	$6.00	McNally, Dave	69T	532	$ .40	$1.60
McLish, Cal	63T	512	$1.75	$7.00	McNally, Dave	70T	20	$ .20	$ .80
McLish, Cal	64T	365	$ .65	$2.60	McNally, Dave	70T	70	$ .50	$2.00
McLish, Cal	73T	377	$ .20	$ .80	McNally, Dave	71T	69	$ .50	$2.00
McLish, Cal	74T	531	$ .25	$1.00	McNally, Dave	71T	320	$ .25	$1.00
McMahon, Don	58T	147	$2.00	$8.00	McNally, Dave	72T	344	$ .10	$ .40
McMahon, Don	59T	3	$1.50	$6.00	McNally, Dave	72T	490	$ .20	$ .80
McMahon, Don	60T	189	$ .75	$3.00	McNally, Dave	73T	600	$ .55	$2.20
McMahon, Don	61T	278	$ .60	$2.40	McNally, Dave	74T	235	$ .10	$ .40
McMahon, Don	62T	483	$1.50	$6.00	McNally, Dave	75T	26	$ .10	$ .40
McMahon, Don	63T	395	$1.00	$4.00	McNamara, John	70T	706	$1.25	$5.00
McMahon, Don	64T	122	$ .50	$2.00	McNamara, John	73T	252	$ .20	$ .80
McMahon, Don	65T	317	$ .50	$2.00	McNamara, John	74T	78	$ .10	$ .40
McMahon, Don	66T	133	$ .50	$2.00	McNamara, John	83TTR	70	$ .01	$ .10
McMahon, Don	67T	7	$ .40	$1.60	McNamara, John	84T	651	$ .01	$ .06
McMahon, Don	68T	464	$ .75	$3.00	McNamara, John	85T	732	$ .01	$ .06
McMahon, Don	69T	616	$ .40	$1.60	McNamara, John	85TTR	84	$ .01	$ .10
McMahon, Don	70T	519	$ .35	$1.40	McNamara, John	86T	771	$ .01	$ .05
McMahon, Don	71T	354	$ .25	$1.00	McNamara, John	87T	368	$ .01	$ .04
McMahon, Don	72T	509	$ .25	$1.00	McNamara, John	88T	414	$ .01	$ .04
McMahon, Don	73T	252	$ .20	$ .80	McNamara, John	90TTR	72	$ .01	$ .05
McMahon, Don	74T	78	$ .10	$ .40	McNamara, John	91T	549	$ .01	$ .03
McMillan, Roy	52T	137	$8.00	$32.00	McNeely, Jeff	92T	618	$ .05	$ .25
McMillan, Roy	53T	259	$11.25	$45.00	McNeely, Jeffrey	92TSC	577	$ .05	$ .20
McMillan, Roy	54T	120	$3.75	$15.00	McNertney, Jerry	64T	564	$2.25	$9.00
McMillan, Roy	55T	181	$6.25	$25.00	McNertney, Jerry	68T	14	$ .35	$1.40
McMillan, Roy	56T	123	$2.50	$10.00	McNertney, Jerry	69T	534	$ .40	$1.60
McMillan, Roy	57T	69	$2.00	$8.00	McNertney, Jerry	70T	158	$ .20	$ .80
McMillan, Roy	58T	360	$1.00	$4.00	McNertney, Jerry	71T	286	$ .25	$1.00
McMillan, Roy	59T	405	$1.00	$4.00	McNertney, Jerry	72T	584	$ .40	$1.60
McMillan, Roy	60T	45	$ .85	$3.40	McNulty, Bill	73T	603	$ .75	$3.00
McMillan, Roy	61T	465	$1.35	$5.40	McQueen, Mike	70T	621	$6.00	$24.00
McMillan, Roy	62T	211	$ .75	$3.00	McQueen, Mike	71T	8	$ .25	$1.00
McMillan, Roy	62TAS	393	$1.25	$5.00	McQueen, Mike	72T	214	$ .10	$ .40
McMillan, Roy	63T	156	$ .50	$2.00	McRae, Brian	91T	222	$ .05	$ .20
McMillan, Roy	64T	238	$ .65	$2.60	McRae, Brian	91TSC	478	$ .10	$1.00
McMillan, Roy	65T	45	$ .35	$1.40	McRae, Brian	92T	659	$ .01	$ .10
McMillan, Roy	66T	421	$ .65	$2.60	McRae, Brian	92TSC	270	$ .01	$ .15
McMillan, Roy	73T	257	$ .50	$2.00	McRae, Brian	93T	49	$ .01	$ .03

TOPPS

Player	Year	No.	VG	EX/MT	Player	Year	No.	VG	EX/MT
McRae, Brian	93TSC	33	$ .01	$ .10	Medich, George	82T	36	$ .01	$ .08
McRae, Hal	68T	384	$2.50	$10.00	Medich, George	82T	78	$ .01	$ .08
McRae, Hal	70T	683	$1.75	$7.00	Medina, Luis	89T	528	$ .01	$ .03
McRae, Hal	71T	177	$ .50	$2.00	Medvin, Scott	89T	756	$ .01	$ .03
McRae, Hal	72T	291	$ .50	$2.00	Meier, Dave	85T	356	$ .01	$ .06
McRae, Hal	72TIA	292	$ .25	$1.00	Mejias, Roman	57T	362	$1.75	$7.00
McRae, Hal	73T	28	$ .35	$1.40	Mejias, Roman	58T	452	$1.00	$4.00
McRae, Hal	74T	563	$ .20	$ .80	Mejias, Roman	59T	218	$1.00	$4.00
McRae, Hal	75T	268	$ .15	$ .60	Mejias, Roman	60T	2	$ .85	$3.40
McRae, Hal	76T	72	$ .15	$ .60	Mejias, Roman	62T	354	$ .75	$3.00
McRae, Hal	77T	340	$ .05	$ .20	Mejias, Roman	63T	432	$1.00	$4.00
McRae, Hal	78T	465	$ .05	$ .20	Mejias, Roman	64T	186	$ .50	$2.00
McRae, Hal	79T	585	$ .03	$ .12	Mejias, Sam	77T	479	$ .05	$ .20
McRae, Hal	80T	185	$ .01	$ .10	Mejias, Sam	78T	576	$ .04	$ .16
McRae, Hal	81T	295	$ .01	$ .08	Mejias, Sam	79T	97	$ .03	$ .12
McRae, Hal	82T	625	$ .01	$ .08	Mejias, Sam	81T	521	$ .01	$ .08
McRae, Hal	83T	25	$ .01	$ .08	Mejias, Sam	82T	228	$ .01	$ .08
McRae, Hal	83T	703	$ .01	$ .08	Mele, Sam	51Tbb	25	$7.50	$30.00
McRae, Hal	84T	96	$ .01	$ .06	Mele, Sam	52T	94	$7.00	$28.00
McRae, Hal	84T	340	$ .01	$ .06	Mele, Sam	54T	240	$3.75	$15.00
McRae, Hal	85T	773	$ .01	$ .06	Mele, Sam	60T	470	$1.25	$5.00
McRae, Hal	86T	415	$ .01	$ .05	Mele, Sam	62T	482	$1.50	$6.00
McRae, Hal	87T	573	$ .01	$ .04	Mele, Sam	63T	531	$2.25	$9.00
McRae, Hal	91TTR	79	$ .01	$ .05	Mele, Sam	64T	54	$ .50	$2.00
McRae, Hal	92T	519	$ .01	$ .03	Mele, Sam	65T	506	$1.25	$5.00
McRae, Hal	93T	507	$ .01	$ .03	Mele, Sam	66T	3	$ .35	$1.40
McRae, Norman	70T	207	$ .20	$ .80	Mele, Sam	67T	418	$ .60	$2.40
McRae, Norman	71T	93	$ .25	$1.00	Melendez, Dan	91TTR	80	$ .05	$ .25
McReynolds, Kevin	87TTR	76	$ .01	$ .15	Melendez, Jose	92T	518	$ .01	$ .03
McReynolds, Kevin	88T	735	$ .01	$ .10	Melendez, Jose	92TSC	342	$ .01	$ .10
McReynolds, Kevin	89T	85	$ .01	$ .03	Melendez, Jose	93T	58	$ .01	$ .03
McReynolds, Kevin	89TRB	7	$ .01	$ .05	Melendez, Jose	93TSC	87	$ .01	$ .10
McReynolds, Kevin	90T	545	$ .01	$ .03	Melendez, Luis	71T	216	$ .25	$1.00
McReynolds, Kevin	91T	105	$ .01	$ .03	Melendez, Luis	72T	606	$ .40	$1.60
McReynolds, Kevin	91TSC	35	$ .05	$ .25	Melendez, Luis	73T	47	$ .10	$ .40
McReynolds, Kevin	92T	625	$ .01	$ .03	Melendez, Luis	74T	307	$ .10	$ .40
McReynolds, Kevin	92TSC	619	$ .01	$ .10	Melendez, Luis	75T	353	$ .10	$ .40
McReynolds, Kevin	92TTR	71	$ .01	$ .05	Melendez, Luis	76T	399	$ .05	$ .25
McReynolds, Kevin	93T	442	$ .01	$ .03	Melton, Bill	69T	481	$ .30	$1.20
McWilliams, Larry	79T	504	$ .03	$ .12	Melton, Bill	70T	518	$ .35	$1.40
McWilliams, Larry	80T	309	$ .01	$ .10	Melton, Bill	71T	80	$ .25	$1.00
McWilliams, Larry	81T	44	$ .01	$ .08	Melton, Bill	72T	90	$ .50	$2.00
McWilliams, Larry	82T	733	$ .01	$ .08	Melton, Bill	72T	183	$ .10	$ .40
McWilliams, Larry	83T	253	$ .01	$ .08	Melton, Bill	72T	495	$ .25	$1.00
McWilliams, Larry	84T	668	$ .01	$ .06	Melton, Bill	72TIA	184	$ .10	$ .40
McWilliams, Larry	85T	183	$ .01	$ .06	Melton, Bill	73T	455	$ .25	$1.00
McWilliams, Larry	86T	425	$ .01	$ .05	Melton, Bill	74T	170	$ .10	$ .40
McWilliams, Larry	87T	564	$ .01	$ .04	Melton, Bill	75T	11	$ .10	$ .40
McWilliams, Larry	88TTR	70	$ .01	$ .05	Melton, Bill	76T	309	$ .05	$ .25
McWilliams, Larry	89T	259	$ .01	$ .03	Melton, Bill	76TTR	309	$ .05	$ .25
McWilliams, Larry	89TTR	80	$ .01	$ .05	Melton, Bill	77T	107	$ .05	$ .20
Meacham, Bobby	84T	204	$ .01	$ .06	Melton, Dave	58T	391	$1.00	$4.00
Meacham, Bobby	85T	16	$ .01	$ .06	Melvin, Bob	86T	479	$ .01	$ .05
Meacham, Bobby	86T	379	$ .01	$ .05	Melvin, Bob	87T	549	$ .01	$ .04
Meacham, Bobby	87T	62	$ .01	$ .04	Melvin, Bob	88T	41	$ .01	$ .04
Meacham, Bobby	88T	659	$ .01	$ .04	Melvin, Bob	89T	329	$ .01	$ .03
Meacham, Bobby	89T	436	$ .01	$ .03	Melvin, Bob	90T	626	$ .01	$ .03
Meacham, Rusty	92TSC	768	$ .01	$ .10	Melvin, Bob	91T	249	$ .01	$ .03
Meacham, Rusty	92TTR	72	$ .01	$ .05	Melvin, Bob	91TSC	312	$ .05	$ .25
Meacham, Rusty	93T	321	$ .01	$ .03	Melvin, Bob	92T	733	$ .01	$ .03
Meadows, Louie	89T	643	$ .01	$ .03	Melvin, Bob	92TSC	642	$ .01	$ .10
Meadows, Louie	90T	534	$ .01	$ .03	Mendoza, Mario	75T	457	$ .10	$ .40
Meads, Dave	87TTR	77	$ .01	$ .05	Mendoza, Mario	78T	383	$ .04	$ .16
Meads, Dave	88T	199	$ .01	$ .04	Mendoza, Mario	79T	509	$ .03	$ .12
Meads, Dave	89T	589	$ .01	$ .03	Mendoza, Mario	80T	652	$ .01	$ .10
Medich, George	73T	608	$1.00	$4.00	Mendoza, Mario	81T	76	$ .01	$ .08
Medich, George	74T	445	$ .10	$ .40	Mendoza, Mario	81TTR	801	$ .01	$ .15
Medich, George	75T	426	$ .10	$ .40	Mendoza, Mario	82T	212	$ .01	$ .08
Medich, George	76T	146	$ .05	$ .25	Mendoza, Reynol	93T	782	$ .05	$ .20
Medich, George	76TTR	146	$ .05	$ .25	Menke, Denis	62T	597	$9.00	$36.00
Medich, George	77T	294	$ .05	$ .20	Menke, Denis	63T	433	$1.00	$4.00
Medich, George	78T	583	$ .04	$ .16	Menke, Denis	64T	53	$ .50	$2.00
Medich, George	79T	657	$ .03	$ .12	Menke, Denis	65T	327	$ .50	$2.00
Medich, George	80T	336	$ .01	$ .10	Menke, Denis	66T	184	$ .50	$2.00
Medich, George	81T	702	$ .01	$ .08	Menke, Denis	67T	396	$ .60	$2.40

TOPPS

Player	Year	No.	VG	EX/MT
Menke, Denis	67T	518	$1.50	$6.00
Menke, Denis	68T	232	$ .35	$1.40
Menke, Denis	69T	487	$ .30	$1.20
Menke, Denis	70T	155	$ .20	$ .80
Menke, Denis	71T	130	$ .25	$1.00
Menke, Denis	72T	586	$ .40	$1.60
Menke, Denis	73T	52	$ .10	$ .40
Menke, Denis	74T	134	$ .10	$ .40
Meoli, Rudy	75T	533	$ .10	$ .40
Meoli, Rudy	76T	254	$ .05	$ .25
Meoli, Rudy	78T	489	$ .04	$ .16
Mercado, Orlando	83TTR	71	$ .01	$ .10
Mercado, Orlando	84T	314	$ .01	$ .06
Mercado, Orlando	85T	58	$ .01	$ .06
Mercado, Orlando	87T	514	$ .01	$ .04
Mercado, Orlando	90TTR	73	$ .01	$ .05
Merced, Orlando	91TTR	81	$ .05	$ .25
Merced, Orlando	92T	637	$ .01	$ .10
Merced, Orlando	92TSC	134	$ .05	$ .20
Merced, Orlando	93T	378	$ .01	$ .03
Mercedes, Henry	93T	602	$ .01	$ .10
Mercedes, Luis	92T	603	$ .01	$ .15
Mercedes, Luis	92TSC	242	$ .05	$ .20
Mercedes, Luis	93T	446	$ .01	$ .03
Merchant, Andy	76T	594	$ .05	$ .25
Mercker, Kent	91T	772	$ .01	$ .03
Mercker, Kent	91TSC	341	$ .05	$ .25
Mercker, Kent	92T	596	$ .01	$ .03
Mercker, Kent	92TSC	147	$ .01	$ .10
Mercker, Kent	93T	144	$ .01	$ .03
Mercker, Kent	93TSC	111	$ .01	$ .10
Merrill, Stump	90TTR	74	$ .01	$ .05
Merrill, Stump	91T	429	$ .01	$ .03
Merriman, Brett	93T	593	$ .01	$ .15
Merritt, Jim	66T	97	$ .35	$1.40
Merritt, Jim	67T	523	$1.50	$6.00
Merritt, Jim	68T	64	$ .35	$1.40
Merritt, Jim	69T	661	$ .40	$1.60
Merritt, Jim	70T	616	$ .50	$2.00
Merritt, Jim	71T	420	$ .50	$2.00
Merritt, Jim	72T	738	$1.25	$5.00
Merritt, Jim	74T	318	$ .10	$ .40
Merritt, Jim	75T	83	$ .10	$ .40
Merritt, Lloyd	58T	231	$1.25	$5.00
Merson, Jack	52T	375	$43.75	$175.00
Merullo, Matt	91TSC	382	$ .05	$ .25
Merullo, Matt	92T	615	$ .01	$ .03
Merullo, Matt	92TSC	404	$ .01	$ .10
Mesa, Jose	91T	512	$ .01	$ .03
Mesa, Jose	91TSC	380	$ .05	$ .25
Mesa, Jose	92T	310	$ .01	$ .03
Mesa, Jose	92TSC	888	$ .01	$ .10
Mesa, Jose	93T	696	$ .01	$ .03
Messersmith, Andy	69T	296	$ .75	$3.00
Messersmith, Andy	70T	72	$ .50	$2.00
Messersmith, Andy	70T	430	$ .05	$1.40
Messersmith, Andy	71T	15	$ .25	$1.00
Messersmith, Andy	72T	160	$ .20	$ .80
Messersmith, Andy	73T	515	$ .25	$1.00
Messersmith, Andy	74T	267	$ .10	$ .40
Messersmith, Andy	75T	310	$ .25	$1.00
Messersmith, Andy	75T	440	$ .10	$ .40
Messersmith, Andy	76T	199	$ .25	$1.00
Messersmith, Andy	76T	201	$ .25	$1.00
Messersmith, Andy	76T	203	$ .30	$1.20
Messersmith, Andy	76T	305	$ .05	$ .25
Messersmith, Andy	77T	80	$ .05	$ .20
Messersmith, Andy	78T	156	$ .04	$ .16
Messersmith, Andy	79T	278	$ .03	$ .12
Metcalf, Tom	64T	281	$ .65	$2.60
Metkovich, George	52T	310	$12.50	$50.00
Metkovich, George	53T	58	$6.25	$25.00
Metkovich, Geroge	91TA53	58	$ .01	$ .15
Metro, Charlie	70T	16	$ .20	$ .80
Mets, Team	63T	473	$25.00	$100.00
Mets, Team	64T	27	$1.75	$7.00
Mets, Team	65T	551	$8.00	$32.00
Mets, Team	66T	172	$1.00	$4.00
Mets, Team	67T	42	$1.25	$5.00
Mets, Team	68T	401	$ .75	$3.00
Mets, Team	70T	1	$3.00	$12.00
Mets, Team	71T	641	$2.50	$10.00
Mets, Team	72T	362	$ .50	$2.00
Mets, Team	73T	389	$ .75	$3.00
Mets, Team	74T	56	$ .25	$1.00
Mets, Team Checklist	75T	421	$ .35	$1.40
Mets, Team Checklist	76T	531	$ .30	$1.20
Mets, Team Checklist	77T	259	$ .25	$1.00
Mets, Team Checklist	78T	356	$ .20	$ .80
Mets, Team Checklist	79T	82	$ .15	$ .60
Mets, Team Checklist	80T	259	$ .10	$ .50
Mets, Team Checklist	81T	681	$ .05	$ .25
Mets, Team Leaders	86T	126	$ .01	$ .05
Mets, Team Leaders	87T	331	$ .01	$ .15
Mets, Team Leaders	88T	579	$ .01	$ .04
Mets, Team Leaders	89T	291	$ .01	$ .10
Metzger, Butch	76T	593	$ .15	$ .60
Metzger, Butch	77T	215	$ .05	$ .20
Metzger, Butch	78T	431	$ .04	$ .16
Metzger, Roger	71T	404	$ .50	$2.00
Metzger, Roger	72T	217	$ .10	$ .40
Metzger, Roger	73T	395	$ .10	$ .40
Metzger, Roger	74T	224	$ .10	$ .40
Metzger, Roger	75T	541	$ .10	$ .40
Metzger, Roger	76T	297	$ .05	$ .25
Metzger, Roger	77T	481	$ .05	$ .20

ROGER METZGER

Player	Year	No.	VG	EX/MT
Metzger, Roger	**78T**	**697**	**$ .04**	**$ .16**
Metzger, Roger	79T	167	$ .03	$ .12
Metzger, Roger	80T	311	$ .01	$ .10
Meulens, Hensley	90T	83	$ .01	$ .10
Meulens, Hensley	91T	259	$ .01	$ .03
Meulens, Hensley	91TSC	503	$ .05	$ .25
Meulens, Hensley	92T	154	$ .01	$ .03
Meulens, Hensley	92TSC	64	$ .01	$ .10
Meulens, Hensley	93T	549	$ .01	$ .03
Meyer, Billy	52T	387	$43.75	$175.00
Meyer, Bob	64T	488	$1.00	$4.00
Meyer, Bob	65T	219	$ .50	$2.00

TOPPS

Player	Year	No.	VG	EX/MT	Player	Year	No.	VG	EX/MT
Meyer, Bob	70T	667	$1.25	$5.00	Mikkelsen, Pete	64T	488	$1.00	$4.00
Meyer, Bob	71T	456	$ .50	$2.00	Mikkelsen, Pete	65T	177	$ .35	$1.40
Meyer, Brian	90T	766	$ .01	$ .03	Mikkelsen, Pete	66T	248	$ .50	$2.00
Meyer, Danny	75T	620	$11.25	$45.00	Mikkelsen, Pete	67T	425	$ .60	$2.40
Meyer, Dan	76T	242	$ .05	$ .25	Mikkelsen, Pete	68T	516	$ .75	$3.00
Meyer, Dan	77T	527	$ .05	$ .20	Miksis, Eddie	52T	172	$7.00	$28.00
Meyer, Dan	78T	57	$ .04	$ .16	Miksis, Eddie	53T	39	$6.25	$25.00
Meyer, Dan	79T	683	$ .03	$ .12	Miksis, Eddie	56T	285	$2.50	$10.00
Meyer, Dan	80T	396	$ .01	$ .10	Miksis, Eddie	57T	.350	$5.00	$20.00
Meyer, Dan	81T	143	$ .01	$ .08	Miksis, Eddie	58T	121	$1.25	$5.00
Meyer, Dan	82T	413	$ .01	$ .08	Miksis, Eddie	59T	58	$1.50	$6.00
Meyer, Dan	82TTR	70	$ .01	$ .10	Miksis, Eddie	91TA53	39	$ .01	$ .15
Meyer, Dan	83T	208	$ .01	$ .08	Milacki, Bob	89T	324	$ .01	$ .15
Meyer, Dan	84T	609	$ .01	$ .06	Milacki, Bob	90T	73	$ .01	$ .03
Meyer, Jack	56T	269	$2.50	$10.00	Milacki, Bob	91T	788	$ .01	$ .03
Meyer, Jack	57T	162	$2.00	$8.00	Milacki, Bob	92T	408	$ .01	$ .03
Meyer, Jack	58T	186	$1.25	$5.00	Milacki, Bob	92TSC	331	$ .01	$ .10
Meyer, Jack	59T	269	$1.00	$4.00	Milacki, Bob	93T	192	$ .01	$ .03
Meyer, Jack	60T	64	$ .85	$3.40	Milbourne, Larry	75T	512	$ .10	$ .40
Meyer, Jack	61T	111	$ .60	$2.40	Milbourne, Larry	78T	366	$ .04	$ .16
Meyer, Joey	88T	312	$ .01	$ .04	Milbourne, Larry	79T	199	$ .03	$ .12
Meyer, Joey	89T	136	$ .01	$ .03	Milbourne, Larry	80T	422	$ .01	$ .10
Meyer, Joey	90T	673	$ .01	$ .03	Milbourne, Larry	81T	583	$ .01	$ .08
Meyer, Russ	52T	339	$43.75	$175.00	Milbourne, Larry	81TTR	802	$ .01	$ .15
Meyer, Russ	56T	227	$3.75	$15.00	Milbourne, Larry	82T	669	$ .01	$ .08
Meyer, Russ	59T	482	$1.00	$4.00	Milbourne, Larry	82TTR	71	$ .01	$ .10
Micelotta, Bob	54T	212	$3.75	$15.00	Milbourne, Larry	83T	91	$ .01	$ .08
Michael, Gene	67T	428	$1.00	$4.00	Milbourne, Larry	83TTR	72	$ .01	$ .10
Michael, Gene	68T	299	$ .35	$1.40	Milbourne, Larry	84T	281	$ .01	$ .06
Michael, Gene	69T	626	$ .40	$1.60	Milbourne, Larry	84TTR	79	$ .01	$ .15
					Milbourne, Larry	85T	754	$ .01	$ .06
					Miles, Jim	69T	658	$ .40	$1.60
					Miles, Jim	70T	154	$ .20	$ .80
					Miley, Mike	76T	387	$ .05	$ .25
					Miley, Mike	77T	257	$ .05	$ .20
					Militello, Sam	92T	676	$ .05	$ .35
					Militello, Sam	93T	624	$ .01	$ .15
					Militello, Sam	93TSC	11	$ .10	$ .50
					Millan, Felix	67T	89	$ .40	$1.60
					Millan, Felix	68T	241	$ .35	$1.40
					Millan, Felix	69T	210	$ .35	$1.40
					Millan, Felix	70T	710	$1.25	$5.00
					Millan, Felix	70TAS	452	$ .35	$1.40
					Millan, Felix	71T	81	$ .25	$1.00
					Millan, Felix	72T	540	$ .40	$1.60
					Millan, Felix	73T	407	$ .25	$1.00
					Millan, Felix	74T	132	$ .10	$ .40
					Millan, Felix	75T	445	$ .10	$ .40
					Millan, Felix	76T	245	$ .05	$ .25
					Millan, Felix	77T	605	$ .05	$ .20
					Millan, Felix	78T	505	$ .04	$ .16
					Miller, Bill	52T	403	$43.75	$175.00
					Miller, Bill	53T	100	$6.25	$25.00
					Miller, Bill	91TA53	100	$ .01	$ .15
					Miller, Bob	52T	187	$7.00	$28.00
					Miller, Bob	54T	241	$3.75	$15.00
					Miller, Bob	55T	9	$2.25	$9.00
					Miller, Bob	55T	157	$4.00	$16.00
					Miller, Bob	56T	263	$2.50	$10.00
					Miller, Bob	56T	334	$2.50	$10.00
					Miller, Bob	57T	46	$2.00	$8.00
					Miller, Bob	58T	326	$1.25	$5.00
					Miller, Bob	59T	379	$1.00	$4.00
					Miller, Bob	60T	101	$ .85	$3.40
					Miller, Bob	61T	314	$ .60	$2.40
					Miller, Bob	62T	293	$ .75	$3.00
					Miller, Bob	62T	572	$7.00	$28.00
					Miller, Bob	63T	261	$ .90	$3.60
					Miller, Bob	64T	394	$1.00	$4.00
					Miller, Bob	65T	98	$ .35	$1.40
					Miller, Bob	66T	208	$ .50	$2.00
					Miller, Bob	67T	461	$1.50	$6.00
					Miller, Bob	68T	534	$ .70	$2.80
					Miller, Bob	69T	403	$ .30	$1.20
					Miller, Bob	70T	47	$ .20	$ .80

Gene Michael SHORTSTOP

Player	Year	No.	VG	EX/MT
Michael, Gene	70T	114	$ .20	$ .80
Michael, Gene	71T	483	$ .50	$2.00
Michael, Gene	72T	713	$1.50	$6.00
Michael, Gene	72T	714	$1.25	$5.00
Michael, Gene	73T	265	$ .20	$ .80
Michael, Gene	74T	299	$ .10	$ .40
Michael, Gene	75T	608	$ .10	$ .40
Michael, Gene	86TTR	73	$ .01	$ .06
Michael, Gene	87T	43	$ .01	$ .04
Michaels, Cass	52T	178	$7.00	$28.00
Mielke, Gary	90T	221	$ .01	$ .10
Mielke, Gary	91T	54	$ .01	$ .03
Mieske, Matt	93T	616	$ .05	$ .25

TOPPS

Player	Year	No.	VG	EX/MT
Miller, Bob	71T	542	$1.00	$4.00
Miller, Bob	72T	414	$ .25	$1.00
Miller, Bob	73T	277	$ .10	$ .40
Miller, Bob	74T	624	$ .10	$ .40
Miller, Bruce	75T	606	$ .10	$ .40
Miller, Bruce	76T	367	$ .05	$ .25
Miller, Darrell	86T	524	$ .01	$ .05
Miller, Darrell	87T	337	$ .01	$ .04
Miller, Darrell	88T	679	$ .01	$ .04
Miller, Darrell	89T	68	$ .01	$ .03
Miller, Dyar	75T	614	$ .10	$ .40
Miller, Dyar	76T	555	$ .05	$ .25
Miller, Dyar	77T	77	$ .05	$ .20
Miller, Dyar	78T	239	$ .04	$ .16
Miller, Dyar	79T	313	$ .03	$ .12
Miller, Dyar	81T	472	$ .01	$ .08
Miller, Dyar	82T	178	$ .01	$ .10
Miller, Eddie	80T	675	$ .01	$ .10
Miller, Ed	81T	192	$ .05	$ .20
Miller, Ed	82T	451	$ .01	$ .08
Miller, John	63T	208	$ .90	$3.60
Miller, John	65T	49	$ .75	$3.00
Miller, John	66T	427	$ .65	$2.60
Miller, John	67T	141	$ .40	$1.60
Miller, John	69T	641	$ .40	$1.60
Miller, Keith	88T	382	$ .01	$ .10
Miller, Keith	89T	268	$ .01	$ .10
Miller, Keith	89T	557	$ .01	$ .10
Miller, Keith	90T	58	$ .01	$ .03
Miller, Keith	91T	719	$ .01	$ .03
Miller, Keith	91TSC	239	$ .05	$ .25
Miller, Keith	92T	157	$ .01	$ .03
Miller, Keith	92TSC	786	$ .01	$ .10
Miller, Keith	92TTR	73	$ .01	$ .05
Miller, Keith	93T	267	$ .01	$ .03
Miller, Kurt	91T	491	$ .05	$ .25
Miller, Larry	65T	349	$ .50	$2.00
Miller, Larry	69T	323	$ .50	$2.00
Miller, Norm	67T	412	$1.00	$4.00
Miller, Norm	68T	161	$ .35	$1.40
Miller, Norm	69T	76	$ .35	$1.40
Miller, Norm	70T	619	$ .50	$2.00
Miller, Norm	71T	18	$ .25	$1.00
Miller, Norm	72T	466	$ .25	$1.00
Miller, Norm	73T	637	$ .60	$2.40
Miller, Norm	74T	439	$ .10	$ .40
Miller, Randy	80T	680	$ .05	$ .20
Miller, Ray	86T	381	$ .01	$ .05
Miller, Rick	72T	741	$2.50	$10.00
Miller, Rick	74T	247	$ .10	$ .40
Miller, Rick	75T	103	$ .10	$ .40
Miller, Rick	76T	302	$ .05	$ .25
Miller, Rick	77T	566	$ .05	$ .20
Miller, Rick	78T	482	$ .04	$ .16
Miller, Rick	79T	654	$ .03	$ .12
Miller, Rick	80T	48	$ .01	$ .10
Miller, Rick	81T	239	$ .01	$ .08
Miller, Rick	81TTR	803	$ .01	$ .15
Miller, Rick	82T	717	$ .01	$ .08
Miller, Rick	83T	188	$ .01	$ .08
Miller, Rick	84T	344	$ .01	$ .06
Miller, Rick	85T	502	$ .01	$ .06
Miller, Rick	86T	424	$ .01	$ .05
Miller, Stu	53T	183	$6.00	$24.00
Miller, Stu	54T	164	$3.75	$15.00
Miller, Stu	56T	293	$3.00	$12.00
Miller, Stu	58T	111	$1.75	$7.00
Miller, Stu	59T	183	$1.00	$4.00
Miller, Stu	60T	378	$ .75	$3.00
Miller, Stu	61T	72	$ .60	$2.40
Miller, Stu	62T	155	$ .60	$2.40
Miller, Stu	63T	286	$ .90	$3.60
Miller, Stu	64T	565	$2.25	$9.00
Miller, Stu	65T	499	$1.25	$5.00
Miller, Stu	66T	265	$ .50	$2.00
Miller, Stu	67T	345	$ .60	$2.40
Miller, Stu	91TA53	183	$ .01	$ .15
Miller, Trever	92T	684	$ .01	$ .10
Millettte, Joe	93T	531	$ .01	$ .03
Milligan, Randy	89TTR	81	$ .01	$ .10
Milligan, Randy	90T	153	$ .01	$ .03
Milligan, Randy	91T	416	$ .01	$ .03
Milligan, Randy	91TSC	80	$ .05	$ .25
Milligan, Randy	92T	17	$ .01	$ .03
Milligan, Randy	92TSC	587	$ .01	$ .10
Milligan, Randy	93T	678	$ .01	$ .03
Milligan, Randy	93TSC	158	$ .01	$ .10
Milliken, Bob	53T	221	$22.50	$90.00
Milliken, Bob	54T	177	$3.75	$15.00
Milliken, Bob	55T	111	$2.25	$9.00
Milliken, Bob	91TA53	221	$ .01	$ .15
Mills, Alan	90TTR	75	$ .01	$ .10
Mills, Alan	91T	651	$ .01	$ .03
Mills, Alan	91TSC	473	$ .05	$ .25
Mills, Alan	92TSC	871	$ .01	$ .10
Mills, Alan	93T	137	$ .01	$ .03
Mills, Brad	82T	118	$ .10	$ .50
Mills, Brad	83T	744	$ .01	$ .08
Mills, Buster	54T	227	$3.75	$15.00
Mills, Dick	71T	512	$ .50	$2.00
Milner, Brian	81T	577	$ .01	$ .08
Milner, Brian	82T	203	$ .10	$1.00
Milner, Eddie	82TTR	72	$ .05	$ .20
Milner, Eddie	83T	449	$ .01	$ .08
Milner, Eddie	84T	34	$ .01	$ .06
Milner, Eddie	85T	198	$ .01	$ .06
Milner, Eddie	86T	544	$ .01	$ .05
Milner, Eddie	87T	253	$ .01	$ .04
Milner, Eddie	87TTR	78	$ .01	$ .05
Milner, Eddie	88T	677	$ .01	$ .04
Milner, John	72T	741	$2.50	$10.00
Milner, John	73T	4	$ .10	$ .40
Milner, John	74T	234	$ .10	$ .40
Milner, John	75T	264	$ .10	$ .40
Milner, John	76T	517	$ .05	$ .25
Milner, John	77T	172	$ .05	$ .20
Milner, John	78T	304	$ .04	$ .16
Milner, John	79T	523	$ .03	$ .12
Milner, John	80T	71	$ .01	$ .10
Milner, John	81T	618	$ .01	$ .08
Milner, John	82T	638	$ .01	$ .08
Minarcin, Rudy	55T	174	$6.25	$25.00
Minarcin, Rudy	56T	36	$2.00	$8.00
Mincher, Don	60T	548	$2.75	$11.00
Mincher, Don	61T	336	$ .60	$2.40
Mincher, Don	62T	386	$1.25	$5.00
Mincher, Don	63T	269	$ .90	$3.60
Mincher, Don	64T	542	$2.25	$9.00
Mincher, Don	65T	108	$ .35	$1.40
Mincher, Don	66T	388	$ .65	$2.60
Mincher, Don	67T	312	$ .60	$2.40
Mincher, Don	68T	75	$ .35	$1.40
Mincher, Don	69T	285	$ .50	$2.00
Mincher, Don	70T	185	$ .20	$ .80
Mincher, Don	71T	680	$1.50	$6.00
Mincher, Don	72T	242	$ .10	$ .40
Minetto, Craig	80T	494	$ .01	$ .10
Minetto, Craig	81T	316	$ .01	$ .08
Mingori, Steve	69T	339	$ .30	$1.20
Mingori, Steve	71T	612	$1.00	$4.00
Mingori, Steve	72T	261	$ .10	$ .40
Mingori, Steve	73T	532	$ .60	$2.40
Mingori, Steve	74T	537	$ .10	$ .40
Mingori, Steve	75T	544	$ .10	$ .40
Mingori, Steve	76T	541	$ .05	$ .25
Mingori, Steve	77T	314	$ .05	$ .20
Mingori, Steve	78T	696	$ .04	$ .16
Mingori, Steve	79T	72	$ .03	$ .12
Mingori, Steve	80T	219	$ .01	$ .10
Minner, Paul	52T	127	$7.00	$28.00

TOPPS

Player	Year	No.	VG	EX/MT
Minner, Paul	53T	92	$4.00	$16.00
Minner, Paul	54T	28	$3.75	$15.00
Minner, Paul	56T	182	$3.75	$15.00
Minner, Paul	91TA53	92	$.01	$.15
Minoso, Orestes	52T	195	$27.50	$110.00
Minoso, Orestes	53T	66	$11.25	$45.00
Minoso, Minnie "Orestes"	56T	125	$5.50	$22.00
Minoso, Minnie	57T	138	$3.50	$14.00
Minoso, Minnie	58T	295	$2.25	$9.00
Minoso, Minnie	59T	80	$2.50	$10.00
Minoso, Minnie	59T	166	$1.75	$7.00
Minoso, Minnie	60T	365	$1.25	$5.00
Minoso, Minnie	61T	42	$.75	$3.00
Minoso, Minnie	61T	380	$1.25	$5.00
Minoso, Minnie	62T	28	$1.25	$5.00
Minoso, Minnie	63T	190	$1.00	$4.00
Minoso, Minnie	64T	538	$2.50	$10.00
Minoso, Minnie	77TRB	232	$.10	$.40
Minoso, Orestes	91TA53	66	$.10	$.50
Minton, Greg	77T	489	$.20	$.80
Minton, Greg	78T	312	$.04	$.16
Minton, Greg	79T	84	$.03	$.12
Minton, Greg	80T	588	$.01	$.10
Minton, Greg	81T	111	$.01	$.08
Minton, Greg	82T	687	$.01	$.08
Minton, Greg	83T	470	$.01	$.08
Minton, Greg	83TRB	3	$.01	$.08
Minton, Greg	84T	205	$.01	$.06
Minton, Greg	85T	45	$.01	$.06
Minton, Greg	86T	310	$.01	$.05
Minton, Greg	87T	724	$.01	$.04
Minton, Greg	87TTR	79	$.01	$.05
Minton, Greg	88T	129	$.01	$.04
Minton, Greg	89T	576	$.01	$.03
Minton, Greg	90T	421	$.01	$.03
Minutelli, Gino	92TSC	452	$.01	$.10
Mirabella, Paul	81T	382	$.01	$.08
Mirabella, Paul	82T	499	$.01	$.08
Mirabella, Paul	83T	12	$.01	$.08
Mirabella, Paul	85T	766	$.01	$.06
Mirabella, Paul	89T	192	$.01	$.03
Miranda, Willie	53T	278	$22.50	$90.00
Miranda, Willie	54T	56	$7.50	$30.00
Miranda, Willie	55T	154	$4.00	$16.00
Miranda, Willie	56T	103	$2.50	$10.00
Miranda, Willie (Willy)	57T	151	$2.00	$8.00
Miranda, Willy	58T	179	$1.25	$5.00
Miranda, Willy	59T	540	$4.00	$16.00
Miranda, Willie	91TA53	278	$.01	$.15
Mitchell, Bobby	71T	111	$.25	$1.00
Mitchell, Bobby	74T	497	$.10	$.40
Mitchell, Bobby	75T	468	$.10	$.40
Mitchell, Bobby	76T	479	$.05	$.25
Mitchell, Bobby	83T	647	$.01	$.08
Mitchell, Bobby	84T	307	$.01	$.06
Mitchell, Craig	76T	591	$.05	$.25
Mitchell, Craig	77T	491	$1.75	$7.00
Mitchell, Craig	78T	711	$.04	$.16
Mitchell, Dale	51Trb	13	$1.75	$7.50
Mitchell, Dale	52T	92	$7.00	$28.00
Mitchell, Dale	53T	26	$4.00	$16.00
Mitchell, Dale	56T	268	$4.00	$16.00
Mitchell, Dale	91TA53	26	$.01	$.15
Mitchell, John	87TTR	80	$.01	$.05
Mitchell, John	88T	207	$.01	$.04
Mitchell, John	91T	708	$.01	$.03
Mitchell, Keith	92T	542	$.01	$.15
Mitchell, Keith	92TSC	551	$.01	$.15
Mitchell, Kevin	86TTR	74	$.15	$1.50
Mitchell, Kevin	87T	653	$.10	$.75
Mitchell, Kevin	87TTR	81	$.10	$.50
Mitchell, Kevin	88T	497	$.01	$.15
Mitchell, Kevin	89T	189	$.01	$.10
Mitchell, Kevin	90T	500	$.01	$.10
Mitchell, Kevin	90TAS	401	$.01	$.10
Mitchell, Kevin	91T	40	$.01	$.10
Mitchell, Kevin	91TSC	250	$.05	$.35
Mitchell, Kevin	92T	180	$.01	$.03
Mitchell, Kevin	92TSC	215	$.05	$.25
Mitchell, Kevin	92TSC	765	$.01	$.10
Mitchell, Kevin	92TTR	74	$.01	$.05
Mitchell, Kevin	93T	217	$.01	$.10
Mitchell, Paul	76T	393	$.05	$.25
Mitchell, Paul	77T	53	$.05	$.20
Mitchell, Paul	78T	558	$.04	$.16
Mitchell, Paul	79T	233	$.03	$.12
Mitchell, Paul	80T	131	$.01	$.10
Mitchell, Paul	81T	449	$.01	$.08
Mitterwald, George	68T	301	$.35	$1.40
Mitterwald, George	69T	491	$.30	$1.20
Mitterwald, George	70T	118	$.20	$.80
Mitterwald, George	71T	189	$.25	$1.00
Mitterwald, George	72T	301	$.10	$.40
Mitterwald, George	72TIA	302	$.10	$.40
Mitterwald, George	74T	249	$.10	$.40
Mitterwald, George	74TTR	249	$.10	$.40
Mitterwald, George	75T	411	$.10	$.40
Mitterwald, George	76T	506	$.05	$.25
Mitterwald, George	77T	124	$.05	$.20
Mitterwald, George	78T	688	$.04	$.16
Mize, John	53T	77	$15.00	$60.00
Mize, John	91TA53	77	$.10	$.75
Mize, Johnny	51Tbb	50	$35.00	$140.00
Mize, Johnny	52T	129	$22.50	$90.00
Mizell, Wilmer	52T	334	$50.00	$200.00
Mizell, Wilmer	53T	128	$4.00	$16.00
Mizell, Wilmer	54T	249	$3.75	$15.00
Mizell, Wilmer	56T	193	$3.75	$15.00
Mizell, Wilmer	57T	113	$2.00	$8.00
Mizell, Wilmer	58T	385	$1.00	$4.00
Mizell, Wilmer	91TA53	128	$.01	$.15
Mizerock, John	87T	408	$.01	$.04
Mlicki, Dave	93T	571	$.01	$.15
Moates, Dave	76T	327	$.05	$.25
Moates, Dave	77T	588	$.05	$.20

JOE **MOELLER**
L. A. DODGERS   PITCHER

Player	Year	No.	VG	EX/MT
Moeller, Joe	63T	53	$.50	$2.00
Moeller, Joe	64T	549	$2.25	$9.00
Moeller, Joe	65T	238	$.50	$2.00

TOPPS

Player	Year	No.	VG	EX/MT	Player	Year	No.	VG	EX/MT
Moeller, Joe	66T	449	$1.50	$6.00	Monday, Rick	81T	726	$ .05	$ .20
Moeller, Joe	67T	149	$ .40	$1.60	Monday, Rick	82T	577	$ .01	$ .08
Moeller, Joe	68T	359	$ .35	$1.40	Monday, Rick	83T	63	$ .01	$ .08
Moeller, Joe	69T	444	$ .30	$1.20	Monday, Rick	84T	274	$ .01	$ .06
Moeller, Joe	70T	97	$ .20	$ .80	Money, Don	69T	454	$ .30	$1.20
Moeller, Joe	71T	288	$ .25	$1.00	Money, Don	70T	645	$1.25	$5.00
Moeller, Ron	61T	466	$1.35	$5.40	Money, Don	71T	49	$ .25	$1.00
Moeller, Ron	63T	541	$2.25	$9.00	Money, Don	72T	635	$ .40	$1.60
Moffitt, Randy	73T	43	$ .10	$ .40	Money, Don	73T	386	$ .10	$ .40
Moffitt, Randy	74T	156	$ .10	$ .40	Money, Don	74T	413	$ .10	$ .40
Moffitt, Randy	75T	132	$ .10	$ .40	Money, Don	75T	175	$ .10	$ .40
Moffitt, Randy	76T	553	$ .05	$ .25	Money, Don	76T	402	$ .05	$ .25
Moffitt, Randy	77T	464	$ .05	$ .20	Money, Don	77T	79	$ .05	$ .20
Moffitt, Randy	78T	284	$ .04	$ .16	Money, Don	78T	24	$ .04	$ .16
Moffitt, Randy	79T	62	$ .03	$ .12	Money, Don	79T	265	$ .03	$ .12
Moffitt, Randy	80T	359	$ .01	$ .10	Money, Don	80T	595	$ .01	$ .10
Moffitt, Randy	81T	622	$ .01	$ .08	Money, Don	81T	106	$ .01	$ .08
Moffitt, Randy	83T	723	$ .01	$ .08	Money, Don	82T	709	$ .01	$ .08
Moffitt, Randy	83TTR	73	$ .01	$ .10	Money, Don	83T	608	$ .01	$ .08
Moffitt, Randy	84T	108	$ .01	$ .06	Money, Don	84T	374	$ .01	$ .06
Moford, Herb	59T	91	$1.50	$6.00	Moneyham, Bill	87T	548	$ .01	$ .04
Mohorcic, Dale	87T	497	$ .01	$ .04	Monge, Sid	76T	595	$ .05	$ .25
Mohorcic, Dale	88T	163	$ .01	$ .04	Monge, Sid	77T	282	$ .05	$ .20
Mohorcic, Dale	89T	26	$ .01	$ .03	Monge, Sid	78T	101	$ .04	$ .16
Moler, Jason	92TTR	75	$ .05	$ .20	Monge, Sid	79T	459	$ .03	$ .12
Molinaro, Bob	79T	88	$ .03	$ .12	Monge, Sid	80T	74	$ .01	$ .10
Molinaro, Bob	81T	466	$ .01	$ .08	Monge, Sid	81T	333	$ .01	$ .08
Molinaro, Bob	82T	363	$ .01	$ .08	Monge, Sid	82T	601	$ .01	$ .08
Molinaro, Bob	83T	664	$ .01	$ .08	Monge, Sid	82TTR	73	$ .01	$ .10
Molitor, Paul	78T	707	$12.50	$50.00	Monge, Sid	83T	564	$ .01	$ .08
Molitor, Paul	79T	24	$3.50	$14.00	Monge, Sid	83TTR	74	$ .01	$ .10
Molitor, Paul	80T	406	$1.75	$7.00	Monge, Sid	84T	224	$ .01	$ .06
Molitor, Paul	81T	300	$ .20	$2.00	Monge, Sid	84TTR	80	$ .01	$ .15
Molitor, Paul	82T	195	$ .15	$1.50	Monge, Sid	85T	408	$ .01	$ .06
Molitor, Paul	83T	630	$ .15	$1.50	Monroe, Zack	59T	108	$1.50	$6.00
Molitor, Paul	84T	60	$ .10	$ .50	Monroe, Zack	60T	329	$ .75	$3.00
Molitor, Paul	85T	522	$ .05	$ .35	Montague, John	75T	405	$ .10	$ .40
Molitor, Paul	86T	267	$ .01	$ .15	Montague, John	78T	117	$ .04	$ .16
Molitor, Paul	87T	741	$ .01	$ .10	Montague, John	79T	337	$ .03	$ .12
Molitor, Paul	88T	465	$ .01	$ .10	Montague, John	80T	253	$ .01	$ .10
Molitor, Paul	89T	110	$ .01	$ .10	Montague, John	81T	652	$ .01	$ .08
Molitor, Paul	90T	360	$ .01	$ .10	Montanez, Willie	71T	138	$ .25	$1.00
Molitor, Paul	91T	95	$ .01	$ .10	Montanez, Willie	72T	690	$1.25	$5.00
Molitor, Paul	91TSC	245	$ .10	$ .40	Montanez, Willie	73T	97	$ .10	$ .40
Molitor, Paul	92T	600	$ .01	$ .03	Montanez, Willie	74T	515	$ .10	$ .40
Molitor, Paul	92TSC	230	$ .01	$ .10	Montanez, Willie	75T	162	$ .10	$ .40
Molitor, Paul	93T	207	$ .01	$ .03	Montanez, Willie	76T	181	$ .05	$ .25
Moloney, Dick	71T	13	$ .25	$1.00	Montanez, Willie	77T	410	$ .05	$ .20
Monbouquette, Bill	59T	173	$1.00	$4.00	Montanez, Willie	78T	38	$ .04	$ .16
Monbouquette, Bill	60T	544	$2.75	$11.00	Montanez, Willie	79T	305	$ .03	$ .12
Monbouquette, Bill	61T	562	$7.50	$30.00	Montanez, Willie	80T	224	$ .01	$ .10
Monbouquette, Bill	62T	580	$3.50	$14.00	Montanez, Willie	81T	559	$ .01	$ .08
Monbouquette, Bill	63T	480	$3.00	$12.00	Montanez, Willie	82T	458	$ .01	$ .08
Monbouquette, Bill	64T	25	$ .50	$2.00	Monteagudo, Aurelio	64T	466	$1.00	$4.00
Monbouquette, Bill	65T	142	$ .35	$1.40	Monteagudo, Aurelio	65T	286	$ .50	$2.00
Monbouquette, Bill	66T	429	$ .65	$2.60	Monteagudo, Aurelio	66T	532	$7.00	$28.00
Monbouquette, Bill	67T	482	$1.50	$6.00	Monteagudo, Aurelio	67T	453	$ .60	$2.40
Monbouquette, Bill	68T	234	$ .35	$1.40	Monteagudo, Aurelio	71T	129	$ .25	$1.00
Monbouquette, Bill	69T	64	$ .35	$1.40	Monteagudo, Aurelio	72T	458	$ .25	$1.00
Monchak, Al	73T	356	$ .20	$ .80	Monteagudo, Aurelio	74T	139	$ .10	$ .40
Monchak, Alex	74T	221	$ .10	$ .40	Monteagudo, Aurelio	74TTR	139	$ .10	$ .40
Monday, Rick	67T	542	$3.00	$12.00	Montefusco, John	76T	30	$ .15	$ .60
Monday, Rick	68T	282	$ .50	$2.00	Montefusco, John	76T	203	$ .30	$1.20
Monday, Rick	69T	105	$ .35	$1.40	Montefusco, John	77T	370	$ .05	$ .20
Monday, Rick	70T	547	$ .50	$2.00	Montefusco, John	78T	142	$ .04	$ .16
Monday, Rick	71T	135	$ .25	$1.00	Montefusco, John	79T	560	$ .03	$ .12
Monday, Rick	72T	730	$1.25	$5.00	Montefusco, John	80T	195	$ .01	$ .10
Monday, Rick	73T	44	$ .20	$ .80	Montefusco, John	81T	438	$ .01	$ .08
Monday, Rick	74T	295	$ .10	$ .40	Montefusco, John	81TTR	804	$ .01	$ .15
Monday, Rick	75T	129	$ .10	$ .40	Montefusco, John	82T	697	$ .01	$ .08
Monday, Rick	76T	251	$ .05	$ .25	Montefusco, John	82TTR	74	$ .01	$ .10
Monday, Rick	77T	360	$ .05	$ .20	Montefusco, John	83T	223	$ .01	$ .08
Monday, Rick	78T	145	$ .04	$ .16	Montefusco, John	84T	761	$ .01	$ .06
Monday, Rick	79T	605	$ .03	$ .12	Montefusco, John	85T	301	$ .01	$ .06
Monday, Rick	80T	465	$ .01	$ .10	Monteleone, Rich	90T	99	$ .01	$ .03

TOPPS

Player	Year	No.	VG	EX/MT
Monteleone, Rich	92TSC	157	$ .01	$ .10
Monteleone, Rich	93T	779	$ .01	$ .03
Montgomery, Bob	71T	176	$ .25	$1.00
Montgomery, Bob	72T	411	$ .25	$1.00
Montgomery, Bob	73T	491	$ .25	$1.00
Montgomery, Bob	74T	301	$ .10	$ .40
Montgomery, Bob	75T	559	$ .10	$ .40
Montgomery, Bob	76T	523	$ .05	$ .25
Montgomery, Bob	77T	288	$ .05	$ .20
Montgomery, Bob	78T	83	$ .04	$ .16
Montgomery, Bob	79T	423	$ .03	$ .12
Montgomery, Bob	80T	618	$ .01	$ .10
Montgomery, Jeff	88T	447	$ .05	$ .35
Montgomery, Jeff	89T	116	$ .01	$ .03
Montgomery, Jeff	90T	638	$ .01	$ .10
Montgomery, Jeff	91T	371	$ .01	$ .03
Montgomery, Jeff	91TSC	369	$ .05	$ .25
Montgomery, Jeff	92T	16	$ .01	$ .03
Montgomery, Jeff	92TSC	12	$ .01	$ .10
Montgomery, Jeff	93T	130	$ .01	$ .03
Montgomery, Jeff	93TSC	125	$ .01	$ .10
Montgomery, Monty	72T	372	$ .10	$ .40
Montgomery, Monty	73T	164	$ .10	$ .40
Monzant, Ray	56T	264	$2.50	$10.00
Monzant, Ray	58T	447	$1.00	$4.00
Monzant, Ray	59T	332	$1.00	$4.00
Monzant, Ray	60T	338	$ .75	$3.00
Monzon, Dan	73T	469	$ .25	$1.00
Monzon, Dan	74T	613	$ .10	$ .40
Moody, Ritchie	93T	438	$ .01	$ .15
Moon, Wally	54T	137	$7.00	$28.00
Moon, Wally	55T	67	$2.25	$9.00
Moon, Wally	56T	55	$2.00	$8.00
Moon, Wally	57T	65	$2.00	$8.00
Moon, Wally	58T	210	$1.25	$5.00
Moon, Wally	59T	530	$4.00	$16.00
Moon, Wally	60T	5	$ .85	$3.40
Moon, Wally	61T	325	$ .60	$2.40
Moon, Wally	62T	52	$1.75	$7.00
Moon, Wally	62T	190	$ .75	$3.00
Moon, Wally	63T	279	$ .90	$3.60
Moon, Wally	64T	353	$ .65	$2.60
Moon, Wally	65T	247	$ .50	$2.00
Moore, Archie	64T	581	$2.25	$9.00
Moore, Balor	71T	747	$1.10	$4.40
Moore, Balor	73T	211	$ .10	$ .40
Moore, Balor	74T	453	$ .10	$ .40
Moore, Balor	75T	592	$ .10	$ .40
Moore, Balor	78T	368	$ .04	$ .16
Moore, Balor	79T	238	$ .03	$ .12
Moore, Balor	80T	19	$ .01	$ .10
Moore, Barry	67T	11	$ .40	$1.60
Moore, Barry	68T	462	$ .75	$3.00
Moore, Barry	69T	639	$ .40	$1.60
Moore, Barry	70T	366	$ .35	$1.40
Moore, Brad	89T	202	$ .01	$ .03
Moore, Charlie	74T	379	$ .25	$1.00
Moore, Charlie	74T	603	$ .10	$ .40
Moore, Charlie	75T	636	$ .10	$ .40
Moore, Charlie	76T	116	$ .05	$ .25
Moore, Charlie	77T	382	$ .05	$ .20
Moore, Charlie	78T	51	$ .04	$ .16
Moore, Charlie	79T	408	$ .03	$ .12
Moore, Charlie	80T	579	$ .01	$ .10
Moore, Charlie	81T	237	$ .01	$ .08
Moore, Charlie	82T	308	$ .01	$ .08
Moore, Charlie	83T	659	$ .01	$ .08
Moore, Charlie	84T	751	$ .01	$ .06
Moore, Charlie	85T	83	$ .01	$ .06
Moore, Charlie	86T	137	$ .01	$ .05
Moore, Charlie	87T	676	$ .01	$ .04
Moore, Charlie	87TTR	82	$ .01	$ .05
Moore, Donnie	78T	523	$ .05	$ .20
Moore, Donnie	79T	17	$ .03	$ .12
Moore, Donnie	84T	207	$ .01	$ .06
Moore, Donnie	85T	699	$ .01	$ .06
Moore, Donnie	85TTR	85	$ .01	$ .10
Moore, Donnie	86T	345	$ .01	$ .05
Moore, Donnie	87T	115	$ .01	$ .04
Moore, Donnie	88T	471	$ .01	$ .04
Moore, Jackie	65T	593	$3.00	$12.00
Moore, Jackie	73T	549	$1.00	$4.00
Moore, Jackie	84TTR	81	$ .01	$ .15
Moore, Jackie	85T	38	$ .01	$ .06
Moore, Jackie	86T	591	$ .01	$ .05
Moore, Junior	78T	421	$ .04	$ .16
Moore, Junior	79T	275	$ .03	$ .12
Moore, Junior	80T	186	$ .01	$ .10
Moore, Kelvin	82T	531	$ .01	$ .08
Moore, Michael	93T	576	$ .10	$ .75
Moore, Mike	83T	209	$ .10	$1.00
Moore, Mike	84T	547	$ .05	$ .20
Moore, Mike	85T	279	$ .01	$ .10
Moore, Mike	85T	373	$ .01	$ .15
Moore, Mike	86T	646	$ .01	$ .10
Moore, Mike	87T	727	$ .01	$ .04
Moore, Mike	88T	432	$ .01	$ .04
Moore, Mike	89T	28	$ .01	$ .03
Moore, Mike	89TTR	82	$ .01	$ .10
Moore, Mike	90T	175	$ .01	$ .03
Moore, Mike	91T	294	$ .01	$ .03
Moore, Mike	91TSC	464	$ .05	$ .25
Moore, Mike	92T	359	$ .01	$ .03
Moore, Mike	92TSC	669	$ .01	$ .10
Moore, Mike	93T	73	$ .01	$ .03
Moore, Ray	55T	208	$6.25	$25.00
Moore, Ray	56T	43	$2.00	$8.00
Moore, Ray	57T	106	$2.00	$8.00
Moore, Ray	58T	249	$1.25	$5.00
Moore, Ray	59T	293	$1.00	$4.00
Moore, Ray	60T	447	$1.25	$5.00
Moore, Ray	61T	289	$ .60	$2.40
Moore, Ray	62T	437	$1.25	$5.00
Moore, Ray	63T	26	$ .50	$2.00
Moorhead, Bob	62T	593	$5.25	$21.00
Moose, Bob	68T	36	$ .35	$1.40
Moose, Bob	69T	409	$ .30	$1.20
Moose, Bob	70T	110	$ .20	$ .80

DONNIE MOORE

TOPPS

Player	Year	No.	VG	EX/MT	Player	Year	No.	VG	EX/MT
Moose, Bob	71T	690	$1.10	$4.40	Moreland, Keith	87T	177	$.01	$.04
Moose, Bob	72T	647	$.40	$1.60	Moreland, Keith	88T	416	$.01	$.04
Moose, Bob	73T	499	$.25	$1.00	Moreland, Keith	88TTR	72	$.01	$.05
Moose, Bob	74T	382	$.10	$.40	Moreland, Keith	89T	773	$.01	$.03
Moose, Bob	75T	536	$.10	$.40	Moreland, Keith	89TTR	83	$.01	$.05
Moose, Bob	76T	476	$.05	$.25	Moreno, Armando	92T	179	$.05	$.20
Mora, Andres	77T	646	$.05	$.20	Moreno, Omar	77T	104	$.05	$.20
Mora, Andres	78T	517	$.04	$.16	Moreno, Omar	78T	283	$.04	$.16
Mora, Andres	79T	287	$.03	$.12	Moreno, Omar	79T	4	$.03	$.12
Morales, Jerry	70T	262	$.20	$.80	Moreno, Omar	79T	607	$.03	$.12
Morales, Jerry	71T	696	$1.10	$4.40	Moreno, Omar	80T	165	$.01	$.10
Morales, Jerry	73T	268	$.10	$.40	Moreno, Omar	80T	204	$.01	$.10
Morales, Jerry	74T	258	$.10	$.40	Moreno, Omar	81T	535	$.01	$.08
Morales, Jerry	75T	282	$.10	$.40	Moreno, Omar	82T	395	$.01	$.08
Morales, Jerry	76T	79	$.05	$.25	Moreno, Omar	83T	485	$.01	$.08
Morales, Jerry	77T	639	$.05	$.20	Moreno, Omar	83TTR	76	$.01	$.10
Morales, Jerry	78T	175	$.04	$.16	Moreno, Omar	84T	16	$.01	$.06
Morales, Jerry	79T	452	$.03	$.12	Moreno, Omar	84T	714	$.01	$.06
Morales, Jerry	80T	572	$.01	$.10	Moreno, Omar	85T	738	$.01	$.06
Morales, Jerry	81T	377	$.01	$.08	Moreno, Omar	86TTR	75	$.01	$.06
Morales, Jerry	81TTR	805	$.01	$.15	Moreno, Omar	87T	214	$.01	$.04
Morales, Jerry	82T	33	$.01	$.08	Moret, Rogelio	71T	692	$1.50	$6.00
Morales, Jerry	83T	729	$.01	$.08	Moret, Rogelio	72T	113	$.10	$.40
Morales, Jose	76T	418	$.05	$.25	Moret, Rogelio	73T	291	$.10	$.40
Morales, Jose	77T	102	$.05	$.20	Moret, Rogelio	74T	590	$.10	$.40
Morales, Jose	77TRB	233	$.05	$.20	Moret, Rogelio	75T	8	$.10	$.40
Morales, Jose	78T	374	$.04	$.16	Moret, Rogelio	76T	632	$.05	$.25
Morales, Jose	79T	552	$.03	$.12	Moret, Rogelio	76TR	632	$.05	$.25
Morales, Jose	80T	218	$.01	$.10	Moret, Rogelio	77T	292	$.05	$.20
Morales, Jose	81T	43	$.01	$.08	Moret, Rogelio	78T	462	$.04	$.16
Morales, Jose	81TTR	806	$.01	$.15	Morgan, Bobby	52T	355	$43.75	$175.00
Morales, Jose	82T	648	$.01	$.08	Morgan, Bobby	53T	85	$4.00	$16.00
Morales, Jose	82TTR	75	$.01	$.10	Morgan, Bobby	56T	337	$2.50	$10.00
Morales, Jose	83TTR	75	$.01	$.10	Morgan, Bobby	58T	144	$1.25	$5.00
Morales, Jose	84T	143	$.01	$.06	Morgan, Bobby	91TA53	85	$.01	$.15
Morales, Rich	69T	654	$.75	$3.00	Morgan, Joe	60T	229	$1.25	$5.00
Morales, Rich	70T	91	$.20	$.80	Morgan, Joe	61T	511	$1.35	$5.40
Morales, Rich	71T	267	$.25	$1.00	Morgan, Joe	89T	714	$.01	$.03
Morales, Rich	72T	593	$.40	$1.60	Morgan, Joe	90T	321	$.01	$.03
Morales, Rich	73T	494	$.25	$1.00	Morgan, Joe	91T	21	$.01	$.03
Morales, Rich	74T	387	$.10	$.40	Morgan, Joe	65T	16	$35.00	$140.00
Moran, Al	63T	558	$3.00	$12.00	Morgan, Joe	66T	195	$10.00	$40.00
Moran, Al	64T	288	$.65	$2.60	Morgan, Joe	67T	337	$6.00	$24.00
Moran, Billy	58T	388	$1.00	$4.00	Morgan, Joe	68T	144	$4.50	$18.00
Moran, Billy	59T	196	$1.00	$4.00	Morgan, Joe	68TAS	364	$2.25	$9.00
Moran, Billy	62T	539	$3.50	$14.00	Morgan, Joe	69T	35	$3.00	$12.00
Moran, Billy	63T	57	$.50	$2.00	Morgan, Joe	70T	537	$3.50	$14.00
Moran, Billy	64T	333	$.65	$2.60	Morgan, Joe	71T	264	$2.50	$10.00
Moran, Billy	65T	562	$1.40	$5.60	Morgan, Joe	72T	132	$1.25	$5.00
Morandini, Mickey	88TTR	71	$.10	$.75	Morgan, Joe	72TTR	752	$10.00	$40.00
Morandini, Mickey	91T	342	$.01	$.10	Morgan, Joe	73T	230	$1.50	$6.00
Morandini, Mickey	91TSC	535	$.10	$.40	Morgan, Joe	74T	85	$1.50	$6.00
Morandini, Mickey	92T	587	$.01	$.03	Morgan, Joe	74TAS	333	$.75	$3.00
Morandini, Mickey	92TSC	369	$.01	$.10	Morgan, Joe	75T	180	$1.75	$7.00
Morandini, Mickey	93T	262	$.01	$.03	Morgan, Joe	76T	197	$.25	$1.00
Morehead, Dave	63T	299	$.90	$3.60	Morgan, Joe	76T	420	$1.50	$6.00
Morehead, Dave	64T	376	$1.00	$4.00	Morgan, Joe	77T	100	$1.25	$5.00
Morehead, Dave	65T	434	$1.00	$4.00	Morgan, Joe	78T	300	$.75	$3.00
Morehead, Dave	66T	135	$.50	$2.00	Morgan, Joe	79T	20	$.25	$1.00
Morehead, Dave	67T	297	$.60	$2.40	Morgan, Joe	80T	650	$.20	$2.00
Morehead, Dave	68T	212	$.35	$1.40	Morgan, Joe	81T	560	$.10	$1.00
Morehead, Dave	69T	29	$.35	$1.40	Morgan, Joe	81TR	807	$.75	$3.00
Morehead, Dave	70T	495	$.35	$1.40	Morgan, Joe	82T	754	$.10	$1.00
Morehead, Dave	71T	221	$.25	$1.00	Morgan, Joe	82TSA	755	$.10	$.50
Morehead, Seth	59T	253	$1.00	$4.00	Morgan, Joe	83T	171	$.01	$.08
Morehead, Seth	60T	504	$1.25	$5.00	Morgan, Joe	83T	603	$.10	$.75
Morehead, Seth	61T	107	$.60	$2.40	Morgan, Joe	83T	604	$.05	$.35
Moreland, Keith	81T	131	$.05	$.25	Morgan, Joe	83TTR	77	$.25	$2.50
Moreland, Keith	82T	384	$.01	$.15	Morgan, Joe	84T	210	$.05	$.35
Moreland, Keith	82TTR	76	$.01	$.10	Morgan, Joe	84T	705	$.01	$.10
Moreland, Keith	83T	619	$.01	$.08	Morgan, Joe	84TTR	82	$.75	$3.00
Moreland, Keith	84T	23	$.01	$.06	Morgan, Joe	85T	352	$.05	$.25
Moreland, Keith	84T	456	$.01	$.06	Morgan, Joe	85TRB	5	$.01	$.10
Moreland, Keith	85T	538	$.01	$.06	Morgan, Mike	80T	671	$.20	$2.00
Moreland, Keith	86T	266	$.01	$.05	Morgan, Mike	83T	203	$.10	$.40

TOPPS

Player	Year	No.	VG	EX/MT	Player	Year	No.	VG	EX/MT
Morgan, Mike	83TTR	78	$ .10	$ .50	Morrison, Jim	80T	522	$ .01	$ .10
Morgan, Mike	84T	423	$ .01	$ .06	Morrison, Jim	81T	323	$ .01	$ .08
Morgan, Mike	86T	152	$ .01	$ .05	Morrison, Jim	82T	654	$ .01	$ .08
Morgan, Mike	87T	546	$ .01	$ .04	Morrison, Jim	82TTR	77	$ .01	$ .10
Morgan, Mike	88T	32	$ .01	$ .04	Morrison, Jim	83T	173	$ .01	$ .08
Morgan, Mike	88TTR	73	$ .01	$ .05	Morrison, Jim	84T	44	$ .01	$ .06
Morgan, Mike	89T	788	$ .01	$ .03	Morrison, Jim	85T	433	$ .01	$ .06
Morgan, Mike	89TTR	84	$ .01	$ .05	Morrison, Jim	86T	553	$ .01	$ .05
Morgan, Mike	90T	367	$ .01	$ .03	Morrison, Jim	87T	237	$ .01	$ .04
Morgan, Mike	91T	631	$ .01	$ .03	Morrison, Jim	88T	751	$ .01	$ .04
Morgan, Mike	91TSC	562	$ .05	$ .25	Morton, Bubba	62T	554	$6.00	$24.00
Morgan, Mike	92T	289	$ .01	$ .03	Morton, Bubba	63T	164	$ .50	$2.00
Morgan, Mike	92TSC	787	$ .01	$ .10	Morton, Bubba	67T	79	$ .40	$1.60
Morgan, Mike	92TTR	76	$ .01	$ .05	Morton, Bubba	68T	216	$ .35	$1.40
Morgan, Mike	93T	373	$ .01	$ .03	Morton, Bubba	69T	342	$ .30	$1.20
Morgan, Mike	93TSC	285	$ .01	$ .10	Morton, Carl	69T	646	$ .40	$1.60
Morgan, Tom	52T	331	$43.75	$175.00	Morton, Carl	70T	109	$ .20	$ .80
Morgan, Tom	53T	132	$6.25	$25.00	Morton, Carl	71T	515	$ .50	$2.00
Morgan, Tom	57T	239	$2.00	$8.00	Morton, Carl	72T	134	$ .10	$ .40
Morgan, Tom	58T	365	$1.00	$4.00	Morton, Carl	73T	331	$ .10	$ .40
Morgan, Tom	59T	545	$4.00	$16.00	Morton, Carl	74T	244	$ .10	$ .40
Morgan, Tom	60T	33	$ .85	$3.40	Morton, Carl	75T	237	$ .10	$ .40
Morgan, Tom	61T	272	$ .60	$2.40	Morton, Carl	76T	328	$ .05	$ .25
Morgan, Tom	62T	11	$ .60	$2.40	Morton, Craig	77T	24	$ .05	$ .20
Morgan, Tom	63T	421	$1.00	$4.00	Morton, Kevin	92T	724	$ .01	$ .03
Morgan, Tom	73T	421	$ .25	$1.00	Morton, Kevin	92TSC	115	$ .01	$ .10
Morgan, Tom	74T	276	$ .10	$ .40	Moryn, Milt	59T	147	$3.00	$12.00
Morgan, Tom	91TA53	132	$ .01	$ .15	Moryn, Walt	57T	16	$2.00	$8.00
Morgan, Vern	73T	49	$ .20	$ .80	Moryn, Walt	58T	122	$1.25	$5.00
Morgan, Vern	74T	447	$ .10	$ .40	Moryn, Walt	59T	488	$1.00	$4.00
Morhardt, Moe	62T	309	$ .75	$3.00	Moryn, Walt	60T	74	$ .85	$3.40
Morlan, John	75T	651	$ .10	$ .40	Moryn, Walt	61T	91	$ .60	$2.40
Morman, Russ	87T	233	$ .01	$ .04	Moschitto, Ross	65T	566	$2.50	$10.00
Morogiello, Dan	84T	682	$ .01	$ .06	Moseby, Lloyd	81T	643	$ .05	$ .25
Morris, Danny	69T	99	$4.50	$18.00	Moseby, Lloyd	82T	223	$ .05	$ .20
Morris, Hal	90T	236	$ .05	$ .20	Moseby, Lloyd	83T	452	$ .01	$ .15
Morris, Hal	90TTR	76	$ .05	$ .20	Moseby, Lloyd	84T	92	$ .01	$ .10
Morris, Hal	91T	642	$ .01	$ .15	Moseby, Lloyd	84T	606	$ .01	$ .06
Morris, Hal	91TSC	339	$ .10	$ .40	Moseby, Lloyd	84TAS	403	$ .01	$ .06
Morris, Hal	92T	773	$ .01	$ .03	Moseby, Lloyd	85T	545	$ .01	$ .10
Morris, Hal	92TSC	63	$ .05	$ .35	Moseby, Lloyd	86T	360	$ .01	$ .05
Morris, Hal	93T	546	$ .01	$ .03	Moseby, Lloyd	87T	210	$ .01	$ .04
Morris, Jack	78T	703	$3.50	$14.00	Moseby, Lloyd	88T	565	$ .01	$ .04
Morris, Jack	79T	251	$1.75	$7.00	Moseby, Lloyd	89T	113	$ .01	$ .03
Morris, Jack	80T	371	$1.00	$4.00	Moseby, Lloyd	90T	779	$ .01	$ .03
Morris, Jack	81T	572	$ .75	$3.00	Moseby, Lloyd	90TTR	77	$ .01	$ .05
Morris, Jack	82T	165	$ .01	$ .15	Moseby, Lloyd	91T	632	$ .01	$ .03
Morris, Jack	82T	450	$ .20	$2.00	Moseby, Lloyd	91TSC	364	$ .05	$ .25
Morris, Jack	82TAS	556	$ .10	$ .50	Moses, Gerry	65T	573	$6.00	$24.00
Morris, Jack	83T	65	$ .10	$ .75	Moses, Gerry	69T	476	$ .50	$2.00
Morris, Jack	84T	136	$ .05	$ .25	Moses, Gerry	70T	104	$ .20	$ .80
Morris, Jack	84T	195	$ .10	$ .75	Moses, Gerry	71T	205	$ .25	$1.00
Morris, Jack	84T	666	$ .05	$ .20	Moses, Gerry	72T	356	$ .10	$ .40
Morris, Jack	85T	610	$ .05	$ .35	Moses, Gerry	73T	431	$ .25	$1.00
Morris, Jack	86T	270	$ .05	$ .35	Moses, Gerry	74T	19	$ .10	$ .40
Morris, Jack	87T	778	$ .05	$ .20	Moses, Jerry	75T	271	$ .10	$ .40
Morris, Jack	88T	340	$ .01	$ .10	Moses, John	84T	517	$ .01	$ .06
Morris, Jack	89T	645	$ .01	$ .10	Moses, John	87T	284	$ .01	$ .04
Morris, Jack	90T	555	$ .01	$ .10	Moses, John	88T	712	$ .01	$ .04
Morris, Jack	91T	75	$ .01	$ .10	Moses, John	89T	72	$ .01	$ .03
Morris, Jack	91TSC	447	$ .10	$ .40	Moses, John	90T	653	$ .01	$ .03
Morris, Jack	91TTR	82	$ .01	$ .10	Moses, John	91T	341	$ .01	$ .03
Morris, Jack	92T	235	$ .01	$ .10	Moses, Wally	60T	459	$1.25	$5.00
Morris, Jack	92TSC	640	$ .01	$ .10	Moskau, Paul	78T	126	$ .04	$ .16
Morris, Jack	92TTR	77	$ .01	$ .05	Moskau, Paul	79T	377	$ .03	$ .12
Morris, Jack	93T	185	$ .01	$ .03	Moskau, Paul	80T	258	$ .01	$ .10
Morris, John	87T	211	$ .01	$ .04	Moskau, Paul	81T	546	$ .01	$ .08
Morris, John	88T	536	$ .01	$ .04	Moskau, Paul	82T	97	$ .01	$ .08
Morris, John	89T	578	$ .01	$ .03	Moss, Les	52T	143	$7.00	$28.00
Morris, John	90T	383	$ .01	$ .03	Moss, Les	57T	213	$2.00	$8.00
Morris, John	92TSC	796	$ .01	$ .10	Moss, Les	58T	153	$1.25	$5.00
Morris, Johnny W.	69T	111	$ .35	$1.40	Moss, Les	59T	453	$1.00	$4.00
Morris, John W.	71T	721	$1.10	$4.40	Mossi, Don	55T	85	$3.50	$14.00
Morris, John W.	75T	577	$ .10	$ .40	Mossi, Don	56T	39	$2.00	$8.00
Morrison, Jim	79T	722	$ .50	$2.00	Mossi, Don	57T	8	$2.00	$8.00

TOPPS

Player	Year	No.	VG	EX/MT
Mossi, Don	58T	35	$2.00	$8.00
Mossi, Don	59T	302	$1.00	$4.00
Mossi, Don	60T	418	$ .75	$3.00
Mossi, Don	61T	14	$ .60	$2.40
Mossi, Don	62T	55	$ .60	$2.40
Mossi, Don	62T	105	$ .60	$2.40
Mossi, Don	63T	218	$ .90	$3.60
Mossi, Don	63T	530	$2.25	$9.00
Mossi, Don	64T	335	$ .65	$2.60
Mossi, Don	66T	74	$ .35	$1.40
Mota, Andy	92T	214	$ .01	$ .10
Mota, Andy	92TSC	166	$ .01	$ .15
Mota, Manny	63T	141	$1.50	$6.00
Mota, Manny	64T	246	$ .75	$3.00
Mota, Manny	65T	463	$1.25	$5.00
Mota, Manny	66T	112	$ .50	$2.00
Mota, Manny	67T	66	$ .40	$1.60
Mota, Manny	68T	325	$ .35	$1.40
Mota, Manny	69T	236	$ .35	$1.40
Mota, Manny	70T	157	$ .25	$1.00
Mota, Manny	71T	112	$ .30	$1.20
Mota, Manny	72T	596	$ .35	$1.40
Mota, Manny	73T	412	$ .25	$1.00
Mota, Manny	74T	368	$ .15	$ .60
Mota, Manny	75T	414	$ .10	$ .40
Mota, Manny	76T	548	$ .05	$ .25
Mota, Manny	77T	386	$ .05	$ .20
Mota, Manny	78T	228	$ .04	$ .16
Mota, Manny	79T	644	$ .05	$ .20
Mota, Manny	80T	104	$ .01	$ .10
Mota, Manny	80THL	3	$ .01	$ .10
Motley, Darryl	82T	471	$ .05	$ .20
Motley, Darryl	85T	561	$ .01	$ .06
Motley, Darryl	86T	332	$ .01	$ .05
Motley, Darryl	87T	99	$ .01	$ .04
Mottola, Chad	93T	56	$ .15	$1.50
Motton, Curt	68T	549	$ .70	$2.80
Motton, Curt	69T	37	$ .35	$1.40
Motton, Curt	70T	261	$ .20	$ .80
Motton, Curt	71T	684	$1.10	$4.40
Motton, Curt	72T	393	$ .10	$ .40
Moyer, Jamie	87T	227	$ .01	$ .10
Moyer, Jamie	88T	36	$ .01	$ .04
Moyer, Jamie	89T	717	$ .01	$ .03
Moyer, Jamie	89TTR	85	$ .01	$ .05
Moyer, Jamie	90T	412	$ .01	$ .03
Moyer, Jamie	91T	138	$ .01	$ .03
Moyer, Jamie	91TSC	481	$ .05	$ .25
Moyer, Jim	72T	506	$ .20	$ .80
Mueller, Don	52T	52	$13.75	$55.00
Mueller, Don	54T	42	$3.75	$15.00
Mueller, Don	56T	241	$3.75	$15.00
Mueller, Don	57T	148	$2.00	$8.00
Mueller, Don	58T	253	$1.25	$5.00
Mueller, Don	59T	368	$1.00	$4.00
Mueller, Willie	80T	668	$ .01	$ .10
Muffett, Billy	58T	143	$2.00	$8.00
Muffett, Billy	59T	241	$1.00	$4.00
Muffett, Billy	61T	16	$ .60	$2.40
Muffett, Billy	62T	336	$ .75	$3.00
Muir, Joe	52T	154	$7.00	$28.00
Mulholland, Terry	87T	536	$ .05	$ .25
Mulholland, Terry	89T	41	$ .01	$ .03
Mulholland, Terry	90T	657	$ .01	$ .03
Mulholland, Terry	91T	413	$ .01	$ .03
Mulholland, Terry	91TSC	58	$ .05	$ .25
Mulholland, Terry	92T	719	$ .01	$ .03
Mulholland, Terry	92TSC	98	$ .01	$ .10
Mulholland, Terry	93T	555	$ .01	$ .03
Mulleavy, Greg	60T	463	$1.25	$5.00
Mullin, Pat	52T	275	$12.50	$50.00
Mulliniks, Rance	78T	579	$ .05	$ .20
Mulliniks, Rance	81T	433	$ .01	$ .08
Mulliniks, Rance	82T	104	$ .01	$ .08
Mulliniks, Rance	82TTR	78	$ .01	$ .10
Mulliniks, Rance	83T	277	$ .01	$ .08
Mulliniks, Rance	84T	762	$ .01	$ .06
Mulliniks, Rance	85T	336	$ .01	$ .06
Mulliniks, Rance	86T	74	$ .01	$ .05
Mulliniks, Rance	87T	537	$ .01	$ .04
Mulliniks, Rance	88T	167	$ .01	$ .04
Mulliniks, Rance	89T	618	$ .01	$ .03
Mulliniks, Rance	90T	466	$ .01	$ .03

Player	Year	No.	VG	EX/MT
Mulliniks, Rance	**91T**	**229**	**$ .01**	**$ .03**
Mulliniks, Rance	92T	133	$ .01	$ .03
Mulliniks, Rance	92TSC	202	$ .01	$ .10
Mullins, Fran	81T	112	$ .01	$ .15
Mullins, Fran	85T	283	$ .01	$ .06
Mumphrey, Jerry	77T	136	$ .20	$ .80
Mumphrey, Jerry	78T	452	$ .04	$ .16
Mumphrey, Jerry	79T	32	$ .03	$ .12
Mumphrey, Jerry	80T	378	$ .01	$ .10
Mumphrey, Jerry	81T	556	$ .01	$ .08
Mumphrey, Jerry	81TTR	808	$ .01	$ .15
Mumphrey, Jerry	82T	175	$ .01	$ .08
Mumphrey, Jerry	82T	486	$ .01	$ .15
Mumphrey, Jerry	83T	81	$ .01	$ .08
Mumphrey, Jerry	83T	670	$ .01	$ .08
Mumphrey, Jerry	84T	45	$ .01	$ .06
Mumphrey, Jerry	85T	736	$ .01	$ .06
Mumphrey, Jerry	86T	282	$ .01	$ .05
Mumphrey, Jerry	86TTR	76	$ .01	$ .06
Mumphrey, Jerry	87T	372	$ .01	$ .04
Mumphrey, Jerry	88T	466	$ .01	$ .04
Munger, Red	51Tbb	14	$7.50	$30.00
Munger, George "Red"	52T	115	$7.00	$28.00
Munoz, Mike	92TSC	441	$ .01	$ .10
Munoz, Mike	93T	379	$ .01	$ .03
Munoz, Mike	93TSC	248	$ .01	$ .10
Munoz, Pedro	91TSC	318	$ .10	$1.00
Munoz, Pedro	92T	613	$ .01	$ .10
Munoz, Pedro	92TSC	541	$ .01	$ .10
Munoz, Pedro	93T	119	$ .01	$ .10
Munoz, Pedro	93TSC	117	$ .01	$ .10
Munson, Thurman	70T	189	$25.00	$100.00
Munson, Thurman	71T	5	$10.00	$40.00
Munson, Thurman	72T	441	$5.00	$20.00
Munson, Thurman	72TIA	442	$2.50	$10.00

TOPPS

Player	Year	No.	VG	EX/MT	Player	Year	No.	VG	EX/MT
Munson, Thurman	73T	142	$2.50	$10.00	Murphy, Dwayne	82T	29	$.01	$.08
Munson, Thurman	74T	340	$2.50	$10.00	Murphy, Dwayne	83T	598	$.01	$.08
Munson, Thurman	75T	20	$2.00	$8.00	Murphy, Dwayne	84T	103	$.01	$.06
Munson, Thurman	76T	192	$.50	$2.00	Murphy, Dwayne	85T	231	$.01	$.06
Munson, Thurman	76T	650	$1.75	$7.00	Murphy, Dwayne	86T	8	$.01	$.05
Munson, Thurman	77T	170	$1.25	$5.00	Murphy, Dwayne	87T	743	$.01	$.04
Munson, Thurman	78T	60	$1.00	$4.00	Murphy, Dwayne	88T	424	$.01	$.04
Munson, Thurman	79T	310	$.75	$3.00	Murphy, Dwayne	89T	667	$.01	$.03
Mura, Steve	79T	725	$.03	$.12	Murphy, Rob	87T	82	$.01	$.10
Mura, Steve	80T	491	$.01	$.10	Murphy, Rob	88T	603	$.01	$.04
Mura, Steve	81T	134	$.01	$.08	Murphy, Rob	89T	446	$.01	$.03
Mura, Steve	82T	641	$.01	$.08	Murphy, Rob	89TTR	86	$.01	$.05
Mura, Steve	82TTR	79	$.01	$.10	Murphy, Rob	90T	268	$.01	$.03
Mura, Steve	83T	24	$.01	$.08	Murphy, Rob	91T	542	$.01	$.03
Mura, Steve	86T	281	$.01	$.05	Murphy, Rob	92T	706	$.01	$.03
Murakami, Masanori	65T	282	$1.25	$5.00	Murphy, Rob	92TSC	663	$.01	$.10
Murcer, Bobby	66T	469	$6.00	$24.00	Murphy, Rob	93TSC	250	$.01	$.10
Murcer, Bobby	67T	93	$.75	$3.00	Murphy, Tom	69T	474	$.30	$1.20
Murcer, Bobby	69T	657	$1.00	$4.00	Murphy, Tom	70T	351	$.35	$1.40
Murcer, Bobby	70T	333	$.35	$1.40	Murphy, Tom	71T	401	$.50	$2.00
Murcer, Bobby	71T	635	$1.25	$5.00	Murphy, Tom	72T	354	$.10	$.40
Murcer, Bobby	72T	86	$.50	$2.00	Murphy, Tom	73T	539	$.60	$2.40
Murcer, Bobby	72T	699	$3.50	$14.00	Murphy, Tom	74T	496	$.10	$.40
Murcer, Bobby	72TIA	700	$1.75	$7.00	Murphy, Tom	74TTR	496	$.10	$.40
Murcer, Bobby	73T	240	$.25	$1.00	Murphy, Tom	75T	28	$.10	$.40
Murcer, Bobby	73T	343	$.10	$.40	Murphy, Tom	76T	219	$.05	$.25
Murcer, Bobby	74T	90	$.15	$.60	Murphy, Tom	77T	396	$.05	$.20
Murcer, Bobby	74TAS	336	$.75	$3.00	Murphy, Tom	78T	103	$.04	$.16
Murcer, Bobby	75T	350	$.20	$.80	Murphy, Tom	79T	588	$.03	$.12
Murcer, Bobby	76T	470	$.15	$.60	Murray, Calvin	92TTR	78	$.10	$1.00
Murcer, Bobby	77T	40	$.10	$.40	Murray, Dale	75T	568	$.10	$.40
Murcer, Bobby	78T	590	$.05	$.20	Murray, Dale	76T	18	$.05	$.25
Murcer, Bobby	79T	135	$.05	$.20	Murray, Dale	77T	252	$.05	$.20
Murcer, Bobby	80T	365	$.01	$.10	Murray, Dale	78T	149	$.04	$.16
Murcer, Bobby	81T	602	$.01	$.08	Murray, Dale	79T	379	$.03	$.12
Murcer, Bobby	82T	208	$.01	$.08	Murray, Dale	80T	559	$.01	$.10
Murcer, Bobby	83T	782	$.01	$.08	Murray, Dale	83T	42	$.01	$.08
Murcer, Bobby	83T	783	$.01	$.08	Murray, Dale	83TTR	79	$.01	$.10
Murff, Red	57T	321	$5.00	$20.00	Murray, Dale	84T	697	$.01	$.06
Murphy, Bill	66T	574	$3.75	$15.00	Murray, Dale	85T	481	$.01	$.06
Murphy, Dale	77T	476	$7.50	$30.00	Murray, Eddie	78T	36	$17.50	$70.00
Murphy, Dale	78T	708	$3.75	$15.00	Murray, Eddie	79T	640	$6.00	$24.00
Murphy, Dale	79T	39	$1.75	$7.00	Murray, Eddie	80T	160	$3.00	$12.00
Murphy, Dale	80T	274	$1.00	$4.00	Murray, Eddie	81T	490	$1.00	$4.00
Murphy, Dale	81T	504	$.15	$1.50	Murray, Eddie	82T	162	$.10	$.50
Murphy, Dale	82T	668	$.15	$1.25	Murray, Eddie	82T	163	$.10	$.50
Murphy, Dale	83T	502	$.05	$.25	Murray, Eddie	82T	390	$.75	$3.00
Murphy, Dale	83T	703	$.01	$.08	Murray, Eddie	82T	426	$.05	$.25
Murphy, Dale	83T	760	$.10	$1.00	Murray, Eddie	83T	21	$.05	$.25
Murphy, Dale	83TAS	401	$.05	$.35	Murray, Eddie	83T	530	$.20	$2.00
Murphy, Dale	84T	126	$.01	$.15	Murray, Eddie	84T	240	$.15	$1.25
Murphy, Dale	84T	133	$.05	$.20	Murray, Eddie	84TAS	397	$.05	$.25
Murphy, Dale	84T	150	$.10	$.75	Murray, Eddie	85T	700	$.10	$.75
Murphy, Dale	84TAS	391	$.05	$.30	Murray, Eddie	85TAS	701	$.05	$.30
Murphy, Dale	85T	320	$.05	$.25	Murray, Eddie	86T	30	$.10	$.50
Murphy, Dale	85TAS	716	$.05	$.25	Murray, Eddie	87T	120	$.05	$.30
Murphy, Dale	86T	600	$.01	$.15	Murray, Eddie	88T	495	$.05	$.20
Murphy, Dale	86TAS	705	$.01	$.15	Murray, Eddie	88TRB	4	$.01	$.10
Murphy, Dale	87T	490	$.05	$.20	Murray, Eddie	89T	625	$.01	$.15
Murphy, Dale	88T	90	$.01	$.10	Murray, Eddie	89TTR	87	$.01	$.15
Murphy, Dale	89T	210	$.01	$.10	Murray, Eddie	90T	305	$.01	$.10
Murphy, Dale	90T	750	$.01	$.10	Murray, Eddie	91T	590	$.01	$.10
Murphy, Dale	91T	545	$.01	$.10	Murray, Eddie	91TAS	397	$.01	$.10
Murphy, Dale	91TSC	243	$.10	$.50	Murray, Eddie	91TSC	177	$.10	$.75
Murphy, Dale	92T	680	$.01	$.03	Murray, Eddie	92T	780	$.01	$.10
Murphy, Dale	92TSC	280	$.05	$.20	Murray, Eddie	92TSC	795	$.05	$.20
Murphy, Dale	93T	445	$.01	$.03	Murray, Eddie	92TTR	79	$.01	$.10
Murphy, Dan	90T	649	$.01	$.10	Murray, Eddie	93T	430	$.01	$.10
Murphy, Danny	61T	214	$.60	$2.40	Murray, Eddie	93TSC	50	$.05	$.25
Murphy, Danny	62T	119	$.60	$2.40	Murray, Larry	80T	284	$.01	$.10
Murphy, Danny	63T	272	$.90	$3.60	Murray, Ray	52T	299	$13.75	$55.00
Murphy, Danny	70T	146	$.20	$.80	Murray, Ray	53T	234	$11.25	$45.00
Murphy, Dwayne	79T	711	$.10	$.40	Murray, Ray	54T	49	$3.75	$15.00
Murphy, Dwayne	80T	461	$.01	$.10	Murray, Ray	91TA53	234	$.01	$.15
Murphy, Dwayne	81T	341	$.01	$.08	Murray, Rich	81T	195	$.01	$.08

TOPPS

Player	Year	No.	VG	EX/MT
Murrell, Ivan	68T	569	$ .70	$2.80
Murrell, Ivan	69T	333	$ .30	$1.20
Murrell, Ivan	70T	179	$ .20	$ .80
Murrell, Ivan	71T	569	$1.00	$4.00
Murrell, Ivan	72T	677	$1.25	$5.00
Murrell, Ivan	73T	409	$ .25	$1.00
Murrell, Ivan	74T	628	$ .10	$ .40
Murtaugh, Danny	59T	17	$1.50	$6.00
Murtaugh, Danny	60T	223	$1.00	$4.00
Murtaugh, Danny	61T	138	$1.00	$4.00
Murtaugh, Danny	61TAS	567	$8.00	$32.00
Murtaugh, Danny	62T	503	$1.50	$6.00
Murtaugh, Danny	63T	559	$2.25	$9.00
Murtaugh, Danny	64T	141	$ .50	$2.00
Murtaugh, Danny	64T	268	$ .65	$2.60
Murtaugh, Danny	70T	532	$ .35	$1.40
Murtaugh, Danny	71T	437	$ .50	$2.00
Murtaugh, Danny	74T	489	$ .10	$ .40
Muser, Tony	73T	238	$ .10	$ .40
Muser, Tony	74T	286	$ .10	$ .40
Muser, Tony	75T	348	$ .10	$ .40
Muser, Tony	76T	537	$ .05	$ .25
Muser, Tony	77T	251	$ .05	$ .20
Muser, Tony	78T	418	$ .05	$ .20
Musial, Stan	58TAS	476	$9.00	$36.00
Musial, Stan	59T	150	$40.00	$160.00
Musial, Stan	59T	470	$5.00	$20.00
Musial, Stan	60T	250	$27.50	$110.00
Musial, Stan	61T	290	$25.00	$100.00
Musial, Stan	62T	50	$27.50	$110.00
Musial, Stan	62T	317	$4.50	$18.00
Musial, Stan	63T	1	$8.00	$32.00
Musial, Stan	63T	138	$8.75	$35.00
Musial, Stan	63T	250	$30.00	$120.00

Player	Year	No.	VG	EX/MT
Musial, Stan	88TTB	665	$ .01	$ .15
Musselman, Jeff	87TTR	83	$ .01	$ .05
Musselman, Jeff	88T	229	$ .01	$ .04
Musselman, Jeff	89T	591	$ .01	$ .03
Musselman, Jeff	90T	382	$ .01	$ .03
Mussina, Mike	92T	242	$ .10	$ .50
Mussina, Mike	92TSC	225	$ .20	$2.00
Mussina, Mike	93T	710	$ .05	$ .25
Mussina, Mike	93TSC	77	$ .10	$1.00
Myatt, George	60T	464	$1.25	$5.00
Myers, Greg	90T	438	$ .01	$ .03
Myers, Greg	91T	599	$ .01	$ .03
Myers, Greg	91TSC	289	$ .05	$ .25
Myers, Greg	92T	203	$ .01	$ .03
Myers, Greg	92TSC	468	$ .01	$ .10
Myers, Greg	93T	637	$ .01	$ .03
Myers, Randy	87T	213	$ .05	$ .20
Myers, Randy	88T	412	$ .01	$ .04
Myers, Randy	89T	610	$ .01	$ .03
Myers, Randy	90T	105	$ .01	$ .03
Myers, Randy	90TTR	78	$ .01	$ .05
Myers, Randy	91T	780	$ .01	$ .03
Myers, Randy	91TSC	275	$ .05	$ .25
Myers, Randy	92T	24	$ .01	$ .03
Myers, Randy	92TSC	805	$ .01	$ .10
Myers, Randy	92TTR	80	$ .01	$ .05
Myers, Randy	93T	302	$ .01	$ .03
Myers, Randy	93TSC	44	$ .01	$ .10
Myrick, Bob	77T	627	$ .05	$ .20
Myrick, Bob	78T	676	$ .04	$ .16
Nabholz, Chris	91T	197	$ .01	$ .15
Nabholz, Chris	91TSC	326	$ .05	$ .35
Nabholz, Chris	92T	32	$ .01	$ .03
Nabholz, Chris	93T	278	$ .01	$ .03
Naehring, Tim	90TTR	79	$ .05	$ .20
Naehring, Tim	91T	702	$ .01	$ .10
Naehring, Tim	91TSC	83	$ .05	$ .35
Naehring, Tim	92T	758	$ .01	$ .03
Naehring, Tim	92TSC	854	$ .01	$ .10
Naehring, Tim	93T	24	$ .01	$ .03
Nagelson, Russ	70T	7	$ .20	$ .80
Nagelson, Russ	71T	708	$1.50	$6.00
Nagy, Charles	88TTR	74	$ .75	$3.00
Nagy, Charles	91T	466	$ .05	$ .35
Nagy, Charles	91TSC	472	$ .20	$2.00
Nagy, Charles	92T	299	$ .01	$ .15
Nagy, Charles	92TSC	389	$ .05	$ .25
Nagy, Charles	93T	730	$ .01	$ .03
Nagy, Mike	70T	39	$ .20	$ .80
Nagy, Mike	71T	363	$ .25	$1.00
Nagy, Mike	72T	488	$ .25	$1.00
Nahorodny, Bill	78T	702	$ .04	$ .16
Nahorodny, Bill	79T	169	$ .03	$ .12
Nahorodny, Bill	80T	552	$ .01	$ .10
Nahorodny, Bill	81T	296	$ .01	$ .08
Nahorodny, Bill	83T	616	$ .01	$ .08
Napoleon, Dan	65T	533	$8.00	$32.00
Napoleon, Dan	66T	87	$ .35	$1.40
Naragon, Hal	56T	311	$2.50	$10.00
Naragon, Hal	57T	347	$5.00	$20.00
Naragon, Hal	58T	22	$2.00	$8.00
Naragon, Hal	59T	376	$1.00	$4.00
Naragon, Hal	60T	231	$ .75	$3.00
Naragon, Hal	61T	92	$ .60	$2.40
Naragon, Hal	62T	164	$1.25	$5.00
Narleski, Ray	55T	160	$5.50	$22.00
Narleski, Ray	56T	133	$2.50	$10.00
Narleski, Ray	57T	144	$2.00	$8.00
Narleski, Ray	58T	439	$1.00	$4.00
Narleski, Ray	59T	442	$1.00	$4.00
Narleski, Ray	60T	161	$ .75	$3.00
Narron, Jerry	80T	16	$ .01	$ .10
Narron, Jerry	81T	637	$ .01	$ .08
Narron, Jerry	82T	719	$ .01	$ .08
Narron, Jerry	85T	234	$ .01	$ .06
Narron, Jerry	86T	543	$ .01	$ .05
Narron, Jerry	87T	474	$ .01	$ .04
Narron, Sam	60T	467	$1.25	$5.00
Narum, Les	64T	418	$1.00	$4.00
Narum, Les	65T	86	$ .35	$1.40
Narum, Les "Buster"	66T	274	$ .50	$2.00
Nash, Cotton	71T	391	$ .25	$1.00
Nash, Jim	67T	90	$ .40	$1.60
Nash, Jim	68T	324	$ .35	$1.40

TOPPS

Player	Year	No.	VG	EX/MT	Player	Year	No.	VG	EX/MT
Nash, Jim	69T	546	$ .40	$1.60	Nelson, Mel	69T	181	$ .35	$1.40
Nash, Jim	70T	171	$ .20	$ .80	Nelson, Ricky	84T	672	$ .01	$ .06
Nash, Jim	71T	306	$ .25	$1.00	Nelson, Ricky	85T	296	$ .01	$ .06
Nash, Jim	72T	401	$ .25	$1.00	Nelson, "Rocky" Glenn	52T	390	$43.75	$175.00
Nash, Jim	73T	509	$ .25	$1.00	Nelson, Rocky	54T	199	$3.75	$15.00
Nastu, Phil	80T	686	$ .01	$ .10	Nelson, Rocky	59T	446	$1.00	$4.00
Navarro, Jaime	91T	548	$ .01	$ .03	Nelson, Rocky	60T	157	$ .75	$3.00
Navarro, Jaime	91TSC	436	$ .10	$ .50	Nelson, Rocky	61T	304	$ .60	$2.40
Navarro, Jaime	92T	222	$ .01	$ .03	Nelson, Roger	68T	549	$ .70	$2.80
Navarro, Jaime	92TSC	87	$ .01	$ .10	Nelson, Roger	69T	279	$ .50	$2.00
Navarro, Jaime	93T	369	$ .01	$ .03	Nelson, Roger	70T	633	$ .50	$2.00
Navarro, Julio	60T	140	$1.25	$5.00	Nelson, Roger	71T	581	$1.00	$4.00
Navarro, Julio	63T	169	$8.00	$32.00	Nelson, Roger	73T	251	$ .10	$ .40
Navarro, Julio	64T	489	$1.00	$4.00	Nelson, Roger	74T	491	$ .10	$ .40
Navarro, Julio	65T	563	$1.40	$5.60	Nelson, Roger	75T	572	$ .10	$ .40
Navarro, Julio	66T	527	$3.75	$15.00	Nen, Dick	64T	14	$ .50	$2.00
Neagle, Denny	92T	592	$ .01	$ .15	Nen, Dick	65T	466	$1.25	$5.00
Neagle, Denny	92TSC	724	$ .01	$ .15	Nen, Dick	66T	149	$ .50	$2.00
Neagle, Denny	92TTR	81	$ .01	$ .05	Nen, Dick	67T	403	$ .60	$2.40
Neagle, Denny	93T	244	$ .01	$ .03	Nen, Dick	68T	591	$ .70	$2.80
Neagle, Denny	93TSC	241	$ .01	$ .10	Nettles, Graig	69T	99	$4.50	$18.00
Neal, Charley	56T	299	$7.00	$28.00	Nettles, Graig	70T	491	$1.25	$5.00
Neal, Charley	57T	242	$2.00	$8.00	Nettles, Graig	71T	324	$ .75	$3.00
Neal, Charley	58T	16	$2.00	$8.00	Nettles, Graig	72T	590	$1.00	$4.00
Neal, Charlie	59T	427	$1.00	$4.00	Nettles, Graig	73T	498	$ .50	$2.00
Neal, Charlie	60T	155	$ .75	$3.00	Nettles, Graig	74T	251	$ .50	$2.00
Neal, Charlie	60TAS	556	$3.50	$14.00	Nettles, Graig	75T	160	$ .30	$1.20
Neal, Charlie	61T	423	$1.00	$4.00	Nettles, Graig	76T	169	$ .25	$1.00
Neal, Charley	62T	365	$1.25	$5.00	Nettles, Graig	77T	2	$ .25	$1.00
Neal, Charlie	63T	511	$1.75	$7.00	Nettles, Graig	77T	20	$ .25	$1.00
Neal, Charlie	64T	436	$1.00	$4.00	Nettles, Graig	78T	250	$ .04	$ .16
Neel, Troy	93T	807	$ .01	$ .15	Nettles, Graig	79T	460	$ .20	$ .80
Neeman, Cal	57T	353	$1.75	$7.00	Nettles, Graig	80T	710	$ .05	$ .20
Neeman, Cal	58T	33	$2.00	$8.00	Nettles, Graig	81T	365	$ .01	$ .15
Neeman, Cal	59T	367	$1.00	$4.00	Nettles, Graig	82T	505	$ .05	$ .20
Neeman, Cal	60T	337	$ .75	$3.00	Nettles, Graig	82TSA	506	$ .01	$ .10
Negray, Ron	56T	7	$2.00	$8.00	Nettles, Graig	83T	635	$ .01	$ .08
Negray, Ron	57T	254	$2.00	$8.00	Nettles, Graig	83T	636	$ .01	$ .08
Neibauer, Gary	69T	611	$ .75	$3.00	Nettles, Graig	84T	175	$ .01	$ .15
Neibauer, Gary	70T	384	$ .35	$1.40	Nettles, Graig	84T	712	$ .01	$ .15
Neibauer, Gary	71T	668	$1.10	$4.40	Nettles, Graig	84T	713	$ .01	$ .15
Neibauer, Gary	72T	149	$ .10	$ .40	Nettles, Graig	84TTR	83	$ .10	$ .85
Neidlinger, Jim	91T	39	$ .01	$ .15	Nettles, Graig	85T	35	$ .01	$ .10
Neiger, Al	61T	202	$ .60	$2.40	Nettles, Graig	86T	450	$ .01	$ .05
Nelson, Bob	56T	169	$2.50	$10.00	Nettles, Graig	87T	205	$ .01	$ .04
Nelson, Dave	69T	579	$ .50	$2.00	Nettles, Graig	87TTR	85	$ .05	$ .20
Nelson, Dave	70T	112	$ .20	$ .80	Nettles, Graig	88T	574	$ .01	$ .04
Nelson, Dave	71T	241	$ .25	$1.00	Nettles, Jim	71T	74	$ .25	$1.00
Nelson, Dave	72T	529	$ .40	$1.60	Nettles, Jim	72T	131	$ .10	$ .40
Nelson, Dave	73T	111	$ .10	$ .40	Nettles, Jim	73T	358	$ .10	$ .40
Nelson, Dave	74T	355	$ .10	$ .40	Nettles, Jim	75T	497	$ .10	$ .40
Nelson, Dave	75T	435	$ .10	$ .40	Nettles, Morris	75T	632	$ .10	$ .40
Nelson, Dave	76T	535	$ .05	$ .25	Nettles, Morris	76T	434	$ .05	$ .25
Nelson, Gene	81TTR	809	$ .01	$ .15	Neville, Dan	65T	398	$1.00	$4.00
Nelson, Gene	82T	373	$ .01	$ .08	Nevin, Phil	91TTR	83	$ .20	$2.00
Nelson, Gene	82TTR	80	$ .01	$ .10	Nevin, Phil	92TTR	82	$ .10	$1.00
Nelson, Gene	83T	106	$ .01	$ .08	Newcombe, Don	56T	235	$13.75	$55.00
Nelson, Gene	85TTR	86	$ .01	$ .10	Newcombe, Don	57T	130	$3.50	$14.00
Nelson, Gene	86T	493	$ .01	$ .05	Newcombe, Don	58T	340	$2.50	$10.00
Nelson, Gene	87T	273	$ .01	$ .04	Newcombe, Don	59T	312	$1.50	$6.00
Nelson, Gene	87TTR	84	$ .01	$ .05	Newcombe, Don	60T	345	$1.25	$5.00
Nelson, Gene	88T	621	$ .01	$ .04	Newcombe, Don	61TMVP	483	$1.35	$5.40
Nelson, Gene	89T	581	$ .01	$ .03	Newcombe, Don	75T	194	$1.50	$6.00
Nelson, Gene	90T	726	$ .01	$ .03	Newcombe, Don	91TA53	320	$ .10	$ .50
Nelson, Gene	91T	316	$ .01	$ .03	Newfield, Marc	91T	529	$ .10	$ .40
Nelson, Gene	91TSC	359	$ .05	$ .25	Newhauser, Don	74T	33	$ .10	$ .40
Nelson, Gene	92T	62	$ .01	$ .03	Newhouser, Hal	53T	228	$35.00	$140.00
Nelson, Gene	92TSC	414	$ .01	$ .10	Newhouser, Hal	55T	24	$4.50	$18.00
Nelson, Jamie	84T	166	$ .01	$ .06	Newhouser, Hal	91TA53	228	$ .10	$1.00
Nelson, Jeff	93T	493	$ .01	$ .03	Newman, Al	87T	323	$ .01	$ .04
Nelson, Jim	71T	298	$ .25	$1.00	Newman, Al	87TTR	86	$ .01	$ .05
Nelson, Mel	63T	522	$1.75	$7.00	Newman, Al	88T	648	$ .01	$ .04
Nelson, Mel	64T	273	$ .65	$2.60	Newman, Al	89T	503	$ .01	$ .03
Nelson, Mel	65T	564	$1.40	$5.60	Newman, Al	90T	19	$ .01	$ .03
Nelson, Mel	66T	367	$ .50	$2.00	Newman, Al	91T	748	$ .01	$ .03

TOPPS

Player	Year	No.	VG	EX/MT
Newman, Al	91TSC	146	$ .05	$ .25
Newman, Al	92T	146	$ .01	$ .03
Newman, Al	92TSC	821	$ .01	$ .10
Newman, Fred	63T	496	$3.00	$12.00
Newman, Fred	64T	569	$2.25	$9.00
Newman, Fred	65T	101	$ .35	$1.40
Newman, Fred	66T	213	$ .50	$2.00
Newman, Fred	67T	451	$ .60	$2.40
Newman, Fred	69T	543	$ .40	$1.60

Player	Year	No.	VG	EX/MT
Newman, Jeff	77T	204	$ .05	$ .20
Newman, Jeff	78T	458	$ .04	$ .16
Newman, Jeff	79T	604	$ .03	$ .12
Newman, Jeff	80T	34	$ .01	$ .10
Newman, Jeff	81T	587	$ .01	$ .08
Newman, Jeff	82T	187	$ .01	$ .08
Newman, Jeff	83T	784	$ .01	$ .08
Newman, Jeff	83TTR	80	$ .01	$ .10
Newman, Jeff	84T	296	$ .01	$ .06
Newman, Jeff	85T	376	$ .01	$ .06
Newman, Ray	72T	667	$1.25	$5.00
Newman, Ray	73T	568	$ .60	$2.40
Newsom, Bobo	53T	15	$5.00	$20.00
Newsom, Bobo	91TA53	15	$ .01	$ .15
Newson, Warren	92T	355	$ .01	$ .03
Newson, Warren	92TSC	512	$ .01	$ .10
Niarhos, Gus	52T	121	$7.00	$28.00
Niarhos, Gus	53T	63	$4.00	$16.00
Niarhos, Gus	91TA53	63	$ .01	$ .15
Nichols, Carl	91T	119	$ .01	$ .03
Nichols, Carl	91TSC	440	$ .05	$ .25
Nichols, Chet	52T	288	$13.75	$55.00
Nichols, Chet	56T	278	$2.50	$10.00
Nichols, Chet	61T	301	$ .60	$2.40
Nichols, Chet	62T	403	$1.25	$5.00
Nichols, Chet	63T	307	$ .90	$3.60
Nichols, Dolan	59T	362	$1.00	$4.00
Nichols, Reid	81T	689	$ .20	$2.00
Nichols, Reid	82T	124	$ .01	$ .08
Nichols, Reid	83T	446	$ .01	$ .08
Nichols, Reid	84T	238	$ .01	$ .06
Nichols, Reid	85T	37	$ .01	$ .06
Nichols, Reid	86T	364	$ .01	$ .05
Nichols, Reid	87T	539	$ .01	$ .04
Nichols, Reid	87TTR	87	$ .01	$ .05
Nichols, Reid	88T	748	$ .01	$ .04
Nichols, Rod	89T	443	$ .01	$ .03
Nichols, Rod	90T	108	$ .01	$ .03
Nichols, Rod	92T	586	$ .01	$ .03
Nichols, Rod	92TSC	534	$ .01	$ .10
Nichols, Rod	93T	372	$ .01	$ .03
Nicholson, Bill	52T	185	$7.00	$28.00
Nicholson, Dave	61T	182	$ .60	$2.40
Nicholson, Dave	62T	577	$6.00	$24.00
Nicholson, Dave	63T	234	$ .90	$3.60
Nicholson, Dave	64T	31	$ .50	$2.00
Nicholson, Dave	65T	183	$ .35	$1.40
Nicholson, Dave	66T	576	$7.00	$28.00
Nicholson, Dave	67T	113	$ .40	$1.60
Nicholson, Dave	69T	298	$ .50	$2.00
Nicosia, Steve	80T	519	$ .01	$ .10
Nicosia, Steve	81T	212	$ .01	$ .08
Nicosia, Steve	82T	652	$ .01	$ .08
Nicosia, Steve	83T	462	$ .01	$ .08
Nicosia, Steve	84T	98	$ .01	$ .06
Nicosia, Steve	85T	191	$ .01	$ .06
Nicosia, Steve	85TTR	87	$ .01	$ .10
Nied, David	93T	444	$ .15	$1.50
Niedenfuer, Tom	83T	477	$ .01	$ .08
Niedenfuer, Tom	84T	112	$ .01	$ .06
Niedenfuer, Tom	85T	782	$ .01	$ .06
Niedenfuer, Tom	86T	56	$ .01	$ .05
Niedenfuer, Tom	87T	538	$ .01	$ .04
Niedenfuer, Tom	87TTR	88	$ .01	$ .05
Niedenfuer, Tom	88T	242	$ .01	$ .04
Niedenfuer, Tom	89T	651	$ .01	$ .03
Niedenfuer, Tom	90T	306	$ .01	$ .03
Niekro, Joe	67T	536	$9.00	$36.00
Niekro, Joe	68T	475	$1.00	$4.00
Niekro, Joe	69T	43	$ .50	$2.00
Niekro, Joe	70T	508	$ .50	$2.00
Niekro, Joe	71T	695	$1.50	$6.00
Niekro, Joe	72T	216	$ .20	$ .80
Niekro, Joe	73T	585	$ .60	$2.40
Niekro, Joe	74T	504	$ .25	$1.00
Niekro, Joe	75T	595	$ .15	$ .60
Niekro, Joe	76T	273	$ .10	$ .40
Niekro, Joe	77T	116	$ .05	$ .20
Niekro, Joe	78T	306	$ .04	$ .16
Niekro, Joe	79T	68	$ .03	$ .12
Niekro, Joe	80T	205	$ .05	$ .20
Niekro, Joe	80T	437	$ .01	$ .10
Niekro, Joe	81T	722	$ .01	$ .08
Niekro, Joe	82T	611	$ .01	$ .15
Niekro, Joe	83T	221	$ .01	$ .08
Niekro, Joe	83T	441	$ .01	$ .08
Niekro, Joe	84T	586	$ .01	$ .06
Niekro, Joe	85T	295	$ .01	$ .06
Niekro, Joe	86T	135	$ .01	$ .05
Niekro, Joe	87T	344	$ .01	$ .04
Niekro, Joe	87TTR	89	$ .01	$ .10
Niekro, Joe	88T	473	$ .01	$ .04
Niekro, Joe	88TRB	5	$ .01	$ .10
Niekro, Phil	64T	541	$55.00	$220.00
Niekro, Phil	65T	461	$12.50	$50.00
Niekro, Phil	66T	28	$5.00	$20.00
Niekro, Phil	67T	456	$4.00	$16.00
Niekro, Phil	68T	7	$ .55	$2.20
Niekro, Phil	68T	257	$1.75	$7.00
Niekro, Phil	69T	355	$1.75	$7.00
Niekro, Phil	70T	69	$1.50	$6.00
Niekro, Phil	70T	160	$1.00	$4.00
Niekro, Phil	71T	30	$1.00	$4.00
Niekro, Phil	72T	620	$1.50	$6.00
Niekro, Phil	73T	503	$1.00	$4.00
Niekro, Phil	74T	29	$ .75	$3.00
Niekro, Phil	75T	130	$ .75	$3.00
Niekro, Phil	75T	310	$ .25	$1.00
Niekro, Phil	76T	435	$ .50	$2.00

TOPPS

Player	Year	No.	VG	EX/MT
Niekro, Phil	77T	615	$ .50	$2.00
Niekro, Phil	78T	10	$ .40	$1.60
Niekro, Phil	78T	206	$ .50	$2.00
Niekro, Phil	79T	595	$ .35	$1.40
Niekro, Phil	80T	205	$ .05	$ .20
Niekro, Phil	80T	245	$ .10	$1.00
Niekro, Phil	81T	387	$ .10	$ .75
Niekro, Phil	82T	185	$ .10	$ .50
Niekro, Phil	83T	410	$ .10	$ .50
Niekro, Phil	83T	411	$ .05	$ .25
Niekro, Phil	83T	502	$ .05	$ .25
Niekro, Phil	84T	650	$ .05	$ .30
Niekro, Phil	84TTR	84	$ .75	$3.00
Niekro, Phil	85T	40	$ .05	$ .25
Niekro, Phil	86T	790	$ .05	$ .20
Niekro, Phil	86TRB	204	$ .01	$ .10
Niekro, Phil	86TTR	77	$ .05	$ .25
Niekro, Phil	87T	694	$ .01	$ .15
Niekro, Phil	88TRB	5	$ .01	$ .10
Nielsen, Jerry	93T	594	$ .01	$ .03
Nielsen, Scott	87T	57	$ .01	$ .04
Nieman, Bob	56T	267	$2.50	$10.00
Nieman, Bob	57T	14	$2.00	$8.00
Nieman, Bob	58T	165	$1.25	$5.00
Nieman, Bob	59T	375	$1.00	$4.00
Nieman, Bob	60T	149	$ .75	$3.00
Nieman, Bob	61T	178	$ .60	$2.40
Nieman, Bob	62T	182	$ .60	$2.40
Niemann, Randy	80T	469	$ .01	$ .10
Niemann, Randy	81T	148	$ .01	$ .08
Niemann, Randy	83T	329	$ .01	$ .08
Niemann, Randy	86TTR	78	$ .01	$ .06
Niemann, Randy	87T	147	$ .01	$ .04
Nieto, Tom	85T	294	$ .01	$ .06
Nieto, Tom	86T	88	$ .01	$ .05
Nieto, Tom	87T	416	$ .01	$ .04
Nieto, Tom	87TTR	90	$ .01	$ .05
Nieto, Tom	88T	317	$ .01	$ .04
Nieves, Juan	86TTR	79	$ .01	$ .06
Nieves, Juan	87T	79	$ .01	$ .04
Nieves, Juan	88T	515	$ .01	$ .04
Nieves, Juan	89T	287	$ .01	$ .03
Nieves, Juan	90T	467	$ .01	$ .03
Nieves, Melvin	93T	658	$ .05	$ .35
Nieves, Melvin	93TSC	89	$ .10	$1.00
Nilsson, Dave	92T	58	$ .05	$ .25
Nilsson, Dave	92TTR	83	$ .05	$ .20
Nilsson, Dave	93T	316	$ .01	$ .10
Nipper, Al	85T	424	$ .01	$ .10
Nipper, Al	86T	181	$ .01	$ .05
Nipper, Al	87T	617	$ .01	$ .04
Nipper, Al	88T	326	$ .01	$ .04
Nipper, Al	88TTR	75	$ .01	$ .05
Nipper, Al	89T	86	$ .01	$ .03
Nischwitz, Ron	62T	591	$12.50	$50.00
Nischwitz, Ron	63T	152	$ .50	$2.00
Nischwitz, Ron	66T	38	$ .35	$1.40
Nixon, Donell	88T	146	$ .01	$ .04
Nixon, Donell	89T	447	$ .01	$ .03
Nixon, Donell	90T	658	$ .01	$ .03
Nixon, Otis	86TTR	80	$ .10	$ .50
Nixon, Otis	87T	486	$ .05	$ .25
Nixon, Otis	89T	674	$ .01	$ .03
Nixon, Otis	90T	252	$ .01	$ .03
Nixon, Otis	91T	558	$ .01	$ .03
Nixon, Otis	91TSC	174	$ .05	$ .25
Nixon, Otis	91TTR	84	$ .01	$ .10
Nixon, Otis	92T	340	$ .01	$ .03
Nixon, Otis	92TSC	882	$ .01	$ .10
Nixon, Otis	93T	333	$ .01	$ .03
Nixon, Russ	58T	133	$2.00	$8.00
Nixon, Russ	59T	344	$1.00	$4.00
Nixon, Russ	60T	36	$ .85	$3.40
Nixon, Russ	61T	53	$ .60	$2.40
Nixon, Russ	62T	523	$6.00	$24.00
Nixon, Russ	63T	168	$ .50	$2.00
Nixon, Russ	64T	329	$ .65	$2.60
Nixon, Russ	65T	162	$ .35	$1.40
Nixon, Russ	66T	227	$ .50	$2.00
Nixon, Russ	67T	446	$ .60	$2.40
Nixon, Russ	68T	515	$ .75	$3.00
Nixon, Russ	69T	363	$ .30	$1.20
Nixon, Russ	83T	756	$ .01	$ .08
Nixon, Russ	84T	351	$ .01	$ .06
Nixon, Russ	88TTR	76	$ .01	$ .05
Nixon, Russ	89T	564	$ .01	$ .03
Nixon, Russ	90T	171	$ .01	$ .03
Nixon, Willard	52T	269	$12.50	$50.00
Nixon, Willard	53T	30	$6.25	$25.00
Nixon, Willard	56T	122	$2.50	$10.00
Nixon, Willard	57T	189	$2.00	$8.00
Nixon, Willard	58T	395	$1.00	$4.00
Nixon, Willard	59T	361	$1.00	$4.00
Nixon, Willard	91TA53	30	$ .01	$ .15
Noboa, Junior	88T	503	$ .01	$ .04
Noboa, Junior	90TTR	80	$ .01	$ .05

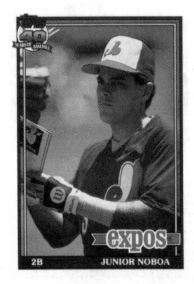

Player	Year	No.	VG	EX/MT
Noboa, Junior	**91T**	**182**	**$ .01**	**$ .03**
Noboa, Junior	92TSC	709	$ .01	$ .10
Noce, Paul	88T	542	$ .01	$ .04
Nokes, Matt	87TTR	91	$ .05	$ .20
Nokes, Matt	88T	645	$ .05	$ .20
Nokes, Matt	88TAS	393	$ .01	$ .10
Nokes, Matt	89T	445	$ .01	$ .03
Nokes, Matt	90T	131	$ .01	$ .06
Nokes, Matt	90TTR	81	$ .01	$ .05
Nokes, Matt	91T	336	$ .01	$ .03
Nokes, Matt	91TSC	64	$ .05	$ .25
Nokes, Matt	92T	748	$ .01	$ .03
Nokes, Matt	92TAS	404	$ .01	$ .03
Nokes, Matt	92TSC	111	$ .01	$ .10
Nokes, Matt	93T	561	$ .01	$ .03
Nokes, Matt	93TSC	189	$ .01	$ .10
Nolan, Gary	68T	196	$ .35	$1.40
Nolan, Gary	69T	581	$ .40	$1.60
Nolan, Gary	70T	484	$ .35	$1.40
Nolan, Gary	71T	75	$ .25	$1.00
Nolan, Gary	72T	475	$ .25	$1.00
Nolan, Gary	73T	260	$ .10	$ .40

TOPPS

Player	Year	No.	VG	EX/MT	Player	Year	No.	VG	EX/MT
Nolan, Gary	74T	277	$ .10	$ .40	Norris, Mike	80T	599	$ .01	$ .10
Nolan, Gary	75T	562	$ .10	$ .40	Norris, Mike	81T	55	$ .01	$ .08
Nolan, Gary	76T	444	$ .05	$ .25	Norris, Mike	82T	370	$ .01	$ .08
Nolan, Gary	77T	121	$ .05	$ .20	Norris, Mike	83T	620	$ .01	$ .08
Nolan, Gary	78T	115	$ .04	$ .16	Norris, Mike	84T	493	$ .01	$ .06
Nolan, Joe	78T	617	$ .04	$ .16	Norris, Mike	85T	246	$ .01	$ .06
Nolan, Joe	79T	464	$ .03	$ .12	North, Bill	73T	234	$ .10	$ .40
Nolan, Joe	80T	64	$ .01	$ .10	North, Bill	74T	345	$ .10	$ .40
Nolan, Joe	81T	149	$ .01	$ .08	North, Bill	75T	121	$ .10	$ .40
Nolan, Joe	82T	327	$ .01	$ .08	North, Bill	75T	309	$ .30	$1.20
Nolan, Joe	82TTR	81	$ .01	$ .10	North, Bill	76T	33	$ .05	$ .25
Nolan, Joe	83T	242	$ .01	$ .08	North, Bill	77T	4	$ .05	$ .20
Nolan, Joe	84T	553	$ .01	$ .06	North, Bill	77T	551	$ .05	$ .20
Nolan, Joe	85T	652	$ .01	$ .06	North, Bill	78T	163	$ .04	$ .16
Nolan, Joe	86T	781	$ .01	$ .05	North, Bill	79T	668	$ .03	$ .12
Nold, Dick	68T	96	$ .35	$1.40	North, Bill	80T	408	$ .01	$ .10
Noles, Dickie	80T	682	$ .01	$ .10	North, Bill	81T	713	$ .01	$ .08
Noles, Dickie	81T	406	$ .01	$ .08	Northey, Ron	52T	204	$7.00	$28.00
Noles, Dickie	82T	530	$ .01	$ .08	Northey, Ron	57T	31	$2.00	$8.00
Noles, Dickie	82TTR	82	$ .01	$ .10	Northey, Scott	70T	241	$ .20	$ .80
Noles, Dickie	83T	99	$ .01	$ .08	Northey, Scott	71T	633	$1.00	$4.00
Noles, Dickie	84T	618	$ .01	$ .06	Northrup, Jim	65T	259	$ .75	$3.00
Noles, Dickie	85T	149	$ .01	$ .06	Northrup, Jim	66T	554	$7.00	$28.00
Noles, Dickie	86T	388	$ .01	$ .05	Northrup, Jim	67T	408	$ .60	$2.40
Noles, Dickie	87T	244	$ .01	$ .04	Northrup, Jim	68T	78	$ .35	$1.40
Noles, Dickie	87TTR	92	$ .01	$ .05	Northrup, Jim	69T	3	$1.00	$4.00
Noles, Dickie	88T	768	$ .01	$ .04	Northrup, Jim	69T	580	$ .40	$1.60
Nolte, Eric	88T	694	$ .01	$ .04	Northrup, Jim	70T	177	$ .20	$ .80
Nordbrook, Tim	76T	252	$ .05	$ .25	Northrup, Jim	71T	265	$ .25	$1.00
Nordbrook, Tim	78T	369	$ .04	$ .16	Northrup, Jim	72T	408	$ .25	$1.00
Nordhagen, Wayne	78T	231	$ .04	$ .16	Northrup, Jim	73T	168	$ .10	$ .40
Nordhagen, Wayne	79T	351	$ .03	$ .12	Northrup, Jim	74T	266	$ .10	$ .40
Nordhagen, Wayne	80T	487	$ .01	$ .10	Northrup, Jim	75T	641	$ .10	$ .40
Nordhagen, Wayne	81T	186	$ .01	$ .08	Norwood, Willie	78T	705	$ .04	$ .16
Nordhagen, Wayne	82T	597	$ .01	$ .08	Norwood, Willie	79T	274	$ .03	$ .12
Nordhagen, Wayne	83T	714	$ .01	$ .08	Norwood, Willie	80T	432	$ .01	$ .10
Noren, Irv	51Tbb	38	$7.50	$30.00	Nossek, Joe	64T	532	$2.50	$10.00
Noren, Irv	52T	40	$13.75	$55.00	Nossek, Joe	65T	597	$1.40	$5.60
Noren, Irv	53T	35	$4.00	$16.00	Nossek, Joe	66T	22	$ .35	$1.40
Noren, Irv	56T	253	$4.50	$18.00	Nossek, Joe	67T	209	$ .50	$2.00
Noren, Irv	57T	298	$5.00	$20.00	Nossek, Joe	69T	143	$ .35	$1.40
Noren, Irv	58T	114	$2.00	$8.00	Nossek, Joe	73T	646	$ .75	$3.00
Noren, Irv	59T	59	$1.50	$6.00	Nossek, Joe	74T	99	$ .10	$ .40
Noren, Irv	60T	433	$ .75	$3.00	Nottebart, Don	60T	351	$ .75	$3.00
Noren, Irv	73T	179	$ .25	$1.00	Nottebart, Don	61T	29	$ .60	$2.40
Noren, Irv	91TA53	35	$ .01	$ .15	Nottebart, Don	62T	541	$6.00	$24.00
Norman, Bill	53T	245	$22.50	$90.00	Nottebart, Don	63T	204	$ .90	$3.60
Norman, Bill	91TA53	245	$ .01	$ .15	Nottebart, Don	64T	434	$1.00	$4.00
Norman, Dan	79T	721	$ .05	$ .20	Nottebart, Don	65T	469	$1.25	$5.00
Norman, Dan	80T	681	$ .75	$3.00	Nottebart, Don	66T	21	$ .35	$1.40
Norman, Dan	83T	237	$ .01	$ .08	Nottebart, Don	67T	269	$ .50	$2.00
Norman, Fred	64T	469	$1.00	$4.00	Nottebart, Don	68T	171	$ .35	$1.40
Norman, Fred	65T	386	$1.00	$4.00	Nottebart, Don	69T	593	$ .40	$1.60
Norman, Fred	70T	427	$ .35	$1.40	Nunez, Clemente	93T	599	$ .01	$ .10
Norman, Fred	71T	348	$ .25	$1.00	Nunez, Ed	85T	34	$ .01	$ .06
Norman, Fred	72T	194	$ .10	$ .40	Nunez, Ed	86T	511	$ .01	$ .05
Norman, Fred	73T	32	$ .10	$ .40	Nunez, Ed	87T	427	$ .01	$ .04
Norman, Fred	74T	581	$ .10	$ .40	Nunez, Ed	88T	258	$ .01	$ .04
Norman, Fred	75T	396	$ .10	$ .40	Nunez, Ed	90T	586	$ .01	$ .03
Norman, Fred	76T	609	$ .05	$ .25	Nunez, Ed	91T	106	$ .01	$ .03
Norman, Fred	77T	139	$ .05	$ .20	Nunez, Ed	91TSC	595	$ .05	$ .25
Norman, Fred	78T	273	$ .04	$ .16	Nunez, Ed	92T	352	$ .01	$ .03
Norman, Fred	79T	47	$ .03	$ .12	Nunez, Ed	92TSC	776	$ .01	$ .10
Norman, Fred	80T	714	$ .01	$ .10	Nunez, Ed	93T	19	$ .01	$ .03
Norman, Fred	81T	497	$ .01	$ .08	Nunez, Jose	88T	28	$ .01	$ .04
Norman, Nelson	80T	518	$ .01	$ .10	Nunn, Howie	59T	549	$4.00	$16.00
Norrid, Tim	79T	705	$ .25	$1.00	Nunn, Howie	61T	346	$ .60	$2.40
Norris, Jim	78T	484	$ .04	$ .16	Nunn, Howie	62T	524	$6.00	$24.00
Norris, Jim	79T	611	$ .03	$ .12	Nuxhall, Joe	52T	406	$62.50	$250.00
Norris, Jim	80T	333	$ .01	$ .10	Nuxhall, Joe	53T	105	$4.50	$18.00
Norris, Jim	81T	264	$ .01	$ .08	Nuxhall, Joe	56T	218	$3.75	$15.00
Norris, Mike	76T	653	$ .10	$ .40	Nuxhall, Joe	57T	103	$2.00	$8.00
Norris, Mike	77T	284	$ .05	$ .20	Nuxhall, Joe	58T	63	$2.00	$8.00
Norris, Mike	78T	434	$ .04	$ .16	Nuxhall, Joe	59T	389	$1.00	$4.00
Norris, Mike	79T	191	$ .03	$ .12	Nuxhall, Joe	60T	282	$1.10	$4.40

TOPPS

Player	Year	No.	VG	EX/MT	Player	Year	No.	VG	EX/MT
Nuxhall, Joe	61T	444	$1.00	$4.00	O'Dell, Billy	55T	57	$2.50	$10.00
Nuxhall, Joe	63T	194	$1.00	$4.00	O'Dell, Billy	57T	316	$5.00	$20.00
Nuxhall, Joe	64T	106	$ .50	$2.00	O'Dell, Billy	58T	84	$2.00	$8.00
Nuxhall, Joe	65T	312	$ .50	$2.00	O'Dell, Billy	59T	250	$1.00	$4.00
Nuxhall, Joe	66T	483	$1.50	$6.00	O'Dell, Billy	60T	303	$ .75	$3.00
Nuxhall, Joe	67T	44	$ .40	$1.60	O'Dell, Billy	61T	96	$ .60	$2.40
Nuxhall, Joe	91TA53	105	$ .01	$ .15	O'Dell, Billy	61T	383	$1.00	$4.00
Nye, Rich	67T	608	$2.25	$9.00	O'Dell, Billy	62T	429	$1.25	$5.00
Nye, Rich	68T	339	$ .35	$1.40	O'Dell, Billy	63T	7	$1.25	$5.00
Nye, Rich	69T	88	$ .35	$1.40	O'Dell, Billy	63T	9	$2.00	$8.00
Nye, Rich	70T	139	$ .20	$ .80	O'Dell, Billy	63T	235	$ .90	$3.60
Nyman, Chris	84T	382	$ .01	$ .06	O'Dell, Billy	64T	18	$ .50	$2.00
Nyman, Gerry	69T	173	$ .35	$1.40	O'Dell, Billy	65T	476	$1.25	$5.00
Nyman, Gerry	70T	644	$1.25	$5.00	O'Dell, Billy	66T	237	$ .50	$2.00
Nyman, Gerry	71T	656	$1.50	$6.00	O'Dell, Billy	67T	162	$ .40	$1.60
Nyman, Nyls	75T	619	$ .10	$ .40	O'Donoghue, John	64T	388	$1.00	$4.00
Nyman, Nyls	76T	258	$ .05	$ .25	O'Donoghue, John	65T	71	$ .35	$1.40
O'Berry, Mike	80T	662	$ .01	$ .10	O'Donoghue, John	66T	501	$1.50	$6.00
O'Berry, Mike	82T	562	$ .01	$ .08	O'Donoghue, John	67T	127	$ .40	$1.60
O'Berry, Mike	84T	184	$ .01	$ .06	O'Donoghue, John	68T	456	$ .35	$1.40
O'Berry, Mike	84TTR	86	$ .01	$ .15	O'Donoghue, John	70T	441	$ .35	$1.40
O'Brien, Bob	72T	198	$1.00	$4.00	O'Donoghue, John	71T	743	$1.50	$6.00
O'Brien, Charlie	88T	566	$ .01	$ .04	O'Malley, Tom	83T	663	$ .01	$ .08
O'Brien, Charlie	89T	214	$ .01	$ .03	O'Malley, Tom	84T	469	$ .01	$ .06
O'Brien, Charlie	90T	106	$ .01	$ .03	O'Malley, Tom	87T	154	$ .01	$ .04
O'Brien, Charlie	91T	442	$ .01	$ .03	O'Malley, Tom	88T	77	$ .01	$ .04
O'Brien, Charlie	91TSC	157	$ .05	$ .25	O'Malley, Tom	90T	504	$ .01	$ .03
O'Brien, Charlie	92T	56	$ .01	$ .03	O'Malley, Tom	91T	257	$ .01	$ .03
O'Brien, Charlie	92TSC	154	$ .01	$ .10	O'Neal, Randy	86T	73	$ .01	$ .05
O'Brien, Charlie	93T	242	$ .01	$ .03	O'Neal, Randy	87T	196	$ .01	$ .04
O'Brien, Charlie	93TSC	128	$ .01	$ .10	O'Neill, Paul	88T	204	$ .05	$ .20
O'Brien, Dan	80T	684	$ .10	$ .75	O'Neill, Paul	89T	604	$ .01	$ .03
O'Brien, Ed	53T	249	$22.50	$90.00	O'Neill, Paul	90T	332	$ .01	$ .10
O'Brien, Eddie	54T	139	$7.00	$28.00	O'Neill, Paul	91T	122	$ .01	$ .03
O'Brien, Eddie	56T	116	$2.50	$10.00	O'Neill, Paul	91TSC	218	$ .05	$ .25
O'Brien, Eddie	57T	259	$2.00	$8.00	O'Neill, Paul	92T	61	$ .01	$ .03
O'Brien, Ed	91TA53	249	$ .01	$ .15	O'Neill, Paul	92TSC	175	$ .01	$ .10
O'Brien, John	53T	223	$11.25	$45.00	O'Neill, Paul	93T	276	$ .01	$ .03
O'Brien, Johnny	54T	139	$7.00	$28.00	O'Neill, Steve	54T	127	$3.75	$15.00
O'Brien, Johnny	55T	135	$2.25	$9.00	O'Neill, Steve	91TA53	307	$ .05	$ .20
O'Brien, Johnny	56T	65	$2.00	$8.00	O'Riley, Don	70T	552	$ .50	$2.00
O'Brien, Johnny	58T	426	$1.00	$4.00	O'Riley, Don	71T	679	$1.10	$4.40
O'Brien, Johnny	59T	499	$1.00	$4.00	O'Toole, Dennis	73T	604	$ .75	$3.00
O'Brien, John	91TA53	223	$ .05	$ .25	O'Toole, Jim	59T	136	$1.00	$4.00
O'Brien, Pete	83TTR	81	$ .10	$ .75	O'Toole, Jim	60T	32	$1.25	$5.00
O'Brien, Pete	84T	534	$ .05	$ .20	O'Toole, Jim	60T	325	$ .75	$3.00
O'Brien, Pete	85T	196	$ .05	$ .20	O'Toole, Jim	61T	328	$ .60	$2.40
O'Brien, Pete	86T	328	$ .01	$ .10	O'Toole, Jim	62T	56	$1.50	$6.00
O'Brien, Pete	87T	17	$ .01	$ .10	O'Toole, Jim	62T	58	$1.50	$6.00
O'Brien, Pete	88T	721	$ .01	$ .06	O'Toole, Jim	62T	60	$2.00	$8.00
O'Brien, Pete	89T	629	$ .01	$ .03	O'Toole, Jim	62T	450	$1.50	$6.00
O'Brien, Pete	89TTR	88	$ .01	$ .05	O'Toole, Jim	63T	70	$ .50	$2.00
O'Brien, Pete	90T	265	$ .01	$ .03	O'Toole, Jim	64T	185	$ .50	$2.00
O'Brien, Pete	90TTR	82	$ .01	$ .05	O'Toole, Jim	65T	60	$ .35	$1.40
O'Brien, Pete	91T	585	$ .01	$ .03	O'Toole, Jim	66T	389	$ .65	$2.60
O'Brien, Pete	91TSC	285	$ .05	$ .25	O'Toole, Jim	67T	467	$1.50	$6.00
O'Brien, Pete	92T	455	$ .01	$ .03	Oates, Johnny	72T	474	$1.50	$6.00
O'Brien, Pete	92TSC	192	$ .01	$ .10	Oates, Johnny	73T	9	$ .15	$ .60
O'Brien, Pete	93T	125	$ .01	$ .03	Oates, Johnny	74T	183	$ .10	$ .40
O'Brien, Syd	69T	628	$ .75	$3.00	Oates, Johnny	75T	319	$ .10	$ .40
O'Brien, Syd	70T	163	$ .20	$ .80	Oates, Johnny	76T	62	$ .05	$ .25
O'Brien, Syd	71T	561	$1.00	$4.00	Oates, Johnny	77T	619	$ .05	$ .20
O'Brien, Syd	72T	289	$ .10	$ .40	Oates, Johnny	78T	508	$ .04	$ .16
O'Connell, Danny	53T	107	$4.00	$16.00	Oates, Johnny	79T	104	$ .03	$ .12
O'Connell, Danny	56T	272	$2.50	$10.00	Oates, Johnny	80T	228	$ .01	$ .10
O'Connell, Danny	57T	271	$5.00	$20.00	Oates, Johnny	81T	303	$ .01	$ .08
O'Connell, Danny	58T	166	$1.25	$5.00	Oates, Johnny	91TTR	85	$ .01	$ .05
O'Connell, Danny	59T	87	$1.50	$6.00	Oates, Johnny	92T	579	$ .01	$ .03
O'Connell, Danny	60T	192	$ .75	$3.00	Oates, Johnny	93T	501	$ .01	$ .03
O'Connell, Danny	61T	318	$ .60	$2.40	Oberkfell, Ken	80T	701	$ .05	$ .20
O'Connell, Danny	62T	411	$1.25	$5.00	Oberkfell, Ken	81T	32	$ .01	$ .08
O'Connell, Danny	91TA53	107	$ .01	$ .15	Oberkfell, Ken	82T	474	$ .01	$ .08
O'Connor, Jack	82T	353	$ .01	$ .08	Oberkfell, Ken	83T	206	$ .01	$ .08
O'Connor, Jack	83T	33	$ .01	$ .08	Oberkfell, Ken	84T	102	$ .01	$ .06
O'Connor, Jack	84T	268	$ .01	$ .06	Oberkfell, Ken	84TTR	85	$ .01	$ .15

TOPPS

Player	Year	No.	VG	EX/MT
Oberkfell, Ken	85T	569	$ .01	$ .06
Oberkfell, Ken	86T	334	$ .01	$ .05
Oberkfell, Ken	87T	627	$ .01	$ .04
Oberkfell, Ken	88T	67	$ .01	$ .04
Oberkfell, Ken	89T	751	$ .01	$ .03
Oberkfell, Ken	90T	488	$ .01	$ .03
Oberkfell, Ken	91T	286	$ .01	$ .03
Oberkfell, Ken	91TSC	414	$ .05	$ .25
Oceak, Frank	60T	467	$1.25	$5.00
Odom, Johnny	65T	526	$35.00	$140.00
Odom, Johnny	67T	282	$ .50	$2.00
Odom, John	68T	501	$ .75	$3.00
Odom, John	69T	195	$ .35	$1.40
Odom, John	70T	55	$ .20	$ .80
Odom, John	71T	523	$ .50	$2.00
Odom, John	72T	557	$ .40	$1.60
Odom, John	72TIA	558	$ .40	$1.60
Odom, John	73T	315	$ .10	$ .40
Odom, John	74T	461	$ .10	$ .40
Odom, John	75T	69	$ .10	$ .40

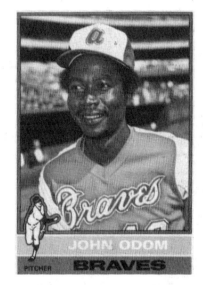

Player	Year	No.	VG	EX/MT
Odom, John	76T	651	$ .05	$ .25
Oelkers, Bryan	87T	77	$ .01	$ .04
Oester, Ron	79T	717	$ .10	$ .40
Oester, Ron	81T	21	$ .01	$ .08
Oester, Ron	82T	427	$ .01	$ .08
Oester, Ron	83T	269	$ .01	$ .08
Oester, Ron	84T	526	$ .01	$ .06
Oester, Ron	84T	756	$ .01	$ .06
Oester, Ron	85T	314	$ .01	$ .06
Oester, Ron	86T	627	$ .01	$ .05
Oester, Ron	87T	172	$ .01	$ .04
Oester, Ron	88T	17	$ .01	$ .04
Oester, Ron	89T	772	$ .01	$ .03
Oester, Ron	90T	492	$ .01	$ .03
Offerman, Jose	91T	587	$ .01	$ .15
Offerman, Jose	91TSC	340	$ .05	$ .35
Offerman, Jose	92T	493	$ .01	$ .03
Offerman, Jose	92TSC	378	$ .01	$ .10
Offerman, Jose	93T	776	$ .01	$ .03
Offerman, Jose	93TSC	129	$ .01	$ .10
Office, Rowland	75T	262	$ .10	$ .40
Office, Rowland	76T	256	$ .05	$ .25
Office, Rowland	77T	524	$ .05	$ .20

Player	Year	No.	VG	EX/MT
Office, Rowland	78T	632	$ .04	$ .16
Office, Rowland	79T	132	$ .03	$ .12
Office, Rowland	80T	39	$ .01	$ .10
Office, Rowland	81T	319	$ .01	$ .08
Office, Rowland	82T	479	$ .01	$ .08
Ogier, Moe	68T	589	$ .70	$2.80
Oglivie, Ben	72T	761	$6.00	$24.00
Oglivie, Ben	73T	388	$ .20	$ .80
Oglivie, Ben	75T	344	$ .10	$ .40
Oglivie, Ben	76T	659	$ .10	$ .40
Oglivie, Ben	77T	122	$ .05	$ .20
Oglivie, Ben	78T	286	$ .04	$ .16
Oglivie, Ben	79T	519	$ .03	$ .12
Oglivie, Ben	80T	53	$ .01	$ .10
Oglivie, Ben	81T	2	$ .10	$ .50
Oglivie, Ben	81T	415	$ .01	$ .08
Oglivie, Ben	82T	280	$ .01	$ .08
Oglivie, Ben	83T	750	$ .01	$ .08
Oglivie, Ben	84T	190	$ .01	$ .06
Oglivie, Ben	85T	681	$ .01	$ .06
Oglivie, Ben	86T	372	$ .01	$ .05
Oglivie, Ben	87T	586	$ .01	$ .04
Ojeda, Bob	82T	274	$ .10	$ .40
Ojeda, Bob	83T	654	$ .01	$ .08
Ojeda, Bob	84T	162	$ .01	$ .06
Ojeda, Bob	84T	786	$ .10	$ .50
Ojeda, Bob	85T	477	$ .01	$ .06
Ojeda, Bob	86T	11	$ .01	$ .05
Ojeda, Bob	86TTR	81	$ .01	$ .06
Ojeda, Bob	87T	746	$ .01	$ .04
Ojeda, Bob	88T	558	$ .01	$ .04
Ojeda, Bob	89T	333	$ .01	$ .03
Ojeda, Bob	90T	207	$ .01	$ .03
Ojeda, Bob	91T	601	$ .01	$ .03
Ojeda, Bob	91TSC	449	$ .05	$ .25
Ojeda, Bob	91TTR	86	$ .01	$ .05
Ojeda, Bob	92T	123	$ .01	$ .03
Ojeda, Bob	92TSC	537	$ .01	$ .10
Ojeda, Bob	93T	338	$ .01	$ .03
Olander, Jim	92T	7	$ .01	$ .10
Olander, Jim	92TSC	274	$ .01	$ .15
Oldis, Bob	53T	262	$20.00	$80.00
Oldis, Bob	54T	91	$3.75	$15.00
Oldis, Bob	55T	169	$6.25	$25.00
Oldis, Bob	60T	361	$ .75	$3.00
Oldis, Bob	61T	149	$ .60	$2.40
Oldis, Bob	62T	269	$ .75	$3.00
Oldis, Bob	63T	404	$1.00	$4.00
Oldis, Bob	91TA53	262	$ .01	$ .15
Olerud, John	90TTR	83	$ .10	$ .50
Olerud, John	91T	168	$ .01	$ .15
Olerud, John	91TSC	482	$ .20	$2.00
Olerud, John	92T	777	$ .01	$ .10
Olerud, John	92TSC	531	$ .10	$ .40
Olerud, John	93T	240	$ .01	$ .10
Olin, Steve	90T	433	$ .01	$ .15
Olin, Steve	91T	696	$ .01	$ .03
Olin, Steve	91TSC	336	$ .05	$ .25
Olin, Steve	92T	559	$ .01	$ .03
Olin, Steve	92TSC	169	$ .01	$ .10
Olin, Steve	93T	167	$ .01	$ .03
Oliva, Pedro "Tony"	63T	228	$12.50	$50.00
Oliva, Tony	64T	116	$3.50	$14.00
Oliva, Tony	65T	1	$3.75	$15.00
Oliva, Tony	65T	340	$3.00	$12.00
Oliva, Tony	66T	216	$1.25	$5.00
Oliva, Tony	66T	220	$ .75	$3.00
Oliva, Tony	66T	450	$2.50	$10.00
Oliva, Tony	67T	50	$1.00	$4.00
Oliva, Tony	67T	239	$1.25	$5.00
Oliva, Tony	68T	165	$ .75	$3.00
Oliva, Tony	68T	480	$8.00	$32.00
Oliva, Tony	68TAS	371	$ .75	$3.00
Oliva, Tony	69T	1	$2.75	$11.00
Oliva, Tony	69T	600	$1.25	$5.00

TOPPS

Player	Year	No.	VG	EX/MT	Player	Year	No.	VG	EX/MT
Oliva, Tony	69TAS	427	$ .50	$2.00	Oliver, Nate	66T	364	$ .50	$2.00
Oliva, Tony	70T	62	$ .75	$3.00	Oliver, Nate	68T	124	$ .35	$1.40
Oliva, Tony	70T	510	$ .75	$3.00	Oliver, Nate	69T	354	$ .30	$1.20
Oliva, Tony	71T	61	$ .75	$3.00	Oliver, Nate	70T	223	$ .20	$ .80
Oliva, Tony	71T	290	$ .75	$3.00	Oliver, Tom	54T	207	$3.75	$15.00
Oliva, Tony	72T	86	$ .50	$2.00	Oliveras, Francisco	91T	52	$ .01	$ .03
Oliva, Tony	72T	400	$ .50	$2.00	Oliveras, Francisco	92TSC	347	$ .01	$ .10
Oliva, Tony	73T	80	$ .30	$1.20	Olivo, Chi Chi	66T	578	$7.00	$28.00
Oliva, Tony	74T	190	$ .25	$1.00	Olivo, Mike	70T	381	$ .35	$1.40
Oliva, Tony	75T	325	$ .25	$1.00	Ollom, Jim	67T	137	$ .50	$2.00
Oliva, Tony	76T	35	$ .25	$1.00	Ollom, Jim	68T	91	$ .35	$1.40
Oliva, Tony	89TTB	665	$ .01	$ .05	Olmsted, Al	81T	244	$ .01	$ .08
Olivares, Ed	62T	598	$17.50	$70.00	Olson, Greg	90TTR	84	$ .01	$ .15
Olivares, Omar	91T	271	$ .01	$ .10	Olson, Greg	91T	673	$ .01	$ .03
Olivares, Omar	92T	193	$ .01	$ .03	Olson, Greg	91TSC	288	$ .05	$ .25
Olivares, Omar	92TSC	386	$ .01	$ .10	Olson, Greg	92T	39	$ .01	$ .03
Olivares, Omar	93T	490	$ .01	$ .03	Olson, Greg	92TSC	675	$ .01	$ .10
Oliver, Al	69T	82	$2.50	$10.00	Olson, Greg	93T	708	$ .01	$ .03
Oliver, Al	70T	166	$ .50	$2.00	Olson, Gregg	89T	161	$ .10	$ .40
Oliver, Al	71T	388	$ .50	$2.00	Olson, Gregg	89TTR	89	$ .05	$ .35
Oliver, Al	72T	575	$ .75	$3.00	Olson, Gregg	90T	655	$ .01	$ .10
Oliver, Al	73T	225	$ .30	$1.20	Olson, Gregg	91T	10	$ .01	$ .03
Oliver, Al	74T	52	$ .25	$1.00	Olson, Gregg	91TSC	156	$ .05	$ .25
Oliver, Al	75T	555	$ .15	$ .60	Olson, Gregg	92T	350	$ .01	$ .03
Oliver, Al	76T	620	$ .25	$1.00	Olson, Gregg	92TSC	293	$ .01	$ .10
Oliver, Al	77T	130	$ .10	$ .40	Olson, Gregg	93T	246	$ .01	$ .03
Oliver, Al	78T	430	$ .10	$ .40	Olson, Karl	52T	72	$13.75	$55.00
Oliver, Al	79T	391	$ .05	$ .20	Olson, Karl	54T	186	$3.75	$15.00
Oliver, Al	80T	260	$ .05	$ .35	Olson, Karl	55T	72	$2.25	$9.00
Oliver, Al	81T	70	$ .01	$ .15	Olson, Karl	56T	322	$2.50	$10.00
Oliver, Al	82T	36	$ .01	$ .08	Olson, Karl	57T	153	$2.00	$8.00
Oliver, Al	82T	590	$ .01	$ .15	Olwine, Ed	87T	159	$ .01	$ .04
Oliver, Al	82TSA	591	$ .01	$ .07	Olwine, Ed	88T	353	$ .01	$ .04
Oliver, Al	82TTR	83	$ .05	$ .25	Ontiveros, Steve	74T	598	$6.00	$24.00
Oliver, Al	83T	111	$ .01	$ .08	Ontiveros, Steve	75T	483	$ .10	$ .40
Oliver, Al	83T	420	$ .01	$ .15	Ontiveros, Steve	76T	284	$ .05	$ .25
Oliver, Al	83T	421	$ .01	$ .08	Ontiveros, Steve	78T	76	$ .04	$ .16
Oliver, Al	83T	701	$ .01	$ .08	Ontiveros, Steve	79T	299	$ .03	$ .12
Oliver, Al	83T	703	$ .01	$ .08	Ontiveros, Steve	80T	514	$ .01	$ .10
Oliver, Al	84T	516	$ .01	$ .06	Ontiveros, Steve	86T	507	$ .01	$ .05
Oliver, Al	84T	620	$ .01	$ .10	Ontiveros, Steve	87T	161	$ .01	$ .04
Oliver, Al	84T	704	$ .01	$ .15	Ontiveros, Steve	88T	272	$ .01	$ .04
Oliver, Al	84TTR	87	$ .05	$ .20	Ontiveros, Steve	89T	692	$ .01	$ .03
Oliver, Al	85T	130	$ .01	$ .10	Ontiveros, Steve	89TTR	90	$ .01	$ .05
Oliver, Al	85TTR	88	$ .01	$ .15	Oquendo, Jose	84T	208	$ .05	$ .20
Oliver, Al	86T	775	$ .01	$ .05	Oquendo, Jose	85T	598	$ .01	$ .10
Oliver, Bob	69T	662	$ .40	$1.60	Oquendo, Jose	86TTR	82	$ .01	$ .06
Oliver, Bob	70T	567	$ .50	$2.00	Oquendo, Jose	87T	133	$ .01	$ .04
Oliver, Bob	71T	470	$ .50	$2.00	Oquendo, Jose	88T	83	$ .01	$ .04
Oliver, Bob	72T	57	$ .10	$ .40	Oquendo, Jose	89T	442	$ .01	$ .03
Oliver, Bob	73T	289	$ .10	$ .40	Oquendo, Jose	90T	645	$ .01	$ .03
Oliver, Bob	74T	243	$ .10	$ .40	Oquendo, Jose	91T	343	$ .01	$ .03
Oliver, Bob	75T	657	$ .10	$ .40	Oquendo, Jose	91TSC	190	$ .05	$ .25
Oliver, Dave	78T	704	$4.50	$18.00	Oquendo, Jose	92T	723	$ .01	$ .03
Oliver, Dave	79T	705	$ .25	$1.00	Oquendo, Jose	92TSC	571	$ .01	$ .10
Oliver, Gene	59T	135	$1.00	$4.00	Oquendo, Jose	93T	535	$ .01	$ .03
Oliver, Gene	60T	307	$ .75	$3.00	Oravetz, Ernie	56T	51	$2.00	$8.00
Oliver, Gene	61T	487	$1.35	$5.40	Oravetz, Ernie	57T	179	$2.00	$8.00
Oliver, Gene	62T	561	$6.00	$24.00	Orioles, Team	56T	100	$7.50	$30.00
Oliver, Gene	63T	172	$ .50	$2.00	Orioles, Team	57T	251	$3.00	$12.00
Oliver, Gene	64T	316	$ .65	$2.60	Orioles, Team	58T	408	$3.50	$14.00
Oliver, Gene	65T	106	$ .35	$1.40	Orioles, Team	59T	48	$5.00	$20.00
Oliver, Gene	66T	541	$76.00	$28.00	Orioles, Team	60T	494	$3.50	$14.00
Oliver, Gene	67T	18	$ .40	$1.60	Orioles, Team	61T	159	$1.75	$7.00
Oliver, Gene	68T	449	$ .35	$1.40	Orioles, Team	62T	476	$3.50	$14.00
Oliver, Gene	69T	247	$ .50	$2.00	Orioles, Team	63T	377	$2.00	$8.00
Oliver, Joe	90T	668	$ .01	$ .15	Orioles, Team	64T	473	$2.50	$10.00
Oliver, Joe	91T	517	$ .01	$ .03	Orioles, Team	65T	572	$7.00	$28.00
Oliver, Joe	91TSC	68	$ .05	$ .25	Orioles, Team	66T	348	$1.25	$5.00
Oliver, Joe	92T	304	$ .01	$ .03	Orioles, Team	67T	302	$1.00	$4.00
Oliver, Joe	92TSC	306	$ .01	$ .10	Orioles, Team	68T	334	$ .75	$3.00
Oliver, Joe	93T	138	$ .01	$ .03	Orioles, Team	70T	387	$ .75	$3.00
Oliver, Joe	93TSC	96	$ .01	$ .10	Orioles, Team	71T	1	$3.00	$12.00
Oliver, Nate	63T	466	$12.50	$50.00	Orioles, Team	72T	731	$2.50	$10.00
Oliver, Nate	65T	59	$ .35	$1.40	Orioles, Team	73T	278	$ .30	$1.20

TOPPS

Player	Year	No.	VG	EX/MT	Player	Year	No.	VG	EX/MT
Orioles, Team	74T	16	$ .25	$1.00	Ortiz, Junior	85T	439	$ .01	$ .06
Orioles, Team Checklist	75T	117	$ .35	$1.40	Ortiz, Junior	86T	682	$ .01	$ .05
Orioles, Team Checklist	76T	73	$ .30	$1.20	Ortiz, Junior	87T	583	$ .01	$ .04
Orioles, Team Checklist	77T	546	$ .25	$1.00	Ortiz, Junior	88T	274	$ .01	$ .04
Orioles, Team Checklist	78T	96	$ .20	$ .80	Ortiz, Junior	89T	769	$ .01	$ .03
Orioles, Team Checklist	79T	689	$ .15	$ .60	Ortiz, Junior	90T	322	$ .01	$ .03
Orioles, Team Checklist	80T	404	$ .10	$ .50	Ortiz, Junior	90TTR	85	$ .01	$ .05
Orioles, Team Checklist	81T	661	$ .05	$ .25	Ortiz, Junior	91T	72	$ .01	$ .03
Orioles, Team Leaders	86T	726	$ .01	$ .05	Ortiz, Junior	91TSC	13	$ .05	$ .25
Orioles, Team Leaders	87T	506	$ .01	$ .04	Ortiz, Junior	92T	617	$ .01	$ .03
Orioles, Team Leaders	88T	51	$ .05	$ .25	Ortiz, Junior	92TSC	727	$ .01	$ .10
Orioles, Team Leaders	89T	381	$ .01	$ .03	Ortiz, Junior	92TTR	84	$ .01	$ .05
Orosco, Jesse	80T	681	$ .75	$3.00	Ortiz, Junior	93T	199	$ .01	$ .03
Orosco, Jesse	83T	369	$ .01	$ .08	Ortiz, Lou	55T	114	$2.25	$9.00
Orosco, Jesse	84T	54	$ .01	$ .06	Orton, John	91T	176	$ .01	$ .03
Orosco, Jesse	84TAS	396	$ .01	$ .06	Orton, John	91TSC	591	$ .05	$ .25
Orosco, Jesse	85T	250	$ .01	$ .06	Orton, John	92TSC	263	$ .01	$ .10
Orosco, Jesse	86T	465	$ .01	$ .05	Osborn, Dan	76T	282	$ .05	$ .25
Orosco, Jesse	87T	704	$ .01	$ .04	Osborn, Don	74T	489	$ .10	$ .40
Orosco, Jesse	88T	105	$ .01	$ .04	Osborne, Donovan	92TTR	85	$ .05	$ .25
Orosco, Jesse	88TTR	77	$ .01	$ .05	Osborne, Donovan	93T	662	$ .01	$ .15
Orosco, Jesse	89T	513	$ .01	$ .03	Osborne, Larry	59T	524	$4.00	$16.00
Orosco, Jesse	89TTR	91	$ .01	$ .05	Osborne, Larry	60T	201	$ .75	$3.00
Orosco, Jesse	90T	636	$ .01	$ .03	Osborne, Larry	61T	208	$ .60	$2.40
Orosco, Jesse	91T	346	$ .01	$ .03	Osborne, Larry	62T	583	$3.50	$14.00
Orosco, Jesse	91TSC	322	$ .05	$ .25	Osborne, Larry	63T	514	$1.75	$7.00
Orosco, Jesse	92T	79	$ .01	$ .03	Osinski, Dan	63T	114	$ .50	$2.00
Orosco, Jesse	93T	289	$ .01	$ .03	Osinski, Dan	64T	537	$2.25	$9.00
Orosco, Jesse	93TSC	37	$ .01	$ .10	Osinski, Dan	65T	223	$ .50	$2.00
Orsino, Johnny	62T	377	$1.25	$5.00	Osinski, Dan	66T	168	$ .50	$2.00
Orsino, Johnny	63T	418	$1.00	$4.00	Osinski, Dan	67T	594	$5.50	$22.00
Orsino, Johnny	64T	63	$ .50	$2.00	Osinski, Dan	68T	331	$ .35	$1.40
Orsino, Johnny	65T	303	$ .50	$2.00					
Orsino, Johnny	66T	77	$ .35	$1.40					
Orsino, Johnny	67T	207	$ .50	$2.00					
Orsulak, Joe	85TTR	89	$ .10	$ .50					
Orsulak, Joe	86T	102	$ .01	$ .15					
Orsulak, Joe	87T	414	$ .01	$ .04					
Orsulak, Joe	88TTR	78	$ .01	$ .05					
Orsulak, Joe	89T	727	$ .01	$ .03					
Orsulak, Joe	90T	212	$ .01	$ .03					
Orsulak, Joe	91T	521	$ .01	$ .03					
Orsulak, Joe	91TSC	191	$ .05	$ .25					
Orsulak, Joe	92T	325	$ .01	$ .03					
Orsulak, Joe	92TSC	135	$ .01	$ .10					
Orsulak, Joe	93T	28	$ .01	$ .03					
Orsulak, Joe	93TSC	92	$ .01	$ .10					
Orta, Jorge	73T	194	$ .20	$ .80					
Orta, Jorge	74T	376	$ .10	$ .40					
Orta, Jorge	75T	184	$ .10	$ .40					
Orta, Jorge	76T	560	$ .05	$ .25					
Orta, Jorge	77T	109	$ .05	$ .20					
Orta, Jorge	78T	42	$ .04	$ .16					
Orta, Jorge	79T	631	$ .03	$ .12					
Orta, Jorge	80T	442	$ .01	$ .10					
Orta, Jorge	81T	222	$ .01	$ .08					
Orta, Jorge	82T	26	$ .01	$ .08					
Orta, Jorge	82TTR	84	$ .01	$ .10					
Orta, Jorge	83T	722	$ .01	$ .08					
Orta, Jorge	83TTR	82	$ .01	$ .10					
Orta, Jorge	84T	312	$ .01	$ .06					
Orta, Jorge	84TTR	88	$ .01	$ .15					
Orta, Jorge	85T	164	$ .01	$ .06					
Orta, Jorge	86T	541	$ .01	$ .05					
Orta, Jorge	87T	738	$ .01	$ .04	Osinski, Dan	69T	622	$ .40	$1.60
Ortega, Phil	62T	69	$ .60	$2.40	Osteen, Claude	59T	224	$1.50	$6.00
Ortega, Phil	63T	467	$3.00	$12.00	Osteen, Claude	60T	206	$ .75	$3.00
Ortega, Phil	64T	291	$ .65	$2.60	Osteen, Claude	62T	501	$1.75	$7.00
Ortega, Phil	65T	152	$ .35	$1.40	Osteen, Claude	63T	374	$1.00	$4.00
Ortega, Phil	66T	416	$ .65	$2.60	Osteen, Claude	64T	28	$ .50	$2.00
Ortega, Phil	67T	493	$1.50	$6.00	Osteen, Claude	65T	570	$2.50	$10.00
Ortega, Phil	68T	595	$ .70	$2.80	Osteen, Claude	66T	270	$ .50	$2.00
Ortega, Phil	69T	406	$ .30	$1.20	Osteen, Claude	67T	330	$ .60	$2.40
Ortiz, Javier	92T	362	$ .01	$ .03	Osteen, Claude	68T	9	$ .75	$3.00
Ortiz, Junior	84T	161	$ .01	$ .06	Osteen, Claude	68T	440	$ .35	$1.40

TOPPS

Player	Year	No.	VG	EX/MT	Player	Year	No.	VG	EX/MT
Osteen, Claude	69T	528	$ .40	$1.60	Owen, Spike	90T	674	$ .01	$ .03
Osteen, Claude	70T	260	$ .25	$1.00	Owen, Spike	91T	372	$ .01	$ .03
Osteen, Claude	71T	10	$ .25	$1.00	Owen, Spike	91TSC	236	$ .05	$ .25
Osteen, Claude	72T	297	$ .10	$ .40	Owen, Spike	92T	443	$ .01	$ .03
Osteen, Claude	72TIA	298	$ .10	$ .40	Owen, Spike	92TSC	221	$ .01	$ .10
Osteen, Claude	73T	490	$ .25	$1.00	Owen, Spike	93T	42	$ .01	$ .03
Osteen, Claude	74T	42	$ .10	$ .40	Owens, J.	93T	606	$ .01	$ .15
Osteen, Claude	74TTR	42	$ .10	$ .40	Owens, Jim	55T	202	$6.25	$25.00
Osteen, Claude	75T	453	$ .10	$ .40	Owens, Jim	56T	114	$2.50	$10.00
Osteen, Claude	76T	488	$ .05	$ .25	Owens, Jim	59T	503	$1.00	$4.00
Osteen, Darrell	66T	424	$1.75	$7.00	Owens, Jim	60T	185	$ .75	$3.00
Osteen, Darrell	67T	222	$ .50	$2.00	Owens, Jim	61T	341	$ .60	$2.40
Osteen, Darrell	68T	199	$ .35	$1.40	Owens, Jim	62T	212	$ .75	$3.00
Ostrowski, Joe	52T	206	$7.00	$28.00	Owens, Jim	63T	483	$3.00	$12.00
Osuna, Al	91T	149	$ .01	$ .15	Owens, Jim	64T	241	$ .65	$2.60
Osuna, Al	92T	614	$ .01	$ .03	Owens, Jim	65T	451	$1.25	$5.00
Osuna, Al	92TSC	68	$ .01	$ .10	Owens, Jim	66T	297	$ .50	$2.00
Osuna, Al	93T	63	$ .01	$ .03	Owens, Jim	67T	582	$2.25	$9.00
Osuna, Al	93TSC	236	$ .01	$ .10	Owens, Jim	73T	624	$1.00	$4.00
Otero, Reggie	60T	459	$1.25	$5.00	Owens, Paul	84T	229	$ .01	$ .06
Otis, Amos	69T	31	$ .75	$3.00	Owens, Paul	85T	92	$ .01	$ .06
Otis, Amos	70T	354	$ .35	$1.40	Ownbey, Rick	83T	739	$ .01	$ .08
Otis, Amos	71T	610	$1.00	$4.00	Oyler, Ray	65T	259	$ .75	$3.00
Otis, Amos	72T	10	$ .20	$ .80	Oyler, Ray	66T	81	$ .35	$1.40
Otis, Amos	73T	510	$ .25	$1.00	Oyler, Ray	67T	352	$ .60	$2.40
Otis, Amos	74T	65	$ .10	$ .40	Oyler, Ray	68T	399	$ .35	$1.40
Otis, Amos	74TAS	337	$ .10	$ .40	Oyler, Ray	69T	178	$ .35	$1.40
Otis, Amos	75T	520	$ .10	$ .40	Oyler, Ray	70T	603	$ .50	$2.00
Otis, Amos	76T	198	$ .15	$ .60	Ozark, Danny	73T	486	$ .25	$1.00
Otis, Amos	76T	510	$ .10	$ .40	Ozark, Danny	74T	119	$ .10	$ .40
Otis, Amos	77T	290	$ .05	$ .20	Ozark, Danny	78T	631	$ .04	$ .16
Otis, Amos	78T	490	$ .04	$ .16	Ozark, Danny	85T	365	$ .01	$ .06
Otis, Amos	79T	360	$ .03	$ .12	Pacella, John	81T	414	$ .01	$ .08
Otis, Amos	80T	130	$ .01	$ .10	Pacella, John	83T	166	$ .01	$ .08
Otis, Amos	81T	585	$ .01	$ .08	Pacheco, Tony	74T	521	$ .10	$ .40
Otis, Amos	82T	725	$ .01	$ .08	Pacillo, Pat	85T	402	$ .01	$ .15
Otis, Amos	82TSA	726	$ .01	$ .07	Pacillo, Pat	87TTR	93	$ .01	$ .05
Otis, Amos	83T	75	$ .01	$ .08	Pacillo, Pat	88T	288	$ .01	$ .04
Otis, Amos	84T	655	$ .01	$ .06	Paciorek, Tom	71T	709	$15.00	$60.00
Otis, Amos	84TTR	89	$ .01	$ .15	Paciorek, Tom	73T	606	$1.00	$4.00
Ott, Billy	65T	354	$ .50	$2.00	Paciorek, Tom	74T	127	$ .10	$ .40
Ott, Ed	76T	594	$ .05	$ .25	Paciorek, Tom	75T	523	$ .10	$ .40
Ott, Ed	77T	197	$ .05	$ .20	Paciorek, Tom	76T	641	$ .05	$ .25
Ott, Ed	78T	28	$ .04	$ .16	Paciorek, Tom	77T	48	$ .05	$ .20
Ott, Ed	79T	561	$ .03	$ .12	Paciorek, Tom	78T	322	$ .04	$ .16
Ott, Ed	80T	383	$ .01	$ .10	Paciorek, Tom	79T	141	$ .03	$ .12
Ott, Ed	81T	246	$ .01	$ .08	Paciorek, Tom	80T	481	$ .01	$ .10
Ott, Ed	81TTR	810	$ .01	$ .15	Paciorek, Tom	81T	228	$ .01	$ .08
Ott, Ed	82T	469	$ .01	$ .08	Paciorek, Tom	82T	336	$ .01	$ .08
Ott, Ed	83T	131	$ .01	$ .08	Paciorek, Tom	82T	678	$ .01	$ .08
Otten, Jim	75T	624	$ .10	$ .40	Paciorek, Tom	82TTR	85	$ .01	$ .10
Otten, Jim	77T	493	$0.25	$ .80	Paciorek, Tom	83T	72	$ .01	$ .08
Otto, Dave	89T	131	$ .01	$ .03	Paciorek, Tom	84T	777	$ .01	$ .06
Otto, Dave	92T	499	$ .01	$ .03	Paciorek, Tom	85T	572	$ .01	$ .06
Otto, Dave	92TSC	461	$ .01	$ .10	Paciorek, Tom	86T	362	$ .01	$ .05
Overmire, Frank	52T	155	$7.00	$28.00	Paciorek, Tom	86TTR	83	$ .01	$ .06
Overy, Mike	77T	489	$ .20	$ .80	Paciorek, Tom	87T	729	$ .01	$ .04
Owchinko, Bob	78T	164	$ .04	$ .16	Pactwa, Joe	76T	589	$ .50	$2.00
Owchinko, Bob	79T	488	$ .03	$ .12	Padres, Team	70T	657	$2.50	$10.00
Owchinko, Bob	80T	79	$ .01	$ .10	Padres, Team	71T	482	$ .75	$3.00
Owchinko, Bob	81T	536	$ .01	$ .08	Padres, Team	72T	262	$ .25	$1.00
Owchinko, Bob	81TTR	811	$ .01	$ .15	Padres, Team	73T	316	$ .30	$1.20
Owchinko, Bob	82T	243	$ .01	$ .08	Padres, Team	74T	226	$ .25	$1.00
Owchinko, Bob	83T	338	$ .01	$ .08	Padres, Team Checklist	75T	146	$ .35	$1.40
Owchinko, Bob	85T	752	$ .01	$ .06	Padres, Team Checklist	76T	331	$ .30	$1.20
Owen, Dave	85T	642	$ .01	$ .06	Padres, Team Checklist	77T	134	$ .25	$1.00
Owen, Larry	82T	502	$ .25	$2.50	Padres, Team Checklist	78T	192	$ .20	$ .80
Owen, Larry	89T	87	$ .01	$ .03	Padres, Team Checklist	79T	479	$ .15	$ .60
Owen, Spike	84T	413	$ .01	$ .15	Padres, Team Checklist	80T	356	$ .10	$ .50
Owen, Spike	85T	84	$ .01	$ .06	Padres, Team Checklist	81T	685	$ .05	$ .25
Owen, Spike	86T	248	$ .01	$ .05	Padres, Team Leaders	86T	306	$ .01	$ .05
Owen, Spike	87T	591	$ .01	$ .04	Padres, Team Leaders	87T	81	$ .01	$ .04
Owen, Spike	88T	733	$ .01	$ .04	Padres, Team Leaders	88T	699	$ .01	$ .10
Owen, Spike	89T	123	$ .01	$ .03	Padres, Team Leaders	89T	231	$ .01	$ .10
Owen, Spike	89TTR	92	$ .01	$ .05	Paepke, Dennis	70T	552	$ .50	$2.00

TOPPS

Player	Year	No.	VG	EX/MT
Pafko, Andy	51Tbb	27	$7.50	$30.00
Pafko, Andy	52T	1	$200.00	$1200.00
Pafko, Andy	54T	79	$3.75	$15.00
Pafko, Andy	56T	312	$2.50	$10.00
Pafko, Andy	57T	143	$2.00	$8.00
Pafko, Andy	58T	223	$1.25	$5.00
Pafko, Andy	59T	27	$1.50	$6.00
Pafko, Andy	60T	464	$1.25	$5.00
Pagan, Dave	75T	648	$.10	$.40
Pagan, Dave	77T	508	$.05	$.20
Pagan, Jose	60T	67	$.85	$3.40
Pagan, Jose	61T	279	$.60	$2.40
Pagan, Jose	62T	565	$3.50	$14.00
Pagan, Jose	63T	545	$2.25	$9.00
Pagan, Jose	64T	123	$.50	$2.00
Pagan, Jose	65T	575	$1.40	$5.60
Pagan, Jose	66T	54	$.35	$1.40
Pagan, Jose	67T	322	$.60	$2.40
Pagan, Jose	68T	482	$.75	$3.00
Pagan, Jose	69T	192	$.35	$1.40
Pagan, Jose	70T	643	$1.25	$5.00
Pagan, Jose	71T	282	$.25	$1.00
Pagan, Jose	72T	701	$1.25	$5.00
Pagan, Jose	72IIA	702	$1.25	$5.00
Pagan, Jose	73T	659	$.60	$2.40
Page, Joe	51Tbb	10	$10.00	$40.00
Page, Joe	52T	48	$18.75	$75.00
Page, Mitchell	78T	55	$.04	$.16
Page, Mitchell	79T	295	$.03	$.12
Page, Mitcholl	80T	586	$.01	$.10
Page, Mitchell	81T	35	$.01	$.08
Page, Mitchell	82T	633	$.01	$.08
Page, Mitchell	83T	737	$.01	$.08
Page, Mitchell	84T	414	$.01	$.06
Pagel, Karl	79T	716	$.03	$.12
Pagel, Karl	80T	676	$.01	$.10
Pagliaroni, Jim	61T	519	$1.35	$5.40
Pagliaroni, Jim	62T	81	$.60	$2.40
Pagliaroni, Jim	63T	159	$.50	$2.00
Pagliaroni, Jim	64T	392	$1.00	$4.00
Pagliaroni, Jim	65T	265	$.50	$2.00
Pagliaroni, Jim	66T	33	$.35	$1.40
Pagliaroni, Jim	67T	183	$.40	$1.60
Pagliaroni, Jim	68T	586	$.70	$2.80
Pagliaroni, Jim	69T	302	$.50	$2.00
Pagliarulo, Mike	85T	638	$.01	$.10
Pagliarulo, Mike	86T	327	$.01	$.10
Pagliarulo, Mike	87T	195	$.01	$.04
Pagliarulo, Mike	88T	435	$.01	$.04
Pagliarulo, Mike	89T	211	$.01	$.03
Pagliarulo, Mike	90T	63	$.01	$.03
Pagliarulo, Mike	91T	547	$.01	$.03
Pagliarulo, Mike	91TSC	522	$.05	$.25
Pagliarulo, Mike	91TTR	87	$.01	$.05
Pagliarulo, Mike	92T	721	$.01	$.03
Pagliarulo, Mike	92TSC	152	$.01	$.10
Pagliarulo, Mike	93T	336	$.01	$.03
Pagnozzi, Tom	88T	689	$.05	$.25
Pagnozzi, Tom	89T	208	$.01	$.03
Pagnozzi, Tom	90T	509	$.01	$.03
Pagnozzi, Tom	91T	308	$.01	$.03
Pagnozzi, Tom	91TSC	223	$.05	$.25
Pagnozzi, Tom	92T	448	$.01	$.03
Pagnozzi, Tom	92TSC	162	$.01	$.10
Pagnozzi, Tom	93T	92	$.01	$.03
Paige, Satchell	53T	220	$120.00	$480.00
Paige, Satchell	91TA53	220	$1.00	$4.00
Paine, Phil	58T	442	$1.00	$4.00
Painter, Lance	93T	738	$.01	$.15
Palacios, Rey	91T	148	$.01	$.03
Palacios, Vicente	88T	322	$.01	$.10
Palacios, Vicente	91T	438	$.01	$.03
Palacios, Vicente	91TSC	443	$.05	$.25
Palacios, Vicente	92T	582	$.01	$.03
Palacios, Vicente	92TSC	486	$.01	$.10
Palica, Erv	52T	273	$12.50	$50.00
Palica, Erv	56T	206	$3.75	$15.00
Pall, Donn	89T	458	$.01	$.10
Pall, Donn	90T	219	$.01	$.03
Pall, Donn	91T	768	$.01	$.03
Pall, Donn	92T	57	$.01	$.03
Pall, Donn	92TSC	184	$.01	$.10
Pall, Donn	93T	707	$.01	$.03
Pall, Donn	93TSC	240	$.01	$.10
Palmeiro, Rafael	87T	634	$.15	$1.50
Palmeiro, Rafael	88T	186	$.05	$.30
Palmeiro, Rafael	89T	310	$.05	$.20
Palmeiro, Rafael	89TTR	93	$.01	$.15
Palmeiro, Rafael	90T	755	$.01	$.15
Palmeiro, Rafael	91T	295	$.01	$.10
Palmeiro, Rafael	91TSC	502	$.10	$.75
Palmeiro, Rafael	92T	55	$.01	$.03
Palmeiro, Rafael	92TSC	516	$.01	$.10
Palmeiro, Rafael	93T	305	$.01	$.03
Palmeiro, Rafael	93TSC	115	$.01	$.15
Palmer, Dave	80T	42	$.05	$.20
Palmer, Dave	81T	607	$.01	$.08
Palmer, Dave	82T	292	$.01	$.08
Palmer, Dave	83T	164	$.01	$.08
Palmer, Dave	84T	750	$.10	$1.00
Palmer, Dave	85T	526	$.01	$.06
Palmer, Dave	86T	421	$.01	$.05
Palmer, Dave	86TTR	84	$.01	$.06
Palmer, Dave	87T	324	$.01	$.04
Palmer, Dave	88T	732	$.01	$.04
Palmer, Dave	88TTR	79	$.01	$.05
Palmer, Dave	89T	67	$.01	$.03
Palmer, Dean	91TTR	88	$.05	$.20
Palmer, Dean	92T	567	$.01	$.10
Palmer, Dean	92TSC	211	$.10	$.75
Palmer, Dean	93T	545	$.01	$.15
Palmer, Dean	93TSC	22	$.05	$.25
Palmer, Jim	66T	126	$45.00	$180.00
Palmer, Jim	67T	475	$27.50	$110.00
Palmer, Jim	68T	575	$15.00	$60.00
Palmer, Jim	69T	573	$11.25	$45.00
Palmer, Jim	70T	68	$.50	$2.00
Palmer, Jim	70T	449	$6.00	$24.00

TOPPS

Player	Year	No.	VG	EX/MT
Palmer, Jim	71T	67	$ .75	$3.00
Palmer, Jim	71T	570	$9.00	$36.00
Palmer, Jim	72T	92	$ .55	$2.20
Palmer, Jim	72T	270	$3.50	$14.00
Palmer, Jim	73T	160	$2.50	$10.00
Palmer, Jim	73T	341	$ .50	$2.00
Palmer, Jim	74T	40	$2.25	$9.00
Palmer, Jim	74T	206	$1.00	$4.00
Palmer, Jim	75T	335	$2.25	$9.00
Palmer, Jim	76T	200	$ .35	$1.40
Palmer, Jim	76T	202	$1.00	$4.00
Palmer, Jim	76T	450	$1.75	$7.00
Palmer, Jim	77T	5	$ .15	$ .60
Palmer, Jim	77T	600	$1.75	$7.00
Palmer, Jim	78T	160	$1.00	$4.00
Palmer, Jim	78T	205	$ .20	$ .80
Palmer, Jim	79T	340	$ .75	$3.00
Palmer, Jim	80T	590	$ .75	$3.00
Palmer, Jim	81T	210	$ .20	$2.00
Palmer, Jim	82T	80	$ .10	$1.00
Palmer, Jim	82TSA	81	$ .10	$ .50
Palmer, Jim	83T	21	$ .05	$ .25
Palmer, Jim	83T	490	$ .10	$1.00
Palmer, Jim	83T	491	$ .10	$ .50
Palmer, Jim	84T	715	$ .05	$ .20
Palmer, Jim	84T	717	$ .05	$ .20
Palmer, Lowell	70T	252	$ .20	$ .80
Palmer, Lowell	71T	554	$1.00	$4.00
Palmer, Lowell	72T	746	$1.25	$5.00
Palys, Stan	58T	126	$1.25	$5.00
Pankovits, Jim	86T	618	$ .01	$ .05
Pankovits, Jim	87T	249	$ .01	$ .04
Pankovits, Jim	88T	487	$ .01	$ .04
Pankovits, Jim	89T	153	$ .01	$ .03
Papi, Stan	79T	652	$ .03	$ .12
Papi, Stan	81T	273	$ .01	$ .08
Papi, Stan	82T	423	$ .01	$ .08
Pappas, Erik	92TSC	442	$ .01	$ .10
Pappas, Milt	58T	457	$1.50	$6.00
Pappas, Milt	59T	391	$1.00	$4.00
Pappas, Milt	60T	12	$ .85	$3.40
Pappas, Milt	60T	399	$ .75	$3.00
Pappas, Milt	61T	48	$ .75	$3.00
Pappas, Milt	61T	295	$ .75	$3.00
Pappas, Milt	62T	55	$ .60	$2.40
Pappas, Milt	62T	75	$ .60	$2.40
Pappas, Milt	63T	358	$ .90	$3.60
Pappas, Milt	64T	45	$ .50	$2.00
Pappas, Milt	65T	270	$ .50	$2.00
Pappas, Milt	66T	105	$ .75	$3.00
Pappas, Milt	67T	254	$ .50	$2.00
Pappas, Milt	68T	74	$ .35	$1.40
Pappas, Milt	69T	79	$ .35	$1.40
Pappas, Milt	70T	576	$ .50	$2.00
Pappas, Milt	71T	441	$ .50	$2.00
Pappas, Milt	72T	208	$ .10	$ .40
Pappas, Milt	73T	70	$ .20	$ .80
Pappas, Milt	74T	640	$ .10	$ .40
Paquette, Craig	92T	473	$ .05	$ .25
Pardo, Al	86T	279	$ .01	$ .05
Paredes, Johnny	89T	367	$ .01	$ .03
Parent, Mark	88TTR	80	$ .01	$ .10
Parent, Mark	89T	617	$ .01	$ .03
Parent, Mark	90T	749	$ .01	$ .03
Parent, Mark	91T	358	$ .01	$ .03
Parent, Mark	92TSC	623	$ .01	$ .10
Paris, Kelly	84T	113	$ .01	$ .06
Parker, Billy	72T	213	$ .20	$ .80
Parker, Billy	73T	354	$ .10	$ .40
Parker, Clay	89TTR	94	$ .01	$ .10
Parker, Clay	90T	511	$ .01	$ .03
Parker, Clay	91T	183	$ .01	$ .03
Parker, Clay	92TSC	631	$ .01	$ .10
Parker, Clay	93TSC	45	$ .01	$ .10
Parker, Dave	74T	252	$6.25	$25.00
Parker, Dave	75T	29	$1.75	$7.00
Parker, Dave	76T	185	$1.00	$4.00
Parker, Dave	77T	270	$ .75	$3.00
Parker, Dave	78T	201	$ .25	$1.00
Parker, Dave	78T	560	$ .75	$3.00
Parker, Dave	79T	1	$ .75	$3.00
Parker, Dave	79T	430	$ .50	$2.00
Parker, Dave	80T	310	$ .20	$2.00
Parker, Dave	81T	640	$ .10	$ .60
Parker, Dave	82T	40	$ .10	$ .50
Parker, Dave	82TAS	343	$ .05	$ .20
Parker, Dave	82TSA	41	$ .05	$ .25
Parker, Dave	83T	205	$ .10	$ .50
Parker, Dave	84T	701	$ .05	$ .20
Parker, Dave	84T	775	$ .05	$ .25
Parker, Dave	84TTR	90	$ .15	$1.50
Parker, Dave	85T	175	$ .05	$ .25
Parker, Dave	86T	595	$ .01	$ .15
Parker, Dave	87T	691	$ .01	$ .15
Parker, Dave	87TAS	600	$ .01	$ .10

Player	Year	No.	VG	EX/MT
Parker, Dave	88T	315	$ .01	$ .10
Parker, Dave	88TTR	81	$ .01	$ .10
Parker, Dave	89T	475	$ .01	$ .03
Parker, Dave	90T	45	$ .01	$ .03
Parker, Dave	90TTR	86	$ .01	$ .05
Parker, Dave	91T	235	$ .01	$ .03
Parker, Dave	91TSC	75	$ .05	$ .25
Parker, Dave	91TTR	89	$ .01	$ .05
Parker, Harry	74T	106	$ .10	$ .40
Parker, Harry	75T	214	$ .10	$ .40
Parker, Rick	90TTR	87	$ .01	$ .05
Parker, Rick	91T	218	$ .01	$ .03
Parker, Rick	92TSC	769	$ .01	$ .10
Parker, Salty	60T	469	$1.25	$5.00
Parker, Salty	73T	421	$ .25	$1.00
Parker, Salty	74T	276	$ .10	$ .40
Parker, Wes	64T	456	$1.50	$6.00
Parker, Wes	65T	344	$ .50	$2.00
Parker, Wes	66T	134	$ .50	$2.00
Parker, Wes	67T	218	$ .50	$2.00
Parker, Wes	68T	533	$ .70	$2.80
Parker, Wes	69T	493	$ .30	$1.20
Parker, Wes	70T	5	$ .20	$ .80

TOPPS

Player	Year	No.	VG	EX/MT
Parker, Wes	71T	430	$.50	$2.00
Parker, Wes	72T	265	$.10	$.40
Parker, Wes	73T	151	$.10	$.40
Parks, Derek	93TSC	74	$.01	$.10
Parks, Jack	55T	23	$2.25	$9.00
Parnell, Mel	51Trb	10	$1.65	$6.60
Parnell, Mel	52T	30	$15.00	$60.00
Parnell, Mel	53T	19	$4.50	$18.00
Parnell, Mel	54T	40	$3.75	$15.00
Parnell, Mel	55T	140	$2.50	$10.00
Parnell, Mel	57T	313	$5.00	$20.00
Parnell, Mel	91TA53	19	$.01	$.15
Parrett, Jeff	88T	588	$.01	$.04
Parrett, Jeff	89T	176	$.01	$.03
Parrett, Jeff	89TTR	95	$.01	$.05
Parrett, Jeff	90T	439	$.01	$.03
Parrett, Jeff	91T	56	$.01	$.03
Parrett, Jeff	91TSC	544	$.05	$.25
Parrett, Jeff	92TSC	834	$.01	$.10
Parrett, Jeff	93T	209	$.01	$.03
Parrett, Jeff	93TSC	99	$.01	$.10
Parrish, Lance	78T	708	$3.75	$15.00
Parrish, Lance	79T	469	$.75	$3.00
Parrish, Lance	80T	196	$.10	$1.00
Parrish, Lance	81T	392	$.10	$.50
Parrish, Lance	82T	535	$.05	$.25
Parrish, Lance	83T	285	$.05	$.20
Parrish, Lance	83TRB	4	$.01	$.15
Parrish, Lance	84T	640	$.05	$.20
Parrish, Lance	85T	160	$.01	$.15
Parrish, Lance	85TAS	708	$.01	$.06
Parrish, Lance	86T	740	$.01	$.15
Parrish, Lance	87T	791	$.01	$.10
Parrish, Lance	87TAS	613	$.01	$.10
Parrish, Lance	87TTR	94	$.01	$.10
Parrish, Lance	88T	95	$.01	$.10
Parrish, Lance	89T	470	$.01	$.03
Parrish, Lance	89TTR	96	$.01	$.10
Parrish, Lance	90T	575	$.01	$.03
Parrish, Lance	91T	210	$.01	$.03
Parrish, Lance	91TSC	166	$.05	$.25
Parrish, Lance	92T	360	$.01	$.03
Parrish, Lance	92TSC	94	$.01	$.10
Parrish, Lance	93T	609	$.01	$.03
Parrish, Lance	93TSC	252	$.01	$.10
Parrish, Larry	76T	141	$.25	$1.00
Parrish, Larry	77T	526	$.20	$.80
Parrish, Larry	78T	294	$.04	$.16
Parrish, Larry	79T	677	$.05	$.20
Parrish, Larry	80T	345	$.01	$.10
Parrish, Larry	81T	15	$.01	$.08
Parrish, Larry	82T	445	$.01	$.08
Parrish, Larry	82TTR	86	$.01	$.10
Parrish, Larry	83T	776	$.01	$.08
Parrish, Larry	84T	169	$.01	$.06
Parrish, Larry	85T	548	$.01	$.06
Parrish, Larry	86T	238	$.01	$.05
Parrish, Larry	87T	629	$.01	$.04
Parrish, Larry	88T	490	$.01	$.04
Parrish, Larry	89T	354	$.01	$.03
Parrott, Mike	79T	576	$.03	$.12
Parrott, Mike	80T	443	$.01	$.10
Parrott, Mike	81T	187	$.01	$.00
Parrott, Mike	82T	358	$.01	$.08
Parsons, Bill	72T	281	$.10	$.40
Parsons, Bill	73T	231	$.10	$.40
Parsons, Bill	74T	574	$.10	$.40
Parsons, Bill	75T	613	$.10	$.40
Parsons, Tom	62T	326	$.75	$3.00
Parsons, Tom	65T	308	$1.50	$6.00
Paschall, Bill	80T	667	$.20	$2.00
Pascual, Camilo	55T	84	$3.50	$14.00
Pascual, Camilo	56T	98	$2.00	$8.00
Pascual, Camilo	57T	211	$2.00	$8.00
Pascual, Camilo	58T	219	$1.25	$5.00
Pascual, Camilo	59T	291	$1.00	$4.00
Pascual, Camillo (Camilo)	59T	413	$1.00	$4.00
Pascual, Camilo	60T	483	$1.25	$5.00
Pascual, Camilo	60TAS	569	$3.50	$14.00
Pascual, Camilo	61T	235	$.60	$2.40
Pascual, Camilo	62T	59	$.60	$2.40
Pascual, Camilo	62T	230	$.75	$3.00
Pascual, Camilo	63T	8	$1.00	$4.00
Pascual, Camilo	63T	10	$1.00	$4.00
Pascual, Camilo	63T	220	$.90	$3.60
Pascual, Camilo	64T	2	$.75	$3.00
Pascual, Camilo	64T	4	$1.25	$5.00
Pascual, Camilo	64T	6	$.75	$3.00
Pascual, Camilo	64T	500	$1.00	$4.00
Pascual, Camilo	65T	11	$.75	$3.00
Pascual, Camilo	65T	255	$.50	$2.00
Pascual, Camilo	66T	305	$.50	$2.00
Pascual, Camilo	67T	71	$.40	$1.60
Pascual, Camilo	68T	395	$.35	$1.40
Pascual, Camilo	69T	513	$.40	$1.60
Pascual, Camilo	70T	254	$.20	$.80
Pasley, Kevin	77T	476	$7.50	$30.00
Pasley, Kevin	78T	702	$.04	$.16
Pasqua, Dan	86T	259	$.01	$.15
Pasqua, Dan	87T	74	$.01	$.04
Pasqua, Dan	88T	691	$.01	$.04
Pasqua, Dan	88TTR	82	$.01	$.05
Pasqua, Dan	89T	558	$.01	$.03
Pasqua, Dan	90T	446	$.01	$.03
Pasqua, Dan	91T	364	$.01	$.03
Pasqua, Dan	91TSC	214	$.05	$.25
Pasqua, Dan	92T	107	$.01	$.03
Pasqua, Dan	92TSC	794	$.01	$.10
Pasqua, Dan	93T	204	$.01	$.03
Pasqua, Dan	93TSC	94	$.01	$.10
Pastore, Frank	80T	677	$.01	$.10
Pastore, Frank	81T	499	$.01	$.08
Pastore, Frank	82T	128	$.01	$.08
Pastore, Frank	83T	658	$.01	$.08
Pastore, Frank	84T	87	$.01	$.06
Pastore, Frank	85T	727	$.01	$.06
Pastore, Frank	86T	314	$.01	$.05
Pastore, Frank	86TTR	85	$.01	$.06
Pastore, Frank	87T	576	$.01	$.04
Pate, Bobby	81T	479	$2.00	$8.00
Patek, Freddie	69T	219	$.75	$3.00
Patek, Freddie	70T	94	$.20	$.80
Patek, Freddie	71T	626	$1.00	$4.00
Patek, Freddie	72T	531	$.40	$1.60
Patek, Freddie	73T	334	$.10	$.40
Patek, Freddie	74T	88	$.10	$.40
Patek, Freddie	75T	48	$.10	$.40
Patek, Freddie	76T	167	$.05	$.25
Patek, Freddie	77T	422	$.05	$.20
Patek, Freddie	78T	204	$.04	$.16
Patek, Freddie	78T	274	$.04	$.16
Patek, Freddie	79T	525	$.03	$.12
Patek, Freddie	80T	705	$.01	$.10
Patek, Freddie	81T	311	$.01	$.08
Patek, Freddie	82T	602	$.01	$.08
Patterson, Bob	88T	522	$.01	$.04
Patterson, Bob	90TTR	88	$.01	$.05
Patterson, Bob	91T	479	$.01	$.03
Patterson, Bob	91TSC	594	$.05	$.25
Patterson, Bob	92T	263	$.01	$.03
Patterson, Bob	92TSC	876	$.01	$.03
Patterson, Bob	93T	299	$.01	$.03
Patterson, Daryl	68T	113	$.35	$1.40
Patterson, Daryl	69T	101	$.35	$1.40
Patterson, Daryl	70T	592	$.50	$2.00
Patterson, Daryl	71T	481	$.50	$2.00
Patterson, Dave	80T	679	$.01	$.10
Patterson, Gil	77T	472	$.05	$.20
Patterson, John	93T	573	$.01	$.03
Patterson, Ken	89T	434	$.01	$.03

TOPPS

Player	Year	No.	VG	EX/MT	Player	Year	No.	VG	EX/MT
Patterson, Ken	90T	156	$ .01	$ .03	Pazik, Mike	76T	597	$ .20	$ .80
Patterson, Ken	91T	326	$ .01	$ .03	Pazik, Mike	77T	643	$ .05	$ .20
Patterson, Ken	92T	784	$ .01	$ .03	Pearce, Jim	55T	170	$3.00	$12.00
Patterson, Ken	92TSC	289	$ .01	$ .10	Pearson, Albie	58T	317	$1.25	$5.00
Patterson, Ken	93TSC	162	$ .01	$ .10	Pearson, Albie	59T	4	$1.50	$6.00
Patterson, Reggie	82T	599	$ .01	$ .08	Pearson, Albie	60T	241	$ .75	$3.00
Pattin, Marty	69T	563	$ .40	$1.60	Pearson, Albie	61T	288	$ .60	$2.40
Pattin, Marty	70T	31	$ .20	$ .80	Pearson, Albie	62T	343	$ .75	$3.00
Pattin, Marty	71T	579	$1.00	$4.00	Pearson, Albie	63T	182	$ .50	$2.00
Pattin, Marty	72T	144	$ .10	$ .40	Pearson, Albie	64T	110	$ .50	$2.00
Pattin, Marty	73T	415	$ .25	$1.00	Pearson, Albie	65T	358	$ .50	$2.00
Pattin, Marty	74T	583	$ .10	$ .40	Pearson, Albie	66T	83	$ .35	$1.40
Pattin, Marty	75T	413	$ .10	$ .40	Pecota, Bill	88T	433	$ .01	$ .10
Pattin, Marty	76T	492	$ .05	$ .25	Pecota, Bill	89T	148	$ .01	$ .03
Pattin, Marty	77T	658	$ .05	$ .20	Pecota, Bill	91T	754	$ .01	$ .03
Pattin, Marty	78T	218	$ .04	$ .16	Pecota, Bill	92T	236	$ .01	$ .03
Pattin, Marty	79T	129	$ .03	$ .12	Pecota, Bill	92TSC	811	$ .01	$ .10
Pattin, Marty	80T	26	$ .01	$ .10	Pecota, Bill	92TTR	86	$ .01	$ .05
Pattin, Marty	81T	389	$ .01	$ .08	Pecota, Bill	93T	517	$ .01	$ .03
Patzke, Jeff	93T	529	$ .10	$ .50	Pecota, Bill	93TSC	148	$ .01	$ .10
Paul, Mike	69T	537	$ .40	$1.60	Peden, Les	53T	256	$22.50	$90.00
Paul, Mike	70T	582	$ .50	$2.00	Peden, Les	91TA53	256	$ .01	$ .15
Paul, Mike	71T	454	$ .50	$2.00	Pedrique, Al	88T	294	$ .01	$ .04
Paul, Mike	72T	577	$ .40	$1.60	Pedrique, Al	89T	566	$ .01	$ .03
Paul, Mike	73T	58	$ .10	$ .40	Pellagrini, Eddie	52T	405	$43.75	$175.00
Paul, Mike	74T	399	$ .10	$ .40	Pellagrini, Eddie	53T	28	$6.25	$25.00
Paula, Carlos	55T	97	$2.25	$9.00	Pellagrini, Eddie	91TA53	28	$ .01	$ .15
Paula, Carlos	56T	4	$2.00	$8.00	Peltier, Dan	92T	618	$ .05	$ .25
Pavletich, Don	59T	494	$1.00	$4.00	Peltier, Dan	93TSC	242	$ .01	$ .10
Pavletich, Don	62T	594	$20.00	$80.00	Pemberton, Rudy	92T	656	$ .05	$ .20
Pavletich, Don	65T	472	$1.25	$5.00	Pena, Alejandro	83TTR	83	$ .10	$ .75
Pavletich, Don	66T	196	$ .50	$2.00	Pena, Alejandro	84T	324	$ .05	$ .20
Pavletich, Don	67T	292	$ .60	$2.40	Pena, Alejandro	85T	110	$ .01	$ .06
Pavletich, Don	68T	108	$ .35	$1.40	Pena, Alejandro	86T	665	$ .01	$ .05
Pavletich, Don	69T	179	$ .35	$1.40	Pena, Alejandro	87T	787	$ .01	$ .04
Pavletich, Don	70T	504	$ .35	$1.40	Pena, Alejandro	88T	277	$ .01	$ .04
Pavletich, Don	71T	409	$ .50	$2.00	Pena, Alejandro	89T	57	$ .01	$ .03
Pavletich, Don	72T	359	$ .10	$ .40	Pena, Alejandro	90T	483	$ .01	$ .03
Pavlik, Roger	93T	223	$ .01	$ .10	Pena, Alejandro	90TTR	89	$ .01	$ .05
Pavlik, Roger	93TSC	193	$ .01	$ .10	Pena, Alejandro	91T	544	$ .01	$ .03
					Pena, Alejandro	91TSC	583	$ .05	$ .25
					Pena, Alejandro	92T	337	$ .01	$ .03
					Pena, Alejandro	92TSC	833	$ .01	$ .10
					Pena, Alejandro	93T	198	$ .01	$ .03
					Pena, Alejandro	93TSC	205	$ .01	$ .10
					Pena, George	73T	601	$ .75	$3.00
					Pena, Geronimo	91T	636	$ .01	$ .10
					Pena, Geronimo	92T	166	$ .01	$ .03
					Pena, Geronimo	92TSC	466	$ .10	$ .40
					Pena, Geronimo	93T	312	$ .01	$ .03
					Pena, Geronimo	93TSC	215	$ .01	$ .10
					Pena, Hipolito	89T	109	$ .01	$ .03
					Pena, Jose	69T	339	$ .30	$1.20
					Pena, Jose	70T	523	$ .35	$1.40
					Pena, Jose	71T	693	$1.50	$6.00
					Pena, Jose	72T	322	$ .10	$ .40
					Pena, Orlando	59T	271	$1.00	$4.00
					Pena, Orlando	63T	214	$ .90	$3.60
					Pena, Orlando	64T	124	$ .50	$2.00
					Pena, Orlando	65T	311	$ .50	$2.00
					Pena, Orlando	66T	239	$ .50	$2.00
					Pena, Orlando	67T	449	$ .60	$2.40
					Pena, Orlando	68T	471	$ .75	$3.00
					Pena, Orlando	74T	393	$ .10	$ .40
					Pena, Orlando	75T	573	$ .10	$ .40
					Pena, Roberto	66T	559	$7.00	$28.00
					Pena, Roberto	69T	184	$ .35	$1.40
					Pena, Roberto	70T	44	$ .20	$ .80
					Pena, Roberto	71T	334	$ .25	$1.00
					Pena, Tony	81T	551	$ .10	$1.00
					Pena, Tony	82T	138	$ .05	$ .25
					Pena, Tony	83T	590	$ .01	$ .15
					Pena, Tony	84T	645	$ .05	$ .20
					Pena, Tony	85T	358	$ .01	$ .10
					Pena, Tony	86T	260	$ .01	$ .10

MIKE PAXTON

Paxton, Mike	78T	216	$ .04	$ .16
Paxton, Mike	79T	122	$ .03	$ .12
Paxton, Mike	80T	388	$ .01	$ .10

TOPPS

Player	Year	No.	VG	EX/MT
Pena, Tony	87T	60	$.01	$.10
Pena, Tony	87TTR	95	$.01	$.10
Pena, Tony	88T	410	$.01	$.10
Pena, Tony	89T	715	$.01	$.03
Pena, Tony	90T	115	$.01	$.03
Pena, Tony	90TTR	90	$.01	$.05
Pena, Tony	91T	375	$.01	$.03
Pena, Tony	91TSC	505	$.05	$.25
Pena, Tony	92T	569	$.01	$.03
Pena, Tony	92TSC	706	$.01	$.10
Pena, Tony	93T	618	$.01	$.03
Pena, Tony	93TSC	164	$.01	$.10
Pendleton, Jim	53T	185	$4.50	$18.00
Pendleton, Jim	54T	165	$3.75	$15.00
Pendleton, Jim	55T	15	$2.25	$9.00
Pendleton, Jim	57T	327	$5.00	$20.00
Pendleton, Jim	58T	104	$2.00	$8.00
Pendleton, Jim	59T	174	$1.00	$4.00
Pendleton, Jim	62T	432	$1.25	$5.00
Pendleton, Jim	91TA53	185	$.01	$.15
Pendleton, Terry	85T	346	$.75	$3.00
Pendleton, Terry	86T	528	$.10	$.50
Pendleton, Terry	87T	8	$.05	$.25
Pendleton, Terry	88T	635	$.01	$.15
Pendleton, Terry	89T	375	$.01	$.10
Pendleton, Terry	90T	725	$.01	$.10
Pendleton, Terry	91T	485	$.01	$.10
Pendleton, Terry	91TSC	327	$.10	$.50
Pendleton, Terry	91TTR	90	$.01	$.10
Pendleton, Terry	92T	115	$.01	$.03
Pendleton, Terry	92TSC	510	$.01	$.10
Pendleton, Terry	93T	650	$.01	$.03
Pennington, Brad	93T	797	$.01	$.15
Pennyfeather, William	93T	819	$.01	$.03
Penson, Paul	54T	236	$3.75	$15.00
Pentz, Gene	77T	308	$.05	$.20
Pentz, Gene	78T	64	$.04	$.16
Penz, Roberto	65T	549	$4.00	$16.00
Pepe, Dave	56T	154	$2.50	$10.00
Pepitone, Joe	62T	596	$15.00	$60.00
Pepitone, Joe	63T	183	$1.00	$4.00
Pepitone, Joe	64T	360	$1.00	$4.00
Pepitone, Joe	65T	245	$.75	$3.00
Pepitone, Joe	66T	79	$.50	$2.00
Pepitone, Joe	67T	340	$.60	$2.40
Pepitone, Joe	68T	195	$.50	$2.00
Pepitone, Joe	69T	589	$.40	$1.60
Pepitone, Joe	70T	598	$.50	$2.00
Pepitone, Joe	71T	90	$.25	$1.00
Pepitone, Joe	72T	303	$.10	$.40
Pepitone, Joe	72TIA	304	$.10	$.40
Pepitone, Joe	73T	580	$.60	$2.40
Pepper, Laurin	55T	147	$2.25	$9.00
Pepper, Laurin	56T	108	$2.50	$10.00
Peraza, Oswald	89T	297	$.01	$.10
Perconte, Jack	81T	302	$1.00	$4.00
Perconte, Jack	82IIH	87	$.01	$.10
Perconte, Jack	83T	569	$.01	$.08
Perconte, Jack	85T	172	$.01	$.06
Perconte, Jack	86T	146	$.01	$.05
Perez, Equardo	93T	494	$.05	$.35
Perez, Marty	71T	529	$1.25	$5.00
Perez, Marty	72T	119	$.10	$.40
Perez, Marty	73T	144	$.10	$.40
Perez, Marty	74T	374	$.10	$.40
Perez, Marty	75T	499	$.10	$.40
Perez, Marty	76T	177	$.05	$.25
Perez, Marty	77T	438	$.05	$.20
Perez, Marty	78T	613	$.04	$.16
Perez, Melido	88TTR	83	$.10	$.50
Perez, Melido	89T	786	$.01	$.10
Perez, Melido	90T	621	$.01	$.03
Perez, Melido	91T	499	$.01	$.03
Perez, Melido	91TSC	232	$.05	$.25
Perez, Melido	92T	129	$.01	$.03
Perez, Melido	92TSC	869	$.01	$.10
Perez, Melido	92TTR	87	$.01	$.05
Perez, Melido	93T	304	$.01	$.03
Perez, Mike	91T	205	$.01	$.10
Perez, Mike	92TSC	798	$.05	$.20
Perez, Mike	92TTR	88	$.01	$.05
Perez, Mike	93T	229	$.01	$.03
Perez, Mike	93TSC	202	$.01	$.10
Perez, Pascual	81T	551	$.10	$1.00
Perez, Pascual	82T	383	$.05	$.20
Perez, Pascual	83TTR	84	$.01	$.10
Perez, Pascual	84T	675	$.01	$.06
Perez, Pascual	85T	106	$.01	$.06
Perez, Pascual	86T	491	$.01	$.10
Perez, Pascual	88T	647	$.01	$.04
Perez, Pascual	89T	73	$.01	$.03
Perez, Pascual	90T	278	$.01	$.03
Perez, Pascual	90TTR	91	$.01	$.05
Perez, Pascual	91T	701	$.01	$.03
Perez, Pascual	91TSC	485	$.05	$.25
Perez, Pascual	92T	503	$.01	$.03
Perez, Tony	65T	581	$37.50	$150.00
Perez, Tony	66T	72	$8.00	$32.00
Perez, Tony	67T	476	$20.00	$80.00
Perez, Tony	68T	130	$3.50	$14.00
Perez, Tony	69T	295	$3.50	$14.00
Perez, Tony	70T	63	$.75	$3.00
Perez, Tony	70T	380	$2.00	$8.00
Perez, Tony	71T	64	$.75	$3.00
Perez, Tony	71T	66	$1.00	$4.00
Perez, Tony	71T	580	$3.00	$12.00
Perez, Tony	72T	80	$1.00	$4.00
Perez, Tony	73T	275	$1.00	$4.00
Perez, Tony	74T	230	$1.00	$4.00
Perez, Tony	75T	560	$.75	$3.00
Perez, Tony	76T	195	$.30	$1.20
Perez, Tony	76T	325	$.50	$2.00
Perez, Tony	77T	655	$.50	$2.00
Perez, Tony	78T	15	$.20	$.80
Perez, Tony	79T	495	$.25	$1.00
Perez, Tony	80T	125	$.10	$1.00
Perez, Tony	81T	575	$.10	$.50
Perez, Tony	82T	255	$.10	$.50
Perez, Tony	82TSA	256	$.05	$.25
Perez, Tony	83T	715	$.10	$.40
Perez, Tony	83T	716	$.05	$.20
Perez, Tony	83TTR	85	$.15	$1.50
Perez, Tony	84T	385	$.05	$.25
Perez, Tony	84T	702	$.05	$.20
Perez, Tony	84T	703	$.05	$.20
Perez, Tony	84T	704	$.01	$.15
Perez, Tony	84TFH	91	$.75	$3.00
Perez, Tony	85T	675	$.01	$.15
Perez, Tony	86T	85	$.05	$.20
Perez, Tony	86TRB	205	$.01	$.10
Perez, Tony	93T	503	$.01	$.03
Perezchica, Tony	92TSC	454	$.01	$.10
Perkins, Broderick	79T	725	$.03	$.12
Perkins, Broderick	81T	393	$.01	$.08
Perkins, Broderick	82T	192	$.01	$.08
Perkins, Broderick	83T	593	$.01	$.08
Perkins, Broderick	83TTR	86	$.01	$.10
Perkins, Broderick	84T	212	$.01	$.06
Perkins, Broderick	85T	609	$.01	$.06
Perkowski, Harry	52T	142	$7.00	$28.00
Perkowski, Harry	53T	236	$11.25	$45.00
Perkowski, Harry	54T	125	$3.75	$15.00
Perkowski, Harry	55T	184	$3.00	$12.00
Perkowski, Harry	91TA53	236	$.01	$.15
Perlman, Jon	89T	476	$.01	$.03
Perlozzo, Sam	78T	704	$4.50	$18.00
Perlozzo, Sam	79T	709	$.25	$1.00
Perranoski, Ron	61T	525	$9.00	$36.00
Perranoski, Ron	62T	297	$.75	$3.00
Perranoski, Ron	63T	403	$1.00	$4.00

TOPPS

Player	Year	No.	VG	EX/MT	Player	Year	No.	VG	EX/MT
Perranoski, Ron	64T	30	$ .50	$2.00	Perry, Jim	72T	220	$ .10	$ .40
Perranoski, Ron	65T	484	$1.25	$5.00	Perry, Jim	72T	497	$ .25	$1.00
Perranoski, Ron	66T	555	$7.00	$28.00	Perry, Jim	73T	385	$ .20	$ .80
Perranoski, Ron	67T	197	$ .50	$2.00	Perry, Jim	74T	316	$ .10	$ .40
Perranoski, Ron	68T	435	$ .35	$1.40	Perry, Jim	75T	263	$ .15	$ .60
Perranoski, Ron	69T	77	$ .35	$1.40	Perry, Pat	87T	417	$ .01	$ .04
Perranoski, Ron	70T	226	$ .20	$ .80	Perry, Pat	88T	282	$ .01	$ .04
Perranoski, Ron	71T	475	$ .50	$2.00	Perry, Pat	89T	186	$ .01	$ .03
Perranoski, Ron	72T	367	$ .10	$ .40	Perry, Pat	90T	541	$ .01	$ .03
Perry, Bob	64T	48	$ .50	$2.00	Perzanowski, Stan	76T	388	$ .05	$ .25
Perry, Gaylord	62T	199	$45.00	$180.00	Pesky, Johnny	51Tbb	5	$10.00	$40.00
Perry, Gaylord	63T	169	$8.00	$32.00	Pesky, Johnny	52T	15	$16.25	$65.00
Perry, Gaylord	64T	468	$10.00	$40.00	Pesky, Johnny	54T	63	$8.00	$32.00
Perry, Gaylord	65T	193	$5.00	$20.00	Pesky, Johnny	63T	343	$ .90	$3.60
Perry, Gaylord	66T	598	$65.00	$260.00	Pesky, Johnny	64T	248	$ .65	$2.60
Perry, Gaylord	67T	236	$3.75	$15.00	Pesky, Johnny	91TA53	315	$ .10	$ .50
Perry, Gaylord	67T	320	$3.75	$15.00	Peters, Frank	68T	409	$ .35	$1.40
Perry, Gaylord	68T	11	$1.00	$4.00	Peters, Gary	60T	407	$1.25	$5.00
Perry, Gaylord	68T	85	$2.50	$10.00	Peters, Gary	61T	303	$ .60	$2.40
Perry, Gaylord	69T	485	$2.50	$10.00	Peters, Gary	63T	522	$1.75	$7.00
Perry, Gaylord	70T	560	$3.50	$14.00	Peters, Gary	64T	2	$ .75	$3.00
Perry, Gaylord	71T	70	$ .75	$3.00	Peters, Gary	64T	130	$ .50	$2.00
Perry, Gaylord	71T	140	$2.00	$8.00	Peters, Gary	65T	9	$ .75	$3.00
Perry, Gaylord	72T	285	$1.75	$7.00	Peters, Gary	65T	430	$1.00	$4.00
Perry, Gaylord	73T	66	$ .35	$1.40	Peters, Gary	66T	111	$ .50	$2.00
Perry, Gaylord	73T	346	$ .30	$1.20	Peters, Gary	67T	233	$ .50	$2.00
Perry, Gaylord	73T	400	$1.00	$4.00	Peters, Gary	67T	310	$ .60	$2.40
Perry, Gaylord	74T	35	$1.00	$4.00	Peters, Gary	68T	8	$ .55	$2.20
Perry, Gaylord	75T	530	$1.00	$4.00	Peters, Gary	68T	210	$ .35	$1.40
Perry, Gaylord	76T	55	$ .75	$3.00	Peters, Gary	68TAS	379	$ .50	$2.00
Perry, Gaylord	76T	204	$ .25	$1.00	Peters, Gary	69T	34	$ .35	$1.40
Perry, Gaylord	77T	152	$ .65	$2.60	Peters, Gary	70T	540	$ .35	$1.40
Perry, Gaylord	78T	686	$ .60	$2.40	Peters, Gary	71T	225	$ .25	$1.00
Perry, Gaylord	79T	5	$ .10	$ .40	Peters, Gary	72T	503	$ .25	$1.00
Perry, Gaylord	79T	321	$ .50	$2.00	Peters, Rick	81T	177	$ .01	$ .08
Perry, Gaylord	80T	280	$ .15	$1.25	Peters, Rick	82T	504	$ .01	$ .08
Perry, Gaylord	81T	582	$ .10	$1.00	Peters, Rick	84T	436	$ .01	$ .06
Perry, Gaylord	81TTR	812	$ .20	$2.00	Peters, Steve	88TTR	84	$ .01	$ .05
Perry, Gaylord	82T	115	$ .10	$ .50	Peters, Steve	89T	482	$ .01	$ .03
Perry, Gaylord	82TTR	88	$ .20	$2.00	Petersen, Matt	93T	497	$ .05	$ .35
Perry, Gaylord	83T	463	$ .10	$ .50					
Perry, Gaylord	83T	464	$ .05	$ .25					
Perry, Gaylord	84T	4	$ .10	$1.00					
Perry, Gaylord	84T	6	$ .10	$ .40					
Perry, Gerald	84TTR	92	$ .05	$ .35					
Perry, Gerald	85T	219	$ .01	$ .06					
Perry, Gerald	86T	557	$ .01	$ .05					
Perry, Gerald	87T	639	$ .01	$ .04					
Perry, Gerald	88T	39	$ .01	$ .04					
Perry, Gerald	89T	130	$ .01	$ .03					
Perry, Gerald	90T	792	$ .01	$ .03					
Perry, Gerald	90TTR	92	$ .01	$ .05					
Perry, Gerald	91T	384	$ .01	$ .03					
Perry, Gerald	91TSC	379	$ .05	$ .25					
Perry, Gerald	92T	498	$ .01	$ .03					
Perry, Gerald	92TSC	338	$ .01	$ .10					
Perry, Gerald	93T	597	$ .01	$ .03					
Perry, Jim	59T	542	$5.50	$22.00					
Perry, Jim	60T	324	$1.25	$5.00					
Perry, Jim	61T	48	$ .75	$3.00					
Perry, Jim	61T	385	$1.25	$5.00					
Perry, Jim	61TAS	584	$8.00	$32.00					
Perry, Jim	62T	37	$ .60	$2.40					
Perry, Jim	62T	405	$1.50	$6.00					
Perry, Jim	63T	535	$3.00	$12.00					
Perry, Jim	64T	34	$ .50	$2.00					
Perry, Jim	65T	351	$ .50	$2.00					
Perry, Jim	66T	283	$ .50	$2.00					
Perry, Jim	67T	246	$ .50	$2.00					
Perry, Jim	68T	393	$ .35	$1.40					
Perry, Jim	69T	146	$ .35	$1.40					
Perry, Jim	70T	70	$ .50	$2.00					
Perry, Jim	70T	620	$1.00	$4.00	Peterson, Adam	90T	299	$ .01	$ .03
Perry, Jim	71T	69	$ .50	$2.00	Peterson, Adam	91T	559	$ .01	$ .03
Perry, Jim	71T	500	$ .50	$2.00	Peterson, Cap	64T	568	$2.25	$9.00

TOPPS

Player	Year	No.	VG	EX/MT	Player	Year	No.	VG	EX/MT
Peterson, Cap	65T	512	$1.25	$5.00	Pfeil, Bobby	70T	99	$ .20	$ .80
Peterson, Cap	66T	349	$ .50	$2.00	Pfeil, Bobby	72T	681	$1.25	$5.00
Peterson, Cap	67T	387	$ .60	$2.40	Pfister, Dan	62T	592	$15.00	$60.00
Peterson, Cap	68T	188	$ .35	$1.40	Pfister, Dan	63T	521	$1.75	$7.00
Peterson, Cap	69T	571	$ .40	$1.60	Pfister, Dan	64T	302	$ .65	$2.60
Peterson, Fritz	66T	584	$3.75	$15.00	Phelps, Ken	85T	582	$ .01	$ .06
Peterson, Fritz	67T	495	$1.50	$6.00	Phelps, Ken	86T	34	$ .01	$ .05
Peterson, Fritz	68T	246	$ .35	$1.40	Phelps, Ken	87T	333	$ .01	$ .04
Peterson, Fritz	69T	46	$ .35	$1.40	Phelps, Ken	88T	182	$ .01	$ .04
Peterson, Fritz	70T	142	$ .20	$ .80	Phelps, Ken	89T	741	$ .01	$ .03
Peterson, Fritz	71T	460	$ .50	$2.00	Phelps, Ken	90T	411	$ .01	$ .03
Peterson, Fritz	72T	573	$ .40	$1.60	Philley, Dave	52T	226	$7.00	$28.00
Peterson, Fritz	72TIA	574	$ .40	$1.60	Philley, Dave	53T	64	$6.25	$25.00
Peterson, Fritz	73T	82	$ .10	$ .40	Philley, Dave	54T	159	$3.75	$15.00
Peterson, Fritz	74T	229	$ .10	$ .40	Philley, Dave	56T	222	$3.75	$15.00
Peterson, Fritz	75T	62	$ .10	$ .40	Philley, Dave	57T	124	$2.00	$8.00
Peterson, Fritz	76T	255	$ .05	$ .25	Philley, Dave	58T	116	$1.25	$5.00
Peterson, Harding	58T	322	$1.25	$5.00	Philley, Dave	59T	92	$1.50	$6.00
Petralli, Geno	86T	296	$ .01	$ .05	Philley, Dave	60T	52	$ .85	$3.40
Petralli, Geno	87T	388	$ .01	$ .04	Philley, Dave	61T	369	$ .60	$2.40
Petralli, Geno	88T	589	$ .01	$ .04	Philley, Dave	62T	542	$6.00	$24.00
Petralli, Geno	89T	137	$ .01	$ .03	Philley, Dave	91TA53	64	$ .01	$ .15
Petralli, Geno	90T	706	$ .01	$ .03	Phillies, Team	56T	72	$6.00	$24.00
Petralli, Geno	91T	78	$ .01	$ .03	Phillies, Team	57T	214	$3.00	$12.00
Petralli, Geno	91TSC	10	$ .05	$ .25	Phillies, Team	58T	134	$3.50	$14.00
Petralli, Geno	92T	409	$ .01	$ .03	Phillies, Team	59T	8	$10.00	$40.00
Petralli, Geno	92TSC	3	$ .01	$ .10	Phillies, Team	60T	302	$2.00	$8.00
Petralli, Geno	93T	332	$ .01	$ .03	Phillies, Team	61T	491	$2.25	$9.00
Petralli, Geno	93TSC	232	$ .01	$ .10	Phillies, Team	62T	294	$1.75	$7.00
Petrocelli, Rico	65T	74	$1.75	$7.00	Phillies, Team	63T	13	$1.00	$4.00
Petrocelli, Rico	66T	298	$ .75	$3.00	Phillies, Team	64T	293	$1.50	$6.00
Petrocelli, Rico	67T	528	$2.25	$9.00	Phillies, Team	65T	338	$1.50	$6.00
Petrocelli, Rico	68T	430	$ .35	$1.40	Phillies, Team	66T	463	$2.75	$11.00
Petrocelli, Rico	69T	215	$ .35	$1.40	Phillies, Team	67T	102	$ .75	$3.00
Petrocelli, Rico	70T	680	$1.25	$5.00	Phillies, Team	68T	477	$1.50	$6.00
Petrocelli, Rico	70TAS	457	$ .35	$1.40	Phillies, Team	70T	436	$ .50	$2.00
Petrocelli, Rico	71T	340	$ .25	$1.00	Phillies, Team	71T	268	$ .50	$2.00
Petrocelli, Rico	72T	30	$ .20	$ .80	Phillies, Team	72T	397	$ .75	$3.00
Petrocelli, Rico	73T	365	$ .10	$ .40	Phillies, Team	73T	536	$1.50	$6.00
Petrocelli, Rico	74T	609	$ .10	$ .40	Phillies, Team	74T	383	$ .25	$1.00
Petrocelli, Rico	75T	356	$ .10	$ .40	Phillies, Team Checklist	75T	46	$ .35	$1.40
Petrocelli, Rico	76T	445	$ .05	$ .25	Phillies, Team Checklist	76T	384	$ .30	$1.20
Petrocelli, Rico	77T	111	$ .05	$ .20	Phillies, Team Checklist	77T	467	$ .25	$1.00
Petry, Dan	80T	373	$ .05	$ .25	Phillies, Team Checklist	78T	381	$ .20	$ .80
Petry, Dan	81T	59	$ .01	$ .15	Phillies, Team Checklist	79T	112	$ .15	$ .60
Petry, Dan	82T	211	$ .01	$ .08	Phillies, Team Checklist	80T	526	$ .10	$ .50
Petry, Dan	82T	666	$ .01	$ .08	Phillies, Team Checklist	81T	682	$ .05	$ .25
Petry, Dan	83T	261	$ .01	$ .08	Phillies, Team Leaders	86T	246	$ .01	$ .15
Petry, Dan	83T	638	$ .01	$ .08	Phillies, Team Leaders	87T	481	$ .01	$ .04
Petry, Dan	84T	147	$ .01	$ .06	Phillies, Team Leaders	88T	669	$ .01	$ .04
Petry, Dan	85T	435	$ .01	$ .06	Phillies, Team Leaders	89T	489	$$ .01	$ .10
Petry, Dan	86T	540	$ .01	$ .05	Phillips, Adolfo	66T	32	$ .35	$1.40
Petry, Dan	87T	752	$ .01	$ .04	Phillips, Adolfo	67T	148	$ .40	$1.60
Petry, Dan	88T	78	$ .01	$ .04	Phillips, Adolfo	68T	202	$ .35	$1.40
Petry, Dan	88TTR	85	$ .01	$ .05	Phillips, Adolfo	69T	372	$ .30	$1.20
Petry, Dan	90T	363	$ .01	$ .03	Phillips, Adolfo	70T	666	$1.25	$5.00
Petry, Dan	90TTR	93	$ .01	$ .05	Phillips, Adolfo	71T	418	$ .50	$2.00
Pettini, Joe	81T	62	$ .01	$ .08	Phillips, Bubba	57T	395	$1.75	$7.00
Pettini, Joe	82T	568	$ .01	$ .08	Phillips, Bubba	58T	212	$1.25	$5.00
Pettini, Joe	83T	143	$ .01	$ .08	Phillips, Bubba	59T	187	$1.00	$4.00
Pettini, Joe	84T	449	$ .01	$ .06	Phillips, Bubba	60T	243	$ .75	$3.00
Pettis, Gary	84TTR	93	$ .05	$ .25	Phillips, Bubba	61T	101	$ .60	$2.40
Pettis, Gary	85T	497	$ .01	$ .15	Phillips, Bubba	62T	511	$1.50	$6.00
Pettis, Gary	86T	604	$ .01	$ .05	Phillips, Bubba	63T	177	$ .50	$2.00
Pettis, Gary	87T	278	$ .01	$ .04	Phillips, Bubba	64T	143	$ .50	$2.00
Pettis, Gary	88T	71	$ .01	$ .04	Phillips, Bubba	65T	306	$ .50	$2.00
Pettis, Gary	88TTR	86	$ .01	$ .05	Phillips, Dick	63T	544	$10.00	$40.00
Pettis, Gary	89T	146	$ .01	$ .03	Phillips, Dick	64T	559	$2.25	$9.00
Pettis, Gary	90T	512	$ .01	$ .03	Phillips, Jack	52T	240	$7.00	$28.00
Pettis, Gary	90TTR	94	$ .01	$ .05	Phillips, Jack	57T	307	$5.00	$20.00
Pettis, Gary	91T	314	$ .01	$ .03	Phillips, Lefty	70T	376	$ .35	$1.40
Pettis, Gary	91TSC	141	$ .05	$ .25	Phillips, Lefty	71T	279	$ .25	$1.00
Pettis, Gary	92T	756	$ .01	$ .03	Phillips, Mike	74T	533	$ .10	$ .40
Pettis, Gary	92TSC	548	$ .01	$ .10	Phillips, Mike	75T	642	$ .10	$ .40
Pevey, Marty	90T	137	$ .01	$ .03	Phillips, Mike	76T	93	$ .05	$ .25

TOPPS

Player	Year	No.	VG	EX/MT
Phillips, Mike	77T	352	$ .05	$ .20
Phillips, Mike	78T	88	$ .04	$ .16
Phillips, Mike	79T	258	$ .03	$ .12
Phillips, Mike	80T	439	$ .01	$ .10
Phillips, Mike	81T	113	$ .01	$ .08
Phillips, Mike	81TTR	813	$ .01	$ .15
Phillips, Mike	82T	762	$ .01	$ .08
Phillips, Taylor	57T	343	$5.00	$20.00
Phillips, Taylor	58T	159	$1.25	$5.00
Phillips, Taylor	59T	113	$1.00	$4.00
Phillips, Taylor	60T	211	$ .75	$3.00
Phillips, Tony	83TTR	87	$1.00	$4.00
Phillips, Tony	84T	309	$ .10	$ .75
Phillips, Tony	85T	444	$ .01	$ .06

Player	Year	No.	VG	EX/MT
Phillips, Tony	**86T**	**29**	**$ .01**	**$ .05**
Phillips, Tony	87T	188	$ .01	$ .04
Phillips, Tony	88T	673	$ .01	$ .04
Phillips, Tony	89T	248	$ .01	$ .03
Phillips, Tony	90T	702	$ .01	$ .03
Phillips, Tony	90TTR	95	$ .01	$ .05
Phillips, Tony	91T	583	$ .01	$ .03
Phillips, Tony	91TSC	41	$ .05	$ .25
Phillips, Tony	91TTR	91	$ .01	$ .15
Phillips, Tony	92T	319	$ .01	$ .03
Phillips, Tony	92TSC	488	$ .01	$ .10
Phillips, Tony	93T	189	$ .01	$ .03
Phillips, Tony	93TSC	5	$ .01	$ .10
Phoebus, Tom	67T	204	$ .50	$2.00
Phoebus, Tom	68T	97	$ .35	$1.40
Phoebus, Tom	69T	185	$ .35	$1.40
Phoebus, Tom	69T	532	$ .40	$1.60
Phoebus, Tom	70T	717	$1.25	$5.00
Phoebus, Tom	71T	611	$1.00	$4.00
Phoebus, Tom	72T	477	$ .25	$1.00
Piatt, Doug	91TTR	92	$ .01	$ .10
Piatt, Doug	92T	526	$ .01	$ .03
Piatt, Doug	92TSC	408	$ .01	$ .10
Piazza, Mike	93T	701	$ .15	$1.50
Picciolo, Rob	78T	528	$ .04	$ .16
Picciolo, Rob	79T	378	$ .03	$ .12
Picciolo, Rob	80T	158	$ .01	$ .10
Picciolo, Rob	81T	604	$ .01	$ .08
Picciolo, Rob	82T	293	$ .01	$ .08
Picciolo, Rob	82TTR	89	$ .01	$ .10
Picciolo, Rob	83T	476	$ .01	$ .08
Picciolo, Rob	84T	88	$ .01	$ .06
Picciolo, Rob	84TTR	94	$ .01	$ .15
Picciolo, Rob	85T	756	$ .01	$ .06
Picciolo, Rob	85TTR	90	$ .01	$ .10
Picciolo, Rob	86T	672	$ .01	$ .05
Pichardo, Hipolito	92TTR	89	$ .01	$ .10
Pichardo, Hipolito	93T	349	$ .01	$ .10
Pichardo, Hipolito	93TSC	211	$ .01	$ .10
Piche, Ron	61T	61	$ .60	$2.40
Piche, Ron	62T	582	$3.50	$14.00
Piche, Ron	63T	179	$ .50	$2.00
Piche, Ron	65T	464	$1.25	$5.00
Pico, Jeff	88TTR	87	$ .01	$ .10
Pico, Jeff	89T	262	$ .01	$ .03
Pico, Jeff	90T	613	$ .01	$ .03
Pico, Jeff	91T	311	$ .01	$ .03
Pierce, Billy	51Tbb	45	$11.25	$45.00
Pierce, Billy	52T	98	$8.00	$32.00
Pierce, Billy	53T	143	$8.00	$32.00
Pierce, Billy	56T	160	$3.50	$14.00
Pierce, Billy	57T	160	$2.50	$10.00
Pierce, Billy	58T	50	$2.25	$9.00
Pierce, Billy	58T	334	$1.25	$5.00
Pierce, Billy	59T	156	$1.50	$6.00
Pierce, Billy	59T	410	$1.00	$4.00
Pierce, Billy	59T	466	$1.50	$6.00
Pierce, Billy	59TAS	572	$8.00	$32.00
Pierce, Billy	60T	150	$ .75	$3.00
Pierce, Billy	60TAS	571	$3.50	$14.00
Pierce, Bill	61T	205	$ .75	$3.00
Pierce, Bill	62T	260	$ .75	$3.00
Pierce, Bill	63T	50	$ .50	$2.00
Pierce, Bill	63T	331	$ .90	$3.60
Pierce, Bill	64T	222	$ .65	$2.60
Pierce, Billy	91TA53	143	$ .01	$ .15
Pierce, Ed	93T	803	$ .01	$ .15
Pierce, Jack	76T	162	$ .05	$ .25
Pierce, Tony	67T	542	$3.00	$12.00
Pierce, Tony	68T	38	$ .35	$1.40
Piersall, Jim	56T	143	$3.75	$15.00
Piersall, Jim	57T	75	$2.50	$10.00
Piersall, Jim	58T	280	$1.75	$7.00
Piersall, Jim	59T	355	$1.50	$6.00
Piersall, Jim	60T	159	$1.25	$5.00
Piersall, Jim	61T	345	$1.00	$4.00
Piersall, Jim	62T	51	$1.50	$6.00
Piersall, Jim	62T	90	$ .75	$3.00
Piersall, Jim	63T	443	$1.25	$5.00
Piersall, Jim	64T	586	$3.00	$12.00
Piersall, Jim	65T	172	$ .50	$2.00
Piersall, Jim	66T	565	$9.00	$36.00
Piersall, Jim	67T	584	$7.00	$28.00
Piersall, Jimmy	91TA53	286	$ .10	$ .50
Pignatano, Joe	58T	373	$1.00	$4.00
Pignatano, Joe	59T	16	$1.50	$6.00
Pignatano, Joe	60T	292	$ .75	$3.00
Pignatano, Joe	60T	442	$1.25	$5.00
Pignatano, Joe	61T	74	$ .60	$2.40
Pignatano, Joe	62T	247	$ .75	$3.00
Pignatano, Joe	73T	257	$ .50	$2.00
Pignatano, Joe	74T	179	$ .40	$1.60
Pilarcik, Al	57T	311	$5.00	$20.00
Pilarcik, Al	58T	259	$1.25	$5.00
Pilarcik, Al	59T	7	$1.50	$6.00
Pilarcik, Al	60T	498	$1.25	$5.00
Pilarcik, Al	61T	62	$ .60	$2.40
Pillette, Duane	52T	82	$7.00	$28.00
Pillette, Duane	53T	269	$22.50	$90.00
Pillette, Duane	54T	107	$3.75	$15.00
Pillette, Duane	55T	168	$6.25	$25.00
Pillette, Duane	91TA53	269	$ .01	$ .15
Pilots, Team	70T	713	$6.00	$24.00
Pina, Horacio	71T	497	$ .50	$2.00

TOPPS

Player	Year	No.	VG	EX/MT	Player	Year	No.	VG	EX/MT
Pina, Horacio	72T	654	$ .40	$1.60	Pirates, Team Checklist	77T	354	$ .25	$1.00
Pina, Horacio	73T	138	$ .10	$ .40	Pirates, Team Checklist	78T	606	$ .20	$ .80
Pina, Horacio	74T	516	$ .10	$ .40	Pirates, Team Checklist	79T	244	$ .15	$ .60
Pina, Horacio	74TTR	516	$ .10	$ .40	Pirates, Team Checklist	80T	551	$ .10	$ .50
Pina, Horacio	75T	139	$ .10	$ .40	Pirates, Team Checklist	81T	683	$ .05	$ .25
Piniella, Lou	64T	167	$7.50	$30.00	Pirates, Team Leaders	86T	756	$ .01	$ .05
Piniella, Lou	68T	16	$1.00	$4.00	Pirates, Team Leaders	87T	131	$ .01	$ .04
Piniella, Lou	69T	394	$1.00	$4.00	Pirates, Team Leaders	88T	231	$ .01	$ .15
Piniella, Lou	70T	321	$ .75	$3.00	Pirates, Team Leaders	89T	699	$ .01	$ .03
Piniella, Lou	71T	35	$ .50	$2.00	Pirtle, Jerry	79T	720	$ .25	$1.00
Piniella, Lou	72T	491	$ .50	$2.00	Pisker, Don	79T	718	$ .03	$ .12
Piniella, Lou	72T	580	$1.00	$4.00	Pisoni, Jim	57T	402	$1.75	$7.00
Piniella, Lou	73T	140	$ .25	$1.00	Pisoni, Jim	59T	259	$1.00	$4.00
Piniella, Lou	74T	390	$ .25	$1.00	Pitler, Jake	52T	395	$43.75	$175.00
Piniella, Lou	74TTR	390	$ .20	$ .80	Pitlock, Skip	71T	19	$ .25	$1.00
Piniella, Lou	75T	217	$ .15	$ .60	Pitlock, Skip	75T	579	$ .10	$ .40
Piniella, Lou	76T	453	$ .20	$ .80	Pittaro, Chris	85TTR	91	$ .01	$ .10
Piniella, Lou	77T	96	$ .20	$ .80	Pittaro, Chris	86T	393	$ .01	$ .05
Piniella, Lou	78T	159	$ .10	$ .40	Pittman, Joe	82T	119	$ .01	$ .08
Piniella, Lou	79T	648	$ .05	$ .20	Pittman, Joe	82TTR	90	$ .01	$ .10
Piniella, Lou	80T	225	$ .05	$ .25	Pittman, Joe	83T	346	$ .01	$ .08
Piniella, Lou	81T	724	$ .05	$ .20	Pizarro, Juan	57T	383	$1.75	$7.00
Piniella, Lou	82T	538	$ .01	$ .15	Pizarro, Juan	59T	188	$1.00	$4.00
Piniella, Lou	83T	307	$ .01	$ .08	Pizarro, Juan	60T	59	$ .85	$3.40
Piniella, Lou	84T	408	$ .01	$ .06	Pizarro, Juan	61T	227	$ .60	$2.40
Piniella, Lou	86TTR	86	$ .01	$ .06	Pizarro, Juan	62T	255	$ .75	$3.00
Piniella, Lou	87T	168	$ .01	$ .04	Pizarro, Juan	63T	10	$1.00	$4.00
Piniella, Lou	88T	44	$ .01	$ .04	Pizarro, Juan	63T	160	$ .50	$2.00
Piniella, Lou	90TTR	96	$ .01	$ .05	Pizarro, Juan	64T	2	$ .75	$3.00
Piniella, Lou	91T	669	$ .01	$ .03	Pizarro, Juan	64T	430	$1.00	$4.00
Piniella, Lou	92T	321	$ .01	$ .03	Pizarro, Juan	65T	9	$ .75	$3.00
Piniella, Lou	93T	512	$ .01	$ .03	Pizarro, Juan	65T	125	$ .35	$1.40
Pinson, Vada	58T	420	$7.50	$30.00	Pizarro, Juan	66T	335	$ .50	$2.00
Pinson, Vada	59T	448	$1.75	$7.00	Pizarro, Juan	67T	602	$2.25	$9.00
Pinson, Vada	60T	32	$1.25	$5.00	Pizarro, Juan	68T	19	$ .35	$1.40
Pinson, Vada	60T	176	$1.25	$5.00	Pizarro, Juan	69T	498	$ .30	$1.20
Pinson, Vada	61T	25	$1.75	$7.00	Pizarro, Juan	71T	647	$1.10	$4.40
Pinson, Vada	61T	110	$1.00	$4.00	Pizarro, Juan	72T	18	$ .10	$ .40
Pinson, Vada	62T	52	$1.75	$7.00	Pizzaro, Juan	62T	59	$ .60	$2.40
Pinson, Vada	62T	80	$1.25	$5.00	Pladson, Gordy	81T	491	$ .01	$ .08
Pinson, Vada	63T	265	$1.00	$4.00	Plantier, Phil	91T	474	$ .10	$ .50
Pinson, Vada	64T	80	$ .75	$3.00	Plantier, Phil	91TSC	459	$1.25	$5.00
Pinson, Vada	64T	162	$ .50	$2.00	Plantier, Phil	92T	782	$ .01	$ .15
Pinson, Vada	65T	355	$1.00	$4.00	Plantier, Phil	92TSC	760	$ .05	$ .35
Pinson, Vada	66T	180	$ .75	$3.00	Plantier, Phil	93T	592	$ .01	$ .03
Pinson, Vada	67T	550	$3.00	$12.00	Plantier, Phil	93TSC	282	$ .05	$ .20
Pinson, Vada	68T	90	$ .75	$3.00	Plaskett, Elmo	63T	549	$2.25	$9.00
Pinson, Vada	69T	160	$ .50	$2.00	Playoff '69, N. L./Game 1	70T	195	$3.50	$14.00
Pinson, Vada	70T	445	$ .50	$2.00	Playoff '69, N. L./Game 2	70T	196	$ .75	$3.00
Pinson, Vada	71T	275	$ .50	$2.00	Playoff '69, N. L./Game 3	70T	197	$5.00	$20.00
Pinson, Vada	72T	135	$ .25	$1.00	Playoff '69, N. L./Mets	70T	198	$2.00	$8.00
Pinson, Vada	73T	75	$ .25	$1.00	Playoff '69, A. L./Game 1	70T	199	$ .50	$2.00
Pinson, Vada	74T	490	$ .20	$ .80	Playoff '69, A. L./Game 2	70T	200	$ .50	$2.00
Pinson, Vada	75T	295	$ .25	$1.00	Playoff '69, A. L./Game 3	70T	201	$ .50	$2.00
Pinson, Vada	76T	415	$ .15	$ .60	Playoff '69, A. L./Orioles	70T	202	$ .50	$2.00
Pirates, Team	56T	121	$7.50	$30.00	Playoffs '70, A. L./Game 1	71T	195	$ .50	$2.00
Pirates, Team	57T	161	$3.00	$12.00	Playoffs '70, A. L./Game 2	71T	196	$ .50	$2.00
Pirates, Team	58T	341	$3.50	$14.00	Playoffs '70, A. L./Game 3	71T	197	$1.00	$4.00
Pirates, Team	59T	528	$11.25	$45.00	Playoffs '70, A. L./Orioles	71T	198	$ .50	$2.00
Pirates, Team	60T	484	$6.25	$25.00	Playoffs '70, N. L./Game 1	71T	199	$ .50	$2.00
Pirates, Team	61T	554	$16.25	$65.00	Playoffs '70, N. L./Game 2	71T	200	$ .50	$2.00
Pirates, Team	62T	409	$2.50	$10.00	Playoffs '70, N. L./Game 3	71T	201	$ .50	$2.00
Pirates, Team	63T	151	$1.00	$4.00	Playoffs '70, N. L./Reds	71T	202	$ .50	$2.00
Pirates, Team	64T	373	$2.50	$10.00	Playoffs '71, N. L.	72T	221	$ .35	$1.40
Pirates, Team	65T	209	$1.00	$4.00	Playoffs '71, A. L.	72T	222	$ .35	$1.40
Pirates, Team	66T	404	$2.00	$8.00	Playoffs '72, A. L.	73T	201	$ .25	$1.00
Pirates, Team	67T	492	$1.50	$6.00	Playoffs '72, N. L.	73T	202	$ .25	$1.00
Pirates, Team	68T	308	$ .75	$3.00	Playoffs '73, A. L.	74T	470	$1.50	$6.00
Pirates, Team	70T	608	$1.25	$5.00	Playoffs '73, N. L.	74T	471	$ .25	$1.00
Pirates, Team	71T	603	$1.75	$7.00	Playoffs '75, N. L. & A. L.	76T	461	$ .25	$1.00
Pirates, Team	72T	1	$1.50	$6.00	Pleis, Bill	62T	124	$ .60	$2.40
Pirates, Team	73T	26	$ .25	$1.00	Pleis, Bill	63T	293	$ .90	$3.60
Pirates, Team	74T	626	$ .25	$1.00	Pleis, Bill	64T	484	$1.00	$4.00
Pirates, Team Checklist	75T	304	$ .35	$1.40	Pleis, Bill	65T	122	$ .35	$1.40
Pirates, Team Checklist	76T	504	$ .30	$1.20	Plesac, Dan	86TTR	87	$ .01	$ .15

TOPPS

Player	Year	No.	VG	EX/MT
Plesac, Dan	87T	279	$ .01	$ .10
Plesac, Dan	88T	670	$ .01	$ .04
Plesac, Dan	89T	740	$ .01	$ .03
Plesac, Dan	90T	490	$ .01	$ .03
Plesac, Dan	91T	146	$ .01	$ .03
Plesac, Dan	91TSC	7	$ .05	$ .25
Plesac, Dan	92T	303	$ .01	$ .03
Plesac, Dan	92TSC	532	$ .01	$ .10
Plesac, Dan	93T	16	$ .01	$ .03
Plesac, Dan	93TSC	24	$ .01	$ .10
Pless, Rance	56T	339	$2.50	$10.00
Plews, Herb	57T	169	$2.00	$8.00
Plews, Herb	58T	109	$2.00	$8.00
Plews, Herb	59T	373	$1.00	$4.00
Plummer, Bill	73T	177	$ .20	$ .80
Plummer, Bill	74T	524	$ .10	$ .40
Plummer, Bill	75T	656	$ .10	$ .40
Plummer, Bill	76T	627	$ .05	$ .25
Plummer, Bill	77T	239	$ .05	$ .20
Plummer, Bill	78T	106	$ .04	$ .16
Plummer, Bill	79T	396	$ .03	$ .12
Plummer, Bill	92T	171	$ .01	$ .03
Plunk, Eric	87T	587	$ .01	$ .04
Plunk, Eric	88T	173	$ .01	$ .04
Plunk, Eric	89T	448	$ .01	$ .03
Plunk, Eric	90T	9	$ .01	$ .03
Plunk, Eric	91T	786	$ .01	$ .03
Plunk, Eric	91TSC	529	$ .05	$ .25

Player	Year	No.	VG	EX/MT
Plunk, Eric	92T	672	$ .01	$ .03
Plympton, Jeff	92TSC	481	$ .01	$ .15
Pocoroba, Biff	76T	103	$ .05	$ .25
Pocoroba, Biff	77T	594	$ .05	$ .20
Pocoroba, Biff	78T	296	$ .04	$ .16
Pocoroba, Biff	79T	555	$ .03	$ .12
Pocoroba, Biff	80T	132	$ .01	$ .10
Pocoroba, Biff	81T	326	$ .01	$ .08
Pocoroba, Biff	82T	88	$ .01	$ .08
Pocoroba, Biff	83T	676	$ .01	$ .08
Pocoroba, Biff	84T	438	$ .01	$ .06
Podbielan, Clarence "Bud"	52T	188	$7.00	$28.00
Podbielan, Bud	53T	237	$11.25	$45.00
Podbielan, Bud	54T	69	$7.50	$30.00
Podbielan, Bud	55T	153	$4.00	$16.00

Player	Year	No.	VG	EX/MT
Podbielan, Bud	56T	224	$3.75	$15.00
Podbielan, Clarence	91TA53	237	$ .01	$ .15
Podres, Johnny	53T	263	$65.00	$260.00
Podres, Johnny	54T	166	$7.00	$28.00
Podres, Johnny	55T	25	$5.00	$20.00
Podres, Johnny	56T	173	$4.00	$16.00
Podres, Johnny	57T	277	$12.50	$50.00
Podres, Johnny	58T	120	$2.25	$9.00
Podres, Johnny	59T	262	$2.00	$8.00
Podres, Johnny	59T	495	$1.00	$4.00
Podres, Johnny	60T	425	$1.25	$5.00
Podres, Johnny	61T	109	$ .75	$3.00
Podres, Johnny	61T	207	$5.00	$20.00
Podres, Johnny	62T	280	$ .75	$3.00
Podres, Johnny	63T	150	$1.00	$4.00
Podres, Johnny	63T	412	$9.00	$36.00
Podres, Johnny	64T	580	$2.50	$10.00
Podres, Johnny	65T	387	$1.25	$5.00
Podres, Johnny	66T	468	$1.50	$6.00
Podres, Johnny	67T	284	$ .75	$3.00
Podres, Johnny	69T	659	$ .75	$3.00
Podres, Johnny	73T	12	$ .20	$ .80
Podres, John	91TA53	263	$ .10	$ .50
Poholsky, Tom	52T	242	$7.00	$28.00
Poholsky, Tom	54T	142	$3.75	$15.00
Poholsky, Tom	56T	196	$3.75	$15.00
Poholsky, Tom	57T	235	$2.00	$8.00
Pointer, Aaron	67T	564	$2.25	$9.00
Pole, Dick	74T	596	$ .10	$ .40
Pole, Dick	75T	513	$ .10	$ .40
Pole, Dick	76T	326	$ .05	$ .25
Pole, Dick	77T	187	$ .05	$ .20
Pole, Dick	78T	233	$ .04	$ .16
Polidor, Gus	88T	708	$ .01	$ .04
Polidor, Gus	90T	313	$ .01	$ .03
Polk, Ron	91TTR	93	$ .01	$ .05
Pollet, Howie	51Trb	7	$1.75	$7.50
Pollet, Howie	52T	63	$13.75	$55.00
Pollet, Howie	53T	83	$6.25	$25.00
Pollet, Howie	54T	89	$3.75	$15.00
Pollet, Howie	55T	76	$2.25	$9.00
Pollet, Howie	56T	262	$2.50	$10.00
Pollet, Howie	60T	468	$1.25	$5.00
Pollet, Howie	91TA53	83	$ .01	$ .15
Polonia, Luis	87TTR	96	$ .05	$ .30
Polonia, Luis	88T	238	$ .05	$ .20
Polonia, Luis	89T	424	$ .01	$ .03
Polonia, Luis	90T	634	$ .01	$ .03
Polonia, Luis	90TTR	97	$ .01	$ .05
Polonia, Luis	91T	107	$ .01	$ .03
Polonia, Luis	91TSC	144	$ .05	$ .25
Polonia, Luis	92T	37	$ .01	$ .03
Polonia, Luis	92TSC	528	$ .01	$ .10
Polonia, Luis	93T	760	$ .01	$ .03
Polonia, Luis	93TSC	100	$ .01	$ .10
Poole, Jim	88TTR	88	$ .01	$ .15
Poole, Jim	92T	683	$ .01	$ .03
Poole, Jim	92TSC	412	$ .01	$ .10
Poole, Jim	93T	793	$ .01	$ .03
Pope, Dave	57T	249	$2.00	$8.00
Popovich, Paul	67T	536	$9.00	$36.00
Popovich, Paul	68T	266	$ .35	$1.40
Popovich, Paul	69T	47	$ .35	$1.40
Popovich, Paul	70T	258	$ .20	$ .80
Popovich, Paul	71T	726	$1.10	$4.40
Popovich, Paul	72T	512	$ .25	$1.00
Popovich, Paul	73T	309	$ .10	$ .40
Popovich, Paul	74T	14	$ .10	$ .40
Popovich, Paul	75T	359	$ .10	$ .40
Popowski, Eddie	73T	131	$ .20	$ .80
Popowski, Eddie	74T	403	$ .10	$ .40
Poquette, Tom	75T	622	$2.75	$11.00
Poquette, Tom	77T	93	$ .05	$ .20
Poquette, Tom	78T	357	$ .04	$ .16
Poquette, Tom	79T	476	$ .03	$ .12

TOPPS

Player	Year	No.	VG	EX/MT
Poquette, Tom	80T	597	$ .01	$ .10
Poquette, Tom	81T	153	$ .01	$ .08
Poquette, Tom	82T	657	$ .01	$ .08
Porter, Chuck	82T	333	$ .01	$ .08
Porter, Chuck	84T	452	$ .01	$ .06
Porter, Chuck	85T	32	$ .01	$ .06
Porter, Chuck	86T	292	$ .01	$ .05
Porter, Darrell	72T	162	$ .25	$1.00
Porter, Darrell	73T	582	$ .75	$3.00
Porter, Darrell	74T	194	$ .10	$ .40
Porter, Darrell	75T	52	$ .10	$ .40
Porter, Darrell	76T	645	$ .05	$ .25
Porter, Darrell	77T	214	$ .05	$ .20
Porter, Darrell	78T	19	$ .04	$ .16
Porter, Darrell	79T	571	$ .03	$ .12
Porter, Darrell	80T	360	$ .01	$ .10
Porter, Darrell	81T	610	$ .01	$ .08
Porter, Darrell	81TTR	814	$ .01	$ .15
Porter, Darrell	82T	447	$ .05	$ .20
Porter, Darrell	82TSA	448	$ .01	$ .10
Porter, Darrell	83T	103	$ .01	$ .08
Porter, Darrell	84T	285	$ .01	$ .06
Porter, Darrell	85T	525	$ .01	$ .06
Porter, Darrell	86T	757	$ .01	$ .05
Porter, Darrell	86TTR	88	$ .01	$ .06
Porter, Darrell	87T	689	$ .01	$ .04
Porter, J. W.	53T	211	$4.50	$18.00
Porter, J. W.	55T	49	$2.25	$9.00
Porter, J. W.	58T	32	$2.00	$8.00
Porter, J. W.	59T	246	$1.00	$4.00
Porter, J. W.	91TA53	211	$ .01	$ .15
Porterfield, Bob	52T	301	$12.50	$50.00
Porterfield, Bob	53T	108	$4.00	$16.00
Porterfield, Bob	56T	248	$3.75	$15.00
Porterfield, Bob	57T	118	$2.00	$8.00
Porterfield, Bob	58T	344	$1.25	$5.00
Porterfield, Bob	59T	181	$1.00	$4.00
Porterfield, Bob	91TA53	108	$ .01	$ .15
Portocarrero, Arnie	58T	465	$1.00	$4.00
Portocarrero, Arnie	59T	98	$1.50	$6.00
Portocarrero, Arnie	60T	254	$ .75	$3.00
Portocarrero, Arnold	54T	214	$3.75	$15.00
Portocarrero, Arnold	55T	77	$2.25	$9.00
Portocarrero, Arnold	56T	53	$2.00	$8.00
Portugal, Mark	87T	419	$ .01	$ .10
Portugal, Mark	89T	46	$ .01	$ .03
Portugal, Mark	90T	253	$ .01	$ .03
Portugal, Mark	91T	647	$ .01	$ .03
Portugal, Mark	91TSC	320	$ .05	$ .25
Portugal, Mark	92T	114	$ .01	$ .03
Portugal, Mark	92TSC	126	$ .01	$ .10
Portugal, Mark	93T	335	$ .01	$ .03
Posada, Leo	61T	39	$ .60	$2.40
Posada, Leo	62T	168	$ .60	$2.40
Posedel, Bill	52T	361	$43.75	$175.00
Posedel, Bill	60T	469	$1.25	$5.00
Post, Wally	52T	151	$8.00	$32.00
Post, Wally	56T	158	$2.50	$10.00
Post, Wally	57T	157	$2.00	$8.00
Post, Wally	58T	387	$1.00	$4.00
Post, Wally	59T	398	$1.00	$4.00
Post, Wally	60T	13	$ .85	$3.40
Post, Wally	61T	378	$1.00	$4.00
Post, Wally	62T	148	$ .60	$2.40
Post, Wally	63T	462	$3.00	$12.00
Post, Wally	64T	253	$ .65	$2.60
Post, Wally	91TA53	294	$ .10	$ .40
Powell, Alonzo	92T	295	$ .01	$ .03
Powell, Alonzo	92TSC	547	$ .01	$ .10
Powell, "Boog" John	62T	99	$5.00	$21.00
Powell, Boog	63T	398	$5.50	$22.00
Powell, Boog	64T	89	$1.00	$4.00
Powell, Boog	65T	3	$5.50	$22.00
Powell, Boog	65T	560	$4.50	$18.00
Powell, Boog	66T	167	$1.00	$4.00

Player	Year	No.	VG	EX/MT
Powell, Boog	67T	230	$ .75	$3.00
Powell, Boog	67T	241	$1.25	$5.00
Powell, Boog	67T	243	$1.25	$5.00
Powell, Boog	67T	521	$1.50	$6.00
Powell, Boog	68T	381	$ .75	$3.00
Powell, Boog	69T	15	$ .75	$3.00
Powell, Boog	70T	64	$1.25	$5.00
Powell, Boog	70T	410	$ .75	$3.00
Powell, Boog	70TAS	451	$ .50	$2.00
Powell, Boog	71T	63	$ .25	$1.00
Powell, Boog	71T	700	$4.50	$18.00
Powell, Boog	72T	250	$ .40	$1.60
Powell, Boog	73T	325	$ .25	$1.00
Powell, Boog	74T	460	$ .20	$ .80
Powell, Boog	75T	208	$ .25	$1.00
Powell, Boog	75T	625	$ .15	$ .60
Powell, Boog	76T	45	$ .15	$ .60
Powell, Boog	77T	206	$ .25	$1.00
Powell, Dennis	87T	47	$ .01	$ .04
Powell, Dennis	88T	453	$ .01	$ .04
Powell, Dennis	89TTR	97	$ .01	$ .05
Powell, Dennis	93TSC	108	$ .01	$ .10
Powell, Grover	64T	113	$ .50	$2.00
Powell, Hosken	79T	656	$ .03	$ .12
Powell, Hosken	80T	471	$ .01	$ .10
Powell, Hosken	81T	137	$ .01	$ .08
Powell, Hosken	82T	584	$ .01	$ .08
Powell, Hosken	82TTR	91	$ .01	$ .10
Powell, Hosken	83T	77	$ .01	$ .08
Powell, Leroy	56T	144	$2.50	$10.00
Power, Ted	84T	554	$ .01	$ .06
Power, Ted	85T	342	$ .01	$ .06
Power, Ted	86T	108	$ .01	$ .05
Power, Ted	87T	437	$ .01	$ .04
Power, Ted	88T	236	$ .01	$ .04
Power, Ted	88TTR	89	$ .01	$ .05
Power, Ted	89T	777	$ .01	$ .03
Power, Ted	90T	59	$ .01	$ .03
Power, Ted	91T	621	$ .01	$ .03
Power, Ted	92TSC	812	$ .01	$ .10
Power, Ted	93TSC	82	$ .01	$ .10
Power, Vic	54T	52	$8.00	$32.00
Power, Vic	55T	30	$2.25	$9.00
Power, Vic	56T	67	$2.00	$8.00
Power, Vic	57T	167	$2.00	$8.00
Power, Vic	58T	406	$1.00	$4.00
Power, Vic	59T	229	$1.00	$4.00
Power, Vic	60T	75	$ .85	$3.40
Power, Vic	61T	255	$ .60	$2.40
Power, Vic	62T	445	$1.25	$5.00
Power, Vic	63T	40	$ .50	$2.00
Power, Vic	64T	355	$ .65	$2.60
Power, Vic	65T	442	$1.00	$4.00
Power, Vic	66T	192	$ .50	$2.00
Powers, John	58T	432	$1.00	$4.00
Powers, John	59T	489	$1.00	$4.00
Powers, Johnny	60T	422	$ .75	$3.00
Pramesa, John	52T	105	$7.00	$28.00
Pratt, Todd	93T	479	$ .01	$ .15
Presko, Joe	52T	220	$7.00	$28.00
Presko, Joe	54T	135	$3.75	$15.00
Presley, Jim	85TTR	92	$ .01	$ .15
Presley, Jim	86T	598	$ .01	$ .10
Presley, Jim	87T	45	$ .01	$ .04
Presley, Jim	88T	285	$ .01	$ .04
Presley, Jim	89T	112	$ .01	$ .03
Presley, Jim	90T	346	$ .01	$ .03
Presley, Jim	90TTR	98	$ .01	$ .05
Presley, Jim	91T	643	$ .01	$ .03
Price, Jimmie	67T	123	$ .40	$1.60
Price, Jimmie	68T	226	$ .35	$1.40
Price, Jimmie	69T	472	$ .30	$1.20
Price, Jimmie	70T	129	$ .20	$ .80
Price, Jimmie	71T	444	$ .50	$2.00
Price, Joe	81T	258	$ .01	$ .08

TOPPS

Player	Year	No.	VG	EX/MT	Player	Year	No.	VG	EX/MT
Price, Joe	82T	492	$ .01	$ .08	Puhl, Terry	81T	411	$ .01	$ .08
Price, Joe	83T	191	$ .01	$ .08	Puhl, Terry	82T	277	$ .01	$ .08
Price, Joe	84T	686	$ .01	$ .06	Puhl, Terry	83T	39	$ .01	$ .08
Price, Joe	85T	82	$ .01	$ .06	Puhl, Terry	84T	383	$ .01	$ .06
Price, Joe	86T	523	$ .01	$ .05	Puhl, Terry	85T	613	$ .01	$ .06
Price, Joe	87T	332	$ .01	$ .04	Puhl, Terry	86T	763	$ .01	$ .05
Price, Joe	88T	786	$ .01	$ .04	Puhl, Terry	87T	693	$ .01	$ .04
Price, Joe	89T	217	$ .01	$ .03	Puhl, Terry	88T	587	$ .01	$ .04
Price, Joe	90T	473	$ .01	$ .03	Puhl, Terry	89T	119	$ .01	$ .03
Price, Joe	91T	127	$ .01	$ .03	Puhl, Terry	90T	494	$ .01	$ .03
Priddy, Bob	64T	74	$ .50	$2.00	Pujols, Luis	79T	139	$ .03	$ .12
Priddy, Bob	65T	482	$1.25	$5.00	Pujols, Luis	81T	313	$ .01	$ .08
Priddy, Bob	66T	572	$3.75	$15.00	Pujols, Luis	82T	582	$ .01	$ .08
Priddy, Bob	67T	26	$ .40	$1.60	Pujols, Luis	83T	752	$ .01	$ .08
Priddy, Bob	68T	391	$ .35	$1.40	Pujols, Luis	84T	446	$ .01	$ .06
Priddy, Bob	69T	248	$ .50	$2.00	Puleo, Charlie	82TTR	94	$ .01	$ .10
Priddy, Bob	70T	687	$1.25	$5.00	Puleo, Charlie	83T	549	$ .01	$ .08
Priddy, Bob	71T	147	$ .25	$1.00	Puleo, Charlie	83TTR	88	$ .01	$ .10
Priddy, Gerry (Jerry)	51Tbb	46	$7.50	$30.00	Puleo, Charlie	84T	273	$ .01	$ .06
Priddy, Jerry	52T	28	$13.75	$55.00	Puleo, Charlie	88T	179	$ .01	$ .04
Priddy, Jerry	53T	113	$6.25	$25.00	Puleo, Charlie	89T	728	$ .01	$ .03
Priddy, Jerry	91TA53	113	$ .01	$ .15	Pulido, Al	87T	642	$ .01	$ .04
Pridy, Todd	93T	441	$ .10	$ .40	Pulliam, Harvey	92T	687	$ .01	$ .10
Prince, Tom	89T	453	$ .01	$ .03	Pulliam, Harvey	92TSC	428	$ .01	$ .15
Prince, Tom	92TSC	332	$ .01	$ .10	Pulsipher, Bill	92TSC	676	$ .05	$ .25
Pritchard, Buddy	58T	151	$1.25	$5.00	Purdin, John	65T	331	$ .50	$2.00
Proctor, Jim	60T	141	$ .75	$3.00	Purdin, John	68T	336	$ .35	$1.40
Proly, Mike	79T	514	$ .03	$ .12	Purdin, John	69T	161	$ .35	$1.40
Proly, Mike	80T	399	$ .01	$ .10	Purdin, John	71T	748	$1.50	$6.00
Proly, Mike	81T	83	$ .01	$ .08	Purkey, Bob	54T	202	$4.50	$18.00
Proly, Mike	81TTR	815	$ .01	$ .15	Purkey, Bob	55T	118	$2.25	$9.00
Proly, Mike	82T	183	$ .01	$ .08	Purkey, Bob	57T	368	$1.75	$7.00
Proly, Mike	82TTR	92	$ .01	$ .10	Purkey, Bob	58T	311	$1.25	$5.00
Proly, Mike	83T	597	$ .01	$ .08	Purkey, Bob	59T	506	$1.00	$4.00
Proly, Mike	84T	437	$ .01	$ .06	Purkey, Bob	60T	4	$ .85	$3.40
Pruitt, Jason	92T	246	$ .01	$ .10	Purkey, Bob	61T	9	$ .60	$2.40
Pruitt, Ron	77T	654	$ .05	$ .20	Purkey, Bob	62T	120	$ .60	$2.40
Pruitt, Ron	78T	198	$ .04	$ .16	Purkey, Bob	62T	263	$ .75	$3.00
Pruitt, Ron	79T	226	$ .03	$ .12	Purkey, Bob	63T	5	$2.00	$8.00
Pruitt, Ron	80T	13	$ .01	$ .10	Purkey, Bob	63T	7	$1.25	$5.00
Pruitt, Ron	81T	442	$ .01	$ .08	Purkey, Bob	63T	350	$ .90	$3.60
Prybylinski, Don	92TSC	748	$ .01	$ .15	Purkey, Bob	64T	480	$1.00	$4.00
Pryor, Greg	79T	559	$ .03	$ .12	Purkey, Bob	65T	214	$ .50	$2.00
Pryor, Greg	80T	164	$ .01	$ .10	Purkey, Bob	66T	551	$7.00	$28.00
Pryor, Greg	81T	608	$ .01	$ .08	Putnam, Eddy	80T	59	$ .01	$ .10
Pryor, Greg	82T	76	$ .01	$ .08	Putnam, Pat	78T	706	$ .04	$ .16
Pryor, Greg	82TTR	93	$ .01	$ .10	Putnam, Pat	79T	713	$ .15	$ .60
Pryor, Greg	83T	418	$ .01	$ .08	Putnam, Pat	80T	22	$ .01	$ .10
Pryor, Greg	84T	317	$ .01	$ .06	Putnam, Pat	81T	498	$ .01	$ .08
Pryor, Greg	85T	188	$ .01	$ .06	Putnam, Pat	82T	149	$ .01	$ .08
Pryor, Greg	86T	773	$ .01	$ .05	Putnam, Pat	83TTR	89	$ .01	$ .10
Pryor, Greg	87T	761	$ .01	$ .04	Putnam, Pat	84T	336	$ .01	$ .06
Puchkov, Yevgeny	93T	633	$ .05	$ .25	Putnam, Pat	84T	636	$ .01	$ .06
Puckett, Kirby	85T	536	$5.00	$20.00	Putnam, Pat	85T	535	$ .01	$ .06
Puckett, Kirby	86T	329	$1.00	$4.00	Pyburn, Jim	57T	276	$5.00	$20.00
Puckett, Kirby	87T	450	$ .10	$1.00	Pyznarski, Tim	87T	429	$ .01	$ .10
Puckett, Kirby	87TAS	611	$ .10	$ .50	Qualls, Jim	69T	602	$ .40	$1.60
Puckett, Kirby	88T	120	$ .05	$ .35	Qualls, Jim	70T	192	$ .20	$ .80
Puckett, Kirby	88TAS	391	$ .01	$ .15	Qualls, Jim	71T	731	$1.50	$6.00
Puckett, Kirby	89T	650	$ .05	$ .35	Qualters, Tom	54T	174	$3.75	$15.00
Puckett, Kirby	89TAS	403	$ .05	$ .20	Qualters, Tom	55T	33	$2.25	$9.00
Puckett, Kirby	90T	700	$ .05	$ .35	Qualters, Tom	58T	453	$1.00	$4.00
Puckett, Kirby	90TAS	391	$ .01	$ .10	Qualters, Tom	59T	341	$1.00	$4.00
Puckett, Kirby	91T	300	$ .05	$ .20	Quantrill, Paul	93T	528	$ .01	$ .15
Puckett, Kirby	91TSC	110	$ .75	$3.00	Queen, Mel	64T	33	$ .50	$2.00
Puckett, Kirby	92T	575	$ .05	$ .20	Queen, Mel	66T	556	$7.00	$28.00
Puckett, Kirby	92TSC	500	$ .10	$1.00	Queen, Mel	67T	374	$ .60	$2.40
Puckett, Kirby	93T	200	$ .01	$ .03	Queen, Mel	68T	283	$ .35	$1.40
Puckett, Kirby	93T	406	$ .01	$ .15	Queen, Mel	69T	81	$ .35	$1.40
Puckett, Kirby	93TSC	283	$ .10	$ .50	Queen, Mel	71T	736	$1.50	$6.00
Pugh, Tim	93T	702	$ .05	$ .35	Queen, Mel	72T	196	$ .10	$ .40
Pugh, Tim	93TSC	265	$ .10	$1.00	Quilici, Frank	66T	207	$ .50	$2.00
Puhl, Terry	78T	553	$ .05	$ .20	Quilici, Frank	68T	557	$ .70	$2.80
Puhl, Terry	79T	617	$ .03	$ .12	Quilici, Frank	69T	356	$ .30	$1.20
Puhl, Terry	80T	147	$ .01	$ .10	Quilici, Frank	70T	572	$ .50	$2.00

TOPPS

Player	Year	No.	VG	EX/MT
Quilici, Frank	71T	141	$ .25	$1.00
Quilici, Frank	73T	49	$ .20	$ .80
Quilici, Frank	74T	447	$ .10	$ .40
Quinones, Luis	87T	362	$ .01	$ .04
Quinones, Luis	88T	667	$ .01	$ .04
Quinones, Luis	90T	176	$ .01	$ .03
Quinones, Luis	91T	581	$ .01	$ .03
Quinones, Luis	92T	356	$ .01	$ .03
Quinones, Luis	92TSC	151	$ .01	$ .10
Quinones, Rey	86TTR	89	$ .01	$ .06
Quinones (nez), Rey	87T	561	$ .01	$ .04
Quinones, Rey	88T	358	$ .01	$ .04
Quinones, Rey	89T	246	$ .01	$ .03
Quinones, Rey	89TTR	98	$ .01	$ .05
Quintana, Carlos	89T	704	$ .01	$ .15
Quintana, Carlos	90T	18	$ .01	$ .03
Quintana, Carlos	91T	206	$ .01	$ .03
Quintana, Carlos	91TSC	12	$ .05	$ .25
Quintana, Carlos	92T	127	$ .01	$ .03
Quintana, Carlos	92TSC	25	$ .01	$ .10
Quirk, Art	62T	591	$12.50	$50.00
Quirk, Art	63T	522	$1.75	$7.00

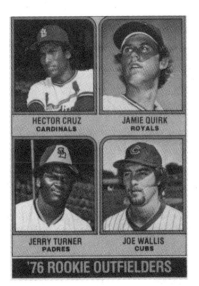

Player	Year	No.	VG	EX/MT
Quirk, Jamie	76T	598	$ .05	$ .25
Quirk, Jamie	77T	163	$ .05	$ .20
Quirk, Jamie	78T	95	$ .04	$ .16
Quirk, Jamie	79T	26	$ .03	$ .12
Quirk, Jamie	80T	248	$ .01	$ .10
Quirk, Jamie	81T	507	$ .01	$ .08
Quirk, Jamie	82T	173	$ .01	$ .08
Quirk, Jamie	83T	264	$ .01	$ .08
Quirk, Jamie	83TTR	90	$ .01	$ .10
Quirk, Jamie	84T	671	$ .01	$ .06
Quirk, Jamie	87T	354	$ .01	$ .04
Quirk, Jamie	88T	477	$ .01	$ .04
Quirk, Jamie	89T	702	$ .01	$ .03
Quirk, Jamie	91T	132	$ .01	$ .03
Quirk, Jamie	91TSC	573	$ .05	$ .25
Quirk, Jamie	92T	19	$ .01	$ .03
Quirk, Jamie	92TSC	83	$ .01	$ .10
Quisenberry, Dan	80T	667	$ .20	$2.00
Quisenberry, Dan	81T	8	$ .05	$ .25
Quisenberry, Dan	81T	493	$ .05	$ .35
Quisenberry, Dan	82T	264	$ .01	$ .15
Quisenberry, Dan	83T	155	$ .01	$ .10
Quisenberry, Dan	83T	708	$ .01	$ .08
Quisenberry, Dan	83TAS	396	$ .01	$ .08
Quisenberry, Dan	84T	3	$ .01	$ .10
Quisenberry, Dan	84T	138	$ .01	$ .10
Quisenberry, Dan	84T	570	$ .01	$ .10
Quisenberry, Dan	84T	718	$ .01	$ .15
Quisenberry, Dan	84TAS	407	$ .01	$ .06
Quisenberry, Dan	85T	270	$ .01	$ .06
Quisenberry, Dan	85TAS	711	$ .01	$ .06
Quisenberry, Dan	86T	50	$ .01	$ .05
Quisenberry, Dan	86TAS	722	$ .01	$ .05
Quisenberry, Dan	87T	714	$ .01	$ .10
Quisenberry, Dan	88T	195	$ .01	$ .04
Quisenberry, Dan	89T	612	$ .01	$ .03
Quisenberry, Dan	90T	312	$ .01	$ .03
Rabb, John	84T	228	$ .01	$ .06
Rabb, John	85T	696	$ .01	$ .06
Rabe, Charley	58T	376	$1.00	$4.00
Radatz, Dick	62T	591	$12.50	$50.00
Radatz, Dick	63T	363	$1.00	$4.00
Radatz, Dick	64T	170	$ .50	$2.00
Radatz, Dick	65T	295	$ .50	$2.00
Radatz, Dick	66T	475	$1.50	$6.00
Radatz, Dick	67T	174	$ .40	$1.60
Radatz, Dick	69T	663	$ .40	$1.60
Rader, Dave	72T	232	$ .10	$ .40
Rader, Dave	73T	121	$ .10	$ .40
Rader, Dave	74T	213	$ .10	$ .40
Rader, Dave	75T	31	$ .10	$ .40
Rader, Dave	76T	54	$ .05	$ .25
Rader, Dave	77T	427	$ .05	$ .20
Rader, Dave	78T	563	$ .04	$ .16
Rader, Dave	79T	693	$ .03	$ .12
Rader, Dave	80T	296	$ .01	$ .10
Rader, Dave	81T	378	$ .01	$ .08
Rader, Doug	67T	412	$1.00	$4.00
Rader, Doug	68T	332	$ .35	$1.40
Rader, Doug	69T	119	$ .35	$1.40
Rader, Doug	70T	355	$ .35	$1.40
Rader, Doug	71T	425	$ .50	$2.00
Rader, Doug	72T	536	$ .40	$1.60
Rader, Doug	73T	76	$ .10	$ .40
Rader, Doug	74T	395	$ .10	$ .40
Rader, Doug	75T	165	$ .10	$ .40
Rader, Doug	76T	44	$ .05	$ .25
Rader, Doug	76TTR	44	$ .05	$ .25
Rader, Doug	77T	9	$ .05	$ .20
Rader, Doug	78T	651	$ .04	$ .16
Rader, Doug	83TTR	91	$ .01	$ .10
Rader, Doug	84T	412	$ .01	$ .06
Rader, Doug	85T	519	$ .01	$ .06
Rader, Doug	89TTR	99	$ .01	$ .05
Rader, Doug	90T	51	$ .01	$ .03
Rader, Doug	91T	231	$ .01	$ .03
Radinsky, Scott	90TTR	99	$ .01	$ .10
Radinsky, Scott	91T	299	$ .01	$ .03
Radinsky, Scott	91TSC	311	$ .05	$ .25
Radinsky, Scott	92T	701	$ .01	$ .03
Radinsky, Scott	93T	550	$ .01	$ .03
Radinsky, Scott	93TSC	275	$ .01	$ .10
Raffensberger, Ken	52T	118	$7.00	$28.00
Raffensberger, Ken	53T	276	$22.50	$90.00
Raffensberger, Ken	54T	46	$3.75	$15.00
Raffensberger, Ken	91TA53	276	$ .01	$ .15
Ragland, Tom	72T	334	$ .10	$ .40
Ragland, Tom	74T	441	$ .10	$ .40
Raich, Eric	76T	484	$ .05	$ .25
Raich, Eric	77T	62	$ .05	$ .20
Raines, Larry	58T	243	$1.25	$5.00
Raines, Tim	81T	479	$2.00	$8.00
Raines, Tim	81TTR	816	$3.00	$12.00
Raines, Tim	82T	70	$ .20	$2.00
Raines, Tim	82T	164	$ .10	$1.00
Raines, Tim	82THL	3	$ .05	$ .35

TOPPS

Player	Year	No.	VG	EX/MT	Player	Year	No.	VG	EX/MT
Raines, Tim	83T	595	$.10	$.75	Ramos, Pedro	65T	13	$.35	$1.40
Raines, Tim	83T	704	$.10	$.75	Ramos, Pedro	66T	439	$.65	$2.60
Raines, Tim	83TAS	403	$.05	$.25	Ramos, Pedro	67T	187	$.40	$1.60
Raines, Tim	84T	134	$.10	$.50	Ramos, Roberto	81T	479	$2.00	$8.00
Raines, Tim	84T	370	$.10	$.50	Ramos, Roberto	82T	354	$.01	$.08
Raines, Tim	84TAS	390	$.05	$.25	Ramos, Bobby "Roberto"	83TTR	93	$.01	$.10
Raines, Tim	85T	630	$.05	$.25	Ramos, Bobby	84T	32	$.01	$.06
Raines, Tim	86T	280	$.01	$.15	Ramos, Bobby	85T	407	$.01	$.06
Raines, Tim	87T	30	$.01	$.15	Ramsdell, Willard	52T	114	$7.00	$28.00
Raines, Tim	88T	720	$.01	$.10	Ramsey, Mike	81T	366	$.01	$.08
Raines, Tim	88TAS	403	$.01	$.10	Ramsey, Mike	82T	574	$.01	$.08
Raines, Tim "Rock"	89T	560	$.01	$.10	Ramsey, Mike	83T	128	$.01	$.08
Raines, Rock	90T	180	$.01	$.10	Ramsey, Mike	84T	467	$.01	$.06
Raines, Rock	91T	360	$.01	$.03	Ramsey, Mike	85T	62	$.01	$.06
Raines, Rock	91TSC	523	$.05	$.25	Rand, Dick	58T	218	$1.25	$5.00
Raines, Rock	91TTR	94	$.01	$.05	Randall, Bob	77T	578	$.05	$.20
Raines, Rock	92T	426	$.01	$.03	Randall, Bob	78T	363	$.04	$.16
Raines, Rock	92TSC	426	$.01	$.10	Randall, Bob	79T	58	$.03	$.12
Raines, Tim	93T	675	$.01	$.03	Randall, Bob	80T	162	$.01	$.10
Raines, Tim	93TSC	43	$.01	$.10	Randle, Lenny	72T	737	$1.25	$5.00
Rainey, Chuck	80T	662	$.01	$.10	Randle, Lenny	73T	378	$.10	$.40
Rainey, Chuck	81T	199	$.01	$.08	Randle, Len	74T	446	$.10	$.40
Rainey, Chuck	82T	522	$.01	$.08	Randle, Len	75T	259	$.10	$.40
Rainey, Chuck	83T	56	$.01	$.08	Randle, Len	76T	31	$.05	$.25
Rainey, Chuck	83TTR	92	$.01	$.10	Randle, Len	77T	196	$.05	$.20
Rainey, Chuck	84T	334	$.01	$.06	Randle, Len	78T	544	$.04	$.16
Rajsich, Dave	79T	710	$.05	$.20	Randle, Len	79T	454	$.03	$.12
Rajsich, Dave	80T	548	$.01	$.10	Randle, Lenny	81T	692	$.01	$.08
Rajsich, Gary	83T	317	$.01	$.08	Randle, Lenny	81TTR	817	$.01	$.15
Rakow, Ed	60T	551	$2.75	$11.00	Randle, Lenny	82T	312	$.01	$.08
Rakow, Ed	61T	147	$.60	$2.40	Randolph, Willie	76T	592	$2.00	$8.00
Rakow, Ed	62T	342	$.75	$3.00	Randolph, Willie	76TTR	592	$.75	$3.00
Rakow, Ed	63T	82	$.50	$2.00	Randolph, Willie	77T	359	$.50	$2.00
Rakow, Ed	64T	491	$1.00	$4.00	Randolph, Willie	78T	620	$.20	$.80
Rakow, Ed	65T	454	$1.25	$5.00	Randolph, Willie	79T	250	$.15	$.60
Ramazzotti, Bob	52T	184	$7.00	$28.00	Randolph, Willie	80T	460	$.10	$.50
Ramirez, Allan	84T	347	$.01	$.06	Randolph, Willie	81T	60	$.05	$.25
Ramirez, Manny	92T	156	$.10	$.75	Randolph, Willie	82T	569	$.01	$.08
Ramirez, Mario	84T	94	$.01	$.06	Randolph, Willie	82TAS	548	$.01	$.07
Ramirez, Mario	85T	427	$.01	$.06	Randolph, Willie	82TSA	570	$.01	$.07
Ramirez, Mario	86T	262	$.01	$.05	Randolph, Willie	83T	140	$.01	$.08
Ramirez, Milt	71T	702	$1.10	$4.40	Randolph, Willie	84T	360	$.01	$.06
Ramirez, Orlando	77T	131	$.05	$.20	Randolph, Willie	85T	765	$.01	$.06
Ramirez, Rafael	81T	192	$.05	$.20	Randolph, Willie	86T	455	$.01	$.05
Ramirez, Rafael	82T	536	$.01	$.08	Randolph, Willie	87T	701	$.01	$.04
Ramirez, Rafael	83T	439	$.01	$.08	Randolph, Willie	88T	210	$.01	$.04
Ramirez, Rafael	84T	234	$.01	$.06	Randolph, Willie	88TAS	387	$.01	$.04
Ramirez, Rafael	85T	647	$.01	$.06	Randolph, Willie	89T	635	$.01	$.03
Ramirez, Rafael	86T	107	$.01	$.05	Randolph, Willie	89TTR	100	$.01	$.05
Ramirez, Rafael	87T	76	$.01	$.04	Randolph, Willie	90T	25	$.01	$.03
Ramirez, Rafael	88T	379	$.01	$.04	Randolph, Willie	90TTR	100	$.01	$.05
Ramirez, Rafael	88TTR	90	$.01	$.05	Randolph, Willie	91T	525	$.01	$.03
Ramirez, Rafael	89T	749	$.01	$.03	Randolph, Willie	91TSC	545	$.05	$.25
Ramirez, Rafael	90T	558	$.01	$.03	Randolph, Willie	91TTR	95	$.01	$.05
Ramirez, Rafael	91T	423	$.01	$.03	Randolph, Willie	92T	116	$.01	$.03
Ramirez, Rafael	91TSC	107	$.05	$.25	Randolph, Willie	92TSC	890	$.01	$.10
Ramirez, Rafael	92TSC	451	$.01	$.10	Randolph, Willie	92TTR	90	$.01	$.05
Ramos, Domingo	84T	194	$.01	$.06	Randolph, Willie	93T	324	$.01	$.03
Ramos, Domingo	85T	349	$.01	$.06	Ranew, Merritt	62T	156	$.60	$2.40
Ramos, Domingo	86T	462	$.01	$.05	Ranew, Merritt	64T	78	$.50	$2.00
Ramos, Domingo	87T	641	$.01	$.04	Ranew, Merritt	66T	62	$.50	$2.00
Ramos, Domingo	88T	206	$.01	$.04	Rangers, Team	72T	668	$3.50	$14.00
Ramos, Domingo	90T	37	$.01	$.03	Rangers, Team	73T	7	$.30	$1.20
Ramos, Domingo	91T	541	$.01	$.03	Rangers, Team	74T	184	$.25	$1.00
Ramos, Pedro	56T	49	$2.00	$8.00	Rangers, Team Checklist	75T	511	$.35	$1.40
Ramos, Pedro	57T	326	$5.00	$20.00	Rangers, Team Checklist	76T	172	$.30	$1.20
Ramos, Pedro	58T	331	$1.25	$5.00	Rangers, Team Checklist	77T	428	$.25	$1.00
Ramos, Pedro	59T	78	$1.50	$6.00	Rangers, Team Checklist	78T	659	$.20	$.80
Ramos, Pedro	59T	291	$1.00	$4.00	Rangers, Team Checklist	79T	499	$.15	$.60
Ramos, Pedro	60T	175	$.75	$3.00	Rangers, Team Checklist	80T	41	$.10	$.50
Ramos, Pedro	61T	50	$.75	$3.00	Rangers, Team Checklist	81T	673	$.05	$.25
Ramos, Pedro	61T	528	$7.50	$30.00	Rangers, Team Leaders	86T	666	$.01	$.05
Ramos, Pedro	62T	485	$1.50	$6.00	Rangers, Team Leaders	87T	656	$.01	$.04
Ramos, Pedro	63T	14	$.50	$2.00	Rangers, Team Leaders	88T	201	$.01	$.04
Ramos, Pedro	64T	562	$2.25	$9.00	Rangers, Team Leaders	89T	729	$.01	$.03

TOPPS

Player	Year	No.	VG	EX/MT
Rapp, Pat	93T	791	$ .01	$ .15
Rapp, Vern	78T	324	$ .04	$ .16
Rapp, Vern	84TTR	95	$ .01	$ .15
Rasmussen, Dennis	85T	691	$ .05	$ .25
Rasmussen, Dennis	86T	301	$ .01	$ .05
Rasmussen, Dennis	87T	555	$ .01	$ .04
Rasmussen, Dennis	88T	135	$ .01	$ .04
Rasmussen, Dennis	88TTR	91	$ .01	$ .05
Rasmussen, Dennis	89T	32	$ .01	$ .03
Rasmussen, Dennis	90T	449	$ .01	$ .03
Rasmussen, Dennis	91T	774	$ .01	$ .03
Rasmussen, Dennis	91TSC	169	$ .05	$ .25
Rasmussen, Dennis	92T	252	$ .01	$ .03
Rasmussen, Dennis	92TSC	749	$ .01	$ .10
Rasmussen, "Eric" Harry	76T	182	$ .05	$ .25
Rasmussen, Eric	77T	404	$ .05	$ .20
Rasmussen, Eric	78T	281	$ .04	$ .16
Rasmussen, Eric	79T	57	$ .03	$ .12
Rasmussen, Eric	80T	531	$ .01	$ .10
Rasmussen, Eric	81T	342	$ .01	$ .08
Rasmussen, Eric	83T	594	$ .01	$ .08
Rasmussen, Eric	84T	724	$ .01	$ .06
Ratliff, Gene	65T	553	$1.40	$5.60
Ratliff, Paul	63T	549	$2.25	$9.00
Ratliff, Paul	70T	267	$ .35	$1.40
Ratliff, Paul	71T	607	$1.00	$4.00
Rau, Doug	73T	602	$ .75	$3.00
Rau, Doug	74T	64	$ .10	$ .40
Rau, Doug	75T	269	$ .10	$ .40
Rau, Doug	76T	124	$ .05	$ .25
Rau, Doug	77T	421	$ .05	$ .20
Rau, Doug	78T	641	$ .04	$ .16
Rau, Doug	79T	347	$ .03	$ .12
Rau, Doug	80T	527	$ .01	$ .10
Rau, Doug	81T	174	$ .01	$ .08
Rau, Doug	81TTR	818	$ .01	$ .15
Rautzhan, Lance	78T	709	$ .04	$ .16
Rautzhan, Lance	79T	373	$ .03	$ .12
Rawley, Shane	79T	74	$ .10	$ .40
Rawley, Shane	80T	723	$ .01	$ .10
Rawley, Shane	81T	423	$ .01	$ .08
Rawley, Shane	82T	197	$ .01	$ .08
Rawley, Shane	82TTR	95	$ .01	$ .10
Rawley, Shane	83T	592	$ .01	$ .08
Rawley, Shane	84T	254	$ .01	$ .06
Rawley, Shane	85T	636	$ .01	$ .06
Rawley, Shane	86T	361	$ .01	$ .05
Rawley, Shane	87T	771	$ .01	$ .04
Rawley, Shane	88T	66	$ .01	$ .04
Rawley, Shane	88TAS	406	$ .01	$ .04
Rawley, Shane	89T	494	$ .01	$ .03
Rawley, Shane	89TTR	101	$ .01	$ .05
Rawley, Shane	90T	101	$ .01	$ .03
Ray, Jim	68T	539	$ .70	$2.80
Ray, Jim	69T	257	$ .50	$2.00
Ray, Jim	70T	113	$ .20	$ .80
Ray, Jim	71T	242	$ .25	$1.00
Ray, Jim	72T	603	$ .40	$1.60
Ray, Jim	73T	313	$ .10	$ .40
Ray, Jim	74T	458	$ .10	$ .40
Ray, Jim	74TTR	458	$ .10	$ .40
Ray, Jim	75T	89	$ .10	$ .40
Ray, Johnny	82T	291	$ .05	$ .25
Ray, Johnny	82TTR	96	$ .05	$ .25
Ray, Johnnie (y)	83T	149	$ .01	$ .15
Ray, Johnny	84T	537	$ .01	$ .10
Ray, Johnny	84TAS	387	$ .01	$ .06
Ray, Johnny	85T	96	$ .01	$ .10
Ray, Johnny	86T	615	$ .01	$ .05
Ray, Johnny	87T	747	$ .01	$ .04
Ray, Johnny	88T	115	$ .01	$ .04
Ray, Johnny	89T	455	$ .01	$ .03
Ray, Johnny	90T	334	$ .01	$ .03
Ray, Johnny	91T	273	$ .01	$ .03
Raydon, Curt	59T	305	$1.00	$4.00

Player	Year	No.	VG	EX/MT
Raydon, Curt	60T	49	$ .85	$3.40
Rayford, Floyd	81T	399	$ .10	$1.00
Rayford, Floyd	83T	192	$ .01	$ .08
Rayford, Floyd	84T	514	$ .01	$ .06
Rayford, Floyd	84TTR	96	$ .01	$ .15
Rayford, Floyd	85T	341	$ .01	$ .06
Rayford, Floyd	86T	623	$ .01	$ .05
Rayford, Floyd	87T	426	$ .01	$ .04
Rayford, Floyd	88T	296	$ .01	$ .04
Raymond, Claude	63T	519	$3.75	$15.00
Raymond, Claude	64T	504	$1.00	$4.00
Raymond, Claude	65T	48	$ .35	$1.40
Raymond, Claude	66T	586	$7.00	$28.00
Raymond, Claude	67T	364	$ .60	$2.40
Raymond, Claude	68T	166	$ .35	$1.40
Raymond, Claude	69T	446	$ .30	$1.20
Raymond, Claude	70T	268	$ .35	$1.40
Raymond, Claude	71T	536	$1.00	$4.00
Razjigaev, Rudy	93T	633	$ .05	$ .25
Ready, Randy	84TTR	97	$ .01	$ .15
Ready, Randy	86T	209	$ .01	$ .05
Ready, Randy	87TTR	97	$ .01	$ .05
Ready, Randy	88T	426	$ .01	$ .04
Ready, Randy	89T	551	$ .01	$ .03
Ready, Randy	89TTR	102	$ .01	$ .05
Ready, Randy	90T	356	$ .01	$ .03
Ready, Randy	91T	137	$ .01	$ .03
Ready, Randy	91TSC	265	$ .05	$ .25
Ready, Randy	92T	63	$ .01	$ .03
Reardon, Jeff	81T	456	$2.00	$8.00
Reardon, Jeff	81TTR	819	$3.50	$14.00

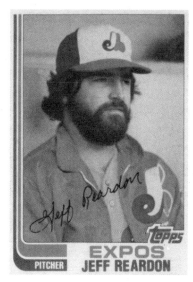

Reardon, Jeff	82T	667	$ .20	$2.00
Reardon, Jeff	83T	290	$ .10	$1.00
Reardon, Jeff	84T	595	$ .10	$ .75
Reardon, Jeff	85T	375	$ .05	$ .25
Reardon, Jeff	86T	35	$ .05	$ .25
Reardon, Jeff	86TAS	711	$ .01	$ .15
Reardon, Jeff	87T	165	$ .01	$ .10
Reardon, Jeff	87TTR	98	$ .05	$ .20
Reardon, Jeff	88T	425	$ .01	$ .10
Reardon, Jeff	89T	775	$ .01	$ .03
Reardon, Jeff	90T	235	$ .01	$ .03
Reardon, Jeff	90TTR	101	$ .01	$ .05

TOPPS

Player	Year	No.	VG	EX/MT	Player	Year	No.	VG	EX/MT
Reardon, Jeff	91T	605	$ .01	$ .03	Reds, Team Leaders	86T	366	$ .01	$ .10
Reardon, Jeff	91TSC	354	$ .05	$ .35	Reds, Team Leaders	87T	281	$ .01	$ .10
Reardon, Jeff	92T	182	$ .01	$ .03	Reds, Team Leaders	88T	81	$ .01	$ .04
Reardon, Jeff	92TRB	3	$ .01	$ .03	Reds, Team Leaders	89T	111	$ .01	$ .03
Reardon, Jeff	92TSC	657	$ .01	$ .10	Redus, Gary	83TTR	94	$ .10	$ .50
Reardon, Jeff	93T	475	$ .01	$ .10	Redus, Gary	84T	475	$ .01	$ .15
Reardon, Jeff	93TSC	161	$ .01	$ .15	Redus, Gary	85T	146	$ .01	$ .06
Reberger, Frank	69T	637	$ .40	$1.60	Redus, Gary	86T	342	$ .01	$ .05
Reberger, Frank	70T	103	$ .20	$ .80	Redus, Gary	86TTR	90	$ .01	$ .06
Reberger, Frank	71T	251	$ .25	$1.00	Redus, Gary	87T	42	$ .01	$ .04
Reberger, Frank	72T	548	$ .40	$1.60	Redus, Gary	87TTR	99	$ .01	$ .05
Reboulet, Jeff	93T	172	$ .01	$ .10	Redus, Gary	88T	657	$ .01	$ .04
Reboulet, Jeff	93TSC	146	$ .01	$ .10	Redus, Gary	89T	281	$ .01	$ .03
Red Sox, Team	56T	111	$7.50	$30.00	Redus, Gary	90T	507	$ .01	$ .03
Red Sox, Team	57T	171	$3.00	$12.00	Redus, Gary	91T	771	$ .01	$ .03
Red Sox, Team	58T	312	$3.50	$14.00	Redus, Gary	91TSC	486	$ .05	$ .25
Red Sox, Team	59T	248	$2.50	$10.00	Redus, Gary	92T	453	$ .01	$ .03
Red Sox, Team	60T	537	$8.00	$32.00	Redus, Gary	92TSC	524	$ .01	$ .10
Red Sox, Team	61T	373	$2.25	$9.00	Reed, Bob	70T	207	$ .20	$ .80
Red Sox, Team	62T	334	$1.75	$7.00	Reed, Bob	71T	732	$1.50	$6.00
Red Sox, Team	63T	202	$1.25	$5.00	Reed, Darren	92TSC	824	$ .01	$ .10
Red Sox, Team	64T	579	$4.50	$18.00	Reed, Darren	92TTR	91	$ .01	$ .05
Red Sox, Team	65T	403	$2.25	$9.00	Reed, Darren	93T	482	$ .01	$ .03
Red Sox, Team	66T	259	$1.00	$4.00	Reed, Howie	65T	544	$1.40	$5.60
Red Sox, Team	67T	604	$28.75	$115.00	Reed, Howie	66T	387	$ .65	$2.60
Red Sox, Team	70T	563	$1.25	$5.00	Reed, Howie	70T	548	$ .50	$2.00
Red Sox, Team	71T	386	$ .50	$2.00	Reed, Howie	71T	398	$ .50	$2.00
Red Sox, Team	72T	328	$ .50	$2.00	Reed, Jeff	87T	247	$ .01	$ .04
Red Sox, Team	73T	596	$1.50	$6.00	Reed, Jeff	87TTR	100	$ .01	$ .05
Red Sox, Team	74T	567	$ .25	$1.00	Reed, Jeff	88T	176	$ .01	$ .04
Red Sox, Team Checklist	75T	172	$ .35	$1.40	Reed, Jeff	89T	626	$ .01	$ .03
Red Sox, Team Checklist	76T	118	$ .30	$1.20	Reed, Jeff	90T	772	$ .01	$ .03
Red Sox, Team Checklist	77T	309	$ .25	$1.00	Reed, Jeff	91T	419	$ .01	$ .03
Red Sox, Team Checklist	78T	424	$ .20	$ .80	Reed, Jeff	91TSC	534	$ .05	$ .25
Red Sox, Team Checklist	79T	214	$ .15	$ .60	Reed, Jeff	92T	91	$ .01	$ .03
Red Sox, Team Checklist	80T	689	$ .10	$ .50	Reed, Jeff	92TSC	487	$ .01	$ .10
Red Sox, Team Checklist	81T	662	$ .05	$ .25	Reed, Jerry	86T	172	$ .01	$ .05
Red Sox, Team Leaders	86T	396	$ .01	$ .05	Reed, Jerry	87T	619	$ .01	$ .04
Red Sox, Team Leaders	87T	306	$ .01	$ .10	Reed, Jerry	88T	332	$ .01	$ .04
Red Sox, Team Leaders	88T	21	$ .01	$ .04	Reed, Jerry	89T	441	$ .01	$ .03
Red Sox, Team Leaders	89T	321	$ .01	$ .03	Reed, Jerry	90T	247	$ .01	$ .03
Redfern, Pete	77T	249	$ .05	$ .20	Reed, Jody	88T	152	$ .05	$ .20
Redfern, Pete	78T	81	$ .04	$ .16	Reed, Jody	89T	734	$ .01	$ .10
Redfern, Pete	79T	113	$ .03	$ .12	Reed, Jody	90T	96	$ .01	$ .03
Redfern, Pete	80T	403	$ .01	$ .10	Reed, Jody	91T	247	$ .01	$ .03
Redfern, Pete	81T	714	$ .01	$ .08	Reed, Jody	91TSC	33	$ .05	$ .25
Redfern, Pete	82T	309	$ .01	$ .08	Reed, Jody	92T	598	$ .01	$ .03
Redfern, Pete	83T	559	$ .01	$ .08	Reed, Jody	92TSC	816	$ .01	$ .10
Redington, Tom	92T	473	$ .05	$ .25	Reed, Jody	93T	103	$ .01	$ .03
Redmond, Wayne	71T	728	$1.10	$4.40	Reed, Rick	92TSC	434	$ .01	$ .10
Redlegs, Team	56T	90	$6.00	$24.00	Reed, Rick	93T	212	$ .01	$ .03
Reds, Team	57T	322	$15.00	$60.00	Reed, Ron	68T	76	$ .35	$1.40
Reds, Team	58T	428	$3.50	$14.00	Reed, Ron	69T	177	$ .35	$1.40
Reds, Team	59T	111	$3.00	$12.00	Reed, Ron	70T	546	$ .35	$1.40
Reds, Team	60T	164	$2.00	$8.00	Reed, Ron	71T	359	$ .25	$1.00
Reds, Team	61T	249	$1.75	$7.00	Reed, Ron	72T	787	$1.75	$7.00
Reds, Team	62T	465	$3.50	$14.00	Reed, Ron	73T	72	$ .10	$ .40
Reds, Team	63T	63	$1.00	$4.00	Reed, Ron	74T	346	$ .10	$ .40
Reds, Team	64T	403	$2.50	$10.00	Reed, Ron	75T	81	$ .10	$ .40
Reds, Team	65T	316	$1.50	$6.00	Reed, Ron	76T	58	$ .05	$ .25
Reds, Team	66T	59	$ .75	$3.00	Reed, Ron	76TTR	58	$ .05	$ .25
Reds, Team	67T	407	$1.25	$5.00	Reed, Ron	77T	243	$ .05	$ .20
Reds, Team	68T	574	$1.75	$7.00	Reed, Ron	78T	472	$ .04	$ .16
Reds, Team	70T	544	$ .75	$3.00	Reed, Ron	79T	177	$ .03	$ .12
Reds, Team	71T	357	$ .75	$3.00	Reed, Ron	80T	609	$ .01	$ .10
Reds, Team	72T	651	$1.25	$5.00	Reed, Ron	81T	376	$ .01	$ .08
Reds, Team	73T	641	$1.50	$6.00	Reed, Ron	82T	581	$ .01	$ .08
Reds, Team	74T	459	$ .25	$1.00	Reed, Ron	83T	728	$ .01	$ .08
Reds, Team Checklist	75T	531	$ .50	$2.00	Reed, Ron	84T	43	$ .01	$ .06
Reds, Team Checklist	76T	104	$ .50	$2.00	Reed, Ron	84TTR	98	$ .01	$ .15
Reds, Team Checklist	77T	287	$ .25	$1.00	Reed, Ron	85T	221	$ .01	$ .06
Reds, Team Checklist	78T	526	$ .20	$ .80	Reed, Steve	93T	461	$ .01	$ .10
Reds, Team Checklist	79T	259	$ .15	$ .60	Reese, Calvin	92T	714	$ .05	$ .20
Reds, Team Checklist	80T	606	$ .10	$ .50	Reese, Dick	65T	597	$1.40	$5.60
Reds, Team Checklist	81T	677	$ .05	$ .25	Reese, Jimmie	73T	421	$ .25	$1.00

TOPPS

Player	Year	No.	VG	EX/MT
Reese, Jimmie	74T	276	$.10	$.40
Reese, Pee Wee	52T	333	$275.00	$1100.00
Reese, Pee Wee	53T	76	$40.00	$160.00
Reese, Pee Wee	56T	260	$37.50	$150.00
Reese, Pee Wee	57T	30	$16.25	$65.00
Reese, Pee Wee	58T	375	$13.25	$55.00
Reese, Pee Wee	91TA53	76	$.15	$1.50
Reese, Rich	67T	486	$1.50	$6.00
Reese, Rich	68T	111	$.35	$1.40
Reese, Rich	69T	56	$.35	$1.40
Reese, Rich	70T	404	$.35	$1.40
Reese, Rich	71T	349	$.25	$1.00
Reese, Rich	72T	611	$.40	$1.60
Regan, Phil	61T	439	$1.00	$4.00
Regan, Phil	62T	366	$.75	$3.00
Regan, Phil	63T	494	$3.00	$12.00
Regan, Phil	64T	535	$2.25	$9.00
Regan, Phil	65T	191	$.35	$1.40
Regan, Phil	66T	347	$.50	$2.00
Regan, Phil	67T	130	$.40	$1.60
Regan, Phil	68T	88	$.35	$1.40
Regan, Phil	69T	535	$.40	$1.60
Regan, Phil	70T	334	$.35	$1.40
Regan, Phil	71T	634	$1.00	$4.00
Regan, Phil	72T	485	$.25	$1.00
Reichardt, Rick	65T	194	$.35	$1.40
Reichardt, Rick	66T	321	$.50	$2.00
Reichardt, Rick	67T	40	$.40	$1.60
Reichardt, Rick	68T	570	$.70	$2.80
Reichardt, Rick	69T	205	$.35	$1.40
Reichardt, Rick	70T	720	$1.75	$7.00
Reichardt, Rick	71T	643	$1.00	$4.00
Reid, Scott	70T	56	$.20	$.80
Reid, Scott	71T	439	$1.00	$4.00
Reimer, Kevin	91T	304	$.01	$.10
Reimer, Kevin	92T	737	$.01	$.03
Reimer, Kevin	92TSC	57	$.01	$.10
Reimer, Kevin	93T	87	$.01	$.03
Reiser, Pete	52T	189	$8.75	$35.00
Reiser, Pete	60T	463	$1.25	$5.00
Reiser, Pete	73T	81	$.25	$1.00
Reitz, Ken	73T	603	$.75	$3.00
Reitz, Ken	74T	372	$.10	$.40
Reitz, Ken	75T	27	$.10	$.40
Reitz, Ken	76T	158	$.05	$.25
Reitz, Ken	76TTR	158	$.05	$.25
Reitz, Ken	77T	297	$.05	$.20
Reitz, Ken	78T	692	$.04	$.16
Reitz, Ken	79T	587	$.03	$.12
Reitz, Ken	80T	182	$.01	$.10
Reitz, Ken	81T	441	$.01	$.08
Reitz, Ken	81TTR	820	$.01	$.15
Reitz, Ken	82T	245	$.01	$.08
Remmerswaal, Win	81T	38	$.01	$.08
Remy, Jerry	76T	229	$.05	$.25
Remy, Jerry	77T	342	$.05	$.20
Remy, Jerry	78T	478	$.04	$.16
Remy, Jerry	79T	618	$.03	$.12
Remy, Jerry	80T	155	$.01	$.10
Remy, Jerry	81T	549	$.01	$.08
Remy, Jerry	82T	25	$.01	$.08
Remy, Jerry	83T	295	$.01	$.08
Remy, Jerry	84T	445	$.01	$.06
Remy, Jerry	85T	761	$.01	$.06
Renick, Rick	68T	301	$.35	$1.40
Renick, Rick	70T	93	$.20	$.80
Renick, Rick	71T	694	$1.50	$6.00
Renick, Rick	72T	459	$.25	$1.00
Reniff, Hal	62T	139	$3.50	$14.00
Reniff, Hal	62T	159	$.75	$3.00
Reniff, Hal	63T	546	$2.25	$9.00
Reniff, Hal	64T	36	$.50	$2.00
Reniff, Hal	65T	413	$1.00	$4.00
Reniff, Hal	66T	68	$.35	$1.40
Reniff, Hal	67T	201	$.50	$2.00
Renko, Steve	70T	87	$.20	$.80
Renko, Steve	71T	209	$.25	$1.00
Renko, Steve	72T	307	$.10	$.40
Renko, Steve	72TIA	308	$.10	$.40
Renko, Steve	73T	623	$.45	$1.80
Renko, Steve	74T	49	$.10	$.40
Renko, Steve	75T	34	$.10	$.40
Renko, Steve	76T	264	$.05	$.25
Renko, Steve	77T	586	$.05	$.20
Renko, Steve	78T	493	$.04	$.16
Renko, Steve	79T	352	$.03	$.12
Renko, Steve	80T	184	$.01	$.10
Renko, Steve	81T	63	$.01	$.08
Renko, Steve	81TTR	821	$.01	$.15
Renko, Steve	82T	702	$.01	$.08
Renko, Steve	83T	236	$.01	$.08
Renko, Steve	83TTR	95	$.01	$.10
Renko, Steve	84T	444	$.01	$.06
Renna, Bill	54T	112	$3.75	$15.00
Renna, Bill	55T	121	$2.25	$9.00
Renna, Bill	56T	82	$2.00	$8.00
Renna, Bill	58T	473	$1.00	$4.00
Renna, Bill	59T	72	$1.50	$6.00

Player	Year	No.	VG	EX/MT
Replogle, Andy	79T	427	$.03	$.12
Repoz, Roger	66T	138	$.50	$2.00
Repoz, Roger	67T	416	$.60	$2.40
Repoz, Roger	68T	587	$.70	$2.80
Repoz, Roger	69T	103	$.35	$1.40
Repoz, Roger	70T	397	$.35	$1.40
Repoz, Roger	71T	508	$.50	$2.00
Repoz, Roger	72T	541	$.40	$1.60
Repulski, Rip	53T	172	$4.50	$18.00
Repulski, Rip	54T	115	$3.75	$15.00
Repulski, Rip	55T	55	$2.25	$9.00
Repulski, Rip	56T	201	$3.75	$15.00
Repulski, Rip	57T	245	$2.00	$8.00
Repulski, Rip	58T	14	$2.00	$8.00
Repulski, Rip	59T	195	$1.00	$4.00
Repulski, Rip	60T	265	$.75	$3.00
Repulski, Rip	61T	128	$.60	$2.40
Repulski, Rip	91TA53	172	$.01	$.15
Rettenmund, Merv	69T	66	$.50	$2.00
Rettenmund, Merv	70T	629	$.50	$2.00

TOPPS

Player	Year	No.	VG	EX/MT
Rettenmund, Merv	71T	393	$ .25	$1.00
Rettenmund, Merv	72T	86	$ .50	$2.00
Rettenmund, Merv	72T	235	$ .10	$ .40
Rettenmund, Merv	73T	56	$ .10	$ .40
Rettenmund, Merv	74T	585	$ .10	$ .40
Rettenmund, Merv	74TTR	585	$ .10	$ .40
Rettenmund, Merv	75T	369	$ .10	$ .40
Rettenmund, Merv	76T	283	$ .05	$ .25
Rettenmund, Merv	77T	659	$ .05	$ .20
Rettenmund, Merv	78T	566	$ .04	$ .16
Rettenmund, Merv	79T	48	$ .03	$ .12
Rettenmund, Merv	80T	402	$ .01	$ .10
Retzer, Ken	62T	594	$20.00	$80.00
Retzer, Ken	63T	471	$3.00	$12.00
Retzer, Ken	64T	277	$ .65	$2.60
Retzer, Ken	65T	278	$ .50	$2.00
Reuschel, Paul	77T	333	$ .05	$ .20
Reuschel, Paul	77T	634	$ .05	$ .25
Reuschel, Paul	78T	663	$ .04	$ .16
Reuschel, Paul	79T	511	$ .03	$ .12
Reuschel, Rick	73T	482	$1.00	$4.00
Reuschel, Rick	74T	136	$ .25	$1.00
Reuschel, Rick	75T	153	$ .15	$ .60
Reuschel, Rick	76T	359	$ .15	$ .60
Reuschel, Rick	77T	530	$ .05	$ .25
Reuschel, Rick	77T	634	$ .05	$ .25
Reuschel, Rick	78T	50	$ .05	$ .25
Reuschel, Rick	79T	240	$ .03	$ .12
Reuschel, Rick	80T	175	$ .01	$ .10
Reuschel, Rick	81T	645	$ .01	$ .08
Reuschel, Rick	81TTR	822	$ .01	$ .15
Reuschel, Rick	82T	405	$ .01	$ .08
Reuschel, Rick	85T	306	$ .01	$ .06
Reuschel, Rick	85TTR	93	$ .01	$ .10
Reuschel, Rick	86T	779	$ .01	$ .05
Reuschel, Rick	87T	521	$ .01	$ .04
Reuschel, Rick	88T	660	$ .01	$ .04
Reuschel, Rick	89T	65	$ .01	$ .03
Reuschel, Rick	90T	190	$ .01	$ .03
Reuschel, Rick	91T	422	$ .01	$ .03
Reuss, Jerry	70T	96	$ .50	$2.00
Reuss, Jerry	71T	158	$ .40	$1.60
Reuss, Jerry	72T	775	$1.25	$5.00
Reuss, Jerry	73T	446	$ .25	$1.00
Reuss, Jerry	74T	116	$ .10	$ .40
Reuss, Jerry	75T	124	$ .15	$ .60
Reuss, Jerry	76T	60	$ .10	$ .40
Reuss, Jerry	77T	645	$ .05	$ .20
Reuss, Jerry	78T	255	$ .04	$ .16
Reuss, Jerry	79T	536	$ .03	$ .12
Reuss, Jerry	80T	318	$ .01	$ .10
Reuss, Jerry	81T	440	$ .01	$ .08
Reuss, Jerry	82T	710	$ .01	$ .08
Reuss, Jerry	83T	90	$ .01	$ .08
Reuss, Jerry	84T	170	$ .01	$ .06
Reuss, Jerry	85T	680	$ .01	$ .06
Reuss, Jerry	86T	577	$ .01	$ .05
Reuss, Jerry	87T	682	$ .01	$ .04
Reuss, Jerry	88T	216	$ .01	$ .04
Reuss, Jerry	89T	357	$ .01	$ .03
Reuss, Jerry	90T	424	$ .01	$ .03
Revenig, Todd	93T	766	$ .01	$ .03
Revering, Dave	78T	706	$ .04	$ .16
Revering, Dave	79T	224	$ .03	$ .12
Revering, Dave	80T	438	$ .01	$ .10
Revering, Dave	81T	568	$ .01	$ .08
Revering, Dave	81TTR	823	$ .01	$ .15
Revering, Dave	82T	109	$ .01	$ .08
Revering, Dave	82TTR	97	$ .01	$ .10
Revering, Dave	83T	677	$ .01	$ .08
Reyes, Gilberto	92T	286	$ .01	$ .03
Reyes, Gilberto	92TSC	173	$ .01	$ .10
Reynolds, Allie	51Trb	6	$3.00	$12.00
Reynolds, Allie	52T	67	$25.00	$100.00
Reynolds, Allie	53T	141	$8.00	$32.00

Player	Year	No.	VG	EX/MT
Reynolds, Allie	91TA53	141	$ .10	$ .50
Reynolds, Archie	71T	664	$1.50	$6.00
Reynolds, Archie	72T	672	$1.25	$5.00
Reynolds, Bob	71T	664	$1.50	$6.00
Reynolds, Bob	72T	162	$ .25	$1.00
Reynolds, Bob	73T	612	$ .75	$3.00
Reynolds, Bob	74T	259	$ .10	$ .40
Reynolds, Bob	75T	142	$ .10	$ .40
Reynolds, Craig	76T	596	$ .15	$ .60
Reynolds, Craig	77T	474	$ .10	$ .40
Reynolds, Craig	78T	199	$ .04	$ .16
Reynolds, Craig	79T	482	$ .03	$ .12
Reynolds, Craig	80T	129	$ .01	$ .10
Reynolds, Craig	81T	617	$ .01	$ .08
Reynolds, Craig	82T	57	$ .01	$ .08
Reynolds, Craig	83T	328	$ .01	$ .08
Reynolds, Craig	84T	776	$ .01	$ .06
Reynolds, Craig	85T	156	$ .01	$ .06
Reynolds, Craig	86T	298	$ .01	$ .05
Reynolds, Craig	87T	779	$ .01	$ .04
Reynolds, Craig	88T	557	$ .01	$ .04
Reynolds, Craig	89T	428	$ .01	$ .03
Reynolds, Craig	90T	637	$ .01	$ .03
Reynolds, Don	79T	292	$ .03	$ .12
Reynolds, Harold	86T	769	$ .05	$ .35
Reynolds, Harold	87T	91	$ .01	$ .10
Reynolds, Harold	88T	485	$ .01	$ .04
Reynolds, Harold	89T	580	$ .01	$ .03
Reynolds, Harold	90T	161	$ .01	$ .03
Reynolds, Harold	91T	260	$ .01	$ .03
Reynolds, Harold	91TSC	217	$ .05	$ .25
Reynolds, Harold	92T	670	$ .01	$ .03
Reynolds, Harold	92TSC	181	$ .01	$ .10
Reynolds, Harold	93T	757	$ .01	$ .03
Reynolds, Harold	93TSC	23	$ .01	$ .10
Reynolds, Ken	71T	664	$1.50	$6.00
Reynolds, Ken	72T	252	$ .10	$ .40
Reynolds, Ken	73T	638	$ .60	$2.40
Reynolds, R. J.	85T	369	$ .01	$ .15
Reynolds, R. J.	86T	417	$ .01	$ .05
Reynolds, R. J.	87T	109	$ .01	$ .04
Reynolds, R. J.	88T	27	$ .01	$ .04
Reynolds, R. J.	89T	658	$ .01	$ .03
Reynolds, R. J.	90T	592	$ .01	$ .03
Reynolds, R. J.	91T	198	$ .01	$ .03
Reynolds, Ronn	86T	649	$ .01	$ .05
Reynolds, Ronn	87T	471	$ .01	$ .04
Reynolds, Shane	93T	522	$ .01	$ .03
Reynolds, Tom	64T	528	$3.00	$12.00
Reynolds, Tom	65T	333	$ .50	$2.00
Reynolds, Tom	67T	487	$1.50	$6.00
Reynolds, Tom	69T	467	$ .30	$1.20
Reynolds, Tommie	70T	259	$ .20	$ .80
Reynolds, Tommie	71T	676	$1.10	$4.40
Reynoso, Armando	92T	631	$ .01	$ .10
Reynoso, Armando	92TSC	763	$ .01	$ .15
Rhode, Dave	91T	531	$ .01	$ .03
Rhode, Dave	91TSC	137	$ .05	$ .25
Rhoden, Rick	75T	618	$ .25	$1.00
Rhoden, Rick	76T	439	$ .20	$ .80
Rhoden, Rick	77T	245	$ .05	$ .20
Rhoden, Rick	78T	605	$ .04	$ .16
Rhoden, Rick	79T	145	$ .03	$ .12
Rhoden, Rick	80T	92	$ .01	$ .10
Rhoden, Rick	81T	312	$ .01	$ .08
Rhoden, Rick	82T	513	$ .01	$ .08
Rhoden, Rick	83T	781	$ .01	$ .08
Rhoden, Rick	84T	485	$ .01	$ .06
Rhoden, Rick	84T	696	$ .01	$ .06
Rhoden, Rick	85T	695	$ .01	$ .06
Rhoden, Rick	86T	232	$ .01	$ .05
Rhoden, Rick	87T	365	$ .01	$ .05
Rhoden, Rick	87TTR	101	$ .01	$ .05
Rhoden, Rick	88T	185	$ .01	$ .04
Rhoden, Rick	89T	18	$ .01	$ .03

TOPPS

Player	Year	No.	VG	EX/MT
Rhoden, Rick	90T	588	$ .01	$ .03
Rhodes, Arthur	92T	771	$ .01	$ .15
Rhodes, Arthur	92TSC	641	$ .05	$ .35
Rhodes, Arthur	93T	554	$ .01	$ .15
Rhodes, "Dusty" Jim	54T	170	$4.50	$18.00
Rhodes, Dusty	55T	1	$10.00	$40.00
Rhodes, Dusty	56T	50	$2.00	$8.00
Rhodes, Dusty	57T	61	$2.00	$8.00
Rhodes, Dusty	91TA53	299	$ .05	$ .20
Rhodes, Karl	91T	516	$ .01	$ .15
Rhodes, Karl	91TSC	52	$ .05	$ .25
Rhodes, Karl	92TSC	241	$ .01	$ .10
Ribant, Dennis	65T	73	$ .35	$1.40
Ribant, Dennis	66T	241	$ .50	$2.00
Ribant, Dennis	67T	527	$1.50	$6.00
Ribant, Denny	68T	326	$ .35	$1.40
Ribant, Dennis	69T	463	$ .30	$1.20

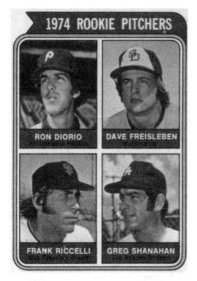

Player	Year	No.	VG	EX/MT
Riccelli, Frank	74T	599	$ .15	$ .60
Riccelli, Frank	80T	247	$ .01	$ .10
Rice, Del	52T	100	$7.00	$28.00
Rice, Del	53T	68	$6.25	$25.00
Rice, Del	57T	193	$2.00	$8.00
Rice, Del	58T	51	$2.00	$8.00
Rice, Del	59T	104	$1.50	$6.00
Rice, Del	60T	248	$ .75	$3.00
Rice, Del	61T	448	$1.35	$5.40
Rice, Del	72T	718	$1.25	$5.00
Rice, Del	91TA53	68	$ .01	$ .15
Rice, Hal	52T	398	$43.75	$175.00
Rice, Hal	53T	93	$4.00	$16.00
Rice, Hal	54T	95	$3.75	$15.00
Rice, Hal	91TA53	93	$ .01	$ .15
Rice, Jim	75T	616	$6.00	$24.00
Rice, Jim	76T	340	$1.75	$7.00
Rice, Jim	77T	60	$1.00	$4.00
Rice, Jim	78T	202	$ .05	$ .20
Rice, Jim	78T	670	$ .75	$3.00
Rice, Jim	79T	2	$ .20	$ .80
Rice, Jim	79T	3	$ .20	$ .80
Rice, Jim	79T	400	$ .50	$2.00
Rice, Jim	80T	200	$ .10	$1.00
Rice, Jim	81T	500	$ .10	$ .50
Rice, Jim	82T	750	$ .05	$ .25

Player	Year	No.	VG	EX/MT
Rice, Jim	83T	30	$ .05	$ .25
Rice, Jim	83T	381	$ .01	$ .08
Rice, Jim	84T	132	$ .05	$ .25
Rice, Jim	84T	133	$ .05	$ .20
Rice, Jim	84T	550	$ .05	$ .20
Rice, Jim	84TAS	401	$ .05	$ .20
Rice, Jim	85T	150	$ .01	$ .15
Rice, Jim	86T	320	$ .01	$ .10
Rice, Jim	87T	480	$ .01	$ .10
Rice, Jim	87TAS	610	$ .01	$ .10
Rice, Jim	88T	675	$ .01	$ .04
Rice, Jim	88TTB	662	$ .01	$ .04
Rice, Jim	89T	245	$ .01	$ .03
Rice, Jim	90T	785	$ .01	$ .03
Richard, J. R.	72T	101	$ .50	$2.00
Richard, J. R.	74T	522	$ .10	$ .40
Richard, J. R.	75T	73	$ .10	$ .40
Richard, J. R.	76T	625	$ .10	$ .40
Richard, J. R.	77T	260	$ .05	$ .20
Richard, J. R.	78T	470	$ .05	$ .20
Richard, J. R.	79T	6	$1.00	$4.00
Richard, J. R.	79T	590	$ .03	$ .12
Richard, J. R.	79TRB	203	$ .03	$ .12
Richard, J. R.	80T	50	$ .01	$ .10
Richard, J. R.	80T	206	$ .75	$3.00
Richard, J. R.	80T	207	$ .01	$ .10
Richard, J. R.	81T	350	$ .01	$ .08
Richard, J. R.	82T	190	$ .01	$ .08
Richard, Lee	72T	476	$ .25	$1.00
Richard, Lee	75T	653	$ .10	$ .40
Richard, Lee	76T	533	$ .05	$ .25
Richards, Gene	77T	473	$17.50	$70.00
Richards, Gene	78T	292	$ .04	$ .16
Richards, Gene	79T	364	$ .03	$ .12
Richards, Gene	80T	616	$ .01	$ .10
Richards, Gene	81T	171	$ .01	$ .08
Richards, Gene	82T	708	$ .01	$ .08
Richards, Gene	83T	7	$ .01	$ .08
Richards, Gene	84T	594	$ .01	$ .06
Richards, Gene	84TTR	99	$ .01	$ .15
Richards, Gene	85T	434	$ .01	$ .06
Richards, Paul	52T	305	$12.50	$50.00
Richards, Paul	60T	224	$ .75	$3.00
Richards, Paul	61T	131	$ .60	$2.40
Richards, Paul	61TAS	566	$8.00	$32.00
Richards, Paul	91TA53	322	$ .05	$ .20
Richardson, Bobby	57T	286	$27.50	$110.00
Richardson, Bobby	58T	101	$5.00	$20.00
Richardson, Bobby	59T	76	$4.00	$16.00
Richardson, Bobby	59T	237	$1.75	$7.00
Richardson, Bobby	60T	405	$2.00	$8.00
Richardson, Bobby	61T	180	$2.00	$8.00
Richardson, Bobby	62T	65	$1.50	$6.00
Richardson, Bobby	63T	173	$20.00	$80.00
Richardson, Bobby	63T	420	$2.00	$8.00
Richardson, Bobby	64T	190	$1.50	$6.00
Richardson, Bobby	65T	115	$1.00	$4.00
Richardson, Bobby	66T	490	$3.00	$12.00
Richardson, Gordon	66T	51	$ .35	$1.40
Richardt, Mike	83T	371	$ .01	$ .08
Richardt, Mike	84T	641	$ .01	$ .06
Richert, Pete	62T	131	$ .60	$2.40
Richert, Pete	63T	383	$1.00	$4.00
Richert, Pete	64T	51	$ .50	$2.00
Richert, Pete	65T	252	$ .50	$2.00
Richert, Pete	66T	95	$ .35	$1.40
Richert, Pete	67T	590	$4.00	$16.00
Richert, Pete	68T	354	$ .35	$1.40
Richert, Pete	69T	86	$ .35	$1.40
Richert, Pete	70T	601	$ .50	$2.00
Richert, Pete	71T	273	$ .25	$1.00
Richert, Pete	72T	649	$ .40	$1.60
Richert, Pete	73T	239	$ .10	$ .40
Richert, Pete	74T	348	$ .10	$ .40
Richert, Pete	74TTR	348	$ .10	$ .40

TOPPS

Player	Year	No.	VG	EX/MT
Richie, Rob	90T	146	$.01	$.03
Rickert, Marv	52T	50	$13.75	$55.00
Ricketts, Dave	65T	581	$37.50	$150.00
Ricketts, Dave	67T	589	$2.25	$9.00
Ricketts, Dave	68T	46	$.35	$1.40
Ricketts, Dave	69T	232	$.50	$2.00
Ricketts, Dave	70T	626	$.50	$2.00
Ricketts, Dave	73T	517	$.25	$1.00
Ricketts, Dick	59T	137	$1.00	$4.00
Ricketts, Dick	60T	236	$.75	$3.00
Rico, Fred	70T	552	$.50	$2.00
Riddle, John	53T	274	$22.50	$90.00
Riddle, John	54T	147	$3.75	$15.00
Riddle, Johnny	55T	98	$2.25	$9.00
Riddle, John	91TA53	274	$.01	$.15
Riddleberger, Denny	71T	93	$.25	$1.00
Riddleberger, Denny	72T	642	$.40	$1.60
Riddleberger, Denny	73T	157	$.10	$.40
Riddoch, Greg	90TTR	102	$.01	$.05
Riddoch, Greg	91T	109	$.01	$.03
Riddoch, Greg	92T	351	$.01	$.03
Ridzik, Steve	57T	123	$2.00	$8.00
Ridzik, Steve	60T	489	$1.25	$5.00
Ridzik, Steve	64T	92	$.50	$2.00
Ridzik, Steve	65T	211	$.50	$2.00
Ridzik, Steve	66T	294	$.50	$2.00
Riggleman, Jim	93T	513	$.01	$.03
Righetti, Dave	82T	439	$.10	$.75
Righetti, Dave	83T	81	$.01	$.08
Righetti, Dave	83T	176	$.05	$.25
Righetti, Dave	84T	5	$.01	$.10
Righetti, Dave	84T	635	$.01	$.15
Righetti, Dave	85T	260	$.05	$.20
Righetti, Dave	86T	560	$.01	$.10
Righetti, Dave	87T	40	$.01	$.10
Righetti, Dave	87TAS	616	$.01	$.10
Righetti, Dave	87TRB	5	$.01	$.04
Righetti, Dave	88T	790	$.01	$.10
Righetti, Dave	89T	335	$.01	$.03
Righetti, Dave	90T	160	$.01	$.03
Righetti, Dave	91T	410	$.01	$.03
Righetti, Dave	91TSC	356	$.05	$.25
Righetti, Dave	91TTR	96	$.01	$.05
Righetti, Dave	92T	35	$.01	$.03
Righetti, Dave	92TSC	107	$.01	$.10
Righetti, Dave	93T	310	$.01	$.03
Rigney, Bill	52T	125	$7.00	$28.00
Rigney, Bill	60T	7	$5.00	$20.00
Rigney, Bill	60T	225	$.75	$3.00
Rigney, Bill	61T	225	$.60	$2.40
Rigney, Bill	62T	549	$6.00	$24.00
Rigney, Bill	63T	294	$.90	$3.60
Rigney, Bill	64T	383	$1.00	$4.00
Rigney, Bill	65T	66	$.35	$1.40
Rigney, Bill	66T	249	$.50	$2.00
Rigney, Bill	67T	494	$1.50	$6.00
Rigney, Bill	68T	416	$.35	$1.40
Rigney, Bill	69T	182	$.35	$1.40
Rigney, Bill	70T	426	$.35	$1.40
Rigney, Bill	71T	532	$1.00	$4.00
Rigney, Bill	72T	389	$.10	$.40
Rigney, Bill	91TA53	328	$.10	$.50
Rijo, Jose	84TTR	100	$2.25	$9.00
Rijo, Jose	85T	238	$.15	$1.25
Rijo, Jose	86T	536	$.05	$.25
Rijo, Jose	87T	34	$.05	$.20
Rijo, Jose	88T	316	$.01	$.10
Rijo, Jose	88TTR	92	$.05	$.25
Rijo, Jose	89T	135	$.01	$.10
Rijo, Jose	90T	627	$.01	$.03
Rijo, Jose	91T	493	$.01	$.03
Rijo, Jose	91TSC	11	$.05	$.25
Rijo, Jose	92T	220	$.01	$.03
Rijo, Jose	92TSC	800	$.01	$.10
Rijo, Jose	93T	165	$.01	$.03
Rijo, Jose	93TSC	233	$.01	$.15
Riles, Earnie	86T	398	$.01	$.10
Riles, Earnie	87T	523	$.01	$.04
Riles, Earnie	88T	88	$.01	$.04
Riles, Ernie (Earnie)	88TTR	93	$.01	$.05
Riles, Ernie	89T	676	$.01	$.03
Riles, Ernie	90T	732	$.01	$.03
Riles, Ernie	91T	408	$.01	$.03
Riles, Ernie	91TSC	432	$.05	$.25
Riles, Ernie	91TTR	97	$.01	$.05
Riles, Ernie	92T	187	$.01	$.03
Riley, George	81T	514	$.01	$.08
Rincon, Andy	81T	244	$.01	$.08
Rincon, Andy	82T	135	$.01	$.08
Ringley, Ron	92TSC	233	$.01	$.10
Rios, Juan	69T	619	$.40	$1.60
Rios, Juan	70T	89	$.20	$.80
Ripken, Billy	88T	352	$.01	$.15
Ripken, Billy	89T	571	$.01	$.03
Ripken, Billy	90T	468	$.01	$.03
Ripken, Billy	91T	677	$.01	$.03
Ripken, Billy	91TSC	222	$.05	$.25
Ripken, Billy	92T	752	$.01	$.03
Ripken, Billy	92TSC	533	$.01	$.10
Ripken, Cal	82T	21	$18.25	$75.00
Ripken, Cal	82TTR	98	$62.50	$250.00
Ripken, Cal	83T	163	$6.00	$24.00
Ripken, Cal	84T	426	$.10	$1.00
Ripken, Cal	84T	490	$2.00	$8.00
Ripken, Cal	84TAS	400	$.20	$2.00
Ripken, Cal	85T	30	$1.00	$4.00
Ripken, Cal	85TAS	704	$.10	$1.00
Ripken, Cal	86T	340	$.25	$2.50
Ripken, Cal	86TAS	715	$.10	$1.00
Ripken, Cal	87T	784	$.10	$1.00
Ripken, Cal	87TAS	609	$.10	$.50
Ripken, Cal	88T	650	$.10	$.50
Ripken Jr., Cal	89T	250	$.10	$.50
Ripken, Cal	90T	570	$.10	$.40
Ripken, Cal	90TAS	388	$.05	$.20
Ripken, Cal	90TRB	8	$.01	$.15

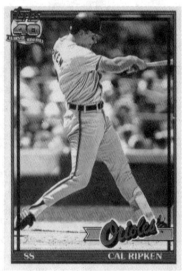

Player	Year	No.	VG	EX/MT
Ripken, Cal	91T	150	$.05	$.25
Ripken, Cal	91TRB	5	$.01	$.15

TOPPS

Player	Year	No.	VG	EX/MT
Ripken, Cal	91TSC	430	$1.00	$4.00
Ripken, Cal	92T	40	$.05	$.35
Ripken, Cal	92TAS	400	$.01	$.15
Ripken, Cal	92TSC	1	$.15	$1.50
Ripken, Cal	92TSC	595	$.10	$1.00
Ripken, Cal	93T	300	$.05	$.20
Ripken, Cal	93TSC	40	$.10	$.75
Ripken Sr., Cal	87TTR	102	$.01	$.10
Ripken Sr., Cal	88T	444	$.01	$.04
Ripley, Allen	79T	702	$.03	$.12
Ripley, Allen	80T	413	$.01	$.10
Ripley, Allen	81T	144	$.01	$.08
Ripley, Allen	82T	529	$.01	$.08
Ripley, Allen	82TTR	99	$.01	$.10
Ripley, Allen	83T	73	$.01	$.08
Rippelmeyer, Ray	61T	276	$.60	$2.40
Rippelmeyer, Ray	62T	271	$.75	$3.00
Rippelmeyer, Ray	73T	486	$.25	$1.00
Rippelmeyer, Ray	74T	119	$.10	$.40
Ritchie, Jay	65T	494	$1.25	$5.00
Ritchie, Wally	87TTR	103	$.01	$.05
Ritchie, Wally	88T	494	$.01	$.04
Ritchie, Wally	92TSC	324	$.01	$.10
Rittwage, Jim	65T	501	$1.25	$5.00
Ritz, Kevin	90T	237	$.01	$.10
Ritz, Kevin	92TSC	337	$.01	$.10
Ritz, Kevin	93T	771	$.01	$.03
Rivera, Ben	93T	622	$.01	$.03
Rivera, Bombo	77T	178	$.05	$.20
Rivera, Bombo	78T	657	$.04	$.16
Rivera, Bombo	79T	449	$.03	$.12
Rivera, Bombo	80T	43	$.01	$.10
Rivera, Bombo	81T	256	$.01	$.08
Rivera, German	85T	626	$.01	$.06
Rivera, Jim	53T	156	$4.00	$16.00
Rivera, Jim	54T	34	$3.75	$15.00
Rivera, Jim	55T	58	$2.25	$9.00
Rivera, Jim	56T	70	$2.00	$8.00
Rivera, Jim	57T	107	$2.00	$8.00
Rivera, Jim	58T	11	$2.00	$8.00
Rivera, Jim	59T	213	$1.00	$4.00
Rivera, Jim	60T	116	$.75	$3.00
Rivera, Jim	61T	367	$.60	$2.40
Rivera, Jim	91TA53	156	$.01	$.15
Rivera, Luis	88TTR	94	$.01	$.10
Rivera, Luis	89T	431	$.01	$.03
Rivera, Luis	90T	601	$.01	$.03
Rivera, Luis	91T	338	$.01	$.03
Rivera, Luis	91TSC	55	$.05	$.25
Rivera, Luis	92T	97	$.01	$.03
Rivera, Luis	92TSC	255	$.01	$.10
Rivera, Luis	93T	296	$.01	$.03
Rivers, Mickey	72T	272	$.25	$1.00
Rivers, Mickey	73T	597	$.75	$3.00
Rivers, Mickey	74T	76	$.10	$.40
Rivers, Mickey	75T	164	$.10	$.40
Rivers, Mickey	76T	85	$.10	$.40
Rivers, Mickey	76T	198	$.15	$.60
Rivers, Mickey	76TTR	85	$.05	$.25
Rivers, Mickey	77T	305	$.05	$.20
Rivers, Mickey	78T	690	$.04	$.16
Rivers, Mickey	79T	60	$.03	$.12
Rivers, Mickey	80T	485	$.01	$.10
Rivers, Mickey	81T	145	$.01	$.08
Rivers, Mickey	82T	704	$.01	$.15
Rivers, Mickey	82TSA	705	$.01	$.07
Rivers, Mickey	83T	224	$.01	$.08
Rivers, Mickey	84T	504	$.01	$.06
Rivers, Mickey	85T	371	$.01	$.06
Rizzuto, Phil	51Trb	5	$8.00	$32.00
Rizzuto, Phil	52T	11	$42.50	$170.00
Rizzuto, Phil	53T	114	$30.00	$120.00
Rizzuto, Phil	54T	17	$17.50	$70.00
Rizzuto, Phil	55T	189	$35.00	$140.00
Rizzuto, Phil	56T	113	$13.75	$55.00

Player	Year	No.	VG	EX/MT
Rizzuto, Phil	61TMVP	471	$4.00	$16.00
Rizzuto, Phil	91TA53	114	$.15	$1.50
Roach, Mel	54T	181	$3.75	$15.00
Roach, Mel	55T	117	$2.25	$9.00
Roach, Mel	59T	54	$1.50	$6.00
Roach, Mel	60T	491	$1.25	$5.00
Roach, Mel	61T	217	$.60	$2.40
Roach, Mel	62T	581	$3.50	$14.00
Roarke, Mike	61T	376	$1.00	$4.00
Roarke, Mike	62T	87	$.60	$2.40
Roarke, Mike	63T	224	$.90	$3.60
Roarke, Mike	64T	292	$.65	$2.60
Robbins, Bruce	80T	666	$.01	$.10
Robbins, Bruce	81T	79	$.01	$.08
Robbins, Doug	88TTR	95	$.01	$.15
Robbins, Doug	92T	58	$.05	$.25
Roberge, Bert	80T	329	$.01	$.10
Roberge, Bert	83T	611	$.01	$.08
Roberge, Bert	85T	388	$.01	$.06
Roberge, Bert	85TTR	94	$.01	$.10
Roberge, Bert	86T	154	$.01	$.05
Roberts, Bip	86TTR	91	$.10	$.75
Roberts, Bip	87T	637	$.10	$.40
Roberts, Bip	89TTR	103	$.01	$.05
Roberts, Bip	90T	307	$.01	$.03
Roberts, Bip	91T	538	$.01	$.03
Roberts, Bip	91TSC	18	$.05	$.25
Roberts, Bip	92T	20	$.01	$.03
Roberts, Bip	92TSC	48	$.01	$.10
Roberts, Bip	92TSC	645	$.01	$.10
Roberts, Bip	92TTR	92	$.01	$.05
Roberts, Bip	93T	219	$.01	$.10
Roberts, Bip	93TSC	30	$.01	$.15
Roberts, Chris	91TTR	98	$.10	$.50
Roberts, Chris	92TTR	93	$.05	$.25
Roberts, Curt	54T	242	$3.75	$15.00
Roberts, Curt	55T	107	$2.25	$9.00
Roberts, Curt	56T	306	$2.50	$10.00
Roberts, Dave	63T	158	$.90	$3.60
Roberts, Dave	66T	571	$7.00	$28.00
Roberts, Dave	69T	536	$.40	$1.60
Roberts, Dave	70T	151	$.20	$.80
Roberts, Dave	71T	448	$.50	$2.00
Roberts, Dave	72T	91	$.50	$2.00
Roberts, Dave	72T	360	$.10	$.40
Roberts, Dave	73T	39	$.10	$.40
Roberts, Dave	73T	133	$.10	$.40
Roberts, Dave	74T	177	$.10	$.40
Roberts, Dave	74T	309	$.10	$.40
Roberts, Dave	75T	301	$.10	$.40
Roberts, Dave	75T	558	$.10	$.40
Roberts, Dave	76T	107	$.05	$.25
Roberts, Dave	76T	649	$.05	$.25
Roberts, Dave	76TTR	649	$.05	$.25
Roberts, Dave	77T	363	$.05	$.20
Roberts, Dave	77T	537	$.05	$.20
Roberts, Dave	78T	501	$.04	$.16
Roberts, Dave	79T	342	$.03	$.12
Roberts, Dave	79T	473	$.03	$.12
Roberts, Dave	80T	93	$.01	$.10
Roberts, Dave	80T	212	$.01	$.10
Roberts, Dave	81T	57	$.01	$.08
Roberts, Dave	81T	431	$.01	$.08
Roberts, Dave	81TTR	824	$.01	$.15
Roberts, Dave	82T	218	$.01	$.08
Roberts, Dave	83T	148	$.01	$.08
Roberts, Leon	75T	620	$11.25	$45.00
Roberts, Leon	76T	292	$.05	$.25
Roberts, Leon	76TTR	292	$.05	$.25
Roberts, Leon	77T	456	$.05	$.20
Roberts, Leon	79T	166	$.03	$.12
Roberts, Leon	80T	507	$.01	$.10
Roberts, Leon	81T	368	$.01	$.08
Roberts, Leon	81TTR	825	$.01	$.15
Roberts, Leon	82T	688	$.01	$.08

TOPPS

Player	Year	No.	VG	EX/MT	Player	Year	No.	VG	EX/MT
Roberts, Leon	83T	89	$ .01	$ .08	Robinson, Brooks	65T	5	$5.50	$22.00
Roberts, Leon	83TTR	96	$ .01	$ .10	Robinson, Brooks	65T	150	$7.00	$28.00
Roberts, Leon	84T	784	$ .01	$ .06	Robinson, Brooks	66T	390	$8.00	$32.00
Roberts, Leon	85T	217	$ .01	$ .06	Robinson, Brooks	67T	1	$5.00	$20.00
Roberts, Robin	52T	59	$35.00	$140.00	Robinson, Brooks	67T	600	$60.00	$240.00
Roberts, Robin	56T	180	$9.50	$38.00	Robinson, Brooks	68T	20	$5.50	$22.00
Roberts, Robin	57T	15	$6.00	$24.00	Robinson, Brooks	68T	530	$3.50	$14.00
Roberts, Robin	58T	90	$6.00	$24.00	Robinson, Brooks	68TAS	365	$2.25	$9.00
Roberts, Robin	59T	156	$1.50	$6.00	Robinson, Brooks	69T	550	$5.50	$22.00
Roberts, Robin	59T	352	$4.00	$16.00	Robinson, Brooks	69TAS	421	$1.75	$7.00
Roberts, Robin	60T	264	$3.75	$15.00	Robinson, Brooks	70T	230	$3.00	$12.00
Roberts, Robin	61T	20	$3.00	$12.00	Robinson, Brooks	70TAS	455	$1.25	$5.00
Roberts, Robin	62T	243	$3.00	$12.00	Robinson, Brooks	71T	300	$4.50	$18.00
Roberts, Robin	63T	6	$1.25	$5.00					
Roberts, Robin	63T	125	$3.00	$12.00					
Roberts, Robin	64T	285	$2.50	$10.00					
Roberts, Robin	65T	15	$2.00	$8.00					
Roberts, Robin	66T	530	$11.25	$45.00					
Roberts, Robin	91TA53	288	$ .10	$ .75					
Robertson, Andre	82T	83	$ .01	$ .15					
Robertson, Andre	83T	281	$ .01	$ .08					
Robertson, Andre	84T	592	$ .01	$ .06					
Robertson, Andre	85T	354	$ .01	$ .06					
Robertson, Andre	86T	738	$ .01	$ .05					
Robertson, Bob	68T	36	$ .35	$1.40					
Robertson, Bob	69T	468	$ .30	$1.20					
Robertson, Bob	70T	664	$1.25	$5.00					
Robertson, Bob	71T	255	$ .25	$1.00					
Robertson, Bob	72T	429	$ .25	$1.00					
Robertson, Bob	72TIA	430	$ .25	$1.00					
Robertson, Bob	73T	422	$ .25	$1.00					
Robertson, Bob	74T	540	$ .10	$ .40					
Robertson, Bob	75T	409	$ .10	$ .40					
Robertson, Bob	76T	449	$ .05	$ .25					
Robertson, Bob	77T	176	$ .05	$ .20					
Robertson, Bob	79T	312	$ .03	$ .12					
Robertson, Jerry	69T	284	$ .50	$2.00					
Robertson, Jerry	70T	661	$1.25	$5.00					
Robertson, Jerry	71T	651	$1.50	$6.00					
Robertson, Jim	54T	149	$3.75	$15.00					
Robertson, Jim	55T	177	$6.25	$25.00					
Robertson, Rich	69T	16	$ .35	$1.40					
Robertson, Rich	70T	229	$ .20	$ .80					
Robertson, Rich	71T	443	$ .50	$2.00					
Robertson, Rich	72T	618	$ .40	$1.60					
Robertson, Sherry	52T	245	$7.00	$28.00	Robinson, Brooks	72T	498	$ .50	$2.00
Robidoux, Billy Jo	86TTR	92	$ .01	$ .06	Robinson, Brooks	72T	550	$5.50	$22.00
Robidoux, Billy Jo	87T	401	$ .01	$ .04	Robinson, Brooks	73T	90	$1.50	$6.00
Robinson, Bill	67T	442	$1.00	$4.00	Robinson, Brooks	74T	160	$1.50	$6.00
Robinson, Bill	68T	337	$ .35	$1.40	Robinson, Brooks	74TAS	334	$ .35	$1.40
Robinson, Bill	69T	313	$ .50	$2.00	Robinson, Brooks	75T	50	$1.25	$5.00
Robinson, Bill	70T	23	$ .20	$ .80	Robinson, Brooks	75T	202	$ .25	$1.00
Robinson, Bill	73T	37	$ .10	$ .40	Robinson, Brooks	76T	95	$1.25	$5.00
Robinson, Bill	74T	174	$ .10	$ .40	Robinson, Brooks	77T	285	$1.00	$4.00
Robinson, Bill	75T	501	$ .10	$ .40	Robinson, Brooks	78TRB	4	$ .25	$1.00
Robinson, Bill	76T	137	$ .05	$ .25	Robinson, Bruce	79T	711	$ .10	$ .40
Robinson, Bill	77T	335	$ .05	$ .20	Robinson, Bruce	81T	424	$ .01	$ .08
Robinson, Bill	78T	455	$ .04	$ .16	Robinson, Craig	74T	23	$ .10	$ .40
Robinson, Bill	79T	637	$ .03	$ .12	Robinson, Craig	74TTR	23	$ .10	$ .40
Robinson, Bill	80T	264	$ .01	$ .10	Robinson, Craig	75T	367	$ .10	$ .40
Robinson, Bill	81T	51	$ .01	$ .08	Robinson, Daniel	93T	599	$ .05	$ .20
Robinson, Bill	82T	543	$ .01	$ .08	Robinson, Dave	71T	262	$ .25	$1.00
Robinson, Bill	82TTR	100	$ .01	$ .10	Robinson, Dewey	80T	664	$ .01	$ .10
Robinson, Bill	83T	754	$ .01	$ .08	Robinson, Dewey	81T	487	$ .01	$ .08
Robinson, Brooks	57T	328	$100.00	$400.00	Robinson, Dewey	82T	176	$ .01	$ .08
Robinson, Brooks	58T	307	$25.00	$100.00	Robinson, Don	79T	264	$ .15	$ .60
Robinson, Brooks	59T	439	$15.00	$60.00	Robinson, Don	80T	719	$ .01	$ .10
Robinson, Brooks	60T	28	$12.50	$50.00	Robinson, Don	81T	168	$ .01	$ .08
Robinson, Brooks	61T	10	$8.75	$35.00	Robinson, Don	82T	332	$ .01	$ .08
Robinson, Brooks	61TAS	572	$22.50	$90.00	Robinson, Don	83T	44	$ .01	$ .08
Robinson, Brooks	62T	45	$9.00	$36.00	Robinson, Don	84T	616	$ .01	$ .06
Robinson, Brooks	62TAS	468	$4.50	$18.00	Robinson, Don	85T	537	$ .01	$ .06
Robinson, Brooks	63T	345	$13.75	$55.00	Robinson, Don	86T	731	$ .01	$ .05
Robinson, Brooks	64T	230	$8.75	$35.00	Robinson, Don	87T	712	$ .01	$ .04
Robinson, Brooks	65T	1	$3.75	$15.00	Robinson, Don	88T	52	$ .01	$ .04

TOPPS

Player	Year	No.	VG	EX/MT
Robinson, Don	89T	473	$ .01	$ .03
Robinson, Don	90T	217	$ .01	$ .03
Robinson, Don	91T	104	$ .01	$ .03
Robinson, Don	91TSC	167	$ .05	$ .25
Robinson, Don	92T	373	$ .01	$ .03
Robinson, Don	92TSC	729	$ .01	$ .10
Robinson, Earl	61T	343	$ .60	$2.40
Robinson, Earl	62T	272	$ .75	$3.00
Robinson, Eddie	51Trb	51	$1.65	$6.60
Robinson, Eddie	52T	32	$13.75	$55.00
Robinson, Eddie	53T	73	$6.25	$25.00
Robinson, Eddie	54T	62	$7.50	$30.00
Robinson, Eddie	56T	302	$2.50	$10.00
Robinson, Eddie	57T	238	$2.00	$8.00
Robinson, Eddie	60T	455	$1.25	$5.00
Robinson, Eddie	91TA53	73	$ .01	$ .15
Robinson, Floyd	62T	454	$1.50	$6.00
Robinson, Floyd	63T	2	$5.00	$20.00
Robinson, Floyd	63T	405	$1.00	$4.00
Robinson, Floyd	64T	195	$ .50	$2.00
Robinson, Floyd	65T	345	$ .50	$2.00
Robinson, Floyd	66T	8	$ .35	$1.40
Robinson, Floyd	66T	199	$ .50	$2.00
Robinson, Floyd	67T	120	$ .40	$1.60
Robinson, Floyd	68T	404	$ .35	$1.40
Robinson, Frank	57T	35	$65.00	$260.00
Robinson, Frank	58T	285	$25.00	$100.00
Robinson, Frank	58T	386	$2.50	$10.00
Robinson, Frank	58TAS	484	$5.50	$22.00
Robinson, Frank	59T	435	$13.75	$55.00
Robinson, Frank	60T	352	$1.75	$7.00
Robinson, Frank	60T	490	$15.00	$60.00
Robinson, Frank	61T	25	$1.75	$7.00
Robinson, Frank	61T	360	$11.00	$44.00
Robinson, Frank	61TAS	581	$22.50	$90.00
Robinson, Frank	62T	54	$2.00	$8.00
Robinson, Frank	62T	350	$11.00	$44.00
Robinson, Frank	62TAS	396	$3.75	$15.00
Robinson, Frank	63T	1	$8.00	$32.00
Robinson, Frank	63T	3	$5.50	$22.00
Robinson, Frank	63T	400	$11.25	$45.00
Robinson, Frank	64T	260	$6.25	$25.00
Robinson, Frank	65T	120	$7.00	$28.00
Robinson, Frank	66T	219	$1.75	$7.00
Robinson, Frank	66T	310	$10.00	$40.00
Robinson, Frank	67T	1	$5.00	$20.00
Robinson, Frank	67T	100	$4.50	$18.00
Robinson, Frank	67T	239	$1.25	$5.00
Robinson, Frank	67T	241	$1.25	$5.00
Robinson, Frank	67T	243	$1.25	$5.00
Robinson, Frank	68T	2	$2.25	$9.00
Robinson, Frank	68T	4	$2.25	$9.00
Robinson, Frank	68T	500	$7.00	$28.00
Robinson, Frank	68T	530	$3.50	$14.00
Robinson, Frank	68TAS	373	$2.50	$10.00
Robinson, Frank	69T	250	$8.00	$32.00
Robinson, Frank	70T	700	$11.25	$45.00
Robinson, Frank	70TAS	463	$1.50	$6.00
Robinson, Frank	71T	640	$10.00	$40.00
Robinson, Frank	72T	88	$ .75	$3.00
Robinson, Frank	72T	100	$1.50	$6.00
Robinson, Frank	72TTR	754	$8.00	$32.00
Robinson, Frank	73T	175	$1.25	$5.00
Robinson, Frank	74T	55	$1.25	$5.00
Robinson, Frank	75T	199	$ .75	$3.00
Robinson, Frank	75T	204	$ .50	$2.00
Robinson, Frank	75T	580	$1.00	$4.00
Robinson, Frank	83T	576	$ .05	$ .35
Robinson, Frank	84T	171	$ .05	$ .25
Robinson, Frank	86TTR	404	$ .01	$ .15
Robinson, Frank	88TTR	96	$ .01	$ .10
Robinson, Frank	89T	774	$ .01	$ .10
Robinson, Frank	90T	381	$ .01	$ .10
Robinson, Frank	91T	639	$ .01	$ .10
Robinson, Humberto	55T	182	$6.25	$25.00
Robinson, Humberto	59T	366	$1.00	$4.00
Robinson, Humberto	60T	416	$1.25	$5.00
Robinson, Jackie	52T	312	$325.00	$1300.00
Robinson, Jackie	53T	1	$150.00	$600.00
Robinson, Jackie	54T	10	$70.00	$280.00
Robinson, Jackie	55T	50	$60.00	$240.00
Robinson, Jackie	56T	30	$40.00	$160.00
Robinson, Jackie	91TA53	1	$1.00	$4.00
Robinson, Jeff D.	84TTR	101	$ .01	$ .15
Robinson, Jeff D.	85T	592	$ .01	$ .06
Robinson, Jeff D.	86TTR	93	$ .01	$ .06
Robinson, Jeff D.	87T	389	$ .01	$ .04
Robinson, Jeff D.	89T	681	$ .01	$ .03
Robinson, Jeff D.	90T	723	$ .01	$ .03
Robinson, Jeff D.	90TTR	103	$ .01	$ .05
Robinson, Jeff D.	91T	19	$ .01	$ .03
Robinson, Jeff D.	91TSC	542	$ .05	$ .25
Robinson, Jeff D.	91TTR	99	$ .01	$ .05
Robinson, Jeff D.	92T	137	$ .01	$ .03
Robinson, Jeff D.	92TSC	756	$ .01	$ .10
Robinson, Jeff M.	87TTR	104	$ .01	$ .05
Robinson, Jeff M.	88T	244	$ .01	$ .04
Robinson, Jeff M.	88T	449	$ .01	$ .10
Robinson, Jeff M.	89T	267	$ .01	$ .10
Robinson, Jeff M.	90T	42	$ .01	$ .03
Robinson, Jeff M.	91T	766	$ .01	$ .03
Robinson, Jeff M.	91TSC	441	$ .05	$ .25
Robinson, Jeff M.	91TTR	100	$ .01	$ .05
Robinson, Jeff M.	92TSC	715	$ .01	$ .10
Robinson, Jerry	63T	466	$12.50	$50.00
Robinson, Ron	86T	442	$ .01	$ .05
Robinson, Ron	87T	119	$ .01	$ .04
Robinson, Ron	88T	517	$ .01	$ .04
Robinson, Ron	89T	16	$ .01	$ .03
Robinson, Ron	90T	604	$ .01	$ .03
Robinson, Ron	90TTR	104	$ .01	$ .05
Robinson, Ron	91T	313	$ .01	$ .03
Robinson, Ron	91TSC	296	$ .05	$ .25
Robinson, Ron	92TSC	739	$ .01	$ .10
Robles, Rafael	69T	592	$ .40	$1.60
Robles, Rafael	70T	573	$ .50	$2.00
Robles, Rafael	71T	408	$ .50	$2.00
Robles, Sergio	73T	601	$ .75	$3.00
Robles, Sergio	74T	603	$ .10	$ .40
Rockett, Pat	78T	502	$ .04	$ .16
Rodgers, Andre	57T	377	$1.75	$7.00
Rodgers, Andre	59T	216	$1.00	$4.00
Rodgers, Andre	60T	431	$ .75	$3.00
Rodgers, Andre	61T	183	$ .60	$2.40
Rodgers, Andre	62T	477	$1.50	$6.00
Rodgers, Andre	63T	193	$ .50	$2.00
Rodgers, Andre	64T	336	$ .65	$2.60
Rodgers, Andre	65T	536	$2.50	$10.00
Rodgers, Andre	66T	592	$3.75	$15.00
Rodgers, Andre	67T	554	$2.25	$9.00
Rodgers, Bob	62T	431	$2.00	$8.00
Rodgers, Bob	63T	280	$1.25	$5.00
Rodgers, Bob	64T	61	$ .50	$2.00
Rodgers, Bob	64T	426	$1.00	$4.00
Rodgers, Bob	65T	342	$ .50	$2.00
Rodgers, Bob	66T	462	$1.50	$6.00
Rodgers, Bob	67T	281	$ .50	$2.00
Rodgers, Bob	68T	433	$ .35	$1.40
Rodgers, Bob	69T	157	$ .35	$1.40
Rodgers, Bob	73T	49	$ .20	$ .80
Rodgers, Bob	74T	447	$ .10	$ .40
Rodgers, Bob	85TTR	95	$ .01	$ .10
Rodgers, Bob	86T	171	$ .01	$ .05
Rodgers, Bob	87T	293	$ .01	$ .04
Rodgers, Bob	88T	504	$ .01	$ .04
Rodgers, Bob	89T	474	$ .01	$ .03
Rodgers, Bob	90T	81	$ .01	$ .03
Rodgers, Bob	91T	321	$ .01	$ .03
Rodgers, Buck "Bob"	92T	21	$ .01	$ .03
Rodgers, Buck	93T	503	$ .01	$ .03

493

TOPPS

Player	Year	No.	VG	EX/MT
Rodriguez, Aurelio	69T	653	$ .75	$3.00
Rodriguez, Aurelio	70T	228	$ .20	$ .80
Rodriguez, Aurelio	71T	464	$ .50	$2.00
Rodriguez, Aurelio	72T	319	$ .10	$ .40
Rodriguez, Aurelio	73T	218	$ .10	$ .40
Rodriguez, Aurelio	74T	72	$ .10	$ .40
Rodriguez, Aurelio	75T	221	$ .10	$ .40
Rodriguez, Aurelio	76T	267	$ .05	$ .25
Rodriguez, Aurelio	77T	574	$ .05	$ .20
Rodriguez, Aurelio	78T	342	$ .04	$ .16
Rodriguez, Aurelio	79T	176	$ .03	$ .12
Rodriguez, Aurelio	80T	468	$ .01	$ .10
Rodriguez, Aurelio	81T	34	$ .01	$ .08
Rodriguez, Aurelio	82T	334	$ .01	$ .08
Rodriguez, Aurelio	82TTR	101	$ .01	$ .10
Rodriguez, Aurelio	83T	758	$ .01	$ .08
Rodriguez, Aurelio	83TTR	97	$ .01	$ .10
Rodriguez, Aurelio	84T	269	$ .01	$ .06
Rodriguez, Eduardo	74T	171	$ .10	$ .40
Rodriguez, Eduardo	75T	582	$ .10	$ .40
Rodriguez, Eduardo	76T	92	$ .05	$ .25
Rodriguez, Eduardo	77T	361	$ .05	$ .20
Rodriguez, Eduardo	78T	623	$ .04	$ .16
Rodriguez, Eduardo	79T	108	$ .03	$ .12
Rodriguez, Eduardo	80T	273	$ .01	$ .10
Rodriguez, Eliseo "Ellie"	69T	49	$ .35	$1.40
Rodriguez, Ellie	70T	402	$ .35	$1.40
Rodriguez, Ellie	71T	344	$ .25	$1.00
Rodriguez, Ellie	72T	421	$ .25	$1.00
Rodriguez, Ellie	73T	45	$ .10	$ .40
Rodriguez, Ellie	74T	405	$ .10	$ .40
Rodriguez, Ellie	75T	285	$ .10	$ .40
Rodriguez, Ellie	76T	512	$ .05	$ .25
Rodriguez, Ellie	77T	448	$ .05	$ .20
Rodriguez, Henry	92T	656	$ .05	$ .20
Rodriguez, Henry	92TSC	268	$ .05	$ .20
Rodriguez, Henry	93T	284	$ .01	$ .03
Rodriguez, Henry	93TSC	226	$ .01	$ .10
Rodriguez, Ivan	91TTR	101	$ .10	$1.00
Rodriguez, Ivan	92T	78	$ .10	$ .40
Rodriguez, Ivan	92TSC	415	$ .15	$1.25
Rodriguez, Ivan	93T	360	$ .01	$ .10
Rodriguez, Rich	91T	573	$ .01	$ .15
Rodriguez, Rich	91TSC	565	$ .10	$ .40
Rodriguez, Rich	92T	462	$ .01	$ .03
Rodriguez, Rich	92TSC	712	$ .01	$ .15
Rodriguez, Rich	93T	693	$ .01	$ .03
Rodriguez, Rich	93TSC	137	$ .01	$ .10
Rodriguez, Rick	88T	166	$ .01	$ .04
Rodriguez, Roberto	68T	199	$ .35	$1.40
Rodriguez, Roberto	69T	358	$ .30	$1.20
Rodriguez, Roberto	71T	424	$ .50	$2.00
Rodriguez, Rosario	91T	688	$ .01	$ .10
Rodriguez, Rosario	92TSC	697	$ .01	$ .15
Rodriguez, Steve	91TTR	102	$ .05	$ .20
Rodriguez, Steve	92TTR	94	$ .01	$ .10
Roe, Preacher	51Trb	16	$3.00	$12.00
Roe, Preacher	52T	66	$25.00	$100.00
Roe, Preacher	53T	254	$20.00	$80.00
Roe, Preacher	54T	14	$5.00	$20.00
Roe, Preacher	91TA53	254	$ .01	$ .15
Roebuck, Ed	55T	195	$8.00	$32.00
Roebuck, Ed	56T	58	$2.00	$8.00
Roebuck, Ed	58T	435	$1.00	$4.00
Roebuck, Ed	60T	519	$2.75	$11.00
Roebuck, Ed	61T	6	$ .60	$2.40
Roebuck, Ed	62T	535	$3.50	$14.00
Roebuck, Ed	63T	295	$ .90	$3.60
Roebuck, Ed	64T	187	$ .50	$2.00
Roebuck, Ed	65T	52	$ .35	$1.40
Roenicke, Gary	80T	568	$ .01	$ .10
Roenicke, Gary	81T	37	$ .01	$ .08
Roenicke, Gary	82T	204	$ .01	$ .08
Roenicke, Gary	83T	605	$ .01	$ .08
Roenicke, Gary	84T	372	$ .01	$ .06
Roenicke, Gary	85T	109	$ .01	$ .06
Roenicke, Gary	86T	494	$ .01	$ .05
Roenicke, Gary	86TTR	94	$ .01	$ .06
Roenicke, Gary	87T	683	$ .01	$ .04
Roenicke, Gary	87TTR	105	$ .01	$ .05
Roenicke, Gary	88T	523	$ .01	$ .04
Roenicke, Ron	82T	681	$1.25	$5.00
Roenicke, Ron	83T	113	$ .01	$ .08
Roenicke, Ron	84T	647	$ .01	$ .06
Roenicke, Ron	86T	63	$ .01	$ .05
Roenicke, Ron	87T	329	$ .01	$ .04
Roenicke, Ron	88T	783	$ .01	$ .04
Roesler, Mike	90T	203	$ .01	$ .10
Rogan, Pat	65T	486	$1.25	$5.00
Rogers, Kenny	89TTR	104	$ .01	$ .10
Rogers, Kenny	90T	683	$ .01	$ .10
Rogers, Kenny	91T	332	$ .01	$ .03
Rogers, Kenny	91TSC	258	$ .05	$ .25
Rogers, Kenny	92T	511	$ .01	$ .03
Rogers, Kenny	92TSC	311	$ .01	$ .10
Rogers, Kenny	93T	169	$ .01	$ .03

Player	Year	No.	VG	EX/MT
Rogers, Kenny	**93TSC**	**55**	**$ .01**	**$ .15**
Rogers, Kevin	93T	822	$ .01	$ .15
Rogers, Lamarr	93T	746	$ .05	$ .20
Rogers, Steve	74T	169	$ .15	$ .60
Rogers, Steve	75T	173	$ .10	$ .40
Rogers, Steve	76T	71	$ .05	$ .25
Rogers, Steve	77T	316	$ .05	$ .20
Rogers, Steve	78T	425	$ .04	$ .16
Rogers, Steve	79T	235	$ .03	$ .12
Rogers, Steve	80T	520	$ .01	$ .10
Rogers, Steve	81T	725	$ .01	$ .08
Rogers, Steve	82T	605	$ .01	$ .08
Rogers, Steve	83T	111	$ .01	$ .08
Rogers, Steve	83T	320	$ .01	$ .08
Rogers, Steve	83T	707	$ .01	$ .08
Rogers, Steve	83TAS	405	$ .01	$ .08
Rogers, Steve	84T	80	$ .01	$ .06
Rogers, Steve	84T	708	$ .05	$ .20
Rogers, Steve	84TAS	394	$ .01	$ .06
Rogers, Steve	85T	205	$ .01	$ .06
Roggenburk, Garry	63T	386	$1.00	$4.00
Roggenburk, Garry	64T	258	$ .65	$2.60

TOPPS

Player	Year	No.	VG	EX/MT
Roggenburk, Garry	66T	582	$3.75	$15.00
Roggenburk, Garry	67T	429	$ .60	$2.40
Roggenburk, Garry	68T	581	$ .70	$2.80
Rogodzinski, Mike	74T	492	$ .10	$ .40
Rogovin, Saul	52T	159	$7.50	$30.00
Rogovin, Saul	57T	129	$2.00	$8.00
Rohde, Dave	92TSC	753	$ .01	$ .10
Rohr, Bill	67T	547	$2.25	$9.00
Rohr, Bill	68T	314	$ .35	$1.40
Rohr, Les	68T	569	$ .70	$2.80
Rojas, Cookie	63T	221	$1.00	$4.00
Rojas, Cookie	64T	448	$1.00	$4.00
Rojas, Cookie	65T	474	$1.25	$5.00
Rojas, Cookie	66T	170	$ .50	$2.00
Rojas, Cookie	67T	595	$5.00	$20.00
Rojas, Cookie	68T	39	$ .35	$1.40
Rojas, Cookie	69T	507	$ .30	$1.20
Rojas, Cookie	70T	569	$ .50	$2.00
Rojas, Cookie	71T	118	$ .25	$1.00
Rojas, Cookie	72T	415	$ .25	$1.00
Rojas, Cookie	73T	188	$ .10	$ .40
Rojas, Cookie	74T	278	$ .10	$ .40
Rojas, Cookie	75T	169	$ .10	$ .40
Rojas, Cookie	76T	311	$ .05	$ .25
Rojas, Cookie	77T	509	$ .05	$ .20
Rojas, Cookie	88TTR	97	$ .01	$ .05
Rojas, Mel	91T	252	$ .01	$ .15
Rojas, Mel	92T	583	$ .01	$ .03
Rojas, Mel	92TSC	489	$ .01	$ .10
Rojas, Mel	93T	341	$ .01	$ .03
Rojas, Minnie	67T	104	$ .40	$1.60
Rojas, Minnie	68T	305	$ .35	$1.40
Rojas, Minnie	69T	502	$ .30	$1.20
Rojek, Stan	52T	163	$7.00	$28.00
Roland, Jim	63T	522	$1.75	$7.00
Roland, Jim	64T	341	$ .65	$2.60
Roland, Jim	65T	171	$ .35	$1.40
Roland, Jim	68T	276	$ .35	$1.40
Roland, Jim	69T	336	$ .30	$1.20
Roland, Jim	70T	719	$1.25	$5.00
Roland, Jim	71T	642	$1.00	$4.00
Roland, Jim	72T	464	$ .25	$1.00
Rolfe, Red	52T	296	$15.00	$60.00
Rollins, Rich	62T	596	$15.00	$60.00
Rollins, Rich	63T	110	$ .50	$2.00
Rollins, Rich	64T	8	$2.00	$8.00
Rollins, Rich	64T	270	$ .65	$2.60
Rollins, Rich	65T	90	$ .35	$1.40
Rollins, Rich	66T	473	$1.50	$6.00
Rollins, Rich	67T	98	$ .40	$1.60
Rollins, Rich	68T	243	$ .35	$1.40
Rollins, Rich	69T	451	$ .30	$1.20
Rollins, Rich	70T	652	$1.25	$5.00
Roman, Bill	65T	493	$1.25	$5.00
Roman, Dan	93T	782	$ .05	$ .20
Romanick, Ron	84TTR	102	$ .01	$ .15
Romaniok, Ron	85T	579	$ .01	$ .06
Romanick, Ron	86T	733	$ .01	$ .05
Romanick, Ron	87T	136	$ .01	$ .04
Romano, John	59T	138	$1.00	$4.00
Romano, Johnny	60T	323	$ .75	$3.00
Romano, Johnny	61T	5	$ .60	$2.40
Romano, Johnny	62T	330	$ .75	$3.00
Romano, Johnny	63T	72	$ .50	$2.00
Romano, Johnny	63T	392	$1.00	$4.00
Romano, Johnny	64T	515	$1.00	$4.00
Romano, Johnny	65T	17	$ .35	$1.40
Romano, Johnny	66T	199	$ .50	$2.00
Romano, Johnny	66T	413	$ .65	$2.60
Romano, Johnny	67T	196	$ .40	$1.60
Romero, Eddie	79T	708	$ .25	$1.00
Romero, Ed	81T	659	$ .01	$ .08
Romero, Ed	82T	408	$ .01	$ .08
Romero, Ed	83T	271	$ .01	$ .08
Romero, Ed	84T	146	$ .01	$ .06
Romero, Ed	85T	498	$ .01	$ .06
Romero, Ed	86T	317	$ .01	$ .05
Romero, Ed	86TTR	95	$ .01	$ .06
Romero, Ed	87T	675	$ .01	$ .04

Player	Year	No.	VG	EX/MT
Romero, Ed	88T	37	$ .01	$ .04
Romero, Ed	89TTR	105	$ .01	$ .05
Romero, Ramon	86T	208	$ .01	$ .05
Romine, Kevin	87T	121	$ .01	$ .04
Romine, Kevin	90TTR	105	$ .01	$ .05
Romine, Kevin	91T	652	$ .01	$ .03
Romo, Enrique	78T	278	$ .04	$ .16
Romo, Enrique	79T	548	$ .03	$ .12
Romo, Enrique	80T	332	$ .01	$ .10
Romo, Enrique	81T	28	$ .01	$ .08
Romo, Enrique	82T	106	$ .01	$ .08
Romo, Enrique	83T	226	$ .01	$ .08
Romo, Vicente	69T	267	$ .50	$2.00
Romo, Vicente	70T	191	$ .20	$ .80
Romo, Vicente	71T	723	$1.50	$6.00
Romo, Vicente	72T	499	$ .25	$1.00
Romo, Vicente	73T	381	$ .10	$ .40
Romo, Vicente	74T	197	$ .10	$ .40
Romo, Vicente	75T	274	$ .10	$ .40
Romo, Vicente	83T	633	$ .01	$ .08
Romonosky, John	59T	267	$1.00	$4.00
Romonosky, John	60T	87	$ .85	$3.40
Roof, Gene	82T	561	$ .01	$ .08
Roof, Phil	63T	324	$1.25	$5.00
Roof, Phil	64T	541	$55.00	$220.00
Roof, Phil	65T	537	$1.50	$6.00
Roof, Phil	66T	382	$ .65	$2.60
Roof, Phil	67T	129	$ .40	$1.60
Roof, Phil	68T	484	$ .75	$3.00
Roof, Phil	69T	334	$ .30	$1.20
Roof, Phil	70T	359	$ .35	$1.40
Roof, Phil	71T	22	$ .25	$1.00
Roof, Phil	72T	201	$ .10	$ .40
Roof, Phil	73T	598	$ .60	$2.40
Roof, Phil	74T	388	$ .10	$ .40
Roof, Phil	75T	576	$ .10	$ .40
Roof, Phil	76T	424	$ .05	$ .25
Roof, Phil	77T	392	$ .05	$ .20
Rooker, Jim	69T	376	$ .50	$2.00

TOPPS

Player	Year	No.	VG	EX/MT
Rooker, Jim	70T	222	$ .20	$ .80
Rooker, Jim	71T	730	$1.10	$4.40
Rooker, Jim	72T	742	$1.25	$5.00
Rooker, Jim	74T	402	$ .10	$ .40
Rooker, Jim	75T	148	$ .10	$ .40
Rooker, Jim	77T	82	$ .05	$ .20
Rooker, Jim	78T	308	$ .04	$ .16
Rooker, Jim	79T	584	$ .03	$ .12
Rooker, Jim	80T	694	$ .01	$ .10
Roomes, Rolando	90T	364	$ .01	$ .03
Root, Charlie	60T	457	$1.25	$5.00
Roque, Jorge	72T	316	$ .10	$ .40
Roque, Jorge	73T	606	$1.00	$4.00
Rosario, Jimmy	72T	366	$ .10	$ .40
Rose, Bobby	92T	652	$ .01	$ .03
Rose, Bobby	92TSC	79	$ .01	$ .10
Rose, Don	73T	178	$ .10	$ .40
Rose, Pete	63T	537	$212.50	$850.00
Rose, Pete	64T	125	$40.00	$160.00
Rose, Pete	65T	207	$40.00	$160.00
Rose, Pete	66T	30	$10.00	$40.00
Rose, Pete	67T	430	$16.25	$65.00
Rose, Pete	68T	230	$10.00	$40.00
Rose, Pete	69T	2	$1.25	$5.00
Rose, Pete	69T	120	$8.75	$35.00
Rose, Pete	69TAS	424	$3.00	$12.00
Rose, Pete	70T	61	$1.25	$5.00
Rose, Pete	70T	580	$16.25	$65.00
Rose, Pete	70TAS	458	$3.00	$12.00
Rose, Pete	71T	100	$10.00	$40.00
Rose, Pete	72T	559	$12.00	$48.00
Rose, Pete	72TIA	560	$6.00	$24.00
Rose, Pete	73T	130	$4.00	$16.00
Rose, Pete	74T	201	$1.00	$4.00
Rose, Pete	79TRB	204	$ .50	$2.00
Rose, Pete	80T	540	$1.00	$4.00
Rose, Pete	80THL	4	$ .15	$1.50
Rose, Pete	81T	180	$ .90	$3.60
Rose, Pete	81TRB	205	$ .10	$1.00
Rose, Pete	82T	636	$ .10	$ .50
Rose, Pete	82T	780	$ .20	$2.00
Rose, Pete	82TAS	337	$ .10	$ .75
Rose, Pete	82THL	4	$ .10	$1.00
Rose, Pete	82TSA	781	$ .10	$1.00
Rose, Pete	83T	100	$ .20	$2.00
Rose, Pete	83T	101	$ .10	$1.00
Rose, Pete	83TAS	397	$ .10	$ .75
Rose, Pete	84T	300	$ .10	$1.00
Rose, Pete	84T	701	$ .05	$ .20
Rose, Pete	84T	702	$ .05	$ .20
Rose, Pete	84TTR	103	$2.00	$8.00
Rose, Pete	85T	547	$ .10	$ .50
Rose, Pete	85T	600	$ .10	$ .50
Rose, Pete	85TRB	6	$ .05	$ .35
Rose, Pete	86T	1	$ .10	$1.00
Rose, Pete (1963-1966)	86T	2	$ .05	$ .30
Rose, Pete (1967-1970)	86T	3	$ .05	$ .30
Rose, Pete (1971-1974)	86T	4	$ .05	$ .30
Rose, Pete (1975-1978)	86T	5	$ .05	$ .30
Rose, Pete (1979-1982)	86T	6	$ .05	$ .30
Rose, Pete (1983-1986)	86T	7	$ .05	$ .30
Rose, Pete	86T	741	$ .05	$ .35
Rose, Pete	86TRB	206	$ .05	$ .25
Rose, Pete	87T	200	$ .05	$ .35
Rose, Pete	87T	393	$ .05	$ .25
Rose, Pete	88T	475	$ .05	$ .25
Rose, Pete	89T	505	$ .01	$ .10
Roseboro, John	58T	42	$3.50	$14.00
Roseboro, John	59T	441	$1.00	$4.00
Roseboro, John	60T	88	$ .85	$3.40
Roseboro, John	60T	292	$ .75	$3.00
Roseboro, John	61T	363	$ .60	$2.40
Roseboro, John	62T	32	$ .60	$2.40
Roseboro, John	62TAS	397	$1.25	$5.00
Roseboro, John	63T	487	$3.00	$12.00
Roseboro, John	64T	88	$ .50	$2.00
Roseboro, John	65T	405	$1.00	$4.00
Roseboro, John	66T	189	$ .50	$2.00
Roseboro, John	67T	365	$ .60	$2.40
Roseboro, John	68T	65	$ .35	$1.40
Roseboro, John	69T	218	$ .35	$1.40
Roseboro, John	70T	655	$1.25	$5.00
Roseboro, John	73T	421	$ .25	$1.00
Roseboro, John	74T	276	$ .10	$ .40
Roselli, Bob	56T	131	$2.50	$10.00
Roselli, Bob	61T	529	$7.50	$30.00
Roselli, Bob	62T	363	$ .75	$3.00
Rosello, Dave	74T	607	$ .10	$ .40
Rosello, Dave	76T	546	$ .05	$ .25
Rosello, Dave	77T	92	$ .05	$ .20
Rosello, Dave	78T	423	$ .04	$ .16
Rosello, Dave	80T	122	$ .01	$ .10
Rosello, Dave	82T	724	$ .01	$ .08
Rosen, Al	51Trb	35	$3.00	$12.00
Rosen, Al	52T	10	$20.00	$80.00
Rosen, Al	53T	135	$8.00	$32.00
Rosen, Al	54T	15	$6.00	$24.00
Rosen, Al	55T	70	$3.50	$14.00
Rosen, Al	56T	35	$2.75	$11.00
Rosen, Al	61TMVP	474	$1.35	$5.40
Rosen, Al	75T	191	$ .35	$1.40
Rosen, Al	91TA53	135	$ .10	$ .50
Rosenberg, Steve	89T	616	$ .01	$ .03
Rosenberg, Steve	90T	379	$ .01	$ .03
Rosenbohm, Jim	93T	667	$ .01	$ .15
Rosenthal, Wayne	92T	584	$ .01	$ .10
Rosenthal, Wayne	92TSC	658	$ .01	$ .10
Ross, Bob	52T	298	$13.75	$55.00
Ross, Bob	54T	189	$3.75	$15.00

Rose, Pete	74T	300	$3.00	$12.00
Rose, Pete	74TAS	336	$ .75	$3.00
Rose, Pete	75T	211	$1.25	$5.00
Rose, Pete	75T	320	$3.75	$15.00
Rose, Pete	76T	240	$3.00	$12.00
Rose, Pete	77T	450	$2.00	$8.00
Rose, Pete	78T	20	$1.00	$4.00
Rose, Pete	78TRB	5	$ .75	$3.00
Rose, Pete	79T	650	$1.10	$4.40

TOPPS

Player	Year	No.	VG	EX/MT
Ross, Gary	69T	404	$ .30	$1.20
Ross, Gary	70T	694	$1.25	$5.00
Ross, Gary	71T	153	$ .25	$1.00
Ross, Gary	73T	112	$ .10	$ .40
Ross, Gary	77T	544	$ .05	$ .20
Ross, Gary	78T	291	$ .04	$ .16
Rossi, Joe	52T	379	$43.75	$175.00
Rossi, Joe	53T	74	$6.25	$25.00
Rossi, Joe	91TA53	74	$ .01	$ .15
Rossiter, Mike	92T	474	$ .05	$ .20
Rossy, Rico	92TSC	629	$ .01	$ .10
Rossy, Rico	93TSC	106	$ .01	$ .10

Player	Year	No.	VG	EX/MT
Rowdon, Wade	87T	569	$ .01	$ .04
Rowe, Don	63T	562	$5.00	$20.00
Rowe, Ken	63T	562	$5.00	$20.00
Rowe, Ken	65T	518	$1.25	$5.00
Rowe, Ralph	73T	49	$ .20	$ .80
Rowe, Ralph	74T	447	$ .10	$ .40
Rowe, Schoolboy	54T	197	$3.75	$15.00
Rowland, Mike	81T	502	$ .01	$ .08
Rowland, Rich	92T	472	$ .01	$ .10
Rowland, Rich	92TSC	508	$ .05	$ .20
Royals, Team	70T	422	$ .50	$2.00
Royals, Team	71T	742	$2.50	$10.00
Royals, Team	72T	617	$1.25	$5.00
Royals, Team	73T	347	$ .30	$1.20
Royals, Team	74T	343	$ .25	$1.00
Royals, Team Checklist	75T	72	$ .35	$1.40
Royals, Team Checklist	76T	236	$ .30	$1.20
Royals, Team Checklist	77T	371	$ .25	$1.00
Royals, Team Checklist	78T	724	$ .20	$ .80
Royals, Team Checklist	79T	451	$ .15	$ .60
Royals, Team Checklist	80T	66	$ .10	$ .50
Royals, Team Checklist	81T	667	$ .05	$ .25
Royals, Team Leaders	86T	606	$ .01	$ .05
Royals, Team Leaders	87T	256	$ .01	$ .10
Royals, Team Leaders	88T	141	$ .01	$ .10
Royals, Team Leaders	89T	789	$ .01	$ .10
Royer, Stan	92TSC	286	$ .05	$ .20
Royer, Stan	93T	820	$ .01	$ .03
Royster, Jerry	76T	592	$2.00	$8.00
Royster, Jerry	77T	549	$ .05	$ .20
Royster, Jerry	78T	187	$ .04	$ .16
Royster, Jerry	79T	344	$ .03	$ .12
Royster, Jerry	80T	463	$ .01	$ .10
Royster, Jerry	81T	268	$ .01	$ .08
Royster, Jerry	82T	608	$ .01	$ .08
Royster, Jerry	83T	26	$ .01	$ .08
Royster, Jerry	84T	572	$ .01	$ .06
Royster, Jerry	85T	776	$ .01	$ .06
Royster, Jerry	85TTR	96	$ .01	$ .10
Royster, Jerry	86T	118	$ .01	$ .05
Royster, Jerry	87T	403	$ .01	$ .04
Royster, Jerry	87TTR	106	$ .01	$ .05
Royster, Jerry	88T	257	$ .01	$ .04
Rozek, Dick	52T	363	$43.75	$175.00
Rozema, Dave	78T	124	$ .04	$ .16
Rozema, Dave	79T	33	$ .03	$ .12
Rozema, Dave	80T	288	$ .01	$ .10
Rozema, Dave	81T	614	$ .01	$ .08
Rozema, Dave	82T	319	$ .01	$ .08
Rozema, Dave	83T	562	$ .01	$ .08
Rozema, Dave	84T	457	$ .01	$ .06
Rozema, Dave	85T	47	$ .01	$ .06
Rozema, Dave	85TTR	97	$ .01	$ .10
Rozema, Dave	86T	739	$ .01	$ .05
Roznovsky, Vic	65T	334	$ .50	$2.00
Roznovsky, Vic	66T	467	$1.50	$6.00
Roznovsky, Vic	67T	163	$ .40	$1.60
Roznovsky, Vic	68T	428	$ .35	$1.40
Roznovsky, Vic	69T	368	$ .30	$1.20
Rucker, Dave	82T	261	$ .01	$ .08
Rucker, Dave	83T	304	$ .01	$ .08
Rucker, Dave	84T	699	$ .01	$ .06
Rucker, Dave	85T	421	$ .01	$ .06
Rucker, Dave	85TTR	98	$ .01	$ .10
Rucker, Dave	86T	39	$ .01	$ .05
Rudi, Joe	69T	587	$1.25	$5.00
Rudi, Joe	70T	102	$ .20	$ .80
Rudi, Joe	71T	407	$ .50	$2.00
Rudi, Joe	72T	209	$ .20	$ .80
Rudi, Joe	73T	360	$ .20	$ .80
Rudi, Joe	74T	264	$ .10	$ .40
Rudi, Joe	75T	45	$ .10	$ .40
Rudi, Joe	76T	475	$ .10	$ .40
Rudi, Joe	77T	155	$ .05	$ .20
Rudi, Joe	78T	635	$ .04	$ .16
Rudi, Joe	79T	267	$ .03	$ .12
Rudi, Joe	80T	556	$ .01	$ .10
Rudi, Joe	81T	701	$ .01	$ .08
Rudi, Joe	81TTR	826	$ .01	$ .15
Rudi, Joe	82T	388	$ .01	$ .08
Rudi, Joe	82TTR	102	$ .01	$ .10
Rudi, Joe	83T	87	$ .01	$ .08
Rudolph, Don	58T	347	$1.25	$5.00
Rudolph, Don	59T	179	$1.00	$4.00
Rudolph, Don	62T	224	$ .75	$3.00
Rudolph, Don	63T	291	$ .90	$3.60
Rudolph, Don	64T	427	$1.00	$4.00
Rudolph, Ken	70T	46	$ .20	$ .80
Rudolph, Ken	71T	472	$ .50	$2.00
Rudolph, Ken	72T	271	$ .10	$ .40
Rudolph, Ken	73T	414	$ .25	$1.00
Rudolph, Ken	74T	584	$ .10	$ .40
Rudolph, Ken	75T	289	$ .10	$ .40
Rudolph, Ken	76T	601	$ .05	$ .25
Ruffcorn, Scott	92T	36	$ .05	$ .20
Ruffin, Bruce	87T	499	$ .01	$ .04
Ruffin, Bruce	88T	268	$ .01	$ .04
Ruffin, Bruce	89T	518	$ .01	$ .03
Ruffin, Bruce	90T	22	$ .01	$ .03
Ruffin, Bruce	91T	637	$ .01	$ .03
Ruffin, Bruce	91TSC	89	$ .05	$ .25
Ruffin, Bruce	92T	307	$ .01	$ .03
Ruffin, Bruce	92TSC	867	$ .01	$ .10
Ruffin, Bruce	92TTR	95	$ .01	$ .05
Ruffin, Bruce	93TSC	270	$ .01	$ .10
Ruhle, Vern	75T	614	$ .10	$ .40

TOPPS

Player	Year	No.	VG	EX/MT
Ruhle, Vern	76T	89	$ .05	$ .25
Ruhle, Vern	77T	311	$ .05	$ .20
Ruhle, Vern	78T	456	$ .04	$ .16
Ruhle, Vern	79T	49	$ .03	$ .12
Ruhle, Vern	80T	234	$ .01	$ .10
Ruhle, Vern	81T	642	$ .01	$ .08
Ruhle, Vern	82T	539	$ .01	$ .08
Ruhle, Vern	83T	172	$ .01	$ .08
Ruhle, Vern	84T	328	$ .01	$ .06
Ruhle, Vern	85T	426	$ .01	$ .06
Ruhle, Vern	85TTR	99	$ .01	$ .10
Ruhle, Vern	86T	768	$ .01	$ .05
Ruhle, Vern	87T	221	$ .01	$ .04
Ruiz, Chico	63T	407	$1.00	$4.00
Ruiz, Chico	64T	356	$ .65	$2.60
Ruiz, Chico	65T	554	$2.50	$10.00
Ruiz, Chico	66T	159	$ .50	$2.00
Ruiz, Chico	67T	339	$ .60	$2.40
Ruiz, Chico	68T	213	$ .35	$1.40
Ruiz, Chico	69T	469	$ .30	$1.20
Ruiz, Chico	70T	606	$ .50	$2.00
Ruiz, Chico	71T	686	$1.50	$6.00
Runge, Paul	85TTR	100	$ .01	$ .10
Runge, Paul	86T	409	$ .01	$ .05
Runge, Paul	89T	38	$ .01	$ .03
Runnells, Tom	91TTR	103	$ .01	$ .05
Runnells, Tom	92T	51	$ .01	$ .03
Runnels, James "Pete"	52T	2	$15.00	$60.00
Runnels, Pete	53T	219	$6.00	$24.00
Runnels, Pete	54T	6	$3.75	$15.00
Runnels, Pete	56T	234	$3.75	$15.00
Runnels, Pete	57T	64	$2.00	$8.00
Runnels, Pete	58T	265	$1.25	$5.00
Runnels, Pete	59T	370	$1.00	$4.00
Runnels, Pete	59T	519	$4.00	$16.00
Runnels, Pete	60T	15	$ .85	$3.40
Runnels, Pete	61T	42	$ .75	$3.00
Runnels, Pete	61T	210	$ .60	$2.40
Runnels, Pete	62T	3	$ .60	$2.40
Runnels, Pete	63T	2	$5.00	$20.00
Runnels, Pete	63T	230	$ .90	$3.60
Runnels, Pete	64T	121	$ .50	$2.00
Runnels, Pete	91TA53	219	$ .01	$ .15
Rush, Bob	52T	153	$7.00	$28.00
Rush, Bob	56T	214	$3.75	$15.00
Rush, Bob	57T	137	$2.00	$8.00
Rush, Bob	58T	313	$1.25	$5.00
Rush, Bob	59T	396	$1.00	$4.00
Rush, Bob	60T	404	$ .75	$3.00
Ruskin, Scott	90TTR	106	$ .01	$ .10
Ruskin, Scott	91T	589	$ .01	$ .03
Ruskin, Scott	92T	692	$ .01	$ .03
Ruskin, Scott	92TSC	777	$ .01	$ .10
Ruskin, Scott	92TTR	96	$ .01	$ .05
Ruskin, Scott	93T	328	$ .01	$ .03
Ruskin, Scott	93TSC	199	$ .01	$ .10
Russell, Bill	70T	304	$ .75	$3.00
Russell, Bill	71T	226	$ .40	$1.60
Russell, Bill	72T	736	$1.75	$7.00
Russell, Bill	73T	108	$ .20	$ .80
Russell, Bill	74T	239	$ .10	$ .40
Russell, Bill	75T	23	$ .10	$ .40
Russell, Bill	76T	22	$ .05	$ .25
Russell, Bill	77T	322	$ .05	$ .20
Russell, Bill	78T	128	$ .04	$ .16
Russell, Bill	79T	546	$ .03	$ .12
Russell, Bill	80T	75	$ .01	$ .10
Russell, Bill	81T	465	$ .01	$ .08
Russell, Bill	82T	279	$ .01	$ .08
Russell, Bill	83T	661	$ .01	$ .08
Russell, Bill	84T	792	$ .01	$ .06
Russell, Bill	85T	343	$ .01	$ .06
Russell, Bill	86T	506	$ .01	$ .05
Russell, Bill	87T	116	$ .01	$ .04
Russell, Jeff	84T	270	$ .05	$ .25
Russell, Jeff	85T	651	$ .01	$ .10
Russell, Jeff	87T	444	$ .01	$ .04
Russell, Jeff	88T	114	$ .01	$ .04
Russell, Jeff	89T	565	$ .01	$ .03
Russell, Jeff	90T	80	$ .01	$ .03
Russell, Jeff	90TAS	395	$ .01	$ .03
Russell, Jeff	91T	344	$ .01	$ .03
Russell, Jeff	91TSC	421	$ .05	$ .25
Russell, Jeff	92T	257	$ .01	$ .03
Russell, Jeff	92TSC	28	$ .01	$ .10
Russell, Jeff	93T	736	$ .01	$ .03
Russell, Jim	52T	51	$13.75	$55.00
Russell, John	86T	392	$ .01	$ .05
Russell, John	87T	379	$ .01	$ .04
Russell, John	88T	188	$ .01	$ .04
Russell, John	90TTR	107	$ .01	$ .05
Russell, John	91T	734	$ .01	$ .03
Russell, John	91TSC	474	$ .05	$ .25
Russell, John	92TSC	846	$ .01	$ .10
Russo, Paul	92T	473	$ .05	$ .25
Ruth, Babe	61T	401	$7.00	$28.00
Ruth, Babe Special 1	62T	135	$3.75	$15.00
Ruth, Babe Special 2	62T	136	$3.75	$15.00
Ruth, Babe Special 3	62T	137	$3.75	$15.00
Ruth, Babe Special 4	62T	138	$3.75	$15.00
Ruth, Babe Special 5	62T	139	$6.00	$24.00
Ruth, Babe Special 6	62T	140	$6.00	$24.00
Ruth, Babe Special 7	62T	141	$3.75	$15.00
Ruth, Babe Special 8	62T	142	$3.75	$15.00
Ruth, Babe Special 9	62T	143	$3.75	$15.00
Ruth, Babe Special 10	62T	144	$3.75	$15.00
Ruth, Babe	73T	1	$6.75	$27.00
Ruth, Babe	73TATL	474	$2.25	$9.00
Ruth, Babe	76TAT	345	$2.50	$10.00
Rutherford, John	52T	320	$50.00	$200.00
Rutherford, John	53T	137	$4.00	$16.00

Player	Year	No.	VG	EX/MT
Rutherford, John	91TA53	137	$ .01	$ .15
Ruthven, Dick	74T	47	$ .10	$ .40
Ruthven, Dick	75T	267	$ .10	$ .40
Ruthven, Dick	76T	431	$ .05	$ .25
Ruthven, Dick	77T	575	$ .05	$ .20
Ruthven, Dick	78T	75	$ .04	$ .16
Ruthven, Dick	79T	419	$ .03	$ .12

TOPPS

Player	Year	No.	VG	EX/MT	Player	Year	No.	VG	EX/MT
Ruthven, Dick	80T	136	$.01	$.10	Ryan, Nolan	78T	400	$7.00	$28.00
Ruthven, Dick	81T	691	$.01	$.08	Ryan, Nolan	78TRB	6	$2.25	$9.00
Ruthven, Dick	82T	317	$.01	$.08	Ryan, Nolan	79T	6	$1.00	$4.00
Ruthven, Dick	83T	484	$.01	$.08	Ryan, Nolan	79T	115	$7.00	$28.00
Ruthven, Dick	83TTR	98	$.01	$.10	Ryan, Nolan	79TRH	417	$.50	$2.00
Ruthven, Dick	84T	736	$.01	$.06	Ryan, Nolan	80T	206	$.75	$3.00
Ruthven, Dick	85T	563	$.01	$.06	Ryan, Nolan	80T	580	$5.00	$20.00
Ruthven, Dick	86T	98	$.01	$.05	Ryan, Nolan	81T	240	$2.75	$11.00
Ryal, Mark	88T	243	$.01	$.04	Ryan, Nolan	82T	66	$.10	$1.00
Ryan, Connie	52T	107	$7.00	$28.00	Ryan, Nolan	82T	90	$2.50	$10.00
Ryan, Connie	53T	102	$4.00	$16.00	Ryan, Nolan	82T	167	$.15	$1.50
Ryan, Connie	54T	136	$3.75	$15.00	Ryan, Nolan	82THL	5	$.75	$3.00
Ryan, Connie	74T	634	$.25	$1.00	Ryan, Nolan	83T	360	$2.25	$9.00
Ryan, Connie	91TA53	102	$.01	$.15	Ryan, Nolan	83T	361	$1.10	$4.40
Ryan, Ken	93T	786	$.05	$.20	Ryan, Nolan	84T	4	$.10	$1.00
Ryan, Mike	65T	573	$6.00	$24.00	Ryan, Nolan	84T	66	$.10	$.50
Ryan, Mike	66T	419	$.65	$2.60	Ryan, Nolan	84T	470	$1.50	$6.00
Ryan, Mike	67T	223	$.50	$2.00	Ryan, Nolan	84T	707	$.10	$1.00
Ryan, Mike	68T	306	$.35	$1.40	Ryan, Nolan	85T	760	$1.00	$4.00
Ryan, Mike	69T	28	$.35	$1.40	Ryan, Nolan	85TRB	7	$.10	$1.00
Ryan, Mike	70T	591	$.50	$2.00	Ryan, Nolan	86T	100	$.25	$2.50
Ryan, Mike	71T	533	$1.00	$4.00	Ryan, Nolan	87T	757	$.10	$1.00
Ryan, Mike	72T	324	$.10	$.40	Ryan, Nolan	88T	250	$.10	$.75
Ryan, Mike	73T	467	$.25	$1.00	Ryan, Nolan	88TRB	6	$.10	$.40
Ryan, Mike	74T	564	$.10	$.40	Ryan, Nolan	88TTB	661	$.05	$.35
Ryan, Nolan	68T	177	$375.00	$1500.00	Ryan, Nolan	89T	530	$.10	$.50
Ryan, Nolan	69T	533	$130.00	$520.00	Ryan, Nolan	89TTR	106	$.15	$1.25
Ryan, Nolan	70T	712	$130.00	$520.00	Ryan, Nolan	90T	1	$.10	$.50
Ryan, Nolan	71T	513	$60.00	$240.00	Ryan, Nolan (Mets)	90T	2	$.05	$.20
Ryan, Nolan	72T	595	$62.50	$250.00	Ryan, Nolan (Angels)	90T	3	$.05	$.20
Ryan, Nolan	73T	67	$3.00	$12.00	Ryan, Nolan (Astros)	90T	4	$.05	$.20
Ryan, Nolan	73T	220	$20.00	$80.00	Ryan, Nolan (Rangers)	90T	5	$.05	$.20
					Ryan, Nolan	91T	1	$.10	$.50
					Ryan, Nolan	91TRB	6	$.05	$.25
					Ryan, Nolan	91TSC	200	$3.25	$13.00
					Ryan, Nolan	92T	1	$.10	$.40
					Ryan, Nolan	92TRB	4	$.05	$.25
					Ryan, Nolan	92TSC	605	$.20	$2.00
					Ryan, Nolan	92TSC	770	$.75	$3.00
					Ryan, Nolan	93T	700	$.10	$.40
					Ryba, Mike	54T	237	$3.75	$15.00
					Saberhagen, Bret	84TTR	104	$3.00	$12.00
					Saberhagen, Bret	85T	23	$.20	$2.00
					Saberhagen, Bret	86T	487	$.10	$.40
					Saberhagen, Bret	86TAS	720	$.01	$.15
					Saberhagen, Bret	87T	140	$.05	$.20
					Saberhagen, Bret	88T	540	$.01	$.10
					Saberhagen, Bret	89T	750	$.01	$.10
					Saberhagen, Bret	90T	350	$.01	$.10
					Saberhagen, Bret	90TAS	393	$.01	$.03
					Saberhagen, Bret	91T	280	$.01	$.10
					Saberhagen, Bret	91TSC	38	$.05	$.35
					Saberhagen, Bret	92T	75	$.01	$.03
					Saberhagen, Bret	92TSC	755	$.01	$.10
					Saberhagen, Bret	92TTR	97	$.01	$.05
					Saberhagen, Bret	93T	600	$.01	$.10
					Sabo, Chris	88TTR	90	$.10	$.75
					Sabo, Chris	89T	490	$.05	$.25
					Sabo, Chris	90T	737	$.01	$.15
					Sabo, Chris	91T	45	$.01	$.10
					Sabo, Chris	91TSC	165	$.05	$.35
					Sabo, Chris	92T	485	$.01	$.03
					Sabo, Chris	92TSC	273	$.05	$.20
					Sabo, Chris	93T	245	$.01	$.03
					Sabo, Chris	93TSC	286	$.01	$.15
					Sackinsky, Brian	93T	647	$.05	$.20
					Sadecki, Ray	60T	327	$1.25	$5.00
					Sadecki, Ray	61T	32	$.60	$2.40
					Sadecki, Ray	62T	383	$1.25	$5.00
					Sadecki, Ray	63T	486	$3.00	$12.00
					Sadecki, Ray	64T	147	$.50	$2.00
					Sadecki, Ray	65T	10	$.75	$3.00
					Sadecki, Ray	65T	230	$.50	$2.00
					Sadecki, Ray	66T	26	$.35	$1.40
					Sadecki, Ray	67T	409	$.60	$2.40

Player	Year	No.	VG	EX/MT
Ryan, Nolan	**74T**	**20**	**$17.50**	**$70.00**
Ryan, Nolan	74T	207	$3.50	$14.00
Ryan, Nolan	75T	312	$3.00	$12.00
Ryan, Nolan	75T	500	$17.50	$70.00
Ryan, Nolan	75THL	5	$5.00	$20.00
Ryan, Nolan	75THL	7	$1.50	$6.00
Ryan, Nolan	76T	330	$15.00	$60.00
Ryan, Nolan	77T	6	$2.50	$10.00
Ryan, Nolan	77T	650	$10.00	$40.00
Ryan, Nolan	77TRB	234	$3.50	$14.00
Ryan, Nolan	78T	206	$.50	$2.00

TOPPS

Player	Year	No.	VG	EX/MT
Sadecki, Ray	68T	494	$ .75	$3.00
Sadecki, Ray	69T	125	$ .35	$1.40
Sadecki, Ray	70T	679	$1.25	$5.00
Sadecki, Ray	71T	406	$ .50	$2.00
Sadecki, Ray	72T	563	$ .40	$1.60
Sadecki, Ray	72TIA	564	$ .40	$1.60
Sadecki, Ray	73T	283	$ .10	$ .40
Sadecki, Ray	74T	216	$ .10	$ .40
Sadecki, Ray	75T	349	$ .10	$ .40
Sadecki, Ray	77T	26	$ .05	$ .20
Sadek, Mike	74T	577	$ .10	$ .40
Sadek, Mike	76T	234	$ .05	$ .25
Sadek, Mike	77T	129	$ .05	$ .20
Sadek, Mike	78T	8	$ .04	$ .16
Sadek, Mike	79T	256	$ .03	$ .12
Sadek, Mike	80T	462	$ .01	$ .10
Sadek, Mike	81T	384	$ .01	$ .08
Sadowski, Bob	62T	595	$5.25	$21.00
Sadowski, Bob	63T	568	$2.25	$9.00
Sadowski, Bob	64T	271	$ .65	$2.60
Sadowski, Bob	65T	156	$ .35	$1.40
Sadowski, Bob	66T	523	$3.75	$15.00
Sadowski, Ed	59T	139	$1.00	$4.00
Sadowski, Ed	60T	403	$ .75	$3.00
Sadowski, Ed	61T	163	$ .60	$2.40
Sadowski, Ed	62T	569	$6.00	$24.00
Sadowski, Ed	63T	527	$2.25	$9.00
Sadowski, Ed	64T	61	$ .50	$2.00
Sadowski, Ted	61T	254	$ .60	$2.40
Saferight, Harry	80T	683	$ .01	$ .10
Sain, John	91TA53	119	$ .10	$ .50
Sain, Johnny	51Tbb	9	$11.25	$45.00
Sain, Johnny	52T	49	$25.00	$100.00
Sain, Johnny	53T	119	$10.00	$40.00
Sain, Johnny	54T	205	$7.00	$28.00
Sain, Johnny	55T	193	$10.00	$40.00
Sain, Johnny	73T	356	$ .20	$ .80
Sain, Johnny	74T	221	$ .10	$ .40
Sakata, Lenn	80T	668	$ .01	$ .10
Sakata, Lenn	81T	287	$ .01	$ .08
Sakata, Lenn	82T	136	$ .01	$ .08
Sakata, Lenn	83T	319	$ .01	$ .08
Sakata, Lenn	84T	578	$ .01	$ .06
Sakata, Lenn	85T	81	$ .01	$ .06
Sakata, Lenn	86T	446	$ .01	$ .05
Sakata, Lenn	88T	716	$ .01	$ .04
Salas, Mark	85TTR	101	$ .01	$ .10
Salas, Mark	86T	537	$ .01	$ .05
Salas, Mark	87T	87	$ .01	$ .04
Salas, Mark	87TTR	107	$ .01	$ .05
Salas, Mark	88TTR	99	$ .01	$ .05
Salas, Mark	89T	384	$ .01	$ .03
Salas, Mark	91T	498	$ .01	$ .03
Salas, Mark	91TSC	456	$ .05	$ .25
Salazar, Argenis	85T	154	$ .01	$ .06
Salazar, Argenis	86TTR	96	$ .01	$ .06
Salazar, Argenis	87T	533	$ .01	$ .04
Salazar, Argenis	88T	29	$ .01	$ .04
Salazar, Argenis	89T	642	$ .01	$ .03
Salazar, Luis	81T	309	$ .05	$ .20
Salazar, Luis	82T	366	$ .01	$ .08
Salazar, Luis	82T	662	$ .01	$ .08
Salazar, Luis	83T	533	$ .01	$ .08
Salazar, Luis	84T	68	$ .01	$ .06
Salazar, Luis	85T	789	$ .01	$ .06
Salazar, Luis	85TTR	102	$ .01	$ .10
Salazar, Luis	86T	103	$ .01	$ .05
Salazar, Luis	87T	454	$ .01	$ .04
Salazar, Luis	87TTR	108	$ .01	$ .05
Salazar, Luis	88T	276	$ .01	$ .04
Salazar, Luis	88TTR	100	$ .01	$ .05
Salazar, Luis	89T	553	$ .01	$ .03
Salazar, Luis	89TTR	107	$ .01	$ .05
Salazar, Luis	90T	378	$ .01	$ .03
Salazar, Luis	91T	614	$ .01	$ .03
Salazar, Luis	91TSC	94	$ .05	$ .25
Salazar, Luis	92T	67	$ .01	$ .03
Salazar, Luis	92TSC	21	$ .01	$ .10
Salazar, Luis	93T	21	$ .01	$ .03
Salkeld, Roger	90T	44	$ .05	$ .20
Salkeld, Roger	92T	676	$ .05	$ .35
Salmon, Chico	64T	499	$1.00	$4.00
Salmon, Chico	65T	105	$ .35	$1.40
Salmon, Chico	66T	594	$3.75	$15.00
Salmon, Chico	67T	43	$ .40	$1.60
Salmon, Chico	68T	318	$ .35	$1.40
Salmon, Chico	69T	62	$ .35	$1.40
Salmon, Chico	70T	301	$ .35	$1.40
Salmon, Chico	71T	249	$ .25	$1.00
Salmon, Chico	72T	646	$ .40	$1.60
Salmon, Tim	93T	20	$ .10	$ .75

Player	Year	No.	VG	EX/MT
Salmon, Tim	**93TSC**	**249**	**$ .75**	**$3.00**
Sambito, Joe	77T	227	$ .05	$ .20
Sambito, Joe	78T	498	$ .04	$ .16
Sambito, Joe	79T	158	$ .03	$ .12
Sambito, Joe	80T	571	$ .01	$ .10
Sambito, Joe	81T	385	$ .01	$ .08
Sambito, Joe	82T	34	$ .01	$ .08
Sambito, Joe	83T	662	$ .01	$ .08
Sambito, Joe	85T	264	$ .01	$ .06
Sambito, Joe	85TTR	103	$ .01	$ .10
Sambito, Joe	86TTR	97	$ .01	$ .06
Sambito, Joe	87T	451	$ .01	$ .04
Sambito, Joe	88T	784	$ .01	$ .04
Samford, Ron	59T	242	$1.00	$4.00
Samford, Ron	60T	409	$ .75	$3.00
Sampen, Bill	90TTR	108	$ .01	$ .15
Sampen, Bill	91T	649	$ .01	$ .03
Sampen, Bill	91TSC	249	$ .05	$ .25
Sampen, Bill	92T	566	$ .01	$ .03
Sampen, Bill	92TSC	277	$ .01	$ .10
Sample, Billy	79T	713	$ .15	$ .60
Sample, Billy	80T	458	$ .01	$ .10
Sample, Billy	81T	283	$ .01	$ .08
Sample, Billy	82T	112	$ .01	$ .08
Sample, Billy	83T	641	$ .01	$ .08
Sample, Billy	84T	12	$ .01	$ .06
Sample, Billy	85T	337	$ .01	$ .06

TOPPS

Player	Year	No.	VG	EX/MT
Sample, Billy	86T	533	$ .01	$ .05
Sample, Billy	86TTR	98	$ .01	$ .06
Sample, Billy	87T	104	$ .01	$ .04
Samuel, Amado	62T	597	$9.00	$36.00
Samuel, Amado	64T	129	$ .50	$2.00
Samuel, Juan	84TTR	105	$ .10	$1.00
Samuel, Juan	85T	265	$ .01	$ .10
Samuel, Juan	85TRB	8	$ .01	$ .10
Samuel, Juan	86T	475	$ .01	$ .15
Samuel, Juan	87T	255	$ .01	$ .10
Samuel, Juan	88T	705	$ .01	$ .04
Samuel, Juan	88TAS	398	$ .01	$ .04
Samuel, Juan	89T	575	$ .01	$ .03
Samuel, Juan	89TTR	108	$ .01	$ .10
Samuel, Juan	90T	85	$ .01	$ .03
Samuel, Juan	90TTR	109	$ .01	$ .05
Samuel, Juan	91T	645	$ .01	$ .03
Samuel, Juan	91TSC	495	$ .05	$ .25
Samuel, Juan	92T	315	$ .01	$ .03
Samuel, Juan	92TSC	11	$ .01	$ .10
Sanchez, Alejandro	86T	563	$ .01	$ .05
Sanchez, Alex	89TTR	109	$ .01	$ .10
Sanchez, Alex	90T	563	$ .01	$ .03
Sanchez, Celerino	73T	103	$ .10	$ .40
Sanchez, Celerino	74T	623	$ .10	$ .40
Sanchez, Israel	89T	452	$ .01	$ .03
Sanchez, Luis	82T	653	$ .10	$1.00

Player	Year	No.	VG	EX/MT
Sanchez, Luis	**83T**	**623**	**$ .01**	**$ .08**
Sanchez, Luis	84T	258	$ .01	$ .06
Sanchez, Luis	85T	42	$ .01	$ .06
Sanchez, Luis	86T	124	$ .01	$ .05
Sanchez, Orlando	82T	604	$ .01	$ .08
Sanchez, Raul	57T	393	$1.75	$7.00
Sanchez, Raul	60T	311	$ .75	$3.00
Sanchez, Rey	92TSC	308	$ .05	$ .25
Sanchez, Rey	92TTR	98	$ .05	$ .20
Sanchez, Rey	93T	292	$ .01	$ .03
Sanchez, Rey	93TSC	36	$ .01	$ .10
Sandberg, Ryne	83T	83	$13.75	$55.00
Sandberg, Ryne	84T	596	$2.00	$8.00
Sandberg, Ryne	85T	460	$1.00	$4.00
Sandberg, Ryne	85TAS	713	$ .10	$1.00
Sandberg, Ryne	86T	690	$ .20	$2.00

Player	Year	No.	VG	EX/MT
Sandberg, Ryne	87T	680	$ .10	$ .75
Sandberg, Ryne	88T	10	$ .10	$ .50
Sandberg, Ryne	89T	360	$ .05	$ .35
Sandberg, Ryne	89TAS	387	$ .01	$ .15
Sandberg, Ryne	90T	210	$ .05	$ .35
Sandberg, Ryne	90TAS	398	$ .01	$ .15
Sandberg, Ryne	91T	740	$ .05	$ .20
Sandberg, Ryne	91TAS	398	$ .01	$ .10
Sandberg, Ryne	91TRB	7	$ .01	$ .10
Sandberg, Ryne	91TSC	230	$ .90	$3.60
Sandberg, Ryne	92T	110	$ .05	$ .25
Sandberg, Ryne	92TAS	387	$ .01	$ .10
Sandberg, Ryne	92TSC	50	$ .10	$1.00
Sandberg, Ryne	92TSC	600	$ .10	$ .50
Sandberg, Ryne	93T	3	$ .05	$ .20
Sandberg, Ryne	93T	402	$ .01	$ .10
Sanders, Deion	89TTR	110	$ .20	$1.75
Sanders, Deion	90T	61	$ .10	$ .40
Sanders, Deion	91TSC	442	$ .20	$2.00
Sanders, Deion	92T	645	$ .01	$ .15
Sanders, Deion	92TSC	15	$ .10	$ .50
Sanders, Deion	93T	795	$ .01	$ .10
Sanders, Ken	66T	356	$ .50	$2.00
Sanders, Ken	71T	116	$ .25	$1.00
Sanders, Ken	72T	391	$ .10	$ .40
Sanders, Ken	73T	246	$ .10	$ .40
Sanders, Ken	74T	638	$ .10	$ .40
Sanders, Ken	75T	366	$ .10	$ .40
Sanders, Ken	76T	291	$ .05	$ .25
Sanders, Ken	77T	171	$ .05	$ .20
Sanders, Reggie	74T	600	$1.25	$5.00
Sanders, Reggie	75T	617	$ .50	$2.00
Sanders, Reggie	92T	283	$ .05	$ .20
Sanders, Reggie	92TSC	865	$ .10	$ .75
Sanders, Reggie	93T	83	$ .01	$ .15
Sanders, Tracy	93T	616	$ .05	$ .25
Sanderson, Scott	79T	720	$ .25	$1.00
Sanderson, Scott	80T	578	$ .10	$ .50
Sanderson, Scott	81T	235	$ .01	$ .08
Sanderson, Scott	82T	7	$ .01	$ .08
Sanderson, Scott	83T	717	$ .01	$ .08
Sanderson, Scott	84T	164	$ .01	$ .06
Sanderson, Scott	84TTR	106	$ .01	$ .15
Sanderson, Scott	85T	616	$ .01	$ .06
Sanderson, Scott	86T	406	$ .01	$ .05
Sanderson, Scott	87T	534	$ .01	$ .04
Sanderson, Scott	88T	311	$ .01	$ .04
Sanderson, Scott	89T	212	$ .01	$ .03
Sanderson, Scott	90T	67	$ .01	$ .03
Sanderson, Scott	90TTR	110	$ .01	$ .05
Sanderson, Scott	91T	728	$ .01	$ .03
Sanderson, Scott	91TTR	104	$ .01	$ .05
Sanderson, Scott	92T	480	$ .01	$ .03
Sanderson, Scott	92TSC	496	$ .01	$ .10
Sanderson, Scott	93T	525	$ .01	$ .03
Sandlock, Mike	53T	247	$11.25	$45.00
Sandlock, Mike	54T	104	$3.75	$15.00
Sandlock, Mike	91TA53	247	$ .01	$ .15
Sands, Charlie	72T	538	$ .40	$1.60
Sands, Charlie	74T	381	$ .10	$ .40
Sands, Charlie	75T	548	$ .10	$ .40
Sandt, Tommy	77T	616	$ .05	$ .20
Sanford, Jack	57T	387	$2.00	$8.00
Sanford, Jack	58T	264	$1.25	$5.00
Sanford, Jack	59T	275	$1.00	$4.00
Sanford, Jack	60T	165	$ .75	$3.00
Sanford, Jack	61T	258	$ .60	$2.40
Sanford, Jack	61T	383	$1.00	$4.00
Sanford, Jack	62T	538	$3.50	$14.00
Sanford, Jack	63T	7	$1.25	$5.00
Sanford, Jack	63T	325	$ .90	$3.60
Sanford, Jack	64T	414	$1.00	$4.00
Sanford, Jack	65T	228	$ .50	$2.00
Sanford, Jack	66T	23	$ .35	$1.40
Sanford, Jack	67T	549	$4.00	$16.00

TOPPS

Player	Year	No.	VG	EX/MT
Sanford, Mo	92T	674	$ .01	$ .15
Sanford, Mo	92TSC	336	$ .01	$ .15
Sanford, Mo	93T	634	$ .01	$ .03
Sanguillen, Manny	68T	251	$1.00	$4.00
Sanguillen, Manny	69T	509	$ .30	$1.20
Sanguillen, Manny	70T	188	$ .20	$ .80
Sanguillen, Manny	71T	62	$ .50	$2.00
Sanguillen, Manny	71T	480	$ .50	$2.00
Sanguillen, Manny	72T	60	$ .20	$ .80
Sanguillen, Manny	73T	250	$ .10	$ .40
Sanguillen, Manny	74T	28	$ .10	$ .40
Sanguillen, Manny	75T	515	$ .10	$ .40
Sanguillen, Manny	76T	191	$ .25	$1.00
Sanguillen, Manny	76T	220	$ .05	$ .25
Sanguillen, Manny	77T	61	$ .05	$ .20
Sanguillen, Manny	78T	658	$ .04	$ .16
Sanguillen, Manny	79T	447	$ .03	$ .12
Sanguillen, Manny	80T	148	$ .01	$ .10
Sanguillen, Manny	81T	226	$ .01	$ .08
Santana, Andres	92TSC	491	$ .01	$ .10
Santana, Rafael	85T	67	$ .01	$ .06
Santana, Rafael	86T	587	$ .01	$ .05
Santana, Rafael	87T	378	$ .01	$ .04
Santana, Rafael	88T	233	$ .01	$ .04
Santana, Rafael	88TTR	101	$ .01	$ .05
Santana, Rafael	89T	792	$ .01	$ .03
Santana, Rafael	90T	651	$ .01	$ .03
Santiago, Benny	87TTR	109	$ .05	$ .35
Santiago, Benny	88T	693	$ .01	$ .10
Santiago, Benny	88TAS	404	$ .01	$ .04
Santiago, Benito "Benny"	88TRB	7	$ .01	$ .06
Santiago, Benny	89T	256	$ .01	$ .03
Santiago, Benny	90T	35	$ .01	$ .03
Santiago, Benny	91T	760	$ .01	$ .03
Santiago, Benny	91TSC	105	$ .05	$ .25
Santiago, Benny	92T	185	$ .01	$ .03
Santiago, Benny	92TSC	130	$ .01	$ .10
Santiago, Benny	93T	220	$ .01	$ .03
Santiago, Benny	93TSC	274	$ .01	$ .10
Santiago, Jose	56T	59	$2.00	$8.00
Santiago, Jose	65T	557	$1.40	$5.60
Santiago, Jose	66T	203	$ .50	$2.00
Santiago, Jose	67T	473	$1.50	$6.00
Santiago, Jose	68T	123	$ .35	$1.40
Santiago, Jose	69T	21	$ .35	$1.40
Santiago, Jose	70T	708	$1.25	$5.00
Santo, Ron	61T	35	$12.50	$50.00
Santo, Ron	62T	170	$3.00	$12.00
Santo, Ron	63T	252	$1.75	$7.00
Santo, Ron	64T	375	$1.50	$6.00
Santo, Ron	65T	6	$1.25	$5.00
Santo, Ron	65T	110	$ .75	$3.00
Santo, Ron	66T	290	$1.00	$4.00
Santo, Ron	67T	70	$ .75	$3.00
Santo, Ron	68T	5	$1.50	$6.00
Santo, Ron	68T	235	$ .75	$3.00
Santo, Ron	68TAS	366	$ .75	$3.00
Santo, Ron	69T	4	$1.00	$4.00
Santo, Ron	69T	570	$1.25	$5.00
Santo, Ron	69TAS	420	$ .50	$2.00
Santo, Ron	70T	63	$ .75	$3.00
Santo, Ron	70T	670	$1.75	$7.00
Santo, Ron	70TAS	454	$ .50	$2.00
Santo, Ron	71T	220	$ .50	$2.00
Santo, Ron	72T	555	$1.00	$4.00
Santo, Ron	72TIA	556	$ .50	$2.00
Santo, Ron	73T	115	$ .25	$1.00
Santo, Ron	74T	270	$ .25	$1.00
Santo, Ron	74TAS	334	$ .35	$1.40
Santo, Ron	74TTR	270	$ .20	$ .80
Santo, Ron	75T	35	$ .15	$ .60
Santorini, Al	69T	592	$ .40	$1.60
Santorini, Al	70T	212	$ .20	$ .80
Santorini, Al	71T	467	$ .50	$2.00
Santorini, Al	72T	723	$1.25	$5.00

Player	Year	No.	VG	EX/MT
Santorini, Al	73T	24	$ .10	$ .40
Santovenia, Nelson	88TTR	102	$ .01	$ .10
Santovenia, Nelson	89T	228	$ .01	$ .03
Santovenia, Nelson	90T	614	$ .01	$ .03
Santovenia, Nelson	91T	744	$ .01	$ .03
Santovenia, Nelson	91TSC	416	$ .05	$ .25
Santovenia, Nelson	92T	732	$ .01	$ .03
Sarmiento, Manny	77T	475	$ .05	$ .20
Sarmiento, Manny	78T	377	$ .04	$ .16
Sarmiento, Manny	79T	149	$ .03	$ .12
Sarmiento, Manny	80T	21	$ .01	$ .10
Sarmiento, Manny	81T	649	$ .01	$ .08

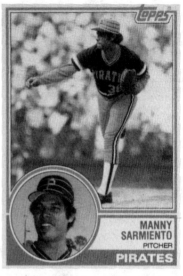

Player	Year	No.	VG	EX/MT
Sarmiento, Manny	83T	566	$ .01	$ .08
Sarmiento, Manny	84T	209	$ .01	$ .06
Sarni, Bill	54T	194	$3.75	$15.00
Sarni, Bill	56T	247	$3.75	$15.00
Sarni, Bill	57T	86	$2.00	$8.00
Sasser, Mackey	88TTR	103	$ .01	$ .15
Sasser, Mackey	89T	457	$ .01	$ .03
Sasser, Mackey	90T	656	$ .01	$ .03
Sasser, Mackey	91T	382	$ .01	$ .03
Sasser, Mackey	91TSC	172	$ .05	$ .25
Sasser, Mackey	92T	533	$ .01	$ .03
Sasser, Mackey	92TSC	249	$ .01	$ .10
Sasser, Mackey	93T	788	$ .01	$ .03
Satriano, Tom	63T	548	$2.25	$9.00
Satriano, Tom	64T	521	$1.00	$4.00
Satriano, Tom	65T	124	$ .35	$1.40
Satriano, Tom	66T	361	$ .50	$2.00
Satriano, Tom	67T	343	$ .60	$2.40
Satriano, Tom	68T	238	$ .35	$1.40
Satriano, Tom	69T	78	$ .35	$1.40
Satriano, Tom	70T	581	$ .50	$2.00
Satriano, Tom	71T	557	$1.00	$4.00
Saucier, Kevin	80T	682	$ .01	$ .10
Saucier, Kevin	81T	53	$ .01	$ .08
Saucier, Kevin	81TTR	827	$ .01	$ .15
Saucier, Kevin	82T	238	$ .01	$ .08
Saucier, Kevin	83T	373	$ .01	$ .08
Sauer, Henry "Hank"	51Tbb	49	$9.00	$36.00
Sauer, Hank	52T	35	$16.25	$65.00
Sauer, Hank	53T	111	$4.50	$18.00
Sauer, Hank	54T	4	$3.75	$15.00

TOPPS

Player	Year	No.	VG	EX/MT
Sauer, Hank	55T	45	$2.25	$9.00
Sauer, Hank	56T	41	$2.00	$8.00
Sauer, Hank	57T	197	$2.00	$8.00
Sauer, Hank	58T	378	$1.00	$4.00
Sauer, Hank	59T	404	$1.00	$4.00
Sauer, Hank	61TMVP	481	$1.35	$5.40
Sauer, Hank	75T	190	$ .15	$ .60
Sauer, Hank	91TA53	111	$ .05	$ .35
Saunders, Dennis	71T	423	$ .50	$2.00
Savage, Jack	90TTR	111	$ .01	$ .05
Savage, Jack	91T	357	$ .01	$ .03
Savage, Ted	62T	104	$ .60	$2.40
Savage, Ted	63T	508	$1.75	$7.00
Savage, Ted	64T	62	$ .50	$2.00
Savage, Ted	67T	552	$4.00	$16.00
Savage, Ted	68T	119	$ .35	$1.40
Savage, Ted	69T	471	$ .30	$1.20
Savage, Ted	70T	602	$ .50	$2.00
Savage, Ted	71T	76	$ .25	$1.00
Saverine, Bob	63T	158	$ .90	$3.60
Saverine, Bob	64T	221	$ .65	$2.60
Saverine, Bob	65T	427	$1.00	$4.00
Saverine, Bob	66T	312	$ .50	$2.00
Saverine, Bob	67T	27	$ .40	$1.60
Saverine, Bob	68T	149	$ .35	$1.40
Sawatski, Carl	53T	202	$4.50	$18.00
Sawatski, Carl	54T	198	$3.75	$15.00
Sawatski, Carl	55T	122	$2.25	$9.00
Sawatski, Carl	58T	234	$1.25	$5.00
Sawatski, Carl	59T	56	$1.50	$6.00
Sawatski, Carl	60T	545	$2.75	$11.00
Sawatski, Carl	61T	198	$ .60	$2.40
Sawatski, Carl	62T	106	$ .60	$2.40
Sawatski, Carl	63T	267	$ .90	$3.60
Sawatski, Carl	64T	24	$ .50	$2.00
Sawatski, Carl	91TA53	202	$ .01	$ .15
Sawyer, Eddie	60T	226	$ .75	$3.00
Sawyer, Rick	77T	268	$ .05	$ .20
Sax, Dave	86T	307	$ .01	$ .05
Sax, Steve	82T	681	$1.25	$5.00
Sax, Steve	82TTR	103	$1.75	$7.00
Sax, Steve	83T	245	$ .10	$ .75
Sax, Steve	84T	610	$ .05	$ .35
Sax, Steve	85T	470	$ .05	$ .25
Sax, Steve	86T	175	$ .01	$ .15
Sax, Steve	87T	769	$ .01	$ .10
Sax, Steve	87TAS	596	$ .01	$ .04
Sax, Steve	88T	305	$ .01	$ .10
Sax, Steve	89T	40	$ .01	$ .03
Sax, Steve	89TTR	111	$ .01	$ .10
Sax, Steve	90T	560	$ .01	$ .03
Sax, Steve	91T	290	$ .01	$ .03
Sax, Steve	91TSC	204	$ .05	$ .25
Sax, Steve	92T	430	$ .01	$ .03
Sax, Steve	92TSC	635	$ .01	$ .10
Sax, Steve	92TTR	99	$ .01	$ .05
Sax, Steve	93T	367	$ .01	$ .03
Scalzitti, Will	93T	476	$ .05	$ .20
Scanlan, Bob	91TTR	105	$ .01	$ .10
Scanlan, Bob	92T	274	$ .01	$ .03
Scanlan, Bob	92TSC	112	$ .01	$ .10
Scanlan, Bob	93T	47	$ .01	$ .03
Scanlon, Pat	78T	611	$ .04	$ .16
Scarbery, Randy	80T	291	$ .01	$ .10
Scarborough, Ray	51Trb	42	$1.65	$6.60
Scarborough, Ray	52T	43	$13.75	$55.00
Scarborough, Ray	53T	213	$4.50	$18.00
Scarborough, Ray	91TA53	213	$ .01	$ .15
Scarce, Mac	73T	6	$ .10	$ .40
Scarce, Mac	74T	149	$ .10	$ .40
Scarce, Mac	75T	527	$ .10	$ .40
Schaal, Paul	65T	517	$1.25	$5.00
Schaal, Paul	66T	376	$ .65	$2.60
Schaal, Paul	67T	58	$ .40	$1.60
Schaal, Paul	68T	474	$ .75	$3.00
Schaal, Paul	69T	352	$ .30	$1.20
Schaal, Paul	70T	338	$ .35	$1.40
Schaal, Paul	71T	487	$ .50	$2.00
Schaal, Paul	72T	177	$ .10	$ .40
Schaal, Paul	72TIA	178	$ .10	$ .40
Schaal, Paul	73T	416	$ .25	$1.00
Schaal, Paul	74T	514	$ .10	$ .40
Schaefer, Jeff	91T	681	$ .01	$ .03
Schaefer, Jeff	92TSC	108	$ .01	$ .10
Schaffer, Jim	62T	579	$6.00	$24.00
Schaffer, Jimmie	63T	81	$ .50	$2.00
Schaffer, Jim	64T	359	$ .65	$2.60
Schaffer, Jimmie	65T	313	$ .50	$2.00
Schaffer, Jimmie	68T	463	$ .75	$3.00
Schaffernoth, Joe	61T	58	$ .60	$2.40
Schaffernoth, Joe	63T	463	$3.00	$12.00
Schaive, John	61T	259	$ .60	$2.40
Schaive, John	62T	529	$6.00	$24.00
Schaive, John	63T	356	$ .90	$3.60
Schatzeder, Dan	78T	709	$ .04	$ .16

Player	Year	No.	VG	EX/MT
Schatzeder, Dan	79T	124	$ .03	$ .12
Schatzeder, Dan	80T	267	$ .01	$ .10
Schatzeder, Dan	81T	417	$ .01	$ .08
Schatzeder, Dan	82T	691	$ .01	$ .08
Schatzeder, Dan	82TTR	104	$ .01	$ .10
Schatzeder, Dan	83T	189	$ .01	$ .08
Schatzeder, Dan	84T	57	$ .01	$ .06
Schatzeder, Dan	85T	501	$ .01	$ .06
Schatzeder, Dan	86T	324	$ .01	$ .05
Schatzeder, Dan	87T	789	$ .01	$ .04
Schatzeder, Dan	88T	218	$ .01	$ .04
Scheffing, Bob	54T	76	$3.75	$15.00
Scheffing, Bob	60T	464	$1.25	$5.00
Scheffing, Bob	61T	223	$ .60	$2.40
Scheffing, Bob	62T	72	$ .60	$2.40
Scheffing, Bob	62T	416	$1.25	$5.00
Scheffing, Bob	63T	134	$ .50	$2.00
Scheib, Carl	52T	116	$7.00	$28.00
Scheib, Carl	53T	57	$6.25	$25.00
Scheib, Carl	54T	118	$3.75	$15.00
Scheib, Carl	91TA53	57	$ .01	$ .15
Scheid, Rich	93T	646	$ .01	$ .15
Scheinblum, Richie	65T	577	$2.50	$10.00

TOPPS

Player	Year	No.	VG	EX/MT
Scheinblum, Richie	68T	16	$1.00	$4.00
Scheinblum, Richie	69T	479	$ .30	$1.20
Scheinblum, Richie	70T	161	$ .20	$ .80
Scheinblum, Richie	71T	326	$ .25	$1.00
Scheinblum, Richie	72T	468	$ .25	$1.00
Scheinblum, Richie	73T	78	$ .10	$ .40
Scheinblum, Richie	74T	323	$ .10	$ .40
Schell, Danny	55T	79	$2.25	$9.00
Scherger, George	73T	296	$ .20	$ .80
Scherger, George	74T	326	$ .25	$1.00
Scherman, Fred	71T	316	$ .25	$1.00
Scherman, Fred	72T	6	$ .10	$ .40
Scherman, Fred	73T	660	$1.00	$4.00
Scherman, Fred	74T	186	$ .10	$ .40
Scherman, Fred	74TTR	186	$ .10	$ .40
Scherman, Fred	75T	252	$ .10	$ .40
Scherman, Fred	76T	188	$ .05	$ .25
Scherrer, Bill	84T	373	$ .01	$ .06
Scherrer, Bill	85T	586	$ .01	$ .06
Scherrer, Bill	86T	217	$ .01	$ .05
Scherrer, Bill	87T	98	$ .01	$ .04
Schilling, Chuck	61T	499	$1.35	$5.40
Schilling, Chuck	62T	345	$ .75	$3.00
Schilling, Chuck	62TAS	467	$1.50	$6.00
Schilling, Chuck	63T	52	$ .50	$2.00
Schilling, Chuck	64T	182	$3.50	$14.00
Schilling, Chuck	64T	481	$1.00	$4.00
Schilling, Chuck	65T	272	$ .50	$2.00
Schilling, Chuck	66T	6	$ .35	$1.40
Schilling, Curt	90T	97	$ .01	$ .15
Schilling, Curt	91T	569	$ .01	$ .03
Schilling, Curt	92T	316	$ .01	$ .03
Schilling, Curt	92TSC	279	$ .01	$ .10
Schilling, Curt	92TTR	100	$ .01	$ .05
Schilling, Curt	93T	421	$ .01	$ .03
Schiraldi, Calvin	86T	210	$ .01	$ .05
Schiraldi, Calvin	87T	94	$ .01	$ .04
Schiraldi, Calvin	88T	599	$ .01	$ .04
Schiraldi, Calvin	88TTR	104	$ .01	$ .05
Schiraldi, Calvin	89T	337	$ .01	$ .03
Schiraldi, Calvin	90T	693	$ .01	$ .03
Schiraldi, Calvin	91T	424	$ .01	$ .03
Schlesinger, Bill	65T	573	$6.00	$24.00
Schlesinger, Bill	68T	258	$ .35	$1.40
Schmidt, Bob	58T	468	$1.00	$4.00
Schmidt, Bob	59T	109	$1.50	$6.00
Schmidt, Bob	60T	501	$1.25	$5.00
Schmidt, Bob	61T	31	$ .60	$2.40
Schmidt, Bob	62T	262	$ .75	$3.00
Schmidt, Bob	63T	94	$ .50	$2.00
Schmidt, Bob	65T	582	$2.50	$10.00
Schmidt, Dave	82T	381	$ .10	$ .50
Schmidt, Dave	82T	418	$ .01	$ .15
Schmidt, Dave	83T	116	$ .01	$ .08
Schmidt, Dave	84T	584	$ .01	$ .06
Schmidt, Dave	85T	313	$ .01	$ .06
Schmidt, Dave	86T	79	$ .01	$ .05
Schmidt, Dave	86TTR	99	$ .01	$ .06
Schmidt, Dave	87T	703	$ .01	$ .04
Schmidt, Dave	87TTR	110	$ .01	$ .05
Schmidt, Dave	88T	214	$ .01	$ .04
Schmidt, Dave	89T	677	$ .01	$ .03
Schmidt, Dave	90T	497	$ .01	$ .03
Schmidt, Dave	90TTR	112	$ .01	$ .05
Schmidt, Dave	91T	136	$ .01	$ .03
Schmidt, Mike	73T	615	$120.00	$480.00
Schmidt, Mike	74T	283	$20.00	$80.00
Schmidt, Mike	75T	70	$15.00	$60.00
Schmidt, Mike	75T	307	$ .50	$2.00
Schmidt, Mike	76T	193	$ .50	$2.00
Schmidt, Mike	76T	480	$7.50	$30.00
Schmidt, Mike	77T	2	$ .25	$1.00
Schmidt, Mike	77T	140	$6.00	$24.00
Schmidt, Mike	78T	360	$4.00	$16.00
Schmidt, Mike	79T	610	$2.25	$9.00
Schmidt, Mike	80T	270	$1.00	$4.00
Schmidt, Mike	81T	2	$ .10	$ .50
Schmidt, Mike	81T	3	$ .10	$ .50
Schmidt, Mike	81T	540	$ .25	$2.50
Schmidt, Mike	81TRB	206	$ .10	$1.00
Schmidt, Mike	82T	100	$ .75	$3.00
Schmidt, Mike	82T	162	$ .10	$ .50
Schmidt, Mike	82T	163	$ .10	$ .50

Player	Year	No.	VG	EX/MT
Schmidt, Mike	82TAS	339	$ .10	$1.00
Schmidt, Mike	82TSA	101	$ .15	$1.50
Schmidt, Mike	83T	300	$ .75	$3.00
Schmidt, Mike	83T	301	$ .15	$1.50
Schmidt, Mike	83TAS	399	$ .10	$1.00
Schmidt, Mike	84T	132	$ .05	$ .25
Schmidt, Mike	84T	700	$ .20	$2.00
Schmidt, Mike	84T	703	$ .05	$ .20
Schmidt, Mike	84TAS	388	$ .10	$ .50
Schmidt, Mike	85T	500	$ .15	$1.50
Schmidt, Mike	85TAS	714	$ .10	$ .50
Schmidt, Mike	86T	200	$ .10	$1.00
Schmidt, Mike	87T	430	$ .10	$ .50
Schmidt, Mike	87TAS	597	$ .05	$ .20
Schmidt, Mike	88T	600	$ .05	$ .35
Schmidt, Mike	89T	100	$ .05	$ .25
Schmidt, Mike	90TTB	662	$ .01	$ .10
Schmidt, Tom	93T	433	$ .10	$ .40
Schmidt, Willard	53T	168	$4.50	$18.00
Schmidt, Willard	56T	323	$2.50	$10.00
Schmidt, Willard	57T	206	$2.00	$8.00
Schmidt, Willard	58T	214	$1.25	$5.00
Schmidt, Willard	59T	171	$1.00	$4.00
Schmidt, Willard	91TA53	168	$ .01	$ .15
Schmitz, Johnny	51Tbb	41	$7.50	$30.00
Schmitz, Johnny	52T	136	$7.00	$28.00
Schmitz, Johnny	54T	33	$3.75	$15.00
Schmitz, Johnny	55T	159	$4.00	$16.00
Schmitz, Johnny	56T	298	$2.50	$10.00
Schneider, Dan	63T	299	$ .90	$3.60
Schneider, Dan	64T	351	$ .65	$2.60
Schneider, Dan	65T	366	$ .50	$2.00
Schneider, Dan	67T	543	$4.00	$16.00
Schneider, Dan	68T	57	$ .35	$1.40
Schneider, Dan	69T	656	$ .40	$1.60

TOPPS

Player	Year	No.	VG	EX/MT
Schneider, Jeff	82T	21	$18.25	$75.00
Schoendienst, Al	51Tbb	6	$30.00	$120.00
Schoendienst, Al	52T	91	$21.25	$85.00
Schoendienst, Al	53T	78	$15.00	$60.00
Schoendienst, Al "Red"	56T	165	$7.50	$30.00
Schoendienst, Red	57T	154	$6.00	$24.00
Schoendienst, Red	58T	190	$5.00	$20.00
Schoendienst, Red	59T	480	$4.00	$16.00
Schoendienst, Red	60T	335	$3.00	$12.00
Schoendienst, Red	61T	505	$4.00	$16.00
Schoendienst, Red	62T	575	$12.50	$50.00
Schoendienst, Red	65T	556	$4.50	$18.00
Schoendienst, Red	66T	76	$1.00	$4.00
Schoendienst, Red	67T	512	$3.00	$12.00
Schoendienst, Red	68T	294	$ .75	$3.00
Schoendienst, Red	69T	462	$ .50	$2.00

Player	Year	No.	VG	EX/MT
Schoendienst, Red	70T	346	$ .75	$3.00
Schoendienst, Red	71T	239	$ .50	$2.00
Schoendienst, Red	72T	67	$ .25	$1.00
Schoendienst, Red	73T	497	$ .50	$2.00
Schoendienst, Red	74T	236	$ .10	$ .40
Schoendienst, Red	90TTR	113	$ .01	$ .05
Schoendienst, Al	91TA53	78	$ .10	$ .75
Schofield, Dick	54T	191	$4.50	$18.00
Schofield, Dick	55T	143	$2.25	$9.00
Schofield, Dick	58T	106	$2.00	$8.00
Schofield, Dick	59T	68	$1.50	$6.00
Schofield, Dick	60T	104	$ .85	$3.40
Schofield, Dick	61T	453	$1.35	$5.40
Schofield, Dick	62T	484	$1.50	$6.00
Schofield, Dick	63T	34	$ .50	$2.00
Schofield, Dick	64T	284	$ .65	$2.60
Schofield, Dick	65T	218	$ .50	$2.00
Schofield, Dick	66T	156	$ .50	$2.00
Schofield, Dick	66T	474	$1.50	$6.00
Schofield, Dick	67T	381	$ .60	$2.40
Schofield, Dick	68T	588	$ .70	$2.80
Schofield, Dick	69T	18	$ .35	$1.40
Schofield, Dick	70T	251	$ .20	$ .80
Schofield, Dick	71T	396	$ .50	$2.00
Schofield, Dick	85T	138	$ .01	$ .10
Schofield Jr., Dick	84TTR	107	$ .05	$ .30
Schofield Jr., Dick	85T	138	$ .01	$ .10
Schofield Jr., Dick	85T	629	$ .01	$ .06
Schofield Jr., Dick	86T	311	$ .01	$ .05
Schofield Jr., Dick	87T	502	$ .01	$ .04
Schofield Jr., Dick	88T	43	$ .01	$ .04
Schofield Jr., Dick	89T	477	$ .01	$ .03
Schofield Jr., Dick	90T	189	$ .01	$ .03
Schofield Jr., Dick	91T	736	$ .01	$ .03
Schofield, Dick	91TSC	59	$ .05	$ .25
Schofield, Dick	92T	230	$ .01	$ .03
Schofield, Dick	92TSC	16	$ .01	$ .10
Schofield, Dick	92TSC	738	$ .01	$ .10
Schofield, Dick	92TTR	101	$ .01	$ .05
Schofield, Dick	93T	79	$ .01	$ .03
Schooler, Mike	88TTR	105	$ .05	$ .20
Schooler, Mike	89T	199	$ .01	$ .10
Schooler, Mike	90T	681	$ .01	$ .03
Schooler, Mike	91T	365	$ .01	$ .03
Schooler, Mike	91TSC	508	$ .05	$ .25
Schooler, Mike	92T	28	$ .01	$ .03
Schooler, Mike	92TSC	313	$ .01	$ .10
Schooler, Mike	93T	258	$ .01	$ .03
Schooler, Mike	93TSC	198	$ .01	$ .10
Schoonmaker, Jerry	56T	216	$3.75	$15.00
Schoonmaker, Jerry	57T	334	$5.00	$20.00
Schourek, Pete	91TTR	106	$ .01	$ .10
Schourek, Pete	92T	287	$ .01	$ .10
Schourek, Pete	92TSC	521	$ .01	$ .10
Schourek, Pete	93T	352	$ .01	$ .03
Schourek, Pete	93TSC	238	$ .01	$ .10
Schreiber, Paul	54T	217	$3.75	$15.00
Schroder, Bob	65T	589	$1.40	$5.60
Schroeder, Bill	84T	738	$ .01	$ .06
Schroeder, Bill	85T	176	$ .01	$ .06
Schroeder, Bill	86T	662	$ .01	$ .05
Schroeder, Bill	87T	302	$ .01	$ .04
Schroeder, Bill	88T	12	$ .01	$ .04
Schroeder, Bill	89T	563	$ .01	$ .03
Schroeder, Bill	90T	244	$ .01	$ .03
Schroeder, Bill	91T	452	$ .01	$ .03
Schroll, Al	59T	546	$4.00	$16.00
Schroll, Al	60T	357	$ .75	$3.00
Schroll, Al	62T	102	$ .60	$2.40
Schrom, Ken	81T	577	$ .01	$ .08
Schrom, Ken	84T	11	$ .01	$ .06
Schrom, Ken	84T	322	$ .01	$ .06
Schrom, Ken	85T	161	$ .01	$ .06
Schrom, Ken	86T	71	$ .01	$ .05
Schrom, Ken	86TTR	100	$ .01	$ .06
Schrom, Ken	87T	635	$ .01	$ .04
Schrom, Ken	88T	256	$ .01	$ .04
Schu, Rick	85TTR	104	$ .01	$ .10
Schu, Rick	86T	16	$ .01	$ .05
Schu, Rick	87T	209	$ .01	$ .04
Schu, Rick	88T	731	$ .01	$ .04
Schu, Rick	89T	352	$ .01	$ .03
Schu, Rick	89TTR	112	$ .01	$ .05
Schu, Rick	90T	498	$ .01	$ .03
Schueler, Ron	73T	169	$ .10	$ .40
Schueler, Ron	74T	544	$ .10	$ .40
Schueler, Ron	74TTR	544	$ .10	$ .40
Schueler, Ron	75T	292	$ .10	$ .40
Schueler, Ron	76T	586	$ .05	$ .25
Schueler, Ron	77T	337	$ .05	$ .20
Schueler, Ron	78T	409	$ .04	$ .16
Schueler, Ron	79T	686	$ .03	$ .12
Schult, Art	53T	167	$4.50	$18.00
Schult, Art	58T	58	$2.00	$8.00
Schult, Art	60T	93	$ .85	$3.40
Schult, Art	91TA53	167	$ .01	$ .15
Schultz, Barney	62T	89	$ .60	$2.40
Schultz, Barney	63T	452	$3.00	$12.00
Schultz, Barney	65T	28	$ .35	$1.40
Schultz, Barney	73T	497	$ .50	$2.00
Schultz, Barney	74T	236	$ .10	$ .40
Schultz, Bob	52T	401	$43.75	$175.00

TOPPS

Player	Year	No.	VG	EX/MT
Schultz, Bob	53T	144	$4.00	$16.00
Schultz, Bob	91TA53	144	$ .01	$ .15
Schultz, Buddy	78T	301	$ .04	$ .16
Schultz, Buddy	79T	532	$ .03	$ .12
Schultz, Buddy	80T	601	$ .01	$ .10
Schultz, Joe	69T	254	$ .50	$2.00
Schultz, Joseph	73T	323	$ .25	$1.00
Schulze, Don	85T	93	$ .01	$ .06
Schulze, Don	86T	542	$ .01	$ .05
Schulze, Don	87T	297	$ .01	$ .04
Schulze, Don	88T	131	$ .01	$ .04
Schurr, Wayne	64T	548	$2.25	$9.00
Schurr, Wayne	65T	149	$ .35	$1.40
Schwall, Don	62T	35	$ .60	$2.40
Schwall, Don	63T	344	$ .90	$3.60
Schwall, Don	64T	558	$2.25	$9.00
Schwall, Don	65T	362	$ .50	$2.00
Schwall, Don	66T	144	$ .50	$2.00
Schwall, Don	67T	267	$ .50	$2.00
Schwartz, Randy	67T	33	$1.00	$4.00
Scioscia, Mike	81T	302	$1.00	$4.00

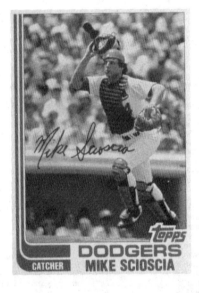

Player	Year	No.	VG	EX/MT
Scioscia, Mike	82T	642	$ .05	$ .25
Scioscia, Mike	83T	352	$ .01	$ .08
Scioscia, Mike	84T	64	$ .01	$ .06
Scioscia, Mike	85T	549	$ .01	$ .06
Scioscia, Mike	86T	468	$ .01	$ .05
Scioscia, Mike	87T	144	$ .01	$ .04
Scioscia, Mike	88T	225	$ .01	$ .04
Scioscia, Mike	89T	755	$ .01	$ .03
Scioscia, Mike	90T	605	$ .01	$ .03
Scioscia, Mike	91T	305	$ .01	$ .03
Scioscia, Mike	91TAS	404	$ .01	$ .03
Scioscia, Mike	91TSC	19	$ .05	$ .25
Scioscia, Mike	92T	13	$ .01	$ .03
Scioscia, Mike	92TSC	140	$ .01	$ .10
Scioscia, Mike	93T	202	$ .01	$ .03
Scioscia, Mike	93TSC	46	$ .01	$ .10
Sconiers, Daryl	82T	653	$ .10	$1.00
Sconiers, Daryl	83TTR	99	$ .01	$ .10
Sconiers, Daryl	84T	27	$ .01	$ .06
Sconiers, Daryl	85T	604	$ .01	$ .06
Sconiers, Daryl	86T	193	$ .01	$ .05
Score, Herb	56T	140	$7.50	$30.00
Score, Herb	57T	50	$4.00	$16.00
Score, Herb	58T	352	$2.00	$8.00
Score, Herb	58TAS	495	$3.50	$14.00
Score, Herb	59T	88	$2.00	$8.00
Score, Herb	60T	360	$1.25	$5.00
Score, Herb	61T	185	$1.00	$4.00
Score, Herb	61T	337	$1.00	$4.00
Score, Herb	62T	116	$ .75	$3.00
Scott, Donnie	85T	496	$ .01	$ .06
Scott, Donnie	85TTR	105	$ .01	$ .10
Scott, Donnie	86T	568	$ .01	$ .05
Scott, Gary	91TSC	596	$ .10	$ .50
Scott, Gary	91TTR	107	$ .01	$ .15
Scott, Gary	92TSC	708	$ .01	$ .10
Scott, Gary	92TTR	102	$ .01	$ .05
Scott, Gary	93T	656	$ .01	$ .03
Scott, George	66T	558	$6.00	$24.00
Scott, George	67T	75	$ .50	$2.00
Scott, George	68T	233	$ .35	$1.40
Scott, George	69T	574	$ .40	$1.60
Scott, George	70T	385	$ .35	$1.40
Scott, George	71T	9	$ .25	$1.00
Scott, George	72T	585	$ .40	$1.60
Scott, George	73T	263	$ .10	$ .40
Scott, George	74T	27	$ .10	$ .40
Scott, George	75T	360	$ .10	$ .40
Scott, George	76T	15	$ .05	$ .25
Scott, George	76T	194	$ .50	$2.00
Scott, George	76T	196	$ .25	$1.00
Scott, George	77T	255	$ .05	$ .20
Scott, George	78T	125	$ .04	$ .16
Scott, George	79T	645	$ .03	$ .12
Scott, George	80T	414	$ .01	$ .10
Scott, John	75T	616	$6.00	$24.00
Scott, John	77T	473	$17.50	$70.00
Scott, John	78T	547	$ .04	$ .16
Scott, Mickey	70T	669	$1.25	$5.00
Scott, Mickey	72T	724	$1.25	$5.00
Scott, Mickey	73T	553	$ .60	$2.40
Scott, Mickey	76T	276	$ .05	$ .25
Scott, Mickey	77T	401	$ .05	$ .20
Scott, Mike	80T	681	$ .75	$3.00
Scott, Mike	81T	109	$ .10	$ .50
Scott, Mike	82T	246	$ .05	$ .25
Scott, Mike	82T	432	$ .05	$ .20
Scott, Mike	83T	679	$ .01	$ .15
Scott, Mike	83TTR	100	$ .05	$ .35
Scott, Mike	84T	559	$ .01	$ .15
Scott, Mike	85T	17	$ .01	$ .10
Scott, Mike	86T	268	$ .01	$ .15
Scott, Mike	87T	330	$ .01	$ .10
Scott, Mike	88T	760	$ .01	$ .04
Scott, Mike	89T	180	$ .01	$ .03
Scott, Mike	90T	460	$ .01	$ .03
Scott, Mike	90TAS	405	$ .01	$ .03
Scott, Mike	91T	240	$ .01	$ .03
Scott, Mike	91TSC	209	$ .05	$ .25
Scott, Rodney	78T	191	$ .04	$ .16
Scott, Rodney	79T	86	$ .03	$ .12
Scott, Rodney	80T	712	$ .01	$ .10
Scott, Rodney	81T	539	$ .01	$ .08
Scott, Rodney	81TRB	204	$ .01	$ .10
Scott, Rodney	82T	259	$ .01	$ .08
Scott, Tim	92TSC	881	$ .05	$ .20
Scott, Tim	93T	166	$ .01	$ .10
Scott, Tim	93TSC	76	$ .01	$ .10
Scott, Tony	78T	352	$ .04	$ .16
Scott, Tony	79T	143	$ .03	$ .12
Scott, Tony	80T	33	$ .01	$ .10
Scott, Tony	81T	165	$ .01	$ .08
Scott, Tony	81TTR	828	$ .01	$ .15
Scott, Tony	82T	698	$ .01	$ .08
Scott, Tony	83T	507	$ .01	$ .08
Scott, Tony	84T	292	$ .01	$ .06
Scott, Tony	85T	733	$ .01	$ .06

TOPPS

Player	Year	No.	VG	EX/MT
Scrivener, Chuck	77T	173	$ .05	$ .20
Scrivener, Chuck	78T	94	$ .04	$ .16
Scudder, Scott	90T	553	$ .01	$ .15
Scudder, Scott	91T	713	$ .01	$ .03
Scudder, Scott	92T	48	$ .01	$ .03
Scudder, Scott	92TSC	644	$ .01	$ .10
Scudder, Scott	93T	248	$ .01	$ .03
Scudder, Scott	93TSC	243	$ .01	$ .10
Scull, Angel	54T	204	$3.75	$15.00
Scurry, Rod	81T	194	$ .01	$ .08
Scurry, Rod	82T	207	$ .01	$ .08
Scurry, Rod	83T	537	$ .01	$ .08
Scurry, Rod	84T	69	$ .01	$ .06
Scurry, Rod	85T	641	$ .01	$ .06
Scurry, Rod	86T	449	$ .01	$ .05
Scurry, Rod	87T	665	$ .01	$ .04
Seanez, Rudy	92TSC	713	$ .01	$ .10
Seanez, Rudy	93T	676	$ .01	$ .03
Searage, Ray	82T	478	$ .01	$ .08
Searage, Ray	86T	642	$ .01	$ .05
Searage, Ray	87T	149	$ .01	$ .04
Searage, Ray	88T	788	$ .01	$ .04
Searage, Ray	90T	84	$ .01	$ .03
Searcy, Steve	89T	167	$ .01	$ .10
Searcy, Steve	90T	487	$ .01	$ .03
Searcy, Steve	91T	369	$ .01	$ .03
Searcy, Steve	91TSC	352	$ .05	$ .25
Searcy, Steve	92T	599	$ .01	$ .03
Searcy, Steve	92TSC	648	$ .01	$ .10
Seaver, Tom	67T	581	$300.00	$1200.00
Seaver, Tom	68T	45	$55.00	$220.00
Seaver, Tom	69T	480	$35.00	$140.00
Seaver, Tom	70T	69	$1.50	$6.00
Seaver, Tom	70T	300	$20.00	$80.00
Seaver, Tom	71T	68	$ .75	$3.00
Seaver, Tom	71T	72	$1.00	$4.00
Seaver, Tom	71T	160	$15.00	$60.00
Seaver, Tom	72T	91	$ .50	$2.00
Seaver, Tom	72T	93	$ .75	$3.00
Seaver, Tom	72T	95	$ .75	$3.00
Seaver, Tom	72T	347	$ .75	$3.00
Seaver, Tom	72T	445	$10.00	$40.00
Seaver, Tom	72TIA	446	$5.00	$20.00
Seaver, Tom	73T	350	$6.50	$26.00
Seaver, Tom	74T	80	$4.50	$18.00
Seaver, Tom	74T	206	$1.00	$4.00
Seaver, Tom	74T	207	$3.50	$14.00
Seaver, Tom	75T	370	$4.50	$18.00
Seaver, Tom	76T	199	$ .25	$1.00
Seaver, Tom	76T	201	$ .25	$1.00
Seaver, Tom	76T	203	$ .30	$1.20
Seaver, Tom	76T	600	$3.50	$14.00
Seaver, Tom	76TRB	5	$ .75	$3.00
Seaver, Tom	77T	6	$2.50	$10.00
Seaver, Tom	77T	150	$2.50	$10.00
Seaver, Tom	78T	450	$1.75	$7.00
Seaver, Tom	79T	100	$ .75	$3.00
Seaver, Tom	80T	500	$1.10	$4.40
Seaver, Tom	81T	220	$ .75	$3.00
Seaver, Tom	82T	30	$ .20	$2.20
Seaver, Tom	82T	165	$ .01	$ .15
Seaver, Tom	82T	756	$ .05	$ .35
Seaver, Tom	82TAS	346	$ .10	$ .75
Seaver, Tom	82TSA	31	$ .10	$1.00
Seaver, Tom	83T	580	$ .20	$2.00
Seaver, Tom	83T	581	$ .10	$1.00
Seaver, Tom	83TTR	101	$2.00	$8.00
Seaver, Tom	84T	246	$ .05	$ .20
Seaver, Tom	84T	706	$ .05	$ .25
Seaver, Tom	84T	707	$ .10	$1.00
Seaver, Tom	84T	708	$ .05	$ .20
Seaver, Tom	84T	740	$ .15	$1.50
Seaver, Tom	84TTR	108	$2.00	$8.00
Seaver, Tom	85T	670	$ .10	$ .50
Seaver, Tom	86T	390	$ .10	$ .50
Seaver, Tom	86TTB	402	$ .05	$ .20
Seaver, Tom	86TTR	101	$ .10	$ .50
Seaver, Tom	87T	425	$ .05	$ .25
Sebra, Bob	87T	479	$ .01	$ .04
Sebra, Bob	88T	93	$ .01	$ .04
Secrest, Charlie	59T	140	$1.00	$4.00
Secrist, Don	69T	654	$ .75	$3.00
Seelbach, Chuck	73T	51	$ .10	$ .40
Seelbach, Chuck	74T	292	$ .10	$ .40
Segui, David	91T	724	$ .01	$ .15
Segui, David	91TSC	50	$ .05	$ .25
Segui, David	92T	447	$ .01	$ .03
Segui, David	92TSC	783	$ .01	$ .10
Segui, David	93T	82	$ .01	$ .03
Segui, Diego	63T	157	$ .50	$2.00
Segui, Diego	64T	508	$1.00	$4.00
Segui, Diego	65T	197	$ .50	$2.00
Segui, Diego	66T	309	$ .50	$2.00
Segui, Diego	68T	517	$ .75	$3.00
Segui, Diego	69T	511	$ .30	$1.20
Segui, Diego	70T	2	$ .20	$ .80
Segui, Diego	71T	67	$ .75	$3.00
Segui, Diego	71T	215	$ .25	$1.00
Segui, Diego	72T	735	$1.25	$5.00
Segui, Diego	73T	383	$ .10	$ .40
Segui, Diego	74T	151	$ .10	$ .40
Segui, Diego	74TTR	151	$ .10	$ .40
Segui, Diego	75T	232	$ .10	$ .40
Segui, Diego	77T	653	$ .05	$ .20
Seitzer, Kevin	87TTR	111	$ .05	$ .20
Seitzer, Kevin	88T	275	$ .01	$ .04
Seitzer, Kevin	89T	670	$ .01	$ .03
Seitzer, Kevin	90T	435	$ .01	$ .03
Seitzer, Kevin	91T	695	$ .01	$ .03
Seitzer, Kevin	91TSC	88	$ .05	$ .25
Seitzer, Kevin	92T	577	$ .01	$ .03
Seitzer, Kevin	92TSC	285	$ .01	$ .10
Seitzer, Kevin	92TSC	820	$ .01	$ .10

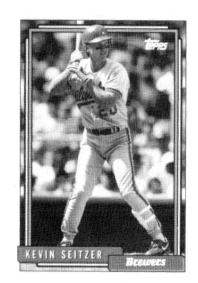

Player	Year	No.	VG	EX/MT
Seitzer, Kevin	92TTR	103	$ .01	$ .05
Seitzer, Kevin	93T	44	$ .01	$ .03
Seitzer, Kevin	93TSC	57	$ .01	$ .10
Sele, Aaron	92T	504	$ .05	$ .35
Sellers, Jeff	87T	12	$ .01	$ .04

TOPPS

Player	Year	No.	VG	EX/MT
Sellers, Jeff	88T	653	$ .01	$ .04
Sellers, Jeff	89T	544	$ .01	$ .03
Sells, Dave	74T	37	$ .10	$ .40
Selma, Dick	66T	67	$ .35	$1.40
Selma, Dick	67T	386	$ .60	$2.40
Selma, Dick	68T	556	$ .70	$2.80
Selma, Dick	69T	197	$ .35	$1.40
Selma, Dick	70T	24	$ .20	$ .80
Selma, Dick	71T	705	$1.50	$6.00
Selma, Dick	72T	726	$1.25	$5.00
Selma, Dick	73T	632	$ .60	$2.40
Sembera, Carroll	66T	539	$3.75	$15.00
Sembera, Carroll	67T	136	$ .40	$1.60
Sembera, Carroll	68T	207	$ .35	$1.40
Sembera, Carroll	69T	351	$ .30	$1.20
Seminara, Frank	92TTR	104	$ .01	$ .15
Seminara, Frank	93T	247	$ .01	$ .03
Seminick, Andy	51Trb	45	$1.65	$6.60
Seminick, Andy	52T	297	$13.75	$55.00
Seminick, Andy	53T	153	$4.00	$16.00
Seminick, Andy	56T	296	$2.50	$10.00
Seminick, Andy	91TA53	153	$ .01	$ .15
Semproch, "Ray" Roman	58T	474	$1.00	$4.00
Semproch, Ray	59T	197	$1.00	$4.00
Semproch, Ray	60T	286	$ .75	$3.00
Semproch, Ray	61T	174	$ .60	$2.40
Senators, Team	57T	270	$12.00	$48.00
Senators, Team	58T	44	$4.50	$18.00
Senators, Team	60T	43	$2.00	$8.00
Senators, Team	62T	206	$1.50	$6.00
Senators, Team	63T	131	$1.00	$4.00
Senators, Team	64T	343	$1.50	$6.00
Senators, Team	65T	267	$1.00	$4.00
Senators, Team	66T	194	$1.00	$4.00
Senators, Team	67T	437	$1.25	$5.00
Senators, Team	70T	676	$2.50	$10.00
Senators, Team	71T	462	$ .75	$3.00

Player	Year	No.	VG	EX/MT
Serafini, Dan	93T	307	$ .01	$ .15
Serena, Bill	52T	325	$43.75	$175.00
Serna, Paul	83T	492	$ .01	$ .08
Serum, Gary	79T	627	$ .03	$ .12
Serum, Gary	80T	61	$ .01	$ .10
Servais, Scott	88TTR	106	$ .05	$ .25
Servais, Scott	92T	437	$ .01	$ .03
Servais, Scott	92TSC	509	$ .01	$ .10
Servais, Scott	93T	36	$ .01	$ .03
Sevcik, John	65T	597	$1.40	$5.60
Severinsen, Al	70T	477	$ .35	$1.40
Severinsen, Al	71T	747	$1.10	$4.40
Severinsen, Al	72T	274	$ .10	$ .40
Severson, Rich	71T	103	$ .25	$1.00
Sexton, Jimmy	79T	232	$ .03	$ .12
Sexton, Jimmy	80T	11	$ .01	$ .10
Sexton, Jimmy	83T	709	$ .01	$ .08
Seyfried, Gordon	64T	499	$1.00	$4.00
Shamsky, Art	65T	398	$1.00	$4.00
Shamsky, Art	66T	119	$ .50	$2.00
Shamsky, Art	67T	96	$ .40	$1.60
Shamsky, Art	68T	292	$ .35	$1.40
Shamsky, Art	69T	221	$ .50	$2.00
Shamsky, Art	70T	137	$ .20	$ .80
Shamsky, Art	71T	445	$ .50	$2.00
Shamsky, Art	72T	353	$ .10	$ .40
Shanahan, Greg	74T	599	$ .15	$ .60
Shannon, Mike	64T	262	$1.25	$5.00
Shannon, Mike	65T	43	$ .35	$1.40
Shannon, Mike	66T	293	$ .50	$2.00
Shannon, Mike	67T	605	$12.50	$50.00
Shannon, Mike	68T	445	$ .35	$1.40
Shannon, Mike	69T	110	$ .35	$1.40
Shannon, Mike	70T	614	$ .50	$2.00
Shannon, Mike	71T	735	$1.50	$6.00
Shantz, Bobby	52T	219	$8.75	$35.00
Shantz, Bobby	53T	225	$27.50	$110.00
Shantz, Bobby	54T	21	$4.00	$16.00
Shantz, Bobby	56T	261	$3.50	$14.00
Shantz, Bobby	57T	272	$7.00	$28.00
Shantz, Bobby	58T	289	$1.50	$6.00
Shantz, Bobby	58T	419	$3.00	$12.00
Shantz, Bobby	59T	222	$1.50	$6.00
Shantz, Bobby	60T	315	$ .75	$3.00
Shantz, Bobby	61T	379	$1.00	$4.00
Shantz, Bobby	61TMVP	473	$1.35	$5.40
Shantz, Bobby	62T	177	$ .60	$2.40
Shantz, Bobby	63T	533	$2.25	$9.00
Shantz, Bobby	64T	278	$ .65	$2.60
Shantz, Bobby	75T	190	$ .15	$ .60
Shantz, Bobby	91TA53	225	$ .05	$ .25
Sharon, Dick	74T	48	$ .10	$ .40
Sharon, Dick	75T	293	$ .10	$ .40
Sharp, Bill	74T	519	$ .10	$ .40
Sharp, Bill	75T	373	$ .10	$ .40
Sharp, Bill	76T	244	$ .05	$ .25
Sharperson, Mike	90T	117	$ .01	$ .03
Sharperson, Mike	91T	53	$ .01	$ .03
Sharperson, Mike	91TSC	541	$ .05	$ .25
Sharperson, Mike	92T	627	$ .01	$ .03
Sharperson, Mike	92TSC	93	$ .01	$ .10
Sharperson, Mike	93T	526	$ .01	$ .03
Shave, John	93T	451	$ .05	$ .25
Shaw, Bob	58T	206	$1.50	$6.00
Shaw, Bob	59T	159	$1.00	$4.00
Shaw, Bob	60T	380	$ .75	$3.00
Shaw, Bob	61T	352	$ .60	$2.40
Shaw, Bob	62T	109	$ .60	$2.40
Shaw, Bob	63T	5	$2.00	$8.00
Shaw, Bob	63T	255	$ .90	$3.60
Shaw, Bob	64T	328	$ .65	$2.60
Shaw, Bob	65T	428	$1.00	$4.00
Shaw, Bob	66T	260	$ .50	$2.00
Shaw, Bob	67T	470	$1.50	$6.00
Shaw, Bob	73T	646	$ .75	$3.00
Shaw, Don	67T	587	$7.00	$28.00
Shaw, Don	68T	521	$ .75	$3.00
Shaw, Don	69T	183	$ .35	$1.40
Shaw, Don	70T	476	$ .35	$1.40
Shaw, Don	71T	654	$1.50	$6.00
Shaw, Don	72T	479	$ .25	$1.00

TOPPS

Player	Year	No.	VG	EX/MT
Shaw, Jeff	92TSC	843	$ .01	$ .10
Shea, Frank	52T	248	$7.00	$28.00
Shea, Frank	53T	164	$4.00	$16.00
Shea, Frank	91TA53	164	$ .01	$ .15
Shea, Steve	69T	499	$ .30	$1.20
Shearer, Ray	58T	283	$1.25	$5.00
Sheets, Larry	85TTR	106	$ .01	$ .15
Sheets, Larry	86T	147	$ .01	$ .05
Sheets, Larry	87T	552	$ .01	$ .04
Sheets, Larry	88T	327	$ .01	$ .04
Sheets, Larry	89T	98	$ .01	$ .03
Sheets, Larry	90T	708	$ .01	$ .03
Sheets, Larry	91T	281	$ .01	$ .03
Sheffield, Gary	89T	343	$ .20	$2.00
Sheffield, Gary	90T	718	$ .10	$ .50
Sheffield, Gary	91T	68	$ .05	$ .25
Sheffield, Gary	91TSC	95	$1.25	$5.00
Sheffield, Gary	92T	695	$ .05	$ .20
Sheffield, Gary	92TSC	309	$ .10	$1.00
Sheffield, Gary	92TSC	766	$ .10	$1.00
Sheffield, Gary	92TTR	105	$ .05	$ .25

Player	Year	No.	VG	EX/MT
Sheffield, Gary	**93T**	**140**	**$ .01**	**$ .15**
Sheffield, Gary	93T	403	$ .01	$ .10
Sheffield, Gary	93TSC	300	$ .10	$ .50
Sheffield, Tony	93T	687	$ .01	$ .15
Shelby, John	83TTR	102	$ .01	$ .10
Shelby, John	84T	86	$ .01	$ .06
Shelby, John	85T	508	$ .01	$ .06
Shelby, John	86T	309	$ .01	$ .05
Shelby, John	87T	208	$ .01	$ .04
Shelby, John	87TTR	112	$ .01	$ .05
Shelby, John	88T	428	$ .01	$ .04
Shelby, John	89T	175	$ .01	$ .03
Shelby, John	91T	746	$ .01	$ .03
Sheldon, Bob	75T	623	$5.25	$21.00
Sheldon, Bob	76T	626	$ .05	$ .25
Sheldon, Roland	61T	541	$10.00	$40.00
Sheldon, Roland	62T	185	$ .60	$2.40
Sheldon, Roland	63T	507	$1.75	$7.00
Sheldon, Roland	65T	254	$ .50	$2.00
Sheldon, Roland	66T	18	$ .35	$1.40
Sheldon, Roland	69T	413	$ .30	$1.20
Shelenback, Jim	67T	592	$5.50	$22.00
Shellenback, Jim	69T	567	$ .40	$1.60

Player	Year	No.	VG	EX/MT
Shellenback, Jim	70T	389	$ .35	$1.40
Shellenback, Jim	71T	351	$ .25	$1.00
Shellenback, Jim	74T	657	$ .10	$ .40
Shepard, Jack	55T	73	$2.25	$9.00
Shepard, Larry	68T	584	$ .70	$2.80
Shepard, Larry	69T	384	$ .30	$1.20
Shepard, Larry	73T	296	$ .20	$ .80
Shepard, Larry	74T	326	$ .25	$1.00
Shepherd, Keith	93T	447	$ .05	$ .20
Shepherd, Ron	87T	643	$ .01	$ .04
Sheridan, Pat	84T	121	$ .01	$ .06
Sheridan, Pat	85T	359	$ .01	$ .06
Sheridan, Pat	86T	743	$ .01	$ .05
Sheridan, Pat	87T	234	$ .01	$ .04
Sheridan, Pat	88T	514	$ .01	$ .04
Sheridan, Pat	89T	288	$ .01	$ .03
Sheridan, Pat	90T	422	$ .01	$ .03
Sherman, Darrell	93T	576	$ .10	$ .75
Sherrill, Tim	91T	769	$ .01	$ .10
Sherrill, Tim	92TSC	822	$ .01	$ .15
Sherry, Larry	60T	105	$1.25	$5.00
Sherry, Larry	61T	412	$1.00	$4.00
Sherry, Larry	61T	521	$1.35	$5.40
Sherry, Larry	62T	435	$1.25	$5.00
Sherry, Larry	63T	565	$2.25	$9.00
Sherry, Larry	64T	474	$1.00	$4.00
Sherry, Larry	65T	408	$1.00	$4.00
Sherry, Larry	66T	289	$ .50	$2.00
Sherry, Larry	67T	571	$4.00	$16.00
Sherry, Larry	68T	468	$ .75	$3.00
Sherry, Norm	60T	529	$4.00	$16.00
Sherry, Norm	61T	521	$1.35	$5.40
Sherry, Norm	62T	238	$ .75	$3.00
Sherry, Norm	63T	316	$ .90	$3.60
Shetrone, Barry	60T	348	$ .75	$3.00
Shetrone, Barry	63T	276	$ .90	$3.60
Shields, Steve	87TTR	113	$ .01	$ .05
Shields, Steve	88T	632	$ .01	$ .04
Shields, Steve	89T	484	$ .01	$ .03
Shifflett, Steve	93T	735	$ .01	$ .03
Shifflett, Steve	93TSC	84	$ .01	$ .10
Shines, Razor	86T	132	$ .01	$ .05
Shipley, Craig	92T	308	$ .01	$ .10
Shipley, Craig	92TSC	374	$ .01	$ .15
Shipley, Craig	93T	601	$ .01	$ .03
Shipley, Craig	93TSC	258	$ .01	$ .10
Shipley, Joe	59T	141	$1.00	$4.00
Shipley, Joe	60T	239	$ .75	$3.00
Shirley, Al	92T	306	$ .05	$ .20
Shirley, Bart	66T	591	$11.25	$45.00
Shirley, Bart	67T	287	$ .60	$2.40
Shirley, Bart	69T	289	$ .50	$2.00
Shirley, Bob	78T	266	$ .04	$ .16
Shirley, Bob	79T	594	$ .03	$ .12
Shirley, Bob	80T	476	$ .01	$ .10
Shirley, Bob	81T	49	$ .01	$ .08
Shirley, Bob	81TTR	829	$ .01	$ .15
Shirley, Bob	82T	749	$ .01	$ .08
Shirley, Bob	82TTR	105	$ .01	$ .10
Shirley, Bob	83T	112	$ .01	$ .08
Shirley, Bob	83TTR	103	$ .01	$ .10
Shirley, Bob	84T	684	$ .01	$ .06
Shirley, Bob	85T	328	$ .01	$ .06
Shirley, Bob	86T	213	$ .01	$ .05
Shirley, Bob	87T	524	$ .01	$ .04
Shockley, Costen	65T	107	$ .75	$3.00
Shopay, Tom	70T	363	$ .35	$1.40
Shopay, Tom	72T	418	$ .25	$1.00
Short, Bill	60T	142	$ .75	$3.00
Short, Bill	61T	252	$ .60	$2.40
Short, Bill	62T	221	$ .75	$3.00
Short, Bill	67T	577	$4.00	$16.00
Short, Bill	68T	536	$ .70	$2.80
Short, Bill	69T	259	$ .50	$2.00
Short, Chris	67T	395	$ .60	$2.40

TOPPS

Player	Year	No.	VG	EX/MT
Short, Chris	68T	7	$ .55	$2.20
Short, Chris	68T	139	$ .35	$1.40
Short, Chris	69T	395	$ .30	$1.20
Short, Chris	70T	270	$ .35	$1.40
Short, Chris	71T	511	$ .50	$2.00
Short, Chris	72T	665	$1.25	$5.00
Show, Eric	82TTR	106	$ .05	$ .25
Show, Eric	83T	68	$ .05	$ .20
Show, Eric	84T	532	$ .01	$ .06
Show, Eric	85T	118	$ .01	$ .06
Show, Eric	86T	762	$ .01	$ .05
Show, Eric	87T	730	$ .01	$ .04
Show, Eric	88T	303	$ .01	$ .04
Show, Eric	89T	427	$ .01	$ .03
Show, Eric	90T	239	$ .01	$ .03
Show, Eric	91T	613	$ .01	$ .03
Show, Eric	91TSC	138	$ .05	$ .25
Show, Eric	92T	132	$ .01	$ .03
Showalter, Buck	92T	201	$ .01	$ .10
Showalter, Buck	93T	510	$ .01	$ .03
Shuba, George	52T	326	$55.00	$220.00
Shuba, George	53T	34	$7.50	$30.00
Shuba, George	91TA53	34	$ .01	$ .15
Shuey, Paul	91TTR	108	$ .10	$ .40
Shumpert, Terry	90TTR	114	$ .01	$ .15
Shumpert, Terry	91T	322	$ .01	$ .03
Shumpert, Terry	91TSC	111	$ .05	$ .25
Shumpert, Terry	92T	483	$ .01	$ .03
Shumpert, Terry	92TSC	165	$ .01	$ .10
Siebern, Norm	58T	54	$2.25	$9.00
Siebern, Norm	59T	308	$1.00	$4.00
Siebern, Norm	60T	11	$ .85	$3.40
Siebern, Norm	61T	119	$ .60	$2.40
Siebern, Norm	61T	267	$ .60	$2.40
Siebern, Norm	62T	127	$ .60	$2.40
Siebern, Norm	62T	275	$ .75	$3.00
Siebern, Norm	63T	2	$5.00	$20.00
Siebern, Norm	63T	430	$1.00	$4.00
Siebern, Norm	64T	145	$ .50	$2.00
Siebern, Norm	65T	455	$1.25	$5.00
Siebern, Norm	66T	14	$ .35	$1.40
Siebern, Norm	67T	299	$ .60	$2.40
Siebern, Norm	68T	537	$ .70	$2.80
Siebert, Paul	75T	614	$ .10	$ .40
Siebert, Sonny	64T	552	$2.25	$9.00
Siebert, Sonny	65T	96	$ .35	$1.40
Siebert, Sonny	66T	197	$ .50	$2.00
Siebert, Sonny	66T	222	$ .75	$3.00
Siebert, Sonny	66T	226	$ .75	$3.00
Siebert, Sonny	67T	95	$ .40	$1.60
Siebert, Sonny	67T	463	$1.50	$6.00
Siebert, Sonny	68T	8	$ .55	$2.20
Siebert, Sonny	68T	295	$ .35	$1.40
Siebert, Sonny	69T	455	$ .30	$1.20
Siebert, Sonny	70T	597	$ .50	$2.00
Siebert, Sonny	71T	710	$5.25	$21.00
Siebert, Sonny	72T	290	$ .10	$ .40
Siebert, Sonny	73T	14	$ .10	$ .40
Siebert, Sonny	74T	548	$ .10	$ .40
Siebert, Sonny	75T	328	$ .10	$ .40
Siebler, Dwight	64T	516	$1.00	$4.00
Siebler, Dwight	65T	326	$ .50	$2.00
Siebler, Dwight	66T	546	$3.75	$15.00
Siebler, Dwight	67T	164	$ .40	$1.60
Sierra, Candy	89T	711	$ .01	$ .03
Sierra, Ruben	87T	261	$ .20	$2.00
Sierra, Ruben	87TRB	6	$ .05	$ .25
Sierra, Ruben	88T	771	$ .05	$ .35
Sierra, Ruben	89T	53	$ .05	$ .35
Sierra, Ruben	90T	185	$ .01	$ .15
Sierra, Ruben	90TAS	390	$ .01	$ .10
Sierra, Ruben	91T	535	$ .01	$ .10
Sierra, Ruben	91TSC	123	$ .20	$2.00
Sierra, Ruben	92T	700	$ .01	$ .10
Sierra, Ruben	92TAS	403	$ .01	$ .10

Player	Year	No.	VG	EX/MT
Sierra, Ruben	92TSC	387	$ .10	$ .50
Sierra, Ruben	93T	440	$ .01	$ .15
Sievers, Roy	51Trb	9	$1.65	$6.60
Sievers, Roy	52T	64	$13.75	$55.00

Player	Year	No.	VG	EX/MT
Sievers, Roy	53T	67	$4.50	$18.00
Sievers, Roy	54T	245	$4.00	$16.00
Sievers, Roy	55T	16	$2.25	$9.00
Sievers, Roy	56T	75	$2.00	$8.00
Sievers, Roy	57T	89	$2.00	$8.00
Sievers, Roy	58T	250	$1.25	$5.00
Sievers, Roy	59T	74	$1.50	$6.00
Sievers, Roy	59T	340	$1.00	$4.00
Sievers, Roy	59T	465	$1.25	$5.00
Sievers, Roy	59TAS	566	$4.00	$16.00
Sievers, Roy	60T	25	$ .85	$3.40
Sievers, Roy	61T	470	$1.35	$5.40
Sievers, Roy	62T	220	$ .75	$3.00
Sievers, Roy	63T	283	$ .90	$3.60
Sievers, Roy	64T	43	$ .50	$2.00
Sievers, Roy	65T	574	$1.40	$5.60
Sievers, Roy	91TA53	67	$ .01	$ .15
Silvera, Al	56T	137	$2.50	$10.00
Silvera, Charlie	52T	168	$8.00	$32.00
Silvera, Charlie	53T	242	$27.50	$110.00
Silvera, Charlie	54T	96	$3.75	$15.00
Silvera, Charlie	55T	188	$3.00	$12.00
Silvera, Charlie	57T	255	$2.00	$8.00
Silvera, Charlie	73T	323	$ .25	$1.00
Silvera, Charlie	74T	379	$ .25	$1.00
Silvera, Charlie	91TA53	242	$ .01	$ .15
Silverio, Tom	72T	213	$ .20	$ .80
Silvestri, Dave	88TTR	107	$ .05	$ .35
Silvestri, Dave	93T	529	$ .10	$ .50
Silvestri, Ken	60T	466	$1.25	$5.00
Silvestri, Ken	73T	237	$ .30	$1.20
Silvestri, Ken	74T	634	$ .25	$1.00
Sima, Al	52T	93	$7.00	$28.00
Sima, Al	53T	241	$11.25	$45.00
Sima, Al	54T	216	$3.75	$15.00
Sima, Al	91TA53	241	$ .01	$ .15
Simmons, Al	91TA53	326	$ .10	$ .50
Simmons, Curt	52T	203	$8.00	$32.00
Simmons, Curt	56T	290	$2.50	$10.00

TOPPS

Player	Year	No.	VG	EX/MT	Player	Year	No.	VG	EX/MT
Simmons, Curt	57T	158	$2.00	$8.00	Sims, Duke	69T	414	$ .30	$1.20
Simmons, Curt	58T	404	$1.00	$4.00	Sims, Duke	70T	275	$ .35	$1.40
Simmons, Curt	59T	382	$1.00	$4.00	Sims, Duke	71T	172	$ .25	$1.00
Simmons, Curt	60T	451	$1.25	$5.00	Sims, Duke	72T	63	$ .10	$ .40
Simmons, Curt	61T	11	$ .60	$2.40	Sims, Duke	73T	304	$ .10	$ .40
Simmons, Curt	62T	56	$1.50	$6.00	Sims, Duke	74T	398	$ .10	$ .40
Simmons, Curt	62T	285	$ .75	$3.00	Sims, Greg	66T	596	$4.50	$18.00
Simmons, Curt	63T	22	$ .50	$2.00	Sinatro, Matt	90TTR	115	$ .01	$ .05
Simmons, Curt	64T	385	$1.00	$4.00	Sinatro, Matt	91T	709	$ .01	$ .03
Simmons, Curt	65T	373	$1.00	$4.00	Sinatro, Matt	92TSC	872	$ .01	$ .10
Simmons, Curt	66T	489	$1.50	$6.00	Singer, Bill	66T	288	$35.00	$140.00
Simmons, Curt	67T	39	$ .40	$1.60	Singer, Bill	67T	12	$ .40	$1.60
Simmons, Curt	91TA53	318	$ .05	$ .20	Singer, Bill	68T	249	$ .35	$1.40
Simmons, Nelson	86T	121	$ .01	$ .05	Singer, Bill	69T	12	$ .75	$3.00
Simmons, Ted	71T	117	$5.00	$20.00	Singer, Bill	69T	575	$ .40	$1.60
Simmons, Ted	72T	154	$ .75	$3.00	Singer, Bill	70T	71	$ .75	$3.00
Simmons, Ted	73T	85	$ .50	$2.00	Singer, Bill	70T	490	$ .35	$1.40
Simmons, Ted	74T	260	$ .50	$2.00	Singer, Bill	71T	145	$ .25	$1.00
Simmons, Ted	75T	75	$ .50	$2.00	Singer, Bill	72T	25	$ .10	$ .40
Simmons, Ted	76T	191	$ .25	$1.00	Singer, Bill	73T	570	$ .60	$2.40
Simmons, Ted	76T	290	$ .25	$1.00	Singer, Bill	74T	210	$ .10	$ .40
Simmons, Ted	77T	470	$ .25	$1.00	Singer, Bill	75T	40	$ .10	$ .40
Simmons, Ted	78T	380	$ .15	$ .60	Singer, Bill	76T	411	$ .05	$ .25
Simmons, Ted	79T	510	$ .20	$ .80	Singer, Bill	76TTR	411	$ .05	$ .25
Simmons, Ted	80T	85	$ .10	$ .40	Singer, Bill	77T	346	$ .05	$ .20
Simmons, Ted	81T	705	$ .05	$ .20	Singleton, Elmer	57T	378	$1.75	$7.00
Simmons, Ted	81TTR	830	$ .10	$ .50	Singleton, Elmer	59T	548	$4.00	$16.00
Simmons, Ted	82T	150	$ .01	$ .15	Singleton, Ken	71T	16	$ .75	$3.00
Simmons, Ted	83T	450	$ .01	$ .15	Singleton, Ken	72T	425	$ .50	$2.00
Simmons, Ted	83T	451	$ .01	$ .08	Singleton, Ken	72TIA	426	$ .25	$1.00
Simmons, Ted	84T	630	$ .01	$ .10	Singleton, Ken	73T	232	$ .20	$ .80
Simmons, Ted	84T	713	$ .01	$ .15	Singleton, Ken	74T	25	$ .15	$ .60
Simmons, Ted	84T	726	$ .01	$ .06	Singleton, Ken	75T	125	$ .15	$ .60
Simmons, Ted	84TAS	404	$ .01	$ .06	Singleton, Ken	76T	175	$ .15	$ .60
Simmons, Ted	85T	318	$ .01	$ .10	Singleton, Ken	77T	445	$ .05	$ .20
Simmons, Ted	86T	237	$ .01	$ .10	Singleton, Ken	78T	65	$ .05	$ .20
Simmons, Ted	86TTR	102	$ .01	$ .06	Singleton, Ken	79T	615	$ .03	$ .12
Simmons, Ted	87T	516	$ .01	$ .04	Singleton, Ken	80T	340	$ .01	$ .10
Simmons, Ted	88T	791	$ .01	$ .10	Singleton, Ken	81T	570	$ .01	$ .08
Simms, Mike	91T	32	$ .01	$ .15	Singleton, Ken	82T	290	$ .01	$ .08
Simms, Mike	91TSC	281	$ .10	$ .50	Singleton, Ken	82TAS	552	$ .01	$ .07
Simms, Mike	92T	463	$ .01	$ .03					
Simms, Mike	92TSC	262	$ .01	$ .10					
Simons, Doug	91TTR	109	$ .01	$ .05					
Simons, Doug	92T	82	$ .01	$ .03					
Simpson, Dick	63T	407	$1.00	$4.00					
Simpson, Dick	64T	127	$ .50	$2.00					
Simpson, Dick	65T	374	$1.25	$5.00					
Simpson, Dick	66T	311	$ .35	$1.40					
Simpson, Dick	67T	6	$ .40	$1.60					
Simpson, Dick	68T	459	$ .75	$3.00					
Simpson, Dick	69T	608	$ .40	$1.60					
Simpson, Harry	52T	193	$7.00	$28.00					
Simpson, Harry	53T	150	$4.00	$16.00					
Simpson, Harry	56T	239	$3.75	$15.00					
Simpson, Harry	57T	225	$2.00	$8.00					
Simpson, Harry	58T	299	$1.25	$5.00					
Simpson, Harry	59T	333	$1.00	$4.00					
Simpson, Harry	60T	180	$ .75	$3.00					
Simpson, Harry	91TA53	150	$ .01	$ .15					
Simpson, Joe	79T	719	$1.50	$6.00					
Simpson, Joe	80T	637	$ .01	$ .10					
Simpson, Joe	81T	116	$ .01	$ .08					
Simpson, Joe	82T	382	$ .01	$ .08					
Simpson, Joe	83T	567	$ .01	$ .08					
Simpson, Joe	83TTR	104	$ .01	$ .10					
Simpson, Joe	84T	219	$ .01	$ .06					
Simpson, Wayne	70T	683	$1.50	$6.00					
Simpson, Wayne	71T	68	$ .75	$3.00					
Simpson, Wayne	71T	339	$ .25	$1.00					
Simpson, Wayne	72T	762	$1.25	$5.00					
Simpson, Wayne	73T	428	$ .25	$1.00					
Sims, Duke	66T	169	$ .50	$2.00	**Singleton, Ken**	**83T**	**85**	**$ .01**	**$ .08**
Sims, Duke	67T	3	$ .40	$1.60	Singleton, Ken	84T	165	$ .01	$ .06
Sims, Duke	68T	508	$ .75	$3.00	Singleton, Ken	85T	755	$ .01	$ .06

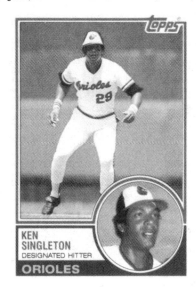

KEN SINGLETON
DESIGNATED HITTER
ORIOLES

TOPPS

Player	Year	No.	VG	EX/MT
Sisk, Doug	83TTR	105	$ .01	$ .10
Sisk, Doug	84T	599	$ .01	$ .06
Sisk, Doug	85T	315	$ .01	$ .06
Sisk, Doug	86T	144	$ .01	$ .05
Sisk, Doug	87T	404	$ .01	$ .04
Sisk, Doug	88T	763	$ .01	$ .04
Sisk, Doug	89T	13	$ .01	$ .03
Sisk, Tommie	63T	169	$8.00	$32.00
Sisk, Tommie	64T	224	$ .65	$2.60
Sisk, Tommie	65T	558	$1.40	$5.60
Sisk, Tommie	66T	441	$ .65	$2.60
Sisk, Tommie	67T	84	$ .40	$1.60
Sisk, Tommie	68T	429	$ .35	$1.40
Sisk, Tommie	69T	152	$ .35	$1.40
Sisk, Tommie	70T	374	$ .35	$1.40
Sisler, Dave	57T	56	$2.00	$8.00
Sisler, Dave	58T	59	$2.00	$8.00
Sisler, Dave	59T	346	$1.00	$4.00
Sisler, Dave	59T	384	$1.00	$4.00
Sisler, Dave	60T	186	$ .75	$3.00
Sisler, Dave	61T	239	$ .60	$2.40
Sisler, Dave	62T	171	$ .60	$2.40
Sisler, Dave	63T	284	$ .90	$3.60
Sisler, Dick	51Tbb	8	$7.50	$30.00
Sisler, Dick	52T	113	$7.00	$28.00
Sisler, Dick	64T	162	$ .50	$2.00
Sisler, Dick	65T	158	$ .35	$1.40
Sisler, George	79TRH	411	$ .15	$ .60
Sisti, Sibby	52T	293	$13.75	$55.00
Sisti, Sibby	53T	124	$4.00	$16.00
Sisti, Sibby	91TA53	124	$ .01	$ .15
Sizemore, Ted	69T	552	$ .50	$2.00
Sizemore, Ted	70T	174	$ .20	$ .80
Sizemore, Ted	71T	571	$1.00	$4.00
Sizemore, Ted	72T	514	$ .25	$1.00
Sizemore, Ted	73T	128	$ .10	$ .40
Sizemore, Ted	74T	209	$ .10	$ .40
Sizemore, Ted	75T	404	$ .10	$ .40
Sizemore, Ted	76T	522	$ .05	$ .25
Sizemore, Ted	77T	366	$ .05	$ .20
Sizemore, Ted	78T	136	$ .04	$ .16
Sizemore, Ted	79T	297	$ .03	$ .12
Sizemore, Ted	80T	81	$ .01	$ .10
Skaggs, Dave	78T	593	$ .04	$ .16
Skaggs, Dave	79T	367	$ .03	$ .12
Skaggs, Dave	80T	211	$ .01	$ .10
Skaggs, Dave	81T	48	$ .01	$ .08
Skeels, Mark	93T	558	$ .05	$ .25
Skeen, Archie	64T	428	$1.00	$4.00
Skidmore, Roe	71T	121	$ .25	$1.00
Skinner, Bob	55T	88	$3.50	$14.00
Skinner, Bob	56T	297	$2.50	$10.00
Skinner, Bob	57T	209	$2.00	$8.00
Skinner, Bob	58T	94	$2.00	$8.00
Skinner, Bob	59T	320	$1.00	$4.00
Skinner, Bob	59T	543	$15.00	$60.00
Skinner, Bob	60T	113	$ .75	$3.00
Skinner, Bob	61T	204	$ .60	$2.40
Skinner, Bob	62T	115	$ .60	$2.40
Skinner, Bob	63T	18	$4.50	$18.00
Skinner, Bob	63T	215	$ .90	$3.60
Skinner, Bob	64T	377	$1.00	$4.00
Skinner, Bob	65T	591	$2.50	$10.00
Skinner, Bob	66T	471	$1.50	$6.00
Skinner, Bob	69T	369	$ .30	$1.20
Skinner, Bob	73T	12	$ .20	$ .80
Skinner, Bob	74T	188	$ .10	$ .40
Skinner, Bob	74T	489	$ .10	$ .40
Skinner, Bob	85T	139	$ .01	$ .10
Skinner, Joel	85T	139	$ .01	$ .10
Skinner, Joel	85T	488	$ .01	$ .06
Skinner, Joel	86T	239	$ .01	$ .05
Skinner, Joel	87T	626	$ .01	$ .04
Skinner, Joel	88T	109	$ .01	$ .04
Skinner, Joel	89T	536	$ .01	$ .03
Skinner, Joel	90T	54	$ .01	$ .03
Skinner, Joel	91T	783	$ .01	$ .03

Player	Year	No.	VG	EX/MT
Skinner, Joel	91TSC	561	$ .05	$ .25
Skinner, Joel	92T	378	$ .01	$ .03
Skinner, Joel	92TSC	278	$ .01	$ .10
Skizas, Lou	57T	83	$2.00	$8.00
Skizas, Lou	58T	319	$1.25	$5.00
Skizas, Lou	59T	328	$1.00	$4.00
Skok, Craig	79T	363	$ .03	$ .12
Skowron, Bill	54T	239	$20.00	$80.00
Skowron, Bill	55T	22	$5.00	$20.00
Skowron, Bill	56T	61	$4.00	$16.00
Skowron, Bill	57T	135	$3.50	$14.00
Skowron, "Moose" Bill	58T	240	$3.00	$12.00
Skowron, Bill	58TAS	477	$1.50	$6.00
Skowron, Bill	59T	90	$3.00	$12.00
Skowron, Bill	59TAS	554	$5.00	$20.00
Skowron, Bill	60T	370	$1.75	$7.00
Skowron, Bill	60TAS	553	$4.00	$16.00
Skowron, Bill	61T	42	$ .75	$3.00
Skowron, Bill	61T	371	$9.00	$36.00
Skowron, Bill	61TAS	568	$10.00	$40.00
Skowron, Bill	62T	110	$1.25	$5.00
Skowron, Bill	63T	180	$1.00	$4.00
Skowron, Bill	64T	445	$1.25	$5.00
Skowron, Bill	65T	70	$ .50	$2.00
Skowron, Bill	66T	199	$ .50	$2.00
Skowron, Bill	66T	590	$11.25	$45.00
Skowron, Bill	67T	357	$ .75	$3.00
Slater, Bob	79T	703	$ .05	$ .20
Slaton, Jim	72T	744	$1.25	$5.00
Slaton, Jim	73T	628	$ .60	$2.40
Slaton, Jim	74T	371	$ .10	$ .40
Slaton, Jim	75T	281	$ .10	$ .40
Slaton, Jim	76T	163	$ .05	$ .25
Slaton, Jim	77T	604	$ .05	$ .20
Slaton, Jim	78T	474	$ .04	$ .16
Slaton, Jim	79T	541	$ .03	$ .12
Slaton, Jim	80T	24	$ .01	$ .10
Slaton, Jim	81T	357	$ .01	$ .08
Slaton, Jim	82T	221	$ .01	$ .08
Slaton, Jim	83T	114	$ .01	$ .08
Slaton, Jim	84TTR	109	$ .01	$ .15

TOPPS

Player	Year	No.	VG	EX/MT
Slaton, Jim	85T	657	$ .01	$ .06
Slaton, Jim	86T	579	$ .01	$ .05
Slaught, Don	84T	196	$ .01	$ .15
Slaught, Don	85T	542	$ .01	$ .06
Slaught, Don	85TTR	107	$ .01	$ .10
Slaught, Don	86T	761	$ .01	$ .05
Slaught, Don	87T	308	$ .01	$ .04
Slaught, Don	88T	462	$ .01	$ .04
Slaught, Don	88TTR	108	$ .01	$ .05
Slaught, Don	89T	611	$ .01	$ .03
Slaught, Don	90T	26	$ .01	$ .03
Slaught, Don	90TTR	116	$ .01	$ .05
Slaught, Don	91T	221	$ .01	$ .03
Slaught, Don	91TSC	358	$ .05	$ .25
Slaught, Don	92T	524	$ .01	$ .03
Slaught, Don	92TSC	545	$ .01	$ .10
Slaught, Don	93T	778	$ .01	$ .03
Slaught, Don	93TSC	127	$ .01	$ .10
Slaughter, Enos	51Tbb	30	$30.00	$120.00
Slaughter, Enos	52T	65	$35.00	$140.00
Slaughter, Enos	53T	41	$22.50	$90.00
Slaughter, Enos	56T	109	$9.00	$36.00
Slaughter, Enos	57T	215	$6.25	$25.00
Slaughter, Enos	58T	142	$6.25	$25.00
Slaughter, Enos	59T	155	$5.00	$20.00
Slaughter, Enos	91TA53	41	$ .10	$1.00
Slaughter, Sterling	64T	469	$1.00	$4.00
Slaughter, Sterling	65T	314	$ .50	$2.00
Slayback, Bill	73T	537	$ .60	$2.40
Slayton, Jim	84T	772	$ .01	$ .06
Slayton, Jim	87T	432	$ .01	$ .04
Sleater, Lou	52T	306	$12.50	$50.00
Sleater, Lou	53T	224	$11.25	$45.00
Sleater, Lou	58T	46	$2.00	$8.00
Sleater, Lou	91TA53	224	$ .01	$ .15
Slocum, Ron	70T	573	$ .50	$2.00
Slocum, Ron	71T	274	$ .25	$1.00
Slocumb, Heathcliff	92T	576	$ .01	$ .03
Slocumb, Heathcliff	92TSC	382	$ .01	$ .10
Slusarski, Joe	88TTR	109	$ .05	$ .25
Slusarski, Joe	92T	651	$ .01	$ .03
Slusarski, Joe	92TSC	782	$ .01	$ .10
Small, Jim	56T	207	$3.75	$15.00
Small, Jim	57T	33	$2.00	$8.00
Smalley Jr., Roy	76T	70	$ .05	$ .25
Smalley Jr., Roy	76T	657	$ .25	$1.00
Smalley Jr., Roy	77T	66	$ .05	$ .20
Smalley Jr., Roy	78T	471	$ .04	$ .16
Smalley Jr., Roy	79T	219	$ .03	$ .12
Smalley Jr., Roy	80T	570	$ .01	$ .10
Smalley Jr., Roy	81T	115	$ .01	$ .08
Smalley Jr., Roy	82T	767	$ .01	$ .08
Smalley Jr., Roy	82TTR	107	$ .01	$ .10
Smalley Jr., Roy	83T	460	$ .01	$ .08
Smalley Jr., Roy	84T	305	$ .01	$ .06
Smalley Jr., Roy	85T	26	$ .01	$ .06
Smalley Jr., Roy	85T	140	$ .01	$ .10
Smalley Jr., Roy	85TTR	108	$ .01	$ .10
Smalley Jr., Roy	86T	613	$ .01	$ .05
Smalley Jr., Roy	87T	744	$ .01	$ .04
Smalley Jr., Roy	88T	239	$ .01	$ .04
Smalley, Roy	51Tbb	17	$7.50	$30.00
Smalley, Roy	52T	173	$7.00	$28.00
Smalley, Roy	54T	231	$3.75	$15.00
Smalley, Roy	57T	397	$1.75	$7.00
Smalley, Roy	76T	70	$ .05	$ .25
Smalley, Roy	85T	140	$ .01	$ .10
Smalley, Roy	91TA53	297	$ .05	$ .20
Smiley, John	87TTR	114	$ .10	$ .75
Smiley, John	88T	423	$ .05	$ .35
Smiley, John	89T	322	$ .01	$ .10
Smiley, John	90T	568	$ .01	$ .03
Smiley, John	91T	143	$ .01	$ .03
Smiley, John	91TSC	471	$ .05	$ .25
Smiley, John	92T	232	$ .01	$ .03
Smiley, John	92TSC	380	$ .01	$ .10
Smiley, John	92TSC	625	$ .01	$ .10
Smiley, John	92TTR	106	$ .01	$ .05
Smiley, John	93T	363	$ .01	$ .03
Smiley, John	93TSC	190	$ .01	$ .15
Smith, Al	54T	248	$4.50	$18.00
Smith, Al	55T	197	$6.25	$25.00
Smith, Al	56T	105	$2.50	$10.00
Smith, Al	57T	145	$2.00	$8.00
Smith, Al	58T	177	$1.25	$5.00
Smith, Al	59T	22	$1.50	$6.00
Smith, Al	60T	428	$ .75	$3.00
Smith, Al	61T	42	$ .75	$3.00
Smith, Al	61T	170	$ .60	$2.40
Smith, Al	62T	410	$1.25	$5.00
Smith, Al	63T	16	$ .50	$2.00
Smith, Al	64T	317	$ .65	$2.60
Smith, Bernie	71T	204	$ .25	$1.00
Smith, Billy	63T	241	$ .90	$3.60
Smith, Billy	78T	666	$ .04	$ .16
Smith, Billy	79T	237	$ .03	$ .12
Smith, Billy	80T	367	$ .01	$ .10
Smith, Billy	82T	441	$ .01	$ .08
Smith, Billy	82T	593	$ .01	$ .08
Smith, Bob G.	58T	226	$1.25	$5.00
Smith, Bob G.	59T	83	$1.50	$6.00
Smith, Bob W.	58T	445	$1.00	$4.00
Smith, Bobby Gene	57T	384	$1.75	$7.00
Smith, Bobby Gene	58T	402	$1.00	$4.00
Smith, Bobby Gene	59T	162	$1.00	$4.00
Smith, Bobby Gene	60T	194	$ .75	$3.00
Smith, Bobby Gene	61T	316	$ .60	$2.40
Smith, Bobby Gene	62T	531	$3.50	$14.00
Smith, Bryn	82T	118	$ .10	$ .50

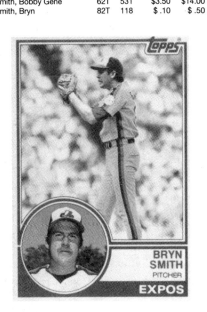

Player	Year	No.	VG	EX/MT
Smith, Bryn	83T	447	$ .01	$ .08
Smith, Bryn	84T	656	$ .01	$ .06
Smith, Bryn	85T	88	$ .01	$ .06
Smith, Bryn	86T	299	$ .01	$ .05
Smith, Bryn	87T	505	$ .01	$ .04
Smith, Bryn	88T	161	$ .01	$ .04
Smith, Bryn	89T	464	$ .01	$ .03
Smith, Bryn	90T	352	$ .01	$ .03

TOPPS

Player	Year	No.	VG	EX/MT
Smith, Bryn	90TTR	117	$ .01	$ .05
Smith, Bryn	91T	743	$ .01	$ .03
Smith, Bryn	91TSC	17	$ .05	$ .25
Smith, Bryn	92T	31	$ .01	$ .03
Smith, Bryn	92TSC	368	$ .01	$ .10
Smith, Bubba	93T	423	$ .10	$ .75
Smith, Charlie	62T	283	$ .75	$3.00
Smith, Charley (ie)	63T	424	$1.00	$4.00
Smith, Charlie	64T	519	$1.00	$4.00
Smith, Charlie	65T	22	$ .35	$1.40
Smith, Charlie	66T	358	$ .50	$2.00
Smith, Charlie	67T	257	$ .50	$2.00
Smith, Charlie	68T	596	$ .70	$2.80
Smith, Charlie	69T	538	$ .40	$1.60
Smith, Dan	93T	607	$ .01	$ .15
Smith, Dave	81T	534	$ .05	$ .20
Smith, Dave	82T	761	$ .01	$ .15
Smith, Dave	83T	247	$ .01	$ .08
Smith, Dave	84T	361	$ .01	$ .06
Smith, Dave	85T	123	$ .01	$ .06
Smith, Dave	86T	408	$ .01	$ .05
Smith, Dave	87T	50	$ .01	$ .04
Smith, Dave	88T	520	$ .01	$ .04
Smith, Dave	89T	305	$ .01	$ .03
Smith, Dave	90T	746	$ .01	$ .03
Smith, Dave	91T	215	$ .01	$ .03
Smith, Dave	91TSC	345	$ .05	$ .25
Smith, Dave	91TTR	110	$ .01	$ .05
Smith, Dave	92T	601	$ .01	$ .03
Smith, Dave	92TSC	219	$ .01	$ .10
Smith, Dick	64T	398	$1.00	$4.00
Smith, Dick	65T	579	$2.50	$10.00
Smith, Dwight	89TTR	113	$ .01	$ .10
Smith, Dwight	90T	311	$ .01	$ .03
Smith, Dwight	91T	463	$ .01	$ .03
Smith, Dwight	91TSC	181	$ .05	$ .25
Smith, Dwight	92T	168	$ .01	$ .03
Smith, Dwight	92TSC	196	$ .01	$ .10
Smith, Dwight	93T	688	$ .01	$ .03
Smith, Dwight	93TSC	278	$ .01	$ .10
Smith, Frank	52T	179	$7.00	$28.00
Smith, Frank	53T	116	$4.00	$16.00
Smith, Frank	54T	71	$7.50	$30.00
Smith, Frank	55T	204	$6.25	$25.00
Smith, Frank	91TA53	116	$ .01	$ .15
Smith, George	65T	483	$1.25	$5.00
Smith, George	66T	542	$3.75	$15.00
Smith, George	67T	444	$ .60	$2.40
Smith, Greg	91T	560	$ .01	$ .03
Smith, Greg	91TSC	554	$ .05	$ .25
Smith, Hal	55T	8	$2.25	$9.00
Smith, Hal	56T	62	$2.00	$8.00
Smith, Hal	56T	283	$3.00	$12.00
Smith, Hal	57T	41	$2.00	$8.00
Smith, Hal	57T	111	$2.00	$8.00
Smith, Hal	58T	257	$1.25	$5.00
Smith, Hal	58T	273	$1.25	$5.00
Smith, Hal	59T	227	$1.00	$4.00
Smith, Hal	59T	497	$1.00	$4.00
Smith, Hal	60T	48	$ .85	$3.40
Smith, Hal	60T	84	$ .85	$3.40
Smith, Hal	61T	242	$ .60	$2.40
Smith, Hal	61T	549	$7.50	$30.00
Smith, Hal	62T	492	$1.50	$6.00
Smith, Hal	63T	153	$ .50	$2.00
Smith, Hal	64T	233	$ .65	$2.60
Smith, Jack	63T	496	$3.00	$12.00
Smith, Jack	64T	378	$1.00	$4.00
Smith, Jimmy	83T	122	$ .01	$ .08
Smith, Keith	78T	710	$ .15	$ .60
Smith, Lee	82T	452	$2.50	$10.00
Smith, Lee	83T	699	$ .75	$3.00
Smith, Lee	84T	176	$ .10	$ .75
Smith, Lee	85T	511	$ .05	$ .35
Smith, Lee	86T	355	$ .05	$ .25

Player	Year	No.	VG	EX/MT
Smith, Lee	87T	23	$ .01	$ .15
Smith, Lee	88T	240	$ .01	$ .10
Smith, Lee	88TTR	110	$ .01	$ .15
Smith, Lee	89T	760	$ .01	$ .03
Smith, Lee	90T	495	$ .01	$ .03
Smith, Lee	90TTR	118	$ .01	$ .05
Smith, Lee	91T	660	$ .01	$ .03
Smith, Lee	91TSC	42	$ .10	$ .40
Smith, Lee	92T	565	$ .01	$ .03
Smith, Lee	92TAS	396	$ .01	$ .10
Smith, Lee	92TSC	180	$ .01	$ .10
Smith, Lee	93T	12	$ .01	$ .03
Smith, Lee	93T	411	$ .01	$ .03
Smith, Lonnie	79T	722	$ .50	$2.00

Player	Year	No.	VG	EX/MT
Smith, Lonnie	81T	317	$ .10	$ .50
Smith, Lonnie	82T	127	$ .05	$ .25
Smith, Lonnie	82TTR	108	$ .05	$ .25
Smith, Lonnie	83T	465	$ .05	$ .20
Smith, Lonnie	83T	561	$ .01	$ .08
Smith, Lonnie	84T	186	$ .01	$ .06
Smith, Lonnie	84T	580	$ .01	$ .15
Smith, Lonnie	85T	255	$ .01	$ .06
Smith, Lonnie	85TTR	109	$ .01	$ .10
Smith, Lonnie	86T	617	$ .01	$ .05
Smith, Lonnie	87T	69	$ .01	$ .04
Smith, Lonnie	88T	777	$ .01	$ .04
Smith, Lonnie	89TTR	114	$ .01	$ .05
Smith, Lonnie	90T	152	$ .01	$ .03
Smith, Lonnie	91T	306	$ .01	$ .03
Smith, Lonnie	91TSC	97	$ .05	$ .25
Smith, Lonnie	92T	467	$ .01	$ .03
Smith, Lonnie	92TSC	282	$ .01	$ .10
Smith, Mayo	55T	130	$2.25	$9.00
Smith, Mayo	56T	60	$2.00	$8.00
Smith, Mayo	67T	321	$ .60	$2.40
Smith, Mayo	68T	544	$1.00	$4.00
Smith, Mayo	69T	40	$ .35	$1.40
Smith, Mayo	70T	313	$ .35	$1.40
Smith, Mike	90T	249	$ .01	$ .03
Smith, Mike	90T	552	$ .01	$ .10
Smith, Ozzie	79T	116	$17.50	$70.00
Smith, Ozzie	80T	393	$4.50	$18.00

TOPPS

Player	Year	No.	VG	EX/MT
Smith, Ozzie	81T	254	$1.25	$5.00
Smith, Ozzie	81TRB	207	$ .10	$1.00
Smith, Ozzie	82T	95	$ .75	$3.00
Smith, Ozzie	82TTR	109	$4.50	$18.00
Smith, Ozzie	83T	540	$ .20	$2.00
Smith, Ozzie	84T	130	$ .10	$1.00
Smith, Ozzie	84TAS	389	$ .05	$ .25
Smith, Ozzie	85T	605	$ .10	$ .75
Smith, Ozzie	85TAS	715	$ .05	$ .25
Smith, Ozzie	86T	730	$ .05	$ .35
Smith, Ozzie	86TAS	704	$ .05	$ .20
Smith, Ozzie	87T	749	$ .05	$ .20
Smith, Ozzie	87TAS	598	$ .01	$ .10
Smith, Ozzie	88T	460	$ .01	$ .10
Smith, Ozzie	88TAS	400	$ .01	$ .10
Smith, Ozzie	89T	230	$ .01	$ .10
Smith, Ozzie	89TAS	389	$ .01	$ .10
Smith, Ozzie	90T	590	$ .01	$ .10
Smith, Ozzie	90TAS	400	$ .01	$ .10
Smith, Ozzie	91T	130	$ .01	$ .10
Smith, Ozzie	91TSC	154	$ .10	$1.00
Smith, Ozzie	92T	760	$ .01	$ .10
Smith, Ozzie	92TSC	680	$ .05	$ .25
Smith, Ozzie	93T	40	$ .01	$ .03
Smith, Paul	54T	11	$3.75	$15.00
Smith, Paul	57T	345	$5.00	$20.00
Smith, Paul	58T	269	$1.25	$5.00
Smith, Pete	64T	428	$1.00	$4.00
Smith, Pete	88TTR	111	$ .10	$ .75
Smith, Pete	89T	537	$ .01	$ .10
Smith, Pete	90T	771	$ .01	$ .03
Smith, Pete	91T	383	$ .01	$ .03
Smith, Pete	91TSC	519	$ .10	$ .50
Smith, Pete	92T	226	$ .01	$ .03
Smith, Pete	92TSC	632	$ .01	$ .10
Smith, Pete	93T	413	$ .01	$ .03
Smith, Pete	93TSC	237	$ .01	$ .10
Smith, Ray	84T	46	$ .01	$ .06
Smith, Reggie	67T	314	$1.75	$7.00
Smith, Reggie	68T	61	$ .50	$2.00
Smith, Reggie	69T	660	$1.00	$4.00
Smith, Reggie	70T	62	$ .75	$3.00
Smith, Reggie	70T	215	$ .50	$2.00
Smith, Reggie	71T	305	$ .50	$2.00
Smith, Reggie	72T	88	$ .75	$3.00
Smith, Reggie	72T	565	$ .40	$1.60
Smith, Reggie	72TIA	566	$ .40	$1.60
Smith, Reggie	73T	40	$ .20	$ .80
Smith, Reggie	74T	285	$ .10	$ .40
Smith, Reggie	75T	490	$ .10	$ .40
Smith, Reggie	76T	215	$ .05	$ .25
Smith, Reggie	77T	345	$ .05	$ .20
Smith, Reggie	78T	168	$ .04	$ .16
Smith, Reggie	79T	465	$ .05	$ .20
Smith, Reggie	80T	695	$ .01	$ .10
Smith, Reggie	81T	75	$ .01	$ .08
Smith, Reggie	82T	545	$ .01	$ .00
Smith, Reggie	82TSA	546	$ .01	$ .07
Smith, Reggie	82TTR	110	$ .01	$ .10
Smith, Reggie	83T	282	$ .05	$ .35
Smith, Reggie	83T	283	$ .01	$ .08
Smith, Roy	85T	381	$ .01	$ .06
Smith, Roy	86T	9	$ .01	$ .05
Smith, Roy	90T	672	$ .01	$ .03
Smith, Roy	91T	503	$ .01	$ .03
Smith, Tommy	74T	606	$ .10	$ .40
Smith, Tommy	75T	619	$ .10	$ .40
Smith, Tommy	77T	14	$ .05	$ .20
Smith, Willie	65T	85	$ .35	$1.40
Smith, Willie	66T	438	$ .65	$2.60
Smith, Willie	67T	397	$ .60	$2.40
Smith, Willie	68T	568	$ .70	$2.80
Smith, Willie	69T	198	$ .35	$1.40
Smith, Willie	70T	318	$ .35	$1.40
Smith, Willie	71T	457	$ .50	$2.00
Smith, Zane	86T	167	$ .01	$ .10
Smith, Zane	87T	544	$ .01	$ .04
Smith, Zane	88T	297	$ .01	$ .04
Smith, Zane	89T	688	$ .01	$ .03
Smith, Zane	90T	48	$ .01	$ .03
Smith, Zane	91T	441	$ .01	$ .03
Smith, Zane	91TSC	260	$ .05	$ .25
Smith, Zane	92T	345	$ .01	$ .03
Smith, Zane	92TSC	807	$ .01	$ .10
Smith, Zane	93T	560	$ .01	$ .03
Smithson, Mike	83TTR	106	$ .01	$ .10
Smithson, Mike	84T	89	$ .01	$ .06
Smithson, Mike	84TTR	110	$ .01	$ .15
Smithson, Mike	85T	483	$ .01	$ .06
Smithson, Mike	86T	695	$ .01	$ .05
Smithson, Mike	87T	225	$ .01	$ .04
Smithson, Mike	88T	554	$ .01	$ .04
Smithson, Mike	89T	377	$ .01	$ .03
Smithson, Mike	90T	188	$ .01	$ .03
Smoltz, John	89T	382	$ .10	$ .50
Smoltz, John	90T	535	$ .05	$ .20
Smoltz, John	91T	157	$ .01	$ .10
Smoltz, John	91TSC	365	$ .15	$1.50
Smoltz, John	92T	245	$ .01	$ .10
Smoltz, John	92TSC	459	$ .05	$ .25
Smoltz, John	93T	35	$ .01	$ .03
Snell, Nate	85TTR	110	$ .01	$ .15
Snell, Nate	86T	521	$ .01	$ .05
Snell, Nate	87T	86	$ .01	$ .04
Snider, Duke	51Trb	38	$16.25	$65.00
Snider, Duke	52T	37	$65.00	$260.00
Snider, Duke	54T	32	$36.25	$145.00
Snider, Duke	55T	210	$130.00	$520.00
Snider, Duke	56T	150	$35.00	$140.00
Snider, Duke	57T	170	$25.00	$100.00
Snider, Duke	57T	400	$50.00	$200.00
Snider, Duke	58T	88	$17.75	$75.00
Snider, Duke	58T	314	$6.00	$24.00
Snider, Duke	58T	436	$17.50	$70.00
Snider, Duke	59T	20	$15.00	$60.00
Snider, Duke	59T	468	$4.00	$16.00
Snider, Duke	60T	493	$15.00	$60.00
Snider, Duke	61T	443	$11.00	$44.00

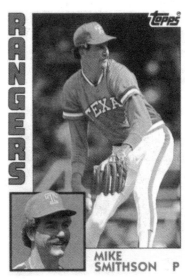

MIKE SMITHSON P

TOPPS

Player	Year	No.	VG	EX/MT
Snider, Duke	62T	500	$12.50	$50.00
Snider, Duke	63T	68	$3.00	$12.00
Snider, Duke	63T	550	$20.00	$80.00
Snider, Duke	64T	155	$8.00	$32.00
Snider, Duke	91TA53	327	$.25	$2.50
Snow, J. T.	93T	422	$.15	$1.50
Snyder, Brian	86T	174	$.01	$.05
Snyder, Cory	85T	403	$.10	$1.00
Snyder, Cory	87T	192	$.01	$.10
Snyder, Cory	88T	620	$.01	$.04
Snyder, Cory	89T	80	$.01	$.03
Snyder, Cory	90T	770	$.01	$.03
Snyder, Cory	91T	323	$.01	$.03
Snyder, Cory	91TSC	488	$.05	$.25
Snyder, Cory	91TTR	111	$.01	$.05
Snyder, Cory	92TSC	772	$.01	$.10
Snyder, Cory	92TTR	107	$.01	$.05
Snyder, Cory	93T	254	$.01	$.03
Snyder, Gene	59T	522	$4.00	$16.00
Snyder, Jerry	57T	22	$2.00	$8.00
Snyder, Jim	88TTR	112	$.01	$.05
Snyder, Jim	89T	44	$.01	$.03
Snyder, Russ	60T	81	$.85	$3.40
Snyder, Russ	61T	143	$.60	$2.40
Snyder, Russ	62T	64	$.60	$2.40
Snyder, Russ	63T	543	$2.25	$9.00
Snyder, Russ	64T	126	$.50	$2.00
Snyder, Russ	65T	204	$.50	$2.00
Snyder, Russ	66T	562	$3.75	$15.00
Snyder, Russ	67T	405	$.60	$2.40
Snyder, Russ	68T	504	$.75	$3.00
Snyder, Russ	69T	201	$.35	$1.40
Snyder, Russ	70T	347	$.35	$1.40
Snyder, Russ	71T	653	$1.50	$6.00
Soderholm, Eric	73T	577	$.60	$2.40
Soderholm, Eric	74T	503	$.10	$.40
Soderholm, Eric	75T	54	$.10	$.40
Soderholm, Eric	76T	214	$.05	$.25
Soderholm, Eric	77T	273	$.05	$.20
Soderholm, Eric	78T	602	$.04	$.16
Soderholm, Eric	79T	186	$.03	$.12
Soderholm, Eric	80T	441	$.01	$.10
Soderholm, Eric	81T	383	$.01	$.08

Player	Year	No.	VG	EX/MT
Soff, Ray	87T	671	$.01	$.04
Sofield, Rick	79T	709	$.25	$1.00
Sofield, Rick	80T	669	$.05	$.30
Sofield, Rick	81T	278	$.01	$.08
Sofield, Rick	82T	42	$.05	$.20
Sojo, Luis	90T	594	$.01	$.10
Sojo, Luis	91T	26	$.01	$.03
Sojo, Luis	91TSC	507	$.05	$.25
Sojo, Luis	91TTR	112	$.01	$.05
Sojo, Luis	92T	206	$.01	$.03
Sojo, Luis	92TSC	373	$.01	$.10
Sojo, Luis	93T	347	$.01	$.03
Sojo, Luis	93TSC	27	$.01	$.10
Solaita, Tony	75T	389	$.10	$.40
Solaita, Tony	76T	121	$.10	$.40
Solaita, Tony	77T	482	$.05	$.20
Solaita, Tony	78T	557	$.04	$.16
Solaita, Tony	79T	18	$.03	$.12
Solaita, Tony	80T	407	$.01	$.10
Solano, Julio	85T	353	$.01	$.06
Solis, Marcelino	59T	214	$1.00	$4.00
Solomon, Eddie	75T	624	$.10	$.40
Solomon, Eddie "Buddy"	78T	598	$.04	$.16
Solomon, Buddy	79T	156	$.03	$.12
Solomon, Buddy	80T	346	$.01	$.10
Solomon, Buddy	81T	298	$.01	$.08
Solomon, Buddy	82T	73	$.01	$.08
Solomon, Buddy	82T	696	$.01	$.08
Sorensen, Lary	78T	569	$.04	$.16
Sorensen, Lary	79T	303	$.03	$.12
Sorensen, Lary	80T	154	$.01	$.10
Sorensen, Lary	81T	379	$.01	$.08
Sorensen, Lary	81TTR	831	$.01	$.15
Sorensen, Lary	82T	689	$.01	$.08
Sorensen, Lary	82TTR	111	$.01	$.10
Sorensen, Lary	83T	48	$.01	$.08
Sorensen, Lary	84T	286	$.01	$.06
Sorensen, Lary	84T	546	$.01	$.06
Sorensen, Lary	84TTR	111	$.01	$.15
Sorensen, Lary	86T	744	$.01	$.05
Sorrell, Bill	66T	254	$32.50	$130.00
Sorrell, Bill	67T	341	$.60	$2.40
Sorrell, Billy	71T	17	$.25	$1.00
Sorrento, Paul	90TTR	119	$.05	$.25
Sorrento, Paul	91T	654	$.01	$.03
Sorrento, Paul	91TSC	408	$.10	$.75
Sorrento, Paul	92T	546	$.01	$.03
Sorrento, Paul	92TSC	707	$.01	$.10
Sorrento, Paul	92TTR	108	$.01	$.05
Sorrento, Paul	93T	264	$.01	$.03
Sorrento, Paul	93TSC	194	$.01	$.10
Sosa, Elias	74T	54	$.10	$.40
Sosa, Elias	75T	398	$.10	$.40
Sosa, Elias	76T	364	$.05	$.25
Sosa, Elias	77T	558	$.05	$.20
Sosa, Elias	78T	694	$.04	$.16
Sosa, Elias	79T	78	$.03	$.12
Sosa, Elias	80T	293	$.01	$.10
Sosa, Elias	81T	181	$.01	$.08
Sosa, Elias	82T	414	$.01	$.08
Sosa, Elias	82TTR	112	$.01	$.10
Sosa, Elias	83T	753	$.01	$.08
Sosa, Elias	83TTR	107	$.01	$.10
Sosa, Elias	84T	503	$.01	$.06
Sosa, Jose	76T	591	$.05	$.25
Sosa, Sammy	90T	692	$.05	$.25
Sosa, Sammy	91T	414	$.01	$.15
Sosa, Sammy	91TSC	6	$.10	$.50
Sosa, Sammy	92T	94	$.01	$.03
Sosa, Sammy	92TSC	628	$.01	$.10
Sosa, Sammy	92TTR	109	$.01	$.05
Sosa, Sammy	93T	156	$.01	$.03
Soto, Mario	78T	427	$.10	$.40
Soto, Mario	80T	622	$.05	$.20
Soto, Mario	81T	354	$.01	$.08

TOPPS

Player	Year	No.	VG	EX/MT
Soto, Mario	82T	63	$.01	$.08
Soto, Mario	83T	215	$.01	$.08
Soto, Mario	83T	351	$.01	$.08
Soto, Mario	84T	160	$.01	$.06
Soto, Mario	84T	756	$.01	$.06
Soto, Mario	85T	495	$.01	$.06
Soto, Mario	86T	725	$.01	$.05
Soto, Mario	87T	517	$.01	$.04
Soto, Mario	88T	666	$.01	$.04
Souchock, Steve	52T	234	$7.00	$28.00
Spahn, Warren	51Trb	30	$13.75	$55.00
Spahn, Warren	52T	33	$58.75	$235.00
Spahn, Warren	53T	147	$37.50	$150.00
Spahn, Warren	54T	20	$25.00	$100.00
Spahn, Warren	55T	31	$21.25	$85.00
Spahn, Warren	56T	10	$20.00	$80.00
Spahn, Warren	57T	90	$16.25	$65.00
Spahn, Warren	58T	270	$15.00	$60.00
Spahn, Warren	58TAS	494	$4.50	$18.00
Spahn, Warren	59T	40	$13.75	$55.00
Spahn, Warren	59TAS	571	$10.00	$40.00
Spahn, Warren	60T	230	$1.75	$7.00
Spahn, Warren	60T	445	$12.50	$50.00
Spahn, Warren	61T	47	$.75	$3.00
Spahn, Warren	61T	200	$8.50	$34.00
Spahn, Warren	61TAS	589	$32.50	$130.00
Spahn, Warren	62T	56	$1.50	$6.00
Spahn, Warren	62T	58	$1.50	$6.00
Spahn, Warren	62T	100	$7.00	$28.00
Spahn, Warren	62T	312	$2.25	$9.00
Spahn, Warren	62TAS	399	$3.50	$14.00
Spahn, Warren	63T	320	$9.50	$38.00
Spahn, Warren	64T	3	$2.50	$10.00
Spahn, Warren	64T	400	$10.00	$40.00
Spahn, Warren	65T	205	$6.50	$26.00
Spahn, Warren	73T	449	$.50	$2.00

Player	Year	No.	VG	EX/MT
Spahn, Warren	91TA53	147	$.15	$1.50
Spangler, Al	60T	143	$.75	$3.00
Spangler, Al	61T	73	$.60	$2.40
Spangler, Al	62T	556	$3.50	$14.00
Spangler, Al	63T	77	$.50	$2.00
Spangler, Al	64T	406	$1.00	$4.00
Spangler, Al	65T	164	$.35	$1.40
Spangler, Al	66T	173	$.50	$2.00
Spangler, Al	68T	451	$.35	$1.40
Spangler, Al	69T	268	$.50	$2.00
Spangler, Al	70T	714	$1.25	$5.00
Spangler, Al	74T	354	$.10	$.40
Spanswick, Bill	64T	287	$7.50	$30.00
Spanswick, Bill	65T	356	$.50	$2.00
Sparma, Joe	64T	512	$2.50	$10.00
Sparma, Joe	65T	587	$1.40	$5.60
Sparma, Joe	66T	267	$.50	$2.00
Sparma, Joe	67T	13	$.40	$1.60
Sparma, Joe	68T	505	$1.00	$4.00
Sparma, Joe	69T	488	$.30	$1.20
Sparma, Joe	70T	243	$.20	$.80
Speake, Bob	56T	66	$2.00	$8.00
Speake, Bob	57T	339	$5.00	$20.00
Speake, Bob	58T	437	$1.00	$4.00
Speake, Bob	59T	526	$4.00	$16.00
Speck, Cliff	87T	269	$.01	$.04
Speckenbach, Paul	64T	548	$2.25	$9.00
Speed, Horace	79T	438	$.03	$.12
Spehr, Tim	92T	342	$.01	$.03
Spehr, Tim	92TSC	96	$.05	$.25
Speier, Chris	72T	165	$.25	$1.00
Speier, Chris	72TIA	166	$.20	$.80
Speier, Chris	73T	273	$.10	$.40
Speier, Chris	73T	345	$.10	$.40
Speier, Chris	74T	129	$.10	$.40
Speier, Chris	74TAS	335	$.15	$.60
Speier, Chris	75T	505	$.10	$.40
Speier, Chris	76T	630	$.05	$.25
Speier, Chris	77T	515	$.05	$.20
Speier, Chris	78T	221	$.04	$.16
Speier, Chris	79T	426	$.03	$.12
Speier, Chris	80T	319	$.01	$.10
Speier, Chris	81T	97	$.01	$.08
Speier, Chris	82T	198	$.01	$.08
Speier, Chris	83T	768	$.01	$.08
Speier, Chris	84T	678	$.01	$.06
Speier, Chris	85T	577	$.01	$.06
Speier, Chris	85TTR	111	$.01	$.10
Speier, Chris	86T	212	$.01	$.05
Speier, Chris	87T	424	$.01	$.04
Speier, Chris	87TTR	115	$.01	$.05
Speier, Chris	88T	329	$.01	$.04
Speier, Chris	89T	94	$.01	$.03
Speier, Chris	90T	753	$.01	$.03
Spence, Bob	71T	186	$.25	$1.00
Spencer, Daryl	56T	277	$2.50	$10.00
Spencer, Daryl	57T	49	$2.00	$8.00
Spencer, Daryl	58T	68	$2.00	$8.00
Spencer, Daryl	59T	443	$1.00	$4.00
Spencer, Daryl	60T	368	$.75	$3.00
Spencer, Daryl	61T	357	$.60	$2.40
Spencer, Daryl	61T	451	$1.35	$5.40
Spencer, Daryl	62T	197	$.75	$3.00
Spencer, Daryl	63T	502	$3.00	$12.00
Spencer, George	52T	346	$43.75	$175.00
Spencer, George	53T	115	$6.25	$25.00
Spencer, George	91TA53	115	$.01	$.15
Spencer, Jim	70T	255	$.20	$.80
Spencer, Jim	71T	78	$.25	$1.00
Spencer, Jim	72T	419	$.25	$1.00
Spencer, Jim	73T	319	$.10	$.40
Spencer, Jim	74T	580	$.10	$.40
Spencer, Jim	75T	387	$.10	$.40
Spencer, Jim	76T	83	$.05	$.25
Spencer, Jim	76TTR	83	$.05	$.25
Spencer, Jim	77T	648	$.05	$.20
Spencer, Jim	78T	182	$.04	$.16
Spencer, Jim	79T	599	$.03	$.12
Spencer, Jim	80T	278	$.01	$.08
Spencer, Jim	81T	435	$.01	$.08
Spencer, Jim	81TTR	832	$.01	$.15
Spencer, Jim	82T	729	$.01	$.08

TOPPS

Player	Year	No.	VG	EX/MT	Player	Year	No.	VG	EX/MT
Sperring, Rob	76T	323	$ .05	$ .25	Spilman, Harry	86T	352	$ .01	$ .05
Sperring, Rob	78T	514	$ .04	$ .16	Spilman, Harry	87T	64	$ .01	$ .04
Spiers, Billy	89TTR	115	$ .01	$ .10	Spilman, Harry	88T	217	$ .01	$ .04
Spiers, Billy	90T	538	$ .01	$ .03	Spinks, Scipio	70T	492	$ .35	$1.40
Spiers, Billy	91T	284	$ .01	$ .03	Spinks, Scipio	71T	747	$1.10	$4.40
Spiers, Billy	91TSC	360	$ .05	$ .25	Spinks, Scipio	72T	202	$ .10	$ .40
Spiers, Billy	92T	742	$ .01	$ .03	Spinks, Scipio	73T	417	$ .25	$1.00
Spiers, Billy	92TSC	379	$ .01	$ .10	Spinks, Scipio	74T	576	$ .10	$ .40
Spiers, Billy	93T	619	$ .01	$ .03	Splittorff, Paul	71T	247	$ .25	$1.00
Spiezio, Ed	67T	128	$ .40	$1.60	Splittorff, Paul	72T	315	$ .10	$ .40
Spiezio, Ed	68T	349	$ .35	$1.40	Splittorff, Paul	73T	48	$ .10	$ .40
Spiezio, Ed	69T	249	$ .50	$2.00	Splittorff, Paul	74T	225	$ .10	$ .40
Spiezio, Ed	70T	718	$1.25	$5.00	Splittorff, Paul	75T	340	$ .10	$ .40
Spiezio, Ed	71T	6	$ .25	$1.00	Splittorff, Paul	76T	43	$ .05	$ .25
Spiezio, Ed	72T	504	$ .25	$1.00	Splittorff, Paul	77T	534	$ .05	$ .20
Spiezio, Wayne	65T	431	$1.25	$5.00	Splittorff, Paul	78T	638	$ .04	$ .16
Spikes, Charlie	73T	614	$12.50	$50.00	Splittorff, Paul	79T	183	$ .03	$ .12
Spikes, Charlie	74T	58	$ .10	$ .40	Splittorff, Paul	80T	409	$ .01	$ .10
Spikes, Charlie	75T	135	$ .10	$ .40	Splittorff, Paul	81T	218	$ .01	$ .08
Spikes, Charlie	76T	408	$ .05	$ .25	Splittorff, Paul	82T	759	$ .01	$ .08
Spikes, Charlie	77T	168	$ .05	$ .20	Splittorff, Paul	83T	316	$ .01	$ .08
Spikes, Charlie	78T	459	$ .04	$ .16	Splittorff, Paul	84T	52	$ .01	$ .06
Spikes, Charlie	80T	294	$ .01	$ .10	Spooner, Karl	55T	90	$3.00	$12.00
Spillner, Dan	75T	222	$ .10	$ .40	Spooner, Karl	56T	83	$2.00	$8.00
Spillner, Dan	76T	557	$ .05	$ .25	Sprague, Ed	69T	638	$ .40	$1.60
Spillner, Dan	77T	182	$ .05	$ .20	Sprague, Ed	72T	121	$ .10	$ .40
Spillner, Dan	78T	488	$ .04	$ .16	Sprague, Ed	75T	76	$ .10	$ .40
Spillner, Dan	79T	359	$ .03	$ .12	Sprague, Ed	88TTR	113	$ .15	$1.50
					Sprague, Ed	91TSC	387	$ .10	$1.00
					Sprague, Ed	92T	516	$ .01	$ .03
					Sprague, Ed	92TSC	445	$ .01	$ .10
					Sprague, Ed	93T	659	$ .01	$ .03
					Sprague, Ed	93TSC	90	$ .01	$ .10
					Spriggs, George	67T	472	$1.50	$6.00
					Spriggs, George	68T	314	$ .35	$1.40
					Spriggs, George	69T	662	$ .40	$1.60
					Spriggs, George	71T	411	$ .50	$2.00
					Spring, Jack	62T	257	$ .75	$3.00
					Spring, Jack	63T	572	$2.25	$9.00
					Spring, Jack	64T	71	$ .50	$2.00
					Springer, Russ	93T	686	$ .01	$ .10
					Sprowl, Bobby	81T	82	$ .01	$ .08
					Sprowl, Bobby	82T	441	$ .01	$ .08
					Squires, Mike	79T	704	$ .15	$ .60
					Squires, Mike	80T	466	$ .01	$ .10
					Squires, Mike	81T	292	$ .01	$ .08
					Squires, Mike	82T	398	$ .01	$ .08
					Squires, Mike	83T	669	$ .01	$ .08
					Squires, Mike	84T	72	$ .01	$ .06
					Squires, Mike	85T	543	$ .01	$ .06
					St. Claire, Ebba	52T	393	$43.75	$175.00
					St. Claire, Ebba	53T	91	$4.00	$16.00
					St. Claire, Ebba	91TA53	91	$ .01	$ .15
					St. Claire, Randy	86T	89	$ .01	$ .05
					St. Claire, Randy	87T	467	$ .01	$ .04
					St. Claire, Randy	88T	279	$ .01	$ .04
					St. Claire, Randy	89T	666	$ .01	$ .03
					St. Claire, Randy	90T	503	$ .01	$ .03
					Stablein, George	81T	356	$ .01	$ .08
					Staehle, Marv	65T	41	$ .35	$1.40

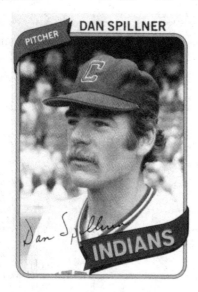

Player	Year	No.	VG	EX/MT	Player	Year	No.	VG	EX/MT
Spillner, Dan	80T	38	$ .01	$ .10	Staehle, Marv	66T	164	$ .50	$2.00
Spillner, Dan	81T	276	$ .01	$ .08	Staehle, Marv	69T	394	$1.00	$4.00
Spillner, Dan	82T	664	$ .01	$ .08	Staehle, Marv	71T	663	$1.10	$4.40
Spillner, Dan	83T	725	$ .01	$ .08	Stafford, Bill	61T	213	$ .60	$2.40
Spillner, Dan	84T	91	$ .01	$ .06	Stafford, Bill	62T	55	$ .60	$2.40
Spillner, Dan	85T	169	$ .01	$ .06	Stafford, Bill	62T	570	$7.00	$28.00
Spillner, Dan	86T	423	$ .01	$ .05	Stafford, Bill	63T	155	$ .50	$2.00
Spilman, Harry	79T	717	$ .10	$ .40	Stafford, Bill	63T	331	$ .90	$3.60
Spilman, Harry	80T	677	$ .01	$ .10	Stafford, Bill	64T	299	$ .65	$2.60
Spilman, Harry	81T	94	$ .01	$ .08	Stafford, Bill	65T	281	$ .50	$2.00
Spilman, Harry	81TTR	833	$ .01	$ .15	Stafford, Jerry	93T	683	$ .01	$ .03
Spilman, Harry	82T	509	$ .01	$ .08	Staggs, Steve	78T	521	$ .04	$ .16
Spilman, Harry	83T	193	$ .01	$ .08	Stahl, Larry	66T	107	$ .35	$1.40
Spilman, Harry	84T	612	$ .01	$ .06	Stahl, Larry	69T	271	$ .50	$2.00
Spilman, Harry	85T	482	$ .01	$ .06	Stahl, Larry	70T	494	$ .35	$1.40

TOPPS

Player	Year	No.	VG	EX/MT
Stahl, Larry	71T	711	$1.50	$6.00
Stahl, Larry	72T	782	$1.25	$5.00
Stahl, Larry	73T	533	$ .60	$2.40
Stahl, Larry	74T	507	$ .10	$ .40
Stahoviak, Scott	92T	66	$ .05	$ .25
Staiger, Roy	76T	592	$2.00	$8.00
Staiger, Roy	77T	281	$ .05	$ .20
Stairs, Matt	92TTR	110	$ .01	$ .10
Staley, Gerry	51Tbb	7	$7.50	$30.00
Staley, Gerald	52T	79	$13.75	$55.00
Staley, Gerald (Gerry)	53T	56	$4.00	$16.00
Staley, Gerald	91TA53	56	$ .01	$ .15
Staley, Jerry	57T	227	$2.00	$8.00
Staley, Jerry	58T	412	$1.00	$4.00
Staley, Jerry	59T	426	$1.00	$4.00
Staley, Gerry (Jerry)	60T	57	$ .85	$3.40
Staley, Jerry	60T	510	$2.75	$11.00
Staley, Jerry	61T	90	$ .60	$2.40
Stallard, Tracy	61T	81	$ .60	$2.40
Stallard, Tracy	62T	567	$6.00	$24.00
Stallard, Tracy	63T	419	$1.00	$4.00
Stallard, Tracy	64T	176	$ .50	$2.00
Stallard, Tracy	65T	491	$1.25	$5.00
Stallard, Tracy	66T	7	$ .35	$1.40
Stallcup, Virgil	52T	69	$13.75	$55.00
Stallcup, Virgil	53T	180	$4.50	$18.00
Stallcup, Virgil	91TA53	180	$ .01	$ .15
Staller, George	73T	136	$ .25	$1.00
Staller, George	74T	307	$ .10	$ .40
Stanek, Al	64T	99	$ .50	$2.00
Stanek, Al	65T	302	$ .50	$2.00
Stanek, Al	66T	437	$ .65	$2.60
Stanfield, Kevin	79T	709	$ .25	$1.00
Stange, Lee	62T	321	$ .75	$3.00
Stange, Lee	63T	246	$ .90	$3.60
Stange, Lee	64T	555	$2.25	$9.00
Stange, Lee	65T	448	$1.25	$5.00
Stange, Lee	66T	371	$ .65	$2.60
Stange, Lee	67T	99	$ .40	$1.60
Stange, Lee	68T	593	$ .70	$2.80
Stange, Lee	69T	148	$ .35	$1.40
Stange, Lee	70T	447	$ .35	$1.40
Stange, Lee	73T	131	$ .20	$ .80
Stange, Lee	74T	403	$ .10	$ .40
Stanhouse, Don	73T	352	$ .10	$ .40
Stanhouse, Don	75T	493	$ .10	$ .40
Stanhouse, Don	77T	274	$ .05	$ .20
Stanhouse, Don	78T	629	$ .04	$ .16
Stanhouse, Don	79T	119	$ .03	$ .12
Stanhouse, Don	80T	517	$ .01	$ .10
Stanhouse, Don	81T	24	$ .01	$ .08
Stanicek, Pete	88TTR	114	$ .01	$ .10
Stanicek, Pete	89T	497	$ .01	$ .03
Stankeiwicz, Andy	92TTR	111	$ .01	$ .15
Stankiewicz, Andy	92T	179	$ .05	$ .20
Stankiewicz, Andy	92TSC	725	$ .01	$ .15
Stankiewicz, Andy	93T	348	$ .01	$ .10
Stankiewicz, Andy	93TSC	105	$ .01	$ .10
Stanky, Eddie	51Trb	48	$2.50	$10.00
Stanky, Eddie	52T	76	$15.00	$60.00
Stanky, Eddie	54T	38	$3.75	$15.00
Stanky, Ed "Eddie"	55T	191	$8.00	$32.00
Stanky, Eddie	66T	448	$1.50	$6.00
Stanky, Eddie	67T	81	$ .40	$1.60
Stanky, Eddie	68T	564	$ .70	$2.80
Stanky, Eddie	91TA53	300	$ .05	$ .20
Stanley, Bob	78T	186	$ .05	$ .20
Stanley, Bob	79T	597	$ .03	$ .12
Stanley, Bob	80T	63	$ .01	$ .10
Stanley, Bob	81T	421	$ .01	$ .08
Stanley, Bob	82T	289	$ .01	$ .08
Stanley, Bob	83T	381	$ .01	$ .08
Stanley, Bob	83T	682	$ .01	$ .08
Stanley, Bob	84T	320	$ .01	$ .06
Stanley, Bob	85T	555	$ .01	$ .06
Stanley, Bob	86T	785	$ .01	$ .05
Stanley, Bob	87T	175	$ .01	$ .04
Stanley, Bob	88T	573	$ .01	$ .04
Stanley, Bob	89T	37	$ .01	$ .03
Stanley, Fred	72T	59	$ .10	$ .40
Stanley, Fred	74T	423	$ .10	$ .40
Stanley, Fred	75T	503	$ .10	$ .40
Stanley, Fred	76T	429	$ .05	$ .25
Stanley, Fred	77T	123	$ .05	$ .20
Stanley, Fred	78T	664	$ .04	$ .16
Stanley, Fred	79T	16	$ .03	$ .12
Stanley, Fred	80T	387	$ .01	$ .10
Stanley, Fred	81T	281	$ .01	$ .08
Stanley, Fred	81TTR	834	$ .01	$ .15
Stanley, Fred	82T	787	$ .01	$ .08
Stanley, Fred	83T	513	$ .01	$ .08
Stanley, Mickey	66T	198	$ .75	$3.00
Stanley, Mickey	67T	607	$9.00	$36.00
Stanley, Mickey	68T	129	$ .50	$2.00
Stanley, Mickey	69T	13	$ .35	$1.40
Stanley, Mickey	70T	383	$ .35	$1.40
Stanley, Mickey	71T	524	$1.00	$4.00
Stanley, Mickey	72T	385	$ .10	$ .40
Stanley, Mickey	73T	88	$ .10	$ .40
Stanley, Mickey	74T	530	$ .10	$ .40
Stanley, Mickey	75T	141	$ .10	$ .40
Stanley, Mickey	76T	483	$ .05	$ .25
Stanley, Mickey	77T	533	$ .05	$ .20
Stanley, Mickey	78T	232	$ .04	$ .16
Stanley, Mickey	79T	692	$ .03	$ .12
Stanley, Mike	87TTR	116	$ .01	$ .05
Stanley, Mike	88T	219	$ .01	$ .04
Stanley, Mike	89T	587	$ .01	$ .03
Stanley, Mike	90T	92	$ .01	$ .03
Stanley, Mike	91T	409	$ .01	$ .03
Stanley, Mike	91TSC	526	$ .05	$ .25
Stanley, Mike	92TSC	741	$ .01	$ .10
Stanley, Mike	93T	359	$ .01	$ .03
Stanton, Leroy	72T	141	$ .10	$ .40
Stanton, Leroy	73T	18	$ .10	$ .40
Stanton, Leroy	74T	594	$ .10	$ .40
Stanton, Leroy	75T	342	$ .10	$ .40

Stange, Lee   71T   311 $ .25 $1.00

TOPPS

Player	Year	No.	VG	EX/MT	Player	Year	No.	VG	EX/MT
Stanton, Leroy	76T	152	$ .05	$ .25	Staub, Rusty	81TTR	835	$ .05	$ .30
Stanton, Leroy	77T	226	$ .05	$ .20	Staub, Rusty	82T	270	$ .01	$ .10
Stanton, Leroy	78T	447	$ .04	$ .16	Staub, Rusty	83T	740	$ .01	$ .08
Stanton, Leroy	79T	533	$ .03	$ .12	Staub, Rusty	83T	741	$ .01	$ .08
Stanton, Mike	82T	473	$ .01	$ .08	Staub, Rusty	84T	430	$ .01	$ .10
Stanton, Mike	82TTR	113	$ .01	$ .10	Staub, Rusty	84T	702	$ .05	$ .20
Stanton, Mike	83T	159	$ .01	$ .08	Staub, Rusty	84T	704	$ .01	$ .15
Stanton, Mike	84T	694	$ .01	$ .06	Staub, Rusty	85T	190	$ .01	$ .06
Stanton, Mike	85T	256	$ .01	$ .06	Staub, Rusty	86T	570	$ .01	$ .05
Stanton, Mike	90T	694	$ .05	$ .20	Stearns, John	76T	633	$ .15	$ .60
Stanton, Mike	91T	514	$ .01	$ .03	Stearns, John	77T	119	$ .05	$ .20
Stanton, Mike	91TSC	413	$ .10	$ .40	Stearns, John	78T	334	$ .04	$ .16
Stanton, Mike	92T	788	$ .01	$ .03	Stearns, John	79T	545	$ .03	$ .12
Stanton, Mike	92TSC	344	$ .01	$ .10	Stearns, John	79TRB	205	$ .03	$ .12
Stanton, Mike	93T	88	$ .01	$ .03	Stearns, John	80T	76	$ .01	$ .10
Stanton, Mike	93TSC	38	$ .01	$ .10	Stearns, John	81T	428	$ .01	$ .08
Stapleton, Dave	81T	81	$ .01	$ .08	Stearns, John	82T	743	$ .01	$ .08
Stapleton, Dave	82T	589	$ .01	$ .08	Stearns, John	83T	212	$ .01	$ .08
Stapleton, Dave	83T	239	$ .01	$ .08	Steels, James	88T	117	$ .01	$ .04
Stapleton, Dave	84T	653	$ .01	$ .06	Steenstra, Kennie	91TTR	113	$ .05	$ .25
Stapleton, Dave	85T	322	$ .01	$ .06	Stefero, John	87T	563	$ .01	$ .04
Stapleton, Dave	86T	151	$ .01	$ .05	Steffen, Dave	81T	626	$ .01	$ .08
Stapleton, Dave	87T	507	$ .01	$ .04	Stegman, Dave	79T	706	$ .03	$ .12
Stargell, Willie	63T	553	$60.00	$240.00	Stegman, Dave	84T	664	$ .01	$ .06
Stargell, Willie	64T	342	$11.00	$44.00	Stegman, Dave	85T	194	$ .01	$ .06
Stargell, Willie	65T	377	$7.00	$28.00	Stein, Bill	76T	131	$ .05	$ .25
Stargell, Willie	66T	99	$1.00	$4.00					
Stargell, Willie	66T	255	$4.50	$18.00					
Stargell, Willie	67T	140	$4.50	$18.00					
Stargell, Willie	67T	266	$1.00	$4.00					
Stargell, Willie	68T	86	$2.75	$11.00					
Stargell, Willie	69T	545	$3.50	$14.00					
Stargell, Willie	70T	470	$2.50	$10.00					
Stargell, Willie	71T	230	$2.50	$10.00					
Stargell, Willie	72T	87	$ .75	$3.00					
Stargell, Willie	72T	89	$ .50	$2.00					
Stargell, Willie	72T	343	$ .40	$1.60					
Stargell, Willie	72T	447	$1.50	$6.00					
Stargell, Willie	72TIA	448	$ .75	$3.00					
Stargell, Willie	73T	370	$1.25	$5.00					
Stargell, Willie	74T	100	$1.00	$4.00					
Stargell, Willie	74T	202	$1.25	$5.00					
Stargell, Willie	74T	203	$1.25	$5.00					
Stargell, Willie	75T	100	$1.00	$4.00					
Stargell, Willie	76T	270	$ .75	$3.00					
Stargell, Willie	77T	460	$ .75	$3.00					
Stargell, Willie	78T	510	$ .75	$3.00					
Stargell, Willie	79T	55	$ .75	$3.00					
Stargell, Willie	80T	610	$ .20	$1.75					
Stargell, Willie	81T	380	$ .10	$1.00					
Stargell, Willie	82T	715	$ .10	$ .75					
Stargell, Willie	82TSA	716	$ .05	$ .30					
Starrette, Herm	64T	239	$ .65	$2.60					
Starrette, Herm	65T	539	$1.40	$5.60					
Starrette, Herm	74T	634	$ .25	$1.00					
Staton, Dave	92T	126	$ .10	$1.00					
Staub, Rusty	63T	544	$10.00	$40.00					
Staub, Rusty	64T	109	$2.00	$8.00					
Staub, Rusty	65T	321	$1.25	$5.00	Stein, Bill	77T	334	$ .05	$ .20
Staub, Rusty	66T	106	$1.00	$4.00	Stein, Bill	78T	476	$ .04	$ .16
Staub, Rusty	66T	273	$ .75	$3.00	Stein, Bill	79T	698	$ .03	$ .12
Staub, Rusty	67T	73	$ .75	$3.00	Stein, Bill	80T	226	$ .01	$ .10
Staub, Rusty	68T	300	$ .75	$3.00	Stein, Bill	81T	532	$ .01	$ .08
Staub, Rusty	69T	230	$ .75	$3.00	Stein, Bill	81TTR	836	$ .01	$ .15
Staub, Rusty	70T	585	$1.00	$4.00	Stein, Bill	82T	402	$ .01	$ .08
Staub, Rusty	71T	560	$1.25	$5.00	Stein, Bill	83T	64	$ .01	$ .08
Staub, Rusty	74T	629	$ .25	$1.00	Stein, Bill	84T	758	$ .01	$ .06
Staub, Rusty	75T	90	$ .25	$1.00	Stein, Bill	85T	171	$ .01	$ .06
Staub, Rusty	76T	120	$ .20	$ .80	Stein, Bill	86T	371	$ .01	$ .05
Staub, Rusty	76TTR	120	$ .10	$ .40	Stein, Randy	79T	394	$ .03	$ .12
Staub, Rusty	77T	420	$ .10	$ .40	Stein, Randy	80T	613	$ .01	$ .10
Staub, Rusty	78T	370	$ .05	$ .20	Steinbach, Terry	87TTR	117	$ .05	$ .25
Staub, Rusty	79T	440	$ .05	$ .20	Steinbach, Terry	88T	551	$ .01	$ .04
Staub, Rusty	80T	660	$ .01	$ .10	Steinbach, Terry	89T	725	$ .01	$ .03
Staub, Rusty	81T	80	$ .01	$ .08	Steinbach, Terry	90T	145	$ .01	$ .03

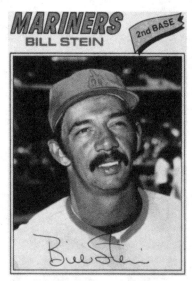

TOPPS

Player	Year	No.	VG	EX/MT
Steinbach, Terry	91T	625	$ .01	$ .03
Steinbach, Terry	91TSC	518	$ .05	$ .25
Steinbach, Terry	92T	234	$ .01	$ .03
Steinbach, Terry	92TSC	22	$ .01	$ .10
Steinbach, Terry	93T	18	$ .01	$ .03
Steinbach, Terry	93TSC	208	$ .01	$ .10
Stelmaszek, Rick	70T	599	$ .75	$3.00
Stelmaszek, Rick	73T	601	$ .75	$3.00
Stelmaszek, Rick	74T	611	$ .10	$ .40
Stelmaszek, Rick	75T	338	$ .10	$ .40
Stengel, Casey	58T	475	$4.50	$18.00
Stengel, Casey	59T	383	$2.00	$8.00
Stengel, Casey	59TAS	552	$8.75	$35.00
Stengel, Casey	60T	227	$5.00	$20.00
Stengel, Casey	62T	29	$4.50	$18.00
Stengel, Casey	63T	43	$1.00	$4.00
Stengel, Casey	63T	233	$4.00	$16.00
Stengel, Casey	64T	324	$3.75	$15.00
Stengel, Casey	64T	393	$1.50	$6.00
Stengel, Casey	65T	187	$3.50	$14.00

CASEY STENGEL — NEW YORK YANKEES

Player	Year	No.	VG	EX/MT
Stengel, Casey	91TA53	325	$ .10	$ .75
Stenhouse, Dave	62T	592	$15.00	$60.00
Stenhouse, Dave	63T	263	$ .90	$3.60
Stenhouse, Dave	64T	498	$1.00	$4.00
Stenhouse, Dave	651	304	$ .50	$2.00
Stenhouse, Dave	85T	141	$ .01	$ .10
Stenhouse, Mike	85T	141	$ .01	$ .10
Stenhouse, Mike	85T	658	$ .01	$ .06
Stenhouse, Mike	85TTR	112	$ .01	$ .10
Stenhouse, Mike	86T	17	$ .01	$ .05
Stennett, Rennie	72T	219	$ .10	$ .40
Stennett, Rennie	73T	348	$ .10	$ .40
Stennett, Rennie	74T	426	$ .10	$ .40
Stennett, Rennie	75T	336	$ .10	$ .40
Stennett, Rennie	76T	425	$ .05	$ .25
Stennett, Rennie	76TRB	6	$ .05	$ .20
Stennett, Rennie	77T	35	$ .05	$ .20
Stennett, Rennie	78T	165	$ .04	$ .16
Stennett, Rennie	79T	687	$ .03	$ .12
Stennett, Rennie	80T	501	$ .01	$ .10
Stennett, Rennie	81T	257	$ .01	$ .08
Stennett, Rennie	82T	84	$ .01	$ .08
Stephen, Buzz	70T	533	$ .35	$1.40

Player	Year	No.	VG	EX/MT
Stephens, Gene	53T	248	$11.25	$45.00
Stephens, Gene	56T	313	$2.50	$10.00
Stephens, Gene	57T	217	$2.00	$8.00
Stephens, Gene	58T	227	$1.25	$5.00
Stephens, Gene	59T	261	$1.00	$4.00
Stephens, Gene	60T	363	$ .75	$3.00
Stephens, Gene	61T	102	$ .60	$2.40
Stephens, Gene	62T	38	$ .60	$2.40
Stephens, Gene	64T	308	$ .65	$2.60
Stephens, Gene	65T	498	$1.25	$5.00
Stephens, Gene	91TA53	248	$ .01	$ .15
Stephens, Verne	51Trb	4	$1.65	$6.60
Stephens, Vern(e)	52T	84	$7.00	$28.00
Stephens, Vern	53T	270	$20.00	$80.00
Stephens, Vern	54T	54	$7.50	$30.00
Stephens, Vern	91TA53	270	$ .01	$ .15
Stephenson, Earl	72T	61	$ .25	$1.00
Stephenson, Jerry	65T	74	$1.75	$7.00
Stephenson, Jerry	66T	396	$ .65	$2.60
Stephenson, Jerry	68T	519	$ .75	$3.00
Stephenson, Jerry	69T	172	$ .35	$1.40
Stephenson, Jerry	71T	488	$ .50	$2.00
Stephenson, John	64T	536	$2.25	$9.00
Stephenson, John	66T	17	$ .35	$1.40
Stephenson, John	67T	522	$1.50	$6.00
Stephenson, John	68T	83	$ .35	$1.40
Stephenson, John	71T	421	$ .50	$2.00
Stephenson, Phil	90T	584	$ .01	$ .03
Stephenson, Phil	91T	726	$ .01	$ .03
Stephenson, Phil	91TSC	420	$ .05	$ .25
Stephenson, Phil	92TSC	684	$ .01	$ .10
Stephenson, Phil	93T	357	$ .01	$ .03
Steve, Lyons	87T	511	$ .01	$ .04
Stevens, Lee	91T	648	$ .01	$ .10
Stevens, Lee	91TSC	293	$ .05	$ .35
Stevens, Lee	92T	702	$ .01	$ .03
Stevens, Lee	92TSC	281	$ .01	$ .10
Stevens, Lee	93T	467	$ .01	$ .03
Stevens, Lee	93TSC	219	$ .01	$ .10
Stevens, Morrie	65T	521	$1.25	$5.00
Stevens, R. C.	58T	470	$1.00	$4.00
Stevens, R. C.	59T	282	$1.00	$4.00
Stevens, R. C.	61T	526	$7.50	$30.00
Steverson, Todd	93T	269	$ .05	$ .20
Stewart, Bunky	55T	136	$2.25	$9.00
Stewart, Dave	82T	213	$1.50	$6.00
Stewart, Dave	83T	532	$ .10	$ .75
Stewart, Dave	84T	352	$ .05	$ .35
Stewart, Dave	85T	723	$ .05	$ .20
Stewart, Dave	86T	689	$ .05	$ .20
Stewart, Dave	87T	14	$ .01	$ .15
Stewart, Dave	88T	476	$ .01	$ .10
Stewart, Dave	89T	145	$ .01	$ .03
Stewart, Dave	90T	270	$ .01	$ .03
Stewart, Dave	91T	580	$ .01	$ .03
Stewart, Dave	91TSC	1	$ .10	$ .50
Stewart, Dave	92T	110	$ .01	$ .03
Stewart, Dave	92TSC	390	$ .01	$ .10
Stewart, Dave	93T	290	$ .01	$ .03
Stewart, Ed	52T	279	$12.50	$50.00
Stewart, Jim	64T	408	$1.00	$4.00
Stewart, Jim	65T	298	$ .50	$2.00
Stewart, Jim	66T	63	$ .35	$1.40
Stewart, Jim	67T	124	$ .40	$1.60
Stewart, Jim	70T	636	$1.25	$5.00
Stewart, Jim	71T	644	$1.50	$6.00
Stewart, Jim	72T	747	$1.25	$5.00
Stewart, Jimmy	73T	351	$ .10	$ .40
Stewart, Sammy	79T	701	$ .03	$ .12
Stewart, Sammy	79TRB	206	$ .03	$ .12
Stewart, Sammy	80T	119	$ .01	$ .10
Stewart, Sammy	81T	262	$ .01	$ .08
Stewart, Sammy	82T	426	$ .05	$ .25
Stewart, Sammy	82T	679	$ .01	$ .08
Stewart, Sammy	83T	347	$ .01	$ .08

TOPPS

Player	Year	No.	VG	EX/MT
Stewart, Sammy	84T	59	$ .01	$ .06
Stewart, Sammy	85T	469	$ .01	$ .06
Stewart, Sammy	86T	597	$ .01	$ .05
Stewart, Sammy	86TTR	103	$ .01	$ .06
Stewart, Sammy	87T	204	$ .01	$ .04
Stewart, Sammy	88T	701	$ .01	$ .04
Stieb, Dave	80T	77	$ .75	$3.00
Stieb, Dave	81T	467	$ .10	$ .75
Stieb, Dave	82T	380	$ .10	$ .50
Stieb, Dave	82T	606	$ .01	$ .10
Stieb, Dave	83T	130	$ .05	$ .35
Stieb, Dave	83T	202	$ .01	$ .08

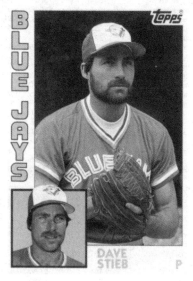

Player	Year	No.	VG	EX/MT
Stieb, Dave	**84T**	**590**	**$ .05**	**$ .20**
Stieb, Dave	84T	606	$ .01	$ .06
Stieb, Dave	85T	240	$ .01	$ .10
Stieb, Dave	86T	650	$ .01	$ .10
Stieb, Dave	87T	90	$ .01	$ .10
Stieb, Dave	88T	775	$ .01	$ .04
Stieb, Dave	89T	460	$ .01	$ .03
Stieb, Dave	90T	320	$ .01	$ .03
Stieb, Dave	91T	460	$ .01	$ .03
Stieb, Dave	91TSC	62	$ .05	$ .25
Stieb, Dave	92T	535	$ .01	$ .03
Stieb, Dave	92TSC	97	$ .01	$ .10
Stieb, Dave	93T	295	$ .01	$ .03
Stieglitz, Al	60T	144	$ .75	$3.00
Stigman, Dick	59T	142	$1.00	$4.00
Stigman, Dick	60T	507	$2.75	$11.00
Stigman, Dick	61T	77	$ .60	$2.40
Stigman, Dick	62T	37	$ .60	$2.40
Stigman, Dick	62T	532	$3.50	$14.00
Stigman, Dick	63T	89	$ .50	$2.00
Stigman, Dick	64T	6	$ .75	$3.00
Stigman, Dick	64T	245	$ .65	$2.60
Stigman, Dick	65T	548	$1.40	$5.60
Stigman, Dick	66T	512	$1.50	$6.00
Stillman, Royle	76T	594	$ .05	$ .25
Stillman, Royle	78T	272	$ .04	$ .16
Stillwell, Kurt	86TTR	104	$ .05	$ .20
Stillwell, Kurt	87T	623	$ .01	$ .15
Stillwell, Kurt	88T	339	$ .01	$ .04
Stillwell, Kurt	88TTR	115	$ .01	$ .05
Stillwell, Kurt	89T	596	$ .01	$ .03

Player	Year	No.	VG	EX/MT
Stillwell, Kurt	90T	222	$ .01	$ .03
Stillwell, Kurt	91T	478	$ .01	$ .03
Stillwell, Kurt	91TSC	189	$ .05	$ .25
Stillwell, Kurt	92T	128	$ .01	$ .03
Stillwell, Kurt	92TSC	650	$ .01	$ .10
Stillwell, Kurt	92TTR	112	$ .01	$ .05
Stillwell, Kurt	93T	84	$ .01	$ .03
Stimac, Craig	81T	356	$ .01	$ .08
Stinson, Bob	70T	131	$ .45	$1.80
Stinson, Bob	71T	594	$1.25	$5.00
Stinson, Bob	72T	679	$1.25	$5.00
Stinson, Bob	74T	653	$ .10	$ .40
Stinson, Bob	75T	471	$ .10	$ .40
Stinson, Bob	76T	466	$ .05	$ .25
Stinson, Bob	77T	138	$ .05	$ .20
Stinson, Bob	78T	396	$ .04	$ .16
Stinson, Bob	79T	252	$ .03	$ .12
Stinson, Bob	80T	583	$ .01	$ .10
Stirnweiss, George	52T	217	$7.00	$28.00
Stobbs, Chuck	52T	62	$13.75	$55.00
Stobbs, Chuck	53T	89	$4.00	$16.00
Stobbs, Chuck	54T	185	$3.75	$15.00
Stobbs, Chuck	55T	41	$2.25	$9.00
Stobbs, Chuck	56T	68	$2.00	$8.00
Stobbs, Chuck	57T	101	$2.00	$8.00
Stobbs, Chuck	58T	239	$1.25	$5.00
Stobbs, Chuck	59T	26	$1.50	$6.00
Stobbs, Chuck	60T	432	$ .75	$3.00
Stobbs, Chuck	61T	431	$1.00	$4.00
Stobbs, Chuck	91TA53	89	$ .01	$ .15
Stock, Milton	52T	381	$43.75	$175.00
Stock, Wes	60T	481	$1.25	$5.00
Stock, Wes	61T	26	$ .60	$2.40
Stock, Wes	62T	442	$1.25	$5.00
Stock, Wes	63T	438	$1.00	$4.00
Stock, Wes	64T	382	$1.00	$4.00
Stock, Wes	65T	117	$ .35	$1.40
Stock, Wes	67T	74	$ .40	$1.60
Stock, Wes	73T	179	$ .25	$1.00
Stoddard, Bob	83T	195	$ .01	$ .08
Stoddard, Bob	84T	439	$ .01	$ .06
Stoddard, Tim	80T	314	$ .01	$ .10
Stoddard, Tim	81T	91	$ .01	$ .08
Stoddard, Tim	82T	457	$ .01	$ .08
Stoddard, Tim	83T	217	$ .01	$ .08
Stoddard, Tim	84T	106	$ .01	$ .06
Stoddard, Tim	84TTR	112	$ .01	$ .15
Stoddard, Tim	85T	693	$ .01	$ .06
Stoddard, Tim	85TTR	113	$ .01	$ .10
Stoddard, Tim	86T	558	$ .01	$ .05
Stoddard, Tim	87T	788	$ .01	$ .04
Stoddard, Tim	88T	359	$ .01	$ .04
Stone, Dean	54T	114	$3.75	$15.00
Stone, Dean	55T	60	$2.25	$9.00
Stone, Dean	56T	87	$2.00	$8.00
Stone, Dean	57T	381	$1.75	$7.00
Stone, Dean	59T	286	$1.00	$4.00
Stone, Dean	62T	574	$3.50	$14.00
Stone, Dean	63T	271	$ .90	$3.60
Stone, George	69T	627	$ .40	$1.60
Stone, George	70T	122	$ .20	$ .80
Stone, George	71T	507	$ .50	$2.00
Stone, George	72T	601	$ .40	$1.60
Stone, George	73T	647	$ .60	$2.40
Stone, George	74T	397	$ .10	$ .40
Stone, George	75T	239	$ .10	$ .40
Stone, George	76T	567	$ .05	$ .25
Stone, Jeff	85T	476	$ .01	$ .06
Stone, Jeff	86T	686	$ .01	$ .05
Stone, Jeff	87T	532	$ .01	$ .04
Stone, Jeff	88T	154	$ .01	$ .04
Stone, Ron	66T	568	$3.75	$15.00
Stone, Ron	68T	409	$ .35	$1.40
Stone, Ron	69T	576	$ .40	$1.60
Stone, Ron	70T	218	$ .20	$ .80

TOPPS

Player	Year	No.	VG	EX/MT
Stone, Ron	71T	366	$ .25	$1.00
Stone, Ron	72T	528	$ .40	$1.60
Stone, Steve	72T	327	$ .25	$1.00
Stone, Steve	73T	167	$ .20	$ .80
Stone, Steve	74T	486	$ .10	$ .40
Stone, Steve	74TTR	486	$ .10	$ .40
Stone, Steve	75T	388	$ .10	$ .40
Stone, Steve	76T	378	$ .05	$ .25
Stone, Steve	77T	17	$ .05	$ .20
Stone, Steve	78T	153	$ .05	$ .20
Stone, Steve	79T	227	$ .03	$ .12
Stone, Steve	80T	688	$ .05	$ .20
Stone, Steve	81T	5	$ .05	$ .25
Stone, Steve	81T	520	$ .01	$ .08
Stone, Steve	82T	419	$ .01	$ .08
Stoneman, Bill	68T	179	$ .35	$1.40
Stoneman, Bill	69T	67	$ .35	$1.40
Stoneman, Bill	70T	398	$ .35	$1.40
Stoneman, Bill	71T	266	$ .25	$1.00
Stoneman, Bill	72T	95	$ .75	$3.00
Stoneman, Bill	72T	610	$ .40	$1.60
Stoneman, Bill	73T	254	$ .10	$ .40
Stoneman, Bill	74T	352	$ .10	$ .40
Stottlemyre Jr., Mel	90T	263	$ .01	$ .10
Stottlemyre Jr., Mel	91T	58	$ .01	$ .03
Stottlemyre, Mel	65T	550	$7.00	$28.00
Stottlemyre, Mel	66T	224	$ .75	$3.00
Stottlemyre, Mel	66T	350	$ .75	$3.00
Stottlemyre, Mel	67T	225	$ .75	$3.00
Stottlemyre, Mel	68T	120	$ .50	$2.00
Stottlemyre, Mel	69T	9	$ .75	$3.00
Stottlemyre, Mel	69T	470	$ .50	$2.00
Stottlemyre, Mel	70T	70	$ .50	$2.00
Stottlemyre, Mel	70T	100	$ .25	$1.00
Stottlemyre, Mel	71T	615	$1.25	$5.00
Stottlemyre, Mel	72T	325	$ .20	$ .80
Stottlemyre, Mel	72T	492	$ .25	$1.00
Stottlemyre, Mel	73T	520	$ .25	$1.00
Stottlemyre, Mel	74T	44	$ .10	$ .40
Stottlemyre, Mel	75T	183	$ .15	$ .60
Stottlemyre, Todd	88TTR	116	$ .10	$ .50
Stottlemyre, Todd	89T	722	$ .01	$ .10
Stottlemyre, Todd	90T	591	$ .01	$ .03
Stottlemyre, Todd	91T	348	$ .01	$ .03
Stottlemyre, Todd	91TSC	564	$ .05	$ .25
Stottlemyre, Todd	92T	607	$ .01	$ .03
Stottlemyre, Todd	92TSC	307	$ .01	$ .10
Stottlemyre, Todd	93T	23	$ .01	$ .03
Stowe, Hal	62T	291	$ .75	$3.00
Strahler, Mike	71T	188	$ .75	$3.00
Strahler, Mike	72T	198	$1.00	$4.00
Strahler, Mike	73T	279	$ .10	$ .40
Strain, Joe	79T	726	$ .05	$ .20
Strain, Joe	80T	538	$ .01	$ .10
Strain, Joe	81T	361	$ .01	$ .08
Strain, Joe	81TTR	837	$ .01	$ .15
Strain, Joe	82T	436	$ .01	$ .08
Straker, Les	87TTR	118	$ .01	$ .05
Straker, Les	88T	264	$ .01	$ .04
Straker, Les	89T	101	$ .01	$ .03
Strampe, Bob	73T	604	$ .75	$3.00
Strange, Doug	90T	641	$ .01	$ .03
Strange, Doug	93TSC	132	$ .01	$ .10
Strawberry, Darryl	83TTR	108	$17.50	$70.00
Strawberry, Darryl	84T	182	$3.00	$12.00
Strawberry, Darryl	85T	278	$ .15	$1.50
Strawberry, Darryl	85T	570	$ .75	$3.00
Strawberry, Darryl	86T	80	$ .10	$1.00
Strawberry, Darryl	87T	460	$ .10	$ .40
Strawberry, Darryl	87TAS	601	$ .05	$ .20
Strawberry, Darryl	88T	710	$ .05	$ .25
Strawberry, Darryl	89T	300	$ .05	$ .25
Strawberry, Darryl	89TAS	390	$ .01	$ .15
Strawberry, Darryl	90T	600	$ .05	$ .20
Strawberry, Darryl	91T	200	$ .01	$ .15

Player	Year	No.	VG	EX/MT
Strawberry, Darryl	91TAS	402	$ .01	$ .10
Strawberry, Darryl	91TSC	301	$ .20	$2.00
Strawberry, Darryl	91TTR	114	$ .01	$ .15
Strawberry, Darryl	92T	550	$ .01	$ .10
Strawberry, Darryl	92TSC	560	$ .10	$ .50
Strawberry, Darryl	93T	450	$ .01	$ .10
Strickland, George	52T	197	$7.00	$28.00
Strickland, George	57T	263	$2.00	$8.00
Strickland, George	58T	102	$2.00	$8.00
Strickland, George	59T	207	$1.00	$4.00
Strickland, George	60T	63	$ .85	$3.40
Strickland, Jim	72T	778	$3.75	$15.00
Strickland, Jim	73T	122	$ .10	$ .40
Striker, Jake	60T	169	$ .75	$3.00
Strittmatter, Mark	93T	746	$ .05	$ .20
Strohmayer, John	71T	232	$ .25	$1.00
Strohmayer, John	72T	631	$ .40	$1.60
Strohmayer, John	73T	457	$ .25	$1.00
Strom, Brent	73T	612	$ .75	$3.00
Strom, Brent	74T	359	$ .10	$ .40
Strom, Brent	75T	643	$ .10	$ .40
Strom, Brent	76T	84	$ .05	$ .25
Strom, Brent	77T	348	$ .05	$ .20
Strom, Brent	78T	509	$ .04	$ .16
Stroud, Ed	67T	598	$5.00	$20.00
Stroud, Ed	68T	31	$ .35	$1.40
Stroud, Ed	69T	272	$ .50	$2.00
Stroud, Ed	70T	506	$ .35	$1.40

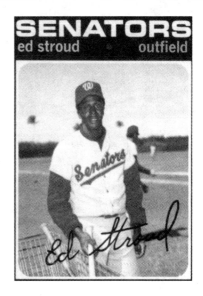

Player	Year	No.	VG	EX/MT
Stroud, Ed	71T	217	$ .25	$1.00
Stroughter, Steve	82TTR	114	$ .01	$ .10
Stuart, Dick	59T	357	$1.50	$6.00
Stuart, Dick	60T	402	$ .75	$3.00
Stuart, Dick	61T	126	$ .60	$2.40
Stuart, Dick	62T	160	$ .60	$2.40
Stuart, Dick	63T	18	$4.50	$18.00
Stuart, Dick	63T	285	$ .90	$3.60
Stuart, Dick	64T	10	$1.00	$4.00
Stuart, Dick	64T	12	$1.25	$5.00
Stuart, Dick	64T	410	$1.00	$4.00
Stuart, Dick	65T	5	$5.50	$22.00
Stuart, Dick	65T	280	$ .50	$2.00
Stuart, Dick	66T	480	$1.50	$6.00
Stuart, Marlin	52T	208	$7.00	$28.00

TOPPS

Player	Year	No.	VG	EX/MT
Stubbs, Franklin	85T	506	$ .01	$ .10
Stubbs, Franklin	86TTR	105	$ .01	$ .06
Stubbs, Franklin	87T	292	$ .01	$ .04
Stubbs, Franklin	88T	198	$ .01	$ .04
Stubbs, Franklin	89T	697	$ .01	$ .03
Stubbs, Franklin	90T	56	$ .01	$ .03
Stubbs, Franklin	90TTR	120	$ .01	$ .05
Stubbs, Franklin	91T	732	$ .01	$ .03
Stubbs, Franklin	91TSC	461	$ .05	$ .25
Stubbs, Franklin	91TTR	115	$ .01	$ .05
Stubbs, Franklin	92T	329	$ .01	$ .03

FRANKLIN STUBBS

Player	Year	No.	VG	EX/MT
Stubbs, Franklin	92TSC	189	$ .01	$ .10
Stubbs, Franklin	93T	124	$ .01	$ .03
Stubbs, Franklin	93TSC	168	$ .01	$ .10
Stubing, Moose	89T	444	$ .01	$ .03
Stuper, John	83T	363	$ .01	$ .08
Stuper, John	84T	49	$ .01	$ .06
Stuper, John	84T	186	$ .01	$ .06
Stuper, John	86T	497	$ .01	$ .05
Sturdivant, Tom	57T	34	$2.00	$8.00
Sturdivant, Tom	58T	127	$1.25	$5.00
Sturdivant, Tom	59T	471	$1.00	$4.00
Sturdivant, Tom	60T	487	$1.25	$5.00
Sturdivant, Tom	61T	293	$ .60	$2.40
Sturdivant, Tom	62T	179	$ .60	$2.40
Sturdivant, Tom	63T	281	$ .90	$3.60
Sturdivant, Tom	64T	402	$1.00	$4.00
Suarez, Ken	66T	588	$3.75	$15.00
Suarez, Ken	68T	218	$ .35	$1.40
Suarez, Ken	69T	19	$ .35	$1.40
Suarez, Ken	70T	209	$ .20	$ .80
Suarez, Ken	71T	597	$1.00	$4.00
Suarez, Ken	72T	483	$ .25	$1.00
Suarez, Ken	74T	39	$ .10	$ .40
Such, Dick	70T	599	$ .75	$3.00
Such, Dick	71T	283	$ .25	$1.00
Sudakis, Bill	69T	552	$ .40	$1.60
Sudakis, Bill	70T	341	$ .35	$1.40
Sudakis, Bill	71T	253	$ .25	$1.00
Sudakis, Bill	72T	722	$1.25	$5.00
Sudakis, Bill	73T	586	$ .60	$2.40
Sudakis, Bill	74T	63	$ .10	$ .40
Sudakis, Bill	74TTR	63	$ .10	$ .40

Player	Year	No.	VG	EX/MT
Sudakis, Bill	75T	291	$ .10	$ .40
Suder, Pete	52T	256	$12.50	$50.00
Sukeforth, Clyde	52T	364	$43.75	$175.00
Sukla, Ed	66T	417	$ .65	$2.60
Sularz, Guy	83T	379	$ .01	$ .08
Sullivan, Frank	55T	106	$2.25	$9.00
Sullivan, Frank	56T	71	$2.00	$8.00
Sullivan, Frank	57T	21	$2.00	$8.00
Sullivan, Frank	58T	18	$2.00	$8.00
Sullivan, Frank	59T	323	$1.00	$4.00
Sullivan, Frank	60T	280	$ .75	$3.00
Sullivan, Frank	61T	281	$ .60	$2.40
Sullivan, Frank	62T	352	$ .75	$3.00
Sullivan, Frank	63T	389	$1.00	$4.00
Sullivan, Haywood	57T	336	$5.50	$22.00
Sullivan, Haywood	58T	197	$1.25	$5.00
Sullivan, Haywood	59T	416	$1.00	$4.00
Sullivan, Haywood	60T	474	$1.25	$5.00
Sullivan, Haywood	61T	212	$ .60	$2.40
Sullivan, Haywood	62T	184	$ .60	$2.40
Sullivan, Haywood	63T	359	$ .90	$3.60
Sullivan, John	65T	593	$3.00	$12.00
Sullivan, John	66T	597	$3.75	$15.00
Sullivan, John	67T	568	$4.00	$16.00
Sullivan, Marc	86T	529	$ .01	$ .05
Sullivan, Marc	87T	66	$ .01	$ .04
Sullivan, Marc	88T	354	$ .01	$ .04
Summers, Champ	76T	299	$ .05	$ .25
Summers, Champ	78T	622	$ .04	$ .16
Summers, Champ	79T	516	$ .03	$ .12
Summers, Champ	80T	176	$ .01	$ .10
Summers, Champ	81T	27	$ .01	$ .08
Summers, Champ	82T	369	$ .01	$ .08
Summers, Champ	82TTR	115	$ .01	$ .10
Summers, Champ	83T	428	$ .01	$ .08
Summers, Champ	84T	768	$ .01	$ .06
Summers, Champ	84TTR	113	$ .01	$ .15
Summers, Champ	85T	208	$ .01	$ .06
Sundberg, Jim	75T	567	$ .25	$1.00
Sundberg, Jim	76T	226	$ .05	$ .25
Sundberg, Jim	77T	351	$ .05	$ .20
Sundberg, Jim	78T	492	$ .04	$ .16
Sundberg, Jim	79T	120	$ .03	$ .12
Sundberg, Jim	80T	530	$ .01	$ .10
Sundberg, Jim	81T	95	$ .01	$ .08
Sundberg, Jim	82T	335	$ .01	$ .08
Sundberg, Jim	83T	665	$ .01	$ .08
Sundberg, Jim	84T	779	$ .01	$ .06
Sundberg, Jim	84TTR	114	$ .01	$ .15
Sundberg, Jim	85T	446	$ .01	$ .06
Sundberg, Jim	85TTR	114	$ .01	$ .10
Sundberg, Jim	86T	245	$ .01	$ .05
Sundberg, Jim	87T	190	$ .01	$ .04
Sundberg, Jim	87TTR	119	$ .01	$ .05
Sundberg, Jim	88T	516	$ .01	$ .04
Sundberg, Jim	89T	78	$ .01	$ .03
Surhoff, B. J.	87T	216	$ .01	$ .15
Surhoff, B. J.	88T	491	$ .01	$ .04
Surhoff, B. J.	89T	33	$ .01	$ .03
Surhoff, B. J.	90T	696	$ .01	$ .03
Surhoff, B. J.	91T	592	$ .01	$ .03
Surhoff, B. J.	91TSC	206	$ .05	$ .25
Surhoff, B. J.	92T	718	$ .01	$ .03
Surhoff, B. J.	92TSC	117	$ .01	$ .10
Surhoff, B. J.	93T	417	$ .01	$ .03
Surkont, Max	52T	302	$12.50	$50.00
Surkont, Max	56T	209	$3.75	$15.00
Surkont, Max	57T	310	$5.00	$20.00
Susce, George	56T	93	$2.00	$8.00
Susce, George	57T	229	$2.00	$8.00
Susce, George	58T	189	$1.25	$5.00
Susce, George	59T	511	$4.00	$16.00
Sutcliffe, Rick	80T	544	$ .75	$3.00
Sutcliffe, Rick	81T	191	$ .05	$ .25
Sutcliffe, Rick	82T	609	$ .05	$ .35

TOPPS

Player	Year	No.	VG	EX/MT
Sutcliffe, Rick	82TTR	116	$ .10	$1.00
Sutcliffe, Rick	83T	141	$ .01	$ .08
Sutcliffe, Rick	83T	497	$ .05	$ .20
Sutcliffe, Rick	83T	707	$ .01	$ .08
Sutcliffe, Rick	84T	245	$ .05	$ .20
Sutcliffe, Rick	84TTR	115	$ .10	$ .40
Sutcliffe, Rick	85T	72	$ .01	$ .06
Sutcliffe, Rick	85TAS	720	$ .01	$ .10
Sutcliffe, Rick	86T	330	$ .01	$ .05
Sutcliffe, Rick	87T	142	$ .01	$ .10
Sutcliffe, Rick	88T	740	$ .01	$ .04
Sutcliffe, Rick	89T	520	$ .01	$ .03
Sutcliffe, Rick	90T	640	$ .01	$ .03
Sutcliffe, Rick	91T	415	$ .01	$ .03
Sutcliffe, Rick	92TSC	700	$ .01	$ .10
Sutcliffe, Rick	92TTR	113	$ .01	$ .05
Sutcliffe, Rick	93T	274	$ .01	$ .03
Sutcliffe, Rick	93TSC	246	$ .01	$ .10
Sutherland, Darrell	66T	191	$ .50	$2.00
Sutherland, Darrell	68T	551	$ .70	$2.80
Sutherland, Gary	67T	587	$7.00	$28.00
Sutherland, Gary	68T	98	$ .35	$1.40
Sutherland, Gary	69T	326	$ .50	$2.00
Sutherland, Gary	70T	632	$ .50	$2.00
Sutherland, Gary	71T	434	$ .50	$2.00
Sutherland, Gary	72T	211	$ .10	$ .40
Sutherland, Gary	73T	572	$ .60	$2.40
Sutherland, Gary	74T	428	$ .10	$ .40
Sutherland, Gary	74TTR	428	$ .10	$ .40
Sutherland, Gary	75T	522	$ .10	$ .40
Sutherland, Gary	76T	113	$ .05	$ .25
Sutherland, Gary	77T	307	$ .05	$ .20
Sutherland, Leo	81T	112	$ .01	$ .15
Sutherland, Leo	82T	599	$ .01	$ .08
Sutko, Glenn	92TSC	559	$ .01	$ .10
Sutter, Bruce	77T	144	$1.00	$4.00
Sutter, Bruce	78T	325	$ .25	$1.00
Sutter, Bruce	79T	457	$ .15	$ .60
Sutter, Bruce	80T	17	$ .10	$ .50
Sutter, Bruce	81T	590	$ .05	$ .25
Sutter, Bruce	81TTR	838	$ .10	$ .50
Sutter, Bruce	82T	168	$ .05	$ .25
Sutter, Bruce	82T	260	$ .01	$ .15
Sutter, Bruce	82TAS	347	$ .01	$ .10
Sutter, Bruce	83T	150	$ .05	$ .25
Sutter, Bruce	83T	151	$ .01	$ .08
Sutter, Bruce	83T	708	$ .01	$ .08
Sutter, Bruce	83TAS	407	$ .01	$ .10
Sutter, Bruce	84T	709	$ .01	$ .06
Sutter, Bruce	84T	730	$ .01	$ .15
Sutter, Bruce	85T	370	$ .01	$ .06
Sutter, Bruce	85TAS	722	$ .01	$ .06
Sutter, Bruce	85TRB	9	$ .01	$ .10
Sutter, Bruce	85TTR	115	$ .01	$ .15
Sutter, Bruce	86T	620	$ .01	$ .05
Sutter, Bruce	87T	435	$ .01	$ .10
Sutter, Bruce	88T	155	$ .01	$ .04
Sutter, Bruce	89T	11	$ .01	$ .03
Sutton, Don	66T	288	$35.00	$140.00
Sutton, Don	67T	445	$8.00	$32.00
Sutton, Don	68T	103	$2.75	$11.00
Sutton, Don	69T	216	$2.00	$8.00
Sutton, Don	70T	622	$3.50	$14.00
Sutton, Don	71T	361	$2.00	$8.00
Sutton, Don	72T	530	$1.25	$5.00
Sutton, Don	73T	10	$ .75	$3.00
Sutton, Don	74T	220	$ .75	$3.00
Sutton, Don	75T	220	$ .75	$3.00
Sutton, Don	76T	530	$ .75	$3.00
Sutton, Don	77T	620	$ .50	$2.00
Sutton, Don	78T	310	$ .50	$2.00
Sutton, Don	79T	170	$ .30	$1.20
Sutton, Don	80T	440	$ .10	$1.00
Sutton, Don	81T	7	$ .05	$ .20
Sutton, Don	81T	605	$ .10	$ .75
Sutton, Don	81TTR	839	$ .20	$2.00
Sutton, Don	82T	305	$ .10	$ .50
Sutton, Don	82TSA	306	$ .05	$ .25
Sutton, Don	83T	145	$ .10	$ .50
Sutton, Don	83T	146	$ .05	$ .25
Sutton, Don	84T	35	$ .05	$ .25
Sutton, Don	84T	715	$ .05	$ .20
Sutton, Don	85T	729	$ .05	$ .25
Sutton, Don	85TRB	10	$ .01	$ .15
Sutton, Don	85TTR	116	$ .10	$ .50
Sutton, Don	86T	335	$ .01	$ .15
Sutton, Don	87T	673	$ .01	$ .15
Sutton, Don	88T	575	$ .01	$ .10
Sutton, Johnny	79T	676	$ .03	$ .12
Sutton, Larry	93T	423	$ .10	$ .75
Sveum, Dale	86TTR	106	$ .01	$ .06
Sveum, Dale	87T	327	$ .01	$ .04
Sveum, Dale	88T	592	$ .01	$ .04
Sveum, Dale	89T	12	$ .01	$ .03
Sveum, Dale	90T	739	$ .01	$ .03
Sveum, Dale	92T	478	$ .01	$ .03
Sveum, Dale	92TSC	687	$ .01	$ .10
Swaggerty, Bill	85T	147	$ .01	$ .06
Swan, Craig	74T	602	$ .10	$ .40
Swan, Craig	76T	494	$ .05	$ .25
Swan, Craig	77T	94	$ .05	$ .20
Swan, Craig	78T	621	$ .04	$ .16
Swan, Craig	79T	7	$ .03	$ .12
Swan, Craig	79T	334	$ .03	$ .12
Swan, Craig	80T	8	$ .01	$ .10
Swan, Craig	81T	189	$ .01	$ .08

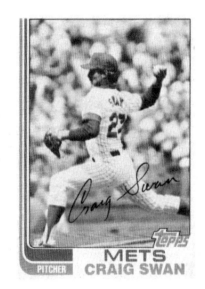

Player	Year	No.	VG	EX/MT
Swan, Craig	82T	592	$ .01	$ .08
Swan, Craig	83T	292	$ .01	$ .08
Swan, Craig	83T	621	$ .01	$ .08
Swan, Craig	84T	763	$ .01	$ .06
Swan, Craig	84TTR	116	$ .01	$ .15
Swan, Russ	90TTR	121	$ .01	$ .15
Swan, Russ	91T	739	$ .01	$ .03
Swan, Russ	91TSC	577	$ .05	$ .25
Swan, Russ	92T	588	$ .01	$ .03
Swan, Russ	92TSC	472	$ .01	$ .10
Swan, Russ	93T	96	$ .01	$ .03
Swan, Russ	93TSC	179	$ .01	$ .10

TOPPS

Player	Year	No.	VG	EX/MT
Swanson, Art	56T	204	$3.75	$15.00
Swanson, Stan	72T	331	$ .10	$ .40
Sweet, Rick	78T	702	$ .04	$ .16
Sweet, Rick	79T	646	$ .03	$ .12
Sweet, Rick	83T	437	$ .01	$ .08
Sweet, Rick	84T	211	$ .01	$ .06
Swift, Billy	85T	404	$ .10	$1.00
Swift, Bill	86T	399	$ .01	$ .10
Swift, Bill	87T	67	$ .01	$ .10
Swift, Bill	88TTR	117	$ .05	$ .20
Swift, Bill	89T	712	$ .01	$ .15
Swift, Bill	90T	574	$ .01	$ .15
Swift, Bill	91T	276	$ .01	$ .10
Swift, Bill	91TSC	372	$ .10	$1.00
Swift, Bill	92T	144	$ .01	$ .10
Swift, Billy	92TSC	243	$ .05	$ .20
Swift, Bill	92TSC	855	$ .01	$ .10
Swift, Bill	92TTR	114	$ .01	$ .05
Swift, Bill	93T	755	$ .01	$ .03
Swift, Bill	**93TSC**	**204**	**$ .01**	**$ .10**
Swift, Bob	52T	181	$7.00	$28.00
Swift, Bob	54T	65	$7.50	$30.00
Swift, Bob	60T	470	$1.25	$5.00
Swindell, Greg	87T	319	$ .10	$ .50
Swindell, Greg	88T	22	$ .05	$ .20
Swindell, Greg	89T	315	$ .01	$ .15
Swindell, Greg	90T	595	$ .01	$ .10
Swindell, Greg	91T	445	$ .01	$ .03
Swindell, Greg	91TSC	428	$ .05	$ .35
Swindell, Greg	92T	735	$ .01	$ .03
Swindell, Greg	92TSC	673	$ .01	$ .10
Swindell, Greg	93T	515	$ .01	$ .10
Swindell, Greg	93TSC	165	$ .01	$ .15
Swisher, Steve	75T	63	$ .10	$ .40
Swisher, Steve	76T	173	$ .05	$ .25
Swisher, Steve	77T	419	$ .05	$ .20
Swisher, Steve	78T	252	$ .04	$ .16
Swisher, Steve	79T	304	$ .03	$ .12
Swisher, Steve	80T	163	$ .01	$ .10
Swisher, Steve	81T	541	$ .01	$ .08
Swisher, Steve	81TTR	840	$ .01	$ .15
Swisher, Steve	82T	764	$ .01	$ .08
Swisher, Steve	83T	612	$ .01	$ .08

Player	Year	No.	VG	EX/MT
Swoboda, Ron	65T	533	$8.00	$32.00
Swoboda, Ron	66T	35	$ .50	$2.00
Swoboda, Ron	67T	186	$ .40	$1.60
Swoboda, Ron	67T	264	$ .50	$2.00
Swoboda, Ron	68T	114	$ .35	$1.40
Swoboda, Ron	69T	585	$ .40	$1.60
Swoboda, Ron	70T	431	$ .35	$1.40
Swoboda, Ron	71T	665	$2.50	$10.00
Swoboda, Ron	72T	8	$ .10	$ .40
Swoboda, Ron	73T	314	$ .10	$ .40
Sykes, Bob	77T	491	$1.25 $1.75	$7.00
Sykes, Bob	79T	569	$ .03	$ .12
Sykes, Bob	80T	223	$ .01	$ .10
Sykes, Bob	81T	348	$ .01	$ .08
Sykes, Bob	82T	108	$ .01	$ .08
Szotkiewicz, Ken	71T	749	$1.10	$4.40
Tabaka, Jeff	93T	586	$ .01	$ .15
Tabb, Jerry	78T	224	$ .04	$ .16
Tabler, Pat	84T	329	$ .01	$ .06
Tabler, Pat	85T	158	$ .01	$ .06
Tabler, Pat	86T	674	$ .01	$ .05
Tabler, Pat	87T	575	$ .01	$ .04
Tabler, Pat	88T	230	$ .01	$ .04
Tabler, Pat	88TTR	118	$ .01	$ .05
Tabler, Pat	89T	56	$ .01	$ .03
Tabler, Pat	90T	727	$ .01	$ .03
Tabler, Pat	91T	433	$ .01	$ .03
Tabler, Pat	92T	333	$ .01	$ .03
Tabler, Pat	92TSC	333	$ .01	$ .10
Tabler, Pat	93TSC	160	$ .01	$ .10
Tackett, Jeff	92TSC	383	$ .01	$ .10
Tackett, Jeff	92TTR	115	$ .01	$ .05
Tackett, Jeff	93T	6	$ .01	$ .03
Tackett, Jeff	93TSC	186	$ .01	$ .10
Talbot, Bob	54T	229	$3.75	$15.00
Talbot, Fred	65T	58	$ .35	$1.40
Talbot, Fred	66T	403	$ .65	$2.60
Talbot, Fred	67T	517	$1.50	$6.00
Talbot, Fred	68T	577	$ .70	$2.80
Talbot, Fred	69T	332	$ .30	$1.20
Talbot, Fred	70T	287	$ .35	$1.40
Talton, Tim	67T	603	$4.00	$16.00
Tamargo, John	79T	726	$ .05	$ .20
Tamargo, John	80T	680	$ .05	$ .20
Tamargo, John	81T	519	$ .01	$ .08
Tanana, Frank	74T	605	$1.25	$5.00
Tanana, Frank	75T	16	$ .50	$2.00
Tanana, Frank	76T	204	$ .25	$1.00
Tanana, Frank	76T	490	$ .25	$1.00
Tanana, Frank	77T	200	$ .20	$ .80
Tanana, Frank	78T	207	$ .04	$ .16
Tanana, Frank	78T	600	$ .10	$ .40
Tanana, Frank	79T	530	$ .10	$ .40
Tanana, Frank	80T	105	$ .05	$ .25
Tanana, Frank	81T	369	$ .05	$ .35
Tanana, Frank	81TTR	841	$ .10	$ .50
Tanana, Frank	82T	792	$ .01	$ .10
Tanana, Frank	82TTR	117	$ .01	$ .10
Tanana, Frank	83T	272	$ .01	$ .08
Tanana, Frank	84T	479	$ .01	$ .06
Tanana, Frank	85T	55	$ .01	$ .06
Tanana, Frank	86T	592	$ .01	$ .05
Tanana, Frank	87T	726	$ .01	$ .04
Tanana, Frank	88T	177	$ .01	$ .04
Tanana, Frank	89T	603	$ .01	$ .03
Tanana, Frank	90T	343	$ .01	$ .03
Tanana, Frank	91T	236	$ .01	$ .03
Tanana, Frank	91TSC	158	$ .05	$ .25
Tanana, Frank	92T	458	$ .01	$ .10
Tanana, Frank	92TSC	416	$ .01	$ .10
Tanana, Frank	93T	53	$ .01	$ .03
Tanana, Frank	93TSC	267	$ .01	$ .10
Tanner, Chuck	55T	161	$8.00	$32.00
Tanner, Chuck	56T	69	$2.75	$11.00
Tanner, Chuck	57T	392	$1.75	$7.00

TOPPS

Player	Year	No.	VG	EX/MT
Tanner, Chuck	58T	91	$2.00	$8.00
Tanner, Chuck	59T	234	$1.00	$4.00
Tanner, Chuck	60T	279	$ .75	$3.00

Player	Year	No.	VG	EX/MT
Tanner, Chuck	71T	661	$1.50	$6.00
Tanner, Chuck	72T	98	$ .20	$ .80
Tanner, Chuck	73T	356	$ .20	$ .80
Tanner, Chuck	74T	221	$ .10	$ .40
Tanner, Chuck	78T	494	$ .04	$ .16
Tanner, Chuck	83T	696	$ .01	$ .08
Tanner, Chuck	84T	291	$ .01	$ .06
Tanner, Chuck	85T	268	$ .01	$ .06
Tanner, Chuck	86T	351	$ .01	$ .05
Tanner, Chuck	86TTR	107	$ .01	$ .06
Tanner, Chuck	87T	593	$ .01	$ .04
Tanner, Chuck	88T	134	$ .01	$ .04
Tapani, Kevin	90T	227	$ .05	$ .35
Tapani, Kevin	91T	633	$ .01	$ .03
Tapani, Kevin	91TSC	161	$ .10	$ .75
Tapani, Kevin	92T	313	$ .01	$ .03
Tapani, Kevin	92TSC	433	$ .01	$ .10
Tapani, Kevin	93T	420	$ .01	$ .03
Tappe, Elvin	55T	129	$2.25	$9.00
Tappe, Elvin	58T	184	$1.25	$5.00
Tappe, Elvin	60T	457	$1.25	$5.00
Tartabull, Danny	86TTR	108	$ .10	$1.00
Tartabull, Danny	87T	476	$ .10	$ .50
Tartabull, Danny	87TTR	120	$ .05	$ .35
Tartabull, Danny	88T	724	$ .01	$ .15
Tartabull, Danny	89T	275	$ .01	$ .10
Tartabull, Danny	90T	540	$ .01	$ .10
Tartabull, Danny	91T	90	$ .01	$ .10
Tartabull, Danny	91TSC	272	$ .05	$ .35
Tartabull, Danny	92T	145	$ .01	$ .10
Tartabull, Danny	92TSC	191	$ .01	$ .15
Tartabull, Danny	92TSC	690	$ .01	$ .15
Tartabull, Danny	92TTR	116	$ .01	$ .05
Tartabull, Danny	93T	330	$ .01	$ .03
Tartabull, Danny	93TSC	85	$ .01	$ .10
Tartabull, Jose	62T	451	$1.75	$7.00
Tartabull, Jose	63T	449	$3.00	$12.00
Tartabull, Jose	64T	276	$ .65	$2.60
Tartabull, Jose	66T	143	$ .50	$2.00
Tartabull, Jose	67T	56	$ .40	$1.60
Tartabull, Jose	68T	555	$ .70	$2.80
Tartabull, Jose	69T	287	$ .50	$2.00
Tartabull, Jose	70T	481	$ .35	$1.40
Tasby, Willie	59T	143	$1.00	$4.00
Tasby, Willie	60T	322	$ .75	$3.00
Tasby, Willie	61T	458	$1.35	$5.40
Tasby, Willie	62T	462	$1.50	$6.00
Tate, Lee	59T	544	$4.00	$16.00
Tate, Randy	76T	549	$ .05	$ .25
Tatum, Jarvis	70T	642	$1.25	$5.00
Tatum, Jarvis	71T	159	$ .25	$1.00
Tatum, Jim	93T	691	$ .05	$ .20
Tatum, Ken	70T	658	$1.25	$5.00
Tatum, Ken	71T	601	$1.00	$4.00
Tatum, Ken	72T	772	$1.25	$5.00
Tatum, Ken	73T	463	$ .25	$1.00
Taubensee, Eddie	92T	427	$ .01	$ .10
Taubensee, Eddie	92TSC	790	$ .05	$ .20
Taubensee, Eddie	92TTR	117	$ .01	$ .10
Taubensee, Eddie	93T	117	$ .01	$ .03
Taussig, Don	62T	44	$ .60	$2.40
Taveras, Alex	77T	474	$ .10	$ .40
Taveras, Frank	74T	607	$ .10	$ .40
Taveras, Frank	75T	277	$ .10	$ .40
Taveras, Frank	76T	36	$ .05	$ .25
Taveras, Frank	77T	538	$ .05	$ .20
Taveras, Frank	78T	204	$ .04	$ .16
Taveras, Frank	78T	685	$ .04	$ .16
Taveras, Frank	79T	165	$ .03	$ .12
Taveras, Frank	80T	456	$ .01	$ .10
Taveras, Frank	81T	343	$ .01	$ .08
Taveras, Frank	82T	782	$ .01	$ .08
Taveras, Frank	82TTR	118	$ .01	$ .10
Taylor, Aaron	93T	786	$ .05	$ .20
Taylor, Bill	54T	74	$7.50	$30.00
Taylor, Bill	55T	53	$2.25	$9.00
Taylor, Bill	58T	389	$1.00	$4.00
Taylor, Bob	58T	164	$1.25	$5.00
Taylor, Bob "Hawk"	61T	446	$1.00	$4.00
Taylor, Bob	62T	406	$1.25	$5.00
Taylor, Bob	63T	481	$3.00	$12.00
Taylor, Bob	64T	381	$1.00	$4.00
Taylor, Bob "Hawk"	65T	329	$ .50	$2.00
Taylor, Bob "Hawk"	68T	52	$ .35	$1.40
Taylor, Brien	92T	6	$ .25	$2.50
Taylor, Brien	93T	742	$ .10	$ .50
Taylor, Bruce	78T	701	$ .04	$ .16
Taylor, Carl	68T	559	$ .70	$2.80
Taylor, Carl	69T	357	$ .30	$1.20
Taylor, Carl	70T	76	$ .20	$ .80
Taylor, Carl	71T	353	$ .25	$1.00
Taylor, Carl	73T	99	$ .10	$ .40
Taylor, Carl	74T	627	$ .10	$ .40
Taylor, Chuck	70T	119	$ .20	$ .80
Taylor, Chuck	71T	606	$1.00	$4.00
Taylor, Chuck	72T	407	$ .25	$1.00
Taylor, Chuck	73T	176	$ .10	$ .40
Taylor, Chuck	74T	412	$ .10	$ .40
Taylor, Chuck	75T	58	$ .10	$ .40
Taylor, Joe	58T	451	$1.00	$4.00
Taylor, Rob	69T	239	$ .50	$2.00
Taylor, Ron	62T	591	$12.50	$50.00
Taylor, Ron	63T	208	$ .90	$3.60
Taylor, Ron	64T	183	$ .50	$2.00
Taylor, Ron	65T	568	$2.50	$10.00
Taylor, Ron	66T	174	$ .50	$2.00
Taylor, Ron	67T	606	$4.00	$16.00
Taylor, Ron	68T	421	$ .35	$1.40
Taylor, Ron	69T	72	$ .35	$1.40
Taylor, Ron	70T	419	$ .35	$1.40
Taylor, Ron	71T	687	$1.50	$6.00
Taylor, Ron	72T	234	$ .10	$ .40
Taylor, Sam	58T	281	$1.25	$5.00
Taylor, Sammy	59T	193	$1.00	$4.00
Taylor, Sammy	60T	162	$ .75	$3.00

TOPPS

Player	Year	No.	VG	EX/MT
Taylor, Sammy	61T	253	$ .60	$2.40
Taylor, Sammy	62T	274	$ .75	$3.00
Taylor, Sammy	63T	273	$ .90	$3.60
Taylor, Scott	93T	456	$ .01	$ .03
Taylor, Terry	89T	597	$ .01	$ .03
Taylor, Todd	91TTR	116	$ .05	$ .20
Taylor, Tony	58T	411	$2.00	$8.00
Taylor, Tony	59T	62	$1.50	$6.00
Taylor, Tony	60T	294	$ .75	$3.00
Taylor, Tony	61T	411	$1.00	$4.00
Taylor, Tony	62T	77	$ .60	$2.40
Taylor, Tony	63T	366	$ .90	$3.60
Taylor, Tony	64T	585	$2.25	$9.00
Taylor, Tony	65T	296	$ .50	$2.00
Taylor, Tony	66T	585	$3.75	$15.00
Taylor, Tony	67T	126	$ .40	$1.60
Taylor, Tony	68T	327	$ .35	$1.40
Taylor, Tony	69T	108	$ .35	$1.40
Taylor, Tony	70T	324	$ .35	$1.40
Taylor, Tony	71T	246	$ .25	$1.00
Taylor, Tony	72T	511	$ .25	$1.00
Taylor, Tony	73T	29	$ .10	$ .40
Taylor, Tony	75T	574	$ .10	$ .40
Taylor, Tony	76T	624	$ .05	$ .25
Taylor, Wade	91TTR	117	$ .01	$ .10
Taylor, Wade	92T	562	$ .01	$ .03
Taylor, Wade	92TSC	667	$ .01	$ .10
Tebbetts, Birdie	52T	282	$13.75	$55.00
Tebbetts, Birdie	58T	386	$2.50	$10.00
Tebbetts, Birdie	62T	588	$3.50	$14.00
Tebbetts, Birdie	63T	48	$ .50	$2.00
Tebbetts, Birdie	64T	462	$1.00	$4.00
Tebbetts, Birdie	65T	301	$ .50	$2.00
Tebbetts, Birdie	66T	552	$7.00	$28.00
Tejada, Wil	89T	747	$ .01	$ .03
Tekulve, Kent	76T	112	$ .35	$1.40
Tekulve, Kent	77T	374	$ .05	$ .25
Tekulve, Kent	78T	84	$ .04	$ .16
Tekulve, Kent	79T	223	$ .03	$ .12
Tekulve, Kent	80T	573	$ .01	$ .10
Tekulve, Kent	81T	695	$ .01	$ .08
Tekulve, Kent	82T	485	$ .01	$ .08
Tekulve, Kent	83T	17	$ .01	$ .08
Tekulve, Kent	83T	18	$ .01	$ .08
Tekulve, Kent	84T	754	$ .01	$ .06
Tekulve, Kent	85T	125	$ .01	$ .06
Tekulve, Kent	85TTR	117	$ .01	$ .10
Tekulve, Kent	86T	326	$ .01	$ .05
Tekulve, Kent	87T	684	$ .01	$ .04
Tekulve, Kent	88T	543	$ .01	$ .04
Tekulve, Kent	89TTR	116	$ .01	$ .05
Telford, Anthony	91T	653	$ .01	$ .15
Telford, Anthony	91TSC	330	$ .05	$ .25
Telford, Anthony	92TSC	557	$ .01	$ .10
Tellmann, Tom	81T	356	$ .01	$ .08
Tellmann, Tom	83TTR	109	$ .01	$ .10
Tellmann, Tom	84T	476	$ .01	$ .06
Tellmann, Tom	85T	112	$ .01	$ .06
Tellmann, Tom	85TTR	118	$ .01	$ .10
Tellmann, Tom	86T	693	$ .01	$ .05
Temple, Johnny	56T	212	$4.50	$18.00
Temple, Johnny	57T	9	$2.00	$8.00
Temple, Johnny	58T	205	$1.25	$5.00
Temple, Johnny	58TAS	478	$1.00	$4.00
Temple, Johnny	59T	335	$1.00	$4.00
Temple, Johnny	60T	500	$1.25	$5.00
Temple, Johnny	61T	155	$ .60	$2.40
Temple, Johnny	62T	34	$ .60	$2.40
Temple, Johnny	63T	576	$3.50	$14.00
Templeton, Garry	77T	161	$ .35	$1.40
Templeton, Garry	78T	32	$ .10	$ .40
Templeton, Garry	79T	350	$ .05	$ .20
Templeton, Garry	80T	587	$ .01	$ .10
Templeton, Garry	80THL	5	$ .05	$ .20
Templeton, Garry	81T	485	$ .01	$ .08
Templeton, Garry	82T	288	$ .01	$ .08
Templeton, Garry	82TTR	119	$ .01	$ .10
Templeton, Garry	83T	505	$ .01	$ .08
Templeton, Garry	84T	615	$ .01	$ .06
Templeton, Garry	85T	735	$ .01	$ .06
Templeton, Garry	86T	90	$ .01	$ .05
Templeton, Garry	87T	325	$ .01	$ .04
Templeton, Garry	88T	640	$ .01	$ .04
Templeton, Garry	89T	121	$ .01	$ .03
Templeton, Garry	90T	481	$ .01	$ .03
Templeton, Garry	91T	253	$ .01	$ .03
Templeton, Garry	91TSC	72	$ .05	$ .25
Templeton, Garry	91TTR	118	$ .01	$ .05
Templeton, Garry	92T	772	$ .01	$ .03
Tenace, Gene	70T	21	$1.50	$6.00
Tenace, Gene	71T	338	$ .25	$1.00
Tenace, Gene	72T	189	$ .20	$ .80
Tenace, Gene	73T	524	$ .25	$1.00
Tenace, Gene	74T	79	$ .10	$ .40
Tenace, Gene	75T	535	$ .10	$ .40
Tenace, Gene	76T	165	$ .05	$ .25

Player	Year	No.	VG	EX/MT
Tenace, Gene	**77T**	**303**	**$ .05**	**$ .20**
Tenace, Gene	78T	240	$ .04	$ .16
Tenace, Gene	79T	435	$ .03	$ .12
Tenace, Gene	80T	704	$ .01	$ .10
Tenace, Gene	81T	29	$ .01	$ .08
Tenace, Gene	81TTR	842	$ .01	$ .15
Tenace, Gene	82T	631	$ .01	$ .08
Tenace, Gene	83T	515	$ .01	$ .08
Tenace, Gene	83TTR	110	$ .01	$ .10
Tenace, Gene	84T	729	$ .01	$ .06
Tepedino, Frank	70T	689	$1.25	$5.00
Tepedino, Frank	71T	342	$ .25	$1.00
Tepedino, Frank	74T	526	$ .10	$ .40
Tepedino, Frank	75T	9	$ .10	$ .40
Terlecky, Greg	77T	487	$ .05	$ .20
Terpko, Jeff	77T	137	$ .05	$ .20
Terrell, Jerry	74T	481	$ .10	$ .40
Terrell, Jerry	75T	654	$ .10	$ .40
Terrell, Jerry	76T	159	$ .05	$ .25
Terrell, Jerry	77T	513	$ .05	$ .20
Terrell, Jerry	78T	525	$ .04	$ .16
Terrell, Jerry	79T	273	$ .03	$ .12

TOPPS

Player	Year	No.	VG	EX/MT
Terrell, Jerry	80T	98	$ .01	$ .10
Terrell, Walt	84T	549	$ .05	$ .20
Terrell, Walt	85T	287	$ .01	$ .10
Terrell, Walt	85TTR	119	$ .01	$ .10
Terrell, Walt	86T	461	$ .01	$ .05
Terrell, Walt	87T	72	$ .01	$ .04
Terrell, Walt	88T	668	$ .01	$ .04
Terrell, Walt	89T	127	$ .01	$ .03
Terrell, Walt	89TTR	117	$ .01	$ .05
Terrell, Walt	90T	611	$ .01	$ .03
Terrell, Walt	91T	328	$ .01	$ .03
Terrell, Walt	91TSC	315	$ .05	$ .25
Terrell, Walt	92T	722	$ .01	$ .03
Terrell, Walt	92TSC	139	$ .01	$ .10
Terrell, Walt	93TSC	223	$ .01	$ .10
Terry, Ralph	57T	391	$2.50	$10.00
Terry, Ralph	58T	169	$2.00	$8.00
Terry, Ralph	59T	358	$1.00	$4.00
Terry, Ralph	60T	96	$ .85	$3.40
Terry, Ralph	61T	389	$1.00	$4.00
Terry, Ralph	62T	48	$ .60	$2.40
Terry, Ralph	63T	8	$1.00	$4.00
Terry, Ralph	63T	10	$1.00	$4.00
Terry, Ralph	63T	315	$ .90	$3.60
Terry, Ralph	64T	458	$1.00	$4.00
Terry, Ralph	65T	406	$1.00	$4.00
Terry, Ralph	66T	109	$ .35	$1.40
Terry, Ralph	67T	59	$ .40	$1.60
Terry, Scott	87T	453	$ .01	$ .04
Terry, Scott	88TTR	119	$ .01	$ .05
Terry, Scott	89T	686	$ .01	$ .03
Terry, Scott	90T	82	$ .01	$ .03
Terry, Scott	91T	539	$ .01	$ .03
Terry, Scott	91TSC	469	$ .05	$ .25
Terry, Scott	92T	117	$ .01	$ .03
Terry, Scott	92TSC	522	$ .01	$ .10
Terwilliger, Wayne	51Trb	14	$1.75	$7.50
Terwilliger, Wayne	52T	7	$13.75	$55.00
Terwilliger, Wayne	53T	159	$4.00	$16.00
Terwilliger, Wayne	54T	73	$7.50	$30.00
Terwilliger, Wayne	55T	34	$2.25	$9.00
Terwilliger, Wayne	56T	73	$2.00	$8.00
Terwilliger, Wayne	59T	496	$1.00	$4.00
Terwilliger, Wayne	60T	26	$ .85	$3.40
Terwilliger, Wayne	91TA53	159	$ .01	$ .15
Tettleton, Mickey	85TTR	120	$1.25	$5.00
Tettleton, Mickey	86T	457	$ .10	$1.00
Tettleton, Mickey	87T	649	$ .01	$ .10
Tettleton, Mickey	88T	143	$ .01	$ .10
Tettleton, Mickey	88TTR	120	$ .05	$ .20
Tettleton, Mickey	89T	521	$ .01	$ .03
Tettleton, Mickey	90T	275	$ .01	$ .03
Tettleton, Mickey	91T	385	$ .01	$ .03
Tettleton, Mickey	91TSC	412	$ .10	$ .40
Tettleton, Mickey	91TTR	119	$ .01	$ .05
Tettleton, Mickey	92T	29	$ .01	$ .03
Tettleton, Mickey	92TSC	195	$ .01	$ .10
Tettleton, Mickey	93T	135	$ .01	$ .03
Tettleton, Mickey	93TSC	31	$ .01	$ .10
Teufel, Tim	84TTR	117	$ .10	$ .40
Teufel, Tim	85T	239	$ .01	$ .15
Teufel, Tim	86T	667	$ .01	$ .05
Teufel, Tim	86TTR	109	$ .01	$ .06
Teufel, Tim	87T	158	$ .01	$ .04
Teufel, Tim	88T	508	$ .01	$ .04
Teufel, Tim	89T	9	$ .01	$ .03
Teufel, Tim	90T	764	$ .01	$ .03
Teufel, Tim	91T	302	$ .01	$ .03
Teufel, Tim	91TSC	43	$ .05	$ .25
Teufel, Tim	91TTR	120	$ .01	$ .05
Teufel, Tim	92T	413	$ .01	$ .03
Teufel, Tim	92TSC	485	$ .01	$ .10
Teufel, Tim	93T	636	$ .01	$ .03
Teufel, Tim	93TSC	213	$ .01	$ .10
Tewksbury, Bob	86TTR	110	$ .10	$ .50
Tewksbury, Bob	87T	254	$ .05	$ .25
Tewksbury, Bob	88T	593	$ .01	$ .04
Tewksbury, Bob	90TTR	122	$ .01	$ .05
Tewksbury, Bob	91T	88	$ .01	$ .03
Tewksbury, Bob	91TSC	417	$ .05	$ .25
Tewksbury, Bob	92T	623	$ .01	$ .03
Tewksbury, Bob	92TSC	258	$ .01	$ .10
Tewksbury, Bob	93T	285	$ .01	$ .03
Thacker, Moe	59T	474	$1.00	$4.00
Thacker, Moe	61T	12	$ .60	$2.40
Thacker, Moe	62T	546	$6.00	$24.00
Theobald, Ron	72T	77	$ .10	$ .40
Theodore, George	74T	8	$ .10	$ .40
Thibdeau, John	69T	189	$ .35	$1.40
Thies, Jake	55T	12	$2.25	$9.00
Thigpen, Bobby	87T	61	$ .05	$ .25
Thigpen, Bobby	88T	613	$ .01	$ .10
Thigpen, Bobby	89T	762	$ .01	$ .03
Thigpen, Bobby	90T	255	$ .01	$ .03
Thigpen, Bobby	91T	420	$ .01	$ .03
Thigpen, Bobby	91TAS	396	$ .01	$ .03
Thigpen, Bobby	91TRB	8	$ .01	$ .03
Thigpen, Bobby	91TSC	256	$ .05	$ .25
Thigpen, Bobby	92T	505	$ .01	$ .03
Thigpen, Bobby	92TSC	224	$ .01	$ .10
Thigpen, Bobby	93T	645	$ .01	$ .03
Thoenen, Dick	68T	348	$ .35	$1.40
Thomas, Andres	86TTR	111	$ .01	$ .06
Thomas, Andres	87T	296	$ .01	$ .04
Thomas, Andres	88T	13	$ .01	$ .04
Thomas, Andres	89T	523	$ .01	$ .03
Thomas, Andres	90T	358	$ .01	$ .03
Thomas, Andres	91T	111	$ .01	$ .03
Thomas, Dan	77T	488	$2.50	$10.00
Thomas, Derrel	72T	457	$ .25	$1.00
Thomas, Derrel	73T	57	$ .10	$ .40

Player	Year	No.	VG	EX/MT
Thomas, Derrel	74T	518	$ .10	$ .40
Thomas, Derrel	75T	378	$ .10	$ .40
Thomas, Derrel	76T	493	$ .05	$ .25
Thomas, Derrel	77T	266	$ .05	$ .20
Thomas, Derrel	78T	194	$ .04	$ .16
Thomas, Derrel	79T	679	$ .03	$ .12
Thomas, Derrel	80T	23	$ .01	$ .10

TOPPS

Player	Year	No.	VG	EX/MT	Player	Year	No.	VG	EX/MT
Thomas, Derrel	81T	211	$ .01	$ .08	Thomas, Gorman	80T	202	$ .05	$ .20
Thomas, Derrel	82T	348	$ .01	$ .08	Thomas, Gorman	80T	623	$ .01	$ .10
Thomas, Derrel	83T	748	$ .01	$ .08	Thomas, Gorman	81T	135	$ .01	$ .08
Thomas, Derrel	84T	583	$ .01	$ .06	Thomas, Gorman	82T	765	$ .01	$ .08
Thomas, Derrel	84TTR	118	$ .01	$ .15	Thomas, Gorman	83T	10	$ .01	$ .10
Thomas, Derrel	85T	448	$ .01	$ .06	Thomas, Gorman	83T	702	$ .05	$ .25
Thomas, Derrel	85TTR	121	$ .01	$ .10	Thomas, Gorman	83TTR	111	$ .01	$ .10
Thomas, Derrel	86T	158	$ .01	$ .05	Thomas, Gorman	84T	515	$ .01	$ .06
Thomas, Frank	56T	153	$3.50	$14.00	Thomas, Gorman	84TTR	119	$ .01	$ .15
Thomas, Frank	57T	140	$2.00	$8.00	Thomas, Gorman	85T	202	$ .01	$ .06
Thomas, Frank	58T	409	$1.00	$4.00	Thomas, Gorman	86T	750	$ .01	$ .05
Thomas, Frank	59T	17	$1.50	$6.00	Thomas, Gorman	87T	495	$ .01	$ .04
Thomas, Frank	59T	490	$1.00	$4.00	Thomas, Keith	53T	129	$6.25	$25.00
Thomas, Frank	60T	95	$ .85	$3.40	Thomas, Keith	91TA53	129	$ .01	$ .15
Thomas, Frank	61T	382	$1.00	$4.00	Thomas, Leroy (Lee)	61T	464	$1.50	$6.00
Thomas, Frank	62T	7	$ .75	$3.00	Thomas, Lee	62T	154	$ .60	$2.40
Thomas, Frank	63T	495	$5.50	$22.00	Thomas, Lee	63T	441	$1.00	$4.00
Thomas, Frank	64T	345	$ .65	$2.60	Thomas, Lee	64T	255	$ .65	$2.60
Thomas, Frank	65T	123	$ .35	$1.40	Thomas, Lee	65T	111	$ .35	$1.40
Thomas, Frank	90T	414	$1.00	$4.00	Thomas, Lee	66T	408	$ .65	$2.60
Thomas, Frank	91T	79	$ .10	$1.00	Thomas, Lee	67T	458	$1.50	$6.00
Thomas, Frank	91TA53	283	$ .05	$ .25	Thomas, Lee	68T	438	$ .35	$1.40
Thomas, Frank	91TSC	57	$6.00	$24.00	Thomas, Roy	78T	711	$ .04	$ .16
Thomas, Frank	92T	555	$ .10	$1.00	Thomas, Roy	79T	563	$ .03	$ .12
Thomas, Frank	92TSC	301	$1.25	$5.00	Thomas, Roy	80T	397	$ .01	$ .10
Thomas, Frank	92TSC	591	$ .20	$2.00	Thomas, Roy	84T	181	$ .01	$ .06
Thomas, Frank	93T	150	$ .10	$ .50	Thomas, Roy	86T	626	$ .01	$ .05
Thomas, Frank	93T	401	$ .05	$ .35	Thomas, Stan	76T	148	$ .05	$ .25
Thomas, Frank	93TSC	200	$ .75	$3.00	Thomas, Stan	77T	353	$ .05	$ .20
Thomas, George	61T	544	$7.50	$30.00	Thomas, Valmy	58T	86	$2.00	$8.00
Thomas, George	62T	525	$3.50	$14.00	Thomas, Valmy	59T	235	$1.00	$4.00
Thomas, George	63T	98	$ .50	$2.00	Thomas, Valmy	60T	167	$ .75	$3.00
Thomas, George	64T	461	$1.00	$4.00	Thomas, Valmy	61T	319	$ .60	$2.40
Thomas, George	65T	83	$ .35	$1.40	Thomasson, Gary	74T	18	$ .10	$ .40
Thomas, George	66T	277	$ .50	$2.00	Thomasson, Gary	75T	529	$ .10	$ .40
Thomas, George	67T	184	$ .40	$1.60	Thomasson, Gary	76T	261	$ .05	$ .25
Thomas, George	69T	521	$ .40	$1.60	Thomasson, Gary	77T	496	$ .05	$ .20
Thomas, George	71T	678	$1.10	$4.40	Thomasson, Gary	78T	648	$ .04	$ .16
Thomas, Gorman	74T	288	$ .35	$1.40	Thomasson, Gary	79T	387	$ .03	$ .12
Thomas, Gorman	75T	532	$ .10	$ .40	Thomasson, Gary	80T	127	$ .01	$ .10
Thomas, Gorman	76T	139	$ .10	$ .40	Thomasson, Gary	81T	512	$ .01	$ .08
					Thome, Jim	92T	768	$ .01	$ .15
					Thome, Jim	92TSC	360	$ .05	$ .25
					Thome, Jim	93T	603	$ .01	$ .03
					Thome, Jim	93TSC	8	$ .01	$ .10
					Thompson, Bobby	79T	336	$ .03	$ .12
					Thompson, Charlie (y)	54T	209	$3.75	$15.00
					Thompson, Charley	57T	142	$2.00	$8.00
					Thompson, Danny	71T	127	$ .25	$1.00
					Thompson, Danny	72T	368	$ .10	$ .40
					Thompson, Danny	73T	443	$ .25	$1.00
					Thompson, Danny	74T	168	$ .10	$ .40
					Thompson, Danny	75T	249	$ .10	$ .40
					Thompson, Danny	76T	111	$ .05	$ .25
					Thompson, Hank	51Trb	32	$1.75	$7.50
					Thompson, Hank	52T	3	$13.75	$55.00
					Thompson, Hank	53T	20	$7.50	$30.00
					Thompson, Hank	54T	64	$8.00	$32.00
					Thompson, Hank	56T	199	$3.75	$15.00
					Thompson, Hank	57T	109	$2.00	$8.00
					Thompson, Hank	91TA53	20	$ .01	$ .15
					Thompson, Jason	77T	291	$ .10	$ .40
					Thompson, Jason	78T	660	$ .04	$ .16
					Thompson, Jason	79T	80	$ .03	$ .12
					Thompson, Jason	80T	150	$ .01	$ .10
					Thompson, Jason	81T	505	$ .01	$ .08
					Thompson, Jason	81TTR	843	$ .01	$ .15
					Thompson, Jason	82T	295	$ .01	$ .08
					Thompson, Jason	83T	730	$ .01	$ .08
					Thompson, Jason	84T	355	$ .01	$ .06
					Thompson, Jason	85T	490	$ .01	$ .06
					Thompson, Jason	86T	635	$ .01	$ .05
					Thompson, Mark	93T	419	$ .05	$ .20
					Thompson, Mike	73T	564	$ .60	$2.40
Thomas, Gorman	77T	439	$ .05	$ .20	Thompson, Mike	76T	536	$ .05	$ .25
Thomas, Gorman	79T	376	$ .05	$ .20					

TOPPS

Player	Year	No.	VG	EX/MT
Thompson, Milt	86T	517	$ .01	$ .15
Thompson, Milt	86TTR	112	$ .01	$ .06
Thompson, Milt	87T	409	$ .01	$ .04
Thompson, Milt	88T	298	$ .01	$ .04
Thompson, Milt	89T	128	$ .01	$ .03
Thompson, Milt	89TTR	118	$ .01	$ .05
Thompson, Milt	90T	688	$ .01	$ .03
Thompson, Milt	91T	63	$ .01	$ .03

Player	Year	No.	VG	EX/MT
Thompson, Milt	**91TSC**	**66**	**$ .05**	**$ .25**
Thompson, Milt	92T	323	$ .01	$ .03
Thompson, Milt	92TSC	447	$ .01	$ .10
Thompson, Rich	85TTR	122	$ .01	$ .10
Thompson, Rich	86T	242	$ .01	$ .05
Thompson, Rich	90T	474	$ .01	$ .03
Thompson, Robby	86TTR	113	$ .05	$ .35
Thompson, Robby	87T	658	$ .01	$ .15
Thompson, Robby	88T	472	$ .01	$ .04
Thompson, Robby	89T	15	$ .01	$ .03
Thompson, Robby	90T	325	$ .01	$ .03
Thompson, Robby	91T	705	$ .01	$ .03
Thompson, Robby	91TSC	77	$ .05	$ .25
Thompson, Robby	92T	475	$ .01	$ .03
Thompson, Robby	92TSC	160	$ .01	$ .10
Thompson, Robby	93T	115	$ .01	$ .03
Thompson, Ryan	93T	547	$ .05	$ .20
Thompson, Scot	79T	716	$ .03	$ .12
Thompson, Scot	80T	574	$ .01	$ .10
Thompson, Scot	81T	395	$ .01	$ .08
Thompson, Scot	83T	481	$ .01	$ .08
Thompson, Scot	85T	646	$ .01	$ .06
Thompson, Scot	86T	93	$ .01	$ .05
Thompson, Tim	58T	57	$2.00	$8.00
Thomson, Bobby	52T	313	$55.00	$220.00
Thomson, Bobby	56T	257	$5.50	$22.00
Thomson, Bobby	57T	262	$2.75	$11.00
Thomson, Bobby	58T	430	$1.50	$6.00
Thomson, Bobby	59T	429	$1.00	$4.00
Thomson, Bobby	60T	153	$ .75	$3.00
Thomson, Bobby	91TA53	330	$ .05	$ .35
Thon, Dickie	80T	663	$ .10	$1.00
Thon, Dickie	81T	209	$ .01	$ .15
Thon, Dickie	81TTR	844	$ .05	$ .25
Thon, Dickie	82T	404	$ .01	$ .08
Thon, Dickie	83T	558	$ .01	$ .08
Thon, Dickie	84T	692	$ .01	$ .06
Thon, Dickie	85T	44	$ .01	$ .06
Thon, Dickie	86T	166	$ .01	$ .05
Thon, Dickie	87T	386	$ .01	$ .04
Thon, Dickie	88TTR	121	$ .01	$ .05
Thon, Dickie	89T	726	$ .01	$ .03
Thon, Dickie	89TTR	119	$ .01	$ .05
Thon, Dickie	90T	269	$ .01	$ .03
Thon, Dickie	91T	439	$ .01	$ .03
Thon, Dickie	91TSC	184	$ .05	$ .25
Thon, Dickie	92T	557	$ .01	$ .03
Thon, Dickie	92TSC	868	$ .01	$ .10
Thon, Dickie	92TTR	118	$ .01	$ .05
Thormodsgard, Paul	78T	162	$ .04	$ .16
Thormodsgard, Paul	79T	249	$ .03	$ .12
Thornton, Andy	74T	604	$1.25	$5.00
Thornton, Andy	75T	39	$ .10	$ .40
Thornton, Andy	76T	26	$ .05	$ .25
Thornton, Andre	78T	148	$ .04	$ .16
Thornton, Andre	79T	280	$ .03	$ .12
Thornton, Andre	80T	534	$ .01	$ .10
Thornton, Andre	81T	388	$ .01	$ .08
Thornton, Andre	82T	746	$ .01	$ .08
Thornton, Andre	83T	640	$ .01	$ .08
Thornton, Andre	84T	115	$ .01	$ .06
Thornton, Andre	85T	475	$ .01	$ .06
Thornton, Andre	86T	59	$ .01	$ .05
Thornton, Andre	87T	780	$ .01	$ .04
Thornton, Lou	86T	488	$ .01	$ .05
Thorpe, Bob	52T	367	$43.75	$175.00
Throedson, Rich	74T	77	$ .10	$ .40
Throneberry, Faye	52T	376	$43.75	$175.00
Throneberry, Faye	53T	49	$4.00	$16.00
Throneberry, Faye	55T	163	$6.25	$25.00
Throneberry, Faye	57T	356	$1.75	$7.00
Throneberry, Faye	59T	534	$4.00	$16.00
Throneberry, Faye	60T	9	$ .85	$3.40
Throneberry, Faye	61T	282	$ .60	$2.40
Throneberry, Faye	91TA53	49	$ .01	$ .15
Throneberry, Marv	58T	175	$3.00	$12.00
Throneberry, Marv	59T	326	$1.00	$4.00
Throneberry, Marv	60T	436	$1.25	$5.00
Throneberry, Marv	61T	57	$1.00	$4.00
Throneberry, Marv	63T	78	$ .90	$3.60
Throop, George	76T	591	$ .05	$ .25
Thurman, Bob	57T	279	$5.00	$20.00
Thurman, Bob	58T	34	$2.00	$8.00
Thurman, Bob	59T	541	$4.00	$16.00
Thurman, Gary	88T	89	$ .01	$ .04
Thurman, Gary	89T	323	$ .01	$ .03
Thurman, Gary	90T	276	$ .01	$ .03
Thurman, Gary	91TSC	306	$ .05	$ .25
Thurman, Gary	92T	494	$ .01	$ .03
Thurman, Gary	92TSC	131	$ .01	$ .10
Thurman, Gary	93TSC	52	$ .01	$ .03
Thurmond, Mark	84T	481	$ .01	$ .10
Thurmond, Mark	85T	236	$ .01	$ .06
Thurmond, Mark	86T	37	$ .01	$ .05
Thurmond, Mark	87T	361	$ .01	$ .04
Thurmond, Mark	88T	552	$ .01	$ .04
Thurmond, Mark	89T	152	$ .01	$ .03
Thurmond, Mark	90T	758	$ .01	$ .03
Tiant, Luis	65T	145	$3.00	$12.00
Tiant, Luis	66T	285	$1.00	$4.00
Tiant, Luis	67T	377	$1.00	$4.00
Tiant, Luis	68T	532	$1.00	$4.00
Tiant, Luis	69T	7	$ .75	$3.00
Tiant, Luis	69T	9	$ .75	$3.00
Tiant, Luis	69T	11	$ .75	$3.00
Tiant, Luis	69T	560	$ .50	$2.00
Tiant, Luis	70T	231	$ .40	$1.60
Tiant, Luis	71T	95	$ .35	$1.40
Tiant, Luis	73T	65	$ .35	$1.40
Tiant, Luis	73T	270	$ .25	$1.00

TOPPS

Player	Year	No.	VG	EX/MT
Tiant, Luis	74T	167	$ .25	$1.00
Tiant, Luis	75T	430	$ .10	$ .40
Tiant, Luis	76T	130	$ .15	$ .60
Tiant, Luis	77T	258	$ .10	$ .40
Tiant, Luis	78T	345	$ .05	$ .20
Tiant, Luis	79T	575	$ .05	$ .20
Tiant, Luis	80T	35	$ .05	$ .20
Tiant, Luis	81T	627	$ .01	$ .15
Tiant, Luis	82T	160	$ .01	$ .08
Tiant, Luis	83T	178	$ .01	$ .08
Tiant, Luis	83T	179	$ .01	$ .08
Tibbs, Jay	85T	573	$ .01	$ .06
Tibbs, Jay	86T	176	$ .01	$ .05
Tibbs, Jay	86TTR	114	$ .01	$ .06
Tibbs, Jay	87T	9	$ .01	$ .04
Tibbs, Jay	88T	464	$ .01	$ .04
Tibbs, Jay	89T	271	$ .01	$ .03
Tibbs, Jay	90T	677	$ .01	$ .03
Tidrow, Dick	72T	506	$ .20	$ .80
Tidrow, Dick	73T	339	$ .10	$ .40
Tidrow, Dick	74T	231	$ .10	$ .40
Tidrow, Dick	75T	241	$ .10	$ .40
Tidrow, Dick	76T	248	$ .05	$ .25
Tidrow, Dick	77T	461	$ .05	$ .20
Tidrow, Dick	78T	179	$ .04	$ .16
Tidrow, Dick	79T	89	$ .03	$ .12
Tidrow, Dick	80T	594	$ .01	$ .10
Tidrow, Dick	81T	352	$ .01	$ .08
Tidrow, Dick	82T	699	$ .01	$ .08
Tidrow, Dick	83T	787	$ .01	$ .08
Tidrow, Dick	83TTR	112	$ .01	$ .10
Tidrow, Dick	84T	153	$ .01	$ .06
Tiefenauer, Bobby	59T	501	$1.00	$4.00
Tiefenauer, Bobby	62T	227	$ .75	$3.00
Tiefenauer, Bobby	64T	522	$1.00	$4.00
Tiefenauer, Bob	65T	23	$ .35	$1.40
Tiefenauer, Bob	68T	269	$ .35	$1.40
Tigers, Team	56T	213	$13.75	$55.00
Tigers, Team	57T	198	$3.00	$12.00
Tigers, Team	58T	397	$3.50	$14.00
Tigers, Team	59T	329	$2.50	$10.00
Tigers, Team	60T	72	$2.00	$8.00
Tigers, Team	61T	51	$1.75	$7.00
Tigers, Team	62T	24	$1.50	$6.00
Tigers, Team	63T	552	$8.00	$32.00
Tigers, Team	64T	67	$1.00	$4.00
Tigers, Team	65T	173	$ .75	$3.00
Tigers, Team	66T	583	$35.00	$140.00
Tigers, Team	67T	378	$1.25	$5.00
Tigers, Team	68T	528	$17.50	$70.00
Tigers, Team	70T	579	$1.25	$5.00
Tigers, Team	71T	336	$ .50	$2.00
Tigers, Team	72T	487	$ .75	$3.00
Tigers, Team	73T	191	$ .30	$1.20
Tigers, Team	74T	94	$ .25	$1.00
Tigers, Team Checklist	75T	18	$ .35	$1.40
Tigers, Team Checklist	76T	361	$ .30	$1.20
Tigers, Team Checklist	77T	621	$ .25	$1.00
Tigers, Team Checklist	78T	404	$ .20	$ .80
Tigers, Team Checklist	79T	66	$ .15	$ .60
Tigers, Team Checklist	80T	626	$ .10	$ .50
Tigers, Team Checklist	81T	666	$ .05	$ .25
Tigers, Team Leaders	86T	36	$ .01	$ .10
Tigers, Team Leaders	87T	631	$ .01	$ .04
Tigers, Team Leaders	88T	429	$ .01	$ .04
Tigers, Team Leaders	89T	609	$ .01	$ .03
Tillman, Bob	62T	368	$ .75	$3.00
Tillman, Bob	63T	384	$1.00	$4.00
Tillman, Bob	64T	112	$ .50	$2.00
Tillman, Bob	65T	222	$ .50	$2.00
Tillman, Bob	66T	178	$ .50	$2.00
Tillman, Bob	67T	36	$ .40	$1.60
Tillman, Bob	68T	174	$ .35	$1.40
Tillman, Bob	69T	374	$ .30	$1.20
Tillman, Bob	70T	668	$1.25	$5.00

Player	Year	No.	VG	EX/MT
Tillman, Bob	71T	244	$ .25	$1.00
Tillotson, Thad	67T	553	$7.50	$30.00
Timlin, Mike	91TTR	121	$ .01	$ .10
Timlin, Mike	92T	108	$ .01	$ .10
Timlin, Mike	92TSC	493	$ .01	$ .10
Timlin, Mike	93T	564	$ .01	$ .03
Timlin, Mike	93TSC	120	$ .01	$ .10
Timmermann, Tom	70T	554	$ .50	$2.00
Timmermann, Tom	71T	296	$ .25	$1.00
Timmermann, Tom	72T	239	$ .10	$ .40
Timmermann, Tom	73T	413	$ .25	$1.00
Timmermann, Tom	74T	327	$ .10	$ .40
Tingley, Ron	89T	721	$ .01	$ .03
Tingley, Ron	93TSC	169	$ .01	$ .10
Tinsley, Lee	92T	656	$ .05	$ .20
Tipton, Joe	52T	134	$7.00	$28.00
Tischinski, Tom	70T	379	$ .35	$1.40
Tischinski, Tom	71T	724	$1.50	$6.00
Tobik, Dave	79T	706	$ .03	$ .12
Tobik, Dave	80T	269	$ .01	$ .10
Tobik, Dave	81T	102	$ .01	$ .08
Tobik, Dave	82T	391	$ .01	$ .08
Tobik, Dave	83T	691	$ .01	$ .08
Tobik, Dave	83TTR	113	$ .01	$ .10
Tobik, Dave	84T	341	$ .01	$ .06
Todd, Jackson	78T	481	$ .04	$ .16

Player	Year	No.	VG	EX/MT
Todd, Jackson	81T	142	$ .01	$ .08
Todd, Jackson	82T	565	$ .01	$ .08
Todd, Jim	75T	519	$ .10	$ .40
Todd, Jim	76T	221	$ .05	$ .25
Todd, Jim	77T	31	$ .05	$ .20
Todd, Jim	78T	333	$ .04	$ .16
Todd, Jim	79T	103	$ .03	$ .12
Todd, Jim	80T	629	$ .01	$ .10
Tolan, Bob	65T	116	$ .50	$2.00
Tolan, Bob	66T	179	$ .50	$2.00
Tolan, Bob	67T	474	$1.50	$6.00
Tolan, Bob	68T	84	$ .35	$1.40
Tolan, Bob	69T	448	$ .30	$1.20
Tolan, Bob	70T	409	$ .35	$1.40
Tolan, Bob	71T	190	$ .25	$1.00
Tolan, Bob	72T	3	$ .10	$ .40
Tolan, Bob	73T	335	$ .10	$ .40

TOPPS

Player	Year	No.	VG	EX/MT
Tolan, Bob	74T	535	$ .10	$ .40
Tolan, Bob	75T	402	$ .10	$ .40
Tolan, Bob	76T	56	$ .05	$ .25
Tolan, Bob	77T	188	$ .05	$ .20
Tolan, Bob	80T	708	$ .01	$ .10
Tolentino, Jose	92T	541	$ .01	$ .10
Toliver, Fred	87T	63	$ .01	$ .04
Toliver, Fred	88T	203	$ .01	$ .04
Toliver, Fred	89T	623	$ .01	$ .03
Toliver, Fred	90T	423	$ .01	$ .03
Tolleson, Wayne	83TTR	114	$ .01	$ .10
Tolleson, Wayne	84T	557	$ .01	$ .06
Tolleson, Wayne	85T	247	$ .01	$ .06
Tolleson, Wayne	86T	641	$ .01	$ .05
Tolleson, Wayne	86TTR	115	$ .01	$ .06
Tolleson, Wayne	87T	224	$ .01	$ .04
Tolleson, Wayne	88T	411	$ .01	$ .04
Tolleson, Wayne	89T	716	$ .01	$ .03
Tolleson, Wayne	90TTR	123	$ .01	$ .05
Tolman, Tim	86T	272	$ .01	$ .05
Tomanek, Dick	58T	123	$1.25	$5.00
Tomanek, Dick	59T	369	$1.00	$4.00
Tomlin, Dave	75T	578	$ .10	$ .40
Tomlin, Dave	76T	398	$ .05	$ .25
Tomlin, Dave	77T	241	$ .05	$ .20
Tomlin, Dave	78T	86	$ .04	$ .16
Tomlin, Dave	79T	674	$ .03	$ .12
Tomlin, Dave	80T	126	$ .01	$ .10
Tomlin, Randy	91T	167	$ .01	$ .15
Tomlin, Randy	91TSC	178	$ .10	$1.00
Tomlin, Randy	92T	571	$ .01	$ .03
Tomlin, Randy	92TSC	661	$ .01	$ .10
Tomlin, Randy	93T	416	$ .01	$ .03
Tomlin, Randy	93TSC	104	$ .01	$ .10
Tompkins, Ron	66T	107	$ .35	$1.40
Tompkins, Ron	68T	247	$65.00	$260.00
Torborg, Jeff	64T	337	$1.50	$6.00
Torborg, Jeff	65T	527	$3.00	$12.00
Torborg, Jeff	66T	257	$ .50	$2.00
Torborg, Jeff	67T	398	$ .60	$2.40
Torborg, Jeff	68T	492	$ .75	$3.00
Torborg, Jeff	69T	353	$ .30	$1.20
Torborg, Jeff	70T	54	$ .20	$ .80
Torborg, Jeff	71T	314	$ .25	$1.00
Torborg, Jeff	72T	404	$ .25	$1.00
Torborg, Jeff	73T	154	$ .10	$ .40
Torborg, Jeff	78T	351	$ .04	$ .16
Torborg, Jeff	89TTR	120	$ .01	$ .05
Torborg, Jeff	90T	21	$ .01	$ .03
Torborg, Jeff	91T	609	$ .01	$ .03
Torborg, Jeff	92T	759	$ .01	$ .03
Torborg, Jeff	93T	509	$ .01	$ .03
Torgeson, Earl	51Tbb	34	$7.50	$30.00
Torgeson, Earl	52T	97	$7.00	$28.00
Torgeson, Earl	56T	147	$2.50	$10.00
Torgeson, Earl	57T	357	$1.75	$7.00
Torgeson, Earl	58T	138	$1.25	$5.00
Torgeson, Earl	59T	351	$1.00	$4.00
Torgeson, Earl	60T	299	$ .75	$3.00
Torgeson, Earl	61T	152	$ .60	$2.40
Torre, Frank	56T	172	$3.50	$14.00
Torre, Frank	57T	37	$2.00	$8.00
Torre, Frank	58T	117	$1.25	$5.00
Torre, Frank	59T	65	$1.50	$6.00
Torre, Frank	60T	478	$1.25	$5.00
Torre, Frank	62T	303	$ .75	$3.00
Torre, Frank	63T	161	$ .50	$2.00
Torre, Joe	62T	218	$5.50	$22.00
Torre, Joe	62T	351	$1.25	$5.00
Torre, Joe	63T	347	$2.00	$8.00
Torre, Joe	64T	70	$1.00	$4.00
Torre, Joe	65T	200	$1.00	$4.00
Torre, Joe	66T	130	$ .75	$3.00
Torre, Joe	67T	350	$1.00	$4.00
Torre, Joe	68T	30	$ .60	$2.40
Torre, Joe	69T	460	$ .75	$3.00
Torre, Joe	70T	190	$ .50	$2.00
Torre, Joe	71T	62	$ .50	$2.00
Torre, Joe	71T	370	$ .75	$3.00
Torre, Joe	72T	85	$ .50	$2.00
Torre, Joe	72T	87	$ .75	$3.00
Torre, Joe	72T	341	$ .10	$ .40
Torre, Joe	72T	500	$ .50	$2.00
Torre, Joe	73T	450	$ .50	$2.00
Torre, Joe	74T	15	$ .25	$1.00
Torre, Joe	75T	209	$ .25	$1.00
Torre, Joe	75T	565	$ .25	$1.00
Torre, Joe	76T	585	$ .15	$ .60
Torre, Joe	77T	425	$ .20	$ .80
Torre, Joe	78T	109	$ .10	$ .40
Torre, Joe	83T	126	$ .01	$ .08
Torre, Joe	84T	502	$ .01	$ .06

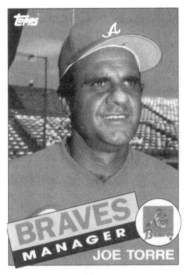

Player	Year	No.	VG	EX/MT
Torre, Joe	**85T**	**438**	**$ .01**	**$ .06**
Torre, Joe	91T	351	$ .01	$ .03
Torre, Joe	92T	549	$ .01	$ .03
Torre, Joe	93T	512	$ .01	$ .03
Torrealba, Pablo	76T	589	$ .50	$2.00
Torrealba, Pablo	77T	499	$ .05	$ .20
Torrealba, Pablo	78T	78	$ .04	$ .16
Torrealba, Pablo	79T	242	$ .03	$ .12
Torres, Felix	62T	595	$5.25	$21.00
Torres, Felix	63T	482	$3.00	$12.00
Torres, Hector	69T	526	$ .40	$1.60
Torres, Hector	70T	272	$ .35	$1.40
Torres, Hector	71T	558	$1.00	$4.00
Torres, Hector	72T	666	$1.25	$5.00
Torres, Hector	76T	241	$ .05	$ .25
Torres, Rusty	72T	124	$ .10	$ .40
Torres, Rusty	73T	571	$ .60	$2.40
Torres, Rusty	74T	499	$ .10	$ .40
Torres, Rusty	77T	224	$ .05	$ .20
Torres, Rusty	80T	36	$ .01	$ .10
Torrez, Mike	68T	162	$ .35	$1.40
Torrez, Mike	69T	136	$ .35	$1.40
Torrez, Mike	70T	312	$ .35	$1.40
Torrez, Mike	71T	531	$1.00	$4.00
Torrez, Mike	73T	77	$ .10	$ .40
Torrez, Mike	74T	568	$ .10	$ .40

TOPPS

Player	Year	No.	VG	EX/MT
Torrez, Mike	75T	254	$ .10	$ .40
Torrez, Mike	76T	25	$ .05	$ .25
Torrez, Mike	77T	365	$ .05	$ .20
Torrez, Mike	78T	645	$ .04	$ .16
Torrez, Mike	79T	185	$ .03	$ .12
Torrez, Mike	80T	455	$ .01	$ .10
Torrez, Mike	81T	525	$ .01	$ .08
Torrez, Mike	82T	225	$ .01	$ .08
Torrez, Mike	82T	786	$ .01	$ .08
Torrez, Mike	83T	743	$ .01	$ .08
Torrez, Mike	83TTR	115	$ .01	$ .10
Torrez, Mike	84T	78	$ .01	$ .06
Toth, Paul	63T	489	$3.00	$12.00
Toth, Paul	64T	309	$ .65	$2.60
Tovar, Cesar	65T	201	$ .50	$2.00
Tovar, Cesar	66T	563	$3.75	$15.00
Tovar, Cesar	67T	317	$ .60	$2.40
Tovar, Cesar	68T	420	$ .35	$1.40
Tovar, Cesar	**69T**	**530**	**$ .40**	**$1.60**
Tovar, Cesar	70T	25	$ .20	$ .80
Tovar, Cesar	71T	165	$ .25	$1.00
Tovar, Cesar	72T	275	$ .10	$ .40
Tovar, Cesar	73T	405	$ .25	$1.00
Tovar, Cesar	74T	538	$ .10	$ .40
Tovar, Cesar	74TTR	538	$ .10	$ .40
Tovar, Cesar	75T	178	$ .10	$ .40
Tovar, Cesar	76T	246	$ .05	$ .25
Tovar, Cesar	77T	408	$ .05	$ .20
Traber, Jim	87T	484	$ .01	$ .04
Traber, Jim	88T	544	$ .01	$ .04
Traber, Jim	89T	124	$ .01	$ .03
Tracewski, Dick	64T	154	$ .50	$2.00
Tracewski, Dick	65T	279	$ .50	$2.00
Tracewski, Dick	66T	378	$ .65	$2.60
Tracewski, Dick	67T	559	$2.25	$9.00
Tracewski, Dick	68T	488	$ .75	$3.00
Tracewski, Dick	69T	126	$ .35	$1.40
Tracewski, Dick	73T	323	$ .25	$1.00
Tracy, Jim	82T	403	$ .01	$ .08
Trammell, Alan	78T	707	$12.50	$50.00
Trammell, Alan	79T	358	$2.50	$10.00
Trammell, Alan	80T	232	$1.00	$4.00
Trammell, Alan	81T	709	$ .10	$1.00
Trammell, Alan	82T	475	$ .10	$1.00
Trammell, Alan	83T	95	$ .10	$1.00
Trammell, Alan	84T	510	$ .10	$ .50
Trammell, Alan	85T	690	$ .05	$ .25
Trammell, Alan	86T	130	$ .05	$ .25
Trammell, Alan	87T	687	$ .01	$ .15
Trammell, Alan	88T	320	$ .01	$ .15
Trammell, Alan	88TAS	389	$ .01	$ .05
Trammell, Alan	89T	770	$ .01	$ .10
Trammell, Alan	89TAS	400	$ .01	$ .05
Trammell, Alan	90T	440	$ .01	$ .10
Trammell, Alan	91T	275	$ .01	$ .10
Trammell, Alan	91TAS	389	$ .01	$ .10
Trammell, Alan	91TSC	63	$ .05	$ .35
Trammell, Alan	92T	120	$ .01	$ .03
Trammell, Alan	92TSC	850	$ .01	$ .10
Trammell, Alan	93T	660	$ .01	$ .03
Travers, Bill	75T	488	$ .10	$ .40
Travers, Bill	76T	573	$ .05	$ .25
Travers, Bill	77T	125	$ .05	$ .20
Travers, Bill	78T	355	$ .04	$ .16
Travers, Bill	79T	213	$ .03	$ .12
Travers, Bill	80T	109	$ .01	$ .10
Travers, Bill	81T	704	$ .01	$ .08
Travers, Bill	81TTR	845	$ .01	$ .15
Travers, Bill	82T	628	$ .01	$ .08
Traynor, Pie	76TAT	343	$ .50	$2.00
Treadway, Jeff	88TTR	122	$ .01	$ .15
Treadway, Jeff	89T	685	$ .01	$ .10
Treadway, Jeff	89TTR	121	$ .01	$ .05
Treadway, Jeff	90T	486	$ .01	$ .03
Treadway, Jeff	91T	139	$ .01	$ .03
Treadway, Jeff	91TSC	497	$ .05	$ .25
Treadway, Jeff	92T	99	$ .01	$ .03
Treadway, Jeff	92TSC	82	$ .01	$ .10
Trebelhorn, Tom	87TTR	121	$ .01	$ .05
Trebelhorn, Tom	88T	224	$ .01	$ .04
Trebelhorn, Tom	89T	344	$ .01	$ .03
Trebelhorn, Tom	90T	759	$ .01	$ .03
Trebelhorn, Tom	91T	459	$ .01	$ .03
Tremel, Bill	55T	52	$2.25	$9.00
Tremel, Bill	56T	96	$2.00	$8.00
Tresh, Tom	62T	31	$4.50	$18.00
Tresh, Tom	63T	173	$20.00	$80.00
Tresh, Tom	63T	470	$11.00	$44.00
Tresh, Tom	64T	395	$1.50	$6.00
Tresh, Tom	65T	440	$1.25	$5.00
Tresh, Tom	66T	205	$ .50	$2.00
Tresh, Tom	67T	289	$ .75	$3.00
Tresh, Tom	68T	69	$ .50	$2.00
Tresh, Tom	69T	212	$ .50	$2.00
Tresh, Tom	70T	698	$1.75	$7.00
Trevino, Alex	80T	537	$ .01	$ .10
Trevino, Alex	81T	23	$ .01	$ .08
Trevino, Alex	82T	368	$ .01	$ .08
Trevino, Alex	82TTR	120	$ .01	$ .10
Trevino, Alex	83T	632	$ .01	$ .08
Trevino, Alex	84T	242	$ .01	$ .06
Trevino, Alex	84TTR	120	$ .01	$ .15
Trevino, Alex	85T	747	$ .01	$ .06
Trevino, Alex	85TTR	123	$ .01	$ .10
Trevino, Alex	86T	444	$ .01	$ .05
Trevino, Alex	86TTR	116	$ .01	$ .06
Trevino, Alex	87T	173	$ .01	$ .04
Trevino, Alex	88T	512	$ .01	$ .04
Trevino, Alex	89T	64	$ .01	$ .03
Trevino, Alex	90T	342	$ .01	$ .03
Triandos, Gus	55T	64	$3.00	$12.00
Triandos, Gus	56T	80	$2.00	$8.00
Triandos, Gus	57T	156	$2.00	$8.00
Triandos, Gus	58T	429	$1.00	$4.00
Triandos, Gus	59T	330	$1.00	$4.00
Triandos, Gus	59TAS	568	$4.00	$16.00
Triandos, Gus	60T	60	$ .85	$3.40
Triandos, Gus	61T	140	$ .60	$2.40

TOPPS

Player	Year	No.	VG	EX/MT
Triandos, Gus	62T	420	$1.25	$5.00
Triandos, Gus	63T	475	$3.00	$12.00
Triandos, Gus	64T	83	$ .50	$2.00
Triandos, Gus	65T	248	$ .50	$2.00
Trice, Bob	54T	148	$3.75	$15.00
Trice, Bob	55T	132	$2.25	$9.00
Trillo, Manny	74T	597	$ .15	$ .60
Trillo, Manny	75T	617	$ .50	$2.00
Trillo, Manny	76T	206	$ .15	$ .60
Trillo, Manny	77T	395	$ .05	$ .20
Trillo, Manny	78T	123	$ .04	$ .16
Trillo, Manny	79T	639	$ .03	$ .12
Trillo, Manny	80T	90	$ .01	$ .10
Trillo, Manny	81T	470	$ .01	$ .08
Trillo, Manny	82T	220	$ .01	$ .08
Trillo, Manny	83T	535	$ .01	$ .08
Trillo, Manny	83TAS	398	$ .01	$ .08
Trillo, Manny	83TRB	5	$ .01	$ .08
Trillo, Manny	83TTR	116	$ .01	$ .10
Trillo, Manny	84T	180	$ .01	$ .06
Trillo, Manny	84TTR	121	$ .01	$ .15
Trillo, Manny	85T	310	$ .01	$ .06
Trillo, Manny	86T	655	$ .01	$ .05
Trillo, Manny	86TTR	117	$ .01	$ .06
Trillo, Manny	87T	732	$ .01	$ .04
Trillo, Manny	88T	287	$ .01	$ .04
Trillo, Manny	89T	66	$ .01	$ .03
Trlicek, Ricky	93TSC	218	$ .01	$ .10
Trombley, Mike	93T	588	$ .01	$ .15
Trout, Dizzy	51Tbb	23	$7.50	$30.00
Trout, Dizzy	52T	39	$13.75	$55.00
Trout, Dizzy	53T	169	$4.50	$18.00
Trout, Dizzy	85T	142	$ .01	$ .10
Trout, Dizzy	91TA53	169	$ .01	$ .15
Trout, Steve	80T	83	$ .05	$ .20
Trout, Steve	81T	552	$ .01	$ .08
Trout, Steve	82T	299	$ .01	$ .08
Trout, Steve	83T	461	$ .01	$ .08
Trout, Steve	83TTR	117	$ .01	$ .10
Trout, Steve	84T	151	$ .01	$ .06
Trout, Steve	85T	142	$ .01	$ .10
Trout, Steve	85T	668	$ .01	$ .06
Trout, Steve	86T	384	$ .01	$ .05
Trout, Steve	87T	750	$ .01	$ .04
Trout, Steve	88T	584	$ .01	$ .04
Trout, Steve	89T	54	$ .01	$ .03
Trowbridge, Bob	58T	252	$1.25	$5.00
Trowbridge, Bob	59T	239	$1.00	$4.00
Trowbridge, Bob	60T	66	$ .85	$3.40
Trucks, Virgil	52T	262	$12.50	$50.00
Trucks, Virgil	53T	96	$6.25	$25.00
Trucks, Virgil	56T	117	$2.50	$10.00
Trucks, Virgil	57T	187	$2.00	$8.00
Trucks, Virgil	58T	277	$1.25	$5.00
Trucks, Virgil	59T	417	$1.00	$4.00
Trucks, Virgil	91TA53	96	$ .01	$ .15
Trujillo, Mike	86T	687	$ .01	$ .05
Trujillo, Mike	87T	402	$ .01	$ .04
Trujillo, Mike	88T	307	$ .01	$ .04
Tsitouris, John	60T	497	$1.25	$5.00
Tsitouris, John	63T	244	$ .90	$3.60
Tsitouris, John	64T	275	$ .65	$2.60
Tsitouris, John	65T	221	$ .50	$2.00
Tsitouris, John	66T	12	$ .35	$1.40
Tsitouris, John	68T	523	$ .75	$3.00
Tucker, Michael	92TTR	119	$ .15	$1.25
Tucker, Scooter	92TTR	120	$ .01	$ .10
Tucker, Scooter	93T	814	$ .01	$ .03
Tudor, John	81T	14	$ .10	$ .50
Tudor, John	82T	558	$ .05	$ .20
Tudor, John	83T	318	$ .01	$ .08
Tudor, John	84T	601	$ .01	$ .06
Tudor, John	84TTR	122	$ .01	$ .15
Tudor, John	85T	214	$ .01	$ .06
Tudor, John	85TTR	124	$ .01	$ .10
Tudor, John	86T	474	$ .01	$ .05
Tudor, John	86TAS	710	$ .01	$ .05
Tudor, John	87T	110	$ .01	$ .04
Tudor, John	88T	792	$ .01	$ .04
Tudor, John	89T	35	$ .01	$ .03
Tudor, John	90TTR	124	$ .01	$ .05
Tufts, Bob	82T	171	$ .20	$2.00
Tunnell, Lee	83TTR	118	$ .01	$ .10
Tunnell, Lee	84T	384	$ .01	$ .06
Tunnell, Lee	85T	21	$ .01	$ .06
Tunnell, Lee	86T	161	$ .01	$ .05
Turley, Bob	54T	85	$7.00	$28.00
Turley, Bob	55T	38	$4.00	$16.00
Turley, Bob	56T	40	$2.75	$11.00
Turley, Bob	57T	264	$3.50	$14.00
Turley, Bob	58T	255	$2.00	$8.00
Turley, Bob	58TAS	493	$1.00	$4.00
Turley, Bob	59T	60	$2.00	$8.00
Turley, Bob	59T	237	$1.75	$7.00
Turley, Bob	59TAS	570	$4.00	$16.00
Turley, Bob	60T	270	$1.25	$5.00
Turley, Bob	61T	40	$ .55	$2.20
Turley, Bob	62T	589	$3.75	$15.00
Turley, Bob	63T	322	$ .90	$3.60
Turner, Jerry	75T	619	$ .10	$ .40
Turner, Jerry	76T	598	$ .05	$ .25
Turner, Jerry	77T	447	$ .05	$ .20
Turner, Jerry	78T	364	$ .04	$ .16
Turner, Jerry	79T	564	$ .03	$ .12
Turner, Jerry	80T	133	$ .01	$ .10
Turner, Jerry	81T	285	$ .01	$ .08
Turner, Jerry	82T	736	$ .01	$ .08
Turner, Jerry	82TTR	121	$ .01	$ .10
Turner, Jerry	83T	41	$ .01	$ .08
Turner, Jim	52T	373	$50.00	$200.00
Turner, Jim	62T	263	$ .75	$3.00
Turner, Jim	73T	116	$ .20	$ .80
Turner, Ryan	93T	537	$ .05	$ .20
Turner, Shane	93T	694	$ .01	$ .03

Player	Year	No.	VG	EX/MT
Turner, Shane	93TSC	97	$ .01	$ .10
Tuttle, Bill	56T	203	$3.75	$15.00
Tuttle, Bill	57T	72	$2.00	$8.00
Tuttle, Bill	58T	23	$2.00	$8.00

TOPPS

Player	Year	No.	VG	EX/MT
Tuttle, Bill	59T	459	$1.00	$4.00
Tuttle, Bill	60T	367	$ .75	$3.00
Tuttle, Bill	61T	536	$7.50	$30.00
Tuttle, Bill	62T	298	$ .75	$3.00
Tuttle, Bill	63T	127	$ .50	$2.00
Tuttle, David	91TTR	122	$ .01	$ .15
Twins, Team	61T	542	$16.25	$65.00
Twins, Team	62T	584	$12.00	$48.00
Twins, Team	63T	162	$1.00	$4.00
Twins, Team	64T	318	$1.50	$6.00
Twins, Team	65T	24	$ .75	$3.00
Twins, Team	66T	526	$17.50	$70.00
Twins, Team	67T	211	$ .75	$3.00
Twins, Team	68T	137	$ .75	$3.00
Twins, Team	70T	534	$ .75	$3.00
Twins, Team	71T	522	$ .75	$3.00
Twins, Team	72T	156	$ .25	$1.00
Twins, Team	73T	654	$1.50	$6.00
Twins, Team	74T	74	$ .25	$1.00
Twins, Team Checklist	75T	443	$ .35	$1.40
Twins, Team Checklist	76T	556	$ .30	$1.20
Twins, Team Checklist	77T	228	$ .25	$1.00
Twins, Team Checklist	78T	451	$ .20	$ .80
Twins, Team Checklist	79T	41	$ .15	$ .60
Twins, Team Checklist	80T	328	$ .10	$ .50
Twins, Team Checklist	81T	669	$ .05	$ .25
Twins, Team Leaders	86T	786	$ .01	$ .05
Twins, Team Leaders	87T	206	$ .01	$ .04
Twins, Team Leaders	88T	609	$ .01	$ .04
Twins, Team Leaders	89T	429	$ .01	$ .03
Twitchell, Wayne	71T	692	$1.50	$6.00
Twitchell, Wayne	72T	14	$ .10	$ .40
Twitchell, Wayne	73T	227	$ .10	$ .40

Twitchell, Wayne	74T	419	$ .10	$ .40
Twitchell, Wayne	75T	326	$ .10	$ .40
Twitchell, Wayne	76T	543	$ .05	$ .25
Twitchell, Wayne	77T	444	$ .05	$ .20
Twitchell, Wayne	78T	269	$ .04	$ .16
Twitchell, Wayne	79T	43	$ .03	$ .12
Tyrone, Jim	74T	598	$6.00	$24.00
Tyrone, Jim	78T	487	$ .04	$ .16
Tyson, Mike	74T	655	$ .10	$ .40
Tyson, Mike	75T	231	$ .10	$ .40

Player	Year	No.	VG	EX/MT
Tyson, Mike	76T	86	$ .05	$ .25
Tyson, Mike	77T	599	$ .05	$ .20
Tyson, Mike	78T	111	$ .04	$ .16
Tyson, Mike	79T	324	$ .03	$ .12
Tyson, Mike	80T	486	$ .01	$ .10
Tyson, Mike	81T	294	$ .01	$ .08
Tyson, Mike	82T	62	$ .01	$ .08
Uecker, Bob	62T	594	$20.00	$80.00
Uecker, Bob	63T	126	$5.00	$20.00
Uecker, Bob	64T	543	$10.00	$40.00
Uecker, Bob	65T	519	$7.50	$30.00
Uecker, Bob	66T	91	$4.00	$16.00
Uecker, Bob	67T	326	$4.00	$16.00
Uhlaender, Ted	66T	264	$ .50	$2.00
Uhlaender, Ted	67T	431	$ .60	$2.40
Uhlaender, Ted	68T	28	$ .35	$1.40
Uhlaender, Ted	69T	194	$ .35	$1.40
Uhlaender, Ted	70T	673	$1.25	$5.00
Uhlaender, Ted	71T	347	$ .25	$1.00
Uhlaender, Ted	72T	614	$ .40	$1.60
Ujdur, Jerry	81T	626	$ .01	$ .08
Ujdur, Jerry	83T	174	$ .01	$ .08
Ullger, Scott	84T	551	$ .01	$ .06
Umbach, Arnie	66T	518	$1.50	$6.00
Umbarger, Jim	76T	7	$ .05	$ .25
Umbarger, Jim	77T	378	$ .05	$ .20
Umbarger, Jim	79T	518	$ .03	$ .12
Umbricht, Jim	60T	145	$ .75	$3.00
Umbricht, Jim	63T	99	$ .50	$2.00
Umbricht, Jim	64T	389	$1.00	$4.00
Underwood, Pat	80T	709	$ .01	$ .10
Underwood, Pat	81T	373	$ .01	$ .08
Underwood, Pat	82T	133	$ .01	$ .08
Underwood, Pat	83T	588	$ .01	$ .08
Underwood, Tom	75T	615	$ .25	$1.00
Underwood, Tom	76T	407	$ .05	$ .25
Underwood, Tom	77T	217	$ .05	$ .20
Underwood, Tom	78T	531	$ .04	$ .16
Underwood, Tom	79T	64	$ .03	$ .12
Underwood, Tom	80T	324	$ .01	$ .10
Underwood, Tom	81T	114	$ .01	$ .08
Underwood, Tom	81TTR	846	$ .01	$ .15
Underwood, Tom	82T	757	$ .01	$ .08
Underwood, Tom	83T	466	$ .01	$ .08
Underwood, Tom	84T	642	$ .01	$ .06
Underwood, Tom	84TTR	123	$ .01	$ .15
Underwood, Tom	85T	289	$ .01	$ .06
Unser, Del	69T	338	$ .30	$1.20
Unser, Del	70T	336	$ .35	$1.40
Unser, Del	71T	33	$ .25	$1.00
Unser, Del	72T	687	$1.25	$5.00
Unser, Del	73T	247	$ .10	$ .40
Unser, Del	74T	69	$ .10	$ .40
Unser, Del	75T	138	$ .10	$ .40
Unser, Del	76T	268	$ .05	$ .25
Unser, Del	77T	471	$ .05	$ .20
Unser, Del	78T	348	$ .04	$ .16
Unser, Del	79T	628	$ .03	$ .12
Unser, Del	80T	27	$ .01	$ .10
Unser, Del	80THL	6	$ .01	$ .10
Unser, Del	81T	566	$ .01	$ .08
Unser, Del	82T	713	$ .01	$ .08
Upham, John	67T	608	$2.25	$9.00
Upshaw, Cecil	67T	179	$ .40	$1.60
Upshaw, Cecil	68T	286	$ .35	$1.40
Upshaw, Cecil	69T	568	$ .40	$1.60
Upshaw, Cecil	70T	295	$ .35	$1.40
Upshaw, Cecil	71T	223	$ .25	$1.00
Upshaw, Cecil	72T	74	$ .10	$ .40
Upshaw, Cecil	73T	359	$ .10	$ .40
Upshaw, Cecil	74T	579	$ .10	$ .40
Upshaw, Cecil	74TTR	579	$ .10	$ .40
Upshaw, Cecil	75T	92	$ .10	$ .40
Upshaw, Willie	79T	341	$ .15	$ .60
Upshaw, Willie	82T	196	$ .01	$ .08

TOPPS

Player	Year	No.	VG	EX/MT
Upshaw, Willie	83T	556	$ .01	$ .08
Upshaw, Willie	84T	453	$ .01	$ .06
Upshaw, Willie	85T	75	$ .01	$ .06
Upshaw, Willie	86T	745	$ .01	$ .05
Upshaw, Willie	87T	245	$ .01	$ .04
Upshaw, Willie	88T	505	$ .01	$ .04
Upshaw, Willie	88TTR	123	$ .01	$ .05
Upshaw, Willie	89T	106	$ .01	$ .03
Upton, Tom	52T	71	$13.75	$55.00
Urban, Jack	58T	367	$1.00	$4.00
Urban, Jack	59T	18	$1.50	$6.00
Uribe, Jose	85TTR	125	$ .01	$ .15
Uribe, Jose	86T	12	$ .01	$ .10
Uribe, Jose	87T	633	$ .01	$ .04
Uribe, Jose	88T	302	$ .01	$ .04
Uribe, Jose	89T	753	$ .01	$ .03
Uribe, Jose	90T	472	$ .01	$ .03
Uribe, Jose	91T	158	$ .01	$ .03
Uribe, Jose	91TSC	267	$ .05	$ .25
Uribe, Jose	92T	538	$ .01	$ .03
Uribe, Jose	92TSC	371	$ .01	$ .10
Uribe, Jose	93T	201	$ .01	$ .03
Urrea, John	78T	587	$ .04	$ .16
Urrea, John	79T	429	$ .03	$ .12
Urrea, John	81T	152	$ .01	$ .08
Urrea, John	81TTR	847	$ .01	$ .15
Urrea, John	82T	28	$ .01	$ .08
Usher, Bob	52T	157	$7.00	$28.00
Usher, Bobby	58T	124	$1.25	$5.00
Vail, Mike	76T	655	$ .05	$ .25
Valdes, Rene	57T	337	$5.00	$20.00
Valdespino, Sandy	65T	201	$ .50	$2.00
Valdespino, Sandy	66T	56	$ .35	$1.40
Valdespino, Sandy	68T	304	$ .35	$1.40
Valdez, Efrain	91T	692	$ .01	$ .10
Valdez, Efrain	91TSC	483	$ .05	$ .25
Valdez, Efrain	92TSC	838	$ .01	$ .10
Valdez, Julio	82T	381	$ .10	$ .50
Valdez, Julio	83T	628	$ .01	$ .08
Valdez, Sergio	90T	199	$ .01	$ .10
Valdez, Sergio	91T	98	$ .01	$ .03
Valdez, Sergio	92TSC	789	$ .01	$ .10
Valdez, Sergio	93TSC	171	$ .01	$ .10
Valdivielso, Jose	56T	237	$3.75	$15.00
Valdivielso, Jose	57T	246	$2.00	$8.00
Valdivielso, Jose	60T	527	$2.75	$11.00
Valdivielso, Jose	61T	557	$7.50	$30.00
Valdivielso, Jose	62T	339	$ .75	$3.00
Valentin, John	93T	424	$ .01	$ .10
Valentin, Jose	93T	804	$ .05	$ .20
Valentine, Bob	71T	188	$ .75	$3.00
Valentine, Bobby	72T	11	$ .25	$1.00
Valentine, Bobby	73T	502	$ .25	$1.00
Valentine, Bobby	74T	101	$ .10	$ .40
Valentine, Bobby	75T	215	$ .10	$ .40
Valentine, Bobby	76T	366	$ .05	$ .25
Valentine, Bobby	77T	629	$ .05	$ .20
Valentine, Bobby	78T	712	$ .05	$ .20
Valentine, Bobby	79T	428	$ .03	$ .12
Valentine, Bobby	80T	56	$ .01	$ .10
Valentine, Bobby	85TTR	126	$ .01	$ .10
Valentine, Bobby	86T	261	$ .01	$ .05
Valentine, Bobby	87T	118	$ .01	$ .04
Valentine, Bobby	88T	594	$ .01	$ .04
Valentine, Bobby	89T	314	$ .01	$ .03
Valentine, Bobby	90T	729	$ .01	$ .03
Valentine, Bobby	91T	489	$ .01	$ .03
Valentine, Bobby	92T	789	$ .01	$ .03
Valentine, Corky	55T	44	$2.25	$9.00
Valentine, Ellis	76T	590	$ .15	$ .60
Valentine, Ellis	77T	52	$ .05	$ .20
Valentine, Ellis	78T	185	$ .04	$ .16
Valentine, Ellis	79T	535	$ .03	$ .12
Valentine, Ellis	80T	395	$ .01	$ .10
Valentine, Ellis	81T	445	$ .01	$ .08
Valentine, Ellis	81TTR	849	$ .01	$ .15
Valentine, Ellis	82T	15	$ .01	$ .08
Valentine, Ellis	83T	653	$ .01	$ .08
Valentine, Ellis	83TTR	120	$ .01	$ .10
Valentine, Ellis	84T	236	$ .01	$ .06
Valentine, Fred	64T	483	$1.00	$4.00
Valentine, Fred	66T	351	$ .50	$2.00
Valentine, Fred	67T	64	$ .40	$1.60
Valentine, Fred	68T	248	$ .35	$1.40
Valentinetti, Vito	57T	74	$2.00	$8.00
Valentinetti, Vito	58T	463	$1.00	$4.00
Valentinetti, Vito	59T	44	$1.50	$6.00
Valenzuela, Fernando	81T	302	$1.00	$4.00
Valenzuela, Fernando	81TTR	850	$ .75	$3.00
Valenzuela, Fernando	82T	166	$ .01	$ .15
Valenzuela, Fernando	82T	510	$ .05	$ .25
Valenzuela, Fernando	82TAS	345	$ .05	$ .20
Valenzuela, Fernando	82THL	6	$ .05	$ .20
Valenzuela, Fernando	83T	40	$ .05	$ .25
Valenzuela, Fernando	83T	681	$ .01	$ .15
Valenzuela, Fernando	84T	220	$ .01	$ .15
Valenzuela, Fernando	85T	440	$ .01	$ .15
Valenzuela, Fernando	86T	630	$ .01	$ .10
Valenzuela, Fernando	86TRB	207	$ .01	$ .10
Valenzuela, Fernando	86TTB	401	$ .01	$ .10
Valenzuela, Fernando	87T	410	$ .01	$ .10
Valenzuela, Fernando	87TAS	604	$ .01	$ .10
Valenzuela, Fernando	88T	780	$ .01	$ .04
Valenzuela, Fernando	89T	150	$ .01	$ .03
Valenzuela, Fernando	90T	340	$ .01	$ .03

Vail, Mike	77T	246	$ .05	$ .20
Vail, Mike	78T	69	$ .04	$ .16
Vail, Mike	79T	663	$ .03	$ .12
Vail, Mike	80T	343	$ .01	$ .10
Vail, Mike	81T	471	$ .01	$ .08
Vail, Mike	81TTR	848	$ .01	$ .15
Vail, Mike	82T	194	$ .01	$ .08
Vail, Mike	83T	554	$ .01	$ .08
Vail, Mike	83TTR	119	$ .01	$ .10
Vail, Mike	84T	766	$ .01	$ .06
Vail, Mike	84TTR	124	$ .01	$ .15
Valarde, Randy	91TSC	438	$ .05	$ .25
Valdes, Marc	92TTR	121	$ .05	$ .20

TOPPS

Player	Year	No.	VG	EX/MT
Valenzuela, Fernando	91T	80	$.01	$.03
Valenzuela, Fernando	91TSC	90	$.05	$.25
Valera, Julio	91T	504	$.01	$.10
Valera, Julio	92TSC	304	$.05	$.20
Valera, Julio	92TSC	646	$.01	$.15
Valera, Julio	92TTR	122	$.01	$.05
Valera, Julio	93T	374	$.01	$.03
Valle, Dave	87TTR	122	$.01	$.15
Valle, Dave	88T	583	$.01	$.04
Valle, Dave	89T	498	$.01	$.03
Valle, Dave	90T	76	$.01	$.03
Valle, Dave	91T	178	$.01	$.03
Valle, Dave	91TSC	32	$.05	$.25
Valle, Dave	92T	294	$.01	$.03
Valle, Dave	92TSC	56	$.01	$.10
Valle, Dave	93T	370	$.01	$.03
Valle, Hector	65T	561	$3.00	$12.00
Valle, Hector	66T	314	$.50	$2.00
Valo, Elmer	51Trb	28	$1.75	$7.50
Valo, Elmer	52T	34	$13.75	$55.00

Player	Year	No.	VG	EX/MT
Valo, Elmer	**53T**	**122**	**$6.25**	**$25.00**
Valo, Elmer	54T	145	$3.75	$15.00
Valo, Elmer	55T	145	$2.25	$9.00
Valo, Elmer	56T	3	$2.00	$8.00
Valo, Elmer	57T	54	$2.00	$8.00
Valo, Elmer	58T	323	$1.25	$5.00
Valo, Elmer	60T	237	$.75	$3.00
Valo, Elmer	61T	186	$.60	$2.40
Valo, Elmer	91TA53	122	$.01	$.15
Van Cuyk, Chris	52T	53	$13.75	$55.00
Van Gorder, Dave	83T	322	$.01	$.08
Van Gorder, Dave	86T	143	$.01	$.05
Van Poppel, Todd	92T	142	$.05	$.20
Van Poppel, Todd	92TSC	129	$.10	$.50
Van Poppel, Todd	93T	673	$.01	$.10
Van Poppel, Todd	93TSC	48	$.05	$.35
Van Slyke, Andy	84T	206	$.25	$2.50
Van Slyke, Andy	85T	551	$.10	$.75
Van Slyke, Andy	86T	683	$.05	$.25
Van Slyke, Andy	87T	33	$.05	$.20
Van Slyke, Andy	87TTR	124	$.05	$.20
Van Slyke, Andy	88T	142	$.01	$.10
Van Slyke, Andy	89T	350	$.01	$.10

Player	Year	No.	VG	EX/MT
Van Slyke, Andy	89TAS	392	$.01	$.06
Van Slyke, Andy	90T	775	$.01	$.10
Van Slyke, Andy	91T	425	$.01	$.10
Van Slyke, Andy	91TSC	118	$.05	$.35
Van Slyke, Andy	92T	545	$.01	$.03
Van Slyke, Andy	92TSC	232	$.01	$.10
Van Slyke, Andy	93T	275	$.01	$.03
Van Slyke, Andy	93T	405	$.01	$.03
Van Slyke, Andy	93TSC	294	$.01	$.15
Vance, Sandy	71T	34	$.25	$1.00
VandeBerg, Ed	82TTR	122	$.01	$.10
VandeBerg, Ed	83T	183	$.01	$.08
VandeBerg, Ed	84T	63	$.01	$.06
VandeBerg, Ed	85T	566	$.01	$.06
VandeBerg, Ed	86T	357	$.01	$.05
VandeBerg, Ed	86TTR	118	$.01	$.06
VandeBerg, Ed	87T	717	$.01	$.04
VandeBerg, Ed	87TTR	123	$.01	$.05
VandeBerg, Ed	88T	421	$.01	$.04
VandeBerg, Ed	89T	242	$.01	$.03
Vander Wal, John	92T	343	$.01	$.15
Vander Wal, John	92TSC	385	$.05	$.25
Vander Wal, John	93T	69	$.01	$.10
Varitek, Jason	92TTR	123	$.10	$.75
Varney, Pete	76T	413	$.05	$.25
Varsho, Gary	89T	613	$.01	$.03
Varsho, Gary	92T	122	$.01	$.03
Varsho, Gary	92TSC	568	$.01	$.10
Varsho, Gary	93T	326	$.01	$.03
Vasquez, Rafael	80T	672	$.01	$.10
Vatcher, Jim	91T	196	$.01	$.10
Vatcher, Jim	92TSC	78	$.01	$.10
Vaughn, Charley	67T	179	$.40	$1.60
Vaughn, Greg	90T	57	$.05	$.20
Vaughn, Greg	91T	347	$.01	$.15
Vaughn, Greg	91TSC	135	$.10	$.50
Vaughn, Greg	92T	572	$.01	$.03
Vaughn, Greg	92TSC	666	$.01	$.10
Vaughn, Greg	93T	153	$.01	$.03
Vaughn, Greg	93TSC	122	$.01	$.10
Vaughn, Mo	91TSC	543	$1.00	$4.00
Vaughn, Mo	91TTR	123	$.05	$.25
Vaughn, Mo	92T	59	$.01	$.03
Vaughn, Mo	92TSC	325	$.10	$.50
Vaughn, Mo	93T	51	$.01	$.03
Veal, Coot	59T	52	$1.50	$6.00
Veal, Coot	61T	432	$1.00	$4.00
Veal, Coot	63T	573	$2.25	$9.00
Veale, Bob	62T	593	$5.25	$21.00
Veale, Bob	63T	87	$.50	$2.00
Veale, Bob	64T	501	$1.00	$4.00
Veale, Bob	65T	12	$1.00	$4.00
Veale, Bob	65T	195	$.35	$1.40
Veale, Bob	66T	225	$1.75	$7.00
Veale, Bob	66T	425	$.65	$2.60
Veale, Bob	67T	238	$1.50	$6.00
Veale, Bob	67T	335	$.60	$2.40
Veale, Bob	68T	70	$.35	$1.40
Veale, Bob	69T	8	$.75	$3.00
Veale, Bob	69T	520	$.40	$1.60
Veale, Bob	70T	236	$.20	$.80
Veale, Bob	71T	368	$.25	$1.00
Veale, Bob	72T	729	$1.25	$5.00
Veale, Bob	73T	518	$.25	$1.00
Vega, Jesus	83T	308	$.01	$.08
Veintidos, Juan	75T	621	$.15	$.60
Velarde, Randy	89T	584	$.01	$.03
Velarde, Randy	90T	23	$.01	$.03
Velarde, Randy	91T	379	$.01	$.03
Velarde, Randy	92T	212	$.01	$.03
Velarde, Randy	92TSC	237	$.01	$.10
Velarde, Randy	93T	174	$.01	$.03
Velarde, Randy	93TSC	32	$.01	$.10
Velasquez, Guillermo	93T	724	$.01	$.10
Velez, Otto	74T	606	$.10	$.40

TOPPS

Player	Year	No.	VG	EX/MT
Velez, Otto	77T	299	$ .05	$ .20
Velez, Otto	78T	59	$ .04	$ .16
Velez, Otto	79T	462	$ .03	$ .12
Velez, Otto	80T	703	$ .01	$ .10
Velez, Otto	81T	351	$ .01	$ .08
Velez, Otto	82T	155	$ .01	$ .08
Venable, Max	81T	484	$ .01	$ .08
Venable, Max	83T	634	$ .01	$ .08
Venable, Max	84T	58	$ .01	$ .06
Venable, Max	86T	428	$ .01	$ .05
Venable, Max	87T	226	$ .01	$ .04
Veneziale, Mike	93T	726	$ .05	$ .20
Ventura, Robin	88TTR	124	$2.50	$10.00
Ventura, Robin	89T	764	$ .15	$1.50
Ventura, Robin	90T	121	$ .10	$ .60
Ventura, Robin	91T	461	$ .05	$ .20
Ventura, Robin	91TSC	274	$ .75	$3.00
Ventura, Robin	92T	255	$ .01	$ .15
Ventura, Robin	92TSC	70	$ .10	$ .50
Ventura, Robin	93T	770	$ .01	$ .15
Ventura, Robin	93TSC	295	$ .05	$ .25
Verbanic, Joe	67T	442	$1.00	$4.00
Verbanic, Joe	68T	29	$ .35	$1.40
Verbanic, Joe	69T	541	$ .40	$1.60
Verbanic, Joe	70T	416	$ .35	$1.40
Veres, Randy	90TTR	125	$ .01	$ .05

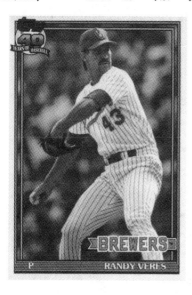

Player	Year	No.	VG	EX/MT
Veres, Randy	91T	694	$ .01	$ .03
Verhoeven, John	77T	91	$ .05	$ .20
Verhoeven, John	78T	329	$ .04	$ .16
Verhoeven, John	81T	603	$ .01	$ .08
Verhoeven, John	82T	281	$ .01	$ .08
Vernon, Mickey	51Tbb	13	$9.00	$36.00
Vernon, Mickey	52T	106	$7.00	$28.00
Vernon, Mickey	56T	228	$3.75	$15.00
Vernon, Mickey	57T	92	$2.00	$8.00
Vernon, Mickey	58T	233	$1.25	$5.00
Vernon, Mickey	59T	115	$1.00	$4.00
Vernon, Mickey	60T	467	$1.25	$5.00
Vernon, Mickey	61T	134	$ .60	$2.40
Vernon, Mickey	62T	152	$ .60	$2.40
Vernon, Mickey	63T	402	$1.00	$4.00
Vernon, Mickey	91TA53	287	$ .05	$ .25
Versalles, Zorro "Zoilo"	61T	21	$1.00	$4.00

Player	Year	No.	VG	EX/MT
Versalles, Zoilo	62T	499	$1.50	$6.00
Versalles, Zoilo	63T	349	$ .90	$3.60
Versalles, Zoilo	64T	15	$ .50	$2.00
Versalles, Zoilo	65T	157	$ .50	$2.00
Versalles, Zoilo	66T	400	$ .65	$2.60
Versalles, Zoilo	67T	270	$ .50	$2.00
Versalles, Zoilo	68T	315	$ .35	$1.40
Versalles, Zoilo	69T	38	$ .35	$1.40
Versalles, Zoilo	70T	365	$ .35	$1.40
Versalles, Zoilo	75T	203	$ .35	$1.40
Veryzer, Tom	75T	623	$5.25	$21.00
Veryzer, Tom	76T	432	$ .05	$ .25
Veryzer, Tom	77T	145	$ .05	$ .20
Veryzer, Tom	78T	633	$ .04	$ .16
Veryzer, Tom	79T	537	$ .03	$ .12
Veryzer, Tom	80T	276	$ .01	$ .10
Veryzer, Tom	81T	39	$ .01	$ .08
Veryzer, Tom	82T	387	$ .01	$ .08
Veryzer, Tom	82TTR	123	$ .01	$ .10
Veryzer, Tom	83T	496	$ .01	$ .08
Veryzer, Tom	83TTR	121	$ .01	$ .10
Veryzer, Tom	84T	117	$ .01	$ .06
Veryzer, Tom	85T	405	$ .01	$ .06
Vezendy, Gerry	65T	509	$1.25	$5.00
Vidal, Jose	67T	499	$1.50	$6.00
Vidal, Jose	68T	432	$ .35	$1.40
Vidal, Jose	69T	322	$ .50	$2.00
Villanueva, Hector	90TTR	126	$ .01	$ .10
Villanueva, Hector	91T	362	$ .01	$ .03
Villanueva, Hector	91TSC	213	$ .05	$ .25
Villanueva, Hector	92T	181	$ .01	$ .03
Villanueva, Hector	92TSC	858	$ .01	$ .10
Villone, Ron	92TTR	124	$ .05	$ .20
Vinson, Chuck	68T	328	$ .35	$1.40
Viola, Frank	83T	586	$1.25	$5.00
Viola, Frank	84T	28	$ .10	$ .50
Viola, Frank	85T	266	$ .05	$ .20
Viola, Frank	85TAS	710	$ .01	$ .10
Viola, Frank	86T	742	$ .05	$ .20
Viola, Frank	87T	310	$ .01	$ .15
Viola, Frank	88T	625	$ .01	$ .10
Viola, Frank	89T	120	$ .01	$ .10
Viola, Frank	89TAS	406	$ .01	$ .05
Viola, Frank	90T	470	$ .01	$ .03
Viola, Frank	91T	60	$ .01	$ .03
Viola, Frank	91TAS	406	$ .01	$ .03
Viola, Frank	91TSC	292	$ .05	$ .25
Viola, Frank	92T	510	$ .01	$ .03
Viola, Frank	92TSC	785	$ .01	$ .10
Viola, Frank	92TTR	125	$ .01	$ .05
Viola, Frank	93T	270	$ .01	$ .03
Viola, Frank	93TSC	147	$ .01	$ .15
Virdon, Bill	56T	170	$3.50	$14.00
Virdon, Bill	57T	110	$2.00	$8.00
Virdon, Bill	58T	198	$2.00	$8.00
Virdon, Bill	59T	190	$1.50	$6.00
Virdon, Bill	59T	543	$15.00	$60.00
Virdon, Bill	60T	496	$1.50	$6.00
Virdon, Bill	61T	70	$ .75	$3.00
Virdon, Bill	62T	415	$1.25	$5.00
Virdon, Bill	63T	55	$ .50	$2.00
Virdon, Bill	64T	495	$1.25	$5.00
Virdon, Bill	65T	69	$ .50	$2.00
Virdon, Bill	72T	661	$1.25	$5.00
Virdon, Bill	73T	517	$ .25	$1.00
Virdon, Bill	78T	279	$ .04	$ .16
Virdon, Bill	83T	516	$ .01	$ .08
Virdon, Bill	84T	111	$ .01	$ .06
Virgil Jr., Ozzie	82T	231	$ .05	$ .35
Virgil Jr., Ozzie	83T	383	$ .01	$ .08
Virgil Jr., Ozzie	84T	484	$ .01	$ .06
Virgil Jr., Ozzie	85T	143	$ .01	$ .10
Virgil Jr., Ozzie	85T	611	$ .01	$ .06
Virgil Jr., Ozzie	86T	95	$ .01	$ .05
Virgil Jr., Ozzie	86TTR	119	$ .01	$ .06

TOPPS

Player	Year	No.	VG	EX/MT
Virgil Jr., Ozzie	87T	571	$ .01	$ .04
Virgil Jr., Ozzie	88T	755	$ .01	$ .04
Virgil, Ozzie	89T	179	$ .01	$ .03
Virgil, Ossie	57T	365	$1.75	$7.00
Virgil, Ossie	58T	107	$2.00	$8.00
Virgil, Ossie	59T	203	$1.00	$4.00
Virgil, Ossie	61T	67	$ .60	$2.40
Virgil, Ozzie (Ossie)	62T	327	$ .75	$3.00
Virgil, Ossie	65T	571	$2.50	$10.00
Virgil, Ozzie (Ossie)	67T	132	$ .40	$1.60
Virgil, Ossie	85T	143	$ .01	$ .10
Vizcaino, Jose	92T	561	$ .01	$ .03
Vizcaino, Jose	92TSC	359	$ .01	$ .10
Vizcaino, Jose	93T	237	$ .01	$ .03
Vizcaino, Jose	93TSC	68	$ .01	$ .10
Vizquel, Omar	89TTR	122	$ .01	$ .15
Vizquel, Omar	90T	698	$ .01	$ .03
Vizquel, Omar	91T	298	$ .01	$ .03
Vizquel, Omar	91TSC	195	$ .05	$ .25
Vizquel, Omar	92T	101	$ .01	$ .03
Vizquel, Omar	92TSC	163	$ .01	$ .10
Vizquel, Omar	93T	68	$ .01	$ .03
Vizquel, Omar	93TSC	67	$ .01	$ .10
Voisard, Mark	93T	476	$ .05	$ .20
Vollmer, Clyde	52T	255	$12.50	$50.00
Vollmer, Clyde	53T	32	$6.25	$25.00
Vollmer, Clyde	91TA53	32	$ .01	$ .15
Von Hoff, Bruce	68T	529	$ .70	$2.80
Von Ohlen, Dave	84T	489	$ .01	$ .06
Von Ohlen, Dave	85T	177	$ .01	$ .06
Von Ohlen, Dave	85TTR	127	$ .01	$ .10
Von Ohlen, Dave	86T	632	$ .01	$ .05
Von Ohlen, Dave	87T	287	$ .01	$ .04
Voss, Bill	66T	529	$5.00	$20.00
Voss, Bill	68T	142	$ .35	$1.40
Voss, Bill	69T	621	$ .40	$1.60
Voss, Bill	70T	326	$ .35	$1.40
Voss, Bill	71T	671	$1.50	$6.00
Voss, Bill	72T	776	$1.25	$5.00
Vossler, Dan	74T	602	$ .10	$ .40
Vuckovich, Pete	77T	517	$ .10	$ .40
Vuckovich, Pete	78T	241	$ .04	$ .16
Vuckovich, Pete	79T	407	$ .03	$ .12
Vuckovich, Pete	80T	57	$ .01	$ .10
Vuckovich, Pete	81T	193	$ .01	$ .08
Vuckovich, Pete	81TTR	851	$ .01	$ .15
Vuckovich, Pete	82T	165	$ .01	$ .15
Vuckovich, Pete	82T	643	$ .01	$ .10
Vuckovich, Pete	82T	703	$ .01	$ .15
Vuckovich, Pete	83T	321	$ .05	$ .20
Vuckovich, Pete	83T	375	$ .01	$ .08
Vuckovich, Pete	83TAS	394	$ .01	$ .08
Vuckovich, Pete	84T	505	$ .01	$ .06
Vuckovich, Pete	85T	254	$ .01	$ .06
Vuckovich, Pete	86T	737	$ .01	$ .05
Vukovich, George	81T	598	$ .01	$ .08
Vukovich, George	82T	389	$ .01	$ .08
Vukovich, George	83T	16	$ .01	$ .08
Vukovich, George	83TTR	122	$ .01	$ .10
Vukovich, George	84T	638	$ .01	$ .06
Vukovich, George	85T	212	$ .01	$ .06
Vukovich, George	86T	483	$ .01	$ .05
Vukovich, John	73T	451	$ .25	$1.00
Vukovich, John	74T	349	$ .10	$ .40
Vukovich, John	75T	602	$ .10	$ .40
Vurks, Ellis	93T	351	$ .01	$ .03
Waddell, Tom	84TTR	125	$ .01	$ .15
Waddell, Tom	85T	453	$ .01	$ .06
Waddell, Tom	86T	86	$ .01	$ .05
Waddell, Tom	87T	657	$ .01	$ .04
Wade, Ben	52T	389	$43.75	$175.00
Wade, Ben	53T	4	$6.25	$25.00
Wade, Ben	54T	126	$3.75	$15.00
Wade, Ben	91TA53	4	$ .01	$ .15
Wade, Gale	55T	196	$6.25	$25.00
Wagner, Gary	66T	151	$ .50	$2.00
Wagner, Gary	67T	529	$1.50	$6.00
Wagner, Gary	68T	448	$ .35	$1.40
Wagner, Gary	69T	276	$ .50	$2.00
Wagner, Gary	70T	627	$ .50	$2.00
Wagner, Gary	71T	473	$ .50	$2.00
Wagner, Hector	92TSC	323	$ .01	$ .10

Wagner, Honus	76TAT	344	$ .75	$3.00
Wagner, Leon	59T	257	$1.50	$6.00
Wagner, Leon	60T	383	$ .75	$3.00
Wagner, Leon	61T	547	$7.50	$30.00
Wagner, Leon	62T	491	$1.50	$6.00
Wagner, Leon	63T	4	$2.00	$8.00
Wagner, Leon	63T	335	$ .90	$3.60
Wagner, Leon	64T	41	$1.25	$5.00
Wagner, Leon	64T	530	$2.25	$9.00
Wagner, Leon	65T	367	$ .50	$2.00
Wagner, Leon	66T	65	$ .35	$1.40
Wagner, Leon	67T	109	$ .60	$2.40
Wagner, Leon	67T	360	$ .60	$2.40
Wagner, Leon	68T	495	$ .75	$3.00
Wagner, Leon	69T	187	$ .35	$1.40
Wagner, Mark	77T	490	$ .05	$ .20
Wagner, Mark	79T	598	$ .03	$ .12
Wagner, Mark	80T	29	$ .01	$ .10
Wagner, Mark	81T	358	$ .01	$ .08
Wagner, Mark	81TTR	852	$ .01	$ .15
Wagner, Mark	82T	443	$ .01	$ .08
Wagner, Mark	83T	144	$ .01	$ .08
Wagner, Mark	85T	581	$ .01	$ .06
Wainhouse, Dave	92TSC	885	$ .01	$ .15
Waitkus, Eddie	51Tbb	51	$7.50	$30.00
Waitkus, Eddie	52T	158	$7.00	$28.00
Waits, Rick	76T	433	$ .05	$ .25
Waits, Rick	77T	306	$ .05	$ .20
Waits, Rick	78T	37	$ .04	$ .16
Waits, Rick	79T	484	$ .03	$ .12
Waits, Rick	80T	168	$ .01	$ .10
Waits, Rick	81T	697	$ .01	$ .08
Waits, Rick	82T	573	$ .01	$ .08
Waits, Rick	83T	779	$ .01	$ .08
Waits, Rick	83TTR	123	$ .01	$ .10
Waits, Rick	84T	218	$ .01	$ .06
Waits, Rick	85T	59	$ .01	$ .06

TOPPS

Player	Year	No.	VG	EX/MT
Waits, Rick	86T	614	$ .01	$ .05
Wakefield, Bill	64T	576	$2.25	$9.00
Wakefield, Bill	65T	167	$ .35	$1.40
Wakefield, Bill	66T	443	$ .65	$2.60
Wakefield, Tim	93T	163	$ .10	$ .50
Wakefield, Tim	93TSC	13	$ .15	$1.50
Walbeck, Matt	93T	812	$ .01	$ .15
Walden, Ronnie	91T	596	$ .01	$ .15
Walewander, Jim	88T	106	$ .01	$ .10
Walewander, Jim	89T	467	$ .01	$ .03
Walk, Bob	81T	494	$ .05	$ .25
Walk, Bob	81TTR	853	$ .10	$ .50
Walk, Bob	82T	296	$ .01	$ .08
Walk, Bob	83T	104	$ .01	$ .08
Walk, Bob	86TTR	120	$ .01	$ .06
Walk, Bob	87T	628	$ .01	$ .04
Walk, Bob	88T	349	$ .01	$ .04
Walk, Bob	89T	504	$ .01	$ .03
Walk, Bob	90T	754	$ .01	$ .03
Walk, Bob	91T	29	$ .01	$ .03
Walk, Bob	91TSC	14	$ .05	$ .25
Walk, Bob	92T	486	$ .01	$ .03
Walk, Bob	92TSC	746	$ .01	$ .10
Walk, Bob	93T	685	$ .01	$ .03
Walkden, Mike	92TSC	852	$ .05	$ .20
Walker, Al "Rube"	52T	319	$43.75	$175.00
Walker, "Rube"	53T	134	$6.25	$25.00
Walker, "Rube"	54T	153	$3.75	$15.00
Walker, "Rube"	55T	108	$2.25	$9.00
Walker, "Rube"	56T	333	$2.50	$10.00
Walker, Al	57T	147	$2.00	$8.00
Walker, Al	58T	203	$1.25	$5.00
Walker, "Rube"	73T	257	$ .50	$2.00
Walker, "Rube"	74T	179	$ .40	$1.60
Walker, Rube	91TA53	134	$ .01	$ .15
Walker, Chico	87T	695	$ .01	$ .04
Walker, Chico	92T	439	$ .01	$ .03
Walker, Chico	92TSC	564	$ .01	$ .10
Walker, Chico	93TSC	114	$ .01	$ .10
Walker, Dixie	53T	190	$4.50	$18.00
Walker, Dixie	91TA53	190	$ .01	$ .15
Walker, Duane	83T	243	$ .01	$ .08
Walker, Duane	84T	659	$ .01	$ .06
Walker, Duane	85T	441	$ .01	$ .06
Walker, Duane	86T	22	$ .01	$ .05
Walker, Greg	83TTR	124	$ .10	$ .50
Walker, Greg	84T	518	$ .05	$ .25
Walker, Greg	85T	623	$ .01	$ .06
Walker, Greg	86T	123	$ .01	$ .05
Walker, Greg	87T	397	$ .01	$ .04
Walker, Greg	88T	764	$ .01	$ .04
Walker, Greg	89T	408	$ .01	$ .03
Walker, Greg	90T	33	$ .01	$ .03
Walker, Harry	60T	468	$1.25	$5.00
Walker, Harry	65T	438	$1.00	$4.00
Walker, Harry	66T	318	$ .50	$2.00
Walker, Harry	67T	448	$ .60	$2.40
Walker, Harry	69T	633	$ .40	$1.60
Walker, Harry	70T	32	$ .20	$ .80
Walker, Harry	71T	312	$ .25	$1.00
Walker, Harry	72T	249	$ .10	$ .40
Walker, Jerry	58T	113	$2.00	$8.00
Walker, Jerry	59T	114	$1.00	$4.00
Walker, Jerry	60T	399	$ .75	$3.00
Walker, Jerry	60T	540	$2.75	$11.00
Walker, Jerry	61T	85	$ .60	$2.40
Walker, Jerry	62T	357	$ .75	$3.00
Walker, Jerry	63T	413	$1.00	$4.00
Walker, Jerry	64T	77	$ .50	$2.00
Walker, Larry	90T	757	$ .10	$1.00
Walker, Larry	91T	339	$ .05	$ .20
Walker, Larry	91TSC	93	$ .75	$3.00
Walker, Larry	92T	531	$ .01	$ .15
Walker, Larry	92TSC	256	$ .10	$ .75
Walker, Larry	93T	95	$ .01	$ .15

Player	Year	No.	VG	EX/MT
Walker, Larry	93T	406	$ .01	$ .10
Walker, Larry	93TSC	299	$ .05	$ .20
Walker, Luke	66T	498	$1.50	$6.00
Walker, Luke	67T	123	$ .40	$1.60
Walker, Luke	68T	559	$ .70	$2.80
Walker, Luke	69T	36	$ .35	$1.40
Walker, Luke	70T	322	$ .35	$1.40
Walker, Luke	71T	68	$ .75	$3.00
Walker, Luke	71T	534	$1.00	$4.00
Walker, Luke	72T	471	$ .25	$1.00
Walker, Luke	73T	187	$ .10	$ .40
Walker, Luke	74T	612	$ .10	$ .40
Walker, Luke	74TTR	612	$ .10	$ .40
Walker, Luke	75T	474	$ .10	$ .40
Walker, Mike	91T	593	$ .01	$ .03
Walker, Shon	93T	658	$ .05	$ .35
Walker, Tom	73T	41	$ .10	$ .40
Walker, Tom	74T	193	$ .10	$ .40
Walker, Tom	75T	627	$ .10	$ .40
Walker, Tom	76T	186	$ .05	$ .25
Walker, Tom	77T	652	$ .05	$ .20
Walker, Tony	87T	24	$ .01	$ .04
Wall, Murray	53T	217	$4.50	$18.00
Wall, Murray	58T	410	$1.00	$4.00
Wall, Murray	59T	42	$1.50	$6.00
Wall, Murray	91TA53	217	$ .01	$ .15
Wall, Stan	76T	584	$ .05	$ .25
Wall, Stan	77T	88	$ .05	$ .20

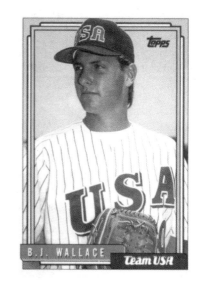

Player	Year	No.	VG	EX/MT
Wallace, B. J.	92TTR	126	$ .10	$1.00
Wallace, B. J.	93T	33	$ .05	$ .25
Wallace, Derek	93T	459	$ .05	$ .20
Wallace, Don	67T	367	$ .60	$2.40
Wallace, Mike	74T	608	$ .10	$ .40
Wallace, Mike	75T	401	$ .10	$ .40
Wallace, Mike	77T	539	$ .05	$ .20
Wallach, Tim	82T	191	$ .15	$1.50
Wallach, Tim	83T	552	$ .05	$ .25
Wallach, Tim	84T	232	$ .05	$ .20
Wallach, Tim	85T	473	$ .01	$ .15
Wallach, Tim	86T	685	$ .01	$ .05
Wallach, Tim	86TAS	703	$ .01	$ .05
Wallach, Tim	87T	55	$ .01	$ .04
Wallach, Tim	88T	560	$ .01	$ .10

TOPPS

Player	Year	No.	VG	EX/MT
Wallach, Tim	88TAS	399	$ .01	$ .04
Wallach, Tim	89T	720	$ .01	$ .03
Wallach, Tim	90T	370	$ .01	$ .03
Wallach, Tim	91T	220	$ .01	$ .03
Wallach, Tim	91TSC	463	$ .05	$ .25
Wallach, Tim	92T	385	$ .01	$ .03
Wallach, Tim	92TSC	340	$ .01	$ .10
Wallach, Tim	93T	570	$ .01	$ .03
Waller, Ty	82T	51	$ .05	$ .25

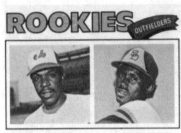

Player	Year	No.	VG	EX/MT
Walling, Denny	77T	473	$17.50	$70.00
Walling, Denny	79T	553	$ .03	$ .12
Walling, Denny	80T	306	$ .01	$ .10
Walling, Denny	81T	439	$ .01	$ .08
Walling, Denny	82T	147	$ .01	$ .08
Walling, Denny	83T	692	$ .01	$ .08
Walling, Denny	84T	36	$ .01	$ .06
Walling, Denny	85T	382	$ .01	$ .06
Walling, Denny	86T	504	$ .01	$ .05
Walling, Denny	87T	222	$ .01	$ .04
Walling, Denny	88T	719	$ .01	$ .04
Walling, Denny	89T	196	$ .01	$ .03
Walling, Denny	90T	462	$ .01	$ .03
Wallis, Joe	76T	598	$ .05	$ .25
Wallis, Joe	77T	279	$ .05	$ .20
Wallis, Joe	78T	614	$ .04	$ .16
Wallis, Joe	79T	406	$ .03	$ .12
Wallis, Joe	80T	562	$ .01	$ .10
Walls, Lee	57T	52	$2.00	$8.00
Walls, Lee	58T	66	$2.00	$8.00
Walls, Lee	59T	105	$1.50	$6.00
Walls, Lee	60T	506	$1.25	$5.00
Walls, Lee	61T	78	$ .60	$2.40
Walls, Lee	62T	129	$1.25	$5.00
Walls, Lee	63T	11	$ .50	$2.00
Walls, Lee	64T	411	$1.00	$4.00
Walsh, Dave	91T	367	$ .01	$ .10
Walter, Gene	86TTR	121	$ .01	$ .06
Walter, Gene	87T	248	$ .01	$ .04
Walter, Gene	89T	758	$ .01	$ .03
Walters, Dan	92TTR	127	$ .01	$ .15
Walters, Dan	93T	273	$ .01	$ .10
Walters, Dan	93TSC	175	$ .01	$ .10
Walters, Ken	60T	511	$2.75	$11.00
Walters, Ken	61T	394	$1.00	$4.00
Walters, Ken	62T	328	$ .75	$3.00
Walters, Ken	63T	534	$2.25	$9.00
Walters, Mike	84T	673	$ .01	$ .06
Walters, Mike	85T	187	$ .01	$ .06
Walton, Bruce	92TSC	563	$ .01	$ .10
Walton, Danny	70T	134	$ .20	$ .80
Walton, Danny	71T	281	$ .25	$1.00
Walton, Danny	73T	516	$ .25	$1.00
Walton, Danny	78T	263	$ .04	$ .16
Walton, Jerome	89TTR	123	$ .01	$ .10
Walton, Jerome	90T	464	$ .01	$ .03
Walton, Jerome	91T	135	$ .01	$ .03
Walton, Jerome	91TSC	162	$ .05	$ .25
Walton, Jerome	92T	543	$ .01	$ .03
Walton, Jerome	92TSC	421	$ .01	$ .10
Walton, Jim	73T	646	$ .75	$3.00
Walton, Jim	74T	99	$ .10	$ .40
Walton, Reggie	82T	711	$ .10	$1.00
Wapnick, Steve	92TSC	554	$ .01	$ .10
Ward, Chris	75T	587	$ .10	$ .40
Ward, Colby	91T	31	$ .01	$ .15
Ward, Duane	87T	153	$ .05	$ .25
Ward, Duane	88T	696	$ .01	$ .04
Ward, Duane	89T	502	$ .01	$ .03
Ward, Duane	90T	28	$ .01	$ .03
Ward, Duane	91T	181	$ .01	$ .03
Ward, Duane	91TSC	363	$ .05	$ .25
Ward, Duane	92T	365	$ .01	$ .03
Ward, Duane	92TSC	781	$ .01	$ .10
Ward, Duane	93T	260	$ .01	$ .03
Ward, Gary	80T	669	$ .05	$ .30
Ward, Gary	81T	328	$ .01	$ .08
Ward, Gary	82T	612	$ .01	$ .08
Ward, Gary	83T	517	$ .01	$ .08
Ward, Gary	84T	67	$ .01	$ .06
Ward, Gary	84TTR	126	$ .01	$ .15
Ward, Gary	85T	414	$ .01	$ .06
Ward, Gary	86T	105	$ .01	$ .05
Ward, Gary	87T	762	$ .01	$ .04
Ward, Gary	87TTR	125	$ .01	$ .05
Ward, Gary	88T	235	$ .01	$ .04
Ward, Gary	89T	302	$ .01	$ .03
Ward, Gary	89TTR	124	$ .01	$ .05
Ward, Gary	90T	679	$ .01	$ .03
Ward, Gary	91T	556	$ .01	$ .03
Ward, Jay	64T	116	$3.50	$14.00
Ward, Jay	65T	421	$1.00	$4.00
Ward, Kevin	92TSC	853	$ .01	$ .10
Ward, Pete	63T	324	$1.25	$5.00
Ward, Pete	64T	85	$ .50	$2.00
Ward, Pete	65T	215	$ .50	$2.00
Ward, Pete	66T	25	$ .35	$1.40
Ward, Pete	67T	143	$ .40	$1.60
Ward, Pete	67T	436	$ .60	$2.40
Ward, Pete	68T	33	$ .35	$1.40
Ward, Pete	69T	155	$ .35	$1.40
Ward, Pete	70T	659	$1.25	$5.00
Ward, Pete	71T	667	$1.10	$4.40
Ward, Preston	53T	173	$4.50	$18.00
Ward, Preston	54T	72	$7.50	$30.00
Ward, Preston	55T	95	$2.25	$9.00
Ward, Preston	56T	328	$2.50	$10.00
Ward, Preston	57T	226	$2.00	$8.00
Ward, Preston	58T	450	$3.00	$12.00
Ward, Preston	59T	176	$1.00	$4.00
Ward, Preston	91TA53	173	$ .01	$ .15
Ward, Turner	91T	555	$ .01	$ .15
Ward, Turner	91TSC	593	$ .05	$ .25
Ward, Turner	92TSC	621	$ .01	$ .15
Warden, Jon	69T	632	$ .40	$1.60
Wardle, Curt	86T	303	$ .01	$ .05
Ware, Jeff	91TTR	124	$ .05	$ .25
Ware, Jeff	92T	414	$ .01	$ .15
Warner, Jack D.	65T	354	$ .50	$2.00

TOPPS

Player	Year	No.	VG	EX/MT
Warner, Jackie	65T	517	$1.25	$5.00
Warner, Jackie	66T	553	$3.75	$15.00
Warren, DeShawn	93T	574	$ .01	$ .15
Warren, Mike	84T	5	$ .01	$ .10
Warren, Mike	84T	338	$ .01	$ .06
Warren, Mike	85T	197	$ .01	$ .06
Warthen, Dan	76T	374	$ .05	$ .25
Warthen, Dan	77T	391	$ .05	$ .20
Warwick, Carl	62T	202	$ .75	$3.00
Warwick, Carl	63T	333	$ .90	$3.60
Warwick, Carl	64T	179	$ .50	$2.00
Warwick, Carl	65T	357	$ .50	$2.00
Warwick, Carl	66T	247	$ .50	$2.00
Washburn, Greg	70T	74	$ .20	$ .80
Washburn, Ray	62T	19	$ .60	$2.40
Washburn, Ray	63T	206	$ .90	$3.60
Washburn, Ray	64T	332	$ .65	$2.60
Washburn, Ray	65T	467	$1.25	$5.00
Washburn, Ray	66T	399	$ .65	$2.60
Washburn, Ray	67T	92	$ .40	$1.60
Washburn, Ray	68T	388	$ .35	$1.40
Washburn, Ray	69T	415	$ .30	$1.20
Washburn, Ray	70T	22	$ .20	$ .80
Washington, Claudell	75T	647	$ .25	$1.00
Washington, Claudell	76T	189	$ .10	$ .40
Washington, Claudell	76T	198	$ .15	$ .60
Washington, Claudell	77T	405	$ .05	$ .20
Washington, Claudell	78T	67	$ .05	$ .20
Washington, Claudell	79T	574	$ .05	$ .20
Washington, Claudell	80T	322	$ .01	$ .10
Washington, Claudell	81T	151	$ .01	$ .08
Washington, Claudell	81TTR	854	$ .01	$ .15
Washington, Claudell	82T	126	$ .01	$ .08
Washington, Claudell	82T	758	$ .01	$ .08
Washington, Claudell	83T	235	$ .01	$ .08
Washington, Claudell	84T	410	$ .01	$ .06
Washington, Claudell	85T	540	$ .01	$ .06
Washington, Claudell	86T	675	$ .01	$ .05
Washington, Claudell	86TTR	122	$ .01	$ .06
Washington, Claudell	87T	15	$ .01	$ .04
Washington, Claudell	88T	335	$ .01	$ .04
Washington, Claudell	89T	185	$ .01	$ .03
Washington, Claudell	89TTR	125	$ .01	$ .05
Washington, Claudell	90T	705	$ .01	$ .03
Washington, Herb	75T	407	$ .10	$ .40
Washington, LaRue	80T	233	$ .01	$ .10
Washington, Ron	82TTR	124	$ .01	$ .10
Washington, Ron	83T	458	$ .01	$ .08
Washington, Ron	84T	623	$ .01	$ .06
Washington, Ron	85T	329	$ .01	$ .06
Washington, Ron	86T	513	$ .01	$ .05
Washington, Ron	87T	169	$ .01	$ .04
Washington, Ron	88TTR	125	$ .01	$ .05
Washington, Team	56T	146	$7.50	$30.00
Washington, Team	59T	397	$2.50	$10.00
Washington Team, N.L.	74T	226	$1.25	$5.00
Washington, U. L.	78T	707	$12.50	$50.00
Washington, U. L.	79T	157	$ .03	$ .12
Washington, U. L.	80T	508	$ .01	$ .10
Washington, U. L.	81T	26	$ .01	$ .08
Washington, U. L.	82T	329	$ .01	$ .08
Washington, U. L.	83T	687	$ .01	$ .08
Washington, U. L.	84T	294	$ .01	$ .06
Washington, U. L.	85T	431	$ .01	$ .06
Washington, U. L.	85TTR	128	$ .01	$ .10
Washington, U. L.	86T	113	$ .01	$ .05
Waslewski, Gary	69T	438	$ .30	$1.20
Waslewski, Gary	70T	607	$ .50	$2.00
Waslewski, Gary	71T	277	$ .25	$1.00
Waslewski, Gary	72T	108	$ .10	$ .40
Wathan, John	77T	218	$ .20	$ .80
Wathan, John	78T	343	$ .04	$ .16
Wathan, John	79T	99	$ .03	$ .12
Wathan, John	80T	547	$ .01	$ .10
Wathan, John	81T	157	$ .01	$ .08
Wathan, John	82T	429	$ .01	$ .08
Wathan, John	83T	746	$ .01	$ .08
Wathan, John	83TRB	6	$ .01	$ .08
Wathan, John	84T	602	$ .01	$ .06
Wathan, John	85T	308	$ .01	$ .06
Wathan, John	86T	128	$ .01	$ .05
Wathan, John	88T	534	$ .01	$ .04
Wathan, John	89T	374	$ .01	$ .03
Wathan, John	90T	789	$ .01	$ .03
Wathan, John	91T	291	$ .01	$ .03
Watkins, Bob	70T	227	$ .30	$1.20
Watkins, Dave	70T	168	$ .20	$ .80
Watson, Allen	92T	654	$ .05	$ .35
Watson, Bob	69T	562	$ .75	$3.00
Watson, Bob	70T	407	$ .35	$1.40
Watson, Bob	71T	222	$ .25	$1.00
Watson, Bob	72T	355	$ .10	$ .40
Watson, Bob	73T	110	$ .10	$ .40
Watson, Bob	74T	370	$ .10	$ .40
Watson, Bob	75T	227	$ .10	$ .40
Watson, Bob	76T	20	$ .05	$ .25
Watson, Bob	77T	540	$ .05	$ .20
Watson, Bob	78T	330	$ .05	$ .20
Watson, Bob	79T	130	$ .03	$ .12
Watson, Bob	80T	480	$ .01	$ .10
Watson, Bob	81T	690	$ .01	$ .08
Watson, Bob	82T	275	$ .01	$ .08
Watson, Bob	82TTR	125	$ .05	$ .20
Watson, Bob	83T	572	$ .01	$ .08
Watson, Bob	84T	739	$ .01	$ .06
Watson, Bob	85T	51	$ .01	$ .06
Watt, Eddie	66T	442	$ .65	$2.60

Player	Year	No.	VG	EX/MT
Watt, Eddie	67T	271	$ .50	$2.00
Watt, Eddie	68T	186	$ .35	$1.40
Watt, Eddie	69T	652	$ .40	$1.60
Watt, Eddie	70T	497	$ .35	$1.40
Watt, Eddie	71T	122	$ .25	$1.00
Watt, Eddie	72T	128	$ .10	$ .40
Watt, Eddie	73T	362	$ .10	$ .40
Watt, Eddie	74T	534	$ .10	$ .40
Watt, Eddie	74TTR	534	$ .10	$ .40
Watt, Eddie	75T	374	$ .10	$ .40
Waugh, Jim	53T	178	$4.50	$18.00

TOPPS

Player	Year	No.	VG	EX/MT
Waugh, Jim	91TA53	178	$ .01	$ .15
Wayne, Gary	90T	348	$ .01	$ .03
Wayne, Gary	91T	207	$ .01	$ .03
Wayne, Gary	91TSC	491	$ .05	$ .25
Wayne, Gary	92TSC	261	$ .01	$ .10
Wayne, Gary	93TSC	10	$ .01	$ .10
Weathers, Dave	93T	739	$ .01	$ .03
Weaver, Earl	69T	516	$2.50	$10.00
Weaver, Earl	70T	148	$ .50	$2.00
Weaver, Earl	71T	477	$ .75	$3.00
Weaver, Earl	72T	323	$ .50	$2.00
Weaver, Earl	73T	136	$ .25	$1.00
Weaver, Earl	74T	306	$ .15	$ .60
Weaver, Earl	78T	211	$ .04	$ .16
Weaver, Earl	83T	426	$ .01	$ .10
Weaver, Earl	85TTR	129	$ .01	$ .15
Weaver, Earl	86T	321	$ .01	$ .05
Weaver, Earl	87T	568	$ .01	$ .04
Weaver, Floyd	65T	546	$1.40	$5.60
Weaver, Floyd	66T	231	$ .50	$2.00
Weaver, Floyd	71T	227	$ .25	$1.00
Weaver, Jim	68T	328	$ .35	$1.40

Player	Year	No.	VG	EX/MT
Weaver, Jim	69T	134	$ .35	$1.40
Weaver, Roger	81T	626	$ .01	$ .08
Webb, Hank	73T	610	$1.25	$5.00
Webb, Hank	75T	615	$ .25	$1.00
Webb, Hank	76T	442	$ .05	$ .25
Webster, Lenny	92T	585	$ .01	$ .03
Webster, Lenny	92TSC	183	$ .01	$ .10
Webster, Lenny	93T	37	$ .01	$ .03
Webster, Mitch	86T	629	$ .01	$ .15
Webster, Mitch	87T	442	$ .01	$ .04
Webster, Mitch	88T	138	$ .01	$ .04
Webster, Mitch	89T	36	$ .01	$ .03
Webster, Mitch	90T	502	$ .01	$ .03
Webster, Mitch	90TTR	127	$ .01	$ .05
Webster, Mitch	91T	762	$ .01	$ .03
Webster, Mitch	91TSC	448	$ .05	$ .25
Webster, Mitch	92T	233	$ .01	$ .03
Webster, Mitch	92TSC	403	$ .01	$ .10
Webster, Ramon	67T	603	$4.00	$16.00
Webster, Ramon	68T	164	$ .35	$1.40
Webster, Ramon	69T	618	$ .40	$1.60

Player	Year	No.	VG	EX/MT
Webster, Ray	59T	531	$4.00	$16.00
Webster, Ray	60T	452	$1.25	$5.00
Wedge, Eric	93T	486	$ .05	$ .25
Weekly, Johnny	62T	204	$ .75	$3.00
Weekly, Johnny	64T	256	$ .65	$2.60
Wegener, Mike	69T	284	$ .50	$2.00
Wegener, Mike	70T	193	$ .20	$ .80
Wegener, Mike	71T	608	$1.00	$4.00
Wegman, Bill	86TTR	123	$ .05	$ .20
Wegman, Bill	87T	179	$ .01	$ .04
Wegman, Bill	88T	538	$ .01	$ .04
Wegman, Bill	89T	768	$ .01	$ .03
Wegman, Bill	90T	333	$ .01	$ .03
Wegman, Bill	91T	617	$ .01	$ .03
Wegman, Bill	91TSC	398	$ .05	$ .25
Wegman, Bill	92T	22	$ .01	$ .03
Wegman, Bill	92TSC	758	$ .01	$ .10
Wegman, Bill	93T	261	$ .01	$ .03
Wehmeier, Herman	51Tbb	110	$7.50	$30.00
Wehmeier, Herman	52T	80	$13.75	$55.00
Wehmeier, Herman	53T	110	$4.00	$16.00
Wehmeier, Herman	54T	162	$3.75	$15.00
Wehmeier, Herman	55T	29	$2.25	$9.00
Wehmeier, Herman	56T	78	$2.00	$8.00
Wehmeier, Herm	57T	81	$2.00	$8.00
Wehmeier, Herm	58T	248	$1.25	$5.00
Wehmeier, Herm	59T	421	$1.00	$4.00
Wehmeier, Herman	91TA53	110	$ .01	$ .15
Wehner, John	92T	282	$ .01	$ .10
Wehner, John	92TSC	831	$ .01	$ .10
Wehner, John	93T	484	$ .01	$ .03
Wehrmeister, Dave	77T	472	$ .05	$ .20
Wehrmeister, Dave	82T	694	$ .01	$ .08
Weik, Dick	54T	224	$3.75	$15.00
Weis, Al	63T	537	$212.50	$850.00
Weis, Al	64T	168	$ .50	$2.00
Weis, Al	65T	516	$1.25	$5.00
Weis, Al	66T	66	$ .35	$1.40
Weis, Al	67T	556	$2.25	$9.00
Weis, Al	68T	313	$ .35	$1.40
Weis, Al	69T	269	$ .50	$2.00
Weis, Al	70T	498	$ .35	$1.40
Weis, Al	71T	751	$4.00	$16.00
Weiss, Walt	88TTR	126	$ .05	$ .25
Weiss, Walt	89T	316	$ .01	$ .03
Weiss, Walt	90T	165	$ .01	$ .03
Weiss, Walt	91T	455	$ .01	$ .03
Weiss, Walt	91TSC	49	$ .05	$ .25
Weiss, Walt	92T	691	$ .01	$ .03
Weiss, Walt	92TSC	248	$ .01	$ .10
Weiss, Walt	93T	580	$ .01	$ .03
Welch, Bob	79T	318	$1.50	$6.00
Welch, Bob	80T	146	$ .10	$1.00
Welch, Bob	81T	624	$ .10	$ .50
Welch, Bob	82T	82	$ .05	$ .25
Welch, Bob	83T	454	$ .05	$ .25
Welch, Bob	84T	306	$ .01	$ .15
Welch, Bob	84T	722	$ .05	$ .20
Welch, Bob	85T	291	$ .01	$ .10
Welch, Bob	86T	549	$ .01	$ .15
Welch, Bob	87T	328	$ .01	$ .10
Welch, Bob	88T	118	$ .01	$ .04
Welch, Bob	88TTR	127	$ .01	$ .05
Welch, Bob	89T	605	$ .01	$ .10
Welch, Bob	90T	475	$ .01	$ .03
Welch, Bob	91T	50	$ .01	$ .03
Welch, Bob	91TAS	394	$ .01	$ .03
Welch, Bob	91TSC	79	$ .05	$ .25
Welch, Bob	92T	285	$ .01	$ .03
Welch, Bob	92TSC	651	$ .01	$ .10
Welch, Bob	93T	705	$ .01	$ .03
Wellman, Bob	52T	41	$13.75	$55.00
Wellman, Brad	84T	109	$ .01	$ .06
Wellman, Brad	85T	409	$ .01	$ .06
Wellman, Brad	86T	41	$ .01	$ .05

TOPPS

Player	Year	No.	VG	EX/MT
Wells, Boomer	82T	203	$ .10	$1.00
Wells, David	88TTR	128	$ .05	$ .20
Wells, David	89T	567	$ .01	$ .10
Wells, David	90T	229	$ .01	$ .03
Wells, David	91T	619	$ .01	$ .03
Wells, David	91TSC	133	$ .05	$ .25
Wells, David	92T	54	$ .01	$ .03
Wells, David	92TSC	721	$ .01	$ .10
Wells, David	93T	458	$ .01	$ .03
Wells, David	93TSC	59	$ .01	$ .10
Welsh, Chris	82T	376	$ .01	$ .08
Welsh, Chris	83T	118	$ .01	$ .08
Welsh, Chris	83TTR	125	$ .01	$ .10
Welsh, Chris	86T	52	$ .01	$ .05
Welsh, Chris	87T	592	$ .01	$ .04
Wendell, Turk	92T	676	$ .05	$ .35
Wenz, Fred	69T	628	$ .75	$3.00

Player	Year	No.	VG	EX/MT
Wenz, Fred	71T	92	$ .25	$1.00
Werhas, John	64T	456	$1.25	$5.00
Werhas, John	65T	453	$1.25	$5.00
Werhas, John	67T	514	$1.50	$6.00
Werle, William	51Trb	33	$1.75	$7.50
Werle, William	52T	73	$13.75	$55.00
Werle, Bill	53T	170	$4.50	$18.00
Werle, Bill	54T	144	$3.75	$15.00
Werle, Bill	91TA53	170	$ .01	$ .15
Werner, Don	78T	702	$ .04	$ .16
Werner, Don	83T	504	$ .01	$ .08
Wert, Don	62T	299	$ .75	$3.00
Wert, Don	64T	19	$ .50	$2.00
Wert, Don	65T	271	$ .50	$2.00
Wert, Don	66T	253	$ .50	$2.00
Wert, Don	67T	511	$1.50	$6.00
Wert, Don	68T	178	$ .35	$1.40
Wert, Don	69T	443	$ .30	$1.20
Wert, Don	70T	33	$ .20	$ .80
Wert, Don	71T	307	$ .25	$1.00
Werth, Dennis	81T	424	$ .01	$ .08
Werth, Dennis	82T	154	$ .01	$ .08
Werth, Dennis	82TTR	126	$ .01	$ .10
Wertz, Vic	51Tbb	40	$10.00	$40.00
Wertz, Vic	52T	244	$7.50	$30.00
Wertz, Vic	53T	142	$7.50	$30.00
Wertz, Vic	56T	300	$2.50	$10.00
Wertz, Vic	57T	78	$2.00	$8.00
Wertz, Vic	58T	170	$1.25	$5.00
Wertz, Vic	59T	500	$1.00	$4.00
Wertz, Vic	60T	111	$ .75	$3.00
Wertz, Vic	61T	173	$ .75	$3.00
Wertz, Vic	61T	340	$ .60	$2.40
Wertz, Vic	62T	481	$1.50	$6.00
Wertz, Vic	63T	348	$ .90	$3.60
Wertz, Vic	91TA53	142	$ .01	$ .15
West, Dave	89T	787	$ .01	$ .10
West, Dave	90T	357	$ .01	$ .03
West, Dave	91T	578	$ .01	$ .03
West, Dave	91TSC	34	$ .05	$ .25
West, Dave	92T	442	$ .01	$ .03
West, Dave	92TSC	398	$ .01	$ .10
West, Dave	93T	652	$ .01	$ .03
Westlake, Wally	51Trb	27	$1.75	$7.50
Westlake, Wally	52T	38	$13.75	$55.00
Westlake, Wally	53T	192	$4.50	$18.00
Westlake, Wally	54T	92	$3.75	$15.00
Westlake, Wally	55T	102	$2.25	$9.00
Westlake, Wally	56T	81	$2.00	$8.00
Westlake, Wally	91TA53	192	$ .01	$ .15
Weston, Mickey	90T	377	$ .01	$ .10
Westrum, Wes	51Trb	37	$1.75	$7.50
Westrum, Wes	52T	75	$13.75	$55.00
Westrum, Wes	54T	180	$3.75	$15.00
Westrum, Wes	56T	156	$2.50	$10.00
Westrum, Wes	57T	323	$5.00	$20.00
Westrum, Wes	60T	469	$1.25	$5.00
Westrum, Wes	66T	341	$ .50	$2.00
Westrum, Wes	67T	593	$4.00	$16.00
Westrum, Wes	91TA53	323	$ .05	$ .20
Wetherby, Jeff	90T	142	$ .01	$ .10
Wetteland, John	90T	631	$ .01	$ .15
Wetteland, John	92TSC	759	$ .01	$ .10
Wetteland, John	93T	231	$ .01	$ .03
Wheat, Leroy	54T	244	$3.75	$15.00
Wheelock, Gary	77T	493	$0.25	$ .80
Wheelock, Gary	78T	596	$ .04	$ .16
Whisenant, Pete	57T	373	$1.75	$7.00
Whisenant, Pete	58T	466	$1.00	$4.00
Whisenant, Pete	59T	14	$1.50	$6.00
Whisenant, Pete	60T	424	$ .75	$3.00
Whisenant, Pete	61T	201	$ .60	$2.40
Whisenton, Larry	79T	715	$ .05	$ .20
Whisenton, Larry	83T	544	$ .01	$ .08
Whitaker, Lou	78T	704	$4.50	$18.00
Whitaker, Lou	79T	123	$1.75	$7.00
Whitaker, Lou	80T	358	$ .75	$3.00
Whitaker, Lou	81T	234	$ .10	$1.00
Whitaker, Lou	82T	39	$ .10	$ .50
Whitaker, Lou	83T	509	$ .10	$ .50
Whitaker, Lou	84T	666	$ .05	$ .20
Whitaker, Lou	84T	695	$ .10	$ .40
Whitaker, Lou	84TAS	398	$ .01	$ .10
Whitaker, Lou	85T	480	$ .05	$ .25
Whitaker, Lou	86T	20	$ .01	$ .15
Whitaker, Lou	87T	661	$ .01	$ .10
Whitaker, Lou	88T	770	$ .01	$ .10
Whitaker, Lou	89T	320	$ .01	$ .03
Whitaker, Lou	90T	280	$ .01	$ .03
Whitaker, Lou	91T	145	$ .01	$ .03
Whitaker, Lou	91TSC	101	$ .05	$ .25
Whitaker, Lou	92T	570	$ .01	$ .03
Whitaker, Lou	92TSC	550	$ .01	$ .10
Whitaker, Lou	93T	160	$ .01	$ .03
Whitaker, Lou	93TSC	135	$ .01	$ .15
Whitaker, Steve	67T	277	$ .50	$2.00
Whitaker, Steve	68T	383	$ .35	$1.40
Whitaker, Steve	69T	71	$ .35	$1.40
Whitaker, Steve	70T	496	$ .35	$1.40
Whitaker, Steve	92T	369	$ .01	$ .10
Whitby, Bill	67T	486	$1.50	$6.00

TOPPS

Player	Year	No.	VG	EX/MT
White, Bill	59T	359	$7.00	$28.00
White, Bill	60T	355	$1.75	$7.00
White, Bill	61T	232	$1.50	$6.00
White, Bill	61T	451	$1.35	$5.40
White, Bill	62T	14	$1.25	$5.00
White, Bill	63T	1	$8.00	$32.00
White, Bill	63T	290	$1.50	$6.00
White, Bill	64T	11	$1.75	$7.00
White, Bill	64T	240	$1.00	$4.00
White, Bill	65T	190	$ .75	$3.00
White, Bill	66T	397	$1.00	$4.00
White, Bill	67T	290	$ .75	$3.00
White, Bill	68T	190	$ .50	$2.00
White, Bill	69T	588	$ .50	$2.00
White, Charlie	55T	103	$2.25	$9.00
White, Devon	87T	139	$ .10	$ .50
White, Devon	88T	192	$ .01	$ .10
White, Devon	89T	602	$ .01	$ .03
White, Devon	90T	65	$ .01	$ .03
White, Devon	91T	704	$ .01	$ .03
White, Devon	91TSC	444	$ .05	$ .25
White, Devon	91TTR	125	$ .01	$ .05
White, Devon	92T	260	$ .01	$ .03
White, Devon	92TSC	41	$ .01	$ .10
White, Devon	93T	387	$ .01	$ .03
White, Frank	74T	604	$1.25	$5.00
White, Frank	75T	569	$ .15	$ .60
White, Frank	76T	369	$ .05	$ .25
White, Frank	77T	117	$ .05	$ .20
White, Frank	78T	248	$ .04	$ .16
White, Frank	79T	439	$ .03	$ .12
White, Frank	80T	45	$ .01	$ .10
White, Frank	81T	330	$ .01	$ .08
White, Frank	82T	645	$ .01	$ .08
White, Frank	82TSA	646	$ .01	$ .07
White, Frank	83T	525	$ .01	$ .08
White, Frank	84T	155	$ .01	$ .06
White, Frank	85T	743	$ .01	$ .06
White, Frank	86T	215	$ .01	$ .05
White, Frank	87T	692	$ .01	$ .04
White, Frank	88T	595	$ .01	$ .04
White, Frank	89T	200	$ .05	$ .20
White, Frank	90T	479	$ .01	$ .03
White, Frank	91T	352	$ .01	$ .03
White, Jerry	76T	594	$ .05	$ .25
White, Jerry	77T	557	$ .05	$ .20
White, Jerry	79T	494	$ .03	$ .12
White, Jerry	80T	724	$ .01	$ .10
White, Jerry	81T	42	$ .01	$ .08
White, Jerry	82T	386	$ .01	$ .08
White, Jerry	83T	214	$ .01	$ .08
White, Jo-Jo	60T	460	$1.75	$7.00
White, Mike	64T	492	$1.25	$5.00
White, Mike	65T	31	$ .35	$1.40
White, Roy	66T	234	$1.75	$7.00
White, Roy	68T	546	$ .75	$3.00
White, Roy	69T	25	$ .35	$1.40
White, Roy	70T	373	$ .35	$1.40
White, Roy	71T	395	$ .50	$2.00
White, Roy	72T	340	$ .20	$ .80
White, Roy	73T	25	$ .20	$ .80
White, Roy	74T	135	$ .10	$ .40
White, Roy	75T	375	$ .15	$ .60
White, Roy	76T	225	$ .05	$ .25
White, Roy	77T	485	$ .05	$ .20
White, Roy	78T	16	$ .04	$ .16
White, Roy	79T	159	$ .03	$ .12
White, Roy	80T	648	$ .01	$ .10
White, Sam	52T	345	$43.75	$175.00
White, Sammy	53T	139	$6.25	$25.00
White, Sammy	56T	168	$2.50	$10.00
White, Sammy	57T	163	$2.00	$8.00
White, Sammy	58T	414	$1.00	$4.00
White, Sammy	59T	486	$1.00	$4.00
White, Sammy	60T	203	$ .75	$3.00
White, Sammy	62T	494	$1.50	$6.00
White, Sammy	91TA53	139	$ .01	$ .15
White Sox, Team	56T	188	$9.00	$36.00
White Sox, Team	57T	329	$12.00	$48.00
White Sox, Team	58T	256	$3.50	$14.00
White Sox, Team	59T	94	$5.00	$20.00
White Sox, Team	60T	208	$2.00	$8.00
White Sox, Team	61T	7	$1.75	$7.00
White Sox, Team	62T	113	$1.50	$6.00
White Sox, Team	63T	288	$2.00	$8.00
White Sox, Team	64T	496	$2.50	$10.00
White Sox, Team	65T	234	$1.00	$4.00
White Sox, Team	66T	426	$2.00	$8.00
White Sox, Team	67T	573	$6.25	$25.00
White Sox, Team	68T	424	$ .75	$3.00
White Sox, Team	70T	501	$ .75	$3.00
White Sox, Team	71T	289	$ .50	$2.00
White Sox, Team	72T	381	$ .50	$2.00
White Sox, Team	73T	481	$ .50	$2.00
White Sox, Team	74T	416	$ .25	$1.00
White Sox, Team Checklist	75T	276	$ .35	$1.40
White Sox, Team Checklist	76T	656	$ .30	$1.20
White Sox, Team Checklist	77T	418	$ .25	$1.00
White Sox, Team Checklist	78T	66	$ .20	$ .80
White Sox, Team Checklist	79T	404	$ .15	$ .60
White Sox, Team Checklist	80T	112	$ .10	$ .50
White Sox, Team Checklist	81T	664	$ .05	$ .25
White Sox, Team Leaders	86T	156	$ .01	$ .05

White Sox, Team Leaders	87T	356	$ .01	$ .04
White Sox, Team Leaders	88T	321	$ .01	$ .04
White Sox, Team Leaders	89T	21	$ .01	$ .03
Whited, Ed	90T	111	$ .01	$ .10
Whitehouse, Len	83TTR	126	$ .01	$ .10
Whitehouse, Len	84T	648	$ .01	$ .06
Whitehouse, Len	85T	406	$ .01	$ .06
Whitehurst, Wally	90T	719	$ .01	$ .03
Whitehurst, Wally	91T	557	$ .01	$ .03
Whitehurst, Wally	91TSC	458	$ .05	$ .25
Whitehurst, Wally	92T	419	$ .01	$ .03
Whitehurst, Wally	92TSC	476	$ .01	$ .10
Whitehurst, Wally	93T	271	$ .01	$ .03
Whiten, Mark	91T	588	$ .05	$ .20
Whiten, Mark	91TSC	452	$ .10	$ .50

TOPPS

Player	Year	No.	VG	EX/MT
Whiten, Mark	91TTR	126	$ .01	$ .15
Whiten, Mark	92T	671	$ .01	$ .03
Whiten, Mark	92TSC	51	$ .05	$ .35
Whiten, Mark	93T	277	$ .01	$ .10
Whiteside, Matt	93T	468	$ .01	$ .15
Whitfield, Fred	63T	211	$ .90	$3.60
Whitfield, Fred	64T	367	$ .65	$2.60
Whitfield, Fred	65T	283	$ .50	$2.00
Whitfield, Fred	66T	88	$ .35	$1.40
Whitfield, Fred	67T	275	$ .50	$2.00
Whitfield, Fred	68T	133	$ .35	$1.40
Whitfield, Fred	69T	518	$ .40	$1.60
Whitfield, Terry	75T	622	$2.75	$11.00
Whitfield, Terry	76T	590	$ .15	$ .60
Whitfield, Terry	78T	236	$ .04	$ .16
Whitfield, Terry	79T	589	$ .03	$ .12
Whitfield, Terry	80T	713	$ .01	$ .10
Whitfield, Terry	81T	167	$ .01	$ .08
Whitfield, Terry	85T	31	$ .01	$ .06
Whitfield, Terry	86T	318	$ .01	$ .05
Whitman, Ryan	93T	558	$ .05	$ .25
Whitmore, Darrell	93T	697	$ .05	$ .20
Whitson, Eddie	79T	189	$ .25	$1.00
Whitson, Eddie	80T	561	$ .01	$ .10
Whitson, Eddie	81T	336	$ .01	$ .08
Whitson, Eddie	82T	656	$ .01	$ .08
Whitson, Eddie	82TTR	127	$ .01	$ .10
Whitson, Eddie	83T	429	$ .01	$ .08
Whitson, Eddie	83TTR	127	$ .01	$ .10
Whitson, Eddie	84T	277	$ .01	$ .06
Whitson, Eddie	85T	762	$ .01	$ .06
Whitson, Eddie	85TTR	130	$ .01	$ .10
Whitson, Eddie	86T	15	$ .01	$ .05

Player	Year	No.	VG	EX/MT
Whitson, Eddie	**87T**	**155**	**$ .01**	**$ .04**
Whitson, Eddie	88T	330	$ .01	$ .04
Whitson, Eddie	89T	516	$ .01	$ .03
Whitson, Eddie	90T	618	$ .01	$ .03
Whitson, Eddie	91T	481	$ .01	$ .03
Whitson, Eddie	91TSC	246	$ .05	$ .25
Whitson, Eddie	92T	228	$ .01	$ .03
Whitson, Eddie	92TSC	172	$ .01	$ .10
Whitt, Ernie	78T	708	$3.75	$15.00
Whitt, Ernie	79T	714	$ .03	$ .12

Player	Year	No.	VG	EX/MT
Whitt, Ernie	81T	407	$ .01	$ .08
Whitt, Ernie	82T	19	$ .01	$ .08
Whitt, Ernie	83T	302	$ .01	$ .08
Whitt, Ernie	84T	506	$ .01	$ .06
Whitt, Ernie	85T	128	$ .01	$ .06
Whitt, Ernie	86T	673	$ .01	$ .05
Whitt, Ernie	87T	698	$ .01	$ .04
Whitt, Ernie	88T	79	$ .01	$ .04
Whitt, Ernie	89T	289	$ .01	$ .03
Whitt, Ernie	90T	742	$ .01	$ .03
Whitt, Ernie	90TTR	128	$ .01	$ .05
Whitt, Ernie	91T	492	$ .01	$ .03
Wickander, Kevin	90T	528	$ .01	$ .03
Wickander, Kevin	91T	246	$ .01	$ .03
Wickander, Kevin	91TSC	572	$ .05	$ .25
Wickander, Kevin	93T	358	$ .01	$ .03
Wicker, Floyd	69T	524	$ .40	$1.60
Wicker, Floyd	71T	97	$ .25	$1.00
Wickersham, Dave	61T	381	$1.00	$4.00
Wickersham, Dave	62T	517	$1.50	$6.00
Wickersham, Dave	63T	492	$3.00	$12.00
Wickersham, Dave	64T	181	$ .50	$2.00
Wickersham, Dave	65T	9	$ .75	$3.00
Wickersham, Dave	65T	375	$1.00	$4.00
Wickersham, Dave	66T	58	$ .35	$1.40
Wickersham, Dave	67T	112	$ .40	$1.60
Wickersham, Dave	68T	288	$ .35	$1.40
Wickersham, Dave	69T	647	$ .40	$1.60
Wickman, Bob	93T	452	$ .05	$ .20
Wickman, Bob	93TSC	53	$ .10	$ .50
Widger, Chris	93T	632	$ .01	$$ .15
Widmar, Al	52T	133	$7.00	$28.00
Widmar, Al	74T	99	$ .10	$ .40
Wieand, Ted	60T	146	$ .75	$3.00
Wiesler, Bob	56T	327	$2.50	$10.00
Wiesler, Bob	57T	126	$2.00	$8.00
Wietelmann, Whitey	73T	12	$ .20	$ .80
Wiggins, Alan	83T	251	$ .01	$ .08
Wiggins, Alan	84T	693	$ .01	$ .06
Wiggins, Alan	85T	378	$ .01	$ .06
Wiggins, Alan	86T	508	$ .01	$ .05
Wiggins, Alan	87TTR	126	$ .01	$ .05
Wight, Bill	52T	177	$7.00	$28.00
Wight, Bill	56T	286	$2.50	$10.00
Wight, Bill	57T	340	$5.00	$20.00
Wight, Bill	58T	237	$1.25	$5.00
Wihtol, Sandy	80T	665	$ .01	$ .10
Wihtol, Sandy	81T	451	$ .01	$ .08
Wilber, Del	52T	383	$43.75	$175.00
Wilborn, Ted	80T	674	$ .01	$ .10
Wilcox, Milt	71T	164	$ .25	$1.00
Wilcox, Milt	72T	399	$ .25	$1.00
Wilcox, Milt	73T	134	$ .10	$ .40
Wilcox, Milt	74T	565	$ .10	$ .40
Wilcox, Milt	75T	14	$ .10	$ .40
Wilcox, Milt	78T	151	$ .04	$ .16
Wilcox, Milt	79T	288	$ .03	$ .12
Wilcox, Milt	80T	392	$ .01	$ .10
Wilcox, Milt	81T	658	$ .01	$ .08
Wilcox, Milt	82T	784	$ .01	$ .08
Wilcox, Milt	83T	457	$ .01	$ .08
Wilcox, Milt	84T	588	$ .01	$ .06
Wilcox, Milt	85T	99	$ .01	$ .06
Wilcox, Milt	86T	192	$ .01	$ .05
Wilfong, Rob	79T	633	$ .03	$ .12
Wilfong, Rob	80T	238	$ .01	$ .10
Wilfong, Rob	81T	453	$ .01	$ .08
Wilfong, Rob	82T	379	$ .01	$ .08
Wilfong, Rob	82TTR	128	$ .01	$ .10
Wilfong, Rob	83T	158	$ .01	$ .08
Wilfong, Rob	84T	79	$ .01	$ .06
Wilfong, Rob	85T	524	$ .01	$ .06
Wilfong, Rob	86T	658	$ .01	$ .05
Wilfong, Rob	87T	251	$ .01	$ .04
Wilhelm, Hoyt	52T	392	$165.00	$660.00

TOPPS

Player	Year	No.	VG	EX/MT
Wilhelm, Hoyt	53T	151	$16.50	$66.00
Wilhelm, Hoyt	54T	36	$11.25	$45.00
Wilhelm, Hoyt	56T	307	$8.25	$33.00
Wilhelm, Hoyt	57T	203	$5.00	$20.00
Wilhelm, Hoyt	58T	324	$4.50	$18.00
Wilhelm, Hoyt	59T	349	$4.25	$17.00
Wilhelm, Hoyt	60T	115	$1.25	$5.00
Wilhelm, Hoyt	60T	395	$3.00	$12.00
Wilhelm, Hoyt	61T	545	$15.00	$60.00
Wilhelm, Hoyt	62T	423	$1.50	$6.00
Wilhelm, Hoyt	62T	545	$15.00	$60.00
Wilhelm, Hoyt	63T	108	$2.50	$10.00
Wilhelm, Hoyt	64T	13	$2.00	$8.00
Wilhelm, Hoyt	65T	276	$2.00	$8.00
Wilhelm, Hoyt	66T	510	$3.25	$13.00
Wilhelm, Hoyt	67T	422	$2.00	$8.00
Wilhelm, Hoyt	68T	350	$1.50	$6.00
Wilhelm, Hoyt	69T	565	$1.75	$7.00
Wilhelm, Hoyt	70T	17	$1.00	$4.00
Wilhelm, Hoyt	71T	248	$1.00	$4.00
Wilhelm, Hoyt	72T	777	$4.50	$18.00
Wilhelm, Hoyt	91TA53	151	$ .10	$ .75
Wilhelm, Hoyt	91TA53	312	$ .10	$1.00
Wilhelm, Jim	80T	685	$ .01	$ .10
Wilkerson, Curt	84TTR	127	$ .01	$ .15
Wilkerson, Curt	85T	594	$ .01	$ .06
Wilkerson, Curt	86T	434	$ .01	$ .05
Wilkerson, Curt	87T	228	$ .01	$ .04
Wilkerson, Curt	88T	53	$ .01	$ .04
Wilkerson, Curt	89T	331	$ .01	$ .03
Wilkerson, Curt	89TTR	126	$ .01	$ .05
Wilkerson, Curt	90T	667	$ .01	$ .03
Wilkerson, Curt	91T	142	$ .01	$ .03
Wilkerson, Curt	91TSC	512	$ .05	$ .25
Wilkerson, Curt	92T	712	$ .01	$ .03
Wilkerson, Curt	92TSC	46	$ .01	$ .10
Wilkerson, Curt	92TSC	849	$ .01	$ .10
Wilkerson, Curt	93TSC	177	$ .01	$ .10
Wilkins, Eric	80T	511	$ .01	$ .10
Wilkins, Eric	81T	99	$ .01	$ .08
Wilkins, Rick	92T	348	$ .01	$ .10
Wilkins, Rick	92TSC	643	$ .01	$ .10
Wilkins, Rick	93T	721	$ .01	$ .03
Wilkins, Rick	93TSC	228	$ .01	$ .10
Wilkinson, Bill	87TTR	127	$ .01	$ .05
Wilkinson, Bill	88T	376	$ .01	$ .04
Wilkinson, Bill	89T	636	$ .01	$ .03
Wilks, Ted	52T	109	$7.00	$28.00
Wilks, Ted	53T	101	$6.25	$25.00
Wilks, Ted	91TA53	101	$ .01	$ .15
Will, Bob	59T	388	$1.00	$4.00
Will, Bob	60T	147	$ .75	$3.00
Will, Bob	61T	512	$1.35	$5.40
Will, Bob	62T	47	$ .60	$2.40
Will, Bob	63T	58	$ .50	$2.00
Willard, Jerry	85T	504	$ .01	$ .06
Willard, Jerry	86T	273	$ .01	$ .05
Willard, Jerry	87T	137	$ .01	$ .04
Willey, "Carlton" (Carl)	58T	407	$1.00	$4.00
Willey, Carl	59T	95	$1.50	$6.00
Willey, Carl	60T	107	$ .85	$3.40
Willey, Carl	61T	105	$ .60	$2.40
Willey, Carl	62T	174	$ .75	$3.00
Willey, Carl	63T	528	$2.25	$9.00
Willey, Carl	64T	84	$ .50	$2.00
Willey, Carl	65T	401	$1.00	$4.00
Willhite, Nick	64T	14	$ .50	$2.00
Willhite, Nick	65T	284	$ .50	$2.00
Willhite, Nick	66T	171	$ .50	$2.00
Willhite, Nick	67T	249	$ .50	$2.00
Williams, Al	81T	569	$ .01	$ .08
Williams, Al	82T	69	$ .01	$ .08
Williams, Al	83T	731	$ .01	$ .08
Williams, Al	84T	183	$ .01	$ .06
Williams, Al	85T	614	$ .01	$ .06
Williams, Bernie	70T	401	$ .35	$1.40
Williams, Bernie	71T	728	$1.10	$4.40
Williams, Bernie	72T	761	$6.00	$24.00
Williams, Bernie	73T	557	$ .60	$2.40
Williams, Bernie	90T	701	$ .05	$ .25
Williams, Bernie	92T	374	$ .01	$ .10
Williams, Bernie	92TSC	260	$ .05	$ .35
Williams, Bernie	93T	222	$ .01	$ .03
Williams, Billy	61T	141	$22.50	$90.00
Williams, Billy	62T	288	$10.00	$40.00
Williams, Billy	63T	353	$6.25	$25.00
Williams, Billy	64T	175	$4.50	$18.00
Williams, Billy	65T	4	$2.00	$8.00
Williams, Billy	65T	220	$3.50	$14.00
Williams, Billy	66T	217	$4.00	$16.00
Williams, Billy	66T	580	$20.00	$80.00

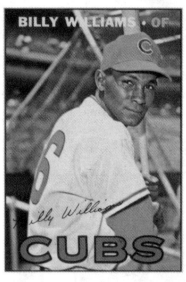

Player	Year	No.	VG	EX/MT
Williams, Billy	**67T**	**315**	**$3.00**	**$12.00**
Williams, Billy	68T	37	$2.50	$10.00
Williams, Billy	69T	4	$1.00	$4.00
Williams, Billy	69T	450	$1.50	$6.00
Williams, Billy	70T	170	$1.50	$6.00
Williams, Billy	71T	64	$ .75	$3.00
Williams, Billy	71T	66	$1.00	$4.00
Williams, Billy	71T	350	$1.50	$6.00
Williams, Billy	72T	439	$1.00	$4.00
Williams, Billy	72TIA	440	$ .50	$2.00
Williams, Billy	73T	61	$ .50	$2.00
Williams, Billy	73T	200	$1.00	$4.00
Williams, Billy	74T	110	$ .75	$3.00
Williams, Billy	74TAS	338	$1.25	$5.00
Williams, Billy	75T	545	$ .75	$3.00
Williams, Billy	76T	525	$ .75	$3.00
Williams, Brian	93T	614	$ .01	$ .10
Williams, Charlie	72T	388	$ .10	$ .40
Williams, Charlie	75T	449	$ .10	$ .40
Williams, Charlie	76T	332	$ .05	$ .25
Williams, Charlie	77T	73	$ .05	$ .20
Williams, Charlie	78T	561	$ .04	$ .16
Williams, Charlie	79T	142	$ .03	$ .12
Williams, Davey	52T	316	$52.50	$210.00
Williams, Davey	53T	120	$6.25	$25.00
Williams, Davey	91TA53	120	$ .01	$ .15
Williams, Dick	52T	396	$60.00	$240.00

TOPPS

Player	Year	No.	VG	EX/MT
Williams, Dick	53T	125	$4.50	$18.00
Williams, Dick	57T	59	$2.50	$10.00
Williams, Dick	58T	79	$2.50	$10.00
Williams, Dick	59T	292	$1.00	$4.00
Williams, Dick	60T	188	$.75	$3.00
Williams, Dick	61T	8	$.75	$3.00
Williams, Dick	62T	382	$1.25	$5.00
Williams, Dick	63T	328	$.90	$3.60
Williams, Dick	64T	153	$.50	$2.00
Williams, Dick	67T	161	$.40	$1.60
Williams, Dick	68T	87	$.35	$1.40
Williams, Dick	69T	349	$.30	$1.20
Williams, Dick	71T	714	$1.50	$6.00
Williams, Dick	72T	137	$.20	$.80
Williams, Dick	73T	179	$.25	$1.00
Williams, Dick	78T	522	$.04	$.16
Williams, Dick	83T	366	$.01	$.08
Williams, Dick	84T	742	$.01	$.06
Williams, Dick	85T	66	$.01	$.06
Williams, Dick	86T	681	$.01	$.05
Williams, Dick	86TTR	124	$.01	$.06
Williams, Dick	87T	418	$.01	$.04
Williams, Dick	88T	104	$.01	$.04
Williams, Dick	91TA53	125	$.01	$.15
Williams, Don	60T	414	$.75	$3.00
Williams, Earl	71T	52	$.25	$1.00
Williams, Earl	72T	380	$.10	$.40
Williams, Earl	73T	504	$.25	$1.00
Williams, Earl	74T	375	$.10	$.40
Williams, Earl	75T	97	$.10	$.40
Williams, Earl	76T	458	$.05	$.25
Williams, Earl	77T	223	$.05	$.20
Williams, Earl	78T	604	$.04	$.16
Williams, Eddie	88T	758	$.01	$.04
Williams, Eddie	89TTR	127	$.01	$.05
Williams, Frank	84TTR	128	$.05	$.20
Williams, Frank	85T	487	$.01	$.06
Williams, Frank	86T	341	$.01	$.05
Williams, Frank	87T	96	$.01	$.04
Williams, Frank	87TTR	128	$.01	$.05
Williams, Frank	88T	773	$.01	$.04
Williams, Frank	89T	172	$.01	$.03
Williams, Frank	89TTR	128	$.01	$.05
Williams, Frank	90T	599	$.01	$.03
Williams, George	63T	324	$1.25	$5.00
Williams, George	64T	388	$1.00	$4.00
Williams, Gerald	92T	656	$.05	$.20
Williams, Gerald	93T	654	$.01	$.15
Williams, Jim A.	70T	262	$.20	$.80
Williams, Jim A.	71T	262	$.25	$1.00
Williams, Jimmy F.	66T	544	$8.00	$32.00
Williams, Jimy	87T	786	$.01	$.04
Williams, Jimy	88T	314	$.01	$.04
Williams, Jimy	89T	594	$.01	$.03
Williams, Ken	88T	559	$.01	$.04
Williams, Ken	89T	34	$.01	$.03
Williams, Ken	89TTR	129	$.01	$.05
Williams, Ken	90T	327	$.01	$.03
Williams, Ken	91T	274	$.01	$.03
Williams, Matt	87TTR	129	$.20	$2.00
Williams, Matt	88T	372	$.10	$1.00
Williams, Matt	89T	628	$.01	$.10
Williams, Matt	90T	41	$.01	$.10
Williams, Matt	91T	190	$.01	$.10
Williams, Matt	91TAS	399	$.01	$.03
Williams, Matt	91TSC	295	$.10	$.50
Williams, Matt	92T	445	$.01	$.10
Williams, Matt	92TSC	582	$.01	$.10
Williams, Matt	93T	225	$.01	$.03
Williams, Matt	93TSC	287	$.10	$.10
Williams, Mike	93T	99	$.01	$.15
Williams, Mitch	86TTR	125	$.05	$.25
Williams, Mitch	87T	291	$.05	$.20
Williams, Mitch	88T	26	$.01	$.10
Williams, Mitch	89T	411	$.01	$.10
Williams, Mitch	89TTR	130	$.01	$.10
Williams, Mitch	90T	520	$.01	$.03
Williams, Mitch	91T	335	$.01	$.03
Williams, Mitch	91TSC	261	$.05	$.25
Williams, Mitch	91TTR	127	$.01	$.05
Williams, Mitch	92T	633	$.01	$.03
Williams, Mitch	92TSC	499	$.01	$.10
Williams, Mitch	93T	235	$.01	$.03
Williams, Mitch	93TSC	180	$.01	$.10
Williams, Reggie	87T	232	$.01	$.04
Williams, Reggie	93T	543	$.01	$.15
Williams, Rick	79T	437	$.03	$.12
Williams, Rick	80T	69	$.01	$.10
Williams, Stan	59T	53	$2.50	$10.00
Williams, Stan	60T	278	$.75	$3.00
Williams, Stan	61T	45	$1.00	$4.00
Williams, Stan	61T	190	$.60	$2.40
Williams, Stan	62T	60	$2.00	$8.00
Williams, Stan	62T	515	$1.50	$6.00
Williams, Stan	63T	42	$.50	$2.00
Williams, Stan	64T	505	$1.00	$4.00
Williams, Stan	65T	404	$1.00	$4.00
Williams, Stan	68T	54	$.35	$1.40
Williams, Stan	69T	118	$.35	$1.40
Williams, Stan	70T	353	$.35	$1.40
Williams, Stan	71T	638	$1.00	$4.00

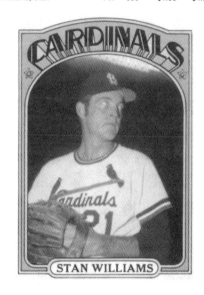

Player	Year	No.	VG	EX/MT
Williams, Stan	72T	9	$.10	$.40
Williams, Ted	54T	1	$157.50	$630.00
Williams, Ted	54T	250	$170.00	$680.00
Williams, Ted	55T	2	$100.00	$400.00
Williams, Ted	56T	5	$75.00	$300.00
Williams, Ted	57T	1	$110.00	$440.00
Williams, Ted	58T	1	$90.00	$360.00
Williams, Ted	58T	321	$10.00	$40.00
Williams, Ted	58TAS	485	$17.50	$70.00
Williams, Ted	69T	539	$1.50	$6.00
Williams, Ted	69T	650	$3.00	$12.00
Williams, Ted	70T	211	$2.00	$8.00
Williams, Ted	71T	380	$1.75	$7.00
Williams, Ted	72T	510	$1.75	$7.00
Williams, Ted	76TAT	347	$1.50	$6.00
Williams, Ted	91TA53	319	$2.50	$10.00
Williams, Walt	67T	598	$5.00	$20.00

TOPPS

Player	Year	No.	VG	EX/MT
Williams, Walt	68T	172	$ .35	$1.40
Williams, Walt	69T	309	$ .50	$2.00
Williams, Walt	70T	395	$ .35	$1.40
Williams, Walt	71T	555	$1.00	$4.00
Williams, Walt	72T	15	$ .10	$ .40
Williams, Walt	73T	297	$ .10	$ .40
Williams, Walt	74T	418	$ .10	$ .40
Williams, Walt	76T	123	$ .05	$ .25
Williamson, Mark	88T	571	$ .01	$ .04
Williamson, Mark	89T	546	$ .01	$ .03
Williamson, Mark	90T	13	$ .01	$ .03
Williamson, Mark	91T	296	$ .01	$ .03

Player	Year	No.	VG	EX/MT
Williamson, Mark	**91TSC**	**20**	**$ .05**	**$ .25**
Williamson, Mark	92T	628	$ .01	$ .03
Williamson, Mark	92TSC	177	$ .01	$ .10
Willis, Carl	87T	101	$ .01	$ .10
Willis, Carl	92TSC	779	$ .01	$ .10
Willis, Carl	93T	747	$ .01	$ .03
Willis, Carl	93TSC	182	$ .01	$ .10
Willis, Jim	54T	67	$7.50	$30.00
Willis, Mike	77T	493	$0.25	$ .80
Willis, Mike	78T	293	$ .04	$ .16
Willis, Mike	79T	688	$ .03	$ .12
Willis, Mike	81T	324	$ .01	$ .08
Willis, Ron	67T	592	$5.50	$22.00
Willis, Ron	68T	68	$ .35	$1.40
Willis, Ron	69T	273	$ .50	$2.00
Willoughby, Jim	73T	79	$ .10	$ .40
Willoughby, Jim	74T	553	$ .10	$ .40
Willoughby, Jim	76T	102	$ .05	$ .25
Willoughby, Jim	77T	532	$ .05	$ .20
Willoughby, Jim	78T	373	$ .04	$ .16
Willoughby, Jim	79T	266	$ .03	$ .12
Wills, Bump	77T	494	$ .35	$1.40
Wills, Bump	78T	23	$ .04	$ .16
Wills, Bump	79T	369	$ .75	$3.00
Wills, Bump	80T	473	$ .01	$ .10
Wills, Bump	81T	173	$ .01	$ .08
Wills, Bump	82T	272	$ .01	$ .08
Wills, Bump	82TTR	129	$ .01	$ .10
Wills, Bump	83T	643	$ .01	$ .08
Wills, Frank	86T	419	$ .01	$ .05
Wills, Frank	87T	551	$ .01	$ .04

Player	Year	No.	VG	EX/MT
Wills, Frank	90TTR	129	$ .01	$ .05
Wills, Frank	91T	213	$ .01	$ .03
Wills, Maury	67T	570	$20.00	$80.00
Wills, Maury	68T	175	$1.00	$4.00
Wills, Maury	69T	45	$ .75	$3.00
Wills, Maury	70T	595	$1.00	$4.00
Wills, Maury	71T	385	$ .75	$3.00
Wills, Maury	72T	437	$ .50	$2.00
Wills, Maury	72TIA	438	$ .25	$1.00
Wills, Maury	75T	200	$1.50	$6.00
Wills, Maury	77TB	435	$ .20	$ .80
Wills, Maury	87TTB	315	$ .01	$ .04
Wills, Ted	61T	548	$7.50	$30.00
Wills, Ted	62T	444	$1.25	$5.00
Wills, Ted	65T	488	$1.25	$5.00
Wilson, Archie	52T	327	$43.75	$175.00
Wilson, Bill D.	54T	222	$3.75	$15.00
Wilson, Bill D.	55T	86	$2.25	$9.00
Wilson, Billy H.	67T	402	$ .60	$2.40
Wilson, Billy H.	69T	576	$ .40	$1.60
Wilson, Billy H.	70T	28	$ .20	$ .80
Wilson, Billy H.	71T	192	$ .25	$1.00
Wilson, Billy H.	72T	587	$ .40	$1.60
Wilson, Billy H.	73T	619	$ .60	$2.40
Wilson, Bob	53T	250	$22.50	$90.00
Wilson, Bob	54T	58	$7.50	$30.00
Wilson, Bob "Red"	56T	92	$2.00	$8.00
Wilson, Bob	57T	19	$2.00	$8.00
Wilson, Bob "Red"	58T	213	$1.25	$5.00
Wilson, Bob "Red"	59T	24	$1.50	$6.00
Wilson, Bob "Red"	60T	379	$ .75	$3.00
Wilson, Bob	91TA53	250	$ .01	$ .15
Wilson, Craig	91T	566	$ .01	$ .10
Wilson, Craig	91TSC	566	$ .05	$ .25
Wilson, Craig	91TTR	128	$ .01	$ .15
Wilson, Craig	92T	646	$ .01	$ .03
Wilson, Craig	92TSC	361	$ .01	$ .10
Wilson, Craig	92TTR	128	$ .01	$ .10
Wilson, Craig	93T	366	$ .01	$ .03
Wilson, Craig	93TSC	88	$ .01	$ .10
Wilson, Dan	91T	767	$ .01	$ .15
Wilson, Dan	91TSC	587	$ .10	$ .40
Wilson, Dan	93T	813	$ .01	$ .03
Wilson, Don	68T	77	$ .35	$1.40
Wilson, Don	69T	202	$ .35	$1.40
Wilson, Don	70T	515	$ .35	$1.40
Wilson, Don	71T	484	$ .50	$2.00
Wilson, Don	72T	20	$ .10	$ .40
Wilson, Don	72T	91	$ .50	$2.00
Wilson, Don	73T	217	$ .10	$ .40
Wilson, Don	74T	304	$ .10	$ .40
Wilson, Don	75T	455	$ .10	$ .40
Wilson, Earl	60T	249	$1.25	$5.00
Wilson, Earl	61T	69	$ .60	$2.40
Wilson, Earl	63T	76	$ .50	$2.00
Wilson, Earl	64T	503	$1.00	$4.00
Wilson, Earl	65T	42	$ .35	$1.40
Wilson, Earl	66T	575	$3.75	$15.00
Wilson, Earl	67T	235	$ .75	$3.00
Wilson, Earl	67T	237	$ .50	$2.00
Wilson, Earl	67T	305	$ .60	$2.40
Wilson, Earl	68T	10	$ .75	$3.00
Wilson, Earl	68T	160	$ .35	$1.40
Wilson, Earl	69T	525	$ .40	$1.60
Wilson, Earl	70T	95	$ .20	$ .80
Wilson, Earl	71T	301	$ .25	$1.00
Wilson, Glenn	83T	332	$ .10	$ .40
Wilson, Glenn	84T	563	$ .01	$ .15
Wilson, Glenn	84TTR	129	$ .05	$ .20
Wilson, Glenn	85T	454	$ .01	$ .06
Wilson, Glenn	86T	736	$ .01	$ .05
Wilson, Glenn	87T	97	$ .01	$ .04
Wilson, Glenn	88T	626	$ .01	$ .04
Wilson, Glenn	88TTR	129	$ .01	$ .05
Wilson, Glenn	89T	293	$ .01	$ .03

TOPPS

Player	Year	No.	VG	EX/MT
Wilson, Glenn	90T	112	$ .01	$ .03
Wilson, Glenn	91T	476	$ .01	$ .03
Wilson, Hack	79TRH	412	$ .15	$ .60
Wilson, Jim	52T	276	$12.50	$50.00
Wilson, Jim	53T	208	$4.50	$18.00
Wilson, Jim	56T	171	$2.50	$10.00
Wilson, Jim	57T	330	$5.00	$20.00
Wilson, Jim	58T	163	$1.25	$5.00
Wilson, Jim	91TA53	208	$ .01	$ .15
Wilson, Mookie	81T	259	$ .15	$1.50
Wilson, Mookie	82T	143	$ .01	$ .08
Wilson, Mookie	83T	55	$ .01	$ .08
Wilson, Mookie	83T	621	$ .01	$ .08
Wilson, Mookie	84T	246	$ .05	$ .20
Wilson, Mookie	84T	465	$ .01	$ .06
Wilson, Mookie	85T	775	$ .01	$ .06
Wilson, Mookie	86T	315	$ .01	$ .05
Wilson, Mookie	87T	625	$ .01	$ .04
Wilson, Mookie	88T	255	$ .01	$ .04
Wilson, Mookie	89T	545	$ .01	$ .03
Wilson, Mookie	90T	182	$ .01	$ .03
Wilson, Mookie	91T	727	$ .01	$ .03

Player	Year	No.	VG	EX/MT
Wilson, Mookie	**91TSC**	**99**	**$ .05**	**$ .25**
Wilson, Mookie	92T	436	$ .01	$ .03
Wilson, Nigel	93T	426	$ .10	$1.00
Wilson, Preston	93T	132	$ .05	$ .35
Wilson, Steve	89TTR	131	$ .01	$ .10
Wilson, Steve	90T	741	$ .01	$ .03
Wilson, Steve	91T	69	$ .01	$ .03
Wilson, Steve	92T	751	$ .01	$ .03
Wilson, Steve	92TSC	626	$ .01	$ .10
Wilson, Steve	93T	133	$ .01	$ .03
Wilson, Trevor	89T	783	$ .01	$ .15
Wilson, Trevor	90T	408	$ .01	$ .03
Wilson, Trevor	91T	96	$ .01	$ .03
Wilson, Trevor	91TSC	212	$ .05	$ .25
Wilson, Trevor	92T	204	$ .01	$ .03
Wilson, Trevor	92TSC	86	$ .01	$ .10
Wilson, Trevor	93T	364	$ .01	$ .03
Wilson, Trevor	93TSC	185	$ .01	$ .10
Wilson, Willie	79T	409	$ .50	$2.00
Wilson, Willie	80T	157	$ .05	$ .35
Wilson, Willie	80T	204	$ .01	$ .10

Player	Year	No.	VG	EX/MT
Wilson, Willie	81T	360	$ .05	$ .25
Wilson, Willie	81TRB	208	$ .01	$ .10
Wilson, Willie	82T	230	$ .01	$ .15
Wilson, Willie	83T	471	$ .01	$ .08
Wilson, Willie	83T	701	$ .01	$ .08
Wilson, Willie	83T	710	$ .01	$ .08
Wilson, Willie	84T	525	$ .01	$ .10
Wilson, Willie	85T	617	$ .01	$ .06
Wilson, Willie	86T	25	$ .01	$ .05
Wilson, Willie	87T	783	$ .01	$ .10
Wilson, Willie	88T	452	$ .01	$ .04
Wilson, Willie	89T	168	$ .01	$ .03
Wilson, Willie	90T	323	$ .01	$ .03
Wilson, Willie	91T	208	$ .01	$ .03
Wilson, Willie	91TSC	378	$ .05	$ .25
Wilson, Willie	91TTR	129	$ .01	$ .05
Wilson, Willie	92T	536	$ .01	$ .03
Wilson, Willie	92TSC	343	$ .01	$ .10
Wilson, Willie	93T	318	$ .01	$ .03
Wiltbank, Ben	79T	723	$ .05	$ .20
Wimmer, Chris	91TTR	130	$ .05	$ .25
Wimmer, Chris	92TTR	129	$ .01	$ .15
Windhorn, Gordon	62T	254	$ .75	$3.00
Wine, Bobby	63T	71	$ .50	$2.00
Wine, Bobby	64T	347	$ .65	$2.60
Wine, Bobby	65T	36	$ .35	$1.40
Wine, Bobby	66T	284	$ .50	$2.00
Wine, Bobby	67T	466	$1.50	$6.00
Wine, Bobby	68T	396	$ .35	$1.40
Wine, Bobby	69T	648	$ .40	$1.60
Wine, Bobby	70T	332	$ .35	$1.40
Wine, Bobby	71T	171	$ .25	$1.00
Wine, Bobby	72T	657	$1.25	$5.00
Wine, Bobby	73T	486	$ .25	$1.00
Wine, Bobby	74T	119	$ .10	$ .40
Wine, Bobby	86T	51	$ .01	$ .05
Wine, Robbie	88T	119	$ .01	$ .04
Winfield, Dave	74T	456	$40.00	$160.00
Winfield, Dave	75T	61	$15.00	$60.00
Winfield, Dave	76T	160	$7.50	$30.00
Winfield, Dave	77T	390	$5.00	$20.00
Winfield, Dave	78T	530	$3.50	$14.00
Winfield, Dave	79T	30	$2.50	$10.00
Winfield, Dave	80T	203	$ .10	$1.00
Winfield, Dave	80T	230	$2.00	$8.00
Winfield, Dave	81T	370	$1.00	$4.00
Winfield, Dave	81TTR	855	$3.00	$12.00
Winfield, Dave	82T	600	$ .75	$3.00
Winfield, Dave	82TAS	553	$ .15	$1.50
Winfield, Dave	83T	770	$ .75	$3.00
Winfield, Dave	84T	460	$ .15	$1.50
Winfield, Dave	84TAS	402	$ .10	$ .50
Winfield, Dave	85T	180	$ .10	$1.00
Winfield, Dave	85TAS	705	$ .10	$ .50
Winfield, Dave	86T	70	$ .10	$ .50
Winfield, Dave	86TAS	717	$ .05	$ .35
Winfield, Dave	87T	770	$ .05	$ .25
Winfield, Dave	88T	510	$ .01	$ .15
Winfield, Dave	88TAS	392	$ .01	$ .10
Winfield, Dave	89T	260	$ .05	$ .20
Winfield, Dave	89TAS	407	$ .01	$ .10
Winfield, Dave	90T	380	$ .01	$ .10
Winfield, Dave	90TTR	130	$ .01	$ .15
Winfield, Dave	91T	630	$ .01	$ .10
Winfield, Dave	91TSC	263	$ .10	$1.00
Winfield, Dave	92T	792	$ .01	$ .10
Winfield, Dave	92TRB	5	$ .01	$ .10
Winfield, Dave	92TSC	745	$ .05	$ .25
Winfield, Dave	92TTR	130	$ .01	$ .15
Winfield, Dave	93T	131	$ .01	$ .10
Winfield, Dave	93TSC	206	$ .05	$ .20
Winkles, Bobby	73T	421	$ .25	$1.00
Winkles, Bobby	74T	276	$ .10	$ .40
Winkles, Bobby	78T	378	$ .04	$ .16
Winn, Jim	85T	69	$ .01	$ .06

TOPPS

Player	Year	No.	VG	EX/MT
Winn, Jim	86T	489	$ .01	$ .05
Winn, Jim	87T	262	$ .01	$ .04
Winn, Jim	87TTR	130	$ .01	$ .05
Winn, Jim	88T	688	$ .01	$ .04
Winningham, Herm	85TTR	131	$ .05	$ .20
Winningham, Herm	86T	448	$ .01	$ .15
Winningham, Herm	87T	141	$ .01	$ .04
Winningham, Herm	88T	614	$ .01	$ .04
Winningham, Herm	89T	366	$ .01	$ .03
Winningham, Herm	90T	94	$ .01	$ .03
Winningham, Herm	91T	204	$ .01	$ .03
Winningham, Herm	91TSC	546	$ .05	$ .25
Winningham, Herm	92T	547	$ .01	$ .03
Winningham, Herm	92TSC	205	$ .01	$ .10
Winningham, Herm	92TSC	883	$ .01	$ .10
Winningham, Herm	92TTR	131	$ .01	$ .05
Winningham, Herm	93T	377	$ .01	$ .03
Wirth, Alan	79T	711	$ .10	$ .40
Wise, Casey	57T	396	$1.75	$7.00
Wise, Casey	58T	247	$1.25	$5.00
Wise, Casey	59T	204	$1.00	$4.00
Wise, Casey	60T	342	$ .75	$3.00
Wise, Rick	64T	561	$3.00	$12.00
Wise, Rick	65T	322	$ .50	$2.00
Wise, Rick	67T	37	$ .40	$1.60
Wise, Rick	68T	262	$ .35	$1.40
Wise, Rick	69T	188	$ .35	$1.40
Wise, Rick	70T	605	$ .50	$2.00
Wise, Rick	71T	598	$1.00	$4.00
Wise, Rick	72T	43	$ .10	$ .40
Wise, Rick	72T	345	$ .10	$ .40
Wise, Rick	72TIA	44	$ .10	$ .40
Wise, Rick	72TTR	756	$1.25	$5.00
Wise, Rick	73T	364	$ .10	$ .40
Wise, Rick	74T	84	$ .10	$ .40
Wise, Rick	74TAS	339	$ .25	$1.00
Wise, Rick	75T	56	$ .10	$ .40
Wise, Rick	76T	170	$ .05	$ .25
Wise, Rick	77T	455	$ .05	$ .20
Wise, Rick	78T	572	$ .04	$ .16
Wise, Rick	79T	253	$ .03	$ .12
Wise, Rick	80T	725	$ .01	$ .10
Wise, Rick	81T	616	$ .01	$ .08
Wise, Rick	82T	330	$ .01	$ .08
Witmeyer, Ron	92TSC	435	$ .05	$ .20
Witt, Bobby	86TTR	126	$ .05	$ .25
Witt, Bobby	87T	415	$ .01	$ .15
Witt, Bobby	88T	747	$ .01	$ .10
Witt, Bobby	89T	548	$ .01	$ .03
Witt, Bobby	90T	166	$ .01	$ .03
Witt, Bobby	91T	27	$ .01	$ .03
Witt, Bobby	91TSC	96	$ .05	$ .25
Witt, Bobby	92T	675	$ .01	$ .03
Witt, Bobby	92TSC	677	$ .01	$ .10
Witt, Bobby	93T	398	$ .01	$ .03
Witt, Bobby	93TSC	150	$ .01	$ .10
Witt, George	59T	110	$1.50	$6.00
Witt, George	60T	298	$ .75	$3.00
Witt, George	61T	286	$ .60	$2.40
Witt, George	62T	287	$ .75	$3.00
Witt, Mike	82T	744	$ .05	$ .25
Witt, Mike	83T	53	$ .05	$ .20
Witt, Mike	83T	651	$ .05	$ .20
Witt, Mike	84T	499	$ .01	$ .06
Witt, Mike	85T	309	$ .01	$ .06
Witt, Mike	87T	760	$ .01	$ .10
Witt, Mike	88T	270	$ .01	$ .10
Witt, Mike	89T	190	$ .01	$ .03
Witt, Mike	90T	650	$ .01	$ .03
Witt, Mike	91T	536	$ .01	$ .03
Witt, Mike	91TSC	466	$ .05	$ .25
Witt, Mike	92T	357	$ .01	$ .03
Witt, Mike	92TSC	848	$ .01	$ .10
Wockenfuss, Johnny	76T	13	$ .05	$ .25
Wockenfuss, Johnny	78T	723	$ .04	$ .16

Player	Year	No.	VG	EX/MT
Wockenfuss, Johnny	79T	231	$ .03	$ .12
Wockenfuss, Johnny	80T	338	$ .01	$ .10
Wockenfuss, Johnny	81T	468	$ .01	$ .08
Wockenfuss, Johnny	82T	629	$ .01	$ .08
Wockenfuss, Johnny	83T	536	$ .01	$ .08
Wockenfuss, Johnny	84T	119	$ .01	$ .06
Wockenfuss, Johnny	84TTR	130	$ .01	$ .15

Player	Year	No.	VG	EX/MT
Wockenfuss, Johnny	85T	39	$ .01	$ .06
Wohlers, Mark	92T	703	$ .01	$ .15
Wohlers, Mark	92TSC	217	$ .05	$ .25
Wohlers, Mark	93T	8	$ .01	$ .03
Wohlers, Mark	93TSC	130	$ .01	$ .10
Wohlford, Jim	73T	611	$ .75	$3.00
Wohlford, Jim	74T	407	$ .10	$ .40
Wohlford, Jim	75T	144	$ .10	$ .40
Wohlford, Jim	76T	286	$ .05	$ .25
Wohlford, Jim	77T	622	$ .05	$ .20
Wohlford, Jim	78T	376	$ .04	$ .16
Wohlford, Jim	79T	596	$ .03	$ .12
Wohlford, Jim	80T	448	$ .01	$ .10
Wohlford, Jim	81T	11	$ .01	$ .08
Wohlford, Jim	82T	116	$ .01	$ .08
Wohlford, Jim	83T	688	$ .01	$ .08
Wohlford, Jim	83TTR	128	$ .01	$ .10
Wohlford, Jim	84T	253	$ .01	$ .06
Wohlford, Jim	85T	787	$ .01	$ .06
Wohlford, Jim	86T	344	$ .01	$ .05
Wohlford, Jim	87T	527	$ .01	$ .04
Wojcik, John	63T	253	$ .90	$3.60
Wojna, Ed	86T	211	$ .01	$ .05
Wojna, Ed	87T	88	$ .01	$ .04
Wolf, Wally	63T	208	$ .90	$3.60
Wolf, Wally	70T	74	$ .20	$ .80
Wolfe, Larry	79T	137	$ .03	$ .12
Wolfe, Larry	80T	549	$ .01	$ .10
Womack, Dooley	66T	469	$6.00	$24.00
Womack, Dooley	67T	77	$ .40	$1.60
Womack, Dooley	68T	431	$ .35	$1.40
Womack, Dooley	69T	594	$ .40	$1.60
Wood, Jake	61T	514	$1.35	$5.40
Wood, Jake	62T	72	$ .60	$2.40
Wood, Jake	62T	427	$1.25	$5.00
Wood, Jake	63T	453	$3.00	$12.00

TOPPS

Player	Year	No.	VG	EX/MT
Wood, Jake	64T	272	$ .65	$2.60
Wood, Jake	65T	547	$2.50	$10.00
Wood, Jake	66T	509	$1.50	$6.00
Wood, Jake	67T	394	$ .60	$2.40
Wood, Ken	52T	139	$7.00	$28.00
Wood, Ted	88TTR	130	$ .05	$ .20
Wood, Ted	92T	358	$ .01	$ .10
Wood, Ted	92TSC	799	$ .05	$ .20
Wood, Ted	93T	698	$ .01	$ .03
Wood, Wilbur	64T	267	$1.25	$5.00
Wood, Wilbur	65T	478	$1.25	$5.00
Wood, Wilbur	67T	391	$ .60	$2.40
Wood, Wilbur	68T	585	$ .70	$2.80
Wood, Wilbur	69T	123	$ .35	$1.40
Wood, Wilbur	70T	342	$ .35	$1.40
Wood, Wilbur	71T	436	$ .50	$2.00
Wood, Wilbur	72T	92	$ .60	$2.40
Wood, Wilbur	72T	94	$ .40	$1.60
Wood, Wilbur	72T	342	$ .10	$ .40
Wood, Wilbur	72T	553	$ .35	$1.40
Wood, Wilbur	72TIA	554	$ .40	$1.60
Wood, Wilbur	73T	66	$ .35	$1.40
Wood, Wilbur	73T	150	$ .20	$ .80
Wood, Wilbur	74T	120	$ .10	$ .40
Wood, Wilbur	74T	205	$ .25	$1.00
Wood, Wilbur	75T	110	$ .10	$ .40
Wood, Wilbur	76T	368	$ .05	$ .25
Wood, Wilbur	77T	198	$ .05	$ .20
Wood, Wilbur	78T	726	$ .05	$ .20
Wood, Wilbur	79T	216	$ .03	$ .12
Woodard, Mike	87T	286	$ .01	$ .04
Woodeshick, Hal	59T	106	$1.50	$6.00
Woodeshick, Hal	60T	454	$1.25	$5.00
Woodeshick, Hal	61T	397	$1.00	$4.00
Woodeshick, Hal	62T	526	$6.00	$24.00
Woodeshick, Hal	63T	517	$1.75	$7.00
Woodeshick, Hal	64T	370	$ .65	$2.60
Woodeshick, Hal	65T	179	$ .35	$1.40
Woodeshick, Hal	66T	514	$1.50	$6.00
Woodeshick, Hal	67T	324	$ .60	$2.40
Woodling, Gene	52T	99	$13.75	$55.00
Woodling, Gene	53T	264	$16.25	$65.00
Woodling, Gene	54T	101	$5.50	$22.00
Woodling, Gene	55T	190	$8.00	$32.00
Woodling, Gene	56T	163	$3.00	$12.00
Woodling, Gene	57T	172	$2.00	$8.00
Woodling, Gene	58T	398	$1.00	$4.00
Woodling, Gene	59T	170	$1.00	$4.00
Woodling, Gene	60T	190	$ .75	$3.00
Woodling, Gene	61T	275	$ .60	$2.40
Woodling, Gene	62T	125	$ .60	$2.40
Woodling, Gene	63T	43	$1.00	$4.00
Woodling, Gene	63T	342	$ .90	$3.60
Woodling, Gene	91TA53	264	$ .05	$ .35
Woods, Alvis	77T	479	$ .05	$ .20
Woods, Alvis	78T	121	$ .04	$ .16
Woods, Alvis	79T	178	$ .03	$ .12
Woods, Alvis	80T	444	$ .01	$ .10
Woods, Alvis	81T	703	$ .01	$ .08
Woods, Alvis	82T	49	$ .01	$ .08
Woods, Alvis	83T	589	$ .01	$ .08
Woods, Gary	77T	492	$ .25	$ .80
Woods, Gary	78T	599	$ .04	$ .16
Woods, Gary	81T	172	$ .01	$ .08
Woods, Gary	82T	483	$ .01	$ .08
Woods, Gary	82TTR	130	$ .01	$ .10
Woods, Gary	83T	356	$ .01	$ .08
Woods, Gary	84T	231	$ .01	$ .06
Woods, Gary	85T	46	$ .01	$ .06
Woods, Gary	86T	611	$ .01	$ .05
Woods, Jim	61T	59	$ .60	$2.40
Woods, Ron	69T	544	$ .40	$1.60
Woods, Ron	70T	253	$ .20	$ .80
Woods, Ron	71T	514	$ .50	$2.00
Woods, Ron	72T	82	$ .10	$ .40
Woods, Ron	73T	531	$ .60	$2.40
Woods, Ron	74T	377	$ .10	$ .40
Woodson, Dick	70T	479	$ .35	$1.40
Woodson, Dick	71T	586	$1.00	$4.00
Woodson, Dick	72T	634	$ .40	$1.60
Woodson, Dick	73T	98	$ .10	$ .40
Woodson, Dick	74T	143	$ .10	$ .40
Woodson, George	69T	244	$ .75	$3.00
Woodson, Kerry	93T	539	$ .01	$ .15
Woodson, Tracy	89T	306	$ .01	$ .03

Player	Year	No.	VG	EX/MT
Woodson, Tracy	93T	457	$ .01	$ .03
Woodward, Rob	87T	632	$ .01	$ .04
Woodward, Woody	64T	378	$1.00	$4.00
Woodward, Woody	65T	487	$1.25	$5.00
Woodward, Woody	66T	49	$ .35	$1.40
Woodward, Woody	67T	546	$4.00	$16.00
Woodward, Woody	68T	476	$ .75	$3.00
Woodward, Woody	69T	142	$ .35	$1.40
Woodward, Woody	70T	296	$ .35	$1.40
Woodward, Woody	71T	496	$ .50	$2.00
World Series '59, Game 1	60T	385	$ .75	$3.00
World Series '59, Game 2	60T	386	$ .75	$3.00
World Series '59, Game 3	60T	387	$ .75	$3.00
World Series '59, Game 4	60T	388	$2.50	$10.00
World Series '59, Game 5	60T	389	$2.50	$10.00
World Series '59, Game 6	60T	390	$ .75	$3.00
World Series '59, Celebration	60T	391	$1.50	$6.00
World Series '60, Game 1	61T	306	$ .90	$3.60
World Series '60, Game 2	61T	307	$10.00	$40.00
World Series '60, Game 3	61T	308	$ .90	$3.60
World Series '60, Game 4	61T	309	$ .75	$3.00
World Series '60, Game 5	61T	310	$ .75	$3.00
World Series '60, Game 6	61T	311	$2.50	$10.00
World Series '60, Game 7	61T	312	$3.00	$12.00
World Series '60, Celebrate	61T	313	$2.00	$8.00
World Series '61, Game 1	62T	232	$1.25	$5.00
World Series '61, Game 2	62T	233	$1.25	$5.00
World Series '61, Game 3	62T	234	$4.50	$18.00
World Series '61, Game 4	62T	235	$2.00	$8.00
World Series '61, Game 5	62T	236	$1.25	$5.00
World Series '61, Celebrate	62T	237	$1.25	$5.00
World Series '62, Game 1	63T	142	$1.50	$6.00
World Series '62, Game 2	63T	143	$1.25	$5.00

TOPPS

Player	Year	No.	VG	EX/MT
World Series '62, Game 3	63T	144	$2.50	$10.00
World Series '62, Game 4	63T	145	$1.25	$5.00
World Series '62, Game 5	63T	146	$1.25	$5.00
World Series '62, Game 6	63T	147	$1.25	$5.00
World Series '62, Game 7	63T	148	$1.25	$5.00
World Series '63, Game 1	64T	136	$3.50	$14.00
World Series '63, Game 2	64T	137	$1.00	$4.00
World Series '63, Game 3	64T	138	$1.00	$4.00
World Series '63, Game 4	64T	139	$1.00	$4.00
World Series '63, Summary	64T	140	$1.00	$4.00
World Series '64, Game 1	65T	132	$.75	$3.00
World Series '64, Game 2	65T	133	$.75	$3.00
World Series '64, Game 3	65T	134	$10.00	$40.00
World Series '64, Game 4	65T	135	$.75	$3.00
World Series '64, Game 5	65T	136	$.75	$3.00
World Series '64, Game 6	65T	137	$.75	$3.00
World Series '64, Game 7	65T	138	$2.00	$8.00
World Series '64, Cards Celeb.	65T	139	$.75	$3.00
World Series '66, Game 1	67T	151	$.75	$3.00
World Series '66, Game 2	67T	152	$1.50	$6.00
World Series '66, Game 3	67T	153	$.75	$3.00
World Series '66, Game 4	67T	154	$.75	$3.00
World Series '66, Celebrate	67T	155	$.75	$3.00
World Series '67, Game 1	68T	151	$1.75	$7.00
World Series '67, Game 2	68T	152	$2.25	$9.00
World Series '67, Game 3	68T	153	$.75	$3.00
World Series '67, Game 4	68T	154	$1.75	$7.00
World Series '67, Game 5	68T	155	$.75	$3.00
World Series '67, Game 6	68T	156	$.75	$3.00
World Series '67, Game 7	68T	157	$.75	$3.00
World Series '67, Cards Celeb.	68T	158	$.75	$3.00
World Series '68, Game 1	69T	162	$1.25	$5.00
World Series '68, Game 2	69T	163	$.75	$3.00
World Series '68, Game 3	69T	164	$1.25	$5.00

World Series '68, Game 4	69T	165	$1.25	$5.00
World Series '68, Game 5	69T	166	$1.75	$7.00
World Series '68, Game 6	69T	167	$.75	$3.00
World Series '68, Game 7	69T	168	$1.25	$5.00
World Series '68, Tigers Celeb.	69T	169	$.75	$3.00
World Series '69, Game 1	70T	305	$.50	$2.00
World Series '69, Game 2	70T	306	$.50	$2.00
World Series '69, Game 3	70T	307	$.50	$2.00
World Series '69, Game 4	70T	308	$.50	$2.00

Player	Year	No.	VG	EX/MT
World Series '69, Game 5	70T	309	$.50	$2.00
World Series '69, Celeb. Mets	70T	310	$1.00	$4.00
World Series '70, Game 1	71T	327	$.50	$2.00
World Series '70, Game 2	71T	328	$.50	$2.00
World Series '70, Game 3	71T	329	$.75	$3.00
World Series '70, Game 4	71T	330	$.50	$2.00
World Series '70, Game 5	71T	331	$1.00	$4.00
World Series '70, Summary	71T	332	$.50	$2.00
World Series '71, Game 1	72T	223	$.25	$1.00
World Series '71, Game 2	72T	224	$.25	$1.00
World Series '71, Game 3	72T	225	$.25	$1.00
World Series '71, Game 4	72T	226	$.75	$3.00
World Series '71, Game 5	72T	227	$.25	$1.00
World Series '71, Game 6	72T	228	$.25	$1.00
World Series '71, Game 7	72T	229	$.25	$1.00
World Series '71, Celebration	72T	230	$.25	$1.00
World Series '72, Game 1	73T	203	$.25	$1.00
World Series '72, Game 2	73T	204	$.25	$1.00
World Series '72, Game 3	73T	205	$.25	$1.00
World Series '72, Game 4	73T	206	$.25	$1.00
World Series '72, Game 5	73T	207	$.25	$1.00
World Series '72, Game 6	73T	208	$.25	$1.00
World Series '72, Game 7	73T	209	$.25	$1.00
World Series '72, Summary	73T	210	$.25	$1.00
World Series '73, Game 1	74T	472	$.35	$1.40
World Series '73, Game 2	74T	473	$1.25	$5.00
World Series '73, Game 3	74T	474	$.35	$1.40
World Series '73, Game 4	74T	475	$.35	$1.40
World Series '73, Game 5	74T	476	$.35	$1.40
World Series '73, Game 6	74T	477	$1.50	$6.00
World Series '73, Game 7	74T	478	$.25	$1.00
World Series '73, Summary	74T	479	$.25	$1.00
World Series '74, Game 1	75T	461	$.75	$3.00
World Series '74, Game 2	75T	462	$.25	$1.00
World Series '74, Game 3	75T	463	$.25	$1.00
World Series '74, Game 4	75T	464	$.25	$1.00
World Series '74, Game 5	75T	465	$.25	$1.00
World Series '74, Summary	75T	466	$.25	$1.00
World Series '75, Reds	76T	462	$.25	$1.00
World Series '76, Reds	77T	411	$.25	$1.00
World Series '76, Yankees	77T	412	$.25	$1.00
World Series '76, Summary	77T	413	$.10	$.40
World Series, Phillies	81T	403	$.01	$.15
World Series, Phillies	81T	404	$.01	$.15
Worrell, Todd	86TTR	127	$.01	$.15
Worrell, Todd	87T	465	$.01	$.04
Worrell, Todd	87TAS	605	$.01	$.10
Worrell, Todd	87TRB	7	$.01	$.04
Worrell, Todd	88T	715	$.01	$.04
Worrell, Todd	89T	535	$.01	$.03
Worrell, Todd	90T	95	$.01	$.03
Worrell, Todd	92TSC	703	$.01	$.10
Worrell, Todd	93T	121	$.01	$.03
Wortham, Rich	80T	502	$.01	$.10
Wortham, Rich	81T	107	$.01	$.08
Worthington, Al	57T	39	$2.00	$8.00
Worthington, Al	58T	427	$1.00	$4.00
Worthington, "Red" Al	59T	28	$1.50	$6.00
Worthington, Al	60T	268	$.75	$3.00
Worthington, Al	63T	556	$2.25	$9.00
Worthington, Al	64T	144	$.50	$2.00
Worthington, Al	65T	216	$.50	$2.00
Worthington, Al	66T	181	$.50	$2.00
Worthington, Al	67T	399	$.60	$2.40
Worthington, Al	68T	473	$.75	$3.00
Worthington, Al	73T	49	$.20	$.80
Worthington, Craig	89T	181	$.01	$.10
Worthington, Craig	90T	521	$.01	$.03
Worthington, Craig	91T	73	$.01	$.03
Worthington, Craig	92TSC	81	$.01	$.10
Worthington, Criag	91TSC	467	$.05	$.25
Wright, Clyde	69T	583	$.40	$1.60
Wright, Clyde	70T	543	$.35	$1.40
Wright, Clyde	71T	67	$.75	$3.00
Wright, Clyde	71T	240	$.25	$1.00

TOPPS

Player	Year	No.	VG	EX/MT
Wright, Clyde	72T	55	$ .10	$ .40
Wright, Clyde	73T	373	$ .10	$ .40
Wright, Clyde	74T	525	$ .10	$ .40
Wright, Clyde	75T	408	$ .10	$ .40
Wright, Clyde	76T	559	$ .05	$ .25
Wright, Ed	52T	368	$43.75	$175.00
Wright, George	83T	299	$ .01	$ .08
Wright, George	84T	688	$ .01	$ .06
Wright, George	85T	443	$ .01	$ .06
Wright, George	86T	169	$ .01	$ .05
Wright, George	86TTR	128	$ .01	$ .06
Wright, Jim	79T	349	$ .03	$ .12
Wright, Jim	81T	526	$ .01	$ .08
Wright, Jim L.	79T	722	$ .50	$2.00
Wright, Jim L.	80T	524	$ .01	$ .10
Wright, Jim L.	82T	362	$ .01	$ .08
Wright, Ken	71T	504	$ .50	$2.00
Wright, Ken	72T	638	$ .40	$1.60
Wright, Ken	73T	578	$ .60	$2.40
Wright, Mel	73T	517	$ .25	$1.00
Wright, Ricky	86TTR	129	$ .01	$ .06
Wright, Ricky	87T	202	$ .01	$ .04
Wright, Tom	54T	140	$3.75	$15.00
Wright, Tom	55T	141	$2.25	$9.00

Player	Year	No.	VG	EX/MT
Wrona, Rick	90T	187	$ .01	$ .03
Wrona, Rick	93TSC	64	$ .01	$ .10
Wyatt, Johnnie	63T	376	$1.00	$4.00
Wyatt, John	64T	108	$ .50	$2.00
Wyatt, Johnnie	65T	590	$1.40	$5.60
Wyatt, John	66T	521	$1.50	$6.00
Wyatt, John	67T	261	$ .50	$2.00
Wyatt, John	68T	481	$ .75	$3.00
Wyatt, Whitlow	60T	464	$1.25	$5.00
Wynegar, Butch	77T	175	$ .20	$ .80
Wynegar, Butch	78T	555	$ .04	$ .16
Wynegar, Butch	79T	405	$ .03	$ .12
Wynegar, Butch	80T	304	$ .01	$ .10
Wynegar, Butch	81T	61	$ .01	$ .08
Wynegar, Butch	82T	222	$ .01	$ .08
Wynegar, Butch	82TTR	131	$ .01	$ .10
Wynegar, Butch	83T	617	$ .01	$ .08
Wynegar, Butch	84T	123	$ .01	$ .06
Wynegar, Butch	85T	585	$ .01	$ .06
Wynegar, Butch	86T	235	$ .01	$ .05
Wynegar, Butch	87T	464	$ .01	$ .04
Wynegar, Butch	88T	737	$ .01	$ .04
Wynn, Early	51Trb	8	$5.00	$20.00
Wynn, Early	52T	277	$50.00	$200.00
Wynn, Early	53T	61	$25.00	$100.00
Wynn, Early	56T	187	$10.00	$40.00
Wynn, Early	57T	40	$5.50	$22.00
Wynn, Early	58T	100	$5.00	$20.00
Wynn, Early	59T	260	$4.00	$16.00
Wynn, Early	60T	1	$10.00	$40.00
Wynn, Early	61T	50	$ .75	$3.00
Wynn, Early	61T	337	$1.00	$4.00
Wynn, Early	61T	455	$3.75	$15.00
Wynn, Early	62T	385	$4.50	$18.00
Wynn, Early	91TA53	61	$ .10	$1.00
Wynn, Jim	64T	38	$1.25	$5.00
Wynn, Jim	65T	257	$ .50	$2.00
Wynn, Jim	66T	520	$1.50	$6.00
Wynn, Jim	67T	390	$ .60	$2.40
Wynn, Jim	68T	5	$1.50	$6.00
Wynn, Jim	68T	260	$ .35	$1.40
Wynn, Jim	69T	360	$ .30	$1.20
Wynn, Jim	70T	60	$ .25	$1.00
Wynn, Jim	71T	565	$1.00	$4.00
Wynn, Jim	72T	770	$1.25	$5.00
Wynn, Jim	73T	185	$ .20	$ .80
Wynn, Jim	74T	43	$ .10	$ .40
Wynn, Jim	74TTR	43	$ .15	$ .60
Wynn, Jim	75T	570	$ .10	$ .40
Wynn, Jim	76T	395	$ .15	$ .60
Wynn, Jim	77T	165	$ .05	$ .20
Wynne, Billy	70T	618	$ .50	$2.00
Wynne, Billy	71T	718	$1.10	$4.40
Wynne, Marvell	84T	173	$ .01	$ .06
Wynne, Marvell	85T	615	$ .01	$ .06
Wynne, Marvell	86T	525	$ .01	$ .05
Wynne, Marvell	87T	37	$ .01	$ .04
Wynne, Marvell	88T	454	$ .01	$ .04
Wynne, Marvell	89T	353	$ .01	$ .03
Wynne, Marvell	90T	256	$ .01	$ .03
Wynne, Marvell	91T	714	$ .01	$ .03
Wyrostek, Johnny	51Tbb	44	$7.50	$30.00
Wyrostek, Johnny	52T	13	$13.75	$55.00
Wyrostek, Johnny	53T	79	$6.25	$25.00
Wyrostek, Johnny	91TA53	79	$ .01	$ .15
Yankees, Team	56T	251	$47.50	$190.00
Yankees, Team	57T	97	$13.75	$55.00
Yankees, Team	58T	246	$12.50	$50.00
Yankees, Team	59T	510	$18.75	$75.00
Yankees, Team	60T	332	$7.50	$30.00
Yankees, Team	61T	228	$8.00	$32.00
Yankees, Team	62T	251	$6.00	$24.00
Yankees, Team	63T	247	$5.00	$20.00
Yankees, Team	64T	433	$4.00	$16.00
Yankees, Team	65T	513	$4.50	$18.00
Yankees, Team	66T	92	$1.00	$4.00
Yankees, Team	67T	131	$1.25	$5.00
Yankees, Team	70T	399	$1.25	$5.00
Yankees, Team	71T	543	$1.75	$7.00
Yankees, Team	72T	237	$ .50	$2.00
Yankees, Team	73T	556	$1.50	$6.00
Yankees, Team	74T	363	$ .25	$1.00
Yankees, Team Checklist	75T	611	$ .35	$1.40
Yankees, Team Checklist	76T	17	$ .30	$1.20
Yankees, Team Checklist	77T	387	$ .25	$1.00
Yankees, Team Checklist	78T	282	$ .25	$1.00
Yankees, Team Checklist	79T	626	$ .15	$ .60
Yankees, Team Checklist	80T	424	$ .10	$ .50
Yankees, Team Checklist	81T	670	$ .05	$ .25
Yankees, Team Leaders	86T	276	$ .01	$ .05
Yankees, Team Leaders	87T	406	$ .01	$ .15
Yankees, Team Leaders	88T	459	$ .01	$ .04
Yankees, Team Leaders	89T	519	$ .01	$ .03
Yastrzemski, Carl	60T	148	$65.00	$260.00

TOPPS

Player	Year	No.	VG	EX/MT
Yastrzemski, Carl	61T	287	$32.50	$130.00
Yastrzemski, Carl	62T	425	$47.50	$190.00
Yastrzemski, Carl	63T	115	$15.00	$60.00
Yastrzemski, Carl	64T	8	$2.00	$8.00
Yastrzemski, Carl	64T	182	$3.50	$14.00
Yastrzemski, Carl	64T	210	$15.00	$60.00
Yastrzemski, Carl	65T	385	$20.00	$80.00
Yastrzemski, Carl	66T	70	$10.00	$40.00
Yastrzemski, Carl	66T	216	$1.25	$5.00
Yastrzemski, Carl	67T	355	$16.25	$65.00
Yastrzemski, Carl	68T	2	$2.25	$9.00
Yastrzemski, Carl	68T	4	$2.25	$9.00
Yastrzemski, Carl	68T	6	$1.75	$7.00
Yastrzemski, Carl	68T	250	$10.00	$40.00
Yastrzemski, Carl	68TAS	369	$3.00	$12.00
Yastrzemski, Carl	69T	1	$2.75	$11.00
Yastrzemski, Carl	69T	130	$7.00	$28.00
Yastrzemski, Carl	69TAS	425	$3.00	$12.00
Yastrzemski, Carl	70T	10	$5.50	$22.00
Yastrzemski, Carl	70TAS	461	$2.75	$11.00
Yastrzemski, Carl	71T	61	$.75	$3.00
Yastrzemski, Carl	71T	65	$.75	$3.00
Yastrzemski, Carl	71T	530	$10.00	$40.00
Yastrzemski, Carl	72T	37	$3.50	$14.00
Yastrzemski, Carl	72TIA	38	$1.75	$7.00
Yastrzemski, Carl	73T	245	$3.75	$15.00
Yastrzemski, Carl	74T	280	$3.00	$12.00
Yastrzemski, Carl	75T	205	$.25	$1.00
Yastrzemski, Carl	75T	280	$2.50	$10.00
Yastrzemski, Carl	76T	230	$2.25	$9.00
Yastrzemski, Carl	77T	480	$1.50	$6.00
Yastrzemski, Carl	77TB	434	$.50	$2.00
Yastrzemski, Carl	78T	40	$1.25	$5.00
Yastrzemski, Carl	79T	320	$.90	$3.60
Yastrzemski, Carl	80T	720	$.20	$1.75
Yastrzemski, Carl	80THL	1	$.25	$2.50
Yastrzemski, Carl	81T	110	$.75	$3.00
Yastrzemski, Carl	82T	650	$.20	$2.00
Yastrzemski, Carl	82TSA	651	$.10	$1.00
Yastrzemski, Carl	83T	550	$.15	$1.50
Yastrzemski, Carl	83T	551	$.10	$.75
Yastrzemski, Carl	84T	6	$.10	$.40
Yastrzemski, Carl	87TTB	314	$.05	$.20
Yaughn, Kip	93T	669	$.01	$.15
Yeager, Steve	73T	59	$.25	$1.00
Yeager, Steve	74T	593	$.10	$.40
Yeager, Steve	75T	376	$.10	$.40
Yeager, Steve	76T	515	$.05	$.25
Yeager, Steve	77T	105	$.05	$.20
Yeager, Steve	78T	285	$.04	$.16
Yeager, Steve	79T	75	$.03	$.12
Yeager, Steve	80T	726	$.05	$.25
Yeager, Steve	81T	318	$.01	$.08
Yeager, Steve	82T	477	$.01	$.08
Yeager, Steve	83T	555	$.01	$.08
Yeager, Steve	84T	661	$.01	$.06
Yeager, Steve	85T	148	$.01	$.06
Yeager, Steve	86T	32	$.01	$.05
Yeager, Steve	86TTR	130	$.01	$.06
Yeager, Steve	87T	258	$.01	$.04
Yelding, Eric	90T	309	$.01	$.03
Yelding, Eric	91T	59	$.01	$.03
Yelding, Eric	91TSC	16	$.05	$.25
Yelding, Eric	92TSC	2	$.01	$.10
Yellen, Larry	64T	226	$.65	$2.60
Yellen, Larry	65T	292	$.50	$2.00
Yett, Rich	87T	134	$.01	$.04
Yett, Rich	88T	531	$.01	$.04
Yett, Rich	89T	363	$.01	$.03
Yett, Rich	90T	689	$.01	$.03
York, Jim	72T	68	$.10	$.40
York, Jim	73T	546	$.60	$2.40
York, Jim	75T	383	$.10	$.40
York, Jim	76T	224	$.05	$.25
York, Mike	91T	508	$.01	$.10

Player	Year	No.	VG	EX/MT
York, Rudy	60T	456	$1.50	$6.00
Yost, Eddie	51Tbb	1	$12.50	$50.00
Yost, Eddie	52T	123	$7.00	$28.00
Yost, Eddie	56T	128	$2.50	$10.00
Yost, Eddie	57T	177	$2.00	$8.00
Yost, Eddie	58T	173	$1.25	$5.00
Yost, Eddie	59T	2	$1.50	$6.00
Yost, Eddie	60T	245	$.75	$3.00
Yost, Eddie	61T	413	$1.00	$4.00
Yost, Eddie	62T	176	$.75	$3.00
Yost, Eddie	73T	257	$.50	$2.00
Yost, Eddie	74T	179	$.40	$1.60
Yost, Ned	79T	708	$.25	$1.00
Yost, Ned	81T	659	$.01	$.08
Yost, Ned	82T	542	$.01	$.08
Yost, Ned	83T	297	$.01	$.08
Yost, Ned	84T	107	$.01	$.06
Yost, Ned	84TTR	131	$.01	$.15
Yost, Ned	85T	777	$.01	$.06
Youmans, Floyd	86T	732	$.01	$.10
Youmans, Floyd	87T	105	$.01	$.04
Youmans, Floyd	88T	365	$.01	$.04
Youmans, Floyd	89T	91	$.01	$.03
Young, Anthony	92T	148	$.01	$.10
Young, Anthony	92TSC	85	$.05	$.20
Young, Anthony	93T	734	$.01	$.03
Young, Bob	52T	147	$7.00	$28.00
Young, Bob	53T	160	$6.25	$25.00
Young, Bobby	54T	8	$3.75	$15.00
Young, Bob	91TA53	160	$.01	$.15
Young, Cliff	92TSC	562	$.01	$.10
Young, Curt	85T	293	$.05	$.30

Young, Curt	86T	84	$.01	$.05
Young, Curt	87T	519	$.01	$.04
Young, Curt	88T	103	$.01	$.04
Young, Curt	89T	641	$.01	$.03
Young, Curt	90T	328	$.01	$.03
Young, Curt	91T	473	$.01	$.03
Young, Curt	92T	704	$.01	$.03
Young, Cy	73TATL	477	$.50	$2.00
Young, Cy	79TRH	416	$.05	$.20
Young, Don	66T	139	$.50	$2.00
Young, Don	69T	602	$.40	$1.60

TOPPS

Player	Year	No.	VG	EX/MT
Young, Don	70T	117	$ .20	$ .80
Young, Eric	93T	145	$ .05	$ .20
Young, Eric	93T	551	$ .05	$ .20
Young, Gerald	88T	368	$ .01	$ .04

Player	Year	No.	VG	EX/MT
Young, Gerald	89T	95	$ .01	$ .03
Young, Gerald	90T	196	$ .01	$ .03
Young, Gerald	91T	626	$ .01	$ .03
Young, Gerald	91TSC	494	$ .05	$ .25
Young, Gerald	92T	241	$ .01	$ .03
Young, Gerald	92TSC	355	$ .01	$ .10
Young, Kevin	93T	494	$ .05	$ .35
Young, Kip	79T	706	$ .03	$ .12
Young, Kip	80T	251	$ .01	$ .10
Young, Matt	83TTR	129	$ .05	$ .25
Young, Matt	84T	235	$ .01	$ .06
Young, Matt	84T	336	$ .01	$ .06
Young, Matt	85T	485	$ .01	$ .06
Young, Matt	86T	676	$ .01	$ .05
Young, Matt	87T	19	$ .01	$ .04
Young, Matt	87TTR	131	$ .01	$ .10
Young, Matt	88T	736	$ .01	$ .04
Young, Matt	90T	501	$ .01	$ .03
Young, Matt	90TTR	131	$ .01	$ .10
Young, Matt	91T	108	$ .01	$ .03
Young, Matt	91TSC	426	$ .05	$ .25
Young, Matt	92TSC	682	$ .01	$ .10
Young, Mike	85T	173	$ .01	$ .10
Young, Mike	86T	548	$ .01	$ .05
Young, Mike	87T	309	$ .01	$ .04
Young, Mike	88T	11	$ .01	$ .04
Young, Mike	89T	731	$ .01	$ .03
Young, Pete	93T	432	$ .01	$ .03
Youngblood, Joel	77T	548	$ .05	$ .20
Youngblood, Joel	78T	428	$ .04	$ .16
Youngblood, Joel	79T	109	$ .03	$ .12
Youngblood, Joel	80T	372	$ .01	$ .10
Youngblood, Joel	81T	58	$ .01	$ .08
Youngblood, Joel	82T	655	$ .01	$ .08
Youngblood, Joel	83T	265	$ .01	$ .08
Youngblood, Joel	83TTR	130	$ .01	$ .10
Youngblood, Joel	84T	727	$ .01	$ .06
Youngblood, Joel	85T	567	$ .01	$ .06
Youngblood, Joel	86T	177	$ .01	$ .05
Youngblood, Joel	87T	759	$ .01	$ .04
Youngblood, Joel	88T	418	$ .01	$ .04
Youngblood, Joel	89T	304	$ .01	$ .03
Yount, Robin	75T	223	$50.00	$200.00
Yount, Robin	76T	316	$13.75	$55.00
Yount, Robin	77T	635	$8.00	$32.00
Yount, Robin	78T	173	$6.00	$24.00
Yount, Robin	79T	95	$3.50	$14.00
Yount, Robin	80T	265	$3.00	$12.00
Yount, Robin	81T	515	$1.25	$5.00
Yount, Robin	82T	435	$ .75	$3.00
Yount, Robin	83T	321	$ .05	$ .20
Yount, Robin	83T	350	$ .75	$3.00
Yount, Robin	83TAS	389	$ .10	$1.00
Yount, Robin	84T	10	$ .20	$2.00
Yount, Robin	85T	340	$ .10	$1.00
Yount, Robin	86T	780	$ .10	$ .75
Yount, Robin	87T	773	$ .05	$ .35
Yount, Robin	88T	165	$ .05	$ .20
Yount, Robin	89T	615	$ .01	$ .15
Yount, Robin	90T	290	$ .01	$ .15
Yount, Robin	90TAS	389	$ .01	$ .10
Yount, Robin	91T	575	$ .01	$ .10
Yount, Robin	91TSC	509	$ .10	$1.00
Yount, Robin	92T	90	$ .01	$ .10
Yount, Robin	92TSC	450	$ .10	$ .50
Yount, Robin	92TSC	607	$ .05	$ .25
Yount, Robin	93T	1	$ .01	$ .10
Yount, Robin	93TSC	173	$ .05	$ .35
Yuhas, Eddie	52T	386	$43.75	$175.00
Yuhas, Ed	53T	70	$6.25	$25.00
Yuhas, Ed	91TA53	70	$ .01	$ .15
Yvars, Sal	52T	338	$43.75	$175.00
Yvars, Sal	53T	11	$6.25	$25.00
Yvars, Sal	91TA53	11	$ .01	$ .15
Zachary, Chris	64T	23	$ .50	$2.00
Zachary, Chris	66T	313	$ .50	$2.00
Zachary, Chris	67T	212	$ .50	$2.00
Zachary, Chris	70T	471	$ .35	$1.40
Zachary, Chris	73T	256	$ .10	$ .40
Zachry, Pat	76T	599	$2.00	$8.00
Zachry, Pat	77T	86	$ .05	$ .20
Zachry, Pat	78T	171	$ .04	$ .16
Zachry, Pat	79T	621	$ .03	$ .12
Zachry, Pat	80T	428	$ .01	$ .10
Zachry, Pat	81T	224	$ .01	$ .08
Zachry, Pat	82T	399	$ .01	$ .08
Zachry, Pat	83T	522	$ .01	$ .08
Zachry, Pat	83TTR	131	$ .01	$ .10
Zachry, Pat	84T	747	$ .01	$ .06
Zachry, Pat	85T	57	$ .01	$ .06
Zahn, Geoff	75T	294	$ .10	$ .40
Zahn, Geoff	76T	403	$ .05	$ .25
Zahn, Geoff	78T	27	$ .04	$ .16
Zahn, Geoff	79T	678	$ .03	$ .12
Zahn, Geoff	80T	113	$ .01	$ .10
Zahn, Geoff	81T	363	$ .01	$ .08
Zahn, Geoff	81TTR	856	$ .01	$ .15
Zahn, Geoff	82T	229	$ .01	$ .08
Zahn, Geoff	83T	547	$ .01	$ .08
Zahn, Geoff	84T	276	$ .01	$ .15
Zahn, Geoff	84T	468	$ .01	$ .06
Zahn, Geoff	85T	771	$ .01	$ .06
Zahn, Geoff	86T	42	$ .01	$ .05
Zamora, Oscar	75T	604	$ .10	$ .40
Zamora, Oscar	76T	227	$ .05	$ .25
Zamora, Oscar	78T	91	$ .04	$ .16
Zanni, Dom	59T	145	$1.00	$4.00
Zanni, Dom	62T	214	$ .75	$3.00
Zanni, Dom	63T	354	$ .90	$3.60
Zanni, Dom	66T	233	$ .50	$2.00
Zarilla, Al	51Trb	49	$1.75	$7.50
Zarilla, Al	52T	70	$13.75	$55.00
Zarilla, Al	53T	181	$4.50	$18.00
Zarilla, Al	91TA53	181	$ .01	$ .15

TOPPS

Player	Year	No.	VG	EX/MT
Zauchin, Norm	55T	176	$6.25	$25.00
Zauchin, Norm	56T	89	$2.00	$8.00
Zauchin, Norm	57T	372	$1.75	$7.00
Zauchin, Norm	58T	422	$1.00	$4.00
Zauchin, Norm	59T	311	$1.00	$4.00
Zavaras, Clint	90T	89	$ .01	$ .10
Zdeb, Joe	78T	408	$ .04	$ .16
Zdeb, Joe	79T	389	$ .03	$ .12
Zeber, George	78T	591	$ .04	$ .16
Zeile, Todd	90T	162	$ .05	$ .20
Zeile, Todd	91T	616	$ .01	$ .10
Zeile, Todd	91TSC	255	$ .10	$ .50
Zeile, Todd	92T	275	$ .01	$ .03
Zeile, Todd	92TSC	544	$ .01	$ .10
Zeile, Todd	93T	428	$ .01	$ .03
Zeile, Todd	93TSC	152	$ .01	$ .10
Zepp, Bill	70T	702	$1.25	$5.00
Zepp, Bill	71T	271	$ .25	$1.00
Zernial, Gus	51Trb	36	$4.50	$18.00
Zernial, Gus	52T	31	$15.00	$60.00
Zernial, Gus	53T	42	$4.50	$18.00
Zernial, Gus	54T	2	$3.75	$15.00
Zernial, Gus	55T	110	$2.25	$9.00
Zernial, Gus	56T	45	$2.00	$8.00
Zernial, Gus	57T	253	$2.00	$8.00
Zernial, Gus	58T	112	$1.25	$5.00
Zernial, Gus	59T	409	$1.00	$4.00
Zernial, Gus	91TA53	42	$ .01	$ .15
Zimmer, Don	55T	92	$9.00	$36.00
Zimmer, Don	56T	99	$4.50	$18.00
Zimmer, Don	57T	284	$8.00	$32.00
Zimmer, Don	58T	77	$3.00	$12.00
Zimmer, Don	59T	287	$1.00	$4.00
Zimmer, Don	60T	47	$ .85	$3.40
Zimmer, Don	61T	493	$1.50	$6.00
Zimmer, Don	62T	478	$2.00	$8.00
Zimmer, Don	63T	439	$1.25	$5.00
Zimmer, Don	64T	134	$ .50	$2.00
Zimmer, Don	65T	233	$ .50	$2.00
Zimmer, Don	73T	12	$ .20	$ .80
Zimmer, Don	74T	403	$ .10	$ .40
Zimmer, Don	78T	63	$ .04	$ .16
Zimmer, Don	88TTR	131	$ .01	$ .05
Zimmer, Don	89T	134	$ .01	$ .03
Zimmer, Don	90T	549	$ .01	$ .03
Zimmer, Don	91T	729	$ .01	$ .03
Zimmerman, Jerry	59T	146	$1.00	$4.00
Zimmerman, Jerry	62T	222	$ .75	$3.00
Zimmerman, Jerry	63T	186	$ .50	$2.00
Zimmerman, Jerry	64T	369	$ .65	$2.60
Zimmerman, Jerry	65T	299	$ .50	$2.00
Zimmerman, Jerry	66T	73	$ .35	$1.40
Zimmerman, Jerry	67T	501	$1.50	$6.00
Zimmerman, Jerry	68T	181	$ .35	$1.40
Zimmerman, Jerry	73T	377	$ .20	$ .80
Zimmerman, Jerry	74T	531	$ .25	$1.00
Zipfel, Bud	63T	69	$ .50	$2.00
Zisk, Richie	72T	392	$ .25	$1.00
Zisk, Richie	73T	611	$ .75	$3.00
Zisk, Richie	74T	317	$ .10	$ .40
Zisk, Richie	75T	77	$ .10	$ .40
Zisk, Richie	76T	12	$ .05	$ .25
Zisk, Richie	77T	483	$ .05	$ .20
Zisk, Richie	78T	110	$ .04	$ .16
Zisk, Richie	79T	260	$ .03	$ .12
Zisk, Richie	80T	620	$ .01	$ .10
Zisk, Richie	81T	517	$ .01	$ .08
Zisk, Richie	81TTR	857	$ .01	$ .15
Zisk, Richie	82T	769	$ .01	$ .08
Zisk, Richie	83T	368	$ .01	$ .08
Zisk, Richie	84T	83	$ .01	$ .06
Zoldak, Sam	52T	231	$7.00	$28.00
Zosky, Eddie	92T	72	$ .01	$ .10
Zosky, Eddie	92TSC	873	$ .01	$ .15
Zosky, Eddie	93T	689	$ .01	$ .03
Zupcic, Bob	92T	377	$ .05	$ .25
Zupcic, Bob	92TSC	839	$ .10	$ .50
Zupcic, Bob	93T	562	$ .01	$ .10
Zupo, Frank	58T	229	$1.25	$5.00
Zuvella, Paul	86T	572	$ .01	$ .05
Zuvella, Paul	86TTR	131	$ .01	$ .06
Zuvella, Paul	87T	102	$ .01	$ .04
Zuverink, George	52T	199	$7.00	$28.00
Zuverink, George	56T	276	$2.50	$10.00
Zuverink, George	57T	11	$2.00	$8.00
Zuverink, George	58T	6	$2.00	$8.00
Zuverink, George	59T	219	$1.00	$4.00
Zweig, Ivan	91TTR	131	$ .05	$ .20

UPPER DECK COMPANY 1989 – 1993

The Upper Deck Company began production of cards in 1989, joining all the other baseball card producers in searching for a share of the collector's market. Promising a better product than had ever been seen before, they actively sought dealer support. An unproved company in an already saturated market caused many dealers to take a "wait and see" attitude. Many who hesitated in ordering wished that they had not done so when the product finally began to arrive. After a slow beginning, the product found wide collector acceptance with the photo-like quality cards.

There are several good things that Upper Deck has done. Card dealers received the first shipments, and candy wholesalers did not get to charge retail prices or allow someone to buy the total allotment for a change.

As I stated in an earlier book, "Distribution and cost (double the other card companies' prices) may be determining factors in the longevity of Upper Deck and collectors will be the ultimate determining factor." Upper Deck proved the point that a superior product will be accepted at higher prices by collectors!

Now comes the race by other card companies to emulate what Upper Deck has done. Fleer's answer to Upper Deck is called Ultra, Donruss premium cards are called Leaf, and Topps has Stadium Club. Now Major League Marketing has finally pushed forward with its premium card called Pinnacle. All in all, Upper Deck created a new image of QUALITY that the other card companies are now copying. That is not bad for the new kid on the block!

In 1991 Upper Deck issued a Final Edition set of 100 cards instead of issuing the extended set as a boxed set. This extended set has its cards listed as UDF in The Upper Deck listing.

1993 Upper Deck cards are being issued in two series. Only the first series of 420 cards are included in my listings, since the second series was unavailable as we went to press.

The listing for each card shown appears immediately following the photograph.

UPPER DECK

Player	Year	No.	VG	EX/MT
Aaron, Hank	91UDHH	1	$ .75	$3.00
Aase, Don	89UD	450	$ .01	$ .08
Aase, Don	90UD	131	$ .01	$ .05
Abbott, Jim	89UD	755	$1.00	$4.00
Abbott, Jim	90UD	645	$ .05	$ .35
Abbott, Jim	91UD	554	$ .05	$ .20
Abbott, Jim	92UD	78	$ .01	$ .10
Abbott, Jim	92UD	86	$ .01	$ .10
Abbott, Jim	92UD	325	$ .01	$ .10
Abbott, Jim	92UD	642	$ .01	$ .15
Abbott, Jim	93UD	30	$ .01	$ .10
Abbott, Jim	93UD	31	$ .01	$ .15
Abbott, Jim	93UD	53	$ .01	$ .10
Abbott, Kyle	91UD	51	$ .05	$ .25
Abbott, Kyle	92UD	8	$ .01	$ .15
Abbott, Kyle	92UD	754	$ .01	$ .05
Abbott, Kyle	93UD	300	$ .01	$ .05
Abbott, Paul	91UD	487	$ .01	$ .15
Abner, Shawn	90UD	301	$ .01	$ .05
Abner, Shawn	91UD	795	$ .01	$ .05
Abner, Shawn	92UD	502	$ .01	$ .04
Acker, Jim	89UD	52	$ .01	$ .08
Acker, Jim	91UD	670	$ .01	$ .05
Agosto, Juan	89UD	251	$ .01	$ .08
Agosto, Juan	90UD	450	$ .01	$ .05
Agosto, Juan	91UD	569	$ .01	$ .05
Agosto, Juan	91UD	788	$ .01	$ .05
Agosto, Juan	92UD	693	$ .01	$ .04
Aguayo, Luis	89UD	156	$ .01	$ .08
Aguilera, Rick	89UD	563	$ .01	$ .08
Aguilera, Rick	90UD	11	$ .01	$ .05
Aguilera, Rick	91UD	542	$ .01	$ .05
Aguilera, Rick	92UD	130	$ .01	$ .04
Aguilera, Rick	93UD	303	$ .01	$ .05
Akerfelds, Darrel	91UD	619	$ .01	$ .05
Aldred, Scott	91UD	7	$ .05	$ .20
Aldrete, Mike	89UD	239	$ .01	$ .08
Aldrete, Mike	89UD	738	$ .01	$ .10
Aldrete, Mike	90UD	415	$ .01	$ .05
Alexander, Doyle	89UD	298	$ .01	$ .08
Alexander, Doyle	90UD	330	$ .01	$ .05
Alexander, Gerald	91UDF	72	$ .01	$ .15
Alexander, Manny	93UD	5	$ .01	$ .15
Alicea, Luis	89UD	281	$ .05	$ .20
Allanson, Andy	89UD	217	$ .01	$ .08
Allanson, Andy	90UD	590	$ .01	$ .05
Allen, Neil	89UD	567	$ .01	$ .08
Allison, Dana	91UD	771	$ .01	$ .15
Allred, Beau	91UD	784	$ .01	$ .10
Alomar, Roberto	89UD	471	$1.25	$5.00
Alomar, Roberto	90UD	346	$ .15	$1.25
Alomar, Roberto	91UD	80	$ .01	$ .15
Alomar, Roberto	91UD	335	$ .10	$ .40
Alomar, Roberto	91UD	763	$ .10	$ .50
Alomar, Roberto	91UDF	83	$ .05	$ .25
Alomar, Roberto	92UD	81	$ .01	$ .15
Alomar, Roberto	92UD	355	$ .05	$ .25
Alomar, Roberto	93UD	42	$ .01	$ .15
Alomar, Roberto	93UD	125	$ .05	$ .25
Alomar, Jr., Sandy	89UD	5	$ .10	$ .75
Alomar, Jr., Sandy	90UD	655	$ .01	$ .10
Alomar, Jr., Sandy	90UD	756	$ .01	$ .10
Alomar, Jr., Sandy	91UD	46	$ .01	$ .10
Alomar, Jr., Sandy	91UD	144	$ .01	$ .15
Alomar, Jr., Sandy	91UDF	81	$ .01	$ .05
Alomar, Jr., Sandy	92UD	81	$ .01	$ .15
Alomar, Jr., Sandy	92UD	156	$ .01	$ .04
Alomar, Sandy	93UD	45	$ .05	$ .25
Alomar, Jr., Sandy	93UD	255	$ .01	$ .05
Alou, Moises	91UD	665	$ .10	$ .40
Alou, Moises	93UD	297	$ .01	$ .10
Alvarez, Jose	89UD	734	$ .01	$ .10
Alvarez, Jose	90UD	634	$ .01	$ .05
Alvarez, Wilson	90UD	765	$ .10	$ .40
Alvarez, Wilson	91UDF	42	$ .01	$ .15
Alvarez, Wilson	92UD	573	$ .01	$ .10
Alvarez, Wilson	93UD	350	$ .01	$ .05
Amaro, Jr., Ruben	92UD	752	$ .01	$ .05
Andersen, Larry	89UD	404	$ .01	$ .08
Andersen, Larry	90UD	407	$ .01	$ .05
Andersen, Larry	91UD	41	$ .01	$ .05
Andersen, Larry	91UD	793	$ .01	$ .05
Andersen, Larry	92UD	587	$ .01	$ .04
Anderson, Allan	89UD	85	$ .01	$ .15

Allan Anderson

Player	Year	No.	VG	EX/MT
Anderson, Allan	**90UD**	**219**	**$ .01**	**$ .05**
Anderson, Allan	91UD	503	$ .01	$ .05
Anderson, Allan	92UD	506	$ .01	$ .04
Anderson, Brady	89UD	408	$ .15	$1.50
Anderson, Brady	90UD	290	$ .05	$ .25
Anderson, Brady	91UD	349	$ .01	$ .15
Anderson, Brady	92UD	185	$ .01	$ .10
Anderson, Brady	93UD	44	$ .05	$ .20
Anderson, Brady	93UD	111	$ .01	$ .05
Anderson, Dave	89UD	89	$ .01	$ .08
Anderson, Dave	90UD	510	$ .01	$ .05
Anderson, Dave	92UD	290	$ .01	$ .04
Anderson, Kent	90UD	691	$ .01	$ .10
Andujar, Joaquin	89UD	79	$ .01	$ .08
Anthony, Eric	90UD	28	$ .10	$ .75
Anthony, Eric	91UD	533	$ .01	$ .10
Anthony, Eric	93UD	183	$ .01	$ .05
Appier, Kevin	90UD	102	$ .10	$ .75
Appier, Kevin	91UD	566	$ .01	$ .10
Appier, Kevin	92UD	159	$ .01	$ .04
Appier, Kevin	93UD	89	$ .01	$ .05
Aquino, Luis	90UD	274	$ .01	$ .10
Aquino, Luis	91UD	504	$ .01	$ .05
Aquino, Luis	92UD	219	$ .01	$ .04
Armas, Tony	89UD	212	$ .01	$ .08
Armas, Tony	90UD	58	$ .01	$ .05
Armstrong, Jack	89UD	257	$ .01	$ .15
Armstrong, Jack	90UD	684	$ .01	$ .10
Armstrong, Jack	91UD	373	$ .01	$ .05
Armstrong, Jack	92UD	296	$ .01	$ .04
Armstrong, Jack	92UD	789	$ .01	$ .05
Arnsberg, Brad	91UD	608	$ .01	$ .05
Arocha, Rene	93UD	3	$ .10	$ .50
Ashby, Alan	89UD	305	$ .01	$ .08

UPPER DECK

Player	Year	No.	VG	EX/MT
Ashby, Andy	91UDF	64	$ .05	$ .25
Ashby, Andy	92UD	19	$ .01	$ .15
Ashley, Billy	93UD	22	$ .05	$ .35
Assenmacher, Paul	89UD	566	$ .01	$ .08
Assenmacher, Paul	90UD	660	$ .01	$ .05
Assenmacher, Paul	91UD	491	$ .01	$ .05

Player	Year	No.	VG	EX/MT
Assenmacher, Paul	**92UD**	**590**	**$ .01**	**$ .04**
Assenmacher, Paul	93UD	320	$ .01	$ .05
Astacio, Pedro	93UD	367	$ .05	$ .35
Atherton, Keith	89UD	599	$ .01	$ .08
August, Don	89UD	325	$ .01	$ .10
August, Don	90UD	295	$ .01	$ .05
Avery, Steve	90UD	65	$ .20	$2.00
Avery, Steve	91UD	365	$ .10	$ .40
Avery, Steve	92UD	41	$ .01	$ .10
Avery, Steve	92UD	475	$ .01	$ .15
Avery, Steve	93UD	246	$ .01	$ .15
Azocar, Oscar	91UD	464	$ .01	$ .10
Backman, Wally	89UD	188	$ .01	$ .08
Backman, Wally	89UD	732	$ .01	$ .10
Backman, Wally	90UD	158	$ .01	$ .05
Backman, Wally	91UD	185	$ .01	$ .05
Backman, Wally	91UD	790	$ .01	$ .05
Backman, Wally	92UD	350	$ .01	$ .04
Baerga, Carlos	90UD	737	$ .75	$3.00
Baerga, Carlos	91UD	125	$ .10	$ .40
Baerga, Carlos	92UD	231	$ .05	$ .25
Baerga, Carlos	93UD	45	$ .05	$ .25
Baerga, Carlos	93UD	174	$ .05	$ .25
Bagwell, Jeff	91UD	702	$ .10	$ .50
Bagwell, Jeff	91UD	755	$ .15	$1.50
Bagwell, Jeff	92UD	276	$ .05	$ .25
Bagwell, Jeff	93UD	256	$ .01	$ .05
Bailes, Scott	89UD	209	$ .01	$ .08
Bailes, Scott	91UD	190	$ .01	$ .05
Baines, Harold	89UD	211	$ .01	$ .10
Baines, Harold	89UD	692	$ .01	$ .10
Baines, Harold	90UD	353	$ .01	$ .05
Baines, Harold	91UD	562	$ .01	$ .05
Baines, Harold	92UD	158	$ .01	$ .04
Baines, Harold	93UD	81	$ .01	$ .05
Balboni, Steve	89UD	111	$ .01	$ .08
Balboni, Steve	90UD	497	$ .01	$ .05
Ballard, Jeff	89UD	595	$ .01	$ .15
Ballard, Jeff	90UD	259	$ .01	$ .05
Ballard, Jeff	91UD	260	$ .01	$ .05
Bankhead, Scott	89UD	316	$ .01	$ .10
Bankhead, Scott	90UD	561	$ .01	$ .15
Bankhead, Scott	91UD	294	$ .01	$ .10
Bankhead, Scott	93UD	329	$ .01	$ .05
Banks, Willie	91UD	74	$ .05	$ .30
Banks, Willie	92UD	14	$ .01	$ .15
Bannister, Floyd	89UD	549	$ .01	$ .08
Bannister, Floyd	90UD	695	$ .01	$ .05
Barberie, Bret	91UDF	67	$ .05	$ .20
Barberie, Bret	92UD	363	$ .01	$ .15
Barfield, Jesse	89UD	149	$ .01	$ .15
Barfield, Jesse	89UD	702	$ .01	$ .10
Barfield, Jesse	90UD	476	$ .01	$ .05
Barfield, Jesse	91UD	485	$ .01	$ .05
Barfield, Jesse	92UD	139	$ .01	$ .04
Barfield, Jesse	92UD	644	$ .01	$ .04
Barfield, John	91UD	629	$ .01	$ .10
Barfield, John	92UD	691	$ .01	$ .04
Barnes, Brian	91UD	12	$ .05	$ .20
Barnes, Brian	92UD	361	$ .01	$ .04
Barnes, Brian	93UD	214	$ .01	$ .05
Barnes, Skeeter	92UD	470	$ .01	$ .04
Barrett, Marty	89UD	173	$ .01	$ .08
Barrett, Marty	90UD	133	$ .01	$ .05
Barrett, Marty	91UD	90	$ .01	$ .05
Bass, Kevin	89UD	425	$ .01	$ .08
Bass, Kevin	90UD	302	$ .01	$ .05
Bass, Kevin	90UD	793	$ .01	$ .05
Bass, Kevin	91UD	287	$ .01	$ .05
Bass, Kevin	92UD	107	$ .01	$ .04
Batiste, Kevin	90UD	115	$ .05	$ .25
Batiste, Kim	92UD	422	$ .01	$ .15
Bautista, Jose	89UD	574	$ .01	$ .10
Bautista, Jose	90UD	8	$ .01	$ .05
Baylor, Don	89UD	601	$ .01	$ .08
Bearse, Kevin	90UD	715	$ .01	$ .15
Beasley, Chris	92UD	614	$ .01	$ .10
Beatty, Blaine	90UD	23	$ .01	$ .15
Beck, Rod	93UD	73	$ .01	$ .05
Bedrosian, Steve	89UD	511	$ .01	$ .08
Bedrosian, Steve	90UD	618	$ .01	$ .05
Bedrosian, Steve	91UD	422	$ .01	$ .05
Bedrosian, Steve	91UD	738	$ .01	$ .05
Bedrosian, Steve	92UD	622	$ .01	$ .04
Belcher, Kevin	91UD	26	$ .01	$ .15
Belcher, Tim	89UD	648	$ .01	$ .15
Belcher, Tim	90UD	547	$ .05	$ .20
Belcher, Tim	91UD	576	$ .01	$ .05
Belcher, Tim	92UD	668	$ .01	$ .04
Belcher, Tim	92UD	761	$ .01	$ .05
Belcher, Tim	93UD	368	$ .01	$ .05
Belinda, Stan	90UD	759	$ .05	$ .25
Belinda, Stan	91UD	161	$ .01	$ .10
Belinda, Stan	92UD	202	$ .01	$ .04
Belinda, Stan	93UD	359	$ .01	$ .05
Bell, Buddy	89UD	112	$ .01	$ .08
Bell, Derek	91UDF	26	$ .10	$ .50
Bell, Derek	92UD	26	$ .01	$ .10
Bell, Derek	93UD	158	$ .01	$ .05
Bell, George	89UD	255	$ .05	$ .25
Bell, George	90UD	95	$ .01	$ .10
Bell, George	90UD	127	$ .01	$ .10
Bell, George	91UD	532	$ .01	$ .15
Bell, George	91UD	725	$ .01	$ .15
Bell, George	91UD	742	$ .01	$ .10
Bell, George	92UD	236	$ .01	$ .04
Bell, George	92UD	724	$ .01	$ .05
Bell, George	93UD	345	$ .01	$ .10
Bell, Jay	89UD	489	$ .01	$ .15
Bell, Jay	90UD	517	$ .01	$ .05
Bell, Jay	91UD	183	$ .01	$ .05
Bell, Jay	92UD	115	$ .01	$ .04

UPPER DECK

Player	Year	No.	VG	EX/MT	Player	Year	No.	VG	EX/MT
Bell, Jay	93UD	103	$ .01	$ .05	Blauser, Jeff	92UD	370	$ .01	$ .04
Bell, Juan	89UD	20	$ .01	$ .15	Blocker, Terry	89UD	399	$ .01	$ .10
Bell, Juan	89UD	747	$ .01	$ .10	Blosser, Greg	91UD	70	$ .05	$ .25
Bell, Juan	91UDF	59	$ .01	$ .05	Blowers, Mike	90UD	767	$ .01	$ .15
Bell, Mike	91UD	644	$ .01	$ .15	Blowers, Mike	91UD	730	$ .01	$ .05
Belle, Joey "Albert"	90UD	446	$ .20	$2.00	Blyleven, Bert	89UD	225	$ .01	$ .10
Belle, Albert	91UD	764	$ .05	$ .25	Blyleven, Bert	89UD	712	$ .01	$ .10
Belle, Albert	92UD	137	$ .01	$ .15	Blyleven, Bert	90UD	527	$ .01	$ .10
Belle, Albert	93UD	45	$ .05	$ .25	Blyleven, Bert	91UD	571	$ .01	$ .05
Belliard, Rafael	89UD	90	$ .01	$ .08	Boddicker, Mike	89UD	542	$ .01	$ .08
Belliard, Rafael	90UD	208	$ .01	$ .05	Boddicker, Mike	90UD	652	$ .01	$ .05
Belliard, Rafael	91UD	706	$ .01	$ .05	Boddicker, Mike	91UD	438	$ .01	$ .05
Belliard, Rafael	92UD	510	$ .01	$ .04	Boddicker, Mike	91UD	719	$ .01	$ .05
Belliard, Rafael	93UD	91	$ .01	$ .05	Boddicker, Mike	92UD	213	$ .01	$ .04
Benavides, Freddie	91UDF	32	$ .01	$ .15	Boever, Joe	90UD	408	$ .01	$ .05
Benedict, Bruce	89UD	121	$ .01	$ .08	Boever, Joe	91UD	430	$ .01	$ .05
Benes, Andy	90UD	55	$ .10	$ .75	Boever, Joe	92UD	402	$ .01	$ .04
Benes, Andy	91UD	275	$ .01	$ .15	Boever, Joe	93UD	310	$ .01	$ .05
Benes, Andy	92UD	323	$ .01	$ .10	Boggs, Wade	89UD	389	$ .10	$ .75
Benes, Andy	93UD	261	$ .01	$ .05	Boggs, Wade	89UD	687	$ .05	$ .25
Benjamin, Mike	90UD	750	$ .01	$ .15	Boggs, Wade	90UD	555	$ .05	$ .35
Benjamin, Mike	91UD	651	$ .01	$ .10	Boggs, Wade	91UD	546	$ .05	$ .20
Benjamin, Mike	92UD	268	$ .01	$ .04					
Benzinger, Todd	89UD	184	$ .01	$ .08					
Benzinger, Todd	89UD	785	$ .01	$ .15					
Benzinger, Todd	90UD	186	$ .01	$ .10					
Benzinger, Todd	91UD	280	$ .01	$ .05					
Benzinger, Todd	91UDF	41	$ .01	$ .05					
Benzinger, Todd	92UD	518	$ .01	$ .04					
Berenguer, Juan	89UD	232	$ .01	$ .08					
Berenguer, Juan	90UD	440	$ .01	$ .05					
Berenguer, Juan	91UD	411	$ .01	$ .05					
Berenguer, Juan	92UD	493	$ .01	$ .04					
Bergman, Dave	89UD	266	$ .01	$ .08					
Bergman, Dave	90UD	381	$ .01	$ .05					
Bergman, Dave	91UD	599	$ .01	$ .05					
Berroa, Geronimo	90UD	531	$ .01	$ .10					
Berry, Sean	91UD	10	$ .05	$ .20					
Berryhill, Damon	89UD	455	$ .01	$ .15					
Berryhill, Damon	90UD	322	$ .01	$ .10					
Berryhill, Damon	91UD	319	$ .01	$ .05					
Berryhill, Damon	92UD	706	$ .01	$ .05					
Bichette, Dante	89UD	24	$ .10	$ .50					
Bichette, Dante	90UD	688	$ .01	$ .10					
Bichette, Dante	91UD	317	$ .01	$ .05					
Bichette, Dante	91UD	712	$ .01	$ .05					
Bichette, Dante	92UD	378	$ .01	$ .04					
Bielecki, Mike	90UD	359	$ .01	$ .05					
Bielecki, Mike	91UD	597	$ .01	$ .05					
Bielecki, Mike	92UD	730	$ .01	$ .05					
Biggio, Craig	89UD	273	$ .15	$1.25					
Biggio, Craig	90UD	104	$ .01	$ .15					
Biggio, Craig	91UD	158	$ .01	$ .05					
Biggio, Craig	92UD	31	$ .01	$ .04					
Biggio, Craig	92UD	162	$ .01	$ .04	Boggs, Wade	91UDF	84	$ .01	$ .15
Biggio, Craig	93UD	114	$ .01	$ .05	Boggs, Wade	92UD	443	$ .01	$ .15
Birtsas, Tim	89UD	638	$ .01	$ .08	Boggs, Wade	92UD	646	$ .01	$ .15
Birtsas, Tim	90UD	137	$ .01	$ .05	Bohanon, Brian	90UD	731	$ .01	$ .15
Bitker, Joe	91UD	797	$ .01	$ .10	Bohanon, Brian	93UD	380	$ .01	$ .05
Bittiger, Jeff	89UD	509	$ .01	$ .08	Bolton, Tom	89UD	545	$ .01	$ .08
Black, Bud	89UD	466	$ .01	$ .08	Bolton, Tom	90UD	351	$ .01	$ .05
Black, Bud	90UD	498	$ .01	$ .05	Bolton, Tom	91UD	86	$ .01	$ .05
Black, Bud	91UD	799	$ .01	$ .05	Bolton, Tom	92UD	110	$ .01	$ .04
Black, Bud	92UD	697	$ .01	$ .04	Bonds, Barry	89UD	440	$ .15	$1.50
Black, Bud	93UD	229	$ .01	$ .05	Bonds, Barry	90UD	227	$ .10	$ .50
Blair, Willie	91UD	427	$ .01	$ .10	Bonds, Barry	91UD	94	$ .01	$ .15
Blankenship, Kevin	89UD	762	$ .01	$ .10	Bonds, Barry	91UD	154	$ .05	$ .25
Blankenship, Kevin	90UD	47	$ .01	$ .10	Bonds, Barry	92UD	134	$ .05	$ .25
Blankenship, Lance	89UD	15	$ .05	$ .20	Bonds, Barry	92UD	711	$ .01	$ .15
Blankenship, Lance	90UD	687	$ .01	$ .05	Bonds, Barry	92UD	721	$ .05	$ .20
Blankenship, Lance	92UD	749	$ .01	$ .05	Bonds, Barry	93UD	210	$ .01	$ .05
Blankenship, Lance	93UD	108	$ .01	$ .05	Bones, Ricky	92UD	623	$ .01	$ .15
Blauser, Jeff	89UD	132	$ .01	$ .15	Bones, Ricky	92UD	762	$ .01	$ .05
Blauser, Jeff	90UD	406	$ .01	$ .05	Bones, Ricky	93UD	328	$ .01	$ .05
Blauser, Jeff	91UD	382	$ .01	$ .05	Bonilla, Bobby	89UD	578	$ .10	$ .50

Wade Boggs

UPPER DECK

Player	Year	No.	VG	EX/MT
Bonilla, Bobby	90UD	16	$ .01	$ .10
Bonilla, Bobby	90UD	366	$ .05	$ .20
Bonilla, Bobby	91UD	152	$ .01	$ .15
Bonilla, Bobby	91UDF	99	$ .01	$ .05
Bonilla, Bobby	92UD	225	$ .01	$ .10
Bonilla, Bobby	92UD	755	$ .01	$ .10
Bonilla, Bobby	93UD	275	$ .01	$ .10
Booker, Greg	89UD	641	$ .01	$ .08
Booker, Rod	89UD	644	$ .01	$ .10
Boone, Bob	89UD	119	$ .01	$ .08
Boone, Bob	89UD	767	$ .01	$ .15
Boone, Bob	90UD	271	$ .01	$ .05
Boone, Bob	91UD	502	$ .01	$ .05
Boone, Bret	92UD	771	$ .10	$ .50
Boone, Bret	93UD	65	$ .05	$ .35
Borders, Pat	89UD	593	$ .10	$ .50
Borders, Pat	90UD	113	$ .01	$ .05
Borders, Pat	91UD	147	$ .01	$ .05
Borders, Pat	92UD	140	$ .01	$ .04
Borders, Pat	93UD	149	$ .01	$ .05
Bordick, Mike	92UD	727	$ .01	$ .05
Bordick, Mike	93UD	189	$ .01	$ .05
Borwning, Tom	92UD	461	$ .01	$ .04
Bosio, Chris	89UD	292	$ .01	$ .08
Bosio, Chris	90UD	293	$ .01	$ .05
Bosio, Chris	91UD	529	$ .01	$ .05
Bosio, Chris	92UD	615	$ .01	$ .04
Boskie, Shawn	90UD	722	$ .05	$ .20
Boskie, Shawn	91UD	471	$ .01	$ .10
Bosley, Thad	89UD	591	$ .01	$ .08
Boston, Daryl	89UD	496	$ .01	$ .08
Boston, Daryl	90UD	529	$ .01	$ .05
Boston, Daryl	91UD	159	$ .01	$ .05
Boston, Daryl	93UD	203	$ .01	$ .05
Boucher, Denis	91UD	761	$ .01	$ .15
Bowen, Ryan	91UDF	45	$ .05	$ .25
Bowen, Ryan	92UD	354	$ .01	$ .15
Boyd, Oil Can	89UD	415	$ .01	$ .15
Boyd, Oil Can	90UD	484	$ .01	$ .05
Boyd, Oil Can	90UD	749	$ .01	$ .05
Boyd, Oil Can	91UD	359	$ .01	$ .05
Boyd, Oil Can	91UDF	51	$ .01	$ .05
Boyd, Oil Can	92UD	559	$ .01	$ .04
Bradley, Phil	89UD	229	$ .01	$ .08
Bradley, Phil	89UD	749	$ .01	$ .10
Bradley, Phil	90UD	194	$ .01	$ .05
Bradley, Phil	91UD	641	$ .01	$ .05
Bradley, Scott	89UD	226	$ .01	$ .08
Bradley, Scott	90UD	383	$ .01	$ .05
Bradley, Scott	91UD	130	$ .01	$ .05
Bradley, Scott	92UD	390	$ .01	$ .04
Braggs, Glenn	89UD	504	$ .01	$ .08
Braggs, Glenn	90UD	456	$ .01	$ .05
Braggs, Glenn	90UD	714	$ .01	$ .05
Braggs, Glenn	91UD	631	$ .01	$ .05
Braggs, Glenn	92UD	341	$ .01	$ .04
Brantley, Jeff	90UD	358	$ .01	$ .10
Brantley, Jeff	91UD	424	$ .01	$ .05
Brantley, Jeff	92UD	581	$ .01	$ .04
Brantley, Mickey	89UD	550	$ .01	$ .08
Bream, Sid	89UD	556	$ .01	$ .08
Bream, Sid	90UD	250	$ .01	$ .05
Bream, Sid	91UD	109	$ .01	$ .05
Bream, Sid	91UD	710	$ .01	$ .05
Bream, Sid	92UD	495	$ .01	$ .04
Bream, Sid	93UD	104	$ .01	$ .05
Brenly, Bob	89UD	479	$ .01	$ .08
Brennan, William	89UD	16	$ .01	$ .10
Brett, George	89UD	215	$ .10	$ .75
Brett, George	89UD	689	$ .05	$ .20
Brett, George	90UD	124	$ .05	$ .25
Brett, George	91UD	525	$ .01	$ .15
Brett, George	92UD	444	$ .01	$ .15
Brett, George	93UD	54	$ .01	$ .15
Brett, George	93UD	56	$ .01	$ .15

Player	Year	No.	VG	EX/MT
Brett, George	93UDSP	5	$2.50	$10.00
Brewer, Rod	93UD	381	$ .01	$ .15
Briley, Greg	89UD	770	$ .05	$ .25
Briley, Greg	90UD	455	$ .01	$ .10
Briley, Greg	91UD	479	$ .01	$ .05
Briley, Greg	92UD	369	$ .01	$ .04
Brock, Greg	89UD	543	$ .01	$ .08
Brock, Greg	90UD	514	$ .01	$ .05
Brock, Greg	91UD	289	$ .01	$ .05
Brock, Lou	91UD	636	$ .05	$ .25
Brogna, Rico	91UD	73	$ .01	$ .15
Brogna, Rico	92UD	74	$ .01	$ .15
Brogna, Rico	93UD	386	$ .01	$ .05
Brookens, Tom	89UD	106	$ .01	$ .08
Brookens, Tom	90UD	138	$ .01	$ .05
Brookens, Tom	91UD	102	$ .01	$ .05
Brooks, Hubie	89UD	122	$ .01	$ .08
Brooks, Hubie	90UD	197	$ .01	$ .05
Brooks, Hubie	90UD	791	$ .01	$ .05
Brooks, Hubie	91UD	217	$ .01	$ .05
Brooks, Hubie	91UD	787	$ .01	$ .05

Player	Year	No.	VG	EX/MT
Brooks, Hubie	**92UD**	**114**	**$ .01**	**$ .04**
Brooks, Hubie	92UD	709	$ .01	$ .05
Brosius, Scott	92UD	312	$ .01	$ .15
Brosa, Terry	92UD	531	$ .01	$ .04
Brothers, Bash	93UD	49	$ .01	$ .15
Brower, Bob	89UD	439	$ .01	$ .08
Brown, Chris	89UD	193	$ .01	$ .08
Brown, Chris	89UD	784	$ .01	$ .10
Brown, Kevin	89UD	752	$ .10	$ .50
Brown, Kevin	90UD	123	$ .05	$ .20
Brown, Kevin	91UD	472	$ .01	$ .05
Brown, Kevin	92UD	578	$ .01	$ .04
Brown, Kevin	93UD	76	$ .01	$ .05
Browne, Jerry	89UD	314	$ .01	$ .08
Browne, Jerry	90UD	426	$ .01	$ .05
Browne, Jerry	91UD	116	$ .01	$ .05
Browne, Jerry	92UD	340	$ .01	$ .04
Browne, Jerry	93UD	129	$ .01	$ .05
Browning, Tom	89UD	617	$ .01	$ .10
Browning, Tom	90UD	189	$ .01	$ .05
Browning, Tom	91UD	633	$ .01	$ .05
Browning, Tom	93UD	270	$ .01	$ .05

UPPER DECK

Player	Year	No.	VG	EX/MT	Player	Year	No.	VG	EX/MT
Brumley, Mike	90UD	312	$ .01	$ .05	Candelaria, John	89UD	248	$ .01	$ .05
Brunansky, Tom	89UD	272	$ .01	$ .08	Candelaria, John	90UD	720	$ .01	$ .05
Brunansky, Tom	90UD	257	$ .01	$ .05	Candelaria, John	91UDF	40	$ .01	$ .05
Brunansky, Tom	90UD	708	$ .01	$ .05	Candelaria, John	92UD	482	$ .01	$ .04
Brunansky, Tom	91UD	163	$ .01	$ .05	Candiotti, Tom	89UD	470	$ .01	$ .08
Brunansky, Tom	92UD	543	$ .01	$ .04	Candiotti, Tom	90UD	388	$ .01	$ .05
Brutcher, Len	91UD	75	$ .01	$ .15	Candiotti, Tom	91UD	218	$ .01	$ .05
Bryant, Scott	91UDF	5	$ .01	$ .15	Candiotti, Tom	91UDF	49	$ .01	$ .05
Buckner, Bill	89UD	639	$ .01	$ .08	Candiotti, Tom	92UD	447	$ .01	$ .04
Buckner, Bill	90UD	252	$ .01	$ .05	Candiotti, Tom	92UD	760	$ .01	$ .05
Buechele, Steve	89UD	418	$ .01	$ .08	Candiotti, Tom	93UD	98	$ .01	$ .05
Buechele, Steve	90UD	685	$ .01	$ .05	Cangelosi, John	89UD	67	$ .01	$ .08
Buechele, Steve	91UD	650	$ .01	$ .05	Cangelosi, John	90UD	370	$ .01	$ .05
Buechele, Steve	92UD	488	$ .01	$ .04	Cano, Jose	90UD	43	$ .01	$ .05
Buechele, Steve	93UD	159	$ .01	$ .05	Canseco, Jose	89UD	371	$ .15	$1.50
Buhner, Jay	89UD	220	$ .05	$ .35	Canseco, Jose	89UD	659	$ .10	$ .50
Buhner, Jay	90UD	534	$ .05	$ .05	Canseco, Jose	89UD	670	$ .10	$ .40
Buhner, Jay	91UD	128	$ .01	$ .05	Canseco, Jose	90UD	66	$ .10	$ .75
Buhner, Jay	92UD	441	$ .01	$ .04	Canseco, Jose	91UD	155	$ .05	$ .35
Buhner, Jay	93UD	55	$ .05	$ .25					
Buhner, Jay	93UD	224	$ .01	$ .05					
Buice, DeWayne	89UD	147	$ .01	$ .08					
Bullinger, Jim	93UD	379	$ .01	$ .05					
Burke, Tim	89UD	456	$ .01	$ .10					
Burke, Tim	90UD	515	$ .01	$ .05					
Burke, Tim	91UD	215	$ .01	$ .05					
Burke, Tim	91UDF	70	$ .01	$ .05					
Burke, Tim	92UD	433	$ .01	$ .04					
Burkett, John	90UD	735	$ .05	$ .20					
Burkett, John	91UD	577	$ .01	$ .05					
Burkett, John	92UD	148	$ .01	$ .04					
Burkett, John	93UD	160	$ .01	$ .05					
Burks, Ellis	89UD	434	$ .01	$ .15					
Burks, Ellis	90UD	343	$ .01	$ .10					
Burks, Ellis	91UD	436	$ .01	$ .10					
Burks, Ellis	92UD	94	$ .01	$ .04					
Burks, Ellis	92UD	525	$ .01	$ .04					
Burks, Ellis	93UD	265	$ .01	$ .05					
Burnitz, Jeromy	92UD	65	$ .01	$ .15					
Burns, Todd	89UD	718	$ .01	$ .10					
Burns, Todd	90UD	689	$ .01	$ .10					
Burns, Todd	91UD	405	$ .01	$ .05					
Bush, Randy	89UD	158	$ .01	$ .08					
Bush, Randy	90UD	493	$ .01	$ .05					
Butler, Brett	89UD	218	$ .01	$ .08					
Butler, Brett	90UD	119	$ .01	$ .05					
Butler, Brett	91UD	270	$ .01	$ .05					
Butler, Brett	91UD	732	$ .01	$ .05					
Butler, Brett	92UD	307	$ .01	$ .04					
Butler, Brett	93UD	259	$ .01	$ .05					
Cabrera, Francisco	90UD	64	$ .05	$ .20					
Cabrera, Francisco	91UD	439	$ .01	$ .05	**Canseco, Jose**	**92UD**	**333**	**$ .01**	**$ .15**
Cadaret, Greg	90UD	549	$ .01	$ .05	Canseco, Jose	92UD	640	$ .01	$ .15
Cadaret, Greg	91UD	343	$ .01	$ .05	Canseco, Jose	92UD	649	$ .01	$ .15
Cadaret, Greg	92UD	412	$ .01	$ .04	Canseco, Jose	93UD	52	$ .05	$ .35
Calderon, Ivan	89UD	650	$ .01	$ .08	Canseco, Jose	93UD	365	$ .05	$ .20
Calderon, Ivan	90UD	503	$ .01	$ .05	Canseco, Ozzie	89UD	756	$ .10	$ .40
Calderon, Ivan	91UD	285	$ .01	$ .05	Canseco, Ozzie	91UD	146	$ .01	$ .10
Calderon, Ivan	91UD	786	$ .01	$ .05	Carman, Don	89UD	409	$ .01	$ .08
Calderon, Ivan	91UDF	96	$ .01	$ .05	Carman, Don	90UD	420	$ .01	$ .05
Calderon, Ivan	92UD	226	$ .01	$ .04	Carman, Don	91UD	288	$ .01	$ .05
Calhoun, Jeff	89UD	33	$ .01	$ .08	Carpenter, Cris	89UD	8	$ .01	$ .15
Caminiti, Ken	89UD	141	$ .01	$ .08	Carpenter, Cris	90UD	523	$ .01	$ .10
Caminiti, Ken	90UD	122	$ .01	$ .05	Carpenter, Cris	92UD	686	$ .01	$ .04
Caminiti, Ken	91UD	180	$ .01	$ .05	Carr, Chuck	91UD	514	$ .01	$ .15
Caminiti, Ken	92UD	279	$ .01	$ .04	Carreon, Mark	90UD	135	$ .01	$ .10
Caminiti, Ken	93UD	305	$ .01	$ .05	Carreon, Mark	92UD	398	$ .01	$ .04
Campbell, Mike	89UD	337	$ .01	$ .08	Carreon, Mark	92UD	739	$ .01	$ .05
Campusano, Sil	89UD	45	$ .01	$ .10	Carter, Gary	89UD	390	$ .05	$ .20
Campusano, Sil	91UD	469	$ .01	$ .05	Carter, Gary	90UD	168	$ .01	$ .05
Canale, George	90UD	59	$ .01	$ .15	Carter, Gary	90UD	774	$ .01	$ .05
Candaele, Casey	89UD	58	$ .01	$ .08	Carter, Gary	91UD	176	$ .01	$ .05
Candaele, Casey	91UD	511	$ .01	$ .05	Carter, Gary	91UD	758	$ .01	$ .05
Candaele, Casey	92UD	387	$ .01	$ .04	Carter, Gary	92UD	267	$ .01	$ .04
Candaele, Casey	93UD	294	$ .01	$ .05	Carter, Gary	92UD	767	$ .01	$ .05

UPPER DECK

Player	Year	No.	VG	EX/MT
Carter, Gary	93UD	219	$ .01	$ .05
Carter, Joe	89UD	190	$ .10	$ .75
Carter, Joe	90UD	53	$ .01	$ .15
Carter, Joe	90UD	375	$ .05	$ .35
Carter, Joe	90UD	754	$ .05	$ .35
Carter, Joe	91UD	226	$ .05	$ .20
Carter, Joe	91UD	765	$ .01	$ .15
Carter, Joe	92UD	224	$ .01	$ .10
Carter, Joe	93UD	41	$ .01	$ .15
Carter, Joe	93UD	42	$ .01	$ .15
Carter, Joe	93UD	223	$ .01	$ .10
Carter, Steve	90UD	368	$ .01	$ .15
Cary, Chuck	89UD	396	$ .01	$ .08
Cary, Chuck	90UD	528	$ .01	$ .05
Cary, Chuck	91UD	409	$ .01	$ .05
Castillo, Braulio	92UD	21	$ .01	$ .10
Castillo, Carmen	89UD	487	$ .01	$ .08
Castillo, Carmen	90UD	281	$ .01	$ .05
Castillo, Frank	91UDF	27	$ .05	$ .25
Castillo, Frank	92UD	526	$ .01	$ .10
Castillo, Frank	93UD	408	$ .01	$ .05
Castillo, Juan	89UD	522	$ .01	$ .08
Castillo, Tony	90UD	551	$ .01	$ .05
Castillo, Tony	91UD	458	$ .01	$ .05
Cecena, Jose	89UD	560	$ .01	$ .10
Cedeno, Andujar	91UD	23	$ .05	$ .25
Cedeno, Andujar	92UD	257	$ .05	$ .20
Cerone, Rick	89UD	152	$ .01	$ .08
Cerone, Rick	90UD	405	$ .01	$ .05
Cerutti, John	89UD	129	$ .01	$ .08
Cerutti, John	90UD	485	$ .01	$ .05
Cerutti, John	91UD	585	$ .01	$ .05
Cerutti, John	92UD	487	$ .01	$ .04
Chamberlain, Wes	91UD	626	$ .05	$ .35
Chamberlain, Wes	92UD	347	$ .01	$ .15
Chamberlain, Wes	93UD	267	$ .01	$ .05
Champarino, Scott	91UD	8	$ .15	$ .15
Chance, Tony	89UD	3	$ .01	$ .10
Charlton, Norm	89UD	783	$ .10	$ .50
Charlton, Norm	90UD	566	$ .01	$ .15
Charlton, Norm	91UD	394	$ .01	$ .05
Charlton, Norm	92UD	677	$ .01	$ .04
Checklist, Rookies (1-26)	89UD	27	$ .01	$ .08
Checklist, Cards (1-100)	89UD	694	$ .01	$ .08
Checklist, Cards (101-200)	89UD	695	$ .01	$ .08
Checklist, Cards (201-300)	89UD	696	$ .01	$ .08
Checklist, Cards (301-400)	89UD	697	$ .01	$ .08
Checklist, Cards (401-500)	89UD	698	$ .01	$ .08
Checklist, Cards (501-600)	89UD	699	$ .01	$ .08
Checklist, Cards (601-700)	89UD	700	$ .01	$ .08
Checklist, Cards (701-800)	89UD	701	$ .01	$ .10
Checklist, Rookies (1-26)	90UD	1	$ .01	$ .05
Checklist, Cards (1-100)	90UD	100	$ .01	$ .05
Checklist, Cards (101-200)	90UD	200	$ .01	$ .05
Checklist, Cards (201-300)	90UD	300	$ .01	$ .05
Checklist, Cards (301-400)	90UD	400	$ .01	$ .05
Checklist, Cards (401-500)	90UD	500	$ .01	$ .05
Checklist, Cards (501-600)	90UD	600	$ .01	$ .05
Checklist, Cards (601-700)	90UD	700	$ .01	$ .05
Checklist, Cards (701-800)	90UD	800	$ .01	$ .05
Checklist, Rookies (1-27)	91UD	1	$ .01	$ .05
Checklist, Prospects (51-76)	91UD	50	$ .01	$ .05
Checklist, Cards (1-100)	91UD	100	$ .01	$ .05
Checklist, Cards (101-200)	91UD	200	$ .01	$ .05
Checklist, Cards (201-300)	91UD	300	$ .01	$ .05
Checklist, Cards (301-400)	91UD	400	$ .01	$ .05
Checklist, Cards (401-500)	91UD	500	$ .01	$ .05
Checklist, Cards (501-600)	91UD	600	$ .01	$ .05
Checklist, Cards (601-700)	91UD	700	$ .01	$ .05
Checklist, Cards (701-800)	91UD	800	$ .01	$ .05
Checklist, Cards (2-21)	91UDF	1	$ .10	$ .50
Checklist, Cards (80-99)	91UDF	79	$ .05	$ .35
Checklist, Cards (1-100)	91UDF	100	$ .01	$ .05
Checklist, Rookies (1-17)	92UD	1	$ .05	$ .25
Checklist, Prospects (52-77)	92UD	51	$ .05	$ .35

Player	Year	No.	VG	EX/MT
Checklist, Cards (1-100)	92UD	100	$ .01	$ .04
Checklist, Cards (101-200)	92UD	200	$ .01	$ .04
Checklist, Cards (201-300)	92UD	300	$ .01	$ .04
Checklist, Cards (301-400)	92UD	400	$ .01	$ .04

Checklist, Cards (401-500)	92UD	500	$ .01	$ .04
Checklist, Cards (501-600)	92UD	600	$ .01	$ .04
Checklist, Diamond Skills	92UD	640	$ .01	$ .15
Checklist, Cards (601-700)	92UD	700	$ .01	$ .04
Checklist, Diamond Skills	92UD	711	$ .01	$ .15
Checklist, Diamond Debuts	92UD	770	$ .05	$ .20
Checklist, Cards (701-800)	92UD	800	$ .01	$ .05
Checklist, Rookies	93UD	1	$ .05	$ .25
Checklist, Community Heroes	93UD	30	$ .01	$ .10
Checklist, Teammates	93UD	41	$ .01	$ .15
Checklist, Cards(1-105)	93UD	105	$ .01	$ .10
Checklist, Cards (106-210)	93UD	210	$ .01	$ .05
Checklist, Cards (211-315)	93UD	315	$ .01	$ .05
Checklist, Cards (316-420)	93UD	420	$ .01	$ .05
Chitren, Steve	91UD	753	$ .01	$ .10
Chitren, Steve	92UD	471	$ .01	$ .04
Cianfrocco, Archi	92UD	772	$ .01	$ .15
Clancy, Jim	89UD	282	$ .01	$ .08
Clancy, Jim	90UD	203	$ .01	$ .05
Clancy, Jim	91UD	682	$ .01	$ .05
Clark, Dave	89UD	517	$ .01	$ .00
Clark, Dave	90UD	449	$ .01	$ .05
Clark, Dave	91UD	314	$ .01	$ .05
Clark, Jack	89UD	346	$ .01	$ .10
Clark, Jack	89UD	773	$ .01	$ .15
Clark, Jack	90UD	342	$ .01	$ .05
Clark, Jack	91UD	331	$ .01	$ .05
Clark, Jack	91UD	735	$ .01	$ .05
Clark, Jack	92UD	521	$ .01	$ .04
Clark, Jerald	89UD	30	$ .05	$ .25
Clark, Jerald	90UD	624	$ .01	$ .05
Clark, Jerald	91UD	624	$ .01	$ .05
Clark, Jerald	92UD	292	$ .01	$ .04
Clark, Jerald	93UD	140	$ .01	$ .05
Clark, Mark	92UD	702	$ .05	$ .25
Clark, Mark	92UD	773	$ .01	$ .10
Clark, Terry	89UD	234	$ .05	$ .20
Clark, Will	89UD	155	$ .15	$1.50
Clark, Will	89UD	678	$ .05	$ .35

UPPER DECK

Player	Year	No.	VG	EX/MT
Clark, Will	90UD	50	$ .05	$ .25
Clark, Will	90UD	556	$ .10	$ .50
Clark, Will	91UD	445	$ .05	$ .25
Clark, Will	91UDF	92	$ .01	$ .15
Clark, Will	92UD	175	$ .05	$ .20
Clark, Will	92UD	718	$ .01	$ .15
Clark, Will	93UD	315	$ .01	$ .05
Clary, Marty	90UD	779	$ .01	$ .05
Clary, Marty	91UD	478	$ .01	$ .15
Clayton, Royce	91UD	61	$ .10	$ .50
Clayton, Royce	91UDF	4	$ .05	$ .35
Clayton, Royce	92UD	2	$ .01	$ .15
Clayton, Royce	93UD	151	$ .01	$ .05
Clemens, Roger	89UD	195	$ .20	$2.00
Clemens, Roger	90UD	57	$ .05	$ .25
Clemens, Roger	90UD	323	$ .10	$ .75
Clemens, Roger	91UD	655	$ .05	$ .35
Clemens, Roger	92UD	545	$ .05	$ .25
Clemens, Roger	92UD	641	$ .01	$ .15
Clemens, Roger	93UD	135	$ .05	$ .25
Cliburn, Stu	89UD	483	$ .01	$ .08
Club, 400 Home Run	92UD	728	$ .01	$ .10
Clutterbuck, Bryan	90UD	239	$ .01	$ .05
Colbrunn, Greg	91UD	15	$ .05	$ .35
Colbrunn, Greg	93UD	342	$ .01	$ .05
Cole, Alex	90UD	751	$ .05	$ .35
Cole, Alex	91UD	654	$ .01	$ .10
Cole, Alex	92UD	197	$ .01	$ .04
Coleman, Vince	89UD	253	$ .01	$ .15
Coleman, Vince	90UD	68	$ .01	$ .05
Coleman, Vince	90UD	223	$ .01	$ .10
Coleman, Vince	91UD	461	$ .01	$ .10
Coleman, Vince	91UD	768	$ .01	$ .10
Coleman, Vince	92UD	131	$ .01	$ .04
Coles, Darnell	89UD	339	$ .01	$ .08
Coles, Darnell	90UD	311	$ .01	$ .05
Collins, Dave	89UD	351	$ .01	$ .08
Colon, Cris	93UD	14	$ .01	$ .10
Combs, Pat	90UD	763	$ .01	$ .10
Combs, Pat	91UD	537	$ .01	$ .05
Combs, Pat	92UD	442	$ .01	$ .04
Concepcion, Dave	89UD	196	$ .01	$ .08
Cone, David	89UD	584	$ .10	$ .50
Cone, David	90UD	224	$ .05	$ .25
Cone, David	91UD	366	$ .01	$ .10
Cone, David	92UD	364	$ .01	$ .04
Cone, David	93UD	335	$ .01	$ .05
Conine, Jeff	91UD	27	$ .05	$ .35
Cook, Dennis	89UD	779	$ .01	$ .15
Cook, Dennis	90UD	71	$ .01	$ .15
Cook, Dennis	91UD	612	$ .01	$ .05
Cook, Dennis	93UD	202	$ .01	$ .05
Coolbaugh, Scott	90UD	42	$ .01	$ .15
Coolbaugh, Scott	91UD	451	$ .01	$ .05
Coolbaugh, Scott	91UDF	37	$ .01	$ .05
Cooper, Scott	91UD	22	$ .10	$ .40
Cooper, Scott	92UD	541	$ .01	$ .15
Cooper, Scott	93UD	57	$ .01	$ .05
Cora, Joey	90UD	601	$ .01	$ .05
Cora, Joey	91UD	291	$ .01	$ .05
Cora, Joey	92UD	359	$ .01	$ .04
Corbett, Sherman	89UD	464	$ .01	$ .08
Cordero, Wilfredo	91UD	60	$ .10	$1.00
Cordero, Wilfredo	92UD	16	$ .05	$ .20
Cordero, Wilfredo	93UD	60	$ .01	$ .15
Cormier, Rheal	92UD	574	$ .05	$ .20
Cormier, Rheal	93UD	79	$ .01	$ .05
Correa, Edwin	89UD	598	$ .01	$ .08
Corsi, Jim	90UD	521	$ .01	$ .05
Costello, John	89UD	625	$ .01	$ .10
Costello, John	90UD	486	$ .01	$ .05
Costo, Tim	91UD	62	$ .05	$ .35
Costo, Tim	93UD	11	$ .01	$ .10
Cotto, Henry	89UD	134	$ .01	$ .08
Cotto, Henry	90UD	207	$ .01	$ .05

Player	Year	No.	VG	EX/MT
Cotto, Henry	91UD	110	$ .01	$ .05
Cotto, Henry	92UD	616	$ .01	$ .04
Cotto, Henry	93UD	411	$ .01	$ .05
Cox, Danny	89UD	535	$ .01	$ .08
Crew, Brew	93UD	43	$ .05	$ .25
Crews, Tim	89UD	611	$ .01	$ .08
Crews, Tim	90UD	670	$ .01	$ .05
Crews, Tim	91UD	596	$ .01	$ .05
Crews, Tim	92UD	687	$ .01	$ .04
Crim, Chuck	89UD	501	$ .01	$ .08
Crim, Chuck	90UD	511	$ .01	$ .05
Crim, Chuck	91UD	391	$ .01	$ .05
Crim, Chuck	92UD	496	$ .01	$ .04
Curtis, Chad	92UD	774	$ .10	$ .40
Curtis, Chad	93UD	235	$ .01	$ .15
Cuyler, Milt	91UD	556	$ .01	$ .15
Cuyler, Milt	92UD	536	$ .01	$ .10
Cuyler, Milt	93UD	162	$ .01	$ .05
Daniels, Kal	89UD	160	$ .01	$ .10
Daniels, Kal	90UD	603	$ .01	$ .05
Daniels, Kal	91UD	166	$ .01	$ .05
Daniels, Kal	92UD	284	$ .01	$ .04
Darling, Ron	89UD	159	$ .01	$ .10
Darling, Ron	90UD	241	$ .01	$ .05
Darling, Ron	91UD	198	$ .01	$ .05
Darling, Ron	91UDF	69	$ .01	$ .05
Darling, Ron	92UD	669	$ .01	$ .04
Darling, Ron	93UD	168	$ .01	$ .05
Darwin, Danny	89UD	97	$ .01	$ .08
Darwin, Danny	90UD	305	$ .01	$ .05
Darwin, Danny	91UD	586	$ .01	$ .05
Darwin, Danny	91UD	705	$ .01	$ .05
Darwin, Danny	92UD	678	$ .01	$ .04
Darwin, Danny	93UD	220	$ .01	$ .05
Dascenzo, Doug	89UD	10	$ .01	$ .15
Dascenzo, Doug	90UD	211	$ .01	$ .05
Dascenzo, Doug	92UD	239	$ .01	$ .04
Dascenzo, Doug	93UD	64	$ .01	$ .05
Daugherty, Jack	90UD	614	$ .01	$ .15
Daugherty, Jack	91UD	284	$ .01	$ .05

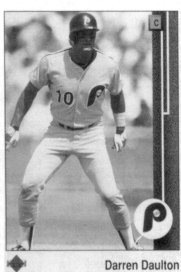

Darren Daulton

Player	Year	No.	VG	EX/MT
Daulton, Darren	89UD	448	$ .05	$ .20
Daulton, Darren	90UD	418	$ .01	$ .05
Daulton, Darren	91UD	408	$ .01	$ .05

UPPER DECK

Player	Year	No.	VG	EX/MT
Daulton, Darren	92UD	429	$ .01	$ .04
Daulton, Darren	93UD	137	$ .01	$ .10
Davidson, Mark	89UD	577	$ .01	$ .08
Davis, Alvin	89UD	105	$ .01	$ .15
Davis, Alvin	89UD	680	$ .01	$ .10
Davis, Alvin	90UD	364	$ .01	$ .10
Davis, Alvin	91UD	457	$ .01	$ .05
Davis, Alvin	92UD	386	$ .01	$ .04
Davis, Chili	89UD	126	$ .01	$ .08
Davis, Chili	90UD	38	$ .01	$ .05
Davis, Chili	91UD	339	$ .01	$ .05
Davis, Chili	91UD	722	$ .01	$ .05
Davis, Chili	92UD	126	$ .01	$ .04
Davis, Chili	93UD	239	$ .01	$ .05
Davis, Eric	89UD	410	$ .05	$ .35
Davis, Eric	89UD	688	$ .05	$ .20
Davis, Eric	90UD	116	$ .01	$ .15
Davis, Eric	91UD	355	$ .01	$ .15
Davis, Eric	92UD	125	$ .01	$ .10
Davis, Eric	92UD	756	$ .01	$ .05
Davis, Glenn	89UD	443	$ .01	$ .15
Davis, Glenn	90UD	245	$ .01	$ .10
Davis, Glenn	91UD	81	$ .01	$ .05
Davis, Glenn	91UD	535	$ .01	$ .10
Davis, Glenn	91UD	757	$ .01	$ .10
Davis, Glenn	92UD	654	$ .01	$ .04
Davis, Glenn	93UD	353	$ .01	$ .05
Davis, Jody	89UD	148	$ .01	$ .08
Davis, Jody	90UD	429	$ .01	$ .05
Davis, John	89UD	548	$ .01	$ .08
Davis, Mark	89UD	268	$ .01	$ .08
Davis, Mark	90UD	431	$ .01	$ .05
Davis, Mark	90UD	710	$ .01	$ .05
Davis, Mark	91UD	589	$ .01	$ .05
Davis, Mark	92UD	607	$ .01	$ .04
Davis, Mike	89UD	146	$ .01	$ .08
Davis, Mike	90UD	258	$ .01	$ .05
Davis, Storm	89UD	153	$ .01	$ .08
Davis, Storm	90UD	292	$ .01	$ .05
Davis, Storm	90UD	712	$ .01	$ .05
Davis, Storm	91UD	639	$ .01	$ .05
Davis, Storm	92UD	499	$ .01	$ .04
Dawson, Andre	89UD	205	$ .10	$ .50
Dawson, Andre	90UD	73	$ .01	$ .15
Dawson, Andre	90UD	357	$ .01	$ .15
Dawson, Andre	91UD	454	$ .01	$ .15
Dawson, Andre	91UD	725	$ .01	$ .15
Dawson, Andre	91UDF	98	$ .01	$ .10
Dawson, Andre	92UD	124	$ .01	$ .10
Dawson, Andre	93UD	308	$ .01	$ .10
Dayley, Ken	89UD	114	$ .01	$ .08
Dayley, Ken	90UD	280	$ .01	$ .05
Dayley, Ken	91UD	628	$ .01	$ .05
Dayley, Ken	91UD	781	$ .01	$ .05
De Los Santos, Luis	89UD	12	$ .01	$ .10
Decker, Steve	91UD	25	$ .05	$ .25
Decker, Steve	92UD	173	$ .01	$ .15
Deer, Rob	89UD	442	$ .01	$ .08
Deer, Rob	90UD	176	$ .01	$ .05
Deer, Rob	91UD	272	$ .01	$ .05
Deer, Rob	91UD	726	$ .01	$ .05
Deer, Rob	92UD	294	$ .01	$ .04
Deer, Rob	93UD	217	$ .01	$ .05
DeJesus, Ivan	89UD	355	$ .01	$ .08
DeJesus, Jose	89UD	769	$ .01	$ .10
DeJesus, Jose	90UD	255	$ .01	$ .05
DeJesus, Jose	91UD	486	$ .01	$ .05
DeJesus, Jose	92UD	631	$ .01	$ .04
DeLeon, Jose	89UD	293	$ .01	$ .08
DeLeon, Jose	90UD	697	$ .01	$ .05
DeLeon, Jose	91UD	220	$ .01	$ .05
DeLeon, Jose	92UD	458	$ .01	$ .04
DeLucia, Rich	91UD	727	$ .01	$ .15
DeLucia, Rich	92UD	637	$ .01	$ .04
Dempsey, Rick	89UD	713	$ .01	$ .10
Dernier, Bob	89UD	340	$ .01	$ .08
Deshaies, Jim	89UD	76	$ .01	$ .08
Deshaies, Jim	90UD	221	$ .01	$ .05
Deshaies, Jim	91UD	208	$ .01	$ .05
Deshaies, Jim	92UD	297	$ .01	$ .04
DeShields, Delino	90UD	702	$ .10	$1.00
DeShields, Delino	90UD	746	$ .15	$1.50
DeShields, Delino	91UD	364	$ .05	$ .25
DeShields, Delino	92UD	36	$ .01	$ .04
DeShields, Delino	92UD	167	$ .01	$ .15
DeShields, Delino	93UD	142	$ .01	$ .15
Devereaux, Mike	89UD	68	$ .10	$ .50
Devereaux, Mike	90UD	681	$ .01	$ .05
Devereaux, Mike	91UD	308	$ .01	$ .05
Devereaux, Mike	92UD	209	$ .01	$ .04
Devereaux, Mike	93UD	167	$ .01	$ .05
Diaz, Bo	89UD	169	$ .01	$ .08
Diaz, Bo	90UD	664	$ .01	$ .05
Diaz, Edgar	91UD	286	$ .01	$ .05
Diaz, Mario	89UD	318	$ .01	$ .10
Diaz, Mike	89UD	606	$ .01	$ .08
Dibble, Rob	89UD	375	$ .10	$ .75
Dibble, Rob	90UD	586	$ .05	$ .20
Dibble, Rob	91UD	635	$ .01	$ .05
Dibble, Rob	92UD	30	$ .01	$ .04
Dibble, Rob	92UD	142	$ .01	$ .04
Dickson, Lance	91UD	9	$ .01	$ .15
Dickson, Lance	91UDF	3	$ .01	$ .15
DiPino, Frank	89UD	61	$ .01	$ .08
DiPino, Frank	90UD	202	$ .01	$ .05
DiPino, Frank	91UD	350	$ .01	$ .05
DiSarcina, Gary	90UD	761	$ .05	$ .35
DiSarcina, Gary	92UD	726	$ .01	$ .05
DiSarcina, Gary	93UD	230	$ .01	$ .05
Donnels, Chris	91UDF	61	$ .01	$ .10
Donnels, Chris	92UD	44	$ .01	$ .15
Dopson, John	89UD	57	$ .01	$ .10
Dopson, John	90UD	671	$ .01	$ .05
Dopson, John	91UD	88	$ .01	$ .05
Dopson, John	93UD	409	$ .01	$ .05
Doran, Bill	89UD	101	$ .01	$ .08
Doran, Bill	90UD	198	$ .01	$ .05
Doran, Bill	91UD	398	$ .01	$ .05

Glenn Davis

UPPER DECK

Player	Year	No.	VG	EX/MT
Doran, Bill	92UD	280	$ .01	$ .04
Doran, Bill	93UD	107	$ .01	$ .05
Dotson, Richard	89UD	80	$ .01	$ .08
Downing, Brian	89UD	485	$ .01	$ .08
Downing, Brian	90UD	146	$ .01	$ .05
Downing, Brian	91UD	231	$ .01	$ .05
Downing, Brian	91UD	770	$ .01	$ .05
Downing, Brian	92UD	483	$ .01	$ .04
Downs, Kelly	89UD	476	$ .01	$ .08
Downs, Kelly	90UD	699	$ .01	$ .05
Downs, Kelly	91UD	441	$ .01	$ .05
Downs, Kelly	92UD	583	$ .01	$ .04
Dozier, D. J.	91UD	3	$ .01	$ .15
Drabek, Doug	89UD	597	$ .01	$ .08
Drabek, Doug	90UD	422	$ .01	$ .05
Drabek, Doug	91UD	278	$ .01	$ .05
Drabek, Doug	92UD	39	$ .01	$ .04
Drabek, Doug	92UD	221	$ .01	$ .04
Dravecky, Dave	89UD	39	$ .01	$ .08
Dravecky, Dave	90UD	679	$ .01	$ .05
Drees, Tom	90UD	3	$ .01	$ .15
Dressendorfer, Kirk	91UD	756	$ .01	$ .15
Dressendorfer, Kirk	92UD	632	$ .01	$ .04
Drummond, Tim	91UD	698	$ .01	$ .15
DuBois, Brian	90UD	78	$ .01	$ .15
Ducey, Rob	89UD	721	$ .01	$ .10
Ducey, Rob	90UD	464	$ .01	$ .05
Duncan, Mariano	90UD	430	$ .01	$ .05
Duncan, Mariano	91UD	112	$ .01	$ .05
Duncan, Mariano	92UD	659	$ .01	$ .04
Duncan, Mariano	92UD	792	$ .01	$ .05
Duncan, Mariano	93UD	201	$ .01	$ .05
Dunne, Mike	89UD	518	$ .01	$ .08
Dunston, Shawon	89UD	107	$ .01	$ .10
Dunston, Shawon	90UD	231	$ .01	$ .10
Dunston, Shawon	91UD	111	$ .01	$ .05
Dunston, Shawon	92UD	35	$ .01	$ .04

Player	Year	No.	VG	EX/MT
Dunston, Shawon	**92UD**	**122**	**$ .01**	**$ .04**
Dunston, Shawon	92UD	714	$ .01	$ .05
Dunston, Shawon	93UD	101	$ .01	$ .05
Durham, Leon	89UD	354	$ .01	$ .08
Dyer, Mike	90UD	374	$ .01	$ .15
Dykstra, Len	89UD	369	$ .01	$ .10
Dykstra, Len	90UD	472	$ .01	$ .10

Player	Year	No.	VG	EX/MT
Dykstra, Lenny	91UD	97	$ .01	$ .05
Dykstra, Lenny	91UD	267	$ .01	$ .05
Dykstra, Lenny	92UD	246	$ .01	$ .04
Dykstra, Lenny	93UD	69	$ .01	$ .05
Easley, Damion	93UD	377	$ .05	$ .25
Eckersley, Dennis	89UD	289	$ .10	$ .40
Eckersley, Dennis	89UD	664	$ .01	$ .15
Eckersley, Dennis	90UD	513	$ .05	$ .20
Eckersley, Dennis	91UD	172	$ .01	$ .15
Eckersley, Dennis	92UD	331	$ .01	$ .10
Eckersley, Dennis	93UD	271	$ .01	$ .10
Edens, Tom	91UD	616	$ .01	$ .10
Edwards, Wayne	90UD	762	$ .01	$ .10
Edwards, Wayne	91UD	697	$ .01	$ .05
Eenhoorn, Robert	91UDF	16	$ .01	$ .15
Eichhorn, Mark	91UD	519	$ .01	$ .05
Eichhorn, Mark	92UD	287	$ .01	$ .04
Eisenreich, Jim	89UD	44	$ .01	$ .08
Eisenreich, Jim	90UD	294	$ .01	$ .05
Eisenreich, Jim	91UD	658	$ .01	$ .05
Eisenreich, Jim	92UD	539	$ .01	$ .04
Eldred, Cal	92UD	477	$ .10	$ .40
Eldred, Cal	93UD	375	$ .05	$ .25
Elster, Kevin	89UD	269	$ .01	$ .08
Elster, Kevin	90UD	187	$ .01	$ .05
Elster, Kevin	91UD	101	$ .01	$ .05
Elster, Kevin	92UD	385	$ .01	$ .04
Elvira, Narciso	91UD	13	$ .01	$ .15
Embree, Alan	93UD	12	$ .05	$ .35
Eppard, Jim	89UD	614	$ .01	$ .10
Ericks, John	91UD	57	$ .01	$ .15
Erickson, Scott	91UD	522	$ .10	$ .40
Erickson, Scott	92UD	89	$ .01	$ .10
Erickson, Scott	92UD	146	$ .01	$ .10
Erickson, Scott	93UD	397	$ .01	$ .05
Esasky, Nick	89UD	299	$ .01	$ .08
Esasky, Nick	89UD	757	$ .01	$ .10
Esasky, Nick	90UD	463	$ .01	$ .05
Esasky, Nick	90UD	758	$ .01	$ .05
Espinoza, Alvaro	90UD	163	$ .01	$ .10
Espinoza, Alvaro	91UD	204	$ .01	$ .05
Espinoza, Alvaro	92UD	119	$ .01	$ .04
Espy, Cecil	89UD	92	$ .01	$ .15
Espy, Cecil	90UD	371	$ .01	$ .05
Evans, Darrell	89UD	394	$ .01	$ .08
Evans, Darrell	90UD	143	$ .01	$ .05
Evans, Dwight	89UD	366	$ .01	$ .08
Evans, Dwight	90UD	112	$ .01	$ .05
Evans, Dwight	91UD	549	$ .01	$ .05
Evans, Dwight	91UD	776	$ .01	$ .05
Evans, Dwight	92UD	248	$ .01	$ .04
Exchange, Pacific Sock	93UD	55	$ .05	$ .25
Family, Royal	93UD	54	$ .01	$ .15
Faries, Paul	91UD	751	$ .01	$ .10
Faries, Paul	92UD	310	$ .01	$ .04
Fariss, Monty	92UD	462	$ .01	$ .15
Farmer, Howard	90UD	753	$ .01	$ .15
Farmer, Howard	91UD	362	$ .01	$ .10
Farr, Steve	89UD	308	$ .01	$ .08
Farr, Steve	90UD	680	$ .01	$ .05
Farr, Steve	91UD	660	$ .01	$ .05
Farr, Steve	91UD	717	$ .01	$ .05
Farr, Steve	92UD	48	$ .01	$ .04
Farr, Steve	93UD	410	$ .01	$ .05
Farrell, John	89UD	468	$ .01	$ .10
Farrell, John	90UD	570	$ .01	$ .05
Farrell, John	91UD	692	$ .01	$ .05
Farrell, Jon	92UD	69	$ .01	$ .10
Fassero, Jeff	92UD	685	$ .01	$ .10
Felder, Mike	89UD	252	$ .01	$ .08
Felder, Mike	90UD	178	$ .01	$ .05
Felder, Mike	91UD	395	$ .01	$ .05
Felder, Mike	92UD	288	$ .01	$ .04
Felder, Mike	93UD	186	$ .01	$ .05
Felix, Junior	89UD	743	$ .10	$ .50

UPPER DECK

Player	Year	No.	VG	EX/MT
Felix, Junior	90UD	106	$.01	$.10
Felix, Junior	91UD	563	$.01	$.15
Felix, Junior	91UD	711	$.01	$.05
Felix, Junior	92UD	303	$.01	$.04
Felix, Junior	93UD	157	$.01	$.05
Fermin, Felix	89UD	88	$.01	$.08
Fermin, Felix	90UD	409	$.01	$.05
Fermin, Felix	91UD	104	$.01	$.05
Fermin, Felix	92UD	160	$.01	$.04
Fernandez, Alex	91UD	645	$.05	$.25
Fernandez, Alex	92UD	551	$.01	$.15
Fernandez, Alex	93UD	362	$.01	$.05
Fernandez, Sid	89UD	168	$.01	$.15
Fernandez, Sid	90UD	261	$.01	$.05
Fernandez, Sid	91UD	242	$.01	$.05
Fernandez, Sid	92UD	671	$.01	$.04
Fernandez, Sid	93UD	361	$.01	$.05
Fernandez, Tony	89UD	139	$.01	$.15
Fernandez, Tony	90UD	130	$.01	$.10
Fernandez, Tony	91UD	126	$.01	$.05
Fernandez, Tony	91UD	754	$.01	$.05
Fernandez, Tony	92UD	272	$.01	$.04
Fetters, Mike	90UD	742	$.01	$.15
Fetters, Mike	91UD	696	$.01	$.15
Fetters, Mike	93UD	193	$.01	$.05
Fielder, Cecil	89UD	364	$.10	$1.00
Fielder, Cecil	90UD	786	$.10	$.40
Fielder, Cecil	91UD	83	$.05	$.20
Fielder, Cecil	91UD	244	$.05	$.25
Fielder, Cecil	91UDF	82	$.01	$.15
Fielder, Cecil	92UD	96	$.01	$.10
Fielder, Cecil	92UD	255	$.01	$.15
Fielder, Cecil	92UD	647	$.01	$.15
Fielder, Cecil	93UD	46	$.01	$.15
Fields, Bruce	89UD	238	$.01	$.08
Finley, Chuck	89UD	632	$.01	$.15
Finley, Chuck	90UD	667	$.01	$.15
Finley, Chuck	91UD	31	$.01	$.05
Finley, Chuck	91UD	437	$.01	$.05
Finley, Chuck	92UD	244	$.01	$.04
Finley, Chuck	93UD	53	$.01	$.10
Finley, Chuck	93UD	77	$.01	$.05
Finley, Steve	89UD	742	$.10	$1.00
Finley, Steve	90UD	602	$.01	$.15
Finley, Steve	91UD	330	$.01	$.05
Finley, Steve	91UD	794	$.01	$.05
Finley, Steve	92UD	368	$.01	$.04
Finley, Steve	93UD	231	$.01	$.05
Firova, Dan	89UD	32	$.01	$.08
Fisher, Brian	89UD	69	$.01	$.08
Fisher, Brian	90UD	97	$.01	$.05
Fisk, Carlton	89UD	609	$.10	$.50
Fisk, Carlton	90UD	367	$.01	$.15
Fisk, Carlton	91UD	29	$.01	$.10
Fisk, Carlton	91UD	643	$.01	$.15
Fisk, Carlton	92UD	571	$.01	$.10
Fisk, Carlton	93UD	272	$.01	$.10
Fitzgerald, Mike	89UD	133	$.01	$.08
Fitzgerald, Mike	90UD	558	$.01	$.05
Fitzgerald, Mike	91UD	516	$.01	$.05
Fitzgerald, Mike	92UD	210	$.01	$.04
Flanagan, Mike	89UD	385	$.01	$.08
Flanagan, Mike	90UD	483	$.01	$.05
Flanagan, Mike	92UD	380	$.01	$.04
Flannery, Tim	89UD	603	$.01	$.08
Fleming, Dave	92UD	4	$.05	$.35
Fleming, Dave	93UD	141	$.05	$.20
Fletcher, Darrin	91UD	428	$.01	$.10
Fletcher, Darrin	92UD	108	$.01	$.04
Fletcher, Scott	89UD	420	$.01	$.08
Fletcher, Scott	90UD	310	$.01	$.05
Fletcher, Scott	91UD	321	$.01	$.05
Fletcher, Scott	92UD	186	$.01	$.04
Foley, Tom	89UD	441	$.01	$.08
Foley, Tom	90UD	489	$.01	$.05
Foley, Tom	91UD	381	$.01	$.05
Foley, Tom	92UD	492	$.01	$.04
Ford, Curt	89UD	309	$.01	$.08
Ford, Curt	90UD	490	$.01	$.05
Fordyce, Brook	91UD	64	$.01	$.15
Fossas, Tony	92UD	503	$.01	$.04
Franco, John	89UD	407	$.01	$.15
Franco, John	90UD	139	$.01	$.05
Franco, John	90UD	709	$.01	$.05
Franco, John	91UD	290	$.01	$.05
Franco, John	92UD	514	$.01	$.04
Franco, John	93UD	321	$.01	$.05
Franco, Julio	89UD	186	$.05	$.20
Franco, Julio	89UD	793	$.01	$.10
Franco, Julio	90UD	82	$.01	$.10
Franco, Julio	90UD	103	$.01	$.10
Franco, Julio	91UD	227	$.01	$.10
Franco, Julio	92UD	241	$.01	$.10
Francona, Terry	89UD	536	$.01	$.08
Francona, Terry	90UD	180	$.01	$.05
Fraser, Willie	89UD	613	$.01	$.08
Fraser, Willie	90UD	85	$.01	$.05
Fraser, Willie	91UD	699	$.01	$.05
Freeman, LaVel	89UD	788	$.01	$.10
Freeman, Marvin	92UD	491	$.01	$.04
Frey, Steve	91UD	397	$.01	$.05
Frohwirth, Todd	90UD	443	$.01	$.05
Frohwirth, Todd	92UD	318	$.01	$.04
Frohwirth, Todd	93UD	191	$.01	$.05
Frye, Jeff	93UD	371	$.01	$.05
Fryman, Travis	91UD	225	$.20	$2.00
Fryman, Travis	92UD	466	$.10	$.40
Fryman, Travis	92UD	643	$.05	$.20
Fryman, Travis	93UD	364	$.05	$.35
Gaetti, Gary	89UD	203	$.01	$.15
Gaetti, Gary	90UD	454	$.01	$.15
Gaetti, Gary	91UD	34	$.01	$.05
Gaetti, Gary	91UD	233	$.01	$.05
Gaetti, Gary	91UD	731	$.01	$.05
Gaetti, Gary	92UD	321	$.01	$.04
Gaetti, Gary	93UD	370	$.01	$.05
Gagne, Greg	89UD	166	$.01	$.08
Gagne, Greg	90UD	217	$.01	$.05

Travis Fryman

UPPER DECK

Player	Year	No.	VG	EX/MT	Player	Year	No.	VG	EX/MT
Gagne, Greg	91UD	415	$ .01	$ .05	Glavine, Tom	90UD	571	$ .10	$ .50
Gagne, Greg	92UD	168	$ .01	$ .04	Glavine, Tom	91UD	480	$ .05	$ .35
Galarraga, Andres	89UD	115	$ .01	$ .15	Glavine, Tom	91UDF	90	$ .10	$ .50
Galarraga, Andres	89UD	677	$ .01	$ .10	Glavine, Tom	92UD	342	$ .05	$ .20
Galarraga, Andres	90UD	356	$ .01	$ .05	Glavine, Tom	92UD	713	$ .01	$ .15
Galarraga, Andres	91UD	456	$ .01	$ .05	Glavine, Tom	93UD	75	$ .05	$ .20
Galarraga, Andres	92UD	474	$ .01	$ .04	Gleaton, Jerry Don	92UD	601	$ .01	$ .04
Galarraga, Andres	92UD	758	$ .01	$ .05	Gomez, Leo	91UD	6	$ .10	$ .50
Gallagher, Dave	89UD	164	$ .01	$ .15	Gomez, Leo	92UD	161	$ .01	$ .15
Gallagher, Dave	90UD	328	$ .01	$ .05	Gomez, Leo	93UD	132	$ .01	$ .05
Gallagher, Dave	91UD	508	$ .01	$ .05	Gonzales, Rene	92UD	729	$ .01	$ .05
Gallagher, Dave	92UD	289	$ .01	$ .04	Gonzales, Rene	93UD	188	$ .01	$ .05
Gallego, Mike	89UD	583	$ .01	$ .08	Gonzalez, German	90UD	352	$ .01	$ .10
Gallego, Mike	90UD	230	$ .01	$ .05	Gonzalez, Jose	89UD	626	$ .01	$ .08
Gallego, Mike	91UD	151	$ .01	$ .05	Gonzalez, Jose	90UD	666	$ .01	$ .10
Gallego, Mike	92UD	193	$ .01	$ .04	Gonzalez, Juan	90UD	72	$2.00	$8.00
Gallego, Mike	92UD	750	$ .01	$ .05	Gonzalez, Juan	91UD	646	$ .10	$1.00
Gant, Ron	89UD	378	$ .15	$1.50	Gonzalez, Juan	92UD	243	$ .10	$ .50
Gant, Ron	90UD	232	$ .10	$ .50	Gonzalez, Juan	93UD	52	$ .05	$ .35
Gant, Ron	91UD	82	$ .01	$ .10	Gonzalez, Luis	91UD	567	$ .10	$ .50
Gant, Ron	91UD	361	$ .05	$ .20	Gonzalez, Luis	91UD	702	$ .10	$ .50
Gant, Ron	92UD	345	$ .01	$ .15	Gonzalez, Luis	92UD	372	$ .05	$ .20
Gant, Ron	93UD	264	$ .01	$ .05	Gooden, Dwight	89UD	565	$ .05	$ .35
Gantner, Jim	89UD	274	$ .01	$ .08	Gooden, Dwight	90UD	62	$ .01	$ .10
Gantner, Jim	90UD	218	$ .01	$ .05	Gooden, Dwight	90UD	114	$ .01	$ .15
Gantner, Jim	91UD	618	$ .01	$ .05	Gooden, Dwight	91UD	224	$ .01	$ .10
Gantner, Jim	92UD	360	$ .01	$ .04	Gooden, Dwight	92UD	84	$ .01	$ .10
Garces, Rich	91UD	741	$ .01	$ .10	Gooden, Dwight	92UD	135	$ .01	$ .10
Garcia, Carlos	92UD	665	$ .05	$ .20	Goodwin, Tom	91UDF	9	$ .05	$ .20
Garcia, Carlos	93UD	334	$ .01	$ .05	Goodwin, Tom	92UD	20	$ .01	$ .10
Garcia, Damaso	90UD	649	$ .01	$ .05	Gordon, Tom	89UD	736	$ .05	$ .25
Garcia, Miguel	90UD	538	$ .01	$ .05	Gordon, Tom	90UD	365	$ .05	$ .25
Gardiner, Mike	91UD	14	$ .01	$ .15	Gordon, Tom	91UD	431	$ .01	$ .05
Gardiner, Mike	92UD	588	$ .01	$ .04	Gordon, Tom	92UD	476	$ .01	$ .04
Gardner, Mark	90UD	743	$ .05	$ .20	Gordon, Tom	93UD	221	$ .01	$ .05
Gardner, Mark	91UD	663	$ .01	$ .15	Gossage, Goose	89UD	452	$ .01	$ .08
Gardner, Mark	92UD	557	$ .01	$ .04	Gott, Jim	89UD	539	$ .01	$ .08
Gardner, Mark	93UD	348	$ .01	$ .05	Gott, Jim	90UD	89	$ .01	$ .05
Gardner, Wes	91UD	214	$ .01	$ .05	Gott, Jim	90UD	701	$ .01	$ .05
Garrelts, Scott	89UD	50	$ .01	$ .08	Gott, Jim	91UD	690	$ .01	$ .05
Garrelts, Scott	90UD	478	$ .01	$ .05	Grace, Mark	89UD	140	$ .10	$1.00
Garrelts, Scott	91UD	443	$ .01	$ .05	Grace, Mark	90UD	128	$ .05	$ .35
Gedman, Rich	89UD	368	$ .01	$ .08					
Gedman, Rich	90UD	402	$ .01	$ .05					
Gedman, Rich	91UD	588	$ .01	$ .05					
George, Chris	92UD	9	$ .01	$ .15					
Geren, Bob	90UD	608	$ .01	$ .10					
Geren, Bob	91UD	202	$ .01	$ .05					
Gerhart, Ken	89UD	426	$ .01	$ .08					
Gibson, Kirk	89UD	633	$ .01	$ .15					
Gibson, Kirk	89UD	662	$ .01	$ .15					
Gibson, Kirk	89UD	666	$ .01	$ .15					
Gibson, Kirk	89UD	676	$ .01	$ .10					
Gibson, Kirk	90UD	264	$ .01	$ .05					
Gibson, Kirk	91UD	634	$ .01	$ .10					
Gibson, Kirk	91UD	737	$ .01	$ .05					
Gibson, Kirk	92UD	180	$ .01	$ .04					
Gibson, Paul	89UD	47	$ .01	$ .15					
Gibson, Paul	90UD	496	$ .01	$ .05					
Gibson, Paul	91UD	579	$ .01	$ .05					
Gibson, Paul	92UD	489	$ .01	$ .04					
Gilkey, Bernard	91UD	16	$ .05	$ .20					
Gilkey, Bernard	92UD	552	$ .01	$ .04					
Gilkey, Bernard	93UD	394	$ .01	$ .05					
Girardi, Joe	89UD	776	$ .05	$ .25					
Girardi, Joe	90UD	304	$ .01	$ .10					
Girardi, Joe	91UD	113	$ .01	$ .05					
Girardi, Joe	92UD	351	$ .01	$ .04					
Gladden, Dan	89UD	400	$ .01	$ .08					
Gladden, Dan	90UD	238	$ .01	$ .05					
Gladden, Dan	91UD	659	$ .01	$ .05					
Gladden, Dan	92UD	332	$ .01	$ .04					
Gladden, Dan	92UD	737	$ .01	$ .05					
Gladden, Dan	93UD	251	$ .01	$ .05					
Glavine, Tom	89UD	360	$ .20	$2.00	Grace, Mark	91UD	99	$ .01	$ .05

UPPER DECK

Player	Year	No.	VG	EX/MT
Grace, Mark	91UD	134	$ .01	$ .15
Grace, Mark	92UD	143	$ .01	$ .10
Grahe, Joe	91UD	657	$ .05	$ .25
Grahe, Joe	92UD	542	$ .01	$ .04
Grahe, Joe	93UD	290	$ .01	$ .05
Grant, Mark	89UD	622	$ .01	$ .08
Grant, Mark	90UD	412	$ .01	$ .05
Grant, Mark	91UD	301	$ .01	$ .05
Gray, Jeff	91UD	685	$ .01	$ .10
Grebeck, Craig	90UD	721	$ .05	$ .25
Grebeck, Craig	92UD	603	$ .01	$ .04
Green, Gary	89UD	722	$ .01	$ .10
Green, Shawn	92UD	55	$ .05	$ .35
Green, Tyler	92UD	68	$ .05	$ .35
Greene, Tommy	90UD	49	$ .10	$ .50
Greene, Tommy	91UDF	62	$ .01	$ .10
Greene, Tommy	92UD	567	$ .01	$ .04
Greene, Willie	93UD	4	$ .05	$ .25
Greenwell, Mike	89UD	432	$ .01	$ .15
Greenwell, Mike	90UD	354	$ .01	$ .15
Greenwell, Mike	91UD	43	$ .01	$ .05
Greenwell, Mike	91UD	165	$ .01	$ .15
Greenwell, Mike	92UD	275	$ .01	$ .10
Greenwell, Mike	93UD	154	$ .01	$ .05
Gregg, Tommy	89UD	751	$ .01	$ .10
Gregg, Tommy	90UD	121	$ .01	$ .10
Griffey, Craig	92UD	85	$ .10	$ .50
Griffey, Jr., Ken	89UD	1	$13.75	$55.00
Griffey, Jr., Ken	90UD	24	$ .10	$ .50
Griffey, Jr., Ken	90UD	156	$1.00	$4.00
Griffey, Jr., Ken	91UD	555	$ .10	$1.00
Griffey, Jr., Ken	91UDF	79	$ .05	$ .35
Griffey, Jr., Ken	91UDF	87	$ .10	$ .50
Griffey, Jr., Ken	92UD	85	$ .10	$ .50
Griffey, Jr., Ken	92UD	424	$ .10	$ .75
Griffey, Jr., Ken	92UD	650	$ .05	$ .35
Griffey, Jr., Ken	93UD	55	$ .05	$ .25
Griffey, Jr., Ken	93UD	355	$ .10	$ .50

Ken Griffey Sr.

Player	Year	No.	VG	EX/MT
Griffey Sr., Ken	**90UD**	**682**	**$ .01**	**$ .10**
Griffey Sr., Ken	91UD	572	$ .05	$ .25
Griffey Sr., Ken	92UD	85	$ .10	$ .50
Griffey Sr., Ken	92UD	335	$ .01	$ .04
Griffin, Alfredo	89UD	631	$ .01	$ .10
Griffin, Alfredo	90UD	338	$ .01	$ .05

Player	Year	No.	VG	EX/MT
Griffin, Alfredo	91UD	119	$ .01	$ .05
Griffin, Alfredo	92UD	282	$ .01	$ .04
Grimsley, Jason	90UD	27	$ .05	$ .20
Grimsley, Jason	92UD	406	$ .01	$ .04
Grissom, Marquis	90UD	9	$ .15	$1.50
Grissom, Marquis	90UD	702	$ .10	$1.00
Grissom, Marquis	91UD	477	$ .05	$ .25
Grissom, Marquis	92UD	455	$ .01	$ .10
Grissom, Marquis	92UD	719	$ .01	$ .10
Grissom, Marquis	93UD	356	$ .01	$ .15
Gross, Greg	89UD	534	$ .01	$ .08
Gross, Kevin	89UD	31	$ .01	$ .08
Gross, Kevin	89UD	719	$ .01	$ .10
Gross, Kevin	90UD	468	$ .01	$ .05
Gross, Kevin	91UD	380	$ .01	$ .05
Gross, Kevin	91UD	713	$ .01	$ .05
Gross, Kevin	92UD	515	$ .01	$ .04
Gross, Kevin	93UD	198	$ .01	$ .05
Ground Breaking, Comiskey Park II	91UD	677	$ .05	$ .20
Gruber, Kelly	89UD	575	$ .01	$ .15
Gruber, Kelly	90UD	111	$ .01	$ .15
Gruber, Kelly	91UD	44	$ .01	$ .05
Gruber, Kelly	91UD	374	$ .01	$ .05
Gruber, Kelly	92UD	324	$ .01	$ .04
Gruber, Kelly	93UD	406	$ .01	$ .05
Guante, Cecilio	89UD	576	$ .01	$ .08
Gubicza, Mark	89UD	202	$ .01	$ .10
Gubicza, Mark	90UD	676	$ .01	$ .05
Gubicza, Mark	91UD	541	$ .01	$ .05
Gubicza, Mark	92UD	459	$ .01	$ .04
Gubicza, Mark	93UD	85	$ .01	$ .05
Guerrero, Pedro	89UD	306	$ .01	$ .08
Guerrero, Pedro(Guerrero)	90UD	244	$ .01	$ .10
Guerrero, Pedro	91UD	98	$ .01	$ .05
Guerrero, Pedro	91UD	327	$ .01	$ .05
Guerrero, Pedro	92UD	357	$ .01	$ .04
Guetterman, Lee	90UD	318	$ .01	$ .05
Guetterman, Lee	91UD	481	$ .01	$ .05
Guetterman, Lee	92UD	610	$ .01	$ .04
Guidry, Ron	89UD	307	$ .01	$ .08
Guillen, Ozzie	89UD	175	$ .01	$ .10
Guillen, Ozzie	90UD	79	$ .01	$ .05
Guillen, Ozzie	90UD	267	$ .01	$ .05
Guillen, Ozzie	91UD	325	$ .01	$ .05
Guillen, Ozzie	92UD	436	$ .01	$ .04
Guillen, Ozzie	93UD	139	$ .01	$ .05
Gullickson, Bill	90UD	799	$ .01	$ .05
Gullickson, Bill	91UD	590	$ .01	$ .05
Gullickson, Bill	92UD	317	$ .01	$ .04
Gullickson, Bill	93UD	398	$ .01	$ .05
Gunderson, Eric	90UD	752	$ .05	$ .20
Gunderson, Eric	91UD	315	$ .01	$ .15
Guthrie, Mark	90UD	436	$ .01	$ .15
Guthrie, Mark	91UD	505	$ .01	$ .05
Guthrie, Mark	92UD	604	$ .01	$ .04
Guthrie, Mark	93UD	099	$ .01	$ .05
Gutierrez, Jackie	89UD	430	$ .01	$ .08
Guzman, Jose	89UD	73	$ .01	$ .08
Guzman, Jose	90UD	617	$ .01	$ .05
Guzman, Jose	92UD	204	$ .01	$ .04
Guzman, Jose	93UD	323	$ .01	$ .10
Guzman, Juan	92UD	625	$ .10	$ .75
Guzman, Juan	93UD	266	$ .05	$ .25
Gwynn, Chris	89UD	607	$ .01	$ .08
Gwynn, Chris	90UD	526	$ .01	$ .05
Gwynn, Chris	91UD	560	$ .01	$ .05
Gwynn, Chris	92UD	83	$ .01	$ .10
Gwynn, Chris	92UD	689	$ .01	$ .04
Gwynn, Tony	89UD	384	$ .10	$1.00
Gwynn, Tony	89UD	683	$ .05	$ .20
Gwynn, Tony	90UD	344	$ .05	$ .35
Gwynn, Tony	91UD	255	$ .01	$ .15
Gwynn, Tony	91UDF	97	$ .01	$ .15
Gwynn, Tony	92UD	83	$ .01	$ .10

UPPER DECK

Player	Year	No.	VG	EX/MT
Gwynn, Tony	92UD	274	$ .01	$ .10
Gwynn, Tony	92UD	717	$ .01	$ .10
Gwynn, Tony	93UD	165	$ .01	$ .15
Hale, Chip	90UD	475	$ .01	$ .15
Hall, Albert	89UD	93	$ .01	$ .08

Drew Hall

Player	Year	No.	VG	EX/MT
Hall, Drew	89UD	324	$ .01	$ .08
Hall, Drew	90UD	631	$ .01	$ .05
Hall, Mel	89UD	538	$ .01	$ .08
Hall, Mel	89UD	729	$ .01	$ .10
Hall, Mel	90UD	458	$ .01	$ .05
Hall, Mel	91UD	392	$ .01	$ .05
Hall, Mel	92UD	291	$ .01	$ .04
Hall, Mel	93UD	291	$ .01	$ .05
Hamelin, Bob	90UD	45	$ .01	$ .15
Hamilton, Darryl	89UD	301	$ .10	$ .40
Hamilton, Darryl	91UD	42	$ .01	$ .05
Hamilton, Darryl	92UD	460	$ .01	$ .04
Hamilton, Darryl	93UD	192	$ .01	$ .05
Hamilton, Jeff	89UD	615	$ .01	$ .08
Hamilton, Jeff	90UD	296	$ .01	$ .05
Hamilton, Jeff	91UD	779	$ .01	$ .05
Hamilton, Joey	92UD	67	$ .10	$ .50
Hammaker, Atlee	89UD	544	$ .01	$ .08
Hammaker, Atlee	90UD	620	$ .01	$ .05
Hammond, Chris	90UD	52	$ .05	$ .35
Hammond, Chris	91UD	748	$ .01	$ .10
Hammond, Chris	92UD	105	$ .01	$ .04
Hammond, Chris	93UD	216	$ .01	$ .05
Haney, Chris	91UDF	23	$ .01	$ .15
Haney, Chris	92UD	662	$ .01	$ .10
Hansen, Dave	91UD	4	$ .01	$ .15
Hanson, Erik	89UD	766	$ .10	$ .50
Hanson, Erik	90UD	235	$ .01	$ .15
Hanson, Erik	91UD	551	$ .01	$ .10
Hanson, Erik	92UD	572	$ .01	$ .04
Hanson, Erik	93UD	338	$ .01	$ .05
Harkey, Mike	89UD	14	$ .01	$ .15
Harkey, Mike	90UD	107	$ .01	$ .15
Harkey, Mike	91UD	475	$ .01	$ .05
Harkey, Mike	92UD	218	$ .01	$ .04
Harnisch, Pete	89UD	744	$ .10	$ .50
Harnisch, Pete	90UD	623	$ .01	$ .10
Harnisch, Pete	91UD	302	$ .01	$ .05
Harnisch, Pete	91UD	772	$ .01	$ .05
Harnisch, Pete	92UD	635	$ .01	$ .04
Harnisch, Pete	93UD	97	$ .01	$ .05
Harper, Brian	89UD	379	$ .01	$ .15
Harper, Brian	90UD	391	$ .01	$ .05
Harper, Brian	91UD	212	$ .01	$ .05
Harper, Brian	92UD	527	$ .01	$ .04
Harper, Brian	93UD	110	$ .01	$ .05
Harris, Donald	92UD	11	$ .01	$ .15
Harris, Gene	90UD	565	$ .01	$ .10
Harris, Greg A.	91UD	509	$ .01	$ .05
Harris, Greg A.	92UD	658	$ .01	$ .04
Harris, Greg A.	93UD	414	$ .01	$ .05
Harris, Greg W.	89UD	724	$ .05	$ .25
Harris, Greg W.	90UD	622	$ .01	$ .10
Harris, Greg W.	91UD	489	$ .01	$ .05
Harris, Greg W.	92UD	306	$ .01	$ .04
Harris, Lenny	89UD	781	$ .05	$ .20
Harris, Lenny	90UD	423	$ .01	$ .10
Harris, Lenny	91UD	239	$ .01	$ .05
Harris, Lenny	92UD	191	$ .01	$ .04
Harris, Lenny	93UD	184	$ .01	$ .05
Harris, Reggie	91UD	672	$ .01	$ .15
Hartley, Mike	91UD	686	$ .01	$ .10
Hartley, Mike	92UD	613	$ .01	$ .04
Harvey, Bryan	89UD	594	$ .10	$ .50
Harvey, Bryan	90UD	686	$ .01	$ .05
Harvey, Bryan	91UD	592	$ .01	$ .05
Harvey, Bryan	92UD	434	$ .01	$ .04
Hassey, Ron	89UD	564	$ .01	$ .08
Hassey, Ron	90UD	195	$ .01	$ .05
Hassey, Ron	91UD	401	$ .01	$ .05
Hatcher, Billy	89UD	344	$ .01	$ .08
Hatcher, Billy	90UD	598	$ .01	$ .05
Hatcher, Billy	90UD	778	$ .01	$ .05
Hatcher, Billy	91UD	114	$ .01	$ .05
Hatcher, Billy	92UD	699	$ .01	$ .04
Hatcher, Mickey	89UD	709	$ .01	$ .10
Hatcher, Mickey	90UD	283	$ .01	$ .05
Hatcher, Mickey	91UD	666	$ .01	$ .05
Hawblitzel, Ryan	92UD	59	$ .05	$ .25
Hawkins, Andy	89UD	495	$ .01	$ .08
Hawkins, Andy	89UD	708	$ .01	$ .10
Hawkins, Andy	90UD	339	$ .01	$ .05
Hawkins, Andy	91UD	333	$ .01	$ .05
Hayes, Charlie	89UD	707	$ .10	$ .40
Hayes, Charlie	90UD	437	$ .01	$ .10
Hayes, Charlie	91UD	269	$ .01	$ .05
Hayes, Charlie	92UD	208	$ .01	$ .04
Hayes, Charlie	92UD	768	$ .01	$ .05
Hayes, Von	89UD	246	$ .01	$ .10
Hayes, Von	90UD	7	$ .01	$ .05
Hayes, Von	90UD	453	$ .01	$ .05
Hayes, Von	91UD	368	$ .01	$ .05
Hayes, Von	92UD	427	$ .01	$ .04
Hayes, Von	92UD	707	$ .01	$ .05
Header, HOF	91UDH	4	$3.50	$14.00
Hearn, Ed	89UD	42	$ .01	$ .08
Heath, Mike	89UD	654	$ .01	$ .08
Heath, Mike	90UD	306	$ .01	$ .05
Heath, Mike	91UD	318	$ .01	$ .05
Heath, Mike	91UD	701	$ .01	$ .05
Heath, Mike	92UD	304	$ .01	$ .04
Heaton, Neal	89UD	99	$ .01	$ .08
Heaton, Neal	90UD	86	$ .01	$ .05
Heaton, Neal	91UD	36	$ .01	$ .05
Heaton, Neal	92UD	417	$ .01	$ .04
Hemond, Scott	90UD	727	$ .01	$ .15
Henderson, Dave	89UD	174	$ .01	$ .15
Henderson, Dave	90UD	206	$ .01	$ .10
Henderson, Dave	91UD	108	$ .01	$ .05
Henderson, Dave	91UDF	88	$ .01	$ .05
Henderson, Dave	92UD	172	$ .01	$ .04
Henderson, Rickey	89UD	210	$ .10	$1.00
Henderson, Rickey	90UD	334	$ .05	$ .35

UPPER DECK

Player	Year	No.	VG	EX/MT
Henderson, Rickey	91UD	444	$ .05	$ .25
Henderson, Rickey	91UD	636	$ .05	$ .25
Henderson, Rickey	91UDF	86	$ .05	$ .20
Henderson, Rickey	91UDSP	2	$1.00	$4.00
Henderson, Rickey	92UD	90	$ .01	$ .10
Henderson, Rickey	92UD	155	$ .01	$ .15
Henderson, Rickey	92UD	640	$ .01	$ .15

Player	Year	No.	VG	EX/MT
Henderson, Rickey	92UD	648	$ .01	$ .15
Henderson, Rickey	92UD	782	$ .01	$ .15
Henderson, Rickey	93UD	136	$ .01	$ .10
Henke, Tom	89UD	264	$ .01	$ .08
Henke, Tom	90UD	282	$ .01	$ .05
Henke, Tom	91UD	149	$ .01	$ .05
Henke, Tom	92UD	395	$ .01	$ .04
Henneman, Mike	89UD	373	$ .01	$ .08
Henneman, Mike	90UD	537	$ .01	$ .05
Henneman, Mike	91UD	386	$ .01	$ .05
Henneman, Mike	92UD	339	$ .01	$ .04
Henneman, Mike	93UD	403	$ .01	$ .05
Henry, Butch	92UD	796	$ .01	$ .05
Henry, Doug	92UD	43	$ .01	$ .10
Henry, Doug	93UD	395	$ .01	$ .05
Henry, Dwayne	89UD	51	$ .01	$ .08
Henry, Dwayne	92UD	430	$ .01	$ .04
Hernandez, Carlos	92UD	707	$ .01	$ .05
Hernandez, Carlos	93UD	148	$ .01	$ .05
Hernandez, Guillermo	89UD	279	$ .01	$ .08
Hernandez, Guillermo	90UD	518	$ .01	$ .05
Hernandez, Jeremy	92UD	42	$ .01	$ .10
Hernandez, Keith	89UD	612	$ .01	$ .10
Hernandez, Keith	90UD	222	$ .01	$ .05
Hernandez, Keith	90UD	777	$ .01	$ .05
Hernandez, Roberto	92UD	7	$ .01	$ .10
Hernandez, Roberto	93UD	352	$ .01	$ .05
Hernandez, Xavier	90UD	26	$ .01	$ .15
Hernandez, Xavier	93UD	319	$ .01	$ .05
Herndon, Larry	89UD	49	$ .01	$ .08
Herr, Tommy	89UD	558	$ .01	$ .08
Herr, Tommy	89UD	720	$ .01	$ .10
Herr, Tommy	90UD	488	$ .01	$ .05
Herr, Tom	91UD	416	$ .01	$ .05
Hershiser, Orel	89UD	130	$ .01	$ .10
Hershiser, Orel	89UD	661	$ .01	$ .15
Hershiser, Orel	89UD	665	$ .01	$ .15
Hershiser, Orel	89UD	667	$ .01	$ .15
Hershiser, Orel	90UD	10	$ .01	$ .05
Hershiser, Orel	90UD	256	$ .01	$ .10
Hershiser, Orel	91UD	524	$ .01	$ .10
Hershiser, Orel	92UD	261	$ .01	$ .04
Hershiser, Orel	93UD	169	$ .01	$ .05
Hesketh, Joe	89UD	60	$ .01	$ .08
Hesketh, Joe	90UD	512	$ .01	$ .05
Hesketh, Joe	92UD	570	$ .01	$ .04
Hetzel, Eric	90UD	673	$ .01	$ .10
Hibbard, Greg	90UD	543	$ .05	$ .25
Hibbard, Greg	91UD	679	$ .01	$ .05
Hibbard, Greg	92UD	420	$ .01	$ .04
Hickerson, Bryan	92UD	667	$ .01	$ .15
Hickey, Kevin	90UD	299	$ .01	$ .05
Higuera, Ted	89UD	424	$ .01	$ .08
Higuera, Ted	90UD	627	$ .01	$ .05
Higuera, Ted	91UD	341	$ .01	$ .05
Higuera, Teddy	92UD	138	$ .01	$ .04
Hill, Donnie	89UD	527	$ .01	$ .08
Hill, Donnie	91UD	211	$ .01	$ .05
Hill, Donnie	92UD	413	$ .01	$ .04
Hill, Glenallen	90UD	776	$ .01	$ .05
Hill, Glenallen	91UD	276	$ .01	$ .05
Hill, Glenallen	91UDF	52	$ .01	$ .05
Hill, Glenallen	92UD	558	$ .01	$ .04
Hill, Ken	90UD	336	$ .10	$ .40
Hill, Ken	91UD	647	$ .01	$ .05
Hill, Ken	92UD	628	$ .01	$ .04
Hill, Ken	92UD	790	$ .01	$ .05
Hill, Ken	93UD	138	$ .01	$ .05
Hillegas, Shawn	89UD	478	$ .01	$ .08
Hillegas, Shawn	90UD	541	$ .01	$ .05
Hinzo, Tommy	89UD	34	$ .01	$ .08
Hitchcock, Sterling	93UD	16	$ .10	$ .50
Hoiles, Chris	91UD	306	$ .05	$ .25
Hoiles, Chris	92UD	183	$ .01	$ .04
Hoiles, Chris	93UD	402	$ .01	$ .05
Hollins, Dave	90UD	785	$ .15	$1.50
Hollins, Dave	91UD	518	$ .01	$ .15
Hollins, Dave	92UD	586	$ .01	$ .04
Hollins, Dave	93UD	153	$ .01	$ .05
Hollins, Jessie	93UD	18	$ .01	$ .15
Holman, Brian	89UD	356	$ .05	$ .20
Holman, Brian	90UD	362	$ .01	$ .05
Holman, Brian	91UD	252	$ .01	$ .05
Holman, Brian	92UD	595	$ .01	$ .04
Holton, Brian	89UD	72	$ .01	$ .08
Holton, Brian	90UD	175	$ .01	$ .05
Honeycutt, Rick	89UD	278	$ .01	$ .08
Honeycutt, Rick	90UD	151	$ .01	$ .05
Honeycutt, Rick	91UD	379	$ .01	$ .05
Honeycutt, Rick	92UD	684	$ .01	$ .04
Horn, Sam	90UD	796	$ .01	$ .05
Horn, Sam	91UD	530	$ .01	$ .05
Horn, Sam	92UD	338	$ .01	$ .04
Horner, Bob	89UD	125	$ .01	$ .08
Horton, Ricky	89UD	629	$ .01	$ .08
Hosey, Steve	92UD	62	$ .05	$ .35
Hosey, Steve	93UD	15	$ .01	$ .15
Hough, Charlie	89UD	437	$ .01	$ .08
Hough, Charlie	90UD	314	$ .01	$ .05
Hough, Charlie	91UD	313	$ .01	$ .05
Hough, Charlie	91UD	792	$ .01	$ .05
Hough, Charlie	92UD	418	$ .01	$ .04
Hough, Charlie	93UD	207	$ .01	$ .05
Housie, Wayne	92UD	664	$ .01	$ .15
Howard, David	92UD	216	$ .01	$ .15
Howard, Steve	91UD	277	$ .01	$ .15
Howard, Tom	89UD	726	$ .05	$ .35
Howard, Thomas	91UDF	39	$ .01	$ .05
Howard, Thomas	92UD	416	$ .01	$ .04
Howard, Thomas	93UD	299	$ .01	$ .05
Howe, Steve	91UDF	31	$ .01	$ .05
Howe, Steve	92UD	630	$ .01	$ .04

UPPER DECK

Player	Year	No.	VG	EX/MT
Howell, Jack	89UD	138	$ .01	$ .08
Howell, Jack	90UD	19	$ .01	$ .05
Howell, Jack	91UD	213	$ .01	$ .05
Howell, Jack	92UD	419	$ .01	$ .10
Howell, Jay	89UD	610	$ .01	$ .08

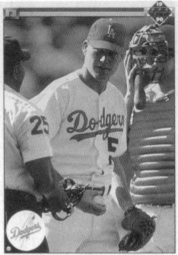
Jay Howell

Player	Year	No.	VG	EX/MT
Howell, Jay	90UD	508	$ .01	$ .05
Howell, Jay	91UD	558	$ .01	$ .05
Howell, Jay	92UD	511	$ .01	$ .04
Howell, Ken	90UD	559	$ .01	$ .05
Howell, Ken	91UD	488	$ .01	$ .05
Howell, Pat	93UD	161	$ .01	$ .10
Howitt, Dann	90UD	747	$ .01	$ .15
Howitt, Dann	91UD	442	$ .01	$ .10
Hrbek, Kent	89UD	213	$ .01	$ .10
Hrbek, Kent	90UD	452	$ .01	$ .05
Hrbek, Kent	91UD	167	$ .01	$ .05
Hrbek, Kent	92UD	334	$ .01	$ .04
Hrbek, Kent	93UD	50	$ .01	$ .15
Hrbek, Kent	93UD	74	$ .01	$ .05
Hubbard, Glenn	89UD	395	$ .01	$ .08
Hudler, Rex	89UD	405	$ .01	$ .08
Hudler, Rex	90UD	411	$ .01	$ .05
Hudler, Rex	91UD	482	$ .01	$ .05
Hudler, Rex	92UD	670	$ .01	$ .04
Hudson, Charles	89UD	586	$ .01	$ .08
Hudson, Charles	90UD	520	$ .01	$ .05
Hulse, David	93UD	374	$ .05	$ .25
Humphreys, Mike	91UDF	35	$ .05	$ .20
Humphreys, Mike	92UD	432	$ .01	$ .04
Hundley, Todd	90UD	726	$ .05	$ .25
Hundley, Todd	91UD	440	$ .01	$ .15
Hundley, Todd	92UD	260	$ .01	$ .10
Hundley, Todd	93UD	293	$ .01	$ .05
Hunter, Brian	91UDF	54	$ .05	$ .35
Hunter, Brian	92UD	366	$ .01	$ .10
Hurst, Bruce	89UD	387	$ .01	$ .08
Hurst, Bruce	89UD	792	$ .01	$ .15
Hurst, Bruce	90UD	433	$ .01	$ .05
Hurst, Bruce	91UD	602	$ .01	$ .05
Hurst, Bruce	92UD	437	$ .01	$ .04
Hurst, Bruce	93UD	304	$ .01	$ .05
Huson, Jeff	90UD	434	$ .01	$ .10
Huson, Jeff	90UD	788	$ .01	$ .05
Huson, Jeff	91UD	195	$ .01	$ .05
Huson, Jeff	92UD	196	$ .01	$ .04
Huson, Jeff	93UD	289	$ .01	$ .05
Incaviglia, Pete	89UD	484	$ .01	$ .15
Incaviglia, Pete	90UD	333	$ .01	$ .05
Incaviglia, Pete	91UD	453	$ .01	$ .05
Incaviglia, Pete	91UD	747	$ .01	$ .05
Incaviglia, Pete	92UD	271	$ .01	$ .04
Incaviglia, Pete	92UD	759	$ .01	$ .05
Innis, Jeff	90UD	562	$ .05	$ .20
Innis, Jeff	92UD	298	$ .01	$ .04
Innis, Jeff	93UD	119	$ .01	$ .05
Jackson, Bo	89UD	221	$ .10	$ .75
Jackson, Bo	90UD	32	$ .05	$ .25
Jackson, Bo	90UD	75	$ .05	$ .35
Jackson, Bo	90UD	105	$ .05	$ .35
Jackson, Bo	91UD	545	$ .05	$ .25
Jackson, Bo	91UD	744	$ .05	$ .25
Jackson, Bo	92UD	555	$ .05	$ .20
Jackson, Chuck	89UD	323	$ .01	$ .08
Jackson, Danny	89UD	640	$ .01	$ .10
Jackson, Danny	90UD	120	$ .01	$ .05
Jackson, Danny	91UD	414	$ .01	$ .05
Jackson, Danny	91UD	723	$ .01	$ .05
Jackson, Danny	92UD	104	$ .01	$ .04
Jackson, Darrin	89UD	214	$ .05	$ .20
Jackson, Darrin	90UD	414	$ .01	$ .05
Jackson, Darrin	92UD	328	$ .01	$ .04
Jackson, Darrin	93UD	258	$ .01	$ .05
Jackson, Mike	89UD	142	$ .01	$ .08
Jackson, Mike	90UD	494	$ .01	$ .05
Jackson, Mike	91UD	496	$ .01	$ .05
Jackson, Mike	92UD	593	$ .01	$ .04
Jackson, Mike	92UD	738	$ .01	$ .05
Jackson, Mike	93UD	170	$ .01	$ .05
Jacoby, Brook	89UD	198	$ .01	$ .08
Jacoby, Brook	90UD	459	$ .01	$ .05
Jacoby, Brook	91UD	137	$ .01	$ .05
Jacoby, Brook	91UDF	78	$ .01	$ .05
Jacoby, Brook	92UD	528	$ .01	$ .04
Jacoby, Brook	93UD	200	$ .01	$ .05
Jaha, John	93UD	177	$ .01	$ .05
James, Chris	89UD	513	$ .01	$ .08
James, Chris	90UD	435	$ .01	$ .05
James, Chris	90UD	798	$ .01	$ .05
James, Chris	91UD	140	$ .01	$ .05
James, Chris	92UD	560	$ .01	$ .04
James, Dion	89UD	587	$ .01	$ .08
James, Dion	90UD	591	$ .01	$ .05
James, Dion	91UD	399	$ .01	$ .05
Javier, Stan	89UD	581	$ .01	$ .08
Javier, Stan	90UD	209	$ .01	$ .05
Javier, Stan	91UD	688	$ .01	$ .05
Javier, Stan	93UD	249	$ .01	$ .05
Jeffcoat, Mike	92UD	597	$ .01	$ .04
Jefferies, Gregg	89UD	9	$ .10	$ .75
Jefferies, Gregg	90UD	166	$ .05	$ .25
Jefferies, Gregg	91UD	95	$ .01	$ .05
Jefferies, Gregg	91UD	156	$ .01	$ .10
Jefferies, Gregg	92UD	133	$ .01	$ .10
Jefferies, Gregg	92UD	725	$ .01	$ .05
Jefferies, Gregg	93UD	54	$ .01	$ .15
Jefferies, Gregg	93UD	176	$ .01	$ .05
Jefferson, Reggie	91UD	746	$ .10	$ .40
Jefferson, Reggie	91UDF	73	$ .05	$ .25
Jefferson, Reggie	92UD	656	$ .05	$ .20
Jeltz, Steve	89UD	219	$ .01	$ .08
Jeltz, Steve	90UD	495	$ .01	$ .05
Jenkins, Fergie	91UDH	3	$3.50	$14.00
Jennings, Doug	89UD	585	$ .01	$ .15
Jimenez, German	89UD	113	$ .01	$ .10
Jody, Davis	89UD	795	$ .01	$ .10
John, Tommy	89UD	230	$ .01	$ .10
Johnson, Chris	91UD	56	$ .01	$ .15
Johnson, Dave	90UD	425	$ .01	$ .10

UPPER DECK

Player	Year	No.	VG	EX/MT
Johnson, Dave	91UD	299	$ .01	$ .05
Johnson, Howard	89UD	582	$ .01	$ .15
Johnson, Howard	90UD	263	$ .01	$ .15
Johnson, Howard	91UD	124	$ .01	$ .10
Johnson, Howard	92UD	37	$ .01	$ .04
Johnson, Howard	92UD	256	$ .01	$ .10
Johnson, Howard	92UD	720	$ .01	$ .05
Johnson, Jeff	92UD	626	$ .01	$ .10
Johnson, Lance	90UD	90	$ .01	$ .05
Johnson, Lance	91UD	248	$ .01	$ .05
Johnson, Lance	92UD	188	$ .01	$ .04
Johnson, Lance	93UD	280	$ .01	$ .05
Johnson, Randy	89UD	25	$ .10	$1.00
Johnson, Randy	90UD	563	$ .01	$ .05
Johnson, Randy	91UD	376	$ .01	$ .05
Johnson, Randy	92UD	164	$ .01	$ .04

Player	Year	No.	VG	EX/MT
Johnson, Randy	**93UD**	**336**	**$ .01**	**$ .05**
Johnson, Wallace	89UD	124	$ .01	$ .08
Jones, Barry	89UD	457	$ .01	$ .08
Jones, Barry	91UD	39	$ .01	$ .05
Jones, Barry	91UD	789	$ .01	$ .05
Jones, Barry	92UD	681	$ .01	$ .04
Jones, Bobby	93UD	19	$ .10	$ .50
Jones, Calvin	92UD	731	$ .01	$ .05
Jones, Chipper	91UD	55	$ .15	$1.50
Jones, Chipper	93UD	24	$ .10	$1.00
Jones, Doug	89UD	540	$ .01	$ .08
Jones, Doug	90UD	632	$ .01	$ .05
Jones, Doug	91UD	216	$ .01	$ .05
Jones, Doug	92UD	798	$ .01	$ .05
Jones, Doug	93UD	171	$ .01	$ .05
Jones, Jimmy	89UD	286	$ .01	$ .08
Jones, Jimmy	92UD	392	$ .01	$ .04
Jones, Kiki	91UD	59	$ .05	$ .20
Jones, Odell	89UD	608	$ .01	$ .08
Jones, Ron	89UD	11	$ .01	$ .15
Jones, Ron	90UD	94	$ .01	$ .05
Jones, Timmy	89UD	348	$ .01	$ .10
Jones, Timmy	90UD	501	$ .01	$ .05
Jones, Tracy	89UD	96	$ .01	$ .08
Jones, Tracy	89UD	798	$ .01	$ .10
Jones, Tracy	90UD	309	$ .01	$ .05
Jordan, Brian	92UD	3	$ .05	$ .35
Jordan, Brian	92UD	702	$ .05	$ .25
Jordan, Michael	91UDSP	1	$2.50	$10.00
Jordan, Ricky	89UD	35	$ .01	$ .15
Jordan, Ricky	90UD	576	$ .01	$ .10
Jordan, Ricky	91UD	160	$ .01	$ .05
Jordan, Ricky	92UD	106	$ .01	$ .04
Jose, Felix	89UD	22	$ .20	$2.00
Jose, Felix	90UD	228	$ .05	$ .25
Jose, Felix	91UD	387	$ .01	$ .15
Jose, Felix	92UD	264	$ .01	$ .10
Jose, Felix	93UD	156	$ .01	$ .05
Joyner, Wally	89UD	573	$ .05	$ .25
Joyner, Wally	89UD	668	$ .01	$ .15
Joyner, Wally	90UD	693	$ .01	$ .15
Joyner, Wally	91UD	575	$ .01	$ .10
Joyner, Wally	92UD	343	$ .01	$ .04
Joyner, Wally	92UD	744	$ .01	$ .05
Joyner, Wally	93UD	54	$ .01	$ .15
Joyner, Wally	93UD	252	$ .01	$ .05
Juden, Jeff	91UD	52	$ .05	$ .20
Juden, Jeff	92UD	6	$ .01	$ .15
Justice, Dave	90UD	711	$1.00	$4.00
Justice, Dave	91UD	363	$ .10	$ .50
Justice, Dave	92UD	29	$ .01	$ .10
Justice, David	92UD	546	$ .05	$ .25
Justice, David	93UD	366	$ .05	$ .20
Kamieniecki, Scott	91UDF	33	$ .05	$ .20
Kamieniecki, Scott	92UD	46	$ .01	$ .10
Karkovice, Ron	89UD	183	$ .01	$ .08
Karkovice, Ron	90UD	69	$ .01	$ .05
Karkovice, Ron	91UD	209	$ .01	$ .05
Karkovice, Ron	92UD	169	$ .01	$ .04
Karkovice, Ron	93UD	199	$ .01	$ .05
Karros, Eric	91UD	24	$ .25	$2.50
Karros, Eric	92UD	534	$ .10	$ .50
Karros, Eric	93UD	385	$ .10	$ .40
Karsay, Steve	91UD	54	$ .10	$ .40
Kelly, Mike	92UD	794	$ .10	$1.00
Kelly, Pat	91UD	76	$ .05	$ .35
Kelly, Pat	92UD	435	$ .01	$ .15
Kelly, Pat	93UD	215	$ .01	$ .05
Kelly, Roberto	89UD	590	$ .10	$ .50
Kelly, Roberto	90UD	193	$ .05	$ .25
Kelly, Roberto	91UD	49	$ .01	$ .05
Kelly, Roberto	91UD	372	$ .01	$ .10
Kelly, Roberto	92UD	577	$ .01	$ .04
Kelly, Roberto	93UD	47	$ .01	$ .15
Kennedy, Terry	89UD	469	$ .01	$ .08
Kennedy, Terry	90UD	397	$ .01	$ .05
Kennedy, Terry	91UD	404	$ .01	$ .05
Kennedy, Terry	92UD	192	$ .01	$ .04
Kent, Jeff	93UD	401	$ .01	$ .10
Key, Jimmy	89UD	291	$ .01	$ .15
Key, Jimmy	90UD	462	$ .01	$ .05
Key, Jimmy	91UD	667	$ .01	$ .05
Key, Jimmy	92UD	302	$ .01	$ .04
Key, Jimmy	93UD	358	$ .01	$ .05
Kiecker, Dana	91UD	507	$ .01	$ .10
Kiely, John	93UD	378	$ .01	$ .05
Kile, Darryl	91UD	774	$ .01	$ .15
Kile, Darryl	92UD	374	$ .01	$ .15
Kile, Darryl	93UD	314	$ .01	$ .05
Kilgus, Paul	89UD	335	$ .01	$ .08
Kilgus, Paul	89UD	797	$ .01	$ .10
Kilgus, Paul	90UD	155	$ .01	$ .05
Killebrew, Harmon	91UDH	1	$3.50	$14.00
King, Eric	89UD	493	$ .01	$ .08
King, Eric	90UD	651	$ .01	$ .05
King, Eric	91UD	281	$ .01	$ .05
King, Eric	91UD	782	$ .01	$ .05
King, Eric	92UD	679	$ .01	$ .04
King, Jeff	90UD	557	$ .01	$ .10
King, Jeff	91UD	687	$ .01	$ .05
King, Jeff	92UD	111	$ .01	$ .04
King, Jeff	93UD	240	$ .01	$ .05

UPPER DECK

Player	Year	No.	VG	EX/MT
Kipper, Bob	89UD	520	$ .01	$ .08
Kipper, Bob	90UD	560	$ .01	$ .05
Kipper, Bob	91UD	407	$ .01	$ .05
Kittle, Ron	89UD	228	$ .01	$ .08
Kittle, Ron	89UD	711	$ .01	$ .10
Kittle, Ron	90UD	790	$ .01	$ .05
Klesko, Ryan	91UDF	1	$ .10	$ .50
Klesko, Ryan	91UDF	8	$ .15	$1.50
Klesko, Ryan	92UD	1	$ .05	$ .25
Klesko, Ryan	92UD	24	$ .10	$ .75
Klesko, Ryan	93UD	376	$ .05	$ .35
Klink, Joe	91UD	468	$ .01	$ .10
Klink, Joe	92UD	530	$ .01	$ .04
Knackert, Brent	91UD	378	$ .01	$ .15
Knepper, Bob	89UD	422	$ .01	$ .08
Knepper, Bob	90UD	599	$ .01	$ .05
Knight, Ray	89UD	259	$ .01	$ .08
Knoblauch, Chuck	91UD	40	$ .10	$1.00
Knoblauch, Chuck	92UD	446	$ .01	$ .15
Knoblauch, Chuck	93UD	254	$ .05	$ .20
Knudson, Mark	91UD	393	$ .01	$ .05
Komminsk, Brad	90UD	428	$ .01	$ .05
Koslofski, Kevin	93UD	351	$ .01	$ .05
Kraemer, Joe	90UD	740	$ .01	$ .15
Kramer, Randy	90UD	519	$ .01	$ .05
Kremers, Jimmy	91UD	262	$ .01	$ .15
Kreuter, Chad	89UD	312	$ .05	$ .20
Kreuter, Chad	90UD	609	$ .01	$ .05
Krueger, Bill	91UDF	60	$ .01	$ .05
Krueger, Bill	92UD	403	$ .01	$ .04
Krueger, Bill	92UD	781	$ .01	$ .05
Kruk, John	89UD	280	$ .01	$ .15
Kruk, John	90UD	668	$ .01	$ .05
Kruk, John	91UD	199	$ .01	$ .05
Kruk, John	92UD	38	$ .01	$ .04
Kruk, John	92UD	326	$ .01	$ .04
Kruk, John	93UD	247	$ .01	$ .05
Krukow, Mike	89UD	46	$ .01	$ .08
Krukow, Mike	90UD	639	$ .01	$ .05
Kunkel, Jeff	89UD	463	$ .01	$ .08
Kunkel, Jeff	90UD	394	$ .01	$ .05
LaCoss, Mike	89UD	48	$ .01	$ .08
LaCoss, Mike	90UD	140	$ .01	$ .05
LaCoss, Mike	91UD	691	$ .01	$ .05
Lake, Steve	90UD	491	$ .01	$ .05
Lamp, Dennis	89UD	503	$ .01	$ .08
Lancaster, Les	89UD	84	$ .01	$ .08
Lancaster, Les	90UD	584	$ .01	$ .05
Lancaster, Les	92UD	481	$ .01	$ .04
Landrum, Bill	90UD	442	$ .01	$ .05
Landrum, Bill	91UD	614	$ .01	$ .05
Landrum, Bill	92UD	636	$ .01	$ .04
Landrum, Ced	92UD	50	$ .01	$ .04
Langston, Mark	89UD	526	$ .05	$ .20
Langston, Mark	90UD	647	$ .01	$ .10
Langston, Mark	90UD	783	$ .01	$ .05
Langston, Mark	91UD	234	$ .01	$ .05
Langston, Mark	92UD	305	$ .01	$ .04
Langston, Mark	93UD	53	$ .01	$ .10
Langston, Mark	93UD	128	$ .01	$ .05
Lankford, Ray	90UD	755	$ .20	$2.00
Lankford, Ray	91UD	346	$ .10	$ .50
Lankford, Ray	92UD	262	$ .01	$ .15
Lankford, Ray	93UD	244	$ .01	$ .15
Lansford, Carney	89UD	562	$ .01	$ .08
Lansford, Carney	90UD	253	$ .01	$ .05
Lansford, Carney	91UD	194	$ .01	$ .05
Lansford, Carney	92UD	682	$ .01	$ .04
LaPoint, Dave	89UD	600	$ .01	$ .08
LaPoint, Dave	89UD	706	$ .01	$ .10
LaPoint, Dave	90UD	507	$ .01	$ .05
LaPoint, Dave	91UD	483	$ .01	$ .05
Larkin, Barry	89UD	270	$ .10	$ .50
Larkin, Barry	90UD	99	$ .01	$ .15
Larkin, Barry	90UD	167	$ .05	$ .25
Larkin, Barry	91UD	353	$ .01	$ .15
Larkin, Barry	92UD	144	$ .01	$ .10
Larkin, Barry	93UD	245	$ .01	$ .10
Larkin, Gene	89UD	580	$ .01	$ .10
Larkin, Gene	90UD	471	$ .01	$ .05
Larkin, Gene	91UD	501	$ .01	$ .05
Larkin, Gene	92UD	187	$ .01	$ .04
Laudner, Tim	89UD	62	$ .01	$ .08
Laudner, Tim	90UD	419	$ .01	$ .05
LaValliere, Mike	89UD	417	$ .01	$ .08
LaValliere, Mike	90UD	578	$ .01	$ .05
LaValliere, Mike	91UD	129	$ .01	$ .05
LaValliere, Mike	92UD	113	$ .01	$ .04
LaValliere, Mike	93UD	120	$ .01	$ .05
Law, Vance	89UD	473	$ .01	$ .08
Law, Vance	90UD	380	$ .01	$ .05
Law, Vance	91UD	760	$ .01	$ .05
Layana, Tim	90UD	717	$ .01	$ .15
Layana, Tim	91UD	396	$ .01	$ .10
Lea, Charlie	89UD	81	$ .01	$ .08

Rick Leach

Player	Year	No.	VG	EX/MT
Leach, Rick	89UD	554	$ .01	$ .08
Leach, Rick	90UD	640	$ .01	$ .05
Leach, Terry	89UD	288	$ .01	$ .08
Leach, Terry	90UD	642	$ .01	$ .05
Leach, Terry	92UD	311	$ .01	$ .05
Leach, Terry	93UD	418	$ .01	$ .05
Leary, Tim	89UD	94	$ .01	$ .08
Leary, Tim	90UD	662	$ .01	$ .05
Leary, Tim	90UD	705	$ .01	$ .05
Leary, Tim	91UD	693	$ .01	$ .05
Lee, Manny	89UD	271	$ .01	$ .08
Lee, Manny	90UD	285	$ .01	$ .05
Lee, Manny "Manuel"	91UD	142	$ .01	$ .10
Lee, Manuel	92UD	118	$ .01	$ .04
Lee, Manuel	93UD	205	$ .01	$ .05
Lee, Mark	92UD	507	$ .01	$ .04
Lee, Terry	91UD	37	$ .01	$ .15
Lefferts, Craig	89UD	541	$ .01	$ .08
Lefferts, Craig	90UD	399	$ .01	$ .05
Lefferts, Craig	90UD	792	$ .01	$ .05
Lefferts, Craig	91UD	228	$ .01	$ .05
Lefferts, Craig	92UD	589	$ .01	$ .04
Lefties, Lethal	93UD	53	$ .01	$ .10

UPPER DECK

Player	Year	No.	VG	EX/MT
Leibrandt, Charlie	89UD	637	$ .01	$ .08
Leibrandt, Charlie	90UD	658	$ .01	$ .05
Leibrandt, Charlie	91UD	460	$ .01	$ .05
Leibrandt, Charlie	92UD	170	$ .01	$ .04
Leiper, Dave	89UD	363	$ .01	$ .08
Leiter, Al	89UD	588	$ .01	$ .15
Leiter, Al	89UD	705	$ .01	$ .10
Leiter, Mark	92UD	319	$ .01	$ .04
Leiter, Mark	93UD	95	$ .01	$ .05
Leius, Scott	91UD	35	$ .01	$ .15
Leius, Scott	92UD	313	$ .01	$ .15
Leius, Scott	93UD	212	$ .01	$ .05
Lemke, Mark	89UD	19	$ .01	$ .15
Lemke, Mark	90UD	665	$ .01	$ .05
Lemke, Mark	91UD	419	$ .01	$ .05
Lemke, Mark	92UD	47	$ .01	$ .04
Lemke, Mark	93UD	109	$ .01	$ .05
Lemon, Chet	89UD	128	$ .01	$ .08
Lemon, Chet	90UD	348	$ .01	$ .05
Lemon, Chet	91UD	389	$ .01	$ .05
Lennon, Patrick	91UDF	43	$ .01	$ .15
Lennon, Patrick	92UD	13	$ .05	$ .20
Leonard, Jeffrey	89UD	263	$ .01	$ .08
Leonard, Jeffrey	89UD	789	$ .01	$ .15
Leonard, Jeffrey	90UD	331	$ .01	$ .05
Leonard, Jeffrey	91UD	107	$ .01	$ .05
Leonard, Mark	91UD	557	$ .01	$ .10
Lewis, Darren	91UD	564	$ .01	$ .15
Lewis, Darren	91UDF	38	$ .01	$ .15
Lewis, Darren	92UD	565	$ .01	$ .15
Lewis, Darren	93UD	173	$ .01	$ .05
Lewis, Mark	91UD	17	$ .05	$ .20
Lind, Jose	89UD	334	$ .01	$ .08
Lind, Jose	90UD	424	$ .01	$ .05
Lind, Jose	91UD	258	$ .01	$ .05
Lind, Jose	92UD	205	$ .01	$ .04
Lind, Jose	93UD	309	$ .01	$ .05
Liriano, Nelson	89UD	109	$ .01	$ .08
Liriano, Nelson	90UD	134	$ .01	$ .05
Liriano, Nelson	91UD	360	$ .01	$ .05
Listach, Pat	92UD	775	$ .10	$1.00
Listach, Pat	93UD	43	$ .05	$ .25
Listach, Pat	93UD	253	$ .10	$ .50
Litton, Greg	90UD	677	$ .01	$ .10
Livingstone, Scott	91UDF	53	$ .05	$ .35
Livingstone, Scott	92UD	538	$ .01	$ .15
Livingstone, Scott	93UD	63	$ .01	$ .05
Lofton, Kenny	91UDF	24	$ .15	$1.50
Lofton, Kenny	92UD	25	$ .05	$ .35
Lofton, Kenny	92UD	766	$ .10	$ .40
Lofton, Kenny	93UD	45	$ .05	$ .25
Lofton, Kenny	93UD	262	$ .05	$ .25
Lombardozzi, Steve	89UD	179	$ .01	$ .08
Long, Bill	89UD	499	$ .01	$ .08
Long, Bill	91UD	495	$ .01	$ .05
Lopez, Javy	93UD	29	$ .10	$ .50
Lovullo, Torey	89UD	782	$ .01	$ .15
Lovullo, Torey	90UD	332	$ .01	$ .10
Luecken, Rick	90UD	621	$ .01	$ .15
Lusader, Scott	91UD	241	$ .01	$ .05
Lynn, Fred	89UD	761	$ .01	$ .15
Lynn, Fred	90UD	247	$ .01	$ .05
Lynn, Fred	90UD	771	$ .01	$ .05
Lynn, Fred	91UD	273	$ .01	$ .05
Lyons, Barry	89UD	176	$ .01	$ .08
Lyons, Barry	90UD	473	$ .01	$ .05
Lyons, Steve	89UD	224	$ .01	$ .08
Lyons, Steve	90UD	390	$ .01	$ .05
Lyons, Steve	91UD	601	$ .01	$ .05
Maas, Kevin	90UD	70	$ .10	$ .50
Maas, Kevin	91UD	375	$ .01	$ .15
Maas, Kevin	92UD	98	$ .01	$ .04
Maas, Kevin	92UD	377	$ .01	$ .15
MacFarlane (f), Mike	89UD	546	$ .05	$ .35
Macfarlane, Mike	90UD	307	$ .01	$ .05
Macfarlane, Mike	91UD	570	$ .01	$ .05
Macfarlane, Mike	92UD	497	$ .01	$ .04
Macfarlane, Mike	93UD	327	$ .01	$ .05
Machado, Julio	90UD	93	$ .01	$ .15
Machado, Julio	91UD	716	$ .01	$ .05
Machado, Julio	92UD	479	$ .01	$ .04
Mack, Shane	89UD	182	$ .01	$ .08
Mack, Shane	91UD	188	$ .01	$ .05
Mack, Shane	92UD	428	$ .01	$ .04
Mack, Shane	93UD	236	$ .01	$ .05
Maddux, Greg	89UD	241	$ .15	$1.50
Maddux, Greg	90UD	213	$ .10	$ .40
Maddux, Greg	91UD	115	$ .05	$ .15
Maddux, Greg	92UD	353	$ .01	$ .10
Maddux, Mike	89UD	338	$ .01	$ .08
Maddux, Mike	92UD	330	$ .01	$ .04
Maddux, Mike	93UD	58	$ .01	$ .05
Magadan, Dave	89UD	388	$ .01	$ .08
Magadan, Dave	90UD	243	$ .01	$ .05
Magadan, Dave	91UD	177	$ .01	$ .05
Magadan, Dave	92UD	112	$ .01	$ .04
Magnante, Mike	93UD	180	$ .01	$ .05
Magrane, Joe	89UD	103	$ .01	$ .15
Magrane, Joe	90UD	242	$ .01	$ .05
Magrane, Joe	91UD	465	$ .01	$ .05
Mahler, Rick	89UD	74	$ .01	$ .08
Mahler, Rick	89UD	760	$ .01	$ .10
Mahler, Rick	90UD	220	$ .01	$ .05
Mahler, Rick	91UD	613	$ .01	$ .05
Mahomes, Pat	92UD	776	$ .05	$ .25
Mahomes, Pat	93UD	337	$ .01	$ .05
Maldonado, Candy	89UD	502	$ .01	$ .08

MARK LEWIS

Player	Year	No.	VG	EX/MT
Lewis, Mark	**92UD**	**235**	**$ .01**	**$ .15**
Lewis, Mark	93UD	88	$ .01	$ .05
Lewis, Scott	91UD	594	$ .01	$ .15
Leyritz, Jim	90UD	723	$ .01	$ .15
Leyritz, Jim	91UD	243	$ .01	$ .10
Leyritz, Jim	92UD	117	$ .01	$ .04
Lieberthal, Mike	91UD	67	$ .05	$ .35
Lilliquist, Derek	89UD	753	$ .05	$ .25
Lilliquist, Derek	90UD	234	$ .01	$ .10
Lilliquist, Derek	91UD	251	$ .01	$ .05
Lilliquist, Derek	93UD	70	$ .01	$ .05

UPPER DECK

Player	Year	No.	VG	EX/MT
Maldonado, Candy	90UD	136	$ .01	$ .05
Maldonado, Candy	90UD	780	$ .01	$ .05
Maldonado, Candy	91UD	138	$ .01	$ .05
Maldonado, Candy	91UD	739	$ .01	$ .05
Maldonado, Candy	91UDF	28	$ .01	$ .05
Maldonado, Candy	92UD	393	$ .01	$ .04
Malone, Chuck	91UD	649	$ .01	$ .15
Mann, Kelly	90UD	33	$ .01	$ .15
Manrique, Fred	89UD	628	$ .01	$ .08
Manrique, Fred	90UD	392	$ .01	$ .05
Manto, Jeff	91UD	238	$ .01	$ .10
Manwaring, Kirt	89UD	500	$ .01	$ .10
Manwaring, Kirt	90UD	457	$ .01	$ .05
Manwaring, Kirt	92UD	740	$ .01	$ .05
Manwaring, Kirt	93UD	179	$ .01	$ .05
Marshall, Mike	89UD	70	$ .01	$ .08
Marshall, Mike	90UD	262	$ .01	$ .05
Marshall, Mike	90UD	781	$ .01	$ .05
Marshall, Mike	91UD	681	$ .01	$ .05
Martin, Al	93UD	340	$ .01	$ .05
Martinez, Carlos	90UD	347	$ .01	$ .15
Martinez, Carlos	91UD	625	$ .01	$ .05
Martinez, Carlos	92UD	598	$ .01	$ .04
Martinez, Carmelo	89UD	365	$ .01	$ .08
Martinez, Carmelo	90UD	592	$ .01	$ .05
Martinez, Carmelo	91UD	92	$ .01	$ .05
Martinez, Carmelo	92UD	696	$ .01	$ .04
Martinez, Chito	91UDF	30	$ .05	$ .20
Martinez, Chito	92UD	672	$ .05	$ .25
Martinez, Dave	89UD	444	$ .01	$ .08
Martinez, Dave	90UD	470	$ .01	$ .05
Martinez, Dave	91UD	186	$ .01	$ .05
Martinez, Dave	92UD	382	$ .01	$ .04
Martinez, Dave	92UD	784	$ .01	$ .05
Martinez, Dave	93UD	400	$ .01	$ .05
Martinez, Dennis	89UD	377	$ .01	$ .08
Martinez, Dennis	90UD	413	$ .01	$ .05
Martinez, Dennis	91UD	385	$ .01	$ .05
Martinez, Dennis "Perfecto"	91UDF	50	$ .01	$ .05
Martinez, Dennis	92UD	365	$ .01	$ .04
Martinez, Dennis	93UD	232	$ .01	$ .05
Martinez, Edgar	89UD	768	$ .15	$1.50
Martinez, Edgar	90UD	532	$ .05	$ .35
Martinez, Edgar	91UD	574	$ .01	$ .05
Martinez, Edgar	92UD	91	$ .01	$ .04
Martinez, Edgar	92UD	367	$ .01	$ .04
Martinez, Pedro	91UDF	2	$ .10	$ .75
Martinez, Pedro	92UD	18	$ .05	$ .25
Martinez, Pedro	92UD	79	$ .01	$ .15
Martinez, Pedro	93UD	324	$ .01	$ .05
Martinez, Ramon	89UD	18	$ .20	$2.00
Martinez, Ramon	90UD	675	$ .05	$ .25
Martinez, Ramon	91UD	78	$ .01	$ .10
Martinez, Ramon	91UD	136	$ .01	$ .15
Martinez, Ramon	92UD	79	$ .01	$ .15
Martinez, Ramon	92UD	346	$ .01	$ .10
Martinez, Ramon	93UD	133	$ .01	$ .05
Martinez, Tino	90UD	37	$ .10	$ .40
Martinez, Tino	91UD	553	$ .01	$ .10
Martinez, Tino	92UD	554	$ .01	$ .10
Martinez, Tino	93UD	287	$ .01	$ .05
Mashers, Motown	93UD	46	$ .01	$ .15
Mathews, Greg	89UD	531	$ .01	$ .08
Mathews, Greg	90UD	678	$ .01	$ .05
Mattingly, Don	89UD	200	$ .15	$1.00
Mattingly, Don	89UD	693	$ .05	$ .25
Mattingly, Don	90UD	191	$ .05	$ .35
Mattingly, Don	91UD	354	$ .01	$ .15
Mattingly, Don	92UD	356	$ .01	$ .15
Mattingly, Don	93UD	47	$ .01	$ .15
Mattingly, Don	93UD	134	$ .01	$ .10
Maurer, Rob	92UD	10	$ .01	$ .15
May, Derrick	90UD	736	$ .10	$ .75
May, Derrick	91UD	334	$ .05	$ .35
May, Derrick	93UD	248	$ .01	$ .05

Randy McCament

Player	Year	No.	VG	EX/MT
Mayne, Brent	91UD	72	$ .05	$ .20
Mazzilli, Lee	89UD	657	$ .01	$ .08
McCament, Randy	**90UD**	**657**	**$ .01**	**$ .15**
McCarty, David	92UD	75	$ .10	$1.00
McCaskill, Kirk	89UD	223	$ .01	$ .08
McCaskill, Kirk	90UD	506	$ .01	$ .05
McCaskill, Kirk	91UD	539	$ .01	$ .05
McCaskill, Kirk	92UD	128	$ .01	$ .04
McCaskill, Kirk	92UD	722	$ .01	$ .05
McClellan, Paul	92UD	563	$ .01	$ .10
McClendon, Lloyd	89UD	446	$ .01	$ .10
McClendon, Lloyd	90UD	398	$ .01	$ .05
McClure, Bob	90UD	81	$ .01	$ .05
McCullers, Lance	89UD	382	$ .01	$ .08
McCullers, Lance	89UD	710	$ .01	$ .10
McCullers, Lance	90UD	615	$ .01	$ .05
McCullers, Lance	91UD	203	$ .01	$ .05
McDonald, Ben	90UD	54	$ .10	$1.00
McDonald, Ben	91UD	446	$ .01	$ .15
McDonald, Ben	92UD	93	$ .01	$ .04
McDonald, Ben	92UD	163	$ .01	$ .15
McDonald, Ben	93UD	276	$ .01	$ .05
McDowell, Jack	89UD	530	$ .10	$1.00
McDowell, Jack	90UD	625	$ .10	$ .40
McDowell, Jack	91UD	323	$ .01	$ .15
McDowell, Jack	92UD	553	$ .01	$ .04
McDowell, Jack	93UD	357	$ .01	$ .05
McDowell, Oddibe	89UD	333	$ .01	$ .08
McDowell, Oddibe	89UD	796	$ .01	$ .15
McDowell, Oddibe	90UD	145	$ .01	$ .05
McDowell, Oddibe	91UD	497	$ .01	$ .05
McDowell, Roger	89UD	296	$ .01	$ .08
McDowell, Roger	90UD	416	$ .01	$ .05
McDowell, Roger	91UD	406	$ .01	$ .05
McDowell, Roger	91UDF	57	$ .01	$ .05
McDowell, Roger	92UD	484	$ .01	$ .04
McDowell, Roger	93UD	250	$ .01	$ .05
McElroy, Chuck	90UD	706	$ .05	$ .20
McElroy, Chuck	91UDF	29	$ .01	$ .05
McElroy, Chuck	92UD	220	$ .01	$ .04
McElroy, Chuck	93UD	130	$ .01	$ .05
McGaffigan, Andy	89UD	359	$ .01	$ .08
McGaffigan, Andy	90UD	597	$ .01	$ .05

UPPER DECK

Player	Year	No.	VG	EX/MT
McGee, Willie	89UD	621	$ .01	$ .08
McGee, Willie	90UD	505	$ .01	$ .05
McGee, Willie	91UD	584	$ .01	$ .05
McGee, Willie	91UD	721	$ .01	$ .05
McGee, Willie	92UD	34	$ .01	$ .04
McGee, Willie	92UD	194	$ .01	$ .04
McGee, Willie	93UD	281	$ .01	$ .05
McGriff, Fred	89UD	572	$ .10	$1.00
McGriff, Fred	89UD	671	$ .05	$ .25
McGriff, Fred	90UD	108	$ .10	$ .40
McGriff, Fred	91UD	565	$ .01	$ .15
McGriff, Fred	91UD	775	$ .01	$ .15
McGriff, Fred	92UD	33	$ .01	$ .10
McGriff, Fred	92UD	344	$ .01	$ .10
McGwire, Mark	89UD	300	$ .15	$1.50
McGwire, Mark	90UD	36	$ .05	$ .25
McGwire, Mark	90UD	171	$ .10	$ .50
McGwire, Mark	91UD	174	$ .05	$ .35
McGwire, Mark	91UD	656	$ .05	$ .25
McGwire, Mark	92UD	153	$ .01	$ .15
McGwire, Marc	93UD	41	$ .01	$ .15
McGwire, Marc	93UD	49	$ .01	$ .15
McGwire, Mark	93UD	420	$ .01	$ .05
McIntosh, Tim	91UD	547	$ .01	$ .15
McKnight, Jeff	90UD	162	$ .01	$ .10

Mark McLemore

Player	Year	No.	VG	EX/MT
McLemore, Mark	**89UD**	**245**	**$ .01**	**$ .08**
McNeely, Jeff	91UDF	20	$ .05	$ .35
McRae, Brian	91UD	543	$ .05	$ .35
McRae, Brian	92UD	157	$ .01	$ .15
McRae, Brian	93UD	238	$ .01	$ .05
McReynolds, Kevin	89UD	367	$ .01	$ .10
McReynolds, Kevin	90UD	265	$ .01	$ .10
McReynolds, Kevin	91UD	105	$ .01	$ .05
McReynolds, Kevin	92UD	362	$ .01	$ .04
McReynolds, Kevin	92UD	742	$ .01	$ .05
McWilliams, Larry	89UD	143	$ .01	$ .08
Meacham, Bobby	89UD	77	$ .01	$ .08
Meacham, Rusty	91UDF	44	$ .01	$ .10
Meacham, Rusty	92UD	453	$ .01	$ .04
Meacham, Rusty	93UD	59	$ .01	$ .05
Meadows, Louie	89UD	401	$ .01	$ .10
Meadows, Louie	90UD	160	$ .01	$ .05
Medina, Luis	89UD	2	$ .01	$ .10

Player	Year	No.	VG	EX/MT
Melendez, Jose	92UD	566	$ .01	$ .10
Melendez, Jose	93UD	288	$ .01	$ .05
Melvin, Bob	89UD	227	$ .01	$ .08
Melvin, Bob	90UD	644	$ .01	$ .05
Melvin, Bob	91UD	310	$ .01	$ .05
Melvin, Bob	92UD	692	$ .01	$ .04
Mercado, Orlando	89UD	624	$ .01	$ .08
Merced, Orlando	91UD	84	$ .10	$ .40
Merced, Orlando	92UD	517	$ .05	$ .20
Merced, Orlando	93UD	150	$ .01	$ .05
Mercedes, Luis	91UD	745	$ .05	$ .35
Mercedes, Luis	92UD	652	$ .05	$ .20
Mercker, Kent	90UD	63	$ .05	$ .20
Mercker, Kent	91UD	642	$ .01	$ .05
Mercker, Kent	92UD	472	$ .01	$ .04
Mercker, Kent	93UD	393	$ .01	$ .05
Merullo, Matt	90UD	67	$ .01	$ .10
Mesa, Jose	91UD	703	$ .01	$ .05
Meulens, Hensley	89UD	746	$ .05	$ .20
Meulens, Hensley	90UD	546	$ .01	$ .15
Meulens, Hensley	91UD	675	$ .01	$ .05
Meulens, Hensley	92UD	606	$ .01	$ .04
Meyer, Brian	90UD	22	$ .01	$ .05
Meyer, Joey	89UD	403	$ .01	$ .08
Micki, Dave	93UD	17	$ .05	$ .20
Mielke, Gary	90UD	612	$ .01	$ .15
Milacki, Bob	89UD	735	$ .05	$ .20
Milacki, Bob	90UD	635	$ .01	$ .10
Milacki, Bob	91UD	328	$ .01	$ .05
Milacki, Bob	92UD	480	$ .01	$ .04
Militello, Sam	93UD	383	$ .05	$ .25
Miller, Darrell	89UD	462	$ .01	$ .08
Miller, Keith	89UD	739	$ .01	$ .10
Miller, Keith	90UD	190	$ .01	$ .05
Miller, Keith	91UD	196	$ .01	$ .05
Miller, Keith	92UD	383	$ .01	$ .04
Miller, Keith	92UD	704	$ .01	$ .05
Miller, Keith	93UD	302	$ .01	$ .05
Miller, Kurt	91UD	68	$ .10	$ .40
Miller, Kurt	92UD	70	$ .01	$ .15
Miller, Kurt	93UD	20	$ .01	$ .05
Milligan, Randy	89UD	559	$ .01	$ .10
Milligan, Randy	89UD	740	$ .01	$ .10
Milligan, Randy	90UD	663	$ .01	$ .05
Milligan, Randy	91UD	548	$ .01	$ .05
Milligan, Randy	92UD	181	$ .01	$ .04
Milligan, Randy	93UD	228	$ .01	$ .05
Mills, Alan	91UD	222	$ .01	$ .15
Mills, Alan	93UD	312	$ .01	$ .05
Minton, Greg	89UD	635	$ .01	$ .08
Minton, Greg	90UD	83	$ .01	$ .05
Mirabella, Paul	89UD	322	$ .01	$ .08
Mitchell, Keith	91UDF	56	$ .05	$ .25
Mitchell, Keith	92UD	80	$ .01	$ .10
Mitchell, Keith	92UD	454	$ .01	$ .15
Mitchell, Kevin	89UD	163	$ .10	$ .40
Mitchell, Kevin	00UD	40	$ .01	$ .10
Mitchell, Kevin	90UD	117	$ .01	$ .15
Mitchell, Kevin	91UD	247	$ .01	$ .15
Mitchell, Kevin	92UD	80	$ .01	$ .10
Mitchell, Kevin	92UD	266	$ .01	$ .10
Mitchell, Kevin	92UD	735	$ .01	$ .05
Mitchell, Kevin	93UD	55	$ .05	$ .25
Mitchell, Kevin	93UD	213	$ .01	$ .05
Mohorcic, Dale	89UD	727	$ .01	$ .10
Mohorcic, Dale	90UD	530	$ .01	$ .05
Molitor, Paul	89UD	525	$ .05	$ .35
Molitor, Paul	89UD	673	$ .01	$ .10
Molitor, Paul	90UD	254	$ .01	$ .10
Molitor, Paul	91UD	324	$ .01	$ .10
Molitor, Paul	92UD	423	$ .01	$ .04
Molitor, Paul	93UD	43	$ .05	$ .25
Molitor, Paul	93UD	333	$ .01	$ .05
Mondesi, Raul	92UD	60	$ .05	$ .35
Montgomery, Jeff	89UD	618	$ .01	$ .15

UPPER DECK

Player	Year	No.	VG	EX/MT
Montgomery, Jeff	90UD	698	$ .01	$ .05
Montgomery, Jeff	91UD	637	$ .01	$ .05
Montgomery, Jeff	92UD	627	$ .01	$ .04
Montgomery, Jeff	93UD	62	$ .01	$ .05
Moore, Kerwin	91UDF	19	$ .05	$ .25
Moore, Mike	89UD	123	$ .01	$ .08
Moore, Mike	89UD	758	$ .01	$ .10
Moore, Mike	90UD	275	$ .01	$ .05
Moore, Mike	91UD	423	$ .01	$ .05
Moore, Mike	92UD	661	$ .01	$ .04
Moore, Mike	93UD	182	$ .01	$ .05
Morandini, Mickey	91UD	18	$ .01	$ .15
Morandini, Mickey	92UD	449	$ .01	$ .04
Morandini, Mickey	93UD	285	$ .01	$ .05
Moreland, Keith	89UD	361	$ .01	$ .08
Moreland, Keith	90UD	401	$ .01	$ .05
Morgan, Mike	89UD	653	$ .01	$ .08
Morgan, Mike	90UD	317	$ .01	$ .05
Morgan, Mike	91UD	578	$ .01	$ .05
Morgan, Mike	92UD	513	$ .01	$ .04
Morgan, Mike	92UD	703	$ .01	$ .05
Morgan, Mike	93UD	106	$ .01	$ .05
Morris, Hal	90UD	31	$ .10	$ .35
Morris, Hal	91UD	351	$ .01	$ .15
Morris, Hal	92UD	121	$ .01	$ .10
Morris, Hal	93UD	121	$ .01	$ .05
Morris, Jack	89UD	352	$ .10	$ .40
Morris, Jack	90UD	573	$ .01	$ .10
Morris, Jack	91UD	45	$ .01	$ .05
Morris, Jack	91UD	336	$ .01	$ .10
Morris, Jack	91UD	736	$ .01	$ .10
Morris, Jack	91UDF	80	$ .01	$ .05
Morris, Jack	92UD	315	$ .01	$ .10
Morris, Jack	92UD	732	$ .01	$ .05
Morris, Jack	93UD	164	$ .01	$ .10
Morrison, Jim	89UD	568	$ .01	$ .08
Morton, Kevin	91UDF	66	$ .01	$ .15
Morton, Kevin	92UD	676	$ .01	$ .10
Moseby, Lloyd	89UD	381	$ .01	$ .08
Moseby, Lloyd	90UD	421	$ .01	$ .05
Moseby, Lloyd	90UD	789	$ .01	$ .05
Moseby, Lloyd	91UD	559	$ .01	$ .05
Moseby, Lloyd	92UD	468	$ .01	$ .04
Moses, John	89UD	242	$ .01	$ .08
Moses, John	90UD	240	$ .01	$ .05
Mota, Andy	91UDF	22	$ .01	$ .10
Mota, Andy	92UD	564	$ .01	$ .15
Moyer, Jamie	89UD	63	$ .01	$ .08
Moyer, Jamie	89UD	791	$ .01	$ .10
Moyer, Jamie	90UD	619	$ .01	$ .05
Moyer, Jamie	91UD	610	$ .01	$ .05
Mulholland, Terry	90UD	474	$ .01	$ .05
Mulholland, Terry	91UD	426	$ .01	$ .05
Mulholland, Terry	92UD	129	$ .01	$ .04
Mulholland, Terry	93UD	279	$ .01	$ .05
Mulliniks, Rance	89UD	43	$ .01	$ .08
Mulliniks, Rance	90UD	132	$ .01	$ .05
Munoz, Pedro	91UD	432	$ .05	$ .35
Munoz, Pedro	92UD	764	$ .01	$ .05
Munoz, Pedro	93UD	341	$ .01	$ .05
Murphy, Dale	89UD	357	$ .05	$ .35
Murphy, Dale	89UD	672	$ .01	$ .15
Murphy, Dale	90UD	533	$ .01	$ .10
Murphy, Dale	91UD	447	$ .01	$ .10
Murphy, Dale	92UD	127	$ .01	$ .10
Murphy, Dale	93UD	32	$ .01	$ .05
Murphy, Rob	89UD	372	$ .01	$ .08
Murphy, Rob	89UD	759	$ .01	$ .10
Murphy, Rob	90UD	461	$ .01	$ .05
Murphy, Rob	91UD	683	$ .01	$ .05
Murphy, Rob	91UD	707	$ .01	$ .05
Murphy, Rob	92UD	639	$ .01	$ .04
Murray, Eddie	89UD	275	$ .10	$ .50
Murray, Eddie	89UD	763	$ .10	$ .40
Murray, Eddie	90UD	277	$ .01	$ .15
Murray, Eddie	91UD	237	$ .01	$ .15
Murray, Eddie	92UD	32	$ .01	$ .10
Murray, Eddie	92UD	265	$ .01	$ .10
Murray, Eddie	92UD	728	$ .01	$ .10
Murray, Eddie	92UD	753	$ .01	$ .10
Murray, Eddie	93UD	115	$ .01	$ .10
Musselman, Jeff	89UD	41	$ .01	$ .08
Musselman, Jeff	90UD	585	$ .01	$ .05
Mussina, Mike	91UD	65	$ .20	$2.00
Mussina, Mike	92UD	675	$ .10	$ .50

Player	Year	No.	VG	EX/MT
Mussina, Mike	93UD	233	$ .10	$ .50
Myers, Greg	90UD	718	$ .01	$ .05
Myers, Greg	91UD	259	$ .01	$ .05
Myers, Greg	92UD	407	$ .01	$ .04
Myers, Randy	89UD	634	$ .01	$ .08
Myers, Randy	90UD	581	$ .01	$ .05
Myers, Randy	90UD	797	$ .01	$ .05
Myers, Randy	91UD	371	$ .01	$ .05
Myers, Randy	92UD	278	$ .01	$ .04
Myers, Randy	92UD	741	$ .01	$ .05
Myers, Randy	93UD	283	$ .01	$ .05
Nabholz, Chris	91UD	538	$ .05	$ .20
Nabholz, Chris	92UD	579	$ .01	$ .04
Nabholz, Chris	93UD	404	$ .01	$ .05
Naehring, Tim	91UD	527	$ .01	$ .15
Naehring, Tim	92UD	523	$ .01	$ .10
Nagy, Charles	91UD	19	$ .10	$ .50
Nagy, Charles	92UD	178	$ .01	$ .10
Nagy, Charles	93UD	243	$ .01	$ .05
Navarro, Jaime	90UD	646	$ .10	$ .50
Navarro, Jaime	91UD	476	$ .01	$ .05
Navarro, Jaime	92UD	633	$ .01	$ .04
Navarro, Jaime	93UD	237	$ .01	$ .05
Neagle, Denny	91UDF	34	$ .05	$ .20
Neagle, Denny	92UD	426	$ .05	$ .20
Neagle, Denny	92UD	748	$ .01	$ .05
Neagle, Denny	93UD	415	$ .01	$ .05
Neidlinger, Jim	91UD	632	$ .01	$ .15
Nelson, Gene	89UD	643	$ .01	$ .08
Nelson, Gene	90UD	80	$ .01	$ .05
Nelson, Gene	91UD	403	$ .01	$ .05
Nelson, Gene	92UD	508	$ .01	$ .04
Nelson, Rob	90UD	51	$ .01	$ .05

UPPER DECK

Player	Year	No.	VG	EX/MT
Nevers, Tom	92UD	53	$ .01	$ .10
Newfield, Marc	91UDF	18	$ .10	$ .75
Newfield, Marc	92UD	51	$ .05	$ .35
Newfield, Marc	92UD	64	$ .05	$ .25
Newman, Al	89UD	197	$ .01	$ .08
Newman, Al	90UD	199	$ .01	$ .05
Newman, Al	91UD	413	$ .01	$ .05
Newman, Al	92UD	293	$ .01	$ .04
Newson, Warren	92UD	621	$ .01	$ .10
Nichols, Rod	90UD	572	$ .01	$ .05
Nichols, Rod	92UD	212	$ .01	$ .04
Nied, Dave	93UD	27	$ .75	$3.00
Niedenfuer, Tom	89UD	488	$ .01	$ .08
Nieves, Juan	89UD	646	$ .01	$ .08
Nieves, Juan	90UD	648	$ .01	$ .05
Nieves, Melvin	93UD	21	$ .10	$ .40
Nilsson, Dave	91UDF	25	$ .10	$ .50
Nilsson, Dave	92UD	57	$ .01	$ .15
Nipper, Al	89UD	494	$ .01	$ .08
Nixon, Otis	89UD	480	$ .01	$ .08
Nixon, Otis	90UD	379	$ .01	$ .05
Nixon, Otis	91UD	520	$ .01	$ .05
Nixon, Otis	91UDF	58	$ .01	$ .05
Nixon, Otis	92UD	451	$ .01	$ .04
Nixon, Otis	93UD	292	$ .01	$ .05
Nokes, Matt	89UD	150	$ .01	$ .08
Nokes, Matt	90UD	226	$ .01	$ .05
Nokes, Matt	90UD	744	$ .01	$ .05
Nokes, Matt	91UD	673	$ .01	$ .05
Nokes, Matt	92UD	295	$ .01	$ .04
Nokes, Matt	93UD	116	$ .01	$ .05
Nosek, Randy	90UD	2	$ .01	$ .15
Novoa, Rafael	91UD	674	$ .01	$ .15
Nunez, Clemente	92UD	701	$ .05	$ .25
Nunez, Jose	90UD	716	$ .01	$ .05
O'Brien, Charlie	90UD	650	$ .01	$ .05
O'Brien, Charlie	91UD	420	$ .01	$ .05
O'Brien, Charlie	92UD	381	$ .01	$ .04
O'Brien, Charlie	93UD	209	$ .01	$ .05
O'Brien, Pete	89UD	54	$ .01	$ .08
O'Brien, Pete	89UD	800	$ .01	$ .15
O'Brien, Pete	90UD	110	$ .01	$ .05
O'Brien, Pete	90UD	719	$ .01	$ .05
O'Brien, Pete	91UD	459	$ .01	$ .05
O'Brien, Pete	92UD	388	$ .01	$ .04
O'Neill, Paul	89UD	428	$ .01	$ .08
O'Neill, Paul	90UD	161	$ .01	$ .10
O'Neill, Paul	91UD	133	$ .01	$ .05
O'Neill, Paul	92UD	464	$ .01	$ .04
Oberkfell, Ken	89UD	313	$ .01	$ .08
Oberkfell, Ken	90UD	360	$ .01	$ .05
Oester, Ron	89UD	287	$ .01	$ .08
Oester, Ron	90UD	118	$ .01	$ .05
Oester, Ron	91UD	611	$ .01	$ .05
Offerman, Jose	90UD	46	$ .05	$ .25
Offerman, Jose	91UD	356	$ .01	$ .10
Offerman, Jose	92UD	532	$ .01	$ .10
Offerman, Jose	93UD	225	$ .01	$ .05
Ojeda, Bob	89UD	386	$ .01	$ .08
Ojeda, Bob	90UD	204	$ .01	$ .05
Ojeda, Bob	91UD	179	$ .01	$ .05
Ojeda, Bob	91UD	715	$ .01	$ .05
Ojeda, Bob	92UD	666	$ .01	$ .04
Olerud, John	90UD	56	$ .15	$1.50
Olerud, John	91UD	145	$ .05	$ .35
Olerud, John	92UD	375	$ .01	$ .15
Olerud, John	93UD	344	$ .01	$ .10
Olin, Steve	90UD	553	$ .05	$ .25
Olin, Steve	91UD	118	$ .01	$ .05
Olin, Steve	92UD	215	$ .01	$ .04
Olin, Steve	93UD	206	$ .01	$ .05
Olivares, Omar	91UD	463	$ .05	$ .25
Olivares, Omar	92UD	478	$ .01	$ .04
Olivares, Omar	93UD	194	$ .01	$ .05
Oliver, Joe	90UD	568	$ .05	$ .20
Oliver, Joe	91UD	279	$ .01	$ .05
Oliver, Joe	92UD	101	$ .01	$ .04
Oliver, Joe	93UD	234	$ .01	$ .05
Oliveras, Francisco	92UD	49	$ .01	$ .04
Olson, Greg	92UD	189	$ .01	$ .04
Olson, Greg	93UD	187	$ .01	$ .05
Olson, Gregg	89UD	723	$ .15	$1.50
Olson, Gregg	90UD	604	$ .01	$ .15
Olson, Gregg	91UD	47	$ .01	$ .05
Olson, Gregg	91UD	303	$ .01	$ .15
Olson, Gregg	91UD	326	$ .01	$ .05
Olson, Gregg	92UD	227	$ .01	$ .04
Olwine, Ed	89UD	435	$ .01	$ .08
Oquendo, Jose	89UD	514	$ .01	$ .08

Jose Oquendo

Player	Year	No.	VG	EX/MT
Oquendo, Jose	90UD	319	$ .01	$ .05
Oquendo, Jose	91UD	193	$ .01	$ .05
Oquendo, Jose	92UD	283	$ .01	$ .04
Oquendo, Jose	93UD	84	$ .01	$ .05
Orosco, Jesse	89UD	87	$ .01	$ .08
Orosco, Jesse	90UD	588	$ .01	$ .05
Orosco, Jesse	91UD	240	$ .01	$ .05
Orosco, Jesse	92UD	580	$ .01	$ .04
Orsulak, Joe	89UD	429	$ .01	$ .08
Orsulak, Joe	90UD	270	$ .01	$ .05
Orsulak, Joe	91UD	506	$ .01	$ .05
Orsulak, Joe	92UD	207	$ .01	$ .04
Orsulak, Joe	93UD	260	$ .01	$ .05
Ortiz, Javier	92UD	657	$ .01	$ .10
Ortiz, Junior	89UD	86	$ .01	$ .08
Ortiz, Junior	90UD	389	$ .01	$ .05
Ortiz, Junior	91UD	170	$ .01	$ .05
Ortiz, Junior	92UD	109	$ .01	$ .04
Orton, John	90UD	672	$ .01	$ .15
Orton, John	93UD	317	$ .01	$ .05
Osborne, Donovan	92UD	702	$ .05	$ .25
Osborne, Donovan	92UD	770	$ .05	$ .20
Osborne, Donovan	92UD	777	$ .05	$ .25
Osborne, Donovan	93UD	347	$ .05	$ .20
Osuna, Al	91UD	752	$ .01	$ .10
Osuna, Al	92UD	259	$ .01	$ .04
Otto, David	89UD	4	$ .01	$ .10
Otto, Dave	92UD	698	$ .01	$ .04
Owen, Larry	89UD	528	$ .01	$ .08

UPPER DECK

Player	Year	No.	VG	EX/MT	Player	Year	No.	VG	EX/MT
Owen, Spike	89UD	161	$ .01	$ .08	Parker, Dave	91UD	733	$ .01	$ .05
Owen, Spike	89UD	717	$ .01	$ .10	Parker, Dave	92UD	522	$ .01	$ .04
Owen, Spike	90UD	291	$ .01	$ .05	Parker, Rick	90UD	732	$ .01	$ .15
Owen, Spike	91UD	189	$ .01	$ .05	Parrett, Jeff	89UD	398	$ .01	$ .15
Owen, Spike	92UD	206	$ .01	$ .04	Parrett, Jeff	89UD	741	$ .01	$ .15
Pagliarulo, Mike	89UD	569	$ .01	$ .08	Parrett, Jeff	90UD	92	$ .01	$ .05
Pagliarulo, Mike	90UD	329	$ .01	$ .05	Parrett, Jeff	91UD	417	$ .01	$ .05
Pagliarulo, Mike	91UD	206	$ .01	$ .05	Parrett, Jeff	93UD	311	$ .01	$ .05
Pagliarulo, Mike	91UD	709	$ .01	$ .05	Parrish, Lance	89UD	240	$ .01	$ .08
Pagliarulo, Mike	92UD	509	$ .01	$ .04	Parrish, Lance	89UD	775	$ .01	$ .10
Pagliarulo, Mike	93UD	306	$ .01	$ .05	Parrish, Lance	90UD	674	$ .01	$ .05
Pagnozzi, Tom	89UD	602	$ .01	$ .08	Parrish, Lance	91UD	552	$ .01	$ .05
Pagnozzi, Tom	91UD	91	$ .01	$ .05	Parrish, Lance	92UD	431	$ .01	$ .04
Pagnozzi, Tom	92UD	379	$ .01	$ .04	Parrish, Lance	93UD	117	$ .01	$ .05
Pagnozzi, Tom	93UD	405	$ .01	$ .05	Parrish, Larry	89UD	36	$ .01	$ .08
Palacios, Ray	89UD	21	$ .01	$ .10	Pasqua, Dan	89UD	204	$ .01	$ .08
Palacios, Vicente	91UDF	71	$ .01	$ .05	Pasqua, Dan	90UD	286	$ .01	$ .05
Pall, Donn	90UD	386	$ .01	$ .05	Pasqua, Dan	91UD	605	$ .01	$ .05
Pall, Donn	91UD	603	$ .01	$ .05	Pasqua, Dan	92UD	281	$ .01	$ .04
Pall, Donn	92UD	592	$ .01	$ .04	Patterson, Bob	93UD	412	$ .01	$ .05
Palmeiro, Rafael	89UD	235	$ .10	$ .75	Patterson, John	92UD	778	$ .01	$ .10
Palmeiro, Rafael	89UD	772	$ .10	$ .75	Patterson, Ken	91UD	283	$ .01	$ .05
Palmeiro, Rafael	90UD	335	$ .05	$ .20	Patterson, Ken	92UD	440	$ .01	$ .04
Palmeiro, Rafael	91UD	30	$ .01	$ .10	Pecota, Bill	89UD	507	$ .01	$ .08
Palmeiro, Rafael	91UD	474	$ .01	$ .15	Pecota, Bill	92UD	240	$ .01	$ .04
Palmeiro, Rafael	92UD	223	$ .01	$ .10	Pecota, Bill	92UD	793	$ .01	$ .05
Palmeiro, Rafael	93UD	52	$ .05	$ .35	Peltier, Dan	91UD	69	$ .05	$ .20
Palmer, David	89UD	515	$ .01	$ .08	Pena, Alejandro	89UD	137	$ .01	$ .08
Palmer, Dean	90UD	74	$ .20	$2.00	Pena, Alejandro	90UD	279	$ .01	$ .05
Palmer, Dean	91UDF	74	$ .05	$ .35	Pena, Alejandro	90UD	703	$ .01	$ .10
Palmer, Dean	92UD	465	$ .05	$ .25	Pena, Alejandro	91UD	388	$ .01	$ .05
Palmer, Dean	93UD	241	$ .01	$ .05	Pena, Alejandro	92UD	694	$ .01	$ .04
Pankovits, Jim	89UD	100	$ .01	$ .08	Pena, Geronimo	91UD	20	$ .01	$ .15
Paredes, Johnny	89UD	477	$ .01	$ .15	Pena, Geronimo	92UD	596	$ .01	$ .04
Parent, Mark	89UD	492	$ .01	$ .10	Pena, Geronimo	93UD	331	$ .01	$ .05
Parent, Mark	90UD	569	$ .01	$ .05	Pena, Tony	89UD	330	$ .01	$ .08
Parent, Mark	91UD	470	$ .01	$ .05	Pena, Tony	90UD	276	$ .01	$ .05
Paris, Kelly	89UD	192	$ .01	$ .08	Pena, Tony	90UD	748	$ .01	$ .05
					Pena, Tony	91UD	652	$ .01	$ .05
					Pena, Tony	92UD	252	$ .01	$ .04
					Pena, Tony	93UD	33	$ .01	$ .05
					Pena, Tony	93UD	185	$ .01	$ .05
					Pendleton, Terry	89UD	131	$ .10	$ .40
					Pendleton, Terry	90UD	469	$ .01	$ .10
					Pendleton, Terry	91UD	484	$ .01	$ .15
					Pendleton, Terry	91UD	708	$ .01	$ .15
					Pendleton, Terry	92UD	229	$ .01	$ .04
					Pendleton, Terry	93UD	163	$ .01	$ .05
					Peraza, Oswald	89UD	651	$ .01	$ .10
					Perez, Eduardo	92UD	52	$ .10	$ .50
					Perez, Melido	89UD	243	$ .05	$ .25
					Perez, Melido	90UD	525	$ .01	$ .05
					Perez, Melido	91UD	623	$ .01	$ .05
					Perez, Melido	92UD	190	$ .01	$ .04
					Perez, Melido	92UD	799	$ .01	$ .05
					Perez, Melido	93UD	326	$ .01	$ .05
					Perez, Mike	91UD	728	$ .01	$ .15
					Perez, Mike	93UD	204	$ .01	$ .05
					Perez, Pascual	89UD	498	$ .01	$ .08
					Perez, Pascual	90UD	487	$ .01	$ .05
					Perez, Pascual	90UD	769	$ .01	$ .05
					Perez, Pascual	91UD	671	$ .01	$ .05
					Perry, Gaylord	91UDH	2	$3.50	$14.00
					Perry, Gerald	89UD	431	$ .01	$ .08
					Perry, Gerald	90UD	101	$ .01	$ .05
					Perry, Gerald	90UD	707	$ .01	$ .05
					Perry, Gerald	91UD	219	$ .01	$ .05
					Perry, Gerald	92UD	690	$ .01	$ .04
					Perry, Pat	89UD	345	$ .01	$ .08
					Peters, Steve	89UD	771	$ .01	$ .15
					Peterson, Adam	92UD	602	$ .01	$ .04
					Petralli, Geno	89UD	482	$ .01	$ .08
					Petralli, Geno	90UD	633	$ .01	$ .05
					Petralli, Geno	91UD	492	$ .01	$ .05
					Petralli, Geno	92UD	599	$ .01	$ .04

Dave Parker

Parker, Dave	89UD	605	$ .01	$ .08
Parker, Dave	90UD	192	$ .01	$ .05
Parker, Dave	90UD	766	$ .01	$ .05
Parker, Dave	91UD	48	$ .01	$ .05
Parker, Dave	91UD	274	$ .01	$ .10

UPPER DECK

Player	Year	No.	VG	EX/MT
Petralli, Geno	93UD	83	$ .01	$ .05
Petry, Dan	89UD	552	$ .01	$ .08
Petry, Dan	90UD	690	$ .01	$ .05
Petry, Dan	91UD	316	$ .01	$ .05
Pettis, Gary	89UD	117	$ .01	$ .08
Pettis, Gary	90UD	385	$ .01	$ .05
Pettis, Gary	90UD	770	$ .01	$ .05
Pettis, Gary	91UD	229	$ .01	$ .05
Pettis, Gary	92UD	179	$ .01	$ .04
Pevey, Marty	90UD	628	$ .01	$ .10
Phelps, Ken	89UD	167	$ .01	$ .08
Phillips, Tony	89UD	267	$ .01	$ .08
Phillips, Tony	90UD	154	$ .01	$ .05
Phillips, Tony	90UD	768	$ .01	$ .05
Phillips, Tony	91UD	131	$ .01	$ .05
Phillips, Tony	92UD	184	$ .01	$ .04
Phillips, Tony	93UD	195	$ .01	$ .05
Piazza, Mike	93UD	2	$1.00	$4.00
Pichardo, Hipolito	93UD	72	$ .01	$ .05
Pico, Jeff	89UD	491	$ .01	$ .15
Pina, Mickey	90UD	764	$ .01	$ .15
Plantier, Phil	91UD	2	$ .10	$ .75
Plantier, Phil	92UD	425	$ .01	$ .15
Plantier, Phil	93UD	274	$ .01	$ .10
Plesac, Dan	89UD	630	$ .01	$ .08
Plesac, Dan	90UD	477	$ .01	$ .05
Plesac, Dan	91UD	322	$ .01	$ .05
Plesac, Dan	92UD	550	$ .01	$ .04
Plunk, Eric	89UD	353	$ .01	$ .08
Plunk, Eric	90UD	630	$ .01	$ .05
Plunk, Eric	91UD	695	$ .01	$ .05
Plunk, Eric	92UD	608	$ .01	$ .04
Plympton, Jeff	92UD	71	$ .01	$ .10
Polidor, Gus	90UD	480	$ .01	$ .05
Polonia, Luis	89UD	162	$ .01	$ .10
Polonia, Luis	90UD	316	$ .01	$ .05
Polonia, Luis	91UD	187	$ .01	$ .05
Polonia, Luis	92UD	147	$ .01	$ .04
Polonia, Luis	93UD	178	$ .01	$ .05
Portugal, Mark	89UD	358	$ .01	$ .08
Portugal, Mark	90UD	502	$ .01	$ .05
Portugal, Mark	91UD	250	$ .01	$ .05
Portugal, Mark	92UD	448	$ .01	$ .04
Portugal, Mark	93UD	99	$ .01	$ .05
Powell, Dennis	90UD	229	$ .01	$ .05
Power, Ted	90UD	340	$ .01	$ .05
Power, Ted	91UD	450	$ .01	$ .05
Power, Ted	92UD	680	$ .01	$ .04
Presley, Jim	89UD	642	$ .01	$ .08
Presley, Jim	90UD	315	$ .01	$ .05
Presley, Jim	90UD	760	$ .01	$ .05
Presley, Jim	91UD	282	$ .01	$ .05
Presley, Jim	91UD	791	$ .01	$ .05
Price, Joe	89UD	505	$ .01	$ .08
Pride, Yankee	93UD	47	$ .01	$ .15
Prince, Tom	00UD	311	$ .01	$ .08
Puckett, Kirby	89UD	376	$ .15	$1.50
Puckett, Kirby	90UD	48	$ .05	$ .20
Puckett, Kirby	90UD	236	$ .10	$ .50
Puckett, Kirby	91UD	544	$ .05	$ .35
Puckett, Kirby	92UD	254	$ .05	$ .20
Puckett, Kirby	93UD	34	$ .05	$ .20
Puckett, Kirby	93UD	50	$ .01	$ .15
Pugh, Tim	93UD	26	$ .10	$ .40
Puhl, Terry	90UD	201	$ .01	$ .05
Puleo, Charlie	89UD	589	$ .01	$ .08
Pulliam, Harvey	92UD	457	$ .05	$ .20
Quinones, Luis	90UD	593	$ .01	$ .05
Quinones, Rey	89UD	508	$ .01	$ .08
Quinones, Rey	89UD	750	$ .01	$ .10
Quintana, Carlos	89UD	26	$ .05	$ .20
Quintana, Carlos	90UD	465	$ .01	$ .05
Quintana, Carlos	91UD	232	$ .01	$ .05
Quintana, Carlos	92UD	421	$ .01	$ .04
Quirk, Jamie	89UD	620	$ .01	$ .08
Quisenberry, Dan	89UD	533	$ .01	$ .08
Quisenberry, Dan	90UD	659	$ .01	$ .05
Radinsky, Scott	90UD	725	$ .05	$ .35
Radinsky, Scott	91UD	621	$ .01	$ .05
Radinsky, Scott	92UD	594	$ .01	$ .04
Radinsky, Scott	93UD	298	$ .01	$ .05
Raines, Tim	89UD	402	$ .01	$ .15
Raines, Tim	90UD	29	$ .01	$ .05
Raines, Tim	90UD	177	$ .01	$ .10
Raines, Tim	91UD	143	$ .01	$ .10
Raines, Tim	91UD	773	$ .01	$ .10
Raines, Tim	92UD	575	$ .01	$ .04
Ramirez, Manny	92UD	63	$ .10	$1.00

Rafael Ramirez

Player	Year	No.	VG	EX/MT
Ramirez, Rafael	89UD	341	$ .01	$ .08
Ramirez, Rafael	90UD	144	$ .01	$ .05
Ramirez, Rafael	91UD	210	$ .01	$ .05
Ramirez, Rafael	92UD	582	$ .01	$ .04
Ramos, Domingo	90UD	150	$ .01	$ .05
Ramos, Domingo	91UD	85	$ .01	$ .05
Ramsey, Fernando	93UD	382	$ .01	$ .15
Randolph, Willie	89UD	237	$ .01	$ .08
Randolph, Willie	89UD	777	$ .01	$ .10
Randolph, Willie	90UD	183	$ .01	$ .05
Randolph, Willie	90UD	704	$ .01	$ .05
Randolph, Willie	91UD	421	$ .01	$ .05
Randolph, Willie	91UD	720	$ .01	$ .05
Randolph, Willie	92UD	211	$ .01	$ .04
Randolph, Willie	92UD	795	$ .01	$ .05
Randolph, Willie	93UD	419	$ .01	$ .05
Rasmussen, Dennis	89UD	645	$ .01	$ .08
Rasmussen, Dennis	90UD	594	$ .01	$ .05
Rasmussen, Dennis	91UD	230	$ .01	$ .05
Rasmussen, Dennis	92UD	439	$ .01	$ .04
Rawley, Shane	89UD	427	$ .01	$ .08
Rawley, Shane	89UD	786	$ .01	$ .10
Rawley, Shane	90UD	438	$ .01	$ .05
Ray, Johnny	89UD	481	$ .01	$ .08
Ray, Johnny	90UD	509	$ .01	$ .05
Ray, Johnny	91UD	678	$ .01	$ .05
Ready, Randy	89UD	474	$ .01	$ .08
Ready, Randy	90UD	404	$ .01	$ .05
Ready, Randy	91UD	540	$ .01	$ .05
Ready, Randy	92UD	408	$ .01	$ .04

UPPER DECK

Player	Year	No.	VG	EX/MT
Reardon, Jeff	89UD	596	$ .05	$ .20
Reardon, Jeff	90UD	417	$ .01	$ .05
Reardon, Jeff	90UD	729	$ .01	$ .10
Reardon, Jeff	91UD	418	$ .01	$ .05
Reardon, Jeff	92UD	501	$ .01	$ .04
Redus, Gary	89UD	419	$ .01	$ .08
Redus, Gary	90UD	248	$ .01	$ .05
Redus, Gary	91UD	38	$ .01	$ .05
Redus, Gary	92UD	519	$ .01	$ .04
Reed, Jeff	89UD	276	$ .01	$ .08
Reed, Jeff	90UD	165	$ .01	$ .05
Reed, Jeff	92UD	299	$ .01	$ .04
Reed, Jerry	89UD	529	$ .01	$ .08
Reed, Jerry	90UD	210	$ .01	$ .05
Reed, Jody	89UD	370	$ .01	$ .15
Reed, Jody	90UD	321	$ .01	$ .05
Reed, Jody	91UD	184	$ .01	$ .05
Reed, Jody	92UD	404	$ .01	$ .04
Reed, Jody	93UD	96	$ .01	$ .05
Reimer, Kevin	91UD	494	$ .01	$ .15
Reimer, Kevin	92UD	201	$ .01	$ .04
Remlinger, Mike	91UDF	36	$ .01	$ .10
Remlinger, Mike	92UD	585	$ .01	$ .04
Renteria, Rich	89UD	547	$ .01	$ .15
Reuschel, Rick	89UD	194	$ .01	$ .08
Reuschel, Rick	90UD	696	$ .01	$ .05
Reuschel, Rick	91UD	249	$ .01	$ .05
Reuss, Jerry	90UD	96	$ .01	$ .05
Reyes, Gilberto	92UD	230	$ .01	$ .04
Reynolds, Craig	89UD	284	$ .01	$ .08
Reynolds, Harold	89UD	249	$ .01	$ .08
Reynolds, Harold	90UD	179	$ .01	$ .05
Reynolds, Harold	91UD	32	$ .01	$ .05
Reynolds, Harold	91UD	148	$ .01	$ .05
Reynolds, Harold	92UD	314	$ .01	$ .04
Reynolds, Harold	93UD	35	$ .01	$ .05
Reynolds, R. J.	89UD	315	$ .01	$ .08
Reynolds, R. J.	90UD	540	$ .01	$ .05
Reynolds, R. J.	91UD	150	$ .01	$ .05
Reynoso, Armando	92UD	674	$ .01	$ .15
Rhoden, Rick	89UD	56	$ .01	$ .08
Rhoden, Rick	90UD	504	$ .01	$ .05
Rhodes, Arthur	91UDF	13	$ .10	$ .50
Rhodes, Arthur	92UD	17	$ .01	$ .10
Rhodes, Arthur	93UD	384	$ .01	$ .10
Rhodes, Karl	91UD	466	$ .01	$ .10
Rhodes, Karl "Tuffy"	91UD	702	$ .10	$ .50
Rice, Jim	89UD	413	$ .01	$ .15
Rice, Jim	90UD	373	$ .01	$ .05
Richie, Rob	90UD	76	$ .01	$ .10
Righetti, Dave	89UD	59	$ .01	$ .08
Righetti, Dave	90UD	479	$ .01	$ .05
Righetti, Dave	91UD	448	$ .01	$ .05
Righetti, Dave	91UD	778	$ .01	$ .05
Righetti, Dave	92UD	171	$ .01	$ .04
Rijo, Jose	89UD	619	$ .01	$ .10
Rijo, Jose	90UD	216	$ .01	$ .05
Rijo, Jose	91UD	298	$ .01	$ .05
Rijo, Jose	92UD	258	$ .01	$ .04
Rijo, Jose	92UD	712	$ .01	$ .05
Rijo, Jose	93UD	226	$ .01	$ .05
Riles, Ernie	89UD	497	$ .01	$ .08
Riles, Ernie	90UD	378	$ .01	$ .05
Riles, Ernest	91UD	780	$ .01	$ .05
Riles, Ernest	92UD	494	$ .01	$ .04
Ripken, Billy	89UD	283	$ .01	$ .08
Ripken, Billy	90UD	184	$ .01	$ .05
Ripken, Billy	91UD	550	$ .01	$ .05
Ripken, Billy	92UD	82	$ .05	$ .25
Ripken, Billy	92UD	250	$ .01	$ .04
Ripken, Billy	93UD	181	$ .01	$ .05
Ripken, Jr., Cal	89UD	467	$ .20	$2.00
Ripken, Jr., Cal	89UD	682	$ .05	$ .50
Ripken, Jr., Cal	90UD	266	$ .10	$1.00
Ripken, Jr., Cal	91UD	347	$ .10	$ .50
Ripken, Jr., Cal	91UDF	85	$ .10	$ .40
Ripken, Jr., Cal	92UD	82	$ .05	$ .25
Ripken, Jr., Cal	92UD	165	$ .05	$ .35
Ripken, Jr., Cal	92UD	645	$ .05	$ .25
Ripken, Jr., Cal	93UD	36	$ .05	$ .25
Ripken, Jr., Cal	93UD	44	$ .05	$ .20
Ritz, Kevin	90UD	98	$ .01	$ .15
Rivera, Ben	93UD	389	$ .01	$ .05
Rivera, Luis	89UD	423	$ .01	$ .10
Rivera, Luis	90UD	482	$ .01	$ .05
Rivera, Luis	91UD	182	$ .01	$ .05
Rivera, Luis	92UD	308	$ .01	$ .04
Roberts, Bip	90UD	303	$ .01	$ .05
Roberts, Bip	91UD	271	$ .01	$ .05
Roberts, Bip	92UD	141	$ .01	$ .04
Roberts, Bip	92UD	763	$ .01	$ .05
Roberts, Bip	93UD	112	$ .01	$ .05
Robidoux, Billy Jo	90UD	782	$ .01	$ .05
Robinson, Don	89UD	523	$ .01	$ .08
Robinson, Don	90UD	616	$ .01	$ .05
Robinson, Don	91UD	402	$ .01	$ .05
Robinson, Jeff D	89UD	332	$ .01	$ .08
Robinson, Jeff D.	90UD	403	$ .01	$ .05
Robinson, Jeff M.	89UD	472	$ .01	$ .15
Robinson, Jeff M.	90UD	552	$ .01	$ .05
Robinson, Jeff M.	91UD	676	$ .01	$ .05
Robinson, Jeff M.	91UD	796	$ .01	$ .05
Robinson, Jeff M.	92UD	320	$ .01	$ .04
Robinson, Ron	89UD	187	$ .01	$ .08
Robinson, Ron	91UD	620	$ .01	$ .10
Robinson, Ron	92UD	198	$ .01	$ .04
Rochford, Mike	90UD	694	$ .01	$ .05
Rodriguez, Ivan	93UD	52	$ .05	$ .35
Rodriguez, Carlos	92UD	77	$ .01	$ .15
Rodriguez, Frankie	91UDF	21	$ .10	$ .75

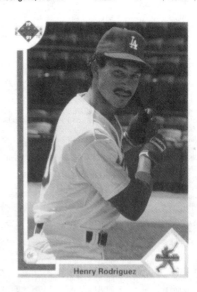
Henry Rodriguez

Player	Year	No.	VG	EX/MT
Rodriguez, Henry	91UD	21	$ .05	$ .25
Rodriguez, Henry	93UD	391	$ .01	$ .05
Rodriguez, Ivan	92UD	245	$ .10	$ .40
Rodriguez, Ivan	93UD	123	$ .05	$ .25
Rodriguez, Rich	91UD	640	$ .01	$ .15
Rodriguez, Rich	92UD	568	$ .01	$ .04
Rodriguez, Rich	93UD	330	$ .01	$ .05
Rodriguez, Ivan	91UDF	55	$ .15	$1.50

UPPER DECK

Player	Year	No.	VG	EX/MT
Rogers, Kenny	90UD	606	$ .01	$ .10
Rogers, Kenny	91UD	606	$ .01	$ .05
Rogers, Kenny	92UD	651	$ .01	$ .04
Rogers, Kenny	93UD	92	$ .01	$ .05
Rogers, Kevin	93UD	8	$ .05	$ .20
Rohde, Dave	91UD	662	$ .01	$ .15
Rojas, Mel	90UD	772	$ .05	$ .20
Rojas, Mel	91UD	357	$ .01	$ .05
Rojas, Mel	92UD	683	$ .01	$ .04
Rojas, Mel	93UD	190	$ .01	$ .05
Romero, Ed	89UD	40	$ .01	$ .08
Romine, Kevin	89UD	524	$ .01	$ .08
Romine, Kevin	90UD	441	$ .01	$ .05
Roomes, Rolando	89UD	6	$ .01	$ .10
Roomes, Rolando	90UD	170	$ .01	$ .05
Rose, Bobby	90UD	77	$ .05	$ .20
Rose, Bobby	92UD	611	$ .01	$ .04
Rosenberg, Steve	89UD	715	$ .01	$ .15
Rosenberg, Steve	90UD	522	$ .01	$ .05
Roysler, Jerry	89UD	433	$ .01	$ .08
Rucker, Dave	89UD	436	$ .01	$ .08
Ruess, Jerry	89UD	151	$ .01	$ .08
Ruffin, Bruce	89UD	319	$ .01	$ .08
Ruffin, Bruce	90UD	580	$ .01	$ .05
Ruffin, Bruce	91UD	410	$ .01	$ .05
Ruffin, Bruce	92UD	309	$ .01	$ .04
Runge, Paul	89UD	55	$ .01	$ .08
Ruskin, Scott	90UD	713	$ .01	$ .15
Ruskin, Scott	91UD	383	$ .01	$ .10
Ruskin, Scott	92UD	384	$ .01	$ .04
Russell, Jeff	89UD	461	$ .01	$ .08
Russell, Jeff	90UD	638	$ .01	$ .05
Russell, Jeff	91UD	648	$ .01	$ .05
Russell, Jeff	92UD	695	$ .01	$ .04
Russell, John	89UD	532	$ .01	$ .08
Russell, John	91UD	191	$ .01	$ .05
Ryan, Nolan	89UD	145	$1.00	$4.00
Ryan, Nolan	89UD	669	$ .10	$1.00
Ryan, Nolan	89UD	774	$1.00	$4.00
Ryan, Nolan	90UD	34	$ .10	$1.00
Ryan, Nolan	90UD	544	$ .15	$1.25
Ryan, Nolan	90UD	734	$ .10	$1.00
Ryan, Nolan	91UD	345	$ .10	$ .75
Ryan, Nolan	91UDSP	2	$1.00	$4.00
Ryan, Nolan	92UD	92	$ .05	$ .20
Ryan, Nolan	92UD	655	$ .10	$ .50
Ryan, Nolan	93UD	37	$ .05	$ .35
Ryan, Nolan	93UD	155	$ .10	$ .50
Saberhagen, Bret	89UD	37	$ .01	$ .15
Saberhagen, Bret	90UD	326	$ .01	$ .10
Saberhagen, Bret	91UD	33	$ .01	$ .05
Saberhagen, Bret	91UD	435	$ .01	$ .10
Saberhagen, Bret	92UD	233	$ .01	$ .04
Saberhagen, Bret	92UD	751	$ .01	$ .05
Saberhagen, Bret	93UD	282	$ .01	$ .05
Sabo, Chris	89UD	180	$ .10	$ .75
Sabo, Chris	89UD	663	$ .05	$ .25
Sabo, Chris	90UD	181	$ .01	$ .15
Sabo, Chris	91UD	77	$ .01	$ .05
Sabo, Chris	91UD	135	$ .01	$ .10
Sabo, Chris	91UDF	94	$ .01	$ .10
Sabo, Chris	92UD	123	$ .01	$ .04
Sabo, Chris	93UD	147	$ .01	$ .05
Salas, Mark	89UD	460	$ .01	$ .08
Salas, Mark	91UD	205	$ .01	$ .05
Salazar, Angel	89UD	222	$ .01	$ .08
Salazar, Luis	89UD	136	$ .01	$ .08
Salazar, Luis	90UD	6	$ .01	$ .05
Salazar, Luis	91UD	311	$ .01	$ .05
Salazar, Luis	92UD	638	$ .01	$ .04
Salkeld, Roger	91UD	63	$ .05	$ .20
Salkeld, Roger	92UD	15	$ .05	$ .20
Salmon, Tim	93UD	1	$ .05	$ .25
Salmon, Tim	93UD	25	$ .75	$3.00
Sampen, Bill	90UD	724	$ .01	$ .15
Sampen, Bill	91UD	661	$ .01	$ .15
Samuel, Juan	89UD	336	$ .01	$ .10
Samuel, Juan	90UD	583	$ .01	$ .05
Samuel, Juan	90UD	795	$ .01	$ .05
Samuel, Juan	91UD	117	$ .01	$ .05
Samuel, Juan	92UD	195	$ .01	$ .04
Sanchez, Alex	90UD	757	$ .01	$ .05
Sanchez, Israel	89UD	326	$ .01	$ .10
Sanchez, Israel	90UD	384	$ .01	$ .05
Sanchez, Rey	92UD	562	$ .01	$ .15
Sandberg, Ryne	89UD	120	$ .15	$1.50
Sandberg, Ryne	89UD	675	$ .05	$ .35
Sandberg, Ryne	90UD	324	$ .10	$ .75
Sandberg, Ryne	91UD	132	$ .10	$ .40
Sandberg, Ryne	91UD	725	$ .05	$ .25
Sandberg, Ryne	91UDF	79	$ .05	$ .35
Sandberg, Ryne	91UDF	93	$ .05	$ .25
Sandberg, Ryne	92UD	145	$ .05	$ .25
Sandberg, Ryne	93UD	38	$ .05	$ .20
Sandberg, Ryne	93UD	175	$ .05	$ .25

Deion Sanders

Player	Year	No.	VG	EX/MT
Sanders, Deion	90UD	13	$ .15	$1.50
Sanders, Deion	91UD	352	$ .05	$ .25
Sanders, Deion	91UD	743	$ .05	$ .25
Sanders, Deion	92UD	247	$ .05	$ .20
Sanders, Deion	92UDСР	3	$2.00	$8.00
Sanders, Deion	93UD	166	$ .01	$ .15
Sanders, Reggie	91UD	71	$ .10	$1.00
Sanders, Reggie	91UDF	1	$ .10	$ .50
Sanders, Reggie	91UDF	11	$ .10	$ .40
Sanders, Reggie	92UD	27	$ .05	$ .25
Sanders, Reggie	93UD	354	$ .01	$ .15
Sanderson, Scott	89UD	342	$ .01	$ .08
Sanderson, Scott	90UD	39	$ .01	$ .05
Sanderson, Scott	90UD	739	$ .01	$ .05
Sanderson, Scott	91UD	582	$ .01	$ .05
Sanderson, Scott	91UD	750	$ .01	$ .05
Sanderson, Scott	92UD	415	$ .01	$ .04
Sanford, Mo	92UD	45	$ .05	$ .25
Santana, Andres	91UD	87	$ .01	$ .15
Santana, Rafael	89UD	216	$ .01	$ .08
Santiago, Benito	89UD	165	$ .01	$ .10
Santiago, Benito	90UD	12	$ .01	$ .05
Santiago, Benito	90UD	325	$ .01	$ .15

UPPER DECK

Player	Year	No.	VG	EX/MT
Santiago, Benito	91UD	467	$ .01	$ .05
Santiago, Benito	91UDF	91	$ .01	$ .05
Santiago, Benito	92UD	253	$ .01	$ .04
Santovenia, Nelson	89UD	380	$ .01	$ .15
Santovenia, Nelson	90UD	432	$ .01	$ .05

Mackey Sasser

Player	Year	No.	VG	EX/MT
Sasser, Mackey	89UD	561	$ .01	$ .10
Sasser, Mackey	90UD	185	$ .01	$ .05
Sasser, Mackey	91UD	103	$ .01	$ .05
Sax, Steve	89UD	53	$ .01	$ .10
Sax, Steve	89UD	748	$ .01	$ .15
Sax, Steve	90UD	18	$ .01	$ .05
Sax, Steve	90UD	172	$ .01	$ .05
Sax, Steve	91UD	462	$ .01	$ .05
Sax, Steve	92UD	358	$ .01	$ .04
Sax, Steve	92UD	743	$ .01	$ .05
Sax, Steve	93UD	369	$ .01	$ .05
Scanlan, Bob	91UDF	48	$ .01	$ .10
Schilling, Curt	91UD	528	$ .01	$ .05
Schilling, Curt	93UD	67	$ .01	$ .05
Schiraldi, Calvin	89UD	82	$ .01	$ .08
Schiraldi, Calvin	90UD	643	$ .01	$ .05
Schmidt, Dave	89UD	447	$ .01	$ .08
Schmidt, Dave	90UD	641	$ .01	$ .05
Schmidt, Dave	91UD	684	$ .01	$ .05
Schmidt, Mike	89UD	406	$ .15	$1.50
Schmidt, Mike	89UD	684	$ .10	$ .50
Schmidt, Mike	90UD	20	$ .10	$ .50
Schofield, Dick	89UD	201	$ .01	$ .08
Schofield, Dick	90UD	669	$ .01	$ .05
Schofield, Dick	91UD	169	$ .01	$ .05
Schofield, Dick	92UD	269	$ .01	$ .04
Schofield, Dick	92UD	791	$ .01	$ .05
Schooler, Mike	89UD	28	$ .01	$ .15
Schooler, Mike	90UD	214	$ .01	$ .10
Schooler, Mike	91UD	638	$ .01	$ .05
Schooler, Mike	92UD	405	$ .01	$ .04
Schourek, Pete	91UD	766	$ .05	$ .20
Schourek, Pete	92UD	673	$ .01	$ .10
Schroeder, Bill	89UD	627	$ .01	$ .08
Schroeder, Bill	90UD	149	$ .01	$ .05
Schu, Rick	89UD	490	$ .01	$ .08
Schulz, Jeff	91UD	607	$ .01	$ .15
Scioscia, Mike	89UD	116	$ .01	$ .08
Scioscia, Mike	90UD	298	$ .01	$ .05
Scioscia, Mike	91UD	139	$ .01	$ .05
Scioscia, Mike	92UD	152	$ .01	$ .04
Scott, Gary	91UD	58	$ .05	$ .25
Scott, Mike	89UD	295	$ .01	$ .15
Scott, Mike	90UD	88	$ .01	$ .05
Scott, Mike	90UD	125	$ .01	$ .05
Scott, Mike	91UD	531	$ .01	$ .05
Scudder, Scott	90UD	164	$ .05	$ .20
Scudder, Scott	91UD	615	$ .01	$ .10
Scudder, Scott	92UD	485	$ .01	$ .04
Scudder, Scott	92UD	787	$ .01	$ .05
Scudder, Scott	93UD	208	$ .01	$ .05
Scurry, Rod	89UD	208	$ .01	$ .08
Seanez, Rudy	91UD	358	$ .01	$ .15
Searcy, Steve	89UD	764	$ .01	$ .15
Searcy, Steve	90UD	575	$ .01	$ .10
Searcy, Steve	91UD	338	$ .01	$ .05
Segui, David	90UD	773	$ .05	$ .20
Segui, David	91UD	342	$ .01	$ .10
Segui, David	92UD	316	$ .01	$ .04
Seitzer, Kevin	89UD	510	$ .05	$ .30
Seitzer, Kevin	90UD	363	$ .01	$ .05
Seitzer, Kevin	91UD	433	$ .01	$ .05
Seitzer, Kevin	92UD	327	$ .01	$ .04
Seitzer, Kevin	92UD	783	$ .01	$ .05
Seitzer, Kevin	93UD	295	$ .01	$ .05
Selleck, Tom	92UDSP	4	$2.50	$10.00
Seminara, Frank	93UD	307	$ .01	$ .05
Servais, Scott	91UDF	68	$ .01	$ .10
Servais, Scott	92UD	561	$ .01	$ .15
Service, Scott	90UD	35	$ .01	$ .10
Sharperson, Mike	91UD	598	$ .01	$ .05
Sharperson, Mike	93UD	316	$ .01	$ .05
Shaw, Jeff	92UD	660	$ .01	$ .04
Sheets, Larry	89UD	254	$ .01	$ .08
Sheets, Larry	90UD	287	$ .01	$ .05
Sheets, Larry	91UD	340	$ .01	$ .05
Sheffield, Gary	89UD	13	$2.50	$10.00
Sheffield, Gary	90UD	157	$ .10	$1.00
Sheffield, Gary	91UD	266	$ .10	$ .40
Sheffield, Gary	92UD	84	$ .01	$ .10
Sheffield, Gary	92UD	234	$ .05	$ .25
Sheffield, Gary	92UD	745	$ .05	$ .25
Sheffield, Gary	93UD	222	$ .05	$ .25
Shelby, John	89UD	75	$ .01	$ .08
Shelby, John	91UD	201	$ .01	$ .05
Sheridan, Pat	89UD	652	$ .01	$ .10
Sheridan, Pat	90UD	460	$ .01	$ .05
Show, Eric	89UD	171	$ .01	$ .08
Show, Eric	90UD	587	$ .01	$ .05
Show, Eric	91UD	293	$ .01	$ .05
Show, Eric	91UD	798	$ .01	$ .05
Shumpert, Terry	90UD	733	$ .01	$ .15
Shumpert, Terry	91UD	521	$ .01	$ .10
Shumpert, Terry	92UD	348	$ .01	$ .04
Sierra, Ruben	89UD	416	$ .10	$1.00
Sierra, Ruben	89UD	686	$ .05	$ .25
Sierra, Ruben	90UD	355	$ .10	$ .40
Sierra, Ruben	91UD	455	$ .05	$ .25
Sierra, Ruben	92UD	176	$ .01	$ .15
Sierra, Ruben	93UD	49	$ .01	$ .15
Sierra, Ruben	93UD	145	$ .05	$ .20
Simmons, Ted	89UD	570	$ .01	$ .08
Simms, Mike	91UD	664	$ .01	$ .15
Simms, Mike	92UD	584	$ .01	$ .04
Simons, Doug	91UDF	63	$ .01	$ .05
Sisk, Doug	89UD	261	$ .01	$ .08
Skalski, Joe	89UD	716	$ .05	$ .10
Skinner, Joel	89UD	328	$ .01	$ .08
Skinner, Joel	90UD	369	$ .01	$ .05
Skinner, Joel	91UD	121	$ .01	$ .05
Skinner, Joel	92UD	199	$ .01	$ .04
Slaught, Don	89UD	178	$ .01	$ .08
Slaught, Don	90UD	152	$ .01	$ .05

UPPER DECK

Player	Year	No.	VG	EX/MT
Slaught, Don	91UD	181	$ .01	$ .05
Slaught, Don	92UD	540	$ .01	$ .04
Slocumb, Heathcliff	91UD	767	$ .01	$ .10
Slocumb, Heathcliff	92UD	569	$ .01	$ .04
Sluggers, Southside	93UD	51	$ .05	$ .35
Slusarski, Joe	91UD	777	$ .01	$ .10
Slusarski, Joe	92UD	663	$ .01	$ .10
Smiley, John	89UD	516	$ .01	$ .08
Smiley, John	90UD	387	$ .01	$ .10
Smiley, John	91UD	669	$ .01	$ .05
Smiley, John	92UD	467	$ .01	$ .04
Smiley, John	92UD	785	$ .01	$ .05
Smiley, John	93UD	268	$ .01	$ .05
Smith, Bryn	89UD	78	$ .01	$ .08
Smith, Bryn	90UD	579	$ .01	$ .05
Smith, Bryn	90UD	794	$ .01	$ .05
Smith, Bryn	91UD	307	$ .01	$ .05
Smith, Bryn	92UD	591	$ .01	$ .04
Smith, Dan	93UD	7	$ .05	$ .25
Smith, Dave	89UD	302	$ .01	$ .08
Smith, Dave	90UD	448	$ .01	$ .05
Smith, Dave	91UD	513	$ .01	$ .05
Smith, Dave	91UD	704	$ .01	$ .05
Smith, Dave	92UD	549	$ .01	$ .04
Smith, Dwight	89UD	780	$ .01	$ .15
Smith, Dwight	90UD	376	$ .01	$ .10

Dwight Smith

Player	Year	No.	VG	EX/MT
Smith, Dwight	91UD	452	$ .01	$ .05
Smith, Greg	90UD	738	$ .01	$ .10
Smith, Lee	89UD	521	$ .01	$ .08
Smith, Lee	90UD	393	$ .01	$ .05
Smith, Lee	91UD	348	$ .01	$ .05
Smith, Lee	92UD	376	$ .01	$ .04
Smith, Lee	93UD	82	$ .01	$ .05
Smith, Lonnie	89UD	731	$ .01	$ .10
Smith, Lonnie	90UD	215	$ .01	$ .05
Smith, Lonnie	91UD	305	$ .01	$ .05
Smith, Lonnie	92UD	301	$ .01	$ .04
Smith, Mark	92UD	66	$ .05	$ .25
Smith, Ozzie	89UD	265	$ .10	$ .50
Smith, Ozzie	89UD	674	$ .01	$ .15
Smith, Ozzie	90UD	225	$ .05	$ .20
Smith, Ozzie	91UD	162	$ .01	$ .15
Smith, Ozzie	91UDF	95	$ .01	$ .10

Player	Year	No.	VG	EX/MT
Smith, Ozzie	92UD	177	$ .01	$ .10
Smith, Ozzie	92UD	716	$ .01	$ .10
Smith, Ozzie	93UD	146	$ .01	$ .10
Smith, Pete	89UD	412	$ .10	$ .40
Smith, Pete	90UD	613	$ .01	$ .05
Smith, Pete	91UD	622	$ .01	$ .05
Smith, Roy	90UD	284	$ .01	$ .05
Smith, Roy	91UD	490	$ .01	$ .05
Smith, Zane	89UD	71	$ .01	$ .08
Smith, Zane	90UD	607	$ .01	$ .05
Smith, Zane	91UD	759	$ .01	$ .05
Smith, Zane	92UD	486	$ .01	$ .04
Smith, Zane	93UD	349	$ .01	$ .05
Smithson, Mike	89UD	38	$ .01	$ .08
Smithson, Mike	90UD	610	$ .01	$ .05
Smoltz, John	89UD	17	$1.00	$4.00
Smoltz, John	90UD	84	$ .01	$ .15
Smoltz, John	90UD	535	$ .05	$ .20
Smoltz, John	91UD	264	$ .01	$ .15
Smoltz, John	92UD	322	$ .01	$ .10
Smoltz, John	93UD	363	$ .01	$ .10
Snider, Van	89UD	23	$ .01	$ .10
Snow, J. T.	93UD	23	$ .75	$3.00
Snyder, Cory	89UD	170	$ .01	$ .10
Snyder, Cory	89UD	679	$ .01	$ .10
Snyder, Cory	90UD	126	$ .01	$ .05
Snyder, Cory	91UD	123	$ .01	$ .05
Snyder, Cory	91UD	724	$ .01	$ .05
Snyder, Cory	92UD	504	$ .01	$ .04
Snyder, Cory	93UD	218	$ .01	$ .05
Sojo, Luis	91UD	297	$ .01	$ .15
Sojo, Luis	91UD	714	$ .01	$ .05
Sojo, Luis	92UD	149	$ .01	$ .04
Sojo, Luis	93UD	94	$ .01	$ .05
Sorrento, Paul	90UD	784	$ .10	$ .40
Sorrento, Paul	91UD	680	$ .01	$ .10
Sorrento, Paul	93UD	196	$ .01	$ .05
Sosa, Sammy	90UD	17	$ .10	$ .50
Sosa, Sammy	91UD	265	$ .01	$ .10
Sosa, Sammy	92UD	438	$ .01	$ .04
Sosa, Sammy	92UD	723	$ .01	$ .05
Sosa, Sammy	93UD	127	$ .01	$ .05
Sox, Boston Cy	93UD	48	$ .01	$ .15
Speier, Chris	89UD	206	$ .01	$ .08
Spiers, Bill	89UD	745	$ .05	$ .20
Spiers, Bill	90UD	237	$ .01	$ .10
Spiers, Bill	91UD	268	$ .01	$ .05
Spiers, Bill	92UD	214	$ .01	$ .04
Spiers, Bill	93UD	325	$ .01	$ .05
Sprague, Ed	91UDF	47	$ .05	$ .35
Sprague, Ed	92UD	242	$ .01	$ .04
St. Claire, Randy	89UD	29	$ .01	$ .08
Stairs, Matt	92UD	786	$ .01	$ .15
Stanicek, Pete	89UD	592	$ .01	$ .10
Stankiewicz, Andy	92UD	779	$ .01	$ .10
Stankiewicz, Andy	93UD	257	$ .01	$ .05
Stanley, Bob	00UD	411	$ .01	$ .08
Stanley, Bob	90UD	654	$ .01	$ .05
Stanley, Mike	89UD	579	$ .01	$ .08
Stanton, Mike	90UD	61	$ .05	$ .35
Stanton, Mike	91UD	749	$ .01	$ .05
Stanton, Mike	92UD	653	$ .01	$ .04
Stanton, Mike	93UD	90	$ .01	$ .05
Stapleton, Dave	89UD	304	$ .01	$ .08
Stars, Latin	93UD	52	$ .05	$ .35
Staton, Dave	91UD	66	$ .05	$ .25
Steal, Iron and	93UD	44	$ .05	$ .20
Steinbach, Terry	89UD	256	$ .01	$ .10
Steinbach, Terry	90UD	246	$ .01	$ .05
Steinbach, Terry	91UD	153	$ .01	$ .05
Steinbach, Terry	92UD	473	$ .01	$ .04
Steinbach, Terry	93UD	278	$ .01	$ .05
Stevens, Lee	91UD	573	$ .05	$ .20
Stevens, Lee	92UD	634	$ .01	$ .04
Stewart, Dave	89UD	185	$ .01	$ .08

UPPER DECK

Player	Year	No.	VG	EX/MT
Stewart, Dave	90UD	272	$ .01	$ .10
Stewart, Dave	91UD	28	$ .01	$ .05
Stewart, Dave	91UD	127	$ .01	$ .10
Stewart, Dave	92UD	547	$ .01	$ .04
Stewart, Dave	93UD	39	$ .01	$ .05
Stieb, Dave	89UD	383	$ .01	$ .08
Stieb, Dave	90UD	605	$ .01	$ .05
Stieb, Dave	91UD	106	$ .01	$ .05
Stieb, Dave	92UD	99	$ .01	$ .04
Stieb, Dave	92UD	136	$ .01	$ .04
Stillwell, Kurt	89UD	616	$ .01	$ .08
Stillwell, Kurt	90UD	361	$ .01	$ .05
Stillwell, Kurt	91UD	587	$ .01	$ .05
Stillwell, Kurt	92UD	329	$ .01	$ .04
Stillwell, Kurt	92UD	705	$ .01	$ .05
Stillwell, Kurt	93UD	152	$ .01	$ .05
Stone, Jeff	89UD	486	$ .01	$ .08
Stottlemyre, Todd	89UD	362	$ .05	$ .20
Stottlemyre, Todd	90UD	692	$ .01	$ .05
Stottlemyre, Todd	91UD	257	$ .01	$ .05
Stottlemyre, Todd	92UD	371	$ .01	$ .04
Stottlemyre, Todd	93UD	413	$ .01	$ .05
Straker, Les	89UD	83	$ .01	$ .08
Strawberry, Darryl	89UD	260	$ .10	$1.00
Strawberry, Darryl	89UD	681	$ .05	$ .25
Strawberry, Darryl	90UD	182	$ .05	$ .25
Strawberry, Darryl	91UD	245	$ .05	$ .25
Strawberry, Darryl	92UD	174	$ .01	$ .15
Stubbs, Franklin	89UD	91	$ .01	$ .08
Stubbs, Franklin	90UD	550	$ .01	$ .05
Stubbs, Franklin	91UD	168	$ .01	$ .05
Stubbs, Franklin	91UD	718	$ .01	$ .05
Stubbs, Franklin	92UD	396	$ .01	$ .04
Stubbs, Franklin	93UD	269	$ .01	$ .05
Sundberg, Jim	89UD	331	$ .01	$ .08
Surhoff, B. J.	89UD	343	$ .01	$ .08
Surhoff, B. J.	90UD	159	$ .01	$ .05
Surhoff, B. J.	91UD	254	$ .01	$ .05
Surhoff, B. J.	92UD	120	$ .01	$ .04
Surhoff, B. J.	93UD	102	$ .01	$ .05
Sutcliffe, Rick	89UD	303	$ .01	$ .10
Sutcliffe, Rick	90UD	109	$ .01	$ .05
Sutcliffe, Rick	91UD	473	$ .01	$ .05
Sutcliffe, Rick	92UD	529	$ .01	$ .04
Sutcliffe, Rick	92UD	708	$ .01	$ .05
Sutcliffe, Rick	92UD	708	$ .01	$ .05
Sutcliffe, Rick	93UD	80	$ .01	$ .05
Sutter, Bruce	89UD	414	$ .01	$ .08
Sveum, Dale	89UD	421	$ .01	$ .08
Sveum, Dale	90UD	499	$ .01	$ .05
Sveum, Dale	92UD	498	$ .01	$ .04
Swan, Russ	92UD	618	$ .01	$ .04
Swift, Bill	89UD	623	$ .10	$1.00
Swift, Bill	90UD	313	$ .01	$ .05
Swift, Bill	91UD	498	$ .01	$ .15
Swift, Bill	92UD	620	$ .01	$ .15
Swift, Bill	92UD	736	$ .01	$ .05
Swift, Bill	93UD	118	$ .01	$ .05
Swindell, Greg	89UD	250	$ .01	$ .15
Swindell, Greg	90UD	574	$ .01	$ .10
Swindell, Greg	91UD	236	$ .01	$ .05
Swindell, Greg	92UD	95	$ .01	$ .04
Swindell, Greg	92UD	336	$ .01	$ .04
Swindell, Greg	92UD	765	$ .01	$ .05
Tabler, Pat	89UD	233	$ .01	$ .08
Tabler, Pat	90UD	142	$ .01	$ .05
Tabler, Pat	92UD	203	$ .01	$ .04
Tanana, Frank	89UD	391	$ .01	$ .08
Tanana, Frank	90UD	516	$ .01	$ .05
Tanana, Frank	91UD	369	$ .01	$ .05
Tanana, Frank	92UD	605	$ .01	$ .04
Tanana, Frank	93UD	68	$ .01	$ .05
Tapani, Kevin	90UD	87	$ .10	$ .75
Tapani, Kevin	91UD	434	$ .01	$ .15
Tapani, Kevin	92UD	624	$ .01	$ .04
Tapani, Kevin	93UD	313	$ .01	$ .05
Tartabull, Danny	89UD	329	$ .05	$ .35
Tartabull, Danny	90UD	656	$ .01	$ .15
Tartabull, Danny	91UD	523	$ .01	$ .15
Tartabull, Danny	91UDF	89	$ .01	$ .10
Tartabull, Danny	92UD	88	$ .01	$ .04
Tartabull, Danny	92UD	237	$ .01	$ .10
Tartabull, Danny	92UD	746	$ .01	$ .05

Player	Year	No.	VG	EX/MT
Tartabull, Danny	**93UD**	**242**	**$ .01**	**$ .05**
Tatum, Jim	93UD	13	$ .05	$ .25
Taubensee, Eddie	92UD	757	$ .01	$ .15
Taubensee, Eddie	93UD	296	$ .01	$ .10
Tekulve, Kent	89UD	207	$ .01	$ .08
Telford, Anthony	91UD	304	$ .01	$ .15
Templeton, Garry	89UD	297	$ .01	$ .08
Templeton, Garry	90UD	288	$ .01	$ .05
Templeton, Garry	91UD	295	$ .01	$ .05
Templeton, Garry	92UD	411	$ .01	$ .04
Terrell, Walt	89UD	475	$ .01	$ .08
Terrell, Walt	89UD	703	$ .01	$ .10
Terrell, Walt	90UD	661	$ .01	$ .05
Terrell, Walt	91UD	320	$ .01	$ .05
Terrell, Walt	92UD	520	$ .01	$ .04
Terry, Scott	90UD	260	$ .01	$ .05
Terry, Scott	92UD	688	$ .01	$ .04
Tettleton, Mickey	89UD	553	$ .01	$ .08
Tettleton, Mickey	90UD	60	$ .01	$ .05
Tettleton, Mickey	90UD	297	$ .01	$ .05
Tettleton, Mickey	91UD	296	$ .01	$ .05
Tettleton, Mickey	91UD	729	$ .01	$ .05
Tettleton, Mickey	92UD	251	$ .01	$ .04
Tettleton, Mickey	93UD	46	$ .01	$ .15
Tettleton, Mickey	93UD	86	$ .01	$ .05
Teufel, Tim	89UD	277	$ .01	$ .08
Teufel, Tim	90UD	492	$ .01	$ .05
Teufel, Tim	91UD	370	$ .01	$ .05
Teufel, Tim	92UD	349	$ .01	$ .04
Teufel, Tim	93UD	61	$ .01	$ .05
Tewksbury, Bob	91UD	630	$ .01	$ .05
Tewksbury, Bob	92UD	512	$ .01	$ .04
Tewksbury, Bob	93UD	318	$ .01	$ .05
Theft, Grand	92UD	782	$ .01	$ .15
Thigpen, Bobby	89UD	647	$ .01	$ .08

UPPER DECK

Player	Year	No.	VG	EX/MT
Thigpen, Bobby	90UD	269	$.01	$.05
Thigpen, Bobby	91UD	93	$.01	$.05
Thigpen, Bobby	91UD	261	$.01	$.05
Thigpen, Bobby	92UD	285	$.01	$.04
Thomas, Andres	89UD	144	$.01	$.08
Thomas, Andres	90UD	212	$.01	$.05
Thomas, Andres	91UD	384	$.01	$.05
Thomas, Frank	91UD	246	$.90	$3.60
Thomas, Frank	92UD	87	$.05	$.35
Thomas, Frank	92UD	166	$.10	$1.00
Thomas, Frank	93UD	51	$.05	$.35
Thomas, Frank	93UD	105	$.01	$.10
Thome, Jim	91UDF	17	$.10	$.40
Thome, Jim	92UD	1	$.05	$.25
Thome, Jim	92UD	5	$.01	$.15
Thome, Jim	93UD	45	$.05	$.25
Thompson, Milt	89UD	317	$.01	$.08
Thompson, Milt	90UD	278	$.01	$.05
Thompson, Milt	91UD	309	$.01	$.05
Thompson, Milt	92UD	397	$.01	$.04
Thompson, Rob	89UD	172	$.01	$.08
Thompson, Robby	90UD	169	$.01	$.05
Thompson, Robby	91UD	178	$.01	$.05
Thompson, Robby	92UD	286	$.01	$.04
Thompson, Robby	93UD	126	$.01	$.05
Thompson, Ryan	93UD	373	$.05	$.25
Thomas, Frank	92UDSP	4	$2.50	$10.00
Thon, Dickie	89UD	258	$.01	$.08
Thon, Dickie	89UD	704	$.01	$.10
Thon, Dickie	90UD	439	$.01	$.05
Thon, Dickie	91UD	449	$.01	$.05
Thon, Dickie	92UD	150	$.01	$.04
Thon, Dickie	92UD	769	$.01	$.05
Thurman, Gary	89UD	347	$.01	$.08
Thurman, Gary	92UD	629	$.01	$.04
Thurmond, Mark	89UD	571	$.01	$.08
Tibbs, Jay	89UD	655	$.01	$.08
Timlin, Mike	91UD	785	$.01	$.15
Timlin, Mike	92UD	409	$.01	$.04
Timlin, Mike	93UD	322	$.01	$.05
Titles, Twin	93UD	50	$.01	$.15
Toliver, Fred	89UD	64	$.01	$.08
Tolleson, Wayne	90UD	320	$.01	$.05
Tomlin, Randy	91UDF	76	$.05	$.35
Tomlin, Randy	92UD	537	$.01	$.04
Tomlin, Randy	93UD	284	$.01	$.05
Torve, Kelvin	89UD	177	$.01	$.08
Traber, Jim	89UD	294	$.01	$.08
Traber, Jim	90UD	268	$.01	$.05
Trade, Blockbuster	93UD	42	$.01	$.15
Trammell, Alan	89UD	290	$.05	$.25
Trammell, Alan	89UD	690	$.01	$.15
Trammell, Alan	90UD	554	$.01	$.15
Trammell, Alan	91UD	223	$.01	$.10
Trammell, Alan	92UD	273	$.01	$.04
Treadway, Jeff	89UD	393	$.01	$.15
Treadway, Jeff	90UD	141	$.01	$.05
Treadway, Jeff	91UD	499	$.01	$.05
Treadway, Jeff	92UD	389	$.01	$.04
Trevino, Alex	89UD	262	$.01	$.08
Trevino, Alex	90UD	205	$.01	$.05
Tribe, Youthful	93UD	45	$.05	$.25
Trillo, Manny	89UD	127	$.01	$.08
Trombley, Mike	93UD	28	$.05	$.25
Tudor, John	89UD	66	$.01	$.08
Tudor, John	90UD	396	$.01	$.05
Tudor, John	91UD	329	$.01	$.05
Turner, Ryan	92UD	710	$.05	$.25
Upshaw, Willie	89UD	157	$.01	$.08
Uribe, Jose	89UD	181	$.01	$.08
Uribe, Jose	90UD	188	$.01	$.05
Uribe, Jose	91UD	207	$.01	$.05
Uribe, Jose	92UD	270	$.01	$.04
Valdez, Rafael	90UD	775	$.01	$.15
Valdez, Rafael	91UD	253	$.01	$.05

Player	Year	No.	VG	EX/MT
Valentin, John	93UD	387	$.01	$.15
Valenzuela, Fernando	89UD	656	$.01	$.10
Valenzuela, Fernando	90UD	445	$.01	$.05
Valenzuela, Fernando	91UD	175	$.01	$.05
Valera, Julio	91UD	534	$.01	$.15
Valera, Julio	92UD	747	$.01	$.05

Player	Year	No.	VG	EX/MT
Valera, Julio	**93UD**	**343**	**$ .01**	**$ .05**
Valle, Dave	89UD	320	$.01	$.08
Valle, Dave	90UD	451	$.01	$.05
Valle, Dave	91UD	595	$.01	$.05
Valle, Dave	92UD	182	$.01	$.04
Valle, Dave	93UD	100	$.01	$.05
Van Poppel, Todd	91UD	53	$.10	$1.00
Van Poppel, Todd	91UDF	12	$.10	$.40
Van Poppel, Todd	92UD	22	$.05	$.25
Van Slyke, Andy	89UD	537	$.05	$.25
Van Slyke, Andy	89UD	685	$.01	$.15
Van Slyke, Andy	90UD	536	$.01	$.15
Van Slyke, Andy	91UD	256	$.01	$.10
Van Slyke, Andy	92UD	132	$.01	$.04
Van Slyke, Andy	92UD	711	$.01	$.15
Van Slyke, Andy	92UD	715	$.01	$.05
Van Slyke, Andy	93UD	124	$.01	$.05
Varsho, Gary	89UD	321	$.01	$.15
Varsho, Gary	92UD	217	$.01	$.04
Vatcher, Jim	91UD	604	$.01	$.15
Vaughn, Greg	90UD	25	$.10	$.35
Vaughn, Greg	91UD	526	$.01	$.10
Vaughn, Greg	92UD	97	$.01	$.04
Vaughn, Greg	92UD	232	$.01	$.10
Vaughn, Maurice "Mo"	91UD	5	$.10	$.50
Vaughn, Mo	92UD	445	$.01	$.15
Vaughn, Mo	93UD	396	$.01	$.05
Velarde, Randy	89UD	189	$.01	$.08
Velarde, Randy	92UD	399	$.01	$.04
Velarde, Randy	93UD	93	$.01	$.05
Ventura, Robin	90UD	21	$.20	$2.00
Ventura, Robin	91UD	263	$.10	$.40
Ventura, Robin	92UD	263	$.01	$.15
Ventura, Robin	93UD	51	$.05	$.35
Ventura, Robin	93UD	263	$.05	$.25
Villanueva, Hector	90UD	741	$.01	$.15
Villanueva, Hector	91UD	171	$.05	$.20

UPPER DECK

Player	Year	No.	VG	EX/MT
Villanueva, Hector	92UD	102	$ .01	$ .04
Viola, Frank	89UD	397	$ .01	$ .15
Viola, Frank	89UD	658	$ .01	$ .15
Viola, Frank	89UD	691	$ .01	$ .10
Viola, Frank	90UD	626	$ .01	$ .10
Viola, Frank	91UD	122	$ .01	$ .10
Viola, Frank	92UD	277	$ .01	$ .04
Viola, Frank	92UD	733	$ .01	$ .05
Viola, Frank	93UD	48	$ .01	$ .15
Viola, Frank	93UD	131	$ .01	$ .05
Virgil, Ozzie	89UD	104	$ .01	$ .08
Vitiello, Joe	92UD	73	$ .05	$ .35
Vitko, Joe	93UD	10	$ .05	$ .20
Vizcaino, Jose	90UD	44	$ .01	$ .15
Vizcaino, Jose	91UD	580	$ .01	$ .05
Vizcaino, Jose	93UD	211	$ .01	$ .05
Vizquel, Omar	89UD	787	$ .05	$ .35
Vizquel, Omar	90UD	233	$ .01	$ .10
Vizquel, Omar	91UD	593	$ .01	$ .05
Vizquel, Omar	92UD	401	$ .01	$ .04
Vizquel, Omar	93UD	301	$ .01	$ .05

Player	Year	No.	VG	EX/MT
Wakefield, Tim	**93UD**	**66**	**$ .10**	**$ .75**
Walewander, Jim	89UD	454	$ .01	$ .08
Walk, Bob	89UD	438	$ .01	$ .08
Walk, Bob	90UD	596	$ .01	$ .05
Walk, Bob	91UD	689	$ .01	$ .05
Walk, Bob	92UD	619	$ .01	$ .04
Walk, Bob	93UD	78	$ .01	$ .05
Walker, Chico	92UD	617	$ .01	$ .04
Walker, Greg	89UD	231	$ .01	$ .08
Walker, Greg	90UD	350	$ .01	$ .05
Walker, Larry	90UD	466	$ .20	$2.00
Walker, Larry	90UD	702	$ .10	$1.00
Walker, Larry	91UD	536	$ .05	$ .35
Walker, Larry	92UD	249	$ .01	$ .04
Walker, Larry	93UD	144	$ .05	$ .20
Walker, Mike	91UD	694	$ .01	$ .10
Wallach, Tim	89UD	102	$ .01	$ .08
Wallach, Tim	90UD	273	$ .01	$ .05
Wallach, Tim	91UD	96	$ .01	$ .05
Wallach, Tim	91UD	235	$ .01	$ .05
Wallach, Tim	92UD	228	$ .01	$ .04
Walling, Denny	89UD	327	$ .01	$ .08
Walter, Gene	89UD	604	$ .01	$ .08

Player	Year	No.	VG	EX/MT
Walters, Dan	93UD	172	$ .01	$ .05
Walton, Jerome	89UD	765	$ .05	$ .20
Walton, Jerome	90UD	345	$ .01	$ .10
Walton, Jerome	91UD	332	$ .01	$ .15
Walton, Jerome	92UD	463	$ .01	$ .04
Ward, Duane	89UD	551	$ .01	$ .08
Ward, Duane	90UD	653	$ .01	$ .05
Ward, Duane	91UD	581	$ .01	$ .05
Ward, Duane	92UD	450	$ .01	$ .04
Ward, Duane	93UD	339	$ .01	$ .05
Ward, Gary	89UD	98	$ .01	$ .08
Ward, Gary	91UD	412	$ .01	$ .05
Ward, Turner	91UD	762	$ .01	$ .15
Washington, Claudell	89UD	310	$ .01	$ .10
Washington, Claudell	89UD	794	$ .01	$ .10
Washington, Claudell	90UD	395	$ .01	$ .05
Washington, Ron	89UD	519	$ .01	$ .08
Wayne, Gary	90UD	372	$ .01	$ .15
Webster, Lenny	90UD	728	$ .05	$ .20
Webster, Mitch	89UD	65	$ .01	$ .08
Webster, Mitch	90UD	153	$ .01	$ .05
Webster, Mitch	90UD	730	$ .01	$ .05
Webster, Mitch	91UD	120	$ .01	$ .05
Wegman, Bill	89UD	445	$ .01	$ .08
Wegman, Bill	90UD	629	$ .01	$ .05
Wegman, Bill	91UD	292	$ .01	$ .05
Wegman, Bill	92UD	612	$ .01	$ .04
Wegman, Bill	93UD	416	$ .01	$ .05
Wehner, John	92UD	469	$ .05	$ .20
Weiss, Walt	89UD	374	$ .01	$ .15
Weiss, Walt	89UD	660	$ .05	$ .25
Weiss, Walt	90UD	542	$ .01	$ .05
Weiss, Walt	91UD	192	$ .01	$ .05
Weiss, Walt	92UD	151	$ .01	$ .04
Weiss, Walt	93UD	122	$ .01	$ .05
Welch, Bob	89UD	191	$ .01	$ .08
Welch, Bob	90UD	251	$ .01	$ .05
Welch, Bob	91UD	425	$ .01	$ .05
Welch, Bob	92UD	452	$ .01	$ .04
Welch, Bob	93UD	407	$ .01	$ .05
Wells, David	90UD	30	$ .01	$ .05
Wells, David	91UD	583	$ .01	$ .05
Wells, David	92UD	116	$ .01	$ .04
Wendell, Turk	92UD	780	$ .01	$ .10
West, David	89UD	7	$ .01	$ .15
West, David	90UD	15	$ .01	$ .05
West, Dave	91UD	377	$ .01	$ .05
West, Dave	92UD	548	$ .01	$ .04
Weston, Mickey	90UD	683	$ .01	$ .10
Wetherby, Jeff	90UD	611	$ .01	$ .15
Wetteland, John	90UD	377	$ .05	$ .35
Wetteland, John	91UD	668	$ .01	$ .05
Wetteland, John	92UD	788	$ .01	$ .05
Wetteland, John	93UD	392	$ .01	$ .05
Whitaker, Lou	89UD	451	$ .01	$ .10
Whitaker, Lou	90UD	41	$ .01	$ .05
Whitaker, Lou	90UD	327	$ .01	$ .05
Whitaker, Lou	91UD	367	$ .01	$ .05
Whitaker, Lou	92UD	516	$ .01	$ .04
Whitaker, Lou	93UD	273	$ .01	$ .05
White, Devon	89UD	110	$ .01	$ .15
White, Devon	90UD	5	$ .01	$ .05
White, Devon	90UD	129	$ .01	$ .05
White, Devon	91UD	517	$ .01	$ .05
White, Devon	91UD	783	$ .01	$ .05
White, Devon	92UD	352	$ .01	$ .04
White, Devon	93UD	346	$ .01	$ .05
White, Frank	89UD	350	$ .01	$ .08
White, Frank	90UD	382	$ .01	$ .05
White, Frank	91UD	568	$ .01	$ .05
White, Rondell	91UDF	10	$ .15	$ .75
White, Rondell	92UD	51	$ .05	$ .35
White, Rondell	92UD	61	$ .05	$ .25
White Sox, 1917 Revisited	91UD	617	$ .01	$ .15
Whited, Ed	90UD	447	$ .01	$ .15

UPPER DECK

Player	Year	No.	VG	EX/MT
Whitehurst, Wally	89UD	737	$.01	$.10
Whitehurst, Wally	90UD	564	$.01	$.05
Whitehurst, Wally	91UD	221	$.01	$.05
Whitehurst, Wally	92UD	414	$.01	$.04
Whiten, Mark	91UD	561	$.05	$.20
Whiten, Mark	91UDF	75	$.01	$.10
Whiten, Mark	92UD	524	$.01	$.15
Whiten, Mark	93UD	227	$.01	$.05
Whiteside, Matt	93UD	390	$.01	$.15
Whitson, Ed	89UD	453	$.01	$.08
Whitson, Ed	90UD	308	$.01	$.05
Whitson, Ed	91UD	312	$.01	$.05
Whitson, Ed	92UD	103	$.01	$.04
Whitt, Ernie	89UD	118	$.01	$.08
Whitt, Ernie	90UD	148	$.01	$.05
Wickman, Bob	92UD	76	$.10	$.40
Wickman, Bob	93UD	372	$.05	$.20
Wilkerson, Curtis	89UD	465	$.01	$.08
Wilkerson, Curtis	90UD	147	$.01	$.05
Wilkerson, Curtis	92UD	490	$.01	$.04
Wilkins, Rick	91UDF	46	$.01	$.10
Wilkins, Rick	92UD	373	$.01	$.15
Williams, Bernie	91UD	11	$.10	$.40
Williams, Bernie	92UD	556	$.01	$.15
Williams, Bernie	93UD	332	$.01	$.05
Williams, Brian	92UD	23	$.05	$.25
Williams, Brian	93UD	286	$.01	$.05
Williams, Eddie	89UD	790	$.01	$.10
Williams, Eddie	90UD	289	$.01	$.10
Williams, Frank	89UD	449	$.01	$.08
Williams, Frank	90UD	539	$.01	$.05
Williams, Gerald	91UDF	15	$.05	$.35
Williams, Gerald	93UD	360	$.01	$.05
Williams, Ken	89UD	506	$.01	$.08
Williams, Ken	89UD	714	$.01	$.10
Williams, Kenny	90UD	249	$.01	$.05
Williams, Kenny	91UD	89	$.01	$.05
Williams, Matt	89UD	247	$.10	$.50
Williams, Matt	90UD	577	$.05	$.20
Williams, Matt	91UD	79	$.01	$.05
Williams, Matt	91UD	157	$.01	$.10
Williams, Matt	92UD	154	$.01	$.10
Williams, Matt	93UD	143	$.01	$.05
Williams, Mitch	89UD	95	$.01	$.08
Williams, Mitch	89UD	778	$.01	$.10
Williams, Mitch	90UD	174	$.01	$.10
Williams, Mitch	91UD	173	$.01	$.05
Williams, Mitch	91UD	769	$.01	$.05
Williams, Mitch	92UD	410	$.01	$.04
Williams, Mitch	93UD	113	$.01	$.05
Williams, Ted	92UDHH	2	$1.00	$4.00
Williamson, Mark	90UD	173	$.01	$.05
Williamson, Mark	91UD	510	$.01	$.05
Williamson, Mark	92UD	609	$.01	$.04
Wilson, Craig	91UD	390	$.01	$.15
Wilson, Dan	91UDF	6	$.05	$.25
Wilson, Dan	92UD	72	$.01	$.15
Wilson, Dan	93UD	6	$.01	$.05
Wilson, Glenn	90UD	410	$.01	$.05
Wilson, Glenn	91UD	515	$.01	$.05
Wilson, Mookie	89UD	199	$.01	$.08
Wilson, Mookie	90UD	481	$.01	$.05
Wilson, Mookie	91UD	512	$.01	$.05
Wilson, Mookie	92UD	391	$.01	$.04
Wilson, Nigel	93UD	9	$.20	$2.00
Wilson, Steve	89UD	799	$.01	$.15
Wilson, Steve	90UD	341	$.01	$.10
Wilson, Steve	91UD	493	$.01	$.05
Wilson, Trevor	89UD	733	$.05	$.35
Wilson, Trevor	90UD	637	$.01	$.10
Wilson, Trevor	91UD	653	$.01	$.05
Wilson, Trevor	92UD	337	$.01	$.04
Wilson, Trevor	93UD	197	$.01	$.05
Wilson, Willie	89UD	244	$.01	$.08
Wilson, Willie	90UD	349	$.01	$.05
Wilson, Willie	91UD	609	$.01	$.05
Wilson, Willie	92UD	238	$.01	$.04
Wilson, Willie	93UD	417	$.01	$.05
Winfield, Dave	89UD	349	$.10	$.75
Winfield, Dave	90UD	337	$.05	$.25
Winfield, Dave	90UD	745	$.05	$.25
Winfield, Dave	91UD	337	$.01	$.15
Winfield, Dave	92UD	28	$.01	$.10
Winfield, Dave	92UD	222	$.01	$.10
Winfield, Dave	92UD	734	$.01	$.10
Winfield, Dave	93UD	40	$.01	$.10
Winningham, Herm	89UD	636	$.01	$.08
Winningham, Herm	90UD	589	$.01	$.05
Winters, Matt	90UD	524	$.01	$.15
Witt, Bobby	89UD	557	$.01	$.08
Witt, Bobby	90UD	636	$.01	$.05
Witt, Bobby	91UD	627	$.01	$.05
Witt, Bobby	92UD	576	$.01	$.04
Witt, Bobby	93UD	87	$.01	$.05
Witt, Mike	89UD	555	$.01	$.08
Witt, Mike	90UD	548	$.01	$.05
Witt, Mike	91UD	429	$.01	$.05
Wohlers, Mark	91UDF	77	$.05	$.35
Wohlers, Mark	92UD	56	$.01	$.10
Wood, Ted	92UD	12	$.01	$.10
Woodson, Kerry	93UD	388	$.01	$.05
Woodson, Tracy	89UD	108	$.01	$.08
Worrell, Todd	89UD	512	$.01	$.08
Worrell, Todd	90UD	467	$.01	$.05
Worthington, Craig	89UD	725	$.01	$.15
Worthington, Craig	90UD	444	$.01	$.10
Worthington, Craig	91UD	141	$.01	$.05
Wrona, Rick	90UD	582	$.01	$.10
Wynne, Marvell	89UD	154	$.01	$.08
Wynne, Marvell	90UD	14	$.01	$.05
Yelding, Eric	90UD	427	$.01	$.10
Yelding, Eric	91UD	197	$.01	$.05
Yelding, Eric	92UD	394	$.01	$.04
Yett, Rich	89UD	728	$.01	$.10
Yett, Rich	90UD	595	$.01	$.05
Youmans, Floyd	89UD	459	$.01	$.08
Youmans, Floyd	89UD	730	$.01	$.10
Young, Anthony	91UDF	65	$.05	$.25
Young, Anthony	92UD	535	$.05	$.25
Young, Anthony	93UD	71	$.01	$.05
Young, Curt	89UD	392	$.01	$.08
Young, Curt	90UD	4	$.01	$.05
Young, Dimitri	91UDF	7	$.15	$1.50
Young, Dmitri	92UD	58	$.10	$.40
Young, Gerald	89UD	135	$.01	$.08
Young, Gerald	90UD	196	$.01	$.05
Young, Matt	90UD	787	$.01	$.05
Young, Matt	91UD	591	$.01	$.05
Young, Matt	91UD	740	$.01	$.05
Young, Matt	92UD	505	$.01	$.04
Young, Mike	89UD	649	$.01	$.08
Youngblood, Joel	89UD	458	$.01	$.08
Yount, Robin	89UD	285	$.10	$.75
Yount, Robin	90UD	91	$.01	$.10
Yount, Robin	90UD	567	$.05	$.25
Yount, Robin	91UD	344	$.01	$.15
Yount, Robin	92UD	456	$.01	$.10
Yount, Robin	93UD	43	$.05	$.25
Yount, Robin	93UDSP	5	$2.50	$10.00
Zancanaro, David	92UD	54	$.01	$.05
Zeile, Todd	89UD	754	$.10	$1.00
Zeile, Todd	90UD	545	$.10	$.50
Zeile, Todd	91UD	164	$.01	$.10
Zeile, Todd	92UD	40	$.01	$.04
Zeile, Todd	92UD	533	$.01	$.10
Zosky, Eddie	91UD	734	$.05	$.20
Zosky, Eddie	91UDF	14	$.01	$.10
Zosky, Eddie	92UD	544	$.01	$.04
Zupcic, Bob	93UD	277	$.01	$.05
Zuvella, Paul	89UD	236	$.01	$.08

Schroeder's ANTIQUES Price Guide

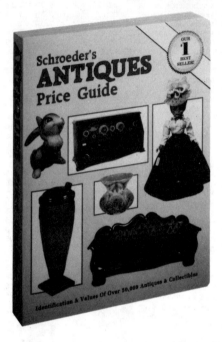

Schroeder's Antiques Price Guide is the #1 best-selling antiques & collectibles value guide on the market today, and here's why . . . More than 300 authors, well-known dealers, and top-notch collectors work together with our editors to bring you accurate information regarding pricing and identification. More than 45,000 items in almost 500 categories are listed along with hundreds of sharp original photos that illustrate not only the rare and unusual, but the common, popular collectibles as well. Each large close-up shot shows important details clearly. Every subject is represented with histories and background information, a feature not found in any of our competitors' publications. Our editors keep abreast of newly-developing trends, often adding several new categories a year as the need arises. If it merits the interest of today's collector, you'll find it in Schroeder's. And you can feel confident that the information we publish is up to date and accurate. Our advisors thoroughly check each category to spot inconsistencies, listings that may not be entirely reflective of market dealings, and lines too vague to be of merit. Only the best of the lot remains for publication. Without doubt, you'll find Schroeder's Antiques Price Guide the only one to buy for reliable information and values.

8½x 11", 608 Pages $12.95

COLLECTOR BOOKS
A Division of Schroeder Publishing Co., Inc.